The Oxford Dictionary of

....

Phrase
and Fable

....

Edited by **Elizabeth Knowles**

OXFORD
UNIVERSITY PRESS

OXFORD
UNIVERSITY PRESS

Great Clarendon Street, Oxford OX2 6DP

Oxford University Press is a department of the University of Oxford.
It furthers the University's objective of excellence in research, scholarship,
and education by publishing worldwide in

Oxford New York

Athens Auckland Bangkok Bogotá Buenos Aires Calcutta
Cape Town Chennai Dar es Salaam Delhi Florence Hong Kong Istanbul
Karachi Kuala Lumpur Madrid Melbourne Mexico City Mumbai
Nairobi Paris São Paulo Shanghai Singapore Taipei Tokyo Toronto Warsaw

with associated companies in Berlin Ibadan

Oxford is a registered trade mark of Oxford University Press
in the UK and in certain other countries

Published in the United States
by Oxford University Press Inc., New York

© Oxford University Press 2000

Database right Oxford University Press (makers)

First published 2000

British Library Cataloguing in Publication Data
Data available

Library of Congress Cataloging in Publication Data
Data available
ISBN 0–19–860219–7

10 9 8 7 6 5 4 3 2 1

Designed by Jane Stevenson
Typeset in Minion and Frutiger
by Interactive Sciences Ltd
Printed in Great Britain
on acid-free paper by
Biddles Ltd
Guildford and King's Lynn

Contents

Introduction

The *Oxford Dictionary of Phrase and Fable* brings together words, names, and phrases with cultural resonance: items from history and religion, mythology, biography, folk customs and superstitions, science and technology, philosophy, and popular culture. Entries justify inclusion by having some figurative or allusive connotation, or by being central to the development of a civilization or culture.

The possibility of producing such a book was first put forward at Oxford in 1927, when the then Secretary to the Delegates, Kenneth Sisam, suggested that Sir Paul Harvey might edit a 'reader's companion to English literature' which would fulfil the role. As Peter Sutcliffe records in *The Oxford University Press: an Informal History* (1978) Sisam, having given a first outline, had additional ideas for entries which ranged from classical mythology, through allusions (which he called 'the really exciting part of the book') to English saints, romantic heroes, and social and sporting events. However, he 'did not at once appreciate that his first thoughts had become Harvey's last'. Sir Paul, taking the original brief as a blueprint, was working through the fifty two plays of Beaumont and Fletcher (poor health meant that he could deal with no more than three five-act plays in a day), and was unable to vary his terms of reference. He was to produce in 1932 the first edition of what has become a central work of reference and scholarship: the *Oxford Companion to English Literature*. Later editions have reinforced the consistency of the original plan, moving the book further away from the broader areas of allusion and reference which Sisam had begun to consider.

In many ways, the delay since 1927 has been beneficial, since the resources available to Oxford lexicographers have never been richer. The current book had its immediate genesis in work done for the phrasal and proverbial sections of the *Oxford Dictionary of Phrase, Saying, and Quotation* (1977). As well as valuable quotations databases, we have electronic access to such texts as the updated *Oxford English Dictionary*, the *New Oxford Dictionary of English*, the *Dictionary of National Biography*, the British National Corpus, and many other sources of information. We thus have the opportunity to sample the range of references likely to be encountered in the English language today, and to bring together the 20,000 items which make up this text. Information from existing resources has where necessary been verified by research, which sometimes brought out unsuspected links between entries—for example, that the Duke of Wellington's charger **Copenhagen** was the grandson of the famous racehorse **Eclipse** ('Eclipse first, the rest nowhere').

Much of the richness and diversity of the book derives directly from the evidence of our quotations files, and the provision of real-life quotations illuminates the contextual background of the words and phrases illustrated. The function of these quotations is to convey the colour and flavour of the way in which the name, word, or phrase illustrated is likely to be used, and to share with our readers the pleasure of direct access to some of the key material on which the entries are based—for example, a reference to 'the *Goldilocks* criterion', and a tribute to 'the Terminator-like efficiency' of biocontrol insects.

The *Oxford Dictionary of Phrase and Fable* for the year 2000 needs to be not simply (as Sisam first envisaged) a reader's companion; it should also be the means of decoding chance-met allusions and references encountered in newspapers and on the airwaves. (What was the **Moon Hoax**? Who are the **Windrush Generation**?) This means that it needs to be thoroughly up to date, covering **Blair Babes** as well as **Busby Babes**, and **Frankenfood** as well as **Frankenstein's monster**. Sometimes a later event emphasizes the resonance of a particular word or name: the significance of **Robben Island** as the prison in which Nelson Mandela was held for many years, was underlined on New Year's Eve 1999 when the ex-President marked the Millennium for South Africa by lighting a candle in his former cell.

The heart of the book is the overall view of figurative usage in the language today: a culturally diverse range of words, phrases, proverbs, and allusions. Many entries link together the ancient and modern worlds. **Gaia**, in Greek mythology the Earth personified as a goddess, is also the name given in James Lovelock's **Gaia hypothesis** for the earth viewed as a vast self-regulating organism. The electronic digital computer used at **Bletchley Park** in the Second World War to break the German codes was named **Colossus**—a name reaching back to classical antiquity and the **Colossus of Rhodes**. Allusions range from figures of classical mythology and history (**Bellerophon**, **Cassandra**, **Chiron**, **Messalina**) and the Bible (**Absalom**, **Job**) to popular culture (**Indiana Jones**, **Bart Simpson**). Many events (often tragic ones) have acquired a particular resonance. The loss of the **Titanic** in 1912 still echoes for us, as does the sinking in 1945 of the American heavy cruiser the **Indianapolis**. Nearer our own time, the **Challenger disaster** evokes more immediate memories.

Proverbs and sayings are an important part of the book, from the traditional **faith will move mountains**, to the modern political slogan, **It's the economy, stupid**. Phrases (although not transparent idioms) are included where there is a story to tell or background information to give: **canteen culture**, **Close Encounter**, **cruel and unusual punishment**, **Founding Father**, **glittering generalities**, **just war**, **poor little rich girl**, **rainbow coalition**, **spoil the Egyptians**, and **the vision thing** are some examples. The core of the book, relating to our stock of figurative language, is further illuminated by a range of entries from the history of ideas and cultural and scientific development, such as **cold fusion**, the **Delian problem**, and the **Red Queen hypothesis**.

Entries in the *Dictionary* range from short definitions for quick access to specific information, to more discursive accounts supported and illustrated by quotations. The book is organized alphabetically, in a word by word sequence of keywords which are distinguished by heavier type. Cross-references to related entries (the keyword being indicated by small type and an arrow) are given where it is felt that explicit direction to that entry will be helpful. Boxed entries (a full list of which will be found at the back of the book) are an enhancement, bringing together sets of items which as individual entries are spread throughout the text. It has been the aim to provide a book in which a discrete piece of information can be quickly traced, but which also allows and encourages browsing.

No dictionary with *Phrase and Fable* in its title can fail to acknowledge a debt to the original conception of such a book as created in 1870 by Ebenezer Cobham Brewer (1810–97), and ancestor of many later editions. Described in the *Dictionary of National Biography* (1917–) as a 'miscellaneous writer', Brewer is uniquely identified as the author of a book which brought together the central matter of 19th-century allusive language, providing factual information as well as what has generally been believed. Brewer's book was very much of its time; not least, in that it rested on a perception of a single western culture. Its readers might be more or less learned, but it could be assumed that they were following one broad path. The early years of the 21st century, however, present us with different challenges.

It has already been said that the present book draws strongly on the resources of Oxford Dictionaries, but individual acknowledgements also need to be made. Susan Ratcliffe, Associate Editor for Oxford Quotations Dictionaries, has made an inestimable contribution by reading, commenting on, and adding to the text, and Susie Dent and Alysoun Owen of the Reference Department have also commented knowledgeably and valuably. I am grateful to the work of many other colleagues, notably John Simpson and the staff of the Oxford English Dictionary, and Judy Pearsall and the staff of Core Dictionaries. John McNeill has been, as always, a valued consultant and adviser. Ralph Bates and Marie G. Diaz verified many references, and the proof-reading was carried out by Kim Allen, Fabia Claris, Carolyn Garwes, Helen Rappaport, and Penny Trumble. All those named (and many unnamed) have a share in the successes of the text; any weaknesses are my own.

To work on a book of this kind has been a pleasure and a privilege; it is hoped that readers will share some of the enjoyment as well as finding the book useful.

ELIZABETH KNOWLES

Oxford, 2000

A The first letter of the modern English alphabet and of the ancient Roman one, corresponding to Greek *alpha* and Hebrew *aleph*.

See also ➤ *who* SAYS *A must say B.*

A 1 excellent, first-rate; in Lloyd's Register of Shipping, used of ships in first-class condition as to hull (A) and stores (1).

Aaron in the bible, the brother of ➤ MOSES and traditional founder of the Jewish priesthood. The first anointed high priest, he acted as a spokesman for his brother after Moses was chosen to lead the Israelites out of Egypt. He was persuaded by the people to make an image of God in the form of a ➤ GOLDEN *calf*, thereby earning Moses' displeasure.

Aaron's beard a name given to the rose of Sharon and other plants, and alluding to the description of Aaron whose beard 'went down to the skirts of his garments' (Psalms 133:2), because of the prominent hairy stamens or the long runners which some of these plants put out.

Aaron's rod the common or great mullein; the name refers to the biblical story (Numbers 17:8) that Aaron's staff flowered when it was placed within the tabernacle, as a sign from God that he was to be the Jewish high priest.

abacot a spurious word found in a number of early dictionaries, such as Bailey, Ash, and Todd, originating in a 15th-century misprint of *bycoket* 'a kind of cap or headdress'.

abacus an oblong frame with rows of wires or grooves along which beads are slid, used for calculating; possibly a development of the classical counting board, it was widely used in Europe in the Middle Ages and is still used in some countries.

The word is this sense dates from the late 17th century; it is recorded in late Middle English, denoting a board strewn with sand on which to draw figures, and comes via Latin from Greek *abax, abak-* 'slab, drawing board', of Semitic origin, and probably related to Hebrew *ʾābāq* 'dust'.

Abaddon a name for the Devil (Revelation 9:11, 'and they had a king over them, which is the angel of the bottomless pit, whose name in the Hebrew tongue is Abaddon, but in the Greek tongue hath his name Apollyon') or for hell. Recorded from late Middle English, *Abaddon* comes via Greek from Hebrew *ʾăbaddōn* 'destruction'. Its use for 'hell' arose in the late 17th century:

> In all her gates Abaddon rues Thy bold attempt.
> — John Milton *Paradise Regained* (1671)

Abba in the New Testament, God as father; in the Syrian Orthodox and Coptic Churches, a title given to bishops and patriarchs. The word comes via Greek from Aramaic *abbā* 'father'.

Abbasid a member of a dynasty of caliphs who ruled in Baghdad from 750 to 1258, named after *Abbas* (566–652), the prophet ➤ MUHAMMAD'S uncle and founder of the dynasty.

abbey see also ➤ *Abbey of* THÉLÈME, ➤ BATTLE *Abbey*, ➤ FONTHILL *Abbey*, ➤ MEDMENHAM *Abbey*, ➤ WESTMINSTER *Abbey*.

Abbey Theatre a theatre in Abbey Street, Dublin, first opened in 1904, staging the work of Irish dramatists such as J. M. Synge and Sean O'Casey. W. B. Yeats was associated with its foundation, and in 1925 it became the first state-subsidized theatre in the English-speaking world.

Abbo of Fleury (?954–1004), French theologian, who was invited to England by Oswald, bishop of Worcester and archbishop of York, to teach in his monastery of Ramsey.

abbot a man who is the head of an abbey of monks. Recorded from Old English (in the form *abbod*) the word comes via ecclesiastical Latin from Greek *abbas* 'father', from Aramaic *abbā* 'father' (see ➤ ABBA).

See also ➤ *Lord of* MISRULE.

Abbotsford the name of Sir Walter Scott's property near Melrose on the Tweed, purchased in 1811.

Abbotsford Club founded in 1834 in memory of Sir Walter Scott, for the purpose of publishing materials bearing on the history or literature of any country dealt with in Scott's writings. It ceased its publications in 1865.

Abdera a Greek city in Thrace whose inhabitants were proverbial for their stupidity, although it was also the birthplace of the philosopher ➤ DEMOCRITUS.

Abdication Crisis the constitutional crisis, resulting from the king of England's determination to marry a divorced woman, ➤ *Wallis* SIMPSON, which culminated in the abdication of ➤ EDWARD *VIII* in 1936.

Abdiel the faithful seraph in Milton's *Paradise Lost* who refused to join in Satan's rebellion; he is not a biblical figure and his name means literally 'servant of God'.

Abecedarian psalm a psalm, like the 119th, with divisions beginning with letters of the alphabet; from Latin *abecedarius* 'alphabetical' (from the names of the letters *a, b, c, d*).

Abednego in Daniel 1:7, the name, meaning 'servant of Nego' (a form of 'Nebo') given by King Nebuchadnezzaar to Azariah, one of those cast into the ➤ BURNING *fiery furnace*.

Abel in the bible, the younger son of Adam and Eve, murdered by his jealous brother ➤ CAIN, after Abel's offering to God of a lamb was accepted by God, while Cain's sheaves were rejected.

Peter **Abelard** (1079–1142), French scholar, theologian, and philosopher. His independence of mind impressed his contemporaries but led to his being twice condemned for heresy.

He lectured in Paris until his academic career was cut short in 1118 by his tragic love affair with his pupil Héloïse, niece of Fulbert, a canon of Notre-Dame. Abelard was castrated at Fulbert's instigation; he entered a monastery, and Héloïse became a nun. Abelard continued his controversial teaching, applying reason to questions of faith, notably to the doctrine of the Trinity. In the early 1130s he and Héloïse put together a collection of their love letters and other correspondence, which was published in 1616. Abelard and Héloïse are buried together in Paris.

take away Aberdeen and twelve miles round, and where are you? Scottish traditional saying; late 19th century.

Aberfan a village in South Wales where, in 1966, a slag heap collapsed, overwhelming houses and a school and killing 28 adults and 116 children.

Abhorrers a nickname given in 1680 to those who signed addresses of *Abhorrence* presented to Charles II, urging the Protestant succession and the exclusion of the Catholic Duke of York.

Abib the first month of the ancient Jewish ecclesiastical year (corresponding to the latter part of March and the early part of April), being the seventh of the civil year. Later called by the Babylonian name *Nisan.*

abigail archaic term for a lady's maid. The term comes from the name of the 'waiting gentlewoman' in Beaumont and Fletcher's popular play of *The Scornful Lady*; so named possibly in biblical allusion to the expression 'thine handmaid' frequently applied to herself by Abigail, future wife of King David (1 Samuel 25:24–31).

abiogenesis a technical term for ➤ SPONTANEOUS *generation*, which was introduced by the English biologist Thomas Henry Huxley (1825–95) in an address to the British Association for the Advancement of Science at Liverpool in September 1870.

Oath of Abjuration an oath disclaiming allegiance to ➤ *James Francis Edward* STUART, son of James II, or his descendants as claimants to the British throne. The Abjuration Act of 1701 made it compulsory for candidates for military or religious office to take the oath; it was reimposed by the Security of the Sovereign Act (1714) and the Treason Act (1766), and in 1778 it was imposed on all Roman Catholics in England as a condition of the removal of various civil disabilities. It was finally abolished in 1858 and replaced by a version of the *Oath of Allegiance.*

abjuration of the realm an oath before a justice or coroner undertaking to leave the country for ever, made by a criminal in order to escape punishment, often after taking sanctuary in a church.

ablaut alternation in the vowels of related word forms, especially in Germanic strong verbs (e.g. in *sing, sang, sung*).

Abner see ➤ L'IL *Abner.*

Abolitionists in the 19th century, supporters of the abolition of the slave-trade; the term is recorded from the early 19th century.

abominable causing moral revulsion; terrible. The word comes (in Middle English) via Old French from Latin *abominabilis*, ultimately from *abominari* 'deprecate', from *ab-* 'away, from' + *omen, omin-* 'omen'. The word was once widely believed to be from *ab-* + Latin *homine* (from *homo* 'human being'), thus 'inhuman, beastly', and until the 17th century frequently spelled *abhominable*. In Shakespeare's *Love's Labours Lost* (1595), Holofernes refers critically to the 'rackers of orthography' who were beginning to write *abominable* for *abhominable*.

Abominable Snowman a popular name for the ➤ YETI, recorded from the early 1920s.

Mount Abora in Coleridge's *Kubla Khan*, the subject of a song by the Abyssinian maid with a dulcimer, perhaps to be identified with *Mount Amara* as referred to in Milton's *Paradise Lost*.

Battle of Aboukir Bay a naval battle in 1798 off Aboukir Bay at the mouth of the Nile, in which the British under Nelson defeated the French fleet. Also called ➤ *Battle of the* NILE.

abracadabra a word said by conjurors when performing a magic trick. The term is recorded from the late 17th century, as a mystical word engraved and used as a charm against illness; it comes from Latin (from a Greek base), and is first recorded in a 2nd-century poem by Q. Serenus Sammonicus. When used as a charm, the word was typically written out in a triangular arrangement, beginning with A on the first line, AB on the second line, and so on.

Abraham in the Bible, the Hebrew patriarch from whom all Jews trace their descent (Genesis 11:27–25:10), and who is directed by God to leave his own country 'unto a land that I will show thee'. In Genesis 22 he is ordered by God to sacrifice his son ➤ ISAAC as a test of faith, a command later revoked.
See also ➤ PLAINS *of Abraham*, ➤ SHAM *Abraham*.

Abraham man originally (in 16th- and 17th-century England) a former or occasional inmate of the Hospital of St. Mary of Bethlehem in London, licensed to beg on his discharge, or a similarly licensed beggar discharged from a charitable institution; in extended usage, a beggar licensed on the basis of insanity or one who pretened to be insane. The name may be connected with the biblical story of the beggar Lazarus (see ➤ LAZARUS²) who when he died was carried by angels into ➤ ABRAHAM's *bosom*.

Abraham's bosom where the righteous dead are said to lie at peace; the term comes from Luke 66:22, 'the beggar died, and was carried by the angels into Abraham's bosom'.

abraxas a term of Gnostic magic of which the etymology is uncertain; it relates to the number 365 (the number of days in a year), and was explained by the 2nd-century Alexandrian Gnostic Basilides as the name of a Supreme Being who presides over 364 (52 x 7) kingdoms of spirits, because the numerical value of the letters of the name is equal to 365.

abroad see also ➤ *the* SCHOOLMASTER *is abroad.*

go abroad and you'll hear news of home proverbial saying, late 17th century; meaning that information about one's immediate vicinity may have become more widely publicized.

Absalom the third and favourite son of ➤ DAVID, who rebelled against his father and was killed; David's lament for him, 'O my son Absalom…would God I had died for thee, O Absalom, my son!' (2 Samuel 19:33) has helped to fix Absalom as the type of a rebellious son who is loved and mourned despite his rebellion.
According to the biblical account, Absalom was killed when he rode beneath an oak tree and the branches caught in his long hair, trapping him, so that he could be dispatched by David's commander ➤ JOAB.

Absalom and Achitophel an allegorical poem (1681) by John Dryden, dealing with the succession crisis centring on the ➤ EXCLUSION *Bill* of 1680; in the poem, *Absalom* stands for the ➤ *Duke of* MONMOUTH, Charles II's illegitimate son, who was put forward by the Protestant party in opposition to the legitimate heir, the Catholic Duke of York, Charles's brother; his counsellor ➤ ACHITOPHEL is the Earl of Shaftesbury.

absence see also ➤ CONSPICUOUS *by one's absence.*

absence makes the heart grow fonder proverbial saying; mid 19th century; 1st century BC in Latin in Propertius, 'passion [is] always warmer towards absent lovers.'

he who is absent is always in the wrong proverbial saying, late Middle English; meaning that someone who is not present cannot defend themselves.

absinthe a green aniseed-flavoured liqueur, originally flavoured with wormwood, although this is now banned owing to its toxicity; in the 19th and early 20th centuries drinking *absinthe* was regarded as a sign of decadence.

> Every culture has its talismanic pleasures and vices, and absinthe was as close as you could come to putting the Belle Époque in a bottle.
> — *Icon Thoughtstyle Magazine* April 1997

absolute zero the lowest temperature that is theoretically possible, at which the particles whose motion constitutes heat would be minimal. It is zero on the Kelvin scale, equivalent to $-273.15°$C.

absquatulate leave abruptly; a North American coinage of the mid 19th century, a blend (simulating a Latin form) of *abscond, squattle* 'depart', and *perambulate.*

days of abstinence in ecclesiastical terminology, days on which the eating of meat was forbidden (cf. ➤ FAST *days*).

absurd see ➤ THEATRE *of the Absurd.*

Abu-Bakr (*c.*573–634), closest adviser and friend of ➤ MUHAMMAD and father of his wife Ayesha (see ➤ AYESHA¹); on Muhammad's death he became the first (Sunni) caliph.

Abu Simbel the site of two huge rock-cut temples in southern Egypt, built during the reign of Ramses II in the 13th century BC and commemorating him and his first wife Nefertari. Following the building of the High Dam at Aswan, the monument was rebuilt higher up the hillside.

Abuna a title given to the Patriarch of the Ethiopian Orthodox Church; the word is Amharic, from Arabic 'our father'.

abundant number a number whose divisors add up to more than its own sum.

Abyla former name (now Jebel Musa) for one of the two rocks forming the ➤ PILLARS *of Hercules.*

St Acacius reputed martyr, of no known date, said to have been put to death with 10,000 companions by a pagan army; he is reputed to have prayed before his death that those venerating their memory would be granted health and strength, and from this he is traditionally counted as one of the ➤ FOURTEEN *Holy Helpers.*

□ **FEAST DAY** His feast day is 22 June.

Académie française a French literary academy with a constant membership of forty, responsible for the standard form of the French language and for compiling and revising a definitive dictionary of the French language. Its tendency is to defend traditional literary and linguistic rules and to discourage innovation. It was founded by Cardinal Richelieu in 1635.

Academy the philosophical school of Plato; *Akadēmeia* was the name of the garden where Plato originally taught, named after the hero *Akadēmos.*

See also ➤ GROVES *of academe.*

Academy award any of a series of awards of the Academy of Motion Picture Arts and Sciences (Hollywood, US) given annually since 1928 for achievement in the film industry in various categories; an ➤ OSCAR.

Acadia a former French colony established in 1604 in the territory now forming Nova Scotia in Canada. It was contested by France and Britain until it was eventually ceded to Britain in 1763; French-speaking Acadians were deported to other parts of North America, especially Louisiana. *Acadie* was the French name for Nova Scotia.

acanthus a conventionalized representation of the leaf of this plant is used especially as a decoration for Corinthian column capitals. The term in this sense dates from the mid 18th century; the name of the plant comes via Latin from Greek *akanthos,* from *akantha* 'thorn', from *akē* 'sharp point'.

accidents see also ➤ *a* CHAPTER *of accidents.*

accidents will happen (in the best regulated families) proverbial saying; mid 18th century.

accidie spiritual or mental sloth; apathy. Recorded from Middle English (figuring in lists of the ➤ SEVEN *deadly sins*), the word comes via Latin from Greek *akēdia* 'listlessness', from *a-* 'without' + *kēdos* 'care'.

accord see ➤ DAYTON *Accord.*

according see ➤ *according to* COCKER, ➤ *according to* GUNTER, ➤ *according to* HOYLE.

accountancy see ➤ CREATIVE *accountancy.*

accountants St ➤ MATTHEW is the patron saint of accountants.

there is no accounting for tastes proverbial saying, late 18th century; a version of the Latin tag *de gustibus non est disputandum* 'there is no disputing about tastes'.

accuses see ➤ *he who* EXCUSES, *accuses himself.*

ace originally, the 'one' on dice; later, a playing card with a single spot on it, ranked as the highest card in its suit in most card games. The term is recorded from Middle English, and comes via Old French from Latin *as* 'unity, a unit'.

an ace caff with quite a nice museum attached advertising slogan for the Victoria and Albert Museum, February 1989.

ace up one's sleeve a powerful hidden advantage; the term is recorded from the 1950s, although the equivalent ➤ CARD *up one's sleeve* is earlier.

Aceldama in the New Testament, a field near Jerusalem purchased with the blood money given to Judas for his betrayal of Jesus, the ➤ POTTER's *field*.

Acephali originally (in the late 16th century) any of various Christian bodies which owned either no leader or no earthly head. In the early 17th century, the word was also used in the context of natural history for supposed races of men or animals without heads. The word comes via medieval Latin from Greek *akephalos* 'headless'.

Achaean of or relating to *Achaea* in ancient Greece; (especially in Homeric contexts) Greek. The Achaeans were among the earliest Greek-speaking inhabitants of Greece, being established there well before the 12th century BC. Some scholars identify them with the Mycenaeans of the 14th–13th centuries BC. The Greek protagonists in the Trojan War are regularly called Achaeans in the *Iliad*, though this may have referred only to the leaders.

Achaemenid a member of the dynasty ruling in Persia from Cyrus I to Darius III (553–330 BC); the name comes from Greek *Akhaimenēs* 'Achaemenes', the reputed ancestor of the dynasty.

Achates a companion of ➤ AENEAS, whose loyalty to his friend was so exemplary as to become proverbial, hence the term ➤ *fidus* ACHATES ('faithful Achates').

fidus Achates a faithful friend and follower; the term is recorded in English from the early 17th century, and is a quotation from Virgil's *Aeneid*.

> Accompanied by three Ethiopian guides and his *fidus Achates*, the Italian Luigi Balugani, Bruce set out for the interior.
> — Frank McLynn *Hearts of Darkness* (1992)

Acherna the ninth brightest star in the sky and the brightest in the constellation Eridanus, visible only in the southern hemisphere. It marks the southern limit of Eridanus, and its name comes from an Arabic word meaning 'end of the river'.

Acheron in Greek mythology, one of the rivers of ➤ HADES.

> The image verges on the acherontic, the look of souls confronting hell.
> — *New York Times* 20 February 1996

achillea a plant of a genus that includes yarrow, supposed to have been used medicinally by ➤ ACHILLES, for whom it is named; Gerard notes in his *Herball* (1597) that, 'This plant *Achillea* is thought to be the very same, wherewith *Achilles* cured the wounds of his soldiers.'

Achilles in Greek mythology, a hero of the ➤ TROJAN *War*, son of Peleus and ➤ THETIS. During his infancy his mother plunged him in the Styx, thus making his body invulnerable except for the heel by which she held him.

When the expedition to Troy was mounted, Thetis tried to protect her son by putting him in the charge of the centaur ➤ CHIRON on the island of Scyros. Odysseus, visiting the island in search of him, found only what appeared to be a group of women, but when a battle-cry was heard one of the girls, the disguised Achilles, revealed himself by seizing sword and shield. Thomas Browne in *Hydriotaphia* (Urn Burial, 1658) gives 'what name Achilles assumed when he hid himself among the women' as the type of a puzzling question, though 'not beyond all conjecture'.

During the Trojan War Achilles withdrew from fighting following a bitter quarrel with ➤ AGAMEMNON. After his friend Patroclus was killed by Hector, Achilles re-entered the battle and killed ➤ HECTOR but was later wounded in the heel by an arrow shot by Paris and died. His armour was seen as an emblem of valour; when it was awarded to ➤ ODYSSEUS, ➤ AJAX committed suicide.

Achilles is one of the central figures of the story of the Trojan War; Homer opens *The Iliad* with the words, 'Achilles' cursed anger sing, O goddess, that son of Peleus, which started a myriad sufferings for the Achaeans.'

Achilles and the tortoise a paradox constructed by the 5th-century Greek philosopher ➤ ZENO, showing that once Achilles has given a tortoise a start he can never overtake it, since each time he arrives where it was, it has already moved on.

Achilles' heel a person's only vulnerable spot; the term is recorded from the early 19th century, and refers to the story of ➤ ACHILLES being plunged into the Styx by his mother to make his body invulnerable, so that the only spot where he could be wounded (and by which he was finally killed) was the heel by which she had held him.

Achilles tendon the tendon attaching the heel to the calf muscle; like ➤ ACHILLES' *heel*, named for the attempt by Thetis to render her son invulnerable by plunging him into the Styx, while grasping him firmly by the heel.

Achitophel in Dryden's allegorical poem ➤ ABSALOM *and Achitophel*, the name given to the earl of Shaftesbury, representing the biblical figure of *Ahitophel*, the friend of David who supported his son's insurrection. In the poem, Achitophel is described as,

> In friendship false, implacable in hate:
> Resolved to ruin or to rule the state.
> — John Dryden *Absalom and Achitophel* (1681)

acid rain rainfall made sufficiently acidic by atmospheric pollution that it causes environmental harm, chiefly to forests and lakes. The main cause is the industrial burning of coal and other fossil fuels, the waste gases from which contain sulphur and nitrogen oxides which combine with atmospheric water to form acids.

acid test a conclusive test for the success or value of something; the reference is to the testing for gold by means of nitric acid.

Acis in Greek mythology, a young shepherd, lover of the sea nymph Galatea (see ➤ GALATEA¹) who was killed out of jealousy by his rival ➤ POLYPHEMUS; as he died, Galatea turned him into a river.

acme the point at which someone or something is best, perfect, or most successful. The word comes (in the late 16th century) from Greek *akmē* 'highest point', and until the 18th century it was often consciously used as a Greek word and often written in Greek letters.

Acmeist denoting or relating to an early 20th century movement in Russian poetry which rejected the values of symbolism in favour of formal technique and clarity of exposition. Notable members were Anna Akhmatova and Osip Mandelstam.

acolyte a person assisting a priest in a religious service or procession; until 1 January 1973, the office of *acolyte* was one of the four Minor Orders of the Roman Catholic Church. Recorded from Middle

English, the word comes via Old French or ecclesiastical Latin, from Greek *akolouthos* 'follower'.

aconite a poisonous plant of the buttercup family, bearing hooded pink or purple flowers and found in temperate regions of the northern hemisphere; an extract of the plant is traditionally used as a poison or in pharmacy, and *aconite* in literary usage may stand for deadly poison.

acorn the fruit of the oak, a smooth oval nut in a rough cup-like base; recorded in Old English in the form *æcern*, the word is of Germanic origin and is related to *acre*; later however it was associated by popular etymology with *oak* and *corn*.

In the UK, an oak-leaf sprig sprig with two acorns is the emblem of the National Trust; the emblem was chosen in 1935 after six designers were invited to submit drawings incorporating a lion, a rose, or an oak, the winner being Joseph Armitage of Lambeth, who chose the oak as being less frequently used in heraldry and easier to reproduce.

See also ➤ *great* OAKS *from little acorns grow.*

acorns were good till bread was found proverbial saying, late 16th century; meaning that until something better is found, what one has will be judged satisfactory.

Acrasia a deceitful enchantress in Spenser's *Faerie Queene* whose home is the luxurious Bower of Bliss; she is the personification of excess or intemperance.

> I fancy the flowers . . . have an Acrasian spell about them.
> — John Keats letter, 1818

acre a unit of land area equal to 4,840 square yards (0.405 hectare). In Old English, *æcer* denoted the amount of land a yoke of oxen could plough in a day; it is a word of Germanic origin, ultimately from an Indo-European root shared by Sanskrit *ajra*, Latin *ager*, and Greek *agros*, 'field'.

See also ➤ GOD's *acre*, ➤ *land of the* BROAD *acres*, ➤ THREE *acres and a cow.*

acre-fight a ghost word; originally glossed in John Cowell's *The Interpreter* (1727 edn.) as 'an old sort of duel fought by single combatants, English and Scotch, between the frontiers of their kingdoms, with sword and lance,' but which in fact appears to be a transliteration of the medieval Latin phrase *acram committere* in the Annals of Burton 1237, where *acram* (for *pugnam*) is a bad translation of Old English *camp* combat, confused with Latin *campus*, French *champ* 'field', and so with English *acre*.

Acres of Diamonds title of a lecture said to have been given over 6,000 times by the American lawyer, clergyman, and educator Russell Herman Conwell (1843–1925); Conwell's view was that opportunities existed for all, and that it was a duty to become wealthy and use the money judiciously for the general good.

acropolis a citadel or fortified part of an ancient Greek city, typically one built on a hill; **the Acropolis** is the name given to the ancient citadel at Athens, containing the Parthenon and other notable buildings, mostly dating from the 5th century BC. The word comes (in the early 17th century) from Greek *akropolis*, from *akron* 'summit' + *polis* 'city'.

acrostic a poem, word puzzle, or other composition in which certain letters in each line form a word or words. The word is recorded from the late 16th century, and comes via French from Greek *akrostikhis*, from *akron* 'end' + *stikhos* 'row, line of verse'.

act see also ➤ *act of* GOD, ➤ *Act of* SETTLEMENT, ➤ *Act of* UNIFORMITY, ➤ *Act of* UNION, ➤ *the* INTOLERABLE *Acts*, ➤ LAND *Acts*, ➤ PLACE *Act*, ➤ REFORM *Act*, ➤ RIOT *Act*, ➤ SIX *Acts*, ➤ TEST *Act*, ➤ THELLUSSON *Act*, ➤ TOLERATION *Act*, ➤ TRUCK *Acts*, ➤ VOLSTEAD *Act*.

Acta Sanctorum a collection of saints' lives, arranged according to the calendar, initiated in early 17th-century Antwerp by a group of Jesuit scholars under the direction of John van Bolland (1596–1665). The series ran to 64 volumes plus supplements (the latter published as 'Analecta Bollandiana').

Actaeon in Greek mythology, a hunter who, because he accidentally saw ➤ ARTEMIS bathing, was changed by her into a stag and killed by his own hounds.

Actes and Monuments title of the martyrology by John Foxe (1516–87); the book, less formally known as *Foxe's Martyrs*, was enormously popular, going through nine editions, each with additional material, between 1563 and 1684. Intended as a history of the Christian Church through the suffering of its martyrs, it focuses in particular on the Protestant martyrs of the 16th and 17th centuries; such famous sayings as the attributed last words of Latimer to Ridley, 'We shall this day light such a candle by God's grace in England, as (I trust) shall never be put out', are to be found in Foxe.

Actian games in ancient Rome, instituted by Octavian (the emperor ➤ AUGUSTUS) in 27 BC to mark his victory in the ➤ *Battle of* ACTIUM.

Action Sermon in the Scottish Presbyterian Church, a sermon preached before Communion.

Action this day annotation as used by Winston Churchill when he returned to office as First Lord of the Admiralty in the wartime Cabinet in 1940.
See also ➤ WINSTON *is back*.

actions speak louder than words proverbial saying, dating from the early 17th century, but first recorded in its current form in the US.

Battle of Actium a naval battle which took place in 31 BC off the promontory of Actium in western Greece, in the course of which Octavian defeated ➤ MARK *Antony*. This cleared the way for Octavian to become sole ruler of Rome as the emperor ➤ AUGUSTUS.

actors St Genesius of Arles, a 4th-century martyr, is the patron saint of actors; according to an apocryphal legend, he was supposed to have been a comic actor who was converted while appearing in anti-Christian satire, and who was then tortured and executed. (An earlier version of the legend makes Genesius a notary, and thus the patron saint of secretaries.)

Actors' Studio an acting workshop in New York City, founded in 1947 by Elia Kazan and others, and a leading centre of method acting.

Acts of the Apostles a New Testament book immediately following the Gospels and relating the history of the early Church, and in particular the missionary journeys of St Paul and others.

acupuncture a system of complementary medicine in which fine needles are inserted in the skin at specific points along what are considered to be lines of energy (meridians), used in the treatment of various physical and mental conditions.
Acupuncture has been practised in China for more than 4,500 years and is increasingly popular in the West. Acupuncturists believe that treatment works by countering an imbalance of energy in the body; recently some scientists have suggested that the needles may stimulate the body's endorphins or naturally occurring painkillers.
The word is recorded from the late 17th century,

and comes from Latin *acu* 'with a needle' + *puncture*.

Adam (in the biblical and Koranic traditions) the name of the first man. According to the Book of Genesis, Adam was created by God as the progenitor of the human race and lived with Eve in the garden of Eden.

In the Bible the Book of Genesis describes how Adam was formed from the dust of the ground and God's breath; Eve, the first woman, was created from one of Adam's ribs as his companion. They lived together in the Garden of Eden until the serpent tempted Eve to eat an apple from the forbidden tree; she persuaded Adam to do the same. As a result of this original sin of disobedience they were both expelled from the garden.

Adam comes from Hebrew *'āḏām* 'man', later taken to be a name.

See also ➤ SECOND *Adam*.

the old Adam the unregenerate condition or character; originally seeing ➤ ADAM as the figure referred to by St Paul in Romans 6:6, 'our old man is crucified with him, that the body of sin might be destroyed.'

When Adam delved and Eve span
Who was then the gentleman?
traditional rhyme associated with the Peasants' Revolt of 1381, and said to have been taken by the priest John Ball as the text of a revolutionary sermon preached at Blackheath, June 1381 (with the crushing of the revolt, John Ball was executed at St Albans on 15 July).

Adam's ale water, as the only drink available in the Garden of Eden; the term is recorded from the mid 17th century.

Adam's apple the projection formed in the neck by the thyroid cartilage. It was so named (in the 18th century) from the notion that a piece of the forbidden fruit became lodged in Adam's throat.

Adam's Bridge a line of shoals lying between NW Sri Lanka and the SE coast of Tamil Nadu in India, separating the Palk Strait from the Gulf of Mannar, traditionally said to be what remains of a causeway built by ➤ RAMA so that his army could cross the strait and rescue his abducted wife ➤ SITA from the demon king of Lanka.

we are all Adam's children (but silk makes the difference) proverbial saying, late 15th century.

Adam's needle popular name for the yucca, recorded from the mid 18th century.

Adam's peak a mountain in Ceylon (Sri Lanka). A rock near the top bears a depression resembling a footprint, which is the focus of religious pilgrimages.

Adam's rib from which ➤ EVE was formed, as in Genesis 2:22, 'And the rib, which the Lord God had taken from man, made he a woman.'

adamant a legendary rock or mineral to which many, often contradictory, properties were attributed, formerly associated with diamond or lodestone. Recorded in Old English, the word comes via Old French and Latin from Greek *adamas, adamant-* 'untameable, invincible', later used to denote the hardest metal or stone, hence diamond.

The phrase *to be adamant* dates from the 1930s, although adjectival use had been implied in such collocations as 'an adamant heart' since the 16th century.

Adamastor in the epic Portuguese poem ➤ *The* LUSIADS, the giant who warns Vasco da Gama that he will wreck ships returning from India at the ➤ CAPE *of Good Hope* (originally known as the *Cape of Storms*).

Adamite a member of a Christian sect advocating nakedness as imitating ➤ ADAM; the term is recorded from the early 17th century.

Adar (in the Jewish calendar) the sixth month of the civil and twelfth of the religious year, usually coinciding with parts of February and March. It is known in leap years as **Second Adar**. Also, an intercalary month preceding this in leap years, also called **First Adar**.

Charles Addams (1912–88), American cartoonist, noted for his macabre and comic drawings, and in particularly for his creation of the ➤ ADDAMS *Family*.

> I see . . . among the women dons, a series of such grotesques . . . from a tall, cadaverous woman with purple hair (really!) to a midget Charles Addams fat creature who has to stand on a stool to get into the soup tureen.
>
> — Sylvia Plath letter, 22 November 1955

Addams Family in the cartoons of ➤ *Charles* ADDAMS, a family of ghouls, ➤ MORTICIA and her husband Gomez, their children Wednesday and Pugsley, and Uncle Fester, whose life in their gothic house on Cemetery Ridge also formed the basis of a television series in the 1960s.

> The mineral deposits . . . tend to contain an Addams Family of heavy metals and sulfur compounds.
> — *High Country News* 19 January 1998

adder a small venomous Eurasian snake which has a dark zigzag pattern on its back, and which is the only poisonous snake in Britain; in biblical and classical translations, *adder* is often used as the word for a poisonous snake. It is also referred to in the Bible (Psalm 58:5) as being deaf, 'like the deaf adder that stoppeth her ear'.

In Old English, the form of the word was *nædre* 'serpent, adder', of Germanic origin. The initial *n* was lost in Middle English by wrong division of *a naddre* (compare *apron, auger*).

if the adder could hear, and the blindworm could see,
neither man nor beast would ever go free. traditional saying, mid 19th century; it was commonly believed that the *blindworm* (the ➤ SLOW-worm) was also poisonous.

adderbolt an old name for a dragonfly, from *adder + bolt* 'the arrow of a crossbow', from the shape of its body.

Joseph Addison (1672–1719), English essayist, poet, dramatist, and Whig politician, noted for his simple, unornamented prose style. In 1711 he founded the *Spectator* with Richard Steele.

Addison of the North nickname of the Scottish lawyer and author Henry Mackenzie (1745–1831), whose writings were held to resemble those of ➤ ADDISON.

as good be an addled egg as an idle bird proverbial saying, late 16th century; meaning that an idle person is of no use.

Addled Parliament dissolved by James I for not passing a single Act between 5 April and 7 June 1614.

Adelphi the name of a group of buildings in London between the Strand and the Thames, laid out by the four brothers, James, John, Robert, and William Adam, and thus called *Adelphi* (from the Greek word for 'brothers'); the name of the theatre in the vicinity of these buildings, at which a certain type of melodrama was prevalent *c.* 1882–1900.

adeptus an epithet for an alchemist professing or believed to have attained the ➤ ARCANUM or great

secret; the word comes from Latin, meaning literally 'having attained'.

Adi Granth the principal sacred scripture of Sikhism. Originally compiled under the direction of Arjan Dev (1563–1606), the fifth Sikh guru, it contains hymns and religious poetry as well as the teachings of the first five gurus. Successive gurus added to the text: the tenth and last guru, Gobind Singh (1666–1708), declared that henceforth there would be no more gurus, the *Adi Granth* taking their place.

The name comes from Sanskrit *ādigrantha*, literally 'first book', based on *grantha* 'literary composition', from *granth* 'to tie'.

Adiaphorists a group of moderate Lutherans who held some Catholic practices condemned by Luther, such as Confirmation and Extreme Unction, to be 'adiaphora' or things regarded as not making an essential difference, and thus matters on which concessions could be made.

Aditi in Hindu belief, a primeval goddess who is the mother of many gods.

admass a term coined by the English writer and critic J. B. Priestley (1894–1984) in 1955 to describe the proliferation of commercial advertising and high-pressure salesmanship.

> I had celebrated their unsophisticated honesty, defending them against the smug contempt of admass man.
> — *Farley Mowat A Whale for the Killing* (1972)

admirable see ➤ CRICHTON.

admiral a commander of a fleet or naval squadron. Recorded from Middle English (denoting an emir or Saracen commander), the word comes via Old French and medieval Latin from Arabic *'amīr* 'commander'. The ending *-al* was from Arabic *-al-* 'of the', used in titles (e.g. *'amīr-al-'umarā* 'ruler of rulers'), later assimilated to the familiar Latinate suffix *-al*.

See also ➤ *Admiral of the* BLUE, ➤ *Admiral of the* RED, ➤ *Admiral of the* WHITE, ➤ YELLOW *admiral*.

Admiral's Cup a yacht-racing competition held every two years since 1957 between international teams of three yachts. The competition consists of inshore stages in the Solent and offshore races across the English Channel and around the Fastnet rock.

admiralty see also ➤ BLACK *Book of the Admiralty*, ➤ DROIT *of Admiralty*.

the price of admiralty the cost of having command of the seas, in a phrase coined by Kipling:

> If blood be the price of admiralty Good God, we ha' paid in full!
> — Rudyard Kipling *Song of the English* (1893)

Admonitioners the Puritans who in 1571 presented 'an admonition' to Parliament, condemning the ceremonies of the Church of England.

St Adomnan (*c*.625–704), abbot of Iona from 679, who is said by Bede to have been the author of a work on 'The Holy Places'; he is also credited with writing an extant work on St Columba.
☐ **FEAST DAY** His feast day is 23 September.

Adonai a Hebrew name for God.

Adonais the name given by Shelley to Keats in the pastoral elegy *Adonais* (1821), written on the death of Keats, and likening him, with other poets who had died young, to the Greek god of beauty and fertility; the origin of the name *Adonais* is unclear, but it may represent the name ➤ ADONIS, or the Hebrew ➤ ADONAI.

Adonia in ancient Greece, an eight-day festival of ➤ ADONIS.

Adonis in classical mythology, a beautiful youth loved by both Aphrodite and Persephone. He was killed by a boar, but Zeus decreed that he should spend the winter of each year in the underworld with Persephone and the summer months with Aphrodite. According to the legend, the rose sprang from the earth where his blood was shed.

In extended usage, an *Adonis* is an extremely handsome young man. In the *Examiner* of 22 March 1812, Leigh Hunt wrote of the Prince Regent, 'This Adonis in loveliness was a corpulent man of fifty'; Hunt and his brother John were prosecuted as a result, and sentenced to two years' imprisonment.

Adoptionist a person maintaining that Jesus Christ is the son of God by adoption only; the term is recorded from the mid 19th century.

Adrastus a mythical Greek king of Argos who was the leader of the army of the ➤ SEVEN *against Thebes* in their attempt to set Polynices on the throne of Thebes.

Adrian IV (*c*.1100–59), pope 1154–9; born *Nicholas Breakspear*. He is the only Englishman to have held this office. He assisted Henry II of England to gain control of Ireland and opposed Frederick I's (Barbarossa's) claims to power.

Adriatic see ➤ MARRIAGE *of the Adriatic*.

cave of Adullam in the Bible, the cave in the hills of Judah in which ➤ DAVID hid from Saul (1 Samuel 22:10), and where his supporters gathered to him.

Adullamite a member of a group of Liberal rebels in the House of Commons in 1866 who were opposed to the Reform Bill; the term comes from a speech by the Liberal politician and reformer John Bright (1811–89) about their leader Robert Lowe:

> The right hon Gentleman . . . has retired into what may be called his political Cave of Adullam—and he has called about him every one that was in distress and every one that was discontented.
> — John Bright speech in the House of Commons, 13 March 1866

adult see ➤ CONSENTING *adult*.

Advaita in Hinduism, a Vedantic doctrine that identifies the individual self (*atman*) with the ground of reality (*brahman*). It is associated especially with the Indian philosopher Shankara (*c*.788–820).

Advance Australia a catchphrase used as a patriotic slogan or motto in Australia, and recorded from the mid 19th century.

Advance Australia Fair the national anthem of Australia, composed *c*.1878 by P. D. McCormick (*c*.1834–1916), a Scot, under the pen-name 'Amicus'. It officially replaced 'God Save the Queen' in 1984.

Advent the first season of the Church year, leading up to Christmas and including the four preceding Sundays. The name is recorded from Old English, and comes from Latin *adventus* 'arrival', in Christian writings applied particularly to the coming of the Saviour.

See also ➤ SEVEN *O's of Advent*.

Advent calendar a calendar made of card containing small numbered flaps, one of which is opened on each day of Advent to reveal a picture appropriate to the season.

Advent candle a candle lit during Advent; especially each candle in a ring of four, lit on successive Sundays in Advent to symbolize the coming of light into the world at Christmas (when a fifth central candle completes the group).

Advent Sunday the first Sunday in Advent; in the Western Church the Sunday closest to St Andrew's

Day (30 November); in the Orthodox Church *Advent Sunday* falls in the middle of November.

Advent wreath a wreath of evergreen foliage in which four candles are set, one to be lit on each Sunday of Advent.

Adventist a member of a sect holding millenarian views; the term is recorded from the mid 19th century.

See also ➤ SECOND *Adventist,* ➤ SEVENTH-*Day Adventist.*

adventurers see ➤ DORCHESTER *Company of Adventurers,* ➤ MERCHANT *Adventurers.*

adventures are to the adventurous proverbial saying; mid 19th century.

the Adversary Satan, the Devil, as in 1 Peter 5:8, 'Your adversary the devil, as a roaring lion, walketh about, seeking whom he may devour.'

Adversity Hume the British radical politician Joseph Hume (1777–1855), who in 1826 moved a motion in Parliament (which was defeated) pressing for an inquiry into the causes of distress throughout the country which he believed presaged a national disaster; he was opposed by the more sanguine Chancellor, ➤ *Prosperity* ROBINSON.

adversity makes strange bedfellows proverbial saying; mid 19th century.

advertisers St Bernardine of Siena (1380–1444), a Franciscan friar famous for his popular preaching, is the patron saint of advertisers.

advocate in the Roman law courts, and in those countries (such as Scotland and France) which retain the Roman law, one whose profession is to plead the cause of someone in a court of justice, a barrister; in the UK, the **Faculty of Advocates** is the society constituting the Scottish Bar.

Recorded from Middle English, the word comes ultimately from Latin *advocare* 'call (to one's aid), summon'.

See also ➤ DEVIL'*s advocate.*

Advocates' Library in Edinburgh, founded by Sir George Mackenzie (1636–91) in 1689 as the library of the Faculty of Advocates, and from 1925 the National Library of Scotland.

advowson in ecclesiastical law, the right to recommend a member of the Anglican clergy for a vacant benefice, or to make such an appointment. The word is recorded from Middle English, in the sense

'patronage of a religious house or benefice' with the obligation to defend it and speak for it, and comes ultimately from Latin *advocare* 'summon'.

adytum the innermost sanctuary of an ancient Greek temple. The word comes via Latin from Greek *aduton,* neuter singular of *adutos* 'impenetrable'.

aedile either of two (later four) Roman magistrates responsible for public buildings and originally also for the public games and the supply of corn to the city. The word comes (in the mid 16th century) from Latin *aedilis* 'concerned with buildings'.

Aegeon in Greek mythology, another name for the giant ➤ BRIAREUS.

Aegeus in Greek mythology, king of Athens and father of ➤ THESEUS, who threw himself into the sea in the (mistaken) belief that his son had been killed by the ➤ MINOTAUR; according to some, this was the origin of the name of the *Aegean Sea.*

Aegir in Scandinavian mythology, the god of the sea.

aegis in classical art and mythology, an attribute of Zeus and Athena (or their Roman counterparts Jupiter and Minerva) usually represented as a goatskin shield. The word (denoting armour or a shield, especially that of a god) is recorded from the early 17th century and comes ultimately from Greek *aigis* 'shield of Zeus'.

Aegisthus in Greek mythology, the lover of his cousin's wife Clytemnestra, who killed her husband ➤ AGAMEMNON; Aegisthus and Clytemnestra were in turn killed by her son ➤ ORESTES.

aegrotat a certificate stating that a university student is too ill to attend an examination; an examination pass awarded to a student having such a certificate. The word comes (in the late 18th century) from Latin, and means literally 'he is sick'.

AEIOU initial letters of a motto adopted as a device by the Emperor Frederick III of Austria in 1440, and unexplained in his lifetime; from papers found after his death, it appears that the letters stood for the Latin phrase *Austriae est Imperare Orbe Universo* 'All the earth is subject to Austria', but many other interpretations have been suggested.

Aelfric (*c.*955–*c.*1020), Anglo-Saxon monk, writer, and grammarian. His chief works are the *Catholic Homilies* (990–2) and the *Lives of the Saints* (993–6), both written in Old English. He also wrote a Latin grammar, which earned him the name *Grammaticus*.

Aelia Capitolina the new city which the Emperor Hadrian built *c*.130 AD on the site of Jerusalem (destroyed by ➤ TITUS in 70 AD).

Aelius see ➤ *Aelius* DONATUS.

Aeneas in classical mythology, a Trojan leader, son of Anchises and Aphrodite, and legendary ancestor of the Romans. When Troy fell to the Greeks he escaped and after wandering for many years eventually reached Italy. The story of his voyage is recounted in Virgil's *Aeneid*.

Aeneid the epic poem by the Roman poet Virgil (70–19 BC) telling the story of Aeneas's wanderings after the fall of Troy, and the settlement in Italy which made him ancestor of the Roman people; the poem opens *Arma virumque cano* [Arms and the man I sing]'.

Aeolian harp a stringed instrument producing musical sounds on exposure to a current of air; the name comes from ➤ AEOLUS, Greek god of the winds.

Aeolian mode in music, the mode represented by the natural diatonic scale A–A (containing a minor 3rd, 6th, and 7th). The term is recorded from the late 18th century, and comes from Latin *Aeolius* 'from Aeolis' (an ancient coastal district of Asia Minor).

Aeolus in Greek mythology, the god of the winds; in Homer's *Odyssey*, a mortal to whom Zeus had given command of the winds, and who in Virgil's *Aeneid* is shown as keeping them imprisoned in a cave.

aeon an age of the universe, an immeasurable time; the personification of an age, and in Neoplatonism, Platonism, and Gnosticism, a power existing from eternity; an emanation or phase of the supreme deity. The word is recorded from the mid 17th century and comes via ecclesiastical Latin from Greek *aiōn*.

aeromancy originally (in late Middle English) a term for divination by air, including augury; in the 17th century, this passed into the idea of weather-forecasting.

Aeschines (*c*.390–*c*.314 BC), Athenian orator and statesman. He opposed Demosthenes' efforts to unite the Greek city states against Macedon, with which he attempted to make peace. Aeschines was tried for treason in 343 but was acquitted, and left Athens for Rhodes in 330.

Aeschylus (*c*.525–*c*.456 BC), Greek dramatist. Aeschylus is best known for his trilogy the *Oresteia* (458 BC, consisting of the tragedies *Agamemnon*, *Choephoroe*, and *Eumenides*), which tells the story of ➤ AGAMEMNON's murder at the hands of his wife Clytemnestra and the vengeance of their son ➤ ORESTES.

Aesculapian snake a long, slender olive-brown to greyish snake found in Europe and SW Asia. In ancient times it was protected owing to its mythical link with the god of healing, ➤ AESCULAPIUS.

Aesculapius in Roman mythology, the god of medicine; equivalent of the Greek ➤ ASCLEPIUS.

Aesir the Norse gods and goddesses collectively, including Odin, Thor, and Balder.

Aesop (6th century BC), Greek storyteller. The moral animal fables associated with him were probably collected from many sources, and initially communicated orally; they were later popularized by the Roman poet Phaedrus, who translated some of them into Latin. Aesop is said to have lived as a slave on the island of Samos.

Aesthetic Movement a literary and artistic movement which flourished in England in the 1880s, devoted to 'art for art's sake' and rejecting the notion that art should have a social or moral purpose. Its chief exponents included Oscar Wilde, Max Beerbohm, Aubrey Beardsley, and others associated with the journal the *Yellow Book*. Their dedication to the ideal of beauty was often carried to extravagant lengths.

The word is recorded from the late 18th century, in the sense 'relating to perception by the senses', and comes ultimately from Greek *aisthesthai* 'perceive'. The sense 'concerned with beauty' was coined in German in the mid 18th century and adopted into English in the early 19th century, but its use was controversial until much later in the century.

St Aethelwold (?908–84), English monk, dean of the monastery of Glastonbury when Dunstan was abbot. He subsequently re-established a monastic house at Abingdon, introducing the strict Benedictine rule from Fleury, and co-operated with Dunstan and Oswald in the Benedictine Reforms of his century. He was also an important figure in the revival of learning, as his pupil Aelfric testifies.

☐ **FEAST DAY** His feast day is 1 August (2 August at Abingdon).

aetites a stone with a loose nucleus, formerly believed to be found in eagles' nests and to have magical and medicinal properties; the name comes via Latin from Greek *aetos* 'eagle'.

affair see ➤ *Affair of the* DIAMOND *Necklace*, ➤ *Affair of the* POISONS.

affluent society a society in which material wealth is widely distributed; often with allusion to the book of that title (1958) by the American economist John Kenneth Galbraith.

afraid with any amazement the words 'be not afraid with any amazement' occur in the marriage service in the *Book of Common Prayer* (1666).

afreet in Arabian and Muslim mythology, a powerful jinn or demon; the word is recorded in English from the late 18th century, and comes from Arabic '*ifrīt.*

ex Africa semper aliquid novi Latin sentence meaning, 'Always something new out of Africa', popular form of the comment in Pliny's *Historia Naturalis*, '*Semper aliquid novi Africam adferre* [Africa always brings [us] something new].'

African American an American of African origin, the currently accepted term in the US for Americans of African origin, having first become prominent in the late 1980s.

Afrikaans a language of southern Africa, derived from the form of Dutch brought to the Cape by Protestant settlers in the 17th century. It is an official language of South Africa, spoken by around 6 million people.

Afrikaner an Afrikaans-speaking white person in South Africa, especially one of Dutch descent.

after a sort, as Costlet served the King proverbial expression, early 18th century; referring to the story of a captain in Cromwell's army who asserted that he served the king 'after a sort'.

after a storm comes a calm proverbial saying; late 14th century.

after dinner rest a while, after supper walk a mile proverbial saying; late 16th century; the implication is that dinner is a heavy meal, while supper is a light one.

aga a former Ottoman title for a military commander or (later) an official of any of various ranks; now, a title of respect for a Turkish landowner.

Aga Khan the spiritual leader of the Khoja branch of Ismalian Muslims. The first Aga Khan was given his title in 1818 by the shah of Persia and subsequently moved with the majority of the Nizaris to the Indian subcontinent.

Aga saga a type of popular novel set in a semi-rural location and concerning the domestic and emotional lives of articulate, middle-class characters, associated particularly with the novels of Joanna Trollope; a book of this genre is a saga of family life against a comfortable background typified by possession of a kitchen with an *Aga* stove, notionally an emblem of middle-class life and representing a sustained cosiness.

Agamemnon in Greek mythology, king of Mycenae and brother of Menelaus, commander-in-chief of the Greek forces in the ➤ TROJAN *War*. On his return home from Troy he was murdered by his wife Clytemnestra and her lover ➤ AEGISTHUS; his murder was avenged by his son ➤ ORESTES and daughter Electra.

brave men lived before Agamemnon proverbial saying, early 19th century; the Roman poet Horace (65–8 BC) has, 'Many brave men lived before Agamemnon's time; but they are all, unmourned and unknown, covered by the long night, because they lack their sacred poet.'

Aganippe in Greek mythology, a fountain at the foot of Mount Helicon, dedicated to the Muses, a source of poetic inspiration.

agape in Christian theology, Christian love, especially as distinct from erotic love or simple affection; a communal meal in token of Christian fellowship, as held by early Christians in commemoration of the ➤ LAST *Supper*. The word is recorded from the early 17th century, and comes from Greek *agapē* 'brotherly love'.

Agapemone an association of men and women established at Spaxton in Somerset by the Reverend Henry James Prince, and a similar establishment conducted by his successor, the Reverend John Hugh Smyth-Pigott, at Clapton, London; in extended (and often derogatory usage) an establishment of this kind, where free love is practised. The name is formed irregularly from Greek *agapē* 'love' + *monē* 'abode'.

Agapetae in the early Church, ascetic women who, having taken vows of virginity, contracted spiritual marriage with monks.

agate a hard semi-transparent variegated chalcedony, usually with colours arranged in bands, which according to Pliny was thought to counteract the bites of spiders and scorpions, and to be able when burnt to avert storms and stop the flow of rivers. There was also said to be an agate of a single colour which could make athletes invincible.

St Agatha a virgin martyr, said to have died at Catania in Sicily. According to later legend, when a pagan consul invoked edicts against Christianity in order to seduce her, she was imprisoned in a brothel and tortured, her breasts being cut off; she died in prison.

She is invoked against fire (especially the eruptions of Mount Etna) and diseases of the breast; she is also patroness of bell-founders. Her emblem in art is a dish with her breasts on it, sometimes mistaken for a dish with two loaves.

□ **FEAST DAY** Her feast day is 5 February.

Agave in classical mythology, the daughter of ➤ CADMUS and Harmonia and mother of Pentheus. In Euripides' *The Bacchae*, she refuses to acknowledge the divinity of ➤ DIONYSUS, and as punishment is driven mad as a ➤ BACCHANT; in their frenzy, she and her companions tear Pentheus apart.

The name *Agave* comes from the Greek word *agauos* 'illustrious'; it is now also the name of a genus of plants of which the chief species is the American Aloe, whose flower-stem (which may be forty feet high) is produced only when the plant arrives at maturity (between the ages of 10 and 70 years).

Agdistis in Phrygian mythology, a mother goddess who is the equivalent of ➤ CYBELE.

age a distinctive period of human history, real or mythical.

See also ➤ *Age of* AQUARIUS, ➤ *age of* CONSENT, ➤ *age of* DISCRETION, ➤ *the age of* MIRACLES *is past*, ➤ *Age of* REASON, ➤ DARK *Ages*, ➤ GOLDEN *Age*, ➤ ICE *Age*, ➤ *if* YOUTH *knew, if age could*, ➤ MIDDLE *Ages*, ➤ ROCK *of Ages*, ➤ STONE *Age*.

Agenor in Greek mythology, king of Tyre, father of ➤ CADMUS and ➤ EUROPA.

Agenda 21 a prioritized agenda for implementing action to safeguard and improve the world environment for the 21st century, which was drafted at the Earth Summit in Rio in 1992.

Agent Orange a defoliant chemical used by the US in the Vietnam War.

> High interest rates work on Birmingham like Agent Orange. No one in any part of the city is enjoying life.
> — Edward Pearce *Election Rides* (1992)

agent provocateur an agent employed to tempt suspected persons into committing an incriminating act; the term is French, and is recorded in English from the late 19th century.

agents see ➤ CROWN *Agents*.

Aggie Weston's informal name for the Royal Sailors' Rest Homes founded by Dame Agnes E. Weston (1840–1918).

Battle of Agincourt a battle in northern France in 1415 during the Hundred Years War, in which the English under Henry V defeated a large French army. The victory, achieved largely by use of the longbow, allowed Henry to occupy Normandy and consolidate his claim to the French throne.

Aglaia in Greek mythology, one of the ➤ THREE *Graces*.

Agnes see also ➤ BLACK *Agnes*.

St Agnes (died *c*.304), Roman martyr, said to have been a Christian virgin who refused to marry, she was martyred during the reign of Diocletian. She is the patron saint of virgins and her emblem is a lamb (Latin *agnus*).

□ **FEAST DAY** Her feast day is 21 January.

Maria Gaetana Agnesi (1718–99), Italian mathematician and philosopher, regarded as the first female mathematician of the Western world. Her major work, produced in 1748, was a comprehensive treatment of algebra and analysis, of which perhaps the most important part was concerned with differential calculus.

Agnoetae a Monophysite sect of the 6th century holding that Jesus was ignorant of some things. The name comes ultimately from Greek *agnoein* 'be ignorant'.

agnostic a person holding the view that nothing can be known of the existence of God or anything beyond material phenomena. The word is recorded from the mid 19th century, and comes from *a-* 'not' + *gnostic* 'of or relating to knowledge'; it was coined by ➤ *Thomas Henry* HUXLEY (1825–95) to describe his own beliefs. R. H. Hutton wrote in a letter of 13 March 1881 that the word was 'Suggested by Prof. Huxley at a party held previous to the formation of the now defunct Metaphysical Society…one evening in 1869, in my hearing. He took it from St. Paul's mention of the altar to "the Unknown God."'

Agnus Dei Latin phrase meaning 'Lamb of God', in the Christian Church a name for Christ, recorded from late Middle English; *Agnus Dei* is used both for an invocation beginning with the words 'Lamb of God' forming a set part of the Mass, and a figure of a lamb bearing a cross or flag, as an emblem of Christ.

agonistes an epithet of a person who takes part in a struggle or contest, a protagonist; used in allusion to Milton's poem *Samson Agonistes* (1671). In ancient Greece, *agōnistēs* meant 'a contestant', coming from *agōn* 'contest'.

agony extreme physical or mental suffering; the final stages of a difficult or painful death. Recorded from Middle English (originally denoting 'mental' anguish alone, as that of Christ in the ➤ *Garden of* GETHSEMANE), the word comes via Old French and late Latin from Greek *agōnia*, from *agōn* 'contest'. The sense of 'physical' suffering dates from the early 17th century.

agony aunt the female author of a newspaper column providing answers to readers' questions about personal difficulties.

agony column originally (in the mid 19th century) the column of a newspaper containing special advertisements, particularly those for missing relatives or friends, and thus containing evidence of great distress. Later (the current meaning), a column in a newspaper or magazine offering advice on personal problems to readers who write in.

the Agony in the Garden the anguish of Christ in the ➤ *Garden of* GETHSEMANE, as in Luke 22:44, 'And being in an agony he prayed more earnestly'; *agony* in this passage is used in Wyclif's translation.

agora in ancient Greece, a public open space used for assemblies and markets; the term **agoraphobia** for extreme or irrational fear of open or public places, leading to panic attacks and reclusive behaviour, derives from this.

Agra a city on the River Jumna in Uttar Pradesh state, northern India. Founded in 1566, Agra was the capital of the Mogul empire until 1658.

Agramant in *Orlando Innamorato* and *Orlando Furioso*, the emperor of Africa, said to be a descendant of Alexander the Great, who leads his armies against Charlemagne.

Agrarian Revolution the transformation of British agriculture during the 18th century, characterized by the enclosure of common land (see ➤ COMMON) and the introduction of technological innovations such as the seed drill and the rotation of crops.

they agree like bells, they want nothing but hanging traditional saying, mid 16th century.

Gnaeus Julius Agricola (AD 40–93), Roman general and governor of Britain 78–84. As governor he completed the subjugation of Wales and defeated the Scottish Highland tribes at the battle of Mons Graupius.

agricultural workers ➤ *St* PHOCAS, St Walstan, an English saint with a local cult in Norfolk among farmers and farm labourers of the Middle Ages, and ➤ *St* ISIDORE *the Farmer*, are the patron saints of agricultural workers.

agrimony a plant of the rose family which bears slender flower spikes and hooked fruits, found in north temperate regions, which was formerly used in herbal medicine and dyeing. The name comes (in late Middle English) via Old French from a Latin alteration of the Greek *argemōnē* 'poppy'.

Marcus Vipsanius Agrippa (63–12 BC), Roman general. Augustus' adviser and son-in-law, he played an important part in the naval victories over Mark Antony, and held commands in western and eastern provinces of the empire.

Ahab a king of ancient Israel who persecuted the prophets, husband of ➤ JEZEBEL, who allowed her persecution and arranged killing of ➤ NABOTH; Ahab was warned by the prophet ➤ ELIJAH that his sin would bring disaster on his dynasty.

Captain Ahab in Herman Melville's novel *Moby Dick* (1851), the whaling captain whose leg has been bitten off by the white whale, ➤ MOBY *Dick*, and who is monomaniacally determined on revenge; his obsession leads, after a three-day pursuit, to the destruction of his ship, the *Pequod*, and the deaths of all but one (see ➤ ISHMAEL) of her crew.

> There are no moral dilemmas for Fergusson, a couthy blend of Captain Ahab and Captain Bligh.
> — *Glasgow Herald* 31 May 1996

Ahasuerus name given in the Hebrew scriptures to the Emperor Xerxes, husband of ➤ ESTHER. *Ahasuerus* is also the name of a king in the Book of Daniel, and is traditionally the name of the ➤ WAN-DERING *Jew*.

Ahaz a king of ancient Israel; the **dial of Ahaz** is the only device for measuring time mentioned in the Bible.

ahimsa in the Hindu, Buddhist, and Jainist tradition, respect for all living things and avoidance of violence towards others. The word comes from Sanskrit, from *a* 'non-, without' + *hiṃsā* 'violence'.

Ahitophel the treacherous counsellor of King David who deserted to ➤ ABSALOM, and hanged himself when Absalom ignored his advice (2 Samuel 17:23).
    See also ➤ ACHITOPHEL.

Ahmed a prince in the Arabian Nights who during a quest meets, falls in love with, and marries the fairy Peri-Banou; he is also the owner of a magic apple with restorative powers which cures a sick princess.

Aholah and **Aholibah** in the Bible (Ezekiel ch. 23), two sisters who personify prostitution, and will be destroyed for their sins; in the prophecy of Ezekiel, Aholah is said to stand for Samaria and Aholibah for Jerusalem.

ahoy an exclamation announcing the sighting of land from a ship. The word comes (in the mid 18th century) from the exclamation *ah* + *hoy*! 'look!'.

Ahriman the evil spirit in the doctrine of ➤ ZORO-ASTRIANISM, the opponent of ➤ AHURA *Mazda*.

Ahura Mazda the creator god of Zoroastrianism, the force for good and the opponent of ➤ AHRIMAN; also called ➤ ORMAZD. The name is Avestan, and means literally 'wise deity'.

St Aidan (d. AD 651), Irish missionary. While a monk in the monastery at Iona he set out to Christianize Northumbria, founding a church and monastery at Lindisfarne in 635 and becoming its first bishop.
    ☐ **FEAST DAY** His feast day is 31 August.

aide-toi, le Ciel t'aidera 'help yourself, and heaven will help you', a line from *Fables* (1668) by the French poet Jean de la Fontaine (1621–95), a version of the proverb ➤ GOD *helps them that help themselves.*

Aids acquired immune deficiency syndrome, a disease in which there is a severe loss of the body's cellular immunity, greatly lowering the resistance to infection and malignancy. Aids was first identified in the early 1980s and now affects millions of people. In the developed world the disease first spread among homosexuals, intravenous drug users, and recipients of infected blood transfusions, before reaching the wider population. This has tended to overshadow a greater epidemic in parts of Africa, where transmission is mainly through heterosexual contact.

Aintree a suburb of Liverpool, site of a racecourse over which the Grand National is run.

air regarded as one of the four ➤ ELEMENTS in ancient and medieval philosophy and in astrology (it is considered essential to the nature of the signs of Gemini, Aquarius, and Libra).
    See also ➤ CASTLES *in the air.*

air travellers St Joseph of Copertino, a 17th-century Franciscan priest born near Brindisi and noted for his levitations, and Our lady of ➤ LORETO, are the patron saints of airmen and airwomen and air passengers.

aircraft see ➤ *one of our aircraft is* MISSING.

airlift see ➤ BERLIN *airlift.*

airport art a work of ethnic art or craft of the type displayed and sold at some airports, viewed dismissively as being copied or mass-produced for the tourist market. **Airport fiction** is a similar term for a type of light, popular fiction sold at airports as ideal for in-flight reading.

airway see ➤ PURPLE *airway.*

aitchbone the buttock or rump bone of cattle, or a cut of beef lying over this. The term is recorded from the late 15th century and comes from dialect *nache* 'rump', ultimately from Latin *natis* 'buttock(s)'; the initial *n* in *a nache bone* was (as in ➤ ADDER) lost by wrong division.

Ajanta Caves a series of caves in the state of Maharashtra, south central India, containing Buddhist frescoes and sculptures dating from the 1st century BC to the 7th century AD.

Ajax in Greek mythology, a hero of the Trojan war, the son of Telamon, king of Salamis; he was proverbial for his size and strength. After the death of

➤ ACHILLES, he quarrelled with Odysseus as to which of them should have Achilles' armour; when it was awarded to Odysseus, Ajax committed suicide.

He is sometimes referred to as **the Greater Ajax** to distinguish him from **the Lesser Ajax**, son of Oileus, leader of the Locrian forces who fought on the Greek side at Troy.

Akali a member of a militant Sikh political group. The name comes from Punjabi, and means literally 'follower of the Immortal One'.

akasha in Hinduism and other religions, a supposed universal etheric field in which a record of past events is imprinted.

Jalaludin Muhammad Akbar (1542–1605), Moghul Emperor from 1556, known as **Akbar the Great**. Akbar expanded the Mogul empire to incorporate northern India and established an efficient but enlightened administration; among his measures were the abolition of slavery and the prohibition of the practice of suttee.

Akela name of the leader of the wolf pack in Kipling's *Jungle Books* (1894–5); he is known as the *Lone Wolf*, and his name comes from Hindi *akelā* 'single, solitary'.

The name is used informally for the adult leader of a group of Cub Scouts (formerly Wolf Cubs).

Akhenaten (14th century BC), Egyptian pharaoh of the 18th dynasty, reigned 1379–1362 BC, who came to the throne as Amenhotep IV. The husband of ➤ NEFERTITI, he introduced the monotheistic solar cult of ➤ ATEN and moved the capital from Thebes to the newly built city of Akhetaten. He was succeeded by his son-in-law, ➤ TUTANKHAMEN, who abandoned the new religion early in his reign.

Akhetaten an ancient Egyptian capital built by Akhenaten in *c.*1375 BC when he established the new worship of the sun disc Aten. It was abandoned four years after his death, when the court returned to the former capital, Thebes.

Akkad the capital city which gave its name to an ancient kingdom traditionally founded by Sargon in north central Mesopotamia. Its site is lost.

Akkadian the extinct language of Akkad, written in cuneiform, with two dialects, Assyrian and Babylonian, widely used from about 3500 BC. It is the oldest Semitic language for which records exist.

Akond title (*Akhund* 'spiritual leader') of Saidu Baba (d. 1877) the ruler and high priest of Swat, a region of the northwestern part of the Indian subcontinent, whose tomb is a major shrine in the area. The English poet Edward Lear, who travelled to India in 1872, had his fancy caught by the title:

> Who, or why, or which, or what,
> Is the Akond of Swat?
> — Edward Lear 'The Akond of Swat' (composed 27 July 1873)

akrasia the state of mind in which someone acts against their better judgement through weakness of will. The word comes (in the early 19th century) from Greek, from *a-* 'without' + *kratos* 'power, strength'. The term is used especially with reference to Aristotle's *Nicomachean Ethics*.

Aksum a town in the province of Tigray in northern Ethiopia, which was a religious centre and the capital of a powerful kingdom between the 1st and 6th centuries AD.

Alabama claims made by the US against Britain for losses caused in the Civil War by British-built Confederate ships, particularly the cruiser *Alabama*, which captured or destroyed 66 ships before being itself sunk in June 1864. The case helped establish international rulings for the limitations on a neutral government in wartime, and in 1872 the tribunal decided that Britain was legally liable for losses caused by the *Alabama* and other ships.

> I can still get angry at the tale
> Of their letting the *Alabama* sail.
> — Alice Duer Miller *The White Cliffs* (1941)

See also ➤ TRENT *affair*.

Aladdin in the Arabian Nights, the name of a poor boy in China who becomes master of a magic lamp (➤ ALADDIN'*s lamp*) and ring; he has a palace built for him by the ➤ SLAVE *of the Lamp*, and marries the Sultan's daughter.

The story first became a pantomime in England in 1788; in 1861 H. J. Byron's dramatization established what are now some of the main pantomime features. Aladdin's mother was named *Widow Twankay* (see ➤ WIDOW *Twankey*), and the magician who tries to steal the lamp was named *Abanazar*.

Aladdin's cave a cave full of treasures revealed to ➤ ALADDIN by a magician; shut inside by the magician, he escapes with the aid of a magic ring (which summons the *Slave of the Ring*) and returns to his mother with the lamp which he has found in the cave (➤ ALADDIN'*s lamp*).

Aladdin's cave is used allusively for a repository of treasures.

> Officers are said to have recovered an Aladdin's Cave of cash, heroin and cocaine—plus several mobile phones.
> — *Daily Star* 2 July 1992

Aladdin's lamp in the story of ➤ ALADDIN, a magic lamp (sought by a magician) which Aladdin finds in the cave of treasure into which he is sent; when he escapes and takes it home, he and his mother discover that rubbing it summons a powerful genie, the ➤ SLAVE *of the Lamp*, who has the power to grant any request.

Alamein see ➤ *Battle of* EL *Alamein.*

Alamo the Franciscan mission which was the site of a desperate and ultimately unsuccessful defence against Santa Ana in the Texan War of Independence; on 6 March 1836, it was captured by Mexican troops, and all the defenders (including ➤ *Davy* CROCKETT) were killed. The sentence on the Alamo memorial in Austin (attributed to Thomas Jefferson Green, 1801–63) reads, 'Thermopylae had her messenger of defeat—the Alamo had none.'

In the battle of San Jacinto, 21 April 1836, where the Texans defeated the Mexican forces and captured Santa Ana, troops used the battle-cry (attributed to Colonel Sidney Sherman) 'Remember the Alamo!'

alant a large hunting-dog of the Middle Ages; a wolfhound; in heraldry also, a short-eared mastiff.

Alaric (*c.*370–410), king of the Visigoths 395–410. Alaric invaded Greece (395–6) and then Italy (400–3), but was checked on each occasion by the Roman general Stilicho. He invaded Italy again in 408 and in 410 captured Rome.

alarm an anxious awareness of danger; a warning of danger. The word is recorded from late Middle English, as an exclamation meaning 'to arms!', and comes via French from Italian *all' arme!* 'to arms!'.

alarums and excursions confused noise and bustle; from a stage direction occurring in slightly varying forms in a number of Shakespeare's history plays, as *3 Henry VI* and *Richard III.*

alastor in Greek mythology, a relentless or avenging spirit, a nemesis; *Alastor* is the name give by Shelley to a poem (1816) which depicts an evil spirit driving a poet to despair and death, because he cannot be satisfied with domestic affection and human sympathy.

St Alban (3rd century), the first British Christian martyr, a native of Verulamium (now St Albans). Alban was converted and baptized by a fugitive priest whom he sheltered. When soldiers searched his house, he put on the priest's cloak and was arrested and condemned to death.
  □ **FEAST DAY** His feast day is 22 June.

Albany an ancient name for the northern part of Scotland, which from the Middle Ages was a royal title; ➤ *Charles Edward* STUART, the *Young Pretender*, styled himself **Count of Albany**, and his illegitimate daughter Charlotte (1753–89) was legitimated by him as **Duchess of Albany**.

In London, *Albany* is the name of an exclusive block of flats in Piccadilly. Built in 1770 on the site of an earlier property by the architect William Chambers (1726–96), in 1791 it was purchased by George III's son Frederick, Duke of York and Albany, after whom it was named York House. In 1802 it was converted into 'residential chambers for bachelor gentlemen', being renamed **Albany House** in 1803.

Albany beef a former name for the flesh of the sturgeon, because the fish was once found in abundance in the waters of the Hudson River around *Albany*, the capital of New York State.

albatross the *albatross* is traditionally believed to bring bad luck, and the word is used for a source of frustration or guilt or an encumbrance, in allusion to Coleridge's poem about the ➤ ANCIENT *Mariner* and his shooting of the bird.

Alberich in German legend, the king of the elves, equivalent of French ➤ OBERON; in the ➤ NIBELUNGENLIED he is the guardian of the Nibelung treasure who is defeated by ➤ SIEGFRIED. In Wagner's ➤ RING *Cycle*, Alberich is a dwarf who steals the Rhinemaidens' gold.

Prince Albert (1819–61), consort to Queen Victoria. Born a prince of Saxe-Coburg-Gotha and first cousin of the queen, he was involved in planning the Great Exhibition of 1851, the profits of which allowed the construction of the Royal Albert Hall (1871). He died prematurely from typhoid fever; Tennyson's dedication to him of the 1862 edition of *Idylls of the King* read:

> Wearing the white flower of a blameless life,
> Before a thousand peering littlenesses,
> In that fierce light which beats upon a throne,
> And blackens every blot.
> — Lord Tennyson *Idylls of the King* (dedication, 1862 ed.)

Albert Memorial a Victorian Gothic memorial (1863–72) to ➤ *Prince* ALBERT in Kensington Gardens, London, designed by George Gilbert Scott, and often held as typifying the grand Victorian style; after being boarded up for a number of years, it was substantially restored in the 1990s.

Albertine designating or pertaining to the elder of the two lines of the house of Frederick the Gentle, Elector of Saxony, which originated with his son Ernest (1441–86) and lost the electoral title to the Albertine line in 1547.

St Albertus Magnus (*c.*1200–80), Dominican theologian, philosopher, and scientist; known as *Doctor Universalis*. A teacher of St Thomas Aquinas, he was a pioneer in the study of Aristotle and contributed significantly to the comparison of Christian theology and pagan philosophy.

 ☐ **FEAST DAY** His feast day is 15 November.

Albigenses the members of a heretic sect in southern France in the 12th–13th centuries, identified with the Cathars. Their teaching was a form of Manichaean dualism, with an extremely strict moral and social code including the condemnation of both marriage and procreation. The heresy spread rapidly until ruthlessly crushed by the elder Simon de Montfort's crusade (1209–31) and by an Inquisition.

 The name is from medieval Latin, from *Albiga*, the Latin name of *Albi*, the town in southern France where the *Albigenses* originated.

albino a person or animal having a congenital absence of pigment in the skin and hair (which are white) and the eyes (which are usually pink). The word comes (in the early 18th century) from Portuguese (originally denoting albinos among African blacks) and Spanish, from Latin *albus* 'white'.

Albion a poetic or literary term for Britain or England (often used in referring to ancient or historical times). Recorded in Old English, the word comes from Latin and is probably of Celtic origin; ultimately related to Latin *albus* 'white', in allusion to the white cliffs of Dover.

 See also ➤ NEW *Albion*, ➤ PERFIDIOUS *Albion*.

album amicorum an 'album of friends', the predecessor of the modern autograph album, popular from the 16th century with travelling students and scholars. Typically an entry would contain a biblical or classical motto, a personal device or coat of arms, a dedication and an autograph. There are many examples in the British Library.

Alcaeus (*c.*620–*c.*580 BC), Greek lyric poet. He invented a new form of lyric metre, the alcaic; he also wrote political odes, drinking songs, and love songs. His works were a model for Horace and the verse of the Renaissance.

Alcatraz a rocky island in San Francisco Bay, California. It was, between 1934 and 1963, the site of a top-security federal prison.

Alcestis in Greek mythology, wife of Admetus, king of Pherae in Thessaly, whose life she saved by consenting to die on his behalf. She was brought back from Hades by Hercules.

alchemilla a genus of herbaceous plants of the rose family; the name comes (in the mid 16th century) from medieval Latin 'lady's mantle', possibly from Arabic *iklīl al-malik*, literally 'crown of the king', influenced by medieval Latin *alchimia* 'alchemy' + the diminutive suffix *-illa*, from the belief of the alchemists that dew from the leaves of this plant could turn base metals to gold.

alchemy the medieval forerunner of chemistry, based on the supposed transformation of matter. It was concerned particularly with attempts to convert base metals into gold or find a universal elixir.

 Alchemy was based on the possible transmutation of all matter, and was far wider in scope than the attempt to turn base metals into gold. It attracted such medieval scholars as Roger Bacon, St Albertus Magnus, and Paracelsus, who was concerned with the search for a chemical therapy for disease. The rise of mechanical philosophy in the 17th century gradually undermined alchemy and it became an aspect of the occult.

 The term comes (in late Middle English) via Old French and medieval Latin from Arabic *alkīmiyā'*, from *al* 'the' + *kīmiyā'* (from Greek *khēmia*, *khēmeia* 'art of transmuting metals').

Alcibiades (*c.*450–404 BC), Athenian general and statesman. He led the unsuccessful Athenian expeditions against Sparta and Sicily during the Peloponnesian War but fled to Sparta after being charged with sacrilege. He later held commands for Athens against Sparta and Persia before being exiled and later assassinated in Phrygia.

Alcina in *Orlando Innamorato* and *Orlando Furioso*, a witch who was mistress of an enchanted garden, and changed her lovers into beasts, stones, and trees.

Alcmene in Greek mythology, the mother by ➤ ZEUS of Hercules.

Alcofribas Nasier the anagrammatic pseudonym used by ➤ RABELAIS for the publication of *Pantagruel* (1532).

alcohol recorded from the mid 16th century, the word comes via French or medieval Latin from Arabic *al-kuḥl* 'the kohl'. In early use the term denoted powders, specifically kohl, and especially those obtained by sublimation; later (in the mid 17th century) the meaning 'a distilled or rectified spirit' developed.

Alcoran an early name (through French) for the ➤ KORAN.

Alcuin (*c*.735–804), English scholar, theologian, and adviser to Charlemagne; also known as *Albinus*. He is credited with the transformation of Charlemagne's court into a cultural centre in the period known as the Carolingian Renaissance. Later, as abbot of Tours he established an important library and school, and developed the type of script known as Carolingian minuscule, which influenced modern roman type.

Alcuin Club founded in 1897 to promote the study of Christian liturgy in general, and in particular the liturgies of the Anglican Communion; it produces one major volume of scholarship a year, and occasional manuals of a practical nature.

Aldebaran the brightest star in the constellation ➤ TAURUS, forming the 'eye of the bull'. The name comes from Arabic, literally 'the follower (of the Pleiades)'.

Aldeburgh a town on the coast of Suffolk, England, which is the setting for an annual music festival (the **Aldeburgh Festival**) established by the composer Benjamin Britten in 1948.

alderman a co-opted member of an English county or borough council, next in status to the Mayor; in North America and Australia, an elected member of a city council. In Old English, *aldorman* (denoting 'a man of high rank') comes from *aldor*, *ealdor* 'chief, patriarch', from *ald* 'old'. Later the sense 'warden of a guild' arose; then, as the guilds became identified with the ruling municipal body, 'local magistrate, municipal officer'.

Aldermaston a village near Reading in southern England, site of the Atomic Weapons Research Establishment. From 1958 to 1963 a march between Aldermaston and London took place each year in protest against the development and production of nuclear weapons.

> You who join in marches on the capital and cultivate an Aldermaston mystique.
> — W. Weaver tr. Umberto Eco's *Misreadings* (1993)

Aldersgate one of the old gates of London. From the old gatehouse the printer John Day (1522–84) issued his editions of Ascham's *The Scholemaster*, Foxe's *Actes and Monuments*, and some of Tyndale's works.

Aldine a book or edition printed by ➤ ALDUS *Manutius* or his successors. The device characteristic of Aldine books is a figure of a dolphin on an anchor.

Aldus Manutius (1450–1515), Italian scholar, printer, and publisher. He printed fine first editions of many Greek and Latin classics at his press in Venice, and pioneered the widespread use of italic type.

ale a drink of pre-Roman origin, originally made like beer but without hops.

> See also ➤ ADAMS's *ale*, ➤ AUDIT *ale*, ➤ BRIDE-*ale*, ➤ CAKES *and ale*, ➤ CHURCH-*ale*, ➤ LAMB-*ale*, ➤ MIDSUMMER *ale*, ➤ WHITSUN *ale*.

ale-silver a rent or tribute paid annually to the Lord Mayor of London by those selling ale within the City.

ale-stake a stake or post set up before an alehouse, with a garland or bush serving as a sign; this may be the origin of the saying, ➤ *good* WINE *needs no bush*.

alec see ➤ SMART *alec*.

Alecto in Greek mythology, one of the ➤ FURIES.

alectoria a precious stone said to be found in the gizzard of cocks; the name comes from Greek *alectōr* 'cock'.

alectryomancy divination by means of a cock with grains of corn.

Aleppo an ancient city in northern Syria, which was formerly an important commercial centre on the trade route between the Mediterranean and the countries of the East; in Shakespeare's *Macbeth*, the First Witch says of the sailor's wife who has offended her, 'her husband's to Aleppo gone, master o' th' Tiger.'

alewife a fish of the herring family, swimming up rivers to spawn; the name is recorded from the mid 17th century, and may come from earlier *alewife* 'woman who keeps an ale house', with reference to the fish's large belly.

Alexander[1] (356–323 BC), king of Macedon 336–323, son of Philip II; known as **Alexander the Great**. He conquered Persia, Egypt, Syria, Mesopotamia, Bactria, and the Punjab; in Egypt he founded the city of Alexandria. According to Plutarch, Alexander wept when he was told that there were an infinite number of worlds, saying, 'Is it not worthy of tears that, when the number of worlds is infinite, we have not yet become lords of a single one?'

After his death from a fever at Babylon his empire quickly fell apart, but he became a model for subsequent imperialist conquerors and the subject of fantastic legends.

> Alexander the Great . . . when he had conquered what was called the Eastern World . . . wept for want of more Worlds to conquer.
> — Isaac Watts *The Improvement of the Mind* (1741)

See also ➤ ALEXANDER *of the North*.

Alexander[2] in Greek mythology, the name given to Paris of Troy (see ➤ PARIS[1]), by the shepherds who brought him up in exile.

St Alexander Nevsky (*c*.1220–63), prince of Novgorod 1236–63. He defeated the Swedes on the banks of the River Neva in 1240, and in 1242 he defeated the Teutonic Knights on the frozen Lake Peipus.

  ☐ **FEAST DAY** His feast day is 30 August or 23 November.

Alexander of Hales (1170/80–1245), English theologian and Franciscan who studied and taught at Paris, and who was called the *Doctor Irrefragabilis* or *Irrefragable Doctor*.

Alexander of the North name given to ➤ CHARLES *XII* of Sweden (1682–1718); James Thomson in *The Seasons* (1744) refers to 'The frantic Alexander of the North'.

Alexander technique a system designed to promote well-being by retraining one's awareness and habits of posture to ensure minimum effort and strain. It is named after Frederick Matthias *Alexander* (1869–1955), the Australian-born actor and elocutionist who developed it.

Alexander the Corrector name assumed by Alexander Cruden (1701–70), editor of the *Biblical Concordance*; the epithet was suggested to him by his previous role as a 'corrector' (a printer's reader who corrected proofs) and reflects the belief he developed that it was his task to reform the nation.

Alexander the Great another name for Alexander, king of Macedon (see ➤ ALEXANDER[1]).

Alexandra limp a manner of walking, in imitation of the limping gait of Alexandra of Denmark (1844–1925), Princess of Wales, adopted by fashionable society in the late 19th century.

Alexandra Rose Day a day in June when rose emblems are sold for charity; it was originally established by Queen Alexandra (1844–1925) to raise money for British hospitals.

Alexandria the chief port of Egypt, founded in 332 BC by Alexander the Great (see ➤ ALEXANDER[1]). Alexandria was a major centre of Hellenistic culture, renowned for its library and for the Pharos lighthouse, and for its schools of literature and philosophy. It was latterly eclipsed by Constantinople.

See also ➤ PLEIADES, ➤ *St* CATHERINE *of Alexandria*, ➤ *St* CLEMENT *of Alexandria*, ➤ *St* CYRIL *of Alexandria*.

Alexandrian Library formed at Alexandria during the reign of the Ptolemies (beginning with Ptolemy Soter, 323–283 BC). It is said to have contained at one time about 400,000 manuscripts, of which a part where accidentally burnt when Julius Caesar was besieged at Alexandria. The story that the library was destroyed by order of the Caliph ➤ OMAR is without foundation.

alexandrine an iambic line of twelve syllables or six feet. The term comes (in the late 16th century) from French, from *Alexandre* (see ➤ ALEXANDER[1]), the subject of an Old French poem in this metre.

St Alexis of Rome according to his legend (which may have no factual basis) this popular saint of the Middle Ages, having left Rome on his wedding night to go on pilgrimage, returned there to live unrecognized as a beggar for seventeen years, and was only identified after death. He is patron saint of hermits and beggars.

  ☐ **FEAST DAY** His feast day is 17 July.

Alf see ➤ *Alf* GARNETT.

Alfadir in Scandinavian mythology, a name for ➤ ODIN, meaning 'All-father'.

Alfar in Scandinavian mythology, the elves.

alfin former name for a chess piece similar in function to the modern-day bishop. Recorded from late Middle English, the word comes via French through Spanish and Portuguese from Arabic *al-fīl* 'elephant', referring to its original shape.

Alfred (849–99), king of Wessex 871–99; known as **Alfred the Great**. Alfred's military resistance saved SW England from Viking occupation, and in 886 he negotiated the boundaries with the Danelaw. A great reformer, he is credited with the foundation of the English navy and with a revival of learning, personally translating Latin texts into English. The legend that, while in disguise and hiding from the Danes, he offered to help a woman by watching her baking cakes, and instead let them burn, is often referred to as a type of simplified historical story.

> One day I gave, as a devoir, the trite little anecdote of Alfred tending cakes . . . to be related with amplifications.
> — Charlotte Brontë *The Professor* (1857)

algebra the part of mathematics in which letters and other general symbols are used to represent numbers and quantities in formulae and equations. Algebra is the generalization of arithmetic to variable or abstract quantities represented by symbols. Modern algebra deals with systems (such as fields, rings, vector spaces, and groups) that consist of elements (typically numbers, vectors, or geometrical transformations) and operations that may be performed with them. Algebra strictly does not include analysis.

Recorded from late Middle English, the word comes via Italian, Spanish, and medieval Latin from Arabic *al-jabr* 'the reunion of broken parts', 'bonesetting', from *jabara* 'reunite, restore'. The original sense, 'the surgical treatment of fractures', probably came via Spanish, in which it survives; the mathematical sense comes from the title of a book, '*ilm al-jabr wa'l-mukābala* 'the science of restoring what is missing and equating like with like' by the 9th-century mathematician *al-Ḵwārizmī* (see ➤ ALGORITHM).

Algonquin Round Table informal meeting place at the *Algonquin* Hotel, New York, for Robert Benchley, Dorothy Parker, Alexander Woollcott, and others.

> A gal who sat around the Algonquin knocking back martinis while banging out sassy quotes.
> — *Washington Post Magazine* 2 May 1993

algorithm a process or set of rules to be followed in calculations or other problem-solving operations, especially by a computer. Recorded from the late 17th century (denoting the Arabic or decimal notation of numbers): it is a variant (influenced by Greek *arithmos* 'number') of Middle English *algorism* which comes via Old French from medieval Latin *algorismus*. The Arabic source, *al-Ḵwārizmī* 'the man of Ḵwārizm' (now Khiva) Abū Ja'far Muhammad ibn Mūsa, is the cognomen of a 9th-century mathematician who was the author of widely translated works on algebra and arithmetic.

Alhambra a fortified Moorish palace, the last stronghold of the Muslim kings of Granada, built between 1248 and 1354 near Granada in Spain. It is an outstanding piece of Moorish architecture with its marble courts and fountains, delicate columns and archways, and wall decorations of carved and painted stucco.

Ali Baba the hero of a story supposed to be from the *Arabian Nights* (but actually first added to the text in a French translation of the early 18th century), who discovered the magic formula (➤ OPEN *sesame*) which opened a cave where forty thieves kept their treasure.

Planning to recover what they had lost, the thieves concealed themselves in Ali Baba's courtyard in forty tall oil jars, but Ali Baba's slave *Morgiana*, discovering their presence, poured boiling oil into the jars and killed them, saving her master.

> A shop like Ali Baba's cave, jammed floor to ceiling with halvah and Turkish delight, hubble-bubble pipes.
> — Nik Cohn *The Heart of the World* (1992)

alibi a claim or piece of evidence that one was elsewhere when an act, typically a criminal one, is alleged to have taken place. The word is recorded from the late 17th century, as an adverb in the sense 'elsewhere', and comes from Latin 'elsewhere'. The noun use dates from the 18th century.

Alice the heroine of two books by Lewis Carroll, *Alice's Adventures in Wonderland* (1865) and *Through the Looking Glass* (1872); as depicted by the illustrator Tenniel, Alice is a child with long straight fair hair held back with a band of ribbon, who meets a bewildering variety of playing-card, chessboard, and other characters in the worlds she finds down a rabbit hole and on the other side of a mirror. The stories were originally told by Carroll (pseudonym of Charles Lutwidge Dodgson, 1832–98) to Alice Liddell, 10-year-old daughter of the Dean of Christ Church, Oxford.

> In this Alice-in-Wonderland system of accounts, a single plank of felled timber shows a higher value than the preservation of a thousand forest species.
> — *Christian Science Monitor* 2 January 1992

alien a hypothetical or fictional being from another world, especially one far distant from the earth; the term has been used since the mid 20th century, and is associated particularly with ➤ UFOs, as in stories about the ➤ ROSWELL incident.

alien priory a monastic establishment owing obedience to a mother-house in a foreign country.

Alighieri see ➤ DANTE *Alighieri*.

alkahest the hypothetical universal solvent sought by alchemists. Recorded from the mid 17th century, the word is sham Arabic, and was probably invented by Paracelsus.

all see also ➤ *All* SAINTS' *Day*, ➤ *All the* TALENTS, ➤ *all* WORK *and no play makes Jack a dull boy*, ➤ *all's for the* BEST *in the best of all possible worlds*, ➤ *all's* WELL *that ends well*.

All Blacks the New Zealand Rugby team, named from the colour of the players' strip; the name was first applied to the team by British journalists at the beginning of the 1905 tour of Britain.

all cats are grey in the dark proverbial saying; mid 16th century; meaning that darkness obscures inessential differences.

all good things must come to an end proverbial saying; mid 15th century.

all human life is there every variety of human experience, used as an advertising slogan for the *News of the World* in the late 1950s; in *The Madonna of the Future* (1879), Henry James wrote, 'Cats and monkeys—monkeys and cats—all human life is there!'

all-singing all-dancing with every possible attribute, able to perform any necessary function; a phrase applied particularly in the area of computer technology, but originally coming from descriptions of show business acts. The term may derive ultimately from a series of posters produced in 1929 to promote the new sound cinema such as that advertising the Hollywood musical *Broadway Melody*,

which proclaimed the words *All talking All singing All dancing*.

it takes all sorts to make a world proverbial saying, early 17th century.

All Souls College an Oxford college founded in 1453 by Archbishop Chichele to offer prayers for the souls of all the faithful departed, originally consisting of a warden and forty fellows, and still with only graduate members.

All Souls' Day a Catholic festival with prayers for the souls of the dead in Purgatory, held on 2 November.

all things are possible with God proverbial saying; late 17th century; originally with biblical allusion to Matthew 19:26, 'Jesus…said unto them, With men this is unpossible, but with God all things are possible.'

all things come to those who wait proverbial saying; early 16th century.

be all things to all men be able or try to please everybody, often with an implication of duplicity; originally probably in allusion to 1 Corinthians 9:22 'I am made all things to all men'.

Allah the name of God among Muslims (and Arab Christians). The name comes from Arabic *'allāh*, contraction of *al-'ilāh* 'the god'.

Allahabad a city in the state of Uttar Pradesh, north central India, which is situated at the confluence of the sacred Jumna and Ganges Rivers, and is a place of Hindu pilgrimage.

allegiance see ➤ PLEDGE *of Allegiance*.

allegory a story, poem, or picture which can be interpreted to reveal a hidden meaning, typically a moral or political one. The word comes (in late Middle English) via Old French and Latin from Greek *allēgoria*, from *allos* 'other' + *-agoria* 'speaking'.

allemande any of a number of German dances, in particular an elaborate court dance popular in the 16th century.

Ethan Allen (1738–89), American soldier. He fought the British in the War of Independence and led the irregular force the *Green Mountain Boys* in their campaign to gain independence for the state of Vermont.

alliance see ➤ QUADRUPLE *Alliance*, ➤ TRIPLE *Alliance*.

alligator a large semiaquatic reptile resembling a crocodile; sometimes taken as a type of strength and ferocity, as in ➤ HALF-*horse, half-alligator*. The name comes from Spanish *el lagarto* 'the lizard', probably based on Latin *lacerta*.

alliteration the rhetorical device of commencing adjacent or closely connected words with the same sound or syllable. The term comes from Latin *ad-* ((expressing addition) + *littera* 'letter'.

Ally Pally an informal name for *Alexandra Palace* in Muswell Hill, North London, the original headquarters of BBC television.

Ally Sloper name of a character in a series of humorous publications, as *Some Playful Episodes in the Career of Ally Sloper* (1873), having a prominent nose and receding forehead and noted for his dishonest and bungling practices.

alma mater the university, school, or college that one once attended. The phrase is recorded from the mid 17th century, in the general sense 'someone or something providing nourishment'; in Latin, literally 'bounteous mother', a title given to various Roman goddesses, notably Ceres and Cybele.

Lawrence Alma-Tadema (1836–1912), Dutch-born British painter known for lush genre scenes set in the ancient world.

> What does Alma-Tadema give? Pipes are blown, torches waved, tambourines banged and rather elegant eurhythmic poses are struck.
> — *Independent* 8 April 1997

Almack's assembly rooms which stood in King Street, St James's, and were celebrated in the 18th and earlier 19th centuries as the scene of social functions. They were founded by one William Almack (or Macall; d. 1781), who appears to have come to London as a valet to the duke of Hamilton. Almack's was replaced as a social centre after 1763 by Willis's Rooms. Almack was also founder of a gaming club, since converted into Brooks's.

Almagest an Arabic version of Ptolemy's astronomical treatise; in the Middle Ages (also with lower-case initial) any celebrated treatise on astrology and alchemy. The word comes from Old French, based on Arabic, from *al* 'the' + Greek *megistē* 'greatest (composition)'.

almanac an annual calendar containing important dates and statistical information such as astronomical data and tide tables. Recorded from late Middle English, the word comes via medieval Latin from Greek, but ultimately is of unknown origin.

See also ➤ CROCKETT *almanacs*, ➤ *Francis* MOORE, ➤ POOR *Richard's Almanack*, ➤ POOR *Robin's Almanack*.

Almanach de Gotha an annual publication giving information about European royalty, nobility, and diplomats, published in *Gotha* 1763–1944 and revived in 1968; the presence of a family in the book was considered to establish aristocratic credentials.

> The *Tatlers* and *Spectators* and *Sketches* of the twenties are one long photographers' tribute to her angelic English loveliness and to the Almanach de Gotha of her misbehaviors.
> — W. M. Spackman *A Presence with Secrets* (1980)

almandine a kind of garnet with a violet tint. The name comes, in late Middle English, via a French alteration of medieval Latin *alabandina (gemma)* '(jewel from) Alabanda', an ancient city in Asia Minor where these stones were cut.

Almesbury a form of the name of *Amesbury* in Wiltshire, according to Malory the site of the sanctuary in which ➤ GUINEVERE took refuge after her adultery with ➤ LANCELOT was revealed.

almighty dollar a phrase expressing the power of money; originally with allusion to the American writer Washington Irving (1783–1859):

> The almighty dollar, that great object of universal veneration throughout our land.
> — Washington Irving 'The Creole Village' in *New Yorker* 12 November 1836

In the early 17th century, Ben Jonson had used a similar image, 'That for which all virtue now is sold, And almost every vice—almighty gold' ('Epistle to Elizabeth, Countess of Rutland', in *Epigrams*, 1616).

Almohad a member of a Berber Muslim movement and dynasty that conquered the Spanish and North African empire of the ➤ ALMORAVIDS in the 12th century, taking the capital Marrakesh in 1147. They were driven out of Spain in 1212 but held on to Marrakesh until 1269.

almond see ➤ JORDAN *almond*.

Almoravid a member of a federation of Muslim Berber peoples that established an empire in Morocco, Algeria, and Spain in the second half of the 11th century. They were in turn driven out by the

➤ ALMOHADS, losing their capital Marrakesh in 1147.

alms money or food given to poor people. Recorded from Old English (in the form *ælmysse*, *ælmesse*), the word comes via Christian Latin from Greek *eleēmosunē* 'compassion', and ultimately from *eleos* 'mercy'.

almshouse a house built originally by a charitable person or organization for poor people to live in.

almucantar a circle on the celestial sphere parallel to the horizon; a parallel of altitude; a telescope mounted on a float resting on mercury, used to determine stellar altitude and azimuth. Recorded from Middle English, the word comes, via medieval Latin or obsolete French, from Arabic *almuḳanṭarāt* 'lines of celestial latitude', based on *al* 'the' + *ḳanṭara* 'arch'.

Alnaschar a beggar in the ➤ ARABIAN *Nights* who destroys his livelihood by indulging in visions of riches and grandeur.

> She . . . was busy with Alnaschar visions of wide expenditure.
> — Elizabeth Gaskell *Ruth* (1853)

aloe originally, the fragrant resin or heartwood of certain oriental trees, as in Psalms 45:8, 'All thy garments smell of myrrh, and aloes, and cassia.' Later, a succulent plant with a rosette of thick tapering leaves and bell-shaped or tubular flowers, which yields a bitter juice; also (usually as *aloes*) the drug obtained from this plant.

aloha a Hawaiian word used in greeting or parting from someone.

Aloha State informal name for Hawaii.

you're never alone with a Strand advertising slogan for *Strand* cigarettes, 1960; the image of loneliness was so strongly conveyed by the solitary smoker that sales were in fact adversely affected.

Alph the river in Xanadu referred to in Coleridge's 'Kubla Khan':

> Where Alph, the sacred river, ran
> Through caverns measureless to man
> Down to a sunless sea.
> — Samuel Taylor Coleridge 'Kubla Khan' (1816)

alpha the first letter of the Greek alphabet (A, α), transliterated as 'a'.

alpha and omega the beginning and the end (*omega* is the last letter of the Greek alphabet, as *alpha* is the first), especially used by Christians as a title for Jesus.

alphabet a set of letters or symbols in a fixed order used to represent the basic set of speech sounds of a language, especially the set of letters from A to Z.

The origin of the alphabet goes back to the Phoenician system of the 2nd millennium BC, from which the modern Hebrew and Arabic systems are ultimately derived. The Greek alphabet, which emerged in 1000–900 BC, developed two branches, Cyrillic (which became the script of Russian) and Etruscan (from which derives the Roman alphabet used in the West).

Recorded from the early 16th century, the word comes via late Latin from Greek *alpha*, *bēta*, the first two letters of the Greek alphabet.

See also ➤ CYRILLIC *alphabet*.

Alpheus in Greek mythology, a river-god who fell in love with the nymph ➤ ARETHUSA. Having fled to Ortygia to escape him, she was turned into a fountain; according to the legend, Alpheus then flowed under the sea to reach the fountain, and this gave rise to the ancient belief that the water of the river Alpheus flowed through the sea without mixing with it.

Alphonsine tables astronomical tables invented in 1252 by Alfonso X 'the Wise' (1221–84), King of Castile; he is supposed to have said, while studying the Ptolemaic system, 'Had I been present at the Creation, I would have given some useful hints for the better ordering of the universe.'

Alsatia name given to the precinct of White Friars in London, formerly a sanctuary for debtors and law-breakers, from the medieval Latin form of *Alsace* as a much-disputed territory.

Alsvid in Scandinavian mythology, the horse that draws the chariot of the moon.

Altamira¹ the site of a cave with Palaeolithic rock paintings, south of Santander in northern Spain, discovered in 1879. The paintings are realistic depictions of deer, wild boar, and especially bison; they are dated to the Upper Magdalenian period.

Altamira² a town in NE Brazil, which in 1989 attracted world attention as the venue of a major protest against the devastation of the Amazonian rainforest.

altar the table in a Christian church at which the bread and wine are consecrated in communion services; a table or flat-topped block used as the focus for a religious ritual, especially for making sacrifices or offerings to a deity. The word comes ultimately from Latin *altus* 'high'.

St Tarsicius, a Roman martyr of the 3rd–4th centuries who was said to have been attacked and killed by a pagan crowd while carrying the sacrament, and who is said to have been very young, is the patron saint of altar servers.

See ➤ *the* HORNS *of the altar.*

alter ego a person's secondary or alternative personality; an intimate and trusted friend. The Latin phrase, meaning literally 'other self', is recorded in English from the mid 16th century.

alternative designating a mode of life, system or knowledge and practice, or organization designedly different from that of the established social order. The word was first used in this sense when the hippie culture of the late 1960s, with its rejection of materialism and traditional Western values, was described as an alternative society. In the 1980s, the term enjoyed a new vogue, as the health and fitness movement became increasingly influential in advocating unconventional medical therapies.

Alternative Service Book a book containing the public liturgy of the Church of England published in 1980 for use as the alternative to the Book of Common Prayer.

Althaea in Greek mythology, mother of Meleager (see ➤ MELEAGER[1]), who when her son killed her brothers threw on to the fire a brand of which the Fates had said that if it were burnt his life would be consumed with it.

Althing the bicameral legislative assembly of Iceland; the word is Icelandic, and comes from Old Norse (literally, 'whole assembly').

alto-relievo a sculpture or carving in high relief; the term comes (in the mid 17th century) from Italian *alto-rilievo*.

Alumbrado a member of the Spanish sect of *Illuminati* or Perfectionists, who arose about 1575, and were suppressed by the Inquisition.

always see ➤ *always a* BRIDESMAID, *never a bride.*

am see also ➤ *am I my* BROTHER'*s keeper.*

am I not a man and a brother inscription on a Wedgwood cameo, composed by the English potter Josiah Wedgwood (1730–95), depicting a kneeling African slave in chains.

amadou a spongy substance made by drying certain bracket fungi and formerly used as an absorbent in medicine, as tinder, and for drying fishing flies. The name comes (in the late 18th century) via French from Latin *amator* 'lover' (because it easily ignites).

Amaimon name of a devil in medieval demonology; in Reginald Scot's *The Discovery of Witchcraft* (1584) he is described as a 'king of the east'. Shakespeare includes *Amaimon*, with *Lucifer* and *Barbason*, in a list of devils' names in *The Merry Wives of Windsor*, and mentions him again in *1 Henry IV*, in a scene in which Falstaff is mocking the supposed prowess of Owen Glendower.

Amalthea in Greek mythology, the she-goat who suckled the infant ➤ ZEUS when he was hidden to protect him from his father ➤ CRONUS; **Amalthea's horn** is another name for the ➤ CORNUCOPIA or horn of plenty.

amanuensis a literary or artistic assistant, in particular one who takes dictation or copies manuscripts. The word comes (in the early 17th century) from Latin, from *(servus) a manu* '(slave) at hand-(writing), secretary' + *-ensis* 'belonging to'.

Mount Amara a place in Abyssinia, where the kings of that country secluded their sons, to protect themselves from sedition.

amaranth in poetic and literary usage, an imaginary flower that never fades, and is thus taken as a type of immortality; the name comes ultimately from Greek *amarantos* 'unfading'.

Tell el-Amarna the site of the ruins of the ancient Egyptian capital Akhetaten, on the east bank of the Nile. A series of cuneiform tablets known as the **Amarna Letters** was discovered on the site in 1887, providing valuable insight into Near Eastern diplomacy of the 14th century BC.

Amaryllis name of a shepherdess in the pastoral poetry of Virgil and Ovid, used by Milton in 'Lycidas' (1638), 'To sport with Amaryllis in the shade'.

Amasis king of Egypt, and friend of ➤ POLYCRATES, said by Herodotus to have warned his friend fruitlessly of the dangers of excessive good fortune.

Amaterasu the principal deity of the Japanese Shinto religion, the sun goddess and ancestor of Jimmu, founder of the imperial dynasty.

amateur a person who engages in a pursuit, especially a sport, on an unpaid basis. Recorded from the late 18th century, the word comes via French and Italian from Latin *amator* 'lover', from *amare* 'to love'.

Amati a family of Italian violin-makers from Cremona. In the 16th and 17th centuries three generations of the *Amatis* (Andrea, *c.*1520–*c.*80 and his sons and grandson Nicolò, 1596–1684) developed the basic proportions of the violin, viola, and cello, refining the body outlines, soundholes, purfling, and scroll. Antonio Stradivari worked in Nicolò's workshop.

amazement see ➤ AFRAID *with any amazement.*

Amazon a member of a legendary race of female warriors believed by the ancient Greeks to exist in Scythia or elsewhere on the edge of the known world; in extended usage, a very tall and strong or athletic woman.

The Amazons, who appear in many Greek legends, were of the Trojans in the ➤ TROJAN *War*, and their queen, Penthesilea, was killed by Achilles. One of the labours of Hercules was to obtain the girdle of Hippolyta, queen of the Amazons.

The name comes (in late Middle English, via Latin) from Greek *Amazōn*, explained by the Greeks as 'breastless' (as if from *a-* 'without' + *mazos* 'breast'), referring to the fable that the Amazons cut off the right breast so as not to interfere with the use of a bow, but probably a folk etymology of an unknown foreign word.

The Amazon river in South America, which initially bore various names after its discovery in 1500, was finally called *Amazon* after a legendary race of female warriors believed to live on its banks.

ambassador an accredited diplomat sent by a state as its permanent representative in a foreign country. The word comes (in late Middle English) via French from Italian *ambasciator*, based on Latin *ambactus* 'servant'. The English poet and diplomat Henry Wotton (1568–1639) provided an early (1604) definition of an ambassador's role, saying that he was 'an honest man sent to lie abroad for the good of his country'.

amber hard translucent fossilized resin originating from extinct coniferous trees of the Tertiary period, typically honey-yellow in colour. It is found chiefly along the southern shores of the Baltic Sea and has been used in jewellery since antiquity. A piece of amber was traditionally used an an amulet to attract lovers.

Amber often contains the bodies of trapped insects (the plot of Michael Crichton's thriller *Jurassic Park* and the 1993 Spielberg film based on it turned on the hypothesis that dinosaur DNA from the blood on which such insects had fed could be recovered from the insect bodies).

When rubbed amber becomes charged with static electricity: the word *electric* is derived from the Greek word for amber.

The word is recorded from late Middle English (also in sense ➤ AMBERGRIS), and comes via Old French from Arabic '*anbar* 'ambergris', later 'amber'.

See also ➤ *a* FLY *in amber.*

ambergris a wax-like substance that originates as a secretion in the intestines of the sperm whale, found floating in tropical seas. It is soft, black, and unpleasant-smelling when fresh, slowly becoming harder, paler, and sweeter-smelling, and used in perfume manufacture.

The word comes (in late Middle English) from Old French *ambre gris* 'grey amber', as distinct from *ambre jaune* 'yellow amber' (the resin).

ambidextrous of a person, able to use the right and left hands equally well. Recorded from the mid 17th century, the term comes from Latin *ambidexter*, from *ambi-* 'on both sides' + *dexter* 'right-handed'.

ambition a strong desire to do or achieve something, typically requiring determination and hard work. The word comes (in Middle English, via Old French) from Latin *ambition(n-)*, from *ambire* 'go around (canvassing for votes)'.

ambo a raised platform in a church from which scriptures and litanies were read. Originally single, by the 6th century they were organized in pairs, one for the Epistles on the south side of the church, and one for the Gospels on the north side.

See also ➤ ARCADES *ambo.*

St Ambrose (*c.*339–97), Doctor of the Church and bishop of Milan. A champion of orthodoxy, he also encouraged developments in church music. He was partly responsible for the conversion of St Augustine of Hippo, and forced the emperor Theodosius to do public penance for a massacre carried out on his orders at Thessalonica; for this Ambrose is sometimes shown with a scourge.

According to legend, when he was a child a swarm of bees settled on his mouth, symbolizing his future eloquence; he may thus be represented by a beehive.

☐ **EMBLEMS** His emblems are a beehive and a scourge.

☐ **FEAST DAY** His feast day is 7 December.

Ambrose's Tavern the scene of the ➤ NOCTES *Ambrosianae*, loosely based on a real Edinburgh tavern of the same name, described by Lockhart.

ambrosia in Greek and Roman mythology, the food of the gods, associated with their immortality. The word comes (in the mid 16th century) via Latin from Greek, 'elixir of life', from *ambrotos* 'immortal'.

Ambrosian Library at Milan, founded in 1609, and originally the private library of Cardinal Borromeo (1564–1631), archbishop of Milan, bequeathed by him to public uses. It was named after ➤ *St* AMBROSE, bishop of Milan.

Ambrosianae see ➤ NOCTES *Ambrosianae*.

Ambrosius Aurelianus in the account of ➤ GILDAS, a 5th-century leader of Romano-British resistance to the Saxons; in the later chronicle of Geoffrey of Monmouth, he is said to have been the elder brother of ➤ UTHER *Pendragon* and to have preceded him as king after defeating and killing ➤ VORTIGERN.

ambsace both aces (= two ones), the lowest possible throw at dice; in figurative usage, bad luck, misfortune. Recorded from Middle English, the word comes via Old French from Latin *ambas* 'both' + *as* 'ace'.

ambush a surprise attack by people lying in wait in a concealed position. Recorded from Middle English, in the sense 'place troops in hiding in order to surprise an enemy', the word comes via Old French *embusche, embuschier*, based on a Latin word meaning 'to place in a wood', related to *bush*.

AMDG abbreviation of the Latin *ad majorem Dei gloriam*, 'to the greater glory of God', motto of the Jesuits.

amen an exclamation, meaning 'so be it', uttered at the end of a prayer or hymn. Recorded from Old English, the word comes via ecclesiastical Latin from Greek *amēn*, from Hebrew 'truth, certainty', used adverbially as expression of agreement, and adopted in the Septuagint as a solemn expression of belief or affirmation.

Amen Corner a site at the west end of ➤ PATER-NOSTER *Row* in London.

Amenhotep the name of four Egyptian pharaohs, the fourth of whom adopted the worship of ➤ ATEN and changed his name to ➤ AKHENATEN.

America the name of a land mass of the western hemisphere, for the modern world first reached by Christopher Columbus, which was apparently coined in M. Waldseemüller *Cosmographiae Introductio* (1507) and coming from *Americus*, modern Latin form of the name of the Italian explorer *Amerigo* Vespucci (1451–1512), who navigated the coast of South America in 1501.

See also ➤ ATHENS *of America*, ➤ UNITED *States*, ➤ VOICE *of America*.

America First a US political slogan denoting patriotic or nationalist commitment, and deriving from a speech by President Woodrow Wilson (1856–1924) opposing American entry into the First World War:

> Our whole duty, for the present . . . is summed up in the motto, 'America First'. Let us think of America before we think of Europe, in order that America may be fit to be Europe's friend when the day of tested friendship comes.
> — Woodrow Wilson speech, 20 April 1915

from this developed **America Firster**, a member or supporter of the **America First Committee**, a Chicago-based organization which opposed the intervention of the US in the Second World War.

America's Cup an international yachting race held every three to four years, named after the yacht *America*, which won it in 1851. The *America*'s owners gave the trophy to the New York Yacht Club as a perpetual international challenge trophy, and it remained in the club's possession for 132 years. An Australian crew won it in 1983, but the Americans won it back in 1987, and held it until 1995, when New Zealand were successful.

American see also ➤ *the American* FABIUS, ➤ DAUGHTERS *of the American Revolution*, ➤ GENERAL *American*, ➤ *House* UN-*American Activities*, ➤ QUIET *American*, ➤ UGLY *American*.

American Civil War the war between the northern US states (usually known as the Union) and the Confederate states of the South, 1861–5.

The war was fought over the issues of slavery and states' rights. The pro-slavery Southern states seceded from the Federal Union following the election of Abraham Lincoln on an anti-slavery platform, but were defeated by the North after failing to gain foreign recognition.

American dream the traditional social ideals of the United States, such as equality, democracy, and material prosperity; the term is recorded from the 1930s.

War of American Independence the war of 1775–83 in which the American colonists won independence from British rule. The war was triggered by resentment of the economic policies of Britain, particularly the right of Parliament to tax the colonies, and by the exclusion of the colonists from participation in political decisions affecting their interests. Following disturbances such as the Boston Tea Party of 1773, fighting broke out in 1775; a year later the Declaration of Independence was signed. The Americans gained the support of France and Spain, and French sea power eventually played a crucial role in the decisive surrender of a British army at Yorktown in 1781.

American Indian a term (now steadily being replaced by ➤ NATIVE *American*) which reflects the belief of Columbus that on reaching America, he had reached the east coast of India.

good Americans when they die go to Paris proverbial saying, mid 19th century; first recorded (attributed to the American epigrammatist Thomas Gold Appleton, 1812–84) in Oliver Wendell Holmes *The Autocrat of the Breakfast Table* (1858), but perhaps best-known from Oscar Wilde's *A Woman of No Importance* (1894).

Americas see ➤ AVENUE *of the Americas*.

Amerindian another term for ➤ AMERICAN *Indian*, used chiefly in anthropological and linguistic contexts.

amethyst a kind of purple or bluish-violet quartz, traditionally supposed to prevent drunkenness. Recorded from Middle English, the word comes via Old French and Latin *amethustos* 'not drunken'.

Amherst College founded in 1821 by Congregationalists in Massachusetts, to offer men an education free of what were regarded as the heretical teachings of Harvard.

Amiatinus Codex the best extant manuscript of the Vulgate, so called from the abbey of *Monte Amiata*, to which it was presented. It was discovered in the 19th century to have been written in England, early in the 8th century, at Wearmouth or Jarrow. It

was probably copied from an Italian original. It is now in the Laurentian Library at Florence.

amicable numbers any pair of numbers having the property that each is the sum of the factors of the other (e.g. 220 and 284).

Amidah a prayer, part of the Jewish liturgy, consisting of a varying number of blessings recited while the worshippers stand. The word is recorded from the late 19th century and comes from Hebrew, literally 'standing'.

Amish the members of a strict Mennonite sect noted for maintaining their traditional culture. The sect was founded by a Swiss preacher, Jakob Amman (or Amen) (*c.*1645–*c.*1730), in the 1690s, and beginning in *c.*1720, the Amish migrated to North America and established major settlements in Pennsylvania, Ohio, and elsewhere.

Ammon Greek and Roman form of the name of the Egyptian god ➤ AMUN.
　　See also ➤ JUPITER *Ammon*.

Ammon's son epithet of ➤ ALEXANDER *the Great*, from the story in Plutarch of Alexander's visit to the temple of Ammon in Egypt, where he was greeted by the high priest as the son of the god. Later, during the campaign in Persia, Cleitas, one of Alexander's commanders and brother of his foster-mother, quarrelling with the king during a drinking bout, accused him of being able to disown his father Philip now that he could call himself the son of Ammon; in the ensuing brawl, Cleitas was killed.

ammonia the name for this colourless pungent gas comes (in the late 18th century) from Latin *sal ammoniacus*, in which the second element represents the Greek word *ammōiakos* 'of Ammon', used as a name for the salt and gum obtained near the temple of ➤ JUPITER *Ammon* at Siwa in Egypt.

ammonite a fossil of a flat-coiled spiral shell, especially one of a later type found chiefly in the Jurassic and Cretaceous periods, typically with intricately frilled suture lines. The name comes from medieval Latin *cornu Ammonis* 'horn of Ammon', from the fossil's resemblance to the ram's horn associated with ➤ JUPITER *Ammon*.

ammunition see ➤ PRAISE *the Lord and pass the ammunition*.

amnesty an official pardon for people who have been convicted of political offences; an undertaking by the authorities to take no action against specified offences or offenders during a fixed period. The term comes (in the late 16th century) via Latin from Greek *amnēstia* 'forgetfulness'; it has thus the same base as *amnesia* 'loss of memory'.

Amnesty International an independent international organization in support of human rights, especially for prisoners of conscience, founded in London in 1961. The organization was awarded the Nobel Peace Prize in 1977.

amok in the phrase **run amok**, behave uncontrollably and disruptively. The word comes (in the mid 17th century) from Portuguese *amouco*, from Malay *amok* 'rushing in a frenzy'. Early use was as a noun denoting a Malay in a homicidal frenzy; the adverb use dates from the late 17th century.

Amos a Hebrew minor prophet (*c.*760 BC), a shepherd of Tekoa, near Jerusalem; also, a book of the Bible containing his prophecies.

Amos and Andy the hardworking *Amos* and his lazy friend *Andy* are characters in an American radio series set in Harlem, New York, from the 1920s to the 1940s, and later transferred to television (1951–66).

ampere a unit of electric current equal to a flow of one coulomb per second, named after the French physicist, mathematician, and philosopher André-Marie *Ampère* (1775–1836), who was one of the founders of the study of electromagnetism and electrodynamics, and who analysed the relationship between magnetic force and electric current.

ampersand the sign &, standing for *and*, as in *Smith & Co*, or Latin *et*, as in *&c.*. The word is recorded from the mid 19th century, and is an alteration of *and per se and* '*&* by itself is *and*', chanted as an aid to learning the sign.

amphibian a cold-blooded vertebrate animal of a class that comprises the frogs, toads, newts, salamanders, and caecilians. They are distinguished by having an aquatic gill-breathing larval stage followed (typically) by a terrestrial lung-breathing adult stage.
    The word is first recorded in the mid 17th century, in the sense 'having two modes of existence or of doubtful nature', and comes via Latin from Greek *amphibion*, noun use of *amphibios* 'living both in water and on land', from *amphi* 'both' + *bios* 'life'.

amphictyony in ancient Greece, an association of states for the common interest (especially as regards

responsibility for a shrine in the vicinity); the word comes from Greek *amphiktiones* 'dwellers around'.

amphigouri a burlesque composition, a piece of nonsense-verse; the word comes (in the early 19th century) from French, and is apparently a humorous formation from Greek *amphi-* 'about, around' + *agoria* 'speaking', on the model of *allégorie* 'allegory'.

Amphion in Greek mythology, one of the two sons of Zeus and ➤ ANTIOPE, who in Homer's *Odyssey* are referred to as founders of Thebes.

amphisbaena a fabled snake with a head at each end, able to move in either direction. The name comes (in late Middle English) via Latin from Greek *amphisbaina*, from *amphis* 'both ways' + *bainein* 'go'.

Amphitrite in Greek mythology, a sea goddess, wife of ➤ POSEIDON and mother of ➤ TRITON.

ampulla a flask for sacred uses such as holding the oil for anointing the sovereign at a coronation. Recorded in this sense from late Middle English, the word is Latin, originally denoting a roughly spherical Roman flask with two handles, and is a diminutive of *amphora*.

amrit a syrup considered divine by Sikhs and taken by them at baptism and in religious observances. The word comes from Sanskrit *amṛta* 'immortal'.

Amritsar a city in the state of Punjab in NW India, founded in 1577 by Ram Das (1534–81), fourth guru of the Sikhs. It became the centre of the Sikh faith and the site of its holiest temple, the ➤ GOLDEN *Temple*. It was the scene of a riot in 1919, in which 400 people were killed by British troops.

Amu Darya a river of central Asia, rising in the Pamirs and flowing into the Aral Sea, which in classical times was known as the ➤ OXUS.

amulet an ornament or small piece of jewellery thought to give protection against evil, danger, or disease. The word is recorded from the late 16th century; it comes from Latin, but is of unknown origin.

Amun a supreme god of the ancient Egyptians, identified with the sun god Ra, and in Greek and Roman times with Zeus. As a national god of Egypt he was associated in a triad with Mut and Khonsu.
    See also ➤ AMMON, ➤ JUPITER *Ammon*.

Roald Amundsen (1872–1928), Norwegian explorer. Amundsen was the first to navigate the

North-West Passage (1903–6), during which expedition he located the site of the magnetic north pole. In 1911 he became the first to reach the South Pole, ahead of the expedition of ➤ *Robert Falcon* SCOTT.

Amurath the name of several Turkish sultans. Amurath in 1574 murdered his brothers on succeeding to the throne, and his successor in 1596 did the same. In Shakespeare's 2 *Henry IV*, the dying king reminds his son:

> This is the English, not the Turkish court;
> Not Amurath an Amurath succeeds,
> But Harry, Harry.
> — William Shakespeare *2 Henry IV* (1597)

Anabaptists the doctrine that baptism should only be administered to believing adults, held by a radical Protestant sect which emerged during the 1520s and 1530s, following the ideas of reformers such as Zwingli. *Anabaptists* also advocated complete separation of Church and state and many of their beliefs are today carried on by the ➤ MENNON-ITES.

Recorded from the mid 16th century, the name comes via ecclesiastical Latin from Greek *anabaptismos*, from *ana-* 'over again' + *baptismos* 'baptism'.

Anacharsis said by Herodotus to have been a Scythian prince of the 6th century BC, who having travelled widely (and according to one account found that in Greece the Spartans were the only people with whom it was possible to hold a sensible conversation), returned to Scythia, and was killed by his own people, perhaps for trying to introduce the worship of the ➤ MAGNA *mater*.

In Plutarch's life of ➤ SOLON, Anacharsis is said to have told the lawgiver that laws were like spiders' webs, and would catch the poor and weak, but easily be broken by the rich and powerful.

See also ➤ *Anarcharsis* CLOOTS.

anaconda a semiaquatic snake of the boa family which may grow to a great size, native to tropical South America. The name is recorded from the mid 18th century, originally denoting a kind of Sri Lankan snake, and represents an unexplained alteration of Latin *anacandaia* 'python', from Sinhalese *henakaṅdayā* 'whip snake', from *hena* 'lightning' + *kaṅda* 'stem'.

Anacreon (*c.*570–478 BC), Greek lyric poet. The surviving fragments of his work include iambic invectives and elegiac epitaphs, but he is most famous for his poetry written in celebration of love and wine.

Anadyomene in Pliny's *Natural History*, an epithet of Aphrodite in a picture by Apelles, shown emerging from the sea; the word is Greek, and means 'rising from the sea'.

anagram a word, phrase, or name formed by rearranging the letters of another, such as *spar*, formed from *rasp*. Recorded from the late 16th century, the word comes via French or modern Latin from Greek *ana-* 'back, anew' + *gramma* 'letter'.

sons of Anak in the Bible (Numbers ch. 13), a race of giants living in the land of Canaan, of whom their spies reported to the Israelites, 'And there we saw the giants, the sons of Anak, which come of the giants: and we were in our own sight as grasshoppers, and so we were in their sight.'

> Even without the backing of rational argument, Mirabelle was a fearsome disputant. With it, she towered like the sons of Anak, and Ursell became as a grasshopper in her sight.
> — Reginald Hill *Singing the Sadness* (1999)

Anancy the name (from Twi *ananse* 'spider') of a trickster spider character found in many folktales of West Africa and the West Indies.

See also ➤ NANCY *story*.

Ananias in the Bible, the husband of ➤ SAPPHIRA, who with his wife was struck dead for attempting to cheat St Peter; his name is used allusively to denote a liar.

> The report [of the trial] was printed under a heading which read: Ananias Also Ran.
> — Josephine Tey *The Franchise Affair* (1948)

anarchy a state of disorder due to absence or non-recognition of authority or other controlling systems. Recorded from the mid 16th century, the term comes via medieval Latin from Greek *anarkhia*, from *anarkhos*, from *an-* 'without' + *arkhos* 'chief, ruler' (also the base of ➤ ARCHON).

Anastasia the youngest daughter (1901–?18) of the last tsar of Russia, now thought to have died with the rest of her family at ➤ YEKATERINBURG; for many years there were rumours that one or more of the family had escaped the massacre, and a number of claimants appeared. One, 'Anna Anderson', who died in the US in 1984, made many efforts to establish her claim, and was believed by many to be Anastasia.

St Anastasia martyr and married virgin, said to have died at Sirmium. By the 5th century she was venerated in Rome as a Roman martyr, perhaps because her cult became conflated with the titulus

Anastasiae, an ancient church by the Circus Maximus. Her name is of interest, deriving from the Greek, *Anastasis*, or Resurrection, although the ➤ GOLDEN *Legend* explains it as referring to her standing on high, raised from vices to virtues.

□ **FEAST DAY** Her feast day is 25 December.

anathema a person or thing accursed or consigned to damnation; the formal act or formula of cursing. The word comes (in the early 16th century) from ecclesiastical Latin 'excommunicated person, excommunication', from Greek *anathema* 'thing devoted to evil, accursed thing', from *anatithenai* 'to set up'.

anathema maranatha these words occur together in 1 Corinthians 16:22, 'If any man love not the Lord Jesus Christ, let him be Anathema Maranatha', and were formerly thought to represent an intensification of *anathema*, but according to modern criticism, they do not belong together, and ➤ MARANATHA represents a distinct sentence.

anatomy the branch of science concerned with the bodily structure of humans, animals, and other living organisms, especially as revealed by dissection and the separation of parts. The term comes (in late Middle English) via Old French and late Latin from Greek *anatomia*, from *ana-* 'up' + *tomia* 'cutting'. Subsequent misdivision gave rise to ➤ ATOMY.

Anaxagoras (*c*.500–*c*.428 BC), Greek philosopher, teaching in Athens. He believed that all matter was infinitely divisible and motionless until animated by mind (*nous*). He also held that whatever a thing changes into is already present in it before the change.

Anaximander (*c*.610–*c*.545 BC), Greek scientist, who lived at Miletus. He is reputed to have drawn the earliest map of the western world, and to have introduced the sundial into Greece. He believed the earth to be cylindrical and poised in space, and is said to have taught that life began in water and that humans originated from fish.

Anaximenes (*c*.546 BC), Greek philosopher and scientist, who lived at Miletus. Anaximenes believed the earth to be flat and shallow, a view of astronomy that was a retrograde step from that of Anaximander. He also proposed a theory of condensation and rarefaction to explain the diversity of natural substances.

ancestor a person, typically one more remote than a grandparent, from whom one is descended. The term comes (in Middle English) via Old French from Latin *antecessor*, from *antecedere*, from *ante* 'before' + *cedere* 'go'.

Anchises in Greek legend, the ruler of Dardanus and father of ➤ AENEAS; according to the *Aeneid*, when Troy fell he was carried out of the burning ruins on his son's shoulders.

anchor a heavy object attached to a cable or chain and used to moor a ship to the sea bottom, typically one having a metal shank with a ring at one end for the cable and a pair of curved and/or barbed flukes at the other; figuratively, a source of security and confidence. An *anchor* in Christian tradition is a symbol of hope, from a passage in Hebrews 6:19, 'Which hope we have as an anchor of the soul'; it is also the emblem of ➤ *St* CLEMENT, who was martyred by being thrown into the sea with an anchor round his neck.

See also ➤ CROWN *and anchor*, ➤ FOUL *anchor*.

the anchor comes home an archaic expression meaning that the anchor is dragged from its hold, and that therefore an enterprise has failed.

anchorite a religious recluse; the name comes (in Middle English via Latin) from ecclesiastical Greek, from *anakhōrein* 'retire'.

Ancien Régime the political and social system in France (the 'old rule') before the Revolution of 1789.

ancient see ➤ *the* ROYAL *and Ancient*.

ancient an obsolete term for an ➤ ENSIGN (by association with *ancien*, an early form of *ancient* 'old'); in Shakespeare's *1 and 2 Henry IV* and *Henry V*, and *Merry Wives of Windsor*, Falstaff's companion Pistol is called **Ancient Pistol**.

ancient demesne land recorded in Domesday Book as belonging to the Crown.

ancient lights the right of access to light of a property, established by custom and used to prevent the construction of buildings on adjacent property which would obstruct such access. Recorded from the mid 18th century, from *lights* meaning 'light from the sky'. In England the sign 'Ancient Lights' was often placed on a house, adjacent to a site where a high building might be erected.

Ancient Mariner eponymous hero of Coleridge's poem, sole survivor of a disastrous voyage in which the ship after a storm is drawn to the South Pole, who stops one of three wedding guests and forces him to listen to his story.

The mariner had shot an ➤ ALBATROSS and brought down a curse on them all. The ship was driven north to the Equator, where they were scorched by the blazing sun; the dead albatross was hung round the mariner's neck as a penance. The rest of the crew died, but the mariner lived on, and was finally released from the burden. Afterward he was compelled constantly to travel and tell his story as an exemplum of divine grace, and the term *Ancient Mariner* is sometimes used allusively to denote the unwanted presence of someone; the Wedding Guest to whom in the poem he recounts his story is held as much by his glittering eye as his skinny hand.

> He took a quiet pleasure . . . watching the innocents drop the book and try to get to the door before he could spear them with his ancient mariner eye.
> — Iain Sinclair *White Chappell Scarlet Tracings* (1987)

Ancient of Days a name for God, from the scriptural title in Daniel 7:9, 'the Ancient of Days did sit, whose garments were white as snow'.

ancile the sacred tutelary shield of ancient Rome, said to have fallen from heaven, on the preservation of which the safety of the city was supposed to depend.

Ancrene Wisse a book of devotional advice, written for three sisters by a chaplain in about 1230.

and now for something completely different catch-phrase popularized by *Monty Python's Flying Circus* (BBC TV programme, 1969–74).

Anderson shelter a small prefabricated air-raid shelter of a type built in the UK during the Second World War; it was named after John *Anderson*, the Home Secretary in 1939–40 when the shelter was adopted.

Andersonville a village in Sumter county, Georgia, which during the American Civil War was the site of a Confederate military prison for Union soldiers; its high death rate was notorious, and after the war the commander, Henry Wirz, was tried by a military tribunal and executed.

Andorra a small autonomous principality in the southern Pyrenees, between France and Spain, whose independence dates from the late 8th century, when ➤ CHARLEMAGNE is said to have granted the Andorrans self-government for their help in defeating the Moors. Andorra retained a feudal system, and was governed jointly by the French head of state and the Spanish bishop of Urgel, until 1993, when a revised constitution was adopted.

andrew see ➤ MERRY *andrew*.

St Andrew an Apostle, the brother of St Peter, and like him a fisherman. The X-shaped cross (the ➤ SALTIRE) became associated with his name during the Middle Ages because he is said to have died by crucifixion on such a cross. St Andrew is the patron saint of Scotland (his relics were supposedly brought to Scotland by ➤ *St* RULE) and Russia. He is often shown in art with a fishing-net.

☐ **FEAST DAY** His feast day is 30 November.

Androcles a runaway slave (in a story by Aulus Gellius, 2nd century AD) who extracted a thorn from the paw of a lion, which later recognized him and refrained from attacking him when he faced it in the arena.

android an automaton resembling a human being; in science fiction, a synthetic human being. The term comes (in the early 18th century, in the modern Latin form) from modern Latin *androides*, from Greek *anēr, andr-* 'man' + the suffix *-oid* denoting form or resemblance.

Andromache in Greek mythology, the wife of ➤ HECTOR. She became the slave of ➤ NEOPTOLEMUS (son of Achilles) after the fall of Troy.

Andromeda in Greek mythology, an Ethiopian princess whose mother ➤ CASSIOPEIA boasted that she herself (or, in some stories, her daughter) was more beautiful than the nereids. In revenge Poseidon sent a sea monster to ravage the country; to placate him Andromeda was fastened to a rock and exposed to the monster, from which she was rescued by ➤ PERSEUS.

Andromeda is also the name of a large northern constellation between Perseus and Pegasus, with few bright stars. It is chiefly notable for the **Andromeda Galaxy** (or **Great Nebula of Andromeda**), a conspicuous spiral galaxy probably twice as massive as our own and located 2 million light years away.

Andromeda strain after the title of a book by Michael Crichton, a hypothetical, novel type of microorganism, especially one created by genetic engineering, whose release into the environment could cause widespread destruction of life.

Andy see ➤ AMOS *and Andy,* ➤ *Andy* CAPP.

Andy Pandy a clown puppet who was one of the central characters of the television series for young children, *Watch with Mother*, from 1950.

> Williams has been playing nauseatingly cute for ages, but achieves a new squashiness here as a chatterbox Andy Pandy.
> — *Time Out* 31 March 1993

anecdote a short amusing or interesting story about a real incident or person. The word comes (in the late 17th century) via French or modern Latin from Greek *anekdota* 'things unpublished', from *an-* 'not' + *ekdotos*, from *ekdidōnai* 'publish'.

Aneirin Welsh poet of the 6th century, to whom the poem *Y Gododdin*, commemorating a British defeat at Catraeth (Catterick) is attributed.

anemone a plant of the buttercup family which typically has brightly coloured flowers and deeply divided leaves. Recorded from the mid 16th century, the name comes from Latin, and is said to be from Greek *anemōnē* 'windflower', literally 'daughter of the wind', from *anemos* 'wind', thought to be so named because the flowers open only when the wind blows.

angary the right of a country at war to seize or destroy neutral property out of military necessity, provided that compensation is paid. Recorded from the late 19th century, the word comes via French from Italian or Latin *angaria* 'forced service', from Greek *angareia*, from *angaros* 'courier' (being liable to serve as the King's messenger), from Persian.

angel a spiritual being more powerful and intelligent than a human being, especially in Jewish, Christian, Muslim, and other theologies, one acting as a messenger, agent, or attendant of God; in Christian angelology, a member of the ninth and lowest order of the ninefold ➤ CELESTIAL *hierarchy*, ranking directly below the archangels. The term is also used for a person regarded as a messenger of God, especially (in biblical translations, as at Revelation 2:1, 'the angel of the church of Ephesus') in the early Church.

An *angel* was also the name given to a former English coin minted between the reigns of Edward IV and Charles I and bearing the figure of the archangel Michael killing a dragon.

An *angel* is the symbol of ➤ *St* MATTHEW and ➤ *St* CECILIA.

Recorded in Old English in the form *engel*, the word comes ultimately via ecclesiastical Latin from Greek *angelos* 'messenger'; it was superseded in Middle English by forms from Old French *angele*.

See also ➤ ANGELS, ➤ FALLEN *angel*, ➤ HELL's *Angel*, ➤ MINISTERING *angel*, ➤ RECORDING *angel*.

Angel Falls a waterfall in the Guiana Highlands of SE Venezuela which is the highest waterfall in the world, with an uninterrupted descent of 978 m (3,210 ft). The falls were discovered in 1935 by the American aviator and prospector James *Angel* (*c*.1899–1956).

the angel in the house a woman who is completely devoted to her husband and family, from the title of a poem (1854–62) by Coventry Patmore. The term is often used pejoratively; in a lecture on 'Professions for Women' (1931), Virginia Woolf asserted that it was the task of women writers to 'kill the Angel in the House'.

Angel of the North a steel sculpture of a winged figure, over 20 metres tall and with a wingspan of 54 metres, created by the British sculptor Antony Gormley (1950–) and assembled on site near the A1 in Gateshead in February 1998; it is positioned to mark the southern entry to Tyneside.

entertain an angel unawares not realize the status of one's guest; the allusion is biblical, to Hebrews 13:2, 'Be not forgetful to entertain strangers: for thereby some have entertained angels unawares.'

the Angelic Doctor another name for ➤ *St* THOMAS *Aquinas*.

the Angelic Hymn another name for the ➤ GLORIA *in excelsis*.

the angelic salutation another name for the ➤ SALUTATION.

angelica a tall aromatic plant of the parsley family, with large leaves and yellowish-green flowers. Native to both Eurasia and North America, it is used in cooking and herbal medicine. The name comes (in the early 16th century) from medieval Latin *(herba) angelica* 'angelic (herb)', so named because it was believed to be efficacious against poisoning and disease.

Fra Angelico the Italian painter Giovanni da Fiesole (*c*.1400–55). His work was intended chiefly for contemplation and instruction, and his simple and direct style shows an understanding of contemporary developments in Renaissance painting, especially perspective.

angels see also ➤ FOOLS *rush in where angels fear to tread*, ➤ *I am on the* SIDE *of the angels*, ➤ *not* ANGLES *but angels*.

City of the Angels an informal name for Los Angeles.

how many angels can dance on the head of a pin? regarded satirically as a characteristic speculation of scholastic philosophy, particularly as exemplified by 'Doctor Scholasticus' (Anselm of Laon, d. 1117) and as used in medieval comedies.

Angels of Mons protective spirits supposedly seen over the First World War battlefield; the origin was in fact a short story, 'The Angel of Mons' (1915) by Arthur Machen (1843–1947), which circulated widely by word of mouth as a factual account.

Angelus a Roman Catholic devotion commemorating the Incarnation of Jesus and including the Hail Mary, said at morning, noon, and sunset; a ringing of church bells announcing this. The word is recorded from the mid 17th century, and comes from the Latin phrase *Angelus domini* 'the angel of the Lord', the opening words of the devotion.

anger see ➤ *never let the* SUN *go down on your anger*.

Angevin any of the Plantagenet kings of England, especially those who were also counts of ➤ ANJOU (Henry II, Richard I, and John), descended from Geoffrey, Count of Anjou. The name comes via French from medieval Latin *Andegavinus*, from *Andegavum* 'Angers', the town in western France which is the former capital of Anjou.

Angkor the capital of the ancient kingdom of Khmer in NW Cambodia, noted for its temples, especially the **Angkor Wat** (mid 12th century); the site was rediscovered in 1860.

angle see also ➤ BLOODY *Angle*.

Angle a member of a Germanic people, originally inhabitants of what is now Schleswig-Holstein, who came to England in the 5th century AD. The Angles founded kingdoms in Mercia, Northumbria, and East Anglia and gave their name to England and the English.

The name comes from Latin *Angli* 'the people of Angul', a district of Schleswig (now in northern Germany), so named because of its angular shape.

angle with a silver hook buy fish instead of catching it, use money as a lure; the expression is recorded in varying forms (as, *fish with a golden hook*) from the mid 16th century.

not Angles but angels translation of Latin *Non Angli sed Angeli*, a comment attributed to ➤ GREGORY *the Great* (AD *c.*540–604), on seeing fair-haired English slaves in Rome; the story is oral tradition, based on Bede's *Historia Ecclesiastica*.

Anglesey an island of North Wales, separated from the mainland by the Menai Strait, which in the 1st century AD was a centre of Druid power and resistance to Roman invasion; in AD 61 it was attacked by Suetonius Paulinus, who killed Druid priests and cut down sacred groves.

Anglican of, relating to, or denoting the Church of England or any Church in communion with it. The name comes (in the early 17th century) from medieval Latin *Anglicanus* (its adoption suggested by *Anglicana ecclesia* 'the English Church' in the Magna Carta), ultimately from the base of ➤ ANGLE.

anglicanum see ➤ OPUS *anglicanum*.

Anglo-Catholicism a tradition within the Anglican Church which is close to Catholicism in its doctrine and worship and is broadly identified with High Church Anglicanism. As a movement, Anglo-Catholicism grew out of the ➤ OXFORD *Movement* of the 1830s and 1840s.

Anglo-Irish of English descent but born or resident in Ireland, or a member of such a family, and associated particularly with the ➤ PROTESTANT *Ascendancy*; in a speech in 1925, Yeats said of the Anglo-Irish stock from which he himself came:

> We . . . are no petty people. We are one of the great stocks of Europe. We are the people of Burke; we are the people of Swift, the people of Emmet, the people of Parnell.
> — William Butler Yeats speech to the Irish Senate, 11 June 1925

Anglo-Irish Agreement an agreement made between Britain and the Republic of Ireland in 1985, admitting the Republic to discussions on Northern Irish affairs and providing for greater cooperation between the security forces in border areas.

Anglo-Saxon relating to or denoting the Germanic inhabitants of England from their arrival in the 5th century up to the Norman Conquest.

Anglo-Saxon Chronicle an early record in English of events in England, from the beginning of the Christian period to 1154.

angora a cat, goat, or rabbit of a long-haired breed; a fabric made from the hair of the angora goat or rabbit. The name comes (in the early 19th century) from the place-name *Angora,* former name (until 1930) of the Turkish capital *Ankara.*

Angria and Gondal imaginary kingdoms invented by the Brontë children, as a further development of games and stories inspired by a box of wooden soldiers brought home by their father in 1826. Early games created the Glass Town Confederacy on the west coast of Africa; the capital city, Glass Town or Verdopolis, owed much in its architecture to the engravings of John Martin (1789–1854). Later Emily and Anne broke away and invented the kingdom of Gondal, which was to provide the setting for many of Emily's poems. Charlotte and Branwell, in 1834, jointly created the kingdom of Angria, of which the principle characters were Alexander Percy, the earl of Northangerland, and Arthur Wellesley, marquis of Douro.

angry see ➤ *a* HUNGRY *man is an angry man.*

angry white male a right-wing or anti-liberal white man, especially a working-class one; the term is first recorded in the US in the early 1990s.

> Now the angry white males are bent on dismantling the new version of Reconstruction.
> — *Guardian* 26 April 1995

angry young man a young man dissatisfied with and outspoken against existing social and political structures, originally, a member of a group of socially conscious writers in the 1950s, including particularly the playwright John Osborne. The phrase, the title of a book (1951) by Leslie Paul, was used of Osborne in the publicity material for his play *Look Back in Anger* (1956), in which the characteristic views were articulated by the anti-hero Jimmy Porter.

Angurvadel in Scandinavian legend, the sword of Frithiof, forged by dwarfs.

anima mundi a power supposed to organize the whole universe and coordinate its parts; the term is recorded in English from the late 16th century, and comes from medieval Latin (as used by ➤ *Peter* ABELARD) meaning literally 'soul of the world', apparently formed to render Greek *psukhē tou kosmou.*

animal individual animals are traditionally held to typify particular qualities, as, the *beaver* and the *bee* as types of industry, the *ox* of strength, and the *wolf*

of savagery. They may also be associated with particular people, as a *dog* is an emblem of ➤ *St* ROCH. ➤ *St* FRANCIS *of Assisi* is the patron saint of animals; the 6th-century Welsh abbot St Beuno, to whose shrine lambs and calves were brought, is the patron saint of sick animals.

The word *animal* is sometimes used to designate a person whose behaviour is regarded as devoid of human attributes or civilizing influences, especially someone who is very cruel, violent, or repulsive.

Animal Farm a fable (1945) by George Orwell which consists of a satire on Russian Communism as it developed under Stalin. The animals of the farm, led by the pigs, revolt against the cruel farmer Mr Jones with the slogan, 'Four legs good, two legs bad', and achieve an apparent life of freedom, but as power corrupts their rulers, they are led to a world in which the slogan is 'All animals are equal but some animals are more equal than others.'

animal, vegetable, and mineral the three traditional divisions into which natural objects have been classified; the classification (earlier in Latin) is first recorded in English in the early 18th century. From the mid 19th century, **animal, vegetable, (or) mineral** became the name of a parlour game in which players had to guess the identity of an object, having been told to which of the three groups it belongs; they are traditionally allowed up to twenty questions, to be answered by 'yes' or 'no'.

> The Lion looked at Alice wearily. Are you animal—or vegetable—or mineral?' he said.
> — Lewis Carroll *Through the Looking-Glass* (1871).

Animula vagula blandula opening words of a Latin poem attributed to the dying Emperor ➤ HADRIAN (AD 76–138):

> *Animula vagula blandula,*
> *Hospes comesque corporis,*
> *Quae nunc abibis in loca*
> *Pallidula rigida nudula,*
> *Nec ut soles dabis iocos!*
>
> — Emperor Hadrian poem

This was translated by Byron:

> Ah! gentle, fleeting, wav'ring sprite,
> Friend and associate of this clay!
> To what unknown region borne,
> Wilt thou now wing thy distant flight?
> No more with wonted humour gay,
> But pallid, cheerless, and forlorn.
> — Lord Byron 'Adrian's Address to his Soul When Dying' (1804)

The lines had earlier been reworked by Alexander Pope in *The Dying Christian to His Soul* (1730), in a poem which substitutes an optimistic Christian vision for Hadrian's bleaker pagan view:

> Vital spark of heav'nly flame!
> Quit, oh quit this mortal frame:
> Trembling, hoping, ling'ring, flying,
> Oh the pain, the bliss of dying!
> — Alexander Pope 'The Dying Christian to his Soul'
> (1730)

Anjou a former province of western France, on the Loire. It was an English possession from 1154, when it was inherited by Henry II as count of Anjou, until 1204, when it was lost to France by King John; it is the origin of the name ➤ ANGEVIN for the dynasty of Plantagenet kings.

ankh an object resembling a cross, but with a loop in place of the upper limb, used in ancient Egyptian art as a symbol of life. Recorded in English from the late 19th century, the word comes from Egyptian, and means literally 'life, soul'.

Ann see ➤ MOTHER *Ann*.

Anna see ➤ *Anna* KARENINA, ➤ *Anna* PAVLOVA.

Anna Comnena (1083–?1148), Byzantine princess and historian, daughter of the Emperor Alexius I Comnenus, and author of *The Alexiad*, a panegyric on his life.

Annales Cambriae a 10th-century series of Welsh annals, of interest for the information they offer about Gildas and some aspects of the legend of Arthur, such as the battle of Badon, which they place in 518, and the battle of Camlan in 539, in which they say Arthur and Mordred were killed.

Annals of the Four Masters a 17th century compilation of earlier Irish chronicles, such as the *Annals of Connacht* and the *Annals of Ulster*; its Irish name is *Annála Ríoghachta Éireann* 'Annals of the Kingdom of Ireland'. It was produced in the 1630s by the Franciscan Michael O'Clery and three collaborators.

Annapurna a ridge of the Himalayas, in north central Nepal, the highest peak of which rises to 8,078 m (26,503 ft); it is named for an aspect of the goddess ➤ PARVATI, and may be referred to as the type of an almost unconquerable height.

> I was standing knee-deep in a bog and he was scaling creative Annapurnas.
> — T. C. Boyle *Budding Prospects* (1984)

Anne (1665–1714), queen of England and Scotland (known as Great Britain from 1707) and Ireland 1702–14. The last of the Stuart monarchs, daughter of the Catholic James II (but herself a Protestant), she succeeded her brother-in-law William III to the throne. As queen she presided over the Act of Union, which completed the unification of Scotland and England. None of her children survived into adulthood, and by the Act of Settlement (1701) the throne passed to the House of Hanover on her death.

See also ➤ *Mrs* MORLEY, ➤ QUEEN *Anne*.

St Anne traditionally the mother of the Virgin Mary, first mentioned by name in the apocryphal gospel of James (2nd century). The extreme veneration of St Anne in the late Middle Ages was attacked by Luther and other reformers. She is the patron saint of Brittany and the province of Quebec in Canada.

☐ **FEAST DAY** Her feast day is 26 July.

anneal heat (metal or glass) and allow it to cool slowly, in order to remove internal stresses and toughen it. The original sense (in Old English, in the form *onǽlan*) was 'set on fire', from *on* + *ǽlan* 'burn, bake', from *āl* 'fire, burning', hence (in late Middle English) 'subject to fire, alter by heating'.

anno domini system of dating from the birth of Christ (see ➤ DIONYSIUS²); the Latin words (abbreviated as AD) mean 'in the year of our Lord'. The term is recorded in English from the late 16th century; from the late 19th century, it has also been used humorously to designated advanced or advancing age.

Annual Register an annual review of the events of the past year, founded by Dodsley and Burke in 1758, which still survives. The first volume appeared on 15 May 1759, and was highly successful; Prior described it as the 'best and most comprehensive of all the periodical works, without any admixture of their trash, or any tediousness of detail'. It also published poetry, literary articles, etc. Burke edited it anonymously for several years.

Annunciation the announcement of the Incarnation, made by Gabriel to Mary; the **Feast of the Annunciation** is celebrated on 25 March, otherwise called *Lady Day*. In art, representations often show Mary sitting with a book on her lap, her pose either shrinking or accepting; Gabriel often holds a lily.

Order of the Annunciation a military order founded by Amadeus VI of Savoy in 1362, under the title 'Knights of the true lover's knot,' and re-named, on the accession of Amadeus VIII to the

Pontificate in 1439, in honour of the Annunciation of the angel Gabriel. Also called *Annunciade.*

annus horribilis a dreadful year; the Latin phrase, modelled on ➤ ANNUS *mirabilis,* was used notably by the Queen in 1992 when looking back on a year which had seen severe marital difficulties for her children and a fire at Windsor Castle:

> 1992 is not a year I shall look back on with undiluted pleasure. In the words of one of my more sympathetic correspondents, it has turned out to be an 'annus horribilis'.
> — Elizabeth II speech at the Guildhall, 24 November 1992

annus mirabilis a remarkable or auspicious year, from modern Latin ('wonderful year') in *Annus Mirabilis: the year of wonders, 1666,* the title of a poem (1667) by Dryden; its subjects were the Dutch War and the Fire of London.

Annwn in Celtic mythology, the underworld, ruled over by ➤ ARAWN. The Welsh counterparts of the ➤ BARGHEST are known as *Cwn Annwn,* 'the Dogs of Hell'.

anorak a socially inept and studious or obsessive person with unfashionable and largely solitary interests. The meaning dates from the 1980s and derives from the anoraks worn by ➤ TRAINSPOTTERS, regarded as typifying this kind of person.

> The Chancellor is an anorak. He has the social skills of a whelk.
> — *Sunday Times* 31 January 1999

the Anschluss the annexation of Austria by Germany in 1938. Hitler had forced the resignation of the Austrian Chancellor by demanding that he admit Nazis into his cabinet. The new Chancellor, a pro-Nazi, invited German troops to enter the country on the pretext of restoring law and order.

St Anselm (*c.*1033–1109), Italian-born philosopher and theologian, Archbishop of Canterbury 1093–1109. He worked to free the Church from secular control and believed that the best way to defend the faith was by intellectual reasoning. His writings include *Cur Deus Homo?* a mystical study on the Atonement, and *Proslogion,* an ontological 'proof' of the existence of God.

☐ **FEAST DAY** His feast day is 21 April.

George Anson (1697–1762), English sailor and explorer, who made a voyage round the world in 1740–4; the account of it, attributed to his chaplain Richard Walter and published in 1748, is the source of Cowper's poem 'The Castaway', which describes the fate of a seaman washed overboard while manning the shrouds.

answer see ➤ *the answer is a* LEMON, ➤ CROSS-*questions and crooked answers,* ➤ DUSTY *answer,* ➤ *a* SOFT *answer turneth away wrath.*

ant the *ant* is proverbial for its industry, often with biblical reference to Proverbs 6:6, 'Go to the ant, thou sluggard; consider her ways, and be wise.'

See also ➤ PHARAOH *ant.*

Antaeus in Greek mythology, a giant, the son of Poseidon and Earth, who compelled all comers to wrestle with him; he gained renewed strength with the ground, and overcame and killed all opponents until he was defeated by Hercules.

> I am essentially a landsman, descended no doubt from Antaeus.
> — Patrick O'Brian *The Nutmeg of Consolation* (1991)

Antarctic of or relating to the south polar region or Antarctica. The name comes (in late Middle English, via Old French or Latin) from Greek *antarktikos* 'opposite to the north', from *ant-*'against' + *arktikos* (see ➤ ARCTIC).

Antares the brightest star in the constellation Scorpius. It is a binary star of which the main component is a red supergiant. The name (which is Greek) means literally 'simulating Mars (Ares)', that is, in colour.

antebellum occurring or existing before a particular war, especially the American Civil War.

antediluvian of or belonging to a time before the biblical Flood; utterly out of date, very antiquated.

antelope a swift-running deer-like ruminant with smooth hair and upward-pointing horns, native to Africa and Asia, and including the gazelles, impala, gnus, and elands. Originally (in late Middle English) this was the name of a fierce mythical creature with long serrated horns, said to live on the banks of the Euphrates; the word comes via Old French and medieval Latin from late Greek *antholops,* of unknown origin and meaning.

antenna either of a pair of long, thin sensory appendages on the heads of insects, crustaceans, and some other arthropods. The word comes (in the mid 17th century) from Latin, alteration of *antemna* 'yard' (of a ship), used in the plural to translate Greek *keraioi* 'horns (of insects)', used by Aristotle.

anthem a musical setting of a religious text to be sung by a choir during a church service, especially in Anglican or Protestant Churches. Recorded from Old English in the form *antefn, antifne* (denoting a composition sung antiphonally), from late Latin *antiphona* 'antiphon, a short sentence sung or recited before or after a psalm or canticle'.

anthemion an ornamental design of alternating motifs resembling clusters of narrow leaves or honeysuckle petals.

Anthemius (6th century AD), Greek mathematician, engineer, and artist; known as **Anthemius of Tralles**. His experiments included study of the effects of compressed steam. In 532 he was chosen by Justinian to design ➤ ST *Sophia* in Constantinople.

anthology a published collection of poems or other pieces of writing; a similar collection of songs or musical compositions issued in one album. The word comes, in the mid 17th century, via French or medieval Latin from Greek *anthologia*, from *anthos* 'flower' + *-logia* 'collection'; in Greek, the word originally denoted a collection of the 'flowers' of verse, i.e. small choice poems or epigrams, by various authors.

In one of his *Essais* (1580), Montaigne commented 'It could be said of me that in this book I have only made up a bunch of other men's flowers, providing of my own only the string that ties them together,' and *Other Men's Flowers* (1944) was the title of an anthology of poetry by the British soldier Lord Wavell.

Anthology Club Boston literary society (*c.*1804–11), devoted to raising the standards of American literature. Despite the scholarly interest in Americana shown by members, they came into conflict with Noah Webster and were viewed as being pro-English. Their reading room was the foundation of the Boston Athenaeum.

Anthony Eden a black Homburg hat, of a type often worn by the British Conservative statesman Anthony Eden (1897–1977).

St Anthony of Egypt (*c.*251–356), Egyptian hermit, the founder of monasticism. During his seclusion in the Egyptian desert he attracted a number of followers whom he organized into a community; his hermit life is also noted for the temptations he underwent, especially from demons in the guise of beautiful women. He is said to have visited, and arranged the burial of, St Paul, the first Christian hermit (see ➤ *St* PAUL²).

In the Middle Ages the belief arose that praying to St Anthony would effect a cure for ergotism, and the Order of Hospitallers of St Anthony (founded at La Motte *c.*1100, with members of the Order wearing black robes marked by a blue tau cross) became a pilgrimage centre. The little bells rung by Hospitallers asking for alms were afterwards hung round the necks of animals as a protection against disease, and pigs which belonged to the Order were allowed to roam free about the streets.

☐ **EMBLEM** His traditional emblems are pigs and bells.

☐ **PATRONAGE** He is the patron saint of basketmakers and swineherds.

☐ **FEAST DAY** His feast day is 17 January.

St Anthony of Padua (1195–1231), Portuguese Franciscan friar, whose charismatic preaching in the south of France and Italy made many converts. He is sometimes shown preaching to fishes (as St Francis is shown with birds), and in one popular legend a mule kneels before him, rejecting a bundle of hay in favour of the consecrated hosts. His devotion to the poor is commemorated by alms known as **St Anthony's bread**; he is invoked to find lost articles; according to a legend a novice borrowed his psalter without permission and was forced by a terrifying apparition to return it.

☐ **EMBLEM** He is often shown with a book and a lily, in the company of the Christ Child; he may also be represented in a nut-tree to mark his preference for solitude.

☐ **FEAST DAY** His feast day is 13 June.

St Anthony's cross another name for the ➤ TAU cross, worn by the Order of Hospitallers of St Anthony of Egypt.

St Anthony's fire inflammation of the skin due to ergot poisoning, reflecting the belief that St Anthony of Egypt could cure the illness.

St Anthony's pig a ➤ TANTONY *pig*.

anthropophagi cannibals, especially in legends or fables; the 'Cannibals that each other eat, The Anthropophagi' were among the wonders with which ➤ OTHELLO fascinated Desdemona. Recorded from the mid 16th century, the word comes via Latin from Greek *anthrōpophagos* 'man-eating'.

anthroposophy a formal educational, therapeutic, and creative system established by Rudolf

Steiner, seeking to use mainly natural means to optimize physical and mental health and well-being.

Anti-Corn-Law League a pressure group formed in Britain in 1838 to campaign for the repeal of the ➤ CORN *Laws*, under the leadership of Richard Cobden and John Bright.

Anti-Rent War in 19th century America, the conflict between the agrarian feudal system with industrial democracy, centred in the Van Rensselaer land-holdings along the Hudson River.

antic hay an absurd dance; the phrase comes originally from Christopher Marlowe's *Edward II* (1593), 'My men, like satyrs…Shall with their goat feet dance an antic hay.'

Antichrist a great personal opponent of Christ, expected by the early Church to appear before the end of the world. The name is recorded from Old English and comes via Old French or ecclesiastical Latin from Greek *antikhristos* 'against Christ'.

antidisestablishmentarianism a factitious long word; although the proper meaning is, opposition to the disestablishment of the Church of England, no actual usage examples have been traced.

Antigone in Greek mythology, daughter of Oedipus and Jocasta, the subject of a tragedy by Sophocles. She was sentenced to death for defying her uncle Creon, king of Thebes, by burying the ritually unburied body of her brother ➤ POLYNICES, but she took her own life before the sentence could be carried out, and Creon's son Haemon, who was engaged to her, killed himself.

antimacassar a piece of cloth put over the back of a chair to protect it from grease and dirt or as an ornament; *Macassar* is a kind of oil formerly used by men to make their hair shine and lie flat.

antimony the chemical element of atomic number 51, a brittle silvery-white semimetal. Antimony was known from ancient times; the naturally occurring black sulphide was used as the cosmetic ➤ KOHL.

antinomian of or relating to the view that Christians are released by grace from the obligation of observing the moral law. Attributed to St Paul by his opponents, this doctrine was held by many Gnostic sects, and also by some radical Protestant groups at the Reformation.

The word is recorded from the mid 17th century,

and comes ultimately from Greek *anti-* 'opposite, against' + *nomos* 'law'.

Antinous[1] in Greek mythology, the chief suitor of ➤ PENELOPE, killed by ➤ ODYSSEUS.

Antinous[2] a young Bithynian favourite of the Emperor Hadrian, renowned for his beauty, who was drowned in the Nile in AD 130; sculptural representations of him were common.

> With her refined Greek profile and ethereal expression, she looks remarkably like the seraphic Antinous.
> — *New Republic* 3 August 1992

Antioch a city in southern Turkey, near the Syrian border, which was the ancient capital of Syria under the Seleucid kings, who founded it *c.*300 BC.

See also ➤ St MARGARET *of Antioch*.

Antiochus III (*c.*242–187 BC), Seleucid king, reigned 223–187 BC, known as **Antiochus the Great**. He restored and expanded the Seleucid empire, regaining the vassal kingdoms of Parthia and Bactria and conquering Armenia, Syria, and Palestine. When he invaded Europe he came into conflict with the Romans, who defeated him on land and sea and severely limited his power.

Antiope in Greek mythology, mother by Zeus of ➤ AMPHION and his brother, legendary founders of Thebes. Imprisoned by her husband's brother for her betrayal of her husband, she was tormented by his wife ➤ DIRCE, but was ultimately revenged by her sons.

the Antipodes Australia and New Zealand (used by inhabitants of the northern hemisphere). The name comes (in late Middle English, via French and late Latin) from Greek *antipodes* 'having the feet opposite', from *anti-* 'against' + *pous, pod-* 'foot'. The term originally denoted the inhabitants of opposite sides of the earth.

antipope a person set up as Pope in opposition to one canonically chosen, and applied particularly to those who resided at ➤ AVIGNON during the ➤ GREAT *Schism*. Recorded from late Middle English (in form *antipape*) the name comes from medieval Latin *antipapa*, on the pattern of ➤ ANTICHRIST.

Anton Piller order in English law, a court order which requires the defendant in proceedings to permit the plaintiff or his or her legal representatives to enter the defendant's premises in order to obtain evidence essential to the plaintiff's case. It was named (in the 1970s) after *Anton Piller*, German manufacturers of electric motors, who were involved in legal proceedings (1975) in which such an order was granted.

Antonine Wall a defensive fortification about 59 km (37 miles) long, built (c.140 AD) across the narrowest part of southern Scotland between the Firth of Forth and the Firth of Clyde. It was intended to mark the frontier of the Roman province of Britain, but in c.181 the wall was breached and the northern tribes forced a retreat to Hadrian's Wall.

Antoninus Pius (86–161), Roman emperor 138–61. The adopted son and successor of Hadrian, he had a generally peaceful and harmonious reign. He extended the empire and the frontier of Britain was temporarily advanced to the Antonine Wall.

Mark Antony (c.83–30 BC), Roman general and triumvir. A supporter of ➤ JULIUS *Caesar*, in 43 he was appointed one of the triumvirate after Caesar's murder. Following the battle of Philippi he took charge of the Eastern Empire, where he established his association with ➤ CLEOPATRA. Quarrels with Octavian (see ➤ AUGUSTUS) led finally to his defeat at the battle of Actium and to his suicide.

antonym a word opposite in meaning to another (e.g. *bad* and *good*).

Anubis in ancient Egyptian theology, the god of mummification, protector of tombs, usually represented as having a jackal's head.

anvil see ➤ *the* CHURCH *is an anvil that has worn out many hammers.*

any port in a storm proverbial saying; mid 18th century.

anyone for tennis? a typical line in a drawing-room comedy; perhaps originally from George Bernard Shaw *Misalliance* (1914) 'Anybody on for a game of tennis?'

Anzac a member of the Australian and New Zealand Army Corps; the acronym is recorded from 1915, in accounts of ➤ GALLIPOLI.

Anzac Day 25 April, commemorating the landings of the corps in the ➤ GALLIPOLI Peninsula on 25 April, 1915.

Anzus an alliance between Australia, New Zealand, and the US, established in 1951 and designed to protect those countries in the Pacific area from armed attack.

Aonia a region of Boeotia in ancient Greece containing Mount Helicon, sacred to the Muses.

> My adventurous song,
> That with no middle flight intends to soar
> Above th' Aonian Mount.
> — John Milton *Paradise Lost* (1667)

Aotearoa Maori name for New Zealand, literally 'land of the long white cloud'.

Apache a member of an American Indian people living chiefly in New Mexico and Arizona; the Apache put up fierce resistance to the European settlers and were, under the leadership of ➤ GERONIMO, the last American Indian people to be conquered. Their reputed ferocity gave rise (in the early 20th century) to the use of *apache* to mean a violent street ruffian, originally in Paris.

The name comes from Mexican Spanish, probably from Zuñi *Apachu*, literally 'enemy'.

apartheid the former South African policy of racial segregation of other groups from the white inhabitants. Adopted by the successful Afrikaner National Party as a slogan in the 1948 election, apartheid extended and institutionalized existing racial segregation. Despite rioting and terrorism at home and isolation abroad from the 1960s onwards, the white regime maintained the apartheid system with only minor relaxation until February 1991.

The word is recorded from the 1940s, and comes from Afrikaans, meaning literally 'separateness'.

ape a large primate that lacks a tail, including the gorilla, chimpanzee, orang-utan, and gibbons; before the introduction of ➤ MONKEY, the word for a monkey, and afterwards still sometimes so used, especially in poetic and literary sources, and when the animal is taken as typifying the ability to imitate human behaviour, especially in an absurd or unthinking way.

See also ➤ BUFFOON *ape*, ➤ NAKED *ape*, ➤ SAY *an ape's paternoster*, ➤ SEDULOUS *ape*.

an ape's an ape, a varlet's a varlet, though they be clad in silk and scarlet proverbial saying, mid 16th century (2nd century AD in Greek); meaning that inward nature cannot be overcome by outward show.

Apelles (4th century BC), Greek painter. He is now known only from written sources, as by Pliny's account of his ➤ VENUS *Anadyomene*, but was highly acclaimed throughout the ancient world. Several Renaissance artists were inspired to try to emulate his works. The saying ➤ NOT *a day without a line* is attributed to him.

lead apes in hell (of a woman) die unmarried; in Shakespeare's *Taming of the Shrew* (1592), the jealous Katharina, accusing their father of favouring her sister, says, 'She is your treasure…I must…for your love to her, lead apes in hell.'

aphorism a concise statement of a scientific principle, typically by a classical author; a pithy observation which contains a general truth. The word comes from the 'Aphorisms of Hippocrates', and was transferred to other sententious statements to the principles of physical science, and then to statements of principles generally.

Aphrodisias an ancient city of western Asia Minor, site of a temple dedicated to Aphrodite. Now in ruins, it is situated 80 km (50 miles) west of Aydin, in modern Turkey.

Aphrodite in Greek mythology, the goddess of beauty, fertility, and sexual love. She is variously described as the daughter of Zeus and Dione, or as being born from the sea. Her cult was of Eastern origin, hence her identification with Astarte and Ishtar. Her Roman equivalent is ➤ VENUS.

The name is Greek, and means literally 'foamborn', from *aphros* 'foam'.

See also ➤ CESTUS[1].

Marcus Gavius Apicius a Roman epicure of the 1st century AD; John Evelyn (1620–1706) uses **Apician** to mean of or pertaining to epicures or to luxurious diet.

Apis in Egyptian mythology, a god depicted as a bull, symbolizing fertility and strength in war.

Apocalypse the complete final destruction of the world, especially as described in the biblical book of Revelation. The word is recorded from Old English, and comes ultimately, via Old French and ecclesiastical Latin, from Greek *apokaluptein* 'uncover, reveal'.

apocalyptic describing or prophesying the complete destruction of the world; resembling the end of the world; momentous or catastrophic; the **apocalyptic number** is another name for ➤ *the* NUMBER *of the beast*, 666.

apocatastasis the Christian doctrine which holds that ultimately all free moral creatures, including devils, will share in the grace of salvation. The doctrine has never enjoyed wide acceptance. Recorded

from the late 17th century, the word comes via Latin from the Greek term for 're-establishment'.

Apocrypha biblical or related writings not forming part of the accepted canon of Scripture. The Old Testament Apocrypha include writings (dating from around 300 BC to AD 100) which appeared in the Septuagint and Vulgate versions but not in the Hebrew Bible; most are accepted by the Roman Catholic and Orthodox Churches as the 'deutero-canonical' books. The New Testament Apocrypha include texts attributed to Apostles and other biblical figures but not regarded as authentic by the Councils of the Church.

Recorded from late Middle English, the word comes from ecclesiastical Latin *apocrypha (scripta)* 'hidden (writings)', ultimately from Greek *apokruptein* 'hide away'. The adjective **apocryphal**, meaning of doubtful authenticity, mythical, fictional, is recorded from the late 16th century.

Apollinaris (*c*.310–*c*.390), bishop of Laodicea in Asia Minor. He upheld the heretical doctrine that Christ had a human body and soul but no human spirit, this being replaced by the divine Logos.

Apollo in Greek mythology, a god, son of Zeus and Leto and brother of ➤ ARTEMIS. He is associated with music, poetic inspiration, archery, prophecy, medicine, pastoral life, and the sun; the sanctuary at ➤ DELPHI was dedicated to him.

Apollo is also the name for the American space programme for landing astronauts on the moon. *Apollo 8* was the first mission to orbit the moon (1968), *Apollo 11* was the first to land astronauts (1969), and five further landings took place up to 1972.

Apollo Belvedere an ancient statue of Apollo, now in the Belvedere Gallery of the Vatican Museum.

Apollodorus (2nd century BC), Athenian grammarian. He was known to have written about the gods, and an extant treatise on mythology, the *Bibliotheca*, was attributed to him. First printed in 1555, this work became widely used, and (indirectly or directly) provided Johnson and Milton with some of their mythological material.

Apollonius of Perga (*c*.260–190 BC), Greek mathematician. In his principal surviving work, *Conics*, he examined and redefined conic sections and was the first to use the terms *ellipse*, *parabola*, and *hyperbola* for these classes of curve. From his astronomical studies he probably originated the concept of epicycles to account for the retrograde motion of the outer planets.

Apollonius of Rhodes (3rd century BC), Greek poet and grammarian. He is known for his *Argonautica*, an epic poem in Homeric style dealing with the expedition of the Argonauts. It was the first such poem to place love (Medea's love for Jason) in the foreground of the action.

Apollyon a name for the Devil, in Revelation 9:11, 'And they had a king over them, which is the angel of the bottomless pit, whose name in the Hebrew tongue is Abaddon, but in the Greek tongue hath his name Apollyon.'

In Bunyan's *Pilgrim's Progress*, Christian has to fight to get past the 'foul fiend' *Apollyon*, who blocks his path.

Recorded from late Middle English (in Wyclif's translation of the Bible) the name comes (via late Latin, in the Vulgate) from Greek *Apolluōn* (translating ➤ ABADDON), and ultimately from *apo-* 'quite' + *ollunai* 'destroy'.

apologia a formal written defence of one's opinions or conduct; the word is Latin, and is recorded from the late 18th century, but its currency is largely due to ➤ *John Henry* NEWMAN's *Apologia pro Vita Sua* (1864), the history of his religious life up to the time of his reception into the Roman Catholic Church in 1845.

apopthegm a concise saying or maxim; an aphorism. The word is recorded from the mid 16th century, and comes ultimately (via French or modern Latin) from Greek *apophthengesthai* 'speak out'.

aposiopesis the rhetorical device of suddenly breaking off in speech; the word comes ultimately (in the late 16th century, via Latin) from Greek *aposiōpan* 'be silent'.

apostasy the abandonment or renunciation of a religious or political belief or principle. The term comes (in Middle English) from ecclesiastical Latin *apostasia*, from a late Greek alteration of Greek *apostasis* 'defection'.

apostate a person who renounces a religious or political belief or principle. Recorded from Middle English, the word comes via ecclesiastical Latin from Greek *apostatēs* 'apostate, runaway slave'.

See also ➤ JULIAN.

Apostle[1] each of the twelve chief disciples of Jesus Christ. The twelve Apostles were Peter, Andrew, James, John, Philip, Bartholomew, Thomas, Matthew, James (the Less), Judas (or Thaddaeus), Simon, and Judas Iscariot. After the suicide of Judas Iscariot his place was taken by Matthias.

The term is also applied to any important early Christian teacher, especially St Paul, and to the first successful Christian missionary in a country or to a people.

Recorded from Old English (in form *apostol*) the word comes via ecclesiastical Latin from Greek *apostolos* 'messenger', from *apostellein* 'send forth'.

See also ➤ ACTS *of the Apostles*, ➤ PILLAR *apostle*, ➤ PRINCE *of the Apostles*, ➤ *Theobald* MATHEW.

Apostles of different countries

NAME	SAINT
Apostle of Germany	St Boniface
Apostle of Spain	St James the Great
Apostle of the Gentiles	St Paul
Apostle of the Indies	St Francis Xavier
Apostles of the Slavs	St Cyril and St Methodius

Apostle[2] a member of an exclusive society in the University of Cambridge (officially 'The Cambridge Conversazione Society') formed in Cambridge in 1820, for the purpose of friendship and formal discussion. During the 19th century members included Arthur Hallam and Tennyson, and the 20th century saw a new age of brilliance, largely inspired by G. E. Moore, with members such as John Maynard Keynes, Bertrand Russell, Leonard Woolf, and E. M. Forster. Members are elected for life.

Apostle spoon a teaspoon with the figure of an Apostle or saint on the handle.

Apostles' Creed a statement of Christian belief used in the Western Church, dating from the 4th century and traditionally ascribed to the twelve Apostles.

Apostolic see ➤ CATHOLIC *and Apostolic Church*.

Apostolic Constitutions a compilation of church doctrines and customs, probably originating in Syria and dating from about the 4th century.

Apostolic Fathers the Christian leaders of the early Church immediately succeeding the Apostles.

Apostolic Majesty a title of the Emperor of Austria as King of Hungary.

apostolic succession (in Christian thought) the uninterrupted transmission of spiritual authority from the Apostles through successive popes and bishops, taught by the Roman Catholic Church but denied by most Protestants.

apothecary a person who prepared and sold medicines and drugs. Recorded from late Middle English, the word comes via Old French and late Latin from Greek *apothēkē* 'storehouse'.

➤ *St* Nicholas *of Myra* is the patron saint of apothecaries.

apotheosis originally (in the late 16th century) this denotes the elevation of someone to divine status, or deification; in later use, the meaning develops of the highest point in the development of something; a culmination or climax. The word comes via ecclesiastical Latin from Greek, from *apotheoun* 'make a god of', from *apo* 'from' + *theos* 'god'.

Appalachian Mountains a mountain system of eastern North America, stretching from Quebec and Maine in the North to Georgia and Alabama in the South. Although not particularly high, the Appalachians served as an effective barrier for some 200 years to westward expansion by early European settlers.

Appalachian Trail a 3,200-km (about 2,000-mile) footpath through the Appalachian Mountains from Mount Katahdin in Maine to Springer Mountain in Georgia.

appeal see ➤ Court *of Appeal.*

appearances are deceptive proverbial saying; mid 17th century.

appellant see ➤ Lords *Appellant.*

appetite comes with eating proverbial saying; mid 17th century, from Rabelais.

Appian Way the principal road southward from Rome in classical times, named after the censor Appius Claudius Caecus, who in 312 BC built the section to Capua; it was later extended to Brindisi.

apple traditionally the fruit with which ➤ Eve was tempted by the serpent.

Apples are an emblem of ➤ St Dorothy.

See also ➤ Adam's *apple*, ➤ big *apple*, ➤ bob *for apples*, ➤ devil's *apple*, ➤ golden *apple*, ➤ love *apple*, ➤ *the* rotten *apple injures its neighbours*, ➤ *small choice in* rotten *apples.*

an apple a day keeps the doctor away proverbial saying; mid 19th century.

Apple Island in Australia, informal name for Tasmania, because of its popular identification as an apple-growing region.

apple-john a kind of apple said to keep two years, and to be perfectly ripe when shrivelled and withered; it was originally so called because it was said to be ripe on St John's day.

the apple never falls far from the tree proverbial saying, mid 19th century; meaning that family characteristics will show themselves.

apple of discord in Greek mythology, the golden apple inscribed 'For the fairest,' said to have been thrown by Eris, the personification of discord, into the assembly of the gods, and contended for by Hera, Athene, and Aphrodite. Paris of Troy (see ➤ Paris¹), chosen by the gods to adjudicate, awarded the apple to Aphrodite; the result was to be the ➤ Trojan *War.*

apple of one's eye a person of whom one is extremely fond and proud, originally denoting the pupil of the eye, considered to be a globular solid body, extended as a symbol of something cherished.

apple of Sodom another name for ➤ Dead *Sea fruit.*

Appleby see ➤ *Sir* Humphrey *Appleby.*

Johnny Appleseed byename for the American nurseryman John Chapman (1774–1845), who sold or gave apple seedlings to pioneers to establish apple trees throughout the midwest; according to legend, *Johnny Appleseed* is a figure who constantly travels planting apple seedlings for others to enjoy.

> Ralph Nader has always wanted to be a Johnny Appleseed, and as he lopes around Orlando with free samples of cereals . . . his moment as an American folk hero seems to have arrived.
> — *Vanity Fair* October 1990

appointment see also ➤ *appointment in* Samarra.

by appointment indicating that a particular manufacturer holds a Royal Warrant for the supply of goods to the sovereign or a particular member of the royal family.

Appomattox the court house at *Appomattox,* Virginia, was the site on 9 April 1865 of the end of the American Civil War, with the formal surrender of the Confederate forces under ➤ *Robert E.* Lee to the Union commander ➤ *Ulysses S.* Grant.

apprentice see ➤ sorcerer*'s apprentice.*

après moi le déluge French phrase meaning, trouble will come after my time; the comment '*Après nous le déluge* [After us the deluge]' is attributed to Madame de Pompadour (1721–64), favourite and mistress of Louis XV of France.

April the fourth month of the year in the northern hemisphere usually considered the second month of spring, often referred to allusively as characterized by changeable weather, with sudden showers and sunshine.
   See also ➤ *in April* Dove*'s flood is worth a king's good*, ➤ March *borrowed from April three days, and they were ill.*

April Fool a person who is the victim of a trick or hoax on April Fool's Day.

April Fool's Day 1 April, in many Western countries traditionally an occasion for playing tricks. This custom has been observed for hundreds of years, but its origin is unknown. It is also called *All Fools' Day.*

April showers bring forth May flowers proverbial saying, mid 16th century; referring to the value of rain during April to early growth.

apron a protective garment, originally *naperon*, the *n* being lost by wrong division.

tied to one's mother's apron strings traditional phrase, meaning that a person who should be grown up is still subject to their mother's dominance; from the mid 16th century, an *apron string* as the fastening of an apron has been used to symbolize the role of the mistress of a household.

apse a large semicircular or polygonal recess in a church, arched or with a domed roof and typically at the church's eastern end. Recorded from the early 19th century, the word comes (in the sense 'either of two points on the orbit of a planet or satellite that are nearest to or furthest from the body round which it moves' from *apsis* (denoting in the early 17th century the orbit of a planet), from Greek *apsis*, *hapsis* 'arch, vault', perhaps from *haptein* 'fasten, join').

Apuleius (born *c.*123 AD), Roman writer, born in Africa. His writings are characterized by an exuberant and bizarre use of language and he is best known for the *Metamorphoses* (*The Golden Ass*), a picaresque novel which recounts the adventures of a man who is transformed into an ass.

aqua fortis an archaic term for nitric acid, as a powerful solvent and corrosive, from Latin, literally meaning 'strong water'.

aqua regia a concentrated mixture of acids able to dissolve 'noble' metals, gold and platinum; the phrase is Latin, and means 'royal water'.

aqua vitae strong alcoholic spirit, especially brandy; the phrase is Latin, and means 'water of life'.

Aquarian a member of an early Christian sect using water instead of wine in the Eucharist.

Aquarius a large constellation (the Water Carrier or Water Bearer); in astrology, the eleventh sign of the ➤ zodiac, which the sun enters about 21 January. The name is from Latin 'of water', used as a noun to mean 'water carrier'.

Age of Aquarius an astrological age which is about to begin, marked by the precession of the vernal equinox into Aquarius, believed by some to herald worldwide peace and harmony.

Aquila a small northern constellation (the Eagle), said to represent the eagle that carried Ganymede to Olympus. It contains the bright star Altair, and some rich star fields of the Milky Way.

aquila non captat muscas Latin saying, recorded in Erasmus, meaning literally 'an eagle does not catch flies'; a great person is not concerned with trivial matters.

Aquilon a former name for the north or north-north-east wind.

Aquinas see ➤ *St* Thomas *Aquinas.*

Aquitaine a region and former province of SW France, on the Bay of Biscay, centred on Bordeaux. A province of the Roman Empire and a medieval duchy, it became an English possession by the marriage of Eleanor of Aquitaine to Henry II, and remained so until 1453.

arabesque an ornamental design consisting of intertwined flowing lines, originally meaning 'in the Arab style'.

Arabia a peninsula of SW Asia, largely desert, lying between the Red Sea and the Persian Gulf and bounded on the north by Jordan and Iraq, which is the original homeland of the Arabs and the historic centre of Islam; in literary use, it may be referred to as a rich and distant eastern land, as in Lady Macbeth's lament, 'All the perfumes of Arabia will not sweeten this little hand.'

Arabia Deserta the ancient Roman designation (in Latin, 'barren Arabia') for the northern part of the Arabian peninsula, excluding the Sinai peninsula, often used in contrast to the more fertile south.

Arabia Felix the ancient Roman designation for the southern part of the Arabian peninsula, often identified partly or wholly with the Yemen. The Latin name means literally 'happy, fertile, or prosperous Arabia', and is thought to come from a Greek translation of the Arabic name for the Yemen, *al-yaman*, which can mean both 'on the right hand side' (i.e. in the south, for one travelling or facing east) or 'fortunate, blessed'. The latter interpretation was adopted in the Greek and Latin translations, perhaps strengthened by the association of the area with the growth of spices, in contrast to the northern, more infertile part of Arabia.

Arabia Petraea the ancient Roman designation for a region in the north-west of the Arabian peninsula, sometimes identified with the Sinai peninsula. The Latin word *petraea* means 'stony', or perhaps 'from (the city of) *Petra*'.

Arabian see also ➤ DARLEY *Arabian*.

Arabian a member of a 3rd century sect in Arabia which held that the soul died with the body, and rose again with it at the resurrection.

Arabian bird a phoenix, a unique specimen; the phrase comes originally from Shakespeare's *Antony and Cleopatra* (1606–7), 'O, Antony! O, thou Arabian bird!'

Arabian Nights a collection of stories and romances written in Arabic. The king of Samarkand has killed all his wives after one night's marriage until he marries ➤ SCHEHERAZADE, who saves her life by entertaining him with stories. The stories include the tales of ➤ ALADDIN and ➤ SINBAD *the Sailor*. The collection is also known as *The Thousand and One Nights*.

Arabic numerals any of the numerals 0, 1, 2, 3, 4, 5, 6, 7, 8, and 9. Arabic numerals reached western Europe (replacing Roman numerals) through Arabia by about AD 1200 but probably originated in India.

Araby an archaic term for ➤ ARABIA.

Arachne a woman of Colophon in Lydia, a skilful weaver who challenged ➤ ATHENE to a contest.

Athene destroyed Arachne's work and Arachne tried to hang herself, but Athene changed her into a spider. The name comes from Greek *arakhnē* 'spider'.

Aragon an autonomous region of NE Spain, bounded on the north by the Pyrenees and on the east by Catalonia and Valencia; capital, Saragossa. Formerly an independent kingdom, which was conquered in the 5th century by the Visigoths and then in the 8th century by the Moors, it was united with Catalonia in 1137 and with Castile in 1479.

Eugene Aram (1704–59), a schoolmaster from Knaresborough, York, whose murder of a friend for many years went undiscovered; he was eventually convicted and hanged, and his story is the subject of Thomas Hood's poem *The Dream of Eugene Aram*:

> Two stern-faced men set out from Lynn,
> Through the cold and heavy mist;
> And Eugene Aram walked between,
> With gyves upon his wrist.
> — Thomas Hood 'The Dream of Eugene Aram' (1829)

In 19th-century literature, Aram was seen as someone who, despite his crime, had an inherent moral worth evinced by his long-term experience of guilt and remorse.

> How Eugene Aram, though a thief, a liar, and a
>   murderer,
> Yet, being intellectual, was amongst the noblest of
>   mankind.
> — C. S. Calverley 'Of Reading' (1861)

Aramaic a branch of the Semitic family of languages, especially the language of Syria used as a lingua franca in the Near East from the 6th century BC, later dividing into varieties one of which included Syriac and Mandaean. It replaced Hebrew locally as the language of the Jews, and though displaced by Arabic in the 7th century AD, it still has about 200,000 speakers in scattered communities.

Aramis name of one of the ➤ THREE *Musketeers* who befriend ➤ D'ARTAGNAN in Dumas' novel.

Aran Islands a group of three islands, Inishmore, Inishmaan, and Inisheer, off the west coast of the Republic of Ireland, traditionally a stronghold of the Gaelic-speaking culture.

Aranyaka each of a set of Hindu sacred treatises based on the Brahmanas, composed in Sanskrit *c*.700 BC. Intended only for initiates, the Aranyakas contain mystical and philosophical material and explications of esoteric rites.

Mount Ararat a pair of volcanic peaks in eastern Turkey, near the borders with Armenia and Iran.

The higher peak, which rises to 5,165 m (16,946 ft), is the traditional site of the resting place of Noah's ark after the Flood (Genesis 8:4).

Arawn in Welsh mythology, the king of ➤ ANNWN, the underworld, who was said to have made a friend of ➤ PWYLL, prince of Dyfed, and to have exchanged kingdoms with him for a year.

arbalest a crossbow with a special mechanism for drawing back and releasing the string. Recorded in Old English in the form *arblast*, the word comes via Old French from late Latin *arcubalista*, from Latin *arcus* 'bow' + *ballista* 'a catapult used in ancient warfare for hurling large stones'.

arbiter elegantiarum a judge of artistic taste and etiquette, a Latin term meaning 'judge of elegance', used by Tacitus to describe ➤ PETRONIUS, arbiter of taste at Nero's court.

Arbor Day a day set apart annually in the US, Australia, New Zealand, and elswhere for the planting of trees.

arbor vitae another term for the evergreen coniferous tree the thuja. Recorded from the mid 16th century, the name comes from a Latin phrase meaning literally 'tree of life', probably with reference to its medicinal use.

Arc see also ➤ *St* JOAN *of Arc*.

Arc de Triomphe a ceremonial arch standing at the top of the Champs Élysées in Paris, commissioned by Napoleon to commemorate his victories in 1805–6. Inspired by the Arch of Constantine in Rome, it was completed in 1836. The Unknown Soldier was buried under the centre of the arch on Armistice Day 1920.

Arcades ambo a phrase from Virgil, meaning in Latin 'both Arcadians', now meaning two persons of the same tastes, profession, or character.

> 'Well, I'm a lawyer too, and a pretty sharp one—*arcades ambo*,' said Johnnie with a coarse laugh.
> — H. Rider Haggard *Colonel Quaritch* (1888)

Arcadia a mountainous district in the Peloponnese of southern Greece. In poetic fantasy it represents a pastoral paradise the home of song-loving shepherds, and in Greek mythology it is the home of Pan.

et in Arcadia ego Latin phrase, meaning literally 'And I too in Arcadia'; a tomb inscription, of disputed interpretation, often depicted in classical paintings, notably by Poussin in 1655.

arcanum a great secret or mystery; one of the supposed great secrets of nature which alchemists tried to discover. Recorded from the late 16th century, the word represents the use as a noun of the neuter of the Latin adjective *arcanus* 'mysterious, secret', from *arcere* 'to shut up', from *arca* 'chest'.

arch see ➤ COURT *of Arches*, ➤ *Arch of* TITUS, ➤ *Arch of* TRAJAN, ➤ DEAN *of the Arches*, ➤ MARBLE *Arch*.

the Arch-poet the name given to the anonymous German writer of Goliardic Latin poetry whose patron was Rainald of Dassel, archchancellor of Frederick Barbarossa (*c.*1123–90).

archaeologists St Damasus, a 4th-century pope who took a keen interest in the collection and housing of papal archives as well as in the relics of Roman martyrs, and ➤ *St* JEROME, are the patron saints of archaeologists.

archangel an angel of greater than ordinary rank; (in traditional Christian angelology) a being of the eighth-highest order of the ninefold celestial hierarchy. The name is recorded from Middle English, and comes via Anglo-Norman French and ecclesiastical Latin, from ecclesiastical Greek *arkhangelos*, from *arkhi-* 'chief' + *angelos* 'messenger, angel'.

archer a person who shoots with a bow and arrow; the constellation and zodiacal sign Sagittarius.

> ➤ *St* GEORGE and ➤ *St* SEBASTIAN are the patron saints of archers.
> See also ➤ FRANC-*archer*.

the Archers a farming soap opera, which has been broadcasting its 'everyday story of country folk' since 1950, and which was originally conceived as a vehicle by which the Ministry of Agriculture could disseminate information. The story has now covered several generations of the *Archer* family and their neighbours; one famous episode, dealing with the death of Grace Archer in a stable fire, being broadcast on 22 September 1955, the night on which Independent Television began transmission.

archetype an original which has been imitated; (in Jungian theory) a primitive mental image inherited from the earliest human ancestors, and supposed to be present in the collective unconscious.

archeus the immaterial principle supposed by the Paracelsians to govern animal and vegetable life; a vital force. It was believed that the chief *archeus* was situated in the stomach, and that subordinate *archei* regulated the action of other organs.

Archie Bunker a man of similar background and prejudices to *Archie Bunker*, a character in a US television comedy series, *All in the Family*, representing a poorly educated white blue-collar worker with strong racist and sexist prejudices.

> His [Senator Sam Ervin's] dropped *g's* and regionalisms . . . are a happy antidote to Archie Bunkerisms.
> — *Time* 25 June 1973

Archilochus (8th or 7th century BC), Greek poet. Acclaimed in his day as equal in stature to Homer and Pindar, he wrote satirical verse and fables and is credited with the invention of iambic metre.

archimage a chief magician or enchanter, a great wizard; the term is used by Spenser in the *Faerie Queene* as the name of the personification of hypocrisy.

archimandrite the superior of a large monastery or group of monasteries in the Orthodox Church.

Archimedean screw an instrument for raising water by the turning of an inclined screw within a cylinder, said to have been invented by ➤ ARCHIMEDES.

Archimedes (*c.*287–212 BC), Greek mathematician and inventor, of Syracuse. He is famous for his discovery of ➤ ARCHIMEDES' *principle* (legend has it that he made this discovery while taking a bath, and ran through the streets shouting 'Eureka!'), and for his assertion (on the action of a lever), 'Give me but one firm spot on which to stand, and I will move the earth.' Among his mathematical discoveries are the ratio of the radius of a circle to its circumference, and formulas for the surface area and volume of a sphere and of a cylinder.

Archimedes' principle a law stating that a body totally or partially immersed in a fluid is subject to an upward force equal in magnitude to the weight of fluid it displaces.

archipelago a group of islands; a sea or stretch of water having many islands. The word comes (in the early 16th century, via Italian) from Greek *arkhi-* 'chief' + *pelagos* 'sea'. The word was originally used as a proper name (*the Archipelago* 'the Aegean Sea'): the general sense arose because the Aegean Sea is remarkable for its large numbers of islands.

architect see also ➤ EVERY *man is the architect of his own fortune.*

architects ➤ St THOMAS *the Apostle* and ➤ *St* BARBARA are the patron saints of architects.

archon the chief magistrate, or, after the time of ➤ SOLON, each of the nine chief magistrates, of ancient Athens. Recorded from the late 16th century, the word comes from Greek *arkhōn* 'ruler'.

Arctic of or relating to the regions around the North Pole. Recorded from late Middle English, the name comes via Old French and Latin from Greek *arktikos*, from *arktos* 'bear, Ursa Major, pole star'.

Arctic Circle the parallel of latitude 66° 33′ north of the equator. It marks the northernmost point at which the sun is visible on the northern winter solstice and the southernmost point at which the midnight sun can be seen on the northern summer solstice.

Arcturus the fourth-brightest star in the sky, and the brightest in the constellation Boötes. It is an orange giant. The name comes from Greek *arktos* 'bear' + *ouros* 'guardian' (because of its position in line with the tail of Ursa Major).

ard-ri in pre-Norman Ireland, the title ('high king') used to describe a powerful Irish king.

the Forest of Arden the home of the banished Duke in Shakespeare's *As You Like It*; it is often understood as representing the actual forest in Warwickshire called Arden and referred to in romance literature, but is actually based on the forest of the Ardennes in the Low Countries (now Belgium).

Fountain of Ardenne a fountain which in Boiardo's *Orlando Innamorato* had the power of changing to hate the love of those who drank its waters.

ardente see also ➤ CHAMBRE *Ardente*, ➤ CHAPELLE *ardente*.

are you now or have you ever been a member of the Communist Party? formal question put to those appearing before the Committee on Un-American Activities during the McCarthy campaign of 1950–4 against alleged Communists in the US government and other institutions; the allusive form *are you now or have you ever been?* derives from this.

are you sitting comfortably? Then we'll begin introduction to stories on *Listen with Mother*, BBC radio programme for small children, 1950–82.

Hannah Arendt (1906–75), German-born American philosopher and political theorist. A pupil of

Heidegger, she established her reputation as a political thinker with one of the first works to propose that Nazism and Stalinism had common roots. In her reports of the trial in Jerusalem of ➤ *Adolf* Eich-mann, she coined the phrase 'the banality of evil'.

Areopagite see ➤ Dionysius[4].

Areopagitica title of Milton's pamphlet on the freedom of the press published in 1644; the title is derived from ➤ Areopagus, and the publication was partly inspired by attempts by Parliament to suppress Milton's own pamphlet on divorce.

Areopagus (in ancient Athens) a hill on which was sited the highest governmental council and later a judicial court. The name comes from Greek *Areios pagos* 'hill of Ares'; the name for the site came to denote the court itself.

Ares in Greek mythology, the war god, son of Zeus and Hera; his Roman equivalent is ➤ Mars.

Arethusa the nymph with whom ➤ Alpheus fell in love, and who was turned into a fountain in her attempt to escape him.

Pietro Aretino (1492–1556), Italian poet, frequently mentioned in English works of the Elizabethan and later periods; he is described by Milton in *Areopagitica* as 'that notorious ribald of Arezzo'.

Guido d'Arezzo (*c.*990–1050), Italian Benedictine monk and musical theorist, to whom the system of naming the notes of a scale by syllables is attributed (see ➤ Gamut).

argent silver as a heraldic tincture. Recorded from late Middle English (denoting silver coins), the word comes via Old French from Latin *argentum* 'silver'.

Argive of or relating to the ancient city of *Argos*; (especially in Homer) Greek.

Argo in Greek mythology, the ship in which Jason and his companions, the ➤ Argonauts, sailed.

Argonauts in Greek mythology, a group of heroes who accompanied ➤ Jason on board the ship *Argo* in the quest for the Golden Fleece. Their story is one of the oldest Greek sagas, known to Homer, and may reflect early explorations in the Black Sea.

Argos a city in the NE Peloponnese of Greece. One of the oldest cities of ancient Greece, it dominated the Peloponnese and the western Aegean in the 7th century bc.

argosy in poetic and literary use, a large merchant ship, originally one from ➤ Ragusa or Venice. Recorded from the late 16th century, the word apparently comes from Italian *Ragusea (nave)* '(vessel of) Ragusa'.

argument from design in Christian theology, the argument that God's existence is demonstrable from the evidence of design in the universe.

Argus in Greek mythology, a vigilant watchman with a hundred eyes, who was set by Hera to watch ➤ Io, and who was killed by Hermes. After his death, his eyes were said to have been transferred by Hera to the eyelike markings on the tail of a peacock. The term **Argus-eyed** is used to mean extremely vigilant, sharp-sighted.

Argyll see ➤ God *bless the Duke of Argyll.*

Ariadne in Greek mythology, the daughter of King Minos of Crete and Pasiphaë. She helped ➤ Theseus to escape from the Minotaur's labyrinth by giving him a ball of thread, which he unravelled as he went in and used to trace his way out again after killing the Minotaur. They fled together but he deserted her on the island of Naxos.

Arianism in Christian theology, the main heresy denying the divinity of Christ, originating with the Alexandrian priest *Arius* (*c.*250–*c.*336). Arianism maintained that the son of God was created by the Father and was therefore neither coeternal nor consubstantial with the Father. It retained a foothold among Germanic peoples until the conversion of the Franks to Catholicism (496).

Ariel the name of a fairy in Shakespeare's *The Tempest*, who has been rescued from the enchantment of the witch Sycorax by ➤ Prospero and who must serve his new master until he is released; Ariel is the airy spirit who contrasts with the gross and animal ➤ Caliban.

The name was given to a satellite of Uranus discovered in 1851, the twelfth closest to the planet and the fourth largest (diameter 1,160 km), and subsequently to a series of six American and British satellites devoted to studies of the ionosphere and X-ray astronomy (1962–79).

Aries a small constellation (the Ram), said to represent the ram whose Golden Fleece was sought by Jason and the Argonauts; in astrology, the first sign of the zodiac, which the sun enters at the vernal equinox (about 20 March).

First Point of Aries the point on the celestial sphere where the path of the sun crosses the celestial equator from south to north in March, marking the zero point of right ascension. Owing to precession of the equinoxes it has moved from Aries into Pisces, and is now approaching Aquarius.

Arimasp any of a mythical race of one-eyed men in northern Europe who tried to take gold guarded by griffins; the name comes via Latin from Greek, and is said to mean in Scythian 'one-eyed'.

Arimathea see ➤ Joseph *of Arimathea*.

Arion[1] a legendary Greek poet and musician of the 7th century BC who is said to have visited Italy and become wealthy; returning home, he was thrown overboard by the seamen who wanted to steal his treasure, but was carried safely to land by a dolphin which had been charmed by the song he was permitted to sing before his death.

Arion[2] in Greek mythology, a magic horse, offspring of Poseidon and Demeter, which belonged to Adrastus, one of the ➤ Seven *against Thebes*; its speed allowed him to escape safely when the attack on Thebes failed.

Ludovico Ariosto (1474–1533), Italian poet. His *Orlando Furioso* (final version 1532), about the exploits of Roland (Orlando) and other knights of Charlemagne, was the greatest of the Italian romantic epics; Spenser used its narrative form as a model for his *Faerie Queene*.

Ariosto of the North in *Childe Harold*, Byron's name for Scott.

Aristarchus[1] (3rd century BC), Greek astronomer; known as **Aristarchus of Samos**. Founder of an important school of Hellenic astronomy, he was aware of the rotation of the earth around the sun and so was able to account for the seasons. Many of his theories were more accurate than those of Ptolemy, which replaced them.

Aristarchus[2] (*c*.217–145 BC), Greek scholar; known as **Aristarchus of Samothrace**. The librarian at Alexandria, he is noted for his editions of the writings of Homer and other Greek authors, and in particular for his rejection of many lines as spurious; from this, the term **aristarch** came to be used to mean 'a severe critic'.

Aristides an Athenian statesman and general of the 5th century BC, known as **Aristides the Just**. He commanded the Athenian army at the battle of Plataea, but came into conflict with ➤ Themistocles and was ostracized. According to a story in Plutarch, one illiterate voter, not recognizing him, requested Aristides himself to write the name 'Aristides' on the sherd that would condemn him; when asked his reason, he said that it was because he was tired of hearing the name 'Aristides the Just'.

Aristippus (late 5th century BC), Greek philosopher; known as **Aristippus the Elder**. He was a pupil of Socrates and is generally considered the founder of the Cyrenaic school, holding that pleasure is the highest good and that virtue is to be equated with the capacity for enjoyment.

Aristophanes (*c*.450–*c*.385 BC), Greek comic dramatist. His surviving plays are characterized by exuberant language and the satirization of leading contemporary figures.

Aristotelian logic the traditional system of logic expounded by Aristotle and developed in the Middle Ages, concerned chiefly with deductive reasoning as expressed in syllogisms.

Aristotle (384–322 BC), Greek philosopher and scientist. A pupil of Plato and tutor to Alexander the Great, he founded a school (the Lyceum) outside Athens. He is one of the most influential thinkers in the history of Western thought and his work was central to Arabic and medieval philosophy. His surviving works cover a vast range of subjects, including logic, ethics, metaphysics, politics, natural science, and physics.

Aristotle's lantern a conical structure of calcareous plates and muscles supporting the rasping teeth of a sea urchin. The term derives from Aristotle's *Historia Animalium*, where the body of the echinus is said to be shaped like the frame of a lantern.

arithmetic the branch of mathematics dealing with the properties and manipulation of numbers. The term comes (in Middle English, via Old French and Latin) from Greek *arithmētikē (tekhnē)* '(art) of counting', from *arithmos* 'number'. Early forms such as *arsmetrike* were influenced by Latin *ars metrica* 'measuring art'.

In the Middle Ages, arithmetic was counted as one of the ➤ seven *liberal arts*, and was one of the subjects of the ➤ quadrivium.

Arjuna a Kshatriya prince in the Mahabharata, one of the two main characters in the Bhagavadgita, the charioteer to whom Krishna gives counsel during the battle.

the ark in the Bible, the ship built by Noah to save his family and two of every kind of animal from the Flood; ➤ NOAH*'s ark.*

Ark of the Covenant the wooden chest which contained the tablets of the laws of the ancient Israelites. Carried by the Israelites on their wanderings in the wilderness, it was cherished by them in the Promised Land; its temporary loss to the Philistines (1 Samuel 4) caused Eli's daughter-in-law to name her son ➤ ICHABOD. The Ark was later placed by Solomon in the Temple at Jerusalem, but was lost when Nebuchadnezzar's forces destroyed the Temple in 586 BC.

The hunt for the lost *Ark of the Covenant* forms the plot of Steven Spielberg's first ➤ *Indiana* JONES film, *Raiders of the Lost Ark* (1981).

Richard Arkwright (1732–92), English inventor and industrialist. In 1767 he patented a water-powered spinning machine capable of producing yarn strong enough to be used as warp. He established several spinning mills despite disputes over patents and opposition to his mechanization.

Arlington National Cemetery the American national burial ground in Arlington County, Virginia, which is the resting place of important soldiers and statesman.

arm see ➤ *the* LONG *arm of the law,* ➤ STRETCH *your arm no further than your sleeve will reach.*

the Armada a Spanish naval invasion force sent against England in 1588 by Philip II of Spain. It was defeated by the English fleet and almost completely destroyed by storms off the Hebrides. The word *armada* comes (in the mid 16th century, meaning 'a fleet of warships') via Spanish and ultimately from Latin *armare* 'to arm'.

Armageddon (in the New Testament) the last battle between good and evil before the Day of Judgement; the place where this will be fought. In extended usage, *Armageddon* means a dramatic and catastrophic conflict, especially one seen as likely to destroy the world or the human race.

The name is Greek, and comes from Hebrew *har mĕgiddōn* 'hill of Megiddo'.

See also ➤ MEGIDDO.

armchair critic one whose views are based on theorizing rather than first-hand experience; *armchair* in this sense is recorded from the 19th century, and

the *Times Register of Events for 1885* refers to Joseph Chamberlain's responding to the expostulations of 'his moderate allies' with sneers at 'the armchair politicians'.

armed at all points prepared in every particular; the expression is recorded from late Middle English, but often refers directly to a First Folio variant reading of Shakespeare's *Hamlet.*

Armenia a landlocked country in the Caucasus of SE Europe. The Armenian homeland fell under Turkish rule from the 16th century, and with the decline of the Ottomans was divided between Turkey, Iran, and Russia. In 1915 the Turks forcibly deported 1,750,000 Armenians to the deserts of Syria and Mesopotamia; more than 600,000 were killed or died on forced marches. Russian Armenia was absorbed into the Soviet Union in 1922, gaining independence as a member of the Commonwealth of Independent States in 1991.

Armenian Church an independent Christian Church established in Armenia since *c.*300 and influenced by Roman and Byzantine as well as Syrian traditions. A small Armenian Catholic Church also exists (see ➤ UNIATE).

Armenteers see ➤ MADEMOISELLE *from Armenteers.*

armillary sphere a model of the celestial globe constructed from rings and hoops representing the equator, the tropics, and other celestial circles, and able to revolve on its axis. The name comes (in the mid 17th century) from modern Latin *armillaris* 'relating to an *armilla*', an astronomical instrument consisting of a hoop fixed in the plane of the equator (sometimes crossed by one in the plane of the meridian), used by the ancient astronomers to show the recurrence of equinoxes and solstices; in Latin, *armilla* means 'bracelet'.

Arminian an adherent of the doctrines of Jacobus Arminius (Latinized name of Jakob Hermandszoon, 1560–1609), a Dutch Protestant theologian who rejected the Calvinist doctrine of predestination. His teachings had a considerable influence on Methodism.

Armistice Day the anniversary of the armistice of 11 November 1918, now replaced by Remembrance Sunday in the UK and Veterans Day in the US.

Armorica an ancient region of NW France between the Seine and the Loire, equating to modern Brittany.

Armory Show popular name for the International Exhibition of painting and sculpture held at the Armory of the 69th Regiment in New York City in 1913; it was organized by the Association of American Painters and Sculptors and helped by the progressive group *The Eight*.

armour see ➤ COAT *armour*, ➤ *knight in* SHINING *armour*.

arms distinctive emblems or devices, originally borne on shields in battle and now forming the heraldic insignia of families, corporations, or counties.
See also ➤ *Arms of* PATRONAGE, ➤ CANTING *arms*, ➤ COAT-*of-arms*, ➤ COLLEGE *of Arms*, ➤ KING *of Arms*, ➤ KINGS *have long arms*.

Armstrong punning name (recorded from the 1920s) identifying the imaginary inventor of non-existent equipment, with reference to the use of physical strength in tasks which might be more easily performed with mechanical assistance.

> This was before traction engines and 'lectric motors what I'm talking about. All we had were our hands, 'Armstrong's Patent' we used to call it.
> — *New Society* 5 August 1976

army see ➤ CHURCH *Army*, ➤ CONTINENTAL *Army*, ➤ DAD's *Army*, ➤ *the* FORGOTTEN *Army*, ➤ RED *Army*, ➤ SALVATION *Army*, ➤ SKELETON *army*, ➤ WHITE *Army*.

an army marches on its stomach proverbial saying; mid 19th century, variously attributed to Frederick the Great and Napoleon.

Arnhem a town in the eastern Netherlands, situated on the River Rhine. During the Second World War, in September 1944, Allied airborne troops made a landing nearby but were overwhelmed by German forces. It was of the plans for this operation (codenamed *Market Garden*) that the British soldier Frederick 'Boy' Browning warned Montgomery, 'I think we might be going a bridge too far.'

Arnold of Rugby (1795–1842), English historian and educator; Headmaster of Rugby School from 1828, and father of the poet Matthew Arnold. Thomas Arnold, 'The Doctor', figures in *Tom Brown's Schooldays*; he himself said, on being appointed Headmaster, 'My object will be, if possible, to form Christian men, for Christian boys I can scarcely hope to make.'

aroint thee avaunt! begone!; the origin is unknown, but its use by Shakespeare, as in 'Aroint thee, witch', popularized it for later writers.

aromatherapy the use of aromatic plant extracts and essential oils for healing and cosmetic purposes.

Arondight the name of ➤ LANCELOT's sword.

arras a wall hanging made of rich tapestry fabric, named after the French town of *Arras*, a centre for tapestry-making.

arrow a weapon consisting of a thin, straight stick with a sharp point, designed to be shot from a bow.
Arrows are the emblem of ➤ *St* EDMUND *the Martyr* and of ➤ *St* SEBASTIAN.
See also ➤ BROAD *arrow*, ➤ TIME's *arrow*.

ars gratia artis Latin phrase meaning ➤ ART *for art's sake*; taken as the motto of Metro-Goldwyn-Mayer film studios, and apparently intended to say 'Art is beholden to the artists'.

arsenic arsenic compounds (and their poisonous properties) have been known since ancient times, and the metallic form was isolated in the Middle Ages. Arsenic occurs naturally in orpiment, realgar, and other minerals, and rarely as the free element; its toxic compounds are widely used as herbicides and pesticides.
Recorded from late Middle English (denoting yellow orpiment, arsenic sulphide), the word comes via French and Latin from Greek *arsenikon* 'yellow orpiment', identified with *arsenikos* 'male', but in fact from Arabic *al-zarnīk* 'the orpiment', based on Persian *zar* 'gold'.
See also ➤ LAVENDER *and old lace*.

art see also ➤ NOBLE *art*.

be art and part in be an accessory or participant in (by *art* in contriving or *part* in executing).

art deco the predominant decorative art style of the 1920s and 1930s, characterized by precise and boldly delineated geometric shapes and strong colours.

art for art's sake used to convey the idea that the chief or only aim of a work of art is the self-expression of the individual artist who creates it.
See also ➤ ARS *gratia artis*.

art is long and life is short proverbial saying; late 14th century; originally from the Greek physician Hippocrates (*c*.460–357 BC), 'Life is short, the art long', often quoted in Latin, *Ars longa, vita brevis*, after Seneca's rendering.

art nouveau a style of decorative art, architecture, and design prominent in western Europe and the

US from about 1890 until the First World War and characterized by intricate linear designs and flowing curves based on natural forms.

arte see also ➤ COMMEDIA *dell'arte*.

Arte Povera an artistic movement that originated in Italy in the 1960s, combining aspects of conceptual, minimalist, and performance art, and making use of worthless or common materials such as earth or newspaper, in the hope of subverting the commercialization of art.

Artegall in Spenser's *Faerie Queene*, the knight who is the champion of Justice and is loved by ➤ BRITOMART; his name may mean 'equal to Arthur'.

Artemis in Greek mythology, a goddess, daughter of Zeus and sister of ➤ APOLLO. She was a huntress and is typically depicted with a bow and arrows, and was also identified with Selene, goddess of the moon; her Roman equivalent is ➤ DIANA.

artemisia an aromatic or bitter-tasting plant of a genus that includes wormwood, mugwort, and sagebrush. Several kinds are used in herbal medicine and many are cultivated for their feathery grey foliage.

The name comes (in Middle English, via Latin) from Greek, 'wormwood' named after the goddess ➤ ARTEMIS, to whom it was sacred.

artesian relating to or denoting a well bored perpendicularly into water-bearing strata lying at an angle, so that natural pressure produces a constant supply of water with little or no pumping. The word comes (in the mid 19th century) from French *artésien*, from *Artois*, where such wells were first made.

the Artesian State an informal name for South Dakota.

the Artful Dodger nickname of Jack Dawkins, a leading member of Fagin's gang of child pickpockets in Dickens's *Oliver Twist*.

> With London's West End shops taken over by artful dodgers by day and cardboard-box dwellers by night, the Dickensian theme rings horribly true.
> — *Artist's & Illustrator's Magazine* December 1993

Arthur a legendary king of Britain, historically perhaps a 5th or 6th century Romano-British chieftain or general. Stories of his life, his court at Camelot, the exploits of his knights such as Lancelot and the quest for the Holy Grail, were developed by Malory, Chrétien de Troyes, and other medieval writers

and became the subject of many legends; the Norman writer Wace mentions the 'Round Table', which enabled the knights to be seated in such a way that none had precedence.

According to the traditional stories Arthur, son of Uther Pendragon, was brought up in ignorance of his birth, but proved his identity as the king's son when he pulled the sword (➤ EXCALIBUR) from the stone. Guided by ➤ MERLIN, he ruled Britain wisely, but in the end his leadership was fatally weakened by the adulterous love of his wife Guinevere and friend Lancelot, and Arthur himself was forced to fight a last battle against his nephew ➤ MORDRED and his supporters. Fatally wounded, he was taken by barge to ➤ AVALON, so that his body was never found; he is thus one of the legendary heroes who may return to his kingdom should the need arise.

See also ➤ *Le* MORTE *D'Arthur*.

Arthur's Seat a hill overlooking Edinburgh from the east, traditionally associated with ➤ ARTHUR.

Arthurian romances the cycle of legends having Arthur as their central character, otherwise known as the ➤ MATTER *of Britain*.

artichoke a European plant cultivated for its large thistle-like flower heads; the unopened flower head of this, of which the heart and the fleshy bases of the bracts are edible. The name comes (in the mid 16th century) via northern Italian and Spanish from Arabic; early popular etymologies included the suggestion that the plant was given to *choking* the garden, or its having a *choke* in its *heart*.

articles see also ➤ *articles of* CONFEDERATION, ➤ SIX *Articles*, ➤ THIRTY-*nine Articles*.

Lords of the Articles prior to the Act of Union in 1706, a standing committee of the Scottish Parliament, who drafted and prepared the measures submitted to the House.

the Articles of War regulations made for the government of the military and naval forces of Great Britain and the United States; the term is recorded from the early 18th century.

artificial intelligence the theory and development of computer systems able to perform tasks normally requiring human intelligence, such as visual perception, speech recognition, decision-making, and translation between languages.

artists ➤ *St* LUKE is the patron saint of artists.

Artois a region and former province of NW France. Known in Roman times as *Artesium*, the area gave its name to a type of well known as the ➤ ARTESIAN well, which was first sunk there in the 12th century.

arts see also ➤ MASTER *of Arts*, ➤ SEVEN *liberal arts*.

Arts and Crafts Movement an English decorative arts movement of the second half of the 19th century which sought to revive the ideal of craftsmanship in an age of increasing mechanization and mass production. William Morris was its most prominent member.

Arundel name of the horse belonging to ➤ BEVIS *of Hampton*.

Arundelian marbles a collection of ancient sculptures presented to the University of Oxford by the Duke of Norfolk in 1667.

Arval Brothers in ancient Rome, a college of 12 priests who offered sacrifices to secure the fertility of the fields. The name comes from Latin *arvum* 'arable land'.

Aryabhata I (476–*c*.550), Indian astronomer and mathematician. His surviving work, the *Aryabhatiya* (499), has sections dealing with mathematics, the measurement of time, planetary models, the sphere, and eclipses. India's first space satellite was named after him.

Aryan relating to or denoting a people speaking an Indo-European language who invaded northern India in the 2nd millennium BC; (in Nazi ideology) relating to or denoting people of Caucasian race not of Jewish descent. The idea that there was an 'Aryan' race corresponding to the parent Indo-European language was proposed by certain 19th-century writers, and was taken up by Hitler and other proponents of racist ideology, but it has been generally rejected by scholars.

as an ancient Roman copper coin; the word is Latin and means 'unit'.

Ascalaphus in Greek mythology, a son of ➤ ACHERON, who betrayed the fact that while in the underworld Persephone had eaten pomegranate seeds, and therefore could not return unscathed to earth. According to Ovid, she turned him into an owl as punishment.

Ascalon the ancient Greek name for *Ashqelon*, an ancient Mediterranean city, situated to the south of modern Tel Aviv, in Israel. A Philistine city state

from the 12th to the 8th century BC, it was conquered by Alexander the Great in 332 BC.

ascendancy see ➤ PROTESTANT *Ascendancy*.

ascendant in astrological belief, the point on the ecliptic at which it intersects the eastern horizon at a particular time, such as that of a person's birth.

Ascension in Christian belief, the ascent of Christ into heaven on the fortieth day after the Resurrection.

Ascension Day the Thursday 40 days after Easter, on which Christ's Ascension is celebrated in the Christian Church.

Ascensiontide the ten-day period between Ascension Day and the eve of Pentecost.

ascents see ➤ SONG *of Ascents*.

asceticism the practice of severe self-discipline and abstention from all forms of indulgence, typically for religious reasons. The term comes (in the mid 17th century, via medieval Latin or Greek) from Greek *askētēs* 'monk', from *askein* 'to exercise'.

Roger Ascham (*c*.1515–68), English humanist scholar and writer, who was tutor to the future Elizabeth I and Latin secretary to Queen Mary and later to Elizabeth. He was noted for his treatise on archery, *Toxophilus* (1545), and *The Scholemaster* (1570), a practical and influential tract on education.

Asclepiad in classical prosody, a measure consisting of a spondee, two (or three) choriambi, and an iambus, named from a Greek poet.

Asclepius in Greek mythology, a hero and god of healing, son of Apollo, often represented bearing a staff with a serpent coiled round it. He sometimes bears a scroll or tablet, probably representing medical learning.

Ascot a town in southern England, south-west of Windsor. Its racecourse is the site of an annual race meeting (**Ascot week**) founded by Queen Anne in 1711.
  See ➤ ROYAL *Ascot*.

Asgard in Scandinavian mythology, a region in the centre of the universe, inhabited by the gods.

ash a tree with silver-grey bark, compound leaves, winged fruits, and hard pale timber, traditionally the wood of which spear-shafts were made.

It has given its name to an Old English runic letter, ᚫ, so named from the word of which it was the first letter.

See also ➤ *beware of an* OAK, *it draws the stroke; avoid an ash, it counts the splash*, ➤ *when the* OAK*'s before the ash, then you will only get a splash.*

Ash Wednesday the first day of Lent in the Western Christian Church, marked by services of penitence, and so named from the custom of marking the foreheads of penitents with ashes on that day.

Ashcan School a group of American realist painters active from *c.*1908 until the First World War, who painted scenes from the slums of New York. The school grew out of the group called 'the Eight'.

Ashendene Press a private press founded by the printer and connoisseur C. J. St John Hornby (1867–1946) in 1895; it remained open until 1935, longer than any other English private press.

Asher (in the Bible) a Hebrew patriarch, son of Jacob and Zilpah (Genesis 30:12, 13); the tribe of Israel traditionally descended from him.

Asherah a Canaanitish goddess; a tree-trunk or wooden post symbolizing this goddess, found in high places devoted to the worship of ➤ BAAL.

ashes see also ➤ DUST *and ashes*, ➤ RISE *from the ashes*, ➤ SACKCLOTH *and ashes.*

the **Ashes** a trophy for the winner of a series of test matches in a cricket season between England and Australia. The name comes from a mock obituary notice published in the *Sporting Times* (2 September 1882), with reference to the symbolical remains of English cricket being taken to Australia after a sensational victory by the Australians at the Oval.

ashes to ashes, dust to dust from the burial service in the *Book of Common Prayer*, 'we therefore commit his body to the ground, earth to earth, ashes to ashes, dust to dust; in sure and certain hope of the Resurrection to eternal life.'

ashet a Scottish and northern English word for a large plate or dish; the word comes (in the mid 16th century) from French *assiette.*

Ashkenazi a Jew of central or eastern European descent. The Ashkenazim became established in the Frankish and other Germanic-speaking kingdoms in the early Middle Ages; subsequently large groups migrated from France and Germany to the Slavic countries from the 12th century onwards. In the 19th century, massive immigration to the US began, and in the 20th century many Ashkenazim moved to Palestine and participated in the foundation of the modern state of Israel. More than 80 per cent of Jews today are Ashkenazim; they preserve Palestinian rather than Babylonian Jewish traditions and some still use Yiddish.

Ashley see also ➤ LAURA *Ashley.*

Ashley Library library formed by the bibliographer and forger T. J. Wise (1859–1937), acquired by the British Museum in 1937.

Elias Ashmole (1617–92), English antiquary. A solicitor from 1638, he showed an insatiable desire for knowledge, studying such diverse topics as alchemy, astrology, Hebrew, and mathematics. His collection of rarities, presented to Oxford University in 1677, formed the nucleus of the ➤ ASHMOLEAN *Museum.*

Ashmolean Museum a museum of art and antiquities in Oxford, founded by Elias Ashmole. It opened in 1683 and was the first public institution of its kind in England. The collection now includes archaeological material, European works of art, and oriental works.

ashram (in the Indian subcontinent) a hermitage, monastic community, or other place of religious retreat; a place of religious retreat or community life modelled on the Indian ashram.

ashrama in Hinduism, any of the four stages of an ideal life, ascending from the status of pupil to the total renunciation of the world.

Ashtaroth biblical name for the Canaanite goddess ➤ ASTARTE.

Ashura the tenth of Muharram, celebrated as a holy day by Sunni Muslims and as a day of mourning (the anniversary of the death of Husain) by Shiite Muslims.

Ashurbanipal king of Assyria *c.*668–627 BC, grandson of Sennacherib. He was responsible for the sacking of Susa and the suppression of a revolt in Babylon. However, Ashurbanipal is chiefly recognized for his patronage of the arts; he established a library of more than 20,000 clay tablets at Nineveh.

Asia the largest of the world's continents, constituting nearly one third of the land mass, lying entirely north of the equator except for some SE Asian islands. It is connected to Africa by the Isthmus of Suez, and borders Europe (part of the same land mass) along the Ural Mountains and across the Caspian Sea.

See also ➤ the LIGHT of Asia, ➤ SEVEN churches of Asia.

asinorum see ➤ PONS asinorum.

ask a silly question and you get a silly answer proverbial saying, early 14th century.

ask no questions and you'll be told no lies proverbial saying, late 18th century.

Aslan name of the lion who is the central character of C. S. Lewis's ➤ NARNIA chronicles, and whose death and resurrection in the first book reflects the Christian theme of the series.

Asmodeus a demon in the apocryphal book of ➤ TOBIT, who has killed the former husbands of Sara on their wedding-nights; in Milton's *Paradise Lost*, described as 'Asmodeus with the fishy fume'.

Asoka emperor of India *c.*269–232 BC, who was converted to Buddhism and established it as the state religion.

Asoka pillar a pillar with four lions on the capital, built by the Emperor Asoka at Sarnath in Uttar Pradesh to mark the spot where the Buddha publicly preached his doctrine, and adopted as a symbol by the government of India.

asp another name for the Egyptian cobra, a large nocturnal African cobra with a thick body and large head; it is particulary associated with ➤ CLEOPATRA, who is said to have committed suicide by allowing herself to be bitten by an asp, and has become a type of venomous poison.

Aspasia a Greek courtesan, lover of ➤ PERICLES and noted for her intellect and supposed political influence.

> The Aspasia of the Coulisse, in so far as she is a psychologic revelation, owes her paternity to the Second Empire.
> — *Harper's Weekly* 24 March 1900

aspen a poplar tree with small rounded long-stalked leaves that tremble in the breeze; it is said to tremble from shame because the Cross was made from its wood.

asperges the rite of sprinkling holy water at the beginning of the Mass, still used occasionally in Catholic churches. The term comes (in the late 16th century) from the first word of the Latin text of Psalms 50(51):9 (literally 'thou shalt purge'), recited before mass during the sprinkling of holy water.

Asphaltic Lake another name for the ➤ DEAD *Sea*.

asphodel an everlasting flower said to grow in the ➤ ELYSIAN *fields*. The name is recorded from late Middle English and comes via Latin from the Greek base of ➤ DAFFODIL.

aspic savoury jelly made with meat stock, used as a garnish, or to contain pieces of food such as meat, seafood, or eggs, set in a mould. The term comes (in the late 18th century) from French, literally 'asp', from the colours of the jelly as compared with those of the snake.

aspidistra a bulbous plant of the lily family, widely grown as a house plant and taken as typifying middle-class gentility and conventionality, particularly with reference to the title of George Orwell's novel *Keep the Aspidistra Flying* (1936).

ass a hoofed mammal of the horse family with long ears and a braying call, a donkey; proverbially taken as a type of patience and stupidity.

See also ➤ BURNELL *the Ass*, ➤ *the* GOLDEN *Ass*, ➤ *the* LAW *is an ass*.

ass-eared an epithet applied to ➤ MIDAS after he had unwisely given judgement against Apollo in a contest of flute-playing.

an ass in a lion's skin a foolish or cowardly person who adopts a heroic pose or appearance; the allusion is to a fable in which a donkey dresses up in the skin of a lion to appear terrible.

Assassins the Nizari branch of Ismaili Muslims at the time of the Crusades, renowned as militant fanatics and popularly supposed to use hashish before going on murder missions. The name comes (in the mid 16th century, from French or medieval Latin) from Arabic ḥašīšī 'hashish-eater'.

See also ➤ OLD *man of the mountains*.

assay the testing of a metal or ore to determine its ingredients and quality. The word is recorded from Middle English, in the general sense 'testing, or a test of, the merit of someone or something', and comes ultimately from Old French *essai* 'trial'.

assay office an establishment for the assaying of ores and metals; in the UK, an institution authorized to award hallmarks to articles made from precious metals. There are currently four in Britain, at London, Birmingham, Sheffield, and Edinburgh.

assembly see ➤ NOTABLES.

asses' bridge another name for the ➤ PONS *asinorum.*

Assisi a town in the province of Umbria in central Italy, famous as the birthplace of St Francis, whose tomb is located there.

    See also ➤ *St* CLARE *of Assisi,* ➤ *St* FRANCIS *of Assisi.*

assisted suicide the suicide of a patient suffering from an incurable disease, effected by the taking of lethal drugs provided by a doctor for this purpose. The concept has been discussed in the debate on euthanasia since the mid-seventies: one expressed view is that the term itself effectively defines euthanasia. **Physician-assisted suicide** identifies more specifically one possible source of assistance, and highlights the area of medical ethics where the strongest debate has occurred, the question of whether or not this assistance is in effect a breach of the Hippocratic Oath.

assizes see ➤ BLOODY *Assizes.*

Assumption the reception of the Virgin Mary bodily into heaven, formally declared a doctrine of the Roman Catholic Church in 1950. The **Feast of the Assumption** is celebrated in the Roman Catholic Church on 15 August.

Assur an ancient city state of Mesopotamia, situated on the River Tigris to the south of modern Mosul. It was the traditional capital of the Assyrian empires, the first of which was established early in the 2nd millennium BC.

Assyria an ancient country in what is now northern Iraq, and which from the early part of the 2nd millennium BC was the centre of a succession of empires; it was at its peak in the 8th and late 7th centuries BC, when its rule stretched from the Persian Gulf to Egypt. It fell in 612 BC to a coalition of Medes and Babylonians.

Fred Astaire (1899–1987), American dancer, singer, and actor, star of a number of film musicals, including *Top Hat* (1935)and *Shall We Dance?* (1937), in a successful partnership with Ginger Rogers. Despite his long career, an early studio official's report on him is said to have read, 'Can't act. Slightly bald. Also dances.'

Astarte a Phoenician goddess of fertility and sexual love who corresponds to the Babylonian and Assyrian goddess Ishtar and who became identified with the Egyptian Isis, the Greek Aphrodite, and others. In the Bible she is referred to as *Ashtaroth* or Ashtoreth and her worship is linked with that of Baal.

asterisk a symbol (*) used to mark printed or written text, typically as a reference to an annotation or to stand for omitted matter. The word comes (in late Middle English) via late Latin from Greek *asteriskos* 'small star'.

Astérix hero of a French comic cartoon, created by the French writer René Goscinny (1924–77) with the illustrator Albert Uderzo, set in Gaul at the time of the Gallic wars; Astérix and his friend Obélix belong to the only tribe unconquered by the Romans, and reflect a sense of French political identity in the face of apparently overwhelming odds.

> Asterix the Gaul, the irrepressible symbol of Gallic defiance.
> — *Daily Telegraph* 4 February 1999

Astley's Amphitheatre a theatrical entertainment, regarded as the first modern circus, founded in London in 1770 by the English theatrical manager and former soldier Philip Astley (1742–1814), who as an equestrian performer was initially the only performer; by 1798 he was allowed to name his now fashionable establishment Astley's Royal Amphitheatre.

> Do what you like—dine where you please—go and have ginger-beer and sawdust at Astley's or psalm-singing with Lady Jane—only don't expect me to busy myself with the boy.
> — William Makepeace Thackeray *Vanity Fair* (1848)

Astolat in the Arthurian Romances, the site of ➤ LANCELOT's meeting with ➤ ELAINE; according to Malory's *Morte D'Arthur,* it is to be identified with Guildford in Surrey.

Nancy Astor (1879–1964), American-born British Conservative politician. She became the first woman to sit in the House of Commons when she succeeded her husband as MP for Plymouth in 1919. She supported causes about which she had deep convictions, such as temperance and women's rights, rather than following the party line.

Astor Place riot a fight between admirers of the American actor Edwin Forrest and the British actor William Charles Macready, both of whom were appearing in New York in 1849. On the evening of 10 May 1849, a mob invaded the Astor Place Opera House where Macready was appearing in *Macbeth,* and in the ensuing violence 31 people were killed, at least 150 were injured, and the theatre was badly damaged.

Astoria a town in northwest Oregon, originally settled as Fort Clatsop by the Lewis and Clark expedition in 1805, and refounded in 1811 as a fur trading post by John Jacob *Astor* (1763–1848).

Astraea a Roman goddess associated with justice, said to have been the last deity to leave the earth, who having lived among humankind during the Golden Age and in retreat in the mountains during the Silver Age, finally left the world for heaven during the evils of the Bronze Age. Her name, which means 'starry maiden', was later used as an epithet of Elizabeth I.

astragali small bones used as dice, or in divination (**astragalomancy**). The word comes (in the mid 16th century) via Latin from Greek *astragalus* 'ankle bone, moulding', also the name of a plant.

astral of or relating to a supposed non-physical realm of existence to which various psychic and paranormal phenomena are ascribed, and in which the physical human body is said to have a counterpart. The word comes (in the early 17th century) from Latin *astralis*, from *astrum* 'star'.

astrolabe an instrument used to make astronomical measurements, typically of the altitudes of celestial bodies, and in navigation for calculating latitude, before the development of the sextant. In its basic form (known from classical times) it consists of a disc with the edge marked in degrees and a pivoted pointer. Recorded from late Middle English, the word comes ultimately (via Old French and medieval Latin) from Greek *astrolabos* 'star-taking'.

astrology the study of movements and relative positions of celestial bodies interpreted as having an influence on human affairs and the natural world. Ancient observers of the heavens developed elaborate systems of explanation based on the movements of the sun, moon, and planets through the constellations of the zodiac, for predicting events and for casting horoscopes. By 1700 astrology had lost intellectual credibility in the West, but continued to have popular appeal. Modern astrology is based on that of the Greeks, but other systems are extant, e.g. that of China.

The term (in full **natural astrology**) originally denoted the practical uses of astronomy, applied in the measurement of time and the prediction of natural phenomena. The commonest sense today (in full **judicial astrology**, relating to human affairs) dates from the mid 16th century.

The word is recorded from late Middle English,

and comes ultimately (via Old French and Latin) from Greek *astron* 'star'.

astronauts St Joseph of Copertino, a 17th-century Franciscan priest born near Brindisi and noted for his levitations, is the patron saint of astronauts.

Astronomer Royal the official title given to an astronomer in charge of one of the royal, or national, observatories of Great Britain.

Astrophel name adopted by Philip Sidney in his sonnet sequence *Astrophel and Stella*; the name means 'star-lover', and the poems give the course of his unhappy love for Stella (the 'star', modelled on ➤ *Penelope* RICH).

Astur in Macaulay's *Lays of Ancient Rome*, one of the chieftains who joins ➤ *Lars* PORSENA and Sextus in their attack on Rome; although fighting for a discredited cause, he is seen as a figure of martial valour and dignity.

> The RSM came in, like Astur the great Lord of Luna, with stately stride . . . from the glittering silver of his stag's head badge to the gloriously polished black of his boots, six and a quarter feet of kilted splendour.
> — George Macdonald Fraser *The General Danced at Dawn* (1970)

Asturias see ➤ PRINCE *of the Asturias*.

asylum the protection granted by a state to someone who has left their native country as a political refugee. Recorded from late Middle English (in the sense 'place of refuge', especially for criminals, the word comes via Latin from Greek *asulon* 'refuge', from *asulos* 'inviolable', from *a-* 'without' + *sulon* 'right of seizure'. Current senses date from the 18th century.

Atahualpa (*c.*1502–33), last Inca ruler, put to death by ➤ *Francisco* PIZARRO; Macaulay gave 'who strangled Atahualpa' as one of the facts which ➤ *every* SCHOOLBOY *knows*.

Atalanta in Greek mythology, a huntress who would marry only someone who could beat her in a foot race. She was beaten when a suitor threw down three golden apples which she stopped to pick up.

> Laurie reached the goal first and . . . his Atalanta came panting up with flying hair.
> — Louisa May Alcott *Little Women* (1869)

See also ➤ MELEAGER[1].

Atalantis former term for a secret or scandalous history, from the short title of a romance of the early

18th century referring to 'the New Atalantis' (probably itself named after Bacon's ➤ *The* New *Atlantis*) satirizing the movers of the Glorious Revolution of 1688.

Atargatis in Assyrian mythology, a fertility goddess, resembling ➤ ASTARTE, and shown as half-fish, half-woman.

Kemal Atatürk (1881–1938), Turkish general and statesman, President 1923–38. He was elected the first President of the Turkish republic, taking the name of Atatürk ('father of the Turks') in 1934. He abolished the caliphate and introduced the adoption of the Roman alphabet for writing Turkish as well as other policies designed to make Turkey a modern secular state.

Ate infatuation, rashness; personified by the Greeks as a destructive goddess, and probably best-known from Shakespeare:

> Caesar's spirit, ranging for revenge,
> With Ate by his side, come hot from hell,
> Shall in these confines, with a monarch's voice
> Cry, 'Havoc!' and let slip the dogs of war.
> — William Shakespeare *Julius Caesar* (1599)

Atellan fables sketches depicting scenes from rustic life, presented on a crude stage with stock characters (the foolish old man, the rogue, the clown), which seem to have been the earliest form of drama to flourish in ancient Rome; it was imported from Campania, and may have originated in the town of Atella.

Aten in Egyptian mythology, the sun or solar disc, the deity of a strong monotheistic cult, particularly during the reign of ➤ AKHENATEN.

Athanasian Creed a summary of Christian doctrine formerly attributed to St Athanasius, but probably dating from the 5th century. It is included in the *Book of Common Prayer* for use at morning prayer on certain occasions.

St Athanasius (*c.*296–373), Greek theologian and upholder of Christian orthodoxy against ➤ ARIANISM. He aided the ascetic movement in Egypt and introduced knowledge of monasticism to the West.
   ☐ **FEAST DAY** His feast day is 2 May.

athanor a type of furnace used by alchemists, able to maintain a steady heat for long periods. The word comes (in the late 15th century) from Arabic, and originally meant 'the baker's oven'.

Atharva Veda a collection of hymns and ritual utterances in early Sanskrit, added at a later stage to the existing Veda material. The name comes from Sanskrit *Atharvan* (the name of Brahma's eldest son, said to be the author of the collection) + *veda* '(sacred) knowledge'.

atheism the theory or belief that God does not exist. The word comes (in the late 16th century, via French) from Greek *atheos*, from *a-* 'without' + *theos* 'god'.

atheling a prince or lord in Anglo-Saxon England. Recorded from Old English (in the form *ætheling*) the word is of West Germanic origin, from a base meaning 'race, family'.

Athelstan (895–939), king of England 925–39. Athelstan came to the thrones of Wessex and Mercia in 924 before effectively becoming the first king of all England. He successfully invaded both Scotland and Wales and inflicted a heavy defeat on an invading Danish army.

the Athenaeum originally the temple of the goddess Athene in ancient Athens, which was used for teaching; the term is used in the names of libraries or institutions for literary or scientific study, especially in *the Athenaeum*, a London club founded in 1824, originally for men of distinction in literature, art, and learning.
   See also ➤ BOSTON *Athenaeum*.

Athene in Greek mythology, the patron goddess of Athens, typically allegorized into a personification of wisdom. Her statues show her as female but fully armed, and in classical times the owl is regularly associated with her. The principal story concerning her is that she sprang, fully armed and uttering her war cry, from the head of Zeus. She is also called ➤ PALLAS. Her Roman equivalent is ➤ MINERVA.

Athens the capital of Greece, originally a flourishing city state of ancient Greece, which was an important cultural centre in the 5th century BC. Athens came under Roman rule in 146 BC, although it remained the focus of the Greek world, and fell to the Goths in AD 267. After its capture by the Turks in 1456 Athens declined to the status of a village, until chosen as the capital of a newly independent Greece in 1834.
   See also ➤ MAID *of Athens,* ➤ TIMON *of Athens.*

Athens of America a name for Boston.

Athens of the North a name for Edinburgh.

athletes ➤ *St* SEBASTIAN is the patron saint of athletes.

Athos name of the eldest and most serious of the ➤ THREE *Musketeers* who befriend ➤ D'ARTAGNAN in Dumas' novel; it is revealed that the murderous agent of Cardinal Richelieu whom they eventually defeat is his estranged and treacherous wife.

Mount Athos a narrow, mountainous peninsula in NE Greece, projecting into the Aegean Sea. It is inhabited by monks of the Orthodox Church, who forbid women and even female animals to set foot on the peninsula.

Atkins see ➤ TOMMY *Atkins*.

Atlanta the state capital of Georgia. Founded at the end of a railway line in 1837, the city was originally called Terminus; in 1843 it was incorporated as Marthasville, and in 1845 its name was finally changed to Atlanta. A Confederate stronghold, its loss to the Union forces under Sherman after a long siege was a turning point in the Civil War; the Southern diarist Mary Chesnut wrote:

> Atlanta is gone. That agony is over. There is no hope but we will try to have no fear.
> — Mary Chesnut diary, 1864

atlantes stone carvings of male figures, used as columns to support the entablature of a Greek or Greek-style building; the word is the plural form of Greek *atlas* (see ➤ ATLAS).

Battle of the Atlantic a succession of sea operations during the Second World War in which Axis naval and air forces attempted to destroy ships carrying supplies from North America to the UK. German U-boats were the main weapon of attack, and about 2,800 Allied, mainly British, merchant ships were lost; the threat was ended by the capture of the U-boats' bases by Allied land forces in 1944.

Atlantic Charter a declaration of eight common principles in international relations drawn up by Churchill and Roosevelt in August 1941 and intended to guide a post-war peace settlement. The charter, which stipulated freely chosen governments, free trade, freedom of the seas, and disarmament of current aggressor states, and condemned territorial changes made against the wishes of local populations, provided the ideological basis for the United Nations organization.

Atlantic Ocean the ocean lying between Europe and Africa to the east and North and South America to the west. The name comes (in late Middle English) via Latin from Greek, from *Atlas, Atlant-*. It originally referred to Mount *Atlas* in Libya, hence to the sea near the west African coast, later extended to the whole ocean.

Atlanticism belief in or support for a close relationship between western Europe and the US, or particularly for Nato.

Atlantis a legendary island, beautiful and prosperous, which was overwhelmed by the sea. As described by Plato, Atlantis was west of the Pillars of Hercules and ruled part of Europe and Africa.
  See also ➤ *the* NEW *Atlantis*.

Atlas in Greek mythology, a Titan who was punished for his part in the revolt against Zeus by being made to support the heavens (a popular explanation of why the sky does not fall). He became identified with the Atlas Mountains. According to a later story Perseus, with the aid of Medusa's head, turned Atlas into a mountain.
  The word *atlas* to designate a collection of maps in a volume, first recorded in the title 'Atlas; or a Geographic Description of the World, by Gerard Mercator and John Hondt' (1636), is said to be derived from a representation of Atlas supporting the heavens placed as a frontispiece to early works of this kind, and to have been first used by Mercator in the 16th century.

Charles Atlas (1893–1972), American bodybuilder, creator of a highly successful mail-order bodybuilding course; its slogan (reflecting the founder's perception of his own unpromising start) was, 'I was a seven-stone weakling.'

> No wonder there were no girl assistants in the 50s—you had to go on a Charles Atlas course to lift one of Cecil's packs.
> — *Photon* April 1997

Atli in Norse legend, the king of the Huns, who marries the Niblung princess Gudrun; she allows him to kill her brothers, Gunnar and Hogni, in revenge for their murder of her husband ➤ SIGURD, but finally kills Atli herself. Atli represents the historical ➤ ATTILA; his Germanic equivalent in the *Nibelungenlied* is *Etzel*.

atman in Hindu philosophy, the spiritual life principle of the universe, especially when regarded as immanent in the real self of the individual. Various strands in Hindu thought differ in the way they regard the relationship (or identity) of the individual atman or 'self' and the universal Atman.

The word comes from Sanskrit *ātman*, literally 'essence, breath'.

atom bomb a bomb which derives its destructive power from the rapid release of nuclear energy by fission of heavy atomic nuclei, causing damage through heat, blast, and radioactivity. It was an *atom bomb* (first tested at ➤ Los *Alamos* in 1945) which was dropped on ➤ Hiroshima.

atomic theory the theory that all matter is made up of tiny indivisible particles or **atoms**, which in ancient times was taught notably by Democritus and Epicurus. According to the modern version, the atoms of each element are effectively identical, but differ from those of other elements, and unite to form compounds in fixed proportions.

atomism a theoretical approach that regards something as interpretable through analysis into distinct, separable, and independent elementary components. Typified by the atomic theory of matter, such an approach is also found, for example, in analyses of time, mental states, logical propositions, language, and society.

atomy a skeleton or emaciated body. The word comes (in the late 16th century) from *anatomy*, taken as *an atomy*.

atonement reparation, in Christian belief the reconciliation of God and mankind through Jesus Christ. The word comes (in the early 16th century, denoting unity or reconciliation, especially between God and man), from *at one* + the suffix *-ment*, influenced by medieval Latin *adunamentum* 'unity', and earlier *onement* from an obsolete verb *one* 'to unite'.

See also ➤ Day *of Atonement*.

Atreus in Greek legend, the son of ➤ Pelops and father of ➤ Agamemnon and Menelaus. He quarrelled with his brother Thyestes and invited him to a banquet at which he served up the flesh of Thyestes' own children, whereupon the sun turned back on its course in horror; the resultant curse on the house of Atreus would in time bring about the murder of his own son.

> It makes me feel as if a tragic doom overhung our family, as it did the house of Atreus.
> — Thomas Hardy *Jude the Obscure* (1895)

Atropos in Greek mythology, one of the three ➤ Fates; her name means literally 'inflexible', and her role was to cut the thread of life spun and measured by her sisters.

> Polly, the Atropos of Personnel, she who had put aside her shears for the flurry of a thousand Forms, she who brooded like Shiva the Destroyer on a world of the lopped.
> — Cynthia Ozick *Puttermesser Papers* (1997)

attack is the best form of defence proverbial saying, late 18th century (usually quoted as 'the best defence is a good offence' in the US).

attainder see ➤ bill *of attainder*.

Attalid a member of a Hellenistic dynasty named after *Attalus I* (reigned 241–197 BC), which flourished in the 3rd and 2nd centuries BC. The Attalid kings established their capital, Pergamum, as a leading cultural centre of the Greek world.

attention deficit disorder any of a range of behavioural disorders occurring primarily in children, including such symptoms as poor concentration, hyperactivity, and learning difficulties; the term is recorded in specialist literature from the 1970s, but came into general awareness and usage in the 1980s and 1990s.

Attic the dialect of Greek used by the ancient Athenians, which was the chief literary form of classical Greek. The word is late 16th century, and comes from Greek *Attikos*.

Attic bird in Milton's *Paradise Regained* (1671), a name for the nightingale.

Attic salt refined, delicate, poignant wit; recorded from the mid 18th century, the phrase is a translation of Latin *sal Atticum*.

Atticus name given to the Roman writer and businessman Titus Pomponius (110–32 BC), friend and correspondent of ➤ Cicero; the name *Atticus* reflected his long residence in Athens.

Atticus was later used by Pope as the name under which he satirized ➤ Addison in the *Epistle to Dr Arbuthnot* (1735).

Attila (406–53), king of the Huns 434–53. He ravaged vast areas between the Rhine and the Caspian Sea, inflicting great devastation on the eastern Roman Empire, before being defeated by the joint forces of the Roman army and the Visigoths at Châlons in 451. He was called the *Scourge of God* (translating Latin *flagellum Dei*) by medieval chroniclers.

> Bing gives us the itch-perfect lowdown on the Attilas of the American workplace ('The Care, Feeding, and Potential Destruction of the Bully').
> — *Esquire* February 1992

See also ➤ ATLI.

Attila Line the boundary separating Greek and Turkish-occupied Cyprus, named after the Attila Plan, a secret Turkish plan of 1964 to partition the country.

Attis in Anatolian mythology, the youthful consort of ➤ CYBELE. His death (after castrating himself) and resurrection were associated with the spring festival and with a sacrifice for the crops; his symbol was the pine tree.

attorney see also ➤ POWER *of attorney*.

Attorney-General the principal legal officer who represents the Crown or a state in legal proceedings and gives legal advice to the government.

attractor see ➤ *the* GREAT *Attractor*.

Attus Navius a legendary Roman augur who in Livy's account was asked by ➤ TARQUINIUS *Priscus* whether the thought then in Tarquinius's mind could be achieved. When Attus said that it could, Tarquinius challenged him to cut through a whetstone with the razor he was holding; Attus cut the stone, and it fell in two.

The story may have been remembered by Robert Peel (1788–1850), when in 1838 he said of ➤ *Robert* WALPOLE, 'So far as the great majority of his audience was concerned, he had blocks to cut, and he chose a fitter instrument than a razor to cut them with.'

aubade a poem or piece of music appropriate to the dawn or early morning. Recorded from the late 17th century, the word comes via French from Spanish *albada*, from *alba* 'dawn'.

John Aubrey (1626–97), English antiquarian and author. He was a pioneer of field archaeology, most of his researches being centred on the earthworks and monuments at Avebury and Stonehenge. He is chiefly remembered for *Brief Lives*, a collection of biographies of eminent people (a bowdlerized edition was first published in 1813).

auburn (chiefly of a person's hair) of a reddish-brown colour. The word comes (in late Middle English) via Old French from Latin *alburnus* 'whitish', from *albus* 'white'.

Sweet Auburn the ideal village, 'loveliest village of the plain' recalled in Goldsmith's *The Deserted Village* (1770), depopulated as a result of the growth of trade and the decline of the countryside.

AUC used to indicate a date reckoned from 753 BC, the year of the foundation of Rome. The letters stand for Latin *ab urbe condita* 'from the foundation of the city' and *anno urbis conditae* 'in the year of the foundation of the city'.

audit ale at Oxford and Cambridge Universities, a term for ale of special quality, originally brewed in various colleges for use on the day of audit; 'the goodly audit ale' is referred to by Byron in *The Age of Bronze* (1823).

Audit Commission (in the UK) an independent body that monitors public spending, especially that by local government, on behalf of the government.

John James Audubon (1785–1851), American naturalist and artist, author of *The Birds of America* (1827–38), in which he portrayed even the largest birds life-size, and painted them in dramatic and sometimes violent action. The book had lasting success, both artistically and as a major contribution to natural history.

Augean stables in Greek mythology, vast stables (belonging to King *Augeas*) which had never been cleaned; this was achieved (as the sixth of his Labours) by ➤ HERCULES, who cleaned them in a day by diverting the River Alpheus to flow through them. The term is often used figuratively to refer to corruption or waste developed over a long period.

> One look would have convinced the most zealous reformer of the sheer impossibility of doing anything with that vast, proliferating Augean stable.
> — George Macdonald Fraser *Quartered Safe out Here* (1992)

auger a tool resembling a large corkscrew, for boring holes in wood. Recorded in Old English in the form *nafogār*, from *nafu* 'the hub of a wheel' + *gār* 'piercer'. The *n* was lost by wrong division of *a nauger* (compare *adder*, *apron*).

Augsburg Confession a statement of the Lutheran position, drawn up mainly by Melancthon and approved by Luther before being presented to the Emperor Charles V at Augsburg on 25 June 1530.

augur in ancient Rome a religious official who observed natural signs, especially the behaviour of birds, interpreting these as an indication of divine approval or disapproval.

The birds might be wild or tame; during the 3rd century BC, in the war with Carthage, the sacred chickens on board the Roman admiral's galley refused to eat the corn offered them, traditionally a sign of bad fortune. The admiral responded by ordering them to be thrown overboard, with the words 'Then let them drink.'

Recorded from late Middle English, the word comes from Latin, meaning 'diviner'.

August the eighth month of the year, in the northern hemisphere usually considered the last month of summer. Recorded from Old English, the name comes from Latin *augustus* 'consecrated, venerable'; named after ➤ AUGUSTUS Caesar, the first Roman emperor.

Augusta a title ('venerable') conferred by the will of the emperor ➤ AUGUSTUS on his wife Livia; after the reign of Domitian, it became the title of the wife of the reigning emperor.

Augustan connected with or occurring during the reign of the Roman emperor Augustus; especially, relating to or denoting Latin literature of this period, including the works of Virgil, Horace, Ovid, and Livy.

Augustan in a literary sense also means relating to or denoting 17th- and 18th-century English literature of a style considered refined and classical, including the works of Pope, Addison, and Swift.

St Augustine of Canterbury (d. *c.*604), Italian churchman. Sent from Rome by Pope Gregory the Great to refound the Church in England in 597, he was favourably received by King Ethelbert, who was afterwards converted, founded a monastery at Canterbury and became its first bishop, but failed to reach agreement with the existing Celtic Church over questions of discipline and practice.
□ **FEAST DAY** His feast day is 26 May.

St Augustine of Hippo (354–430), Doctor of the Church; his early life was marked by a series of spiritual crises, and he is known for a famous prayer in his *Confessions*, 'Give me chastity and continency—but not yet.' Augustine was baptized by St Ambrose in 386 and henceforth lived a monastic life. He became bishop of Hippo in North Africa in 396. His writings, such as *Confessions* and the *City of God*, dominated subsequent Western theology.
□ **FEAST DAY** His feast day is 28 August.

Augustinian a member of a religious order observing a rule derived from the writings of St Augustine of Hippo.

Augustus (63 BC–AD 14), the first Roman emperor; also called (until 27 BC) *Octavian.* He was adopted by the will of his great-uncle ➤ JULIUS *Caesar* and gained supreme power by his defeat of ➤ MARK *Antony* in 31 BC. (Cicero had said of the young Octavian, 'The young man should be praised, decorated, and got rid of.')

In 27 BC he was given the title *Augustus* ('venerable') and became in effect the first Roman emperor. His rule was marked abroad by a series of expansionist military campaigns and at home by moral and religious reforms; according to Suetonius, he 'could boast [of Rome] that he had inherited brick and left it marble'.

Auld Alliance informal term for the political relationship of France and Scotland between the 14th and the 16th century.

Auld Kirk informal name for the ➤ CHURCH *of Scotland.*

auld lang syne Scottish phrase meaning, times long past. The phrase was popularized as the title and refrain of a song by Robert Burns (1788), now traditionally sung on New Year's Eve.

Auld Reekie an informal name for Edinburgh, recorded from the early 19th century and meaning literally 'Old Smoky'.

Aulis the port in Boeotia where Agamemnon offered his daughter ➤ IPHIGENIA as a sacrifice to Artemis when the Greek fleet was becalmed on the way to Troy.

aunt see also ➤ AGONY *aunt,* ➤ WELSH *aunt.*

Aunt Edna Terence Rattigan's name for a typical female theatregoer of conventional tastes, 'a nice respectable, middle-class, middle-aged, maiden lady, with time on her hands and the money to help her pass it.'

Aunt Sally a game in which players throw sticks or balls at a wooden dummy; in figurative usage, a person or thing subjected to much criticism, especially one set up as an easy target for it.

Auntie an informal term for the BBC regarded as a conservative institution; when in 1997 Gerald Kaufman, as chairman of the House of Commons natural heritage select committee, wished to convey the view that the BBC's governors should be replaced by a modern board of management, he commented, 'It is about time that Auntie started power-dressing.'

Aurangzeb (1618–1707), Mogul emperor of Hindustan 1658–1707, who increased the Mogul empire to its greatest extent, and who assumed the title Alamgir ('Conqueror of the World'). His reign was a period of great wealth and splendour, but rebellions and wars weakened the empire and it declined sharply after his death. Dryden's tragedy *Aureng-Zebe* (produced 1675) was remotely based on the events by which Aurangzeb wrested the Mogul empire from his father and brothers.

aurea see ➤ LEGENDA *Aurea*.

Aurelian (*c*.215–75), Roman emperor 270–5. Originally a common soldier, he rose through the ranks and was elected emperor by the army. He quelled rebellions and repelled invaders, built new walls round Rome, and established the state worship of the sun; he was assassinated by his own officers.

Aurelianus see ➤ AMBROSIUS *Aurelianus*.

Marcus Aurelius (121–80), Roman emperor 161–80. The adopted successor of Antoninus Pius, he was occupied for much of his reign with wars against invading Germanic tribes. His *Meditations*, a collection of aphorisms and reflections, are evidence of his philosophical nature.

aureole a circle of light or brightness depicted in art around the head or body of a person represented as holy.

Auriga a large northern constellation (the Charioteer), said to represent a man holding a whip. It includes the bright star Capella, several bright variable stars and star clusters, and is crossed by the Milky Way.

aurochs a large wild Eurasian ox that was the ancestor of domestic cattle. It was probably exterminated in Britain in the Bronze Age, and the last one was killed in Poland in 1627.

Aurora in Roman mythology, the goddess of the dawn, equivalent of the Greek ➤ Eos. Most of the stories about her tell of handsome men being kidnapped to live with her.

From the early 18th century, aurora has been used to designate a natural electrical phenomenon characterized by the appearance of streamers of reddish or greenish light in the sky, especially near the northern or southern magnetic pole. The effect is caused by the interaction of charged particles from the sun with atoms in the upper atmosphere. In northern and southern regions it is respectively called **aurora borealis** or **northern lights** and **aurora australis** or **southern lights**.

Auschwitz a Nazi concentration camp in the Second World War, near the town of Oświęcim (Auschwitz) in Poland. It may be referred to as a symbol of the Holocaust; the Italian novelist Primo Levi (1919–87) said of the year he spent there, 'Our language lacks words to express this offence, the demolition of a man.'

The German slogan '*Arbeit macht frei* [Work liberates]', originally inscribed on the gates of ➤ DACHAU, was subsequently also placed on those of Auschwitz.

Ausonia ancient and poetic name for Italy, named for *Auson*, son of Odysseus, who was said to have settled there.

auspices originally, the observation of bird-flight in divination; later, a divine or prophetic token. In ancient Rome, an *auspex* (from Latin *avis* 'bird' + -*specere* 'to look') observed the flight of birds to take omens for the guidance of affairs; a flight of birds was the omen which established ➤ ROMULUS rather than his brother Remus as king.

Auster in Latin writing, the south wind.
See also ➤ BLACK *Auster*.

Battle of Austerlitz a battle in 1805 near the town of Austerlitz (now in the Czech Republic), in which Napoleon defeated the Austrians and Russians.

Austin Friars another name for ➤ AUGUSTINIAN Friars.

Australia an island country and continent of the southern hemisphere. The name comes (via French) from Latin *australis* in the phrase *Terra Australis* 'the southern land', the name given, from the 16th century, to the supposed southern continent and islands lying in the Great Southern Ocean.
See also ➤ ADVANCE *Australia*, ➤ ADVANCE *Australia Fair*.

Order of Australia an order instituted in 1975 to honour Australians for outstanding achievement and divided into four classes: Companion (AC), Officer (AO), Member (AM), and Medal of the Order of Australia (OAM). A fifth class of Knight or Dame, above Companion, was abolished in 1986.

Australia Day a national public holiday in Australia, commemorating the founding on 26 January 1788 of the colony of New South Wales.

Australian Capital Territory an area of New South Wales ceded to the Commonwealth of Australia as the site of Canberra and its immediate environs; formerly known as *Capital Territory*.

Austrian lip another name for the ➤ HABSBURG *lip*.

War of the **Austrian** Succession a group of several related conflicts (1740–8), involving most of the states of Europe, that were triggered by the death of the Emperor Charles VI and the accession of his daughter ➤ MARIA *Theresa* in 1740 to the Austrian throne.

aut see ➤ *aut* CAESAR *aut nihil*.

the **Authentics** a title given (in the early 17th century) to a collection of the New Constitutions of Justinian.

Authorized Version an English translation of the Bible made in 1611 at the order of James I and still widely used, though never formally 'authorized'. Also called the *King James Bible*.

authors ➤ *St* FRANCIS *de Sales* is the patron saint of authors.

auto-da-fé the burning of a heretic by the Spanish Inquisition; the phrase is recorded in English from the early 18th century, and comes from Portuguese, literally 'act of faith'.

Autocrat of the Breakfast-Table name under which Oliver Wendell Holmes (1809–94) wrote a series of articles, originally published in the *Atlantic Monthly*.

Autolycus in Greek mythology, a son of Hermes celebrated for his craft as a thief, who stole the flocks of his neighbours and mingled them with his own.

In Shakespeare's *The Winter's Tale*, the roguish but charming pedlar *Autolycus* is so named because he is a 'snapper up of unconsidered trifles'.

autumn the season after summer and before winter, when crops and fruits are gathered and leaves fall, in the northern hemisphere from September to November and in the southern hemisphere from March to May. The name is recorded from late Middle English, and comes ultimately (perhaps via Old French) from Latin *autumnus*.

Auxerre see ➤ *St* GERMANUS.

Avalon in Arthurian legend, the place to which Arthur was conveyed after death; in Welsh mythology, the kingdom of the dead.

Avar a member of a nomadic equestrian people from central Asia who built up a large kingdom in SE Europe from the 6th century but were conquered by Charlemagne (791–9).

avatar in Hindu belief, a manifestation of a deity or released soul in bodily form on earth; an incarnate divine teacher. The word comes from Sanskrit *avatāra* 'descent'.

ave Latin greeting, meaning 'hail, be well'; according to Suetonius' *Lives of the Caesars*, gladiators in the arena saluted the Roman emperor with the words, '*Ave Caesar, morituri te salutant* [Hail Caesar, those who are about to die salute you].'

ave atque vale Latin, meaning 'hail and farewell!'; the poet Catullus, in a poem to his dead brother, wrote, '*Atque in perpetuum, frater, ave atque vale* [And so, my brother, hail, and farewell for evermore!].'

Ave Maria a Latin prayer to the Virgin Mary used in Catholic worship. The first line is adapted from Luke 1:28; the second was added in the Middle Ages. The name comes from the opening words, literally 'hail, Mary!'

Avebury a village in Wiltshire, site of one of Britain's major henge monuments of the late Neolithic period. The monument consists of a bank and ditch containing the largest known stone circle, with two smaller circles and other stone settings within it. It is the centre of a complex ritual landscape that also contains a stone avenue, chambered tombs, ➤ SILBURY *Hill*, and various other monuments.

Avenue of the Americas a name for Sixth Avenue, New York.

averages see ➤ LAW *of averages*.

Avernus a lake near Naples in Italy, which fills the crater of an extinct volcano, described by Virgil and other Latin writers as the entrance to the underworld; *Avernus* may also be used for the underworld itself. The name was said to come from Greek and mean 'birdless (lake)', because the poisons rising from it were believed to kill birds flying over it.

Averroës (*c*.1126–98), Spanish-born Islamic philosopher, judge, and physician. His extensive body of work includes writings on jurisprudence, science, philosophy, and religion. His highly influential commentaries on Aristotle sought to reconcile Aristotle with Plato and the Greek philosophical tradition with the Arabic.

Avesta the sacred writings of Zoroastrianism, compiled in the 4th century, and written in an ancient Iranian language closely related to Vedic Sanskrit.

Aveyron see ➤ WILD *Boy of Aveyron*.

Avicenna (980–1037), Persian-born Islamic philosopher and physician; Arabic name ibn-Sina. His philosophical system, drawing on Aristotle but in many ways closer to Neoplatonism, was the major influence on the development of scholasticism. His *Canon of Medicine*, which combined his own knowledge with Roman and Arabic medicine, was a standard medieval medical text.

Avignon a city on the Rhône in SE France, which from 1309 until 1377 the residence of the popes during their exile from Rome and was papal property until the French Revolution.

Ávila see ➤ *St* TERESA *of Ávila*.

avis see ➤ RARA *avis*.

Avogadro's constant the number of atoms or molecules in one mole of a substance, equal to 6.023 × 10²³, and named after the Italian chemist and physicist Amedeo Avogadro (1776–1856). His law, formulated in 1811, and stating that equal volumes of gases at the same temperature and pressure contain equal numbers of molecules, was used to derive both molecular weights and a system of atomic weights.

Avon see ➤ *the* BARD *of Avon*.

Avril see ➤ POISSON *d'Avril*.

awe see ➤ DAYS *of Awe*.

awkward squad composed of recruits and soldiers who need further training; first recorded in Robert Burns's 'Don't let the awkward squad fire over me', shortly before his death in 1796.

axe an emblem of several saints as the instrument of their martyrdom: ➤ JOHN *the Baptist*, ➤ BONIFACE, ➤ MAGNUS, ➤ OLAF, ➤ WINEFRIDE, ➤ *Thomas* MORE, and ➤ *John* FISHER.

axinomancy divination by means of an axe-head.

the Axis the alliance of Germany and Italy formed before and during the Second World War, later extended to include Japan and other countries.

ayatollah a high-ranking religious leader among Shiite Muslims, chiefly in Iran. The word comes (in the 1950s) via Persian from Arabic, literally 'token of God'.

Ayers Rock a red rock mass in Northern Territory, Australia, south-west of Alice Springs. The largest monolith in the world, it is 348 m (1,143 ft) high and about 9 km (6 miles) in circumference.

In 1980 it was the site of a famous mystery, the disappearance of a nine-week-old girl said to have been carried off by a dingo; the child's body was never found, and although her mother was tried and convicted of her murder in 1982, the verdict was later quashed. In 1995 an inquest concluded that an open verdict was the only possible finding.

Ayers Rock is named after Sir Henry Ayers, Premier of South Australia in 1872–3; its Aboriginal name is *Uluru*.

Ayesha¹ name of the youngest wife of Muhammad, who nursed him in his last illness, and who is traditionally depicted as a model of piety.

Ayesha² name of the central character of Rider Haggard's *She* (1887), the mysterious and long-lived queen who is otherwise known as She-who-must-be-obeyed.

the Ayrshire Poet a name for Robert Burns.

Ayurveda the traditional Hindu system of medicine, which is based on the idea of balance in bodily systems and uses diet, herbal treatment, and yogic breathing.

azalea a deciduous flowering shrub with clusters of brightly coloured, sometimes fragrant, flowers. The name comes (in the mid 18th century) from modern Latin from Greek, feminine of *azaleos* 'dry', because the shrub flourishes in dry soil.

Azania an alternative name for South Africa, proposed in the time of apartheid by some supporters of majority rule for the country. The word comes from Greek (taken from classical geography), probably based on Arabic *Zanj*, denoting a black African.

azimuth the direction of a celestial object from the observer, expressed as the angular distance from the north or south point of the horizon to the point at which a vertical circle passing through the object intersects the horizon. Recorded from late Middle English (denoting the arc of a celestial circle from the zenith to the horizon) the word comes from Old French *azimut* from Arabic *as-samt*, from *al* 'the' + *samt* 'way, direction'.

azoth the alchemists' name for mercury, as the essential first principle of all metals. Also, the universal remedy of Paracelsus.

Azrael in Jewish and Muslim mythology, the angel who severs the soul from the body.

Aztec a member of the American Indian people dominant in Mexico before the Spanish conquest of the 16th century. The Aztecs arrived in the central valley of Mexico after the collapse of the Toltec civilization in the 12th century. Their rich and elaborate civilization centred on the city of Tenochtitlán, which boasted vast pyramids, temples, and palaces with fountains. Aztec rulers (the last and most famous of whom was Montezuma) tended to be despotic, and captives taken in war were offered as sacrifices to the gods.

The name comes via French or Spanish from Nahuatl *aztecatl* 'person of Aztlan', their legendary place of origin.

azure the heraldic term for blue. Recorded from Middle English (denoting a blue dye) the word comes via Old French and medieval Latin from Arabic *al* 'the' + *lāzaward* (from Persian *lāžward* 'lapis lazuli').

Bb

B the second letter of the modern English alphabet and of the ancient Roman one, corresponding to Greek *beta*, Hebrew *beth*, used symbolically to denote the second of two or more hypothetical persons or things.

See also ➤ *who* SAYS *A must say B*, ➤ *not know a B from a* BATTLEDORE.

ba in ancient Egyptian belief, the soul of a person or god, which survived after death but which had to be sustained with offerings of food. It was typically represented as a human-headed bird. See also ➤ KA.

ba gua a Chinese religious motif incorporating the eight trigrams of the *I Ching*, typically arranged octagonally around a symbol denoting the balance of yin and yang, or around a mirror; this motif regarded in feng shui as a pattern determining the significance and auspicious qualities of spatial relationships.

Baader-Meinhof Group another name for ➤ RED *Army Faction*.

Baal a male fertility god whose cult was widespread in ancient Phoenician and Canaanite lands and was strongly resisted by the Hebrew prophets. The name comes from Hebrew *ba'al* 'lord'.

Baalbek a town in eastern Lebanon, site of the ancient city of Heliopolis. Its principal monuments date from the Roman period; they include the Corinthian temples of Jupiter and Bacchus and private houses with important mosaics.

Baath Party a pan-Arab socialist party founded in Syria in 1943. Different factions of the Baath Party hold power in Syria and Iraq. The name comes from an Arabic word meaning 'resurrection, renaissance'.

Baba Yaga a celebrated witch of Russian folklore, the 'Bony-legged One', who lives in a house on chicken-legs and flies about in a mortar, using a pestle as oar and a broom to sweep away her tracks.

Babar the elephant hero of a series of picture-books, written and drawn by Jean de Brunhoff (1899–1937) and then by his son Laurent (1925–   ); *Babar* as a young elephant has lived with people, but has returned to the jungle to become king of the elephants with his cousin and wife Celeste.

Charles Babbage (1791–1871), English mathematician, inventor, and pioneer of machine computing. He designed a mechanical computer with ➤ *Ada, Countess of* LOVELACE, which would both perform calculations and print the results, but was unable to complete it in his lifetime. His analysis of the postal service led to the introduction of the penny post.

Babbitt a term for a materialistic, complacent, and conformist businessman, from the name George *Babbitt*, the protagonist of the novel *Babbitt* by Sinclair Lewis.

> The Republican party . . . stretches from Main Street to Wall Street, encompassing complacent, small-town Babbitts and corporate CEOs.
> — *Mother Jones* September 1992

Tower of Babel in the Bible, a tower built in an attempt to reach heaven, which God frustrated by confusing the languages of its builders so that they could not understand one another (Genesis 11:1–9). The story was probably inspired by the Babylonian ziggurat, and may be an attempt to explain the existence of different languages.

> The noise, like the smells, was similarly overwhelming—it was a veritable Tower of Babel.
> — J. M. Dillard *The Lost Years* (1989)

babes see also ➤ BUSBY *Babes*, ➤ MILK *for babes*, ➤ *out of the* MOUTHS *of babes*—.

babes in the wood inexperienced people in a situation calling for experience; the reference is to the two children in a 16th-century ballad, the *Children in the Wood*, whose wicked uncle wishes to steal their inheritance. Abandoned in a forest, the children die of starvation and the robins cover their bodies with leaves; the uncle and his accomplice are subsequently brought to justice.

Babi Yar the name of a deep ravine to the north of Kiev in the Ukraine, site of the mass-killing of Jews by SS squads between 1941 and 1943. *Babi Yar* has become a symbol of the Holocaust, and was the subject of a poem by ➤ YEVTUSHENKO.

Babieca the name of ➤ *El* CID's horse, said to have carried his master's dead body on its last journey from Valencia to Burgos; the horse survived for two more years (during which time no one could ride him), and was buried by the gates of the monastery at Valencia, with two elm trees planted on his grave. The name means informally 'stupid', and reflects the story that El Cid as a boy chose what appeared to be a clumsy and awkward colt, which grew into his famous horse.

Babism a religion founded in 1844 by the Persian Mirza Ali Muhammad of Shiraz (1819–50, popularly known as 'The Bab'), who taught that a new prophet would follow Muhammad. Babism developed into Baha'i when Baha'ullah claimed to be this prophet.

Babrius a Greek writer of fables who lived probably in the second century AD but about whom nothing is known. The fables, which exist today in two books (of which the second is incomplete), are based on the fables of Aesop with some apparently original additions.

Babur (1483–1530), first Mogul emperor of India *c*.1525–30, descendant of Tamerlane. He invaded India *c*.1525 and conquered the territory from the Oxus to Patna. A Muslim, he instigated the policy of religious toleration towards his non-Muslim subjects which was continued by later Mogul emperors.

baby see also ➤ BEANIE *Baby,* ➤ *don't* THROW *the baby out with the bathwater.*

baby boomer a person born during the temporary marked increase in the birth rate following the Second World War.

Babylon an ancient city in Mesopotamia, the capital of Babylonia in the 2nd millennium BC under Hammurabi. The city (of which only ruins now remain) lay on the Euphrates and was noted by Classical writers for its luxury, its fortifications, and its legendary Hanging Gardens. The name is also given in Revelation to the mystical city of the Apocalypse, and it is taken as the type of a great and decadent city.

The name is also used (chiefly among Rastafarians) as a contemptuous or dismissive term for aspects of white culture seen as degenerate or oppressive, especially the police.

See also ➤ *the* HANGING *Gardens of Babylon,* ➤ *the* MODERN *Babylon,* ➤ WHORE *of Babylon.*

Babylonia an ancient region of Mesopotamia, formed when the kingdoms of Akkad in the north and Sumer in the south combined in the first half of the 2nd millennium BC. Babylonia was dominated by Assyria, formerly its dependency, from the 14th to the 7th century BC. The throne was held by the Chaldeans from 625 to 539 BC, and Babylonia was conquered by Cyrus the Great of Persia in 539 BC.

Babylonian Captivity the captivity of the Israelites in Babylon, lasting from their deportation by Nebuchadnezzar in 586 BC until their release by Cyrus the Great in 539 BC. Its allusive force as a type of grieving exile has been strengthened by the first line of Psalm 137 in the Book of Common Prayer, 'By the waters of Babylon we sat down and wept'.

baccalaureate a university bachelor's degree. The word comes (in the mid 17th century) from French *baccalauréat* or medieval Latin *baccalaureatus,* from *baccalaureus* 'bachelor'. The earlier form *baccalarius* was altered by wordplay to conform with *bacca lauri* 'laurel berry', because of the laurels awarded to scholars.

Bacchae in ancient Greece, priestesses or female devotees of the Greek god Bacchus; ➤ BACCHANTS.

Bacchanalia the Roman festival of Bacchus, typified by scenes of drunken revelry and celebration.

bacchants priestesses or female devotees of the god Bacchus. They are depicted wearing the skins of fawns or panthers and wreaths of ivy, oak, or fir, each carrying a thyrsus. As described by Euripides in *The Bacchae,* they roam the mountains with music and dancing, and inspired by the god to frenzy, uproot trees, and catch and tear apart wild animals.

Bacchus in Greek mythology, another name for ➤ DIONYSUS.

Johann Sebastian Bach (1685–1750), German composer. An exceptional and prolific baroque composer, he produced works ranging from violin concertos, suites, and the six *Brandenburg Concertos* (1720–1) to clavier works and sacred cantatas. Large-scale choral works include *The Passion according to St John* (1723), *The Passion according to St Matthew* (1729), and the *Mass in B minor* (1733–8).

Bach flower remedies preparations of the flowers of various plants used in a system of complementary medicine intended to relieve ill health by influencing underlying emotional states, named after Edward *Bach* (1886–1936), British physician.

Back Bay reclaimed western addition of the city of Boston, on the south bank of the Charles River, which since the mid 19th century has been a fashionable residential district.

> Can't that Boston woman write anything without sticking Back Bay into it?
> — *American Mercury* July 1926

back of beyond a term (first recorded in Sir Walter Scott's *The Antiquary*, 1816, as a humorous phrase for some very out of the way place), used in Australia for the far inland regions remote from large towns or closely settled districts, the backblocks.

back of Bourke the remote and sparsely populated inland of Australia; *Bourke* is a town in New South Wales.

back slang slang in which words are spoken as though they were spelled backwards (e.g. *redraw* for *warder*).

back to basics a political catchphrase of the early 1990s, embodying a conscious return to what are seen as fundamental principles of self-respect, decency, and honesty. The use of the phrase derived from a speech made by John Major, then Prime Minister, to the Conservative Party Conference in 1993, when he said that 'It is time to get back to basics: to self-discipline and respect for the law, to consideration for others.' The emphasis was on personal responsibility, but in the public mind *back to basics* was associated with a call to return to the perceived moral values of an earlier era. It was accordingly used ironically in situations in which members of the Party were deemed to have fallen short of the aspirations embodied in the phrase.

backbencher in Britain, a Member of Parliament who does not hold office in the government or opposition, and who occupies the benches behind the front bench on either side of the house.

backroom boys people who provide vital scientific and technical support for those in the field who become public figures; the expression derives from Lord Beaverbrook:

> Now who is responsible for this work of development on which so much depends? To whom must the praise be given? To the boys in the back rooms. They do not sit in the limelight. But they are the men who do the work.
> — Lord Beaverbrook in *Listener* 27 March 1941

backs see also ➤ *the* BEAST *with two backs*.

the **Backs** in Cambridge, the college gardens which back on to the River Cam; the name is recorded from the late 19th century.

backwoodsman a member of the House of Lords who rarely, if ever, attends meetings of that body, but is prepared on occasion to assert his political rights. The term is recorded from the early 20th century.

backyard see ➤ NOT *in my backyard*.

bacon in early use, *bacon* was used to mean not just the cured meat from the back and sides of a pig, but also fresh pork, the meat most readily available to the rural population; from this, the word was used to mean a rustic, a clown.

Recorded from Middle English, the word comes via Old French from a Germanic word meaning 'ham, flitch', related to *back*.

Francis Bacon (1561–1626), English statesman and philosopher, described by Izaak Walton as 'the great Secretary of Nature and all learning, Sir Francis Bacon'. As a scientist he advocated the inductive method; his views were instrumental in the founding of the Royal Society in 1660.

Roger Bacon (*c*.1214–94), English philosopher, scientist, and Franciscan friar. Most notable for his work in the field of optics, he emphasized the need for an empirical approach to scientific study. He eventually fell foul of his own order, which imprisoned him for 'suspect novelties'.

See also ➤ BRAZEN *head*.

Bacon's Rebellion a rebellion led by a Virginia planter, Nathaniel *Bacon* (1647–76), against the arbitrary rule of the crown authorities.

Baconian philosophy the inductive method of reasoning associated with the English statesman and philosopher ➤ *Francis* BACON (1561–1626), whose radical philosophical beliefs proved very influential in the century following his death.

Baconian theory the theory, first promulgated in the late nineteenth century, that Francis Bacon (as the head of a group including Raleigh and Spenser) was the true author of the plays attributed to Shakespeare, and that a great system of thought was concealed in them by ciphers. The American writer Delia Salter Bacon (1811–59) was one of the earliest and most enthusiastic proponents of the theory.

Bactria an ancient country in central Asia, corresponding to the northern part of modern Afghanistan. Traditionally the home of Zoroaster, it was the seat of a powerful Indo-Greek kingdom in the 3rd and 2nd centuries BC.

bad see also ➤ *a bad* PENNY *always turns up.*

the Bad epithet applied to a number of medieval rulers, as Charles the Bad, king of Navarre (1332–87).

bad excuse is better than none proverbial saying, mid 16th century.

bad hair day a day on which everything seems to go wrong, characterized as a day on which one's hair is particularly unmanageable; an expression which became current in the 1990s.

bad money drives out good proverbial saying, early 20th century; known as ➤ GRESHAM'*s law.*

bad news travels fast proverbial saying, late 16th century.

a bad workman blames his tools proverbial saying, early 17th century; late 13th century in French.

Baden-Baden a spa town in the Black Forest, which was a fashionable resort in the 19th century.

badge see ➤ DOGGETT'*s Coat and Badge.*

badger a heavily built nocturnal mammal, typically with a grey and black coat and striped head, living in an extensive burrow system. The formerly popular sport of **badger-baiting** involved setting dogs to attack and draw out the animal defending its burrow or a substitute shelter, and this has given rise to various figurative uses.

Badger State an informal name for Wisconsin.

Badlands a barren plateau region of the western US, mainly in North and South Dakota and Nebraska.

Badminton the Duke of Beaufort's country seat in SW England, which has given its name (*badminton*) to a game with rackets in which a shuttlecock is played back and forth across a net which was developed from the old game of battledore and shuttlecock in the 1870s by British officers in India, and to a mixture of claret, soda, and sugar, fashionable as a summer drink in the mid 19th century.

Badminton is also well known for its annual horse trials.

Battle of Badon Hill an ancient British battle (the location of which is uncertain), in AD 516, in which the forces of King Arthur successfully defended themselves against the Saxons. Another source implies that the battle was fought *c.*500, but does not connect it with Arthur.

Karl Baedeker (1801–59), German publisher, who in 1827 started his own publishing firm in Koblenz. He is remembered chiefly for the series of guidebooks to which he gave his name and which are still published today.

Baedeker raids in the Second World War, raids carried out by the Luftwaffe in April and May 1942 on places of cultural and historical importance in Britain.

William Baffin (*c.*1584–1622), English navigator and explorer, the pilot of several expeditions in search of the North-West Passage 1612–16. He discovered the largest island of the Canadian Arctic in 1616; this and the strait between it and Greenland are named after him.

bag see ➤ BOTTOM *of the bag,* ➤ PETTY *Bag.*

bag and baggage with all one's belongings, completely. Originally, this was a military phrase denoting all the property of an army collectively, and of the soldiers individually, and to march out **with bag and baggage** indicated that an army or a commander was making an honourable retreat, without surrender of any possessions.

bag lady a homeless woman who carries her possessions around in shopping bags; the phrase was first recorded in the US in the 1970s.

Bag o'Nails traditional name for an inn, representing an alteration of *Bacchanals.*

Baggins the family name of the ➤ HOBBITS, Bilbo and Frodo, who in Tolkien's *The Hobbit* and *Lord of the Rings* come into possession of the One Ring of power.

Baghdad the capital of modern-day Iraq, on the River Tigris, which was a thriving city under the Abbasid caliphs, notably ➤ HARUN *ar-Rashid,* in the 8th and 9th centuries.

Baha'i a monotheistic religion founded in the 19th century as a development of ➤ BABISM, emphasizing the essential oneness of humankind and of all religions and seeking world peace.

Baikonur a mining town in central Kazakhstan. The world's first satellite (1957) and the first manned space flight (1961) were launched from the former Soviet space centre nearby.

bailey the outer wall of a castle and a court enclosed by it. Recorded from Middle English, the word probably comes from Old French *baile* 'palisade, enclosure'.

See also ➤ MOTTE-*and-bailey*.

Bailey bridge a temporary bridge of lattice steel designed for rapid assembly from prefabricated standard parts, used especially in military operations, named after D. *Bailey* (1901–85), the English engineer who designed it.

bailie a municipal officer and magistrate in Scotland. The word comes via Old French from the base of ➤ BAILIFF.

bailiff a person who performs certain actions under legal authority, in particular, a sheriff's officer who executes writs and processes and carries out distraints and arrests; the sovereign's representative in a district, especially the chief officer of a hundred; the first civil officer in the Channel Islands. The word is recorded from Middle English, and comes ultimately (via Old French) from Latin *bajulus* 'carrier, manager'.

See also ➤ BUM-*bailiff*.

bailiwick an informal term for one's sphere of operations or particular area of interest, deriving from the legal sense 'the jurisdiction of a bailie or bailiff'.

Baily's beads in astronomy, a string of bright points seen at the edge of the darkened moon at the beginning or end of totality in an eclipse of the sun, caused by the unevenness of the lunar topography.

Bairam either of two annual Muslim festivals, the *Greater Bairam*, held at the end of the Islamic year, and the *Lesser Bairam*, held at the end of Ramadan.

bairns see ➤ FOOLS *and bairns should never see half-done work.*

Bajazet ruler of the Ottomans (1389–1402), who overran the provinces of the eastern Empire and besieged Constantinople, but was defeated and taken prisoner by Timor (➤ TAMERLANE).

bake-meat pastry, a pie; the expression is now best known from Shakespeare's *Hamlet*, 'The funeral bake-meats Did coldly furnish forth the marriage tables.'

as you bake, so shall you brew proverbial saying, late 16th century.

baker see also ➤ *the* BUTCHER, *the baker, the candlestick-maker,* ➤ *the* OWL *was a baker's daughter,* ➤ PULL *Devil, pull baker.*

Baker day a dated term for ➤ INSET *day*, named after Kenneth *Baker*, the Conservative Education Secretary (1986–9) who introduced the practice.

Baker Street Irregulars the gang of street urchins who appear in three of the ➤ *Sherlock* HOLMES stories, and who are used by Holmes for carrying messages and maintaining surveillance on suspected persons; Holmes lived at 221b Baker Street.

baker's dozen a group of thirteen; the expression comes (in the late 16th century) from the former bakers' custom of adding an extra loaf to a dozen sold to a retailer, this representing the latter's profit.

bakers ➤ *St* ELIZABETH *of Hungary* and St Zita, a 13th-century Luccan serving-maid who was said to have had her loaves baked by angels while she herself was in an ecstatic trance, are the patron saints of bakers.

Balaam a non-Israelite prophet whose story is related in the biblical book of *Numbers*. In allusive use he is often taken as an example of an evil diviner who would sell his prophetic powers to the highest bidder, although his powers are questionable: although supposedly a seer, he is repeatedly unable to see the divine messenger that is visible even to his donkey. The animal is finally granted the power of speech by God to address her master, and it is suggested in Lockhart's *Life of Scott* (1839) that this is the origin of the (archaic) journalist's slang usage *Balaam* to mean 'superfluous or trivial material used to fill up a column'.

A passage from Balaam's final oracle was quoted in the first telegraph message, 'What God hath wrought!' (*Numbers* 23:23).

Balaam basket an editor's container for unwanted material.

Battle of Balaclava a battle of the Crimean War, fought between Russia and an alliance of British, French, and Turkish forces in and around the port of Balaclava (now Balaklava) in the southern Crimea in 1854. The battle ended inconclusively; it is chiefly remembered as the scene of the ➤ CHARGE *of the Light Brigade.*

Le **Balafré** nickname, meaning 'the Scarred' of the French soldier and politician François, Duc de Guise (1519–43).

balance see also ➤ CHECKS *and balances,* ➤ WEIGHED *in the balance and found wanting.*

Balance the zodiacal sign or constellation Libra.

balance of nature a state of equilibrium produced by the interaction of living organisms, ecological balance; the phrase is recorded from the early 20th century.

balance of power a situation in which states of the world have roughly equal power. The phrase in this sense is recorded from the early 18th century, in 'Your glorious design of re-establishing a just balance of power in Europe' (*London Gazette*, 1701), and is associated with the political aspirations of ➤ *Robert* WALPOLE (1676–1745); in 1752 the economist David Hume wrote an essay entitled 'Of the balance of power'.

Vasco Núñez de Balboa (1475–1519), Spanish explorer. In 1511 Balboa joined an expedition to Darien (in Panama) as a stowaway, but rose to command it after a mutiny. In 1513 he reached the western coast of the isthmus of Darien (Panama), thereby becoming the first European to see the Pacific Ocean.

balcony a platform enclosed by a wall or balustrade on the outside of a building, with access from an upper-floor window or door. Between the early 17th and early 19th centuries, the word was usually pronounced with the stress on the second syllable, but the modern pronunciation occurs in Swift.

the Bald epithet applied to a number of medieval rulers, as, **Charles the Bald** (823–77), king of the Franks and Holy Roman Emperor.

baldachin a ceremonial canopy of stone, metal, or fabric over an altar, throne, or doorway. Recorded from the late 16th century (denoting a rich brocade of silk and gold thread) the word comes ultimately from Italian *Baldacco* 'Baghdad', place of origin of the original brocade.

Balder in Scandinavian mythology, a son of Odin and god of the summer sun. He was invulnerable to all things except mistletoe, with which the god Loki, by a trick, induced the blind god Hödur to kill him.

baldfaced (of an animal) having a white patch on the forehead; an inn at Kingston in Surrey named

the **Baldfaced Stag** is said to have been the headquarters of the highwayman Jerry Abershaw (177?–95).

Baldwin (1058?–1118), crusader, first king of Jerusalem (1100–18), brother of ➤ GODFREY *of Bouillon.*

> It speaks to him of Baldwin, and Tancred, the princely Saladin, and great Richard of the Lion Heart.
> — Mark Twain *The Innocents Abroad* (1869)

bale is highest when boot is nighest proverbial saying, Middle English; another version of 'it is always darkest before dawn' (*bale* = need, *boot* = help).

Cristóbal Balenciaga (1895–1972), Spanish couturier, whose garments were noted for their simplicity, elegance, and boldness of design. In the 1950s he contributed to the move away from the tight-waisted New Look originated by Christian Dior to a looser, semi-fitted style, which culminated in 1957 with a chemise ('the sack').

Arthur James Balfour (1848–1930), British Conservative statesman, Prime Minister 1902–5. In 1917, in his capacity as Foreign Secretary, Balfour issued the declaration in favour of a Jewish national home in Palestine that came to be known as the Balfour Declaration.

Balfour was nephew of the Conservative statesman Lord Salisbury, a relationship which may have given rise to the expression ➤ BOB'*s your uncle.*

See also ➤ BLOODY *Balfour.*

Mr Balfour's poodle the House of Lords; from the title of a book by Roy Jenkins *Mr Balfour's Poodle. An account of the struggle between the House of Lords and the government of Mr Asquith* (1954); ultimately in allusion to Lloyd George:

> The leal and trusty mastiff which is to watch over our interests, but which runs away at the first snarl of the trade unions . . . A mastiff? It is the right hon. Gentleman's poodle.
> — David Lloyd George speech in the House of Commons, 26 June 1907

Balisard in Ariosto's *Orlando Furioso,* the name of Ruggiero's sword.

Balius in the *Iliad,* the name of one of Achilles' horses, a son of the harpy Podarge and Zephyr.

Balkan Wars two wars of 1912–13 that were fought over the last European territories of the Ottoman Empire. In 1912 Bulgaria, Serbia, Greece, and Montenegro forced Turkey to give up Albania and Macedonia, leaving the area around Constantinople

(Istanbul) as the only Ottoman territory in Europe. The following year Bulgaria disputed with Serbia, Greece, and Romania for possession of Macedonia, which was partitioned between Greece and Serbia.

the Balkans the countries occupying the part of SE Europe lying south of the Danube and Sava Rivers, forming a peninsula bounded by the Adriatic and Ionian Seas in the west, the Aegean and Black Seas in the east, and the Mediterranean in the south. The peninsula was taken from the Byzantine Empire by the Ottoman Turks in the 14th and 15th centuries, and parts remained under Turkish control until 1912–13. After the First World War the peninsula was divided between Greece, Albania, Bulgaria, and Yugoslavia (which broke up in 1991–3), with Turkey retaining only a small area including Constantinople (Istanbul).

The term **Balkanize** meaning 'divide (a region or body) into smaller mutually hostile states or groups' is recorded from the 1920s; earlier, the German statesman Otto von Bismarck had prophesied, 'If there is ever another war in Europe, it will come out of some damned silly thing in the Balkans.'

Balkis the name of the queen of Sheba in Arabic literature.

ball-flower an architectural ornament resembling a ball within the petals of a flower.

ballad a poem or song narrating a story in short stanzas. Traditional ballads are typically of unknown authorship, having been passed on orally from one generation to the next as part of the folk culture. Recorded from the late 15th century (denoting a light, simple song), the word comes via Old French from Provençal *balada* 'to dance', from late Latin. The sense 'narrative poem' dates from the mid 18th century, and was used by Johnson in the *Rambler*.

Ballarat a mining and sheep-farming centre in Victoria, Australia, which is the site of the discovery in 1851 of the largest gold reserves in Australia.
See also ➤ Eureka.

ballet see ➤ Bolshoi *Ballet*.

Ballingreich see ➤ goodman.

when the balloon goes up when the action or trouble starts, probably with allusion to the release of a balloon to mark the start of an event.

ballot a procedure by which people vote secretly on a particular issue. The word is recorded from the mid 16th century, and originally denoted a small coloured ball placed in a container to register a vote; it comes from Italian *ballotta*, diminutive of *balla* 'ball'.

the ballot is stronger than the bullet familiar form given to a quotation from a speech by Abraham Lincoln, 18 May 1858: 'To give victory to the right, not bloody bullets, but peaceful ballots only, are necessary.'

balls see ➤ *three* golden *balls*.

balm in Gilead comfort in distress, succour; originally with reference to Jeremiah 8:22, 'Is there no balm in Gilead?'

> 'My garden was smashed flat,' he continued mournfully, 'but so was Dora's,' he added in a tone which indicated that there was yet balm in Gilead.
> — L. M. Montgomery *Anne of Avonlea* (1909)

Balmoral Castle a holiday residence of the British royal family, on the River Dee in Scotland. The estate was bought in 1847 by Prince Albert, who rebuilt and refurbished the castle.

> Despite its crenellated battlements, round towers and embrasures, it didn't begin to rank with the Windsors and Balmorals of this world.
> — Alistair MacLean *When Eight Bells Toll* (1966)

Balmung in the *Nibelungenlied*, a sword made for ➤ Siegfried by Wieland.

baloney foolish or deceptive talk, nonsense. The word is said to be a corruption of *Bologna*, from *Bologna sausage*, but the connection remains conjectural.

Balor the chief of the Fomors in Gaelic mythology. One of his eyes had the power of destroying whatever it looked on. The eye was put out and Balor himself slain by Lugh, the sun-god, at the great battle of Moytura.

balsam an aromatic resinous substance, such as balm, exuded by various trees and shrubs and used as a base for certain fragrances and medical preparations. In the 17th and 18th centuries, the word was also applied by alchemists to a healthful preservative essence, of oily and softly penetrative nature, conceived by Paracelsus to exist in all organic bodies.

Balthasar the traditional name of one of the ➤ Magi.

Balthazar a very large wine bottle, equivalent in capacity to sixteen regular bottles. The name comes, in the 1930s, from the king of Babylon (otherwise ➤ BELSHAZZAR), who 'made a great feast … and drank wine before a thousand' (Daniel 5:1).

Baltic see ➤ *the* EYE *of the Baltic.*

Baltic Exchange an association of companies, based in London, whose members are engaged in numerous international trading activities, especially the chartering of vessels to carry cargo. The name comes from *Virginia and Baltic,* one of many coffee houses where shipowners and merchants met in London in the 18th century, the coffee house being so named by association with areas of much of the trade.

In April 1992, the Baltic Exchange building in London was seriously damaged by an IRA bomb, an event which brought into question the advisability of establishing a ➤ RING *of steel* around the City of London.

Bamberg Bible another name for the ➤ THIRTY-*Six-Line Bible,* which was printed at Bamberg in Bavaria.

Bambi eponymous name of the young deer in Felix Salten's story for children (1923); filmed by Disney in 1942, the story became widely known, and *Bambi* is used to refer to the wide-eyed and consciously appealing look and manner of a young and timid animal.

bambocciade a painting of rustic and grotesque scenes, especially from low life. Recorded from the early 19th century, the term comes ultimately via French from Italian *bamboccio* 'child, simpleton, puppet', nickname of the painter Peter de Laer.

bamboo curtain a political and economic barrier between China and non-Communist countries, on the model of ➤ IRON *curtain.*

bamboozle an informal term meaning, cheat or fool. Of unknown origin, and recorded from the early 18th century, it is mentioned in 1710 by Swift in the *Tatler* no. 230 (on 'the continual Corruption of our English Tongue') among other slang terms recently invented or brought into vogue.

Bamian a city in central Afghanistan, near which are the remains of two colossal statues of Buddha and the ruins of the city of Ghulghuleh, which was destroyed by Genghis Khan *c.*1221.

Bampton Lectures an annual series of eight divinity lectures to be preached at the University Church in Oxford, founded by the English divine John Bampton (1690–1751).

ban[1] originally (in Old English, in form *bannan*) 'summon by official proclamation', of Germanic origin; reinforced in Middle English by Old Norse *banna* 'curse, prohibit', the verb came to mean 'officially or legally prohibit'.

ban[2] a governor or viceroy in certain military districts in Hungary, Slavonia, and Croatia under the Austro-Hungarian Empire; the word comes from Persian *bān* 'lord, master, keeper', and was brought into Europe by the Avars who ruled in Slavonic countries subject to Hungary.

ban the bomb US anti-nuclear slogan, adopted from 1953 onwards by the Campaign for Nuclear Disarmament.

Banagher name of a town in Ireland, apparently noted as a 'rotten borough', and recorded in the proverb, 'That beats Banagher, and Banagher beats the Devil.'

banana republic a small state dependent on foreign capital, typically as a result of the domination of the economy by a single trade, and hence politically unstable; the name was particularly used of Central American states.

Bananaland in Australia, an informal name for Queensland.

Banbury an Oxfordshire town formerly noted for the number and fervour of its Puritan inhabitants, as for its cakes and cheese. Philemon Holland's translation of Camden's *Britannia* (1610) notes, 'The fame of this town is for zeal, cheese, and cakes,' although Thomas Fuller in *Oxford* (1662) says that he cannot find the words in Camden's original (Latin) text, and regrets that 'the error is continued out of design to nick the town of Banbury, as reputed then a place of precise people.'

> To Banbury came I, O profane one!
> Where I saw a Puritane-one
> Hanging of his cat on Monday
> For killing of a mouse on Sunday.
> — Richard Brathwaite *Barnabee's Journal* (1638)

See also ➤ SHEPHERD *of Banbury.*

Banbury cake a flat pastry with a spicy currant filling, originally made in Banbury.

thin as Banbury cheese very thin; in Shakespeare's *The Merry Wives of Windsor* (1597), Slender is addressed as 'You Banbury cheese'.

Banbury Cross a market cross in Banbury, referred to in the nursery rhyme, 'Ride a cock-horse to Banbury Cross, To see a fine lady upon a white horse.' The original Cross was in fact destroyed at the end of the 16th century; the *Oxford Dictionary of Nursery Rhymes* notes that 'A Jesuit priest wrote in January 1601, "The inhabitants of Banbury being far gone in Puritanism, in a furious zeal tumultuously assailed the Cross that stood in the market place, and so defaced it that they scarcely left one stone upon another." '

banco an exclamation used in baccarat, chemin de fer, and similar games to express a player's willingness to meet the banker's whole stake single-handed. Recorded from the late 18th century, the word comes via French from Italian.

Bancroft Library the collection of regional materials formed by the American bookseller and historian Hubert Howe Bancroft (1831–1918), and sold by him to the University of California (Berkeley) in 1905. The library continues to collect in the areas of the western part of North America (emphasizing California) and Mexico and Central America; it now holds other rare materials on campus, including the manuscripts and other papers of Mark Twain.

band see ➤ Sacred *Band*.

Band of Hope a name given (from about 1847) to associations of young people who pledged themselves to temperance; the name is first recorded in a temperance song of 1847 by J. Tunnicliff, 'The Band of Hope shall be our name, the Temperance star our guide.'

Bandar-log in Kipling's *Jungle Books*, the monkey people, who talk constantly of their abilities and their plans but who achieve nothing, taken as the type of irresponsible chattering people. Their motto 'What the Bandar-log think now the Jungle will think tomorrow' is a version of the proverbial ➤ *what* Manchester *says today, the rest of England says tomorrow.*

> That is just what the *Bandar Log* overlook, when they jabber about the dreadful industrial upheaval that is coming with peace.
> — Ian Hay *Carrying On* (1917)

bandersnatch a fierce mythical creature immune to bribery and capable of moving very fast. The name was coined by Lewis Carroll in *Through the Looking Glass* (1871), and is probably a portmanteau word.

> No one ever influenced Tolkien—you might as well try to influence a bandersnatch.
> — C. S. Lewis letter, 15 May 1959

bandit see ➤ Beltway *Bandit*.

bandog a fighting dog bred for its strength and ferocity by crossing aggressive breeds. Recorded from Middle English, a *bandog* was originally a dog kept on a chain or 'band'; the term was then generalized to cover any ferocious dog, such as a mastiff or bloodhound. The practice of breeding these cross-breeds for secret dog-fights has led to its being revived and specialized in meaning.

bands a collar with two hanging strips, worn by certain lawyers, clerics, and academics as part of their formal dress.

bandwagon a large wagon capable of carrying the band in a procession; in figurative use, a particular activity or cause that has suddenly become fashionable, and which is seen as having a momentum which carries its proponents forward.
See also ➤ climb *on the bandwagon.*

bang see ➤ big *bang.*

Bangorian controversy a religious controversy raised by a sermon preached before the king in 1717 by Benjamin Hoadly, Bishop of *Bangor*, directed against the ➤ Nonjurors who had refused to take the oath of allegiance to the Crown.

bank see also ➤ beetle *bank*, ➤ break *the bank*, ➤ Left *Bank*, ➤ man *who broke the bank*, ➤ piggy *bank*, ➤ Right *Bank*, ➤ South *Bank*, ➤ West *Bank*.

bank holiday a day on which banks are officially closed, kept as a public holiday; traditionally, bills payable on these days are paid on the following day.
    Certain Saints' days and anniversaries, to the number in all of about 33 days per annum, were kept as Holidays at the Bank of England. In 1834 these holidays were reduced to Good Friday, the 1st of May, 1st of November, and Christmas Day. The list was subsequently revised and enlarged in 1871 (when Easter Monday, Whit Monday, the first Monday in August, and the 26th of December (Boxing Day) were established as bank holidays in England and Ireland, and New Year's Day, the first Monday in May, the first Monday in August, and Christmas Day in Scotland); further revisions and additions have followed, as, the abolition of Whit Monday and the establishment of the Late Spring Bank Holiday.

bankers ➤ St MATTHEW, the former tax-collector, is the patron saint of bankers.

bankrupt a person or organization declared in law to be unable to pay their debts, initially (in the mid 16th century) used for someone who has reduced himself to penury by spendthrift ways, and who was seen as a criminal debtor; Thomas More in his *Apology* (1533) refers to bankrupts who 'have wasted and misspent their own'. The current sense is recorded from the early 18th century; originally only a trader could be made a *bankrupt*, while other persons became *insolvent*, but the legal distinction, abolished in the US in 1841 and in England in 1869, had long before disappeared in popular use.

The word comes from Italian *banca rotta* 'broken bench' (the change in ending was due to association with Latin *-rupt* 'broken'). Johnson in his *Dictionary* suggested that the term derived from the reported custom of breaking the bench of an Italian money-changer who had become insolvent; however, *rotta* was also used to mean 'wrecked' (of a ship), with the figurative senses 'discomfited, defeated, interrupted, stopped'.

Joseph Banks (1743–1820), English botanist. He accompanied Captain James Cook on his first voyage to the Pacific, and helped to establish the Royal Botanic Gardens at Kew. His collections later became part of the British Museum.

Bankside the south side of the Thames opposite London, in medieval times the site of the brothel district (suppressed in 1546).

> The punks of the bankside a penny a time.
> — James Joyce *Ulysses* (1922)

Bannatyne Club founded in 1823, under the presidency of Sir Walter Scott, for the publication of old Scottish documents. The club was dissolved in 1861. George Bannatyne (1545–1608), in whose honour it was named, was the compiler in 1568 of a large collection of Scottish poems.

banner a flag on a pole used as the standard of a king, knight, or army; a banner is the emblem of the saints seen as military figures, ➤ St GEORGE, ➤ St JAMES *the Great*, and ➤ St MAURICE.

banneret a knight who commanded his own troops in battle under his own banner. The word comes (in Middle English) from Old French *baneret*, literally 'bannered'.

Battle of Bannockburn a battle which took place near Stirling in central Scotland in 1314, in which the English army of Edward II, advancing to break the siege of Stirling Castle, was defeated by the Scots under Robert the Bruce; his victory allowed the Bruce, as ➤ ROBERT I, to re-establish Scotland as a separate kingdom.

> We Scots have Bannockburn as our World War Two; football matches with England are wars of liberation.
> — *M8* December 1990

banns a notice read out on three successive Sundays in a parish church, announcing an intended marriage and giving the opportunity for objections. Recorded from Middle English, the word represents the plural of *ban* 'proclamation'.

See also ➤ FORBID *the banns*.

banquet an elaborate and formal evening meal for many people, typically followed by speeches and often marking a state occasion. The word comes (in the late 15th century) from French as a diminutive of *banc* 'table'; in the early 16th century, the senses of 'a slight repast between meals' and 'a course of sweetmeats, fruit, and wine, sometimes served as a separate entertainment' were also recorded.

Banqueting House a hall in Whitehall Palace designed (1622) by Inigo Jones; it was from a window in the *Banqueting House* that Charles I stepped onto the scaffold for his execution, and his body was laid out in the hall the following night.

Banquo a character in Shakespeare's *Macbeth* who is murdered on Macbeth's orders, and whose ghost subsequently appears at Macbeth's banqueting table, invisible to all except Macbeth himself; he embodies both a reminder of Macbeth's guilt, and the warning that his usurpation of power will ultimately fail.

> Imre Nagy was his Banquo and he was always Macbeth.
> — *New York Review of Books* 14 November 1996

banshee in Irish legend, a female spirit whose wailing warns of a death in the house. Recorded from the late 17th century, the term comes from Irish *bean sidhe*, from Old Irish *ben side* 'woman of the fairies'.

> In Ireland long ago every family that had the least pretension to respectability had a banshee of its own. Without one its members would be regarded as not Irish at all, only upstarts.
> — Edmund Lenihan *Aoibheall the Banshee* (1991)

bantam a chicken of a small breed, the cock of which is noted for its aggression. It is apparently named after the province of *Bantam* in Java, although the fowl is not native there.

> This advice meshed with Truman's bantam-cock personality.
> — G. H. Clarfield & W. M. Wiecek *Nuclear America* (1984)

bantamweight a weight in boxing and other sports intermediate between flyweight and featherweight. In the amateur boxing scale it ranges from 51 to 54 kg.

banting a former method of slimming which involved avoiding fat, starch, and sugar in food; the term is recorded from the mid 19th century, and comes from the name of William *Banting* (1797–1878), a London undertaker, who in 1863, having achieved a satisfactory loss of weight by his regime, published 'A Letter on Corpulence, addressed to the Public' embodying the system he had followed. The publication caught the public interest, and a number of editions followed, while the derived verb 'to bant' became well-known.

bantling a young child, a brat; the word (recorded from the late 16th century) may come from German *Bänkling* 'bastard' from *Bank* 'bench'.

banyan an Indian fig tree, the branches of which produce aerial roots which later become accessory trunks, so that a mature tree may cover several hectares in this manner; one Indian politician used the image of such a tree to describe the difficulty of finding a successor to Jawarharlal Nehru:

> The Prime Minister is like the great banyan tree. Thousands shelter beneath it, but nothing grows.
> — Sadashiv Kanoji Patil in J. K. Galbraith *A Life in Our Times* (1981)

Recorded from the late 16th century, the word comes via Portuguese from Gujarati *vāṇiyo* 'man of the trading caste', from Sanskrit. Originally denoting a Hindu merchant, the term was applied, by Europeans in the mid 17th century, to a particular tree under which such traders had built a pagoda.

banyan day naval slang (recorded from the mid 18th century) for a day on which no meat is served, originally with reference to the vegetarianism of *banyans*, or Hindus of the trading caste.

banzai a Japanese battle cry; a form of greeting used to the Japanese emperor. In Japanese, the word means literally 'ten thousand years (of life to you)'.

From the 1980s, the word has been used to designate extremely fast driving, especially in motor racing; a **banzai lap** is a lap of a course taken particularly rapidly.

baobab a short tree with a very thick trunk and large edible fruit, living to a great age. The word comes (in the mid 17th century) probably from an African language, and is first recorded in Latin (1592) in a treatise on the plants of Egypt by Prosper Alpinus, Italian botanist.

Baphomet the idol allegedly worshipped by the Knights Templars; the name was said to have been formed kabbalistically by writing backward *tem.o.h.p.ab*, an abbreviation of *templi omnium hominum pacis abbas* 'abbot' or 'father of the temple'.

baptism in the Christian Church, the religious rite of sprinkling water on a person's head or of immersing them in water, symbolizing purification or regeneration and admission to the Christian Church. In many denominations, baptism is performed on young children and is accompanied by name-giving.

Recorded from Middle English, the word comes via Old French and ecclesiastical Latin from ecclesiastical Greek *baptismos* 'ceremonial washing', from *baptizein* 'immerse, baptize'.

baptism of blood the death by violence of unbaptized martyrs, regarded as a form of baptism.

baptism of fire a difficult or painful new undertaking or experience, from the original sense of 'a soldier's first battle'.

Baptist[1] epithet of St ➤ JOHN *the Baptist.*

Baptist[2] a member of a Protestant Christian denomination advocating baptism only of adult believers by total immersion. Baptists form one of the largest Protestant bodies and are found throughout the world and especially in the US.

bar[1] in heraldry, a charge in the form of a narrow horizontal stripe across the shield.

bar[2] in a court of law, the barrier or rail at which a prisoner stands. In the Inns of Court, formerly, a barrier or partition separating the seats of the benchers from the rest of the hall, to which students, after they had reached a certain standing, were 'called' (long popularly understood to refer to that in a court of justice, beyond which the King's or Queen's Counsel (and Serjeants-at-Law) have place, but not ordinary barristers).

The *bar* denotes the profession of barrister; in British usage, barristers collectively.

See also ➤ BENCH *and Bar,* ➤ CALLED *to the Bar,* ➤ CALLED *within the Bar.*

bar[3] in horse racing, except the horses indicated (used when stating the odds); the expression is recorded from the mid 19th century.

Bar Cochba the leader of a Jewish rebellion in Palestine in AD 132, the purpose of which was to resist the project of the Emperor Hadrian to rebuild Jerusalem as a Graeco-Roman city, with a temple of Jupiter on the site of the former Jewish Temple. The name Bar Cochba means 'son of a star', and this lead to his being identified as the subject of the prophecy in *Numbers* 24:17 'there shall come a star out of Jacob'; according to Christian sources, echoed in rabbinic literature, he claimed to be, and was accepted as, the Messiah.

The name Bar Cochba is found only in some rabbinic and in Christian sources; most Jewish sources call him Bar Koziba ('son of a liar'). Recent finds of some of his letters in the Judaean desert show that his real name was Simeon bar Kosiba.

bar mitzvah the religious initiation ceremony of a Jewish boy who has reached the age of 13 and is regarded as ready to observe religious precepts and eligible to take part in public worship. The term comes from Hebrew *bar miṣwāh*, literally 'son of the commandment'.

See also ➤ BAT *mitzvah*.

Barabbas the prisoner released by ➤ PILATE to the crowd instead of Jesus. The description in John's Gospel 'Now Barabbas was a robber' was famously modified by the Scottish poet Thomas Campbell (1777–1844):

> Now Barabbas was a publisher
> — Samuel Smiles *A Publisher and his Friends* (1891)

In allusive terms Barabbas's name is also used to convey the sense of evil being chosen over good, as in the 1926 comment by the French dramatist Jean Cocteau 'If it has to choose who is to be crucified the crowd will always save Barabbas.'

Baratarian a member of a band of privateers and smugglers which inhabited the area of *Barataria* Bay, an inlet of the Gulf of Mexico in Louisiana, south of New Orleans, in the early nineteenth century.

barathrum a pit or gulf (from Greek *barathron*); in 17th century English, often used for the abyss, hell, as in Jonson's *Every Man in his Own Humour* (1601), 'Let gross opinion sink and be damned As deep as Barathrum'. Figurative usage often includes the idea of hell as an insatiable maw, as in *The Man*

in the Moone (c.1609) 'a bottomless Barathrum, a merciless moneymonger'.

Barathrum was also the name given to a deep pit in ancient Athens into which criminals condemned to death were thrown, but in English this is recorded only from the 19th century.

barb[1] a piece of vertically pleated linen cloth worn over or under the chin, as by nuns; the word is recorded from Middle English, and comes via Old French from Latin *barba* 'beard'. From this developed (in late Middle English) the current sense of a sharp projection near the end of an arrow, fishhook, or similar object, which is angled away from the main point so as to make extraction difficult.

barb[2] a small horse of a hardy breed originally from North Africa. Recorded from the mid 17th century, the name comes via French from Italian *barbero* 'of ➤ BARBARY[1]'.

See also ➤ *the* GODOLPHIN *Barb*.

St Barbara a supposed virgin-martyr, whose cult became very popular in the later Middle Ages. According to the *Golden Legend* she was shut up in a tower by her father, and while he was away became a Christian; she ordered a third window to be made in the building in honour of the Holy Trinity. At her father's instigation she was tried and condemned to death for her Christianity; by some accounts, her father was her executioner. On her death, he was struck by lightning and died.

☐ **EMBLEM** The usual emblem for Barbara is a tower, although she may also be shown with a sword as the instrument of her execution.

☐ **PATRONAGES** Because of the manner of her father's death she is the patron of those in danger of sudden death, first by lightning and then by mines or cannon-balls, and she is therefore patron saint of miners and gunners; as builder of a tower, she is also patron saint of architects. She is also taken as one of the ➤ FOURTEEN *Holy Helpers*.

Barbara, celarent opening words (*Barbara*, 'barbarous things', *Celarent*, 'they might hide') of a 12th-century Latin hexameter verse of scholastic philosophy incorporating the mnemonic names of 19 valid syllogisms; the vowels signify quantity and quality, and most of the remaining letters also have significance.

Barbara is taken as a mnemonic for its three *a*'s, A indicating a universal affirmative proposition.

barbarian in ancient times, a member of a community or tribe not belonging to one of the great civilizations (Greek, Roman, and Christian). The term is recorded from Middle English, as an adjective used depreciatively to denote a person with different speech and customs, and comes via Old French and Latin from Greek *barbaros* 'foreign'.

Barbarossa[1] nickname ('Redbeard') of the Emperor ➤ FREDERICK I.

Barbarossa was the code name for the military operation in which Hitler's armies launched their invasion of the Soviet Union in 1941.

Barbarossa[2] (c.1483–1546), Barbary pirate, born *Khair ad-Din*, notorious for his successes against Christian vessels in the eastern Mediterranean.

Barbary[1] a former name (also **Barbary States**) for the [Saracen] countries of North and NW Africa, together with Moorish Spain. The area was noted between the 16th and 18th centuries as a haunt of pirates.

Barbary[2] in Shakespeare's *Richard II*, the name of Richard's horse ('roan Barbary'), presumably alluding to its breed.

Barbary Coast A nickname for a district of San Francisco (the ➤ TENDERLOIN) regarded as the main centre for vice and corruption. The original *Barbary Coast* was the Mediterranean coast of North Africa from Morocco to Egypt, taken as the home of the corsairs and a source of violence and danger.

Barbason name of a fiend referred to in Shakespeare's *Merry Wives of Windsor* and *Henry V* ('I am not Barbason, you cannot conjure me').

The name apparently derives from Reginald Scot's description of a fiend called 'Marbas, alias Barbas', who

> appeareth in the form of a mighty lion, but at the commandment of a conjuror cometh up in the form of a man and answereth fully as touching anything which is hidden or secret.
> — Reginald Scot *The Discovery of Witchcraft* (1584)

It has been suggested that Shakespeare's form of the name comes either from confusion with a Gascon called Barbason who, according to Holinshed, fought hand to hand with Henry V at Harfleur, or that in *Merry Wives of Windsor* he deliberately added a syllable so that the name matched those of the other two devils mentioned (*Amaimon* and *Lucifer*).

barbecue a meal or gathering at which food is cooked outside on a rack. The word comes from Spanish *barbacoa*, perhaps ultimately a use of Arawak 'wooden frame on posts', and the original sense was 'wooden framework for sleeping on, or for storing meat or fish to be dried on'.

barbed steed a horse which has been armed or caparisoned. *Barbed* here is a 16th-century variant of *barded*, from *bard* 'armour for the breast and flanks of a warhorse'. The expression occurs notably in the opening speech of Shakespeare's *Richard III* ('And now instead of mounting barbed steeds'), and was also used and perhaps reinforced by Scott in *Ivanhoe*.

barber a person who cuts men's hair and shaves or trims beards as an occupation; formerly also, a regular practitioner in surgery and dentistry. The Company of Barber-surgeons was incorporated by Edward IV in 1461; under Henry VIII the title was altered to 'Company of Barbers and Surgeons', and barbers were restricted to the practice of dentistry; in 1745 they were divided into two distinct corporations.

barber's pole a pole painted with spiralling red and white stripes and hung outside barbers' shops as a business sign.

barbershop a popular style of close harmony singing, usually for four male voices. The expression dates from the early 20th century, but there are earlier references to *barber's music*, apparently harsh discordant music, like that formerly produced by customers waiting their turn in a barber's shop, where a musical instrument was provided for their amusement.

> My Lord called for the lieutenant's cittern, and with two candlesticks, with money in them, for symbols, we made barber's music.
> — Samuel Pepys diary 5 June (1660)

Barbican the complex of high-rise buildings around the **Barbican Centre** in the City of London. A *barbican* is the outer defence of a city or castle, especially a double tower above a gate or drawbridge; it is recorded from the 17th century as being retained as the name of a street in London. Recorded from Middle English, the word probably comes ultimately from Arabic.

Barbie doll trademark name for a doll representing a conventionally attractive and fashionably dressed young woman, used allusively for a woman who is attractive in a glossily artificial way, but who is considered to lack sense and character.

Barbizon School a mid 19th-century school of French landscape painters who reacted against classical conventions and based their art on direct study of nature. Led by Théodore Rousseau, the group included Charles Daubigny and Jean-François Millet.

Barchester the fictional cathedral city of the county of ➤ BARSETSHIRE, featuring in the novels of the Anglican Church by Anthony Trollope and (in the 20th century) Angela Thirkell; M. R. James also used it as the setting for one of his ghost stories, 'The Stalls of Barchester Cathedral'.

> The world of Barchester, a Grantlyesque world of gentlemanly assumptions and comforts.
> — Joanna Trollope *The Choir* (1988)

bard a poet, traditionally one reciting epics and associated with a particular oral tradition. Recorded from Middle English, the word is of Celtic origin (*bàrd* in Scottish Gaelic, *bard* in Irish and Welsh). In Scotland in the 16th century it was a derogatory term for an itinerant musician, but was later romanticized by Sir Walter Scott:

> The last of all the bards was he
> Who sung of Border chivalry.
> — Sir Walter Scott *The Lay of the Last Minstrel* (1805)

the Bard of Avon a name for Shakespeare, recorded from the late 19th century.

bardolatry excessive admiration of Shakespeare, first recorded in 1901 in George Bernard Shaw's Preface to *Three Plays for Puritans*, 'So much for Bardolatry!'

Bardolph in Shakspeare's *Henry IV* parts 1 and 2, Falstaff's red-nosed companion (see ➤ BUBUKLE); he is said in *Henry V* to have been hanged for robbing a French church shortly before Agincourt, but in *The Merry Wives of Windsor* he becomes tapster at the Garter Inn.

> If beauty is a matter of fashion, how is it that wrinkled skin, grey hair, hairy backs and Bardolph-like noses have never been 'in fashion'?
> — *Frontiers: Penguin Popular Science* (1994)

Brigitte Bardot (1934–), French actress, whose film *And God Created Woman* (1956) established her reputation as a youthful international sex symbol with blonde hair and pouting lips; in later years, ceasing to make films, she has become chiefly concerned with animal welfare.

> Cut to moody, blue-toned music video of a fifteen-year-old Paradis, now with full-scale, petulant Bardot lips.
> — Camille Paglia *Vamps and Tramps* (1994)

Barebones Parliament the nickname of Cromwell's Parliament of 1653, from one of its members, Praise-God *Barbon*, an Anabaptist leather

seller of Fleet Street. It replaced the ➤ RUMP *Parliament*, but was itself dissolved within a few months.

barefoot see ➤ *the* SHOEMAKER's *son always goes barefoot.*

barefooted (of a friar or nun) shoeless or wearing sandals as the only footwear, ➤ DISCALCED.

Willem Barents (d. 1597), Dutch explorer. The leader of several expeditions in search of the North-East Passage to Asia, Barents discovered Spitsbergen and reached Novaya Zemlya, off the coast of which he died; the **Barents Sea** is named after him.

bargain see ➤ *the* BEST *of a hard bargain,* ➤ *it takes* TWO *to make a bargain.*

Bargello a kind of embroidery worked on canvas in stitch patterns suggestive of flames, named after the *Bargello* Palace in Florence, Italy, from designs on furniture from the palace.

barghest a demonic spirit, said to appear in the form of a large dog, and to guard the graves of those who have died by violence.

Barisal guns booming sounds of unknown origin heard in *Barisal*, a town in Bangladesh and certain other regions, especially on the water.

bark see also ➤ DOGS *bark, but the caravan goes on,* ➤ JESUITS' *bark,* ➤ PERUVIAN *bark,*

do not put your hand between the bark and the tree proverbial saying, mid 16th century; advising against intervening in another's family affairs.

his bark is worse than his bite traditional saying, mid 17th century.

bark up the wrong tree pursue a misguided course of action; originally US (mid 19th century), referring to a dog which has mistaken the tree in which a quarry has taken refuge.

barker a tout at an auction or fairground sideshow who calls out to passers-by to attract custom. The original sense (in late Middle English) is 'a person or animal that barks; a noisy protestor'; the current sense, for someone seeking to attract rather than repel, is recorded from the late 17th century.

a barking dog never bites proverbial expression recorded from the 16th century, and 13th century in French; *bark* is contrasted with *bite* in a number of traditional phrases, especially *his bark is worse than his bite.*

Barkis in Dickens's *David Copperfield*, the carrier who is the suitor of David's nurse Peggotty, to whom he sends the message 'Barkis is willin' '.

Sts Barlaam and Joasaph two subjects of a popular medieval legend, in which it was prophesied of the infant Joasaph, son of an Indian king, that he would be converted to Christianity. To avert this, he is shut up in a palace to protect him from dangerous knowledge. Guided by a revelation, a monk Barlaam visits the prince in disguise, and converts him. His father tries to win him back by arranging a public disputation, but in the end is converted himself. For a time Joasaph ruled the kingdom with his father, but later retired to the wilderness with Barlaam.

The story is an exhortation to renunciation of the world, and is in fact of Buddhist origin.

barleycorn a grain of barley, formerly constituting a unit of measurement. **John Barleycorn** (recorded from the 17th century) is the personification of barley, especially as the grain from which malt liquor is made.

Barmecide illusory or imaginary, and therefore disappointing. The word comes from Arabic *Barmakī*, the name of a prince in the ➤ ARABIAN *Nights*, who gave a beggar a feast consisting of ornate but empty dishes.

St Barnabas one of the earliest Christian disciples at Jerusalem; an Apostle, but not one of the original twelve (see ➤ APOSTLE[1]). A Jewish Cypriot and a Levite, he was originally called Joseph; the name Barnabas means 'son of consolation'. He introduced Paul to the other apostles, and with him undertook the first missionary journey, which began in Cyprus. Later Paul and Barnabas quarrelled and separated; Barnabas returned to Cyprus and evangelized it. According to legend, he was martyred at Salamis in 61 AD.

 ❑ **FEAST DAY** His feast day is 11 June.
See also ➤ BARNABY *bright.*

Barnabite a member of a small religious order founded in 1530, named from its church of St *Barnabas* in Milan.

Barnaby bright, Barnaby bright
The longest day and the shortest night
traditional rhyme, mid 17th century. In the ➤ OLD

Style calendar St Barnabas' Day, 11 June, was reckoned the longest day on the year. Spenser alludes to this in his *Epithalamion* (1595) 'This day the sun is in his chiefest height, With Barnaby the bright', and the rhyme itself is recorded in J. Howell *Proverbs* (1659).

Barnaby Rudge eponymous hero of the novel by Dickens set at the time of the ➤ GORDON *Riots.* Barnaby, a simple-minded boy, has a pet raven ('Grip') for his constant companion.

> There comes Poe, with his raven, like Barnaby Rudge,
> Three-fifths of him genius, and two-fifths sheer fudge.
> — James Russell Lowell 'A Fable for Critics' (1848)

barnacle goose an arctic goose which, because its breeding grounds were long unknown, was believed to hatch from the shell of the crustacean to which it gave its name, or, according to another story, from the fruit of a particular tree growing by the seashore, from which the birds were said to hatch as the fruit dropped into water.

Barnard's Inn one of the ➤ INNS *of Chancery*, belonging to ➤ GRAY'*s Inn* and existing from *c.*1454; it was originally named for and owned by the *Mackworth* family, and the name *Barnard* was derived from a later tenant called Lionel Barnard. *Barnard's Inn* was bought by the Mercer's Company in 1892, and from 1894–1959 was the Mercer's School; the original building was demolished in 1931, and a replica erected.

Barnardine in Shakespeare's *Measure for Measure* a prisoner (awaiting execution) who 'apprehends death no more dreadfully but as a drunken sleep; careless, reckless, and fearless of what's past, present, or to come'.

Thomas John Barnardo (1845–1905), Irish-born doctor and philanthropist. He founded the East End Mission for destitute children in 1867, the first of many such homes. Now known as Dr Barnardo's Homes, they cater chiefly for those with physical and mental disabilities.

Barnburner an adherent of a section of the Democratic Party in New York State in the 1840s, whose zeal for reform was so intense that it was said that they were prepared to 'burn the barn to get rid of the rats'. (Cf. ➤ ROOT *and branch.*)

barnstorm (chiefly in North America), tour rural districts giving theatrical performances, originally often in barns; in extended usage, make a rapid tour of (an area), typically as part of a political campaign.

Phineas Taylor Barnum (1810–91), American showman. He billed his circus, opened in 1871, as 'The Greatest Show on Earth'; ten years later he founded the Barnum and Bailey circus with his former rival Anthony Bailey (1847–1906). The Barnum circus was enormously popular (Winston Churchill, likening Ramsay Macdonald to 'The Boneless Wonder', recalled being taken to it as a child); Barnum himself is said to have coined the phrase, 'There's a sucker born every minute.'

> The roller-coaster tour has visitors tilting up and down ramps and walkways past such Barnumesque spectacles as the Hupfield Phonoliszt, a rotating violin with 1,350 horsehair strings.
> — *Yippy Yi Yea* April 1995

Barnum effect in psychology, the tendency to accept as true types of information such as character assessments or horoscopes, even when the information is so vague as to be worthless. The term comes from ➤ *Phineas Taylor* BARNUM; the word *Barnum* was in use from the mid 19th century as a noun in the sense 'nonsense, humbug'.

baron a member of the lowest order of the British nobility. Baron is not used as a form of address, barons usually being referred to as 'Lord'. Also, a similar member of a foreign nobility.

Recorded from Middle English, the word comes via Old French from medieval Latin *baro, baron-* 'warrior', and is probably of Germanic origin.

See also ➤ COURT *baron*, ➤ LAST *of the Barons*.

baron of beef a joint of beef consisting of two sirloins joined at the backbone. The term is first recorded in Samuel Johnson's *Dictionary* (1755).

baron of the Cinque Ports in historical usage, a freeman of the ➤ CINQUE PORTS, who had feudal service of bearing the canopy over the head of the sovereign on the day of coronation; also, until the Reform Bill of 1832, a burgess returned by these ports to Parliament.

baronet a member of the lowest hereditary titled British order, with the status of a commoner but able to use the prefix 'Sir'. The term originally denoted a gentleman, not a nobleman, summoned by the king to attend parliament; the current order was instituted in the early 17th century.

Barons' War the English civil war of 1264–7 between forces led by Henry III and Simon de Montfort respectively.

baroque relating to or denoting a style of European architecture, music, and art of the 17th and 18th centuries that followed mannerism and is characterized by ornate detail. In architecture the period is exemplified by the palace of Versailles and by the work of Wren in England. Major composers include Vivaldi, Bach, and Handel; Caravaggio and Rubens are important baroque artists.

The word comes (in the mid 18th century) from French, originally denoting a pearl of irregular shape.

Barr body a strongly heterochromatic body just inside the membrane of on-dividing cell nuclei in females, representing a condensed, inactive X chromosome and diagnostic of genetic femaleness. It is named after the Canadian anatomist M. L *Barr* (1908–), who with E. G. Bertram first reported it.

barrack jeer loudly at someone. Probably deriving from Northern Irish dialect meaning 'brag, boast', although an Australian alteration of the Aboriginal word *borak* 'banter' has been suggested.

barrack-room lawyer a person who likes to give authoritative-sounding opinions on subjects in which they are not qualified, especially legal matters. The term comes originally from military slang.

barrel See also ➤ CRACKER-*barrel*.

barrel of salt a barrel of salt is the emblem of St Rupert, 8th-century bishop of Worms and Salzburg, who encouraged the development of salt-mines near Salzburg.

barrelhouse a cheap or disreputable bar; an unrestrained and unsophisticated style of jazz. The name comes (in the late 19th century) from the rows of barrels along the walls of such a bar.

barricade an improvised barrier erected across a street or other thoroughfare, particularly in ➤ *Day of the* BARRICADES; the word is recorded from the late 16th century, and comes via French from Spanish *barrica*, related to *barrel* (since barrels were often used in the construction of barricades).

Day of the Barricades during the ➤ FRENCH *Wars of Religion*, 12 May 1588, the day on which the people of Paris rose in support of Guise and the Catholic League against Henri III, and blockaded the streets with casks filled with earth and paving stones. The word, in the earlier form *barricado*, is recorded from the late 16th century, and comes ultimately from Spanish *barrica*, related to *barrel*, since barrels were (as on this occasion) often used in their construction.

barrister a person called to the *bar* and entitled to practise as an advocate, particularly in the higher courts; the word is recorded from late Middle English, and may be formed on the pattern of *minister*.

Barrowist a follower of Henry Barrowe, one of the founders of Congregationalism, executed in 1593 for nonconformity with the Church of England.

Barry see ➤ *Marie Jeanne* Du *Barry*.

bars see ➤ STARS *and Bars*.

Barsetshire a fictional county, 'pleasant, green, tree-becrowded', created by Anthony Trollope for a series of novels and also used by Angela Thirkell; its cathedral city is ➤ BARCHESTER. *Barsetshire* may now be used allusively for an idealized rural county.

> Too often the adjective 'Proustian' evokes a kind of decadent Barsetshire.
> — *Spectator* 10 January 1958

See also ➤ BORSETSHIRE.

Bart Simpson in the American cartoon series *The Simpsons* (1990–, created by Matt Groening), the mischievous and sometimes aggressive 10-year-old son of ➤ HOMER *J. Simpson*, whose characteristic introduction of himself runs, 'I'm Bart Simpson: who the hell are you?'

> His contempt for authority is reminiscent of Bart Simpson.
> — *Esquire* November 1995

St Bartholomew an apostle of the 1st century AD, whose apostolate is said to have included India and Armenia. He was martyred by being flayed alive.

In England, the cult of St *Bartholomew* was given impetus by the gift in the 11th century by Emma, wife of King Canute, of an arm of St Bartholomew to Canterbury Cathedral, a relic which was regarded as a sensational and valuable acquisition. From 1133 to 1855, a great fair was held annually at West Smithfield on the saint's feast day. This provides the setting for Jonson's play *Bartholomew Fair* (1614, performed 1631), in which the various protagonists visit the fair.

The name 'Bartholomew' was applied to various goods on sale at the fair; a **Bartholomew baby** is a puppet or doll sold at the fair, and **Bartholomew pig**

refers to the roast pork available there (one of Jonson's characters, the ranting Puritan Zeal-for-the-land Busy, has come to the fair for the express purpose of eating *Bartholomew pig*).

◻ **FEAST DAY** His feast day is 24 August.

◻ **EMBLEM** His traditional emblem is a flaying-knife.

◻ **PATRONAGE** He is the patron saint of tanners.

the Massacre of St Bartholomew the name given to the massacre of Huguenots throughout France ordered by Charles IX at the instigation of his mother Catherine de Médicis, began on the morning of the feast of St Bartholomew, 24 August 1572. In Protestant writing, this became proverbial as a type of savagery and betrayal.

bartizan a battlemented parapet or an overhanging corner turret at the top of a castle or church tower. The word comes (in the early 19th century) from a Scots variant of *bratticing* 'temporary breastwork or parapet', and was revived and reinterpreted by Sir Walter Scott.

John Bartlett (1820–1905), owner of the University Book Store at Cambridge, Massachusetts, a meeting place for Harvard academics. His reference book *Familiar Quotations* was first published in 1855; 'Ask John Bartlett' had been the customary saying in Cambridge when a book or quotation was wanted.

Dick Barton special agent hero, originally of a radio series for children, broadcast between 1946 and 1951, and later appearing on television and films; *Dick Barton* was noted for his upright moral character as well as for his struggle with a range of criminal adversaries.

John Bartram (1699–1777), first American-born botanist, described, with the Philadelphia gardens he established, in Crèvecœur's *Letters from an American Farmer*. He was appointed Botanist to the King in 1765.

Baruch the scribe of the prophet ➤ JEREMIAH, who 'wrote from the mouth of Jeremiah all the words of the Lord, which he had spoken unto him' (Jeremiah 36:4); he was sent by his master to read Jeremiah's prophecies in the Temple, against the king's wishes. *Baruch* is also the name of a book of the Apocrypha, attributed in the text to his authorship, 'And these are the words of the book, which Baruch the son of Nerias…wrote in Babylon' (Baruch 1:1).

Bashaba title of a chief or king among the (now extinct) Abnaki people of Maine.

bashi-bazouk in historical usage, a mercenary of the Turkish irregulars, notorious for pillage and brutality. Recorded from the mid 19th century, the name comes from modern Turkish, literally 'one whose head is turned'.

Basic English a simplified form of English limited to 850 selected words, intended for international communication.

basics See ➤ BACK *to basics*.

basil an aromatic plant of the mint family, the leaves of which are used as a culinary herb. In Keats' poem 'Isabella, or the Pot of Basil', based on a story in the *Decameron*, Isabella, whose lover has been murdered by her brothers, hides his severed head in a pot with a plant of basil over it, and mourns over it. The guilty brothers, stealing the pot, find the head and take flight into banishment.

Recorded from late Middle English, the name comes via Old French and medieval Latin from Greek *basilikos* 'royal' (see ➤ BASILICA), perhaps because the plant was used in some royal unguent or medicine. In Latin, the name was confused with *basiliscus*, on the supposition that the plant was an antidote to the poison of a ➤ BASILISK.

St Basil (*c*.330–79), Doctor of the Church, bishop of Caesarea; known as **St Basil the Great**. Brother of St Gregory of Nyssa, he staunchly opposed Arianism and put forward a monastic rule which is still the basis of monasticism in the Eastern Church.

◻ **FEAST DAY** His feast day is 14 June.

Basilian a monk or nun of the order following the monastic rule of St Basil the Great.

basilica a large oblong hall or building with double colonnades and a semicircular apse, used in ancient Rome as a law court or for public assemblies. The name was then applied to a building of this type used as a Christian Church; in Rome, it designated specifically the seven churches founded by Constantine. *Basilica* is also the name given to certain churches granted special privileges by the Pope.

Recorded from the mid 16th century, the word comes from Latin, literally 'royal palace', and from Greek *basilikē*, feminine of *basilikos* 'royal', from *basileus* 'king'.

Basilike see ➤ EIKON *Basilike*.

basilisk a mythical reptile with a lethal gaze or breath, hatched by a serpent from a cock's egg. In figurative or allusive use, the idea of a lethal gaze is paramount, as in **basilisk eye**, **basilisk stare**.

The name comes ultimately from Greek *basiliskos* 'little king, serpent', from *basileus* 'king', and Pliny suggests that it is so called from a spot, resembling a crown, on its head; medieval writers gave it 'a certain comb or coronet'.

> A basilisk stare that would have plunged a normal man into silence.
> — Martin Cruz Smith *Rose* (1996)

Basin State informal name for Utah.

Basin Street a street in the Storyville district of New Orleans, particularly associated with early jazz, as in the title of 'Basin Street Blues' (Spencer Williams, 1928).

Basingstoke a town in Hampshire, taken in *Ruddigore* as the type of an essentially comic name.

> Some word that teems with hidden meaning—like Basingstoke.
> — W. S. Gilbert *Ruddigore* (1887)

John Baskerville (1706–75), English printer, designer of the typeface which is named after him; after his death his types were sold to Beaumarchais for his edition of Voltaire (1784–9).

the Hound of the Baskervilles in Conan Doyle's story of this name (1902), a ghostly and savage hound believed to haunt, and hunt to their deaths, the Dartmoor family of Baskerville, in revenge for an ancestor's crimes. Despite an initially alarming story of the marks on the ground where the dead body of Sir Charles Baskerville has been found ('Mr Holmes, they were the footprints of a gigantic hound!') ➤ *Sherlock* HOLMES demonstrates that the legend is being exploited by an unrecognized descendant who hopes to inherit the family estate.

basket see also ➤ BALAAM *basket*, ➤ *don't put all your* EGGS *in one basket*, ➤ MOSES *basket*.

basket case a person or thing regarded as useless or unable to cope, originally a US slang expression for a soldier who had lost all four limbs, and was so unable to move independently.

Basket Maker a member of a culture of the southwestern US, forming the early stages of the Anasazi culture, from the 1st century BC until *c*.700 AD. The name comes from the basketry and other woven fragments found in early cave sites.

basket-makers ➤ St ANTHONY *of Egypt* is the patron saint of basket-makers.

basket of bread a basket of bread is the emblem of ➤ St NICHOLAS *of Tolentino*.

basket of fruit and flowers a basket of fruit and flowers is the emblem of ➤ St DOROTHY.

Basque a member of a people living in the Basque Country of France and Spain. Culturally one of the most distinct groups in Europe, the Basques were largely independent until the 19th century; the Basque separatist movement ETA is carrying on an armed struggle against the Spanish government. The Basque language is not known to be related to any other language.

The name comes via French from Latin *Vasco*, the same base as *Gascon*.

bassarid a Thracian bacchanal; a ➤ BACCHANT. The word comes from Greek, literally meaning 'fox', probably from the traditional dress of fox-skins.

bastard a person born of parents not married to each other. In the past the word *bastard* was the standard term in both legal and non-legal use for 'an illegitimate child'. Today, however, it has little importance as a legal term and is retained today in this older sense only as a term of abuse.

Bastard slip is a dated term for a shoot or sucker springing from the base of a plant, and Thomas More in his *History of Richard III* relates that when in June 1483 a sermon was preached at St Paul's Cross which asserted the invalidity of Edward IV's marriage to Elizabeth Woodville, and the consequent illegitimacy of their children, the text was taken from the Book of Wisdom, 'Bastard slips shall not take deep root'.

The word is recorded from Middle English, and comes via Old French from medieval Latin, probably ultimately from *bastum* 'packsaddle' (cf. ➤ BATMAN), which can be compared with Old French *fils de bast*, literally 'packsaddle son' (i.e. the son of a mule driver who uses a packsaddle for a pillow and is gone by morning).

baste beat, thrash. Recorded from the mid 16th century: perhaps a figurative use of *baste* 'pour fat or juices over meat during cooking in order to keep it moist'.

Bastet in Egyptian mythology, a goddess usually shown as a woman with the head of a cat, wearing one gold earring.

Bastille a fortress in Paris built in the 14th century and used in the 17th–18th centuries as a state prison. Its storming by the mob on 14 July 1789 marked the start of the French Revolution; the anniversary of this event (**Bastille Day**) is kept as a national holiday in France.

The name comes (via Old French) from Provençal *bastida*, from *bastir* 'build'.

bat a nocturnal flying mammal, in poetic use often associated with the coming of night and darkness, as in Shakespeare's *Macbeth*, 'Ere the bat hath flown his cloistered flight'. They have also a sinister association with vampires, notably in the tradition established by Bram Stoker:

> Bats usually wheel about, but this one seemed to go straight on.
> — Bram Stoker *Dracula* (1897)

See also ➤ FLITTERMOUSE, ➤ REARMOUSE.

bat mitzvah in Judaism, a religious initiation ceremony for a Jewish girl aged twelve years and one day, regarded as the age of religious maturity. The word comes from Hebrew *baṭ miṣwāh* 'daughter of commandment', suggested by ➤ BAR *mitzvah*.

Bâtard see ➤ *Le* GRAND *Bâtard*.

Batavian of or relating to the ancient Germanic people who inhabited the island of Betuwe between the Rhine and the Waal (now part of the Netherlands).

H. M. Bateman (1887–1970), Australian-born British cartoonist, who is known for the series of cartoons entitled 'The Man Who …', which illustrated a variety of offences against established custom.

> You wouldn't have listened either, because accompanying us, like something out of an H. M. Bateman cartoon, was a gleaming troupe of nubilia.
> — *Independent on Sunday* 16 February 1997

Batesian mimicry mimicry in which an edible animal is protected by its resemblance to one avoided by predators, named after Henry W. *Bates* (1825–92), the English naturalist who first described it.

Bath a spa town in south west England, originally founded by the Romans as *Aquae Sulis*; the legendary prince ➤ BLADUD is said to have discovered the hot springs. The Roman city was a ruin by Anglo-Saxon times, and it is thought that the Old English poem 'The Ruin', which describes a devastated city, refers to it.

In the 18th century, Bath became a fashionable resort, with ➤ *Beau* NASH as master of ceremonies;

it was visited by many writers, and is the subject of frequent literary allusions.

See also ➤ WIFE *of Bath.*

Order of the Bath (in the UK) an order of knighthood, so called from the ceremonial bath which originally preceded installation. It has four classes of membership, which are: Knight or Dame Grand Cross of the Order of the Bath (GCB), Knight or Dame Commander (KCB/DCB), and Companion (CB).

See also ➤ KNIGHT *of the Bath.*

Bath King of Arms the herald or marshal of the ➤ *Order of the* BATH.

Bath Oliver trademark term for a kind of unsweetened biscuit, named after Dr William *Oliver* of Bath (1695–1764).

Bathia in the Talmud, the name of the Egyptian princess said to have found ➤ MOSES in the bulrushes.

bathos an effect of anticlimax created by an unintentional lapse in mood from the sublime to the trivial or ridiculous. The word comes from Greek, literally 'depth', and is first recorded in the Greek sense in the mid 17th century; the current sense was introduced by Alexander Pope in the early 18th century, in his satire *Peri Bathous, or the art of sinking in poetry.* The title was a parody of Longinus' essay *On the Sublime.*

Bathsheba in the Bible, the beautiful wife of ➤ URIAH the Hittite, seen bathing by ➤ DAVID; desiring her, the king arranged for Uriah's death in battle, and married the widow. Bathsheba subsequently became the mother of David's heir, ➤ SOLOMON.

Batman an American cartoon character, by day the millionaire socialite Bruce Wayne but at night a cloaked and masked figure, the *Caped Crusader,* fighting crime in Gotham City (New York), often assisted by *Robin the Boy Wonder.* First appearing in 1939 in a comic strip by artist Bob Kane (1916–) and writer Bill Finger (1917–74), Batman has since featured in a popular 1960s TV series and two major films (1989 and 1992).

See also ➤ GOTHAM.

batman an officer's personal servant, an orderly. Recorded from the mid 18th century and originally denoting an orderly in charge of the *bat horse* 'packhorse' which carried the officer's baggage, the word

comes ultimately from medieval Latin *bastum* 'packsaddle', the same base as ➤ BASTARD.

Batrachomyomachia the 'battle of the frogs and mice', a short Greek mock-epic poem in Homeric style, describing a one-day war between the frogs and the mice in a story deriving from one of Aesop's fables. The fighting is brought to an end by Zeus at the request of Athena; having failed with thunderbolts, he sends crabs to quell the strife.

bats see ➤ PARLIAMENT *of bats.*

battalions see ➤ PROVIDENCE *is always on the side of the big battalions.*

battels at Oxford and Cambridge, a college account for food and accommodation expenses. Recorded from the late 16th century, the term may come from dialect *battle* 'nourish', from an earlier adjective 'nutritious', ultimately related to *batten* 'improve in condition, grow fat'.

batten down the hatches prepare for a difficulty or crisis; literally, secure a ship's tarpaulins over the hatchways with *battens* or strips of wood or metal.

Battenberg name of a family of German counts who died out in the 14th century; in 1858, the name was revived for the offspring of a morganatic marriage of a prince of the German state of Hesse. In 1917 the members of the family who were connected with the British royal family and lived in England, renounced the German title of prince of Battenberg and took instead the surname *Mountbatten.*

battle see also ➤ BATTLES, ➤ WAGER *of battle.*

Battle Abbey an abbey founded by William the Conqueror near the site of the ➤ *Battle of* HASTINGS, in fulfilment of his vow before the battle that he would build an abbey if he achieved victory. The church was consecrated in 1094.

The Battle Abbey Roll a roll of names purporting to show the names of families that came over to England with William the Conqueror. The original roll is not extant, and the 16th-century versions (by Leland, Holinshed, and Duchesne) are all said to be faulty, and to contain names which should not be there.

Battle Hymn of the Republic the title of Julia Ward Howe's poem, which became one of the most popular songs of the Union forces during the American Civil War, is said to have been suggested to her by the editor of the *Atlantic Monthly,* J. T.

Fields, when both were visiting the Union troops in 1861. The 'Battle Hymn' was first published in the *Atlantic Monthly* in February, 1862.

Battle in the Clouds the battle of Lookout Mountain, 1863, which took place near Chattanooga, Tennessee, during the American Civil War, and which was an important victory for the Union forces.

Battle of Britain a series of air battles fought over Britain (August–October 1940), in which the RAF successfully resisted raids by the numerically superior German air force.

Battle of the Books a prose satire (written 1697) by Jonathan Swift, dramatizing the conflict between ancient and modern learning; the dispute is summed up by one of the representatives of classical learning (Aesop) as being between the 'sweetness and light' of the ancient world, and the 'dirt and poison' of the modern. The resultant battle, although fierce, is inconclusive, although the ancient world is seen as having the advantage.

Battle of the Bulge an unofficial name for the campaign in the Ardennes, December 1944–January 1945, when German forces attempted to break through Allied lines and almost succeeded in doing so.

battle of the frogs and mice another name for the ➤ Batrachomyomachia.

Battle of the Giants another name for the ➤ Gigantomachy.

Battle of the Kegs a humorous ballad of the American Revolution, composed by Francis Hopkinson and published in 1778. The American forces had attempted to attack British shipping at Philadelphia by floating kegs containing combustible material down the Delaware River, and the poem describes the panic which ensued among the British forces, and their belief that the kegs were filled with armed rebels.

Battle of the Spurs in 1513, between the French and the victorious forces of Henry VIII of England and the Emperor Maximilian.

Battle of the Standard a battle which took place in 1138, between the English and the Scots; a contemporary chronicler, Richard of Hexham, describes the 'standard' as the mast of a ship, with flags at the top, mounted on a machine which was brought into the field. He quotes a Latin couplet written on the occasion which says that the standard

was so called from 'stand', because 'it was there that valour took its stand to conquer or die'.

Battle of the Standards a name given to the American presidential contest of 1896, between the Republican William McKinley (1843–1901) and the Democrat William Jennings Bryan (1840–1925), in which a key issue was Democratic opposition to an exclusive gold standard; it was in the speech which won him the Democratic presidential nomination that Bryan had proclaimed, 'You shall not crucify mankind upon a cross of gold.'

battleaxe a battleaxe is the emblem of *St Olaf* (➤ Olaf *II Haraldsson* of Norway), who was killed in battle.

Battleborn State informal name for the state of Nevada, which was admitted to the Union during the American Civil War (October, 1864).

battlebus a bus or coach used as a mobile operational centre during an election campaign; the term derives from the British general election of 1983, when the Liberal Party used such a vehicle.

battledore a game played with a shuttlecock and rackets, a forerunner of badminton, also known as **battledore and shuttlecock**. Recorded from late Middle English, as a word for a wooden paddle-shaped implement formerly used in washing clothes for beating and stirring, *battledore* may come ultimately from Provençal *batedor* 'beater'.

not know a B from a battledore be completely illiterate or ignorant; the saying is based on the resemblance in shape of the paddle-shaped battledore to a horn-book, from which children traditionally learned to read.

battles see also ➤ Conn *of the Hundred Battles*.

Battles ■ See box opposite.

bauble a small showy trinket or decoration; previously also, a baton used as an emblem by jesters, the sense used by Oliver Cromwell at the dismissal of the ➤ Rump *Parliament*, 20 April 1653, 'Take away that fool's bauble, the mace.'

The word comes (in Middle English) from Old French *baubel* 'a child's toy', although the ultimate origin is unknown.

Baucis in a story told by Ovid, the wife of a good old countryman Philemon. They entertained the gods ► Zeus and ► Hermes as hospitably as their poverty allowed when the gods, who had visited the earth in disguise, were rejected by the rich. For this, the couple were saved from a flood which covered the district, and their dwelling was transformed into a temple of which they became the first priest and priestess. They were also granted their request to die at the same time, and were then turned into trees whose boughs intertwined.

The story was used by Swift in his poem *Baucis and Philemon* (1709); in this version, the couple entertain two hermits, their cottage becomes a church, and Philemon (in an elevation described with some irony) the parson.

Battles

Battle	War		Battle	War
Battle of Aboukir Bay	Napoleonic Wars, 1798		Battle of Marengo	Napoleonic Wars, 1800
Battle of Actium	Second Roman Triumvirate, 31 BC		Battle of Marston Moor	English Civil War, 1644
			Battle of Naseby	English Civil War, 1645
Battle of Agincourt	Hundred Years War, 1415		Battle of Navarino	Greek War of Independence, 1827
Battle of Austerlitz	Napoleonic Wars, 1805			
Battle of Badon Hill	Saxon invasion, early 6th century		Battle of Nechtansmere	Northumbrian invasion, 685
			Battle of Oudenarde	War of the Spanish Succession, 1708
Battle of Balaclava	Crimean War, 1854			
Battle of Bannockburn	Anglo-Scottish War, 1314		Battle of Passchendaele	First World War, 1917
Battle of Blenheim	War of the Spanish Succession, 1704		Battle of Plataea	Persian Wars, 479 BC
			Battle of Prestonpans	Jacobite Rising, 1745
Battle of Borodino	Napoleonic Wars, 1812		Battle of Ramillies	War of the Spanish Succession, 1706
Battle of Bosworth Field	Wars of the Roses, 1485			
Battle of the Boyne	Glorious Revolution, 1689		Battle of Roncesvalles	Charlemagne's rearguard and the Basques, 778
Battle of Britain	Second World War, 1940			
Battle of Crécy	Hundred Years War, 1346		Battle of Saratoga	War of American Independence, 1777
Battle of Culloden	Jacobite Rising, 1745			
Battle of Edgehill	English Civil War, 1642		Battle of Sedan	Franco-Prussian War, 1870
Battle of El Alamein	Second World War, 1942		Battle of Sedgemoor	Monmouth's Rebellion, 1685
Battle of Flodden Field	Anglo-Scottish War, 1513		Battle of Stalingrad	Second World War, 1942–3
Battle of Gettysburg	American Civil War, 1863		Battle of Trafalgar	Napoleonic Wars, 1805
Battle of Hastings	Norman Conquest, 1066		Battle of Verdun	First World War, 1916
Battle of Jutland	First World War, 1916		Battle of Vimy Ridge	First World War, 1917
Battle of Lepanto	Christian-Turkish naval battle, 1571		Battle of Waterloo	Napoleonic Wars, 1815
			Battle of Wounded Knee	Sioux Rising, 1890
Battle of Little Bighorn	Sioux Wars, 1876		Battle of Ypres	First World War, 1914, 1915, and 1917
Battle of Malplaquet	War of the Spanish Succession, 1709			

Bauhaus a school of applied arts established by Walter Gropius in Weimar in 1919 and noted for its refined functionalist approach to architecture and industrial design. The socialist principles on which Bauhaus ideas rested incurred the hostility of the Nazis and, after moving to Berlin in 1932, the school was closed in 1933.

Bavaria a state of southern Germany, formerly an independent kingdom, which became part of the German Empire in 1871.
See also ► Ludwig II.

bawbee in Scottish usage, a coin of low value, originally a silver coin worth three (later six) Scottish pennies. Recorded from the mid 16th century, the word comes from the name of the laird of *Sillebawby*, mint-master under James V of Scotland.

Bawtry in a traditional ballad, home of a saddler who on hearing of a hue and cry called attention to himself by leaving his drink behind him in an ale-house, and was apprehended and hanged.

Baxterian a follower of the Puritan divine Richard Baxter (1615–91), whose doctrinal teaching amalgamated the Arminian doctrine of free grace with the Calvinistic doctrine of election.

bay see also ► *Bay of* Pigs.

bay a wreath of leaves from the bay laurel or bay tree was the traditional way of marking recognition of the prowess of a victor or poet (see also ➤ POET *Laureate*). From this, bay leaves or *bays* symbolize public recognition, as in Marvell's lines 'How vainly men themselves amaze, To win the palm, the oak, or bays.'

Bay trees were also seen from classical times as having a protective role; in his *Natural History* (AD 77) Pliny notes that 'Thunder never strikes the laurel', and that 'The laurel…guards the portals of our emperors and pontiffs.' In later tradition, bay trees (like ➤ ROWANS) might be planted as a protection against witches, and a bay tree withering was taken as a portent of evil, as in Shakespeare's *Richard II*, ''Tis thought the King is dead, we will not stay; The bay-trees in our country [Wales] are all withered.'

Bay leaves have also been used as a traditional method of divination; the belief that bay leaves fastened to or placed under the pillow will result in dreaming of one's future spouse is recorded from the early 18th century.

See also ➤ FLOURISH *like a green bay tree*, ➤ LAUREL.

Bay Psalm Book the metrical version of the Psalms produced at Cambridge, Massachusetts (the ➤ BAY *State*) in 1640, the first book to be printed in British America.

Bay State informal name for the state of Massachusetts (the original colony was sited around Massachusetts Bay).

Bay Street the moneyed interests of Toronto, especially as opposed to other regions of Canada (*Bay Street* is a street in Toronto where the headquarters of many financial institutions are located).

> Government leaders went to Bay Street and Wall Street.
> — *Harrowsmith* June 1994

Bayard[1] name of the magic bright bay-coloured horse given by Charlemagne to Renaud (or Rinaldo), one of the four sons of Aimon. *Bayard* was formerly used as a mock-heroic name for any horse, and also as a type of blind recklessness.

Bayard[2] the French soldier Pierre du Terrail, Chevalier de *Bayard* (1473–1524), became known as the knight 'sans peur et sans reproche' (fearless and above reproach).

Bayes' theorem a theorem describing how the conditional probability of each of a set of possible causes for a given observed outcome can be computed from knowledge of the probability of each

cause and the conditional probability of the outcome of each cause. It is named after Thomas *Bayes* (1702–61), English mathematician.

Bayeux Tapestry a fine example of medieval English embroidery, executed between 1066 and 1077, probably at Canterbury, for Odo, bishop of Bayeux and half-brother of William the Conqueror, and now exhibited at Bayeux in Normandy. In seventy-nine scenes, accompanied by a Latin text and arranged like a strip cartoon, it tells the story of the Norman Conquest and the events leading up to it; these include a representation of ➤ HALLEY'*s comet*, the appearance of which as causing predictions of disaster prior to the Battle of Hastings is noted in the Anglo-Saxon Chronicle. It is an important historical record, relating incidents not recorded elsewhere.

a bayonet is a weapon with a worker at each end British pacifist slogan (1940).

Bayou State informal name for Mississippi.

Bayreuth a town in Bavaria where Wagner made his home from 1874 and where he is buried. Festivals of his operas are held regularly there in a theatre specially built (1872–6) to house performances of *Der Ring des Nibelungen*.

the Bays the 2nd Dragoon Guards, or **Queen's Bays** (now incorporated in the 1st Queen's Dragoon Guards), who originally rode bay horses.

BC before Christ (used to indicate that the date is before the Christian era).

be there for someone be available to support or comfort someone while they are experiencing difficulties or adversities; the expression became popular in the late 1980s as encapsulating a view of personal support and sympathy offered readily in time of need.

be what you would seem to be proverbial saying, late Middle English; earlier in classical sources, as Aeschylus *Seven against Thebes*, 'he wishes not to appear but to be the best.' In *Catilina*, Roman historian Sallust (86–35 BC) says of Cato, 'He preferred to be rather than to seem good.'

Beachcomber pseudonym of the British journalist and humorous writer J. B. Morton (1893–1975).

Beachy Head name of a chalk headland on the Sussex coast, noted for the number of suicides which have taken place by jumping over the cliff there. It is also, in Chesterton's poem, one of the points of the type of a rambling journey:

> A merry road, a mazy road, and such as we did tread
> The night we went to Birmingham by way of Beachy
> Head.
> — G. K. Chesterton 'The Rolling English Road' (1914)

beacon a signal fire lighted on a pole, a hill, or other high place, allowing for warnings to be passed by a chain of such fires; the maintenance of beacons was one of the means of national defence against a possible Spanish invasion in late 16th-century England. From this, *beacon* came to mean a conspicuous hill suitable for the site of a signal fire (frequently occurring in place-names, as **Brecon Beacons, Dunkery Beacon**).

Recorded from Old English (in form *bēacn*) meaning 'sign, portent', the word is of West Germanic origin and is related to *beckon*.

See also ➤ BELISHA *beacon*.

Beacon Hill a noted residential district in Boston, originally named for the elevation where in 1635 a signal was placed to warn against possible Indian attacks; in 1795 the State House was placed on the summit.

bead originally meaning 'prayer', current senses derive from the use of a rosary, each bead representing a prayer.

See also ➤ BAILY's *beads*, ➤ St CUTHBERT's *beads*, ➤ St MARTIN's *beads*, ➤ WORRY *beads*.

beadle a ceremonial officer of a church, college, or similar institution. Originally (from Old English to the late 17th century) a person who makes a proclamation, a town crier; later (now historical), a parish officer appointed by the vestry to keep order in church and punish petty offenders, the role of ➤ Mr BUMBLE in Dickens's *Oliver Twist*.

beadsman historical term for a pensioner provided for by a benefactor in return for prayers, especially one living in an almshouse.

beagle a small hound of a breed with a short coat, used for hunting hares. Recorded from the late 15th century, the word may come from Old French *beegueule* 'open-mouthed', from *beer* 'open wide' + *gueule* 'throat'.

HMS *Beagle* was the name of the ship of ➤ *Charles* DARWIN's voyage of 1831–6 around the southern hemisphere; the **Beagle Channel** through the islands of Tierra del Fuego at the southern tip of South America was named after her.

beak-head a Romanesque architectural ornament consisting of a bird, animal, or human head with a beak or tongue extending downwards. Each beak-head is cut as a wedge and is designed to sit in an arch.

Beaker folk a late Neolithic and early Bronze Age European people (*c.*2700–1700 BC), named after distinctive waisted pots (**Beaker ware**) that were associated with their burials and appear to have been used for alcoholic drinks. It is now thought that the Beaker folk were not a separate race, but that the use of such pots spread as a result of migration, trade, and fashion.

on one's beam-ends at the end of one's financial resources; *beam-ends* the ends of a ship's beams; *on her beam-ends* (of a ship) on its side, almost capsizing.

a beam in one's eye a fault that is greater in oneself than in the person with whom one is finding fault, in allusion to *Matthew* 7:3 'Why beholdest thou the mote that is in thy brother's eye, but considerest not the beam that is in thine own eye?'

bean from early times, the broad bean was a staple foodstuff (see also ➤ BEANFEAST), and there are various traditional rhymes recommending the best time of planting, as in ➤ CANDLEMAS *day, put beans in the clay.*

Beans as an article of diet are associated particularly with Leicestershire, both in the epithet 'Bean-belly Leicestershire', and in the saying 'Shake a Leicestershire man by the collar, and you shall hear the beans rattle in his belly.'

Beans were traditionally used in casting ballots, and the Latin tag *Abstineto a fabis* 'Abstain from beans' is understood as an injunction to abstain from meddling in affairs of state by casting one's vote in an election. The followers of ➤ PYTHAGORAS abstained from eating beans, although the reason for this is not known.

beanfeast a celebratory party with plenty of food and drink; originally, an annual dinner given by an employer to his employees, at which beans and bacon were regarded as an indispensable dish. The term is recorded from the early 19th century.

Beanie Baby US trademark name for any of a variety of soft toy animals stuffed with beans, frequently treated as a collectable item, and highly popular in the 1990s.

beanstalk see ➤ JACK *and the Beanstalk*.

bear[1] a *bear* is the type of an uncouth and savage creature. In medieval usage, also taken as symbolizing sloth and gluttony.

From the late 18th century, **the Bear** has been used to denote Russia.

A *bear* is the emblem of St Gall, a 7th-century Irish monk and hermit living in what is now Switzerland, and the Russian St Seraphim (1759–1833), who while living as a hermit cared for bears and other wild animals.

See also ➤ Congleton *rare, Congleton rare, sold the Bible to pay for a bear,* ➤ Great *Bear,* ➤ lick *into shape,* ➤ Little *Bear,* ➤ Rupert *Bear,* ➤ sell *the skin before one has caught the bear,* ➤ Smokey *Bear,* ➤ teddy *bears' picnic,* ➤ Yogi *Bear.*

bear[2] in Stock Exchange usage, a person who sells shares hoping to buy them back again later at a lower price. The term (applied to the stock thus sold) is recorded from the early 18th century, and was common at the time of the ➤ South *Sea Bubble.* The dealer is this kind of stock was known as the **bearskin jobber**, and it seems likely that the original phrase was 'sell the bearskin', and that it derived from the proverbial advice 'not to sell the skin before one has caught the bear'.

The associated *bull* is of later date, and may perhaps have been suggested by the existence of *bear* in this sense.

bear and forbear proverbial saying, late 16th century.

bear and ragged staff crest of the Earls of Warwick, showing a bear with a staff having projecting stumps or knobs; the bear is said to derive from *Arthgal,* a legendary Earl of Warwick, who because his name meant 'bear' took the animal as his badge; the *ragged staff* refers to the story that his son killed a giant with a young ash tree, which he tore up by the roots.

Bear Bible printed at Basle in 1569, decorated with the symbol of a bear on the title page.

bear garden a scene of uproar and confusion; a *bear garden* was originally (like the ➤ Paris *garden*) a place set apart for baiting of bears with dogs for sport, and such areas were also often used for other rough sports.

bear leader in the 18th century, a humorous name for a rich young man's travelling tutor, seen as one managing a somewhat uncouth charge.

bear market a market in which share prices are falling encouraging selling.

beard a growth of hair on the chin and lower cheeks of a man's face; in allusive use, taken as evidence of age, experience, or virility.

See also ➤ Aaron*'s beard,* ➤ *it is* merry *in hall when beards wag all,* ➤ old *man's beard,* ➤ *a* red *beard and a black head, catch him with a good trick and take him dead,* ➤ singeing *of the king of Spain's beard.*

beard the lion in his den attack someone on their own ground or subject; partly from the idea of taking a lion by the tuft of hair on its chin, partly from the use of *beard* to mean 'face'.

Aubrey Beardsley (1872–98), English artist and illustrator, associated with art nouveau and the Aesthetic movement. He is known for original and controversial illustrations, such as those for Oscar Wilde's *Salome* (1894). He became artistic editor of *The Yellow Book* in 1894.

> The governess is a Decadent artist, joining moral and aesthetic extremes, evil with beauty, a Beardsleyesque black and white.
> — Camille Paglia *Sexual Personae* (1990)

beast an animal, especially a large or dangerous four-footed one; in figurative usage, an inhumanly cruel, violent, or depraved person. From late Middle English (in Wyclif's translation of the Bible), **the Beast** was a name for Antichrist (see also ➤ *the* mark *of the beast,* ➤ *the* number *of the beast*).

See also ➤ Beauty *and the Beast,* ➤ Blatant *Beast,* ➤ *the* Glatysant *Beast,* ➤ mark *of the beast,* ➤ *the* Questing *Beast,* ➤ *the* nature *of the beast.*

Beast of Belsen byname for Josef Kramer (1906–45), German commandant of Belsen concentration camp from December 1944. Notorious for his cruelty, at the end of the Second World War he was tried before a British military tribunal and executed in November 1945.

Beast of Bodmin Moor name given to a panther-like creature supposedly living in the Bodmin Moor area; despite reports of such feral cats from the early 1990s, no conclusive proof for their existence has yet been demonstrated.

Beast of Bolsover nickname of the Labour politician Dennis Skinner (1932–), MP for Bolsover in Derbyshire and noted for his abrasive manner and left-wing views.

the beast with two backs a man and woman in the act of sexual intercourse; originally as a quotation from Shakespeare's *Othello* (1602–4), in Iago's warning to Desdemona's father, 'Your daughter and the Moor are now making the beast with two backs.' Earlier Rabelais had had, '*faire la bête à deux dos* [do the two-backed beast together]'.

beat generation a movement of young people in the 1950s and early 1960s who rejected conventional society, valuing free self-expression and favouring modern jazz. Among writers associated with the movement were Jack Kerouac (1922–69) and Allen Ginsberg (1926–97); the phrase itself was supposedly coined by Kerouac in the course of a conversation.

beat the bounds trace out the boundaries of a parish, striking certain points with rods; the custom is recorded from the late 16th century.

beat the bush (while another takes the birds) proverbial expression, late Middle English; the reference is to rousing birds that fly into a net held by someone else, meaning that one is expending labour of which others gain the fruit.

beat the Dutch say or do something extraordinary; the term is recorded from the late 18th century, and is from the US.

if you can't beat them, join them proverbial saying; mid 20th century.

beatific vision the first sight of the glories of heaven; the direct experience of God by those in heaven.

beatification in the Roman Catholic Church, declaration by the Pope that a dead person is in a state of bliss, constituting the first step towards canonization and permitting public veneration.

beatitude supreme blessedness; **His/Your Beatitude** is a title given to patriarchs in the Orthodox Church. The word is recorded from late Middle English, and comes via Old French or Latin, from Latin *beatus* 'blessed'.

the Beatitudes the blessings listed by Jesus in the Sermon on the Mount (Matthew 3:5–11):

> Blessed are the poor in spirit: for theirs is the kingdom of heaven. Blessed are they that mourn: for they shall be comforted. Blessed are the meek: for they shall inherit the earth. Blessed are they which do hunger and thirst after righteousness: for they shall be filled. Blessed are the merciful: for they shall obtain mercy. Blessed are the pure in heart: for they shall see God. Blessed are they which are persecuted for righteousness' sake: for theirs is the kingdom of heaven.
> — Bible (AV) Matthew ch. 3, v. 5–11

the Beatles a pop and rock group from Liverpool consisting of George Harrison, John Lennon, Paul McCartney, and Ringo Starr. Remembered for the quality and stylistic diversity of their songs (mostly written by Lennon and McCartney), they achieved success with their first single 'Love Me Do' (1962) and went on to produce albums such as *Sergeant Pepper's Lonely Hearts Club Band* (1967).

beatnik a young person in the 1950s and early 1960s belonging to a subculture associated with the ► BEAT *generation*. The word was formed in the 1960s on the pattern of *sputnik*, perhaps influenced by US use of Yiddish *-nik*, denoting someone or something who acts in a particular way.

Cecil Beaton (1904–80), English photographer famous for his fashion features and portraits of celebrities, particularly the British royal family. He later diversified into costume and set design, winning two Oscars for the film *My Fair Lady* (1964).

Beatrice[1] name given by ► DANTE *Alighieri* in *Vita nuova* and *The Divine Comedy* to the woman with whom he had fallen in love at his first sight of her; in *The Divine Comedy* she is his guide for his spiritual journey. While her identity is not certainly known, she is generally identified with Bice Portinari, who married Simone de' Bardi and died in 1290.

> Vanna is Beatrice taking you through the circles of ignorance, encouraging and applauding you every time you decipher one of the riddles of the universe.
> — Marshall Blonsky *American Mythologies* (1992)

Beatrice[2] the spirited heroine of Shakespeare's *Much Ado About Nothing* (1598–9), who says of herself, 'There was a star danced, and under that I was born.'

beau a rich, fashionable young man, a dandy; sometimes used in a personal appellation, as in **Beau Brummell**, **Beau Nash**. Recorded from the late 17th century, the word comes from French, literally 'handsome', from Latin *bellus*.

See also ► *Beau* NASH, ► *George* BRUMMELL.

Beau Geste nickname of Michael Geste (punning on *beau geste* a noble and generous act) who in P. G.

Wren's romantic adventure novel (1924) of this title runs away to enlist in the French Foreign Legion to spare his family the distress of a wrongful accusation against him.

> I didn't take seriously his flippant suggestion that he could always escape retribution, like a latter-day Beau Geste, by enlisting in the French Foreign Legion.
> — Don McCullin *Unreasonable Behaviour* (1990)

beau ideal one's highest or ideal type of excellence or beauty; the perfect model; from a French phrase, *beau idéal*, literally 'ideal beauty', but here misunderstood as 'beautiful ideal'.

beau sabreur a handsome swordsman, the sobriquet given to Joachim Murat (1767–1815), Napoleon's marshal and brother-in-law, king of Naples.

Beauclerk a learned man, a scholar, given posthumously as a byname to Henry I (1068–1135).

Beaufort scale a scale of wind speed based on a visual estimation of the wind's effects, ranging from force 0 (less than 1 knot or 1 kph, 'calm') to force 12 (64 knots or 118 kph and above, 'hurricane'). It is sometimes extended to higher numbers, especially in the US.

Recorded from the mid 19th century, it is named after Francis Beaufort (1774–1857), the English admiral and naval hydrographer who devised it.

Beaujolais nouveau a Beaujolais wine sold in the first year of a vintage; the name is recorded from the early 1970s, when the popularity of this drink led to the development of a new sport in the hotel and catering world: the race to be the first to have the new year's vintage in stock. Some wine bars and restaurants even went to the lengths of having stocks flown in by helicopter; in due course, signboards saying 'The Beaujolais Nouveau has arrived' became a common sight on pavements.

beauty see also ➤ BLACK *Beauty*, ➤ CAMBERWELL, ➤ SLEEPING *Beauty*.

Beauty and the Beast a fairy story by the French writer for children Madame de Beaumont (1711–80), translated into English in 1757. In the story Beauty, the youngest daughter of a merchant, goes to live in the Beast's palace and agrees to marry him; she discovers that he is a prince who has been put under a spell, which is destroyed by her love for him, and her ability to see his true worth beneath the hideous exterior.

beauty draws with a single hair proverbial saying, late 16th century.

beauty is in the eye of the beholder proverbial saying, mid 18th century; 3rd century BC in Greek.

beauty is only skin deep proverbial saying, early 17th century.

beauty without cruelty slogan for Animal Rights.

beaver[1] a large semiaquatic rodent noted for its habit of gnawing through tree-trunks to make dams, often taken from this as a type of industry. Recorded from Old English (in form *beofor*) and of Germanic origin, the word comes ultimately from an Indo-European root meaning 'brown'.

beaver[2] the lower part of the face guard of a helmet in a suit of armour; in Shakespeare's *1 Henry IV* (1597), describing the young Henry, Prince of Wales, before armed for battle, Sir Richard Vernon says, 'I saw young Harry, with his beaver on.'

Recorded from the late 15th century, the word comes from Old French *bavier* 'bib', from *baver* 'slaver'.

the Beaver nickname given to Lord Beaverbrook (1879–1964).

Beaver State informal name for Oregon.

bebop a type of jazz originating in the 1940s and characterized by complex harmony and rhythms. It is associated particularly with the cerebral style of playing of Charlie Parker, Thelonious Monk, and Dizzy Gillespie.

St Thomas à Becket (*c*.1118–70), English prelate and statesman, Archbishop of Canterbury 1162–70. Initially a friend and supporter of Henry II, as archbishop he came into open opposition with the king, whose reported words 'Will no one rid me of this turbulent priest?' are said to have sent four knights to assassinate Becket in his cathedral. Henry was obliged to do public penance at Becket's tomb, which became a major centre of pilgrimage until its destruction under Henry VIII (1538).

☐ **FEAST DAY** His feast day is 29 December.

William Beckford (1759–1844), English writer and collector. Having inherited a large fortune, he travelled in Europe, collecting works of art and curios, and created and decorated Fonthill Abbey, a Gothic extravaganza, which in the end he was forced to sell.

As an author he is remembered for the oriental romance *Vathek* (1786, originally written in French).

Becky Sharp the scheming anti-heroine of Thackeray's *Vanity Fair* (1847–8), who despite her wit and charm is unscrupulous in her pursuit of material gain.

> If it's not Essex girl, it's Worcester Woman. If it's not the Bridget Jones of the Nineties, it's the Becky Sharp of the new millennium.
> — *Independent on Sunday* 31 January 1999

bed see also ➤ *as you* MAKE *your bed, so you must lie on it,* ➤ *bed of* JUSTICE, ➤ EARLY *to bed and early to rise, makes a man healthy, wealthy and wise,* ➤ GREAT *Bed of Ware.*

bed and breakfast sell (shares) after hours one evening and buy them back as soon as possible the following day, in order to establish a loss for tax purposes.

lady of the bedchamber (in the UK) a female attendant to the queen or queen mother, ranking in the royal household above woman of the bedchamber.

Bedchamber Crisis on Robert Peel's first taking office as Prime Minister in 1839, he requested that some of the Whig ladies of the bedchamber be replaced by Tories. When Queen Victoria (as queen regnant) refused the request, Peel resigned, and Melbourne came back into office.

Beddgelert alternative form of the name of the village of ➤ BETHGELERT.

St Bede (*c.*673–735), English monk, theologian, and historian, known as **The Venerable Bede**, who lived and worked at the monastery in Jarrow on Tyneside. Bede wrote *The Ecclesiastical History of the English People* (completed in 731), a primary source for early English history.
 ☐ **FEAST DAY** His feast day is 27 May.

bedel in some British universities, an official with largely ceremonial duties. Recorded from late Middle English, the word is an archaic spelling of *beadle.*

Bedell Bible a translation of the Bible into Irish, prepared under the direction of Bishop William Bedell (1571–1642).

Bedevere in the Arthurian romances, one of the few who survives the final battle against Mordred; he was charged by the dying Arthur with the duty of throwing the sword ➤ EXCALIBUR back into the lake,

and after twice failing to carry out the task, finally did so.

bedfellows see ➤ ADVERSITY *makes strange bedfellows.*

Bedford Coffee-House a coffee-house which stood at the north-east corner of Covent Garden. It described itself as 'the emporium of wit, the seat of criticism and the standard of taste', and gained in popularity in the 1730s with the decline of Button's; it was freqented by actors and others, including Garrick, Sheridan, and Hogarth.

bedlam a scene of uproar or confusion, deriving ultimately from *Bedlam,* a corruption of *Bethlehem,* in the name of the 'Hospital of St Mary of Bethlehem', founded by the Sheriff of London in Bishopsgate in 1247 for the housing of the clergy of St Mary of Bethlehem when they visited Britain. The house is mentioned as a hospital for the sick in 1330, and lunatics are stated to have been there in 1402. On the ➤ DISSOLUTION *of the monasteries* it passed to the London civic authorities and in 1547 became a royal foundation. Its place was taken in 1675 by a new hospital in Moorfields, and this again was transferred to the Lambeth Road in 1815. The site now houses the Imperial War Museum.
 The use of 'bedlam' as a general term to mean an asylum for the insane is recorded from the mid 17th century.
 See also ➤ TOM *o' Bedlam.*

Bedouin a nomadic Arab of the desert; the word comes (via Old French) from Arabic *badawīn* 'dwellers in the desert', from *badw* 'desert'.

bedpost see ➤ DEVIL*'s bedpost.*

bedstraw see ➤ LADY*'s bedstraw.*

bee as a social insect producing honey, the bee is traditionally taken as the type of an industrious and productive worker. (In the fourth book of Virgil's *Georgics,* the bees are treated with affectionate irony as exemplars of the ideal citizen body). Its economic value was also recognized from earliest times: for non-tropical antiquity, bee-keeping had the same importance as sugar production does now, and the Athenian statesman Solon (*c.*630–*c.*560 BC) introduced a law regulating bee-keeping.
 There are also a number of superstitions concerning bees. When buying or selling bees, they should be exchanged for other goods rather than paid for with money. Pliny advises that the person who takes the honey from a hive should be well washed and

clean, and the belief is recorded from the nineteenth century that bees will not thrive in a quarrelsome atmosphere.

Bees are also associated with various beliefs to do with death, as in the tradition that a swarm settling on dead wood is a sign of impending death. The tradition of 'telling the bees' that the owner of their hive has died is a long-established one, as is the belief that on the owner's death the hive should be lifted or turned; in both cases it is believed that this will avert the death or disappearance of the bees.

See also ➤ BEES, ➤ BUSY *bee*, ➤ QUEEN *bee*.

bee-keepers ➤ *St* AMBROSE, ➤ *St* BERNARD, and the 6th-century Irish-born monk St Modomnoc, who was the bee-keeper in the Pembrokeshire monastery of Menevia, are the patron saints of bee-keepers.

beef see also ➤ BARON *of beef*, ➤ WHERE*'s the beef.*

the Beef-steak Club founded about 1876; the members used to dine in a room at Toole's Theatre, and moved, when this was demolished, to Green Street, Leicester Square. There was an earlier club of the same name.

the Sublime Society of Beef Steaks was founded in 1735 by J. Rich, the manager of the Covent Garden theatre. The society, which included many eminent persons, used to meet and dine in a room at the theatre, the name being derived from the beefsteaks served. When Covent Garden Theatre was burnt, the Society moved to the Bedford Coffee-House, and later to the Lyceum Theatre.

beefcake attractive men with well-developed muscles; the slang term is modelled on the earlier *cheesecake* for an attractive woman.

beefeater a Yeoman Warder or Yeoman of the Guard in the Tower of London. The word is recorded from the early 17th century, originally as a derogatory term for a well-fed servant: the current sense dates from the late 17th century.

beehive an emblem of ➤ *St* AMBROSE, from the story that a swarm of bees, symbolizing his future eloquence, settled on him as a child.

Beehive State informal name for Utah.

beeline a straight line between two points, originally with reference to the straight line supposedly taken instinctively by a bee when returning to the hive.

Beelzebub a name for the Devil, recorded in English from early times; Milton in *Paradise Lost*, however, uses it as the name of one of the fallen angels. The name comes originally from late Latin translating a Hebrew word meaning 'lord of the flies', recorded in 2 Kings 1:2 as the name of a Philistine god, and a Greek word meaning 'the Devil', from Matthew 12:24.

been there, done that used to express past experience of or familiarity with something, especially something now regarded as boring or unwelcome; the extension 'and got the T-shirt' reinforces the notion of a jaded tourist who has relentlessly visited sites and bought souvenirs.

beer see also ➤ he that DRINKS *beer, thinks beer,* ➤ LIFE *isn't all beer and skittles,* ➤ SMALL *beer,* ➤ TURKEY, *heresy, hops, and beer came into England all in one year.*

beer money an allowance of money to servants, instead of beer; the term is recorded from the early 19th century.

Beersheba see also ➤ *from* DAN *to Beersheba.*

bees see also ➤ the BIRDS *and the bees.*

bees are the emblem of ➤ *St* AMBROSE and ➤ *St* JOHN *Chrysostom.*

where bees are, there is honey proverbial saying, early 17th century.

beetle see also ➤ DEATH-*watch beetle,* ➤ SHARD-*beetle.*

beetle (of a person's eyebrows) project or overhang. The word is recorded (as an adjective, meaning 'shaggy and projecting') from the mid 16th century, a back-formation from **beetle-browed**. The verb was used by Shakespeare as a nonce-word in *Hamlet* (1601), in a reference to 'The dreadful summit of the cliff That beetles o'er his base into the sea'; it was then adopted by later writers.

beetle bank a strip of land, usually in the centre of a field, sown with perennial grasses and other plants to create an environment in which aphid-eating insects can thrive.

Mrs Beeton (1836–65), English author on cookery, famous for her best-selling *Book of Cookery and Household Management* (1861), first published serially in a women's magazine, contained over 3,000 recipes and articles, as well as sections giving advice on legal and medical matters.

Befana in Italian legend, the name of a beneficent fairy who fills children's shoes with toys on Twelfth Night.

beg the question assume the truth of an argument or proposition to be proved, without arguing it. The original meaning belongs to the field of logic and is a translation of Latin *petitio principii*, literally meaning 'laying claim to a principle', i.e. assuming something that ought to be proved first.

beggar ➤ St ALEXIS *of Rome*, ➤ St MARTIN *of Tours*, and the French-born St Benedict Labre (1748–83), who after living as a pilgrim visiting shrines on the way to Rome, spent his last nine years there as a homeless person among the destitute, are the patron saints of beggars.

See also ➤ *if* WISHES *were horses then beggars would ride*, ➤ MOCK-*Beggar Hall*, ➤ SEA-*beggar*, ➤ STURDY *beggar*, ➤ SUE *a beggar and catch a louse*.

beggar-my-neighbour a card game for two players in which the object is to acquire one's opponents cards; the name is recorded from the mid 18th century.

set a beggar on horseback and he'll ride to the Devil proverbial saying, late 16th century; meaning that a person unused to power will make unwise use of it.

the Beggar's Opera a low-life ballad opera (1728) by John Gay (1685–1732), combining burlesque and political satire in its story of the highwayman ➤ MACHEATH who is betrayed by the informer ➤ PEACHUM. In the 20th century, Bertolt Brecht's version of Gay's work, *The Threepenny Opera* (*Die Dreigroschenoper*, 1928) was one of the theatrical successes of Weimar Germany.

beggars can't be choosers proverbial saying, mid 16th century; in its original form, it ran 'beggars should not be choosers.'

begging friar another name for a ➤ MENDICANT.

Beghard a member of one of the lay brotherhoods which arose in the Low Countries in the 13th century in imitation of the female ➤ BEGUINES; the use of the name was often derogatory. From the 14th century they were denounced by Popes and Councils, and persecuted by the Inquisition; in the 17th century such of them as still survived were absorbed in the ➤ THIRD *Order* of the Franciscans.

beginner's luck good luck traditionally said to attend a beginner; the expression is recorded from the late 19th century.

beginning see ➤ *a* GOOD *beginning makes a good ending*.

beglerbeg the governor of a province of the Ottoman Empire, in rank next to the grand vizier. Recorded in English from the mid 16th century, the word is Turkish, and means 'bey of beys'.

Beguine a member of a lay sisterhood in the Low Countries, formed in the 12th century and not bound by vows; members were allowed to leave their societies for marriage. They were protected by Pope John XXII (*c.*1245–1334), when he persecuted the male Beguins or Beghards, and are still represented by small communities existing in the Netherlands, with an organization somewhat similar to some Anglican sisterhoods.

The name is said in a 12th-century chronicle to derive from the nickname of ➤ LAMBERT, a priest of Liège, 'who was called Lambert le Bègue (because he was a stammerer)…because he was the first to arise and preach to them by his word and example the reward of chastity'.

beguine a popular dance of Caribbean origin, similar to the foxtrot; the name comes (in the 1930s) from West Indian French, from French *béguin* 'infatuation'.

begum a Muslim woman of high rank, now used (with capital initial) as the title of a married Muslim woman, equivalent to *Mrs.* The word comes from Urdu *begam*, from eastern Turkish *bigim* 'princess', feminine of *big* 'prince'.

behemoth a huge or monstrous creature. The name comes from a Hebrew word occurring several times in the Old Testament and generally translated as 'beast'; however, in Job 40:15, the Authorized Version has 'behemoth'. The animal mentioned in Job is probably the hippopotamus, but the word came to be used generally for a particularly large and strong animal, as in Milton's *Paradise Lost*, 'Behemoth biggest born of earth'.

> Firms that once lined LaSalle Street . . . are being supplanted rapidly by international financial behemoths from the Pacific Rim to Europe.
> — *Tribune* (Chicago) 21 July 1994

See also ➤ LEVIATHAN.

Behistun a village in western Iran, originally on the road from Ecbatana to Babylon, site of important cuneiform inscriptions in Old Persian, Elamite, and Babylonian.

beholder see ➤ BEAUTY *is in the eye of the beholder*.

bejan a freshman at a Scottish university. Recorded from the mid 17th century, the term comes from French *bec jaune* 'yellow beak' (in allusion to young birds), and was adopted from the University of Paris.

Bel an alternative form of the name of the god ➤ Baal, occurring most frequently in the stories of ➤ Bel *and the Dragon*.

Bel and the Dragon two stories included as a single item in the Apocrypha. The first relates how the prophet ➤ Daniel convinced the Babylonian king that the offerings of food and drink which were daily set before the image of Bel (➤ Baal) were not really eaten by the god but were secretly removed by the priests. As a result, the priests were executed and the image destroyed.

In the second story, which is apparently based on an ancient Semitic myth, Daniel obtained the king's consent to attack a dragon, and killed it by feeding it with cakes made of pitch, fat, and hair. This so enraged the people that they insisted that Daniel should be cast into a den of seven lions. With the help of the prophet Habakkuk, who was miraculously transported from Judaea to feed him, he was saved from death and freed. In consequence the king became a worshipper of Yahweh.

Sir Toby Belch in Shakespeare's *Twelfth Night* (1601), a roistering knight, disreputable uncle to Olivia, who argues for the ➤ cakes *and ale* of life against the Puritanism of ➤ Malvolio.

> At present I share Balliol with one ... man ... who rather repels me at meals by his ... habit of shewing satisfaction with the food: Sir Toby Belch was not in it.
> — Aldous Huxley letter, October 1915

beldam a malicious and ugly woman, especially an old one; a witch. Recorded from late Middle English (originally in the sense 'grandmother'), the word comes from Old French *bel* 'beautiful' + *dam* 'mother'.

Belgae an ancient Celtic people inhabiting Gaul north of the Seine and Marne Rivers, eventually defeated by Julius Caesar in the Gallic Wars of 58–51 BC. At the beginning of the 1st century BC some of the Belgae had crossed to southern England, where they established kingdoms around Colchester, Winchester, and Silchester; their numbers were swelled by Belgae fleeing the Romans.

Belial the personification of evil, used from early times as a name for the Devil, and by Milton as the name of the fallen angel who represents impurity:

> Belial came last, than whom a spirit more lewd
> Fell not from heaven.

Following biblical use, the name is often used in the phrase *sons of Belial*. It comes from a Hebrew word meaning 'worthlessness'.

believe nothing of what you hear, and only half of what you see proverbial saying, mid 19th century.

believing see ➤ seeing *is believing*.

Belisarius outstanding general of the 6th century Roman emperor ➤ Justinian, his greatest victories being the recovery of Africa from the Vandals in 533, and Italy from the Ostrogoths in 540. Towards the end of his life he fell from favour and was accused of a conspiracy against Justinian; there was a tradition that his eyes were put out and that he ended his life as a beggar on the streets of Constantinople.

Belisha beacon in the UK, an orange ball containing a flashing light, mounted on a striped post on the pavement at each end of a zebra crossing, named (in the 1930s) after Leslie Hore-*Belisha* (1893–1957), British politician, Minister of Transport when the beacons were introduced.

bell a bell is the emblem of ➤ St Anthony *of Egypt* and the 6th-century Breton abbot St Winwaloe, of whom it was said that at the sound of his bell, fishes would follow him.

See also ➤ as the fool *thinks, so the bell clinks*, ➤ bells, ➤ Canterbury *bell*, ➤ division *bell*, ➤ Gabriel *bell*, ➤ hanging *in the bell-ropes*, ➤ Liberty *Bell*, ➤ Lutine *Bell*, ➤ pancake-*bell*, ➤ pardon-*bell*, ➤ passing *bell*, ➤ sacring *bell*, ➤ sanctus *bell*.

Currer Bell the pseudonym under which Charlotte Brontë (1816–55) originally published her work; her sister Emily (1818–48) used the name *Ellis Bell* and Anne (1820–49) was *Acton Bell*.

ring the bell be the best of the lot (in allusion to a fairground strength-testing machine).

bell, book, and candle the formulaic requirements for laying a curse on someone, with allusion to the closing words of the rite of excommunication, 'Do to the book, quench the candle, ring the bell', meaning that the service book is closed, the candle put out (by being dashed to the floor), and the passing bell rung, as a sign of spiritual death.

bell-founders St ➤ AGATHA is the patron saint of bell-founders, perhaps through a misinterpretation of the emblem with which she is most commonly represented, her severed breasts lying upturned on a plate.

Bell Harry name of the central tower of Canterbury Cathedral, designed by the English master mason John Wastell (1458–c.1515), on the orders of Cardinal Morton.

bell sheep in Australia and New Zealand, a sheep caught by the shearer just before the bell rings to signal the end of a shift, which he is allowed to shear.

bell the cat take the danger of a shared enterprise upon oneself, from the fable in which mice proposed hanging a bell around a cat's neck so as to be warned of its approach; the nickname 'Bell-the-Cat' was popularly given to the 16th century Scottish Earl of Angus who is said to have used the phrase when asserting his readiness to lead the Scottish nobles in a revolt against King James III's low-born favourites.

belladonna deadly nightshade; a drug prepared from the leaves and root of this plant. The name comes (in the mid 18th century) via modern Latin from Italian *bella donna* 'fair lady', perhaps from the use of its juice to add brilliance to the eyes by dilating the pupils.

bellarmine a large glazed drinking-jug in the form of a pot-bellied burlesque likeness of Cardinal Robert Bellarmine (1542–1627), originally designed by the Protestant party in the Netherlands, who regarded the Jesuit theologian Bellarmine, who from 1570 to 1576 had been Professor of Theology at Louvain, as a significant opponent.

belle époque the period of settled and comfortable life preceding the First World War. The phrase is French, and means literally 'fine life'.

La Belle Province an informal name for Quebec, in French literally 'the Beautiful Province'.

Bellerophon in Greek mythology, an ancient Corinthian hero, said in some accounts to be the son of ➤ POSEIDON. Anteia, wife of Proetus king of Argus, fell in love with him, and when he rejected her accused him publicly of trying to seduce her (cf. ➤ POTIPHAR's wife). Proetus, unwilling to violate

the laws of hospitality, sent Bellerophon to the king of Lycia, with a sealed letter requesting the king to kill Bellerophon. The king set him a number of tasks likely to prove fatal, such as killing the ➤ CHIMAERA and defeating the ➤ AMAZONS, but Bellerophon with the help of the winged horse ➤ PEGASUS was always successful. He was finally reconciled to the king, and married his daughter.

Afterwards Bellerophon incurred the anger of the gods by his presumption in trying to ride Pegasus to heaven, but the horse threw him. He ended his life as a lonely outcast.

> That election may well show that not all the forces in the Ukraine are Chimeras. Somewhere in Ukraine's life there may emerge a Bellerophon—a hero ready to slay the monster that has long terrorized the land.
> — *National Review* 4 April 1994

Bellerus in Milton's *Lycidas*, an invented person from whom *Bellerium*, or Bolerium, the Roman name of Land's End, in Cornwall, is said to derive.

belli see ➤ CASUS *belli*.

Fabian Gottlieb Bellingshausen (1778–1852), Russian explorer, who in 1819–21 became the first to circumnavigate Antarctica; the **Bellingshausen Sea** is named after him.

bellman historical term for a town crier, a man employed to go round the streets of a town and make public announcements, to which he attracted attention by ringing a bell. The *bellman* also announced deaths, and called on the faithful to pray for the souls of the departed.

Bellona the Roman goddess of war, sometimes thought of as the wife or sister of Mars (➤ MACBETH is referred to as 'that Bellona's bridegroom' in recognition of his military prowess). She was seen as delighting in the carnage of battle and it is possible that she was associated with human sacrifice; it is recorded that in 47 BC, while destroying by decree a temple of Isis, workers also pulled down the walls of the adjoining temple of Bellona and found pots filled with human flesh.

a bellowing cow soon forgets her calf proverbial saying, late 19th century; meaning that the person who laments most loudly is the one who is soonest comforted.

bells see also ➤ *born within sound of* Bow *Bells*, ➤ CAP *and bells*, ➤ SMELLS *and bells*.

bells and whistles in computing, speciously attractive but superfluous facilities, with allusion to the various bells and whistles of old fairground organs.

ring the bells backward ring them beginning with the bass bell, in order to give alarm of fire or invasion, or express dismay; the expression is recorded from the early 16th century.

fable of the belly a version of a fable by Aesop in which the head, limbs, and other organs of the body object that all the belly does is receive the food which they provide, told by Menenius Agrippa to the rebellious plebeians in Shakespeare's *Coriolanus* to demonstrate that the role of the senate is to 'digest things rightly' for the good of the whole state.

the belly wants ears proverbial expression, mid 16th century; meaning that a person distracted by hunger will not listen to argument; the view 'a hungry belly has no ears' was expressed by the Roman statesman Cato the Elder (234–149 BC).

belomancy divination by means of arrows; the word comes (in the mid 17th century) from Greek *belos* 'dart'.

beloved see ➤ *the beloved* PHYSICIAN.

beloved disciple the anonymous and idealized disciple in St John's Gospel, described as the one 'whom Jesus loved', and traditionally often identified as St John the Evangelist.

below stairs the basement of a house, formerly as the part occupied by servants.

below the belt unfair or unfairly; disregarding the rules, from the notion of an unfair and illegal blow in boxing; Margot Asquith (1864–1945) made a direct allusion to the origin of the phrase when she said of Lloyd George, 'He cannot see a belt without hitting beneath it.'

below the gangway in the House of Commons, below the cross-passage halfway down the British House of Commons which gives access to the back benches.

below the salt at the lower end of the table, among the less distinguished guests; a large salt-cellar (the *salt*), often made of precious metal, was traditionally placed in the middle of a long dining-table, marking the division between those regarded as more or less favoured guests.

Belphegor the Septuagint and Vulgate form of the Moabitish 'Baal-peor' mentioned in Numbers 25. Machiavelli in his *Novella di Belfagor* (*c*.1518) gives the name to a devil sent into the world by Pluto to discover if it is true, as many of those arriving in hell assert, that they have been sent there by their wives, and the name *Belphegor* is sometimes used generally for a devil or demon.

> A brewage so composed can only be fitting for the stomachs of Belphegor and his brethren.
> — *Athenaeum* 26 April 1856

Belphoebe in Spenser's *Faerie Queene*, a chaste huntress who partly symbolizes Queen Elizabeth.

Belsen a Nazi concentration camp in the Second World War, near the village of Belsen in north western Germany, the liberation of which at the end of the Second World War provided the Allied countries with horrific and graphic pictures of what had been done to its inmates; the English scientist Janet Vaughan (1899–1993) working there as a doctor in 1945, wrote to a friend, 'I am here—trying to do science in hell.'

See also ➤ BEAST *of Belsen,* ➤ *Anne* FRANK.

Belshazzar's feast the feast made by Belshazzar, the son of ➤ NEBUCHADNEZZAR and the last king of Babylonia, at which his doom was foretold by the writing on the wall, interpreted by ➤ DANIEL. Belshazzar was killed in the sack of Babylon by Cyrus in 538 BC.

See also ➤ WEIGHED *in the balance and found wanting,* ➤ WRITING *on the wall.*

belt see ➤ BELOW *the belt,* ➤ CHASTITY *belt,* ➤ LONSDALE *belt,* ➤ ORION, ➤ RUST *Belt.*

Beltane an ancient Celtic festival celebrated on May Day, marked by bonfires being kindled on the hills. Beltane was also traditionally one of the quarter-days in Scotland, the others being ➤ HALLOWMAS, ➤ CANDLEMAS, and ➤ LAMMAS. The name comes from the Celtic name for the day which marked the beginning of summer.

In recent times, *Beltane* has been celebrated as a modern Pagan festival.

The name is recorded from late Middle English, and comes from Scottish Gaelic *bealltainn.*
See also ➤ IMBOLC, ➤ SAMHAIN.

belted wearing the distinctive cincture of an earl or knight. In Sir Walter Scott's *Lay of the Last Minstrel,* **Belted Will** is the name given to Lord William

Howard (1563–1640), warden of the Western Marches.

Beltway Washington DC, especially as representing the perceived insularity of the US government, from a transferred use by association with the ring road encircling Washington.

> Spreading the government around a bit ought to reduce that self-feeding and self-regarding Beltway culture that Washington-phobes claim to dislike so much.
> — *Time* 20 January 1992

Beltway Bandit in US slang, a company or individual, frequently one employed by a US government agency, hired by a corporation to assist in securing government contracts.

> A consulting contract worth probably $300,000 or so to some Beltway Bandit.
> — Tom Clancy *Rainbow Six* (1998)

Belus in Greek mythology, king of Egypt, a son of the god ➤ POSEIDON. He is said to have been the ancestor of several royal houses in Greece and Africa.

belvedere a summer house or open-sided gallery, typically at rooftop level, commanding a fine view; the word comes (in the late 16th century) from Italian, literally 'fair sight'.

See also ➤ APOLLO *Belvedere*.

Belvedere Torso a Greek sculpture fragment of a male nude, believed to have been copied by the Athenian sculptor Apollonius from a 2nd-century original; the pose of the torso influenced Michelangelo and was much studied in the Late Renaissance and Baroque periods.

bema the altar part or sanctuary in ancient and Orthodox churches. Recorded in English from the late 17th century, the word comes from Greek *bēma* 'a step or raised place', the term used for the platform from which orators spoke in ancient Athens.

Bembo a typeface modelled on that used in the Aldine edition of the tract *De Aetna* by the Italian cardinal and scholar Pietro *Bembo* (1470–1547).

ben see ➤ BIG *Ben*, ➤ BUT *and ben*, ➤ RARE *Ben*.

ben trovato of an anecdote, invented but plausible. The phrase is Italian, and means literally 'well found'; The saying *Se non è vero, è molto ben trovato* 'if it is not true, it is a happy invention' was apparently a common saying in the 16th century, being

found for example in the writings (1585) of the Italian philosopher Giordano Bruno.

Benares former name for ➤ VARANASI, a holy city for Hindus.

bench see also ➤ CROSS *bench*.

Bench the office of a judge or magistrate, from the *bench* as a judge's seat in a law court (recorded in this sense from Middle English); from this comes the expression **raised to the Bench**, meaning, elevated to the dignity of a judge.

Bench and Bar judges and barristers collectively.

bencher in the UK, a senior member of any of the Inns of Court, who form for each Inn a self-elective body, managing its affairs, and traditionally possessed the privilege of 'calling to the bar'.

benchmark a standard or point of reference against which things may be compared or assessed; a *benchmark* was originally a surveyor's mark cut in a wall, pillar, or building and used as a reference point in measuring altitudes.

The mark consists of a series of wedge-shaped incisures, in the form of the 'broad-arrow' with a horizontal bar through its apex; when the spot is below sea-level, as in mining surveys, the mark is inverted. The horizontal bar is the essential part, the broad arrow being added (originally by the Ordnance Survey) as an identification. In taking a reading, an angle-iron is held with its upper extremity inserted in the horizontal bar, so as to form a temporary bracket or *bench* for the support of the levelling-staff, which can thus be placed on absolutely the same base on any subsequent occasion.

bend in heraldry, an ordinary in the form of a broad diagonal stripe from top left (dexter chief) to bottom right (sinister base) of a shield or part of one.

bend sinister in heraldry, a broad diagonal stripe from top right to bottom left of a shield (a supposed sign of bastardy).

Bendigo a former gold-mining town in the state of Victoria, Australia, which was originally called Sandhurst, but was renamed after a local boxer who had adopted the nickname of a well-known English prizefighter, William Thompson (1811–80).

Bendis a Thracian moon-goddess, whose worship was introduced to ancient Greece. In the time of Plato her festival, the Bendideia, was celebrated annually at Peiraeus with torch races on horseback and a solemn procession, and is the occasion of Plato's dialogue *The Republic*. In Samothrace her worship became involved with the ➤ MYSTERIES.

the Benedicite the canticle used in the Anglican service of matins beginning 'O all ye works of the Lord, bless ye the Lord'. It is also called 'The Song of the Three Holy Children', the text being taken from that book of the Apocrypha.

Benedick a newly married man, especially one who had been regarded as a sworn bachelor, from the name of the hero in Shakespeare's *Much Ado About Nothing*, who against his own will falls in love with and marries Beatrice; the usage probably develops from the mocking question, 'How dost thou, Benedick the married man?'

St Benedict (*c*.480–*c*.550), Italian hermit. He established a monastery at ➤ MONTE *Cassino* and his *Regula Monachorum* (known as the Rule of St Benedict) formed the basis of Western monasticism.

   ☐ **FEAST DAY** His feast day is 11 July (formerly 21 March).

Benedictine a monk or nun of a Christian religious order following the rule of St Benedict, established *c*.540. The Rule of St Benedict was gradually adopted by most Western monastic houses, sometimes with their own modifications. Benedictines were also known as *Black Monks* from the colour of their habits.

   The liqueur benedictine, based on brandy, is named from its being originally made by Benedictine monks in France.

Benediction a service in which the congregation is blessed with the Blessed Sacrament, held mainly in the Roman Catholic Church.

benedictional a book containing the forms of episcopal benedictions formerly in use.

Benedictus an invocation beginning *Benedictus qui venit in nomine Domini* (Blessed is he who comes in the name of the Lord) forming a set part of the Mass.

benefice a permanent Church appointment, typically that of a rector or vicar, for which property and income are provided in respect of pastoral duties.

benefit see also ➤ BROCK's *benefit*.

benefit of clergy the exemption of the English clergy and nuns from the jurisdiction of the ordinary civil courts, granted in the Middle Ages but abolished in 1827.

benevolence a forced loan or contribution levied by certain English monarchs without the consent of Parliament (first demanded by Edward IV in 1473 as a token of goodwill).

Benin an African kingdom powerful in the 14th–17th centuries; in 1975, the name was adopted for the former *Dahomey*, a modern state of West Africa.

Benjamin a Hebrew patriarch, the youngest and favourite son of ➤ JACOB, whose elder brothers were forced by their unrecognized brother ➤ JOSEPH, whom they had wronged, to take back to Egypt with them: in Genesis 43:36, Jacob laments, 'Joseph is not, and Simeon is not, and ye will take Benjamin away.'

   In Egypt, an accusation of the theft of a cup is arranged against Benjamin, and it seems that Jacob will indeed lose him; however, this is the dramatic opening to Joseph's forgiveness of, and reconciliation with, the other brothers.

   Benjamin gave his name to the smallest tribe of Israel, traditionally descended from him.

> The new uncle being my granny's Benjamin.
> — Anthony Hope *Half and Half Tragedy* (1913)

Benjamin's portion the largest portion of something, with allusion to Genesis 63:34, in which Joseph, giving food to his brothers, gives to Benjamin (the only one who is innocent of wrongdoing against him) five times the amount he has given to the others.

Bent's Fort trading post on the Arkansas River, founded (*c*.1829) by the frontiersmen Charles and William Bent; it became the most famous of the mountain trading posts.

Jeremy Bentham (1748–1832), English philosopher and jurist, the first major proponent of utilitarianism. Bentham was concerned to reform the law, arguing that the proper object of all legislation and conduct was to secure 'the greatest happiness of the greatest number'.

   He left his body for dissection; his skeleton, dressed in his usual clothes, is kept in University College London.

   See also ➤ PANOPTICON.

Beowulf a legendary Scandinavian hero whose exploits are celebrated in an eponymous Old English poem; in the first part, as a young warrior, he destroys the monster ➤ GRENDEL and Grendel's mother, and in the second part, as an old king, he kills (but is also killed by) a dragon which is ravaging his country.

> The hell of our ancient Northern-European ancestors, of the Vikings, the Danes, the Jutes, of Beowulf and the monster-haunted meres—the hell of eternal cold.
> — Alistair Maclean *H.M.S. Ulysses* (1955)

Berchta a mother goddess of German mythology, typically dressed in white (her name means 'bright') and triple-headed; she was traditionally patron of spinners, because at the end of the year she was said to finish off unfinished work; however on Twelfth Night she might also spoil and tangle flax as a punishment.

Berchtesgarden a town in southern Germany in the Bavarian alps, site of Hitler's fortified retreat.

Berenice's hair the northern constellation *Coma Berenices*, named after an Egyptian queen of the 3rd century BC, wife of Ptolemy III. She dedicated her hair as an offering for the safe return of her husband from an expedition, and the hair was stolen and according to legend, placed in the heavens.
See also ➤ COMA *Berenices.*

Bergamasque a dance resembling a tarantella, named from the Italian province of *Bergamo* in northern Italy; such a dance forms the climax of the mechanicals' entertainment in Shakespeare's *Midsummer Night's Dream.*

bergamot[1] a dessert pear of a rich and sweet variety. Recorded from the early 17th century, the name comes via French and Italian from Turkish *begarmudu* 'prince's pear', from *beg* 'prince' + *armud* 'pear' + the possessive suffix *-u.*

bergamot[2] a tree bearing a dwarf variety of Seville orange, used in cosmetics and as flavouring in Earl Grey tea. Recorded from the late 17th century, it is named after the city and province of *Bergamo* in northern Italy.

Bergerac see ➤ CYRANO *de Bergerac.*

Vitus Bering (1681–1741), Danish navigator and explorer, who led several Russian expeditions aimed at discovering whether Asia and North America were connected by land. He sailed along the coast of Siberia and in 1741 reached Alaska from the east but

died on the return journey; the **Bering Sea** and **Bering Strait** are named after him.

> And you'll not weight him by the heels and dump him overside,
> But carry him up to the sand-hollows to die as Bering died.
> — Rudyard Kipling 'The Rhyme of the Three Sealers' (1893)

George Berkeley (1685–1753), Irish philosopher and bishop. He argued that material objects exist solely by being perceived, so there are only minds and mental events. Since God perceives everything all the time, objects have a continuous existence in the mind of God. Notable works: *A Treatise Concerning the Principles of Human Knowledge* (1710).

Berlin the capital of Germany, which at the end of the Second World War was occupied by the Allies and divided into two parts: **West Berlin**, comprising the American, British, and French sectors, later a state of the Federal Republic of Germany despite forming an enclave within the German Democratic Republic; and **East Berlin**, the sector of the city occupied by the USSR and later capital of the German Democratic Republic.

Between 1961 and 1989 the ➤ BERLIN *Wall* separated the two parts; it was in West Berlin in 1963 that President Kennedy gave a speech with the celebrated words, '*Ich bin ein Berliner* [I am a Berliner]'. The two halves of Berlin were reunited in 1990; occupation formally ended in 1994.

Berlin airlift an operation by British and American aircraft to airlift food and supplies to Berlin in 1948–9, while Russian forces blockaded the city to isolate it from the West and terminate the joint Allied military government of the city. After the blockade was lifted the city was formally divided into East and West Berlin.

Berlin Wall a fortified and heavily guarded wall built in 1961 by the communist authorities on the boundary between East and West Berlin, chiefly to curb the flow of East Germans to the West. Regarded as a symbol of the division of Europe into the communist countries of the East and the democracies of the West, it was opened in November 1989 after the collapse of the communist regime in East Germany and subsequently dismantled.

Bermoothes the 'still-vexed Bermoothes', (the Bermudas, originally named after the Spanish sailor Juan Bermúdez, who sighted the islands early in the

16th century) are referred to in Shakespeare's *The Tempest.*

Bermuda Triangle an area of the western Atlantic Ocean where a large number of ships and aircraft are said to have mysteriously disappeared; the name is recorded from the 1960s.

> Here, in me, in this Bermuda Triangle of the soul, the fine discriminations that are a prerequisite for moral health disappear into empty air and silence and are never heard of again.
> — John Banville *Athena* (1995)

Bern see ➤ DIETRICH *von Bern.*

St Bernard of Aosta (*c.*996–*c.*1081), French monk who founded two hospices for travellers in the Alps. The St Bernard passes, where the hospices were situated, and St Bernard dogs are named after him, and he is patron saint of mountaineers.
□ **FEAST DAY** His feast day is 28 May.

St Bernard of Clairvaux (1090–1153), French theologian and monastic reformer. He was the first abbot of Clairvaux and his monastery became one of the chief centres of the Cistercian order.
□ **FEAST DAY** His feast day is 20 August.

St Bernadette (1844–79), French peasant girl, born Marie Bernarde Soubirous. Her visions of the Virgin Mary in Lourdes in 1858 led to the town's establishment as a centre of pilgrimage. Bernadette later became a nun and she was canonized in 1933.
□ **FEAST DAY** Her feast day is 18 February.

Bernadotte family name of the present royal house of Sweden, founded by Jean Baptiste Jules Bernadotte (1763–1844), French soldier, king of Sweden (as Charles XIV) 1818–44. One of Napoleon's marshals, he was adopted by Charles XIII of Sweden in 1810 and later became king.

Berne Convention an international copyright agreement of 1886, later revised. The US has never been party to it.

Bernicia an Anglian kingdom founded in the 6th century AD, extending from the Tyne to the Forth and eventually united with Deira to form Northumbria.

Gian Lorenzo Bernini (1598–1680), Italian baroque sculptor, painter, and architect. A major figure of the Italian baroque, Bernini used a variety of materials to fuse sculpture, architecture, and painting into a decorative whole. He became architect to St

Peter's in 1629, and his work includes the great canopy over the altar and the colonnade round the piazza at St Peter's, Rome.

Bernoulli the name of a Swiss family that produced many eminent mathematicians and scientists, including Jakob Bernoulli (1654–1705), a professor of mathematics at Basle, who made discoveries in calculus, which he used to solve minimization problems, and contributed to geometry and the theory of probabilities.

His brother Johann (1667–1748), was also professor of mathematics at Basle and contributed to differential and integral calculus.

Johann's son Daniel (1700–82) was professor of mathematics at St Petersburg and then holder successively of the chairs of botany, physiology, and physics at Basle. Although his original studies were in medicine, his greatest contributions were to hydrodynamics and mathematical physics.

Berossus a priest at Babylon in the 3rd century BC who wrote a history of Babylon which transmitted Babylonian history and astronomy to the Greek world.

Berry a former province and medieval duchy of France; Jean, duc de Berry (1340–1416), son of John II of France, was the patron who commissioned the *Très riches heures du duc de Berry.*

berserk out of control with anger or excitement, wild or frenzied (as in *gone berserk*); originally as a noun denoting a wild Norse warrior who fought with frenzy, from the Old Norse *berserkr*, probably from *bjorn* 'bear' and *serkr* 'coat' (indicating that the berserk had taken on the savagery of a bear), but also possibly from *berr* 'bare', meaning a warrior who fought without armour.

Bertha see ➤ BIG *Bertha*

Bertie see ➤ BURLINGTON *Bertie,* ➤ *Bertie* WOOSTER.

Alphonse Bertillon (1853–1914), French criminologist. He devised a system of body measurements for the identification of criminals, which was widely used until superseded by fingerprinting at the beginning of the 20th century.

beryl a transparent pale green, blue, or yellow mineral consisting of a silicate of beryllium and aluminium, sometimes used as a gemstone. In early sources, *beryl* is used as a type of perfect clarity, as crystal now is.

Bes in Egyptian mythology, a grotesque god depicted as having short legs, an obese body, and an almost bestial face, who dispelled evil spirits.

Bess see also ➤ BLACK *Bess,* ➤ GOOD *Queen Bess.*

Bess of Hardwick nickname of Elizabeth Talbot (1518–1608), Countess of Shrewsbury, by whom the great Elizabethan house of Hardwick Hall in Derbyshire was built; the architect was Robert Smythson, and the house was described in a popular rhyme as 'Hardwick Hall, more glass than wall' in recognition of its array of windows.

Friedrich Wilhelm Bessel (1784–1846), German astronomer and mathematician. He determined the positions of some 75,000 stars, obtained accurate measurements of stellar distances, and following a study of the orbit of Uranus, predicted the existence of an eighth planet.

Bessy one of the stock characters, a man dressed as a woman, in the medieval sword-dance and in the mummers' play.

best see also ➤ *the best* DOCTORS *are Dr Diet, Dr Quiet, and Dr Merryman,* ➤ *the best thing since* SLICED *bread,* ➤ HOPE *for the best and prepare for the worst.*

the best club in London the House of Commons; in Dickens's *Our Mutual Friend* (1865), Mr Twemlow says of it, 'I think…that it is the best club in London.'

all's for the best in the best of all possible worlds proverbial saying, early 20th century; originally from Voltaire'a *Candide* (1759), in which Pangloss habitually says, 'In this best of possible worlds…all is for the best.'

the best is the enemy of the good proverbial saying, mid 19th century; often attributed to Voltaire, in the form '*le mieux est l'ennemi du bien*' (*Contes,* 1772), the notion in fact derives from an Italian proverb quoted in his *Dictionnaire philosophique* (1770 ed.), '*Le meglio è l'inimico del bene.*'

the best-laid schemes of mice and men gang aft agley proverbial saying, late 18th century; originally from Robert Burns 'To a Mouse' (1786).

make the best of a bad bargain proverbial advice, late 16th century; encouraging one to look for the least discouraging element in a poor situation.

the best of friends must part proverbial saying, early 17th century.

the best of men are but men at best proverbial saying, late 17th century.

the best things come in small packages proverbial saying, late 19th century.

the best things in life are free proverbial saying, early 20th century.

it is best to be on the safe side proverbial saying, mid 17th century.

bestiary a descriptive or anecdotal treatise on various kinds of animal, especially a medieval work with a moralizing tone.

bet see ➤ *bet like the* WATSONS.

beta the second letter of the Greek alphabet (**B, β**), transliterated as 'b'.

beta test a trial of machinery, software, or other products, in the final stages of its development, carried out by a party unconnected with its development.

bête noire a person or thing that one particularly dislikes. Recorded in English from the mid 19th century, the phrase is French, and means literally 'black beast'.

Beth Din a Jewish court of law composed of three rabbinic judges, responsible for matters of Jewish religious law and the settlement of civil disputes between Jews. The name comes from Hebrew *bēt dīn,* literally 'house of judgement'.

bethel a hallowed spot, a place where God is worshipped; originally with reference to Genesis 28:19, from the story of Jacob who set up a pillar on the spot on which he had dreamed of seeing a ladder reaching up to heaven, 'And he called the name of that place Beth-el.'

Bethesda in the bible (John 5:2–4), the name of a healing pool, perhaps representing *Bethzatha,* and understood to mean 'house of grace'.

Bethgelert a village at the foot of Snowdon (also called *Beddgelert*), site of the home of Llewelyn the Great; the name of the village (in a story invented in 1784 by the village landlord) supposedly deriving from its being the burial-place of Llewelyn's hound Gelert. According to the story, the hound was wrongly suspected of having killed the prince's son and was killed in revenge by his master; it was then revealed that the child was safe in hiding, and that the bloodstains on the hound came from a wolf which it had slain in defence of the child.

Bethlehem a small town to the south of Jerusalem, in the West Bank, which was first mentioned in Egyptian records of the 14th century BC. It was the native city of King David and is the reputed birthplace of Jesus. It contains a church built by Constantine in 330 over the supposed site of Christ's birth.

See also ➤ BEDLAM.

Bethlehemite a member of an order of monks existing in England in the 13th century; they wore a five-rayed star on the breast, in memory of the star which announced the nativity of Christ at Bethlehem.

better a dinner of herbs than a stalled ox where hate is proverbial saying, mid 16th century; originally from the Bible.

better a good cow than a cow of a good kind proverbial saying, early 20th century; meaning that good character is more important than distinguished lineage.

better be an old man's darling than a young man's slave proverbial saying, mid 16th century.

better be envied than pitied proverbial saying, mid 16th century; 5th century BC in Greek.

better be out of the world than out of the fashion proverbial saying, mid 17th century.

better be safe than sorry proverbial saying, mid 19th century.

better dead than red a cold-war slogan claiming that the prospect of nuclear war is preferable to that of a communist society.

better late than never proverbial saying, early 14th century; 1st century BC in Greek.

better 'ole in a 1915 cartoon, *Old Bill* (see ➤ *Old Bill*[1]), while taking shelter from bombardment in a shell-hole, advised his complaining friend, 'If you know of a better 'ole, go to it.'

better one house spoiled than two proverbial saying, late 16th century (of two wicked or foolish people joined in marriage).

better red than dead a slogan of nuclear disarmament campaigners, late 1950s.

the better the day, the better the deed proverbial saying, early 17th century.

better the devil you know than the devil you don't know proverbial saying, mid 19th century.

it is better to be born lucky than rich proverbial saying, mid 17th century.

it is better to give than to receive proverbial saying, late 14th century.

'tis better to have loved and lost than never to have loved at all proverbial saying, early 18th century; originally from William Congreve *The Way of the World* (1700), 'Say what you will, 'tis better to be left, than never to have lov'd.'

it is better to travel hopefully than to arrive proverbial saying, late 19th century; from Robert Louis Stevenson.

better to wear out than to rust out proverbial saying, mid 16th century.

better wed over the mixen than over the moor proverbial saying, early 17th century; meaning that it is better to marry a neighbour than a stranger (a *mixen* is a midden).

Betty see also ➤ *Betty* BOOP, ➤ *all my* EYE *and Betty Martin*.

Betty Crocker a fictitious character, exhibiting conservative values and a consistently cheerful demeanour, purporting to be the presenter or writer of a series of radio programmes, newspaper articles, and books on cooking, distributed in the United States from 1924 onwards. The name was first used in 1921 as the signatory to letters sent to prizewinners in a promotional competition.

between see ➤ *between* SCYLLA *and Charybdis*, ➤ *between the* BARK *and the tree*.

between two stools one falls to the ground proverbial saying, late 14th century.

Beulah in the prophecies of Isaiah (ch. 62, v. 4), a name to be given to Israel when she is at one with God: 'thou shalt be called Hephzibah, and thy land Beulah: for the Lord delighteth in thee, and thy land shall be married.' (*Beulah* in Hebrew means 'married'.)

In Bunyan's *Pilgrim's Progress*, the **Land of Beulah** is a pleasant and fertile country beyond the Valley of the Shadow of Death, and within sight of the

Heavenly City; the name may thus be used for heaven itself:

> I'm weary and tired o' Milton, and longing to get away to the land o' Beulah.
>
> — Elizabeth Gaskell *North and South* (1855)

In Blake's writing, *Beulah* stands for a state of light, which is symbolized by the moon.

William Henry Beveridge (1879–1963), British economist and social reformer, born in India. He was chairman of the committee which prepared the Beveridge Report, which formed the basis of much of the social legislation on which the welfare state in the UK is founded.

> Want is one only of five giants on the road of reconstruction . . . the others are Disease, Ignorance, Squalor and Idleness.
>
> — William Henry Beveridge *Social Insurance and Allied Services* (1942)

Beverley see ➤ St JOHN *of Beverley*.

Beverly Hills a largely residential city in California, on the NW side of the Los Angeles conurbation, famous as the home of many film stars.

Bevin boy during the Second World War, a young man of age for National Service selected by lot to work as a miner; the term comes from the name of the Labour politician Ernest *Bevin* (1881–1951), Minister of Labour and National Service, 1940–5.

Bevis of Hampton hero of a popular verse romance of that title of the late 13th or early 14th century, in which the hero, betrayed and sold into slavery in the East, fights to redeem himself and avenge his murdered father with the help of his sword Morglay and his horse Arundel.

bevy a company of ladies, roes, quails, or larks.

Thomas Bewick (1753–1828), English artist and wood engraver, noted especially for the animal studies in such books as *A History of British Birds* (1797, 1804).

bey the governor of a district or province in the Ottoman empire, also formerly used in Turkey and Egypt as a courtesy title. The word is Turkish, the modern form of *beg* 'prince, governor'.

beyond see also ➤ BACK *of beyond*, ➤ *beyond the* BLACK *stump*.

beyond the veil in the unknown state of being after death; the phrase is originally a figurative reference to the veil which in the Jewish Temple separated the main body of the Temple from the

tabernacle, and derives particularly from Tyndale's translation of the Bible.

Bezaleelian worthy or typical of a skilful craftsman seen as resembling *Bezaleel*, who in Exodus 31:4 was commanded by God 'To devise cunning works, to work in gold, and in silver, and in brass'.

bezant a gold or silver coin, originally minted at Byzantium (later Constantinople, the modern Istanbul), widely used in the currency of medieval Europe. Also in heraldry, a gold roundel representing such a coin.

Recorded from Middle English, the word comes via Old French from Latin *Byzantius* 'Byzantine'.

bezoar a concretion with a hard nucleus found in the stomach or intestines of certain animals (chiefly ruminants), formerly believed to be antidotal. Bezoar is also the name for a wild goat with flat scimitar-shaped horns, found from Greece to Pakistan. It is the ancestor of the domestic goat and is the best-known source of the above stony concretions.

Recorded from the late 15th century (in the general sense 'stone or concretion'), the word comes via French and Arabic from Persian *pādzahr* 'antidote'.

Bhagavadgita a sacred Hindu poem composed between the 2nd century BC and the 2nd century AD and incorporated into the ➤ MAHABHARATA. Presented as a dialogue between the Kshatriya prince Arjuna and his divine charioteer Krishna, it stresses the importance of doing one's duty and of faith in God.

Bhagwan a guru or revered person (often used as a proper name or form of address); a title for a venerated deity in human form. The word comes via Hindi from the Sanskrit root *bhaj* 'adore'.

Bharatanatyam a classical dance form of southern India. The name comes from Sanskrit *bharatanātya*, literally 'the dance of Bharata', from *Bharata*, reputed to be the author of the *Nātyaśāstra*, a manual of dramatic art.

Bhopal a city in central India, the capital of the state of Madhya Pradesh. In December 1984 leakage of poisonous gas from an American-owned pesticide factory in the city caused the death of about 2,500 people.

> Consider the consequences of another Bhopal-like eco-catastrophe.
>
> — Alvin Toffler *Powershift* (1990)

Biafra a state proclaimed in 1967, when part of eastern Nigeria, inhabited chiefly by the Ibo people, sought independence from the rest of the country. In the ensuing civil war the new state's troops were overwhelmed by numerically superior forces, and by 1970 it had ceased to exist.

Bianchi the *Whites*, in the Middle Ages one of two factions into which the ➤ GUELPHS split.

Biarritz a seaside resort in SW France, on the Bay of Biscay, which was made fashionable after 1854 by Napoleon III and the Empress Eugénie; Biarritz was later visited by Queen Victoria and Edward VII and became especially popular with British visitors.

bib see ➤ *one's best bib and* TUCKER.

the Bible the Christian scriptures, consisting of the Old and New Testaments; the Jewish scriptures, consisting of the Torah or Law, the Prophets, and the Hagiographa or Writings.

The Bible is traditionally regarded by Christians as having divine authority, though they disagree on how it should be interpreted. The medieval Catholic Church suppressed translations of the Latin text into the vernacular, and only at the Reformation did they become widely available; among English translations the Authorized or King James Version of 1611 made a lasting impression on English culture. Since the 19th century, the methods of critical scholarship have been applied to the Bible as a historical text, though fundamentalist belief in its literal truth has become prominent in the 20th century.

See also ➤ CONGLETON *rare, Congleton rare, sold the Bible to pay for a bear.*

Bible: named translations ■ See box.

Bible Belt those areas of the southern and middle western United States and western Canada where Protestant fundamentalism is widely practised.

Bible-box a large flat-lidded box, especially of the 17th century, able to hold a family Bible.

Biblia Pauperum block books constituting largely pictorial books of devotion of the medieval period. Also called *poor man's Bible.*

bibliomancy the practice of foretelling the future by interpreting a randomly chosen passage from a book, especially the Bible. See also ➤ SORTES.

Bibliothèque nationale the national library of France, in Paris, which receives a copy of every book and periodical published in France.

Bible: named translations

Bamberg Bible	Kralitz Bible
Bear Bible	Matthew's Bible
Bedell Bible	Mazarin Bible
Bishops' Bible	New English Bible
Breeches Bible	Pfister's Bible
Bug Bible	Placemakers' Bible
Cannon's Bible	Polyglot Bible
Coverdale's Bible	Printers' Bible
Cranmer's Bible	Rhemish Bible
Denial Bible	She Bible
Discharge Bible	Sin On Bible
Douay Bible	Standing Fishes Bible
Ears to Ear Bible	Taverner's Bible
Forty-two-line Bible	Thirty-six-line Bible
Genevea Bible	Treacle Bible
Good News Bible	Tyndale's Bible
Great Bible	Unrighteous Bible
Gutenberg Bible	Vinegar Bible
He Bible	Wicked Bible
Jerusalem Bible	Wife-hater Bible
Judas Bible	Zurich Bible
King James Bible	

bidding prayer a prayer in the form of an invitation by a minister or leader of a congregation to pray about something.

Biedermeier denoting or relating to a style of furniture and interior decoration current in Germany in the period 1815–48, characterized by restraint, conventionality, and utilitarianism; the term was also used to mean dully conventional and bourgeois in appearance or outlook. The word comes from the name of Gottlieb *Biedermaier*, a fictitious German provincial schoolmaster and poet created by L. Eichrodt (1854).

Bifrost in Scandinavian mythology, the bridge connecting heaven and earth.

Big Apple an informal name for New York City.

big bang the explosion of dense matter which according to current cosmological theories marked the origin of the universe. In the beginning a fireball of radiation at extremely high temperature and density, but occupying a tiny volume, is believed to have formed. This expanded and cooled, extremely fast at first, but more slowly as subatomic particles condensed into matter which later accumulated to form galaxies and stars. The galaxies are currently still retreating from one another. What was left of the original radiation continued to cool and has been detected as a uniform background of weak microwave radiation.

In the UK, *Big Bang* is the name given to the introduction in 1986 of major changes in trading in the Stock Exchange, principally involving widening of membership, relaxation of rules for brokers, and computerization.

Big Ben the great clock tower of the Houses of Parliament in London and its bell, named after Sir Benjamin Hall (1802–67), commissioner of public works at the time of its construction; *Big Ben* was designed by the English lawyer and mechanician Edmund Beckett, Lord Grimthorpe (1816–1905).

Big Bend National Park a US national park in a bend of the Rio Grande, in the desert lands of southern Texas on the border with Mexico, in which were discovered, in 1975, fossil remains of the pterosaur.

Big Bertha military nickname for a large-bore German gun or mortar used in the First World War, named after Frau *Bertha* Krupp von Bohlen und Halbach, owner of the Krupp steel works in Germany from 1903 to 1943.

Big Blue informal name for the computer company IBM, at the time of its market dominance.

Big Blue Machine in Canada, informal name for the Ontario Progressive Conservative party, especially during the premiership of William Davis (1971–85), or for the group of people responsible for the party's campaigns and political organization.

Big Board in the US, informal name for the New York Stock Exchange.

Big Brother a person or organization exercising total control over people's lives, from the head of state in George Orwell's novel *1984* (1949); his apparently benevolent but actually ruthlessly omnipotent rule is summed up by the slogan, 'Big Brother is watching you.'

big cheese an important person. The phrase dates from the 1920s, and *cheese* probably comes via Urdu from Persian *čīz* 'thing'; *the cheese* was used earlier to mean 'first-rate' (i.e. *the* thing).

Big-endian in Swift's *Gulliver's Travels* (1726), a member of the faction (opposed to the ➤ Small-*endians*) who believed that eggs should be broken at the larger end before they are eaten.

> It is computed, that eleven thousand persons have, at several times, suffered death, rather than submit to break their eggs at the smaller end. Many large volumes have been published upon this controversy: but the books of the Big-Endians have been long forbidden, and the whole party rendered incapable by law of holding employments.
> — Jonathan Swift *Gulliver's Travels* (1726) 'A Voyage to Lilliput'

big fish eat little fish proverbial saying, early 13th century.

big five a name given by hunters to the five largest and most dangerous of the African mammals: rhinoceros, elephant, buffalo, lion, and leopard.

big fleas have little fleas upon their backs to bite them,
and little fleas have lesser fleas, and so *ad infinitum*
proverbial saying, mid 18th century, from Jonathan Swift 'On Poetry' (1733).

Big Smoke an informal term for London; also called ➤ *the* Smoke.

big stick a display of force or power, especially in international diplomacy; the phrase is associated particularly with Theodore Roosevelt (1858–1919), who in a letter of 26 January 1900 commented, 'I have always been fond of the West African proverb: "Speak softly and carry a big stick; you will go far".'

big white chief an important person, the senior member of a group; the name is a humorous one modelled on the supposed speech of American Indians.

Bigfoot a large, hairy ape-like creature resembling a yeti, supposedly found in NW America, so named because of the size of its footprints. (It is also known by the Salish name *Sasquatch*.)

> Enter a weird beast, unknown to Johnson's modest handbook of shibbiology until several American readers assured him that, like Bigfoot, it really does exist: the *Genitive-Apostrophe-S*.
> — *Economist* 21 December 1996

the bigger they are, the harder they fall proverbial saying, early 20th century; (similar formations in earlier related proverbs from the late 15th century).

Biggles a fictional aviator and war hero Major James Bigglesworth, DSO, MC in a series of books

for children by Captain W. E. Johns, published between the 1930s and 1970s; he typifies the adventurous hero who is as morally upright as he is daring.

> Microlight flying will appeal to the Biggles factor in
> most adults.
> — *Times* 7 March 1981

bigwig an important person, especially in a particular sphere; recorded from the early 18th century,
the term comes from the large wigs worn at that
period by important men.

Bikini an atoll in the Marshall Islands, in the western Pacific, used by the US between 1946 and 1958 as
a site for testing nuclear weapons.

The *bikini* as a two-piece swimsuit for women
was so named because of the supposed 'explosive'
effect created by the garment.

Steve Biko (1946–77), South African radical leader.
He was banned from political activity in 1973; after
his death in police custody he became a symbol of
heroic resistance to apartheid.

Bilbo forename of the ➤ HOBBIT **Bilbo Baggins**,
who is the hero of Tolkien's *The Hobbit*, and who
appears in *The Lord of the Rings*.

bilbo a slender sword having a blade of notable
temper and elasticity; the name comes (in the mid
16th century) from an alteration of *Bilbao* in Spain,
where such swords were made. The weapon was associated with violent action, as in Congreve's The
Old Bachelor (1693), 'Bilbo's the word, and slaughter will ensue.'

bile a bitter greenish-brown alkaline fluid which
aids digestion and is secreted by the liver and stored
in the gall bladder, and which was formerly regarded as one of the four ➤ HUMOURS of the body.

bilk obtain or withold money from someone by deceit or without justification. Recorded from the mid
17th century, *bilk* was originally a term used in crib-
bage, meaning 'spoil one's opponent's score'.

Bill a pet form of the given name *William*; in Britain, an informal term for the police, recorded from
the 1960s, and shortened from *Old Bill*.

See also ➤ *Bill* SIKES, ➤ BUFFALO *Bill*, ➤ PECOS
Bill.

bill a draft of a proposed law presented to parliament for discussion; the word is recorded from
Middle English (denoting a written list or catalogue) and is probably based ultimately on medieval
Latin *bulla* 'seal, sealed document'.

Old Bill[1] a grumbling veteran soldier, typically having a large moustache (with allusion to a cartoon
character created during the war of 1914–18 by Bruce
Bairnsfather (1888–1959), British cartoonist).

Old Bill[2] informal name for the police, the ➤ BILL.
This may have originated from the cartoon character's being depicted in police uniform and giving
advice on wartime security on posters during the
war of 1939–45.

bill of attainder an act formerly introduced in
Parliament for the purpose of making a person subject to *attainder*, the forfeiture of land and civil
rights suffered as a consequence of a sentence of
death for treason or felony, without judicial process.

bill of health a certificate relating to the incidence
of infectious disease on ship or in port at time of
sailing; from this comes the phrase **a clean bill of
health** to mean a declaration or confirmation that
someone is healthy or that something is in good
condition.

Bill of Rights a legal statement of the rights of a
class of people, in particular: the English constitutional settlement of 1689, confirming the deposition
of James II and the accession of William and Mary,
guaranteeing the Protestant succession, and laying
down the principles of parliamentary supremacy;
the first ten amendments to the Constitution of the
US, ratified in 1791.

billabong in Australia, a branch of a river forming
a backwater or stagnant pool, made by water flowing from the main stream during a flood. Recorded
from the mid 19th century, the word comes from
Wiradhuri *bilabang* (originally as the name of the
Bell River, New South Wales), from *billa* 'water' +
bang 'channel that is dry except after rain'.

billet see ➤ *every* BULLET *has its billet*.

billet-doux a dated term for a love letter; recorded
from the late 17th century, the phrase is French, and
means literally 'sweet note'.

Billingsgate a London fish market dating from
the 16th century, traditionally noted for vituperative
language. (In 1982 the market moved to the Isle of
Dogs in the East End.)

> Mr. Osborne . . . cursed Billingsgate with an emphasis
> quite worthy of the place.
> — William Makepeace Thackeray *Vanity Fair* (1848)

Billy see ➤ *Billy* BUNTER, ➤ BLUE *Billy*, ➤ SILLY
Billy.

billy goat informal name for a male goat, recorded from the mid 19th century.

Billy the Kid William H. Bonney (1859–81), American outlaw; born *Henry McCarty*; known as **Billy the Kid**. A notorious robber and murderer, he was captured by Sheriff Pat Garrett in 1880, and was shot and killed by Garrett after he escaped.

billycock a kind of bowler hat; the term is recorded from the mid 19th century, and the hat is said to be named after *William Coke*, nephew of Thomas William Coke, Earl of Leicester (1752–1842).

bimbo an attractive but unintelligent or frivolous young woman. The term came into English (from Italian, 'little child, baby') in the early 1920s as a derogatory term for a person of either sex; P. G. Wodehouse wrote in the 1940s about 'bimbos who went about the place making passes at innocent girls after discarding their wives'. The sense of stupid or 'loose' woman was however developing, and in the late 1980s the term enjoyed a new vogue in the media; journalists claimed that the *bimbo* was epitomized by young women who were prepared to 'kiss and tell', ending their affairs with the rich and famous by selling their stories to the popular press.
    See also ➤ HIMBO.

bimetallism a system of allowing the unrestricted currency of two metals (e.g. gold and silver) as legal tender at a fixed ratio to each other; *bimetallism* was the subject of the ➤ BATTLE *of the Standards* in 1896 between the US presidential contenders William McKinley and William Jennings Bryan.

Bimini an island in the Bahamas, according to Indian legend the site of the ➤ FOUNTAIN *of Youth* sought by Ponce de Leon.

binary notation a system of numerical notation which has 2 rather than 10 as a base.

bind see ➤ SAFE *bind*.

Alfred Binet (1857–1911), French psychologist. He devised a mental age scale which described performance in relation to the average performance of students of the same physical age, and with the psychiatrist Théodore Simon (1873–1961) was responsible for a pioneering system of intelligence tests.

bingo a game in which players mark off numbers on cards as the numbers are drawn randomly by a caller, the winner being the first person to mark off all their numbers.

biodiversity the variety of plant and animal life in the world or in a particular habitat. A high level of biodiversity is usually considered to be important and desirable.

Biosphere 2 an artificial habitat created in the Arizona desert into which 8 experimenters were sealed between September 1991 and September 1993. The idea was to test whether an artificial environment could be created and sustained independently of life on earth (seen as *Biosphere 1*), partly as an ecological experiment and partly to determine whether space habitats or colonies on other worlds were practicable.

biotechnology the exploitation of biological processes for industrial and other purposes, especially the genetic manipulation of micro-organisms for the production of antibiotics and hormones.

biotecture the use of living plants as an integral part of the design of buildings.

Bircher a member or supporter of the ➤ JOHN *Birch Society*, an extreme right-wing and anti-communist American organization founded in 1958, and named after John Birch, a USAF officer and 'first casualty of the cold war', killed by Chinese communists in 1945.

bird a warm-blooded egg-laying vertebrate animal distinguished by the possession of feathers, wings, a beak, and especially by being able to fly. Birds probably evolved in the Jurassic period from small dinosaurs that may already have been warm-blooded.
    Birds are an emblem of ➤ St FRANCIS *of Assisi*.
    The word is recorded in Old English (in the form *brid*) denoting 'chick, fledgling'; its ultimate origin is unknown.
    See also ➤ ATTIC *bird*, ➤ *Bird of* WASHINGTON, ➤ BIRDS, ➤ BLUE *bird of happiness*, ➤ DAULIAN *bird*, ➤ DEVIL*'s bird*, ➤ *the* EARLY *bird catches the worm*, ➤ *in vain the* NET *is spread in the sight of the bird*, ➤ *it's an* ILL *bird that fouls its own nest*, ➤ OOZLUM *bird*, ➤ RARE *bird*, ➤ *St* MARTIN*'s bird*, ➤ WAKON-*bird*, ➤ WHITE *bird*.

the bird has flown the prisoner or fugitive has escaped; the expression was famously used by Charles I of his failed attempt to arrest the ➤ FIVE *Members* in the House of Commons, 4 January 1642, when he found that the men had escaped, 'I see all the birds are flown.'

a bird in the hand is worth two in the bush proverbial saying, mid 15th century; 13th century in Latin.

a bird never flew on one wing proverbial saying, early 18th century.

Bird of Freedom the emblematic bald eagle of the US; the phrase is recorded from the mid 19th century.

bird of ill omen someone regarded as bringing misfortune.

bird of Jove the eagle, which in classical mythology was sacred to Jove.

bird of Juno the peacock, which in classical mythology was sacred to Juno.

bird of passage a migratory bird, and thus a term for a transient visitor, someone who passes through or visits a place without staying for long.

Bird Woman nickname of the Shoshone Indian woman Sacagawea (1787–1812?), who acted as interpreter, peacemaker, and guide to the ➤ LEWIS *and Clark expedition*.

bird's-eye view a general view from above, as of a landscape; figuratively, a résumé of a subject.

bird's nest soup in Chinese cookery, made from the dried gelatinous coating of the nests of swifts and other birds.

Birdcage Walk in St James's Park, Westminster, perhaps named from the aviary kept there in the 17th century by Charles II.

birdie in golf, a score of one stroke under par at a hole; the term comes from US slang *bird*, denoting any first-rate thing.

birds see also ➤ PIGS *may fly, but they are very unlikely birds*, ➤ STYMPHALIAN *birds*, ➤ *you cannot* CATCH *old birds with chaff*.

the birds and the bees informal term for basic facts about sex and reproduction as told to a child.

there are no birds in last year's nest proverbial saying, early 17th century.

birds in their little nests agree proverbial saying, early 18th century.

birds of a feather flock together proverbial saying, mid 16th century.

little birds that can sing and won't sing must be made to sing proverbial saying, late 17th century.

Birmingham derogatory term used for supporters of the ➤ EXCLUSION *Bill* in 1680, in allusion to the counterfeit coins once made in Birmingham; the implication was that the anti-Catholic stance assumed by the Whig party was hypocritical.

birth see ➤ *Virgin* BIRTH.

Birthday Honours in Britain, the titles and decorations awarded on a sovereign's official birthday.

Birtism the policies introduced into the BBC in the 1990s by John *Birt* as Director-General, characterized by an emphasis on the explanatory function of broadcasting and a market-based approach to the elements of programme-making; for those opposed to the policies, *Birtism* was used to sum up an attitude seen as ultimately inimical to creativity.

bis dat, qui cito dat Latin proverb meaning, 'He gives twice who gives quickly'.

bishop[1] a senior member of the Christian clergy, usually in charge of a diocese and empowered to confer holy orders.

➤ *St* AMBROSE and St Charles Borromeo (1538–84), archbishop of Milan, are the patron saints of bishops.

In chess, a bishop is a piece, typically with its top shaped like a mitre, that can move in any direction along a diagonal on which it stands. Each player starts the game with two bishops, one moving on white squares and the other on black.

Recorded in Old English (in form *biscop*, *bisceop*) the word comes from Greek *episkopos* 'overseer'.

See also ➤ BOY *bishop*, ➤ *the* FIGHTING *Bishop*, ➤ FLYING *bishop*, ➤ MISSIONARY *bishops*, ➤ *St* NICHOLAS*'s bishop*, ➤ SEVEN *Bishops*, ➤ TITULAR *bishop*.

bishop[2] file and tamper with the teeth of a horse so as to deceive as to age. Recorded from the early 18th century, the term apparently comes from the name of someone initiating the practice.

bishop[3] murder by drowning; from name of a man named Bishop who with a confederate drowned a boy in Bethnal Green in 1831 to sell his body for dissection. The term is first used by Barham in the *Ingoldsby Legends*:

> I Burked the papa,
> now I'll Bishop the son.
>   — R. H. Barham *Ingoldsby Legends* (1840)

the bishop has put his foot in it the milk or porridge is burnt, the meat is overcooked; the phrase is first recorded in the writings of ➤ *William* TYNDALE (*c*.1494–1536), in which he explains that the expression is used 'because the bishops burn who they lust and whosoever displeaseth them'.

Bishops' Bible an edition of the Bible published in 1568 under the direction of Archbishop Parker, and intended to counteract the popularity of the Calvinist ➤ GENEVA *Bible*.

Otto von Bismarck (1815–98), Prussian minister and German statesman, Chancellor of the German Empire 1871–90; known as the **Iron Chancellor**. He was the driving force behind the unification of Germany, orchestrating wars with Denmark (1864), Austria (1866), and France (1870–1) in order to achieve this end. As Chancellor of the new German Empire (1871–90) he continued to dominate the political scene, attempting to break the influence of the Catholic Church at home while consolidating Germany's position as a European power.

The name Bismarck is also used for ➤ BLACK *velvet*, in reference to the German Chancellor's reported liking for the drink.

bissextile containing the **bissextus** or extra day which the ➤ JULIAN *calendar* inserts in ➤ LEAP *years*.

bit see ➤ *the* BITER *bit*, ➤ DEVIL's *bit*.

have the bit between one's teeth be ready to tackle a problem in a determined or independent way; the allusion is to a horse which is out of its rider's control.

the bitch goddess material or worldly success; the term was coined by the philosopher William James (1842–1910), who in a letter to H. G. Wells, 11 September 1906, referred to 'the moral flabbiness born of the exclusive worship of the bitch-goddess *success*'.

bite see also ➤ DEAD *men don't bite*, ➤ *every* DOG *is allowed one bite*, ➤ *his* BARK *is worse than his bite*.

bite one's thumb at insult by making the gesture of biting one's thumb; in Shakespeare's *Romeo and Juliet* (1595), in a scene between two quarrelling servants, one when challenged says to the other, 'I do not bite my thumb at you, sir; but I bite my thumb, sir.'

bite the bullet behave stoically; the reference is to a wounded soldier undergoing surgery without the aid of anaesthetics.

bite the dust fall and die, come to an unfortunate end; the expression is recorded from the mid 18th century.

bite the hand that feeds one injure a benefactor; the expression is recorded from the late 18th century, and is first recorded in Edmund Burke's *Thoughts on the Cause of the Present Discontents* (1770), in a reference to the proposition 'that we set ourselves to bite the hand that feeds us', so that 'with insanity we oppose the measures…whose sole object is our own peace and prosperity'.

the biter bit a person who has damaged another has in turn been similarly damaged; *biter* in this phrase means a deceiver (the sense is otherwise obsolete).

Bithynia the ancient name for the region of NW Asia Minor west of ancient Paphlagonia, bordering the Black Sea and the Sea of Marmara.

bitten see ➤ ONCE *bitten, twice shy*.

bitter-ender (in southern African history) a Boer who refused to surrender towards the end of the Second Boer War. The expression probably entered South African English at approximately the same time that *bitter-einder* entered South African Dutch (there is a misconception that *bitter-ender* was derived from Afrikaans).

black of the very darkest colour due to the absence of or complete absorption of light; the opposite of white. *Black* in western countries has traditionally been worn as a sign or mourning, and in figurative use the word has traditionally implied foreboding, evil, or melancholy.

The use of *black* to refer to African peoples (and their descendants) dates back at least to the late 14th century. Although the word has been in continuous use ever since, other terms have enjoyed prominence too: in the US *coloured* was the term adopted in preference by emancipated slaves following the American Civil War, and *coloured* was itself superseded in the US in the early 20th century by *Negro* as the term preferred by prominent black American campaigners such as Booker T. Washington. In Britain on the other hand, *coloured* was the most widely used and accepted term in the 1950s and early 1960s. With the civil rights and Black Power movements of the 1960s, *black* was adopted by Americans of African origin to signify a sense of racial pride, and it remains the most widely used and generally accepted term in Britain today.

See also ➤ ALL *Blacks*, ➤ *Black* AUSTER, ➤ *Black* DAHLIA, ➤ *the black* OX, ➤ *the* DEVIL *is not so black as he is painted*, ➤ MEN *in black*, ➤ PENNY *black*, ➤ TWO *blacks don't make a white.*

Black Act in the early 18th century, a severe law passed against poaching and trespassing (poachers who blackened their faces were known as *blacks*).

Black Agnes name for Agnes, Countess of Dunbar and March (1312–69), celebrated for her successful defence of Dunbar Castle against the English in January 1337–8.

Black and Tans an armed force recruited by the British government to suppress insurrection in Ireland in 1921, so called from their wearing a mixture of black constabulary and khaki military uniforms. Their harsh methods caused an outcry in Britain and America.

Black Auster in Macaulay's *Battle of Lake Regillus* (1842), name of the horse belonging to Herminius.

Black Beauty name of the horse which is the central character in Anna Sewell's novel of this name (1877); the book tells the story, in autobiographical form, of the Black Beauty's treatment by a variety of owners, and Anna Sewell said of it that its special aim was 'to induce kindness, sympathy, and an understanding treatment of horses'.

black belt a black belt worn by an expert in judo, karate, and other martial arts. Also, a person qualified to wear this.

Black Bess supposedly the name of the highwayman ➤ *Dick* TURPIN's horse, deriving from the version of Turpin's story given by Harrison Ainsworth in his novel *Rookwood* (1834).

black bile in medieval science and medicine, one of the four bodily ➤ HUMOURS, believed to be associated with a *melancholy* temperament.

Recorded in English from the late 18th century, the term is a translation of Greek *melankholia* 'melancholy', from *melas, melan-* 'black' + *kholē* 'bile',

an excess of which was formerly believed to cause depression.

black book an official book bound in black; the distinctive name of various individual books of public note, sometimes referring to the colour of the binding. The name was also given to an official return prepared during the reign of Henry VIII, containing the reports of the visitors upon the abuses in the monasteries.

A *black book* is also one in which there is a record of punishments, giving rise to the figurative phrase **to be in someone's black books**.

the Black Book of Carmarthen a Welsh manuscript of the 12th century, containing a collection of ancient Welsh poetry with a number of references to King ➤ ARTHUR.

Black Book of the Admiralty a code of rules for the government of the Navy, said to have been compiled in the reign of Edward III.

Black Book of the Exchequer containing an official account of the royal revenues at the time of its compilation in the 12th century.

black box any complex piece of equipment, typically a unit in an electronic system, with contents which are mysterious to the user; specifically now, a flight recorder in an aircraft.

black bun rich fruit cake in a pastry case, traditionally eaten in Scotland at New Year.

Black Canons another name for the black-cloaked ➤ AUGUSTINIANS.

black cap a cap (actually a small piece of black cloth) formerly worn by a judge when passing sentence of death.

Black Carib a language derived from Island Carib with borrowings from Spanish, English, and French, spoken in isolated parts of Central America by descendants of people transported from the Lesser Antilles.

black-coat worker a person in a clerical or professional, rather than an industrial or commercial, occupation.

Black Country a district of the Midlands with much heavy industry, traditionally regarded as blackened by the smoke and dust of the coal and iron trades.

Black Death the great epidemic of bubonic plague that killed a large proportion of the population of Europe in the mid 14th century. It originated in central Asia and China and spread rapidly through Europe, carried by the fleas of black rats, reaching England in 1348 and killing between one third and one half of the population in a matter of months.

The name 'black death' is modern, and was apparently introduced into English history by Mrs. Penrose (Mrs. Markham) in her *History of England* for children (1823), and into medical literature by Babington's translation of Hecker's *Der Schwarze Tod* in 1833.

black diamond a name for coal, as consisting (like diamonds) of carbon, and implying its value as a fuel; the term dates from the mid 19th century.

Black Dick nickname of Richard, Earl Howe (1726–99), admiral of the fleet who commanded the victorious British forces at the Battle of the ➤ GLORIOUS *First of June.*

black dog a metaphorical representation of melancholy or depression, used particularly by Samuel Johnson to describe his attacks of melancholia:

> The black dog I hope always to resist, and in time to drive, though I am deprived of almost all those that used to help me . . . When I rise my breakfast is solitary, the black dog waits to share it, from breakfast to dinner he continues barking, except that Dr Brocklesby for a little keeps him at a distance . . . Night comes at last, and some hours of restlessness and confusion bring me again to a day of solitude. What shall exclude the black dog from a habitation like this?
> — Samuel Johnson letter to Mrs Thrale, 28 June 1783

In the 20th century, the term has been associated with Winston Churchill, who used the phrase 'black dog' when alluding to his own periodic bouts of depression.

black doll traditionally the sign of a marine store or *dolly-shop.*

Black Douglas byname of James Douglas (1286?–1330), Scottish champion and supporter of Robert Bruce, and afterwards of several senior representatives of his branch of the Douglas family.

After the death of King Robert, the ➤ BLACK *Douglas* took his heart on pilgrimage to the Holy Land to fulfil a vow made by the king to go on crusade. Going first to Spain, he took service with the king of Castile against the Moorish kingdom of Granada, and was killed in battle there; he is said to have thrown the heart of Bruce ahead of him, with the words 'Onward as thou wert wont, Douglas will follow.'

black earth another name for ➤ CHERNOZEM.

black economy the part of a country's economic activity which is unrecorded and untaxed by its government.

black flag a pirate's ensign, characteristically thought to feature a white skull and crossbones on a black background.

Black Friar a ➤ DOMINICAN friar, named for the black habits worn by the order.

Black Friday a name for various Fridays regarded as disastrous, such as 6 December 1745, when the landing of the Young Pretender was announced in London, and 11 May 1866, which saw a commercial panic at the failure of Overend, Gurney, & Co.

black frost frost which does not have a white surface.

Black Hand a name given to several secret societies or associations, such as a Spanish revolutionary society of anarchists of the 19th century.

Black Hills a range of mountains in east Wyoming and west South Dakota, which includes the sculptured granite face of ➤ *Mount* RUSHMORE. The Black Hills were considered sacred territory by the Sioux; discovery of gold there in 1874, and the subsequent gold rush, led to war in 1876, and the ➤ *Battle of* LITTLE *Bighorn.* The Hunkpapa Sioux leader ➤ SITTING *Bull* (c.1831–90) is reported to have said, 'The Black Hills belong to me. If the whites try to take them, I will fight.'

black hole a region of space having a gravitational field so intense that no matter or radiation can escape; informally, a place where money or lost items are thought of as going, never to be seen again.

Black holes are probably formed when a massive star exhausts its nuclear fuel and collapses under its own gravity. If the star is massive enough no known force can counteract the increasing gravity, and it will collapse to a point of infinite density. Before this stage is reached, within a certain radius (the event horizon) light itself becomes trapped and the object becomes invisible.

Black Hole of Calcutta a dungeon 6 metres (20 feet) square in Fort William, Calcutta, where perhaps as many as 146 English prisoners were confined overnight following the capture of Calcutta by the nawab of Bengal in 1756. Only 23 of them were still alive the next morning.

black information information held by banks, credit agencies, or other financial institutions about people who are considered bad credit risks.

black is beautiful slogan of American civil rights campaigners, mid-1960s.

Black Jew another term for ➤ FALASHA.

black letter an early, ornate, bold style of type, distinguished from Roman type (which subsequently became established), and still in regular use in Germany.
    See also ➤ GOTHIC *type*.

black-letter day an inauspicious or unlucky day, the opposite of a ➤ RED-*letter day*.

black magic magic involving the supposed invocation of evil spirits for evil purposes.

black mamba a highly venomous slender olive-brown to dark grey snake that moves with great speed and agility. Native to eastern and southern Africa, it is the largest poisonous snake on the continent, and may be taken as the type of a venomous and aggressive snake.

Black Maria a police vehicle for transporting prisoners. The term originated (in the mid 19th century) in the US, and the name is said to come from a black woman, *Maria* Lee, who kept a boarding house in Boston and helped police in escorting drunk and disorderly customers to jail.

black market an illegal traffic or trade in officially controlled or scarce commodities.

black mass a travesty of the Roman Catholic Mass in worship of the Devil.

Black Monday a Mondy regarded as unlucky; in particular, Easter Monday (probably so called because Mondays in general were held to be unlucky; th: tradition that a day of rejoicing is naturally followed by calamity may also be involved).
    The name is also given to Monday 19 October 1987, when massive falls in the value of stocks on Wall Street triggered similar falls in markets around the world.

Black Monk a member of the ➤ BENEDICTINES, from the black habits worn by Benedictine Orders.

black Muslim a member of the ➤ NATION *of Islam*.

Black Nell name of a horse belonging to ➤ *Wild Bill* HICKOK.

Black Panther a member of a militant political organization set up in the US in 1966 to fight for black rights. From its peak in the late 1960s it declined in the 1970s after internal conflict and the arrest of some of its leaders.

black people St Peter Claver (1580–1654), a Spanish Jesuit priest who worked particularly at Cartagena (now Colombia) when it was the centre of the slave trade, is the patron saint of missionary enterprises among black people.

Black Pope an informal term for the General of the ➤ JESUITS, recorded from the late 19th century.

Black Power a movement in support of rights and political power for black people, especially prominent in the US in the 1960s and 1970s.

Black Prince name given to Edward, Prince of Wales (1330–76), eldest son of Edward III of England, who was responsible for the English victory at Poitiers in 1356. He predeceased his father, but his son became king as Richard II.
    The name is recorded from the mid 16th century, but although it has been suggested that it refers either to the colour of his armour or to the savagery of some of his deeds, there is no clear evidence as to the origin.
    See also ➤ WIN *one's spurs*.

Black Prince's ruby a large red gem which is in fact a spinel with a smaller ruby inserted, now set in the Maltese cross at the front of the British imperial state crown. The jewel was given to the ➤ BLACK *Prince* by Pedro the Cruel, king of Castile, after the battle of Najéra in 1367; later, it was worn by Henry V at Agincourt in 1415.

Black Rod the chief usher of the Lord Chamberlain's department of the royal household, who is also usher to the House of Lords; his full title is **Gentleman Usher of the Black Rod**.

Black Sash a women's anti-apartheid movement in South Africa, established in the late 1950s.

Black Saturday a particularly unlucky Saturday; in Scotland, Saturday 10 September 1547, the date of the Battle of Pinkie, where an English army led by the Duke of Somerset defeated the Scots.
    The name is also given in Scotland to Saturday 4 August 1621, the date on which the articles of Perth to enforce episcopal observances were passed by the Scottish Parliament.

Black Sea a tideless almost landlocked sea bounded by Ukraine, Russia, Georgia, Turkey, Bulgaria, and Romania, connected to the Mediterranean through the Bosporus and the Sea of Marmara.

black section in the British Labour Party, a proposed, officially recognized grouping of non-white members at constituency level, designed to represent the interests of non-whites. The formation of *black sections* was first proposed in the early 1980s, but the suggestion was criticized as a form of reverse apartheid by the trade unions, and was finally rejected by the National Executive Committee and the party conference in 1987.

black sheep a member of a family or group who is regarded as a disgrace to it. The term is recorded from the late 18th century, and the saying 'there is a black sheep in every flock' is proverbial.

black spot in Stevenson's *Treasure Island* (1883), a summons to one regarded as a traitor who is 'tipped the black spot'.

Black Stone the sacred reddish-black stone built into the outside wall of the ➤ KAABA and ritually touched by Muslim pilgrims.

beyond the black stump in Australia, beyond the limits of settled, and therefore civilized, life; from the use of a fire-blackened stump as a marker when giving directions to travellers.

black swan a thing or kind of person that is extremely rare, a ➤ RARA *avis.* The phrase is originally from the *Satires* of the Roman writer Juvenal (AD *c.*60–*c.*130), '*Rara avis in terris nigroque simillima cycno* [A rare bird on this earth, like nothing so much as a black swan].'

Black Thursday a particularly unlucky Thursday; in Australia, 6 February 1851, a day on which devastating bushfires occurred in Victoria.

Black Tom nickname of Thomas Wentworth, Lord Strafford (also called **Black Tom Tyrant**), associated with the belief that as Lord Lieutenant of Ireland he was prepared in 1640 to bring the Irish army over to England for the king's use (see also ➤ STRAFFORDIAN).

The nickname *Black Tom* was also given to the Puritan general Thomas Fairfax (1612–71), in this case from his dark complexion.

black velvet a drink consisting of a mixture of stout and champagne; also known as *Bismarck,* in

reference to the German Chancellor's reported liking for it.

Black Watch the Royal Highland Regiment. In the early 18th century the term *Watch* was given to certain companies of irregular troops in the Highlands; *Black Watch* referred to some of these companies raised *c.*1729–30, distinctive by their dark-coloured tartan.

Black Wednesday 16 September 1992, the day on which the UK withdrew sterling from the European Exchange Rate Mechanism as a result of adverse economic circumstances. The affair was embarrassing, and damaging, to the Conservative Government, although Conservatives opposed to closer ties with Europe called the day *White Wednesday* to signal their pleasure at the withdrawal.

black widow a highly venomous American spider which has a black body with red markings; it is taken as a type of venomous and dangerous creature.

blackball reject a candidate for membership of a private club, typically by means of a secret ballot. The term is recorded from the late 18th century, and comes from the practice of registering an adverse vote by placing a black ball in a ballot box.

blackberry a prickly climbing shrub of the rose family which bears an edible soft fruit consisting of a cluster of soft purple-black drupelets, and which grows extensively in the wild (also called ➤ BRAMBLE); the fruit of this plant.

Blackberries are proverbially taken as the type of something plentiful.

In some regions, it was traditionally thought unlucky to pick blackberries after a certain date, such as Michaelmas (29 September) or All Saints' Day (1 November), as it was believed that after that date the fruit had been spoiled by the Devil or other malefic powers.

Blackberry Summer a spell of fine weather at the end of September or beginning of October when blackberries are ripening.

blackbird the *blackbird* is noted for its song; it is also the emblem of the 7th-century Irish monk ➤ *St* KEVIN.

In the 19th century, *blackbird* was also a slang term for a black or Polynesian captive on a slave ship.

blackboard jungle a school noted for indiscipline; the term comes from the title of a novel (1954) by Evan Hunter, later filmed.

blackface the make-up used by a non-black performer playing a black role; the term is recorded from the late 19th century.

Blackfoot a member of a confederacy of North American Indian peoples of the north-western plains. The Blackfoot confederacy was made up of three closely related tribes: the Blackfoot proper or Siksika, the Bloods, and the Peigan.

blackguard a man who behaves in a dishonourable or contemptible way. The term originated (in the early 16th century) as two words, *black guard*, denoting a body of attendants or servants, especially the menials who had charge of kitchen utensils, but the exact significance of the epithet 'black' is uncertain. The sense 'scoundrel, villain' dates from the mid 18th century, and was formerly considered highly offensive.

Blackheath a district of open land in southeast London; the site in 1381 of a revolutionary sermon preached by John Ball which took as its text the rhyme '➤ *When* ADAM *delved and Eve span*'.

blackjack a gambling card game in which players try to acquire cards with a face value totalling 21 and no more.

blackleg a person who continues working when fellow workers are on strike. The term is recorded in this sense from the mid 19th century, but the origin of the name remains unknown.

blacklist a list of people or groups regarded as unacceptable or untrustworthy and often marked down for punishment or execution; the term is recorded from the early 17th century.

blackmail the action of demanding money from someone in return for not revealing compromising information about them; the term originally denoted protection money exacted from farmers and landowners in the English and Scottish border country in the 16th and 17th centuries.

blackout a period when all lights must be turned out or covered to prevent their being seen by the enemy during an air raid.

blackshirt a member of a Fascist organization, in particular, (in Italy) a member of a paramilitary group founded by ➤ *Benito* MUSSOLINI, and (in the UK) a supporter of Oswald Mosley's British Union of Fascists, founded in 1932.

blacksmith see also ➤ *the* HARMONIOUS *Blacksmith*, ➤ *the* LEARNED *blacksmith*.

blacksmiths ➤ *St* DUNSTAN and ➤ *St* ELOI are the patron saints of blacksmiths.

Blackstone used informally to refer to *Commentaries on the Laws of England* (1765–9), an exposition of English law by William Blackstone (1723–80).

blackthorn winter a spell of cold weather at the time in early spring when the blackthorn flowers (the *blackthorn* is a thorny Eurasian shrub which bears its white flowers before the leaves appear).

blade a dashing, pleasure-seeking fellow. The term is recorded from the late 16th century, and probably refers to such a man as the wielder of a sword.

Bladud a legendary British prince, according to Geoffrey of Monmouth, the father of ➤ *King* LEAR, and supposedly the discoverer of the hot springs at ➤ BATH.

Blair Babes informal term for the record number of Labour women MPs elected to Parliament in May 1997 when Labour took office under Tony Blair; in later use, *Blair Babe* often implies one who is seen as particularly ➤ ON-*message* in relation to New Labour.

Blaise according to Malory and Tennyson, the magician who in Arthurian legend was ➤ MERLIN's master and teacher.

St Blaise an Armenian bishop and martyr of the 4th century, one of the ➤ FOURTEEN *Holy Helpers*, who was said to have been martyred by being torn with combs for carding wool before he was beheaded.

He is said at the intervention of the boy's mother to have healed a boy who had a fishbone stuck in his throat; when Blaise was afterwards in prison, the woman brought him food and candles.

   ◻ **EMBLEM** His emblems are a comb (for carding wool) and a candle.

   ◻ **PATRONAGE** He is the patron saint of woolcombers and those with illnesses of the throat.

   ◻ **FEAST DAY** His feast day is 3 February.

Blake see also ➤ SEXTON *Blake*.

William Blake (1757–1827), English artist and poet. Blake's poems mark the beginning of romanticism and a rejection of the Age of Enlightenment. His watercolours and engravings, like his writings, were only fully appreciated after his death.

Jean Pierre François Blanchard (1753–1809), French balloonist. Together with the American John Jeffries (1744–1819), he made the first crossing of the English Channel by air, flying by balloon, on 7 January 1785, and was the first to fly a balloon in the US. Blanchard was among the earliest to experiment with parachuting; he was killed making practice jumps by parachute from a balloon.

blank verse verse without rhyme, especially the iambic pentameter of unrhymed heroic, the regular measure of English dramatic and epic poetry.

born on the wrong side of the blanket a dated term denoting illegitimacy, recorded from the late 18th century.

Blarney Stone an inscribed stone in the wall of *Blarney* Castle, near Cork, which is difficult of access but which is said to give the gift of persuasive speech to anyone who kisses it; from this comes *blarney* as a word for flattering or cajoling talk.

blasphemy the action or offence of speaking sacrilegiously about God or sacred things; profane talk. Recorded from Middle English, the word comes via Old French and ecclesiastical Latin from Greek *blasphēmia* 'slander, blasphemy'.

Blatant Beast in Spenser's *Faerie Queene*, a monster, the personification of the calumnious voice of the world, begotten of Envy and Detraction. Sir Calidore pursues it, finds it despoiling monasteries and defiling the Church, overcomes it and chains it up. But finally it breaks through the chain, 'So now he raungeth through the world again.'

blatherskite a person who talks at great length without making much sense. The 17th-century Scottish song *Maggie Lauder*, by F. Semphill, in which the word occurs, was popular with American troops during the War of Independence, and the term was adopted into American colloquial speech.

Blaue Reiter a group of German expressionist painters formed in 1911, based in Munich. The group, who included Wassily Kandinsky, Jean Arp, and Paul Klee, were stylistically diverse but shared a desire to portray the spiritual side of life. The name, which in German means 'blue rider', is the title of a painting by Kandinsky.

Helena Blavatsky (1831–91), Russian spiritualist, born in Ukraine. In 1875 she co-founded the Theosophical Society in New York, together with the American Henry Steel Olcott.

blaxpoitation the exploitation of black people, especially with regard to stereotyped roles in films.

blaze a white spot or stripe on the face of a mammal or bird. The word is recorded from the mid 17th century and is ultimately of Germanic origin, related to German *Blässe* 'blaze' and *blass* 'pale', and probably also to *blemish*.
  Blaze was also used in the mid 17th century for a white mark made on a tree, usually by cutting off a slice of bark, to indicate a path; from this comes the later *blaze a trail* and *trailblazer*.

a bleating sheep loses a bite proverbial saying, late 16th century.

Blenheim a battle in 1704 in Bavaria, near the village of Blindheim, in which the English, under the Duke of Marlborough, defeated the French and the Bavarians.
  The name was given to the Duke of Marlborough's seat at Woodstock near Oxford, a stately home designed by Vanbrugh. The house and its estate were given to the first Duke of Marlborough in honour of his victory at *Blenheim*.

Louis Blériot (1872–1936), French aviation pioneer. Trained as an engineer, he built one of the first successful monoplanes in 1907, and on 25 July 1909 he became the first to fly the English Channel (Calais to Dover), in a monoplane of his own design.

bless see ➤ *not have a* PENNY *to bless oneself with.*

blessed see also ➤ *blessed are the* DEAD *that the rain rains on,* ➤ ISLANDS *of the Blessed.*

blessed is he who expects nothing, for he shall never be disappointed proverbial saying, early 18th century.

Blessed Virgin Mary a title given to ➤ MARY as the mother of Jesus.

single blessedness a humorous expression for the state of being unmarried, originally a quotation from Shakespeare's *Midsummer Night's Dream*:

> But earthlier happy is the rose distilled,
> Than that which withering on the virgin thorn
> Grows, lives, and dies, in single blessedness.
> — William Shakespeare *A Midsummer Night's Dream* (1595–6)

blessing God's favour and protection or a prayer asking for this; in the Christian Church, a blessing given with three fingers symbolizes the Trinity.

See also ➤ OUT *of God's blessing into the warm sun,* ➤ TORONTO *blessing.*

blessings brighten as they take their flight proverbial saying, mid 18th century.

Bletchley Park near Milton Keynes in Buckinghamshire, during the Second World War the centre of British codebreaking activity, where the ➤ ENIGMA code was broken.

See also ➤ COLOSSUS.

William Bligh (1754–1817), British naval officer, captain of HMS *Bounty.* In 1789, on a voyage to the West Indies, part of his crew, led by the first mate Fletcher Christian, mutinied and Bligh was set adrift in an open boat, arriving safely at Timor, nearly 6,400 km (4,000 miles) away, a few weeks later.

See also ➤ MUTINY *on the Bounty.*

Blighty an informal and often affectionate term for Britain or England, chiefly as used by soldiers of the First and Second World Wars (in the First World War, a wound which was sufficiently serious to merit being shipped home to Britain was known as a *Blighty*).

The term was first used by soldiers serving in India, and is an Anglo-Indian alteration of Urdu *bilāyatī* 'foreign, European', from Arabic *wilāyat, wilāya* 'dominion, district'.

Blimp a pompous, reactionary type of person, deriving from the character, **Colonel Blimp**, invented by cartoonist David Low (1891–1963), used in anti-German or anti-government drawings before and during the Second World War.

> I was in serious danger of turning into one of the Colonel Blimp types who sat around me in considerable numbers, eating cornflakes or porridge with their blimpish wives.
> — Bill Bryson *Notes from a Small Island* (1995)

blind ➤ St LUCY, ➤ St DUNSTAN, the archangel Raphael (see ➤ RAPHAEL[1]), and ➤ St THOMAS *the Apostle* are the patron saints of the blind.

See also ➤ *a* DEAF *husband and a blind wife are always a happy couple,* ➤ *in the* COUNTRY *of the blind the one-eyed man is king,* ➤ LOVE *is blind,* ➤ NOTHING *so bold as a blind mare,* ➤ SAND-*blind.*

blind as a bat completely blind, a simile recorded from the late 16th century; earlier comparisons of this kind were to *beetles* and *moles,* the common

point being that all were seen as creatures who habitually moved in darkness.

there's none so blind as those who will not see proverbial saying, mid 16th century.

turn a blind eye pretend not to notice, said to be in allusion to ➤ *Horatio* NELSON, who lifted a telescope to his blind eye at the Battle of Copenhagen (1801), thus not seeing the signal to 'discontinue the action'.

Blind Freddie in Australia, the type of an unperceptive person; the name is recorded from the mid 20th century, and may be the nickname of a Sydney hawker.

the Blind Harper nickname of the blind Welsh musician John Parry (d. 1782), who played before the poet Thomas Gray to such effect that Gray said that his 'tunes of a thousand years old' had helped Gray to finish his poem 'The Bard' (1757).

when the blind lead the blind, both shall fall into the ditch proverbial saying, late 9th century.

the Blind Magistrate John Fielding (1722–80), Bow Street magistrate and brother of the novelist and magistrate Henry Fielding, who although being blind from birth was first assisting magistrate to his brother, and then after Henry's death holder of the office in his own right. A traditional story said that he knew more than three thousand thieves by their voices, although the origin of this is uncertain.

blind man's buff a game in which a blindfold player tries to catch others while being pushed about by them; *buff* here means a buffet or blow.

a blind man's wife needs no paint proverbial saying, mid 17th century.

blind with science confuse by the use of long or technical words or involved explanations; expression is recorded from the 1930s.

blindworm another name for the ➤ SLOW-*worm,* traditionally believed to be both blind and venomous (a 'blindworm's sting' was included with the 'adder's fork' in the cauldron prepared by Macbeth's witches).

See also ➤ *if the* ADDER *could hear, and the blindworm could see.*

bliss see ➤ *where* IGNORANCE *is bliss, 'tis folly to be wise.*

the **Blitz** the German air raids on Britain in 1940; the word dates from that year, and is an abbreviation of ➤ BLITZKRIEG.

blitzkrieg an intense military campaign intended to bring about a swift victory. The word comes from German, and means literally 'lightning war'.

block see also ➤ a CHIP off the old block.

put one's head on the block put one's standing or reputation at risk by proceeding with a particular course of action, an informal expression ultimately referring to the executioner's block.

block book a book printed from engraved wooden blocks.

Bloggs see ➤ JOE Bloggs.

Blondel legendary troubador who in medieval chronicles is said to have discovered Richard I in the castle of Durrenstein, where he had been imprisoned by the Duke of Austria, by singing below the castle windows.

Blondie the curly-haired heroine of an American strip cartoon by Chic Young (1901–73) which first appeared in 1930; *Blondie* was first the girlfriend, and later the wife, of Dagwood Bumstead for whom the ➤ DAGWOOD *sandwich* is named.

> Even Blondie, after sixty years as a supermom, is looking for a job.
> — *New Yorker* 9 December 1991

Blondin (1824–97), French acrobat, famous for walking across a tightrope suspended over ➤ NIAGARA *Falls* on several occasions.

blood in medieval science and medicine, *blood* was regarded as one of the four bodily humours, believed to be associated with a confident and optimistic, or *sanguine*, temperament.

Blood is traditionally used to denote the killing of a person, or guilt for a death, as in **blood on one's hands**.

See also ➤ BLUE *blood*, ➤ CORRUPTION *of blood*, ➤ DRAGON's *blood*, ➤ FIELD *of Blood*, ➤ NELSON's *blood*, ➤ one's (own) FLESH *and blood*, ➤ PIGEON's *blood*, ➤ PRECIOUS *blood*, ➤ SACRED *Blood*.

Colonel Blood (1618?–80), Irish-born adventurer, who in 1671 attempted to steal the Crown Jewels.

Blood and Guts nickname of US General George Patton (1885–1945), commander of the 3rd Army in the Second World War, noted for his forthright and dominant personality, whose force played a decisive part in the ➤ BATTLE *of the Bulge*.

blood and iron military force as distinguished from diplomacy; the phrase is a translation of German *Blut und Eisen*, and is particularly associated with ➤ *Otto von* BISMARCK:

> This policy cannot succeed through speeches, and shooting-matches, and songs; it can only be carried out through blood and iron.
> — Otto von Bismarck speech in the Prussian House of Deputies, 28 January (1886)

In a speech on 30 December 1862, Bismarck had used the form 'Iron and blood'.

blood and soil a Nazi catchphrase, translating German *Blut und Boden*, summing up the centrality of race and land to Nazi ideology.

> The success of Fascist blood-and-soil ideology.
> — W. H. Auden *I Believe* (1940)

blood-and-thunder designating a story which features bloodshed and violence; the term is recorded from the mid 19th century.

you cannot get blood from a stone proverbial saying, mid 17th century.

blood is thicker than water proverbial saying, early 19th century (12th century in German), meaning that in the end family ties will always count.

the **blood of the martyrs is the seed of the Church** proverbial saying, mid 16th century, meaning that persecution causes the Church to grow; the 3rd century early Christian writer Tertullian has, 'As often as we are mown down by you, the more we grow in numbers; the blood of Christians is the seed.'

blood, toil, tears and sweat Winston Churchill's summary of what in May 1940 he could offer the country for its immediate future:

> I have nothing to offer but blood, toil, tears and sweat.
> — Winston Churchill speech in the House of Commons, 13 May 1940

blood will have blood proverbial saying, late Middle English, meaning that killing will provoke further killing; ultimately, the saying refers to Genesis 9:6, 'Whoso sheddeth man's blood, by man shall his blood be shed.'

blood will tell proverbial saying, mid 19th century; meaning that family characteristics or heredity will in the end be dominant.

Bloodless Revolution another term for the
➤ GLORIOUS *Revolution*.

bloodstone a type of green chalcedony spotted or
streaked with red, used as a gemstone, which was
formerly supposed to have the power of staunching
bleeding.

bloodthirsty eager for bloodshed, a word first recorded in Coverdale's translation of the Bible (1525),
Psalms 25:9, 'O destroy not my soul with the sinners, nor my life with the bloodthirsty.'

bloodwite in Anglo-Saxon England, a fine for
shedding blood paid to an alderman or king.

bloody see also ➤ *the* DARK *and bloody ground*,
➤ RAWHEAD *and bloody bones.*

bloody adjective used informally to express anger,
annoyance, or shock; recorded in English from the
mid 17th century, the origin of the term is uncertain,
but it is thought to have a connection with the
'bloods' (aristocratic rowdies) of the late 17th and
early 18th centuries. From the mid 18th century
until quite recently, *bloody* used as a swear word was
regarded as unprintable, probably from the mistaken belief that it implied a blasphemous reference
to the blood of Christ, or that the word was an alteration of 'by Our Lady'; hence the shock occasioned
in Shaw's play when Eliza uses the words 'Not
bloody likely' (see ➤ PYGMALION).

Bloody Angle an area of the battlefield of
Spotsylvania, one of the most hard-fought hand-
to-hand encounters (1864) of the American Civil
War.

Bloody Assizes the trials of the supporters of the
Duke of Monmouth after their defeat at the Battle of
Sedgemoor, held in SW England in 1685. The government's representative, Judge ➤ JEFFREYS, sentenced several hundred rebels to death and about
1,000 others to transportation to America as plantation slaves.

Bloody Balfour nickname given to ➤ *Arthur James
BALFOUR* (1848–1930) as Irish Chief Secretary in
1887, when two rioters were killed during the prosecution for conspiracy of the nationalist William
O'Brien (1852–1928).

the **Bloody** Eleventh nickname of the 11th Foot,
later the Devonshire Regiment; the name was given
after their heavy losses in the battle of Salamanca in
the Peninsular Wars, 22 July 1812.

Bloody Friday 21 July 1972, the day when a number
of people were killed and injured by bombs in Belfast.

Bloody Hand in heraldry, the armorial device or
➤ RED *Hand* of Ulster.

Bloody Mary nickname of Mary Tudor (1516–87),
in reference to the series of religious persecutions
taking place in her reign.

Bloody Sunday a name for various Sundays
marked by violence and bloodshed, especially 30
January 1972 in Northern Ireland, when 13 civilians
were killed during the dispersal of marchers by British troops in the Bogside.

Bloody Thursday 5 July 1934, when 3 people were
killed on the San Francisco Waterfront during industrial conflict surrounding the longshoremen's
strike.

the **Bloody** Tower in the Tower of London, supposedly site of the murder of the ➤ PRINCES *in the
Tower.*

bloom see ➤ *when the* FURZE *is in bloom, my love's
in season*, ➤ *when the* GORSE *is out of bloom, kissing's
out of fashion.*

bloomers historical term for women's and girls'
loose-fitting trousers, gathered at the knee or, originally, the ankle. The name comes (in the mid 19th
century) from Mrs Amelia J. *Bloomer* (1818–94), an
American social reformer who advocated a similar
garment.

Bloomingdale's a fashionable New York department store.

> I nip out for an hour at Bloomingdale's. It is the perfect
> salve for my wounded ego.
> — *New York Magazine* 2 April 1990

Bloomsbury Gang a section of the Whig party of
1765, led by the 4th Duke of Bedford, whose London
house was in Bloomsbury.

Bloomsbury Group a group of writers, artists,
and philosophers living in or associated with
Bloomsbury in the early 20th century. Members of
the group, which included Virginia Woolf, Lytton
Strachey, Vanessa Bell, Duncan Grant, and Roger
Fry, were known for their unconventional lifestyles
and attitudes and were a powerful force in the
growth of modernism.

Bloomsday the 16th of June, on which celebrations take place in Ireland and other countries to

mark the anniversary of the events in James Joyce's *Ulysses*.

blot see also ➤ *blot on one's* ESCUTCHEON.

blot one's copybook tarnish one's good reputation; a *copybook* was a book in which copies were written or printed for pupils to imitate.

blow see ➤ JOE *Blow*.

blow the gaff reveal a plot or secret; the term is recorded from the early 19th century, but the origin is unknown.

blow the whistle on bring an illicit activity to an end by informing on the person responsible; term *whistleblower* for such an informant comes (in the 1970s) from this.

Blowing Stone a rough sarsen stone in Kingston Lisle, Oxfordshire, with holes which when blown through emit a moaning sound.

blue of a colour intermediate between green and violet, as of the sky or sea on a sunny day.
  Blue was traditionally seen as the colour of constancy, as well as the colour of sorrow and anguish, and of plagues and hurtful things. It is also associated with the male sex (as *pink* is with the female sex).
  Politically, the colour was associated with the Scottish Presbyterian or Whig party in the 17th century, and later with the Tory, and then Conservative, party.
  At Oxford and Cambridge Universities, a *blue* is a person who has represented Cambridge (a **Cambridge Blue**) or Oxford (an **Oxford Blue**) in a particular sport.
  The informal sense of blue to mean 'obscene, indecent, profane' developed in the mid 19th century.
  See also ➤ BIG *Blue*, ➤ BOLT *from the blue*, ➤ CLEAR *blue water*, ➤ COVENTRY *blue*, ➤ LIGHT *blue*, ➤ LIGHT *the blue touch paper and retire immediately*, ➤ NATTIER *blue*, ➤ OXFORD *blue*, ➤ PRUSSIAN *blue*, ➤ *the* THIN *blue line*, ➤ THREE *blue balls*, ➤ TRUE-*blue*, ➤ WILD *blue yonder*.

Admiral of the Blue in the British navy, former title of the Admiral of the Blue squadron (one of the three divisions of the Royal Navy made in the 17th century).

blue are the hills that are far away proverbial saying, late 19th century, meaning that a distant view lends enchantment; the thought is echoed in

Housman's line from *A Shropshire Lad* (1896) 'What are those blue remembered hills'.

Blue Billy nickname of the British admiral William Cornwallis (1744–1819).

blue bird of happiness embodiment of the concept in Maurice Maeterlinck's visionary play *The Blue Bird* (*L'Oiseau Bleu*), first produced in London in 1910. In the play two children set out on a search for 'the bird that is blue' to cure the sick child of an old woman; when, after many disappointments, they find themselves back at home, they offer their own pet bird, and discover as they do so that it is blue.

blue blood that which is traditionally said to flow in the veins of old and aristocratic families; the term is a translation of Spanish *sangre azul*, attributed to Castilian families who claimed to have no admixture of Moorish, Jewish, or other foreign blood. The expression may have originated in the blueness of the veins of people of fair complexion as compared with those of dark skin.

Blue Boar heraldic cognizance of Richard Duke of York (1411–60), father of Edward IV and Richard III.

Blue Bonnets Scots soldiery (also called *Blue Caps*), from the broad round horizontally flattened bonnet or cap of blue woollen material, formerly widely worn in Scotland.

blue book in the UK, a report bound in a blue cover and issued by Parliament or the Privy Council; in the US, an official book listing government officials.

blue box[1] chiefly in the US, an electronic device used to access long-distance telephone lines illegally.

blue box[2] a blue plastic box for the collection of recyclable household materials.

blue-chip denoting companies or their shares considered to be a reliable investment, though less secure than gilt-edged stock. The term comes (in the early 20th century) from the US; from the *blue chip* used in gambling games, which usually has a high value.

Blue Coat a student at a charity school with a blue uniform which represents the blue coat traditionally worn by an almoner; the name is particularly associated with Christ's Hospital School, whose uniform is a long dark blue gown fastened at the waist with a belt, and bright yellow stockings.

blue-collar worker a manual worker, particularly in industry; the term is recorded (originally in the US) from the 1950s.

blue-eyed boy a person highly regarded by someone and treated with special favour; the term is first recorded in a novel by P. G. Wodehouse in 1924.

blue flag a European award for beaches based on cleanliness and safety.

blue for a boy blue as a colour is traditionally associated with the male sex; this expression is recorded from the early 20th century.

Blue Hen's Chickens inhabitants of the state of Delaware. The term is said to have come from a company in the American War of Independence, led by a Captain Caldwell of Delaware, who were known in Carolina firstly as 'Caldwell's gamecocks', and then 'the blue hen's chickens' and the 'blue chickens'. From this, the name 'Blue Hen' was given to the state.

Blue John a blue or purple banded variety of fluorite found in Derbyshire.

blue law in colonial New England, a strict puritanical law, particularly one preventing entertainment or leisure activities on a Sunday; currently in North America, a law prohibiting certain activities, such as shopping, on a Sunday.

Blue Monday a name for the Monday before Lent.

once in a blue moon very rarely; a moon that is blue is something that is seldom or never seen. In the early 16th century, to say 'that the moon is blue' is recorded as the type of a fantastic statement.

Blue Nile one of the two principal headwaters of the ➤ NILE. Rising from Lake Tana in NW Ethiopia, it flows some 1,600 km (1,000 miles) southwards then north-westwards into Sudan, where it meets the White Nile at Khartoum.

blue-pencil censor or make cuts in a manuscript; a blue 'lead' pencil was traditionally used for marking corrections and deletions.

Blue Peter a blue flag with a white square in the centre, raised by a ship about to leave port.

From 1958, *Blue Peter* has been the name of a television magazine series for children which combines education and entertainment with successful charitable appeals; it is known particularly for the catchphrase 'Here's one I made earlier' as the culmination to directions for making a model out of empty yoghurt pots, coat-hangers, and similar domestic items.

> Look at the market full of young designers wrapped in lycra selling extravagantly large pieces of jewellery made the same way you used to make sea shell encrusted plant pot holders for your mum during your Blue Peter period.
> — Jane Owen *Camden Girls* (1997)

Blue Riband[1] a badge worn by members of the Order of the Garter (also called *Blue Ribbon*).

Blue Riband[2] a trophy for the ship making the fastest eastward sea crossing of the Atlantic Ocean on a regular commercial basis (also called *Blue Ribbon*).

Blue Ribbon Army a temperance organization; the term is recorded from the late 19th century.

Blue Ribbon of the turf the Derby; the term was used by Disraeli in his memoir *Lord George Bentinck* (1852).

blue shift in astronomy, the displacement of the spectrum to shorter wavelengths in the light coming from distant celestial objects moving towards the observer.

blue-sky ignoring possible difficulties; hypothetical, not yet practicable or profitable in the current state of knowledge or technological development.

blue-sky law a law relating to the practice of dealing in doubtful or worthless securities. The term is recorded from the early 20th century, and is supposed to allude to a person who is ready to sell the 'blue sky' to a credulous buyer.

Bluebeard a character in a tale by Charles Perrault, who killed several wives in turn for disobeying his order to avoid a locked room which contained the bodies of his previous wives. His last wife, left in his castle on her own with her sister, explores and opens the fatal room, as Bluebead on returning discovers; in the nick of time, she is rescued by her brothers, who arrive and kill Bluebeard.

His name is often used allusively to refer to the uncontrollable curiosity which has brought them to their death.

> Be bold, be bold, but not *too* bold—there is no Bluebeard's locked room so fearful as the face in the mirror.
> — Julie Burchill *Goodbye Cruel World* (1989)

bluebottle a nickname for someone whose official dress was blue, as a beadle or a policeman; the use is recorded from the early 17th century.

Bluegrass State informal name for Kentucky; *bluegrass* here is a bluish-green grass which was introduced into North America from northern Europe, and which is widely grown for fodder, especially in Kentucky and Virginia.

bluejacket a sailor in the navy, especially as used to distinguish a seaman from a marine.

Bluemantle one of four pursuivants of the English College of Arms.

Bluenose informal name for a person from Nova Scotia; recorded from the mid 19th century.

blueprint a design plan or other technical drawing. The term comes (in the late 19th century) from the original process in which prints were composed of white lines on a blue ground or of blue lines on a white ground.

blues melancholic music of black American folk origin, typically in a 12-bar sequence. It developed in the rural southern US towards the end of the 19th century, finding a wider audience in the 1940s, as blacks migrated to the cities. This urban blues gave rise to rhythm and blues, and rock and roll.

the blues feelings of melancholy, sadness, or depression. The term is recorded from the mid 18th century, and comes elliptically from *blue devils* 'depression or delirium tremens'.

Blues and **Royals** a regiment of the Household Cavalry, formed from the amalgamation (1969) of the Royal Horse Guards (also known as the *Blues*) and the *Royal* Dragoons.

Blueshirts popular name for the Army Comrades Association, an Irish political organization for ex-soldiers of the Free State in 1932, and modelling itself on European fascist movements.

bluestocking an intellectual or literary woman. The term is recorded from the late 17th century and was originally used to describe a man wearing blue worsted (instead of formal black silk) stockings; extended to mean 'in informal dress'. Later the term denoted a person who attended the literary assemblies held (*c.*1750) by three London society ladies, where some of the men favoured less formal dress. The women who attended became known as **blue-stocking ladies** or **blue-stockingers**.

bluey in Australia and New Zealand, a bundle of possessions carried by a bushman, originally so called because the outer covering was generally a blue blanket.

bluff an attempt to deceive someone into believing that one can or is going to do something. The word is recorded from the late 17th century (originally in the sense 'blindfold, hoodwink'): from Dutch *bluffen* 'brag', or *bluf* 'bragging'. The current sense (originally US, mid 19th century) originally referred to bluffing in the game of poker.

Johann Friedrich Blumenbach (1752–1840), German physiologist and anatomist. He is regarded as the founder of physical anthropology, though his approach has since been much modified. He classified modern humans into five broad categories (Caucasian, Mongoloid, Malayan, Ethiopian, and American) based mainly on cranial measurements.

Blunderbore in the story of ➤ JACK *the Giant-Killer*, a Cornish giant, brother of ➤ CORMORAN.

blurb a short description of a book, film, or other product written for promotional purposes and appearing on the cover of a book or in an advertisement. The term is said to have been coined in 1907 by the American humorist Gelett Burgess (1866–1951), in a comic book jacket featuring an attractive young woman whom he named 'Miss Blinda Blurb'; the first recorded example of *blurb* in its current sense is from Burgess in *Burgess Unabridged* (1914), in which he defines the word as 'an inspired testimonial…abounding in agile adjectives and adverbs'.

Enid Blyton (1897–1968), English writer of children's fiction. Her best-known creation for young children is the character Noddy, who first appeared in 1949; her books for older children include the series of *Famous Five* and *Secret Seven* adventure stories. Her popularity with her readers has been phenomenal and long-lasting, although her books have been severely criticized (and at one point were destocked from libraries) for their simplistic storylines, stereotypical characters, and limited vocabulary. More recently it has been found that her stories, with their direct narrative line, are particularly accessible to those with reading difficulties.

> I had not given a thought to skiing lessons since primary school, when I read a children's novel in which a wholesome bunch of Blytonesque youngsters pitch up at a remote Swiss chalet.
> — *Times Educational Supplement* 18 July 1997

bo tree a fig tree native to India and SE Asia, regarded as sacred by Buddhists. Recorded from the mid 19th century, the name represents Sinhalese *bōgaha* 'tree of knowledge' (Buddha's enlightenment having occurred beneath such a tree), from

Sanskrit *budh* 'understand thoroughly' + *gaha* 'tree'.

boa a constrictor snake which bears live young and may live to great size, native to America, Africa, Asia, and some Pacific islands. The *boa* is first mentioned in the writings of Pliny, who wrongly derives the name from the Latin *bos* 'ox'.

Boadicea another name for ➤ BOUDICCA.

Boanerges 'sons of thunder', the byname given by Jesus to James and John, the sons of Zebedee, who wanted to call down fire on the Samaritans.

boar more fully the **wild boar**, a tusked Eurasian wild pig from which domestic pigs are descended, exterminated in Britain in the 17th century. In allusive use, **the Boar** is Richard III, whose emblem was a ➤ WHITE *Boar*.
   See also ➤ BLUE *Boar*, ➤ CALYDONIAN *boar*, ➤ CHILD *on a boar*, ➤ WHITE *Boar*.

boar's head traditionally served at a feast on Christmas day.

Boar's Head Inn a tavern in Eastcheap, celebrated in connection with ➤ FALSTAFF, and said to have been destroyed in the Great Fire, immediately rebuilt, and finally demolished in the 19th century.

board see also ➤ BIG *Board*.

Board of Green Cloth a department of the Royal Household, consisting of the Lord Steward and his subordinates, so called from the green-covered table at which its business was originally transacted.

Board of Trade a now nominal British government department within the Department of Trade and Industry concerned with commerce and industry. The title of **President of the Board of Trade**, revived in the 1990s by the Conservative politician Michael Heseltine when Secretary of State for Industry, was at an earlier period commemorated in a sardonic rhyme by the English writer and humorist A. P. Herbert (1890–1971):

> This high official, all allow,
> Is grossly overpaid;
> There wasn't any Board, and now
> There isn't any Trade.
>   — A. P. Herbert 'The President of the Board of Trade'
> (1922)

boat a boat is the emblem of ➤ St SIMON, ➤ St JUDE, and the 7th-century French abbot St Bertin,

whose monastery of Sithiu (Saint-Bertin) in northern France was originally accessible only by water.
   See also ➤ BRIDGE *of boats*, ➤ BURN *one's boats*, ➤ WADE *'s boat*.

Boatswain name of ➤ BYRON's pet Newfoundland dog, who died of madness 18 November 1808 and who was buried at Newstead Abbey with an inscription composed by the poet:

> Near this spot are deposited the remains of one who possessed beauty without vanity, strength without insolence, courage without ferocity, and all the virtues of Man, without his vices.
>   — Lord Byron 'Inscription on the Monument of a
> Newfoundland Dog' (1808)

Franz Boas (1858–1942), German-born American anthropologist. A pioneer of modern anthropology, he developed the linguistic and cultural components of ethnology. He did much to overturn the theory that Nordic peoples constitute an essentially superior race; his writings were burnt by the Nazis.

Boaz see also ➤ JACHIN *and Boaz*.

Boaz in the Old Testament, the name of the wealthy landowner who became the second husband of ➤ RUTH.

bob see also ➤ COCKEYE *bob*.

bob[1] a change of order in bell-ringing; used in names of change-ringing methods, as **plain bob**. The term is recorded from the late 17th century, and may be connected with *bob* meaning 'sudden movement up and down'.

bob[2] in British usage, a shilling; more generally, used with reference to a large but unspecified amount of money. The term is recorded from the late 18th century but the origin is unknown.

bob for apples try to catch floating or hanging apples with one's mouth alone, as a game, traditionally played at ➤ HALLOW'EEN.

Bob's your uncle everything is all right. Popular etymology suggests that the term derives from the political advancement of ➤ *Arthur James* BALFOUR (1848–1930), who was nephew to the Conservative statesman Robert, Lord Salisbury, and who became first Chief Secretary for Ireland and then (in 1902) Prime Minister; the problem with this explanation is that the phrase is not recorded until the 1930s.

Bobadill a braggart who pretends to prowess, from the name of a character in Ben Jonson's *Every Man in His Humour* (1598), a boastful cowardly soldier who associates with and impresses callow younger men.

> That Bobadillian method of contest.
> — Thomas Carlyle *The French Revolution* (1837)

bobbery noise, noisy disturbance. Recorded from the early 19th century, the word is of Anglo-Indian origin, and represents an alteration of Hindi *Bāp re!* 'O father!', an exclamation of surprise or dismay.

Bobbing John a nickname of John Erskine, Earl of Mar (1675–1732), a leader of the Jacobite rebellion of 1715, who had previously vacillated in his allegiance to the exiled Stuarts and had initially been a Hanoverian supporter; a contemporary account judged him to be 'a man of good sense but bad morals'. A Jacobite song of 1715 runs, 'Hey for Bobbing John, and his Highland quorum!'

bobby see also ➤ GREYFRIARS *Bobby*.

bobby informal term for a police officer, deriving (in the mid 19th century) from a pet form of *Robert*, given name of the politician ➤ *Robert* PEEL, founder of the modern police force.

bobby-dazzler a person or thing considered remarkable or excellent. Recorded from the mid 19th century (originally as northern English dialect) the second element is related to *dazzle*; the origin of the first element is unknown.

bobby-soxer dated US term for an adolescent girl; *bobby socks* were socks which reached just about the ankle, worn in the 1940s by girls in their teens.

bobtail see ➤ RAGTAG *and bobtail*.

Bocardo the prison in the old North Gate of the city of Oxford, pulled down in 1771, where in 1554 the Protestant martyrs Cranmer, Ridley, and Latimer were housed before their trial and execution. Earlier, in 1535, describing the effect of the new learning in Oxford, Richard Layton had written to Thomas Cromwell on his visitation to Oxford University, 'We have set Dunce [➤ *John* DUNS *Scotus*] in Bocardo, and have utterly banished him Oxford for ever, with all his blind glosses.'

Giovanni Boccaccio (1313–75), Italian writer, poet, and humanist. He is most famous for the *Decameron* (1348–58), a collection of a hundred tales told by ten young people who have moved to the country to escape the Black Death.

the Boche informal and dated term for Germans, especially German soldiers, considered collectively. The word is French soldiers' slang, originally in the sense 'rascal', later used in the First World War meaning 'German'.

bodach in Scottish and Irish use, a ghost, a spectre.

Bode's law in astronomy, a formula by which the distances of the first seven planets from the sun are roughly derived in terms of powers of two. It is named after Johann E. Bode (1747–1826), the German astronomer who drew attention to the law, which was discovered earlier by his countryman, Johann D. Titius (1729–96).

Bodhgaya a village in the state of Bihar, NE India, where the Buddha attained enlightenment. A ➤ BO *tree* there is said to be a descendant of the tree under which he meditated.

bodhisattva in Mahayana Buddhism, a person who is able to reach nirvana but delays doing so through compassion for suffering beings.

bodice-ripper a sexually explicit romantic novel or film, especially one with a historical setting with a plot featuring the seduction of the heroine. The term is recorded from 1980, and reflects a focus of popular women's fiction which was then commercially very successful. In the 1990s the term was extended to novels with a contemporary setting, gay novels, and biographical works with sexual revelations: books in which the emphasis on sexual seduction remained, while the element of costume drama was lost, so that the ripping of the bodice was no more than notional.

bodies see also ➤ CORPORATIONS *have neither bodies to be punished nor souls to be damned*, ➤ SEVEN *bodies terrestrial*.

know where the bodies are buried have the security deriving from personal knowledge of an organization's confidential affairs and secrets.

bodkin originally, a dagger, a stiletto; this sense, obsolete from the mid 17th century, is likely still to be encountered in Shakespeare's *Hamlet* (1601) 'For who would bear the whips and scorns of time…When he himself might his quietus make With a bare bodkin?'
  Recorded from Middle English, the word may be of Celtic origin, related to Irish *bod*, Welsh *bidog*, Scottish Gaelic *biodag* 'dagger'.

Bodleian Library the library of Oxford University, one of six copyright libraries in the UK. The first library was founded in the 14th century, but was refounded by ➤ *Sir Thomas* BODLEY.

Thomas Bodley (1545–1613), English scholar and diplomat, who became a fellow of Merton College in 1564, lecturing in Greek. In 1585 he became an ambassador to Queen Elizabeth I. He refounded and greatly enlarged the Oxford University library, which was renamed the ➤ BODLEIAN in 1604.

Bodmin see ➤ BEAST *of Bodmin Moor.*

Giambattista Bodoni (1740–1813), Italian printer. He designed a typeface characterized by extreme contrast between uprights and diagonals, which is named after him.

body and soul the corporeal and spiritual entities that make up a person; the term is traditionally often used in the context of the difficulty of sustaining existence, as in 'keep body and soul together'.

body corporate a formal term for a ➤ CORPOR- ATION.

body language the conscious and unconscious movements and postures by which attitudes and feelings are communicated.

Body of Liberties the first written laws of Massachusetts, based on common law and resembling the Bill of Rights. This code of 100 basic laws was drafted by Nathaniel Ward and adopted by the General Court (December 1641). It was replaced in 1648 by *The Book of General Laws and Libertyes.*

body piercing the piercing of holes in parts of the body other than the ear lobes in order to insert rings or other decorative objects; the term became generally current in the 1980s, when the practice became fashionable.

body politic the people of a nation, state, or society considered collectively as an organized group of citizens; the term is recorded from the early 16th century.

bodyline in cricket, persistent short-pitched fast bowling on the leg side, threatening the batsman's body, especially as employed by England (and in particular, the English bowler ➤ *Harold* LARWOOD) in the Ashes series in Australia in 1932–3.

bodysnatcher a person who illicitly disinterred corpses for dissection, for which there was no legal provision until 1832, a ➤ RESURRECTION *man.*

Boeotia a region of ancient Greece, of which the chief city was Thebes, according to legend founded by ➤ CADMUS. *Boeotia* was traditionally proverbial among Athenians for the dullness and stupidity of its inhabitants, something which both Cicero and Horace attributed to the dampness of the prevailing atmosphere.

Boer a member of the Dutch and Huguenot population which settled in southern Africa in the late 17th century. The Boers were Calvinist in religion and fiercely self-sufficient. Conflict with the British administration of Cape Colony after 1806 led to the Great Trek of 1835–7 and the Boer Wars, after which the Boer republics of Transvaal and Orange Free State became part of the Republic of South Africa. The Boers' present-day descendants are the Afrikaners.

Boer Wars two wars fought by Great Britain in southern Africa between 1880 and 1902. The first war (1880–1) began with the revolt of the Boer settlers in Transvaal against British rule and ended with the establishment of an independent Boer Republic under British suzerainty. The second (1899–1902) was caused by the Boer refusal to grant equal rights to recent British immigrants and by the imperialist ambitions of Cecil Rhodes. The British eventually won through superior numbers and the employment of concentration camps to control the countryside.

Boethius (*c.*480–524), Roman statesman and philosopher, best known for *The Consolation of Philosophy,* which he wrote while in prison on a charge of treason. He argued that the soul can attain happiness in affliction by realizing the value of goodness and meditating on the reality of God.

boffin informal term for a person engaged in scientific or technical research; the word is recorded from the Second World War, and seems to have been first applied by members of the Royal Air Force to scientists working on radar, but the origin is unknown.

bog see ➤ SERBONIAN *bog.*

bog-standard ordinary or basic. The term probably comes from an alteration of *box-standard,* an informal term for a motorcycle or other mechanical device which has no modifications, but which is in the condition in which it came out of the manufacturer's box.

Humphrey Bogart (1899–1957), American actor, who made his name by playing ruthless gangsters; in later films, such as *Casablanca* (1942), he portrays characters who while still tough and ruthless, are ultimately guided by moral and heroic principles.

> Those Humphrey Bogart moments that require us to choose between striker or scab, resistance fighter or quisling.
> — *Esquire* January 1996

bogey an evil or mischievous spirit. Recorded from the mid 19th century, as a proper name for the Devil, the word is probably related to *bogle*.

In golf, *bogey* denotes a score of one stroke over par at a hole, and may come from *Bogey* (the Devil) regarded as an imaginary player.

boggart in Scotland and northern England, an evil or mischievous spirit; the word is recorded from the late 16th century, and is related to *bogey* and *bogle*.

Bogomil a member of a heretical medieval Balkan sect professing a modified form of ➤ Manichae-ism. The name is recorded from the mid 19th century, and comes from medieval Greek *Bogomilos*, from *Bogomil*, literally 'beloved of God', the name of the person who first disseminated the heresy, from Old Church Slavonic.

bogtrotter an offensive colloquial term for an Irish person; originally (in the late 17th century) designating those living in regions not subject to English rule, the *wild Irish*.

Bohemia a region forming the western part of the Czech Republic. Formerly a Slavic kingdom, it fell under Austrian rule in 1526, and became a province of the newly formed Czechoslovakia by the Treaty of Versailles in 1919.

In Shakespeare's *The Winter's Tale* (1610–11), ➤ Perdita is abandoned as an infant on the coast of Bohemia, and later marries the king's son.

From the mid 19th century, *Bohemia* was also used to designate the community of social ➤ Bohe-mians or the milieu in which they lived.

See also ➤ Queen *of Hearts*.

Bohemian a person who has informal and unconventional social habits, especially an artist or writer. The word comes (in the mid 19th century) from French *bohémien* 'gypsy', because gypsies were thought to come from ➤ Bohemia, or because they perhaps entered the West through Bohemia.

Niels Bohr (1885–1962), Danish physicist and pioneer in quantum physics. Bohr's theory of the structure of the atom incorporated quantum theory for the first time, and is the basis for present-day quantum-mechanical models. After fleeing from Nazi persecution in the 1930s Bohr helped to develop the atom bomb in Britain and then in the US. He won the Nobel Prize for Physics (1922).

boiling point the temperature at which a liquid boils and turns to vapour; in figurative usage, the point at which anger or excitement breaks out into violent expression.

Bokmål one of two standard forms of the Norwegian language, a modified form of Danish.

the Bold epithet of Philip III of France (1245–85) and Charles, Duke of Burgundy (see ➤ Charles *le Téméraire*).

to boldly go explore freely, unhindered by fear of the unknown; from the brief given to the Starship *Enterprise* in ➤ Star *Trek*:

> These are the voyages of the starship *Enterprise*. Its five-year mission . . . to boldly go where no man has gone before.
> — Gene Roddenberry *Star Trek* (television series, from 1964)

Bolingbroke surname given to Henry IV of England (1367–1413), who was born at his father's castle of *Bolingbroke* in Lincolnshire, and from this was sometimes called **Henry of Bolingbroke**.

Simón Bolívar (1783–1830), Venezuelan patriot and statesman; known as **the Liberator**. He succeeded in driving the Spanish from Venezuela, Colombia, Peru, and Ecuador, although his dream of a South American federation was never realized. Upper Peru was named *Bolivia* in his honour.

Bollandist a member of a group of Jesuits who edited the ➤ Acta *Sanctorum*, a critical edition of the lives of the saints, based on early manuscripts and first edited by John van *Bolland* (1596–1665).

Bollingen Prize in Poetry established (1948) by the Bollingen Foundation, financed by Paul Mellon and named by him for the Swiss home of the psychoanalyst Jung. The award was originally given annually for the highest achievement in American poetry issued the preceding year, but became a biennial award after 1963.

Bollinger trademark name for a type of champagne, named after the *Bollinger* family, who produce it.

Bollywood the Indian popular film industry, based in Bombay; the word is recorded from the 1970s, and is a blend of *Bombay* and *Hollywood*.

Bolognese school the school of painting centred on *Bologna* in northern Italy between the 15th and 17th centuries.

Bolshevik a member of the majority faction of the Russian Social Democratic Party, which was renamed the Communist Party after seizing power in the October Revolution of 1917. The name is Russian, from *bol'she* 'greater', with reference to the greater faction.

Bolshoi Ballet a Moscow ballet company, established since 1825 at the Bolshoi Theatre, where it staged the first production of Tchaikovsky's *Swan Lake* (1877).

Bolsover see ➤ BEAST *of Bolsover*.

bolt a short, heavy arrow shot from a crossbow, often used in proverbial phrases, such as ➤ *a* FOOL*'s bolt is soon shot*.

a bolt from the blue a sudden or unexpected piece of news, with reference to the unlikelihood of a thunderbolt coming from a clear blue sky.

bomb a container filled with explosive or incendiary material, designed to explode on impact or when detonated by a timing, proximity, or remote-control device. Recorded from the late 17th century, the word probably comes, via French and Italian, from Latin *bombus* 'booming, humming'.

From the 1950s, **the Bomb** was used, especially by campaigners for nuclear disarmament, for the atomic or hydrogen bomb.

See also ➤ BAN *the bomb*, ➤ SMART *bomb*.

Bomba nickname of Ferdinand II (1810–59), king of the ➤ Two *Sicilies* from 1830, who was given the nickname after heavy bombardment of Sicilian towns by his forces while repressing a rebellion in 1848.

bombast high-sounding language with little meaning, used to impress people. The word is recorded in this sense from the late 16th century, and has been popularly supposed to derive from the name of ➤ PARACELSUS Bombast von Hohenheim, but it in fact represents a figurative use of *bombast* denoting 'raw cotton or cotton wool used as padding', which comes ultimately (via French) from an alteration of medieval Latin *bombyx* 'silkworm'.

Bombay duck the bummalo (fish), especially when dried and eaten as an accompaniment with curries. Recorded from the mid 19th century, the phrase comes from an alteration of *bummalo* by association with *Bombay* in India, from which the fish were exported.

bombazine a twilled dress fabric of worsted and silk or cotton, especially a black kind formerly used for mourning clothes. The word (which comes via French and medieval Latin) is based ultimately on Greek *bombux* 'silkworm'.

bomber see ➤ BROWN *Bomber*.

Bon a Japanese Buddhist festival held annually in August to honour the dead; also called *Festival of the Dead* and *Lantern Festival*.

City of Bon-accord an informal Scottish name for Aberdeen; *bon-accord* in Scottish usage (from French) means 'good will, fellowship'.

Bon Gaultier the pseudonym (taken from Rabelais) under which W. E. Aytoun and T. Martin published in 1845 *A Book of Ballads*, a collection of parodies and light poems. Among the authors parodied are Tennyson and Elizabeth Barrett Browning.

Bona Dea a Roman fertility goddess (in Latin, the 'good goddess'), worshipped exclusively by women, and sometimes identified with ➤ FAUNA. It was during the festival of the *Bona Dea* that the scandal occurred that caused Caesar to divorce his wife, giving rise to the expression ➤ CAESAR*'s wife must be above suspicion*.

bona fide genuine, real. The phrase comes from Latin, and means literally 'good faith'.

bona fides a person's honesty and sincerity of intention; informally, documentary evidence showing that a person is what they claim to be; credentials. The phrase comes from Latin, and means literally 'good faith'.

bonanza a situation or event which creates a sudden increase in wealth, good fortune, or profits. Recorded from the early 19th century (originally in the US, especially with reference to success when mining) the word comes from Spanish, literally 'fair weather, prosperity', from Latin *bonus* 'good'.

Bonaparte a Corsican family including the three actual or titular rulers of France named ➤ NAPOLEON; during the Napoleonic Wars, the informal *Boney* was often used as a disparaging reference to Napoleon I.

St **Bonaventura** (1221–74), Franciscan theologian; known as **the Seraphic Doctor**. Appointed minister general of his order in 1257, he was made cardinal bishop of Albano in 1273. He wrote the official biography of St Francis and had a lasting influence as a spiritual writer.

☐ **FEAST DAY** His feast day is 15 (formerly 14) July.

bonaventure in nautical usage, former term for a lateen sail carried on an extra mizen mast, or the mast itself. Recorded from the late 15th century, the word comes ultimately from Italian *bonaventura* 'good fortune', and was commonly found as a ship's name, with its Italian meaning; the *Edward Bonaventure* was the only ship which returned safely from the first voyage of the English to Russia in 1553.

bond see ➤ *an* ENGLISHMAN's *word is his bond.*

James Bond a British secret agent in the spy novels of Ian Fleming (1908–64), and subsequently in the films based on them. *Bond*, known also by his code name 007, is noted for his daring, his sexual success, and (especially in the films) the number of gadgets with which he pursues his secret service activities.

> They could opt for a touch of the James Bond and buy a pistol disguised as a pen.
> — *Sunday Telegraph* 4 February 1996

See also ➤ M, ➤ Q, ➤ SHAKEN, *not stirred.*

Bondi a coastal resort in New South Wales, Australia, a suburb of Sydney. It is noted for its popular beach.

bone as the most lasting parts of the body, *bones* are traditionally used for 'mortal remains', as in Shakespeare's epitaph:

> Good friend, for Jesu's sake forbear
> To dig the dust enclosed here.
> Blest be the man that spares these stones,
> And curst be he that moves my bones.
> — inscription on William Shakespeare's grave at Stratford-on-Avon, probably composed by himself.

In proverbial usage, a *bone* is the type of something hard and dry.

See also ➤ DEVIL's *bones*, ➤ *a* DOG *that will fetch a bone will carry a bone*, ➤ FUNNY *bone*, ➤ HARD *words break no bones*, ➤ NAPIER's *bones*, ➤ *the* NEARER *the bone, the sweeter the meat*, ➤ RAG-*and-bone man*, ➤ RAWHEAD *and bloody bones*, ➤ *what's* BRED *in the bone will come out in the flesh*, ➤ *while two* DOGS *are fighting for a bone, the third runs away with it.*

point the bone at (of an Australian Aboriginal) cast a spell on (someone) so as to cause their sickness or death. The expression refers to an Aboriginal ritual, in which a bone is pointed at a victim.

a **bone** in her mouth water foaming before a ship's bows; the expression is recorded from the early 17th century.

bone of contention a subject or issue over which there is continuing disagreement; proverbially, a bone thrown between two dogs is the type of something which causes a quarrel.

throw the bones in southern Africa, use divining bones (a set of carved dice or bones used by traditional healers in divination) to foretell the future or discover the source of a difficulty by studying the pattern they form when thrown on the ground.

Boney a traditional English informal name for ➤ NAPOLEON *I*, used during the Napoleonic Wars.

bonfire recorded from late Middle English, the term originally denoted a large open-air fire on which *bones* were burnt (sometimes as part of a celebration), also one for burning heretics or proscribed literature. Dr Johnson in his *Dictionary* accepted the mistaken idea that the word came from French *bon* 'good'.

Dietrich Bonhoeffer (1906–45), German Lutheran theologian and pastor. He was an active opponent of Nazism both before and during the Second World War and was involved in the German resistance movement. Arrested in 1943, he was sent to Buchenwald concentration camp and later executed.

Boniface an archaic term for an innkeeper, from the name of the jovial innkeeper in Farquhar's *Beaux' Stratagem* (1707).

> I knew a burly Boniface who for many years kept a public-house in one of our rural capitals.
> — Ralph Waldo Emerson *The Conduct of Life* (1860)

St **Boniface** (680–754), Anglo-Saxon missionary, born *Wynfrith*, known as the *Apostle of Germany*. He was sent to Frisia and Germany to spread the Christian faith and was appointed Primate of Germany in 732; he was martyred in Frisia.

☐ **EMBLEM** His emblem is an axe, as the instrument of his martyrdom.

☐ **FEAST DAY** His feast day is 5 June.

bonkbuster a type of popular novel characterized by frequent explicit sexual encounters between the usually glamorous and wealthy characters. The term is recorded from the 1980s, and comes from the slang *bonk* 'an act of sexual intercourse' on the pattern of *blockbuster*.

The *bonkbuster* is likely to have a contemporary setting, its seduction scenes lacking the romanticism lent by the period setting of the ➤ BODICE-*ripper*; the characters, like those in ➤ SEX-*and-shopping* novels, tend to be glamorous and wealthy.

bonne bouche an appetizing item of food, especially something sweet eaten at the end of a meal. The phrase is French, and means literally 'a good taste in the mouth'.

bonnet a soft, round brimless hat like a beret, especially as worn by men and boys in Scotland; in heraldry, the velvet cap within a coronet. The word comes (in late Middle English, via French) from medieval Latin *abonnis* 'headgear'.

The current main sense, a woman's or child's hat tied under the chin, typically with a brim framing the face, is recorded from the late 15th century.

See also ➤ BLUE *Bonnets*, ➤ PHRYGIAN *bonnet*.

bonnet piece a gold coin of James V of Scotland, on which the sovereign is shown wearing a bonnet.

bonnet rouge the red cap worn as a symbol of liberty in the French Revolution.

William H. Bonney name of the American outlaw known as ➤ BILLY *the Kid*.

Bonnie and Clyde title of Warren Beatty's film (1967) about the 1930s American gangsters *Bonnie* Parker and her partner *Clyde* Barrow, who were eventually ambushed and shot dead at a police roadblock in 1934.

> The couple are soon on the run pursued by all and sundry—a modern day Bonnie and Clyde.
> — *Film Focus* December 1994

Bonnie Dundee nickhame of John Graham of Claverhouse, Viscount *Dundee*, Scottish royalist and Jacobite leader, killed in 1689 at the battle of Killiecrankie.

Bonnie Prince Charlie name given by his supporters to the young ➤ *Charles Edward* STUART.

boodle see ➤ *the whole* KIT *and boodle*.

boogie-woogie a style of jazz played on the piano with a strong, fast beat; the term is recorded from the early 20th century (in the US, where *boogie* meant 'party'); the ultimate origin is unknown.

Boojum an imaginary dangerous animal, invented by Lewis Carroll in his nonsense poem *The Hunting of the Snark*:

> But oh, beamish nephew, beware of the day,
> If your Snark be a Boojum! For then
> You will softly and suddenly vanish away,
> And never be met with again!
> — Lewis Carroll *The Hunting of the Snark* (1876)

The name is used allusively for an otherwise unspecified danger.

> It was long before the day of antibiotics, our modern prescription of keeping at least one sort of Boojum at bay.
> — *New York Review of Books* 15 February 1996

book a *book* is the emblem of ➤ *St* ANNE, ➤ *St* AUGUSTINE, ➤ *St* BERNARD, and other saints.

Recorded from Old English (in form *bōc*, originally meaning also 'a document or charter'), the word is of Germanic origin, and is probably related to *beech* (on which runes were carved).

See also ➤ BELL, *book, and candle*, ➤ *Book of the* DUN *Cow*, ➤ DOMESDAY *Book*, ➤ EMBLEM *book*, ➤ *a* GREAT *book is a great evil*, ➤ SIBYLLINE *books*, ➤ *a* TURN-*up for the book*, ➤ YELLOW *book*,

you can't tell a book by its cover proverbial saying, early 20th century.

the Book of Books the Bible, often with reference to its use in the administration of oaths.

Book of Canons a collection of canons enacted by early church councils, published in 1610 and probably dating from the late 4th or early 5th century.

Book of Changes English name for the ➤ I *Ching*.

Book of Common Prayer the official service book of the Church of England, compiled by Thomas Cranmer and others, first issued in 1549, and largely unchanged since the revision of 1662.

book of hours a book of prayers appointed for particular canonical hours or times of day, used by Roman Catholics for private devotions and popular especially in the Middle Ages, when they were often richly illuminated.

Book of Kells an 8th-century illuminated manuscript of the Gospels, now kept in the library of Trinity College, Dublin, and produced either in the scriptorium of Iona or at *Kells* in County Meath, where the community moved after attack by Vikings in the early 9th century.

book of life the record of those achieving salvation; originally, with biblical reference, as in Revelation 20:12, 'And I saw the dead, small and great, stand before God; and the books were opened: and another book was opened, which is the book of life.'

In South Africa, the *Book of Life* is a name given to the comprehensive personal identity document, introduced originally for whites only (in general use since 1986).

Book of the Dead a collection of ancient Egyptian religious and magical texts, selections from which were often written on or placed in tombs.

The name (in full **Tibetan Book of the Dead**) is also given to a Tibetan Buddhist text recited during funerary rites, describing the passage from death to rebirth.

Booker Prize a literary prize awarded annually for a novel published by a British or Commonwealth citizen during the previous year, financed by the multinational company Booker McConnell.

bookkeepers ➤ *St* Matthew, as a tax-collector is the patron saint of bookkeepers and those who keep financial records.

bookland in Anglo-Saxon England, an area of common land granted by written charter (*bōc* or book) to a private owner.

Books of Discipline two documents, adopted in 1561 and 1581 respectively, constituting the original standards of the polity and government of the Reformed Church of Scotland, and also dealing with schools, universities, and other matters.

booksellers ➤ *St* John *of God* is the patron saint of booksellers.

Booksellers' Row a name that was given to the old Holywell Street, which ran parallel to the Strand between St Clement Dane's and St Dunstan's, before the formation of the Aldwych at the end of the 19th century; so called from the number of second-hand booksellers that had shops there.

bookworm a person who seems to find their chief sustenance in reading, and is always poring over books; the word in this sense is recorded from the early 17th century, while the literal use meaning, the larva of a wood-boring beetle which feeds on the paper and glue in books, is not recorded until the mid 19th century.

George Boole (1815–64), English mathematician, responsible for ➤ Boolean algebra. The study of mathematical or symbolic logic developed mainly from his ideas.

Boolean denoting a system of algebraic notation used to represent logical propositions by means of the binary digits 0 (false) and 1 (true), especially in computing and electronics.

boomer see ➤ baby *boomer*.

boomerang a curved flat piece of wood that can be thrown so as to return to the thrower, traditionally used by Australian Aboriginals as a hunting weapon.

boon companion a close friend with whom one enjoys spending time. The expression is recorded from the mid 16th century, originally in the sense 'good fellow' denoting a drinking companion; *boon* comes (via French) from Latin *bonus* 'good'.

boondoggle an unnecessary, wasteful, or fraudulent project. The term, which is recorded from the 1930s, is of unknown origin.

Daniel Boone (*c*.1734–1820), American pioneer. Boone made trips west from Pennsylvania into the unexplored area of Kentucky, organizing settlements and successfully defending them against hostile American Indians.

Betty Boop the heroine of a number of short cartoon films produced by Max Fleischer (1883–1972), and appearing in a newspaper strip from 1934; she was wide-eyed, dressed in skimpy clothing, and had a garter on her left leg. She was said to have been based on a popular singer of the 1920s, Helen Kane, known for adding 'boop-boop-a-doop' when singing 'I Wanna be Loved by You'.

> In the self-animating conceit of being poised between one kind of reality and another, the characters are like Betty Boop.
>
> — *New Yorker* 5 June 1989

boot see also ➤ bale *is highest when boot is nighest.*

boot a boot is the emblem of the English priest John Schorne (d. *c*.1315), centre of a popular cult, who was said to have trapped the Devil in his boot.

See also ➤ Puss *in Boots*, ➤ seven-*leagued boots.*

boot and saddle a cavalry signal to mount, from an alteration of French *boute-selle* 'place-saddle'.

Boötes a northern constellation (the Herdsman), said to represent a man holding the leash of two dogs (Canes Venatici) while driving a bear (Ursa Major). It contains the bright star Arcturus.

John Wilkes Booth (1838–65), American actor and assassin of ➤ *Abraham* LINCOLN, who shot the president in Ford's Theatre, Washington, DC. Booth initially escaped, but was pursued to Virginia, where he refused to surrender and was shot dead.

It was reported that, having shot Lincoln, Booth exclaimed '*Sic semper tyrannis*! The South is avenged', although the second part of the statement does not appear in any contemporary source, and is possibly apocryphal.

William Booth (1829–1912), English religious leader, founder and first general of the Salvation Army. A Methodist revivalist preacher, he worked actively to improve the condition of the poor, attending to both their physical and spiritual needs. In 1865 he established a mission in the East End of London which later became the Salvation Army.

In his book *In Darkest England* (1890), Booth coined the phrase the ➤ SUBMERGED *tenth* for that part of the population living permanently in poverty.

bootlegger a smuggler of liquor. The word is recorded from the late 19th century, and comes from the smugglers' practice of concealing bottles in their boots.

bootless archaic term meaning (of a task or undertaking) ineffectual, useless; the word represents Old English *bōtlēas* 'not able to be compensated for by payment'.

Boots Library a circulating library established at the end of the 19th century by Nottingham businessman and philanthropist Jesse Boot (1850–1931). Unlike Mudie's it catered largely for provincial and suburban subscribers, and by the mid-1930s was the largest of its kind, with over 400 branches; in Betjeman's poem, it epitomizes middle-class England:

> Think of what our Nation stands for,
> Books from Boots' and country lanes.
> — John Betjeman 'In Westminster Abbey' (1940)

Lizzie Borden took an axe
And gave her mother forty whacks;
When she saw what she had done
She gave her father forty-one!
popular rhyme in circulation after the acquittal of

Lizzie *Borden*, in June 1893, from the charge of murdering her father and stepmother at Fall River, Massachusetts on 4 August 1892.

the Border the boundary and adjoining districts between Scotland and England, which especially between the 15th and the 17th centuries was a lawless area requiring particular management. The term seems to have originated in Scotland, where the border with England, being the only one it had, became known as *the* border. The political importance of the Border disappeared after James VI of Scotland inherited the English crown in 1603.

Border States in the US, an informal name for Delaware, Maryland, Virginia, Kentucky, and Missouri.

Boreas in Roman and Greek mythology, the god of the north wind.

Borgia the family name of Rodrigo *Borgia* (1431–1503), later Pope Alexander VI, and his illegitimate children Cesare and Lucrezia; their traditional reputation was for ruthless ambition, and they were popularly believed to be skilled in poisoning.

> Pope Innocent X was not a nice man, he was something of a Borgian figure.
> — *Guardian* 12 October 1996

Cesare Borgia (*c.*1476–1507), Italian statesman, cardinal, and general. The illegitimate son of Cardinal Rodrigo Borgia (later Pope Alexander VI) and brother of Lucrezia Borgia, he was captain general of the papal army from 1499, and became master of a large portion of central Italy until he was defeated at Naples in 1504. Machiavelli takes him in *The Prince* as the model of a successful ruler.

> I'm . . . so dismissive of consensus-building and cooperation that I make Cesare Borgia look like a softy.
> — *Saturday Night* October 1995

Lucrezia Borgia (1480–1519), Italian noblewoman, sister of Cesare Borgia. She married three times, according to the political alliances useful to her family; after her third marriage in 1501 she established herself as a patron of the arts.

bork obstruct (someone, especially a candidate for public office) by systematically defaming or vilifying them. The word comes from the name of Robert *Bork* (born 1927), an American judge whose nomination to the Supreme Court (1987) was rejected following unfavourable publicity for his allegedly extreme views.

Martin Borman (1900–*c*.1945), German Nazi politician, who succeeded Hess as Party chancellor in 1941. Considered to be Hitler's closest collaborator, he disappeared at the end of the Second World War; he was sentenced to death *in absentia* at the Nuremberg trials in 1945. His skeleton, exhumed in Berlin, was identified in 1973.

born see also ➤ *born on the wrong side of the* BLANKET, ➤ *born within sound of* Bow *Bells*, ➤ *a* POET *is born, not made*, ➤ *to the* MANNER *born*.

born in the purple born into an imperial or royal family as a ➤ PORPHYROGENITE; ➤ PURPLE was originally the dye used for fabric worn by an emperor or senior magistrate in Rome or Byzantium.

if you're **born** to be hanged then you'll never be drowned proverbial saying, late 16th century; mid 14th century in French.

born under a lucky star naturally fortunate; a proverbial phrase reflecting belief in planetary influences on one's fortunes.

born with a silver spoon in one's mouth born in affluence; a traditional phrase which in the 20th century was notably reworked by the American Democratic politician Ann Richards on President George Bush, 'he was born with a silver foot in his mouth.'

Borobudur a Buddhist monument in central Java, built *c*.800. It consists of five square successively smaller terraces, one above the other, surmounted by three galleries and a stupa.

Battle of Borodino a battle in 1812 at Borodino, a village to the west of Moscow, at which Napoleon's forces defeated the Russian army under Prince Kutuzov (1745–1813). This allowed the French to advance to Moscow, but the heavy losses that they suffered at Borodino contributed to their eventual defeat; ➤ TALLEYRAND, on hearing of the outcome, is said to have commented, 'This is the beginning of the end.'

borough a town (as distinct from a city) with a corporation and privileges granted by royal charter; formerly, a town sending representatives to Parliament. From the late 18th century **the Borough** was used for Southwark in London.

Originally (in Old English, in form *burg*, *burh*) the word meant a fortress, a fortified town; later, a town, district or large village with some form of municipal organization.

See also ➤ POCKET *borough*, ➤ ROTTEN *borough*.

borough-English in medieval England, tenure whereby the youngest son of a family inherited all lands and tenements; the term is a partial translation of Anglo-Norman French *tenure en Burgh Engloys* 'tenure in (an) English borough', and according to Blackstone, it was so named because it was a custom which prevailed in certain boroughs, and it was English as distinguished from French.

Francesco Borromini (1599–1667), Italian architect, who worked mostly in Rome; his buildings include the churches of S. Carlo alle Quattro Fontane (1641) and S. Ivo della Sapienza (1643–60). A leading figure of the Italian baroque, especially influential in Austria and southern Germany, he used subtle architectural forms and much sculptural decoration.

borrow take and use something that belongs to someone else with the intention of returning it; originally, take something on security given for its safe return.

George Borrow (1803–81), English writer. His travels in England, Europe, Russia, and the Far East, sometimes in the company of gypsies provided material for the picaresque narrative *Lavengro* (1851) and its sequel *The Romany Rye* (1857).

borrowed days in Scottish tradition, the last three days of March (Old Style), said to have been borrowed from April and to be particularly stormy; in Cheshire, the *borrowed days* referred to the first eleven days of May, and were so called because in Old Style they would have belonged to April.

See also ➤ MARCH *borrowed from April three days, and they were ill*.

borrowed plumes a borrowed display likely to make the wearer appear pretentious or laughable, often with reference to the fable in which the jay or jackdaw assumes the peacock's plumes.

borrowed time an unexpected extension of time, especially of one's span of life; the expression **living on borrowed time** is recorded from the late 19th century.

the Borrowers central characters in a series of children's stories by Mary Norton, beginning with *The Borrowers* (1952); they are a family of tiny people who live under the floorboards in an old house and survive by 'borrowing' objects from the household (the 'human beans') overhead, and their survival undiscovered by those on whom their way of life depends is constantly perilous.

he that goes a-borrowing goes a-sorrowing proverbial saying, late 15th century.

Borscht Belt a resort area in the Catskill Mountains, in the state of New York, frequented chiefly by Jewish people of eastern European origin.

Borsetshire the county in which the long-running radio soap opera ➤ *the* ARCHERS is set; the county town is *Borchester*, and the name is an alteration of ➤ BARSETSHIRE.

borstal former custodial institution for young offenders, named after the village of *Borstal* in southern England, where the first of these was established.

Hieronymus Bosch (*c.*1450–1516), Dutch painter. Bosch's highly detailed works are typically crowded with half-human, half-animal creatures and grotesque demons in settings symbolic of sin and folly. His individual style prefigures that of the surrealists.

> His larger canvases . . . anticipate more of a Boschian inferno than Elysian fields.
> — *Church Times* 22 January 1999

bosh something regarded as absurd or untrue; nonsense. Recorded from the mid 19th century, the word comes from Turkish *boş* 'empty, worthless', and was originally popularized by the frequency of its occurrence in the novel *Ayesha* (1834) by the traveller and writer James Morier.

Boskop a town in South Africa, in North-West Province, where a skull fossil was found in 1913. The fossil is undated and morphologically shows no primitive features. At the time this find was regarded as representative of a distinct 'Boskop race' but is now thought to be related to the San–Nama (Bushman–Hottentot) types.

Bosnian of or belonging to Bosnia-Herzegovina, a former constituent republic of Yugoslavia, which declared independence in 1992. Ethnic conflict among Croats, Muslims, and Serbs quickly reduced the republic to a state of civil war, and the terms **Bosnian Muslims** and **Bosnian Serbs** to distinguish the chief antagonists were increasingly heard.

bosom see also ➤ VIPER *in one's bosom*.

bosom friend a specially intimate or dear friend; the term is recorded from the late 16th century.

Bosporus a strait connecting the Black Sea with the Sea of Marmara, and separating Europe from the Anatolian peninsula of western Asia; Istanbul (originally Byzantium and then Constantinople) is located at its south end. Its name, meaning 'cow's passage', is said to derive from the legend that ➤ Io crossed it in her flight from Hera's vengeance.

Boston the state capital of Massachusetts, founded *c.*1630 and named after Boston in Lincolnshire; its traditional profile of social exclusivity was summed up in a verse by the American oculist John Collins Bossidy (1860–1928):

> And this is good old Boston,
> The home of the bean and the cod,
> Where the Lowells talk to the Cabots
> And the Cabots talk only to God.
> — John Collins Bossidy verse spoken at Holy Cross College alumni dinner in Boston, Massachusetts, 1910, in *Springfield Sunday Republican* 14 December 1924

See also ➤ BRAHMIN, ➤ PROPER *Bostonian*.

Boston Athenaeum association of Boston literary men, founded in 1805 as an outgrowth of the ➤ ANTHOLOGY *Club* and modelled on the Liverpool Athenaeum of England.

Boston Stump informal name for the church tower of Boston, Lincolnshire, perhaps because, although lofty and a conspicuous sea-mark, it has no spire.

Boston Tea Party a violent demonstration in 1773 by American colonists prior to the War of American Independence. Colonists boarded vessels in Boston harbour and threw the cargoes of tea into the water in protest at the imposition of a tax on tea by the British Parliament, in which the colonists had no representation.

James Boswell (1740–95), Scottish author, companion and biographer of Samuel Johnson. He is known for *Journal of a Tour to the Hebrides* (1785), which describes his travels with Samuel Johnson in 1773, and for *The Life of Samuel Johnson* (1791), which gives a vivid and intimate portrait of Johnson and an invaluable panorama of the age and its personalities. His name may be used to designate a person who, as a constant companion or attendant, witnesses and records the life of another.

See also ➤ LUES *Boswelliana*.

Bosworth Field a battle of the Wars of the Roses fought in 1485 near Market Bosworth in Leicestershire. Henry Tudor defeated and killed the Yorkist king ➤ RICHARD *III*, enabling him to take the throne as Henry VII.

botanomancy divination by means of plants.

Botany Bay an inlet of the Tasman Sea in New South Wales, Australia, just south of Sydney, which was the site of Captain James Cook's landing in 1770 and of an early British penal settlement.

It was named by Cook after the large variety of plants collected there by his companion, Sir Joseph Banks.

> The loss of America what can repay?
> New colonies seek for at Botany Bay.
> — John Freeth 'Botany Bay' in *New London Magazine* (1786)

Botany wool merino wool, especially from Australia; named after ➤ BOTANY *Bay*, from which the wool originally came.

bothy in Scotland, a small hut or cottage, especially one for housing farm labourers or for use as a mountain refuge. Recorded from the late 18th century, the word is obscurely related to Irish and Scottish Gaelic *both*, *bothan*, and perhaps to *booth*.

botony in heraldry, (of a cross) having the end ornamented with three projections like buds.

Sandro Botticelli (1445–1510), Italian painter, who worked in Renaissance Florence under the patronage of the Medicis. Botticelli is best known for his mythological works such as *Primavera* (*c*.1478) and *The Birth of Venus* (*c*.1480). His work was neglected until the 19th century, when it had a significant influence on the Pre-Raphaelites.

> Her thin brown hair would've been mousy on another girl, but it accentuated her Botticellian frailty.
> — *Esquire* February 1994

bottle a glass or plastic container, characteristically with a narrow neck, used for storing drinks or other liquids. Recorded from late Middle English, the word originally denoted a leather bottle, and comes via Old French from medieval Latin *butticula*, diminutive of 'cask, wineskin'.

See also ➤ PILGRIM *bottle*.

bottom drawer household linen stored by a woman in preparation for her marriage, originally as in the lowest drawer of a chest of drawers; the term is recorded from the late 19th century. A corresponding US term was a ➤ HOPE *chest*.

Bottom the Weaver in Shakespeare's *A Midsummer Night's Dream* (1595–6), the blustering leader of the mechanicals to whom Puck gives an ass's head and with whom ➤ TITANIA, enchanted by a magic herb, falls in love.

> It almost touched her—not in the way of love but of gratitude. He was still to her like Bottom with the ass's head, or the Newfoundland dog gambolling out of water.
> — Anthony Trollope *Ayala's Angel* (1881)

bottomless pit an unfathomable place, Hell; in Revelation 9:11, ➤ ABADDON is called 'the angel of the bottomless pit'.

Boudicca (d. AD 62), a queen of the Britons, ruler of the Iceni tribe in eastern England; also known as **Boadicea**. Boudicca led her forces in revolt against the Romans and sacked Colchester, St Albans, and London before being defeated by the Roman governor Suetonius Paulinus.

bouget in heraldry, an ancient water vessel consisting of a yoke with two leather pouches or skins attached.

bough see ➤ KISSING *bough*.

Boulangist in 19th-century France, a member of a political party formed by General Georges E. J. M. Boulanger (1837–91), advocating a policy of anti-German militarism.

boulle brass, tortoiseshell, or other material cut to make a pattern and used for inlaying furniture. The name comes (in the early 19th century) from French *boule*, from the name of André Charles *Boulle* (1642–1732), French cabinetmaker. The variant *buhl* is apparently a modern Germanized spelling.

bouncing bomb the bomb designed by ➤ *Barnes* WALLIS and used in the ➤ DAMBUSTERS' *raid* on the Ruhr valley dams; the bomb when dropped was designed to bounce along the surface of the water before impacting on the dam itself.

bounds see ➤ BEAT *the bounds*.

bountiful see ➤ LADY *Bountiful*.

bounty see ➤ MUTINY *on the Bounty*.

Nicolas Bourbaki a pseudonym of a group of mathematicians, mainly French, attempting to give a complete account of the foundations of pure mathematics. Their first publication was in 1939.

The group was named, humorously, after a defeated French general of the Franco-Prussian War (1870–1).

Bourbon the surname of a branch of the royal family of France. The Bourbons ruled France from

1589, when Henry IV succeeded to the throne, until the monarchy was overthrown in 1848, and reached the peak of their power under Louis XIV in the late 17th century. Members of this family have also been kings of Spain (1700–1931, and since 1975).

➤ TALLEYRAND is said to have commented of the Bourbons in exile, during the Napoleonic period, 'They have learnt nothing, and forgotten nothing' (a similar remark was made by the French general Charles François du Périer Dumouriez in 1795 of the courtiers surrounding the exiled Louis XVIII).

bourbon a kind of American whisky distilled from maize and rye, named after *Bourbon* County, Kentucky.

bourgeois see ➤ ÉPATER *les bourgeois*.

Bourke see ➤ BACK *of Bourke*.

bourn a destination, a goal; in poetic usage, a realm. Originally (in the early 16th century) the word meant a boundary between fields, a frontier; it seems likely that the later senses developed from interpretations of Shakespeare's *Hamlet* 'Something after death—The undiscover'd country, from whose bourn No traveller returns'.

boustrophedon of written words, from right to left and from left to right in alternate lines. Recorded from the early 17th century, the word comes from Greek, and means literally 'as an ox turns in ploughing', from *bous* 'ox' + *-strophos* 'turning'.

bovarism domination by an unreal or romantic conception of oneself, from the name of the principal character of Flaubert's *Madame Bovary* (1857).

Bovril a trademark term for a concentrated essence of beef diluted with hot water to make a drink. The word comes (in the late 19th century) from Latin *bos, bov-* 'ox'; the second element may represent *vril*, an imaginary form of energy described in E. Bulwer-Lytton's novel *The Coming Race* (1871).

bow see also ➤ *bow of* PROMISE, ➤ CUPID's *bow*, ➤ ULYSSES' *bow*.

Clara Bow 1905–65), American actress and one of the most popular stars and sex symbols of the 1920s, who was known as the 'It Girl'.

born within sound of Bow Bells born within City bounds, ➤ COCKNEY; the bells referred to are those of Bow Church or St Mary-le-Bow, formerly St Mary of the Arches, in Cheapside, London, so

called from the 'bows' or arches supporting its steeple.

bow down in the house of Rimmon pay lip-service to a principle, sacrifice one's principles for the sake of conformity; originally with reference to 2 Kings 5:18, the verse in which ➤ NAAMAN, believing in the God of Israel who had healed him, explained to Elijah that he must still accompany his master the king of Syria to the temple of ➤ RIMMON, and thus 'bow myself in the house of Rimmon'.

Bow Street Runner the popular name for a London policeman during the first half of the 19th century; *Bow Street* in London, near Covent Garden, is the site of the principal metropolitan police court. The *Bow Street Runners* were nicknamed *Redbreasts* for the bright scarlet waistcoats they habitually wore.

bow-wow an imitation of a dog's bark; Boswell in his *Journal of a Tour to the Hebrides* (1785) referred to 'Dr. Johnson's…bow-wow way' as characteristic of the way in which his memorable sayings were delivered, and in 1826 Sir Walter Scott, comparing himself with Jane Austen, said, 'the Big Bow-Wow strain I can do myself like any now going; but the exquisite touch, which renders ordinary commonplace things and characters interesting…is denied to me.'

bow-wow theory in the 19th century, a derogatory term for the theory that human speech originated in animal sounds.

bowdlerize remove material that is considered improper or offensive from (a text), especially with the result that the text becomes weaker or less effective. The word comes from the name of Dr Thomas *Bowdler* (1754–1825), who published an expurgated edition of Shakespeare in 1818.

> It certainly is my wish, and it has been my study, to exclude from this publication whatever is unfit to be read aloud by a gentleman to a company of ladies.
> — Thomas Bowdler preface to *The Family Shakespeare* (1818)

bowels of mercy innate compassion; the *bowels* were traditionally regarded as the seat of tender and sympathetic emotions, as in Colossians 3:12, 'Put on therefore, as the elect of God…bowels of mercies, kindness, humbleness of mind.'

Bowery a street and district in New York associated with drunks and vagrants. The name derives from the fact that it once ran through Peter

Stuyvesant's farm, or *bouwerie*, as it was called by the Dutch settlers.

Jim Bowie (1789–1836), American frontiersman; full name **James Bowie**. He shared command of the garrison that resisted the Mexican attack on the Alamo, where he died.

> The traditional values upheld by Santa Anna . . . are closer to the Buchanan brigades than the values of live-and-let-live Texans like Jim Bowie.
> — *New York Times* 19 August 1992

bowie knife a long knife with a blade double-edged at the point, named after ➤ *Jim* BOWIE.

bowl see ➤ GOLDEN *bowl*.

bowler a man's hard felt hat with a round dome-shaped crown, which since the 1920s has been a symbol of civilian life after retirement from the army; the name comes (in the mid 19th century) from William *Bowler*, the English hatter who de-signed it in 1850.

those who play at bowls must look out for rubbers proverbial saying, mid 18th century; a *rubber* here is an alteration of *rub*, an obstacle or im-pediment to the course of a bowl.

bowstring the string of an archer's bow, trad-itionally made of three strands of hemp, and in Ot-toman Turkey used for strangling offenders.

box see ➤ BLACK *box*, ➤ CHRISTMAS *box*, ➤ *the* DIS-PATCH *Box*, ➤ *in the* WRONG *box*, ➤ PANDORA*'s box*.

Box and Cox used to refer to an arrangement whereby people or things make use of the same ac-commodation or facilities at different times, accord-ing to a strict arrangement. The expression comes from the title of a play (1847) by J. M. Morton, in which two characters, John *Box* and James *Cox*, un-knowingly become tenants of the same room.

box-day in Scotland, a day appointed in the Court of Session for the lodgement of papers ordered to be deposited in the Court.

box the compass recite the compass points in cor-rect order; the phrase is recorded from the mid 18th century, and box may come from Spanish *bojar* 'sail round', from Middle Low German *bōgen* 'bend', from the base of *bow*.

Boxer[1] a member of a fiercely nationalistic Chinese secret society which flourished in the 19th century. In 1899 the society led a Chinese uprising against Western domination which was eventually crushed

by a combined European force, aided by Japan and the US. The name translates Chinese *yì hé quán*, lit-erally 'righteous harmony fists'.

Boxer[2] in Orwell's *Animal Farm* (1945), the name of the carthorse who is a type of simple and hard-working loyalty (his credo is 'I must work harder'), but who is rewarded by being sent to the knacker's when no longer physically able to work.

Boxgrove man a fossil hominid of the Middle Pleistocene period, whose fragmentary remains were found at *Boxgrove* near Chichester, SE Eng-land, in 1993 and 1995. Dated (controversially) to about 500,000 years ago, it is one of the earliest known humans in Europe.

Boxing Day the first day (strictly, the first week-day) after Christmas day, on which Christmas-boxes were traditionally given.

boy see also ➤ BLUE *for a boy*, ➤ OLD *boy network*.

boy bishop one of the choirboys formerly elected at the annual 'Feast of Boys' in certain cathedrals, to walk in a procession of the boys to the altar of the Innocents or of the Holy Trinity, and perform the office on the eve and day of the Holy Innocents, the boys occupying the canons' stalls in the cathedral during the service. Provision for this is made in the Sarum Office.

The custom dates from the 13th century, and lasted until the Reformation. Boy bishops were ap-pointed also in religious houses and in schools.

you can take the boy out of the country but you can't take the country out of the boy pro-verbial saying, mid 20th century.

never send a boy to do a man's job proverbial saying, mid 20th century.

boyar a member of the old aristocracy in Russia, next in rank to a prince. Recorded in English from the late 16th century, the word comes from Russian *boyarin* 'grandee'.

boycott withdraw from commercial or social rela-tions with (a country, organization, or person) as a punishment or protest, from the name of Captain Charles C. *Boycott* (1832–97), an Irish land agent so treated in 1880, in an attempt instigated by the Irish Land League to get rents reduced. The practice was described, in detail, in a speech by the nationalist leader ➤ *Charles Stewart* PARNELL (1846–91):

> When a man takes a farm from which another has been evicted, you must show him on the roadside when you meet him; you must show him in the streets of the town; you must show him in the fair and the market-place; and even in the house of worship, by leaving him severely alone—by putting him into a moral Coventry, by isolating him from his kind as if he were a leper of old.
> — Charles Stewart Parnell speech, 19 September 1880

Robert Boyle (1627–91), Irish-born scientist. A founder member of the Royal Society, Boyle put forward a view of matter based on particles which was a precursor of the modern theory of chemical elements. He is best known for his experiments with the air pump, which led to the law named after him.

Boyle's law a law stating that the pressure of a given mass of an ideal gas is inversely proportional to its volume at a constant temperature.

Battle of the Boyne a battle fought near the River Boyne in Ireland in 1690, in which the Protestant army of William of Orange, the newly crowned William III, defeated the Catholic army (including troops from both France and Ireland) led by the recently deposed James II. The battle is celebrated annually (on 12 July) in Northern Ireland as a victory for the Protestant cause.

boys ➤ *St* NICHOLAS *of Myra* and the 16th-century Italian Jesuit St Aloysius Gonzaga (1568–91), noted for his early piety, are the patron saints of boys.

two boys are half a boy, and three boys are no boy at all proverbial saying, mid 20th century; meaning that the more boys there are present, the less work will be done.

three boys in a tub three boys in a tub is the emblem of ➤ *St* NICHOLAS *of Myra*.

boys will be boys proverbial saying, early 17th century.

Boys' Brigade the oldest of the national organizations for boys in Britain, founded in 1883 with the aim of promoting 'Christian manliness', discipline, and self-respect. Companies are now also found in the US and in Commonwealth countries; each is connected with a church.

Boz the pseudonym used by Charles Dickens in his *Pickwick Papers* and contributions to the *Morning Chronicle*; in his preface to the Pickwick Papers (1847), Dickens explained that he had taken the name from a younger brother's mispronunciation of the nickname 'Moses'.

Bozzy nickname of the Scottish author and biographer ➤ *James* BOSWELL (1740–95).

La Brabançonne the national anthem of Belgium, 'The Song of Brabant', originally written in the nationalist revolt of 1830, which established the independence of Belgium from the Netherlands. The song was first written in French by the Belgian actor Jenneval (Louis-Alexandre Dechet); the current Flemish version was written in 1860 by Charles Rogier (1800–85). The music was composed by François van Campenhout (1779–1848).

Brabant a former duchy in western Europe, lying between the Meuse and Scheldt Rivers, the capital of which was Brussels; it is now divided into two provinces in two countries: North Brabant in the Netherlands, of which the capital is 's-Hertogenbosch; and Brabant in Belgium, of which the capital remains Brussels.

Bradbury a term for the former one-pound note, from the name of John S. *Bradbury*, British Secretary to the Treasury, 1913–19.

James Bradley (1693–1762), English astronomer. Bradley was appointed Astronomer Royal in 1742. He discovered the aberration of light and also observed the oscillation of the earth's axis, which he termed *nutation*. His star catalogue was published posthumously.

Bradshaw a timetable of all passenger trains in Britain, issued 1839–1961. It was named after its first publisher, George *Bradshaw* (1801–53), printer and engraver. In Conan Doyle's *The Valley of Fear* (1915) Sherlock Holmes noted it as one of the 'standardized books which anyone may be supposed to possess'; he concluded, however, that it was otherwise unsuitable for conveying a coded message:

> The vocabulary of Bradshaw is nervous and terse, but limited. The selection of words would hardly lend itself to the sending of general messages.
> — Arthur Conan Doyle *The Valley of Fear* (1915)

Brag is a good dog, but Holdfast is better proverbial saying, late 16th century; meaning that perseverance is a better quality than ostentation.

Braganza the dynasty that ruled Portugal from 1640 until the end of the monarchy in 1910 and Brazil (on its independence from Portugal) from 1822 until the formation of a republic in 1889.

braggadocio boastful or arrogant behaviour. The word comes (in the late 16th century) from

Braggadocchio, the name of a braggart in Spenser's *Faerie Queene*.

Bragi in Scandinavian mythology, the god of poetry.

Tycho Brahe (1546–1601), Danish astronomer. He built an observatory equipped with precision instruments, but despite demonstrating that comets follow sun-centred paths he adhered to a geocentric view of the planets.

Brahma the creator god in Hinduism, who forms a triad with Vishnu and Shiva. Brahma was an important god of late Vedic religion, but has been little worshipped since the 5th century AD and has only one major temple dedicated to him in India today.

Brahman a member of the highest Hindu caste, that of the priesthood.

Brahmana in Hinduism, any of the lengthy commentaries on the Vedas, composed in Sanskrit *c.*900–700 BC and containing expository material relating to Vedic sacrificial ritual.

Brahmanism the complex sacrificial religion that emerged in post-Vedic India (*c.*900 BC) under the influence of the dominant priesthood (Brahmans), an early stage in the development of Hinduism. It was largely as a reaction to Brahman orthodoxy that religions such as Buddhism and Jainism were formed.

Brahmin a socially or culturally superior person, especially one from New England, and in particular ➤ BOSTON.

> Boston Brahmins are not described in bodily terms at all.
> — *Raritan* Spring 1990

Braille a form of written language for the blind, in which characters are represented by patterns of raised dots that are felt with the fingertips, developed by ➤ *Louis* BRAILLE.

Louis Braille (1809–52), French educationist. Blind from the age of 3, by the age of 15 he had developed his own system of raised-point reading and writing, which was immediately accepted by his fellow students at the Institute des Jeunes Aveugles in Paris, and which was officially adopted two years after his death.

brain drain the emigration of highly trained or qualified people from a particular country; the term was used particularly in the UK in the 1960s in relation to scientists moving to the US.

Brainiac a superintelligent alien character of the 1950s ➤ SUPERMAN comic strip. The name represents a blend of *brain* and *maniac*.

In North America, *brainiac* is used informally for an exceptionally intelligent person.

brains trust a group of experts who give impromptu answers to questions on topics of general or current interest in front of an audience or on the radio.

The name *Brain Trust* was given in 1933 to a group of experts appointed to advise the US president Franklin Roosevelt on political and economic matters; from the 1940s in Britain, the *Brains Trust* referred to a BBC (radio) programme.

brainstorm a moment in which one is suddenly unable to think clearly or act sensibly; a spontaneous group discussion to produce ideas and ways of solving problems. *Brainstorm*, according to the context, can mean either an attack on the brain, by which its functions are disturbed, or an attack by the brain which successfully concentrates those functions on a given problem.

brainwash pressurize (someone) into adopting radically different beliefs by using systematic and often forcible means; the term is recorded from the 1950s, and was particularly associated with the activities of totalitarian, and especially Communist, states.

brainwave an electrical impulse in the brain; a sudden clever idea. The term is recorded from the mid 19th century, originally as a technical term.

Joseph Bramah (1748–1814), English inventor. One of the most influential engineers of the Industrial Revolution, Bramah is best known for his hydraulic press, used for heavy forging. His other inventions included machine tools, a beer engine, a machine for numbering banknotes, and a water closet.

Bramantip a mnemonic of scholastic philosophers, A indicating a universal affirmative proposition, I a particular affirmative proposition.

bramble a prickly scrambling shrub of the rose family, especially a ➤ BLACKBERRY; in traditional belief, it was lucky to pass under a shoot of bramble which had rooted at both ends.

Matthew Bramley an English butcher in whose garden the English cooking apple now named after him is said to have first grown, *c.*1850.

Bran[1] in Welsh mythology, a king of the island of Britain who, when mortally wounded, ordered that his head should be cut off and kept as it would have miraculous powers; the oracular head was said to have been buried in London, where (until dug up) it was a protection against invasion. The name *Bran* means 'raven'.

Bran[2] in James Macpherson's epic poem (1763) about the legendary hero ➤ FINGAL, the name of the hero's dog; a proverbial use of the name, 'If it be not Bran, it is Bran's brother', is recorded in Walter Scott's novel *Waverley* (1814).

branch see ➤ RED *Branch*, ➤ ROOT *and branch*.

Constantin Brancusi (1876–1957), Romanian sculptor, who spent much of his working life in France. His sculpture represents an attempt to move away from a representational art and to capture the essence of forms by reducing them to their ultimate, almost abstract, simplicity.

a **brand from the burning** a rescued person, a convert; originally with biblical allusion, as to Amos 4:11, 'ye were as a firebrand plucked out of the burning', and Zechariah 3:2, 'is this not a brand plucked out of the fire?'

brand new completely or conspicuously new; the term is recorded from the late 16th century, and means 'as if fresh and glowing from the furnace'.

Brand X a name used for an unidentified brand contrasted unfavourably with a product of the same type which is being promoted; the term is recorded from the 1930s.

Brandenburg Gate one of the city gates of Berlin (built 1788–91), the only one that survives. After the construction of the ➤ BERLIN *Wall* in 1961 it stood in East Berlin, a conspicuous symbol of a divided city. It was reopened in December 1989.

> The Wall was down, the borders open and the *Sekt* flowed freely as half a million people celebrated at the Brandenburg Gate.
>
> — *Twenty Twenty* Spring 1991

Brands Hatch a motor-racing circuit near Farningham in Kent.

branks an instrument of punishment for a scolding woman, consisting of an iron framework for the head and a sharp metal gag for restraining the

tongue. Recorded from the mid 16th century, the origin of the word is uncertain; it may be compared with German *Pranger* 'a pillory or bit for a horse' or Dutch *prang* 'a fetter'.

Georges Braque (1882–1963), French painter. His collages, which introduced commercial lettering and fragmented objects into pictures to contrast the real with the 'illusory' painted image, were the first stage in the development of synthetic cubism.

Brasenose College a college of Oxford University, properly the 'King's Hall and College of Brasenose', which was granted its charter in 1509, replacing an earlier hall. In the 14th century a number of the students had moved to Stamford, where they lived in 'Brasenose Hall', on the door of which was a bronze knocker in the shape of an animal mask with a large snout (the 'brazen nose'). The knocker, which was acquired by the College in 1890, is probably the origin of the Hall's name, although it has been suggested that the origin is actually Latin *brasinium* 'brewery'.

brass a yellow alloy of copper and zinc; the word is recorded from Old English (in form *bræs*),but is of unknown origin. *Brass* is traditionally taken as a type of hardness or insensitivity; impudence, effrontery, nerve.

Formerly (from late Middle English to the late 18th century), *brass* was used for copper or bronze coin; from the late 16th century, it has been used informally to mean 'cash'.

In the UK, the word also denotes a memorial, typically a medieval one, consisting of a flat piece of inscribed brass, laid in the floor or set into the wall of a church.

See also ➤ BRAZEN, ➤ CORINTHIAN *brass*, ➤ *where there's* MUCK *there's brass*.

brass hat an army officer of high rank (having gold braid on the cap); the term may be used pejoratively, to indicate someone seen as out of touch with the fighting forces.

cold enough to freeze the balls off a brass monkey bitterly cold; the phrase comes (in the late 19th century) from a type of brass rack or 'monkey' in which cannonballs were stored and which contracted in very cold weather, ejecting the balls.

the brass ring in North America, an informal expression for success, typically regarded as a reward for ambition or hard work, originally with reference to the reward of a free ride given on a merry-go-round to the person hooking a brass ring suspended over the horses.

brass rubbing an image created by rubbing heelball or chalk over paper laid on an engraved brass memorial tablet to reproduce its design.

get down to brass tacks come to the essential details, reach the real matter in hand; the term, which is originally US, is recorded from the late 19th century.

brat pack a rowdy and ostentatious group of young celebrities, typically as of a mid-1980s group of film stars who were seen as having a rowdy, fun-loving, and pampered lifestyle and a spoilt attitude to society.

brave see also ➤ *brave men lived before* AGAMEMNON, ➤ *the* BRAVEST *of the brave*, ➤ FORTUNE *favours the brave*.

brave a dated term for an American Indian warrior; the word in this sense is recorded from the early 19th century.

none but the brave deserve the fair proverbial saying, late 17th century; originally from Dryden:

> Happy, happy, happy, pair!
> None but the brave,
> None but the brave,
> None but the brave deserves the fair.
> — John Dryden *Alexander's Feast* (1697)

brave new world used to refer, often ironically, to a new and hopeful period in history resulting from major changes in society, from the title of a satirical novel by Aldous Huxley (1932), originally with reference to Miranda's words in Shakespeare's *The Tempest*, on first encountering other human beings:

> How many goodly creatures are there here!
> How beauteous mankind is! O brave new world,
> That has such people in't.
> — William Shakespeare *The Tempest* (1611)

Braveheart name given to the 13th-century Scottish hero ➤ *William* WALLACE in the film (1995) of this name, in which he is shown courageously fighting and dying for Scottish independence. *Braveheart* may now be used allusively to encapsulate a view of Scottish nationalism maintained against English oppression.

> If Scotland is to live up to its Braveheart vision.
> — *Sunday Herald* (Glasgow) 10 October 1999

the bravest of the brave nickname of Marshal ➤ NEY, from Napoleon's comment on him when Ney commanded the rearguard on the retreat from Moscow in 1812.

Vicar of Bray the protagonist of an 18th-century song who kept his benefice from Charles II's reign to George I's by changing his beliefs to suit the times.

> In good King Charles's golden days,
> When loyalty no harm meant;
> A furious High-Churchman I was,
> And so I gained preferment.
> Unto my flock I daily preached,
> Kings are by God appointed,
> And damned are those who dare resist,
> Or touch the Lord's Anointed.
> And this is law, I will maintain,
> Unto my dying day, Sir,
> That whatsoever King shall reign,
> I will be the Vicar of Bray, sir!
> — 'The Vicar of Bray' in *British Musical Miscellany* (1734)

brazen in archaic or literary use, resembling or made of brass; (of music) harsh in sound; (of a person or their behavious) impudent, shameless (frequently in **brazen-faced**).

brazen age a mythological age, said by classical writers such as the Greek poet Hesiod of the 8th century BC, to come after the silver age and before the iron age.

brazen bull an instrument of torture belonging to Phalaris, tyrant of Acragas in mid 6th-century Sicily, who was said to have had a bull of brass, designed by ➤ PERILLUS, in which his enemies were roasted to death.

brazen head in various legends, a head made of brass which can speak and is omniscient. The plot of Robert Greene's play *Frier Bacon, and Frier Bongay* (1594), based on the legends surrounding ➤ *Roger* BACON and ➤ *Thomas* BUNGAY, centres on the brazen head which they make and, with the help of the Devil, endow with speech; because Bacon's servant fears to wake him when the head speaks the words 'Time was', 'Time is' and 'Time is past', the oracular powers are lost and the head shatters.

brazen horse in Chaucer's 'Squire's Tale', a magic horse given to ➤ CAMBUSCAN, king of Tartary, which was capable of flying safely and swiftly to any destination.

breach of promise the action of breaking a sworn assurance to do something, formerly especially to marry someone.

breach of the peace an act of violent or noisy behaviour that causes a public disturbance and is considered a criminal offence.

bread food made of flour, water, and yeast mixed together; in general usage, essential food; the means of subsistence, one's livelihood.

See ➤ ACORNS *were good till bread was found,* ➤ BASKET *of bread,* ➤ *the best thing since* SLICED *bread,* ➤ BREAKING *of bread,* ➤ BUTTER *one's bread on both sides,* ➤ LOAVES *of bread,* ➤ MAN *cannot live by bread alone,* ➤ SINGING *bread.*

one cannot live by bread alone people have spiritual as well as physical needs; originally with biblical allusion to Deuteronomy 8:3, 'that he might make thee know that man doth not live by bread alone', and Matthew 4:4, 'Man shall not live by bread alone.'

bread and butter a person's livelihood or main source of income, typically as earned by routine work; the phrase in this sense is first recorded in a letter by Jonathan Swift:

> Your quarrelling with each other upon the subject of bread and butter is the most usual thing in the world.
> — Jonathan Swift letter, 12 August 1732

From the early 20th century (originally in the US), the term **bread-and-butter letter** has been used for a letter conveying conventional thanks for hospitality.

bread and cheese plain or needful food, victuals, living; the phrase with this general sense is recorded from the late 16th century.

Bread and Cheese Club an informal social club founded in New York, *c.*1822, by J. Fenimore Cooper, and growing out of impromptu meetings of his circle of friends.

bread and circuses a diet of entertainment or political policies on which the masses are fed to keep them happy; the phrase is a translation of Latin *panem et circenses* in the work of the Roman satirist Juvenal (AD *c.*60–*c.*130), 'Only two things does he [the modern citizen] anxiously wish for—bread and circuses.'

bread and salt on which an oath was traditionally taken.

bread and water a frugal diet that is eaten in poverty, chosen in abstinence, or given as a punishment.

bread and wine the consecrated elements used in the celebration of the Eucharist; the sacrament of the Eucharist.

bread is the staff of life traditional saying, mid 17th century.

the bread never falls but on its buttered side proverbial saying, mid 19th century.

the bread of idleness food or sustenance for which one has not worked; after Proverbs 31:27 'She…eateth not the bread of idleness.'

cast one's bread upon the waters do good without expectation of reward; with biblical allusion to Ecclesiastes 11:1, 'Cast thy bread upon the waters: for thou shalt find it after many days.'

break a butterfly on a wheel employ disproportionate force in the achievement of an aim; the wheel here is one on which the bodies of criminals were broken as a method of execution. The phrase is first used by Pope:

> Satire or sense, alas! can Sporus feel?
> Who breaks a butterfly upon a wheel?
> — Alexander Pope 'An Epistle to Dr Arbuthnot' (1735)

On 1 June 1967, after the rock star Mick Jagger had been arrested for cannabis possession, the *Times* published a leader (written by William Rees-Mogg) headed 'Who breaks a butterfly on a wheel?', criticizing what was seen as the inappropriate severity of the measure.

break one's duck in cricket, score one's first run (in allusion to the origin of ➤ DUCK as resembling a *duck's egg* in shape).

break the bank in gambling, exhaust the bank's resources or limit of payment, win spectacularly.

break the mould make impossible the repetition of a certain type of creation; put an end to a pattern of events or behaviour by setting markedly different standards. Originally with reference to Ariosto's *Orlando Furioso* (1532), 'Nature made him and then broke the mould'.

breakfast see ➤ AUTOCRAT *of the Breakfast-Table,* ➤ BED *and breakfast,* ➤ HOPE *is a good breakfast,* ➤ SING *before breakfast.*

breaking and entering (in North American, and formerly also British, legal use) the crime of entering a building by force so as to commit burglary.

breaking of bread in the Christian Church, a name for the Eucharist.

Nicholas Breakspear name of the only English pope, ➤ ADRIAN *IV.*

breast *breasts* (on a dish) are the emblem of ➤ St AGATHA.

The *breast* is also used for a person's chest regarded as the seat of the emotions, and the repository of consciousness, designs, and secrets. The phrase **make a clean breast of**, meaning make a full disclosure or confession, is recorded from the mid 18th century.

breath in archaic usage, the power of breathing, life. The word is recorded from Old English (in form *brǣþ* 'smell, scent'), and is of Germanic origin, related to brood.

the **breath of life** a necessity; originally with biblical allusion to the literal sense, as in Genesis 2:7, 'And the Lord God…breathed into his nostrils the breath of life.'

Bertolt Brecht (1898–1956), German dramatist, producer, and poet. His interest in combining music and drama led to collaboration with Kurt Weill, for example in *The Threepenny Opera* (1928), an adaptation of John Gay's *The Beggar's Opera*. Brecht's later drama, written in exile after Hitler's rise to power, uses techniques of theatrical alienation and includes *Mother Courage* (1941) and *The Caucasian Chalk Circle* (1948).

what's bred in the bone will come out in the flesh proverbial saying, late 15th century (earlier in medieval Latin); meaning that inherent characteristics will in the end become apparent.

Breda a manufacturing town in the SW Netherlands. It is noted for the **Compromise of Breda** of 1566, a protest against Spanish rule over the Netherlands; the 1660 manifesto of Charles II (who lived there in exile), stating his terms for accepting the throne of Britain; and the **Treaty of Breda**, which ended the Anglo-Dutch war of 1665–7.

Breeches Bible a popular name for the ➤ GENEVA *Bible.* of 1560, so named because the word *breeches* is used in Genesis 3:7 for the garments made by Adam and Eve.

Brehon law the code of law prevailing in Ireland before the English conquest; a *brehon* was a judge in ancient Ireland.

Jacques Brel (1929–78), Belgian singer and composer. He gained a reputation in Paris as an original songwriter whose satirical wit was balanced by his idealism and hope.

Bren gun a lightweight quick-firing machine gun used by the Allied forces in the Second World War. The name comes from a blend of *Brno* (a town in the Czech Republic where it was originally made) and *Enfield* in England (site of the Royal Small Arms Factory where it was later made).

St Brendan (*c.*486–*c.*575), Irish abbot. The legend of the 'Navigation of St Brendan' (*c.*1050), describing his voyage with a band of monks to a promised land (possibly Orkney or the Hebrides), was widely popular in the Middle Ages.

- ☐ **EMBLEM** His emblem is a whale.
- ☐ **FEAST DAY** His feast day is 16 May.

  Poor Kingsley Porter—how strange that he shd have had a sort of pre-Saxon death in the search (figuratively speaking) of a mysterious Western isle. There is something very Thule-an & St Brendan-ish about it.
  — Edith Wharton letter, 25 July 1933

Brent Spar name of the redundant oil installation which Shell UK in 1995 planned for deep sea disposal; ➤ GREENPEACE activists, claiming that toxic chemicals from the installation would damage the deep sea enviroment, prevented the process with the combination of a flotilla of small boats and a successful public relations campaign.

Brer see ➤ *Brer* FOX, ➤ *Brer* RABBIT.

Bretwalda lord of the Britons, lord of Britain; in the Anglo-Saxon Chronicle, a title given to King Egbert, and (retrospectively) to some earlier Anglo-Saxon kings, and occasionally assumed by later ones.

breviary a book containing the service for each day, to be recited by those in orders in the Roman Catholic Church. The word is recorded from late Middle English (when it also denoted an abridged version of the psalms), and comes from Latin *breviarium* 'summary, abridgement', ultimately from *brevis* 'short, brief'.

brevity is the soul of wit proverbial saying, early 17th century; originally as a quotation from Shakespeare's *Hamlet* (1601).

brew see also ➤ *as you* BAKE, *so shall you brew.*

as you brew, so shall you bake proverbial saying, late 16th century.

brewpub an establishment, typically one including a restaurant, selling beer brewed on the premises. Introduced in North America in the 1980s, they contributed, with *microbreweries*, to reversing the traditional notion of a brewery as producing beer to be sold over as wide an area as possible through a number of outlets.

Brewster Sessions magistrates' sessions for the issue of licences to permit trade in alcoholic liquor (a *brewster* is a brewer, originally a female one).

Brian Boru (d. 1014), king of Munster, who after successfully establishing his dominance as high king was finally killed in battle against the Norse at Clontarf; he is seen as the type of an early Irish warrior king.

> Our colonel comes from Brian's race,
> His wounds are in his breast and face.
> — Thomas Davis 'Clare's Dragoons' (1845)

Briareus in Greek mythology, a giant with a hundred hands, one of three giants who aided Zeus against the ➤ TITANS.

brick see ➤ *I found* ROME *brick, I leave it marble.*

brickfielder in Australia, a dry north wind, typically accompanied by dust. Recorded from the early 19th century, the term comes from the name of *Brickfield* Hill, the site (now part of central Sydney) of a former brickworks, associated with dust.

bricklayers ➤ *St* STEPHEN is the patron saint of bricklayers.

you cannot make bricks without straw proverbial saying, mid 17th century; meaning that nothing can be made or achieved if one does not have the correct materials. Originally the reference is biblical, to Exodus 5:7, 'Ye shall no more give the people straw to make brick, as heretofore: let them go and gather straw for themselves.'

bridal in Old English (in form *brȳd-ealu*) this meant 'wedding feast', from *brȳd* 'bride' + *ealu* 'ale-drinking'. The current sense 'of or concerning a bride or a newly married couple' is recorded from late Middle English, and since the late 16th century has been associated with adjectives ending in *-al*.

See also ➤ BRIDE-*ale.*

bride see also ➤ *always a* BRIDESMAID, *never a bride.*

St Bride another name for ➤ *St* BRIDGET.

bride-ale traditional term for a wedding celebration with drinking of ale, a wedding-feast.

See also ➤ BRIDAL.

Bride of the Sea a name for Venice, emphasizing her traditional role as a sea power.

See also ➤ MARRIAGE *of the Adriatic.*

happy is the bride that the sun shines on proverbial saying, mid 17th century.

bridegroom a man about to be married or very recently married. In Old English the form of the

word was *brȳdguma*, with the second element representing *guma* 'man'; the later change was due to association with *groom.*

Brides in the Bath name given in the popular press to the case of George Joseph Smith, who between 1912 and 1914 bigamously married and drowned in the bath three women, whose lives he had previously insured; arrested (initially for falsifying an entry in the marriage register) early in 1915, he was tried, convicted, and executed for murder later in the same year.

always a bridesmaid, never a bride proverbial saying, early 20th century.

bridewell archaic term for a prison or reform school for petty offenders. Recorded from the mid 16th century, the word comes from *St Bride's Well* in the City of London, near which such a building stood.

bridge see ➤ ASSES' *bridge,* ➤ BAILEY *bridge,* ➤ *don't* CROSS *the bridge till you come to it,* ➤ *everyone* SPEAKS *well of the bridge that carries him across,* ➤ *painting the* FORTH *Bridge,* ➤ RAINBOW *Bridge,* ➤ TOWER *Bridge,* ➤ VERRAZANO-*Narrows Bridge,* ➤ WATER *under the bridge.*

Bridge Fraternity from the 12th century, a confraternity of laymen dedicated to the building or maintenance of a bridge, especially one carrying a pilgrimage route over a river. The best-known example of such a fraternity is that of the bridge of Avignon, founded by St-Bénézet in the late 12th century and linking Avignon with Villeneuve on the opposite bank of the Rhone.

bridge of boats a bridge formed by mooring boats side by side across a river; the **bridge of boats** over the river Rhône at Arles was in use throughout the 2nd and 3rd centuries AD.

it is good to make a bridge of gold to a flying enemy proverbial saying, late 16th century, meaning that it is wiser to give passage to an enemy in flight, who may be desperate; the idea is attributed to Aristides (480 BC), who warned ➤ THEMISTOCLES against destroying the bridge of boats which the Persian king Xerxes had constructed across the Hellespont for the invasion of Greece.

Bridge of Sighs in Venice, a bridge connecting the Doge's palace with the state prison originally crossed by prisoners on their way to torture or execution.

bridgebuilders ➤ St JOHN *Nepomuk* and St Benezet (*c*.1163–84), who as a shepherd boy at Avignon, *c*.1178, was instructed in a vision to build a bridge over the river Rhone, are the patron saints of bridgebuilders.

James Bridger (1804–81), Virginia-born fur trader, frontiersman, and guide in the Far West, who is the hero of many folk legends.

St Bridget of Ireland (d. *c*.525), Irish abbess. She was venerated in Ireland as a virgin saint and noted in miracle stories for her compassion; her cult soon spread over most of western Europe. It has been suggested that she may represent the Irish goddess Brig. She is also called *Bride*, *Brigid*, and *Mary of the Gael*.

 ☐ **PATRONAGE** She is patron of dairymaids.
 ☐ **EMBLEM** Her emblems are a cheese and a cow.
 ☐ **FEAST DAY** Her feast day is 1 February.

St Bridget of Sweden (*c*.1303–73), Swedish nun and visionary. She experienced her first vision of the Virgin Mary at the age of 7. After her husband's death she was inspired by further visions to devote herself to religion, and she founded the Order of *Bridgettines* (*c*.1346) at Vadstena in Sweden. She is also called *Birgitta*.

 ☐ **FEAST DAY** Her feast day is 23 July.

bridle see ➤ SCOLD's *bridle*.

Bridport dagger the gallows; *Bridport* was famous for hemp, from which execution ropes were made.

brief see ➤ DOCK *brief*.

Brigadoon a fictional Highland village (in the 1947 musical of this title by Lerner and Loewe), which since the 18th century has been under an enchantment so that it comes to life for only one day every hundred years; the name is used allusively for a representation of an idealized Scotland, or for something characterized by its infrequent appearance or occurrence.

> A fleeting Brigadoon embodiment of a dreamland.
> — Paul Theroux *Translating LA* (1994)

Brigadore in Spenser's *Faerie Queene*, the horse of Sir Guyon, stolen by ➤ BRAGGADOCHIO.

bright see also ➤ BARNABY *bright*.

John Bright (1811–89), English Liberal politician and reformer. A noted orator, Bright was the leader, along with Richard Cobden, of the campaign to repeal the ➤ CORN *Laws*, and was a vociferous opponent of the ➤ CRIMEAN *War*, of which he said in the House of Commons in February 1855, 'The angel of death has been abroad throughout the land; you may almost hear the beating of his wings.' He was also closely identified with the 1867 Reform Act.

 See also ➤ ADULLAMITE, ➤ MOTHER *of Parliaments*.

bright young thing an enthusiastic, ambitious, and self-consciously fashionable young person, a term originally applied in the 1920s to a member of a young fashionable set noted for exuberant and outrageous behaviour.

Brighton a resort town on the south coast of England, which was patronized by the Prince of Wales (later George IV), and is noted for its Regency architecture; the clergyman and wit Sydney Smith (1771–1845) said of **Brighton Pavilion** as built for the Prince that it 'looks as if St Paul's had slipped down to Brighton and pupped'.

brilliant cut a circular cut for diamonds and other gemstones in the form of two many-faceted pyramids joined at their bases, the upper one truncated near its apex.

brimstone see ➤ FIRE *and brimstone*.

James Brindley (1716–72), pioneering English canal-builder. He designed some 600 km (375 miles) of waterway with a minimum of locks, cuttings, or tunnels, connecting most of the major rivers of England. Carlyle refers to him thus:

> The ineloquent Brindley, behold he has chained seas together.
> — Thomas Carlyle *Past and Present* (1843)

bring see ➤ *bring home the* BACON.

brinkmanship the art or practice of pursuing a dangerous policy to the limits of safety before stopping, especially in politics. The term derives from an interview with the American international lawyer and politician John Foster Dulles (1888–1959):

> The ability to get to the verge without getting into the war is the necessary art . . . We walked to the brink and we looked it in the face.
> — John Foster Dulles in *Life* 16 January 1956

Marquise de Brinvilliers (*c*.1630–76), French aristocrat executed for a number of poisonings; those murdered included her father and two of her brothers.

> Some said that she might be a Brinvilliers, others a Cleopatra . . . They who took the Brinvilliers side of the controversy were men so used to softness and flattery from women as to have learned to think that a woman silent, arrogant, and hard of approach, must be always meditating murder.
>
> — Anthony Trollope *The Eustace Diamonds* (1873)

Briseis in Greek mythology the slave girl who during the siege of Troy was taken from ➤ ACHILLES by ➤ AGAMEMNON; from this came the anger of Achilles which is the theme of the *Iliad*.

all shipshape and Bristol fashion in good order, neat and clean. Recorded from the mid 19th century, the term was originally in nautical use, referring to the commercial prosperity of Bristol, when its shipping was in good order.

Brit award each of a number of prizes awarded annually by the British Phonographic Industry for outstanding service to the music business.

Britain the island containing England, Wales, and Scotland, and including the small adjacent islands. The name is recorded from Old English (in form *Breoton,* from Latin *Brittones* 'Britons'), but it became a largely historical term until revived in the mid 16th century, as the possible union of England and Scotland became a subject of political concern.

See also ➤ COUNT *of Britain,* ➤ LITTLE *Britain,* ➤ *the* MATTER *of Britain.*

Britannia the personification of Britain, usually depicted as a helmeted woman with shield and trident. The figure had appeared on Roman coins and was revived with the name *Britannia* on the coinage of Charles II (the first model being Charles's favourite Frances Stuart (1647–1702), later Duchess of Richmond).

In the 20th century, *Britannia* was the name of the British royal yacht, launched in 1953 and taken out of service in 1997.

See also ➤ COOL *Britannia,* ➤ RULE *Britannia.*

British Academy an institution founded in 1901 for the promotion of historical, philosophical, and philological studies.

British disease a fault or disorder considered typical of the British as a nation, especially (in the 1970s) proneness to industrial unrest.

British Empire a former empire consisting of Great Britain and its possessions, dominions, and dependencies.

Colonization of North America and domination of India began in the 17th century. A series of small colonies, mostly in the West Indies, were gained during the late 17th–early 19th centuries, and Australia, New Zealand, various parts of the Far East, and large areas of Africa were added in the 19th century. Self-government was granted to Canada, Australia, New Zealand, and South Africa in the mid 19th century, and most of the remaining colonies have gained independence since the end of the Second World War.

Order of the British Empire (in the UK) an order of knighthood instituted in 1917 and divided into five classes, each with military and civilian divisions. The classes are: Knight or Dame Grand Cross of the Order of the British Empire (GBE), Knight or Dame Commander (KBE/DBE), Commander (CBE), Officer (OBE), and Member (MBE). The two highest classes entail the awarding of a knighthood.

British English English as used in Great Britain, as distinct from that used elsewhere.

British Expeditionary Force a British force made available by the army reform of 1908 for service overseas. Such forces were sent to France in 1914, at the outbreak of the First World War and 1939, early in the Second World War (this force was evacuated from Dunkirk in 1940).

British India that part of the Indian subcontinent administered by the British from 1765, when the East India Company acquired control over Bengal, until 1947, when India became independent and Pakistan was created. By 1850 British India was coterminous with India's boundaries in the west and north and by 1885 it included Burma in the east. The period of British rule was known as the ➤ RAJ.

British Library the national library of Britain, containing the former library departments of the British Museum. The principal copyright library, it was established separately from the British Museum in 1972, and moved into its own premises in 1997.

British Lion the lion as the national emblem of Great Britain; in figurative usage, the British nation. The term is first recorded in Dryden:

> Such mercy from the British Lion flows.
>
> — John Dryden *The Hind and the Panther* (1687)

In sport, the *British Lions* are a touring international rugby union team representing the British Isles.

British Museum a national museum of antiquities in London. Established with public funds in 1753, it includes among its holdings the ➤ MAGNA *Carta*, the ➤ ELGIN *Marbles*, and the ➤ ROSETTA *Stone*.

British warm a short thick overcoat or duffel coat, worn especially by army officers.

Britomart in Spenser's *Faerie Queene*, the female knight of chastity, who falls in love with an image of Artegall seen in a magic mirror. She is the daughter of Ryence, King of Britain, and the most powerful of several types of Queen Elizabeth in the poem.

Britpop pop music by a loose affiliation of British groups of the mid 1990s, typically influenced by the Beatles and other British groups of the 1960s and perceived as a reaction against American grunge music.

Brittany a region and former duchy of NW France, forming a peninsula between the Bay of Biscay and the English Channel. It was occupied in the 5th and 6th centuries by Britons fleeing the Saxons, and was an independent duchy from 1196 until 1532, when it was incorporated into France.
See also ➤ MAID *of Brittany*.

land of the broad acres a traditional name for Yorkshire.

broad arrow a mark resembling a broad arrow-head, formerly used on British prison clothing and other government property.

Broad Church a tradition or group within the Anglican Church favouring a liberal interpretation of doctrine; the phrase came into vogue around 1848, and according to the Master of Balliol, Benjamin Jowett, was first proposed in his hearing by the poet Arthur Hugh Clough (1819–61). In 1850 Dean Stanley used broad in this sense in an article in the Edinburgh Review:

> There is no need . . . for minute comparison of the particular formularies of the Church to prove . . . that it is, by the very conditions of its being, not High or Low, but Broad.
> — Dean Stanley in *Edinburgh Review* July 1850

In general usage, *Broad Church* means a group, organization, or doctrine which allows for and caters to a wide range of opinions and people.

broad-piece a twenty-shilling piece of the reigns of James I and Charles I, which was broader and thinner than succeeding coinage.

broad Scotch lowland Scots.

broadcasters ➤ *St* GABRIEL is the patron saint of broadcasters.

broadcloth clothing fabric of fine twilled wool or worsted, or plain-woven cotton. Recorded from late Middle English, the term originally denoted cloth made 72 inches wide, as opposed to 'strait' cloth, 36 inches wide. The term now implies quality rather than width.

Broadmoor a special hospital near Reading in southern England for the secure holding of patients regarded as both mentally ill and potentially dangerous. It was established in 1863.

the Broads a network of shallow freshwater lakes, traversed by slow-moving rivers, in Norfolk and Suffolk. They were formed by the gradual natural flooding of medieval peat diggings.

broadside a firing of all the guns from one side of a warship.

Broadway a street traversing the length of Manhattan, New York. It is famous for its theatres, and its name has become synonymous with show business (it is also known informally as the ➤ GREAT *White Way*).
See also ➤ OFF-*Broadway*.

Brobdingnag in Swift's *Gulliver's Travels* (1726), a land where everything is of huge size.

> The Beetle was never designed to accommodate . . . a pram that looked like it'd been made for export to Brobdingnag.
> — J. Torrington *Swing Hammer Swing!* (1992)

Broceliande a legendary region adjoining Brittany, in the Arthurian legends, where Merlin lies.

brock the badger; recorded from Old English, but actually of Celtic origin, with cognates in Cornish, Welsh, Irish and Scottish Gaelic, and Breton. It survives in place-names such as **Brockenhurst** in Hampshire, and Beatrix Potter gave the name **Tommy Brock** to the badger in her children's stories.

Brock's benefit a spectacular display of pyrotechnics, from the name of the public fireworks display held annually at the Crystal Palace, London, from 1865 to 1936, from C. T. *Brock*, firework manufacturer.

Brocken the highest of the Harz Mountains of north central Germany. It is noted for the phenomenon of the ➤ BROCKEN *spectre* and for witches' revels which reputedly took place there on Walpurgis night.

Brocken spectre a magnified shadow of an observer, typically surrounded by rainbow-like bands, thrown on to a bank of cloud in high mountain areas when the sun is low. The phenomenon was first reported on the ➤ BROCKEN.

Broederbond a secret society in South Africa (founded in 1918) promoting the interests of and restricted in membership to male, Protestant Afrikaners. The name is Afrikaans, and comes from *broeder* 'brother' + *bond* 'league'.

brogue a marked accent, especially Irish or Scottish, when speaking English. Recorded from the early 18th century, the term may come allusively from *brogue* 'a rough shoe of untanned leather, formerly worn in parts of Ireland and the Scottish Highlands', referring to the rough footwear of Irish peasants.

if it ain't broke, don't fix it proverbial saying, late 20th century.

broken reed someone not to be relied on; originally often with biblical allusion to Isaiah 36:6, 'Lo, thou trustest in the staff of this broken reed.'

broker see ➤ HONEST *broker*.

bromide a trite and unoriginal idea or remark, especially one intended to soothe or placate; *bromide* here is a figurative use of the (dated) meaning, a sedative preparation containing potassium bromide.

Brompton cocktail a powerful painkiller and sedative consisting of a vodka or other liquor laced with morphine and sometimes also cocaine. Recorded from the late 20th century, the term is said to come from the name of *Brompton* Hospital, London, where the mixture was invented for cancer patients.

the Bronx a borough in the north-east of New York City; named after Jonas *Bronck*, a Dutch settler who purchased land there in 1641. A **Bronx cheer** is a sound of derision or contempt made by blowing through closed lips with the tongue between them.

Bronze Age a prehistoric period that followed the Stone Age and preceded the Iron Age, when weapons and tools were made of bronze rather than stone.

The Bronze Age began in the Near East and SE Europe in the late 4th and early 3rd millennium BC. It is associated with the first European civilizations, the beginnings of urban life in China, and the final stages of some Meso-American civilizations, but did not appear in Africa and Australasia at all.

Brooklyn a borough of New York City, at the south-western corner of Long Island. The Brooklyn Bridge (1869–83) links Long Island with lower Manhattan.

Brooklynese an uncultivated form of New York speech associated especially with the borough of ➤ BROOKLYN.

Brooks's a London club founded by Almack in the middle of the 18th century. It was originally in Pall Mall, and the present clubhouse dates from 1778. In its early days it was a noted gambling centre, and was much associated with the names of Charles James Fox and Sheridan.

broom a flowering shrub with long, thin green stems, small or few leaves, and a profusion of flowers, a sprig of which (in Latin *planta genista*) was said to have been worn as a crest as by Geoffrey of Anjou, and to be the origin of the name ➤ PLANTAGENET. The word is recorded from Old English (in the form *brōm*) and is of Germanic origin, ultimately related to ➤ BRAMBLE.
From late Middle English, *broom* has also meant a long-handled brush of bristles or twigs, used for sweeping; this is the emblem of ➤ *St* MARTHA, St Petronilla, an early Roman martyr whose fictional legend makes her the daughter of ➤ *St* PETER, and St Zita, a 13th-century Luccan serving-maid.
See also ➤ NEW *brooms sweep clean*.

broomstick a brush with twigs at one end and a long handle, on which witches were traditionally said to fly.
See also ➤ MARRY *over the broomstick*.

broose a traditional race by young men present at country weddings in Scotland, the course being from the bride's former home to the bridegroom's house. The origin of the term is unknown.

broth see ➤ *too many* COOKS *spoil the broth*, ➤ VIPER-*broth*.

brother a man or boy in relation to other sons and daughters of his parents; a fellow member of the same calling. Recorded from Old English (in form *brōþor*), the word is of Germanic origin and comes ultimately from an Indo-European root shared by Latin *frater*.

See also ➤ AM *I not a man and a brother*, ➤ BIG *Brother*.

Brother Jonathan America personified. Recorded from the early 19th century, the term is said to come from the name applied to Jonathan Trumbull, Governor of New York, by George Washington, and to have been used originally with biblical reference to 2 Samuel 1:26, 'my brother Jonathan: very pleasant hast thou been unto me'.

am I my brother's keeper? an expression of rejection for natural ties; originally a biblical quotation, from the response of ➤ CAIN to God when asked the whereabouts of the murdered Abel (Geneis 4:9).

City of Brotherly Love an informal name for Philadelphia.

Brothers' Club a club founded by Bolingbroke in 1711 at the inspiration of Swift to 'advance conversation and friendship' and assist deserving authors and wits. It was composed of members of the Tory Ministry and some of their supporters, and included Swift, Prior, and Arbuthnot.

brougham a horse-drawn carriage with a roof, four wheels, and an open driver's seat in front, named after Lord *Brougham* (1778–1868), who designed the carriage.

brown see also ➤ KNEES *up, Mother Brown*.

brown originally, dusky, dark. The word is recorded in this sense from Old English (in form *brūn*, of Germanic origin) and is now found only in poetic use:

> I watch the twilight falling brown.
> — Lord Tennyson *To the Reverend F. D. Maurice* (1854)

From Middle English, *brown* has the current sense, of a colour produced by mixing red, yellow, and black, as of dark wood or rich soil.

Capability Brown name given to the English landscape gardener Lancelot Brown (1716–83). He evolved an English style of natural-looking landscape parks, as at Blenheim and Chatsworth.

Father Brown in the stories of G. K. Chesterton (1874–1936), a Roman Catholic priest who is also an amateur detective, and who solves crimes through apparent paradoxes and inspired common sense.

John Brown (1800–59), American abolitionist. In 1859 he was executed after raiding a government arsenal at Harpers Ferry in Virginia, intending to arm black slaves and start a revolt. He became a hero of the abolitionists in the Civil War; he is commemorated in the song 'John Brown's Body'.

Brown Bomber nickname of the boxer Joe Louis (1914–81).

Brown, Jones, and Robinson an alternative expression for ➤ TOM, *Dick, and Harry*.

Browne see also ➤ SAM *Browne*.

Thomas Browne (1605–82), English author and physician. He achieved prominence with *Religio Medici* (1642), a collection of opinions on a vast number of subjects connected with religion. *Hydriotaphia (Urn Burial*, 1658), a study of burial customs, is a notable example of Browne's elaborately ornate language.

Brownian motion in physics, the erratic random movement of microscopic particles in a fluid, as a result of continuous bombardment from molecules of the surrounding medium, named (in the late 19th century) after Robert *Brown* (1773–1858), the Scottish botanist who first observed the motion.

brownie especially in Scottish folklore, a benevolent elf supposedly haunting houses and doing housework secretly. The name is a diminutive of *brown*; a 'wee brown man' often appears in Scottish ballads and fairy tales, and may be compared with the Old Norse *svartálfar*, the dark elves of the Edda.

Brownies (now **Brownie Guides**) are members of junior branch of the Guides' Association, for girls aged between about 7 and 10; they wear a brown uniform.

Brownist an adherent or supporter of the ecclesiastical principles of the Puritan Robert Brown (*c*.1550–*c*.1633), who preached *c*.1578 denouncing the parochial system and ordination, whether by bishops or by presbytery. After 1580 he, with Robert Harrison, collected a congregation at Norwich, which they called 'the church', but which was familiarly known as 'the Brownists'. He finally submitted to the bishop of Peterborough and became for 40 years rector of Achurch in Northamptonshire. He is regarded as the founder of Congregationalism.

Brownshirt a member of a Nazi militia founded by Hitler in Munich in 1921, with brown uniforms resembling those of Mussolini's Blackshirts. They aided Hitler's rise to power, but were eclipsed by the SS after the ➤ NIGHT *of the Long Knives* in June 1934.

James Bruce (1730–94), Scottish explorer. In 1770 he was the first European to discover the source of the Blue Nile, although his *Travels to Discover the Sources of the Nile* (1790), recounting his expedition, was dismissed by his contemporaries as fabrication.

Robert the Bruce (1274–1329), Scottish nationalist leader, from 1306, ➤ ROBERT *I*, King of Scotland.

Bruegel the name of a family of Flemish artists, Pieter Bruegel the Elder (1525–69), who produced landscapes, religious allegories, and satires of peasant life, Peter Bruegel the Younger (1564–1638), known as **Hell Bruegel**, who is noted for his paintings of devils, and Jan Bruegel (1568–1623), son of Pieter Bruegel the Elder, known as **Velvet Bruegel**, who was a celebrated painter of flowers, landscapes, and mythological scenes.

Bruges a city in NW Belgium, capital of the province of West Flanders, which until the 15th century was a centre of the Flemish textile trade.

Bruges Group a political pressure group formed with the intention of arguing against British participation in the creation of a federal European state. The name alludes to a speech given in Bruges by Margaret Thatcher, then British Prime Minister, in September 1988.

bruin a bear, especially in children's fables; from Dutch *bruin* 'brown', used as a name for the bear in the 13th-century fable *Reynard the Fox*.

Brum an informal name for Birmingham, a shortened form of ➤ BRUMMAGEM.

Brumaire the second month of the French republican calendar (1793–1805), originally running from 22 October to 20 November. The name is French, from *brume* 'mist'.

brumby in Australia, a wild or unbroken horse. The word is recorded from the late 19th century, but the origin is unknown.

Brummagem cheap, showy, or counterfeit. The term comes (in the mid 17th century) from a dialect form of *Birmingham*, England, with reference to counterfeit coins and cheap plated goods once made there.

George Brummell (1778–1840), English dandy, known as **Beau Brummell**. He was the arbiter of British fashion for the first decade and a half of the

19th century, owing his social position to his friendship with the Prince Regent. His remedies for style included, 'No perfumes, but very fine linen, plenty of it, and country washing.'

Brunhild in the *Nibelungenlied*, the wife of Gunther, who instigated the murder of Siegfried. In the Norse versions she is *Brynhild*, a Valkyrie whom ➤ SIGURD (the counterpart of Siegfried) wins by penetrating the wall of fire behind which she lies in an enchanted sleep; his death comes about because he is later tricked into forgetting her and marrying the Nibelung princess Gudrun.

Isambard Kingdom Brunel (1806–59), English engineer, son of ➤ *Marc Isambard* BRUNEL. He was chief engineer of the Great Western Railway. His achievements include designing the Clifton suspension bridge (1829–30) and the first transatlantic steamship, the *Great Western* (1838), and the *Great Eastern* (1858), the world's largest ship until 1899.

Marc Isambard Brunel (1769–1849), French-born English engineer, father of ➤ *Isambard Kingdom* BRUNEL. He introduced mass-production machinery to Portsmouth dockyard, an early example of automation; and designed other machines for woodworking, boot-making, knitting, and printing. He also worked to construct the first tunnel under the Thames (1825–43).

Filippo Brunelleschi (1377–1446), Italian architect. He is especially noted for the dome of Florence cathedral (1420–61), which he raised without the use of temporary supports; it is the largest dome in the world in diameter. Brunelleschi revived Roman architectural forms, and is often credited with the Renaissance 'discovery' of perspective.

Giordano Bruno (1548–1600), Italian philosopher. He was a follower of Hermes Trismegistus and a supporter of the heliocentric Copernican view of the solar system, envisaging an infinite universe of numerous worlds moving in space. Bruno was tried by the Inquisition for heresy and burned at the stake.

St Bruno (*c*.1032–1101), German-born French churchman. In 1084 he withdrew to the mountains of Chartreuse and founded the ➤ CARTHUSIAN order at La Grande Chartreuse.
 □ **FEAST DAY** His feast day is 6 October.

Brunswick a former duchy and state of Germany, mostly incorporated into Lower Saxony, more fully **Brunswick-Wolfenbüttel**. In earlier times Hanover constituted the electorate of **Brunswick-Lüneburg**, whence the name **line of Brunswick** for English sovereigns from George I.

Brunswick clubs Irish Protestant organizations opposing the Catholic Emancipation Act of 1829; the first of them was founded by Charles, Duke (1823–31) of Brunswick in 1828.

brush the bushy tail of a fox.

Brussels the capital of Belgium and of the Belgian province of Brabant; the headquarters of the European Commission is located there.

> The recent wave of hostility to interference from 'Brussels' has badly dented the commission's self-confidence.
> — *Economist* 10 October 1992

The Brut a rhyming chronicle of ➤ BRUTUS, legendary founder of the British race, and his descendants.

brutum fulmen a mere noise; an ineffective act, an empty threat. Recorded from the early 17th century, the phrase comes from Latin (Pliny), meaning literally 'unfeeling thunderbolt'.

Brutus legendary Trojan hero, great-grandson of Aeneas and supposed ancestor of the British people. In medieval legend he was said to have brought a group of Trojans to England and founded *Troynovant* or New Troy (London).

Lucius Junius Brutus legendary founder of the Roman Republic. Traditionally he led a popular uprising after the rape of ➤ LUCRETIA, against the king (his uncle) and drove him from Rome. He and the father of Lucretia were elected as the first consuls of the Republic (509 BC).

Marcus Junius Brutus (85–42 BC), Roman senator. With Cassius he led the conspirators who assassinated Julius Caesar in 44. They were defeated by Caesar's supporters, Antony and Octavian, at the battle of Philippi in 42, after which he committed suicide.

Bryn Mawr College founded in 1880 near Philadelphia by the Society of Friends; it is an important non-sectarian college for women.

Brythonic denoting, relating to, or belonging to the southern group of Celtic languages, consisting of Welsh, Cornish, and Breton. They were spoken in Britain before and during the Roman occupation, surviving as Welsh and Cornish after the Anglo-Saxon invasions, and being taken to Brittany by emigrants.

BSE bovine spongiform encephalopathy, a disease of cattle which affects the central nervous system, causing agitation and staggering, and is usually fatal. It is believed to be caused by an agent such as a prion and to be related to ➤ CREUTZFELDT–*Jakob disease* in humans.

The disease (informally called *mad cow disease* because of the symptoms of falling and staggering) was first identified in the UK in late 1986, and in the wake of extreme public anxiety as to the infection spreading to humans through the eating of infected meat, the US and several European countries banned imports of British beef. By the end of 1999, while the European Commission appeared satisfied with the measures taken, countries such as France and Germany were still unwilling to accept the reintroduction of British beef.

BTW an abbreviation for the phrase *by the way*: one of a number of abbreviations used in various online communities, such as bulletin boards and the Internet.

bubble a commercial scheme or enterprise that is unstable and unlikely to last; the term in this sense is recorded from the 17th century onwards, especially as in ➤ MISSISSIPPI *bubble*, ➤ SOUTH *Sea Bubble*.

bubble and squeak cooked cabbage fried with cooked potatoes and often meat; the name, which is recorded from the late 18th century, refers to the sounds made in cooking the dish.

Bubbles popular name for the portrait by John Everett Millais of his grandson, William James (1881–1973) as a four-year-old boy blowing bubbles; the picture became widely known when it was used in an advertisement by Pears' soap, and William James (in later life an Admiral of the Fleet) acquired *Bubbles* as a permanent nickname.

bubbly an informal term for champagne, recorded from the 1920s.

bubonic plague the commonest form of plague in humans, characterized by fever, delirium, and the formation of buboes. The plague bacterium is transmitted by rat fleas. Epidemics occurred in Europe throughout the Middle Ages (notably as the ➤ BLACK *Death* and the ➤ GREAT *Plague* of 1665–6); the disease is still endemic in parts of Asia.

bucca in Cornish legend, an elf or goblin. The name comes from Cornish, 'hobgoblin, bugbear, scarecrow'.

buccaneer a pirate, originally one operating in the Caribbean. The word is recorded from the mid 17th century, originally denoting European hunters in the Caribbean; it comes ultimately from French *boucan* 'a frame on which to cook or cure meat', from Tupi *mukem*.

Bucentaur the state barge used by the Doge of Venice for the ➤ MARRIAGE *of the Adriatic* on Ascension Day.

The name comes ultimately from Italian *bucentoro*, and may be taken from the figurehead of the vessel, representing a mythical creature, half man and half ox, perhaps from Greek *bous* 'ox' + *kentauros* 'centaur'. Alternatively, *bucentoro* may be from Venetian Italian, literally 'barge of gold'.

Bucephalus the favourite horse of Alexander the Great, who tamed the horse as a boy and took it with him on his campaigns until its death, after a battle, in 326 BC. The name in Greek means literally 'ox-headed'.

Alexander Buchan (1829–1907), Scottish meteorologist, who produced maps and tables of atmospheric circulation, and of ocean currents and temperatures, based largely on information gathered on the voyage of HMS *Challenger* in 1872–6.

John Buchan (1875–1940), Scottish novelist. His adventure stories feature recurring heroes such as Richard Hannay and often involve elaborate cross-country chases; characterization is simple and the moral standard of his heroes is high.

Buchenwald a Nazi concentration camp in the Second World War, near the village of Buchenwald in eastern Germany.

Buchmanism another name for ➤ MORAL *Rearmament*, from the name of Frank Buchman (1878–1961), American evangelist and founder of the Oxford Group.

buck archaic term for a fashionable and typically hellraising young man. Recorded from the early 18th century, the word initially implied spirited conduct rather than elegance of dress; the meaning of a young man regarded as being fashionable dates from the early 19th century.

pass the buck shift the responsibility for something to someone else; the *buck* here is an article placed as a reminder in front of a player whose turn it is to deal at poker.

Harry Truman (1884–1974), as President of the US, had on his desk the unattributed motto, **the buck stops here**.

Buck House an informal name for Buckingham Palace, recorded from the early 1920s.

Buck's Fizz champagne or sparkling white wine mixed with orange juice. The name comes (in the 1930s) from the name *Buck's Club*, in London.

buckboard an open horse-drawn carriage with four wheels and seating that is attached to a plank stretching between the front and rear axles. The word is recorded from the mid 19th century, and the first element comes from *buck* 'body of a cart'.

Buckeye State informal name for the state of Ohio, so called from the abundance of buckeye trees, an American tree related to the horse chestnut, with showy red or white flowers.

Master of the Buckhounds an officer of the Royal Household (a *buckhound* is a staghound of a small breed, formerly used for hunting fallow deer).

Duke of Buckingham[1] George Villiers (1592–1628), 1st Duke, influential favourite of James I (by whom he was nicknamed 'Steenie') and Charles I; deeply unpopular, he was assassinated by John Felton (1595?–1628). In Dumas' *The Three Musketeers*, he is portrayed as the lover of Anne of Austria.

Duke of Buckingham[2] George Villiers (1628–87), 2nd Duke, a prominent figure at the court of Charles II, was one of the five members of the ➤ CABAL, and was represented as the treacherous Zimri in Dryden's *Absalom and Achitophel*.

Buckingham Palace the London residence of the British sovereign since 1837, adjoining St James's Park, Westminster. It was built for the Duke of Buckingham in the early 18th century and bought by George III in 1761, and redesigned by John Nash for George IV *c.*1821–30; the facade facing the Mall was redesigned in 1913.

William Buckland (1784–1856), English geologist. He helped to redefine geology, correlating deposits and associated fossils with former conditions, and developed the idea of an ice age. He was the first to describe and name a dinosaur (*Megalosaurus*), in 1824.

Buckley's chance in Australia, a slim chance, no chance at all. The expression is sometimes said to be from the name of William *Buckley* (died 1856), who, despite dire predictions as to his chances of survival, lived with the Aboriginals for many years.

buckram coarse linen or other cloth stiffened with gum or paste, and used typically as interfacing and in bookbinding. Originally (in Middle English) this denoted a kind of fine linen or cotton cloth; the word comes from Old French *boquerant*, perhaps ultimately from Bukhoro in central Asia.

See also ➤ MEN *in buckram*.

buckshee free of charge; the word is originally soldiers' slang from the First World War, and represents an alteration of *baksheesh*.

Buddha a title given to the founder of Buddhism, Siddartha Gautama (*c*.563–*c*.460 BC). Born an Indian prince in what is now Nepal, he renounced wealth and family to become an ascetic, and after achieving enlightenment while meditating, taught all who came to learn from him.

Buddhism a widespread Asian religion or philosophy, founded by Siddartha Gautama in NE India in the 5th century BC.

Buddhism has no god, and gives a central role to the doctrine of karma. The 'four noble truths' of Buddhism state that all existence is suffering, that the cause of suffering is desire, that freedom from suffering is nirvana, and that this is attained through the 'eightfold path' of ethical conduct, wisdom, and mental discipline (including meditation). There are two major traditions, Theravada and Mahayana.

See also ➤ ESOTERIC *Buddhism*, ➤ MAHAYANA, ➤ THERAVADA, ➤ TIBETAN *Buddhism*.

buddy a close friend, especially a person who befriends and helps another with an incapacitating disease, typically Aids.

budget an estimate of income and expenditure for a set period of time; (with capital initial) an annual or other regular estimate of national revenue and expenditure put forward by a finance minister, including details of changes in taxation.

The word comes (in late Middle English) from Old French *bougette*, diminutive of *bouge* 'leather bag', from Latin *bulga* 'leather bag, knapsack', of Gaulish origin.

Budget originally meant a pouch or wallet, and later its contents. In the mid 18th century, the Chancellor of the Exchequer, in presenting his annual statement, was said 'to open the budget'. In the late 19th century the use of the term was extended from governmental to private or commercial finances.

buff see also ➤ BLIND *man's buff*.

buff a yellowish-beige colour; a stout dull leather with a velvety surface.

Originally (from the mid 16th to the early 18th century) *buff* meant 'a buffalo or other wild ox'; from the late 16th century, it also came to mean 'ox-hide' or (in the late 18th century) 'colour of oxhide'.

Buff probably comes via French and Italian from late Latin *bufalus* 'buffalo'.

Buffalo Bill (1846–1917), American showman, born *William Frederick Cody*. He gained his nickname for killing 4,280 buffalo in eight months to feed the Union Pacific Railroad workers, and subsequently devoted his life to his travelling Wild West Show.

Comte de Buffon (1707–88), French naturalist. A founder of palaeontology, he emphasized the unity of all living species, minimizing the apparent differences between animals and plants. He produced a compilation of the animal kingdom, the *Histoire Naturelle*, which had reached thirty-six volumes by the time of his death.

bug see also ➤ MILLENNIUM *bug*.

Bug Bible a name given to versions of the English Bible (Coverdale's and Matthew's) in which the words in Psalm 91:5 are translated, 'thou shalt not be afraid for any bugs by night'.

bug-eyed monster an extra-terrestrial monster with bulging eyes.

> Young space cadets, for instance, dislike meeting Bems—for bug-eyed Monsters.
> — Arthur Koestler *The Trail of the Dinosaur* (1953)

Buggins' turn a system by which appointments or awards are made in rotation rather than by merit, from *Buggins*, used to represent a typical surname.

Bugs Bunny an American cartoon rabbit with prominent teeth who first appeared in Warner Brothers' films in 1938.

> The outer petals are tipped with green, but the most distinguishing feature is its long, divided Bugs Bunny ear-like spathe.
> — *Garden* March 1991

builders the Spanish-born Dominican friar St Vincent Ferrer (1350–1419) is the patron saint of builders.

building see ➤ SICK *building syndrome*.

built see ➤ *built on* SAND.

Bulgar a member of a Slavic people who settled in what is now Bulgaria in the 7th century; the name comes from medieval Latin *Bulgarus*, from Old Church Slavonic *Blŭgarinŭ*.

bulimia an emotional disorder involving distortion of body image and an obsessive desire to lose weight, in which bouts of extreme overeating are followed by depression and self-induced vomiting, purging, or fasting.

> It gives you a feeling of comfort. It's like having a pair of arms around you, but it's temporary. Then you're disgusted at the bloatedness of your stomach, and then you bring it all up again.
> — Diana, Princess of Wales interview on *Panorama*, BBC1 TV, 20 November 1995

bull[1] a bull is the emblem of ➤ St LUKE, ➤ St FRIDESWIDE, and ➤ St THOMAS *Aquinas*; **the Bull** is the zodiacal sign and constellation ➤ TAURUS.

On the Stock Exchange, a person who buys shares hoping to sell them at a higher price later; the term is recorded from the early 18th century.

In Egyptian mythology, the god ➤ APIS was depicted as a bull, symbolizing fertility and strength in war.

The word dates from late Old English (in form *bula*, recorded in place names), and comes from Old Norse *boli*.

See also ➤ BRAZEN *bull*, ➤ COCK-*and-bull story*, ➤ *the* FARNESE *Bull*, ➤ GENEVA *bull*, ➤ JOHN *Bull*, ➤ RED *rag to a bull*, ➤ WAR *of the Brown Bull*, ➤ WATER-*bull*.

bull[2] a papal edict. Recorded from Middle English, the word comes via Old French from Latin *bulla* 'bubble, rounded object', in medieval Latin, 'seal or sealed document'. Also called *papal bull*.

See also ➤ *the* GOLDEN *Bull*.

like a bull at a gate with the angry vigour of a bull charging a restraining ('five-barred') gate; the expression is recorded from the late 19th century.

bull-baiting the practice of setting dogs to harass a bull, popular as an entertainment in medieval Europe.

bull by the horns implying a firm grasp of a difficult issue; the expression is recorded from the early 18th century.

bull in a china shop a clumsy person in a situation calling for adroit movement; the phrase is recorded from the mid 19th century.

bull market a market in which share prices are rising, encouraging buying.

bull-roarer a sacred object of Australian Aboriginal ceremony and ritual, so called because of a fancied resemblance to a child's toy. A *bull-roarer* consists of a flat oval carved piece of wood, pointed at each end and pierced at one end; a string is threaded through the hole so that the bull-roarer can be swung round, making a booming noise. It is also known as a *churinga*.

Bull Run a small river in eastern Virginia, scene of two Confederate victories, in 1861 and 1862, during the American Civil War.

bulldog a dog of a sturdy smooth-haired breed with a large head and powerful protruding lower jaw, a flat wrinkled face, and a broad chest; a *bulldog* has traditionally been taken as the symbol of what are regarded as British characteristics of pluck and stubbornness, and may generally denote a person noted for courageous or stubborn tenacity.

At Oxford and Cambridge Universities, *bulldog* is used informally for an official who assists the proctors, especially in disciplinary matters.

Bulldog Drummond hero of a series of novels by Sapper (H. C. McNeile, 1888–1937); the former Captain Drummond is a large, ugly, xenophobic, but charming ex-army officer who despite his apparent brainlessness defeats a succession of fiendishly clever international crooks with a blend of violence and daring.

> I wandered through sleeping, low-lit streets threaded with fog, just like in a Bulldog Drummond movie.
> — Bill Bryson *Notes from a Small Island* (1995)

bullet see also ➤ *the* BALLOT *is stronger than the bullet*, ➤ BITE *the bullet*.

every bullet has its billet proverbial saying, late 16th century; meaning that Fate will determine who is to be killed.

bulletin a short official statement or broadcast summary of news; a regular newsletter or printed report issued by an organization or society. Recorded from the mid 17th century (denoting an official warrant in some European countries), the word comes via French from the Italian diminutive of *bulletta* 'passport', diminutive of *bulla* 'seal, bull'.

bullfight a public spectacle, especially in Spain, at which a bull is baited, and finally killed by a ➤ MATADOR. The term is recorded in English from the mid 18th century, having superseded the earlier (late 17th century) *bull-feast*.

bullring an arena where bullfights take place; in England, sometimes used for the land on which *bull-baiting* took place, still surviving in place names such as the Bullring in Birmingham.

bullseye the centre of the target in sports such as archery, shooting, and darts; a shot that hits the centre of such a target; in figurative use, something that achieves exactly the intended effect.

bully[1] a person who uses strength or influence to harm or intimidate others who are weaker. Recorded from the mid 16th century (probably coming from Middle Dutch *boele* 'lover'), the original use was as a term of endearment applied to either sex; later becoming a familiar form of address to a male friend. (In Shakespeare's *A Midsummer Night's Dream* (1595–6), ➤ BOTTOM is called 'sweet bully Bottom'.) The current sense dates from the late 17th century.

bully[2] especially in North America, informal term meaning very good; first-rate. The word is recorded from the late 16th century, originally meaning 'admirable, gallant, jolly', and coming from ➤ BULLY[1]. The current sense dates from the mid 19th century.
See also ➤ *bully* PULPIT.

a bully is always a coward proverbial saying, early 19th century.

bum-bailiff a bailiff empowered to collect debts; recorded from the early 17th century, the name comes from the association of an approach from behind.

Bumble the beadle in Dickens's *Oliver Twist*, a type of the consequential, domineering parish official.

> Is a reintroduction of the parish workhouse next . . . ?
> Poor relief, with shades of Bumble the Beadle and
> Oliver Twist, must look appealing in its cheapness and
> efficiency.
> — *ATA Mag: Alberta Teachers' Association* November
> 1993

bummaree a self-employed licensed porter at Smithfield meat market in London; the word is recorded from the late 18th century, but the origin is unknown.

bump in rowing, (in races on narrow rivers where boats make a spaced start one behind another) the point at which a boat begins to overtake or touch the boat ahead, thereby defeating it and so being started ahead of it in the next race; a series of such rowing contests takes place at Oxford and Cambridge Universities, and a successful outcome is celebrated by a **Bump supper**.

bumper a flat race for inexperienced horses which are intended for future racing in hurdles or steeplechases. The word is said to be from an earlier racing term *bumper* 'amateur rider'.

Natty Bumppo real name of *Leatherstocking*, the hero of *The Pioneers* (1823) and four other novels (the *Leatherstocking* series) of American frontier life by James Fenimore Cooper (1789–1851); his name may be used for the type of a frontiersman of the period, with particular reference to tracking skills.

> You didn't have to be Natty Bumppo to see that the
> road had been in disuse for some time.
> — T. C. Boyle *Budding Prospects* (1984)

Bunbury a fictitious excuse for making a visit or avoiding an obligation, from the name of an imaginary person (so used) in Oscar Wilde's *The Importance of Being Earnest*.

> Stekel was notorious among the Wednesday crowd for
> his desire to be the midst of every conversation, often
> inventing a patient afflicted with the disorder of the
> week—Ernest Jones called this Bunbury figure 'Stekel's
> Wednesday patient'—so as to be able to contribute to
> the evening's discussion.
> — Marjorie Garber *Vice Versa* (1995)

Buncombe the name of the county in North Carolina from which the word ➤ BUNKUM derives.

bungalow a low house, having only one storey or, in some cases, upper rooms set in the roof. The word comes (in the late 17th century) from Hindi *banglā* 'belonging to Bengal'.

Thomas Bungay (fl. 1290), *Friar Bungay*, a Franciscan, who was divinity lecturer of his Order in Oxford and Cambridge. He was popularly accounted a magician and is frequently referred to in that capacity; he features in this role in Robert Greene's play *Frier Bacon and Frier Bongay* (see ➤ *brazen* HEAD).

bungee-jumping the sport of leaping from a bridge, crane, or other high place while secured by a long nylon-cased rubber band around the ankles; *bungee-jumping* became popular in the early 1980s, its practitioners purportedly being attracted to it for the adrenalin rush it provides. *Bungee* is recorded from the 1930s, denoting an elasticated cord for launching a glider, but the ultimate origin is unknown.

Bunker Hill the first pitched battle (1775) of the War of American Independence (actually fought on Breed's Hill near Boston, Massachusetts). Although the British won, the good performance of the untrained Americans gave considerable impetus to the Revolution.

bunkum nonsense. Recorded from the mid 19th century, originally as *buncombe*, the word comes from *Buncombe* County in North Carolina, mentioned in an inconsequential speech made by its congressman, Felix Walker, solely to please his constituents (*c.*1820).

bunny a child's term for a rabbit. The word is recorded from the early 17th century, originally used as a term of endearment to a person, later as a pet name for a rabbit; it comes from dialect *bun* 'squirrel, rabbit', also used as a term of endearment, of unknown origin.

See also ➤ BUGS *Bunny*.

bunny girl a club hostess, waitress, or photographic model, wearing a skimpy costume with ears and a tail suggestive of a rabbit.

Bunraku Japanese puppet drama, particularly as practised by the Bunraku-za marionette company.

Billy Bunter a schoolboy character, noted for his fatness and gluttony, in stories by Frank Richards (pseudonym of Charles Hamilton 1876–1961).

> Strawson, whose fat, self-satisfied Billy Bunter form waddled towards me at that moment.
> — Angus Wilson *Old Men at the Zoo* (1961)

John Bunyan 1628–88), English writer. A Nonconformist, he was imprisoned twice for unlicensed preaching and during this time wrote his spiritual autobiography *Grace Abounding* (1666), and began his major work *The Pilgrim's Progress* (1678–84), an allegory recounting the spiritual journey of its hero Christian (see ➤ CHRISTIAN²).

> Just as Oliver Cromwell aimed to bring about the kingdom of God on earth and founded the British Empire, so Bunyan wanted the millennium and got the novel.
> — Christopher Hill *A Turbulent, Seditious, and Factious People: John Bunyan and his Church, 1628–1688* (1988)

Paul Bunyan name of a legendary figure of the lumber camps of the northwestern US, a giant lumberjack proverbial for his size, strength, and vitality, and with the ability to create lakes and rivers; he is said to have been responsible for the Grand Canyon

and the Black Hills. Originally a figure of oral folklore, the first Paul Bunyan stories were published in 1910 by James MacGillivray in 'The Round River Drive' (*Detroit News-Tribune*, 24 July, 1910).

Paul Bunyan was the subject of an operetta by Benjamin Britten, for which the libretto was written by W. H. Auden.

bunyip in Australia, a mythical amphibious monster said to inhabit inland waterways. The name comes from an aboriginal word.

buppie informal term for a young urban black professional; a black ➤ YUPPIE.

Burana see ➤ CARMINA *Burana*.

Buraq in the Koran (Sura 17), the horse-like creature which is given by Gabriel to ➤ MUHAMMAD to carry him on a night journey through the heavens to Jerusalem; it is larger than a donkey but smaller than a horse, and has a woman's head and a peacock's tail.

burb a suburb or suburban area; the usage is recorded from the late 1970s in US English, especially in **the burbs**, a somewhat dismissive term for a location seen as conventional and boring.

Richard Burbage (*c.*1567–1619), English actor. He was the creator of most of Shakespeare's great tragic roles: Hamlet, Othello, Lear, and Richard III, and was also associated with the building of the Globe Theatre.

Burbank a city in southern California, on the north side of the Los Angeles conurbation, which is a centre of the film and television industries.

burble make a continuous murmuring noise; speak in an unintelligible or silly way, especially at unnecessary length. Recorded from Middle English as an imitative formation meaning 'to bubble', the current senses date from Lewis Carroll in the late 19th century:

> And as in uffish thought he stood,
> The Jabberwock, with eyes of flame,
> Came whiffling through the tulgey wood,
> And burbled as it came!
> — Lewis Carroll *Through the Looking-Glass* (1872)

burden a load, typically a heavy one; in figurative use, a duty or misfortune that causes hardship, anxiety, or grief; a nuisance. Recorded from Old English (in form *byrthen*) the word is of West Germanic origin, related to *bear* 'carry'.

Burden is also used for the refrain or chorus of a song; the word in this sense is partly confused with *bourdon*, from Old French, meaning 'drone', of imitative origin.

See also ➤ GOD *makes the back to the burden*, ➤ WHITE *man's burden*.

burden of proof the obligation to prove one's assertion; the term (translating Latin *onus probandi* in Roman law) is recorded from the late 16th century.

Bureau of State Security full name of **BOSS**, the former South African intelligence and security organization under apartheid.

bureaucracy a system of government in which most of the important decisions are taken by state officials rather than by elected representatives.

Guy Burgess (1911–63), British Foreign Office official and spy. Acting as a Soviet agent from the 1930s, he worked for MI5 while ostensibly employed by the BBC. After the war he worked at the British Embassy in Washington, under Kim Philby; charged with espionage in 1951, he fled to the USSR with Donald Maclean.

Burgess Shale a stratum of sedimentary rock exposed in the Rocky Mountains in British Columbia, Canada. The bed, dated to the Cambrian period (about 540 million years ago), is rich in well-preserved fossils of early marine invertebrates, many of which represent evolutionary lineages unknown in later times.

Lord Burghley William Cecil (1520–98), 1st Baron, English statesman. Secretary of State to Queen Elizabeth I 1558–72 and Lord High Treasurer 1572–98, he was the queen's most trusted councillor and minister and the driving force behind many of her government's policies.

burglary entry into a building illegally with intent to commit a crime such as theft. In English law before 1968, burglary was a crime under statute and in common law; since 1968 it has been a statutory crime only.

John Burgoyne (1722–92), English general and dramatist; known as **Gentleman Johnny.** He surrendered to the Americans at Saratoga (1777) in the War of American Independence.

Burgundy a region and former duchy of east central France, centred on Dijon. Under a series of strong dukes Burgundy achieved considerable independence from imperial control in the later Middle Ages, before being absorbed by France when King Louis XI claimed the duchy in 1477.

Jean Buridan (*c*.1295–*c*.1358) French philosopher who studied under William of Ockham, said to have constructed the paradox of **Buridan's ass**, whereby a hungry and thirsty donkey, placed between a bundle of hay and a pail of water, would die of hunger and thirst because there was no reason for him to choose one resource over the other.

buried see ➤ *know where the* BODIES *are buried.*

buried in woollen buried in a woollen shroud, as required by an act of Charles II for the encouragement of woollen manufacture.

Edmund Burke (1729–97), British man of letters and Whig politician. Burke wrote on the issues of political emancipation and moderation, notably with respect to Roman Catholics and the American colonies. His *Reflections on the Revolution in France* (1790) called on European leaders to resist the new regime.

John Burke (1787–1848), Irish genealogical and heraldic writer. He compiled *Burke's Peerage* (first published in 1826), a genealogical guide to peers and baronets.

Robert Burke (1820–61), Irish explorer. He led a successful expedition from south to north across Australia in the company of William Wills and two others—the first white men to make this journey. On the return journey, however, Burke, Wills, and a third companion died of starvation.

William Burke (1792–1829), Irish murderer. He was a bodysnatcher operating in Edinburgh with his accomplice *William Hare*, and was convicted of murdering those whose bodies he subsequently sold for dissection. He gave his name to the verb *burke* meaning, 'kill secretly by suffocation or strangulation', as Burke is said to have killed his victims.

Burlington Bertie the type of a man-about-town, personified in the song (1915) by W. F. Hargreaves, popularized by the music-hall performer Vesta Tilley:

> I'm Burlington Bertie
> I rise at ten thirty and saunter along like a toff,
> I walk down the Strand with my gloves on my hand,
> Then I walk down again with them off.
> — W. F. Hargreaves 'Burlington Bertie from Bow'
> (1915)

Burlington refers to the luxurious *Burlington Arcade* in the fashionable area of Piccadilly, London.

Burma Road a route linking Lashi in Burma to Kunming in China. Completed in 1939, it was built by the Chinese in response to the Japanese occupation of the Chinese coast, to serve as a supply route to the interior.

burn, baby, burn black extremist slogan in use during the Los Angeles riots, August 1965.

burn in effigy subject an image (of a person) to burning as the punishment desired for the original (formerly done in the case of a prisoner who had fled from justice).

burn one's boats destroy one's means of retreat, do something which makes it impossible to return to an earlier state; the term is recorded (in figurative use) from the late 19th century.

burn one's fingers (especially in a financial context) suffer unpleasant consequences as a result of one's actions, discouraging one from trying a similar action again.

burn the candle at both ends draw on one's resources from two directions; especially, overtax one's strength by going to bed late and getting up early. The expression is recorded in English from the mid 18th century, but is found earlier in French.

burn the midnight oil read or work late into the night, supposedly by lamplight; a related image is found in the expression ➤ SMELL *of the lamp*.

Edward Burne-Jones (1833–98), English painter and designer. His work, which included tapestry and stained-glass window designs, reflected his interest in medieval and literary themes and is typical of the later Pre-Raphaelite style.

Burnell the Ass the hero of the *Speculum Stultorum* by Wireker. Burnell, who represents the monk who is dissatisfied with his lot, is an ass who wants a longer tail. He goes to Salerno and Paris to study, and finally loses his tail altogether. In the course of his travels he hears the tale that Chaucer alludes to in 'The Nun's Priest's Tale', in which the priest's son Gandulf breaks a cock's leg by throwing a stone at it. Later, on the morning when he is to be ordained, the cock fails to crow in time to rouse him and he loses his benefice.

burning see ➤ *a* BRAND *from the burning*, ➤ *burning* MARL.

burning bush in Exodus 3:2, a bush which 'burned with fire, and…was not consumed', seen by ➤ MOSES on Mount Horeb, and constituting a sign from God that he was to lead the Israelites out of Egypt.

burning fiery furnace in Daniel ch. 3, the fire into which the three Hebrew exiles in Babylon, Shadrach, Meshach, and Abednego, were cast by King Nebuchadnezzar because they refused to worship pagan images, and in which they were preserved unharmed.

See also ➤ SONG *of the Three Holy Children.*

burning of the clavie a ceremony for Hogmanay held in the village of Burghead on the Moray Firth in Scotland (*clavie* here is a beam of wood).

Robert Burns (1759–96), Scottish poet, best known for poems such as 'The Jolly Beggars' (1786) and 'Tam o' Shanter' (1791), and for old Scottish songs which he collected, including 'Auld Lang Syne' and 'Ye Banks and Braes'.

Burns Night 25 January, the birthday of ➤ *Robert* BURNS, when celebrations are held in Scotland and elsewhere.

a burnt child dreads the fire proverbial saying, mid 13th century.

burnt offering an offering burnt on an altar as a religious sacrifice, originally in biblical use, as in Job 1:5, 'Job…offered burnt offerings according to the number of them all.'

Aaron Burr (1756–1836), American Democratic Republican statesman. In 1804, while Vice-President, he killed his rival Alexander Hamilton in a duel. He then plotted to form an independent administration in Mexico and was tried for treason but acquitted.

bursars ➤ *St* JOSEPH is the patron saint of bursars.

Cyril Burt (1883–1971), English psychologist. Using studies of identical twins, he claimed that intelligence is inherited, but he was later accused of fabricating data.

Richard Burton (1821–90), English explorer, anthropologist, and translator of the *Arabian Nights* (1885–8), the *Kama Sutra* (1883), and *The Perfumed Garden* (1886). He and John Hanning Speke were the first Europeans to see Lake Tanganyika (1858).

bury one's head in the sand ignore unpleasant realities; the expression alludes to the traditional belief that the ➤ OSTRICH if pursued would bury its head in the sand, through incapacity to distinguish between seeing and being seen.

bury the hatchet end a quarrel or conflict and become friendly; the allusion is to an American Indian custom of burying a hatchet or tomahawk to mark the conclusion of a peace treaty.

Busby Babes informal name given to the young football players recruited for Manchester United by Matt *Busby* (1909–94), the Scottish-born football manager. An air crash at Munich airport in 1958 killed most of the side, but he reconstructed the team and won the European Cup in 1968.

bush see also ➤ BEAT *the bush (while another takes the birds)*, ➤ *a* BIRD *in the hand is worth two in the bush*➤, BURNING *bush*, ➤ *good* WINE *needs no bush*, ➤ SYDNEY *or the bush.*

the bush especially in Australia and Africa, wild or uncultivated country. The term is recorded from the late 18th century, and may represent a direct adoption of Dutch *bosch* 'bush' in regions which were originally Dutch colonies.

Bush Brotherhood an Anglican missionary organization founded to provide a peripatetic ministry in remote areas of the Australian bush.

bush lawyer in Australia and New Zealand, a layman who fancies he has a knowledge of the law, an argumentative person.

bush telegraph an informal network by means of which information is conveyed in remote areas; the term is originally Australian, and refers to bushrangers' confederates who disseminated intelligence as to the movements of the police.

bushel in Britain, a measure of capacity equal to 8 gallons (equivalent to 36.4 litres), used for corn, fruit, liquids, etc.; in the US, a measure of capacity equal to 64 US pints (equivalent to 35.2 litres), used for dry goods. The word is recorded from Middle English, and comes from Old French *boissel*, perhaps ultimately of Gaulish origin.

hide one's light under a bushel keep quiet about one's talents or accomplishments, originally with reference to Matthew 5:15, 'Neither do men light a candle, and put it under a bushel, but on a candlestick.'

bushido the code of honour and morals developed by the Japanese ➤ SAMURAI. The word is Japanese, and comes from *bushi* 'samurai' + *dō* 'way'.

bushranger in 19th-century Australia, an escaped convict or outlaw living in the bush, often by resort to robbery.

bushwhacker one who lives in wild uncultivated country; in the American Civil War, an irregular combatant with a group who had taken to the woods.

the busiest men have the most leisure proverbial saying, late 19th century.

business a person's regular occupation, trade, or profession; the practice of making one's living by engaging in commerce; in the theatre, actions other than dialogue performed by actors.

Recorded from Old English (in the form *bisignis*) in the sense 'anxiety', the sense 'state of being busy' was used from Middle English down to the 18th century, but is now differentiated as *busyness*. The use 'appointed task' dates from late Middle English, and from it all the other current senses have developed.

See also ➤ EVERYBODY'*s business is nobody's business*, ➤ PUNCTUALITY *is the soul of business.*

business before pleasure proverbial saying, mid 19th century.

Busiris in Greek mythology, a king of Egypt who sacrificed to Zeus all strangers landing on his shores in the hope of ending a drought; he was killed by Hercules.

busk play music or otherwise perform for voluntary donations in a street or subway. The word is recorded from the mid 17th century in nautical use in the sense 'cruise about, tack' (from obsolete French *busquer* 'seek', via Italian or Spanish, and ultimately of Germanic origin). The term in English later came to mean 'go about selling things', and hence (in the mid 19th century) 'go about performing'.

buskin a thick-soled laced boot worn by an ancient Athenian tragic actor to gain height; **the buskin** denotes the style or spirit of tragic drama. The word is recorded from the early 16th century, designating a calf-length boot; it probably comes via Old French from Middle Dutch *broseken*, but the ultimate origin is unknown.

See also ➤ SOCK *and buskin.*

busman's holiday a holiday or form of recreation that involves doing the same thing that one does at work; the term is recorded from the late 19th century, when excursions by bus were a popular form of holiday.

Frances Mary Buss (1827–94), English educationist. She was in charge of the North London Collegiate School for Ladies (1850–94) and was the first to use the title headmistress. She also co-founded a training college for women teachers in Cambridge, and campaigned for higher education for women with her friend Dorothea Beale. Together they were the subject of a popular rhyme:

> Miss Buss and Miss Beale
> Cupid's darts do not feel.
> How different from us,
> Miss Beale and Miss Buss.
>
> — rhyme, c.1884

Buster name of a cross-breed Staffordshire bull terrier belonging to the Labour MP Roy Hattersley, who in 1996 was fined for allowing his dog to kill a greylag goose in a royal park. *Buster's Diaries* (Roy Hattersley, 1998) subsequently put the dog's side of the story.

busy bee an industrious person; an expression deriving from the *bee* taken as the type of a busy worker.

but and ben in Scottish usage, a two-roomed cottage, a small or humble home; from *but* the outer room of a two-roomed house; *ben* the parlour of a two-roomed house with only one outer door, opening into the kitchen.

butcher see also ➤ *Butcher* CUMBERLAND, ➤ *it is possible for a* RAM *to kill a butcher.*

the Butcher of Lyons nickname of Klaus Barbie (1913–91), head of the Gestapo in Lyons between 1942 and 1944, regarded as responsible for the deaths of 4,000 people and the deportation of over 7,000 others. He was extradited from Bolivia to France in 1983 and in 1987 was tried in Lyons for 'crimes against humanity'; he was sentenced to life imprisonment.

the butcher, the baker, the candlestick-maker people of all trades; from the nursery rhyme 'Rub-a-dub-dub, Three men in a tub.'

Butlin's popular holiday camps founded by Sir William ('Billy') Butlin (1899–1980) in 1936 at Skegness, taken as the type of an establishment offering organized leisure and entertainment.

> I think I speak for the whole village when I say that we're not some kind of Butlins holiday camp for every ne'er do well who can get his hands on a caravan.'
>
> — P. Gregory *Perfectly Correct* (1996)

Butskellism the adoption of economic policies broadly acceptable to both political parties, from a blend of the names of R. A. *Butler* (Conservative Chancellor of the Exchequer 1951–5) and H. T. N. *Gaitskell* (Labour Chancellor of the Exchequer 1950–1 and subsequently Shadow Chancellor).

butter see also ➤ BREAD *and butter.*

butter one's bread on both sides be wasteful or luxurious; the expression is recorded from the early 19th century.

buttercup the name is recorded from the 18th century, superseding the earlier *butterflower*: the traditional explanation of the names was that cows by eating the plant gave its yellow colouring to butter, but in fact all kinds are poisonous and generally avoided by livestock.

buttered see ➤ the BREAD *never falls but on its buttered side.*

William Butterfield (1814–1900), English architect, an exponent of the Gothic revival. Associated with the Oxford Movement, he mainly designed and restored churches. His mature style uses hard, angular forms and patterned, coloured brickwork. Notable building: Keble College, Oxford (1867–83).

> Red, white, and blue brick, with a huge roof, tiled, striped, and Butterfieldian.
>
> — Nikolaus Pevsner *Cambridgeshire* (1970)

butterfingers informal term for a clumsy person, especially one who fails to hold a catch at cricket; the expression is recorded from the mid 19th century.

butterflower an earlier (late 16th-century) name for the ➤ BUTTERCUP.

butterfly an insect with two pairs of large wings that are covered with microscopic scales, typically brightly coloured and held erect when at rest; in transferred usage, a showy or frivolous person.
See also ➤ BREAK *a butterfly on a wheel.*

the butterfly effect the effect of a very small change in the initial conditions of a system which makes a significant difference to the outcome; the term derives from the title of a paper (1979) by the American meteorologist Edward Lorenz (1917–), 'Predictability: Does the flap of a butterfly's wings in Brazil set off a tornado in Texas?'

butterfly kiss a caress consisting of a fluttering of the eyelashes against the cheek.

float like a butterfly, sting like a bee summary of Muhammad Ali's boxing strategy (probably originated by his aide Drew 'Bundini' Brown).

Buttermere see ➤ MAID *of Buttermere*.

Button's Coffee House a coffee house, the rival of Will's, which stood in Russell Street, Covent Garden; Button was an old servant of Addison's, and the house was frequented by Dryden, Addison, Steele, and Pope. It declined in popularity after Addison's death and Steele's retirement to Wales.

Buttons a nickname for a liveried pageboy; especially, in the pantomime of ➤ CINDERELLA, the page who serves Cinderella's father and has an unrequited love for Cinderella herself; the character was first introduced in the 19th century, after Rossini's Cinderella opera *La Cenerentola* (1817) became well known.

buy in the cheapest market and sell in the dearest proverbial saying, late 16th century.

let the buyer beware proverbial saying, early 16th century; the Latin tag *caveat emptor* is also found.

the buyer has need of a hundred eyes, the seller of but one proverbial saying, mid 17th century.

buzzard a large hawklike bird of prey with broad wings and a rounded tail, often seen soaring in wide circles. The buzzard, despite its appearance, could not be used in falconry, and from this arose the figurative sense of 'a worthless, stupid, or ignorant person', as well as the expression **between hawk and buzzard**.

   Recorded from late Middle English, the word comes from Old French *busard*, based on Latin *buteo* 'falcon'.

buzzword a technical word or phrase that has become fashionable, typically as a slogan.

by see ➤ *by a long* CHALK, ➤ *by* APPOINTMENT, ➤ *by* HOOK *or by crook*, ➤ *by* RETURN *of post*,

by-law a regulation made by a local authority or corporation; a rule made by a company or society to control the actions of its members. The term is recorded from Middle English, and probably comes from obsolete *byrlaw* 'local law or custom', from Old Norse *býr* 'town', but associated with *by*.

Byblos an ancient Mediterranean seaport, situated on the site of modern Jebeil, to the north of Beirut in Lebanon. An important trading centre with strong links with Egypt, it became a thriving Phoenician city in the 2nd millennium BC, and was particularly noted for the export of papyrus and cedar wood.

Bycorne in the poem *Chichevache and Bycorne* by John Lydgate (?1370–1449), the proper name of a fabulous animal, which habitually fed on patient husbands, and grew fat from the abundance of this diet, while his mate *Chichevache* fed on patient wives, and was correspondingly lean.

Bye Plot the less important of two plots (the other was the ➤ MAIN *Plot*) against the government of James I uncovered in 1603; also known as ➤ WATSON*'s plot*.

Byerley Turk with the ➤ GODOLPHIN *Barb* and the ➤ DARLEY *Arabian*, one of the three founding sires of the Thoroughbred, imported to improve the stock in the 18th century.

byline a line in a newspaper naming the writer of an article.

Lord Byron George Gordon (1788–1824), English poet, who had an instantaneous success in *Childe Harold's Pilgrimage* (1812); he said of himself, 'I awoke one day and found myself famous.' In 1815 there were rumours of an incestuous relationship with his half-sister, his wife left him, and debts associated with his ancestral home increased. Ostracized and embittered, he left England permanently and stayed with Shelley in Geneva, finally settling in Italy. Though criticized on moral grounds, Byron's poetry, with its dark and moody heroes, exerted considerable influence on the romantic movement, particularly on the Continent. In 1824 he joined the fight for Greek independence, but died of malaria before seeing serious battle.

Byzantine regarded as typifying the politics and bureacratic structure of the ➤ BYZANTINE *Empire*; in particular, (of a system or situation) excessively complicated and typically involving a great deal of administrative detail; characterized by deviousness or underhand procedure.

   Byzantine is also used to designate an ornate artistic and architectural style which developed in the Byzantine Empire and spread to Italy, Russia, and elsewhere. The art is generally rich and stylized (as in religious icons) and the architecture is typified by many-domed, highly decorated churches.

Byzantine Empire the empire in SE Europe and Asia Minor formed from the eastern part of the Roman Empire.

The Roman Empire was divided in AD 395 by the Emperor Theodosius between his sons; Constantinople (Byzantium) became the capital of the Eastern Empire in 476, with the fall of Rome. In 1054 theological and political differences between Constantinople and Rome led to the breach between Eastern and Western Christianity (see ➤ GREAT *Schism*).

After about 1100 the empire gradually declined; the loss of Constantinople to the Ottoman Turks in 1453 was the end of the empire, although its rulers held Trebizond (Trabzon) until 1461.

Byzantium an ancient Greek city, founded in the 7th century BC, at the southern end of the Bosporus, site of the modern city of Istanbul. It was rebuilt by Constantine the Great in AD 324–30 as Constantinople.

Cc

C the third letter of the modern English alphabet and of the ancient Roman one, originally corresponding to Greek *gamma*, Semitic *gimel*.

Ça ira French for 'things will work out', refrain of 'Carillon national', popular song of the French Revolution (*c.* July 1790), translated by William Doyle; the phrase is believed to originate with Benjamin Franklin, who may have uttered it in 1776 when asked for news of the American Revolution.

cab-drivers ➤ *St* FIACRE is the patron saint of cab-drivers.

Cabal in the mid 17th century, the name given to a committee of five ministers under Charles II, whose surnames happened to begin with C, A, B, A, and L (Clifford, Arlington, Buckingham, Ashley, and Lauderdale).

The word *cabal* (denoting the ➤ KABBALAH) is recorded from the late 16th century, and comes ultimately via French from medieval Latin *cabala*.

Cabala see ➤ KABBALAH.

Cabbage Garden in Australia, an informal name for the state of Victoria.

Cabbagetown in Canada, an informal term for a depressed urban area; an inner-city slum. The expression comes from the nickname of a depressed area of Toronto, where the inhabitants were said to exist on a diet of cabbage.

Cabbala see ➤ KABBALAH.

Cabeiri in ancient Greece, a group of gods (apparently non-Greek in origin) on whom, together with a mother goddess, a mystery cult was centred; they are instanced in *Middlemarch* as one of the subjects of Mr Casaubon's fruitless studies:

> Mr Casaubon himself was lost . . . in an agitated dimness about the Cabeiri, or in an exposure of other mythologists' ill-considered parallels.
> — George Eliot *Middlemarch* (1872)

the Cabinet in the UK, Canada, and other Commonwealth countries, the committee of senior ministers responsible for controlling government policy; (in the US) a body of advisers to the President, composed of the heads of the executive departments of the government.

Cabinet was first used in the early 17th century for the private room in which confidential advisers of the sovereign or chief ministers of a country meet; the current sense is recorded from the mid 17th century.

See also ➤ KITCHEN *cabinet*, ➤ SHADOW *cabinet*.

cable the chain of a ship's anchor; in nautical usage, a length of 200 yards (182.9 metres) or (in the US) 240 yards (219.4 metres).

the whole caboodle the whole number or quantity of people or things in question. Recorded from the mid 19th century (originally US), and perhaps from the phrase ➤ *the whole* KIT *and boodle*, in the same sense.

caboshed in heraldry (of the head of a stag, bull, or other animal) shown full face with no neck visible.

Cabot the name of two Italian explorers and navigators, the elder of whom, **John Cabot** (*c.*1450–*c.*98), sailed from Bristol in 1497 in search of Asia, but in fact landed on the mainland of North America (the site of his arrival is uncertain). Returning to Bristol, he undertook a second expedition in 1498 from which he never returned.

His son **Sebastian Cabot** (*c.*1475–1557) accompanied his father on his voyage in 1497 and made further voyages after the latter's death, most notably to Brazil and the River Plate (1526).

ca'canny dated term for the policy of deliberately limiting output at work; the term (recorded from the late 19th century) is a Scots expression, meaning 'proceed warily'.

cachet see ➤ LETTRE *de cachet*.

cacique in Latin America or the Spanish-speaking Caribbean, a native chief. The word is recorded from the mid 16th century, and comes (via Spanish or French) from Taino.

cacodemon a malevolent spirit or person. The word is recorded from the late 16th century and comes from Greek, from *kakos* 'bad' + *daimōn* 'spirit'.

cacoethes an urge to do something inadvisable; the word is recorded from the mid 16th century, and comes via Latin from Greek *kakoēthes*, from *kakos* 'bad' + *ēthos* 'disposition'.

cacoethes scribendi an incurable passion for writing; the phrase is originally a quotation from the Roman satirist Juvenal (AD *c*.60–*c*.130), '*Tenet insanabile multos Scribendi cacoethes et aegro in corde senescit* [Many suffer from the incurable disease of writing, and it becomes chronic in their sick minds].'

cacology archaic term for a bad choice of words or poor pronunciation. Recorded from the late 18th century, the word comes via late Latin from Greek *kakologia* 'vituperation' from *kakos* 'bad'.

Cacus in Roman mythology, a fire-breathing monster, son of Vulcan, who according to Virgil's *Aeneid* lived in a cave below the Aventine and preyed on the country round about; he was killed by Hercules after stealing some of the cattle, formerly belonging to Geryon, which Hercules was taking back to Greece.

cad a man who behaves dishonourably, especially towards a woman. The word is recorded from the late 18th century, and originally denoted a passenger picked up by the driver (the *caddie*) of a horse-drawn coach for personal profit.

George and Richard Cadbury (1839–1922) and (1835–99), English cocoa and chocolate manufacturers and social reformers. As committed Quakers, they were concerned with improving their employees' working and living conditions, and established a new factory and housing estate at Bournville.

Cadbury Code a code of practice regulating the corporate governance of all listed companies, issued in 1992 by a Committee, chaired by Sir George Adrian Hayhurst *Cadbury* (1929–), a director of the Bank of England 1970–94; the Committee had been set up as a result of the wide public concern generated by the discovery in 1991 of the misappropriation of the company pension funds of Mirror Group Newspapers.

caddie a person who carries a golfer's clubs and provides other assistance during a match. Recorded (as a Scots term) from the mid 17th century, and

coming from French *cadet*, the original term denoted a gentleman who joined the army without a commission, intending to learn the profession and follow a military career, later coming to mean 'odd-job man'. The current sense dates from the late 18th century.

See also ➤ CAD.

Jack Cade (d. 1450), Irish rebel. In 1450 he assumed the name of *Mortimer* (suggesting links with the royal family) and led the Kentish rebels against Henry VI. They occupied London for three days and executed the treasurer of England and the sheriff of Kent. Cade died of a wound received in an attempt to capture him.

cadet archaic term for a younger son or daughter; designating a junior branch of a family. The word is recorded from the early 17th century and comes via French from Gascon dialect *capdet*, a diminutive based on Latin *caput* 'head'. The notion 'little head' or 'inferior head' gave rise to that of 'younger, junior'.

Brother Cadfael in the popular detective stories of Ellis Peters (1913–95), a former crusader who is a Benedictine monk of the 12th-century abbey of Shrewsbury, later home to the shrine of ➤ St WINEFRIDE; Cadfael uses his worldly knowledge and herbalist's skills, as well as his faith, to resolve mysteries in the abbey and the town.

> If only one could withdraw to a place that is, yet never was: to Shrewsbury Abbey, but in the 1140s, as depicted by the detective writer Ellis Peters. There would be safety within those walls, peace and healing round the brazier in Brother Cadfael's herby garden shed.
> — *Church Times* 8 November 1996

cadge *cadge* is recorded from the early 17th century, in the dialect sense 'carry about', a backformation from the noun *cadger*. This dates from the late 15th century denoting (in northern English and Scots) an itinerant dealer, whence the verb sense 'hawk, peddle', giving rise to the current verb senses 'ask or obtain something to which one is not entitled' from the early 19th century.

In falconry, a *cadge* is a padded wooden frame on which hooded hawks are carried to the field; the word here is apparently an alteration of *cage*, perhaps confused with the dialect verb *cadge* 'carry about'.

Cadiz a city and port on the coast of SW Spain, which was important in the 16th to 18th centuries as the headquarters of the Spanish fleet. In 1587 Sir

Francis Drake burnt the ships of Philip II at anchor there (an enterprise which he described as 'the singeing of the King of Spain's beard').

Cadmean letters supposedly the Phoenician letters with which ➤ CADMUS taught the Boeotians the art of writing, and from which the Greek alphabet is said to be derived.

Cadmean victory a victory gained at too great a cost; a proverbial expression (like ➤ PYRRHIC *victory*) deriving from the fact that in Theban mythology success was often followed by disaster.

Cadmus in Greek mythology, the brother of ➤ EUROPA and traditional founder of Thebes in Boeotia. He killed a dragon which guarded a spring, and when (on Athene's advice) he sowed the dragon's teeth there came up a harvest of armed men; he disposed of the majority by setting them to fight one another, and the survivors formed the ancestors of the Theban nobility.

See also ➤ *the necklace of* HARMONIA.

caduceus an ancient Greek or Roman herald's wand, typically one with two serpents twined round it, carried by the messenger god Hermes or Mercury. The word comes from Latin, from Doric Greek *karukeion* for Greek *kērux* 'herald'.

Caecias in Greek mythology, the north-east wind personified.

Caedmon (7th century), Anglo-Saxon monk and poet, said to have been an illiterate herdsman inspired in a vision to compose poetry on biblical themes. The only authentic fragment of his work is a song in praise of the Creation, quoted by Bede.

Caen a city and river port in Normandy in northern France, on the River Orne, which is the burial place of William the Conqueror. The town was the scene of fierce fighting between the Germans and the Allies in June and July 1944.

Caerleon a town in South Wales, the tradional seat of Arthur, as in Tennyson's *Idylls of the King*:

> Arthur on the Whitsuntide before
> Held court at old Caerleon upon Usk.
> — Lord Tennyson *The Marriage of Geraint* (1859)

It is probably to be identified with *Carlioun*, which in Malory's *Morte D'Arthur* is said to be where Arthur was crowned and held his court.

Caernarfon a town in NW Wales on the shore of the Menai Strait. Its 13th-century castle was the birthplace of Edward II.

Caesar a title of Roman emperors, especially those from Augustus to Hadrian. Recorded from the Middle English, the word comes from Latin *Caesar*, family name of the Roman statesman ➤ *Gaius* JULIUS *Caesar*.

aut Caesar, aut nihil Latin motto meaning, Caesar or nothing; inscribed on the sword of ➤ *Cesare* BORGIA (1476–1507).

Caesar's wife must be above suspicion proverbial saying, late 18th century; with reference to the story in Plutarch's *Caesar* of how Caesar divorced his wife Pompeia after the scandal surrounding the affair in which Clodius, who was in love with Pompeia, smuggled himself into the house in which the women of Caesar's household were celebrating the festival of the ➤ BONA *Dea*. Caesar refused to bring charges against Clodius, but divorced Pompeia; when questioned, he replied 'I thought my wife ought not even to be under suspicion'.

Caesarea an ancient port on the Mediterranean coast of Israel, founded in 22 BC by Herod the Great on the site of a Phoenician harbour and named in honour of the Roman emperor Augustus Caesar. Caesarea became one of the principal cities of Roman Palestine, but it later declined as its harbour silted up.

Caesarea Philippi a city in ancient Palestine, on the site of the present-day village of Baniyas in the Golan Heights. It was the site of a Hellenistic shrine to the god Pan and then of a temple built towards the end of the 1st century BC by Herod the Great and named in honour of the Roman emperor Augustus Caesar.

Caesarean section a surgical operation for delivering a child by cutting through the wall of the mother's abdomen. The term is recorded from the early 17th century, and the name is said to come from the story that Julius Caesar was delivered by this method.

Café Royal a French-style café-restaurant at 68 Regent Street, which was for several decades from the 1880s onwards the haunt of artists and writers and the scene of many artistic gatherings, scandals, and celebrations. Its habitués included Whistler, Wilde, Crowley, Beerbohm, and Shaw.

Count Cagliostro assumed name of an Italian adventurer, Giuseppe Balsamo (1743–95), who posed successfully as an alchemist and magician in late 18th-century Paris society; he was banished after his involvement in the ➤ *Affair of the* DIAMOND *Necklace*. In 1789 he was arrested in Rome, and spent his final years in prison.

> To me he has always been a political Cagliostro. Now a conjuror is I think a very pleasant fellow to have among us if we know he is a conjuror—but a conjuror who is believed to do his tricks without sleight of hand is a dangerous man.
>
> — Anthony Trollope *Phineas Redux* (1874)

Cagoulard a member of a secret French right-wing organization in the 1930s; the name is French, and means literally 'wearer of a monk's cowl'.

Caiaphas name of the Jewish high priest at the time of the trial and execution of Jesus; in John 11:50, when the possibility that the crowds flocking to Jesus will provoke Roman intervention is discussed by the chief priests and Pharisees, it is Caiaphas who says, 'It is expedient for us, that one man should die for the people, and that the whole nation perish not.'

> Worldly institutions, operating the Caiaphatic ethic, throw people on the human scrapheap of unemployment, in order that the company may not perish.
>
> — *Church Times* 12 February 1999

Cain in the Bible, the eldest son of Adam and Eve, and murderer of his brother Abel after Abel's offering to God of a lamb was accepted by God, while Cain's sheaves were rejected. Cain is the first murderer of humankind, and from this becomes a fugitive and outcast.

curse of Cain the fate of someone compelled to lead a wandering life; in Genesis 4:11–12, after the killing of Abel, God tells Cain that he is 'cursed from the earth' and that he will be 'a fugitive and a vagabond…in the earth'.

the land God gave to Cain a name for Labrador, referring to Cain's banishment by God to a desolate land 'east of Eden'. The term derives from a remark attributed to the French navigator and explorer Jacques Cartier (1491–1557), on first discovering the northern shore of the Gulf of St Lawrence (now Labrador and Quebec), 'I am rather inclined to believe that this is the land God gave to Cain.'

mark of Cain placed on Cain by God, initially as a sign that he should not be killed or harmed, later taken as identifying him as a murderer.

Cainite a member of a 2nd-century sect professing reverence for Cain and other wicked Scriptural characters.

Cajun a member of any of the largely self-contained communities in the bayou areas of southern Louisiana formed by descendants of French Canadians, speaking an archaic form of French and known for their lively folk music and spicy cooking. The name comes from an alteration of *Acadian* (see ➤ ACADIA).

cake see also ➤ BANBURY *cake*, ➤ LAND *of Cakes*, ➤ *my cake is* DOUGH, ➤ POMFRET *cake*, ➤ PONTEFRACT *cake*, ➤ SOUL *cake*, ➤ *you cannot* HAVE *your cake and eat it*.

cakes and ale merrymaking, good things; originally, a quotation from Shakespeare's *Twelfth Night* (1601) ,'Dost thou think, because thou art virtuous, there shall be no more cakes and ale?'

cakewalk a strutting dance popular at the end of the 19th century, developed from an American black contest in graceful walking which had a cake as a prize.

Calabria a region of SW Italy, forming the 'toe' of the Italian peninsula. The name was formerly applied by the Byzantines to the eastern promontory forming the 'heel', but was transferred to the 'toe' in the west when the area was seized by the Lombards *c.*700 AD.

Calais a port in northern France. Captured by Edward III in 1347 after a long siege, it remained an English possession until it was retaken by the French in 1558. Queen ➤ MARY *Tudor*, who died that year, is reported in *Holinshed's Chronicles* to have said, 'When I am dead and opened, you shall find 'Calais' lying in my heart.'

Calamity Jane (*c.*1852–1903), American frontierswoman, noted for her skill at shooting and riding; born *Martha Jane Canary*.

> A blonde voluptuous piece comes on and twirls a gun like Calamity Jane.
>
> — Steven Berkoff *Coriolanus in Deutschland* (1992)

Calchas in Homer's *Iliad*, the seer of the Greek forces at the siege of Troy.

> I can picture the probable domestic anxiety in the house of Calchas when in pursuit of his calling he found it necessary to stand up to the king of men, Agamemnon!
>
> — W. M. Kirkland *The Joys of Being a Woman* (1918)

calculate determine (the amount or number of something) mathematically. Recorded from late Middle English, the word comes from late Latin calculat- 'counted', ultimately from *calculus* 'a small pebble (as used on an abacus)'.

Calcutta see ➤ BLACK *Hole of Calcutta*.

caldarium a hot room in an ancient Roman bath.

Randolph **Caldecott** (1846–86), English graphic artist and watercolour painter. He is best known for his illustrations for children's books, and a medal awarded annually for the illustration of American children's books is named after him.

Caledonia the Roman name for northern Britain, later applied poetically or rhetorically to Scotland, as in Scott's *The Lay of the Last Minstrel* (1805), 'O Caledonia! stern and wild'.

Caledonian Canal a system of lochs and canals crossing Scotland from Inverness on the east coast to Fort William on the west. Built by Thomas Telford, it was opened in 1822. It traverses the Great Glen, part of its length being formed by Loch Ness.

calendar a chart or series of pages showing the day, weeks, and months of a particular year, or giving particular seasonal information. Recorded from Middle English, the word comes via Old French from Latin *kalendarium* 'account book', from *kalendae*: see ➤ CALENDS.

See also ➤ ADVENT *calendar*, ➤ FRENCH *Republican calendar*, ➤ GREGORIAN *calendar*, ➤ JEWISH *calendar*, ➤ JULIAN *calendar*, ➤ NEWGATE *Calendar*, ➤ ROMAN *calendar*, ➤ SHEPHERD's *calendar*.

calender a member of a mendicant order of dervishes in Persia. The name comes (in the early 17th century) from Persian *qalandar*, of unknown origin.

calends the first day of the month in the ancient Roman calendar. Recorded from Old English (denoting an appointed time) the word comes via Old French from Latin *kalendae, calendae* 'first day of the month' (when accounts were due and the order of days was proclaimed), and is related to Latin *calare* and Greek *kalein* 'call, proclaim'.

See also ➤ *at the* GREEK *Calends*, ➤ CALENDAR.

calenture feverish delirium, formerly supposed to afflict sailors in the tropics, in which the sea is mistaken for green fields; recorded from the late 16th century, the word comes via French from Spanish *calentura* 'fever', ultimately from Latin *calentem* 'hot, burning'.

calepin an obsolete term for a dictionary, recorded from the mid 16th to the mid 17th centuries, and taking its name from the Augustinian friar

Ambrosio *Calepino*, of *Calepio* in Italy, author of a famous Latin dictionary, first published in 1502, and going through many editions in the 16th century.

calf see also ➤ DIVINITY *calf*, ➤ *the* GOLDEN *calf*, ➤ *kill the* FATTED *calf*.

calf love another term for ➤ PUPPY *love*.

calfskin a calf's skin as the type of clothing worn by fools or jesters; Shakespeare's *King John* (1591–8) has, 'Hang a calf's skin on those recreant limbs!'

> He settled down to enjoy some heavenly guying of a fool by a clever devil who knew how to wear the calfskin.
> — Clemence Dane *The Flower Girls* (1954)

Caliban in Shakespeare's *The Tempest*, the brutish and degraded son of the witch Sycorax, who has been forced to serve ➤ PROSPERO; in contrast to the 'airy spirit' ➤ ARIEL, he typifies a gross and animal nature. His name may represent either 'Carib' or 'cannibal'.

> The nineteenth century dislike of Realism is the rage of Caliban seeing his own face in the glass.
> — Oscar Wilde *The Picture of Dorian Gray* (1891) preface

Caliburn in the chronicle of Geoffrey of Monmouth, the name of King Arthur's sword; ➤ EXCALIBUR is an alteration of it.

Calicut a seaport in the state of Kerala in SW India, on the Malabar Coast, which in the 17th and 18th centuries became a centre of the textile trade with Europe; the cotton fabric *calico* originated there and is called after it.

Caligula (AD 12–41), Roman emperor 37–41, born *Gaius Julius Caesar Germanicus*. He gained the nickname *Caligula* ('little boot') as an infant on account of the miniature military boots he wore.

Caligula's brief reign, which began when he succeeded Tiberius and ended with his assassination, became notorious for its tyrannical excesses. He made his horse ➤ INCITATUS a consul, and expressed the wish 'that the Roman people had but one neck'; on another occasion, he ordered, 'Strike him so that he can feel he is dying.'

> In his own diocese, a bishop . . . has virtual Caligulan powers.
> — *New York Review of Books* 28 May 1998

caliph the chief Muslim civil and religious ruler, regarded as the successor of Muhammad. The caliph ruled in Baghdad until 1258 and then in Egypt until the Ottoman conquest of 1517; the title was then held by the Ottoman sultans until it was abolished in 1924 by ➤ *Kemal* ATATÜRK.

Calixtine a member of a section of the Hussites, who maintained that in the Mass the cup as well as the bread should be administered to the laity; an Utraquist. Recorded from the early 18th century, the word comes ultimately (via French and medieval Latin) from Latin *calix* 'cup'.

call see also ➤ *call a* SPADE *a spade.*

called see ➤ MANY *are called but few are chosen.*

be called to the Bar be admitted as a barrister.

be called within the Bar be appointed as a Queen's (or King's) Counsel.

caller herring in Scotland and northern England, fresh herring; *caller* (which dates from late Middle English) is an alteration of *calver* 'fresh', perhaps coming from a Germanic base meaning 'be cold'.

Callicrates (5th century BC), Greek architect. He was the leading architect in Periclean Athens, and with Ictinus designed the Parthenon (447–438 BC); other structures attributed to him include the Ionic temple of Athena Nike on the Acropolis in Athens (448–after 421 BC).

calligraphy decorative handwriting or handwritten lettering. Recorded from the early 17th century, the word comes from Greek *kalligraphia*, from *kalligraphos* 'person who writes beautifully', from *kallos* 'beauty' + *graphein* 'write'.

Callimachus (*c.*305–*c.*240 BC), Greek poet and scholar. He is famed for his hymns and epigrams, and was head of the library at Alexandria. He compiled a critical catalogue of the existing Greek literature of his day.

Calliope in Greek and Roman mythology, the Muse of epic poetry. The name comes from Greek *Kalliopē*, literally 'having a beautiful voice'.

Callippic cycle a period of 76 years, equal to 4 Metonic cycles, at the end of which, by omission of one day, the phases of the moon recur at the same day and hour. It is named after *Callippus*, a Greek astronomer of the 4th century BC.

Callisto in Greek mythology, a nymph, an attendant of Artemis, who was the lover of Zeus and mother of his son Arcas; she was turned into a bear either by Zeus to save her from the anger of his wife Hera or by Hera and Artemis in vengeance; later she was placed as a constellation in the heavens by Zeus (see also ➤ URSA *Major*).

In astronomy, *Callisto* is one of the Galilean moons of Jupiter, the eighth-closest satellite to the planet, icy with a dark, cratered surface.

calomel mercurous chloride, a white powder formerly used as a purgative. The name, which is modern Latin, is recorded from the late 17th century, and may come from Greek *kalos* 'beautiful' + *melas* 'black', perhaps because it was originally obtained from a black mixture of mercury and mercuric chloride.

caloyer a Greek monk, especially a monk of the order of St Basil. Recorded from the late 16th century, the word comes via French and Italian from ecclesiastical Greek *kalogēros*, from *kalos* 'beautiful' + *gērōs*, *-as* 'old age'.

Calpe in Greek mythology, name of one of the ➤ PILLARS *of Hercules.*

caltrop a spiked metal ball thrown on the ground to impede wheeled vehicles or (formerly) cavalry horses; a heraldic representation of this. The word in this sense is recorded from late Middle English, and was probably adopted from French.

Caltrop is recorded from Old English (in form *calcatrippe*), originally with the sense of a plant which tended to catch and entangle the feet; later, it developed its current sense of a creeping plant with woody carpels that typically have hard spines and resemble military caltrops. It derives from medieval Latin *calcatrippa*, from *calx* 'heel' or *calcare* 'to tread' + a word related to *trap*.

calumet a tobacco-pipe with a bowl of clay or stone, and a long reed stem carved and ornamented with feathers, used among North American Indians as a symbol of peace or friendship. Recorded from the late 17th century, the word comes via French from late Latin *calamellus* 'little reed', diminutive of Latin *calamus* (referring to the pipe's reed stem).

Calvary the hill outside Jerusalem on which Jesus was crucified. The name comes from late Latin *calvaria* 'skull', translation of Greek *golgotha* 'place of a skull' (Matthew 27:33).

The word calvary is also used to designate a sculpture or picture representing the scene of the Crucifixion.

See also ➤ GOLGOTHA.

Calvary cross in heraldry, a cross mounted on a pyramid of three grises or steps.

Calves' Head Club an association formed at the end of the 17th century to ridicule Charles I, calves' heads being used to represent the monarch and his courtiers on the anniversary of his execution. The club was suppressed in 1735.

John Calvin (1509–64), French Protestant theologian and reformer. On becoming a Protestant in the early 1530s he fled to Switzerland, where he attempted to reorder society on reformed Christian principles and established the first Presbyterian government, in Geneva. His *Institutes of the Christian Religion* (1536) was the first systematic account of reformed Christian doctrine.

Calvinism the Protestant theological system of John Calvin and his successors, which develops Luther's doctrine of justification by faith alone into an emphasis on the grace of God and centres on the doctrine of predestination.

Calydon a Greek town in Aetolia, in Greek mythology ruled over by Meleager (see ➤ Meleager[1]), and ravaged by the ➤ Calydonian *boar*.

Calydonian boar a monstrous wild boar sent by Artemis to ravage Calydon in Aetolia; the boar was hunted down and killed by ➤ Meleager.

Calypso in Greek mythology, a nymph who kept the shipwrecked Odysseus on her island, Ogygia, for seven years; she released him in the end on the orders of Zeus. Her name is Greek, meaning literally 'she who conceals'.

calypso a kind of West Indian (originally Trinidadian) music in syncopated African rhythm, typically with words improvised on a topical theme. The word is recorded from the 1930s, but is of unknown origin.

Cam and Isis the rivers on which the universities of Cambridge and Oxford stand, in literary use often taken together as personifications of their respective universities.

Camacho in *Don Quixote*, a rich farmer of La Mancha, who prepares a splendid feast in anticipation of his wedding with Quiteria, but who is in the end deprived of his bride by a rival.

> Rounds of beef, hams, fillets of veal, and legs of mutton bobbed, indiscriminately with plum puddings, up and down in a great boiler, from which a steam arose . . . reminding one exceedingly of Camacho's wedding.
> — Elizabeth Gaskell *The Cumberland Sheep-Shearers* (1853)

Camaldolite a member of a religious order founded by St Romuald at Camaldoli in the Appennines, at the beginning of the 11th century.

Camargue a region of the Rhône delta in SE France, characterized by numerous shallow salt lagoons. The region is known for its white horses and as a nature reserve.

Camber according to legend one of the sons of Brutus (Brut), the legendary first king of Britain. Camber is supposed to have given his name to *Cambria* (Wales), but this is in fact a Latinized derivative of *Cymry* (Welshmen).

Camberwell a district in London which has given its name to the **Camberwell beauty**, a migratory butterfly with deep purple yellow-bordered wings, which is a rare visitor to Britain; in the 19th century, when Camberwell was still a village, the first specimens were captured there.

Cambria the Latin name for Wales, a variant of Cumbria, from Welsh ➤ Cymry.

     See also ➤ Annales *Cambriae*.

Cambridge Platonists a group of Anglican divines who had close connections with Cambridge University and tried to promote a rational form of Christianity in the tradition of Hooker and Erasmus. The group included Benjamin Whichcote (1609–83), appointed provost of King's College by Parliament (1644) and dispossessed at the Restoration.

Cambridge University a university at Cambridge in England, first established when a group of students migrated from Oxford to Cambridge in 1209 and formally founded in 1230. The university comprises a federation of thirty-one colleges, the oldest of which, Peterhouse, was founded in 1284. Colleges for women were founded in the mid 19th century.

     The distinctive colour associated with Cambridge is ➤ light *blue*.

     See also see ➤ Apostle[2].

Cambuscan in Chaucer's 'Squire's Tale', a king of Tartary, owner of the magic ➤ brazen *horse*.

Cambyses (d.522 BC), king of Persia 529–522 BC, son of Cyrus. He is chiefly remembered for his conquest of Egypt in 525 BC, and as the subject of a play by Preston which became proverbial for its bombastic grandiloquence: it is alluded to by Shakespeare:

> I must speak in passion, and I will do it in King Cambyses' vein.
> — William Shakespeare *1 Henry IV* (1597)

Camden Society founded in 1838 in honour of the antiquary and historian William *Camden*

(1551–1653), for the purpose of publishing documents relating to the early history and literature of the British empire. In 1897 it was amalgamated with the Royal Historical Society.

Camden Town Group a group of artists active in London in the period 1911–1913, lead by Walter Sickert and Spencer Frederick Gore, generally considered to be the earliest British exponents of post-impressionism; in 1913 they merged into the larger ➤ LONDON *Group.*

camel the *camel* can survive for long periods without food or drink, chiefly by using up the fat reserves in its hump; from this comes the name ➤ SHIP *of the desert.*

Camels are the emblem of the 4th-century Egyptian martyr St Mennas, probably because pilgrims to his shrine arrive by camel.

The British engineer Alec Issigonis (1908–88) once used the image of the camel to explain his dislike of working through committees: 'A camel is a horse designed by a committee.'

See also ➤ *it is the* LAST *straw that breaks the camel's back,* ➤ STRAIN *at a gnat and swallow a camel.*

camelopard an archaic name for a giraffe, coming (in late Middle English) via Latin from Greek *kamēlopardalis,* from *kamēlos* 'camel' + *pardalis* 'female panther or pard'; the second element derives from the comparison of a giraffe's spotted skin to that of a leopard.

Camelot in Arthurian legend, the place where King Arthur held his court, variously identified as Caerleon in Wales, Camelford in Cornwall, Cadbury Castle in Somerset, and (by Thomas Malory) Winchester in Hampshire.

In extended usage, *Camelot* is a place associated with glittering romance and optimism; it is also often used for the White House of ➤ *John Fitzgerald* KENNEDY's presidency.

> Don't let it be forgot
> That once there was a spot
> For one brief shining moment that was known
> As Camelot.
>
> — Alan Jay Lerner 'Camelot' (1960 song)

camera see also ➤ CANDID *camera.*

camera a chamber or round building; especially in names of buildings, such as the ➤ RADCLIFFE *Camera. Camera* is recorded in English from the late 17th century denoting a council or legislative chamber in Italy or Spain, the treasury department of the papal curia; the word comes from Latin 'vault, arched chamber', from Greek *kamara* 'object with an arched cover'.

in camera in private, in particular taking place in the private chambers of a judge, with the press and public excluded; the term comes from late Latin, 'in the chamber'.

Cameronian a follower of Richard *Cameron* (1648–80), a noted Scottish Covenanter and field preacher, who rejected the indulgence granted to nonconforming ministers and formally renounced allegiance to Charles II. His followers afterwards constituted the 'Reformed Presbyterian Church of Scotland'.

Cameronian Regiment a name given to the old 26th Regiment of Foot in the British Army (later the 1st Battalion of the Scottish Rifles), formed originally of the Cameronians and other Presbyterians who rallied to the cause of William III, and fought at the Battle of Killiecrankie in 1689 where the Jacobite leader Graham of Claverhouse (see ➤ BONNIE *Dundee*) was killed.

Camford a fictional equivalent of the universities of Oxford and Cambridge; an alternative (though less popular) term for ➤ OXBRIDGE.

Camilla in the *Aeneid,* a maiden-warrior of the Volsci, who fights with the forces ranged against Aeneas, and is killed in battle.

Don Camillo the Italian parish priest who is the hero of a number of stories by Giovanni Guareschi (1908–68), in which he is pitted against his former Partisan ally the Communist mayor of the village.

Marcus Furius Camillus (d. *c.*365 BC), Roman statesman and general, who according to Livy was regarded as the second founder of Rome after its occupation by Brennus and his Gauls *c.*390 BC.

camisado a night attack, originally one in which the attackers wore shirts over their armour as a means of mutual recognition; the word is recorded from the mid 16th century, and comes ultimately (via Spanish) from late Latin *camisia* 'shirt, nightgown'.

Camisard a member of the French Protestant insurgents who rebelled against the persecution that followed the revocation of the Edict of Nantes; recorded from the early 18th century, the word comes

(via French) from the late Latin base of
➤ CAMISADO.

Camlann according to the 9th-10th-century
Annales Cambriae the place of the battle in 537 in
which Arthur and Medraut (Mordred) fell. It may
possibly be Slaughter or Bloody Bridge on the River
Camel, near Camelford in Cornwall; Malory, a very
long time after the historical sources, says the battle
was near Salisbury and the sea.

camlet originally, a costly eastern fabric; later, a
light cloth used for cloaks and similar garments. Recorded from late Middle English, the word comes
ultimately, via Old French, from Arabic *ḳamla(t)*
'nap, pile of velvet', by Westerners popularly associated with *camel*, as if the material were made of
camel's hair.

the Camorra a secret criminal society originating
in Naples and Neapolitan emigrant communities in
the 19th century. Some members later moved to the
US and formed links with the Mafia. The name is
Italian, and may come from Spanish *camorra* 'dispute, quarrel'.

Camp name of a bulldog belonging to Sir Walter
Scott; when he died in 1809, Scott gave up an engagement on the grounds of having lost 'a dear old
friend'.
    See also ➤ MAIDA.

Camp David the country retreat of the President of
the US, in the Appalachian Mountains in Maryland.
President Carter hosted talks there between the
leaders of Israel and Egypt which resulted in the
Camp David agreements (1978) and the
Egypt–Israel peace treaty of 1979.
    Originally established and named *Shangri-La* in
1942 by President Franklin Roosevelt, *Camp David*
was renamed in 1953 by President Dwight Eisenhower after his grandson David.

camp follower a civilian who works in or is attached to a military camp; in extended usage, a person who is nominally attached to a group but is not
fully committed or does not make a substantial contribution to its activities.

Campaign for Nuclear Disarmament a British
organization which campaigns for the abolition of
nuclear weapons worldwide and calls for unilateral
disarmament. Founded in 1958 under the presidency of Bertrand Russell, it was revived in 1979 to
oppose the siting of US cruise missiles in Britain.
With the improvement in East–West relations and

the break-up of the Soviet Union, the organization
has had a lower public profile.

campaign wig a close-fitting wig with a curled
forehead, in the late 17th century worn for travelling.

Campania territory in ancient Italy south of Latium, lying between the Apennines and the Tyrrhenian Sea, and extending south to the Surrentine
promontory (Sorrento). A volcanic plain, it is exceptionally fertile, and many wealthy Romans had
villas there.

campanile an Italian bell tower, especially a free-
standing one. Recorded from the mid 17th century,
the word is from Italian, and comes from *campana*
'bell'.

Campaspe in the eponymous prose comedy by
Lyly, published in 1584 and based on a story in
Pliny's *Natural History*, a beautiful Theban captive
desired by Alexander, whose portrait is painted by
➤ APELLES. Apelles and Campaspe fall in love, and
Alexander resigns his claims to her.

the Campbells are Comin' traditional song
which may date from the early 18th century, and
celebrate the victory of John Campbell, Duke of
Argyll, over the Jacobite forces at Sheriffmuir (1715).

Campeador a name (Spanish for 'Champion')
given to the medieval Spanish hero the ➤ CID.

campion a plant of the pink family, typically having pink or white flowers with notched petals. Recorded from the mid 16th century, the name may be
related to *champion*. It was originally used for the
rose campion, whose name in Latin (*Lychnis
coronaria*) and Greek (*lukhnis stephanōmatikē*)
means 'campion fit for a crown', and which was said
in classical times to have been used for victors' garlands.

St Edmund Campion (1540–81), English Jesuit
priest and martyr. He was ordained a deacon in the
Church of England in 1569 but went abroad, becoming a Catholic and a Jesuit priest in 1573. Returning
to England in 1580, he was arrested, charged with
conspiracy against the Crown, tortured, and executed. He was canonized in 1970.
    ☐ **FEAST DAY** His feast day is 1 December.

Campus Martius in ancient Rome, a park and recreation ground (the 'field of Mars') outside the city

walls which was where the Roman legions exercised. It was originally the site of an altar to Mars.

he who can, does; he who cannot, teaches proverbial saying, early 20th century; from George Bernard Shaw.

a can of worms a complex and largely uninvestigated matter (especially one likely to prove problematic or scandalous); the term is recorded from the 1960s.

Cana an ancient small town in Galilee, where Christ is said to have performed his first miracle by changing water into wine during a marriage feast (John 2:1–11).

Canaan the biblical name for the area of ancient Palestine west of the River Jordan, the Promised Land of the Israelites, who conquered and occupied it during the latter part of the 2nd millennium BC.

Order of Canada an order instituted in 1967 to honour Canadians for outstanding achievement and divided into three classes: Companion (CC), Officer (OC), and Member (CM).

Canada Day 1 July, observed as a public holiday in Canada to mark the day in 1867 when four of the former colonial provinces were united under one government as the Dominion of Canada (formerly called *Dominion Day*).

Canaletto (1697–1768), Italian painter. Working chiefly in his native city of Venice, he was especially popular with the English aristocracy, who commissioned his paintings of Venetian festivals and scenery as mementoes of their grand tour.

canard an unfounded rumour or story. Recorded from the mid 19th century, the word comes from French, literally 'duck', also 'hoax', from Old French *caner* 'to quack'. One suggested origin is the expression *vendre un canard à moitié* 'half-sell a duck', with the implication that a half-sale is no sale at all, and therefore the vendor has been fooled. Alternatively, the expression has been attributed to a made-up story about ducks, which was believed by many, and came to exemplify public credulity.

Le Canard Enchaîné ('The Chained Duck') is the title of a famous French satirical weekly newspaper, founded in 1916.

canary in the 19th century, domestic *canaries* were often kept in coal mines; by succumbing to any build up of gas, they gave warning to miners of potential danger.

> Many scientists suspect that amphibians are the world's equivalent of the miner's canary . . . If they're declining then the health of our environment is also declining.
> — *Canadian Geographic* July 1992

Canary Islands a group of islands in the Atlantic Ocean, off the NW coast of Africa, whose name comes (via French and Spanish) from Latin *Canaria (insula)* '(island) of dogs', from *canis* 'dog', one of the islands being noted in Roman times for large dogs.

cancan a lively, high-kicking stage dance originating in 19th-century Parisian music halls and performed by women in long skirts and petticoats. The word is recorded from the mid 19th century, and comes from French, from the child's word for *canard* 'duck', from Old French *caner* 'to quack'.

Cancer a constellation (the Crab), said to represent a crab crushed under the foot of Hercules. It is most noted for the globular star cluster of Praesepe or the Beehive.

In astrology, *Cancer* is the fourth sign of the zodiac, which the sun enters at the northern summer solstice (about 21 June).

See also ➤ TROPIC.

cancer a disease caused by an uncontrolled division of abnormal cells in a part of the body. Recorded from Old English, the word comes from Latin, 'crab or creeping ulcer', translating Greek *karkinos*, said to have been applied by ➤ GALEN to such tumours because the swollen veins around them resembled the limbs of a crab. ➤ CANKER was the usual form until the 17th century.

Candace in biblical times, a title of queen mothers who ruled Ethiopia; in Acts 8:27, the apostle Philip converts and baptizes the chamberlain of one of these queens.

Candaules (d. *c*.685 BC), king of Lydia, said by Herodotus to have been killed by his successor ➤ GYGES.

candid frank, open, outspoken. The word is recorded from the mid 17th century meaning 'white', from Latin *candidus* 'white', subsequent early senses were 'pure', 'innocent', 'unbiased', and finally 'frank'.

candid camera the technique of photographing or filming people without their knowledge, chiefly in situations set up for the amusement of television viewers.

candidate a person who applies for a job or is nominated for election. The word is recorded from the early 17th century, and comes from Latin *candidatus* 'white-robed', also denoting a candidate for office (who traditionally wore a white toga), from *candidus* 'white'.

Candide the naive hero of Voltaire's novel *Candide* (1759) who through the misfortunes he encounters rejects the unfounded optimism of his tutor Dr ➤ PANGLOSS in favour of the practical philosophy inherent in the phrase 'we must cultivate our garden.'

> An anti-Candide, his 'garden' cultivated to exhaustion, puts his 'estate' behind him.
> — John Barth *Once Upon a Time* (1994)

candle a candle is the emblem of ➤ *St* GENEVIEVE, ➤ *St* BLAISE, and ➤ *St* GUDULE.

See also ➤ BELL, *book, and candle*, ➤ BURN *the candle at both ends*, ➤ CORPSE-*candle*, ➤ HOLD *a candle to the Devil*, ➤ PASCHAL *candle*, ➤ ROMAN *candle*, ➤ SELL *by the candle*, ➤ SOUL-*candle*, ➤ TACE *is Latin*.

candlelight see ➤ *never* CHOOSE *your women or your linen by candlelight*.

Candlemas a Christian festival held on 2 February to commemorate the purification of the Virgin Mary (after childbirth, according to Jewish law) and the presentation of Christ in the temple. Candles were traditionally blessed at this festival.

if Candlemas day be sunny and bright, winter will have another flight;
if Candlemas day be cloudy with rain, winter is gone, and won't come again
traditional rhyme, late 17th century.

Candlemas day, put beans in the clay; put candles and candlesticks away proverbial saying, late 17th century.

candlestick see ➤ *the* BUTCHER, *the baker, the candlestick-maker*.

canephora in ancient Greece, each of the maidens who carried on their heads baskets bearing sacred objects used at certain feasts; a caryatid representing or resembling such a figure.

canicular days another name for the ➤ DOG *days*; canicular comes from Latin *canicularis* 'pertaining to the Dog Star', from *canicula*, diminutive of *canis* 'dog'.

canicular period a period of 1460 full years, containing 1461 of the ancient Egyptian ordinary years of 365 days, the ➤ SOTHIC period.

canicular year the ancient Egyptian year computed from one rising of the Dog Star to the next, the ➤ SOTHIC year.

canker a necrotic fungal disease of apple and other trees that results in damage to the fruit. The word is recorded from Middle English (denoting a tumour), and comes via Old French *chancre*, from Latin *cancer* 'crab' (see ➤ CANCER).

Canmore nickname of ➤ MALCOLM *III* of Scotland (from Gaelic *Ceann-mor* 'great head').

Cannae a village in Apulia in Italy, the scene of a great defeat inflicted on the Romans by ➤ HANNIBAL in 216 BC.

canned (especially of music, laughter, or applause) pre-recorded and therefore considered to be lacking in freshness and spontaneity.

cannibal a person who eats the flesh of other human beings. The word is recorded from the mid 16th century and comes from Spanish *Canibales* (plural), variant (recorded by Columbus) of *Caribes*, the name of a West Indian people reputed to eat humans (see ➤ CARIB).

Anthropologists distinguish two categories of cannibalism among humans: **endocannibalism**, in which the remains of relatives or other members of one's own group are consumed, generally out of respect and reverence; and **exocannibalism**, in which the remains of one's enemies are consumed, as a form of ritualized vengeance or with the aim of absorbing the vitality or other qualities of vanquished foes. There are also recorded instances of disasters in which survivors of a stranded group of travellers have been forced to resort to cannibalism to avoid starvation; the ➤ DONNER *Party* was one such example of this.

cannon a large, heavy piece of artillery, typically mounted on wheels, formerly used in warfare; recorded from late Middle English, the word comes via French from Italian *cannone* 'large tube', from *canna* 'cane, reed'.

A cannon is the emblem of ➤ *St* BARBARA.

Cannon Bible another name for the ➤ ZURICH *Bible*, from the cannon in a woodcut of Christ being led away from judgement.

canoe see ➤ JOHN *Canoe*.

canon[1] originally, a Church decree or law; later (from late Middle English), a general law, rule, principle, or criterion by which something is judged. Recorded from Old English, the word comes via Latin from Greek *kanōn* 'rule'; it was reinforced in Middle English by Old French *canon*.

From Middle English, the word also designated (in the Roman Catholic Church) the part of the Mass containing the words of consecration (also known as the **canon of the Mass**).

From late Middle English, *canon* has also designated a collection or list of sacred books accepted as genuine; from the late 19th century the term was extended to cover the works of a particular author or artist that are recognized as genuine, and then a list of literary works considered to be permanently established as being of the highest quality.

In music, a *canon* is a piece in which the same melody is begun in different parts successively, so that the imitations overlap; **in canon** means with different parts successively beginning the same melody. This sense is recorded from the late 16th century.

canon[2] originally (in the Roman Catholic Church), a member of certain orders of clergy that live communally according to an ecclesiastical rule in the same way as monks (also as **canon regular** or **regular canon**).

Later (from the mid 16th century), a member of the clergy who is on the staff of a cathedral, especially one who is a member of the chapter. The position is frequently conferred as an honorary one.

The word is recorded from Middle English and comes via Old French from Latin *canonicus* 'according to rule', ultimately from the base of ➤ CANON[1].

See also ➤ BLACK *Canons*, ➤ BOOK *of Canons*.

canon law ecclesiastical law, especially (in the Roman Catholic Church) that laid down by papal pronouncements.

canoness in the Roman Catholic Church, a member of certain religious orders of women living communally according to an ecclesiastical rule in the same way as nuns.

canonical age in the Christian Church, the age according to ➤ CANON *law* at which a person may seek ordination or undertake a particular duty.

canonical dress dress worn by the clergy as prescribed by ➤ CANON *law*.

canonical epistles an alternative name for the ➤ CATHOLIC *Epistles*.

canonical hour each of the times of daily prayer appointed in the breviary; each of the seven offices (matins with lauds, prime, terce, sext, nones, vespers, and compline) appointed for these times.

In the Church of England, the time (now usually between 8 a.m. and 6 p.m.) during which a marriage may lawfully be celebrated.

canonical obedience the obedience owed by a member of the clergy to a bishop or other clerical superior according to canon law.

canonist an expert in canon law; St Raymond of Pennafort (*c*.1180–1275), Spanish Dominican friar who took his doctorates in canon and civil law at Bologna, is the patron saint of canonists.

canonization in the Roman Catholic Church, the official declaration that a dead person is a saint; the process typically involves a rigorous investigation of the life and record of the prospective saint and any cult surrounding them. In the early Church, sanctity was often established through the growth of a spontaneous cult; in the late 12th century, it was declared that the formal pronouncement of the Church was required for public veneration.

Recorded from late Middle English, the word comes from late Latin *canonizare* 'admit as authoritative' (in medieval Latin 'admit to the list of recognized saints'), from Latin *canon* (see ➤ CANON[1]).

Canopic jar a covered urn used in ancient Egyptian burials to hold the entrails and other visceral organs from an embalmed body. The lids, originally plain, were later modelled as the human, falcon, dog, and jackal heads of the four sons of Horus, protectors of the jars.

The name comes (via Latin) from *Canopus*, the name of a town in ancient Egypt.

Canopus the pilot of the fleet of King Menelaus in the Trojan War.

Canopus is also the name of the second-brightest star in the sky, and the brightest in the constellation ➤ CARINA. It is a supergiant, visible only to observers in the southern hemisphere.

canopy an ornamental cloth covering or held up over something, especially a throne or bed. Recorded from late Middle English, the word comes from medieval Latin *canopeum* 'ceremonial canopy', alteration of Latin *conopeum* 'mosquito net over a bed', from Greek *kōnōpeion* 'couch with mosquito curtains', from *kōnōps* 'mosquito'.

Canossa a town in Modena, Italy, where in 1077 the Emperor Henry IV (1050–1106), who had been excommunicated during his struggle with the papacy, was forced to recant and do penance before Pope Gregory VII.

we will not go to Canossa an assertion made by the German Chancellor ➤ *Otto von* BISMARCK in a speech to the Reichstag, 14 May 1872 during his quarrel with Pope Pius IX regarding papal authority over German subjects, in allusion to the Emperor Henry IV's submission to Pope Gregory VII at Canossa in Modena in 1077.

cant hypocritical and sanctimonious talk, typically of a moral, religious, or political nature. The word is recorded from the early 16th century in the sense 'musical sound, singing' (the probable origin is Latin *cantare* 'to sing'). In the mid 17th century this gave rise to the senses 'whining manner of speaking' and 'form of words repeated mechanically' (for example a beggar's plea), hence 'jargon' (of beggars and other such groups).

Cantab of Cambridge University; the term comes from Latin *Cantabrigiensis*, from *Cantabrigia* 'Cambridge'.

Cantate Psalm 98 (97 in the Vulgate) used as a canticle (e.g. as an alternative to the Magnificat at Evening Prayer in the Church of England); *cantate* is Latin for 'sing ye', and is the first word of the psalm.

Cantate Sunday the fourth Sunday after Easter so called because the introit for that day is taken from the ➤ CANTATE.

canteen culture in the UK, a set of conservative and discriminatory attitudes said to exist within the police force, characterized by resistance to the introduction of modern managerial standards and practices, and at its most extreme associated with male chauvinist and racist views. The phrase reflects the supposition that the canteen is the place where those of like mind foregather to reinforce one another's prejudices.

canter a pace of a horse between a trot and a gallop, with not less than one foot on the ground at any time. The word is recorded from the early 18th century (as a verb), and is short for *Canterbury pace* or

Canterbury gallop, from the supposed easy pace of medieval pilgrims to ➤ CANTERBURY.

Canterbury a city in Kent, SE England, the seat of the Archbishop of Canterbury. St Augustine established a church and monastery there in 597, and it became a place of medieval pilgrimage, to the shrine of ➤ *St Thomas à* BECKET.

Canterbury bell a southern European bellflower, grown for ornament, named with reference to the bells on pilgrims' horses.

Canterbury gallop the pace of mounted pilgrims; a slow easy gallop.

Canterbury tale a story told on a pilgrimage (originally one of Chaucer's cycle of linked tales told by a group of pilgrims); a long tedious story.

canticle a hymn or chant, typically with a biblical text, forming a regular part of a church service. The word is recorded from Middle English and comes from Latin *canticulum* 'little song'.

The **Canticles** or **Canticle of Canticles** is another name for the ➤ SONG *of Songs* (especially in the Vulgate).

canting arms in heraldry, arms containing an allusion to the name of the bearer; canting here means 'speak, say (in a particular way)'.

canting crew beggars and similar groups sharing a particular jargon; the term is recorded from the late 17th century.

Canuck a Canadian, especially a French Canadian (chiefly used by Canadians themselves and often derogatory in the US). The word apparently comes from *Canada*.

Canute (d. 1035), Danish king of England 1017–35, Denmark 1018–35, and Norway 1028–35, son of Sweyn I. After Edmund Ironside's murder, Canute became king of England and presided over a relatively peaceful period. He is remembered for the legend of his demonstrating to fawning courtiers his inability to stop the rising tide; this has become distorted in folklore to suggest that Canute really expected to turn back the tide.

canvass solicit votes from (electors in a constituency). The word is recorded from the early 16th century, in the sense 'toss in a *canvas* sheet (as a sport or punishment)'. Later extended senses include 'criticize, discuss' (mid 16th century) and 'propose for discussion'; hence 'seek support for'.

cap see also ➤ BLACK *cap*, ➤ DUNCE's *cap*, ➤ JOHN *Knox cap*, ➤ JULIET *cap*, ➤ LIBERTY *cap*.

cap follow (an anecdote, witticism, or quotation) with a more apposite one; the expression is recorded from the late 16th century.

cap-à-pie from head to foot, fully armed, fully ready; the phrase (from Old French) is recorded in English from the early 16th century.

cap and bells the insignia of the professional jester.

cap and feather days the days of childhood; recorded from the early 19th century.

cap and gown traditional formal garb of a university student.

if the cap fits, wear it proverbial saying, mid 18th century.

cap of liberty a conical cap given to Roman slaves on emancipation, often used as a Republican symbol.

cap of maintenance a cap or hat worn as a symbol of dignity, or carried before a monarch on ceremonial occasions.

cap verses reply to one previously quoted with another, that begins with the final or initial letter of the first, or that rimes or otherwise corresponds with it.

capability see ➤ *Capability* BROWN.

cape see also ➤ *Cape* HORN.

Cape of Good Hope a mountainous promontory south of Cape Town, South Africa, near the southern extremity of Africa; originally known as the *Cape of Storms*.
See also ➤ ADAMASTOR.

Cape doctor in South Africa, the strong prevailing SE wind in Western Cape Province.

Cape of Storms original name of the ➤ CAPE *of Good Hope*.

Capel Court a lane in London which until 1973 led to the ➤ STOCK *Exchange*, sometimes used allusively (in *Punch*, 1845, Thackeray refers to 'all the stags' [those applying for an allocation of shares in a joint-stock concern with a view to immediate sale for profit] in Capel Court').

Capernaite a derogatory term for a believer in transubstantiation, used especially in theological controversy of the 16th and 17th centuries, and taken from the name of *Capernaum* in Galilee (with reference to John 6:52, in a passage about Jesus's teaching in the synagogue at Capernaum, 'How can this man give us his flesh to eat?').

Capetian name of the dynasty ruling France 987–1328, founded by Hugh *Capet* (938–96), king of France 987–96.

capful of wind enough wind to fill a sail, supposedly under the control of a particular person who has summoned it (see ➤ WHISTLE *for a wind*).

capital cross a Greek cross having each extremity terminated in an ornament like a Tuscan capital.

capital gain a profit from the sale of property or an investment; **capital gains tax** a tax levied on profit from the sale of property or an investment.

capital punishment the legally authorized killing of someone as punishment for a crime; *capital* here meant originally 'involving the loss of the head', coming ultimately from Latin *caput* 'head'.

capital ship a large warship such as a battleship or aircraft carrier.

Capitol in ancient Rome, the temple of Jupiter Optimus Maximus on the Saturnian or Tarpeian (afterwards called Capitoline) Hill in ancient Rome; the name is sometimes applied to the whole hill, including the citadel. The *Capitol* in literary terms is often seen as a symbol of Rome. The 18th-century historian Edward Gibbon, describing in his *Memoirs* the genesis of his *Decline and Fall of the Roman Empire*, says, 'It was at Rome…as I sat musing amidst the ruins of the Capitol…that the idea of writing the decline and fall of the city first started to my mind.'
    In the US, *Capitol* (usually **the Capitol**) is the name of the seat of the US Congress in Washington DC. The term in an American context in fact goes back to the late 17th century; in 1699 an act was passed in the Virginia Assembly 'directing the Building the Capitol and the City of Williamsburgh'.

Capitol Hill the region around the Capitol in Washington DC (often as an allusive reference to the US Congress itself).

capitulary a royal ordinance under the Merovingian dynasty. Recorded from the mid 17th century, the word comes via late Latin *capitularius*, from Latin *capitulum* in the sense 'section of a law'.

capon a castrated domestic cock fattened for eating. The term, recorded from late Old English, comes from Old French, based on Latin *capo*, *capon-*.

Al Capone (1899–1947), American gangster, of Italian descent. Although he was indirectly responsible for many murders, including the ➤ *St* VALENTINE's *Day Massacre*, it was for federal income tax evasion that he was eventually imprisoned in 1931.

Andy Capp cloth-capped working-class hero of the popular cartoon strip, created in 1957 by the British cartoonist Reg Smythe (1917–98).

Cappadocia an ancient region of central Asia Minor, between Lake Tuz and the Euphrates, north of Cilicia. It was an important centre of early Christianity.

capped chosen as a member of a particular soccer, rugby, or cricket team, especially a national one in an international competition.

Capri an island off the west coast of Italy, south of Naples, to which the Roman emperor Tiberius (42 BC–AD 37) retired in AD 26, never returning to Rome. The satirist Juvenal said of Tiberius's letter to the Roman Senate, which in AD 31 caused the downfall of the formerly favoured and powerful Sejanus, 'A huge wordy letter came from Capri.'

Capricorn the tenth sign of the zodiac (the Goat), which the sun enters at the northern winter solstice (about 21 December).
    Recorded from Old English, the name comes from Latin *capricornus*, from *caper, capr-* 'goat' + *cornu* 'horn', on the pattern of Greek *aigokēros* 'goat-horned, Capricorn'.
    See also ➤ TROPIC.

Capsian of, relating to, or denoting a Palaeolithic culture of North Africa and southern Europe, noted for its microliths. It is dated to *c.*8000–4500 BC, named from Latin *Capsa* (now *Gafsa* in Tunisia) where objects from this culture were found.

Captain see also ➤ *Captain* HOOK, ➤ *Captain* KIDD, ➤ CAPTAIN *Marvell*, ➤ CAPTAIN *Moonlight*.

Captain Cooker in New Zealand, a wild boar. The term is recorded from the late 19th century, and apparently refers to the explorer Captain James Cook, who brought domesticated pigs (from which the wild boar is supposedly descended) to New Zealand.

captivity see ➤ BABYLONIAN *Captivity*.

Capuchin a friar belonging to a branch of the Franciscan order that observes a strict rule drawn up in 1529. The name is recorded from the late 16th century, and comes via obsolete French from Italian *cappuccino*, from *cappuccio* 'hood, cowl', from *cappa* 'covering for the head', the friars being so named because of their sharp-pointed hoods.

Capulet in Shakespeare's *Romeo and Juliet*, the name of the Veronese noble house (the Cappelletti) to which Juliet belongs, hostile to the family of the Montagues (the Montecchi).

> And they were freighted, apparently, with an internal feud of Montague and Capulet proportions.
> — *Post* (Denver) 2 January 1994

caput mortuum in alchemy, the residue remaining after distillation or sublimation. The phrase is Latin, and means literally 'dead head'.

would you buy a used car from this man? campaign slogan directed against ➤ *Richard* NIXON, 1968, despite which he won the presidential election.

Caracalla nickname of Aurelius Antoninus (188–217), Roman emperor 211–17; the name *Caracalla* derived from the long hooded Celtic cloak which he made fashionable. In 212 he granted Roman citizenship to all free inhabitants of the Roman Empire.

Caradoc Celtic form of the name of the British chieftain ➤ CARATACUS.

Caran d'Ache pseudonym (a transliteration of the Russian word for pencil) of Emmanuel Poiré, Russian-born French caricaturist and illustrator (1858–1909), noted for his early development of the strip cartoon, and for his strong crisp line drawings.

carat a measure of the purity of gold, pure gold being 24 carats; later also, a unit of weight for precious stones and pearls, now equivalent to 200 milligrams.
    Recorded from late Middle English, the word comes via French from Italian *carato*, from Arabic *ḳīrāṭ* (a unit of weight), from Greek *keration* 'fruit of

the carob' (also denoting a unit of weight), diminutive of *keras* 'horn', with reference to the elongated seed pod of the carob.

Caratacus (1st century AD), British chieftain, son of Cymbeline. He took part in the resistance to the Roman invasion of AD 43 and when defeated fled to Yorkshire, where he was handed over to the Romans in AD 51. His Celtic name is *Caradoc*, and he is also known as *Caractacus*.

Caravaggio (*c*.1571–1610), Italian painter. An influential figure in the transition from late mannerism to baroque, he made use of naturalistic realism and dramatic light and shade.

caravan a group of people, especially traders or pilgrims, travelling together across a desert in Asia or North Africa. The word is recorded from the late 15th century, and comes via French from Persian *kārwān*.
  See also ➤ DOGS *bark, but the caravan goes on.*.

carbon dating the determination of the age of an organic object from the relative proportions of the carbon isotopes carbon-12 and carbon-14 that it contains. The ratio between them changes as radioactive carbon-14 decays and is not replaced by exchange with the atmosphere.

Carbonari the members of a secret republican association in the kingdom of Naples in the early 19th century, during the French occupation under ➤ *Joachim* MURAT, with the design of introducing a republican government. The name comes from Italian 'colliers, charcoal-burners', an appellation assumed by the society.

the Carboniferous the fifth period of the Palaeozoic era, between the Devonian and Permian periods. The Carboniferous lasted from about 363 to 290 million years ago. During this time the first reptiles and seed-bearing plants appeared, and there were extensive coral reefs and coal-forming swamp forests.

carborundum see ➤ NIL *carborundum illegitimi.*

carcake a small cake baked with eggs, eaten on Shrove Tuesday in parts of Scotland; the first syllable represents 'care, sorrow'.

where the carcase is, there shall the eagles be gathered together proverbial saying, mid 16th century; ultimately with biblical allusion to Matthew 24:28, 'Wheresoever the carcase is, there shall the eagles be gathered together.'

Carchemish an ancient city on the upper Euphrates, north-east of Aleppo. It was a Hittite stronghold, annexed by Sargon II of Assyria in 717 BC.

card see also ➤ COURT *card*, ➤ LUCKY *at cards, unlucky in love*, ➤ PLAY *the — card*, ➤ RED *card*, ➤ YELLOW *card*.

a card up one's sleeve a plan in reserve, a hidden advantage; the expression was notably used by the British politician Henry Labouchere (1831–1912), who commented on William Ewart Gladstone's frequent appeals to a higher power that he 'did not object to the old man always having a card up his sleeve, but…did object to his insinuating that the Almighty had placed it there'.

cardboard city an urban area where homeless people congregate under makeshift shelters made from cardboard boxes; the term dates from the 1980s, and is sometimes written with capital initials, as though it were a place-name in its own right.

cardigan the *cardigan* was named (in the mid 19th century) after James Thomas Brudenel, 7th Earl of *Cardigan* (1797–1868), leader of the Charge of the Light Brigade, whose troops first wore such garments.

cardinal a leading dignitary of the Roman Catholic Church. Cardinals are nominated by the Pope, and form the Sacred College which elects succeeding popes (now invariably from among their own number). The word is recorded from Old English and comes from Latin *cardinalis*, from *cardo, cardin-* 'hinge'; the derivation reflects the notion of the important function of such priests as 'pivots' of church life.
  Cardinals wear a deep scarlet cassock with a wide-brimmed red hat; the **cardinal's hat** is often taken as a symbol of his office, and is the emblem of ➤ *St* BONAVENTURA, ➤ *St* JEROME, and ➤ *St* ROBERT *Bellarmine.*
  See also ➤ COLLEGE *of Cardinals.*

cardinal humour each of the four chief ➤ HUMOURS of the body.

cardinal number a number denoting quantity (one, two, three, etc.) as opposed to an ordinal number (first, second, third, etc.).

cardinal point each of the four main points of the compass (north, south, east, and west).

cardinal virtues the chief moral attributes of scholastic philosophy: justice, prudence, temperance, and fortitude, identified by the classical philosophers and adopted by Christian moral theologians.

care see also ➤ COMMUNITY *care*.

care killed the cat proverbial expression, late 16th century, which may be compared with ➤ CURIOSITY *killed the cat*; the meaning of *care* has shifted somewhat from 'worry, grief' to 'care, caution'.

Care Sunday the fifth Sunday in Lent; formerly also, the Sunday preceding Good Friday; Care here means 'sorrow, trouble, grief'.

careful see ➤ *if you can't be* GOOD, *be careful*.

cares see ➤ CHILDREN *are certain cares, but uncertain comforts*.

caret a mark (^, ʌ) placed below the line to indicate a proposed insertion in a printed or written text. The word comes (in the late 17th century) from Latin, meaning literally 'is lacking'.

Mother Carey's chicken a sailors' name (now dated) for the storm petrel; it is recorded from mid 18th century, but the origin is unknown.

Mother Carey's goose a name for the giant petrel.

Carey Street a street in London, formerly the location of the Bankruptcy Department of the Supreme Court, used allusively to indicate a state of bankruptcy.

carfax a place where four roads or streets meet (now usually in place-names). The word is recorded from Middle English, and comes ultimately, via Anglo-Norman French, Old French, and popular Latin, from Latin *quadri-* 'four' + *furca* 'fork'.

cargo cult in the Melanesian Islands, a system of belief based around the expected arrival of ancestral spirits in ships bringing cargoes of food and other goods.

Caria an ancient region of SW Asia Minor, south of the Maeander River and north-west of Lycia.

Carib a member of an indigenous South American people living mainly in coastal regions of French Guiana, Suriname, Guyana, and Venezuela; the language of this people, the only member of the Cariban family of languages still spoken by a substantial number of people (around 20,000).

The Caribs were in the process of colonizing the Lesser Antilles from the mainland, displacing Arawak peoples, when their expansion was halted by the arrival of the Spaniards, who all but wiped them out; a few hundred remain on Dominica.

The name comes from Spanish *caribe*, from Haitian Creole. Compare with ➤ CANNIBAL.

See also ➤ BLACK *Carib*.

Mr Carker the sinister manager of the Dombey shipping house in Dickens's *Dombey and Son* (1848), who in the end betrays his master's trust and destroys himself; he is noted for the hypcritical smile which shows his white and glistening teeth.

> Flashing his Carker-teeth in terrible smiles.
> — Lyndall Gordon *Charlotte Brontë* (1994)

carline[1] chiefly in Scottish usage, an old woman, a witch; the word is recorded from Middle English, and comes from Old Norse *carling*. It was used by James I and VI (1566–1625) in a comment on the wives of Scottish judges, 'I made the carles lords, but who made the carlines ladies?'

carline[2] a thistle-like European plant with a purplish stem and seeds that carry a tuft of silky down. The flower heads bear shiny persistent straw-coloured bracts. The name comes (in the late 16th century) via French from medieval Latin *carlina*, perhaps ultimately from Latin *carduus* thistle, altered by association with *Carolus Magnus* (➤ CHARLEMAGNE), to whom its medicinal properties were said to have been revealed.

Carling Sunday another name for ➤ CARE *Sunday*, the fifth Sunday of Lent, on which it was customary to eat *carlings*, dried or parched peas. The name may come ultimately from the first element in *Care Sunday*.

Carlioun in Malory's *Morte D'Arthur*, the city where Arthur was crowned and held his court; it is probably to be identified with ➤ CAERLEON.

Carlism a Spanish conservative political movement originating in support of Don *Carlos*, brother of Fernando VII (died 1833), who claimed the throne in place of Fernando's daughter Isabella. The movement supported the Catholic Church and opposed centralized government; it was revived in support of the Nationalist side during the Spanish Civil War.

Carlovingian another term for ➤ CAROLINGIAN. The name comes from French, and is formed from *Karl* 'Charles' on the pattern of *Merovingian*.

Thomas Carlyle (1795–1881), Scottish historian and political philosopher. He established his reputation as a historian with his *History of the French Revolution* (1837). Influenced by German Romanticism, many of his works, including *Sartor Resartus* (1833–4), celebrate the force of the 'strong, just man' as against the degraded masses.

carmagnole title of a popular French revolutionary song of 1793; a carmagnole was also a kind of dress much worn by supporters of the Jacobins in the French Revolution, originally a Piedmontese peasant dress, characterized by a short-skirted coat with rows of buttons, worn with a red cap, and a red, white, and blue waistcoat.

Carmarthen see ➤ BLACK *Book of Carmarthen*.

Mount Carmel a group of mountains near the Mediterranean coast in NW Israel, which in the Bible is the scene of the defeat of the priests of Baal by the prophet ➤ ELIJAH.

Carmelite a friar or nun of a contemplative Catholic order dedicated to Our Lady. The Carmelite order of friars was founded during the Crusades *c*.1154 by St Berthold at Mount Carmel; the order of nuns was established in 1452. A reform movement in the late 16th century, led by St Teresa of Ávila and St John of the Cross, led to the formation of the stricter 'discalced' orders.

Carmen the seductive Spanish gipsy girl who is the eponymous heroine of Bizet's opera (1875).

> A Carmen-like ankylosaurus dances with a rose in her teeth, and hard rock dinosaurs blare bedrock music.
> — *Publishers' Weekly* 2 November 1990

Carmen Sylva pseudonym used as a poet by Queen Elisabeth of Romania (1843–1916).

Carmina Burana a compilation of 228 Latin and German songs, probably written about 1230, discovered in the monastery of Benediktbeuern in 1803. It contains works of three kinds, corresponding to the categories of poetry written by the 12th-century troubadours: moral-satirical poems, love poems; and poems of camaraderie, many of them drinking songs.

Carnaby Street a street in the West End of London, which became famous in the 1960s as a centre of the popular fashion industry.

> Some days the streets of midtown Manhattan recall Saturdays on Carnaby Street and the King's Road in London when they were the shopping meccas of the youthquake.
> — *New York Times* 18 October 1992

Carnac the site in Brittany of nearly 3,000 megalithic stones dating from the Neolithic period. They include single standing stones (menhirs), dolmens, and long avenues of grey monoliths arranged in order of height.

carnal relating to physical, especially sexual, needs and activities; recorded from late Middle English, the word comes from Christian Latin *carnalis*, from *caro, carn-* 'flesh'.

Andrew Carnegie (1835–1919), Scottish-born American industrialist and philanthropist, who after building up a fortune in the steel industry in the US, retired from business in 1901 and devoted his wealth to charitable purposes, in particular libraries, education, and the arts. The saying 'From shirtsleeves to shirtsleeves in three generations' is sometimes attributed to him, but has not been found in his writings.

carnival a period of public revelry at a regular time each year, as during the week before Lent in Roman Catholic countries, involving processions, music, dancing, and the use of masquerade. Recorded from the mid 16th century, the word comes via Italian from medieval Latin *carnevelamen*, *carnelevarium* 'Shrovetide', from Latin *caro, carn-* 'flesh' + *levare* 'put away'.

Nicolas Carnot (1796–1832), French scientist. His work in analysing the efficiency of steam engines was posthumously recognized as being of crucial importance to the theory of thermodynamics.

carol a religious folk song or popular hymn, particularly one associated with Christmas. The word is recorded from Middle English; it comes from Old French, but is of ultimately unknown origin.

Carolingian of or relating to the Frankish dynasty, founded by ➤ CHARLEMAGNE's father Pepin III, that ruled in western Europe from 750 to 987 in succession to the ➤ MEROVINGIAN dynasty.

Carolingian is also used specifically to designate a style of minuscule script developed in France during the time of Charlemagne, on which modern lower-case letters are largely based.

The name is an alteration of earlier ➤ CAROLINGIAN, by association with medieval Latin *Carolus* 'Charles'.

Carolingian Renaissance a period during the reign of Charlemagne and his successors that was marked by achievements in art, architecture, learning, and music. Credit for stimulating this renaissance is traditionally given to Charlemagne's adviser Alcuin.

carolus a gold piece of the reign of Charles I of Great Britain.

Wallace Hume Carothers (1896–1937), American industrial chemist. He developed the first successful synthetic rubber, neoprene, and the synthetic fibre Nylon 6.6. He committed suicide before nylon had been commercially exploited.

carousel originally (from the mid 17th century) a tournament in which groups of knights took part in chariot races and other demonstrations of equestrian skills; later (from the late 17th century), a merry-go-round, a roundabout. The word comes via French from Italian.

Vittore Carpaccio (*c.*1455–1525), Italian painter noted especially for his paintings of Venice. His use of red pigments, resembling raw meat, has given his name to *carpaccio*, an Italian hors d'oeuvre consisting of thin slices of raw beef or fish served with a sauce.

Carpathian wizard in Milton's *Comus*, a term used for ➤ PROTEUS, who according to Virgil lived in the *Carpathian* Sea and herded flocks of sea-lions with his shepherd's crook.

carpe diem Latin phrase meaning 'seize the day!', used as an exclamation to urge someone to make the most of the present time and give little thought to the future; originally it is a quotation from the Roman poet Horace, '*Dum loquimur, fugerit invida Aetas: carpe diem, quam minimum credula postero* [While we're talking, envious time is fleeing: seize the day, put no trust in the future].'

a carpenter is known by his chips proverbial saying, mid 16th century.

carpenters ➤ *St* JOSEPH is the patron saint of carpenters.

carpet see also ➤ MAGIC *carpet*.

on the carpet being severely reprimanded by someone. The expression comes from the earlier meaning of *carpet* in the sense of 'table covering', referring to the 'carpet of the council table' before which one would be summoned for reprimand.

carpet knight archaic term for someone who avoids hard work in favour of leisure activities or philandering; the original reference was a contemptuous one to a knight whose exploits took place in a carpeted chamber or a lady's boudoir rather than on the field of battle.

carpetbagger in the US in the 19th century, a person from the northern states who went to the South after the Civil War to profit from Reconstruction, of whom it was said that their 'property qualification' consisted merely of the contents of the carpet-bag they had brought with them.

In extended usage, the term now denotes a political candidate who seeks election in an area where they have no local connections.

> Hillary Clinton has given her Senate election campaign a much-needed fillip with a breezy television appearance in which she traded one-liners with a New York chat show host who had ridiculed her as a 'carpetbagger from Arkansas'.
> — *Daily Telegraph* 14 January 2000

Carracci the name of a family of Italian painters comprising the brothers Annibale (1560–1609) and Agostino (1557–1602) and their cousin Ludovico (1555–1619). Together they established a teaching academy at Bologna, while Annibale became famed for his frescoes on the ceiling of the Farnese Gallery in Rome and for his invention of the caricature.

Carrara a town in Tuscany in NW Italy, famous for the white marble quarried there since Roman times.

carrel a small cubicle with a desk for the use of a reader or student in a library; formerly, a small enclosure or study in a cloister. Recorded from the late 16th century, the word is apparently related to *carol* in the old sense 'ring'.

carriage dog an archaic name for a Dalmatian, dogs which were formerly trained to run behind carriages as guard dogs.

carriage trade archaic term for those customers of sufficient wealth or social standing to maintain a private carriage.

Lewis Carroll (1832–98), English writer; pseudonym of *Charles Lutwidge Dodgson*. He wrote the children's classics *Alice's Adventures in Wonderland* (1865) and *Through the Looking Glass* (1871), which were inspired by Alice Liddell, the young daughter of the dean at the Oxford college where Carroll was a mathematics lecturer.

carronade a short large-calibre cannon, formerly in naval use, and first made at *Carron* near Falkirk in Scotland.

carry see also ➤ *carry* COALS *to Newcastle*.

Kit Carson (1809–68), Kentucky-born frontiersman and guide, who is the subject of many frontier legends; in the last years of his life he was involved in military action against the Navajo people.

Rachel Carson (1907–64), American zoologist, a pioneer ecologist and popularizer of science. She is noted especially for *The Sea Around Us* (1951) and *Silent Spring* (1963), an attack on the indiscriminate use of pesticides.

> She had read her . . . Rachel Carson and she knew how horrible pesticides and things were.
> — Richard Lowe and William Shaw *Travellers* (1993)

in the cart in serious trouble or difficulty, probably deriving from the historical sense of a *cart* as used for conveying convicts to the gallows and for the public exposure of offenders.

put the cart before the horse reverse the proper order of things; the expression is recorded from the early 16th century.

Cartagena a port in SE Spain. Originally named Mastia, it was refounded as *Carthago Nova* ('New Carthage') by Hasdrubal in *c*.225 BC, as a base for the Carthaginian conquest of Spain. It has a fine natural harbour and has been a naval port since the 16th century.

carte blanche complete freedom to act as one wishes, from the original literal sense (recorded from the early 18th century) of a blank sheet of paper to be filled in as a person wishes.

carte de visite a small photographic portrait mounted on a card, originally designed to be used as a visiting card, although the custom never caught on.

Cartesian of or relating to the ideas of the philosopher *Descartes*, deriving from *Cartesius*, the Latinized form of his name.
See also ➤ DUALISM.

Cartesian coordinates numbers which indicate the location of a point relative to a fixed reference point (the origin), being its shortest (perpendicular) distances from two fixed axes (or three planes defined by three fixed axes) which intersect at right angles at the origin.

Carthage an ancient city on the coast of North Africa near present-day Tunis. Founded by the Phoenicians *c*.814 BC, Carthage became a major force in the Mediterranean, and came into conflict with Rome in the Punic Wars. It was finally destroyed by the Romans in 146 BC; at the time it was decreed that the destruction should be complete, with no houses or crops surviving, although in the 1st century ➤ BC it was to be refounded by Julius Caesar.
See also ➤ DELENDA *est Carthago*.

Carthaginian faith another term for ➤ PUNIC *faith*.

Carthaginian peace a peace settlement which imposes very severe terms on the defeated side, as that imposed by Rome on Carthage.

Carthago see ➤ DELENDA *est Carthago*.

Carthusian a monk or nun of an austere contemplative order founded by ➤ St BRUNO in 1084.

cartomancy fortune telling by interpreting a random selection of playing cards.

Sydney Carton the cynical barrister in Charles Dickens's *A Tale of Two Cities* who redeems his wastrel life by deliberately taking the place of a man sentenced to death; on the steps of the guillotine, his last thoughts are, 'It is a far, far better thing that I do, than I have ever done; it is a far, far better rest that I go to, than I have ever known.' He is taken as a type of heroic self-sacrifice.

> Sydney Carton . . . was small-time stuff compared with you, Bertie.
> — P. G. Wodehouse *The Code of the Woosters* (1938)

cartoon originally (from the late 16th century) a full-size drawing made by an artist as a preliminary design for a painting or other work of art; the word comes (via Italian *cartone*) from Latin *carta* from Greek *khartēs* 'papyrus leaf'.
From the mid 19th century, the term has been extended to a simple drawing showing the features of its subjects in a humorously exaggerated way, especially a satirical one in a newspaper or magazine.

cartouche an oval or oblong enclosing a group of Egyptian hieroglyphs, typically representing the name and title of a monarch.

carucate a measure of land equivalent to the area that could be ploughed in a year by one plough and eight oxen; a plough-land. The word comes (in late Middle English) from medieval Latin, from *caruca* 'coach, chariot', in early Gaul applied to the wheel plough.

See also ➤ OXGANG.

Enrico Caruso (1873–1921), Italian operatic tenor. His voice combined a brilliant upper register with a baritone-like warmth. He appeared in both French and Italian opera and was the first major tenor to be recorded on gramophone records, becoming a household name even among those who never attended operatic performances.

caryatid a stone carving of a draped female figure, used as a pillar to support the entablature of a Greek or Greek-style building. The name comes (in the mid 16th century) via French and Italian from Latin *caryatides* from Greek *karuatides*, plural of *karuatis* 'priestess of Artemis at Caryae', from *Karuai* (Caryae) in Laconia.

Louis Casabianca (1755–98), a Corsican naval officer who perished with his little son at the Battle of Aboukir Bay, an event commemorated in the poem *Casabianca* (1849) by Mrs Hemans, with its famous opening line 'The boy stood on the burning deck.'

Giovanni Jacopo Casanova (1725–98), Italian adventurer. He is famous for his memoirs describing his sexual encounters and other exploits.

Mr Casaubon the bachelor scholar in George Eliot's Middlemarch (1871–2) who becomes Dorothea's husband; he is initially admired by his wife for his breadth of knowledge, but it becomes clear that his intellectual life is limited to pedantry, and that his projected great work on comparative religions will never be written.

Casbah see ➤ COME *with me to the Casbah*.

case see also ➤ CIRCUMSTANCES *alter cases*, ➤ HARD *cases make bad law*.

the case is altered, quoth Plowden traditional saying apparently referring to the English jurist Edmund Plowden (1518–85). According to tradition, Plowden, who was defending a man prosecuted for hearing Mass, elicited the fact that the service had been performed by a layman, who had assumed the guise of a priest in order to inform on those present. At this, Plowden said, 'The case is altered: no priest, no mass', and succeeded in getting his client acquitted.

Roger Casement (1864–1916), Irish diplomat and nationalist. In 1914 he sought German support for an Irish uprising, and was subsequently hanged by the British for treason. His diaries reveal his homosexuality and were used to discredit a campaign for his reprieve.

cash for questions designating or relating to a series of incidents in the mid-1990s in which several Conservative MPs were alleged to have accepted money from private individuals in return for tabling specific questions in the House of Commons.

See also ➤ SLEAZE *factor*.

Casket Letters letters supposed to have been passed between Mary Queen of Scots and Bothwell, and to have established her complicity in the murder of Darnley. They were repudiated by the queen as forgeries, but it was threatened that they would be used as evidence against her. They disappeared before the end of the 16th century and have never been recovered.

Caslon a kind of roman typeface first introduced in the 18th century, named after William *Caslon* (1692–1766), English type founder.

Caspar see also ➤ *Caspar* MILQUETOAST.

Caspar traditionally the name of one of the three ➤ MAGI.

Cassandra in Greek mythology, a daughter of the Trojan king Priam, who was given the gift of prophecy by Apollo. When she cheated him, however, he turned this into a curse by causing her prophecies, though true, to be disbelieved. After the fall of Troy, she became the slave of Agamemnon; having prophesied his death, she was killed with him by Clytemnestra.

From 1935 *Cassandra* was also the pen-name of the *Daily Mirror* journalist William Connor (1909–67); according to the *Dictionary of National Biography*, 'his column became what has been called "the whipping post, stocks and ducking stool for jacks-in-office, muddling magistrates, indiscreet politicians and erring judges"'. Cassandra's support for criticism of ➤ P. G. WODEHOUSE's wartime broadcasts from France while interned by the Germans was extremely influential; his 'vitriolic' style, on the other hand, often annoyed the government, as in his contribution to the caption, 'The price of petrol has been raised by a penny (Official)', beneath a cartoon showing a torpedoed sailor, face black with oil, lying on a raft in an empty sea.

> Weather forecasters are false prophets. Their position is the reverse of Cassandra's.
> — Charles Higson *Getting Rid of Mr Kitchen* (1996)

cassation see ➤ COURT *of Cassation*.

Cassibelan another name for ➤ CASSIVELLAUNUS.

Cassidy see ➤ HOPALONG *Cassidy*.

Cassiopeia in Greek mythology, the wife of Cepheus, king of Ethiopia, and mother of ➤ ANDROMEDA. She boasted that she herself (or, in some versions, her daughter) was more beautiful than the nereids, thus incurring the wrath of Poseidon.

In astronomy, *Cassiopeia* is a constellation near the north celestial pole, recognizable by the conspicuous 'W' pattern of its brightest stars.

Cassivellaunus king of Britain, brother and successor of Lud, who according to Geoffrey of Monmouth's *History* led the resistance to Julius Caesar's second invasion. In Shakespeare's *Cymbeline* he appears as *Cassibelan*.

Cassiterides 'the tin islands', a name used by the Greeks in classical times for lands in the north-west of Europe which produced tin, probably referring particularly to the south-west of England and the Scilly Isles.

Gaius Cassius (d. 42 BC), Roman general, one of the main leaders of the conspiracy in 44 BC to assassinate Julius Caesar. He and Brutus were defeated by Caesar's supporters, Antony and Octavian, at the battle of Philippi, in the course of which he committed suicide.

Plutarch's *Life* of Caesar notes that when Caesar was warned of a possible plot against him by Antony and Dolabella, 'he said that he did not fear such fat, luxurious men, but rather the pale, lean fellows,' meaning Cassius and Brutus.' This was used by Shakespeare in his description of Cassius as having, 'a lean and hungry look'.

> Mr Blank, smaller and more Cassius-like in physique.
> — *Harper's Magazine* May 1859

cassock a full-length garment of a single colour worn by certain Christian clergy, members of church choirs, and others having some particular office or role in a church. The word comes (in the mid 16th century) via French *casaque* 'long coat' from Italian *casacca* 'riding coat', probably ultimately from Turkic *kazak* 'vagabond' (see ➤ COSSACK).

cast see also ➤ *cast one's* BREAD *upon the waters*.

ne'er cast a clout till May be out proverbial saying, early 18th century; warning against leaving off old or warm clothes until the end of the month of May (the saying is sometimes mistakenly understood to refer to may blossom).

cast the first stone be the first to make an accusation (used to emphasize that a potential critic is not wholly blameless); the original reference is to John 8:7, and the saying of Jesus to those who wanted to stone a woman who had committed adultery, 'He that is without sin among you, let him first cast a stone at her.'

Castalia a spring on Mount Parnassus, sacred in antiquity to Apollo and the Muses.

caste each of the hereditary classes of Hindu society, distinguished by relative degrees of ritual purity or pollution and of social status. Castes are traditionally defined by occupation, but may also be linked to geographical location and dietary customs. There are four basic classes or varnas in Hindu society: *Brahman* (priest), *Kshatriya* (warrior), *Vaisya* (merchant or farmer), and *Sudra* (labourer).

Recorded in English from the mid 16th century (in the general sense 'race, breed'), the word comes from Spanish and Portuguese *casta* 'lineage, race, breed', feminine of *casto* 'pure, unmixed', from Latin *castus* 'chaste'.

Castel Gandolfo the summer residence of the pope, situated on the edge of Lake Albano near Rome.

Castile a region of central Spain, on the central plateau of the Iberian peninsula, formerly an independent Spanish kingdom. The marriage of Isabella of Castile to Ferdinand of Aragon in 1469 linked these two powerful kingdoms and led eventually to the unification of Spain.

castle a large building or group of buildings fortified against attack with thick walls, battlements, towers, and in many cases a moat. The word is recorded from late Old English and comes from Anglo-Norman French and Old Northern French *castel*, from Latin *castellum*, diminutive of *castrum* 'fort'.

See also ➤ DOUBTING *Castle*, ➤ *an* ENGLISHMAN's *home is his castle*, ➤ KING *of the Castle*, ➤ MAIDEN *Castle*.

the Castle the former Irish viceregal government and administration, of which Dublin Castle was the seat; in 1813 the Irish nationalist leader Daniel

O'Connell referred critically to 'a newspaper in the pay of the Castle'.

It is said that when in 1922 Michael Collins arrived at Dublin Castle for the handover by British forces and was told by the British officer in charge that he was seven minutes late, he replied, 'We've been waiting seven hundred years, you can have the seven minutes.'

the Castle of Indolence in James Thomson's poem of this name (1748), the castle into which the wizard Indolence entices weary pilgrims.

> Safe-lodged in some . . . superstitious or voluptuous Castle of Indolence, they can slumber through, in stupid dreams.
> — Thomas Carlyle *Sartor Resartus* (1831)

Castle Perilous in Malory's *Morte D'Arthur*, the castle of the lady Lyonesse in which she is held captive before her release by Gareth.

Lord Castlereagh (1769–1822), Robert Stewart, British Tory statesman. Born in Ulster, he had a continuing interest in Irish affairs. He became Foreign Secretary in 1812 and represented Britain at the Congress of Vienna (1814–15), playing a central part in reviving the Quadruple Alliance; he committed suicide apparently as a result of pressure of work. Despite his diplomatic skill, he was seen domestically as embodying harsh repressive government, and is thus famously commemorated by Shelley:

> I met Murder on the way—
> He had a mask like Castlereagh—
> Very smooth he looked, yet grim,
> Seven bloodhounds followed him.
> — Percy Bysshe Shelley 'The Mask of Anarchy' (1819)

castles in Spain visionary unattainable schemes; the expression is recorded from late Middle English, and it is possible that *Spain*, as the nearest Moorish country to Christendom, was taken as the type of a region in which the prospective castle-builder had no standing.

castles in the air an alternative expression to ➤ CASTLES *in Spain*; the phrase in this form is recorded from the late 16th century.

Castor and Pollux in Greek mythology, the twin sons of ➤ JUPITER and ➤ LEDA and brothers of ➤ HELEN, the ➤ DIOSCURI.

casus belli an act or situation provoking or justifying war. The phrase is Latin, and comes from *casus* 'case', and *belli* 'of war'; it is recorded in English from the mid 19th century.

cat the *cat* has been traditionally associated with witchcraft, and in Christian art a cat may be shown in a picture as emblematic of sinful human nature; cat may also be used informally for a malicious or spiteful woman.

In ancient Egypt, cats were regarded as sacred animals; the goddess ➤ BASTET is shown with a cat's head.

See also ➤ BELL *the cat*, ➤ CARE *killed the cat*, ➤ CATS, ➤ CHESHIRE *cat*, ➤ CURIOSITY *killed the cat*, ➤ FAT *cat*, ➤ GIB *cat*, ➤ *no* ROOM *to swing a cat*, ➤ *there are more* WAYS *of killing a cat than choking it with cream*, ➤ TOUCH *not the cat but a glove*.

put the cat among the pigeons stir up trouble; the expression is recorded from the early 18th century, and the idea of the destructive potential of a cat inside a pigeon-loft is explained as standing for a man getting among women.

Cat and Mouse Act informal name for the 1913 act passed, during the suffragette campaign, to allow for the temporary release of prisoners on hunger strike and their subsequent rearrest; a cartoon of the period showed the body of a suffragette in the jaws of a cat.

a cat has nine lives a proverbial belief; recorded from the mid 16th century.

cat i' the adage in Shakespeare's *Macbeth*, Lady Macbeth uses the image in scorn of her husband's irresolution; the reference is to the proverb ➤ *the* CAT *would eat fish, but would not wet her feet*.

a cat in gloves catches no mice proverbial saying, late 16th century.

a cat may look at a king proverbial expression, mid 16th century.

cat o' nine tails a rope whip with nine knotted cords, formerly used (especially at sea) to flog offenders.

the cat, the rat, and Lovell our dog, Rule all England under the hog hostile rhyme describing the rule of Richard III, whose personal emblem was a ➤ WHITE *Boar*, and his three favourites, William Catesby ('the cat'), Richard Ratcliffe ('the rat'), and Lord Lovell, whose crest was a dog; the rhyme is recorded from the early 16th century in Robert Fabyan's *Chronicles*, and is attributed to the English landowner and conspirator against Richard, William Collingbourne (d. 1484).

the **cat** would eat fish but would not wet her feet proverbial saying, early 13th century.

when the **cat's away the mice will play** proverbial saying, early 17th century.

cat's cradle a child's game in which a loop of string is put around and between the fingers and complex patterns are formed.

cat's paw a person who is used by another, typically to carry out an unpleasant or dangerous task, and originally with allusion to the fable of a monkey which asked a cat to extract its roasted chestnuts from the fire.

catacomb an underground cemetery consisting of a subterranean gallery with recesses for tombs, as constructed by the ancient Romans. Recorded from Old English, the word comes from late Latin *catumbas*, the name of the subterranean cemetery under the Basilica of St Sebastian on the Appian Way near Rome, in or near which the relics of the apostles Peter and Paul were said to have been placed in the 3rd century.

The term *catacombs* was subsequently given to other subterranean cemeteries in Rome (redis-covered in the late 16th century), especially as trad-itional places of refuge for early Christians in times of persecution.

Catalan a Romance language closely related to Castilian Spanish and Provençal, widely spoken in ➤ CATALONIA (where it has official status alongside Castilian Spanish) and in Andorra, the Balearic Is-lands, and parts of southern France.

Catalonia an autonomous region of NE Spain having a strong separatist tradition; the normal lan-guage for everyday purposes is Catalan, which has also won acceptance in recent years for various of-ficial purposes.

in the **catbird seat** in a superior or advantageous position. A **catbird** is a long-tailed American song-bird of the mockingbird family, with mainly dark grey or black plumage and catlike mewing calls, and this expression is said to be an allusion to a baseball player in the fortunate position of having no strikes and therefore three balls still to play (a reference made in James Thurber's short story *The Catbird Seat*).

catch a crab get one's oar jammed under water, as if it were being held down by a crab; miss the water with the stroke.

you cannot **catch** old birds with chaff proverbial saying, late 15th century.

catch-22 a dilemma or difficult circumstance from which there is no escape because of mutually con-flicting or dependent conditions. The term comes from the title of a novel (1961) by Joseph Heller, in which the main character feigns madness in order to avoid dangerous combat missions, but his desire to avoid them is taken to prove his sanity:

> There was only one catch and that was Catch-22, which specified that a concern for one's own safety in the face of dangers that were real and immediate was the process of a rational mind . . . Orr would be crazy to fly more missions and sane if he didn't, but if he was sane he had to fly them. If he flew them he was crazy and didn't have to; but if he didn't want to he was sane and had to.
>
> — Joseph Heller *Catch-22* (1961)

catching's before hanging proverbial saying, early 19th century.

catchphrase a well-known sentence or phrase, typically one that is associated with a particular famous person or fictional character.

catechism a summary of the principles of Chris-tian religion in the form of questions and answers, used for the instruction of Christians. The word is recorded from the early 16th century and comes via ecclesiastical Latin from ecclesiastical Greek *katēkhizein* 'instruct orally, make hear'.

See also ➤ SHORTER *Catechism*.

catechumen a Christian convert under instruc-tion before baptism. Recorded from late Middle English, the word comes via ecclesiastical Latin from ecclesiastical Greek *katēkhoumenos* 'being in-structed', from *katēkhizein* 'instruct orally, make hear'.

cater-cornered in North America, situated diag-onally opposite someone or something. The expres-sion dates from the mid 19th century, and comes from dialect *cater* 'diagonally', from *cater* denoting the four on dice, from French *quatre* 'four'.

cater-cousin archaic term for an intimate friend; recorded from the early 16th century, the origin of *cater* here is uncertain, although it may derive from *cater* 'buyer of provisions', with reference to people sharing lodgings.

cateran historical term for a warrior or raider from the Scottish highlands. The word is recorded from Middle English (originally in the plural or as a collective singular denoting the peasantry as fighters); it comes from Scottish Gaelic *ceathairne* 'peasantry'.

caterpillar the larva of a butterfly or moth, which has a segmented worm-like body with three pairs of true legs and several pairs of leg-like appendages. The term was formerly used to mean a rapacious person or one who preys on society, as in Shakespeare's *Richard II* (1595), 'the caterpillars of the commonwealth'.

The word is recorded from late Middle English, and perhaps comes from a variant of Old French *chatepelose*, literally 'hairy cat', influenced by obsolete *piller* 'ravager'. The association with 'cat' is found in other languages, e.g. Swiss German *Teufelskatz* (literally 'devil's cat'), Lombard *gatta* (literally 'cat').

Caterpillar Club founded by Leslie Leroy Irvin in 1922 for those whose lives had been saved by agency of parachute.

caters in bell-ringing, a system of change-ringing using nine bells, with four pairs changing places each time. The word comes (in the late 19th century) from French *quatre* 'four'.

Cathar a member of a heretical medieval Christian sect which professed a form of Manichaean dualism and sought to achieve great spiritual purity. The name is recorded in English from the mid 17th century, and comes from medieval Latin *Cathari* (plural), from Greek *katharoi* 'the pure'.

catharsis the process of releasing, and thereby providing relief from, strong or repressed emotions. The notion of 'release' through drama derives from Aristotle's *Poetics*.

The word comes from Greek *katharsis*, from *kathairein* 'cleanse', from *katharos* 'pure'.

Cathay the name by which China (also called *Khitai*) was known to medieval Europe. The name comes from medieval Latin *Cataya, Cathaya*, from Turkic *Khitāy*.

cathedral the principal church of a diocese, with which the bishop is officially associated. Recorded from Middle English (as an adjective, the noun being short for *cathedral church* 'the church which contains the bishop's throne'), the word comes via Latin from Greek *kathedra* 'seat'.

Catherine de' Medici (1519–89), queen of France, who ruled as regent (1560–74) during the minority reigns of her three sons, Francis II, Charles IX, and

Henry III; she is seen as a main instigator of ➤ *the Massacre of St* Bartholomew (1572).

St Catherine of Alexandria (d. *c.*307), early and probably legendary Christian martyr. According to tradition she opposed the persecution of Christians under the emperor Maxentius and refused to recant or to marry the emperor; when pagan philosophers were sent to dispute with her she converted them. She is traditionally regarded as one of the ➤ Fourteen *Holy Helpers*.

She is said to have been tortured on a spiked wheel (destroyed by her angelic protectors) and finally beheaded; the **Catherine wheel** subsequently became her emblem.

◻ **EMBLEM** Her emblems are a Catherine wheel and a sword, and a palm-branch as a symbol of her virginity.

◻ **FEAST DAY** Her feast day is 25 November.

St Catherine of Siena (1333?–80), Sienese virgin and member of the Dominican Third Order, who was a noted spiritual leader of the 14th century, and who was popularly believed to have contributed significantly to the ending of the ➤ Great *Schism* and the return of the papacy to Rome from Avignon. She is the patron saint of Italy, and was declared a Doctor of the Church in 1970.

◻ **EMBLEM** Her usual emblem is a lily.

◻ **FEAST DAY** Her feast day was 30 April; from 1969 it has been 29 April.

Catherine the Great (1729–96), empress of Russia. Born a princess of Anhalt-Zerbst, she became empress (as **Catherine II**) after her husband, Peter III, was deposed; her attempted social and political reforms were impeded by the aristocracy. She formed alliances with Prussia and Austria, and made territorial advances at the expense of the Turks and Tartars.

Catherine wheel a firework in the form of a flat coil which spins when fixed to something solid, and lit; it is named for the spiked wheel which was one of the instruments of martyrdom of ➤ *St* Catherine *of Alexandria*.

Catholic of or including all Christians; of or relating to the historic doctrine and practice of the Western Church; ➤ Roman *Catholic*. The term is recorded from late Middle English and comes via Old French or late Latin from Greek *katholikos* 'universal', from *kata* 'in respect of' + *holos* 'whole'.

Catholic and Apostolic Church another name for the ➤ Irvingites.

Catholic Association founded by the Irish nationalist Daniel O'Connell (1775–1847) to promote ➤ CATHOLIC *Emancipation*.

Catholic Church the Church universal, the whole body of Christians; also, the Church of Rome.

Catholic Emancipation the granting of full political and civil liberties to Roman Catholics in Britain and Ireland. This was effected by the Catholic Emancipation Act of 1829, which repealed restrictive laws, including that which barred Catholics from holding public office.

Catholic Epistle a name for the 'general' epistles of James, Peter, Jude, and 1 John, as not being addressed to particular churches or persons. The second and third epistles of John are now also regarded as belonging to this group.

Catholic King a title given to the king of Spain.

Catholic League in 16th-century France, the party headed by the Guise family, the ➤ HOLY *League*.

catholicon an electuary supposed to be capable of evacuating all humours from the body, a universal remedy, a panacea; the term was used in French in the 16th century by the French Ambrose Paré (*c.*1510–90), and is referred to in the translators' preface to the Authorized Version (1611), 'Men talk much…of Catholicon the drug, that it is instead of all purges.'

Catholicos the Patriarch of the Armenian or the Nestorian Church.

Catiline (*c.*108–62 BC), Roman nobleman and conspirator. In 63 BC his planned uprising was discovered by Cicero, whose speech in the Senate, including the question, 'How long will you abuse our patience, Catiline?' was the signal for Catiline to leave Rome. In the suppression of the uprising his fellow conspirators were executed and Catiline himself died in battle in Etruria.

Marcus Porcius Cato (234–149 BC), Roman statesman, orator, and writer, known as **Cato the Elder** or **Cato the Censor**. As censor he initiated a vigorous programme of reform, and attempted to stem the growing influence of Greek culture; he was also an implacable enemy of Carthage, ending every speech he made in the Senate with the words ➤ DELENDA *est Carthago*.

Cato Street Conspiracy a plot by a group of conspirators led by Arthur Thistlewood (1770–1820) to assassinate participants at a cabinet dinner given by Lord Harrowby in February 1822, as a preliminary to revolution. The attempt failed, and Thistlewood and four of his accomplices were hanged.

cats see also ➤ ALL *cats are grey in the dark,* ➤ KEEP *no more cats than will catch mice,* ➤ KILKENNY *cats,* ➤ *wanton* KITTENS *make sober cats.*

cattle see ➤ HURRY *no man's cattle,* ➤ PARK *cattle.*

Catullus (*c.*84–*c.*54 BC), Roman poet. His one book of verse contains poems in a variety of metres on a range of subjects. He is best known for his love poems.

Caucasian in the racial classification as developed by Blumenbach and others in the 19th century, *Caucasian* (or **Caucasoid**) included peoples whose skin colour ranged from light (in northern Europe) to dark (in parts of North Africa and India). Although the classification is outdated and the categories are now not generally accepted as scientific, the term *Caucasian* has acquired a more restricted meaning. It is now used, especially in the US, as a synonym for 'white or of European origin'.

El Caudillo title ('the Leader') assumed by General ➤ FRANCO in 1937.

Caudine Forks name given to a narrow pass in the mountains near Capua, where the Roman army was defeated by the Samnites in 321 BC.

caudle a warm drink consisting of thin gruel mixed with wine or ale, sweetened and spiced, given chiefly to sick people. The word is recorded from Middle English, and comes ultimately from Latin *caldu*m 'hot drink'.

caul part of the amniotic membrane enclosing a fetus, occasionally found on a child's head at birth, and thought to bring good luck. The word is recorded from Middle English, and may come from Old French *cale* 'head covering', although recorded earlier in English.

cauldron of oil a cauldron of oil is the emblem of ➤ St JOHN *the Evangelist.*

cause see also ➤ *the* DOUGLAS *Cause,* ➤ FIRST *Cause.*

the good old cause in 17th century England, applied particularly to Puritan beliefs and principles, as in Milton's *The Ready and Easy Way to Establish a Free Commonwealth* (2nd ed., 1660), 'What I have spoken, is the language of that which is not called amiss, *The good old Cause.*' The usage was later reinforced by Wordsworth:

> Plain living and high thinking are no more:
> The homely beauty of the good old cause
> Is gone.
> — William Wordsworth 'O friend! I know not which way
> I must look' (1807)

rebel without a cause a person who is dissatisfied with society but does not have a specific aim to fight for, from the title of a US film, starring ➤ *James* DEAN, released in 1955.

> The road-tripping, law-breaking guy or girl from the wrong side of the tracks is the latest Hollywood incarnation of the rebel without a cause.
> — *This Magazine* November 1994

causeway see ➤ GIANT's *Causeway.*

causewayed camp a type of Neolithic settlement in southern Britain, visible as an oval enclosure surrounded by concentric ditches that are crossed by several causeways. It is believed that such camps may have had a ritual function.

Cavalier a supporter of Charles I in the Civil War of 1642–9, a 17th-century Royalist. The word in this sense is recorded from the mid 17th century and is a special usage of the more general, 'a horseman; a lively military man; a courtly or fashionable gentleman, a gallant, especially as an escort to a lady'; ultimately it derives (perhaps through French) from Italian *cavaliere* from Latin *caballus* 'horse'.

The term as applied to the king's supporters by their opponents was originally derogatory; the critical force survives, for example, in the speech made by the English soldier John Lambert (1619–83) in the Parliament of 1656 supporting the rule of the major-generals, 'The quarrel is now between light and darkness, not who shall rule, but whether we shall live or be preserved or no. Good words will not do with the cavaliers.'

The term was later increasingly used to indicate a style of life and social custom opposed to the repressive practices of the ➤ ROUNDHEADS.

See also ➤ LAUGHING *Cavalier.*

Cavalier Parliament a name for the first Parliament of Charles II, following the Restoration in 1660 and noted for its support of the restored monarchy.

cave see ➤ ADULLAM, ➤ AJANTA *Caves,* ➤ ALADDIN's *cave,* ➤ CORYCIAN *Cave,* ➤ FINGAL's

Cave, ➤ IDOLS *of the tribe, cave, market, and theatre,* ➤ KING's *Cave,* ➤ MAMMOTH *Cave.*

caveat emptor the principle that the buyer alone is responsible for checking the quality and suitability of goods before a purchase is made; the phrase is Latin and means, 'let the buyer beware.'

Edith Cavell (1865–1915), English nurse. During the First World War she helped Allied soldiers to escape from occupied Belgium. She was subsequently executed by the Germans and became a heroine of the Allied cause. It was reported that on the evening of her execution, she had said, 'I realize that patriotism is not enough. I must have no hatred or bitterness towards anyone.'

cavern see ➤ KENT's *Cavern.*

caviar to the general a good thing unappreciated by the ignorant; the phrase is originally a quotation from Shakespeare's *Hamlet* (1601), 'The play, I remember, pleased not the million; 'twas caviar to the general.'

Count Cavour (1810–61), Italian statesman. In 1847 Cavour founded the newspaper *Il Risorgimento* to further the cause of Italian unification under Victor Emmanuel II; he later became Premier of Piedmont (1852–59; 1860–1), and in 1861 became the first Premier of a unified Italy.

Cawnpore earlier variant spelling of *Kanpur* in northern India, the site of a massacre of British soldiers and European families in July 1857, during the Indian Mutiny.

William Caxton (*c.*1422–91), the first English printer. He printed the first book in English in 1474 and went on to produce about eighty other texts.

St Cecilia (2nd or 3rd century), Roman martyr. According to legend, she took a vow of celibacy but when forced to marry converted her husband to Christianity and both were martyred. She was first confined in a hot bathroom in an attempt to suffocate her; later she was beheaded. She is the patron saint of church music.

❑ **EMBLEM** She is typically shown with an organ or with a lute.

❑ **FEAST DAY** Her feast day is 22 November.

celebrity novel a novel written by or ascribed to a famous person and designed to sell on the strength of that person's fame; *celebrity novels,* for which large advances were often paid, are associated particularly with the 1980s.

Celestial City in Bunyan's ➤ PILGRIM*'s Progress*, the object of Christian's journey, heaven.

Celestial Empire the Chinese Empire; the name is recorded in English from the early 19th century.

celestial hierarchy in Christian theology, each of three divisions of angelic beings (each comprising three orders) in the ninefold celestial system described in a 4th-century work formerly attributed to Dionysius the Areopagite (see ➤ DIONYSIUS[4]) and now to ➤ PSEUDO-*Dionysius*; angels collectively, the angelic host.

Celestial Hierarchy

NAME	ORDER
seraphs	first
cherubs	second
thrones	third
dominations	fourth
virtues	fifth
powers	sixth
principalities	seventh
archangels	eighth
angels	ninth

Celestine a member of a reformed branch of the Benedictine order, founded by Pope Celestine V in the 13th century.

Benvenuto Cellini (1500–71), Italian goldsmith and sculptor, the most renowned goldsmith of his day. His work is characterized by its elaborate virtuosity; the salt cellar of gold and enamel which he made while working for Francis I of France typifies the late Renaissance style. His autobiography is famous for its racy style and its vivid picture of contemporary Italian life.

Anders Celsius (1701–44), Swedish astronomer, best known for his temperature scale. He was professor of astronomy at Uppsala, and in 1742 he advocated a metric temperature scale with 100° as the freezing point of water and 0° as the boiling point; however, the thermometer which was actually introduced at the Uppsala Observatory had its scale reversed.

Celt a member of a group of peoples inhabiting much of Europe and Asia Minor in pre-Roman times. Their culture developed in the late Bronze Age around the upper Danube, and reached its height in the La Tène culture (5th to 1st centuries BC) before being overrun by the Romans and various Germanic peoples.

Celtic the language group of the Celts, constituting a branch of the Indo-European family and including Irish, Scottish Gaelic, Welsh, Breton, Manx, Cornish, and several extinct pre-Roman languages such as Gaulish.

Celtic Church the Christian Church in the British Isles from its foundation in the 2nd or 3rd century until its assimilation into the Roman Catholic Church (664 in England; 12th century in Wales, Scotland, and Ireland).

Celtic cross a Latin cross with a circle round the centre.

Celtic fringe the Highland Scots, Irish, Welsh, and Cornish in relation to the rest of Britain; the term, often regarded as derogatory, is recorded from the late 19th century.

Celtic Sea the part of the Atlantic Ocean between southern Ireland and SW England.

Celtic tiger the Irish economy seen as a successor to the earlier ➤ TIGER *economies*.

> At the risk of a horrible mixed metaphor, we can say that the Celtic Tiger needs a human face and a human heart.
> — Cahal Daly in *Irish Times* 10 January 1998 'This Week They Said'

Celtic twilight the romantic fairy tale atmosphere of Irish folklore and literature; the term derives originally from W. B. Yeats's name for his collection of writings (1893) based on Irish folk-tales.

cemetery a burial ground, especially one not in a churchyard, ultimately from the Greek verb *koiman* 'put to sleep'.

See also ➤ ARLINGTON *Cemetery*.

Cenci name of a 16th-century Italian family; the execution of **Beatrice Cenci** in 1599 for the murder of her father was the subject of Shelley's play *The Cenci* (1819–21).

cenotaph a monument to someone buried elsewhere, especially one commemorating people who died in a war; **the Cenotaph** is the name of the war memorial in Whitehall, London, designed by Sir Edwin Lutyens and erected in 1919–20. The word is recorded from the early 17th century and comes ultimately, via French and late Latin, from Greek *kenos* 'empty' + *taphos* 'tomb'.

censer a container in which incense is burnt, typically during a religious ceremony.

censor originally (in ancient Rome), either of two magistrates who held censuses and supervised public morals. Later, in extended use, an official who examines material that is about to be published, such as books, films, news, and art, and suppresses any parts that are considered obscene, politically unacceptable, or a threat to security.

Les Cent Nouvelles Nouvelles a collection of French tales, loosely modelled on Boccacio's ➤ DE-CAMERON, and written down probably between 1464 and 1467.

centaur in Greek mythology, a creature with the head, arms, and torso of a man and the body and legs of a horse. They are said to have been defeated by the ➤ LAPITHS in the battle after the wedding of Pirithous, when they tried to carry off the bride and other women; in classical Greek thought they may have symbolized animal nature.

The name comes via Latin from Greek *kentauros*, the Greek name for a Thessalonian tribe of expert horsemen; of unknown ultimate origin.

See also ➤ CHIRON, ➤ NESSUS, ➤ SAGITTARY.

centaury a widely distributed herbaceous plant of the gentian family, typically having pink flowers, some kinds of which are used in herbal medicine. Recorded from late Middle English, the name is ultimately based on Greek *kentauros* 'centaur', because its medicinal properties were said to have been discovered by the centaur ➤ CHIRON.

Centennial State informal name for Colorado, which was admitted as a state in the centennial year (1876) of the existence of the United States.

cento a literary work made up of quotations from other authors. Recorded from the early 17th century (and also meaning, a piece of patchwork), the word is from Latin, literally 'patchwork garment'.

Central Park a large public park in the centre of Manhattan in New York City, which was established in the mid 19th century and which employed landscape techniques to incorporate existing natural features.

centumvir in ancient Rome, any of a body of (originally 105) judges appointed to decide common causes among the Roman people.

centuriator see ➤ *Centuriator of* MAGDEBURG.

centurion the commander of a century (a company, originally of a hundred men) in the ancient Roman army.

century of the common man the 20th century; the term derives from a speech by the American Democratic politician Henry Wallace (1888–1965), made during the Second World War:

> The century on which we are entering—the century which will come out of this war—can be and must be the century of the common man.
> — Henry Wallace speech, 8 May 1942

Cephalus in Greek mythology, the husband of ➤ PROCRIS, whose jealous wife, hiding in a thicket to watch him, was mistaken by him for an animal and accidentally killed.

Cepheus king of Ethiopia, husband of ➤ CASSIOPEIA and father of ➤ ANDROMEDA, for whom a constellation near the north celestial pole is named.

Cerberus in Greek mythology, a monstrous watchdog with three (or in some accounts fifty) heads, which guarded the entrance to Hades. Cerberus could be appeased with a cake, as by Aeneas, or lulled to sleep (as by Orpheus) with lyre music; one of the twelve labours of Hercules was to bring him up from the underworld.

Cerealia ancient Roman games in honour of the goddess ➤ CERES.

cerecloth cloth made waterproof by smearing or impregnation with wax, especially as then used for wrapping a corpse, a winding-sheet. The term is recorded from late Middle English and comes from earlier *cered cloth*, from *cere* 'to wax', from Latin *cerare*, from *cera* 'wax'.

ceremony a formal religious or public occasion, typically one celebrating a particular event, achievement, or anniversary. The word is recorded from late Middle English and comes from Old French *ceremonie* or Latin *caerimonia* 'religious worship', (plural) 'ritual observances'.

See also ➤ MASTER *of Ceremonies*.

Ceremony of the Keys the formal procedure in which the gates of the Tower of London are locked each night.

cereology the study or investigation of ➤ CROP *circles*; the term is recorded from the late 20th century, and derives from ➤ CERES.

Ceres in Roman mythology, the corn goddess, the equivalent of the Greek ➤ DEMETER.

In astronomy, *Ceres* is the name of the first asteroid to be discovered, found by G. Piazzi of Palermo on 1 January 1801.

Ceridwen in Welsh mythology, the goddess of poetic inspiration, an enchantress said to live beneath a lake; her magic cauldron conferred the gift of second sight.

Cerinthian an adherent of *Cerinthus*, a Gnostic of the 1st century AD who is usually presented as antagonistic to the Apostle John.

Miguel de Cervantes (1547–1616), Spanish novelist and dramatist. His most famous work is *Don Quixote* (1605–15), a satire on chivalric romances that greatly influenced the development of the novel. It tells the story of an amiable knight who imagines himself called upon to roam the world in search of adventure on his horse Rosinante, accompanied by the shrewd squire Sancho Panza.

Cerynitian hind a hind with gilded horns, sacred to Artemis, living in the land of the Hyperboreans, captured by Hercules as the fourth of his Labours.

Cesarewitch a horse race run annually over two miles at Newmarket, England. The name comes from Russian *tsesarevich* 'heir to the throne', in honour of the Russian Crown prince (later Alexander II) who attended the inaugural race in 1839.

cestus[1] a (bridal) belt or girdle for the waist, especially that of Aphrodite or Venus. The word comes via Latin from Greek *kestos*, literally 'stitched'.

cestus[2] a covering for the hand made of thongs of bull-hide loaded with metallic strips, used by boxers in ancient Rome. The word comes from Latin *caestus*, from *caedere* 'strike'.

Cetshwayo (*c.*1826–84), Zulu king. He became ruler of Zululand in 1873 and was involved in a series of battles with the Afrikaners and British; he was deposed as leader after the capture of his capital by the British in 1879.

Cetus a large northern constellation (the Whale), said to represent the sea monster which threatened ➤ ANDROMEDA.

Chaco War a boundary dispute in 1932–5 between Bolivia and Paraguay, triggered by the discovery of oil in the northern part of the Gran Chaco, in which Paraguay eventually forced Bolivia to sue for peace and gained most of the disputed territory; casualties on both sides were heavy.

Chad in full **Mr Chad**. The figure of a human head looking over a wall, with a caption protesting against some omission or shortage, and usually beginning 'Wot, no—?'

St Chad (d. 672), first bishop of Mercia and Lindsey at Lichfield, for whom there was an early and popular cult; it was said by Bede that if the faithful put dust from his shrine into water, the drink was medicinal for people and animals.
　□ **FEAST DAY** His feast day is 2 March.
　See also ➤ DAVID *and Chad: sow peas good or bad.*

Chad-farthing at Lichfield, a term used for dues paid to the Church, apparently named for ➤ *St* CHAD.

chador a large piece of dark-coloured cloth, typically worn by Muslim women, wrapped around the head and upper body to leave only the face exposed. The word is recorded in English from the early 17th century, and comes via Urdu from Persian *čādar* 'sheet or veil'.

chaff the husks of corn or other seed separated by winnowing or threshing; traditionally taken as the type of something worthless, as in **separate the wheat from the chaff**, 'distinguish valuable people or things from worthless ones'.
　Recorded from Old English (in the form *cæf*, *ceaf*), the word probably comes from a Germanic base meaning 'gnaw'.
　See also ➤ *a* KING'*s chaff is worth more than other men's corn,* ➤ *you cannot* CATCH *old birds with chaff.*

chagan the title of the king of the Avars in the 6th and 7th centuries. The word comes ultimately (via medieval Latin and Byzantine Greek) from Old Turkish *ḳaġan* 'king, monarch'.

Chagatai name of a dynasty founded by *Chaghatai*, a son of Genghis Khan, which reigned in Transoxiana 1227–1358, later used to designate the literary Turkic language of central Asia between the 15th and 19th centuries.

chain a jointed measuring line consisting of linked metal rods; the length of such a measuring line (66 ft).

a chain is no stronger than its weakest link proverbial saying, mid 19th century.

chair see ➤ PERILOUS *Chair.*

Council of Chalcedon the fourth ecumenical council of the Christian Church, held in 451 at Chalcedon, a former city on the Bosporus in Asia Minor, now part of Istanbul.

Chalcedonian a person upholding the decrees of the Council of Chalcedon (AD 451), especially those regarding the nature of Christ, which were eventually accepted by all except the ➤ MONOPHYSITE Churches.

chalcedony a microcrystalline type of quartz occurring in several different forms including onyx and agate. The word comes (in late Middle English) from Latin *chalcedonius* (often believed to mean 'stone of Chalcedon', but this is doubtful), which in the Vulgate represents Greek *khalkēdōn*, the name (in Revelation 21:19) of the precious stone forming the third foundation of the New Jerusalem.

Chaldea an ancient country in what is now southern Iraq, inhabited by the Chaldeans. The name comes from Greek *Khaldaia*, from Akkadian *Kald*, the name of a Babylonian tribal group.

Chaldean a member of an ancient people who lived in Chaldea *c*.800 BC and ruled Babylonia 625–539 BC. They were renowned as astronomers and astrologers.

Chaldees see ➤ UR *of the Chaldees.*

chalice see also ➤ POISONED *chalice.*

chalice a chalice is the emblem of St Richard of Chichester (1197–1253), who is said once to have dropped the chalice at Mass without the wine being spilt, ➤ St HUGH *of Lincoln*, and other saints.

not by a long chalk by no means, not at all, with reference to the chalk used for marking up scores in competitive games.

chalk and cheese the types of two completely different things; the proverbial contrast between these two substances is recorded from late Middle English.

chalk and talk classroom instruction making substantial use of the blackboard.

challenge a call to someone to participate in a competitive situation; the original meaning in Middle English was 'accusation', from the Latin *calumnia* 'calumny'.

See also ➤ MEET *the challenge—make the change.*

Challenger Disaster the accident in which the US space shuttle *Challenger* was destroyed on takeoff in January 1986, exploding in mid-air and killing all seven astronauts on board (the crew members included a science teacher who had won a national competition to participate, and who had been going to give a lesson from space to her class). Shuttle missions were subsequently suspended until September 1988, while more rigorous safety systems were instituted.

> We will never forget them, nor the last time we saw them this morning, as they prepared for the journey and waved goodbye and 'slipped the surly bonds of earth' to 'touch the face of God.'
> — Ronald Reagan broadcast from the Oval Office after the loss of *Challenger*, 28 January 1986

Chalybean pertaining to the Chalybes, an ancient people of Asia Minor famous for their skill in working iron; the term is first recorded in Milton's Samson Agonistes (1671), in a reference to 'Chalybean tempered steel'.

cham an autocrat, a dominant critic; chiefly used in ➤ GREAT *Cham*. The word is recorded from late Middle English, and comes ultimately, via French, from Turkic *ḵān* 'khan'.

chamber see ➤ Chamber *of* DEPUTIES, ➤ *the* GILDED *Chamber*.

Chamber of Horrors the name given in the mid 19th century to a room in Madame Tussaud's waxwork exhibition which showed especially notorious murderers and their victims as well as scenes of execution.

chamberlain historical term for an officer who managed the household of a monarch or noble. The term is recorded from Middle English (denoting a servant in a bedchamber) and comes via Old French and Old Saxon from Latin *camera* 'vault'.

See also ➤ LORD *Great Chamberlain of England*.

Chambre Ardente in France in the 16th and 17th centuries, a court set up to try cases of heresy and witchcraft (as in the ➤ *Affair of the* POISONS); the name means literally 'burning court'.

chameleon a small slow-moving Old World lizard with a prehensile tail, long extensible tongue, protruding eyes that rotate independently, and a highly developed ability to change colour. It has become the type of a changeable or inconstant person.

The name is recorded from Middle English, and comes via Latin from Greek *khamaileōn*, from *khamai* 'on the ground' + *leōn* 'lion'.

Champ de Mars the park in Paris by the Seine, laid out in 1765, and named after the Roman ➤ CAMPUS *Martius*.

champagne a white sparkling wine from Champagne in NE France, first produced there in about 1700, and regarded as a symbol of luxury and associated with celebration.

Champagne Charlie a man noted for living a life of luxury and excess, from the name of a popular song, first performed in 1868.

champagne socialist in the UK, a derogatory term for a person who espouses socialist ideals while enjoying a wealthy and luxurious lifestyle.

Champion of England the person whose duty it was to ride armed into Westminster Hall on Coronation Day, and formally issue a challenge to any disputing the right of succession. Also called **king's champion, queen's champion**.

champions see also ➤ SEVEN *Champions*.

Samuel de Champlain (1567–1635), French explorer and colonial statesman. He established a settlement at Quebec in 1608, developing alliances with the native peoples, and was appointed Lieutenant Governor in 1612. **Lake Champlain**, which he reached in 1609, is named after him.

Jean-François Champollion (1790–1832), French Egyptologist. A pioneer in the study of ancient Egypt, he is best known for his success in deciphering some of the hieroglyphic inscriptions on the ➤ ROSETTA *Stone* in 1822.

Champs Élysées an avenue in Paris, leading from the Place de la Concorde to the Arc de Triomphe. It is noted for its fashionable shops and restaurants.

Charlie Chan fictional Chinese-American detective working for the Honolulu police force, created by the American writer Earl Derr Biggers (1884–1933), and first appearing in a series of six novels from 1925.

> Would weigh about a hundred and sixty pounds. Fat face, Charlie Chan moustache, thick soft neck.
> — Raymond Chandler *The Big Sleep* (1939)

Chan Chan the capital of the pre-Inca civilization of the Chimu. Its extensive adobe ruins are situated on the coast of north Peru.

chance see also ➤ BUCKLEY*'s chance*.

chancel the part of a church near the altar, reserved for the clergy and choir, and typically separated from the nave by steps or a screen. The word is recorded from Middle English, and comes (via Old French) from Latin *cancelli* 'crossbars'.

chancellor a senior state or legal official; in some European countries, such as Germany, the head of the government. Recorded from late Old English, the word comes (via Old French) from late Latin *cancellarius* 'porter, secretary' (originally a court official stationed at the grating separating public from judges), from *cancelli* 'crossbars'.
See also ➤ IRON *Chancellor*, ➤ LORD *Chancellor*.

Chancellor of the Duchy of Lancaster in the UK, a member of the government legally representing the Crown as Duke of Lancaster, typically a cabinet minister employed on non-departmental work.

Chancellor of the Exchequer the finance minister of the United Kingdom, who prepares the nation's annual budgets.

Battle of Chancellorsville a Confederate victory of the American Civil War, 2–4 May 1863, in which however ➤ *Stonewall* JACKSON was fatally wounded, being shot by his own men.

Chancery in the UK, the Lord Chancellor's court, the highest court of judicature next to the House of Lords; but, since the Judicature Act of 1873 a division of the High Court of Justice. It formerly consisted of two distinct tribunals, one ordinary, being a court of common law, the other extraordinary, being a court of equity. To the former belonged the issuing of writs for a new parliament, and of all original writs. The second proceeded upon rules of equity and conscience, moderating the rigour of the common law, and giving relief in cases where there was no remedy in the common-law courts; it is in this role that it is shown in Dickens's *Bleak House*, presiding over the apparently interminable case of the ➤ JARNDYCE estate, and entangling the many hopeless claimants who expect a judgement shortly.
The expression **in chancery**, referring to the head of a boxer or wrestler held under an opponent's head and being pummelled, derives from the tenacity and absolute control which the Court of Chancery was believed to exert, and to the certainty of cost and loss to property which was 'in chancery'.

Raymond Chandler (1888–1959), American novelist, remembered as the creator of the private detective ➤ *Philip* MARLOWE, and noted for his tough realistic style and settings ranging across social boundaries. He is said to have advised aspiring thriller writers, 'When in doubt have a man come through the door with a gun in his hand.'

> His world is a sprawling Chandleresque landscape that reaches from the dusty, segregated neighborhoods of the L.A. basin to the fancy houses in the canyons.
> — *Esquire* June 1994

Chandragupta Maurya (*c.*325–297 BC), Indian emperor. He founded the Mauryan empire and annexed provinces deep into Afghanistan from Alexander's Greek successors. The empire continued to expand after his death, but ended in 185 BC.

Subrahmanyan **Chandrasekhar** (1910–95), Indian-born American astronomer. He suggested how some stars could eventually collapse to form a dense white dwarf, provided that their mass does not exceed an upper limit (the **Chandrasekhar limit**).

Lon Chaney (1883–1930), American actor. He played a wide variety of deformed villains and macabre characters in more than 150 films, including *The Hunchback of Notre Dame* (1923). He became known as 'the Man of a Thousand Faces'.

> His Chaney-like rendering of the village idiot in *Ryan's Daughter*.
> — *Films in Review* August 1971

change see also ➤ CHOP *and change*, ➤ NOUS *avons changé tout cela*, ➤ SEA *change*, ➤ TIMES *change and we with time*, ➤ WIND *of change*.

don't change horses in mid-stream proverbial saying, mid 19th century.

a change is as good as a rest proverbial saying, late 19th century.

changeling a child believed to have been secretly substituted by fairies for the parents' real child in infancy; the term is first recorded from the late 16th century.

changes see also ➤ BOOK *of Changes*.

ring the changes vary the ways of expressing, arranging, or doing something, with allusion to bell-ringing and the different orders in which a peal of bells may be rung.

Channel see also ➤ CHOPS *of the Channel*.

Channel Country an area of SW Queensland and NE South Australia, watered intermittently by natural channels, where rich grasslands produced by the summer rains provide grazing for cattle.

Channel Islands a group of islands in the English Channel off the NW coast of France, of which the largest are Jersey, Guernsey, and Alderney. Formerly part of the dukedom of Normandy, they have owed allegiance to the English Crown since the Norman Conquest in 1066.

Channel Tunnel a railway tunnel under the English Channel, linking the coasts of England and France, opened in 1994 and 49 km (31 miles) long. The name considerably predates the actual tunnel, as the idea was discussed in the 19th century; the *Times* of 25 June 1869 carried a report on a 'project for a submarine tunnel between Dover and a point near Cape Blanc-nez, on the French coast'. The humorous blend *Chunnel*, referring to such a project, is found from the 1920s.

chanson de geste a medieval French historical verse romance, typically one connected with ➤ CHARLEMAGNE. The phrase is French, and means literally 'song of heroic deeds', from *chanson* 'song' and *geste* from Latin *gesta* 'actions, exploits'.

Chant du départ popular French revolutionary song by the French poet and radical politician Marie-Joseph de Chénier (1744–1811).

Chanticleer a name given to a domestic cock, especially in fairy tales and medieval poems. The name is recorded from Middle English, and comes from Old French *Chantecler*, the name of the cock in the fable *Reynard the Fox*, from *chanter* 'sing, crow' + *cler* 'clear'.

Chantrey bequest fund established with money left by the sculptor Francis Legatt *Chantrey* (1781–1841) to the Royal Academy, with the view of establishing a national collection by the purchase of works of sculpture and painting by artists residing in Great Britain at the time of execution.

chantry a chapel, altar, or other part of a church endowed for a priest or priests to celebrate masses for the founder's soul; a chapel, altar, or other part of a church endowed for such a purpose. The word is recorded from late Middle English, and comes from Old French *chanterie*, from *chanter* 'to sing'.

chaos originally, denoting a gaping void or chasm, later extended to formless primordial matter; in current usage, complete disorder and confusion. In Greek mythology, *Chaos* is sometimes personified as the first created being, from which came the primeval deities Gaia, Tartarus, Erebus, and Nyx.

Recorded from the late 15th century, the word

comes via French and Latin from Greek *khaos* 'vast chasm, void'.

chaos theory the branch of mathematics that deals with complex systems whose behaviour is highly sensitive to slight changes in conditions, so that small alterations can give rise to strikingly great consequences, as in the ➤ BUTTERFLY *effect*.

chapbook a small pamphlet containing tales, ballads, or tracts, sold by pedlars; (chiefly in North America) a small paper-covered booklet, typically containing poems or fiction. The term is recorded from the early 19th century, and the first element comes from *chapman*, archaic term for a pedlar.

chape historical term for the point of a scabbard. The term is recorded from Middle English, in the general sense 'plate of metal overlaying or trimming something', and comes from Old French, literally 'cape, hood', from late Latin *cappa* 'cap'.

chapel a small building for Christian worship; part of a large church or cathedral with its own altar and dedication. The word is recorded from Middle English and comes via Old French from medieval Latin *cappella*, diminutive of *cappa* 'cap or cape' (the first chapel being a sanctuary in which ➤ *St* MARTIN's cloak was preserved).

See also ➤ FATHER *of the chapel*, ➤ SISTINE *Chapel*.

chapel of ease a chapel situated for the convenience of parishioners living a long distance from the parish church; the term is recorded from the mid 16th century.

Chapel of the Rolls the chapel attached to the ➤ ROLLS in Chancery Lane.

Chapel Royal the body of clergy, singers, and musicians employed by the English monarch for religious services, now based at St James's Palace, London. Among members of the Chapel Royal have been Thomas Tallis, William Byrd, and Henry Purcell.

chapelle ardente a chamber prepared for the lying-in-state of a distinguished person, and lit up with candles and torches; the phrase is French, and means literally 'burning chapel'.

chaperon a person who accompanies and looks after another person or group of people; a dated term for an older woman responsible for the decorous behaviour of a young unmarried girl at social occasions. The word is recorded from late Middle

English, denoting a hood or cap, regarded as giving protection, and comes from French *chaperon* 'hood', ultimately from late Latin *cappa* 'cap'.

chaplain a member of the clergy attached to a private chapel, institution, ship, regiment, etc. The word comes (in Middle English via Old French) from medieval Latin *cappellanus*, originally denoting a custodian of the cloak of St Martin, from *cappella*, originally 'little cloak' (see also ➤ CHAPEL).

Charlie **Chaplin** (1889–1977), English film actor and director. He directed and starred in many short silent comedies, mostly playing a bowler-hatted tramp, a character which was his trademark for more than twenty-five years. A master of mime who combined pathos with slapstick clowning, he was best suited to the silent medium; he is on record as saying, 'All I need to make a comedy is a park, a policeman and a pretty girl.'

> He seems to be a sensitive, shy man, lean and ductile, with a Chaplinesque ability to show by limb and eye what he is experiencing.
>
> — *Descant* Summer 1991

George **Chapman** (*c*.1560–1634), English poet and dramatist. He is chiefly known for his translations of Homer; the complete *Iliad* and *Odyssey* were published in 1616, and are commemorated in Keats's sonnet 'On First Looking into Chapman's Homer' (1817).

Chappaquiddick Island a small island off the coast of Massachusetts, the scene of a car accident in 1969 involving Senator Edward Kennedy in which his assistant Mary Jo Kopechne drowned.

> A curse hanging over Victor Emmanuel's head, like some kind of royal Chappaquiddick.
>
> — *Vanity Fair* February 1992

chapter the governing body of a religious community, especially a cathedral, or a knightly order. The term is recorded from Middle English, and comes via Old French from Latin *capitulum*, diminutive of *caput* 'head'.

chapter and verse an exact reference or authority; originally, the exact reference to a passage of Scripture (the usage is recorded from the early 17th century). **Chapter and verse** divisions to the scriptures are of comparatively late date; Jewish scholars of the 6th to 10th centuries AD (*Masoretes*) divided books into verses, and the New Testament was divided into chapters by ➤ *Stephen* LANGTON (*c*.1150–1228). Verses appeared in the Greek and Latin editions of the New Testament produced in

Geneva in 1551, and then in the English ➤ GENEVA *Bible* of 1560.

Chapter 11 protection from creditors given to a company in financial difficulties for a limited period to allow it to reorganize. It is named with allusion to chapter 11 of the US bankruptcy code.

chapter house a building used for the meetings of the canons of a cathedral or other religious community.

a chapter of accidents a series of unfortunate events; the term is recorded from the late 18th century.

Chapter of Myton a battle during the Scots invasion of northern England in 1319, in which the Scots forces defeated the English at Myton-on-Swale in Yorkshire.

charades a game in which players guess a word or phrase from a written or acted clue given for each syllable and for the whole item. Recorded from the late 18th century, the word comes from French, from modern Provençal *charrado* 'conversation', from *charra* 'chatter', perhaps of imitative origin.

charge see also ➤ COMMUNITY *charge*.

charge in heraldry, a device or bearing placed on a shield or crest.

Charge of the Light Brigade a British cavalry charge in 1854 during the Battle of Balaclava in the Crimean War. A misunderstanding between the commander of the Light Brigade and his superiors led to the British cavalry being destroyed. The charge was immortalized in verse by Alfred Tennyson.

The English soldier Lord George Paget (1818–80), who was the second-in-command at the charge, commented afterwards, 'As far as it engendered excitement the finest run in Leicestershire could hardly bear comparison.' The view of the French general Pierre Bosquet (1810–61), was, '*C'est magnifique, mais ce n'est pas la guerre* [It is magnificent, but it is not war].'

Charing Cross a locality in the City of Westminster, London, containing the site (on what is now the south side of Trafalgar Square) of a cross erected to commemorate the last resting place of the coffin of Eleanor of Castile, queen of Edward I, on its journey from Nottinghamshire, where she died in 1290, to Westminster.

The original cross (the final one of 12 which marked the stages of the coffin's journey) was destroyed in the 17th century, and an equestrian statue of Charles I now stands in its place. A bronze plaque in the pavement behind the statue (placed there in 1955) marks the official centre of London, from which mileages are measured.

Charing represents a name recorded from the Anglo-Saxon period, rather than an alteration of *chère reine*, as is sometimes suggested.

chariot a two-wheeled vehicle drawn by horses, used in ancient warfare and racing; the term is recorded from late Middle English, and comes via Old French *char* 'cart' from Latin *carrus* 'wheeled vehicle'.

charitable societies ➤ St ELIZABETH *of Hungary* and ➤ St VINCENT *de Paul* are the patron saints of charitable societies.

charity archaic term for love of humankind, typically in a Christian context; recorded from late Old English, the word comes via Old French from Latin *caritas*, from *carus* 'dear'.

The current main sense of an organization set up to provide help and raise money for those in need is recorded from the late 16th century.

charity begins at home proverbial saying, late 14th century.

Charity Commission in the UK, a board established to control charitable trusts.

charity covers a multitude of sins proverbial saying, early 17th century; sometimes, with biblical allusion to 1 Peter 4:8, 'For charity shall cover the multitude of sins.'

charivari a cacophonous mock serenade, typically performed by a group of people in derision of an unpopular person or in celebration of a marriage. The term is recorded from the mid 17th century, and comes from French (of unknown origin); it was taken as the title of a Parisian satirical journal, of which the full title of *Punch* (1841) was an imitation, 'Punch, or the London Charivari'.

charlatan a person falsely claiming to have a special knowledge or skill. The word is recorded from the early 17th century, denoting an itinerant seller of supposed remedies; it comes via French from Italian *ciarlatano*, from *ciarlare* 'to babble'.

Charlemagne (742–814), king of the Franks 768–814 and Holy Roman emperor (as Charles I) 800–814; the name comes from *Carolus Magnus*

'Charles the Great'. As the first Holy Roman emperor Charlemagne promoted the arts and education, and his court became the cultural centre of the ➤ CAROLINGIAN *Renaissance*, the influence of which outlasted his empire.

Charlemagne's wagon another name for ➤ CHARLES's *Wain*.

Charles I (1600–49), king of England, Scotland, and Ireland, son of James I, reigned 1625–49. His reign was dominated by the deepening religious and constitutional crisis that resulted in the English Civil War 1642–9. After the battle of Naseby, Charles tried to regain power in alliance with the Scots, but his forces were defeated in 1648 and he was tried by a special Parliamentary court and beheaded.

See also ➤ KING *Charles's head*, ➤ *the* MARTYR *King*, ➤ REMEMBER.

Charles II (1630–85), king of England, Scotland, and Ireland, son of Charles I, reigned 1660–85. Charles was restored to the throne after the collapse of Cromwell's regime and displayed considerable adroitness in handling the difficult constitutional situation, in particular the crisis centring on the ➤ EXCLUSION *Bill*, although continuing religious and political strife dogged his reign.

See also ➤ MERRY *Monarch*.

Charles V (1500–58), Holy Roman emperor 1519–56, and king of Spain (through his mother, daughter of Ferdinand and Isabella) 1500–58. His reign was characterized by the struggle against Protestantism in Germany, rebellion in Castile, and war with France (1521–44). Exhausted by these struggles, Charles handed Naples, the Netherlands, and Spain over to his son Philip II and the imperial Crown to his brother Ferdinand, and retired to a monastery.

Charles VII (1403–61), king of France 1422–61. At the time of his accession much of northern France was under English occupation. After the intervention of ➤ JOAN *of Arc*, however, the French experienced a dramatic military revival, Charles was crowned at previously occupied ➤ REIMS, and the defeat of the English ended the Hundred Years War.

Charles XII (1682–1718), king of Sweden 1697–1718. In 1700 he embarked on the Great Northern War against Denmark, Poland-Saxony, and Russia. Initially successful, in 1709 he embarked on an expedition into Russia which ended in the destruction of his army at Poltava and his internment until 1715. He is sometimes called the *Alexander of the North*.

Charles le Téméraire (1433–77, Duke of ➤ BURGUNDY from 1467, killed in battle at Nancy in 1477, after which the duchy was absorbed by France. Also known as **Charles the Bold** and **Charles the Rash**.

Charles Martel Frankish ruler of the eastern part of the Frankish kingdom from 715 and the whole kingdom from 719, grandfather of ➤ CHARLEMAGNE. His rule marked the beginning of Carolingian power.

Charles the Bold another name for ➤ CHARLES le *Téméraire*.

Charles the Rash another name for ➤ CHARLES le *Téméraire*.

Charles's Wain the Plough in Ursa Major. It is called in Old English *Carles wægn* 'the wain of Carl (Charlemagne)', perhaps because the star Arcturus was associated with King Arthur, with whom Charlemagne was connected in legend.

Charleston a city and port in South Carolina; the bombardment in 1861 of Fort Sumter, in the harbour, by Confederate troops marked the beginning of the American Civil War.

The *charleston*, a lively dance of the 1920s which involved turning the knees inwards and kicking out the lower legs, was named for the city.

Charlie see ➤ BONNIE *Prince Charlie*, ➤ CHAMPAGNE *Charlie*, ➤ *Charlie* CHAN, ➤ *Charlie* CHAPLIN.

Charlotte Dundas a paddle steamer launched in 1802 on the River Clyde, the first vessel to use steam propulsion commercially.

charm an object, act, or saying believed to have magic power. The word is recorded from Middle English, in the senses 'incantation or magic spell', and comes via Old French from Latin *carmen* 'song, verse'.

charm offensive a campaign of flattery, friendliness, and cajolement designed to achieve the support or agreement of others; the term is recorded from the late 1970s, and was originally associated particularly with politicians attempting to win 'hearts and minds' in support for a particular cause.

See also ➤ PRAWN *cocktail offensive*.

charming see ➤ PRINCE *Charming*.

Charon in Greek mythology, an old man who ferried the souls of the dead across the Rivers ➤ STYX and ➤ ACHERON to ➤ HADES; he received a fee of one obol for each soul.

In astronomy, *Charon* is the name of the only satellite of Pluto, discovered in 1978, with a diameter (1,190 km) that is more than half that of Pluto.

> There is something about a small ferry that . . . conjures up images not only of old-fashioned American colorfulness but also of dark yearning and Charon-related going-to-hellness.
> — *Atlantic* April 1991

charter a written grant by the sovereign or legislative power of a country, by which a body such as a borough, company, or university is created or its rights and privileges defined; a written constitution or description of an organization's functions; in the UK, a written statement of the rights that a specified group of people has or should have. Recorded from Middle English, the word comes via Old French from Latin *chartula*, diminutive of *charta* 'paper' from Greek *khartēs* 'papyrus leaf'.

See also ➤ ATLANTIC *Charter*, ➤ CITIZEN's *Charter*.

Great Charter another name, recorded from the 16th century, for ➤ MAGNA *Carta*.

People's Charter the document embodying the principles and demands of ➤ CHARTISM; the name is first used in an address of 1838 by the Chartist William Lovett (1800–77), 'In the course of a few weeks this Bill will be prepared and printed for circulation, under the title of "The People's Charter".'

Charter Mark in the UK, an award granted to institutions for exceptional public service under the terms of the ➤ CITIZEN's *Charter*.

Charter School a school established by the ➤ CHARTER *Society*.

Charter Society founded in 1733 in Ireland, to provide Protestant education for the Catholic poor in Ireland.

Charterhouse archaic term for a ➤ CARTHUSIAN monastery; in the UK, *Charterhouse* is now the name of a charitable institution, later a public school, founded on the site of the Carthusian monastery in London (later moved to Godalming, Surrey).

The name is recorded from late Middle English, and comes ultimately from (Old) French *Chartreuse* (from medieval Latin *Carthusia*), with assimilation of the second element to *house*.

Chartism a UK parliamentary reform movement of 1837–48, the principles of which were set out in a manifesto called *The People's Charter* and called for universal suffrage for men, equal electoral districts, voting by secret ballot, abolition of property qualifications for MPs, and annual general elections.

Chartres a city in northern France, noted for its Gothic cathedral with fine stained glass.

Chartreuse in France and French-speaking countries, a ➤ CARTHUSIAN monastery.

The drink *chartreuse*, a pale green or yellow liqueur made from brandy and aromatic herbs, is named after *La Grande Chartreuse*, the Carthusian monastery near Grenoble, where the liqueur was first made.

Charybdis in Greek mythology, a dangerous whirlpool in a narrow channel of the sea, opposite the cave of the sea-monster ➤ SCYLLA.

See also ➤ *between* SCYLLA *and Charybdis*.

chase see also ➤ *a* STERN *chase is a long chase*.

chase in British place names, an area of unenclosed land formerly reserved for hunting; in archaic usage, **beast of the chase** (or **bird of the chase**) denotes an animal traditionally hunted for sport across open country.

chase the dragon take heroin by heating it on a piece of folded tin foil and inhaling the fumes. The term is said to be translated from Chinese, and to arise from the fact that the fumes and the molten heroin powder move up and down the piece of tin foil with an undulating movement resembling the tail of the dragon in Chinese myths.

chastity belt historical term for a garment or device designed to prevent the woman wearing it from having sexual intercourse.

chasuble a sleeveless outer vestment worn by a Catholic or High Anglican priest when celebrating Mass, typically ornate and having a simple hole for the head. Recorded from Middle English, the word comes via Old French from late Latin *casubla*, alteration of *casula* 'hooded cloak or little cottage', diminutive of *casa* 'house'.

chateau a large French country house or castle, often giving its name to wine made in its neighbourhood. The term is recorded in English from the mid 18th century; the French word *chateau* comes (via Old French *chastel*) from Latin *castellum* (see ➤ CASTLE).

chatelaine archaic term for a woman in charge of a large house; recorded from the mid 19th century, the word is French, feminine of *chatelain* 'castellan', from medieval Latin *castellanus* from Latin *castellum* (see ➤ CASTLE).

Chattanooga a city in Tennessee, site of a battle (1863) in the American Civil War which contributed to the success of the Union cause.

chattel in law, an item of property other than freehold land, including tangible goods (**chattels personal**) and leasehold interests (**chattels real**); generally, a personal possession. Recorded from Middle English, the word comes via Old French from medieval Latin *capitale*, and ultimately from Latin *capitalis*, from *caput* 'head'.

See also ➤ GOODS *and chattels*.

chattering classes educated people, especially those in academic, artistic, or media circles, considered as a social group given to the expression of liberal opinions about society and culture. The term is recorded from the 1980s.

Lady Chatterley a sexually promiscuous woman, especially one attracted to a man considered socially inferior, with allusion to the character in D. H. Lawrence's novel *Lady Chatterley's Lover* (originally published in Italy in 1928, but not available in England in unexpurgated form until 1960), which tells the story of Constance Chatterley's affair with the gamekeeper Mellors.

Thomas Chatterton (1752–70), English poet, chiefly remembered for his fabricated poems professing to be those of a 15th-century monk. He committed suicide at the age of 17; his tragic life was much romanticized by Keats and Wordsworth.

> I thought of Chatterton, the marvellous boy,
> The sleepless soul that perished in its pride.
> — William Wordsworth 'Resolution and Independence' (1807)

Geoffrey Chaucer (*c*.1342–1400), English poet. His most famous work, the *Canterbury Tales* (*c*.1387–1400), is a cycle of linked tales told by a group of pilgrims. His skills of characterization, humour, and versatility established him as the first great English poet.

> The worshipful father and first founder and embellisher of ornate eloquence in our English, I mean Master Geoffrey Chaucer.
> — William Caxton epilogue to Caxton's edition (*c*.1478) of Chaucer's translation of Boethius *De Consolacione Philosophie*

Guy de Chauliac (*c*.1300–68), French physician, who was private physician to three successive popes in Avignon from 1342. His *Chirurgia Magna* (1363) was the first work to describe many surgical techniques, and remained the standard work in Europe until at least the 17th century.

chautauqua in North America, an institution that provided popular adult education courses and entertainment in the late 19th and early 20th centuries; it is named for *Chautauqua*, a county in the southwestern part of the state of New York, where the summer schools were originally held.

chauvinism exaggerated or aggressive patriotism; excessive or prejudiced support or loyalty for one's own cause, group, or sex. The word dates from the late 19th century and is named after Nicolas *Chauvin*, a Napoleonic veteran noted for his extreme patriotism, popularized as a character by the Cogniard brothers in *Cocarde Tricolore* (1831).

Chavín a civilization that flourished in Peru *c*.1000–200 BC, uniting a large part of the country's coastal region in a common culture. It is named after the town and temple complex of *Chavín* de Huantar in the northern highlands, where the civilization was centred.

it is as cheap sitting as standing proverbial saying, mid 17th century.

cheap obsolete word meaning a market or marketplace, surviving in place-names as *Cheapside*, *Chepstow*, *Chipping Campden*. Recorded from Old English (in form *cēap*) the word comes via Germanic from Latin *caupo* 'small tradesman, innkeeper'.

Cheapside in the City of London, the street which originally ran along the south side of the main market.

cheat act dishonestly or unfairly in order to gain an advantage. The word comes from a late Middle English shortening of the original sense of *escheat* in the sense 'land that reverted to the feudal lord when the tenant died leaving no one eligible to succeed under the terms of the grant'.

cheats never prosper proverbial saying, early 19th century.

check see ➤ *take a* RAIN *check*.

Checkers name of a spaniel belonging to Richard Nixon's children, which became famous when in 1952 Nixon was accused of surreptitiously accepting money for his vice-presidential campaign. In a high-profile speech on television Nixon asserted his family's modest means and financial independence and probity, but admitted accepting a spaniel as a gift:

And our little girl, Tricia, the six-year-old, named it Checkers. And you know, the kids love the dog, and I just want to say this right now, that regardless of what they do about it, we're going to keep it.
— Richard Nixon speech, 23 September 1952

The **Checkers speech** may be referred to as a type of political broadcast resting on a personal appeal.

[Clinton] had ruled out the Checkers speech approach to the character issue.
— *New Republic* 25 May 1992

checkmate in chess, a position in which a player's king is directly attacked by an opponent's piece or pawn and has no possible move to escape the check. The attacking player thus wins the game.

Recorded from Middle English, the term comes from Old French *eschec mat*, from Arabic *šāh mā*, from Persian *šāh māt* 'the king is dead'.

checks and balances counterbalancing influences by which an organization or system is regulated, typically those ensuring that power in political institutions is not concentrated in the hands of particular individuals or groups. The term is first recorded in the writings of the American statesman John Adams (1735–1826):

The checks and balances of republican governments have been in some degree adapted by the courts of princes.
— John Adams *A Defence of the Constitutions of Government of the United States of America* (1787–8)

cheek by jowl close together, side by side; the phrase comes from a use of *jowl* in the sense 'cheek'; the phrase was originally *cheek by cheek*.

turn the other cheek refrain from retaliating when one has been attacked or insulted, originally with biblical allusion to Matthew 5:39, 'whosoever shall smite thee on thy right cheek, turn to him the other also'.

cheese see also ➤ BIG *cheese*, ➤ BREAD *and cheese*, ➤ CHALK *and cheese*, ➤ CHESHIRE *Cheese*, ➤ *thin as* BANBURY *cheese*,

cheese a food made from the pressed curds of milk, firm and elastic or soft and semi-liquid in texture. The word is recorded from Old English (in form *cēse*), and is of West Germanic origin, ultimately from Latin *caseus*.

A *cheese* is the emblem of St Juthwara, a reputed

British virgin martyr with a cult in the south west of England, and ➤ *St* BRIDGET *of Ireland*.

Cheesemongers nickname of the First Life Guards; the term derived in the 19th century from the sneering remark that the regiments were composed 'not of gentlemen but of cheesemongers'.

cheesewring see ➤ DEVIL'*s cheesewring*.

chela a follower and pupil of a guru; the word comes from Hindi *celā*.

Chelsea pensioner in the UK, an inmate of the Chelsea Royal Hospital for old or disabled soldiers; the hospital was originally founded by Charles II in 1682, and the pensioners are characterized by their scarlet coats.

Chemosh in 1 Kings 11:7, a Moabite god ('the abomination of Moab') to whom Solomon built an altar; he is referred to in Milton's *Paradise Lost* as 'Chemos, the obscene dread of Moab's sons'.

Chenab a river of northern India and Pakistan, which rises in the Himalayas and flows through Himachal Pradesh and Jammu and Kashmir, to join the Sutlej River in Punjab. It is one of the five rivers that gave Punjab its name.

Cheops (fl. early 26th century BC), Egyptian pharaoh of the 4th dynasty; Egyptian name *Khufu*. He commissioned the building of the Great Pyramid at Giza.

clerk of the cheque an officer of the royal household keeping the roll of royal staff and having control of the yeomen of the guard.

chequebook journalism the practice of paying a large amount of money to someone so as to acquire the exclusive right to publish their story in a particular newspaper.

Chequers a Tudor mansion in Buckinghamshire which serves as a country seat of the British Prime Minister in office; it was left to the nation for this purpose by the British politician and philanthropist Lord Lee of Fareham (1868–1947).

Chernobyl a town near Kiev in Ukraine where, in April 1986, an accident at a nuclear power station resulted in a serious escape of radioactive material, and the subsequent contamination of Ukraine, Belarus, and other parts of Europe.

The cancer rate rivals Bhopal's and Chernobyl's.
— *New York Times* 27 June 1995

See also ➤ CULTURAL *Chernobyl*.

chernozem a fertile black soil rich in humus, with a lighter lime-rich layer beneath. Such soils typically occur in temperate grasslands such as the Russian steppes and North American prairies. The word comes (in the mid 19th century) from Russian, from *chërnyĭ* 'black' + *zemlya* 'earth'.

cherry a small, soft round stone fruit that is typically bright or dark red, and which is taken as a type of something red. The name is recorded from Middle English and comes from Old Northern French *cherise*, from medieval Latin *ceresia*, based on Greek *cerasos* 'cherry tree, cherry' The final -s was lost because *cherise* was interpreted as plural.

See ➤ *a* SECOND *bite at the cherry,* ➤ TWO *bites at the cherry.*

Cherry-breeches nickname of the 11th Hussars, or *Cherrypickers,* from their crimson trousers.

cherry fair a fair held in cherry orchards for the sale of the fruit, formerly used as a symbol of the shortness of life and the fleeting nature of its pleasures.

cherry-pick selectively choose (as the most beneficial or profitable items or opportunities) from what is available. The expression is probably a backformation from *cherry picker,* a hydraulic crane with a platform at the end, for raising and lowering people working at a height, with the idea of someone being raised to a position of advantage for picking the best fruit on a tree.

As the term has become more familiar there has been a further shift in emphasis: a *cherry-picker* may now be a person who selects favourable figures and statistics in order to present biased data.

a cherry year, a merry year; a plum year, a dumb year proverbial saying, late 17th century.

the Cherrypickers alternative nickname for the 11th Hussars or ➤ CHERRY-*breeches.*

Chersonese ancient name for the Gallipoli peninsula; the name (recorded from the early 17th century) comes via Latin from Greek *khersonēsos* 'peninsula', from *khersos* 'dry' + *nēsos* 'island'. It survives also in more modern poetic use, as in Patrick Shaw-Stewart's First World War poem:

> Achilles came to Troyland,
> And I, to Chersonese.
> — Patrick Shaw-Stewart poem (1916)

cherub a winged angelic being described in biblical tradition as attending on God, represented in ancient Middle Eastern art as a lion or a bull with eagles' wings and a human face and regarded in Christian angelology as an angel of the second highest order of the ninefold celestial hierarchy; the plural form is **cherubim**.

In art, the word denotes a representation of a cherub, depicted as a chubby, healthy-looking child with wings; the plural form is **cherubim** or **cherubs**.

Recorded from Old English (in form *cherubin*), the word comes ultimately, via Latin and Greek, from Hebrew *kĕrūb,* plural *kĕrūbīm.* A rabbinic folk etymology, which explains the Hebrew singular form as representing Aramaic *kĕ-rabyā* 'like a child', led to the representation of the cherub as a child.

Cherubims a nickname of the eleventh Hussars (also called ➤ CHERRY-*breeches* and *Cherrypickers*).

Cheshire cat a cat depicted with a broad fixed grin, as popularized through Lewis Carroll's *Alice's Adventures in Wonderland* (1865). The origin is unknown, but it is said that *Cheshire* cheeses used to be marked with the face of a smiling cat.

Cheshire Cheese name of an eating-house in Fleet Street where the Rhymers' Club met for several years in the 1880s and 1890s; it is described by Yeats in his autobiography *The Trembling of the Veil* (1922).

chess a board game of strategic skill for two players, played on a chequered board. Each player begins the game with a king, a queen, two bishops, two knights, two rooks (or 'castles'), and eight pawns, which are moved and capture opposing pieces according to precise rules. The object is to put the opponent's king under a direct attack from which escape is impossible (*checkmate*). Recorded from Middle English, the word comes from Old French *esches,* plural of *eschec* 'a check'.

chestnut a glossy hard brown edible nut, which may be roasted and eaten, and the large European tree that produces this. *Chestnut* also denotes a deep reddish-brown colour, or a horse of a reddish-brown or yellowish-brown colour, with a brown mane and tail.

an old chestnut a joke, story, or subject that has become tedious and uninteresting because of its age and repetition; the expression is recorded from the late 19th century and the origin is unknown, although it has been suggested that it derives from a scene in W. Dimond's *The Broken Sword* (1816), 'this is the twenty-seventh time I have heard you relate this story, and you invariably said, a chestnut, till now.'

pull someone's chestnuts out of the fire succeed in a hazardous undertaking for someone else's benefit, with reference to the fable of a monkey using a ➤ CAT's *paw* to extract roasting chestnuts from a fire.

chevalier historical term for a knight; a member of certain orders of knighthood or of modern French orders such as the Legion of Honour. Recorded from late Middle English (denoting a horseman or mounted knight) the word comes via Old French and medieval Latin, from Latin *caballus* 'horse'.

the Young Chevalier a name given to ➤ *Charles Edward* STUART (1720–88), son of ➤ *James Francis Edward* STUART, and otherwise known as the ➤ YOUNG *Pretender*.

Chevalier de St George a name given to ➤ *James Francis Edward* STUART (1688–1766), father of ➤ *Charles Edward* STUART, and otherwise known as the *Chevalier* and the ➤ OLD *Pretender*.

chevet in large churches, an apse with an ambulatory giving access behind the high altar to a series of chapels set in bays. The style was developed in 12th-century France. The term is recorded from the early 19th century, and comes from French, literally 'pillow', from Latin *capitium*, from *caput* 'head'.

chew see ➤ BITE *off more than one can chew*.

chi[1] the twenty-second letter of the Greek alphabet (**X, χ**), transliterated as 'kh' or 'ch'.

chi[2] the circulating life force whose existence and properties are the basis of much Chinese philosophy and medicine. The word comes from Chinese *qì*, literally 'air, breath'.

chi-ro a monogram of *chi* (X) and *rho* (P) as the first two letters of Greek *Khristos* Christ.

Chian wine wine from the island of *Chios* in the Aegean, highly regarded in classical times.

Chiang Kai-shek (1887–1975), Chinese statesman and general, President of China 1928–31 and 1943–9 and of Taiwan 1950–75. He tried to unite China by military means in the 1930s but was defeated by the communists. Forced to abandon mainland China in 1949, he set up a separate Nationalist Chinese State in Taiwan.

chiaroscuro the treatment of light and shade in drawing and painting; an effect of contrasted light and shadow created by light falling unevenly or from a particular direction on something. Recorded from the mid 17th century, the word comes from Italian, from *chiaro* 'clear bright' (from Latin *clarus*) + *oscuro* 'dark, obscure' (from Latin *obscurus*).

chiasmus a rhetorical or literary figure in which words, grammatical constructions, or concepts are repeated in reverse order, in the same or a modified form. The word is modern Latin, recorded in English from the mid 19th century, and comes from Greek *chiasma* 'crosspiece, cross-shaped mark', from *khiazein* 'mark with the letter chi'.

Chibcha a member of a native people of Colombia whose ancient civilization was destroyed by Europeans. The name is American Spanish, and comes from Chibcha *zipa* 'chief, hereditary leader'.

chic see ➤ RADICAL *chic*.

Chicago a city in Illinois, on Lake Michigan, selected as a terminal for the new Illinois and Michigan canal, and developed during the 19th century as a major grain market and food-processing centre. During the Prohibition period, Chicago was a noted centre for gang warfare.

chicane a sharp double bend created to form an obstacle on a motor-racing track or a road. The word is recorded, in the sense 'chicanery, trickery' from the late 17th century; it comes from French *chicane* 'quibble', of unknown origin.

Chichén Itzá a site in northern Yucatán, Mexico, the centre of the Mayan empire after AD 918.

Chichevache proper name of a fabulous monster said to feed only on patient wives, and from the scarcity of its diet, to be always lean and hungry; it is contrasted with the ➤ BYCORNE.

chicken a *chicken* may symbolize something in need of shelter and protection, as in Jesus's lament for Jerusalem (see ➤ HEN), and Macduff's grief for his children in Shakespeare's *Macbeth* (see ➤ at one FELL *swoop*); it is also a type of timidity. The word is recorded from Old English (in form *cīcen, cȳen*), and is of Germanic origin, probably related to *cock*.

See also ➤ BLUE *Hen's Chickens*, ➤ CURSES, *like chickens, come home to roost*, ➤ *don't* COUNT *your chickens before they are hatched*, ➤ MAY *chickens come cheeping*, ➤ *Mother* CAREY's *chicken*, ➤ PHARAOH's *chicken*, ➤ *the* RUBBER *chicken circuit*.

chicken-and-egg denoting a situation in which each of two things appears to be necessary to the other. Either it is impossible to say which came first or it appears that neither could ever exist.

why did the chicken cross the road? traditional puzzle question, to which the answer is, to get to the other side; recorded from the mid 19th century.

chief cook and bottle-washer a person who performs a variety of important but routine tasks.

child see also ➤ EAGLE *and child,* ➤ INNER *child,* ➤ *it is a* WISE *child that knows its own father,* ➤ PRAISE *the child, and you make love to the mother,* ➤ SPARE *the rod and spoil the child.*

give me a child for the first seven years, and you may do what you like with him afterwards traditionally regarded as a Jesuit maxim; recorded in *Lean's Collectanea* volume 3 (1903).

Monday's child is fair of face,
Tuesday's child is full of grace,
Wednesday's child is full of woe,
Thursday's child has far to go,
Friday's child is loving and giving,
Saturday's child works hard for his living,
And the child that is born of the Sabbath day,
Is bonny, and blithe, and good and gay.
traditional rhyme, mid 19th century.

the child is the father of the man proverbial saying, early 19th century; from Wordsworth's 'My heart leaps up when I behold' (1807), but perhaps also with allusion to Milton's *Paradise Regained* (1671), 'The childhood shows the man.'

Child of God a person who has achieved this position by creation, or by regeneration and adoption; the phrase is recorded from Middle English.

child on a boar a child on a boar is the emblem of ➤ *St* CYRICUS.

Child Support Agency in the UK, a government agency responsible for the assessment and collection of compulsory child maintenance payments from absent parents.

Childe archaic or literary word for a youth of noble birth, typically forming part of a name, as *Childe Harold.* The word is recorded from late Old English, and is a variant of *child.*

Childe Roland hero of a poem by Browning, 'Childe Roland to the Dark Tower came', the title deriving from a snatch of song recited by Edgar in Shakespeare's *King Lear*; in the poem, the narrator is a knight errant crossing a nightmare landscape who finally reaches the Dark Tower and sets the ➤ SLUGHORN to his lips, but the outcome and the reason for his journey are unknown.

> The fancy made him smile—of Childe Roland bearing a slug-horn to his lips with an arm as feeble as his was.
> — Jack London *The Red One* (1918)

Childermas old name for the feast of the Holy Innocents, 28 December. The name is recorded from Old English, in form *childramæsse,* from *cildra* 'of children' and *mæsse* 'Mass'.

children see also ➤ *Children of* PAUL's, ➤ *the* DEVIL's *children have the devil's luck,* ➤ HEAVEN *protects children, sailors, and drunken men,* ➤ SONG *of the Three Holy Children.*

children ➤ *St* NICHOLAS *of Myra* and ➤ *St* LAMBERT are the patron saints of children.

children and fools tell the truth proverbial saying, mid 16th century.

children are certain cares, but uncertain comforts proverbial saying, mid 17th century.

Children in the Wood another name for the ➤ BABES *in the Wood.*

the children of Israel the Jewish people, as people whose descent is traditionally traced from the patriarch Jacob (also called *Israel*), each of whose twelve sons became the founder of a tribe.

children should be seen and not heard proverbial saying, early 15th century.

Children's Crusade a movement in 1212 in which tens of thousands of children (mostly from France and Germany) embarked on a crusade to the Holy Land. Most of the children never reached their destination; arriving at French and Italian ports, many were sold into slavery.

chiliarch especially in ancient Greece, a commander of a thousand men; the word is recorded from the late 16th century, and comes via late Latin from Greek *khiliarkhēs,* from *khilioi* 'thousand'.

chiliast another term for a person who holds ➤ MILLENARIAN beliefs; the word is recorded from the late 16th century, and comes via late Latin from Greek *khiliastēs,* from *khilias* 'a thousand years', from *khilioi* 'thousand'.

Chillingham name of a park in Northumberland, one of several parks in Britain in which white ➤ PARK *cattle* are maintained.

Chillon a castle on the lake of Geneva in which the ➤ PRISONER *of Chillon* was held in captivity.

Chilon name of an ephor at Sparta in the 6th century BC, famous for his wisdom and accounted one of the ➤ SEVEN *Sages*.

Chiltern Hundreds in the UK, a Crown manor, whose administration is a nominal office for which an MP applies as a way of resigning from the House of Commons.

The holding of an office of profit under the Crown became a disqualification in 1707, and in 1740 the Stewardship of a royal manor was used in order to create a disqualification, when Sir Watkin Wynn took the Stewardship of H. M. Lordship and Manor of Bromfield and Yale (which was again taken in 1749). In 1742 Lord Middlesex took the Head Stewardship of H. M. Honour of Otford in Kent, and in January 1750–51 John Pitt, MP for Wrexham, took the Stewardship of the *Chiltern Hundreds*, which has come to be the ordinary form, except when a second resignation takes place before this is vacant.

chimera in Greek mythology, a fire-breathing female monster with a lion's head, a goat's body, and a serpent's tale; any mythical animal with parts taken from various animals. In extended usage, the term may be used for a thing which is hoped or wished for but in fact is illusory or impossible to achieve.

Chimera is also now used in biology for an organism containing a mixture of genetically different tissues, formed by processes such as fusion of early embryos, grafting, or mutation.

chimes see ➤ WESTMINSTER *chimes*, ➤ WHITTINGTON *chimes*.

china see also ➤ *all* LOMBARD *Street to a China orange*, ➤ BULL *in a china shop*, ➤ *not for all the* TEA *in China*,

China syndrome a hypothetical sequence of events following the meltdown of a nuclear reactor, in which the core melts through its containment structure and deep into the earth. It takes its name from *China* as being on the opposite side of the earth from a reactor in the US.

china wedding in the US, a 20th wedding anniversary.

Chinatown a district of any non-Chinese town, especially a city or seaport, in which the population is predominantly of Chinese origin.

Chindit a member of the Allied forces behind the Japanese lines in Burma (now Myanmar) in 1943–5. The name comes from Burmese *chinthé*, a mythical creature.

Chinese Chippendale a style of Chippendale furniture combining square and angular outlines with Chinese motifs.

Chinese Gordon nickname of ➤ *Charles George* GORDON (1833–85), who first made his name by crushing the Taiping Rebellion (1863–4) in China.

Chinese wall an insurmountable barrier to understanding (alluding to the ➤ GREAT *Wall of China*); on the Stock Exchange, a prohibition against the passing of confidential information from one department of a financial institution to another.

Chinese water torture a form of torture whereby a constant drip of water is caused to fall on to the victim's head.

Chinese whispers a game in which a message is distorted by being passed around in a whisper; also known as *Russian scandal*.

chinoiserie the imitation or evocation of Chinese motifs and techniques in Western art, furniture, and architecture, especially in the 18th century.

chinook a warm dry wind which blows down the east side of the Rocky Mountains at the end of winter. The name is from an attributive use of *Chinook*, a member of an American Indian people originally inhabiting the region around the Columbus River in Oregon.

Chinook Jargon an extinct pidgin composed of elements from Chinook, an extinct Penutian language of the Chinook people, Nootka, English, French, and other languages, formerly used in the Pacific North-West of North America.

chintz printed multicoloured cotton fabric with a glazed finish, used especially for curtains and upholstery. The word is recorded from the early 17th century, as *chints*, plural of *chint*, denoting a stained or painted calico cloth imported from India, from Hindi *chīṃṭ* 'spattering, stain'.

chip see also ➤ CLIPPER *chip*.

a **chip** off the old block someone resembling their father or mother, especially in character and behaviour; the term is recorded from the early 17th century, and was notably used by Edmund Burke (1729–97) of the younger Pitt's maiden speech, when he commented, 'Not merely a chip of the old "block", but the old block itself.'

a **chip** on one's shoulder a deeply ingrained grievance, typically about a particular thing. The phrase (originally US) is recorded from the 19th century, and may originate in a practice described in the *Long Island Telegraph* (Hempstead, New York), 20 May 1830, 'When two churlish boys were *determined* to fight, a *chip* would be placed on the shoulder of one, and the other demanded to knock it off at his peril.'

Thomas **Chippendale** (1718–79), English furniture-maker and designer. He produced furniture in a neoclassical vein, with elements of the French rococo, chinoiserie, and Gothic revival styles, and his book of furniture designs *The Gentleman and Cabinetmaker's Director* (1754) was immensely influential.

See also ➤ CHINESE *Chippendale*.

chips see also ➤ *a* CARPENTER *is known by his chips*.

have had one's **chips** be beaten, be finished; *chips* here are gambling chips with which a stake is placed.

Mr **Chips** nickname of the schoolmaster hero, Mr Chipping, of James Hilton's novel *Good-bye, Mr Chips* (1934); he spends his professional life in the same school, and despite his unimpressive looks and manner is in the end regarded with respect and affection by pupils and colleagues.

> He wasn't a kindly Mr. Chips, and never would be, yet he respected grit and determination, spending long hours with those who had trouble in his classes.
> — Robert James Waller *Slow Waltz in Cedar Bend* (1993)

when the **chips** are down when it comes to the point; *chips* here are gambling chips with which a stake is placed.

chiromancy the prediction of a person's future from the lines on the palms of their hands; palmistry.

Chiron in Greek mythology, a learned ➤ CENTAUR who acted as teacher to Jason, Achilles, and many other heroes.

In astronomy, *Chiron* is the name of asteroid 2060, discovered in 1977, which is unique in having an orbit lying mainly between the orbits of Saturn and Uranus. It is believed to have a diameter of 370 km.

> The old sea-Chiron, thinking perhaps that for the nonce he had sufficiently instructed his young Achilles . . . would commit himself to nothing further.
> — Herman Melville *Billy Budd* (written 1891)

Chisholm Trail running from the Red River in eastern Texas to Southern Kansas, for more than 20 years following the Civil War it provided owners of Texas range cattle with an outlet to the Indian Territory and successive railheads of the westward-building railroads.

chivalry the medieval knightly system with its religious, moral, and social code; knights, noblemen, and horsemen of that system collectively. Recorded from Middle English, the word comes, via Old French *chevalerie* and medieval Latin, from late Latin *caballarius* 'horseman' (see ➤ CHEVALIER).

See also ➤ *the* FLOWER *of Chivalry*.

chivvy tell (someone) repeatedly to do something. Recorded from the late 18th century, the word probably comes from the ballad *Chevy Chase*, celebrating a skirmish (probably the battle of Otterburn, 1388) on the Scottish border (but often mistakenly thought to be a place name). Originally a noun denoting a hunting cry, the term later meant 'a pursuit', hence the verb 'to chase, worry' (mid 19th century).

Chladni figures the patterns formed when a sand-covered surface is made to vibrate. The sand collects in the regions of least motion. They are named (in the early 19th century) after Ernst *Chladni* (1756–1827), German physicist.

Chloe in the classical Greek story by Longus, the shepherdess loved by ➤ DAPHNIS.

chocolate a food preparation in the form of a paste or solid block made from roasted and ground cacao seeds, typically sweetened and eaten as confectionery. The word is recorded from the early 17th century, in the sense 'a drink made from chocolate', and comes via French or Spanish from Nahuatl *chocolatl* 'food made from cacao seeds', influenced by unrelated *cacaua-atl* 'drink made from cacao'.

Chocolate was a fashionable drink in the 17th and 18th centuries, with **chocolate-houses** established for its supply.

Choctaw the Muskogean language of an American Indian people now living mainly in Mississippi, closely related to Chickasaw and now almost extinct, sometimes taken as the type of an unknown or difficult language.

> He had a good many private expressions that were Choctaw to those that did not know him.
> — John Buchan *The Courts of the Morning* (1929)

choir an organized body of singers performing or leading in the musical parts of a church service; that part of a church appropriated to singers; especially the chancel of a cathedral, minster, or large church.

Choir may also denote a company of angels, especially any of the nine orders in medieval angelology.

The word is recorded from Middle English (in form *quer, quere*), from Old French *quer*, from Latin *chorus*. The spelling change in the 17th century, which means that now the older variant *quire* is found only in the reference in the Book of Common Prayer to 'Quires and Places where they sing', was due to association with Latin *chorus* and modern French *choeur*.

See also ➤ RULER *of the choir*.

choler in medieval science and medicine, one of the four bodily ➤ HUMOURS, identified with bile, believed to be associated with a peevish or irascible, or *choleric*, temperament. Also known as *yellow bile*.

Recorded from late Middle English (also denoting diarrhoea), the word comes from Old French *colere* 'bile, anger', from Latin *cholera* 'diarrhoea' (from Greek *kholera*), which in late Latin acquired the senses 'bile or anger', from Greek *kholē* 'bile'.

never choose your women or your linen by candlelight proverbial saying, late 16th century.

choosers see ➤ BEGGARS *can't be choosers*.

chop and change change one's tactics, vacillate, be inconstant; an alliterative phrase in which *chop* has lost its original meaning of 'barter' and is now taken as 'change, alter'.

Chops of the Channel the entrance from the Atlantic Ocean to the English Channel; the *Chops* here are the jaws or mouth of the Channel.

chopsocky kung fu or a similar martial art, especially as depicted in violent action films. The term dates from the 1970s, and may be a humorous formation on *chop suey*.

choragus in ancient Greek drama, the leader of a chorus; at Athens, the chorus-master who defrayed the cost of bringing out the chorus.

Chorasmian waste poetic term for the desert land south of the Sea of Aral and around the lower

course of the Oxus river; the name refers to the *Chorasmii*, a people of Sogdiana.

touch a chord affect or stir someone's emotions, with figurative reference to the emotions being the 'strings' of the mind visualized as a musical instrument.

choriambus a metrical foot consisting of two short (or unstressed) syllables between two long (or stressed) ones. The word is recorded from the late 18th century and comes via late Latin from Greek *khoriambos*, from *khoreios* 'of the dance' + *iambos* (see ➤ IAMBUS).

chortle laugh in a breathy, gleeful way, chuckle; a word coined by Lewis Carroll in *Through the Looking Glass* (1871), probably a blend of *chuckle* and *snort*.

chorus in ancient Greek tragedy, a group of performers who comment on the main action, typically speaking and moving together; a single character who speaks the prologue and other linking parts of the play, especially in Elizabethan drama.

The word is recorded from the mid 16th century (denoting a character speaking the prologue and epilogue in a play and serving to comment on events), and comes via Latin from Greek *khoros*.

chosen people those selected by God for a special relationship with him, especially the people of Israel, the Jews.

Chouan a member of an irregular force maintaining a partisan resistance in the west of France against the Republican and Bonapartist governments. The name may be from that of Jean *Chouan*, said to be one of their leaders, or from *chouan* as an older form of *chat-huant* a species of owl.

chough a black bird of the crow family, having a long red bill and red feet. The bird appears on the arms of the county of Cornwall, and according to Cornish legend became the home for King Arthur's spirit after his death.

chrestomathy a selection of passages from an author or authors, designed to help in learning a language. The word is recorded from the mid 19th century and comes from Greek *khrēstomatheia*, from *khrēstos* 'useful' + *-matheia* 'learning'.

Chrétien de Troyes (12th century), French poet. His courtly romances on Arthurian themes include

Lancelot (*c.*1177–81) and *Perceval* (1181–90, unfinished).

chrism a mixture of oil and balsam, consecrated and used for anointing at baptism and other rites of the Catholic, Orthodox, and Anglican Churches. The word is recorded from Old English, and comes via medieval and ecclesiastical Latin from Greek *khrisma* 'anointing', from *khriein* 'anoint'.

chrisom a white robe put on a child at baptism, and used as its shroud if it died within the month. The word is recorded from Middle English and is an alteration of *chrism*, representing a popular sound with two syllables.

Christ the title, also treated as a name, given to Jesus of Nazareth; the Messiah as prophesied in the Hebrew scriptures. The name is recorded in Old English (in form *Crīst*), from Latin *Christus*, from Greek *Khristos*, noun use of an adjective meaning 'anointed', from *khriein* 'anoint', translating Hebrew *māšīah* 'Messiah'.
   See also ➤ CHURCHES *of Christ*, ➤ DISCIPLES *of Christ*, ➤ IMITATION *of Christ*.

Christ's cross me speed a formula said before repeating the alphabet; the figure of a cross preceded the alphabet in horn-books (see also ➤ CRISS-*cross*).

Christ's Hospital a boys' school founded in London in 1552 for poor children, now a public school at Horsham, Sussex, whose pupils wear long dark blue belted gowns and yellow stockings (see also ➤ BLUE *Coat*).

Christ's thorn a thorny shrub popularly supposed to have formed Christ's crown of thorns, in particular either of two shrubs related to the buckthorn.

Christadelphian a member of a Christian sect, founded in America in 1848, which claims to return to the beliefs and practices of the earliest disciples and holds that Christ will return in power to set up a worldwide theocracy beginning at Jerusalem. The name comes from late Greek *Khristadelphos* 'in brotherhood with Christ', from *Khristos* 'Christ' + *adelphos* 'brother'.

Christendom the worldwide body or society of Christians; the Christian world. The word is recorded from Old English (in form *crīstendōm*), and comes from *crīsten* 'Christian' + -*dōm* 'domain'.
   See also ➤ WISEST *Fool in Christendom*.

Christian[1] of, relating to, or professing Christianity; believing in Jesus *Christ* and his teachings; having or showing qualities associated with Christians, especially those of decency, kindness, and fairness. The term is recorded from late Middle English, and comes directly from Latin *Christianus*.

Christian[2] the central character of the first part of Bunyan's ➤ *The* PILGRIM*'s Progress* (1678–84), which recounts the story of his journey to the Celestial City.

Fletcher Christian (*c.*1764–*c.*1793), English seaman and mutineer. As first mate under Captain Bligh on HMS *Bounty*, in April 1789 Christian seized the ship and cast Bligh and others adrift. In 1790 the mutineers settled on Pitcairn Island, where Christian was probably killed by Tahitians.

Christian Brothers a Roman Catholic lay teaching order, originally founded in France in 1684.

Most Christian King epithet of the king of France.

Christian name a forename, especially one given at baptism. In official contexts, the term has largely given way to alternatives such as *given name*, *first name*, and *forename*, in recognition of the fact that English-speaking societies have many religions and cultures, not just Christian ones.

Christian science the beliefs and practices of the Church of Christ Scientist, a Christian sect founded by Mary Baker Eddy in 1879. Members hold that only God and the mind have ultimate reality, and that sin and illness are illusions which can be overcome by prayer and faith.

Christiana the central character of the second part of Bunyan's ➤ *The* PILGRIM*'s Progress*, the wife of Christian, who with her children sets out to follow her husband's path to the Celestial City.

Christianity the religion based on the person and teachings of Jesus of Nazareth, or its beliefs and practices. Christianity is today the world's most widespread religion, with more than a billion members, mainly divided between the Roman Catholic, Protestant, and Eastern Orthodox Churches. It originated among the Jewish followers of Jesus of Nazareth, who believed that he was the promised Messiah (or 'Christ'), but the Christian Church soon became an independent organization, largely through the missionary efforts of St Paul. In 313 Constantine ended official persecution in the Roman Empire and in 380 Theodosius I recognized it as the state religion. There are highly disparate views on the extent to which Christian belief may be adapted to take account of modern science or of non-Christian cultures.

See also ➤ MUSCULAR *Christianity.*

Christians see also ➤ MALABAR *Christians.*

Agatha **Christie** (1890–1976), English writer of detective fiction. Her novels are characterized by brisk, humorous dialogue and ingenious plots; many of them feature the Belgian ➤ *Hercule* POIROT or the resourceful ➤ *Miss* MARPLE in an idealized Home Counties setting.

Christingle a lighted candle symbolizing Christ as the light of the world, held by children especially at a special Advent service originating in the Moravian Church. Recorded from the 1950s, the name probably comes from German dialect *Christkindl* 'Christ-child, Christmas gift'.

Christmas the annual Christian festival celebrating Christ's birth, held on 25 December (one of the quarter days in England, Wales, and Ireland); the name is recorded from Old English, in form *Crīstes* 'Christ's' *mæsse* 'Mass'.

See also ➤ — SHOPPING *days to Christmas*, ➤ *the* DEVIL *makes his Christmas pies of lawyers' tongues and clerks' fingers*, ➤ *a* DOG *is for life, not just for Christmas*, ➤ FATHER *Chrismas*, ➤ *the* TWELVE *days of Christmas*, ➤ WHITE *Christmas.*

Christmas box originally, a box, usually of earthenware, in which contributions of money were collected at Christmas by apprentices; the box being broken when full and the money shared. Later, a present or gratuity given at Christmas to tradespeople or those held to have performed a regular service (such as delivering post) for a person without direct payment from them. The practice gave rise to the name ➤ BOXING *Day* for the day on which such presents were generally given.

Christmas card a decorative greetings card sent at Christmas; the custom began in England in the 1860s. The term may be used to refer to a conventionally pretty scene reminiscent of such a card.

Christmas Day the day on which the festival of Christmas is celebrated, 25 December.

Christmas stocking a real or ornamental stocking hung up by children on Christmas Eve for Father Christmas to fill with presents.

Christmas tree an evergreen (especially spruce) or artificial tree set up and decorated with lights, tinsel, and other ornaments as part of Christmas celebrations. The custom was originally German, but spread to England after its introduction into the royal household in the early years of the reign of Queen Victoria.

St Christopher a legendary 3rd-century Christian martyr, adopted as the patron saint of travellers, since it is said that he once carried Christ in the form of a child across a river; he was traditionally a giant, and is often shown as such in art, carrying the Christ-child on his shoulder. He is also one of the ➤ FOURTEEN *Holy Helpers.*

His image was often placed in wall-paintings on the north wall of churches opposite the porch so that he would be seen by those who entered; there was a tradition that anyone seeing an image of the saint would not die that day, and he was invoked against water, tempest, plague, and sudden death.

☐ **FEAST DAY** His feast day is 25 July.

Christopher Robin name of the little boy in A. A. Milne's stories about the bear ➤ WINNIE-*the-Pooh* and other toys, shown in the illustrations with long hair and wearing a smock; the original *Christopher Robin* was Milne's son.

> With his Christopher Robin blond hair, delicate frame and quiet manner, Jarrett belies the stereotype of the midget-brained surfing behemoth.
> — *Toronto Life* August 1994

Christy Minstrels name of a troupe of minstrels imitating black musicians, originated in New York in the late 19th century by George *Christy.*

Chronicles the name of two books of the Bible, recording the history of Israel and Judah until the return from Exile (536 BC).

chronogram a phrase, sentence, or inscription, in which certain letters (usually distinguished by size or appearance from the rest) express by their numerical values a date or epoch. An example was given (in the *Athenaeum* No. 2868) of a pamphlet issued in 1666 when it was feared that a day of national humiliation would succeed an engagement between the English and Dutch navies; instead of the imprint of the year, the page had 'LorD haVe MerCIe Vpon Vs'. The capitalized letters in Roman numerals added up to 1666 (L=50 + D=500 + V=5 + M=1000 + C=100 + I=1 + V=5 + V=5).

chrysanthemum a popular plant of the daisy family, having brightly coloured ornamental flowers and existing in many cultivated varieties. In some parts of Europe it is a favourite funeral flower and is thus associated with All Souls' Day; in Japan, it is the crest of the imperial family.

Chrysanthemum Throne the throne of Japan; the chrysanthemum is the crest of the imperial family.

Chrysaor in Spenser's *Faerie Queene*, the sword of Justice, wielded by ➤ ARTEGALL.

chryselephantine of ancient Greek sculpture, overlaid with gold and ivory. The word (recorded from the early 19th century) comes from Greek *khruselephantinos*, from *khrusos* 'gold' + *elephas, elephant-* 'elephant' or 'ivory'.

chrysoprase a golden-green precious stone, mentioned in the New Testament (Revelation 21:20) as one of the precious stones in the wall of the New Jerusalem, perhaps a variety of beryl; in the Middle Ages, believed to have the faculty of shining in the dark. Now, an apple-green variety of chalcedony containing nickel, used as a gemstone.

The word is recorded from Middle English, and comes via Old French and Latin from Greek *khrusoprasos*, from *khrusos* 'gold' + *prason* 'leek'.

Chrysostom see ➤ St JOHN *Chrysostom*.

chthonic concerning, belonging to, or inhabiting the underworld. The word is recorded from the late 19th century, and comes from Greek *khthōn* 'earth'.

Chubb a lock with a device for fixing the bolt immovably to prevent it from being picked, named (in the mid 19th century) after Charles *Chubb* (1773–1845), the London locksmith who invented it.

chuck in the towel give up, admit defeat; from boxing, throw the towel used to wipe a contestant's face into the middle of the ring as an acknowledgement of defeat.

chum an informal and now dated term for a close friend, originally Oxford University slang, and probably deriving from *chamber-fellow*. Cf. ➤ CRONY.

Chunnel from the late 1920s, a humorous name for the projected ➤ CHANNEL *Tunnel*.

church a building used for public Christian worship. Also (with upper case initial) a particular Christian organization, typically one with its own clergy, buildings, and distinctive doctrines; **the Church**, the hierarchy of clergy of such an organization, especially the Church of England or the Roman Catholic Church.

The word is recorded from Old English (in form *cir(i)ce, cyr(i)ce*), ultimately based on medieval Greek *kurikon*, from Greek *kuriakon (dōma)* 'Lord's (house)', from *kurios* 'master or lord'.

See also ➤ DOCTOR *of the Church*, ➤ EASTERN *Church*, ➤ *he is a* GOOD *dog who goes to church*, ➤ MOTHER *Church*, ➤ *the* NEARER *the church, the further from God*, ➤ NOTE *of the Church*, ➤ PRINCE *of the Church*, ➤ SEVEN *churches of Asia*, ➤ *where* GOD *builds a church, the Devil will build a chapel*, ➤ WORLD *Council of Churches*.

church-ale in former times, a periodic festive gathering held in connection with a church.

Church Army a voluntary Anglican organization concerned with social welfare. It was founded in 1882 on the model of the Salvation Army, for evangelistic purposes.

Church Commissioners a body managing the finances of the Church of England.

Church Invisible the Church composed of those members known only to God, as distinguished from the ➤ VISIBLE *Church*. Also called the *Church Mystical*.

the Church is an anvil that has worn out many hammers proverbial saying, early 20th century.

Church Militant the whole body of living Christian believers, regarded as striving to combat evil here on earth.

church mouse a mouse living in a church, proverbially taken as a type of poverty, as in **poor as a church mouse**.

Church of England the English branch of the Western Christian Church, which combines Catholic and Protestant traditions, rejects the Pope's authority, and has the monarch as its titular head. The English Church was part of the Catholic Church until the Reformation of the 16th century; after Henry VIII failed to obtain a divorce from Catherine of Aragon he repudiated papal supremacy, bringing the Church under the control of the Crown.

Church of Scotland the national (Presbyterian) Christian Church in Scotland. In 1560 John Knox reformed the established Church along Presbyterian lines, but there were repeated attempts by the Stuart monarchs to impose episcopalianism, and the Church of Scotland was not finally established as Presbyterian until 1690.

church-planting the practice of establishing a core of Christian worshippers in a parish, with the intention that they should develop into a thriving congregation. The practice developed in the mid 1980s among evangelical congregations; such groups may be seen as offshoots from a parent church where the original congregation has grown too large, but the introduction of such a core into an existing congregation whose practices are more traditional has been more controversial.

church-scot in the Anglo-Saxon period, a custom of corn collected on St Martin's day; extended to other contributions in kind and money made for the support of the clergy, or demanded as a traditional ecclesiastical due.

Church Slavonic the liturgical language used in the Orthodox Church in Russia, Serbia, and some other countries. It is a modified form of Old Church Slavonic.

Church triumphant the portion of the Church which has overcome the world, and entered into glory.

Churches of Christ a number of Protestant denominations, chiefly in the US, originating in the Disciples of Christ but later separated over doctrinal issues.

Churching of Women the formal thanksgiving by women after childbirth, based on the Jewish rite of Purification and first mentioned in a letter of St Augustine of Canterbury to St Gregory the Great.

churel in the Indian subcontinent: the malevolent ghost of a woman who has died in childbirth, believed to spread disease.

churn supper another name for a ➤ HARVEST *supper*.

Churrigueresque of or relating to the lavishly ornamented late Spanish baroque style, characteristic or suggestive of the architecture of José Benito

Churriguera (1650–1723), a Spanish architect who worked in this style.

ci-devant in the language of Revolutionary France, a person of rank, a former nobleman or noblewoman. The expression is from French, and is used to indicate that someone or something once possessed a specified characteristic but no longer does so; it means literally, 'heretofore'.

Colley Cibber (1671–1757), English comic actor, dramatist, and theatre manager, noted for his adaptation (1700) of Shakespeare's *Richard III* (see ➤ PERISH *the thought* and ➤ RICHARD*'s himself again*); after his much-ridiculed appointment as Poet Laureate in 1730 he wrote an *Apology for the Life of Mr Colley Cibber, Comedian* (1740).

ciborium a receptacle shaped like a shrine or a cup with an arched cover, used in the Christian Church for the reservation of the Eucharist. Also, a canopy over an altar in a church, standing on four pillars. Recorded from the mid 16th century, the word comes via medieval Latin from Greek *kibōrion* 'seed vessel of the water lily or a cup made from it'; it is probably also influenced by Latin *cibus* 'food'.

Marcus Tullius Cicero (106–43 BC), Roman statesman, orator, and writer. As an orator and writer Cicero established a model for Latin prose; his surviving works include speeches, treatises on rhetoric, philosophical works, and letters. He was a supporter of Pompey against Julius Caesar (according to Plutarch, he was 'the man who is thought to have been the first to see beneath the surface of Caesar's public policy and to fear it, as one might fear the smiling surface of the sea'); in the *Philippics* (43 BC) he attacked Mark Antony, who had him put to death.

cicerone a guide who gives information about antiquities and places of interest to sightseers, from Italian and apparently originally in humorous allusion to the eloquence and learning of ➤ CICERO.

El Cid (*c*.1043–99), Count of Bivar, Spanish soldier. A champion of Christianity against the Moors, in 1094 he captured Valencia, which he went on to rule. He is immortalized in the Spanish *Poema del Cid* (12th century) and in Corneille's play *Le Cid* (1637).

cider an alcoholic drink made from fermented apple juice. In early translations of biblical passages or allusions to them, it was used to render Latin *sicera* 'strong drink' of the Vulgate.

Recorded from Middle English, the word comes via Old French and ecclesiastical Latin from ecclesiastical *sikera*, from Hebrew *šēķār* 'strong drink'.

close but no cigar of an attempt which is almost but not quite successful, referring to a cigar offered in congratulation.

Cilicia an ancient region on the coast of SE Asia Minor, corresponding to the present-day province of Adana, Turkey.

Cilician Gates a mountain pass in the Taurus Mountains of southern Turkey, historically forming part of a route linking Anatolia with the Mediterranean coast.

Cimmerian relating to or denoting members of an ancient nomadic people who overran Asia Minor in the 7th century BC, conquered Phrygia *c.*676 BC and terrorized Ionia, but were gradually destroyed by epidemics and wars. In Greek mythology, relating to or denoting members of a mythical people who lived in perpetual mist and darkness near the land of the dead.

cinchona an evergreen South American tree or shrub with fragrant flowers, the bark of which is a source of ➤ QUININE and other medicinal alkaloids. The word is recorded from the mid 18th century, and comes from modern Latin, named after the Countess of *Chinchón* (died 1641), who introduced the drug into Spain.

Lucius Quinctius Cincinnatus a legendary Roman hero of the 5th century BC who, according to tradition, was called from the plough to be dictator when the Roman army was blockaded by the Italian tribe of the Aequi. He is taken as a type of the heroic soldier called from peaceful pursuits to save his country; the name **Cincinnatus of the West** was applied by Byron to George Washington ('Ode to Napoleon Bonaparte', 1814).

> It was General de Gaulle, the Cincinnatus from a country retreat at Colombey-les-Deux-Eglises, who was then restored to power by the forces of the Right.
> — Thomas Pakenham *The Scramble for Africa* (1991)

Cinderella a girl in various traditional European fairy tales. In the version by Charles Perrault she is exploited as a servant by her stepmother and stepsisters but enabled by a fairy godmother to attend a royal ball. She meets and captivates ➤ PRINCE *Charming* but has to flee at midnight, leaving the prince to identify her by the glass slipper which she leaves behind.

> Family planning remains a Cinderella issue, at the bottom of the male-dominated political agenda.
> — *She* May 1991

Cinque Ports a group of medieval ports in Kent and East Sussex in SE England, which were formerly allowed trading privileges in exchange for providing the bulk of England's navy. The five original Cinque Ports were Hastings, Sandwich, Dover, Romney, and Hythe; later Rye and Winchelsea were added.
See also ➤ BARON *of the Cinque Ports.*

cinquecento the 16th century as a period of Italian art, architecture, or literature, with a reversion to classical forms. The term comes from Italian, literally '500' (shortened from *milcinquecento* '1500') used with reference to the years 1500–99.

cinquefoil an ornamental design of five lobes arranged in a circle, as in architectural tracery or heraldry.

cipher a secret or disguised way of writing; a code. The term comes (in late Middle English, in the senses 'symbol for zero' and 'arabic numeral') from Old French, based on Arabic *ṣifr* 'zero'.

Circe in Greek mythology, an enchantress who lived with her wild animals on the island of Aeaea. When Odysseus visited the island his companions were changed into pigs by her potions, but he protected himself with the herb ➤ MOLY, and forced her to restore his men into human beings.

> At one and the same time woman is a sexually desired wife, a tabooed Madonna and a dangerous Circe, whose magic is dangerous to the man.
> — *British Journal of Psychiatry* August 1968

circenses see ➤ PANEM *et circenses.*

circle see also ➤ CORN *circle,* ➤ CROP *circle,* ➤ MAGIC *circle,* ➤ SQUARE *the circle.*

the wheel has come full circle the situation has returned to what it was in the past, as if completing a cycle, with reference to Shakespeare's *King Lear,* by association with the wheel fabled to be turned by Fortune and representing mutability.

circle of Ulloa a luminous ring or white rainbow sometimes appearing in alpine regions opposite the sun during foggy weather, named for the 18th-century Spanish explorer of South America Antonio de Ulloa (1716–95).

circuit in the UK, a regular journey made by a judge around a particular district to hear cases in court; a district of this type; also, a group of local Methodist Churches forming an administrative unit.

circuit rider in North America, historical term for a clergyman who travelled on horseback from church to church, especially within a rural Methodist circuit.

circular see ➤ COURT *circular*.

circulating library a library with books lent for a small fee to subscribers; the first circulating library was set up in Edinburgh in the early 18th century, and in the 18th and 19th centuries the system proved extremely popular, with the rise of such establishments as ➤ MUDIE*'s Lending Library*; the success of ➤ BOOTS *Library* extended into the 20th century. The *circulating library* was particularly associated with a taste for popular fiction; it was condemned by a character in Sheridan's *The Rivals* (1775) as 'an evergreen tree of diabolical knowledge', and by the early 19th century, Edward Denham in Jane Austen's *Sanditon* could point out, 'I am no indiscriminate novel-reader. The mere trash of the common circulating library, I hold in the highest contempt.'

Circumcellion a member of a group of vagabond monks roving from place to place, characterized by violence and fanaticism. The name dates from the mid 16th century, and comes from Latin *circum* 'around' + *cella* 'cell', with reference to their habitual wandering.

Circumlocution Office the type of a government department, satirized in Dickens's *Little Dorrit* (1857), in which the establishment is shown as run purely for the benefit of its incompetent and obstructive officials, typified by the Barnacle family.

circumstances alter cases proverbial saying, late 17th century.

circus see also ➤ BREAD *and circuses*, ➤ MONTY *Python's Flying Circus*, ➤ SANGER*'s Circus*,

cisalpine on this (the Roman) side of the Alps; south of the Alps.

cist in ancient Greece, a small receptacle for sacred utensils carried in procession at the celebration of mystic festivals.

Cistercian a member of an order founded as a stricter branch of the Benedictines, the reforms

being particularly associated with the influence of ➤ St BERNARD *of Clairvaux*, who was particularly critical of elaborate decoration in ecclesiastical buildings:

> In the cloister, under the eyes of the brethren who read there, what profit is there in those ridiculous monsters, in that marvellous and deformed beauty, that beautiful deformity? To what purpose are those unclean apes, those fierce lions, those monstrous centaurs, those half-men, those striped tigers, those fighting knights, those hunters winding their horns . . . For God's sake, if men are not ashamed of these follies, why at least do they not shrink from the expense?
> — St Bernard of Clairvaux letter to William, abbot of St-Thierry, *c.*1125

The monks are now divided into two observances, the strict observance, whose adherents are known popularly as Trappists, and the common observance, which has certain relaxations.

The name comes (via French) from *Cistercium*, the Latin name of *Cîteaux* near Dijon in France, where the order was founded.

cities see also ➤ *the* TWIN *Cities*.

Cities of the Plain Sodom and Gomorrah; the original reference is to Genesis 13:12, 'Lot dwelled in the cities of the plain.'

citizen see also ➤ JOHN *Citizen*.

Citizen King nickname of Louis Philippe (1773–1850), King of the French; his father, Philippe d'Orléans (1747–93), who had initially supported the French Revolution against his cousin Louis XVI, had taken the name ➤ ÉGALITÉ, and Louis Philippe had fought with the revolutionary army before defecting to Austria in 1793. Thomas Carlyle in *The French Revolution* (1837) refers to him as 'young Égalité'.

Citizen's Charter a document setting out the rights of citizens, especially a British government document of 1991, guaranteeing citizens the right of redress where a public service fails to meet certain standards.

city a large town, specifically in the UK, one created by charter and containing a cathedral; **the City** designates the financial and commercial institutions located in the **City of London**.

Recorded from Middle English, the word comes via Old French from Latin *civitas*, from *civis* 'citizen'. Originally denoting a town, and often used as a Latin equivalent to Old English *burh* 'borough', the term was later applied to foreign and ancient cities and to the more important English boroughs. The connection between city and cathedral grew up under the Norman kings, as the episcopal sees (many had been established in villages) were removed to the chief borough of the diocese.

See also ➤ CARDBOARD *city*, ➤ CELESTIAL *City*, ➤ QUEEN *City*, ➤ SALT *Lake City*

City nicknames

NAME	CITY
City of Bon-accord	Aberdeen
City of Dreaming Spires	Oxford
City of Elms	New Haven, Connecticut
City of Magnificent Distances	Washington, DC
City of the Angels	Los Angeles, California
City of the Tribes	Rome
City of the Violated Treaty	Limerick
City of the Violet Crown	Athens
Crescent City	New Orleans
Empire City	New York City
the Eternal City	Rome
Forbidden City	Beijing; Lhasa
Forest City	Cleveland, Ohio
Granite City	Aberdeen
Monumental City	Baltimore, Maryland
Mormon City	Salt Lake City, Utah
Quaker City	Philadelphia, Pennsylvania
Soul City	Harlem
Windy City	Chicago

The City of Dreadful Night title of a poem (1874) by the Scottish writer James Thomson (1834–72), which evokes the nightmare landscape of a despairing and half-ruined city.

> Three years later, Murrow sat in one of the fifteen Lancasters that flew through shrapnel-ridden skies to turn Berlin into 'a city of dreadful night'.
> — *New York Review of Books* 15 February 1996

City of God Paradise, perceived as an ideal community in Heaven; the Christian Church. The phrase is a translation of Latin *Civitas Dei*, by St Augustine.

City of London the part of London situated within the ancient boundaries and governed by the Lord Mayor and the Corporation.

city of refuge by Mosaic law, a walled town set apart for the protection of those who had accidentally committed manslaughter.

civic crown in ancient Rome, a garland of oak leaves and acorns, given to one who saved the life of a fellow-citizen in war; the phrase is a translation of Latin *corona civica*.

a civil question deserves a civil answer proverbial saying, mid 19th century.

civil war a war between citizens of the same country, especially (frequently with capital initials) in England (1642–9), America (1861–5), or Spain (1936–9).

civility see also ➤ *there is* NOTHING *lost by civility*.

civility costs nothing proverbial saying, early 18th century.

the end of civilization as we know it the complete collapse of ordered society; supposedly a cinematic cliché, and actually used in the film *Citizen Kane* (1941) 'a project which would mean the end of civilization as we know it.'

civis Romanus sum Latin for, 'I am a Roman citizen', the formal statement of Roman citizenship.

Civvy Street in British informal usage, civilian as opposed to Service life.

clack-dish a wooden dish with a lid traditionally carried and rattled or 'clacked' by beggars.

Clactonian of, relating to, or denoting a Lower Palaeolithic culture represented by flint implements found at Clacton-on-Sea in SE England, dated to about 250,000–200,000 years ago.

Claddagh ring a ring in the form of two hands clasping a heart, traditionally given in Ireland as a token of love. It is called after a small fishing village on the edge of Galway city.

claimant see ➤ TICHBORNE *claimant*.

Clairvaux see ➤ *St* BERNARD *of Clairvaux*.

clairvoyance the supposed faculty of perceiving things or events in the future or beyond normal sensory contact. Recorded from the mid 19th century, the word comes from French, from *clair* 'clear' + *voir* 'to see'.

clam a marine bivalve mollusc with shells of equal size, the type of something which silently withdraws into itself from contact with another. The name is recorded from the early 16th century and apparently comes from earlier *clam* 'a clamp', from Old English *clam*, *clamm* 'a bond or bondage'.

clameur de haro in the law of Normandy and the Channel Isles, a cry of ➤ HARO constituting an appeal to the Duke of Normandy.

clan a group of close-knit and interrelated families (especially associated with families in the Scottish

Highlands). The word is recorded from late Middle English, and comes from Scottish Gaelic *clann* 'offspring, family', from Old Irish *cland*, from Latin *planta* 'sprout'.

clan badge a sprig of a plant worn as the symbol of a Scottish clan.

Clan Na Gael an Irish-American revolutionary organization formed to pursue Irish independence after the defeat of the Fenian rising of 1867.

Clapham omnibus the **man on the Clapham omnibus** as the type of the average man; the phrase is attributed, in the *Law Reports* of 1903, to the English judge Lord Bowen (1853–94), although the *Journal for the Society of Arts*, 1857, on the 'true Londoner's nature', refers to 'your dog-collar'd occupant of the knife-board of a Clapham omnibus'.

Clapham Sect an early 19th-century group noted for evangelical opinions and philanthropic activity; some of the chief members lived at *Clapham* in south-west London.

like the clappers very fast; *the clappers* are a contrivance in a mill for striking or shaking the hopper so as to make the grain move down to the millstones.

claptrap nonsense; originally from a theatrical device of the 18th century designed to elicit applause. The term in its current sense is first recorded in Byron's *Don Juan* (1819) 'that air Of clap-trap, which your recent poets prize'.

claque a group of people hired to applaud (or heckle) a performer or public speaker; a group of sycophantic followers. The word comes (in the mid 19th century) from French, from *claquer* 'to clap'; the practice of paying members of an audience for their support originated at the Paris opera.

John Clare (1793–1864), English poet, who wrote in celebration of the natural world, and whose work is notable for its use of the poet's own dialect and grammar; his popularity became part of a vogue for rural poetry and 'ploughman' poets. In 1837 he was certified insane and spent the rest of his life in an asylum.

St Clare of Assisi (1194–1253), Italian saint and abbess. With St Francis she founded the order of Poor Ladies of San Damiano ('Poor Clares'), of which she was abbess. In 1958 she was declared the patron saint of television, on the grounds that she miraculously experienced the Christmas midnight mass in the Church of St Francis in Assisi when on her deathbed.

□ **EMBLEM** She is often shown with a pyx or monstrance, in reference to the story that when Assisi was in danger from the army of the Emperor Frederick II, which included Saracen troops, Clare (who was ill) was carried to the wall of the city holding a pyx with the Sacrament, and the attacking forces fled.

□ **FEAST DAY** Her feast day is 11 (formerly 12) August.

See also ➤ Poor *Clare*.

Clarenceux in heraldry, (in the UK) the title given to the second King of Arms, with jurisdiction south of the Trent. Recorded from Middle English and coming from Anglo-Norman French, the position is named after the dukedom of *Clarence* created for the second son of Edward II, married to the heiress of *Clare* in Suffolk.

Constitutions of Clarendon a body of propositions drawn up at the Council of Clarendon in the reign of Henry II (1164), defining the limits of civil and ecclesiastical jurisdiction in England.

Lord Clarendon (1609–74), Edward Hyde, English statesman and historian, chief adviser to Charles II and Chancellor of Oxford University 1660–7. He shifted his allegiance from the Roundheads on the outbreak of the Civil War, becoming royal adviser and accompanying King Charles I to Oxford. A number of buildings in Oxford are named after him. His *History of the Rebellion and Civil Wars in England* was published posthumously (1702–4).

Clarendon Code the common name of four Acts passed in England when Edward Hyde, Lord Clarendon, was Charles II's chief adviser, all intended to curb the powers and liberties of dissenters and noncomformists.

Clarendon Press an imprint of Oxford University Press, named from the Clarendon Building which was designed by Hawksmoor as the new printing-house; the imprint was first used in 1713 for a selection of verses in honour of Queen Anne.

clarendon type a thick-faced condensed type, in capital and small letters, made in many sizes.

claret a red wine from Bordeaux, or wine of a similar character made elsewhere; the term (recorded from late Middle English) originally denoted a light red or yellowish wine, as distinct from a red or white, and comes from Old French *(vin) claret* and medieval Latin *claratum (vinum)* 'clarified (wine)', from Latin *clarus* 'clear'.

From the mid 17th century, *claret* has been used to denote the colour of the wine in its modern sense, a deep purplish-red.

William Clark (1770–1838), American explorer. With Meriwether Lewis, he commanded an expedition (1804–6) across the North American continent.

See also ➤ LEWIS *and Clark expedition.*

classes see ➤ CHATTERING *classes.*

classic race in the UK, each of the five main flat races of the horse-racing season, namely the Two Thousand and the One Thousand Guineas, the Derby, the Oaks, and the St Leger.

Classical Mythology: Greek and Roman deities

GREEK DEITY	ROMAN EQUIVALENT
Aphrodite	Venus
Ares	Mars
Artemis	Diana
Athene	Minerva
Eirene	Pax
Hephaestus	Vulcan
Hera	Juno
Hermes	Mercury
Poseidon	Neptune
Zeus	Jupiter

---

classicism the following of ancient Greek or Roman principles and style in art and literature, generally associated with harmony, restraint, and adherence to recognized standards of form and craftsmanship, especially from the Renaissance to the 18th century.

the classics the works of ancient Greek and Latin writers and philosophers.

Claude Lorraine (1600–82), French painter. His paintings became so popular that he recorded them in the form of sketches in his *Liber Veritatis* (*c.*1635) to guard against forgeries. Although the influence of the late mannerists is evident in his early landscapes, his mature works (such as *Ascanius and the Stag*, 1682) concentrate on the poetic power of light and atmosphere.

Claudius (10 BC–AD 54), Roman emperor from AD 41, proclaimed emperor after the murder of his nephew Caligula. His reign was noted for its restoration of order after Caligula's decadence and for its expansion of the Empire, in particular the invasion of Britain in AD 43. His fourth wife, Agrippina, is said to have poisoned him with a dish of mushrooms.

Claus see ➤ SANTA *Claus.*

clause see ➤ CONSCIENCE *clause.*

Clause Four a clause in the Labour Party constitution containing an affirmation of the Party's commitment to the common ownership of industry and services (this specific point was originally introduced in 1918 as clause 3d and revised in 1929 under Clause 4, which has thereafter dealt also with the Party's other aims):

> To secure for the workers by hand or by brain the full fruits of their industry and the most equitable distribution thereof that may be possible upon the basis of the common ownership of the means of production, distribution, and exchange.
> — Labour Party Constitution (1918, revised 1929)

In the 1995, the modernization of ➤ NEW *Labour* reached the point at which (despite left-wing opposition) *Clause Four* could be replaced.

> Those who seriously believe we cannot improve on words written for the world of 1918 when we are now in 1995 are not learning from our history but living it.
> — Tony Blair in *Independent* 11 January 1995

Karl von Clausewitz (1780–1831), Prussian general and military theorist. His study *On War* (1833) had a marked influence on strategic studies in the 19th and 20th centuries. He is particularly associated with the saying 'War is the continuation of politics by other means', the usual rendering of the statement in *On War* (1832–4), 'War is nothing but a continuation of politics with the admixture of other means.'

Rudolf Clausius (1822–88), German physicist, one of the founders of modern thermodynamics. He was the first, in 1850, to formulate the second law of thermodynamics, developing the concept of a system's available thermal energy and coining the term *entropy* for it.

clavie see ➤ BURNING *of the clavie.*

clay see ➤ FEET *of clay.*

claymore a broadsword used by Scottish Highlanders, either two-edged, or basket-hilted and single-edged (a form introduced in the 16th century). The name comes from Gaelic *claidheamh* 'sword' + *mór* 'great'.

Clayton's in Australian and New Zealand usage, largely illusory; existing in name only. The expression comes (in the 1980s) from the proprietary name of a soft drink marketed using the line 'It's the drink I have when I'm not having a drink'.

clean free from ceremonial defilement, according to Mosaic Law and similar religious codes; (of an animal) not prohibited under such codes and fit to be used for food.

cleanliness is next to godliness proverbial saying, late 18th century.

clear see ➤ *the* COAST *is clear.*

clear blue water the ideological gap between the British Conservative and Labour parties. The phrase, from a blend of *clear water*, the distance between two boats, and *blue water*, the open sea, with a play on *blue* as the traditional colour of the British Conservative party, is recorded from 1994. It was given a satirical twist by the Conservative politician Geoffrey Howe at that year's Party Conference, when he warned that 'Wrapping ourselves in the Union Jack in the pursuit of a populist chimera would simply be a prelude to burial at sea—the clear blue water somewhere out in the mid-Atlantic.'

The phrase quickly became a cliché of modern political life; in 1996 John Major made allusive use of it in a Commons debate, speaking of the *clear red water* which lay between himself and the Labour leader, Tony Blair.

clearances see ➤ HIGHLAND *clearances.*

Cleisthenes (*c.*570 BC–*c.*508 BC), Athenian statesman. His reforms consolidated the Athenian democratic process begun by Solon and influenced the policies of Pericles. He sought to undermine the power of the nobility by passing laws which made citizenship of a locality politically more important than membership of a kinship group.

Georges Clemenceau (1841–1929), French statesman, Prime Minister 1906–9 and 1917–20. At the Versailles peace talks he pushed hard for a punitive settlement with Germany, but failed to obtain all that he demanded (notably the River Rhine as a frontier).

St Clement of Alexandria (*c.*150–*c.*215), Greek theologian. He was head of the catechetical school at Alexandria (*c.*190–202), but was forced to flee from Roman imperial persecution. His main contribution to theological scholarship was to relate the ideas of Greek philosophy to the Christian faith.

   □ **FEAST DAY** His feast day is 5 December.

St Clement of Rome (1st century AD), pope (bishop of Rome) *c.*88–*c.*97, probably the third after St Peter; he wrote an epistle *c.*96 to the Church at Corinth, insisting that certain deposed presbyters be reinstated.

In later tradition he became the subject of a variety of legends; one held that he was martyred by being thrown into the sea with an anchor round his neck. He is also patron of Trinity House, the authority responsible for lighthouses and lightships.

   □ **FEAST DAY** His feast day is 23 November.

Clementines the constitutions collected by Pope Clement V (1264–1314), forming the seventh book of the decretals. Also, certain apocryphal writings once attributed to Clement of Rome, a bishop of the early Church (fl. *c.*AD 96).

Cleopatra (69–30 BC), queen of Egypt from 47 BC, the last Ptolemaic ruler. After a brief liaison with Julius Caesar she formed a political and romantic alliance with Mark Antony. Their ambitions ultimately brought them into conflict with Rome, and she and Antony were defeated at the battle of Actium in 31. She is reputed to have committed suicide by allowing herself to be bitten by an asp.

> Rhetorics and sentimentality were always his fatal Cleopatras.
> — *New York Review of Books* 2 February 1995

Cleopatra's Needles a pair of granite obelisks erected at Heliopolis by Tuthmosis III *c.*1475 BC. They were taken from Egypt in 1878, one being set up on the Thames Embankment in London and the other in Central Park, New York. They have no known historical connection with Cleopatra.

Cleopatra's nose taken as the type of a single feature a change in which would have been of immeasurable influence; the reference is to a comment by the French mathematician, physicist, and moralist Blaise Pascal (1623–62), 'Had Cleopatra's nose been shorter, the whole face of the world would have changed.'

> Historians call it the Cleopatra's nose theory—the theory that history is shaped mainly by contingent events, such as the alluring shape of an Egyptian queen's proboscis.
> — *Economist* 31 October 1992

clerestory the upper part of the nave, choir, and transepts of a large church, containing a series of windows. It is clear of the roofs of the aisles and admits light to the central parts of the building.

clergy the body of all people ordained for religious duties, especially in the Christian Church. Recorded from Middle English, the word comes via Old French, based on ecclesiastical Latin *clericus* 'clergyman', from Greek *klērikos* 'belonging to the Christian clergy', from *klēros* 'lot, heritage' (Acts 1:26, 'And they gave forth their lots, and the lot fell upon Matthias', in the account of the choosing of a twelfth apostle to replace Judas).

See also ➤ BENEFIT *of clergy*.

clergymen's sons always turn out badly proverbial saying, late 19th century.

clerihew a short comic or nonsensical verse in two rhyming couplets with lines of unequal length, and referring to a famous person; the term dates from the 1920s, and the form is named after the English writer Edmund *Clerihew* Bentley (1875–1956), who invented it.

clerk see also ➤ *clerk of the* CHEQUE, ➤ PARSON-*and-clerk*, ➤ St NICHOLAS'*s clerks*, ➤ SIX *Clerks*, ➤ TREASON *of the clerks*.

Clerk of the Closet in the UK, the sovereign's principal chaplain.

Clerk of the House a senior official in the House of Commons.

Clerk of the Weather an imaginary functionary humorously supposed to control the state of the weather.

Cleveland bay a bay horse of a strong breed originating in the north of England. Cleveland bays were formerly popular carriage horses.

click a speech sound produced as a type of plosive by sudden withdrawal of the tongue from the soft palate, front teeth, or back teeth and hard palate, occurring in some southern African and other languages. A **click language** is one in which such sounds are used.

Clifden nonpareil a large European moth of mostly subdued coloration, with a pale blue band on the underwing, named (in the mid 18th century) after *Clifden* (now *Cliveden*), a village in Buckinghamshire, where it was first observed.

> This curious Fly was found by Mr Davenport, sticking against the Body of an Ash Tree, near Cleifden, in Buckinghamshire.
> — B. Wilkes *English Moths and Butterflies* (1749)

cliffhanger a dramatic and exciting ending to an episode of a serial, leaving the audience in suspense

and anxious not to miss the next episode; originally (in the US in the 1930s) a *cliffhanger* was a serial film in which each episode ended in a desperate situation.

cliffs see ➤ WHITE *cliffs of Dover*.

climacteric a supposedly critical stage in human life, especially occurring at ages that are multiples of seven years. The word is recorded from the mid 16th century, in the sense 'constituting a critical period in life', and comes ultimately, via French or Latin, from Greek *klimaktēr* 'critical period', from *klimax* 'ladder, climax'.

climb on the bandwagon seek to join the party or group that is likely to succeed.

hasty climbers have sudden falls proverbial saying, mid 15th century.

clink an informal word for prison, recorded from the early 16th century and originally denoting a particular prison in Southwark, London.

Clio in Greek mythology, the Muse of history; the name comes from Greek *kleiein* 'celebrate'.

clipper a fast sailing ship, especially one of 19th-century design with concave bows and raked masts.

Clipper chip a microchip developed by the US Government, and proposed as a compulsory standard for data encryption technology, which inserts an identifying code into encrypted transmissions that allows them to be deciphered by a third party with access to a Government-held key.

Clitumnus a spring near Spoleto, renowned in classical antiquity; it was described by Virgil and the younger Pliny, and visited by the emperors Caligula and Flavius Honorius.

Lord Clive (1725–74), British general and colonial administrator; known as **Clive of India**. In 1757 he recaptured Calcutta, following the Black Hole incident, and gained control of Bengal. He served as governor of Bengal 1765–7, reforming the colony's administration, but was implicated in the East India company's corruption scandals. Although officially exonerated (his comment during Parliamentary cross-examination was, 'By God, Mr Chairman, at the moment I stand astonished at my own moderation'), he committed suicide.

Cliveden Set the group of right-wing politicians and journalists who met regularly in the 1930s at *Cliveden*, Lord Astor's country house.

Cloacina name for a supposed Roman goddess of the sewers; in ancient Rome, the *Cloaca Maxima* was the main sewer (originally an open watercourse but later covered over).

cloak see also ➤ WOMEN *beneath a cloak.*

cloak a cloak is the emblem of ➤ *St* MARTIN *of Tours.*

cloak-and-dagger involving or characteristic of mystery, intrigue, or espionage; the term is recorded from the early 19th century as a translation of French *de cape de d'épée* or Spanish *de capa y espada,* relating particularly to dramas or stories of intrigue or melodramatic adventure, in which the principal characters are likely to be cloaked and armed with swords or daggers.

clock a device for measuring time, ultimately (through Middle Low German and Middle Dutch) from medieval Latin *clocca* 'bell'.

See also ➤ *by* SHREWSBURY *clock,* ➤ JACK *of the clock,* ➤ SETTLER'*s clock.*

from clogs to clogs is only three generations proverbial saying, late 19th century.

cloister a covered walk in a convent, monastery, college, or cathedral, often with a wall on one side and a colonnade open to a quadrangle on the other. The word is recorded from Middle English (in the sense 'place of religious seclusion', and comes via Old French from Latin *claustrum, clostrum* 'lock, enclosed place', from *claudere* 'to close'.

Clonmacnoise the remains in county Galway, above the Shannon river, of one of the most important Irish monasteries, founded in the mid-6th century, which by the 8th century was a major centre of art and learning.

Anacharsis Cloots pseudonym of the Prussian-born French revolutionary Jean, baron de Cloots (1755–94), who was guillotined after the downfall of Hébert and at the instigation of Robespierre.

close see also ➤ *close but no* CIGAR.

Close Encounter term used for a supposed encounter with a UFO, and divided into categories, from a **Close Encounter of the First Kind** (sighting but no physical evidence), through Second (physical evidence left) and Third (extra-terrestrials beings observed) to a **Close Encounter of the Fourth Kind,** which involves abduction by aliens. The expression was popularized by the science-fiction film *Close Encounter of a Third Kind* (1977).

close season a period between specified dates when fishing or the killing of particular game is officially forbidden.

closet see also ➤ CLERK *of the Closet.*

closet drama a play to be read rather than acted; *closet* here means a room for private study, especially in reference to theories and ideas rather than practical measures.

closure in a legislative assembly, a procedure for ending a debate and taking a vote. The term in this sense is recorded in English from the late 19th century; when in 1882 rules providing for this procedure were first introduced into the House of Commons, the principle was referred to as *clôture,* the name applied to it in the French Assembly.

See also ➤ KANGAROO *closure.*

cloth see also ➤ CUT *your coat according to your cloth.*

the cloth the clergy, the clerical profession; the expression is recorded from the early 18th century, and derives from the earlier (mid 17th century) use of *cloth* to mean the profession of a minister or clergyman, as marked by their professional garb.

cloth of gold fabric made of gold threads interwoven with silk or wool.

See also ➤ FIELD *of the Cloth of Gold.*

cloth of state an embroidered cloth erected over a throne or chair as a sign of rank, a canopy.

clothes make the man proverbial saying, early 15th century.

Clotho in Greek Mythology, one of the three ➤ FATES; the name in Greek means literally 'she who spins', and traditionally Clotho spun the thread of life, which was then measured by Lachesis, and cut by Atropos.

clothworkers ➤ *St* HOMOBONUS is the patron saint of clothworkers.

cloud see also ➤ LAND *of the Long White Cloud,* ➤ MAGELLANIC *Clouds.*

cloud cuckoo land a state of unrealistic or absurdly over-optimistic fantasy. The phrase is recorded in English from the late 19th century, and is a translation of Greek *Nephelokokkugia,* the name of the city built by the birds in Aristophanes' comedy *Birds,* from *nephelē* 'cloud' + *kokkux* 'cuckoo'.

every cloud has a silver lining proverbial saying, mid 19th century.

on cloud nine extremely happy, with reference to a notional ten-part classification of clouds in which 'nine' was next to the highest.

the Cloud of Unknowing a mystical prose work of the 14th century, regarded as one of the most admired products of the Middle English mystical tradition.

Clouet two French court portrait painters, Jean (c.1485–1541) and his son François (c.1516–72). Jean Clouet worked as court painter to Francis I; the monarch's portrait in the Louvre is attributed to him. François succeeded his father as court painter, and is chiefly known for his undated portraits of Elizabeth of Austria (now in the Louvre) and Mary, Queen of Scots (now in the Wallace Collection in London).

Inspector **Clouseau** bungling French policeman played (with a consciously unconvincing French accent) by Peter Sellars in *The Pink Panther* (1963) and subsequent films.

> Waiters with inspired Clouseau accents rushed to place a large plant-pot on our table . . . replacing it only seconds later with an empty bread-basket.
> — *Punch* 16 July 1986

clove the dried flower bud of a tropical tree, used as a pungent aromatic spice. The name comes (in Middle English) from Old French *clou de girofle*, literally 'nail of gillyflower' (from its shape), ➤ GILLYFLOWER being originally the name of the spice and later applied to the similarly scented pink.

cloven hoof a divided hoof, as that of a goat, ascribed to a satyr, the god Pan, or to the Devil; in extended usage, the mark of an inherently evil nature.

> It is no use telling me that there are bad aunts and good aunts. At the core, they are all alike. Sooner or later, out pops the cloven hoof.
> — P. G. Wodehouse *The Code of the Woosters* (1938)

clover a herbaceous plant of the pea family, which has dense globular flower heads and leaves which are typically three-lobed; a **four-leaved clover** is a traditional symbol of luck.

See also ➤ PIGS *in clover.*

Clovis[1] (465–511), king of the Franks from 481. He extended Merovingian rule to Gaul and Germany after victories at Soissons (486) and Cologne (496), making Paris his capital. After his conversion to Christianity he championed orthodoxy against the Arian Visigoths, finally defeating them in the battle of Poitiers (507). He is traditionally regarded as

founder of the French nation, and *Louis* as the Christian name of many early kings of France derives from *Clovis.*

Clovis[2] a Palaeo-Indian culture of Central and North America, dated to about 11,500–11,000 years ago and earlier. The culture is distinguished by heavy leaf-shaped stone spearheads (**Clovis points**), often found in conjunction with the bones of mammoths. The culture was first found near *Clovis* in eastern New Mexico, US.

clown originally, an unsophisticated country person, a rustic; the word is first recorded in the mid 16th century, and is perhaps of Low German origin.

From the early 16th century, the term denoted a fool or jester as a stage character (perhaps originally representing a rustic buffoon); later, it was extended to one of the characters in a pantomime or harlequinade, and finally to a comic entertainer in a circus, wearing a traditional costume and exaggerated make-up.

club[1] a thick heavy stick or staff for use as a weapon; **prentices and clubs** is recorded from the mid 16th century as the rallying cry of London apprentices.

A club is the emblem of ➤ *St* CHRISTOPHER, ➤ *St* JUDE, ➤ *St* MAGNUS, ➤ *St* SIMON, and ➤ *St* JAMES *the Less,*

In cards, *clubs* form one of the four suits, marked with the conventional reprentation of a trefoil leaf in black; *club* here is a translation of the Spanish name *basto*, or Italian *bastone*, the symbol shown on Spanish cards; the design on English cards is taken from the French, where the name is *trèfle* 'trefoil'.

See also ➤ CLUB[2].

club[2] an association or organization dedicated to a particular interest or activity; the premises of such an organization. The word derives obscurely from ➤ CLUB[1], and the earliest (mid 17th-century) senses include 'a social meeting the expenses of which are jointly defrayed' and 'a secret society, especially with a political object'.

The current sense is recorded from the late 17th century, and associated particularly with the establishment of London clubs in the 18th and 19th centuries. *Clubbable*, meaning sociable, was used approvingly by Dr Johnson of Boswell, and by the late 19th century the word *Clubland* was being used for the vicinity of St James's in London, an area where there are many clubs.

See also ➤ *the* BEST *club in London.*

clue a piece of evidence or information used in the detection of a crime or the solving of a mystery; ultimately a variant of *clew* meaning 'a ball of thread', and in particular that used by Theseus to guide himself through the ➤ LABYRINTH.

Cluedo trademark name for a board game based on solving a murder committed in country house by one of a set of stock characters, invented by Anthony E. Platt in 1944; the six potential murderers are, ➤ *Reverend* GREEN, ➤ *Colonel* MUSTARD, ➤ *Mrs* PEACOCK, ➤ *Professor* PLUM, ➤ *Miss* SCARLET, and ➤ *Mrs* WHITE, and players are required to accuse a named character in a specific location and with a particular weapon.

> I've never played Cluedo, but I'm sure you could insist the butler dunnit.
> — *Daily Telegraph* 18 December 1998

Cluniac of or relating to a reformed Benedictine monastic order founded at *Cluny* in eastern France in 910.

clunk, click, every trip road safety campaign promoting the use of seat-belts, 1971.

Cluny a Benedictine monastery in eastern France, founded in 910 and introducing a period of monastic reform based on strict observance of the Benedictine Rule; the abbey was subject only to the pope, and all future Cluniac foundations, or priories, remained directly subject to the original mother house.

The abbey church, built between 1088 and 1130, and famous for its size and magnificence, was badly damaged in the French Revolution and effectively demolished in the 19th century.

cluricaune in Irish mythology, an elf having the appearance of a tiny old man, a ➤ LEPRECHAUN.

Clyde see also ➤ BONNIE *and Clyde*.

Clyde a river in western central Scotland which flows from the Southern Uplands to the Firth of Clyde, formerly famous for the shipbuilding industries along its banks.

Clydesdale a horse of a heavy, powerful breed, used for pulling heavy loads, a ➤ SHIRE *horse*.

Clydesider a member of a group of the Labour Party and the Independent Labour Party which was associated with Glasgow and the neighbouring industrial area along the ➤ CLYDE.

Clym of the Clough name of a northern English outlaw, a famous archer, companion of Adam Bell

and William of Cloudesley. They lived in the forest of Engelwood, not far from Carlisle, and are supposed to have been contemporary with Robin Hood's father.

Clytemnestra in Greek mythology, the wife of ➤ AGAMEMNON. She conspired with her lover Aegisthus to murder Agamemnon on his return from the Trojan War, and was murdered in retribution by her son Orestes and her daughter Electra.

Clytie in classical mythology, a water nymph who fell in love with Apollo; pining away, she became rooted in the ground, and her face became a sunflower, following the sun on its daily course. The image is used by William Blake in *Songs of Innocence and Experience* (1789–94), 'Ah Sunflower, weary of time, Who countest the steps of the sun.'

coach a horse-drawn carriage, especially a closed one, deriving through French from Hungarian *kocsi (szekér)* '(wagon)' from *Kocs*, a town in Hungary.
See also ➤ DEVIL*'s coach-horse*.

drive a coach and horses through make (legislation) useless; the idea of a coach and six horses as the type of something very large which could fill or make a hole is recorded from the late 17th century, and the Irish Jacobite lawyer Stephen Rice (1637–1715) is reported to have said 'I will drive a coach and six horses through the Act of Settlement.'

coachmen St Richard of Chichester (1197–1253) is the patron saint of the guild of coachmen at Milan, perhaps because according to his legend he drove carts on his family farm.

Coade stone a kind of artificial stone, otherwise known as *lithodipyra* or 'stone twice fired', made at a factory in Lambeth which was taken over in 1769 by the *Coade* family; it was manufactured until the mid 19th century, and was said to have greater frost and heat resistance than natural stone. It was very popular for statues, monuments, and decorative work.

coal see also ➤ WHITE *coal*.

haul someone over the coals reprimand someone severely; the original reference is to the treatment of heretics, as in a comment attributed to Cardinal Allen (1532–94), 'St Augustine, that knew best how to fetch an heretic over the coals'.

heap coals of fire on a person's head cause remorse by returning good for evil; the reference is originally biblical, to Romans 12:20, 'if thine enemy hunger, feed him…for in so doing thou shalt heap coals on fire on his head.'

carry coals to Newcastle provide a commodity already in abundant supply; the expression 'as common as coals from Newcastle' is recorded from the early 17th century, and 'carry coals to Newcastle' from the mid 17th century.

the Coalsack a dark nebula of dust near the Southern Cross that gives the appearance of a gap in the stars of the Milky Way.

coast see also ➤ BARBARY *Coast*.

the coast is clear there is no danger of being observed or caught; the expression is recorded from the 16th century, and refers to the expectation that a sea-coast would be guarded against landing or attack.

coat see also ➤ CUT *your coat according to your cloth*, ➤ DOGGETT'*s Coat and Badge*, ➤ HOLY *Coat*, ➤ TRAIL *one's coat*.

coat armour originally (from Middle English to the 17th century) a coat of arms; later (from the late 17th century), heraldic arms.

coat-card obsolete term for a ➤ COURT *card*.

coat of arms a coat or vest embroidered with heraldic arms, a herald's tabard; the distinctive heraldic bearings or shield of a person, family, corporation, or country.

coat of mail a jacket covered with or composed of metal rings or plates, which served as as armour.

coat of many colours in the Bible, given to ➤ JOSEPH by his father Jacob (Genesis 37:3, 'Now Israel loved Joseph more than all his children, because he was the son of his old age: and he made him a coat of many colours'). The gift increased the jealousy of his brothers, who took it from him when they sold it into slavery; later, having torn it and stained it with blood, they offered it to Jacob as a proof that Joseph was dead.

cob a powerfully built, short-legged horse; the word in this sense is recorded from the early 19th century, and is first recorded in Middle English denoting a strong man or leader; the underlying general sense appears to be 'stout, rounded, sturdy'.

cobalt a hard silvery-white magnetic metal, obtained chiefly as a by-product from nickel and copper ores. The word derives from German *Kobalt*

'imp, demon', from the belief that cobalt was harmful to the ores with which it occurred.

William Cobbett (1763–1835), English writer and political reformer. He started his political life as a Tory, but later became a radical and in 1802 founded the periodical *Cobbett's Political Register*. *Rural Rides*, his account of his travels on horseback to observe rural conditions between 1822 and 1826, was published in 1830.

See also ➤ GREAT *Wen*.

cobbler ➤ *St* CRISPIN and ➤ *St* CRISPINIAN are the patron saints of cobblers.

let the cobbler stick to his last proverbial saying, mid 16th century, meaning that people should only concern themselves with things they know something about; translating Latin *ne sutor ultra crepidam*, and attributed by Pliny originally to the the Greek artist Apelles (fl. 325 BC) when a cobbler criticized not just his representation of a shoe, but also the rest of the picture.

See also ➤ ULTRACREPIDARIAN.

the cobbler to his last and the gunner to his linstock proverbial saying, mid 18th century.

Richard Cobden (1804–65), English political reformer, one of the leading spokesmen of the free-trade movement in Britain. From 1838, together with ➤ *John* BRIGHT, he led the Anti-Corn Law League in its successful campaign for the repeal of the Corn Laws (1846).

Cobham's plot another name for the ➤ MAIN *Plot*, in which Henry Brooke, Lord Cobham (d. 1619) was a chief conspirator (although convicted, he was not executed).

cock the male bird of a domestic fowl, proverbially protective of its hens and noted for aggression; the cock tradionally crows at first light or ➤ COCKCROW, and is used in ➤ COCKFIGHTING.

A *cock* is the emblem of ➤ *St* PETER and ➤ *St* VITUS.

See also ➤ *there's many a* GOOD *cock come out of a tattered bag*.

cock-a-doodle-doo used to represent the sound made by a cock when it crows, and from this also a child's name for a cock.

cock-a-hoop extremely and obviously pleased, especially about a triumph or success; the expression dates from the mid 17th century, and comes from the phrase *set cock a hoop*, of unknown origin, apparently denoting the action of turning on the tap and allowing liquor to flow (prior to a drinking session).

cock and bull story an incredible tale, a false story; the expression 'talk of a cock and a bull' is recorded from the early 17th century, and apparently refers to an original story or fable, now lost.

cock-and-pie formerly used in an asseveration; dating from the mid 16th century, the reference is supposed to be to the ordinal of the Roman Catholic Church, with *cock* standing for 'God' and *pie* a collection of rules in the pre-Reformation Church to show how to deal with the concurrence of more than one service or office on the same day.

Cock Lane Ghost a supposed ghost to which were attributed mysterious noises heard at 33 Cock Lane, Smithfield, in 1762, and which were discovered to be due to the imposture of one William Parsons and his daughter. Dr Johnson took part in the investigation of the mystery, and wrote a brief 'Account of the Detection of the Imposture in Cock-Lane', published in *The Gentleman's Magazine* (February 1762).

Cock of the North in a Jacobite song of *c.*1715, nickname given to the Duke of Gordon (cf. ➤ COCKALORUM).

cock-of-the-walk a person whose supremacy in a particular circle or sphere is undisputed; the phrase is recorded from the mid 19th century.

cock-penny a customary payment at Shrovetide, formerly made to the schoolmaster in certain schools in the north of England, originally to defray ➤ COCKFIGHTING or ➤ COCK-*throwing* expenses.

cock robin a familiar name for a male robin, especially in nursery rhymes.

cock-throwing throwing sticks and other missiles at a cock tied to a post to knock it down or kill it, as a sport formerly practised especially at Shrovetide.

every cock will crow upon his own dunghill proverbial saying, mid 13th century; in Latin in 1st century AD.

that cock won't fight that won't do; the expression, which refers to cockfighting, is recorded from the late 18th century, and was notably used by Lord Beaverbrook (1879–1964) to Winston Churchill

when discussing their support for Edward VIII during the ➤ ABDICATION *crisis* of 1936, 'Our cock won't fight.'

cockade a rosette or knot of ribbons worn in a hat as a badge of office or party, or as part of a livery. Recorded from the mid 17th century, the word comes from French *cocarde*, originally in *bonnet à la coquarde*, from the feminine of obsolete *coquard* 'saucy'.

The cockade worn in the hat by coachmen and livery servants of persons serving under the Crown is a rosette of black leather, originally the distinctive badge of the House of Hanover, as the ➤ WHITE *cockade* was of the House of Stuart and its adherents.

Cockaigne an imaginary land of idleness and luxury. Recorded from Middle English, the word comes from Old French *cocaigne*, as in *pais de cocaigne* 'fool's paradise', ultimately from Middle Low German *kokenje* 'small sweet cake', diminutive of *koke* 'cake'.

> A single lava of ice exploding in the air in the shape of a mushroom, an exquisite eruption in a land of Cockaigne.
> — William Weaver tr. Umberto Eco's *The Island of the Day Before* (1994)

cockalorum a self-important little man; in a Jacobite song of *c.*1715 (see also ➤ BOBBING *John*), a nickname for Lord Huntly, son of the Duke of Gordon, the ➤ COCK *of the North*:

> Hey for Sandy Don!
> Hey for Cockalorum!
> Hey for Bobbing John,
> And his Highland quorum!
> — Jacobite song (*c.*1715)

cockatrice a ➤ BASILISK; in heraldry, a mythical animal depicted as a two-legged dragon (or ➤ WYVERN) with a cock's head.

Recorded from late Middle English, the word comes via Old French from Latin *calcatrix* 'tracker' (from *calcare* 'to tread or track'), translating Greek *ikhneumōn* 'tracker', see ➤ ICHNEUMON.

> Joshua's eyes were fixed on the old woman as if she were a cockatrice.
> — Walter M. Miller *A Canticle for Leibowitz* (1959)

John Douglas Cockcroft (1897–1967), English physicist. In 1932 he succeeded (with E. T. S. Walton) in splitting the atom, ushering in the whole field of nuclear and particle physics.

cockcrow a poetic or literary term for dawn, as signalled by the crowing of a cock; reference may also be made to the story of ➤ *St* PETER's denial, of which Jesus had warned him (Matthew 26:34), 'before the cock crow, thou shalt deny me thrice.'

cocker a small spaniel of a breed with a silky coat, named (in the early 19th century) because the dog was bred to flush game birds such as *woodcock*, for shooting.

according to Cocker reliably, correctly; recorded from the early 19th century, and deriving from the name of Edward *Cocker* (1631–75), English arithmetician, reputed author of a popular text, *Arithmetick*.

cockerel see ➤ GOLDEN *Cockerel Press*.

cockeye bob in Australia and New Zealand, informal name for a cyclone or thunderstorm. Recorded from the late 19th century, it is probably an alteration of an Aboriginal word.

cockfighting the sport (now illegal in the UK and some other countries) of setting two cocks, typically armed with long steel spurs, to fight each other; references to the sport are found from late Middle English.

cockle a mollusc with a strong ribbed shell; the shell itself became the symbol of St ➤ JAMES *the Great* and his shrine of Santiago de Compostela.

cockle-hat a hat with a cockle-shell or scallop-shell in it, worn by pilgrims, especially those travelling to ➤ SANTIAGO *de Compostela*.

cockles see also ➤ HOT *cockles*.

cockles of one heart one's deepest feelings; recorded from the late 17th century, and perhaps deriving from a perceived resemblance in shape between a heart and a cockle-shell.

Cockney a native of East London, traditionally one born within hearing of Bow Bells; the dialect or accent typical of such a person.

The word is recorded from late Middle English, denoting a pampered child; the origin is uncertain, but it is apparently not the same word as Middle English *cokeney* 'cock's egg', denoting a small misshapen egg (probably from cock + obsolete *ey* 'egg'). A later sense was 'a town-dweller regarded as affected or puny', from which the current sense arose in the early 17th century.

See also ➤ MOCKNEY.

Cockney School a disparaging term applied by John Gibson Lockhart (1794–1854) and others to the

poetry of Leigh Hunt, Hazlitt, and Keats:

> If I may be permitted to have the honour of christening it, it may henceforth be referred to by the designation of The Cockney School.
> — John Gibson Lockhart in *Blackwood's Magazine* October 1817

King of Cockneys a kind of Master of the Revels, who in the 16th century was chosen by the students at Lincoln's Inn on Childermas Day (28 December).

cockpit a place for holding cockfights; in figurative usage, the place where a contest is fought out. The word is also recorded from the late 16th century used for a theatre:

> Can this cockpit hold
> The vasty fields of France?
> — William Shakespeare *Henry V* (1599)

The Cockpit was the name of a 17th-century London theatre, built on the site of a cockpit, and was later used for a block of buildings on or near the site of a cockpit built by Henry VII, used from the 17th century as government offices, and from this used informally for 'the Treasury' and 'the Privy Council chambers'.

In the early 18th century the term was in nautical use, denoting an area in the aft lower deck of a man-of-war where the wounded were taken, later coming to mean the 'pit' or well in a sailing yacht from which it was steered.

the cockpit of Europe Belgium, as a part of Europe on which European conflicts have frequently been fought; the idea is first recorded in the writings of the Anglo-Welsh man of letters James Howell (*c*.1594–1666):

> The Netherlands have been for many years, as one may say, the very cockpit of Christendom.
> — James Howell *Instructions for Foreign Travel* (1642)

cockshy a target for throwing sticks or stones at as a game, originally from the sport of ➤ COCK-*throwing*.

cocksure presumptuously or arrogantly confident, the first element from archaic *cock* as a euphemism for *God*.

cocktail an alcoholic drink consisting of one or more spirits mixed with fruit juice, lemonade, cream, or other ingredients. The original use was as an adjective describing a creature with a tail like that of a cock, specifically a horse with a docked tail; hence (because hunters and coach-horses were generally docked) a racehorse which was not a thoroughbred, having a cock-tailed horse in its pedigree. The current sense of an alcoholic drink is perhaps analogous, from the idea of an adulterated spirit.

See also ➤ BROMPTON *cocktail,* ➤ MOLOTOV *cocktail.*

Cocytus in Greek mythology, one of the rivers of Hades. It was also the name of a tributary of the Acheron in Epirus.

> Our own log-boat being too heavy and far too valuable to be ventured upon this Cocytus.
> — Sir Walter Scott diary, 19 August 1814

cod war any of several disputes between Britain and Iceland in the period 1958–76, concerning fishing rights in waters around Iceland.

code originally (in Roman law, from Middle English) any of the systematic collections of statutes made by or for the later emperors, especially that of Justinian; later (from the mid 18th century), a systematic collection or digest of laws; a body of laws so arranged as to avoid inconsistency and overlapping. The word comes from Latin ➤ CODEX.

From the early 19th century *code* has also denoted a system of military or other signals used to ensure secrecy; a system of words, letters, figures, or symbols used to represent others, especially for the purposes of secrecy.

See also ➤ CADBURY *Code,* ➤ CLARENDON *Code,* ➤ COUNTRY *code,* ➤ THEODOSIAN *Code.*

Code Napoléon the French legal code drawn up under Napoleon I in 1804.

codex an ancient manuscript text in book form. The word comes (in the late 16th century, denoting a collection of statutes or set of rules) from Latin, literally 'block of wood', later denoting a block split into leaves or tablets for writing on, hence a book.

See also ➤ AMIATINUS *Codex.*

codswallop nonsense. Recorded from the 1960s, and sometimes said to be named after Hiram *Codd,* who invented a bottle for fizzy drinks (1875); the derivation remains unconfirmed.

coelacanth a large bony marine fish with a three-lobed tail fin and fleshy pectoral fins, found chiefly around the Comoro Islands near Madagascar. It is thought to be related to the ancestors of land vertebrates and was known only from fossils until one was found alive in 1938.

The name is recorded from the mid 19th century, and comes via the modern Latin genus name from Greek *koilos* 'hollow' + *akantha* 'spine' (because its fins have hollow spines).

coenobite a member of a monastic community; the word is recorded from late Middle English and comes via Old French or ecclesiastical Latin, and late Latin, from Greek *koinobion* 'convent', from *koinos* 'common' + *bios* 'life'.

Coeur de Lion nickname (French, literally 'heart of a lion') of ➤ RICHARD *I* of England (1157–99).

coffee a hot drink made from the roasted and ground bean-like seeds of a tropical shrub. Recorded from the late 16th century, the word comes via Turkish from Arabic *ḳahwa,* probably via Dutch *koffie.*

> Coffee, (which makes the politician wise,
> And see thro' all things with his half-shut eyes).
> — Alexander Pope *The Rape of the Lock* (1714)

Coffee House an establishment serving coffee and refreshments; they were first introduced during the Commonwealth, the first recorded in England being in Oxford in 1650, and the first in London in 1652. They were much frequented in the 17th and 18th centuries for political and literary discussions and for the circulation of news; Swift in *The Conduct of the Allies* (1711) says, 'It is the folly of too many, to mistake the echo of a London coffee-house for the voice of the kingdom,' and in 1876 Disraeli decried accounts of Bulgarian atrocities with the words, 'Coffee house babble'.

Coffee Houses in London

Bedford Coffee-House	Slaughter's Coffee House
Button's Coffee House	Tom's Coffee House
Don Saltero's Coffee House	Will's Coffee House

---

coffin a long, narrow box, typically of wood, in which a dead body is buried or cremated. The word is recorded from Middle English (in the general sense 'box, chest, casket') and comes from Old French *cofin* 'little basket or case', via Latin from Greek *kophinos* 'basket'.

coffin corner in American football, the corner formed by the goal line and sideline.

Coffin Texts texts inscribed on the inside of coffins during the Middle Kingdom in Egypt.

coffin-wood elm wood, as customarily used for making coffins, and thus an unlucky wood to fell.

> We ain't goin' to lay any axe-iron to coffinwood here.
> — Rudyard Kipling *Actions and Reactions* (1909)

the cogito in philosophy, the principle establishing the existence of a being from the fact of its thinking or awareness. The word in Latin means 'I

think', and comes from Descartes's formula,
➤ COGITO, *ergo sum.*

cogito, **ergo sum** I think, therefore I am; Latin formula ('I think or am thinking, therefore I am' of the French philosopher and mathematician René Descartes (1596–1650). The formulation was first made in French, as '*Je pense, donc je suis*' in *Le Discours de la méthode* (1637); it is now generally quoted from the 1641 Latin edition.

cognizance in heraldry, a distinctive device or mark, especially an emblem or badge formerly worn by retainers of a noble house.

Ferdinand Julius Cohn (1828–98), German botanist, a founder of bacteriology and the first to devise a systematic classification of bacteria into genera and species.

coif a white cap worn by lawyers as a distinctive mark of their profession, especially, and later only, that worn by a serjeant-at-law; **the coif** thus became the term for the position of serjeant-at-law.

shuffle off this mortal coil die; originally a quotation from Shakespeare's *Hamlet* (1601), 'When we have shuffled off this mortal coil.'

coin a flat, usually round piece of metal with an official stamp, used as money. The word is recorded from Middle English, in the sense 'cornerstone', later 'angle or wedge' (senses now spelled *quoin*), coming from Old French *coin* 'wedge, corner, die', *coigner* 'to mint', from Latin *cuneus* 'wedge'.

In late Middle English the term denoted a die for stamping money, or a piece of money produced by such a die.

Coke of Norfolk name given to Thomas William Coke, Earl of Leicester (1752–1842). When he began to farm his estate of Holkham, he annually invited farmers from the neighbouring districts to examine his farm and discuss its management; these meetings became the Holkham sheepshearing gatherings, the last of which was held in 1821.

Jean Baptiste Colbert (1619–83), French statesman, chief minister to Louis XIV 1665–83. He was responsible for reforming the country's finances and the navy, and for boosting industry and commerce. His reforms, however, could not keep pace with Louis's spending on war and court extravagance, and by the end of Louis's reign the French economy was again experiencing severe problems.

According to an account in the *Journal*

Oeconomique April 1751, Colbert, *c.*1664, assembled a number of representatives of commerce to ask what he could best do for them; 'the most rational and the least flattering among them answered him in one word: "Laissez-nous-faire." '

colcannon an Irish and Scottish dish of cabbage and potatoes boiled and pounded. The origin of the second element is uncertain, but it is said that cannonballs were used to pound such vegetables as spinach. In parts of Canada, especially Newfoundland, the term is used for a dish of various vegetables, usually including cabbage, traditionally eaten on Halloween.

Colchester a town in Essex, famous for its oysters, sometimes called **Colchesters** or **Colchester natives**.

colchicum a plant of a genus including the autumn crocuses, especially meadow saffron, which has analgesic properties. The name comes via Latin from Greek *kolkhikon* 'of Colchis', alluding to the skills as a poisoner of the sorceress ➤ MEDEA of Colchis in classical mythology.

Colchis an ancient region south of the Caucasus mountains at the eastern end of the Black Sea. In classical mythology it was the goal of Jason's expedition for the ➤ GOLDEN *Fleece*, and the home of ➤ MEDEA.

cold see also ➤ *as the* DAY *lengthens, so the cold strengthens,* ➤ *cold enough to freeze the balls off a* BRASS *monkey,* ➤ *cold* OBSTRUCTION, ➤ FEED *a cold and starve a fever,* ➤ REVENGE *is a dish that can be eaten cold.*

Cold Comfort Farm a novel (1932) by Stella Gibbons, which depicts the fated, poverty-stricken, and generally uncomfortable rural lives of the Starkadder family and their matriarch, Aunt Ada Doom; the book was written as a parody of the work of such regional writers as Mary Webb (1881–1927).

See also ➤ *something* NASTY *in the woodshed.*

cold dark matter matter consisting of massive particles of low energy, which is believed by some scientists to exist in the universe but which has not yet been directly observed.

cold fusion nuclear fusion occurring at or close to room temperature. Claims for its discovery in 1989 are generally held to have been mistaken.

cold hands, warm heart proverbial saying, early 20th century.

cold turkey the abrupt and complete cessation of taking a drug to which one is addicted; the phrase derives from one of the symptoms, the development of 'goose-flesh' on the skin from a sudden chill, caused by this.

cold war a state of political hostility existing between the Soviet bloc countries and the Western powers after the Second World War, characterized by threats, violent propaganda, subversive activities, and other measures short of open warfare. The term was famously used in 1947 by the American financier and presidential advisor Bernard Baruch (by his own account, 'cold war' was suggested to him by H. B. Swope, former editor of the *New York World*):

> Let us not be deceived—we are today in the midst of a cold war.
> — Bernard Baruch speech to South Carolina Legislature, 16 April 1947

Colditz a medieval castle near Leipzig in Germany, used as a top-security camp for Allied prisoners in the Second World War.

> Three weeks, secretly gettin' all me things ready. It's been like livin' in bleedin' Colditz with a tunnel beneath the floorboards.
> — Willy Russell *Shirley Valentine* (1986)

Coldstream Guards in the British army, one of five regiments of Foot Guards; the regiment is named for *Coldstream* in the Scottish borders, where it was first raised, *c.*1650, and which supported Charles II in the Restoration of 1660.

Cole see ➤ OLD *King Cole*.

Samuel Taylor Coleridge (1772–1834), English poet, critic, and philosopher. His *Lyrical Ballads* (1798), written with William Wordsworth, marked the start of English romanticism and included 'The Rime of the Ancient Mariner'. During the latter part of his life he wrote little poetry but contributed significantly to critical and philosophical literature.

Colin Clout the name adopted by Spenser in *The Shepheardes Calendar* and *Colin Clouts come home again.*

coliseum a large theatre, cinema, or stadium; the name recorded from the late 19th century, is an alteration of Latin *colosseum* (see ➤ COLOSSEUM).

collaboration traitorous cooperation with an enemy; the term was particularly used of those in occupied countries who cooperated with the Axis forces in the Second World War.

collapse see ➤ *collapse of* STOUT *party.*

collar of esses a chain consisting of a series of S's: the former badge of the House of Lancaster, still used in the costumes of some officials.

collect in church use, a short prayer, especially one assigned to a particular day or season. The word is recorded from Middle English, and comes via Old French from Latin *collecta* 'gathering', feminine past participle of *colligere* 'gather together'.

college an educational institution or establishment. Also, an organized group of professional people with particular aims, duties, and privileges, as in, **Royal College of Physicians**. The word is recorded from late Middle English, and comes via Old French from Latin *collegium* 'partnership, association', from *collega* 'partner in office', from *col-* 'together with' + *legare* 'depute'.

See also ➤ SACRED *College.*

College of Arms in the UK, a corporation which officially records and grants armorial bearings. Formed in 1484, it comprises three Kings of Arms, six heralds, and four pursuivants.

College of Cardinals the body of cardinals of the Roman Catholic Church, founded in the 11th century and since 1179 responsible for the election of the Pope. Also called the ➤ SACRED *College.*

collegiate church a church endowed for a chapter of canons but without a bishop's see; in the US and Scotland, a church or group of churches established under two or more pastors.

collegiate Gothic a style of neo-Gothic architecture used for some US university buildings.

Collins a letter of thanks for hospitality or entertainment, sent by a departed guest, from **Mr Collins**, the pompous young clergyman in Jane Austen's *Pride and Prejudice* (1813), whose letter of thanks after spending a few days with the Bennets was 'written with all the solemnity of gratitude which a twelvemonth's abode in the family might have prompted'.

> The amateur composer even of a Collins or bread-and-butter letter realizes that his mother tongue is a stubborn means for the communication of gratitude.
> — Walter de la Mare *Pleasures and Speculations* (1940)

Michael Collins (1890–1922), Irish nationalist leader and politician. A member of Parliament for Sinn Fein, he was one of the negotiators of the Anglo-Irish Treaty of 1921. He commanded the Irish Free State forces in the civil war and became head of state but was assassinated ten days later.

Collyridian a member of a sect idolatrously offering cakes to the Blessed Virgin, which consisted mainly of women and originated in Thrace in the 4th century AD.

Cologne a German city on the Rhine, famous in the Middle Ages for its shrine of the Wise Men of the East, commonly called the **Three Kings of Cologne** (see ➤ *the* THREE *Kings*).

Colón the chief port of Panama, at the Caribbean end of the Panama Canal. It was founded in 1850 by the American William Aspinwall (1807–55), after whom it was originally named, but was renamed in 1903 after Christopher Columbus, *Colón* being the Spanish form of his surname.

colonel a rank of officer in the army and in the US air force, above a lieutenant colonel and below a brigadier or brigadier general. The word is recorded from the mid 16th century and comes from obsolete form *coronel* (earlier form of *colonel*), from Italian *colonnello* 'column of soldiers', from *colonna* 'column', from Latin *columna*. The form *coronel*, source of the modern pronunciation, was usual until the mid 17th century.

colonial goose in Australia and New Zealand, stuffed boned roast leg of mutton.

colony see also ➤ CROWN *Colony*, ➤ LOST *Colony*, ➤ THIRTEEN *Colonies*.

colophon a publisher's emblem or imprint, especially one on the title page of a book; formerly also, a statement at the end of a book, typically with a printer's emblem, giving information about its authorship and printing.

The word is recorded from the early 17th century (denoting a finishing touch), and comes via late Latin from Greek *kolophōn* 'summit or finishing touch'.

Colorado a river which rises in the Rocky mountains of northern Colorado and flows generally south-westwards to the Gulf of California, passing through the Grand Canyon. Also, the state in the central US named from this river, part of which was acquired by the ➤ LOUISIANA *Purchase* in 1803 and the rest ceded by Mexico in 1848. It became the 38th state in 1876, from which it is known as the ➤ CENTENNIAL *State*.

Colosseum the name since medieval times of the *Amphitheatrum Flavium*, a vast amphitheatre in

Rome, begun *c*.75 AD; the name is Latin, and is the neuter of *colosseus* 'gigantic'.

Epistle to the Colossians a book of the New Testament, an epistle of St Paul to the Church at Colossae in Phrygia.

colossus a person or thing of enormous size, importance or ability; the word is this sense is recorded from the early 17th century, and derives from the ➤ COLOSSUS *of Rhodes.*

Colossus was the name given to the electronic digital computer, one of the first of its kind, which was developed at ➤ BLETCHLEY *Park* in the Second World War to break German codes, the use of which was said to have shortened the war by two years.

Colossus of Rhodes a huge bronze statue of the sun god Helios, one of the Seven Wonders of the World. Built *c*.292–280 BC, it stood beside the harbour entrance at Rhodes for about fifty years. *Colossus* comes via Latin from Greek *kolossos*, applied by Herodotus to the statues of Egyptian temples.

colour the property possessed by an object of producing different sensations in the eye as a result of the way it reflects or emits light; one, or any mixture, of the constituents into which light can be separated in a spectrum or rainbow, sometimes including (loosely) black and white.

In ➤ HERALDRY, the major conventional colours as used in coats of arms (especially as opposed to metals, furs, and stains) have their own names.

See also ➤ COAT *of many colours*, ➤ FOUR-*colour problem*, ➤ FUNDAMENTAL *colours*, ➤ HAUL *down one's colours*, ➤ LITURGICAL *colours*, ➤ NAIL *one's colours to the mast*, ➤ PRIMARY *colour*, ➤ REGIMENTAL *colour*, ➤ SAIL *under false colours*, ➤ TROOP *the colour.*

colt a young uncastrated male horse, in particular one less than four years old. Recorded from Old English, the word may be related to Swedish *kult*, applied to boys or half-grown animals.

See also ➤ *a* RAGGED *colt may make a good horse.*

Samuel Colt (1814–62), American inventor. He is remembered chiefly for the revolver named after him, which he patented in 1836; it was adopted by the US army in 1846. The revolver was highly influential in the development of small arms in the 19th century.

John Coltrane (1926–67), American jazz saxophonist. He was a leading figure in avant-garde jazz, bridging the gap between the harmonically dense jazz of the 1950s and the free jazz that evolved in the 1960s.

St Columba (*c.*521–97), Irish abbot and missionary. He established the monastery at Iona in *c.*563, and converted the Picts to Christianity. St Columba contributed significantly to the literature of Celtic Christianity. A famous early comment on copyright, 'To every cow her calf, to every book its copy' is attributed to him.

☐ **FEAST DAY** His feast day is 9 June.

Columbine a character in Italian *commedia dell'arte*, the mistress of ➤ HARLEQUIN; the name comes via French from Italian *Colombina*, feminine of *colombino* 'dovelike', from *colombo* 'dove'.

Christopher Columbus (1451–1506), Italian-born Spanish explorer. He persuaded the Spanish monarchs, Ferdinand and Isabella, to sponsor an expedition to sail across the Atlantic in search of Asia and to prove that the world was round. In 1492 he set sail with three small ships and discovered the New World (in fact various Caribbean islands). He made three further voyages between 1493 and 1504, in 1498 discovering the South American mainland.

See also ➤ KNIGHT *of Columbus.*

Columbus Day in the US, a legal holiday commemorating the discovery of the New World by Christopher Columbus in 1492. It is observed by most states on the second Monday of October.

column see also ➤ DODGE *the column,* ➤ DUKE *of York's Column,* ➤ FIFTH *column,* ➤ NELSON'S *Column,* ➤ TRAJAN'S *Column.*

Coma Berenices a small inconspicuous northern constellation (*Berenice's Hair*), said to represent the tresses of Queen ➤ BERENICE.

Comanche a member of an American Indian people of the south-western US. The Comanche were among the first to acquire horses (from the Spanish) and resisted white settlers fiercely.

comb a comb (for carding wool) is the emblem of ➤ *St* BLAISE.

come see also ➤ EASY *come, easy go,* ➤ LIGHT *come, light go,* ➤ QUICKLY *come, quickly go.*

Come-outer in 19th-century New England, a member of a mystic movement (originating at Cape Cod) holding that ministers and creeds are unnecessary and that the only source of divine truth is God speaking directly to the heart.

come with me to the Casbah a line often attributed to Charles Boyer in the film *Algiers* (1938), but not found there.

the Comeback Kid Bill Clinton's description of himself after coming second in the New Hampshire primary in the 1992 presidential election (since 1952, no presidential candidate had won the election without first winning in New Hampshire); his subsequent career, in which he won a second term and survived impeachment, demonstrated the appropriateness of the name.

Comédie Française the French national theatre (used for both comedy and tragedy), in Paris, founded in 1680 by Louis XIV, and reconstituted by Napoleon I in 1803. It is organized as a cooperative society in which each actor holds a share or part-share.

comedy professional entertainment consisting of jokes and satirical sketches, intended to make an audience laugh. Recorded from late Middle English (as a genre of drama, also denoting a narrative poem with a happy ending, as in Dante's *Divine Comedy*), the word comes via Old French and Latin from Greek *kōmōidia*, from *kōmōidos* 'comic poet', from *kōmos* 'revel' + *aoidos* 'singer'.

See also ➤ *the* DIVINE *Comedy,* ➤ NEW *Comedy,* ➤ RESTORATION *comedy.*

comedy of manners a play, novel, or film that gives a satirical portrayal of behaviour in a particular social group.

comforter see ➤ JOB'S *comforter.*

comfrey a Eurasian plant of the borage family, which has large hairy leaves and clusters of purplish or white bell-shaped flowers, traditionally valued for its medicinal properties. Recorded from Middle English, the name comes ultimately via Anglo-Norman French from Latin *confervere* 'heal' (literally 'boil together'), referring to its medicinal use.

coming see also ➤ SECOND *Coming.*

coming events cast their shadows before them proverbial saying, early 19th century.

command see also ➤ *he that cannot* OBEY, *cannot command.*

Command Paper (in the UK) a document laid before Parliament by order of the Crown, though in practice by the government.

Commander of the Faithful one of the titles of a caliph, first assumed (*c.*640) by Omar I.

commandment a divine rule, especially one of the ➤ TEN *Commandments.*
See also ➤ ELEVENTH *commandment.*

commando a soldier specially trained for carrying out raids; a unit of such troops. The term is recorded from the late 18th century (denoting a militia, originally consisting of Boers in South Africa); it comes ultimately from Portuguese *commanda*r 'to command'.

commedia dell'arte an improvised kind of popular comedy in Italian theatres in the 16th–18th centuries, based on stock characters. Actors adapted their comic dialogue and action according to a few basic plots (commonly love intrigues) and to topical issues.

commendation ninepence a bent ninepenny piece used as a love token.

Commendatore a knight of an Italian order of chivalry.

comment see ➤ NO *comment.*

Committee of Public Safety a French governing body set up in April 1793, during the Revolution. Consisting of nine (later twelve) members, it was at first dominated by Danton, but later came under the influence of Robespierre, when it initiated the Terror. The Committee's power ended with the fall of Robespierre in 1794, and it was dissolved in 1795.

Committee of the Whole House the whole House of Commons when sitting as a committee.

Committee of Ways and Means a committee of the House of Commons or of the US House of Representatives.

common see also ➤ CENTURY *of the common man.*

common a piece of open land for public use, especially in a village or town, and often traditionally used for pasturage; the ➤ ENCLOSURE of such land to make it private property was a policy in Britain in the 18th and early 19th centuries.

> The fault is great in man or woman
> Who steals a goose from off a common;
> But what can plead that man's excuse
> Who steals a common from a goose?
> — in *The Tickler Magazine* 1 February 1821

See also ➤ RIGHT *of common.*

Common Entrance in the UK, an examination taken, usually at 13, by pupils wishing to enter public schools.

the Common Era another term for ➤ *the* CHRISTIAN *Era.*

common fame is seldom to blame proverbial saying, mid 17th century.

common law the part of English law that is derived from custom and judicial precedent rather than statutes, and often contrasted with *statute law*; the body of English law as adopted and adapted by the different States of the US.

Common Market a name for the European Economic Community or European Union, used especially in the 1960s and 1970s.

common or garden ordinary; originally a humorous substitute for 'common', 'ordinary'. The phrase is recorded in it literal sense ('the Common or Garden Nightshade') from the mid 17th century; this extended usage dates from the late 19th century.

Common Pleas historical term for a court for hearing civil cases between subjects or citizens not involving Crown or state.

Common Prayer the Church of England liturgy, originally set forth in the ➤ BOOK *of Common Prayer.*

common sense originally, an 'internal' sense which was regarded as the common bond or centre of the five senses, in which the various impressions received were reduced to the unity of a common consciousness.

Common Serjeant (in the UK) a circuit judge of the Central Criminal Court with duties in the City of London.

commoner originally, a citizen, a burgess. Later, a member of the common people, anyone below the rank of peer.

Great Commoner a nickname for the elder ➤ *William* PITT (1708–78).

commons see also ➤ DOCTORS' *Commons,* ➤ HOUSE *of Commons.*

commonwealth the body politic; a nation, viewed as a community in which everyone has an interest. The term is recorded from late Middle English, originally as two words, denoting public welfare.

The Commonwealth is the name given to the republican period of government in Britain between the execution of Charles I in 1649 and the Restoration of Charles II in 1660.

Commonwealth (also called **Commonwealth of Nations**) is also now used for an international association consisting of the UK together with states that were previously part of the British Empire, and dependencies. The British monarch is the symbolic head of the Commonwealth.

See also ➤ IDEAL *commonwealth,* ➤ NEW *Commonwealth.*

Commonwealth Day the second Monday in March, celebrating the British Commonwealth. It was instituted to commemorate assistance given to Britain by the colonies during the Boer War (1899–1902).

commonwealth of learning learned people collectively; the phrase is recorded from the mid 17th century.

Communard an adherent of the Paris Commune of 1871.

the Commune the group which seized the municipal government of Paris in the French Revolution and played a leading part in the Reign of Terror until suppressed in 1794.

The Commune is also the name given to the municipal government organized on communalistic principles elected in Paris in 1871. It was soon brutally suppressed by government troops. Also called **the Paris Commune**.

communications see ➤ EVIL *communications corrupt good manners.*

communion the service of Christian worship at which bread and wine are consecrated and shared; the ➤ EUCHARIST.

communion of saints a fellowship between Christians living and dead.

communism a theory or system of social organization in which all property is vested in the community and each person contributes and receives according to their ability and needs.

The most familiar form of communism is that established by the Bolsheviks after the Russian Revolution of 1917, and it has generally been understood in terms of the system practised by the former USSR and its allies in eastern Europe, in China since 1949, and in some developing countries such as Cuba, Vietnam, and North Korea. Communism embraced

a revolutionary ideology in which the state would wither away after the overthrow of the capitalist system. In practice, however, the state grew to control all aspects of communist society. Communism in eastern Europe collapsed in the late 1980s and early 1990s against a background of failure to meet people's economic expectations, a shift to more democracy in political life, and increasing nationalism such as that which led to the break-up of the USSR.

See also ➤ ARE *you now or have you ever been a member of the Communist Party?.*

community care long-term care for the mentally ill, the elderly, and people with disabilities which is provided within the community rather than in hospitals or institutions, especially as implemented in the UK under the National Health Service and Community Care Act of 1990.

community charge (in the UK) a tax, introduced by the Conservative government in 1990 (1989 in Scotland), levied locally on every adult in a community. It was replaced in 1993 by the council tax. Informally called the ➤ POLL *tax.*

Comnena see ➤ ANNA *Comnena.*

Comnenus name of an imperial Byzantine dynasty of the 11th and 12th centuries.

Companion of Honour in the UK, a member of an order of knighthood founded in 1917.

Companion of Literature in the UK, a holder of an honour awarded by the Royal Society of Literature and founded in 1961.

company see ➤ JOHN *Company,* ➤ MISERY *loves company,* ➤ TWO *is company, but three is none,* ➤ WHITE *Company.*

a man is known by the company he keeps proverbial saying, mid 16th century.

the company makes the feast proverbial saying, mid 17th century.

comparisons are odious proverbial saying, mid 15th century.

compass an instrument containing a magnetized pointer which shows the direction of magnetic north and bearings from it. The use of the compass for navigation at sea was reported from China *c.*1100, western Europe 1187, Arabia *c.*1220, and Scandinavia *c.*1300, although it probably dates from much earlier. Since the early 20th century the magnetic compass has been superseded by the gyrocompass as primary equipment for ships and aircraft.

The word is recorded in Middle English in various senses ('measure', 'artifice', 'circumscribed area', and 'pair of compasses') which also occur in Old French, from which the word comes, but their development and origin are uncertain. The transference of sense to the magnetic compass is held to have occurred in the related Italian word *compasso*, from the circular shape of the compass box.

See also ➤ BOX *the compass*.

compassion fatigue indifference to charitable appeals on behalf of those who are suffering, experienced as a result of the frequency or number of such appeals.

comping the practice of entering competitions, especially those promoting consumer products.

compital in ancient Rome, pertaining to crossroads, and especially designating shrines of domestic gods placed at street corners; the **Compitalia** was an annual festival in honour of these gods.

complementary medicine any of a range of medical therapies that fall beyond the scope of scientific medicine but may be used alongside it in the treatment of disease and ill health. Examples include acupuncture and osteopathy.

he that complies against his will is of his own opinion still proverbial saying, late 17th century; originally from Samuel Butler *Hudibras* (1678).

compline the seventh and last of the daytime canonical hours of prayer; the office, originally directed to be said immediately before retiring for the night, appointed for this hour.

Complutensian Polyglot the earliest complete Polyglot Bible, published at Alcalá in the early part of the 16th century, at the expense of Cardinal Ximenes.

composition see ➤ FALLACY *of composition*.

Compostela the Spanish city of ➤ SANTIAGO *de Compostela*, which has been from the medieval period a pilgrimage centre for its shrine of ➤ St JAMES *the Great*.

compromise see ➤ MISSOURI *Compromise*.

computer a device which is capable of receiving information (data) in a particular form and of performing a sequence of operations in accordance with a predetermined but variable set of procedural instructions (program) to produce a result in the form of information or signals. Most computers operate electronically and manipulate data in digital form.

The power of the digital computer lies in its ability to carry out different tasks according to its programming, without any structural change. Successive generations of computer have become progressively smaller and faster as vacuum tubes have been replaced first by transistors and then by integrated circuits. Originally huge and expensive tools of scientific research, they now include handheld machines for personal use, and are widely used for the storage, processing, transfer, and presentation of information, and for the control of mechanical and electronic systems.

Comstock lode a very rich lode of silver and gold discovered in Nevada in 1858 by the American prospector H. T. P. Comstock (1820–70).

> One of the greatest honey pots since the Comstock Lode.
> — *Post* (Denver) 11 June 1995

Comstockery excessive opposition to supposed immorality in the arts; prudery. The word comes from the name of Anthony *Comstock* (1844–1915), member of the New York Society for the Suppression of Vice.

Comus revelry personified; the term comes from Milton's *Masque of Comus* (1637), in which Comus himself is a pagan god of Milton's invention.

Comyn see ➤ *the* RED *Comyn*.

Conall Cernach warrior of the Ulster cycle, protector of Ulster during the boyhood of Cuchulain.

Conan see also ➤ *Arthur Conan* DOYLE.

Conan in the legends relating to ➤ FINN, a figure resembling ➤ THERSITES.

Conan the Barbarian sword and sorcery fantasy hero, otherwise known as **Conan of Cimmeria**, noted for his strength, fighting skills, and enjoyment of physical pleasures; the character was originally created by the American writer Robert E. Howard (1906–36), and in the 1982 film was played by Arnold Schwarzenegger.

> Marc Singer plays a cross between Conan The Barbarian and Dr Dolittle, a muscle-bound meathead who has the power to talk to and control all animals.
> — *TV Quick* 7 June 1997

concealed land term for land withheld from the sovereign without proper title, used especially of land that had been in monastic possession before the Reformation.

conception see ➤ IMMACULATE *Conception.*

Conceptionist a member of a Catholic order founded in France in the 18th century and named in honor of the ➤ IMMACULATE *Conception.*

the Concert of Europe the chief European powers acting together, used particularly of post-Napoleonic Europe.

> My third sound principle is to take care to cultivate and maintain to the utmost the concert of Europe, to keep the Powers of Europe together.
> — William Ewart Gladstone *Speech at Midlothian* (1880)

concert pitch a standard for the tuning of musical instruments, internationally agreed in 1960, in which the note A above middle C has a frequency of 440 Hz; figuratively, a state of readiness, efficiency, and keenness.

conch a tropical marine mollusc with a robust spiral shell which may bear long projections and have a flared lip; a shell of this kind blown like a trumpet to produce a hollow-sounding musical note, often depicted as played by Tritons and other mythological figures.

Conchubar mac Nessa Red Branch king of the Ulster cycle; uncle of ➤ CUCHULAIN, his jealous revenge brings about the death of ➤ DEIRDRE and the sons of Uisneach.

conclamation a loud calling out of many together, especially of loud lamentation for the dead.

conclave in the Roman Catholic Church, the assembly of cardinals for the election of a pope; the meeting place for such an assembly. The word is recorded from late Middle English (denoting a private room) and comes via French from Latin *conclave* 'lockable room', from *con-* 'with' + *clavis* 'key'.

concoction see ➤ *an* ERROR *in the first concoction.*

Concord a town in NE Massachusetts; battles there and at ➤ LEXINGTON in April 1775 marked the start of the War of American Independence. During the mid-19th century, Concord was the home of the Transcendentalist movement, whose leaders included Emerson, Thoreau, and Hawthorne.

concordance an alphabetical list of the words (especially the important ones) present in a text or body of texts, usually with citations of the passages concerned or with the context displayed on a computer screen.

concordat an agreement or treaty, especially one between the Vatican and a secular government relating to matters of mutual interest.

Concorde a supersonic airliner, the only one to have entered operational service, able to cruise at twice the speed of sound. Produced through Anglo-French cooperation, it made its maiden flight in 1969 and has been in commercial service since 1976, with British Airways and Air France.

> Pheasants aspiring to reach Concordean altitudes.
> — *Field* January 1990

concrete jungle a city or an area of a city with a high density of large, unattractive, modern buildings and which is perceived as an unpleasant living environment.

concrete number a number of specified people or objects as opposed to a number in the abstract (for example, seven men or days as distinct from the abstract number seven).

concrete poetry poetry in which the meaning or effect is conveyed partly or wholly by visual means, using patterns of words or letters and other typographical devices.

concrete universal in idealist philosophy, an abstraction which is manifest in a developing or organized set of instances, so having the qualities of both the universal and the particular.

concubine in polygamous societies (and chiefly in historical and biblical use), a woman who lives with a man but has lower status than his wife or wives.

conditions see ➤ MADRID *conditions.*

condottiere a leader or a member of a troop of mercenaries, especially in medieval Italy. The word is Italian, and comes from *condotto* 'troop under contract', from *condotta* 'a contract'.

conduct unbecoming unsuitable or inappropriate behaviour; the phrase comes from *Articles of War* (1872) 'Any officer who shall behave in a scandalous manner, unbecoming the character of an officer and a gentleman shall…be CASHIERED'; the Naval Discipline Act, 10 August 1860 uses the words 'conduct unbecoming the character of an Officer'.

Conestoga wagon in North America, a large wagon used for long-distance travel. It is named (in the early 18th century) after *Conestoga*, a town in Pennsylvania.

coney a rabbit; originally the preferred term (now superseded by *rabbit*) and still in use in heraldry, and for the animal's fur. In the 16th and 17th centuries, **coney-catching** was a term for duping or deceiving a gullible victim.

Coney Island a resort and amusement park on the Atlantic coast in Brooklyn, New York City, on the south shore of Long Island.

> It out-Coneyed Coney Island. There were all of fourteen million trippers.
> — S. J. Perelman letter, *c.*June 1964

confarreation the highest and most solemn form of marriage among the patricians of ancient Rome, made by offering a cake made of spelt in the presence of the ➤ PONTIFEX *Maximus* or ➤ FLAMEN *Dialis* and ten witnesses.

Recorded from the late 16th century, the word comes from Latin, and ultimately from *confarreare* 'unite in marriage by offering bread', from *con-* 'with' + *farreum* 'spelt-cake'.

Confederate States the eleven Southern states which seceded from the United States in 1860–1, thus precipitating the American Civil War.

Confederate States		
Alabama	Mississippi	Virginia
Arkansas	North Carolina	
Florida	South Carolina	
Georgia	Tennessee	
Louisiana	Texas	

articles of confederation those adopted by the thirteen original colonies at the ➤ CONTINENTAL *Congress* of 1777.

Confederation of British Industry (in the UK) an organization to promote the prosperity of British business. The organization was founded in 1965 (combining earlier associations), has a membership of about 50,000 companies, and provides its members with a wide range of services and practical advice and voices the views of the management side of industry in the UK. It is often abbreviated to **CBI**.

Confederation of the Rhine the union of certain German states under the protection of Napoleon Bonaparte from 1806 to 1813.

Conference on Disarmament a committee with forty nations as members that seeks to negotiate

multilateral disarmament. It was constituted in 1962 as the **Committee on Disarmament** (with eighteen nations as members) and adopted its present title in 1984. It meets in Geneva.

confess and be hanged proverbial saying, late 16th century.

confessed see ➤ *a* FAULT *confessed is half redressed*.

confessio a tomb in which a martyr or confessor is buried, and, by extension, the whole structure erected over it; also, the crypt or shrine under the high-altar, or the part of the altar, in which the relics are placed.

confession a formal admission of one's sins with repentance and desire of absolution, especially privately to a priest as a religious duty.

Confession is also used for a statement of faith setting out essential religious doctrine (also called **confession of faith**); (with capital initial) the religious body or Church sharing a confession of faith.

See also ➤ AUGSBURG *Confession*, ➤ WESTMINSTER *Confession*.

confession is good for the soul proverbial saying, mid 17th century.

confessional see ➤ SEAL *of the confessional*.

confessor see ➤ *St* EDWARD *the Confessor*.

confetti small pieces of coloured paper traditionally thrown over a bride and bridegroom by their wedding guests after the marriage ceremony has taken place. The term is recorded from the early 19th century, and originally denoted the real or imitation sweets thrown during Italian carnivals; it comes from Italian, literally 'sweets', from Latin *confectum* 'something prepared'.

Confiteor a form of prayer confessing sins, used in the Roman Catholic Mass and some other sacraments. The word is Latin, 'I confess', from the formula *Confiteor Deo Omnipotenti* 'I confess to Almighty God'.

confraternity a brotherhood, especially with a religious or charitable purpose.

Confucianism a system of philosophical and ethical teachings founded by ➤ CONFUCIUS and developed by Mencius.

Confucius (551–479 BC), Chinese philosopher. He worked for the government and later took up the

role of an itinerant sage. His ideas about the importance of practical moral values, collected by his disciples in the *Analects*, formed the basis of the
philosophy of ➤ CONFUCIANISM.

confusable a word or phrase that is easily confused with another in meaning or usage, such as
mitigate, which is often confused with *militate*.

confusion of tongues the confusion of languages
of the builders of the ➤ TOWER *of Babel*; the phrase
is recorded from late Middle English.

confusion worse confounded complete confusion, deriving from a usage by Milton in *Paradise
Lost*:

> With ruin upon ruin, rout on rout,
> Confusion worse confounded.
> — John Milton *Paradise Lost* (1667)

congé an unceremonious dismissal or rejection of
someone. The term is recorded from late Middle
English in the general sense 'permission to do
something' (coming via Old French *congie* from
Latin *commeatus* 'leave of absence'); it is now usually treated as equivalent to modern French.

congius an ancient Roman liquid measure of one
eighth of an amphora, equal in modern terms to
about 6 imperial pints.

**Congleton rare, Congleton rare,
sold the Bible to pay for a bear.**
traditional rhyme, celebrating the story that the
clerk of *Congleton* in Cheshire sold their church
bible to pay for a town bear for bear-baiting. From
this the people of Congleton were called **Congleton
bears**.

Congregationalism a system of organization
among Christian churches whereby individual local
churches are largely self-governing.

Congress the national legislative body of the
United States, which meets at the Capitol in Washington DC; it was established by the Constitution of
1787 and is composed of the Senate and the House
of Representatives.
   See also ➤ CONTINENTAL *Congress*, ➤ LIBRARY *of
Congress*.

Congreve rocket for use in war, invented in 1808
by Colonel William Congreve (1772–1828). He is said
also to have invented the **Congreve match**.

conjure call upon (a spirit or ghost) to appear by
means of a magic ritual; the word in this sense is
recorded from Middle English, and the meaning

'make (something) appear unexpectedly or seemingly by magic' develops from it. The phrase **a name
to conjure with**, used to indicate that one believes a
person to be important within a particular sphere of
activity, reflects both senses.

conker the hard shiny dark brown nut of a horse
chestnut tree; in plural, a children's game in which
each has a conker on the end of a string and takes
turns in trying to break another's with it.
   Conker is recorded from the mid 19th century as a
dialect word denoting a snail shell, with which the
game, or a similar form of it, was originally played;
it may originally have come from *conch*, but it is associated with (and frequently spelled as) *conquer* in
the 19th and early 20th centuries, and an alternative
name for the game was *conquerors*.

Conn of the Hundred Battles a legendary pre-
Christian Gaelic king of Tara.

> The tribal images of many Irish heroes and heroines of
> antiquity, Cuchulin, Conn of hundred battles.
> — James Joyce *Ulysses* (1922)

Connacht a province in the south-west of Ireland;
with Ulster, Munster, and Leinster one of the traditional four divisions of the island. Also called *Connaught*.

Hell or Connaught summary of the choice
offered to the Catholic population of Ireland, transported to the western counties of ➤ CONNACHT to
make room for settlers, traditionally attributed to
➤ *Oliver* CROMWELL.

Connecticut a state in the north-eastern US,
which was one of the original thirteen states of the
Union, and ratified the draft US Constitution in
1788.

Connecticut Wits a literary group of the late 18th
century, centred at Hartford (and known also as the
Hartford Wits). They modelled themselves on the
Augustan wits, but retained the intellectual and
spiritual conservatism of Connecticut.

Maureen Connolly (1934–69), American tennis
player; known as **Little Mo**. She was 16 when she first
won the US singles title and 17 when she took the
Wimbledon title; she retained these titles for a further two years each. In 1953 she became the first
woman to win the grand slam before being forced to
retire in 1954 after a riding accident.

Conqueror an epithet of various rulers, especially
William, duke of Normandy and (after 1066) king of
England (see ➤ WILLIAM *I*).

came over with the Conqueror of a family, be old and distinguished; supposedly, be identified as one of the Norman families accompanying William of Normandy to England.

> After all, the Woosters did come over with the Conqueror . . . and a fat lot of good it is coming over with Conquerors, if you're simply going to wind up being given the elbow by Aberdeen terriers.
> — P. G. Wodehouse *The Code of the Woosters* (1938)

conquistador a conqueror, especially one of the Spanish conquerors of Mexico and Peru in the 16th century.

conscience see also ➤ COURT *of Conscience*, ➤ PRICK *of conscience*, ➤ *a* QUIET *conscience sleeps in thunder*, ➤ SOUL *and conscience*.

prisoner of conscience a person detained or imprisoned because of his or her religious or political beliefs; the term is recorded from the early 1960s, and is particularly associated with the campaigns of ➤ AMNESTY *International*.

conscience clause a clause that makes concessions to the consciences of those affected by a law, especially one providing for the withdrawal of children in public schools from religious teaching disapproved by their parents.

conscience makes cowards of us all proverbial saying, early 17th century; originally from Shakespeare's *Hamlet*.

conscience money money paid because of feelings of guilt, especially about a payment that one has evaded.

conscientious objector a person who for reasons of conscience refuses to conform to the requirements of law, especially one who objects to serving in the armed forces. The term is recorded from the late 19th century, but came to prominence with national conscription in the First World War, when those claiming to be *conscientious objectors* had to establish their status before a tribunal; the derogatory shortening *conchy* dates from this period.

In *Good-bye to All That* (1928) Robert Graves records that the writer Lytton Strachey, appearing before a tribunal, was asked by the Chairman what he would do if he saw a German soldier trying to violate his sister, and replied, 'I would try to get between them.'

conscript fathers the body of Roman senators; a translation of Latin *patres conscripti*, the collective

title by which the Roman senators were addressed (used also as a title by the Venetian senate).

consent see also ➤ SILENCE *means consent*.

age of consent the age at which a person's consent to sexual intercourse is valid in law.

consenting adult an adult who willingly agrees to engage in a sexual act.

conservationists ➤ *St* FRANCIS *of Assisi* is the patron saint of conservationists.

conservative averse to change or innovation and holding to traditional attitudes and values, typically in relation to politics or religion. The name was first used in its political sense in 1830 by the politician John Wilson Croker, suggesting that the Tory Party might be termed the ➤ CONSERVATIVE *Party*.

Conservative Judaism a form of Judaism, particularly prevalent in North America, which seeks to preserve Jewish tradition and ritual but has a more flexible approach to the interpretation of the law than Orthodox Judaism.

Conservative Party a political party promoting free enterprise and private ownership, in particular a major British party that since the Second World War has been in power 1951–64, 1970–4, and 1979–97. It emerged from the old Tory Party under Sir Robert Peel in the 1830s and 1840s.

The name was first used by John Wilson Croker in 1830:

> Attached to what is called the Tory, and which might with more propriety be called the Conservative, party.
> — John Wilson Croker in *Quarterly Review* January 1830

The new name immediately largely took the place of the term ➤ TORY (originally reproachful), which had been in use for nearly 150 years. (Measures tending to preserve cherished political conditions had before this been sometimes spoken of as *conservatory*.) Preference for *Conservative* occasionally implied disavowal of the reactionary tendencies which had sometimes been associated with earlier Toryism.

conservators of the peace applied in a general sense to the Sovereign, Lord Chancellor, Lord Treasurer, Lord High Constable, the Justices of the King's Bench, the Master of the Rolls, and others.

consistory in the Roman Catholic Church the council of cardinals, with or without the Pope. In the Church of England, a court presided over by a bishop, for the administration of ecclesiastical law in a diocese.

consolamentum the spiritual baptism of the Cathars.

Consolidated Fund the account held by the Exchequer of the British government at the Bank of England into which public monies (such as tax receipts) are paid and from which major payments are made, other than those dependent on periodic parliamentary approval.

Consols British government securities without redemption date and with fixed annual interest; the term dates from the late 18th century, and is a contraction of *consolidated annuities*.

conspicuous by one's absence obviously not present in a place where one or it should be, from a speech made by the British Whig statesman Lord John Russell (1792–1878):

> Among the defects of the Bill, which were numerous, one provision was conspicuous by its presence and another by its absence.
> — Lord John Russell speech to the electors of the City of London, April 1859

Lord John attributed the coinage to a passage in Tacitus, relating to the funeral, in AD 22, of Junia, sister of Brutus and widow of Cassius:

> The effigies of twenty highly distinguished families headed the procession. But Cassius and Brutus were the most gloriously conspicuous—precisely because their statues were not to be seen.
> — Tacitus *Annals*

conspiracy see ➤ CATO *Street Conspiracy*.

constable the governor of a royal castle; formerly, the highest-ranking official in a royal household. Recorded from Middle English, the word comes via Old French from Latin *comes stabuli* 'count (head officer) of the stable'.

The use of *constable* to mean 'an officer of the peace' is also recorded from Middle English; the current sense of the lowest rank of police officer dates from the mid 19th century.

See also ➤ LORD *High Constable*, ➤ OUTRUN *the constable*.

Constable of England one of the chief functionaries in the English royal household, who together with the Earl Marshal was the judge of the Court of Chivalry. Also called *Lord High Constable*.

Constable of France the principal officer of the household of the early French kings, who ultimately rose to be commander-in-chief of the army in the absence of the monarch.

Constable of Scotland a chief officer in the Scottish royal household, having powers of jurisdiction in respect of all transgressions committed within four miles of the king's person, the parliament or privy council.

Council of Constance the 16th ecumenical council of the Roman Catholic Church (1414–18), which brought to an end the ➤ GREAT *Schism*.

constant see ➤ AVOGADRO's *constant*, ➤ PLANCK's *constant*.

constant dropping wears away a stone proverbial saying, mid 13th century, earlier in Greek.

Constantine (*c*.274–337), Roman emperor; known as **Constantine the Great**. He was the first Roman emperor to be converted to Christianity and in 324 made Christianity a state religion, though paganism was also tolerated. In 330 he moved his capital from Rome to Byzantium, renaming it *Constantinopolis* (➤ CONSTANTINOPLE). In the Orthodox Church he is venerated as a saint.

See also ➤ DONATION *of Constantine*.

Constantinople the former name for Istanbul from AD 330 (when it was given its name by Constantine the Great) to the capture of the city by the Turks in 1453. *Constantinople* is the anglicized form of *Constantinopolis*, 'city of Constantine'.

Constituent Assembly the parliamentary assembly of revolutionary France, set up in 1789 under the formal name of *Assemblée Nationale Constituante*; it was replaced by the Legislative Assembly in 1791.

The name Constituent Assembly was subsequently used for the body elected in 1917 in the first phase of the Russian Revolution; it was dissolved in 1918 by the Bolsheviks.

the Constitution the basic written set of principles and precedents of federal government in the US, which came into operation in 1789 and has since been modified by twenty-six amendments.

See also ➤ CONSTITUTIONS *of Clarendon*, ➤ *the* FATHER *of the Constitution*.

Constitution State informal name for Connecticut, where the draft US Constitution was ratified in 1788.

consubstantiation the doctrine, especially in Lutheran belief, that the substance of the bread and wine coexists with the body and blood of Christ in the Eucharist. It was formulated in opposition to the doctrine of ➤ TRANSUBSTANTIATION.

consul in ancient Rome, one of the two annually elected chief magistrates who jointly ruled the republic; any of the three chief magistrates of the first French republic (1799–1804). The word derives ultimately from Latin *consulere* 'take counsel'.

See also ➤ FIRST *Consul*.

consumption dated term for a wasting disease, especially pulmonary tuberculosis.

contango on the British Stock Exchange, the normal situation in which the spot or cash price of a commodity is lower than the forward price; formerly, a percentage paid by a buyer of stock to postpone transfer to a future settling day.

Recorded from the mid 19th century, the word is probably an arbitrary formation on the pattern of Latin verb forms ending in *-o* in the first person singular, perhaps with the idea 'I make contingent'.

contango day on the British Stock Exchange, the eighth day before a settling day.

contemplative a person whose life is devoted primarily to prayer, especially in a monastery or convent.

contempt see also ➤ FAMIILIARITY *breeds contempt*.

contempt of court the offence of being disobedient to or disrespectful of a court of law and its officers.

contemptibles see ➤ OLD *Contemptibles*.

continent see ➤ DARK *Continent*.

Continental Army in the US, the army raised by the Continental Congress of 1775, with George Washington as commander.

Continental Congress in the US, each of the three congresses held by the American colonies in revolt against British rule in 1774, 1775, and 1776 respectively. The second Congress, convened in the wake of the battles at Lexington and Concord, created a Continental Army, which fought and eventually won the ➤ *War of* AMERICAN *Independence*.

Continental Divide the main series of mountain ridges in North America, chiefly the crests of the Rocky Mountains, which form a watershed separating the rivers flowing eastwards into the Atlantic Ocean or the Gulf of Mexico from those flowing westwards into the Pacific.

continental drift the gradual movement of the continents across the earth's surface through geological time.

The reality of continental drift was confirmed in the 1960s, leading to the theory of plate tectonics. It is believed that a single supercontinent called Pangaea broke up to form Gondwana and Laurasia, which further split to form the present-day continents. South America and Africa, for example, are moving apart at a rate of a few centimetres per year.

Continental Sunday Sunday as a day of recreation (as held to be customary in Continental Europe) rather than of rest and worship.

Continental System the plan of Napoleon Bonaparte for cutting off Great Britain from all connexion, political, commercial, and personal, with the continent of Europe; instituted by the Berlin Decree of 19th November, 1806, which declared the British Islands in a state of blockade, forbad all commerce with them, and ordered the arrest of all British subjects on the continent.

continuous creation the creation of matter as a continuing process throughout time, especially as postulated in steady state theories of the universe.

Contra a member of a guerrilla force in Nicaragua which opposed the left-wing Sandinista government 1979–90, and was supported by the US for much of that time.

contraries see ➤ DREAMS *go by contraries*.

contredanse a French form of country dance, originating in the 18th century and related to the quadrille; the word comes from French, and is an alteration of English *country dance*, by association with *contre* 'against, opposite'.

conundrum a question asked for amusement, typically one with a pun in its answer; a riddle; a confusing and difficult problem or question. The word is of unknown origin, but is first recorded (in the late 16th century) in a work by Thomas Nashe, as a term of abuse for a crank or pedant, later coming to denote a whim or fancy, also a pun. Current senses date from the late 17th century.

conventicle a secret or unlawful religious meeting of people with nonconcormist views; the **Conventicles Acts** were two acts of Charles II, 'to prevent and suppress seditious Conventicles'.

Convention parliament an assembly of the Houses of Parliament meeting without the summons of the Sovereign, as that of 1660, which restored Charles II, and that of 1688, which declared the throne abdicated by James II.

conversation see ➤ CRIMINAL *conversation*.

conversus former term for a lay-brother in a Benedictine monastery.

Convocation in the Church of England, a representative assembly of clergy of the province of Canterbury or York.

Captain James Cook (1728–79), English explorer. On his first expedition to the Pacific (1768–71), he charted the coasts of New Zealand and New Guinea as well as exploring the east coast of Australia and claiming it for Britain. He made two more voyages to the Pacific before being killed in a skirmish with native people in Hawaii.
   See also ➤ CAPTAIN *Cooker*.

Thomas Cook (1808–92), English founder of the travel firm Thomas Cook. In 1841 he organized the first publicly advertised excursion train in England; the success of this venture led him to organize further excursions both in Britain and abroad, laying the foundations for the tourist and travel-agent industry.

Cook's tour a rapid tour of many places; named after the travel firm founded by ➤ *Thomas* COOK.

> Persinger took me on a Cook's tour of his neuroscientific theories.
> — *Independent on Sunday* 2 July 1995

Cookie Monster a member of the ➤ MUPPETS, a large blue friendly creature characterized by its sweet tooth and voracious appetite.

> [The] White House budget director . . . warns that federal spending is 'the ultimate Cookie Monster', capable of gobbling up everything in its path.
> — *Independent on Sunday* 28 January 1990

cooks ➤ *St* LAWRENCE and ➤ *St* MARTHA are the patron saints of cooks.

too many cooks spoil the broth proverbial saying, late 16th century.

cool as a cucumber completely calm; the term is recorded from the mid 18th century.

Cool Britannia Britain, perceived as a stylish and fashionable place; especially (in the late 1990s) as represented by the international success of and interest in contemporary British art, popular music,
film, and fashion. The term was widely used but not universally liked; in 1998 the veteran Labour politician Tony Benn commented dryly, 'When I think of Cool Britannia, I think of old people dying of hypothermia.'

Coon a nickname for a member of the old Whig party of the United States, which at one time had the *raccoon* as an emblem.

cooper a craftsman who makes and repairs wooden vessels formed of staves and hoops, as casks, barrels, buckets, and tubs. The word is recorded from Middle English, and comes ultimately (via Middle Dutch and Middle Low German) from Latin *cupa* 'tub, vat'.

James Fenimore Cooper (1789–1851), American novelist. He is renowned for his tales of American Indians and frontier life, in particular *The Last of the Mohicans* (1826).

> They try to move stealthily through the underbrush like Fenimore Cooper's Indians.
> — *Prairie Fire* Autumn 1992

See also ➤ *the Last of the* MOHICANS, ➤ *Natty* BUMPPO.

Cooperative Wholesale Society a British co-operative society, the largest in the world, formed in 1863. It acts as a manufacturer, wholesaler, and banker for the numerous cooperative retail societies by which it is owned and controlled.

Copenhagen name of the Duke of Wellington's chestnut charger, which he rode during the Peninsular campaign and at Waterloo. Wellington said of him, 'There may have been many faster horses, no doubt many handsomer, but for bottom and endurance I never saw his fellow.'
   Copenhagen, who was the grandson of the famous racehorse ➤ ECLIPSE, was buried at Stratfield Saye with full military honours. He figures in the equestrian statue of Wellington opposite the entrance of Apsley House in London.

Copernican system the theory that the sun is the centre of the solar system, with the planets (including the earth) orbiting round it.

Nicolaus Copernicus (1473–1543), Polish astronomer. He proposed a model of the solar system in which the planets orbited in perfect circles around the sun, and his work ultimately led to the overthrow of the established geocentric cosmology. He published his astronomical theories in *De Revolutionibus Orbium Coelestium* (1543).

King **Cophetua** a legendary African king who fell in love with and married a beggar girl; the story is told in one of the ballads in Percy's *Reliques* (1765), and was the subject of one of Burne-Jones's best-known Pre-Raphaelite paintings, *King Cophetua and the Beggar Maid* (1884).

> Her discoloured, old blue frock and her broken boots seemed only like the romantic rags of King Cophetua's beggar-maid.
> — D. H. Lawrence *Sons and Lovers* (1913)

copper a red-brown metal, the earliest metal to be used by humans, first by itself and then later alloyed with tin to form bronze; it was associated by alchemists with the planet Venus.

Recorded from Old English (in form *copor*, *coper*), the word is ultimately based on late Latin *cuprum*, from Latin *cyprium aes* 'Cyprus metal', so named because Cyprus was the chief source.

See also ➤ UP *to a point, Lord Copper*.

Copper Age the Chalcolithic period, especially in SE Europe, when weapons were made of copper.

copper-bottomed thoroughly reliable, certain not to fail; figuratively, from earlier usage referring to the copper sheathing of the bottom of a ship.

copperhead a stout-bodied venomous snake with coppery-pink or reddish brown coloration, which has become the type of secret or unexpected hostility, since unlike the rattlesnake it strikes without warning. During the American Civil War, *Copperhead* was a derogatory nickname among Unionists for a Northern sympathizer with the Secessionists of the South.

Copt a native Egyptian in the Hellenistic and Roman periods; a member of the Coptic Church. The word comes via French *Copte* or modern Latin *Coptus*, from Arabic *al-ḳibṭ, al-ḳubṭ* 'Copts', and ultimately (via Coptic) from Greek *Aiguptios* 'Egyptian'.

Coptic the language of the Copts, which represents the final stage of ancient Egyptian. It now survives only as the liturgical language of the Coptic Church.

Coptic Church the native Christian Church in Egypt, traditionally founded by St Mark, and adhering to the Monophysite doctrine rejected by the Council of Chalcedon. Long persecuted after the Muslim Arab conquest of Egypt in the 7th century, the Coptic community now make up about 5 per cent of Egypt's population.

copybook a book containing models of handwriting for learners to imitate.

See also ➤ BLOT *one's copybook*.

copyright the exclusive legal right, given to the originator or their assignee for a fixed number of years, to print, publish, perform, film, or record literary, artistic, or musical material, and to authorize others to do the same.

copyright library a library entitled to a free copy of each book published in the UK. The copyright libraries in the British Isles are the British Library, the Bodleian Library, Cambridge University Library, the National Library of Wales, the National Library of Scotland, and the library of Trinity College, Dublin.

coral a hard stony substance secreted by certain marine coelenterates as an external skeleton, typically forming large reefs in warm seas; the precious red variety of this, used in jewellery.

Coral Sea a part of the western Pacific lying between Australia, New Guinea, and Vanuatu, the scene of a naval battle between US and Japanese carriers in 1942.

coranto the name ('current of news') applied to periodical news-pamphlets issued between 1621 and 1641 (their publication was interrupted 1632–8) containing foreign intelligence taken from foreign papers. They were one of the earliest forms of English journalism, and were followed by the newsbook.

corban an offering or sacrifice made to God by the ancient Hebrews; the treasury of the Temple at Jerusalem (the earliest sense in English) as where such offerings were placed. The word comes ultimately via popular Latin and New Testament Greek from Hebrew *qorbān* 'offering'.

corbel a projection jutting out from a wall to support a structure above it; a **corbel table** is a projecting course of bricks or stones resting on corbels. Recorded from late Middle English, the word comes from Old French, diminutive of *corp* 'crow', from Latin *corvus* 'raven', perhaps because of the shape of a corbel, resembling a crow's beak.

corbie in Scottish usage, a raven, crow, or rook; the word is recorded from late Middle English, and comes, like ➤ CORBEL, from Old French *corp* 'crow'.

corbie messenger one who returns too late or not at all, with reference to Genesis 8:7, and the raven sent out from the ark 'which went to and fro, until the waters were dried up from the earth', in contrast to the dove, which returned to the ark when she could find no resting-place.

Corcovado a high peak on the south side of Rio de Janeiro; a gigantic statue of Christ, 40 m (131 ft) high, named 'Christ the Redeemer', stands on its summit.

Charlotte Corday 1768–93), French political assassin. She became involved with the Girondists and in 1793 assassinated the revolutionary leader Jean Paul Marat in his bath; she was found guilty of treason and guillotined four days later.

> You were a very terrible person, a sort of Charlotte Corday in a schoolgirl's dress; a ferocious patriot.
> — Joseph Conrad *Nostromo* (1904)

Cordelia in Shakespeare's play, the youngest of the three daughters of King ➤ LEAR, who is rejected by her father as ungrateful when she refrains from extravagant statements of her love for him, but who unlike her elder sisters is loyal to him; she is seen as a figure of loving duty and self-sacrifice.

> In her attempt to shatter the Cordelia-like silence of Nicole Stewart and Elizabeth Rosen, Garner seeks out their young feminist supporters.
> — *New Yorker* 7 July 1997

Cordelier a Franciscan Observant; so named from the knotted cord (Old French *cordelle* 'small rope') which these friars wore around the waist.

The *Cordeliers* were one of the political clubs of the French Revolution; the name derived from the meeting-place of the club, a former convent of the Franciscan Cordeliers.

Cordoba a city in Andalusia, southern Spain. Founded by the Carthaginians, it was under Moorish rule from 711 to 1236, and as capital of the most powerful of the Arab states in Spain, it was a centre of learning and culture, and was renowned for its architecture, particularly the Great Mosque.

See also ➤ CORDOVAN.

cordon bleu a cook of the highest class. The term (in French, literally 'blue ribbon') is recorded from the mid 18th century; the blue ribbon once signified the highest order of chivalry in the reign of the Bourbon kings.

cordon sanitaire a guarded line preventing anyone from leaving an area infected by a disease and thus spreading it; the term is recorded from the 19th century.

cordovan a kind of soft leather made originally from goatskin and now from horsehide; the word is recorded from the late 16th century, and comes from *Cordova*, a variant of ➤ CORDOBA, where it was originally made.

corduroy a thick cotton fabric with velvety ribs; the word is recorded from the late 18th century, and probably comes from *cord* 'ribbed fabric' + *duroy*, denoting a kind of lightweight worsted formerly made in the West of England; the ultimate origin is unknown, although the word is sometimes wrongly explained as representing a supposed French *corde du roi* 'king's cord'.

corduroy road historical term for a road made of tree trunks laid across a swamp; the term is first recorded in the US in the early 19th century.

cordwainer a shoemaker (still used in the names of guilds); the word is recorded from Middle English, and comes ultimately from Old French *cordewan* 'of Cordoba' (see ➤ CORDOVAN).

Marie Corelli (1855–1924), English writer of romantic fiction. The sales of her novels *Thelma* (1887), *Barabbas* (1893), and *The Sorrows of Satan* (1895) broke all existing records for book sales, although popularity was not matched by critical acclaim.

Corineus in the Middle English poem *The Brut*, a Roman ally of ➤ BRUTUS who wrestled with and defeated ➤ GOGMAGOG.

Corinth a city on the north coast of the Peloponnese, Greece, a prominent city state in ancient Greece, which was celebrated for its artistic adornment, and which became a type of luxury and licentiousness.

Corinthian[1] relating to or denoting the lightest and most ornate of the classical orders of architecture (used especially by the Romans), characterized by flared capitals with rows of acanthus leaves.

Corinthian[2] from the proverbial luxury and licentiousness of Corinth, *Corinthian* was used from the late 16th century for a wealthy (and profligate) man. In the early 19th century the term was extended to mean a man of fashion, and finally, a wealthy amateur of sport.

Corinthian brass an alloy, said to be of gold, silver, and copper, produced at ➤ CORINTH, and much prized in ancient times as the material of costly ornaments.

Epistle to the Corinthians either of two books of the New Testament, epistles of St Paul to the Church at Corinth.

Gaius Marcius Coriolanus (5th century BC), Roman general, who got his name from the capture of the Volscian town of Corioli, but whose pride, despite his military prowess and fame, was so offensive to the people of Rome that he was banished. According to legend, he subsequently led a Volscian army against the city and was only turned back by the pleas of his mother and wife.

> He was not a Coriolanus but a democratic technician.
> — Saul Bellow *It All Adds Up* (1994)

Cormoran a Cornish giant killed by ➤ JACK *the Giant-killer.*

cormorant a rather large diving bird with a long neck, long hooked bill, short legs, and mainly dark plumage, which is taken as the type of an insatiably greedy or rapacious person. The name is recorded from Middle English, and comes via Old French from medieval Latin *corvus marinus* 'sea-raven'.

corn see also ➤ *after* LAMMAS *corn ripens as much by night as by day,* ➤ ANTI-*Corn-Law-League,* ➤ PHARAOH's *corn,* ➤ SARACEN *corn.*

corn circle another term for a ➤ CROP *circle.*

corn dolly a symbolic or decorative model of a human figure, made of plaited straw.

corn in Egypt a plentiful supply; from Genesis 42:2 'Behold, I have heard that there is corn in Egypt: get you down thither and buy for us from thence.'

Corn Law Rhymer a name for Ebenezer Elliott (1781–1849), the Yorkshire poet and former Chartist whose opposition to the Corn Laws became his consuming interest, and who was the author of the 'Corn-law Rhymes (1831).

Corn Laws in the UK, a series of 19th-century laws introduced to protect British farmers from foreign competition by allowing grain to be imported only after the price of home-grown wheat had risen above a certain level. They had the unintended effect of forcing up bread prices and were eventually repealed in 1846.

cornage a feudal 'service', being a form of rent fixed by the number of horned cattle; also called *horngeld.* The term comes from via Old French from

Latin *cornu* 'horn', and was formerly widely misunderstood, and explained as a duty to blow a horn to warn of a border incursion or other danger.

Pierre Corneille (1606–84), French dramatist, generally regarded as the founder of classical French tragedy.

Cornelia (2nd century BC), mother of the Gracchi, famous in her day and after as the ideal Roman matron, distinguished for her virtue and her accomplishments.

corner see ➤ COFFIN *corner,* ➤ *the* FOUR *corners of the earth,* ➤ POETS' *Corner,* ➤ PUSS *in the corner.*

cornerstone a stone that forms the base of a corner of a building, joining two walls; an important quality or feature on which a particular thing depends or is based (often in biblical allusions, as in Isaiah 28:16, 'I lay in Zion…a precious corner stone, a sure foundation').

Cornhusker State an informal name for Nebraska.

Cornish see also ➤ *By* TRE, *Pol, and Pen, you shall know the Cornish men.*

Cornish the ancient Celtic language of Cornwall, belonging to the Brythonic branch of the Celtic language group. It gradually died out in the 17th and 18th centuries, although attempts have been made to revive it.

Cornish hug a special 'lock' used in ➤ CORNISH *wrestling.*

Cornish wrestling a local form of wrestling in which contestants, wearing loose canvas jackets, try to throw their opponent by grappling, tripping, and other techniques.

cornstalk a former nickname for a non-Aboriginal native of Australia, recorded from the early 19th century.

cornucopia a symbol of plenty consisting of a goat's horn overflowing with flowers, fruit, and corn. The word comes (in the early 16th century) from late Latin, from Latin *cornu copiae* 'horn of plenty', a mythical horn able to provide whatever is desired, in Greek mythology supposedly the horn of the goat ➤ AMALTHEA which suckled Zeus.

Duchy of Cornwall an estate vested in the Prince of Wales, consisting of properties in Cornwall and elsewhere in SW England.

coronach in Scotland or Ireland, a funeral song; the word is recorded from the early 16th century and was originally Scots, denoting the outcry of a crowd, from Scottish Gaelic *corranach* (Irish *coranach*), from *comh-* 'together' + *rànach* 'outcry'.

coronary gold money awarded in lieu of a crown to a victorious Roman general (translating Latin *coronarium aurum*).

Coronation stone another name for the ➤ STONE *of Scone.*

Coronation Street a fictitious street in, and the title of, a television soap opera (1960–) set in a working-class street in the middle of an industrial city in the north of England.

> The one thing you have a job to find in Manchester is the one thing you might reasonably expect to see—row after row of huddled Coronation Streets.
> — Bill Bryson *Notes from a Small Island* (1995)

coroner an official who holds inquests into violent, sudden, or suspicious deaths, and (in Britain) inquiries into cases of treasure trove. Formerly also, an official responsible for safeguarding the private property of the Crown. The name is recorded from Middle English, and comes ultimately from Anglo-Norman French *corune* 'a crown', reflecting the Latin title *custos placitorum coronae* 'guardian of the pleas of the crown'.

coronet a relatively simple crown, now especially as worn by lesser royalty and peers or peeresses (in Shakespeare's *Julius Caesar* (1599), Casca, describing the crown offered by Antony to Caesar, says, ''Twas not a crown neither, 'twas one of these coronets').

corporal see ➤ *the* LITTLE *Corporal,* ➤ SEVEN *corporal works of mercy.*

corporations have neither bodies to be punished nor souls to be damned proverbial saying, mid 17th century.

corposant an appearance of ➤ *St* ELMO*'s fire* on a mast, rigging, or other structure; the word is recorded from the mid 16th century and comes from Old Spanish, Portuguese, and Italian *corpo santo* 'holy body'.

corpse-candle a lambent flame seen in a churchyard or over a grave, and believed to appear as an omen of death, or to indicate the route of a coming funeral.

corpus a collection of written texts, especially the entire works of a particular author or a body of writing on a particular subject. The word (Latin, literally 'body') is recorded from late Middle English denoting an animal or human body; the textual sense dates from the early 18th century.

Corpus is now also used for a collection of written or spoken material in machine-readable form, assembled for the purpose of studying linguistic structures and frequencies.

See also ➤ HABEAS *corpus.*

Corpus Christi a feast of the Western Christian Church commemorating the institution of the Eucharist, observed on the Thursday after Trinity Sunday. The name is Latin, and means literally, 'body of Christ'.

corpus delicti the facts and circumstances constituting a breach of a law; the phrase is Latin, and means literally 'body of offence'.

corpuscular philosophy a term for the theory of matter put forward by ➤ *Robert* BOYLE (1627–91); in 1667 he published 'Origin of Forms and Qualities (According to the Corpuscular Philosophy)'.

correction see ➤ HOUSE *of correction.*

corrector see ➤ ALEXANDER *the Corrector.*

Antonio Correggio (*c.*1494–1534), Italian painter. The soft, sensual style of his devotional and mythological paintings influenced the rococo of the 18th century. He is best known for his frescoes in Parma cathedral.

the corridors of power the senior levels of government or administration, where covert influence is regarded as being exerted and significant decisions are made, from the title of C. P. Snow's novel *The Corridors of Power* (1964).

corroboree an Australian Aboriginal dance ceremony which may take the form of a sacred ritual or an informal gathering. The word comes from Dharuk *garaabara*, denoting a style of dancing.

corruption of blood the effect of attainder by which the person attainted could neither inherit, retain, nor transmit land.

corsair a privateer, especially one operating along the southern shore of the Mediterranean in the 17th century; the word comes (in the mid 16th century, via French) from medieval Latin *cursarius*, from *cursus* 'a raid, plunder'.

Byron's poem *The Corsair* (1814) told the story of a pirate chief, Conrad, whose chivalry and courage in the end outweigh his vices; the poem had great popular success, and Jane Austen, writing to her sister Cassandra in March 1814 notes, 'I have read the Corsair, mended my petticoat, & have nothing else to do.'

the Corsican a name for Napoleon Bonaparte, who was born in Corsica; he was also called by his enemies the **Corsican ogre**.

corsned in Anglo-Saxon law, a piece of bread of about an ounce weight consecrated by exorcism (*panis conjuratus*) which an accused person was required to swallow as a trial of his guilt or innocence.

Cortana in the legends of Charlemagne, name of a sword belonging to ➤ OGIER *the Dane*; every wound that it inflicted was mortal.

Cortes the legislative assembly of Spain and formerly of Portugal. The name is from Spanish and Portuguese, plural of *corte* 'court'.

Hernando Cortés (1485–1547), first of the Spanish conquistadores. Cortés overthrew the Aztec empire, conquering its capital, Tenochtitlán, in 1519 and deposing the emperor, Montezuma. In 1521 he destroyed Tenochtitlán completely and established Mexico City as the new capital of Mexico (then called New Spain), serving briefly as governor of the colony. Keats takes him as the type of an explorer looking at previously unknown lands, although in fact it was ➤ BALBOA rather than Cortés who was the first European to see the Pacific Ocean.

> Then felt I like some watcher of the skies
> When a new planet swims into his ken;
> Or like stout Cortez when with eagle eyes
> He stared at the Pacific.
> — John Keats 'On First Looking into Chapman's Homer'
> (1817)

Corunna a port in NW Spain. It was the point of departure for the Armada in 1588 and the site of a battle in 1809 in the Peninsular War, at which British forces under Sir John Moore defeated the French. Moore, who was killed in the battle, was buried in the city; the subject of a poem by the Irish writer Charles Wolfe (1791–1823):

> We buried him darkly at dead of night,
> The sods with our bayonets turning.
> — Charles Wolfe 'The Burial of Sir John Moore at
> Corunna' (1817)

Corvinus epithet of Matthias I, king of Hungary (1458–90), deriving from the raven (Latin *corvus*) on his escutcheon.

Corybant a priest of the fertility and nature goddess Cybele, whose worship involved wild dances and ecstatic states; the word **corybantic**, meaning wild, frenzied, derives from the name.

Corycian Cave a large cave on Mount Parnassus, the home of the nymphs, daughters of Pleistos, who were supposed to live there.

Corydon a shepherd who figures in the *Idylls* of Theocritus and the *Eclogues* of Virgil, and whose name has become conventional in pastoral poetry.

> 'Gad, what a debauched Corydon!' said my lord.
> — William Makepeace Thackeray *Vanity Fair* (1848)

coryphaeus in ancient Greek drama, the leader of a chorus; the word comes (in the early 17th century) from Greek *koruphaios* 'chief, chorus-leader', from *koruphē* 'head, top'.

Cosa Nostra a US criminal organization resembling and related to the Mafia. The name is Italian, meaning literally 'our affair'.

Cosimo de' Medici (1389–1464), Italian statesman and banker; known as **Cosimo the Elder**. He laid the foundations for the Medici family's power in Florence, becoming the city's ruler in 1434 and using his considerable wealth to promote the arts and learning.

Cosmati name of a family of architects, sculptors, and mosaicists living in Rome in the 13th century; **Cosmati work**, a style of mosaic in which marble slabs are surrounded with borders made up of small pieces of marble and glass, is named after them.

cosmos the universe seen as a well-ordered whole; from the the Greek word *kosmos* 'order, ornament, world, or universe', so called by Pythagoras or his disciples from their view of its perfect order and arrangement.

Cossack a member of a people of southern Russia, Ukraine, and Siberia, noted for their horsemanship and military skill. The Cossacks had their origins in the 15th century when refugees from religious persecution, outlaws, adventurers, and escaped serfs banded together in settlements for protection. Under the tsars they were allowed considerable autonomy in return for protecting the frontiers; with the collapse of Soviet rule Cossack groups have reasserted their identity in both Russia and Ukraine.

The name comes through Russian from Turkic

kazak 'vagabond, nomad', a word which is ultimately also the base of ➤ CASSOCK.

Costa del Crime humorous term for a coastal holiday resort supposedly inhabited by criminals beyond the reach of an extradition treaty; the term is pseudo-Spanish, modelled on *Costa del Sol* 'coast of the sun', a resort region on the Mediterranean coast of southern Spain.

Costa Geriatrica humorous term for a coastal holiday resort area largely frequented or inhabited by elderly people; the expression dates from the 1970s, and is pseudo-Spanish, literally 'geriatric coast'.

costard a kind of cooking apple of large ribbed variety; the word is mentioned freqently between the 14th and the 17th centuries, after which the term passes out of general use, atlthough still retained by fruit growers for apples derived from the original *costard*.

costermonger a dated British term for a person who sells goods, especially fruit and vegetables, from a handcart in the street. The word is recorded from the early 16th century, when it denoted an apple seller, and comes from ➤ COSTARD.

costmary an aromatic plant of the daisy family, formerly used in medicine and in flavouring ale prior to the use of hops. The name is recorded from late Middle English, and comes from obsolete *cost* (via Latin, Greek, and Arabic from Sanskrit *kuṣṭha*, denoting an aromatic plant) + *Mary*, the mother of Christ (with whom it was associated in medieval times because of its medicinal qualities).

cotillion a dance with elaborate steps and figures, in particular, an 18th-century French dance based on the contredanse. In the US, a *cotillion* is a formal ball, especially one at which debutantes are presented. The word is recorded from the early 18th century, and comes from French *cotillon* 'petticoat dance'.

cottage see ➤ LOVE *in a cottage*.

King Cotton cotton as the dominant commercial crop of the southern American states personified.

cotton famine the failure of the supply of cotton to the English cotton-mills during the American Civil War.

Cotton State informal name for Alabama.

Cottonian library the collection of Robert *Cotton* (1570–1631), deposited in the British Museum in 1753.

Cottonopolis nickname for the city of Manchester, in NW England, once a centre of the British cotton trade.

Cotys name of a Thracian goddess (also called *Cotytto*) whose worship was adopted in Corinth and perhaps Athens.

couch potato a person who takes little or no exercise and watches a lot of television. The term was coined in the US from a pun on *boob tube* as a slang expression for television; someone given to continuous viewing was a *boob tuber*, and the cartoonist Robert Armstrong drew the most familiar tuber, a potato, reclining on a couch watching TV. Following this, a club was formed called The Couch Potatoes, and the name was later registered as a trademark.

See also ➤ MOUSE *potato*.

couchant in heraldry, (of an animal) lying with the body resting on the legs and the head raised.

couché in heraldry, (of a shield) shown tilted, with the sinister corner uppermost.

Emile Coué (1857–1926), French psychologist, who propounded a system of psychotherapy using usually optimistic auto-suggestion; the sentence 'Every day, in every way, I am getting better and better' was to be said 15 to 20 times, morning and evening.

cough see ➤ LOVE *and a cough cannot be hid*.

coughs and sneezes spread diseases. Trap the germs in your handkerchief. Second World War health slogan, 1942.

council see also ➤ *Council of* CHALCEDON, ➤ *Council of* CONSTANCE, ➤ *Council of* TRENT, ➤ NICAEA.

Council of Ten the ruling body of the the Venetian Republic.

councils of war never fight proverbial saying, mid 19th century.

counsel see also ➤ NIGHT *brings counsel*.

counsel any of the advisory declarations of Christ and the Apostles, in medieval theology reckoned to be twelve, given as a means of attaining greater moral perfection.

counsel of perfection advice designed to guide one towards moral perfection (sometimes with reference to Matthew 19:21, 'If thou wilt be perfect, go and sell all that thou hast, and give to the poor'); ideal but impracticable advice.

Counsellor of State a member of a group of people appointed to act for the British monarch during a temporary absence abroad.

count a foreign nobleman whose rank corresponds to that of an earl; the term is recorded from late Middle English, and comes via Old French from Latin *comes*, *comit-* 'companion, overseer, attendant', in late Latin, 'person holding a state office'.

See also ➤ *Count* PALATINE.

Count of Britain one of two generals of the Roman province of Britannia in the 4th century.

Count of the Saxon Shore one of two generals of the Roman province of Britannia in the 4th century.

count out the House bring a sitting of the House of Commons to a close on counting the number of members present and finding it less than forty, the number required to 'make a house'; this must be done by the Speaker when attention is drawn to the matter.

don't count your chickens before they are hatched proverbial saying, late 16th century.

Counter-Reformation the reform of the Church of Rome in the 16th and 17th centuries which was stimulated by the Protestant Reformation. Measures to oppose the spread of the Reformation were resolved on at the ➤ *Council of* TRENT (1545–63) and the Jesuit order became the spearhead of the Counter-Reformation, both within Europe and abroad. Although most of northern Europe remained Protestant, southern Germany and Poland were brought back to the Roman Catholic Church.

counties see ➤ SIX *Counties*, ➤ TWENTY-*six Counties*.

counting see ➤ COUNTING *of the omer*.

country see also ➤ *country* MOUSE, ➤ GOD *made the country and man made the town*, ➤ *you can take the* BOY *out of the country but you can't take the country out of the boy.*

go to the country test public opinion by dissolving Parliament and holding a general election; the term is first recorded in a novel by Disraeli:

> What with church and corn together, and the Queen Dowager, we may go to the country with as good a cry as some other persons.
>
> — Benjamin Disraeli *Sybil* (1845)

Country Code a set of guidelines to be observed when walking, driving, or riding in the countryside.

country dance a traditional type of social English dance, in particular one performed by couples facing each other in long lines.

in the country of the blind, the one-eyed man is king proverbial saying, early 16th century.

happy is the country that has no history proverbial saying, early 19th century.

county a territorial division of some countries, forming the chief unit of local administration.

See also ➤ *County* PALATINE.

coup d'état a sudden, violent, and illegal seizure of power from a government; the phrase (French, literally 'blow of state') came into general use in the 19th century, but is recorded from the mid 17th century. The shorter *coup* is now frequently used.

coupon a voucher entitling the holder to a discount off a particular product; especially in wartime, a detachable ticket entitling the holder to a ration of food, clothes, or other goods. The word is recorded from the early 19th century, originally denoting a detachable portion of a stock certificate to be given up in return for payment of interest.

In 1918, *coupon* developed the transferred sense of a recommendation given to a parliamentary candidate by a party leader, in reference to the rationing system which had been in force during the war.

Coupon election informal name for the British general election of 1918, in which candidates for constituencies were given recommendations or 'coupons' by party leaders.

courage see ➤ DUTCH *courage*.

courant in heraldry, (of an animal) represented as running.

the course of true love never did run smooth proverbial saying, late 16th century; originally from Shakespeare's *A Midsummer Night's Dream*.

court a body of people presided over by a judge, judges, or a magistrate, and acting as a tribunal in civil and criminal cases; the establishment, retinue, and courtiers of a sovereign. The word is recorded from Middle English, and comes via Old French from Latin *cohors*, *cohort-* 'yard or retinue'.

See ➤ CONTEMPT *of court*, ➤ CROWN *Court*, ➤ KANGAROO *court*.

court baron the assembly of the freehold tenants of a manor under the presidency of the lord or his steward.

court card a playing card that is a king, queen, or jack of a suit. The term dates from the mid 17th century, and is an alteration of coat card, so named because of the decorative dress of the figures depicted.

court circular a daily report of the activities and public engagements of royal family members, published in some newspapers.

court dress formal clothing worn at a royal court; official clothing worn in a court of law by those in the legal profession.

court hand a notoriously illegible style of handwriting used in English law courts until banned in 1731; the Act in question stated that all proceedings should 'be written in such a common legible Hand and Character, as the Acts of Parliament are usually ingrossed in…and not in any Hand commonly called Court Hand, and in Words at Length and not abbreviated'.

court martial a judicial court for trying members of the armed services accused of offences against military law.
    See also ➤ DRUMHEAD *court martial*.

Court of Appeal a court of law that hears appeals against both civil and criminal judgements from the Crown Courts, High Court, and County Courts.

Court of Arches the ecclesiastical court of appeal for the province of Canterbury, so named because it was formerly held at the church of St Mary-le-Bow, famous for its arched crypt.

Court of Cassation in France, the name of the supreme court of appeal (French, *Cour de cassation*) as having the power in the last resort to alter, or cancel, or quash (*casser*) decisions of the other courts which are wrong in form or law.

Court of Conscience a small debt court; in figurative use, the conscience as a moral tribunal.

court of honour a court or tribunal for determining questions concerning the laws or principles of honour, as the courts of chivalry said formerly to have existed in Europe.

court of love an institution said to have existed in southern France in the Middle Ages, a tribunal composed of lords and ladies deciding questions of love and gallantry; such an institution in medieval literature.

Court of Peculiars a branch of the ➤ COURT *of Arches*, which had jurisdiction over the peculiars of the Archbishop of Canterbury.

Court of Piepowders a summary court formerly held at fairs and markets to administer justice among itinerant dealers and others temporarily present; *piepowder* is recorded from Middle English denoting a dusty-footed man or wayfarer, and comes via Anglo-Norman French from Anglo-Latin *pedepulverosus* 'dusty-footed', from Latin *pes, ped-* 'foot' + *pulvis, pulver-* 'dust'.

Court of Requests a former court of record, held by the Lord Privy Seal and the Masters of Requests for the relief of persons petitioning the king.

Court of St James's the British sovereign's court; St James's Palace was the chief royal residence between 1660 and 1837, when Queen Victoria moved to Buckingham Palace. It is currently the official London residence of the Prince of Wales.

Court of Session the supreme civil court in Scotland.

court plaster sticking plaster, originally black and in the 18th century used by ladies at court for beauty spots.

Samuel Courtauld (1876–1947), English industrialist. He was a director of his family's silk firm and a collector of French Impressionist and post-Impressionist paintings. He presented his collection to the University of London, endowed the **Courtauld Institute of Art**, and bequeathed to it his house in Portman Square, London.

courtesy title a title given to someone, especially the son or daughter of a peer, that has no legal validity.

courtly love a highly conventionalized medieval tradition of love between a knight and a married noblewoman, first developed by the troubadours of Southern France and extensively employed in European literature of the time. The love of the knight for his lady was regarded as an ennobling passion and the relationship was typically unconsummated.

cousin a child of one's uncle or aunt (more fully, one's **first cousin**); someone belonging to the same extended family. The word is recorded from Middle English, and comes via Old French from Latin *consobrinus* 'mother's sister's child', from *con-*

'with' + *sobrinus* 'second cousin' (from *soror* 'sister').

There are various phrases to indicate the degree of kinship, as **first cousin once removed**, a child of one's first cousin, or one's parent's first cousin, and **second cousin**, a child of one's parent's first cousin.

See ➤ CATER-*cousin*, ➤ *cross* COUSINS, ➤ KISSING *cousin*.

cousin german an old-fashioned term for cousin; *german* here comes from Old French *germain*, from Latin *germanus* 'genuine, of the same parents'.

cove a dated term meaning 'fellow, chap', perhaps deriving from Romany *kova* 'thing or person'.

coven a group or gathering of witches who meet regularly; the word is a variant of *covin* (archaic term for fraud, deception; in Middle English, denoting a company or band), and comes via Old French from Latin *convenium*, from *convenire* 'assemble'.

covenant see also ➤ DAY *of the Vow*, ➤ DEED *of covenant*, ➤ LAND *of the Covenant*, ➤ SOLEMN *League and Covenant*.

New Covenant in Christian theology, the covenant between God and the followers of Christ.

Old Covenant in Christian theology, the covenant between God and Israel in the Old Testament.

Covenant of Grace in theology, one of the two relations represented as subsisting between God and Man, before the Fall of Man and since the Atonement.

Covenant of Works in theology, one of the two relations represented as subsisting between God and Man, before the Fall of Man and since the Atonement.

Covenant Theology in the US, another name for ➤ FEDERAL *Theology*.

Covenanter an adherent of the National Covenant (1638) or the Solemn League and Covenant (1643), upholding the organization of the Scottish Presbyterian Church.

Covent Garden a district in central London, originally the convent garden of the Abbey of Westminster. It was the site for 300 years of London's chief fruit and vegetable market, which in 1974 was moved to Nine Elms, Battersea. The first Covent Garden Theatre was opened in 1732; and was several

times destroyed and reconstructed. Since 1946 it has been the home of the national opera and ballet companies, based at the Royal Opera House (built 1888).

send to Coventry refuse to associate with or speak to, perhaps deriving from the extreme unpopularity of soldiers stationed in *Coventry*, who were cut off socially by the citizens, or because Royalist prisoners were sent there during the Civil War, the city being staunchly Parliamentarian.

Coventry blue the best quality of blue dye, taken as a type of reliability; the term originally denoted a kind of blue thread manufactured at Coventry.

Miles Coverdale (1488–1568), English biblical scholar. He translated the first complete printed English Bible (1535), published in Zurich while he was in exile for preaching against confession and images. He also edited the Great Bible of 1539 by the printer Richard Grafton.

Coverdale's Bible the first complete printed English Bible (1535), translated by ➤ *Miles* COVERDALE.

Sir Roger de Coverley a character described in *The Spectator*, a country gentleman whose greatgrandfather supposedly invented the country dance called after him; he is shown as a typical 18thcentury country squire.

cow a *cow* is the emblem of ➤ *St* BRIDGET *of Ireland* and St Perpetua, a 3rd-century martyr of Carthage, who was gored by a mad heifer in her martyrdom.

In Egyptian mythology, the goddess ➤ HATHOR may be represented as a cow; in Greek mythology, ➤ Io was turned into a heifer by Zeus to protect her from Hera.

See also ➤ *a* BELLOWING *cow soon forgets her calf*, ➤ BETTER *a good cow than a cow of a good kind*, ➤ *Book of the* DUN *Cow*, ➤ DUN *Cow of Dunsmore*, ➤ *it is idle to* SWALLOW *the cow and choke on the tail*, ➤ SACRED *cow*, ➤ THREE *acres and a cow*, ➤ THREE *things are not to be trusted; a cow's horn, a dog's tooth, and a horse's hoof*, ➤ *the* TUNE *the old cow died of*.

cow parsley a European hedgerow plant of the parsley family, which has fern-like leaves and large heads of tiny white flowers, giving the appearance of lace. There is a traditional belief that bringing the flowers indoors may lead to a death.

why buy a cow when milk is so cheap? proverbial saying, mid 17th century.

cowabunga used to express delight or satisfaction. This fanciful word, recorded from the 1960s, was popularized by cartoons and the films *Teenage Mutant Ninja Turtles*; it was also recently used as surfers' slang.

coward a person who lacks the courage to do or endure dangerous things, possibly deriving from the Latin *cauda* 'tail', with reference to a frightened animal with its tail between its legs.

See also ➤ *a* BULLY *is always a coward*, ➤ CONSCIENCE *makes cowards of us all*.

cowards die many times before their death proverbial saying, late 16th century; often with allusion to Shakespeare's *Julius Caesar*, 'Cowards die many times before their deaths: The valiant never taste of death but once.'

cowboy a mounted man who tends and herds cattle, especially in the western US and as represented in westerns and novels.

Cowes a town on the Isle of Wight, southern England, which is internationally famous as a yachting centre.

Cowichan sweater in Canada, a thick sweater made with unbleached wool and decorated with symbols taken from the mythology of the Cowichan Indians of southern Vancouver Island.

cowl a large loose hood, especially one forming part of a monk's habit. Recorded from Old English (in form *cugele*, *cūle*) the word comes from ecclesiastical Latin *cuculla*, from Latin *cucullus* 'hood of a cloak'.

the cowl does not make the monk proverbial saying, late 14th century.

cowslip a European primula with clusters of drooping fragrant yellow flowers in spring, growing on dry grassy banks and in pasture. Balls made of cowslip flowers were traditionally used as a method of love divination.

coxcomb a vain and conceited man, ultimately from a variant of *cockscomb*, and referring to the design of a jester's cap.

coxswain the steersman of a ship's boat (originally the *cock* or *cockboat*).

coyote a wolf-like wild dog native to North America; the term **coyote diggings** was given to the small lateral shafts sunk by miners in California, resembling the holes of the coyote.

Coyote State informal name for South Dakota.

cozen to cheat or trick, recorded from the late 16th century, and perhaps through Italian ultimately from Latin *cocio* 'dealer'.

CQD the original ➤ SOS for shipping, used in the last signals sent by the ➤ TITANIC.

crab a crustacean with a broad carapace, stalked eyes, and five pairs of legs, the first pair of which are modified as pincers. With capital initial, the zodiacal sign or constellation ➤ CANCER.

See also ➤ CATCH *a crab*.

crack of dawn very early in the morning; the term (originally US) is recorded from the late 19th century.

crack of doom a thunder peal announcing the Day of Judgement; originally often as a quotation from Shakespeare's *Macbeth*, 'What, will the line stretch out to the crack of doom?'

cracker-barrel in North American usage (especially of a philosophy), plain, simple, and unsophisticated; with reference to the barrels of soda crackers once found in country stores, around which informal discussions would take place between customers.

the Craft the brotherhood of ➤ FREEMASONS; the expression is recorded from late Middle English.

Crail capon a Scottish term for a haddock.

crambo a game in which a player gives a word or line of verse to which each of the other players must find a rhyme. The word comes (in the early 17th century, denoting a particular fashion in drinking) from earlier *crambe* 'cabbage', used figuratively to denote something distasteful that is repeated, apparently from Latin *crambe repetita* 'cabbage served up again', applied by Juvenal to any distasteful repetition.

See also ➤ DUMB *crambo*.

cramp ring a ring held to be efficacious against cramp, falling sickness, and similar ailments, especially one of those which in pre-Reformation times was blessed on Good Friday for this purpose.

Thomas Cranmer (1489–1556), English Protestant cleric and martyr. After helping to negotiate Henry

VIII's divorce from Catherine of Aragon, he was appointed the first Protestant Archbishop of Canterbury in 1532. He was responsible for liturgical reform and the compilation of the Book of Common Prayer (1549). In the reign of Mary Tudor Cranmer was tried for treason and heresy and burnt at the stake.

Cranmer's Bible the 1540 edition of the ➤ GREAT *Bible*.

crannock a dry measure formerly in use in Wales, the west of England, and Ireland.

crannog an ancient fortified dwelling constructed in a lake or marsh in Scotland or Ireland. The name is recorded from the early 17th century and comes from Irish *crannóg*, Scottish Gaelic *crannag* 'timber structure', from *crann* 'tree, beam'.

crape black silk or imitation silk, formerly used for mourning clothes.

craps a gambling game played with two dice, chiefly in North America, perhaps deriving from *crab's eyes*, denoting the lowest throw (two ones) at dice.

crash see ➤ WALL *Street Crash*.

Marcus Licinius Crassus (*c*.115–53 BC), Roman politician. After defeating Spartacus in 71 BC, Crassus joined Caesar and Pompey in the First Triumvirate in 60. In 55 he was made consul and given a special command in Syria, where, after some successes, he was defeated and killed.

cravat a short, wide strip of fabric worn by men wound the neck and tucked inside an open-necked shirt. The term comes (through French) from Serbo-Croat, because of the scarf worn by Croatian mercenaries in France in the 17th century.

craven contemptibly lacking in courage; cowardly, perhaps ultimately (via Anglo-Norman French) from Old French 'crushed, overwhelmed', based on Latin *crepare* 'burst'.

Crazy Horse (*c*.1849–77), Sioux chief; Sioux name **Ta-Sunko-Witko**. A leading figure in the resistance to white settlement on American Indian land, he was at the centre of the confederation that defeated General Custer at Little Bighorn (1876). He surrendered in 1877 and was killed in custody.

a creaking door hangs longest proverbial saying, late 17th century.

the Creation the bringing into of existence of the universe, especially when regarded as an act of God.
   See also ➤ CONTINUOUS *creation*.

creation science the reinterpretation of scientific knowledge in accord with belief in the literal truth of the Bible, especially regarding the origin of matter, life, and humankind.

creationism the belief that the universe and living organisms originate from specific acts of divine creation, as in the biblical account, rather than by natural processes such as evolution.

creative accountancy the exploitation of loopholes in financial regulation in order to gain advantage or present figures in a misleadingly favourable light.

creature an animal, as distinct from a human being; originally, 'something created'.

Battle of Crécy a battle between the English and the French in 1346 near the village of Crécy-en-Ponthieu in Picardy, at which the forces of Edward III defeated those of Philip VI. It was the first major English victory of the Hundred Years War.

credence table a small table placed on the right hand of the high altar, for holding articles used in the service of the mass.

credibility gap an apparent difference between what is said or promised and what happens or is true.

give credit where credit is due proverbial saying, late 18th century.

credo a statement of the beliefs or aims which guide someone's actions; (with capital initial) a creed of the Christian Church in Latin. The word is Latin, literally 'I believe'.

credo quia impossibile popular summary of a saying by the Latin Church father Tertullian (AD *c*.160–*c*.225), '*Certum est quia impossibile est* [It is certain because it is impossible].'

the Creed a formal statement of Christian beliefs, especially the Apostles' Creed or the Nicene Creed.
   See also ➤ APOSTLES' *Creed*, ➤ ATHANASIAN *Creed*, ➤ NICENE *Creed*.

creeping to the Cross an informal term for the Adoration of the Cross, in the Roman Catholic Service for Good Friday.

Cremona a town in Lombardy, where the art of violin-making reached its highest perfection in the 17th and early 18th century.

Cremorne Gardens pleasure gardens in Chelsea, which were a popular place of entertainment during the middle of the 19th century, but which became notorious for irregularities and were closed in 1877.

Creole a person of mixed European and black descent, especially in the Caribbean; descendant of Spanish or other European settlers in the Caribbean or Central or South America; a white descendant of French settlers in Louisiana and other parts of the southern US.

Creole also denotes a mother tongue formed from the contact of a European language (especially English, French, Spanish, or Portuguese) with local languages (especially African languages spoken by slaves in the W. Indies), usually through an earlier pidgin stage.

The name comes via French and Spanish, probably from Portuguese *crioulo* 'black person born in Brazil, home-born slave', from *criar* 'to breed', from Latin *creare* 'produce, create'.

Creon name (meaning 'prince') given to several figures in Greek myth, especially the king of Corinth with whom Jason and Medea took refuge, and the brother of ➤ Jocasta, who became ruler of Thebes, and who as king was responsible for the death of ➤ Antigone.

crescent the curved sickle shape of the waxing or waning moon; in heraldry, the representation of this as a charge or a cadence mark for a second son in England.

The Crescent symbolizes the political power of Islam or of the Ottoman Empire.

See also ➤ Fertile *Crescent*, ➤ Red *Crescent*.

Crescent City a name for New Orleans, which is built on a curve of the Mississippi.

cresset a metal container of oil, grease, wood, or coal set alight for illumination and typically mounted on a pole, ultimately from Old French variant of *graisse* 'oil, grease'.

Cressida in medieval legends of the Trojan War, the daughter of Calchas, a Trojan priest. She was faithless to her lover Troilus, a son of Priam.

Crest in the UK, a computer system for buying and selling shares, introduced in 1996. The name is an arbitrary formation.

Cresta Run a hazardously winding, steeply banked channel of ice built each year at the Cresta Valley, St Moritz, Switzerland, as a tobogganing course, on which competitors race on light toboggans in a characteristic head-first position. Such a run was first built in 1884.

crestfallen sad and disappointed, from the original use referring to a mammal or a bird having a fallen or drooping crest.

Cretan bull the bull captured by Hercules as the seventh of his Labours; it may have been either the bull which became the father of the ➤ Minotaur, or the one which carried ➤ Europa to Crete.

Crete a Greek island in the eastern Mediterranean, noted for the remains of the Minoan civilization which flourished there in the 2nd millennium BC.

See also ➤ Dictys *Cretensis*.

cretin dated term for a person who is deformed and mentally handicapped because of congenital thyroid deficiency, originally (through French) from Swiss French *crestin* 'Christian' (from Latin *Christianus*), here used to mean 'human being', apparently as a reminder that, though deformed, *cretins* were human and not animals.

Creutzfeldt–Jakob disease a fatal degenerative disease affecting nerve cells in the brain, causing mental, physical, and sensory disturbances such as dementia and seizures. It is believed to be caused by prions and hence to be related to BSE and other spongiform encephalopathies such as kuru and scrapie.

Crewian oration a Latin oration delivered by the Public Orator at Oxford at the commemoration of the benefactors of the university, named after Nathaniel *Crew* (1633–1721), third Lord Crew of Stene and bishop of Durham, and established by his bequest.

James Crichton (1560–*c*.85), Scottish adventurer, known as **the Admirable Crichton**, an accomplished swordsman, poet, and scholar. He served in the French army and made a considerable impression on French and Italian universities with his skills as a polyglot orator. The epithet which became traditional was first applied to him in Johnstone's *Heroes Scoti* (1603) '*Iacobus Critonius Clunius, Musarum* *pariter ac Martis alumnus, omnibus in studiis, ipsis etiam Italis admirabilis*'; it first appeared in English in Urquhart's *Jewel* (1652) 'The admirable Crichtoun…did…present himself to epilogate this his almost extemporanean Comedie.'

The phrase **Admirable Crichton** was used as the title of a play by James Barrie (1914), in which the manservant Crichton, cast away with his employers on a desert island, becomes the natural leader of the party through his innate authority and skills; subsequent allusive uses often refer to the play.

> Inspector Neele raised his eyebrows. 'The admirable Miss Crichton.' 'I find one must *know* how to do everything oneself.'
> — Agatha Christie *A Pocket Full of Rye* (1953)

cricket an open-air game played on a large grass field with ball, bats, and two wickets, between teams of eleven players, the object of the game being to score more runs than the opposition; in the informal phrase **not cricket**, *cricket* is taken as exemplifying fairness and rectitude.

crime see also ➤ POVERTY *is not a crime.*

crime doesn't pay American proverb, a slogan of the FBI and the cartoon detective ➤ *Dick* TRACY.

Crimean War a war (1853–6) between Russia and an alliance of Great Britain, France, Sardinia, and Turkey. Russian aggression against Turkey led to war, with Turkey's European allies intervening to destroy Russian naval power in the Black Sea in 1854 and eventually capture the fortress city of Sebastopol in 1855 after a lengthy siege. In Britain the war was chiefly remembered for the deficiencies in the British army's medical services exposed by the work of Florence Nightingale and others.

criminal conversation adultery, especially as formerly constituting grounds for the recovery of legal damages by a husband from his wife's adulterous partner.

criosphinx a sphinx with a ram's head, one of three types of the Egyptian sphinx.

Hawley Harvey Crippen (1862–1910), American-born British murderer; known as **Doctor Crippen**. Crippen poisoned his wife at their London home and sailed to Canada with his former secretary; his arrest on board ship was achieved through the intervention of radio-telegraphy, the first case of its use

in apprehending a criminal; Crippen was later hanged.

Cripplegate a street in the City of London, thought to derive from an Old English term meaning 'covered way' referring to a postern gate to the Barbican; it was later popularly said to refer to the number of *cripples* who assembled to beg in the vicinity of St Giles's Church there, since St Giles is patron saint of the lame.

crisis a time of intense difficulty or danger; originally (in Middle English) denoting the turning point of a disease. The general sense 'decisive point' dates from the early 17th century.

See also ➤ BEDCHAMBER *Crisis.*

St Crispin 3rd-century martyr, probably of Roman origin, who according to his legend preached in Gaul with his brother **Crispinian**; they are said to have supported themselves by shoemaking, and became patron saints of cobblers, shoemakers, and leather-workers.

☐ **FEAST DAY** Their feast day is 25 October.

St Crispin's day 25 October, on which the Battle of Agincourt took place, and which is referred to by Henry V in Shakespeare's play:

> Then will he strip his sleeve and show his scars,
> And say, 'These wounds I had on Crispin's day.'
> — William Shakespeare *Henry V* (1599)

St Crispin's lance a name for a shoemaker's awl.

St Crispinian 3rd-century martyr, brother of ➤ *St* CRISPIN.

criss-cross a pattern of intersecting straight lines or paths, originating (in the 17th century) in *Christ-cross*, the figure of a cross preceding the alphabet in a hornbook.

critic see ➤ ARMCHAIR *critic.*

Cro-Magnon man the earliest form of modern human in Europe, associated with the Aurignacian flint industry. Their appearance *c.*35,000 years ago marked the beginning of the Upper Palaeolithic and the apparent decline and disappearance of Neanderthal man; the group persisted at least into the Neolithic period. The name comes from *Cro-Magnon*, a hill in the Dordogne, France, where remains were found in 1868.

> Some of the pictures of progress painted by 'netizens render modern-day society practically Cro-Magnon.
> — *Internet Underground* March 1996

croaking see ➤ *the croaking* RAVEN *bodes misfortune.*

Benedetto Croce (1866–1952), Italian philosopher and politician. In his 'Philosophy of Spirit' he denied the physical reality of a work of art and identified philosophical endeavour with a methodological approach to history. A former Minister of Education, he helped to rebuild democracy in Italy after the fall of Mussolini.

Davy Crockett (1786–1836), American frontiersman, soldier, and politician. He was a member of the House of Representatives 1827–35 and cultivated the image of a rough backwoods legislator. On leaving politics he returned to the frontier, where he took up the cause of Texan independence and was killed at the siege of the ➤ ALAMO.

Crockett almanacs popular pamphlets issued at irregular intervals by various publishers, supposedly by Davy Crockett or his heirs; about 50 appeared between 1835 and 1856. Beside the standard features of an almanac, they generally contain legends and stories of oral tradition about such figures as Daniel Boone and Kit Carson, or mythical creatures such as the sea serpent of Cape Cod.

Crockford informal name for **Crockford's Clerical Directory**, a reference book of Anglican clergy in the British Isles first issued in 1860.

Crockford's a famous gambling club established in 1827 at 50 St James's Street, London, by William Crockford (1775–1844); it is now in Curzon Street. Crockford was originally a fishmonger; he amassed £1,200,000 out of the club in a few years.

crocodile from the legend which gives rise to the phrase ➤ CROCODILE *tears*, a person making a hypocritical or malicious show of sorrow.

In Barrie's *Peter Pan,* ➤ *Captain* HOOK is stalked by, and finally falls victim to, the crocodile which has previously bitten off his hand.

crocodile tears tears or expressions of sorrow that are insincere, said to be so named from a belief that crocodiles wept while devouring or alluring their prey; the 16th-century account in *Hakluyt* (1600) of John Hawkins's voyages notes that 'his nature is ever when he would have his prey, to cry and sob like a Christian body, to provoke them to come to him, and then he snatcheth at them'.

Croesus (6th century BC), last king of Lydia *c.*560–546 BC. Renowned for his great wealth, he subjugated the Greek cities on the coast of Asia Minor before being overthrown by Cyrus the Great. At this point Croesus' fate becomes unclear; Cyrus is said to have cast him on a pyre from which he was saved by the miraculous intervention of Apollo.

> He is over seventy now and has his hair and teeth still and as rich as Croesus.
> — Barry Unsworth *Sacred Hunger* (1992)

cromlech in Wales, a megalithic tomb consisting of a large flat stone laid on upright ones, a ➤ DOLMEN. In Brittany, the term denotes a circle of standing stones. The name comes via French from Breton *krommlec'h.*

Samuel Crompton (1753–1827), English inventor of the spinning mule. He lacked the means to obtain a patent and sold his rights to a Bolton industrialist for £67; the House of Commons subsequently gave him £5,000 in compensation.

Oliver Cromwell (1599–1658), English general and statesman, ➤ LORD *Protector of the Commonwealth* 1653–8. Cromwell was the leader of the victorious Parliamentary forces (or Roundheads) in the English Civil War. As head of state he styled himself Lord Protector, and refused Parliament's offer of the Crown in 1657. His rule was notable for its puritan reforms in the Church of England. He was briefly succeeded by his son Richard (1626–1712), who was forced into exile in 1659.

See also ➤ *Hell or* CONNAUGHT, ➤ REGICIDE, ➤ RUSSET, ➤ WARTS *and all.*

Thomas Cromwell (*c.*1485–1540), English statesman, chief minister to Henry VIII 1531–40. He presided over the king's divorce from Catherine of Aragon (1533) and his break with the Roman Catholic Church as well as the dissolution of the monasteries and the 1534 Act of Supremacy. He fell from favour over Henry's marriage to Anne of Cleves and was executed on a charge of treason.

Cronian Sea in Milton's *Paradise Lost* (1667), the frozen sea of the north, seen as belonging to ➤ CRONUS.

croning a ceremony (frequently with a religious or spiritual element) performed, typically on her 60th birthday, to celebrate a woman's passing into old age; the term, originally US, is recorded from the early 1990s.

Cronus in Greek mythology, the supreme god until dethroned by ➤ ZEUS. The youngest son of Uranus (Heaven) and Gaia (Earth), Cronus overthrew and castrated his father and then married his sister

Rhea. Because he was fated to be overcome by one of his male children, Cronus swallowed all of them as soon as they were born, but when Zeus was born, Rhea deceived him and hid the baby away.

crony a close friend or companion. Recorded from the mid 17th century (originally as Cambridge university slang) the word comes from Greek *khronios* 'long-lasting' (here used to mean 'contemporary'), from *khronos* 'time'.

The word gained a high profile in the summer of 1998, when the Conservative leader William Hague used it in the House of Commons to describe what he saw as the undesirable influence of lobbyists:

> Feather-bedding, pocket-lining, money-grabbing cronies.
> — William Hague speech in the House of Commons, 8 July 1998

crook see ➤ *by* HOOK *or by crook.*

Crookback a nickname for ➤ RICHARD *III* as having a hunchback, as in Shakespeare's *3 Henry VI* (1592); Robert Fabyan's *Chronicle* (1494) records that it was earlier applied to Edmund of Lancaster (1245–96), who is also known as *Crouchback.*

croon hum or sing in a soft, low voice, especially in a sentimental manner. The use of *croon* in standard English was probably popularized by Robert Burns, as in *Tam o' Shanter* (1790), 'Whiles crooning o'er some auld Scots sonnet', and is now associated particularly with singers of the 1930s.

crop see also ➤ *good* SEED *makes a bad crop.*

crop circle an area of standing crops which have been flattened in the form of a circle or more complex form. No general cause of *crop circles* has been identified although various natural and unorthodox explanations have been put forward; many are known to have been hoaxes.

crop-eared of a Roundhead in the English Civil War, having the hair cut very short; the term was probably intended by their opponents to associate them with those whose ears had been cut off as a punishment.

Croppy a supporter of the Irish Insurrection of 1798, whose short hair signalled his sympathy with the French Revolution; the term is recorded from *c.*1798, especially as a derogatory term in Loyalist songs such as 'Croppies lie down'.

Croquemitaine name of a child-eating monster of French nursery stories, the 'Lord of Fear'; he is a tall, gaunt, and pallid figure of nightmare and the traditional defences against him are a clear conscience and a good digestion.

croquet a game played on a lawn, in which wooden balls are driven through a series of square-topped hoops by means of mallets; perhaps ultimately from a dialect form of French *crochet* 'hook'.

cross see also ➤ *cross the* RUBICON, ➤ *why did the* CHICKEN *cross the road.*

cross a mark, object, or figure formed by two short intersecting lines or pieces; especially (with capital initial), **the Cross** on which Christ was crucified, or a representation of this.

A *cross* is the emblem of ➤ *St* HELENA and ➤ *St* PHILIP.

See also ➤ CHARING *Cross,* ➤ CHRIST'*s cross me speed,* ➤ CREEPING *to the Cross,* ➤ CRISS-*cross,* ➤ ELEANOR *Cross,* ➤ EXALTATION *of the Cross,* ➤ FIERY *cross,* ➤ GENEVA *cross,* ➤ GEORGE *Cross,* ➤ INVENTION *of the Cross,* ➤ IRON *Cross,* ➤ MILITARY *Cross,* ➤ PAUL'*s cross,* ➤ RED *cross,* ➤ *St* ANTHONY'*s cross,* ➤ *St* GEORGE'*s cross,* ➤ *St* JOHN *of the Cross,* ➤ *St* PATRICK'*s cross,* ➤ SOUTHERN *Cross,* ➤ STATIONS *of the Cross,* ➤ VICTORIA *Cross,* ➤ *the* WAY *of the Cross,* ➤ WEEPING *Cross.*

Cross: specific forms

Calvary cross	Lorraine cross
capital cross	Maltese cross
Celtic cross	papal cross
cross potent	patriarchal cross
cross saltire	rosy cross
Greek cross	tau cross
Jerusalem cross	Teutonic cross
Latin cross	

---

cross and pile archaic term for the obverse and reverse side of a coin; head and tail.

cross bench a seat in the House of Lords occupied by a member who is independent of any political party; the term is recorded from the mid 19th century.

cross cousins each of two cousins who are children of a brother and sister.

cross keys keys borne crosswise, as in the papal arms.

cross-legged of the effigy of a knight shown with one leg laid over the other; the popular tradition that this represents a crusader, although long-enduring, is unhistorical, since the first such effigies are not found until *c.*1250 (when the era of the Crusades was drawing to a close), and the style continued for another 80 or so years.

cross of Lorraine another term for the ➤ LORRAINE *cross*.

cross potent in heraldry, having the limbs terminating in potents or crutch-heads.

at cross purposes with a misunderstanding of each other's meaning or intention, perhaps from *play at cross-purposes* take part in a parlour-game in which unrelated questions and answers were linked.

cross-questions and crooked answers a parlour game, recorded from the late 18th century, in which questions and answers which have nothing to do with one another are connected.

cross saltire a cross shaped like the letter X; this is the emblem of ➤ *St* ANDREW.

cross someone's palm with silver pay someone before having one's fortune told, originally by describing a cross on the fortune-teller's hand with a silver coin.

don't cross the bridge till you come to it proverbial saying, mid 19th century.

cross the floor in the British House of Commons, to change one's party allegiance, literally by moving across the *floor* or open space which divides the Government and the Opposition benches.

cross upside down a cross upside down is the emblem of ➤ *St* PETER, who was crucified head downwards.

crossbill a thickset finch with a crossed bill and red plumage, said in a medieval fable to derive from the bird's having attempted to pull the nails from the cross at Christ's crucifixion.

crossbones see ➤ SKULL *and crossbones*.

crosses see also ➤ NOUGHTS *and crosses*.

crosses are ladders that lead to heaven proverbial saying, early 17th century.

crossing the line informal expression for crossing the ➤ EQUATOR.

crossroads the place where two roads cross or intersect, formerly used as a burial-place for suicides; the *Examiner* of 23 November 1812 records that after a verdict of ➤ FELO *de se* brought in by the jury at an inquest, 'The body…was…buried in a

cross-road, with the customary ceremonies.'
     See also ➤ DIRTY *work at the crossroads.*

crossword a puzzle consisting of a grid of squares and blanks into which words crossing vertically and horizontally are written according to clues.

Crostarie another name for the ➤ FIERY *cross*, from Gaelic *cros-tàraidh, -tàra* cross of gathering.

Croton see ➤ MILO *of Croton.*

Crouchback nickname of Edmund of Lancaster (1245–96), who had a hunchback; he is also called ➤ CROOKBACK.

Crouchmas former name for the festival of the ➤ INVENTION *of the Cross*, observed on 3 May; *Crouch* here means 'Cross'.

crow a large perching bird with mostly glossy black plumage, a heavy bill, and a raucous voice; figurative uses may refer to carrion crows feeding on the bodies of the dead, and the bird is also taken as a type of blackness.
     A *crow* is the emblem of ➤ *St* ANTHONY *of Egypt* and St Paul the first hermit (see ➤ *St* PAUL²), who were brought by a loaf of bread by a crow or raven.
     See also ➤ EAT *crow*, ➤ JIM *Crow*, ➤ ONE *for the mouse, one for the crow.*

white crow a rare thing or event, a *rara avis*; the expression is recorded from the 16th century.

as the crow flies as directly as possible; the expression is recorded from the early 19th century.

Crow rate a reduced rate for transporting grain by rail from western to eastern Canada, legislated by the Crow's Nest Pass Agreement (1897), which ensured a subsidy to the Canadian Pacific Railway. This agreement was terminated in 1995.

crow steps the steplike projections on the sloping part of a gable, common in Flemish architecture and 16th- and 17th-century Scottish buildings.

Crowland see ➤ RAMSEY, *the rich of gold and fee.*

Aleister Crowley (1875–1947), son of a rich brewer turned Plymouth Brethren; Crowley was a diabolist who claimed to be the Beast from the Book of Revelation. He joined the Order of the Golden Dawn, a group of theosophists involved in Cabbalistic magic, of which Yeats was a member, and precipitated its dissolution when it rejected his claims to ascend to a higher spiritual grade.

crown a circular ornamental headdress worn by a monarch as a symbol of authority, usually made of or decorated with precious metals and jewels.

A *crown* is the emblem of ➤ *St* LOUIS, ➤ *St* OLAF, ➤ *St* WENCESLAS, and other royal saints.

The word is recorded from Middle English, and comes ultimately (via Anglo-Norman French and Old French) from Latin *corona* 'wreath, chaplet'.

See also ➤ *City of the* VIOLET *Crown*, ➤ CIVIC *crown*, ➤ IRON *Crown of Lombardy*, ➤ JEWEL *in the crown*, ➤ MURAL *crown*, ➤ OLIVE *crown*, ➤ PLEAS *of the Crown*, ➤ TRIPLE *crown*.

Crown Agents a body appointed by the British government to provide commercial and financial services, originally to British colonies, now to foreign governments and international bodies. It is responsible to the Minister for Overseas Development and its full title (as re-established in 1979) is the Crown Agents for Overseas Governments and Administrations.

crown and anchor a gambling game played with three dice each bearing a crown, an anchor, and the four card suits, and played on a board similarly marked.

Crown Colony a British colony whose legislature and administration is controlled by the Crown, represented by a governor. Some British dependencies within the Commonwealth still retain the designation, with varying degrees of self-government.

Crown Court in England and Wales, a court of criminal jurisdiction, which deals with serious offences and appeals referred from the magistrates' courts.

Crown jewels the crown and other ornaments and jewellery worn or carried by the sovereign on certain state occasions; the phrase is first recorded in English in the 17th century, in Milton's *Eikonoklastes* (1649), in which he described Queen Henrietta Maria's journey to Holland at the beginning of the Civil War 'where she pawned and set to sale the crown jewels'.

Crown of St Stephen the crown of the sovereigns of Hungary, which according to tradition was presented to ➤ *St* STEPHEN *of Hungary* by Pope Sylvester II.

crown of the sun a gold écu much current in England in the 15th–16th centuries.

crown of thorns with which Christ was crowned in mockery, as recounted in John 19:2, 'And the soldiers platted a crown of thorns, and put it on his head.' The *crown of thorns* is one of the ➤ *Instruments of the* PASSION, and may be used figuratively to indicate undeserved humiliation and suffering; the Labour politician Aneuran Bevan (1897–1960), commenting on his own position in the Labour Party of the mid 1950s, is reported as saying, 'Damn it all, you can't have the crown of thorns *and* the thirty pieces of silver.'

Crown prince in some countries, a male heir to a throne.

Crown princess in some countries, a female heir to a throne, or the wife of a Crown prince.

Crown Prosecution Service in England and Wales, an independent organization which decides whether cases brought by the police proceed to the criminal court. Its head is the Director of Public Prosecutions, with each region having its own Chief Crown Prosecutor.

crowning glory a woman's hair; perhaps originally with an echo of 1 Corinthians 11:15, 'if a woman have long hair, it is a glory unto her.'

crozier a hooked staff carried by a bishop as a symbol of pastoral office, originally denoting the person who carried a processional cross in front of an archbishop. Recorded from Middle English, the word comes partly from Old French *croisier* 'cross-bearer', from *croix* 'cross' based on Latin *crux*; reinforced by Old French *crocier* 'bearer of a bishop's crook'.

cru in France, a vineyard or group of vineyards, especially one of recognized superior quality. The word comes from French *crû*, literally 'growth'.

crucial decisive or critical; the sense 'decisive' is from Francis Bacon's Latin phrase *instantia crucis* 'crucial instance', which he explained as a metaphor from a *crux* or fingerpost marking a fork at a crossroad; Newton and Boyle took up the metaphor in *experimentum crucis*.

crucifer a person carrying a cross or crucifix in a procession.

crucifix a representation of a cross with a figure of Christ on it. The word is recorded from Middle English and comes via Old French and ecclesiastical Latin, from Latin *cruci fixus* 'fixed to a cross'.

crucifixion the execution of a person by nailing or binding them to a cross; practised by the ancient

Greeks and Romans, and considered particularly ig-
nominious; **the Crucifixion**, the killing of Jesus
Christ in such a way.

Alexander Cruden (1701–70), born in Aberdeen,
established a bookshop in London in 1732 and in
1737 published his *Biblical Concordance*; its later editions (1761 and 1769) remain standard works of reference. His eccentricities verged on insanity, and he
believed himself in later life called upon to reform
the nation.

See also ➤ ALEXANDER *the Corrector*.

the Cruel epithet applied to Pedro of Castile
(1334–69).

cruel and unusual punishment a term for punishment which is seen to exceed the bounds of what
is regarded as an appropriate penal remedy for a civilized society; it derives from the Eighth Amendment (1791) to the Constitution of the United States,
which says that, 'Excessive bail shall not be required,
nor excessive fines imposed, nor cruel and unusual
punishment inflicted.'

The question of over-harsh punishment was
much debated at this period; Gibbon in *The Decline
and Fall of the Roman Empire* (1776–88) putting forward the view, 'Whenever the offence inspires less
horror than the punishment, the rigour of penal law
is obliged to give way to the common feelings of
mankind.'

Cruella De Vil the wicked central character of
Dodie Smith's *One Hundred and One Dalmatians*
(1956), who steals Dalmatian puppies for their fur.

> She'd vroom up at midnight, like a crazed Cruella De Vil
> after the puppies had started their long journey home.
> — *Globe & Mail Report on Business* April 1993

cruelty see ➤ BEAUTY *without cruelty*, ➤ THEATRE
of Cruelty.

cruets are the emblems of ➤ St JOSEPH *of Arimathea* and ➤ St VINCENT *of Saragossa*.

Charles Cruft (1852–1939), English showman, who
in 1886 initiated the first dog show in London. The
Cruft's shows, held annually, have helped to raise
standards in dog breeding.

George Cruikshank (1792–1878), English painter,
illustrator, and caricaturist. The most eminent political cartoonist of his day, he was known for exposing the private life of the Prince Regent. His later
work includes illustrations for Charles Dickens's

Sketches by Boz (1836), and a series of etchings supporting the temperance movement.

cruise missile a low-flying missile which is guided
to its target by an on-board computer; the deploy-
ment of *cruise missiles* at the US airbase at
➤ GREENHAM *Common*, Berkshire, became the
focus for continuing protest in the 1970s and 1980s.

Crusade a medieval military expedition, one of a
series made by Europeans to recover the Holy Land
from the Muslims in the 11th, 12th, and 13th centuries. The First Crusade (1096–9) resulted in the
capture of Jerusalem and the establishment of **Crusader** states in the Holy Land, but the second
(1147–9) failed to stop a Muslim resurgence, and Jerusalem fell to Saladin in 1187. The third (1189–92)
recaptured some lost ground but not Jerusalem,
while the fourth (1202–4) was diverted against the
Byzantine Empire, which was fatally weakened by
the resultant sack of Constantinople. The fifth
(1217–21) was delayed in Egypt, where it accomplished nothing, and although the sixth (1228–9) resulted in the return of Jerusalem to Christian hands
the city was lost to the Turks in 1244. The seventh
(1248–54) ended in disaster in Egypt, while the
eighth and last (1270–1) petered out when its leader,
Louis IX of France, died on his way east.

The transferred use of *crusade* to mean a vigorous
movement or enterprise against poverty or a similar
social evil dates from the late 18th century, and is
first recorded in the writings of Thomas Jefferson,
'Preach, my dear Sir, a crusade against ignorance.'

See also ➤ CHILDREN'*s Crusade*.

Caped Crusader a name for the cartoon character
➤ BATMAN in his role as fearless crimefighter.

> Isotretinoin, a drug derived from vitamin A . . . is the
> caped crusader of the acne world, the last hope of the
> truly desperate.
> — *Independent* 29 November 1995

cruse see ➤ WIDOW'*s cruse*.

Robinson Crusoe the hero of Daniel Defoe's novel
Robinson Crusoe (1719), who survives a shipwreck
and lives on a desert island; the story is said to be
based on that of ➤ *Alexander* SELKIRK.

See also ➤ MAN *Friday*.

crusty a young person who is homeless or travels
constantly, has a shabby appearance, and rejects
conventional values. The term began to be used in
the early 1990s, and the culture associated with
crusties is also associated with New Age travellers.

crutch a crutch is the emblem of ➤ *St* GILES, who was traditionally lame.

Crutched Friars an order of mendicant friars established in Italy by 1169, which spread to England, France, and the Low Countries in the 13th century and was suppressed in 1656; the name comes (from obsolete *crouch* 'cross') from their bearing or wearing a cross, first on the top of their staves, and then on their habits, first in scarlet and then in blue.

crux a cross (from Latin); the term is recorded from the mid 17th century, chiefly in *crux ansata* ('cross with a handle'), a word for ➤ ANKH. From the early 18th century, the figurative use of the decisive or most important point at issue is recorded.

The *Crux* is the name of the smallest constellation (the Cross or Southern Cross), but the most familiar one to observers in the southern hemisphere.

cry see ➤ *cry* WOLF, ➤ HUE *and cry*, ➤ MUCH *cry, little wool*, ➤ SING *before breakfast, cry before night.*

don't cry before you're hurt proverbial saying; mid 16th century.

it is no use crying over spilt milk proverbial saying; mid 17th century.

cryonics the practice or technique of deep-freezing the bodies of those who have died of an incurable disease, in the hope of a future cure. The term is a contraction of cryogenics, the branch of physics dealing with the production and effects of very low temperatures.

Interest in the technique is recorded from the 1960s, although shortly before his death in 1996 ➤ *Timothy* LEARY announced that he had abandoned plans to have his head preserved by the cryonics movement, saying, 'I was worried that I would wake up in 50 years surrounded by people with clipboards.'

cryptography the art of writing or solving codes; the term is recorded from the mid 17th century.

crystal originally, ice, or a clear and transparent mineral resembling ice; a form of quartz (especially **rock-crystal**) having these qualities, which in ancient and medieval belief was thought to be congealed water or ice which had been 'petrified' by some natural process. *Crystal* was believed to have magic powers, and is taken as the type of something characterized by purity and clarity. The word is recorded from late Old English, and comes via French and Latin from Greek *krustallos* 'ice, crystal'.

From the early 17th century, *crystal* developed the sense in chemistry of a piece of a homogeneous solid substance having a natural geometrically regular form with symmetrically arranged plane faces.

crystal-gazing looking intently into a crystal ball with the aim of seeing images relating to future or distant events.

crystal healing the use of the supposed healing powers of crystals in alternative medicine.

Crystal Palace a large building of prefabricated iron and glass resembling a giant greenhouse, designed by Joseph Paxton for the Great Exhibition of 1851 in Hyde Park, London, and re-erected at Sydenham near Croydon; it was accidentally burnt down in 1936.

crystal wedding in the US, a 15th wedding anniversary.

crystalline sphere in ancient and medieval astronomy, a transparent sphere of the heavens postulated to lie between the fixed stars and the ➤ PRIMUM MOBILE and to account for the precession of the equinox and other motions.

crystallomancy divination by means of a crystal.

Cuban Missile Crisis an international crisis in October 1962, the closest approach to nuclear war at any time between the US and the USSR. When the US discovered Soviet nuclear missiles on Cuba, President John F. Kennedy demanded their removal and announced a naval blockade of the island; the Soviet leader Khrushchev acceded to the US demands a week later.

cube see ➤ RUBIK's *cube.*

cubism an early 20th-century style and movement in art, especially painting, in which perspective with a single viewpoint was abandoned and use was made of simple geometric shapes, interlocking planes, and, later, collage.

cubit an ancient measure of length, approximately equal to the length of a forearm. It was typically about 18 inches or 44 cm, though there was a **long cubit** of about 21 inches or 52 cm. The word comes (in Middle English) from Latin *cubitum* 'elbow, forearm, cubit'.

Cuchulain in Irish mythology, ➤ RED *Branch* hero of the Ulster cycle, and nephew of ➤ CONCHUBAR; he defends Ulster against the forces of the queen of Connaught, but at last (through the enmity of the

➤ Morrigan) is killed fighting heroically against overwhelming odds.

cucking stool a chair to which disorderly women were tied and then ducked into water or subjected to public ridicule as a punishment.

cuckold the husband of an adulteress, often regarded as an object of derision, ultimately derived from Old French *cucu* 'cuckoo', from the cuckoo's habit of laying its egg in another bird's nest.

cuckoo many cuckoos lay their eggs in the nests of small songbirds; the cuckoo fledgling, once hatched, pushes the songbird fledglings out of the nest, giving rise to the phrase **cuckoo in the nest** for an unwelcome intruder in a place or situation.

In Britain the first call of the cuckoo (a migratory bird) is traditionally a sign of spring.

See ➤ cloud *cuckoo land*.

cuckoo-flower a spring-flowering herbaceous plant with pale lilac flowers, growing in damp meadows and by streams; it is so named because it flowers at the time of year when the cuckoo is first heard calling.

cuckoo spit whitish froth found in compact masses on leaves and plant stems, exuded by the larvae of froghoppers, but traditionally believed to have been left by the cuckoo.

cucumber a long, green-skinned fruit with watery flesh, usually eaten raw in salads or pickled, taken as the type of something remaining cool under all circumstances.

cuddy informal (chiefly Scottish) name for a donkey, perhaps a pet form of the given name *Cuthbert*, once popular in Scotland and northern England.

cui bono who stands, or stood, to gain (from a crime, and so might have been responsible for it)? The phrase is Latin, and means 'to whom (is it) a benefit?'

Ely Culbertson (1891–1955), American bridge player. An authority on contract bridge, he revolutionized the game by formalizing a system of bidding. This helped to establish this form of the game in preference to auction bridge.

culchie in Ireland, a derogatory term for a country bumpkin, apparently an alteration of *Kiltimagh* (Irish *Coillte Mach*), the name of a country town in County Mayo, Ireland.

Culdee an Irish or Scottish monk of the 8th to 12th centuries, living as a recluse usually in a group of thirteen (on the analogy of Christ and his Apostles). The tradition ceased as the Celtic Church was brought under Roman Catholic rule.

The name is recorded from late Middle English, and comes from medieval Latin *culdeus*, alteration, influenced by Latin *cultores Dei* 'worshippers of God' of *kelledei* (plural, found in early Scottish records), from Old Irish *céle dé*, literally 'companion of God'.

Cullinan diamond the largest diamond known, presented by the people of the Transvaal to Edward VII as a birthday gift in 1907; two sections of it were set in the king's crown. The stone was named after Sir Thomas *Cullinan*, who had discovered the mine three years earlier.

Battle of Culloden the last pitched battle on British soil, and the final engagement of the Jacobite uprising of 1745–6, fought on *Culloden* moor near Inverness. The Hanoverian army under the Duke of Cumberland crushed the small and poorly supplied Jacobite army of Charles Edward Stuart, and a ruthless pursuit after the battle effectively prevented any chance of saving the Jacobite cause.

Nicholas Culpeper (1615–54), English herbalist. His *Complete Herbal* (1653) popularized herbalism and, despite embracing ideas of astrology and the doctrine of signatures, was important in the development of botany and pharmacology.

cult originally, homage paid to a divinity; later, a system of religious veneration and devotion directed towards a particular figure or object. The word comes (in the early 17th century, perhaps via French) from Latin *cultus* 'worship', from *cult-* 'inhabited, cultivated, worshipped'.

More recently, *cult* has been used for a relatively small group of people having religious beliefs or practices regarded by others as strange or sinister.

See also ➤ cargo *cult*.

cultivate one's garden attend to one's own affairs; after Voltaire (1694–1778) '*Il faut cultiver notre jardin* [We must cultivate our garden]', typifying the practical philosophy adopted by ➤ Candide.

cultural Chernobyl a cultural disaster; an event which is considered to be detrimental to the culture of a particular country, used originally and chiefly with reference to the opening of the Euro Disney theme park near Paris in April 1992. The phrase is a translation of French *Tchernobyl Culturel* (as used by the theatre director Ariane Mnouchkine) from the name *Chernobyl*, a city in Ukraine where in April 1986 an explosion at a nuclear power station resulted in a serious leak of radioactivity.

Cultural Revolution a political upheaval in China 1966–8 intended to bring about a return to revolutionary Maoist beliefs. Largely carried forward by the ➤ RED *Guard*, it resulted in attacks on intellectuals, a large-scale purge in party posts, and the appearance of a personality cult around Mao Zedong. It led to considerable economic dislocation and was gradually brought to a halt by premier Zhou Enlai.

culture see ➤ CANTEEN *culture*, ➤ DEPENDENCY *culture*, ➤ ENTERPRISE *culture*, ➤ TWO *cultures*.

culture shock the feeling of disorientation experienced by a person who finds himself or herself in a notably unfamiliar or uncongenial cultural environment; the term is recorded from the 1940s.

culture vulture humorous term for a person who is very interested in the arts, especially to an obsessive degree.

culver a pigeon, especially the woodpigeon; ultimately deriving from the Latin *columbula* diminutive of *columba* 'dove, pigeon'.

culverkeys a popular name of various plants, the flowers of which suggest a bunch of keys, as the bluebell and the cowslip; *culver* here means a dove or pigeon.

Cumaean designating the ➤ SIBYL of Virgil's *Aeneid*, who had her seat near Cumae, an ancient city on the Italian coast near Naples.

Butcher Cumberland William Augustus, Duke of *Cumberland* (1721–65), English military commander and third son of George II, gained great notoriety for the severity of his suppression of the Jacobite clans in the aftermath of his victory at the ➤ *Battle of* CULLODEN.

Although the victory was initially popular in England, reports of Cumberland's repressive measures were less well received, and according to a letter (1746) of Horace Walpole's, when it was proposed to make Cumberland a freeman of a city company, an alderman said, 'Then let it be of the Butchers.' In the same year a caricature was published showing him dressed as a calf in butcher's dress.

Cumbria an ancient kingdom of northern Britain; since 1974 the name has been used for a modern

county of NW England, formed largely from the former counties of Westmorland and Cumberland.

Cunarder a ship belonging to the *Cunard* Line, founded by Samuel Cunard (1787–1865) as the first regular steamship line for transatlantic passenger traffic.

cunctator a person who acts tardily, a delayer, often used with reference to Quintus Fabius Maximus *Cunctator*, Roman general in the war against Hannibal, whose delaying tactics were successful in wearing down his enemies' forces without the risk of a pitched battle.

cuneiform denoting or relating to the wedge-shaped characters used in the ancient writing systems of Mesopotamia, Persia, and Ugarit, surviving mainly impressed on clay tablets. The name comes ultimately (via French or modern Latin) from Latin *cuneus* 'wedge'.

cunning originally (in Middle English) the word meant (possessing) erudition or skill and had no implication of deceit; a **cunning man** or **cunning woman** was one who possessed such skill or learning. The sense 'deceitfulness' dates from late Middle English.

cup see also ➤ DIOGENES *cup*, ➤ *the* LAST *drop makes the cup run over*, ➤ FULL *cup, steady hand*.

cup a cup is the emblem of ➤ St JOHN *the Evangelist* and ➤ *St* BENEDICT.

cup-and-ring denoting marks cut in megalithic monuments consisting of a circular depression surrounded by concentric rings.

cup-bearer a person who serves wine, especially in a royal or noble household.

Cup Final the final match in a sports competition in which the winners are awarded a cup.

let this cup pass from me an appeal to be released from an ordeal; the allusion is to Christ in the Garden of Gethsemane, and his prayer 'If it be possible, let this cup pass from me' (Matthew 26:39). The implication is generally that the ordeal cannot be escaped, and must be endured.

he that will to Cupar maun to Cupar proverbial saying, early 18th century; *Cupar* is a town in Scotland.

cupboard see also ➤ SKELETON *in the cupboard*.

cupboard love affection that is feigned in order to obtain something; the expression is recorded from the mid 18th century, but there is a mid-17th century example of 'all for the love of a cupboard', in which the *cupboard* represents the food it contains.

Cupid in Roman mythology, the god of love, son of Venus. He is represented as a naked winged boy with a bow and arrows, with which he wounds his victims.

Cupid's bow a shape like that of the double-curved bow often shown carried by Cupid, especially at the top edge of a person's upper lip.

curate a member of the clergy engaged as assistant to a vicar, rector, or parish priest. The word is recorded from Middle English, and comes from medieval Latin *curatus*, from Latin *cura* 'care'.

curate's comfort a cake-stand with two or more tiers.

curate's egg a thing that is partly good and partly bad, from a cartoon in *Punch* (1895) depicting a meek curate who, given a stale egg at the bishop's table, assures his host that 'parts of it are excellent'.

cure see ➤ NO *cure, no pay*, ➤ PREVENTION *is better than cure*.

what can't be cured must be endured proverbial saying, late 16th century.

Curetonian the Syriac version of the Gospels discovered and edited by the Revd William *Cureton* (1808–64).

curfew a regulation requiring people to remain indoors between specified hours, typically at night. Originally denoting a regulation requiring people to extinguish fires at a fixed hour in the evening, or a bell rung at that hour, from Old French *cuevrefeu*, from *cuvrir* 'cover' + *feu* 'fire'. The current sense dates from the late 19th century.

Curia the papal court at the Vatican, by which the Roman Catholic Church is governed. It comprises various Congregations, Tribunals, and other commissions and departments.

The word is recorded from the mid 19th century, and comes from Latin *curia*, denoting a division of an ancient Roman tribe, also (by extension) the senate of cities other than Rome; later the term came to denote a feudal or Roman Catholic court of justice, whence the current sense.

Marie Curie (1867–1934), Polish-born French physicist, and her husband **Pierre Curie** (1859–1906)

French physicist, pioneers of radioactivity. Working together on the mineral pitchblende, they discovered the elements polonium and radium, for which they shared the 1903 Nobel Prize for Physics with A.-H. Becquerel. After her husband's accidental death Marie received another Nobel Prize (for chemistry) in 1911 for her isolation of radium. She died of leukaemia, caused by prolonged exposure to radioactive materials.

curiosa curiosities, especially erotic or pornographic books or articles.

curiosity killed the cat proverbial saying, early 20th century.

curiouser and curiouser more and more curious, increasingly strange (originally as a quotation from Lewis Carroll's *Alice in Wonderland* (1865), ' "Curiouser and curiouser!" cried Alice').

curlew a large wading bird of the sandpiper family, with a long downcurved bill, brown streaked plumage, and frequently a distinctive ascending two-note call. In early translations of the Bible, the name is used to represent the Greek word for a quail.

curling a game played on ice, especially in Scotland and Canada, in which large round flat stones are slid across the surface towards a mark. Members of a team use brooms to sweep the surface of the ice in the path of the stone to control its speed and direction.

curmudgeon a bad-tempered or surly person. Of unknown origin, although a correspondent of Dr Johnson attempted to assign an etymology to it based on the fusion of *coeur* 'heart' and *méchant* 'evil'; this was misunderstood by Ash in his dictionary.

the Curragh a level stretch of open ground in County Kildare, Ireland, famous for its racecourse and military camp.

Curragh mutiny informal name for the event at the Curragh camp in March 1914, when 60 cavalry officers stationed there resigned their commissions in the belief that they were to be used to force Ulster to accept Home Rule.

currant a small dried fruit made from a small seedless variety of grape originally grown in the eastern Mediterranean and much used in cookery.

Originally in Middle English as *raisons of Corauntz*, translating Anglo-Norman French *raisins de Corauntz* 'grapes of Corinth' (the original source).

currency see ➤ SINGLE *currency*.

curry favour ingratiate oneself with someone through obsequious behaviour, from an alteration of Middle English *curry favel*, from the name (*Favel* or *Fauvel*) of a chestnut horse in a 14th-century French romance who became a symbol of cunning and duplicity; hence 'to rub down Favel' meant to use the cunning which he personified.

curse a solemn utterance intended to invoke a supernatural power to inflict harm or punishment on someone or something. The word is recorded from Old English, but the origin is unknown.

See ➤ *curse of* CAIN.

curse of Scotland a name given to the nine of diamonds in a pack of cards, perhaps because it resembled the armorial bearings of Lord Stair, nine lozenges on a saltire, the number and shape of the spots being identical, and their arrangement similar. The first Earl of Stair was the object of much execration, especially from the adherents of the Stuarts, for his share in sanctioning the Massacre of Glencoe in 1692, and subsequently for the influential part played by him in bringing about the Union with England in 1707. An opponent said of him that he was 'at the bottom of the Union', and 'so he may be styled the Judas of the Country'.

curses, like chickens, come home to roost proverbial saying, late 14th century.

cursitor each of twenty-four officers of the Court of Chancery who until 1835 made out all writs *de cursu*, i.e. of the common official course or routine, for their respective counties.

Cursitor Baron a baron of the former Court of Exchequer appointed for fiscal rather than legal expertise.

cursive written with the characters joined. The term dates from the late 18th century, and comes via medieval Latin from Latin *curs*- 'run'.

Cursor Mundi a northern poem dating from about 1300, surviving in seven manuscripts of about 24,000 short lines. It is founded on the works of late 12th-century Latin writers who wrote various pseudo-histories made up of hagiographic, legendary, and biblical material.

curtain see ➤ BAMBOO *curtain*, ➤ IRON *curtain*.

curtal friar a friar with a short ('curtal' or shortened) habit; in some ballads of Robin Hood, the term is applied to Friar Tuck.

curtana the unpointed sword carried in front of English sovereigns at their coronation to represent mercy. The name is recorded from Middle English and comes from Anglo-Latin *curtana (spatha)* 'shortened (sword)', from Old French *cortain*, the name of a sword belonging to ➤ ROLAND (the point of which was damaged when it was thrust into a block of steel), from *cort* 'short', from Latin *curtus* 'cut short'.

Curthose nickname of Robert II, Duke of Normandy (1054?–1134), eldest son of William the Conqueror; the name means 'short boot' or 'short legging'.

Curtmantle nickname, meaning 'Short Mantle' of Henry II (1133–89), king of England.

curule denoting or relating to the authority exercised by the senior magistrates in ancient Rome, chiefly the consul and praetor, who were entitled to use the *sella curulis* ('curule seat', a kind of folding chair).

The word is recorded from the early 17th century and comes from Latin *curulis*, from *currus* 'chariot' (in which the chief magistrate was conveyed to the seat of office), from *currere* 'to run'.

Cush in the Bible, the eldest son of Ham and grandson of Noah (Genesis 10:6).

Cush is also the name of the southern part of ancient Nubia, first mentioned in Egyptian records of the Middle Kingdom. In the Bible it is the country of the descendants of Cush.

cusp in astrology, the initial point of an astrological house.

Custer's Last Stand popular name for the fight between the American cavalry and the Sioux at Little Bighorn in Montana in 1876, in which George Armstong *Custer* was killed.

custodiet see ➤ QUIS *custodiet ipsos custodes*.

the **customer** is always right proverbial saying, early 20th century.

custos rotulorum in England and Wales, the principal Justice of the Peace of a county, who has nominal custody of the records of the commission of the peace. The function is usually fulfilled by the Lord Lieutenant. The phrase is Latin.

custumal a written account of the customs of a manor or other local community or large establishment.

cut see also ➤ *most* UNKINDEST *cut of all*, ➤ *a* SHORT *cut is often the longest way round.*

don't **cut** off your nose to spite your face proverbial saying, mid 16th century.

cut the mustard chiefly in North America, succeed; come up to expectations, meet requirements; *mustard* means the real thing, the genuine article.

cut your coat according to your cloth proverbial saying, mid 16th century.

St **Cuthbert** (d. 687), English monk, who lived as a hermit on Farne Island before becoming bishop of Lindisfarne. After Viking raids on Lindisfarne at the end of the 9th century, Cuthbert's body was taken by the monks seeking a new home for the community; after years of travel, they settled at Durham, where Cuthbert's shrine now is.
    ◻ **FEAST DAY** His feast day is 20 March.

St **Cuthbert's** beads detached and perforated joints of fossil crinoids found along the Northumbrian coast.

St **Cuthbert's** duck the eider duck, which breeds on the Farne Islands.

cutpurse an archaic term for a pickpocket, with reference to stealing by cutting purses suspended from a waistband.

Moll Cutpurse nickname of Mary Frith (1584–1659), on whose life Middleton and Dekker's *The Roaring Girl* (1611) was based.

Cutty Sark the only survivor of the British tea clippers, launched in 1869 and now preserved as a museum ship at Greenwich, London.
    The name comes from Robert Burns's *Tam o' Shanter*, a poem about a Scottish farmer chased by a young witch who wore only her 'cutty sark' (= short shift).

cutty-stool in Scotland, a stool on which an offender was publicly rebuked during a church service; *cutty* here means 'low'.

Cybele a mother goddess worshipped especially in Phrygia and later in Greece (where she was associated with Demeter), Rome, and the Roman provinces, with her consort ➤ ATTIS.

Cyberia the space of virtual reality, especially viewed as a 'global village' or sphere of spiritual human interaction. The name comes from *cyber-*, combining form meaning, 'relating to electronic communications networks and virtual reality', suggested by *Siberia*.

cyberpunk a genre of science fiction set in a lawless subculture of an oppressive society dominated by computer technology.

Cyclades a large group of islands in the southern Aegean Sea, regarded in antiquity as circling around the sacred island of Delos.

cycle see also ➤ CALLIPPIC *cycle*, ➤ METONIC *cycle*.

cycle of the moon another name for the ➤ METONIC *cycle*.

cycle of the sun another name for the ➤ SOLAR *cycle*.

cyclic poet any of the writers of the ➤ EPIC *cycle*.

Cyclops a member of a race of savage one-eyed giants, said to have been the builders of the walls of Mycenae. In the Odyssey, ➤ ODYSSEUS escaped death by blinding the one-eyed ➤ POLYPHEMUS. The name comes via Latin from Greek *Kuklōps*, literally 'round-eyed', from *kuklos* 'circle' + *ōps* 'eye'.

Cyclopean of an ancient style of masonry in which the stones are of immense size and more or less irregular shape; found in Greece, Italy, and elsewhere, and once said to be the work of the ➤ CYCLOPS.

cygnet a young swan; the word comes (in late Middle English) from Anglo-Norman French *cignet*, diminutive of Old French *cigne* 'swan', based on Latin *cycnus*, from Greek *kuknos*.

Cygnus a prominent northern constellation (the Swan), said to represent a flying swan that was the form adopted by Zeus on one occasion.

Cymbeline (d. *c*.42 AD), British chieftain. A powerful ruler, he made Camulodunum (Colchester) his capital, and established a mint there. He was the subject of a medieval fable used by Shakespeare for his play *Cymbeline*.

Cymru the Welsh name for Wales.
See also ➤ PLAID *Cymru*.

Cymry the Welsh name for the Welsh.

Cynewulf (late 8th–9th centuries), Anglo-Saxon poet. Modern scholarship attributes four poems to him: *Juliana, Elene, The Fates of the Apostles,* and *Christ II*. Each of these is inscribed with his name in runes in Anglo-Saxon collections.

cynghanedd an intricate system of alliteration and rhyme in Welsh poetry.

Cynic a member of a school of ancient Greek philosophers founded by Antisthenes, marked by an ostentatious contempt for ease and pleasure. The movement flourished in the 3rd century BC and revived in the 1st century AD.

The name is recorded in English from the mid 16th century, and comes via Latin *cynicus*, from Greek *kunikos*; probably originally from *Kunosarges*, the name of a gymnasium where Antisthenes taught, but popularly taken to mean 'doglike, churlish', *kuōn, kun-*, 'dog' becoming a nickname for a Cynic.

cynosure a person or thing that is the centre of attention or admiration. The term comes (in the late 16th century, via French or Latin) from Greek *kunosoura* 'dog's tail' (also 'Ursa Minor'), and originally denoted the constellation Ursa Minor, or the pole star which it contains, long used as a guide by navigators.

Cynthia a name for ➤ ARTEMIS or Diana, from Mount Cynthus in Delos, where Artemis was born, and used poetically to denote the moon.

cypherpunk a person who uses encryption when accessing a computer network in order to ensure privacy, especially from government authorities.

cypress an evergreen coniferous tree with small rounded woody cones and flattened shoots bearing small scale-like leaves, used as a symbol of mourning.

St Cyprian (d. 258), Carthaginian bishop and martyr. The author of a work on the nature of true unity

in the Church in its relation to the episcopate, he was martyred in the reign of the Roman emperor Valerian.

☐ **FEAST DAY** His feast day is 16 September.

Cyprus an island in the eastern Mediterranean, famous in ancient times for the worship of ➤ APHRODITE or Venus; in the 18th and 19th centuries, *Cyprian* designated a prostitute.

Cyrano de Bergerac (1619–55), French soldier, duellist, and writer. He is chiefly remembered for the large number of duels that he fought (many on account of his proverbially large nose), as immortalized in a play by Edmond Rostand (*Cyrano de Bergerac,* 1897).

Cyrene an ancient Greek city in North Africa, near the coast in Cyrenaica, which from the 4th century BC was a great intellectual centre, with a noted medical school, and gave its name to the Cyrenaic school of philosophy founded by ➤ ARISTIPPUS.

See also ➤ SIMON *of Cyrene*.

St Cyricus reputed 4th-century martyr, said to have been put to death as a child with his mother Julitta, and traditionally counted as one of the ➤ FOURTEEN *Holy Helpers*. He may be shown as a naked child riding a boar, reflecting the story that he appeared to Charlemagne in a dream promising to save his life on a boar-hunt if the king would clothe him; this was interpreted by the bishop of Nevers as meaning that the king should repair the roof of the cathedral of St Cyr.

☐ **PATRONAGE** He is patron saint of children.

☐ **FEAST DAY** His feast day is 16 June (15 July in the Eastern Church).

St Cyril (826–69), Greek missionary. The invention of the ➤ CYRILLIC *alphabet* is ascribed to him. He and his brother, St *Methodius*, were sent to Moravia where they taught in the vernacular, which they adopted also for the liturgy, and circulated a Slavic version of the scriptures.

☐ **FEAST DAY** His feast day (in the Eastern Church) is 11 May; (in the Western Church) is 14 February.

St Cyril of Alexandria (d. 444), Doctor of the Church and patriarch of Alexandria. A champion of orthodoxy, he is best known for his vehement opposition to the views of the patriarch of Constantinople, Nestorius, whose condemnation he secured at the Council of Ephesus in 431. His extensive writings include a series of theological treatises, sermons, and letters.

□ **FEAST DAY** His feast day is 9 February.

Cyrillic alphabet used by many Slavic peoples, chiefly those with a historical allegiance to the Orthodox Church. Ultimately derived from Greek uncials, it is now used for Russian, Bulgarian, Serbian, Ukrainian, and some other Slavic languages.

Cyrus the Great (d. *c.*530 BC), king of Persia 559–530 BC and founder of the Achaemenid dynasty, father of Cambyses. He defeated the Median empire in 550 BC and went on to conquer Asia Minor, Babylonia, Syria, Palestine, and most of the Iranian plateau. He is said to have ruled with wisdom and moderation, maintaining good relations with the Jews (whom he freed from the Babylonian Captivity) and the Phoenicians.

Cyrus the Younger (d. 401 BC), Persian prince. On the death of his father, Darius II, in 405 BC, Cyrus led an army of mercenaries against his elder brother, who had succeeded to the throne as Artaxerxes II. His campaign is recounted by the historian Xenophon.

Cytherea another name for ➤ APHRODITE, from Latin *Cythera* 'Kithira', the name of an Ionian island.

czar an outdated variant of ➤ TSAR.

Dd

D the fourth letter of the modern English alphabet and of the ancient Roman one, corresponding to Greek *delta*, Hebrew *daleth*.

D-Day the day on which a particular operation is scheduled to begin; especially, (an anniversary of) 6 June 1944, when Allied forces invaded German-occupied northern France.

In Britain, *D-Day* was later also used for 15 February 1971, the day on which decimal currency came into official use.

Vasco da Gama (*c*.1469–1524), Portuguese explorer. He led the first European expedition round the Cape of Good Hope in 1497, sighting and naming Natal on Christmas Day before crossing the Indian Ocean and arriving in Calicut in 1498. He returned to Calicut (1502–3) to avenge a massacre of Portuguese settlers and also established colonies in Mozambique.

dacha a country house or cottage in Russia, typically used as a second or holiday home.

Dachau a Nazi concentration camp in southern Bavaria, from 1933 to 1945, in allusive use, a place of desolation; the slogan '*Arbeit macht frei* [Work liberates]' was inscribed on its gates (and later on those of ▶ AUSCHWITZ).

Dacia an ancient country of SE Europe in what is now NW Romania. It was annexed by Trajan in AD 106 as a province of the Roman Empire.

dactyl a metrical foot consisting of one stressed syllable followed by two unstressed syllables or (in Greek and Latin) one long syllable followed by two short syllables. Recorded from late Middle English, the word comes via Latin from Greek *daktulos*, literally 'finger', the three bones of the finger corresponding to the three syllables.

Idaean Dactyls in Greek mythology, magical smiths, living on either the Phrygian or the Cretan Mount Ida.

Dad's Army a name for the Second World War ▶ HOME *Guard*, from the title of the popular television series, written by Jimmy Perry and David Croft and first appearing in 1968, featuring the Home Guard of 'Walmington-on-Sea', led by the pompous bank manager Captain Mainwaring and his upper-class subordinate Sergeant Wilson, and featuring a range of men from the elderly butcher Corporal Jones to the young and naive Private Pike.

> The auxiliaries were a sort of 'Dad's Army' combination of older men and younger ones who lacked the experience for incorporation into active units.
> — Mark Urban *Big Boys' Rules* (1992)

Dada an early 20th-century international movement in art, literature, music, and film, repudiating and mocking artistic and social conventions and emphasizing the illogical and absurd. Dada was launched in Zurich in 1916 by Tristan Tzara and others, soon merging with a similar group in New York. It favoured montage, collage, and the ready-made, which all emphasize the anti-rational and the arbitrariness of creative form. The name is French, literally 'hobby-horse', the title of a review which appeared in Zurich in 1916.

Richard Dadd (1817–86), English painter. After killing his father while suffering a mental breakdown, he was confined in asylums, where he produced a series of visionary paintings, including *The Fairy Feller's Master-stroke* (1855–64).

daddy-long-legs an informal name for an insect with very long thin legs; in Britain, a crane fly, in North America, a harvestman.

In Jean Webster's novel *Daddy-Long-Legs* (1912), this is the playful name given by the young and orphaned heroine to the anonymous benefactor whom she eventually marries.

Daedalus in Greek mythology, a craftsman, considered the inventor of carpentry, who is said to have built the ▶ LABYRINTH for Minos, king of Crete. Minos imprisoned him and his son ▶ ICARUS, but they escaped using wings which Daedalus made and fastened with wax. Icarus, however, flew too near the sun and was killed.

daemon in ancient Greek belief, a divinity or supernatural being of a nature between gods and humans; an inner or attendant spirit or inspiring force. The word is recorded from the mid 16th century, and until the 19th century represented the common spelling of *demon*.

Daemon is the term used by Rudyard Kipling for his authorial inspiration:

> Let us now consider the Personal Daemon of Aristotle and others, of whom it has been truthfully written . . . : This is the doom of the Makers—their Daemon lives in their pen.
> If he be absent or sleeping, they are even as other men . . . Mine came to me early when I sat bewildered among other notions, and said, 'Take this and no other.' I obeyed and was rewarded.
>
> — Rudyard Kipling *Something of Myself* (1937)

daffodil a bulbous European plant which typically bears bright yellow flowers with a long trumpet-shaped centre. The name is recorded from the mid 16th century and comes from late Middle English *affodill* (the initial *d*- is unexplained), from medieval Latin *affodilus*, a variant of Latin *asphodilus* (see ➤ ASPHODEL). In poetry, the *daffodil* is associated with the approach of spring.

dagger a short knife with a pointed and edged blade, used as a weapon, which is the emblem of ➤ *St* EDWARD *the Martyr*, St Peter the Martyr, a 13th-century Dominican friar and priest born in Verona, who was attacked and killed while travelling from Como to Milan (he was wounded in the head with an axe, while the friar who was with him was stabbed), St Olaf (see ➤ OLAF *II Haraldsson*), and ➤ *St* WENCESLAS.

In printing, *dagger* is another name for an ➤ OBELUS.

See also ➤ BRIDPORT *dagger*, ➤ CLOAK-*and-dagger*.

dagger of lath the weapon worn by Vice in a morality play.

dagoba a stupa or dome-shaped structure containing Buddhist relics.

Dagobert the name of several ➤ MEROVINGIAN kings.

Dagon in the Bible, a national deity of the ancient Philistines, represented as a fish-tailed man. The name comes via Latin and Greek from Hebrew *dāgōn*, perhaps from *dāgān* 'corn', but said (according to folk etymology) to be from *dāg* 'fish'.

Louis-Jacques-Mandé Daguerre (1789–1851), French physicist, painter, and inventor of the first practical photographic process. He went into partnership with Joseph-Nicéphore Niépce (1765–1833)

to improve the latter's heliography process, and in 1839 he presented his *daguerreotype* process to the French Academy of Sciences.

Dagwood sandwich in North America, a thick sandwich with a variety of fillings, named (in the 1970s) after *Dagwood* Bumstead, a comic-strip character, suitor and later husband of ➤ BLONDIE, who makes and eats this type of sandwich.

Black Dahlia name given in press reports to the victim of a notorious and unsolved American murder case, in which the mutilated body of a young actress was discovered in Los Angeles in 1947.

Dáil the lower House of Parliament in the Republic of Ireland, composed of 166 members (called **Teachti Dála**). It was first established in 1919, when Irish republicans proclaimed an Irish state.

daimyo in feudal Japan, one of the great lords who were vassals of the shogun; the word comes from Japanese, from *dai* 'great' + *myō* 'name'.

dairymaids ➤ *St* BRIDGET *of Ireland* is the patron saint of dairymaids.

daisy a small European grassland plant which has flowers with a yellow disc and white rays, and which is associated with spring; in informal use (chiefly US) something regarded as first-rate or charming.

See also ➤ *it is not* SPRING *until you can plant your foot upon twelve daisies.*

Dalai Lama the spiritual head of Tibetan Buddhism and, until the establishment of Chinese communist rule, the spiritual and temporal ruler of Tibet. Each Dalai Lama is believed to be the reincarnation of the bodhisattva Avalokitesvara, reappearing in a child when the incumbent Dalai Lama dies. The present Dalai Lama, the fourteenth incarnation, escaped to India in 1959 following the invasion of Tibet by the Chinese and was awarded the Nobel Peace Prize in 1989.

The name is from Tibetan, literally 'ocean monk', so named because he is regarded as 'the ocean of compassion'.

Dalek in science fiction, a member of a race of hostile alien machine-organisms which appeared in the BBC television serial *Dr Who* from 1963; they are characterized by their staccato mechanical utterance, and their catch-phrase, 'Exterminate! Exterminate!'

The name is an invented word, coined by the

author Terry Nation after a volume of an encyclopedia covering the alphabetical sequence *dal–lek*.

> 'Two minutes 'til we go live people,' announces the officious dalek over the tannoy.
> — *MOJO* February 1995

Arthur Daley Cockney con-man noted for his cunning and frequently unsuccessful deals, a central character in the TV series *Minder* (1979–85 and 1988–94).

> London's art dealers are a tough breed. Behind the hauteur of most W1 *antiquaires* lies business acumen that would not shame Arthur Daley.
> — *Daily Telegraph* 5 December 1995

Salvador Dali (1904–89), Spanish painter. A surrealist, he portrayed dream images with almost photographic realism against backgrounds of arid Catalan landscapes.

> In the eerie blue light from the mercury-vapour lamp, the croissants took on a Daliesque look.
> — Paul Bowdring *Consolation of Pastry* (1994)

Dallas a city in NE Texas where President John F. Kennedy was assassinated in November 1963.

Dallas was also the title of a glitzy US soap (1978–91) featuring members of the warring and oil-rich Ewing family of Southfork Ranch, Texas.

Dalmatia an ancient region in what is now SW Croatia, comprising mountains and a narrow coastal plain along the Adriatic, together with offshore islands, which once formed part of the Roman province of Illyricum. *Dalmatian* dogs are so named because they are believed to have originated in Dalmatia in the 18th century.

dalmatic a wide-sleeved long, loose vestment open at the sides, worn by deacons and bishops, and by monarchs at their coronation. Recorded from late Middle English, the word comes via Old French *dalmatique* or late Latin *dalmatica*, from *dalmatica* *(vestis)* '(robe) of (white) Dalmatian wool', from *Dalmaticus* 'of Dalmatia'.

Dalriada an ancient Gaelic kingdom in northern Ireland whose people (the Scots) established a colony in SW Scotland from about the late 5th century. By the 9th century Irish Dalriada had declined but the people of Scottish Dalriada gradually acquired dominion over the whole of Scotland.

John Dalton (1766–1844), English chemist, father of modern atomic theory. He defined an atom as the smallest part of a substance that could participate in a chemical reaction and argued that elements are composed of atoms. He stated that elements combine in definite proportion and produced the first table of comparative atomic weights. Dalton also gave the first detailed description of colour blindness (**daltonism** derives from his name).

Dalton plan a system of education in which pupils are made responsible for the completion of assignments over fairly long periods, named (in the early 20th century) after *Dalton*, Massachusetts, where the first school used the plan.

daltonism a term for a form of colour blindness named after ➤ *John* DALTON.

Damascene of or relating to the city of ➤ DAMASCUS, and particularly used in the phrase **Damascene conversion**, in allusion to the conversion of St Paul on the ➤ *road to* DAMASCUS.

Damascus was famous for its metalworking, and *damascene* is also used to mean relating to or denoting a process of inlaying a metal object with gold or silver decoration.

Damascus the capital of Syria, a city which has existed for over 4,000 years, and which was famous for metalworking; it was on the ➤ *road to* DAMASCUS that St Paul was converted.

See also ➤ *St* JOHN *of Damascus*.

road to Damascus in the Bible, it was while Saul of Tarsus was travelling to Damascus in pursuit of Christians that he experienced the vision in which he heard the question, 'Saul, Saul, why persecutest thou me?', and was temporarily struck blind; when he recovered his sight, he became a convert (see ➤ *St* PAUL[1]) to the cause which he had formerly persecuted.

The term *road to Damascus* is now used for a sudden and complete personal conversion to a cause or principle which one has formerly rejected; Margaret Thatcher employed it in 1989 when commenting on Neil Kinnock as leader of the Labour Party:

> You don't reach Downing Street by pretending you've travelled the road to Damascus when you haven't even left home.
> — Margaret Thatcher in *Independent* 14 October 1989

Damascus steel steel made with a wavy surface pattern produced by hammer-welding strips of steel and iron followed by repeated heating and forging, used chiefly for knife and sword blades. Such items were often marketed, but not necessarily made, in Damascus during the medieval period.

damask a figured, lustrous woven fabric, with a pattern visible on both sides, originally produced in ➤ DAMASCUS.

damask rose a sweet-scented rose of an old variety (or hybrid) that is typically pink or light red in colour. The petals are very soft and velvety and are used to make attar.

Dambusters' raid informal name for the Second World War raid by 617 Squadron of the RAF, May 1943, on the Möhne and Eder dams in the Ruhr valley in Germany, using the ➤ BOUNCING *bomb* designed by ➤ *Barnes* WALLIS.

dame see ➤ *Dame* DURDEN, DAME PARTLET, ➤ PAIX *des Dames*.

Robert Francis Damiens (1715–57), attempted assassin of Louis XV of France; his execution, in the course of which he was dismembered, is described in detail by one of the revolutionaries in Dickens's *Tale of Two Cities* (1859).

> If a commoner gave a noble even so much as a Damiens-scratch which didn't kill or even hurt, he got Damiens' dose for it just the same; they pulled him to rags and tatters with horses, and all the world came to see the show.
> — Mark Twain *A Connecticut Yankee at the Court of King Arthur* (1889)

damn in Christian belief, to be **damned** is to be condemned by God to suffer eternal punishment in hell. The word comes (in Middle English, via Old French) from Latin *dam(p)nare* 'inflict loss on', from *damnum* 'loss, damage'.

damn with faint praise commend so feebly as to imply disapproval; from Pope's 'An Epistle to Dr Arbuthnot' (1735): 'Damn with faint praise, assent with civil leer, And without sneering, teach the rest to sneer.'

damnosa hereditas an inheritance or tradition bringing more burden than profit; a Latin phrase, meaning an inheritance that causes loss.

Damocles a legendary courtier who extravagantly praised the happiness of Dionysius I, ruler of Syracuse. To show him how precarious this happiness was, Dionysius seated him at a banquet with a sword hung by a single hair over his head. The

sword of Damocles is now used to refer to a precarious situation.

> Large blocks have fallen in the waterfall area and more hang damocles-like over the river waiting to obliterate oblivious gorge walkers.
> — *On the Edge* June 1998

Damon a legendary Syracusan of the 4th century whose friend *Pythias* (also called Phintias) was sentenced to death by Dionysius I. Damon stood bail for Pythias, who returned just in time to save him, and was himself reprieved.

> To many on the Hall board . . . Giamatti and Vincent are a modern Damon and Pythias. They are heroic figures—one the stout, earthy, charismatic intellectual; the other, the brilliant businessman and gentle compromiser.
> — Thomas Boswell *Cracking the Show* (1994)

William Dampier (1652–1715), English explorer and adventurer. He is notable for having sailed round the world twice. In 1683 he set out from Panama, crossing the Pacific and reaching England again in 1691; in 1699 the government commissioned him to explore the NW coast of Australia.

damsel archaic or poetic term for a young unmarried woman; also in the humorous **damsel in distress** for a young woman in difficulties. Recorded from Middle English, the word comes from Old French *dam(e)isele*, based on Latin *domina* 'mistress'.

Dan see also ➤ *Dan* DARE, ➤ DESPERATE *Dan*.

Dan¹ in the Bible, a Hebrew patriarch, son of Jacob and Bilhah, or the the tribe of Israel traditionally descended from him. *Dan* is also the name of an ancient town in the north of Canaan, where the tribe of Dan settled, and which marked the northern limit of the ancient Hebrew kingdom of Israel (see ➤ *from* DAN *to Beersheba*).

Dan² a former honorific, the equivalent of 'Master', or 'Sir'; later poetic and archaic uses probably derive from Spenser's 'Dan Chaucer, well of English undefiled' in *The Faerie Queene* (1596).

from Dan to Beersheba proverbial expression indicating a farthest extremity; *Dan* in biblical times marked the farthest northern point of the ancient Hebrew kingdom, and *Beersheba* the southern point.

> What profits it to have a covenanted State and a purified Kirk if a mailed Amalekite can hunt our sodgers from Dan to Beersheba?
> — John Buchan *Witch Wood* (1927)

Danae in Greek mythology, the daughter of Acrisius, king of Argos. An oracle foretold that she would bear a son who would kill her father, and in an attempt to evade this, Acrisius imprisoned her. Zeus visited her in the form of a shower of gold and she conceived ➤ PERSEUS, who killed Acrisius by accident.

Danaids in Greek mythology, the daughters of Danaus, king of Argos, who were compelled to marry the sons of his brother Aegyptus. Apart from one, Hypermnestra, who helped her husband to escape, the sisters murdered their husbands on the wedding night, and were punished in Hades by being set to fill a leaky jar with water.

dance see also ➤ GIANTS' *Dance*, ➤ PYRRHIC *dance*, ➤ St VITUS's *dance*.

they that dance must pay the fiddler proverbial saying, mid 17th century.

dance of death a medieval allegorical representation in which a personified Death leads people to the grave, designed to emphasize the equality of all before death.

dance the Tyburn jig be hanged; recorded from the late 17th century.

dancers ➤ St VITUS is the patron saint of dancers.

dandelion a widely distributed weed of the daisy family, with a rosette of jagged leaves, large bright yellow flowers followed by globular heads of seeds with downy tufts, and stems containing a milky latex. The name (recorded from late Middle English) comes from French *dent-de-lion*, translation of medieval Latin *dens lionis* 'lion's tooth', because of the jagged shape of the leaves.

Dandie Dinmont a terrier of a breed from the Scottish Borders, with short legs, a long body, and a rough coat; named after a farmer who owned a special breed of terriers portrayed in Sir Walter Scott's *Guy Mannering*.

dandiprat archaic term for a small boy or an insignificant person; the word is recorded from the early 16th century, denoting a coin worth three half-pence.

dandy a man unduly devoted to style, smartness, and fashion in dress and appearance; perhaps a shortened form of 17th-century *Jack-a-dandy* 'conceited fellow' (the last element representing *Dandy*, a pet form of the given name *Andrew*).

Dane a Viking invader of the British Isles in the 9th–11th centuries; the term in this sense, broadly covering all Norse invaders of the period and not just those coming from Denmark, is recorded from Old English.

See also ➤ OGIER *the Dane*.

Danegeld a land tax levied in Anglo-Saxon England during the reign of King Ethelred to raise funds for protection against Danish invaders; the term is also given to taxes collected for national defence by the Norman kings until 1162. The word is now often used allusively with reference to the likelihood that buying off an enemy will ensure their return for further payment, a view popularized in a poem by Kipling:

> And that is called paying the Dane-geld;
> But we've proved it again and again,
> That if once you have paid him the Dane-geld
> You never get rid of the Dane.
> — Rudyard Kipling 'What Dane-geld means' (1911)

Danelaw the part of northern and eastern England occupied or administered by Danes from the late 9th century until after the Norman Conquest.

danewort a dwarf elder with a strong, unpleasant smell and berries yielding a blue die that was formerly used to colour leather. The name derives from the folklore that the plant sprang up where Danish blood was spilt in battle.

danger see ➤ *the post of* HONOUR *is the post of danger*.

dangerous see ➤ DELAYS *are dangerous*.

Daniel a Hebrew prophet (6th century BC), who spent his life as a captive at the court of Babylon. In the Bible he interpreted the dreams of ➤ NEBUCHADNEZZAR and was delivered by God from the lions' den into which he had been thrown as the result of a trick.

In the apocryphal Book of ➤ SUSANNA he is portrayed as a wise judge, a role recalled by Shylock in his initial praise of ➤ PORTIA as 'a Daniel come to judgement'.

See also ➤ GODLIKE *Daniel*.

Dannebrog the national flag of Denmark. The word is Danish, and means literally 'Danish cloth'.

Order of Dannebrog a Danish order of knighthood, founded in 1219, revived in 1671, and regulated by various later statutes.

danse macabre another (French) term for the ➤ DANCE *of death*.

Dante Alighieri (1265–1321), Italian poet, whose reputation rests chiefly on *The Divine Comedy* (*c.*1309–20), an epic poem describing his spiritual journey through Hell and Purgatory and finally to Paradise. His love for *Beatrice* Portinari is described in *Vita nuova* (*c.*1290–4).

Georges Danton (1759–94), French revolutionary. A noted orator, he won great popularity in the early days of the French Revolution. He was initially an ally of Robespierre but later revolted against the severity of the Revolutionary Tribunal and was executed on Robespierre's orders; he is said to have told the executioner, 'Thou wilt show my head to the people: it is worth showing.'

Danube a river which rises in the Black Forest in SW Germany and flows into the Black Sea; it is the second-longest river in Europe after the Volga, and the cities of Vienna, Budapest, and Belgrade are situated on it.

Danube School a group of landscape painters working in the Danube region in the early 16th century. Its members included Altdorfer and Cranach the Elder.

Daphne in Greek mythology, a nymph who was turned into a laurel bush to save her from the amorous pursuit of Apollo.

Daphnis in Greek mythology, a Sicilian shepherd who, according to one version of the legend, was struck with blindness for his infidelity to the nymph Echenais. He consoled himself with pastoral poetry, of which he was the inventor.

dapple grey of a horse, grey or white with darker ring-like markings; dapple may be related to Old Norse *depill* 'spot'.

darbies an informal archaic term for handcuffs, from an allusive use of *Father Darby's bands*, a rigid from of agreement which put debtors in the power of moneylenders, possibly from the name of a 16th-century usurer.

Darby and Joan a devoted old married couple, living in placid domestic harmony, from a poem (1735) in the *Gentleman's Magazine*, which contained the lines 'Old Darby, with Joan by his side…They're never happy asunder.'

Darbyite a member of the Plymouth Brethren (and especially, the Exclusive Brethren), from the name John *Darby* (1800–82), founder of the sect.

Dardanelles a narrow strait between Europe and Asiatic Turkey (called the ➤ HELLESPONT in classical times), linking the Sea of Marmara with the Aegean Sea, which in 1915 was the scene of an unsuccessful attack on Turkey by Allied troops (see ➤ GALLIPOLI).

Dardanus in Greek mythology, ancestor of the kings of Troy, son of Zeus and Electra, daughter of the Titan Atlas. In the Trojan war, the enmity of Zeus' wife Hera towards the Trojans in part originated from her jealousy of Electra.

Dan Dare in a comic strip (1950–67) in *The Eagle*, the heroic Space Fleet Colonel who defended the universe against the ➤ MEKON and his evil allies.

Virginia Dare (b. 1587), the first white child to be born in America, who disappeared with other members of the ➤ LOST *Colony*.

daric a gold coin of ancient Persia, said to have been named after ➤ DARIUS.

Darien a sparsely populated province of eastern Panama, but originally designating the whole of the Isthmus of Panama; famously mentioned by Keats in his reference to 'stout Cortes…Silent upon a peak in Darien' (although it was ➤ BALBOA and not ➤ CORTÉS who was the first to see the Pacific here). At the end of the 17th century an unsuccessful attempt was made by Scottish settlers to establish a colony here, with the aim of controlling trade between the Atlantic and Pacific Oceans.

Darius (*c.*550–486 BC), king of Persia 521–486 BC, known as **Darius the Great**. He divided the empire into provinces, governed by satraps, developed commerce, built a network of roads, and connected the Nile with the Red Sea by canal. After a revolt by the Greek cities in Ionia he invaded Greece but was defeated at ➤ MARATHON.
  Darius was also the name of the last Achaemenid king of Persia (553–330 BC), defeated and dethroned by Alexander the Great (see ➤ ALEXANDER[1]).

dark see also ➤ COLD *dark matter*, ➤ LEAP *in the dark*.

Dark Ages the period in western Europe between the fall of the Roman Empire and the high Middle Ages, *c.*500–1100 AD, during which Germanic tribes swept through Europe and North Africa, often attacking and destroying towns and settlements. It is traditionally viewed as being a time of unenlightenment, though scholarship was kept alive in the monasteries and learning was encouraged at the courts of Charlemagne and Alfred the Great.

the dark and bloody ground a name for Kentucky, popularized by the American poet Theodore O'Hara (1820–67):

> Sons of the dark and bloody ground.
> — Theodore O'Hara 'The Bivouac of the Dead (1847)

The phrase is sometimes said to be the meaning of Kentucky as an Indian term, but this has been questioned; alternatively, it is said to derive from a warning given by a Cherokee chief in the late 18th century, that the land was already 'a bloody ground' from earlier hunting and fighting, and that it would be dark for prospective settlers.

it was a dark and stormy night one variant of an opening line intended to convey a threatening and doom-laden atmosphere; in this form used by the novelist Edward Bulwer-Lytton (1803–73) in his novel *Paul Clifford* (1830).

Dark Continent a name given to Africa at a time when it was little known to Europeans, first recorded in H. M. Stanley's *Through the Dark Continent* (1878).

dark horse a person about whom little is known, especially someone whose abilities or potential for success is concealed. The term is originally racing slang, denoting a horse about whose racing powers little is known, and is first recorded in the mid 19th century.

Dark Lady the woman to whom a number of Shakespeare's sonnets were written; the Elizabethan scholar A. L. Rowse suggested that she may have been Emilia Lanier (1569–1645), but she has never been certainly identified; an alternative name is that of Mary Fitton (1578–1647).

dark of the moon the time near to a new moon when there is no moonlight.

dark star a starlike object which emits little or no visible light. Its existence is inferred from other evidence, such as the eclipsing of other stars.

darkest hour is just before the dawn proverbial saying, mid 17th century.

darkness see ➤ PRINCE *of Darkness.*

Darley Arabian with the Byerley Turk and the Godolphin Barb, one of the three founding sires of

the Thoroughbred, imported to improve the stock in the 18th century.

Grace Darling (1815–42), English heroine. The daughter of a lighthouse keeper on the Farne Islands, in September 1838 she and her father rowed through a storm to rescue the survivors of the wrecked ship *Forfarshire.*

Mr Darling father of Wendy and her brothers, whose neglect of his children leads to their temporary loss in the Never-Never Land when they follow ➤ PETER *Pan.*

darning see ➤ DEVIL*'s darning-needle.*

darshan in the Indian subcontinent, the opportunity or occasion of seeing a holy person or the image of a deity.

Dart see ➤ RIVER *of Dart.*

D'Artagnan the young and dashing Gascon in Dumas' novel *Les Trois Mousquetaires* (1844), who despite initially giving offence by his impetuous ways is befriended by the ➤ THREE *Musketeers,* Athos, Porthos, and Aramis, and with their help defeats the machinations of Cardinal Richelieu.

> Lieutenant MacKenzie's cry of 'There goes the D'Artagnan of D Company; his father was the finest swordsman in France.'
> — George MacDonald Fraser *McAuslan in the Rough* (1974)

Darth Vader in the ➤ STAR *Wars* trilogy, the former ➤ JEDI who has betrayed his allegiance to serve the Empire, and who is the father of ➤ LUKE *Skywalker;* he is characterized by his ruthless aggression, and by the black cloak, armour, and concealing vizor in which he is always clothed. Although he is initially the villain of the trilogy, he is ultimately redeemed, turning his destructive powers on the Emperor to save his son. (The first film of a second trilogy, *The Phantom Menace* (1999), set at an earlier period, focuses on the young *Anakim Skywalker,* who will become *Darth Vader.*)

> Thousands of Darth Vader-like riot police, sheathed in black armor with scabbards.
> — *Nation* 30 March 1998

Dartmoor a moorland district in Devon that was a royal forest in Saxon times and is now a national park; it is also the site of **Dartmoor Prison.**

Charles Darwin (1809–82), English natural historian and geologist, proponent of the theory of evolution by natural selection. Darwin was the naturalist on HMS *Beagle* for her voyage around the southern hemisphere (1831–6), during which he collected the material which became the basis for his ideas on natural selection. His works *On the Origin of Species* (1859) and *The Descent of Man* (1871) had a fundamental effect on our concepts of nature and humanity's place within it.

Erasmus Darwin (1731–1802), English physician, scientist, inventor, and poet. Darwin is chiefly remembered for his scientific and technical writing, much of which appeared in the form of long poems. These include *The Botanic Garden* (1789–91) and *Zoonomia* (1794–96), which proposed a Lamarckian view of evolution. He was the grandfather of Charles Darwin and Francis Galton.

Darwinism the theory of the evolution of species by natural selection adavnced by ➤ *Charles* DARWIN.

Dasein in Hegelian philosophy, existence, determinate being; in existentialism, human existence, the being of a person in the world. The word is from German *dasein* 'exist'.

Dick Datchery the name assumed by one of the characters in Dickens's unfinished novel *Edwin Drood*; his identity is not revealed.

date the day of the month or year as specified by a number; the word is recorded from Middle English and comes via Old French from medieval Latin *data*, feminine past participle of *dare* 'give', from the Latin formula used in dating letters, *data (epistola)* '(letter) given or delivered', to record a particular time or place.

Date Line an imaginary North–South line through the Pacific Ocean, adopted in 1884, to the east of which the date is a day earlier than it is to the west. It lies chiefly along the meridian furthest from Greenwich (i.e. longitude 180°), with diversions to pass around some island groups. Also called **International Date Line**.

date rape rape by a person that the victim is dating, or with whom he or she has gone on a date; the term, first recorded in the 1970s, came to prominence in the 1980s, and was given first publicity by a number of high-profile trials in the US.

datum line in surveying, an assumed surface used as a reference for the measurement of heights and depths.

daughter see also ➤ DUKE *of Exeter's daughter*, ➤ JAIRUS's *daughter*, ➤ *like* MOTHER, *like daughter*,

➤ *my* SON *is my son till he gets him a wife*, ➤ *when your daughter is stolen, shut* PEPPER *Gate.*

daughter of Zion in the Bible, Jerusalem, as in Isaiah 10:32, 'he shall shake his hand against the daughter of Zion, the hill of Jerusalem.'

Daughters of the American Revolution in the US, a patriotic society whose aims include encouraging education and the study of US history and which tends to be politically conservative. Membership is limited to female descendants of those who aided the cause of independence. It was first organized in 1890.

Daulian bird a nightingale, from the story of ➤ PROCNE, the 'woman of Daulis', who was changed into a nightingale.

Honoré Daumier (1808–78), French painter and lithographer. From the 1830s he worked as a cartoonist for periodicals such as *Charivari*, where he produced lithographs satirizing French society and politics.

dauphin title of the eldest son of the king of France, from the family name of the lords of the *Dauphiné* (first used in this way in the 14th century), ultimately a nickname meaning 'dolphin'.

Le Grand Dauphin Louis (1661–1711), eldest son of Louis XIV, who died in the lifetime of his father.

David see also ➤ CAMP *David*, ➤ DRUNK *as David's sow*, ➤ MAGEN *David*.

David (d. *c.*962 BC), king of Judah and Israel. In the biblical account he was the youngest son of Jesse, who killed the Philistine Goliath and, on ➤ SAUL's death, became king, making Jerusalem his capital; he was the father of ➤ ABSALOM and (by his marriage with ➤ BATHSHEBA), ➤ SOLOMON. He is traditionally regarded as the author of the Psalms, though this has been disputed.

It was a traditional Jewish belief that the Messiah would be descended from David, and in Matthew 9:27 two blind men seeking healing from Jesus address him as 'Son of David'. Although the term was not widely used in the early Church, it is found in later writings, as in Milton's *Paradise Regained* (1671), 'O Son of David, Virgin-born'.

Elizabeth David (1913–92), British cookery writer who played a leading role in introducing Mediterranean cuisine to Britain in the 1950s and 1960s.

Jacques-Louis David (1748–1825), French painter, famous for neoclassical paintings such as *The Oath* *of the Horatii* (1784) and *The Intervention of the Sabine Women* (1799). He became actively involved in the French Revolution, voting for the death of Louis XVI and supporting Robespierre.

St **David** (6th century), Welsh monk, who since the 12th century has been regarded as the patron saint of Wales. Little is known of his life, but it is generally accepted that he transferred the centre of Welsh ecclesiastical administration from Caerleon to Mynyw (now St David's); he also established a number of monasteries and churches.

☐ **FEAST DAY** His feast day is 1 March.

David and Chad: sow peas good or bad proverbial advice, mid 17th century; advising that early March is the best time for sowing.

Bette Davis (1908–89), American actress. She established her Hollywood career playing a number of strong, independent female characters in such films as *Dangerous* (1935) and *Jezebel* (1938). Her flair for suggesting the macabre and menacing emerged in later films, such as *Whatever Happened to Baby Jane?* (1962).

Davis Cup an annual tennis championship for men, first held in 1900, between teams from different countries. It is named after Dwight F. *Davis* (1879–1945), the American doubles champion who donated the trophy.

Davis Strait a sea passage separating Greenland from Baffin Island and connecting Baffin Bay with the Atlantic Ocean, named after John *Davis* (1550–1605), the English explorer who sailed through it in 1587.

Humphry Davy (1778–1829), English chemist, a pioneer of electrochemistry. He discovered nitrous oxide (laughing gas) and the elements sodium, potassium, magnesium, calcium, strontium, and barium. He also identified and named the element chlorine, determined the properties of iodine, and demonstrated that diamond was a form of carbon. In 1815 he invented the miner's safety lamp.

Davy Jones's locker the bottom of the sea, especially regarded as the grave of those drowned at sea, from an extension of the early 18th-century *Davy Jones*, denoting the evil spirit of the sea.

Richard Dawkins (1941–), English biologist. Dawkins's book *The Selfish Gene* (1976) did much to popularize the theory of sociobiology. In *The Blind Watchmaker* (1986, a title deriving from the writing

of ➤ *William* PALEY) Dawkins discussed evolution by natural selection and suggested that the theory could answer the fundamental question of why life exists:

> [Natural selection] has no vision, no foresight, no sight at all. If it can be said to play the role of watchmaker in nature, it is the *blind* watchmaker.
> — Richard Dawkins *The Blind Watchmaker* (1986)

dawn see ➤ CRACK *of dawn*, ➤ *the* DARKEST *hour is just before dawn*.

dawn man an extinct primitive man, formerly especially ➤ PILTDOWN *man*.

dawn raid in Stock Exchange usage, an attempt to acquire a substantial portion of a company's shares at the start of a day's trading, typically as a preliminary to a takeover bid.

dawn redwood a coniferous tree with deciduous needles, known only as a fossil until it was found growing in SW China in 1941.

James Dawson (1717?–46), one of eight Jacobite officers belonging to the Manchester regiment of volunteers, who were hanged, drawn, and quartered on Kennington Common, 30 July 1746. As **Jemmy Dawson**, his story is told in a ballad by Shenstone.

day see also ➤ *the* BETTER *the day, the better the deed*, ➤ DAYS, ➤ *every* DOG *has his day*, ➤ *I have* LOST *a day*, ➤ YEAR *and a day*.

Doris Day (1924–), American actress and singer. She became a film star in the 1950s with roles in light-hearted musicals, comedies, and romances such as *Calamity Jane* (1953) and *Pillow Talk* (1959).

as the **day** lengthens, so the cold strengthens proverbial saying, early 17th century.

Day of Atonement another term for ➤ YOM *Kippur*.

Day of Judgement another term for ➤ JUDGEMENT *Day*.

day of obligation in the Roman Catholic Church, a day on which all are required to attend Mass.

day of reckoning the time when past mistakes or misdeeds must be punished or paid for, a testing time when the degree of one's success or failure will be revealed; with allusion to Judgement Day, on which (in some beliefs) the judgement of mankind is expected to take place.

day of rest a day in the week set aside from normal work or activity, typically Sunday on religious grounds.

Day of the Vow in South Africa (1980–95), 16 December, a public holiday commemorating the vow made by a Voortrekker group to keep the day holy should they defeat the Zulu army at the Battle of Blood River on that day in 1838.

Formerly called *Dingaan's Day*, it was named *Day of the Covenant* in 1952 and *Day of the Vow* in 1980; it was replaced by the *Day of Reconciliation* in 1995.

**be the day weary or be the day long,
at last it ringeth to evensong.**
proverbial saying, early 16th century.

day-star the morning star, (in poetic use) the sun; figuratively, someone or something regarded as the precursor of a new era.

daylight saving the achieving of longer evening daylight, especially in summer, by setting the clocks an hour ahead of the standard time; the originator of the system was the English builder William Willett (1865–1915), who is said to have had the idea in summer 1907 when returning from a morning ride over a Kentish common and seeing how many blinds were still down in the larger houses. The first Daylight Saving Bill was introduced into the House of Commons in the following March, but did not become law until (as a wartime measure) 1916. From 1907 until his death, Willett worked to promote his idea; he wrote and published 19 editions (in English and other languages) of a pamphlet entitled *The Waste of Daylight*.

In 1925 a new Summer Time Act established what had been seen as a temporary measure, and two years later an area of Pett's Wood near Chislehurst in Kent, said to be where the idea had first occurred to Willett, was purchased and handed over to public ownership in his memory.

days see ➤ ANCIENT *of Days*, ➤ BORROWED *days*, ➤ *days of* ABSTINENCE, ➤ DOG *days*, ➤ EGYPTIAN *days*, ➤ *an* EIGHT *days*, ➤ *give us back our* ELEVEN *days*, ➤ GOOD *old days*.

Days of Awe another term for ➤ HIGH *Holidays*.

days of grace the period of time allowed by law for the payment of a bill of exchange or an insurance premium after it falls due.

dayspring a poetic and literary term for dawn; sometimes with biblical reference to Luke 1:78, 'the dayspring from on high hath visited us,' in allusion to the nativity of John the Baptist.

Dayton Accord an agreement on measures to achieve the ending of hostilities in former Yugoslavia, reached in Dayton, Ohio, on 21 November 1995 and signed by the Presidents of Bosnia, Croatia, and Serbia on 14 December 1995 in Paris. At the press conference in Dayton on 21 November, President Izetbegović of Bosnia said, 'And to my people I say, this may not be a just peace, but it is more just than a continuation of war.'

de facto Latin phrase, meaning, in fact, whether by right (*de jure*) or not.

Charles de Gaulle (1890–1970), French general and statesman, head of government 1944–6, President 1959–69. A wartime organizer of the Free French movement, he is remembered particularly for his assertive foreign policy and for quelling the student uprisings and strikes of May 1968.

de gustibus non est disputandum Latin tag meaning, 'there is no disputing about tastes'; the English version is, *there is no accounting for tastes*.

Cecil B. de Mille (1881–1959), American film producer and director, famous for his spectacular epics; an anonymous clerihew of 1938, sometimes attributed to Nicolas Bentley, ran:

> Cecil B. de Mille
> Rather against his will,
> Was persuaded to leave Moses
> Out of 'The Wars of the Roses'.
> — Anonymous in J. W. Carter (ed.) *Clerihews* (1938)

He founded the Jesse L. Lasky Feature Play Company (later Paramount) with Samuel Goldwyn in 1913 and chose the then little-known Los Angeles suburb of Hollywood as a location for their first film, *The Squaw Man* (1914). He is said, when Adolph Zukor protested at the increasing costs of *The Ten Commandments*, to have retorted, 'What do you want me to do? Stop shooting now and release it as *The Five Commandments*?'

de Morgan's laws two laws in Boolean algebra and set theory which state that AND and OR, or union and intersection, are dual. They are used to simplify the design of electronic circuits. Named (in the early 20th century) after Augustus de *Morgan* (1806–71), English mathematician, they were already known (by logicians) as principles in the Middle Ages.

de mortuis nil nisi bonum Latin tag meaning, speak nothing but good of the dead.

Christine de Pisan (*c.*1364–*c.*1430), Italian writer, resident in France from 1369. The first professional woman writer in France, she is best known for her works in defence of women's virtues and achievements, such as *Le Livre des trois vertus* (1406).

de profundis a heartfelt cry of appeal expressing one's deepest feelings of sorrow and anguish, from the opening words (Latin, 'from the depths') of Psalm 130. *De Profundis* was the title of Oscar Wilde's prose apologia, begun while he was in prison as a letter to Lord Alfred Douglas, and published in 1905.

Thomas De Quincey (1785–1859), English essayist and critic. After first taking opium for toothache at Oxford, he became a lifelong addict. He achieved fame with his *Confessions of an English Opium Eater* (1822), a study of his addiction to opium and its psychological effects, ranging from euphoria to nightmares.

Eamon de Valera (1882–1975), American-born Irish statesman, Taoiseach (Prime Minister) 1937–48, 1951–4, and 1957–9 and President of the Republic of Ireland 1959–73. He was involved in the Easter Rising, the leader of Sinn Fein 1917–26 and the founder of the Fianna Fáil Party in 1926. As President of the Irish Free State from 1932, de Valera was largely responsible for the new constitution of 1937 which created the state of Eire.

Lloyd George said of him, 'Negotiating with de Valera…is like trying to pick up mercury with a fork', to which de Valera responded, 'Why doesn't he use a spoon?'

deacon in Catholic, Anglican, and Orthodox Churches, an ordained minister ranking below that of priest (now, except in the Orthodox Church, typically in training for the priesthood). In some Protestant Churches, a *deacon* is a lay officer appointed to assist a minister, especially in secular affairs; in the early Church, a deacon was an appointed minister of charity.

➤ *St* Lawrence and ➤ *St* Stephen are the patron saints of deacons.

The word is recorded from Old English (in form *diacon*) and comes via ecclesiastical Latin from Greek *diakonos* 'servant', in ecclesiastical Greek 'Christian minister'.

See also ➤ Paul *the Deacon*, ➤ Seven *Deacons*.

dead see also ➤ Book *of the Dead*, ➤ Festival *of the Dead*, ➤ *it's* ill *waiting for dead man's shoes*,

➤ *never* speak *ill of the dead*, ➤ *the* quick *and the dead*.

let the dead bury the dead proverbial saying, early 19th century; with ultimate biblical allusion to Matthew 8:22, 'Jesus said unto him, Follow me, and let the dead, bury their dead.'

Dead End Kids in *Dead End* (1937) and subsequent films, a group of tough slum-dwelling youngsters living in poverty and on the edge of a criminal life likely to represent their future.

> Before I had the good fortune to be employed by yours truly, I was what you would call a dead-end kid.
> — Peter Carey *The Tax Inspector* (1991)

Dead Heart the arid interior of Australia; the term is first recorded in 1906.

dead man walking in the United States, a condemned prisoner making the final journey to the execution chamber.

dead man's fingers a fungus that produces clumps of dull black, irregular, finger-like fruiting bodies at the bases of dead tree stumps.

dead man's handle especially in a diesel or electric train, a lever which acts as a safety device by shutting off power when not held in place by the driver.

dead men don't bite proverbial saying, mid 16th century; 1st century AD in Greek.

dead men tell no tales proverbial saying, mid 17th century.

Dead Sea a salt lake or inland sea in the Jordan valley, on the Israel–Jordan border. Its surface is 400 m (1,300 ft) below sea level. The name is recorded from Middle English, and is a translation of Latin *mare mortuum*, Greek (in the writings of Aristotle) *hē nekra thalassa*. The term was used by the Greeks and Romans for the Arctic Ocean in the North of Europe, perhaps because it was regarded as devoid of life or movement.

Dead Sea fruit a legendary fruit, of attractive appearance, which dissolved into smoke and ashes when held (also called *apple of Sodom*); figuratively, a hollow disappointing thing. The fruit are described in the *Travels* attributed to the 14th-century ➤ *John de* Mandeville:

> There beside [the Dead Sea] grow trees that bear full fair apples, and fair of colour to behold, but whoso breaketh them or cutteth them in two, he shall find within them coals and cinders.
> — John de Mandeville *Travels* ch. 13 (*c.*1400)

Dead Sea Scrolls a collection of Hebrew and Aramaic manuscripts discovered in pottery storage jars in caves near Qumran between 1947 and 1956. Thought to have been hidden by the Essenes or a similar Jewish sect shortly before the revolt against Roman rule AD 66–70, the scrolls include texts of many books of the Old Testament; they are some 1,000 years older than previously known versions.

blessed are the dead that the rain rains on proverbial saying, early 17th century.

dead white European male a writer, philosopher, or other significant figure whose importance and talents may have been exaggerated by virtue of his belonging to a historically dominant gender and ethnic group. The acronym **DWEM** is also used.

deadline historical term for a line drawn around a prison, beyond which prisoners were liable to be shot.

deadly see ➤ SEVEN *deadly sins.*

Deadwood Dick sobriquet of Richard W. Clarke (1845–1930), English-born frontiersman of South Dakota, who was known as an Indian fighter and express guard for the Black Hills gold shipments. His exploits were the subject of a number of dime novels.

deaf see also ➤ DIALOGUE *of the deaf.*

there's none so deaf as those who will not hear proverbial saying, mid 16th century.

a deaf husband and a blind wife are always a happy couple proverbial saying, late 16th century.

Deal see also ➤ *a* DOVER *shark and a Deal savage.*

Deal, Dover, and Harwich,
the devil gave with his daughter in marriage:
and, by a codicil to his will,
he added Helvoet and the Brill.
traditional rhyme, late 18th century.

dean the head of the chapter of a cathedral or collegiate church. Recorded from Middle English, the word comes via Old French from late Latin *decanus* 'chief of a group of ten', from *decem* 'ten'.

James Dean (1931–55), American actor, who although he starred in only three films before dying in a car accident, became a cult figure closely identified with the title role of *Rebel Without a Cause* (1955), symbolizing for many the disaffected youth of the post-war era, and giving a phrase to the language.

> The Lower East Side is the land of designer knockoffs, and these boys are imitation James Deans.
> — Samual Freedman *Small Victories* (1990)

See also ➤ *rebel without a* CAUSE.

Dean of Faculty the president of the Faculty of Advocates in Scotland.

Dean of guild an officer of a medieval guild who summoned members to attend meetings; in Scotland, the head of the guild or merchant company of a royal burgh, latterly usually a member of the town council.

Dean of peculiars a member of the clergy invested with the charge of a church or parish exempt from the jurisdiction of the diocese in which it lies.

Dean of the Arches the lay judge of the Court of Arches having jurisdiction over thirteen London parishes exempt from the authority of the Bishop of London.

Dean of the Sacred College the senior member of the Sacred College, usually the oldest of the Cardinal Bishops, who presides in the consistory in the absence of the Pope.

dean's list in North American usage, a list of students recognized for academic achievement during a term by the dean of the college they attend.

dear see ➤ FAR-*fetched and dear-bought is good for ladies.*

Dear John letter a letter from a woman to a man, terminating a personal relationship.

deasil in Scotland, in the direction of the sun's apparent course, considered as lucky; clockwise; the opposite of ➤ WIDDERSHINS. Recorded from the late 18th century, the word comes from Scottish Gaelic.

Death the personification of the power that destroys life, often represented in art and literature as a skeleton or an old man holding a scythe.

See also ➤ DANCE *of death,* ➤ *a* FATE *worse than death,* ➤ *the* KISS *of death,* ➤ NOTHING *is certain but death and taxes,* ➤ *the* SHADOW *of death,* ➤ *there is a* REMEDY *for everything except death,* ➤ WALL *of Death.*

death duty in the UK, a tax levied on property after the owner's death (replaced officially in 1975 by capital transfer tax and in 1986 by inheritance tax).

death futures life insurance policies of terminally ill people, purchased by a third party at less than their mature value as a form of short-term investment.

death in the pot a biblical phrase, from the story of a famine in Gilgal during which a pottage containing poisonous herbs was made by Elisha's servant for the sons of the prophets; when they cried out, 'O thou man of God, there is death in the pot' (2 Kings 5:40), Elisha added meal to the dish, and they were able to eat it safely.

death is the great leveller proverbial saying, early 18th century.

Death-or-Glory-Boys in the British army, a nickname for the 17th Regiment of Lancers, from the regimental badge of a death's head with the words 'or glory'.

death pays all debts proverbial saying, early 17th century.

death row especially with reference to the US, a prison block or section for prisoners sentenced to death.

till death us do part for as long as each of a couple live, from the marriage service in the *Book of Common Prayer*.

Death Valley a deep arid desert basin below sea level in SE California and SW Nevada, the hottest and driest part of North America.

death warrant an official order for the execution of a condemned person.

death-watch beetle a small beetle whose larvae bore into dead wood and structural timbers, causing considerable damage. The adult makes a tapping sound like a watch ticking, formerly believed to portend death.

death's head a human skull as a symbol of mortality.

Debatable Land a former name for the tract of country between the Rivers Esk and Sark on the border between England and Scotland.

Deborah a biblical prophet and leader who inspired the Israelite army to defeat the Canaanites. The 'Song of Deborah', a song of victory attributed to her, is thought to be one of the oldest sections of the Bible.

John Debrett (*c*.1750–1822), English publisher. He compiled *The Peerage of England, Scotland, and Ireland* (first issued in 1803), which is regarded as the authority on the British nobility.

> I was silly enough to believe that having my name in Debrett's and Burke's would act as some sort of talisman.
> — Benedicta Leigh *The Catch of Hands* (1991)

debt see also ➤ DEATH *pays all debts,* ➤ OUT *of debt, out of danger,* ➤ SPEAK *not of my debts unless you mean to pay them.*

debt of honour a debt that is not legally recoverable, especially a sum lost in gambling.

Decalogue another name for the ➤ TEN *Commandments*; the name is recorded from late Middle English, and comes via French and ecclesiastical Latin from Greek *dekalogos (biblos)* '(book of) the Ten Commandments', from *hoi deka logoi* 'the Ten Commandments' (literally 'the ten sayings').

Decameron a work by Boccaccio, written between 1348 and 1358, containing a hundred tales supposedly told in ten days by a party of ten young people who had fled from the Black Death in Florence. The work was influential on later writers such as Chaucer and Shakespeare.

decan in astrology, each of three equal ten-degree divisions of a sign of the zodiac.

decanal relating to or denoting the south side of the choir of a church, the side on which the dean sits.

Decapolis in biblical times, a league of 10 ancient Greek cities formed in Palestine after the Roman conquest of 63 BC; the cities were Scythopolis, Hippos, Gadara, Raphana, Dion, Pelia, Gerasa, Philadelphia, Canatha, and Damascus.

decathlon an athletic event taking place over two days, in which each competitor takes part in the same prescribed ten events (100 metres sprint, long jump, shot-put, high jump, 400 metres, 110 metres hurdles, discus, pole vault, javelin, and 1,500 metres).

December the twelfth month of the year, in the northern hemisphere usually considered the first month of winter. The name is recorded from Middle English, and comes from Latin, from *decem* 'ten', being originally the tenth month of the Roman year.

See also ➤ MAN *of December.*

Decembrist a member of a group of Russian revolutionaries who in December 1825 led an unsuccessful revolt against Tsar Nicholas I. The leaders were executed and later came to be regarded as martyrs by the Left.

decemvir in ancient Rome, either of two bodies of magistrates appointed in 451 and 450 BC respectively to draw up a code of laws, who were in the meantime entrusted with the supreme government of Rome.

decimal relating to or denoting a system of numbers and arithmetic based on the number ten, tenth parts, and powers of ten.
　See also ➤ DEWEY *decimal classification*.

decimate kill one in every ten of (a group of people) as a punishment for the whole group; kill, destroy, or remove a large proportion of. In Middle English the term *decimation* denoted the levying of a tithe, and later the tax imposed by Cromwell on the Royalists (1655). The verb *decimate* originally alluded to the Roman punishment of executing one man in ten of a mutinous legion.
　Historically, the meaning of the word *decimate* is 'kill one in every ten of (a group of people)'. This sense has been more or less totally superseded by the later, more general sense 'kill or destroy (a large proportion of)', as in *the virus has decimated the population*. Some traditionalists argue that this and other later senses are incorrect, but it is clear that this is now part of standard English.

decision theory the mathematical study of strategies for optimal decision-making between options involving different risks or expectations of gain or loss depending on the outcome.

Decius Gaius Messius Quintus Trajanus (*c*.201–51), Roman emperor from 249, the first Roman emperor to promote systematic persecution of Christians in the empire, although popular protest eventually forced him to reverse this policy shortly before the end of his reign. Decius was killed resisting a Gothic invasion of Moesia.

deck a pack of cards. The term, originally current in English, is now chiefly North American.

declaration see also ➤ DOWNING *Street Declaration*, ➤ RIGHTS *of man*, ➤ UNILATERAL *Declaration of Independence*.

Declaration of Independence a document declaring the US to be independent of the British Crown, signed on 4 July 1776 by the Congressional representatives of thirteen states, including Thomas Jefferson, Benjamin Franklin, and John Adams.

Declaration of Indulgence in the UK, any of a number of proclamations of religious liberties made by the two Stuart kings Charles II and James II, especially those of 1662, 1672, and 1687–8.

Declaration of Rights a statute passed by the English parliament in 1689, which first established the joint monarchy of William and Mary and which was designed to ensure that the Crown would not act without Parliament's consent. It was later incorporated into the Bill of Rights.

Decorated denoting a stage of English Gothic church architecture typical of the 14th century (between Early English and Perpendicular), with increasing use of decoration and geometrical, curvilinear, and reticulated tracery.

Decoration Day in the US, another term for ➤ MEMORIAL *Day*.

decree nisi in English law, an order by a court of law that states the date on which a marriage will end, unless a good reason to prevent a divorce is produced. The phrase is recorded from the late 19th century; *nisi* is Latin, meaning 'unless'.

decretal the collection of papal decrees forming part of canon law.

Decretum a collection of decisions and judgements in canon law. The word is from Latin, literally 'something decreed'.

decuman gate in ancient Rome, the chief entrance to a camp, or that farthest from the enemy; the term meant literally, belonging to the tenth cohort.

Richard Dedekind (1831–1916), German mathematician, one the founders of abstract algebra and modern mathematics. He provided a workable description of the properties of real numbers as a foundation on which analysis could be based. He is remembered also for his theory of rings of algebraic integers, and for introducing collections of numbers as entities that may be studied by set theory.

Feast of Dedication another name for ➤ HANUKKAH.

John Dee (1527–1608), English alchemist, mathematician, and geographer. He aided in the first English translation of Euclid's works, and was Elizabeth

I's astrologer; in later life he absorbed himself in alchemy and acquired notoriety as a sorcerer.

deed of **covenant** an agreement to pay a regular amount of money, particularly when this enables the recipient (typically a charity) to reclaim any tax paid by the donor on the amount.

deed poll in English law a legal deed made and executed by one party only, especially to formalize a change of a person's name; the term originates in the parchment having been 'polled' or cut even, not indented as in the case of a deed made between two parties.

deemster a judge (of whom there are two) in the Isle of Man judiciary.

the **Deep South** the south-eastern region of the US regarded as embodying traditional Southern culture and traditions.

Deep Throat codename (from the title of a pornographic film, 1972) given in the ➤ WATERGATE affair to the journalists' principal anonymous informant; from this, *deep throat* is used to mean a person working for an organization who anonymously supplies information on misconduct to an outside source. The original *Deep Throat* has never been publicly identified.

> She interviewed a great many people, including some anonymous Deep Throats.
> — Richard Ellmann *Life of Sim Botchit* (1978)

deer a hoofed grazing or browsing animal, with branched bony antlers that are shed annually and typically born only by the male (the ➤ STAG), sometimes taken as a type of swiftness.

See also ➤ SMALL *deer*.

defence see ➤ ATTACK *is the best form of defence.*

Defender a member of an 18th-century Irish Catholic society, formed to resist the Orangemen.

Defender of the Faith a title conferred on Henry VIII by Pope Leo X in 1521. It was recognized by Parliament as an official title of the English monarch in 1544, and has been borne by all subsequent sovereigns.

Defenestration of Prague in 1618, the throwing by Protestant citizens of Catholic officials from the windows of Hradčany Castle, an event which contributed to the outbreak of the Thirty Years War.

deferent in the Ptolemaic system of astronomy, the large circular orbit followed by the centre of the small epicycle in which a planet was thought to move.

Daniel Defoe (1660–1731), English novelist and journalist. His best-known novel, *Robinson Crusoe* (1719), is loosely based on the true story of the shipwrecked sailor ➤ *Alexander* SELKIRK; it has a claim to being the first English novel.

defrock deprive (a person in holy orders) of ecclesiastical status.

degree an academic rank conferred by a college or university after examination or after completion of a course, or conferred as an honour on a distinguished person.

degrees see also ➤ SONG *of Degrees*.

prohibited degrees the number of steps of consanguinity or affinity within which marriage is not allowed.

dei see ➤ FLAGELLUM *dei*, ➤ OPUS *dei*.

Dei gratia Latin phrase meaning, by the grace of God.

Deianira in Greek mythology, the wife of ➤ HERCULES, who was tricked into smearing poison on a garment which caused his death.

Deipara Mother of God (as a title of the Virgin Mary); a late Latin word meaning 'God-bearing', the equivalent of Greek *theotokos*.

Deiphobus in Greek mythology, a son of Priam, who married Helen after the death of Paris, and was killed by ➤ MENELAUS after the fall of Troy.

deipnosophist a person skilled in the art of dining and table talk, from Greek *deipnosophistēs*, used in plural as the title of a work by Atheneus (3rd cent. AD), describing long discussions at a banquet, from *deipnon* 'dinner' + *sophistēs* 'wise man'.

Deira a northern Anglo-Saxon kingdom in Britain which at the end of the 7th century AD united with Bernicia to form Northumbria.

Deirdre in Irish mythology, a tragic heroine (**Deirdre of the Sorrows**) of whom it was prophesied that her beauty would bring banishment and death to heroes. King ➤ CONCHUBAR of Ulster wanted to marry her, but she fell in love with Naoise, son of Usnach, who with his brothers carried her off to Scotland. They were lured back by Conchubar and treacherously slain, and Deirdre took her own life.

deity a god or goddess; (often as *the Deity*) God. The word is recorded from Middle English, denoting the divine nature of God, and comes via Old French from ecclesiastical Latin *deitas* (translating Greek *theotēs*), from *deus* 'god'.

delays are dangerous proverbial saying, late 16th century.

Delectable Mountains in Bunyan's ➤ PILGRIM*'s Progress*, the country within sight of the Celestial City.

House of Delegates in the US, the lower house of the legislature in Virginia, West Virginia, and Maryland.

delenda est Carthago the words, calling for the complete destruction of ➤ CARTHAGE, with which ➤ CATO the Elder ended every speech in the Senate.

Delft a town in the Netherlands, in the province of South Holland, which was the home of the painters Pieter de Hooch and Jan Vermeer, and which is noted for its pottery, a tin-glazed earthenware, typically decorated by hand in blue on a white background.

Delhi a Union Territory in north central India, containing the cities of Old and New Delhi. **Old Delhi**, a walled city on the River Jumna, was made the capital of the Mogul empire in 1638 by Shah Jahan (1592–1666). **New Delhi**, the capital of India, was built 1912–29 to replace Calcutta as the capital of British India.

Delian League an alliance of ancient Greek city states, dominated by Athens, that joined in 478–447 BC against the Persians. The league was disbanded on the defeat of Athens in the Peloponnesian War (404 BC), but again united under Athens' leadership against Spartan aggression in 377–338 BC. Also called the *Athenian empire*.

Delian problem the problem of finding geometrically the side of a cube having twice the volume of a given cube (from the Delian oracle's pronouncement that a plague in Athens would cease if the cubical altar to Apollo were doubled in size).

Delilah in the Bible, a woman who betrayed her husband ➤ SAMSON to the Philistines by revealing to them that the secret of his strength lay in his long hair.

> Breaches of faith between men and women have been around since Delilah scissored Samson.
> — *New York Times* 12 February 1992

Delinquent in Parliamentarian usage, a person who assisted Charles I or Charles II, by arms, money, or personal service, in levying war, 1642–60.

delirium an acutely disturbed state of mind characterized by restlessness, illusions, and incoherence of thought and speech, occurring in fever, intoxication, and other disorders. The word comes from Latin, from *delirare* 'deviate, be deranged' (literally 'deviate from the furrow', from *de-* 'away' + *lira* 'ridge between furrows').

Great Deliverer a name for William III of Great Britain (1650–1702), as preserving the Protestant succession from the son of the Catholic James II.

Della Cruscan of or relating to the Academy della Crusca in Florence, an institution established in 1582, with the purity of the Italian language as its chief interest. The name *Accademia della Crusca* 'Academy of the bran' referred to the 'sifting' of the language.

Luca della Robbia (1400–82), Italian sculptor and ceramicist, who is best known for his relief panels in Florence cathedral and his colour-glazed terracotta figures. Luca invented vitreous glazes to colour terracotta figures, thus making it possible for polychromatic sculpture to be used in outdoor settings without suffering from the effects of damp.

Delos a small Greek island in the Aegean Sea, regarded as the centre of the Cyclades. In classical times it was considered to be sacred to Apollo, and according to legend was the birthplace of Apollo and Artemis.

Delphi one of the most important religious sanctuaries of the ancient Greek world, dedicated to Apollo and situated on the lower southern slopes of Mount Parnassus above the Gulf of Corinth. Thought of as the navel of the earth, it was the seat of the ➤ DELPHIC *oracle*.

Delphic oracle the oracle of Apollo at Delphi, regarded as particularly holy; the characteristic riddling responses to a wide range of questions were delivered by the ➤ PYTHIA, and have given rise to the use of *Delphic* to mean deliberately obscure or ambiguous.

Delphin designating an edition of Latin classics prepared for the use of the dauphin, son of Louis XIV of France. The word comes from the Latin phrase *ad usum Delphini* 'for the use of the Dauphin'.

delta the fourth letter of the Greek alphabet (**Δ**, **δ**), transliterated as 'd'.

The word is used for a triangular tract of sediment deposited at the mouth of a river, typically where it diverges into several outlets. Originally (in the mid 16th century) the term was applied specifically as **the Delta** (of the River Nile), from the shape of the Greek letter.

Delta Force an elite American military force whose main responsibilities are rescue operations and special forces work.

deluge see also ➤ APRÈS *moi le déluge*, ➤ OGYGIAN *deluge*.

the Deluge another name for the biblical ➤ FLOOD, recorded in Genesis ch. 6–8.

line of demarcation a dividing line, originally that dividing the New World between the Spanish and the Portuguese, decreed by Pope Alexander VI in 1493.

Demeter in Greek mythology, the corn goddess, daughter of Cronus and Rhea, and mother of ➤ PERSEPHONE. She is associated with Cybele, and her symbol is an ear of corn. The Eleusinian mysteries were held in honour of her. Roman equivalent ➤ CERES.

demi-monde a group of people considered to be on the fringes of respectable society; in 19th century France, the class of women considered to be of doubtful social standing and morality. The phrase is French, literally 'half-world'.

demi-vierge a woman who behaves licentiously while remaining a virgin, from French (literally 'half-virgin') from *Les demi-vierges* (1874), a novel by M. Prévost.

demijohn a bulbous narrow-necked bottle holding from 3 to 10 gallons of liquid, typically enclosed in a wicker cover. The word probably comes from an 18th-century alteration of French *dame-jeanne* 'Lady Jane', by association with *demi-* 'half-sized' and the given name *John*.

demiurge a being responsible for the creation of the universe, in particular (in Platonic philosophy) the Maker or Creator of the world. The word comes via ecclesiastical Latin from Greek *dēmiourgos* 'craftsman'.

democracy a system of government by the whole population or all the eligible members of a state, typically through elected representatives. The word is recorded from the late 16th century, and comes via French and late Latin from Greek *dēmokratia*, from *dēmos* 'the people' + *kratia* 'power'.

Democrat see ➤ YELLOW-*dog Democrat*.

Democratic Party one of the two main US political parties (the other being the Republican Party), which follows a broadly liberal programme, tending to support social reform and minority rights.

Democritus (*c*.460–*c*.370 BC), Greek philosopher. He developed the atomic theory originated by his teacher, Leucippus, which explained natural phenomena in terms of the arrangement and rearrangement of atoms moving in a void.

Demogorgon the name of a mysterious and terrible infernal deity, first mentioned in the 5th century, and described as the primordial God of ancient mythology in the *Repertorium* of Conrad de Mure (1273), and following this in Boccaccio's *Genealogia Deorum*, on which subsequent references in Ariosto, Milton, Shelley, and other writers seem to be based.

demon an evil spirit or devil, especially one thought to possess a person or act as a tormentor in hell; the word is recorded from Middle English, and comes partly via medieval Latin and Latin from Greek *daimōn* 'deity, genius', and partly (in this sense) from Latin *daemonium* 'lesser or evil spirit', from Greek diminutive of *daimōn*.

From late Middle English, the word was also used for a divinity or supernatural being (in ancient Greek belief) of a nature between gods and humans, an inner or attendant spirit or inspiring force, for which ➤ DAEMON is now the standard spelling.

See also ➤ MAXWELL'*s demon*, ➤ PRINCE *of demons*.

Demos the common people of an ancient Greek state; the populace as a political unit, especially in a democracy.

Demosthenes (384–322 BC), Athenian orator and statesman, who according to Plutarch overcame an initial stammer by training himself to speak with pebbles in his mouth. He is best known for his political speeches on the need to resist the aggressive tendencies of Philip II of Macedon (the *Philippics*). The Greeks were defeated by Philip at the battle of Chaeronea in 338 BC and Demosthenes committed suicide after the failure of an Athenian revolt against Macedon.

denarius an ancient Roman silver coin, originally worth ten asses.

dene-hole an ancient excavation of a kind found in chalk-formations in England and France, consisting of a narrow shaft sunk down to the chalk, and there widening out into one or more chambers.

Denial Bible an edition of 1792, in which at Luke 22:34 the name Philip appears instead of Peter for the disciple who would deny Jesus.

denim a hard-wearing cotton twill fabric, typically blue, used for jeans, overalls, and other clothing; the word comes from the French *serge de Nimes*, denoting a kind of serge from the manufacturing town of Nimes.

St Denis (died *c*.250), Italian-born French bishop, patron saint of France; Roman name *Dionysius*. According to tradition he was one of a group of seven missionaries sent from Rome to convert Gaul; he became bishop of Paris and was martyred in the reign of the emperor Valerian. He was beheaded, and according to legend subsequently walked two leagues carrying his own head, a story which is said to have prompted Mme du Deffand's comment, ➤ *il n'y a que le* PREMIER *pas qui coûte*. He is taken as one of the ➤ FOURTEEN *Holy Helpers*.
☐ **FEAST DAY** His feast day is 9 October.

Denmark Street the world of composers and publishers of popular music, Tin Pan Alley, from the name of a street in London.

Dennis the Menace a cartoon character introduced in 1951 in the children's comic the *Beano*, a destructive boy with black-and-red striped jersey, boots, and black hair, who with his dog Gnasher terrorizes teachers, other children, and anyone else they may encounter.
  In contrast, a US *Dennis the Menace*, created by Hank Ketcham and also appearing in 1951, is a dynamic five-year-old who is not aggressive and who exhausts his parents only by his energy; disasters which ensue are accidental rather than planned.

> You used to be Dennis the Menace, north London's very own berserker, the wild man of Tottenham.
> — Charles Higson *Full Whack* (1995)

dentists St Apollonia, a 3rd-century martyr whose sufferings included having her teeth wrenched from her jaws, is the patron saint of dentists.

Deo gratias Latin for, thanks be to God.

deoch-and-doris in Scotland and Ireland, a final drink taken before parting, from the Scottish Gaelic *deoch an doruis* 'drink at the door'.

deodand historical term for a thing forfeited to the Crown for a religious or charitable use, as having caused a human death. The word comes ultimately from Latin *Deo dandum* 'thing to be given to God'.

dependency culture a way of life characterized by dependency on state benefits.

the Deposition the taking down of the body of Christ from the Cross.

the Depression the financial and industrial slump of 1929 and subsequent years, also known as **the Great Depression**.

Chamber of Deputies the lower house of Parliament of the French Third Republic, of Italy, and some other countries.

Derby an annual flat horse race for three-year-olds, founded in 1780 by the 12th Earl of Derby. The race is run on Epsom Downs in England in late May or early June.
  In North American usage, a *derby* is a bowler hat, said to be from American demand for a hat of the type worn at the Epsom Derby.
  See also ➤ KENTUCKY *Derby*, ➤ KIPLINGCOTES *Derby*.

Derby Day the day on which the annual race is run.

Derby dog a dog appearing on the racecourse after this has been cleared; taken proverbially as something sure to turn up or come in the way. The term is recorded from the mid 19th century.

Derbyshire neck an old name for goitre, formerly endemic in parts of Derbyshire.

derrick a kind of crane with a movable pivoted arm for moving and lifting heavy weights, originally meaning a hangman or the gallows, from *Derrick* the surname of a London hangman.

Jacques Derrida (1930–), French philosopher and critic, the most important figure in deconstruction. He rejected structuralist assumptions about meaning, pointing out the ambiguity and contradiction in meaning between presentation and content in texts.

derring-do action displaying heroic courage. The term comes (in the late 16th century) from late Middle English *dorryng do* 'daring to do', used by Chaucer, and, in a passage by Lydgate based on Chaucer's work, misprinted in 16th-century editions as *derrynge do*; this was misinterpreted by Spenser to mean 'manhood, chivalry', and subsequently taken up and popularized by Sir Walter Scott.

dervish a Muslim (specifically Sufi) religious man who has taken vows of poverty and austerity. Dervishes first appeared in the 12th century; they were noted for their wild or ecstatic rituals. The name comes via Turkish from Persian *darvīš* 'religious mendicant'.

See also ➤ WHIRLING *dervish.*

Lord Derwentwater's lights a local name for the aurora borealis, said to have appeared specially bright on the night of the execution of the Jacobite Earl of *Derwentwater* (1689–1716).

desaparecido especially in South America, a person who has disappeared, presumed killed by members of the armed services or the police. The word is Spanish, and means literally 'disappeared'.

descamisado an extreme liberal in the Spanish Revolutionary War of 1820–3; a revolutionary, a very poor person. The word is Spanish, and means literally 'shirtless'.

René Descartes (1596–1650), French philosopher, mathematician, and man of science. Aiming to reach totally secure foundations for knowledge, he concluded that everything was open to doubt except his own conscious experience, and his existence as a necessary condition of this: '*Cogito, ergo sum*' (I think, therefore I am). From this certainty he developed a dualistic theory regarding mind and matter as separate though interacting. In mathematics Descartes developed the use of coordinates to locate a point in two or three dimensions.

the Descent the descent of Christ into hell.

Deseret the Mormon name for Utah (meaning 'honeybee').

desert see also ➤ SHIP *of the desert.*

the Desert Fathers the hermits living an ascetic life in 4th-century Egypt, whose lives became the pattern for Christian community monasticism.

Desert Island Discs a popular radio progamme (1942–), originally created by Roy Plomley (1914–85), in which the chosen celebrity 'castaway' chooses eight records with which to be marooned on a desert island, together with one luxury and one book besides the Bible and Shakespeare.

the Desert Rats the 7th British armoured division (with a jerboa as its badge) in the North African desert campaign of 1941–2.

desert rose a dense shrub with pinkish-lilac flowers and black spotted leaves and fruit. Native to arid regions of Australia, it is the floral emblem of the Northern Territory of Australia.

Desert Storm Operation *Desert Storm* was the name of the Allied Forces' land campaign in the 1991 Gulf War; **Desert Storm syndrome** is another term for ➤ GULF *War Syndrome.*

designer drug a synthetic analogue of an illegal drug, especially one devised to circumvent drug laws; a fashionable artificial drug.

desperate cases ➤ St JUDE and St Rita of Cascia (1377–1447), a widow and Augustinian nun who had endured 18 years of marriage to a violent and unfaithful husband, are the patron saints of desperate cases.

Desperate Dan the enormous stubble-chinned cowboy in a cartoon strip in the *Dandy* comic, noted for his fondness for cow pies containing the whole animal.

> The Nissan looks like something Desperate Dan ought to drive; squat, long, chrome-bedecked and gargoyled.
> — *Farmers Weekly* 22 November 1996

desperate diseases must have desperate remedies proverbial saying, mid 16th century.

Destiny the power or agency supposed to pretermine events, personfied as a goddess; **the Destinies,** the three Fates of mythology.

See also ➤ MAN *of Destiny,* ➤ MANIFEST *destiny.*

detectorist a person who uses a metal detector for a hobby, something which has grown in popularity since the 1970s. A number of interesting finds have been made, but archaeologists have expressed concern that in excavating the buried metal evidence may be damaged or vital provenance relating to the artefacts lost.

determinism the doctrine that all events, including human action, are ultimately determined by causes regarded as external to the will. Some philosophers have taken determinism to imply that individual human beings have no free will and cannot be held morally responsible for their actions.

Detroit a major industrial city and Great Lakes shipping centre in NE Michigan, which is the centre of the US automobile industry, containing the headquarters of Ford, Chrysler, and General Motors—whence its nickname 'Motown' (short for 'motor town'). In the 1960s it was also an important centre for rock and soul music.

detur any of several prizes of books given annually at Harvard University, from Latin, meaning 'let there be given', the first word of the accompanying inscription.

Deucalion in Greek mythology, the son of ➤ PRO-METHEUS. With his wife Pyrrha he survived a flood sent by Zeus to punish human wickedness; they were then instructed to throw stones over their shoulders, and these turned into humans to repopulate the world.

deuce a thing representing, or represented by, the number two; the word is recorded from the late 15th century, and comes from Old French *deus* 'two', from Latin *duos*.

In tennis, *deuce* is the score of 40 all in a game, at which each player needs two consecutive points to win the game.

deus absconditus a god who is hidden from human perception, from Latin, literally 'hidden god'; sometimes with reference to Isaiah 45:15, 'Verily thou art a God that hidest thyself.'

deus ex machina an unexpected power or event saving a seemingly hopeless situation, especially as a contrived plot device in a play or novel. The phrase is modern Latin, a direct translation of Greek *theos ek mēkhanēnēs* 'god from the machinery', since in Greek theatre, actors representing gods were suspended above the stage, the denouement of the play being brought about by their intervention.

Deutero-Isaiah the supposed later author of Isaiah 40–55 (from Greek *deuteros* 'second').

Deuteronomy the fifth book of the Bible, containing a recapitulation of the Ten Commandments and much of the Mosaic law.

Deva name of the Roman legionary fortress on the site of which Chester stands.

deva a member of a class of divine beings in the Vedic period, which in Indian religion are benevolent and in Zoroastrianism are evil. The word is from Sanskrit, literally 'shining one', later 'god'.

Devanagari the alphabet used for Sanskrit, Hindi, and other Indian languages. The name comes from Sanskrit, literally 'divine town script', from *deva* 'god' + *nāgarī* (from *nagara* 'town'), an earlier name of the script.

Devi in Hindu mythology, the supreme goddess, often identified with Parvati and Sakti.

devil in Christian and Jewish belief, the supreme spirit of evil, Satan. The name is recorded from Old English (in form *dēofol*) and comes ultimately via late Latin from Greek *diabolos* 'accuser, slanderer' (used in the Septuagint to translate Hebrew *śāṭān* 'Satan'), from *diaballein* 'to slander'.

The Devil is traditionally represented with horns, cloven hooves, and a forked tail, all signs of his demonic origin.

See also ➤ BETTER *the devil you know than the devil you don't know*, ➤ DEAL, *Dover, and Harwich, the devil gave with his daughter in marriage*, ➤ FOR-EIGN *devil*, ➤ HASTE *is from the devil*, ➤ *he who* SUPS *with the devil should have a long spoon*, ➤ HOLD *a candle to the Devil*, ➤ HOME *is home as the Devil said when he found himself in the Court of Session*, ➤ *an* IDLE *brain is the Devil's workshop*, ➤ *if it* RAINS *when the sun is shining, the devil is beating his wife*, ➤ *it is easier to* RAISE *the Devil than to lay him*, ➤ NEEDS *must when the devil drives*, ➤ PARSLEY *seed goes nine times to the Devil*, ➤ PRINTER'*s devil*, ➤ PULL *Devil, pull baker*, ➤ ROBERT *the Devil*, ➤ *say the* DEVIL'*s paternoster*, ➤ TALK *of the Devil and he is bound to appear*, ➤ TELL *the truth and shame the Devil*, ➤ *what is* GOT *over the Devil's back is spent under his belly*, ➤ *where* GOD *builds a church the Devil will build a chapel*, ➤ WHITE *Devil*, ➤ *the* WORLD, *the flesh, and the devil*, ➤ YOUNG *saint, old devil.*

devil among the tailors an altercation; the phrase is recorded from the 19th century.

devil and his dam traditional expression for the Devil and a woman who is even worse.

the devil can quote scripture for his own ends proverbial saying, late 16th century.

the devil dances in an empty pocket proverbial saying, late Middle English.

the **devil** finds work for idle hands to do proverbial saying, early 18th century.

why should the **devil** have all the best tunes proverbial saying, mid 19th century; attributed to the English evangelist Rowland Hill (1744–1833), and referring to the fact that many hymns were sung to popular secular tunes.

give the **devil** his due proverbial saying, late 16th century.

the **devil** is not so black as he is painted proverbial saying, mid 16th century.

the **devil** looks after his own proverbial saying, early 18th century.

the **devil** makes his Christmas pies of lawyers' tongues and clerks' fingers proverbial saying, late 16th century.

the **devil** on two sticks another term for ➤ DI-ABOLO.

he looks as the **devil** over Lincoln perhaps referring to Lincoln College, Oxford, or to a carving in Lincoln Cathedral, which shows a demonic figure crouched on a person's shoulder; the expression is recorded from the mid 16th century.

the **devil** rides on a fiddlestick proverbial saying, late 16th century.

the **devil** take the hindmost proverbial saying, early 17th century.

the **devil** to pay proverbial saying, early 18th century; supposed to refer to the alleged bargains made with Satan, and the inevitable payment to be made to him in the end, but it has also been attributed to the difficulty of 'paying' or caulking the seam called the 'devil', near a ship's keel, whence the expanded form 'the devil to pay and no pitch hot'. However, there is no evidence that this is the original sense, and it has never affected the general use of the proverb.

the **Devil** was sick, the Devil a monk would be. the Devil was well, the devil a monk was he. proverbial saying, early 17th century, variant of a medieval Latin proverb

devil's advocate a person appointed by the Roman Catholic Church to challenge a proposed beatification or canonization, or the verification of a miracle.

devil's bedpost a name for the four of clubs.

devil's bird a bird distinguished by its wailing cry, taken as an evil omen.

devil's bit any of a number of wild plants with a very short rootstock, said in folklore to have been bitten off by the devil.

devil's bones a name for dice, recorded from the mid 17th century.

devil's bridge a natural formation of stone, supposedly built by the devil.

devil's cheesewring a rocky outcrop near Lynton, held to resemble a cheesepress.

the **devil's** children have the devil's luck proverbial saying, late 17th century.

devil's coach-horse a large black predatory rove beetle which raises its hind end and opens its jaws in a threatening manner when disturbed.

devil's darning needle a name for dragonfly, also called a *darner*.

devil's dozen thirteen.

devil's fourposter a name for the four of clubs.

devil's guts an invasive climbing or twining plant, especially a member of the convolvulus family.

Devil's Island a rocky island off the coast of French Guiana, used from 1852 as a penal settlement, especially for political prisoners. The last prisoner was released in 1953.

the **Devil's** Own a nickname of the 88th Foot (**the Devil's own Connaught boys**); also of the Inns of Court Rifle Corps of Volunteers.

devil's Parliament a name for the parliament (in Latin, *Parliamentum diabolicum*) held by Henry VI at Coventry in 1459, which attainted the Duke of York, his son the Earl of March, afterwards Edward IV, and their chief followers.

devil's picture books playing cards; recorded from the late 18th century.

the **Devil's** Punchbowl a large natural formation in Surrey.

the **Devil's** Tower a natural volcanic formation in Wyoming.

Devonshire dumpling a native or inhabitant of Devonshire, a county of SW England.

dew tiny drops of water that form on cool surfaces at night, when atmospheric vapour condenses, but which were formerly believed to descend from the heavens, as in Daniel 4:23, 'Hew the tree down, and destroy it; yet leave the stump of the roots thereof in the earth…and let it be wet with the dew of heaven.' *Dew* in literary use is thus referred to as something that refreshes.

> Sleep, that healing dew of heaven.
>   — Percy Bysshe Shelley *The Cenci* (1819)

See also ➤ MAY *dew*.

dew-cup traditional term for an early morning allowance of beer for harvesters.

dew pond a shallow pond, especially an artificial one, occurring on downs where the water supply from springs or surface drainage is inadequate; so named because such ponds were originally thought to be fed by dew.

dewclaw a rudimentary inner toe present in some dogs; the name, recorded from the late 16th century, may refer to the fact that while the other claws come in contact with the soil, or press the grass to the ground, this only brushes the dewy surface.

Dewey decimal classification an internationally applied decimal system of library classification which uses a three-figure code from 000 to 999 to represent the major branches of knowledge, and allows finer classification to be made by the addition of further figures after a decimal point. The system was devised in the late 19th century by the American librarian Melvil *Dewey* (1851–1931).

Dewi Welsh name for ➤ *St* DAVID.

Dewitt a former term meaning 'kill by mob violence'; it comes (in the late 17th century) from the surname of the two brothers John and Cornelius *De Witt*, Dutch statesmen, opponents of William III as Stadtholder of the United Provinces, who were murdered by a mob in 1672.

dexter in heraldry, of, on, or towards the right-hand side (in a coat of arms, from the bearer's point of view, i.e. the left as it is depicted). The opposite of ➤ SINISTER. The term is recorded from the mid 16th century and comes from Latin, 'on the right'.

dey (the title of) any of the supreme rulers of Algiers, 1710–1830, originally the commanding officers of the janissaries of Algiers under the Ottoman Empire. Also, (the title of) the local ruler of Tunis or Tripoli under nominal Ottoman suzerainty. The word comes from Turkish *dayı* maternal uncle, used also as a courtesy title.

dharma in Indian religion, the eternal law of the cosmos, inherent in the very nature of things. In Hinduism, *dharma* is seen as the cosmic law both upheld by the gods and expressed in right behaviour by humans, including adherence to the social order. In Buddhism, it is interpreted as universal truth or law, especially as proclaimed by the Buddha. In Jainism, it is conceived both as virtue and as a kind of fundamental substance, the medium of motion.

The word comes from Sanskrit, literally 'decree or custom'.

dhyana in Hindu and Buddhist practice, profound meditation which is the penultimate stage of yoga.

diabolo a game in which a two-headed top is thrown up and caught with a string stretched between two sticks; the name comes (in the early 20th century) from Italian, from ecclesiastical Latin *diabolus* 'devil'; the game was formerly called *devil on two sticks*.

Diabolus the name of the Devil (from ecclesiastical Latin) in Bunyan's *The Holy War* (1682); he leads his hosts of **Diabolonians** against the stronghold of ➤ MANSOUL.

diaconicon a building or room adjoining a church, where vestments, ornaments, and other things used in the church service are kept; a sacristy. The word comes from Greek *diakonikon*, from the base of ➤ DEACON.

diadem a jewelled crown or headband worn as a symbol of sovereignty. Recorded from Middle English, the word comes via Old French and Latin from Greek *diadēma* 'the regal headband of the Persian kings', from *diadein* 'bind round'.

Diadochi the six Macedonian generals of Alexander the Great (Antigonus, Antipater, Cassander, Lysimachus, Ptolemy, and Seleucus), among whom his empire was eventually divided after his death in 323 BC. The word comes from Greek *diadokhoi* 'successors'.

diaeresis a mark (¨) placed over a vowel to indicate that it is sounded separately, as in *naïve*, *Brontë*.

Sergei Diaghilev (1872–1929), Russian ballet impresario. In 1909 he formed the Ballets Russes, which he directed until his death, with Nijinsky, and later Massine, as his star performer. He transformed the European ballet scene, pooling the talents of leading choreographers, painters, and composers of his day.

dial the face of a clock or watch that is marked to show units of time. The word is recorded from Middle English, denoting a mariner's compass, and comes from medieval Latin *diale* 'clock dial', based on Latin *dies* 'day'.

See also ➤ Ahaz.

dialectic enquiry into metaphysical contradictions and their solutions. The ancient Greeks used the term to refer to various methods of reasoning and discussion in order to discover the truth. More recently, Kant applied the term to the criticism of the contradictions which arise from supposing knowledge of objects beyond the limits of experience, e.g. the soul. Hegel applied the term to the process of thought by which apparent contradictions (which he termed thesis and antithesis) are seen to be part of a higher truth (synthesis).

The word is recorded from late Middle English, and comes via Old French or Latin from Greek *dialektikē (tekhnē)* '(art) of debate', from *dialegesthai* 'converse with'.

dialectical materialism the Marxist theory (adopted as the official philosophy of the Soviet communists) that political and historical events result from the conflict of social forces and are interpretable as a series of contradictions and their solutions. The conflict is seen as caused by material needs.

dialogue of the deaf a discussion in which each party is unresponsive to what the others say; the expression is a translation of French *dialogue de sourds*.

diamond a precious stone consisting of a clear and colourless crystalline form of pure carbon, the hardest naturally occurring substance, taken as a type of brilliance or excellence. The word is recorded from Middle English, and comes via Old French from medieval Latin *diamas, diamant-*, variant of Latin *adamans*, from the base of adamant.

Diamond is also used for a figure with four straight sides of equal length forming two opposite acute angles and two opposite obtuse angles, a rhombus, and *diamonds* are thus one of the four suits in a conventional pack of playing cards, denoted by a red figure of such a shape.

Diamond was the name of Isaac Newton's dog,

which according to a (probably apocryphal) story knocked over a candle which set fire to some papers and thereby destroyed the finished work of some years; he was said to have been reproached with the words, 'O Diamond! Diamond! thou little knowest the mischief done!'

See also ➤ Acres *of Diamonds*, ➤ black *diamond*.

Diamonds: famous stones

Cullinan diamond	Koh-i-noor
Florentine diamond	Pitt diamond
Hope diamond	Sancy diamond

---

diamond cuts diamond proverbial saying, early 17th century.

Diamond Head a volcanic crater overlooking the port of Honolulu on the Hawaian island of Oahu.

Diamond Jim nickname of James Buchanan Brady (1856–1917), an American millionaire who started his career as a bellboy, and who was noted for his fondness for jewellery, especially diamonds.

diamond jubilee the 60th anniversary of a notable event, especially a sovereign's accession or the foundation of an organization.

Affair of the Diamond Necklace a scandal in 18th century France concerning ➤ Marie Antoinette's supposed purchase of a valuable necklace and subsequent denial of any knowledge of the matter.

Although the affair was an attempt by a French adventuress to acquire the necklace by a pretence of acting on behalf of the Queen, and Marie Antoinette was not involved, the Queen's innocence was not believed, and the scandal contributed materially to her unpopularity.

Diamond Pitt appellation of Thomas Pitt (1653–1726), East India merchant and governor of Madras, and owner of the ➤ Pitt *diamond*.

the Diamond Sculls an annual single-scull race at Henley Royal Regatta, instituted in 1844, for which the prize was a gold pin ornamented with gold sculls and a drop diamond.

Diamond State informal name for the state of Delaware, said to be so named because it was seen as small in size but of great importance.

diamond wedding the sixtieth anniversary of a wedding.

Diana an early Italian goddess associated with hunting, virginity, and, in later literature, the moon, the Roman equivalent of the Greek goddess ➤ Ar-temis.

> Frances emerged from the study: a tall, thin Diana of a young woman with boyishly cropped hair.
> — Janet Malcolm *The Silent Woman* (1994)

See also ➤ Mirror *of Diana*.

Diana of Ephesus a statue of the goddess particularly venerated at Ephesus; her Temple there was one of the ➤ Seven *Wonders of the World*.

great is Diana of the Ephesians in the Bible (Acts 19:28) the cry of a crowd at Ephesus protesting against the preaching of the apostles Paul and Barnabas; according to the account given in Acts, the people had been worked up by a silversmith named Demetrius, who traded in silver models of Diana's shrine and was concerned for his livelihood.

Diana, Princess of Wales (1961–97), former wife of Prince Charles. The daughter of the 8th Earl Spencer, she married Prince Charles in 1981; the couple were divorced in 1996, having had two children. She became a popular figure through her charity work and glamorous media appearances, and her death in a car crash in Paris gave rise to intense national mourning.

See also ➤ *the* People's *Princess*, ➤ Queen *of Hearts*, ➤ Taj *Mahal*.

Dianetics a system developed by the founder of the Church of Scientology, L. Ron Hubbard, which aims to relieve psychosomatic disorder by cleansing the mind of harmful mental images. The word comes from Greek *dianoētikos* 'relating to thought'.

diapason an organ stop sounding a main register of flue pipes, typically of eight-foot pitch; in poetic and literary usage, the entire compass, range, or scope of something; a grand swelling burst of harmony.

The word is recorded from late Middle English (denoting the interval of an octave), and comes via Latin from Greek *dia pasōn (khordōn)* 'through all (notes)'.

Bartolomeu Dias (*c.*1450–1500), Portuguese navigator and explorer. He was the first European to round the Cape of Good Hope (1488), thereby establishing a sea route from the Atlantic to Asia. He

later accompanied Vasco da Gama on the first European expedition to Asia by this route.

the diaspora Jews living outside Israel; the dispersion of the Jews beyond Israel.

The main diaspora began in the 8th–6th centuries bc, and even before the sack of Jerusalem in ad 70 the number of Jews dispersed by the diaspora was greater than that living in Israel. Thereafter, Jews were dispersed even more widely throughout the Roman world and beyond (for example, into India). The term embraces concerns about cultural assimilation and loss of Jewish identity which are at the centre of the movement of Zionism.

The word is Greek, and comes from *diaspeirein* 'disperse', from *dia* 'across' + *speirein* 'scatter'. The term originated in the Septuagint (Deuteronomy 28:25) in the phrase *esē diaspora en pasais basileias tēs gēs* 'thou shalt be a dispersion in all kingdoms of the earth'.

diatessaron an arrangement of the four Gospels as one narrative; the word comes via Old French and Latin from Greek *dia tessarōn* 'composed of four'.

Fra Diavolo nickname of the Italian brigand Michele Pezza (1771–1806). He fought against the French occupation of Naples, and in folk legends appears as a popular guerrilla leader.

dice a small cube with each side having a different number of spots on it, ranging from one to six, thrown and used in gambling and other games involving chance.

The word is originally the plural of *die*, recorded from Middle English and coming via Old French from Latin *datum* 'something given or played'.

See also ➤ *the* die *is cast*.

Dick see also ➤ Black *Dick*, ➤ Deadwood *Dick*, ➤ *Dick* Barton, ➤ *Dick* Datchery, ➤ Dirty *Dick*, ➤ Moby *Dick*, ➤ Mocha *Dick*, ➤ Queen *Dick*, ➤ Tumbledown *Dick*, ➤ Tom, *Dick, and Harry*.

queer as Dick's hatband proverbial expression, recorded from the late 18th century.

Charles Dickens (1812–70), English novelist. His novels are notable for their satirical humour and treatment of contemporary social problems, including the plight of the urban poor and the corruption and inefficiency of the legal system.

The term **Dickensian** is used especially in suggesting the poor social conditions or comically repulsive characters that the novels of Charles Dickens portray.

> Whatever Crystal Palace was like, it is a safe bet that Olympia was worse. The gloom of its vast caverns . . . seemed at times to have been built around some Dickensian pea-souper.
> — *Field* February 1990

dictator in ancient Rome, a chief magistrate with absolute power, appointed in an emergency; in extended usage (from the late 16th century), a ruler with total power over a country, typically one who has obtained power by force.

dictatorship of the proletariat the Communist ideal of proletarian supremacy following the overthrow of capitalism and preceding the classless state.

Dictys Cretensis Dictys of Crete, said to have accompanied Idomeneus (leader of the Cretans) to the Trojan War, and to have written a diary of the events.

Didache a Christian text (also called the *Teaching of the Twelve Apostles*) compiled in Egypt or Syria in the 2nd century, and dealing with morals and ethics, church practice, and the prospect of the Second Coming.

Jeremy **Diddler** a character in the farce *Raising the Wind* (1803) by the Irish dramatist James Kenney (1780–1849). Diddler constantly borrowed and failed to repay small sums of money, and his name probably gives rise to *diddle* 'cheat or swindle (someone)' the name may in turn have been based on an earlier verb *diddle* 'walk unsteadily, swerve'.

Denis Diderot (1713–84), French philosopher, writer, and critic. A leading figure of the Enlightenment in France, he was principal editor of the *Encyclopédie* (1751–76), through which he disseminated and popularized philosophy and scientific knowledge.

didgeridoo an Australian Aboriginal wind instrument in the form of a long wooden tube, traditionally made from a hollow branch, which is blown to produce a deep resonant sound, varied by rhythmic accents of timbre and volume.

didicoi a gypsy; an itinerant tinker. Perhaps an alteration (in the mid 19th century) of Romany *dik akei* 'look here'.

Dido in the *Aeneid*, the queen and founder of Carthage, who fell in love with the shipwrecked Aeneas and killed herself when he deserted her.

Didyma an ancient sanctuary of Apollo, site of one of the most famous oracles of the Aegean region, close to the west coast of Asia Minor; the name is said to come from Greek 'twin', and to refer to the two springs there.

Didymus the Greek word for 'twin', an epithet of St Thomas the apostle.

die see also ➤ COWARDS *die many times before their deaths*, ➤ *see* NAPLES *and die*, ➤ YOUNG *men may die, but old men must die*.

the die is cast an event has happened or a decision has been taken that cannot be changed; the saying is originally a translation of Caesar's words at the crossing of the ➤ RUBICON, meaning that in figurative terms the dice for his gamble had been thrown (the saying is often quoted in Latin, '*iacta alea est*', but the words were originally spoken in Greek).

you can only die once proverbial saying, mid 15th century.

the Diehards in the British army, a name for the 57th Regiment of Foot, said to derive from the battle of Albuera (May 1811) in the Peninsular Wars, when the Regiment, defending an important position, was adjured by its commanding officer, 'Die hard! 57th, die hard!'

Dien Bien Phu a village in NW Vietnam, in 1954 the site of a French military post which was captured by the Vietminh after a 55-day siege; a significant defeat for French forces in the war (1946–54) in Indo-China.

> The buzzwords for Yugoslavia in the Pentagon are 'quagmire' and 'Dien Bien Phu'.
> — *New Yorker* 24 August 1992

Dieppe a channel port in northern France, which in August 1942 was the scene of an unsuccessful amphibious raid by a joint force of British and Canadian troops to destroy the German-held port and airfield. The raid ended disastrously, with two thirds of the Allied troops being killed.

Dies Irae a Latin hymn sung in a Mass for the dead; from the opening words (literally, 'day of wrath') of the hymn.

dies non a day on which no legal business can be done, or which does not count for legal or other purposes. The phrase is Latin, short for *dies non-judicus* 'non-judicial day'.

Diet of Worms a meeting of the Holy Roman emperor Charles V's imperial diet at Worms in 1521, at which Martin Luther was summoned to appear. Luther committed himself there to the cause of Protestant reform, and his teaching was formally condemned in the Edict of Worms.

Dietrich von Bern in the *Nibelungenlied*, the name given to ➤ THEODORIC, a great king of the Ostrogoths (*c*.454–526), who invaded Italy and decisively defeated Odoacer at Verona (Bern) in 489. He was the hero of the German epics of the 13th century and of the Teutonic race in general, and the centre round which clustered many legends.

Dieu et mon droit French phrase meaning, God and my right, the motto of the British monarchs from the time of Henry VI.

difference in heraldry, alter (a coat of arms) to distinguish members or branches of a family.

different see also ➤ AND *now for something completely different.*

different strokes for different folks proverbial saying, late 20th century.

the difficult is done at once, the impossible takes a little longer proverbial saying, late 19th century.

Digambara a member of one of two principal sects of Jainism, which was formed as a result of doctrinal schism in about AD 80 and continues today in parts of southern India. The sect's adherents reject property ownership and usually do not wear clothes.

digamma the sixth letter of the early Greek alphabet (Ϝ, ϝ), probably pronounced as 'w'. It became obsolete before the Classical period.

the Digest the compendium of Roman law compiled in the reign of ➤ JUSTINIAN.

Digger a member of a group of radical dissenters formed in England in 1649 as an offshoot of the ➤ LEVELLERS, believing in a form of agrarian communism in which common land would be made available to the poor; they first asserted their principles at St George's Hill, Walton-on-Thames, in Surrey in 1649, where they began to dig up the land and plant crops. The Diggers were suppressed by the authorities, and their leader, Gerrard Winstanley (fl. 1648–52) imprisoned.

digger in Australia and New Zealand, an informal term for a man, especially a private soldier. The term derived (in the early 20th century) from *digger*

'miner', reinforced by association with the digging of trenches on the battlefields.

digit any of the numerals from 0 to 9, especially when forming part of a number; the word comes from Latin *digitus* 'finger, toe', and the sense arose from the practise of counting on one's fingers.

dilemma a situation in which a difficult choice has to be made between two or more alternatives, especially ones that are equally undesirable. The word is recorded from the early 16th century, denoting a form of argument involving a choice between equally unfavourable alternatives; it comes via Latin from Greek *dilēmma*, from *di-* 'twice' + *lēmma* 'premise'.

See also ➤ *on the* HORNS *of a dilemma.*

dilettante a person who cultivates an area of interest, such as the arts, without real commitment or knowledge. The word is recorded from the mid 18th century, and comes from Italian 'person loving the arts', from *dilettare* 'to delight', from Latin *delectare.*

Society of the Dilettanti a society, originally founded about 1732 as a dining society by some gentlemen of wealth and position who had travelled in Italy, which soon devoted itself to the patronage of the fine arts. It has chiefly encouraged the study of classical archaeology.

diligence historical term for a public stagecoach; the word is recorded from the late 17th century, and comes from French, shortened from *carrossse de diligence* 'coach of speed'.

diligence is the mother of good luck proverbial saying, late 16th century.

dilligrout a kind of pottage which was offered to the British monarch on coronation day by the lord of the manor of Addington, Surrey (now part of London). The word is recorded from the mid 17th century, but the origin is unknown.

dime in North America, a ten-cent coin. The word in this sense is recorded from the late 18th century; in its original sense, 'a tithe or tenth part', it comes via Old French *disme* from Latin *decima pars* 'tenth part'.

dimension see ➤ FOURTH *dimension.*

dimissory in the Christian Church, denoting formal permission from a bishop (**letters dimissory**) for a person from one diocese to be ordained in another, or (formerly) for an ordained person to leave one diocese for another.

The word is recorded (as a plural noun) from late Middle English, and comes from late Latin *dimissorius*, from *dimiss-* 'sent away'. The adjective dates from the late 16th century, the original sense being 'valedictory'.

dimity a hard-wearing cotton fabric woven with stripes or checks, and derived through Italian or medieval Latin from Greek *dimitos*, from *di-* 'twice' + *mitos* 'warp, thread'

dine with Duke Humphrey go hungry, an expression recorded from the late 16th century. The origin is not clear, but in the 17th century it was associated with Old St. Paul's, London, and said of those who, while others were dining, passed their time walking in that place, or sitting in 'the chair of Duke Humphrey', or 'at Duke Humphrey's table'. According to Stowe, the monument of Sir John Beauchamp there was 'by ignorant people misnamed to be' that of Humphrey Duke of Gloucester, son of Henry IV (who was really buried at St. Albans); alternatively, it was suggested that an adjacent part of the church was known as *Duke Humphrey's Walk*.

Thomas Fuller, in his *History of the University of Cambridge* (1655) and *Worthies* (1662) gives a different explanation, suggesting that initially the reference to dining with 'the chair of Duke Humphrey' meant reading books in a stationer's shop in St Paul's churchyard, but that after the death of Humphrey of Gloucester, 'when many of his former Alms-men were at a losse for a meals meat', saying *dine with Duke Humphrey* came to mean, going hungry.

dine with St Giles and the Earl of Murray go hungry; a Scottish equivalent to ➤ DINE *with Duke Humphrey*, apparently relating to the tomb of the Earl of Murray who was buried in St Giles's Church, Edinburgh.

Ding an sich in Kant's philosophy, German phrase meaning, a thing as it is in itself, not mediated through perception by the senses or conceptualization, and therefore unknowable.

Dinmont see ➤ DANDIE *Dinmont*.

dinner see ➤ AFTER *dinner rest a while, after supper walk a mile*, ➤ BETTER *a dinner of herbs than a stalled ox where hate is*.

dinosaur a fossil reptile of the Mesozoic era, often reaching an enormous size; in extended usage, a person or thing that is outdated or has become obsolete because of failure to adapt to changing circumstances.

Dinosaurs were all extinct by the end of the Cretaceous period (65 million years ago), the most popular theory being that the extinctions were in fact the result of the impact of a large meteorite.

The word is recorded from the mid 19th century, and comes from modern Latin *dinosaurus* from Greek *deinos* 'terrible' + *sauros* 'lizard'. It was coined by the English anatomist and palaeontologist ➤ *Richard* OWEN.

Diocletian (245–313), Roman emperor 284–305. Faced with mounting military problems, in 286 he divided the empire between himself in the east and Maximian in the west. Diocletian insisted on the maintenance of Roman law in the provinces and launched the final persecution of the Christians (303); he abdicated in 305.

Diogenes (*c*.400–*c*.325 BC), Greek philosopher. The most famous of the ➤ CYNICS, he lived ascetically in Athens (according to legend, he lived in a tub) and was accordingly named *Kuōn* ('the dog'), from which the Cynics were then said to have derived their name. According to one story, he used to walk round Athens by day with a light, explaining that he was looking for an honest man. He emphasized self-sufficiency and the need for natural, uninhibited behaviour, regardless of social conventions.

Plutarch records that Alexander the Great once asked Diogenes if he lacked anything:

> 'Yes,' said he, 'that I do: that you stand out of my sun a little.'
>
> — Plutarch *Parallel Lives* (tr. Thomas North, 1579)

Alexander is supposed to have commented 'If I were not Alexander, I would be Diogenes.'

> I . . . become a penny-ante Diogenes, searching endlessly for an honest game.
>
> — J. Varley *Steel Beach* (1991)

Diogenes cup the cup-like cavity formed in the palm of the hand by arching the fingers and bending the thumb and little finger toward each other; from a story that the Cynic substituted this for a cup in raising water to his mouth.

Diomedes in Greek mythology, one of the ➤ SEVEN *against Thebes*, who was later one of the leaders of the Greek forces in the Trojan War; in medieval developments of the story, it is Diomedes with whom ➤ CRESSIDA falls in love and betrays Troilus.

horses of Diomedes in Greek mythology, the man-eating horses of *Diomedes*, a Thracian and son of Ares, which were captured as one of the ➤ *Labours of* HERCULES.

Dione in Greek mythology, the consort of Zeus at Dodona, the only seat of her cult, and by him the mother of Aphrodite.

Dionne Quintuplets five Canadian sisters, Émilie, Yvonne, Cécile, Marie, and Annette, who were born on 28 May 1934; they were the first documented set of quintuplets to survive birth. In 1935 they were made wards of the Canadian government, and in their early years were international celebrities and a major tourist attraction.

Dionysian period said to have been introduced by Dionysius Exiguus (see ➤ DIONYSIUS²) for calculating the date of Easter.

Dionysius see also ➤ PSEUDO-*Dionysius*.

Dionysius¹ the name of two rulers of Syracuse. Dionysius I (*c.*430–367 BC, ruled 405–367) was known as **Dionysius the Elder**. A tyrannical ruler, he waged three wars against the Carthaginians for control of Sicily, later becoming the principal power in Greek Italy after the capture of Rhegium (386) and other Greek cities in southern Italy. His son, Dionysus II (*c.*397–*c.*344 BC, ruled 367–357 and 346–344) was known as **Dionysius the Younger**. He lacked his father's military ambitions and signed a peace treaty with Carthage in 367. Despite his patronage of philosophers, he resisted the attempt by Plato to turn him into a philosopher king.

Dionysius² (d. *c.*556), Scythian monk and scholar, also known as **Dionysius Exiguus**. He is famous for introducing the system of dates BC and AD that is still in use today, accepting 753 AUC as the year of the Incarnation; this has since been shown to be mistaken. He is said to have taken the nickname *Exiguus* ('little') as a sign of humility.

Dionysius³ (1st century BC), Greek historian, literary critic, and rhetorician, also known as **Dionysius of Halicarnassus**. He lived in Rome from 30 BC and is best known for his detailed history of the city, written in Greek; this covers the period from the earliest times until the outbreak of the first Punic War (264 BC).

Dionysius⁴ (1st century AD), Greek churchman, also known as **Dionysius the Areopagite**. His conversion by St Paul is recorded in Acts 17:34 and according to tradition he went on to become the first bishop of Athens. He was later confused with St Denis and with a mystical theologian, Pseudo-Dionysius the Areopagite, who exercised a profound influence on medieval theology.

Dionysus in Greek mythology, a god, son of ➤ ZEUS and Semele; his worship entered Greece from Thrace *c.*1000 BC. Originally a god of the fertility of nature, associated with wild and ecstatic religious rites, in later traditions he is a god of wine who loosens inhibitions and inspires creativity in music and poetry. Also called ➤ BACCHUS.

Diophantus (fl. prob. *c.*250 AD), Greek mathematician. Diophantus was the first to attempt an algebraical notation, showing in *Arithmetica* how to solve simple and quadratic equations. His work led to Pierre de Fermat's discoveries in the theory of numbers.

Christian Dior (1905–57), French couturier. His first collection (1947), featured narrow-waisted tightly fitted bodices and full pleated skirts; this became known as the New Look. He later created the first A-line garments and built up a range of quality accessories.

Dioscuri in Greek and Roman mythology the twins Castor and Pollux, born to ➤ LEDA after her seduction by Zeus, and brothers of ➤ HELEN. Castor was mortal, but Pollux was immortal; at Pollux's request they shared his immortality between them, spending half their time below the earth in Hades and the other half on Olympus. They are often identified with the constellation Gemini.

The name comes from Greek *Dioskouroi* 'sons of Zeus'.

Diotrephes archaic term for a person who loves pre-eminence among others, especially in a congregation, from a man named in 3 John 9, 'I wrote unto the church: but Diotrephes, who loveth to have the pre-eminence among them, receiveth us not.'

> A man may figure as the Diotrephes of a Meeting.
> — Robert Southey *Sir Thomas More* (1829)

diphthong a sound formed by the combination of two vowels in a single syllable, in which the sound begins as one vowel and moves towards another (as in *coin*, *loud*, and *side*). Also, a digraph representing the sound of a diphthong or single vowel (as in *feat*); a compound vowel character; a ligature (such as æ).

Recorded from late Middle English, the word comes via French and late Latin from Greek *diphthongos*, from *di-* 'twice' + *phthongos* 'voice, sound'.

diploma a certificate awarded by an educational establishment to show that someone has successfully completed a course of study; an official document or charter. The word is recorded from the mid 17th century, in the sense 'state paper', and comes via Latin from Greek *diplōma* 'folded paper', from *diploun* 'to fold', from *diplous* 'double'.

diplomat an official representing a country abroad; in extended usage, a person who can deal with people in a sensitive and effective way. The word is recorded from the early 19th century, and comes from French, as a back-formation from *diplomatique* 'diplomatic', from Latin *diploma* (see ➤ DIPLOMA).

> A diplomat ... is a person who can tell you to go to hell in such a way that you actually look forward to the trip.
> — Caskie Stinnett *Out of the Red* (1960)

diplomatic bag a container in which official mail is sent to or from an embassy, which is not subject to customs inspection.

diplomatic edition an edition exactly reproducing an original version. *Diplomatic* in this sense is recorded from the late 18th century, and is probably due to the publication of the *Codex Juris Gentium Diplomaticus* (1695), a collection of public documents, many of which dealt with international affairs.

diplomatic immunity the privilege of exemption from certain laws and taxes granted to diplomats by the state in which they are working.

the Dipper in the US, an informal name for *the Plough* (see ➤ PLOUGH), taking its shape to represent a ladle for dipping up water.

diptych an ancient writing tablet consisting of two hinged leaves with waxed inner sides for writing on with a stylus; the word is recorded in English in this sense from the early 17th century.

Diptychs in the early Church were tablets recording a list of the living and the dead who were prayed for at the Eucharist; the word also denoted the names themselves, and the intercessions in the course of which they were introduced.

From the early 19th century, *diptych* has been used for a painting, especially an altarpiece, on two hinged wooden panels which may be closed like a book.

The word comes via late Latin from late Greek

diptukha 'pair of writing tablets', from Greek *diphtukhos* 'folded in two'.

Dipylon a double gateway in which the two gates are placed side by side, on the north-west side of Athens. The name is also used to designate a style of Greek pottery found during excavations near this site, or the designs found on such pottery.

Dircaean swan a name for the Greek poet ➤ PINDAR, who was born at Thebes (in Greek literature, symbolized by the spring ➤ DIRCE).

Dirce in Greek mythology, wife of the regent of Thebes and tormentor of the imprisoned ➤ ANTIOPE, put to death in revenge by Antiope's sons; they are said to have tied her to the horns of a bull so that she was dragged to death. After her death she was changed into the spring named for her, and which in Greek literature symbolizes Thebes.

Directoire of or relating to a neoclassical decorative style intermediate between the more ornate Louis XVI style and the Empire style, prevalent during the French ➤ DIRECTORY (1795–9).

the Directory the French revolutionary government in France 1795–9, comprising two councils and a five-member executive. It maintained an aggressive foreign policy, but could not control events at home and was overthrown by Napoleon Bonaparte.

dirge a lament for the dead, especially one forming part of a funeral rite. The word comes (in Middle English, denoting the Office for the Dead), from Latin *dirige!* (imperative) 'direct!', the first word of an antiphon (Psalm 5:8) used in the Latin Office for the Dead.

dirt see also ➤ *we must* EAT *a peck of dirt before we die.*

throw dirt enough and some will stick proverbial saying, mid 17th century.

Dirty Dick nickname of Nathaniel Bentley (1735?–1809), who kept a warehouse in Leadenhall Street which was the first glazed hardware shop in London; despite his early dandyism, the dirt of his premises was proverbial.

the Dirty Half-hundred in the British army, the 50th Foot (1st Battalion Royal West Kent), from the fact that, during the Peninsula war, the men wiped their faces with their black facings.

you dirty rat frequently attributed to James Cagney in a gangster part, but not found in this precise form in any of his films.

the Dirty Shirts in the British army, the 101st Foot (1st Battalion Munster Fusiliers), from the fact that they fought in their shirtsleeves at Delhi in 1857.

dirty water will quench fire proverbial saying, mid 16th century.

dirty work at the crossroads dishonourable, illicit, or underhand behaviour. The term (recorded from the early 20th century) may reflect a view of *crossroads* as a sinister place, where suicides were traditionally buried.

Dis in Roman mythology, the ruler of the Underworld, equivalent of the Greek Pluto (see ➤ PLUTO¹) or Hades; the name, as coming from *Dives* 'rich', may be a translation for *Pluto*.

> Proserpine gathering flowers
> Herself a fairer flower by gloomy Dis
> Was gathered.
> — John Milton *Paradise Lost* (1667)

disarmament see ➤ CAMPAIGN *for Nuclear Disarmament*, ➤ CONFERENCE *on Disarmament*.

discalced denoting or belonging to one of several strict orders of Catholic friars or nuns who go barefoot or are shod only in sandals. The word is recorded from the mid 17th century, and is a variant, influenced by French, of earlier *discalceated*, and from Latin *discalceatus*, from *dis-* (expressing removal) + *calceatus* (from *calceus* 'shoe').

Discharge Bible an edition of 1806 in which 1 Timothy 5:21, 'I charge thee before God', has 'discharge' for 'charge'.

disciple a personal follower of Christ during his life, especially one of the twelve Apostles; in extended usage, a follower or pupil of a teacher, leader, or philosophy.

The word is recorded from Old English, and comes from Latin *discipulus* 'learner', from *discere* learn.

See also ➤ BELOVED *disciple*.

Disciples of Christ a Protestant denomination, originating among American Presbyterians in the early 19th century and found chiefly in the US, which rejects creeds and regards the Bible as the only basis of faith.

discipline in its original meaning, punishment undergone as a form of penance, mortification by scourging oneself; the word is recorded in this sense from Middle English, and comes via Old French from Latin *disciplina* 'instruction, knowledge', from the base of *disciple*.

See also ➤ BOOKS *of Discipline*.

Discipline of the Secret the practice ascribed to the early Church of excluding catechumens and pagans from certain doctrines and rites; the term is a translation of modern Latin *disciplina arcana*, a term of post-Reformation controversy.

discord disagreement between people; lack of harmony. Recorded from Middle English, the word comes via Old French from Latin *discordare*, and ultimately from *dis-* (expressing negation, reversal) + *cor, cord-* 'heart'.

See also ➤ APPLE *of discord*.

age of discretion the age at which one is considered fit to manage one's affairs or take responsibility for one's actions; the phrase is recorded from the mid 19th century.

discretion is the better part of valour proverbial saying, late 16th century; often with allusion to Shakespeare's *1 Henry IV*.

Discworld the universe which provides the setting for the fantasy novels of Terry Pratchett (1948–), a disc resting on the backs of four elephants, in turn standing on the shell of a giant turtle swimming through space.

disease see ➤ COUGHS *and sneezes spread diseases*, ➤ CREUTZFELD–*Jakob disease*, ➤ DESPERATE *diseases must have desperate remedies*, ➤ LIFE *is a sexually transmitted disease*.

disgrace see ➤ POVERTY *is no disgrace, but it is a great inconvenience*.

disjecta membra scattered fragments, especially of a written work; the phrase is Latin, an alteration of *disjecti membra poetae*, as used by the poet Horace, 'in our case you would not recognize, as you would in the case of Ennius, the limbs, even though you had dismembered him, of a poet.'

the dismal science economics; a humorous term coined by Thomas Carlyle (1795–1881).

Dismas traditionally, the name of the penitent thief (the unrepentant thief is said to have been named *Gestas*) crucified with Jesus, to whom the promise was made in Luke 23:43, 'Today shalt thou be with me in paradise.' The name is found in the apocryphal Gospel of Nicodemus.

Walt Disney (1901–66), American animator and film producer. He made his name with the creation of cartoon characters such as Mickey Mouse, Donald Duck, Goofy, and Pluto. *Snow White and the Seven Dwarfs* (1937) was the first full-length cartoon feature film with sound and colour.

Disney is said to have commented in his last illness, 'Fancy being remembered around the world for the invention of a mouse!'

Disneyland a fantastic or fanciful place, a never-never land, from the name of the large amusement park set up by the Disney Corporation near Los Angeles.

> He drew the draperies on the bay and the glittering Disneylandish conglomeration of shops and restaurants.
>
> — Greg Bear *The Forge of God* (1987)

the Dispatch Box a box in the British House of Commons for official documents next to which Ministers stand when speaking.

mentioned in dispatches distinguished by having one's actions commended in an official military dispatch.

dispensation in Christian theology, a divinely ordained order prevailing at a particular period of history, as, **the Mosaic dispensation**.

Benjamin Disraeli (1804–81), British Tory statesman; Prime Minister 1868 and 1874–80. He was largely responsible for the introduction of the second Reform Act (1867), which doubled the electorate, and introduced measures to improve public health and working conditions in factories. He also ensured that Britain bought a controlling interest in the ➤ SUEZ *Canal* (1875) and made Queen Victoria Empress of India.

He wrote a number of novels, including *Sybil* (1845) which drew on his experience of political life, and is said to have addressed the Queen (after the publication of her *Leaves from the Journal of our Life in the Highlands* in 1868) with the words, 'We authors, Ma'am.' He told Matthew Arnold, 'Everyone likes flattery, and when you come to Royalty you should lay it on with a trowel.' In 1997, Tony Blair, speaking at the Queen's golden wedding celebrations, and reporting her injunction, 'Please don't

be too effusive,' commented, 'I am from the Disraeli school of Prime Ministers in their relations with the Monarch.'

See also ➤ PRIMROSE *League*, ➤ Two *Nations*.

Dissenter in historical British usage, a member of a non-established Church, a Nonconformist.

dissociation of sensibility T. S. Eliot's term for a separation of thought from feeling which he held to be first manifested in poetry of the later seventeenth century:

> In the seventeenth century a dissociation of sensibility set in, from which we have never recovered; and this dissociation, as is natural, was due to the influence of the two most powerful poets of the century, Milton and Dryden.
>
> — T. S. Eliot 'The Metaphysical Poets (1921)

dissolution of the monasteries the abolition of monasteries in England and Wales by Henry VIII under two Acts (1536, 1539), in order to replenish his treasury by vesting monastic assets in the Crown and to establish royal supremacy in ecclesiastical affairs.

distaff a stick or spindle on to which wool or flax is wound for spinning; in extended usage, used as modifier, as in ➤ DISTAFF *side*, to mean of or concerning women. The word is recorded from Old English (in form *distæf*); the first element is apparently related to Middle Low German *dise, disene* 'distaff, bunch of flax', the second is *staff*. The extended sense arose because spinning was traditionally done by women.

See also ➤ *have* TOW *on one's distaff*.

distaff side the female side of a family; also called *spindle side*.

St Distaff's day the day after Twelfth Day or the Feast of the Epiphany, on which day (7 January) women resumed their spinning and other ordinary employments after the holidays.

distance see also ➤ *City of* MAGNIFICENT *Distances*.

distance lends enchantment to the view proverbial saying, late 18th century; originally a quotation from the Scottish poet Thomas Campbell (1777–1844):

> 'Tis distance lends enchantment to the view, And robes the mountain in its azure hue.
>
> — Thomas Campbell *Pleasures of Hope* (1799)

a distinction without a difference an artificially created distinction, where no real difference exists; the phrase is recorded from the late 16th century.

dithyramb a wild choral hymn of ancient Greece, especially one dedicated to ➤ Dionysus; in extended usage, a passionate or inflated speech, poem, or other writing.

dittany any of a number of aromatic herbaceous or shrubby plants, especially (also **dittany of Crete**) a dwarf shrub with white woolly leaves and pink flowers, traditionally believed to have great healing properties, and to have the power to expel weapons.

The name is recorded from late Middle English, and comes via Old French or medieval Latin, from Latin *dictamnus*, *dictamnum*, from Greek *diktamnon*, perhaps from *Diktē*, the name of a mountain in Crete.

ditto used in accounts and lists to indicate that an item is repeated (often indicated by two apostrophes under the word or figure to be repeated). The word is recorded from the early 17th century in the sense 'the aforesaid month', and comes from Tuscan dialect, variant of Italian *detto* 'said', from Latin *dictus* 'said'.

divan historical term for a legislative body, council chamber, or court of justice in the Ottoman Empire or elsewhere in the Middle East. The word is recorded from the late 16th century, and comes via French or Italian from Turkish *dīvān*, from Persian *dīwān* 'anthology, register, court, or bench' (compare ➤ DIWAN).

As a piece of furniture, a *divan* was originally (early 18th century) a low bench or raised section of floor used as a long seat against the wall of a room, common in Middle Eastern countries; European imitation of this led to the sense 'low flat sofa or bed' (late 19th century).

Dives a poetic or literary term for a rich man, deriving (in late Middle English) from late Latin, used in the Vulgate translation of the Bible, in the story in Luke ch. 16 of the rich man and the beggar Lazarus (see ➤ LAZARUS).

> 'There must be rich and poor,' Dives says, smacking his claret.
> — William Makepeace Thackeray *Vanity Fair* (1848)

divide see also ➤ CONTINENTAL *Divide*.

divide separate or be separated into two groups for voting; the word in this sense is recorded from the *Original Journals of the House of Commons* of 1554,

'Upon the question for the bill the House did divide.'

divide and rule proverbial saying, early 17th century, translating Latin *divida et impera*; meaning that government control is more easily exercised if possible opponents are separated into factions.

divided see ➤ *a* HOUSE *divided cannot stand*.

divination the practice of seeking knowledge of the future or the unknown by supernatural means.

divine of, from, or like God or a god; the word is recorded from late Middle English, and comes via Old French from Latin *divinus*, from *divus* 'godlike' (related to *deus* 'god').

The **Divine Comedy** an epic poem, by ➤ DANTE (*c*.1309–20) describing his spiritual journey through Hell and Purgatory (with Virgil as guide) and finally to Paradise (with Beatrice as guide).

Divine Office in the Christian Church, the series of services of prayers and psalms said (or chanted) daily by Catholic priests, members of religious orders, and other clergy.

divine right of kings the doctrine that kings derive their authority from God not their subjects, from which it follows that rebellion is the worst of political crimes. It was enunciated in Britain in the 16th century under the Stuarts and is also associated with the absolutism of Louis XIV of France.

> The Right Divine of Kings to govern wrong.
> — Alexander Pope *The Dunciad* (1742)

divining rod a stick or rod, typically forked, used for ➤ DOWSING.

divinity see also ➤ MARROW *Controversy*.

divinity calf a dark brown calf leather with blind tooling, traditionally used for binding theological works.

division bell in Britain, a bell rung in Parliament to announce an imminent *division* of members into two groups to vote for or against a bill.

division of labour the assigning of different parts of a task or manufacturing process to different people. The term is recorded from the late 18th century, in Adam Smith's *On the Wealth of Nations* (1776).

division sign in mathematics, the sign ÷, placed between two numbers showing that the first is to be divided by the second, as in $6 \div 3 = 2$; the sign was invented by the English mathematician John Pell (1611–85).

divorce see ➤ VELVET *divorce*.

divus Latin, meaning 'godlike'; after the time of Augustus, this title was conferred on deceased Roman emperors to indicate their divine status.

Diwali a Hindu festival with lights, held in the period October to November, to celebrate the new season at the end of the monsoon. It is particularly associated with Lakshmi, the goddess of prosperity, and marks the beginning of the financial year in India.

The name comes from Hindi *dīvālī*, from Sanskrit *dīpāvali* 'row of lights', from *dīpā* 'lamp' + *vali* 'row'.

diwan a central finance department, chief administrative office, or regional governing body in Islamic societies; a chief treasury official, finance minister, or Prime Minister in some Indian states.

The word is Urdu, and comes from Persian *dīwān* (compare ➤ DIVAN).

Dixie an informal name for the Southern states of the US. It was used in the song 'Dixie' (1859), a marching song popular with Confederate soldiers in the American Civil War. The ultimate origin is uncertain, although it has been suggested that the name comes from French *dix* 'ten' on ten-dollar notes printed before the Civil War by the Citizens Bank of Louisiana, and circulating in the Southern States.

See also ➤ HEART *of Dixie*.

Dixiecrat in the US, informal name for any of the Southern Democrats who seceded from the Democratic party in 1948 in opposition to its policy of extending civil rights.

Dixieland a kind of jazz with a strong two-beat rhythm and collective improvisation, which originated in New Orleans in the early 20th century.

Dizzy a contemporary nickname for ➤ *Benjamin* DISRAELI (1804–81); it is recorded that when after a successful vote in the House of Commons, Disraeli refused a supper party at the Carlton to go home, his wife told people proudly, 'Dizzy came home to *me*.'

djinn an alternative spelling for ➤ JINN.

do as I say, not as I do proverbial saying, mid 16th century.

do as you would be done by proverbial saying, late 16th century; in Charles Kingsley's *The Water-Babies* (1863), Mrs *Doasyouwouldbedoneby* is the motherly and benevolent figure who is contrasted with her stern sister, Mrs *Bedonebyasyoudid*.

do right and fear no man proverbial saying, mid 15th century.

do unto others as you would they should do unto you proverbial saying, early 10th century.

dobbin a dated pet name for a draught horse or farm horse; recorded from the late 16th century, it is a pet form of the given name *Robert*.

In Thackeray's *Vanity Fair* (1847–8), William *Dobbin* is the name of Amelia's steadfast admirer, seen as a figure of patience and long-suffering.

dobby a spirit or apparition attached to a particular house or locality, especially, a household brownie.

dobby-horse a wooden figure of a horse, used in folk-plays or fairgrounds.

Docetae a group of 2nd-century Christian heretics believing in Gnostic doctrine (*Docetism*) that Christ's body was not human but either a phantasm or of real but celestial substance, and that therefore his sufferings were only apparent. The name comes from medieval Latin, based on Greek *dokein* 'seen'.

dock brief a brief given directly to a barrister selected from a panel of those present by a prisoner in the dock, without the agency of a solicitor.

in dock, out nettle a charm uttered in applying dock-leaves to nettle-stings; formerly also, a proverbial expression for changeableness and inconstancy.

docken Scottish term for the plant dock, as the type of something worthless.

doctor originally (in Middle English) a person skilled in, and therefore entitled to teach or speak authoritatively on, any branch of knowledge, a learned person; the word comes via Old French from Latin *doctor* 'teacher', from *docere* 'teach'.

From this developed the senses of ➤ DOCTOR *of the Church*, and (with capital initial) a person holding the highest university degree; the sense of *doctor* as an authority on medicine or surgery gave rise to the current meaning of a qualified medical practitioner.

➤ *St* LUKE, and St Cosmas and St Damian, martyrs of the early Church said in a late legend to have been twin brothers who were doctors, are patron saints of doctors of medicine.

See also ➤ an APPLE *a day keeps the doctor away*, ➤ CAPE *doctor*, ➤ *doctor* SOLIDUS, ➤ *Doctor* WHO, ➤ SPIN *doctor*.

Doctor: traditional epithets

NAME	PERSON
Angelic Doctor	St Thomas Aquinas (1225–74)
Invincible Doctor	William of Ockham (1285–1347/9)
Irrefragable Doctor	Alexander of Hales (c. 1186–1245)
Mellifluous Doctor	St Bernard of Clairvaux (1090–1153)
Merciless Doctor	John Haighton (1755–1826)
Resolute Doctor	John Baconthorpe (d. 1346)
Seraphic Doctor	St Bonaventura (1221–74); St Teresa of Ávila (1515–82)
Subtle Doctor	John Duns Scotus (c. 1265–1308)
Universal Doctor	St Albertus Magnus (c. 1200–80); Alain de Lille (1114–1203)

Doctor of the Church any of the early Christian theologians regarded as especially authoritative in the Western Church (particularly St Augustine of Hippo, St Jerome, St Ambrose, and St Gregory the Great), or those later so designated by the Pope (e.g. St Thomas Aquinas, St Teresa of Ávila).

the best doctors are Dr Diet, Dr Quiet, and Dr Merryman proverbial saying, mid 16th century; referring to an appropriate regime for someone who is ill.

Doctors' Commons (the site of) a London building occupied by the former College of Doctors of Laws, in which legal business relating to wills, marriage licences, and divorce proceedings was transacted. The name referred originally to the common table and dining-hall of the Association or College of Doctors of Civil Law in London, formed in 1509 by civilians entitled to plead in the Court of Arches.

Dodge City a city in SW Kansas. Established in 1872 as a railhead on the Santa Fe Trail, it rapidly gained a reputation as a rowdy frontier town.

> Even those strongholds of Dodge City-style showdowns—medical negligence claims, are not to be spared his reforming zeal.
> — *Counsel* March 1996

dodge the column shirk a duty, avoid work; *column* here means the usual formation of troops for marching.

dodger see ➤ the ARTFUL *Dodger*.

dodo a large extinct flightless bird with a stout body, stumpy wings, a large head, and a heavy hooked bill, which was found on Mauritius until the end of the 17th century. The name, recorded from the early 17th century, comes from Portuguese *doudo* 'simpleton', because the bird had no fear of man and was easily killed.

Dodona site of a famous oracle of Zeus at Epirus in ancient Greece, situated in a grove of oaks.

doe a doe is the emblem of St Withburga (d. *c.*743), an English princess who was said to have founded a community at East Dereham, and who was buried there; according to William of Malmesbury, she had a tame doe which gave her milk.

John Doe chiefly in the US, an anonymous party, typically the plaintiff, in a legal action. Recorded from the 18th century, *John Doe* was originally in legal use as a name of a fictitious plaintiff, corresponding to *Richard Roe*, used to represent the defendant.

dog a *dog* is the emblem of ➤ *St* DOMINIC, ➤ *St* ROCH, ➤ *St* EUSTACE, ➤ *St* HUBERT, and ➤ *St* BERNARD *of Aosta*.

➤ *St* HUBERT is the patron saint of healthy dogs and St Sithney, a Cornish saint who is said to have chosen his patronage rather than have charge of young women, is the patron saint of mad dogs.

The nickname of ➤ DIOGENES was **the Dog**.

See also ➤ *a* BARKING *dog never bites*, ➤ BLACK *dog*, ➤ BRAG *is a good dog, but Holdfast is better*, ➤ CARRIAGE *dog*, ➤ *the* CAT, *the rat, and Lovell the dog, rule all England under the hog*, ➤ DERBY *dog*, ➤ DOGS, ➤ HAIR *of the dog that bit you*, ➤ *he is a* GOOD *dog who goes to church*, ➤ HEARING *dog*, ➤ *is thy* SERVANT *a dog*, ➤ *it is a* POOR *dog that's not worth whistling for*, ➤ *it is easy to find a* STICK *to beat a dog*, ➤ *like* HUNT*'s dog that will neither go to church nor stay at home*, ➤ *a* LIVE *dog is better than a dead lion*, ➤ LOVE *me, love my dog*, ➤ *the* QUICK *brown fox jumps over the lazy dog*, ➤ R *is the dog's letter*, ➤ SEA *dog*, ➤ SHAGGY-*dog story*, ➤ *there are more* WAYS *of killing a dog than choking it with butter*, ➤ *there are more* WAYS *of killing a dog than hanging it*, ➤ THREE *things are not to be trusted; a cow's horn, a dog's tooth, and a horse's hoof*, ➤ *why* KEEP *a dog and bark yourself?*, ➤ *a* WOMAN, *a dog, and a walnut tree*, ➤ YELLOW-*dog Democrat*, ➤ *you can't* TEACH *an old dog new tricks*.

Dogs

NAME	OWNER
Boatswain	Lord Byron
Bran	Fingal
Buster	Roy Hattersley
Checkers	Richard Nixon
Diamond	Isaac Newton
Fala	Franklin Roosevelt
Flush	Elizabeth Barrett Browning
Gnasher	Dennis the Menace
Greyfriars Bobby	John Grey
Gromit	Wallace
Maera	Erigone
Nana	the Darling family
Orthrus	Geryon
Snoopy	Charlie Brown
Snowy	Tintin

give a dog a bad name and hang him proverbial saying, early 18th century.

**I am His Highness's dog at Kew,
Pray tell me, Sir, whose dog are you?**
epigram said to have been engraved on the collar of a dog given by the poet Alexander Pope to the Prince of Wales.

dog days the hottest period of the year (reckoned in antiquity from the heliacal rising of ➤ SIRIUS, the Dog Star).

dog does not eat dog proverbial saying, mid 16th century.

dog eat dog a situation of fierce competition in which people are willing to harm each other in order to succeed.

every dog has his day proverbial saying, mid 16th century.

dog in the manger a person who is inclined to prevent others from having or using things that one does not need oneself, from the fable of the dog that lay in a manger to prevent the ox and horse from eating the hay.

every dog is allowed one bite proverbial saying, early 20th century.

a dog is for life, not just for Christmas slogan of the National Canine Defence League.

dog Latin a debased form of Latin; the term is recorded from the late 18th century, and represents a derogatory use of *dog*.

the dog returns to its vomit proverbial saying, late fourteenth century; ultimately with biblical allusion to Proverbs 26:11, 'As a dog returneth to his vomit: so a fool returneth to his folly.'

dog rose a delicately scented Eurasian wild rose with pink or white flowers, which commonly grows in hedgerows, the root of which was in classical times thought to cure the bite of a mad dog.

Dog Star the star ➤ SIRIUS. The name is a translation of Greek *kuon* or Latin *canicula* 'small dog', both names of the star; so named as it appears to follow at the heels of Orion (the hunter).

a dog that will fetch a bone will carry a bone proverbial saying, early 19th century.

dog-tooth a small pointed architectural ornament or moulding forming one of a series radiating like petals from a raised centre, typical of Romanesque and Early English styles.

dog-whipper an official formerly employed to whip dogs out of a church or chapel; the word was later sometimes locally used for a sexton or beadle.

dogaressa the wife of a ➤ DOGE.

Dogberry a foolish constable in Shakespeare's *Much Ado About Nothing* (1598–9), used allusively for an ignorant and self-important official.

> All the saloons and major restaurants of Baltimore were closed last night as a mark of respect to the dead Roosevelt . . . It was silly, but it gave a lot of Dogberries a chance to annoy their betters.
> — H. L. Mencken diary, 15 April 1945

doge formerly the chief magistrate of Venice or Genoa. The word is recorded from the mid 16th century, and comes via French from Venetian Italian *doze*, based on Latin *dux, duc-* 'leader'.

it's dogged as does it proverbial saying, mid 19th century.

doggerel comic verse composed in irregular rhythm; verse or words that are badly written or expressed. Recorded from late Middle English (as an adjective describing such verse), apparently from *dog* used contemptuously, as in ➤ DOG *Latin*.

Doggett's Coat and Badge an orange livery with a silver badge offered as a trophy in an annual rowing contest among Thames watermen in London. It was instituted in 1715 by an Irish comic actor,

Thomas Doggett (1620–1721). The contest is the oldest sculling race in the world.

dogs see also ➤ *if you* LIE *down with dogs, you will get up with fleas,* ➤ *let* SLEEPING *dogs lie,* ➤ *the more I see of* MEN, *the more I like dogs,* ➤ *rain* CATS *and dogs.*

while two dogs are fighting for a bone, a third runs away with it proverbial saying, late 14th century.

dogs bark, but the caravan goes on proverbial saying, late 19th century.

the dogs of war the havoc accompanying military conflict, originally a quotation from Shakespeare's *Julius Caesar*

> Caesar's spirit, ranging for revenge,
> With Ate by his side, come hot from hell,
> Shall in these confines, with a monarch's voice
> Cry, 'Havoc!' and let slip the dogs of war.
> — William Shakespeare *Julius Caesar* (1599)

dogwatch either of two short watches on a ship (4–6 or 6–8 pm); the name refers to the light sleeping of dogs, and the difficulty of telling whether, when their eyes are shut, they are asleep or not.

doh the first and eighth note of a major scale.

doily a small ornamental mat made of lace or paper with a lace pattern, put on a plate under cakes or other sweet food. The word comes from *Doiley* or *Doyley,* the name of a 17th-century London draper. The word originally denoted a woollen material used for summer wear, said to have been introduced by this draper. The current sense (originally *doily napkin*) dates from the early 18th century.

Robert Doisneau (1912–94), French photographer, best known for his photos of the city and inhabitants of Paris, which he began taking in the 1930s. His photojournalism includes pictures taken during the liberation of Paris in 1944.

dolce stil nuovo a name (in Italian, literally 'sweet new style') for the courtly poetry of ➤ DANTE and other Italian poets of the 13th and 14th centuries.

dolce vita a life of heedless pleasure and luxury; the phrase, Italian, for 'sweet life', may have been popularized in English by Federico Fellini's film *La Dolce Vita* (1960).

doldrums the condition of a ship making no headway; a region of calms, sudden storms, and light unpredictable winds near the Equator; in figurative usage, a state or period of little activity or progress in affairs. The word is recorded (as *doldrum* 'dull, sluggish person') from the late 18th century, and may come from *dull,* on the pattern of *tantrums.*

dole originally, a part or division of a whole; one's share or portion; fate or lot in life. Later (from Middle English) the distribution of charitable gifts. The word is recorded from Old English (in form *dāl*), and is of Germanic origin.

The sense 'unemployment benefit' dates from the early 20th century.

See also ➤ HAPPY *man, happy dole,* ➤ TICHBORNE *dole.*

doleful see ➤ *the Doleful* EVENSONG.

doll see ➤ BARBIE *doll,* ➤ BLACK *doll.*

dollar the basic monetary unit of the US, Canada, Australia, and certain other countries. The word comes through early Flemish or Low German from German *T(h)aler,* short for *Joachimsthaler,* a coin from the silver-mine of *Joachimsthal* ('Joachim's valley'), now *Jáchymov* in the Czech Republic. The term was later applied to a coin used in the Spanish-–American colonies, which was also widely used in the British North American colonies at the time of the American War of Independence, and was adopted as the name of the US monetary unit in the late 18th century.

See also ➤ ALMIGHTY *dollar.*

Engelbert Dollfuss (1892–1934), Austrian statesman, Chancellor of Austria 1932–4. From 1933 Dollfuss attempted to block Austrian Nazi plans to force the *Anschluss* by governing without Parliament. He was assassinated by Austrian Nazis.

dolly see also ➤ CORN *dolly.*

Dolly name given to the lamb which in 1997 was successfully cloned by British scientists; the implications for possible commercial exploitation prompted the American Republican politician John Marchi (1948–) to say, 'We ought not to permit a cottage industry in the God business.'

Dolly Varden a large hat with one side drooping and with a floral trimming, from the name of a character in Dickens's *Barnaby Rudge* (1841), who wore a similar hat.

dolmen a megalithic tomb with a large flat stone laid on upright ones, found chiefly in Britain and France. The word is recorded from the mid 19th century and comes from French, perhaps via Breton from Cornish *tolmen* 'hole of a stone'.

dolphin a small gregarious toothed whale which typically has a beak-like snout and a curved fin on the back. Dolphins have become well known for their sociable nature and high intelligence.

Dolphin is used for a dolphin-like creature depicted in heraldry or art, typically with an arched body and fins like a fish; in early Christian art, used as an emblem of love, diligence, or swiftness.

Dom a title prefixed to the name of some Roman Catholic dignitaries and Benedictine and Carthusian monks, coming from Latin *dominus* 'master'.

Domdaniel a fabled submarine hall where a magician or sorcerer met with his disciples, introduced in the French 'Continuation of the Arabian Nights' (1788–93) by Dom Chaves and M. Cazotte, and from this adopted by Southey in *Thalaba* (1801). It is not clear whether 'Daniel' is intended to refer to the Hebrew prophet, or to 'a great Grecian sage' of that name who appears in the tale of 'the Queen and the Serpents' in the *Arabian Nights*.

Domdaniel is placed by Cazotte 'under the sea near Tunis', and by Southey 'under the roots of the ocean', and used by Carlyle in the sense of 'infernal cave' and 'den of iniquity'.

> Spain was as a black Domdaniel.
> — Thomas Carlyle *Cromwell* (1845)

Millennium Dome a large building resembling a giant dome erected at Greenwich in London to house a national exhibition celebrating British achievements at the millennium. *The Dome* was formally opened to visitors by invitation on New Year's Eve 1999, and subsequently to the general public; reactions to its exhibitions, such as the *Body Zone* and the *Spirit Zone*, and to its planned blend of entertainment and instruction, continue mixed.

Dome of the Rock an Islamic shrine in Jerusalem, for Muslims the third most holy place after Mecca and Medina. Built in the area of Solomon's temple, the shrine dates from the end of the 7th century. It surrounds the sacred rock on which, according to tradition, Abraham prepared to sacrifice his son Isaac and from which the prophet Muhammad made his miraculous midnight ascent into heaven (the Night Journey).

Domesday Book a comprehensive record of the extent, value, ownership, and liabilities of land in England, made in 1086 by order of William I. The name was apparently a popular one applied during the 12th century because the book was regarded as a final authority (with allusion to *doomsday* 'the Day of Judgement'); it is sometimes referred to as *Doomsday Book*.

dominations (in traditional Christian angelology) the fourth-highest order of the ninefold ➤ CELESTIAL *hierarchy*.

St Dominic (*c*.1170–1221), Spanish priest and friar; Spanish name *Domingo de Guzmán*. In 1216 he founded the Order of Friars Preachers at Toulouse in France; its members became known as ➤ DOMINICANS or Black Friars.

❑ **EMBLEM** In art his usual emblems are a lily or a black and white dog, from the punning *Domini canis* 'hound of God'.

❑ **FEAST DAY** His feast day is 8 August.

dominical letter any of the seven letters A–G used in Church calendars to indicate the date (1–7 January) on which the first Sunday in the year falls, and hence in dating movable feasts. (*Dominical* here means 'of Sunday as the Lord's day', and comes via late Latin, from Latin *dominicus*, from *dominus* 'lord, master'.)

Dominican a member of the Roman Catholic order of preaching friars founded by St ➤ DOMINIC, or of a religious order for women founded on similar principles.

Dominion historical term for each of the self-governing territories of the British Commonwealth. See also ➤ OLD *Dominion*.

domino any of 28 small oblong pieces marked with 0–6 pips in each half, used to play the game of **dominoes**, in which each piece is laid down to form a line, each player in turn trying to find and lay down a piece with a value matched by that of a piece at either end of the line already formed. This meaning dates from the early 19th century; in an earlier sense, the word meant a loose cloak, worn with a mask for the upper part of the face at masquerades. It is originally recorded in the late 17th century, from French, denoting a hood worn by priests in winter, and is probably ultimately based on Latin *dominus* 'lord, master'.

domino effect the effect of the ➤ DOMINO *theory*. The term derived from a speech by President Eisenhower in 1954 on the possibility of the spread of communist rule:

> You have broader considerations that might follow what you might call the 'falling domino' principle. You have a row of dominoes set up. You knock over the first one, and what will happen to the last one is that it will go over very quickly. So you have the beginning of a disintegration that would have the most profound influences.
>
> — Dwight Eisenhower speech, 7 April 1954

domino theory the theory that a political event in one country will cause similar events in neighbouring countries, like a falling domino causing an entire row of upended dominoes to fall.

Don see also ➤ *Don* CAMILLO, ➤ *Don* JUAN, ➤ *Don* QUIXOTE.

don a university teacher, especially a senior member of a college at Oxford or Cambridge; originally, a transferred colloquial use of the word as a Spanish title prefixed to a male forename.

Don Saltero's Coffee House a coffee house founded by John Salter, one-time servant of Sir Hans Sloane, about 1690; it stood in Cheyne Walk, Chelsea, and Salter (encouraged by Sloane) turned it into a museum of curios, in which he also operated as a barber and tooth-drawer. The coffee house was still in existence when Carlyle moved into Cheyne Walk in 1834, although it lost its eccentric character after Salter's death *c*.1728.

Donald Duck a Walt Disney cartoon character, an irascible duck with a high quacking voice who likes his own way; he first appeared in 1934, and Clarence Nash (1904–85) spoke the soundtrack for his voice.

> Almost everyone has heard the 'Donald Duck' voice produced after someone breathes helium from a balloon.
>
> — *Discover Diving* April 1993

Donatello (1386–1466), Italian sculptor. He was one of the pioneers of scientific perspective, and is especially famous for his lifelike sculptures, including the bronze *David* (*c*.1430–60). He later reacted against classical principles, evolving a style in which distortion is used to convey dramatic and emotional intensity, such as his wooden *St Mary Magdalene* (*c*.1455).

Donation of Constantine the grant by which the emperor ➤ CONSTANTINE supposedly conferred on Pope Sylvester I (314–35) and his successors spiritual supremacy over the other Christian patriarchs; the document was a forgery of the 9th century, but in the Middle Ages was widely regarded as important to claims of papal power in Europe.

Donation of Pepin the undertaking by the Carolingian king Pepin III to win for the papacy lands which had been conquered by the Lombards; these lands became the foundation of the Papal States.

Donatist a member of a schismatic Christian group in North Africa, formed in 311, who held that only those living a blameless life belonged in the Church. They survived until the 7th century, and were named after *Donatus* (d. *c*.355), a Christian prelate in Carthage and the group's leader.

Aelius Donatus (4th century), Roman grammarian. The *Ars Grammatica*, containing his treatises on Latin grammar, was the sole textbook used in schools in the Middle Ages.

what's done cannot be undone proverbial saying, mid 15th century; earlier in Greek.

donjon the great tower or innermost keep of a castle. The word is recorded from Middle English, and is a variant of *dungeon*.

donkey the *donkey* was used as a beast of burden, and traditionally taken as a type of stupidity.

A *donkey*, representing the deliberate eschewing of a horse that might have symbolized martial and worldly power, was the animal on which Jesus rode into Jerusalem on Palm Sunday.

The word was originally pronounced to rhyme with *monkey*, and may come from *dun* 'dull greyish-brown', or from the given name *Duncan*.

See also ➤ *a* PENNY *more and up goes the donkey*.

donkeys' years informal expression for a very long time, recorded from the early 20th century, and with punning allusion to the length of a donkey's ears; perhaps the origin of ➤ YONKS.

Donner Party a wagon train of emigrants who set out across the plains for California in 1846, and who after taking a new cutoff south of the Great Salt Lake, were so delayed that they were blocked by early snows in the Sierra Nevada. They camped at what is now called Donner Lake, and during the succeeding winter about half the party died; when the survivors were brought out in the spring by rescue parties from California, it was found that some of them had resorted to cannibalism.

Donnybrook Fair an annual fair once held in a what is now a suburb of Dublin; *donnybrook* may now be used to indicate uproar and confusion.

donzel archaic term for a young man who has not been knighted, a squire; the word is recorded from the late 16th century, and comes ultimately, via Italian, from a diminutive of Latin *dominus* 'lord, master'.

doolally temporarily deranged or feeble-minded; the expression was originally (in Indian army slang) **doolally tap**, from *Deolali* (the name of a town near Bombay) + Urdu *tap* 'fever'.

doom death, destruction, or some other terrible fate; in Christian belief, an archaic name for the Last Judgement. The word is recorded from Old English (in form *dōm*), and originally denoted 'statute, judgement'; it is of Germanic origin, from a base meaning 'put in place'.

See also ➤ CRACK *of doom.*

doomsday the last day of the world's existence; Judgement Day. From this, the nickname **Doomsday Sedgwick** was given to the puritan and mystic William Sedgwick (1610?–69?), who following the prophecy of a woman in the neighbourhood of Swaffham Prior, Cambridge, proclaimed the near advent of the day of judgement in 1646. Nothing happened on the appointed day, but during the following night there was a considerable storm.

Doomsday Book is sometimes found as a variant of Domesday Book.

door see also ➤ *a* CREAKING *door hangs longest,* ➤ HOLY *Door,* ➤ *keep the* WOLF *from the door,* ➤ OPPORTUNITY *never knocks twice at any man's door,* ➤ SIN *lieth at the door,* ➤ *when* ONE *door shuts, another opens.*

a door must either be shut or open proverbial saying, mid 18th century.

Doors an American rock group formed in 1965 and associated with the drug culture and psychedelia of the late 1960s. The group revolved around the flamboyant personality of lead singer Jim Morrison and is remembered for dramatic songs such as 'Light My Fire' (1967) and 'Riders on the Storm' (1971).

Doors of Perception a book (1954) by Aldous Huxley recommending experimental drug-taking; the American rock star Jim Morrison named the ➤ DOORS from this title. The phrase originally comes from Blake's *The Marriage of Heaven and Hell* (1790–3), 'If the doors of perception were cleansed everything would appear to man as it is, infinite.'

doppelgänger an apparition or double of a living person. The word (recorded from the mid 19th century) comes from German, literally 'double-goer'.

Dopper in South Africa, a member of the Gereformeerde Kerk, a strictly orthodox Calvinistic denomination, usually regarded as very old-fashioned in ideas, manners, and dress. The word is Afrikaans, of unknown origin.

Doppler effect in physics, an increase (or decrease) in the frequency of sound, light, or other waves as the source and observer move towards (or away from) each other. The effect causes the sudden change in pitch noticeable in a passing siren, as well as the red shift seen by astronomers. It is named for the Austrian physicist Johann Christian *Doppler* (1803–53), who discovered it.

Dora see also ➤ SISTER *Dora.*

Dora acronym personifying the **Defence of the Realm Act**, first passed in August 1914, which provided the British Govenment with wide powers during the 1914–18 war.

Dorado see ➤ EL *Dorado.*

Dorcas name of a woman in Acts 9:36, described as 'full of good works and almsdeeds which she did', after whom the **Dorcas society** of women in a church whose aim is to make and provide clothing for the poor is named.

Dorchester Company of Adventurers a joint stock company which attempted to establish a permanent fishing and farming colony on Cape Ann in 1623. When the colony failed, the settlers came first under the temporary rules of John Endecott, and were then organized as the New England Company for a Plantation in Massachusetts Bay, which became the Massachusetts Bay Company.

Gustave Doré (1832–83), French book illustrator, known for his woodcut illustrations of books such as Dante's *Inferno* (1861), Cervantes' *Don Quixote* (1863), and the Bible (1865–6); he produced so many of these that at one time he employed more than forty block cutters.

Dorian a member of a Hellenic people speaking the Doric dialect of Greek, thought to have entered Greece from the north *c.*1100 BC. They settled in the Peloponnese and later colonized Sicily and southern Italy.

Dorian mode the mode represented by the natural diatonic scale D-D (containing a minor 3rd and minor 7th).

Doric[1] relating to or denoting a classical order of architecture characterized by a plain, sturdy column and a thick square abacus resting on a rounded moulding.

Doric[2] the ancient Greek dialect of the Dorians, and in extended usage, any broad or rustic dialect, especially that spoken in the north-east of Scotland.

Dormition in the Orthodox Church, the passing of the Virgin Mary from earthly life; the feast held in honour of this on 15 August, corresponding to the Assumption in the Western Church.

dormouse the *dormouse*, some kinds of which are noted for spending long periods of hibernation, is used from the mid 16th century as the type of a sleepy or dozing person, and sleepiness is the overriding characteristic of the Dormouse in Carroll's *Alice in Wonderland*. The first element of the word is associated with French *dormir* or Latin *dormire* 'to sleep'.

dornick any of various fabrics, such as a silk or wool fabric formerly used for hangings, carpets, and vestments, and a linen fabric used in Scotland for tablecloths and napkins, which were originally manufactured at *Doornik*, the Flemish name for *Tournai*.

St Dorothy (d. *c.*313), a virgin martyr during the persecution of Diocletian. She is said to have been taunted on her way to execution by Theophilus, a young lawyer who asked her to send him fruits from the paradise to which she believed she was going. She agreed to do so, and after her death an angel brought him a basket holding three apples and three roses; this converted him, and he too was executed.
· □ **EMBLEM** Her emblem is a basket of fruit and flowers.
· □ **FEAST DAY** Her feast day is 6 February.

Dory see ➤ JOHN *Dory*.

doryphore a pedantic and annoyingly persistent critic. Recorded from the 1950s, the word was introduced by Harold Nicolson from French, literally meaning 'Colorado beetle', from Greek *doruphoros* 'spear-carrier'.

Fyodor Dostoevsky (1821–81), Russian novelist. Dostoevsky's novels reveal his psychological insight, savage humour, and concern with the religious, political, and moral problems posed by human suffering.

dot the i's and cross the t's ensure that all details are correct; the phrase is recorded from the mid 19th century.

Dotheboys Hall in Dickens's *Nicholas Nickleby*, the harsh and desolate school of which Mr Squeers is the headmaster:

> EDUCATION.—At Mr Wackford Squeers's Academy, Dotheboys Hall, at the delightful village of Dotheboys, near Greta Bridge in Yorkshire, Youth are boarded, clothed, booked, furnished with pocket-money, provided with all necessaries, instructed in all languages living and dead, mathematics, orthography, geometry, astronomy, trigonometry, the use of the globes, algebra, single stick (if required), writing, arithmetic, fortification, and every other branch of classical literature. Terms, twenty guineas per annum. No extras, no vacations, and diet unparalleled.
> — Charles Dickens *Nicholas Nickleby* (1839)

Douai a town in northern France which in the Middle Ages was ruled successively by Flanders, Burgundy, Austria, and Spain; in the 16th and 17th centuries it was a centre for English Roman Catholics in exile.

Douay Bible an English translation of the Bible formerly used in the Roman Catholic Church, completed at Douai in France early in the 17th century.

double Dutch language that is impossible to understand, gibberish. The term is recorded from the late 19th century, although *high Dutch*, in the same sense, is earlier.

double-headed eagle another term for the ➤ TWO-*headed eagle*.

double helix a pair of parallel helices intertwined about a common axis, especially that in the structure of the DNA molecule; the structure was originally proposed by Francis Crick (1916–) and James D. Watson (1928–), broadly explaining how genetic information is carried in living organisms and how genes replicate.

Double Summer Time daylight saving time in which clocks are set two hours ahead of standard time, used in Britain during the Second World War.

double whammy a twofold blow or setback; a figurative use of 'two blows resulting in a knockout'. The original (US) sense of whammy was 'an evil influence', and in the 1950s was particularly associated with the comic strip L'il Abner; a *double whammy* in this context was an intense and powerful look which had a stunning effect on its victims.

Double whammy in its current sense entered the language through modern politics, being given a high profile by Conservative campaigning in the British general election of 1992, with campaign posters on tax policy using the slogan, 'Labour's double whammy'.

doublethink the acceptance of or mental capacity to accept contrary opinions or beliefs at the same time, especially as a result of political indoctrination, coined by George Orwell in his novel *Nineteen Eighty-Four* (1949).

doubloon former name for a Spanish gold coin, so named because the coin was worth double the value of a pistole.

when in doubt, do nowt proverbial saying, mid 19th century.

Doubting Castle in Bunyan's *Pilgrim's Progress* (1678), the castle of Giant Despair.

> The Bastille was to be either the prize or the prison of the assailants. The downfall of it included the idea of the downfall of Despotism; and this compounded image was become as figuratively united as Bunyan's Doubting Castle and Giant Despair.
> — Thomas Paine *The Rights of Man* (1791)

doubting Thomas a person who is sceptical and refuses to believe something without proof, from biblical allusion to the apostle ➤ *St* THOMAS, who declared that he would not believe that Christ had risen unless he had seen and touched his wounds.

my cake is dough my project has failed; a proverbial expression recorded from the mid 16th century.

doughboy a United States infantryman, especially one in the First World War. The term is said to have been applied in the Civil War to the large globular brass buttons on the infantry uniform; it has also been suggested that it derives from the use of pipe clay 'dough' to clean the white belts worn by infantrymen.

doughnutting in a parliamentary debate, the practice of clustering around a speaker during a televised debate to make them appear well supported or to give the impression that the debate is well attended.

Douglas see ➤ BLACK *Douglas*.

the Douglas Cause the case in which Archibald Douglas (1748–1827) defended his right to inherit the Douglas estates as the son of Lady Jane Douglas; the Duke of Hamilton (the next heir) alleging that he was not Lady Jane's true son. The case was heard by the Scottish law lords over a period of 5 years (1762–7); the casting vote was finally given against Douglas, but was subsequently reversed by the House of Lords.

the Douglas larder the destruction by the ➤ BLACK *Douglas* (1286?–1330) of his own castle, having seized it by a stratagem from the English garrison.

dove a stocky seed- or fruit-eating bird with a small head, short legs, and a cooing voice, which is traditionally a symbol of peace.

In Christian art, a dove often stands for the Holy Spirit, as in Luke 3:22, in the account of Jesus being baptized by John in Jordan, 'And the Holy Spirit descended in a bodily shape like a dove upon him.' The dove in biblical terms is also associated with an olive branch as a messenger of peace and deliverance, as in the account in Genesis 8:8–12, of the dove sent out from the ark by Noah, which returned from its second flight with an olive leaf in its beak, 'so Noah knew that the waters were abated from the earth'.

A dove is the emblem of ➤ *St* AMBROSE, ➤ *St* DAVID, ➤ *St* GREGORY, and the Welsh-born St Samson, 6th-century bishop of Dol in Brittany.

In 20th century political usage, a *dove* is a person who (unlike a *hawk*) advocates peaceful or conciliatory policies, especially in foreign affairs.

See also ➤ TURTLE *dove*.

**in April Dove's flood
is worth a king's good.**
traditional rhyme about the river Dove, between Staffordshire and Derbyshire; the springtime flooding was seen as beneficial to the fields.

dovecotes see ➤ FLUTTER *the dovecotes*.

Dover see also ➤ DEAL, *Dover, and Harwich, the devil gave with his daughter in marriage*, ➤ JACK *of Dover*, ➤ WHITE *cliffs of Dover*.

Treaty of Dover made in 1670 between Charles II and Louis XIV; there were in fact two treaties, in the second and secret one of which Charles promised to declare himself a Catholic in return for a French subsidy.

a Dover shark and a Deal savage local saying, late 18th century; implying an equality of savagery among the fishermen of both ports.

Dow Jones Index an index of figures indicating the relative price of shares on the New York Stock Exchange, based on the average price of selected stocks. It is named from *Dow Jones & Co, Inc.*, a financial news agency founded by Charles H. *Dow* (1851–1902) and Edward D. *Jones* (c.1855–1920), American economists whose company compiled the first average of US stock prices in 1884.

down see ➤ *down* MEMORY *lane.*

Downing Street a street in Westminster, London, between Whitehall and St James's Park. No. 10 (since the time of Sir Robert Walpole) is the official residence of the Prime Minister; No. 11 is the home of the Chancellor of the Exchequer, and the Foreign and Commonwealth Office is also situated in the street. *Downing Street* is often used to personify the Prime Minister's immediate circle as distinct from the Parliamentary party.

> Downing Street is said to be unconvinced by Mr Prescott's green tax proposal.
> — *Sunday Telegraph* 25 January 1998

Downing Street Declaration a joint agreement between the British and Irish governments, formulated in 1993, forming the basis of a peace initiative in Northern Ireland.

Dowsabel an English form (through French) of the female name *Dulcibella*, perhaps used first in a pastoral song, and thus coming to mean a sweetheart, a lover.

dowsing a technique for searching for underground water, minerals, ley lines, or anything invisible, by observing the motion of a pointer (traditionally a forked stick or *divining rod*, now often paired bent wires) or the changes in direction of a pendulum, supposedly in response to unseen influences.

doxographer a writer who collected and recorded the opinions of the ancient Greek philosophers.

doxology a liturgical formula of praise to God. The word is recorded from the mid 17th century, and comes via medieval Latin from Greek *doxologia*, from *doxa* 'appearance, glory', from *dokein* 'seem'.

Arthur Conan Doyle (1859–1930), Scottish novelist and short-story writer, chiefly remembered for his creation of the private detective Sherlock Holmes. Holmes first appeared (with his friend Dr Watson, the narrator of the stories) in *A Study in Scarlet* (1887), and featured in more than fifty stories

and in novels such as *The Hound of the Baskervilles* (1902).

dozen a group or set of twelve.
> See also ➤ BAKER*'s dozen*, ➤ DEVIL*'s dozen*, ➤ LONG *dozen.*

Dr see ➤ *Dr* JEKYLL, ➤ *Dr* PRESTO, ➤ *Dr* SLOP.

Drachenfels a hill in western Germany on the east bank of the Rhine, which in German legend was the home of the dragon killed by ➤ SIEGFRIED.

> I feel as though I'd set a mousetrap and caught the Dragon from Drachenfels instead.
> — Manning Coles *The Fifth Man* (1946)

Draco¹ (7th century BC), Athenian legislator. His codification of Athenian law was notorious for its severity in that the death penalty was imposed even for trivial crimes, giving rise to the adjective **draconian**.

> You have a soft place in your heart yourself, you know—you're not a Draco, a Jeffreys.
> — George Eliot *Middlemarch* (1872)

Draco² a large northern constellation (the Dragon), stretching around the north celestial pole and said to represent the dragon killed by Hercules. It has no bright stars.

draconites a fabled precious stone supposed to have been formed in the brain of a dragon.

Dracula the Transylvanian vampire in Bram Stoker's novel *Dracula* (1897). The name is a variant of *Drakula*, *Dragwlya*, names given to Vlad Ţepeş (Vlad the Impaler), a 15th-century prince of Wallachia renowned for his cruelty.

> Consensus scares him the way garlic scares Count Dracula.
> — *American Spectator* March 1994

dragon a mythical monster like a giant reptile. In European tradition the dragon is typically fire-breathing and tends to symbolize chaos or evil, whereas in the Far East it is usually a beneficent symbol of fertility, associated with water and the heavens.

In medieval Norse and Germanic legends, *dragons* are often shown as guardians of treasure-hoards terrorizing the surrounding countryside; the dragon killed by ➤ BEOWULF in his final battle is a typical example.

A *dragon* is the emblem of ➤ *St* GEORGE, ➤ *St* MARGARET *of Antioch*, ➤ *St* MARTHA, St Sylvester (d. 335), Pope from 314 to 335, and the 6th-century Welsh-born St Armel, Breton abbot who is said to have captured a dragon and disposed of it by ordering it to plunge into the river below Mont-Saint-Armel.

Dragon is also used for any of (originally) four Asian countries, South Korea, Taiwan, Singapore, and Hong Kong, which developed booming economies based on high-technology exports.

The word is recorded from Middle English (also denoting a large serpent), and comes via Old French and Latin from Greek *drakōn* 'serpent'.

See also ➤ Bel *and the Dragon,* ➤ chase *the dragon,* ➤ Fafnir, ➤ red *dragon,* ➤ Rouge *Dragon,* ➤ Welsh *dragon.*

dragon boat a traditional type of Chinese rowing boat, decorated at the prow and stern with figures of the head and tail of a dragon, used in racing at an annual Spring festival, said to originate in ancient China.

According to legend, this derives from what occurred when the followers of a statesman who had drowned himself as a protest against the corruption of the court took out their boats to search for his body. In order to drive away fish which might eat the body, they beat drums and hit the water with their paddles. In the modern sport, the time for the paddle-strokes is given to the crew by a drum beaten by the helmsman sitting on a raised seat in the prow.

Dragon Hill a site near Faringdon in Oxfordshire, supposedly where St George killed the dragon.

Dragon Lady a domineering, powerful, or belligerent woman; from the name of a villainous Asian female character in the comic strip 'Terry and the Pirates', drawn by the American cartoonist Milton Caniff (1907–1988).

> Ms. Munn likes to project the image of a Dragon Lady, to the point of tacking the title to her office door. She cherishes a reputation for outspokenness.
> — *New Yorker* 21 October 1991

the Dragon of Wantley a monster whose legend is recounted in a 17th-century ballad which is a satire on earlier verse romances, and which depicts a Yorkshire dragon which devoured children and cattle, and which was killed by Moore of Moore Hall. The ballad was printed in Percy's *Reliques,* with a note indicating that the story represents a quarrel over tithes, with the dragon representing Sir Francis Wortley in his conflict with the parishioners.

> The remains of this extensive wood are still to be seen ... Here haunted of yore the fabulous Dragon of Wantley.
> — Sir Walter Scott *Ivanhoe* (1819)

dragon ship a Viking longship ornamented with a beaked prow.

dragon's blood a red gum or powder that is derived from the fruit of certain palm trees and from the stem of the dragon tree and related plants.

dragon's head in astronomy, archaic term for the descending node of the moon's orbit; in heraldry, the tincture tenné or tawny when blazoning is by the heavenly bodies.

dragon's teeth the teeth of the dragon killed by ➤ Cadmus in Greek legend, which when sown in the ground sprouted up as armed men; the expression **sow dragon's teeth**, meaning take action that (perhaps unintentionally) brings trouble about, derives from this.

dragonnade any of a series of persecutions directed by Louis XIV against French Protestants, in which troops (*dragons* or 'dragoons') were quartered upon them; from this, the term is used more widely for any persecution carried out with troops.

here be dragons alluding to a traditional indication of early map-makers that a region was unexplored and potentially dangerous.

dragoon a member of any of several cavalry regiments in the household troops of the British army; earlier, a mounted infantryman armed with a carbine. The word originally denoted a kind of carbine or musket, thought of as breathing fire, from French *dragon.*

Francis Drake (*c.*1540–96), English sailor and explorer. He was the first Englishman to circumnavigate the globe (1577–80), in his ship the *Golden Hind,* and his raid on Cadiz in 1587 delayed the sailing of the Armada by destroying its supply ships.

> These zones ... have commanded the respect and fear of sailors since the time of Francis Drake.
> — D. G. Campbell *Crystal Desert* (1992)

Drake Passage an area of ocean, named after ➤ *Francis* Drake, noted for its violent storms, connecting the South Atlantic with the South Pacific and separating the southern tip of South America (Cape Horn) from the Antarctic Peninsula.

Drake's drum in the poem by Henry Newbolt (1862–1938), supposedly a relic of ➤ *Francis* Drake, which will give warning in times of national danger.

drakes see also ➤ ducks *and drakes.*

dramatic unities the three dramatic principles requiring limitation of the supposed time of a drama to that occupied in acting it or to a single day (**unity of time**), use of one scene throughout (**unity of place**), and concentration on the development of a single plot (**unity of action**). The principles are derived from a Renaissance interpretation of Aristotle's *Poetics*.

dramatis personae the characters of a play, novel, or narrative; the participants in a series of events. Recorded from the mid 18th century, the phrase is from Latin, literally 'persons of the drama'.

Drang nach Osten the former German policy of eastward expansion, especially that espoused under Nazi rule. The phrase is German, literally 'pressure towards the east'.

drápa an Old Icelandic heroic and laudatory poem.

The Drapier's Letters a series of pamphlets written by ➤ *Jonathan* Swift under the guise of the 'Drapier', a Dublin draper, protesting against the introduction of ➤ Wood's *halfpence* into Ireland and their likely effect on the Irish economy; as a result, the coinage had to be withdrawn and Wood compensated by the government.

Draupnir in Scandinavian mythology, the gold ring belonging to ➤ Odin which produced nine further rings every night.

draw the longbow make exaggerated statements about one's own achievements, boast; the term is recorded from the early 19th century.

Drawcansir a character in Buckingham's *The Rehearsal* (1671), a blustering bragging figure who in the last scene is made to enter a battle and to kill all the combatants on both sides.

The name is formed as a parody on *Almanzor* in Dryden's *Conquest of Granada*, perhaps intended to suggest *draw*ing a *can* of liquor.

> Is England alone to be the Drawcansir of the world, and to bully not only her enemies, but her friends?
> — Benjamin Franklin in *The London Chronicle* 18 August 1768

drawing room a room in a private house in which guests can be received and entertained, originally (denoting a private room attached to a more public one) a shortening of *withdrawing-room* 'a room to withdraw to'.

whosoever **draws** his sword against the prince must throw the scabbard away proverbial saying, early 17th century.

dreadlocks a Rastafarian hairstyle in which the hair is washed but not combed and twisted while wet into tight braids or ringlets hanging down on all sides.

dreadnought a type of battleship introduced in the early 20th century, larger and faster than its predecessors and equipped entirely with large-calibre guns. The term comes from the name of Britain's HMS *Dreadnought*, which was the first to be completed (1906).

The popular slogan 'We want eight, and we won't wait', on the construction of dreadnoughts, is recorded from 1909, and in the same year Lloyd George used the dreadnought as a standard of comparison for the suggested cost of the aristocracy:

> A fully-equipped duke costs as much to keep up as two Dreadnoughts; and dukes are just as great a terror and they last longer.
> — David Lloyd George speech at Newcastle, 9 October 1909

dream see also ➤ American *dream*, ➤ pipe *dream*.

dream of a funeral and you hear of a marriage proverbial saying, mid 17th century.

City of Dreaming Spires a name for Oxford, deriving originally from a poem by Matthew Arnold:

> And that sweet City with her dreaming Spires.
> — Matthew Arnold 'Thyrsis' (1866)

dreams see also ➤ morning *dreams come true*.

dreams go by contraries proverbial saying, early 15th century.

dree one's weird submit to one's destiny; *dree*, a Scottish or archaic word meaning 'endure', is recorded from Old English (in form *drēogan*) and is of Germanic origin; related to Old Norse *drȳgja* 'practise, perpetrate'.

dreidel a small four-sided spinning top with a Hebrew letter on each side, used by Jewish people; a gambling game played with such a top, especially at Hanukkah.

Dresden[1] a city in eastern Germany, the capital of Saxony, on the River Elbe. Famous for its baroque architecture, it was almost totally destroyed by Allied bombing in 1945, and is sometimes referred to as a type of complete destruction of this kind.

> Inflicting a 'Dresden' on a nation of 10 million people
> was grossly out of proportion to the problem.
> — *Independent* 10 June 1999

Dresden² porcelain ware with elaborate decoration and delicate colourings, made originally at Dresden (see ➤ DRESDEN¹) and (since 1710) at nearby Meissen.

> How bored she was with that face! Fair hair, big blue
> eyes, little pouting mouth, pink and white complexion.
> Like a doll. Yet Chris approved. 'A Dresden
> Shepherdess,' he'd called her.
> — D. Devine *Illegal Tender* (1970)

dress-down Friday in the US a day, typically a Friday, on which it is considered acceptable for office workers to dress more casually ('dress down') in the workplace.

Alfred Dreyfus (1859–1935), French army officer, of Jewish descent. In 1894 he was falsely accused of providing military secrets to the Germans; his trial and imprisonment caused a major political crisis in France. He was eventually rehabilitated in 1906. Notable among his supporters was the novelist Émile Zola, whose famous open letter to the President of the French Republic in connection with the affair was entitled, '*J'accuse* [I accuse].'

drink see ➤ EAT, *drink, and be merry,* ➤ *you can take a* HORSE *to the water but you can't make him drink.*

he that drinks beer, thinks beer proverbial saying, early 19th century.

dripping see ➤ *a* DRIPPING *June sets all in tune.*

drive see also ➤ *drive a* COACH *and horses through.*

drive-by shooting a shooting carried out from a passing vehicle; the term is recorded in the US from the early 1980s, and was linked particularly with rival teenage gangs and with the drug culture. The term *drive-by* soon began to be used figuratively, especially in implying a hit-and-run approach to a subject, as in **drive-by documentary** and **drive-by journalism**.

drive gently over the stones proverbial saying, early 18th century; traditional advice to the inexperienced.

you can drive out Nature with a pitchfork, but she keeps on coming back proverbial saying, mid 16th century; originally, with reference to the Epistles of the Roman poet Horace (65–8 BC), '*Naturam expelles furca, tamen usque recurret* [You may drive out nature with a pitchfork, yet she'll be constantly running back].'

driven snow snow piled into drifts or made smooth by the wind, taken as a type of purity.

> I'm as pure as the driven slush.
> — Tallulah Bankhead in *Saturday Evening Post* 12 April
> 1947

Drogheda a port in the NE Republic of Ireland, where in 1649 the inhabitants were massacred after refusing to surrender to Oliver Cromwell's forces.

> Hazlerigg looked more than usually like the Great
> Protector—in one of his Drogheda and Wexford
> moods.
> — Michael Gilbert *They Never Looked Inside* (1948)

droit de seigneur the alleged right of a medieval feudal lord to have sexual intercourse with a vassal's bride on her wedding night. The phrase is French, literally 'lord's right'.

droit of Admiralty a right by which proceeds arising from wrecks or the seizure of enemy ships could be claimed by the Court of Admiralty and are now paid into the Exchequer.

drone a male bee in a colony of social bees, which does no work but can fertilize a queen; in figurative usage (from the early 16th century), a person who does no useful work and lives off others.

Drones Club in the stories of P. G. Wodehouse, the club frequented by Bertie Wooster and his friends:

> In the heart of London's clubland there stands a tall and
> grimly forbidding edifice known to taxi-drivers and the
> elegant young men who frequent its precincts as the
> Drones Club. Yet its somewhat austere exterior belies
> the atmosphere of cheerful optimism and bonhomie
> that prevails within. For here it is that young gallants of
> Mayfair forgather for the pre-luncheon bracer and to
> touch lightly on the topics of the day.
> — P. G. Wodehouse *Eggs, Beans, and Crumpets* (1940)

drop see also ➤ *drop* SERENE, ➤ *drop the* PILOT, ➤ PRINCE *Rupert's drop.*

dropping see ➤ CONSTANT *dropping wears away a stone.*

dróttkvætt a complex verse-form used by the court poets of early Scandinavia; the syllabic pattern and internal rhyme-scheme make it likely that early poems were transmitted to later generations without much alteration. The word is Old Norse, and means 'court poem'.

Drottningholm the winter palace of the Swedish royal family, on an island to the west of Stockholm. It was built in 1662 for Queen Eleonora of Sweden.

a **drowning** man will clutch at a straw proverbial saying, mid 16th century.

drug a substance which has a physiological effect when ingested or otherwise introduced into the body; the word is recorded from Middle English, and comes from Old French *drogue*, and perhaps ultimately from Middle Dutch *droge vat*, literally 'dry vats', referring to the contents (i.e. dry goods).

See also ➤ DESIGNER *drug*, ➤ RECREATIONAL *drugs*.

Druid a priest, magician, or soothsayer in the ancient Celtic religion; the word is first recorded from the mid 16th century in English sources, in Golding's translation of Caesar's *Martiall Exploytes in Gallia* (1565), and comes from Latin *druidae*, *druides* (plural), from Gaulish, related to Irish *draoidh* 'magician'.

According to Pliny the elder, *mistletoe* was the sacred plant of the Druids, who cut it ritually with a golden sickle as part of their sacrificial ceremonies. The popular association of druids with oak groves derives largely from Pliny's account.

The use of *Druid* for a member of a group claiming to represent or be derived from this religion is recorded from the early 18th century.

Druid stone name for the stone of which the megalithic monument Stonehenge on Salisbury Plain in Wiltshire is made.

United Ancient Order of Druids a secret benefit society founded in London in 1781, and having lodges called *groves*.

drum see also ➤ DRAKE's *drum*, ➤ LAMBEG *drum*, ➤ MARCH *to a different drum*.

drum-and-trumpet history history in which undue prominence is given to battles and wars, a derogatory term recorded from the late 19th century:

> Whatever the worth of the present work may be, I have striven throughout that it should never sink into a 'drum and trumpet history'.
> — J. R. Green *A Short History of the English People* (1928)

drum someone out expel or dismiss with ignominy, with allusion to the formal military drum beat accompanying dismissal from a regiment.

drumhead court martial carried out by an army in the field, originally round an upturned drum, for

summary treatment of offences during military operations.

Drummond see ➤ BULLDOG *Drummond*.

Drummond light another term for ➤ LIMELIGHT (from the inventor, Captain T. *Drummond*, Royal Engineers, c.1825).

drunk as David's sow very drunk; informal term recorded from the early 18th century.

drunken see also ➤ HEAVEN *protects children, sailors, and drunken men*

drunken Helot in allusion to the statement by Plutarch that Helots were, on certain occasions, forced to appear in a state of drunkenness as an object lesson to Spartan youth.

drunken Parliament name for the Scottish parliament which met after the Restoration on 1 January 1661.

Drury Lane the site in London of the Theatre Royal, one of London's most famous theatres, where ➤ *Nell* GWYN is said to have sold oranges. While under ➤ SHERIDAN's managament in the late 18th century, it was demolished and rebuilt; the new theatre, however, burned down in 1809, and it was said that Sheridan was found watching it, drinking a glass of wine, saying, 'A man may surely be allowed to take a glass of wine by his own fireside.'

The present and fourth theatre on this site, dating from 1812, was not particularly successful until the 1880s, when it became famous for its melodramas and spectacles.

> The leading lady is not a heroine of the Drury Lane type; nor does the villain forge or assassinate.
> — George Bernard Shaw *The Quintessence of Ibsenism* (1891)

Druze a member of a political and religious sect of Islamic origin, living chiefly in Lebanon and Syria. The Druze broke away from the Ismaili Muslims in the 11th century; they are regarded as heretical by the Muslim community at large.

The name comes from French, and derives from Arabic *durūz* (plural), from the name of one of their founders, Muhammad ibn Ismail *al-Darazī* (died 1019).

dryad in folklore and Greek mythology, a nymph inhabiting a tree, especially an oak tree, or a wood; the word comes via Old French and Latin from Greek *druas, druad-*, from *drus* 'tree'.

Dr Jonas Dryasdust a fictional antiquarian to whom Sir Walter Scott pretended to dedicate *Ivanhoe* (1819) and other novels; from this, a writer or student of antiquities, history, or statistics, who is concerned with the driest and most uninteresting details.

John Dryden (1631–1700), English poet, critic, and dramatist of the Augustan Age, nicknamed 'Glorious John' by Sir Walter Scott.

See also ➤ ABSALOM *and Achitophel,* ➤ ANNUS *mirabilis,* ➤ *the* NOBLE *savage.*

Marie Jeanne Du Barry (1743–93), French courtier and mistress of Louis XV. During the French Revolution she was arrested by the Revolutionary Tribunal and guillotined.

the Dual Monarchy Austria-Hungary, especially between 1867 and 1918.

dualism a theory or system of thought that regards a domain of reality in terms of two independent principles, especially mind and matter (**Cartesian dualism**). Also, the religious doctrine that the universe contains opposed powers of good and evil, especially seen as balanced equals; in Christian theology, the doctrine that Christ had two coexisting natures, human and divine.

dub make (someone) a knight by the ritual touching of the shoulder with a sword; the word comes from Old French *adober* 'equip with armour'.

Alexander Dubček (1921–92), Czechoslovak statesman, First Secretary of the Czechoslovak Communist Party 1968–9. Dubček was the driving force behind the political reforms of 1968, (the ➤ PRAGUE *Spring*) which prompted the Soviet invasion of Czechoslovakia in 1968 and his removal from office. After the collapse of communism in 1989 he was elected speaker of the Federal Assembly in the new Czechoslovak parliament.

Dublin the capital city of the Republic of Ireland, situated on the Irish Sea at the mouth of the River Liffey, built on the site of a Viking settlement, and noted for its 18th-century architecture. The name comes from Irish *dubh* 'black' + *linn* 'pool', in reference to the dark waters of the Liffey by which the first settlement was made. Ptolemy recorded the Celtic name in the 2nd century AD as *Eblana* (now used in literary imprints).

The current Irish name of the city is *Baile Átha Cliath* meaning 'town of the hurdle ford', describing the material (*cliath* 'woven withy, hurdle') used for fording rivers in ancient times.

ducat a gold coin formerly current in most European countries. The origin is Italian *ducato*, referring to a silver coin minted by the Duke of Apulia in 1190.

Duccio (*c.*1255–*c.*1320), Italian painter, founder of the Sienese school of painting, building on elements of the Byzantine tradition. The only fully documented surviving work by him is the *Maestà* for the high altar of Siena cathedral (completed 1311).

Il Duce the title, in Italian 'the Leader', assumed by Benito Mussolini in 1922.

duchess the wife or widow of a duke; a woman holding a rank equivalent to duke in her own right. The word is recorded from late Middle English, and comes via Old French from medieval Latin *ducissa*, from the Latin base of *duke*.

See also ➤ *the* FLYING *Duchess.*

duchy see ➤ *Duchy of* CORNWALL.

duck see also ➤ BOMBAY *duck,* ➤ BREAK *one's duck,* ➤ DONALD *Duck,* ➤ *St* CUTHBERT's *duck.*

duck in cricket, a batsman's score of nought. From a shortening of *duck's egg*, used for the figure o because of its similar outline.

ducking stool a chair fastened to the end of a pole, used formerly to plunge offenders into a pond or river as a punishment, and used particularly for disorderly women, scolds, and dishonest tradesmen.

duckling see ➤ UGLY *duckling.*

ducks and drakes a game of throwing flat stones so that they skim along the surface of water; in figurative use, **play ducks and drakes with** trifle with; treat frivolously or wastefully.

ductus litterarum the general shape and formation of letters and their combinations in manuscripts, the study of which may enable the restoration of true readings in a corrupt text. The phrase is Latin, from *ductus* 'conduct' + *litterarum* 'of letters'.

Duessa in Spenser's *Faerie Queene*, the daugher of Deceit and Shame, standing for falsity in general, but in particular alluding to the Roman Catholic Church and Mary, Queen of Scots; she is contrasted with Una, who stands for single-minded adherence to true religion.

> The impression of this figure of Margaret—with all Margaret's character taken out of it, as completely as if some evil spirit had got possession of her form—was so deeply stamped upon his imagination, that when he wakened he felt hardly able to separate the Una from the Duessa.
>
> — Elizabeth Gaskell *North and South* (1854)

duke a male holding the highest hereditary title in the British and certain other peerages; (chiefly historical) in some parts of Europe, a male ruler of a small independent state. Recorded from Old English (denoting the ruler of a duchy) the word comes via Old French from Latin *dux, duc-* 'leader'.

See also ➤ DINE with Duke Humphrey, ➤ IRON *Duke*, ➤ the PROUD *duke*.

Duke of Exeter's daughter an instrument of torture supposedly invented by a Duke of Exeter.

Duke of York's Column in London, at the top of Waterloo Steps, erected in memory of Frederick Duke of York, second son of George III.

Dukhobor a member of a Russian Christian sect similar to the Society of Friends, many members of which migrated to Canada in 1899 after persecution for refusing military service. The name comes from Russian, from *dukh* 'spirit' + *borets* 'wrestler'.

dulce et decorum est pro patria mori Latin for, 'lovely and honourable it is to die for one's country'; originally a quotation from the *Odes* of Horace, and used with an ironic edge by the First World War poet Wilfred Owen (1893–1918):

> The old Lie: Dulce et decorum est
> Pro patria mori.
>
> — Wilfred Owen 'Dulce et Decorum Est'

Dulcinea the name given by ➤ *Don* QUIXOTE to his mistress in Cervantes's romance; more generally, a sweetheart, a lover.

Dulcinist a member of a religious sect who opposed the papacy and rejected marriages, oaths, and rites and ceremonies generally.

John Foster Dulles (1888–1959), American Republican statesman and international lawyer. He was the US adviser at the founding of the United Nations in 1945 and negotiated the peace treaty with Japan in 1951. As Secretary of State at the height of the cold war (1953–9) he urged the stockpiling of nuclear arms to deter Soviet aggression, and is associated with the policy of ➤ BRINKMANSHIP.

dum spiro spero Latin motto, 'while I breathe I hope'.

dum vivimus vivamus Latin motto, 'while we live let us live'.

Alexandre Dumas (1802–70), French novelist and dramatist, known as **Dumas père**. Although he was a pioneer of the romantic theatre in France, his reputation now rests on his historical adventure novels *The Three Musketeers* (1844–5) and *The Count of Monte Cristo* (1844–5).

See also ➤ THREE *Musketeers*.

dumb see also ➤ IT *takes 40 dumb animals to make a fur coat, but only one to wear it.*

dumb crambo a game in which one side has to guess a word chosen by the other side, after being given a word which rhymes with it; the term is first recorded in the early 19th century.

the dumb ox a nickname for ➤ St THOMAS *Aquinas*; according to Butler's *Lives of the Saints* (1756) given to him by his schoolfellows because they thought his habitual silence indicated stupidity. ➤ ALBERTUS *Magnus* is said to have commented, 'We call him the dumb ox, but he will give such a bellow of learning as will be heard all over the world.'

dumdum a kind of soft-nosed bullet that expands on impact and inflicts laceration, from *Dum Dum*, name of a town and arsenal near Calcutta, India, where such bullets were first produced.

dumpling see ➤ DEVONSHIRE *dumpling*.

dun make persistent demands on (someone), especially for payment of a debt. First recorded (in the early 17th century) as a noun, from *Dunkirk* privateer. An alternative (18th-century) explanation derived it from the name of *Joe Dun*, said to have been a bailiff in Lincoln.

Book of the Dun Cow a fragmentary Irish manuscript of the 11th century, containing stories from Irish mythology, and in particular the deeds of Cuchulain.

Dun Cow of Dunsmore a monstrous creature said in an early 14th-century verse romance to have been killed by the medieval hero ➤ GUY *of Warwick*.

Dunblane a town in Scotland which in March 1996 was the scene of a tragedy when sixteen pupils of the local primary school with their teacher were shot to death by a ➤ SPREE *killer*; their headmaster was quoted as saying, 'Evil visited us yesterday. We don't know why.' Public pressure subsequently resulted in a change on handgun law.

dunce a foolish or ignorant person; originally an epithet for a follower of ➤ *John* DUNS *Scotus*, whose adherents were ridiculed by 16th-century humanists and reformers as enemies of learning.

See also ➤ PARLIAMENT *of dunces*.

dunce's cap a paper cone formerly put on the head of a *dunce* at school as a mark of disgrace; the expression is recorded from the mid 19th century.

The Dunciad the epic of dunces; title of a mock-heroic satire by Alexander Pope (1688–1744) which was inspired by criticism of Pope's edition of Shakespeare, and which ridicules Cibber and other writers.

Dundas see ➤ CHARLOTTE *Dundas*, ➤ STARVATION *Dundas*.

Dundee see ➤ BONNIE *Dundee*.

Dundreary long side-whiskers worn without a beard, from the name of Lord *Dundreary*, a character in T. Taylor's comedy *Our American Cousin* (1858).

Dunfermline a city in Fife, Scotland, near the Firth of Forth. A number of Scottish kings, including Robert the Bruce, are buried in its Benedictine abbey, and the opening of the ballad *Sir Patrick Spens*, 'The king sits in Dunfermline town Drinking the blude-red wine' emphasizes the traditional connection with Scottish royalty.

dunghill see ➤ *every* COCK *will crow upon his own dunghill*.

Dunker a member of the German Baptist Brethren, a sect of Baptist Christians founded in 1708 but living in the US since the 1720s. The name comes from Pennsylvanian German, from *dunke* 'to dip'.

Dunkirk a port of northern France, which in the Middle Ages was a centre of privateering activity. In modern times, *Dunkirk* was the scene of the evacuation of the British Expeditionary Force in 1940. Forced to retreat to the Channel by the German breakthrough at Sedan, 335,000 Allied troops were evacuated by warships, requisitioned civilian ships, and a host of small boats, under constant attack from the air.

The expression **Dunkirk spirit** is used (sometimes ironically) for the refusal to surrender or despair in a time of crisis.

Dunmow flitch a side of bacon awarded at Great Dunmow in Essex on Whit Monday to any married couple who will swear that they have not quarrelled or repented of their marriage vows for at least a year and a day. The custom was instituted in Great Dunmow; the earliest evidence for it is 1244, though its origin may be earlier.

John Duns Scotus (*c.*1265–1308), Scottish theologian and scholar. A profoundly influential figure in the Middle Ages, he was the first major theologian to defend the theory of the Immaculate Conception, and opposed ➤ St THOMAS *Aquinas* in arguing that faith was a matter of will rather than something dependent on logical proofs.

In the 16th century his name, through his followers the *Scotists*, became associated with a scholasticism characterized by hair-splitting and useless distinctions, which was seen as inimical to the new learning; from this developed the word ➤ DUNCE.

John Dunstable (*c.*1390–1453), English composer. He was a significant early exponent of counterpoint.

Dunstable way a proverbial type of plainness and directness, recorded from the mid 16th century; apparently referring originally to the road from London (Edgware Road) to Dunstable in Bedfordshire, a part of the ancient Roman Road called Watling Street, notable for its long, straight, and even stretches.

St Dunstan (*c.*909–88), Anglo-Saxon prelate. As Archbishop of Canterbury he introduced the strict Benedictine rule into England and succeeded in restoring monastic life. He is traditionally said to have been a metalworker.

❑ **PATRONAGE** He is patron of blacksmiths, goldsmiths, jewellers, and locksmiths, and of the blind.

❑ **EMBLEM** His emblems are tongs and pincers; he is sometimes shown holding the devil by the nose with a pair of tongs.

❑ **FEAST DAY** His feast day is 19 May.

duodecimo a size of book in which each leaf is one twelfth of the size of the printing sheet. The word is recorded from the mid 17th century, and comes from Latin (*in*) *duodecimo* '(in) a twelfth'.

Auguste Dupin detective created by Edgar Allan Poe in *The Murders in the Rue Morgue* (1841) and other stories, noted for his powers of logic and deduction.

Dame Durden from a traditional song, a name for a housewife; in Dickens's *Bleak House* (1853), when

Esther Summerson takes over the household keys for her guardian Mr Jarndyce, she is nicknamed *Dame Durden*.

Durga in Hindu mythology, a fierce goddess, wife of Shiva, often identified with Kali. She is usually depicted riding a tiger or lion and slaying the buffalo demon, and with eight or ten arms.

durgah in the Indian subcontinent, the tomb and shrine of a Muslim holy man.

Durham a city on the River Wear, famous for its 11th-century cathedral, which contains the tomb of the Venerable ➤ BEDE as well as the shrine of ➤ *St* CUTHBERT.

Durindana the sword of Roland or Orlando, which had been that of Hector of Troy. Also called *Durandal*.

Eleanora Duse (1858–1924), Italian actress, best known for her tragic roles, particularly in plays by Ibsen and Gabriele d'Annunzio.

> She is an actress—the Dixie Duse, I call her.
> — Gore Vidal *Palimpsest* (1995)

Dussehra the tenth and final day of the Hindu festival of Navaratri. In southern India it especially commemorates the victory of the god Rama over the demon king Ravana.

dust see ➤ ASHES *to ashes, dust to dust,* ➤ BITE *the dust.*

dust and ashes used to convey a feeling of great disappointment of disillusion about something; originally with allusion to the legend of the ➤ DEAD *Sea fruit.*

shake the dust off one's feet depart indignantly or disdainfully; originally with allusion to Matthew 10:14, 'And whosoever shall not receive you, nor hear your words, when ye depart out of that house or city, shake off the dust of your feet.'

dusty answer an unsatisfactory reply; perhaps originally as a quotation from George Meredith (1828–1909):

> Ah, what a dusty answer gets the soul
> When hot for certainties in this our life!
> — George Meredith *Modern Love* (1862)

dusty-foot archaic term for a wayfarer or traveller; the term is recorded from late Middle English, and is a translation of medieval Latin *pede pulverosus* 'dusty of foot' (see ➤ COURT *of Piepowders*).

Dutch of or relating to the Netherlands or its people or their language; from Middle Dutch 'Dutch, Netherlandish, German', the English word originally denoted speakers of both High and Low German, but became more specific after the United Provinces adopted the Low German of Holland as the national language on independence in 1579.

See also ➤ DOUBLE *Dutch,* ➤ PENNSYLVANIA *Dutch.*

Dutch courage strength or confidence gained from drinking alcohol; the term is recorded from the early 19th century, and referred to the belief that the Dutch were heavy drinkers.

Dutch Reformed Church a branch of the Protestant Church in the Netherlands, formed during the Reformation. It was disestablished in 1798 and replaced in 1816 by the Netherlands Reformed Church. It is the dominant branch of the Protestant Church among Afrikaners in South Africa.

Dutch uncle a person giving firm but benevolent advice; the expression is recorded from the mid 19th century, and may imply only that the person concerned is not an actual relative.

Dutchman see ➤ *the* FLYING *Dutchman.*

Dutchman's breeches a small patch of blue sky, traditionally said by sailors to be just enough to make a pair of breeches for a Dutchman.

duty see ➤ DEATH *duty,* ➤ MAILS *and duties.*

duumvir in ancient Rome, each of two magistrates or officials holding a joint office. The word is from Latin, from *duum virum* 'of the two men'.

dwarf in folklore or fantasy, a member of a mythical race of short, stocky human-like creatures who are generally skilled in mining and metalworking.

See also ➤ BLACK *Dwarf,* ➤ SEVEN *Dwarfs.*

DWEM acronym for ➤ DEAD *white European male.*

> Some of PC's greatest excesses, from mandatory bilingualism to the labelling of Shakespeare and Milton as DWEMs.
> — *Guardian* 13 January 1995

dwt a former abbreviation meaning 'pennyweight', from Latin *denarius* 'penny'.

dybbuk in Jewish folklore, a malevolent wandering spirit that enters and possesses the body of a living person until exorcized.

dyed in the wool unchanging in a particular belief or opinion, originally with allusion to the fact that yarn was dyed in the raw state, producing a more even and permanent colour.

dyers ➤ *St* MAURICE is the patron saint of dyers.

dying ➤ *St* BARBARA, ➤ *St* JOSEPH, and ➤ *St* MARGARET *of Antioch* are the patron saints of the dying.

dyke see also ➤ DEVIL'*s Dyke*, ➤ FEBRUARY *fill dyke be it black or be it white*, ➤ OFFA'*s Dyke*.

put one's finger in the dyke attempt to stem the advance of something undesirable, from a story of a small Dutch boy who saved his community from flooding, by placing his finger in a hole in a dyke.

Dymoke surname of an ancient English family who between the 14th and the 19th centuries held the hereditary office of *king's champion*.

St Dymphna (*c.*7th century), said to have been the daughter of a Celtic or British king whose own father fell in love with her. She fled to Antwerp, and then nearby Gheel, with her confessor, but her father traced them there and killed them when she refused to commit incest. She is the patron saint of those with mental illness.

□ **FEAST DAY** Her feast day is 15 May.

dynasty a line of hereditary rulers of a country; a period of time when a country is ruled by such a line. The word comes (in late Middle English) via French on late Latin, from Greek *dunasteia* 'lordship, power'.

See also ➤ *the* SIX *Dynasties.*

Dynasties of Europe

NAME	COUNTRY
Bernadotte	Sweden
Bonaparte	France
Bourbon	France
Braganza	Portugal; Brazil
Capet	France
Grimaldi	Monaco
Habsburg	Austria; Spain
Hanover	Britain
Hohenstaufen	Austria
Hohenzollern	Spain
Plantagenet	England
Romanov	Russia
Stuart	Britain; Scotland
Tudor	England
Valois	France
Vasa	Sweden
Windsor	Britain
Wittelsbach	Bavaria

Ee

E the fifth letter of the modern English alphabet. and of the ancient Roman one, representing the Semitic ⅎ (= h), but adopted by the Greeks (and from them by the Romans) as a vowel.

E-boat in the Second World War, an enemy torpedo boat.

E-number a code number preceded by the letter E, denoting food additives numbered in accordance with EU directives.

eagle a large bird of prey with a massive hooked bill and long broad wings, renowned for its keen sight and powerful soaring flight, traditionally regarded as the ➤ KING *of birds*. In the 15th-century *Boke of St Albans*, the eagle is listed in falconry as the bird for an emperor.

An *eagle* is the emblem of ➤ St JOHN *the Evangelist*.

The figure of an eagle was used as an ensign in the Roman and French imperial armies; a figure of a bald eagle is the emblem of the United States, from which **the Eagle** may mean the US.

See also ➤ DOUBLE-*headed eagle*, ➤ SPREAD *eagle*, ➤ THEBAN *eagle*, ➤ *thy* YOUTH *is renewed like the eagle's*, ➤ *where the* CARCASE *is, there shall the eagles be gathered together*.

two-headed eagle emblem of the empires of Austria and Russia.

eagle and child the crest of the Stanley family; adopted by Sir John Stanley (1350?–1414), and probably taken from the crest of the Latham family whose heiress he had married. Legends to explain the crest include the story that the founder of the house had been discovered as a child unharmed below an eagle's eyrie.

Eagle of the Broken Covenant a name for ➤ ELEANOR *of Aquitaine* (*c*.1122–1204), deriving from a prophecy of ➤ MERLIN in Geoffrey of Monmouth's chronicles, interpreted as referring to Eleanor and her third son (later Richard I), who rebelled against his father with his mother's support.

eagle-stone another name for ➤ AETITES.

eagles don't catch flies proverbial saying, mid 16th century.

Ealing Studios a film studio in Ealing, West London, active 1929–55, but remembered chiefly for the comedies it made in the post-war decade.

ear see also ➤ *have a* WOLF *by the ears*, ➤ *have the right* SOW *by the ear*, ➤ JEW's *ear*, ➤ WALLS *have ears*, ➤ WAR *of Jenkins's Ear* .

Ears to Ear Bible an edition of 1810, in which Matthew 13:34 has 'Who hath ears to ear, let him hear'.

Amelia Earhart (1898–1937), American aviator. In 1932 she became the first woman to fly across the Atlantic solo. Her aircraft disappeared over the Pacific Ocean during a subsequent round-the-world flight.

earl a British nobleman ranking above a viscount and below a marquess. The word originally denoted a man of noble rank, as opposed to a *churl*; also specifically a hereditary nobleman directly above the rank of thane. It was later an equivalent of ➤ JARL and, under Canute and his successors, applied to the governor of divisions of England such as Wessex and Mercia. In the late Old English period, as the Saxon court came increasingly under Norman influence, the word was applied to any nobleman bearing the continental title of ➤ COUNT.

Earl Grey a kind of China tea flavoured with bergamot, probably named after the 2nd *Earl Grey* (1764–1845), said to have been given the recipe by a Chinese mandarin.

Earl Marshal in the United Kingdom, the officer presiding over the College of Arms, with ceremonial duties on various royal occasions.

the **early** bird catches the worm proverbial saying, mid 17th century.

Early English denoting the earliest stage of English Gothic church architecture, typical of the late 12th and 13th centuries and marked by the use of pointed arches and simple lancet windows without tracery.

the **early** man never borrows from the late man proverbial saying, mid 17th century.

early to bed and early to rise, makes a man healthy, wealthy, and wise proverbial saying, late 15th century.

Wyatt Earp (1848–1929), American gambler and marshal. He is famous for the gunfight at the OK Corral (1881), in which Wyatt with his brothers and his friend Doc Holliday fought the Clanton brothers at Tombstone, Arizona. Wyatt collaborated in writing his biography (published 1931), which presents a fictionalized portrait of him as a heroic frontiersman.

> Throwing his gun up, like Wyatt Earp on an on-day.
> — *Field* March 1995

earth the planet on which we live; the world. The earth is the third planet from the sun in the solar system, orbiting between Venus and Mars at an average distance of 149.6 million km from the sun, and has one natural satellite, the moon; it is believed to have formed about 4,600 million years ago. The earth, which is three-quarters covered by oceans and has a dense atmosphere of nitrogen and oxygen, is the only planet known to support life.

See also ➤ the ENDS *of the earth,* ➤ FRIENDS *of the Earth,* ➤ MOTHER *Earth,* ➤ *the* SALT *of the earth.*

Earth Summit an unofficial name for the United Nations Conference on Environment and Development, held in Rio de Janeiro in Brazil in 1992.

the **earthly** paradise the garden of Eden; an ideal or idyllic place, typically one of great natural beauty.

earthquake a sudden violent shaking of the ground, typically causing great destruction, as a result of movements within the earth's crust or volcanic action. In Greek mythology, ➤ POSEIDON was god of earthquakes, and one of his epithets was 'earth-shaker'.

earwig a small elongated insect with a pair of terminal appendages that resemble pincers; it was probably so named because it was once thought to crawl into the human ear.

ease see ➤ CHAPEL *of ease.*

east the direction towards the point of the horizon where the sun rises at the equinoxes, on the right-hand side of a person facing north, or the point on the horizon itself.

In a Christian church, *east* designates the end that contains the (high) altar, traditionally but not necessarily the geographical east.

The word is recorded from Old English (in form *ēst-*) and is of Germanic origin; it comes ultimately from an Indo-European root shared by Latin *aurora,* Greek *auōs* 'dawn'.

See also ➤ RAIN *from the east: wet two days at least,* ➤ *when the* WIND *is in the east, 'tis neither good for man nor beast.*

East End the part of London east of the City as far as the River Lea, including the Docklands; traditionally having a high immigrant population, and marked by poverty.

East India Company a trading company (informally, ➤ JOHN *Company*) formed in 1600 to develop commerce in the newly colonized areas of SE Asia and India. In the 18th century it took administrative control of Bengal and other areas of India, and held it until the British Crown took over in 1858 in the wake of the Indian Mutiny.

East Indiaman a trading ship belonging to the East India Company.

East Indies archaic name for the whole of SE Asia to the east of and including India.

East is East a saying suggesting that there is an uncrossable barrier between two groups of people from different cultures, deriving from a poem by Rudyard Kipling in *Barrack-Room Ballads* (1892), 'Oh, East is East, and West is West, and never the twain shall meet.'

> East is east and west is west, and it will be a long time before fishermen from the bookends of Canada agree on delicate matters of taste over a plate of oysters.
> — *English Today* October 1994

East Side a part of Manhattan in New York City, lying between the East River and Fifth Avenue.

east, west, home's best proverbial saying, mid 19th century.

Easter the most important and oldest festival of the Christian Church, celebrating the resurrection of Christ and held (in the Western Church) between 21 March and 25 April, on the first Sunday after the first full moon following the northern spring equinox.

The name is recorded from Old English (in form *ēastre*) and is of Germanic origin, related to *east*. According to Bede the word is derived from *Ēastre*, the name of a goddess associated with spring.

when Easter day lies in our Lady's lap then, O England, beware a clap
traditional warning of ill fortune when Easter and Lady Day coincide.

Easter egg an artificial chocolate egg or decorated hard-boiled egg given at Easter, especially to children.

Easter Rising the uprising in Dublin and other cities in Ireland against British rule, Easter 1916. It ended with the surrender of the protesters, some of whose leaders were subsequently executed, but was a contributory factor in the establishment of the Irish Free State (1921).

Easter Sepulchre a recess in certain medieval churches for keeping the Eucharistic elements from Good Friday until the Easter festivities.

Easter term a term in the courts of law, formerly movable and occurring between Easter and Whitsuntide, but now fixed within a certain period; in the older universities, a term formerly occurring between Easter and Whitsuntide and now included in the Trinity term; in some universities and schools, the term between Christmas and Easter.

Eastern bloc the countries of eastern and central Europe which were under Soviet domination from the end of the Second World War until the collapse of the Soviet communist system in 1989–91.

Eastern Church another name for the ➤ ORTHO-DOX *Church*.

Eastern Empire the eastern part of the Roman Empire, after its division in AD 395.

Eastern Time the standard time in a zone including the eastern states of the US and parts of Canada, specifically **Eastern Standard Time**, standard time based on the mean solar time at the meridian 75° W, five hours behind GMT, and **Eastern Daylight Time**, Eastern time during daylight saving time, six hours behind GMT.

easy come, easy go proverbial saying, mid 17th century.

easy does it proverbial saying, mid 19th century.

you are what you eat proverbial saying, mid 20th century; equivalent proverb in German.

we must eat a peck of dirt before we die proverbial saying, mid 18th century.

eat crow in North American usage, be humiliated by having to admit one's mistakes or defeats.

eat, drink, and be merry traditional saying; originally with biblical allusion to Luke 12:19, 'eat, drink, and be merry', an injunction to the soul inviting the response from God, 'Thou fool, this night thy soul shall be required of thee.'

eat humble pie make a humble apology and accept humiliation. *Humble pie* is from a pun based on *umbles* 'offal', considered as inferior food.

eat no fish refrain from following Roman Catholic practices, as in eating fish rather than meat on Fridays.

eat one's terms in the course of studying for the Bar, be required to dine a certain number of times in the Hall of one of the Inns of Court.

eat salt with be a guest of; *salt* here is taken as a type of a necessary adjunct to food, and thus as a symbol of hospitality.

he that would eat the fruit must climb the tree proverbial saying, early 18th century.

eat to live, not live to eat proverbial saying, late 14th century.

eavesdropper a person who listens secretly to a conversation, originally meaning ' a person who listens from under the eaves', from the obsolete noun *eavesdrop* 'the ground on to which water drips from the eaves', probably ultimately from Old Norse *upsardropi*, from *ups* 'eaves' + *dropi* 'a drop'.

Ebenezer the name of the memorial stone set up by Samuel after the victory of Mizpeh, when the Israelites recovered the ark of the Lord from the Philistines (1 Samuel 7–12); in Hebrew the name means 'the stone of help', and from this the term has come to be used for a Nonconformist chapel.

Ebionite a member of a Christian sect of the 1st to 3rd centuries which held that Jesus was a mere man, and that the Mosaic law was binding on Christians; the name comes via Latin from Hebrew *ebyōn* 'poor', probably originally implying 'one who is poor in spirit'.

Ebla a city in ancient Syria, situated to the southwest of Aleppo. It became very powerful in the mid 3rd millennium BC, when it dominated a region corresponding to modern Lebanon, northern Syria, and SE Turkey. It was a thriving trading city and centre of scholarship, as testified in some 15,000 cuneiform tablets discovered among the city's ruins in 1975.

Eblis in ➤ *William* BECKFORD's *Vathek* (1786), the prince of darkness to whose realm Vathek is banished after he has impiously challenged Mohammed and brought about his own damnation; in later literature, the term 'son of Eblis' is found as an objurgation. The name probably represents ➤ IBLIS.

Ebonics American black English regarded as a language in its own right rather than as a dialect of standard English; the name is a blend of *ebony* and *phonics*.

ebony heavy blackish or very dark brown timber from a mainly tropical tree, traditionally taken as the type of intense blackness. The name is recorded from late Middle English and comes from earlier *ebon* (via Old French and Latin from Greek *ebenos* 'ebony tree'), perhaps on the pattern of *ivory*.

Eboracum Roman name for York; from this, the ecclesiastical title of the Archbishop of York is *Ebor*.

Ecce Homo a representation of Christ wearing the crown of thorns, from the words of Pontius Pilate to the Jews, 'behold the man', after Jesus was crowned with thorns (John 19:5, 'Then came Jesus forth, wearing the crown of thorns, and the purple robe. And Pilate saith unto them, Behold the man!').

ecce signum Latin phrase meaning, 'behold the sign'.

> My sword hack'd like a hand-saw—ecce signum!
> — William Shakespeare *1 Henry IV* (1597)

Ecclesia the Church, especially as personified in medieval art.

Ecclesiastes a book of the Bible traditionally attributed to Solomon, consisting largely of reflections on the vanity of human life.

Ecclesiastical Commissioners the members of a body, subordinate to the Privy Council, which managed the estates and revenues of the Church of England from 1835 to 1948.

Ecclesiasticus a book of the Apocrypha containing moral and practical maxims, probably composed or compiled in the early 2nd century BC.

Echidna the name of a mythical creature which gave birth to the many-headed Hydra; the word comes from the Greek *ekhidna* 'viper'.

echites formerly another name for ➤ AETITES; the word comes from Greek *ekhis* viper, because the colour and patterning of the stone was thought to resemble the snake.

Echo in Greek mythology, a nymph deprived of speech by Hera in order to stop her chatter, and left able only to repeat what others had said; she fell in love with ➤ NARCISSUS, and on being rejected by him, wasted away with grief until there was nothing left of her but her voice. In another account she was vainly loved by the god Pan, who finally caused some shepherds to go mad and tear her to pieces; Earth hid the fragments, which could still imitate other sounds.

Eckhardt a figure in German legend, who in the legend of ➤ TANNHÄUSER is a courtier of the Venusberg; during Thursday of Shrovetide, he is said to be seen escorting a procession of those who have recently died.

Eclectics a class of ancient philosophers who did not belong to or found any recognized school of thought but selected such doctrines as they wished from various schools. The name comes, in the late 17th century, from Greek *eklektikos*, from *eklegein* 'pick out'.

Eclipse a famous racehorse of the 18th century and one of the ancestors of all thoroughbred racehorses throughout the world. The **Eclipse Stakes**, run annually at Sandown Park near London since 1886, is named in the horse's honour, and the comment of the Irish racehorse-owner Dennis O'Kelly (*c*.1720–87), 'Eclipse first, the rest nowhere', has become a saying indicating pre-eminence.

See also ➤ COPENHAGEN.

eclipse an obscuring of the light from one celestial body by the passage of another between it and the observer or between it and its source of illumination; in figurative usage, a loss of significance, power, or prominence in relation to another person or thing.

Eclipses were traditionally considered ominous; in Shakespeare's *Macbeth*, the witches add to their cauldron 'slips of yew Slivered in the moon's eclipse'. On the other hand, the Jewish ethical work *Orchoth Zaddikkim* ('The Ways of the Righteous', *c*.15th century) points out, 'men are more wont to be astonished at the sun's eclipse than at his unfailing rise.' Total eclipses, however, such as that in August 1999, continue to exert a fascination for many people.

The word is recorded from Middle English, and comes via Old French and Latin from Greek *ekleipsis*, from *ekleipein* 'fail to appear, be eclipsed', from *ek* 'out' + *leipein* 'to leave'.

> Today's total eclipse of the Sun will almost certainly be watched by more people than any before. It will send a shiver down the spines of many millions of neck-craners in cities and in fields and on mountain tops across Europe, the Middle East and Asia.
> — *Independent* 11 August 1999

ecliptic in astronomy, a great circle on the celestial sphere representing the sun's apparent path during the year, so called because lunar and solar eclipses can only occur when the moon crosses it.

eclogue a short poem, especially a pastoral dialogue; the word comes (in late Middle English, via Latin) from Greek *eklogē* 'selection', from *eklegein* 'pick out'.

ecological footprint something which has had a permanent and damaging effect on the surrounding environment.

ecologists ➤ St FRANCIS *of Assisi* is the patron saint of ecologists.

economical with the truth used euphemistically to describe a person or statement that lies or deliberately withholds information. The expression comes from a statement given in evidence by Sir Robert Armstrong, British cabinet secretary, in the 'Spycatcher' trial (1986), conducted to prevent publication of a book by a former MI5 employee:

> It contains a misleading impression, not a lie. It was being economical with the truth.
> — Robert Armstrong in *Daily Telegraph* 19 November 1986

The expression 'over-economical with the truth' had been applied to Harold Wilson by the Earl of Dalkeith in the House of Commons, 4 July 1968; in 1992, under cross-examination at the Old Bailey during the Matrix Churchill case, the Conservative politician Alan Clark (1928–99) referred to, 'Our old friend economical…with the *actualité*'.

The theological phrase *economy of truth* (i.e. sparing use of truth) is of long-standing, and was used by the 18th-century politician Edmund Burke:

> Falsehood and delusion are allowed in no case whatsoever: But, as in the exercise of all the virtues, there is an economy of truth.
> — Edmund Burke *Two letters on Proposals for Peace* (1796)

economy the wealth and resources of a country or region, especially in terms of the production and consumption of goods and services. The word is recorded from the late 15th century, in the sense 'management of material resources'; it comes via French or Latin from Greek *oikonomia* 'household management'. The current sense dates from the 17th century.

It's the economy, stupid slogan on a sign put up at the 1992 Clinton presidential campaign headquarters by campaign manager James Carville; it is frequently now quoted as summarizing the view that economic concerns are paramount with the electorate.

écorcheur in medieval France, a mercenary who terrorized the countryside, a ➤ ROUTIER; the word in French means literally 'flayer'.

ecstasy an emotional or religious frenzy or trance-like state, originally one involving an experience of mystic self-transcendence. The word is recorded from late Middle English, and comes via Old French and late Latin from Greek *ekstasis* 'standing outside oneself'.

The extended sense of *ecstasy* to mean an overwhelming feeling of great happiness or joyful excitement, now the current meaning, is recorded from the early 16th century.

Ecstasy is now also the name of an illegal amphetamine-based synthetic drug with euphoric and hallucinatory effects, originally produced as an appetite suppressant.

ectoplasm a supernatural viscous substance that is supposed to exude from the body of a medium during a spiritualistic trance and form the material for the manifestation of spirits.

Sir Ector in Malory's *Morte D'Arthur*, the knight who is Arthur's foster-father.

ecumenical originally (from the late 16th century), belonging to the universal Church; later, promoting or relating to unity among the world's Christian Churches, as in **ecumenical movement**, a movement for the reunification of the various branches of the Christian Church worldwide.

The word comes via late Latin from Greek *oikoumenikos* from *oikoumenē* 'the (inhabited) earth'.

ecumenical council any of various representative councils of the church worldwide (since the 9th century, of the Roman Catholic Church alone) whose decisions are considered authoritative.

Ecumenical Patriarch a title of the Orthodox Patriarch of Constantinople.

ecumenists ➤ *St* CYRIL and his brother St Methodius, and St Josaphat (1580–1623), archbishop of Polotsk, are the patron saints of ecumenists.

Edda either of two 13th-century Icelandic books, the **Elder** or **Poetic Edda** (a collection of Old Norse poems on Norse legends) and the **Younger** or **Prose Edda** (a handbook to Icelandic poetry by Snorri Sturluson). The Eddas are the chief source of knowledge of Scandinavian mythology.

Mary Baker Eddy (1821–1910), American religious leader and founder of the Christian Science movement. Long a victim to various ailments, she believed herself cured by a faith healer, Phineas Quimby, and later evolved her own system of spiritual healing.

Eddystone Rocks a rocky reef off the coast of Cornwall, SW of Plymouth. The reef was the site of the earliest lighthouse (1699) built on rocks fully exposed to the sea.

Eden see also ➤ ANTHONY *Eden*, ➤ *the* LUCK *of Eden Hall*.

Eden the place (more fully, the **Garden of Eden**) where Adam and Eve lived in the biblical account of the Creation, from which they were expelled for disobediently eating the fruit of the tree of knowledge.

The name comes from late Latin (Vulgate), Greek *Ēdēn* (Septuagint), and Hebrew ʿĒḏen, perhaps related to Akkadian *edinu*, from Sumerian *eden* 'plain, desert', but believed to be related to Hebrew ʿēḏen 'delight'.

Battle of Edgehill the first pitched battle of the English Civil War (1642), fought at the village of Edgehill in the west Midlands. The Parliamentary army attempted to halt the Royalist army's march on London; the battle ended with no clear winner and with heavy losses on both sides.

Edict of Milan a proclamation made by the Emperor Constantine in 313 by which Christianity was given legal status within the Empire.

Edict of Nantes an edict issued by Henry IV of France in 1598, granting toleration to the Protestants (revoked by Louis XIV in 1685).

Edinburgh the capital of Scotland, lying on the southern shore of the Firth of Forth, nicknamed the *Athens of the North* in allusion to its academic and intellectual traditions, and to the predominantly neoclassical style of architecture in its city centre. The city grew up round the 11th-century castle built by Malcolm III on a rocky ridge which dominates the landscape.

Edinburgh Festival an international festival of the arts held annually in Edinburgh since 1947. In addition to the main programme a flourishing fringe festival has developed.

Edinburgh Review an influential political and literary quarterly periodical (1802–1929), described by Thomas Carlyle as 'a kind of Delphic oracle'.

Thomas Edison (1847–1931), American inventor. He took out the first of more than a thousand patents at the age of 21. His inventions include automatic telegraph systems, the carbon microphone for telephones, the phonograph, and the carbon filament lamp. His definition of genius, 'one per cent inspiration, ninety-nine per cent perspiration' is often quoted.

editio princeps the first printed edition of a book; the phrase is Latin, and comes from *editio(n-)* 'edition' and *princeps* 'leader, chief' (from *primus* 'first').

Edmund see also ➤ *St Edmund* CAMPION.

Edmund II (*c*.980–1016), son of Ethelred the Unready, reigned 1016; known as **Edmund Ironside**. Edmund led the resistance to Canute's forces in 1015, but was eventually defeated and forced to divide the kingdom with Canute. On Edmund's death Canute became king of all England.

St Edmund of Abingdon (*c*.1175–1240), English churchman and teacher, Archbishop of Canterbury 1234–40; born **Edmund Rich**; the Oxford college St Edmund Hall takes its name from him.
☐ **FEAST DAY** His feast day is 16 November.

St Edmund the Martyr (*c*.841–70), king of East Anglia 855–70. After the defeat of his army by the invading Danes in 870, tradition holds that he was captured and shot with arrows for refusing to reject the Christian faith or to share power with his pagan conqueror.
☐ **EMBLEM** Arrows, for his martyrdom, and a wolf, said to have guarded the saint's head after his death, are the emblems of St Edmund.
☐ **FEAST DAY** His feast day is 20 November.

Edna see ➤ AUNT *Edna*, ➤ *Dame Edna* EVERAGE.

over Edom will I cast out my shoe proverbial saying, from Psalm 60:7, referring to the ancient region of *Edom*, south of the Dead Sea, traditionally believed to be inhabited by the descendants of Esau.

Edward I (1239–1307), king of England, reigned 1272–1307; known as *the Hammer of the Scots*. His campaign against Prince Llewelyn ended with the annexation of Wales in 1284, but he failed to conquer Scotland, where resistance was led by Sir William Wallace and later Robert the Bruce.

Edward II (1284–1327), king of England, son of Edward I, who in 1314 was defeated by Robert the Bruce at Bannockburn. In 1326 Edward's wife, Isabella of France, and her lover, Roger de Mortimer, invaded England; Edward was deposed in favour of his son and murdered.

Edward III (1312–77), king of England, son of Edward II, who in 1330 took control of his kingdom, banishing Isabella and executing Mortimer. He supported Edward de Baliol, the pretender to the Scottish throne, and started the ➤ HUNDRED *Years War.*

Edward IV (1442–83), king of England, who as the Yorkist leader became king after defeating the Lancastrian Henry VI. Edward was briefly forced into exile in 1470–1 by the Earl of Warwick but regained his position with victory at Tewkesbury in 1471.

Edward V (1470–*c*.1483), king of England, son of Edward IV, reigned 1483 but not crowned. Edward and his brother Richard (known as the *Princes in the Tower*) were probably murdered and the throne was taken by their uncle, Richard III.

Edward VI (1537–53), king of England, son of Henry VIII, reigned 1547–53. His reign saw the establishment of Protestantism as the state religion. He was succeeded by his elder sister, Mary I.

Edward VII (1841–1910), king of England, son of Queen Victoria, reigned 1901–10. Although he played little part in government on coming to the throne, his popularity helped revitalize the monarchy. The ➤ ENTENTE *Cordiale* was established in his reign, and he was nicknamed **Edward the Peacemaker**. The word **Edwardian** generally refers to things characteristic of his reign.

Edward VIII (1894–1972), king of England, son of George V, reigned 1936 but not crowned. Edward abdicated eleven months after coming to the throne in order to marry the American divorcee Mrs ➤ *Wallis* SIMPSON; he was subsequently known as the *Duke of Windsor*. He had been enormously popular as Prince of Wales, but his father was said to have prophesied, 'After I am dead, the boy will ruin himself in twelve months.'

St Edward the Confessor (*c*.1003–66), son of Ethelred the Unready and his second wife Emma of Normandy, king of England 1042–66. Famed for his piety, Edward rebuilt Westminster Abbey, where he was eventually buried.

☐ **EMBLEM** He is sometimes shown with a ring which according to legend he gave to a beggar; subsequently English pilgrims in the Holy Land (or India) encountered an old man who said that he was St John the Apostle, and who gave them back the ring, telling them to return it to the king, and warn him that he would die in six months' time.

☐ **FEAST DAY** His feast day is 13 October.

Edward the Elder (*c*.870–924), son of Alfred the Great, king of Wessex 899–924. His military successes against the Danes made it possible for his son Athelstan to become the first king of all England in 925.

St Edward the Martyr (*c*.963–78), son of Edgar, king of England 975–8. Edward was faced by a challenge for the throne from supporters of his half-brother, Ethelred, who eventually had him murdered at Corfe Castle in Dorset.

☐ **EMBLEM** His emblem is a dagger, symbol of his martyrdom.

☐ **FEAST DAY** His feast day is 18 March.

Edwardian of, relating to, or characteristic of the reign of King ➤ EDWARD *VII* (1841–1910), king from 1901.

Eelam the proposed homeland of the Tamil people of Sri Lanka, for which the Tamil Tigers separatist group have been fighting since the early 1980s.

effect see ➤ *the* BUTTERFLY *effect,* ➤ DOMINO *effect.*

effectual calling in Christian theology, the action of the Holy Spirit in instilling Christian faith.

effectual grace in Christian theology, the special grace given to those elected to salvation.

effigy see ➤ BURN *in effigy.*

Égalité name of Philippe, Duc d'Orleans (1747–93), who renounced his title and voted for the death of his cousin, Louis XVI; he was however himself later guillotined.

See also the ➤ CITIZEN *King.*

Egeria in Roman religion, an Italian water-nymph, to whom pregnant women sacrificed to secure easy delivery, and who was said to be the consort and adviser of Numa Pompilius, the legendary second king of Rome (715–673 BC), whom she used to meet by night at the Porta Capena and instruct in statesmanship and religion. Her name may be used allusively for a woman regarded as a patroness and adviser.

> She has a sort of Egeria look.
> — Harold Nicolson diary, 9 December 1932.

egg it was traditionally thought that if a hen laid a very small egg is was unlucky; it was sometimes called a *cock's egg*, and believed capable of hatching a cockatrice or basilisk. Superstition also attached to the question of which end of a boiled egg should be opened; Sir Thomas Browne in *Vulgar Errors* (1650) notes that it was thought unlucky to crack an egg at the smaller end (see also ➤ BIG-*endian*).

See also ➤ *as good be an* ADDLED *egg as an idle bird*, ➤ CHICKEN-*and-egg*, ➤ CURATE's *egg*, ➤ *don't* TEACH *your grandmother to suck eggs*, ➤ EASTER *egg*, ➤ EGGSHELL, ➤ GO *to work on an egg*, ➤ MUNDANE *egg*, ➤ NEST *egg*, ➤ NUREMBERG *egg*, ➤ ORPHIC *egg*, ➤ PASCH-*egg*, ➤ PHILOSOPHER's *egg*, ➤ ROC's *egg*, ➤ *there is* REASON *in the roasting of eggs*, ➤ *you cannot make an* OMELETTE *without breaking eggs*.

Egg Saturday a former name for the Saturday before Shrove Tuesday, traditionally a time of celebration before the rigours of Lent.

Egg Sunday a former name for the Sunday before Shrove Tuesday.

kill the goose that lays the golden eggs destroy a reliable and valuable source of income; the allusion is to one of Aesop's fables, in which a man killed the goose which laid a single golden egg each day in the belief that he would find a number of eggs inside it, and instead through greed lost his source of wealth.

don't put all your eggs in one basket proverbial saying, mid 17th century; reworked by Mark Twain in *Pudd'nhead Wilson* (1894) as, 'Put all your eggs in the one basket, and—WATCH THAT BASKET.'

sure as eggs is eggs without doubt, certainly; recorded from the late 17th century.

eggshell the thin, hard outer layer of an egg, especially a hen's egg, traditionally a type of worthlessness or fragility. *Eggshells* were also believed to be used in casting spells, and it was thought necessary to crush or break them to prevent this, as recorded by Pliny the Elder (23–79):

> There is no one . . . who does not dread being spellbound by means of evil imprecations; and hence the practice, after eating eggs or snails, of immediately breaking the shells, or piercing them with a spoon.
> — Pliny *Natural History*

In the late 16th century, Scot in his *Discoverie of Witchcraft* (1584) recorded the belief that witches could sail in eggshells.

ego a person's sense of self-esteem or self-importance; in metaphysics, a conscious thinking subject; in psychoanalysis, the part of the mind that mediates between the conscious and the unconscious and is responsible for reality testing and a sense of personal identity. The term is recorded from the early 19th century, and comes from Latin, literally 'I'.

See also ➤ ALTER *ego*, ➤ *et in* ARCADIA *ego*.

egotistical sublime a phrase coined by Keats to describe his version of Wordsworth's distinctive genius:

> As to the poetical character itself, (I mean that sort of which, if I am any thing, I am a member; that sort distinguished from the Wordsworthian or egotistical sublime; which is a thing *per se* and stands alone) it is not itself—it has no self . . . It has as much delight in conceiving an Iago as an Imogen.
> — John Keats letter to Richard Woodhouse, 27 October 1818

Egypt the ancient kingdoms of Upper and Lower Egypt were ruled successively by thirty-one dynasties, which may be divided into the Old Kingdom, the Middle Kingdom, and the New Kingdom. Egypt was a centre of Hellenistic culture and then a Roman province before coming under Islamic rule and then becoming part of the Ottoman Empire (modern Egypt became independent in 1922).

Gypsies derive their name from the popular belief that they originated in Egypt, and ➤ *St* MARY *of Egypt* was sometimes referred to informally as *Mary Gypsy*.

See also ➤ *St* ANTHONY *of Egypt*, ➤ CORN *in Egypt*, ➤ PLAGUES *of Egypt*.

Egyptian days a former term for 24 evil or unlucky days of the medieval calendar (perhaps connected with the ➤ PLAGUES *of Egypt*).

spoil the Egyptians a phrase meaning, profit from the wealth or belongings of another (*spoil* here means plunder or despoil); with biblical allusion to Exodus 12:37, 'And the Lord gave the people favour in the sight of the Egyptians, so that they lent unto them such things as they required. And they spoiled the Egyptians.'

> Easing a world of such misproud priests as thou art of their jewels . . . is a lawful spoiling of the Egyptians.
> — Sir Walter Scott *Ivanhoe* (1819)

Adolf Eichmann (1906–62), German Nazi administrator who was responsible for administering the concentration camps. After the war he went into hiding in Argentina, but in 1960 he was traced by Israeli agents and executed after trial in Israel. It was in writing on the trial that ➤ *Hannah* ARENDT coined the phrase, 'the banality of evil':

> It was as though in those last minutes he was summing up the lessons that this long course in human wickedness had taught us—the lesson of the fearsome, word-and-thought-defying *banality of evil*.
> — Hannah Arendt *Eichmann in Jerusalem* (1963)

Alexandre Gustave Eiffel (1832–1923), French engineer, best known as the designer and builder of the Eiffel Tower and architect of the inner structure of the Statue of Liberty.

Eiffel Tower a wrought-iron structure erected in Paris for the World Exhibition of 1889. With a height of 300 metres (984 ft), it was the tallest man-made structure for many years.

Eiger a mountain peak in the Bernese Alps in central Switzerland, which rises to 3,970 m (13,101 ft), the north face of which is often taken as the type of something bleak and forbidding.

> A face like the north face of the Eiger.
> — *She* May 1991

eight the word is recorded from Old English (in form *ehta, eahta*) and is of Germanic origin; it comes from an Indo-European root shared by Latin *octo* and Greek *oktō*.

The Eight is the name given to a group of American realist painters who exhibited together in 1908, united by a concern to involve painting with the realities of contemporary, especially urban, life.

See also ➤ PIECE *of eight*.

behind the eight ball (chiefly in North America) at a disadvantage; in a variety of the game of pool, the black ball is numbered eight.

an eight days formerly, a week; recorded from Middle English.

eighteen in Britain, *eighteen* is now the age at which a person legally reaches adult status (the former age was twenty-one).

See also ➤ REVOLUTIONS *of 1848*, ➤ WAR *of 1812*.

eightfold path in Buddhism, the path to nirvana, comprising eight aspects in which an aspirant must become practised.

eighth see ➤ *eighth* WONDER *of the world*.

Eights Week at Oxford University, the week in the summer term when races are held between the eight-oared rowing boats (**Eights**) of the different colleges.

Eikon Basilike a book, published about the date of his execution, claiming to be meditations by ➤ CHARLES *I*, and for a long time so regarded; the title is Greek, and means literally 'royal image'. It was exceedingly popular, going through 49 editions, to the extent that a reply by Parliament was thought necessary, and ➤ EIKONOKLASTES published in the same year. *Eikon Basilike*, subtitled 'the Portraiture of his Sacred Majesty in his Solitudes and Sufferings', did a great deal to reinforce the figure of Charles as the ➤ MARTYR *King*.

Eikonoklastes a book, 'the Image-breaker', by John Milton, issued in 1649 by Parliament as a detailed refutation of the picture of Charles I given in ➤ EIKON *Basilike*.

Albert Einstein (1879–1955), German-born American theoretical physicist, founder of the theory of relativity; **an Einstein**, a genius.

Einstein is often regarded as the greatest scientist of the 20th century. In 1905 he published his special theory of relativity and in 1915 he succeeded in incorporating gravitation in his general theory of relativity, which was vindicated when one of its predictions was observed during the solar eclipse of 1919. However, Einstein searched without success for a unified field theory embracing electromagnetism, gravitation, relativity, and quantum mechanics. He influenced the decision to build an atom bomb but after the war he spoke out passionately against nuclear weapons.

His name is used allusively (an sometimes ironically) for a highly intelligent person.

> Who was the Einstein . . . that put technical support on a 900 line?
> — *Macworld* September 1991

Eire the Gaelic name for Ireland, the official name of the Republic of Ireland from 1937 to 1949.

Eirene in Greek mythology, the goddess of peace; her Roman equivalent is Pax.

eisteddfod a competitive festival of music and poetry in Wales, in particular the annual **National Eisteddfod**. The word is from Welsh, and means literally 'session', from *eistedd* 'sit'.

eke-name an additional name, a ➤ NICKNAME.

Ekka in Australia, informal name (from an alteration of *exhibition*) for the Queensland Royal Show ('Brisbane Exhibition'), held each August.

el see also ➤ *Tell el-*AMARNA, ➤ *El* CID.

Battle of El Alamein a battle of the Second World War fought in 1942 at El Alamein in Egypt, 90 km (60 miles) west of Alexandria. The German Afrika Korps under Rommel was halted in its advance towards the Nile by the British 8th Army under Montgomery, giving a decisive British victory.

El Djem a town in eastern Tunisia, noted for its well-preserved Roman amphitheatre.

El Dorado the name of a fictitious country or city abounding in gold, formerly believed to exist somewhere in the region of the Orinoco and Amazon Rivers; the name is first recorded in English in the title of Raleigh's *Discoverie of Guiana, with a relation of the Great and Golden City of Manoa (which the Spanish call El Dorado)* (1596).

The belief, which led Spanish conquistadors to converge on the area in search of treasure and Sir ➤ *Walter* RALEIGH to lead his second expedition up the Orinoco, appears to have originated in rumours of an Indian ruler who ritually coated his body with gold dust and then plunged into a sacred lake while his subjects threw in gold and jewels. The name comes from Spanish, and means literally 'the gilded one'.

> Then there are the real prospectors who 'go bush'. Some . . . become semi-hermits, scrubbing up for a visit to the pub on Friday night then retreating to the quiet forest in their lonely quest for El Dorado.
> — *Food & Travel* April 1998

El Greco (1541–1614), Cretan-born Spanish painter; born Domenikos Theotokopoulos. El Greco's portraits and religious works are characterized by distorted perspective, elongated figures, and strident use of colour.

> The elder of the two had an eerie, long, thin El Greco face.
> — John Lanchester *The Debt to Pleasure* (1996)

El Niño an irregularly occurring and complex series of climatic changes affecting the equatorial Pacific region and beyond every few years, characterized by the appearance of unusually warm, nutrient-poor water off northern Peru and Ecuador, typically in late December. The name is from Spanish, literally 'the (Christ) child', because of the occurrence near Christmas.

Elaine in Arthurian romances, the name of the maiden who falls in love with Lancelot and dies of unrequited love; in Malory's *Morte D'Arthur* she is the *Maid of Astolat* (Tennyson's *Lady of Shalott*).

élan vital in the philosophy of Henri Bergson (1859–1941), an intuitively perceived life-force; any mysterious life-force, especially once supposed to have caused the variations from which new species have emerged.

Elba a small island off the west coast of Italy, famous as the place of Napoleon's first exile (1814–15).

Elbrus a peak in the Caucasus mountains, on the border between Russia and Georgia, which rises to 5,642 m (18,481 ft), and is the highest mountain in Europe.

elder see also ➤ PROTOCOLS *of the Learned Elders*, ➤ RULING *elder*.

elder a small tree or shrub with pithy stems, typically having white flowers and bluish-black or red berries, and sometimes believed to be unlucky: according to legend, ➤ JUDAS *Iscariot* hanged himself on an elder, and the tree is associated with witches. Pliny's *Natural History*, on the other hand, says that elder has prophylactic and curative properties, and it was also believed that elder could protect against lightning.

the Elder used to distinguish between two related famous people with the same name, as **Pitt the Elder, Pliny the Elder**.

Elder Brother each of the thirteen senior members of ➤ TRINITY *House*.

Eleanor Cross any of the stone crosses erected by Edward I to mark the stopping places of the cortège that brought the body of his queen, Eleanor of Castile (1246–90), from Nottinghamshire to London in 1290. Three of the twelve crosses survive.

Eleanor of Aquitaine (*c*.1122–1204), daughter of the Duke of Aquitaine, queen of France 1137–52 and of England 1154–89. She was married to Louis VII of France from 1137; in 1152, with the annulment of their marriage, she married the future Henry II of England. Her ten children included the monarchs Richard I and John; she acted as regent (1190–4) while Richard was away on the Crusades.

Eleatic of or relating to *Elea*, an ancient Greek city in SW Italy, or the school of philosophers which flourished there in about the 5th century BC, including Xenophanes, Parmenides, and Zeno.

elecampane a plant which has yellow daisy-like flowers with long slender petals and bitter aromatic roots that are used in herbal medicine; a 19th-century source noted 'Elecampane has been prescribed since the time of Hippocrates.'

The name is recorded from late Middle English and comes from medieval Latin *enula* (from Greek *helenion* 'elecampane') + *campana* probably meaning 'of the fields'.

election see ➤ Coupon *Election*, ➤ Khaki *Election*.

Elector a German prince entitled to take part in the election of the Holy Roman Emperor. There were originally seven Electors; subsequently electorates were created for Bavaria (1623–1778), Hanover (from 1708), and Hesse-Kassel (from 1803). The role officially terminated with the abolition of the ➤ Holy *Roman Empire* in 1806.

Electors: seven original Electors

Archbishop of Cologne	Count Palatine of the Rhine
Archbishop of Mainz	Margrave of Brandenburg
Archbishop of Trier	King of Bohemia
Duke of Saxony	

Great Elector a nickname for ➤ Frederick *William* (1620–88), Elector of Brandenburg.

electoral college a body of electors chosen or appointed by a larger group, as, the princes who elected the Holy Roman Emperor, or (in the US) a body of people representing the states of the US, who formally cast votes for the election of the President and Vice-President.

Electra in Greek mytholgy, the daughter of ➤ Agamemnon and ➤ Clytemnestra, sister of Orestes. She persuaded her brother Orestes to kill Clytemnestra and Aegisthus (their mother's lover) in revenge for the murder of Agamemnon. Her name is used in **Electra complex**, a dated term in psychoanalysis for the Oedipus complex as manifested in young girls.

Electra is also the name of one of the ➤ Pleiades, daughter of the Titan Atlas and mother by Zeus of ➤ Dardanus, ancestor of the kings of Troy.

electric of, worked by, charged with, or producing electricity. The word comes (in the mid 17th century, via modern Latin) from Latin *electrum* 'amber' from Greek *ēlektron*, because rubbing amber causes electrostatic phenomena.

electuary a medicinal substance mixed with honey or another sweet substance, probably (through late Latin) from Greek *ekleikhein* 'lick up'.

elegant variation the stylistic fault of deliberately avoiding repetition by using different words for the same thing.

elegantiarum see ➤ Arbiter *elegantiarum*.

elegiac couplet a pair of lines consisting of a dactylic hexameter and a pentameter, especially in Greek and Latin verse.

elegy in Greek and Roman poetry, a poem written in elegiac couplets, as notably by Catullus and Propertius; in modern literature, a poem of serious reflection, typically a lament for the dead. The word is recorded from the early 16th century and comes via French or Latin from Greek *elegeia*, from *elegos* 'mournful poem'.

element any of the four substances (earth, water, air, and fire) regarded as the fundamental constituents of the world in ancient and medieval philosophy. The word is recorded from Middle English (denoting fundamental constituents of the world or celestial objects) and comes via Old French from Latin *elementum* 'principle, rudiment', translating Greek *stoikheion* 'step, component part'.

In late Middle English, *elements* denoted the letters of the alphabet; from this developed the sense of the rudiments of learning, the first principles of a subject.

From the mid 16th century, *element* (usually in plural) has also denoted the bread or wine used in the Christian Eucharist.

Elementary, my dear Watson supposedly said by Sherlock Holmes to ➤ Dr Watson, although the remark in this form is not found in any of Conan Doyle's stories; the nearest thing to it is an exchange in *The Memoirs of Sherlock Holmes* (1894):

> 'Excellent,' I cried. 'Elementary,' said he.
> — Arthur Conan Doyle *The Memoirs of Sherlock Holmes* (1894) 'The Crooked Man'

The misquotation 'Elementary, my dear Watson' is first recorded in P. G. Wodehouse's *Psmith, Journalist* (1915).

The Elements ➤ EUCLID's fundamental treatise on geometry.

elenchus the Socratic method of eliciting truth by question and answer, especially as used to refute an argument (also called **Socratic elenchus**).

elephant the *elephant* is the largest living land animal, and is taken as a type of something of great size and weight. The Indian elephant was traditionally used as a beast of burden and in the ancient world (as, notably, by ➤ HANNIBAL when he crossed the Alps in 219–18 BC) as a mount in war.

Elephant is also used for a size of paper, typically 28 x 23 inches (approximately 711 x 584 mm).

In the US, the elephant is the emblem of the Republican Party.

The word is recorded from Middle English, and comes via Old French and Latin from Greek *elephas, elephant-* 'ivory, elephant'.

See also ➤ KING *of the White Elephant*, ➤ PINK *elephants*, ➤ WHITE *elephant*.

Order of the Elephant the highest Danish order of knighthood, the membership of which is limited to the monarch, princes of the royal blood, and 30 Knights chosen by the monarch. It was first founded in the 12th century, and re-established in the 15th. The Order was originally associated with an Order dedicated to the Virgin Mary, with a medallion of the Virgin and a smaller medallion with three nails of the Cross, on a chain of alternate elephants and spurs. From the coronation of Frederick II (1559) an elephant has been the badge of the Order.

see the elephant in the US, see the world, get experience of life; an *elephant* is taken here as the type of something remarkable.

elephant and castle a public-house sign which has given its name to the main crossroads of Southwark in London; it is popularly said to be a corruption of *Infanta de Castile*, but in fact is probably adopted from the arms of the Worshipful Company of Cutlers, whose trade included the importation of elephants' tusks (in heraldry, the elephant is shown with a crenellated round tower on its back).

the Elephant Man nickname of Joseph Carey Merrick (1862–90), who as a result of what is now thought to be Proteus syndrome had an enormous head with bone protruding from his forehead and mouth, and folds of spongy flesh covered with skin resembling a cauliflower hanging from his head, chest, and back. In adult life the only way in which he could support himself was by allowing himself to be exhibited as a freak ('The Elephant Man, Half-a-Man and Half-an-Elephant'); when changing public taste made this unprofitable, he was in 1886 abandoned by his manager, who also robbed him. Through the efforts of the surgeon Sir Frederick Treves, he was finally given sanctuary in the London Hospital, where he spent the few remaining years of his life.

elephantine book a book of classical antiquity composed of ivory leaves or tablets.

Eleusinian mysteries the annual rites performed by the ancient Greeks at the village of Eleusis in honour of Demeter and Persephone.

Eleusis a village near Athens which in classical times was a town famous for its cult of the corn goddess Demeter.

Eleutherian an epithet of Zeus as protector of political freedom.

elevation in the Christian Church, the raising of the consecrated elements for adoration at Mass.

eleven the word is recorded from Old English (in form *endleofon*), and comes from the base of *one* + a second element, probably expressing the sense 'left over' and occurring also in *twelve*.

The phrase **the Eleven** is used to designate the original Apostles, without ➤ JUDAS.

See also ➤ CHAPTER *11*.

give us back our eleven days slogan protesting against the adoption of the Gregorian Calendar in 1752; it became particularly well-known from Hogarth's depiction, 'An Election Entertainment', of the rowdy election in Oxfordshire in 1754 in which one of the candidates was the son of the astronomer, Lord Macclesfield, regarded as virtual author of the bill introducing the change. Hogarth shows the Whigs with a placard captured from a Tory mob; the legend on the placard reads, 'Give us back our eleven days'.

eleven-plus in the UK, an examination taken at the age of 11–12 to determine the type of secondary school a child should enter; the examination is now limited to a few local education authority areas.

elevenses a short break for light refreshments, usually with tea or coffee, taken about eleven o'clock in the morning; the word is recorded from the late 18th century.

eleventh see also ➤ the BLOODY *Eleventh.*

eleventh commandment humorous term for a rule to be observed as strictly as the ten commandments, recorded from the mid 19th century, and often defined as, 'Thou shalt not be found out.'

at the eleventh hour at the latest possible moment; originally with reference to the story in Matthew ch. 20 of the labourers who were hired 'about the eleventh hour' to work in the vineyard, and who were given the same payment as those who had worked all day.

elf a supernatural creature of folk tales, typically represented as a small, delicate, elusive figure in human form with pointed ears, magical powers, and a capricious nature. The word is recorded from Old English and is of Germanic origin; related to German *Alp* 'nightmare'.

elf-arrow a flint arrowhead (regarded as an elves' weapon).

elf-fire another name for *ignis fatuus* or ➤ WILL *o' the wisp.*

elf-locks a tangled mass of hair, as said to have been tangled by supernatural agency.

elf-shot a disease, especially of livestock, attributed to the agency of elves.

Elgin Marbles a collection of classical Greek marble sculptures and architectural fragments, chiefly from the frieze and pediment of the ➤ PARTHENON in Athens, brought to England by the diplomat and art connoisseur Thomas Bruce (1766–1841), the 7th Earl of Elgin. Their original exhibition in London had an enormous impact, it being the first time authentic classical Greek sculpture had been on public display.

In the 20th century, debate over whether or not the sculptures should be returned to Greece intensified, and was given fresh impetus by the revelation in 1999 that cleaning in the 1930s had damaged the surface of the artefacts.

Eli in the Bible, the priest who acted as a teacher to the prophet ➤ SAMUEL, and whose successor Samuel became.

Elia the pseudonym adopted by ➤ *Charles* LAMB in his *Essays of Elia* (1823) and *Last Essays of Elia* (1833); the name was that of an Italian clerk who had formerly worked at the South Sea House with Lamb's brother John.

Elijah (9th century BC), a Hebrew prophet in the time of ➤ AHAB and Jezebel who maintained the worship of Jehovah against that of Baal and other pagan gods. He is said to have been miraculously fed by ravens, to have raised a widow's son from the dead, and to have been carried to heaven in a chariot of fire (1 Kings 17–2 Kings 2).

His successor as the prophet of Israel was ➤ ELISHA, something signalled in 2 Kings 2:13, when after Elisha had seen the fiery chariot go up to heaven, 'He took up also the mantle of Elijah that fell from him.'

> This was the poet he had prophesied, the literary Messiah for whom he had served as an Elijah or John the Baptist.
> — Harold Bloom *The Western Canon* (1994)

George Eliot the pseudonym of the English novelist Mary Ann Evans (1819–80). Her novels of provincial life are characterized by their exploration of moral problems and their development of the psychological analysis that marks the modern novel.

Between about 1854 and his death in 1878 she lived with G. H. Lewes in union that could not be regularized as he had a wife living; this was something that distressed her fellow-author Mrs Gaskell when she first heard rumours of the true identity of the author of Adam Bede:

> It is a noble grand book, whoever wrote it—but Miss Evans' life taken at the best construction, does so jar against the beautiful book that one cannot help hoping against hope.
> — Elizabeth Gaskell letter to George Smith, 4 August 1859

Elisha (9th century BC), a Hebrew prophet, disciple and successor of ➤ ELIJAH, who invited ➤ JEHU to lead the revolt against the house of Ahab, and who healed ➤ NAAMAN of his leprosy.

Elissa another name of ➤ DIDO, queen of Carthage, by which she was said to have been known at Tyre, where her father was king.

elixir a magical or medicinal potion; in alchemy, a preparation which was supposed to be able to change metals into gold. The word is recorded from late Middle English and comes via medieval Latin from Arabic *al-'iksīr*, and ultimately from Greek *xērion* 'powder for drying wounds'.

elixir of life an alchemical preparation supposedly able to prolong life indefinitely; the phrase is a translation of medieval Latin *elixir vitae.*

Elizabeth I (1533–1603), daughter of Henry VIII, queen of England and Ireland 1558–1603. Succeeding her Catholic sister Mary I, Elizabeth re-established a moderate form of Protestantism as the state religion. Her reign was dominated by the threat of a Catholic restoration and by war with Spain, culminating in the Armada of 1588. Although frequently courted, she never married.

See also ➤ QUEEN *Elizabeth's pocket pistol.*

St Elizabeth in the Bible, the wife of ➤ ZACHARIAS and mother of John the Baptist; she is said to have been the cousin of the Virgin Mary (see ➤ *the* VISITATION).

□ **FEAST DAY** Her feast day (jointly with Zacharias) is 5 November.

St Elizabeth of Hungary (1207–31), princess. Married happily to the Landgrave of Thuringia and early widowed, she devoted her life to the poor; she is patron saint of charitable societies. Roses are her emblem.

□ **FEAST DAY** Her feast day is 17 (formerly 19) November.

elk test a test of the stability and handling of a motor vehicle when swerving sharply, as if to avoid a sudden obstruction in the road; the term is recorded from the late 1990s as describing a practice in Scandinavian countries.

ell a former measure of length (equivalent to six hand breadths) used mainly for textiles, locally variable but typically about 45 inches in England and 37 inches in Scotland.

The word is recorded from Old English (in form *eln*) and is of Germanic origin, from an Indo-European root shared by Latin *ulna* ('humerus'). Like the ➤ CUBIT, the measure was originally linked to the length of the human arm or forearm.

See also ➤ *give him an* INCH *and he'll take an ell.*

Ellis Island an island in the bay of New York, formerly the site of a fort, that from 1892 until 1943 served as an entry point for immigrants to the US, and later (until 1954) as a detention centre for people awaiting deportation. The island is named after Samuel Ellis, a Manhattan merchant who owned it in the 1770s.

ellops in Milton's *Paradise Lost*, a kind of snake. The word is also used by classical writers (such as Pliny) for a kind of fish.

every elm has its man proverbial saying, early 20th century; perhaps referring to the readiness of the tree to drop its branches on the unwary (see also ➤ COFFIN-*wood*).

St Elmo another name for ➤ *St* ERASMUS (d. *c*.300), patron saint of sailors.

St Elmo's fire a phenomenon in which a luminous electrical discharge appears on a ship or aircraft during a storm, regarded as a sign of protection given by St Elmo.

City of Elms a name for New Haven, Connecticut (also called *Elm City*).

Elohim a name for God used frequently in the Hebrew Bible.

Elohist the postulated author or authors of parts of the Hexateuch in which God is regularly named Elohim.

Eloi (*c*.588–660), bishop of Noyon, pioneer apostle in much of Flanders. He was a skilled metalworker, and is patron saint of goldsmiths, blacksmiths, and farriers.

□ **EMBLEM** His main emblem is a horseshoe, though like ➤ *St* DUNSTAN he is also shown holding the Devil by the nose with a pair of pincers.

□ **FEAST DAY** His feast day is 1 December, and the feast of his translation is 25 June.

eloquent see ➤ OLD *man eloquent.*

Elsinore a port on the NE coast of the island of Zealand, Denmark. It is the site of the 16th-century Kronborg Castle, which is the setting for Shakespeare's *Hamlet.*

Elul (in the Jewish calendar) the twelfth month of the civil and sixth of the religious year, usually coinciding with parts of August and September.

Elysée Palace a building in Paris which has been the official residence of the French President since 1870. It was built in 1718 for the Comte d'Evreux and was occupied by Madame de Pompadour, Napoleon I, and Napoleon III.

See also ➤ CHAMPS *Élysées.*

the Elysian fields another name for ➤ ELYSIUM.

Elysium in Greek mythology, the place at the ends of the earth to which certain favoured heroes were conveyed by the gods after death. The name comes via Latin from Greek *Elusion* (*pedion*) '(plain) of the blessed'.

Elzevir a family of Dutch printers, fifteen of whose members were active 1581–1712. Louis (*c*.1542–1617) founded the business *c*.1580. His sons Bonaventure (1583–1652) and Abraham (1592–1652) managed the firm in its prime, when it published elegant editions of the works of classical authors (1634–6) and a series on countries called *Petites Républiques* (1625–49).

em in printing, a unit for measuring the width of printed matter, equal to the height of the type size being used.

emancipation see also ➤ CATHOLIC *Emancipation*.

Emancipation Proclamation (in the American Civil War) the announcement made by President Lincoln on 22 September 1862 emancipating all black slaves in states still engaged in rebellion against the Federal Union with effect from the beginning of 1863. Although implementation was strictly beyond Lincoln's powers, the declaration turned the war into a crusade against slavery.

embarras de richesse(s) a superfluity of something, more than one needs or wants; a French phrase, meaning 'embarrassment of riches', from *L'embarras des richesses* (1726), title of comedy by Abbé d'Allainval.

Ember day any of a number of days reserved for fasting and prayer in the Western Christian Church. *Ember days* traditionally comprise the Wednesday, Friday, and Saturday following St Lucy's Day (13 December), the first Sunday in Lent, Pentecost (Whitsun), and Holy Cross Day (14 September), though other days are observed locally. They date back at least to 5th-century Rome, probably originating in agricultural festivals, though they have long been associated with ordinations.

Ember is recorded from Old English (in form *ymbren*), perhaps an alteration of *ymbryne* 'period', from *ymb* 'about' + *ryne* 'course', perhaps influenced in part by ecclesiastical Latin *quatuor tempera* 'four periods' (on which the equivalent German *Quatember* is based).

ember goose a regional name for the great northern diver, recorded from the late 17th century; the name comes from Norwegian *immer, imbre*.

emblem a heraldic device or symbolic object as a distinctive badge of a nation, organization, or family. The word is recorded from the late 16th century (as a verb), and comes from Latin *emblema* 'inlaid work, raised ornament', from Greek *emblēma* 'insertion', from *emballein* 'throw in, insert'.

emblem book a book of a kind popular in medieval and Renaissance Europe, containing drawings accompanied by allegorical interpretations.

emerald a bright green precious stone, in modern use consisting of a chromium-rich variety of beryl; a type of brilliant green. In heraldry, *emerald* is the name given to the tincture vert in the fanciful blazon of arms of peers. Recorded from Middle English, the word comes via Old French and Latin from Greem (*s*)*maragdos* (see also ➤ SMARAGD) from Hebrew *bāreqet* 'emerald', from *bāraq* 'flash, sparkle'.

Emerald Isle a name for Ireland, perhaps from the prevailing green of its countryside; first recorded in a nationalist poem by William Drennan (1754–1820):

> Nor one feeling of vengeance presume to defile
> The cause, or the men, of the Emerald Isle.
> — William Drennan *Erin* (1795)

Emesa a city in ancient Syria, on the River Orontes on the site of present-day Homs. It was famous for its temple to the sun god Elah-Gabal. Ruled by priest-kings throughout the period of the Roman Empire, Emesa fell to the Muslims in AD 636.

emigrants St Frances Xavier Cabrini (1850–1917), Italian-born American nun who was the first US citizen to be canonized, is the patron saint of emigrants. She had founded an order of missionary sisters in 1880 and initially intended to go to China, but she was told by Pope Leo XIII to 'go west, not east', and accordingly she travelled to the United States in 1889.

émigré a person who has left their own country to settle in another, especially for political reasons. The word came into English in the 18th century, and originally denoted a person escaping the French Revolution.

Emily's list a group whose purpose is to further the political candidature of women, from the acronym for *Early Money Is Like Yeast*; in this context, *yeast* is punningly seen as the agent which makes the dough rise. The organization was founded in the US in 1985.

eminence a title given to a Roman Catholic cardinal, or used in addressing him.

See also ➤ GREY *eminence.*

éminence grise a person who exercises power or influence in a certain sphere without holding an official position. The term was originally applied to Cardinal Richelieu's grey-cloaked private secretary, Père Joseph (1577–1638).

eminent domain the right of a government or its agent to expropriate private property for public use, with payment of compensation. In the UK it is used chiefly of international law, whereas in the US it is used of federal and state governments.

emir originally (now only archaic) a male descendant of Muhammad; later, a title of various Muslim (mainly Arab) rulers, (in historical usage) a Muslim (usually Arab) military commander or local chief. The word is recorded in English from the late 16th century, and comes via French from Arabic *'amīr* 'commander'.

emma see ➤ *Emma* PEEL, ➤ PIP *emma.*

Emmanuel the name (also **Immanuel**) given to Christ as the deliverer of Judah prophesied by Isaiah, as in Isaiah 7:14 'Behold, a virgin shall conceive, and bear a son, and shall call his name Immanuel', Isaiah 8:8, 'the stretching out of his wings shall fill the breadth of thy land, O Immanuel', and Matthew 1:23, 'Behold, a virgin shall be with child, and shall bring forth a son, and they shall call his name Emmanuel, which being interpreted is, God with us.'

In Bunyan's *Holy War* (1682), Emmanuel is the opponent of ➤ DIABOLUS for the possession of ➤ MANSOUL.

emmet a dialect word for an ant; now in British regional use, a humorous term for a holidaymaker or a tourist.

Emmy in the US, a statuette awarded annually to an outstanding television programme or performer.

emoticon a representation of a facial expression such as a smile or frown, formed by various combinations of keyboard characters and used in electronic communications to convey the writer's feelings or intended tone. The word is recorded from the 1990s, and is a blend of *emotion* and *icon.*

Empedocles (*c.*493–*c.*433 BC), Greek philosopher, born in Sicily. He taught that the universe is composed of fire, air, water, and earth, which mingle

and separate under the influence of the opposing principles of Love and Strife. According to legend he leapt into the crater of Mount Etna in order that he might be thought a god.

emperor a sovereign ruler of great power and rank, especially one ruling an empire. The word is recorded from Middle English (especially representing the title given to the head of the Roman Empire), and comes via Old French from Latin *imperator* 'military commander', from *imperare* 'to command'.

See also ➤ LEAGUE *of the Three Emperors.*

empire see also ➤ CELESTIAL *Empire,* ➤ EASTERN *Empire,* ➤ *the* EVIL *Empire,* ➤ FIRST *Empire,* SECOND *Empire.*

Empire City informal name for New York City.

Empire Day former name of ➤ COMMONWEALTH *Day,* originally 24 May, the birthday of Queen Victoria, and instituted as a memorial given by the former colonies to Britain during the Boer War.

Empire State informal name for the state of New York.

Empire State Building a skyscraper on Fifth Avenue, New York City, which was for several years the tallest building in the world. When first erected, in 1930–1, it measured 381 m (1,250 ft); the addition of a television mast in 1951 brought its height to 449 m (1,472 ft).

> This undersea precipice, known as the Florida Escarpment, stands more than four times as high as the Empire State Building.
>
> — *Scientific American* June 1997

Empire State of the South informal name for the state of Georgia.

Empire style a style of furniture, decoration, or dress fashionable during the First or (less commonly) the Second Empire in France. The decorative style was neoclassical but marked by an interest in Egyptian and other ancient motifs probably inspired by Napoleon's Egyptian campaigns.

Empty Quarter alternative name for Rub' al Khali, a vast desert in the Arabian peninsula, extending from central Saudi Arabia southwards to Yemen and eastwards to the United Arab Emirates and Oman.

empty sacks will never stand upright proverbial saying, mid 17th century; meaning that those in an extremity of need cannot survive.

empty vessels make the most sound proverbial saying, mid 15th century; meaning that foolish and empty-headed people make the most noise.

Empusa in classical mythology, an evil spirit or demon supposed to be sent by Hecate.

> Empusa's crew, so naked-new they may not face the fire,
> But weep that they bin too small to sin to the height of their desire.
> — Rudyard Kipling 'Tomlinson' (1891)

the empyrean heaven, in particular the highest part of heaven, thought by the ancients to be the realm of pure fire and by early Christians to be the abode of God and the angels. The word is recorded from late Middle English (as an adjective, meaning belonging to or deriving from heaven), and comes via medieval Latin from Greek *empurios*, from *en-* 'in' + *pur* 'fire' The noun dates from the mid 17th century.

en in printing, a unit of measurement equal to half an em and approximately the average width of typeset characters, used especially for estimating the total amount of space a text will require.

enaluron in heraldry, a bordure charged with birds, usually eight in number.

Encaenia an annual celebration at Oxford University in memory of founders and benefactors. The name is recorded from the late 17th century, and comes via Latin from Greek *enkainia* 'dedication festival' (based on *kainos* 'new').

Enceladus in Greek mythology, a giant killed by Athena. His name was used for a satellite of Saturn, the eighth closest to the planet and probably composed mainly of ice, discovered by W. Herschel in 1789.

enchanter's nightshade a woodland plant with small white flowers and fruit with hooked bristles, native to Eurasia and the eastern US, so called (from the late 16th century) because it was believed by early botanists to be the herb used by ➤ CIRCE to charm Odysseus' companions.

enchantment see ➤ DISTANCE *lends enchantment to the view*, ➤ LAND *of Enchantment*.

enchiridion a book containing essential information on a subject. Recorded from late Middle English, the word comes via late Latin from Greek *enkheiridion*, from *en-* 'within' + *kheir* 'hand' + the diminutive suffix *-idion*.

enclosure the process or policy of fencing in waste or common land so as to make it private property, as pursued in much of Britain in the 18th and early 19th centuries.

See also ➤ AGRARIAN *Revolution*.

pour encourager les autres French expression meaning, as an example to others; originally, a quotation from Voltaire on the execution of Admiral John Byng in 1757, for neglect of duty in failing to relieve Minorca when blockaded by a French fleet, '*Dans ce pays-ci il est bon de tuer de temps en temps un amiral pour encourager les autres* [In this country [England] it is thought well to kill an admiral from time to time to encourage the others].'

Encratite a member of any of several early Christian sects who carried ascetic practices to extremes. Recorded from the late 16th century, the word comes via late Latin from patristic Greek *egkratitai*, from *egkrates* 'self-controlled, continent'.

encyclical a papal letter sent to all bishops of the Roman Catholic Church. The word is recorded (as an adjective) from the mid 17th century, and comes via late Latin from Greek *enkuklios* 'circular, general'.

encyclopedia a book or set of books giving information on many subjects or on many aspects of one subject and typically arranged alphabetically. Recorded from the mid 16th century, the word is modern Latin, from pseudo-Greek *enkuklopaideia* for *enkuklios paideia* 'all-round education'.

The first true encyclopedias were by Roman writers such as Cato, Varro, and Pliny the Elder, with articles grouped under main topics. Medieval encyclopedias were generally in Latin, but after the Renaissance similar works were produced in vernacular languages and an alphabetical arrangement came to be adopted. The first book to be called an encyclopedia appeared in 1559. The 18th century saw the publication of the *Cyclopaedia* of Ephraim Chambers (1728) and the great French *Encyclopédie* (1751–76), under the direction of Diderot, whose contributors included Voltaire, Jean-Jacques Rousseau, and other brilliant but controversial writers. The *Encyclopaedia Britannica* began in Scotland in 1768–71 as a dictionary of the arts and sciences; its second edition, in ten volumes, added history and biography and the current (15th) edition is the largest encyclopedia in the English language. The *Encyclopaedia Britannica* has been based in Chicago since 1941.

end see also ➤ *at the end of the* RAINBOW, ➤ DEAD *End Kids,* ➤ *the end of* CIVILIZATION *as we know it.*

the end crowns the work proverbial saying, early 16th century.

the end justifies the means proverbial saying, late 16th century; earlier in Latin, by the Roman poet Ovid, *'exitus acta probat* [the outcome justifies the deeds].'

the end of the world the termination of life on earth; figuratively, a calamitous matter or situation (usually in negative contexts, as, *it's not the end of the world*).

Enderby Land a part of Antarctica claimed by Australia, named by its discoverer, the English navigator John Biscoe (1794–1843), after the London whaling firm *Enderby* Brothers, where he was employed.

Endor see ➤ WITCH *of Endor.*

the ends of the earth the most remote parts of the world.

Endura the physical privations (frequently fatal) undergone by the Cathars after *consolamentum* to prevent recontamination of the soul.

Endymion a remarkably beautiful young man, loved by the Moon (Selene); well-known tradition claims that he had fifty daughters by Selene. According to one story, he was put in an eternal sleep by Zeus for having fallen in love with Hera, and was then visited every night by Selene.

enemy see ➤ *the* BEST *is the enemy of the good,* ➤ *the* GOOD *is the enemy of the best,* ➤ PUBLIC *enemy number one,* ➤ *take heed of* RECONCILED *enemies (and of meat twice boiled),* ➤ *there is no* LITTLE *enemy.*

Enfants sans Souci in medieval France, an association of the merchants, craftsmen, and students of Paris, founded for the purpose of staging theatrical entertainments and other amusements; the name means literally, 'Children without Care'.

engineers St Ferdinand of Castile (1199–1252) is the patron saint of engineers.

England inhabited from at least Palaeolithic times, and with extensive Neolithic and Bronze Age cultures, England was conquered by the Romans in the first century AD, when it was inhabited by Celtic peoples, and was a Roman province until the early 5th century. During the 3rd–7th centuries Germanic-speaking tribes, traditionally known as Angles, Saxons, and Jutes, established a number of independent kingdoms. England emerged as a distinct political entity in the 9th century before being conquered by William, Duke of Normandy, in 1066.

See also ➤ CHAMPION *of England,* ➤ CHURCH *of England,* ➤ CONSTABLE *of England,* ➤ *the Garden of* ENGLAND, ➤ LADY *of England,* ➤ *the* MATTER *of England,* ➤ MERRY *England,* ➤ MIDDLE *England,* ➤ YOUNG *England.*

England is the paradise of women, the hell of horses, and the purgatory of servants proverbial saying, late 16th century; a similar proverb in French is found applied to Paris in the mid 16th century.

England's difficulty is Ireland's opportunity proverbial saying, mid 19th century.

Englander see ➤ LITTLE *Englander.*

English the Germanic language spoken in England which takes its name from the Angles (who first committed their dialect to writing) and was extended to refer to all the dialects of the vernacular, Saxon and Jutish too.

See also ➤ BASIC *English,* ➤ BOROUGH-*English,* ➤ BRITISH *English,* ➤ EARLY *English,* ➤ *the English* SOLOMON, ➤ ESTUARY *English,* ➤ FATHER *of English Poetry,* ➤ OXFORD *English,* ➤ ROCK *English,* ➤ WORLD *English.*

the English are a nation of shopkeepers proverbial saying, early 19th century; attributed to Napoleon, but a similar usage is found earlier in the writings of Adam Smith (1732–90):

> To found a great empire for the sole purpose of raising up a people of customers, may at first sight appear a project fit only for a nation of shopkeepers. It is, however, a project altogether unfit for a nation of shopkeepers; but extremely fit for a nation whose government is influenced by shopkeepers.
> — Adam Smith *Wealth of Nations* (1776)

English Pale that part of Ireland (see ➤ PALE¹) over which England exercised jurisdiction before the whole country was conquered. Centred on Dublin, it varied in extent at different times from the reign of Henry II until the full conquest under Elizabeth I. The term was also used for a small area round Calais, the only part of France remaining in English hands after the Hundred Years War. It was recaptured by France in 1558.

one Englishman can beat three Frenchmen proverbial saying, late 16th century.

an **Englishman's home is his castle** proverbial saying, late 16th century.

an **Englishman's word is his bond** proverbial saying, early 16th century.

Englishry the fact of being an Englishman, used chiefly in the legal phrase **presentment of Englishry**: the offering of proof that a person who had been killed was an Englishman, and that therefore the fine levied (under the Norman kings) on a hundred or township for the murder of a 'Frenchman' or Norman, could not be imposed.

enigma a riddle, usually one involving metaphor; in figurative usage, a person or thing that is mysterious, puzzling, or difficult to understand; the word is recorded from the mid 16th century, and comes via Latin from Greek *ainigma*, from *ainissesthai* 'speak allusively', from *ainos* 'fable'. It was famously used by Winston Churchill in a broadcast of 1941 to describe Russia, 'a riddle wrapped in a mystery inside an enigma'.

Enigma was the name of the German encoding machines used for vital strategic messages in the Second World War; with the assistance of a machine smuggled out of Germany, British cryptographers working at ➤ BLETCHLEY *Park* on the project code-named *Ultra* broke the German codes. The story of Enigma remained an official secret until the ban on publication was lifted in 1974.

See also ➤ COLOSSUS.

Eniwetok an uninhabited island in the North Pacific, one of the Marshall Islands. Cleared of its native population, it was used by the US as a testing ground for atom bombs from 1948 to 1954.

the **Enlightenment** a European intellectual movement of the late 17th and 18th centuries emphasizing reason and individualism rather than tradition. It was heavily influenced by 17th-century philosophers such as Descartes, Locke, and Newton, and its prominent exponents include Kant, Goethe, Voltaire, Rousseau, and Adam Smith.

ennead a set of nine, in particular, each of the six divisions in Porphyry's collection of Plotinus' works, each of which contains nine books.

Enniskillen a town in Northern Ireland, noted in loyalist tradition for the defence by its townsmen against the supporters of the deposed King James II in 1689. The old spelling *Inniskilling* is preserved as a regimental name in the British army, commemorating this.

In November 1987, on Remembrance Day, a bomb exploded at the war memorial in Enniskillen, killing eleven people.

Quintus Ennius (293–169 BC), Roman poet and dramatist. He was largely responsible for the creation of a native Roman literature based on Greek models. Of his many works (surviving only in fragments) the most important was the *Annals* (undated), a hexametric epic on the history of Rome.

Enoch[1] in the Bible, the eldest son of Cain, and the first city built by Cain (Genesis 4:17), named after him.

Enoch[2] a Hebrew patriarch, father of Methuselah; he is said in the Bible to have lived for 365 years, and may be cited as a type of extreme longevity.

Enoch is also said to have ascended to heaven without dying, as in Genesis 5:24, 'And Enoch walked with God: and he was not; for God took him.' By this story he is sometimes linked with ➤ ELIJAH, who ascended to heaven in a fiery chariot, and ➤ St JOHN *the Evangelist*, whose later legend also says that he was taken up to heaven without dying.

Two works ascribed to him, the *Book of Enoch* and the *Book of the Secrets of Enoch*, date from the 2nd–1st centuries BC and 1st century AD respectively. A third treatise likewise dates from the Christian era.

> A year with Will Scott would make a dayfly feel like Enoch.
> — Dorothy Dunnett *The Game of Kings* (1961)

enough is as good as a feast proverbial saying, late 14th century.

ENSA an organization which served to arrange variety entertainment for the British armed services during the Second World War; the name is an acronym for *Entertainments National Service Organization*.

ensign a military or naval standard; a flag, especially one flown at the stern of a vessel to show its nationality (in Britain, each of three such flags with the union flag in one corner). The word is recorded from late Middle English, and comes via Old French from Latin *insignia* 'signs of office'.

From the late 16th century, *ensign* has also been used for a standard-bearer (now historical), and from this for an infantry officer of the lowest commissioned rank, a second lieutenant (now only in the Foot Guards) and an officer in the Yeomen of the Guard. *Ensign* now also denotes an officer of the lowest commissioned rank in the US navy.

See also ➤ ANCIENT, ➤ RED *ensign*, ➤ WHITE *ensign*.

entail a settlement of the inheritance of property over a number of generations so that it remains within a family or other group; *entailed* property was traditionally often settled on a male heir. Recorded from late Middle English (also as **intail**), the word comes from *en-*, *in-* + Old French *taille* 'notch, tax', from *taillier* 'to cut', based on Latin *talea* 'twig, cutting'.

entasis in architecture, a slight convex curve in the shaft of a column, introduced to correct the visual illusion of concavity produced by a straight shaft.

entente see also ➤ *the* LITTLE *Entente*.

the Entente Cordiale the understanding between Britain and France reached in 1904, forming the basis of Anglo-French cooperation in the First World War.

enterprise culture a capitalist society in which entrepreneurs are given particular encouragement; the term came to prominence in the UK in the early 1980s, when it was suggested that the *enterprise culture* was modelled on the spirit of free enterprise which characterized US society.

enthusiasm originally (as a derogatory term), religious fervour supposedly resulting directly from divine inspiration, typically involving speaking in tongues and wild, uncoordinated movements of the body. The word is recorded in this sense from the early 17th century, and comes via French or late Latin from Greek *enthousiasmos*, from *enthous* 'possessed by a god, inspired' (based on *theos* 'god').

The principal current sense of intense and eager enjoyment, interest, or approval, is recorded from the early 18th century.

envelope see ➤ PUSH *the envelope*.

envied see ➤ BETTER *be envied*.

Environmentally Sensitive Area in the UK, an area officially designated as containing landscapes or wildlife that would be threatened by unrestricted development.

Eocene of, relating to, or denoting the second epoch of the Tertiary period, between the Palaeocene and Oligocene epochs. The Eocene epoch lasted from 56.5 to 35.4 million years ago. It was a time of rising temperatures, and there was an abundance of mammals, including the first horses, bats, and whales.

The term is recorded from the mid 19th century, and comes from Greek *ēōs* 'dawn' + *kainos* 'new'.

Eolithic of, relating to, or denoting a period at the beginning of the Stone Age, preceding the Palaeolithic and characterized by the earliest crude stone tools.

The term is recorded from the late 19th century, and comes via French from Greek *ēōs* 'dawn' + *lithikos* (from *lithos* 'stone').

Eonism a term for transvestism, especially by a man, named after Charles d'Éon (1728–1810), a French adventurer who wore women's clothes.

Eos in Greek mythology, the goddess of the dawn, whose Roman equivalent was ➤ AURORA.

epact the number of days by which the solar year exceeds the lunar year. The word is recorded from the mid 16th century, denoting the age of the moon in days at the beginning of the calendar year, and comes via French and late Latin from Greek *epaktai* (*hēmerai*) 'intercalated (days)', from *epagein* 'bring in'.

eparch in the Orthodox church, the chief bishop of a province or **eparchy**; the word is recorded from the mid 17th century, denoting the governor of an administrative division of Greece, and comes from Greek *eparkhos*, from *epi* 'above' + *arkhos* 'ruler'.

épater les bourgeois shock people who have attitudes or views perceived as conventional or complacent; the comment '*Il faut épater le bourgeois* [One must astonish the bourgeois]' is attributed to Baudelaire; the phrase is also attributed to Privat d'Anglemont (*c.*1820–59) in the form '*Je les ai épatés, les bourgeois* [I flabbergasted them, the bourgeois].'

epaulette an ornamental shoulder piece on an item of clothing, typically on the coat or jacket of a military uniform. The term comes through French from Latin *spatula* in the late Latin sense 'shoulder blade'.

ephebe in ancient Greece, a young man of 18–20 years undergoing military training; the word comes via Latin from Greek *ephēbos*, from *epi* 'near to' + *hēbē* 'early manhood'.

ephemera things that exist or are used or enjoyed for only a short time; items of collectable memorabilia, typically written or printed ones, that were originally expected to have only short-term usefulness or popularity.

Recorded in English from the late 16th century as the plural of *ephemeron*, from Greek, neuter of *ephēmeros* 'lasting only a day'. As a singular noun the word originally denoted a plant said by ancient writers to last only one day, or an insect with a short lifespan, and hence was applied (late 18th century) to a person or thing of short-lived interest. Current use has been influenced by plurals such as *trivia* and *memorabilia*.

Epistle to the Ephesians a book of the New Testament ascribed to St Paul consisting of an epistle to the Church at Ephesus.

Ephesus an ancient Greek city on the west coat of Asia Minor, in present-day Turkey, site of the temple of Diana, one of the Seven Wonders of the World. It was an important centre of early Christianity; St Paul preached there and St John is traditionally said to have lived there.

See also ➤ DIANA *of Ephesus*, ➤ *great is* DIANA *of the Ephesians*

ephialtes an evil spirit supposed to cause nightmares; nightmare. Recorded from late Middle English (and now rare or obsolete), the word comes from Greek (in Greek mythology, *Ephialtes* was also the name of one of the giants who took part in the war against Zeus and the gods of Olympus).

ephor in ancient Greece, any of the five senior Spartan magistrates; the word comes from Greek *ephoros* 'overseer'.

epic a long poem, typically one derived from ancient oral tradition, narrating the deeds and adventures of heroic or legendary figures or the past history of a nation. The word comes via Latin from Greek *epikos*, from *epos* 'word, song', related to *eipein* 'say'.

Epictetus (*c*.55–*c*.135 AD), Greek philosopher, who preached the common brotherhood of man and advocated a Stoic philosophy. His teachings were published posthumously in the *Enchiridion*.

Epicureanism an ancient school of philosophy, founded in Athens by Epicurus. The school rejected determinism and advocated hedonism (pleasure as the highest good), but of a restrained kind: mental pleasure was regarded more highly than physical, and the ultimate pleasure was held to be freedom

from anxiety and mental pain, especially that arising from needless fear of death and of the gods.

Epicurus (341–270 BC), Greek philosopher, founder of Epicureanism. His physics is based on Democritus' theory of a materialist universe composed of indestructible atoms moving in a void, unregulated by divine providence.

epicycle a small circle whose centre moves round the circumference of a larger one, used in the Ptolemaic system to describe planetary orbits.

Epidaurus an ancient Greek city and port on the NE coast of the Peloponnese, site of a temple dedicated to Asclepius and a well-preserved Greek theatre dating from the 4th century BC.

epigram a pithy saying or remark expressing an idea in a clever and amusing way; a short poem, especially a satirical one, having a witty or ingenious ending.

epileptics ➤ *St* DYMPHNA and ➤ *St* VITUS are the patron saints of epileptics.

Epimenides a semi-legendary Cretan poet and prophet supposedly living between the 7th and 6th centuries BC, and credited with the creation of ➤ *the* LIAR *paradox*. He is said to be the person referred as having made the assertion that all Cretans were liars in Titus 1:12 'One of themselves; even a prophet of their own'.

epinicion in ancient Greece, an ode sung in honour of a victor in the games; a song of triumph.

the Epiphany the manifestation of Christ to the Gentiles as represented by the ➤ MAGI; the festival commemorating this on 6 January. The name is recorded from Middle English, and comes ultimately from Greek *epiphainein* 'reveal'.

episcopacy the government of a Church by bishops. The word comes (in the mid 17th century) from ecclesiastical Latin *episcopatus* 'episcopate, the office of a bishop', on the pattern of *prelacy*.

Episcopal Church the Anglican Church in Scotland and the US.

episode an event or group of events occurring as part of a sequence; an incident or period considered in isolation. The word dates from the late 17th century, and originally denoted a section between two choric songs in Greek tragedy.

Epistle in the Christian Church, a book of the New Testament in the form of a letter from an Apostle.

Epistle also denotes an extract from an Epistle (or another New Testament book not a Gospel) that is read in a church service.

See also ➤ CANONICAL *epistles,* ➤ CATHOLIC *Epistle.*

Epistle side the south end of an altar, from which the Epistle is traditionally read (opposite to the north or *Gospel* side).

epitaph a phrase or form of words written in memory of a person who has died, especially as an inscription on a tombstone. The word is recorded from late Middle English, and comes via Old French and Latin from Greek *epitaphion* 'funeral oration'.

epithalamium a song or poem celebrating a marriage. The word is recorded from the late 16th century, and comes via Latin from Greek *epithalamion,* from *epi* 'upon' + *thalamos* 'bridal chamber'.

epoch a period of time in history or a person's life, typically one marked by notable events or particular characteristics. The word is recorded from the early 17th century, originally in the Latin form *epocha,* and in the general sense of a date from which succeeding years are numbered; it comes ultimately from Greek *epokhē* 'stoppage, fixed point of time'.

epode a form of lyric poem written in couplets, in which a long line is followed by a shorter one. Also, the third section of an ancient Greek choral ode, or of one division of such an ode.

Eppur si muove Italian for 'But it does move'; supposedly said by ➤ GALILEO after his formal recantation, that the earth moves around the sun, in 1632.

epsilon the fifth letter of the Greek alphabet (E, ε), transliterated as 'e'.

Epsom Downs site of the racecourse, near the town of *Epsom* in Surrey, where the annual Derby and Oaks horse races are held.

Epsom salts crystals of hydrated magnesium sulphate used as a purgative or for other medicinal use; named after the town of *Epsom* in Surrey, where it was first found occurring naturally.

Jacob Epstein (1880–1959), American-born British sculptor. A founder member of the vorticist group, he later had great success in his modelled portraits of the famous, in particular his *Einstein* (1933). Many of his works aroused violent criticism for their use of distortion and alleged obscenity.

all animals are equal, but some animals are more equal than others final slogan promulgated by the pigs in Orwell's fable ➤ ANIMAL *Farm.*

equality in mathematics, the condition of being equal in number or amount; a symbolic expression of the fact that two quantities are equal, an equation.

Equality State an informal name for Wyoming, the first state in the US to introduce women's suffrage.

equals see ➤ FIRST *among equals.*

equation of time the difference between mean solar time (as shown by clocks) and apparent solar time (indicated by sundials), which varies with the time of year.

equator a line notionally drawn on the earth equidistant from the poles, dividing the earth into northern and southern hemispheres and constituting the parallel of latitude 0°. The term is recorded from late Middle English, and comes from medieval Latin *aequator,* in the phrase *circulus aequator diei et noctis* 'circle equalizing day and night'.

equerry an officer of the British royal household who attends or assists members of the royal family; formerly, an officer of the household of a prince or noble who had charge over the stables. The word is recorded from the early 16th century, and comes from Old French *esquierie* 'company of squires, prince's stables', from Old French *esquier* 'esquire', perhaps associated with Latin *equus* 'horse'. The historical sense is apparently based on Old French *esquier d'esquierie* 'squire of stables'.

equilibrium see ➤ NASH *equilibrium.*

equinox the time or date (twice each year) at which the sun crosses the celestial equator, when day and night are of equal length (about 22 September and 20 March).

Equuleus a small northern constellation (the Foal or Little Horse), perhaps representing the brother of Pegasus.

era a long and distinct period of history with a particular feature or characteristic. The word is recorded from the mid 17th century and comes from late Latin *aera,* denoting a number used as a basis of reckoning, an epoch from which time is reckoned, plural of *aes aer-* 'money, counter'.

See ➤ *the* COMMON *Era.*

era of Nabonassar a Babylonian era, employed in astronomy, commencing 747 BC.

era of the Hegira the Muslim era, reckoned from the year of Muhammad's departure from Mecca in AD 622.

Desiderius Erasmus (*c*.1469–1536), Dutch humanist and scholar. He was the foremost Renaissance scholar of northern Europe, paving the way for the Reformation with his satires on the Church, including the *Colloquia Familiaria* (1518). However, he opposed the violence of the Reformation and condemned Luther in *De Libero Arbitrio* (1523).

St Erasmus 4th-century bishop of Formiae and martyr, also known as ➤ *St* ELMO; he is one of the ➤ FOURTEEN *Holy Helpers*, and is patron saint of sailors. Because of this, a windlass became his emblem; the iconography was later misunderstood, and it was thought to be an instrument of torture with which his intestines were wound out of him.
　　❑ **FEAST DAY** His feast day is 2 June.

Erastianism the doctrine that the state should have supremacy over the Church in ecclesiastical matters, wrongly attributed to the Swiss theologian and physician *Erastus* (Thomas Lieber, 1524–83). Professor of medicine at Heidelberg from 1558, he opposed the imposition of a Calvinistic system of Church government in the city.

Erato in Greek and Roman mythology, the Muse of lyric poetry and hymns. The name is Greek, and means literally 'lovely'.

Eratosthenes (*c*.275–194 BC), Greek scholar, geographer, and astronomer. The first systematic geographer of antiquity, he accurately calculated the circumference of the earth and attempted (less successfully) to determine the size and distance of the sun and of the moon.

Erebus in Greek mythology, the primeval god of darkness, son of Chaos; also taken as the proper name of a dark region between Earth and Hades, and as such a type of a place of blackness and gloom.
　　Erebus was also the name of one of the two ships of Sir James Ross's expedition to the Antarctic in 1838 (the other was called *Terror*); Mount Erebus, a volcanic peak on Ross Island, Antarctica, the world's most southerly active volcano, is named for it.

> 　It is as black as Erebus down here.
> 　　　　　　　— Rosemary Sutcliff *Outcast* (1967)

Erech biblical name for ➤ URUK.

Erechtheum a marble temple of the Ionic order built on the Acropolis in Athens *c*.421–406 BC, with shrines to Athene, Poseidon, and Erechtheus, a legendary king of Athens. A masterpiece of the Ionic order, it is most famous for its southern portico, in which the entablature is supported by six caryatids.

eremite a Christian hermit or recluse; the word is recorded from Middle English, and comes via Old French from late Latin *eremita*, from the base of ➤ HERMIT.

Erewhon an anagram of 'nowhere', used as the title of a satirical novel by Samuel Butler published anonymously in 1872; *Erewhon* in the story is the name of a previously undiscovered country, in which morality is equated with health and good looks, and crime with illness.

Eric the Red (*c*.940–*c*.1010), Norse explorer, father of ➤ LEIF *Ericsson*. He left Iceland in 982 in search of land to the west, exploring Greenland and establishing a Norse settlement there in 986.

Erichthonius in Greek mythology, a king of Athens, usually said to be the son of Hephaestus, whose semen fell on the earth as he struggled to rape Athena. Gaia (Earth) gave birth to the child and Athena took him and hid him in a chest which she gave to the daughters of Cecrops, king of Athens, to guard. They were forbidden to open the chest, but disobeying, they saw either the child in serpent form or attended by serpents: terrified, they leaped to their deaths from the Acropolis.
　　Erichthonius became king of Athens and received from Athena two drops of the Gorgon's blood, one of which poisoned and the other healed. He was later worshipped at Athens in the form of a snake.

Eridanus a long straggling southern constellation (the River), said to represent the river into which ➤ PHAETHON fell when struck by Zeus' thunderbolt.

Lake Erie one of the five Great Lakes of North America, situated on the border between Canada and the US. It is linked to Lake Huron by the Detroit River and to Lake Ontario by the Welland Ship Canal and the Niagara River, which is its only natural outlet.

Erin a poetic and literary name for Ireland, derived ultimately from *Érainn*, a name given to one of the ancient peoples of Ireland, which was extended to include the population of the whole island.

Erinyes in Greek mythology, the Furies.

erl-king in Germanic mythology, a bearded giant or goblin believed to lure little children to the land of death. The term comes from German 'alder-king', a mistranslation of Danish *ellerkonge* 'king of the elves'.

ermine a stoat, especially in its white winter coat. The word comes through Old French, and probably derives ultimately from medieval Latin *(mus) Armenius* 'Armenian (mouse)'.

    Ermine also denotes the white fur of the stoat, used for trimming garments, especially the ceremonial robes of judges or peers; in heraldry, it is fur represented as black spots on a white ground, as a heraldic tincture (the spots represent the dark tips of the ermines' tails, and are usually elaborated into short vertical lines with small curved projections, often with (usually three) smaller dots above).

Ernestine designating or pertaining to the elder of the two lines of the house of Frederick the Gentle, Elector of Saxony, which originated with his son *Ernest* (1441–86), and lost the electoral title to the ➤ ALBERTINE line in 1547.

Ernie in the UK, the computer that randomly selects the prizewinning numbers of Premium Bonds.

Eros in Greek mythology, the god of love, son of Aphrodite; his Roman equivalent is ➤ CUPID. The name comes via Latin from Greek, literally 'sexual love'.

    A winged statue of *Eros* over the fountain in Piccadilly Circus, London, made by Sir Alfred Gilbert (1854–1934), was erected as a memorial to the philanthropist the Earl of Shaftesbury, and unveiled in 1893.

to err is human (to forgive divine) proverbial saying, late 14th century.

errant see ➤ KNIGHT *errant*.

an error in the first concoction a fault in the initial stage; *concoction* here means the first of three stages of digestion formerly recognized.

Erse the Scottish or Irish Gaelic language; the name is an early Scots form of *Irish*.

Erté (1892–1990), Russian-born French fashion designer and illustrator. During the First World War his garments became internationally famous through his decorative magazine illustrations, and in the 1920s he became a noted art deco designer,

moving into the design of household items and fabrics, and creating elaborate *tableaux vivants* for Broadway shows such as the *Ziegfeld Follies*.

Ertebølle a late Mesolithic culture in the western Baltic (4th millennium BC), the final phases of which show Neolithic influence in the form of permanent coastal fishing and collecting sites and the use of skin boats.

Erymanthian boar a monstrous boar, living on Mount Erymanthus in Arcadia and ravaging the surrounding countryside, which Hercules captured as the second of his Labours.

Esalen an institute in California which promotes an alternative way of life and teaches psychological and physiotherapeutic techniques aimed at increasing self-awareness and potential.

Esau in the Bible, the elder of the twin sons of Isaac and Rebecca, who sold his birthright to his brother Jacob for a ➤ MESS *of pottage*, and was later tricked out of his father's blessing by his brother. The smooth-skinned Jacob deceived Isaac, who was blind, by using animal skins so that to his father's touch he felt like Esau, a 'hairy man'; despite Isaac's words, 'The voice is Jacob's voice, but the hands are the hands of Esau', he gave the blessing to his younger son.

eschatology the part of theology concerned with death, judgement, and the final destiny of the soul and of humankind.

M. C. Escher (1898–1972), Dutch graphic artist. His prints are characterized by their sophisticated use of visual illusion. From the 1940s his work took on a surrealist flavour, for example, staircases that appear to lead both up and down in the same direction.

> One chase sequence manages to thrill by making Mega-City One look like a vertiginous M. C. Escher dreamworld.
> — *Entertainment Weekly* 14 July 1995

Escorial a monastery and palace in central Spain, near Madrid, built in the late 16th century by Philip II, and encompassing the royal mausoleum.

escutcheon a shield or emblem bearing a coat of arms. The word comes (in the late 15th century) from Anglo-Norman French *escuchon*, based on Latin *scutum* 'shield'.

blot on one's escutcheon a stain on one's reputation or character; a figurative phrase recorded from the late 17th century.

escutcheon of pretence a small shield within a coat of arms, bearing another coat or device to which the bearer has a claim, especially one to which a man's wife is heiress.

Esdras either of two books of the Apocrypha. The first is mainly a compilation from Chronicles, Nehemiah, and Ezra; the second is a record of angelic revelation.

Eskimo In recent years, the word *Eskimo* (an Algonquian word, perhaps meaning 'people speaking a different language') has come to be regarded as offensive (partly through the associations of the now discredited folk etymology 'one who eats raw flesh'). The peoples inhabiting the regions from NW Canada to western Greenland prefer to call themselves *Inuit*. The term *Eskimo*, however, continues to be the only term which can be properly understood as applying to the people as a whole and is still widely used in anthropological and archaeological contexts.

esoteric intended for or likely to be understood by only a small number of people with a specialized knowledge or interest. The word is recorded from the mid 17th century, and comes from Greek *esōterikos*, from the comparative of *esō* 'within'.

Esoteric Buddhism a system of theosophical doctrines alleged to have been transmitted by an inner circle of Buddhists.

Esperanto an artificial language devised in 1887 as an international medium of communication, based on roots from the chief European languages. It retains the structure of these languages and has the advantage of grammatical regularity and ease of pronunciation. The name *Dr Esperanto* was used as a pen-name by the inventor of the language, Ludwik L. Zamenhof (1858–1917), Polish physician; the literal sense is 'one who hopes' (based on Latin *sperare* 'to hope').

esprit de l'escalier used to refer to the fact that a witty remark or retort often comes to mind after the opportunity to make it has passed. The (French) phrase means literally 'wit of the staircase' (i.e. a witty remark coming to mind on the stairs leading away from a gathering), and was coined by the French philosopher and man of letters Denis Diderot (1713–84).

Esquipulas a town in SE Guatemala, near the border with Honduras. Noted for the image of the 'Black Christ of Esquipulas' in its church, the town is a centre of pilgrimage.

esquire a young nobleman who, in training for knighthood, acted as an attendant to a knight. Recorded from late Middle English, the word comes via Old French from Latin *scutarius* 'shield-bearer', from *scutum* 'shield'.

From being a courtesy title given to such a person, esquire in British usage became a polite title appended to a man's name when no other title is used, typically in the address of a letter or other documents, as in *J. C. Pearson Esquire*.

essay a short piece of writing on a particular subject. The term was apparently taken from Montaigne, whose *Essais* were published in 1580; the first recorded use in English is Francis Bacon's *Essays* (1597).

Essene a member of an ancient Jewish ascetic sect of the 2nd century BC–2nd century AD in Palestine, who lived in highly organized groups and held property in common. The Essenes are widely regarded as authors of the Dead Sea Scrolls.

esses see ➤ COLLAR *of esses*.

Essex girl a derogatory term applied to a type of young woman, supposedly to be found in and around Essex, and variously characterized as unintelligent, promiscuous, and materialistic. While ➤ ESSEX *man* is regarded primarily as a type of political supporter, *Essex girl* is seen primarily in social terms, and is typically the butt of politically incorrect jokes.

Essex man a derogatory term for a type of British Conservative voter, in London and the south-east of England (and particularly the county of Essex) in the late 1980s. *Essex man* is characterized as a brash, amoral, self-made young businessman, of right-wing views and few or no cultural or intellectual interests, devoted to the acquisition of goods and material wealth.

Est-il possible French, literally 'Is it possible'; a nickname (from the frequency with which he uttered the remark) of George of Denmark (1653–1708), consort of Queen Anne. It was said that when in 1688, the prince was one of those to desert his father-in-law James II for William of Orange, the king exclaimed, 'So Est-il possible is gone too.'

the Established Church a Church officially recognized by the state as the national Church. The use of established in this sense is first recorded in English in 1660, in a declaration to Parliament by the newly-restored Charles II, 'We need not profess the high affection and esteem we have for the Church of England, as it is established by law.'

the **Establishment** a group in a society exercising power and influence over matters of policy or taste, and seen as resisting change. The term is recorded intermittently from the 1920s, but in British English derives its current use from an article in the *Spectator* of 1955:

> By the 'Establishment' I do not mean only the centres of official power—though they are certainly part of it—but rather the whole matrix of official and social relations within which power is exercised.
> — Henry Fairlie in *The Spectator* 23 September 1955

estate a class or order regarded as forming part of the body politic, in particular (in Britain), one of the three groups (**the three estates**) constituting Parliament, now the Lords Spiritual (the heads of the Church), the Lords Temporal (the peerage), and the Commons. Also called **estate of the realm**.
See also ➤ the FOURTH *estate*.

Estates General another term for ➤ STATES *General*.

Esther in the Bible, a Jewish woman chosen on account of her beauty by the Persian king Ahasuerus (generally supposed to be Xerxes I) to be his queen. She used her influence with him to save her kinsman ➤ MORDECAI and the Israelites in captivity from persecution, particularly at the hands of the king's chief minister, ➤ HAMAN.
Esther is also the book of the Bible containing an account of these events; a part survives only in Greek and is included in the Apocrypha.
See also ➤ HADASSAH.

Estotiland a supposed land off the coast of Labrador, mentioned in Heylyn's *Cosmographia* (1652); in *Paradise Lost* (1667) Milton refers to 'the low sun…which had forbid the snow From cold Estotiland'.

Estuary English in the UK, a type of accent identified as spreading outwards from London and containing features of both received pronunciation and London speech.

et see ➤ et in ARCADIA *ego*.

ET a creature from outer space, stranded on earth, who is befriended by Californian children in Spielberg's film (1982) of that name; the letters stand for *extra-terrestrial*, and he communicates his longing to return to his planet with the line 'ET phone home'.

> A reliable pager can help you . . . know when to make like ET and phone home.
> — *Road King* June 1995

eta the seventh letter of the Greek alphabet (**H, η**), transliterated as 'e' or 'ē'.

L'État, c'est moi French, literally 'I am the state'; attributed to Louis XIV (1638–1715) before the Parlement de Paris, 13 April 1655, but probably apocryphal.

eternal see also ➤ the eternal FITNESS of things, ➤ HOPE springs eternal.

the Eternal an everlasting or universal spirit, not subject to time, as represented by God; recorded from the late 16th century.

the Eternal City a name for the city of Rome; a translation of Latin *urbs aeterna*, occurring in Ovid and Tibullus, and frequently found in the official documents of the Empire.

eternal triangle a relationship between three people, typically a couple and the lover of one of them, involving sexual rivalry.

eternity ring a ring given as a symbol of lasting affection, typically having an unbroken circle of gems set into it.

Etesian wind another name for ➤ MELTEMI; the term is recorded from the early 17th century, and comes from Latin *etesius* 'annual'.

eth an Old English letter, ð or Ð. It was superseded by the digraph *th*, but is now used as a phonetic symbol.

Ethanim in the Jewish calendar, another name for ➤ TISHRI; the name comes from a Hebrew phrase meaning 'month of steady-flowing rivers'.

Ethelred II (*c.*969–1016), king of England 978–1016; known as **Ethelred the Unready**. Ethelred's inability to confront the Danes after he succeeded his murdered half-brother St Edward the Martyr led to his payment of tribute to prevent their attacks. In 1013 he briefly lost his throne to the Danish king Sweyn I.

St Etheldreda (d. 679), English princess and queen, foundress and abbess of Ely. She is the patron saint of Ely, and the word *tawdry* derives from a contraction of *St Audrey*, a later form of her name, in reference to the cheap laces and other finery sold at the annual fair in her honour.

☐ **EMBLEM** It is said that in a time of famine the Ely community was supplied with milk by two does, and Etheldreda may be shown with them.

☐ **FEAST DAY** Her feast day is 23 June.

ethic see ➤ PROTESTANT *ethic.*

ethical foreign policy the conduct of foreign policy according to ethical as well as national considerations; since the British general election of 1997, the aspiration has been particularly associated with the incumbency of Robin Cook as Foreign Secretary, but its precise application in individual cases has been controversial.

ethical investment investment in companies that meet ethical criteria specified by the investor, typically excluding the armaments and tobacco industries.

Ethiopia a country in NE Africa, on the Red Sea. It is the oldest independent country in Africa, having a recorded civilization that dates from the 2nd millennium BC.

ethnic cleansing the mass expulsion or killing of members of one ethnic or religious group in an area by those of another. The term has been in use since the early 1990s, as conflict spread in the former Yugoslavia; it became particularly associated with the bitter fighting between Bosnian Serbs and Bosnian Muslims in Bosnia, and most recently with events in ➤ KOSOVO.

etin in Scottish folklore, a giant.

Mount Etna a volcano in eastern Sicily, which is the highest and most active volcano in Europe; it was traditionally said to be Vulcan's workshop, and in classical times eruption were also explained as the struggles of giants imprisoned by Zeus beneath the mountain.

See also ➤ EMPEDOCLES.

Eton College a boys' public school in southern England, on the River Thames opposite Windsor, founded in 1440 by Henry VI to prepare scholars for King's College, Cambridge.

Etrog any of the statuettes by the Canadian sculptor S. Etrog (1933–), formerly awarded anually for achievement in Canadian film-making.

Etruria an ancient state of western Italy, situated between the Rivers Arno and Tiber and corresponding approximately to modern Tuscany and parts of Umbria. It was the centre of the Etruscan civilization, which was at its height *c.*500 BC and was an important influence on the Romans, who had subdued the Etruscans by the end of the 3rd century BC.

Etruscan the language of ancient Etruria, which was written in an alphabet derived from Greek but is not related to any known language.

the Ettrick Shepherd name for the Scottish poet James Hogg (1770–1835), who began herding sheep at the age of seven and in adult life worked as a shepherd.

etymology the study of the origin of words and the way in which their meanings have changed throughout history. The word is recorded from late Middle English, and comes via Old French and Latin from Greek *etumologia*, from *etumologos* 'student of etymology', and ultimately from *etumos* 'true'.

Etzel in the *Nibelungenlied* the equivalent of the Norse ➤ ATLI.

Eucharist the Christian service, ceremony, or sacrament commemorating the Last Supper, in which bread and wine are consecrated and consumed. Also, the consecrated elements, especially the bread.

From the earliest times Christians have blessed and shared bread and wine in commemoration of the Last Supper (recorded in the first three Gospels and 1 Corinthians 10–11) and of the self-sacrifice of Christ. The bread and wine are referred to as the body and blood of Christ, though much theological controversy has focused on how substantially or symbolically this is to be interpreted.

The word is recorded from late Middle English, and comes via Old French, based on ecclesiastical Greek *eukharistia* 'thanksgiving'.

Euchite a member of a 4th-century Christian sect which believed that salvation could be gained only through incessant prayer; the name comes ultimately from Greek *eukhē* 'prayer'.

Euchologion a book of prayers or religious rites, in particular, a book of the Orthodox Church containing the Eucharistic rites and other liturgical matter.

euchre a North American card game for two to four players, played with the thirty-two highest cards, the aim being to win at least three of the five tricks played.

Euclid (*c.*300 BC), Greek mathematician. His great work *Elements of Geometry*, which covered plane geometry, the theory of numbers, irrationals, and solid geometry, was the standard work until other kinds of geometry were discovered in the 19th century.

Euclidean geometry the geometry of ordinary experience, based on the axioms of Euclid, especially the one stating that parallel lines do not meet.

eudaemonism a system of ethics that bases moral value on the likelihood of actions producing happiness.

Eudist a member of the Congregation of Jesus and Mary, founded for secular clergy by St Jean *Eudes* (1601–80), French missioner, and now concerned chiefly with secondary education in France, Canada, and other French-speaking countries.

Eugene see ➤ *Eugene* ARAM.

Euhemerus (*c.*316 BC), Sicilian writer, who maintained that the gods and goddesses of Greek mythology were deified men and women; from this, comes the word *Euhemerism*, meaning a method of mythological interpretation regarding myths as traditional accounts of real incidents in human history.

Till Eulenspiegel a German peasant (in English, *Owlglass*) of the 14th century whose jokes were the subject of a 16th-century collection of satirical tales.

> We have learned to respect the tricksters, the Till Eulenspiegels of our civilized condition.
> — *New York Review of Books* 27 March 1997

Eumaeus in Homer's *Odyssey*, the faithful swineherd of Odysseus; he entertained Odysseus in his hut when the latter returned to Ithaca and afterwards helped him to destroy the suitors.

Eumenides in Greek mythology, a name given to the Furies. The Eumenides ('the Kindly Ones') probably originated as well-disposed deities of fertility, whose name was given to the Furies either by confusion or euphemistically.

Eunomian a follower of *Eunomius*, 4th-century bishop of Cyzicus on the Sea of Marmara, who developed an extreme form of Arianism.

eunuch a man who has been castrated, especially (in the past) one employed to guard the women's living areas at an oriental court. The word is recorded from Old English, and comes via Latin from Greek *enoukhos*, literally 'bedroom work'.

eupatrid in ancient Greece, a member of the hereditary aristocracy of Athens; a person of noble descent.

euphemism a mild or indirect word or expression substituted for one considered to be too harsh or blunt when referring to something unpleasant or embarrassing. The word is recorded from the late 16th century, and comes from Greek *euphēmismos*, from *euphēmizein* 'use auspicious words'.

Euphrates a river of SW Asia which rises in the mountains of eastern Turkey and flows through Syria and Iraq to join the Tigris, forming the Shatt al-Arab waterway.

euphuism an artificial, highly elaborate way of writing or speaking. Recorded from the late 16th century, the word comes from late 16th century: from *Euphues*, the name of a character in John Lyly's prose romance of the same name (1578–80), from Greek *euphuēs* 'well endowed by nature'. It originally referred to a conversational and literary style popular in the late 16th and early 17th centuries in imitation of Lyly's work, which was characterized by alliteration, antitheses, and similes referring to nature and mythology.

Eureka the name of a lead in the Ballarat goldfield, site of the **Eureka stockade**, scene of a clash between gold-miners and the police and military at Ballarat in 1854, now a symbol of republicanism.

eureka a cry of joy or satisfaction when one finds or discovers something. Recorded from the early 17th century, and said to have been uttered by Archimedes when he hit upon a method of determining the purity of gold (Greek *heurēka* 'I have found it').

Eureka flag a blue flag bearing a white cross with a star at the end of each arm, first raised at the *Eureka stockade* (see ➤ EUREKA); it is also known as the *Southern Cross*.

Euripides (480–*c.*406 BC), Greek dramatist. His nineteen surviving plays show important innovations in the handling of traditional myths, such as the introduction of realism, an interest in feminine psychology, and the portrayal of abnormal and irrational states of mind.

Euro the single European currency, introduced in parts of the European Union in 1999.

Euro-sceptic a person who is opposed to increasing the powers of the European Union.

Europa in Greek mythology, a princess of Tyre who was courted by Zeus in the form of a bull. She was carried off by him to Crete, where she bore him three sons (Minos, Rhadamanthus, and Sarpedon). The continent of *Europe* is said to be named after her, although Herodotus thinks this is unlikely since she was a Phoenician, and not from mainland Europe.

In astronomy, *Europa* is one of the Galilean moons of Jupiter, the sixth-closest satellite to the planet, having a network of dark lines on a bright icy surface (diameter 3,138 km).

Europe see ➤ *the* COCKPIT *of Europe*, ➤ CONCERT *of Europe*, ➤ *the* GARDEN *of Europe*, ➤ SICK *Man of Europe*, ➤ YOUNG *Europe*.

European see also ➤ DEAD *white European male*.

European Union an economic and political association of certain European countries as a unit with internal free trade and common external tariffs. The European Union was created on 1 November 1993, with the coming into force of the Maastricht Treaty. It encompasses the old European Community (EC) together with two intergovernmental 'pillars' for dealing with foreign affairs and with immigration and justice. The terms **European Economic Community** (EEC) and **European Community** (EC) continue to be used loosely to refer to what is now the European Union.

Eurostar trademark name for the high-speed passenger rail service that links London with various European cities via the Channel Tunnel.

Eurotrash informal term for rich European socialites, especially those living or working in the United States.

Eurus in Latin literature, the east or south-east wind.

Euryale the name of one of the three ➤ GORGONS.

Euryalus in Virgil's *Aeneid*, the close friend and companion of Nisus (see ➤ NISUS²).

Eurydice in Greek mythology, the wife of Orpheus. After she was killed by a snake Orpheus secured her release from the underworld on the condition that he did not look back at her on their way back to the world of the living. But Orpheus did look back, whereupon Eurydice disappeared.

Eusebius (*c.*264–*c.*340 AD), bishop and Church historian; known as **Eusebius of Caesaria**. His *Ecclesiastical History* is the principal source for the history of Christianity (especially in the Eastern Church) from the age of the Apostles until 324.

St Eustace a possibly legendary martyr who is traditionally regarded as one of the ➤ FOURTEEN *Holy Helpers* and is the patron of hunters; he is shown (like ➤ *St* HUBERT) confronting a hart or stag with a crucifix in its antlers.

According to his unhistorical legend, he was a Roman general named Placidas who in the time of Trajan became a convert to Christianity and changed his name to Eustace; with his wife and children he was martyred by being roasted to death in a brazen bull.

◻ **FEAST DAY** His feast day is 20 September (in the East, 2 November).

Euston Road relating to or denoting a group of English post-Impressionist realistic painters of the 1930s, from the name of a road in London, site of a former School of Drawing and Painting (1938–9).

Euterpe in Greek and Roman mythology, the Muse of flutes. The name is Greek, and means literally 'well-pleasing'.

euthanasia the painless killing of a patient suffering from an incurable and painful disease or in an irreversible coma. The practice is illegal in most countries, although euthanasia in cases where the patient has given active consent is accepted in practice in the Netherlands.

The word is recorded from the early 17th century (in the sense 'easy death'), and comes from Greek, from *eu* 'well' + *thanatos* 'death'.

Eutopia a place of ideal happiness or good order, often wrongly regarded as the correct form of ➤ UTOPIA, which has largely superseded it.

Euxine Sea the 'hospitable' sea, the euphemistic Greek name for the stormy Black Sea.

evangel archaic term for the Christian gospel; any of the four Gospels. The word is recorded from Middle English, and comes via French and ecclesiastical Latin from Greek *euangelion* 'good news', from *euangelos* 'bringing good news'.

evangelical of or according to the teaching of the gospel or the Christian religion; in particular, of or denoting a tradition within Protestant Christianity emphasizing the authority of the Bible, personal conversion, and the doctrine of salvation by faith in the Atonement. Conservative evangelicalism is closely associated with Christian fundamentalism; there also exists a strand of liberal evangelicalism, which takes a critical approach to the Bible while still asserting the importance of the believer's relationship with God.

the **Evangelical** Prophet Isaiah, viewed as prophesying the life of Christ and anticipating gospel doctrines in his writing.

Evangelist the writer of one of the four Gospels (Matthew, Mark, Luke, or John); ➤ St JOHN is also known as **St John the Evangelist**.

evangelistary a book containing the portions of the Gospels that form part of the liturgy.

Arthur Evans (1851–1941), English archaeologist. His excavations at ➤ KNOSSOS (1899–1935) resulted in the discovery of the Bronze Age civilization of Crete, which he named Minoan after the legendary Cretan king Minos.

Edith Evans (1888–1976), English actress. She appeared in a wide range of Shakespearean and contemporary roles but is particularly remembered as Lady Bracknell in Oscar Wilde's *The Importance of Being Earnest.*

Evans's in the NW corner of the Piazza, Covent Garden, originally the residence of the earl of Orford (d. 1727), converted into a hotel in 1774. In 1844 it passed under the management of one Paddy Green and became famous for its musical parties and suppers; Thackeray's 'Cave of Harmony' is partly drawn from it.

Eve in the Bible, the first woman, companion of ➤ ADAM and mother of Cain and Abel; she was formed by God from a rib from Adam's side, and is shown in Genesis as yielding to the temptation of the serpent, and subsequently persuading Adam to eat the fruit of the tree of knowledge.

See also ➤ when ADAM *delved and Eve span.*

John Evelyn (1620–1706), English diarist and writer. He is remembered chiefly for his *Diary* (published posthumously in 1818), which describes his travels abroad, his contemporaries, and such important historical events as the Great Plague and the Great Fire of London.

evensong in the Christian Church, a service of evening prayers, psalms, and canticles, conducted according to a set form, especially that of the Anglican Church. The word is recorded from Old English (in form *æfensang*), originally applied to the pre-Reformation service of vespers.

See also ➤ *be the* DAY *weary or be the day long, at last it ringeth to evensong.*

the **Doleful Evensong** another name for the ➤ FATAL *Vespers.*

events see ➤ COMING *events cast their shadows before them.*

ever and anon occasionally; an archaic and poetic phrase originally used in Shakespeare's *Love's Labour's Lost,* 'Ever and anon, they made a doubt.'

the **Ever-Memorable** contemporary epithet of the scholar and divine John Hales (1584–1656), noted for his breadth of learning.

Dame Edna Everage Australian 'Housewife Superstar', a character created by the comedian Barry Humphries (1934–), first appearing on British television in the late 1970s, and noted for her flamboyant outfits and self-adulatory accounts of her lifestyle and family.

Mount Everest a mountain in the Himalayas, on the border between Nepal and Tibet. Rising to 8,848 m (29,028 ft), it is the highest mountain in the world; it was first climbed in 1953 by Sir Edmund Hillary and Tenzing Norgay.

Everglades a vast area of marshland and coastal mangrove in southern Florida, part of which is protected as a national park.

Evergreen State informal name for the State of Washington.

every man for himself proverbial saying, late 14th century.

every man for himself, and God for us all proverbial saying, mid 16th century.

every man for himself, and the Devil take the hindmost proverbial saying, early 16th century.

every man has his price proverbial saying, mid 18th century; the English Whig statesman Robert Walpole (1676–1745) is reported as saying of fellow parliamentarians, 'All those men have their price.'

every man is the architect of his own fortune proverbial saying, mid 16th century; earlier in Latin.

every man to his taste proverbial saying, late 16th century.

every man to his trade proverbial saying, late 16th century.

everybody loves a lord proverbial saying, mid 19th century.

what **everybody** says must be true proverbial saying, late 14th century.

everybody's business is nobody's business proverbial saying, early 17th century.

Everyman the name of the principal character in a 15th-century morality play, to whom Knowledge makes the promise, 'Everyman, I will go with thee, and be thy guide.'

everything see also ➤ *a* PLACE *for everything, and everything in its place.*

everything has an end proverbial saying, late 14th century.

evidence the available body of facts or information indicating whether a belief or proposition is true or valid; in legal usage, information given personally, drawn from a document, or in the form of material objects, tending or used to establish facts in a legal investigation or admissible as testimony in a law court. The word is recorded from Middle English and comes via Old French from Latin *evidentia*, from *evident*- 'obvious to the eye or mind'.

See also ➤ *what the* SOLDIER *said isn't evidence.*

evil see also ➤ IDLENESS *is the root of all evil,* ➤ KING*'s evil,* ➤ MONEY *is the root of all evil,* ➤ SEE *no evil, hear no evil, speak no evil.*

evil communications corrupt good manners proverbial saying, early 15th century, with biblical allusion.

evil doers are evil dreaders proverbial saying, mid 16th century.

the **Evil** Empire a term for the former Soviet Union, deriving from a speech by Ronald Reagan in 1983, when in the context of 'nuclear freeze proposals' he warned that his hearers should not 'ignore the facts of history and the aggressive impulses of an evil empire'. The name is often used allusively of a political approach focusing exclusively on the perceived dangers from a particular direction.

> While we have had our eyes glued to the world's keyholes to see what the 'Evil Empire' was doing, other nations in the Western World have been hurtling past us.
> — Philip Slater *A Dream Deferred* (1991)

the **evil** eye a gaze or stare superstitiously believed to cause material harm; the expression in this sense is recorded from the late 18th century.

the **Evil** One the Devil; as used in Milton's *Paradise Lost* (1667), 'That space the Evil one abstracted stood From his own evil'.

never do **evil** that good may come of it proverbial saying, late 16th century, with biblical allusion.

of two **evils**, choose the least proverbial saying, late 14th century; earlier in Greek, in Aristotle's *Nicomachean Ethics*, 'we must as a second-best course, it is said, take the least of the evils,' and Latin, in Cicero's *De Officiis*, 'of evils choose the least.'

ewe lamb a person's most cherished possession; originally with biblical allusion to 2 Samuel 12, 'But the poor man had nothing, save one little ewe lamb', the words with which the prophet Nathan rebuked ➤ DAVID for taking the wife of Uriah the Hittite from him.

Ewing name of the dysfunctional oil-rich Texas family around whom the television soap ➤ DALLAS was centred.

> They like to think of themselves as decorous and cosmopolitan, far removed from the gold-Cadillac-driving real-life Ewings who have made 'Texas rich' synonymous with profligate yahoodom.
> — *Spy* May 1992

ex see also ➤ *ex pede* HERCULEM.

ex cathedra with the full authority of office (especially that of the Pope, implying infallibility as defined in Roman Catholic doctrine). The phrase is Latin, 'from the teacher's chair', from *ex* 'from' and *cathedra* 'seat' (from Greek *kathedra*).

ex gratia (especially with reference to the paying of money) done from a sense of moral obligation rather than because of any legal requirement. The phrase is Latin, and means literally, 'from favour'.

ex libris used as an inscription on a bookplate to show the name of the book's owner. The phrase is Latin, and means literally 'out of the books or library (of someone)'.

exaltation in astrology, the position of a planet in the zodiac in which it exerts great influence.

Exaltation of the Cross a feast observed in the Roman Catholic and Orthodox Churches on 14 September in honour of the Cross of Christ, to commemorate either the exposition of the supposed True Cross in 629 after its recovery from the Persians, or the dedication by Constantine in 335 of the basilica built on the site of the Holy Sepulchre.

examination see ➤ Previous *Examination*.

example is better than precept proverbial saying, early 15th century.

exarch in the Orthodox Church, a bishop lower in rank than a patriarch and having jurisdiction wider than the metropolitan of a diocese. Also, a governor of a distant province under the Byzantine emperors. The word is recorded from the late 16th century, and comes via ecclesiastical Latin from Greek *exarkhos*, from *ex-* 'out of' + *arkhos* 'ruler'.

Exarchist a supporter of the Exarch of Bulgaria against the Patriarch of Constantinople during the schism of 1872–1945.

Excalibur in Arthurian legend, King Arthur's magic sword, which according to legend he drew from the stone in which it was embedded to prove that he was the true king; by another account, it was given him by the Lady of the Lake. In Malory's *Morte D'Arthur*, when the king is mortally wounded, he tells Sir Bedivere to throw the sword back into the lake; when he finally obeys, an arm in white samite emerges from the water to catch and take the sword.

Excalibur is also the name of the database, installed in 1996 at Labour Party headquarters, which was held to have contributed materially to the party's ability in Opposition to mount a swift rebuttal of government claims.

excelsior the Latin motto ('higher') on the seal of the State of New York (adopted by the senate of that state 16 March 1778), the accompanying device being a rising sun.

In his poem 'Excelsior' (1841), the American poet Henry Wadsworth Longfellow used the word as a refrain meaning 'upwards', as an injunction or aspiration ('A voice replied, far up the height, Excelsior!'). When it was pointed out that this was not grammatically correct, he is said to have suggested that the word might stand for a longer phrase, '*Scopus meus excelsior est* [My goal is higher].'

In modern use, the word is likely to be either an allusion to Longfellow, or to be used in the names of hotels, newspapers, and manufactured products to indicate superior quality.

the Excelsior State an informal name for New York State, from the motto on its seal.

the exception proves the rule proverbial saying, mid 17th century; originally this meant that the recognition of something as an exception proved the existence of a rule, but it is now more often used or understood as justifying divergence from a rule.

there is an exception to every rule proverbial saying, late 16th century.

exchange see also ➤ Baltic *Exchange*, ➤ Royal *Exchange*.

a fair exchange is no robbery proverbial saying, mid 16th century.

Exchequer in the UK, the former government office responsible for collecting revenue and making payments on behalf of the sovereign, auditing official accounts, and trying legal cases relating to revenue. The original sense was 'chessboard', and current senses derive from the department of state established by the Norman kings to deal with the royal revenues, named *Exchequer* from the chequered tablecloth on which accounts were kept by means of counters.

See also ➤ Black *Book of the Exchequer*, ➤ Red *Book of the Exchequer*.

Exchequer Chamber any of a number of former courts of appeal whose functions were amalgamated in the Court of Appeal in 1873. Formerly also, an assembly of all the judges to decide points of law, defunct since the 18th century.

Exclusion Bill a bill of 1680 seeking to bar James Duke of York (the future James II, brother of ➤ Charles *II*) from the succession, on the grounds of his being a Roman Catholic; those opposed to him supported Charles's illegitimate son, the ➤ *Duke of* Monmouth, as representing a Protestant succession.

excommunicate officially exclude someone from participation in the sacraments and services of the Christian Church. The word is recorded from late Middle English, and comes from ecclesiastical Latin *excommunicat-* 'excluded from communication with the faithful'.

excubitor in ancient Rome, a member of one of the four companies into which the imperial guard was divided; the word is Latin, and means literally 'watchman'.

excursions see ➤ ALARUMS *and excursions.*

excuse see ➤ *a* BAD *excuse is better than none.*

he who **excuses, accuses himself** proverbial saying, early 17th century; earlier in Latin.

exegesis critical explanation or interpretation of a text, especially of scripture. The word is recorded from the early 17th century, and comes from Greek *exēgēsis*, from *exēgeisthai* 'interpret'.

exequatur an official recognition by a government of a consul, agent, or other representative of a foreign state, authorizing them to exercise office. The word is Latin, literally 'let him or her perform'.

Exeter see also ➤ DUKE *of Exeter's daughter.*

The **Exeter** Book a major manuscript of Old English poetry, containing some of the most famous shorter poems, such as *The Wanderer* and The *Seafarer*; it dates from *c.*940, and was given by Bishop Leofric (d. 1072) to Exeter Cathedral, where it remains.

Exeter Hall a building in the Strand, London, erected in 1830–1, used chiefly for religious and philanthropic assemblies till 1907, and sometimes referred to allusively for a type of evangelism.

> We must be patient, and let the Exeter-Hallery and other tragic Tomfoolery rave itself out.
> — Thomas Carlyle *Latter-day Pamphlets* (1858)

exhibition see ➤ GREAT *Exhibition.*

existentialism a philosophical theory or approach which emphasizes the existence of the individual person as a free and responsible agent determining their own development through acts of the will.

The term denotes recurring themes in modern philosophy and literature rather than a single school of thought. Generally taken to originate with Kierkegaard and Nietzsche, existentialism tends to be atheistic (although there is a strand of Christian existentialism deriving from the work of Kierkegaard), to disparage scientific knowledge, and to deny the existence of objective values, stressing instead the reality and significance of human freedom and experience. The approach was developed chiefly in 20th-century Europe, notably by Martin Heidegger, Jean-Paul Sartre, Albert Camus, and Simone de Beauvoir.

Exocet a French-made guided anti-ship missile, used particularly in the Falklands War, and sometimes in figurative use; the name comes (in the 1970s) from French, from Greek *ekōkoitos* 'fish that comes up on the beach' (literally 'out of bed').

> Mr Yentob compared *Who Wants To Be A Millionaire*—which has won audiences of up to 19 million—to an 'Exocet missile through the schedules'.
> — *Daily Telegraph* 23 March 1999

Exodus the second book of the Bible, which recounts the departure of the Israelites from slavery in Egypt, their journey across the Red Sea and through the wilderness led by ➤ MOSES, and the giving of the ➤ TEN *Commandments*. The events have been variously dated by scholars between about 1580 and 1200 BC.

exon each of the four officers acting as commanders of the Yeomen of the Guard. The word represents the pronunciation of the French *exempt* 'free from', because these officers were exempt from normal duties.

Exon Domesday an abstract of the ➤ DOMESDAY *Book* covering SW England, and kept at Exeter Cathedral.

exorcize originally, conjure up or command an evil spirit; later, drive out or attempt to drive out an evil spirit from a person or place in which it is believed to be present. Recorded from late Middle English, the word comes via French or ecclesiastical Latin from Greek *exorkizein*, from *ex-* 'out' + *horkos* 'oath'. The specific sense of driving out an evil spirit dates from the mid 16th century.

expect see also ➤ BLESSED *is he who expects nothing, for he shall never be disappointed,* ➤ *nobody expects the* SPANISH *Inquisition.*

what can you **expect** from a pig but a grunt? proverbial saying, mid 18th century.

experience is the best teacher proverbial saying, mid 16th century.

experience is the father of wisdom proverbial saying, mid 16th century.

experience keeps a dear school proverbial saying, mid 18th century.

expressionism a style of painting, music, or drama in which the artist or writer seeks to express emotional experience rather than impressions of the external world. Expressionists characteristically reject traditional ideas of beauty or harmony and use distortion, exaggeration, and other non-naturalistic devices in order to emphasize and express the inner world of emotion. The paintings of El Greco and Grünewald exemplify expressionism in this broad sense, but the term is also used of a late 19th and 20th century European and specifically German movement tracing its origins to Van Gogh, Edvard Munch, and James Ensor, which insisted on the primacy of the artist's feelings and mood, often incorporating violence and the grotesque.

extispicy in ancient Rome, inspection of the entrails of sacrificial victims in order to predict the future; haruspicy.

extra see ➤ GO *the extra mile.*

extreme sports performed in a hazardous environment and involving great physical risk, such as parachuting or white-water rafting; *extreme sports* became a fashionable leisure activity in the early 1990s.

extreme unction in the Roman Catholic Church, a former name for the sacrament of anointing of the sick, especially when administered to the dying.

extremes meet proverbial saying, mid 18th century; mid 17th century in French.

extremity see ➤ MAN's *extremity is God's opportunity.*

extropy the pseudoscientific principle that life will expand indefinitely and in an orderly, progressive way throughout the entire universe by the means of human intelligence and technology; the word (recorded from the 1980s) comes from *ex-* 'out' + a shortened form of *entropy.*

Exultet the Latin hymn beginning *Exultet jam angelica turba caelorum*, sung in the Roman Catholic Church at the blessing of the paschal candle on Easter Eve.

Exxon Valdez name of the oil tanker which ran aground off the Alaskan coast in 1989, causing considerable environmental damage and giving rise to the development of the ➤ VALDEZ *Principles.*

> The environmental prophets seize on every calamity—for instance Exxon Valdez—as proof of our sinful ways.
> — Julian Symon in *Guardian* 16 March 1995

eyas a young hawk, especially (in falconry) an unfledged nestling taken from the nest for training. The word (originally *nyas*) is recorded from the late 15th century, and comes from French *niais*, based on Latin *nidus* 'nest'. The initial n was lost by wrong division of *a nyas.*

eye *eyes* (on a dish) are the emblem of ➤ St LUCY, who was blinded during her martyrdom.

See also ➤ APPLE *of one's eye*, ➤ ARGUS-*eyed*, ➤ *a* BEAM *in one's eye*, ➤ BEAUTY *is in the eye of the beholder*, ➤ *the* BUYER *has need of a hundred eyes, the seller of but one*, ➤ *the* EVIL *eye*, ➤ FIELDS *have eyes and woods have ears*, ➤ *in the* TWINKLING *of an eye*, ➤ MOTE *in a person's eye*, ➤ POPE's *eye*, ➤ RED-*eye flight*, ➤ *the* SCALES *fall from someone's eyes*, ➤ SEEING *Eye*, ➤ THIRD *eye*, ➤ *turn a* BLIND *eye*, ➤ *turn a* NELSON *eye*, ➤ WALL *eye.*

all my eye and Betty Martin nonsense; said in a letter of 1781 to be 'a sea phrase', although the identity of *Betty Martin* is unexplained.

please your eye and plague your heart proverbial saying, early 17th century.

eye-catcher in 18th-century landscape design, an architectural feature such as a sham ruin or a monument, intended to draw the eye in a particular direction.

eye-diseases ➤ St LUCY is the patron saint of eye-diseases.

what the eye doesn't see, the heart doesn't grieve over proverbial saying, mid 16th century; earlier in Latin.

an eye for an eye and a tooth for a tooth used to refer to the belief that retaliation in kind is the appropriate way to deal with an offence or crime, with biblical allusion to Exodus 21:23–4, 'And if any mischief follow, thou shalt give life for life, Eye for eye, tooth for tooth.'

the eye of a master does more work than both his hands proverbial saying, mid 18th century.

eye of a needle the type of a minute gap through which it is difficult to pass; mainly with echoes of Jesus's saying, 'it is easier for a camel to go through the eye of a needle, than for a rich man to enter into the kingdom of heaven' (Matthew 19:24).

the eye of day poetic term for the sun.

the eye of Greece Athens, so named in Milton's *Paradise Regained* (1671), 'Athens, the eye of Greece, mother of arts And eloquence'.

the eye of the Baltic a name for Gotland, an island in the Baltic.

the eye of the storm the calm region at the centre of a storm.

the eye of the wind the direction from which the wind is blowing.

eye rhyme a similarity between words in spelling but not in pronunciation, for example *love* and *move*.

an eye to the main chance consideration for one's own interests; *main chance* literally, in the game of hazard, a number (5, 6, 7, or 8) called by a player before throwing the dice.

eye tooth a canine tooth, especially one in the upper jaw; figuratively, the type of something precious that might be given or hazarded for a particular gain.

eyeball to eyeball face to face with someone, especially in an aggressive way; the expression is particularly associated with the US politician Dean Rusk (1909–94) as Secretary of State on the

➤ CUBAN *Missile Crisis*, 24 October 1962, 'We're eyeball to eyeball, and I think the other fellow just blinked.'

eyes and no eyes traditional saying, mid 18th century; expressing the difference between an observant and an unobservant person.

the eyes are the window of the soul proverbial saying, mid 16th century.

Ezekiel a Hebrew prophet of the 6th century BC who prophesied the forthcoming destruction of Jerusalem and the Jewish nation and inspired hope for the future well-being of a restored state. Also, a book of the Bible containing his prophecies.

> It identified him with a sustained severity of tone, with . . . citations of biblical and Sophoclean anguish, so that he became an Ezekiel or at least a Tiresias.
> — Richard Ellmann *Golden Codgers* (1973)

Ezra a Jewish priest and scribe who played a central part in the reform of Judaism in the 5th or 4th century BC, continuing the work of Nehemiah and forbidding mixed marriages. Also, a book of the Bible telling of Ezra, the return of the Jews from Babylon, and the rebuilding of the Temple.

Ff

F the sixth letter of the modern English alphabet and of the ancient Roman one, corresponding to Greek *digamma* (Ϝ), Semitic *waw*.

See also ➤ *the* THREE *F's*.

the Fab Four George Harrison, John Lennon, Paul McCartney, and Ringo Starr; the four members of the pop and rock group ➤ *the* BEATLES.

Peter Carl Fabergé (1846–1920), Russian goldsmith and jeweller, of French descent. He is famous for the intricate Easter eggs that he made for Tsar Alexander III and other royal households.

> All the best things are like that: a fine confusion and combination of colours and textures and shapes and surprises. Take Fabergé eggs.
> — *British Airways High Life* October 1993

Fabian employing a cautiously persistent and dilatory strategy to wear out an enemy, after the manner of the Roman general and statesman ➤ FABIUS.

Fabian Society an organization of socialists aiming at the gradual rather than revolutionary achievement of socialism, founded in 1884 and named after ➤ FABIUS.

Fabius (d. 203 BC), Roman general and statesman, known as **Fabius Cunctator**. After Hannibal's defeat of the Roman army at Cannae in 216 BC, Fabius successfully pursued a strategy of caution and delay in order to wear down the Carthaginian invaders. This earned him his nickname, which means 'delayer'.

the American Fabius an informal name for George Washington, likening his tactics to those of the Roman general and statesman.

fable a short story, typically with animals as characters, conveying a moral; a story, typically a supernatural one incorporating elements of myth and legend. Recorded from Middle English, the word comes via Old French from Latin *fabula* 'story', from *fari* 'speak'.

See also ➤ *fable of the* BELLY.

fabliau a metrical tale, typically a bawdily humorous one, of a type found chiefly in early French poetry.

Jean Henri Fabre (1823–1915), French entomologist, who became well known for his meticulous observations of insect behaviour, notably the life cycles of dung beetles, oil beetles, and solitary bees and wasps; he wrote popular works such as *The Sacred Beetle and Others* (translated 1918).

Gaius Fabricius Luscinus Roman soldier and statesman of the 3rd century BC, who was admired in later times as a type of the antique Roman virtues of austerity and incorruptibility, refusing to profit personally from his public role. He was said to have refused bribes from ➤ PYRRHUS, and at his death to have left his daughters unprovided with dowries (they were afterwards given by the Senate).

> The days of true heroism are over, when a citizen fought for his country like a Fabricius or a Washington, and then returned to his farm to let his virtuous fervour run in a more placid, but not a less salutary, stream.
> — Mary Wollstonecraft *The Rights of Women* (1792)

the face that launched a thousand ships the face of ➤ HELEN, seeing her as the cause of the Trojan War; originally as a quotation from Marlowe's *Doctor Faustus* (1604), 'Was this the face that launched a thousand ships, And burnt the topless towers of Ilium?'

fact is stranger than fiction proverbial saying, mid 19th century.

faction in ancient Rome, a company or organization of contractors for the chariot races in the circus.

Factory Acts (in the UK) a series of laws regulating the operation of factories, designed to improve the working conditions of employees, especially women and children. The most important was that of 1833, which set a minimum age of 9 years and a maximum of eight hours a day for child employees and which also instituted inspectors to ensure compliance with these regulations.

the factory king nickname of Richard Oastler (1789–1861), who worked to improve conditions in Yorkshire factories.

factotum an employee who does all kinds of work; the term dates from the mid 16th century, where it is found in Robert Greene's use *Johannes factotum* 'John do-it-all' or 'Jack of all trades'.

facts are stubborn things proverbial saying, early 18th century.

faerie a poetic or literary word for fairyland, a pseudo-archaism introduced by Edmund Spenser (*c.*1552–99) in his allegorical poem *The Faerie Queene*, celebrating Queen Elizabeth.

Fafnir in Scandinavian and Germanic mythology, in the story of the Volsungs and Nibelungs, the dragon who guards a hoard of gold and is killed by ➤ Sigurd (Siegfried).

faggot a bundle of sticks or twigs bound together as fuel, in the 16th century used particularly with reference to the burning of heretics; it was said that those who had recanted were required to wear the emblem of a faggot on their sleeve, as a sign of the punishment to which they had been liable.

Fagin in Dickens's *Oliver Twist* (1838), the master of the gang of pickpockets led by the ➤ Artful *Dodger*; his name is used allusively for a criminal who systematically recruits and organizes child thieves.

> Police believe that the 'Fagin' at the centre of this operation runs a school for thieves in Santiago, Chile.
> — *Globe & Mail* (Toronto) 23 November 1991

Fahrenheit of or denoting a scale of temperature on which water freezes at 32° and boils at 212° under standard conditions, named (in the mid 18th century) after Gabriel Daniel *Fahrenheit* (1686–1736), German physicist.

faience glazed ceramic ware, in particular decorated tin-glazed earthenware of the type which includes delftware and maiolica. Recorded from the late 17th century, the term originally denoted pottery made at *Faenza*, a town in northern Italy.

failure see ➤ success *has many fathers while failure is an orphan.*

faint heart never won fair lady proverbial saying, mid 16th century.

fair see also ➤ cherry *fair*, ➤ Donnybrook *Fair*, ➤ *if Saint* Paul*'s day be fair and clear, it will betide a happy year*, ➤ turn *about is fair play*, ➤ Vanity *Fair*, ➤ Widecombe *Fair*.

the Fair epithet applied to ➤ Philip *the Fair*, king of France (*le Bel*), and other rulers.

fair and softly goes far in a day proverbial saying, mid 14th century.

a fair field and no favour proverbial saying, late 17th century.

all's fair in love and war proverbial saying; early 17th century.

Fair Isle multicoloured geometric designs used in woollen knitwear, as traditionally made on *Fair Isle*, one of the Shetland Islands, lying about halfway between Orkney and Shetland.

fair maid of February a name for the snowdrop.

fair maid of France a kind of crowfoot.

the Fair Maid of Kent sobriquet of Joan (1328–85), daughter of Edmund Earl of Kent, and wife of her cousin Edward, the ➤ Black *Prince*; although the phrase is not found in contemporary sources, she is called '*cette jeune damoiselle de Kent*' in Froissart's *Chronicle*.

fair play's a jewel proverbial saying, early 19th century.

Fair Rosamond name given to Rosamond de Clifford (d. 1176?), said to have been a mistress of Henry II; according to later chroniclers, the king concealed her in a maze at Woodstock to protect her from Queen Eleanor's jealousy. In an elaboration of the legend, Eleanor finds her rival by using a silken thread to guide herself through the maze, and then offers Rosamond the choice of a dagger or a bowl of poison.

Fairbanks the name of two American actors. Douglas (Elton) (1883–1939) co-founded United Artists in 1919 and became famous for his swashbuckling film roles. His son Douglas (1909–, known as **Douglas Fairbanks Jr**) played similar roles.

> I'd neither the intention nor the expectation of doing a Douglas Fairbanks on the outer battlements of the Dubh Sgeir castle.
> — Alistair Maclean *When Eight Bells Toll* (1966)

Thomas Fairfax (1612–71), English Parliamentary general. He was appointed commander of the New Model Army in 1645 and won the Battle of Naseby. In 1650 he was replaced by Oliver Cromwell for refusing to march against the Scots, who had proclaimed the future Charles II king. Fairfax later helped to secure the restoration of Charles II.

fairy a small imaginary being of human form that has magical powers, especially a female one. The word is recorded from Middle English (denoting fairyland, or fairies collectively), and comes via Old French from Latin *fata* 'the Fates'.

Fairies were traditionally seen as impinging on the mortal world with dangerous effect, but the perception of them as powerful beings inhabiting a parallel world to that of humankind gradually dwindled, and by the 17th century they were largely figures of a literary tradition.

In the 20th century, the question of whether fairies might exist was raised by Arthur Conan Doyle, who published *The Coming of the Fairies* (1921), based on the experiences of two Yorkshire schoolgirls from Cottingley who had apparently been visited by, and taken photographs of, fairies. Conan Doyle, a keen believer in the supernatural, was convinced, although (as was revealed in 1983 by the original authors) the photographs had in fact been faked by the two girls.

fairy dart a flint arrowhead, supposedly as used by the fairies.

fairy godmother a female character in some fairy stories who has magical powers and brings unexpected good fortune to the hero or heroine; the term is recorded from the mid 19th century.

fairy money money or gold given by fairies to mortals is said to turn to dried leaves and crumble rapidly away; John Locke uses the image in his *Essay concerning Human Understanding* (1690), 'Such borrowed wealth, like fairy-money…will be but leaves and dust when it comes to use.'

fairy of the mine a goblin supposed to inhabit mines; the term is used by Milton in *Comus* (1634), 'No goblin or swart faery of the mine, Hath hurtful power o'er true virginity.'

fairy ring a circular area of grass that is darker in colour than the surrounding grass due to the growth of certain fungi. They were popularly believed to have been caused by fairies dancing.

fairy tale denoting something regarded as resembling a fairy story in being magical, idealized, or extremely happy.

faith see also ➤ ATTIC *faith*, ➤ CARTHAGINIAN *faith*, ➤ DEFENDER *of the Faith*, ➤ PUNIC *faith*.

St Faith (3rd century?), virgin and martyr; her shrine at Conques was a popular centre, and she was invoked by Crusaders and pilgrims.
   ◻ EMBLEM She is shown with a sword or a bundle of rods.
   ◻ FEAST DAY Her feast day is 6 October.

faith will move mountains proverbial saying, late 19th century; originally with biblical allusion to Matthew 17:28, 'If ye have faith as a grain of mustard-seed, ye shall say unto this mountain; Remove to yonder place; and it shall remove.'

faithful see also ➤ COMMANDER *of the Faithful*, ➤ FATHER *of the Faithful*, ➤ OLD *Faithful*.

Most Faithful King epithet of the king of Portugal.

fakir a Muslim (or, loosely, a Hindu) religious ascetic who lives solely on alms. The word is recorded from the early 17th century, and comes via French from Arabic *faḳīr* 'needy man'.

Fala name of a Scotch terrier belonging to Franklin Roosevelt, which in 1944 was in the news when it was reported that the dog had been left on an Aleutian island and that a destroyer had been sent back for it. Roosevelt (in his dog's name) firmly countered stories of the waste of taxpayers' money, saying publicly that while he did not resent attacks on his family, Fala did, and as a Scottie was particularly annoyed by the Republicans' suggestion that his master would have sanctioned this outlay: 'His Scotch soul was furious. He has not been the same dog since.'

Falabella a horse of a miniature breed, the adult of which does not usually exceed 75 cm in height; it is named after Julio *Falabella* (d. 1981), an Argentinian breeder.

Falange the Spanish Fascist movement that merged with traditional right-wing elements in 1937 to form the ruling party, the Falange Española Tradicionalista, under General Franco. It was formally abolished in 1977. The name is Spanish, and comes from Latin *phalang-*, *phalanx* 'body of infantry, phalanx'.

Falasha a member of a group of people in Ethiopia who hold the Jewish faith but use Ge'ez rather than Hebrew as a liturgical language. The Falashas were not formally recognized as Jews until 1975, and many of them were airlifted to Israel in 1984–5 and after. Also called ➤ BLACK *Jew*.

The name is Amharic, and means literally 'exile, immigrant'.

falchion a broad, slightly curved sword with the cutting edge on the convex side. The word is recorded from Middle English (in form *fauchon*) and comes via Old French from Latin *falx*, *falc-* 'sickle'.

The -l- was added in the 16th century to conform with the Latin spelling.

Falcidian law in ancient Rome, a law (instituted by P. Falcidius) which ordained that a Roman citizen must leave at least a quarter of his estate to his legal heirs.

falcon a bird of prey with long pointed wings and a notched beak, characteristically catching prey by diving on it. In the traditional sport of falconry, the 15th-century *Boke of St Albans* lists the birds appropriate to different ranks.

In Egyptian mythology, the god ➤ Horus is represented as having the head of a falcon.

The name is recorded from Middle English (in form *faucon*, originally denoting any diurnal bird of prey used in falconry), and comes via Old French, from late Latin *falco*, from Laxin *falx, falc-* 'scythe' (or of Germanic origin, related to Dutch and German). The -l- was added in the 15th century to conform with the Latin spelling.

See also ➤ peregrine *falcon*.

Falconry: hierarchy of birds

Bird	Rank
eagle	emperor
gyrfalcon	king
peregrine	prince
saker	knight
merlin	lady
goshawk	yeoman
sparrowhawk	priest
musket	holy water clerk
kestrel	knave

faldstool a folding chair used by a bishop when not occupying the throne or when officiating in a church other than his own; a small movable folding desk or stool for kneeling at prayer.

Falernian in ancient Rome, a celebrated wine from the *ager Falernus* in Campania.

Falkirk a town in central Scotland, where Edward I defeated the Scots under ➤ *William* Wallace in 1298.

Falkland Islands a group of islands in the South Atlantic, forming a British Crown Colony, originally occupied and colonized by Britain in 1832–3, following the expulsion of an Argentinian garrison. Argentina refused to recognize British sovereignty and

continues to refer to the islands by their old Spanish name, the Malvinas.

Falklands War an armed conflict between Britain and Argentina in 1982, which came about when on the orders of General Galtieri's military junta, Argentinian forces invaded the Falkland Islands in the South Atlantic in support of their claim to sovereignty. In response Britain sent a task force of ships and aircraft, which forced the Argentinians to surrender six weeks after its arrival.

fall see also ➤ *the* bigger *they are, the harder they fall*, ➤ pride *goes before a fall*.

the Fall[1] the lapse of humankind into a state of sin, ascribed in traditional Jewish and Christian theology to the disobedience of Adam and Eve as described in Genesis; also called **the Fall of Man**.

the Fall[2] in North America, autumn; the expression derives from the earlier **fall of the leaf**, first recorded in Roger Ascham's *Toxophilus* (1545), 'Spring time, summer, fall of the leaf, and winter'.

fall by the wayside fail to persist in an endeavour or undertaking; with biblical allusion to the ➤ *parable of the* sower, in which some of the seed 'fell by the way side' and was eaten by birds.

the Fall Line in the US, the zone demarcating the Piedmont from the Atlantic coastal plain.

fall of the leaf autumn; see ➤ *the* Fall[2].

fall on stony ground of words or a suggestion be ignored or badly received; with biblical allusion to the ➤ *parable of the* sower, in which some seed 'fell upon stony places' and withered away.

fallacy see also ➤ pathetic *fallacy*.

fallacy of composition the error of assuming that what is true of a member of a group is true for the group as a whole.

fallen angel in Christian, Jewish, and Muslim tradition, an angel who rebelled against God and was cast out of heaven.

falling sickness an archaic term for epilepsy; in Shakespeare's *Julius Caesar*, the expression is used of Caesar.

falling star a meteor or shooting star.

false dawn a promising sign which comes to nothing; literally, a transient light which precedes the true dawn by about an hour, especially in eastern countries.

false friend a word or expression that has a similar form to one in a person's native language, but a different meaning (for example English *magazine* and French *magasin* 'shop').

false memory an apparent recollection of an event which did not actually occur, especially one of childhood sexual abuse arising from suggestion during psychoanalysis; in the 1990s the question of whether buried memory of this kind could be recovered through psychoanalysis was strongly debated, with proponents of the theory using the term *recovered memory* to demonstrate the belief that such recollections could be rooted in fact.

Sir John Falstaff the fat, jolly, and debauched knight who is a main character in Shakespeare's *Henry IV* (parts 1 and 2) and the *Merry Wives of Windsor*. Greedy and cowardly, despite his joviality, Falstaff is shown as the boon companion of Prince Hal, but is rejected when the prince becomes king.

It has been suggested that Falstaff was modelled on the historical Sir John Oldcastle (d. 1417), a Lollard, originally a friend of Henry V, whose religious and political beliefs sundered him from the king, and finally resulted in his execution.

> His travelling companion—a blustery, almost Falstaffian junk-food addict.
> — *New York Times Book Review* 31 May 1998

fame see ➤ COMMON *fame*, ➤ HALL *of Fame*.

familiar a demon (also called a **familiar spirit**) supposedly attending and obeying a witch, often said to assume the form of an animal.

familiarity breeds contempt proverbial saying, late 14th century; 5th century AD in Latin.

Familist a member of the Christian sect the ➤ FAMILY *of Love*.

family see also ➤ *the family that* PRAYS *together stays together*.

family bible a bible designed to be used at family prayers, typically one with space on its flyleaves for recording important family events.

Family Compact[1] the name given to each of three agreements between the French and Spanish branches of the House of Bourbon in the 18th century.

Family Compact[2] the oligarchy which ruled Upper Canada in the early 19th century.

Family of Love a Christian sect of the 16th and 17th centuries which asserted the importance of love and the necessity for absolute obedience to any government.

family tree a diagram showing the relationship between people in several generations of a family.

famine see also ➤ COTTON *famine*, ➤ POTATO *Famine*.

the Famine Queen derogatory nickname for Queen Victoria, coined by Maud Gonne (1867–1953) in relation to the ➤ POTATO *Famine*.

the Famous Five four children, Julian, Dick, Anne, and their cousin 'George' (Georgina), with their dog Timmy, in a series of adventure stories (1942–63) by ➤ *Enid* BLYTON.

famous for fifteen minutes enjoying a brief period of fame before fading back into obscurity; coined by the American artist Andy Warhol, who predicted in 1968 that 'In the future everybody will be world famous for fifteen minutes.'

famous last words said as an ironic comment on or reply to an overconfident assertion that may well be proved wrong by events; recorded from the late 1940s.

famulus an assistant or servant, especially one working for a magician or scholar. Recorded from the mid 19th century, the word is Latin, meaning 'servant'.

fan a person who has a strong interest in or admiration for a particular sport, art form, or famous person; from an abbreviation of ➤ FANATIC.

fanatic a person filled with excessive and rigidly single-minded zeal or enthusiasm, especially for an extreme religious or political cause. The word is recorded (as an adjective) from the mid 16th century, from French *fanatique* or Latin *fanaticus* 'of a temple, inspired by a god', from *fanum* 'temple'. The adjective originally described behaviour or speech that might result from possession by a god or demon, hence the earliest sense of the noun 'a religious maniac' (mid 17th century).

fancy originally (in late Middle English) capricious or arbitrary preference, individual taste; later (in the late 16th century) imagination; the aptitude for the invention of illustrative or decorative imagery. The word is a contraction of *fantasy*.

From the mid 18th century, **the Fancy**, was used

for enthusiasts for a particular sport, especially boxing or racing.

See also ➤ FOOTLOOSE *and fancy-free*.

Fannie Mae in the US, the Federal National Mortgage Association, a corporation (now privately owned) which trades in mortgages.

Lord Fanny a contemptuous nickname for Lord Hervey (1696–1743), given him by Pope in his 'Imitation of the First Satire of the Second Book of Horace' (1733).

sweet **Fanny** Adams a nautical term for tinned meat or stew; apparently from the name of a murder victim, Fanny Adams, *c.*1870, whose body was said to have been mutilated.

trip the light **fantastic** humorous term meaning, to dance; originally, with allusion to Milton:

Come, and trip it as ye go
On the light fantastic toe.
— John Milton 'L'Allegro' (1645)

fantasy the faculty or activity of imagining things, especially things which are impossible or improbable. Recorded from late Middle English, the word comes via Old French and Latin from Greek *phantasia* 'imagination, appearance', later 'phantom', from *phantazein* 'make visible'. From the 16th to the 19th centuries the spelling *phantasy* was also used.

From the late 1940s, *fantasy* has been used specifically to denote a genre of imaginative fiction involving magic and adventure, especially in a setting other than the real world.

fantasy football a competition in which participants select imaginary teams from among the players in a league and score points according to the actual performance of their players.

FAQ a text file containing a list of questions and answers relating to a particular subject, especially one giving basic information for users of an Internet newsgroup. The expression comes from the acronym for *frequently asked questions*.

Far East China, Japan, and other countries of East Asia; the phrase came into use in the mid 19th century, though in a letter of January 1616, the English diplomat Thomas Roe had noted of lodestones that 'they are in the far east countries'.

far-fetched and dear-bought is good for ladies proverbial saying, mid 14th century.

Michael **Faraday** (1791–1867), English physicist and chemist, who contributed significantly to the field of electromagnetism, discovering electromagnetic induction and demonstrating electromagnetic rotation (the key to the electric dynamo and motor). Faraday also discovered the laws of electrolysis and set the foundations for the classical field theory of electromagnetic behaviour.

It is said that when Gladstone asked him about the usefulness of electricity, he responded, 'Why sir, there is every possibility that you will soon be able to tax it!'

Faraday cage an earthed metal screen surrounding a piece of equipment in order to exclude electrostatic influences.

fare the money a passenger on public transport has to pay; this stems from an earlier meaning, 'a journey for which a price is paid'.

Cape **Farewell** the northernmost point of South Island, New Zealand, which was named by Captain James Cook as the last land sighted before he left for Australia in March 1770.

Farmer George nickname of George III (1738–1820), king of England; interested in agriculture, he was lampooned in satires and caricatures as having farmed for profit.

Farnese the Italian family ruling the duchy of Parma and Piacenza from 1545 to 1731.

Alessandro **Farnese** (1545–92), Duke of Parma, Italian general and statesman. While in the service of Philip II of Spain he acted as Governor General of the Netherlands (1578–92). He captured Antwerp in 1585, securing the southern Netherlands for Spain.

the **Farnese** Bull a marble group executed by Apollonius of Tralles (2nd century BC) and his brother Tauriscus. The work shows Zethus and Amphion, the sons of Antiope, tying ➤ DIRCE to the horns of a wild bull for her cruel treatment of their mother.

the **Farnese** Hercules a copy (by Glycon of Athens) of the statue of Hercules by the Greek sculptor ➤ LYSIPPUS, excavated in 1540 from the Baths of Caracalla in Rome and initially in the possession of the *Farnese* family; Samuel Taylor Coleridge refers to 'the idealized figures of the Apollo Belvidere, and the Farnese Hercules' in *Biographia Litteraria* (1817).

faro a gambling card game in which players bet on the order in which the cards will appear. The name comes (in the early 18th century) from French *pharaon* 'Pharaoh', said to have been the name of the king of hearts.

farrago a confused mixture; the word comes originally from Latin 'mixed fodder', from *far* 'corn'.

farriers ➤ *St* ELOI is the patron saint of farriers.

farthing a former monetary unit and coin of the UK, withdrawn in 1961, equal to a quarter of an old penny. Recorded from Old English (in form *fēorþing*), the word comes from *fēorþa* 'fourth', perhaps on the pattern of Old Norse *fjórðungr* 'quarter'.

See also ➤ CHAD-*farthing*.

farthingale a hooped petticoat or circular pad of fabric around the hips, formerly worn under women's skirts to extend and shape them. The word comes through French from Spanish *verduga* 'rod, stick', which reference to the cane originally used for the hoop holding out the petticoat.

fasces in ancient Rome, a bundle of rods with a projecting axe blade, carried by a lictor as a symbol of a magistrate's power; the word is Latin, plural of *fascis* 'rod'.

fascism an authoritarian and nationalistic right-wing system of government and social organization.

The term Fascism was first used of the totalitarian right-wing nationalist regime of Mussolini in Italy (1922–43), and the regimes of the Nazis in Germany and Franco in Spain were also Fascist. Fascism tends to include a belief in the supremacy of one national or ethnic group, a contempt for democracy, an insistence on obedience to a powerful leader, and a strong demagogic approach.

The name comes from Italian *fascismo*, from *fascio* 'bundle, political group', from Latin *fascis* 'rod'.

fash oneself Scottish term for, feel upset or worried; from early modern French *fascher*, based on Latin *fastus* 'disdain, scornful contempt'.

fashion see ➤ BETTER *be out of the world than out of fashion*.

fast abstain from all kinds of food or drink, especially as a religious observance.

Fasti in ancient Rome, a calendar or calendars showing the permitted days for legal and public business, festivals, games, and anniversaries.

fasting see ➤ *it's ill speaking between a* FULL *man and a fasting*.

fat see also ➤ LAUGH *and be fat*, ➤ *the* OPERA *isn't over till the fat lady sings*.

the Fat a nickname of Charles III of France (839–88) and other rulers.

fat cat a wealthy and powerful person, especially a businessman or politician; the term is recorded from the late 1920s in the US, but has become frequent in the UK since the early 1990s, in relation particularly to what are perceived as inflated salaries paid to senior executives of formerly nationalized industries.

the fat is in the fire in early use (mid 17th century) indicating the complete failure of a plan; now, indicating that something has happened that will cause an explosion of anger or recrimination.

the fat of the land the best of everything as one's resource for living; originally with reference to Genesis 45:18, 'Ye shall eat the fat of the land.'

Fata Morgana a mirage; originally (in Italian) 'fairy Morgan', referring to a mirage seen in the Strait of Messina between Italy and Sicily and attributed to ➤ MORGAN *le Fay*, whose legend and reputation were carried to Sicily by Norman settlers.

Al Fatah a Palestinian political and military organization founded in 1958 by Yasser Arafat and others to bring about the establishment of a Palestinian state. It has dominated the Palestine Liberation Organization since the 1960s, despite challenges from more extreme groups.

fatal causing death; originally (in Middle English) with the meanings 'destined by fate' and 'ominous'.

the fatal necklace another name for ➤ *the necklace of* HARMONIA.

the Fatal Sisters another name for ➤ *the* FATES, Clotho, Lachesis, and Atropos.

the fatal thread the thread of life, as spun and cut by ➤ *the* FATES.

the Fatal Vespers a service at Blackfriars in London, on 26 October 1623, when the greater part of a Roman Catholic congregation were killed by the falling-in of the floor. Also called *the Doleful Evensong*.

a fate worse than death rape; the term is recorded from the early 19th century, although earlier in the mid 17th century Dorothy Osborne in a letter refers to 'the Roman courage, when they killed themselves to avoid misfortunes that were infinitely worse than death.'

the Fates in Greek and Roman mythology, the three goddesses who preside over the birth, life, and death of humans. Each person was thought of as a spindle, around which the three Fates (Clotho, Lachesis, and Atropos) would spin the thread (eventually to be measured off and cut) of human destiny.

father see also ➤ *the* CHILD *is the father of the man*, ➤ *Father* BROWN, ➤ *Father* TIME, ➤ FATHERS, ➤ FOUNDING *Father*, ➤ HOLY *Father*, ➤ SERAPHIC *Father*, ➤ *the* WISH *is father to the thought*.

father a man in relation to his natural children; recorded in Old English (in form *fæder*) and of Germanic origin, the word comes from an Indo-European root shared by Latin *pater* and Greek *patēr*.

In Christian belief, **the Father** is used for the first person of the Trinity, God.

➤ *St* JOSEPH is the patron saint of fathers.

Father Christmas an imaginary figure said to bring presents for children on the night before Christmas Day. He is conventionally pictured as a jolly old man from the far north, with a long white beard and red garments trimmed with white fur.

The origins of Father Christmas are obscure. His conventionalized image is comparatively recent; in late medieval Europe he became identified with St Nicholas (Santa Claus); in England Father Christmas was a personification of Christmas, a genial red-robed old man who appeared in many 16th-century masques and in mummers' plays. There was a great revival of the celebration of Christmas in the 19th century and Father Christmas acquired (from St Nicholas) the association of present-bringing.

like father, like son proverbial saying, mid 14th century; earlier in Latin.

Father of English Poetry a name for ➤ *Geoffrey* CHAUCER, given him by John Dryden.

the Father of History a name for ➤ HERODOTUS.

the Father of Lies the Devil, Satan; originally with biblical allusion to John 8:44, 'for he is a liar, and the father of it'.

the Father of Reform a name for the political reformer John Cartwright (1740–1824), who advocated annual parliaments and universal suffrage, and founded the Society for Constitutional Information.

father of the chapel in the UK, the shop steward of a printers' trade union; a *chapel* in this sense was originally a printers' workshop or printing office, and then a meeting or association of the journeymen in a printing office for arranging affairs and settling disagreements among themselves.

the Father of the Constitution a name for the American Democratic Republican statesman James Madison (1751–1836), fourth president of the United States, who played a leading part in drawing up the US Constitution (1787).

Father of the Faithful a name for the patriarch Abraham, after Romans 4:11, 'that he might be the father of all them that believe'. In Muslim usage, *Father of the Faithful* is a title for the Caliph.

Father of the House of Commons the member with the longest continuous service.

the Father of Waters informal name for the the ➤ MISSISSIPPI.

Father's Day a day of the year on which fathers are particularly honoured by their children, especially with gifts and greetings cards. It was first observed in the state of Washington in 1910; in the US and Britain, it is usually the third Sunday in June, in Australia, the first Sunday in September.

the Fatherland Germany, especially during the period of Hitler's control.

fathers see also ➤ APOSTOLIC *Fathers*, ➤ CONSCRIPT *fathers*, ➤ *the* DESERT *Fathers*, ➤ LAND *of my Fathers*, ➤ LIMBO *of the fathers*, ➤ PILGRIM *Fathers*.

the Fathers of the Church early Christian theologians (in particular of the first five centuries) whose writings are regarded as especially authoritative.

Fatiha the short first sura of the Koran, used by Muslims as an essential element of ritual prayer. The word comes from Arabic *al-Fātiḥah* 'the opening (sura)'.

Fatima[1] (*c*.606–32 AD), youngest daughter of the prophet Muhammad and wife of the fourth caliph, Ali. The descendants of Muhammad trace their lineage through her; she is revered especially by Shiite Muslims as the mother of the imams Hasan and Husayn.

Fatima[2] name of the last and surviving wife of
➤ BLUEBEARD.

Fátima[3] a village in Portugal, where in 1917 it was
reported that apparitions of the Virgin Mary appeared; it is now the site of a Marian shrine.

Fatimid a member of a dynasty which ruled in
parts of northern Africa, Egypt, and Syria from 909
to 1171, and founded Cairo as its capital in 969; the
dynasty is said to descend from *Fatima* (see
➤ FATIMA[1]), youngest daughter of the prophet Muhammad.

kill the fatted calf produce one's best food to
celebrate, especially at a prodigal's return, with biblical allusion to the story of the **prodigal son** (see
➤ PRODIGAL), in which the father, welcoming the
return of his son with a feast, tells his servants,
'bring hither the fatted calf, and kill it' (Luke 15:23).

fatwa a ruling on a point of Islamic law given by a
recognized authority. In 1989 a fatwa calling for the
death of the British novelist Salman Rushdie was issued by Ayatollah Khomeini following the publication of Rushdie's novel *The Satanic Verses*.

faubourg a suburb, especially one in Paris. The
term, which is French, was earlier *faux-bourg* 'false
borough'), perhaps an alteration of *forsborc*, literally
'outside the town', but perhaps based on Middle
High German *phâlburgere* 'burghers of the pale', i.e.
people living outside the city wall but still inside the
palisade.

Faugh-a-Balaghs a name for the Royal Irish Fusiliers; from Irish *fág an bealach* 'clear the way', the
regimental war-cry, as used at the battle of Barrosa
in 1811.

fault in geology, an extended break in a rock formation, marked by the relative displacement and
discontinuity of strata on either side of a particular
plane.
See also ➤ SAN *Andreas fault*.

a fault confessed is half redressed proverbial
saying, mid 16th century.

faun in Roman mythology, one of a class of lustful
rural gods, represented as a man with a goat's horns,
ears, legs, and tail. The word is recorded from late
Middle English, and comes from the name of the
pastoral god ➤ FAUNUS.

fauna the animals of a particular region, habitat,
or geological period. The term is recorded from the
late 18th century, and is a modern Latin application

of *Fauna*, the name of a rural goddess, sister of
➤ FAUNUS.

Fauntleroy see ➤ LITTLE *Lord Fauntleroy*.

Faunus in Roman mythology, an ancient Italian
pastoral god, grandson of Saturn, associated with
wooded places.

Faust (d. *c.*1540), German astronomer and necro-
mancer. Reputed to have sold his soul to the Devil,
he became the subject of dramas by Marlowe and
Goethe, an opera by Gounod, and a novel by
Thomas Mann.

> Has Southern California made a Faustian bargain with a
> devil wearing Ray Bans?
> — *Coloradoan* (Fort Collins) 23 January 1994

fauvism a style of painting with vivid expressionistic and non-naturalistic use of colour that flourished in Paris from 1905 and, although short-lived,
had an important influence on subsequent artists,
especially the German expressionists. Matisse was
regarded as the movement's leading figure.
The name comes from French *fauvisme*, from
fauve 'wild beast'. The name originated from a remark of the French art critic Louis Vauxcelles at the
Salon of 1905; coming across a quattrocento-style
statue in the midst of works by Matisse and his associates, he is reputed to have said, '*Donatello au milieu des fauves!*' ('Donatello among the wild beasts').

Favonius in Roman mythology, the west wind,
also known as Zephyrus, and associated with
springtime.

favour see also ➤ CURRY *favour*, ➤ GRACE *and favour*, ➤ KISSING *goes by favour*.

favour a thing such as a badge or knot of ribbons
that is given or worn as a mark of liking or support.

most favoured nation the nation to which a State
has granted by treaty and other agreements the
greatest political or commercial privileges, especially that to which the State accords the lowest scale
of import duties.

favourite son in the US, a person who has en-
deared himself particularly to his country or State,
especially, a candidate for presidential or other high
office who has the support of the constituency or
the political leaders of his own State.

Guy Fawkes (1570–1606), English conspirator,
who was hanged for his part in the ➤ GUNPOWDER
Plot of 5 November 1605. The occasion is commemorated annually on Bonfire Night with fireworks,

bonfires, and the burning of a *guy*, named after Guy Fawkes.

fay a poetic and literary word for a fairy; recorded from late Middle English, and coming via Old French from Latin *fata* 'the Fates'.

See also ➤ MORGAN *le Fay*.

Fayum the name of a province in upper Egypt used to designate articles discovered there, in particular funerary portraits of the early Christian period.

fear the Greeks bearing gifts proverbial saying, late 19th century; originally from Virgil, as ➤ LAOCOON's words of warning on the ➤ TROJAN *Horse*, 'I fear the Greeks even when they bring gifts.'

feast see also ➤ BELSHAZZAR's *feast*, ➤ *the* COMPANY *makes the feast*, ➤ ENOUGH *is as good as a feast*, ➤ MOVABLE *feast*, ➤ SKELETON *at the feast*.

feast day a day on which a celebration, especially an annual Christian one, is held; a day dedicated to a particular saint.

feast of reason intellectual discussion, as complementary to genial conversation; the phrase comes originally from Pope's *Satires of Horace* (1733), 'the feast of reason and the flow of soul'.

feather see also ➤ BIRDS *of a feather flock together*, ➤ CAP *and feather days*, ➤ FINE *feathers make fine birds*, ➤ PEACOCK's *feather*, ➤ PRINCE *of Wales' feathers*, ➤ TAR *and feather*.

show the white feather behave in a cowardly fashion (a white feather in the tail of a game bird is a mark of bad breeding). During the First World War, *white feathers* were sometimes sent or given to men as a sign that they should be on active service; it is recorded that the politician John Davidson (1889–1970), who had been asked to stay at the Colonial Office instead of joining up as he wished to do, was on one occasion sent a white feather.

a feather in one's cap an achievement to be proud of; literally, a decoration or mark of honour.

featherweight a weight in boxing and other sports intermediate between bantamweight and lightweight. In the amateur boxing scale it ranges from 54 to 57 kg.

Febronian of or pertaining to 'Justinus Febronius' (J. N. von Hontheim of Trier, Germany) or his doctrine (published in 1763) that national Roman Catholic Churches should be as far as possible independent of Rome.

February the second month of the year in the northern hemisphere, usually considered the last month of winter. The name is recorded from Middle English (in form *feverer*), and comes via Old French from Latin *februarius*, from *februa*, the name of a purification feast held in this month. The spelling change in the 15th century was due to association with the Latin word.

See also ➤ FAIR *maid of February*.

February fill dyke be it black or be it white proverbial saying, mid 16th century; meaning that February is a month likely to bring heavy rain (black) or snow (white).

February Revolution the first phase of the ➤ RUSSIAN *Revolution*.

if in February there be no rain, 'tis neither good for hay nor grain proverbial saying, early 18th century; meaning that a drought in February will be damaging to crops later in the year.

fecit Latin for 'made it', a word appearing in an inscription of a silversmith or other craftsman, as for example '*Omar Ramsden me fecit* [Omar Ramsden made me].'

fedayeen Arab guerrillas operating especially against Israel. Recorded from the 1950s, the word comes from the plural of Arabic *fidā'ī* 'one who gives his life for another or for a cause', from *fadā* 'to ransom someone' The singular *fedai* (from Arabic and Persian *fidā'ī*) had previously been used (late 19th century) to denote an Ismaili Muslim assassin.

Federal designating the Northern States in the American Civil War.

Federal Bureau of Investigation an agency of the US federal government that deals principally with internal security and counter-intelligence and that also conducts investigations in federal law enforcement. It was established in 1908 as a branch of the Department of Justice, but was substantially reorganized under the controversial directorship (1924–72) of ➤ *J. Edgar* HOOVER.

Federal Theology the system based on the doctrine of covenants made by God with Adam as representing mankind, and with Christ as representing the Church.

Federalist Party an early political party in the US, joined by George Washington during his presidency

(1789–97) and in power until 1801. The party's emphasis on strong central government was extremely important in the early years after independence, but by the 1820s it had been superseded by the Democratic Republican Party.

fee formerly, a legal term for an estate of land, especially one held on condition of feudal service.

fee-faw-fum the first line of doggerel spoken by the giant in the fairy tale 'Jack the Giant Killer' (➤ JACK *and the Beanstalk*) on seeing Jack; in Shakespeare's *King Lear* (1605–6), Edgar, playing at being mad, says, 'His word was still, "Fie, foh, and fum, I smell the blood of a British man." '

feeble see ➤ FORCIBLE-*feeble*.

feed a cold and starve a fever proverbial saying, mid 19th century (probably intended as two separate admonitions, but sometimes interpreted to mean that if you feed a cold you will have to starve a fever later).

feeding frenzy an aggressive and competitive group attack on prey by a number of sharks or piranhas; in figurative use, an episode of frantic competition or rivalry for something, often referring to media excitement over a news story.

the Feeding of the Five Thousand in the Bible (Mark ch. 6), the miracle by which Jesus fed the five thousand who had gathered to hear him on the only food which they had, five loaves and two fishes; when everyone had eaten, the fragments filled twelve baskets.

feel-good causing a feeling of happiness and well-being, especially in material contexts; in the 1990s, the presence or absence of a **feel-good factor** was frequently referred to in discussions of economic recovery as affecting a government's popularity, and therefore its political fortunes.

Feel-good in its current sense is recorded from the early 1970s, but prior to that Dr Feelgood had been a name adopted in 1962 by the blues pianist 'Piano Red' (William Perryman), who broadcast and recorded under this sobriquet. Later the term was used (with negative connotations) as a term for a physician providing short-term palliatives rather than a more effective treatment or cure.

feet of clay a fundamental flaw or weakness in a person otherwise revered, with biblical allusion to a dream of ➤ NEBUCHADNEZZAR, in which a magnificent idol has feet 'part of iron and part of clay'; Daniel interprets this to signify a future kingdom that

will be 'partly strong, and partly broken', and will eventually fall.

Robert 'Beau' Feilding (1651?–1712), who in 1705 contracted a bigamous marriage with the Duchess of Cleveland, and who died at Scotland Yard 12 May 1712. Steele described him as 'Orlando' in the *Tatler* (1709, nos. 50 and 51).

feis in ancient Ireland, an assembly of kings and chiefs, formerly believed to be a kind of early Celtic parliament.

felix culpa the sin of Adam viewed as fortunate, because it brought about the blessedness of the Redemption; the phrase is Latin, and means 'happy fault'.

Dr John Fell (1625–86), dean of Christ Church, Oxford, and bishop of Oxford, remembered also as promoter of the Oxford University Press, and as the subject of an undergraduate verse by Thomas Brown (1663–1704):

> I do not love thee, Dr Fell.
> The reason why I cannot tell;
> But this I know, and know full well,
> I do not love thee, Dr Fell.

at one fell swoop at a single blow, in one go. *Swoop* here denotes the sudden pouncing of a bird of prey from a height on its quarry, especially with allusion to Shakespeare *Macbeth*, when Macduff hears of the murder of his wife and children 'What, all my pretty chickens and their dam, at one fell swoop?'

fellow a member of a learned society; in the UK, an incorporated senior member of a college.

felo de se suicide. From Anglo-Latin, literally 'felon of himself'; suicide was formerly a criminal act in the UK.

the female of the species is more deadly than the male proverbial saying, early 20th century; originally from a poem (1919) by Kipling.

feminazi a contemptuous term, a blend of *feminist* and *Nazi*, for a radical feminist; the word is recorded from the US in the early 1990s, and was initially used particularly in the abortion debate by opponents of the pro-choice movement.

feminie womankind; in early use (late Middle English, as in Chaucer), the Amazons and their country.

feminine rhyme a rhyme between stressed syllables followed by one or more unstressed syllables (e.g. *stocking/shocking, glamorous/amorous*).

feminism the advocacy of women's rights on the ground of the equality of the sexes. The issue of rights for women first became prominent during the French and American revolutions in the late 18th century; Mary Wollstonecraft's *A Vindication of the Rights of Woman* was published in 1792. In Britain it was not until the emergence of the suffragette movement in the late 19th century that there was significant political change. A 'second wave' of feminism arose in the 1960s, with an emphasis on unity and sisterhood; seminal figures included Betty Friedan and Germaine Greer.

fen-fire another name for will-o'-the-wisp.

fence see ➤ GOOD *fences make good neighbours,* ➤ *make a* VIRGINIA *fence.*

fencible historical term for a soldier belonging to a British militia which could be called up only for service on home soil; recorded from Middle English, the word originally denoted 'fit or suitable for defence', and was a shortening of *defensible.*

feng shui in Chinese thought, a system of laws considered to govern spatial arrangement and orientation in relation to the flow of energy (*chi*), and whose favourable or unfavourable effects are taken into account when siting and designing buildings.

The term is Chinese, from *fēng* 'wind' and *shuǐ* 'water'.

Fenian a member of the Irish Republican Brotherhood, a 19th-century revolutionary nationalist organization among the Irish in the US and Ireland. The Fenians staged an unsuccessful revolt in Ireland in 1867 and were responsible for isolated revolutionary acts against the British until the early 20th century, when they were gradually eclipsed by the IRA.

The name comes from Old Irish *féne,* the name of an ancient Irish people, confused with *fiann, fianna* 'band of warriors', the source of ➤ FIANNA *Fáil*'s name.

fennel an aromatic yellow-flowered European plant of the parsley family, with feathery leaves; the name, recorded from Old English (in form *finule, fenol*) comes ultimately from the Latin diminutive of *faenum* 'hay'.

Fenrir in Norse mythology, the wolf, son of Loki, which will devour Odin at ➤ RAGNARÖK. Fenrir was

originally shackled by the gods, in the process of which he bit off the hand of ➤ TYR, but at Ragnarök he will break his bonds to join in the attack on the gods.

the Fens the flat low-lying areas of eastern England, mainly in Lincolnshire, Cambridgeshire, and Norfolk, formerly marshland but largely drained for agriculture since the 17th century.

ferae naturae the legal term for undomesticated or wild animals; the phrase is Latin, meaning 'belonging to the wild part of nature'.

Ferdinand of Aragon (1452–1516), king of Castile 1474–1516 and of Aragon 1479–1516; known as **Ferdinand the Catholic**. His marriage to Isabella of Castile in 1469 ensured his accession (as Ferdinand V) to the throne of Castile with her. Ferdinand subsequently succeeded to the throne of Aragon (as Ferdinand II) and was joined as monarch by Isabella. They instituted the Spanish Inquisition in 1478 and supported Columbus's expedition in 1492. Their capture of Granada from the Moors in the same year effectively united Spain as one country. Their daughter, Catherine of Aragon, became the first wife of Henry VIII of England.

Ferdinand the Bull the central character of Munro Leaf's book for children *The Story of Ferdinand* (1936), a young Spanish bull who likes to sit under a tree and sniff at flowers; when he is stung by a bee, he gives the mistaken impression of being fierce, and is sent to the bullring. When there, he refuses to fight, but instead smells the flowers in the hats of the women spectators; in the end, he is taken home again.

Fergus mac Roich in the Ulster cycle, the stepfather of Conchubar, who leaves court after the betrayal of ➤ DEIRDRE and the sons of Usna.

ferial in the Christian Church, denoting an ordinary weekday, as opposed to one appointed for a festival or fast; (of a service) for use on a ferial day.

The term comes (in late Middle English) from Latin *feria* 'holiday'; in late Latin, the word was used with a prefixed ordinal number to mean 'day of the week' (e.g. *secunda feria* 'second day, Monday'), but Sunday (Dominicus) and Saturday (Sabbatum) were usually referred to by their names; hence *feria* came to mean 'ordinary weekday'.

Pierre de Fermat (1601–65), French mathematician. His work on curves led directly to the general methods of calculus introduced by Newton and

Leibniz. He is also recognized as the founder of the theory of numbers.

Fermat's last theorem a conjecture by Fermat that if n is an integer greater than 2, the equation $x^n + y^n = z^n$ has no positive integral solutions. Fermat apparently noted in the margin of his copy of *Diophantus' Arithmetica* 'I have a truly marvellous demonstration of this proposition which this margin is too narrow to contain', but his proof has never been found, and *Fermat's last theorem* may be cited as an example of an unsolved problem. In 1995 a general proof was published by the Princeton-based British mathematician Andrew Wiles.

> They occasionally address famous outstanding problems like Fermat's Last Theorem or the Riemann Hypothesis.
> — J. L. Casti *Paradigms Lost* (1989)

fernyear dialect term for last year; formerly also, in past years, in olden times. *Fern* here means 'ancient'.

Ferrara a city in northern Italy, capital of a province of the same name, which grew to prominence in the 13th century under the rule of the powerful Este family.

Enzo Ferrari (1898–1988), Italian car designer and manufacturer. In 1929 he founded the company named after him, producing a range of high-quality sports and racing cars. Since the early 1950s Ferraris have won the greatest number of world championship Grands Prix of any car.

Ferris wheel a fairground ride consisting of a giant vertical revolving wheel with passenger cars suspended on its outer edge, named (in the late 19th century) after George W. G. *Ferris* (1859–96), the American engineer who invented it.

ferronnière an ornamental chain with a central jewel, worn around the head, from French, meaning 'frontlet, coronet worn on the forehead', after Leonardo da Vinci's portrait *La belle ferronnière*.

FERT letters inscribed on the collar of the ➤ *Order of the* ANNUNCIATION, founded in 1362 by Amadeus VI of Savoy; *Fert* (Latin 'he bears') is the motto of the House of Savoy, but it has been suggested that the letters may stand for Latin '*Fortitudo eius Rhodum tenuit* [His courage held Rhodes]', referring to the assistance given to the Order of St John in defending Rhodes earlier in the 14th century.

Fertile Crescent a crescent-shaped area of fertile land in the Middle East extending from the eastern Mediterranean coast through the valley of the Tigris and Euphrates Rivers to the Persian Gulf. It was the centre of the Neolithic development of agriculture (from 7000 BC), and the cradle of the Assyrian, Sumerian, and Babylonian civilizations.

fertility cult a pagan religious system of some agricultural societies in which seasonal rites are performed with the aim of ensuring good harvests and the future well-being of the community.

fess in heraldry, an ordinary in the form of a broad horizontal stripe across the middle of the shield; **in fess**, across the middle third of the field.

Festina lente Latin saying, 'make haste slowly'; words attributed to the emperor ➤ AUGUSTUS, meaning that caution should be mingled with speed.

Festival of Britain a festival celebrated with lavish exhibitions and shows throughout Britain, especially at the South Bank in London (see ➤ SKYLON), in May 1951 to mark the centenary of the ➤ GREAT *Exhibition* of 1851.

Festival of Lights another name for ➤ HANUKKAH and ➤ DIWALI.

Festival of the Dead another term for the Japanese Buddhist festival of ➤ BON.

fetch the apparition or double of a living person, formerly believed to be a warning of that person's impending death. The word is recorded from the late 17th century, but the origin is unknown.

fetish an inanimate object worshipped for its supposed magical powers or because it is considered to be inhabited by a spirit. Recorded from the early 17th century, and originally denoting an object used by the peoples of West Africa as an amulet or charm, the word comes through French from Portuguese 'charm, sorcery', from an adjective meaning 'made by art', from Latin *facticius* 'made by art'.

fetterlock a D-shaped fetter for tethering a horse by the leg, now only as represented as a heraldic charge; the **falcon and fetterlock** was one of the badges of the House of York.

fettle condition, as in *in fine fettle*. In Middle English as a verb meaning 'prepare oneself for battle, gird up', from dialect *fettle* 'strip of material, band'; the word is of Germanic origin, and is related to German *Fessel* 'chain, band'.

feu follet French, literally 'frolicsome fire', for ➤ WILL-*o'*-*the-wisp*.

feudalism the dominant social system in medieval Europe, in which the nobility held lands from the Crown in exchange for military service, and vassals were in turn tenants of the nobles, while the peasants (villeins or serfs) were obliged to live on their lord's land and give him homage, labour, and a share of the produce, notionally in exchange for military protection.

fever see also ➤ FEED *a cold and starve a fever*, ➤ YELLOW *fever*.

the Few in Britain, the RAF pilots who took part in the Battle of Britain; the name alludes to a speech made by Winston Churchill on the Battle of Britain in the House of Commons, 20 August 1940, 'Never in the field of human conflict was so much owed by so many to so few.'

fey originally (in Old English, in form *fǣge*) fated to die soon; the word is of Germanic origin, and related to German *feige* 'cowardly'.
  The original meaning is still current in Scottish usage, but from the early 19th century the word has developed a more general sense of giving an impression of vague unworldliness, having supernatural powers of clairvoyance.

Georges Feydeau (1862–1921), French dramatist, whose name has become a byword for French bedroom farce.

> Ottoline was determined to keep her affair with Russell safe from Bloomsbury's prying eyes and she and Russell went to Feydeauesque lengths to keep their secret dark.
> — *New York Review of Books* 7 October 1993

St Fiacre (d. *c*.670), Irish-born hermit living in France; he is said to have been a skilled horticulturist, but to have been of a misogynistic nature (his patronage of those suffering from venereal disease may be linked to this).
  Fiacre is the name of a small four-wheeled carriage for public hire, named after the *Hôtel de St Fiacre* in Paris, where such vehicles were first hired out.
  ☐ **PATRONAGE** He is patron of gardeners, those suffering from venereal disease, and taxi-drivers.
  ☐ **EMBLEM** His emblem is a spade.
  ☐ **FEAST DAY** His feast day is 30 August (1 September in France and Ireland).

Fianna Fáil one of the two main political parties of the Republic of Ireland. Larger and traditionally more republican than its rival Fine Gael, it was formed in 1926 in opposition to the Anglo-Irish Treaty of 1921 by Eamon de Valera together with some of the moderate members of Sinn Fein.
  The name comes from Irish *fianna* 'band of warriors' (applied to the followers of Finn MacCool), and *Fáil* genitive of *Fál* an ancient name for Ireland. The phrase *Fianna Fáil* was used in 15th-century poetry in the neutral sense 'people of Ireland', but the founders of the political party interpreted it to mean 'soldiers of destiny'.
  See also ➤ FENIAN.

fiat a formal authorization or proposition, a decree; from Latin, 'let it be done'.

Leonardo Fibonacci (*c*.1170–*c*.1250), Italian mathematician; known as **Fibonacci of Pisa**. Fibonacci popularized the use of the 'new' Arabic numerals in Europe through such works as *Liber Abaci* (1202, revised 1228). He made many original contributions in complex calculations, algebra, and geometry, and pioneered number theory and indeterminate analysis, discovering the **Fibonacci series**.

Fibonacci series a series of numbers in which each number (**Fibonacci number**) is the sum of the two preceding numbers. The simplest is the series 1, 1, 2, 3, 5, 8, etc.

Johann Gottlieb Fichte (1762–1814), German philosopher. A pupil of Kant, he postulated that the ego is the basic reality; the world is posited by the ego in defining and delimiting itself. His political addresses had some influence on the development of German nationalism and the overthrow of Napoleon.

Marsilio Ficino (1433–99), Italian philosopher and theologian, whose writings influenced the Florentine Platonist Renaissance.

fico archaic term for an insulting gesture in which the thumb is thrust between two of the closed fingers or into the mouth.

fiction see ➤ FACT *is stranger than fiction*, ➤ LEGAL *fiction*, ➤ TRUTH *is stranger than fiction*.

fiddle in Old English as *fithele*, denoting a violin or similar instrument (originally not an informal or depreciatory term) and based on Latin *vitulari* 'celebrate a festival, be joyful', perhaps from *Vitula*, the name of a Roman goddess of joy and victory.
  See also ➤ there's many a GOOD *tune played on an old fiddle*.

fiddle while Rome burns be concerned with relatively trivial matters while ignoring the serious or disastrous events going on around one; the original reference is to the behaviour of the emperor Nero, who according to Suetonius sang the whole of 'The Sack of Ilium' in his preferred stage costume to celebrate the beauty of the flames as Rome burned.

The first use of *fiddle* in this allusion is found in George Daniel's *Trinarchodia* (1649), 'let Nero fiddle out Rome's obsequies'.

fiddler see ➤ *they that* DANCE *must pay the fiddler.*

Fiddler's Green the sailor's Elysium, traditionally a place of wine, women, and song; the term is recorded from the early 19th century.

fiddlestick see ➤ *the* DEVIL *rides on a fiddlestick.*

Fidei Defensor Latin for ➤ DEFENDER *of the Faith.*

fidus see ➤ *fidus* ACHATES.

fief another term for ➤ FEE.

field see also ➤ *the* ELYSIAN *fields,* ➤ *a* FAIR *field and no favour,* ➤ FLOOD *and field,* ➤ FRESH *fields and pastures new,* ➤ KILLING *field,* ➤ POTTER's *field.*

Field of Blood another name for ➤ ACELDAMA.

Field of the Cloth of Gold the scene of a meeting between Henry VIII of England and Francis I of France near Calais in 1520, for which both monarchs erected elaborate temporary palaces, including a sumptuous display of golden cloth. Little of importance was achieved, although the meeting symbolized Henry's determination to play a full part in European dynastic politics.

fields have eyes and woods have ears proverbial saying, early 13th century.

fiend an evil spirit or demon; the fiend (in archaic use) the Devil. Recorded from Old English (in form *fēond*), meaning 'an enemy, a devil, a demon', and of Germanic origin.

fiery see also ➤ BURNING *fiery furnace.*

fiery cross a wooden cross, charred and dipped in blood, used among Scottish clans to summon men to battle. The term is also now used for a burning wooden cross carried as a symbol by the ➤ KU *Klux Klan.*

See also ➤ CROSTARIE.

fifteen the name **The Fifteen** is given to the Jacobite rebellion of 1715.

See also ➤ FAMOUS *for fifteen minutes.*

Fifteen O's fifteen meditations on the Passion of Christ composed by St Bridget, each beginning with 'O Jesu' or a similar invocation.

fifth see also ➤ PLEASE *to remember the Fifth of November.*

take the fifth in the US, exercise the right guaranteed by the Fifth Amendment to the Constitution of refusing to answer questions in order to avoid incriminating oneself; the Amendment (1791) states that, 'no person…shall be compelled in any criminal case to be a witness against himself'.

fifth column a group within a country at war who are sympathetic to or working for its enemies. The term dates from the Spanish Civil War, when General Mola, leading four columns of nationalist troops towards Madrid in 1936, declared that he had a fifth column inside the city.

fifth force a hypothetical force counteracting or modifying the effect of gravity, postulated to explain some apparently anomalous observations. Recent experiments have suggested that it does not exist.

fifth-generation denoting a proposed new class of computer or programming language employing artificial intelligence.

Fifth Monarchy the last of the five great kingdoms predicted in the Book of Daniel (Daniel 2:44, 'And in the days of these kings shall the God of heaven set up a kingdom, which shall never be destroyed'); in the 17th century, this was identified with the millennial reign of Christ predicted in the apocalypse.

Fifth-Monarchy-Man a member of a 17th-century sect expecting the immediate second coming of Christ and believing that it was the duty of Christians to be prepared to assist in establishing his reign by force, and in the meantime to repudiate all other government; John Evelyn in his diary for 1657 refers to them as 'desperate zealots, called the fifth monarchy-men'.

Fifth Republic the republican regime established in France with de Gaulle's introduction of a new constitution in 1958.

smite under the fifth rib strike to the heart, kill; originally with biblical allusion to 2 Samuel 2:23, 'Abner with the hinder end of the spear smote him under the fifth rib…and he fell down there, and died.'

fifth wheel an extra wheel for a four-wheeled vehicle; a superfluous person or thing. This originally denoted a horizontal turntable over the front axle of a carriage as an extra support to prevent its tipping.

Fifty-four forty or fight slogan of the Democratic Party in the US presidential campaign of 1844, in which the Oregon boundary definition was an issue (in 1846 the new Democratic president, James K. Polk, compromised on the 49th parallel with Great Britain).

fifty-year rule in the UK, a rule that public records may be open to inspection after a lapse of fifty years. Superseded in the UK in 1968 by the thirty-year rule.

fig a soft pear-shaped fruit with sweet dark flesh and many small seeds, eaten fresh or dried, which in a number of phrases, such as *not give a fig for*, is taken as the type of something of little value.

In Mark ch. 11, Jesus sees a fig-tree with leaves but no fruit and says to it, 'No man eat fruit of thee hereafter for ever'; the tree subsequently withers. It is in fact usual for the leaves of this tree to appear before the fruit; but the 'barren fig tree' is being used as an image of Israel's failure to respond spiritually to God.

In the 16th and 17th centuries, *fig* (also called **Italian fig** or **Spanish fig**) sometimes denoted a poisoned fig as a method of secret killing.

fig leaf a leaf of a fig tree, often used for concealing the genitals in paintings and sculpture; with particular reference to the story of Adam and Eve, when having eaten of the tree of the knowledge of good and evil and become ashamed of their nakedness, 'they sewed fig leaves together, and made themselves aprons' (Genesis 3:7).

Fig Sunday a dialect name for ➤ PALM *Sunday*.

Figaro the central character, a barber turned valet who both assists and circumvents his master Count Almaviva, of *The Barber of Seville* (1775) and *The Marriage of Figaro* (1784) by the French dramatist Pierre de Beaumarchais (1732–99); they inspired operas by Rossini and Mozart. Figaro was popularly seen as resisting the aristocratic abuse of personal power.

The French daily newspaper *Le Figaro*, originally founded in Paris in 1826 to comment on the arts, was named after him.

fight see ➤ *that* COCK *won't fight*, ➤ WAR *will cease when men refuse to fight.*

Fighting French a name given to the ➤ FREE *French* armed forces during the German occupation of France in the Second World War.

the Fighting Bishop an epithet of Henry Despencer, bishop of Norwich (d. 1406), who put down insurrection in Norfolk during the Peasants' Revolt in arms; he is also called the *Warlike Bishop*.

he that fights and runs away lives to fight another day proverbial saying, mid 16th century; earlier in the writings of the Greek comic dramatist Menander (342–*c*.292 BC), 'a man who flees will fight again.'

figurehead a carving, typically a bust or a full-length figure, set at the prow of an old-fashioned sailing ship.

figures see ➤ CHLADNI *figures.*

Filarete (1400–69), name (from Greek, and meaning 'lover of virtue') adopted by the Italian architect and writer Antonio Averlino, author of the influential *Trattato d'Architettura*, which describes a model Renaissance city named *Sforzinda*.

filbert a cultivated hazel tree that bears edible oval nuts. Recorded from Middle English, the name comes via Anglo-Norman French *philbert* from dialect French *noix de filbert*, so named because it is ripe about 20 August, the feast day of St *Philibert*), 7th-century Gascon abbot who was the founder of Jumièges.

In 1915, the word was used punningly in the popular comic song *Gilbert the Filbert* by Wimpers, with the lines, 'I'm Gilbert, the Filbert, The Colonel of the Knuts'.

file see ➤ RANK *and file.*

filibuster an action such as prolonged speaking which obstructs progress in a legislative assembly in a way that does not technically contravene the required procedures.

The word comes from French *flibustier*, first applied to pirates who pillaged the Spanish colonies in the West Indies. In the mid 19th century (via Spanish *filibustero*), the term denoted American adventurers who incited revolution in several Latin

American states. The verb was used to describe tactics intended to sabotage US congressional proceedings.

Filioque the word inserted in the Western version of the Nicene Creed to assert the doctrine of the procession of the Holy Ghost from the Son as well as from the Father, which is not admitted by the Eastern Church. It was one of the central issues in the Great Schism of 1054.

Filioque is Latin, literally 'and from the Son'.

fill-dyke a traditional epithet for the month of ➤ FEBRUARY, because of the likelihood of heavy rain or snow.

fimbriated in heraldry, (of a charge) bordered with a narrow band or edge.

fin de siècle French phrase meaning relating to or characteristic of the end of a century, especially the 19th century, seen as characteristically advanced, modern, or decadent.

final see ➤ CUP *Final*.

Finality Jack a nickname for Lord John Russell (1792–1878), when in 1837 he earned the hostility of radical politicians by declaring that it was impossible for him to take part in further measures of electoral reform.

financial year a year as reckoned for taxing or accounting purposes, for example the British tax year, reckoned from 6 April.

find see ➤ SEEK *and ye shall find*.

finders keepers (losers weepers) proverbial saying, early 19th century.

findings keepings proverbial saying, mid 19th century.

fine art creative art, especially visual art whose products are to be appreciated primarily or solely for their imaginative, aesthetic, or intellectual content.

fine feathers make fine birds proverbial saying, late 16th century.

Fine Gael one of the two major political parties of the Republic of Ireland (the other being ➤ FIANNA *Fáil*). Founded in 1923 as *Cumann na nGaedheal*, it changed its name in 1933. It has advocated the concept of a united Ireland achieved by peaceful means.

The name is Irish, and means literally 'tribe of Gaels'.

fine words butter no parsnips proverbial saying, mid 17th century.

one's finest hour the time of one's greatest achievement; now particularly associated with a speech by Winston Churchill:

> Let us therefore brace ourselves to our duty, and so bear ourselves that, if the British Commonwealth and its Empire lasts for a thousand years, men will still say, 'This was their finest hour.'
> — Winston Churchill speech in the House of Commons, 18 June 1940

Fingal a character in an epic poem by the Scottish poet James Macpherson (1736–96), based on the legendary Irish hero ➤ FINN *mac Cool* but fictionally transformed and depicted as fighting both the Norse invaders and the Romans (under Caracalla) from an invented kingdom in NW Scotland.

Fingal's Cave a cave on the island of Staffa in the Inner Hebrides, noted for the clustered basaltic pillars that form its cliffs. It is said to have been the inspiration of Mendelssohn's overture *The Hebrides* (also known as *Fingal's Cave*), but in fact he noted down the principal theme before his visit to Staffa.

finger see also ➤ BURN *one's fingers*, ➤ DEAD *man's fingers*, ➤ GREEN *fingers*, ➤ MEDICAL *finger*, ➤ PHYSICIAN *finger*, ➤ put one's FINGER *in the dyke*, ➤ RING *finger*, ➤ WEDDING-*finger*.

have a finger in every pie be involved in a large and varied number of activities or enterprises; the expression in this form is recorded from the late 19th century, but the image of a finger (earlier hand) in a pie indicating involvement dates back to the mid 16th century.

finger of God an image (after Exodus 8:19) of God's intervention in human affairs; in astrology, an aspect between three planets where one is quincunx to each of the other two, which are sextile to each other.

fingerpost a post at a road junction from which signs project in the direction of the place or route indicated.

fingerprint an impression or mark made on a surface by a person's fingertip, especially as used for identifying individuals from the unique pattern of whorls and lines.

all fingers and thumbs awkward, clumsy; earliest in the mid 16th century as, 'each finger is a thumb'.

fingers crossed a gesture intended to avert bad luck; recorded from the early 20th century.

fingers were made before forks proverbial saying, mid 18th century (the form 'God made hands before knives' is found in the mid 16th century).

at one's fingertips especially of information, readily available; recorded from the late 19th century.

finisher of the law in the 18th and 19th centuries, a term for a hangman, an executioner.

Mike Fink (1770?–1823?), keelboatman on the Ohio and Mississippi rivers, whose tall tales made him as fabulous as ➤ *Paul* Bunyan; stories derived from oral sources made their way into print.

Finlandization the process or result of being obliged for economic reasons to favour, or at least not oppose, the interests of the former Soviet Union despite not being politically allied to it. The word is a translation of German *Finnlandisierung*, referring to the case of Finland after 1944.

Huckleberry Finn name of the character created by Mark Twain, introduced in *The Adventures of Tom Sawyer* (1876), and central to its sequel, *The Adventures of Huckleberry Finn* (1884). Son of the town drunkard, Huckleberry Finn is shown as brave and resourceful, but cramped by the confines of civilization.

> The once-idolized figure of the hacker, that jeans-clad Huck Finn of the circuit boards, is becoming an anachronism.
> — *American Book Review* April 1991

Finn mac Cool in Irish mythology, the warrior hero of a cycle of legends about a band of warriors defending Ireland. Father of the legendary Irish warrior and bard ➤ Ossian, he is supposed to have lived in the 3rd century AD.

Finnish the language of the Finns. It is a Finno-Ugric language related to Estonian, and more distantly to Hungarian, and is noted for its morphological complexity.

Fionnuala in Irish mythology, a princess, one of the four ➤ *Children of* Lir, who were turned into swans by their stepmother's enchantment.

Firbolg in Irish mythology, an early colonizing people of Ireland.

fire one of the four elements in ancient and medieval philosophy and in astrology (considered essential to the nature of the signs Aries, Leo, and Sagittarius).

See also ➤ *a* burnt *child dreads the fire*, ➤ elf-*fire*, ➤ *the* fat *is in the fire*, ➤ fen-*fire*, ➤ friendly *fire*, ➤ Great *Fire*, ➤ Greek *fire*, ➤ *heap* coals *of fire on a person's head*, ➤ *if you* play *with fire you'll get burnt*, ➤ Kentish *fire*, ➤ *no* smoke *without fire*, ➤ out *of the frying pan*, ➤ Promethean *fire*, ➤ *pull someone's* chestnuts *out of the fire*, ➤ *St* Anthony*'s fire*, ➤ *St* Elmo*'s fire*, ➤ set *the Thames on fire*, ➤ wandering *fire*.

fire and brimstone torment in hell; often with biblical allusion, as in Revelation 19:20, 'These both were cast alive into a lake of fire burning with brimstone.'

fire and sword burning and slaughter, especially by an invading army; in Scottish law before the Union, **letters of fire and sword** denoted an order authorizing a sheriff to dispossess a tenant or proceed against a delinquent with any means in his power.

never fire first according to accounts by Voltaire and others, the French commander at the battle of Fontenoy in 1745 assured the British commander, Lord Charles Hay (d. 1760), that the French guards never fired first.

fire is a good servant but a bad master proverbial saying, early 17th century.

the Fire of London the huge and devastating fire which destroyed some 13,000 houses over 400 acres of London between 2 and 6 September 1666, having started in a bakery in Pudding Lane in the City of London; perhaps the best-known account of it is in Samuel Pepys's diary.

fire worship the treatment of fire as a god; especially in ➤ Zoroastrianism.

firedrake in Germanic mythology, a dragon; the creature which ➤ Beowulf encounters in his final battle is described as '*frēcne fȳrdraca* [terrible firedrake]'.

firefighters ➤ *St* Agatha and ➤ *St* Lawrence are the patron saints of firefighters.

fireman see ➤ visiting *fireman*.

fireship a ship loaded with burning material and explosives and set adrift to ignite and blow up an enemy's ships.

fireside chats in the US, the informal broadcasts made by ➤ *Franklin* ROOSEVELT during his presidency on topics of national interest.

firkin a small cask used chiefly for liquids, butter, or fish; a unit of liquid volume equal to half a kilderkin (usually 9 imperial gallons or about 41 litres). The word is recorded from Middle English (in form *ferdekyn*), and probably comes from the Middle Dutch diminutive of *vierde* 'fourth' (a *firkin* originally contained a quarter of a barrel).

firmament the heavens or the sky, especially when regarded as a tangible thing; recorded from Middle English, the word comes ultimately from Latin *firmare* 'fix, settle'.

first see ➤ CAST *the first stone,* ➤ GLORIOUS *First of June,* ➤ *on the* FIRST *of March, the crows begin to search.*

first among equals recognized by the other members of a group as their effective leader; a translation of ➤ PRIMUS *inter pares.*

first catch your hare proverbial saying, early 19th century, early 14th century in Latin; often attributed to the English cook Hannah Glasse (fl. 1747), but her directions are, 'Take your hare when it is cased'; 'cased' here means 'skinned'.

First Cause in philosophy, a supposed ultimate cause of all events, which does not itself have a cause, identified with God.

first come, first served proverbial saying, late 14th century, late 13th century in French.

First Consul the title held by Napoleon Bonaparte (see ➤ NAPOLEON) from 1799 to 1804, when he became Emperor of France; a painting by Ingres, 'Bonaparte as First Consul' (1804), is notable for the imagery which associates the figure of the portrait with ancient Rome.

first-day cover an envelope bearing a stamp or set of stamps postmarked on their day of issue.

the first duty of a soldier is obedience proverbial saying, mid 19th century.

First Empire the period of the reign of Napoleon I as emperor of the French (1804–15).

First Fleet the eleven British ships under the command of Arthur Phillip (1738–1814), sailor and first governor of New South Wales, which arrived in Australia in January 1788.

first-foot the first person to cross a threshold in the New Year, in accordance with a Scottish custom; it is traditionally thought lucky for the *first-foot* to be a dark-haired man.

First Four Ships the first European settlers' ships that arrived in New Zealand in 1840.

first fruits the first agricultural produce of a season, especially when given as an offering to God; originally with biblical allusion as to Numbers 18:12, 'the first fruits of them which they shall offer unto the Lord'.

First Gentleman in Europe a nickname of ➤ GEORGE *IV,* referring to his role as a leader of fashion and good manners; the name was however applied satirically by Cruikshank in a caricature (1820) which showed the 'First Gentleman in Europe' recovering from a debauch.

The name *first gentleman of Europe* had in the 17th century been applied admiringly by the political economist William Petty to the Catholic and Royalist Irish peer the Duke of Ormonde (1610–88).

first impressions are the most lasting proverbial saying, early 18th century.

First Lady the wife of the President of the US; the term is recorded from the mid 19th century, and has gradually come into official use (it is said that Jacqueline Kennedy in the 1960s asserted, 'The one thing I do not want to be called is First Lady. It sounds like a saddle horse').

A number of *First Ladies,* such as Eleanor Roosevelt, have been notable figures in their own right; Nancy Reagan commented of the role, 'If the President has a bully pulpit, then the First Lady has a white glove pulpit…more refined, restricted, ceremonial, but it's a pulpit all the same.'

first light the time when light first appears in the morning; dawn.

First Nations in Canada, a term used for Canadian Indians, in recognition of their original status as indigenous inhabitants of countries which were later colonized.

first past the post denoting an electoral system in which a candidate or party is selected by achievement of a simple majority.

first post in the British armed forces, the first of two bugle calls giving notice of the hour of retiring at night.

First Republic the republican regime in France from the abolition of the monarchy in 1792 until Napoleon's accession as emperor in 1804.

First State informal name for Delaware.

it is the first step that is difficult proverbial saying, late 16th century.
  See also ➤ *ce n'est que le* PREMIER *pas qui coûte.*

first things first proverbial saying, late 19th century.

there is always a first time proverbial saying, late 16th century.

First World the industrialized capitalist countries of western Europe, North America, Japan, Australia, and New Zealand.

First World War a war (1914–18) in which the Central Powers (Germany and Austria–Hungary, joined later by Turkey and Bulgaria) were defeated by an alliance of Britain and its dominions, France, Russia, and others, joined later by Italy and the US.

fish the cold-blooded *fish* is taken as a type of something cold and unfeeling; proverbially also associated with heavy drinking. From an early period its flesh, especially when dried or salted, has taken the place of meat during times of fasting or abstinence.
  In Christian art, a *fish* is a symbol of Christ, and sometimes also of the newly baptized and of the Eucharist; it is often found in paintings in the catacombs. The reason for the symbolism is not wholly clear, although it may derive from the Greek letters of 'Jesus Christ, Son of God, Saviour' read as *ikhthus* 'fish'.
  A *fish* is an emblem of the 9th-century Cornish hermit St Neot, whose legend refers to a fish which although repeatedly eaten continued to provide food, St Zeno, 4th-century bishop of Verona, who is sometimes shown as a fisherman, ➤ *St* ANTHONY *of Padua*, and the 7th-century English princess St Eanswith.

The Fish or **The Fishes** are names given to the zodiacal sign or constellation Pisces.
  See also ➤ BIG *fish eat little fish,* ➤ *the* CAT *would eat fish but would not wet her feet,* ➤ EAT *no fish,* ➤ KEEP *your own fish-guts for your own sea-maws,* ➤ KETTLE *of fish,* ➤ LITTLE *fish are sweet,* ➤ LOAVES *and fishes,* ➤ *St* PETER*'s fish.*

the fish always stinks from the head downwards proverbial saying, late 16th century.

fish and guests stink after three days proverbial saying, late 16th century.

fish-day a fast-day on which fish rather than meat is eaten.

there are as good fish in the sea as ever came out of it proverbial saying, late 16th century.

fish in troubled waters take advantage of disturbance or trouble to gain one's end; recorded from the mid 16th century.

neither fish nor fowl nor good red herring of indefinite character and difficult to identify or classify; with original reference to dietary restrictions in times of fasting and abstinence.

make fish of one and flesh of another traditional saying, early 18th century; meaning to make an invidious distinction, to show partiality.

fish royal a fish such as a sturgeon which if caught belongs to the sovereign.

all is fish that comes to the net proverbial saying; early 16th century.

St John Fisher (1469–1535), English churchman. In 1504 he became bishop of Rochester and earned the disfavour of Henry VIII by opposing his divorce from Catherine of Aragon. When he refused to accept the king as supreme head of the Church, he was condemned to death.
  ❑ **FEAST DAY** His feast day is 22 June.

Fisher King in medieval legends of the ➤ *Holy* GRAIL, a wounded king in whose castle the Grail is kept, and who will only be healed when the right question about the Grail is asked.

fisher of men an evangelist; originally with biblical allusion to Matthew 4:19, 'And he saith unto them, Follow me, and I will make you fishers of men.'

Fisherman's ring a seal-ring worn by the Pope, showing St Peter drawing in his net full of fish.

fishermen ➤ *St* ANDREW, ➤ *St* PETER, ➤ *St* SIMON, St Zeno, 4th-century bishop of Verona, who is sometimes shown as a fisherman, ➤ *St* NICHOLAS *of Myra*, and ➤ *St* MAGNUS are the patron saints of fishermen.

fishwife a woman who sells fish, taken as typified by a coarse-mannered woman who is prone to shouting and abuse (the association of fish-selling with vituperative language is also found in ➤ BILLINGSGATE).

fist see ➤ MAILED *fist*.

fitché in heraldry, (of a cross) having its lower limb tapered to a point.

the eternal fitness of things the natural appropriateness of the existing order of things, what is fitting or appropriate; originally with reference to the ethical theories of the English divine Samuel Clarke (1675–1729).

fittest see ➤ SURVIVAL *of the fittest*.

fitz a son (originally from Anglo-Norman French). Chiefly in patronymic designations surviving as an element in surnames (*Fitzgerald*), and sometimes used for the illegitimate son of a prince (*Fitzclarence*, *Fitzroy*).

five recorded from Old English (in form *fíf*) and of Germanic origin, the word comes from an Indo-European root shared by Latin *quinque* and Greek *pente*.

See also ➤ BIG *five*, ➤ *the* FAMOUS *Five*, ➤ *the* FEEDING *of the Five Thousand*, ➤ FORTUNE 500.

five Ks in Sikh belief, the five signs, *kangha* (comb), *kara* (steel bangle), *kesh* (uncut hair, covered by a turban, and beard), *kirpan* (short sword) and *kuccha* (short trousers, originally for riding) which show allegiance to the ➤ KHALSA.

Five Members the members of the Long Parliament, Pym, Hampden, Haselrig, Holles, and Strode, whose arrest was unsuccessfully attempted by Charles I on 4 January 1642 in the House of Commons; having been warned in advance, they had escaped. The event contributed materially to the final break between king and Parliament.

See also ➤ *the* BIRD *has flown*.

Five Nations[1] the Iroquois confederacy as originally formed, including the Mohawk, Oneida, Seneca, Onondaga, and Cayuga peoples.

Five Nations[2] an annual international rugby union championship involving England, France, Ireland, Scotland, and Wales; in 2000, the *Five Nations* became *Six Nations* when Italy joined the championship.

Five Pillars of Islam the five duties expected of every Muslim—profession of the faith in a prescribed form, observance of ritual prayer, giving alms to the poor, fasting during the month of Ramadan, and performing a pilgrimage to Mecca.

the Five Towns in the novels of Arnold Bennett, Tunstall, Burslem, Hanley, Stoke-on-Trent, and Longton, now forming the federated borough of Stoke-on-Trent. They are represented in the novels by Turnhill, Bursley, Hanbridge, Knype, and Longshaw.

flabellum a fan carried in religious ceremonies, especially to keep insects away from the consecrated host.

flag a national flag is often taken as the essential symbol of the country concerned, as in the US *Pledge of Allegiance*:

> I pledge allegiance to the flag of the United States of America and to the republic for which it stands, one nation under God, indivisible, with liberty and justice for all.
>
> — Francis Bellamy *The Pledge of Allegiance to the Flag* (1892)

The word is recorded from the mid 16th century, perhaps from obsolete *flag* 'drooping', of unknown ultimate origin.

See also ➤ QUARANTINE *flag*, ➤ RED *flag*, ➤ TRADE *follows the flag*, ➤ WHITE *flag*, ➤ YELLOW *flag*.

flag captain the captain of a flagship.

Flag Day in the US, 14 June, the anniversary of the adoption of the ➤ STARS *and Stripes* in 1777.

flag of convenience a flag of a country under which a ship is registered in order to avoid financial charges or restrictive regulations in the owner's country.

flag of truce a white flag indicating a desire for a truce.

flagellant a person who subjects themselves to flogging as a religious discipline, especially as a member of a sect which arose in the 13th century.

flagellum dei Latin for ➤ *the* SCOURGE *of God*.

Protestant flail a short staff weighted with lead said to have been carried as a defensive weapon by Protestants at the time of the so-called ➤ POPISH *plot* (1678–81).

flamboyant of or denoting a style of French Gothic architecture marked by wavy flamelike tracery and ornate decoration.

flame a vitriolic or abusive message sent via electronic mail, typically in quick response to another message.

flamen in ancient Rome, a priest serving a particular deity.

Flamen Dialis in ancient Rome, the *flamen* of Jupiter.

flaming sword traditionally held by the angel in the expulsion from Paradise, originally as in Genesis 3:24, 'So he drove out the man; and he placed at the east of the garden of Eden Cherubims, and a flaming sword which turned every way, to keep the tree of life.'

Flaminian Way in ancient Italy, the road from Rome (the *Via Flaminia*) leading north to Rimini.

Flanders a region in the south-western part of the Low Countries, now divided between Belgium (where it forms the provinces of East and West Flanders), France, and the Netherlands. It was a powerful medieval principality and the scene of prolonged fighting during the First World War, when Allied troops held the sector of the Western Front round the town of Ypres.

Flanders Mare a nickname of Anne of Cleves (1515–57), fourth wife of Henry VIII, whom the king divorced; according to Smollett's *A Complete History of England* (3rd ed., 1759), 'The King found her so different from her picture…that…he swore they had brought him a Flanders mare.'

Flanders poppy a red poppy, used as an emblem of the Allied soldiers who fell in the First World War.

flapper in the 1920s, a fashionable young woman intent on enjoying herself and flouting conventional standards of behaviour; the actress Mrs Patrick Campbell (1865–1940) said ruefully of the theatre of 1927, 'I'm out of a job. London wants flappers, and I can't flap.'

flapper vote a derogatory term for the parliamentary vote granted to women of 21 and over in 1928.

Flash Gordon spaceman hero of the comic strip created by the American cartoonist Alex Raymond in 1934, who in order to save the world from extinction is sent to the planet Mongo to defeat the forces of the evil emperor Ming.

> Now the president's on TV, he's Flash Gordon.
> — Kate Green *Night Angel* (1989)

a flash in the pan a promising start followed by failure, a one-off success; originally referring to an ineffective ignition of powder in a gun.

Flashman a character in *Tom Brown's Schooldays* (1857) by Thomas Hughes, revived from 1969 in a series of humorous novels by George Macdonald Fraser. Flashman is a bully and a coward (as in the original novel), and his reputation as a hero is entirely undeserved, but his saving grace appears to be that he is free from the hypocrisy of many of the more moral characters around him.

> The young cricketers of Marlborough and Radley may include the odd Tom Brown, but there will always be Flashmans.
> — *Daily Telegraph* 23 July 1997

flatline die; with reference to the continuous straight line displayed on a heart monitor, indicating death. The term is recorded in a medical context in the early 1980s, but came to general prominence with the release of the film *The Flatliners* (1990). The film tells the story of a group of medical students who dangerously exploit their ability to control the heart rate by helping each other to *flatline* in order to experience the first few seconds after the moment of death, before being revived (the participants, or **flatliners**, were considerably chastened by the experience).

flattery see ➤ IMITATION *is the sincerest form of flattery*.

Flavian a member of a dynasty (AD 69–96) of Roman emperors including ➤ VESPASIAN and his sons Titus and Domitian.

Flavius see ➤ *Flavius* JOSEPHUS.

flavour of the month a person or thing that enjoys a short period of great popularity; the term originated as a marketing ploy in US ice-cream parlours in the 1940s, when a particular ice-cream flavour would be singled out for the month or week for special promotion.

flea the *flea* is taken as the type of something small and contemptible, or as a sign of dirt and degradation.

See also ➤ BIG *fleas have little fleas upon their backs to bite them,* ➤ *if you* LIE *down with dogs, you will get up with fleas,* ➤ NOTHING *should be done in haste but gripping a flea.*

fleadh a festival of Irish or Celtic music, dancing, and culture.

fleece see ➤ *the* GOLDEN *Fleece.*

fleet see also ➤ FIRST *Fleet,* ➤ FLOGGING *round the fleet.*

the Fleet a stream (now covered) flowing into the Thames between Ludgate Hill and Fleet Street, and the prison that stood near it.

Fleet marriage a wedding performed clandestinely by a **Fleet parson**, any of a number of disreputable clergymen to be found in or around the Fleet prison ready to perform such marriages.

Fleet prison a former London prison in the neighbourhood of the present Farringdon Street, alongside the Fleet river. It was built in the time of Richard I, and long afterwards served as a place of imprisonment for persons condemned by the Star Chamber. After the abolition of the latter in 1640, it served mainly as a debtors' prison, until demolished in 1848, and it figures as such in Dickens's novels, notably *Pickwick Papers.*

Fleet Street a street in central London in which the offices of national newspapers were located until the mid 1980s (often used to refer to the British Press).

> A careful reading of the News of the World story suggests that it is nothing more than a classic Fleet Street spoiler.
> — *Guardian* 3 October 1994

Alexander Fleming (1881–1955), Scottish bacteriologist. In 1928, while investigating the body's defences against infection, Fleming discovered the effect of penicillin on bacteria. Twelve years later Howard Florey and Ernst Chain established its therapeutic use as an antibiotic. Fleming won the Nobel Prize for Physiology or Medicine in 1945, shared with Florey and Chain.

Fleming's left-hand rule a mnemonic concerning the behaviour of a current-carrying conductor in a magnetic field, according to which the directions of the magnetic field, the current, and the force exerted on the conductor are indicated respectively by the first finger, second finger, and thumb of the left hand when these are held out perpendicular to each other.

Fleming's right-hand rule a mnemonic concerning the behaviour of a conductor moving in a magnetic field, according to which the directions of the magnetic field, the induced current, and the motion of the conductor are indicated respectively by the first finger, second finger, and thumb of the right hand when these are held out perpendicular to each other. It was invented in 1900 by the English electrical engineer John Ambrose *Fleming* (1849–1945).

the flesh the human body and its physical needs and desires, especially as contrasted with the mind or the soul.

See also ➤ *make* FISH *of one and flesh of another,* ➤ *one's* POUND *of flesh,* ➤ *the* WORLD, *the flesh, and the devil.*

one flesh intimately united, especially by virtue of marriage; originally with allusion to Genesis 2:24, 'Therefore shall a man…cleave unto his wife: and they shall be one flesh.'

flesh and blood used to emphasize that a person is a physical, living being with human emotions or frailties, often in contrast to something abstract, spiritual, or mechanical; **one's own flesh and blood**, a near relative or one's close family.

flesh and fell archaic expression for the whole substance of the body; *fell* here means the human skin.

fleshly school of poetry a group of late 19th-century poets associated with Dante Gabriel Rossetti; the term was coined in the *Contemporary Review* of October 1871 by the Scottish writer Robert Buchanan.

Fletcherism the practice of thorough mastication as advocated by the US author Horace *Fletcher* (1849–1919).

fleur-de-lis a stylized lily composed of three petals bound together near their bases. It is especially known from the former royal arms of France, in which it appears in gold on a blue field. Recorded from Middle English, the term comes from Old French *flour de lys* 'flower of the lily'.

fleuron a flower-shaped ornament, used especially on buildings, coins, and books.

flexible friend a credit card, from the advertising slogan, 'Access—your flexible friend'.

flibbertigibbet a frivolous, flighty, or excessively talkative person; recorded from late Middle English, and probably imitative of idle chatter.

Flibbertigibbet is also the name a name for a devil or fiend, the 'foul field Flibbertigibbet' which Edgar, pretending insanity as 'poor Tom' in Shakespeare's *King Lear* claims to have seen. Sir Walter Scott later used the name in *Kenilworth* (1821) for the impish character Dickie Sludge.

flies see ➤ *as the* CROW *flies*, ➤ EAGLES *don't catch flies*, ➤ *a* SHUT *mouth catches no flies*.

Matthew Flinders (1774–1814), English explorer. He explored the coast of New South Wales (1795–1800) and circumnavigated Australia (1801–3) for the Royal Navy, charting much of the west coast of the continent for the first time.

flitch see ➤ DUNMOW *flitch*.

flittermouse an old-fashioned term for a bat; recorded from the mid 16th century, and formed on the pattern of Dutch *vledermuis* or German *Fledermaus*.

flixweed a Eurasian plant with small yellow flowers and finely divided leaves, which was formerly thought to cure dysentery or *flux* (from the obsolete form *flix*).

Floberge in the legends of Charlemagne, name of a sword belonging to Renaud of Montauban (in *Orlando Furioso*, he becomes ➤ RINALDO, and his sword is *Fusberta*).

floccinaucinihilipilification the action or habit of estimating something as worthless. (The word is used chiefly as a curiosity.)

flocks and herds sheep and cattle, one's possessions generally; originally often with biblical allusion, as in Genesis 46:32, 'their flocks, and their herds, and all that they have.'

Battle of Flodden (Field) a decisive battle of the Anglo-Scottish war of 1513, at Flodden, a hill near the Northumbrian village of Branxton. A Scottish army under James IV was defeated by a smaller but better-led English force under the Earl of Surrey (sent northwards by Henry VIII, who was on campaign in France) and suffered heavy losses, including the king and most of his nobles.

flog a dead horse waste energy on a lost cause or unalterable situation; the use of *dead horse* as a something which is no longer of use, and which cannot be revived, is recorded from the mid 17th century.

flogging round the fleet the former Naval punishment of being flogged alongside each vessel in the fleet.

the Flood the biblical flood said in Genesis ch. 6–9 to have been brought by God upon earth because of the wickedness of the human race, and from which only ➤ NOAH and his family were saved; in extended usage, marking a period of time preceded by extreme antiquity, as in *antediluvian, before the Flood.*

See also ➤ RAINBOW.

flood and field archaic or poetic expression for sea and land; the whole world.

floor see ➤ CROSS *the floor*.

Flora in Roman mythology, the goddess of flowering plants.

Floréal the eighth month of the French Republican calendar (1793–1805), originally running from 20 April to 19 May. The name is French, and comes from Latin *floreus* 'flowery'.

floreat used before a name to express one's desire that the specified institution or person will flourish. The word is Latin for 'let flourish', originally used in *floreat Etona*, the motto of Eton College.

Florence a city in west central Italy, the capital of Tuscany, on the River Arno, which was a leading centre of the Italian Renaissance from the 14th to the 16th century, especially under the rule of the Medici family during the 15th century.

Florentine diamond a clear, pale-yellow stone of Indian origin, which was once owned by Charles the Bold of Burgundy; in the 16th century, the stone came into the possession of Pope Julius II and the Medici family.

Florida a state forming the peninsula of the southeastern US. Explored by Ponce de Leon in 1513, it was purchased from Spain by the US in 1819, and became the 27th state of the Union in 1845. The name comes from Ponce de Leon's landing on the peninsula during the Easter season (Spanish *Pascua florida* 'flowering Easter') and being impressed by the abundant vegetation.

florin an English gold coin of the 14th century, worth six shillings and eight old pence; a former British coin and monetary unit worth two shillings.

The word comes via Old French from Italian

fiorino, diminutive of *fiore* 'flower', from Latin *flos, flor-*. The word originally denoted a gold coin issued in Florence, bearing a *fleur-de-lis* (the city's emblem) on the reverse.

See ➤ GRACELESS *florin*.

John Florio (*c*.1553–1625), English lexicographer, of Italian descent. He produced an Italian–English dictionary entitled *A Worlde of Wordes* (1598) and translated Montaigne's essays into English (1603).

florists ➤ *St* DOROTHY and the Peruvian St Rose of Lima (1586–1617) are the patron saints of florists.

Florizel the prince of Bohemia, in Shakespeare's *The Winter's Tale*; as a young man, George, Prince of Wales, afterwards George IV, signed his letters to the actress Mary Robinson (see ➤ PERDITA) 'Florizel'.

flotsam the wreckage of a ship or its cargo found floating on or washed up by the sea (as distinguished from ➤ JETSAM, goods or material thrown overboard and washed ashore). **Flotsam and jetsam** is used generally for useless or discarded objects.

flourish like a green bay tree develop vigorously in a congenial environment, whether or not this is deserved; originally with reference to Psalm 37:5 in the Book of Common Prayer, 'I myself have seen the ungodly in great power: and flourishing like the green bay-tree.'

flow of soul genial conversation, as complementary to intellectual discussion; the phrase comes originally from Pope's *Satires of Horace* (1733), 'the feast of reason and the flow of soul'.

flower see also ➤ BACH *flower remedies*, ➤ BASKET *of fruit and flowers*, ➤ HUNDRED *Flowers*, ➤ LANGUAGE *of flowers*, ➤ ROGATION *flower*, ➤ SAY *it with flowers*.

the Flower of Chivalry a name given to several distinguished knights, including Sir David Brechin (d. 1321) and Sir William Douglas (1300?–53), the Knight of Liddesdale.

flower people hippies, especially in the 1960s, who wore flowers as symbols of peace and love.

flower power the ideas of the flower people, especially the promotion of peace and love as means of changing the world.

no flowers by request an intimation that no flowers are desired at a funeral; the writer and humourist Alfred Ainger (1837–1904) used the phrase at a dinner for contributors in 1897 to sum

up the principles on which the *Dictionary of National Biography* was being compiled.

the Flowery Kingdom a name (a translation from Chinese) for the Chinese Empire.

Fluellen a Welsh soldier in Shakespeare's *Henry V*; mocked by Pistol for wearing a ➤ LEEK on St David's day, he forces the Englishman to eat it. His name represents the Welsh proper name *Llewelyn*.

Flush name of Elizabeth Barrett's spaniel; she took the dog with her when she eloped with Robert Browning.

flush in poker or brag, a hand of cards all of the same suit; ultimately (through French) from Latin *flux* 'a flow'. The use in cards can be compared with the English *run*.

See also ➤ ROYAL *flush*.

flutter the dovecotes cause alarm, throw into confusion or excitement; perhaps originally as a quotation from Shakespeare:

> If you have writ your annals true, 'tis there,
> That, like an eagle in a dove-cote, I
> Fluttered your Volscians in Corioli:
> Alone I did it.
> — William Shakespeare *Coriolanus* (1608)

fly the *fly* is traditionally taken as a type of something insignificant, and also referred to as an insect that will settle on decaying matter.

a fly in amber a curious relic of the past, preserved into the present; alluding to the fossilised bodies of insects often found trapped in amber.

The image was given a different slant by Michael Crichton's thriller *Jurassic Park* (1990) and the Spielberg film based on it, in which the DNA essential to the recreation of dinosaurs was retrieved from the animal's blood supposedly fossilized with the insect that had fed from it.

a fly in the ointment a minor irritation that spoils the success or enjoyment of something; originally with biblical allusion to Ecclesiastes 10:1, 'Dead flies cause the ointment of the apothecary to send forth a stinking savour.'

a fly on the wall an unnoticed observer of a particular situation; the phrase is first recorded in the mid 20th century.

fly-the-garter a game in which players jump from one side of a 'garter' or line of stones over the back of one of their number; first recorded in a letter of 1818 by Keats, 'I must…make Wordsworth and

Coleman play at leap-frog, or keep one of them down a whole half-holiday at fly-the-garter.'

flying bishop in the Anglican Church in the UK, a bishop opposed to the ordination of women priests, who is authorized to act as bishop to clergy outside his own diocese, should they be similarly opposed, and their own bishop willing to ordain women.

the Flying Duchess Mary, Duchess of Bedford (1865–1937), an early aviator who was lost on a solo flight over the North Sea in 1937.

the Flying Dutchman a legendary spectral ship supposedly seen in the region of the Cape of Good Hope and presaging disaster; the name is also used for the captain of this ship, said to have been condemned to sail the seas for ever.

> Aden is a port of call for the Flying Dutchman or the Ancient Mariner: if it did not exist, Mary Shelley, or Gustav Doré, would have dreamed it up.
> — Tim Mackintosh-Smith *Yemen* (1997)

flying picket a person who, with others, travels to picket any workplace where there is an industrial dispute.

flying saucer a disc-shaped flying craft supposedly piloted by aliens, a UFO; the term is recorded from the late 1940s.

Flying Scotsman an LNER steam locomotive of Sir Nigel Gresley's A3 Pacific design, once used as the daily express train between London (King's Cross) and Edinburgh, and now preserved.

flying squad a division of a police force or other organization which is capable of reaching an incident quickly; the term is recorded from the late 1920s, and the rhyming slang *Sweeney Todd* from the mid 1930s.

Errol Flynn (1909–59), Australian-born American actor. His usual role was the swashbuckling hero of romantic costume dramas in films such as *Captain Blood* (1935) and *The Adventures of Robin Hood* (1938).

FOB acronym for a *friend of Bill Clinton*, especially one of his close circle of advisers and contacts; the term is recorded from 1992, the year in which he won his first presidential election, and was applied particularly to those who had been associated with him during his term as Governor of Arkansas.

Foggy Bottom in the US, a nickname for the State Department, from the traditional name of a swampy piece of land in Washington near Hamburg village.

> Like all noncitizens aspiring to marry into Foggy Bottom, I had to be screened.
> — Bette Bao Lord *Legacies* (1990)

foil a thin leaf of metal placed under a precious stone to increase its brilliance; in architecture, a leaf-shaped curve formed by the cusping of an arch or circle.

Folger Shakespeare Memorial Library a library in Washington DC, dedicated in 1932 as the gift of Henry Clay Folger (1857–1930) and his wife, which contains the greatest collection in the US of Shakespeareana; this includes 79 copies of the First Folio.

Folies-Bergère a variety theatre in Paris, opened in 1869, known for its lavish productions featuring nude and semi-nude female performers.

> Young men's dreams . . . of setting up an island casino at The Drome with *Folies Bergère* girls.
> — Alan Warner *These Demented Lands* (1997)

folio an individual leaf of paper or parchment, either loose as one of a series or forming part of a bound volume, which is numbered on the recto or front side only.

Recorded from late Middle English, the word comes from Latin, ablative of *folium* 'leaf', in medieval Latin used in references to mean 'on leaf so-and-so'. The original sense of *in folio* (from Italian *in foglio*) was 'in the form of a full-sized sheet or leaf folded once (designating the largest size of book)'.

folklore the traditional beliefs, customs, and stories of a community, passed through the generations by word of mouth; a body of popular myth and beliefs relating to a particular place, activity, or group of people.

follow-my-leader a children's game in which the participants must copy the actions and words of a person who has been chosen as leader.

he that follows freits, freits will follow him proverbial saying, early 18th century; *freits* here are troubles.

folly a costly ornamental building with no practical purpose, especially a tower or mock-Gothic ruin built in a large garden or park.

Folsom a Palaeo-Indian culture of Central and North America, dated to about 10,500–8,000 years ago. The culture is distinguished by fluted stone projectile points or spearheads (**Folsom points**), the discovery of which (in 1926) forced a radical re-thinking of the date at which humans first inhabited the New World. The name comes (in the early 20th century) from *Folsom*, New Mexico, the area where remains were first found.

Fomors the sea-giants of Gaelic mythology. They are represented as more ancient than the gods (the ➤ Tuatha *Dé Danann*) and as having been ousted by them and destroyed at the battle of Moytura.

fons et origo the source and origin of something; the phrase is Latin, originally as *fons et origo mali* 'the source and origin of evil'.

font in printing, a set of type of one particular face and size. The word is recorded from the late 16th century, denoting the action or process of casting or founding, and comes from French *fonte*, from *fondre* 'to melt'.

Fontevraud in France, the site of a major Bene-dictine abbey of the 11th and 12th centuries; Henry II of England, Eleanor of Aquitaine, and their son Richard I are buried there.

Margot Fonteyn (1919–91), English ballet dancer. She danced all the classical ballerina roles and cre-ated many new ones for the Royal Ballet. In 1962 she began a celebrated partnership with Rudolf Nur-eyev, dancing with him in *Giselle* and *Romeo and Juliet*. In 1979 she was named *prima ballerina assoluta*, a title given only three times in the history of ballet.

Fonthill Abbey the Gothic house in Wiltshire of ➤ *William* Beckford; he is said to have spent over a quarter of a million of it in the course of sixteen years, but when he was forced through debts in 1822 to sell the property, and the public were admitted, Hazlitt described it as, 'a desert of magnificence, a glittering waste of laborious idleness, a cathedral turned into a toyshop, an immense museum of all that is most curious and costly, and at the same time most worthless.'

fool see also ➤ April *Fool*, ➤ at forty *every man is a fool or his own physician*, ➤ children *and fools tell the truth*, ➤ fortune *favours fools*, ➤ *Paradise of* Fools, ➤ *the* Ship *of Fools*, ➤ Wisest *Fool in Chris-tendom*,

fool historical term for a jester or clown, especially one retained in a great household; the term in this sense is recorded from late Middle English.

a **fool** and his money are soon parted proverbial saying, late 16th century.

a **fool** at forty is a fool indeed proverbial saying, early 16th century, from Edward Young (1683–1765).

there's no **fool** like an old fool proverbial saying, mid 16th century.

a **fool** may give a wise man counsel proverbial saying, mid 14th century.

as the **fool** thinks, so the bell clinks traditional saying, late Middle English; meaning that a foolish person believes what he wishes to believe.

a **fool's** bolt is soon shot proverbial saying, Mid-dle English; meaning that a fool has little power of perseverance.

fool's gold a brassy yellow mineral that can be mistaken for gold, especially pyrite.

Feast of Fools a burlesque festival which in the Middle Ages was sometimes celebrated in churches on New Year's Day.

All Fools' Day a humorous term for 1 April as a day for testing the credulity of others; recorded from the early 18th century, and probably modelled on *All Saints' Day* and *All Souls' Day*.

fools and bairns should never see half-done work proverbial saying, early 18th century.

fools ask questions that wise men cannot an-swer proverbial saying, mid 17th century.

fools build houses and wise men live in them proverbial saying, late 17th century.

fools for luck proverbial saying, mid 19th century.

fools rush in where angels fear to tread pro-verbial saying, early 18th century; from Pope's *An Essay on Criticism* (1711).

foolscap a size of paper, about 330 x 200 (or 400) mm. It is said to be named from a former water-mark representing a fool's cap.

foot see also ➤ *the* bishop *has put his foot in it*, ➤ boot *is on the other foot*, ➤ dusty *-foot*, ➤ *one* white *foot, buy him*.

foot a unit of linear measure equal to 12 inches (30.48 cm), so named because it was originally based on the length of a man's foot.

football see ➤ fantasy *football*.

footloose and fancy-free unencumbered with responsibilities; an elaboration of *footloose* which is recorded in this sense from the late 19th century.

footman see ➤ RUNNING *footman.*

footprint see ➤ ECOLOGICAL *footprint.*

Footsie informal term for the trademark ➤ FTSE *index.* Recorded from the 1980s, the expression is a fanciful elaboration of *FTSE,* influenced by *footsie.*

forbear see ➤ BEAR *and forbear.*

Forbidden City an area of Beijing (Peking) containing the former imperial palaces, to which entry was forbidden to all except the members of the imperial family and their servants.

The name *Forbidden City* is also given to Lhasa in Tibet, which as the centre of Tibetan Buddhism was closed to foreign visitors until the 20th century.

forbidden fruit the fruit forbidden to Adam in the garden of Eden; with reference to Genesis 2:17, 'But of the tree of the knowledge of good and evil, thou shalt not eat of it.' The term *forbidden fruit,* recorded from the mid 17th century, often implies its attraction.

forbid the banns raise an objection to an intended marriage, especially in church following the reading of the ➤ BANNS.

force see ➤ DELTA *Force.*

forcible-feeble a person disguising feebleness under a show of force; with allusion to one of Falstaff's reluctant recruits in Shakespeare's *2 Henry IV* (1597), who is addressed as 'Most forcible Feeble'.

Henry Ford (1863–1947), American motor manufacturer. A pioneer of large-scale mass production, he founded the Ford Motor Company, which in 1909 produced his famous Model T, of which he is reported to have said, 'Any customer can have a car painted any colour that he wants so long as it is black.'

Ford Foundation created in 1936 by Henry Ford and his son Edsel; after their deaths it became the world's largest philanthropic endowment.

Fordism the use in manufacturing industry of the methods pioneered by Henry Ford, typified by large-scale mechanized mass production.

forecastle the forward part of a ship below the deck, traditionally used as the crew's living quarters; also called (reflecting the pronunciation) **fo'c's'le.**

Foreign and Commonwealth Office the British government department dealing with foreign affairs; also (and earlier) known as the **Foreign Office.**

foreign devil in China, a foreigner, especially a European, a translation of Chinese *(faan) kwai ló* '(foreign) devil fellow'; the term is recorded in English from the mid 19th century.

Foreign Legion a military formation of the French army founded in the 1830s to fight France's colonial wars. Composed, except for the higher ranks, of non-Frenchmen, the Legion was famed for its audacity and endurance. Its most famous campaigns were in French North Africa in the late 19th and early 20th centuries. Although its original purpose has been lost, it is still in existence, in greatly reduced form.

In the 19th and early 20th centuries, the *Foreign Legion* provided the background for a number of romantic British adventures stories, as Ouida's *Under Two Flags* (1867) and P. G. Wren's *Beau Geste* (1924), in which upper-class Englishmen wrongly suspected of crime joined the ranks of the Legion under an alias.

> I didn't take seriously his flippant suggestion that he could always escape retribution, like a latter-day Beau Geste, by enlisting in the French Foreign Legion.
> — Don McCullin *Unreasonable Behaviour* (1990)

Foreign Secretary in the UK, the government minister who heads the Foreign and Commonwealth Office; the role was famously referred to by the Labour politician Aneurin Bevan in 1957, when speaking against a motion proposing unilateral nuclear disarmament at the Labour Party Conference, 'If you carry this resolution you will send Britain's Foreign Secretary naked into the conference chamber.'

forelock see ➤ *take* TIME *by the forelock.*

forest originally, a wooded area, especially owned by the monarch, kept for hunting and having its own laws and officers; the term is recorded from Middle English (also denoting any uncultivated land) and comes via Old French from Latin *forestis (silva),* literally '(wood) outside'.

See also ➤ *Forest of* ARDEN, ➤ NEW *Forest.*

Forest City an informal name for Cleveland, Ohio.

Forest Lawn in California, a large cemetery outside Los Angeles, noted for its landscaping and elaborate statuary; the name is sometimes used allusively.

This is Forest Lawnese for saying that it is a replica of the fabulous Washington statue.
— Paul Theroux *Translating LA* (1994)

forest laws in Britain, laws relating to the government of the royal forests, enacted by William I and other Norman kings; they were administered by *forest courts*.

foretold see ➤ LONG *foretold, long last; short notice, soon past*.

forewarned is forearmed proverbial saying, early 16th century.

Forfar a town in eastern Scotland which is noted for its castle, the meeting place in 1057 of an early Scottish Parliament and the home of several Scottish kings. **Forfarshire** was, from the 16th century until 1928, the name of what is now Angus.

forgery a forged or copied document, signature, banknote, or work of art; notable forgers have included Dr Dodd (1729–77), the ➤ MACARONI *Parson* executed in 1777, ➤ *William Henry* IRELAND (1777–1835), ➤ *Thomas James* WISE (1859–1937), ➤ *Tom* KEATING (1917–84), and ➤ *Hans van* MEEGEREN (1889–1947).

forget-me-not a low-growing plant of the borage family, which typically has blue flowers and is a popular ornamental. The name, which is mid 16th-century, translates the Old French name *ne m'oubliez mye*; the plant was said to have the virtue of ensuring that the wearer of the flower would never be forgotten by a lover.

forgive see ➤ *to* ERR *is human (to forgive divine)*, ➤ *to* KNOW *all is to forgive all*.

the Forgotten Army the British army in Burma after the fall of Rangoon in 1942 and the evacuation west, and the subsequent cutting by the Japanese of the supply link from India to Nationalist China, said to derive from Lord Louis Mountbatten's encouragement to his troops after taking over as supreme Allied commander in South-East Asia, 'You are not the Forgotten Army—no one's even heard of you.'

the Forgotten Man a phrase coined by William Graham Sumner in a speech at Yale University in 1885:

The forgotten man works and votes—generally he prays—but his chief business in life is to pay . . . Who

and where is the forgotten man in this case, who will have to pay for it all?
— William Graham Summer *The Forgotten Man* (1885)

The term was later used by Franklin Roosevelt when in a radio broadcast of 1932 he referred to 'the forgotten man at the bottom of the economic pyramid'.

fork see also ➤ CAUDINE *Forks*, ➤ FINGERS *were made before forks*, ➤ MORTON's *Fork*, ➤ SILVER-*fork*.

fork in ancient Rome, the *furca* or yoke under which defeated enemies were made to pass as a token of submission.

Forkbeard nickname of Sweyn I (d.1014), king of Denmark and England, father of ➤ CANUTE.

forked cap in the 16th and 17th centuries, a (derogatory) term for mitre.

forked lightning lightning that is visible in the form of a zigzag or branching line across the sky.

forked tongue a lying or deceitful tongue (frequently in **with a forked tongue**); the reference is to the forked tongue of a snake as a symbol of deceit.

forlorn hope a persistent or desperate hope that is unlikely to be fulfilled. Recorded from the mid 16th century, the phrase comes from Dutch *verloren hoop* 'lost troop', originally denoting a band of soldiers picked to begin an attack, many of whom would not survive; the current sense (mid 17th century), derives from a misunderstanding of the etymology.

form criticism analysis of the Bible by tracing the history of its content of parables, psalms, and other literary forms.

form follows function guiding principle taught by proponents of the architectural Modernist movement; the phrase was coined by the American architect Louis Henri Sullivan (1856–1924).

Simon Forman (1552–1611), physician and astrologer, who in his *Booke of Plaies* (preserved in a manuscript in the Bodleian Library, Oxford) records and comments on visits to performances of Shakespeare's *Macbeth* and *The Winter's Tale* at the Globe theatre in 1611 and to an unspecified *Cymbeline*.

George Formby (1904–61), English comedian. He became famous for his numerous musical films in the 1930s in which he projected the image of a Lancashire working lad and accompanied his songs on the ukulele.

former see ➤ *Former* PROPHETS.

Formosa former name for Taiwan, an island off the south-east coast of China where the Nationalist Chinese State was set up by ➤ CHIANG *Kai-shek* in 1949; the name is from Portuguese and means 'beautiful'. The literary impostor ➤ *George* PSALMANAZAR (1679?–1763) presented himself as a native of *Formosa*, compiling a catechism in its supposed language.

Formula One an international form of motor racing, whose races are called Grand Prix.

fort see also ➤ BENT's *Fort*.

Fort Knox a US military reservation in Kentucky, famous as the site of the depository (built in 1936) which holds the bulk of the nation's gold bullion in its vaults.

> We are sort of the Fort Knox for plants.
> — *Agricultural Research* September 1998

Fortean of, relating to, or denoting paranormal phenomena; the word comes from the name of Charles H. *Fort* (1874–1932), American student of paranormal phenomena.

painting the Forth Bridge the steel structure of the *Forth Bridge* in Scotland has required constant repainting; this is consequently an expression for undertaking a task that can never be completed.

forties see also ➤ HUNGRY *forties*, ➤ *the* ROARING *forties*.

the Forties the central North Sea between Scotland and southern Norway, so called from its prevailing depth of forty fathoms or more. The area is an important centre of North Sea oil production.

Fortnum and Mason a luxury grocery store in Piccadilly, London, founded in 1707, and sometimes referred to allusively for the quality traditionally typified by its merchandise.

> I . . . can only look on all of it as real Woolworth stuff (in contrast to, say, Mozart, who is vintage Fortnum and Mason).
> — *Guardian* 21 March 1974

fortunate see also ➤ JOHN *the Fortunate*.

the Fortunate Islands originally (translating Latin *Fortunatae Insulae*) a name for fabulous islands in the Western Ocean, the abode of the blessed dead; later, a name for the Canary Isles.

Fortunatus's purse the subject of a 15th-century romance, in which the beggar *Fortunatus* is given by

Fortune a purse from which he can take ten pieces of gold whenever he wishes; however, because he has chosen wealth over long life, he dies just as he has reached the height of worldly success.

> Most of us, not possessing the purse of Fortunatus, have to get our furnishings a little at a time
> — *American Woman* August 1920

Fortune chance or luck as a power in human affairs, often personified as a goddess; the word comes (in Middle English, via Old French) from Latin *Fortuna*, the name of a goddess personifying luck or chance. The emblem of Fortune is a wheel, indicating mutability.

See also ➤ SOLDIER *of fortune*, ➤ WHEEL *of Fortune*.

fortune favours fools proverbial saying, mid 16th century.

fortune favours the brave proverbial saying, late 14th century.

Fortune 500 in the US, an annual list of the five hundred most profitable US industrial corporations, published in *Fortune* magazine.

Fortune's wheel another term for the ➤ WHEEL *of Fortune*.

forty the name **The Forty** is given to the members of the Académie Française; also called **the Forty Immortals**.

See also ➤ *a* FOOL *at forty is a fool indeed*, ➤ FORTIES, ➤ LIFE *begins at forty*, ➤ RULE 43.

at forty every man is a fool or his own physician traditional saying; an early version (giving thirty as the key age) is attributed to the emperor Tiberius by Tacitus in the *Annals*, 'He had always a sneer for the arts of the physicians, and for men who, after thirty years of life, needed the counsel of a stranger in order to distinguish things salutary to their system from things deleterious.' Plutarch in his *Moralia* says, 'I have heard that Tiberius Caesar once said that a man over sixty who holds out his hand to a physician is ridiculous.'

the Forty-five an informal name for the Jacobite rebellion of 1745.

forty hours in the Roman Catholic Church the continuous exposition of the Host for forty hours, used as an occasion of special devotion or intercession.

Forty Martyrs of England and Wales name given to a group of English and Welsh Roman Catholics canonized in 1970 as representing those martyred for their faith between 1535 and 1679.

□ **FEAST DAY** Their feast day is 25 October.

forty-niner a seeker for gold in the Californian gold rush of 1849.

forty-ninth parallel the parallel of latitude 49° north of the equator, especially as forming the boundary between Canada and the US west of the Lake of the Woods.

forty stripes save one forty stripes were laid down by Jewish law as the maximum punishment to be inflicted; it became customary for the punishment to be set at the maximum number 'save one'.

Forty-two-line Bible printed at Mainz 1453–5, and sometimes attributed to Johann Gutenberg (the name comes from the number of lines in each column).

forty years on opening words of the Harrow school song by the English schoolmaster E. E Bowen (1836–1901):

> Forty years on, when afar and asunder
> Parted are those who are singing to-day.
> — E. E. Bowen 'Forty Years On' (Harrow School Song, published 1886)

The words were used by Alan Bennett as the title of a satirical comedy (1968) set in an English public school.

forum in an ancient Roman city, a public square or marketplace used for judicial and other business.

Fosse Way an ancient road in Britain, so called from the *fosse* or ditch that used to run along each side of it. It ran from Axminster to Lincoln, via Bath and Leicester (about 300 km, 200 miles), and marked the limit of the first stage of the Roman occupation (mid 1st century AD).

Jean Bernard Léon Foucault (1819–68), French physicist. He is chiefly remembered for the huge pendulum (**Foucault's pendulum**) which he hung from the roof of the Panthéon in Paris in 1851 to demonstrate the rotation of the earth. He also invented the gyroscope and was the first to determine the velocity of light reasonably accurately.

foul anchor an anchor that has become entangled with a rope or cable, as the badge of the British Admiralty.

Founding Father a member of the convention that drew up the constitution of the US in 1787.

Early use of the phrase is particularly associated with US president Warren G. Harding (1865–1923), who in his inaugural address of 1921 referred to his 'belief in the divine inspiration of the founding fathers'.

fountain see also ➤ *Fountain of* ARDENNE.

Fountain of Youth a mythical fountain which according to legend had the power of renewing youth; it was said in the 12th-century French work *Roman d'Alisandre* to have been a sidestream of the Euphrates in which Alexander the Great and his army bathed, and were restored to the prime of life.

The belief in the existence of such a fountain was widespread in the Middle Ages. After the discovery of America it was said to be in the Bahamas, and the Spanish explorer ➤ *Juan* PONCE *de León*, discoverer of Florida, was authorized in 1512 to look for and settle ➤ BIMINI, the island where the *Fountain of Youth* was said to be.

four recorded from Old English (in form *fēower*) and of Germanic origin, the word comes from an Indo-European root shared by Latin *quattuor* and Greek *tessares*.

See also ➤ ANNALS *of the Four Masters*, ➤ CLAUSE *Four*, ➤ *the* FAB *Four*, ➤ FIRST *Four Ships*, ➤ GANG *of Four*.

four-colour problem a mathematical problem to prove that any plane map can be coloured with only four colours so that no two same-coloured regions have a common boundary.

the four corners of the earth the ends of the earth; *four corners* is traditionally used to indicate the limits or scope of something.

four eyes see more than two proverbial saying, late 16th century.

the four freedoms the four essential human freedoms as proclaimed in a speech to Congress by Franklin D. Roosevelt in 1941: freedom of speech and expression, freedom of worship, freedom from want, and freedom from fear.

Four-H club in North America, a club for the instruction of young people in citizenry and agriculture (from supposedly improving head, heart, hands, and health).

the Four Horsemen of the Apocalypse War, Famine, Death, and Pestilence; they are traditionally identified with the riders of the white, red, black, and pale horses seen in Revelation:

> And I looked, and behold a pale horse: and his name
> that sat on him was death, and Hell followed with him.
> And power was given unto them over the fourth part of
> the earth, to kill with the sword, and with hunger, and
> with death, and with the beasts of the earth.
> — Bible (AV) Revelation ch. 6, v. 8

the **Four** Hundred in the 19th century, the members of the highest social group in New York.

four-letter word any of several short words referring to sexual or excretory functions, regarded as coarse or offensive; the term is recorded from the 1920s.

the **Four Maries** the four ladies-in-waiting of Mary Queen of Scots who were brought up with the Queen, Mary Beaton, Mary Fleming, Mary Livingstone, and Mary Seton; in a traditional and unhistorical ballad 'The Queen's Maries', they are named as Mary Beaton, Mary Seton, Mary Carmichael, and Mary Hamilton, who tells her story on the eve of her execution for killing her illegitimate child:

> Yestreen the Queen had four Maries,
> The night she'll hae but three;
> There was Marie Seaton, and Marie Beaton,
> And Marie Carmichael, and me.
> — Anonymous 'The Queen's Maries'

four-minute men in the First World War in the US, members of a volunteer organization who gave talks four minutes in duration to church congregations and cinema and theatre audiences to increase support for the war in Europe.

four-minute mile a mile run by an athlete in four minutes or less, first achieved by Roger Bannister in 1954.

four noble truths the four central beliefs containing the essence of Buddhist teaching; they are that human life is characterized by frustration and suffering, that the cause of this is desire and greed, that desire must therefore be got rid of, and that following the ➤ EIGHTFOLD *path* is the way to achieve this.

the **four seas** the seas surrounding the British Isles; the expression **within the four seas** traditionally meant within the boundaries of Great Britain.

Jean Fourier (1768–1830), French mathematician. His studies involved him in the solution of partial differential equations by the method of separation of variables and superposition; this led him to analyse the series and integrals that are now known by

his name. **Fourier series** are used widely for describing periodic phenomena and for solving many partial differential equations.

Fourierism a system for the reorganization of society into self-sufficient cooperatives, in accordance with the principles of the French socialist Charles *Fourier* (d. 1837).

fourposter see ➤ DEVIL's *fourposter*.

Fourteen Holy Helpers a group of saints, also known as the *Auxiliary Saints*, whose intercessory powers in human affairs, especially illness, were regarded as particularly effective; their collective cult was especially strong in the Rhineland between the 14th and 16th centuries.

Fourteen Holy Helpers

Saint	Feast Day
Acacius	8 May
Barbara	4 December
Blaise	3 February
Catherine of Alexandria	25 November
Christopher	25 July
Cyricus	8 August
Denis	9 October
Erasmus	2 June
Eustace	20 September
George	23 April
Giles	1 September
Margaret of Antioch	20 July
Pantaleon	27 July
Vitus	15 June

Fourteen Points set out by US President Woodrow Wilson (1856–1924) in a speech to the US Congress, 8 January 1918, as the basis for peace negotiations in the First World War; the first point was 'Open covenants of peace, openly arrived at'.

fourth dimension a postulated spatial dimension additional to those determining length, area, and volume; the phrase is recorded from the late 19th century, and is now also used in physics to denote time as analogous to linear dimensions.

the **fourth** estate the press; a group regarded as having power in the land equivalent to that of one of the three Estates of the Realm, the Crown, the House of Lords, and the House of Commons. The term derives from a usage by Macaulay:

> The gallery in which the reporters sit has become a
> fourth estate of the realm.
> — Lord Macaulay *Essay Contributed to the Edinburgh
> Review* (1843) 'Hallam'.

the **Fourth** of July in the US, ➤ INDEPENDENCE *Day*.

the **Fourth** of June the birthday of George III (1738–1820), speech day at Eton because of his interest in the school.

Fourth Party a group of politicians (1880–5) led by Lord Randolph Churchill, forming a party independent of the three existing political parties.

Fourth Republic the republican regime in France between the end of the Second World War (1945) and the introduction of a new constitution by Charles de Gaulle in 1958.

Fourth World those countries and communities considered to be the poorest and most underdeveloped of the Third World.

fowl see ➤ *neither* FISH *nor fowl nor good red herring*.

Fowler short title for *Modern English Usage* (1926), the moderately prescriptive guide to style and idiom by the English lexicographer and grammarian H. W. *Fowler* (1858–1933).

the **Fowler** nickname of Henry I (876–936), king of Germany from 919.

fox the *fox* is proverbial for its artfulness and cunning; in Ben Jonson's play, the miser who deceives those around him with promises of wealth is named *Volpone* (in Italian, 'Fox'). It figures in a number of fables, such as that giving rise to the expression ➤ SOUR *grapes*.

See also ➤ *the* QUICK *brown fox jumps over the lazy dog*, ➤ REYNARD *the Fox*, ➤ SWAMP *Fox*.

Brer Fox in the stories of 'Uncle Remus', the determined enemy of ➤ *Brer* RABBIT, who despite his own strength and cunning is in the end always outwitted by him.

Charles James Fox (1749–1806), British statesman. He became a Whig MP in 1768, supporting American independence and the French Revolution, and collaborated with Lord North to form a coalition government (1783–4), but then remained in opposition until 1806, when he took office again as Foreign Secretary and passed an anti-slavery bill through Parliament.

George Fox (1624–91), English preacher and founder of the Society of Friends (Quakers). He taught that truth is the inner voice of God speaking to the soul and rejected priesthood and ritual. Despite repeated imprisonment, he established a society called the 'Friends of the Truth' (*c*.1650), which later became the Society of Friends.

Fox Sisters Margaret *Fox* (1836–93), with her sisters Katherine and Leah, conducted a series of sensational seances in upstate New York; although they were later discredited, they inaugurated a vogue for spiritualism.

Foxe's Martyrs informal name for *Actes and Monuments*, the martyrology by the Protestant divine John *Foxe* (1516–87).

foxfire the phosphorescent light emitted by certain fungi on decaying timber.

foxglove a tall plant with erect spikes of pinkish-purple (or white) flowers shaped like the fingers of gloves, which is a source of the drug digitalis.

fractal a curve or geometrical figure, each part of which has the same statistical character as the whole. Such figures are described mathematically as having fractional dimensions. They are useful in modelling structures (such as eroded coastlines or snowflakes) in which similar patterns recur at progressively smaller scales, and in describing partly random or chaotic phenomena such as crystal growth, fluid turbulence, and galaxy formation.

fragile X syndrome an inherited condition characterized by an X chromosome that is abnormally susceptible to damage, especially by folic acid deficiency. Affected individuals tend to be mentally handicapped.

Jean-Honoré Fragonard (1732–1806), French painter in the rococo style. He is famous for landscapes and for erotic canvases such as *The Swing* (*c*.1766) and *The Progress of Love* (1771).

Fraktur a German style of black-letter type. The name comes from Latin *fractura* 'fracture', because of its angularity.

franc the basic monetary unit of France, Belgium, Switzerland, Luxembourg, and several other countries, equal to 100 centimes. The name comes via Old French from Latin *Francorum Rex* 'king of the Franks', the legend on gold coins struck in the 14th century in the reign of Jean le Bon.

franc-archer a member of a body of archers established by Charles VII, and exempted from taxes in consideration of their services. The name in French means literally 'free archer'.

franc-tireur a member of a corps of light infantry, originating in the wars of the French Revolution, and having an organization distinct from that of the regular army; the name is recorded from the early 19th century, and comes from French *franc* 'free' + *tireur* 'shooter'.

France the name of the modern country derives ultimately from the *Franks* (see ➤ FRANK) who settled it.

See ➤ CONSTABLE *of France*, ➤ FAIR *maid of France*, ➤ *the* MATTER *of France*, ➤ SHE-*Wolf of France*.

Francesca da Rimini the wife of Giovanni Malatesta of *Rimini*, who fell in love with her husband's younger brother Paolo and was put to death with him; her story is told in the fifth canto of Dante's *Inferno*. Her name is used for its rhyming effect by W. S. Gilbert in Patience (1881), 'Francesca di Rimini, miminy, piminy, *Je-ne-sais-quoi* young man!', but more seriously, **Paolo and Francesca** are referred to a type of doomed and sinful pair of lovers.

> He was swayed by some power . . . like that great wind of Hell which drove Paolo and Francesca ceaselessly on.
> — W. Somerset Maugham *Of Human Bondage* (1915)

Francis see also ➤ *St Francis* XAVIER.

St Francis de Sales (1567–1622), French bishop. One of the leaders of the Counter-Reformation, he was bishop of Geneva 1602–22 and co-founder of the Order of the Visitation, an order of nuns (1610). The Salesian order (founded in 1859) is named after him.
　☐ **FEAST DAY** His feast day is 24 January.

St Francis of Assisi (*c*.1181–1226), Italian monk, founder of the Franciscan order. Born into a wealthy family, he renounced his inheritance and devoted himself to his religious calling. He soon attracted followers, founding the Franciscan order in 1209 and drew up its original rule (based on complete poverty). He is revered for his generosity, simple faith, humility, and love of nature, and is often shown preaching to the birds.
　☐ **FEAST DAY** His feast day is 4 October.

Franciscan a friar, sister, or lay member of a Christian religious order founded in 1209 by St Francis of Assisi or based on its rule, and noted for its preachers and missionaries.

The extremely austere rule written by ➤ *St* FRANCIS *of Assisi* in 1209 was modified in 1221 and received papal approval in 1223, but divergences of practice led to the separation of the Friars Minor of the Observance (the Observants) and the Friars Minor Conventual (the Conventuals) in 1517, and to the foundation of the stricter Friars Minor Capuchin (the ➤ CAPUCHINS) in 1529. The order of Franciscan nuns was founded by ➤ *St* CLARE (*c*.1212) under the direction of St Francis; they are known as 'Poor Clares'. There is also a third order of lay associates (tertiaries), and a Franciscan order within the Anglican Church.

Noted Franciscans include ➤ *St* ANTHONY *of Padua*, ➤ *St* BONAVENTURA, ➤ *Roger* BACON, and ➤ WILLIAM *of Occam*.

Franco-Prussian War the war of 1870–1 between France (under Napoleon III) and Prussia, in which Prussian troops advanced into France and decisively defeated the French at Sedan. The defeat marked the end of the French Second Empire. For Prussia, the proclamation of the new German Empire at Versailles was the climax of Bismarck's ambitions to unite Germany.

franglais a blend of French and English, either French speech that makes excessive use of English expressions, or unidiomatic French spoken by an English person. Recorded from the 1960s, the word was coined in French from a blend of *français* 'French' and *anglais* 'English'.

Frank a member of a Germanic people that conquered Gaul in the 6th century and controlled much of western Europe for several centuries afterwards. Also (in the eastern Mediterranean region), a person of western European nationality or descent.

The name is recorded from Old English (in form *Franca*) and is of Germanic origin, perhaps from the name of a weapon and related to Old English *franca* 'javelin'; it is ultimately related to *France* and *French*.

frank an official mark or signature on a letter or parcel, especially to indicate that postage has been paid or does not need to be paid. The term was originally used in the early 18th century to mean the superscribed signature of a member or parliament or other eminent person entitled to send letters free of charge (ultimately from *frank* meaning 'free').

Anne Frank (1929–45), German Jewish girl known for her diary, which records the experiences of her family living for two years in hiding from the Nazis in occupied Amsterdam. They were eventually betrayed and sent to concentration camps; Anne and her sister died in ➤ BELSEN, and of the family only the father Otto Frank survived the war.

> I want to go on living even after death!
> — Anne Frank diary, 4 April 1944

frankalmoign a feudal tenure in England by which a religious body could hold land perpetually, usually in return for praying for the soul of the donor and his descendants.

Frankenfood a derogatory term for food derived from genetically-modified produce, a shortening of *Frankenstein food*; the word is recorded from 1992, and more recently *Frankenscience* has also been recorded.

> Ever since Mary Shelley's baron rolled his improved human out of the lab, scientists have been bringing such good things to life. If they want to sell us Frankenfood, perhaps it's time to gather the villagers, light some torches, and head to the castle.
> — Paul Lewis in *New York Times* 16 June 1992

Frankenstein a character in the novel *Frankenstein, or the Modern Prometheus* (1818) by Mary Shelley. Baron Frankenstein is a scientist who creates and brings to life a manlike monster which eventually turns on him and destroys him; *Frankenstein* is not the name of the monster itself, as is often assumed, and sometimes suggested in allusive use.

In the 1990s, the name has been used by opponents of the development of genetically-modified crops in the expressions **Frankenstein food** or ➤ FRANKENFOOD.

> The Frankenstein monsters of pollution, overcrowding, global warming, and techno-ennui—our creations, not nature's—are out of control.
> — *New Yorker* 6 October 1997

Frankfurt School a school of philosophy of the 1920s, whose adherents were involved in a reappraisal of Marxism, particularly in terms of the cultural and aesthetic dimension of modern industrial society. Principal figures include Theodor Adorno, Max Horkheimer, and Herbert Marcuse.

frankincense an aromatic gum resin obtained from an African tree and burnt as incense; traditionally used in the Jewish Temple. It was one of the gifts, with gold and myrrh, brought by the ➤ MAGI to the infant Jesus, and because it was also used by magicians and sorcerers may symbolize their submission to him.

The word is recorded from late Middle English, and comes from Old French *franc encens*, literally 'high-quality incense'.

franklin a landowner of free but not noble birth in the 14th and 15th centuries in England. The word is recorded from Middle English, and comes from Anglo-Latin *francalanus*, from *francalis* 'held without dues'.

Benjamin Franklin (1706–90), American statesman, inventor, and scientist. A wealthy printer and publisher, he was one of the signatories to the peace between the US and Great Britain after the War of American Independence. His main scientific achievements were the formulation of a theory of electricity, which introduced positive and negative electricity, and a demonstration of the electrical nature of lightning. This led to the invention of the lightning conductor, as reflected in the inscription for a bust of Franklin composed by the French economist and statesman A. R. J. Turgot (1727–81):

> *Eripuit coelo fulmen, sceptrumque tyrannis.* He snatched the lightning shaft from heaven, and the sceptre from tyrants.
> — A. R. J. Turgot inscription for a bust of Benjamin Franklin

John Franklin (1786–1847), Arctic explorer and author of two *Narratives* of voyages to the Polar Sea. His final voyage of discovery in *Erebus* and *Terror* in search of the North-West Passage, began in 1845, and resulted in disaster. Numerous relief expeditions were sent out including one organized by his widow which found a record of the expedition proving that Franklin had discovered the North-West Passage.

frankpledge in Anglo-Saxon law, each of the mutually responsible members of a *tithing*, or company of ten householders; the **view of frankpledge** was the name given to a court held periodically for the production of the members of a tithing or later of a hundred or a manor.

Franz Josef (1830–1916), emperor of Austria 1848–1916 and king of Hungary 1867–1916. He gave Hungary equal status with Austria in 1867. His annexation of Bosnia–Herzegovina (1908) contributed to European political tensions, and the assassination in Sarajevo of his heir apparent, Archduke Franz Ferdinand, precipitated the First World War.

frater historical term for the dining room or refectory of a monastery; the word is recorded from Middle English and comes from Old French, from a shortening of *refreitor*, from late Latin *refectorium* 'refectory'.

Fred see ➤ Fred KARNO.

Freddie see ➤ BLIND *Freddie.*

Frederick I (*c.*1123–90), king of Germany and Holy Roman emperor 1152–90; known as **Frederick Barbarossa** ('Redbeard'). He made a sustained attempt to subdue Italy and the papacy, but was eventually defeated at the battle of Legnano in 1176. He drowned while on his way to the Third Crusade.

Frederick II (1712–86), king of Prussia from 1740, known as **Frederick the Great**. His campaigns in the War of the Austrian Succession (1740–8) and the Seven Years War (1756–63) succeeded in considerably strengthening Prussia's position; by the end of his reign he had doubled the area of his country. He was also a distinguished patron of the arts.

Frederick William (1620–88), Elector of Brandenburg 1640–88; known as **the Great Elector**. His programme of reconstruction and reorganization following the Thirty Years War brought stability to his country and laid the basis for the expansion of Prussian power in the 18th century. In his foreign policy he sought to create a balance of power by the formation of shifting strategic alliances.

free see also ➤ *the* BEST *things in life are free*, ➤ LAND *of the Free*, ➤ WEE *Free.*

Free Church a Christian Church which has dissented or seceded from an established Church; the term is recorded from the mid 16th century.

Free Church of Scotland a strict Presbyterian Church organized by dissenting members of the established Church of Scotland in 1843. In 1900 its majority amalgamated with the United Presbyterian Church to form the United Free Church; its name was retained by the minority group, nicknamed the *Wee Free Kirk.*

free company a group of mercenaries; the use of free companion as a member of such a company is first recorded in Scott's *Ivanhoe* (1819).

Free French an organization of French troops and volunteers in exile formed under General de Gaulle in 1940. Based in London, the movement continued the war against the Axis Powers after de Gaulle appealed by radio from London for French resistance to the Franco-German armistice. Apart from organizing forces that opposed the Axis powers in French Equatorial Africa, Lebanon, and elsewhere, and co-operated with the French Resistance, its French National Committee (established in 1941) eventually developed into a provisional government for liberated France. The Free French were also involved in the liberation of Paris in 1944.

there's no such thing as a free lunch proverbial saying, mid 20th century; the variant **there ain't no such thing as a free lunch** can be expressed by the acronym *tanstaafl.*

Free Stater a member of the Irish Free State army, used particularly in the period of the civil war with anti-Treaty forces following the establishment of the Irish Free State in 1921.

free trade international trade left to its natural course without tariffs, quotas, or other restrictions. The term is first recorded in the early 19th century, in Cobbett's *Rural Rides* (1823) quoting a newspaper reference to an attempt to 'inculcate in the mind of the Bourbons wise principles of free trade'. The related *freedom of trade* had been used earlier, in Adam Smith's *Wealth of Nations* (1776).

free verse poetry that does not rhyme or have a regular rhythm; also called (from French) *vers libre.*

freebooter a pirate or lawless adventurer; the word is recorded from the late 16th century and comes from Dutch, from *vrij* 'free' + *buit* 'booty'.

freedom see also ➤ BIRD *of Freedom*, ➤ *the* FOUR *freedoms*, ➤ PRESIDENTIAL *Medal.*

Freedom of the Rule liberty granted to a Scottish advocate to plead at the English bar.

freedom ride in the US, an organized ride in buses or other public transport as a demonstration against racial segregation; the term was used particularly in the context of civil rights demonstrations of the 1960s.

freedom song in South Africa, a song or chant sung at protest gatherings and demonstrations, strongly political in content and typically in a formulaic call-and-response style.

Freedom Trail a historic route through Boston, Massachusetts, which begins and ends at Faneuil Hall, where Bostonians met to protest against British 'taxation without representation' (see ➤ BOSTON *Tea Party*) in the months preceding the War of American Independence.

freelance working for different companies at different times rather than being permanently employed by one company; originally (as two words) denoting a mercenary.

Mrs Freeman the name adopted by Sarah Churchill, duchess of Marlborough, in her correspondence with Queen Anne (➤ *Mrs* MORLEY).

Freemason a member of an international order established for mutual help and fellowship, which holds elaborate secret ceremonies.

The original *free masons* were itinerant skilled stonemasons of the 14th century, who are said to have recognized fellow craftsmen by secret signs, while the *accepted masons* were honorary members of the fraternity who began to be admitted early in the 17th century. Modern freemasonry is usually traced to the formation of the Grand Lodge in London in 1717; members are typically professionals and businessmen. Freemasons have sometimes been criticized for their secrecy, for supposed occult elements in their rituals, or for alleged corruption in business, professional, or government matters.

freezing point the temperature at which a liquid turns into a solid when cooled. It is constant for any particular liquid at a given pressure.

Gottlob Frege (1848–1925), German philosopher and mathematician, founder of modern logic. He developed a logical system for the expression of mathematics (the foundations for Bertrand Russell's work). He also worked on general questions of philosophical logic and semantics and devised his influential theory of meaning, based on his use of a distinction between what a linguistic term refers to and what it expresses.

Freischütz in German legend, a marksman or 'freeshooter' who makes a pact with the powers of evil to obtain bullets which will go wherever he chooses; *Der Freischütz* (1821) is the title of an opera by Carl Maria von Weber (1784–1824).

freits ➤ *he that* FOLLOWS *freits, freits will follow him.*

John Charles Frémont (1813–90), American explorer and politician. He was responsible for exploring several viable routes to the Pacific across the Rockies in the 1840s.

French see also ➤ *the* FIGHTING *French,* ➤ FREE *French.*

French leave absence from work or duty without permission, said to derive from the French custom of leaving a dinner or ball without saying goodbye to the host or hostess. The phrase was first recorded

in the late 18th century; the equivalent French expression is *filer à l'Anglaise*, literally 'to escape in the style of the English'.

French Republican Calendar a reformed calendar officially introduced by the French Republican government on 5 October 1793, and taken to have started on the equinox of 22 September 1792, the day of the proclamation of the Republic. It had twelve months of thirty days each (divided into three weeks of ten days), running from *Vendemiaire* to *Fructidor*, and with five days of festivals at the year's end (six in leap years). It was abandoned under the Napoleonic regime and the Gregorian calendar was formally reinstated on 1 January 1806.

French Republican Calendar: months

MONTH	ORIGINAL DATES
Vendemiare	22 September to 21 October
Brumaire	22 October to 20 November
Frimaire	21 November to 20 December
Nivose	21 December to 19 January
Pluviose	20 January to 18 February
Ventose	19 February to 20 March
Germinal	21 March to 19 April
Floréal	20 April to 19 May
Prairial	20 May to 18 June
Messidor	19 June to 18 July
Thermidor	19 July to 17 August
Fructidor	18 August to 16 September

French Revolution the overthrow of the Bourbon monarchy in France (1789–99). The profound political and social effects of the French Revolution mark a turning point in French history. It was the first of a series of European political upheavals, in which various groups in French society found common cause in opposing the feudal structure of the state, with its privileged Establishment and discredited monarchy. The Revolution began with the meeting of the legislative assembly (the States General) in May 1789, when the French government was already in crisis; the Bastille was stormed in July of the same year.

The Revolution became steadily more radical and ruthless with power increasingly in the hands of the Jacobins and Robespierre, who in 1793 gained control of the Committee of Public Safety, a governing body originally dominated by Danton. Louis XVI's execution in January 1793 was followed by Robespierre's Reign of Terror (September 1793–July

1794). The Revolution failed to produce a stable form of republican government and after several different forms of administration the last, the Directory, was overthrown by Napoleon in 1799.

French Wars of Religion a series of religious and political conflicts in France (1562–98) involving the Protestant Huguenots on one side and Catholic groups on the other. The wars were complicated by interventions from Spain, Rome, England, the Netherlands, and elsewhere, and were not brought to an end until the defeat of the Holy League and the settlement of the Edict of Nantes.

fresco a painting done rapidly in watercolour on wet plaster on a wall or ceiling, so that the colours penetrate the plaster and become fixed as it dries; this method of painting, used in Roman times and by the great masters of the Italian Renaissance including Giotto, Masaccio, Piero della Francesca, Raphael, and Michelangelo.

The word is recorded from the late 16th century and comes from Italian, literally 'cool, fresh'. It was first recorded in the phrase *in fresco*, representing Italian *affresco* 'on the fresh (plaster)'.

fresh fields and pastures new new areas of activity, from a misquotation of Milton's 'Lycidas' (1638), 'Tomorrow to fresh woods and pastures new.'

Sigmund Freud (1856–1939), Austrian neurologist and psychotherapist. He was the first to emphasize the significance of unconscious processes in normal and neurotic behaviour, and was the founder of psychoanalysis as both a theory of personality and a therapeutic practice. He proposed the existence of an unconscious element in the mind which influences consciousness, and of conflicts in it between various sets of forces. Freud also stated the importance of a child's semi-consciousness of sex as a factor in mental development; his theory of the sexual origin of neuroses aroused great controversy.

Frey in Scandinavian mythology, the god of fertility and dispenser of rain and sunshine.

Freya in Scandinavian mythology, the goddess of love and of the night, sister of Frey.

friar a member of any of certain religious orders of men, especially the four mendicant orders (Augustinians, Carmelites, Dominicans, and Franciscans). The word is recorded from Middle English, and comes via Old French from Latin *frater* 'brother'.

See also ➤ BLACK *Friar,* ➤ CRUTCHED *Friars,* ➤ CURTAL *friar,* ➤ *Friar* TUCK, ➤ GREY *Friar,* ➤ WHITE *Friar.*

Friar Minor a Franciscan friar, so named because the Franciscans regard themselves of humbler rank than members of other orders.

Friar Rush the proper name (German *Rausch*) of the hero of a popular story, which tells of the adventures of a demon disguised as a friar.

friar's lantern a name for the *ignis fatuus* or will o' the wisp.

Friday the day of the week before Saturday and following Thursday, recorded in Old English and named for the Germanic goddess *Frigga*, as a translation of the late Latin *Veneris dies* 'day of the planet Venus'.

Friday, in memory of ➤ GOOD *Friday,* was traditionally a day of fasting and abstinence in the Christian Church; it is also often traditionally regarded as an unlucky day, with Friday 13th being particularly perilous.

In Islamic belief, Friday is regarded as the day of the week on which Adam was created (as in Genesis 1:26–7).

See also ➤ DRESS-*down Friday,* ➤ GIRL *Friday,* ➤ MAN *Friday,* ➤ *Monday's* CHILD *is fair of face.*

Fridays	
Black Friday	6 December 1745; 11 May 1866
Bloody Friday	21 June 1972
Good Friday	Friday before Easter Sunday

St Frideswide (*c.*680–727), Anglo-Saxon princess, virgin and patron of Oxford; she was first abbess of a double monastery founded on the site of what is now Christ Church Cathedral. Her cult was locally popular and her shrine was restored under Mary I, but in 1558 it was desecrated when through the agency of a Calvinist divine who wished to suppress the cult, her relics were mixed with those of the wife of one of the fellows.

❑ **FEAST DAY** Her feast days are 19 October and 12 February (the date of her translation).

friend see also ➤ *the* BEST *of friends must part,* ➤ BOSOM *friend,* ➤ FALSE *friend,* ➤ FLEXIBLE *friend,* ➤ SAVE *us from our friends.*

Friend a member of the ➤ RELIGIOUS *Society of Friends,* a Quaker; the name is recorded from the late 17th century.

a friend in need is a friend indeed proverbial saying, mid 11th century; 5th century BC in Greek.

friendly fire weapon fire coming from one's own side that causes accidental injury or death to one's own forces.

friendly society in the UK, a mutual assurance providing sickness benefits, life assurance, and pensions, originally the name of a particular fire-insurance company operating *c*.1700.

Friends of the Earth an international pressure group established in 1971 to campaign for a better awareness of and response to environmental problems.

Frigga in Scandinavian mythology, the wife of Odin and goddess of married love and of the hearth, sometimes identified with ➤ FREYA. ➤ FRIDAY is named after her.

frigidarium a cold room in an ancient Roman bath.

Frimaire the third month of the French Republican calendar (1793–1805), originally running from 21 November to 20 December. The name comes from the French *frimas* 'hoar frost'.

fringe see also ➤ CELTIC *fringe*, ➤ *the* LUNATIC *fringe*.

fringe as worn by orthodox Jews, in accordance with the command given by God to Moses in Numbers 15:38, 'Speak unto the children of Israel, and bid them that they make them fringes in the borders of their garments throughout their generations.' The fringes were to act as a reminder of the Ten Commandments.

frippery showy or unnecessary ornament in architecture, dress, or language. Recorded from the mid 16th century (denoting old or second-hand clothes), ultimately from Old French *frepe* 'rag', of unknown origin.

Frisia an ancient region of NW Europe, consisting of the Frisian Islands and parts of the mainland corresponding to the modern provinces of Friesland and Groningen in the Netherlands and the regions of Ostfriesland and Nordfriesland in NW Germany. *Frisian* is the Germanic language most closely related to English and Dutch.

Martin **Frobisher** (*c*.1535–94), English explorer, who in 1576 led an unsuccessful expedition in search of the North-West Passage. Frobisher served in Sir Francis Drake's Caribbean expedition of 1585–6 and played a prominent part in the defeat of the Spanish Armada.

frock now chiefly a woman's or girl's dress, but originally a loose outer garment, in particular a long gown with flowing sleeves worn by monks, priests, or clergy (this sense is preserved in *defrock*), and a labourer's smock-frock.

Frodo forename of the ➤ HOBBIT **Frodo Baggins** (nephew of ➤ BILBO), who is one of the central characters of *The Lord of the Rings*, and who ultimately succeeds in his quest to destroy the One Ring. Tolkien had originally chosen another name for his character; his notes on the first draft of the book read, 'Bingo Bolger-Baggins a bad name. Let Bingo = Frodo.'

Friedrich Froebel (1782–1852), German educationist and founder of the kindergarten system. Believing that play materials, practical occupations, and songs are needed to develop a child's real nature, he opened a school for young children in 1837, later naming it the *Kindergarten* ('children's garden'). He also established a teacher-training school.

frog the word *frog* was used as as a general term of abuse in Middle English, and was applied specifically to the Dutch in the 17th century; its application to the French (late 18th century) is partly alliterative, partly from the reputation of the French for eating frogs' legs.

Allusions are also found to a traditional fairy story, recorded by the ➤ GRIMM brothers, in which a frog in a pool returns a princess's lost golden ball in return for her promise that he may live with and be loved by her. When he claims the reward her father makes her keep her promise; the frog eats from her plate and sleeps in her room. In the original story it is when she has thrown him against the wall that he turns into his real shape, that of a handsome prince, who is now her lover and husband; the usual version is that it is when she kisses him that the enchantment is broken and he is restored.

> I don't mean I've done a sudden transformation. I'm not a frog that's been kissed by a princess.
> — Julian Barnes *Talking it Over* (1991)

See also ➤ KERMIT *the Frog*.

have a **frog** in one's throat lose one's voice or find it hard to speak because of hoarseness; the expression is recorded from the early 20th century.

Jean Froissart (1333?–*c*.1400), French chronicler and poet. He travelled widely in Western Europe, collecting material for his future histories. In 1361 he was received in England by Edward III, and visited Scotland. In 1366 he accompanied the Black Prince to Bordeaux, and in 1368 the duke of Clarence to Milan. He revisited England in 1394–5. His chronicles record the chivalric exploits of the nobles of England and France from 1325 to 1400.

Fronde a series of civil wars in France 1648–53, in which the nobles whose power had been weakened by the policies of Cardinal Richelieu rose in rebellion against Mazarin and the court during the minority of Louis XIV. Although some concessions were obtained after the rebellion of the Parliament in 1648, the nobles were not successful in curbing the power of the monarchy.

The word is French, from the name for a type of sling used in a children's game played in the streets of Paris at this time.

frondeur a rebel during the Fronde; in general usage, a political rebel.

front bench in the UK, the foremost seats in the House of Commons, occupied by the members of the cabinet and shadow cabinet.

frost giants in Scandinavian mythology, the enemies of Thor.

Fructidor the twelfth month of the French Republican calendar (1793–1805), originally running from 18 August to 16 September. Also, the purge of conservative deputies that took place on the eighteenth day of this month (4 September) in 1797.

fruit see also ➤ BASKET *of fruit and flowers*, ➤ DEAD *Sea fruit*, ➤ FIRST *fruits*, ➤ FORBIDDEN *fruit*, ➤ *he that would* EAT *the fruit must climb the tree*, ➤ SEPTEMBER *blow soft, till the fruit's in the loft*, ➤ STOLEN *fruit*, ➤ *a* TREE *is known by its fruit*.

when all fruit fails, welcome haws proverbial saying, early 18th century; used of someone taking an older or otherwise unsuitable lover.

frumentation in ancient Rome, a general charitable distribution of corn.

frumious angrily ferocious, a nonsense word invented by Lewis Carroll in *Through the Looking-glass* (1871) to describe the ➤ BANDERSNATCH, and later explained by him as a blend of *fuming* and *furious*.

Elizabeth Fry (1780–1845), English Quaker prison reformer, a leading figure in the early 19th-century campaign for penal reform. She concerned herself particularly with conditions in Newgate and other prisons, the plight of convicts transported to Australia, and the vagrant population in London and the south-east.

frying see ➤ OUT *of the frying pan*.

FTSE index a figure (published by the *Financial Times*) indicating the relative prices of shares on the London Stock Exchange, especially (also **FTSE 100 index**) one calculated on the basis of Britain's one hundred largest public companies.

See also ➤ FOOTSIE.

Dr Fu Manchu a moustached Chinese master-criminal created by the British writer Sax Rohmer (1883?–1959), first appearing in the novel *Dr Fu Manchu* (1913) and subsequently in several films (in *The Mask of Fu Manchu*, 1932, he was played by Boris Karloff).

> He wore a dastardly Fu Manchu mustache that basically told the world: *This Is One Crazy Dude.*
> — *Show* September 1990

Klaus Fuchs (1911–88), German-born British physicist. He was a communist who fled Nazi persecution. During the 1940s he passed to the USSR secret information acquired while working on the development of the atom bomb in the US, and while engaged in research in Britain, where he held a senior post in the Atomic Energy Research Establishment at Harwell. He was imprisoned from 1950 to 1959.

Vivian Fuchs (1908–99), English geologist and explorer. He led the Commonwealth Trans-Antarctic Expedition (1955–8), making the first overland crossing of the Antarctic. His party met Sir Edmund Hillary's New Zealand contingent, approaching from the opposite direction, at the South Pole.

fudge and mudge in politics, reach a makeshift solution by glossing over differences or blurring distinctions; prevaricate or temporize. The expression was first recorded in a speech at the Labour Party Conference on 2 October 1980 by British politician David Owen, when he said of the leadership of James Callaghan, 'We are fed up with fudging and mudging, with mush and slush. We need courage, conviction, and hard work.'

fudge factor a figure included in a calculation to account for some unquantified but significant phenomenon or to ensure a desired result.

Fugger name of a dynasty of German merchant bankers of the 15th and 16th centuries constituting a major influence on European economics and politics of the period.

Führer 'Leader', the title assumed by Adolf Hitler in 1934.

Mount Fuji a dormant volcano in the Chubu region of Japan, with a symmetrical, conical, snow-capped peak. Regarded by the Japanese as sacred, it has been celebrated in art and literature for centuries.

William Fulbright (1905–95), American senator. His name designates grants awarded under the Fulbright Act of 1946, which authorized funds from the sale of surplus war materials overseas to be used to finance exchange programmes of students and teachers between the US and other countries. The scheme was later supported by grants from the US government.

full see also ➤ *the full* MONTY.

full cup, steady hand proverbial saying, early 11th century.

it's ill speaking between a full man and a fasting proverbial saying, mid 17th century.

Thomas Fuller (1608–61), English cleric and historian. He is chiefly remembered for *The History of the Worthies of England* (1662), a description of the counties with short biographies of local personages.

out of the fullness of the heart the mouth speaks proverbial saying, late 14th century; originally with biblical allusion to Matthew 12:34, 'Out of the abundance of the heart the mouth speaketh.'

Robert Fulton (1765–1815), American pioneer of the steamship. He constructed a steam-propelled 'diving-boat' in 1800, which submerged to a depth of 7.6 m (25 ft), and in 1806 he built the first successful paddle steamer, the *Clermont*. Eighteen other steamships were subsequently built, inaugurating the era of commercial steam navigation.

fum in China, a fabulous bird, equivalent to a phoenix, one of the former symbols of imperial dignity.

fun run an uncompetitive run, especially for sponsored runners in support of a charity. The first such runs took place in the US in the 1970s as a way of bringing together people who had taken up jogging or long-distance running recreationally. By the mid 1980s such events had become widely popular, with large races such as the annual London Marathon in the UK attracting thousands of participants.

function see ➤ FORM *follows function*.

functionalism belief in or stress on the practical application of a thing, in particular, (in the arts) the doctrine that the design of an object should be determined solely by its function, rather than by aesthetic considerations, and that anything practically designed will be inherently beautiful.

Although similar ideas are found in ancient Greek thought and in 18th-century aesthetic theory, it was not until the 20th century that functionalism was established as a new aesthetic. In the 20th century, functionalism has been particularly influential on architecture, where it is associated particularly with figures such as Le Corbusier (who defined a house as 'a machine for living in'), Frank Lloyd Wright, and Mies van der Rohe. Functionalism had a strong impact on industrial design (e.g. of furniture) of the 1930s and after. Functionalism is associated with 19th-century sociologists such as Émile Durkheim and early 20th-century anthropologists such as Bronisław Malinowski.

functional food a food containing health-giving additives, first developed in Japan; the term is recorded from the early 1990s, and is a translation of Japanese *kinoseishokuhin*. Food products of this kind were promoted strongly in Western markets in the 1990s, leading to the development of the alternative term ➤ NUTRACEUTICALS.

fund see ➤ CONSOLIDATED *Fund*.

fundamental colours originally, the seven colours of the spectrum, red, orange, yellow, green, blue, indigo, and violet; now, the three colours, red, green, and violet, out of which all the others are produced.

fundamentalism a form of Protestant Christianity which upholds belief in the strict and literal interpretation of the Bible, including its narratives, doctrines, prophecies, and moral laws. Also, strict maintenance of ancient or fundamental doctrines of any religion or ideology, notably Islam.

Modern Christian fundamentalism arose from

American millenarian sects of the 19th century, and has become associated with reaction against social and political liberalism and rejection of the theory of evolution. Islamic fundamentalism appeared in the 18th and 19th centuries as a reaction to the disintegration of Islamic political and economic power, asserting that Islam is central to both state and society and advocating strict adherence to the Koran (*Qur'an*) and to Islamic law (*sharia*), supported if need be by jihad or holy war.

fundie a member of the radical, as opposed to the pragmatic, wing of the Green movement; often contrasted with *realo*. The term comes (in the 1980s) from German, from an abbreviation of *Fundamentalist* 'fundamentalist'.

funeral ➤ *St* JOSEPH *of Arimathea* is the patron saint of funeral directors.

See also ➤ DREAM *of a funeral and you hear of a marriage*.

one funeral makes many proverbial saying, late 19th century.

funny bone the part of the elbow over which passes the ulnar nerve, which may cause numbness and pain along the forearm and hand if knocked; so called from the sensation if it is struck.

fur see ➤ IT *takes 40 dumb animals to make a fur coat, but only one to wear it.*

Furby a small electronic furry toy animal, which is capable of responding to external stimuli by moving and 'speaking' a vocabulary composed of English and an invented language.

the Furies in Greek mythology, spirits of punishment, often represented as one of three goddesses (Alecto, Megaera, and Tisiphone) with hair composed of snakes, who executed the curses pronounced upon criminals, tortured the guilty with stings of conscience, and inflicted famines and pestilences. The Furies were identified at an early date with the ➤ EUMENIDES.

furlong an eighth of a mile, 220 yards. Recorded from Old English (in form *furlang*), the word comes from *furh* 'furrow' + *lang* 'long'. The word originally denoted the length of a furrow in a common field (formally regarded as a square of ten acres). It

was also used as the equivalent of the Roman *stadium*, one eighth of a Roman mile, whence the current sense.

furnace see ➤ BURNING *fiery furnace*.

furphy in Australia and New Zealand, a rumour or story, especially one that is untrue or absurd. The word comes from the First World War, from the name painted on water and sanitary carts manufactured by the *Furphy* family of Shepparton, Victoria.

furrow see ➤ PLOUGH *a lonely furrow*.

furry a festival held annually at Helston, Cornwall on the eighth of May; (more fully *furry dance*) a distinctive communal dance performed at this (also called *floral dance*).

when the furze is in bloom, my love's in tune proverbial saying, mid 18th century.

Fusberta in Ariosto's *Orlando Furioso*, the name of the hero ➤ RINALDO's sword (in the earlier Charlemagne cycle, he is *Renaud* and his sword is *Floberge*).

fusion see ➤ COLD *fusion*.

fustian thick hard-wearing twilled cloth with a short nap, usually dyed in dark colours. It was sometimes used to cover pillows and cushions, and the implication that the language was 'padded' may have given rise to the sense of 'pompous or pretentious speech or writing'.

Recorded from Middle English, the word comes via Old French from medieval Latin *fustaneum*, from (*pannus*) *fustaneus* 'cloth from Fostat', a suburb of Cairo.

futhark the runic alphabet; from its first six letters, *f, u, th, a* (or *o*), *r, k*.

future see also ➤ DEATH *futures*, ➤ WAVE *of the future*.

future shock a state of distress or disorientation due to rapid social or technological change; coined by the American writer Alvin Toffler (1928–):

> Culture shock is relatively mild in comparison with a much more serious malady that might be called 'future shock'. Future shock is the dizzying disorientation brought on by the premature arrival of the future.
> — Alvin Toffler in *Horizon* Summer 1965

Futurism an artistic movement begun in Italy in 1909, which violently rejected traditional forms so as to celebrate and incorporate into art the energy and dynamism of modern technology. Launched by Filippo Marinetti, it had effectively ended by 1918 but was widely influential, particularly in Russia on figures such as Malevich and Mayakovsky.

fuzzy in computing and logic, of or relating to a form of set theory and logic in which predicates may have degrees of applicability, rather than simply being true or false. It has important uses in artificial intelligence and the design of control systems.

fylfot a swastika; the name may perhaps come from from *fill-foot* 'pattern filling the foot of a painted window', a meaning suggested by a passage in a late 15th-century manuscript, but otherwise not recorded in early sources.

fyrd the English militia before 1066.

Gg

G the seventh letter of the modern English alphabet and of the ancient Roman one, originally corresponding to a differentiated form of C.

G-man an FBI agent; *G* is here the initial letter of *government*.

G-string a garment consisting of a narrow strip of cloth that covers the genitals and is attached to a waistband, worn as underwear or by striptease performers.

gaberdine originally (in the early 16th century) a loose long upper garment, associated particularly with Jews (Shylock in The *Merchant of Venice* tells the Christians who revile him 'You…spit upon my Jewish gaberdine') and beggars; the word comes from Old French and perhaps ultimately from Middle High German *wallevart* 'pilgrimage', with original meaning 'garment worn by a pilgrim'.

The current textile sense of a smooth, durable twill-woven cloth, or a raincoat made of this, dates from the early 20th century.

Gabriel in the Bible, the archangel who foretold the birth of Jesus to the Virgin Mary (Luke 1:26–38), and who also appeared to Zacharias, father of John the Baptist, and to Daniel; in Islam, the archangel who revealed the Koran to the Prophet Muhammad.

Gabriel bell another name for the ➤ ANGELUS, from Gabriel's role in the Annunciation.

Gabriel's hounds wild geese, from their yelping call.

Gadarene swine the pigs into which Jesus cast the demons that had possessed a madman (see ➤ LEGION²), and which as a result ran down a steep cliff into the sea and were killed; from this, *Gadarene* means involving or engaged in a headlong or potentially disastrous rush to do something.

Gadarene comes from New Testament Greek *Gadarēnos* 'inhabitant of Gadara' (see Mark ch. 8).

> What is needed are proper experiments and a somewhat less Gadarene rush hoping for instant profits from soya beans.
>
> — Steve Jones in *Times Higher Education Supplement* 27 August 1999

gadroon a decorative edging on metal or wood formed by parallel rounded strips (reeding) like inverted fluting. The word is recorded from the late 17th century, and comes from French *godron*, probably related to *goder* 'pucker'.

Gadsden Purchase an area in New Mexico and Arizona, near the Rio Grande, which was purchased from Mexico in 1853 by the American diplomat James *Gadsden* (1788–1858), with the intention of ensuring a southern railroad route to the Pacific.

Gaekwar the title of the hereditary ruler of Baroda, a state in India until 1960, when it became part of Gujarat.

Gael see ➤ CLAN *na Gael*.

Gaelic a Celtic language spoken in the highlands and islands of western Scotland, brought from Ireland in the 5th and 6th centuries AD and now spoken by about 40,000 people; also (more fully **Irish Gaelic**) another term for the Irish language.

Gaelic League a movement founded in 1893 to revive Irish language and culture.

the Gaeltacht a region of Ireland in which the vernacular language is Irish.

gaff see ➤ BLOW *the gaff*.

Yuri Gagarin (1934–68), Russian cosmonaut, who in 1961 made the first manned space flight, completing a single orbit of the earth in 108 minutes.

gagging order in the UK, informal term for an official order forbidding public discussion of a specified subject, in print or by broadcasting. In the 1960s, considerable attention was paid to the appropriate circumstances for issuing a *Defence notice*, or *D-notice*, a formal request from the Services, Press and Broadcasting Committee that news editors should observe a ban on specified subjects with a bearing on national security. The development of modern communication techniques has made it less easy for outright prohibitions of this kind to be sustained, but in the 1990s public attentions was once more drawn to the principles involved, and the informal term *gagging order* began to be used, and to be applied also in cases where the principle involved is one of personal privacy rather than national security.

See also ➤ MARY *Bell order.*

Gaia in Greek mythology, the Earth personified as a goddess, daughter of Chaos. She was the mother and wife of Uranus (Heaven); their offspring included the Titans and the Cyclops.

In the hypothesis put forward by James Lovelock, *Gaia* is now used for the earth viewed as a vast self-regulating organism.

> Gaia is a tough bitch. People think the earth is going to die and they have to save it, that's ridiculous . . . There's no doubt that Gaia can compensate for our output of greenhouse gases, but the environment that's left will not be happy for any people.
> — Lynn Margulis in *New York Times Biographical Service*
> January 1996

Gaia hypothesis the theory, put forward by the English scientist James Lovelock (1919–) in 1969, that living matter on the earth collectively defines and regulates the material conditions necessary for the continuance of life. The principle is demonstrated by a computer model *Daisyworld*, showing how competition for territory on a planet between two species of daisy, dark and light, results in the successful regulation of the temperature of the planet to what would be beneficial to plants of both species. The planet, or rather the biosphere, is thus likened to a vast self-regulating organism.

Gaiety Girl a chorus girl or performer in a musical show, originally and especially at the *Gaiety*, a former London theatre famous for its musicals.

the gaiety of nations general gaiety or amusement; originally as a quotation from Samuel Johnson on the death of the actor David Garrick in *Lives of the Poets* (1779–81), 'that stroke of death, which has eclipsed the gaiety of nations and impoverished the public stock of harmless pleasure'.

gain see ➤ one man's LOSS *is another man's gain.*

Thomas Gainsborough (1727–88), English painter. He was famous for his society portraits, including *Mr and Mrs Andrews* (1748) and *The Blue Boy* (c.1770), and for landscapes such as *The Watering Place* (1777).

gaiters see ➤ all GAS *and gaiters.*

gala a social occasion with special entertainments or performances; the word is recorded from the

early 17th century (in the sense 'showy dress') and comes via Italian and Spanish from Old French *gale* 'rejoicing'.

In the UK, *gala* is the name given to the traditional annual celebration of the northern mining communities, as in the *Durham Miners' Gala*.

Galahad the noblest of King Arthur's knights, son of ➤ *Sir* LANCELOT, renowned for immaculate purity and destined to find the Holy Grail.

> We have set forth, politically, on such a high and Galahad quest of holy liberty.
> — D. H. Lawrence *Sea and Sardinia* (1921)

Galapagos Islands a Pacific archipelago on the equator, west of Ecuador. The islands are noted for their abundant wildlife, including giant tortoises and many other endemic species. They were the site of Charles Darwin's observations of 1835, which helped him to form his theory of natural selection. Fragments of pottery found there, made by the Chimu Indians, indicate that the islands were visited by people who travelled from the mainland of South America before the Spanish conquest.

Galatea[1] in Greek mythology, a sea nymph courted by the Cyclops ➤ POLYPHEMUS, who in jealousy killed his rival Acis.

Galatea[2] in Greek mythology, the name given to the statue fashioned by ➤ PYGMALION and brought to life.

Galatia an ancient region in central Asia Minor, settled by invading Gauls (the **Galatians**) in the 3rd century BC. In 64 BC it became a protectorate of Rome and, in 25 BC, with the addition of some further territories, it became a province of the Roman Empire.

Epistle to the Galatians a book of the New Testament, an epistle of St Paul to the Church in Galatia.

galaxy a system of millions or billions of stars, together with gas and dust, held together by gravitational attraction; **the Galaxy**, the galaxy of which the solar system is a part, the ➤ MILKY *Way*; in figurative usage, a large or impressive group of people.

The name is recorded from Middle English, referring to the Milky Way, and comes via Old French and medieval Latin from Greek *galaxias (kuklos)* 'milky (vault)', from *gala, galakt-* 'milk'.

Galba (*c.*3 BC–AD 69), Roman emperor AD 68–9. The successor to Nero, he aroused hostility by his severity and parsimony and was murdered in a conspiracy organized by his successor Otho in the *Year of the Four Emperors*.

The Roman historian Tacitus said of him, 'He seemed much greater than a private citizen while he still was a private citizen, and by everyone's consent capable of reigning if only he had not reigned.'

Galen (129–99), Greek physician. He attempted to systematize the whole of medicine, making important discoveries in anatomy and physiology. His works became influential in Europe when retranslated from Arabic in the 12th century. The word **galenical**, meaning (of a medicine) made of natural rather than synthetic components, derives from his name.

galère a coterie; a (usually undesirable) group of people, an unpleasant situation. The word is French, literally 'galley', and comes here from a usage in Molière's play *Les Fourberies de Scapin* (1672), '*Que diable allait-il faire dans cette galère?* [What the devil was he doing in that galley?]'

the Galilean Jesus as an inhabitant of ➤ GALILEE, often with derogatory implication; the dying words attributed to Julian the Apostate (AD *c*.332–363) are, '*Vicisti, Galilaee* [You have won, Galilean].'

Galilean moons the four largest satellites of Jupiter (Callisto, Europa, Ganymede, and Io), discovered by ➤ GALILEO in 1610 and independently by the German astronomer Simon Marius (1573–1624).

Galilee a northern region of ancient Palestine, west of the River Jordan, associated with the ministry of Jesus.

The word *galilee* is also used for a porch or chapel at the entrance to a church; perhaps alluding to Galilee as an outlying portion of the Holy Land, or with reference to the phrase in Matthew 4:15, 'Galilee of the Gentiles'.

Galileo Galilei (1564–1642), Italian astronomer and physicist, one of the founders of modern science. He discovered the constancy of a pendulum's swing, formulated the law of uniform acceleration of falling bodies, and described the parabolic trajectory of projectiles. He applied the telescope to astronomy and observed craters on the moon, sunspots, Jupiter's moons, and the phases of Venus. His acceptance of the Copernican system was rejected by the Catholic Church, and under threat of

torture from the Inquisition he publicly recanted his heretical views (see also ➤ EPPUR *si muove*).

galimatias confused language, meaningless talk, gibberish. Recorded from the mid 17th century, but of unknown origin.

gall bile; proverbial for its bitterness, and in biblical allusion associated with ➤ WORMWOOD; the **gall of bitterness** is the extremity of bitterness.

gallery see ➤ PLAY *to the gallery*.

Gallia the Latin name for Gaul, as in Caesar's *De Bello Gallico*, '*Gallia est omnis divisa in partes tres* [Gaul as a whole is divided into three parts]'.

Gallic Wars Julius Caesar's campaigns 58–51 BC, which established Roman control over Gaul north of the Alps and west of the River Rhine (Transalpine Gaul). During this period Caesar twice invaded Britain (55 and 54 BC). Largely disunited, the Gauls combined in 53–52 BC under the chieftain Vercingetorix (d. *c*.46 BC) but were eventually defeated.

Gallican of or relating to the ancient Church of Gaul or France; in particular, of or holding a doctrine (reaching its peak in the 17th century) which asserted the freedom of the Roman Catholic Church in France and elsewhere from the ecclesiastical authority of the papacy.

gallimaufry a confused jumble or medley of things. The word is recorded from the mid 16th century, and from archaic French *galimafrée* 'unappetizing dish', perhaps from Old French *galer* 'have fun' + Picard *mafrer* 'eat copious quantities'.

Gallio a person who is indifferent, from the name of a Roman proconsul of Achaia, whose refusal to take action is recorded in Acts 18:17: 'And Gallio cared for none of these things'.

Gallipoli a major campaign of the First World War which took place on the Gallipoli peninsula, on the European side of the Dardanelles, in 1915–16.

In early 1915, after a naval attempt to force the Dardanelles had failed, the Allies (with heavy involvement of troops from Australia and New Zealand) invaded the peninsula, hoping to remove Turkey from the war and open supply lines to Russia's Black Sea ports. The campaign reached stalemate and became bogged down in trench warfare. After each side had suffered a quarter of a million casualties, the Allies evacuated the peninsula without further loss in January 1916.

galloglass a member of a special class of soldiers or retainers maintained by Irish chiefs. The word is recorded from the late 15th century, and comes from Irish *gallóglach*, from *gall* 'foreigner' + *óglach* 'youth, servant, warrior', from *óg* 'young'.

gallop see ➤ CANTERBURY *gallop*.

gallows a structure, typically of two uprights and a crosspiece, for the hanging of criminals; the word is recorded from Old English (in form *galga*, *gealga*) and is of Germanic origin.

See also ➤ PIT *and gallows*.

Gallup poll trademark name for an assessment of public opinion by the questioning of a representative sample, typically as a basis for forecasting votes in an election. It is named after George H. *Gallup* (1901–84), the American statistician who devised the method.

galosh a waterproof overshoe, typically made of rubber. The word is originally Middle English (denoting a type of clog) and comes via Old French from late Latin diminutive of Latin *gallica* (*solea*) 'Gallic (shoe)'

Francis Galton (1822–1911), English scientist, who founded eugenics and introduced methods of measuring human mental and physical abilities. He also pioneered the use of fingerprints as a means of identification.

galumph move in a clumsy, ponderous, or noisy manner. The word was coined (in the sense 'prance in triumph') by Lewis Carroll in *Through the Looking Glass* (1871), perhaps as a blend of *gallop* and *triumph*.

game see also ➤ PLAY *the game*.

game wild mammals or birds hunted for sport or food, often within a restricted season; the word in this sense dates from Middle English, and comes from *game* meaning sport derived from the hunting, shooting, or catching of animals.

The hunting of *game* is regulated by **game laws**, often associated with repressive measures against poaching; in 1769 ➤ BLACKSTONE noted disapprovingly that 'Though the forest-laws are now mitigated…yet from this root has sprung up a bastard slip known by the name of the game-law.' The notorious ➤ BLACK *Act* dealt severely with poachers;

the clergyman Sydney Smith commented in 1823, 'the game laws have been carried to a pitch of oppression which is a disgrace to the country.'

the Gamecock State an informal name for South Carolina; a *gamecock* is a cock bred and trained for cockfighting, traditionally a type of aggressive competition, as in John Gay's *Fables* (1727), 'No author ever spar'd a brother, Wits are gamecocks to one another.'

gamekeeper see ➤ *an old* POACHER *makes the best gamekeeper*.

gamesmanship the art of winning games by using various ploys and tactics to gain a psychological advantage. The term derives from the title of Stephen Potter's humorous book (1947), 'The theory and practice of gamesmanship or the art of winning games without actually cheating'.

gamma the third letter of the Greek alphabet (Γ, γ), transliterated as 'g'.

gammadion an arrangement of shapes of capital gamma (Γ), especially of four, as a swastika or a hollow Greek cross.

gammer an archaic term for an old countrywoman; the word dates from the late 16th century, and is probably a contraction of *godmother*, by association with *grandmother*.

Gammer Gurton's Needle the second English comedy in verse, which is written in rhymed long doggerel, and deals farcically with the losing and finding of the needle used to mend the garments of Hodge, Gammer Gurton's man.

gammon nonsense, rubbish. First recorded in the early 18th century; the origin is uncertain, but the term was first used in criminals' slang in *give gammon* 'give cover to (a pickpocket)' and *keep in gammon* 'distract (a victim) for a pickpocket'.

gammon and spinach nonsense, humbug; with a pun on *gammon* 'bacon, ham'. The words *gammon and spinach* are part of the refrain to the song 'A frog he would a-wooing go', and the term is used by Dickens: Miss Mowcher in *David Copperfield* (1850) says, 'What a world of gammon and spinnage it is, though, ain't it!', and in *Bleak House* (1853) the cage birds belonging to Miss Flite, one of those hopelessly enmired in a Chancery suit, are named 'Hope, Joy, Youth, Peace, Rest, Life, Dust, Ashes, Waste, Want, Ruin, Despair, Madness, Death, Cunning,

Folly, Words, Wigs, Rags, Sheepskin, Plunder, Precedent, Jargon, Gammon, and Spinach'.

Sarah Gamp in Dickens's *Martin Chuzzlewit* (1844), a monthly nurse with a fondness for gin who carried a large cotton umbrella; *gamp* from this is a dated British term for an umbrella, especially a large unwieldy one.

> The mouthpiece is a good way from his mouth. Perhaps he applies the instrument to his lips when he is so dispoged, like Sarah Gamp did with the gin bottle in *Martin Chuzzlewit*.
> — *New Scientist* 14 December 1991

See also ➤ *Mrs* HARRIS.

gamut a complete scale of musical notes; the compass or range of a voice or instrument. Earlier, a scale consisting of seven overlapping hexachords, containing all the recognized notes used in medieval music, covering almost three octaves from bass G to treble E. The word comes from medieval Latin *gamma ut*, originally the name of the lowest note in the medieval scale (bass G an octave and a half below middle C), then applied to the whole range of notes used in medieval music. The Greek letter Γ (gamma) was used for bass G, with *ut* indicating that it was the first note in the lowest of the hexachords or six-note scales.

Notes in each hexachord were named using syllables of a Latin hymn for St John the Baptist's Day, in which each line began on the next note of the scale: '*Ut* quant laxis *re*sonare fibris *Mi*ra gestorum *fa*muli tuorum, *Sol*ve polluti *la*bii reatum, Sancte Iohannes.' A seventh note, *si*, was added later, from the initial letters of Sancte Iohannes. The scheme was adapted in the 19th century to form solmization systems such as the Tonic Sol-fa.

The system of naming the notes of a scale by syllables is attributed to ➤ *Guido d'*AREZZO (*c*.990–1050).

Ganapati another name for the Hindu god ➤ GANESH.

gandharva in Hinduism, any of a class of minor deities or genii of the sky, often represented as celestial musicians, and depicted in a variety of presiding or attendant roles.

Mahatma Gandhi (1869–1948), Indian nationalist and spiritual leader. He became prominent in the opposition to British rule in India, pursuing a policy of non-violent civil disobedience. He never held government office, but was regarded as the country's supreme political and spiritual leader; he was assassinated by a Hindu following his agreement to the creation of the state of Pakistan.

> Havel is a sort of Euro-Gandhi: shy and selfless, yet insuperably stubborn; seemingly egoless, yet devoid of moral doubt.
> — *Vanity Fair* August 1991

Gandolfo see ➤ CASTEL *Gandolfo*.

Ganelon in the romances of Charlemagne, a traitorous count who plans the defeat of the rearguard at ➤ RONCESVALLES.

Ganesh in Hinduism, an elephant-headed deity, son of Shiva and Parvati. Worshipped as the remover of obstacles and patron of learning, he is invoked at the beginning of literary works, rituals, or any new undertaking. He is usually depicted coloured red, with a pot belly and one broken tusk, riding a rat.

Gang of Four in China, a group of four associates, including Mao Zedong's wife, involved in implementing the Cultural Revolution. They were among the groups competing for power on Mao's death in 1976, but were arrested and imprisoned.

In the UK, the name was applied to a group of four Labour MPs (Shirley Williams, Roy Jenkins, David Owen, and William Rodgers) who broke away from the Labour Party in 1981 to form the Social Democratic Party.

Ganges a river of northern India and Bangladesh, which rises in the Himalayas and flows some 2,700 km (1,678 miles) south-east to the Bay of Bengal, where it forms the world's largest delta. The river is regarded by Hindus as sacred.

gangway see ➤ BELOW *the gangway*.

Ganymede in Greek mythology, a Trojan youth who was so beautiful that he was carried off to be Zeus' cup-bearer.

In astronomy, *Ganymede* is one of the Galilean moons of Jupiter, the seventh-closest satellite to the planet and the largest satellite in the solar system.

gap year a period of one academic year taken as a break from formal education by a student between leaving school and taking up a place at a college or university.

gaps see ➤ GOD *of the gaps*.

Garamond a typeface much used in books, named (in the mid 19th century) after Claude *Garamond* (1499–1561), French type founder.

garbage in, garbage out used to express the idea that in computing and other spheres, incorrect or poor quality input will always produce faulty output (often abbreviated as **GIGO**).

Greta Garbo (1905–90), Swedish-born American actress, noted for such films as *Mata Hari* (1931), *Grand Hotel* (1932), in which she spoke the line 'I want to be alone', and *Anna Karenina* (1935). After her retirement in 1941 she lived as a recluse.

> This is not to say . . . Julia pulled a Greta Garbo and demanded to be left alone.
> — *Daily Telegraph* 18 March 1996

garden see also ➤ the AGONY *in the Garden,* ➤ BEAR *garden,* ➤ COMMON *or garden,* ➤ COVENT *Garden,* ➤ CREMORNE *Gardens,* ➤ CULTIVATE *one's garden,* ➤ *Garden of* GETHSEMANE, ➤ *the* HANGING *Gardens of Babylon,* ➤ *if you would be* HAPPY *for a week,* ➤ KNOT *garden,* ➤ PARIS *garden,* ➤ RANELAGH *Gardens.*

the **Garden** the philosophy or school of the Greek philosopher ➤ EPICURUS, who taught in a garden.

garden city a new town designed as a whole with much open space and greenery; the term is recorded from the late 19th century, and in 1899 Ebenezer Howard (1850–1928), later founder of Letchworth and Welwyn garden cities, formed the Garden City Association. In 1902 he republished an earlier work under the title *Garden Cities of Tomorrow.*

the **Garden of Earthly Delights** title of a painting by ➤ *Hieronymus* BOSCH, a triptych showing (with many surreal images) the lost earthly paradise with the creation of Eve followed by the Temptation and finally the Fall.

the **Garden of England** informal name for the English counties of Kent and Worcestershire, in recognition of their fertility.

the **Garden of Europe** an informal name for Italy.

Garden State an informal name for New Jersey.

gardeners ➤ *St* FIACRE and ➤ *St* PHOCAS are the patron saints of gardeners.

gardyloo beware of the water: a warning formerly shouted in Edinburgh before dirty water or slops were thrown from a window into the street; the act of throwing out such water or slops. The expression apparently comes from *gare de l'eau,* pseudo-French for *gare l'eau* 'beware of the water'.

Gargantua a voracious giant in Rabelais' book of the same name (1534); *gargantuan,* meaning enormous, is derived from the name.

Giuseppe Garibaldi (1807–02), Italian patriot and military leader of the Risorgimento. After involvement in the early struggles in the north of Italy in the 1830s and 1840s, with his volunteer force of 'Red Shirts' he captured Sicily and southern Italy from the Austrians in 1860–1, thereby playing a key role in the establishment of a united kingdom of Italy, but failed to conquer the papal territories around French-held Rome.

garland see ➤ VIRGIN*'s garland.*

Garland Day in Devonshire, traditionally celebrated on the anniversary of the Restoration, 29 May 1660.

Garland Sunday in Ireland, the last Sunday of July, on which a pilgrimage is traditionally made to Croagh Patrick in County Mayo. Of medieval origin (and at a date close to the Celtic festival of ➤ LUGHNASA), the pilgrimage was formally revived in 1903.

garlic a strong-smelling pungent-tasting bulb, used as a flavouring in cookery and in herbal medicine, which is traditionally a protection against evil, especially (perhaps since the publication of Bram Stoker's *Dracula*) vampires:

> I had laid over the clamps of those doors garlic, which the Un-Dead cannot bear.
> — Bram Stoker *Dracula* (1897)

The name is recorded from Old English (in form *gārlēac*), from *gār* 'spear (because the shape of a clove resembles the head of a spear) + *lēac* 'leek'.

garment see ➤ SILENCE *is a woman's best garment.*

All Sir Garnet all as it should be, highly satisfactory; the term, recorded from the late 19th century, refers to the British soldier Sir Garnet Wolseley (1833–1933). The leader of several successful military expeditions, he was regarded as the ideal of the modern professional soldier, and was the model for the 'modern Major-General' in Gilbert and Sullivan's *The Pirates of Penzance* (1879); the actor George Grossmith made himself up as Wolseley to sing the song.

Alf Garnett central character of the television series *Till Death Us Do Part* (1964–74), characterized by the extremity of his right-wing, xenophobic, and racist views, and intolerance of any opinion but his own.

> When it came to anything foreign, I was a super patriot, well to the right of Alf Garnett. My country could do no wrong.
> — Don McCullin *Unreasonable Behaviour* (1990)

Garratt see ➤ the Mayor *of Garratt*.

Garraway's a celebrated coffee-house in Change Alley, Cornhill, founded by one Thomas Garway, a tea, coffee, and tobacco merchant, in the 17th century. It was a meeting-place of dealers in stocks and shares, notably in the days of the South Sea Company, and contained an auction room referred to in *The Tatler*.

David Garrick (1717–79), English actor and dramatist. He was a notably versatile actor and the manager of the Drury Lane Theatre, and was equally successful in tragic and comic roles in both Shakespearean and contemporary plays.

See also ➤ the GAIETY *of nations*.

Garrick Club founded in 1831 as a club in which 'actors and men of education and refinement might meet on equal terms'. Its original premises were at 35 King Street. Barham, D'Orsay, and Samuel Rogers were among its first members. It was much frequented by Thackeray and possesses a famous collection of portraits of actors and actresses and theatrical memorabilia.

Garsington Manor the Oxfordshire home of Ottoline Morrell from 1915 to 1927, where she and her husband entertained many distinguished guests from the political and artistic worlds.

garter a band worn around the leg to keep up a stocking or sock, the badge of the ➤ *Order of the* GARTER. The word is recorded from Middle English and comes from Old French, from *garet* 'bend of the knee, calf of the leg', probably of Celtic origin.

Order of the Garter the highest order of English knighthood, founded by Edward III *c.*1344. According to tradition, the garter was that of the Countess of Salisbury, which the king placed on his own leg after it fell off while she was dancing with him. The king's comment to those present, '*Honi soit qui mal y pense*' (shame be to him who thinks evil of it), was adopted as the motto of the order.

The *Garter* as the badge of the Order is a ribbon of dark-blue velvet, edged and buckled with gold, and bearing the above words embroidered in gold, and is worn below the left knee; garters also form part of the ornament of the collar worn by the Knights. Presentation is in the sovereign's personal gift.

The 19th-century Prime Minister Lord Melbourne (1779–1848) is said to have remarked, 'I like the Garter: there is no damned merit in it.'

Garter King of Arms in the UK, the principal King of Arms of the English ➤ COLLEGE *of Arms*.

Garuda in Hindu mythology, an eagle-like being that serves as the mount of ➤ VISHNU.

all gas and gaiters a satisfactory state of affairs; originally recorded in Dickens's *Nicholas Nickleby* (1839) 'All is gas and gaiters.'

gasconade poetic and literary term for extravagant boasting. Recorded from the mid 17th century, the word comes from French *gasconnade*, from *gasconner* 'talk like a Gascon, brag'.

Gascony a region and former province of SW France, in the northern foothills of the Pyrenees, which having united with Aquitaine in the 11th century, was held by England between 1154 and 1453.

Gascons were traditionally said to be braggarts and boasters as well as impetuous (➤ D'ARTAGNAN in *The Three Musketeers* is a Gascon).

Pierre Gassendi (1592–1655), French astronomer and philosopher. He is best known for his atomic theory of matter, which was based on his interpretation of the works of Epicurus, and he was an outspoken critic of Aristotle. He observed a new comet, a lunar eclipse, and a transit of Mercury (confirming Kepler's theories), and he coined the term *aurora borealis*.

Gastronia strike a sensational and ultimately unsuccessful strike of textile workers in Gastronia, NC, in 1929; in the ensuing violence, the local chief of police was killed.

gate see also ➤ BRANDENBURG *Gate*, ➤ BULL *at a gate*, ➤ CILICIAN *Gates*, ➤ DECUMAN *gate*, ➤ *the* GOLDEN *Gate*, ➤ IRON *Gate*, ➤ IVORY *gate*, ➤ KISSING *gate*, ➤ PEARLY *Gates*, ➤ TRAITORS' *Gate*.

-gate combining form used in nouns denoting an actual or alleged scandal, especially one involving a cover-up. The usage derives from the ➤ WATERGATE scandal in the US, 1972.

gate of horn in Greek mythology, the gate through which false dreams pass (as opposed to the ➤ IVORY *gate* for true dreams).

the **Gate** of Tears meaning of the Arabic name of the Strait of Mandib, connecting the Red Sea with the Gulf of Aden and the Indian Ocean, from the dangers involved in its navigation.

Gath see ➤ TELL *it not in Gath*.

Gatha any of seventeen poems attributed to Zoroaster which are the most ancient texts of the Avesta.

gathering see ➤ *here we go gathering* NUTS *in May*.

gathering an (annual) assembly of dancing, piping, or sporting contests held in various parts of the Scottish Highlands.

Gatling gun a rapid-fire, crank-driven gun with clustered barrels. The first practical machine gun, it was officially adopted by the US army in 1866. It is named after Richard J. *Gatling* (1818–1903), its American inventor.

gaudeamus igitur opening words of a students' song, *Gaudeamus igitur, juvenes dum sumus*, modern Latin for, 'Then let us then rejoice, while we are young', from a medieval students' song traced back to 1267, but revised in the 18th century.

Antonio Gaudi (1853–1926), Spanish architect. He was a leading but idiosyncratic exponent of art nouveau, working chiefly in Barcelona, and is known especially for his ornate and extravagant church of the Sagrada Familia (begun 1884); it was unfinished at his death and is still under construction.

gaudy a celebratory dinner or entertainment held by a college for old members. The term is recorded from the mid 16th century (in the sense 'rejoicing, a celebration') from Latin *gaudium* 'joy', or from *gaude* 'rejoice!'.

gaudy night a ➤ GAUDY; originally as a quotation from Shakespeare's *Antony and Cleopatra* (1606–7), 'Let's have one other gaudy night', and reinforced by the title of Dorothy L. Sayers's detective novel (1935), set in a fictional Oxford women's college.

Gaul an ancient region of Europe, corresponding to modern France, Belgium, the south Netherlands, SW Germany, and northern Italy. The area south of the Alps was conquered in 222 BC by the Romans, who called it **Cisalpine Gaul**. The area north of the Alps, known as **Transalpine Gaul**, was taken by Julius Caesar between 58 and 51 BC; the southern province of Transalpine Gaul became known as **Gallia Narbonensis**.

See also ➤ GALLIA.

Gauleiter a political official governing a district under Nazi rule; in general use, an overbearing official. The word comes (in the 1930s) from German, from *Gau* 'administrative district' + *Leiter* 'leader'.

Gaullism the principles and policies of ➤ *Charles* DE *Gaulle*, characterized by their conservatism, nationalism, and advocacy of centralized government.

Gaultier see ➤ BON *Gaultier*.

Gaunt see ➤ JOHN *of Gaunt*.

gauntlet see also ➤ RUN *the gauntlet*.

throw down the gauntlet issue a challenge, from the medieval custom of issuing a challenge by throwing one's *gauntlet*, or armoured glove, to the ground; whoever picked it up (**take up the gauntlet**) was deemed to have accepted the challenge.

Karl Friedrich Gauss (1777–1855), German mathematician, astronomer, and physicist, who laid the foundations of number theory, and in 1801 he rediscovered the lost asteroid Ceres using advanced computational techniques. He applied rigorous mathematical analysis to geometry, geodesy, electrostatics, and electromagnetism, and discovered non-Euclidean geometry and quaternions.

Siddhartha Gautama name of the ➤ BUDDHA.

Gavel Act a statute (1704) enforcing the practice of English ➤ GAVELKIND on Irish Catholics, but allowing the eldest son to inherit the whole estate if he conformed to the Church of Ireland.

gavelkind a system of inheritance in which a deceased person's land was divided equally among all male heirs. Recorded from Middle English, the word comes from obsolete *gavel* 'payment, rent' + *kind* 'group, kin'.

gavroche a Parisian street urchin, from the name of a gamin in Victor Hugo's novel *Les Misérables* (1862).

Gawain in Arthurian legend, one of the knights of the Round Table who sought for the Holy Grail. He is Arthur's nephew, and is the hero of the medieval poem *Sir Gawain and the Green Knight*.

gay homosexual; a sense of the word recorded from the 1930s and becoming established in the 1960s as the term preferred by homosexual men to describe themselves. It is now the standard accepted word throughout the English-speaking world, and as a result the centuries-old other senses of gay meaning either 'carefree' or 'bright and showy' have more or less dropped out of natural use, despite concerted attempts by some to keep them alive.

gay gene a sequence or sequences of DNA which, when present in the human X-chromosome, may predispose towards homosexuality. Whether such a gene in fact exists is still a matter of debate, as are the moral and ethical questions attendant on research in this area.

Gay Gordons name for a traditional Scottish dance, popular in old-time and modern dancing; the *Gay Gordons* is also recorded as a name for the Gordon Highlanders, and in particular the 2nd Battalion, the 92nd Highlanders.

gay plague Aids, so called because when first identified it seemed to be spreading rapidly and uncontrollably amongst homosexual men.

the gay science the art of poetry; from Provençal *gai saber.*

gayatri a Vedic metre comprising three octosyllabic lines; a hymn or verse composed in this metre, especially the verse of the Rig-veda repeated daily as a prayer by brahmins.

Gayomart in Zoroastrian belief, the first created being, ancestor of humankind. He was destroyed by ➤ AHRIMAN, and his body became the Earth's metals and minerals.

Gaza Strip a strip of territory in Palestine, on the SE Mediterranean coast, including the town of Gaza. Administered by Egypt from 1949, and occupied by Israel from 1967, it became a self-governing enclave under the PLO–Israeli accord of 1994 and elected its own legislative council in 1996.

the Gazelle boy name given by a French writer, Jean-Claude Armen, to a young boy whom he reported having seen running with a herd of wild gazelles in the Spanish Sahara in the 1960s. The assumption (according to the theory of ➤ WILD *Children*) was that the boy had been reared by the animals, but despite some further reported sightings no additional evidence was forthcoming.

gazette a journal or newspaper, especially the official one of an organization or institution. The word comes through French from Italian *gazzetta*, originally Venetian *gazeta de la novità* 'a halfpennyworth of news' (because the news-sheet sold for a *gazeta*, a Venetian coin of small value).

See also ➤ LONDON *Gazette.*

gazetted announced or published in an official gazette; especially with reference to an appointment.

gazetteer a geographical index or dictionary. The original (17th-century) meaning was 'journalist', and the current meaning comes from a late 17th-century publication called *The Gazetteer's: or, Newsman's Interpreter: Being a Geographical Index.*

gazump make an offer for a house that is higher than that made by someone whose offer has already been accepted by the seller, and thus succeed in acquiring the property.

The word is recorded from the 1920s in the (archaic) sense 'swindle'; it comes from Yiddish *gezumph* 'overcharge'. The current meaning dates from the 1970s.

gazunder lower the amount of an offer that one has made to the seller of a property, typically just before the exchange of contracts. The term is recorded from the late 1980s (when the boom in the UK housing market collapsed), and is a blend of *gazump* and *under.*

Geber (*c.*721–*c.*815), Arab chemist; Latinized name of *Jabir ibn Hayyan.* Many works are attributed to him, but his name was used by later writers. He was familiar with many chemicals and laboratory techniques, including distillation and sublimation.

Geechee an English creole spoken by blacks in parts of South Carolina and Georgia, from the name of the *Ogeechee* River, in Georgia, US.

geese see also ➤ *like* MACFARLANE*'s geese that liked their play better than meat,* ➤ *on Saint* THOMAS *the Divine kill all turkeys, geese, and swine,* ➤ SACRED *geese,* ➤ WILD *geese.*

all one's geese are swans one characteristically exaggerates the merits of undistinguished persons or things; the use of *goose* and *swan* to point up such a contrast dates back to the 16th century (in early use, *crow* was also used in place of *goose*).

Gehazi in the Bible, the servant of Elisha who, when his master has healed ➤ NAAMAN of leprosy, surreptitiously follows the Syrian to claim the reward which the prophet has refused; he is punished for his dishonesty by himself becoming a leper.

Kipling used the figure of Gehazi to represent Rufus Isaacs in his bitter poem on the ➤ MARCONI *scandal.*

Gehenna in Judaism and the New Testament, hell. The name comes via ecclesiastical Latin from Greek *geenna*, from Hebrew *gē' hinnōm* 'hell', literally 'valley of Hinnom', a place near Jerusalem where children were sacrificed to Baal, as in Jeremiah 19:6, 'this place shall no more be called Tophet, nor The valley of the son of Hinnom, but The valley of slaughter.'

Lou Gehrig (1903–41), American baseball player; known as **the Iron Horse**. He played a record 2,130 major-league games for the New York Yankees from 1925 to 1939; his stamina earned him his nickname. He died from a form of motor neuron disease now often called **Lou Gehrig's disease**.

Geist the spirit of an individual or group. The word is German, and is related to *ghost*.

Gelalaean of or pertaining to the calendar instituted by Jalal ad-Din in 1079. The name derives from Persian *Gelal ed-din* 'Glory of the Faith' or *Jalāl ad-Dawla* 'Glory of the Dynasty', titles of Malik-Shah, Seljuk Sultan of Khorasan and reformer of the Persian calendar.

Gelderland a province of the Netherlands, on the border with Germany; capital, Arnhem. Formerly a duchy, the province was variously occupied by the Spanish, the French, and the Prussians until 1815, when it joined the newly united kingdom of the Netherlands.

Gemara a rabbinical commentary on the Mishnah, forming the second part of the Talmud. The name comes from Aramaic *gĕmārā* 'completion'.

Gem State an informal name for Idaho.

Gemeinschaft social relations between individuals, based on close personal and family ties; community. Contrasted with ➤ GESELLSCHAFT.

Gemini a northern constellation (the Twins), said to represent the twins Castor and Pollux, the ➤ DIOSCURI, whose names are given to its two brightest stars. Also, in astrological thought, the third sign of the zodiac, which the sun enters about 21 May.
   Gemini was also the name of a series of twelve manned American orbiting spacecraft, launched in the 1960s in preparation for the Apollo programme.
   Gemini comes from Latin, and means 'twins'.

gendarme a paramilitary police officer in France and other French-speaking countries. The word (originally denoting a mounted officer in the army) comes from French *gens d'armes* 'men of arms'.

gender the state of being male or female. The word has been used since the 14th century primarily as a grammatical term, referring to the classes of noun in Latin, Greek, German, and other languages designated as *masculine, feminine,* or *neuter*. It has also been used since the 14th century in the sense 'the state of being male or female', but this did not become a common standard use until the mid 20th century. Although the words *gender* and *sex* both have the sense 'the state of being male or female', they are typically used in slightly different ways: *sex* tends to refer to biological differences, while *gender* tends to refer to cultural or social ones.

gene see ➤ GAY *gene,* ➤ *the* SELFISH *gene*.

genealogy a line of descent traced continuously from an ancestor. The word is recorded from Middle English and comes via Old French and late Latin from Greek *genealogia*, from *genea* 'race, generation'.

general see also ➤ CAVIAR *to the general*.

General American the accent of English with which people speak in the greater part of the US, excluding New England, New York, and the South.

General Strike the strike of May 1926 in the UK, called by the Trades Union Congress in support of the mineworkers.

General Synod the highest governing body of the Church of England, an elected assembly of three houses (bishops, clergy, and laity).

General Thanksgiving a form of thanksgiving in the Book of Common Prayer or the Alternative Service Book.

general warrant a warrant for the arrest of the person or people suspected of an offence, no individual being named or described. According to Blackstone, the practice of issuing general warrants, founded on some clauses in the Acts (of Charles II) for regulating the press, was inadvertently continued after those Acts expired in 1694, and (except during the last four years of Queen Anne) remained down to 1763. In that year the arrest of John Wilkes on a general warrant raised the question of the legality of such warrants. In 1765 the Court of King's Bench decided that they were illegal, and in 1766 this was affirmed by a vote of the House of Commons.

generalissimo the commander of a combined military force consisting of army, navy, and air force units. The word comes from Italian, and is recorded in English from the early 17th century. The term was used during the Civil War; Queen ➤ HENRIETTA-*Maria*, who in 1642 arrived at Newark with a small Royalist army, described herself as 'her she-majesty generalissima'.

generalities see ➤ GLITTERING *generalities*.

generation see ➤ *from* CLOGS *to clogs is only three generations*, ➤ LOST *generation*.

the generation gap differences of outlook or opinion between people of different generations; the term is recorded from the 1960s.

Generation X the generation born after that of the ➤ BABY *boomers* (roughly from the early 1960s to mid 1970s), typically perceived to be disaffected and directionless. The term was popularized by Douglas Coupland's book *Generation X: tales for an accelerated culture* (1991), although it had been coined much earlier, in the title of a book (1964) by Charles Hamblett and Jane Deverson.

it takes three generations to make a gentleman proverbial saying, early 19th century.

generous see ➤ *be* JUST *before you're generous*.

Genesis the first book of the Bible, which includes the stories of the creation of the world, ➤ NOAH's *ark*, the ➤ *Tower of* BABEL, and the patriarchs ➤ ABRAHAM, Isaac, ➤ JACOB, and Joseph.

The name, recorded from late Old English, comes via Latin from Greek, 'generation, creation, nativity, horoscope', from the base of *gignesthai* 'be born or produced'. The name was given to the first book of the Old Testament in the Greek translation (the Septuagint), hence in the Latin translation (the Vulgate).

genetic engineering the deliberate modification of the characteristics of an organism by manipulating its genetic material. The phrase is recorded from 1969, and in 1980 the US Supreme Court ruled that engineered living organisms were patentable: this made the infant biotech field potentially enormously profitable. The field has attracted enormous and continuing controversy, most recently in the area of ➤ GM *crops*.

See also ➤ DOLLY.

genetic fingerprinting the analysis of DNA from samples of body tissues or fluids in order to identify individuals. Patterns can be identified which are believed to be specific to the person or animal from which the sample came.

Geneva bands two white cloth strips attached to the collar of some Protestant's clerical dress, as originally worn by Calvinists in Geneva.

Geneva Bible an English translation of the Bible published in 1560 by Protestant scholars working in Europe.

Geneva bull nickname of the presbyterian divine Stephen Marshall (1594?–1655), noted for his preaching.

Geneva Convention an international agreement first made at Geneva in 1864 and later revised, governing the status and treatment of captured and wounded military personnel and civilians in wartime.

Geneva cross a red cross as distinguishing hospitals, first-aid stations, and ambulances in war.

Geneva gown a long loose black gown worn by (especially Calvinist) clergy and academics.

Geneva Protocol any of various protocols drawn up in Geneva, especially that of 1925 limiting chemical and bacteriological warfare.

St Genevieve (d. *c.*500), French nun, and patroness of Paris, who is said to have helped save the city from Attila and the Huns by fasting and prayer.
  ☐ **EMBLEM** Her emblem is a candle, sometimes shown with the devil, who is said to have blown it out when she went to pray in the church at night.
  ☐ **FEAST DAY** Her feast day is 3 January.

Genghis Khan (1162–1227), founder of the Mongol empire; born *Temujin*. He took the name Genghis Khan ('ruler of all') in 1206 after uniting the nomadic Mongol tribes, and by the time of his death his empire extended from China to the Black Sea; his grandson Kublai Khan completed the conquest of China.

In allusive use his name stands for a figure of savage conquest; he is said to have asserted that, 'Happiness lies in conquering one's enemies, in driving them in front of oneself, in taking their property, in savouring their despair, in outraging their wives and daughters.'

See also ➤ *somewhere to the* RIGHT *of Genghis Khan*.

genie a spirit of Arabian folklore, as traditionally depicted imprisoned within a bottle or oil lamp, and capable of granting wishes when summoned; figuratively, an agent of power or change which is or may be released from containment.

Recorded from the mid 17th century (denoting a guardian or protective spirit), the word comes via French from Latin base of ➤ GENIUS. *Génie* was adopted in the current sense by the 18th-century French translators of *The Arabian Nights' Entertainments*, because of its resemblance in form and sense to Arabic *jinnī* ➤ JINN.

Genist a member of a sect of ancient Jews who claimed pure-blooded descent from Abraham because they had not taken foreign wives during the Babylonian Captivity.

genius exceptional intellectual or creative power or other natural ability. The word is recorded from late Middle English, and comes from Latin, meaning 'attendant spirit present from one's birth, innate ability or inclination', from the root of *gignere* 'beget'. The original sense 'tutelary spirit attendant on a person' gave rise in the late 16th century to a sense 'a person's characteristic disposition', which led to the meaning 'a person's natural ability', and finally (in the mid 17th century) 'exceptional natural ability'.

genius is an infinite capacity for taking pains proverbial saying, late 19th century.

genius loci the presiding god or spirit of a particular place; originally with reference to Virgil *Aeneid* 'He prays to the spirit of the place and to Earth'; later with *genius* taken as referring to the body of associations connected with or inspirations derived from a place, rather than to a tutelary deity.

Alexander Pope in *Epistles to Several Persons* (1731) has a related phrase, 'Consult the genius of the place in all.'

Genizah a room attached to an ancient synagogue in Cairo, where vast quantities of fragments of biblical and other Jewish manuscripts were discovered in 1896–8.

Genoa a seaport on the NW coast of Italy, which was the birthplace of ➤ *Christopher* COLUMBUS.

genocide the deliberate killing of a large group of people, especially those of a particular race or nation. The term is recorded from the 1940s, in relation to Nazi rule in occupied Europe.

genome see ➤ HUMAN *Genome Project*.

genre painting a style of painting depicting scenes from ordinary life, especially domestic situations. Genre painting is associated particularly with 17th-century Dutch and Flemish artists.

Genro a body of personal counsellors to the Japanese throne, who dominated the government from 1889 to the 1930s.

gens in ancient Rome, a group of families who shared a name and claimed a common origin; the word is Latin, from the root of *gignere* 'to beget'.

Gentile a person who is not Jewish. The name is recorded from late Middle English and comes from Latin *gentilis* 'of a family or nation, of the same clan' (used in the Vulgate to refer to non-Jews) from *gens, gent-* 'family, race', from the root of *gignere* 'to beget'.

See also ➤ APOSTLE *of the Gentiles*.

gentle archaic term for someone regarded as noble or having the qualities attributed to noble birth; courteous, chivalrous. The word comes (in Middle English, via Old French), from Latin *gentilis* 'of the same clan', from the same base as ➤ GENTILE.

gentle breeze a light wind of force 3 on the Beaufort scale (7–10 knots or 13–19 kph).

the gentle craft humorous term (in the 16th and 17th centuries) for shoemaking, and later for angling.

the gentle sex women; the term is recorded from the late 16th century.

the Gentle Shepherd nickname applied to George Grenville (1712–70), after an exchange with the elder Pitt in the House of Commons. During a debate on the imposition of a cider tax, in March 1763, he intervened in defence of the proposition, and reminded the house that the recent war had made the imposition of new taxes a necessity, and he 'wished gentlemen would show him *where* to lay them.' Pitt, mimicking his languid mode of speech, responded by quoting the refrain of an old song, 'Gentle shepherd, tell me where!'; he then rose to attack Grenville bitterly.

gentleman a man of good social position, especially one of wealth and leisure; the word is recorded from Middle English (denoting a man of noble birth), and was a translation of Old French *gentilz hom*. In later use the term denoted a man of a good family (especially one entitled to a coat of arms) but not of the nobility.

See also ➤ FIRST *Gentleman in Europe*, ➤ *it takes three* GENERATIONS *to make a gentleman*, ➤ LITTLE *gentleman in black velvet*, ➤ WALKING *gentleman*, ➤ *When* ADAM *delved and Eve span, Who was then the gentleman*.

gentleman of fortune an adventurer; as first used in Robert Louis Stevenson's *Treasure Island* (1883), a pirate.

gentleman of the road a highwayman.

gentleman-ranker a well-born or educated man serving as a private soldier; the term is used in Kipling's stories and poems of military life.

Gentleman Usher of the Black Rod the full title of ➤ BLACK *Rod*.

gentleman's agreement an arrangement or understanding which is based upon the trust of both or all parties, rather than being legally binding.

genuflect lower one's body briefly by bending one knee to the ground, typically in worship or as a sign of respect. The word comes from ecclesiastical Latin *genuflectere*, from Latin *genu* 'knee' + *flectere* 'to bend'.

Geoffrey of Monmouth (*c.*1100–*c.*1154), Welsh chronicler. His *Historia Regum Britanniae* (*c.*1139; first printed in 1508), an account of the kings of Britain, was a major source for English literature but is now thought to contain little historical fact.

geomancy divination from the configuration of a handful of earth or random dots.

The term is also used for the art of placing or arranging buildings or other sites auspiciously.

geometry the branch of mathematics concerned with the properties and relations of points, lines, surfaces, solids, and higher dimensional analogues; in the Middle Ages, one of the subjects of the ➤ QUADRIVIUM.

See also ➤ EUCLIDEAN *geometry,* ➤ RIEMANNIAN *geometry.*

Geordie a person from Tyneside; the English dialect or accent typical of people from Tyneside. The term is recorded from the mid 19th century and represents a diminiutive of the given name *George.*

George see also ➤ CHEVALIER *de St George,* ➤ FARMER *George,* ➤ let GEORGE *do it.*

George a jewel bearing the image of St George, forming part of the insignia of the ➤ *Order of the* GARTER.

St George patron saint of England; he is reputed in legend to have slain a dragon, and may have been martyred near Lydda in Palestine some time before the reign of Constantine. His cult did not become popular until the 6th century, and he probably became patron saint of England in the 14th century. He is taken as one of the ➤ FOURTEEN *Holy Helpers.*
 ☐ **FEAST DAY** His feast day is 23 April.

George I (1660–1727), elector of Hanover and king of England, great-grandson of James I, who succeeded to the British throne as a result of the ➤ *Act of* SETTLEMENT (1701). Unpopular in England as a foreigner who never learned English, he left administration to his ministers.

George II (1683–1760), king of England, son of George I; he depended heavily on his ministers, although he took an active part in the War of the Austrian Succession (1740–8). His later withdrawal from active politics allowed the development of constitutional monarchy.

George III (1738–1820), king of England, grandson of George II; nicknamed **Farmer George**. He exercised considerable political influence, but it declined from 1788 after bouts of mental illness, as a result of which his son was made regent in 1811.

George IV (1762–1830), king of England (*Prince Regent* from 1811), son of George III, nicknamed the *First Gentleman in Europe.* Known as a patron of the arts and *bon viveur,* he gained a bad reputation which was further damaged by his attempt to divorce his estranged wife Caroline of Brunswick just after coming to the throne.

George V (1865–1936), king of England, son of Edward VII; he exercised restrained but important influence over British politics, playing an especially significant role in the formation of the government in 1931.

George VI (1894–1952), king of England, son of George V, who came to the throne on the abdication of his elder brother Edward VIII. Despite a retiring disposition he became a popular monarch, gaining respect for the staunch example he and his family set during the London Blitz.

George Cross in the UK and Commonwealth countries, a decoration for bravery awarded especially to civilians, instituted in 1940 by King George VI and taking precedence over all other medals and decorations except the Victoria Cross.

George Cross Island a name for Malta, which was awarded the George Cross in recognition of the bravery of its inhabitants in the Second World War.

George Medal in the UK and Commonwealth countries, a medal for bravery awarded especially to civilians, instituted with the George Cross in 1940.

St George's cross a red vertical cross on a white background.

Georgia a state of the south-eastern US, on the Atlantic coast, founded as an English colony in 1732 and named after George II, which became one of the original thirteen states of the Union (1788).

In the American Civil War the march by ➤ SHERMAN's army which crushed the Confederate forces was made through Georgia.

Georgian green a slightly yellowish green popular in the 18th and early 19th centuries.

Gerald of Wales English name for ➤ GIRALDUS *Cambrensis*.

John Gerard (1545–1612), English herbalist. Gerard was qualified as a barber-surgeon in London and soon developed an interest in plants, particularly those with medicinal properties. He was curator of the physic garden of the College of Surgeons and published his *Herball*, containing over 1,800 woodcuts, in 1597. It became the best-known English herbal.

St Germain-en-Laye site of a royal chateau to the west of Paris which was the final home of the exiled ➤ JAMES *II*.

German see also ➤ HIGH *German*.

German Empire an empire in German-speaking central Europe, created by Bismarck in 1871 after the Franco-Prussian War by the union of twenty-five German states under the Hohenzollern king of Prussia.

Forming an alliance with Austria–Hungary, the German Empire became the greatest industrial power in Europe and engaged in colonial expansion in Africa, China, and the Far East. Tensions arising with other colonial powers led to the First World War, after which the German Empire collapsed and the Weimar Republic was created.

germane relevant to a subject under consideration, a sense that arises from a usage in Shakespeare's *Hamlet* (1601), 'the phrase would be more germane to the matter if we could carry a cannon by our sides.'

St Germanus of Auxerre (d. 446), bishop of Auxerre; he was leader of the British force which won the ➤ HALLELUJAH *Victory* over the Picts and Saxons, and his shrine became a famous pilgrimage centre.

Germany see ➤ APOSTLE *of Germany*.

Germinal the seventh month of the French Republican calendar (1793–1805), originally running from 21 March to 19 April. The name is French, from Latin *germen, germin-* 'sprout, seed'.

Geronimo (*c*.1829–1909), Apache chief. He led his people in resistance to white encroachment on tribal reservations in Arizona before surrendering in 1886.

His name is used as an exclamation used to express exhilaration, especially when leaping from a great height or moving at speed. The expression dates from the Second World War, and was adopted as a slogan by American paratroopers.

gerrymander manipulate the boundaries (of an electoral constituency) so as to favour one party or class. Recorded from the early 19th century, and deriving from the name of Governor Elbridge *Gerry* of Massachusetts + *salamander*, from the supposed similarity between a salamander and the shape of a new voting district on a map drawn when he was in office (1812), the creation of which was felt to favour his party: the map (with claws, wings, and fangs added), was published in the Boston *Weekly Messenger*, with the title *The Gerry-Mander*.

St Gertrude of Nivelles (626–59), daughter of Pepin of Landen, abbess of Nivelles. She is represented in art with mice as her emblem, and has been invoked against pests of rats and mice, by travellers and pilgrims, and as a patroness of the recently dead, on the popular belief that the journey to the next world took three days, the first night of which was spent under the care of Gertrude. Fine weather on her feast-day was regarded as a signal for beginning garden work.
   ☐ **EMBLEM** Her emblem is a mouse.
   ☐ **FEAST DAY** Her feast day is 17 March.

Geryon in Greek mythology, a three-headed or three-bodied giant, living on an island in the far west; he owned a great herd of fine cattle, and it was one of the ➤ *Labours of* HERCULES to steal them and drive them back to Greece.

Gesellschaft social relations based on impersonal ties, as duty to a society or organization. Contrasted with ➤ GEMEINSCHAFT. The word is German, meaning 'companionship'.

Gessler the tyrannical Austrian governor in the story of the legendary Swiss hero ➤ *William* TELL.

Gesta Danorum the 13th-century history of Denmark by ➤ SAXO *Grammaticus*.

Gesta Romanorum a compilation of stories and anecdotes in Latin, probably made in England in the 14th century.

gestalt in psychology, an organized whole that is perceived as more than the sum of its parts; the word is German (recorded in English from the 1920s), and means literally 'form, shape'.

gestalt psychology a movement in psychology founded in Germany in 1912, seeking to explain perceptions in terms of gestalts rather than by analysing their constituents.

gestalt therapy a psychotherapeutic approach developed by Fritz Perls (1893–1970). It focuses on insight into gestalts in patients and their relations to the world, and often uses role playing to aid the resolution of past conflicts.

Gestapo the German secret police under Nazi rule. It ruthlessly suppressed opposition to the Nazis in Germany and occupied Europe and sent Jews and others to concentration camps. From 1936 it was headed by Heinrich Himmler. The name is German, from *Geheime Staatspolizei* 'secret state police'.

Gestas traditionally the name of the impenitent thief, who with the penitent ➤ DISMAS was crucified with Jesus.

geste see ➤ BEAU *Geste*, ➤ CHANSON *de geste*.

get see ➤ *what you* SEE *is what you get*, ➤ *get down to* BRASS *tacks*, ➤ *the* MORE *you get, the more you want*.

Garden of Gethsemane a garden between Jerusalem and the Mount of Olives, where Jesus went with his disciples after the Last Supper, and where he was betrayed; in allusion, a place of suffering and endurance.

> I can be brave in the day, but nights are my Gethsemane.
> — Sandra Cisneros *Woman Hollering Creek* (1991)

See also ➤ *the* AGONY *in the Garden*.

Jean Paul Getty (1892–1976), American industrialist. He made a large fortune in the oil industry and

was also a noted art collector. He founded the J. Paul Getty Museum in Los Angeles.

Battle of Gettysburg a decisive battle of the American Civil War, fought near the town of Gettysburg in Pennsylvania in July 1863. A Union army under General Meade repulsed the Confederate army of General Lee and forced him to abandon his invasion of the north.

Gettysburg address a speech delivered on 19 November 1863 by President Abraham Lincoln at the dedication of the national cemetery on the site of the Battle of Gettysburg, opening with the words:

> Fourscore and seven years ago our fathers brought forth upon this continent a new nation, conceived in liberty, and dedicated to the proposition that all men are created equal.
> — Abraham Lincoln opening words of the address at Gettysburg, 19 November 1863

Although the speech is now taken as a classic piece of oratory, there was some immediate contemporary criticism, which contrasted its concision unfavourably with the two-hour address by Edward Everett (1794–1865) which had succeeded it. Everett himself took a different view, writing to Lincoln on the following day, 'I should be glad if I could flatter myself that I came as near the central idea of the occasion in two hours as you did in two minutes.'

the 'Ghan in Australia, the train running between Adelaide and Alice Springs.

ghat a level place on the edge of a river where Hindus cremate their dead. Also called **burning-ghat**.

Ghazi often as an honorific title, a Muslim fighter against non-Muslims. The word comes from Arabic *al-ġā*, participle of *ġazā* 'invade, raid'.

Ghaznavid a member of a Turkish Muslim dynasty founded in Ghazna, Afghanistan, in AD 977. The dynasty extended its power into Persia and the Punjab, but in the 11th century fragmented under pressure from the Seljuk Turks, and was finally destroyed in 1186.

Ghent a city in Belgium, capital of the medieval principality of Flanders, which was formerly known in English as Gaunt (surviving in names, e.g. ➤ JOHN *of Gaunt*).

ghetto a part of a city, especially a slum area, occupied by a minority group or groups; originally, the Jewish quarter in a city. Recorded from the early

17th century, the word may come from Italian *getto* 'foundry' (because the first ghetto was established in 1516 on the site of a foundry in Venice), or from Italian *borghetto*, diminutive of *borgo* 'borough'.

Ghibelline a member of one of the two great political factions in Italian medieval politics, traditionally supporting the Holy Roman emperor against the Pope and his supporters, the Guelphs, during the long struggle between the papacy and the Empire. The name may come ultimately from German *Waiblingen*, an estate belonging to Hohenstaufen emperors.

Lorenzo Ghiberti (1378–1455), Italian sculptor and goldsmith. His career was dominated by his work on two successive pairs of bronze doors for the baptistery in Florence. The second, more famous, pair (1425–52) depicts episodes from the Bible laid out on carefully constructed perspective stages.

Ghirlandaio (*c.*1448–94), Italian painter; the name means 'garland-maker', and refers to the skill of his goldsmith father in metal garland-work. He is noted for his religious frescoes, particularly *Christ Calling Peter and Andrew* (1482–4) in the Sistine Chapel, Rome. He painted in a naturalistic style that included detailed portraits of leading contemporary citizens.

ghost an apparition of a dead person which is believed to appear or become manifest to the living, typically as a nebulous image and (as with ➤ HAM-LET's father) attempting to right a wrong done in life; this sense of the word is recorded from late Middle English.

The word is recorded from Old English (in form *gāst*) in the sense 'spirit, soul', and is of Germanic origin; the *gh*- spelling occurs first in Caxton, and was probably influenced by Flemish *gheest*.

See also ➤ COCK *Lane Ghost*, ➤ HOLY *Ghost*, ➤ SAMPFORD *ghost*.

give up the ghost die; *ghost* here is in the sense of 'spirit, soul'.

Ghost Dance an American Indian religious cult of the second half of the 19th century, based on the performance of a ritual dance, lasting sometimes for several days, which, it was believed, would drive away white people, bring the dead back to life, and restore the traditional lands and way of life. Advocated by the Sioux chief Sitting Bull, the cult was

central to the uprising that was crushed at the Battle of Wounded Knee.

the ghost in the machine the mind viewed as distinct from the body, a term coined by the philosopher Gilbert Ryle for a viewpoint which he regarded as completely misleading:

> Such in outline is the official theory. I shall often speak of it, with deliberate abusiveness, as 'the dogma of the Ghost in the machine'.
> — Gilbert Ryle *The Concept of Mind* (1949)

ghost town a deserted town with few or no remaining inhabitants; typically one which was previously at the centre of a gold-mining site where the vein is now exhausted.

the ghost walks money is available and salaries will paid. The phrase has been has been explained by the story that an actor playing the ghost of Hamlet's father refused to 'walk again' until the cast's overdue salaries had been paid.

ghost word a word recorded in a dictionary or other reference work which is not actually used. The term is first recorded in a paper entitled 'Report upon "Ghost-words" ' by the philologist W. W. Skeat (1835–1912), in which he warned against such inclusions:

> We should jealously guard against all chances of giving any undeserved record of words which had never any real existence, being mere coinages due to the blunders of printers or scribes, or to the perfervid imaginations of ignorant or blundering editors.
> — W. W. Skeat in *Transactions of the Philological Society* 1885–7

ghostbuster a person who claims to be able to banish ghosts and poltergeists. The term (probably a conscious echo of the earlier *gangbuster*) was first recorded in 1920, but derived its late 20th-century popularity from the 1984 film *Ghostbusters*, about three specialists trying to contain a paranormal outbreak in Manhattan; the supernatural element represented not so much the disembodied spirit of a dead person, as the kind of destructive supernatural entity represented by a poltergeist.

ghoul an evil spirit or phantom, especially one supposed to rob graves and feed on dead bodies. Recorded from the late 18th century, the word comes from Arabic *ḡūl*, a desert demon believed to rob graves and devour corpses.

Ghulghuleh a ruined ancient city near Bamian in central Afghanistan. It was destroyed by ➤ GENGHIS *Khan c.*1221.

GI a private soldier in the US army, originally (denoting equipment supplied to US forces) an abbreviation of *government issue* (or *general issue*).

giant an imaginary or mythical being of human form but superhuman size, often seen as at war with the gods; in Greek mythology, it was the giants who rebelled unsuccessfully against ➤ ZEUS and the gods of Olympus, and in Scandinavian mythology, the frost giants were the particular enemies of ➤ THOR.

Giant has also been used for an abnormally tall or large person; Charles Byrne (1761–83), whose skeleton was acquired for his museum by the English anatomist and surgeon John Hunter (1728–93), was known as the **Irish giant**.

In astronomy, *giant* is the name for a star of relatively great size and luminosity compared to ordinary stars of the main sequence, and 10–100 times the diameter of the sun.

See also ➤ FROST *giants*, ➤ JACK *the Giant-Killer*, ➤ LITTLE *Giant*.

Giant Despair in Bunyan's *Pilgrim's Progress*, a giant who imprisons Christian and Hopeful in ➤ DOUBTING *Castle*.

> For any redeeming feature it presented to their eyes, they might have entered . . . on the grim domains of Giant Despair.
> — Charles Dickens *Martin Chuzzlewit* (1844)

giant order in architecture, an order whose columns extend through more than one storey.

Giant Pope in Bunyan's *Pilgrim's Progress*, a giant who was formerly a figure of terror and tyranny, but who is 'grown crazy and stiff in his joints that he can now do little more that sit in his cave's mouth, grinning at pilgrims as they go by, and biting his nails, because he cannot come at them.'

Giant's Causeway a geological formation of basalt columns, dating from the Tertiary period, on the north coast of Northern Ireland. It was once believed to be the end of a road made by a legendary giant to Staffa in the Inner Hebrides, where there is a similar formation.

Dr Johnson's comment on the Causeway (in October 1779) was that it was 'worth seeing…but not worth going to see.'

the War of the Giants another name for the ➤ GIGANTOMACHY.

Giants' Dance in the chronicle of Geoffrey of Monmouth, the stones brought from Ireland by the magician Merlin to be set up as Stonehenge.

Giants' Ring a prehistoric settlement south of Belfast.

giaour archaic and derogatory term for a non-Muslim, especially a Christian.

gib cat a male cat, a tomcat; recorded from the mid 16th century.

gibbet an upright post with an arm on which the bodies of executed criminals were left hanging as a warning or deterrent to others; the gallows. The word is recorded from Middle English, and comes from Old French *gibet* 'staff, cudgel, gallows', diminutive of *gibe* 'club, staff', and probably of Germanic origin.

Edward Gibbon (1737–94), English historian. He is best known for his multi-volume work *The History of the Decline and Fall of the Roman Empire* (1776–88), chapters of which aroused controversy for their critical account of the spread of Christianity.

Grinling Gibbons (1648–1721), Dutch-born English sculptor. He is famous for his decorative carvings, chiefly in wood, of fruit and flowers, small animals, and cherubs' heads; as in the choir stalls of St Paul's Cathedral, London.

> He did too much . . . He out-Grinling'd Gibbons with his verbal garlands.
> — Clemence Dane *The Flower Girls* (1954)

Orlando Gibbons (1583–1625), English composer and musician. He became a chamber musician to King James I in 1619 and the organist of Westminster Abbey from 1623. He composed mainly sacred music, although he is also known for madrigals such as *The Silver Swan* (1612).

Gibeonite any of the inhabitants of *Gibeon*, who in Joshua 9:27 were condemned by Joshua to be 'hewers of wood and drawers of water' for the Israelites; a drudge.

> The Mac-Couls . . . were a sort of Gibeonites or hereditary servants to the Stewarts of Appin.
> — Sir Walter Scott *Waverley* (1814)

Rock of Gibraltar a rocky headland at the eastern end of the Strait of Gibraltar, captured by the British during the War of the Spanish Succession in 1704 and formally ceded by the Peace of Utrecht (1713–14); traditionally one of the ➤ PILLARS *of Hercules*.

Gibson Desert a desert region in Western Australia, to the south-east of the Great Sandy Desert. The first European to cross it (1876) was Ernest Giles, who named it after his companion Alfred *Gibson*, who went missing on an earlier expedition.

Gibson girl a girl typifying the fashionable ideal of the late 19th and early 20th centuries, as represented in the work of Charles D. *Gibson* (1867–1944), American artist and illustrator.

Gideon in the Bible, an Old Testament warrior and judge of Israel, under whose leadership (Judges ch. 6–8) the Midianites were conquered.

See also ➤ *the* SWORD *of the Lord and of Gideon.*

Gideons International an international Christian organization of business and professional people, founded in 1899 in the US with the aim of spreading the Christian faith by placing bibles in hotel rooms and hospital wards.

gift see also ➤ *the gift of* TONGUES, ➤ SEVEN *gifts of the Holy Spirit.*

never look a gift horse in the mouth proverbial saying, early 16th century; referring to the fact that it is by a horse's teeth that its age is judged.

Gigantomachy in Greek mythology, the struggle between the gods and the giants, ending with the defeat of the giants.

Gigantopithecus a very large fossil Asian ape of the Upper Miocene to Lower Pleistocene.

Humphrey Gilbert (*c.*1539–83), English explorer. He led an unsuccessful attempt to colonize the New World in 1578–9. On a second voyage he claimed Newfoundland for Elizabeth I in 1583, but was lost when his ship foundered in a storm on the way home.

William Gilbert (1544–1603), English physician and physicist. He discovered how to make magnets, and coined the term *magnetic pole*. His book *De Magnete* (1600) is an important early work on physics.

William Schwenck Gilbert (1836–1911), English dramatist, best known as a librettist who collaborated on light operas with the composer Arthur Sullivan; the term **Gilbertian** is used to mean resembling or reminiscent of a characteristically ludicrous or paradoxical situation in a Gilbert and Sullivan opera.

Gilbertine a member of the English religious order for men and women founded by St *Gilbert* of Sempringham (*c.*1083–1189).

gild the lily embellish excessively, add ornament where none is needed, from an alteration of Shakespeare:

> To gild refinèd gold, to paint the lily . . .
> Is wasteful and ridiculous excess.
> — William Shakespeare *King John* (1591–8)

The conflated expression *gild the lily* is recorded from the early 20th century.

gild the pill make something unpleasant seem more acceptable (pills were traditionally coated with gilt to make them more attractive).

Gildas British historian of the 6th century whose Latin work, *De Excidio et Conquestu Britanniae*, refers to the British victory over the Saxons at the ➤ *Battle of* BADON *Hill* (although he does not mention Arthur).

the Gilded Chamber an informal name for the House of Lords.

gilded spurs a traditional emblem of knighthood.

gilded youth young people of wealth, fashion, and flair (translating French *jeunesse dorée*).

Gilderoy a Scottish robber and cattle-thief, subject of a traditional ballad, said to have been hanged higher than other criminals because of the wickedness of his crimes; **higher than Gilderoy's kite** means, extremely high, out of sight.

Gilead see ➤ BALM *in Gilead.*

Giles personal forename as the generic name for a farmer.

St Giles (d. *c.*710), hermit, living in Provence, whose shrine became an important pilgrimage centre in the Middle Ages. According to his legend, a hind that was being hunted took refuge with him; Giles was wounded and lamed by the arrow shot at it. He is patron of the lame, lepers, and (because of the hind that he sheltered) of nursing mothers. He is also patron of blacksmiths, and churches dedicated to him are often found near to smithies where travellers could have their horses shod.

Many churches, including St Giles at Cripplegate in London, were dedicated to him, and there were two annual medieval fairs, at Winchester and Oxford, of which St Giles' Fair Oxford survives as a funfair, set up for two days each year in the wide street of St Giles' in the city centre.

In Germany, he was regarded as one of the ➤ FOURTEEN *Holy Helpers.*

☐ **FEAST DAY** His feast day is 1 September.
See also ➤ DINE *with St Giles and the Earl of Moray.*

Gilgamesh a legendary king of the Sumerian city state of Uruk who is supposed to have ruled sometime during the first half of the 3rd millennium BC. He is the hero of the Babylonian epic of Gilgamesh, one of the best-known works of ancient literature, which recounts his exploits in an ultimately unsuccessful quest for immortality. It contains an account of a flood that has close parallels with the biblical story of Noah.

gill see also ➤ *every* HERRING *must hang by its own gill.*

Eric Gill (1882–1940), English sculptor, engraver, and typographer. His best-known sculptures are the relief carvings *Stations of the Cross* (1914–18) at Westminster Cathedral and the *Prospero and Ariel* (1931) on Broadcasting House in London. He designed the first sans serif typeface, Gill Sans. He illustrated many books for the Golden Cockerell Press, and designed printing types for the Monotype Corporation.

Dizzy Gillespie (1917–93), American jazz trumpet player and bandleader. He was a virtuoso trumpet player and a leading exponent of the bebop style.

gillie in Scotland, a man or boy who attends someone on a hunting or fishing expedition; originally, a Highland chief's attendant. The word comes from Scottish Gaelic *gille* 'lad, servant', and is also found in the term *gilliewetfoot*, denoting a servant who carried the chief over a stream, used as a contemptuous name by Lowlanders for the follower of a Highland chief.

Gillies Hill the Scottish victory at Bannockburn was confirmed by a charge of about 2,000 Scots down *Gillies Hill*, which overlooked the battlefield to the west.

James Gillray (1757–1815), caricaturist. He used his mordant wit and political independence to show up the abuses and vices of Parliament and the royal family, and his often vicious caricatures of Napoleon helped to rouse the patriotism of the country to the threat of invasion.
See also ➤ OLD *Lady of Threadneedle Street.*

gillyflower any of a number of fragrant flowers, such as the wallflower or white stock; (in archaic use) a clove-scented pink or carnation. The word comes via Old French and medieval Latin from Greek *karuophullon* (from *karuon* 'nut' + *phullon* 'leaf'). The ending was altered by association with flower, but *gilliver* survived in dialect.

gilt see also ➤ GINGERBREAD.

gilt-edged relating to or denoting stocks or securities ('paper') that are regarded as extremely reliable investments; *gilt-edged* was originally used literally of writing-paper or the pages of books.

gimmick a trick or device intended to attract attention, publicity, or trade. Of unknown origin, but possibly an approximate anagram of *magic*, the original sense being 'a piece of magicians' apparatus'.

gin a clear alcoholic spirit distilled from grain or malt and flavoured with juniper berries, from an abbreviation of *geneva*, Dutch form of the plant's name, from Latin through Old French.

ginger a hot fragrant spice made from the rhizome of a SE Asian plant; figuratively, spirit, mettle.

ginger group a highly active faction within a party or movement that presses for stronger action on a particular issue.

gingerbread cake made with treacle or syrup and flavoured with ginger, which was traditionally made in decorative forms which were then gilded; **take the gilt off the gingerbread** thus means, strip something of its attractions.

gingerly in a careful or cautious manner. The original (early 16th-century) sense is 'daintily, mincingly'): this may come from Old French *gensor* 'delicate', ultimately from Latin *genitus* '(well)-born'.

Ginnunagap in Scandinavian mythology, the abyss between Niflheim and Muspelheim.

ginseng a plant tuber credited with various tonic and medicinal properties, especially in the Far East. The name is recorded from the mid 17th century, and comes from Chinese *rénshēn*, from *rén* 'man' + *shēn*, a kind of herb (because of the supposed resemblance of the forked root to a person).

Gioconda smile an enigmatic smile, reminiscent of *La Gioconda*, a portrait (also known as *Mona Lisa*) by Leonardo da Vinci (1452–1519) of the wife of

Francesco del *Giocondo*, noted for the sitter's enigmatic smile.

> Noelle gave Tandy her Gioconda smile.
> — J. Gunn *Joy Machine* (1996)

Giorgione Italian painter, (*c.*1478–1510). An influential figure in Renaissance art, he introduced the small easel picture in oils intended for private collectors.

Giotto (*c.*1267–1337), Italian painter. He rejected the flat, formulaic, and static images of Italo-Byzantine art in favour of a more naturalistic style showing human expression. Notable works include the frescoes in the Arena Chapel, Padua (1305–8) and the church of Santa Croce in Florence (*c.*1320).

Giotto's O the perfect circle supposedly drawn freehand by ➤ GIOTTO.

> I saw . . . that the practical teaching of the masters of Art was summed up by the O of Giotto.
> — John Ruskin *Queen of Air* (1869)

Giralda name of the square tower of Seville Cathedral; originally, part of the Moorish mosque.

Giraldus Cambrensis (*c.*1146–1220), Welsh cleric and chronicler; he is the author of *Topographia Hibernica*, which covers the natural history, marvels, and early events of Ireland, and the *Iterarium Cambriae* on the topography of Wales. He is also known as **Gerald of Wales**.

gird up one's loins prepare and strengthen oneself for what is to come; originally with biblical allusion, as in 2 Kings 4:29, 'Gird up thy loins, and take my staff in thy hand.'

girl a female child, a young woman; the word, recorded from Middle English, originally denotetd a child or young person of either sex, and is perhaps related to Low German *gör* 'child'.

➤ *St* AGNES, ➤ *St* CATHERINE *of Alexandria*, ➤ *St* NICHOLAS *of Myra*, and ➤ *St* URSULA are the patron saints of girls.

girl Friday a female helper, especially a junior office worker or a personal assistant to a business executive; recorded from 1940, as an alteration of ➤ MAN *Friday*.

Girl Guide a member of the ➤ GUIDES *Association*.

giro a system of electronic credit transfer used in Europe and Japan, largely involving banks, post offices, and public utilities; a cheque or payment by such a system, especially a social security payment.

The term is recorded from the late 19th century, and comes via German from Italian, 'circulation of money'.

Girondist a member of the French moderate republican Party in power during the Revolution 1791–3, so called because the party leaders were the deputies from the department of the *Gironde* in SW France. The revolutionary Pierre Vergniaud (1753–93), executed with other Girondists, said, 'There was reason to fear that the Revolution, like Saturn, might devour in turn each one of her children.'

Giunta in the Venetian republic, a number of patricians chosen to act as advisers in special emergencies; later, the co-opted members of the council which ran the affairs of the State. The name is Italian, from *giugnere* 'to join', and is related to *junta*.

give see also ➤ *give us back our* ELEVEN *days*.

give a thing, and take a thing, to wear the devil's gold ring proverbial saying, late 16th century; a schoolchildren's rhyme, chanted when a person gives something and then asks for it back.

give and take is fair play proverbial saying, late 18th century.

he gives twice who gives quickly proverbial saying, mid 16th century.

Giza a city south-west of Cairo in northern Egypt, on the west bank of the Nile, site of the Pyramids and the Sphinx.

gladiator in ancient Rome, a man trained to fight with weapons against other men or wild animals in an arena; usually a slave or prisoner trained for the purpose. The word is Latin, and comes from *gladius* 'sword'; it was used by Cicero as a term of abuse in his denunciation of Catiline.

William Ewart Gladstone (1809–98), British Liberal statesman, Prime Minister 1868–74, 1880–5, 1886, and 1892–4, known as the **GOM** (for *Grand Old Man*). At first a Conservative minister, he later joined the Liberal Party, becoming its leader in 1867. His ministries saw the introduction of elementary education, the passing of the Irish Land Acts and the third Reform Act, and his campaign in favour of Home Rule for Ireland.

A noted orator, he was described by his political rival Disraeli as 'A sophistical rhetorician, inebriated with the exuberance of his own verbosity;'

Queen Victoria is said to have complained, 'He speaks to Me as if I was a public meeting.'

Gladstone bag a bag like a briefcase having two equal compartments joined by a hinge, named after the 19th-century statesman ➤ *William Ewart* GLAD-STONE, who was noted for the amount of travelling he undertook when electioneering.

Glagolitic denoting or relating to an alphabet based on Greek minuscules, formerly used in writing some Slavic languages. The alphabet is of uncertain origin, and was introduced in the 9th century, at about the same time as the Cyrillic alphabet, which has superseded it except in some Orthodox Church liturgies.

Glasgow a city in Scotland on the River Clyde, which was formerly a major shipbuilding centre.

Glasgow magistrate in Scotland, humorous term for a herring; perhaps because in the 17th century herring were cured there by Walter Gibson, a merchant who was also Provost of the city.

glasnost in the former Soviet Union, the policy or practice of more open consultative government and wider dissemination of information, initiated by leader Mikhail Gorbachev from 1985.

The word comes from Russian *glasnost'*, literally 'the fact of being public'.

glass see also ➤ PROSPECTIVE *glass*.

glass ceiling an unacknowledged barrier to advancement in a profession, especially affecting women and members of minorities. The term was originally (in the early 1980s) coined to denote an invisible but impenetrable barrier enshrining prejudices which were not openly admitted, but as the concept became more familiar, the figurative associations were developed: a *glass ceiling* was taken as something that could be broken.

those who live in glass houses shouldn't throw stones proverbial saying, mid 17th century.

Glastonbury a town in Somerset which is the legendary burial place of King Arthur and Queen Guinevere, and the site of a ruined abbey held by legend to have been founded by ➤ JOSEPH *of Arimathea*. It was identified in medieval times with the mythical ➤ AVALON.

Glastonbury chair a kind of folding armchair, supposedly designed after a chair owned by the last Abbot of Glastonbury (executed 1539).

Glastonbury thorn a winter-flowering form of hawthorn, said to have sprung up at Glastonbury from the staff of ➤ JOSEPH *of Arimathea*; it is traditionally said to flower on Christmas Day according to the Old Style calendar.

the Glatysant Beast the creature in Malory's *Morte D'Arthur* which is the original of Spenser's 'blatant beast'. The word is from an Old French word meaning 'baying', 'barking'.

Glaucus a legendary fisherman of ancient Greece who noticed that a fish which he had caught was restored to life after contact with a particular herb; eating the herb himself, he was turned into a sea god and acquired the power of prophecy.

> By scaly Triton's winding shell,
> And old soothsaying Glaucus' spell.
> — John Milton *Comus* (1637)

Gleipnir in Scandinavian mythology, name of the magic shackle with which ➤ FENRIR was bound by the gods; it was forged by the dwarfs from the sound of a cat's footfall, the beard of a woman, the roots of a mountain, the sinews of a bear, the breath of a fish, and the spittle of a bird.

Massacre of Glencoe a massacre in 1692 of members of the Jacobite MacDonald clan by Campbell soldiers, which took place near Glencoe in the Scottish Highlands.

The MacDonald clan failed to swear allegiance to William III, making them liable to military punishment. Soldiers from the Campbell clan, who had been billeted on the MacDonalds for twelve days, murdered the MacDonald chief and about thirty of his followers, while the rest of the clan escaped. The chief of the Campbell clan, which had a long-standing feud with the MacDonalds, was held responsible, although the massacre was almost certainly instigated by the government.

See also ➤ CURSE *of Scotland*.

Glendalough in Wicklow, the remains, consisting of a round tower, a ruined cathedral, and several stone churches, of an important early monastic settlement, founded by ➤ *St* KEVIN in the 7th century and with a notably picturesque setting in the 'valley of the two lakes'.

Owen Glendower (*c*.1354–*c*.1417), Welsh chief. He proclaimed himself Prince of Wales and led a national uprising against Henry IV, allying himself with Henry's English opponents, including Henry Percy. He continued fighting against the English until his death.

glengarry a brimless boat-shaped hat with a cleft down the centre, typically having two ribbons hanging at the back, worn as part of Highland dress. The term is recorded from the mid 19th century, and comes from the name of *Glengarry*, a valley in the Highlands of Scotlad.

glimpses of the moon the earth by night, sublunary scenes (originally with reference to the scene in Shakespeare's *Hamlet* in which Hamlet addresses his father's ghost, 'That thou, dead corse again in complete steel, Revisit'st thus the glimpses of the moon.'

Knight of Glin one of three hereditary Irish titles (the others being the ➤ *Knight of* KERRY and the ➤ WHITE *Knight*); the title, belonging to the Fitzgerald family, is recorded from the 15th century.

glitterati the fashionable set of people engaged in show business or some other glamorous activity. Recorded from the 1950s (in the US), the word is a blend of *glitter* and *literati*.

glittering generalities platitudes, clichés, superficially convincing but empty phrases; the phrase is first recorded in a letter from the American lawyer Rufus Choate (1799–1859), 'Its constitution the glittering and sounding generalities of natural right which make up the Declaration of Independence.'

all that glitters is not gold proverbial saying, early 13th century.

global warming the gradual increase in the overall temperature of the earth's atmosphere due to the greenhouse effect caused by increased levels of carbon dioxide, CFCs, and other pollutants.

globe a globe is the emblem of ➤ *St* HENRY and ➤ *St* LOUIS.

globe of fire a globe of fire is the emblem of ➤ *St* MARTIN *of Tours*.

Globe Theatre a theatre in Southwark, London, erected in 1599, where many of Shakespeare's plays were first publicly performed by Richard Burbage and his company. Shakespeare had a share in the theatre and also acted there; it has been suggested that the reference in Prospero's speech in *The Tempest* to 'the great globe itself' may contain a punning allusion to the theatre.

It caught fire in 1613 from a discharge of stage gunfire during a play, and was destroyed, although it was rebuilt in 1614 and used until all London theatres were closed on the outbreak of the Civil War in 1642.

The theatre's site was rediscovered in 1989 and a reconstruction of the original theatre was opened in 1997.

use of the globes the learning or teaching of geography and astronomy by using terrestrial and celestial globes.

gloria see also ➤ SIC *transit gloria mundi*.

Gloria a Christian liturgical hymn or formula beginning (in the Latin text) with *Gloria* 'Glory'.

Gloria in excelsis the hymn beginning *Gloria in excelsis Deo* ('Glory to God in the highest'), forming a set part of the Mass.

Gloria Patri the doxology beginning *Gloria Patris* ('Glory be to the Father'), used after psalms and in formal prayer, such as the rosary.

Gloriana a name for Queen Elizabeth I, which is used for the character representing her in Spenser's *Faerie Queene*. Benjamin Britten's opera composed for the coronation of Elizabeth II (1952), was entitled *Gloriana*.

the Glorious First of June name given to a decisive naval victory of 1 June 1794, when the British navy under Lord Howe defeated French revolutionary forces off Ushant; the name is first recorded in the title (1794), 'Songs, Duets, Choruses…In a New and Appropriate Entertainment. Called *The Glorious First of June*.'

Glorious John a nickname for ➤ *John* DRYDEN (1631–1700), first recorded in Scott:

> 'You forget glorious John,' said Mordaunt. 'Ay, glorious you may well call him.'
> — Walter Scott *The Pirate* (1821)

the Glorious Revolution the events (1688–9) that led to the replacement, in 1689, of James II by his daughter Mary II and her husband William of Orange (who became William III) as joint monarchs. The bloodless 'revolution' greatly enhanced the constitutional powers of Parliament, with William and Mary's acceptance of the conditions laid down in the Bill of Rights.

The term is first recorded in a sermon preached on 5 November 1716, which coupled the discovery of the ➤ GUNPOWDER *Plot* with the *Glorious Revolution* as examples of divine intervention.

the Glorious Twelfth 12 August, on which the grouse-shooting season opens; the term is recorded from the late 19th century.

the glorious uncertainty of the law an ironic phrase which according to the *Gentleman's Magazine* of August 1830 was first used at a dinner of the Judges and Counsel about 1756, when after the toast of 'the glorious memory of King William' had been drunk. One of those present, a Mr Wilbraham, proposed 'the glorious uncertainty of the law', in sarcastic allusion to Lord Chief Justice Mansfield's customary overruling of former decisions.

glory see also ➤ CROWNING *glory*, ➤ DEATH-or-Glory-Boys, ➤ HAND *of glory*, ➤ LAND *of Hope and Glory*, ➤ OLD *Glory*, ➤ QUEEN *of glory*.

glossolalia the phenomenon of (apparently) speaking in an unknown language, especially in religious worship. It is practised especially by Pentecostal and charismatic Christians.

Gloucestershire see ➤ *sure as* GOD's *in Gloucestershire*.

glove traditionally as a token of a pledge, or a challenge to battle, as in **throw down the glove, take up the glove** (a *glove* here is a gauntlet).

A *glove* as a type of something that fits or suits perfectly is recorded from the late 18th century.

The expressions **handle without gloves** and **take the gloves off**, recorded from the early 19th century and meaning, treat without mercy or forbearance, refer to boxing-gloves, and the notion of bare-knuckle fighting as being particularly vicious.

See also ➤ *a* CAT *in gloves catches no mice*.

glove money extraordinary rewards formerly given to officers of English courts, in particular, money given by a sheriff to other officers in a county in which there were no offenders left for execution.

Glyndebourne Festival an annual festival of opera, held at the estate of Glyndebourne near Lewes, East Sussex. The original opera house was built by the owner of the estate, John Christie (1882–1962), who founded the festival in 1934. A new opera house was opened in 1994.

GM abbreviation for *genetically-modified*, much used in the debate on crops produced in this way;

the term is recorded from the mid 1990s, and the expression **GM-free** is now found.

gnat see ➤ STRAIN *at a gnat and swallow a camel.*

gnome a legendary dwarfish creature supposed to guard the earth's treasures underground; now popularly represented in a small garden ornament in the form of a bearded man with a pointed hat.

The word is recorded from the mid 17th century, and comes via French from modern Latin *gnomus*, a word used by Paracelsus as a synonym of *Pygmaeus*, denoting a mythical race of very small people said to inhabit parts of Ethiopia and India.

gnomes of Zurich informal term for Swiss financiers, regarded as having a sinister influence; the phrase was popularized by Harold Wilson (1916–95):

> All these financiers, all the little gnomes in Zurich and the other financial centres about whom we keep on hearing.
> — Harold Wilson speech in the House of Commons, 12 November 1956

gnomic expressed in or of the nature of short, pithy maxims or aphorisms. Recorded from the early 19th century (**gnomical** in the same sense dates from the early 16th century), the word comes from Greek *gnōmikos*, ultimately formed as English *gnome* (late 16th century), 'thought, judgement, opinion', from Greek *gnōme* in same sense, from *gnōmai* 'sayings, maxims', from the base of *gignōskein* 'know'.

gnosis knowledge of spiritual mysteries. Recorded from the late 16th century, the word comes from Greek *gnōsis* 'knowledge', related to *gignōskein* 'know'.

Gnosticism a prominent heretical movement of the 2nd-century Christian Church, partly of pre-Christian origin. Gnostic doctrine taught that the world was created and ruled by a lesser divinity, the demiurge, and that Christ was an emissary of the remote supreme divine being, esoteric knowledge (*gnosis*) of whom enabled the redemption of the human spirit.

go see also ➤ *go to the* COUNTRY.

go further and fare worse proverbial saying, mid 16th century.

go the extra mile make an extra effort, do more than is strictly asked or required. In a revue song

(1957) by Joyce Grenfell, 'Ready…To go the extra mile', but perhaps ultimately in allusion to Matthew 5:41 'And whosoever shall compel thee to go a mile, go with him twain.'

go to work on an egg advertising slogan for the British Egg Marketing Board, from 1957; perhaps written by Fay Weldon or Mary Gowing.

go west, young man first recorded in *Hints toward Reforms* (1850) by Horace Greeley (1811–72), American founder and editor of the *New York Times*, 'Go West, young man, and grow up with the country.' In the following year, 'Go West, young man, go West!' was used in an editorial in the *Terre Haute* [Indiana] *Express*.

The American writer Nathanael West (1903–40), asked by William Carlos Williams why he had chosen the name 'West' as a pseudonym, replied, 'Horace Greeley said, "Go West, young man." So I did.'

goal see ➤ SCORE *an own goal.*

goalposts see ➤ MOVE *the goalposts.*

goat the *goat* is taken as the symbol of a (damned) sinner (often with biblical allusion to Matthew 25:32–3, as in ➤ SEPARATE *the sheep from the goats*); it is also traditionally a type of lustfulness and folly.

The Goat is a name for the zodiacal sign Capricorn or the constellation Capricornus.

The word is recorded from Old English (in form *gāt*, meaning 'female goat'), and is of Germanic origin, ultimately related to Latin *haedus* 'kid'.

See also ➤ SCAPEGOAT.

Goat and Compasses a public house sign, said to represent an alteration of the words *Great God Encompassing*; it has been suggested that public feeling against the Puritan text 'God encompasseth us' over private doorways encouraged the change.

goat-god a name for the god Pan, who is typically represented with the legs and hooves of a goat.

goatsucker another term for the nightjar, because the bird was thought to suck goats' udders.

gobbledegook informal language that is meaningless or made unintelligible by excessive use of abstruse technical terms, nonsense. Originally (1940s) US, and probably imitative of a turkey's gobble.

Gobelins a tapestry and textile factory in Paris, established by the Gobelin family *c.*1440 and taken

over by the French Crown in 1662. It was highly successful in the late 17th and 18th centuries, when designs by leading French painters were used, and tapestry panels became used as alternatives to oil paintings. A **Gobelin tapestry** is a tapestry made at this factory, or one which imitates this.

Gobi Desert a barren plateau of southern Mongolia and northern China; in allusive use, a type of remote emptiness and desolation.

> His notion [that] … you could stand in the middle of the Gobi Desert with a cellular phone and be connected to the world.
>
> — *Vanity Fair* October 1996

Comte de Gobineau (1816–82), French writer and anthropologist. His stated view that the races are innately unequal and that the white Aryan race is superior to all others later influenced the ideology and policies of the Nazis.

goblin a mischievous, ugly, dwarf-like creature of folklore. The word is Middle English and from Old French *gobelin*, possibly related to German (see ➤ KOBOLD) or Greek *kobalos* 'mischievous goblin'. In medieval Latin *Gobelinus* occurs as the name of a mischievous spirit, said to haunt Évreux in northern France in the 12th century.

God in Christianity and other monotheistic religions, the creator and ruler of the universe and source of all moral authority, the supreme being. In certain other religions (with lower-case initial), a superhuman being or spirit worshipped as having power over nature or human fortunes; a deity.

See also ➤ ALL *things are possible with God,* ➤ *by the* GRACE *of God,* ➤ CHILD *of God,* ➤ CITY *of God,* ➤ FINGER *of God,* ➤ GODS, ➤ LAMB *of God,* ➤ *the land God gave to* CAIN, ➤ *little* TIN *god,* ➤ MAN *proposes, God disposes,* ➤ MAN's *extremity is God's opportunity,* ➤ *the* MILLS *of God grind slowly, yet they grind exceeding small,* ➤ MOTHER *of God,* ➤ OUT *of God's blessing into the warm sun,* ➤ *put your trust in God, and keep your* POWDER *dry,* ➤ St JOHN *of God,* ➤ *the* SCOURGE *of God,* ➤ SERVANT *of the servants of God,* ➤ SWORD *of God,* ➤ TRUCE *of God.*

act of God an instance of uncontrollable natural forces in operation (often used in insurance claims, as being exempted from cover given).

you cannot serve God and Mammon proverbial saying, mid 16th century; with biblical allusion to Matthew 6:24, 'No man can serve two masters…Ye cannot serve God and mammon.'

See also ➤ MAMMON.

God bless the Duke of Argyll Scottish saying, mid 19th century; said originally to be uttered when shrugging the shoulders, and to be related to iron posts set up in Glasgow to mark the duke's property, which could be leant or rubbed against.

where God builds a church, the Devil will build a chapel proverbial saying, mid 16th century.

god from the machine a ➤ DEUS *ex machina*.

God helps them that help themselves proverbial saying, mid 16th century; early 15th century in French.

God made the country and man made the town proverbial saying, mid 17th century.

God makes the back to the burden proverbial saying, early 19th century.

God never sends mouths but He sends meat proverbial saying, late 14th century.

God of the gaps God as an explanation for phenomena not yet explained by science; God thought of as acting only in those spheres not otherwise accounted for. The phrase itself is recorded from the mid 20th century, deriving from earlier (critical) accounts of this mode of thought.

> Only disaster awaits the religion which . . . tries to fit God into the gaps left by scientific study.
> — C. E. Raven *Creator Spirit* (1927)

God save the mark an exclamatory phrase which originally probably served as a formula to avert an evil omen; *mark* here may mean 'sign' or 'omen', although it was apparently also used by a midwife when a child was born with a birthmark.

God save the Queen (or King) the British national anthem. Evidence suggests a 17th-century origin for the complete words and tune of the anthem. The ultimate origin is obscure: the phrase 'God save the King' occurs in various passages in the Old Testament, while as early as 1545 it was a watchword in the navy, with 'long to reign over us' as a countersign.

God sends meat, but the Devil sends cooks proverbial saying, mid 16th century.

God tempers the wind to the shorn lamb proverbial saying, mid 17th century.

God's acre a churchyard; early 17th century, from German *Gottesacker*.

sure as God's in Gloucestershire traditional saying, mid 17th century; meaning without doubt, certainly, and perhaps referring to the relic of Christ's blood kept before the Dissolution of the Monasteries in the shrine at Hailes Abbey.

God's in his heaven; all's right with the world proverbial saying, from early 16th century in the form 'God is where he was'; now largely replaced by this quotation from Robert Browning's *Pippa Passes* (1841).

Goddam a person given to swearing, as in the Middle Ages, an Englishman as described by the French, and in the 17th century, a Cavalier as described by the Puritans.

goddess see also ➤ *the* BITCH *goddess*, ➤ *the Goddess of* REASON, ➤ *the* WHITE *Goddess*.

godfather in literal use, a male godparent, who presents a child at baptism, responding on their behalf and promising to take responsibility for their religious education; the term is recorded from Old English, and in late Middle English was extended to a male sponsor at the consecration of a church bell.

From the 1960s, the word has also denoted a person directing an illegal organization, especially a leader of the American mafia; the usage derives from the film *The Godfather* (1972) by Francis Ford Coppola, based on the novel (1969) by Mario Puzo, and centring on *Don Corleone*, the sinister head of a Mafia 'family', whose customary remark is, 'I'll make him an offer he can't refuse.'

Godfrey of Bouillon (d. 1100), duke of lower Lorraine and leader of the First Crusade in which Jerusalem was captured; he is often taken as the type of a Christian knight and war-leader, and is traditionally one of the ➤ NINE *Worthies*.

Lady Godiva (d. 1080), English noblewoman, wife of Leofric, Earl of Mercia. According to a 13th-century legend, she agreed to her husband's proposition that he would reduce unpopular taxes only if she rode naked on horseback through the marketplace of Coventry. In later versions of the story, all the townspeople refrained from watching, except for *Peeping Tom*, who was struck blind in punishment.

Godlike Daniel a nickname given by his admirers to ➤ *Daniel* WEBSTER (1782–1852).

godliness see ➤ CLEANLINESS *is next to godliness*.

the **Godolphin** Barb with the ➤ BYERLEY *Turk* and the ➤ DARLEY *Arabian*, one of the three founding sires of the Thoroughbred, imported to improve the stock in the 18th century.

gods see also ➤ HOUSEHOLD *gods*, ➤ *in the* LAP *of the gods*, ➤ TAKE *the goods the gods provide*, ➤ TWILIGHT *of the gods*.

whom the gods love die young proverbial saying, mid 16th century.

the gods send nuts to those who have no teeth proverbial saying, early 20th century.

whom the gods would destroy, they first make mad proverbial saying, early 17th century; earlier in Greek.

William Godwin (1756–1836), English social philosopher and novelist. He advocated a system of anarchism based on a belief in the goodness of human reason and on his doctrine of extreme individualism. His ideological novel *Caleb Williams* (1794) was an early example of the crime and detection novel. In 1797 he married ➤ *Mary* WOLLSTONECRAFT; the couple's daughter was ➤ *Mary* SHELLEY.

Godwottery an affected quality of archaism, excessive fussiness, and sentimentality. Recorded from the 1930s, from the line 'A garden is a lovesome thing, God wot!', in T. E. Brown's poem *My Garden* (1876).

Godzilla a Jurassic dinosaur which has survived by living in the depths of the ocean, and which has been disturbed and mutated by atom bomb tests into a dragonlike monster capable of devastating Tokyo. *Godzilla* (originally called *Gojira*) appeared in 1955, in the first of a series of Japanese films.

> The mind needs monsters. It needs its Grendels and Krakens and Godzillas . . . to embody all that is dangerous and deathlike in the imagination.
> — *Times* 6 October 1999

Joseph Goebbels (1897–1945), German Nazi leader and politician. From 1933 Goebbels was Hitler's Minister of Propaganda, with control of the press, radio, and all aspects of culture, and manipulated these in order to further Nazi aims. He committed suicide rather than surrender to the Allies.

Hermann Goering (1893–1946), German Nazi leader and politician. Goering was responsible for the German rearmament programme, founder of the Gestapo, and from 1936 until 1943 directed the

German economy. Sentenced to death at the Nuremberg war trials, he committed suicide in his cell.

what goes around comes around proverbial saying, late 20th century; of US origin.

Johann Wolfgang von Goethe (1749–1832), German poet, dramatist, and scholar. Involved at first with the *Sturm und Drang* movement, Goethe changed to a more measured and classical style, as in the 'Wilhelm Meister' novels (1796–1829). He had interests in philosophy, physics, and biology and was also director of the Weimar Theatre 1791–1817.

goety witchcraft or magic performed by the invocation and employment of evil spirits; necromancy. The word is recorded from the mid 16th century, and comes via late Latin from Greek *goēteia* 'witchcraft'.

Gog and Magog in the Bible, the names of enemies of God's people. In Ezekiel 38–9, Gog is apparently a ruler from the land of Magog, while in Revelations 20:8, **Gog and Magog** are nations under the dominion of Satan.

In medieval legend, **Gog and Magog** are opponents of Alexander the Great, living north of the Caucasus.

The names are also used for two giant statues standing in Guildhall, London, from the time of Henry V (destroyed in 1666 and 1940; replaced in 1708 and 1953), representing either the last two survivors of a race of giants supposed to have inhabited Britain before Roman times, or ➤ GOGMAGOG, chief of the giants, and Corineus, an ally of the legendary Trojan hero ➤ BRUTUS.

Gogmagog in the chronicle of Geoffrey of Monmouth, the chief of the giants occupying Britain before the arrival of ➤ BRUTUS and the Trojans, and who was defeated and killed in a wrestling-match with Brutus's ally ➤ CORINEUS. The **Gogmagog Hills** near Cambridge are said to be named after him.

Goidelic of, relating to, or denoting the northern group of Celtic languages, including Irish, Scottish Gaelic, and Manx. Speakers of the Celtic precursor of the Goidelic languages are thought to have invaded Ireland from Europe *c.*1000 BC, spreading into Scotland and the Isle of Man from the 5th century AD onwards.

when the going gets tough, the tough get going proverbial saying, mid 20th century; particularly associated with the American financier and diplomat Joseph P. Kennedy (1888–1969), father of President Kennedy, and used by him as a family saying.

Golconda a source of wealth, advantages, or happiness; from the name of a city near Hyderabad, India, famous for its diamonds.

> The economists and statisticians will be set to work to gather in the orthographic Golconda.
> — Steven Pinker *The Language Instinct* (1994)

gold a yellow precious metal, the chemical element of atomic number 79, valued especially for use in jewellery and decoration, and to guarantee the value of currencies; taken as a type of something that is precious, beautiful, or brilliant.

The bullseye of an archery target is known as the *gold*.

The word is recorded from Old English, and is of Germanic origin, from an Indo-European root shared by *yellow*.

See also ➤ *all that* GLITTERS *is not gold*, ➤ CORONARY *gold*, ➤ FIELD *of the Cloth of Gold*, ➤ FOOL*'s gold*, ➤ *it is good to make a bridge of* GOLD *to a flying enemy*, ➤ RED *gold*, ➤ STREETS *paved with gold*.

crock of gold a large but distant or imaginary reward, with allusion to the story of a *crock of gold* supposedly to be found by anyone reaching the end of a rainbow.

gold-beater's skin a membrane used to separate leaves of gold during beating.

gold brick chiefly in the US, a thing that looks valuable, but is in fact worthless; from the confidence trickster's practice of preparing a block of base metal with a corner of gold to look like a brick-shaped piece of gold.

Gold Coast a former name (until 1957) for Ghana, so called because it was an important source of gold.

Gold Collar a classic greyhound race, inaugurated in 1933, run annually in September at the Catford track in south London, originally in May, now in September.

gold disc a framed golden disc awarded to a recording artist or group for sales of a recording exceeding a specified high figure. The figure varies from year to year and between countries; typical recent figures are, for a single, 500,000 in the UK or one million in the US, and for an album, 250,000 in the UK or 500,000 in the US.

Gold Key the office of the ➤ GROOM *of the Stole*, a *gold key* being the formal mark of the office.

gold may be bought too dear proverbial saying, mid 16th century.

gold standard the system by which the value of a currency was defined in terms of gold, for which the currency could be exchanged. The gold standard was generally abandoned in the Depression of the 1930s.

Gold Stick in the UK, a ceremonial officer in the Sovereign's household, entitled to carry a gilt rod on state occasions. The office is now held by the colonels of the senior household regiments in England and Scotland.

Goldberg see ➤ RUBE *Goldberg*.

golden see also ➤ *kill the goose that lays the golden* EGGS.

golden age an idyllic, often imaginary past time of peace, prosperity, and happiness; originally, the Greek and Roman poets' name for the first period of history, when the human race lived in an ideal state, and which was succeeded by the silver, brazen, and iron ages.

golden apple in Greek mythology, *golden apple* may be a fruit from the apples of the ➤ HESPERIDES, the ➤ APPLE *of discord*, or one of the apples thrown down to distract ➤ ATALANTA.

The phrase is also an archaic term for the ➤ ORB in the British Regalia, seen as resembling an apple in being smooth and round, and is recorded in the late 16th century as an alternative name for the tomato.

the Golden Ass a prose narrative (*Metamorphoses*) of the 2nd century by ➤ APULEIUS, a picaresque novel which recounts the adventures of a man who is transformed into an ass, and which depicts in particular the practices of ancient religious mysteries.

three golden balls the traditional sign of a pawnbroker, sometimes said to be derived from the coat of arms of the Medici family, or from the three bags of gold given to three girls for dowries by ➤ St NICHOLAS *of Myra*, who through this has become patron saint of pawnbrokers.

the Golden Bough title of a book (1890–1915) by the Scottish anthropologist James George Frazer, proposing an evolutionary theory of the development of human thought, from the magical and religious to the scientific, and focusing particularly on the figure of the sacrificial king who dies and is reborn.

The title of the book came from Virgil's *Aeneid*, 'the double tree that bears the golden bough' in Dryden's translation (1697); Aeneas is told by the Sibyl that he must find and pick the branch before he can safely journey to the underworld.

the golden bowl is broken a biblical metaphor for death, deriving from Ecclesiastes:

> Or ever the silver cord be loosed, or the golden bowl be broken, or the pitcher be broken at the fountain, or the wheel broken at the cistern.
> — Bible (Authorized Version) Ecclesiastes 12:1

The image was later picked up by Blake in 'Thel's Motto' (1789), 'Can wisdom be put in a silver rod? Or love in a golden bowl?', and was used by Henry James as the title of his last novel (*The Golden Bowl*, 1904), in which a gilded crystal bowl with a flaw in it is central to the plot, and symbolizes the key relationships of the main characters.

the Golden Bull a decree (*Aurea Bulla*) issued by the Emperor Charles IV in 1356 to regulate the election and coronation of an emperor.

the golden calf in the Bible, an image of gold in the shape of a calf, made by Aaron in response to the Israelites' plea for a god while they awaited Moses' return from Mount Sinai, where he was receiving the ➤ TEN *Commandments* (Exodus 32), and which Moses destroyed; in extended usage, a false god, especially wealth as an object of worship.

Golden Cockerel Press a private press founded in 1920 at Waltham St Lawrence, Berkshire, by Harold Taylor, and taken over in 1924 by Robert Gibbings (1889–1958), wood-engraver, illustrator, and writer of travel books. The Golden Cockerel type was designed by Eric Gill, who was associated with the press from 1924 and designed one of its most celebrated productions, *The Four Gospels* (1941).

the Golden Fleece in Greek mythology, the fleece of the golden-fleeced ram which rescued Helle and her brother (see ➤ HELLESPONT), which was guarded by an unsleeping dragon, and sought and won by ➤ JASON with the help of ➤ MEDEA.

Order of the Golden Fleece an order of knighthood instituted at Bruges in 1430 by Philip the Good, duke of Burgundy. The right of investiture in the order of the Golden Fleece belonged (after 1700) to the sovereigns of Austria and Spain.

the Golden Gate a deep channel connecting San Francisco Bay with the Pacific Ocean, spanned by the Golden Gate suspension bridge (completed 1937).

golden goal in some soccer and hockey competitions, the first goal scored during extra time which ends the match and gives victory to the scoring side.

golden goose in a traditional fairytale, a goose which laid golden eggs; it was killed in an attempt to possess the source of this wealth, which as a result was lost. The phrase is now used for a continuing source of wealth or profit that may be exhausted if it is misused.

See also ➤ *kill the goose that lays the golden* EGGS.

golden handcuffs used to refer to benefits, typically deferred payments, provided by an employer to discourage an employee from taking employment elsewhere.

golden handshake a substantial payment given to someone who is made redundant or retires early.

golden hello a substantial payment made by an employer to a keenly sought recruit.

the Golden Hind the ship in which Francis Drake circumnavigated the globe in 1577–80, named by Drake in honour of his patron, Sir Christopher Hatton (1540–91), whose crest was a golden hind.

the Golden Horde the Tartar and Mongol army, led by descendants of ➤ GENGHIS *Khan*, that overran Asia and parts of eastern Europe in the 13th century and maintained an empire until around 1500 (so called from the richness of the leader's camp).

the Golden Horn a curved inlet of the Bosporus forming the harbour of Istanbul.

golden jubilee the fiftieth anniversary of a significant event, in particular, the fiftieth anniversary of a sovereign's accession.

a golden key can open any door proverbial saying, late 16th century.

the Golden Legend a medieval collection of saints' lives and similar stories, written in the 13th century by Jacobus de Voragine (1230–98), Archbishop of Genoa; an English version was published by Caxton in 1483. The title is a translation of Latin *Legenda Aurea.*

golden mean the ideal moderate position between two extremes; originally as a translation of Latin *aurea mediocritas,* from Horace's *Odes.*

golden-mouthed an epithet of ➤ *St* JOHN *Chrysostom,* who is referred to as 'the golden mouth' from late Middle English.

golden number the number showing a year's place in the ➤ METONIC *cycle* and used to fix the date of Easter for that year; the *golden number* for any year AD is found by adding 1 to the number of the year and dividing the result by 19; the remainder is the golden number for that year (if there is no remainder, the golden number is 19). The term is a translation of medieval Latin *aureus numerus,* so called from its importance in calculating the date of Easter, and not as sometimes suggested because it appeared in calendars in letters of gold.

golden parachute a large payment or other financial compensation guaranteed to a company executive if they should be dismissed as a result of a merger or takeover.

golden rose an ornament of wrought gold, blessed by the pope on the fourth Sunday in Lent, and usually sent as a mark of favour to some notable Roman Catholic personage, city, or church. The ornament has been of various forms; the design finally adopted is a thorny branch with several leaves and flowers, surmounted by a principal rose—all of pure gold.

The *Golden Rose* is also an award presented at the International Television Festival at Montreux for successful light entertainment programmes.

golden rule a basic principle which should always be followed to ensure success in general or in a particular activity; the term is sometimes specifically used of the injunction given by Jesus in Matthew 7:12, 'whatsoever ye would that men should do to you, do ye even so to them.'

golden sand of the River Pactolus in Lydia, containing particles of gold said to be due to ➤ MIDAS's having bathed there.

golden section the division of a line so that the whole is to the greater part as that part is to the smaller part (i.e. in a ratio of 1 to ½ ($\sqrt{5}$ + 1)), a proportion which is considered to be particularly pleasing to the eye.

Although the proportion has been known since the 4th century ➤ BC, and occurs in Euclid, the name *golden section* (now the usual term) is not recorded before the 19th century.

golden share a share in a company that gives control of at least 51 per cent of the voting rights, especially when held by the government.

the Golden State an informal name for California.

Golden Temple the Sikh temple at Amritsar in the Punjab, the holiest of the Sikh faith and an important pilgrimage site, which in 1919 was the scene of a riot in which 400 people were killed by British troops. In 1984 the building was occupied by a group of Sikh extremists, and sustained some damage when they were forcibly removed by Indian troops.

the Golden Triangle the area at the meeting-point of Myanmar (Burma), Laos, and Thailand, where much opium is grown.

the Golden Vale a name for the Vale of Tipperary.

golden wedding the fiftieth anniversary of a wedding.

Goldilocks heroine of the children's story *The Three Bears,* in which she eats and sleeps in their house without leave, and chooses the possessions of the smallest bear as being neither too large nor too small for her, but 'just right'; the essential story goes back to 1837, but the version in which *Goldilocks* is first named as the intruder is in John Hassall's *Old Nursery Stories and Rhymes* (*c.*1904).

Goldilocks is now used allusively to designate something regarded as falling in the centre of a range of possible values or conditions, rather than leaning to one extreme or the other.

> Only Earth occupies the comfortable middle ground, satisfying the Goldilocks criterion: not too hot, not too cold, just right.
> — *New Scientist* 18 September 1999

goldsmiths ➤ *St* DUNSTAN and ➤ *St* ELOI are the patron saints of goldsmiths.

Samuel Goldwyn (1882–1974), Polish-born American film producer, who with Louis B. Mayer founded the film company Metro-Goldwyn-Mayer (MGM) in 1924, and who is famous for such 'Goldwynisms' as 'Include me out' and 'a definite maybe' (a number of the colourful and contradictory comments attributed to him are likely to be apocryphal).

golem in Jewish legend, a clay figure brought to life by magic; an automaton or robot. The word is recorded from the late 19th century, and comes via Yiddish from Hebrew *gōlem* 'shapeless mass'.

Golgotha the site of the crucifixion of Jesus; Calvary. The name comes from late Latin, via Greek from an Aramaic form of Hebrew *gulgoleth* 'skull'; as in Matthew 27:33, 'And they were come to unto a place called Golgotha, that is to say, a place of a skull.'

goliard any of a class of educated jesters or buffoons specializing in the writing of satirical Latin verse, who flourished chiefly in the 12th and 13th centuries in Germany, France, and Britain.

The word comes via Old French 'glutton' from Latin *gula* 'gluttony', although in the 12th and 13th centuries *goliards* were supposed to be named after a poet called *Golias*, given the titles of *episcopus* and *archipoeta*, and regarded by ➤ GIRALDUS *Cambrensis* as a real person.

Goliath in the Bible, a Philistine giant and warrior, according to legend killed by David (1 Samuel 17) armed only with a sling and 'five smooth stones'; the contest between the young David and Goliath is often taken as a type of apparently unequal combat.

According to another tradition, the giant killed by David was originally unnamed, and Goliath was killed by Elhanan (2 Samuel 21:19).

Victor Gollancz (1893–1967), British publisher and philanthropist, founder of the charity War on Want. A committed socialist, Gollancz campaigned against the rise of Fascism in the 1930s and founded the Left Book Club (1936). He also organized aid for First World War refugees.

golliwog a soft doll with bright clothes, a black face, and fuzzy hair. From *Golliwogg*, the name of a doll character in books by Bertha Upton (died 1912), American writer, perhas a blend of the exclamation *golly* and *pollywog* 'tadpole'.

Gollum in Tolkien's *The Hobbit* and ➤ LORD *of the Rings*, a repulsive but pitiful figure, the former hobbit who, having come into possession of the One Ring (his 'precious') is possessed by it. When he is tricked out of the ring he is reduced to an entity obsessively bent on recovery; in the end he is destroyed with it.

GOM Grand Old Man, a name originally applied to ➤ *William Ewart* GLADSTONE.

gomer[1] in American military slang, an inept or stupid colleague, especially a trainee. The name may come from *Gomer* Pyle, US television character, portrayed as an ignorant hill-billy.

gomer[2] a derogatory term (amongst members of the medical profession) for a difficult or unrewarding patient; especially an elderly one. The term may come from the initial letters of *get out of my emergency room*.

Gomorrah a town in ancient Palestine, probably south of the Dead Sea. According to Genesis 19:24, it was destroyed by fire from heaven, along with ➤ SODOM, for the wickedness of its inhabitants.

gompa a Tibetan temple or monastery (from Tibetan *gōn-pa*, *gōm-pa* 'a solitary place, a hermitage').

de Goncourt surname of two brothers, Edmond (1822–96) and Jules (1830–70), French novelists and critics. Working together, the brothers wrote art criticism, realist novels and social history. In his will Edmond provided for the establishment of the Académie Goncourt, which awards the annual ➤ PRIX *Goncourt*.

Gondal an imaginary island kingdom in the juvenilia of the Brontës; invented and written about by Emily and Anne, while Charlotte and Branwell set their characters and stories in ➤ ANGRIA.

Gondwana a vast continental area believed to have existed in the southern hemisphere and to have resulted from the break-up of Pangaea in Mesozoic times. It comprised the present Arabia, Africa, South America, Antarctica, Australia, and the peninsula of India.

The name is recorded from the late 19th century, originally denoting any of a series of rocks in India, especially fluviatile shales and sandstones, from the name of a region in central northern India, from Sanskrit *goṇḍavana* 'forest of Gond'.

gone with the wind from Ernest Dowson 'I have forgot much, Cynara, gone with the wind' (1896); subsequently popularized by the title of Margaret Mitchell's novel (1936) on the American Civil War.

gonfalon a banner or pennant, especially one with streamers, hung from a crossbar; such a banner as the standard of some Italian republics.

gonfalonier a standard-bearer, in particular, the Pope's standard-bearer. Formerly also, any of various officials or magistrates in the Italian city-states.

good see also ➤ ALL *good things must come to an end*, ➤ BETTER *a good cow than a cow of a good kind*, ➤ *can any good thing come out of* NAZARETH, ➤ *good* AMERICANS *when they die go to Paris*, ➤ *the good old* CAUSE, ➤ *good* SAMARITAN, ➤ *good* WINE *needs no bush*, ➤ *the* GREAT *and the good*, ➤ IT*'s good to talk*, ➤ *never do* EVIL *that good may come of it*, ➤ *the* SOVEREIGN *good*, ➤ *you've* NEVER *had it so good*.

the Good epithet of a number of royal personages of the Middle Ages, as, **Philip the Good**, Duke of Burgundy (1396–1467).

if you can't be good, be careful proverbial saying, early 20th century.

a good beginning makes a good ending proverbial saying, early 14th century.

the Good Book informal name for the Bible.

there's many a good cock come out of a tattered bag proverbial saying, late 19th century; the reference is to cockfighting.

the good die young proverbial saying, late 17th century.

he is a good dog who goes to church proverbial saying, early 19th century.

Good Duke Humphrey nickname of Humphrey of Gloucester (1391–1447), used in Shakespeare's *2 Henry VI*; see also ➤ DINE *with Duke Humphrey*.

good fences make good neighbours proverbial saying, mid 17th century.

Good Friday the Friday before Easter Sunday, on which the Crucifixion of Christ is commemorated in the Christian Church. It is traditionally a day of fasting and penance.

Good Friday agreement an agreement between the British and Irish governments and the main political parties of Northern Ireland, reached at Stormont Castle, Belfast, on Good Friday (10 April) 1998, and passed by public referenda in Northern Ireland and the Irish Republic on 22 May 1998, setting out proposals for the securing of peace in Northern Ireland, including provisions for the formation of new political assemblies and commitments regarding such issues as the release of prisoners and the decommissioning of the weapons of paramilitary organizations. A Northern Irish

Assembly was set up in the autumn of 1999, but after disagreements on the role of decommissioning was suspended in February 2000.

Good Gray Poet sobriquet of the American poet Walt Whitman (1819–92), first applied to him in a book of this title (1866) by his friend, the journalist William O'Connor.

a good horse cannot be of a bad colour proverbial saying, early 17th century.

the only good Indian is a dead Indian proverbial saying, mid 19th century.

the good is the enemy of the best proverbial saying, early 20th century.

a good Jack makes a good Jill proverbial saying, early 17th century.

good men are scarce proverbial saying, early 17th century.

good mother lizard a name applied to the *maiasaur*, a large duck-billed dinosaur, the remains of which were found as a presumed nest containing numerous young. This was interpreted to mean that the dinosaurs provided parental care after their young hatched, much as birds do today, and the name *good mother lizard* was given in acknowledgement (in implied contrast to the 'tyrant lizard' or *tyrannosaur*).

a good name is better than a golden girdle proverbial saying, Middle English; originally with reference to Proverbs 22:1, 'A good name is rather to be chosen than great riches.'

the good neighbours former term for fairies or witches, recorded from the late 16th century.

Good News Bible a translation of the Bible in simple everyday English, published 1966–76 by the United Bible Societies.

good ol' boy in the US, a (typically white) male from the Southern States of America, regarded as one of a group conforming to a social and cultural masculine stereotype.

the good old days the past, regarded as better than the present; recorded from the late 19th century (the equivalent **good old times** dates from the early 19th century).

Good Parliament name given to the parliament which met in 1376, and endeavoured to reform financial abuses. A number of ministers and officials were impeached, although the achievements of the Parliament were ephemeral.

Good Queen Bess a nickname for Elizabeth I.

the Good Regent a nickname for James Stewart, Earl of Moray (d. 1570), illegitimate elder brother of Mary Queen of Scots, and Regent of Scotland from 1567 after Mary's flight to England.

the Good Shepherd a name for Jesus Christ, with allusion to John 10:16, 'there shall be one fold, and one shepherd' (see also ➤ SHEPHERD).

there's a good time coming proverbial saying, early 19th century.

a good time was had by all title of a collection of poems published in 1937 by Stevie Smith (1902–71), taken from the characteristic conclusion of accounts of social events in parish magazines.

there's many a good tune played on an old fiddle proverbial saying, early 20th century.

one good turn deserves another proverbial saying, early 15th century.

goodbye farewell; a contraction of *God be with you!* with *good* substituted for the first element.

goodfella a gangster, especially a member of a Mafia 'family'; the term was popularized by the film *Goodfellas* (1990) by Martin Scorsese, in which a reliable member of the Mafia is seen as a *good fellow* by his associates.

Goodfellow see ➤ ROBIN *Goodfellow*.

gooding the custom in some areas of collecting alms on St Thomas's Day (21 December).

goodman an archaic, chiefly Scottish, term for a male head of a household; the **Goodman of Ballingreich** was an incognito used by James V of Scotland.

goods see also ➤ ILL *gotten goods*.

goods and chattels all kinds of personal property; a *chattel* is a movable possession.

goodwife an archaic, chiefly Scottish, term for the female head of a household, from which the synonymous ➤ GOODY derives.

Goodwin Sands an area of sandbanks in the Strait of Dover. Often exposed at low tide, the sandbanks are a hazard to shipping.

See also ➤ TENTERDEN *steeple is the cause of Goodwin Sands*.

Goodwood a racecourse in West Sussex, near Chichester, which is the scene of an annual summer race meeting.

goody an archaic term for an elderly woman of humble station: a pet form of ➤ GOODWIFE, often prefixed to a surname, as in ➤ GOODY *Two-Shoes*.

Goody Two-shoes a nursery story dating from the 18th century, in which the orphaned heroine survives adversity, and while setting a constant good example becomes both rich and beloved. The term is used today for a girl or woman who is regarded as priggishly moral.

> While you sit and sweat in the rush hour, your green goody-twoshoes colleagues, will be able to have an extra half an hour in bed, smugly overtake you on the inside and arrive at work before you.
>
> — *Independent* 4 May 1998

goodyear a malevolent power, an evil spirit; from a (mid 16th-century) imprecation, as in '*what the goodyear*?', perhaps originally representing elliptical *I hope for a good year*.

Charles Goodyear (1800–60), American inventor. He developed the process of the vulcanization of rubber, after accidentally dropping some rubber mixed with sulphur and white lead on to a hot stove.

goofer in the US, a (magic) spell; a practitioner of magic (of African origin, perhaps related to Mende *ngafa* 'spirit, devil').

googly in cricket, an off break bowled with an apparent leg-break action. The word is recorded from the early 20th century, but the origin is unknown.

Goon any of the members of the cast of a British radio show of the 1950s and 1960s, the **Goon Show**, including Spike Milligan, Harry Secombe, and Peter Sellers, noted for its zany and surrealist humour, and such catchphrases as 'You rotten swines. I told you I'd be deaded.'

Goon is recorded from the mid 19th century meaning 'a silly, foolish, or eccentric person', perhaps from dialect *gooney* 'booby', influenced by the subhuman cartoon character 'Alice the *Goon*', created by E. C. Segar (1894–1938), American cartoonist. Allied prisoners-of-war in the Second World War referred to their German guards as 'goons'.

goose the *goose* is proverbially contrasted with the *swan* as being the clumsier, less elegant, and less distinguished bird; it is also traditionally taken as a type of stupidity and folly.

A *goose* is the emblem of St Werburga, a Mercian princess and nun (d. *c.*700), who in her legend is said to have brought a goose back to life, ➤ *St* Bridget *of Ireland*, and ➤ *St* Martin *of Tours*.

See also ➤ barnacle *goose*, ➤ colonial *goose*, ➤ ember *goose*, ➤ geese, ➤ golden *goose*, ➤ *kill the goose that lays the golden* eggs, ➤ Michaelmas *goose*, ➤ *Mother* Carey's *goose*, ➤ Mother *Goose*, ➤ wild *goose chase*.

royal game of goose a game played with counters on a board divided into sections, some of which had a goose depicted on them.

Goose Fair in Nottingham and other English towns, a fair held at Michaelmas, when geese are in season.

goose-girl a girl employed to tend geese, in fairy stories the type of the peasant girl who marries a prince.

goose-step a military marching step in which the legs are not bent at the knee, especially associated with German militarism.

gooseberry as the first fruit of the summer, *gooseberries* were often traditionally eaten at Whitsun or at village feasts and celebrations.

Children were traditionally told that babies were found under gooseberry bushes.

In British informal use, someone who *plays gooseberry* is a third person who stays in the company of two people, especially lovers, who would prefer to be alone; the usage comes from *gooseberry-picker*, referring to an activity as a pretext for the lovers to be together.

The word is recorded from the mid 16th century; the first element perhaps from *goose*, or based on Old French *groseille*, altered because of an unexplained association with the bird.

See also ➤ Cape *gooseberry*.

gopher a burrowing rodent with fur-lined pouches on the outside of the cheeks, found in North and Central America. The word may come from Canadian French *gaufre* 'honeycomb', because the gopher 'honeycombs' the ground with its burrows.

Gopher is the name of a menu-based system which allows users of the Internet to search for and retrieve documents on topics of interest. The name comes from the gopher mascot of the University of Minnesota, US, where the system was invented.

Gopher State informal name for Minnesota.

gopher wood in the Bible the timber from which Noah's ark was made, from an unidentified tree (Genesis 6:14, 'Make thee an ark of gopher wood').

gopi in Hinduism, any of the milkmaids of Brindavan, companions of Krishna.

gopura in southern India, the great pyramidal tower over the entrance gate to a temple precinct. The name comes from Sanskrit *gopura* 'city gate', from *go* 'cow, cattle' + *pura* 'city, quarter'.

Mikhail Gorbachev (1931–), Soviet statesman, General Secretary of the Communist Party of the USSR 1985–91 and President 1988–91. His foreign policy brought about an end to the cold war, while within the USSR he introduced major reforms known as ➤ glasnost and ➤ perestroika. He resigned following an attempted coup and at a time of the Soviet republics' desire for autonomy.

There was great enthusiasm for him in Western Europe during the period of his reforms; with terms such as **Gorbymania** and **Gorby fever** used in the press to describe the reaction to his trips outside the Soviet Union.

Gorbals a district of Glasgow on the south bank of the River Clyde, formerly noted for its slums and tenement buildings.

cut the Gordian knot solve or remove a problem in a direct or forceful way, rejecting gentler or more indirect methods. The expression comes from the legend that *Gordius*, king of Gordium, tied an intricate knot and prophesied that whoever untied it would become the ruler of Asia. It was cut through with a sword by Alexander the Great.

Gordium an ancient city of Asia Minor (now NW Turkey), the capital of Phrygia in the 8th and 9th centuries BC. According to legend the city was founded by Gordius, who tied the knot cut by Alexander the Great during his expedition of 334 BC.

Gordon see also ➤ Flash *Gordon*, ➤ Gay *Gordons*.

Charles George Gordon (1833–85), British general and colonial administrator. He made his name by crushing the Taiping Rebellion (1863–4) in China, from which he was known as **Chinese Gordon**. In 1884 he fought Mahdist forces in Sudan led by Muhammad Ahmad, the ➤ Mahdi, but was trapped at Khartoum and killed.

Gordon Bennett expressing surprise, incredulity, or exasperation. The word is probably an alteration of gorblimey, after James *Gordon Bennett* (1841–1918), American publisher and sports sponsor.

Gordon Riots a series of anti-Catholic riots in London in June 1780 in which about 300 people were killed. The riots were provoked by a petition presented to Parliament by Lord George *Gordon* (1751–93) against the relaxation of restrictions on the holding of landed property by Roman Catholics.

Gordonstoun a public school in Scotland founded in 1934 by the German educationist Kurt Hahn, and attended by Charles, Prince of Wales.

gore a triangular or tapering piece of material used in making a garment, sail, or umbrella. Ultimately the word (which in Old English meant 'a triangular piece of land') is probably related to Old English *gār* 'spear', a spearhead being triangular.

gorgio the gypsy name for a non-gypsy (from Romany *gorjo*).

Gorgon in Greek mythology, each of three sisters, Stheno, Euryale, and Medusa, with snakes for hair, who had the power to turn anyone who looked at them to stone. ➤ MEDUSA was killed by Perseus, and the winged horse ➤ PEGASUS is said to have sprung from her blood.

In extended usage, *gorgon* is used for a fierce, frightening, or repulsive woman.

gorilla a powerfully built great ape with a large head and short neck, found in the forests of central Africa, which is the largest living primate. The name comes from an alleged African word for a wild or hairy person, found in the Greek account of the voyage of the Carthaginian explorer Hanno in the 5th or 6th century BC; adopted in 1847 as the specific name of the ape.

Maxim Gorky (1868–1936), Russian writer and revolutionary, who after the Revolution was honoured as the founder of the new, officially sanctioned socialist realism.

Gorlois in Arthurian legend, the duke of Cornwall who is the first husband of ➤ IGRAINE.

Gormenghast in the fantasy novels of Mervyn Peake (1911–68), *Gormenghast* (1946) and its two sequels, the fantastic and crumbling castle which is the family seat of the doomed Earls of Groan.

> A psychiatric hospital of Gormenghastian horror where dissident voices were silenced.
> — *Independent of Sunday* 5 March 1995

when the gorse is out of bloom, kissing's out of fashion proverbial saying, mid 19th century.

Gorsedd a council of Welsh or other Celtic bards and Druids, especially as meeting daily before the eisteddfod. The word is Welsh, and means 'mound, throne, assembly'.

Goschens a colloquial name for consols after their conversion from 3 to 2¾ per cent by G. J. *Goschen* (Chancellor of the Exchequer) in 1888 (later to 2½).

Goschen had been appointed as Chancellor in 1886 when Lord Randolph Churchill suddenly resigned the office; Churchill afterwards said ruefully, 'All great men make mistakes. Napoleon forgot Blücher, I forgot Goschen.'

goshawk a large short-winged hawk, resembling a large sparrowhawk, which in the 15th-century *Boke of St Albans* is listed in falconry as the bird for a yeoman. The name is recorded from Old English (in form *gōshafoc*) and comes from *goose* + *hawk*.

Goshen a place of plenty or of light, from the name of the fertile land allotted to the Israelites in Egypt, in which (Exodus 10:23 implies) there was light during the plague of darkness.

> I should have thought them the one Goshen in your desert . . . them and the presents.
> — Rhoda Broughton *Belinda* (1883)

Gospel the record of Christ's life and teaching in the first four books of the New Testament; each of these books. The four Gospels ascribed to St Matthew, St Mark, St Luke, and St John all give an account of the ministry, crucifixion, and resurrection of Christ, though the Gospel of John differs greatly from the other three. There are also several apocryphal gospels of later date.

The word comes from Old English *gōdspel* 'good news', translating ecclesiastical Latin *bona annuntiatio* used to gloss *evangelium*, from Greek *euangelion* 'good news'; after the vowel was shortened in Old English, the first syllable was mistaken for *god* 'God'.

See also ➤ SYNOPTIC *Gospels*.

the gospel according to— the authorized account given by—.

Gospel side in a church, the north side of the altar, at which the Gospel is read, opposite to the ➤ EPISTLE *side*.

gossamer a fine, filmy substance consisting of cobwebs spun by small spiders, which is seen especially in autumn. The word apparently comes (in

Middle English) from *goose summer*, perhaps from the time of year around St Martin's summer, i.e. early November, when geese were eaten (gossamer being common then).

gossip casual or unconstrained conversation or reports about other people, typically involving details which are not confirmed as being true. In late Old English, *godsibb* meant 'godfather, godmother, baptismal sponsor', literally, 'a person related to one in God', from *god* 'God' + *sibb* 'a relative'. In Middle English the sense was 'a close friend, a person with whom one gossips', and from this came the sense 'a person who gossips', and finally (in the early 19th century), 'idle talk'.

what is got over the Devil's back is spent under his belly proverbial saying, late 16th century; meaning that what is gained improperly will be spent on folly and debauchery.

Goth a member of a Germanic people that invaded the Roman Empire from the east between the 3rd and 5th centuries. The eastern division, the Ostrogoths, founded a kingdom in Italy, while the Visigoths went on to found one in Spain.

Gotha see ➤ ALMANACH *de Gotha*.

Gotham a village in Nottinghamshire associated with the folk tale *The Wise Men of Gotham*, in which the inhabitants of the village demonstrated cunning by feigning stupidity.

Gotham is now also a nickname for New York City, used originally by Washington Irving and later associated with the ➤ BATMAN stories.

See also ➤ WISE *Men of Gotham*.

Gothic of or in the style of architecture prevalent in western Europe in the 12th–16th centuries (and revived in the mid 18th to early 20th centuries), characterized by pointed arches, rib vaults, and flying buttresses, together with large windows and elaborate tracery. English Gothic architecture is divided into Early English, Decorated, and Perpendicular.

The word comes via French or late Latin from *Gothi* 'the Goths', and was used in the 17th and 18th cents to mean 'not classical' (i.e. not Greek or Roman), and hence to refer to medieval architecture which did not follow classical models and a typeface based on medieval handwriting.

See also ➤ COLLEGIATE *Gothic*, ➤ GOTHICK, ➤ STRAWBERRY *Hill*.

gothic novel an English genre of fiction popularized in the 18th to early 19th centuries by Mrs Radcliffe and others, characterized by an atmosphere of mystery and horror and having a pseudo-medieval setting; in Jane Austen's *Northanger Abbey* (1818), the heroine Catherine Morland's fondness for such novels leads her to suspect her lover's father of having murdered his wife.

> Charming as were all Mrs Radcliffe's works, and charming even as were the works of her imitators, it was not in them that human nature, at least in the midland counties of England, was to be looked for. Of the Alps and Pyrenees, with their pine forests and their vices, they might give a faithful delineation; and Italy, Switzerland, and the South of France, might be as fruitful in horrors as they were there represented. Catherine dared not doubt beyond her own country, and even of that, if hard pressed, would have yielded the northern and western extremities. But in the central part of England there was surely some security . . . in the laws of the land, and the manners of the age.
> — Jane Austen *Northanger Abbey* (1818)

Gothic revival the reintroduction of a Gothic style of architecture towards the middle of the 19th century.

Gothic type a typeface with lettering derived from the angular style of handwriting with broad vertical downstrokes used in western Europe from the 13th century, including Fraktur and black-letter typefaces.

Gothick a pseudo-archaic spelling of ➤ GOTHIC in the sense belonging to or redolent of the Dark Ages; portentously gloomy or horrifying.

Götterdammerung in Germanic mythology, the downfall of the gods. The word comes from German, literally 'twilight', popularized by Wagner's use of the word as the title of the last opera of the Ring cycle.

Frederick W. Goudy (1865–1947), American type designer and printer, founder of the Village Press in 1903 in Illinois. In 1903 he moved it to New York, where until its destruction by fire in 1939 it was known for expressing the character of the text in its design and printing of books. Goudy also designed some 100 new type faces.

John Gould (1804–81), English bird artist. He produced many large illustrated volumes, though it is believed that many of the finest plates were actually drawn by Gould's wife and other employed artists.

Stephen Jay Gould (1941–), American palaeontologist. A noted popularizer of science, he has studied modifications of Darwinian evolutionary theory, proposed the concept of punctuated equilibrium, and written on the social context of scientific theory.

gourd see ➤ JONAH's *gourd*.

gourmand a person who enjoys eating and often eats too much. Also, a connoisseur of good food.

The words *gourmand* and *gourmet* overlap in meaning but are not identical. Both can be used to mean 'a connoisseur of good food' but *gourmand* is more usually used to mean 'a person who enjoys eating and often eats too much'.

gout a disease in which defective metabolism of uric acid causes arthritis, especially in the smaller bones of the feet, deposition of chalk-stones, and episodes of acute pain. The word comes through Old French from medieval Latin *gutta* 'drop', because gout was believed to be caused by the dropping of diseased matter from the blood into the joints.

Government House in British usage, the official residence of a governor, especially in a colony or Commonwealth state that regards the British monarch as head of state.

the government shall be upon his shoulder in Isaiah 9:6, the prophecy of the Messiah, 'For unto us a child is born…and the government shall be upon his shoulder.'

Governor General the chief representative of the Crown in a Commonwealth country of which the British monarch is head of state.

Gower see ➤ MORAL *Gower*.

gowk an awkward or foolish person. Originally (from Old Norse *gaukr*) a word for a cuckoo.

gowk storm a spring gale which occurs at the time of the cuckoo's arrival.

gown the members of a university as distinct from the permanent residents of a town; usually in ➤ TOWN *and gown*.

See also ➤ CAP *and gown*.

Goya (1746–1828), Spanish painter and etcher. He is famous for his works treating the French occupation of Spain (1808–14), including *The Shootings of May 3rd 1808* (painting, 1814) and *The Disasters of War* (etchings, 1810–14), depicting the cruelty and horror of war.

> It's a Goyaesque vision where animals are dominant and humans submissive.
> — *Big Issue* 26 August 1996

the Gracchi Tiberius Sempronius *Gracchus* (*c.*163–133 BC) and his brother Gaius Sempronius (*c.*153–121 BC), Roman tribunes. They were responsible for radical social and economic legislation, especially concerning the redistribution of land to the poor. This led eventually to their deaths, as the legislation was passed against the wishes of the senatorial class.

See also ➤ CORNELIA.

grace in Christian belief, the free and unmerited favour of God, as manifested in the salvation of sinners and the bestowal of blessings.

Grace in Christian usage also denotes a short prayer of thanks said before or after a meal.

The word is also used as a form of description or address for a duke, duchess, or archbishop: **Her Grace, the Duchess of Omnium, Your Grace**.

See also ➤ COVENANT *of Grace*, ➤ DAYS *of grace*, ➤ HERB *of grace*, ➤ KNIGHT *of Grace*, ➤ PILGRIMAGE *of Grace*, ➤ SAVING *grace*, ➤ YEAR *of grace*.

act of grace a privilege or concession that cannot be claimed as a right.

W. G. Grace (1848–1915), English cricketer and doctor. In a first-class career that lasted until 1908, he made 126 centuries, scored 54,896 runs, and took 2,864 wickets. He twice captained England in test matches against Australia (1880 and 1882). He was a popular draw; according to one account, when he was unexpectedly bowled first ball, the umpire called 'not out', and the bowler was told, 'They have paid to see Dr Grace bat, not to see you bowl.'

grace and favour denoting accommodation occupied by permission of a sovereign or government.

grace note an extra note added as an embellishment and not essential to the harmony or melody.

by the grace of God through God's favour, especially (translating Latin *Dei gratia*) appended to the formal statement of a monarch's title, and formerly to that of some ecclesiastical dignitaries.

graceless florin a florin issued in 1849, from which the letters DG [*Dei gratia*] had been omitted; also called the *godless florin*.

Graces see ➤ *the* THREE *Graces*.

Cape Gracias a Dios a cape forming the easternmost extremity of the Mosquito Coast in Central America, on the border between Nicaragua and Honduras. It was so named (in Spanish, literally 'thanks (be) to God') by Columbus, who, becalmed off the coast in 1502, was able to continue his voyage with the arrival of a following wind.

grade a mark indicating the quality of a student's work; the word is recorded from the early 16th century, coming from French, or from Latin *gradus* 'step', and was originally used as a unit of measurement of angles (a degree of arc), the term later referred to degrees of merit or quality.

Gradgrind a person lacking warm feelings and imagination and interested only in facts, seen as resembling Thomas *Gradgrind*, character in Charles Dickens's novel *Hard Times* (1854); his views on education are expressed by the words, 'Now, what I want is, Facts…Facts alone are wanted in life.'

> A great many bricks of Gradgrind fact, whether laudatory or dismissive, are bound to destroy the fluid nature of human lives.
> — *New Yorker* 8 May 1995

gradual in the Western Christian Church, a response sung or recited between the Epistle and Gospel in the Mass; the name comes (in the mid 16th century) from the earlier *gradual* adjective, from medieval Latin *gradualis*, from Latin *gradus* 'step'. The original sense of the adjective was 'arranged in degrees'; the noun refers to the altar steps in a church, from which the antiphons were sung.

gradual psalms fifteen psalms (120–134), each of which is entitled in the Authorized Version 'Song of Degrees', in the Revised Version 'Song of Ascents'.

gradus a manual of classical prosody formerly used in schools to help in writing Greek and Latin verse. Recorded from the mid 18th century, the name comes from the Latin title *Gradus ad Parnassum* 'Step(s) to Parnassus', the title of one such manual.

Graecia see ▶ MAGNA *Graecia*.

Graecism the Greek spirit, style, or mode of expression, especially as imitated in a work of art; the adoption or imitation of any of these.

graf a German nobleman corresponding in rank to a European count or British earl.

graffiti writing or drawings scribbled, scratched, or sprayed illicitly on a wall or other surface in a public place. The term is recorded from the mid 19th century, and comes from Italian (plural), from *graffio* 'a scratch'.

Graham Land the northern part of the Antarctic Peninsula, the only part of Antarctica lying outside the Antarctic Circle. Discovered in 1831–2 by the English navigator John Biscoe (1794–1843), it now forms part of British Antarctic Territory, but is claimed also by Chile and Argentina.

Grahamism the vegetarian principles of Sylvester *Graham* (1794–1851), US advocate of dietary reform.

Holy Grail in medieval legend, the cup or platter (also called simply the *Grail*) used by Christ at the Last Supper, and in which Joseph of Arimathea received Christ's blood at the Cross. Quests for it undertaken by medieval knights are described in versions of the Arthurian legends written from the early 13th century onward; it is the immaculately pure ▶ GALAHAD, accompanied by Bors and Perceval, who is destined to find the *Holy Grail*. In figurative usage, the term is used for a thing which is being earnestly pursued or sought after.

The word comes via Old French *graal*, from medieval Latin *gradalis* 'dish'.

a grain of mustard seed a small thing capable of vast development, from the great height attained by black mustard in Palestine, as in Matthew 13:31 'a mustard seed…indeed is the least of all seeds: but when it is grown, it is the greatest among herbs.'

Grainne in the legends relating to the Irish hero Finn, the daughter of King Cormac. Finn, though a great warrior and hunter, was unfortunate in love. He sought to marry Grainne, but she fell in love with Finn's nephew Diarmait O'Duibhne and eloped with him. The long story of their flight and Finn's unsuccessful pursuit ends in Finn's temporary acceptance of the situation; but Finn finally caused the death of Diarmait.

Gram in Norse legend, the name of ▶ SIGURD's sword.

gramarye originally (in Middle English), grammar; (from the late 15th century), occult learning; magic, necromancy. The word was revived in literary use by Sir Walter Scott, and comes via Anglo-Norman French from the base of *grammar*.

grammar the whole system and structure of a language or of languages in general, usually taken as consisting of syntax and morphology (including inflections) and sometimes also phonology and semantics; *grammar* was one of the ▶ SEVEN *liberal arts*.

Recorded from late Middle English, the word

comes via Old French and Latin from Greek *grammatikē (tekhnē)* '(art) of letters', from *gramma, grammat-* 'letter of the alphabet, thing written'.

grammar school in the UK, a state secondary school to which pupils are admitted on the basis of ability; since 1965 most have been absorbed into the comprehensive school system. The name originally denoted a class of schools founded in the 16th century or earlier for the teaching of Latin; after the Education Act of 1944, a *grammar school* was any secondary school with a 'liberal' curriculum including languages, history, literature, and the sciences, as distinct from technical or modern schools.

Grammy each of a number of annual awards given by the American National Academy of Recording Arts and Sciences for achievement in the record industry.

Comte de Gramont French nobleman resident at Charles II's court; his *Memoirs*, compiled in French by his brother-in-law Anthony Hamilton and translated in 1714, are an important source for the history of the Restoration court.

El Gran Capitán nickname ('The Great Captain') of the Spanish military leader Gonzalo Fernández de Córdoba (1453–1515), noted for his military exploits in support of the king of Naples against the French.

Granada a city in Andalusia in southern Spain. Founded in the 8th century, it became the capital of the Moorish kingdom of Granada in 1238, and was the last Moorish stronghold to fall in the reconquest of Spain in 1492. It is the site of the Alhambra palace.

granary a region producing large quantities of corn; the word comes (in the late 16th century) from Latin, from *granum* 'grain'.

the Marquis of Granby a public-house sign, commemorating John Manners, Marquis of Granby (1721–70), noted for his military prowess and in command of the British forces during the ➤ SEVEN *Years War*.

grand see also ➤ *Grand Ole* OPRY, ➤ *Grand* REMONSTRANCE, ➤ *Le Grand* DAUPHIN, ➤ *the Grand* TURK.

Grand Alliance a defensive alliance formed in 1689 between Britain, the Netherlands, and the Holy Roman emperor against the expansionist policies of France.

Grand Canal a series of waterways in eastern China, extending from Beijing southwards to Hangzhou, between the Yangtze and the Yellow River. Its original purpose was to transport rice from the river valleys to the cities, and its construction proceeded in stages between 486 BC and AD 1327.

The name is also given to the main waterway of Venice in Italy, which is lined on each side by fine palaces and spanned by the Rialto Bridge.

Grand Canyon a deep gorge in Arizona, formed by the Colorado River, which is about 440 km (277 miles) long, 8 to 24 km (5 to 15 miles) wide, and, in places, 1,800 m (6,000 ft) deep.

> The current welfare system is structured so that when earned income exceeds a certain level there is a sudden loss in welfare benefits . . . . This so-called 'cliff effect' looks more like a Grand Canyon.
> — *Colorodoan* (Fort Collins) 28 March 1993

Grand Canyon State informal name for Arizona.

Grand Fleet the main British naval fleet, either that based at Spithead in the 18th century or that based at Scapa Flow in the First World War.

Grand Guignol a dramatic entertainment of a sensational or horrific nature, originally a sequence of short pieces as performed at the *Grand Guignol* theatre in Paris. From the name of the bloodthirsty puppet ➤ GUIGNOL.

Grand Inquisitor the director of the court of Inquisition, especially in Spain and Portugal.

Grand Monarque a name (the 'Great Monarch') for ➤ LOUIS *XIV* (1638–1715), king of France from 1643.

Grand National an annual horse race established in 1839, a steeplechase run over a course of 4 miles 856 yards (about 7,200 metres) with thirty jumps, at Aintree, Liverpool, in late March or early April.

Grand Old Duke of York Frederick, Duke of York (1763–1827), commander-in-chief of the British army, as commemorated in the nursery rhyme:

> Oh, the grand old Duke of York,
> He had ten thousand men;
> He marched them up to the top of the hill,
> And he marched them down again.
> — Anonymous nursery rhyme, recorded from the late 19th century

The rhyme is recorded with a number of variants (as, 'the brave old Duke of York'); however, the instance of military indecision has not been traced, and it seems likely that the verse is a hostile adaptation of an earlier rhyme about the king of France.

Although forced to resign in 1809 because of his involvement with an adventuress, Mary Anne Clarke, who had made money from her relationship with him by promising to recommend those who paid her for promotion, York was generally a successful commander-in-chief, who had instituted needed reforms.

See also ➤ Duke *of York's Column.*

Grand Old Man a nickname for ➤ *William Ewart* Gladstone, often abbreviated to *GOM.*

Grand Old Party in the US, the Republican Party; a term recorded from the late 19th century.

Grand Penitentiary in the Roman Catholic Church, a cardinal presiding over the penitentiary.

Grand Pensionary the first minister of the state or province of Holland and Zeeland between 1619 and 1794.

Grand Prix (de Paris) an international horse race for three-year-olds, founded in 1863 and run annually in June at Longchamps, Paris.

Grand Seignior a name for the Sultan of Turkey; the term (French for 'great lord') is recorded from the late 16th century.

grand slam the winning of each of a group of major championships or matches in a particular sport in the same year, in particular in tennis, golf, or rugby union; *grand slam* here is a transferred use from cards, especially bridge, referring to the bidding and winning of all thirteen tricks.

grand tour a cultural tour of Europe conventionally undertaken, especially in the 18th century, by a young man of the upper classes as a part of his education.

Grande Armée Napoleon's main army, from the campaign of 1805 to that of 1814.

La Grande Mademoiselle a name for the tall and wealthy French princess Anne de Montpensier (1627–93), cousin of Louis XIV, formally known as 'Mademoiselle' as her father, brother of Louis XIII, had the designation 'Monsieur'.

grandfather clock a clock in a tall free-standing wooden case, driven by weights; the name derives from the popular song *Grandfather's Clock* (1876) by H. C. Work, with the lines, 'My grandfather's clock was too large for the shelf, So it stood ninety years on the floor.'

Sir Charles Grandison hero of Richardson's novel of that name (1753), intended by the author to represent his ideal of a perfect gentleman, and characterized by a stately and formal courtesy and chivalric magnanimity; the term **Grandisonian** was coined in the 1820s to designate a manner or deportment held to reflect these qualities.

> A man of scrupulous veracity, correctness and integrity, a kind of Grandisonian style of magnanimity, both in substance and manner, visible in all his conduct.
> — Thomas Carlyle letter, 13 April 1859

grandma see ➤ *Grandma* Moses.

grandmother see ➤ *don't* teach *your grandmother to suck eggs.*

grange originally a grange was an outlying farm with tithe barns belonging to a monastery or feudal lord (the term was also used for a barn). It comes (in Middle English, with the sense 'granary, barn' through Old French, from medieval Latin *granica (villa)* 'grain house or farm', based on Latin *granum* 'grain'.

Granger States an informal name for Wisconsin, Illinois, Minnesota, and Iowa, referring to their capacity for producing grain.

grangerize illustrate (a book) by later insertion of material, especially prints cut from other works. From the name of the English biographer James *Granger* (1723–76), who in 1769 published a 'Biographical History of England', with blank leaves for the reception of engraved portraits or other pictorial illustrations of the text. The filling up of a 'Granger' became a favourite hobby, and afterwards other books were treated in the same manner.

Grani in Norse legend, the name of ➤ Sigurd's horse, on whose back Fafnir's treasure was loaded; in Old Norse poetry, gold can thus be called 'Grani's burden'.

Granite City informal name for Aberdeen.

Granite State informal name for New Hampshire.

granny dumping the abandonment of a elderly relative in a public place such as a hospital or nursing home, usually because of an inability to meet the cost of providing proper care; it was observed in the US in the early 1990s that a number of elderly and confused patients, apparently brought for treatment to a hospital emergency room, were then abandoned by those responsible for them.

Granny Smith a dessert apple of a bright green variety with crisp sharp-flavoured flesh, originating in Australia. It is named after Maria Ann (*Granny*) Smith (*c*.1801–1870), who first produced such apples.

Ulysses S. Grant (1822–85), American general and 18th President of the US 1869–77, who as supreme commander of the Unionist armies, defeated the Confederate army in 1865 with a policy of attrition; in May 1864 he sent a dispatch to Washington from his headquarters in the field which read, 'I purpose to fight it out on this line, if it takes all summer.'

It was Grant who accepted Robert E. Lee's surrender at ➤ APPOMATTOX, and who is said to have prevented his men from cheering with the words, 'The war is over—the rebels are our countrymen again.'

Grantchester a village south of Cambridge, home of the First World War poet Rupert Brooke (1887–1915), and celebrated for his nostalgic poem 'The Old Vicarage, Grantchester' (1915), which asks the nostalgic question 'Stands the Church clock at ten to three? And is there honey still for tea?'

Granth short for ➤ ADI *Granth*.

Grantha a southern Indian alphabet dating from the 5th century AD, used by Tamil brahmans for the Sanskrit transcriptions of their sacred books.

grapes see ➤ SOUR *grapes*.

grapeshot ammunition consisting of a number of small iron balls fired together from a cannon.

on the grapevine referring to the circulation of rumours and unofficial information; the term apparently derives a usage in the American Civil War, and is a shortening of 'a dispatch by grapevine telegraph'.

Grasmere a village in Cumbria, beside a small lake of the same name, where ➤ *William* WORDSWORTH and his sister Dorothy lived from 1799.

grasp the nettle tackle a difficulty boldly (in allusion to the fact that a nettle stings when touched lightly, but not when grasped firmly); the idea of the *nettle* representing a difficult or perilous situation is found in Shakespeare's 2 *Henry IV* (1597), 'Out of this nettle, danger, we pluck this flower safety.'

grass *grass* is taken as a type of something green; the word may also mean the season when the grass grows, spring and early summer.

In literary or poetic use, *grass* is often referred to as growing over and covering graves and battlefields:

> Pile the bodies high at Austerlitz and Waterloo.
> Shovel them under and let me work—
> I am the grass; I cover all.
> — Carl Sandburg 'Grass' (1918)

The image may also cover the idea of a formerly prosperous community returning to the wilderness; in 1932 the US President Herbert Hoover, warning against tariff proposals, said, 'The grass will grow in the streets of a hundred cities, a thousand towns.'

The word is recorded in Old English (in form *græs*) and is of Germanic origin, ultimately related to *green* and *grow*.

See also ➤ SNAKE *in the grass*.

while the grass grows, the steed starves proverbial saying, mid 14th century; meaning that by the time hopes or expectations can be satisfied, it may be too late.

the grass is always greener on the other side of the fence proverbial saying, mid 20th century.

grass roots the most basic level of an activity or organization, a figurative use recorded from the early 20th century, and now particularly applied in politics to the rank-and-file of a political organization.

grass widow a woman whose husband is away often or for a prolonged period. In the early 16th century, the word denoted an unmarried woman with a child, perhaps from the idea of the couple having lain on the *grass* instead of in bed. The current sense dates from the mid 19th century,

grasshopper the *grasshopper* is sometimes taken as a type of something frivolous and trivial, as in the passage by Edmund Burke (1729–97):

> Because half a dozen grasshoppers under a fern make the field ring with their importunate chink, whilst thousands of great cattle, reposed beneath the shadow of the British oak, chew the cud and are silent, pray do not imagine that those who make the noise are the only inhabitants of the field.
> — Edmund Burke *Reflections on the Revolution in France* (1790)

In biblical translations, *grasshopper* is sometimes used for locust, as in Ecclesiastes 12:1, 'the grasshopper shall be a burden, and desire shall fail.'

A *grasshopper* was also the personal emblem of the 16th-century financier ➤ *Thomas* GRESHAM; his house in Lombard Street was known as 'the Sign of the Grasshopper', and the badge was later used by Martin's Bank, which originated in Gresham's trading there.

grassy knoll in conspiracy theories of the death of ➤ *John Fitzgerald* KENNEDY, it is suggested that the real assassin was an unidentified gunman on a *grassy knoll* overlooking the route of the motorcade in Dallas.

> Normally buttoned-up auto industry analysts sound like conspiracy buffs surveying the grassy knoll.
> — *New York Times* 24 October 1993

gratia see ➤ DEI *gratia*.

gratias see ➤ DEO *gratias*.

Grattan's Parliament name given to the independent Irish parliament in Dublin set up in 1782 and terminating in 1800 with the Act of Union, named for the Irish politician and nationalist Henry Grattan (1746–1820), to whose efforts the establishment of legislative independence was largely attributed, and looked back to by later nationalists such as ➤ *Charles Stewart* PARNELL as a golden age.

gravamen in the Anglican Church, a memorial from the Lower House of Convocation to the Upper House representing the existence of disorders and grievances within the Church; the term is recorded from the early 17th century, and comes from late Latin, literally 'physical inconvenience'.

From the mid 19th century, *gravamen* has been used (chiefly in legal contexts) to mean the essence or most serious part of a complaint or accusation.

grave see also ➤ PASSAGE *grave*, ➤ WHITE *man's grave*.

gravel-blind almost completely blind (originally, 'more than sand-blind', in Lancelot Gobbo's description of his father):

> This is my true-begotten father, who, being more than sand-blind, high-gravel blind, knows me not.
> — William Shakespeare *The Merchant of Venice* (1596–8)

graven image an idol, in allusion to the second commandment in Exodus 20:2, 'Thou shalt not make unto thee any graven image.'

graveyard shift a work shift that runs through the early morning hours, typically covering the period between midnight and 8 a.m.; a group of employees working such a shift. The term is originally nautical, and has been explained as referring to the number of disasters that occur during this time.

Gray's Inn one of the Inns of Court in London, originating in the late 13th century with those who came to study law under Reginald de Grey of Wilton; his manor house, just outside the City of London, became the first hostel of the society. The precise date at which the Honourable Society of Gray's Inn was founded is not known, but by the 16th century it was well established, with such notable members as William Cecil, Lord Burleigh and Francis Walsingham. The reign of Elizabeth I was a particularly successful period for *Gray's Inn*, and a toast to 'the pious, glorious and immortal memory of Good Queen Bess' is still drunk on special guest nights.

Gray's Inn for walks,
Lincoln's Inn for a wall,
The Inner Temple for a garden,
And the Middle Temple for a hall.
traditional rhyme, mid 17th century; on the four ➤ INNS *of Court*.

greasy pole a pole covered with an oily substance to make it more difficult to climb or walk along, used especially as a form of entertainment; used to refer to the difficult route to the top of someone's profession. The term is notably attributed to Disraeli on becoming Prime Minister, 'I have climbed to the top of the greasy pole.'

great see also ➤ *the* DEPRESSION, ➤ *Great* CHARTER, ➤ *Great* COMMONER, ➤ *Great* DELIVERER, ➤ GREAT *Elector*, ➤ *Great* HARRY, ➤ GREAT *Magician*, ➤ *great* OAKS *from little acorns grow*.

the Great an epithet applied to a number of rulers, as **Alfred the Great**, **Catherine the Great**, and saints, such as **St James the Great**.

the great and the good people in a given sphere regarded as particularly worthy and admirable; the term is first recorded in the mid 19th century in a reference to 'the great and the good throughout the world' as eulogists for Benjamin Franklin, but is now often used ironically.

Great Attractor a massive grouping of galaxies in the direction of the constellations Hydra and Centaurus, whose gravitational pull is thought to be responsible for deviations in the velocity of other galaxies.

Great Bear in astronomy, the constellation ➤ URSA *Major*, named from the story in Greek mythology that the nymph Callisto was turned into a bear and placed as a constellation in the heavens by Zeus.

Great Bed of Ware an English Elizabethan four-poster bed, now in the Victoria and Albert Museum, and proverbially taken as a type of something of great size; the Protestant divine William Jenkyn (1613–85) wrote in 1648 in a polemic against his fellow divine John Goodwin, 'Solid matter lodgeth in his great book of words, as a child of two days old in the great bed of Ware.'

Great Bible the edition of the English Bible which Thomas Cromwell ordered in 1538 to be set up in every parish church. It was the work of Miles Coverdale, and was first issued in 1539.

a great book is a great evil proverbial saying, early 17th century; earlier in Greek in the writings of the Hellenistic poet and scholar Callimachus (*c.*305–*c.*240 BC).

Great Cham of Literature a nickname for ➤ *Samuel* JOHNSON (1709–84), coined by the writer Tobias Smollett (1721–71) in a letter of 16 March 1759 to John Wilkes.

great circle a circle on the surface of a sphere which lies in a plane passing through the sphere's centre. As it represents the shortest distance between any two points on a sphere, a great circle of the earth is the preferred route taken by a ship or aircraft.

Great Council under the Norman kings of England, the assembly of tenants-in-chief and great ecclesiastics, out of which the House of Lords originated.

Great Divide another name for the ➤ CONTINENTAL *Divide* or Great Dividing Range.

Great Exhibition the first international exhibition of the products of industry, promoted by Prince Albert and held in the Crystal Palace in London in 1851.

Great Fire another name for the ➤ FIRE *of London.*

the great game spying; the term in this sense is first recorded in Rudyard Kipling's *Kim* (1901), 'When he comes to the Great Game he must go alone—alone, and at peril of his head.'

a great gulf fixed an unbridgeable difference; originally with biblical allusion to Luke 16:26, 'Between us and you there is a great gulf fixed,' in the words of Abraham to ➤ DIVES in the story of the rich man and Lazarus, the beggar.

great hundred archaic expression meaning, one hundred and twenty.

Great Lake State informal name for Michigan.

Great Lakes a group of five large interconnected lakes in central North America, consisting of Lakes Superior, Michigan, Huron, Erie, and Ontario, and constituting the largest area of fresh water in the world. Lake Michigan is wholly within the US, and the others lie on the Canada–US border. Connected to the Atlantic Ocean by the St Lawrence Seaway, the Great Lakes form an important commercial waterway.

Great Leap Forward an unsuccessful attempt made under Mao Zedong in China 1958–60 to hasten the process of industrialization and improve agricultural production by reorganizing the population into large rural collectives and adopting labour-intensive industrial methods.

the great majority the dead; often in **join the great majority**, die, originally from the poet Edward Young (1683–1765) 'Death joins us to the great majority.' The same idea is found earlier in the writing of the 1st-century AD Roman satirist Petronius, '*Abiit ad plures* [He's gone to join the majority].'

great minds think alike proverbial saying, early 17th century.

Great Mogul a title given to the Mogul emperor of Delhi; recorded in English from the late 16th century.

Great Mother another name for the ➤ MOTHER *Goddess.*

Great Northern War a conflict 1700–21 in which Russia, Denmark, Poland, and Saxony opposed Sweden. The war resulted in Sweden losing her imperial possessions in central Europe, and Russia under Peter the Great becoming a major power in the Baltic.

great omission a name for the section of St Mark's Gospel, 6:45–8:26, which is omitted by St Luke.

Great Plague a serious outbreak of bubonic plague in England in 1665–6, in which about one fifth of the population of London died, and which was the last major outbreak in Britain. The diarist Samuel Pepys notes of this time in London:

> I saw a dead corpse in a coffin lie in the close unburied—and a watch is constantly kept there, night and day, to keep the people in—the plague making us cruel as dogs one to another.
> — Samuel Pepys diary, 4 September 1665

Pepys also records that at the height of the plague passers-by 'would breathe in the faces…of well people going by', so that if they themselves were infected the infection would be passed on.

Great Plains a vast area of plains to the east of the Rocky Mountains in North America, extending from the valleys of the Mackenzie River in Canada to southern Texas.

Great Rebellion the Royalist name for the English Civil War of 1642–51, recorded from the early 18th century.

Great Schism the breach between the Eastern and the Western Churches, traditionally dated to 1054 and becoming final in 1472. The excommunications of 1054 were abolished as an ecumenical gesture in 1965.
   The name is also used for the period 1378–1417, when the Western Church was divided by the creation of antipopes.

Great Seal a seal used for the authentication of state documents of the highest importance. That of the UK is held by the Lord Chancellor and that of the US by the Secretary of State.

Great Spirit the supreme god in the traditional religion of many North American Indians, a translation of Ojibwa *kitchi manitou.*

Great Synagogue a Jewish council of 120 members, said to have been founded and presided over by Ezra after the return from the Babylonian captivity.

Great Tom of Lincoln a bell in Lincoln Cathedral; *Tom* was frequently used as a name for an exceptionally large bell.

Great Tom of Oxford a bell in Tom Tower, Christ Church, Oxford.

Great Trek the northward migration 1835–7 of large numbers of Boers, discontented with British rule in the Cape, to the areas where they eventually founded the Transvaal Republic and Orange Free State.

Great Unknown a nickname for Sir Walter Scott (1771–1832), as the anonymous author of the Waverley novels (well known as a poet, he did not acknowledge authorship of the novels until 1827).

great unwashed the lower classes, the rabble; a derogatory term recorded from the mid 19th century.

Great Wall of China a fortified wall in northern China, extending some 2,400 km (1,500 miles) from

Kansu province to the Yellow Sea north of Beijing. It was first built *c.*210 BC, as a protection against nomad invaders. The present wall dates from the Ming dynasty. Although principally a defensive wall, it served also as a means of communication: for most of its length it was wide enough to allow five horses to travel abreast.

Great War another name for the ➤ FIRST *World War*; the term in this sense is recorded from 1914.

Great Wen an archaic nickname for London, a phrase originally coined by Cobbett:

> But what is to be the fate of the great wen of all? The monster, called 'the metropolis of the empire'?
> — William Cobbett *Rural Rides* (1821)

Great White Way a nickname for Broadway in New York City, with reference to the brilliant street illumination.

great year another name for the ➤ PLATONIC *year.*

Great Zimbabwe a complex of stone ruins in a fertile valley in Zimbabwe, south of Harare, discovered by Europeans in 1868. They are the remains of a city which was the centre of a flourishing civilization in the 14th and 15th centuries. The buildings consist of an acropolis, a stone enclosure, and other scattered remains. The circumstances of its eventual decline and abandonment are unknown.

the greater the sinner, the greater the saint proverbial saying, late 18th century.

the greater the truth, the greater the libel proverbial saying, late 18th century.

the Greatest Show on Earth the title under which the American showman ➤ *Phineas Taylor* BARNUM billed his circus when it opened in 1871.

Grecian a boy in the highest class at Christ's Hospital, the Bluecoat School.

Grecian bend an affected way of walking in which the body is bent forward from the hips, prevalent in the late 19th century.

Grecian coffee-house a coffee house which stood in Devereux Court, Essex Street, Strand, and was frequented by Addison, Steele, and Goldsmith, and by many fellows of the Royal Society, which gave it a reputation for learning. It was announced in No. 1 of *The Tatler* that all learned articles would proceed from the Grecian.

Grecian nose a straight nose that continues the line of the forehead without a dip.

Greco see ➤ EL *Greco*.

Greece see ➤ *the eye of* GREECE.

Greek Anthology a compilation of Greek epigrams, songs, epitaphs, and rhetorical exercises, based on a collection made by Meleager of Gadara, *c.*60 BC, and subsequently augmented; the fullest form is a compilation made by a 10th-century AD Byzantine scholar Constantine Cephalas. An abridgement prepared by a 14th-century Byzantine scholar Maximus Planudes was influential during the Renaissance.

at the Greek Calends never; the *Greek Calends* will never come as the Greeks did not use calends in reckoning time. The term is recorded from the mid 17th century, when William Drummond of Hawthornden (1585–1649) reflected that 'That gold, plate, and all silver given to the Mint-house in these late Troubles, shall be paid at the Greek Calends.'

Greek Church another name for the ➤ GREEK *Orthodox Church.*

Greek cross a cross of which all four arms are of equal length.

Greek Fathers the ➤ FATHERS *of the Church* who wrote in Greek.

Greek fire a combustible composition emitted by a flame-throwing weapon, and used to set light to enemy ships, which was first used by the Greeks besieged in Constantinople (673–8). It ignited on contact with water, and was probably based on naphtha and quicklime.

Greek gift a gift made to conceal an act of treachery; the allusion is to the ➤ TROJAN *Horse,* and to the warning *timeo Danaos et dona ferentes* 'I fear the Greeks even when they bring gifts.'

See also ➤ FEAR *the Greeks bearing gifts.*

Greek key a pattern of interlocking right-angled spirals.

when Greek meets Greek, then comes the tug of war proverbial saying, late 17th century; originally in Nathaniel Lee's *The Rival Queens* (1677), 'When Greeks joined Greeks, then was the tug of war.'

Greek Orthodox Church the Eastern Orthodox Church which uses the Byzantine rite in Greek, in particular the national Church of Greece.

Greek Revival a necoclassical movement in architecture and the arts, occurring in Europe and North America in the late 18th and early 19th centuries.

all Greek to me completely unintelligible; Greek for unintelligible language or gibberish is recorded from from the late 16th century, as in Shakespeare's *Julius Caesar* (1599) when Casca, having said that Cicero spoke Greek, adds, 'those that understood him smiled at one another and shook their heads; but, for mine own part, it was Greek to me.'

green of the colour between blue and yellow in the spectrum; coloured like grass or emeralds. Green is traditionally the colour of jealousy, and also symbolized youth and immaturity.

In 20th century use, *green* (often with a capital initial) means concerned with or supporting protection of the environment as a political principle.

See also ➤ *believe that the* MOON *is made of green cheese,* ➤ BOARD *of Green Cloth,* ➤ FIDDLER'*s Green,* ➤ GEORGIAN *green,* ➤ JACK-*in-the-green,* ➤ KENDAL *Green,* ➤ LINCOLN *green,* ➤ LITTLE *green man,* ➤ RUB *of the green,* ➤ USHER *of the Green Rod,* ➤ WEARING *of the Green,* ➤ WIGS *on the green.*

Reverend Green one of the six stock characters constituting the murderer and suspects in the game of ➤ CLUEDO.

green belt an area of open land around a city, on which building is restricted.

A *green belt* also marks a level of proficiency in judo, karate, or other martial arts below that of a brown belt.

Green Beret a British commando or a member of the US Army Special Forces.

Green Book in England and Wales, a book setting out the procedural rules of the county courts, bound in green.

green card in the US, a permit allowing a foreign national to live and work permanently in the US.

Green Cross code a road-safety drill taught to children.

the **green**-eyed **monster** jealousy personified; originally from Iago's warning in Shakespeare's *Othello*:

> O! beware, my lord, of jealousy;
> It is the green-eyed monster which doth mock
> The meat it feeds on.
> — William Shakespeare *Othello* (1602–4)

green fingers natural ability in growing plants; recorded from the 1930s.

the **Green** Island a name for Ireland.

the **Green** Linnets a name for the 39th Foot, later the Dorsetshire Regiment, from the green facings on their uniform.

green man a man dressed up in greenery to represent a wild man of the woods or seasonal fertility. A carved image of this is often seen in medieval English churches, as a human face with branches and foliage growing out of the mouth.

Green Mountain Boys an irregular militia organized to defend the New Hampshire Grants of Vermont against New York land-jobbers, led by Ethan Allen; in the American War of Independence they took a leading part in the capture of Fort Ticonderoga from British forces.

Green Mountain State informal name for Vermont.

Green Paper in the UK, a preliminary report of government proposals that is published in order to provoke discussion.

Green Party an environmentalist political party. Green Parties arose in Europe in the early 1970s, since when they have achieved a certain amount of electoral success, particularly in Germany. The Green Party in Britain was founded in 1973 as the Ecology Party, changing its name in 1985.

green ribbon a ribbon of green colour worn as the badge of the King's Head Club, consisting of supporters of the ➤ *Duke of* MONMOUTH (1679–85).

green room a room in a theatre or studio in which performers can relax when they are not performing. The name probably derives from the room's originally being painted green. The first reference to it is in a play by Colley Cibber:

> I do know London pretty well, and the Side-box, Sir, and behind the Scenes, ay, and the Green Room and all the Girls, and Women-Actresses there.
> — Colley Cibber *Love Makes Man* (1701)

green shoots signs of growth or renewal, especially of economic recovery. The expression in this context derives from a misquotation, 'the green shoots of recovery', of a speech made by the Conservative politician Norman Lamont when Chancellor:

> The green shoots of economic spring are appearing once again.
> — Norman Lamont speech at the Conservative Party Conference, 9 October 1991

Green Thursday another name for Maundy Thursday, perhaps referring to the practice of giving green branches to penitents who had made their confession on Ash Wednesday.

a **green** Yule makes a fat churchyard proverbial saying, mid 17th century.

Kate **Greenaway** (1846–1901), English artist. She is known especially for her illustrations of children's books such as *Mother Goose* (1881). An annual award for the best children's book illustration in Britain is named after her.

greenback in the US, an informal name for a dollar bill.

Greeneland the seedy politically unstable and dangerous world said to be the typical setting for the characters in the novels of Graham *Greene* (1904–91).

greener see ➤ *the* GRASS *is always greener on the other side of the fence.*

greenery-yallery of or in the style of the 19th-century Aesthetic Movement (used to convey the idea of affectation); originally as a quotation from Gilbert and Sullivan:

> A greenery-yallery, Grosvenor Gallery,
> Foot-in-the-grave young man!
> — W. S. Gilbert *Patience* (1881)

greengage a sweet greenish fruit resembling a small plum; the tree bearing this fruit. Named after Sir William *Gage*, the English botanist who introduced it to England.

Greenham Common a village near Newbury, Berkshire, the site of a US cruise missile base which became a focus for anti-nuclear protests in the 1980s.

greenhorn a person who is new to or inexperienced at a particular activity.

greenhouse effect the trapping of the sun's warmth in a planet's lower atmosphere due to the greater transparency of the atmosphere to visible radiation from the sun than to infrared radiation emitted from the planet's surface.

On earth the increasing quantity of atmospheric carbon dioxide from the burning of fossil fuels, together with the release of other gases, is causing an increased greenhouse effect and leading to global warming. A greenhouse effect involving CO_2 is also responsible for the very high surface temperature of Venus.

Greenland a large island lying to the north-east of North America and mostly within the Arctic Circle, of which only 5 per is habitable; explored by ➤ ERIC *the Red* at the end of the 10th century, it was said to have been so named by its discoverer 'because it would induce settlers to go there, if the land had a good name'.

greenmail in Stock Exchange usage, the practice of buying enough shares in a company to threaten a takeover, forcing the owners to buy them back at a higher price in order to retain control.

Greenpeace an international organization that campaigns actively but non-violently for conservation of the environment and the preservation of endangered species. The name is said to have been coined from a meeting of the Don't Make a Wave Committee, which preceded the formation of Greenpeace, when the Canadian environmentalist Bill Darnell said, 'Make it a *green* peace.'

greensickness archaic name for *chlorosis*, an anaemia caused by iron deficiency, especially in adolescent girls, causing a pale, faintly greenish complexion, a common diagnosis in the 19th century.

greenwash to mislead with a false statement of the environmental credentials of a person, company, or product; to create a misleading environmental image.

Greenwich a London borough on the south bank of the Thames, the original site of the Royal Greenwich Observatory. The buildings at Greenwich, together with many of the old instruments, now form part of the National Maritime Museum, and reclaimed land at Greenwich forms the site of the ➤ MILLENNIUM *Dome*.

See also ➤ ROYAL *Greenwich Observatory*.

Greenwich Mean Time the mean solar time at the Greenwich meridian, adopted as the standard time in a zone that includes the British Isles.

Greenwich meridian the prime meridian, which passes through the former Royal Observatory at Greenwich. It was adopted internationally as the zero of longitude in 1884.

Greenwich Village a district of New York City on the lower west side of Manhattan, traditionally associated with writers, artists, and musicians.

Gregorian calendar the calendar introduced in 1582 by Pope Gregory XIII, as a modification of the Julian calendar.

To bring the calendar back into line with the solar year, 10 days were suppressed, and centenary years were only made leap years if they were divisible by 400. Scotland adopted the Gregorian calendar in 1600, but England and Wales did not follow suit until 1752 (by which time 11 days had to be suppressed). At the same time New Year's Day was changed from 25 March to 1 January, and dates using the new calendar were designated 'New Style'.

Gregorian chant church music sung as a single vocal line in free rhythm and a restricted scale (plainsong), in a style developed for the medieval Latin liturgy, and named after St Gregory the Great, who is said to have standardized it.

Gregorian epoch the time from which the Gregorian calendar dates (1582).

Gregorian telescope an early reflecting telescope in which light reflected from a concave elliptical secondary mirror passes through a hole in the primary mirror. It was rendered obsolete by the introduction of Newtonian and Cassegrain telescopes. It is named after James *Gregory* (1638–75), the Scottish mathematician who invented it.

Gregorian tree a former name for the gallows, called after *Gregory* Brandon, hangman of London in the reign of James I; he was succeeded by his son Richard (d. 1649), executioner of Charles I, who was known as *Young Gregory*.

St Gregory (*c.*540–604), pope (as Gregory I) from 590 and Doctor of the Church, also known as **St Gregory the Great**. An important reformer, he did much to establish the temporal power of the papacy. He sent St Augustine to England to lead the country's conversion to Christianity, and is also credited with the introduction of Gregorian chant.

 □ **FEAST DAY** His feast day is 12 March.

Gregory VII (*c.*1020–85), pope from 1073, who asserted the power of the papacy and hierarchy and insisted on clerical celibacy; in his conflict with the

Holy Roman Emperor Henry IV (1050–1106) he was at first successful, so that Henry was forced to do penance at ➤ CANOSSA in 1077; finally deposed in 1084, Gregory died at Salerno, his last words being, 'I have loved justice and hated iniquity; therefore I die in exile.'

See also ➤ HILDEBRANDINE.

St Gregory of Nazianus (329–89), Doctor of the Church, bishop of Constantinople. With St Basil and St Gregory of Nyssa he was an upholder of Orthodoxy against the Arian and Apollinarian heresies, and influential in restoring adherence to the Nicene Creed.

◻ **FEAST DAY** His feast day is (in the Eastern Church) 25 and 30 January; (in the Western Church) 2 January (formerly 9 May).

St Gregory of Nyssa (c.330–395), Doctor of the Eastern Church, bishop of Nyssa in Cappadocia. The brother of St Basil, he was an Orthodox follower of Origen and joined with St Basil and St Gregory of Nazianus in opposing Arianism.

◻ **FEAST DAY** His feast day is 9 March.

St Gregory of Tours (c.540–94), Frankish bishop and historian. He was elected bishop of Tours in 573; his writings provide the chief authority for the early Merovingian period of French history.

◻ **FEAST DAY** His feast day is 17 November.

Gregynog Press a private press founded in 1923 at Gregynog Hall, near Newtown, Montgomeryshire, and endowed by Miss Gwendoline and Miss Margaret Davies as part of their plan to establish an arts and crafts centre. It excelled in the fineness of its bindings, and survived until 1940. It was revived in 1974.

gremlin an imaginary mischievous sprite regarded as responsible for an unexplained problem or fault, especially a mechanical or electronic one. From the 1940s, originally as RAF slang, and perhaps suggested by *goblin*.

grenadier originally, a soldier armed with *grenades*; now, a member of the **Grenadier Guards**, in the UK the first regiment of royal household infantry.

Grendel in the Old English epic poem *Beowulf*, the water monster who nightly attacks Heorot, the hall built by Hrothgar, king of Denmark, and each night kills and eats one of Hrothgar's thanes. Grendel is of the race of ➤ CAIN, living away from humankind but drawn by savagery and greed to the hall where the king's men feast.

He ravages Heorot over many years, but is mortally wounded in his fight with the hero ➤ BEOWULF and his severed arm nailed up as a trophy. Grendel's mother then comes to Heorot to avenge her son; she kills Hrothgar's most valued thane, but is in her turn destroyed by Beowulf in her underwater lair.

> Presently the culprit broke surface, looking like Grendel's mother, to be disqualified for wrestling and ungentlemanly conduct.
> — George Macdonald Fraser *The General Danced at Dawn* (1970)

Thomas Gresham (c.1519–79), English financier. He founded the Royal Exchange in 1566 and served as the chief financial adviser to the Elizabethan government; his emblem, a ➤ GRASSHOPPER, was later used by Martin's Bank.

Gresham's Law the tendency for money of lower intrinsic value to circulate more freely than money of higher intrinsic and equal nominal value (often expressed as 'Bad money drives out good').

Gretchen in Goethe's *Faust* (1808), name of the simple girl seduced by Faust; in extended usage, a girl held to resemble her, a typically German girl or woman.

Gretel see ➤ HANSEL *and Gretel*.

Gretna Green a village in Scotland just north of the English border near Carlisle, formerly a popular place for runaway couples from England to be married without the parental consent required in England for people under a certain age.

Place de Grève in Paris, the former site of public executions; ➤ *Robert François* DAMIENS was put to death there, and the first guillotine was erected there for the execution of a highwayman in April 1792.

grey see also ➤ EARL *Grey*, ➤ *the grey* MARE *is the better horse*.

Lady Jane Grey (1537–54), niece of Henry VIII, queen of England 9–19 July 1553. In 1553, to ensure a Protestant succession, John Dudley, the Duke of Northumberland, forced Jane to marry his son and persuaded the dying Edward VI to name Jane as his successor. She was quickly deposed by forces loyal to Edward's (Catholic) sister Mary, who had popular support, and executed the following year. She is sometimes referred to as the *Nine Days' Queen*.

Despite her youth she was known for her learning; in *The Schoolmaster* (1570) her former tutor Roger Ascham records her as saying, 'One of the greatest benefits that God ever gave me is that he sent me so sharp and severe parents and so gentle a schoolmaster.'

little grey cells the expression used by Agatha Christie's detective ➤ *Hercule* POIROT to describe his intelligence.

> 'This affair must all be unravelled from within.' He tapped his forehead. 'These little grey cells. It is "up to them"—as you say over here!'
> — Agatha Christie *The Mysterious Affair at Styles* (1920)

grey economy the part of the economy consisting of transactions which are not taxed or accounted for in official statistics.

grey eminence another term for ➤ ÉMINENCE *grise*.

Grey Friar a Franciscan friar, so named because of the colour of the order's habit.

grey market an unofficial market or trade in something, especially unissued shares or controlled or scarce goods.

grey matter the darker tissue of the brain and spinal cord, consisting mainly of nerve cell bodies and branching dendrites; informally, intelligence.

Greyfriars Bobby name of a famous Skye terrier belonging to a Scottish shepherd, John Grey; after his master's death in 1858, the dog spent the last fourteen years of his life in the Greyfriars Kirkyard, where John Grey was buried. He was fed by local people, and after his death, Baroness Burdett Coutts had a statue of him set up in the churchyard to mark his loyalty.

> The Man was offended. 'Well, thanks for standing by me,' he said. Who does he think I am, Greyfriars Bobby?
> — Roy Hattersley *Buster's Diaries* (1998)

the Scots Greys the 2nd Dragoons, raised in 1681 as the Royal Regiment of Dragoons, and originally wearing a grey uniform.

gridiron a gridiron is the emblem of ➤ *St* LAWRENCE and ➤ *St* VINCENT *of Saragossa*.

gridlock a traffic jam affecting a whole network of intersecting streets, which in the early 1990s developed the figurative use of a situation in which no progress can be made. In US politics it was used particularly to denote the situation in which legislation makes no progress, either because of conflicts within Congress, or because of disagreements between Congress and the Administration. A high-profile instance is recorded in 1992, when just after the election of President Clinton the Republican

Robert Dole said dryly, 'A little gridlock might be good from time to time.'

griffin a mythical creature with the head and wings of an eagle and the body of a lion, typically depicted with pointed ears and with the eagle's legs taking the place of the forelegs. The ancient Greeks believed that they lived in Scythia, guarding the gold for which that country was renowned.

grig a small eel; a grasshopper or cricket. Chiefly in **as merry as a grig**.

Grim Reaper a personification of death in the form of a cloaked skeleton wielding a large scythe; *reaper* in this sense is recorded from the mid 19th century.

Grim the Collier a character in *Grim the Collier of Croyden*, a comedy by William Haughton (*c.*1575–1605), who has given his name to a kind of hawkweed, grown in gardens, with orange or red flowers and calyces covered with black hairs.

Grimaldi name of the ruling dynasty of the principality of Monaco.

Francesco Maria Grimaldi (1618–63), Italian physicist and astronomer, who discovered the diffraction of light and verified Galileo's law of the uniform acceleration of falling bodies, and drew a detailed map of the moon (naming features after astronomers and physicists).

Joseph Grimaldi (1779–1837), English circus entertainer, who created the role of the circus clown. He performed at Covent Garden, where he became famous for his acrobatic skills; the term *Joey* for a clown is an abbreviation of his name.

grimalkin a cat (used especially in reference to its characteristically feline qualities); in the opening scene of Shakespeare's *Macbeth*, the witches are apparently called away by fiends or familiars addressed by them as 'Paddock' and 'Graymalkin'.

The word is recorded from the late 16th century, and comes from *grey* + *Malkin* (pet form of the given name *Matilda*).

grimgribber legal jargon, learned gibberish, from *Grimgribber*, an imaginary estate invented by a sham lawyer in Richard Steele's play *The Conscious Lovers* (1722).

Jacob and Wilhelm Grimm (1785–1863 and 1786–1859), German philologists and folklorists. In 1852 the brothers jointly inaugurated a dictionary of

German on historical principles, which was eventually completed by other scholars in 1960. They also compiled an anthology of German fairy stories, based on oral folk tales, which appeared in three volumes between 1812 and 1822, and their name may be used allusively in this context to indicate a somewhat sinister atmosphere of magic and danger.

> 'Is that it? asked Globus. 'Are the Grimms' fairy stories over for the day? Excellent.'
> — Robert Harris *Fatherland* (1992)

Grimm's law the observation that certain Indo-European consonants (mainly stops) undergo regular changes in the Germanic languages which are not seen in others such as Greek or Latin. Examples include *p* becoming *f* so that Latin *pedem* corresponds to English *foot* and German *Fuss*. The principle was set out by Jacob Grimm in his German grammar (2nd edition, 1822).

grimoire a book of magic spells and incantations. Recorded from the mid 19th century, the word comes from French, and is an alteration of *grammaire* 'grammar'.

grimpen a marshy area, from the dangerous *Grimpen* Mire on Dartmoor, in which the villain is finally swallowed up, in Conan Doyle's *The Hound of the Baskervilles* (1902).

Grímr a byname of Odin, perhaps preserved in place-names such as *Grim's Dyke*. The name is related to the Norse word for a hood, figuratively night, and probably refers to stories of Odin travelling in disguise.

gripe former name for a griffin or vulture; the name comes ultimately via Latin *gryps*, *gryph-* from the base of *griffin*.

grisaille a method of painting in grey monochrome, typically to imitate sculpture; a painting or stained-glass window in this style. The word comes (in the mid 19th century) from French, from *gris* 'grey'.

Griselda the heroine of Chaucer's *Clerk's Tale*, the model of a patient wife who is persecuted and ultimately apparently rejected by her husband. The story comes from Boccaccio.

all is grist that comes to the mill proverbial saying; mid 17th century; **grist to the mill** is a phrase used to denote useful experience, material, or knowledge. *Grist* is corn that is ground to make flour.

grith in Anglo-Saxon England, security, peace, or protection guaranteed under specific limits of time or place; (more fully **church-grith**) sanctuary, security within the precincts of a church.

groaning an archaic term for a woman's lying-in, used attributively for food and drink provided for attendants and visitors.

groat any of various medieval European coins, in particular an English silver coin worth four old pence, issued between 1351 and 1662; often taken as the type of something of little or no value, as in *not care a groat*.

The word comes from Middle Dutch *groot* or Middle Low German *grōte* 'great, thick', hence 'thick penny'.

Grobian in German writers of the 15th and 16th centuries, an imaginary person taken as the type of boorish behaviour, from medieval Latin *Grobianus*, his supposed personal name, from German *grob* 'coarse, rude'.

grockle a holidaymaker at an English resort, especially one in the West Country. An invented word, originally a fantastic creature in a children's comic, adopted arbitrarily and popularized by the film *The System* (1962).

grog spirits (originally rum) mixed with water. The word, which is mid 18th century, is said to be from *Old Grog*, the reputed nickname (because of his grogram cloak) of Admiral Vernon (1684–1757), who in 1740 first ordered diluted (instead of neat) rum to be served out to sailors.

Grolier the name of a famous French book collector, Jean *Grolier* de Servin, Vicomte d'Aiguisy (1479–1565), used to designate the interlacing geometrical designs adorning the bindings of his books. The **Grolier Club**, founded in New York in 1884 for the study and promotion of 'the arts pertaining to the production of books' is named after him.

Gromit name of the faithful and silent dog belonging to the cheese-loving inventor ➤ WALLACE in Nick Park's claymation films of his two plasticine figures; despite his inability to speak, *Gromit* ably conveys his views through expression and the movement of his long dark ears.

grommet an eyelet placed in a hole in a sheet or panel to protect or insulate a rope or cable passed through it or to prevent the sheet or panel from being torn; the term is now also used for a tube surgically implanted in the eardrum, typically to drain fluid from the middle ear. Originally (in nautical use) it meant, a circle of rope used as a fastening.

Groom of the Stole a high officer of a royal household ranking next below the vice-chamberlain; *stole* here is a variant of *stool* in the sense of 'commode, privy'.

groom-porter in the royal household, the holder of an office (abolished under George III) whose principal function was to regulate gaming.

Groperland an informal name for Western Australia.

Walter Gropius (1883–1969), German-born American architect. He was the first director of the Bauhaus School of Design (1919–28) and a pioneer of the international style. He settled in the US in 1938, where he was professor of architecture at Harvard University until 1952.

Robert Grosseteste (*c*.1175–1253), English churchman, philosopher, and scholar, whose experimental approach to science, especially in optics and mathematics, inspired his pupil ➤ *Roger* BACON.

Grosvenor Gallery a gallery in Bond Street, London, for the exhibition of pictures of the modern school, erected by Coutts Lindsay in 1876. It was especially associated for a time with the aesthetic movement, and Bunthorne in Gilbert and Sullivan's *Patience* describes himself as

> A greenery-yallery, Grosvenor Gallery
> Foot-in-the-grave young man.

The Gallery closed in 1890.
See also ➤ GREENERY-*yallery*.

George Grosz (1893–1959), German painter and draughtsman. His satirical drawings and paintings characteristically depict a decadent society in which gluttony and depraved sensuality are juxtaposed with poverty and disease.

grotesque comically or repulsively ugly or distorted. The word (recorded in English from the mid 16th century) comes through French from Italian *opera* or *pittura grottesca* 'work or painting resembling that found in a grotto'; 'grotto' here probably denoted the rooms of ancient buildings in Rome which had been revealed by excavations, and which contained murals in the grotesque style.

Hugo Grotius (1583–1645), Dutch jurist and diplomat. His legal treatise *De Jure Belli et Pacis* (1625) established the basis of modern international law.

Groucho see ➤ *I am a* MARXIST *of the Groucho tendency*

ground bass a short musical theme, usually in the bass, which is constantly repeated as the other parts of the music vary.

groundhog North American term for the woodchuck, a marmot with a heavy body and short legs.

Groundhog Day in the US, 2 February, when the groundhog is said to come out of its hole at the end of hibernation. If the animal sees its shadow—i.e. if the weather is sunny—it is said to portend six weeks more of winter weather.

groundling a spectator or reader of inferior taste; originally a member of the part of a theatre audience that traditionally stood in the pit beneath the stage, with reference to Hamlet's words to the players in Shakespeare's *Hamlet* (1601), 'it offends me to the soul to hear a robustious periwig-pated fellow tear a passion to tatters, to very rags, to split the ears of the groundlings.'

groundswell a build-up of opinion or feeling in a large section of the population, likened to a large or extensive swell in the sea.

group see also ➤ BRUGES *Group*.

Group of Seven a group of Canadian landscape painters, officially established in 1920, who formed the first major national movement in Canadian art. Their work exhibited a bold and colourful expressionistic style.

The name is also given to a group of seven leading industrial nations outside the former communist bloc, consisting of the US, Japan, Germany (originally West Germany), France, the UK, Italy, and Canada.

Group of Seventy-Seven a term for the developing countries of the world.

Group of Three the three largest industrialized economies (the US, Germany, and Japan).

grove a small wood or group of trees, often deliberately planted; in older biblical translations, as 2 Kings 21:1 'a graven image of the grove', sometimes used erroneously to render Hebrew *'ăšērāh* and *'ēšel*, now understood to mean 'sacred tree' and 'tamarisk' respectively.

George Grove (1820–1900), English musicologist. He was the founder and first editor of the multi-volume *Dictionary of Music and Musicians* (1879–89) and served as the first director of the Royal College of Music (1883–94).

groves of academe the academic world; originally as a quotation from the *Epistles* of the 1st-century ad Roman poet Horace, '*Atque inter silvas Academi quaerere verum* [And seek for truth in the groves of Academe].'

growlery after Dickens's use in *Bleak House*, place to growl or be grumpy in; a private sitting-room or study.

> Sit down, my dear,' said Mr. Jarndyce. 'This, you must know, is the Growlery. When I am out of humour, I come and growl here'.
> — Charles Dickens *Bleak House* (1853)

Grub Street used in reference to a world or class of impoverished journalists and writers, from the name of a street (later Milton Street) in Moorgate, London, inhabited by such authors in the 17th century. The allusion is first recorded in the mid 17th century, in the writings of the Anglican churchman and writer Jeremy Taylor (1616–67), in a reference to 'the quintessence of Grub Street'.

grubstake an amount of material, provisions, or money supplied to an enterprise (originally a prospector for ore) in return for a share in the resulting profits.

gruelling extremely tiring and demanding, from the verb *gruel* 'exhaust, punish', from an old phrase *get one's gruel* 'receive one's punishment', and thus ultimately from the noun *gruel* 'a thin liquid food of oatmeal or other meal boiled in milk or water'.

Grumbletonian a member of the Country Party in 17th-century English politics, allegedly motivated by dissatisfied personal ambition. The name comes from *grumble* after ➤ MUGGLETONIAN and similar forms.

Mrs Grundy a person with very conventional standards of propriety, from the name of a person repeatedly mentioned in T. Morton's comedy *Speed the Plough* (1798), often in the phrase 'What will Mrs Grundy say?', which became a popular catchphrase.

> Freedom, openness, chic—one can almost hear the grumblings of Ms. and Mr. Grundys on both the right and the left.
> — Marjorie Garber *Vice Versa* (1995)

Guadalcanal an island in the western Pacific, the largest of the Solomon Islands, which during the Second World War was the scene of the first major US offensive against the Japanese (August 1942).

> He understood history when it happened to him. (He didn't mistake Guadalcanal for just another day's work.)
> — Carol Bly *Letters from the Country* (1981)

guard see ➤ PRAETORIAN *guard*, ➤ RED *Guard*, ➤ UP *Guards and at them*, ➤ VARANGIAN *guard*, ➤ WHITE *Guard*, ➤ YEOMAN *of the Guard*.

guardant in heraldry (especially of an animal), depicted with the body sideways and the face towards the viewer.

guardian angel a spirit that is thought to watch over and protect a person or place; recorded from the mid 17th century.

Guardian of the Poor former name for a member of a board elected to administer the poor laws in a parish or district.

Giuseppe Guarneri (1687–1744), Italian violin-maker; known as *del Gesù*. He is the most famous of a family of three generations of violin-makers based in Cremona. He is noted for the attention he gave to the tone quality of his instruments, which do not conform to any standard shape or dimensions.

gubbins miscellaneous items. The term comes (in the mid 16th century with the sense 'fragments') from obsolete *gobbon* 'piece, slice', probably related to *gobbet*.

Gudrun in Norse legend, sister of Gunnar, the wife of ➤ SIGURD and later of Atli (Attila the Hun); the Norse equivalent of Kriemhild in the *Nibelungenlied*. In both Norse and Germanic versions of the story, she is ultimately a figure of vengeance, bringing about the death of the brothers who have killed her husband.

In saga literature, *Gudrun* is also the name of the remorseless heroine of the Old Icelandic *Laxdæla Saga*, who is loved by Kjartan but marries his foster-brother Bolli, and who in the end incites Bolli to kill Kjartan; when her husband comes to her with news of Kjartan's death, she says bleakly, 'The morning work has been unequal; I have spun twelve ells of yarn, and you have killed Kjartan.' On her deathbed she reflects, 'I did the worst to him I loved the most', although it is unclear whether she means Bolli or Kjartan.

St Gudule (*c.*648–712), virgin, patron of Brussels. She habitually prayed in the early morning, and it was said that when she was praying the devil blew out the candle, which was then reignited by divine power; she is often shown with a candle.

☐ **FEAST DAY** Her feast day is 8 January.

Guebre a Zoroastrian; the word comes via French from Persian, from the base of *giaour*.

Guelph a member of one of two great factions in Italian medieval politics, traditionally supporting the Pope against the Holy Roman emperor (supported by the ➤ GHIBELLINES). The name comes through Italian *Guelfo* from Middle High German *Welf*, the name of the founder of one of the two great rival dynasties in the Holy Roman Empire, a princely family of Swabian origin from which the British royal house is descended through George I.

The name *Welf* is believed to have been adopted into political use in Italy from its reputed use as a war cry (at the battle of Weinsburg in 1140) by partisans of Henry the Lion, Duke of Bavaria, who belonged to this family, and fought against the Emperor Conrad III; it was thus adopted as a name for the adversaries of the Hohenstaufen emperors.

Otto von Guericke (1602–86), German engineer and physicist. He was the first to investigate the properties of a vacuum, and he devised the Magdeburg hemispheres to demonstrate atmospheric pressure.

Guernica a town in the Basque Provinces of northern Spain, to the east of Bilbao. Formerly the seat of a Basque parliament, it was bombed in 1937, during the Spanish Civil War, by German planes in support of Franco, an event depicted in a famous painting by Picasso.

> The massacre of the innocents in a Baghdad basement . . . could become, for Arabs certainly and for some Westerners as well, the Guernica of the Gulf war.
> — Brian Macarthur (ed.) *Despatches from the Gulf War* (1991)

guerrilla a member of a small independent group taking part in irregular fighting, typically against larger regular forces. The word, which comes from the Spanish diminutive of *guerra* 'war', was introduced into English during the Peninsular War of the early 19th century.

guests see ➤ FISH *and guests stink after three days.*

Les Gueux French for 'ragamuffins, beggars', a name first given in contempt to the Protestant nobles who opposed Margaret of Parma, Regent of the Netherlands, and afterwards adopted by various bodies of Dutch and Flemish partisans in the wars

with the Spaniards in the 16th century. See also ➤ SEA-*beggar*.

Che Guevara (1928–67), Argentinian revolutionary and guerrilla leader. He played a significant part in the Cuban revolution (1956–9) and became a government minister under Castro. He was captured and executed by the Bolivian army while training guerrillas for a planned uprising in Bolivia.

Meyer Guggenheim (1828–1905), Swiss-born American industrialist, who with his seven sons established large mining and metal-processing companies. His son Solomon (1861–1949) set up several foundations providing support for the arts, including the **Guggenheim Museums** in New York and Bilbao.

Guides Association (in the UK) an organization for girls, corresponding to the ➤ SCOUT *Association*, established in 1910 by Lord Baden-Powell with his wife and sister. The three sections into which it is divided, originally Brownies, Guides, and Rangers, are now called Brownie Guides (7–11 years), Guides (10–16 years), and Ranger Guides (14–19 years). Similar organizations exist in many countries worldwide under the aegis of the World Association of Girl Guides and Girl Scouts, formed in 1928.

Guido see ➤ *Guido d'*AREZZO.

Guignol the bloodthirsty chief character in a French puppet show of that name which is similar to Punch and Judy, which has given its name to ➤ GRAND *Guignol*.

guild a medieval association of craftsmen or merchants, often having considerable power.

Guilds are first mentioned in Old English pre-Conquest documents, but they had a strong religious focus, with their objects including the provision of masses for the souls of deceased members, and the payment of *wergild* in cases of justifiable homicide. **Merchant guilds**, incorporated societies of the merchants of a town or city, having exclusive rights of trading within the town, are not found in pre-Conquest England, although they were known on the Continent, and were later introduced to England (in many English towns, and in the royal burghs of Scotland, the merchant guild became the governing body of the town).

The **trade guilds**, which in England came to prominence in the 14th century, were associations of persons exercising the same craft, formed for the purpose of protecting and promoting their common interests. They are historically represented in London by the Livery Companies, although these are not ordinarily known as guilds.

See also ➤ DEAN *of guild.*

guillotine a machine with a heavy blade sliding vertically in grooves, used for beheading people. The device was named after Joseph-Ignace *Guillotin* (1738–1814), the French physician who recommended its use for executions in 1789; its introduction was intended as a humanitarian measure for relatively painless killing (previously the right to death by decapitation had been limited to the nobility). The first guillotine was set up in the ➤ *Place de* GRÈVE in Paris. It was informally called *Louison* and *Louisette*, after Dr Antoine *Louis* who designed the machine; later it became known also as *la Veuve* 'the Widow'.

The term *guillotine* is used in parliament for a procedure used to prevent delay in the discussion of a legislative bill by fixing times at which various parts of it must be voted on.

guilty see also ➤ WE *are all guilty,* ➤ WE *name the guilty men.*

a guilty conscience needs no accuser. proverbial saying, late 14th century; earlier in Latin.

guinea a former British gold coin that was first minted in 1663 from gold imported from West Africa, with a value that was later fixed at 21 shillings. It was replaced by the sovereign from 1817.

It was named after *Guinea* in West Africa as being intended for the *Guinea trade* and made with gold from that source; the first coins were minted 'in the name and for the use of the Company of Royal Adventurers of England trading with Africa'; these pieces were to bear for distinction the figure of a little elephant.

guinea pig a domesticated tailless South American cavy, originally raised for food. It no longer occurs in the wild and is now typically kept as a pet or for laboratory research; in extended use, *guinea pig* means a person or thing used as a subject for experiment.

Guinevere in Arthurian legend, the wife of King ➤ ARTHUR and lover of ➤ LANCELOT. In the Arthurian cycle she is seen through her love for Lancelot as one of the key figures in the ultimate destruction of Arthur's kingdom, by providing an opening which can be exploited by the traitor ➤ MORDRED. Guinevere, who survives her husband's death, traditionally repented her sins and became a nun.

Guinness trademark name for a brand of stout manufactured by the Irish firm of Guinness; the well-known advertising slogan 'Guinness is good for you' was adopted in 1929, reputedly as representing the reply universally given to researchers asking people why they drank Guinness.

guiser a mummer in a folk play performed especially at Christmas or Halloween; recorded from the late 15th century, the word comes from the archaic verb *guise* 'dress fantastically'.

Gujranwala a city in Pakistan, in Punjab province, north-west of Lahore. It was the birthplace of the Sikh ruler Ranjit Singh, and was an important centre of Sikh influence in the early 19th century.

Gulag a system of labour camps maintained in the Soviet Union from 1930 to 1955 in which many people died. Besides ordinary criminals, inmates included dissident intellectuals, political opponents, and members of ethnic minorities; the word became widely known in the west in the 1960s and 1970s with the translation of Alexander Solzhenitsyn's works, notably *The Gulag Archipelago.*

The word is Russian, from *G(lavnoe) u(pravlenie ispravitel' no-trudovykh) lag(ereĭ)* 'Chief Administration for Corrective Labour Camps'.

See also ➤ *the* LAOGAI.

Gulbarga a city in south central India, in the state of Karnataka, which was formerly the seat of the Bahmani kings of the Deccan (1347–*c.*1424).

Calouste Sarkis Gulbenkian (1869–1955), Turkish-born British oil magnate and philanthropist, of Armenian descent. He founded the Gulbenkian Foundation, to which he left his large fortune and art collection.

gules red, as a heraldic tincture. The word comes (in Middle English) from Old French *goles* (plural of *gole* 'throat', from Latin *gula*), used to denote pieces of red-dyed fur used as a neck ornament.

gulf see also ➤ GREAT *gulf fixed.*

Gulf Stream a warm ocean current which flows from the Gulf of Mexico parallel with the American coast towards Newfoundland, continuing across the Atlantic Ocean towards NW Europe as the North Atlantic Drift.

Gulf War the war of January and February 1991 in which an international coalition of forces assembled in Saudi Arabia under the auspices of the United Nations forced the withdrawal of Saddam Hussein's Iraqi forces from Kuwait, which they had invaded and occupied in August 1990.

Gulf War syndrome a medical condition affecting many veterans of the 1991 Gulf War, causing fatigue, chronic headaches, and skin and respiratory disorders. Its origin is uncertain, though it has been attributed to exposure to a combination of pesticides, vaccines, and other chemicals.

Gulistan Persian for 'The Rose Garden', title of a 13th-century Persian poem by the poet Sa'di (1213–91).

gull a credulous person, a dupe, a fool, possibly a transferred used of the word meaning 'an unfledged bird'. Dekker's *The Gull's Hornbook* (1609) is a satirical book of manners directed against fops and gallants of the day.

Gullah a member of a black people living on the coast of South Carolina and nearby islands. Also, the Creole language of this people, having an English base with elements from various West African languages. The name may come from a shortening of *Angola*, or from *Gola*, the name of an agricultural people of Liberia and Sierra Leone.

Gummidge a peevish, self-pitying, and pessimistic person, given to complaining, from the name of Mrs *Gummidge*, a character in Dickens's *David Copperfield* (1850) who says of herself, 'I am a lone lorn creetur…and everythink goes contrairy with me.'

> It's true I've felt rather Gummidgey and 'low' and disheartened these last two years.
> — D. H. Lawrence letter, 9 March 1928

Worzel Gummidge a talking scarecrow with straw hair who is the central character of a series of children's books by Barbara Euphan Todd (d. 1976); the stories were later televised.

In the satirical *Dear Bill* letters by Richard Ingram and John Wells, published in *Private Eye* and purporting to record the thoughts of Denis Thatcher during his wife's tenure as Prime Minister, the nickname *Worzel Gummidge* was given to Michael Foot, perhaps because his white hair was thought to resemble the scarecrow's.

gun a weapon incorporating a metal tube from which bullets, shells, or other missiles are propelled by explosive force, typically making a characteristic loud, sharp noise. The word is recorded from Middle English, and may be a pet form of the Scandinavian name *Gunnhildr*, from *gunnr* + *hildr*, both meaning 'war'.

See also ➤ HAVE *gun, will travel.*

gun money a name given to money coined by James II in Ireland in 1689, from the metal of old guns. The derogatory association of base money with Catholic rule was a Protestant tradition; the Irish judge Jonah Barrington (1760–1834) recorded in his *Recollections* (1827) the Orange toast, 'The glorious, pious, and immortal memory of the great and good King William—not forgetting Oliver Cromwell who assisted in redeeming us from Popery, Slavery, Arbitrary Power, Brass Money, and Wooden Shoes.'

gun room a dated term for a set of quarters for midshipmen or other junior officers in a warship.

gunboat diplomacy foreign policy that is supported by the use or threat of military force, a term now associated particularly with British imperial power, as in Bevan's criticism of Winston Churchill:

> He does not talk the language of the 20th century but that of the 18th. He is still fighting Blenheim all over again. His only answer to a difficult situation is send a gun-boat.
> — Aneurin Bevan speech at the Labour Party Conference, 2 October 1951

Gunga Din central character in the poem (1892) by Kipling, the Indian water-carrier who is killed bringing water to fighting soldiers; allusive use typically refers to the line, 'You're a better man that I am, Gunga Din!'

Gunn see ➤ MARTHA *Gunn.*

Gunnar in Norse legend, the brother of Gudrun; eqivalent of Gunther in the *Nibelungenlied*. In the Norse stories, he brings about the death of his brother-in-law ➤ SIGURD, who having helped him by magic to win Brynhild has betrayed the secret, and is himself killed by Atli, at the instigation of Gudrun.

gunner see also ➤ let the COBBLER *stick to his last and the and the gunner to his linstock.*

gunner's daughter the gun to which a sailor, especially a boy serving on a warship, was lashed for flogging.

See also ➤ KISS *the gunner's daughter.*

the **Gunningiad** Horace Walpole's satirical name for the Gunnings; originally an impoverished Irish family, their fortunes were founded on the beauty and resulting social success of two sisters, Maria (1733–60), who married the Earl of Coventry, and Elizabeth (1734–90), who married first the Duke of Hamilton, and after his death the Duke of Argyll.

gunpowder an explosive consisting of a powdered mixture of saltpetre, sulphur, and charcoal. The earliest known propellant explosive, gunpowder (which originated in China) has now largely been superseded by high explosives, although it is still used for quarry blasting and in fuses and fireworks.

Its introduction can be taken as a type of technological advance; Francis Bacon in *Novum Organum* (1620) said of 'printing, gunpowder, and the mariner's needle [the compass]' that 'these three have changed the whole face and state of things throughout the world.' Thomas Carlyle in 1838 wrote of 'The three great elements of modern civilization, Gunpowder, Printing, and the Protestant Religion.'

Gunpowder Plot a conspiracy by a small group of Catholic extremists to blow up James I and his Parliament on 5 November 1605. The plot was uncovered when Lord Monteagle was sent an anonymous letter telling him to stay away from the House on the appointed day. Guy Fawkes was arrested in the cellars of the Houses of Parliament the day before the scheduled attack and betrayed his colleagues under torture. The leader of the plot, Robert Catesby, was killed resisting arrest and the rest of the conspirators were captured and executed. The plot is commemorated by the traditional searching of the vaults before the opening of each session of Parliament, and by bonfires and fireworks, with the burning of an effigy of ➤ *Guy* FAWKES, one of the conspirators, annually on 5 November.

See also ➤ PLEASE *to remember the Fifth of November, Gunpowder Treason and Plot.*

according to Gunter in the US, reliably, correctly; the allusion is to the mathematician Edmund *Gunter* (see ➤ GUNTER's *chain*).

Gunter's a famous London confectioner's and caterer's, established in the reign of George III and noted particularly for their ice-creams; Thackeray's *Vanity Fair* (1848) refers to 'the annual ball with supper from Gunter's (who...supplies most of the first-rate dinners which J. gives)', and in

Maugham's *Of Human Bondage* (1915) a character is described as giving 'the same nice little dinner parties, with veal creams and ices from Gunters, as she did twenty years ago.'

Gunter's chain a former measuring instrument 66 ft (20.1 m) long, subdivided into 100 links, each of which is a short section of wire connected to the next link by a loop. It has now been superseded by the steel tape and electronic equipment. It was named after Edmund *Gunter* (1581–1626), the English mathematician who devised it.

Gunther in the *Nibelungenlied*, the husband of Brunhild and brother of Kriemhild, by whom he was beheaded in revenge for Siegfried's murder; equivalent of the Norse ➤ GUNNAR.

Gupta a Hindu dynasty established in AD 320 by Chandragupta I in Bihar. At one stage it ruled most of the north of the Indian subcontinent, but it began to disintegrate towards the end of the 5th century, only northern Bengal being left by the middle of the 6th century.

George Gurdjieff (1877–1949), Russian spiritual leader and occultist. He founded the Institute for the Harmonious Development of Man in Paris (1922). His thought was published posthumously as *All and Everything* (1950) and *Meetings with Remarkable Men* (1963).

gurdwara a Sikh place of worship; the word comes via Punjabi from Sanskrit *guru* 'teacher' + *dvāra* 'door'.

Gurkha a member of any of several peoples of Nepal noted for their military prowess; in particular, a member of a regiment in the British army established specifically for Nepalese recruits in the mid 19th century. *Gurkha* is the name of a locality, from the Sanskrit word for 'cowherd', used as an epithet of their patron deity.

Gurmukhi the script used by Sikhs for writing Punjabi; the word comes via Punjabi from Sanskrit *guru* 'teacher' + *mukha* 'month'.

guru a Hindu spiritual teacher. Also, each of the ten first leaders of the Sikh religion. The word comes from Sanskrit meaning 'weighty, grave', hence 'elder, teacher'.

Gustavus Adolphus (1594–1632), king of Sweden 1611–32. His repeated victories in battle made Sweden a European power, and in 1630 he intervened on the Protestant side in the Thirty Years War. His domestic reforms laid the foundation of the modern state.

gustibus see ➤ DE *gustibus non est disputandum.*

Gut-tide a time for feasting, and in particular, Shrove Tuesday, as preceding the rigours of Lent.

Johannes Gutenberg (*c.*1400–68), German printer. He was the first in the West to print using movable type, introduced typecasting using a matrix, and was the first to use a press. By *c.*1455 he had produced what later became known as the Gutenberg Bible.

Gutenberg Bible the edition of the Bible (Vulgate version) completed by Johannes Gutenberg in about 1455 in Mainz, Germany. Printed in Latin in three volumes in 42-line columns, it is the first complete book extant in the West and is also the earliest to be printed from movable type. There are about forty copies still in existence. Also called the ➤ FORTY-*two-line Bible.*

St Guthlac (*c.*673–714), hermit of Crowland, whose cult had great popularity in pre-Conquest England. He is represented with a scourge, as a weapon against diabolical attacks.

□ **FEAST DAY** His feast day is 11 April; the date of his translation is 30 August.

guts see also ➤ BLOOD *and Guts,* ➤ DEVIL*'s guts.*

gutter press reporters or newspapers engaging in sensational journalism, especially accounts of the private lives of public figures; the usage is recorded from the late 19th century.

The English writer and journalist Gerald Priestland (1927–91) commented, 'Journalists belong in the gutter because that is where the ruling classes throw their guilty secrets.'

Gustavo Gutiérrez (1928–), Peruvian theologian. He was an important figure in the emergence of ➤ LIBERATION *theology* in Latin America, outlining its principles in *A Theology of Liberation* (1971).

guy a figure representing ➤ *Guy* FAWKES, burnt on a bonfire on Guy Fawkes' Night, and often displayed by children begging for money for fireworks.

The original *guys* were figures paraded about in the streets on the anniversary of the ➤ GUNPOWDER *Plot.*

See also ➤ *a* PENNY *for the guy.*

Thomas Guy (*c.*1645–1724), who set up as a bookseller in 1668 and was one of the Oxford University printers, 1679–92. He greatly increased his fortune by selling his South Sea company stock, and left £200,000 for the endowment of **Guy's Hospital** in Southwark, as well as other charitable bequests.

Guy Fawkes Night another term for ➤ BONFIRE *Night.*

Guy of Warwick hero of an early 14th-century verse romance, who among other exploits killed the ➤ DUN *Cow.*

Eleanor Gwyn (1650–87), English actress and mistress to Charles II, called 'pretty witty Nell' by Samuel Pepys; Charles himself in his last illness is said to have requested, 'Let not poor Nelly starve.'

She was generally popular; when at Oxford during the ➤ POPISH *Plot* her coach was mobbed by a crowd who had mistaken her for Charles's disliked French Catholic mistress, the Duchess of Portsmouth, she addressed them, 'Pray, good people, be civil. I am the Protestant whore.'

Gwynedd a former principality of North Wales. Powerful in the mid 13th century under Llewelyn, it was finally subjugated by the English forces of Edward I in 1282, following Llewelyn's death.

Gyges (*c.*685–*c.*657 BC), king of Lydia, who became king on killing his predecessor ➤ CANDAULES. According to Herodotus, he was the favourite officer of Candaules, who being proud of his wife's beauty insisted that Gyges should see the queen naked while remaining hidden. When the queen, sensing his presence, offered him the choice of dying himself or killing the king and taking the kingdom (with her as his queen), he chose the latter course.

Plato in the *Republic* tells the story that Gyges won the queen and the kingdom by means of a magic ring of invisibility, to illustrate the view that men are not virtuous when they need not fear the consequences of their actions.

gymnosophist a member of an ancient Hindu sect who wore very little clothing and were given to asceticism and contemplation; they were known to the Greeks through the reports of the companions of Alexander. Recorded from late Middle English, the word comes ultimately (via French and Latin) from *gumnos* 'naked' + *sophistēs* 'teacher of philosophy, sophist'.

gyp a college servant at the Universities of Cambridge and Durham. The word (recorded from the mid 18th century) may come from the obsolete *gippo* 'menial kitchen servant', originally denoting a man's short tunic, from obsolete French *jupeau*.

gypsy a member of a travelling people with dark skin and hair, speaking a language (Romany) related to Hindi, and traditionally living by seasonal work, itinerant trade, and fortune telling. Gypsies are now found mostly in Europe, parts of North Africa, and North America, but are believed to have originated in the Indian subcontinent. They have at various times been subjected to persecution and forced migration, notably in Nazi Germany.

The word (originally *gipcyan*) dates from the mid 16th century, and is short for *Egyptian*, because gypsies were popularly supposed to have come from Egypt.

See also ➤ KING *of the Gypsies*, ➤ *St* MARY *of Egypt*.

gypsywort a white-flowered Eurasian plant of the mint family, which grows in damp habitats, so named because it was reputed to have been used by gypsies to stain the skin brown.

gyre-carline Scottish term for a witch, a hag; the first element represents Old Norse *gýgr* 'ogress'.

gyrfalcon the largest falcon, found in arctic regions and occurring in several colour forms, one of which is mainly white. In the 15th-century *Boke of St Albans*, the *gyrfalcon* is listed in falconry as the bird for a king.

Recorded from Middle English, the word comes from Old French, and is of Germanic origin. The first element is probably related to Old High German *gēr* 'spear'; the spelling *gyr-* arose from a mistaken idea that the bird's name came from Latin *gyrare* 'revolve'.

gyromancy divination by inference from the point at which a person walking round and round a marked circle fell down from dizziness.

gytrash an apparition, usually in the form of a large dog or other animal; the term is from northern dialect, and is first recorded in Charlotte Brontë's *Jane Eyre* (1847), as the subject of stories told by the nursemaid Bessie.

Hh

H the eighth letter of the modern English alphabet and of the ancient Roman one, representing a Semitic letter adopted by Greek as H, originally the eighth and later, after the omission of Ϝ, the seventh letter of the alphabet.

ha-ha a ditch with a wall on its inner side below ground level, forming a boundary to a park or garden without interrupting the view. Recorded from the early 18th century, from French, it is said to represent a cry of surprise on suddenly encountering such an obstacle.

Habakkuk a Hebrew minor prophet, probably of the 7th century BC; also, a book of the Bible containing his prophecies.

Voltaire is said to have been accused of misrepresenting facts in the prophet's history, and to have replied, '*Habacuc était capable de tout* [Habbakuk was capable of anything].'

Habdalah a Jewish religious ceremony or formal prayer marking the end of the Sabbath; the name comes from Hebrew *haḇdālāh* 'separation, division'.

habeas corpus a writ requiring a person under arrest to be brought before a judge or into court, especially to secure the person's release unless lawful grounds are shown for their detention.

Recorded from late Middle English, the phrase is from Latin, literally 'thou shalt have the body (in court)'.

haberdasher a dealer in dressmaking and sewing goods; in early use the term denoted a dealer in a variety of household goods, later also specifically a hatter. Ultimately the word is probably based on Anglo-Norman French *hapertas*, perhaps the name of a fabric.

Jürgen Habermas (1929–), German social philosopher. A leading figure of the Frankfurt School, he developed its cultural reappraisal of Marxism and is especially noted for his work on communication theory.

habit a long, loose garment worn by a member of a religious order; **the habit** is used to mean the monastic order or profession.

habits see ➤ OLD *habits die hard*.

haboob a violent and oppressive wind blowing in summer in Sudan and elsewhere, bringing sand from the desert.

Habsburg one of the principal dynasties of central Europe from medieval to modern times.

Taking their name from a castle in Aargau, Switzerland, the family established a hereditary monarchy in Austria in 1282, gradually extending its power, more often by marriage than by conquest, and secured the title of Holy Roman emperor from 1452, reaching its peak of power under Emperor Charles V. Austrian and Spanish branches were created when Charles divided the territories between his son Philip II and his brother Ferdinand; the Habsburgs ruled Spain 1504–1700, while Habsburg rule in Austria ended with the collapse of Austria–Hungary in 1918.

Habsburg lip a term for the prominent lower lip and chin characteristic of the Habsburg family, and said to be the result of inbreeding. Also called *Austrian lip*.

háček a diacritic mark (ˇ) placed over a letter to indicate modification of the sound in Slavic and other languages.

hack a writer or journalist producing dull, unoriginal work. Recorded in this sense from the late 17th century, and coming from the use of the word to mean 'a horse for ordinary riding'; ultimately, an abbreviation of ➤ HACKNEY.

one's hackles rise the hairs on the back of one's neck are thought of as being raised in anger or hostility; *hackles* are the long feathers on the neck of a fighting cock, or the erectile hairs along the back of a dog, which rise when the animal is angry.

hackney a horse or pony of a light breed with a high-stepping trot, used in harness. The word is Middle English, and probably comes from *Hackney* in East London, where horses were pastured. The term originally denoted an ordinary riding horse (as opposed to a war horse or draught horse), especially one available for hire.

The word is the origin of **hackneyed** meaning 'unoriginal and trite', and ultimately of ➤ HACK for a dull and uninspired journalist.

what you've never had you never miss proverbial saying, early 20th century.

Hadassah an American Zionist women's organization, founded in 1912, which contributes to welfare work in Israel. The name comes from Hebrew *hădassāh* 'myrtle', the name of the biblical character ➤ ESTHER (Esther 2:7, 'Hadassah, that is, Esther, his uncle's daughter').

haddock a silvery-grey fish of North Atlantic coastal waters, which has a mark on each side of the neck, traditionally said to be the mark of St Peter's thumb and finger when he caught the fish whose mouth contained the tribute-money (see ➤ *St* PETER's *fish*).

Hades in Greek mythology, the underworld; the abode of the spirits of the dead. Also, the god of the underworld (also called *Pluto*, see ➤ PLUTO¹), one of the sons of Cronus.

Hadith a collection of traditions containing sayings of the prophet Muhammad which, with accounts of his daily practice (the Sunna), constitute the major source of guidance for Muslims apart from the Koran. The name comes from Arabic *ḥadīt* 'tradition'.

Hadrian (AD 76–138), Roman emperor from 117. The adopted successor of ➤ TRAJAN, he toured the provinces of the Empire and secured the frontiers. The building of Hadrian's Wall was begun just after his visit to Britain.

Hadrian's Wall a Roman defensive wall across northern England, stretching from the Solway Firth in the west to the mouth of the River Tyne in the east (about 120 km, 74 miles). It was begun in AD 122, after the emperor Hadrian's visit, to defend the province of Britain against invasions by tribes from the north. The wall was built of stone and was 2.5–3 m thick, with forts and fortified posts at intervals along its length. After Hadrian's death the frontier

was advanced to the ➤ ANTONINE *Wall*, which the Romans proved unable to hold; after being overrun and restored several times Hadrian's Wall was abandoned *c*.410 AD.

Ernst Haeckel (1834–1919), German biologist and philosopher. He popularized Darwin's theories and saw evolution as providing a framework for describing the world, with the German Empire representing the highest evolved form of a civilized nation. He developed the recapitulation theory of ontogenesis (now discredited) and is said to have coined the word *ecology*.

Hafiz (*c*.1325–*c*.90), 14th-century lyric Persian poet. The word 'hafiz' means 'one who knows the Koran by heart'.

Haftorah a short reading from the Prophets which follows the reading from the Law in a Jewish synagogue. The word comes from Hebrew *haptārāh* 'dismissal'.

hag a witch, especially one in the form of an ugly old woman. The word is Middle English, and is perhaps from an Old English word related to Dutch *heks* and German *Hexe* 'witch'.

hag-ridden afflicted by a nightmare, supposedly through being ridden by a hag or witch.

hag-stone a stone with a hole in it, hung at the head of one's bed to protect the occupant against a nightmare.

Haganah an underground defence force comprising a group of Jewish settlers in Palestine and playing a leading part in the creation of the State of Israel in 1948.

Hagar in the Bible and in Islamic tradition, the Egyptian slave who is mother of ➤ ISHMAEL (Ismail) by Abraham. Driven out of Abraham's household by his wife Sarah, she and her son take flight into the desert, where their lives are saved by an angel who reveals to them the existence of a well.

Hagarene archaic term for a reputed descendant of ➤ HAGAR, a Saracen.

Haggadah the text recited at the Seder on the first two nights of the Jewish Passover, including a narrative of the Exodus. Also, a legend, parable, or anecdote used to illustrate a point of the Law in the Talmud.

The name comes from Hebrew *Haggādāh* 'tale, parable'.

Haggai a Hebrew minor prophet of the 6th century. Also, a book of the Bible containing his prophecies of a glorious future in the Messianic age.

haggard a hawk caught for training as a wild adult of more than twelve months. Recorded from the mid 16th century (used in falconry), the word comes from French, and is perhaps related to *hedge*, later influenced by *hag*.

The original notion was of a bird which had fended for itself and might be half-starved as well as untamed; from this developed the usage of *haggard* to mean looking exhausted and unwell.

Henry Rider Haggard (1856–1925), English novelist. He is famous for adventure novels, many of which have an African setting, such as *King Solomon's Mines* (1885) and *She* (1889).

> I'm more like a Rider Haggard explorer dying in a cave and mapping the treasure he has discovered in his own blood.
> — Clemence Dane *The Flower Girls* (1954)

haggis a Scottish dish consisting of a sheep's or calf's offal mixed with suet, oatmeal, and seasoning and boiled in a bag, traditionally one made from the animal's stomach. The word is recorded from late Middle English and probably comes from earlier *hack, hew*.

Hagia Sophia another name for ➤ SANTA *Sophia*. The name is Greek, literally 'holy wisdom'.

hagigah in Judaism, the peace-offering brought by pilgrims to the Temple at the three great feasts of Passover, Pentecost, and Tabernacles.

Hagiographa the books of the Bible comprising the last of the three major divisions of the Hebrew scriptures, other than the Law and the Prophets. The books of the Hagiographa are: Ruth, Psalms, Job, Proverbs, Ecclesiastes, Song of Solomon, Lamentations, Daniel, Esther, Ezra–Nehemiah, and Chronicles. Also called *the Writings*.

hagioscope another term for ➤ SQUINT in a church.

haham a person learned in Jewish law; a wise man; among Sephardic Jews, a rabbi; the spiritual head of a Sephardic community.

haiku a Japanese poem of seventeen syllables, in three lines of five, seven, and five, traditionally evoking images of the natural world. The form originated in the 16th century.

hail a shout or call used to attract attention. Middle English, from an obsolete adjective *hail* 'healthy' occurring in greetings and toasts (see ➤ WASSAIL).

Hail Mary a prayer to the Virgin Mary used chiefly by Roman Catholics, beginning with part of Luke 1:28. Also called ➤ AVE *Maria*.

Haile Selassie (1892–1975), emperor of Ethiopia 1930–74. In exile in Britain during the Italian occupation of Ethiopia (1936–41), he was restored to the throne by the Allies and ruled until deposed by a military coup. He is revered by the ➤ RASTAFARIAN religious sect.

hair a hair is traditionally used as the type of something of extremely small magnitude, value, or measure, the slightest thing, the least degree. The sword over ➤ DAMOCLES's head is suspended by a single hair.

In classical and biblical stories a person's hair may have sacred significance; ➤ BERENICE's *hair* was dedicated as an offering for her husband's safe return from war, and Nisus, king of Megara (see ➤ NISUS[1]) was vulnerable to betrayal when his daughter Scylla cut off his lock of purple hair. In the Bible, ➤ SAMSON's strength lay in his hair, and ➤ ABSALOM, admired for his long hair, was able to be killed when it caught in the branches of a tree.

See also ➤ BAD *hair day*, ➤ BEAUTY *draws with a single hair*, ➤ RED *hair*, ➤ STRAWS *in one's hair*.

hair of the dog that bit you an alcoholic drink taken to cure a hangover, from the former belief that such a hair was an efficacious remedy against the bite of a mad dog.

hair shirt a shirt of haircloth, formerly worn by penitents and ascetics.

hairdressers ➤ St MARY *Magdalene* is the patron saint of hairdressers for women, and ➤ St MARTIN *de Porres*, and St Cosmas and St Damian, martyrs of the early Church said in a late legend to have been twin brothers, are the patron saints of hairdressers for men.

haji a Muslim who has been to Mecca as a pilgrim.

hajj the Muslim pilgrimage to Mecca which takes place in the last month of the year, and which all Muslims are expected to make at least once during their lifetime. The word comes from Arabic *(al-) ḥajj* '(the Great) Pilgrimage'.

haka a Maori ceremonial war dance involving chanting, an imitation of which is performed by New Zealand rugby teams before a match.

Hakenkreuz a swastika, especially in its clockwise form as a Nazi symbol. The word is German, from *Haken* 'hook' + *Kreuz* 'cross'.

Richard Hakluyt (*c.*1552–1616), English geographer and historian. He compiled *Principal Navigations, Voyages, and Discoveries of the English Nation* (1598), a collection of accounts of great voyages of discovery which inspired further discovery and colonization.

Halacha Jewish law and jurisprudence, based on the Talmud.

halal denoting or relating to meat prepared as prescribed by Muslim law. The word comes (in the mid 19th century) from Arabic *ḥalāl* 'according to religious law'.

halcyon days a period of time in the past that was idyllically happy and peaceful. The *halcyon* is a mythical bird said by ancient writers to breed in a nest floating at sea at the winter solstice, charming the wind and waves into calm.

Hale–Bopp a periodic comet which passed close to the sun in the spring of 1997 and was one of the brightest of the 20th century. It was exceptionally large and active, has a period of just over 4,000 years, and was the first comet to exhibit a sodium tail. Named after Alan Hale and Thomas Bopp, the American astronomers who discovered it (independently of each other).

Hales see ➤ ALEXANDER *of Hales.*

half see also ➤ *the* DIRTY *Half-hundred,* ➤ *half* NELSON, ➤ SIX *of one and half a dozen of the other.*

half a loaf is better than no bread proverbial saying, mid 16th century.

half-blue a person who has represented Oxford or Cambridge University in a minor sport or as a second choice in any sport.

the half is better than the whole proverbial saying, mid 16th century.

half mast the position of a flag which is being flown some way below the top of its staff as a mark of respect for a person who has died.

one half of the world does not know how the other half lives proverbial saying, early 17th century.

half the truth is often a whole lie proverbial saying, mid 18th century.

halfpence see ➤ WOOD's *halfpence.*

halfway house a compromise between two different or opposing views or courses of action; originally, an inn midway between two towns or stages of a journey, and so considered a convenient stopping-place.

Halicarnassus an ancient Greek city on the SW coast of Asia Minor, at what is now the Turkish city of Bodrum. It was the birthplace of the historian Herodotus and is the site of the Mausoleum of Halicarnassus (see ➤ MAUSOLEUM), one of the ➤ SEVEN *Wonders of the World.*

See also ➤ DIONYSIUS[3].

Halifax see ➤ *from Hell,* HULL, *and Halifax.*

hall see also ➤ LIBERTY *Hall,* ➤ MOCK-*Beggar Hall.*

Hall of Fame a national memorial in New York City containing busts and memorials honouring the achievements of famous Americans.

Hall of Mirrors one of the rooms (in French, the *Galerie des Glaces*) in the State Apartments of the palace of Versailles, constructed at the end of the 17th century with 17 mirrors opposite 17 windows, and lit by glass chandeliers; it was in the ➤ HALL *of Mirrors* that the ➤ *Treaty of* VERSAILLES was signed in 1919.

Hallé Orchestra British symphony orchestra, founded in Manchester in 1858 by Sir Charles *Hallé*, German-born pianist and conductor, who settled in Manchester in 1848.

Hallel a portion of the service for certain Jewish festivals, consisting of Psalms 113–118. The word comes from Hebrew *hallēl* 'praise'.

hallelujah God be praised (uttered in worship or as an expression of rejoicing). From Old English, via ecclesiastical Latin from Greek *allēlouia* (in the Septuagint), or (from the 16th century) directly from Hebrew *hallĕlūyāh* 'praise ye the Lord'.

Hallelujah Chorus a musical composition based on the word 'hallelujah', especially that in the oratorio 'Messiah' by G. F. Handel (1685–1759), German-born musician.

Hallelujah Victory supposedly that gained over a pagan army by newly converted Bretons, led by ➤ GERMANUS, bishop of Auxerre, in 429; their battle-cry was 'Hallelujah!'

Edmond Halley (1656–1742), English astronomer and mathematician. He is best known for identifying a bright comet (later named after him), and for successfully predicting its return. Halley was a Fellow of the Royal Society, Astronomer Royal, and friend of Newton, the publication of whose *Principia* was due largely to him.

Halley's Comet a periodical comet with an orbital period of about 76 years, its reappearance in 1758–9 having been predicted by Edmond Halley. It was first recorded in 240 BC and last appeared, rather faintly, in 1985–6, when the European space probe Giotto took close-up photographs of the nucleus.
    See also ➤ BAYEUX *tapestry*.

hallmark a mark stamped on articles of gold, silver, or platinum by the British assay offices, certifying their standard of purity. Recorded from the early 18th century, and the word refers to *Goldsmiths' Hall* in London, where articles were tested and stamped with such a mark.

don't halloo till you are out of the wood proverbial saying, late 18th century.

Halloween the night of 31 October, the eve of All Saints' Day. Halloween is of pre-Christian origin, being associated with the Celtic festival Samhain, when ghosts and spirits were thought to be abroad. Adopted as a Christian festival, it gradually became a secular rather than a Christian observance, involving dressing up and the wearing of masks. These secular customs were popularized in the US in the late 19th century and later developed into the custom of children playing trick or treat.
    The name is recorded from the late 18th century, and is a contraction of *All Hallows Even* 'All Saints Eve'; *hallow* here means a holy person or saint.

All Hallows Day 1 November, ➤ *All* SAINTS' *Day*.

All Hallows Eve 31 October, ➤ HALLOWEEN.

All Hallows summer another name for ➤ *St* MARTIN'*s summer*.

Hallstatt a cultural phase of the late Bronze Age and early Iron Age in Europe (*c*.1200–600 BC in temperate continental areas), preceding the La Tène period. It is generally equated with the Urnfield complex and is associated with the early Celts.

halo a disc or circle of light shown surrounding or above the head of a saint or holy person to represent their holiness, recorded in this sense from the mid 19th century. (From the 6th century, living persons were shown with a square halo.) The word dates from the mid 16th century (denoting a circle of light round the sun), and comes via medieval Latin and Latin from Greek *halōs* 'disc of the sun and moon'.

halutzim Jewish pioneers who entered Palestine from 1917 onwards to build it up as a Jewish State.

Ham in the Bible, a son of Noah, traditional ancestor of the Hamites and the people of Canaan. In Genesis Ham is said (in contrast to his brothers) to have mocked his father when Noah was drunk; in return Noah prophesied that he would be 'the lowest of slaves' to his brothers.

ham an excessively theatrical actor. The term (originally US, from the late 19th century) may be from the first syllable of *amateur* (compare with the US slang term *hamfatter* 'inexpert performer').

hamadryad in Greek and Roman mythology, a nymph who lives in a tree and dies when the tree dies. The word comes via Latin from Greek *Hamadruas*, from *hama* 'together' + *drus* 'tree'.

hamadryas a large Arabian and NE African baboon, the male of which has a silvery-grey cape of hair and a naked red face and rump. It was regarded as sacred in ancient Egypt.

Haman in the Bible, the chief minister of ➤ AHASUERUS, who plotted a massacre of the Jews and was hanged on the gallows he prepared for the ➤ MORDECAI (Esther 7:10); the gallows was said to be fifty cubits high, and the expression **hang as high as Haman** became proverbial.

hamartia a fatal flaw leading to the downfall of a tragic hero or heroine. Recorded from the late 18th century, the word comes from Greek meaning 'fault, failure, guilt'; it was used in Aristotle's *Poetics* with reference to ancient Greek tragedy.

Hamas a Palestinian Islamic fundamentalist movement that has become a focus for Arab resistance in the Israeli-occupied territories. It opposes peace with Israel and has come into conflict with the more moderate Palestine Liberation Organization.

Hambledon Club a famous cricket club of the early days of the game. It flourished about 1750–91, being supported by wealthy patrons of cricket, and played its matches on Broadhalfpenny and Wind-mill Downs in Hampshire.

Hambletonian (b. 1849), name of an American harness racehorse from which most present-day harness racers are descended.

hamburger a round patty of minced beef, fried or grilled and typically served in a bread roll. From German, from the name of the port of *Hamburg*.

Hamelin a medieval market town in Lower Saxony, which in the legend of the ➤ PIED *Piper* was infested with a plague of rats.

hamesucken in Anglo-Saxon and Scottish law, the crime of committing an assault on a person in his or her own house or dwelling-place.

Hamhung an industrial city in eastern North Korea, which was the centre of government of NE Korea during the Yi dynasty of 1392–1910.

Hamilcar (*c*.270–229 BC), Carthaginian general, father of ➤ HANNIBAL. He fought Rome in the first Punic War and negotiated the terms of peace after Carthaginian defeat. From 237 he and Hannibal were engaged in the conquest of Spain.

Alexander Hamilton (*c*.1757–1804), American Federalist politician. He established the US central banking system as First Secretary of the Treasury under Washington (1789–95), and advocated strong central government. He was killed in a duel with Aaron Burr.

Emma Hamilton (*c*.1765–1815), English beauty and mistress of Lord Nelson. She met Lord Nelson while married to Sir William Hamilton, the British ambassador to Naples. She had a daughter by Nelson in 1801 and lived with him after her husband's death in 1803.

Hamiltonian of or pertaining to James *Hamilton* (1769–1831) or his system of teaching languages by word-for-word translation, with instruction in grammar left to a later stage.

Hamite a member of a group of North African peoples, including the ancient Egyptians and Berbers, supposedly descended from ➤ HAM, son of Noah.

Hamitic of or denoting a hypothetical language family formerly proposed to comprise Berber, ancient Egyptian, the Cushitic languages, and the

Chadic languages. These are now recognized as independent branches of the Afro-Asiatic family.

Hamlet a legendary prince of Denmark, hero of a tragedy by Shakespeare. The story is based on one in Saxo Grammaticus's *Historiae Danicae*, in which the young prince is opposed to the usurping uncle who has murdered Hamlet's father and married his mother.

In Shakespeare's play, Hamlet, adjured by his father's ghost to seek revenge, is torn between hatred of his usurping uncle and love for his mother; in allusive use, his name may indicate not only tragedy but also an ultimately fatal indecision.

> But not in a Hamlet-like way, in which seeing both sides causes you torture inside.
> — Aaron Copland and Vivian Perlis *Copland: 1900–1942* (1984)

See also ➤ OPHELIA, ➤ POLONIUS.

Hamlet without the Prince a performance or event taking place without the principal actor or central figure. The phrase derives from an account given in the *Morning Post* of September 1775, of a theatrical company in which the actor who was to play the hero ran off with the innkeeper's daughter; when the play was announced, the audience was told 'the part of Hamlet to be left out, for that night.'

hammer a hammer is the emblem of St Apollonia, a 3rd-century martyr whose sufferings included having her teeth wrenched from her jaws, and ➤ *St* ELOI.

In Scandinavian mythology, a hammer, *Mjǫllnir*, was the weapon of the god ➤ THOR.

See also ➤ *the* CHURCH *is an anvil that has worn out many hammers.*

the Hammer personal epithet (translating ➤ MARTEL) of a number of military and political figures of the Middle Ages.

hammer and sickle the symbols of the industrial worker and the peasant used as the emblem of the former USSR and of international communism.

when all you have is a hammer, everything looks like a nail proverbial saying, late 20th century (chiefly North American).

be hammered on the Stock Exchange, be declared a defaulter, from the practice of striking three strokes with a mallet on the side of a rostrum in the

Stock Exchange before a formal declaration of default.

Dashiell Hammett (1894–1961), American novelist, who developed the hard-boiled style of detective fiction in works such as *The Maltese Falcon* (1930) and *The Thin Man* (1932).

John Hampden (1594–1643), English parliamentarian and one of the ➤ Five *Members*, who was killed in action at Thame; in Clarendon's *History of the Rebellion*, it is said of him that 'He had a head to contrive, a tongue to persuade, and a hand to execute any mischief.' The 18th-century poet Gray, however, takes him as a type of courage in the face of the abuse of power:

> Some village-Hampden that with dauntless breast
> The little tyrant of the fields withstood.
> — Thomas Gray *Elegy Written in a Country Churchyard*
> (1751)

Hampden club any of a series of clubs founded by the political reformer John Cartwright (1740–1824), named after ➤ *John* HAMPDEN.

Hampshire hog a native of Hampshire, a county on the coast of southern England.

Hampstead a residential suburb of NW London, sometimes referred to as characterizing a fashionably left-wing lifestyle.

Hampton Court a palace on the north bank of the Thames in the borough of Richmond-upon-Thames, London. It was built by Cardinal Wolsey as his private residence but later presented by him to Henry VIII, and was a favourite royal residence until the reign of George II. Its gardens contain a well-known maze. William III had part of it rebuilt by Sir Christopher Wren and the gardens laid out in formal Dutch style.

Hampton Court Conference held by James I at Hampton Court in January 1604 with the Anglican bishops and representatives of puritan ministers; it was at this meeting that James's policy 'No bishop, no king' was formulated.

hamza in Arabic script, a symbol representing a glottal stop. The word is Arabic, literally 'compression'.

Han the Chinese dynasty that ruled from 206 BC until AD 220 with only a brief interruption. During this period Chinese rule was extended over Mongolia, administration was in the hands of an organized civil service, Confucianism was recognized as the state philosophy, and detailed historical records were kept.

Hanafi a follower of the school of Islamic law founded by the jurist Abū *Hanīfa* (c.699–767).

Hanaper the department of the Chancery into which fees were paid for the sealing and enrolment of charters and other documents. The word originally meant a case or basket for a *hanap*, a drinking-vessel or wine-cup, especially an ornate one, and thus came to be used more generally for a repository for plate or treasure.

Hancock see ➤ JOHN *Hancock*.

hand from the mid 16th century, a linear measure, now used only of a horse's height, and equal to four inches; a hand-breadth.

See also ➤ *a* BIRD *in the hand is worth two in the bush*, ➤ BITE *the hand that feeds one*, ➤ BLACK *Hand*, ➤ BLOOD *on one's hands*, ➤ BLOODY *Hand*, ➤ COLD *hands, warm heart*, ➤ COURT *hand*, ➤ *the* DEVIL *finds work for idle hands to do*, ➤ LAYING *on of hands*, ➤ MANY *hands make light work*, ➤ RED *hand*.

hand of glory originally, a French charm made from a mandrake root; the phrase is a translation of French *main de gloire*, an alteration of the original *mandragore* 'mandrake'. Later, the term came to mean a charm made from the hand of an executed criminal.

one hand for oneself and one for the ship proverbial saying, late 18th century; meaning, hold on with one hand, and work the ship with the other.

the hand that rocks the cradle rules the world proverbial saying, mid 19th century; originally from the American poet William Ross Wallace (d. 1881):

> For the hand that rocks the cradle
> Is the hand that rules the world.
> — William Ross Wallace 'What rules the world' (1865)

The proverb was notably reworked by Mary Robinson when elected President of Ireland in 1990, paying tribute to the women of Ireland in her victory speech; 'Instead of rocking the cradle, they rocked the system.'

put one's hand to the plough set out on a task from which one will not be deflected; originally with biblical allusion to Luke 9:62, 'No man, having put his hand to the plough, and looking back, is fit for the kingdom of God.'

one hand washes the other proverbial saying, late 16th century; earlier in Greek.

handfast a former term for a betrothal or marriage contract, especially one sealed by a handshake.

handle see ➤ DEAD *man's handle.*

hands across the sea promoting closer international links; the expression is recorded from the late 19th century.

handsaw see ➤ *know a* HAWK *from a handsaw.*

handsome see also ➤ PHILIP *the Handsome.*

handsome is as handsome does proverbial saying, late 16th century.

W. C. Handy (1873–1958), American blues musician. He set up a music-publishing house in 1914, and his transcriptions of traditional blues helped establish the pattern of the modern twelve-bar blues.

hang see also ➤ *give a* DOG *a bad name and hang him,* ➤ *give a man* ROPE *enough and he will hang himself,* ➤ *hang up one's* STOCKING.

hang a thief when he's young, and he'll no' steal when he's old proverbial saying, early 19th century.

Hang Seng index a figure indicating the relative price of shares on the Hong Kong Stock Exchange, named after the *Hang Seng Bank* in Hong Kong, where it was devised.

hanged see also ➤ CONFESS *and be hanged,* ➤ *if you're* BORN *to be hanged then you'll never be drowned,* ➤ *never mention* ROPE *in the house of a man who has been hanged.*

hanged, drawn, and quartered in allusion to the traditional mode of execution for traitors, by which prisoners were drawn on a hurdle to the place of execution, and after being hanged were disembowelled while still alive; their bodies were then quartered, for display in different places. The sentence was carried out on ➤ *William* WALLACE 1305, and on the regicide Thomas Harrison in 1660; the occasion was described by Pepys:

> I went out to Charing Cross, to see Major-general Harrison hanged, drawn, and quartered; which was done there, he looking as cheerful as any man could do in that condition.
> — Samuel Pepys diary, 13 October 1660

one might as well be hanged for a sheep as a lamb proverbial saying, late 17th century.

hanging see also ➤ CATCHING*'s before hanging.*

hanging and wiving go by destiny proverbial saying, mid 16th century.

the Hanging Gardens of Babylon legendary terraced gardens at Babylon, watered by pumps from the Euphrates, whose construction was ascribed to Nebuchadnezzar (*c.*600 BC). They were one of the ➤ SEVEN *Wonders of the World.*

hanging in the bell-ropes traditional reference to the period of time during which a couple's banns were to be called.

hangman an executioner who hangs condemned people; the term **common hangman** was also used for the public executioner. Some official hangmen left their mark on the language, as Gregory Brandon in ➤ GREGORIAN *tree,* the London executioner from whose surname the word ➤ DERRICK comes, and ➤ *Jack* KETCH, whose name became a generic term for an executioner.

From the mid 20th century *hangman* has also denoted a game for two in which one player tries to guess the letters of a word, and failed attempts are recorded by drawing a gallows and someone hanging on it, line by line.

hangul the Korean phonetic alphabet, also called *onmun.*

hanif among Muslims, a follower of the original and true (monotheistic) religion (Arabian *ḥanīf* is an epithet applied to Abraham in the Koran).

Hannibal (247–182 BC), Carthaginian general. In the second Punic War he attacked Italy via the Alps, which he crossed with elephants; he repeatedly defeated the Romans, but failed to take Rome itself. After being recalled to Africa he was defeated at Zama by Scipio Africanus in 202.

See also ➤ VINEGAR.

Hanoi Jane nickname given to the American actress Jane Fonda (1937–), who campaigned against American involvement in the Vietnam War, and who in 1972 visited Hanoi to denounce the US bombing campaigns against North Vietnam.

Hanover a former state and province in northern Germany. It was an electorate of the Holy Roman Empire 1692–1806, ruled by the Guelph dynasty, and from 1866 until 1945 was a province of Prussia. In 1714 the Elector of Hanover succeeded to the British throne as George I, and from then until the accession of Victoria (1837) the same monarch ruled both Britain and Hanover.

With the accession of Victoria (1837) to the British throne, however, Hanover passed to her uncle, Ernest, Duke of Cumberland (1771–1851), the Hanoverian succession being denied to a woman as long as a male member of the Guelph family survived. The British royal house from 1714 to the death of Queen Victoria in 1901 was known as **the House of Hanover**.

The heraldic badge of Hanover, a *white horse*, was formerly represented in the ➤ ROYAL *Arms* of the United Kingdom.

the Hanoverians any of the British sovereigns from George I to Victoria.

Hansard the official verbatim record of debates in the British, Canadian, Australian, or New Zealand parliament. It is named after Thomas C. *Hansard* (1776–1833), an English printer whose company originally printed it.

Hanse a medieval guild of merchants; **the Hanse**, the ➤ HANSEATIC *League*. The word is recorded from Middle English, and comes from Old French *hanse* 'guild, company', from Old High German *hansa* 'company, troop'.

Hanseatic League a medieval association of north German cities, formed in 1241 and surviving until the 19th century. In the later Middle Ages it included over 100 towns and functioned as an independent political power, but it began to collapse in the 17th century, and only Hamburg, Bremen, and Lübeck remained when it disbanded in the 19th century.

hansel a gift given at the beginning of the year or to mark an acquisition or the start of an enterprise, supposedly to bring good luck. The word is Middle English (denoting luck), apparently related to Old English *handselen* 'giving into a person's hands' and Old Norse *handsal* 'giving of the hand to seal a promise', from *hand* + an element related to *sell*; the notion of luck, however, is not present in these words.

Hansel and Gretel central characters in one of Grimm's fairy stories; a brother and sister who are abandoned in the forest, and who when starving find their way to a cottage made of bread and cakes. The witch who owns it traps them as they begin to eat; she locks Hansel in a cage, planning to fatten him up and eat him, but in the end Gretel by a trick burns the witch in her own oven and rescues her brother.

> The axons also sense the presence of specific molecules on the glial surfaces on which they creep, and can steer themselves like Hansel and Gretel following the trail of bread crumbs.
> — Steven Pinker *The Language Instinct* (1994)

hansom a two-wheeled horse-drawn cab accommodating two inside, with the driver seated behind. It is named after Joseph A. *Hansom* (1803–82), English architect, patentee of such a cab in 1834.

Hanukkah a lesser Jewish festival, lasting eight days from the 25th day of Kislev (in December) and commemorating the rededication of the Temple in 165 BC by the Maccabees after its desecration by the Syrians. It is marked by the successive kindling of eight lights.

Hanuman a semi-divine being of monkey-like form, whose exploits are described in the ➤ RAMA-YANA; he helps Rama rescue his wife Sita from the demon king of Lanka.

The name *hanuman* also denotes a pale-coloured langur monkey of the Indian subcontinent, venerated by Hindus.

hapax legomenon a term of which only one instance of use is recorded. The phrase comes (in the mid 17th century) from Greek 'a thing said once', from *hapax* 'once' and the passive participle of *legein* 'to say'.

haplography the inadvertent omission of a repeated letter or letters in writing (e.g. writing *philogy* for *philology*).

haplology the omission of one occurrence of a sound or syllable which is repeated within a word, e.g. in *February* pronounced as *Febr'y*.

happy see also ➤ *happy is the* BRIDE *the sun shines on*, ➤ *happy is the* COUNTRY *that has no history*.

Happy Birthday to you title of a song (1935) by the American educationist Pattie S. Hill (1868–1946), traditionally sung to someone on their birthday, inserting the relevant name into the line 'Happy birthday, dear—, happy birthday to you.'

happy-clappy belonging to or characteristic of a Christian group whose worship is marked by enthusiasm and spontaneity; the term is an informal and mildly disparaging one for a style of worship associated with the evangelical movement which has come to prominence in the last 20 years, and dramatizes the division between a traditional and formulaic approach to worship and one which is more spontaneous and informal.

happy families a children's card game played with special cards in sets of four, each depicting members of a 'family', the object being to acquire as many sets as possible.

if you would be **happy** for a week take a wife; if you would be happy for a month kill a pig; but if you would be happy all your life plant a garden proverbial saying, mid 17th century.

happy hunting ground a place where success or enjoyment is obtained, originally referring to the optimistic hope of American Indians for good hunting grounds in the afterlife.

happy man, happy dole proverbial saying, mid 16th century; meaning, may happiness be his portion.

call no man **happy** till he dies proverbial saying, mid 16th century; earlier in classical Greek, and traditionally said by the Athenian statesman ➤ SOLON to ➤ CROESUS.

hara-kiri ritual suicide by disembowelment with a sword, formerly practised in Japan by samurai as an honourable alternative to disgrace or execution; figuratively, ostentatious or ritualized self-destruction. The word comes (in the mid 19th century) from colloquial Japanese, from *hara* 'belly' + *kiri* 'cutting'.

haram a Muslim sacred place, forbidden to non-Muslims; the word comes from Arabic *ḥarām* 'forbidden'.

Harappa an ancient city of the Indus valley civilization (*c.*2600–1700 BC), in northern Pakistan. The site of the ruins was discovered in 1920.

harbinger a person or thing that announces or signals the approach of another; originally, a person who provided lodging, later one who went ahead to find lodgings for an army or for a nobleman and his retinue, hence (mid 16th century), a herald.

Recorded from Middle English, the word comes via Old French *herberge* 'lodging' from Old Saxon '*heriberga* 'shelter for an army, lodging', from *heri* 'army' + a Germanic base meaning 'fortified place', related to *harbour*.

hard-boiled denoting a tough, realistic style of detective fiction set in a world permeated by corruption and deceit.

hard cases make bad law proverbial saying, mid 19th century.

hard words break no bones proverbial saying, late 17th century.

harder see ➤ the BIGGER *they are the harder they fall.*

Keir **Hardie** (1856–1915), Scottish Labour politician. A miner before becoming an MP in 1892, he became the first leader of both the Independent Labour Party (1893) and the Labour Party (1906). Although he remained an MP until his death, his pacifism isolated him from his Labour colleagues during the First World War.

Hardwick see ➤ BESS *of Hardwick.*

Hardy See also ➤ KISS *me, Hardy,* ➤ LAUREL *and Hardy.*

Thomas **Hardy** (1840–1928), English novelist and poet. Much of his work deals with the struggle against the indifferent force that inflicts the sufferings and ironies of life, especially his *Wessex* novels.

> His marriage had already degenerated into a condition of Hardyesque misery.
> — *Guardian* 11 June 1994

hare a fast-running, long-eared mammal that resembles a large rabbit, having very long hind legs and typically found in grassland or open woodland. It is taken as a type of a fleet-footed and timid animal, and was traditionally supposed to sleep with its eyes open; hares were also associated with witchcraft, and witches were believed to be able to take the shape of a hare.

See also ➤ FIRST *catch your hare,* ➤ *if you* RUN *after two hares you will catch neither,* ➤ MAD *as a March hare,* ➤ MARCH *hare,* ➤ *you cannot* RUN *with the hare and hunt with the hounds.*

William **Hare** (fl. 1829), Irish bodysnatcher and confederate of ➤ *William* BURKE; he turned king's evidence to save his life when Burke was convicted for murder and executed.

hare and hounds a game, especially a paperchase, in which a group of people chase another person or group across the countryside.

the **hare** and the tortoise in one of Aesop's fables, typifying the defeat of ability by persistence; the hare lost the race between them through over-confidence in its superiority of speed, because it allowed itself over the course of the race to be distracted from reaching the goal.

Hare Krishna a member of the International Society for Krishna Consciousness, a religious sect based mainly in the US and other Western countries. Its devotees typically wear saffron robes, favour celibacy, practise vegetarianism, and chant mantras based on the name of the Hindu god Krishna.

Haredi a member of any of various Orthodox Jewish sects characterized by strict adherence to the traditional form of Jewish law and rejection of modern secular culture, many of whom do not recognize the modern state of Israel as a spiritual authority. The name is from Hebrew, literally 'one who trembles (in awe at the word of God)'.

Harefoot nickname of ➤ HAROLD I, king of England.

harelip another term (now considered offensive) for a cleft lip; from a perceived resemblance to the mouth of a hare.

harem the separate part of a Muslim household reserved for wives, concubines, and female servants; the women living there. In extended usage, the word also denotes the wives (or concubines) of a polygamous man, and thus a group of female animals sharing a single mate.

The word comes (in the mid 17th century) from Arabic *ḥaram*, *ḥarīm*, literally 'prohibited, prohibited place', and from this 'sanctuary, women's quarters, women'.

James Hargreaves (1720–78), English inventor. A pioneer of the Lancashire cotton industry, he invented the spinning jenny (*c.*1764). His success in speeding up the spinning process caused opposition and in 1768 his house and machinery were destroyed by a mob.

Harijan a member of a hereditary Hindu group of the lowest social and ritual status, an ➤ UNTOUCHABLE. The word comes from Sanskrit *harijana*, literally 'a person dedicated to Vishnu', from *Hari* 'Vishnu' + *jana* 'person'. The term was adopted and popularized by ➤ GANDHI.

hark back mention or remember something from the past; originally a hunting term, used of hounds retracing their steps to find a lost scent.

Harleian of or belonging to Robert *Harley*, Earl of Oxford (1661–1724) and his son Edward Harley, and

especially designating or pertaining to their library of books and manuscripts now deposited in the British Library.

The Harleian Miscellany a reprint of a selection of rare pamphlets and tracts from the Harleian manuscripts, issued 1744–6.

Harlem a district of New York City, situated to the north of 96th Street in NE Manhattan. It has a large black population and in the 1920s and 1930s was noted for its nightclubs and jazz bands.

Harlem Renaissance a movement in US literature in the 1920s which centred on Harlem and was an early manifestation of black consciousness in the US. The movement, stimulated by W. E. B. Du Bois's magazine *Crisis*, included writers such as Langston Hughes and Zora Neale Hurston.

Harlequin a mute character in traditional pantomime, typically masked and dressed in a diamond-patterned costume, in the Italian *commedia dell' arte* the lover of ➤ COLUMBINE.

The name (recorded from the 16th century) comes from obsolete French, from earlier *Herlequin* (or *Hellequin*), the name of the leader of a legendary troop of demon horsemen; perhaps ultimately related to Old English *Herla cyning* 'King Herla', a mythical figure sometimes identified with Woden.

harlequinade the section of a traditional pantomime in which Harlequin played a leading role. It originated in the Italian *commedia dell'arte* as a sequence of narrative dances, but became a mere epilogue to the presentation of a fairy tale, which eventually displaced it altogether.

Harley Street a street in central London where many eminent physicians and surgeons have consulting rooms.

the necklace of Harmonia in Greek mythology, made by the god Hephaestus, and given as a wedding present to *Harmonia*, daughter of Ares and Aphrodite, by her husband ➤ CADMUS. It brought harm to all who subsequently owned it, and is also known as *the fatal necklace*.

The Harmonious Blacksmith an informal name for the air and variations in Handel's fifth harpsichord suite.

Harmonist a member of a communistic religious body in the United States, founded by George Rapp of Würtemberg in 1803; they settled in Pennsylvania, and founded a town called *Harmony* (from which the name comes) and another town called *Economy*.

harmony an arrangement of the four Gospels, or of any parallel narratives, which presents a single continuous narrative text.

haro see ➤ CLAMEUR *de haro*.

Harold I (d. 1040), king of England from 1035, called **Harold Harefoot**. An illegitimate son of Canute, he came to the throne when his half-brother Hardecanute (Canute's legitimate heir) was king of Denmark and thus absent when Canute died. When a third royal claimant was murdered a year later, Harold was formally recognized as king.

Harold II (*c*.1019–66), reigned 1066, the last Anglo-Saxon king of England. Succeeding Edward the Confessor, he was faced with two invasions within months of his accession. He resisted his half-brother Tostig and the Norse king Harald Hardrada at Stamford Bridge, but was killed and his army defeated by William of Normandy at the Battle of Hastings.

harp a musical instrument, roughly triangular in shape, consisting of a frame supporting a graduated series of parallel strings, played by plucking with the fingers. The modern orchestral harp has an upright frame, with pedals which enable the strings to be retuned to different keys. The harp is an emblem of Ireland.

See also ➤ JEW's *harp*, ➤ WELSH *harp*.

harper see ➤ *the* BLIND *Harper*.

Harpers Ferry a small town in Jefferson County, West Virginia, at the junction of the Potomac and Shenandoah Rivers. It is famous for a raid in October 1859 in which ➤ *John* BROWN and a group of abolitionists captured a Federal arsenal located there.

Harpocrates Greek name for the Egyptian god ➤ HORUS.

harpy in Greek and Roman mythology, a rapacious monster described as having a woman's head and body and a bird's wings and claws or (as in Virgil's *Aeneid*) depicted as a bird of prey with a woman's face; in extended usage, a grasping unscrupulous woman.

Harrington in the 17th century, a brass farthing token, coined by John, Lord Harrington (d. 1613) under a patent granted him by James I in 1613.

Arthur Travis Harris (1892–1984), British Marshal of the RAF; known as **Bomber Harris**, who as Commander-in-Chief of Bomber Command (1942–5) in the Second World War organized mass bombing raids against Dresden (see ➤ DRESDEN[1]) and other German towns which resulted in large-scale civilian casualties.

The policy was challenged in the House of Lords by George Bell, Bishop of Chichester, who said of the saturation bombing of Berlin in 1944, 'The policy is obliteration, openly acknowledged. This is not a justifiable act of war.' Harris's own view, however, (echoing Bismarck's assessment that the Balkans were 'not worth the healthy bones of a single Pomeranian grenadier') was that he 'would not regard the whole of the remaining cities of Germany as worth the bones of one British grenadier.'

Mrs Harris in Dickens's *Martin Chuzzlewit* (1844), the imaginary but much-quoted friend of ➤ *Sarah* GAMP, who quarrels bitterly and finally with her associate Betsey Prig when Betsey utters the 'memorable and tremendous words: "I don't believe there's no sich a person!"'

Harrods a prestigious department store which originated when Charles Henry Harrod (1800–85), English grocer and tea merchant, took over a shop in Knightsbridge, London, in 1853. This was subsequently expanded by his son, Charles Digby Harrod (1841–1905).

Harrow School a boys' public school in NW London, founded under Queen Elizabeth I in 1571; pupils are known as *Harrovians*.

Harrowing of Hell in medieval Christian theology, the defeat of the powers of evil and the release of its victims by the descent of Christ into hell after his death. It is a subject of mystery plays and of Orthodox icons; in medieval religious art Christ is shown treading down the gates of hell to release the souls of the faithful who have died before his Coming.

Harrowing here comes from *harrow*, a by-form of the verb *to harry*.

Harry see also ➤ BELL *Harry*, ➤ LIGHT *Horse Harry*, ➤ OLD *Harry*, ➤ TOM, *Dick, and Harry*.

Great Harry name of a Tudor warship launched in 1514.

Harry Tate stage-name of R. M. Hutchinson (1872–1940), music-hall comedian, used to designate anything incompetent or disorderly.

hart an adult male deer, especially a red deer over five years old. In Christian iconography, the hart can symbolize a soul longing for the water of baptism, in allusion to Psalm 42, 'Like as the hart desireth the water-brooks: so longeth my soul after thee, O God.' A hart can also stand as an image of Christ as the adversary of Satan, since the Bestiaries attribute to deer the power of finding and killing snakes.

A *hart* (or stag), sometimes with a cross in its antlers, is the emblem of ➤ St EUSTACE and ➤ St HUBERT.

See also ➤ WHITE *hart*.

hart royal traditionally, a hart that has been hunted by a king or queen and has escaped.

J. R. Hartley central character in a 1980s television advertisement for ➤ YELLOW *Pages*, an elderly man who is shown patiently ringing a succession of secondhand bookshops asking if they have '*Fly Fishing* by J. R. Hartley'. It is only when he is finally successful and has to give his name that his identity as the author of the wanted book is revealed.

In August 1999 an advertisement for Internet bookselling in British newspapers read 'We could have saved J. R. Hartley a lot of time and trouble.'

Norman Hartnell (1901–79), English couturier. He is remembered especially as the dressmaker to Queen Elizabeth II (whose coronation gown he designed) and the Queen Mother.

hartshorn aqueous ammonia solution used as smelling salts, formerly prepared from the horns of deer.

Harun ar-Rashid (763–809), fifth Abbasid caliph of Baghdad 786–809. The most powerful of the Abbasid caliphs, he was made famous by his portrayal in the *Arabian Nights*, and is known particularly for his custom of walking the streets of his city in disguise.

haruspex in ancient Rome, a religious official who interpreted omens by inspecting the entrails of sacrificial animals. The word comes from Latin, from an unrecorded element meaning 'entrails' (related to Sanskrit *hirā* 'artery') + -*spex* (from *specere* 'look at').

Harvard University the oldest American university, founded in 1636 at Cambridge, Massachusetts. It is named after John *Harvard* (1607–38), an English settler who bequeathed his library and half his estate to the university.

harvest festival a celebration of the annual harvest, especially (in Britain) one held in schools and as a service in Christian churches, to which gifts of food are brought for the poor.

harvest home the gathering in of the final part of the year's harvest; a festival marking the end of the harvest period.

harvest moon the full moon that is seen nearest to the time of the autumn equinox.

William Harvey (1578–1657), English physician, discoverer of the circulation of the blood. In *De Motu Cordis* (1628) Harvey described the motion of the heart and concluded that the blood left through the arteries and returned to the heart through the veins after it had passed through the flesh. Harvey also studied embryology and animal locomotion.

Harwich see ➤ DEAL, *Dover, and Harwich, the devil gave with his daughter in marriage.*

Harz Mountains a range of mountains in central Germany, the highest of which is the ➤ BROCKEN. The region is the source of many legends about witchcraft and sorcery.

Hasdrubal[1] (d. 221 BC), Carthaginian general. He accompanied his father-in-law, Hamilcar, to Spain in 237 and advanced the Carthaginian boundary to the Ebro.

Hasdrubal[2] (d. 207 BC), Carthaginian general. The younger brother of ➤ HANNIBAL, he was left in command of Carthaginian forces in Spain after Hannibal departed for Italy in 218. He was killed in battle while crossing the Alps to join Hannibal.

Hashemite a member of an Arab princely family claiming descent from *Hashim*, great-grandfather of Muhammad; the official name for Jordan, ruled by a branch of this dynasty, is the **Hashemite Kingdom of Jordan**.

Hasid a member of a strictly orthodox Jewish sect in Palestine in the 3rd and 2nd centuries BC which opposed Hellenizing influences on their faith and supported the Maccabean revolt. The name comes from Hebrew *ḥāsīd* 'pious'.

Hasidism a mystical Jewish movement founded in Poland in the 18th century in reaction to the rigid academicism of rabbinical Judaism. The movement, which emphasized the importance of religious enthusiasm, had a strong popular following; it was inspired by Israel ben Eliezer (*c*.1700–60), called *Baal-Shem-Tov* (Hebrew for 'master of the good name') because of his reputation as a miraculous healer. Denounced in 1781 as heretical, the movement declined sharply in the 19th century, but fundamentalist communities developed from it, and *Hasidism* is still influential in Jewish life, particularly in Israel and New York.

Hasmonean of or relating to the Jewish dynasty established by the Maccabees. The name comes via modern Latin from Greek *Asamonaios*, the grandfather of Mattathias, head of the Maccabees in the 2nd century BC.

haste see also ➤ MARRY *in haste and repent at leisure.*

haste is from the devil proverbial saying, mid 17th century.

more haste, less speed proverbial saying, mid 14th century; *speed* here meant originally success rather than swiftness.

haste makes waste proverbial saying, late 14th century.

make haste slowly proverbial saying, late 16th century.
  See also ➤ FESTINA *lente.*

Battle of Hastings a decisive battle which took place in 1066, on a ridge called *Senlac*, just north of the town of Hastings, East Sussex. William the Conqueror (➤ WILLIAM *I*) defeated the forces of the Anglo-Saxon king ➤ HAROLD *II*; Harold died in the battle, leaving the way open for William to seize London and the vacant throne and leading to the subsequent Norman Conquest of England. ➤ BATTLE *Abbey* was founded by William to give thanks for his victory.

Warren Hastings (1732–1818), British colonial administrator. India's first Governor General (1774–84), he introduced vital administrative reforms. He was later impeached for corruption but acquitted after a seven-year trial.

hasty see ➤ *hasty* CLIMBERS *have sudden falls.*

hat see also ➤ CARDINAL'*s hat,* ➤ COCKLE-*hat,* ➤ PILGRIM'*s hat,* ➤ RED *hat,* ➤ SCARLET *hat.*

hat-trick three successes of the same kind, especially consecutive ones within a limited period, originally referring in cricket to the club presentation of a new hat (or some equivalent) to a bowler taking three wickets successively.

hatches see ➤ BATTEN *down the hatches.*

hatches, matches, and dispatches informal term for the official announcement of births, marriages, and deaths in a newspaper.

hatchet see ➤ BURY *the hatchet.*

hatchment a large tablet, typically diamond-shaped, bearing the coat of arms of someone who has died, displayed in their honour. The word is recorded from the early 16th century, and probably comes from obsolete French *hachement*, from Old French *acesmement* 'adornment'.

hatha yoga a system of physical exercises and breathing control used in yoga; the term comes from Sanskrit *haṭha* 'force' + *yoga.*

Anne Hathaway (*c.*1557–1623), the wife of Shakespeare, whom she married in 1582. They had three children, a daughter (Susannah) and a twin daughter and son (Judith and Hamnet).

Hathor in Egyptian mythology, a sky goddess, the patron of love and joy, represented variously as a cow, with a cow's head or ears, or with a solar disc between a cow's horns. Her name means 'House of Horus'.

Hatshepsut (d. 1482 BC), Egyptian queen of the 18th dynasty, reigned *c.*1503–1482 BC. On the death of her husband Tuthmosis II she became regent for her nephew Tuthmosis III; she then named herself Pharaoh and was often portrayed as male.

hatter see ➤ MAD *as a hatter.*

Hatto (*c.*850–913), archbishop of Mainz, and Carolingian statesman who according to hostile Saxon legend was an oppressor of the poor, and in punishment was eaten alive by a plague of mice in the ➤ MOUSE *Tower* near Bingen. (In other accounts he was struck by lightning, or thrown into Etna by the devil.)

horse and hattock a supposed call by witches to be on their way (a **hattock** was a fairy hat); at the trial of the Scottish witch Isobel Gowdie in 1662, she is said to have confessed that 'I had a little horse, and would say, 'Horse and Hattock, in Devil's name.'

Hau-Hauism a 19th-century Maori religion promising eternal salvation from the white man.

haul see also ➤ *haul someone over the* COALS.

haul down one's colours admit defeat (*colours* a naval or military flag).

haurient in heraldry (of a fish or marine creature), depicted swimming vertically, typically with the head upwards.

Hauteclaire in the *Song of Roland*, the sword ('Highbright') belonging to the paladin Oliver.

have see also ➤ *have had one's* CHIPS, ➤ *have the* BIT *between one's teeth*.

have gun, will travel supposedly characteristic statement of a hired gunman in a western; popularized as the title of an American television series (1957–64).

what you have, hold proverbial saying, mid 15th century.

you cannot have your cake and eat it proverbial saying, mid 16th century.

havelock a cloth covering for a military cap, with a neck-flap to give protection from the sun, named after Sir Henry *Havelock* (1795–1857), major-general of the British army in India.

haven see ➤ SAFE *haven*.

haversack a small, stout bag carried on the back or over the shoulder, used especially by soldiers and walkers. The word comes through French from obsolete German *Habersack*, denoting a bag used by soldiers to carry oats as horse feed, from dialect *Haber* 'oats' + *Sack* 'sack, bag'.

havoc widespread destruction. The word was originally used in the phrase *cry havoc* (Old French *crier havot*) 'to give an army the order *havoc*', which was the signal for plundering.

Hawcubite a member of a band of violent young men frequenting the London streets in the early 18th century; the origin of the name is unknown.

Lord Haw-haw nickname given to ➤ *William* JOYCE (1906–46), who made propaganda broadcasts in English from Nazi Germany; the nickname referred to his drawling nasal delivery, thought to mimic the 'haw-haw' quality supposedly typical of upper-class speech.

Hawaii a state of the US comprising a group of over twenty islands in the North Pacific. First settled by Polynesians, Hawaii was discovered by Captain James Cook in 1778. It was annexed by the US in 1898 and became the 50th state in 1959. Formerly called the *Sandwich Islands*, it came to be known as Hawaii, after the largest of the islands, in the 19th century.

hawk a diurnal bird of prey with broad rounded wings and a long tail, typically taking prey by surprise with a short chase; in falconry, any diurnal bird of prey, used in falconry.

Hawk is also used to denote a person who advocates an aggressive or warlike policy, especially in foreign affairs; the opposite of a *dove*.

> I don't consider myself dovish and I certainly don't consider myself hawkish. Maybe I would describe myself as owlish—that is, wise enough to understand that you want to do everything possible to avoid war.
> — H. Norman Schwarzkopf III in *New York Times* 28 January 1991

See also ➤ IGNOBLE *hawk*, ➤ NOBLE *hawk*.

know a hawk from a handsaw have ordinary discernment, chiefly with allusion to Shakespeare's *Hamlet*, when ➤ HAMLET, who has been feigning madness, says, 'I am but mad north-north-west; when the wind is southerly, I know a hawk from a handsaw.' (*Handsaw* is generally taken as an alteration of *heronshaw*, a heron.)

Hawkeye nickname of the tracker ➤ *Natty* BUMPPO in J. Fenimore Cooper's novels of American frontier life; the character **Hawkeye Pierce** in ➤ MASH is said to have been named after him.

Hawkeye State informal name for Iowa.

Stephen Hawking (1942–), English theoretical physicist, whose main work has been on space–time, quantum mechanics, and black holes. While still a student he developed a progressive disabling neuromuscular disease: confined to a wheelchair, unable to write, and with severely impaired speech, he carries out his mathematical calculations mentally and communicates them in a developed form. Hawking's life and work are a triumph over severe physical disability, and his book *A Brief History of Time* (1988) proved a popular best-seller.

Hawkins see also ➤ SADIE *Hawkins day*.

John Hawkins (1532–95), English sailor. Involved in the slave trade and privateering, he later helped build up the fleet which defeated the Spanish Armada in 1588.

hawks will not pick out hawks' eyes proverbial saying, late 16th century.

Hawkshaw name of a detective in the play *The Ticket-of-Leave Man* by Tom Taylor (1817–80), English dramatist; also portrayed in the comic strip

Hawkshaw the Detective by Augustus Charles ('Gus') Mager (1878–1956), American cartoonist.

Nicholas Hawksmoor (1661–1736), English architect. Having become a clerk to Sir Christopher Wren in 1679, in 1690 he went on to work with Vanbrugh at Castle Howard and Blenheim Palace. In 1711 he was commissioned to design six London churches, including St Mary Woolnooth (1716–24) and St George's, Bloomsbury (1716–30).

hawthorn a thorny shrub or tree of the rose family, with white, pink, or red blossom and small dark red fruits (haws), and which in Britain was typically used for hedging; it was traditionally believed that bringing hawthorn blossom, or *may*, into the house was unlucky.

See also ➤ ne'er CAST *a clout till May be out.*

Nathaniel Hawthorne (1804–64), American novelist and short-story writer. Much of his fiction explores guilt, sin, and morality, as notably in the novel *The Scarlet Letter.*

Hawthorne effect the alteration of behaviour by the subjects of a study due to their awareness of being observed. The term comes (in the 1960s) from *Hawthorne*, the name of one of the Western Electric Company's plants in Chicago, where the phenomenon was first observed in the 1920s.

hay see ➤ MAKE *hay while the sun shines.*

Friedrich August von Hayek (1899–1992), Austrian-born British economist. Strongly opposed to Keynesian economics, he was a leading advocate of the free market, linking state economic control with the loss of individual liberty in his most notable book, *The Road to Serfdom* (1944).

Haymarket Riot a riot in Haymarket Square, Chicago, in 1886, which broke out during a mass protest against the killing of strikers by police, when a bomb was thrown and several policemen injured and killed.

haystack see ➤ LOOK *for a needle in a haystack.*

Hazchem denoting a system of labelling hazardous chemicals, especially during transportation.

William Hazlitt (1778–1830), English essayist and critic. His diverse essays, collected in *Table Talk* (1821), were marked by a clarity and conviction which brought new vigour to English prose writing.

He Bible the first of two issues of the Bible printed in 1611, in which the last words of Ruth 3:15 are, 'and

he went into the city', where the ➤ SHE *Bible* has, 'and she went into the city'.

head a *head* (held in the hands) is the emblem of ➤ St DENIS, ➤ St OSWALD, and other saints who were beheaded at martyrdom.

See also ➤ BRAZEN *head,* ➤ BURY *one's head in the sand,* ➤ CALVES' *Head Club,* ➤ DEATH's *head,* ➤ *the* FISH *always stinks from the head downwards,* ➤ KING *Charles's head,* ➤ NAG's *head,* ➤ *put one's head on the* BLOCK, ➤ SARACEN's *head,* ➤ SPEAKING *head,* ➤ TWO *heads are better than one,* ➤ *where* MACGREGOR *sits is the head of the table.*

Head Centre in 19th-century Ireland, title of the leader of the ➤ FENIANS.

headaches St Gereon, a 4th-century martyr of Cologne who was beheaded, and ➤ St STEPHEN are the patron saints of those suffering from headaches.

headhunting the practice among some peoples of collecting the heads of dead enemies as trophies, extended to the practice of identifying and approaching a suitable person employed elsewhere to fill a business position.

heads I win, tails you lose proverbial saying, mid 19th century; the reference is to the obverse (*head*) and reverse (*tail*) of a coin which is being tossed to decide a chance. **Heads or tails** (which is earlier) is similarly used.

headsman term for a man who was responsible for beheading condemned prisoners; an executioner.

heal see ➤ PHYSICIAN, *heal thyself.*

healer see ➤ TIME *is a great healer.*

healing see ➤ CRYSTAL *healing.*

health see also ➤ BILL *of health,* ➤ SMOKING *can seriously damage your health.*

health an expression of friendly feeling towards a companion before drinking; recorded from the early 17th century.

heap see ➤ *heap* COALS *of fire on a person's head.*

hear see also ➤ BELIEVE *nothing of what you hear, and only half of what you see,* ➤ *if the* ADDER *could hear, and the blindworm could see.*

hear all, see all, say nowt, tak'all, keep all, gie nowt, and if tha ever does owt for nowt do it for thysen proverbial saying, early 15th century.

hearing dog a dog trained to alert the deaf or hard of hearing to such sounds as the ringing of an alarm, doorbell, or telephone.

hearse a vehicle for conveying the coffin at a funeral. The word comes in Middle English from Anglo-Norman French *herce* 'harrow, frame', from Latin *hirpex* 'a kind of large rake', from Oscan *hirpus* 'wolf' (with reference to the teeth). The earliest recorded sense in English is 'latticework canopy placed over the coffin (whilst in church) of a distinguished person', but this probably arose from the late Middle English sense 'triangular frame (shaped like the ancient harrow) for carrying candles at certain services'. The current sense dates from the mid 17th century.

William Randolph Hearst (1863–1951), American newspaper publisher and tycoon. His introduction of features such as large headlines and sensational crime reporting revolutionized American journalism. He was the model for the central character of Orson Welles's film *Citizen Kane* (1941).

heart the *heart* is traditionally regarded as the centre of a person's thoughts and emotions, especially love or compassion.

The heart is stylistically represented by two equal curves meeting at a point at the bottom and a cusp at the top; such *hearts* are emblematic of love.

Hearts are one of the four suits in a conventional pack of playing cards, denoted by a stylized red figure of a heart.

See also ➤ COCKLES *of one's heart*, ➤ COLD *hands, warm heart*, ➤ DEAD *Heart*, ➤ FAINT *heart never won fair lady*, ➤ HOME *is where the heart is*, ➤ HOPE *deferred makes the heart sick*, ➤ if it were not for HOPE, *the heart would break*, ➤ *it is a* POOR *heart that never rejoices*, ➤ LONELY *heart*, ➤ *out of the* FULLNESS *of the heart the mouth speaks*, ➤ *please your* EYE *plague your heart*, ➤ PURPLE *Heart*, ➤ *the* QUEEN *of Hearts*, ➤ SACRED *Heart*, ➤ *a* SONG *in one's heart*, ➤ SEARCHER *of men's hearts*, ➤ *the* WAY *to a man's heart is through his stomach*, ➤ WEAR *one's heart on one's sleeve*.

heart disease ➤ St JOHN *of God* is the patron saint of those suffering from heart disease.

Heart of Dixie informal name for Alabama.

Heart of Midlothian name for the old Edinburgh Tolbooth, or prison, taken by Scott as the title of a novel (1818), set in 18th-century Edinburgh and opening with the ➤ PORTEOUS *riot*.

heart of oak the solid central part of an oak tree as the traditional timber for ships. The phrase was popularized by the 18th-century song, 'Heart of oak are our ships, heart of oak are our men.'

heart's-blood archaic term for the blood, as being necessary for life; vital energy or force.

just a heartbeat away from the Presidency the vice-president's position; from Adlai Stevenson (1900–65), speech at Cleveland, Ohio, 23 October 1952, 'The Republican party did not have to…encourage the excesses of its Vice-Presidential nominee [Richard Nixon]—the young man who asks you to set him one heart-beat from the Presidency of the United States.'

hearts and minds people as represented by their emotions and intellect; originally with biblical allusion to Philippians 4:7, 'And the peace of God, which passeth all understanding, shall keep your hearts and minds through Christ Jesus.'

The term is now used to denote emotional or intellectual support or commitment; an early example of this sense is found in a letter of 13 February 1818 from the American statesman John Adams (1735–1826), 'The Revolution was effected before the war commenced. The Revolution was in the hearts and minds of the people.' In the 20th century the phrase was used particularly in the context of public opposition to the Vietnam War.

heartsease a wild European pansy which typically has purple and yellow flowers, and which has given rise to a series of hybrids from which most garden pansies were developed. The origin of the word is uncertain, the term being applied by herbalists to both the pansy and the wallflower in the 16th century.

if you don't like the heat get out of the kitchen proverbial saying, mid 20th century; particularly associated with ➤ *Harry S.* TRUMAN.

Heath Robinson ingeniously or ridiculously overcomplicated in design or construction; the term comes from the name of the English cartoonist and illustrator William Heath *Robinson* (1872–1944), who lampooned the machine age by inventing absurdly complicated 'Heath Robinson contraptions' to perform elementary or ridiculous actions.

heathen a person who does not belong to a widely held religion (especially one who is not a Christian, Jew, or Muslim) as regarded by those who do. Recorded from Old English and of Germanic origin, the word is generally regarded as a specifically Christian use of a Germanic adjective meaning 'inhabiting open country', from the base of *heath*.

take to the heather in Scottish usage, become an outlaw.

heaven a place regarded in various religions as the abode of God (or the gods) and the angels, and of the good after death, often traditionally depicted as being above the sky.

See also ➤ CROSSES *are ladders that lead to heaven,* ➤ GOD'*s in his heaven; all's right with the world,* ➤ *in* SEVENTH *heaven,* ➤ MARRIAGES *are made in heaven,* ➤ PENNIES *from heaven,* ➤ QUEEN *of heaven,* ➤ SEVEN *heavens,* ➤ SON *of Heaven.*

heaven protects children, sailors, and drunken men proverbial saying, mid 19th century.

heavenly body a planet, star, or other celestial body.

heavenly host a literary or biblical term for the angels.

make heavy weather of perform (an apparently simple task) clumsily or ineptly, exaggerate the difficulty or burden presented by (a problem). The phrase *heavy weather* has the specific nautical meaning of violent wind accompanied by heavy rain or rough sea.

Hebe in Greek mythology, the daughter of Hera and Zeus, and cup-bearer of the gods.

In astronomy, *Hebe* is the name of asteroid 6, discovered in 1847.

Hebrew a member of an ancient people living in what is now Israel and Palestine and, according to biblical tradition, descended from the patriarch Jacob, grandson of Abraham. After the Exodus (*c.*1300 BC) they established the kingdoms of Israel and Judah, and their scriptures and traditions form the basis of the Jewish religion. Also, the Semitic language of this people, in its ancient or modern form.

Hebrew is written from right to left in a characteristic alphabet of twenty-two consonants, the vowels sometimes being marked by additional signs. From about AD 500 it was almost entirely restricted to Jewish religious use, but it was revived as a spoken language in the 19th century and, with a vocabulary extended by borrowing from contemporary languages, is now the official language of the state of Israel.

Hebrew Bible the sacred writings of Judaism, called by Christians the Old Testament, and comprising the Law (Torah), the Prophets, and the Hagiographa or Writings.

Epistle to the Hebrews a book of the New Testament, traditionally included among the letters of St Paul but now generally held to be non-Pauline.

Hebron a Palestinian city on the West Bank of the Jordan. It is one of the most ancient cities in the Middle East, probably founded in the 18th century BC, and as the home of Abraham it is a holy city of both Judaism and Islam.

Hecate in Greek mythology, a goddess of dark places, often associated with ghosts and sorcery and worshipped with offerings at crossroads. She is frequently identified with ➤ ARTEMIS and Selene; her name means 'the distant one'.

hecatomb in ancient Greece or Rome, a great public sacrifice, originally of a hundred oxen; figuratively, an extensive loss of life for some cause. The word comes (in the late 16th century, via Latin) from Greek *hekatombē* (from *hekaton* 'hundred' + *bous* 'ox').

Hector in Greek mythology, a Trojan warrior and prince of Troy, eldest son of ➤ PRIAM and Hecuba and husband of Andromache. He was killed by ➤ ACHILLES, who dragged his body behind his chariot three times round the walls of Troy.

Hecuba in Greek mythology, queen of Troy, the wife of ➤ PRIAM and mother of children including ➤ HECTOR, Paris, Cassandra, and Troilus; after the fall of Troy and the death of Priam she became a slave. She is taken as the type of a bereft and mourning woman, as to be portrayed by the players in *Hamlet*:

> For Hecuba!
> What's Hecuba to him or he to Hecuba
> That he should weep for her?
> — William Shakespeare *Hamlet* (1601)

hedge-priest archaic and derogatory term for an illiterate or uneducated priest, regarded as of inferior status.

hedge-school a school held by a hedge-side or in the open air, especially in Ireland in the 18th and 19th centuries.

hedgehog a nocturnal insectivorous Old World mammal with a spiny coat and short legs, able to roll itself into a ball for defence. In the Bestiaries it is said to gather fruit for its young by impalement on its spines; it may thus be taken to exemplify prudence, or as an image of the Devil harvesting unwary souls.

hedonism the pursuit of pleasure; sensual self-indulgence; the ethical theory that pleasure (in the sense of the satisfaction of desires) is the highest good and proper aim of human life. Recorded from the mid 19th century, the word comes from Greek *hēdonē* 'pleasure'.

heel see ➤ ACHILLES' *heel*, ➤ HIGH *Heels and Low Heels.*

Uriah Heep obsequious and treacherous character in Dickens's *David Copperfield* (1850), characterized by the exaggerated self-denigration of his frequent remark 'We are so very 'umble.'

Georg Wilhelm Friedrich Hegel (1770–1831), German philosopher. In his *Science of Logic* (1812–16) Hegel described the three-stage process of dialectical reasoning, on which Marx based his theory of dialectical materialism. He believed that history, the evolution of ideas, and human consciousness all develop through idealist dialectical processes as part of the Absolute or God coming to know itself.

Hegira ➤ MUHAMMAD's departure from Mecca to Medina in AD 622, prompted by the opposition of the merchants of Mecca and marking the consolidation of the first Muslim community. The name comes (via medieval Latin) from Arabic *hijra* 'departure', from *hajara* 'emigrate'.

See also ➤ ERA *of the Hegira.*

Martin Heidegger (1889–1976), German philosopher. In *Being and Time* (1927) he examined the ontology of Being, in particular human existence as involvement with a world of objects (*Dasein*). His writings on *Angst* (dread) as a fundamental part of human consciousness due to radical freedom of choice and awareness of death had a strong influence on existentialist philosophers such as Sartre.

Heidelberg man a type of prehistoric man indicated by a prehistoric jaw found at Mauer near Heidelberg in 1907. The term may be used allusively of someone regarded as notably uncivilized or uncouth.

> Telfer found him crouched on a ledge, like a disgruntled Heidelberg man.
> — George MacDonald Fraser *McAuslan in the Rough* (1974)

Heidi eponymous heroine of the story (1881) of an orphaned Swiss girl by Johanna Spyri, who from the age of five is brought up in idyllic alpine surroundings; when taken to a more prosperous city life she pines until returned to the mountains.

Heil Hitler used by the Germans or their supporters during the Nazi regime as a greeting or an acclamation of the supremacy of Hitler.

Heimdall in Scandinavian mythology, the watchman of the gods, said to have been the son of nine mothers.

Heimskringla the sagas of the Norse kings, compiled by the Icelandic historian and poet ➤ SNORRI *Sturluson* (1179–1241); the stories cover the period from mythical times to the late 12th century, and the narrative focuses particularly on ➤ OLAF *I Tryggvason* and ➤ OLAF *II Haraldsson.* The title is taken from *Kringla heimsins* 'orb of the world', the opening words of the book.

heir apparent an heir whose claim cannot be set aside by the birth of another heir.

heir presumptive a person whose claim can be set aside by the birth of another heir.

heirs see ➤ WALNUTS *and pears you plant for your heirs.*

Werner Heisenberg (1901–76), German mathematical physicist and philosopher. He developed a system of quantum mechanics based on matrix algebra in which he stated his famous uncertainty principle (1927). For this and his discovery of the allotropic forms of hydrogen he was awarded the 1932 Nobel Prize for Physics.

Hel in Scandinavian mythology, the underworld and the goddess who ruled it, daughter of ➤ LOKI, and sister of ➤ FENRIR and the ➤ MIDGARD's *serpent.*

Das Heldenbuch 'The Book of Heroes', a collection of German metrical romances of the 13th century.

Helen in Greek mythology, the daughter of Zeus and Leda, born from an egg. In the Homeric poems she was the outstandingly beautiful wife of ➤ MENELAUS, and her abduction by Paris (to whom she had been promised, as a bribe, by Aphrodite) led to the Trojan War. Helen has a non-Greek name and is probably in origin an ancient pre-Hellenic goddess connected with vegetation and fertility.

See also ➤ *the* FACE *that launched a thousand ships.*

St Helena (*c.*255–*c.*330 AD), Roman empress and mother of Constantine the Great. In 326 she visited the Holy Land and founded basilicas on the Mount of Olives and at Bethlehem. She is credited with the finding of the cross on which Christ was crucified.

☐ **FEAST DAY** Her feast day is 21 May in the Eastern Church, and 18 August in the Western Church.

Mount Helicon a mountain in Boeotia, central Greece, to the north of the Gulf of Corinth, which was believed by the ancient Greeks to be the home of the Muses.

Heliogabalus (AD 204–22), Roman emperor 218–22. He took his name from the Syro-Phoenician sun god *Elah-Gabal,* of whom he was a hereditary priest. He became notorious for his dissipated lifestyle and neglect of state affairs; he and his mother were both murdered.

Heliopolis an ancient Egyptian city situated near the apex of the Nile delta at what is now Cairo. It was an important religious centre and the centre of sun worship, and was the original site of the obelisks known as Cleopatra's Needles.

Heliopolis was also the ancient Greek name for ➤ BAALBEK.

The name is Greek, from *hēlios* 'sun' + *polis* 'city'.

Helios in Greek mythology, the sun personified as a god, father of ➤ PHAETHON. He is generally represented as a charioteer driving daily from east to west across the sky. In Rhodes he was the chief national god.

heliotrope a plant of the borage family, cultivated for its fragrant purple or blue flowers which are used in perfume. Recorded in Old English, the name was originally applied to various plants whose flowers turn towards the sun. It comes via Latin from Greek *hēliotropion* 'plant turning its face to the sun'.

hell a place regarded in various religions as a spiritual realm of evil and suffering, often traditionally depicted as a place of perpetual fire beneath the earth where the wicked are punished after death.

See also ➤ *from Hell,* HULL, *and Halifax, Good Lord, deliver us,* ➤ *the* HARROWING *of Hell,* ➤ *he that would go to* SEA *for pleasure would go to hell for a pastime,* ➤ *Hell or* CONNAUGHT, ➤ *lead* APES *in hell,* ➤ *the* ROAD *to hell is paved with good intentions,* ➤ VICAR *of Hell.*

Hell-fire Clubs associations of reckless and profligate young ruffians who were a nuisance to London chiefly in the early 18th century. There was a later and more famous Hell-fire Club, founded about 1745, at Medmenham Abbey.

hell hath no fury like a woman scorned proverbial saying, late 17th century; originally from Congreve.

all hell let loose a state of utter confusion and uproar, utter pandemonium; originally after Milton, 'Wherefore with thee Came not all hell broke loose?'

Hell's Angel a member of any of a number of gangs ('chapters') of male motorcycle enthusiasts, first formed in California in the 1950s and originally notorious for lawless behaviour.

Hell's Canyon a chasm in Idaho, cut by the Snake River and forming the deepest gorge in the US. Flanked by the Seven Devils Mountains, the canyon drops to a depth of 2,433 m (7,900 ft).

hell's kitchen an area or place regarded as very disreputable or unpleasant, in particular, a district of New York City once regarded as the haunt of criminals.

Hellas Greek name for Greece.

hellebore a poisonous winter-flowering Eurasian plant of the buttercup family, typically having coarse divided leaves and large white, green, or purplish flowers; originally (in Old English) the name denoted any of various plants supposed to cure madness.

Hellen in Greek mythology, the son or brother of Deucalion and ancestor of all the Hellenes or Greeks.

Hellene an ancient Greek.

Hellenic the branch of the Indo-European language family comprising classical and modern Greek.

Hellenistic of or relating to Greek history, language, and culture from the death of Alexander the Great to the defeat of Cleopatra and Mark Antony by Octavian in 31 BC. During this period Greek culture flourished, spreading through the Mediterranean and into the Near East and Asia and centring on Alexandria in Egypt and Pergamum in Turkey.

Hellespont the ancient name for the Dardanelles, named after the legendary Helle, who fell into the strait and was drowned while escaping with her brother Phrixus from their stepmother, Ino, on a golden-fleeced ram.

See also ➤ *the* GOLDEN *Fleece*.

hellhound a hound or dog from hell; in Greek and Roman mythology, ➤ CERBERUS. In extended usage, *hellhound* is used for a fiend, or fiendish person; in the last scene of Shakespeare's *Macbeth*, the wronged Macduff addresses his enemy as 'hell-hound'.

helmet a piece of armour for the head, usually made of metal; *helmet*, and the archaic *helm*, are of Germanic origin, and come from an Indo-European root, meaning 'to cover or hide'.

In Greek mythology, ➤ PERSEUS was lent by Pluto a helmet which made him invisible when he set out to kill the gorgon Medusa.

See also ➤ MAMBRINO'*s helmet*.

Joannes Baptista van Helmont (1577–1644), Belgian chemist and physician. He made early studies on the conservation of matter, was the first to distinguish gases, and coined the word *gas*.

Héloïse (1098–1164), French abbess, chiefly remembered for her tragic love affair with ➤ *Peter* ABELARD, whose pupil she had been; after the birth of a son, the two were secretly married, but when the affair came to light her uncle had Abelard castrated. He became a monk while Héloïse entered a convent; she later became abbess of Paraclete.

helot a member of a class of serfs in ancient Sparta, intermediate in status between slaves and citizens. The name comes via Latin from Greek *Heilōtes* (plural), traditionally taken as referring to Helos, a Laconian town whose inhabitants were enslaved.

See also ➤ DRUNKEN *Helot*.

hemispheres see ➤ MAGDEBURG *hemispheres*.

hemlock a highly poisonous European plant of the parsley family, with a purple-spotted stem, fern-like leaves, small white flowers, and an unpleasant smell. In ancient Greece, the poison obtained from this plant was a method of execution; ➤ SOCRATES was put to death in this way.

hemp the fibre of the cannabis plant, extracted from the stem and used to make rope, especially with reference to execution by hanging. The name is recorded from Old English (in form *henep*, *hænep*)

and is of Germanic origin; it is related to Greek *kannabis*.

hen a female bird, especially of a domestic fowl. While a hen may be taken as the type of a foolish woman, a hen with her chickens may symbolize Christ, in allusion to Jesus's words in Matthew:

> O Jerusalem, Jerusalem, thou that killest the prophets, and stonest them which are sent unto thee, how often would I have gathered thy children together, even as a hen gathereth her chickens under her wings, and ye would not!
> — Bible (AV) Matthew ch. 23 v. 37

See also ➤ BLUE *Hen's Chickens*, ➤ SCARCE *as hen's teeth*.

hendiadys the expression of a single idea by two words connected with 'and', e.g. *nice and warm*, when one could be used to modify the other, as in *nicely warm*.

Jimi Hendrix (1942–70), American rock guitarist and singer. Remembered for the flamboyance and originality of his improvisations, he greatly widened the scope of the electric guitar.

Hengist and Horsa (d. 488 and d. 455), semi-mythological Jutish leaders. According to Bede the brothers were invited to Britain by the British king ➤ VORTIGERN in 449 to assist in defeating the Picts and later established an independent Anglo-Saxon kingdom in Kent.

Henley see also ➤ ORATOR *Henley*.

Henley Royal Regatta the oldest rowing regatta in Europe, inaugurated in 1839 at Henley-on-Thames, Oxfordshire, as a result of the interest aroused locally by the first Oxford and Cambridge Boat Race, which took place at Henley in 1829. The regatta is held annually in the first week in July.

Robert Henri (1865–1929), American painter, who as an advocate of realism, believed that the artist must be a social force. The Ashcan School of painters was formed largely as a result of his influence.

Henri IV (1553–1610), king of France 1589–1610; known as **Henri of Navarre**. Although leader of Huguenot forces in the latter stages of the French Wars of Religion, on succeeding the Catholic Henry III he became Catholic himself in order to guarantee peace; the comment 'Paris is well worth a Mass' has been attributed to him. He established religious freedom with the ➤ EDICT *of Nantes* (1598) and restored order after the prolonged civil war before being assassinated in 1610.

Henrietta Maria (1609–69), daughter of Henri IV of France, queen consort of ➤ CHARLES I of England 1625–49. Her Roman Catholicism heightened public anxieties about the court's religious sympathies and was a contributory cause of the English Civil War. From 1644 she lived mainly in France.

Henry see also ➤ HOORAY *Henry*.

Henry I (1068–1135), king of England, youngest son of William I, reigned 1100–35. His only son drowned in 1120, and although Henry extracted an oath of loyalty to his daughter Matilda from the barons in 1127, his death was followed almost immediately by the outbreak of civil war.

Henry II (1133–89), king of England, son of Matilda, reigned 1154–89. The first Plantagenet king, he restored order after the reigns of Stephen and Matilda. Opposition to his policies on reducing the power of the Church was led by ➤ *Thomas à* BECKET, who was eventually murdered by four of Henry's knights.

Henry III (1207–72), king of England, son of John, reigned 1216–72. His ineffectual government caused widespread discontent, ending in Simon de Montfort's defeat and capture of Henry in 1264. Although he was restored a year later, real power resided with his son, who eventually succeeded him as Edward I.

Henry IV (1367–1413), king of England, son of John of Gaunt, reigned 1399–1413; known as **Henry Bolingbroke**. He overthrew Richard II, establishing the Lancastrian dynasty. His reign was marked by rebellion in Wales under Owen Glendower and in the north, under the Percy family.

Henry V (1387–1422), king of England, son of Henry IV, reigned 1413–22. He renewed the Hundred Years War soon after coming to the throne and defeated the French at ➤ AGINCOURT in 1415.

Henry VI (1421–71), king of England, son of Henry V, reigned 1422–61 and 1470–1. He was unfit to rule effectively on his own due to a recurrent mental illness; after intermittent civil war with the House of York (the ➤ WARS *of the Roses*), Henry was deposed in 1461 by Edward IV. He briefly regained his throne following a Lancastrian uprising.

Henry VII (1457–1509), king of England, the first Tudor king, who inherited the Lancastrian claim to the throne through his mother, a great-granddaughter of John of Gaunt. He defeated Richard III at Bosworth Field and eventually established an unchallenged Tudor dynasty.

Henry VIII (1491–1547), king of England, son of Henry VII, reigned 1509–47. Henry had six wives, two of whom he had executed and two of whom he divorced. His efforts to divorce his first wife, Catherine of Aragon, which were opposed by the pope, led to England's break with the Roman Catholic Church and indirectly to the establishment of Protestantism. Henry's ensuing dissolution of the monasteries not only destroyed most of the remaining vestiges of the old religious Establishment but also changed the pattern of land ownership.

Henry VIII: Queens

Catherine of Aragon	1485–1536 (divorced)
Anne Boleyn	1507–36 (executed)
Jane Seymour	c.1509–37
Anne of Cleves	1515–57 (divorced)
Catherine Howard	c.1521–42 (executed)
Katherine Parr	1512–48

Henry the Fowler (*c*.876–936), king of the Germans 919–36. As duke of Saxony, he was elected king by the nobles of Saxony and Franconia. He waged war successfully against the Slavs in Brandenburg, the Magyars, and the Danes, from whom he gained the territory of Schleswig in 934.

Henry the Navigator (1394–1460), Portuguese prince. The third son of John I of Portugal, he organized many voyages of discovery, most notably south along the African coast, thus laying the foundation for Portuguese imperial expansion round Africa to the Far East.

Hentenian designating editions of the Vulgate prepared at Louvain by John *Henten* or Hentenius (1499–1566), theologian of the Dominican order.

G. A. Henty (1832–1902), English writer and novelist, remembered particularly as the author of stories for boys, mainly based on military history, such as *With Clive in India* (1884). The didactic influence, conveyed largely through the manly characters of the heroes, is supported by strong narrative and an appearance of historical fidelity.

Hans Werner Henze (1926–   ), German composer and conductor, whose work sometimes reflects his left-wing ideals, as in *The Raft of the Medusa* (1968) (a requiem for Che Guevara).

hepatoscopy divination by examination of the liver of an animal.

Hephaestus in Greek mythology, the god of fire and of craftsmen, son of Zeus and Hera, and husband of Aphrodite. He was a divine metalworker who was lame as the result of having interfered in a quarrel between his parents. His Roman equivalent is ➤ VULCAN.

George Hepplewhite (d. 1786), English cabinet-maker and furniture designer. The posthumously published book of his designs, *The Cabinetmaker and Upholsterer's Guide* (1788), contains almost 300 designs, characterized by light and elegant lines, which sum up neoclassical taste.

The Heptameron a compilation of stories made by Marguerite d'Angoulême, queen of Navarre (1492–1549), in imitation of Boccaccio's *Decameron*.

heptarchy the seven kingdoms of the Angles and the Saxons believed to have been established in Britain in the 7th–8th century.

The term appears to have been introduced by 16th century historians, in accordance with their notion that there were seven Angle and Saxon kingdoms so related that one of their rulers had always the supreme position of King of the Angle-kin (*Rex gentis Anglorum*), 'so that in the Heptarchy itself there seems always to have been a Monarchy' (Camden).

Heptarchy: the kingdoms

East Anglia	Northumbria
Essex	Sussex
Kent	Wessex
Mercia	

Heptateuch the first seven books of the Bible (Genesis to Judges) collectively.

heptathlon an athletic event, in particular one for women, in which each competitor takes part in the same prescribed seven events (100 metres hurdles, high jump, shot-put, 200 metres, long jump, javelin, and 800 metres).

Hera in Greek mythology, a powerful goddess, the wife and sister of Zeus and the daughter of Cronus and Rhea. She was worshipped as the queen of heaven and as a marriage goddess. Her Roman equivalent is ➤ JUNO. Her name comes from Greek *Hēra* 'lady', feminine of *hērōs* 'hero', perhaps used as a title.

Heracleid any of the descendants of Heracles (➤ HERCULES) from whom the Dorian aristocracy of the Peloponnese claimed descent.

Heracles Greek form of ➤ HERCULES.

Heraclitus (*c*.500 BC), Greek philosopher. He believed that fire is the origin of all things and that permanence is an illusion, everything being in a (harmonious) process of constant change.

Heraclius (d. 641), emperor of the Eastern Empire from 610, who defeated the Persian Chosroes and recaptured the wood of the Cross; he became through this a hero of medieval legend.

herald an official employed to oversee state ceremonial, precedence, and the use of armorial bearings, and (historically) to make proclamations, carry ceremonial messages, and oversee tournaments.

In the UK, a *herald* is an official of the College of Arms or the Lyon Court ranking above a pursuivant.

See also ➤ SNOWDON *herald*, ➤ WINDSOR *herald*.

Heraldry: colours

HERALDIC TINCTURE	COLOUR
azure	blue
gules	red
purpure	purple
sable	black
vert	green

heraldry the system by which coats of arms and other armorial bearings are devised, described, and regulated.

Heralds' College informal name for the ➤ COLLEGE *of Arms*.

herb any plant with leaves, seeds, or flowers used for flavouring, food, medicine, or perfume. The word (which is Middle English) comes via Old French from Latin *herba* 'grass, green crops, herb'. Although *herb* has always been spelled with an *h*, pronunciation without it was usual until the 19th century and is still standard in the US.

See also ➤ BETTER *a dinner of herbs than a stalled ox where hate is*.

herb bennet another term for the plant wood avens. The name comes (in late Middle English via Old French) from medieval Latin *herba benedicta* 'blessed herb', apparently first applied to a plant thought to ward off the Devil.

herb Gerard ground elder, which was formerly used to treat gout. It is named after St *Gerard* of Toul (*c*.935–94), invoked against gout.

herb of grace the plant rue; the name is supposed to derive (like the synonymous *herb of repentance*), from the coincidence of the name with the noun and verb rue 'repent, repentance'. The name is probably now best-known from Shakespeare, as in *Richard II*: 'I'll set a bank of rue, sour herb of grace.'

herb Paris a European woodland plant of the lily family, which has a single unbranched stem bearing a green and purple flower above four unstalked leaves. The name translates medieval Latin *herba paris*, probably literally 'herb of a pair', referring to the resemblance of the four leaves to a true-love knot.

herb Robert a common cranesbill with pungent-smelling red-stemmed leaves and pink flowers, native to north temperate regions. The name translates medieval Latin *herba Roberti*, variously supposed to refer to *Robert* Duke of Normandy, St *Robert*, or St *Rupert*.

Herculaneum an ancient Roman town, near Naples, on the lower slopes of Vesuvius. The volcano's eruption in AD 79 buried it deeply under volcanic ash, along with Pompeii, and thus largely preserved it until its accidental rediscovery by a well-digger in 1709. The first excavations were begun in 1738.

Hercule see ➤ HERCULE *Poirot*.

ex pede Herculem inferring the whole of something from an insignificant part; alluding to the story that Pythagoras calculated Hercules's height from the size of Hercules's foot.

Hercules in Greek and Roman mythology, a hero (the Greek form of his name is *Heracles*) of superhuman strength and courage; he is usually armed with a club. The son of Zeus and Alcmene, in his cradle he strangled two snakes which Hera had sent to kill him; in adult life he performed twelve immense tasks or 'labours' (the **Labours of Hercules**) imposed on him, and after death was ranked among the gods. His death came about through one of his deeds: the dying centaur Nessus, whom he had killed, tricked Hercules's wife Deianeira into smearing his blood on her husband's robe. The centaur's blood was a poison which consumed Hercules with fire.

In astronomy, *Hercules* is a large northern constellation, said to represent the kneeling figure of Hercules. It contains the brightest globular cluster in the northern hemisphere, but no bright stars.

See also ➤ *the* FARNESE *Hercules*, ➤ PILLARS *of Hercules*.

Hercules: Labours of Hercules	
LABOUR	NUMBER
Nemean lion	first
Hydra	second
Erymanthian boar	third
Cerynitian hind	fourth
Stymphalian birds	fifth
Augean stables	sixth
Cretan bull	seventh
horses of Diomedes	eighth
girdle of the Amazon	ninth
cattle of Geryon	tenth
golden apples of the Hesperides	eleventh
capture of Cerberus	twelfth

Hercules' knot a kind of knot, attributed to Hercules, very difficult to undo.

Hercules Romanus name taken by the emperor Commodus (AD 141–92), who proclaimed himself to be an incarnation of Hercules; there is a marble bust of Commodus portrayed as Hercules and carrying a club in the Capitoline museum at Rome.

Hercynian originally used by the ancient writers (Latin *Hercynia silva*) to designate an area of forested mountains in central Germany; later (from the late 19th century) applied in geology to the Harz Mountains formed in the Hercynian period.

herds see ➤ FLOCKS *and herds*.

here see ➤ *here be* DRAGONS.

here's one I made earlier catch-phrase popularized by children's television programme *Blue Peter*, from 1963, as a culmination to directions for making a model out of empty yoghurt pots, coat-hangers, and similar domestic items.

heresy belief or opinion contrary to orthodox religious (especially Christian) doctrine. Recorded from Middle English, the word comes via Old French and Latin from Greek *hairesis* 'choice' (in ecclesiastial Greek 'heretical sect'), from *haireomai* 'choose'.

See also ➤ TURKEY, *heresy, hops, and beer came into England all in one year*.

heretic a person believing in or practising religious heresy. The word (recorded from Middle English) comes from Old French via ecclesiastical Latin from Greek *hairetikos* 'able to choose'.

hereticate make a heretic of, especially as a derogatory term to denote the ceremony of deathbed inauguration said to have been practised by the ➤ ALBIGENSES.

Hereward the Wake (11th century), semi-legendary Anglo-Saxon rebel leader. A leader of Anglo-Saxon resistance to William I's new Norman regime, he is thought to have been responsible for an uprising centred on the Isle of Ely in 1070. *The Wake* apparently means 'the watchful one'.

Hergest see ➤ RED *Book of Hergest*.

heriot a tribute paid to a lord out of the belongings of a tenant who died, often consisting of a live animal or, originally, military equipment that he had been lent during his lifetime. The word comes from Old English, from *here* 'army' + *geatwa* 'trappings'.

heritage valued objects and qualities such as historic buildings, unspoilt countryside, and cultural traditions that have been passed down from previous generations.
See also ➤ WORLD *Heritage Site*.

herm a squared stone pillar with a carved head on top (typically of ➤ HERMES), used in ancient Greece as a boundary marker or a signpost.

Hermaphrodite in Greek mythology, a son of Hermes and Aphrodite, with whom the nymph Salmacis fell in love and prayed to be forever united. As a result Hermaphroditus and Salmacis became joined in a single body which retained characteristics of both sexes.

Hermas see ➤ SHEPHERD *of Hermas*.

hermeneutics the branch of knowledge that deals with interpretation, especially of the Bible or literary texts.

Hermes in Greek mythology, the son of Zeus and Maia, the messenger of the gods, and god of merchants, thieves, and oratory. He was portrayed as a herald equipped for travelling, with broad-brimmed hat, winged shoes, and a winged rod. His Roman equivalent is ➤ MERCURY.
He was also associated with fertility, and from early times was represented by a stock or stone (a ➤ HERM), generally having a human head carved at the top and a phallus halfway up it. As patron of flocks and herds, he may be shown carrying a lamb or a calf, and thus may be taken as the equivalent of Christ as the Good Shepherd.

Hermes Trismegistus a legendary figure regarded by Neoplatonists and others as the author of certain works on astrology, magic, and alchemy. Latin *Trismegistus* means 'thrice-greatest Hermes', in reference to ➤ THOTH, identified with ➤ HERMES.

Hermetic of or relating to an ancient occult tradition encompassing alchemy, astrology, and theosophy.

hermetic seal an airtight seal (originally as used by alchemists).

hermit a person living in solitude as a religious discipline; the word is recorded from Middle English, and comes via Old French and late Latin, from Greek *erēmitēs*, from *erēmos* 'solitary'.
➤ *St* ANTHONY *of Egypt*, ➤ *St* GILES, and St Hilarion (*c*.291–*c*.371), who became a hermit in Palestine, are the patron saints of hermits.
Hermit was the name of a colt belonging to Henry Chaplin (1840–1923), which won the Derby by a neck at starting odds of 66 to 1 against.
See also ➤ PETER *the Hermit*.

Herne the Hunter a spectral hunter said to have been in medieval times a keeper in Windsor Forest who hanged himself from the tree known as Herne's (or later Falstaff's) oak, and thereafter haunted the forest; the origins of the story are uncertain, though it bears some resemblance to the tale of the Wild Huntsman.

hero see ➤ NO *man is a hero to his valet*.

Hero in Greek mythology, priestess of Aphrodite at Sestos on the European shore of the Hellespont, whose lover Leander, a youth of Abydos on the opposite shore, swam the strait nightly to visit her. One stormy night he was drowned and Hero in grief threw herself into the sea.

Hero of Alexandria (1st century AD), Greek mathematician and inventor. His surviving works are important as a source for ancient practical mathematics and mechanics. He described a number of hydraulic, pneumatic, and other mechanical devices designed both for utility and amusement, including elementary applications of the power of steam.

Herod (*c*.74–4 BC), ruled 37–4 BC, known as **Herod the Great**. He built the palace of Masada and rebuilt the Temple in Jerusalem. According to the New Testament, Jesus was born during his reign, and he ordered the ➤ MASSACRE *of the Innocents* (Matthew 2:16).

See also ➤ OUT-*Herod Herod.*

Herod Agrippa I (10 BC–AD 44), grandson of Herod the Great, king of Judaea AD 41–4. He imprisoned St Peter and put St James the Great to death.

Herod Agrippa II (AD 27–*c*.93), son of Herod Agrippa I, king of various territories in northern Palestine 50–*c*.93. He presided over the trial of St Paul (Acts 25:13 ff.).

Herod Antipas (22 BC–*c*.40 AD), son of Herod the Great, tetrarch of Galilee and Peraea 4 BC–AD 40. He married Herodias and was responsible for the beheading of John the Baptist. According to the New Testament (Luke 23:7), Pilate sent Jesus to be questioned by him before the Crucifixion.

Herodias in the Bible, the wife of Herod Antipas, by a second marriage denounced as incestuous by John the Baptist, and mother of Salome.

Herodotus (5th century BC), Greek historian. Known as 'the Father of History'. He was the first historian to collect his materials systematically, test their accuracy to a certain extent, and arrange them in a well-constructed and vivid narrative.

heroic age the period in Greek history and legend before the Trojan War and its aftermath, in which the legends of the heroes were set.

heroic couplet (in verse) a pair of rhyming iambic pentameters, much used by Chaucer and the poets of the 17th and 18th centuries such as Alexander Pope.

heroic verse a type of verse used for epic or heroic subjects, such as the hexameter, iambic pentameter, or alexandrine.

heroon originally, a temple dedicated to a hero, often over his supposed tomb; later, a sepulchral monument in the form of a small temple. The term was applied particularly to the mausoleum of the Comnenian emperors in 11th- and 12th-century Byzantium.

Herophilus (4th–3rd centuries BC), Greek anatomist. He is regarded as the father of human anatomy for his fundamental discoveries concerning the anatomy of the brain, eye, and reproductive organs. Herophilus also studied the physiology of nerves,

arteries, and veins. Some of his terms are still in use although none of his works survive.

Herrenvolk the German nation as considered by the Nazis to be innately superior to others. The word is German, and means literally 'master race'.

herring a fairly small silvery fish which is most abundant in coastal waters and is of great commercial importance in many parts of the world; according to a late 16th-century saying, **Of all the fish in the sea, the herring is the king**.

A sea-battle fought at Rouvrai, 12 February 1429, between the French and the English, was popularly known as the Battle of the Herrings.

See also ➤ CALLER *herring,* ➤ KING *of the herrings,* ➤ *neither* FISH *nor fowl nor good red herring,* ➤ RED *herring,* ➤ SHOTTEN *herring.*

every herring must hang by its own gill proverbial saying, early 17th century; meaning that one should be self-reliant.

herringbone an arrangement or design consisting of columns of short parallel lines, with all the lines in one column sloping one way and all the lines in the next column sloping the other way so as to resemble the bones in a fish, used especially in the weave of cloth or the placing of bricks.

John Herschel (1792–1871), English astronomer and physicist, son of William. He extended the sky survey to the southern hemisphere, carried out pioneering work in photography, and made contributions to meteorology and geophysics.

William Herschel (1738–1822), German-born British astronomer. His cataloguing of the skies resulted in the discovery of the planet Uranus. He was the first to appreciate the great remoteness of stars and developed the idea that the sun belongs to the star system of the Milky Way.

Hershey bar a brand of American chocolate bar, produced by the company founded by the American manufacturer and philanthropist Milton Snavely Hershey (1857–1945); in 1903 he established a factory in Pennsylvania which became the world's largest chocolate manufacturing plant, and the centre of the company town of *Hershey.*

herstory history viewed from a female or specifically feminist perspective. The term is recorded from the 1970s.

Hertfordshire kindness traditional saying, mid 17th century; explained as referring to a reputation for the return of favours received, and in particular to drinking the health of the person who has just drunk yours.

Hesiod (*c*.700 BC), Greek poet. One of the earliest known Greek poets, he wrote the *Theogony*, a hexametric poem on the genealogies of the gods, and *Works and Days*, which gave moral and practical advice and was the chief model for later ancient didactic poetry.

he who hesitates is lost proverbial saying, early 18th century; originally (in Addison's *Cato* (1713)), 'the woman that deliberates is lost'.

Hesped a funeral oration pronounced over the dead at a Jewish memorial service.

Hesperia 'Land of the West', a poetical name applied by the Greeks to Italy, and by the Romans to Spain or regions beyond it.

the Hesperides a group of nymphs, the daughters of Hesperus (or, in earlier versions, of Night and Hades), who were guardians, with the aid of a watchful dragon, of a tree of ➤ GOLDEN *apples* (given to Hera by Gaia) in a garden located beyond the Atlas Mountains at the western border of Oceanus, the river encircling the world. One of the labours of ➤ HERCULES was to fetch the golden apples.

Hesperus the planet Venus, the evening star.

Rudolf Hess (1894–1987), German Nazi politician, deputy leader of the Nazi Party 1934–41. In 1941, secretly and on his own initiative, he parachuted into Scotland to negotiate peace with Britain. He was imprisoned for the duration of the war and, at the Nuremberg war trials, sentenced to life imprisonment in Spandau prison, Berlin, where he died.

Hessian in 19th-century America, a military or political hireling, a mercenary, from the employment of Hessian troops by the British government in the American War of Independence. During the War of Secession, it was again used in the South as a term of obloquy for the Federal soldiers.

Hesvan in the Jewish calendar, the second month of the civil and eighth of the religious year, usually coinciding with parts of October and November.

Hesychast a member of a movement dedicated to interior prayer, originating among the Orthodox monks of Mount Athos in the 14th century. The

word comes (in the mid 19th century) from late Greek *hēsukhastēs* 'hermit', from *hēsukhazein* 'be still'.

hetaera a courtesan or mistress, especially one in ancient Greece akin to the modern geisha.

heuristic enabling a person to discover or learn something for themselves; in computing, proceeding to a solution by trial and error or by rules that are only loosely defined.

hex a magic spell, a curse. The word comes (in the mid 19th century, as a verb) via Pennsylvanian German, from German *hexen* (verb), *Hexe* (noun).

hexameron the six days of the Creation; an account (as contained in Genesis) of this period.

Hexateuch the first six books of the Bible (Genesis to Joshua) collectively.

hey see also ➤ *Hey*, JOHNNIE *Cope*.

hey, hey, LBJ, how many kids have you killed today? anti-Vietnam marching slogan, during the presidency of Lyndon Baines Johnson.

Georgette Heyer (1902–74), English novelist. She is noted especially for her historical novels, which include numerous Regency romances such as *Regency Buck* (1935).

Thor Heyerdahl (1914–), Norwegian anthropologist. He is noted for his ocean voyages in primitive craft to demonstrate his theories of cultural diffusion, the best known of which was that of the balsa raft *Kon-Tiki* from Peru to the islands east of Tahiti in 1947, while in 1969 he successfully crossed from Morocco to Central America in a papyrus boat (*Ra II*).

Hezbollah an extremist Shiite Muslim group which has close links with Iran, created after the Iranian revolution of 1979 and active especially in Lebanon. The name comes from Arabic *ḥizbullāh* 'Party of God'.

Hiawatha a legendary 16th-century North American Indian teacher and chieftain, hero of a narrative poem by Henry Wadsworth Longfellow called *The Song of Hiawatha* (1855).

hibakusha in Japan, a survivor of either of the atomic explosions at Hiroshima or Nagasaki in 1945.

Hibernia Latin name for Ireland, from an alteration of *Iverna*, from Greek *I(w)ernē*, of Celtic origin; related to Irish *Éire*, *Éirinn* 'Ireland'.

hic jacet literary term for an epitaph; Latin for 'here lies', the first two words of a Latin epitaph.

hiccius doccius a formula uttered by a juggler when performing a trick; a feat of dexterity, a clever trick. The phrase may be an alteration of *hicce est doctus* 'here is the learned man', or a nonsense formula simulating Latin.

James Butler Hickok (1837–76), American frontiersman and marshal; known as **Wild Bill Hickok**. The legend of his invincibility in his encounters with frontier desperadoes became something of a challenge to gunmen, and he was eventually murdered at Deadwood, South Dakota.

hickory see ➤ OLD *Hickory*.

hidden agenda a secret motivation or bias behind a statement or policy, an ulterior motive, a person's real but concealed aims and intentions.

hide see also ➤ *hide one's light under a* BUSHEL.

hide a former measure of land used in England, typically equal to between 60 and 120 acres, being the amount that would support a family and its dependants.

those who hide can find proverbial saying, early 15th century.

Hieracite a follower of the teachings of *Hierax* (fl. *c*.AD 300), an Egyptian ascetic who denied bodily resurrection and believed in the necessity of celibacy for Christian perfection.

hierarchy see ➤ CELESTIAL *hierarchy*.

hieroglyph a stylized picture of an object representing a word, syllable, or sound, as found in ancient Egyptian and certain other writing systems.

Hieronymite of or pertaining to ➤ St JEROME (d. 420), the author of the Latin Vulgate translation of the Bible and one of the Doctors of the Church.

higgledy-piggledy in confusion or disorder. The expression comes (in the late 16th century) from a rhyming jingle, probably with reference to the irregular herding together of pigs.

high see also ➤ TOBY.

High Church of or adhering to a tradition within the Anglican Church emphasizing ritual, priestly authority, sacraments, and historical continuity with Catholic Christianity.

High Court of Parliament in the UK, a formal term for Parliament.

high day the day of a religious festival; frequently in **high days and holidays**.

High German the standard literary and spoken form of German, originally used in the highlands in the south of Germany. The establishment of this form as a standard language owes much to the biblical translations of Martin Luther in the 16th century.

High Heels and Low Heels names of opposing religious factions in Swift's *Gulliver's Travels*.

High Holidays the Jewish festivals of Yom Kippur and Rosh Hashana.

High Mass a Roman Catholic or Anglo-Catholic mass with full ceremonial, including music and incense and typically having the assistance of a deacon and subdeacon.

high muck-a-muck a person in a position of authority, especially one who is overbearing or conceited. The term, recorded from the 19th century, may come from Chinook *hiyu* 'plenty' + *muckamuck* 'food', from Nootka *ḥayo* 'ten' + *maṙhoṙmaq-* 'choice wheatmeal', with *high* substituted for *hiyu*.

high places in the Bible, a place of worship or sacrifice (often idolatrous) on a hill or high ground; the altar and other appointments for this kind of worship.

high priest the chief priest of the historic Jewish religion.

the high seas the open ocean, especially that not within any country's jurisdiction.

high street the main street of a town, especially as the traditional site for most shops, banks, and other businesses.

high table a table in a dining hall, typically on a platform, for the most important people, such as the fellows of a college.

high treason the crime of betraying one's country, ➤ TREASON against the sovereign or state.

higher mathematics advanced mathematics, such as number theory and topology, as taught at university level.

the higher the monkey climbs the more he shows his tail proverbial saying, late 14th century.

Highland clearances the forced removal of crofters from their land in the Highlands of Scotland in the late 18th and early 19th centuries. The clearances, carried out by landlords wanting to install sheep and deer on their estates, led to extreme hardship as well as to widespread emigration to North America and elsewhere.

Highland Games a meeting for athletic events, playing of the bagpipes, and dancing, held in the Scottish Highlands or by Scots elsewhere. The most famous gathering is that held annually at Braemar.

Highland Mary to whom a number of Robert Burns's poems are addressed; she was Mary Campbell, with whom he was in love, and who died of fever in 1786.

the Highlands the mountainous part of Scotland, to the north of Glasgow and Stirling, often associated with Gaelic culture.

highness a title (as **His Highness, Your Royal Highness**) given to a person of princely or royal rank.
   See also ➤ SERENE *Highness*.

highwayman a man, typically on horseback, who held up travellers at gunpoint in order to rob them; ➤ *Dick* TURPIN is a famous example. The term is recorded from the mid 17th century.

hikayat in classical Malay literature, a prose narrative combining fact and romance.

St Hilary (*c*.315–*c*.367), French bishop. In *c*.350 he was appointed bishop of Poitiers, in which position he became a leading opponent of Arianism; he was named a Doctor of the Church in 1851.
   ◻ **FEAST DAY** His feast day is 13 January.

Hilary term a university term beginning in January; a term or session of the High Court beginning in January. The name comes from ➤ *St* HILARY, whose feast is on 13 January.

St Hilda (*c*.614–80), English abbess. Related to the Anglo-Saxon kings of Northumbria, she founded a monastery for both men and women at Whitby around 658, and was one of the leaders of the Celtic Church delegation at the Synod of Whitby, but accepted the decision in favour of Roman rather than Celtic customs.
   ◻ **FEAST DAY** Her feast day is 17 November.
   See also ➤ LADY *Margaret Hall for ladies*.

Hildebrandine of, pertaining to, or resembling the policy of *Hildebrand* (Pope ➤ GREGORY *VII*, 1073–85), who asserted the power of the papacy and hierarchy and insisted on clerical celibacy.

St Hildegard of Bingen (1089–1179), German abbess, scholar, composer, and mystic. A nun of the Benedictine order, she became Abbess of Diessem in 1136, later moving her community to Bingen. She wrote scientific works, poetry, and music, and described her mystical experiences in *Scivias*.
   ◻ **FEAST DAY** Her feast day is 17 September.

Hildesheim a city in Lower Saxony, site of a Benedictine monastery founded by ➤ BERNARD *of Clairvaux*.

hill see also ➤ BLUE *are the hills that are far away*, ➤ *City of the* SEVEN *Hills*, ➤ SEVEN *Hills*.

the Hill in North America, informal name for the US Senate, or the Canadian federal parliament or government.

Octavia Hill (1838–1912), English housing reformer and co-founder of the National Trust (1895). An active campaigner for the improvement of housing for the poor, she met John Ruskin while working for a Christian Socialist association. In 1864 Ruskin provided financial assistance for Octavia Hill to fund the first of several housing projects, the purchase and refurbishment of three London slum houses.

Rowland Hill (1795–1879), English educationist, administrator, and inventor, chiefly remembered for his introduction of the penny postage-stamp system in 1840. He was initially a teacher who introduced a system of self-government at his school in Birmingham and wrote on the challenges of mass education; in the 1830s he invented a rotary printing-press.

hill folk in the writings of Scott, a name for the ➤ CAMERONIANS.
   Hills are traditionally a place of worship, and associated with the supernatural, and *hill folk* is also used for supernatural people who in folk belief live inside hollow hills.

Edmund Hillary (1919–), New Zealand mountaineer and explorer. In 1953 Hillary and Tenzing Norgay were the first people to reach the summit of

Mount Everest, as members of a British expedition. Hillary later led the New Zealand contingent of the Commonwealth Trans-Antarctic Expedition (1955–8) organized by Vivian Fuchs.

hillbilly an unsophisticated country person, as associated originally with the remote regions of the Appalachians.

Hillsborough a football stadium in Sheffield, England, home of Sheffield Wednesday Football Club, which was the scene of Britain's worst sports disaster when, on 15 April 1989, 95 Liverpool fans died in a crush at an FA Cup semi-final match between Liverpool and Nottingham Forest.

> There was so much that could and should have been done, and nothing ever was, and everyone trundled along for year after year after year, for a hundred years, until Hillsborough.
> — Nick Hornby *Fever Pitch* (1992)

himbo an attractive but unintelligent man; the word, an alteration of *bimbo*, was a journalistic creation of the 1980s.

Heinrich Himmler (1900–45), German Nazi leader, chief of the SS (1929–45) and of the Gestapo (1936–45). He established and oversaw the systematic genocide of over 6 million Jews and other disfavoured groups between 1941 and 1945. Captured by British forces in 1945, he committed suicide by swallowing a cyanide capsule.

Hinayana a name given by the followers of Mahayana Buddhism to the more orthodox schools of early Buddhism. The tradition died out in India, but it survived in Ceylon (Sri Lanka) as the Theravada school and was taken from there to other regions of SE Asia.

hind a female deer, especially a red deer or sika in and after the third year.

A *hind* is the emblem of ➤ *St* EUSTACE, ➤ *St* GILES, and ➤ *St* HUBERT; ➤ *St* ETHELDREDA, who is said to have been brought milk by two does, may also be shown with them.

According to Plutarch, the Roman general Quintus Sertorius (fl. 87–73 BC), while in his province of Spain, had a tame white hind which (in order to impress the native peoples) he asserted had been given to him by the goddess Diana and had oracular powers.

See also ➤ CERYNITIAN *hind*, ➤ *the* GOLDEN *Hind*.

Hindenburg name of a German airship, the largest ever built, intended to provide a luxury passenger service across the Atlantic; on 6 May 1937, while landing in New Jersey from its inaugural flight, the *Hindenburg* burst into flames and was completely destroyed, with 36 of the 97 people aboard being killed. The disaster marked the end of the use of rigid airships as a means of commercial transport.

> It was an event seen and heard by millions. In some uncanny way, the destruction of the Hindenburg came to symbolize the end of an era of innocence in which there was still hope of avoiding war.
> — Ronald A. Mayer *The 1937 Newark Bears* (1980)

Paul Ludwig von Beneckendorff und von Hindenburg (1847–1934), German Field Marshal and statesman, President of the Weimar Republic 1925–34. Elected President in 1925 and re-elected in 1932, he reluctantly appointed Hitler as Chancellor in 1933; he is reported to have said in 1932, 'That man for a Chancellor? I'll make him a postmaster and he can lick the stamps with my head on them.'

Hindenburg Line in the First World War, a German fortified line of defence on the Western Front to which Paul von *Hindenburg* directed retreat and which was not breached until near the end of the war; it was also called the ➤ SIEGFRIED *Line*.

hindmost see ➤ *the* DEVIL *take the hindmost*.

Hinduism a major religious and cultural tradition of the Indian subcontinent, which developed from Vedic religion.

Hinduism is practised primarily in India, Bangladesh, Sri Lanka, and Nepal. It is a diverse family of devotional and ascetic cults and philosophical schools, all sharing a belief in reincarnation and involving the worship of one or more of a large pantheon of gods and goddesses, including ➤ BRAHMA, ➤ SHIVA, and ➤ VISHNU (incarnate as Rama and Krishna), ➤ KALI, Durga, Parvati, and ➤ GANESH. Hindu society was traditionally based on a caste system.

Hindustan former name for the Indian subcontinent in general, more specifically that part of India north of the Deccan, especially the plains of the Ganges and Jumna Rivers.

Hindustani a group of mutually intelligible languages and dialects spoken in NW India, principally Hindi and Urdu. *Hindustani* was the usual term in the 18th and 19th centuries for the native language of NW India. The usual modern term is *Hindi* (or *Urdu* in Muslim contexts), although *Hindustani* is still used to refer to the dialect of Hindi spoken around Delhi, which is widely used throughout India as a lingua franca.

Hindutva a very strong or aggressive sense of Hindu identity, seeking the creation of a Hindu state.

Hinnom the valley of *Hinnom* is the literal name of the biblical ➤ GEHENNA.

> A sulphurous smell filled the air; then all was silent, and black as a cave in Hinnom.
> — Thomas Hardy *Far From the Madding Crowd* (1874)

smite **hip and thigh** punish unsparingly, originally with biblical allusion to Judges 15:8 of Samson and the Philistines, 'He smote them hip and thigh with a great slaughter.'

Hipparchus (*c.*170–after 126 BC), Greek astronomer and geographer. He is best known for his discovery of the precession of the equinoxes and is credited with the invention of trigonometry. Hipparchus constructed the celestial coordinates of 800 stars, indicating their relative brightness, but rejected Aristarchus' hypothesis that the sun is the centre of the planetary system.

hippocampus a mythical sea-monster, half horse and half fish or dolphin, represented as drawing the chariot of Neptune.

hippocentaur another name for a ➤ CENTAUR.

hippocras wine flavoured with spices. The word, which is late Middle English, comes from Old French translating medieval Latin *vinum Hippocraticum* 'Hippocratic wine', so called because it was strained through a filter called ➤ HIPPOCRATES' *sleeve.*

Hippocrates (*c.*460–377 BC), Greek physician, traditionally regarded as the father of medicine. His name is associated with the medical profession's ➤ HIPPOCRATIC *oath* from his attachment to a body of ancient Greek medical writings, probably none of which was written by him. This collection is so varied that physicians have been able to find within it notions that agreed with their own ideas of what medicine and doctors should be.

Hippocrates' sleeve a conical bag of cotton, linen, or flannel, used as a filter.

Hippocratic oath an oath stating the obligations and proper conduct of doctors, formerly taken by those beginning medical practice. Parts of the oath are still used in some medical schools.

Hippocrene the name of a fountain (literally, 'the fountain of the horse') on Mount Helicon sacred to the Muses, which according to legend was produced by a stroke of ➤ PEGASUS' hoof; *Hippocrene* allusively means poetic inspiration, as in Keats's *Ode to a Nightingale* (1820), 'O for a beaker…Full of the true, the blushful Hippocrene.'

hippodrome in ancient Greece or Rome, a course for chariot or horse races.

hippogriff a mythical creature with the body of a horse and the wings and head of an eagle, born of the union of a male griffin and a filly.

Hippolyta queen of the Amazons given in marriage to ➤ THESEUS by ➤ HERCULES, who had conquered her and taken away her girdle, the achievement being one of his twelve labours. She had a son by Theseus called ➤ HIPPOLYTUS. According to another version she was slain by Hercules, and it was her sister Antiope who was the wife of Theseus.

Hippolytus the son of Theseus and ➤ HIPPOLYTA, banished and cursed by his father after being accused by his stepmother ➤ PHAEDRA of rape. He was killed when a sea monster, sent by Poseidon in response to the curse, frightened his horses as he drove his chariot along a seashore.

hippomanes a growth said by Pliny to occur on the head of a newborn foal, used in antiquity as an aphrodisiac.

Hippomenes in Greek mythology, the successful suitor of ➤ ATALANTA, who won his race with her by dropping three ➤ GOLDEN *apples* which distracted her attention.

hippy especially in the 1960s, a person of unconventional appearance, typically having long hair and wearing beads, associated with a subculture involving a rejection of conventional values and the taking of hallucinogenic drugs. The name comes from *hip* meaning 'following the latest fashion, understanding, aware'.

hiragana the more cursive form of kana (syllabic writing) used in Japanese, primarily used for function words and inflections.

Hiram in the Bible, name of a king of Tyre, who supplied many of the building materials for Solomon's Temple.

Hiram is also the name of a skilled worker in the building of the Temple of Solomon, a figure in the legends of freemasonry.

hircocervus a mythical animal, half goat, half stag.

hire see ➤ *the* LABOURER *is worthy of his hire.*

Hiren former term for a seductive woman, a prostitute, from the name of a character in Peele's play *The Turkish Mahamet and Hyrin the fair Greek* (*a.* 1594): the word is an alteration of *Irene*, French *Irène*.

hiring fair a regional fair for the hiring of farm servants, traditionally held at Whitsun and Martinmas.

Hirohito (1901–89), emperor of Japan 1926–89. Regarded as the 124th direct descendant of Jimmu, he refrained from involvement in politics, though he was instrumental in obtaining Japan's agreement to the unconditional surrender which ended the Second World War. In 1946 the new constitution imposed by America obliged him to renounce his divinity and become a constitutional monarch.

hirondelle in heraldry, a swallow.

Hiroshima a city on the south coast of the island of Honshu, western Japan, capital of Chugoku region, which was the target of the first atom bomb, dropped by the United States on 6 August 1945 and resulting in the deaths of about one third of the city's population of 300,000. Together with a second attack, on ➤ NAGASAKI three days later, this led to Japan's surrender and the end of the Second World War.
 See also ➤ HIBAKUSHA.

Hisperic designating a variety of medieval Latin, of which the group of documents entitled *Hisperica Famina* (probably of the 6th century) is a notable example, characterized by a highly artificial vocabulary, with many borrowed words.

Historia Ecclesiastica Gentis Anglorum the most famous work of Bede, finished in 731, is a Latin history of the English people, in five books, from the invasion of Julius Caesar, beginning with a description of Britain, and ending with an account of the state of the country in 731.
 The author draws on Pliny and other Latin authors, and on Gildas and probably the *Historia Britonum* of Nennius. In the second book, in connection with the consultation between Edwin of Northumbria and his nobles whether they shall accept the gospel as preached by Paulinus, occurs the famous simile of the life of man as a sparrow flying out of the night into the lighted hall, and out again into the night.

historiated of an initial letter in an illuminated manuscript, decorated with designs representing scenes from the text.

historical materialism another term for ➤ DIALECTICAL *materialism.*

history see ➤ DRUM-*and-trumpet history,* ➤ FATHER *of History,* ➤ *happy is the* COUNTRY *that has no history.*

history of the Four Kings a name (recorded from the mid 18th century) for a pack of cards.

history repeats itself proverbial saying, mid 19th century.

hit for six in cricket, hit the ball or bowler for six runs; figuratively, defeat soundly in an argument.

hitch one's wagon to a star set oneself high aspirations; first recorded in Ralph Waldo Emerson's *Society and Solitude* (1870), 'Hitch your wagon to a star…Let us not fag in paltry works.'

Alfred Hitchcock (1899–1980), English film director. Acclaimed in Britain for films such as *The Thirty-Nine Steps* (1935), he moved to Hollywood in 1939, where his first film was *Rebecca* (1940). Among his later works, notable for their suspense and their technical ingenuity, are the thrillers *Strangers on a Train* (1951), *Psycho* (1960), with its famous shower murder, and *The Birds* (1963).

Shere Hite (1942–), American feminist. She published her research into sex, gender definition, and private life in the ground-breaking work *The Hite Report on Female Sexuality* (1976), based on the responses of thousands of people to anonymous questionnaires.

Adolf Hitler (1889–1945), Austrian-born Nazi leader, Chancellor of Germany 1933–45. He co-founded the National Socialist German Workers' (Nazi) Party in 1919, and came to prominence through his powers of oratory. While imprisoned for an unsuccessful putsch in Munich (1923–4) he wrote *Mein Kampf* (1925), an exposition of his political ideas. Becoming Chancellor in 1933, he established the totalitarian Third Reich. His expansionist foreign policy precipitated the Second World War, while his fanatical anti-Semitism led to the Holocaust.

See also ➤ HEIL *Hitler*, ➤ FÜHRER, ➤ MEIN *Kampf*, ➤ NIGHT *of the long knives*, ➤ THOUSAND-*Year Reich.*

Hitler diaries in April 1983, it was announced that Hitler's diaries had been discovered; initially accepted as genuine (extracts were published in the *Sunday Times*), it was soon demonstrated that they were forgeries.

Hitler moustache a small square moustache like that worn by Adolf Hitler.

Hitler salute another term for ➤ NAZI *salute.*

Hittite a member of an ancient people who established an empire in Asia Minor and Syria that flourished from *c.*1700 to *c.*1200 BC. Also, a subject of this empire or one of their descendants, including a Canaanite or Syrian people mentioned in the Bible (11th to 8th century BC).

HIV abbreviation for *human immunodeficiency virus*, a retrovirus which causes ➤ AIDS.

Ho Chi Minh (1890–1969), Vietnamese communist statesman, President of North Vietnam 1954–69. He led the Vietminh against the Japanese during the Second World War, fought the French until they were defeated in 1954 and Vietnam was divided into North and South Vietnam, and deployed his forces in the guerrilla struggle that became the Vietnam War.

ho-ho bird a mythical Chinese bird resembling a pheasant, frequently used as an emblem of courage.

hoarstone an ancient boundary stone, supposedly one that is grey with lichen; the word now survives only in place names.

hob a sprite or hobgoblin. In Middle English the word meant 'country fellow', and was a pet form of *Rob*, short for *Robin* or *Robert*, often referring specifically to ➤ ROBIN *Goodfellow.*

Meindert Hobbema (1638–1709), Dutch landscape painter. A pupil of Jacob van Ruisdael, he was one of the last 17th-century Dutch landscape painters. He was particularly admired by the painter John Crome of Norwich ('Old Crome', 1768–1821); Crome's last words are reported as, 'Hobbema, my dear Hobbema, how I have loved you!'

Thomas Hobbes (1588–1679), English philosopher. Hobbes was a materialist, claiming that there was no more to the mind than the physical motions discovered by science, and he believed that human action was motivated entirely by selfish concerns, notably fear of death. In *Leviathan* (1651) he argued that absolute monarchy was the most rational, hence desirable, form of government.

hobbit a member of an imaginary race similar to humans, of small size and with hairy feet, in stories by ➤ J. R. R. TOLKIEN. The name was invented by Tolkien in his story *The Hobbit* (1937), and said by him to mean 'hole-dweller'.

hobby an activity done regularly in one's leisure time for pleasure. From pet forms of the given name *Robin*, originally in the sense 'a small horse or pony'. The word later came to denote a toy horse or hobby horse, and hence 'a pastime, something done for pleasure'.

hobby horse a model of a horse or a horse's head, typically of wicker, used in morris dancing or pantomime; traditionally, the framework was fastened about the waist of one of the morris dancers, so that the *hobby horse* became one of the characters. The phrase **the hobby horse is forgot**, which occurs in Shakespeare's *Love's Labour's Lost*, is apparently a quotation from an old ballad.

hobgoblin in mythology and fairy stories, a mischievous imp or sprite; fearsome mythical creature, a bogey.

hobnob mix socially, especially with those of perceived higher social status. The word comes (in the 19th century) from archaic *hob or nob, hob and nob*, probably meaning 'give and take', used by two people drinking to each other's health, from dialect *hab nab* 'have or not have'.

Hobson-Jobson assimilation of adopted foreign words to the sound-pattern of the adopting language, from the title of a famous collection (1886) of Anglo-Indian words by Yule & Burnell, representing an alteration (by British hearers) of Arabic *Yā Ḥasan! Yā Ḥusayn!* O Hasan! O Husain!, a cry used by Muslims at the ceremonies held at ➤ MUHARRAM.

Hobson's choice a choice of taking what is available or nothing at all, named (in the mid 17th century) after Thomas *Hobson* (1554–1631), a Cambridge carrier who hired out horses, giving the customer the 'choice' of the one nearest the door or none at all.

hock see also ➤ *from* SODA *to hock.*

Hock designating days of or events connected with the beginning of the second week after Easter, formerly important for the payment of rents, the collection of money (often by roughly humorous methods) for parish purposes, and as the beginning of the summer half of the rural year. The origin of the name is unknown.

Hock Monday the second Monday after Easter Sunday.

Hock-money money collected for parish purposes during Hocktide.

Hock Tuesday the second Tuesday after Easter Sunday.

David **Hockney** (1937–), English painter and draughtsman. He is best known for his association with pop art and for his Californian work of the mid 1960s, such as *A Bigger Splash* (1967) which depicts flat, almost shadowless architecture, lawns, and swimming pools.

Hocktide the period comprising the second Monday and Tuesday after Easter Sunday.

hocus-pocus deception, trickery (words often used by a person performing conjuring tricks). The expression comes (in the early 17th century)from *hax pax max Deus adimax*, a pseudo-Latin phrase used as a magic formula by conjurors.

hodden grey in Scottish usage, typical rustic clothing made of grey hodden (a coarse woollen cloth) that has not been dyed; the term was popularized by the Scottish poet Allan Ramsay (1686–1758), 'But Meg, poor Meg! maun with the shepherds stay, And tak what God will send in hodden grey.'

Hodegetria an iconographical depiction of the Virgin and Child in which the Virgin with her right hand indicates the Child, who is on her left arm; the word is Greek, and means 'The Indicator of the Way'.

According to tradition the arrangement follows that of a painting originally attributed to St Luke, but the earliest surviving example is probably to be assigned to the 7th century. Sometimes, in the process of copying, the Child was transferred from the Virgin's left arm to the right and she indicates Him with her left hand, but there is no particular significance in this variant.

Hodge used as a name for a typical English agricultural labourer; a pet name of the given name *Roger.*

Hodge was the name of Dr Johnson's cat, and the subject of an anecdote recounted by Boswell:

> When I observed he was a fine cat, saying, 'Why yes, Sir, but I have had cats whom I liked better than this'; and then as if perceiving Hodge to be out of countenance, adding, 'but he is a very fine cat, a very fine cat indeed.'
> — James Boswell *Life of Samuel Johnson* (1791)

Jimmy **Hoffa** (1913–*c*.75), American trade union leader. President of the Teamsters union from 1957, he was imprisoned in 1967–71 for attempted bribery of a federal court judge, fraud, and looting pension funds. His sentence was commuted by President Nixon and he was given parole in 1971 on condition that he resigned as president of the union. He disappeared in 1975, and is thought to have been murdered.

E. T. A. Hoffmann (1776–1822), German novelist, short-story writer, and music critic. His extravagantly fantastic stories provided the inspiration for Offenbach's opera *Tales of Hoffmann* (1881).

hog a domesticated pig, especially a castrated male reared for slaughter; often taken as a type of undiscriminating greed. The word is recorded from Old English (in form *hogg, hocg*), perhaps of Celtic origin and related to Welsh *hwch* and Cornish *hoch* 'pig, sow'.

See ➤ *the* CAT, *the rat, and Lovell the dog, rule all England under the hog,* ➤ HAMPSHIRE *hog.*

go the whole hog informal expression meaning, do something completely or thoroughly; of several origins suggested, one interprets *hog* as the American slang term for a ten cent piece; another refers the idiom to one of William Cowper's poems (1779), which discusses Muslim uncertainty about which parts of the pig are acceptable as food, leading to the 'whole hog' being eaten, because of confusion over Muhammad's teaching.

William **Hogarth** (1697–1764), English painter and engraver. Notable works include his series of engravings on 'modern moral subjects', such as *A Rake's Progress* (1735) and *Marriage à la Mode* (1743–5), which satirized the vices of both high and low life in 18th-century England.

Hogarth Press founded in 1917 by Leonard and Virginia Woolf at their home, Hogarth House in

Richmond; their earliest publications included Katherine Mansfield's *Prelude* (1918) and T. S. Eliot's *Poems* (1919), and their policy was to publish new and experimental work, and translations.

Hogen Mogen in the mid 17th century, the States General of the Netherlands, or the members of this. From Dutch *Hoogmogendheiden* High Mightinesses, the title of the States General.

James Hogg (1770–1835), Scottish poet. A shepherd in the Ettrick Forest whose poetic talent was discovered by Sir Walter Scott, he is best known today for his prose work *The Confessions of a Justified Sinner* (1824). He became known as the **Ettrick Shepherd**.

Hogmanay in Scotland, New Year's Eve, and the celebrations that take place at this time. Also, a gift of cake etc. demanded by children at Hogmanay. The word is recorded from the early 17th century, and perhaps comes from an Anglo-Norman French form of Old French *aguillanneuf* 'last day of the year, new year's gift'.

Hogs Norton, where pigs play the organ proverbial reference to an Oxfordshire village, supposedly inhabited by rustic and clownish people.

Hogwarts in the books of J. T. Rowling, the school for wizards attended by ➤ *Harry* POTTER.

Hohenstaufen a German dynastic family, some of whom ruled as Holy Roman emperors between 1138 and 1254, among them ➤ FREDERICK *I* (Barbarossa).

Hohenzollern a German dynastic family from which came the kings of Prussia from 1701 to 1918 and German emperors (of whom the last was ➤ WILHELM *II*) from 1871 to 1918.

hoi polloi the masses; the common people; from Greek (literally, 'the many'; *hoi* is the Greek word for the definite article 'the').

hoist see ➤ *hoist with one's own* PETARD.

hoity-toity haughty, snobbish; in archaic use, frolicsome. The word comes (in the mid 17th-century sense 'boisterous or silly behaviour') from the obsolete *hoit* 'indulge in riotous mirth'.

hokey-cokey a communal dance performed in a circle with synchronized shaking of the limbs in turn, accompanied by a simple song.

hokey-pokey dated term for ice cream sold on the street, especially by Italian street vendors; the origin of the term is unknown.

Katsushika Hokusai (1760–1849), Japanese painter and wood engraver, who represented aspects of Japanese everyday life in his woodcuts, and who strongly influenced European Impressionist artists.

Hans Holbein (1497–1543), German painter and engraver; known as **Holbein the Younger**. He became a well-known court portraitist in England and was commissioned by Henry VIII to supply portraits of the king's prospective brides, including the ➤ FLANDERS *Mare*, Anne of Cleves.

Holborn a district of London through which ran the road to ➤ TYBURN, as noted in Swift's poem 'Clever Tom Clinch':

> As clever Tom Clinch, while the rabble was bawling,
> Rode stately through Holborn to die in his calling.
> — Jonathan Swift 'Clever Tom Clinch' (*a.* 1745)

See also ➤ *he will* RIDE *backwards up Holborn Hill*.

hold a candle to the Devil serve or assist a wicked person, be active in wickedness.

Holdfast see ➤ BRAG *is a good dog but Holdfast is better*.

hole-in-the-wall in the UK, informal term for an automatic cash dispenser installed in the outside wall of a bank; the term became current in the mid 1980s, when use of the machines became generally available. The term is not used in this sense in the US, where a *hole-in-the-wall* is likely to be a small restaurant, and where a cash dispensing machine is known as an *automated teller machine* or *ATM*.

Holger Danske Danish name for ➤ OGIER *the Dane*.

Holi a Hindu spring festival celebrated in February or March in honour of Krishna.

holiday a day or festivity or recreation; originally, a *holy day* (Old English *hāligdæg*).

See also ➤ BUSMAN*'s holiday,* ➤ ROMAN *holiday*.

holier than thou characterized by an attitude of self-conscious virtue and piety, from Isaiah 65:5 'Stand by thyself, come not near to me; for I am holier than thou.'

Raphael Holinshed (d. *c.*1580), English chronicler. Although the named compiler of *The Chronicles of England, Scotland, and Ireland* (1577), Holinshed wrote only the *Historie of England* and had help with the remainder. The revised (1587) edition was used by Shakespeare.

Holland the name of a former province of the Netherlands, earlier *Holtlant* (from *holt* 'wood' + *-lant* 'land'). *Holland* is also the name of a kind of smooth, hard-wearing linen fabric, used chiefly for window blinds and furniture covering, which was made there.

Philemon Holland (1552–1637), English schoolmaster and noted classicist; he was responsible for translations of Livy, Pliny, Plutarch, Suetonius, Xenophon, and Camden's *Britannia*, and Thomas Fuller named him the ➤ TRANSLATOR *General* of his age.

Mother Holle in Germanic mythology, an ancient goddess of death who is an aspect of the mother goddess ➤ HULDA. She appears in one of Grimms' fairy stories as an old woman for whom a young girl does housework, especially making the down from the bed fly so that snow falls in the world above. The girl works so hard that when she is sent home she is rewarded with a shower of gold, but her lazy younger sister is punished for idleness with a shower of pitch.

Herman Hollerith (1860–1929), American engineer. He invented a tabulating machine using punched cards for computation, an important precursor of the electronic computer, and founded a company that later expanded to become the IBM Corporation.

hollow square a body of infantry drawn up in a square with a space in the middle.

holly a widely distributed evergreen shrub, typically having prickly dark green leaves, small white flowers, and red berries; the branches, foliage, and berries of this plant are traditionally used as decorations at Christmas.

The holly as an evergreen tree is used as an image of fidelity in a song attributed to Henry VIII, 'As the holly groweth green And never changeth hue, So I am, ever hath been, unto my lady true.'

Buddy Holly (1936–59), American rock-and-roll singer, guitarist, and songwriter. He recorded such hits as 'That'll be the Day' with his band, The Crickets, before going solo in 1958. He was killed in an aircraft crash.

hollyhock a tall Eurasian plant of the mallow family, with large showy flowers. The name comes (in Middle English) from *holy* + obsolete *hock* 'mallow'

and originally denoted the marsh mallow which has medicinal uses (hence, perhaps, the use of 'holy'); the current sense dates from the mid 16th century.

Hollywood a district of Los Angeles, the principal centre of the American film industry; the American film industry and the lifestyles of the people associated with it.

Sherlock Holmes an extremely perceptive private detective in stories by ➤ *Arthur Conan* DOYLE; presented through the eyes of his friend and colleague ➤ *Dr* WATSON, Holmes is shown as embodying the powers of rational deduction, unaffected by his occasional indulgence in cocaine. His duel with his arch-enemy Professor ➤ MORIARTY appeared to lead to his death in the ➤ REICHENBACH *Falls*, but Doyle was forced by popular demand to allow the detective to emerge unscathed.

holmgang by Old Norse custom, a duel to the death; the word means 'going to the holm', the *holm* being an island on which such duels were traditionally fought.

the Holocaust the mass murder of Jews under the German Nazi regime during the period 1941–45. More than 6 million European Jews, as well as members of other persecuted groups, such as gypsies and homosexuals, were murdered at concentration camps such as Auschwitz.

The word holocaust was originally recorded in Middle English denoting a Jewish sacrificial offering which is burnt completely on an altar; from this it was extended to mean a sacrifice on a large scale, and then a complete destruction or massacre. (It comes ultimately from Greek *holokauston*, from *holos* 'whole' + *kaustos* 'burnt'.) The specific application was introduced by historians during the 1950s, probably as an equivalent to Hebrew *ḥurban* and *shoah* 'catastrophe' (used in the same sense); but it had been foreshadowed by contemporary references to the Nazi atrocities as a 'holocaust' in the sense of slaughter on a large scale.

Holofernes in the Apocrypha, the Assyrian general of Nebuchadnezzar's forces, who was killed by ➤ JUDITH.

In 16th-century literature, Holofernes is also the name of the great doctor in theology (**Tubal Holofernes**) who in Rabelais' *Gargantua* (1534) taught the young Gargantua, and of the pedantic schoolmaster in Shakespeare's *Love's Labour's Lost* (1595).

holus-bolus all at once, perhaps originally pseudo-Latin for 'whole bolus, whole lump'.

holy see also ➤ *Holy* GRAIL.

Holy Alliance a loose alliance of European powers pledged to uphold the principles of the Christian religion. It was proclaimed at the Congress of Vienna (1814–15) by the emperors of Austria and Russia and the king of Prussia and was joined by most other European monarchs. Its influence was not great, but it is often seen as a symbol of conservatism and autocratic principles in Europe.

holy ampoule another name for ➤ *la* SAINTE *ampoule*.

the Holy City Jerusalem; (in Christian tradition) Heaven.

Holy Coat a term for the seamless garment worn by Jesus, for which the soldiers at the Crucifixion cast lots, as in John 19:23–4, 'The coat was without seam, woven from the top throughout. They said therefore among themselves, let us not rend it, but cast lots for it.'

Holy Cross Day the day on which the feast of the ➤ EXALTATION *of the Cross* is held, 14 September.

holy day a day consecrated or set apart for religious observance; also called **holy day of obligation**.

holy death ➤ *St* JOSEPH is the patron saint of those who have a holy death.

Holy Door the door in the facade of St Peter's, Rome, which is nearest to the Vatican. It is normally sealed with brickwork, except during the ➤ HOLY *Year*, when it is opened for the passage of those wishing to gain the Indulgence of the Holy Year.

Holy Family Christ as a child with Mary and Joseph (and often also others such as John the Baptist or St Anne), especially as a subject for a painting.

Holy Father a name for the Pope.

Holy Ghost another term for the ➤ HOLY *Spirit*. See also ➤ SIN *against the Holy Ghost*.

Order of the Holy Ghost a French order of Knighthood (*ordre du Saint-Esprit*), instituted by Henry III in 1578.

holy herb in early herbals, a name for vervain, traditionally regarded as having medicinal properties.

Holy Innocents' Day a Christian festival commemorating the ➤ MASSACRE *of the Innocents*, 28 December.

Holy Island another name for ➤ LINDISFARNE, which from the 7th century until its sack by Vikings was an important religious centre.

Holy Island is also the name of a small island off the western coast of ➤ ANGLESEY in North Wales.

Holy Lance the spear with which the side of Jesus was pierced at the Crucifixion; a relic of this was later said to be kept in the ➤ SAINTE *Chapelle* in Paris.

Holy Land a region on the eastern shore of the Mediterranean, in what is now Israel and Palestine, revered by Christians as the place in which Christ lived and taught, by Jews as the land given to the people of Israel, and by Muslims.

Holy League any of various European alliances sponsored by the papacy during the 15th, 16th, and 17th centuries. They include the League of 1511–13, formed by Pope Julius II to expel Louis XII of France from Italy, the French Holy League (also called the Catholic League) of 1576 and 1584, a Catholic extremist league formed during the French Wars of Religion, and the Holy (or Catholic) League of 1609, a military alliance of the German Catholic princes.

Holy Maid of Kent name given to Elizabeth Barton (*c*.1506–34), a domestic servant from Aldington in Kent, who *c*.1525 began to report visions which she had experienced. She was at first given some official support by the Church, but endangered herself by publicly intervening in the matter of Henry VIII's divorce from Catherine of Aragon, prophesying that it would result in his death. She was executed at Tyburn on 20 April 1534, having confessed that her visions were not genuine.

Holy Name especially in the Catholic Church, the name of Jesus as an object of formal devotion.

holy of holies the inner chamber of the sanctuary in the Jewish Temple in Jerusalem, separated by a veil from the outer chamber. It was reserved for the presence of God and could be entered only by the High Priest on the Day of Atonement.

Holy Office the ecclesiastical court of the Roman Catholic Church established as the final court of appeal in trials of heresy. Formed in 1542 as part of the Inquisition, it was renamed the Sacred Congregation for the Doctrine of the Faith in 1965.

holy orders the sacrament or rite of ordination as a member of the clergy, especially in the grades of bishop, priest, or deacon.

holy place a place revered as holy, typically one to which religious pilgrimage is made, and especially any of the sites associated with Jesus.

Holy Roman Empire the empire set up in western Europe following the coronation of Charlemagne as emperor in the year 800. It was created by the medieval papacy in an attempt to unite Christendom under one rule. At times the territory of the empire was extensive and included Germany, Austria, Switzerland, and parts of Italy and the Netherlands. The title of emperor, which had largely belonged to German dynasties since Otto I's coronation in 962, was formally abolished in 1806.

In 1756, Voltaire commented memorably on it as 'This agglomeration which was called and which still calls itself the Holy Roman Empire, was neither holy nor Roman, nor an empire.'

Holy Rood Day the day on which the feast of the Invention of the Cross is held, 3 May. Also, another term for ➤ HOLY *Cross Day.*

Holy Saturday the Saturday preceding Easter Sunday.

Holy Scripture the sacred writings of Christianity contained in the Bible.

Holy See the papacy or the papal court; those associated with the Pope in the government of the Roman Catholic Church at the Vatican.

Holy Sepulchre the place in which the body of Jesus was laid after being taken down from the Cross. Also, the church in Jerusalem erected over the traditional site of this tomb.

See also ➤ KNIGHT *of the Holy Sepulchre.*

Holy Spirit in Christian belief, the third person of the Trinity; God as spiritually active in the world. In Christian art, the Holy Spirit is often represented as a ➤ DOVE.

See also ➤ SEVEN *gifts of the Holy Spirit.*

Holy Spirit Association for the Unification of World Christianity another name for ➤ UNIFICATION *Church.*

Holy Thursday (chiefly in the Roman Catholic Church) Maundy Thursday; (in the Anglican Church) Ascension Day.

holy war a war declared or waged in support of a religious cause; *The Holy War* is the title of an allegory (1682) by John Bunyan, depicting the battle for the city of ➤ MANSOUL between Emmanuel and ➤ DIABOLUS.

holy water water blessed by a priest and used in religious ceremonies.

Holy Week the week before Easter, starting on Palm Sunday.

holy Willie a pious hypocrite; from Burns's poem 'Holy Willie's Prayer' (1785).

Holy Writ the Bible; writings or sayings of unchallenged authority.

Holy Year in the Roman Catholic Church, a period of remission from the penal consequences of sin, granted under certain conditions for a year usually at intervals of twenty-five years.

hom the juice of the soma plant as a sacred drink of the Parsees.

homburg a man's felt hat having a narrow curled brim and a tapered crown with a lengthwise indentation, named after *Homburg,* a town in western Germany, where such hats were first worn.

home see also ➤ CHARITY *begins at home,* ➤ EAST, *west, home's best,* ➤ *an* ENGLISHMAN'*s home is his castle,* ➤ *go* ABROAD *and you'll hear news of home,* ➤ *there is no* PLACE *like home,* ➤ WHO *goes home,* ➤ *a* WOMAN'*s place is in the home.*

home alone (of a child) left at home unsupervised during parental absence. The expression was popularized by the film *Home Alone* (1990), starring the child actor Macaulay Culkin in the story of a little boy who, accidentally left behind when his parents and siblings went on holiday, was left alone at home to fend for himself against all odds.

Home Counties the English counties surrounding London, into which London has extended. They comprise chiefly Essex, Kent, Surrey, and Hertfordshire.

Home Guard the British citizen army organized in 1940 to defend the UK against invasion, finally disbanded in 1957.

See also ➤ DAD'*s Army.*

home is home, as the Devil said when he found himself in the Court of Session proverbial saying, early 19th century.

home is home though it's never so homely proverbial saying, mid 16th century.

home is where the heart is proverbial saying, late 19th century.

home, James, and don't spare the horses traditional saying, recorded (as *Home, James*) from the 1920s; *Home James, and don't spare the horses* was a song-title of 1934.

Home Office the British government department dealing with domestic affairs, including law and order, immigration, and broadcasting, in England and Wales.

home of lost causes a name for Oxford; originally a quotation from Matthew Arnold:

> Whispering from her towers the last enchantments of the Middle Age . . . Home of lost causes, and forsaken beliefs, and unpopular names, and impossible loyalties!
> — Matthew Arnold *Essays in Criticism* (First Series, preface, 1865)

home rule the government of a colony, dependent country, or region by its own citizens, in particular as advocated for Ireland 1870–1914.

The campaign for Irish home rule was one of the dominant forces in British politics in the late 19th and early 20th centuries, particularly in that Irish nationalists, under ➤ *Charles Stewart* PARNELL and later John Redmond, frequently held the balance of power in the House of Commons. (➤ GLADSTONE, a supporter of Home Rule, wrote in his diary of 10 April 1887, 'One prayer absorbs all others: Ireland, Ireland, Ireland.')

A Home Rule Act was finally passed in 1914 but was suspended until after the First World War; in the spring of that year, John Redmond was asked by a priest from Tipperary if anything could now rob them of Home Rule and answered, 'A European war might do it.' After the ➤ EASTER *Rising* of 1916 and Sinn Fein's successes in the general election of 1918, and following three years of unrest and guerrilla warfare (1918–21) a Treaty was signed in 1921, establishing the Irish Free State and the province of Northern Ireland.

Home Secretary in the UK, the Secretary of State in charge of the Home Office.

Home Service one of the original programme services of the BBC (renamed *Radio 4*).

home shopping shopping carried out from one's own home by ordering goods advertised in a catalogue or on a television channel, or by using various electronic media.

Home, sweet home title of a popular song by the American songwriter J. H. Payne (1791–1852), from *Clari, or, the Maid of Milan* (opera, 1823).

homeless the French-born St Benedict Labre (1748–83), who after living as a pilgrim visiting shrines on the way to Rome, spent his last nine years there as a homeless person among the destitute, is the patron saint of the homeless.

homeopathy a system of complementary medicine in which disease is treated by minute doses of natural substances that in a healthy person would produce symptoms of disease. It is often contrasted with ➤ ALLOPATHY.

Homer (8th century BC), Greek epic poet. He is traditionally held to be the author of the *Iliad* and the *Odyssey*, though modern scholarship has revealed the place of the Homeric poems in a pre-literate oral tradition. In later antiquity Homer was regarded as the greatest poet, and his poems were constantly used as a model and source by others.

Homer J. Simpson in the American cartoon series *The Simpsons* (1990–, created by Matt Groening), the beer-loving and often frustrated safety inspector of the Springfield Nuclear Power Plant who is the patriarch of the dysfunctional Simpson family and father of ➤ BART *Simpson*.

> Sometimes you have to hit yourself on the forehead and utter a Homer Simpson 'doh'.
> — *PC Week* 2 February 1999

Homer sometimes nods proverbial saying, late fourteenth century; from Horace:

> I'm aggrieved when sometimes even excellent Homer nods.
> — Horace *Ars Poetica*

Homeric of or in the style of Homer or the epic poems ascribed to him; of Bronze Age Greece as described in these poems.

Homeric laughter irrepressible laughter, proverbially like that of Homer's gods in the *Iliad* as they watched lame Hephaestus hobbling.

homespun of cloth or yarn, made or spun at home; in figurative usage, simple and unsophisticated.

Homo the genus of primates of which modern humans (*Homo sapiens*) are the present-day representatives. The genus *Homo* is believed to have existed for at least two million years, of which *H. sapiens* has occupied perhaps the last 400,000 years, and modern humans (*H. sapiens sapiens*) first appeared in the Upper Palaeolithic. Among several extinct species are *H. habilis*, *H. erectus*, and *H. neanderthalensis*, known from remains found at Olduvai Gorge in East Africa, and elsewhere.

Homo sapiens the primate species to which modern humans belong; humans regarded as a species.

homoeoteleuton a rhetorical figure consisting in the use of a series of words with the same or similar endings.

homonym each of two or more words having the same written form but of different meaning and origin.

Homoousion the doctrine that the first and second persons of the Trinity are of identical essence or substance.

homunculus a small or or diminutive person, a dwarf; in earlier use, a foetus considered as a fully formed human being.

honest broker an impartial mediator in international, industrial, or other disputes. Recorded from the late 19th century, the term is a translation of German *ehrlicher Makler* with reference to the Prussian statesman ➤ *Otto von* BISMARCK, under whom Germany was united.

honesty is the best policy proverbial saying, early 17th century.

honey see ➤ LAND *of milk and honey*, ➤ *where* BEES *are there is honey*.

honey catches more flies than vinegar proverbial saying, mid 17th century.

honi soit qui mal y pense French phrase meaning, 'shame on him who thinks evil of it' (the motto of the ➤ *Order of the* GARTER).

Honiton lace lace consisting of floral sprigs hand sewn on to fine net or joined by lacework; named for the town of *Honiton* in Devon.

honorificabilitudinitatibus the long word in Shakespeare's *Love's Labour's Lost*, in which Baconians see a cryptogram indicating that Bacon was the author of the works attributed to Shakespeare.

honour see also ➤ BIRTHDAY *Honours*, ➤ COMPANION *of Honour*, ➤ COURT *of honour*, ➤ DEBT *of honour*, ➤ PEACE *with honour*, ➤ *a* PROPHET *is not without honour save in his own country*.

there is honour among thieves proverbial saying, early 19th century.

the post of honour is the post of danger proverbial saying, mid 16th century.

Honourable used as a title indicating eminence or distinction, given to certain high officials, the children of certain ranks of the nobility, and MPs.

Honourable Artillery Company a regiment in the British Army, originally founded in 1537 as the *Guild of St George*, a guild of archers and handgunners.

The Honourable Corps of Gentlemen at Arms in the UK, the sovereign's bodyguard.

honours of war privileges granted to a capitulating force, for example that of marching out with colours flying.

hooch alcoholic liquor, especially inferior or illicit whisky, a late 19th-century abbreviation of *Hoochinoo*, the name of an Alaskan Indian people who made liquor.

Hood see also ➤ ROBIN *Hood*.

hoof see ➤ CLOVEN *hoof*.

Captain Hook the dark and sinister pirate captain with a steel hook in place of his right hand, who in Barrie's *Peter Pan* is the mortal enemy of Peter, but who in the end falls victim to the crocodile which stalks him.
  See also ➤ CROCODILE, ➤ PETER *Pan*.

hook, line, and sinker used to emphasize that someone has been completely deceived or tricked (with allusion to the taking of bait by a fish).

by hook or by crook by one means or another; the expression is of longstanding, but there is no clear evidence for the origin.

Robert Hooke (1635–1703), English scientist. He formulated the law of elasticity (➤ HOOKE's *law*), proposed an undulating theory of light, introduced the term *cell* to biology, postulated elliptical orbits for the earth and moon, and proposed the inverse square law of gravitational attraction. He also invented or improved many scientific instruments and mechanical devices, and designed a number of buildings in London after the Great Fire.

Hooke's law a law stating that the strain in a solid is proportional to the applied stress within the elastic limit of that solid.

Joseph Hooker (1817–1911), English botanist and pioneer in plant geography. Hooker applied Darwin's theories to plants and, with George Bentham (1800–84), he produced a work on classification, *Genera Plantarum* (1862–83). He introduced the cultivation of rhododendrons to Britain and became director of Kew Gardens in 1865.

hooligan a violent young troublemaker, typically one of a gang, perhaps from *Hooligan*, the surname of a fictional rowdy Irish family in a music-hall song of the 1890s, also of a character in a cartoon.

Hooray Henry a boisterous but ineffectual young upper-class man, often regarded as belonging to the same group as ➤ SLOANE *Rangers*.

Hoosier State informal name for Indiana; Hoosier (of unknown origin) means a native or inhabitant of Indiana.

J. Edgar Hoover (1895–1972), American lawyer and director of the FBI 1924–72. He reorganized the FBI into an efficient, scientific law-enforcement agency, but came under criticism for the organization's role during the McCarthy era and for its reactionary political stance in the 1960s. Hoover's knowledge, and files, were legendary; Lyndon Johnson once said of him, 'Better to have him inside the tent pissing out, than outside pissing in.'

Hooverville in the US, a shanty town built by unemployed and destitute people during the Depression of the early 1930s, named after Herbert *Hoover* (1874–1964), during whose presidency such accommodation was built.

hop-o'-my-thumb a dwarf, a pygmy; the original *Hop o' my Thumb* was the central character of a fairy story by Perrault, the minute youngest child of a poor faggot-maker who through his wit and daring saves his six elder (and larger) brothers from an ogre, and who steals the ogre's ➤ SEVEN-*league boots*.

Hopalong Cassidy a limping fictional cowboy, created by the writer Clarence E. Mulford, who wearing black clothes and riding a white horse was played in a series of films (and later a television series) by the American actor William Boyd (1898–1972).

hope one of the three theological virtues.
See also ➤ BAND *of Hope*, ➤ *he that* LIVES *in hope dances to an ill tune*, ➤ LAND *of Hope and Glory*, ➤ THEOLOGY *of hope*.

Bob Hope (1903–), British-born American comedian. He often adopted the character of a cowardly incompetent, cheerfully failing to become a romantic hero, as in the series of *Road* films (1940–62).
In 1998, when erroneous reports of Bob Hope's death were marked by tributes to him in Congress, Hope was quoted as saying, 'Well, I'm still here,' a modern version of Mark Twain's 'Reports of my death have been greatly exaggerated.'

hope chest a chest containing household linen and clothing stored by a woman in preparation for her marriage.

hope deferred makes the heart sick proverbial saying, late 14th century; originally with biblical allusion.

Hope diamond a rare sapphire blue diamond, now on display in the Smithsonian institute, which was purchased by the London banker Thomas Henry *Hope* in 1830.

hope for the best and prepare for the worst proverbial saying, mid 16th century.

hope is a good breakfast but a bad supper proverbial saying, mid 17th century.

hope springs eternal proverbial saying, mid 18th century, from Pope:
> Hope springs eternal in the human breast:
> Man never Is, but always To be blest.
> — Alexander Pope *An Essay on Man* Epistle 1 (1733)

if it were not for hope, the heart would break proverbial saying, mid 13th century.

Hope Theatre on Bankside, Southwark, built in 1613 by Henslowe as a bear-garden, with a movable stage on which plays could be performed. Jonson's *Bartholomew Fair* was acted there in 1614.

hopeless cases ➤ *St* JUDE is the patron saint of hopeless cases.

Gerard Manley Hopkins (1844–89), English poet. Becoming a Jesuit in 1868, he wrote little poetry until 1876, when a shipwreck inspired him to write 'The Wreck of the Deutschland'. Like his poems 'Windhover' and 'Pied Beauty' (both 1877), it makes use of Hopkins's 'sprung rhythm' technique. His work was published posthumously as *Poems* (1918).

hops see ➤ TURKEY, *heresy, hops, and beer came into England all in one year.*

Horace (65–8 BC), Roman poet of the Augustan period. A notable satirist and literary critic, he is best known for his *Odes*, much imitated by later ages, especially by the poets of 17th-century England. In the style of earlier Greek lyric poets, they celebrate friendship, love, good wine, and the contentment of a peaceful rural life. His other works include *Satires* and *Ars Poetica*.

horde see ➤ *the* GOLDEN *Horde.*

horizon-blue a light shade of blue, the colour of the French Army uniform during and after the war of 1914–18 (translating French *bleu horizon*).

horlogion in the Orthodox Church, a liturgical book containing the offices for the canonical hours, corresponding more or less to the Western breviary.

horn in biblical and derived uses a *horn* is taken as an emblem of power and might, a means of defence or resistance.

In Christian iconography (except as in the ➤ HORNS *of Moses*), the representation of *horns* on the head of a person or supernatural being are a sign of evil.

Horns were fancifully said to be worn by a cuckold.

Recorded from Old English and of Germanic origin, the word comes from an Indo-European root shared by Latin *cornu* and Greek *keras*.

See also ➤ AMALTHEA'*s horn*, ➤ BULL *by the horns*, ➤ GATE *of horn*, ➤ *the* GOLDEN *Horn*, ➤ *make a* SPOON *or spoil a horn*.

Cape Horn the southernmost point of South America, on a Chilean island south of Tierra del Fuego. The region is notorious for its storms, and until the opening of the Panama Canal in 1914 constituted the only sea route between the Atlantic and Pacific Oceans. It was named after *Hoorn*, the birthplace of the Dutch navigator William C. Schouten who discovered it in 1616.

hornbook a former teaching aid consisting of a leaf of paper showing the alphabet, and often the ten digits and the Lord's Prayer, mounted on a wooden tablet and protected by a thin plate of horn.

Horn of Africa a peninsula of NE Africa, comprising Somalia and parts of Ethiopia, and lying between the Gulf of Aden and the Indian Ocean.

horn of plenty another name for a ➤ CORNUCOPIA.

Horner see ➤ JACK *Horner.*

hornpipe a lively dance associated with sailors, typically performed by one person; a piece of music for such a dance. The word denotes a wind instrument made of horn, played to accompany dancing.

make horns at hold the fist with two fingers extending like a pair of horns, as an insulting gesture.

on the horns of a dilemma faced with a decision involving equally unfavourable alternatives.

horns of Moses in traditional art, Moses may be represented with horns, based on a misreading of the passage describing his descent from Mount Sinai, in which the Hebrew word for 'rays of light' as surrounding his head has been mistranslated.

the horns of the altar the projections, resembling a horn, at each corner of the altar in the Jewish Temple.

horoscope in astrology, a forecast of a person's future, typically including a delineation of character and circumstances, based on the relative positions of the stars and planets at the time of that person's birth.

Horsa see ➤ HENGIST *and Horsa.*

horse the *horse*, used for riding, racing, and to carry and pull loads, is taken as a type of strength.

➤ *St* GILES and St Hippolytus, a Roman martyr of the 3rd century said to have been torn apart by wild horses, are the patron saints of horses.

See also ➤ BRAZEN *horse,* ➤ CRAZY *Horse,* ➤ DARK *horse,* ➤ DOBBY-*horse,* ➤ FLOG *a dead horse,* ➤ *a* GOOD *horse cannot be of a bad colour,* ➤ HOBBY *horse,* ➤ *horse and* HATTOCK, ➤ HORSES, ➤ *if* TWO *ride on a horse, one must ride behind,* ➤ *it is too late to shut the* STABLE *door after the horse has bolted,* ➤ *Lou* GEHRIG, ➤ *the* MAN *who is born in a stable is not a horse,* ➤ *never look a* GIFT *horse in the mouth,* ➤ *one man may* STEAL *a horse, while another may not look over a hedge,* ➤ PALE *horse,* ➤ PRZEWALSKI's *horse,* ➤ PUT *the cart before the horse,* ➤ RIDE *a-cock-horse,* ➤ SHIRE *horse,* ➤ *a* SHORT *horse is soon curried,* ➤ STALKING *horse,* ➤ STRAIGHT *from the horse's mouth,* ➤ TELL *that to the horse marines,* ➤ *there is* NOTHING *so good for the inside of a man as the outside of a horse,* ➤ THREE *things are not to be trusted; a cow's horn, a dog's tooth, and a horse's hoof,* ➤ TROJAN *horse,* ➤ WATER-*horse,* ➤ WHITE *Horse,* ➤ WOODEN *horse.*

Horses

NAME	RIDER
Arundel	Bevis of Hampton
Babieca	El Cid
Barbary	Richard II
Bayard	Rinaldo
Black Auster	Herminius
Black Bess	Dick Turpin
Black Nell	Wild Bill Hickok
Brigadore	Sir Guyon
Bucephalus	Alexander the Great
Copenhagen	Duke of Wellington
Grani	Sigurd
Incitatus	Caligula
Kantaka	Prince Gautama
Pegasus	Bellerophon; Perseus
Ronald	Lord Cardigan
Rosinante	Don Quixote
Silver	the Lone Ranger
Sorrel	William III
Traveller	Robert E. Lee
White Surrey	Richard III

horse chestnut a deciduous tree with large leaves of five leaflets, conspicuous sticky winter buds, and upright conical clusters of white, pink, or red flowers. It bears nuts (conkers) enclosed in a fleshy case. The name (which is late 16th century) translates (now obsolete) botanical Latin *Castanea equina*; its fruit is said to have been an Eastern remedy for chest diseases in horses.

Horse Guards in the UK, the mounted squadrons provided from the Household Cavalry for ceremonial duties.

horse latitudes a belt of calm air and sea occurring in both the northern and southern hemispheres between the trade winds and the westerlies.

Horse-marines a name for the 17th Lancers, two troops of whom were once employed as marines during fighting in the West Indies.

See also ➤ TELL *that to the horse marines.*

you can take a horse to water but you cannot make him drink proverbial saying, late 12th century.

horseback see ➤ *set a* BEGGAR *on horseback and he'll ride to the Devil.*

horseleech a large predatory leech of freshwater and terrestrial habitats which feeds on carrion and small invertebrates, which it swallows whole; in figurative use, a rapacious, insatiable person, sometimes with biblical allusion, as to Proverbs 30:15, 'The horseleech hath two daughters, crying Give, give.'

horsemen see ➤ *the* FOUR *Horsemen of the Apocalypse.*

horsepower an imperial unit of power equal to 550 foot-pounds per second (about 750 watts); the power of an engine measured in terms of this.

horses see also ➤ *don't* CHANGE *horses in midstream,* ➤ *drive a* COACH *and horses through,* ➤ HOME, *James, and don't spare the horses,* ➤ *if* WISHES *were horses, then beggars would ride,* ➤ *if you can't* RIDE *two horses at once. you shouldn't be in the circus,* ➤ WHITE *horses.*

horses for courses proverbial saying, late 19th century.

horseshoe a shoe for a horse formed of a narrow band of iron in the form of an extended circular arc and secured to the hoof with nails, traditionally regarded as bringing good luck.

horsiculture the commercial development of farmland for the pasturing of horses or for equestrian activities; the term is recorded from the late 1970s, and is associated with the impact of the *set-aside* policy which required farmers to leave a proportion of their cultivable land fallow.

Horst Wessel Song the official song of the Nazi Party in Germany. The tune was that of a music-hall song popular with the German army in the First World War; the words were written by *Horst Wessel* (1907–30), a member of Hitler's Storm Troops killed by political enemies and regarded as a Nazi martyr.

Horus in Egyptian mythology, a god regarded as the protector of the monarchy, and typically represented as a falcon-headed man. He assumed various aspects: in the myth of Isis and Osiris he was the posthumous son of the latter, whose murder he avenged, and in this aspect he was known to the Greeks as Harpocrates, most often represented as a chubby infant with a finger held to his mouth.

hosanna especially in biblical, Judaic, and Christian use, used to express adoration, praise, or joy. The word comes via Greek from Rabbinical Hebrew *hōšaʿnā*, abbreviation of biblical *hōšīʿā-nnā* 'save, we pray' (Psalm 118:25).

Hosanna Sunday an old name for Palm Sunday.

Hosea a Hebrew minor prophet of the 8th century ➤ BC; a book of the Bible containing his prophecies.

hospital originally, a house for the reception and entertainment of pilgrims, travellers, or strangers; any of the establishments of the ➤ KNIGHTS *Hospitallers*. Also, a charitable institution for the housing and maintenance of the needy; an asylum for the destitute, infirm, or aged (now chiefly in surviving proper names).

St Camillus of Lellis (1550–1614), founder of the Ministers of the Sick, and ➤ St JOHN *of God* are the patron saints of hospitals.

See also ➤ CHRIST'*s Hospital*.

hospital blues the uniform worn by wounded soldiers in the wars of 1914–18 and 1939–45.

Hospital Sunday the Sunday nearest to St Luke's day (18 October).

hospitaller a member of a charitable order, originally the ➤ KNIGHTS *Hospitallers*.

See also ➤ St JULIAN.

hospodar a governor of Wallachia and Moldavia under the Ottoman Porte. The word comes via Romanian from Ukrainian *hospodar*, related to Russian *gospodar'*, from *gospod'* 'lord'.

host see also ➤ *he that* RECKONS *without his host must reckon again*, ➤ LORD *of Hosts*.

host the bread (often **the Host**) consecrated in the Eucharist.

A *host* (in a monstrance) is the emblem of ➤ *St* CLARE *of Assisi*.

Recorded from Middle English, the word comes via Old French from Latin *hostia* 'victim'.

hot button a topic or issue that is highly charged emotionally or politically; the term is recorded in the US as a marketing term from the early 1970s.

hot cockles a traditional game in which one player is blindfolded and has to guess which of the others struck him or her.

hot cross bun a bun marked with a cross and containing dried fruit, traditionally eaten on ➤ GOOD *Friday*.

hot-desking the practice in an office of allocating desks to workers when they are required or on a rota system, rather than giving each worker their own desk; the usage as a working practice is recorded from the early 1990s.

hotchpot the reunion and blending together of properties for the purpose of securing equal division, especially of the property of an intestate parent. The word comes (originally as a variant of *hotchpotch*, a mixture of odds and ends) from Anglo-Norman French.

Hotspur archaic term for a rash or reckless person; first recorded and best known as, the nickname of Henry Percy (1364–1403), son of the Earl of Northumberland, who was killed in battle at Shrewsbury during a rebellion against Henry IV.

Hottentot used to refer to Khoikhoi peoples of South Africa and Namibia. The term comes from Dutch, perhaps a repetitive formula in a Nama dancing-song, transferred by Dutch sailors to the people themselves, or from German *hotteren-totteren* 'stutter' (with reference to their click language).

The word *Hottentot* is first recorded in the late

17th century and was a name applied by white Europeans to the Khoikhoi. It is now regarded as offensive with reference to people and should always be avoided in favour of *Khoikhoi* or the names of the particular peoples. The only standard use for *Hottentot* in modern use is in the names of animals and plants.

Harry Houdini (1874–1926), Hungarian-born American magician and escape artist. In the early 1900s he became famous for his ability to escape from all kinds of bonds and containers, from prison cells to aerially suspended straitjackets.

hound a dog of a breed used for hunting, especially one able to track by scent. Recorded from Old English (in the form *hund*) in the general sense of 'dog', the word is of Germanic origin, and comes from an Indo-European root shared by Greek *kuōn, kun-* 'dog'.

See also ➤ GABRIEL'*s hounds,* ➤ HARE *and hounds,* ➤ ORION'*s hound,* ➤ PHARAOH *hound,* ➤ WISH-*hounds,* ➤ *you cannot* RUN *with the hare and hunt with the hounds.*

hour see also ➤ *at the* ELEVENTH *hour,* ➤ *book of* HOURS, ➤ CANONICAL *hour,* ➤ *the* DARKEST *hour is just before dawn,* ➤ FORTY *hours,* ➤ *improve the* SHINING *hour,* ➤ PLANETARY *hour,* ➤ *their* FINEST *hour,* ➤ THREE *Hours,* ➤ *the* WITCHING *hour.*

the hour is come, but not the man proverbial saying; the earliest use found to date is in Walter Scott. In *Guy Mannering* (1815), he has 'The hour's come, and the man,' and in *The Heart of Midlothian* (1818) there is a chapter heading, 'The hour's come, but not the man.'

one hour's sleep before midnight is worth two after proverbial saying, mid 17th century.

hourglass an invertible device with two connected glass bulbs containing sand that takes an hour to pass from the upper to the lower bulb. An **hourglass figure** is one supposedly shaped like such a device; when Arthur Miller and Marilyn Monroe were married in 1956, *Variety* reportedly carried the headline, 'Egghead weds hourglass'.

houri a beautiful young woman, especially one of the virgin companions of the faithful in the Muslim Paradise. The word (recorded from the 18th century) comes through Persian from Arabic, meaning 'having eyes with a marked contrast of black and white'.

house see also ➤ *the* ANGEL *in the house,* ➤ BETTER *one house spoiled than two,* ➤ CLERK *of the House,* ➤ COUNT *out the House,* ➤ *House of* DELEGATES, ➤ HOUSES, LEADER *of the House,* ➤ LEARNING *is better than house and land,* ➤ LORETO.

House a family or family lineage, especially a noble or royal one; a dynasty.

the House informal name for several establishments; the college of Christ Church at Oxford University is known as *the House.*

In the UK, *the House* is also an informal name for the Stock Exchange, and (more recently) has been in common use for Covent Garden Opera House.

when house and land are gone and spent, then learning is most excellent proverbial saying, mid 18th century.

house church a charismatic Church independent of traditional denominations.

a house divided cannot stand proverbial saying, mid 11th century; originally from the Bible.

House of Commons in the UK, the elected chamber of Parliament.

See also ➤ FATHER *of the House of Commons.*

house of correction an institution where vagrants and minor offenders were confined and set to work.

house of God a place of religious worship, especially a church.

House of Keys in the Isle of Man, the elected chamber of Tynwald.

House of Lords in the UK, the chamber of Parliament which until 1999 was composed of hereditary and life peers and bishops; reform of the method of selecting the chamber is currently under way.

House of Representatives the lower house of the US Congress and other legislatures.

the House that Jack built a nursery accumulation of great antiquity, possibly based on an old Hebrew original, a hymn in Sepher Haggadah, beginning 'A kid my father bought for two pieces of money', 'then came the cat and ate the kid, etc.', 'then came the dog and bit the cat, etc.', ending with the Angel of Death who killed the butcher who slew the ox, etc.; and the Holy One who slew the Angel of Death. That the English version is an early one is indicated by the reference to the 'priest, all shaven and shorn'.

housecarl a member of the bodyguard of a Danish or English king or noble. Recorded from Old English (in form *hūscarl*), the word comes from Old Norse *húskarl* 'manservant', (plural) 'retinue, bodyguard'.

the Household the establishment and affairs of a royal household.

Household Cavalry in the British army, the two cavalry regiments with responsibility for guarding the monarch and royal palaces (and otherwise acting as part of the Royal Armoured Corps).

household gods gods presiding over a household, especially (in Roman History) the ➤ LARES and ➤ PENATES.

Household Troops in the British army, troops whose formal duty is to guard the sovereign.

housel former term for the administration or receiving of the Eucharist; recorded from Old English (in form *hūsl*), the word comes from Gothic *hunsl* 'sacrifice, offering'.

houses see also ➤ FOOLS *build houses and wise men live in them*, ➤ *a* PLAGUE *on all their houses*, ➤ *those who live in* GLASS *houses shouldn't throw stones.*

Houses of Parliament in the UK, the Houses of Lords and Commons regarded together, or the building where they meet (the Palace of Westminster).

housetops see ➤ PROCLAIM *from the housetops.*

housewife ➤ *St* MARTHA and St Zita, a 13th-century Luccan serving-maid, are the patron saints of housewives.

A. E. Housman (1859–1936), English poet and classical scholar. He is now chiefly remembered for the poems collected in *A Shropshire Lad* (1896), a series of nostalgic verses largely based on ballad forms.

Houston an inland port of Texas, linked to the Gulf of Mexico by the Houston Ship Canal. Since 1961 it has been a centre for space research and manned space flight, and is the site of the NASA Space Centre; when difficulties arose on the Apollo 13 space mission, 14 April 1970, the message from the astronaut James Lovell was, 'Houston, we've had a problem.'

It is named after Samuel *Houston* (1793–1863), an American politician and military leader who led the struggle to win control of Texas and make it part of the US.

Houyhnhnm the name (intended to suggest the neigh of a horse) of a fictional race of reasoning horses in Swift's *Gulliver's Travels* (1726).

John Howard (1726–90), English philanthropist and prison reformer. His tour of British prisons in 1773 culminated in two Acts of Parliament setting down sanitary standards; his work *The State of Prisons in England and Wales* (1777) gave further impetus to the movement for improvements in prisons, and the **Howard League for Penal Reform** (established 1844) is named after him.

Leslie Howard (1893–1943), English actor. He was best known for his roles as the archetypal English gentleman in films such as *The Scarlet Pimpernel* (1935) and *Pygmalion* (1938). He died returning from Lisbon to London when his plane was shot down by German aircraft.

Howe see also ➤ JACKY *Howe.*

Elias Howe (1819–67), American inventor. In 1846 he patented the first sewing machine. Its principles were adapted by Isaac Merrit Singer and others in violation of Howe's patent rights, and it took a seven-year litigation battle to secure the royalties.

according to Hoyle according to plan or the rules. The expression comes (in the early 20th century) from Edmond *Hoyle* (1672–1769), English writer on card games.

Hrimfaxi in Scandinavian mythology, the name, 'Rime-mane', of the horse of the night.

Hubbard see ➤ OLD *Mother Hubbard.*

Edwin Hubble (1889–1953), American astronomer. He studied galaxies and devised a classification scheme for them. In 1929 he proposed what is now known as ➤ HUBBLE*'s law* with its constant of proportionality (➤ HUBBLE*'s constant*).

Hubble Space Telescope an orbiting astronomical observatory launched in 1990. The telescope's fine high-resolution images are far better than can be obtained from the earth's surface.

Hubble's constant the ratio of the speed of recession of a galaxy (due to the expansion of the universe) to its distance from the observer. The reciprocal of the constant is called *Hubble time* and represents the length of time for which the universe has been expanding, and hence the age of the universe.

Hubble's law a law stating that the red shifts in the spectra of distant galaxies (and hence their speeds of recession) are proportional to their distance.

St Hubert (d. 727), bishop of Maastricht and Liège; he is said to have converted to Christianity when, hunting on a Good Friday, he found himself confronted by a stag with a crucifix in its antlers (a similar story is told of ➤ *St* EUSTACE). He is the patron of huntsmen, and his supposed hunting-horn is in the Wallace Collection.

   □ **FEAST DAY** His feast day is 30 May, and his translation 3 November.

hubris in Greek tragedy, excessive pride towards or defiance of the gods, leading to ➤ NEMESIS; in extended usage, excessive pride or self-confidence.

Huckleberry see ➤ *Huckleberry* FINN.

hudibrastic in the metre or manner of *Hudibras*, a mock-heroic satirical poem by Samuel Butler, published 1663–78.

Henry Hudson (*c.*1565–1611), English explorer. He discovered the North American bay, river, and strait which bear his name. In 1610 he attempted to winter in Hudson Bay, but his crew mutinied and set Hudson and a few companions adrift, never to be seen again.

Jeffrey Hudson (1619–82), dwarf, who was presented to Charles I and Henrietta Maria by the Duke of Buckingham; he remained in the royal service, and followed the queen to France in 1644. He appears with Henrietta Maria in a portrait of her by Van Dyke.

Hudson River school a group of 18th-century American painters who rejected the tradition of aristocratic portraiture in favour of romantic depictions of the American landscape.

Hudson's Bay blanket a durable woollen blanket, typically with a coloured border, originally sold by the ➤ HUDSON's *Bay Company* and frequently used as material for coats.

Hudson's Bay Company a British colonial trading company set up in 1670 and granted all lands draining into Hudson Bay for purposes of commercial exploitation, principally trade in fur. The company amalgamated with the rival North-West Company

in 1821 and handed over control to the new Canadian government in 1870; it is now a Canadian retail and wholesale operation.

hue and cry a loud cry calling for the pursuit and capture of a criminal. In former English law, the cry had to be raised by the inhabitants of a hundred in which a robbery had been committed, if they were not to become liable for the damages suffered by the victim.

hug see ➤ CORNISH *hug*.

Hugh see also ➤ LADY *Margaret Hall for ladies*.

Little St Hugh (d. 1255), a boy of nine, also known as **Hugh of Lincoln**, whose murdered body was discovered in a well; the rumour spread that he had been the victim of ritual murder carried out by the Jewish community in Lincoln, and as a result 19 Jews were executed. The story is recounted in Chaucer's 'Prioress's Tale', and represents a popular form of anti-Semitic belief of the period.

   □ **FEAST DAY** His feast day is 27 August.

St Hugh of Cluny (1024–1109), abbot of ➤ CLUNY; a monk at Cluny from about *c.*1040, he became abbot in 1049, and it was during the period of his rule that the great expansion of Cluny took place.

   □ **FEAST DAY** His feast day is 29 April.

St Hugh of Lincoln (*c.*1140–1200), Carthusian monk and bishop, noted for his scholarship, who revived the learning of the Lincoln schools. He was proverbial for his justice, as for his care for the sick and oppressed; he was also the friend and critic of three Angevin kings, Henry II, Richard, and John.

   □ **EMBLEM** He is sometimes shown with a tame swan (from his manor at Stow), and with a chalice ornamented with the child Jesus.

   □ **FEAST DAY** His feast day is 17 November and his translation, 6 October.

Howard Hughes (1905–76), American industrialist, film producer, and aviator. He made his fortune through the Hughes Tool Company, made his debut as a film director in 1926, and from 1935 to 1938 broke many world aviation records. For the last twenty-five years of his life he lived as a recluse.

   The Howard Hughes of pop rarely goes out in public.
   — *Newsweek* 6 September 1993

Huguenot a French Protestant of the 16th–17th centuries. Largely Calvinist, the Huguenots suffered severe persecution at the hands of the Catholic majority, and many thousands emigrated from France.

   The name is French, an alteration (by association

with the name of a Geneva burgomaster, Besançon *Hugues*) of *eiguenot*, from Dutch *eedgenot*, from Swiss German *Eidgenoss* 'confederate', from *Eid* 'oath' + *Genoss* 'associate'.

huia an extinct New Zealand wattlebird with glossy black plumage, the female having a much longer and more curved bill than the male. The tail feathers were formerly prized by Maoris, and the last huia was seen in 1907.

hula a dance performed by Hawaiian women, characterized by six basic steps, undulating hips, and gestures symbolizing or imitating natural phenomena or historical or mythological subjects.

Hulda in Germanic mythology, the goddess of marriage and fertility; an aspect of the triple mother goddess who may also be personified as ➤ BERCHTA and ➤ *Mother* HOLLE, the ancient goddess of death.

the Incredible Hulk a character created in Marvel Comics in 1962; a green-skinned monster into which, because of a laboratory accident which has altered his body chemistry, a mild-mannered research scientist metamorphoses when enraged.

> And what about that green coat of his . . . He looks like the Incredible Hulk's little boy!
> — J. Sullivan *Only Fools and Horses* (BBC TV camera script, 1989)

the hulks old ships stripped of fittings and permanently moored, which during the 18th and 19th centuries were used as prisons; in Dickens's David *Copperfield* (1861), the convict Magwitch has escaped from the hulks.

from Hell, Hull, and Halifax, Good Lord, deliver us proverbial saying, late 16th century.

Monsieur Hulot the comically inept character introduced in the films of ➤ *Jacques* TATI; *Monsieur Hulot* is particularly characterized by his walk, tilted forward on his toes and taking long strides, and by the raincoat which is too short for him and the umbrella which he always carries.

huma a mythical bird, similar to the phoenix, supposed to bring luck to any person over whom it hovers on its restless flights.

human see also ➤ ALL *human life is there*, ➤ MILK *of human kindness*, ➤ *to* ERR *is human, to forgive divine*, ➤ UNIVERSAL *Declaration of Human Rights*.

Human Genome Project an international project to study the entire genetic material of a human being.

human shield a person or group of people held near a potential target to deter attack; the term was used particularly of western hostages in Iraq during the Gulf War.

Humanae Vitae encyclical issued by Pope Paul VI in 1968, condemning artificial means of birth control.

humanism an outlook or system of thought attaching prime importance to human rather than divine or supernatural matters. Humanist beliefs stress the potential value and goodness of human beings, emphasize common human needs, and seek solely rational ways of solving human problems.

Humanism (often with capital initial) denotes a Renaissance cultural movement which turned away from medieval scholasticism and revived interest in ancient Greek and Roman thought.

humanitarian originally, a person believing in the humanity but not the divinity of Christ; later, a person concerned with human welfare.

humanities learning or literature concerned with human culture, especially literature, history, art, music, and philosophy.

Humber in Geoffrey of Monmouth's chronicle, name of a king of the Huns said to have invaded Britain about 1000 BC.

Humbert Humbert the stepfather of ➤ LOLITA, in Nabokov's novel, who has an affair with his sexually precocious stepdaughter.

> A size 7 poured into her size 5 Calvins, . . . Richard Avedon's camera ogled her like an invisible Humbert Humbert.
> — *Entertainment Weekly* 23 June 1995

humble see ➤ EAT *humble pie*.

Hume see also ➤ ADVERSITY *Hume*.

David Hume (1711–76), Scottish philosopher, economist, and historian. He rejected the possibility of certainty in knowledge and claimed that all the data of reason stem from experience. In economics he attacked mercantilism and anticipated the views of Adam Smith.

Humint covert intelligence-gathering by agents or others.

humours in medieval science and medicine, the four chief fluids of the body, ➤ BLOOD, ➤ PHLEGM, *yellow bile* (➤ CHOLER), and ➤ BLACK *bile* (*melancholy*), that were thought to determine a person's physical and mental qualities by the relative proportions in which they were present. Also called ➤ CAR-DINAL *humours.*

Humphrey see also ➤ DINE *with Duke Humphrey,* ➤ GOOD *Duke Humphrey.*

Sir Humphrey Appleby in the television series *Yes Minister* (1980–2) and *Yes Prime Minister* (1986–88) by Jonathan Lynn and Antony Jay, the subtle Permanent Secretary (and ultimately Cabinet Secretary) whose Civil Service wiles usually thwart the political initiatives of the Minister (and later Prime Minister) Jim Hacker, to whom he is nominally responsible.

Humpty-Dumpty the egg-like nursery-rhyme character who fell off a wall and could not be put together again; the rhyme was originally a riddle to which the answer was 'egg', and is recorded from the first half of the 19th century.

The detective story writer P. D. James once explained her long-term fascination with her chosen genre by saying, 'I had an interest in death from an early age. It fascinated me. When I heard "Humpty Dumpty sat on a wall,' I thought, 'Did he fall or was he pushed?" '

Humpty-Dumpty is a character in Carroll's *Through the Looking-Glass* (1872), who says to Alice, 'When *I* use a word…it means just what I choose it to mean—neither more nor less.'

Hun a member of a warlike Asiatic nomadic people who invaded and ravaged Europe in the 4th–5th centuries; their famous leader was ➤ ATTILA.

In extended usage, *Hun* denotes a reckless or uncivilized destroyer of something; it is also (especially in military contexts during the First and Second World Wars) a derogatory term for a German.

hundred in Anglo-Saxon England, a *hundred* was a subdivision of a county or shire, having its own court.

See also ➤ CHILTERN *Hundreds,* ➤ CONN *of the Hundred Battles.*

Hundred Days the period of the restoration of Napoleon Bonaparte, after his escape from Elba, ending with his abdication on 22 June 1815; the immediate source was a speech delivered by Louis de Chabrol de Volvic, prefect of Paris, to Louis XVIII in 1815.

hundred-eyed in Greek mythology, the epithet of ➤ ARGUS.

Hundred Flowers a period of debate in China 1956–7, when, under the slogan 'Let a hundred flowers bloom and a hundred schools of thought contend', citizens were invited to voice their opinions of the communist regime. It was forcibly ended after social unrest and fierce criticism of the government, with those who had voiced their opinions being prosecuted.

hundred-handed in Greek mythology, the epithet of three sons of Uranus, the giant ➤ BRIAREUS and his brothers.

Hundred Years War a war between France and England, conventionally dated 1337–1453.

The war consisted of a series of conflicts in which successive English kings attempted to dominate France, and began when Edward III claimed the throne of France following the death of the last Capetian king. Despite an early string of English military successes, most notably Crécy and Poitiers, the House of Valois retained its position, and in the reign of Edward's son, Richard II, hostilities ceased almost completely. In 1415 England, under Henry V, delivered a crushing victory at Agincourt and occupied much of northern France, but once again proved unable to consolidate the advantage. Under the regency of Henry VI, control of conquered territory was gradually lost to French forces, revitalized in the first instance by Joan of Arc. With the exception of Calais, all English conquests had been lost by 1453.

hundredth see ➤ OLD *Hundredth.*

hundredweight a unit of weight equal to one twentieth of an imperial or metric ton.

Hungary see ➤ *St* ELIZABETH *of Hungary.*

hunger drives the wolf out of the wood proverbial saying, late 15th century.

hunger is the best sauce proverbial saying, early 16th century.

hunger march a march undertaken by a group of people in protest against unemployment or poverty, especially any of those by unemployed workers in Britain during the 1920s and 1930s.

Hungerford a country town in Berkshire, England, where in August 1987 a survivalist named Michael Ryan massacred fourteen people in an episode of ➤ SPREE *killing* before committing suicide; the event is sometimes taken as the type of this kind of massacre.

> The psychopathic gunmen—what he called the 'Hungerford element'—. . . would not give up their activities whatever the political solution.
> — Antony Beevor *Inside the British Army* (1990)

hungry forties the decade beginning in 1840, characterized in the British Isles by much poverty and unemployment.

a hungry man is an angry man proverbial saying, mid 17th century.

hunt see also ➤ ORATOR *Hunt.*

hunt the pursuit and killing of a wild animal for sport or food, especially the pursuit on horseback of a fox or deer, using hounds; an association of people who meet regularly to hunt, especially with hounds. The question of whether hunting should be made illegal is currently a matter of political debate in Britain.

In bell-ringing, *hunt* denotes the moving of the place of a bell in a simple progression. This sense is probably based on the idea of the bells pursuing one another.

hunt the slipper a parlour game in which all the players but one sit in a ring and pass a slipper covertly from one to another, the remaining player standing in the middle and trying to guess who has it.

like Hunt's dog that will neither go to church nor stay at home proverbial saying, mid 17th century.

Hunter see also ➤ HERNE *the Hunter,* ➤ MIGHTY *hunter.*

John Hunter (1728–93), Scottish anatomist, regarded as a founder of scientific surgery. He also made valuable investigations in pathology, physiology, dentistry, and biology. His large museum collection of comparative anatomy was eventually passed to the Royal College of Surgeons in London.

hunter-gatherer a member of a nomadic people who live chiefly by hunting and fishing, and harvesting wild food. All humans probably lived in this way before the Neolithic period, but now only a few groups remain.

hunter's moon the first full moon after a harvest moon.

hunting see ➤ HAPPY *hunting ground.*

hunting pink scarlet as worn by foxhunters; a scarlet riding-coat or the material from which it is made. It has been suggested that huntsmen took the colour because Henry II declared foxhunting a royal sport.

Countess of Huntingdon (1707–91), Selena Hastings, English religious leader. A follower of the evangelical preacher George Whitefield, she was instrumental in introducing Methodism to the upper classes and established many chapels and a training college for ministers.

Huntingdonian a member of the Calvinistic Methodist sect founded by Selina, Countess of *Huntingdon* (1707–91).

Huntington Beach a city on the Pacific coast, to the south of Long Beach, in southern California, which is noted as a surfing locality.

huntsman ➤ *St* EUSTACE and ➤ *St* HUBERT are the patron saints of huntsmen.

See also ➤ WILD *Huntsman.*

Huon of Bordeaux hero of a French 13th-century *chanson de geste,* who kills the son of Charlemagne in an affray, and to redeem his life has to make a journey to Babylon; he is assisted by the magic powers of ➤ OBERON.

hurdy-gurdy a musical instrument with a droning sound played by turning a handle, which is typically attached to a rosined wheel sounding a series of drone strings, with keys worked by the left hand.

Hurlothrumbo a burlesque by Samuel Johnson (1691–1773), a Manchester dancing master, which had such a popular success when produced at the Haymarket that a **Hurlothrumbo Society** was formed, and the words **mere Hurlothrumbo** briefly became a catchphrase.

hurricane a storm with a violent wind, in particular a tropical cyclone in the Caribbean. The word comes from Spanish *huracán,* probably from Taino *hurakán* 'god of the storm' (Taino, now extinct, was a Caribbean language of the Arawakan group).

hurry no man's cattle proverbial saying, early 19th century.

hurt see ➤ *don't* CRY *before you're hurt.*

husband a married man considered in relation to his wife. The word is late Old English, in the senses 'male head of a household' and 'manager, steward', from Old Norse *húsbóndi* 'master of a house', from *hús* 'house' + *bóndi* 'occupier and tiller of the soil'; the original sense of the verb 'to husband' was 'till, cultivate'.

See also ➤ *a* DEAF *husband and a blind wife are always a happy couple.*

ship's husband an agent appointed by a ship's owners to see that a ship in port is well provided in all respects.

the husband is always the last to know proverbial saying, early 17th century.

husbandmen ➤ *St* GEORGE is the patron saint of husbandmen.

husbandry the care, cultivation, and breeding of crops and animals; management and conservation of resources. The word comes (in Middle English) from *husband* in the obsolete sense of 'farmer'.

hush-hush especially of an official plan or project, highly secret or confidential. The term is first recorded during the First World War, the first reference being (in 1916) to 'hush-hush Tanks'.

John Huss (*c.*1372–1415), Bohemian religious reformer. A rector of Prague University, he supported the views of Wyclif, attacked ecclesiastical abuses, and was excommunicated in 1411. He was later tried and burnt at the stake; on seeing an aged peasant bringing a bundle of twigs to throw on the pile, he exclaimed '*O sancta simplicitas!* [O holy simplicity!].'

Hussite a member or follower of the religious movement begun by John Huss. After Huss's execution the Hussites took up arms against the Holy Roman Empire and demanded a set of reforms that anticipated the Reformation. Most of the demands were granted (1436), and a Church was established that remained independent of the Roman Catholic Church until 1620. An early Protestant group that arose among the Hussites, the Bohemian Brethren, is thought to have formed the basis of the Moravian Church.

hussy an impudent or immoral girl or woman; the original late Middle English sense was 'housewife', of which the word is a contraction.

hustings a meeting at which candidates in an election address potential voters. In late Old English, *husting* meant 'deliberative assembly, council'; the word came from Old Norse *húthing* 'household assembly held by a leader', from *hús* 'house' + *thing*

'assembly, parliament'. In Middle English, *hustings* was applied to the highest court of the City of London, presided over by the Recorder of London. Subsequently it denoted the platform in the Guildhall where the Lord Mayor and aldermen presided, and (early 18th century) a temporary platform on which parliamentary candidates were nominated; hence the sense 'electoral proceedings'.

Hutchinsonian[1] a follower of Mrs Anne *Hutchinson* (1591–1643), who emigrated from England to Massachusetts, where she founded an Antinomian sect, was banished from the colony, and eventually massacred by Indians at Hell Gate, New York county, with all but one of her family.

Hutchinsonian[2] a follower of John *Hutchinson* (1674–1737), whose chief work, *Moses's Principia* (1724), maintained that Hebrew was the primitive language of mankind and the key to all knowledge. It was written as an attack on Isaac Newton's *Principia*, and is thought to have influenced Smart.

Hutterite a member of either an Anabaptist Christian sect established in Moravia in the early 16th century, or a North American community holding similar beliefs and practising a very old-fashioned communal way of life. The name comes from Jacob *Hutter* (d. 1536), a Moravian Anabaptist.

James Hutton (1726–97), Scottish geologist, whose description of the processes that have shaped the surface of the earth, although controversial at the time, is now accepted as showing that it is very much older than had previously been believed.

Thomas Henry Huxley (1825–95), English biologist. A surgeon and leading supporter of Darwinism, he coined the word ➤ AGNOSTIC to describe his own beliefs.

Christiaan Huygens (1629–95), Dutch physicist, mathematician, and astronomer. His wave theory of light enabled him to explain reflection and refraction. He also patented a pendulum clock, improved the lenses of his telescope, discovered a satellite of Saturn, and recognized the nature of Saturn's rings, which had eluded Galileo.

Hy Brasil in Irish mythology, the name of a magical island situated off the west coast of Ireland.

hyacinth a bulbous plant of the lily family, native to western Asia, with strap-like leaves and a compact spike of bell-shaped fragrant flowers, which are sometimes used in perfumery; the flower is supposed to have sprung from the blood of ➤ HYACINTHUS.

Hyacinthus a beautiful boy whom the god Apollo loved but killed accidentally with a discus. From his blood Apollo caused the hyacinth to spring up.

Hyades in Greek mythology, the daughters of Atlas and sisters of the Pleiades who nursed the infant Dionysus; as a reward, they were placed as stars in the head of the constellation Taurus. In another version of the story, they were changed into stars by Zeus out of compassion for their bitter mourning for their brother Hyas.

The name of the constellation comes from Greek *Huades*, by folk etymology from *huein* 'to rain' (in reference to their weeping), but perhaps from *hus* 'pig', the Latin name of the constellation being *Suculae* 'little pigs'.

Hyblean sweet, mellifluous; from the name of *Hybla*, a town in Sicily celebrated for the honey produced on the neighbouring hills.

Mr Hyde the evil personality assumed by ➤ *Dr* JEKYLL in R. L. Stevenson's story 'Strange Case of Dr Jekyll and Mr Hyde' (1886).

> Mike began to go wrong . . . reawakening a kind of Mr. Hyde who'd slumbered peacefully within him during the good years.
> — *New York Magazine* 23 June 1997

Hyde Park the largest British royal park, in west central London, between Bayswater Road and Kensington Road. It contains the Serpentine, Marble Arch, the Albert Memorial, and Speakers' Corner.

Hydra in Greek mythology, a many-headed snake whose heads grew again as they were cut off, killed by ➤ HERCULES as the second of his Labours; in figurative usage, a thing which is hard to overcome or resist because of its pervasive or enduring quality or its many aspects.

In astronomy, *Hydra* is the name of the largest constellation (the Water Snake or Sea Monster), said to represent the creature killed by Hercules. Its few bright stars are close to the celestial equator.

hyena a doglike African mammal with forelimbs that are longer than the hindlimbs and an erect mane, noted as a scavenger but also an effective hunter. The expression **laugh like a hyena**, which has become proverbial, refers to its characteristic cry, and it may also be taken as a type of contemptible and repellent creature.

Recorded from Middle English, the word comes via Latin from Greek *huaina*, feminine of *hus* 'pig'; the transference of the term probably being because the animal's mane was thought to resemble a hog's bristles.

Hygeia in Greek mythology, the goddess of health, daughter of Asclepius.

Hyksos a people of mixed Semitic and Asian descent who invaded Egypt and settled in the Nile delta c.1640 BC. They formed the 15th and 16th dynasties of Egypt and ruled a large part of the country until driven out c.1532 BC.

The name comes from Greek *Huksōs* (interpreted by Manetho as 'shepherd kings' or 'captive shepherds'), from Egyptian *heqa khoswe* 'foreign rulers'.

Hylas in Greek mythology, a king's son taken as his companion on the expedition of the Argonauts by Hercules; he was drowned when a water-nymph who had fallen in love with him drew him into her fountain.

hyleg in astrology, the giver of life in a nativity. Recorded from the early 17th century, the word comes from Persian *haylāj* 'celestial indicator of the length of a newborn child's life'.

Hymen originally a cry (*Hymen Hymeniae*) used at ancient Greek weddings, and understood (rightly or wrongly) as an invocation of a handsome young man of that name who had been happily married.

Mount Hymettus a mountain in Attica, famous in ancient times for its honey and marble.

hymn a religious song or poem, typically of praise to God or a god. Recorded from Old English, the word comes via Latin from Greek *humnos* 'ode or song in praise of a god or hero', used in the Septuagint to translate various Hebrew words, and hence in the New Testament and other Christian writings.

See also ➤ *the* ANGELIC *Hymn*, ➤ BATTLE *Hymn of the Republic*, ➤ SERAPHIC *Hymn*.

hyoscine a poisonous plant alkaloid used as an antiemetic in motion sickness and as a preoperative medication for examination of the eye. It became notorious as the poison used by Crippen.

Hypatia (*c*.370–415), Greek philosopher, astronomer, and mathematician. Head of the Neoplatonist school at Alexandria, she wrote several learned treatises as well as devising inventions such as an astrolabe. She was murdered by a Christian mob opposed to her Neoplatonist philosophy.

Hyperborean in Greek mythology, a member of a race worshipping Apollo and living in a land of sunshine and plenty beyond the north wind.

Hyperion in Greek mythology, one of the Titans, father of the sun, moon, and dawn. In Shakespeare's *Hamlet*, Hamlet uses his name as the type of a glorious and handsome king when comparing his murdered father to his usurping uncle, 'So excellent a king: that was, to this, Hyperion to a satyr.'

In Astronomy, *Hyperion* is the name of a satellite of Saturn, the sixteenth closest to the planet, discovered in 1848 and having an irregular shape.

Hypermnestra in Greek mythology, one of the ▶ DANAIDS, the only one who did not murder her husband on their wedding night.

hypnale a snake whose bite was supposed to induce a fatal sleep.

Hypnos in Greek mythology, the god of sleep, son of Nyx (Night).

hypnosis the induction of a state of consciousness in which a person apparently loses the power of voluntary action and is highly responsive to suggestion or direction. Its use in therapy, typically to recover suppressed memories or to allow modification of behaviour by suggestion, has been revived but is still controversial.

hypocrisy the practice of claiming to have higher standards or beliefs than is the case. The word comes (in Middle English, via Old French and ecclesiastical Latin) from Greek *hupokrisis* 'acting of a theatrical part'.

hyponym a word whose meaning implies or is included in that of another (e.g. *scarlet* and *tulip*, in relation to *red* and *flower* respectively).

hypostatic union in Christian theology, the combination of divine and human natures in the single person of Christ.

hypothec in the law of Scotland, the Channel Islands, and ancient Rome: a creditor's right established over a debtor's property that continues in the debtor's possession.

Hyrcanian of or pertaining to Hyrcania, an ancient region bordering the Caspian Sea which was noted for its wildness; in Shakespeare's *Macbeth*, the 'Hyrcan tiger' is cited as a type of savagery.

hyssop in biblical use, a wild shrub of uncertain identity whose twigs were used for sprinkling in ancient Jewish rites of purification.

hysterica passio hysteria; the phrase is Latin for 'hysteric passion', and is recorded from the early 17th century.

hysteron proteron a figure of speech in which what should come last is put first, i.e. an inversion of the natural order, for example '*I die! I faint! I fail!*'.

I the ninth letter of the modern English alphabet, representing the Semitic consonant *yod*, which was adopted by Greek as *iota*, representing a vowel. In the 17th century a differentiation was made in the Roman alphabet, the consonant being represented by J, j (in its origin merely a variant form of I, i in certain positions), and the vowel by I, i.

See also ➤ DOT *the i's and cross the t's*, ➤ *I am His Highness's* DOG *at Kew*

I Ching an ancient Chinese manual of divination based on eight symbolic trigrams and sixty-four hexagrams, interpreted in terms of the principles of yin and yang. It was included as one of the 'five classics' of Confucianism. Its English name is *Book of Changes*, a translation of the original Chinese *yijing*.

I'm all right, Jack expressing selfish complacency and unconcern for others; recorded from the early 20th century, originally in nautical use.

Iago in Shakespeare's *Othello* (1602–4), the Machiavellian villain who as an apparently loyal subordinate so poisons ➤ OTHELLO's mind that he kills his innocent wife and attempts to have her supposed lover murdered. Allusions to *Iago* refer to his single-minded desire for negativism and destruction, as well as to the malice and innuendo with which he achieves his ends.

iambus a metrical foot consisting of one short (or unstressed) syllable followed by one long (or stressed) syllable. The word, which is Latin, comes from Greek *iambos* 'iambus, lampoon', from *iaptein* 'attack verbally' (because the iambic trimeter was first used by Greek satirists).

Iapetus in Greek mythology, one of the Titans, son of Gaia and Uranus, and brother of Atlas; by the Renaissance writers he was sometimes identified with ➤ JAPHETH, son of Noah.

Iberian peninsula the extreme SW peninsula of Europe, containing present-day Spain and Portugal. It was colonized by Carthage until the third Punic War (149–146 BC), after which it came increasingly under Roman influence. It was invaded by the Visigoths in the 4th–5th centuries AD and by the Moors in the 8th century. The name comes from *Iberia*, the ancient name of the peninsula (in Latin, literally 'the country of the *Iberes*', from Greek *Ibēres* 'Spaniards').

ibis a large wading bird with a long downcurved bill, long neck, and long legs, in Egyptian mythology, associated particularly with the god ➤ THOTH.

See also ➤ SACRED *ibis*.

Iblis in Muslim belief, the Devil; the name means one who has nothing to expect from the mercy of God.

See also ➤ EBLIS.

Henrik Ibsen (1828–1906), Norwegian dramatist. He is is credited with being the first major dramatist to write tragedy about ordinary people in prose. Ibsen's later works, such as *The Master Builder* (1892), deal increasingly with the forces of the unconscious and were admired by Sigmund Freud.

Icaria an ideal republic described in a work (*Voyage en Icarie*, 1840) by the French communist Etienne Cabet (1788–1856), afterwards taken as the name of several communistic settlements, established by Cabet at Nauvoo and elsewhere in the US.

Icarian Sea an old name for the Aegean Sea, into which ➤ ICARUS fell to his death.

Icarius in Greek mythology, an inhabitant of Attica who entertained the god Dionysus and received from him the gift of wine. He gave some to his neighbours who, feeling the effects, assumed that he had poisoned them, and killed him.

Icarius was also the name of the father of ➤ PENELOPE.

Icarus in Greek mythology, the son of ➤ DAEDALUS, who escaped from Crete using wings made by his father but was killed when he flew too near the sun and the wax attaching his wings melted so that he fell into the sea, and was drowned. The fall of

Icarus was the subject of a painting by Pieter Bruegel the Elder (*c.*1525–69), which in turn was the subject of Auden's poem 'Musée des Beaux Arts' (1940).

Icarus is used allusively to denote someone who is over-ambitious in their aspirations.

> He was Icarus now, and on the very verge of challenging gravity, or God, depending how one looked at it.
>
> — Jenny Diski *Happily Ever After* (1991)

ice see also ➤ *the* RICH *man has his ice in the summer and the poor man gets his in the winter.*

Ice Age the series of glacial episodes during the Pleistocene period.

ice saints in the Netherlands and German-speaking regions of Europe, a name for saints whose days fall during the cold period of the ➤ BLACKTHORN *winter* in early May.

iceberg a large floating mass of ice detached from a glacier or ice sheet and carried out to sea; the loss of the ➤ TITANIC was due to the ship's striking an iceberg.

See also ➤ TIP *of the iceberg.*

Iceland an island country in the North Atlantic, lying just south of the Arctic Circle, settled by Norse colonists in the 9th century; Icelandic prose sagas written about the early settlers and their descendants form a substantial part of Old Norse literature, and many of the Norse court poets of the 10th and 11th centuries were Icelanders by birth.

See also ➤ SNAKES *in Iceland.*

iceman a name for a prehistoric human or hominid, the frozen remains of whom are discovered preserved in (especially) glacial ice; the term has been particularly associated with the body of a man discovered in 1991 in the mountains of the Tyrol on the Italo-Austrian border.

The first newspaper reports suggested that it was the body of a medieval man; initial archaeological views selected the Bronze Age. However, carbon dating, and the analysis of skin and bone samples, soon made it clear that *Iceman* came from a much earlier period, perhaps as early as 3300 BC.

Iceni a tribe of ancient Britons inhabiting an area of SE England in present-day Norfolk and Suffolk. Their queen, ➤ BOUDICCA, led an unsuccessful rebellion against the Romans in AD 60.

Ich dien German, meaning 'I serve'; the motto of the Prince of Wales, adopted with the crest of ostrich feathers after the battle of Crécy (1346), from

John of Luxembourg, King of Bohemia, who was killed in the battle.

The motto is spelt *ich diene* on the tomb of the Black Prince, Edward Prince of Wales, at the time of his burial at Canterbury in 1376.

Ichabod in the Bible, the name given by ➤ ELI's daughter-in-law to her son, used as an expression of regret, in allusion to 1 Samuel (she named the child Ichabod, saying, 'the glory is departed from Israel'), in the account of the capture of the ➤ ARK *of the Covenant* of God by the Philistines.

ichneumon another name for the Egyptian mongoose, venerated in ancient Egypt because it destroyed the eggs of crocodiles. The name comes via Latin from Greek *ikhneumōn* 'tracker'.

ichor in Greek mythology, the fluid which flows like blood in the veins of the gods.

Ichthus Latin transliteration of Greek for 'fish', which in its Greek form is an acrostic standing for 'Jesus Christ, Son of God, Saviour'.

Icknield Way an ancient pre-Roman track which crosses England in a wide curve from Wiltshire to Norfolk.

icon a painting of Christ or another holy figure, typically in a traditional style on wood, venerated and used as an aid to devotion in the Byzantine and other Eastern Churches.

In computing, an *icon* is a symbol or graphic representation on a VDU screen of a program, option, or window, especially one of several for selection.

The word is recorded from the mid 16th century in the sense 'simile' and from the late 16th century in the sense 'likeness, image' (see ➤ EIKON *Basilike*); it comes via Latin from Greek *eikōn* 'likeness, image'. Current senses date from the mid 19th century onwards.

iconoclast a destroyer of images used in religious worship, in particular, a supporter of the 8th- and 9th-century movement in the Byzantine Church which sought to abolish the veneration of icons and other religious images. The word is recorded from the mid 17th century, and comes via medieval Latin from ecclesiastical Greek *eikonoklastēs*, from *eikōn* 'likeness' + *klan* 'to break'. The title of Milton's *Eikonoklastes* (1649) can be seen as an early use.

In extended use, the word denotes someone who attacks cherished beliefs or institutions.

Ictinus (5th century BC), Greek architect. He is said to have designed the Parthenon in Athens with the architect ➤ CALLICRATES and the sculptor ➤ PHIDIAS between 448 and 437 BC.

id the part of the mind in which innate instinctive impulses and primary processes are manifest. The word comes from Latin (literally, 'that'), translating German *es*. It was first used in this sense by Freud, following use in a similar sense by his contemporary, Georg Groddeck.

Ida a mountain in central Crete, the highest peak in the island associated in classical times with the god Zeus, who is said in some legends to have been born in a cave there.

Ida was also the name of a range of mountains in southern Phrygia where Paris of Troy was exposed as a child, in an attempt to avert the destruction he was prophesied to bring on Troy; he was brought up by shepherds there.

In astronomy, *Ida* is the name of asteroid 243, which is 52 km long and has a tiny moon (Dactyl).

See also ➤ *Idaean* DACTYLS.

Idalian of or belonging to the ancient town of *Idalium* in Cyprus, where the goddess Aphrodite was worshipped.

idea see ➤ *the* YOUNG *idea*.

ideal see ➤ BEAU *ideal*.

ideal commonwealth an imaginary state, as conceived by various philosophical writers, especially in the 16th and 17th centuries.

ideal gas in chemistry, a hypothetical gas whose molecules occupy negligible space and have no interactions, and which consequently obeys the gas laws exactly.

idealism in philosophy, any of various systems of thought in which the objects of knowledge are held to be in some way dependent on the activity of mind.

identikit a trademark name for a picture of a person, especially one sought by the police, reconstructed from typical facial features according to witnesses' descriptions.

ides in the ancient Roman calendar, a day falling roughly in the middle of each month (the 15th day of March, May, July, and October, and the 13th of other months) from which other dates were calculated.

See also ➤ CALENDS, ➤ NONES.

beware the Ides of March according to Plutarch (and used in Shakespeare's *Julius Caesar*) a warning given by a soothsayer to Julius Caesar that he would be in great danger on the Ides of March. When the day arrived, Caesar, meeting the fortune-teller on his way to the senate, said to him, 'The Ides of March are come,' to which the reply was, 'Yes, they are come, but they are not past.'

idle see ➤ *the* DEVIL *finds work for idle hands to do*.

an idle brain is the devil's workshop proverbial saying, early 17th century.

idle people have the least leisure proverbial saying, late 17th century.

idleness see ➤ *the* BREAD *of idleness*.

idleness is the root of all evil proverbial saying, early 15th century.

Ido an artificial universal language developed from Esperanto; the name is recorded from the early 19th century, from Ido, literally 'offspring'.

idol an image or representation of a god used as an object of worship; in extended usage, a person or thing that is greatly admired, loved, or revered. Recorded from Middle English, the word comes via Old French from Latin *idolum* 'image, form', used in ecclesiastical Latin in the sense 'idol', ultimately from Greek *eidos* 'form, shape'.

idols of the tribe, cave, market, and theatre four classes of fallacies referred by Bacon (1620) respectively to limitations of human mind, prejudices of idiosyncrasy, influence of words, philosophical and logical prepossessions.

Idomeneus in Greek mythology, king of Crete, son of Deucalion and descendant of Minos. He was forced to kill his son after vowing to sacrifice the first living thing that he met on his return from the Trojan war.

Idris[1] in Welsh mythology, a giant living on the mountain ridge of **Cader Idris** in Snowdonia (the name means, literally, 'Chair of Idris').

Idris[2] in Islamic tradition, a prophet, mentioned in the Koran; he is said not to have died, but to have been taken directly to Paradise. In Jewish tradition, he is sometimes identified with ➤ ENOCH.

According to later Islamic legend, he is credited

with being the first to use pens and sew garments, and to have been the first astronomer and chronologist, as well as skilled in medicine. He is regarded as patron of tailors.

Idun in Scandinvian mythology, the goddess who was the guardian of the magic apples of youth; when (through the machinations of ➤ LOKI) she and her apples were captured by the giants, the gods began to age, until Loki was forced to rescue Idun.

if see ➤ *if* IFS *and ands were pots and pans,* ➤ *if it ain't* BROKE, *don't fix it,* ➤ *if the* CAP *fits, wear it,* ➤ *if you can't* BEAT *them, join them,* ➤ *if you're* BORN *to be hanged then you'll never be drowned.*

IFOR (abbreviation for) the name of the (United Nations) Implementation Force, the force that replaced Unprofor in Bosnia.

if ifs and ands were pots and pans, there'd be no work for tinkers' hands proverbial saying, mid 19th century; traditional response to an overoptimistic conditional expression, in which *ands* is the plural form of *and* 'if'.

Iftar the meal eaten by Muslims after sunset during Ramadan.

Father Ignatius name taken by the preacher Joseph Leycester Lyne (1837–1908), who formed a community at Claydon, near Ipswich, in 1862, and who in 1869 built Llanthony Abbey.

St Ignatius Loyola (1491–1556), Spanish theologian and founder of the Society of Jesus, who after sustaining a leg wound as a soldier, renounced military life and turned to prayer and mortification. In 1534 he founded the Society of Jesus and became its first general. His *Spiritual Exercises* (1548), an ordered scheme of meditations, is still used in the training of ➤ JESUITS.
   ☐ **FEAST DAY** His feast day is 31 July.

ignipotent ruling or having power over fire (from a Virgilian epithet for ➤ VULCAN).

ignis fatuus a ➤ WILL-*o'-the-wisp*. Recorded in English from the mid 16th century, the phrase is modern Latin, literally 'foolish fire' (because of its erratic movement).

ignoble hawk in falconry, any of the short-winged hawks (e.g. the goshawk and sparrowhawk) which chase or rake after their prey instead of swooping down on it (the practice of a ➤ NOBLE *hawk*).

ignoramus an ignorant or stupid person. The word is recorded from the late 16th century, as the endorsement made by a grand jury on an indictment considered backed by insufficient evidence to bring before a petty jury; it is from Latin, literally 'we do not know' (in legal use 'we take not notice of it'), from *ignorare* 'to ignore'. The modern sense may derive from the name of a character in George Ruggle's *Ignoramus* (1615), a satirical comedy exposing lawyers' ignorance.

ignorance see ➤ INVINCIBLE *ignorance.*

time of ignorance the period of Arab history prior to the teaching of Muhammad.

where ignorance is bliss, 'tis folly to be wise proverbial saying, mid 18th century; originally from Gray:

> Thought would destroy their paradise.
> No more; where ignorance is bliss,
> 'Tis folly to be wise.
> — Thomas Gray *Ode on a Distant Prospect of Eton College* (1747)

ignorance of the law is no excuse for breaking it proverbial saying, early 15th century.

Ignorantine a member of a religious order, the Brethren of Saint-Jean-de-Dieu, founded in 1495 to minister to the sick poor; they were introduced into France by Marie de Medici, and subsequently devoted themselves to the instruction of the poor. They applied the name of *Ignorantine* to themselves as a sign of humility.

ignoratio elenchi a logical fallacy which consists in apparently refuting an opponent while actually disproving something not asserted; any argument which is irrelevant to its professed purpose. The phrase is Latin, literally 'ignorance of the elenchus'.

ignotum per ignotius an explanation which is harder to understand than what it is meant to explain. The phrase is Latin, literally 'the unknown through something more unknown'.

Igraine in Arthurian legend, the mother by ➤ UTHER *Pendragon* of ➤ ARTHUR; she was the wife of Gorlois of Cornwall, and Uther took on the form of Gorlois by Merlin's magic.

ihram the purified state into which a Muslim must enter before performing a pilgrimage, during which actions such as sexual intercourse, shaving, and cutting one's nails are forbidden; the costume worn at this time consists of two lengths of seamless typically white fabric, one worn about the hips, the other over the shoulders or sometimes only over the left shoulder. The word is Arabic, ultimately from *ḥarama* 'forbid'.

IHS Jesus; the letters, from late Latin, represent Greek as an abbreviation of the name of Jesus used in manuscripts and also as a symbolic or ornamental monogram. Later they are often taken as an abbreviation of various Latin phrases, notably *Iesus Hominum Salvator* 'Jesus Saviour of Men', *In Hoc Signo (vinces)* 'in this sign (thou shalt conquer)', and *In Hac Salus* 'in this (cross) is salvation'.

IHS tablet a tablet with the monogram IHS is the emblem of the Franciscan friar St Bernardino of Siena (1380–1444), noted for his preaching, who would customarily hold up a plaque with IHS on it at the end of a sermon.

ikebana the art of Japanese flower arrangement, with formal display according to strict rules.

il see ➤ *Il* DUCE.

Iliad a Greek hexameter epic poem in twenty-four books, traditionally ascribed to Homer.

  The poem tells of the climax of the Trojan War between Greeks and Trojans. The greatest of the Greek heroes, ➤ ACHILLES, retires to his tent enraged by a perceived insult. In his absence his close friend Patroclus is killed by the Trojan hero Hector; at this the grief-stricken Achilles takes the field and kills Hector.

Iliad in a nutshell in allusion to a copy of Homer's *Iliad* which was supposedly small enough to be enclosed in the shell of a nut; it is used to suggest great condensation, brevity, or limitation.

Ilium the alternative name for ➤ TROY, especially the 7th-century BC Greek city.

of that ilk in Scottish usage, of the place or estate of the same name, as in *Sir Iain Moncreiffe of that Ilk*; the word is recorded from Old English (in the form *ilca*, in sense 'same'), and is of Germanic origin, related to *alike*.

ill see ➤ BIRD *of ill omen*.

it's an ill bird that fouls its own nest proverbial saying, mid 13th century.

ill gotten goods never thrive proverbial saying, early 16th century.

he that has an ill name is half hanged proverbial saying, late 14th century.

it's ill waiting for dead men's shoes proverbial saying, mid 16th century.

ill weeds grow apace proverbial saying, late 15th century.

it's an ill wind that blows nobody any good proverbial saying, mid 16th century.

Illuminati a name given to a sect of 16th-century Spanish heretics (the *Alumbrados*) who claimed special religious enlightenment.

  Illuminati is also used to represent German *Illuminaten*, a Bavarian secret society founded in 1776, holding deistic and republican principles and organized like the Freemasons.

  The name is Latin, literally 'the enlightened ones'.

the Illustrious an epithet of a number of rulers, as **Henry the Illustrious**, 13th-century Margrave of Baden.

Illyria an ancient region along the east coast of the Adriatic Sea, including Dalmatia and what is now Montenegro and northern Albania, subsequently the Roman province of *Illyricum*, and later divided into the provinces of Dalmatia and Pannonia. It was overrun by the Huns and the Visigoths between the 3rd and 5th centuries AD.

  The name was revived, as the **Illyrian Provinces**, in 1809 after Napoleon's defeat of the Austrians and the annexation of the region to France. The region was reclaimed by Austria in 1814, retaining its identity as the kingdom of Illyria until 1849.

image see ➤ GRAVEN *image*, ➤ WAXEN *image*.

imagism a movement in early 20th-century English and American poetry which sought clarity of expression through the use of precise images. The movement derived in part from the aesthetic philosophy of T. E. Hulme and involved Ezra Pound, James Joyce, Amy Lowell, and others.

Imam a title of various Muslim leaders, especially of one succeeding Muhammad as leader of Shiite Islam. The word comes from Arabic *'imām* 'leader', from *'amma* 'lead the way'.

imambara in the Indian subcontinent, a building in which Shiite Muslims assemble at the time of Muharram, and the gardens and courtyards surrounding it.

Imbolc an ancient Celtic festival celebrated on the second day of February. The name is a Celtic word, literally 'in the belly or womb', the festival being dedicated to women and fertility.

imbongi in traditional African society, a poet employed to compose poems praising a chief.

imbroccata a downward pass or thrust in fencing.

Imhotep (fl. 27th century BC), Egyptian architect and scholar. He probably designed the step pyramid built at Saqqara for the 3rd-dynasty pharaoh Djoser. Later deified, he was worshipped as the patron of architects, scribes, and doctors, while in Greece he was identified with the god ➤ ASCLEPIUS.

imitation is the sincerest form of flattery proverbial saying, early 19th century.

Imitation of Christ English name for ➤ THOMAS *à Kempis*'s manual of spiritual devotion *De Imitatione Christi*.

Immaculate Conception the doctrine that God preserved the Virgin Mary from the taint of original sin from the moment she was conceived. The belief was much disputed in the Middle Ages, but was generally accepted by Roman Catholics from the 16th century; it was defined as a dogma of the Roman Catholic Church in 1854. The **Feast of the Immaculate Conception** is celebrated on 8 December.

Immaculate Heart of Mary the heart of the Virgin Mary as an object of devotion in the Roman Catholic Church.

Immaculate Lamb a name for Jesus, recorded from late Middle English and translating Latin *agnus immaculatus*.

immanence philosophy a theory developed in Germany in the late 19th century that reality exists only through being immanent in conscious minds.

immolate kill or offer as a sacrifice, especially by burning. The word comes from the Latin *immolat-* 'sprinkled with sacrificial meal'.

immortal the name **the Immortals** was a title for the royal bodyguard of ancient Persia, because their number was always the same.

See also ➤ *the* FORTY, ➤ *the Immortal* MEMORY.

Immortal Dreamer a nickname of John Bunyan, in allusion to the dream-setting of *Pilgrim's Progress*:

> So I awoke, and behold it was a dream.
> — John Bunyan *Pilgrim's Progress* pt 1 (1678)

immram any of various stories of fabulous sea voyages written in Ireland between the late 8th and 11th centuries.

imp a small, mischievous devil or sprite. The word is recorded in Old English (in form *impa*, *impe*) in the sense 'young shoot, scion', *impian* 'to graft', based on Greek *emphuein* 'to implant'. In late Middle English, the noun denoted a descendant, especially of a noble family, and later a child of the devil or a person regarded as such; hence a 'little devil' or mischievous child (early 17th century).

The verb *imp* in falconry, meaning repair a damaged feather in (the wing or tail of a trained hawk) by attaching part of a new feather, retains the original meaning 'to graft'.

See also ➤ LINCOLN *imp*.

impale in heraldry, display (a coat of arms) side by side with another on the same shield, separated by a vertical line; (of a coat of arms) adjoin (another coat of arms) in this way.

impanation the medieval and Reformation doctrine that the body of Christ is present within the Eucharistic bread and does not replace it.

imperator in ancient Rome, commander (a title conferred under the Republic on a victorious general and under the Empire on the emperor); later, confined to the head of the state, in whose name the victories were won, and thus becoming the equivalent of its English representative, *emperor*.

From the ancient Roman Emperors, it was continued as the Latin title of the Emperors of the East and West, and so of all monarchs who claimed 'imperial' rank or position.

The word is Latin, from *imperare* 'to order, command'.

imperial see also ➤ PRINCE *Imperial*.

imperial of, relating to, or denoting the system of non-metric weights and measures (the ounce, pound, stone, inch, foot, yard, mile, acre, pint, gallon, etc.) formerly used for all measures in the UK, and still used for some. Also, (of a size of paper) measuring (in the UK) 762 × 559 mm (30 × 22 inches).

Imperial Conference any of a series of conferences for the Prime Ministers of British dominions, held in London between 1907 and 1946.

Imphal the capital of the state of Manipur in the far north-east of India, lying close to the border with Burma (Myanmar), which was the scene of an important victory in 1944 by Anglo-Indian forces over the Japanese.

impluvium the square basin in the centre of the atrium of an ancient Roman house, which received rainwater from an opening in the roof.

impossibile see ➤ CREDO *quia impossibile.*

impossible see ➤ *the* DIFFICULT *is done at once, the impossible takes a little longer.*

Impressionism a style or movement in painting originating in France in the 1860s, characterized by a concern with depicting the visual impression of the moment, especially in terms of the shifting effect of light and colour.

The Impressionist painters repudiated both the precise academic style and the emotional concerns of Romanticism, and their interest in objective representation, especially of landscape, was influenced by early photography. Impressionism met at first with suspicion and scorn, but soon became deeply influential. Its chief exponents included Monet, Renoir, Pissarro, Cézanne, Degas, and Sisley.

impressions see ➤ FIRST *impressions are the most lasting.*

imprimatur an official licence issued by the Roman Catholic Church to print an ecclesiastical or religious book; from the Latin 'let it be printed'.

Imprint a typeface derived from Caslon, named after the periodical for which it was designed.

impropriate grant (an ecclesiastical benefice) to a corporation or person as their property; place (tithes or ecclesiastical property) in lay hands.

improve see ➤ *improve the* SHINING *hour.*

Impuritan an opponent of Puritanism; in the 17th century a derogatory term with a play on the sense of 'a person who is impure'.

the In and Out nickname of the Naval and Military Club in Piccadilly, London, from the words 'In' and 'Out' painted on the pillars of the approach to the courtyard.

in extremis at the point of death; Latin, from *in* 'in' + *extremis*, ablative plural of *extremus* 'outermost'.

in flagrante delicto in the very act of wrongdoing, especially in an act of sexual misconduct; Latin, 'in the heat of the crime' (literally, 'in blazing crime').

in loco parentis (of a teacher or other adult responsible for children) in the place of a parent; Latin.

in medias res into the middle of a narrative; without preamble; into the midst of things; Latin.

in memoriam in memory of (a dead person); Latin. The phrase was used by Tennyson in *In Memoriam A. H. H.*, a poem, published in 1850, written in memory of his friend Arthur Hallam, who died suddenly in 1833 at the age of 22.

in petto undisclosed, secretly (especially of the appointment of cardinals not named as such); the phrase is Italian, literally 'in the breast'.

in puris naturalibus in a natural state; stark naked; Latin.

in statu pupillari under guardianship, especially as a pupil; Latin.

in vino veritas under the influence of alcohol, a person tells the truth; Latin, literally 'truth in wine'.

inaugurate begin or introduce (a system, policy, or period); admit (someone) formally to office. The word, which is late 16th century, comes from Latin *inaugurat-* 'interpreted as omens (from the flight of birds)', based on *augurare* 'to augur'.

Inca a member of a South American Indian people living in the central Andes before the Spanish conquest. Also, the supreme ruler of this people.

The Incas arrived in the Cuzco valley in Peru *c.*1200 AD. When the Spanish invaded in the early 1530s, the Inca empire covered most of modern Ecuador and Peru, much of Bolivia, and parts of Argentina and Chile. Inca technology and architecture were highly developed despite a lack of wheeled vehicles and of writing. Their descendants, speaking Quechua, still make up about half of Peru's population.

the Incarnation in Christian theology, the embodiment of God the Son in human flesh as Jesus Christ; the word comes ultimately from ecclesiastical Latin *incarnat-* 'made flesh', from *in-* 'into' + *caro, carn-* 'flesh'.

incense a gum, spice, or other substance that is burned for the sweet smell it produces, and the smoke or perfume from this, especially as part of a religious ceremonial.

inch a unit of linear measure equal to one twelfth of a foot. The word is recorded from late Old English (in form *ynce*) and comes from Latin *uncia* 'twelfth part', from *unus* 'one' (probably denoting a unit).

give him an inch and he'll take an ell traditional saying, mid 16th century; meaning that undue advantage will be taken of a slight concession.

Inchcape Rock a sandstone reef in the North Sea, off the mouth of the River Tay in Scotland. A lighthouse designed by the Scottish civil engineers Robert Stevenson (1772–1850) and John Rennie was built there in 1807–c.1811.

incipit a manuscript, early printed book, or chanted liturgical text; the word is Latin, literally '(here) begins'.

Incitatus the name of ➤ CALIGULA's horse, made a consul by the emperor. The action became proverbial; when the American politician John Randolph of Roanoke (1773–1833) complained of John Quincy Adams's appointment of Richard Rush as Secretary of the Treasury, he said, 'Never were abilities so much below mediocrity so well rewarded; no, not when Caligula's horse was made Consul.'

incognito an assumed or false identity. The word comes (in the mid 17th century) from Italian, literally 'unknown'.

incorruptible see ➤ *the* SEA-*green Incorruptible.*

incredible see ➤ *the Incredible* HULK.

incubation in ancient Greece, the practice of sleeping in a temple or sacred place in the expectation of visions or revelations.

incubus a male demon believed to have sexual intercourse with sleeping women. Recorded from Middle English, the word is a late Latin form of Latin *incubo* 'nightmare', from *incubare* 'lie on'.

incunabula the early stages of the development of something; in particular, early printed books, especially those printed before 1501. The word comes from Latin, meaning literally 'swaddling clothes'.

indaba a conference between members of southern African native peoples.

act of indemnity a parliamentary act granting exemption from the penalties attached to any unconstitutional or illegal proceeding; in English history, applied particularly to acts of 1660 and 1690, exempting those who had taken arms or acted against Charles II and William III respectively from any penal consequences.

indenture a deed of contract of which copies were made for the contracting parties with the edges indented for identification; in particular, an agreement binding an apprentice to a master, or a contract by which a person agreed to work for a set period for a landowner in a British colony in exchange for passage to the colony.

independence see ➤ DECLARATION *of Independence,* ➤ UNILATERAL *Declaration of Independence.*

Independence Day another term for ➤ FOURTH *of July.*

Independence Hall a building in Philadelphia where the US Declaration of Independence was proclaimed and outside which the Liberty Bell is kept.

Independency in the Christian Church, the principle that each local congregation is autonomous and responsible to God alone; Congregationalism.

Independent a member or adherent of a Church holding the principle of Independency; a Congregationalist.

Independent Labour Party a British socialist political party formed in 1893 under the leadership of Keir Hardie. It was instrumental in the formation of the Labour Party in 1906, but tension between the two parties grew in the 1930s over the questions of pacifism and support for communism, and by the early 1950s the Independent Labour Party had lost all its parliamentary representation.

index see ➤ Dow *Jones index,* ➤ FTSE *index,* ➤ HANG *Seng index,* ➤ NIKKEI *index.*

Index Expurgatorium a list of passages to be deleted from a book before it was considered fit for reading by Roman Catholics; a list of authors considered fit to read only after the removal of objectionable matter from their works, later included in the *Index Librorum Prohibitorum.*

Index Librorum Prohibitorum an official list of books which Roman Catholics were forbidden to read or which were to be read only in expurgated editions, as contrary to Catholic faith or morals. The first Index was issued in 1557; it was revised at intervals until abolished in 1966.

India a country in southern Asia (occupying the greater part of the Indian subcontinent) much of which was united under a Muslim sultanate based around Delhi from the 12th century until incorporated in the Mogul empire in the 16th century. Colonial intervention began in the late 17th century, particularly by the British; in 1765 the ➤ EAST *India Company* acquired the right to administer Bengal. In 1858, after the ➤ INDIAN *Mutiny,* the Crown took over the Company's authority, and in 1876 Queen Victoria was proclaimed Empress of India. Independence was won in 1947, at which time India was partitioned, Pakistan being created from mainly Muslim territories in the north-east (now Bangladesh) and the north-west.

The name comes via Latin from Greek *India,* from *Indos,* the name of the River Indus, from Persian *Hind,* from Sanskrit *sindhu* 'river', specifically 'the Indus', also 'the region around the Indus'. Both the Greeks and the Persians extended the name to include all the country east of the Indus.

See also ➤ BRITISH *India,* ➤ EAST *India Company.*

India House the office of the ➤ EAST *India Company* in London.

India paper originally, a soft, absorbent paper imported from China and used for proofs of engravings. Later, the term was used for **Oxford India paper,** a very thin, tough, opaque printing paper made by the Oxford University Press in imitation of paper from the East, used especially for Bibles.

Indiaman a ship engaged in trade with India or the East or West Indies, especially an East Indiaman.

Indian a member of the indigenous peoples of America, an **American Indian.**

The native peoples of America came to be described as *Indian* as a result of Christopher Columbus and other voyagers in the 15th–16th centuries believing that, when they reached the east coast of America, they had reached part of India by a new route. The terms *Indian* and *Red Indian* are today regarded as old-fashioned and inappropriate, recalling, as they do, the stereotypical portraits of the Wild West. *American Indian,* however, is well established, although the preference where possible is to make reference to specific peoples, as *Apache, Delaware,* and so on.

See also ➤ AMERICAN *Indian,* ➤ *the only* GOOD *Indian is a dead Indian.*

Indian Bible the first complete Bible to be printed in North America.

Indian ink deep black ink containing dispersed carbon particles, used especially in drawing and technical graphics. The term, which is mid 17th century, was originally applied to Chinese and Japanese pigments prepared in solid blocks and imported to Europe via India.

Indian Mutiny a revolt of Indians against British rule, 1857–8.

Discontent with British administration resulted in widespread mutinies in British garrison towns, with accompanying massacres of white soldiers and inhabitants. After a series of sieges (most notably that of Lucknow) and battles, the revolt was put down; it was followed by the institution of direct rule by the British Crown in place of the ➤ EAST *India Company* administration.

Indian National Congress a broad-based political party in India, founded in 1885 and the principal party in government since independence in 1947. It developed a powerful central organization under Mahatma Gandhi in the 1920s and dominated the independence movement in the following decade. Following splits in the party the Indian National Congress (I), formed by Indira Gandhi as a breakaway group, was confirmed in 1981 as the official Congress party.

Indian rope-trick the supposed feat, performed in the Indian subcontinent, of climbing an upright, unsupported length of rope.

Indian summer a period of unusually dry, warm weather occurring in late autumn. The name is generally attributed to the fact that the region in which the meteorological conditions in question were originally noticed was still occupied by indigenous American peoples, although other more specific explanations have been attempted.

Indiana see ➤ *Indiana* JONES.

Indianapolis see also ➤ INDY.

Indianapolis name of an American heavy cruiser which in 1945 was torpedoed in Japanese waters and sank; of 1,196 men aboard, only 316 survived, many of them dying by dehydration or shark attack through the ensuing five days before they were rescued. The *Indianapolis* involved the greatest loss of life in American naval history, and became an enduring legend; in the film *Jaws* (1975) the shark-hunter Quint explains his hatred of sharks as deriving from the hours he spent in the water after the *Indianapolis* sank watching his friends being killed.

At a subsequent court martial, the captain was convicted of negligence through failing to zigzag in hostile waters and therefore hazarding the ship. In recent years, however, the declassification of Navy documents has suggested that crucial warnings of enemy activity in the area were not given for fear of revealing that the Americans had broken the Japanese codes. A campaign for legislation to quash the conviction is currently under way.

Indies an archaic term for the East Indies.

indigo a tropical plant of the pea family, which was formerly widely cultivated as a source of dark blue dye; the dark blue dye obtained from this plant; a colour between blue and violet in the spectrum.

Indo-European of or relating to the family of languages spoken over the greater part of Europe and Asia as far as northern India.

The Indo-European languages have a history of over 3,000 years. Their unattested, reconstructed ancestor, Proto-Indo-European, is believed to have been spoken well before 4000 BC in a region somewhere to the north or south of the Black Sea. The family comprises twelve branches: Indic (including Sanskrit and its descendants), Iranian, Anatolian (including Hittite and other extinct languages), Armenian, Hellenic (Greek), Albanian (or Illyrian), Italic (including Latin and the Romance languages), Celtic, Tocharian (an extinct group from central Asia), Germanic (including English, German, Dutch, and the Scandinavian languages), Baltic, and Slavic (including Russian, Czech, Bulgarian, and Serbo-Croat).

indolence see ➤ the CASTLE *of Indolence.*

Indra in Hinduism, the warrior king of the heavens, god of war and storm, to whom many of the prayers in the Rig Veda are addressed. His weapons are the thunderbolt and lightning, his helpers are the Maruts. His role in later Hinduism is small.

induct formally introduce (a member of the clergy) into possession of a benefice. The word (recorded from late Middle English) comes from Latin *inducere* 'to lead in'.

indulgence see also ➤ DECLARATION *of Indulgence.*

indulgence in the Roman Catholic Church, a grant by the Pope of remission of the temporal punishment in purgatory still due for sins after absolution. The unrestricted sale of indulgences by ➤ PARDONERS was a widespread abuse during the later Middle Ages.

Indus a river of southern Asia, flowing from Tibet through Kashmir and Pakistan to the Arabian Sea. Along its valley an early civilization flourished from

*c.*2600 to 1760 BC, whose economic wealth was derived from well-attested sea and land trade with the rest of the Indian subcontinent. In the early 2nd millennium its power declined, probably because of incursions by the Aryans.

industrial see ➤ MILITARY-*industrial complex.*

Industrial Revolution the rapid development of industry that occurred in Britain in the late 18th and 19th centuries, brought about by the introduction of machinery.

Preceded by major changes in agricultural methods which freed workers for the factories, Britain's industrial revolution was made possible by the rise of modern industrial methods, with steam power replacing the use of muscle, wind, and water, the growth of factories, and the mass production of manufactured goods. The textile industry was the prime example of industrialization, and created a demand for machines, and for tools for their manufacture, which stimulated further mechanization. Improved transport was needed, provided by canals, roads, railways, and steamships; construction of these required a large labour force, and the skills acquired were exported to other countries. It made Britain the most powerful industrial country in the world but radically changed the face of British society, throwing up large cities (particularly in the Midlands) as the population shifted from the countryside, and causing or exacerbating a series of profound social and economic problems.

industrie see ➤ CHEVALIER *d'industrie.*

industry see ➤ CONFEDERATION *of British Industry.*

Indy a form of motor racing in which cars are driven round a banked, regular oval circuit which allows for racing at exceptionally high speeds. It takes place chiefly in the US, and is named (from the 1950s) from *Indianapolis* in Indiana, where the principal *Indy* event, an annual 500-mile (804.5-km) motor race, known as the **Indy 500**, is held.

Ine (d. 726), king of Wessex, who extended the prestige and power of the throne and developed an extensive legal code.

inexpressibles a dated colloquialism for breeches or trousers; recorded from the late 18th century.

infallibility in the Roman Catholic Church, the doctrine (also called **papal infallibility**) that in specified circumstances the Pope is incapable of error in pronouncing dogma; the assertion that infallibility attached to his definitions in matters of faith and morals was made by the Vatican Council of 1870.

infangthief in Anglo-Saxon law, the right of the lord of a manor to try and to punish a thief caught within the limits of his demesne. Recorded from Old English (in form *infangenþēof*) the word means literally 'thief seized within'.

infant a very young child or baby. Recorded from late Middle English, the word comes through Old French from Latin *infant-* 'unable to speak'. In the late 16th and early 17th centuries it is also used to mean a young man of noble or gentle birth.

See also ➤ *the infant* PHENOMENON, ➤ LIMBO *of infants.*

infanta a daughter of the ruling monarch of Spain or Portugal, especially the eldest daughter who was not heir to the throne.

infante the second son of the ruling monarch of Spain or Portugal.

infanticide the killing of a newborn child, which in some societies (as in ancient Greece, by exposure) has in certain circumstances been sanctioned; in law, the crime of a mother killing her child within a year of birth.

infantry soldiers marching or fighting on foot; foot soldiers collectively.

inferiority complex an unrealistic feeling of general inadequacy caused by actual or supposed inferiority in one sphere, sometimes marked by aggressive behaviour in compensation.

infernal of, relating to, or characteristic of hell or the underworld. Recorded from late Middle English, the word comes via Old French and Christian Latin, from Latin *infernus* 'below, underground', used by Christians to mean 'hell', on the pattern of *inferni* (masculine plural) 'the shades' and *inferna* (neuter plural) 'the lower regions'.

Inferno hell (with reference to Dante's ➤ DIVINE *Comedy*).

infidel a person who does not believe in religion or who adheres to a religion other than one's own. The word originally denoted a person of a religion other than one's own, specifically a Muslim (to a Christian), a Christian (to a Muslim), or a Gentile (to a Jew).

influenza a highly contagious viral infection of the respiratory passages causing fever, severe aching, and catarrh, and often occurring in epidemics. The word comes (in the mid 18th century) from Italian, literally 'influence', from medieval Latin *influentia*. The Italian word also has the sense 'an outbreak of an epidemic', hence 'epidemic'. It was applied specifically to an influenza epidemic which began in Italy in 1743, later adopted in English as the name of the disease.

See also ➤ SPANISH *flu.*

infobahn a high speed computer network, especially the Internet.

information superhighway an extensive electronic network such as the Internet, used for the rapid transfer of information such as sound, video, and graphics in digital form.

infotainment broadcast material which is intended both to entertain and to inform.

infralapsarian a Calvinist holding the view that God's election of only some to everlasting life was not originally part of the divine plan, but a consequence of the Fall of Man.

infula in the Christian Church, either of the two ribbons on a bishop's mitre. The term comes (in the early 17th century) from Latin, denoting a woollen fillet worn by a priest or placed on the head of a sacrificial victim.

Jan Ingenhousz (1730–99), Dutch scientist. He is best known for his work on photosynthesis, in which he discovered that sunlit green plants take in carbon dioxide, fix the carbon, and 'restore' the air (oxygen).

Ingvaeonic the hypothetical language from which the earliest recorded dialects of West Germanic (except Old High German) descended.

ink a coloured fluid or paste used for writing, drawing, printing, or duplicating. The word dates from Middle English, and comes via Old French and late Latin from Greek *enkauston*, denoting the purple ink used by Roman emperors for signatures, from *enkaiein* 'burn in'.

Inkatha a mainly Zulu political party and organization in South Africa, founded in 1928 and revived in 1975 by Chief Buthelezi. It has a professed aim of racial equality and universal franchise in South Africa, but progress towards political reform was obstructed by violent clashes between Inkatha factions and members of the rival ANC. The name comes from Zulu *inkhata* 'crown of woven grass', a tribal emblem symbolizing the force unifying the Zulu nation.

inkhorn term a word or expression used only in academic writing.

inkosi a Zulu ruler, chief, or high official.

Inmarsat an international organization founded in 1978 that provides telecommunication services, as well as distress and safety communication services, to the world's shipping, aviation, and offshore industries.

inn a public house, typically one in the country, in some cases providing accommodation; earlier, a house providing accommodation, food, and drink, especially for travellers.

The word is Old English, in the sense 'dwelling place, lodging', and is of Germanic origin. In Middle English it was used to translate Latin *hospitium* hospice, denoting a house of residence for students: this sense is preserved in the names of some buildings formerly used for this purpose, notably *Gray's Inn* and *Lincoln's Inn*, two of the ➤ INNS *of Court*. The current sense dates from late Middle English.

See also ➤ BOAR*'s Head Inn*.

inner child a person's supposed original or true self, especially when regarded as damaged or concealed by negative childhood experiences; the term is associated particularly with theories developed in the 1980s, according to which 'getting in touch with' one's *inner child* is seen as a healing process whereby damage done in the past can be assuaged, and a key step towards achieving true well-being taken.

inner city the area near the centre of a city, especially when associated with social and economic problems.

Inner House (of the Court of Session) (in Scotland) either of two law courts that correspond to the Court of Appeal in England and Wales, each presided over by three judges.

inner light personal spiritual revelation; a source of enlightenment within oneself.

Inner Temple one of the two ➤ INNS *of Court* on the site of the Temple in London, the other being the ➤ MIDDLE *Temple*.

innings in cricket, each of two or four divisions of a game during which one side has a turn at batting;

in transferred use, a period during which a person or group is active or effective.

Inniskilling a soldier of a regiment originally raised for the defence of *Enniskillen* in 1689, later the 5th Royal Inniskilling Dragoon Guards.

See also ➤ *the* SKINS.

the Innocents the young children killed by Herod in the ➤ MASSACRE *of the Innocents* after the birth of Jesus.

Innocents' Day a Christian festival commemorating the ➤ MASSACRE *of the Innocents*, 28 December.

Inns of Chancery the buildings in London formerly used as hostels for law students.

Inns of Court the four legal societies having the exclusive right of admitting people to the English bar; the sets of buildings in London occupied by these societies.

the Inquisition an ecclesiastical tribunal established by Pope Gregory IX *c*.1232 for the suppression of heresy, at a time when certain heretical groups were regarded by the Church as enemies of society. It was active chiefly in northern Italy and southern France, becoming notorious for the use of torture; condemned heretics who refused to recant were handed over to the civil authorities and could be burned at the stake. In 1542 the papal Inquisition was reinstituted to combat Protestantism, eventually becoming an organ of papal government.

See also ➤ SPANISH *Inquisition*.

inquisitor see also ➤ GRAND *Inquisitor*.

Inquisitor General the head of the ➤ SPANISH *Inquisition*.

INRI an abbreviation for Jesus of Nazareth, King of the Jews (a traditional representation in art of the inscription over Christ's head at the Crucifixion). The letters are the initials of the Latin phrase *Iesus Nazarenus Rex Iudaeorum*.

insane root a term used in Shakespeare's *Macbeth* for a plant which would affect the senses, perhaps henbane or hemlock, described as 'the insane root That takes the reason prisoner'.

inscape the unique inner nature of a person or object as shown in a work of art, especially a poem, originally as used in the poetic theory of ➤ *Gerard Manley* HOPKINS.

INSET day a day in term-time used for training teachers in British state schools. The term is an acronym from *in-service education and training.*

insider dealing the illegal practice of trading on the stock exchange to one's own advantage through having access to confidential information; the term came particularly to prominence in the 1980s, with the exposure and prosecution of a number of prominent individuals both in the US and the UK.

inspector see ➤ *Inspector* CLOUSEAU, ➤ *Inspector* MORSE.

instrumentalism the pragmatic philosophy of the American philosopher John Dewey (1859–1952), holding that thought is an instrument designed to solve practical problems over a wide range and that truth is not final and static but changes as these problems change.

instruments see ➤ *Instruments of the* PASSION.

insult speak to or treat with disrespect or scornful abuse. The word dates from the mid 16th century, in the sense 'exult, act arrogantly', from Latin *insultare* 'jump or trample on'.

integer a whole number; a number which is not a fraction. The word is recorded from the early 16th century, as an adjective meaning 'entire, whole', and comes from Latin, 'intact, whole'.

The German mathematician Leopold Kronecker (1823–91) commented, 'God made the integers, all the rest is the work of man.'

intelligence see also ➤ ARTIFICIAL *intelligence.*

intelligence quotient a number representing a person's reasoning ability (measured using problem-solving tests) as compared to the statistical norm or average for their age, taken as 100. Abbreviated as **IQ**.

intelligentsia intellectuals or highly educated people as a group, especially when regarded as possessing culture and political influence. The word comes (in the early 20th century) from Russian *intelligentsiya*, from Polish *inteligencja*, from Latin *intelligentia.*

Intelsat an international organization of more than 100 countries, formed in 1964, which owns and operates the worldwide commercial communications satellite system.

intercalary of a day or month, inserted in the calendar to harmonize it with the solar year, e.g. 29 February in leap years.

interdict in the Roman Catholic Church, a sentence debarring a person, or especially a place, from ecclesiastical functions and privileges; in English history, referring particularly to the papal interdict laid on England in 1208 as a result of King John's refusal to accept the election of ➤ *Stephen* LANGTON as Archbishop of Canterbury.

Interlingua an artificial international language formed of elements common to the Romance languages, designed primarily for scientific and technical use.

International any of four associations founded to promote socialist or communist action.

The First International was formed by Karl Marx in London in 1864 as an international working men's association and was dissolved twelve years later after internal wrangling between Marxists and anarchists. The Second International was formed in Paris in 1889 to celebrate the 100th anniversary of the French Revolution and, although gravely weakened by the First World War, still survives as a loose association of social democrats.

The Third International, also known as the Comintern, was formed by the Bolsheviks in 1919 to further the cause of world revolution. Active if seldom effective between the wars, it was abolished in 1943 as a gesture towards the Soviet Union's war allies. The Fourth International, a body of Trotskyist organizations, was formed in 1938 in opposition to the policies of the Stalin-dominated Third International.

International Brigade a group of volunteers (mainly from Europe and the US) which was raised internationally by foreign communist parties and which fought on the Republican side in the Spanish Civil War.

International Court of Justice a judicial court of the United Nations which replaced the Cour Permanente de Justice in 1945 and meets at The Hague.

International Phonetic Alphabet an internationally recognized set of phonetic symbols developed in the late 19th century, based on the principle of strict one-to-one correspondence between sounds and symbols.

international style a functional style of 20th-century architecture, so called because it crossed national and cultural barriers. It is characterized by the use of steel and reinforced concrete, wide windows, uninterrupted interior spaces, simple lines, and strict geometric forms.

the **Internationale** a revolutionary song composed in France in the late 19th century. It was adopted by French socialists and subsequently by others, and was the official anthem of the USSR until 1944.

Internet an international computer network providing electronic mail and information from computers in educational institutions, government agencies, and industry, accessible to the general public via modem links.

Interpol an organization based in Paris that co-ordinates investigations made by the police forces of member countries into crimes with an international dimension. Originally, the name was the telegraphic address of the International Criminal Police Commission, founded in 1923.

the **Interregnum** the period in English history from the execution of ➤ CHARLES *I* in 1649 to the Restoration of ➤ CHARLES *II* in 1660.

intestinal disease ➤ St ERASMUS is the patron saint of those suffering from intestinal disease.

intestines intestines are the emblem of ➤ St ERASMUS.

intichiuma sacred ceremonies performed by some Central Australian Aboriginals with the purpose of increasing the number of totemic plants or animals and thus ensuring a good food supply.

intifada the Palestinian uprising against Israeli occupation of the West Bank and Gaza Strip, beginning in 1987. The word comes from Arabic *intifāḍa* 'an uprising' (literally 'a jumping up as a reaction to something') from *intifaḍa* 'be shaken, shake oneself'.

the **Intolerable** Acts derogatory term for four measures enacted by the British Parliament in 1774 against the American colonies, by which the harbour of Boston was closed until restitution was made for the tea destroyed at the ➤ BOSTON *Tea Party*, the charter of the Massachusetts colony was

abrogated, British officials charged with capital offences as a result of carrying out law enforcement could elect to go to England or another colony for trial, and new arrangements for billeting British troops on American households were made.

intrapreneur a manager within a company who promotes innovative product development and marketing.

Inuit the members of an indigenous people of northern Canada and parts of Greenland and Alaska.

The peoples inhabiting the regions from NW Canada to western Greenland prefer to be called *Inuit* rather than *Eskimo*, and this term now has official status in Canada. By analogy, the term *Inuit* is also used, usually in an attempt to be politically correct, as a synonym for *Eskimo* in general. However, this latter use, in including people from Siberia who are not Inupiaq-speakers, is, strictly speaking, not accurate.

Les **Invalides** founded by Louis XIV in 1670 as a military hospital, and later the resting place of Napoleon Bonaparte and others.

invalids ➤ St ROCH is the patron saint of invalids.

invecked in heraldry, bordered by or (of an edge) consisting of a series of small convex lobes; scalloped.

invention see also ➤ NECESSITY *is the mother of invention.*

Invention of the Cross a festival, held on 3 May (Holy Rood Day), commemorating the reputed finding of the Cross of Christ by ➤ St HELENA, mother of the emperor Constantine, in AD 326 (*invention* here meant 'coming upon, finding').

investigative journalism journalism which involves inquiring intensively into and seeking to expose malpractice, the miscarriage of justice, or other controversial issues. The term came to prominence in the US in the 1970s with the reporting of ➤ WATERGATE; in the US, it has subsequently been associated particularly with television and radio, and a range of 'watchdog' programmes.

The American politician Lawton Chiles (1930–), commenting on the phenomenon, said in 1991, 'You are misunderstood, maligned, viewed by the press as a Pulitzer Prize ready to be won.'

Investiture Controversy a conflict, lasting from 1076 to 1122, over whether bishops and abbots could be invested by lay overlords; the essential issue was the relationship between empire and papacy.

Invincible Doctor nickname of ➤ WILLIAM *of Ockham* (1285–1347/9), translation of the Latin phrase *Doctor Invincibilis*.

invincible ignorance in theological terms, ignorance which the person concerned does not have the means to overcome; the term is a translation of scholastic Latin *ignorantia invinciblis*, in the *Summa Theologiae* of ➤ THOMAS *Aquinas*.

invisibility in a number of legends, conferred on the wearer by an article of clothing, as the ring of ➤ GYGES or the magic coat of ➤ JACK *the Giant-killer*.

invisible see also ➤ CHURCH *Invisible*.

the invisible the unseen world; God.

the Invisible Man the central character of H. G. Wells's novel of that name (1897), about a scientist who discovers (in the end, disastrously for himself) how to make himself invisible; because he can only appear visible by wearing clothing, the typical image of him is shrouded in a big coat with hat and heavy gloves.

invita Minerva when one is not in the mood; without inspiration (a Latin phrase meaning 'Minerva (the goddess of wisdom) unwilling').

invulnerability in a number of legends, supposedly conferred upon a recipient; there is usually one fatal weakness which brings about destruction, as in the story of ➤ ACHILLES' *heel*, and the mistletoe twig which brings about the death of ➤ BALDER.

inyanga in South Africa, a traditional healer or diviner, especially one specializing in herbalism.

Io in Greek mythology, a priestess of Hera who was loved by ➤ ZEUS. Trying to protect her from the jealousy of Hera, Zeus turned Io into a heifer. Hera sent a gadfly to torture the heifer, which then fled across the world and finally reached Egypt, where Zeus turned her back into human form.

The *Bosporus* ('cow's passage') and the *Ionian* Sea are reputed to have been crossed by Io, and derive their names from her story.

Iona a small island in the Inner Hebrides, off the west coast of Mull. It is the site of a monastery founded by St Columba in about 563, which became the centre for Celtic Christian missions in Scotland.

Ionia in classical times, the central part of the west coast of Asia Minor, which had long been inhabited by Hellenic people (the Ionians) and was again colonized by Greeks from the mainland from about the 8th century BC.

Ionian a member of an ancient Hellenic people inhabiting Attica, parts of western Asia Minor, and the Aegean islands in pre-classical times. They were apparently displaced from some areas by the Dorians in the 11th or 12th century BC but retained their settlements in Attica, especially Athens, where they were responsible for some of the greatest achievements of classical Greece. They also colonized the islands that became known as the Ionian Islands.

Ionian mode in music, the mode represented by the natural diatonic scale C–C (the major scale).

Ionic relating to or denoting a classical order of architecture characterized by a column with scroll shapes (volutes) on either side of the capital.

iota the ninth letter of the Greek alphabet (I, ι), transliterated as 'i'.

iota subscript in Greek, a small iota written beneath a long vowel, forming the second element of a diphthong but not pronounced and not always represented in transliteration.

IOU a signed document acknowledging a debt, representing a pronunciation of *I owe you*.

Iphigenia in Greek mythology, the daughter of ➤ AGAMEMNON, who was obliged to offer her as a sacrifice to Artemis when the Greek fleet was becalmed on its way to the Trojan War. However, in some accounts, Artemis saved her life and took her to Tauris in the Crimea, where she became a priestess until rescued by her brother Orestes.

ipse dixit a dogmatic and unproven statement. From Latin, literally 'he himself said it', translating Greek *autos epha*, a phrase used of Pythagoras by his followers.

ipsissima verba the precise words; the phrase is Latin.

Muhammad Iqbal (1875–1938), Indian poet and philosopher, generally regarded as the father of Pakistan. As president of the Muslim League in 1930, he advocated the creation of a separate Muslim state in NW India; the demands of the League led ultimately to the establishment of Pakistan in 1947.

IRA abbreviation for the ➤ IRISH *Republican Army.*

irae see ➤ DIES *Irae.*

Iran–Iraq War the war of 1980–8 between Iran and Iraq in the general area of the Persian Gulf. It ended inconclusively after great hardship and loss of life on both sides.

Irangate a US political scandal of 1987 involving the covert sale by the US of arms to Iran. The proceeds of the arms sales were used by officials to give arms to the anti-communist Contras in Nicaragua, despite Congressional prohibition. The sale occurred during the presidency of Ronald Reagan, at a time when official relations between the countries were suspended (and while Iran was at war with Iraq), and was followed by the release of American hostages held in the Middle East.

IRB the Irish Republican Brotherhood.

Ireland an island of the British Isles, lying west of Great Britain, which was inhabited by Celts from about the 6th century BC. English invasions began in the 12th century under Henry II, although the whole of the island was not conquered until the time of the Tudors.

Revolts against English rule led to English and Scottish families being settled on confiscated land; in parts of Ulster the descendants of Protestant settlers form a majority. After an unsuccessful rebellion in 1798, union of Britain and Ireland followed in 1801. In 1921 Ireland was partitioned by the Anglo-Irish Treaty.

In nationalist tradition and literature, Ireland is often personified, as *Dark Rosaleen* and the *Seanbhean bocht* or *Shan Van Vocht* (the 'Little Old Woman'); the *Four Green Fields* of her domain are the provinces of Ulster, Munster, Leinster, and Connacht.

See also ➤ YOUNG *Ireland.*

William Henry Ireland (1777–1835), literary forger and author of two supposedly lost Shakespeare plays. He produced his first forgeries at the age of 17, while working as a clerk in a lawyer's office with access to parchment and old deeds, and an exhibition

was arranged in 1794 by his delighted and credulous father. The play *Vortigern and Rowena,* produced by Kemble in 1795, was however jeered by the audience, and in the following year Ireland confessed to having forged the 'discovered' manuscripts.

St Irenaeus (*c.*130–*c.*200 AD), Greek theologian, the author of *Against Heresies* (*c.*180), a detailed attack on Gnosticism.
   □ **FEAST DAY** His feast day is (in the Eastern Church) 23 August; (in the Western Church) 28 June.

irenics a part of Christian theology concerned with reconciling different denominations and sects; the word comes from Greek *eirēnikos,* from *eirēnē* 'peace'.

Irgun a right-wing Zionist organization founded in 1931. During the period when it was active (1937–48) it carried out violent attacks on Arabs and Britons in its campaign to establish a Jewish state; it was disbanded after the creation of Israel in 1948.

Iris in Greek mythology, the goddess of the rainbow, who acted as a messenger of the gods.

Irish see also ➤ SCOTS-*Irish.*

Irish box an EU-designated fishing ground located largely in Irish territorial waters.

Irish Free State the name for southern Ireland from 1921 until 1937.

Irish rat according to legend, Irish rats could be killed or driven away by rhyming.

Irish Republican Army the military arm of Sinn Fein, aiming for union between the Republic of Ireland and Northern Ireland. The IRA was formed during the struggle for independence from Britain in 1916–21; in 1969 it split into Official and Provisional wings. The Official IRA became virtually inactive, while the Provisional IRA stepped up the level of violence against military and civilian targets in Northern Ireland, Britain, and Europe. The IRA declared a ceasefire in 1994 and another in 1997.

Irish Sweepstake a sweepstake on the results of certain major horse races, authorized since 1930 by the government of the Republic of Ireland in order to benefit Irish hospitals. It is the largest international lottery.

Irishman see ➤ UNITED *Irishman.*

iroha the Japanese kana or syllabary (a Japanese word, from the opening syllables *i, ro, ha* or (formerly) *fa* in one method of listing).

iron see ➤ BLOOD *and iron,* ➤ *Lou* GEHRIG, ➤ NEW *off the irons,* ➤ RING *of iron,* ➤ STRIKE *while the iron is hot.*

iron age originally, the Greek and Roman poets' name for the last and worst period of human history, succeeding the gold, silver, and brazen ages; in allusive reference, an age of wickedness, cruelty, or oppression.

In archaeology, the *Iron Age* denotes a prehistoric period that followed the Bronze Age, when weapons and tools came to be made of iron. It is conventionally taken as beginning in the early 1st millennium BC, but iron-working began with the Hittites in Anatolia in *c.*1400 BC. Its arrival in Britain was associated with the first Celtic immigrants in about the 6th century BC. In much of Europe it ended at the Roman period, but outside the Roman Empire it continued to the 4th–6th centuries AD.

Iron-arm epithet of several rulers and soldiers, including Baldwin I (d. 879), the first ruler of Flanders.

Iron Chancellor nickname of the German statesman ➤ *Otto von* BISMARCK (1815–98), Chancellor of the German Empire (1871–90).

Iron Cross the highest German military decoration for bravery, originally awarded in Prussia (instituted 1813) and revived by Hitler in 1939.

Iron Crown of Lombardy the hereditary crown of the ancient kings of Lombardy, so called from having a circlet of iron inserted, reputed to have been made from one of the nails of the Cross.

Iron Curtain a notional barrier separating the former Soviet bloc and the West prior to the decline of communism that followed the political events in eastern Europe in 1989. The phrase is particularly associated with a speech by Winston Churchill in 1946, 'From Stettin in the Baltic to Trieste in the Adriatic an iron curtain has descended across the Continent,' although the term in relation to the Soviet Union and her sphere of influence is recorded intermittently from 1920.

Iron Duke a nickname of the ➤ *Duke of* WELLINGTON (1769–1852), recorded from the mid 19th century.

the iron entered into his soul from the Latin *ferrum pertransit animam ejus*, a mistranslation in the Vulgate of the Hebrew, literally 'his person entered into the iron', i.e., he was placed in chains or fetters.

Iron Gate a gorge through which a section of the River Danube flows, forming part of the boundary between Romania and Serbia. Navigation was improved by means of a ship canal constructed through it in 1896.

Iron Guard a fascist Romanian political party that was founded in 1927 and ceased to exist after the Second World War.

Iron-hand nickname of the German knight Götz von Berlichingen (1480–1562), whose artificial iron hand replaced one that had been shot away, and whose life exploits in battle against various feudal rulers were the subject of a play by Goethe.

an iron hand in a velvet glove ruthlessness disguised by courtesy; recorded in Carlyle's *Latter-day Pamphlets* (1850), 'Soft of speech and manner, yet with an inflexible rigour of command..."iron hand in a velvet glove", as Napoleon defined it.'

Iron Lady the nickname of Margaret Thatcher (1925–), given her in January 1976 by the Soviet defence ministry newspaper *Red Star*, which accused her of trying to revive the Cold War; she immediately responded to the name:

> I stand before you tonight in my red chiffon evening gown, my face softly made up, my fair hair gently waved . . . the Iron Lady of the Western World! Me? A cold war warrior? Well, yes—if that is how they wish to interpret my defence of values and freedoms fundamental to our way of life.
> — Margaret Thatcher speech, 31 January 1976

iron maiden in historical contexts, an instrument of torture consisting of a coffin-shaped box lined with iron spikes.

the Man in the Iron Mask a political prisoner in France at the time of Louis XIV, said by some to be a brother of the king, who was made to wear a mask supposedly of iron; he died in the Bastille in 1703, and his identity is still disputed.

ironclad a 19th-century warship with armour plating; the term was originally used particularly of such ships during the American Civil War (see ➤ MONITOR).

Ironside nickname of Edmund II, king of England (c.998–1016); the name is noted in the *Anglo-Saxon Chronicle* as given him for his bravery.

Ironsides a nickname for ➤ Oliver CROMWELL. In the English Civil War, Cromwell's cavalry troopers were called Ironsides by their Royalist opponents in allusion to their hardiness in battle.

Iroquois a member of a former confederacy of six American Indian peoples (Mohawk, Oneida, Seneca, Onondaga, Cayuga, and Tuscarora) who lived mainly in southern Ontario and Quebec and northern New York State.

irredentism in 19th-century Italian politics, an advocate of the return to Italy of all Italian-speaking districts subject to other countries.

Irrefragable Doctor nickname of the theologian ➤ ALEXANDER *of Hales* (c.1186–1245).

irregular see ➤ BAKER *Street Irregulars*.

Irus in Homer's *Odyssey*, the beggar who fights with the returning Odysseus.

Henry Irving (1838–1905), English actor-manager. He managed the Lyceum Theatre from 1878 to 1902, during which period he entered into a celebrated acting partnership with Ellen Terry.

Washington Irving (1783–1859), American writer. He is best known for *The Sketch Book of Geoffrey Crayon, Gent* (1819–20), which contains such tales as 'Rip Van Winkle' and 'The Legend of Sleepy Hollow'. He served as US ambassador to Spain in 1842–6.

Irvingite a member of the *Catholic Apostolic Church*, which followed the teachings of Edward Irving (1792–1834), who was originally a minister of the Church of Scotland.

is your journey *really* necessary? 1939 slogan, coined to discourage Civil Servants from going home for Christmas.

Isaac in the Bible, a Hebrew patriarch, son of ➤ ABRAHAM and Sarah and father of ➤ JACOB and Esau, whom Abraham was commanded by God to sacrifice. Because of his obedience to God, Isaac was spared; a ram caught in a thicket nearby was substituted for the boy.

Isabella greyish yellow, a light buff colour; a traditional story, which derives the word from the Archduchess Isabella who refused to change her linen until the siege of Ostend (1601–4) was ended, is chronologically impossible, as the earliest use of the word predates the siege.

Isabella I (1451–1504), queen of Castile 1474–1504 and of Aragon 1479–1504. Her marriage in 1469 to Ferdinand of Aragon helped to join together the Christian kingdoms of Castile and Aragon, marking the beginning of the unification of Spain. They instituted the Spanish Inquisition (1478) and supported Columbus's famous expedition of 1492.

Isabella of France (1292–1358), daughter of Philip IV of France and wife of Edward II of England (1308–27), known as the **She-Wolf of France**. After returning to France in 1325, she organized an invasion of England in 1326 with her lover Roger de Mortimer, murdering Edward and replacing him with her son, Edward III. Edward took control in 1330, executing Mortimer and sending Isabella into retirement.

isagogics introductory study, especially of the literary and external history of the Bible prior to exegesis.

Isaiah a major Hebrew prophet of Judah in the 8th century BC, who taught the supremacy of the God of Israel and emphasized the moral demands on worshippers. Also, a book of the Bible containing his prophecies (and, it is generally thought, those of at least one later prophet).
See also ➤ DEUTERO-*Isaiah*.

Isaurian a native or inhabitant of *Isauria*, an ancient country in Asia Minor, between Cilicia and Phrygia, in particular, any of a line of emperors of the Eastern Roman Empire.

Iseult a princess in medieval legend. According to one account, she was the sister or daughter of the king of Ireland, the wife of King Mark of Cornwall, and loved by ➤ TRISTRAM. In another account, she was the daughter of the king of Brittany and wife of Tristram.

Ishmael in the Bible, a son of ➤ ABRAHAM and ➤ HAGAR, his wife Sarah's maid, driven away with his mother after the birth of Isaac (Genesis 16:12, 'His hand will be against every man, and every man's hand against him'). *Ishmael* (or Ismail) is also important in Islamic belief as the traditional ancestor of Muhammad and of the Arab peoples.

In allusive use, *Ishmael* denotes an outcast; the doomed narrator of Melville's *Moby Dick* (1851) opens the book with the words, 'Call me Ishmael.'

Ishtar a Babylonian and Assyrian goddess of love and war whose name and functions correspond to those of the Phoenician goddess ➤ ASTARTE.

St Isidore of Seville (*c.*560–636), Spanish archbishop and Doctor of the Church; also called *Isidorus Hispalensis*. He is noted for his *Etymologies*, an encyclopedic work used by many medieval authors.

   □ **FEAST DAY** His feast day is 4 April.

St Isidore the farmer (*c.*1080–1130), Spanish patron of Madrid, and of farmers; he worked as a labourer on a farm near Madrid, and according to one legend was once seen being assisted in his ploughing by a second team of white oxen driven by angels.

   □ **EMBLEM** His emblem is a sickle.

   □ **FEAST DAY** His feast day is 15 May.

Isis see ➤ CAM *and Isis*.

Isis in Egyptian mythology, a goddess of fertility, wife of Osiris and mother of ➤ HORUS. Her worship spread to western Asia, Greece, and Rome, where she was identified with various local goddesses, and became the focus of one of the major mystery religions, involving enactment of the myth of the death and resurrection of ➤ OSIRIS.

Islam the religion of the Muslims, a monotheistic faith regarded as revealed through Muhammad as the Prophet of Allah.

Founded in the Arabian peninsula in the 7th century AD, Islam is now the professed faith of nearly a billion people worldwide, particularly in North Africa, the Middle East, and parts of Asia. The ritual observances and moral code of Islam were said to have been given to Muhammad as a series of revelations, which were codified in the Koran. Islam is regarded by its adherents as the last of the revealed religions, and Muhammad is seen as the last of the prophets, building on and perfecting the examples and teachings of Abraham, Moses, and Jesus. There are two major branches in Islam, ➤ SUNNI and ➤ SHIA.

The name comes from Arabic *'islām* 'submission', from *'aslama* 'submit (to God)'.

See also ➤ FIVE *Pillars of Islam*.

Islamic Jihad a Muslim fundamentalist terrorist group within the Shiite Hezbollah association.

island see also ➤ CONEY *Island*, ➤ DESERT *Island Discs*, ➤ DEVIL'*s Island*, ➤ *the* FORTUNATE *Islands*, ➤ GEORGE *Cross Island*, ➤ *the* GREEN *Island*, ➤ HOLY *Island*.

Islands of the Blessed (in classical mythology) a land, traditionally located near the place where the sun sets, to which the souls of the good were taken to enjoy a life of eternal bliss.

isles see ➤ LORD *of the Isles*.

Islington person a term used to denote a middle-class, socially aware person with left-wing views, characteristics supposedly typical of Islington residents, and harking back to the *parlour pink* of a previous generation. *Islington person* is seen as a typical supporter of ➤ NEW *Labour* who, while rejecting the brash self-interest of ➤ ESSEX *man*, is nevertheless similarly insulated by material wealth from the harshest pressures of modern society.

Ismaili a member of a branch of Shiite Muslims that seceded from the main group in the 8th century because of their belief that Ismail, the son of the sixth Shiite imam, should have become the seventh imam. The Ismailis eventually split into many sects, of which the best known is the Nizari sect, headed by the ➤ AGA *Khan*.

Isocrates (436–338 BC), Athenian orator whose written speeches are among the earliest political pamphlets; they advocate the union of Greeks under Philip II of Macedon and a Panhellenic crusade against Persia.

Israel the Hebrew nation or people. According to tradition they are descended from the patriarch Jacob (also named *Israel*), whose twelve sons became founders of the twelve tribes. Also called **children of Israel**.

Israel was also used as the name of the northern kingdom of the Hebrews (*c.*930–721 BC), formed after the reign of Solomon, whose inhabitants were carried away to captivity in Babylon.

The name comes from Hebrew *Yiśrā'ēl* 'he that strives with God', from the story of Jacob's wrestling at Penuel with a man by whom he was given an angelic blessing, in Genesis 32:28, 'Thy name shall be no more Jacob, but Israel; for as a prince hast thou power with God and with men, and hath prevailed.'

See also ➤ CHILDREN *of Israel*, ➤ LOST *Tribes of Israel*, ➤ TRIBES *of Israel*, ➤ TWELVE *Tribes of Israel*.

Israfel in Muslim tradition, the angel of music, who will sound the trumpet on the Day of Judgement.

Issachar in the Bible, a Hebrew patriarch, son of Jacob and Leah (Genesis 30:18); the tribe of Israel traditionally descended from him.

issuant in heraldry, (of the upper part of an animal) shown rising up or out from another bearing, especially from the bottom of a chief or from behind a fess.

Istanbul a port in Turkey on the Bosporus, lying partly in Europe, partly in Asia, formerly the Roman city of ➤ CONSTANTINOPLE (330–1453), and built on the site of the ancient Greek city of ➤ BYZANTIUM. It was captured by the Ottoman Turks in 1453 and was the capital of Turkey from that time until 1923. The name is Turkish, from Greek *eis tēn polin* 'into the city'.

Isthmian games games held by the ancient Greeks every other year near the *Isthmus* of Corinth.

Sir Isumbras hero of a verse-romance of the early 14th century, a knight who having sinned through arrogance was offered a choice between suffering in youth and old age. Having chosen youth, he loses his wife and family and is imprisoned for 21 years by the Saracens, but in the end his sins are expiated, and his family and possessions restored.

Sir Isumbras at the Ford, showing the knight in old age on horseback and carrying two children across a stream, was the subject of a painting (1857) by Millais which was severely criticized by Ruskin for its freedom of technique. The picture was later parodied by the artist Frederick Sandys, in a lithograph which showed *Sir Isumbras* as Millais himself, mounted on a donkey, and carrying his fellow ➤ PRE-*Raphaelites* Rossetti and Holman Hunt.

it sex appeal; the term is first recorded of the mysterious 'Mrs Bathurst' in Kipling's *Traffics and Discoveries* (1904), ''Tisn't beauty, so to speak…It's just it. Some women'll stay in a man's memory if they once walk down a street.' The usage was reinforced by the romantic novelist Elinor Glyn in her novel *It* (1927).

The American actress Clara Bow (1905–65), who starred in the film of Glyn's novel, was subsequently known as the ➤ IT *Girl*.

it could be you advertising slogan for the British national lottery, 1994.

It girl from the original application to the actress Clara Bow (1905–65) as star of the film *It* (1927), an actress or model, regarded as vivacious and outgoing, and having particular sex appeal; in later use, *It girl* also denotes a young woman typifying the latest fashion and social success.

it takes 40 dumb animals to make a fur coat, but only one to wear it slogan of an anti-fur campaign poster, sometimes attributed to David Bailey (1938–).

it'll play in Peoria catch-phrase of the Nixon administration (early 1970s) meaning 'it will be acceptable to middle America', but originating in a standard music hall joke of the 1930s.

it's good to talk advertising slogan for British Telecom.

italic of the sloping kind of typeface used especially for emphasis or distinction and in foreign words; (of handwriting) modelled on 16th-century Italian handwriting, typically cursive and sloping and with elliptical or pointed letters.

Italic school the school of philosophy founded in Magna Graecia by ➤ PYTHAGORAS in the 6th century BC.

Italic version a Latin translation of the Bible used prior to the time of ➤ *St* JEROME and the preparation of the ➤ VULGATE.

Italiot an inhabitant of any of the Greek colonies in ancient Italy.

Italy see ➤ YOUNG *Italy*.

itch see ➤ SEVEN *year itch*.

itching palm avarice; originally with reference to Shakespeare's *Julius Caesar*, in a scene in which Brutus accuses Cassius of being ready to take bribes:

> Let me tell you, Cassius, you yourself
> Are much condemned to have an itching palm.
> — William Shakespeare *Julius Caesar* (1599)

Ithaca an island off the western coast of Greece in the Ionian Sea, the legendary home of ➤ ODYSSEUS.

ITMA title of a British radio comedy series (1939–49); *ITMA* was originally the acronym for a newspaper headline of May 1939:

> It's that man again . . . ! At the head of a cavalcade of
> seven black motor cars Hitler swept out of his Berlin
> Chancellery last night on a mystery journey.
> — *Daily Express* 2 May 1939

Ivan the Terrible name given to Ivan IV (1530–84),
grand duke of Muscovy and first tsar of Russia. He
captured Kazan, Astrakhan, and Siberia, but the
Tartar siege of Moscow and the Polish victory in the
Livonian War (1558–82) left Russia weak and divided. In 1581 he killed his eldest son Ivan in a fit of
rage, the succession passing to his mentally handicapped second son Fyodor.

Ivanhoe the hero of Scott's novel (1819) of that
name, a knight of noble Saxon lineage at the time of
the Crusades; he becomes a friend and supporter of
Richard the Lionheart, despite the traditional enmity between Normans and Saxons, which Scott
presents as having survived from the 11th century.
Popular in its day, evidence of its enduring appeal
was apparently given in November 1996 when Tony
Blair selected it as his chosen book on ➤ DESERT *Island Discs.*

St Ivo of Brittany (*c.*1235–1303), a Breton lawyer
who was ordained as a priest towards the end of his
life; he is patron of lawyers and judges.
  ☐ **FEAST DAY** His feast day is 19 May.

ivory gate in classical belief, the gate through
which true dreams pass; in Virgil's *Aeneid*, it is said
that the spirits of the dead send true dreams to humankind through the *ivory gate*, and false dreams
through the *gate of horn.*

ivory shoulder in Greek mythology, the child Pelops was killed by his father Tantalus and offered as
food to the gods to see if they could tell that this was
not the flesh of an animal. Demeter, grieving for
Persephone, ate part of the shoulder, but the other
gods, realizing the deception, brought Pelops back
to life, and replaced the missing shoulder with one
of ivory.

ivory tower a state of privileged seclusion or separation from the facts and practicalities of the real
world; the term is recorded from the early 20th century, translating French *tour d'ivoire*, used by the
writer Sainte-Beuve (1804–69), '*Et Vigny plus secret,
Comme en sa tour d'ivoire, avant midi rentrait* [And
Vigny more discreet, as if in his ivory tower, returned before noon].'

ivy a woody evergreen climbing plant, typically
having shiny, dark green five-pointed leaves, which

in classical times was sacred to Bacchus (the
➤ THYRSUS was sometimes wreathed with ivy). A
branch or bush of ivy was the traditional sign of a
vintner's shop or tavern, giving rise to the expression ➤ *Good* WINE *needs no bush.*

Ivy was sometimes regarded as unlucky, and is
traditionally opposed to the *holly* at times of celebration.

Ivy League a group of long-established universities
in the eastern US having high academic and social
prestige. It includes Harvard, Yale, Princeton, and
Columbia. The term refers to the ivy traditionally
growing over the walls of these establishments.

Iwo Jima a small volcanic island, the largest of the
Volcano Islands in the western Pacific. During the
Second World War it was the heavily fortified site of
a Japanese airbase, and its attack and capture in
1944–5 was one of the severest US campaigns. It was
returned to Japan in 1968.

The photograph of the American Marines raising
the flag at Iwo Jima on 23 February 1945 became one
of the most famous images of the Pacific War; the
event is commemorated by the Marines' Memorial
near ➤ ARLINGTON.

> Memories of the awful splendors of Belleau Wood and
> Iwo Jima.
> — *Atlantic* September 1992

Ixion in Greek mythology, a king punished by Zeus
for attempting to seduce Hera by being pinned to a
fiery wheel that revolved unceasingly through the
underworld.

ixora any of various various evergreen shrubs or
small trees of the genus *Ixora*, of the madder family,
mostly native to tropical Africa and Asia, which bear
compact corymbs of white or brightly coloured
flowers. The name, which is modern Latin, comes
from Portuguese *Iswara* from Sanskrit *īśvara* 'lord,
master', epithet of Hindu deities, the flowers of certain species being used as votive offerings.

Iyyar in the Jewish calendar, the eighth month of
the civil and second of the religious year, usually coinciding with parts of April and May.

Izvestia a Russian daily newspaper founded in 1917
as the official organ of the Soviet government. It has
continued to be published independently since the
collapse of communist rule and the break-up of the
Soviet Union. The name is from Russian *izvestiya*
'news'.

J j

J the tenth letter of the modern English alphabet, originally a modification of the letter I. In the 17th century the two forms of the letter came to be differentiated, i remaining for the vowel and j being used for the consonant, with the capital form of the latter, J, being introduced.

J'accuse title of the open letter written by Émile Zola to the President of the French Republic protesting at the trial and conviction of ➤ *Alfred* DREYFUS.

J'Ouvert in the Caribbean, the official start of carnival, at dawn on the Monday preceding Lent. The name is French Creole, from French *jour ouvert* 'day opened'.

jabberwocky invented or meaningless language, nonsense, from the title of a nonsense poem in Lewis Carroll's *Through the Looking Glass* (1871), about the monstrous *Jabberwock*.

Jachin and **Boaz** names of the bronze pillars at the entrance to Solomon's Temple, made by ➤ HIRAM and described in 1 Kings 7:15–22; their purpose was to act as the symbolical gateposts of the Temple, indicating that beyond them lay sacred ground.

jacinth in early use, a gem of a blue colour, probably a sapphire, mentioned in Exodus 28:19 as being in the high priest's breastplate, and in Revelation 21:20 a stone in the wall of the New Jerusalem; the name comes (in Middle English) from an Old French or medieval Latin alteration of Latin *hyacinthus* 'hyacinth'. In modern usage, *jacinth* denotes a reddish-orange gem variety of zircon.

Jack pet name of the given name John. The term was originally (in late Middle English) used to denote an ordinary man, and in the mid 16th century, a youth, hence the ➤ KNAVE in cards, and the use of the word to denote a male animal. The word is also used for a number of devices saving human labour, as if one had a helper. The general sense of 'labourer' arose in the early 18th century, and since the mid 16th century, the notion of 'smallness' has arisen.

See also ➤ *all* WORK *and no play makes Jack a dull boy*, ➤ FINALITY *Jack*, ➤ *a* GOOD *Jack makes a good Jill*, ➤ *the* HOUSE *that Jack built*, ➤ *Jack* KETCH, ➤ RADICAL *Jack*, ➤ SIXTEEN-*string Jack*, ➤ UNION *Jack*, ➤ YELLOW *jack*.

Jack-a-Lent a figure of a man, set up to be pelted (as an 'Aunt Sally') during Lent.

Jack Amend-all nickname given to ➤ *Jack* CADE.

Jack and Jill a nursery rhyme, in which *Jack and Jill*, who go up a hill for water, both fall down, with Jack breaking his crown and Jill tumbling after; it has been suggested that the origin is political, with Jack and Jill representing Henry VII's ministers Empson and Dudley, who were executed soon after Henry VIII's accession. An alternative explanation is that the rhyme is of Scandinavian origin, in the story of two children (Hjuki and Bil) who were stolen by the moon while drawing water.

Jack and Jill party in North American usage, a party held for a couple soon to be married, to which both men and women are invited.

Jack and the Beanstalk a fairy story, recorded from the mid 18th century, about a poor boy who sells his mother's cow for a handful of beans; she throws them angrily away, but the ones that have fallen into the garden root and grow into an enormous plant. Jack climbs the beanstalk, and discovers a ferocious giant; with magic help, he first steals from the giant and then by a trick contrives his death.

A beanstalk is proverbially fast-growing, but in this story it may also represent the Norse world-ash ➤ YGGDRASIL.

> It looked as though every small business venture led to a crock of gold and property prices would grow like Jack's beanstalk.
>
> — *Independent* 16 December 1991

Jack Frost a personification of frost; recorded from the early 19th century.

every Jack has his **Jill** proverbial saying, early 17th century.

Little Jack Horner subject of a nursery rhyme about a boy eating a 'Christmas pie' who 'put in his thumb, And pulled out a plum.' The origin is dubiously attributed to a *Jack Horner* who was steward to the abbot of Glastonbury in the reign of Henry VIII and by a trick acquired the deeds of the manor of Mells at the dissolution of the monasteries, took them to the king, and was handsomely rewarded: the Horner family still holds the manor.

jack-in-a-bottle a local name for the long-tailed tit.

jack-in-office a self-important minor official; the term is recorded from the early 18th century.

jack in the basket a type of warning beacon, used at sea or in rivers to mark sandbanks or other hidden dangers.

jack-in-the-box a toy consisting of a box containing a figure on a spring which pops up when the lid is opened; the term is recorded from the early 18th century.

Jack-in-the-green a man or boy enclosed in a wooden or wicker pyramidal framework covered with leaves, in traditional May Day celebrations.

Jack is as good as his master proverbial saying, early 18th century.

jack of all trades and master of none traditional saying, early 17th century; meaning that a person who tries to master too many skills will learn none of them properly.

Jack of Dover in Chaucer's *Prologue*, the name of a dish, probably a pie that had been cooked and reheated.

Jack of Newbury John Winchcombe, alias Smallwood (d. 1520), a clothier of Newbury, whose wealth inspired the authors of numerous chapbook stories. According to legend he led 100 or 250 men, equipped at his own expense, at the battle of Flodden Field, and entertained Henry VIII and Catherine of Aragon in his house.

jack-o'-lantern originally, a man with a lantern, a night watchman; from this, an ignis fatuus or ➤ WILL-*o-the-*wisp. The term in these senses is recorded from the 17th century.

From the mid 19th century, *jack-o'-lantern* has also been used (originally in the US) for a lantern made from a hollowed-out pumpkin or turnip in which holes are cut to represent facial features, typically made at Halloween.

Jack of the clock a figure of a man which strikes the bell on the outside of a clock; the use of *Jack* in this sense is recorded from the late 15th century, and in Shakespeare's *Richard III* (1591), in the quarrel between the king and Buckingham, Richard turns on the duke with the words, 'like a Jack thou keepst the stroke Betwixt thy begging and my meditation'.

Jack Russell a terrier of a small working breed with short legs, named after the Revd John *(Jack) Russell* (1795–1883), an English clergyman famed in fox-hunting circles as a breeder of such terriers.

Jack Sprat in the 16th and 17th centuries, a name for a very small man, a dwarf; in the nursery rhyme, recorded from the late 17th century, *Jack Sprat* is the husband who 'could eat no fat', while his wife 'could eat no lean'.

Jack tar informal name for a sailor, recorded from the late 18th century.

Jack the Giant-Killer a nursery tale of Northern origin, known in England from very early times. Jack was the son of a Cornish farmer, and lived in the days of King Arthur, who by his ingenuity acquired a coat that made him invisible, shoes which gave him great speed in running, and a magic sword. With the help of these, he destroyed all the giants in the land.

Jack the Ripper an unidentified 19th-century English murderer. In 1888 at least six prostitutes were brutally killed in the East End of London, the bodies being mutilated in a way that indicated a knowledge of anatomy. The authorities received taunting notes from a person calling himself *Jack the Ripper* and claiming to be the murderer, but the cases remain unsolved despite a wide variety of names being suggested.

jackal a slender long-legged wild dog that feeds on carrion, game, and fruit, and hunts in packs, found in Africa and southern Asia; it was traditionally supposed to go in front of the lion and hunt up prey for him, and from this was called **the lion's provider**. (Kipling used the myth in *The Jungle Books* in his picture of the jackal, Tabaqui, hunting food for his master, the tiger Sher Khan.) The animal was described by Topsell in *The History of Four-footed Beasts* (1607) as 'the second kind of hyaena'.

The name is recorded in English from the early

17th century; by the end of the century, it was used to denote a person seen as behaving like a jackal, especially one in a subservient relation to another. More recently, it has acquired connotations of cunning and treachery, as in the byname of the assassin on whom Frederick Forsyth's thriller *The Day of the Jackal* (1971), about a plot to assassinate General de Gaulle, was based.

jackanapes an impertinent person. The word dates from the early 16th century, originally as *Jack Napes*: perhaps from a playful name for a tame ape, the initial *n-* by elision of *an ape*, and the final -*s* as in surnames such as *Hobbes*: hence applied to a person whose behaviour resembled that of an ape.

jackaroo a young man working on a sheep or cattle station to gain experience. The word (recorded from the late 19th century) is an alteration of an Aboriginal (Queensland) term for *dhugai-iu* 'wandering white man', by blending *jack* and *kangaroo*.

jackass a male ass or donkey; the word is recorded from the early 18th century, and from the early 19th century has also denoted a stupid person, a fool.

jackboot a large leather military boot reaching to the knee, used as a symbol of cruel or authoritarian behaviour or rule, and now particularly associated with German soldiers during the Nazi regime.
   In the mid 18th century, in the early years of George III's reign, when the influence of his mother the Princess Dowager of Wales and his leading minister John, Earl of Bute was deeply unpopular, the emblem of a *jackboot* (with a petticoat for the Princess) was used to lampoon Bute; it is recorded in 1765 that members of the Lords and Commons on their way to Parliament were mobbed with the cry, 'Wilkes and Liberty and no Jack Boot'.

jackdaw a small grey-headed crow that typically nests in tall buildings and chimneys, noted for its inquisitiveness, its ability to mimic the sound of words, and its propensity to steal bright objects.
   The *jackdaw* is also mentioned allusively in reference to the fable of a jackdaw which decked itself out in peacock's feathers to impress the other birds.

the Jackdaw of Rheims title of a poem in R. H. Barham's *The Ingoldsby Legends* (1840), in which a jackdaw steals the cardinal's ring and is cursed by bell, book, and candle; the working of the curse on the bird reveals the thief.

jackpot a large cash prize in a game or lottery, especially one that accumulates until it is won. The term was originally used in a form of poker, where the pool or pot accumulated until a player could open the bidding with two jacks or better.

jackrabbit a hare found on the prairies and steppes of North America, sometimes taken as a type of swift-footedness. The name is a contraction of *jackass-rabbit*, so called from its long ears.

Andrew Jackson (1767–1845), American general and Democratic statesman, 7th President of the US 1829–37; known as **Old Hickory**. He defeated a British army at New Orleans in 1815 and invaded Florida, then held by the Spanish, in 1818. As President he replaced an estimated 20 per cent of those in public office with Democrat supporters, a practice that became known as the spoils system. The state capital of Mississippi, originally known as *Le Fleur's Bluff*, is named after him.

Thomas Jonathan Jackson (1824–63), American Confederate general; known as **Stonewall Jackson** (see ➤ STONEWALL¹). During the American Civil War he made his mark as a commander at the first battle of Bull Run in 1861 and later became the deputy of Robert E. Lee.

jackstone a small round pebble or star-shaped piece of metal or plastic used in tossing or catching games; the game played with these.

jackstraw another name for ➤ SPILLIKIN.

Jacky Howe in Australia, a (navy or black) sleeveless singlet worn especially by shearers and rural workers. It is named after John Robert *Howe* (?1861–1920), a champion Queensland shearer of the 1890s.

Jacob see also ➤ *Jacob* MARLEY.

Jacob in the Bible, a Hebrew patriarch, the younger of the twin sons of ➤ ISAAC and Rebecca, who persuaded his brother ➤ ESAU to sell him his birthright and tricked him out of his father's blessing (Genesis 25, 27).
   Jacob married his cousin ➤ RACHEL and (through the deception of their father, his uncle ➤ LABAN) her sister Leah; it was Rachel's children, his youngest sons ➤ JOSEPH and ➤ BENJAMIN who were dearest to him. His twelve sons became the founders of the twelve tribes of ancient Israel.

Jacob sheep a four-horned sheep of a piebald breed, kept as an ornamental animal or for its wool, and named originally from the story in Genesis

30:40, in which Jacob, who has herded his uncle Laban's cattle and sheep, is given the speckled and brown animals for his portion.

Jacob's ladder a ladder reaching up to heaven, seen in a dream by Jacob (Genesis 28:12), when he saw the angels of God ascending and descending; it was in the same dream that God spoke to him and promised to him and his descendants the land on which he was then lying. When he woke in the morning he set up the stone which had been his pillow to mark the place, which was later named ➤ BETHEL.

Jacob's staff a rod with a sliding cursor formerly used for measuring distances and heights. Originally (in the 16th century) denoting a pilgrim's staff, with allusion to St James (*Jacobus* in ecclesiastical Latin), whose symbols are a pilgrim's staff and a scallop shell.

Jacob's stone a name given to the ➤ STONE *of Scone*, said to have been the stone used by Jacob for a pillow when he had the dream of Jacob's ladder.

Jacobean of or relating to the reign of James I of England; (of furniture) in the style prevalent during the reign of James I, especially being the colour of dark oak.

Jacobethan (especially of architecture) displaying a combination of Elizabethan and Jacobean styles.

Jacobin a member of a democratic club established in Paris in 1789. The Jacobins were the most radical and ruthless of the political groups formed in the wake of the French Revolution, and in association with Robespierre they instituted the Terror of 1793–4.

The term was applied to the Dominicans in Old French from their church in Paris, St Jacques (Latin, *Jacobus*), near which they built their first convent; the latter eventually became the headquarters of the French revolutionary group.

Jacobite[1] a member of the Syrian Orthodox Church (Monophysite); the name comes (in late Middle English) from medieval Latin *Jacobita*, from the name of *Jacobus* Baradaeus, a 6th-century Syrian monk.

Jacobite[2] a supporter of the deposed ➤ JAMES *II* and his descendants in their claim to the British throne after the Revolution of 1688. Drawing most of their support from Catholic clans of the Scottish Highlands, Jacobites made attempts to regain the

throne in 1689–90, 1715, 1719, and 1745–6, finally being defeated at the Battle of Culloden.

The Jacobites traditionally had a number of toasts and emblems to indicate their sympathies; they would drink to the ➤ KING *over the Water* or the ➤ LITTLE *gentleman in black velvet,* and silver or glassware might be marked with a rose, or the Latin word *Fiat* ('let it be done').

Jacobus the unofficial name for an English gold coin, struck in the reign of James I. It was originally issued in 1603, under the name of the *Sovereign,* and in 1604 there was a second issue, known as the *Unite.*

Jacobus de Voragine (*c.*1230–*c.*98), archbishop of Genoa and author of the ➤ GOLDEN *Legend.*

jacquard an apparatus with perforated cards, fitted to a loom to facilitate the weaving of figured and brocaded fabrics. Also, a fabric made on a loom with such a device, with an intricate variegated pattern. The name comes from Joseph M. *Jacquard* (1787–1834), French weaver and inventor.

jacquerie a communal uprising or revolt, especially the revolt of the peasants of northern France against the nobles in 1357–8; the term is recorded from the early 16th century, and comes from Old French, literally 'villeins', from *Jacques,* a given name formerly used to mean 'peasant' in France.

jactitation of marriage archaic term for the false declaration that one is married to a specified person.

jacuzzi trademark name for a large bath with a system of underwater jets to massage the body. It is named after the Italian-born American inventor Candido *Jacuzzi* (*c.*1903–86).

jade a hard, typically green stone used for ornaments and implements and consisting of the minerals jadeite or nephrite. The word is recorded from the late 16th century, and comes via French from Spanish *piedra de ijada* 'stone of the flank' (i.e., stone for colic, which it was believed to cure).

Jael in the Bible (Judges 4:17) the woman who killed the commander of the Canaanite army, Sisera; when he was in flight after a defeat, she sheltered him in her tent, but when he was asleep she killed him by hammering a nail into his temples.

Jaffa a city and port on the Mediterranean coast of Israel which has been inhabited since prehistoric times. Jaffa was a Byzantine bishopric until captured by the Arabs in 636; later, it was a stronghold of the Crusaders. Its biblical name is ➤ JOPPA.

Jagannatha another name for ➤ JUGGERNAUT.

Jainism a non-theistic religion founded in India in the 6th century BC by the Jina Vardhamana Mahavira as a reaction against the teachings of orthodox Brahmanism, and still practised there. The Jain religion teaches salvation by perfection through successive lives, and non-injury to living creatures, and is noted for its ascetics.

The name *Jain*, for an adherent of Jainism, comes via Hindi from Sanskrit *jaina* 'of or concerning a *Jina* (a great Jain teacher or holy man, literally 'victor')', from *ji-* 'conquer' or *iyā* 'overcome'.

Jairus's daughter in the New Testament, a synagogue leader's daughter who was raised from the dead by Jesus. According to the story, by the time that Jesus reached her house, she appeared to have died; he said to the mourners (Mark 5:39), 'the damsel is not dead, but sleepeth.' When he took her hand and spoke to her, she woke up.

Jalal ad-Din ar-Rumi (1207–73), Persian poet and Sufi mystic, founder of the order of whirling dervishes; also called **Mawlana**. He wrote much lyrical poetry and an influential epic on Sufi mystical doctrine.

jalousie a blind or shutter made of a row of angled slats. The name comes (in the mid 18th century) from French, literally 'jealousy', from Italian *geloso* 'jealous', also (by extension) 'screen', associated with the screening of women from view in the Middle East.

jam tomorrow and jam yesterday, but never jam today proverbial saying, late 19th century; from Lewis Carroll:

> The rule is, jam to-morrow and jam yesterday—but never jam today.
> — Lewis Carroll *Through the Looking-Glass* (1872)

In the 1960s, this was reworked by the Labour politician Tony Benn (1925–), 'Some of the jam we thought was for tomorrow, we've already eaten.'

Jambres see ➤ JANNES *and Jambres.*

James see ➤ COURT *of St James's,* ➤ HOME, *James, and don't spare the horses,* ➤ James BOND.

Jesse James (1837–82), American outlaw, who joined with his brother Frank (1843–1915) and others to form a notorious band of outlaws which specialized in bank and train robberies and inspired many westerns. In April 1882, while living in Missouri under the name of Thomas Howard, he was shot in the back of the head by a former gang member, Robert Ford, in return for an amnesty and a reward; the contemporary *Ballad of Jesse James* (1882) referred to 'the dirty little coward That shot Mr Howard.'

> Jesse James is the manifestation of romantic lawlessness, a psychic inheritance of the pioneers and vigilantes.
> — *American Mercury* February 1927

James I (1566–1625), son of Mary, Queen of Scots, king of Scotland (as James VI) 1567–1625, and of England and Ireland 1603–25. He inherited the throne of England from Elizabeth I, as great-grandson of Margaret Tudor, daughter of Henry VII. His declaration of the divine right of kings and his intended alliance with Spain made him unpopular with Parliament.

James II (1633–1701), son of Charles I, king of England, Ireland, and (as James VII) Scotland 1685–8. His Catholic beliefs led to the rebellion of the Duke of Monmouth in 1685 and to James' later deposition in favour of William of Orange and Mary II. Attempts to regain the throne resulted in James's defeat at the Battle of the Boyne in 1690. He died in exile in France.

St James the Great an Apostle, son of Zebedee and brother of John. He was put to death by Herod Agrippa I; afterwards, according to a Spanish tradition, his body was taken to ➤ SANTIAGO *de Compostela*, which became a major pilgrimage centre. He is traditionally seen in Spanish iconography as leading the Christian Reconquest against the Moors.

☐ **EMBLEM** The emblems of St James are a scallop shell and a pilgrim's hat.

☐ **FEAST DAY** His feast day is 25 July.

St James the Less an Apostle; he is said to have been martyred by being beaten to death with a fuller's club. He may be identical with the James who was a leader of the early Christian Church at Jerusalem, also known as **the Lord's brother**.

☐ **EMBLEM** His emblem is a fuller's club.

☐ **FEAST DAY** His feast day (in the Eastern Church) is 9 October; (in the Western Church) is 1 May.

Jameson Raid an abortive raid into Boer territory made in 1895–6 by pro-British extremists led by Dr L. S. Jameson (1853–1917) in an attempt to incite an uprising among recent, non-Boer immigrants. The raid seriously heightened tension in South Africa and contributed to the eventual outbreak of the Second Boer War.

Jamestown a British settlement established in Virginia in 1607, during the reign of King James I. Built on a marshy and unhealthy site, it was abandoned when the state capital of Virginia was moved to Williamsburg at the end of the 17th century.

Jamshid a legendary early king of Persia, reputed inventor of the arts of medicine, navigation, and iron-working. According to legend he was king of the peris (or fairies) who was condemned to assume human form for boasting of his immortality, and ruled Persia for 700 years.

Jan Mayen a barren and virtually uninhabited island in the Arctic Ocean between Greenland and Norway, annexed by Norway in 1929, which is named after Jan *May*, the Dutch sea captain who claimed the island for his company and his country in 1614.

Jane see also ➤ CALAMITY *Jane*, ➤ HANOI *Jane*.

Jane the heroine of a *Daily Mirror* strip cartoon created by Norman Pett, originating in 1932, but particularly remembered for her Second World War adventures (which often involved loss of her clothing).

Janglish another name for ➤ JAPLISH.

janissary a member of the Turkish infantry forming the Sultan's guard between the 14th and 19th centuries. The word is recorded from the early 16th century, and comes from French *ianissaire*, based on Turkish *yeniçeri*, from *yeni* 'new' + *çeri* 'troops'.

Jannes and Jambres in rabbinic tradition, the names given to two of the Egyptian magicians who withstood Moses (Exodus ch. 7 and 8), and who were said in some stories to have the power of flight; they are referred to by St Paul in 2 Timothy 3:8.

Cornelius Otto Jansen (1585–1638), Flemish Roman Catholic theologian and founder of Jansenism. A strong opponent of the Jesuits, he proposed a reform of Christianity through a return to St Augustine. To this end he produced *Augustinus* (1640), a four-volume study of St Augustine's teachings.

Jansenism a Christian movement of the 17th and 18th centuries, based on Jansen's writings and characterized by moral rigour and asceticism. It was the subject of papal condemnation and of persecution in France, but was tolerated in the Netherlands. Its most famous adherent was Pascal.

St Januarius (d. *c*.305), bishop of Benevento and martyr. He is patron saint of Naples, where his relics are preserved; they include a phial of his blood which is said to liquefy.
☐ **FEAST DAY** His feast day is 16 November.

January the first month of the year, in the northern hemisphere usually considered the second month of winter. The name (recorded from Old English) comes from Latin *Januarius (mensis)* 'month of Janus', the Roman god who presided over doors and beginnings.
See also ➤ MAY *and January*.

Janus in Roman mythology, an ancient Italian deity, guardian of doorways and gates and protector of the state in time of war; he is usually represented with two faces, so that he looks both forwards and backwards. In ancient Rome the doors of the shrine of Janus in the Forum were closed in times of peace; according to Livy between the time of ➤ NUMA and his own day, this happened only twice, once after the First Punic War (241 BC) and after Octavian's victory at Actium (31 BC).

Japanimation animated cartoons produced in Japan, noted for their high-tech productions and sexually explicit storylines.

Japheth in the Bible, a son of Noah, traditional ancestor of the peoples living round the Mediterranean. His name is probably to be connected with that of ➤ IAPETUS, a Titan in Greek mythology.

Japlish a blend of Japanese and English, either Japanese speech that makes liberal use of English expressions or unidiomatic English spoken by a Japanese.

jar of ointment a jar of ointment is the emblem of ➤ *St* MARY *Magdalene* and ➤ *St* MARY *of Egypt*.

jargon special words or expressions used by a particular profession or group that are difficult for others to understand. The word is recorded from late Middle English, originally in the sense 'twittering, chattering', later 'gibbering' (from Old French, of unknown origin). The modern sense dates from the mid 17th century.

jarl a Norse or Danish chief; the word is from Old Norse, literally 'man of noble birth', related to earl.

Jarndyce v. **Jarndyce** the Chancery suit around which the plot of Dickens's *Bleak House* (1853) revolves, and which over the years has destroyed the happiness and lives of most members of the family involved as they become obsessed with pursuing their claims and waiting for the long-expected judgement; in the end, the costs of the case are found to have consumed the whole property.

Jarrow a town in NE England, on the Tyne estuary. From the 7th century until the Viking invasions its monastery was a centre of Northumbrian Christian culture; the Venerable Bede lived and worked there. Its name is associated with a series of hunger marches to London by the unemployed during the Depression of the 1930s.

Jason in Greek mythology, the son of the king of Iolcos in Thessaly, and leader of the ➤ ARGONAUTS in the quest for the ➤ GOLDEN *Fleece*, during which Jason has to perform such tasks as yoking a pair of fire-breathing bulls for ploughing, and sowing the dragon's teeth of ➤ CADMUS, from which spring up armed men. Assisted by the sorceress ➤ MEDEA, whom he marries, he is successful in his quest, but later when he deserts her for Creusa, daughter of the king of Corinth, Medea takes vengeance by killing the princess as well as her own children by Jason.

Jasper see also ➤ *Jasper* PETULENGRO.

jasper originally, any bright-coloured chalcedony other than carnelian; now, an opaque reddish-brown variety of chalcedony. In the Bible, jasper is the name of a stone in the high-priest's breastplate (Exodus 28:20); it is also one of the stones in the wall of the New Jerusalem (21:18).

Jataka any of the various stories of the former lives of the Buddha found in Buddhist literature. The name comes from Sanskrit *jātaka* 'born under'.

jatha an armed parade, especially of Sikhs.

jaundiced affected or tinged with jealousy or resentment, bitter; the usage, recorded from the early 18th century, related to the early belief that jealousy was associated with the medical condition *jaundice*, characterized by yellowing of the skin or whites of the eyes, and typically caused by obstruction of the bile duct, by liver disease, or by excessive breakdown of red blood cells.

jaunty nautical slang for the master-at-arms on a ship, perhaps an alteration of French *gendarme*.

Java man a fossil hominid of the Middle Pleistocene period, whose remains were found in Java in 1891.

Javan the Hebrew name for Ionia; used in some translations of the Bible for Ionia and the Greek region of Asia Minor.

jaw-jaw talk, especially at length, engage in lengthy and pointless discussion; the term was most famously used by Winston Churchill in a speech at the White House in 1954 when he said, 'To jaw-jaw is always better than to war-war.'

Jawi originally, the Malay vernacular. Now, the Malay language written in Arabic script.

Jaws of Life American trademark term for a hydraulic apparatus used to pry apart the wreckage of crashed vehicles in order to free people trapped inside.

jazz a type of music of black American origin characterized by improvisation, syncopation, and usually a regular or forceful rhythm, emerging at the beginning of the 20th century. Brass and woodwind instruments and piano are particularly associated with jazz, although guitar and occasionally violin are also used; styles include Dixieland, swing, bebop, and free jazz.

Jedburgh justice summary justice, such as that meted out to Border reivers at *Jedburgh* in southern Scotland in the 16th century; the term *Jeddart justice* is also used.

Jedi in ➤ STAR *Wars*, the name given to the mystical knightly order, trained to use the Force, whose powers have been misused and their order almost destroyed by the renegade ➤ DARTH *Vader*.

jeep a small, sturdy motor vehicle with four-wheel drive, especially one used by the military. The name dates from the Second World War, and comes from the initials *GP* standing for *general purpose*, influenced by 'Eugene the Jeep', a creature of great resourcefulness and power represented in the *Popeye* comic strip.

Jeeves the resourceful and influential valet of ➤ *Bertie* WOOSTER in the novels of ➤ P. G. WODEHOUSE.

Thomas Jefferson (1743–1826), American Democratic Republican statesman, 3rd President of the US 1801–9. He played a key role in the American leadership during the War of Independence and was the principal drafter of the ➤ DECLARATION *of Independence* (1776). While President, Jefferson secured the ➤ LOUISIANA *Purchase* (1803).

Judge Jeffreys (*c*.1645–89), Welsh judge and Chief Justice of the King's Bench from 1683, who took part in the ➤ POPISH *Plot* prosecutions and later became infamous for his brutal sentencing at the ➤ BLOODY *Assizes*.

Jehoshaphat a king of Judah in the mid 9th century BC.

Jehovah a form of the Hebrew name of God used in some translations of the Bible. The name comes from medieval Latin *Iehouah*, *Iehoua*, from Hebrew *YHWH* or *JHVH*, the consonants of the name of God, with the inclusion of vowels taken from *'ăḏōnāy* 'my lord'.

Jehovah's Witness a member of a fundamentalist Christian sect (the Watch Tower Bible and Tract Society) founded in the US by Charles Taze Russell (1852–1916), denying many traditional Christian doctrines (including the divinity of Christ) but preaching the Second Coming of Christ, and refusing military service and blood transfusion on religious grounds.

Jehu (842–815 BC), king of Israel, who at the invitation of Elisha led the revolt against the house of Ahab and had ➤ JEZEBEL killed; he was noted for his furious chariot-driving.

> It was one of those old, black, hearselike contraptions
> . . . driven by elderly Jehus with walrus moustaches.
> — Thomas Wolfe *You Can't Go Home Again* (1934)

Dr Jekyll the central character of Robert Louis Stevenson's story *The Strange Case of Dr Jekyll and Mr Hyde* (1886). He discovers a drug which creates a separate personality (appearing in the character of ➤ *Mr* HYDE) into which Jekyll's evil impulses are channelled. The term **Jekyll-and-Hyde** is often used to describe someone with violent and unpredictable changes of mood and personality.

Gertrude Jekyll (1843–1932), English horticulturalist and garden designer. Forced to abandon painting because of her failing eyesight, Jekyll turned to garden design. She designed over 300 gardens for buildings designed by Edwin Lutyens, promoting colour design in garden planning and 'wild' gardens.

jelly see ➤ ROYAL *jelly*.

Mrs Jellyby a character in Dickens's *Bleak House* (1853), who ignores and neglects her children

through her interest in 'Borrioboola Gha' in Africa, and who has become a type for ambitious philanthrophy which fails to see needs at close range.

Jemmy see ➤ *Jemmy* TWITCHER.

War of Jenkins's Ear a naval war between England and Spain (1739). It was precipitated by a British sea captain, Robert Jenkins, who appeared before Parliament to produce what he claimed was his ear, cut off by the Spanish while they were carrying out a search of his ship in the Caribbean. His story was probably at least partially fabricated.

Edward Jenner (1749–1823), English physician, the pioneer of vaccination. Jenner deliberately infected people with small amounts of cowpox as he believed it would protect them from catching smallpox. The practice was eventually accepted throughout the world, leading to the widespread use of vaccination for other diseases and eventually to the eradication of smallpox in the late 20th century.

jennet a small Spanish horse. The name comes (in late Middle English) via French from Spanish *jinete* 'light horseman', from Spanish Arabic *Zenāta*, the name of a Berber people famous for horsemanship.

jenneting an early ripening apple, so called from French *Jeannet* pet-form of Jean 'John', as in Norman French *pome de Jeannet* 'John's apple', because it was usually ripe by St John's Day, 24 June. In the 18th century, the first element was sometimes explained as representing the name of the month (as in *Juniting*).

Jephthah in the Bible, a judge of Israel who sacrificed his daughter in consequence of a vow that if victorious in battle he would sacrifice the first living thing that met him on his return. A similar rash promise was made by ➤ IDOMENEUS in Greek mythology.

jeremiad a long, mournful complaint or lamentation, a list of woes, as uttered by the prophet ➤ JEREMIAH.

Jeremiah (*c*.650–*c*.585 BC), a Hebrew major prophet who foresaw the fall of Assyria, the conquest of his country by Egypt and Babylon, and the destruction of Jerusalem. The biblical ➤ LAMENTATIONS are traditionally ascribed to him.

In extended usage, a *Jeremiah* is a person who complains continually or foretells disaster.

Jeremy see ➤ *Jeremy* DIDDLER.

Jerez a town in Andalusia, Spain; it is the centre of the sherry-making industry and its name is the origin of the word ➤ SHERRY.

Jericho a town in Palestine, in the West Bank north of the Dead Sea, which has been occupied from at least 9000 BC. According to the Bible, Jericho was a Canaanite city destroyed by the Israelites after they crossed the Jordan into the Promised Land; its walls were flattened by the shout of the army and the blast of the trumpets.

Occupied by the Israelis since the Six Day War of 1967, in 1994 Jericho was the first area given partial autonomy under the PLO–Israeli peace accord.

See also ➤ ROSE *of Jericho.*

jerk prepare (pork or chicken) by marinating it in spices and barbecuing it over a wood fire. The word comes (in the early 18th century) from Latin American Spanish *charquear*, ultimately from Quechua *echarqui* 'dried flesh'.

jerkwater of or associated with small, remote, and insignificant rural settlements. The term, which is mid 19th century, refers to the need for early railway engines to be supplied with water in remote areas, by dipping a bucket into a stream and 'jerking' it out by rope.

jeroboam a wine bottle with a capacity four times larger than that of an ordinary bottle. It is named after *Jeroboam*, a king of Israel 'who made Israel to sin'.

St Jerome (*c.*342–420), Doctor of the Church. He was secretary to Pope Damasus in Rome (382–5) before settling in Bethlehem, where he ruled a newly founded monastery and devoted his life to study. He is chiefly known for his compilation of the ➤ VULGATE.

In art Jerome is often shown in cardinal's dress, or with the lion from whose paw (according to legend) he removed a thorn; he may also have a stone in his hand as a sign of penance.

☐ **FEAST DAY** His feast day is 30 September.

Jerry see also ➤ TOM *and Jerry.*

Jerry informal term for a German (especially in military contexts); the word is recorded from 1919.

jerry-built badly or hastily built with materials of poor quality. The term is mid 19th century, and is sometimes said to be from the name of a firm of builders in Liverpool, or to allude to the walls of

Jericho, which fell down at the sound of Joshua's trumpets.

Jersey Lily nickname of the Jersey-born actress 'Lillie' Langtry (1852–1929), famous for her beauty; her portrait by Millais was entitled 'A Jersey Lily'.

Jerusalem the holy city of the Jews, sacred also to Christians and Muslims, lying in the Judaean hills about 30 km (20 miles) from the River Jordan.

The city was captured from the Canaanites by King David of the Israelites (*c.*1000 BC), who made it his capital. As the site of the Temple, built by Solomon (957 BC), it became also the centre of the Jewish religion. Since then it has shared the troubled history of the area—destroyed by the Babylonians in 586 BC and by the Romans in AD 70, refounded by Hadrian as a Gentile city (AD 135) under the name of Aelia Capitolina, destroyed again by the Persians in 614, and fought over by Saracens and Crusaders in the Middle Ages.

From 1099 it was the capital of a Crusader kingdom, which persisted as a political entity until 1291, even though Jerusalem itself was captured by Saladin in 1187. Suleiman the Magnificent rebuilt its walls (1542). From 1947 the city was divided between the states of Israel and Jordan until the Israelis occupied the whole city in June 1967 and proclaimed it the capital of Israel. It is revered by Christians as the place of Christ's death and resurrection, and by Muslims as the site of the Dome of the Rock.

See also ➤ NEW *Jerusalem,* ➤ NEXT *year in Jerusalem!*

Jerusalem artichoke a knobbly edible tuber with white flesh, eaten as a vegetable; the tall North American plant, closely related to the sunflower, which produces this tuber. Recorded from the early 17th century, *Jerusalem* is an alteration of Italian *girasole* 'sunflower'.

Jerusalem Bible a modern English translation of the Bible by mainly Roman Catholic scholars, published in 1966 and revised (as the **New Jerusalem Bible**) in 1985.

Jerusalem Chamber a room in Westminster Abbey in which Henry IV died, 20 March 1413.

Jerusalem cross a cross with arms of equal length each ending in a bar; a cross potent.

Jerusalem Delivered title of an epic poem by the Italian poet Torquato Tasso (1544–95) about the capture of Jerusalem by ➤ GODFREY *of Bouillon* and other crusaders.

Jerusalem letters letters or symbols tattooed on the arm or body, such as pilgrims or visitors to Jerusalem sometimes bore in testimony or memory of their visit.

Jerusalem pony a donkey (in allusion to Jesus's riding into Jerusalem on ➤ PALM *Sunday* on a donkey).

jessant in heraldry, (of a charge, as a branch or flower) represented as held in or issuing from the mouth of an animal.

Jesse in the Bible, the father of ➤ DAVID (1 Samuel 16), represented as the first in the genealogy of Jesus Christ.

Jesse tree a representation in carving or stained glass of the genealogy of Jesus as a tree with Jesse at the base and intermediate descendants on branching scrolls of foliage.

Jesse window a church window showing Jesus' descent from Jesse, typically in the form of a Jesse tree.

jest see ➤ *many a* TRUE *word spoken in jest*.

Jesu archaic form of ➤ JESUS, coming (in Middle English) from Old French. *Jesus* became the usual spelling in the 16th century, but *Jesu* was often retained in translations of the Bible, reflecting Latin vocative use.

Jesuit a member of the *Society of Jesus*, a Roman Catholic order of priests founded by ➤ *St* IGNATIUS *Loyola*, St Francis Xavier, and others in 1534, to do missionary work. The order was zealous in opposing the Reformation. Despite periodic persecution it has retained an important influence in Catholic thought and education.

By their enemies the Jesuits were accused of teaching that the end justifies the means, and the lax principles of casuistry put forward by a few of their moralists were ascribed to the order as a whole, thus giving rise to **jesuitical** in the sense dissembling or equivocating, in the manner once associated with Jesuits.

Jesuits' bark an archaic term for cinchona bark, introduced into Europe from the Jesuit Missions in South America.

Jesus the central figure of the Christian religion. He conducted a mission of preaching and healing (with reported miracles) in Palestine in about AD 28–30, which is described in the Gospels, as are his arrest, death by crucifixion, and Resurrection from the dead. His followers considered him to be the Christ or Messiah and the Son of God, and belief in his Resurrection became a central tenet of Christianity.

The name comes from Christian Latin *Iesus*, from Greek *Iēsous*, from a late Hebrew or Aramaic analogous formation based on *Yĕhōšûă* 'Joshua'.

See also ➤ *Jesus* PSALTER.

jetsam unwanted material or goods that have been thrown overboard from a ship and washed ashore, especially material that has been discarded to lighten the vessel. Recorded from the late 16th century, originally as *jetson*: a contraction of *jettison*.

See also ➤ FLOTSAM.

jeunesse dorée French term for ➤ GILDED *youth*.

Jew a member of the people and cultural community whose traditional religion is Judaism and who trace their origins to the ancient Hebrew people of Israel.

The name is Middle English and comes via Old French and Latin from Greek *Ioudaios*, via Aramaic from Hebrew *yĕhūdī*, from *yĕhūdāh* 'Judah'.

See also ➤ BLACK *Jew*, ➤ WANDERING *Jew*.

Jew's ear a common fungus with a brown rubbery cup-shaped fruiting body, growing on dead or dying trees in both Eurasia and North America. It is a mistranslation (from the mid 16th century) of medieval Latin *auricula Judae* 'Judas's ear', from its shape, and because it grows on the elder, which was said to be the tree from which Judas Iscariot hanged himself.

Jew's harp a small lyre-shaped musical instrument held between the teeth and struck with a finger. It can produce only one note, but harmonics are sounded by the player altering the shape of the mouth cavity. The name of the instrument is an ancient one, but no connection with Jews has been established with certainty.

jewel in the crown the best in a particular class of assets, traditionally used in the context of British colonial possessions.

jewels see ➤ CROWN *jewels*.

jewellers ➤ *St* ELOI is the patron saint of jewellers.

Jewish calendar a complex ancient calendar in use among Jewish people. It is a lunar calendar adapted to the solar year, normally consisting of twelve months but having thirteen months in leap years, which occur seven times in every cycle of nineteen years. The years are reckoned from the Creation (which is placed at 3761 BC); there are 12 months, with an intercalary month (First Adar) being added in leap years. The religious year begins with Nisan and ends with Adar, while the civil year begins with Tishri and ends with Elul.

Jewish calendar: months			
Nisan	Thammuz	Tishri	Tebet
Iyyar	Ab	Hesvan	Sebat
Sivan	Elul	Kislev	Adar

Jewish New Year another term for ➤ ROSH *Hashana*.

Jewry Jews collectively; formerly also, a Jewish quarter in a town or city.

Jews' myrtle a name for *butcher's broom*, from the tradition that the crown of thorns was made from its branches.

Jezebel (fl. 9th century BC), a Phoenician princess, traditionally the great-aunt of ➤ DIDO and in the Bible the wife of ➤ AHAB king of Israel. She was denounced by Elijah for introducing the worship of Baal into Israel, and was finally killed at the order of ➤ JEHU (2 Kings 10:30–37).

According to the story, when Jezebel heard that Jehu had come, she 'painted her face, and tired her head' and looked down from the window at him. At Jehu's order, she was thrown down from the window, and (following a prophecy made by Elijah) the dogs ate her body all except her skull, her feet, and the palms of her hands. Her use of cosmetics was especially condemned by Puritan England.

Jezreel in the Bible, the capital of Israel in the reign of Ahab; Naboth's vineyard was near to it, and it was in Jezreel that Jezebel was put to death, and of which Elijah had prophesied, 'In the portion of Jezreel shall dogs eat the flesh of Jezebel.' ➤ HOSEA later prophesied (Hosea 1:5) that guilt for the blood of Jezreel would fall on the house of Jehu, and that the nation of Israel would be destroyed in the valley of Jezreel.

Jezreelite a member of a sect founded by James White (1840–85) under his assumed name of James Jershom *Jezreel*; he had originally been a follower of ➤ *Joanna* SOUTHCOTT, and the initials of his new name were supposed to represent *Joanna* Southcott,

John Wroe (1782–1863), founder of the 'Christian Israelites', and *James* White; the use of ➤ JEZREEL may also refer to Hosea's prophecy.

Jhelum a river which rises in the Himalayas and flows through the Vale of Kashmir into Punjab, where it meets the Chenab River. It is one of the five rivers that gave Punjab its name. In ancient times it was called the Hydaspes.

jig see also ➤ DANCE *the Tyburn jig*.

jiggery-pokery deceitful or dishonest behaviour; the term (which is late 19th century) is probably a variant of Scots *joukery-pawkery*, from *jouk* 'dodge, skulk'.

jihad a holy war undertaken by Muslims against unbelievers. The name comes from Arabic *jihād*, literally 'effort', expressing, in Muslim thought, struggle on behalf of God and Islam.
See also ➤ ISLAMIC *Jihad*.

Jill see ➤ *every* JACK *has his Jill*, ➤ JACK *and Jill*.

Jim see also ➤ DIAMOND *Jim*, ➤ SUNNY *Jim*.

Jim Crow the name of a black character in a 19th-century plantation song, with the refrain 'Wheel about and turn about and jump Jim Crow'; the name was also used in the stage presentation of a song and dance act first performed by Thomas D. Rice (1808–60). From the mid 20th century, *Jim Crow* was also used to denote racial discrimination, especially through segregation of black people in the US.

Jim Crow laws laws which formerly ensured the segregation of black people in the US.

Jim'll fix it catch-phrase of a BBC television series (1975–94) for children starring Jimmy Savile in which participants had their wishes fulfilled.

Francisco Jiménez de Cisneros (1436–1517), Spanish cardinal and statesman, regent of Spain 1516–17, also known in English by the variant spelling **Ximenes**. He was Grand Inquisitor for Castile and Léon from 1507 to 1517, during which time he undertook a massive campaign against heresy, having some 2,500 alleged heretics put to death.

Jimmy Woodser an informal Australian expression for a person who drinks alone or for a drink taken on one's own, from a line in the poem 'Jimmy Wood' (1892) by Barcroft Boake: 'Who drinks alone, drinks toast to Jimmy Wood, sir.'

Jin name of two Chinese dynasties (in English, also called *Chin*).

A dynasty that ruled Manchuria and northern China AD 1115–1234.

A dynasty that ruled China AD 265–420, commonly divided into **Western Jin** (265–317) and **Eastern Jin** (317–420).

Jina in ➤ JAINISM, a great teacher who has attained liberation from karma; a carving or statue of such a teacher.

jingo a dated, chiefly derogatory expression for a vociferous supporter of policy (**jingoism**) favouring war, especially in the name of patriotism.

Originally (in the late 17th century) a conjuror's word, *by jingo* occurred in a popular song adopted by those supporting the sending of a British fleet into Turkish waters to resist Russia in 1878. The chorus ran: 'We don't want to fight, yet by Jingo! if we do, We've got the ships, we've got the men, and got the money too'.

jinn in Arabian and Muslim mythology, an intelligent spirit of lower rank than the angels, able to appear in human and animal forms and to possess humans, and having supernatural powers.

The name influenced the adoption from French of ➤ GENIE.

Muhammad Ali Jinnah (1876–1948), Indian statesman and founder of Pakistan. He headed the Muslim League in its struggle with the Hindu-oriented Indian National Congress over Indian independence. His fear that Muslims would be excluded from office led him to campaign for a separate Muslim state, and in 1947 he became the first Governor General and President of Pakistan.

jitterbug a fast dance popular in the 1940s, performed chiefly to swing music.

jive a lively style of dance popular especially in the 1940s and 1950s, performed to swing music or rock and roll.

Recorded from the 1920s (in the US, originally denoting meaningless or misleading speech).

Jix nickname of the British politician William Joynson-Hicks (1865–1932); his name was originally *Hicks*, but he added Joynson when he married Grace *Joynson*, daughter of a Manchester silk-manufacturer.

Joab in the Bible, commander of ➤ DAVID's army, who put ➤ ABSALOM to death: 'And he took three darts in his hand, and thrust them through the heart of Absalom, while he was yet alive in the midst of the oak.'

St Joachim in Christian tradition, the husband of St Anne and father of the Virgin Mary. He is first mentioned in an apocryphal work of the 2nd century, and then rarely referred to until much later times; scenes such as the marriage of Joachim and Anne are shown in medieval art.

☐ **FEAST DAY** In the Eastern Church the feast of St Joachim and St Anne is on 9 September; in the Western Church the feast of St Joachim was on 16 August, but is now (with St Anne) on 26 July.

Joan see also ➤ DARBY *and Joan.*

Pope Joan according to a legend widely believed in the Middle Ages, a woman in male disguise who (*c.*1100) became a distinguished scholar and then pope, reigned for more than two years, and died after giving birth to a child during a procession.

St Joan of Arc (*c.*1412–31), French national heroine, known as the **Maid of Orleans**. She led the French armies against the English in the Hundred Years War, relieving besieged Orleans (1429) and ensuring that Charles VII could be crowned in previously occupied Reims. Captured by the Burgundians in 1430, she was handed over to the English, convicted of heresy, and burnt at the stake. She was canonized in 1920.

☐ **FEAST DAY** Her feast day is 30 May.

Joasaph see ➤ *Sts* BARLAAM *and Joasaph.*

Job in the Bible, a prosperous man whose patience and piety were tried by undeserved misfortunes, and who, in spite of his bitter lamentations, remained confident in the goodness and justice of God; also, the book of the Bible recounting his story.

Job is shown initially as a man who is wealthy and upright, surrounded by his family; he is reduced from this to sitting among ashes scraping with potsherds at the boils that afflict him, while his wife urges him to 'Curse God, and die.' Despite this, and the comforting of his friends which only aggravates his sense of despair, he remains true to his belief in God, and is in the end restored and justified.

> I feel like Job and will rejoice in the deadly blasts of whatever comes.
> — Sylvia Plath letter, 29 April 1956

poor as Job very poor. Job after his possessions are taken from him becomes a type of abject poverty;

proverbial allusions to him are recorded from late Middle English.

Job's comforter a person who aggravates distress under the guise of giving comfort, with allusion to the story of the biblical patriarch, in which three friends who came to comfort him only increased his sense of injustice and wrong.

jobber in the UK, a principal or wholesaler who dealt only on the Stock Exchange with brokers, not directly with the public. On the UK Stock Exchange the term *jobber* was officially replaced by *broker-dealer* in 1986, broker-dealers being entitled to act as both agents and principals in share dealings.

jobsworth an official who upholds petty rules even at the expense of humanity or common sense. The expression comes from the supposedly characteristic response of such a person, 'It's more than my job's worth (not) to'.

Jocasta in Greek mythology, a Theban woman, the wife of ➤ LAIUS and mother and later wife of ➤ OEDIPUS. When she discovered that she had committed incest with her son, she hanged herself.

Jocism an organization, *Jeunesse Ouvrière Chrétienne* 'Christian working youth' aimed at spreading Christianity amongst working people, set up by Joseph Cardijn in Belgium in 1924 and later extended to other parts of Europe; the name comes from the initial letters of the organization.

jockey a person who rides in horse races, especially as a profession. Recorded from the late 16th century, the word is originally a diminutive of *Jock*, Scots form of the given name Jack, taken as the name for an ordinary man, lad, or underling; from this, the word came to mean 'mounted courier', thus giving rise (in the late 17th century) to the current sense.

Another early use 'horse-dealer' (long a byword for dishonesty) probably gave rise to the verb sense 'manipulate', whereas the main verb sense 'struggle *for* something' probably relates to the behaviour of jockeys manoeuvring for an advantageous position during a race.

Jockey Club an organization whose stewards are the central authority for the administration of horse racing in Britain. It was founded in 1750.

Jockey of Norfolk nickname of John Howard, Duke of Norfolk (*c.*1430–85), supporter of Richard III, who was killed at ➤ BOSWORTH; there is a tradition (recorded in Shakespeare's play) that before the battle he received a written warning, 'Jockey of

Norfolk be not too bold, for Dickon thy master is bought and sold.'

jodhpurs full-length trousers worn for horse riding, which are close-fitting below the knee and have reinforced patches on the inside of the leg. They are named after the former princely state of *Jodhpur*, where similar garments are worn by Indian men as part of everyday dress.

Jodrell Bank the site in Cheshire of one of the world's largest radio telescopes, with a fully steerable dish 76 m (250 ft) in diameter.

Joe an ordinary man (pet form of the given name *Joseph*); the usage is recorded from the mid 19th century.
See also ➤ UNCLE *Joe*, ➤ VINEGAR *Joe*.

Joe Bloggs in British usage, a name for a hypothetical average man.

Joe Blow in North American usage, a name for a hypothetical average man.

Joe Public a name for a hypothetical representative member of the general public, or the general public personified.

Joe Sixpack chiefly in the US, a name for a hypothetical ordinary working man; *Sixpack* refers to a pack of six cans of beer held together with a plastic fastener.

joey[1] in Australia, a young kangaroo, wallaby, or possum; the name comes from Aboriginal *joè*.

joey[2] a silver threepenny bit. The word is a diminutive of the pet name *Joe*: the derivation remains unknown. The term (originally London slang) denoted a fourpenny piece in the 19th century.

Joel a Hebrew minor prophet of the 5th or possibly 9th century BC; a book of the Bible containing his prophecies.

Johannes a Portuguese gold coin minted by *Joannes* or João V (1703–50), current in New England and later also Ireland.

johar the sacrificial burning of Rajput women to avoid their being captured by an enemy. The word comes via Hindi from Sanskrit *jatu-griha* 'house built of combustible materials'.

John the English given name which represents Latin and Greek *Johannes*; in English usage, it was traditionally taken as the representative proper name for a footman, butler, waiter, messenger, or someone in a similar role.

See also ➤ APPLE-*john*, ➤ BLUE *John*, ➤ BOBBING *John*, ➤ DEAR *John letter*, ➤ GLORIOUS *John*, ➤ *John* DOE, ➤ LITTLE *John*, ➤ LONG *John Silver*, ➤ PRESTER *John*, ➤ *St John* FISHER.

St John an Apostle, son of Zebedee and brother of ➤ *St* JAMES *the Great*, known as *St John the Evangelist* or *St John the Divine*, said to have been persecuted under Domitian but to have survived into old age.

St John was present at the Crucifixion and it was to him that care of the Virgin Mary was confided by the dying Jesus; he is traditionally identified with the ➤ BELOVED *disciple*.

He has traditionally been credited with the authorship of the fourth Gospel, Revelation, and three epistles of the New Testament.

In Christian art he is represented with a book (for the Gospel) and his symbol of an eagle; he may also be shown with a cup holding a viper, recalling the challenge to him by a priest of Diana at Ephesus to drink poisoned wine.

☐ **FEAST DAY** His feast day is 27 December.

John-a-Nokes a fictitious name for one of the parties in a legal action (the other often being named as ➤ JOHN-*a-Stiles*).

John-a-Stiles a fictitious name for one of the parties in a legal action (the other often being named as ➤ JOHN-*a-Nokes*).

John Barleycorn a personification of barley, or of malt liquor; the term is recorded from the early 17th century, in the title of a ballad of 'the bloody murther of Sir John Barleycorn'.

John Birch Society an extreme right-wing American organization founded in 1958 by Robert Welch, and named after a USAF officer killed in 1945, sometimes referred to as 'the first casualty of the Cold War'.

John Bull a personification of England or the typical Englishman, represented as a stout red-faced farmer in a top hat and high boots. The name is that of a character representing the English nation in John Arbuthnot's satire *Law is a Bottomless Pit; or, the History of John Bull* (1712).

John Bull's Other Island an ironic description of Ireland deriving from Leon Paul Blouet's *John Bull and his Island* (1884) and used by Shaw as the title of a play (1904) written at the request of Yeats 'as a patriotic contribution to the repertory of the Irish Literary Theatre'.

John Canoe in the West Indies, an elaborately masked dancer in a celebration held at Christmas; this celebration.

St John Chrysostom (*c.*347–407), Doctor of the Church, bishop of Constantinople. He attempted to reform the corrupt state of the court, clergy, and people; this offended many, including the Empress Eudoxia, who banished him in 403. His name means 'golden-mouthed' in Greek.

☐ **EMBLEM** His emblem is a bee.

☐ **FEAST DAY** His feast day is 27 January.

John Citizen a hypothetical ordinary man.

John Company a nickname for the ➤ EAST *India Company*, taken over from the name *Jan Kompanie*, by which the Dutch East India Company and Dutch government were traditionally known in the East Indies; a translation (1785) of Sparrman's *Voyage to the Cape of Good Hope* notes that the Dutch as traders in this area had represented their company as 'one individual powerful prince, by the Christian name of *Jan* or *John*', and that from this the writer had told his interpreter to say 'that we were the children of *Jan Company*'.

John Dory originally, a humorous version of a proper name; later, an edible dory (fish) of the eastern Atlantic and Mediterranean, with a black oval mark on each side. In the early 17th century, there was a popular ballad on the career of *John Dory*, supposedly the captain of a French privateer.

John Hancock informal American expression for a personal signature, perhaps from the American Revolutionary leader *John Hancock* (1737–93), the first of the signatories to the ➤ DECLARATION *of Independence*.

John Knox cap name for an academic cap as worn in Scottish universities, taken as the typical headgear of ➤ *John* KNOX.

St John Lateran the cathedral church of Rome, dedicated to St John the Baptist and St John the Evangelist, forming part of the ➤ LATERAN complex, and originally founded in the 4th century by ➤ CONSTANTINE.

John o'Groats a village at the extreme NE point of the Scottish mainland, said to be named after *John de Groat* and his two brothers, who came from Holland with a royal letter of protection and built a house on the site in the 16th century.

See also ➤ *from* LAND's *End to John o'Groats.*

St **John** of Beverley (d. 721), bishop of York, who is reputed to have shown special care for the poor and handicapped.

☐ **FEAST DAY** His feast day is 7 May, and his translation, 25 October.

St **John** of Damascus (*c.*675–*c.*749), Syrian theologian and Doctor of the Church. A champion of image worship against the iconoclasts, he wrote the influential encyclopedic work on Christian theology *The Fount of Wisdom.*

☐ **FEAST DAY** His feast day is 4 December.

John of Gaunt (1340–99), son of ➤ EDWARD *III*; he was effective ruler of England during the final years of his father's reign and the minority of Richard II. His son Henry Bolingbroke later became King ➤ HENRY *IV.* His title of Duke of *Lancaster* gave the name Lancastrian to one of the two sides in the 15th-century dynastic struggle of the ➤ WARS *of the Roses.*

Gaunt represents an Anglicization of his birthplace of ➤ GHENT.

See also ➤ *House of* LANCASTER.

St **John** of God (1495–1550), Portuguese founder of the Brothers Hospitallers, who fought as a mercenary for Spain against the French and Turks and later worked as a shepherd and a pedlar. He is patron of hospitals and the sick, and also of booksellers and printers.

☐ **FEAST DAY** His feast day is 8 March.

St **John** of Nepomuk (*c.*1345–93), priest and martyr, who was put to death by Wenceslas IV of Bohemia by being thrown into the river Moldau. He was later regarded as a martyr for the seal of the confession, since the story grew up that he had incurred the king's anger for refusing to reveal the contents of the queen's confession.

☐ **FEAST DAY** His feast day is 16 May.

St **John** of the Cross (1542–91), Spanish mystic and poet. A Carmelite monk and priest, he joined with St Teresa of Ávila in founding the 'discalced' Carmelite order in 1568. He also wrote mystical poems.

☐ **FEAST DAY** His feast day is 14 December.

John Sobieski (1624–96), king of Poland (as **John** III) 1674–96. In 1683 he relieved Vienna when it was besieged by the Turks, thereby becoming the hero of the Christian world.

St **John** the Baptist Jewish preacher and prophet, son of ➤ St ELIZABETH and ➤ ZACHARIAS, seen as the forerunner of Jesus: 'There was a man sent from God, whose name was John…He was not that Light, but was sent to bear witness of that Light' (John 1:6–8).

In *c.*27 AD he was preaching and baptizing on the banks of the River Jordan, and among those whom he baptized was Christ; John is reported to have said, 'I saw the Spirit descending like a dove, and it abode with him' (John 1:32).

He was beheaded by Herod Antipas after denouncing the latter's marriage to Herodias, the wife of Herod's brother Philip, and at the request of Herodias's daughter ➤ SALOME.

During his ministry John is said to have lived in the desert wearing camel's hair and eating locusts and wild honey (Matthew 3:4), and this is how he is typically represented.

☐ **FEAST DAY** His feast day is 24 June.

St **John** the Divine another name for ➤ St JOHN.

See also ➤ REVELATION *of St John the Divine.*

St **John** the Evangelist another name for ➤ St JOHN.

John the Fortunate (1604–56), John IV, king of Portugal (reigned 1640–56). The founder of the Braganza dynasty, he expelled a Spanish usurper and proclaimed himself king.

John the Great (1357–1433), John I, king of Portugal (reigned 1385–1433). Reinforced by an English army, he defeated the Castilians at Aljubarrota (1385), winning independence for Portugal. He established an Anglo-Portuguese alliance (1386), brought peace and prosperity and encouraged voyages of discovery.

John the Painter nickname of the incendiary James Aitken (1752–77); he had originally been apprenticed to a house-painter, and is said while in America to have taken part in the ➤ BOSTON *Tea Party.* In the belief that it would further America's cause, he planned to attack British dockyards, and set fire to the rope house at Portsmouth and warehouses at Bristol. Arrested, charged, and convicted, he was hanged at Portsmouth, and his body afterwards hung in chains at the mouth of the harbour.

Hey, Johnnie Cope Jacobite song celebrating the defeat of Sir John Cope at the ➤ *Battle of* PRESTONPANS in 1745, when Cope's force was surprised and routed; the first line of the song runs, 'Hey, Johnnie Cope, are ye waukin' yet?'

Johnny Reb in the American Civil War, a Unionist name for a Confederate soldier.

Amy Johnson (1903–41), English aviator, who in 1930 became the first woman to fly solo to Australia, although her time was three days short of the record. She later set a record with her solo flight to Tokyo (1931) and broke the solo-flight record to Cape Town (1932). She joined the Auxiliary Air Force in 1939, but was lost when her plane disappeared in a flight over the Thames estuary.

Andrew Johnson (1808–75), American Democratic statesman, 17th President of the US 1865–9. His lenient policy towards the Southern states after the American Civil War led him to be impeached by the Republican majority in Congress; he was acquitted by a single vote.

Earvin Johnson (1959–), American basketball player; known as **Magic Johnson**. He played for the Los Angeles Lakers from 1979 to 1991, winning the NBA's Most Valuable Player of the Year award three times. After being diagnosed HIV-positive he won an Olympic gold medal in 1992 and then returned to the Lakers.

Jack Johnson (1878–1946), American boxer. He was the first black world heavyweight champion (1908–15).

Lyndon Baines Johnson (1908–73), American Democratic statesman, 36th President of the US 1963–9, known as 'LBJ'. As Vice-President, he succeeded to the Presidency on Kennedy's assassination; in his first speech to Congress he said, 'All I have I would have given gladly not to be standing here today.'

As Majority Leader in the Senate he had been noted for his political prowess and earthy speech; as President he directed his energies to the campaign of social and economic reform which would build the 'Great Society'. He was largely successful, but the increasing involvement of the US in the ➤ VIET-NAM *War* undermined his popularity and he refused to seek re-election.

Pussyfoot Johnson informal name for the American temperance supporter W. E. Johnson (1862–1945); the term ➤ PUSSYFOOT derived from this.

Samuel Johnson (1709–84), English lexicographer, writer, critic, and conversationalist; known as **Dr Johnson**. A leading figure in the literary London of his day, he formed the Literary Club, which

numbered Edmund Burke, Oliver Goldsmith, Joshua Reynolds, David Garrick, and Johnson's biographer ➤ *James* BOSWELL among its members. His *A Dictionary of the English Language*, published in 1755, was and remains a landmark of lexicography.

Known as the ➤ GREAT *Cham* in the literary world, his physical characteristics were famously described by Macaulay:

> The gigantic body, the huge massy face, seamed with the scars of disease, the brown coat, the black worsted stockings, the grey wig with the scorched foretop, the dirty hands, the nails bitten and pared to the quick.
> — Lord Macaulay *Essays Contributed to the Edinburgh Review* (1843)

johnnycake a North American term for maize flour bread typically baked or fried on a griddle, perhaps an alteration of *journey cake*.

Jean de Joinville (*c*.1224–1317), French chronicler, author of the *Histoire de Saint Louis*, which provides a detailed account of the Seventh Crusade (1248–54).

joker a playing card, typically bearing the figure of a jester, used in some games as a wild card; in the US, *joker* denotes a clause unobtrusively inserted in a bill or document and affecting its operation in a way not immediately apparent.

In the ➤ BATMAN stories, the *Joker* is one of Batman's villainous opponents.

joker in the pack a person whose behaviour is unexpected or unpredictable.

jolly informal name for a Royal Marine, recorded from the early 19th century.

Jolly Roger a pirate's flag with a white skull and crossbones on a black background; the term is recorded from the late 18th century.

Jonah in the Bible, a Hebrew minor prophet, who was called by God to preach in Nineveh, but disobeyed and attempted to escape by sea; in a storm he was thrown overboard as a bringer of bad luck and swallowed by a great fish (traditionally, a whale), only to be saved and finally succeed in his mission.

The name *Jonah* is proverbially used for someone likely to bring bad luck, particularly at sea.

Jonah's gourd in the Authorized Version and other translations, a plant which grows quickly to shade the prophet is called a *gourd*:

> And the Lord God prepared a gourd, and made it come up over Jonah, that it might be a shadow over his head, to deliver him from his grief.
>
> — Bible (AV) Jonah ch. 4 v. 6

Jonathan in the Bible, a son of ➤ SAUL, noted for his friendship with ➤ DAVID and killed with his father at the battle of Mount Gilboa by the Philistines. David famously lamented his friend, 'I am distressed for thee, my brother Jonathan: very pleasant hast thou been unto me' (2 Samuel 1:26).

See also ➤ BROTHER *Jonathan*.

Jonathan's a coffee-house in Change Alley, Cornhill, referred to in The *Tatler* and The *Spectator* as a mart for stock-jobbers.

Jones see also ➤ BROWN, *Jones, and Robinson*, ➤ DAVY *Jones's locker*, ➤ DOW *Jones Index*, PAUL Jones.

Daniel Jones (1881–1967), British phonetician. He developed the International Phonetic Alphabet from 1907 and went on to invent the system of cardinal vowels.

Indiana Jones an archaeologist, played by Harrison Ford in the film *Raiders of the Lost Ark* (1981, by Steven Spielberg) and its two sequels; a mild-mannered academic in the classroom, on the trail of a lost treasure such as the ➤ ARK *of the Covenant* or the ➤ HOLY *Grail* he is transformed into a daring adventurer armed with a bullwhip.

> These people want to be Indiana Jones without the discipline of having to study for it . . . They are robbing ancient cultures of their achievements.
>
> — *Daily Telegraph* 7 August 1999

Inigo Jones (1573–1652), English architect and stage designer. He introduced the Palladian style to England; notable buildings include the Queen's House at Greenwich (1616) and the Banqueting Hall at Whitehall (1619). He also pioneered the use of the proscenium arch and movable stage scenery in England.

John Paul Jones (1747–92), Scottish-born American admiral. He became famous for his raids off the northern coasts of Britain during the War of American Independence, and is said when asked on 23 September 1779 whether he had lowered his flag, as his ship was sinking, to have replied, 'I have not yet begun to fight.'

keep up with the Joneses try to maintain the same social and material standards as one's friends and neighbours; the expression derives from a comic-strip title, 'Keeping up with the Joneses—by Pop' in the New York *Globe*, 1913.

jongleur in the Middle Ages, an itinerant minstrel. The word is French, a variant of *jougleur* 'juggler', earlier *jogleor* 'pleasant, smiling', from Latin *joculator* 'joker'.

Ben Jonson (1572–1637), English dramatist and poet. With his play *Every Man in his Humour* (1598) he established his 'comedy of humours', whereby each character is dominated by a particular obsession. He became the first Poet Laureate in the modern sense.

Janis Joplin (1943–70), American singer. She died from a heroin overdose just before her most successful album, *Pearl*, and her number-one single 'Me and Bobby McGee' were released.

In 1969 her hopes that her photograph would appear on the cover of *Newsweek* were frustrated by the death of former President Eisenhower, of which she said bitterly, 'Fourteen heart attacks and he had to die in my week. In MY week.'

Joppa biblical name for ➤ JAFFA.

Jordan a river flowing southward for 320 km (200 miles) from the Anti-Lebanon Mountains through the Sea of Galilee into the Dead Sea. John the Baptist baptized Christ in the River Jordan. It is regarded as sacred not only by Christians but also by Jews and Muslims.

The crossing of Jordan is taken figuratively (after Numbers 33:51, in reference to the Israelites passing over Jordan to the land of Canaan) to symbolize death; the usage was reinforced by John Bunyan in the second part of *Pilgrim's Progress* (1684) in the story of Mr Standfast's crossing the river, when 'the trumpets sounded for him on the other side'.

jordan almond a high-quality almond of a variety grown chiefly in SE Spain. The name, which is late Middle English, apparently comes from French or Spanish *jardin* 'garden'.

jorum a large bowl or jug which was used for serving drinks such as tea or punch. The word (which is early 18th century) may come from the biblical figure *Joram*, who 'brought with him vessels of silver, and vessels of gold' to King David (2 Samuel 8:10).

Jorvik Viking name for York; the name is now used in the title of the *Jorvik Viking Centre*, founded by the York Archaelogical Trust and recreating for visitors the streets of the Viking city of York as established through archaeological exploration.

Joseph in the Bible, a Hebrew patriarch, son of ➤ JACOB. He was given a coat of many colours by his father, whose favourite he was, and he exacerbated his brothers' jealousy by dreams which predicted his dominance over them, as by their sheaves in the harvest field bowing down to the sheaf of Joseph.

Sold by them into captivity in Egypt and at risk from the machinations of ➤ POTIPHAR's wife, he attained high office in Egypt, finding favour with Pharaoh by his interpretation of the dream of seven fat and seven lean cattle, and seven full and seven thin ears of corn, as a warning against a coming famine.

The story is ultimately one of reconciliation, when his brothers come to Egypt to buy corn and are in Joseph's power; in the end the whole family of Jacob settles in Egypt.

St Joseph husband of the Virgin Mary. A carpenter of Nazareth, and by later tradition already elderly, he was betrothed to Mary at the time of the Annunciation. In Christian art, representations of the Nativity often show St Joseph a little apart from the main group, with his chin on his hand.

□ **FEAST DAY** His feast day is 19 March.

Joseph of Arimathea a member of the council at Jerusalem who, after the Crucifixion, asked Pilate for Christ's body, which he buried in his own tomb. He is also known from the medieval story that he came to England with the ➤ HOLY *Grail* and built the first church at ➤ GLASTONBURY.

Josephine (1763–1814), Empress of France 1804–9. She married Napoleon in 1796. Their marriage proved childless and she was divorced by Napoleon in 1809. She is remembered in the (probably apocryphal) words attributed to Napoleon, 'Not tonight, Josephine' (the phrase, current by the early 20th century, does not appear in contemporary sources).

Josephite a member of a party formed among Russian Orthodox monks in the 16th century, who defended the holding of property by monastic communities. They are named after St *Joseph* (1439–1515), Abbot of Volokolamsk, Russian reformer.

Flavius Josephus (*c*.37–*c*.100), Jewish historian, general, and Pharisee. His *Jewish War* gives an eyewitness account of the events leading up to the Jewish revolt against the Romans in 66, in which he was

a leader. His *Antiquities of the Jews* is a history running from the Creation to 66.

Joshua (fl. *c*.13th century BC), the Israelite leader who succeeded ➤ MOSES; he led his people into the Promised Land, and captured ➤ JERICHO. Also, the sixth book of the Bible, named for him, telling of the conquest of Canaan and its division among the twelve tribes of Israel.

Joshua tree a yucca which grows as a tree and has clusters of spiky leaves, native to arid regions of south-western North America. The name apparently comes (in the mid 19th century) from the plant's being likened to a man brandishing a spear, with reference to Joshua 8:18 ('and Joshua stretched out his hand with the spear towards the city').

Josiah in the Bible, a king of Judah who put an end to the worship of idols and restored strict religious observance.

joss a Chinese religious statue or idol. The word, which is early 18th century, comes from Javanese *dejos*, from obsolete Portugues *deos*, and ultimately from Latin *deus* 'god'.

jot a very small amount; via Latin, from Greek *iōta*, the smallest letter of the Greek alphabet.

nor one jot or tittle not the smallest amount; after Matthew 5:18, 'Till heaven and earth pass, one jot or one tittle shall in no wise pass from the law'; *tittle* here comes from the medieval Latin for 'small stroke, accent' (see ➤ TITTLE).

Jotun in Scandinavian mythology, a member of the race of giants, enemies of the gods.

Jotunheim in Scandinavian mythology, a region of the universe, inhabited by giants.

jouk and let the jaw go by proverbial saying, early 18th century; *jouk* here is a Scottish word meaning 'stoop or duck' and *jaw* means 'a rush of water', and the tenor of the advice is to be cautious when danger threatens.

James Prescott Joule (1818–89), English physicist. Joule established that all forms of energy were interchangeable—the first law of thermodynamics. The Joule–Thomson effect, discovered with William Thomson, later Lord Kelvin, in 1852, led to the development of the refrigerator and to the science of cryogenics. Joule also measured and described the heating effects of an electric current passing through a resistance.

Joule–Thomson effect the change of temperature of a gas when it is allowed to expand without doing any external work. The gas becomes cooler if it was initially below a certain temperature (the *inversion temperature*), or hotter if initially above it.

Monsieur Jourdain the central character of Molière's *Le Bourgeois Gentilhomme* (1671), to whom it is revealed that for forty years he has 'been speaking prose without knowing it'.

journalism see ➤ CHEQUEBOOK *journalism*.

journalists ➤ St FRANCIS *de Sales* is the patron saint of journalists.

journey an act of travelling from one place to another. The word dates from Middle English, and the earliest senses, 'day, a day's travel, a day's work' come from Old French, based on Latin *diurnum* 'daily portion'.
    See also ➤ IS *your journey really necessary*, ➤ NIGHT *Journey*, ➤ SABBATH *day's journey*.

journeyman a trained worker who is employed by someone else; in its original sense (in late Middle English) the word meant someone who was not bound by indentures, but was paid by the day.

Jove another name for ➤ JUPITER; the name comes from Latin *Jov-*, stem of Old Latin *Jovis*, replaced later by *Jupiter*. The dated English exclamation **by Jove** is recorded from the late 16th century.
    See also ➤ BIRD *of Jove*.

Jove but laughs at lovers' perjury proverbial saying, mid 16th century.

jovial cheerful and friendly, with reference to the supposed influence of the planet *Jupiter* on those born under it.

Jovinianist a follower or adherent of *Jovinian*, a 4th-century Milanese monk who denied the superiority of virginity over marriage and the particular merit of abstinence, holding that all forms of Christian living are equally rewarded in heaven.

jowl see ➤ CHEEK *by jowl*.

joy see ➤ SEVEN *joys of Mary*, ➤ TRAVELLER*'s joy*.

joy of a planet in astrology, the fact or condition of a planet being in the house where it is most powerful.

James Joyce (1882–1941), Irish writer. One of the most important writers of the modernist movement, he made his name with *Dubliners* (short stories, 1914). His novel *Ulysses* (1922) revolutionized the structure of the modern novel and developed the stream-of-consciousness technique.

William Joyce (1906–46), nicknamed ➤ *Lord* HAW-*Haw*, wartime broadcaster from Nazi Germany, executed for treason.

Joyous Gard the castle of Lancelot in Arthurian legend. It is situated somewhere in the north, and Malory says it has been variously identified as Alnwick or Bamburgh (near Berwick-on-Tweed). Tristram once keeps Iseult there for three years; after Lancelot has to surrender Guinevere it is renamed 'Dolorous Gard'.

Don Juan legendary Spanish lover and hero of a number of stories, the type of a heartless seducer. According to a Spanish story first dramatized by Gabriel Téllez (1584–1641), he was Don Juan Tenorio of Seville.

juba a dance originating among plantation slaves in the southern US, featuring rhythmic handclapping and slapping of the thighs.

jube a rood-loft or screen and gallery dividing the choir of a church from the nave. The word comes from Latin meaning 'bid' or 'order', and is said to be from the words *Jube, domine, benedicere*, said from it by the deacon before the reading of the Gospel.

Jubilate Psalm 100, beginning *Jubilate deo* 'rejoice in God', especially as used as a canticle in the Anglican service of matins.

jubilee a special anniversary of an event, especially one celebrating twenty-five or fifty years of a reign or activity.
    In Jewish history, a jubilee is a year of emancipation and restoration, kept every fifty years; in the Roman Catholic Church, it is a period of remission from the penal consequences of sin, granted by the Roman Catholic Church under certain conditions for a year, usually at intervals of twenty-five years.
    Recorded from late Middle English, the word comes via Old French from late Latin *jubilaeus (annus)* '(year) of jubilee', based on Hebrew *yōḇēl*, originally 'ram's-horn trumpet', with which the jubilee year was proclaimed.
    See also ➤ DIAMOND *jubilee*.

Book of Jubilees a Jewish apocryphal text which reinterprets the narrative of Genesis in terms of a scheme of dating related to Jewish law and ceremonial.

Judaea the southern part of ancient Palestine, corresponding to the former kingdom of Judah. The Jews returned to the region after the Babylonian Captivity, and in 165 BC the Maccabees again established it as an independent kingdom. It became a province of the Roman Empire in 63 BC, and was subsequently amalgamated with Palestine.

Judah in the Bible, a Hebrew patriarch, the fourth son of Jacob. Also, the tribe of Israel traditionally descended from him, the most powerful of the twelve tribes of Israel.

Judah is also the name given to the southern part of ancient Palestine, occupied by the tribe of Judah. After the reign of Solomon (*c.*930 BC) it formed a separate kingdom from Israel.

Judaism the monotheistic religion of the Jews. For its origins Judaism looks to the biblical covenant made by God with Abraham, and to the laws revealed to Moses and recorded in the Torah (supplemented by the rabbinical Talmud), which established the Jewish people's special relationship with God.

Since the destruction of the Temple in Jerusalem in AD 70, the rituals of Judaism have centred on the home and the synagogue, the chief day of worship being the Sabbath (sunset on Friday to sunset on Saturday), and the annual observances including Yom Kippur and Passover.

See also ➤ CONSERVATIVE *Judaism,* ➤ ORTHODOX *Judaism,* ➤ REFORM *Judaism.*

Judas one of the twelve Apostles; full name **Judas Iscariot,** who betrayed Christ to the Jewish authorities in return for ➤ THIRTY *pieces of silver;* the Gospels leave his motives uncertain. Overcome with remorse, he later committed suicide by hanging, and was buried in the ➤ POTTER's *field.*

Judas Bible an early 17th century translation in which *Judas* appears as a misprint for *Jesus.*

Judas-coloured of hair, red, from the medieval tradition that Judas Iscariot had red hair and beard.

Judas goat an animal used to lead others in a flock or herd to destruction, as in a slaughterhouse.

Judas kiss an act of betrayal, especially one disguised as a gesture of friendship, with biblical allusion to the betrayal of Christ, when in

➤ GETHSEMANE Judas identified their quarry to the soldiers with a kiss of greeting.

Judas Maccabaeus (d. *c.*161 BC), Jewish leader. Leading a Jewish revolt in Judaea against Antiochus IV Epiphanes from around 167, he recovered Jerusalem and dedicated the Temple anew, and protected Judaism from Hellenization. He is the hero of the two books of the Maccabees in the Apocrypha.

Judas tree a Mediterranean tree of the pea family, with purple flowers that typically appear before the rounded leaves; according to popular belief, Judas hanged himself on a tree of this kind.

Judas window a small aperture in a door (in some old houses, or in prison cells), through which a person can look without being noticed from the other side; a peep-hole.

St Jude an Apostle, supposed brother of James; also known as *Judas.* Thaddaeus (mentioned in St Matthew's Gospel) is traditionally identified with him. According to tradition, he was martyred in Persia with St Simon.

He may be shown holding a club, as the instrument of his martyrdom; otherwise he is seen holding a fish (while St Simon has a ship).

☐ **FEAST DAY** His feast day (with St Simon) is 28 October.

Judenrat a council representing a Jewish community, especially in German-occupied territory during the Second World War. The word is German, and means 'Jewish council'.

judge a public officer appointed to decide cases in a law court, proverbially taken as a type of gravity and sobriety. ➤ St Ivo *of Brittany* is the patron saint of judges.

The office of a judge is referred to as the ➤ BENCH; in the UK, a judge formally wears scarlet robes trimmed with ermine, sometimes alluded to as symbolizing the office.

In ancient Israel, a *judge* was a leader having temporary authority in the period between Joshua and the kings.

The word comes (in Middle English, via Old French) from Latin *judex,* judic-, from *jus* 'law' + *dicere* 'to say'.

See also ➤ JUDGES.

Judge Advocate General an officer in supreme control of the courts martial in the armed forces, excluding (in the UK) the navy.

no one should be judge in his own case proverbial saying, mid 15th century.

judge not, that ye be not judged proverbial saying, late 15th century; with biblical allusion to the words of Jesus in Matthew 7:1.

judgement see ➤ DAY *of Judgement*, ➤ LAST *Judgement*.

Judgement Day the time of the ➤ LAST *Judgement*; the end of the world.

judgement in default judgement awarded to the plaintiff on the defendant's failure to plead.

Judgement of Solomon in the Bible, the arbitration of king ➤ SOLOMON over a baby claimed by two women. He proposed cutting the baby in half, and then gave it to the woman who showed concern for its life, recognizing that the true mother was the one who would relinquish the child rather than have it harmed.

Judges the seventh book of the Bible, describing the conquest of Canaan under the leaders called 'judges' in an account that is parallel to that of the Book of Joshua and is probably more accurate historically. The book includes the stories of Deborah, Jael, Gideon, Jephthah, and Samson.

Judges' Rules in English law, rules regarding the admissibility of an accused's statements as evidence.

Judicial Committee of the Privy Council (in the UK) a court made up of members of the House of Lords and others, which considers appeals made to the Sovereign in Council concerning decisions of some Commonwealth courts outside the UK.

Judith in the Apocrypha, a rich Israelite widow who saved the town of Bethulia from Nebuchadnezzar's army by seducing the besieging general ➤ HOLOFERNES and cutting off his head while he slept. Also, a book of the Apocrypha recounting the story of Judith.

Judy the wife of Punch in the ➤ PUNCH *and Judy* show.

Jugendstil German term for ➤ ART *nouveau*; the word is German, from *Jugend* 'youth' + *Stil* 'style'.

Juggernaut in Hinduism, the form of Krishna worshipped in Puri, Orissa, where in the annual festival his image is dragged through the streets on a heavy chariot; devotees are said formerly to have thrown themselves under its wheels.

The word *juggernaut*, meaning a large heavy vehicle, comes in extended usage from this.

The name comes via Hindi from Sanskrit *Jagannātha* 'Lord of the World'.

juggler a person who continuously tosses into the air and catches a number of objects so as to keep at least one in the air while handling the others, especially as a professional entertainer; the word was originally recorded (in late Old English) in the sense 'magician, wizard', and developed through 'a conjuror, a person performing feats of dexterity' to the current sense. In figurative usage, a *juggler* is a trickster.

The word comes (like ➤ JONGLEUR) via Old French from Latin *joculator*, from *joculari* 'to jest', from *joculus* diminutive of *jocus* ' joke'.

Jugurtha (d.104 BC), joint king of Numidia *c.*118–104. His attacks on his royal partners prompted intervention by Rome and led to the outbreak of the **Jugurthine War** (112–105). He was eventually captured by the Roman general Marius and executed in Rome.

Julia set a set of complex numbers which do not converge to any limit when a given mapping is repeatedly applied to them. In some cases the result is a connected fractal set.

The term is recorded from the 1970s, and is named after Gaston M. *Julia* (b. 1893), Algerian-born French mathematician.

Julian the Apostate (*c.*331–63 AD), Roman emperor from 360 AD, nephew of Constantine. He restored paganism as the state cult in place of Christianity, but this move was reversed after his death on campaign against the Persians; his last words are said to have been, ➤ VICISTI, *Galilaee*.

St Julian the Hospitaller an almost certainly entirely mythical saint, who was later associated with historical figures of this name; according to a 13th-century legend, he was a young nobleman who when out hunting encountered a hart which prophesied that he would kill his own parents.

When through an accident this happened, he embarked on a life of penance, building a hospital by a river-crossing, and helping travellers to cross the river. Finally he was told that his penance was acceptable to God.

□ **PATRONAGE** He is the patron of innkeepers, boatmen, and travellers.

Julian calendar a calendar introduced by the authority of Julius Caesar in 46 BC, in which the year consisted of 365 days, every fourth year having 366 days. It was superseded by the Gregorian calendar, though it is still used by some Orthodox Churches. Dates in the Julian calendar are sometimes designated 'Old Style'.

Julian of Norwich (*c.*1342–*c.*1413), English mystic. She is said to have lived as a recluse outside St Julian's Church, Norwich. She is chiefly associated with the *Revelations of Divine Love* (*c.*1393), a description of a series of visions she had in which she depicts the Holy Trinity as Father, Mother, and Lord, and in which she makes the assertion 'Sin is behovely [necessary], but all shall be well and all shall be well and all manner of thing shall be well.'

Julian year (the average length of) a year of the Julian calendar.

Juliet the heroine of Shakespeare's *Romeo and Juliet* (1595), sometimes taken as a type of doomed young love.

Juliet cap a type of women's small ornamental cap, typically made of lace or net and often worn by brides. Recorded from the early 20th century, it is so named because it forms part of the usual costume of the heroine of Shakespeare's *Romeo and Juliet*.

julio an Italian silver coin of small denomination, struck by Pope *Julius* II (1503–13).

Julius Caesar (100–44 BC), Roman general and statesman. He established the First Triumvirate with ➤ Pompey and Crassus (60), and became consul in 59, obtaining command of the provinces of Illyricum, Cisalpine Gaul, and Transalpine Gaul. Between 58 and 51 he fought the Gallic Wars, subjugating Transalpine Gaul and defeating ➤ Vercingetorix, invading Britain (55–54), and acquiring immense power.

Resentment at this on the part of Pompey and other powerful Romans led to civil war; in 49 BC Caesar crossed the ➤ Rubicon into Italy, and next year Pompey was defeated at ➤ Pharsalia.

Julius Caesar was made dictator of the Roman Empire and initiated a series of reforms, including the introduction of the Julian calendar; in Egypt he had a brief liaison with ➤ Cleopatra. Hostility to Caesar's autocracy culminated in his murder on the ➤ Ides (15th) of March in a conspiracy led by ➤ Brutus and Cassius.

July the seventh month of the year, in the northern hemisphere usually considered the second month of summer. The name is recorded from Middle English, and comes from Latin *Julius (mensis)* '(month) of July', named after Julius Caesar.

See ➤ the Fourth *of July,* ➤ a swarm *in May is worth a load of hay.*

the July monarchy a name for the monarchy (1830–48) of ➤ Louis *Philippe,* king of the French, who became king in the ➤ July *Revolution* of 1830.

the July Revolution the revolution of 1830 in which Charles X of France was overthrown and by which ➤ Louis *Philippe* gained the throne as king of the French.

jumart a fictitious hybrid animal, said to be born of a mating between a bull and a mare or she-ass, or between a horse or ass and a cow.

Jumbo name of an elephant at London Zoo, sold in 1882 to the Barnum and Bailey circus; the word had originally denoted a large and clumsy person.

Jumna a river of northern India, which rises in the Himalayas and flows in a large arc southwards and south-eastwards, through Delhi, joining the Ganges below Allahabad. Its source (Yamunotri) and its confluence with the Ganges are both Hindu holy places. Its Hindu name is *Yamuna.*

June the sixth month of the year, in the northern hemisphere usually considered the first month of summer. Recorded from Middle English, the word comes via Old French from Latin *Junius (mensis)* '(month) of June', variant of *Junonius* 'sacred to Juno'.

See also ➤ the Fourth *of June,* ➤ Glorious *First of June,* ➤ a swarm *in May is worth a load of hay.*

a dripping June sets all in tune proverbial saying, mid 18th century; meaning that rain in June is beneficial to all crops and plants.

June War Arab name for ➤ Six *Day War.*

Carl Jung (1875–1961), Swiss psychologist. Jung originated the concept of introvert and extrovert personality, and of the four psychological functions of sensation, intuition, thinking, and feeling. He collaborated with Sigmund Freud in developing the psychoanalytic theory of personality, but later disassociated himself from Freud's preoccupation with sexuality as the determinant of personality, preferring to emphasize a mystical or religious factor in the unconscious.

Jungfrau a mountain in the Swiss Alps, taken as a type of a distant snowy peak.

> We saw Queen Mary looking like the Jungfrau, white and sparkling in the sun.
> — Henry ('Chips') Channon diary, 22 June 1937

Junggramatiker the members of a late 19th-century school of historical linguists who held that phonetic changes (sound laws) operate without exceptions.

jungle see ➤ BLACKBOARD *jungle*, ➤ CONCRETE *jungle*, ➤ LAW *of the jungle.*

Junius pseudonymous author of a series of letters that appeared in the *Public Advertiser* between 1769 and 1772, attacking among others the duke of Grafton, Lord Mansfield, and George III himself.

Junius see also ➤ *Lucius Junius* BRUTUS.

junk old or discarded articles considered useless or of little value. The usage dates from the mid 19th century; originally (in late Middle English) it denoted an old or inferior rope.

Junkanoo chiefly in Jamaica, Belize, and the Bahamas, a masquerade held at Christmas, consisting of a street procession of characters in traditional costumes and dancing to drums, bells, and whistles.

Junker a German nobleman or aristocrat, especially a member of the Prussian aristocracy. The word comes from German, ultimately from Middle High German *junc* 'young' + *herre* 'lord'.

junket a dish of sweetened and flavoured curds of milk, often served with fruit. Also, an extravagant trip or celebration.

In late Middle English, the word (from Old French *jonquette* 'rush basket', from *jonc* 'rush', from Latin *juncus*) denoted a rush basket, especially one for fish (this remained in dialect use); the term also denoted a cream cheese, formerly made in a rush basket or served on a rush mat. A later extended sense 'feast, merrymaking' gave rise to the second sense current today.

Juno in Roman mythology, the most important goddess of the Roman state, wife of ➤ JUPITER. She was originally an ancient Italian goddess. Her Greek equivalent is ➤ HERA.

See also ➤ BIRD *of Juno.*

junta a military or political group that rules a country after taking power by force; earlier (in the early 17th century) a deliberative or administrative council in Spain or Portugal. The word comes from Spanish and Portuguese, from Latin *juncta*, feminine past participle of *jungere* 'join'.

Jupiter in Roman mythology, the chief god of the Roman state religion, giver of victory, originally a sky god associated with thunder and lightning. His wife was Juno. Also called *Jove*. His Greek equivalent is ➤ ZEUS. The name is Latin, from *Jovis pater*, literally 'Father Jove'.

In astronomy, *Jupiter* is the name given to the largest planet in the solar system, a gas giant which is the fifth in order from the sun and one of the brightest objects in the night sky.

Jupiter Ammon as worshipped in the Egyptian western desert, where the cult of the Egyptian god ➤ AMUN was linked with Jupiter.

Jurassic the second period of the Mesozoic era, between the Triassic and Cretaceous periods. The Jurassic lasted from about 208 to 146 million years ago. Large reptiles, including the largest known dinosaurs, were dominant on both land and sea. Ammonites were abundant, and the first birds (including Archaeopteryx) appeared.

The name comes from French *jurassique*, from the Jura mountains on the border of France and Switzerland.

Jurassic Park title of a thriller (1990) by Michael Crichton and the Spielberg film based on it, in which dinosaurs were cloned from fossil DNA to stock a theme park; the result was carnage as the systems for control and safety failed. *Jurassic Park* is now referred to as a type of environment where savagery prevails.

> In the Jurassic Park of the Balkans, the mutant beasts of old-style communism and atavistic nationalism have taken on a new lease of life—the dinosaurs rule.
> — *Observer* 29 December 1996

jurist the Franciscan preacher St John of Capistrano (1386–1456), a noted student of theology, is the patron saint of jurists.

jury a body of people (typically twelve in number, giving rise to the expression ➤ TWELVE *good men and true*) sworn to give a verdict in a legal case on the basis of evidence submitted to them in court. The word is recorded from late Middle English, and comes from Old French *juree* 'oath, inquiry', from Latin *jurata*, feminine past participle of *jurare* 'swear'.

See also ➤ PACK *a jury.*

the jury is still out the final decision has not been given; referring to the custom that a jury in court retires to consider its verdict.

jury-rigged of a ship, having temporary makeshift rigging; *jury* perhaps based on Old French *ajurie* 'aid'.

jus gentium international law; Latin, literally 'law of nations'.

jus primae noctis a term for ➤ DROIT *de seigneur*; Latin, literally 'right of the first night'.

the Just epithet of several rulers and lawgivers, as the 5th-century Athenian statesman ➤ ARISTIDES.

be just before you're generous proverbial saying, mid 18th century.

just war in the Middle Ages, a debate among moral theologians on the circumstances in which participation in war by Christians could be justified led to St Thomas Aquinas's laying down three conditions which a *just war* must meet: it had to be authorized by the sovereign, the cause must be just, and those engaging in it must have the intention of advancing good or avoiding evil. In the 16th century a fourth condition was added by the Spanish theologian Francisco de Vitoria (d. 1546), saying that the war must be fought by 'proper means'.

The phrase is recorded in English from the late 15th century; it was used most recently in the debate on the Allied action against Serbia in May 1999.

just when you thought it was safe to go back in the water advertising copy for the film *Jaws 2* (1978), featuring the return of the great white shark in its role as maneater.

justice see ➤ JEDBURGH *justice*, ➤ KNIGHT *of Justice*, ➤ POETIC *justice*.

bed of justice a bed (in French, *lit de justice*) adorned in a particular way in the French king's bedchamber, where he gave receptions; the throne of the king in the Parliament of Paris; also, a sitting of this parliament at which the king was present. As the king sometimes convened the parliament to enforce the registration of his own decrees, the term came to be chiefly or exclusively applied to sessions held for this purpose.

Justice of the Peace in the UK, a lay magistrate appointed to hear minor cases, grant licences, etc., in a town, county, or other local district.

justiciar a regent and deputy presiding over the court of a Norman or early Plantagenet king of England. Also, either of two supreme judges in medieval Scotland.

St Justin (*c.*100–165), Christian philosopher; known as **St Justin the Martyr**. According to tradition he was martyred in Rome together with some of his followers. He is remembered for his *Apologia* (*c.*150).

□ **FEAST DAY** His feast day is 1 June.

Justinian (483–565), Byzantine emperor 527–65, husband of ➤ THEODORA. Through his general ➤ BELISARIUS he regained North Africa from the Vandals, Italy from the Ostrogoths, and Spain from the Visigoths. He codified Roman law in ➤ *the* DIGEST (529) and carried out a building programme throughout the Empire, of which St Sophia at Constantinople (532) was a part.

Jute a member of a Germanic people that (according to Bede) joined the Angles and Saxons in invading Britain in the 5th century, settling in a region including Kent and the Isle of Wight. They may have come from Jutland.

Battle of Jutland a major naval battle in the First World War, fought between the British Grand Fleet under Admiral Jellicoe and the German High Seas Fleet in the North Sea west of Jutland on 31 May 1916. Although the battle was indecisive the German fleet never again sought a full-scale engagement, and the Allies retained control of the North Sea.

Juvenal (*c.*60–*c.*140), Roman satirist. His sixteen verse satires present a savage attack on the vice and folly of Roman society, chiefly in the reign of the emperor Domitian.

juvenilia works produced by an author or artist while still young; the word is recorded from the early 17th century, and comes from Latin, from the neuter plural of *juvenilis*, from *juvenis* 'young, a young person'.

Famous examples of juvenilia include the chronicles of ➤ ANGRIA and ➤ GONDAL compiled by the Brontë children.

Kk

K the eleventh letter of the modern English alphabet and the tenth of the ancient Roman one, corresponding to Greek *kappa*, Phoenician and general Semitic *kaph*.

See also ➤ *the* Five *Ks*.

K 2 the highest mountain in the Karakoram range, on the border between Pakistan and China. It is the second-highest peak in the world, and was discovered in 1856 and named K2 because it was the second peak to be surveyed in the Karakoram range. It was also formerly known as *Mount Godwin-Austen* after Col. H. H. Godwin-Austen, who first surveyed it.

ka in ancient Egypt, the supposed spiritual part of an individual human being or god, which survived (with the soul) after death and could reside in a statue of the person.

ka me, ka thee traditional saying implying mutual help or mutual flattery; recorded from the mid 16th century.

Kaaba a square stone building in the centre of the Great Mosque at ➤ Mecca, the site most holy to Muslims and towards which they must face when praying. It stands on the site of a pre-Islamic shrine said to have been built by Abraham, and a sacred Black Stone is set in its south-eastern corner.

kabaddi a sport of Indian origin played by teams of seven on a circular sand court. The players attempt to tag or capture opponents and must hold their breath while running, repeating the word 'kabaddi' to show that they are doing so.

kabaka the traditional ruler of the Baganda people of Uganda.

Kabbalah the ancient Jewish tradition of mystical interpretation of the Bible, first transmitted orally and using esoteric methods (including ciphers). It reached the height of its influence in the later Middle Ages and remains significant in ➤ Hasidism.

kabloona among Inuit people, a person who is not a member of the Inuit; a white person. The word comes from Inuit *kabluna* 'big eyebrow'.

kabuki a form of traditional Japanese drama with highly stylized song, mime, and dance, now performed only by male actors, using exaggerated gestures and body movements to express emotions, and including historical plays, domestic dramas, and dance pieces.

Kabul the capital of Afghanistan, situated in the north-east of the country, with a strategic position commanding the mountain passes through the Hindu Kush, especially the Khyber Pass. It was capital of the Mogul empire 1504–1738 and in 1773 replaced Kandahar as capital of an independent Afghanistan. It suffered severe damage in the conflict that followed the Soviet invasion of Afghanistan in 1979.

kachina a deified ancestral spirit in the mythology of Pueblo Indians; a person who represents such a spirit in ceremonial dances.

Kaddish an ancient Jewish prayer sequence regularly recited in the synagogue service, including thanksgiving and praise and concluding with a prayer for universal peace; a form of this prayer sequence recited for the dead. The word comes from Aramaic *qaddīš* 'holy'.

Kaffir chiefly in South African usage, an insulting and contemptuous term for a black African. The word *Kaffir* is first recorded in the 16th century (as *Caffre*) and was originally simply a descriptive term for a particular ethnic group. Now it is always a racially abusive and offensive term when used of people, and in South Africa its use is actionable. Some mining authorities and other employers in South Africa adopted the term *fanakalo* as an alternative to *Kaffir*.

Franz Kafka (1883–1924), Czech novelist, who wrote in German. His work is characterized by its portrayal of an enigmatic and nightmarish reality where the individual is perceived as lonely, perplexed, and threatened.

kagura a form of traditional sacred music and dance performed at Shinto festivals.

kahuna in Hawaii, a wise man or shaman.

Kai Lung the Chinese sage and storyteller who is the central character of a series of stories by Ernest Bramah (1868–1942).

k'ai shu the usual script used for the Chinese language, suitable for everyday purposes.

Kairouan a city in NE Tunisia which is a Muslim holy city and a place of pilgrimage.

kaiser the German Emperor, the Emperor of Austria, or the head of the Holy Roman Empire; in British usage, **the Kaiser** refers particularly to ➤ WILHELM *II* of Germany (1859–1941), especially in the context of the First World War.

The word is originally recorded from Middle English (in form *cayser*), from Old Norse *keisari*, based on Latin *Caesar*; the modern English form (early 19th century) derives from German *Kaiser*.

the Kaiser's War a name for the First World War.

kaizen a Japanese business philosophy of continuous improvement of working practices and personal efficiency.

Kalahari Desert a high, vast, arid plateau in southern Africa north of the Orange River, comprising most of Botswana with parts in Namibia and South Africa.

Kalevala a collection of Finnish legends transmitted orally until published in the 19th century, and now regarded as the Finnish national epic.

Kaleyard School a group of late 19th-century fiction writers, including J. M. Barrie, who described local town life in Scotland in a romantic vein and with much use of the vernacular.

Kaleyard in Scots means literally 'kitchen garden'.

Kalgoorlie a gold-mining town in Western Australia. Gold was discovered there in 1887, leading to a gold rush in the 1890s.

Kali in Hinduism, the most terrifying goddess, wife of ➤ SHIVA, often identified with Durga, and in her benevolent aspect with Parvati. She is typically depicted as black, naked, old, and hideous, with a necklace of skulls, a belt of severed hands, and a protruding bloodstained tongue. The ➤ THUGS were her devotees.

> It's your own hunger, not some she-demon with gaping jaws. It's your own fear, not Kali.
> — Kate Green *Night Angel* (1989)

Kalidasa (probably fl. 5th century AD), Indian poet and dramatist. He is best known for his drama *Sakuntala*, the love story of King Dushyanta and the maiden Sakuntala.

Union of the Kalmar the treaty which joined together the Crowns of Denmark, Sweden, and Norway in 1397, dissolved in 1523.

kalon the ideal good; the *summum bonum*. Recorded from the mid 18th century, the word comes from Greek.

kalpa in Hindu and Buddhist tradition, an immense period of time, reckoned as 4,320 million human years, and considered to be the length of a single cycle of the cosmos (or 'day of Brahma') from creation to dissolution.

Kama the Hindu god of love, typically represented as a youth with a bowl of sugar cane, a bowstring of bees, and arrows of flowers.

Kama Sutra an ancient Sanskrit treatise on the art of love and sexual technique; the name comes from Sanskrit, from *kāma* 'love' + *sūtra* 'thread'.

kamerad especially in the First World War, used by a German-speaking soldier notifying to an enemy a wish to surrender; the word is German for 'comrade'.

kami a divine being in the Shinto religion.

kamikaze in the Second World War, a Japanese aircraft loaded with explosives and making a deliberate suicidal crash on an enemy target. The word, which is Japanese, comes from *kami* 'divinity' + *kaze* 'wind', originally referring to the gale that, in Japanese tradition, destroyed the fleet of invading Mongols in 1281.

kana the system of syllabic writing used for Japanese, having two forms, hiragana and katakana.

kanaka former term for a Pacific Islander employed as an indentured labourer in Australia, especially in the sugar and cotton plantations of Queensland.

kanban a Japanese manufacturing system in which the supply of components is regulated through the use of a card displaying a sequence of specifications and instructions, sent along the production line. Also, a card of this type.

Kanchenjunga a mountain in the Himalayas, on the border between Nepal and Sikkim, which is the world's third-highest mountain. The name is Tibetan, meaning literally 'the five treasures of the snows', referring to the five separate peaks of the summit.

Kandahar a city in southern Afghanistan, which from 1748 was Afghanistan's first capital after independence, until being replaced by Kabul in 1773.

Wassily Kandinsky (1866–1944), Russian painter and theorist. A pioneer of abstract art, he urged the expression of inner and essential feelings in art, rather than the representation of surface appearances. In 1911 he co-founded the Munich-based *Blaue Reiter* group of artists, and later taught at the Bauhaus (1922–33).

Kandy a city in Sri Lanka, which was the capital (1480–1815) of the former independent kingdom of Kandy and contains one of the most sacred Buddhist shrines, the Dalada Maligava (Temple of the Tooth).

kangaroo a large plant-eating marsupial with a long powerful tail and strongly developed hind-limbs that enable it to travel by leaping, found only in Australia and New Guinea. The word, recorded from the late 18th century, is the name of a specific kind of kangaroo in an extinct Aboriginal language of North Queensland.

kangaroo closure in the UK, a parliamentary closure involving the selection by a committee chairperson of some amendments and the exclusion of others.

kangaroo court an unofficial court held by a group of people in order to try someone regarded, especially without good evidence, as guilty of a crime or misdemeanour.

kangha a comb worn in the hair as one of the five distinguishing signs of the Sikh ➤ KHALSA, symbolizing cleanliness.

kanji a system of Japanese writing using Chinese characters, used primarily for content words.

Kanpur a city in Uttar Pradesh, northern India, on the River Ganges, also known as *Cawnpore*. It was the site of a massacre of British soldiers and European families in July 1857, during the Indian Mutiny.

Immanuel Kant (1724–1804), German philosopher. In the *Critique of Pure Reason* (1781) he countered Hume's sceptical empiricism by arguing that

any affirmation or denial regarding the ultimate nature of reality ('noumenon') makes no sense. All we can know are the objects of experience ('phenomena'), interpreted by space and time and ordered according to twelve key concepts. Kant's *Critique of Practical Reason* (1788) affirms the existence of an absolute moral law—the categorical imperative.

Kantaka name of the white horse belonging to Prince Siddhartha Gautama, later the ➤ BUDDHA, on which he rode when he left his palace to renounce his worldly life. *Kantaka* was born on the same day as his master and died mourning for his departure; he is said to have been reborn as a god.

kapellmeister a leader of a chamber ensemble or orchestra, originally as attached to a German court. The word comes (in the mid 19th century) from German, from *Kapelle* 'court orchestra' (from medieval Latin *capella* 'chapel') + *Meister* 'master'.

kappa the tenth letter of the Greek alphabet (**K, κ**), transliterated as 'k'.

kapu in Hawaiian traditional culture and religion, a set of rules and prohibitions for everyday life.

kara a steel bangle worn on the right wrist as one of the five distinguishing signs of the Sikh ➤ KHALSA, symbolizing loyalty, commitment, and unity with God.

Vuk Stefanović Karadžić (1787–1864), Serbian writer, grammarian, lexicographer, and folklorist. He modified the Cyrillic alphabet for Serbian written usage and compiled a Serbian dictionary in 1818. Widely claimed to be the father of modern Serbian literature, he collected and published national folk stories and poems.

Karaite a member of a Jewish sect founded in the 8th century and located chiefly in the Crimea and nearby areas, and in Israel, which rejects rabbinical interpretation in favour of a literal interpretation of the scriptures.

Recorded from the early 18th century, the name comes from Hebrew *Qārā'īm* 'Scripturalists', from *qārā'* 'read'.

Karakorum an ancient city in central Mongolia, now ruined, which was the capital of the Mongol empire, established by Genghis Khan in 1220. The capital was moved by Kublai Khan to Khanbaliq (modern Beijing) in 1267, and Karakorum was destroyed by Chinese forces in 1388.

karanga a Maori ritual chant of welcome.

karaoke a form of entertainment, offered typically by bars and clubs, in which people take turns to sing popular songs into a microphone over pre-recorded backing tracks. The term comes (in the 1970s) from Japanese, and means literally 'empty orchestra'.

karate an oriental system of unarmed combat using the hands and feet to deliver and block blows, widely practised as a sport. It was formalized in Okinawa in the 17th century, and popularized via Japan after about 1920. Karate is performed barefoot in loose padded clothing, with a coloured belt indicating the level of skill, and involves mental as well as physical training.

The word is Japanese, from *kara* 'empty' + *te* 'hand'.

Karbala a city in southern Iraq, which is a holy city for Shiite Muslims, being the site of the tomb of Husayn, grandson of Muhammad, who was killed there in AD 680.

Anna Karenina the tragic heroine of Tolstoy's novel of that name (1875–7), whose unhappy love affair with Count Vronsky, and the pressures of a hypocritical society, end in her killing herself by throwing herself in front of a train.

Karitane trained or administered according to the principles of child care and nutrition advocated by the Royal New Zealand Society for the Health of Women and Children (the Plunket Society). The name comes (in the early 20th century) from the name of a township in New Zealand.

Boris Karloff (1887–1969), British-born American actor. His name is chiefly linked with horror films, such as the monster in *Frankenstein* (1931), and *The Body Snatcher* (1945).

In the UK in the 1990s, the name *Doris Karloff* was applied to the Conservative politician Ann Widdecombe, who as a Home Office minister was held by some to embody a capacity for terror equivalent to that evoked by Karloff's traditional roles.

karma in Hinduism and Buddhism, the sum of a person's actions in this and previous states of existence, viewed as deciding their fate in future existences. The word comes from Sanskrit *karman* 'action, effect, fate'.

karma yoga in Hinduism, the discipline of selfless action as a way to perfection.

Karmathian a member of a Muslim sect founded in the 9th century, and named after *Karmat*, founder of the sect.

Karnak a village in Egypt on the Nile, now largely amalgamated with Luxor. It is the site of the northern complex of monuments of ancient Thebes, including the great temple of ➤ AMUN.

Fred Karno (1866–1941), comedian; his 'Army' was the company which gave a solid start or valuable experience to many comedians, and which later became known as a type of chaotic organization ('We are Fred Karno's army, the ragtime infantry', perhaps referring to 'Kitchener's Army', was one of the trench songs of the First World War).

Karoo an elevated semi-desert plateau in South Africa; the name comes from *Khoikhoi*, literally 'hard, dry'.

karoshi in Japan, death caused by overwork or job-related exhaustion; recorded from the late 1980s, the word is Japanese, from *ka* 'excess' + *rō* 'labour' + *shi* 'death'.

karuna in Buddhism, loving compassion.

the kasbah in a North African city, the area surrounding the citadel, typically the old part of a city; the word figures in a famous supposed film line, ➤ COME *with me to the Casbah*.

kashrut the body of Jewish religious laws concerning such things as the suitability of food and the use of ritual objects. The word is Hebrew, literally 'legitimacy in religion'.

katabasis a military retreat (with reference to that of the 10,000 Greeks from Asia under ➤ XENOPHON, as narrated in his work the *Anabasis*); a descent into the underworld. The word is Greek, from *kata* 'down' + *basis* 'going'.

katakana the more angular form of kana (syllabic writing) used in Japanese, primarily used for words of foreign origin.

katana a long, single-edged sword used by Japanese ➤ SAMURAI.

Kathak a type of northern Indian classical dance, with alternating passages of mime and dancing; a member of a northern Indian caste of storytellers and musicians.

The word comes from Sanskrit *kathaka* 'professional storyteller', from *kathā* 'story'.

Kathakali a form of dramatic dance of southern India, based on Hindu literature and characterized by masks, stylized costume and make-up, and frequent use of mime. The name comes from Malayalam, from Sanskrit *kathā* 'story' + Malayalam *kaḷi* 'play'.

katharevousa a heavily archaized form of modern Greek used in traditional literary writing, as opposed to the form which is spoken and used in everyday writing (called demotic).

Recorded from the early 20th century, the word comes from modern Greek, literally 'purified', ultimately from Greek *katharos* 'pure'.

kathenotheism Vedic polytheism, in which each god in turn for a period of time is considered single and supreme.

Kattern old name for the feast day of ➤ *St* CATH-ERINE *of Alexandria*, 25 November, especially as celebrated by lacemakers in the Midlands.

katun a period of twenty years, each of 360 days, in the calendar of the Mayan Indians.

Katzenjammer Kids cartoon drawn by Rudolf Dirks in 1897 for the *New York Journal*, featuring Hans and Fritz, two incorrigible children; the name *Katzenjammer* came from German *Katzen* (combining form of *Katze* 'cat') + *Jammer* 'distress'.

kavadi a decorated arch carried on the shoulders as an act of penance in Malaysian Hindu religious practice.

Kawi the classic or poetic language of Java and Bali, in which the ancient indigenous language is mixed with many words of Sanskrit origin.

Sir Kay in the Arthurian legend (as in Malory), Arthur's steward, a brave but churlish knight, foster-brother of Arthur, whose rough manners are sometimes explained by his having been brought up by a nurse while Arthur was reared by Kay's own mother.

Edmund Kean (1787–1833), English actor. Achieving fame as Shylock at London's Drury Lane theatre in 1814, he became renowned for his interpretations of Shakespearean tragic roles, notably those of Macbeth and Iago. Coleridge said of him, 'To see him

act, is like reading Shakespeare by flashes of lightning.'

Tom Keating (1917–84), artist, restorer, and faker, who came to public notice in 1976 when it was revealed that thirteen water-colours attributed to Samuel Palmer were in fact by Keating; he said later that his purpose was fooling the experts rather than making money, and that in the end it was the point that the joke should become public knowledge. His trial in 1979 was halted because of his ill-health, but he became something of a public figure, broadcasting on his favourite artists with great success.

Buster Keaton (1895–1966), American actor and director. His deadpan face and acrobatic skills made him one of the biggest comedy stars of the silent-film era. He starred in and directed films including *The Navigator* (1924), and *The General* (1926).

John Keats (1795–1821), English poet. A principal figure of the romantic movement, he wrote all of his most famous poems, including 'La Belle Dame sans Merci', 'Ode to a Nightingale', and 'Ode on a Grecian Urn', in 1818 (published in 1820). Keats was noted for his spiritual and intellectual contemplation of beauty. He died in Rome of tuberculosis.

John Keble (1792–1866), English churchman. His sermon on national apostasy (1833) is generally held to mark the beginning of the ➤ OXFORD *Movement*, which he founded with John Henry Newman and Edward Pusey. Politically, it failed to win support for its idea that the law of the land need not coincide with the Church's teaching; theologically, however, the work of Keble's followers did much to revive traditional Catholic teaching, as well as to define and mould the Church of England.

Kedar in the Bible, the name of a son of ➤ ISH-MAEL, and of the nomadic tribe descended from him; in Psalm 120:5 'the tents of Kedar' are seen as a place of exile and barbarism, and Isaiah prophesies 'all the glory of Kedar shall fail.'

Christine Keeler (1942–), English model and showgirl. She achieved notoriety with her affair with the Conservative cabinet minister ➤ *John* PRO-FUMO in 1963 when she was also mistress of a Soviet attaché. Profumo resigned and Keeler was imprisoned on related charges.

keelhaul in former naval practice, punish someone by dragging them through the water under the keel of a ship, either across the width or from bow to stern.

keen wail in grief for a dead person; from Irish *caoinim* 'I wail'.

Charles Samuel Keene (1823–91), English illustrator and caricaturist. He is remembered for his work in the weekly journal *Punch* from 1851.

why keep a dog and bark yourself? proverbial saying, late 16th century.

keep a thing seven years and you'll always find a use for it proverbial saying, early 17th century.

keep no more cats than will catch mice proverbial saying, late 17th century.

keep taking the tablets supposedly traditional advice from a doctor, especially when little change in the patient's condition is envisaged.

keep your own fish-guts for your own sea-maws proverbial saying, early 18th century.

keep your shop and your shop will keep you proverbial saying, early 17th century.

keeper see ➤ *am I my* BROTHER's *keeper?*, ➤ FINDERS *keepers (losers weepers)*.

Keeper of the Great Seal an officer in England and Scotland (in England now the Lord Chancellor) who has the custody of the Great Seal.

Keeper of the Privy Seal in England, former name for the Lord Privy Seal; a similar officer in Scotland and the Duchy of Cornwall.

Helen Keller (1880–1968), American writer, social reformer, and academic. Blind and deaf from the age of nineteen months, she learned how to read, type, and speak with the help of a tutor; describing the moment at which communication through words was made, she said, 'The mystery of language was revealed to me. I knew then that 'w-a-t-e-r' meant the wonderful cool something that was flowing over my hand.' She went on to champion the cause of blind and deaf people throughout the world.

Kellogg Pact a treaty renouncing war as an instrument of national policy, signed in Paris in 1928 by representatives of fifteen nations. It grew out of a proposal made by the French Premier Aristide Briand (1862–1932) to Frank B. Kellogg (1856–1937), US Secretary of State. Also called **Kellogg–Briand Pact**.

Kells see ➤ BOOK *of Kells*.

Ned Kelly (1855–80), Australian outlaw. Leader of a band of horse and cattle thieves and bank raiders operating in Victoria, he was eventually hanged in Melbourne. He became a folk hero, and the expression **game as Ned Kelly** meaning 'very brave' is proverbial.

Kelmscott the name of *Kelmscott* House, Hammersmith (named after Kelmscott Manor, Kelmscott, Oxfordshire), the home of ➤ *William* MORRIS (1834–1896), used in the name of the Kelmscott Press, which was founded there by him in 1890 and worked until 1898, printing limited editions of fine books.

kelpie a water spirit of Scottish folklore, typically taking the form of a horse, reputed to delight in the drowning of travellers. The word (recorded from the late 17th century) may come from Scottish Gaelic *cailpeach, colpach* 'bullock, colt'.

The later derived sense of a sheepdog of an Australian breed, originally bred from a Scottish collie, apparently comes from the name of a particular bitch, *King's Kelpie* (*c.*1879).

William Thomson Kelvin (1824–1907), British physicist and natural philosopher. He is best known for introducing the absolute scale of temperature. He also restated the second law of thermodynamics and was involved in the laying of the first Atlantic cable, for which he invented several instruments.

Kelvin scale a scale of temperature with absolute zero as zero, and the triple point of water as exactly 273.16 degrees (equivalent to 0° Celsius).

Kemal see ➤ *Kemal* ATATÜRK.

Fanny Kemble (1809–93), English actress. The daughter of Charles Kemble and the niece of Sarah Siddons, she was a success in both Shakespearean comedy and tragedy, playing such parts as Portia, Beatrice, Juliet, and Lady Macbeth.

John Philip Kemble (1757–1823), English actor-manager, brother of Sarah Siddons. Noted for his performances in Shakespearean tragedy, he was manager of Drury Lane (1788–1803) and Covent Garden (1803–17) theatres. His younger brother *Charles Kemble* (1775–1854) was also a successful actor-manager.

Margery Kempe (*c.*1373–*c.*1440), English mystic. From about 1432 to 1436 she dictated one of the first autobiographies in English, *The Book of Margery*

Kempe. It gives an account of her series of pilgrimages, as well as details of her mystic self-transcendent visions.

Kempeitai the Japanese military secret service in the period 1931–45.

Kempis see ➤ Thomas à *Kempis*.

Kendal Green a kind of rough green woollen cloth; the green colour of this cloth. Kendal in Cumbria (formerly Westmorland) was a noted centre for cloth-weaving, and *Rymer's Foedera* has a letter of protection, of the year 1331, to John Kempe of Flanders, who established cloth-weaving there.

St Kenelm (d. 812 or 821), a prince of the Mercian royal family, who may have died in battle against the Welsh, and was buried at Winchcombe. In the later **Kenelm Legend** of the 11th century, he is said to have been murdered in infancy on the orders of a jealous sister; the whereabouts of his body was later revealed by a document in Old English, dropped by a dove on to the high altar of St Peter's, Rome, which was read by English pilgrims.

    ☐ **FEAST DAY** His feast day is 17 July.

John Fitzgerald Kennedy (1917–63), 35th President of the US 1961–3, known as *JFK*. The youngest man ever to be elected US President (at 43), he gained a reputation as an advocate for civil rights. In foreign affairs, despite the ➤ *Bay of* Pigs fiasco, and particularly after the ➤ Cuban *Missile Crisis*, he was seen as a glamorous and popular world leader.

    He was assassinated while riding in a motorcade through Dallas, Texas, in November 1963; Lee Harvey Oswald was charged with his murder, but was himself shot before he could stand trial. Oswald was said to be the sole gunman by the Warren Commission (1964), but the House of Representatives Assassinations Committee (1979) concluded that more than one gunman had been involved; the affair remains the focus for a number of conspiracy theories, as those involving the ➤ grassy *knoll*.

Kenneth I (d. 858), king of Scotland *c*.844–58; known as **Kenneth MacAlpin**. He is traditionally viewed as the founder of the kingdom of Scotland, which was established following his defeat of the Picts in about 844.

Kensal Green the first London cemetery (as distinct from a churchyard), opened in 1832, and used allusively as a symbol of death and burial.

> For there is good news yet to hear and fine things to be seen,
> Before we go to Paradise by way of Kensal Green.
> — G. K. Chesterton 'The Rolling English Road' (1914)

Kensington a fashionable residential district in central London. Part of the borough of Kensington and Chelsea, it contains Kensington Palace (the birthplace of Queen Victoria), Kensington Gardens, and the Victoria and Albert Museum, Natural History Museum, and Science Museum.

Kent one of the kingdoms of Anglo-Saxon England, probably covering much the same area as the modern county in SE England.

    See also ➤ Fair *Maid of Kent*, ➤ Holy *Maid of Kent*.

Man of Kent a native or inhabitant of the county of Kent living to the east of the River Medway; distinguished from a ➤ Kentish *man*.

William Kent (*c*.1685–1748), English architect and landscape gardener. Chiefly remembered for his landscape gardens at Stowe House in Buckinghamshire (*c*.1730), he also promoted the Palladian style of architecture in England and is renowned for such works as the Treasury (1733–7) and Whitehall (1734–6).

Kent's Cavern a large limestone cave near Torquay, Devon, in which were found human and animal bones from a very early period, first discovered in the early 19th century.

Kentish fire a prolonged volley of rhythmic clapping, either as applause or as a demonstration of impatience or dissent (said to have originated in reference to meetings held in Kent in 1828–9 in opposition to the Catholic Relief Bill).

Kentish man a native or inhabitant of Kent living west of the River Medway; distinguished from a ➤ Man *of Kent*.

St Kentigern (d. 612), monk and bishop, evangelist of Strathclyde and Cumbria, and associated particularly with Glasgow; he is said to have been the illegitimate grandson of a British prince, and is also known by his pet name of *Mungo*. His later legends include the story that when the queen was told by her husband to find within three days a ring which he had thrown out to sea, he comforted her by telling her that the ring had been returned in a salmon caught by one of his monks; from this, a ring and a

fish appear on the arms of the city of Glasgow.
□ **FEAST DAY** His feast day is 13 January.

Kentucky Derby an annual horse race for three-year-olds at Louisville, Kentucky. First held in 1875, it is the oldest horse race in the US.

Kentucky Tragedy a celebrated 19th-century American murder, also known as the *Beauchamp case*, in which an attorney, Jerome Beauchamp, stabbed to death Solomon P. Sharp, former seducer of his wife Ann Beauchamp, and solicitor-general of Kentucky. After a long trial marked by corruption on both sides, Beauchamp was condemned to death. His wife died in their subsequent attempt at a suicide pact, but Beauchamp was hanged.

Johannes Kepler (1571–1630), German astronomer. His analysis of Tycho Brahe's planetary observations led him to discover the three laws governing orbital motion. The first two laws recognized the elliptical orbits of the planets; in *Harmonices Mundi* (1620) he expounded the third law of planetary dynamics, relating the distances of the planets from the sun to their orbital periods.

Kepler's laws three theorems describing orbital motion. The first law states that planets move in elliptical orbits with the sun at one focus. The second states that the radius vector of a planet sweeps out equal areas in equal times. The third law relates the distances of the planets from the sun to their orbital periods.

kermes a red dye used, especially formerly, for colouring fabrics and manuscripts; the dried bodies of a female scale insect (the **oak kermes**), which are crushed to yield this dye.
    Recorded from the late 16th century (denoting the small evergreen oak on which the insect forms berry-like galls), the word comes via French from Arabic *ḳirmiz*, related to *crimson*.

kermis a summer fair held in towns and villages in the Netherlands; in the US, a fair or carnival, especially one held to raise money for a charity. The term, dating from the late 16th century, originally denoted a mass on the anniversary of the dedication of a church, when a fair was held, from *kerk* 'church' + *mis* 'Mass'.

Kermit the Frog the name of the bright green frog who is one of the central characters of ➤ *the* MUPPETS.

kern in the Middle Ages, a light-armed Irish foot soldier. The word comes (in late Middle English, via Irish) from Old Irish *ceithern* 'band of foot soldiers'.

Knight of Kerry one of three hereditary Irish titles (the others being the ➤ *Knight of* GLIN and the ➤ WHITE *Knight*); the title, belonging to the Fitzgerald family, is recorded from the 15th century.

kersey a kind of coarse, ribbed cloth with a short nap, woven from short-stapled wool, probably named from *Kersey*, a town in Suffolk where woollen cloth was made.

kerygma the preaching of the Gospels; the element of proclamation as contrasted with *didache* (teaching) in the communication of the Christian gospel.

kesh the uncut hair and beard worn as one of the five distinguishing signs of the Sikh ➤ KHALSA, symbolizing dedication.

kestrel a small falcon that hovers with rapidly beating wings while searching for prey on the ground; figuratively (in archaic use), a contemptible person. In falconry, a *kestrel* is traditionally the bird flown by a knave.

Jack Ketch (1663–86), public executioner. His name became notorious on account of his barbarity at the executions of William Lord Russell, the ➤ *Duke of* MONMOUTH (who is said to have requested, 'Do not hack me as you did my Lord Russell'), and other political offenders, and from that (and perhaps partly also from association with the verb *catch*) it was given to the hangman in the puppet-play of Punchinello, which was introduced from Italy shortly after his death; finally, *Jack Ketch* became a generic term for an executioner.

kethib a traditional reading in the Hebrew text of the Old Testament and Hebrew Scriptures which is unintelligible or unsuitable for public reading and for which another word or passage is substituted.

kettle see also ➤ *the* POT *calling the kettle black*.

kettle of fish originally (in late 18th-century Scotland) an expression for a kettle of fish cooked during a boating excursion or picnic, and thus applied to the picnic itself. The ironical use **a pretty kettle of fish!** is likely to be an extension of this.

> Well, Mr Baldwin! *this* is a pretty kettle of fish!
> — Queen Mary said on 17 November 1936, after
> Edward VIII had told her he was prepared to give up the
> throne to marry Mrs Simpson

St Kevin (d. *c.*618), founder and abbot of the monastic settlement ➤ GLENDALOUGH in County Wicklow. One later legend associates him with a blackbird, which is said to have laid one of her eggs on his outstretched hands while he was at prayer; Kevin remained in the same position until the egg had hatched.

☐ **FEAST DAY** His feast day is 3 June.

Kew see also ➤ *I am His Highness's* DOG.

Kew Gardens the Royal Botanic Gardens at Kew, in Richmond, London. Developed by the mother of George III with the aid of Sir Joseph Banks, the gardens were presented to the nation in 1841 and are now an important botanical institution.

kewpie American trademark name for a type of doll (also called **kewpie doll**) characterized by a large head, big eyes, chubby cheeks, and a curl or topknot on top of its head. The name comes (in the early 20th century) from an alteration of *Cupid.*

> He pops up his lid in a kewpie-doll expression of surprise-pleasure.
> — *New York Review of Books* 25 June 1992

key a key (representing one's own key to a house) is often used as a symbol on a coming-of-age card.

Keys are the emblem of ➤ *St* PETER, St Petronilla, an early Roman martyr whose fictional legend makes her the daughter of ➤ *St* PETER, ➤ *St* MARTHA, and St Zita, a 13th-century Luccan serving-maid.

See also ➤ CEREMONY *of the Keys,* ➤ CROSS *keys,* ➤ GOLD *Key,* ➤ *a* GOLDEN *key can open any door,* ➤ HOUSE *of Keys,* ➤ POWER *of the keys,* ➤ PUBLIC *key,* ➤ *St* PETER's *keys.*

Key Stage in the UK, any of the four fixed stages into which the national curriculum is divided, each having its own prescribed course of study. At the end of each stage, pupils are required to complete standard assessment tasks.

St Keyne (?6th century), traditionally one of the daughters of Brychan, the Welsh patriarch whose children were Christian pioneers of South Wales and Cornwall. In a popular legend (celebrated by Southey in his poem 'The Well of St Keyne') she confers mastery in a marriage on the first partner of the two to drink from her well.

☐ **FEAST DAY** Her feast day is 8 (or 7) October.

John Maynard Keynes (1883–1946), English economist. An adviser to the Treasury during both world wars, he laid the foundations of modern macroeconomics with *The General Theory of Employment, Interest and Money* (1936), in which he argued that full employment is determined by effective demand and requires government spending on public works to stimulate this. His theories influenced Roosevelt's decision to introduce the American New Deal.

In 1917 he had written to his friend Duncan Grant, 'I work for a Government I despise for ends I think criminal.' Towards the end of his life he was to say of Britain in the Second World War, 'We threw good housekeeping to the winds. But we saved ourselves and helped save the world.'

Keystone Kops bumbling police characters in films made by Keystone, a US film company formed in 1912, remembered for its silent slapstick comedy films.

> Once the Keystone Kops-like operation was in the air, another failing . . . was noted.
> — Laurie Garrett *The Coming Plague* (1995)

Keystone State informal name for Pennsylvania, as being the seventh or central one of the original thirteen states.

khaki a textile fabric of a dull brownish-yellow colour, in particular a strong cotton fabric used in military clothing. Dating from the mid 19th century, the word comes from an Urdu word meaning 'dust-coloured'.

Khaki Election informal name for the British general election of 1900, used in reference to the South African War of 1899–1902, and later also applied to the general elections, such as 1918, in which military action was a key issue. The usage seems to derive from an electioneering speech:

> Are you . . . going to . . . vote solid for our Government? Or may I put it in another way . . . will you vote khaki?
> — G. Faber speech in *Yorkshire Herald* 5 January 1900

Khaldi the supreme god in the ancient Armenian kingdom of Urartu.

Khalistan the name given by Sikh nationalists to a proposed independent Sikh state; the name may be compared with Arabic *khālsa* 'pure, real, proper'.

Khalsa the body or company of fully initiated Sikhs, to which devout orthodox Sikhs are ritually admitted at puberty. The Khalsa was founded in 1699 by the last Guru (Gobind Singh). Members show their allegiance by five signs (called the *five*

Ks). Men take the additional name *Singh* 'lion', and women the name *Kaur* 'princess'.

Khalsa: the Five Ks

kanga	comb
kara	steel bangle
kesh	uncut hair, covered by a turban, and beard
kirpan	short sword
kuccha	short trousers, originally for riding

khamsin an oppressive hot southerly wind, which blows in Egypt at intervals for about 50 days in March, April, and May, and fills the air with sand from the desert. The name comes (in the late 17th century) from Arabic *ḳamsīn*, from *ḳamsūn* 'fifty' (being the approximate duration in days).

khan a title given to rulers and officials in central Asia, Afghanistan, and certain other Muslim countries; especially, any of the successors of ➤ GENGHIS *Khan*, supreme rulers of the Turkish, Tartar, and Mongol peoples and emperors of China in the Middle Ages.

The word comes (in late Middle English, via Old French and medieval Latin) from Turkic *ḳān* 'lord, prince'.

Khartoum the capital of Sudan, situated at the junction of the Blue Nile and the White Nile. Originally established in 1821 as an Egyptian army camp, it developed into a garrison town. In 1885 a British and Egyptian force under the command of ➤ *General* GORDON was besieged in Khartoum for ten months by the Mahdists, who eventually stormed the garrison, killing most of the defenders, including Gordon. It remained under the control of the Mahdists until they were defeated by the British in 1898 and the city was recaptured by General Kitchener, who later took the title, *Kitchener of Khartoum.*

Khazar a member of a Turkic people who occupied a large part of southern Russia from the 6th to the 11th centuries and who converted to Judaism in the 8th century.

Khedive the title of the viceroy of Egypt under Turkish rule 1867–1914. The word comes via French and Ottoman Turkish from Persian *ḳadiw* 'prince' (variant of *ḳudaiw* 'minor god', from *ḳudā* 'god').

Khlyst a member of a sect of ascetic Russian Christians, formed in the 17th century, who believed that Christ could be reincarnated in human beings

through their suffering. The name comes from Russian, literally 'whip'.

Khmer an ancient kingdom in SE Asia which reached the peak of its power in the 11th century, when it ruled over the entire Mekong valley from the capital at Angkor. It was destroyed by Siamese conquests in the 12th and 14th centuries.

Khmer Rouge a communist guerrilla organization which opposed the Cambodian government in the 1960s and waged a civil war from 1970, taking power in 1975. Under Pol Pot the Khmer Rouge undertook a forced reconstruction of Cambodian society, involving mass deportations from the towns to the countryside and mass executions (see ➤ KILLING *field*). More than two million died before the regime was overthrown by the Vietnamese in 1979. Khmer Rouge forces have continued a programme of guerrilla warfare from bases in Thailand.

Khoja a member of a Muslim sect found mainly in western India. The word is recorded from the early 17th century, originally in the sense 'Muslim scribe or teacher'.

Ruhollah Khomeini (1900–89), Iranian Shiite Muslim leader; known as **Ayatollah Khomeini**. He returned from exile in 1979 to lead an Islamic revolution which overthrew the shah. He established Iran as a fundamentalist Islamic republic and relentlessly pursued the Iran–Iraq War 1980–8, and in 1989 issued a fatwa condemning Salman Rushdie, author of *The Satanic Verses.*

Khonsu a moon god worshipped especially at Thebes, a member of a triad as the divine son of Amun and Mut. His name means 'he who crosses'.

khutbah a form of sermon, consisting of homily and supplication, delivered in mosques before the mid-day Friday prayer, at the time of the two main Muslim festivals, and on other exceptional occasions.

Khyber Pass a mountain pass in the Hindu Kush, on the border between Pakistan and Afghanistan. The pass was for long of great commercial and strategic importance, the route by which successive invaders entered India, and was garrisoned by the British intermittently between 1839 and 1947.

ki-mon in Japanese tradition (taken from Chinese geomancy): the north-east, the traditional source of evil.

kibbutz a communal settlement in Israel, typically a farm.

kiblah the direction of the ➤ Kaaba (the sacred building at Mecca), to which Muslims turn at prayer. The word comes (in the mid 17th century) from Arabic *ḳibla* 'that which is opposite'.

kickshaw a fancy but insubstantial cooked dish, especially one of foreign origin. Recorded from the late 16th century, the word comes from French *quelque chose* 'something', and the French spelling was common in the 17th century.

kid a young goat, taken as a type of young and frisky animal; in extended usage (from the 17th century) a child, a young person.

See also ➤ Billy *the Kid*, ➤ Dead *End Kids*, ➤ Katzenjammer *Kids*.

William Kidd (1645–1701), Scottish pirate, known as **Captain Kidd**. Sent to the Indian Ocean in 1695 in command of an anti-pirate expedition, Kidd became a pirate himself. In 1699 he went to Boston in the hope of obtaining a pardon, but was arrested and later hanged in London.

kiddush a ceremony of prayer and blessing over wine, performed by the head of a Jewish household at the meal ushering in the Sabbath (on a Friday night) or a holy day, or at the lunch preceding it.

kidnap take someone away illegally by force, typically to obtain a ransom; the word dates from the late 17th century, and the second element represents the slang *nap* 'nab, seize'.

kidney temperament, nature, as in **of the same kidney**. The *kidneys* were anciently thought to control disposition and temperament.

Kiel Canal a man-made waterway in NW Germany, running westwards from Kiel to Brunsbüttel at the mouth of the Elbe. It connects the North Sea with the Baltic and was constructed in 1895 to provide the German navy with a shorter route between these two seas.

Søren Kierkegaard (1813–55), Danish philosopher. A founder of existentialism, he affirmed the importance of individual experience and choice and believed one could know God only through a 'leap of faith', and not through doctrine.

Kievan of or pertaining to the Ukrainian city of *Kiev*, especially in the historical period (*c*.900–*c*.1150) when it dominated European Russia.

kilderkin a cask for liquids or other substances, holding 16 or 18 gallons; this amount as a unit of measurement.

Mount Kilimanjaro an extinct volcano in northern Tanzania. It has twin peaks, the higher of which, Kibo, is the highest mountain in Africa.

Kilkenny cats two cats from Kilkenny in Ireland which, according to legend, fought until only their tails remained.

kill see also ➤ kill the FATTED *calf*, ➤ *kill the goose that lays the golden* EGGS.

killcrop an insatiable child, supposed in folklore to be a fairy changeling.

killer see ➤ SERIAL *killer*.

killing field a place where a heavy loss of life has occurred, typically as the result of massacre or genocide during a time of warfare or violent civil unrest. The term is particularly associated with Cambodia under the rule of Pol Pot and the ➤ Khmer *Rouge* in the late 1970s, where mass deportations from the towns to the countryside were followed by mass executions in what became known as *the killing fields*. Events in Cambodia, and in particular the scale of killing, were reported by a number of Western journalists, but it was with the release in 1984 of the film *The Killing Fields* that the phrase passed into the language.

killing no murder proverbial saying, mid 17th century; originally, the title of a pamphlet by Edward Sexby (d. 1658), which was an apology for tyrannicide and which was ironically dedicated to Oliver Cromwell. Captured and imprisoned, Sexby died in the Tower of London on 13 January 1658.

Kilroy mythical person, popularized by American servicemen in the Second World War, who left such inscriptions as 'Kilroy was here' on walls all over the world.

Of the many unverifiable accounts of the source of the term, one claims that James J. *Kilroy* of Halifax, Massachusetts, a shipyard employee, wrote 'Kilroy was here' on sections of warships after inspection; the phrase is said to have been reproduced by shipyard workers who entered the armed services.

kilt a knee-length skirt of pleated tartan cloth, traditionally worn by men as part of Scottish Highland dress (and now also worn by women and girls). The wearing of the *kilt* was proscribed for a time after the Jacobite rising of 1745, as part of the policy to erode distinctive Highland practices.

Kim hero of Kipling's picaresque novel of that name (1901), the orphaned son of an Irish soldier, who grows up as an Indian and becomes the chela of a Buddhist lama from Tibet; found by his father's old regiment, he is educated and later recruited into the British secret service, at the end of the book still managing to combine the two sides of his life.

Kim's game a memory-testing game in which players try to remember as many as possible of a set of objects briefly shown to them; from the game with jewels played by ➤ KIM in Kipling's novel.

Kimberley a city in South Africa, in the province of Northern Cape, which has been a diamond-mining centre since the early 1870s.

kin see ➤ KITH *and kin,* ➤ NEXT *of kin.*

kindergarten an establishment where children below the age of compulsory education play and learn; a nursery school. The word, which dates from the mid 19th century, is from German, literally 'children's garden'.

king the male ruler of an independent state, especially one who inherits the position by right of birth.

➤ *St* EDWARD *the Confessor,* ➤ *St* LOUIS, and St Henry (973–1024), Holy Roman Emperor from 1002, are the patron saints of *kings.*

In chess, the king is the most important piece, of which each player has one, which the opponent has to checkmate in order to win. The king can move in any direction, including diagonally, to any adjacent square that is not attacked by an opponent's piece or pawn. In cards, the king is the highest-ranking court card.

See also ➤ *all* STUARTS *are not sib to the king,* ➤ *a* CAT *may look at a king,* ➤ CATHOLIC *King,* ➤ *the* CITIZEN *King,* ➤ ERL-*king,* ➤ *the* FACTORY *king,* ➤ GOD *save the Queen (or King),* ➤ *King* COTTON, ➤ *King* LOG, ➤ *king of* COCKNEYS, ➤ *king of* SHREDS *and patches,* ➤ *King* PELLAM, ➤ *King* PELLES, ➤ *King* PHILIP's *War,* ➤ KINGS, ➤ *the* MARTYR *King,* ➤ OLD *King Cole,* ➤ PEARLY *king,* ➤ *the* RAILWAY *King,* ➤ *the* SAILOR *King,* ➤ SLAVE *King,* ➤ SUN *King.*

Kings:	
titles conferrred by the Pope	
TITLE	SOVEREIGN
Most Catholic King	King of Spain
Most Christian King	King of France
Most Faithful King	King of Portugal
Most Religious King	King of England

every man a king slogan of the populist American Democratic politician Huey Long (1893–1935) in his successful campaign to be Governor of Louisiana in 1928; Long later took the slogan as the title of his autobiography (1933). He declared for the presidency in 1934, but was assassinated in the following year.

See also ➤ KINGFISH, ➤ SUI *generis.*

king and country the objects of allegiance for a patriot whose head of State is a king, recorded from the early 17th century. The phrase received particular public attention when in February 1933 the Oxford Union debated the motion 'That this House will in no circumstances fight for its King and Country'; the motion was passed by 275 votes to 153.

Your King and Country need you caption for a recruiting advertisement of 1914, showing Lord ➤ KITCHENER with pointing finger (the comment 'Kitchener is a great poster' is attributed to Margot Asquith (1864–1945), British political hostess and wife of H. H. Asquith). The recruiting slogan was coined by Eric Field, July 1914.

the king can do no wrong proverbial saying, mid 17th century.

King Charles's head an obsession resembling that of Dickens's character 'Mr Dick' in *David Copperfield* (1850):

> Mr. Dick had been for upwards of ten years endeavouring to keep King Charles the First out of the Memorial; but he had been constantly getting into it, and was there now.
> — Charles Dickens *David Copperfield* (1850)

King Charles spaniel a spaniel of a small breed, typically with a white, black, and tan coat, favoured by ➤ CHARLES II.

King Country in 19th-century New Zealand, an extensive region in the North Island formerly allotted to the Maoris under a king, later a source of dispute with the ➤ KINGITES when the grant was revoked.

King James Bible another name for the ➤ AUTHORIZED *Version,* dedicated to ➤ JAMES I.

King Kong a huge ape-like monster featured in the film *King Kong* (1933); captured and brought to New York, it escapes, climbing the Empire State Building with Fay Wray in its grasp before being shot down from besieging aeroplanes.

> He was shown holding a model of an early bi-plane, which made him look rather like King Kong swatting away attacking craft.
> — Bill Bryson *Notes from a Small Island* (1995)

King of Arms in the UK, a chief herald. Those now at the College of Arms are the Garter, Clarenceux, and Norroy and Ulster Kings of Arms; the Lyon King of Arms has jurisdiction in Scotland.

See also ➤ BATH *King of Arms*, ➤ GARTER *King of Arms*, ➤ ULSTER *King of Arms*.

King of Bath a nickname for Richard 'Beau' Nash (1674–1762), a leader of society in Bath and unofficial master of ceremonies who presided over the fashionable Assembly Rooms.

king of beasts a name for the lion; its supposed rank in the hierarchy of animals is recorded from classical times.

king of birds the eagle (used in reference to the bird's perceived grandeur); one of Aesop's fables tells how the ➤ WREN attempted to steal the title.

King of Kings in the Christian Church, used as a name or form of address for God. Also, a title assumed by certain kings who rule over lesser kings.

king of men in classical literature, an epithet of ➤ ZEUS, and of ➤ AGAMEMNON.

King of Rome title born by the son (1811–32) of Napoleon I, who had gone into exile as a child with his mother, Marie-Louise of Austria, and died young; he was latterly known by the Austrian title of Duke of Reichstadt.

king of Spain's trumpeter dated informal name for a donkey braying; recorded from the late 18th century (the equivalent *Portugal trumpeter* dates from the mid 17th century).

King of Terrors Death personified; originally with biblical allusion to Job 18:14, 'His confidence…shall bring him to the king of terrors.'

King of the Castle a children's game in which the object is to beat one's rivals to an elevated position at the top of a mound or other high place.

King of the Gypsies title given to Bampfylde Moore Carew (1693–1770), who born of a Devon family joined a group of gypsies and travelled with them; he was later said to have been elected as the gypsy chief or king.

king of the herrings another term for the allis shad and oarfish.

King of the May a young man chosen to preside over traditional May or springtime celebrations, especially those held on May Day (the terms *May King* and *May Lord* are also used).

King of the Romans the prospective head of the ➤ HOLY *Roman Empire*; the title was assumed after selection by the seven Electors and coronation at Aachen, but prior to coronation as Emperor by the Pope at Rome.

King of the White Elephant a title of the king of Siam.

King of the World English meaning of 'Shah Jehan', the title assumed by the fifth of the Mogul emperors of Delhi.

the King over the Water Jacobite name for the exiled ➤ JAMES *II*, 'over the water' in France, and later for his son and grandson. Jacobites were said to drink a secret toast to the Stuart king by passing their glasses over a bowl of water as a signal.

King's Bench in the reign of a king, the term for Queen's Bench.

king's bounty in the UK, a sum of money given from royal funds to a mother who had had a multiple birth of three or more.

King's Cave on the west coast of Arran in Scotland, supposedly where Robert the Bruce found shelter.

a king's chaff is worth more than other men's corn proverbial saying, early 17th century.

King's Champion another term for the ➤ CHAMPION *of England*.

King's colour in the UK, in the reign of a king, the term for Queen's colour.

King's Counsel in the UK, in the reign of a king, the term for Queen's Counsel.

King's County the former name of the Irish county of Offaly in the province of Leinster.

King's Crag in Fife in Scotland, supposedly so called because of the death there in a riding accident of Alexander III (1249–86).

King's English another term for Queen's English.

King's evidence in the reign of a king, the term for Queen's evidence.

king's evil scrofula, in England and France formerly held to be curable by the royal touch. The practice of touching for the *king's evil* continued from the time of Edward the Confessor to the death of Queen Anne in 1714 (➤ *Samuel* JOHNSON, as a child of three, was touched for the disease by Queen

Anne in 1712). The Office for the ceremony has not been printed in the Prayer-book since 1719.

king's friends in the 18th century, the name given to a political group which supported George III in his attempts to increase the power of the Crown.

King's Guide in the UK, in the reign of a king, the term for Queen's Guide.

King's highway in the UK, in the reign of a king, the term for Queen's highway.

King's Messenger in the UK, in the reign of a king, the term for Queen's Messenger.

King's peace in the UK, in the reign of a king, the term for Queen's peace.

King's Proctor in the UK, in the reign of a king, the term for Queen's Proctor.

King's Regulations in the UK, in the reign of a king, the term for Queen's Regulations.

King's Remembrancer in the UK, in the reign of a king, the term for Queen's Remembrancer.

King's scholar in the UK, in the reign of a king, the term for Queen's scholar.

King's Scout in the UK, in the reign of a king, the term for Queen's Scout.

king's shilling a shilling formerly given to a recruit when enlisting in the army during the reign of a king.

King's speech in the UK, in the reign of a king, the term for Queen's Speech.

kingdom see also ➤ the FLOWERY *Kingdom.*

Kingdom Come the next world, Heaven; the term comes from the clause *thy kingdom come* in the Lord's Prayer, and may be used informally to denote a time which seems infinitely distant.

Kingfish nickname of the American Democratic politician Huey Long (1893–1935), who is reported to have said of himself, 'For the present you can just call me the Kingfish.'

Kingite in 19th-century New Zealand, a follower of the Maori king to whom the ➤ KING *Country* was allotted.

Warwick the Kingmaker Richard Neville, Earl of *Warwick* (1428–71), English statesman. During the Wars of the Roses he fought first on the Yorkist side,

helping Edward IV to gain the throne (1461), and then on the Lancastrian side, briefly restoring Henry VI to the throne (1470). Warwick was killed at the battle of Barnet.

kings see also ➤ DIVINE *right of kings,* ➤ HISTORY *of the Four Kings,* ➤ PHILOSOPHER *kings,* ➤ SHEPHERD *Kings,* ➤ *the* SPORT *of kings,* ➤ *the* THREE *Kings,* ➤ VALLEY *of the Kings.*

Kings the name of two books of the Bible, recording the history of Israel from the accession of Solomon to the destruction of the Temple in 586 BC. In the Septuagint and Vulgate, these are called the third and fourth books of Kings, the two books of Samuel being called the first and second books of Kings.

kings have long arms proverbial saying, mid 16th century.

Alfred Charles Kinsey (1894–1956), American zoologist and sex researcher. He carried out pioneering studies into sexual behaviour by interviewing large numbers of people. His best-known work, *Sexual Behaviour in the Human Male* (1948, also known as the *Kinsey Report*), was controversial but highly influential.

Rudyard Kipling (1865–1936), English novelist, short-story writer, and poet. He was born in India, where he worked as a journalist 1882–9, and set many of his writings in the India of the Raj, and much of his best-known work is regarded as epitomizing the British colonial spirit. Of his vast and varied output, Kipling is perhaps now primarily known for his tales for children, notably *The Jungle Book* (1894) and the *Just So Stories* (1902). In 1907 he became the first English writer to be awarded the Nobel Prize for literature.

Kiplingcotes Derby a local race of 4½ miles, run over a course on the Yorkshire wolds and said to be the oldest flat race in Great Britain. The race is said to have been initiated in 1519 by a group of hunting gentleman; the first record of a race is found in 1555, run at Kiplingcotes Ashe at Shrovetide. The prize, the East Yorkshire Plate, was formerly known as the **Kiplingcotes Plate**.

kippa a skullcap worn by Orthodox male Jews.

kirin a mythical beast of composite form resembling a unicorn, frequently portrayed in Japanese pottery and art.

the **Kirk (of Scotland)** the Church of Scotland as distinct from the Church of England or from the Episcopal Church in Scotland.

See also ➤ AULD *Kirk*.

Kirk session the lowest court in the Church of Scotland, composed of the minister and elders of the parish.

Kirke see ➤ *Kirke's* LAMBS.

kirn a feast held on the completion of a harvest, a harvest home; the last handful of corn cut on the harvest-field.

kirpan a short sword or knife with a curved blade, worn (sometimes in miniature form) as one of the five distinguishing signs of the Sikh ➤ KHALSA, symbolizing power and freedom.

kirtle see ➤ NEAR *is my kirtle, but nearer is my smock.*

Kislev in the Jewish calendar, the third month of the civil and ninth of the religious year, usually coinciding with parts of November and December.

kismet fate, destiny. The word comes (in the early 19th century, via Turkish) from Arabic *ḳismat* 'division, portion, lot', from *ḳasama* 'to divide'.

kiss touch with the lips as a sign of love, sexual desire, reverence, or greeting; the associations of intimacy and trust make a betrayal such as the ➤ JUDAS *kiss* more shocking.

See also ➤ BUTTERFLY *kiss*.

kiss and tell recount one's sexual exploits, especially to the media regarding a famous person; in US politics from the mid 1970s, the revealing of confidential information gained through any close or privileged relationship.

kiss-in-the-ring a children's game in which all the players stand in a ring with hands joined except for one who runs round and touches one of the opposite sex, who then pursues and tries to kiss him or her.

Kiss me, Hardy said to have been the dying words of ➤ NELSON at the battle of Trafalgar, 21 October 1805, addressed to his flag captain, Thomas Masterman Hardy (1769–1839).

the kiss of death a seemingly kind or well-intentioned action, look, or association, which brings disastrous consequences; the association is with the kiss of betrayal given to Jesus by ➤ JUDAS.

the kiss of life the mouth-to-mouth method of artificial respiration.

kiss of peace a ceremonial kiss as part of a religious ceremony, especially in the Eucharist.

kiss the book kiss a Bible, New Testament, or Gospels, while taking an oath.

kiss the gunner's daughter be lashed to the breech of a gun for flogging, an old naval punishment.

kiss the pope's toe kiss the golden cross of the sandal on the pope's right foot, as a mark of respect.

Henry Kissinger (1923–), German-born American statesman and diplomat, Secretary of State 1973–7, who in an era of ➤ SHUTTLE *diplomacy* helped negotiate the withdrawal of US troops from South Vietnam, for which he shared the Nobel Peace Prize. He later restored US diplomatic relations with Egypt in the wake of the Yom Kippur War.

kissing see ➤ MISTLETOE, ➤ *when the* GORSE *is out of bloom, kissing's out of fashion*

kissing bough a Christmas wreath or ball of evergreens hung from the ceiling, under which a person may be kissed.

kissing cousin a relative who is not a close cousin, but who is known well enough to be given a kiss in greeting.

kissing gate a small gate hung in a U- or V-shaped enclosure, letting one person through at a time.

kissing goes by favour proverbial saying, early 17th century.

when the kissing has to stop when the honeymoon period finishes; when one is forced to recognize harsh realities, originally with reference to Browning:

> What of soul was left, I wonder, when the kissing had to stop?
> — Robert Browning 'A Toccata of Galuppi's' (1855)

kissogram a novelty greeting or message delivered by a man or woman who accompanies it (often dressed in a particular costume) with a kiss, pre-arranged as a humorous surprise for the recipient.

Kiswa the black cloth covering the walls of the ➤ KAABA, made annually in Egypt and brought to Mecca with the pilgrimage caravan, now usually made of black brocade with the Islamic creed outlined in the weave and a gold-embroidered band bearing Koranic texts.

the whole kit and boodle everything. The word *kit* comes (in Middle English) from Middle Dutch *kitte* 'wooden vessel'. The original sense 'wooden tub' was later applied to other containers; the use denoting a soldier's equipment (late 18th century) probably arose from the idea of a set of articles packed in a container. *Boodle* in the early 17th century denoted a pack or crowd, and came from Dutch *boedel, boel* 'possessions, disorderly mass'.

kit-cat a canvas of a standard size (typically 36 × 28 in., 91.5 × 71 cm), especially as used for a life-size portrait showing the sitter's head, shoulders, and one or both hands. The name comes from a series of portraits of the members of the ➤ KIT-*Cat Club*.

Kit-Cat Club an association of prominent Whigs and literary figures founded in the early part of the 18th century. According to Alexander Pope its members included Richard Steele, Joseph Addison, William Congreve, and John Vanbrugh. It was named after *Kit* (= Christopher) *Cat* or *Catling*, who kept the pie house in Shire Lane, by Temple Bar, the original meeting place of the club.

kitchen see also ➤ HELL*'s kitchen*, ➤ *if you don't like the* HEAT *get out of the kitchen*.

kitchen cabinet a group of unofficial advisers (originally of the president of the US, in the mid 19th century) popularly believed to have greater influence than elected or appropriate officials; a private or unofficial group of advisers thought to be unduly influential.

kitchen-sink in art forms, characterized by great realism in the depiction of drab or sordid subjects. The term is most used of post-war British drama, such as John Osborne's *Look Back in Anger* (1956) and Arnold Wesker's *Roots* (1959), which uses working-class domestic settings rather than the drawing rooms of conventional middle-class drama, and of a short-lived school of British social realist painters.

Lord Kitchener (1850–1916), **Kitchener of Khartoum**, British soldier and statesman. At the outbreak of the First World War he was made Secretary of State for War. He had previously defeated the Mahdist forces at Omdurman in 1898, served as Chief of Staff in the Second Boer War, and been Commander-in-Chief (1902–9) in India.

In the capacity of Secretary of State for War, he was responsible for organizing the large volunteer army which eventually fought the war on the Western Front. His commanding image appeared on recruiting posters urging ➤ *Your* KING *and Country need you.* He was drowned when the ship taking him to Russia was sunk by a mine.

kite a medium to large long-winged bird of prey which typically has a forked tail and frequently soars on updraughts of air; rare in Britain until recent years, the **red kite** has recently been successfully reintroduced. The name is recorded from Old English (in form *cȳta*), and is probably of imitative origin and related to German *Kauz* 'screech owl'.

From the mid 16th century, kite was used figuratively for a person preying on others, a rapacious person, a sharper.

Kitemark a trademark name for an official kite-shaped mark on goods approved by the British Standards Institution (a *kite* here is a quadrilateral figure with two pairs of equal sides, and symmetrical only about its diagonals).

kith and kin one's relations. The word kith is Old English, and the original senses were 'knowledge', 'one's native land', and 'friends and neighbours'. The phrase *kith and kin* originally denoted one's country and relatives; later one's friends and relatives.

kitsch art, objects, or design considered to be in poor taste because of excessive garishness or sentimentality, but sometimes appreciated in an ironic or knowing way. The word comes (in the 1920s) from German.

wanton kittens make sober cats proverbial saying, early 18th century.

Kitty Hawk a town on a narrow sand peninsula on the Atlantic coast of North Carolina. It was there that, in 1903, the Wright brothers made the first powered aeroplane flight.

kiva a chamber, built wholly or partly underground, used by male Pueblo Indians for religious rites.

Kiwanis Club a North American society of business and professional men formed for the maintenance of commercial ethics and as a social and charitable organization.

kiwi a flightless New Zealand bird with hair-like feathers, having a long downcurved bill with sensitive nostrils at the tip, a national emblem of New Zealand; from the early 20th century, used informally for a New Zealander.

Klan see ➤ KU *Klux Klan.*

Martin Heinrich Klaproth (1743–1817), German chemist, one of the founders of analytical chemistry. He discovered three new elements (zirconium, uranium, and titanium) in certain minerals, and contributed to the identification of others. A follower of Lavoisier, he helped to introduce the latter's new system of chemistry into Germany.

Paul Klee (1879–1940), Swiss painter, resident in Germany from 1906. He joined Kandinsky's *Blaue Reiter* group in 1912 and later taught at the Bauhaus (1920–33). His work is characterized by his sense of colour and moves freely between abstraction and figuration. Although some of his paintings have a childlike quality, his later work became increasingly sombre, as in *A Tiny Tale of a Tiny Dwarf* (1925), and were labelled 'degenerate' by the Nazi regime.

Calvin Klein (1942–), American fashion designer, known for his understated fashions for both men and women.

Klondike a tributary of the Yukon River, in Yukon Territory, NW Canada, which rises in the Ogilvie mountains and flows 160 km (100 miles) westwards to join the Yukon at Dawson. It gave its name to the surrounding region, which became famous when gold was found in nearby Bonanza Creek in 1896. In the ensuing gold rush of 1897–8 thousands settled in the area to mine gold. and the town of Dawson was established. Within ten years the area was exhausted and the population dramatically decreased.

Klosters a fashionable Alpine winter-sports resort in eastern Switzerland, near the Austrian border.

knaidel a type of dumpling eaten especially in Jewish households during Passover.

knave another term for the 'jack' in cards. The word originally (in Old English) meant 'boy, servant', and then generally someone of low social status; in Middle English, the sense of 'dishonest or unscrupulous man' developed. The playing-card sense is recorded from the middle of the 16th century.

In Dickens's *Great Expectations*, Estella is scornful of Pip's use of 'jack':

> 'He calls the knaves, Jacks, this boy,' said Estella with disdain, before our first game was out.
>
> — Charles Dickens *Great Expectations* (1861)

on the knees of the gods alternative expression for ➤ *in the* LAP *of the gods.*

Knees up, Mother Brown a popular song by H. Weston, B. Lee, and I. Taylor, traditionally sung while dancing by raising each knee in turn; this has given rise to *knees-up* meaning a party, a lively gathering.

Knesset the parliament of modern Israel, established in 1949. It consists of 120 members elected every four years.

Knickerbocker a New Yorker, taken as a descendant of the original Dutch settlers in New York. The term comes from Diedrich *Knickerbocker,* pretended author of W. Irving's *History of New York* (1809).

The term knickerbockers for loose-fitting breeches gathered at the knee or calf is said to have arisen from the resemblance of knickerbockers to the knee breeches worn by Dutch men in Cruikshank's illustrations in Irving's book.

knife a knife is the emblem of ➤ *St* BARTHOLOMEW, St Peter the Martyr, a 13th-century Dominican friar and priest born in Verona, who was attacked and killed while travelling from Como to Milan (he was wounded in the head with an axe, while the friar who was with him was stabbed), and ➤ *St* WILLIAM *of Norwich.*

knight in the Middle Ages, a man who served his sovereign or lord as a mounted soldier in armour; a man raised by a sovereign to honourable military rank after service as a page or a squire.

➤ *St* GEORGE and ➤ *St* JAMES *the Great* are the patron saints of knights.

In the UK, a *knight* is a man awarded a non-hereditary title by the sovereign in recognition of merit or service and entitled to use the honorific 'Sir' in front of his name.

Knight is also a dated term for a member of the class of equites in ancient Rome, or a citizen of the second class in ancient Athens (called *hippeus* in Greek), seen in comparison with medieval knights.

In chess, a *knight* is a piece, typically with its top shaped like a horse's head, that moves by jumping to the opposite corner of a rectangle two squares by three. Each player starts the game with two knights.

The word is recorded from Old English (in the

form *cniht*, denoting 'boy, youth, servant') and is of West Germanic origin.

See also ➤ CARPET *knight,* ➤ *knight in* SHINING *armour,* ➤ *Knight of* GLIN, ➤ *Knight of* KERRY, ➤ REDCROSSE *Knight,* ➤ TEUTONIC *Knights,* ➤ WHITE *knight.*

knight errant a medieval knight wandering in search of chivalrous adventures.

Knight of Columbus a member of a society of Roman Catholic men founded at New Haven, Connecticut, in 1882.

Knight of Grace a knight of the Order of the ➤ KNIGHTS *Hospitallers,* of the lower rank of the Order.

Knight of Justice a knight of the Order of the ➤ KNIGHTS *Hospitallers,* possessing full privileges.

Knight of La Mancha another name for ➤ *Don* QUIXOTE.

Knight of Pythias a member of a charitable and religious North American society founded in 1864.

Knight of the Bath a member of the ➤ *Order of the* BATH.

Knight of the Holy Sepulchre a member of a secular confraternity, later a religious order, composed of those knighted during the Crusades, especially at the Holy Sepulchre itself.

Knight of the Round Table a member of the brotherhood of knights who were followers of ➤ *King* ARTHUR.

the **Knight of the Rueful Countenance** another name for ➤ *Don* QUIXOTE.

knight of the shire a gentleman representing a shire or county in Parliament, originally, a parliamentary member chosen from those holding the rank of knight.

the **Knight of the Swan** another name for ➤ LOHENGRIN.

Knight of Windsor any of a small number of military officers who have pensions and apartments in Windsor Castle.

knight service in the Middle Ages, the tenure of land by a knight on condition of performing military service.

Knights Hospitallers a military and religious order founded as the Knights of the Order of the Hospital of St John of Jerusalem in the 11th century.

Originally protectors of pilgrims, they also undertook the care of the sick. During the Middle Ages they became a powerful and wealthy military force, with foundations in various European countries; their military power ended when Malta was surrendered to Napoleon (1798). In England, the order was revived in 1831 and was responsible for the foundation of the St John Ambulance Brigade in 1888.

Knights Templars a religious and military order for the protection of pilgrims to the Holy Land, founded as the Poor Knights of Christ and of the Temple of Solomon in 1118.

The order became powerful and wealthy, but its members' arrogance towards rulers, together with their wealth and their rivalry with the Knights Hospitallers, led to their downfall; the order was suppressed in 1312, many of its possessions being given to the Hospitallers. The Inner and Middle Temple in London are on the site of the Templars' English headquarters.

Knightsbridge a district in the West End of London, to the south of Hyde Park, noted for its fashionable and expensive shops.

knitbone another name for comfrey, with allusion to its supposed healing properties.

knobkerrie a short stick with a knobbed head, traditionally used as a weapon by the indigenous peoples of South Africa.

knocks see ➤ SCHOOL *of hard knocks.*

Knole sofa a sofa with adjustable sides allowing conversion into a bed, named (in the mid 20th century) after *Knole* Park, Kent, site of the original sofa (*c.*1605–20) from which others were designed.

Knossos the principal city of Minoan Crete, the remains of which are situated on the north coast of Crete. Excavations by Sir Arthur Evans from 1900 onwards revealed the remains of a luxurious and spectacularly decorated complex of buildings, which he named the Palace of Minos, with frescoes of landscapes, animal life, and the sport of bull-leaping. The city site was occupied from Neolithic times until *c.*1200 BC; Crete was overrun by the Mycenaeans in *c.*1450 BC, but the palace survived until the 14th or early 13th century BC.

knot see ➤ *cut the* GORDIAN *knot,* ➤ HERCULES' *knot,* ➤ PORTER's *knot,* ➤ STAFFORD *knot,* ➤ TRUE-*love knot.*

knot a unit of speed equivalent to one nautical mile per hour, used especially of ships, aircraft, or winds. This comes from the use of the word to mean a length marked by knots on a log line, as a measure of speed.

knot garden a formal garden laid out in an intricate design; *knot* was used from the late 15th century to denote a flower-bed laid out in a fanciful or ornate shape.

knotgrass a common Eurasian plant of the dock family, with jointed creeping stems and small pink flowers; an infusion of it was formerly thought to inhibit growth, and in Shakespeare's *Midsummer Night's Dream* (1595–6), Helena in their quarrel addresses the shorter Hermia as 'You dwarf; you minimus, of hindering knotgrass made'.

know see also ➤ *know where the* BODIES *are.*

...but I know a man who can advertising slogan for the Automobile Association.

to know all is to forgive all proverbial saying, early 20th century.

you should know a man seven years before you stir his fire proverbial saying, early 19th century.

what you don't know can't hurt you proverbial saying, late 16th century.

Know-nothing a member of a political party in the United States, called also the American party, prominent during the years 1853–56; so named because, having been originally organized as a secret society, its members, to preserve this character, professed to outsiders complete ignorance regarding it. The chief principle of the party was that none but native citizens should be permitted to share in the government. It disappeared about 1859.

know thyself proverbial saying, late fourteenth century; inscribed in Greek on the temple of Apollo at Delphi; Plato in *Protagoras* ascribes the saying to the ➤ SEVEN *Sages.*

you never know what you can do till you try proverbial saying, early 19th century.

knowledge see ➤ *a* LITTLE *knowledge is a dangerous thing,* ➤ TREE *of knowledge.*

knowledge is power proverbial saying, late 16th century; originally from Francis Bacon.

known see ➤ *a man is known by the* COMPANY.

Knox see also ➤ FORT *Knox.*

John Knox (*c.*1505–72), Scottish Protestant reformer. Knox played a central part in the establishment of the Church of Scotland within a Scottish Protestant state, and as a fiery orator led opposition to the Catholic Mary, Queen of Scots when she returned to rule in her own right in 1561; apart from his disapproval of her Catholicism, he had in 1558 issued a pamphlet entitled 'The first blast of the trumpet against the monstrous regiment [rule] of women'.

See also ➤ JOHN *Knox cap.*

Knox Version a translation (1945–9) of the ➤ VULGATE by the English theologian and writer Ronald Knox (1888–1957), which was accepted for use in the Roman Catholic Church.

knur and spell a traditional game resembling trapball, in which a wooden ball or hard knot of wood (the *knur*) is struck with a bat.

kobold in Germanic mythology, a spirit who haunts houses or lives underground in caves or mines.

koftgari a kind of damascene work of the Indian subcontinent, in which a pattern traced on steel is inlaid with gold. The word comes (in the late 19th century) from Urdu and Persian *kuft-garī* 'beaten work'.

Koh-i-noor a famous Indian diamond, one of the treasures belonging to Aurangzeb, which has a history going back to the 14th century. It passed into British possession on the annexation of Punjab in 1849, and was set in the queen's state crown for the coronation of George VI (1937). The name comes from Persian, meaning 'mountain of light'.

Kohima Memorial memorial at Kohima in the far north-east of India to the Burma campaign of the Second World War; it carries the epitaph:

> When you go home, tell them of us and say,
> 'For your tomorrow we gave our today.'
> — from an epitaph composed by John Maxwell
> Edmonds (1875–1958) for use on First World War
> memorials

koine the common language of the Greeks from the close of the classical period to the Byzantine era.

koinonia Christian fellowship or communion, with God or, more commonly, with fellow Christians.

Theo Kojak a New York policeman played by Telly Savalas (1924–94) in the television series (1973–8) of that name, characterized by his wisecracking, bald head, and habit of sucking lollipops, as by his catch-phrase, 'Who loves ya, baby?'

Kol Nidre an Aramaic prayer annulling vows made before God, sung by Jews at the opening of the Day of Atonement service on the eve of ➤ YOM *Kippur*. The name comes from Aramaic *kol niḏrē* 'all the vows' (the opening words of the prayer).

Komsomol an organization for communist youth in the former Soviet Union. The name comes from Russian *Kommunisticheskiĭ Soyuz Molodëzhi* 'Communist League of Youth'.

Kon-Tiki the raft made of balsa logs in which Thor Heyerdahl sailed from the western coast of Peru to the islands of Polynesia in 1947. It was named after an Inca god.

Kondratiev each of a series of cycles or waves of economic contraction and expansion lasting about fifty years, postulated by the Russian economist Nikolai D. *Kondratiev* (1892–*c.*1935) in the 1920s.

Konya an ancient Phrygian settlement, which became the capital of the Seljuk sultans towards the end of the 11th century.

the Kop a high bank of terracing at certain soccer grounds where spectators formerly stood, notably at Liverpool Football Club. The name comes from *Spion Kop*, site of a Boer War battle in which troops from Lancashire led the assault (Liverpool then being part of Lancashire).

kopeck a monetary unit of Russia and some other countries of the former USSR, equal to one hundredth of a rouble. The name comes from Russian *kopeĭka*, diminutive of *kop′ë* 'lance' (from the figure on the coin (1535) of Tsar Ivan IV, bearing a lance instead of a sword).

koppa a letter in the early Greek alphabet, later displaced by *kappa*; it survives as a numeral (= 90).

koradji in Australia, an Aboriginal medicine man.

Koran the Islamic sacred book, believed to be the word of God as dictated to Muhammad by the archangel Gabriel and written down in Arabic. The Koran consists of 114 units of varying lengths, known as *suras*; the first sura is said as part of the ritual prayer. These touch upon all aspects of human existence, including matters of doctrine, social organization, and legislation. The Koran was traditionally held by Muslims to be untranslatable,

although versions or interpretations in other languages are available.

kore an archaic Greek statue of a young woman, standing and clothed in long loose robes. The word comes from Greek *korē* 'maiden'.

Korean War the war of 1950–3 between North and South Korea. UN troops, dominated by US forces, countered the invasion of South Korea by North Korean forces by invading North Korea, while China intervened on the side of the North. Peace negotiations were begun in 1951, and the war ended two years later with the restoration of previous boundaries.

Koreish the tribe which inhabited Mecca in the time of Muhammad and to which he belonged.

koru a stylized fern-leaf motif in Maori carving and tattooing.

Thaddeus Kosciusko (1746–1817), Polish soldier and patriot. After fighting for the Americans during the War of American Independence, he led a nationalist uprising against Russia in Poland in 1794, defeating a large Russian force at Racławice. Captured and imprisoned by the Russians (1794–6), he eventually moved to France.

Koshare a member of a Pueblo Indian clown society representing ancestral spirits in rain and fertility ceremonies.

kosher of food, or premises in which food is sold, cooked, or eaten, satisfying the requirements of Jewish law.

　　Restrictions on the foods suitable for Jews are derived from rules in the books of Leviticus and Deuteronomy. Animals must be slaughtered and prepared in the prescribed way, in which the blood is drained from the body, while certain creatures, notably pigs and shellfish, are forbidden altogether. Meat and milk must not be cooked or consumed together, and separate utensils must be kept for each. Strict observance of these rules is today confined mainly to Orthodox Jews.

　　The word comes (in the mid 19th century) from Hebrew *kāšēr* 'proper'.

Kosovo an autonomous province of Serbia bordering on Albania, the majority of whose people are of Albanian descent, and which in 1999 was subjected to ➤ ETHNIC *cleansing* by Serbian paramilitary forces, resulting in the bombing of Belgrade by

Nato. (Debate on the ethics of the Allies' action included considerations of whether or not it fell within the definition of a ➤ JUST *war*.)

Lajos Kossuth (1802–94), Hungarian statesman and patriot. He led the 1848 insurrection against the Habsburgs, but after brief success the uprising was crushed and he began a lifelong exile.

August von Kotzebue (1761–1819), German dramatist. His many plays were popular in both Germany and England. He was a political informant to Tsar Alexander I and was assassinated by the Germans.

His son **Otto von Kotzebue** (1787–1846) was a navigator and explorer; he discovered an inlet of NW Alaska (Kotzebue Sound) now named after him.

kouros an archaic Greek statue of a young man, standing and often naked. The word is from Greek, the Ionic form of *koros* 'boy'.

kowtow kneel and touch the ground with the forehead in worship or submission as part of traditional Chinese custom. The word comes from Chinese *kētóu*, from *kē* 'knock' + *tóu* 'head'.

Richard von Krafft-Ebing (1840–1902), German physician and psychologist. He established the relationship between syphilis and general paralysis and pioneered the systematic study of aberrant sexual behaviour.

Krakatoa a small volcanic island in Indonesia, lying between Java and Sumatra, scene of a great eruption in 1883 which destroyed most of the island.

kraken an enormous mythical sea monster said to appear off the coast of Norway.

Kralitz Bible a version of the Bible in Czech, published at *Kralitz* by the Moravian Church, 1579–93.

kramat a Muslim holy place or place of pilgrimage.

the Kremlin the citadel in Moscow housing the Russian and (formerly) USSR government. The name is recorded from the mid 17th century, and comes via French from Russian *kreml'* 'citadel'.

Kremlinology the study and analysis of Soviet or Russian policies.

kreutzer a small silver or copper coin, originally stamped with a cross and formerly current in parts of Germany and in Austria.

kriegspiel a war game in which blocks representing armies or other military units are moved about on maps.

Kriemhild in the *Nibelungenlied*, a Burgundian princess, wife of Siegfried and later of Etzel (Attila the Hun), whom she marries in order to be revenged on her brothers for Siegfried's murder. Her Norse equivalent is ➤ GUDRUN.

Krishna in Hindu belief, one of the most popular gods, the eighth and most important avatar or incarnation of Vishnu.

He is worshipped in several forms: as the child god whose miracles and pranks are extolled in the Puranas; as the divine cowherd whose erotic exploits, especially with his favourite, Radha, have produced both romantic and religious literature; and as the divine charioteer who preaches to Arjuna on the battlefield in the *Bhagavadgita*.

See also ➤ HARE *Krishna*.

Kriss Kringle in parts of the US, Santa Claus; the name is probably an alteration of German *Christkindl* 'Christmas present, (informal) Christ-child'.

Kristallnacht the occasion of concerted violence by Nazis throughout Germany and Austria against Jews and their property on the night of 9–10 November 1938. The (German) word means literally 'night of crystal', referring to the broken glass produced by the smashing of shop windows.

Peter Kropotkin (1842–1921), Russian prince and anarchist. Imprisoned in 1874, he escaped abroad in 1876 and did not return to Russia until after the Revolution. His works include *Modern Science and Anarchism* (1903).

Paulus Kruger (1825–1904), South African soldier and statesman, President of Transvaal (1883–99), know as **Oom Paul**. He led the Afrikaners to victory in the First Boer War in 1881. His refusal to allow equal rights to non-Boer immigrants was one of the causes of the Second Boer War. Forced to flee the country, he died in exile in Switzerland.

Kruger telegram sent by Kaiser Wilhelm II of Germany to President Kruger, 3 January 1896, after the failure of the ➤ JAMESON *Raid*; the intention was to demonstrate to Britain the dangers of political isolation, but the effect was to arouse considerable anti-German feeling.

Alfred Krupp (1812–87), German arms manufacturer. His company played a pre-eminent part in German arms production from the 1840s through to the end of the Second World War.

kryptonite in science fiction, an alien mineral with the property of depriving ➤ SUPERMAN of his powers.

Kshatriya a member of the second of the four great Hindu castes, the military caste. The traditional function of the Kshatriyas is to protect society by fighting in wartime and governing in peacetime.

Ku Klux Klan an extremist right-wing secret society in the US. The Ku Klux Klan was originally founded in the southern states after the Civil War to oppose social change and black emancipation by violence and terrorism. Although disbanded twice, it re-emerged in the 1950s and 1960s and continues at a local level. Members disguise themselves in white robes and hoods, and often use a burning cross as a symbol of their organization.

Kuan Yin in Chinese Buddhism, the goddess of compassion.

Kublai Khan (1216–94), Mongol emperor of China, grandson of Genghis Khan. With his brother Mangu (then Mongol Khan) he conquered southern China (1252–9). After Mangu's death in 1259 he completed the conquest of China, founded the Yuan dynasty, and established his capital on the site of the modern Beijing.

kuccha short trousers ending above the knee, worn as one of the five distinguishing signs of the Sikh ➤ KHALSA, symbolizing loyalty and discipline.

kudos praise and honour received for an achievement. Recorded from the late 18th century, the word is Greek and means 'praise'.

Kufic an early angular form of the Arabic alphabet found chiefly in decorative incriptions. Recorded from the early 18th century, the word comes from the name *Kufa*, a city south of Baghdad, because the script was attributed to the city's scholars.

kukri a curved knife broadening towards the point, used by Gurkhas.

kulak a peasant in Russia wealthy enough to own a farm and hire labour. Emerging after the emancipation of serfs in the 19th century the kulaks resisted Stalin's forced collectivization, but millions were arrested, exiled, or killed.

Kultur German civilization and culture (sometimes used derogatorily to suggest elements of racism, authoritarianism, or militarism).

Kulturkampf a conflict from 1872 to 1887 between the German government (headed by Bismarck) and the papacy for the control of schools and Church appointments, in which Bismarck was forced to concede to the Catholic Church.

Kumbh Mela a Hindu festival and assembly, held once every twelve years at four locations in India, at which pilgrims bathe in the waters of the Ganges and Jumna Rivers. The name comes from Sanskrit, meaning literally 'pitcher festival'.

kumkum a red powder used ceremonially, especially by Hindu women to make a small distinctive mark on the forehead.

kundalini in yoga, latent female energy believed to lie coiled at the base of the spine.

kung fu a primarily unarmed Chinese martial art resembling karate; the word comes from Chinese gongfu, from *gong* 'merit' + *fu* 'master'. *Kung fu* became popular in the West during the 1970s, largely through the films of Bruce Lee.

Kuomintang a nationalist party founded in China under Sun Yat-sen in 1912, and led by Chiang Kai-shek from 1925. It held power from 1928 until the Communist Party took power in October 1949 and subsequently formed the central administration of Taiwan.

kurdaitcha in Australia, the use among Aboriginals of a bone in spells intended to cause sickness or death; a man empowered to point the bone at a victim.

kurgan a prehistoric burial mound or barrow of a type found in southern Russia and the Ukraine.

Kushan a member of an Iranian dynasty which invaded the Indian subcontinent and established a powerful empire in the north-west between the 1st and 3rd centuries AD.

kusti a cord worn round the waist by Parsees, consisting of seventy-two threads to represent the chapters of one of the portions of the Zend-Avesta.

Kutaisi an industrial city in central Georgia, which is one of the oldest cities in Transcaucasia, and which has been the capital of various kingdoms, including Colchis and Abkhazia.

kwai-lo in China, a foreigner, especially a European; the term means literally 'foreign devil'.

Kwanzaa a secular festival observed by many African Americans from 26 December to 1 January as a celebration of their cultural heritage and traditional values. The name comes from Kiswahili *matunda ya kwanza*, literally 'first fruits (of the harvest)'.

kylin a mythical composite animal, often figured on Chinese and Japanese ceramics. Recorded from the mid 19th century, the name comes from Chinese *qilin*, from *qi* 'male' + *lin* 'female'.

Kyrie a short repeated invocation (in Greek or in translation) used in many Christian liturgies, especially at the beginning of the Eucharist or as a response in a litany. The word comes from Greek *Kuriē eleēson* 'Lord, have mercy'.

L l

L the twelfth letter of the modern English alphabet and the eleventh of the ancient Roman one, corresponding to Greek *lambda* and ultimately Semitic *lamed*.

L is the Roman numeral for 50. Originally, this was a symbol identified with the letter *L* because of coincidence of form. In ancient Roman notation, *L* with a stroke above denoted 50,000.

L is also the sign for pounds sterling, from the initial letter of Latin *librae* 'pounds'.

La see also ➤ KNIGHT *of La Mancha*.

Jean de La Bruyère (1645–96), French writer and moralist. He is known for his *Caractères* (1688), based on a translation of the *Characters* of Theophrastus and exposing the vanity and corruption of human behaviour by satirizing Parisian society.

Jean de La Fontaine (1621–95), French poet. He is chiefly remembered for his *Fables* (1668–94), drawn from oriental, classical, and contemporary sources; they include such tales as 'The Cicada and the Ant' and 'The Crow and the Fox'. He also wrote *Contes et nouvelles* (1664–74), a collection of bawdy verse tales drawn from Ariosto, Boccaccio, and others.

Duc de La Rochefoucauld (1613–80), François de Marsillac, French writer and moralist. The author of *Réflexions, ou sentences et maximes morales* (1665), he was a supporter of the queen mother Marie de Médicis in plotting against Richelieu, and later joined the uprising of the nobles (known as the ➤ FRONDE, 1648–53) against Mazarin and the court when Louis XIV was a minor.

La Rochelle a port on the Atlantic coast of western France, which in the 17th century was a noted Huguenot stronghold. Having supported the English invasion of Ré, La Rochelle was besieged and finally conquered by the forces of Louis XIII and Richelieu. Many of its inhabitants starved to death during the siege.

Sieur de La Salle (1643–87), René-Robert Cavelier, French explorer, who sailed down the Ohio and Mississippi Rivers to the sea from Canada in 1682, naming the Mississippi basin *Louisiana* in honour

of Louis XIV. In 1684 he led an expedition to establish a French colony on the Gulf of Mexico, but was murdered when his followers mutinied.

La Scala an opera house in Milan built 1776–8 by the Empress Maria Theresa (at the time of Austria's control of Milan) on the site of the church of Santa Maria della Scala.

Georges de La Tour (1593–1652), French painter. He is best known for his nocturnal religious scenes and his subtle portrayal of candlelight.

laager a camp or encampment formed by a circle of wagons; an entrenched position or viewpoint that is defended against opponents. The word comes from Afrikaans and ultimately from Dutch *leger, lager* 'camp'. It is recorded in South African sources from the mid 19th century, but gradually the figurative use has become dominant.

Laban in the Bible, the father of Leah and ➤ RACHEL and uncle of ➤ JACOB, who tricked his nephew into marrying the elder sister Leah, and having to serve another seven years for Rachel.

labarum Constantine the Great's imperial standard, which bore Christian imagery (a monogram of the first two letters of Greek *Christos*) fused with the military symbols of the Roman Empire.

Labor Day US and Australian spelling of ➤ LABOUR *Day*

labour see also ➤ DIVISION *of labour*, ➤ MOUNTAIN *in labour*.

Labour Day a public holiday or day of festivities held in honour of working people, in many countries on 1 May, in the US and Canada on the first Monday in September.

Labour isn't working caption on a poster showing a long queue outside an unemployment office; British Conservative Party slogan, 1978.

labour of love work undertaken either from fondness for the work itself, or from desire to benefit persons whom one loves. The term was originally used (in the late 17th century) as a direct quotation from St Paul's Epistle to the Thessalonians: 'Your work of faith and labour of love'.

Labour Party a left-of-centre political party formed to represent the interests of ordinary working people, in particular a major British party that since the Second World War has been in power 1945–51, 1964–70, 1974–9, and since 1997. Arising from the trade union movement at the end of the 19th century, it replaced the Liberals as the country's second party after the First World War.
    See also ➤ NEW *Labour*, ➤ OLD *Labour*.

Labour Weekend in New Zealand, the weekend including Labour Day.

the labourer is worthy of his hire proverbial saying, late 14th century, deriving originally from Luke 10:7, and first used as a saying by Chaucer.

labouring see ➤ *ply the labouring* OAR.

labours see also ➤ HERCULES.

labours of the month in the Middle Ages, seasonal occupations associated with particular months, and often represented in sculpture and illumination.

Labours of the Month	
MONTH	**OCCUPATION**
January	Janus (sometimes also sitting at a table feasting)
February	man warming himself by a fire
March	pruning (usually vines); sometimes also digging
April	man in foliage
May	knight on horseback
June	mowing (haymaking)
July	harvesting (reaping)
August	threshing grain (occasionally fruit-picking)
September	treading grapes (occasionally picking grapes)
October	beating acorns from trees (sometimes filling casks)
November	slaughtering hogs (sometimes animals feeding from a manger)
December	feasting

labret an object such as a small piece of shell, bone, or stone inserted into the lip as an ornament in some cultures.

labrys the sacred double-headed axe of ancient Crete.

the Labyrinth in Greek mythology, the intricate maze constructed by ➤ DAEDALUS for the Cretan king Minos to house the ➤ MINOTAUR; Theseus, using a ball of thread, made his way through its passages to kill the monster.

lace see ➤ LAVENDER *and old lace*.

Lacedaemon an area of ancient Greece comprising the city of Sparta and its surroundings; **Lacedaemonian** thus means Spartan, or (of speech or correspondence) laconic. In the British army, the 46th Foot were known as **the Lacedaemonians**, from the reputed devotion of an early Colonel of the regiment to Spartan discipline.

laches a legal expression for unreasonable delay in making an assertion or claim, such as asserting a right, claiming a privilege, or making an application for redress, which may result in refusal. The word dates from late Middle English (in the sense 'slackness, negligence') and comes via Old French from Latin *laxus* 'loose, lax'; the current sense is recorded from the 16th century.

Lachesis in Greek mythology, one of the three ➤ FATES. Traditionally, *Clotho* holds the distaff, *Lachesis* spins the thread of life, and *Atropos* cuts the thread.

lachrymal vase in ancient Rome and other cultures, a phial for holding the tears of mourners at a funeral.

Lackland a nickname for King John of England, used in reference to the lands lost during his reign. The phrase is recorded from the late 16th century, and translates the Latin *Sine Terra* and Anglo-Norman French *Sanz Tere* (both meaning 'without land') of earlier chroniclers.

laconic (of a person, speech, or style of writing) using very few words. The term comes (in the mid 16th century, in the sense 'Laconian, Spartan) via Latin from Greek from *Lakōn* 'Sparta', the Spartans being known for their terse speech.

lacuna an unfilled space or interval; a gap; a missing portion in a book or manuscript. The word comes (in the mid 17th century) from Latin, 'pool', from *lacus* 'lake'.

ladder a ladder is the emblem of the monk and abbot *St John Climacus* (d. 649), author of the treatise *The Ladder of Paradise* from which his name comes (*Climacus* means 'ladder'), in which he developed the concept of the ladder as an image of spiritual life.

See also ➤ CROSSES *are ladders that lead to heaven*, ➤ JACOB'*s ladder*, ➤ SNAKES *and ladders*.

ladies See also ➤ LORDS *and ladies*, ➤ *the Ladies of* LLANGOLLEN.

ladies who lunch women who organize and take part in fashionable lunches to raise funds for charitable projects, from 'The Ladies who Lunch', 1970 song by Stephen Sondheim (1930–) 'A toast to that invincible bunch…Let's hear it for the ladies who lunch.'

Ladies' Gallery a public gallery in the House of Commons, reserved for women to attend debates.

Ladies' Mile another name for ➤ ROTTEN *Row*. The earliest reference is from a novel by Mary Elizabeth Braddon:

> The mighty tide of fashion's wonderful sea, surging westward, under the dusty elms and lindens of the Lady's Mile.
>
> — M. E. Braddon *Lady's Mile* (1866)

Ladino the language of some Sephardic Jews, especially formerly in Mediterranean countries. It is based on medieval Spanish, with an admixture of Hebrew, Greek, and Turkish words, and is written in modified Hebrew characters.

St Ladislaus (*c*.1040–95), king of Hungary (as Ladislaus I) 1077–95. He extended Hungarian power, established order in his kingdom, and advanced the spread of Christianity.

☐ **FEAST DAY** His feast day is 27 June.

ladle a *ladle* is the emblem of ➤ *St* MARTHA, seen as the epitome of housewifely virtues.

Ladon in Greek mythology, the dragon guarding the ➤ GOLDEN *apples* of the Hesperides, which was eventually killed by Hercules.

lady in Old English the word (in the form *hlǣfdīge*) denoted a woman to whom homage or obedience is due, such as the wife of a lord or the mistress of a household, and also (specifically) the Virgin Mary;

it comes from *hlāf* 'loaf' + a Germanic base meaning 'knead', related to *dough*.

See also ➤ BAG *lady*, ➤ DARK *Lady*, ➤ FIRST *Lady*, ➤ IRON *Lady*, ➤ *Lady* CHATTERLEY, ➤ *Lady* MACBETH, ➤ *lady of the* BEDCHAMBER, ➤ LOATHLY *Lady*, ➤ OLD *Lady of Threadneedle Street*, ➤ SILVER *Lady*, ➤ WHITE *lady*.

Our Lady the Virgin Mary.

See also ➤ *Our Lady's* PSALTER, ➤ *when* EASTER *day lies in Our Lady's lap*.

Lady Bountiful a patronizingly generous woman, named from a character in Farquhar's *The Beaux' Stratagem*.

> 'I enjoy my work,' Miriam said, steadfastly smiling. The old woman snorted. 'Lady Bountiful,' she said spitefully.
>
> — Philippa Gregory *Perfectly Correct* (1994)

Lady chapel a chapel in a church or cathedral, typically to the east of the high altar in a cathedral, to the south in a church, dedicated to the Virgin Mary.

Lady Day 25 March (the feast of the Annunciation), a quarter day in England, Wales, and Ireland.

Lady Luck the personification of Fortune.

Lady Margaret Hall for ladies,
St Hugh's for girls,
St Hilda's for wenches,
Somerville for women.
Oxford saying, *c*.1930s.

Lady of England title of Matilda, daughter of Henry I, as sovereign of England.

Order of Our Lady of Ransom another name for the Order of ➤ MERCEDARIANS.

the Lady of Shalott the name given by Tennyson to ➤ ELAINE, the Maid of Astolat, who died of unrequited love for Lancelot. In Tennyson's poem she is imprisoned in her tower by a magic spell, which compels her to watch in a mirror the scenes outside which she then depicts in her weaving. The mirror cracks, and the curse falls on her, when she looks directly out of the window, and sees Lancelot; she dies as her barge carries her down the river to Camelot.

the Lady of the Lake in the Arthurian romances, the sorceress who gives the sword Excalibur to Arthur.

the Lady of the Lamp a popular name for ➤ *Florence* NIGHTINGALE (1820–1910), referring to her work as a nurse in the Crimean War; this image of her in the wards at night is first alluded to by Long-fellow in *The Courtship of Miles Standish* (1858), 'A Lady with a Lamp shall stand in the great history of the land, A noble type of good, Heroic woman-hood.'

Our Lady of the Snows name given by Kipling to Canada in his poem on the Canadian Preferential Tariff, 1897.

lady's bedstraw a yellow-flowered plant, the flowers of which were formerly used in Britain to curdle the milk in cheesemaking and (as it smells of hay when dried) to make a mattress for sleeping on. The plant was also called **Our Lady's bedstraw**, and is one of a number of plant names such as *lady's mantle*, *lady's slipper*, and *lady's smock*, to reflect an allusion to the Virgin Mary, often in reference to the beauty and delicacy of the flowers.

ladybird the *ladybird* is traditionally regarded as lucky, and its name ('Our Lady's bird') associates it with the Virgin Mary.

Ladysmith a town in eastern South Africa, in KwaZulu/Natal, founded in the early 19th century and named after the wife of the governor of Natal, Sir Harry Smith (1787–1860). It was subjected to a four-month siege by Boer forces during the Second Boer War, and was finally relieved on 28 February 1900 by Lord Roberts.

Laertes in Greek mythology, the father of Odysseus, who survives to see his son come home to Ithaca.

In Shakespeare's *Hamlet*, *Laertes* is the name of ► OPHELIA's brother, who avenges his sister's death by killing Hamlet in the duel in which he himself is also killed.

Laetare Sunday the fourth Sunday of Lent. The name comes from Latin *Laetare* 'Rejoice', the opening word of the Introit, and the day marks the point at which the rigours of Lent are temporarily relaxed. It is also known as Mothering Sunday and Refreshment Sunday.

laeti a class of non-Roman cultivators under the later Roman Empire, who occupied lands for which they paid tribute.

Marquis de Lafayette (1757–1834), French soldier and statesman. He fought alongside the American colonists in the War of Independence and commanded the National Guard (1789–91) in the French Revolution, and the abiding force of his name was

demonstrated in the First World War by the American soldier Charles E. Stanton (1859–1933)'s '*Lafayette, nous voilà!* [Lafayette, we are here]' at the tomb of Lafayette in Paris, on the Fourth of July, 1917.

Lag b'Omer a Jewish festival held on the 33rd day of the Omer (the period between Passover and Pentecost), traditionally regarded as celebrating the end of a plague in the 2nd century.

Lagado a city in Swift's *Gulliver's Travels*, where the experiments on cucumbers were conducted.

> He had been eight years upon a project for extracting sun-beams out of cucumbers, which were to be put into vials hermetically sealed, and let out to warm the air in raw inclement summers.
> — Jonathan Swift *Gulliver's Travels* (1726) 'A Voyage to Laputa'

lagan (in legal contexts) goods or wreckage lying on the bed of the sea.

lager lout in the UK, a young (usually affluent) man who typically spends leisure time drinking large quantities of lager or other beer as one of a group in a pub, and who takes part in rowdy, aggressive, or boorish group behaviour.

The term originated in 1988 with the criticism by the Conservative politician John Patten, then a Home Office Minister, of the **lager culture** which meant that young men who might have been expected to behave respectably had nothing better to do than drink beer and behave disruptively; the term *lager louts* itself appeared shortly afterwards.

Joseph Louis de Lagrange (1736–1813), Italian-born French mathematician. He is remembered for his proof that every positive integer can be expressed as a sum of at most four squares, and for his work on mechanics and its application to the description of planetary and lunar motion.

Lagrangian point one of five points in the plane of orbit of one body around another (e.g. the moon around the earth) at which a small third body can remain stationary with respect to both.

R. D. Laing (1927–89), Scottish psychiatrist. He became famous for his controversial views on madness and in particular on schizophrenia, linking what society calls insanity with politics and family structure.

laissez-faire a policy or attitude of leaving things to take their own course, without interfering; abstention by governments from interfering in the workings of the free market.

The remark '*Laissez-nous-faire* [Allow us to do

it]', dated *c.*1664, is recorded in a source of the mid 18th century:

> Monsieur Colbert assembled several deputies of commerce at his house to ask what could be done for commerce; the most rational and the least flattering among them answered him in one word: 'Laissez-nous-faire'.
>
>   — in *Journal Oeconomique* Paris 1751

The expression became particularly associated with 18th-century political economists, as d'Argenson and Quesnay.

Laius in Greek mythology, a king of Thebes, husband of Jocasta and father of ➤ OEDIPUS, of whom it was prophesied that he would be killed by his own son. Laius accordingly ordered that the child should be exposed, but Oedipus was rescued and brought up in ignorance of his birth. When a man, he met Laius, quarrelled with him, and killed him; he subsequently married the widowed Jocasta.

lake see also ➤ LADY *of the Lake.*

Asphaltic Lake another name for ➤ *the* DEAD *Sea.*

Lake District a region of lakes and mountains in Cumbria. Earlier also called *Lakeland,* the term *Lake District,* first used by Wordsworth in 1835, has become dominant.

Lake Poets the poets Samuel Taylor Coleridge, Robert Southey, and William Wordsworth, who lived in and were inspired by the Lake District; they are also known as the *Lake School.* Both terms are first recorded in the *Edinburgh Review* of 1816; the pejorative *Lakers,* however, antedates them by two years.

Lakshmi in Hindu belief, the goddess of prosperity, consort of Vishnu. She assumes different forms (e.g. ➤ RADHA, ➤ SITA) in order to accompany her husband in his various incarnations.

René Lalique (1860–1945), French jeweller, famous for his art nouveau brooches and combs and his decorative glassware.

Lallans a distinctive Scottish literary form of English, based on standard older Scots. The name comes (as an adjective in the early 18th century) from a Scots variant of *Lowlands,* with reference to a central Lowlands dialect.

lallation imperfect speech, especially the repetition of meaningless sounds by babies. Recorded from the mid 17th century, the word comes from Latin *lallare* 'sing a lullaby'.

lama an honorific title applied to a spiritual leader in Tibetan Buddhism, whether a reincarnate lama (such as the ➤ DALAI *Lama*) or one who has earned the title in life.

See also ➤ DALAI *Lama,* ➤ PANCHEN *Lama.*

Jean Baptiste de Lamarck (1744–1829), French naturalist. He was an early proponent of organic evolution, although his theory is not widely accepted today. He suggested that species could have evolved from each other by small changes in their structure, and that the mechanism of such change (not now generally considered possible) was that characteristics acquired in order to survive could be passed on to offspring.

Apparent support for Lamarck's theories came when the Austrian zoologist Paul Kammerer (1880–1926) appeared to demonstrate the development of nuptial pads on the forefeet of *midwife toads*; it was however shown that the specimens had been injected with ink to produce the dark swellings claimed as nuptial pads. Kammerer committed suicide shortly afterwards.

lamb a *lamb* symbolizes youth and innocence; in Christian art it is emblematic of Jesus Christ (the **Lamb of God**).

A *lamb* is the emblem of ➤ *St* AGNES and ➤ *St* JOHN *the Baptist.*

See also ➤ EWE *lamb,* ➤ IMMACULATE *Lamb,* ➤ PASCHAL *lamb,* ➤ GOD *tempers the wind to the shorn lamb,* ➤ LARRY *the Lamb,* ➤ MARCH *comes in like a lion, and goes out like a lamb.*

Charles Lamb (1775–1834), English essayist and critic. He devoted much of his life to caring for his sister Mary, who suffered from a recurrent mental illness and in a fit of insanity in 1796 had killed their mother; together they wrote *Tales from Shakespeare* (1807), to make the stories of Shakespeare's plays familiar to the young.

Charles Lamb was also the author of the miscellaneous *Essays of Elia.* Lamb worked at South Sea House, and the pseudonym *Elia* was apparently the name of an Italian clerk formerly employed there.

lamb-ale an annual celebration at lamb-shearing.

Lamb of God a title of Jesus Christ (see John 1:29). Compare with ➤ AGNUS *Dei.*

lamb's wool a drink consisting of hot ale mixed with the pulp of roasted apples, and sugared and spiced.

lambda the eleventh letter of the Greek alphabet (Λ, λ), transliterated as 'l'.

Lambeg drum a large drum of a type traditionally beaten by ➤ ORANGEMEN on ceremonial occasions, named after *Lambeg*, a village near Belfast, Northern Ireland.

Lambert 12th-century priest of Liège, nicknamed *le Bègue* ('the Stammerer'), who founded the ➤ BEGUINE order.

St Lambert (*c*.635–*c*.705), bishop of Maastricht and patron of Liège; he was venerated as a martyr because his violent death was attributed by later biographers to his having reproved the Frankish ruler Pepin II (687–714) for adultery with the mother of his son ➤ CHARLES *Martel*.

His feast day is referred to in Shakespeare's *Richard II* as the day appointed for the tournament between Mowbray and Bolingbroke:

> Be ready, as your lives shall answer it,
> At Coventry, upon Saint Lambert's day.
>
> — William Shakespeare *Richard II* (1595)

□ **FEAST DAY** His feast day is 17 September.

Lambeth Books a name sometimes given to the symbolic poems which Blake wrote and etched while living at Lambeth, a borough of London, on the south bank of the Thames (1780–1800). They include *America*, *Europe*, and *The Song of Los*.

Lambeth Conference an assembly of bishops from the Anglican Communion, usually held every ten years (since 1867) at Lambeth Palace and presided over by the Archbishop of Canterbury.

Lambeth Palace a palace in the London borough of Lambeth, the residence of the Archbishop of Canterbury since 1197.

Lambeth Quadrilateral the essence of Anglicanism as charted by four essential principles (see ➤ QUADRILATERAL²), originally enunciated in 1870 and approved by the Lambeth Conference of 1888 as a basis for the reunion of the Christian Church.

Lambeth Walk a social dance with a walking step, popular in the late 1930s, created for the review *Me and My Girl* and named after a street in Lambeth.

lambrequin a cloth covering the back of a medieval knight's helmet, represented in heraldry as the mantling. The word comes via French from the Dutch diminutive of *lamper* 'veil'.

Kirke's Lambs the 2nd foot, commanded by Colonel Kirke (1646?–91), known for its savagery and so called ironically from its badge of a *paschal lamb*. The regiment was raised for service at Tangier, and Macaulay suggests this may have been the origin of the badge:

> As they had been levied for the purpose of waging war on an infidel nation, they bore on their flag a Christian emblem, the Paschal Lamb . . . These men, the rudest and most ferocious in the English army, were called Kirke's Lambs.
>
> — Lord Macaulay *History of England* (1849)

Kirke and his men became notorious during the suppression of Monmouth's rebellion; stories circulated of the number of people he had executed, and it was said that, having set up his headquarters at the White Hart in Taunton, he used the inn signpost as a gallows.

Iamdan a person learned in Jewish law; a Talmudic scholar.

lame duck an ineffectual or unsuccessful person or thing, originally (in the mid 18th century) Stock Exchange slang for one who could not meet his financial engagements, a defaulter. The term is first recorded in a letter from Horace Walpole of 1761, in which he asks, 'Do you know what a Bull, and a Bear, and a Lame Duck are?'

Lamentations a book of the Bible (in full **the Lamentations of Jeremiah**) telling of the desolation of Judah after the fall of Jerusalem in 586 BC.

lamia a mythical monster supposed to have the body of a woman, and to prey on human beings and suck the blood of children. The word is used in early translations of the Bible for Isaiah 34:15 (where the Authorized Version has 'screech owl', with marginal alternative 'night monster' and Lamentations 4:3 (where the Authorized Version has 'sea monsters' or 'sea calves'). *Lamia* comes via Latin from Greek, denoting a carnivorous fish or mythical monster.

In Keats's poem of this name, the serpent *Lamia* is transformed into a beautiful woman and wins the love of Lycius. At their wedding feast in Corinth her real nature is recognized by the sage Apollonius: he challenges her by her name, and she reverts to her true form, vanishing with a shriek of anguish.

Lammas the first day of August (also called **Lammas Day**), formerly observed as harvest festival, and one of the quarter-days in Scotland. The first element represents Old English *hlāf* 'loaf', but the word was later interpreted as if it represented *lamb* + *mass*.

latter Lammas a day that will never come; the equivalent of the Greek calends.

after Lammas corn ripens as much by night as by day traditional saying, recorded from the late 17th century.

Lammas growth in forestry, a shoot produced by a tree in summer, after a pause in growth; it is the equivalent of German *Johannestrieb* 'St John's shoot', in allusion to St John the Baptist's day, 24 June.

lamp See ➤ ALADDIN*'s lamp*, ➤ *the* LADY *of the Lamp*, ➤ SANCTUARY *lamp*, ➤ SLAVE *of the Lamp*, ➤ SMELL *of the lamp*.

lamplighter a person employed to light street gaslights by hand, often used allusively with reference to the rapidity with which the lamplighter ran on his rounds, or climbed the ladders formerly used to reach the street lamps.

lampoon a speech or text criticizing someone or something by using ridicule, irony, or sarcasm. The word comes (in the mid 17th century) from French, said to be from *lampons* 'let us drink' (used as a refrain), from *lamper* 'gulp down', nasalized form of *laper* 'to lap (liquid)' It is first recorded in the writings of John Evelyn:

> Here they still paste up their drolling lampoons and scurrilous papers.
>
> — John Evelyn *Memoirs* (1645)

lamprey an eel-like aquatic vertebrate which has a sucker mouth with horny teeth and a rasping tongue, and which attaches itself to other fish and sucks their blood; it is also a food fish, and is traditionally said to have caused the death of Henry I:

> King Henry being in Normandy, after some writers, fell from or with his horse, whereof he caught his death; but Ranulphe says he took a surfeit by eating of a lamprey, and thereof died.
>
> — Robert Fabyan *The New Chronicles of England and France* (1516)

House of Lancaster the English royal house descended from ➤ JOHN *of Gaunt*, Duke of Lancaster, that ruled England from 1399 (Henry IV) until 1461 (the deposition of Henry VI) and again on Henry's brief restoration in 1470–1. With the red rose as its emblem it fought the Wars of the Roses with the ➤ *House of* YORK, both houses being branches of the Plantagenet line. Lancaster's descendants, the Tudors, eventually prevailed through Henry VII's accession to the throne in 1485.

The **Duchy of Lancaster** is now an estate vested in the Crown, consisting of properties in Lancashire and elsewhere in England.

See also ➤ CHANCELLOR *of the Duchy of Lancaster*, ➤ TIME-*honoured Lancaster*.

Lancaster House Agreement an agreement which brought about the establishment of the independent state of Zimbabwe, reached in September 1979 at Lancaster House in London.

Lancasterian System the education system for schools devised by Joseph Lancaster (1778–1838), in which the older and more able pupils were appointed as monitors to teach the younger ones.

Lancastrian a follower of the House of Lancaster or of the Red Rose party supporting it in the Wars of the Roses.

lance a lance is the emblem of ➤ St JUDE, ➤ St THOMAS *the Apostle*, St Gereon, a 4th-century martyr of Cologne, and ➤ *St* MAURICE.

See also ➤ HOLY *Lance*, ➤ *St* CRISPIN*'s lance*.

lance-knight a mercenary foot-soldier, especially one armed with a lance or pike. The first element originally represented 'land'.

Lancelot in Arthurian legend, the most famous of Arthur's knights, father of ➤ GALAHAD; he is one of the most significant figures of the cycle, since it is the revelation of his adulterous love for ➤ GUINEVERE that forces him into exile and allows the traitor ➤ MORDRED opportunity to rebel against Arthur.

Lancelot is seen as a type of flawed courage; he is one of Arthur's greatest knights, but he is not judged pure enough to find the ➤ HOLY *Grail* which will be his son's reward.

Lancer originally, a soldier of a cavalry regiment armed with lances; now, a soldier belonging to a regiment that still retains this title, as *the Queen's Royal Lancers*.

lancers a quadrille for eight or sixteen pairs, fashionable in the mid 19th century.

land see also ➤ DEBATABLE *Land*, ➤ *the land God gave to* CAIN, ➤ *land of the* BROAD *acres*, ➤ *the* PROMISED *Land*.

Land Acts a series of British parliamentary acts concerning land tenure in Ireland, passed in 1870, 1881, 1903, and 1909, intended to give tenants greater security and further rights.

land girl in the UK, a woman doing farm work, especially during the Second World War.

every land has its own law proverbial saying, early 17th century.

Land League an Irish organization formed in 1879 to campaign for tenants' rights. Its techniques included the use of the boycott against anyone taking on a farm from which the tenant had been evicted. The Land Act of 1881 met many of the League's demands.

Land of Beulah another name for ➤ BEULAH.

Land of Cakes an informal name for Scotland; *cakes* here are thin pieces of oaten bread.

Land of Enchantment an informal name for New Mexico.

Land of Hope and Glory the song written by A. C. Benson (1862–1925) to a melody by Edward Elgar:

> Land of Hope and Glory, Mother of the Free,
> How shall we extol thee who are born of thee?
> Wider still and wider shall thy bounds be set;
> God who made thee mighty, make thee mightier yet.
> — A. C. Benson 'Land of Hope and Glory' (1902)

Benson's song was written to be sung as the Finale to Elgar's *Coronation Ode* (1902); it became very popular as a patriotic song, and is now particularly associated with the Last Night of the Proms.

land of milk and honey in the Bible, the land promised to the Israelites, 'a land flowing with milk and honey' (Exodus 3:8). A *land of milk and honey* may now be used generally to suggest a place of prosperity and contentment, but there may also be a suggestion that this is a future state to be achieved.

> Robson has made it quite clear that promotion back to English football's land of milk and honey is his priority this season.
> — *Sunday Telegraph* 25 January 1998

Land of my Fathers Wales, from the title '*Hen Wlad fy Nhadau* [Land of my Fathers]', taken from the opening words of the first verse of the Welsh national anthem by Evan James (1809–78). According to the *Dictionary of National Biography*, Evan James wrote a three-verse song in Welsh one Sunday evening in 1856, and shortly afterwards his son James James (1832–1902) composed the music for it. It was first sung publicly by James James at an eisteddfod in 1857, and was an immediate popular success; by the 1880s it was being sung as a national anthem at the close of meetings.

Land of Nod after the murder of Abel, ➤ CAIN was exiled by God:

> And Cain went out from the presence of the Lord, and dwelt in the land of Nod, on the east of Eden.
> — Bible (Authorized Version, 1611) Genesis ch. 4, v. 16

From the mid 18th century, the phrase has been used punningly to mean sleep; the place of Cain's exile, and its desolate nature, is more likely to be described as ➤ *the land God gave to* CAIN.

Land of Opportunity an informal name for Arkansas.

Land of the Covenant another name for ➤ CANAAN, the land promised by God through his covenant with the Israelites.

Land of the Free an informal name for the United States, taken from the poem by the American lawyer and verse-writer Francis Scott Key (1779–1843), which was adopted as the US national anthem in 1931:

> 'Tis the star-spangled banner; O long may it wave
> O'er the land of the free, and the home of the brave!
> — Francis Scott Key 'The Star-Spangled Banner' (1814)

See also ➤ STAR-*Spangled Banner*.

land of the leal in Scottish usage, the home of the blessed dead, Heaven; the *leal* are those who have been loyal and faithful in life.

Land of the Little Sticks Canada (from Chinook *stik* 'wood, tree, forest', the subarctic tundra region of northern Canada, characterized by its stunted vegetation).

Land of the Long White Cloud New Zealand (translating the Maori name ➤ AOTEAROA).

Land of the Midnight Sun any of the most northerly European countries, where the sun can be seen at midnight during the summer.

Land of the Rising Sun Japan; a translation of Japanese *Nippon*, which comes from *nichi* 'the sun' + *pon, hon* 'source'. *Nippon* is recorded in English from the early 17th century, but *Land of the Rising Sun* is not found until the mid 19th century.

do a land-office business in informal American usage, do a lot of successful trading. The expression looks back to the period at which new lands were being made available to settlers, and land-offices dealing with sales and settlement of new lands accordingly to a great deal of business.

you buy land, you buy stones; you buy meat, you buy bones proverbial saying, late 17th century; meaning that every purchase has its drawbacks.

from Land's End to John o'Groats from one end of Britain to the other; *Land's End* is a rocky promontory in SW Cornwall, forming the westernmost point of England, and by road is approximately 876 miles from *John o'Groats*, a village at the extreme NE point of the Scottish mainland.

landnám land-taking, especially with reference to the Norse colonization of Iceland; the saga of the settlement of Iceland is known as *Landnámabok*.

landscape all the visible features of an area of countryside or land, often considered in terms of their aesthetic appeal; a picture representing this. The term was in fact introduced (in the late 16th century, from Dutch) to denote a picture of natural scenery; it then came to mean a view or prospect of such scenery, and finally, a tract of land with its distinguishing characteristics and features.

landscape gardening the art and practice of laying out grounds in a way which is ornamental or which imitates natural scenery, a style popularized in the 18th century by practitioners such as Capability Brown (1716–83) and Humphrey Repton (1752–1818).

Edwin Henry Landseer (1802–73), English painter and sculptor. He is best known for his animal subjects such as *The Monarch of the Glen* (1851), and the name **Landseer Newfoundland** designates a breed of black and white Newfoundland dog of a type once painted by him. As a sculptor he is chiefly remembered for the bronze lions in Trafalgar Square (1867).

landsknecht a member of a class of mercenary soldiers in the German and other continental armies in the 16th and 17th centuries. The word is German, meaning literally 'soldier of the land', and originally it denoted mercenary footsoldiers of the imperial territory as distinguished from the Swiss, but it was soon applied more widely. An etymological association of the first syllable with *lance* brought about the development of the term *lance-knight*, and its restriction to men armed with a lance or similar weapon.

Landsmål another term for ➤ NYNORSK.

Karl Landsteiner (1868–1943), Austrian-born American physician. In 1930 Landsteiner was awarded a Nobel Prize for devising the ABO system of classifying blood, which made it possible for blood transfusions to be carried out successfully. He was also the first to describe the ➤ RHESUS *factor* in blood.

lane see ➤ *it is a* LONG *long lane that has no turning*, ➤ PETTICOAT *Lane*.

Lanfranc (1005?–89), Pavian-born scholar and cleric, prior of Bec and Caen, and counsellor of William the Conqueror, who in 1070 was appointed Archbishop of Canterbury by the new king.

William Langland (*c*.1330–*c*.1400), English poet. A minor friar, he devoted much of his life to writing and rewriting *Piers Plowman* (*c*.1367–70), a long allegorical poem in alliterative verse which takes the form of a spiritual pilgrimage.

langsuir in Malaysian folklore: a female vampire with a whinnying cry, that preys on newborn children.

Stephen Langton (*c*.1150–1228), English prelate, Archbishop of Canterbury 1207–15; 1218–28. A champion of the English Church, he was involved in the negotiations leading to the signing of Magna Carta.

Lillie Langtry (1853–1929), British actress, known as the **Jersey Lily** from her place of birth. She made her stage debut in 1881 and later became the mistress of the Prince of Wales, later Edward VII.

language see also ➤ BODY *language*.

language of flowers a set of symbolic meanings attached to different flowers when they are given or arranged.

langue d'oc the form of medieval French spoken south of the Loire, generally characterized by the use of *oc* to mean 'yes', and forming the basis of modern Provençal.

langue d'oïl the form of medieval French spoken north of the Loire, generally characterized by the use of *oïl* to mean 'yes', and forming the basis of modern French.

lanner a falcon with a dark brown back and buff cap, found in SE Europe, the Middle East, and Africa; in falconry, the female of this bird. Recorded from late Middle English, the word comes from Old French *lanier*, perhaps a noun use of 'cowardly', from a derogatory use of *lanier* 'wool merchant', from Latin *lanarius*, from *lana* 'wool'.

lanneret in falconry, a male lanner, which is smaller than the female.

lansquenet an archaic variant of
➤ LANDSKNECHT. Also, a gambling game of German origin which involved betting on cards turned up by the dealer; in the *London Gazette* of 1687, the playing of this game in private houses was forbidden.

> Each day she dreaded to hear that he had lost everything at lansquenet.
> — M. Collins *The Prettiest Woman in Warsaw* (1885)

lantern a lantern is the emblem of ➤ *St* LUCY and ➤ *St* GUDULE.
  See also ➤ ARISTOTLE*'s lantern*, ➤ FRIAR*'s lantern*, ➤ JACK-*o'-lantern*.

Lantern Festival another name for the Japanese Buddhist festival of ➤ BON.

Lanzarote the most easterly of the Canary Islands. A series of volcanic eruptions in about 1730 dramatically altered the island's landscape, creating an area of volcanic cones in the south-west known as the 'Mountains of Fire'; it is also now a popular holiday resort.

> Clubbing in Corfu or largin' it in Lanzarote, things can suddenly go cringingly wrong.
> — *Just Seventeen* 14 August 1996

Lao-tzu (fl. 6th century BC), Chinese philosopher traditionally regarded as the founder of Taoism and author of the Tao-te-Ching, its most sacred scripture.

Lao's mirror as described in Goldsmith's *Citizen of the World* (1762), a mirror, belonging to an empress of China, which reflected the mind as well as the face.

Laocoon in Greek mythology, a Trojan priest who, with his two sons, was crushed to death by two great sea serpents as a penalty for warning the Trojans against the ➤ TROJAN *Horse*. A marble sculpture in the Vatican Museum, attributed by Pliny to Agesander, Athenodorus, and Polydurus of Rhodes, depicts the death of Laocoon and his sons, and in allusive use his name often reflects the idea of someone struggling within enveloping coils.

> I'm feeling like Laocoon. I'm feeling like a professional contortionist who's tied himself into seventy knots and forgotten how to undo them.
> — Nicholas Blake *The Case of the Abominable Snowman* (1941)

Laodamia in Greek mythology, the wife of Protesilaus, prince of Thessaly, who in the Trojan War was the first of the Greeks to leap ashore, and subsequently the first to be killed. Laodamia was plunged into such grief at his death that the gods allowed him to return to her for three hours; when he left her again she killed herself. Wordsworth's poem *Laodamia* (1814) is based on this story.

Laodicean lukewarm or half-hearted, especially with respect to religion or politics; from *Laodicea* in Asia Minor, with reference to the early Christians there described in Revelations 3:15 as being 'lukewarm, neither cold nor hot'.

the laogai in China, a system of labour camps, many of whose inmates are political dissidents. The name comes from Chinese, meaning 'reform through labour', and is recorded from English from the 1990s.
  In 1996 the Chinese-born American activist, Harry Wu, said, 'I want to see the word *laogai* in every dictionary in every language in the world. I want to see the laogai ended.' He went on to draw a parallel with the word *gulag*, suggesting that it was only as in the mid 1970s that the word became known that pressure for the system to end began to grow.

in the lap of the gods beyond human control; from Homer *The Iliad* 'It lies in the lap of the gods.'

lapis lazuli a bright blue metamorphic rock consisting largely of lazurite, used for decoration and in jewellery, and from which the pigment ➤ ULTRAMARINE was originally made.

Lapith in Greek mythology, a member of a Thessalian people who fought and defeated the centaurs; the battle between them after the wedding feast of the Lapith king Pirithous, when the centaurs tried to carry off the bride and other Lapith women, was a favourite topic for Greek sculptors.

lapsus calami a Latin phrase meaning a slip of the pen.

lapsus linguae a Latin phrase meaning a slip of the tongue.

Laputa[1] the flying island in Swift's *Gulliver's Travels*, whose inhabitants were addicted to visionary projects; the term **Laputan** is now used to indicate pointless intellectual effort.

> To that seriously endangered species, the intelligent general reader of science fiction and fantasy, such squabbles are exercises in Laputan pointlessness.
> — *Interzone* June 1999

Laputa[2] in John Buchan's novel *Prester John* (1910), the Reverend John *Laputa* is the central character who reveals himself to be the 'heir of John', and leader of an unsuccessful Zulu uprising.

lapwing traditional allusions to the *lapwing* refer to its crested head, its technique of distracting an enemy from its nest by crying loudly at a distance from it, or by offering itself as quarry to be followed, and to the belief that the newly-hatched lapwing runs about with its head in the shell.

larder originally (in Middle English) *larder* denoted a store of meat, probably bacon; the word comes via Old French from Latin *laridum*, related to Greek *larinos* 'fat'.
   See also ➤ *the* DOUGLAS *larder*.

lares gods of the household worshipped in ancient Rome in conjunction with Vesta and the penates; the phrase **lares and penates** is used to mean the home.
   See also ➤ PENATES.

lark the lark's song is delivered on the wing, and traditional allusions refer to its early singing, the strength and sweetness of its song, and the height to which it soars above its nest.
   See also ➤ *if the* SKY *falls we shall catch larks*.

lark-silver in medieval Ireland, an annual payment due to the Crown from tenants of the Honour of Clare.

Pierre Larousse (1817–75), French lexicographer and encyclopedist. He edited the fifteen-volume *Grand dictionnaire universel du XIX* *siècle* (1866–76), which aimed to treat every area of human knowledge. In 1852 he co-founded the publishing house of Larousse.

Larry the Lamb in the ➤ TOYTOWN stories of S. G. Hulme Beatman (1886–1932), the well-meaning but ineffectual lamb whose customary bleating apology is, 'I'm only a little lamb.'

Lars see ➤ *Lars* PORSENA.

larva the active immature form of an insect, especially one that differs greatly from the adult and forms the stage between egg and pupa. The word comes from Latin 'ghost, mask', and in the 17th century was used to denote a disembodied spirit or ghost.

Harold Larwood (1904–95), English cricketer. A fearsome fast bowler for Nottinghamshire, in the 1932–3 MCC tour of Australia he bowled fast short-pitched ➤ BODYLINE deliveries, and was involved in controversy when several of the home batsmen were badly injured.

Las Vegas a city in southern Nevada noted for its casinos and nightclubs.

Lascaux the site of a cave in the Dordogne, France, which is richly decorated with Palaeolithic wall paintings of animals dated to the Magdalenian period. Discovered in 1940, the cave was closed in 1963 to protect the paintings, a replica later being opened nearby.

lash see ➤ *a* LASH *of scorpions*.

Lassie name of the loyal and intelligent collie which is the central character in a series of films, originally created by Eric Knight in the children's story *Lassie Come Home* (1940), in which a poor Yorkshire couple have to sell their son's much-loved collie. The actor Roddy McDowall (1928–98) who played the boy, said of the dog (actually a male) which appeared with him in the film, 'Lassie was a lot smarter than a lot of people I know.'

Orlando de Lassus (*c*.1532–94), Flemish composer. A notable composer of polyphonic music, he wrote over 2,000 secular and sacred works.

last see also ➤ CUSTER's *Last Stand*, ➤ *the Last of the* MOHICANS, ➤ *the last* ROSE, ➤ *let the* COBBLER *stick to his last*.

Last Day the final day of the world, on which the ➤ LAST *Judgement* will take place.

the last drop makes the cup run over proverbial saying, mid 17th century.

Last Judgement the judgement of humankind expected in some religious traditions to take place at the end of the world.

The Last of the Barons title of a novel by Bulwer-Lytton (1843) about Richard Neville, Earl of Warwick (1428–71), known as ➤ *Warwick the* KINGMAKER.

last post in the British armed forces, the second of two bugle calls giving notice of the hour of retiring at night, played also at military funerals and acts of remembrance.

last rites in the Christian Church, rites administered to a person who is about to die.

it is the last straw that breaks the camel's back proverbial saying, mid 17th century.

Last Supper the supper eaten by Jesus and his disciples on the night before the Crucifixion, as recorded in the New Testament and commemorated by Christians in the Eucharist.

the four last things in Christian belief, death, judgement, heaven, and hell, as studied in eschatology.

last trump the trumpet blast that in some religious beliefs is thought will wake the dead on Judgement Day.

Last words ■ See box opposite.

late see ➤ the EARLY *man never borrows from the late man*, ➤ BETTER *late than never*, ➤ *the late* UNPLEASANTNESS.

late Latin Latin of about AD 200–600.

Lateran the site in Rome containing the cathedral church of Rome (a basilica dedicated to St John the Baptist and St John the Evangelist) and the Lateran Palace, where the popes resided until the 14th century.
See also ➤ St JOHN *Lateran*.

Lateran Council any of five general councils of the Western Church held in the Lateran Palace in 1123, 1139, 1179, 1215, and 1512–17. The council of 1215 condemned the ➤ ALBIGENSES as heretical and clarified the Church doctrine on transubstantiation, the Trinity, and the Incarnation.

Lateran Treaty a concordat signed in 1929 in the Lateran Palace between the kingdom of Italy (represented by Mussolini) and the Holy See (represented by Pope Pius XI), which recognized as fully sovereign and independent the papal state under the name Vatican City.

lath see ➤ DAGGER *of lath*.

lathe any of the ancient divisions of Kent.

latifundium a large landed estate or ranch in ancient Rome or more recently in Spain or Latin America, typically worked by slaves.

Latin the language of ancient Rome and its empire, widely used historically as a language of scholarship and administration.
Latin is a member of the Italic branch of the Indo-European family of languages. After the decline of the Roman Empire it continued to be a medium of communication among educated people throughout the Middle Ages in Europe and elsewhere, and remained the liturgical language of the Roman Catholic Church until the reforms of the second Vatican Council (1962–5); it is still used for scientific names in biology and astronomy. The Romance languages are derived from it.
See also ➤ DOG *Latin*, ➤ LATE *Latin*, ➤ LAW *Latin*, ➤ LOW *Latin*, ➤ MEDIEVAL *Latin*, ➤ PIG *Latin*, ➤ QUARTIER *Latin*, ➤ ROGUES' *Latin*, ➤ SILVER *Latin*, ➤ TACE *is Latin for a candle*, ➤ THIEVES' *Latin*, ➤ VULGAR *Latin*.

Latin America the parts of the American Continent where Spanish or Portuguese is the main national language, i.e., Mexico and Brazil, in effect, the whole of Central and South America including many of the Caribbean islands.

Latin Church the Christian Church which originated in the Western Roman Empire, giving allegiance to the Pope of Rome, and historically using Latin for the liturgy; the Roman Catholic Church as distinguished from Orthodox and Uniate Churches.

Latin cross a plain cross in which the vertical part below the horizontal is longer than the other three parts.

Latin Quarter the district of Paris (the *Quartier Latin*) on the left or south bank of the Seine, where Latin was spoken in the Middle Ages, and where students and artists live and the principal university buildings are situated.

Latin rights in ancient Rome, a set of privileges, falling short of full citizenship, enjoyed by inhabitants of Latium and from 89 BC on extended to people outside Italy.

Latin rite a religious ceremonial using Latin, especially in the Roman Catholic Church.

Latin square an arrangement of letters or symbols that each occur n times, in a square array of n^2 compartments so that no letter appears twice in the same row or column.

Last words

All my possessions for a moment of time	Elizabeth I (1533–1603)
All this buttoning and unbuttoning	18th-century suicide note
Be of good comfort Master Ridley, and play the man. We shall this day light such a candle by God's grace in England, as (I trust) shall never be put out	Hugh Latimer (c.1485–1555)
Bugger Bognor	George V (1865–1936)
Come closer, boys. It will be easier for you	Erskine Childers (1870–1922)
Crito, we owe a cock to Aesculapius; please pay it and don't forget it	Socrates (469–399 BC)
Die, my dear Doctor, that's the last thing I shall do!	Lord Palmerston (1784–1865)
Don't let the awkward squad fire over me	Robert Burns (1759–96)
An emperor ought to die standing	Vespasian (AD 9–79)
Farewell, my friends, I go to glory	Isadora Duncan (1878–1927)
For God's sake look after our people	Robert Falcon Scott (1868–1912)
For my name and memory, I leave it to men's charitable speeches, and to foreign nations, and the next ages	Francis Bacon (1561–1626)
Give Dayrolles a chair	Lord Chesterfield (1694–1773)
God save Ireland!	the Manchester Martyrs, William Allen, Michael Larkin, and William O'Brien (all d. 1867)
God will pardon me, it is His trade	Heinrich Heine (1797–1856)
Greetings, we win!	Pheidippides (d. 490 BC)
How's the Empire?	George V (1865–1936)
I am about to take my last voyage, a great leap in the dark	Thomas Hobbes (1588–1679)
I am going to seek a great perhaps…Bring down the curtain, the farce is played out	François Rabelais (c.1494–c.1553)
I am just going outside and may be some time	Lawrence Oates (1880–1912)
I die happy	Charles James Fox (1749–1806)
I find, then, I am but a bad anatomist	Wolfe Tone (1763–98)
I have a long journey to take, and must bid the company farewell	Walter Raleigh (c.1552–1618)

I have loved justice and hated iniquity: therefore I die in exile	Pope Gregory VII (c.1020–85)
I only regret that I have but one life to lose for my country	Nathan Hale (1755–76)
I will die like a true-blue rebel. Don't waste any time in mourning—organize	Joe Hill (1879–1915)
I'm tired, and I have to go to sleep	Allen Ginsberg (1912–97)
If this is dying, then I don't think much of it	Lytton Strachey (1880–1932)
It's been so long since I've had champagne	Anton Chekhov (1860–1904)
Let not poor Nelly starve	Charles II (1630–85)
Lord, open the King of England's eyes!	William Tyndale (c.1494–1536)
Love? What is it? Most natural painkiller. What there is…LOVE	William S. Burroughs (1914–97)
More light!	Johann Wolfgang von Goethe (1749–1832)
My design is to make what haste I can to be gone	Oliver Cromwell (1599–1658)
Now God be praised, I will die in peace	James Wolfe (1727–59)
Now I'll have eine kleine Pause	Kathleen Ferrier (1912–53)
O liberty! O liberty! what crimes are committed in thy name!	Mme Roland (1754–93)
Oh, my country! how I leave my country!	William Pitt (1759–1806)
On the contrary	Henrik Ibsen (1828–1926)
One of us must go	Oscar Wilde (1854–1900)
See in what peace a Christian can die	Joseph Addison (1672–1719)
So little done, so much to do	Cecil Rhodes (1853–1902)
Strike the tent	Robert E. Lee (1807–70)
Tell them I've had a wonderful life	Ludwig Wittgenstein (1889–1951)
Tell them to stand up for Jesus	Dudley Atkins Tyng (d. 1858)
Thank God, I have done my duty	Horatio Nelson (1758–1805)
They couldn't hit an elephant at this distance	John Sedgwick (d. 1864)
This hath not offended the king	Thomas More (1478–1535)
This, this is the end of earth. I am content	John Quincy Adams (1767–1848)
Thomas—Jefferson—still surv—	John Adams (1735–1826)

Last words

Turn up the lights; I don't want to go home in the dark	O. Henry (1862–1910)	What *is* the answer?…what is the question?	Gertrude Stein (1874–1946)
Vicisti, Galilaee [You have won, Galilean]	Julian the Apostate (AD c.332–363)	Why fear death? It is the most beautiful adventure in life	Charles Frohman (1860–1915)
We are all going to Heaven, and Vandyke is of the company	Thomas Gainsborough (1727–88)	Why not? Why not? Why not? Yeah	Timothy Leary (1920–96)
Well, I've had a happy life	William Hazlitt (1778–1830)	Would to God this wound had been for Ireland	Patrick Sarsfield (c.1655–93)
What an artist dies with me!	Nero (AD 37–68)		

Latinus in Roman mythology, king of ➤ LATIUM, and father of Lavinia whom ➤ AENEAS married.

Latitudinarian any of a group of 17th-century divines who, while attached to episcopal government and liturgical forms of worship, regarded them basically as not of fundamental importance.

Latium an ancient region of west central Italy, west of the Apennines and south of the River Tiber. Settled during the early part of the 1st millennium BC by a branch of the Indo-European people known as the *Latini*, it had become dominated by Rome by the end of the 4th century BC; it is now part of the modern region of Lazio.

Latona in Roman mythology, ➤ LETO.

latria in the Roman Catholic Church, supreme worship allowed to God alone.

latter see also ➤ *latter* LAMMAS, ➤ *Latter* PROPHETS.

Latter-Day Saints the Mormons' name for themselves.

lau a water monster reputed to live in the swamps of the Nile valley.

William Laud (1573–1645), English prelate, Archbishop of Canterbury 1633–45. His attempts to restore some pre-Reformation practices in England and Scotland aroused great hostility and were a contributory cause of the English Civil War. He was impeached by Parliament in 1640, imprisoned in the Tower of London, and finally tried and executed for treason.

laudator temporis acti a person who holds up the past as a golden age, from Latin *laudator temporis acti (se puero)* 'a praiser of past times,

(when he himself was a boy)' in Horace's *Ars Poetica*.

Harry Lauder (1870–1950), Scottish music-hall comedian. He became highly popular singing songs, many of which were his own compositions, such as 'I Love a Lassie' and 'Roamin' in the Gloamin'', and entertained troops at home and abroad in both world wars.

lauds a service of morning prayer in the Divine Office of the Western Christian Church, traditionally said or chanted at daybreak, though historically it was often held with matins on the previous night.

Recorded from Middle English, the name comes from the frequent use, in Psalms 148–150, of the Latin imperative *laudate!* 'praise ye!'

laugh and be fat proverbial saying, late 16th century.

laugh and the world laughs with you; weep and you weep alone proverbial saying, late 19th century; originally as a quotation from the American poet Ella Wheeler Wilcox (1855–1919):

> Laugh and the world laughs with you;
> Weep, and you weep alone;
> For the sad old earth must borrow its mirth,
> But has trouble enough of its own.
> — Ella Wheeler Wilcox 'Solitude'.

let them laugh that win proverbial saying, mid 16th century.

Laughing Cavalier popular name for a portrait of an unknown man by the Dutch painter Franz Hals (c.1580–1666); the name is not contemporary, but began to be used in the late 19th century. In 1913, the romantic novelist Baroness Orczy published a book, *The Laughing Cavalier*, purporting to show that the sitter was the direct ancestor of her hero Sir Percy Blakeney, the ➤ SCARLET *Pimpernel*.

laughing gas a non-technical term for nitrous oxide. The gas, originally discovered by Sir Humphrey Davy (1778–1829), which was used particularly in dentistry as an anaesthetic, produces exhilaration when first inhaled.

laughing philosopher a name for the Greek philosopher ➤ DEMOCRITUS, from his custom of laughing at everything.

he **laughs** best who laughs last proverbial saying, early 17th century.

he who **laughs** last, laughs longest proverbial saying, early 20th century.

Laura ➤ PETRARCH's name for the woman in praise of whom his sonnet sequence is written.

laura a group of huts or cells inhabited by reclusive monks in Egypt and the Middle East. In the Orthodox Church, a monastery consisting of separate cells; a large monastery. The word comes from Greek meaning 'lane, passage, alley'.

Laura Ashley of a garment or fabric, characteristic of the style of the British fashion and textile designer *Laura Ashley* (1925–85), typically having a small floral pattern.

> Her mind was room-by-room Laura Ashley wallpaper: tiny, unopened pastel buds arranged in straight rows.
> — Margaret Atwood *Wilderness Tips* (1991)

Laurasia a vast continental area believed to have existed in the northern hemisphere and to have resulted from the break-up of Pangaea in Mesozoic times. It comprised the present North America, Greenland, Europe, and most of Asia north of the Himalayas.

laureate see ➤ POET *Laureate*.

laurel the foliage of the bay tree woven into a wreath or crown and worn on the head as an emblem of victory or mark of honour in classical times. The word is often found in the plural, as in **look to one's laurels**, be concerned about losing one's preeminence, and **rest on one's laurels**, cease to strive for further glory.

In classical times (as recorded by Pliny), laurel was believed to avert lightning.

Laurel may also be used in numismatics to designate an English gold coin, first coined in 1619, on which the sovereign's head was shown with a wreath of laurel.

Laurel and Hardy an American comedy duo consisting of **Stan Laurel** (1890–1965) and **Oliver Hardy** (1892–1957). In many slapstick comedy films from 1927 onwards, British-born Stan Laurel played the scatterbrained and often tearful innocent, Oliver Hardy his pompous, overbearing, and frequently exasperated friend, characterized by the catchphrase, 'Another fine mess you've gotten me into.'

laurel-man a term recorded in Swift's writings for someone opposed to the Hanoverian succession.

Laurence laziness personified, a lazy person (**lazy Laurence** is also used); this association of the personal name with the quality is first recorded in the proverbial **Laurence bids wages**, meaning that the attractions of idleness are tempting.

It has been suggested that there is an allusion to the heat prevalent around the time of the feast of ➤ *St* LAWRENCE (10 August). Another conjecture is that there was a joke to the effect that when the martyr St Lawrence told his torturers to turn him round on his gridiron, it was because he was too lazy to move by himself.

In the US, *laurence* is also used for the shimmering effect that can be seen on a road or other surface on a hot day; this may again derive from the association of St Lawrence with heat.

Laurentian Library name of the library in Florence founded in the 15th century by Lorenzo (Laurentius) de' Medici. When the Medici were expelled from Florence the collection was purchased by the Medici Pope Leo X and taken to Rome; he added to it, and intended that it should be returned to Florence. This was done by the Medici Pope Clement VII.

Annie Laurie (1682–1764), daughter of Sir Robert Laurie of Maxwelton, and subject of the Scottish ballad written by her rejected suitor William Douglas.

Laurin in Germanic legend, name of a dwarf king in the Tyrol, noted for his cunning, who defends his rose garden against intrusion. *Laurin* is captured by the hero ➤ DIETRICH *von Bern*, who has heard of the rose garden; ultimately he is baptized, and becomes a thane of Dietrich's.

lavabo (in the Roman Catholic Church) a towel or basin used for the ritual washing of the celebrant's hands at the offertory of the Mass. The word comes (in the mid 18th century) from Latin, literally 'I will wash', in *Lavabo inter innocentes manus meas* 'I will wash my hands in innocence' (Psalm 26:6), which was recited at the washing of hands in the Roman rite.

lavender a small aromatic evergreen shrub of the mint family, with narrow leaves and bluish-purple flowers, which has been widely used in perfumery and medicine since ancient times.

It was customary to place the flowers and stalks of lavender among linen or other clothes as a preservative against moths during storage, and from this comes the phrase **lay up in lavender**, meaning preserve carefully for future use.

lavender and old lace the title of a novel (1902) by Myrtle Reed, later dramatized, used to denote a gentle and old-fashioned style; the phrase was reworked in Joseph Kesselring's play *Arsenic and Old Lace* (1941), featuring two respectable spinster sisters who are given to poisoning their lodgers.

lavender list informal name for the draft of Harold Wilson's last honours list, supposedly first drawn up by his secretary Marcia Falkender on a sheet of lavender notepaper, and later regarded as having some names of questionable merit.

Lavengro Romany name (meaning 'philologist' or 'word-master') given to Romany rye who is the eponymous hero of George Borrow's story (1851).

laver a basin or similar container used for washing oneself; (in biblical use) a large brass bowl for Jewish priests' ritual ablutions.

Antoine Laurent Lavoisier (1743–94), French scientist, regarded as the father of modern chemistry. He caused a revolution in chemistry by his description of combustion as the combination of substances with air, or more specifically the gas oxygen. He was guillotined in the French Revolution because of his involvement in the collection of indirect taxes.

law see also ➤ *every* LAND *has its own law,* ➤ *the* GLORIOUS *uncertainty of the law,* ➤ JOUK *and let the law go by,* ➤ *the* LONG *arm of the law,* ➤ MYRMIDON, ➤ NECESSITY *knows no law,* ➤ POSSESSION *is nine points of the law,* ➤ SCROLL *of the Law.*

law an individual rule as part of a legal system or set of rules may be informally designated by a prefixed word or name, as in ➤ IGNORANCE *of the law is no excuse for breaking it,* ➤ LEMON *law,* ➤ LINDBERGH *law,* ➤ LYDFORD *law,* ➤ MAINE *Law,* ➤ MEGAN's *law,* ➤ MURPHY's *Law,* ➤ OHM's *law,* ➤ PARKINSON's *law,* ➤ PLANCK's *law,* ➤ POYNINGS' *law,* ➤ VERNER's *law.*

one law for the rich and another for the poor proverbial saying, mid 19th century.

the law is an ass proverbial saying, most famously associated with Dickens' Mr Bumble:

> 'If the law supposes that,' said Mr Bumble . . . 'the law is a ass—a idiot.'
> — Charles Dickens *Oliver Twist* (1838)

law Latin the non-standard Latin of early English statutes.

law lord in the United Kingdom, a member of the House of Lords qualified to perform its legal work; a term first recorded in a letter of Edmund Burke's of 1773, in which he comments that 'The measure…will not be opposed in council by any great law-lord of the kingdom.'

law merchant a former system of rules for the regulation of trade and commerce, differing in some respects from common law, and administered through special courts such as the ➤ COURT *of Piepowders.*

law of averages the supposed principle that future events are likely to turn out so that they balance any past deviation from a presumed average. The term is recorded from the 19th century, and derives initially from a comment by the historian Henry Thomas Buckle (1821–62):

> The great advance made by the statisticians consists in applying to these inquiries [into crime] the doctrine of averages, which no one thought of doing before the eighteenth century.
> — H. T. Buckle *The History of Civilization in England* (1857)

The first (sceptical) reference to 'Mr Buckle's "Law of Averages" ' is found in 1875, and from then on the term became established.

law of nations international law, a body of rules established by custom or treaty and recognized by nations as binding in their relations with one another. *Law of nations,* a translation of the Latin phrase *jus gentium,* was originally used to denote rules common to the law of all nations. The transition to the current sense developed particularly through the appeal to 'the law of nations' in such matters as the treatment of ambassadors or the obligation to observe treaties.

law of the jungle the supposed code of survival in jungle life, originally shown favourably in Kipling's *Jungle Books*:

> Now this is the Law of the Jungle—as old and as true as the sky;
> And the Wolf that shall keep it may prosper, but the Wolf that shall break it must die.
> — Rudyard Kipling *The Second Jungle Book* (1895) 'The Law of the Jungle'

The term is now used to embody the principle that those who are strong and apply ruthless self-interest will be most successful.

> At the beer tank the law of the jungle prevailed, the stronger shoving the weaker.
> — Bessie Head *Tales of Tenderness and Power* (1989)

Law Officer (in England and Wales) the Attorney General or the Solicitor General, or (in Scotland) the Lord Advocate or the Solicitor General for Scotland.

Law Society the professional body responsible for regulating solicitors in England and Wales, established in 1825.

lawn fine linen or cotton fabric used for making clothes, especially the sleeves of a bishop, from which it is used allusively. It is probably named from the French city of *Laon*, important for linen manufacture.

D. H. Lawrence (1885–1930), English novelist, poet, and essayist. His work is characterized by its condemnation of industrial society and by its frank exploration of sexual relationships, as in *Lady Chatterley's Lover*, originally published in Italy in 1928, but not available in England in unexpurgated form until 1960.

St Lawrence (d.258), Roman martyr and deacon of Rome. According to tradition, Lawrence was ordered by the prefect of Rome to deliver up the treasure of the Church; when in response to this order he presented the poor people of Rome to the prefect, he was roasted to death on a gridiron. Feast day, 10 August.

□ **EMBLEM** His traditional emblem is a gridiron.

□ **FEAST DAY** His feast day is 10 August.

T. E. Lawrence (1888–1935), British soldier and writer, known as **Lawrence of Arabia**. From 1916 onwards he helped to organize the Arab revolt against the Turks in the Middle East, contributing to General Allenby's eventual victory in Palestine in 1918. Lawrence described this period in *The Seven Pillars of Wisdom* (1926). In 1922, seeking anonymity, he enlisted in the RAF as **Aircraftsman Shaw**. He was killed in a motorcycle accident.

See also ➤ LIMELIGHT.

Thomas Lawrence (1769–1830), English painter. He achieved success with his full-length portrait (1789) of Queen Charlotte, the wife of King George III, and by 1810 he was recognized as the leading portrait painter of his time.

laws see also ➤ CORN *Laws*, ➤ NUREMBERG *laws*, ➤ PENAL *Laws*, ➤ NEWTON's *laws of motion*.

laws of war the rules and conventions, recognized by civilized nations, which limit belligerents' action.

lawyer see also ➤ BARRACK-*room lawyer*, ➤ BUSH *lawyer*, ➤ *the* DEVIL *makes his Christmas pies of lawyers' tongues and clerks' fingers*, ➤ PENANG *lawyer*, ➤ PHILADELPHIA *lawyer*.

a man who is his own lawyer has a fool for a client proverbial saying, early 19th century.

lay not ordained into or belonging to the clergy. Recorded from Middle English, the word comes from Old French via late Latin and ultimately from Greek *laos* 'people'.

lay brother a man who has taken the vows of a religious order but is not ordained or obliged to take part in the full cycle of liturgy and is employed in ancillary or manual work.

St Gerard Majella (d. 1755), an Italian Redemptorist lay brother, is the patron saint of *lay brothers*.

lay-overs for meddlers proverbial saying, late 18th century; a traditional response to an impertinent question, *lay-overs* being light smacks given as a punishment for meddling.

lay reader in the Anglican Church, a layperson licensed to preach and to conduct some religious services, but not licensed to celebrate the Eucharist.

lay sister a woman who has taken the vows of a religious order but is not obliged to take part in the full cycle of liturgy and is employed in ancillary or manual work.

➤ *St* MARTHA is the patron saint of lay sisters.

lay vicar another name for a ➤ VICAR *choral*.

Layamon (late 12th century), English poet and priest. He wrote the verse chronicle known as the *Brut*, a history of England which introduces for the first time in English the story of King Arthur.

laying on of hands in religious usage, the deliberate touching of someone in blessing or ordination.

lazar an archaic term for a poor and diseased person, especially one afflicted by an unpleasant disease such as leprosy. The word is recorded from Middle

English and comes from Latin *lazarus*, with biblical allusion to the beggar covered with sores whose story is told in Luke 16:20 (see ➤ LAZARUS²).

lazaretto an isolation hospital for people with infectious diseases, especially leprosy or plague; a building or ship used for quarantine.

Lazarist a member of the Congregation of the Mission, a Catholic organization founded at the priory of St Lazare in Paris by St Vincent de Paul to preach to the rural poor and train candidates for the priesthood.

Lazarus¹ in the Bible, the brother of Martha and Mary, raised from the dead by Jesus. According to the story in John, ch. 11, Lazarus had died and been buried before Jesus reached him; he was raised not just from the dead, but from the tomb, and has thus become a type for an unlooked-for resurrection.

> A new cocktail of drugs has made life better for many Aids patients in Europe and America: people who once were preparing to die now call it 'the Lazarus syndrome.'
>
> — *Guardian* 27 April 1999

Lazarus² in the Bible, a beggar covered with sores, who was refused help by the rich man Dives, but who on death entered heaven when Dives was denied. The word ➤ LAZAR comes from his name.

lazy see ➤ LONG *and lazy, little and loud.*

Le Corbusier (1887–1965), French architect and town planner, born in Switzerland. A pioneer of the international style, he developed theories on functionalism, the use of new materials and industrial techniques, and the Modulor, a modular system of standard-sized units.

J. Sheridan Le Fanu (1814–73), Irish novelist. He is best known for his stories of mystery, suspense, and the supernatural such as *The House by the Churchyard* (1861) and *Uncle Silas* (1864).

Le Mans an industrial town in NW France, which is the site of a motor-racing circuit, on which a 24-hour endurance race (established in 1923) is held each summer.

André Le Nôtre (1613–1700), French landscape gardener. He designed many formal gardens, including the parks of Vaux-le-Vicomte and Versailles, begun in 1655 and 1662 respectively. These incorporated his ideas on geometric formality and equilibrium.

Urbain Le Verrier (1811–77), French mathematician. His analysis of the motions of the planets suggested that an unknown body was disrupting the orbit of Uranus; the same conclusion was reached almost simultaneously by John Couch Adams. Le Verrier prompted the German astronomer Johann Galle (1812–1910) to investigate, and the planet Neptune was discovered in 1846.

lead see also ➤ *lead* APES *in hell.*

lead a heavy bluish-grey soft ductile metal, in alchemy associated with Saturn, and proverbial for its heaviness and low value.
See also ➤ SWING *the lead.*

Leadenhall Street the East India Company, from the name of a street in the City of London, which from 1648 to 1861 contained the Company's headquarters.

leader see also ➤ *the* LOST *Leader,* ➤ TAKE *me to your leader.*

Leader of the House a member of the government officially responsible for initiating business in the British Parliament.

leaderene a female leader, especially an autocratic one, originally a humorous or ironic name for Margaret Thatcher, while Leader of the Opposition, and later Prime Minister.

leading question a question that prompts or encourages the answer wanted.

leaf see also ➤ FALL *of the leaf,* ➤ MAPLE *leaf.*

leaf a single thickness of paper, especially in a book with each side forming a page, seen as resembling the leaf of a plant in being flat and thin.
See also ➤ TURN *over a new leaf.*

the League a league formed in France 1576 under the direction of the Catholic House of Guise, to prevent the accession of the Huguenot Henri of Navarre to the French throne (he succeeded as Henri IV in 1589, and is said to have indicated his readiness to accept the Catholic faith with the words '*Paris vaut bien une messe* [Paris is well worth a mass]').
See also ➤ HOLY *League.*

League of Arab States an organization of Arab states, founded in 1945 in Cairo, whose purpose is to ensure cooperation among its member states and protect their independence and sovereignty.

the League of Nations an association of countries established in 1919 by the Treaty of Versailles to promote international cooperation and achieve international peace and security. Although the League greatly assisted post-war economic reconstruction, it failed in its prime purpose through the refusal of member nations to put international interests before national ones, It was powerless to stop Italian, German, and Japanese expansionism leading to the Second World War, and was replaced by the United Nations in 1945.

League of the Three Emperors the *Dreikaiserbund*, an alliance made towards the end of the 19th century between Germany, Austria-Hungary, and Russia, at the instigation of the German Chancellor Bismarck; the intention was to agree each empire's sphere of influence over the Balkans, and to isolate France.

Leah in the Bible, the eldest daughter of ➤ LABAN and sister of ➤ RACHEL, who by a trick became the first wife of ➤ JACOB.

Leakey a family of eminent Kenyan archaeologists and anthropologists. **Louis Leakey** (1903–72), pioneered the investigation of human origins in East Africa. He began excavations at Olduvai Gorge and together with his wife Mary discovered the remains of early hominids and their implements, including *Australopithecus* or *Zinjanthropus boisei* in 1959. British-born **Mary Leakey** (1913–96), discovered *Homo habilis* and *Homo erectus* at Olduvai in 1960.

leaks see ➤ LITTLE *leaks sink the ship.*

leal an archaic Scottish term meaning 'loyal and honest'; it was famously used by David Lloyd George in describing the House of Lords as being 'the right hon. Gentleman's [Arthur Balfour's] poodle', rather than 'the leal and trusty mastiff which is to watch over our interests'.

See also ➤ LAND *of the leal.*

Leander in Greek mythology, a young man, the lover of the priestess Hero, who swam nightly across the Hellespont to visit her, and who was drowned while so doing.

Leander Club the oldest amateur rowing club in the world, founded early in the 19th century, now based in Henley-on-Thames. Membership is a mark of distinction in the rowing world, and a large proportion of its members are former Oxford and Cambridge oarsmen.

Leaning Tower of Pisa the circular bell tower of Pisa cathedral, which leans about 5 m (17 ft) from the perpendicular over its height of 55 m (181 ft).

leap see also ➤ GREAT *Leap Forward,* ➤ LOOK *before you leap.*

a leap in the dark a daring step or enterprise whose consequences are unpredictable; in Vanbrugh's The Provoked Wife (1697), one of the characters, contemplating marriage, says:

> So, now I am in for Hobbes's voyage, a great leap in the dark.

The allusion is to Hobbes's attributed last words:

> I am about to take my last voyage, a great leap in the dark.

leap year a year, occurring once every four years, which has 366 days including 29 February as an intercalary day. The term, recorded from late Middle English, probably comes from the fact that feast days after February in such a year fell two days later than in the previous year, rather than one day later as in other years, and could be said to have 'leaped' a day.

According to tradition, a woman may propose to a man on 29 February.

Lear a legendary early king of Britain, the central figure in Shakespeare's tragedy *King Lear*, mentioned by the chronicler Geoffrey of Monmouth. In Shakespeare's play, Lear divides his kingdom between his two elder daughters, Goneril and Regan, and is driven to madness by their neglect and mistreatment of him; he may be taken as the proverbial figure of a parent faced with an ungrateful child:

> How sharper than a serpent's tooth it is
> To have a thankless child!
> — William Shakespeare *King Lear* (1605-6)

Edward Lear (1812–88), English humorist and illustrator. He wrote *A Book of Nonsense* (1845) and *Laughable Lyrics* (1877), and also published illustrations of birds and of his travels around the Mediterranean. He is particularly associated with the ➤ LIMERICK, which he popularized in his *Book of Nonsense*, although he did not invent the form.

learn See ➤ *it is* NEVER *too late to learn,* ➤ LIVE *and let learn,* ➤ NEVER *too old to learn.*

the learned blacksmith a nickname of the American pacifist Elihu Burritt (1810–79), in recognition of his early life. Burritt, an autodidact who taught himself many languages, organized a number of peace congresses in European cities from 1848.

learning see also ➤ COMMONWEALTH *of learning*, ➤ REVIVAL *of learning*, ➤ *there is no* ROYAL *road to learning*.

learning is better than house and land proverbial saying, late 18th century.

See also ➤ *when* HOUSE *and land are gone and spent*, then learning is most excellent.

Timothy Leary (1920–96), American psychologist and drug pioneer. After experimenting with consciousness-altering drugs including LSD, he was dismissed from his teaching post at Harvard University in 1963 and became a figurehead for the hippy drug culture.

> If you take the game of life seriously, if you take your nervous system seriously, if you take your sense organs seriously, if you take the energy process seriously, you must turn on, tune in and drop out.
> — Timothy Leary lecture, June 1966, in *The Politics of Ecstasy* (1968)

See also ➤ LAST *words*.

least said, soonest mended proverbial saying, mid 15th century.

there is nothing like leather proverbial saying, late 17th century, deriving from one of Aesop's fables.

leather medal originally in the US, a derisory award, a booby prize.

> He ought to get a leather medal with a putty rim for all the plans he invents.
> — James Joyce *Ulysses* (1922)

leather or prunella something to which one is completely indifferent, the type of something that is of no importance. The term derives from a misinterpretation of Pope's lines:

> Worth makes the Man, and want of it the Fellow;
> The rest, is all but Leather or Prunella.
> — Alexander Pope *Essay on Man* (1734)

In Pope's poem, a distinction is being drawn between the trade of a cobbler (*leather*) and the profession of a clergyman (*prunella* as the material from which a clerical gown is made). The phrase was however taken to denote something of no value.

leather-workers ➤ *St* CRISPIN and ➤ *St* CRISPINIAN are the patron saints of leather-workers.

leatherneck an informal term for a US marine, with allusion to the leather lining inside the collar of a marine's uniform.

Leatherstocking nickname of ➤ *Natty* BUMPPO, the hero of *The Pioneers* (1823) and four other novels of American frontier life by James Fenimore Cooper (1789–1851).

> Leatherstocking treads the soft sod of the trackless forest in an awful silence.
> — Timothy Mo *An Insular Possession* (1986)

leave no stone unturned try every possible expedient; the expression is used by Pliny in his Letters, 'my method is to feel my way and try everything—in fact I "leave no stone unturned".' The term was said by the sophist Zenobius to derive from a story of hidden Persian treasure.

leaven a substance such as yeast which is added to dough to make it ferment and rise; in figurative use, a pervasive influence that modifies something or transforms it for the better, as in Matthew 13:33:

> The kingdom of heaven is like unto leaven, which a woman took and hid in three measures of meal, till the whole was leavened.
> — Bible (AV) Matthew ch. 13, v. 33

Although the term is now used to denote a force for good, it was originally used also to warn against bad influences, as in Matthew 16:6 'Take heed and beware of the leaven of the Pharisees.'

The phrase **of the same leaven** designates someone of the same sort or character.

See also ➤ OLD *leaven*.

Lebensraum the territory which a state or nation believes is needed for its natural development, originally with reference to Germany. The word is German, and means literally 'living space'.

Charles Lebrun (1619–90), French painter, designer, and decorator. He was prominent in the development and institutionalization of French art and was a leading exponent of French classicism. In 1648 he helped to found the Royal Academy of Painting and Sculpture, becoming its director in 1663; from this position he laid the basis of academicism.

Charles Leconte de Lisle (1818–94), French poet and leader of the Parnassians. His poetry often draws inspiration from mythology, biblical history, and exotic Eastern landscape.

Hannibal Lecter the psychopathic genius who is the serial-killer anti-hero of *The Silence of the Lambs* (1988, film 1991) and other books by Thomas Harris (1940–). Dr Lecter is otherwise known as **Hannibal the Cannibal**, and his 'I'm having an old friend for dinner' is to be taken in its literal sense.

lectern a tall stand with a sloping top to hold a book or notes, and from which someone, typically a preacher or lecturer, can read while standing up. Recorded from Middle English, the word comes via Old French from medieval Latin *lectrum*, from *legere* 'to read'.

lectionary a list or book of portions of the Bible appointed to be read at divine service.

lectisternium in ancient Rome, a sacrificial banquet at which food was set before images of gods, placed on couches.

Leda in Greek mythology, the wife of Tyndareus king of Sparta. She was loved by Zeus, who visited her in the form of a swan; among her children were the ➤ Dioscuri, ➤ Helen, and Clytemnestra.

lee shore a shore lying on the leeward side of a ship (the side sheltered from the wind), on to which a ship could be blown in foul weather.

Bruce Lee (1941–73) American actor. An expert in kung fu, he starred in a number of martial arts films, such as *Enter the Dragon* (1973).

Christopher Lee (1922–), English actor. His reputation is chiefly based on the horror films that he made for the British film company Hammer, which include *Dracula* (1958).

Gypsy Rose Lee (1914–70), American striptease artist. In the 1930s she became famous on Broadway for her sophisticated striptease act.

Robert E. Lee (1807–70), American general, commander of the Confederate army of Northern Virginia for most of the American Civil War. His invasion of the North was repulsed at the Battle of Gettysburg (1863) and he surrendered at ➤ Appomattox in 1865.
See also ➤ Traveller.

leech¹ an term (now archaic or humorous) for a doctor or healer. Recorded from Old English, the word was later often understood as a transferred use of ➤ leech², sometimes with an indication of rapacity:

> Grudging the leech his growing bill.
> — W. M. Praed *Poems* (1864)

Leechcraft is similarly used for the art of healing.

leech² an aquatic or terrestrial annelid worm with suckers at both ends. Many species are bloodsucking parasites, especially of vertebrates (*leeches* were traditionally used in medicine to draw off blood) and others are predators, giving rise to the transferred sense of a person who extorts profit from or sponges on others.

leek the *leek* is a national emblem of Wales, and is traditionally worn on St David's day (1 March). No clear reason for the association with ➤ *St* David has been identified, although some sources suggest that it derives from a battle in which Welsh forces led by David wore leeks as a badge, and Fluellen in Shakespeare's Henry V explains it as a memorial to a battle fought in France under the Black Prince, in which 'Welshmen did good service in a garden where leeks did grow, wearing leeks in their Monmouth caps'.

Proverbial usages refer to it as the type of something worthless (as in **not worth a leek**) or allude to its colour; the description of Pyramus in the burlesque mechanicals' play in Shakespeare's *Midsummer Night's Dream* includes the line, 'His eyes were green as leeks'.

eat one's leek submit to humiliation under compulsion; the allusion is to the scene in Shakespeare's *Henry V,* in which Pistol, who has jeered at Fluellen for wearing the leek on St David's day, is forced by Fluellen to eat it, with the words, 'if you can mock a leek, you can eat a leek'.

leet a yearly or half-yearly court of record held by the lords of certain manors (also called **court leet**); the jurisdiction of such a court.

Antoni van Leeuwenhoek (1632–1723), Dutch naturalist. He developed a lens for scientific purposes and was the first to observe bacteria, protozoa, and yeast. He accurately described red blood cells, capillaries, striated muscle fibres, spermatozoa, and the crystalline lens of the eye, but his work only became known towards the end of his life.

left¹ on, towards, or relating to the side of a human body or of a thing which is to the west when the person or thing is facing north. The original meaning (in Old English) was 'weak', the left-hand side being regarded as the weaker side of the body.
See also ➤ sinister.

left² of or relating to a person or group favouring radical, reforming, or socialist views. The usage is first recorded in English in Carlyle's account (in *The French Revolution*, 1837), and originated in the

French National Assembly of 1789, in which the nobles were seated on the President's right and the commons on his left; this ceremonial grouping soon came to reflect political views.

Left Bank a district of the city of Paris, situated on the left bank of the River Seine, to the south of the river, an area noted for its intellectual and artistic life.

left brain the left-hand side of the human brain, which is believed to be associated with linear and analytical thought.

left-handed marriage a morganatic marriage (it was customary, in such marriages in Germany, for the bridegroom to give the bride his left hand instead of his right).

legacy software in computing, software or hardware that has been superseded but is difficult to replace because of its wide use.

legal fiction an assertion accepted as true, though probably fictitious, to achieve a useful purpose in legal matters.

legal tender coins or banknotes that must be accepted if offered in payment of a debt.

legate a member of the clergy, especially a cardinal, representing the Pope; a **legate a latere** is a papal legate of the highest class, with full powers.

legend a traditional story sometimes popularly regarded as historical but not authenticated. This sense dates from the early 17th century; in Middle English, the word was used to denote the story of a saint's life, and came via Old French from medieval Latin *legenda* 'things to be read'.
   See also ➤ *the* GOLDEN *Legend*.

Legenda Aurea Latin name for the ➤ *the* GOLDEN *Legend*.

legion[1] a division of 3,000–6,000 men, including a complement of cavalry, in the ancient Roman army.
   See also ➤ THEBAN *Legion*, ➤ THUNDERING *Legion*.

legion[2] great in number, many, as in **their name is legion**. This usage dates from the late 17th century, from the story in Mark 5:9 of the madman healed by Jesus, who when asked his name had replied, 'My name is Legion, for we are many.'

Legion of Honour a French order of distinction (the *légion d'honneur*), founded in 1802 by Napoleon, conferred especially for civil and military services.

legion of the lost people who are destitute or abandoned; the phrase was probably popularized through Kipling's usage:

> To the legion of the lost ones, to the cohort of the
>   damned,
> To my brethren in their sorrow overseas,
> Sings a gentleman of England cleanly bred, machinely
>   crammed,
> And a trooper of the Empress, if you please.
> — Rudyard Kipling *Barrack-Room Ballads* (1892)
>   'Gentleman-Rankers'

legionnaires' disease a form of bacterial pneumonia first identified after an outbreak at an American Legion meeting in 1976. It is spread chiefly by water droplets through air conditioning and similar systems.

legist a member of a group of legal philosophers in the early Han dynasty in China.

legitimist in France, a supporter of the elder Bourbon line, driven from the throne when Charles X abdicated in 1830, and opposed to both the Bonapartists and the Orleanists, who in July 1830 recognized Louis-Philippe as King of the French.

Lego trademark name for a construction toy consisting of interlocking plastic building blocks.

> My father and the other scientists at the lab are playing
> about with living cells as if they were pieces of Lego.
> — V. Alcock *Monster Garden* (1988)

legs see also ➤ *everyone* STRETCHES *his legs according to the length of his coverlet*, ➤ *there goes more to a* MARRIAGE *than four bare legs in a bed*.

Gottfried Wilhelm Leibniz (1646–1716), German rationalist philosopher, mathematician, and logician. He argued that the world is composed of single units (monads), each of which is self-contained but acts in harmony with every other, as ordained by God, and so this world is the best of all possible worlds. Leibniz also made the important distinction between necessary and contingent truths and devised a method of calculus independently of Newton.

Ludwig Leichhardt (1813–48), Australian explorer, born in Prussia. After emigrating to Australia in 1841, he began a series of geological surveys; he disappeared during an attempt at a transcontinental crossing.

Leiden a city in the west Netherlands, north-east of The Hague. It is the site of the country's oldest university, founded in 1575.

Leif Ericsson Norse explorer, son of Eric the Red. He sailed westward from Greenland (*c*.1000) and reputedly discovered land (variously identified as Labrador, Newfoundland, or New England), which he named Vinland because of the vines he claimed to have found growing there.

leitmotif a recurrent theme throughout a musical or literary composition, associated with a particular person, idea, or situation, originally associated particularly with the musical drama of Wagner.

lemming a small, short-tailed, thickset rodent related to the voles, found in the Arctic tundra. The Norway lemming is noted for its fluctuating populations and periodic mass migrations, and from this *lemming* is used to denote a person who unthinkingly joins a mass movement, especially a headlong rush to destruction.

Lemnos a Greek island in the northern Aegean Sea, where in Greek mythology Hephaestus is said to have fallen when thrown out of heaven; its extinct volcano was said to be his forge.

In later legend, Lemnos was associated with two massacres. Firstly, the women of Lemnos offended Aphrodite and in conseqence were deserted by their husbands; in revenge, they killed all the men on the island, and married the ➤ Argonauts who spent a year on Lemnos in their travels; their children became the next generation on the island. Secondly, the Pelasgians settled in Lemnos when driven out of Attica; they brought a number of captive Athenian women with them who bore their children. The children grew up speaking the Attic dialect with their mothers, and the Pelasgians grew suspicious of them: the women and children were murdered by them.

the answer is a lemon the response is unsatisfactory; a *lemon* here is taken as the type of something unsatisfactory, perhaps referring to the least valuable symbol in a fruit machine.

lemon law informal term in the US for a law designed to provide redress for buyers of faulty or substandard cars; the expression *hand someone a lemon*, meaning pass off a sub-standard article as being of good value, is recorded from the early 20th century.

lempira the basic monetary unit of Honduras, equal to 100 centavos. It is named after *Lempira*, a 16th-century Indian chieftain who opposed the Spanish conquest of Honduras.

Lemuria[1] a festival in ancient Rome marking the period when the spirits of dead members of a household (the *lemures*) were believed to haunt their former homes; the most dangerous were those who had died young, and who thus particularly resented the living.

Lemuria[2] a hypothetical continent stretching from Africa to south-east Asia, formerly supposed to have existed in the Jurassic period.

Ninon de Lenclos (1620–1705), French courtesan. She was a famous wit and beauty who advocated a form of Epicureanism in her book *La Coquette vengée* (1659), and later presided over one of the most distinguished literary salons of the age.

Lend-Lease an arrangement made in 1941 whereby the US supplied military equipment and armaments to the UK and its allies, originally as a loan in return for the use of British-owned military bases.

lend your money and lose your friend proverbial saying, late 15th century.

length begets loathing proverbial saying, mid 18th century.

Vladimir Ilich Lenin (1870–1924), the principal figure in the Russian Revolution and first Premier of the Soviet Union 1918–24.

Lenin was the first political leader to attempt to put Marxist principles into practice. In 1917 he established Bolshevik control after the overthrow of the tsar, and in 1918 became head of state (Chairman of the Council of People's Commissars). With Trotsky he defeated counter-revolutionary forces in the Russian Civil War, but was forced to moderate his policies to allow the country to recover from the effects of war and revolution.

Leningrad between 1924 and 1991, the name given to St Petersburg.

John Lennon (1940–80), English pop and rock singer, guitarist, and songwriter. A founder member of the Beatles, he wrote most of their songs in collaboration with Paul McCartney. He was assassinated outside his home in New York.

lens a piece of glass or other transparent substance with curved sides for concentrating or dispersing light rays. The word comes (in the late 17th century) from the Latin word for 'lentil', because of the similarity in shape.

as much akin as Lenson Hill to Pilsen Pen Dorsetshire saying, referring to Lewesdon Hill and Pillesden Hill.

Lent the period preceding Easter which in the Christian Church is devoted to fasting, abstinence, and penitence in commemoration of Christ's fasting in the wilderness. In the Western Church it runs from Ash Wednesday to Holy Saturday, and so includes forty weekdays. The name comes from a Middle English abbreviation of ➤ LENTEN.

See also ➤ MID-*Lent Sunday.*

lent lily the European wild daffodil, which typically has pale creamy-white outer petals.

Lent term in the UK, the university term in which Lent falls.

Lenten of, in, or appropriate to Lent. Old English *lencten* 'spring, Lent', of Germanic origin, is related to *long*, perhaps with reference to the lengthening of the day in spring; it is now interpreted as coming directly from *Lent* + the suffix *-en.*

Lenten fare food appropriate to Lent, especially that without meat.

Lenten rose a hellebore that is cultivated for its flowers which appear in late winter or early spring.

Leo a large constellation (the Lion), said to represent the lion slain by Hercules. *Leo* is also the fifth sign of the zodiac, which the sun enters about 23 July.

St Leo (d. 461), pope from 440 and Doctor of the Church; known as **Leo the Great.** He defined the doctrine of the Incarnation at the Council of Chalcedon (451) and extended the power of the Roman see to Africa, Spain, and Gaul. He persuaded the Huns to retire beyond the Danube and secured concessions from the Vandals when they captured Rome.

◻ **FEAST DAY** His feast day is (in the Eastern Church) 18 February; (in the Western Church) 11 April.

St Leonard (?6th century), Frankish noble and hermit, who became one of the most popular saints of western Europe in the Middle Ages.

◻ **PATRONAGE** He was patron especially of pregnant women and captives such as prisoners of war.

◻ **FEAST DAY** His feast day is 6 November.

Leonardo da Vinci (1452–1519), Italian painter, scientist, and engineer. His paintings are notable for their use of the technique of *sfumato* and include *The Virgin of the Rocks* (1483–5), *The Last Supper* (1498), and the enigmatic *Mona Lisa* (1504–5). He devoted himself to a wide range of other subjects, from anatomy and biology to mechanics and hydraulics: his nineteen notebooks include studies of the human circulatory system and plans for a type of aircraft and a submarine.

Leonidas king of Sparta, commander of the Greeks at the battle of ➤ THERMOPYLAE in 480 BC, where he and all his men were killed.

Leonine City the part of Rome in which the Vatican stands, walled and fortified by Pope Leo IV.

Leonine verse (of medieval Latin verse) in hexameter or elegiac metre with internal rhyme; (of English verse) with internal rhyme. The term may come from *Leo* as the name of a medieval poet, but his identity is not known.

leopard the leopard was originally (as in Pliny's *Natural History*) regarded as a hybrid between a lion and a 'pard'. In heraldry, *leopard* means both the spotted leopard as a heraldic device, and a lion passant guardant as in the arms of England.

the leopard does not change his spots proverbial saying, mid 16th century; originally with biblical allusion to Jeremiah 13:23, 'Can the Ethiopian change his skin, or the leopard his spots?'

Battle of Lepanto a naval battle fought in 1571 close to the port of Lepanto at the entrance to the Gulf of Corinth. The Christian forces of Rome, Venice, and Spain, under the leadership of Don John of Austria, defeated a large Turkish fleet, ending for the time being Turkish naval domination in the eastern Mediterranean.

leper a person suffering from leprosy; in figurative use, a person who is avoided or rejected by others for moral or social reasons.

➤ *St* GILES is the patron saint of *lepers.*

Marcus Aemilius Lepidus (died *c.*13 BC), Roman statesman and triumvir. A supporter of Julius Caesar in the civil war against Pompey, he was elected consul in 46, and appointed one of the Second Triumvirate with Octavian and Antony in 43. He retired from public life following a failed revolt in Sicily against Octavian in 36.

leprechaun in Irish folklore, a small mischievous sprite. The word is Irish, and comes ultimately from Old Irish *lu* 'small' + *corp* 'body'.

leprosy a contagious disease that affects the skin, mucous membranes, and nerves, causing discoloration and lumps on the skin and, in severe cases, disfigurement and deformities. Leprosy, now mainly confined to tropical Africa and Asia, was common in medieval Europe, and those afflicted by it were forced to live apart from the community.

Traditional allusions tend to refer to the pallor of the skin in someone suffering from the illness: the Life-in-Death figure in Coleridge's *The Rime of the Ancient Mariner* (1798) is described as having skin that is 'white as leprosy'.

Leptis Magna an ancient seaport and trading centre on the Mediterranean coast of North Africa, near present-day Al Khums in Libya. Founded by the Phoenicians, it became one of the three chief cities of Tripolitania and was later a Roman colony under Trajan. Most of its impressive remains date from the reign of Septimius Severus (AD 193–211), a native of the city.

Lesbian from or relating to Lesbos, a Greek island in the eastern Aegean, off the coast of NW Turkey; its artistic golden age of the late 7th and early 6th centuries BC produced the poets Alcaeus and ➤ SAPPHO, and the sense of *lesbian* to mean a homosexual woman derives from the association with Sappho, who expressed affection for women in her poetry.

Lesbian rule a mason's rule made of lead, which could be bent to fit the curves of a moulding; used figuratively for a principle of judgement that is pliant and accommodating.

lese-majesty the insulting of a monarch or other ruler; treason. Recorded from Middle English, the phrase comes directly from French *lèse-majesté*, and ultimately from Latin *laesa majestas* 'injured sovereignty'.

less is more proverbial saying, mid 19th century; first recorded in the poetry of Browning:

> Well, less is more, Lucrezia:
> I am judged.
> — Robert Browning 'Andrea del Sarto' (1855)

More recently, it has been associated with the architect and designer Mies van der Rohe (1886–1969).

Ferdinand de Lesseps (1805–94), French diplomat. From 1854 onwards, while in the consular service in Egypt, he devoted himself to the project of the Suez Canal. Work began in 1859 and it was opened in 1869. In 1881 he embarked on the building of the Panama Canal, but the project was abandoned in 1889.

lesson see ➤ PROPER *lesson*.

Lestrigonians in the *Odyssey*, a cannibal people of southern Italy.

let George do it let someone else do the work or take the responsibility; a colloquial expression recorded from the early 20th century.

let the train take the strain British Rail advertising slogan, 1970 onwards.

let well alone proverbial saying, late 16th century.

Lethe in Greek mythology, a river in Hades whose water when drunk made the souls of the dead forget their life on earth. The name comes via Latin from Greek *lēthē* 'forgetfulness'.

Leto in Greek mythology, the daughter of a Titan, mother (by Zeus) of ➤ ARTEMIS and ➤ APOLLO. Her Roman name is *Latona*.

letter see also ➤ CADMEAN *letters*, ➤ CASKET *letters*, ➤ DEAR *John letter*, ➤ DOMINICAL *letter*, ➤ *the* DRAPIER's *Letters*, ➤ NUNDINAL *letter*, ➤ JERUSALEM *letters*, ➤ LISLE *Letters*, ➤ *the* PASTON *Letters*, ➤ PASTORAL *letter*, ➤ POISON *pen letter*, ➤ PYTHAGOREAN *letter*, ➤ R *is the dog's letter*, ➤ SAMIAN *letter*, ➤ SCARLET *letter*, ➤ RED-*letter day*, ➤ ZINOVIEV *letter*

letter missive a letter from the monarch to a dean and chapter nominating a person to be elected bishop.

letter of marque a licence to fit out an armed vessel and use it in the capture of enemy merchant shipping and to commit acts which would otherwise have constituted piracy.

letters patent an open document issued by a monarch or government conferring a patent or other right.

lettre de cachet a warrant issued in the France of the *ancien régime* for the imprisonment of a person without trial at the pleasure of the monarch.

Leucothea in Greek mythology, a sea-goddess, originally Ino, daughter of Cadmus, persecuted by Hera for fostering the child ➤ DIONYSUS, son of Zeus and Ino's sister ➤ SEMELE. When her husband Athamas in a fit of madness killed one of their two sons, Ino threw herself into the sea with the other boy; she was transformed into the sea-goddess *Leucothea*, and her son ➤ MELICERTES became the sea-god Palaemon.

the Levant an archaic name for the eastern part of the Mediterranean with its islands and neighbouring countries. The name comes from French, literally 'rising', the present participle of *lever* 'to lift', used as a noun in the sense 'point of sunrise, east'. Recorded from the late 15th century, the word originally meant more generally the countries of the east, with **High Levant** another term for the Far East.

The archaic term *levant* 'run away, typically leaving unpaid debts' may come from this; there is comparabale expression in French *faire voile en Levant*, literally 'set sail for the Levant.'

levanter a strong easterly wind in the Mediterranean region.

levee a reception or assembly of people, in particular, a reception of visitors just after rising from bed, as held by the sovereign in pre-revolutionary France (the word comes from French *lever* 'rise'); an afternoon assembly for men held by the British monarch or their representative.

level playing field a state or condition of parity or impartiality, fair play (a playing field which is not level may be held to offer unfair advantages to the home side). In the 1980s the image became increasingly popular in the worlds of business and politics, although a number of instances suggest scepticism that the implied equality of opportunity is to be readily achieved.

leveller see ➤ DEATH *is the great leveller.*

Leveller an extreme radical dissenter in the English Civil War (1642–9), wishing to *level* all differences of rank, and calling for the abolition of the monarchy, social and agrarian reforms, and religious freedom; they were ultimately suppressed by Cromwell.

The name was applied to the ➤ WHITEBOYS in 18th-century Ireland, in relation to their activities in levelling park walls and breaking down fences.

leveret a young hare in its first year. Recorded from late Middle English, the world comes from an Anglo-Norman French diminutive of *levre* 'hare'.

Viscount Leverhulme (1851–1925), English industrialist and philanthropist, who with his brother manufactured soap under the trade name Sunlight; their company, Lever Bros., came to form the basis

of the international corporation Unilever. Leverhulme founded the model village Port Sunlight for his company's workers; he is also remembered for his comment on the value of advertising, 'Half the money I spend on advertising is wasted, but the trouble is I don't know which half.'

Levi (in the Bible) a Hebrew patriarch, son of Jacob and Leah (Genesis 29:34); the tribe of Israel traditionally descended from him.

See also ➤ LEVITE.

Levi's trademark name for a type of denim jeans or overalls reinforced with rivets. They are named after *Levi* Strauss, original US manufacturer in the 1860s.

leviathan in biblical use, a sea monster, identified in different passages with the whale and the crocodile (e.g. Job 41, Psalm 74:14), and with the Devil (after Isaiah 27:1).

> There go the ships, and there is that Leviathan: whom thou hast made to take his pastime therein.
> — Book of Common Prayer Psalm 104, v.26

The name was subsequently used by Hobbes in his 1651 political study, and from this the word may be used allusively for an absolute monarch or state.

> By art is created that great Leviathan, called a commonwealth or state, (in Latin *civitas*) which is but an artificial man . . . and in which, the sovereignty is an artificial soul.
> — Thomas Hobbes *Leviathan* (1651) introduction

levitation the act of rising and hovering in the air by means of supposed magical powers.

Levite a member of the Hebrew tribe of Levi, especially of that part of it which provided assistants to the priests in the worship in the Jewish temple.

Levitical (in Judaism, of rules concerning codes of conduct, temple rituals, etc.) derived from the biblical Book of Leviticus; the **Levitical degrees** are the degrees of consanguinity within which marriage is forbiddenin Leviticus 18:6–18.

Leviticus the third book of the Bible, containing details of law and ritual.

Lewis and Clark expedition an expedition mounted in 1803–4 for the purpose of exploring a land route to the Pacific; the expedition, under Meriwether Lewis (1774–1809) and William Clark (1770–1838), followed the Missouri River to its source, travelled through the Rockies, and followed the Columbia River to the Pacific; Lewis was rewarded for the success of the expedition by being made governor of Louisiana Territory.

lex talionis the law of retaliation, whereby a punishment resembles the offence committed in kind and degree; a Latin phrase recorded in English from the late 16th century.

Lexington a residential town north-west of Boston, Massachusetts, which was the scene in 1775 of the first battle in the War of American Independence. The American revolutionary leader Samuel Adams (1722–1803), hearing gunfire at Lexington on 19 April 1775, is said to have exclaimed, 'What a glorious morning is this' (traditionally quoted as, 'What a glorious morning for America').

Lexiphanes a person who uses bombastic phraseology, from Greek *Lexiphanēs* 'phrase-monger' (title of one of Lucian's dialogues).

ley line a supposed straight line connecting three or more prehistoric or ancient sites, sometimes regarded as the line of a former track and associated by some with lines of energy and other paranormal phenomena. Recorded from the 1920s, *ley* is a variant of *lea* 'an open area of grassy or arable land'.

Lhasa the capital of Tibet, situated in the northern Himalayas. Its inaccessibility and the hostility of the Tibetan Buddhist priests to foreign visitors—to whom Lhasa was closed until the 20th century— earned it the title of the ➤ FORBIDDEN *City*. The spiritual centre of Tibetan Buddhism, Lhasa was the seat of the ➤ DALAI *Lama* until 1959, when direct Chinese administration was imposed on the city.

li shu in Chinese calligraphy, a form of script developed during the Han dynasty and widely adopted for official and educational purposes.

Lia Fáil a stone pillar on the Hill of Tara in Ireland, said to be the inauguration stone of the Irish high kings.

a liar ought to have a good memory proverbial saying, mid 16th century; 1st century AD in Latin.

the liar paradox the paradox involved in a speaker's statement that he or she is lying or is a (habitual) liar, as in the statement by a Cretan that all Cretans are liars; by this definition, if he is a Cretan, then what he says cannot be true, and Cretans are honest.

libation a drink poured out as an offering to a deity.

libel a published false statement that is damaging to a person's reputation; a written defamation. The

word is recorded from Middle English (in the general sense 'a document, a written statement'), and comes via Old French from Latin *libellus*, diminutive of *liber* 'a book'.

Liber Albus a collection of records of the City of London compiled by John Carpenter (?1370–?1441), town clerk of London from 1417 to 1438.

Liber pontificalis a collection of papal histories, begun in the 4th century and continued in a variety of forms until the death of Martin V (d. 1431).

liberal see also ➤ SEVEN *liberal arts*, ➤ SOCIAL *and Liberal Democrats*.

Liberal a member of a political party favouring free trade and gradual political and social reform that tends towards individual freedom or democracy.

Liberal Unionist a member of a group of British Liberal MPs who left the party in 1886 because of Gladstone's support for Irish Home Rule. Led by Joseph Chamberlain from 1891, they formed an alliance with the Conservative Party in Parliament, and merged officially with them in 1909 as the Conservative and Unionist Party.

liberation theology a movement in Christian theology, developed mainly by Latin American Roman Catholics, which attempts to address the problems of poverty and social injustice as well as spiritual matters. It interprets liberation from social, political, and economic oppression as an anticipation of ultimate salvation.

Liberation Tigers of Tamil Eelam another name for the ➤ TAMIL *Tigers*.

the Liberator epithet applied to ➤ *Simón* BOLÍVAR and the Irish nationalist leader Daniel O'Connell (1775–1847).

Liberia a country on the Atlantic coast of West Africa, which was founded in 1822 as a settlement for freed slaves from the US, and was proclaimed independent in 1847.

liberties see also ➤ BODY *of Liberties*.

liberties in England before 1850, a district within the limits of a county, but exempt from the jurisdiction of the sheriff and having a separate commission of the peace. The **liberties of a city** was the area beyond the bounds of a city which was subject to the control of the municipal authority, and the **liberties of a prison** (especially the Fleet and the Marshalsea in London), the area outside the prison within which prisoners were sometimes allowed to live.

libertine a person, especially a man in sexual matters, who behaves without moral principles or a sense of responsibility; a freethinker. The term comes (in late Middle English, denoting a freed slave or the son of one) from Latin *libertinus* 'freedman', from *liber* 'free'. In the mid 16th century, imitating French *libertin*, the term denoted a member of any of various antinomian sects in France.

liberty See also ➤ CAP *of liberty*, ➤ SONS *of liberty*, ➤ TREE *of liberty*.

Statue of Liberty a statue at the entrance to New York harbour, a symbol of welcome to immigrants, representing a draped female figure carrying a book of laws in her left hand and holding aloft a torch in her right; it is inscribed with lines by the American poet Emma Lazarus (1849–87):

> Give me your tired, your poor,
> Your huddled masses yearning to breathe free,
> The wretched refuse of your teeming shore,
> Send these, the homeless, tempest-tossed, to me:
> I lift my lamp beside the golden door.
> — Emma Lazarus 'The New Colossus' (1883)

Dedicated in 1886, it was designed by Frédéric-Auguste Bartholdi and was the gift of the French, commemorating the alliance of France and the US during the War of American Independence. The formal title of the statue is *Liberty Enlightening the World*.

See also ➤ TEMPEST-*tossed*.

Liberty Bell a bell in Philadelphia first rung on 8 July 1776 to celebrate the first public reading of the Declaration of Independence. It bears the legend 'Proclaim liberty throughout all the land unto all the inhabitants thereof' (Leviticus 25:10).

It cracked irreparably when rung for George Washington's birthday in 1846 and is now housed near Independence Hall, Philadelphia.

liberty cap another term for the ➤ CAP *of liberty*.

Liberty Enlightening the World formal title of the ➤ *Statue of* LIBERTY.

Liberty Hall a place where one may do as one likes. The phrase comes originally from Goldsmith:

> This is Liberty-hall, gentlemen. You may do just as you please.
> — Oliver Goldsmith *She Stoops to Conquer* (1773)

Libitina the ancient Italian goddess of funerals; registers of the dead were kept in her temple at Rome.

Libra a small constellation (the Scales or Balance), said to represent the pair of scales which is the symbol of justice. It contains no bright stars. Also, the seventh sign of the zodiac, which the sun enters at the northern autumnal equinox (about 23 September).

librarians ➤ *St* JEROME is the patron saint of *librarians*.

library a building or room containing collections of books, periodicals, and sometimes films and recorded music for people to read, borrow, or refer to. The earliest libraries found include collections of Assyrian clay tablets at Tell el-Amarna in Egypt; Aristotle's personal library was the basis of the Alexandrian Library founded by Ptolemy I of Egypt, and many national libraries have personal collections as their basis. In the 19th century, the free library was increasingly seen as a key facility that should be made available:

> What a sad want I am in of libraries, of books to gather facts from! Why is there not a Majesty's library in every county town? There is a Majesty's jail and gallows in every one.
> — Thomas Carlyle letter, 18 May 1832

In literary use, the library is often seen as conducive to serious thought; in Jane Austen's *Pride and Prejudice* (1813), Mr Bennet sees his library as the one room in his house that is free of 'folly and conceit', and a character in F. Scott Fitzgerald's *The Great Gatsby* (1925) reflects that ' I've been drunk for about a week now, and I thought it might sober me up to sit in a library.'

See also ➤ ADVOCATES' *Library*, ➤ ALEXANDRIAN *Library*, ➤ AMBROSIAN *Library*, ➤ ASHLEY *Library*, ➤ BANCROFT *Library*, ➤ BODLEIAN *Library*, ➤ BOOTS *Library*, ➤ BRITISH *Library*, ➤ CIRCULATING *Library*, ➤ COPYRIGHT *Library*, ➤ COTTONIAN *Library*, ➤ FOLGER *Shakespeare Memorial Library*, ➤ LAURENTIAN *Library*, ➤ LONDON *Library*, ➤ MUDIE'S *Library*.

Library of Congress the US national library, in Washington DC. It was established in 1800, originally for the benefit of members of the US Congress, and was at first housed in the Capitol, moving to its present site in 1897.

Lichfield town in central England, in Staffordshire north of Birmingham, which was the birthplace of Samuel Johnson. Lichfield is also mentioned notably in the journal of George Fox

(1624–91), founder of the Society of Friends (the Quakers), who on seeing the spires of Lichfield in 1651 recorded, 'I…espied three steeple-house spires, and they struck at my life.'

lick into shape make presentable, originally with reference to the supposed practice of bears with their young. According to early bestiaries, bear-cubs were born without form, and were then licked into shape by their mothers; a bear may thus be taken as a symbol of the Church shaping human nature.

lictor in ancient Rome, an officer attending the consul or other magistrate, bearing the fasces, and executing sentence on offenders.

Lide a name for the month of March (now only in dialectal use). Recorded from Old English, the name is from the same base as *loud*.

lido a public open-air swimming pool or bathing beach, from the name of a famous beach resort near Venice. The first use of the name in Britain is in 1930, in a report in the *Morning Post* recording that 'the question of the safety of bathers in the Serpentine 'Lido' was raised at an inquest…yesterday.'

lie detector an instrument for determining whether a person is telling the truth by testing for physiological changes considered to be associated with lying, but generally not accepted for judicial purposes.

if you lie down with dogs, you will get up with fleas proverbial saying, late 16th century.

lie in state of the corpse of a person of national importance, be laid in a public place of honour before burial.

lies see ➤ the FATHER *of Lies*.

lieutenant a deputy or substitute acting for a superior; recorded from late Middle English, the word comes from Old French, from *lieu* 'place' and *tenant* 'holding'. In the normal British pronunciation the first syllable sounds like *lef-*, while in the US, it rhymes with *do*. It is not clear where the British pronunciation comes from, but it seems likely that at some point before the 19th century, the *u* was read and pronounced as a *v*, which later became an *f*. (In 1793, the philologist and lexicographer John Walker (1732–1807) expressed the hope that 'the regular sound, *lewtenant*' would in time become current.)

Lieutenant of the Tower (in the UK) the acting commandant of the Tower of London.

life see also ➤ ART *is long and life is short*, ➤ BOOK *of life*, ➤ *the* BREATH *of life*, ➤ *a* DOG *is for life, and not just for Christmas*, ➤ ELIXIR *of life*, ➤ *the life of* RILEY, ➤ LINE *of life*, ➤ STAFF *of life*, ➤ THREAD *of life*, ➤ TREE *of life*, ➤ *the* WEB *of life*.

life begins at forty proverbial saying, mid 20th century, from the title of a book:

> Life begins at forty. This is the revolutionary outcome of our New Era . . . Today it is half a truth. Tomorrow it will be an axiom.
> — Walter B. Pitkin *Life begins at Forty* (1932)

Life Guards in the British army, a regiment of the Household Cavalry.

life is a sexually transmitted disease graffito found on the London Underground.

life isn't all beer and skittles proverbial saying, mid 19th century.

while there's life there's hope proverbial saying, mid 16th century; earlier in Greek and Latin. The saying is reworked in a modern political quotation by the Labour politician Richard Crossman (1907–74), who is said to have commented on the death of the Labour leader Hugh Gaitskell in 1963, 'While there is death there is hope.'

lifeline in palmistry, a line on the palm of the hand which supposedly indicates one's length of life. The word is recorded in this sense from the late 19th century; the earlier term was *line of life*.

LIFFE (abbreviation for) the London International Financial Futures Exchange.

light see ➤ CHARGE *of the Light Brigade*, ➤ DRUMMOND *light*, ➤ HIDE *one's light under a bushel*, ➤ SWEETNESS *and light*.

light at the end of the tunnel a long-awaited sign that a period of hardship or adversity is nearing an end. The expression was given an ironic extension by the American poet Robert Lowell (1917–77):

> If we see light at the end of the tunnel,
> It's the light of the oncoming train.
> — Robert Lowell 'Since 1939' (1977)

This image was reinforced by the American writer Paul Dickson (1939–):

> Rowe's Rule: the odds are five to six that the light at the end of the tunnel is the headlight of an oncoming train.
> — Paul Dickson in *Washingtonian* November 1978

light blue the distinctive colour associated with Eton and Cambridge (as opposed to the dark blue of Harrow and Oxford), originally particularly associated with sporting contests.

light come, light go proverbial saying, late 14th century.

Light Horse Harry nickname of the American cavalry officer Henry Lee (1756–1818), father of the Confederate Commander ➤ *Robert E.* LEE; *light horse* are light-armed cavalry.

light infantry having light weapons and thus able to manoeuvre at speed; the light division in the British army was introduced under Sir John Moore (1761–1809) and developed particularly during the Peninsular War.

the Light of Asia a name for the ➤ BUDDHA, deriving from Edwin Arnold's epic poem *The Light of Asia* (1879), which associated the Buddha with Jesus Christ and brought his story to a western audience; *the Light of Asia* is not an eastern term for the Buddha.

the Light of the World Jesus Christ, *Lux Mundi*; the phrase is biblical, as in John 8:12, 'I am the light of the world'; it was famously used by the Pre-Raphaelite artist Holman Hunt as the title of his picture (1851–3) of Jesus Christ, illustrating Revelation 3:20, 'Behold, I stand at the door and knock.'

light the blue touch paper and retire immediately traditional instruction for lighting fireworks.

light year a unit of astronomical distance equivalent to the distance that light travels in one year, which is 9.4607×10^{12} km (nearly 6 million million miles). The expression is now often used figuratively.

> They are a million light years away from the football yobbo and the lager lout.
> — B. MacArthur *Despatches from the Gulf War* (1991)

lighthouse the ➤ PHAROS of Alexandria was one of the Seven Wonders of the World.

In early Christian iconography, in which the Church is often portrayed as a ship, a *lighthouse* is a symbol for the safe guidance of the soul through life.

the lighthouse of the Mediterranean a name for the volcano ➤ STROMBOLI, which has been in a state of continuous mild eruption throughout history.

lightning proverbial as a type of swift movement.
See also ➤ *Benjamin* FRANKLIN, ➤ SHEET *lightning*.

lightning never strikes twice in the same place proverbial saying, mid 19th century.

lights see ➤ ANCIENT *lights*, ➤ FESTIVAL *of Lights*, ➤ *Lord* DERWENTWATER'*s lights*, ➤ NORTHERN *Lights*, ➤ SOUTHERN *Lights*.

ligure in the Bible, a kind of precious stone, worn on the high priest's breastplate (Exodus 28:19). The word appeared in Greek in many different forms, one of which, adopted in late Latin as *lyncurius*, was connected with the medieval belief that the stone was a concretion of the urine of the lynx. It may in fact ultimately be from the same source as *azure* and *(lapis) lazuli*.

Liguria a coastal region of NW Italy, which extends along the Mediterranean coast from Tuscany to the border with France; capital, Genoa. In ancient times Liguria extended as far as the Atlantic seaboard. A coastal strip around Genoa, designated the **Ligurian Republic** in 1797 after Napoleon's Italian campaign, was annexed to France between 1805 and 1815.

Lihyanite an early form of Arabic known only from north Arabian inscriptions of the 2nd and 1st centuries BC, written in a southern Semitic alphabet.

like breeds like proverbial saying, mid 16th century.

like will to like proverbial saying, late 14th century.

Likert scale in psychology, a scale used to represent people's attitudes to a topic, named (in the mid 20th century) after Rensis *Likert* (1903–81), American psychologist.

Likud a coalition of right-wing Israeli political parties, formed in 1973, that won power in the Israeli elections of 1977 and governed under Menachem Begin until 1984. Likud returned to power in 1996 under Benjamin Netanyahu. The name is a Hebrew word, meaning literally 'consolidation, unity'.

Li'l Abner an American cartoon character created by Al Capp in 1934; the good-natured but simple Abner and his hillbilly family, including a much-loved pig, counterpoint the commonly encountered human failings of stupidity and greed.

See also ➤ DOUBLE *whammy,* ➤ SADIE *Hawkins day,* ➤ SKUNKWORKS.

lilac the fragrant violet, pink, or white blossom of the *lilac* is widely believed to produce misfortune if picked or taken indoors.

Recorded from the early 17th century, the name comes from obsolete French, via Spanish and Arabic, from Persian *līlak,* variant of *nīlak* 'bluish', from *nīl* 'blue'.

Lili Marlene a German song (1917) by Hans Leip (1893–1983) which was popular with both German and Allied soldiers during the Second World War. The song, with its image of Lili Marlene standing beneath the lantern by the barrack gate, became known to Allied troops after it was broadcast to them by Nazi propaganda radio in North Africa in 1941, and an English version of the lyrics was written by Tommie Connor. Leip said that the song was based on two girls he knew called Lili and Marlene.

Otto Lilienthal (1848–96), German pioneer in the design and flying of gliders. His early flying experiments involved running downhill into the wind wearing precisely constructed wings connected to a tail, and subsequently with the addition of a small motor to flap the wings. Working with his brother, he made over 2,000 flights in various gliders before being killed in a crash.

Lilith a female demon of Jewish folklore, who tries to kill newborn children. In the Talmud she is the first wife of Adam, dispossessed by Eve.

Lilliburlero an anti-Jacobite song ridiculing the Irish, popular at the end of the 17th century especially among soldiers and supporters of William III during the Revolution of 1688:

> Ara! but why does King James stay behind?
> Lilli burlero bullen a la
> Ho! by my shoul 'tis a Protestant wind
>   — Thomas Wharton 'A New Song' (written 1687)

After 'A New Song' became a successful propaganda weapon against James II, Wharton is said to have boasted that 'I sang a king out of three kingdoms.'

With different words the song has remained associated with the Orange Party, as 'The Protestant Boys'.

Lilliput in Swift's *Gulliver's Travels,* the imaginary country inhabited by people 6 inches (15 cm) high; the term **Lilliputian** for a trivial or very small person or thing derives from this.

When Gulliver is shipwrecked on the island of

Lilliput, the inhabitants attempt to constrain him by tying him down with a network of ropes; this image is often referred to in allusions to Gulliver and Lilliput.

> We will eliminate thousands of other regulations that hamstring federal employees, to cut the final Lilliputian ropes on the federal grant.
>   — *Insight* 11 October 1993

lily the *lily* with its trumpet-shaped flowers on a long slender stem and fragrant scent is often of symbolic importance; white lilies stand for purity, and an orange lily is an emblem of the ➤ ORANGE *Order.* In heraldry, the lilies of the ➤ FLEUR-*de-lis* represent France.

A *lily* is the emblem of ➤ *St* ANTHONY *of Padua,* ➤ *St* CATHERINE *of Siena,* and ➤ *St* DOMINIC. In representations of the ➤ ANNUNCIATION, Gabriel is often shown holding a lily.

See also ➤ GILD *the lily,* ➤ JERSEY *Lily,* ➤ LENT *lily.*

lily of the field in biblical translations, the **lilies of the field** may be any of a number of conspicuous Palestinian flowers, variously identified as a lily, tulip, anemone, and gladiolus:

> Consider the lilies of the field . . . they toil not, neither do they spin, yet even Solomon in all his glory was not arrayed like one of these.
>   — Bible (AV) Matthew ch. 6, v. 28

lily of the valley a European plant of the lily family, with broad leaves and arching stems of fragrant white bell-shaped flowers. In the Bible, the phrase is used to translate the Vulgate's *lilium convallium* (Song of Solomon), an unidentified plant.

limberham former term for a foolish man who keeps a mistress, like the hero of Dryden's play *Mr Limberham;* the word originally meant 'a supple-jointed person', and in figurative use, someone who is obsequious.

limbo in some Christian beliefs, the supposed abode of the souls of unbaptized infants, and of the just who died before Christ's coming.

Limbo of infants, translating Latin *limbus infantum,* was the name for the abode of unbaptized children.

Limbo of the fathers, translating Latin *limbus patrum,* was the name for the abode of the just who died before Christ's coming.

The name is recorded from late Middle English, and comes from the medieval Latin phrase *in limbo,* from *limbus* 'hem, border, limbo'. From the mid seventeenth century the use of the term widened to cover a place or situation resembling limbo; it is now generally used for an uncertain period of awaiting a decision or resolution; an intermediate state or condition.

Limehouse make a fiery political speech, as David Lloyd George (1863–1945) did at Limehouse in east London in 1909, when as Chancellor presiding over his first budget he attacked privilege as embodied by 'the Dukes'.

limelight the intense white light produced by heating lime in an oxyhydrogen flame, formerly used in theatres to light up important players and scenes and so direct attention to them; **the limelight** is now used to mean the focus of public attention, as in the comment on the supposedly retiring ➤ *T. E.* LAWRENCE attributed to Lord Berners, 'He's always backing into the limelight'.

limerick a humorous five-line poem with a rhyme scheme *aabba*, popularized by ➤ *Edward* LEAR and closely associated with him. It is said to be named from the chorus 'will you come up to Limerick?', sung between improvised verses at a gathering.

Treaty of Limerick signed (reputedly on the ➤ TREATY *Stone* at Limerick) by Jacobite and Williamite forces in Ireland in 1691. Limerick had been the last Jacobite stronghold, and by the terms of the treaty its defenders under Patrick Sarsfield were offered free passage to France. Those who went abroad in this manner were to form the ➤ IRISH *Brigade*.

Limey an American and Australian informal derogatory term for a British person. It dates from the late 19th century, and is said to derive from the former enforced consumption of lime juice in the British navy in order to prevent scurvy.

limited edition an edition of a book, or reproduction of a print or object, limited to a specific number of copies.

limmu the year of office to which an Assyrian eponym gave his name; the office of an Assyrian eponym. The word is Assyrian, meaning 'period, circuit, administrative year'.

Thomas Linacre (*c.*1460–1524), English physician and classical scholar. In 1518 he founded the College of Physicians in London, and became its first president. He translated Galen's Greek works on medicine and philosophy into Latin, reviving studies in anatomy, botany, and clinical medicine in Britain.

His students of Greek included Thomas More and probably Erasmus.

Lincoln see also ➤ *he looks as the* DEVIL *over Lincoln.*

Abraham Lincoln (1809–65), American Republican statesman, 16th President of the US 1861–5. His election as President on an anti-slavery platform helped precipitate the ➤ AMERICAN *Civil War;* he was assassinated by ➤ *John Wilkes* BOOTH shortly after the war ended. Lincoln was noted for his succinct, eloquent speeches, including the ➤ GETTYSBURG address of 1863. The town of Lancaster in Nebraska, founded in 1856, was made state capital and renamed *Lincoln* in his honour in 1867.

See also ➤ GETTYSBURG *address.*

Lincoln green bright green woollen cloth originally made at Lincoln, a city in eastern England which is the county town of Lincolnshire.

Lincoln imp a grotesque carving in the choir of Lincoln cathedral, showing a figure with large ears and one knee crossed over the other, and traditionally said to have been turned to stone by the painted angels of the Angel Choir. More recently the *Lincoln Imp* has become a symbol of good luck, perhaps because Edward VII, who had been presented with a gold scarf-pin of the Imp, was said to have been wearing it in 1896 when his horse Persimmon won the Derby.

Lincoln Memorial a monument in Washington DC to Abraham Lincoln, designed by Henry Bacon (1866–1924) and dedicated in 1922. Built in the form of a Greek temple, the monument houses a large statue of Lincoln.

Lincoln's Inn one of the Inns of Court in London, on the site of what was originally the palace of Ralph Neville (d. 1244), bishop of Chichester and Chancellor, and which later became the property of Henry de Lacy, earl of Lincoln (1249?–1311). When the property was made available to students of the law it was thus called *Lincoln's Inn.*

James Lind (1716–94), Scottish physician. He laid the foundations for the discovery of vitamins by performing experiments on scurvy in sailors. After his death the Royal Navy officially adopted the practice of giving lime juice to sailors.

Jenny Lind (1820–87), Swedish soprano, who was known as *the Swedish nightingale* for the purity and agility of her voice.

Lindabrides a lady-love, a sweetheart, a mistress, from a lady in the 16th-century romance *Mirror of Knighthood*.

Charles Lindbergh (1902–74), American aviator. In 1927 he made the first solo transatlantic flight in a single-engined monoplane, *Spirit of St Louis*. He moved to Europe with his wife to escape the publicity surrounding the kidnap and murder of his two-year-old son in 1932.

Lindbergh law in the US, a law making kidnapping a federal offence if the victim is taken across a state line or if ransom demands are sent by post. The law was passed by Congress in response to the kidnapping and death of the infant son of ➤ *Charles* LINDBERGH.

linden another name for the lime tree, especially in North America. The word comes from Old English (as an adjective in the sense 'made of wood from the lime tree'), but has been reinforced by obsolete Dutch *lindenboom* and German *Lindenbaum*.

Before the Second World War, the fashionable avenue **Unter den Linden**, named for the lime trees planted in its central promenade, was the centre of Berlin's social and cultural life.

Lindisfarne a small island off the coast of Northumberland, north of the Farne Islands. Linked to the mainland by a causeway exposed only at low tide, it is the site of a church and monastery founded by St Aidan in 635, which was a missionary centre of the Celtic Church. The sacking of Lindisfarne at the end of the 8th century was one of the first indicators of the coming Viking raids on Britain.

Lindisfarne Gospels a manuscript of the four gospels which was probably written to mark the canonization of St Cuthbert in 698; the illuminations and decorative capitals show elements of Celtic and Byzantine design. The Lindisfarne Gospels are now in the Cottonian collection in the British Library.

lindworm a monstrous and evil serpent or dragon of Scandinavian mythology, from Danish and Swedish *lindorm* 'a kind of mythical serpent'. In heraldry, a *lindworm* is shown as a dragon or wyvern, but without wings.

line see also ➤ DATE *Line*, ➤ DATUM *line*, ➤ *the* FALL *Line*, ➤ HOOK, *line and sinker*, ➤ LEY *line*, ➤ LINE *of demarcation*, ➤ *the line of least* RESISTANCE, ➤ MASON–*Dixon Line*, ➤ PLIMSOLL *line*, ➤ SHIP *of*

the line, ➤ *the* THIN *blue line*, ➤ *the* THIN *red line*, ➤ WALLACE'*s line*.

line a connected series of military fieldworks or defences facing an enemy force, often given a specific name.

See also ➤ ATTILA *Line*, ➤ HINDENBURG *line*, ➤ MAGINOT *Line*, ➤ SIEGFRIED *Line*.

the Line informal term for the equator, dating from the late 16th century.

See also ➤ CROSSING *the line*.

up the line to the battle-front; the term is especially associated with the First World War.

line engraving the art or technique of engraving by lines incised on the plate, as distinguished from etching and mezzotint, and especially popular in the 19th century.

line of battle originally, a battle formation of warships in line ahead; now, a disposition of troops for action in battle.

line of life in classical mythology, the thread spun and cut by the Fates, determining the length of a person's life, the ➤ THREAD *of life*.

See also ➤ LIFELINE.

Linear A the earlier of two related forms of writing discovered at Knossos in Crete between 1894 and 1901, found on tablets and vases dating from *c*.1700 to 1450 BC and still largely unintelligible.

Linear B a form of Bronze Age writing discovered on tablets in Crete, dating from *c*.1400 to 1200 BC. In 1952 it was shown by Michael Ventris and John Chadwick to be a syllabic script composed of linear signs, derived from Linear A and older Minoan scripts, representing a form of Mycenaean Greek.

linen see ➤ *one does not* WASH *one's dirty linen in public*.

ling chih a motif on Chinese ceramic ware, especially a representation of the fungus *Polyporus lucidus*, symbolizing longevity or immortality.

lingam a symbol of divine generative energy, especially a phallus or phallic object as a symbol of Shiva. The word comes from Sanskrit *linga*, literally 'mark, (sexual) characteristic'.

Lingua Franca a mixture of Italian with French, Greek, Arabic, and Spanish, formerly used in the Levant; *lingua franca* now denotes a language that is adopted as a common language between speakers whose native languages are different.

Recorded from the late 17th century, the phrase comes from Italian, and means literally 'Frankish tongue'.

lingworm a fabulous serpent of Scandinavian mythology; the word is first found in William Morris's translation of the *Völsunga Saga* (1870) in a description of the dragon Fafnir, and represents Old Norse *lyngormr* 'heather serpent'.

link see ➤ *a* CHAIN *is no stronger than its weakest link,* ➤ MISSING *link.*

links a golf course, especially one on grass-covered sandy ground near the sea. In Scots usage the word originally denoted comparatively level or undulating ground near the seashore, covered with turf or coarse grass; it derives ultimately from Old English *hlinc* 'rising ground'.

Linnaean system the classification system for plants and animals devised by the Swedish botanist Carolus Linnaeus (1707–78). He devised an authoritative classification system for flowering plants involving binomial Latin names (later superseded by that of Antoine Jussieu), and also a classification method for animals. His work provides a sound starting point for zoological and botanical nomenclature.

linnets see ➤ *the* GREEN *Linnets.*

lion the *lion* is traditionally taken as the type of strength, majesty, and courage, the 'king of beasts'., and has been used as an epithet of successful and warlike rulers, as in ➤ COEUR *de Lion* and ➤ WILLIAM *the Lion.*

A *lion* is the emblem of ➤ *St* MARK and ➤ *St* JEROME.

See also ➤ *an* ASS *in a lion's skin,* ➤ BEARD *the lion in his den,* ➤ BRITISH *Lion,* ➤ *a* LIVE *dog is better than a dead lion,* ➤ MARCH *comes in like a lion, and goes out like a lamb,* ➤ *a* MOUSE *may help a lion,* ➤ PRIDE *of lions,* ➤ SEA *lion,* ➤ NEMEAN *lion,* ➤ TWIST *the lion's tail.*

a lion in the way a danger or obstacle, especially an imaginary one; the reference is a biblical one, to Proverbs 26:13, 'the slothful man saith, There is a lion in the way'. The variant **a lion in the path** is also used.

lion of St Mark a winged lion emblematic of St Mark the Evangelist; one of the four animals of the ➤ TETRAMORPH.

Lion of the North ➤ GUSTAVUS *Adolphus* (1594–1632), king of Sweden.

Lion Sermon an annual sermon to be given at the church of St Catherine Cree, Leadenhall Street, London, on 16 October, as laid down in a bequest by John Gayer (d. 1649), lord mayor of London. The story ran that he had once been lost in a desert, when a lion had passed without hurting him in consequence of his prayers and vows of charity.

the lion's mouth a place of great danger, originally with biblical allusion, as in Proverbs 22:21 'Save me from the lion's mouth', and Timothy 4:17, 'I was delivered out of the mouth of the lion'.

the lion's provider the ➤ JACKAL, from the traditional belief that the jackal went before the lion to hunt up his prey.

lion's share the largest or principal portion, originally with reference to a fable of Aesop.

lioncel in heraldry, a young or small lion; in particular, each of two or more lions appearing together in arms.

lions things of note worth seeing in a particular place; the usage derived from the practice of taking visitors to see the lions which used to be kept in the Tower of London.

throw to the lions put in an unpleasant or dangerous situation, originally with reference to the practice in imperial Rome of throwing religious and political dissidents, especially Christians, to wild beasts as a method of execution.

The earliest use in English appears to be in a sermon by the Puritan divine Thomas Adams (*fl.* 1612–53), in which he noted that although the Christians had fought in Aurelius's army, the cry was still '*Christianos ad leones*,—Throw the Christians to the lions'. The Latin phrase is recorded in Tertullian's *Apologeticus*, in which he says that misfortunes such as flood, drought, famine, or pestilence evoke this immediate response.

Lions Club a worldwide charitable society devoted to social and international service, taking its membership primarily from business and professional groups.

lip see ➤ HABSBURG *lip.*

Lipari Islands a group of seven volcanic islands in the Tyrrhenian Sea, off the NE coast of Sicily, and in Italian possession. Believed by the ancient Greeks to be the home of the wind-god ➤ AEOLUS, the islands were formerly known as the *Aeolian Islands*.

Lipizzaner a horse of a fine white breed used especially in displays of dressage. The name comes (in the early 20th century) from German, from *Lippiza*, site of the former Austrian Imperial stud near Trieste; the stud is now based in Vienna.

Fra Filippo Lippi (*c.*1406–69), Italian painter. He was a pupil of Masaccio, whose influence can be seen in the fresco *The Relaxation of the Carmelite Rule* (*c.*1432); his later style is more decorative and less monumental than his early work. He is the subject of Robert Browning's monologue poem *Fra Lippo Lippi* (1855).

> Lippo Lippi's girl-Madonna's, with the maladive sensuality of their tired faces.
> — Rupert Brooke, letter October 1907

lipstick lesbian a lesbian of glamorous or manifestly feminist appearance. The phrase is recorded from the mid 1980s, and has been particularly associated with the choice of many politically active women to look and to dress in a style which represents a conscious breaking away from what is thought of as the conventional stereotype of lesbianism.

Children of Lir in Irish mythology, Fionnuala and her three brothers, the children of King Lir, who were changed into swans for nine hundred years by their stepmother's enchantment; when they were finally restored to human form, they were baptized by a priest, who had befriended them as swans, before dying of their extreme age.

liripipe a long tail hanging from the back of a hood, especially in medieval or academic dress. Recorded from the early 17th century, the word comes from medieval Latin *liripipium* 'tippet of a hood, cord'.

Lisbon according to the legend preserved in the ➤ LUSIADS of Luis de Camoëns (1524–80), *Lisbon* in Portugal derives its name from its legendary founder *Ulysses* (the city is called *Ulysippo* or *Olisipo* in early Latin sources).

Lisieux see ➤ St TERESA *of Lisieux*.

Lisle Letters a collection of some 3,000 letters written to and from Arthur Plantagenet, Viscount Lisle (an illegitimate son of Edward IV), his family and household, while he was lord deputy of Calais from 1533 to 1540. They give a vivid picture of the political and domestic life of the time.

list see ➤ DEAN's *list*, ➤ EMILY's *list*.

listeners never hear any good of themselves proverbial saying, mid 17th century.

Joseph Lister (1827–1912), English surgeon, inventor of antiseptic techniques in surgery. He realized the significance of Louis Pasteur's germ theory in connection with sepsis and in 1865 he used carbolic acid dressings on patients who had undergone surgery. Later he introduced a carbolic spray in the operating theatre. After about 1883 aseptic rather than antiseptic techniques became popular, though Lister believed in the use of both.

Franz Liszt (1811–86), Hungarian composer and pianist. He was a key figure in the romantic movement; many of his piano compositions combine lyricism with great technical complexity, while his twelve symphonic poems (1848–58) created a new musical form.

the Litany in the Christian Church, a series of petitions for use in church services or processions, usually recited by the clergy and responded to in a recurring formula by the people.

literae humaniores the honours course in classics, philosophy, and ancient history at Oxford University. Recorded in English from the mid 18th century, the phrase is Latin, and means literally 'the more humane studies' (that is, the humanities, secular learning as opposed to divinity).

literature see ➤ COMPANION *of Literature*.

litotes ironical understatement in which an affirmative is expressed by the negative of its contrary (e.g. *I shan't be sorry* for *I shall be glad*). Recorded from the late 16th century, the word comes via late Latin from Greek, ultimately from *litos* 'plain, meagre'.

little see also ➤ *little* BIRDS *that can't sing and won't sing must be made to sing*, ➤ *little* GREY *cells*, ➤ *Little* MAGICIAN, ➤ *Little* TICH, ➤ *little* TIN *god*.

Little Bear the constellation Ursa Minor.

Battle of Little Bighorn a battle in which General George Custer and his forces were defeated by Sioux warriors on 25 June 1876, popularly known as ➤ CUSTER's *Last Stand*. It took place in the valley of the Little Bighorn River in Montana.

Little Britain a former name for Brittany, recorded in early chronicles and romances.

the **Little Corporal** a nickname for Napoleon, noted for his small stature.

there is no little enemy proverbial saying, mid 17th century.

Little England beyond Wales the English-speaking area of Pembrokeshire (Dyfed); a name first recorded in Camden's *Britannia* (1586).

Little Englander a person who opposes an international role or policy for England (or, in practice, for Britain). The term dates from the late 19th century, and is currently often used in relation to opposition to Europe.

> Little Englanders . . . relish every opportunity to decry what they call 'meddling by Brussels Eurocrats'.
> — *Earth Matters* Autumn 1992

the Little Entente a treaty between Romania, Czechoslovakia, and Yugoslavia, formed after the First World War.

little fish are sweet proverbial saying, early 19th century; meaning that small gifts are always acceptable.

little gentleman in black velvet the mole, as a Jacobite toast, referring to the belief that William III's death resulted from the king's being thrown from his horse when it stumbled on a molehill.

Little Giant a sobriquet of the American lawyer and politician Stephen A. Douglas (1813–61), leader of the Democratic party, who was only 5 feet 4 inches in height. Douglas is remembered particularly for a series of seven debates with Abraham Lincoln on the issue of slavery during the 1858 senatorial campaign in Illinois; he won the senatorial race, but lost to Lincoln in the presidential campaign two years later.

Little Gidding a manor in Huntingdonshire where Nicholas Ferrar (1592–1637) and his family established, 1625–42, a religious community of some forty members, following a systematic rule of private devotion, public charity, and study. The house was visited by Charles I, Crashaw, and George Herbert, but it was raided by Cromwell's soldiers in 1646, and the community dispersed. T. S. Eliot celebrates it in 'Little Gidding', one of the *Four Quartets.*

little-go a former informal term for the first examination for the BA degree at Oxford and Cambridge. The final examination was known as *great-go.*

little green man an imaginary being from outer space. The expression is not recorded until the mid-20th century; the earliest literal use of the phrase, in Kipling's *Puck of Pook's Hill* (1906), refers to a Pictish warrior who is tattooed green.

every little helps proverbial saying, early 17th century.

Little John one of the companions of Robin Hood in the legends relating to that outlaw; he is noted for his great height and his prowess with a quarterstaff.

a little knowledge is a dangerous thing proverbial saying, early 18th century; originally in allusion to Pope:

> A little learning is a dangerous thing;
> Drink deep, or taste not the Pierian spring:
> — Alexander Pope *An Essay on Criticism* (1711)

Little League in North America, organized baseball played by children aged between 8 and 12.

little leaks sink the ship proverbial saying, early 17th century.

little local difficulty a euphemistic description of an acute political problem, famously used by Harold Macmillan (1894–1986) as Prime Minister, before leaving for a Commonwealth tour, following the resignation of the Chancellor of the Exchequer and other members of the Cabinet:

> I thought the best thing to do was to settle up these little local difficulties, and then turn to the wider vision of the Commonwealth.
> — Harold Macmillan statement at London Airport, 7 January 1958

Little Lord Fauntleroy an excessively good-mannered or elaborately dressed young boy, from the name of the boy hero of Frances Hodgson Burnett's novel *Little Lord Fauntleroy* (1886), who wore velvet suits with lace collars, and had his hair in ringlets.

Little Mary a dated euphemism for the stomach, deriving from Barrie's play of that name (1903).

Little Masters a group of 16th-century Nuremberg engravers, followers of Dürer, who worked small-dimension plates with biblical, mythological, and genre scenes.

Little Parliament the assembly of 120 members, nominated by Cromwell and his Council, which sat from 4 July to 12 December 1653.

little people a name for small supernatural creatures such as fairies and leprechauns; recorded from the early 18th century.

little pitchers have large ears proverbial saying, mid 16th century, meaning that children overhear what is not meant for them (a pitcher's *ears* are its handles).

a little pot is soon hot proverbial saying, mid 16th century, meaning that a small person quickly becomes angry or passionate.

Little Red Book informal name for *Quotations from Chairman Mao Zedong* (published in English in 1966).

Little Red Riding-hood heroine of the nursery story by the French writer Charles Perrault (1628–1703), in which a woodcutter's daughter is menaced by a wolf which has eaten her grandmother and is lying in wait, disguised as the grandmother, for Red Riding Hood herself.

Little Rhody informal name for Rhode Island.

little strokes fell great oaks proverbial saying, early 15th century.

little thieves are hanged, but great ones escape proverbial saying, mid 17th century.

little things please little minds proverbial saying, late 16th century.

Little Venice an area of London at the west end of Regent's Canal.

Émile Littré (1801–81), French lexicographer and philosopher. He was the author of the major *Dictionnaire de la langue française* (1863–77) and a history of the French language (1862). A follower of Auguste Comte, he became the leading exponent of positivism after Comte's death.

liturgical colours the colours used in ecclesiastical vestments and hangings for an altar, varying according to the season, festival, or kind of service. These have varied over the centuries, but now generally conform to the system established in 1570, with violet for Advent and Lent, white and gold for Christmas, Epiphany, Easter Sunday, and Trinity Sunday, red for Passion Sunday and Pentecost, and green for the rest of the year.

liturgy a form or formulary according to which public religious worship, especially Christian worship, is conducted. **The Liturgy** designates the Communion office of the Orthodox Church, and is also an archaic term in the Anglican Church for the Book of Common Prayer.

Recorded from the mid 16th century, the word comes via French or late Latin from Greek *leitourgia* 'public service, worship of the gods', and since the mid 19th century *liturgy* has also been used to denote a public office or duty performed voluntarily by a rich Athenian in ancient Greece.

lituus in ancient Rome, the crooked staff or wand carried by an augur.

live and learn proverbial saying, early 17th century.

live and let live proverbial saying, early 17th century.

if you want to live and thrive, let the spider run alive proverbial saying, mid 19th century.

a live dog is better than a dead lion proverbial saying, late 14th century; ultimately with biblical allusion to Ecclesiastes 9:4, 'For to him that is joined to all the living there is hope: for a living dog is better than a dead lion.'

they that live longest, see most proverbial saying, early 17th century.

come live with me and you'll know me proverbial saying, early 20th century.

liver the *liver* was anciently supposed to be the seat of love and violent emotion; it was the source of one of the four humours (➤ CHOLER) of early physiology.

A light coloured liver was traditionally supposed to show a deficiency of choler, and thus indicate a lack of spirit or courage; the expressions **white-livered** and **yellow-livered**, meaning cowardly, derive from this.

In the ancient world, the liver of a sacrificed animal was examined for omens, as reflected in Shakespeare's *Troilus and Cressida*:

> The gods are deaf to hot and peevish vows;
> They are polluted off'rings, more abhorr'd
> Than spotted livers in the sacrifice.
>
> — William Shakespeare *Troilus and Cressida* (1602)

Liverpool Poets the name given to a group of three poets, Adrian Henri (1932–), Roger McGough (1937–), and Brian Patten (1946–), who came together in the 1960s in the period of the Liverpool euphoria generated partly by the success of the Beatles. The combined form of their work was pop, 'underground', urban, anti-academic, good-humoured, and vocal: poetry was conceived by them as a medium for public rather than private consumption, a performance art.

livery a special uniform worn by a servant, an official, or a member of a City Company. The original sense was 'the dispensing of food, provisions, or clothing to servants', and the sense of a special uniform arose because medieval nobles provided matching clothes to distinguish their own servants from those of others.

livery company in the UK, any of the London City companies, which formerly had distinctive costumes. Descended from medieval craft guilds, the companies are now largely social and charitable organizations; none is now a trading company, though some still have some involvement with the operation of their original trade; several support public schools (e.g. Merchant Taylors, Haberdashers), and collectively they are involved in various forms of technical education.

A member of such a company is known as a **liveryman**.

he who lives by the sword dies by the sword proverbial saying, early 17th century, with biblical allusion to Matthew 26:52 'All they that take the sword shall perish with the sword.'

he that lives in hope dances to an ill tune proverbial saying, late 16th century; meaning that hoping for something better may constrain one's freedom of action.

he lives long who lives well proverbial saying, mid 16th century.

living will a written statement detailing a person's desires regarding their medical treatment in circumstances in which they are no longer able to express informed consent, especially an *advance directive*, a prior statement of refusal to permit certain specific types of medical treatment.

The concept of the *living will* was first discussed in legal circles in the US in the late 1960s, and the documents themselves had acquired legal status in most states by the end of the 1980s. Interest in the idea developed later in the UK, but by the mid 1990s it had become accepted, as a result of a number of court cases reaffirming common law, that the wishes of a patient could be binding on doctors.

David Livingstone (1813–73), Scottish missionary and explorer. He went to Bechuanaland as a missionary in 1841. On extensive travels, he discovered Lake Ngami (1849), the Zambezi River (1851), and

the Victoria Falls (1855). In 1866 he went in search of the source of the Nile, and was found in poor health by Henry Morton Stanley in 1871; Stanley greeted him with the famous words, 'Dr Livingstone, I presume?'

Livy (59 BC–AD 17), Roman historian. His history of Rome from its foundation to his own time contained 142 books, of which thirty-five survive (including the earliest history of the war with Hannibal).

lizard *lizards* were traditionally believed to be poisonous, and a 'lizard's leg' was one of the ingredients in the cauldron prepared by the three witches in *Macbeth*; the belief is also suggested by the proverb, 'Whom a serpent has stung, a lizard alarms'.

See also ➤ GOOD *mother lizard*.

Lizzie see ➤ TIN *Lizzie*.

the Ladies of Llangollen Lady Eleanor Butler (?1739–1829) and Miss Sarah Ponsonby (?1735–1831), two devoted friends who left their families (against strong opposition) to set up a lifelong residence together in Plas Newydd in Llangollen Vale. Their house, adorned in Gothic style, became a place of admiration and curiosity far beyond its neighbourhood, visited by distinguished guests, including Wordsworth.

Llaregyb the setting for Dylan Thomas's play *Under Milk Wood*; the name in reverse intentionally suggests 'bugger all'.

Llewelyn name of two medieval princes of Gwynedd in North Wales, **Llewelyn the Great** (1173–1240), who established himself powerfully in his principality, and his grandson (d. 1282), who proclaimed himself prince of all Wales in 1258, and was recognized by Henry III in 1265. His refusal to pay homage to Edward I led the latter to invade and subjugate Wales (1277–84); Llewelyn died in an unsuccessful rebellion.

Lloyd Morgan's canon the principle that the behaviour of an animal should not be interpreted in terms of a higher psychological process if it can be explained in terms of a lower one, from the name of *Lloyd Morgan* (1852–1936), British psychologist.

Lloyd's an incorporated society of insurance underwriters in London, made up of private syndicates. Founded in 1871, Lloyd's originally dealt only in marine insurance. It is named after the coffee house of Edward Lloyd (fl. 1688–1726), in which underwriters and merchants congregated and where ➤ LLOYD*'s List* was started in 1734.

Lloyd's List a daily newsletter relating to shipping, published in London from 1734.

Lloyd's Register a classified list of merchant ships over a certain tonnage, published annually in London; the corporation that produces this list and lays down the specifications for ships on which it is based. Also called **Lloyd's Register of Shipping**.

loaf see ➤ HALF *a loaf is better than no bread,* ➤ *a* SLICE *off a cut loaf isn't missed,* ➤ LOAVES *and fishes,* ➤ LOAVES *of bread.*

Loamshire name given to an imaginary rural county, much used in novels and plays; the **Loamshires** are supposedly a regiment from this county. The name is first recorded in George Eliot's novel *Adam Bede* (1859).

Loathly Lady a traditional ballad figure, an apparently ugly woman whose beauty is restored when at last she has found a husband and the enchantment laid on her is dispelled. The story is told by the ➤ WIFE *of Bath* in the *Canterbury Tales*; the knight who has married the *loathly lady* has to answer the question, 'what do women most desire?', and his wife regains youth and beauty at the correct answer, 'sovereignty'.

loaves and fishes personal profit as a motive for religious profession or public service, with biblical allusion to John 6:26, and the story of the miracle by which Jesus and his disciples fed a crowd of five thousand with 'five loaves, and two fishes'.

loaves of bread *loaves of bread* are the emblem of ➤ *St* PHILIP and ➤ *St* NICHOLAS *of Tolentino*.

lobby in the UK, any of several large halls in the Houses of Parliament in which MPs may meet members of the public. The verb *to lobby*, meaning to seek to influence a politician or public official on an issue, derives (originally in the US) from the practice of frequenting the lobby of a house of legislature to influence its members into supporting a cause.

lobby correspondent in the UK, a senior political journalist of a group receiving direct but unattributable briefings from the government.

lobscouse a stew formerly eaten by sailors, consisting of meat, vegetables, and ship's biscuit. The word is recorded from the early 18th century, but is of unknown origin; ➤ SCOUSE derives from it.

lobster in the 17th century, *lobster* was used as a contemptuous term for a soldier in a regiment of Roundhead cuirassiers, so named from their wearing complete suits of armour. In later times it became a general (derogatory) term for a soldier, from the characteristic red coat, compared with the colour of the lobster's shell when cooked.

local option a choice available to a local administration to accept or reject national legislation (e.g. concerning the sale of alcoholic liquor).

Locarno Pact a series of agreements made in Locarno in 1925 between the UK, Germany, France, Belgium, Poland, and Czechoslovakia in an attempt to ensure the future peace of Europe. The Pact guaranteed the common borders of France, Germany, and Belgium and the demilitarization of the Rhineland, as specified by the Treaty of Versailles.

Loch Ness Monster a large creature alleged to live in the deep waters of Loch Ness. Reports of its existence date from the time of St Columba (6th century); the number of sightings increased after the construction of a major road alongside the loch in 1933, but, despite recent scientific expeditions, there is still no proof of its existence.

Lochiel title of the chief of Clan Cameron, from *Lochiel* in Inverness; Donald Cameron (1695?–1748), chief from 1719 and one of the leading adherents of the Young Pretender, ➤ *Charles Edward* STUART, and who was exiled after the failure of the 1745 rising, was known as 'the Gentle Lochiel'.

Lochinvar the hero of a ballad included in the fifth canto of Scott's *Marmion*. His fair Ellen is about to be married to 'a laggard in love and a dastard in war', when the brave Lochinvar arrives at the bridal feast, claims a dance with her, and, as they reach the door, swings the lady on to his horse, and rides off with her.

> The young Lochinvar business was rather out of my usual line.
> — John Buchan *The Island of Sheep* (1936)

Lochow an earlier form of *Lochawe* in Argyll, Scotland, part of the hereditary lands of clan Campbell; the saying **it is a far cry to Lochow**, first recorded by Scott, implies that the Campbells' domains lie beyond the reach of invaders.

lock see also ➤ *the* RAPE *of the Lock*.

lock, stock, and barrel including everything completely (the allusion is to the complete mechanism of a firearm).

John Locke (1632–1704), English philosopher, a founder of empiricism and political liberalism. His *Two Treatises of Government* (1690) argues that the authority of rulers has a human origin and is limited. In *An Essay concerning Human Understanding* (1690) he argued that all knowledge is derived from sense-experience.

locker see ➤ Davy *Jones's locker,* ➤ a shot *in the locker.*

Lockerbie a town in SW Scotland, in Dumfries and Galloway, where in 1988 the wreckage of an American airliner, destroyed by a terrorist bomb, crashed on the town, killing all those on board and eleven people on the ground.

Locket's a fashionable ordinary, or tavern, in Charing Cross, frequently alluded to in the drama of the 17th–18th centuries, so named from Adam Locket, the landlord.

Lockhart by folk etymology, a surname deriving from a member of the family's having brought back the heart of Sir James Douglas (*c.*1286–1330) from Spain where he was killed in battle against the Moors; the family subsequently adopted the device of a heart within a fetterlock.

locksmith see ➤ love *laughs at locksmiths.*

Norman Lockyer (1836–1920), English astronomer. His spectroscopic analysis of the sun led to his discovery of a new element, which he named *helium.* Lockyer also studied possible astronomical alignments in ancient monuments such as Stonehenge. He founded both the Science Museum in London and the scientific journal *Nature,* which he edited for fifty years.

loco-foco an invented name for a self-igniting cigar or match, used in 19th-century America to designate the 'Equal Rights' or Radical section of the Democratic Party; the name came from a rowdy meeting at Tammany Hall, during which the gas lights were extinguished, and the room at once re-lighted by the candles and *loco-foco* matches which the Equal Rights supporters had with them.

Locrian mode in music, the mode represented by the natural diatonic scale B–B (containing a minor 2nd, 3rd, 6th, and 7th, and a diminished 5th). It is named (from *Locris,* a division of ancient Greece) after an ancient Greek mode, but is not identifiable with it.

Locrine according to Geoffrey of Monmouth, the eldest son of ➤ Brutus and father of ➤ Sabrina; he was king of Logres as his inherited third of his father's kingdom. He was the subject of a play (1595) once attributed to Shakespeare and published in the third Folio (1664), and one by Swinburne.

locum informal shortening of **locum tenens**, a person who stands in temporarily for someone else of the same profession, especially a cleric or doctor. The Latin phrase **locum tenens** is recorded in English from the mid 17th century and comes from medieval Latin, meaning literally 'one holding a place'.

locus classicus a passage considered to be the best known or most authoritative on a particular subject; the phrase comes from Latin, and means literally 'classical place'.

locus poenitentiae a place of repentance, in law, an opportunity allowed by law to a person to recede from some engagement, so long as some particular step has not been taken; the allusion is originally biblical, to Hebrews 12:17, where it is said of ➤ Esau that, trying to reverse the agreement whereby he had sold his birthright, 'he found no place of repentance.'

locus standi a recognized position; in law, a right to be heard in court. A Latin phrase, meaning literally 'place of standing', recorded in English from the mid 19th century.

locust the *locust* is usually solitary, but from time to time there is a population explosion and it migrates in vast swarms which cause extensive damage to crops. It is taken as a type of devouring and destructive propensities.

locust years years of poverty and hardship, a phrase coined by Winston Churchill in his *History of the Second World War* (1948) to describe Britain in the 1930s. The allusion is a biblical one:

> I will restore to you the years that the locust hath eaten.
> — Bible (AV) Joel ch. 2, v. 25

Locusta in ancient Rome, a noted poisoner of Gallic origin who was employed by the younger Agrippina to kill Claudius and Britannicus; she was eventually executed by Galba.

lode a vein of metal ore in the earth. This sense dates from the early 17th century; it derives ultimately from Old English *lād* 'way, course'. The term denoted a watercourse in late Middle English and a lodestone in the early 16th century.

See also ➤ COMSTOCK *lode*.

lodestar a star that is used to guide the course of a ship, especially the pole star. The word is recorded from Middle English, and the first element means 'way, course'. The figurative use developed early and was popular up to the 17th century; it was then revived in the early 19th century.

lodestone a piece of magnetite or other naturally magnetized mineral, able to be used as a magnet. Recorded from the early 16th century, the word means literally 'way-stone', from the use of the magnet in guiding mariners.

lodge a branch or meeting place of an organization such as the Freemasons or the Orange Order. The term probably derives from the late Middle English use of *lodge* to mean the workshop of a body of 'free masons' (see ➤ FREEMASON); this usage is first recorded in Robert Plot's *Natural History of North Staffordshire* (1686), in which he refers to 'a meeting (or Lodge as they term it in some places)'.

log an apparatus for determining the speed of a ship, originally one consisting of a float attached to a knotted line that is wound on a reel, the distance run out in a certain time being used as an estimate of the vessel's speed. The word ➤ LOGBOOK derives from this.

King Log in Aesop's fable, the antithesis of ➤ *King* STORK in his rule over the frogs. According to the story, the frogs asked for a king, and were first of all given a log by Jupiter. Demanding a more active king, they were given a stork, who ate many of them. The two kings are referred to allusively as types of inertia and excessive activity.

log cabin a hut built of whole or split logs; in North America taken (as typical of a settler's cabin) as symbolizing the humblest origins from which a person might rise to eminence. The biography of James Garfield (1831–81), American Republican statesman and 20th President of the US, was entitled *From Log-cabin to White House* (1910, by William Roscoe Thayer).

logan stone a rocking or moving stone; *logan* comes from *logging* (from dialect *log* 'to rock').

logbook an official record of events during the voyage of a ship or aircraft, originally an account of her rate of progress as indicated by the ➤ LOG.

at loggerheads in dispute with. The origin may be a use of *loggerhead* in the late 17th-century sense 'long-handled iron instrument for heating liquids and tar', perhaps wielded as a weapon. The earlier *go to loggerheads* is found from the late 17th century.

logic reasoning conducted or assessed according to strict principles of validity; a particular system or codification of the principles of proof and inference. In the Middle Ages, *logic* was one of the ➤ SEVEN *liberal arts*.

See also ➤ ARISTOTELIAN *logic*.

logic bomb in computing, a set of instructions secretly incorporated into a program so that if a particular condition is satisfied they will be carried out, usually with harmful effects.

logic chopping the practice of engaging in excessively pedantic argument. The expression *chop logic* is recorded from the early 16th century, and originally meant 'exchange or bandy logical arguments'; in later use, *chop* was wrongly understood as meaning 'cut, split'.

logical positivism a form of positivism, developed by members of the Vienna Circle, which considers that the only meaningful philosophical problems are those which can be solved by logical analysis.

logion a saying attributed to Christ, especially one not recorded in the canonical Gospels. The word comes from Greek, 'oracle', from *logos* 'word'.

Logos[1] in theology, the Word of God, or principle of divine reason and creative order, identified in the Gospel of John with the second person of the Trinity incarnate in Jesus Christ.

Logos[2] in Jungian psychology, the principle of reason and judgement, associated with the animus.

Logres in Geoffrey of Monmouth's chronicle, the part of Brutus's kingdom assigned to his eldest son Locrine, i.e. England. It is the usual term for Arthur's kingdom in medieval romance from Chrétien de Troyes onwards.

logrolling the practice of exchanging favours, especially in politics by reciprocal voting for each other's proposed legislation. Recorded from the early 19th century, the expression is North American, and derives from the proverbial phrase *you roll my log and I'll roll yours*.

Lohengrin in medieval French and German romances, the son of Perceval (Parsifal). He was summoned from the temple of the Holy Grail and taken in a boat drawn by swans to Antwerp, where he rescued Elsa of Brabant from a forced marriage; he was ready to marry her himself, providing that she did not ask who he was. Elsa broke this condition and he was carried away in the swan-boat back to the Grail castle.

The story of Lohengrin, sometimes called the *Swan Knight*, is the subject of an opera by Wagner (1850).

loins see ➤ GIRD *up one's loins.*

Lok Sabha the lower house of the Indian Parliament.

Loki in Scandinavian mythology, a mischievous and sometimes evil god who contrived the death of Balder and was punished by being bound to a rock. He was the father of Fenrir, the Midgard's serpent, and Hel.

Lolita the sexually precocious heroine of Nabokov's novel (1958) who has an affair with her stepfather Humbert; *Lolita* is now often used allusively.

> A look that was pure Lolita; baby doll dresses, socks and skirts.
> — *Sunday Times* 6 March 1994

Lollard a follower of John Wyclif. The Lollards believed that the Church should aid people to live a life of evangelical poverty and imitate Christ. Official attitudes to the Lollards varied considerably, but they were generally held to be heretics and often severely persecuted. Their ideas influenced the thought of John Huss, who in turn influenced Martin Luther.

The word was originally a derogatory term, derived from a Dutch word meaning 'mumbler', based on *lollen* 'to mumble'.

Lombard a member of a Germanic people who invaded Italy in the 6th century, and who settled in what became **Lombardy**. The name of this people comes from Italian *lombardo*, representing late Latin *Langobardus*, of Germanic origin, from the base of the adjective *long* + the ethnic name *Bardi*. The name *Longobard* is now also used by modern scholars.

In the Middle Ages, the term *Lombard* was used for bankers and money-lenders from Lombardy, and from this was applied generally to anyone engaged in banking and money-lending.

Lombard Street a street in the City of London containing many of the principal London banks, so named because it was formerly occupied by bankers from Lombardy. (There is a street in Paris similarly called the *Rue des Lombards.*)

all Lombard Street to a China Orange at very long odds; an expression dating from the early 19th century, although a *China orange* taken as the type of something worthless is recorded earlier.

Lomé Convention an agreement on trade and development aid, reached in Lomé in 1975, between the EC and forty-six African, Caribbean, and Pacific Ocean states, aiming for technical cooperation and the provision of development aid. Further agreements have been signed by a larger group.

London the capital of the United Kingdom, situated in SE England on the River Thames. The name comes from the Latin form *Londinium*, first recorded in Tacitus; the ultimate origin is unexplained, although it was formerly thought that the first element reflected a Celtic word for 'wild'.

See also ➤ *the* BEST *club in London*, ➤ CITY *of London*, ➤ *the* FIRE *of London*, ➤ NINE *Worthies of London*, ➤ TOWER *of London*.

London Eye name given to the *Millennium Wheel*, an observation wheel erected on the banks of the Thames in London between County Hall and Jubilee Gardens and opened to the public in February 2000; its passenger-carrying capsules are designed to give a 25-mile view across the London skyline.

London Gazette an official journal containing lists of government appointments and promotions, names of bankrupts, and other public notices. The first such journal published in England was the *Oxford Gazette*, the first number of which appeared in November 1665, when the Court was at Oxford during the Great Plague. Numbers 22 and 23 were printed in London, and with Number 24 the title was changed to the *London Gazette*. Official journals for Scotland and Ireland were published separately, with the *Edinburgh Gazette* first issued in 1690, and the *Dublin Gazette* in 1705.

London Group an association of English artists formed in 1913 from members of the ➤ CAMDEN *Town Group* and other alliances. The *London Group* comprised Impressionist and Post-Impressionist painters as well as more radical artists.

London Library a library founded in 1840, largely at the instigation of Thomas Carlyle, with the suport of many eminent men of letters of the day. It opened on 3 May 1841, in two rooms in Pall Mall, with a stock of 3,000 volumes; initial subscribers included Dickens, Macaulay, and Macready. It moved to its present premises in St James's Square in 1845.

London particular a dense fog of a kind formerly affecting London; *London fog* had been used by Maria Edgeworth in a letter of 1830 ('It is so very dark in a thick London fog that I can scarcely see what I write'), but *London particular* is first recorded in Dickens's *Bleak House*:

> 'This is a London particular.' I had never heard of such a thing. 'A fog, miss,' said the young gentleman.
> — Charles Dickens *Bleak House* (1853)

London stone a large stone set into the wall of Number 111, Cannon Street. It is mentioned as significant by William Camden (1551–1623), although its precise history and meaning is unknown:

> That great stone call'd London-stone: this I take to have been a milestone (such a one stood in the Forum at Rome) from which all the journeys were begun; since it stood in the middle of the City.
> — William Camden *Britannia* (1695)

Londonderry a city and port on the River Foyle in Northern Ireland, giving its name to the county in which it lies. Built on the site of an abbey founded by St Columba in AD 546, It was formerly called Derry, a name still used by many. In 1613 it was granted to the City of London for colonization and became known as Londonderry. In 1689 it resisted a siege by James II for 105 days before being relieved; the 'No Surrender!' slogan of the defenders became a motto of Protestant Ulster.

Lone Ranger a character created originally for American radio in 1933, as a masked enforcer of law in the American West, who (assisted by the Indian *Tonto*) constantly intervenes on the side of right, but never reveals his identity. Episodes ended with his call to his white horse, 'Hi-yo, Silver, away!'

Lone Star State an informal name for Texas.

lone wolf a wolf living by itself rather than in a pack, and thus a person who prefers to act alone. In its literal sense, the term may well have been popularized by the character of the wolf Akela in Kipling's *Jungle Books*.

lonely heart a person looking for a lover or friend by advertising in a newspaper; Nathaniel West's 1933 novel *Miss Lonelyhearts* was the story of a journalist whose job it was to write a daily agony column.

long see also ➤ LAND *of the Long White Cloud*.

long and lazy, little and loud; fat and fulsome, pretty and proud proverbial saying, late 16th century; categorizing physical and temperamental characteristics in women.

the long arm of the law the far-reaching power of the law, especially as represented by the police; *strong arm of the law*, similarly dating from the late 19th century, is also found.

long dozen thirteen.

long foretold, long last; short notice, soon past proverbial saying, mid 19th century.

Long John Silver the one-legged pirate who is the anti-hero of Stevenson's *Treasure Island* (1883).

it is a long long lane that has no turning proverbial saying, mid 19th century.

Long March the epic withdrawal of the Chinese communists from SE to NW China in 1934–5, over a distance of 9,600 km (6,000 miles). 100,000 people, led by Mao Zedong, left the communist rural base (the Jiangxi Soviet) after it was almost destroyed by the Kuomintang; 20,000 people survived the journey to reach Yan'an in Shaanxi province.

Long Meg and her Daughters a Bronze Age circle of standing stones near Little Selkeld in Cumberland.

Long Meg of Westminster a woman who wore men's clothes and whose exploits were famous in the 16th century; her name is used allusively with reference to masculine attributes in a woman, and in particular to great height.

Long Parliament the English Parliament which sat from November 1640 to March 1653, was restored for a short time in 1659, and finally voted its own dissolution in 1660. It was summoned by Charles I and sat through the English Civil War and on into the interregnum which followed.

long pig a translation of a term formerly used in some Pacific Islands for human flesh as food.

a long pull, a strong pull, and pull all together proverbial saying; early 19th century.

long purples dialect term for any of several plants with long spikes or racemes of purple flowers, as early purple orchid or purple loosestrife; *long purples* are first mentioned in Shakespeare's *Hamlet* as being among the flowers gathered by Ophelia.

Long Tom informal name for a gun of large size and long range, recorded from the mid 19th century.

long word there are a number of factitious terms which occur chiefly as instances of long words rather than in actual usage; *pneumonoultramicroscopicsilicovolcanoconiosis* is an example.

longbow a large bow drawn by hand and shooting a long feathered arrow. It was the chief weapon of English armies from the 14th century until the introduction of firearms.

See also ➤ DRAW *the longbow*.

Longchamp in Paris, the racecourse at the end of the Bois de Boulogne, where the Prix de l'Arc de Triomphe is run.

longest see also ➤ BARNABY *bright, Barnaby bright The longest day.*

the longest way round is the shortest way home proverbial saying, mid 17th century; meaning that not trying to take a short cut is often the most effective way.

Longinus[1] traditionally the name of the Roman soldier who pierced Jesus in the side with his spear at the Crucifixion.

Longinus[2] (fl. 1st century AD), Greek scholar. He is the supposed author of a Greek literary treatise *On the Sublime*, concerned with the moral function of literature, which influenced Augustan writers such as Dryden and Pope.

Longshanks a nickname of Edward I, king of England. His height was noted in early chronicles, and there is a reference to 'Great Edward Longshanks' issue' in Marlowe's *Edward II* (1593).

Longwood name of the house on St Helena in which Napoleon lived in exile and where he died in 1821.

Lonsdale belt an ornate belt awarded to a professional boxer winning a British title fight. A fighter winning three title fights in one weight division is given a belt to keep. It is named after the fifth Earl of Lonsdale, Hugh Cecil Lowther (1857–1944), who presented the first one.

look see also ➤ LOOK *to one's laurels.*

look before you leap proverbial saying, mid 14th century.

lookers-on see most of the game proverbial saying, early 16th century.

looking-glass being or involving the opposite of what is normal or expected; the allusion is to Lewis Carroll's *Through the Looking Glass* (1871), in which Alice climbs through the looking glass and encounters the Red and White Queens and other chessboard characters.

> We'd entered a looking-glass world where trains ran the wrong way, signals pointed downwards for go and the tracks were miles apart.
> — N. Whittaker *Platform Souls* (1995)

loon in North America, a large diving bird with a sleek black or grey head, a straight pointed bill, and short legs set far back under the body; the bird's actions when escaping from danger have given rise to the the use of *loon* to mean 'a silly or foolish person'.

loosestrife any of a number of tall plants which bear upright spikes of flowers and grow by water and in wet ground. The name comes (in the mid 16th century) from *loose* + *strife*, taking the Greek name *lusimakheion* (actually from *Lusimakhos*, the name of its discoverer) to be directly from *luein* 'undo' + *makhē* 'battle'. The misinterpretation is of long standing; Pliny, although giving Lysimachus as the discoverer, also says that oxen are made to eat it because it makes them more willing to draw together when pulling a cart.

lord a peer of the realm; a man of noble rank or high office. The word comes from Old English *hlāford*, from *hlāfweard* 'bread-keeper'.

See also ➤ EVERYBODY *loves a lord*, ➤ Lord *of* MISRULE, ➤ Lords *of the* ARTICLES, ➤ NEW *lords, new laws*, ➤ PRAISE *the Lord and pass the ammunition*, ➤ SHEPHERD *Lord*, ➤ YEAR *of Our Lord.*

Our Lord a name for Christ.

Lord Advocate the principal law officer of the Crown in Scotland.

Lord Chamberlain (in the UK) the official in charge of the royal household, formerly the licenser of plays. Also called **Lord Chamberlain of the Household**.

Lord Chancellor in the UK, the highest officer of the Crown, who presides in the House of Lords, the Chancery Division, or the Court of Appeal. Also called **Lord High Chancellor**.

See also ➤ WOOLSACK.

Lord Chief Justice (in the UK) the officer presiding over the Queen's Bench Division and the Court of Appeal (Criminal Division).

Lord Commissioner the representative of the Crown at the General Assembly of the Church of Scotland. Also called **Lord High Commissioner**.

Lord Great Chamberlain of England the hereditary holder of a ceremonial office whose responsibilities include attendance on the monarch at a coronation.

Lord High Admiral a title of the British monarch, originally the title of an officer who governed the Royal Navy and had jurisdiction over maritime causes.

Lord High Chancellor another name for the ➤ LORD *Chancellor*.

Lord High Commissioner another name for the ➤ LORD *Commissioner*.

Lord High Constable the ➤ CONSTABLE *of England* and ➤ CONSTABLE *of Scotland* were also known as *Lord High Constable*.

Lord Jim the central character in Joseph Conrad's novel of this name (1900), a disgraced chief mate whose life at a trading station on a remote Malayan island is an attempt to redeem himself from his former moment of cowardice.

> Let us pray . . . that William does not consider pulling a Lord Jim and fleeing his conscience all over the tropics.
> — Amanda Cross *The James Joyce Murder* (1967)

Lord Lieutenant in the UK, the chief executive authority and head of magistrates in each county. Before 1921, the title was also used for the viceroy of Ireland.

Lord Mayor's Day 9 November, the day on which the Lord Mayor of London goes in procession with the Aldermen and other city dignitaries to and from Westminster, where he receives from the Lord Chancellor the assent of the Crown to his election. The procession is known as the **Lord Mayor's show**.

lord of creation a name for mankind seen as having dominance over the created world; the reference is to Genesis, and God's promise to Adam and Eve:

> And God blessed them, and God said unto them, Be fruitful, and multiply, and replenish the earth, and subdue it: and have dominion over the fish of the sea, and over the fowl of the air, and over every living thing that moveth upon the earth.
> — Bible (AV) Genesis ch. 1, v. 28

Lord of Hosts God; a title of Jehovah in the Old Testament, sometimes referring to the heavenly hosts, and sometimes to the armies of Israel.

Lord of the Isles title of the early lords of Argyll as rulers of the Western Isles; the title forfeited in 1493, and was merged in the Crown of Scotland in 1540. *The Lord of the Isles* is the title of a poem by Sir Walter Scott (1815), which recounts the romance of the Lord of the Isles and Edith of Lorn against the story of Robert Bruce's fight to win Scotland.

lord of the manor in medieval England, a feudal lord in whom jurisdiction over the land he held was vested.

Lord of the Rings in Tolkien's trilogy *The Lord of the Rings* (1954–5), sequel to *The Hobbit* (1937), a title of Sauron, the Dark Lord, referring to the rings of power made for dwarves, elves, and men, and especially to the One Ring which confers magical powers, including invisibility, on its holder.

Lord Ordinary (in Scotland) any of the judges of the Outer House of the Court of Session.

Lord President of the Council (in the UK) the cabinet minister presiding at the Privy Council.

Lord Privy Seal in the UK, a senior cabinet minister without specified official duties.

Lord Protector of the Commonwealth title of Oliver Cromwell, established in an Act of 1653, stating that 'From and after the six and twentieth day of December 1653 the Name, Style, Title and Teste of the Lord Protector…of the Commonwealth, of England, Scotland, and Ireland…shall be used.'

The title was born by Oliver Cromwell ('His Highness the Lord Protector') until his death in 1658, and then by his son Richard Cromwell 1658–9.

Lord Provost the head of a municipal corporation or borough in certain Scottish cities.

Lord's a cricket ground in St John's Wood, north London, headquarters since 1814 of the Marylebone Cricket Club (MCC), named after the cricketer Thomas *Lord* (1755–1832).

the Lord's Day a Christian name for Sunday, recorded since the late 12th century; in the 17th and 18th centuries, *Lord's day* was widely used (not exclusively among Puritans) as an ordinary name for the day.

Lord's Prayer the prayer taught by Jesus to his disciples, as recorded in Matthew 6.9–13; the term is a translation of Latin *oratio Dominica*, and is first recorded in the Book of Common Prayer of 1549.

Lord's Supper a term (translating Latin *cena Dominica*) for Holy Communion, first recorded in English in Wycliff's translation of the Bible in 1382.

Lord's Table a communion table, an altar; the term is first used in Coverdale's translation of the Bible (1535), in 1 Corinthians 10:21, 'Ye cannot be partakers of the Lord's table, and of the table of devils.'

lords and ladies another term for wild arum; the name has been explained as referring to the dark and light spikes of the flower, the dark spikes being the lords and the light, the ladies.

There was a traditional belief that adders obtained their poison from the berries of this plant, and the dark spots on the leaves were said to have been stained with the blood of Christ.

In the fens, *lords and ladies* were associated with St Withburga (d. *c*.743), an English princess who was said to have founded a community at East Dereham, and who was buried there. Her body was stolen at the end of the 10th century by the monks of Ely, and during their journey, they rested at Brandon. Nuns of Thetford, who had brought the wild arum over with them from Normandy, came down to the river and laid the flowers on the saint's body. Some plants fell into the river and began to grow, and soon the banks of the river as far as Ely were covered with the plants.

Lords Appellant a group of nobles who brought charges of treason against certain supporters of Richard II in 1388.

Lords of Session (in Scotland) the judges of the Court of Session.

Lords spiritual the bishops in the House of Lords.

Lords temporal the members of the House of Lords other than bishops.

Lorelei in German legend, a beautiful woman with long blonde hair who sat on the *Lorelei* rock on the bank of the Rhine, in the Rhine gorge near Sankt Goarshausen, and with her singing lured boatmen to distraction. The name is often used allusively.

> Both are the Lorelei song of a dependency forged from decades of federal subsidies, work projects and heroics.
> — *High Country News* 27 May 1996

Lorelei is also the name of the gold-digging heroine of Anita Loos's comic novel *Gentlemen Prefer Blondes* (1925).

Lorenzo de' Medici (1449–92), Italian statesman and scholar, also known as **Lorenzo the Magnificent**. A patron of the arts and humanist learning, he supported Botticelli, Leonardo da Vinci, and Michelangelo among others. He was also a noted poet and scholar in his own right.

See also ➤ LAURENTIAN *library*.

Loreto a town in eastern Italy, near the Adriatic coast to the south of Ancona, which is the site of the **House of Loreto** (or *Holy House*), said to be the home of the Virgin Mary and to have been brought from Nazareth by angels in 1295.

loriner archaic term for a maker of small iron objects, especially bits, spurs, stirrups, and mountings for horse's bridles. The word, which comes via Old French *lorain* 'harness strap' from Latin *lorum* 'strap', survives only in the title of a London livery company.

Lorraine a medieval kingdom (corresponding to the modern region of NE France) which extended from the North Sea to Italy. The name comes from Latin *Lotharingia*, from *Lothair*, the name of a Frankish king (825–69).

Lorraine later became an important French duchy of the House of Guise.

Lorraine cross a cross with one vertical and two horizontal bars. It was the symbol of Joan of Arc, and in the Second World War was adopted by the Free French forces of General de Gaulle. Also called ➤ CROSS OF *Lorraine*.

Los Alamos a town in northern New Mexico, which has been a centre for nuclear research since the 1940s, when it was the site of the development of the first atomic and hydrogen bombs; it was after watching the explosion of the first atomic bomb at Los Alamos on 16 July 1945 that the physicist Robert Oppenheimer (1904–67) commented, 'I remembered the line from the Hindu scripture, the *Bhagavad Gita*…"I am become death, the destroyer of worlds." '

> Even the detonation at Los Alamos did not hold implications as frightening as cloning.
> — N. Freedman *Joshua* (1973)

los von Rom a policy seeking to reduce the political influence of the Roman Catholic Church in Austria and Germany at the end of the 19th century; the movement concerned with this. The phrase is German, meaning literally 'free from Rome'.

what you lose on the swings you gain on the roundabouts proverbial saying, early 20th century.

you cannot lose what you never had proverbial saying, late 16th century.

one man's loss is another man's gain proverbial saying, early 16th century.

there's no great loss without some gain proverbial saying, mid 17th century.

I have lost a day in Suetonius *Lives of the Caesars* he attributes to the Roman emperor Titus (AD 39–81, emperor from AD 78), the remark '*Amici, diem perdidi* [Friends, I have lost a day]', on reflecting that he had done nothing to help anybody all day.

lost articles ➤ *St* ANTHONY *of Padua* is the patron saint of those who are trying to find what is lost.

Lost Colony an early British settlement on Roanoke Island, founded in 1587, which had mysteriously disappeared by 1590; the only trace found was the word *Croatoan* carved on a tree. Among those missing was *Virginia Dare* (b. 1587), the first white child to be born in America.

lost generation the generation reaching maturity during and just after the First World War, a high proportion of whose men were killed during those years. The expression was applied by Gertrude Stein to disillusioned young American writers, such as Ernest Hemingway, Scott Fitzgerald, and Ezra Pound, who went to live in Paris in the 1920s, in the words 'You are all a lost generation.'

The phrase was apparently borrowed (in translation) from a French garage mechanic, whom Stein heard address it disparagingly to an incompetent apprentice; Ernest Hemingway subsequently took it as his epigraph to *The Sun Also Rises* (1926).

The Lost Leader the title of a poem by Robert Browning (1845) on Wordsworth's acceptance of the office of Poet Laureate, condemning the poet's abandonment of radical principles with the lines 'Just for a handful of silver he left us, Just for a riband to stick in his coat'.

Lost Sunday another name for Septuagesima Sunday.

Lost Tribes of Israel the ten tribes of Israel taken away *c.*720 BC by Sargon II to captivity in Assyria (2 Kings 17:6), from which they are believed never to have returned, while the tribes of Benjamin and Judah remained.

Lot[1] in the Bible, the nephew of Abraham, who was allowed to escape from the destruction of Sodom (Genesis 19). His wife, who disobeyed orders and looked back, was turned into a pillar of salt.

Lot[2] in Arthurian legend, king of Orkney, brother-in-law of Arthur and husband of Morgawse, and father of Gawain and his brothers; ➤ LOTHIAN is said to be named after him.

Lotharingia an ancient duchy of northern Europe, situated between the Rhine and the Scheldt from Frisia to the Alps. The name ➤ LORRAINE derives from this.

Lothario a man who behaves selfishly and irresponsibly in his sexual relationships with women, from a character in Rowe's *Fair Penitent* (1703).

> Their father was a Lothario who deserted their mother when they were eight and nine so he could play the field and sleep with thousands.
> — *Cosmopolitan* September 1996

Lothian a region of central Scotland, supposedly named from King Lot of Arthurian legend (see ➤ LOT[2]).

Lotka-Volterra of or relating to a mathematical model which uses coupled differential equations to describe and predict the variation of two interacting populations, especially a predator and a prey species.

Lotophagi in Greek mythology, the ➤ LOTUS-*eaters*.

lottery see ➤ MARRIAGE *is a lottery*.

lotus in Greek mythology, a legendary plant whose fruit induces a dreamy forgetfulness and an unwillingness to depart.

Lotus is also the name of either of two large water lilies, a red-flowered Asian lily, the flower of which is a symbol in Asian art and religion, and a white- or blue-flowered lily regarded as sacred in ancient Egypt.

The word is recorded from the late 15th century, denoting a type of clover or trefoil described by Homer as food for horses; it comes via Latin from Greek *lōtos*, and is of Semitic origin. The term was used by classical writers to denote various trees and plants. This legendary plant, mentioned by Homer, was thought by later Greek writers to be *Ziziphus lotus*, a relative of the jujube.

lotus-eater a person who spends their time indulging in pleasure and luxury rather than dealing with practical concerns. The *lotus-eaters* or *Lotophagi* in

Greek mythology were a people who lived on the fruit of the lotus, said to cause a dreamy forgetfulness and an unwillingness to depart.

Lotophagi is recorded in English from the early 17th century, but the first use of *lotus-eater* is in the title of a poem by Tennyson, *The Lotos-eaters* (1832). **Lotus-eating** and the verb **lotus-eat** are now a part of the mainstream language.

> A scathing documentary about the rich lotus-eaters on the Thirties Riviera.
> — *Independent* 28 May 1999

lotus-land a place or state concerned solely with, or providing, idle pleasure and luxury.

lotus position a cross-legged position for meditation, with the feet resting on the thighs.

Lotus Sutra one of the most important texts in Mahayana Buddhism, significant particularly in China and Japan and given special veneration by the Nichiren sect.

Louis the name of eighteen kings of France, etymologically representing the name of ➤ CLOVIS, who as king of the Franks was seen as founder of the French kingdom.

St Louis (1214–70), king of France (as **Louis IX**) from 1226. He conducted two unsuccessful crusades, dying of plague in Tunis during the second. The ➤ SAINTE *Chapelle* in Paris was built by him as a shrine for the relic of Christ's Crown of Thorns given him by the Emperor Baldwin.

He is regarded as patron of the French kings; when Louis XVI was executed in 1793, his Irish-born confessor the Abbé Edgeworth de Firmont, watching him mount the steps of the guillotine, called out to him, '*Fils de Saint Louis, montez au ciel* [Son of Saint Louis, ascend to heaven].'

☐ **FEAST DAY** His feast day is 25 August.

Louis XI (1423–83), son of Charles VII, reigned 1461–83. He continued his father's work in laying the foundations of a united France ruled by an absolute monarchy. His long struggle with Charles the Rash, Duke of Burgundy, ended with France's absorption of much of Burgundy's former territory along her border.

Louis XIV (1638–1715), reigned 1643–1715; known as **the Sun King**. His reign represented the high point of the Bourbon dynasty and of French power in Europe, and in this period French art and literature flourished. His almost constant wars of expansion

united Europe against him, however, and gravely weakened France's financial position.

Louis XVI (1754–93), reigned 1774–92. His minor concessions and reforms in the face of the emerging French Revolution proved disastrous. As the Revolution became more extreme, he was executed with his wife, Marie Antoinette, and the monarchy was abolished.

Louis Philippe (1773–1850), king of France 1830–48, son of Philippe d'Orleans (see ➤ ÉGALITÉ). After the restoration of the Bourbons he became the focus for liberal discontent and was made king, replacing Charles X in the ➤ JULY *Revolution*. His regime was gradually undermined by radical discontent and eventually overthrown.

See also ➤ CITIZEN *King*.

Louisiana a state in the southern US, on the Gulf of Mexico. Louisiana, named in honour of Louis XIV of France, originally denoted the large region of the Mississippi basin claimed for France by the explorer La Salle in 1682. It was sold by the French to the US in the Louisiana Purchase of 1803. The smaller area now known as Louisiana became the 18th state in 1812.

Louisiana Purchase the territory sold by France to the US in 1803, comprising the western part of the Mississippi valley and including the modern state of Louisiana. The area had been explored by France, ceded to Spain in 1762, and returned to France in 1800.

loup-garou in France and French-speaking countries, a werewolf.

Lourdes a town in SW France, at the foot of the Pyrenees, which has been a major place of Roman Catholic pilgrimage since in 1858 a young peasant girl, Marie Bernarde Soubirous (St Bernadette), claimed to have had a series of visions of the Virgin Mary.

Louvre the principal museum and art gallery of France, in Paris, housed in the former royal palace built by Francis I and later extended. (Philip Augustus had first established a royal residence here in the late 12th century.) The royal collections, from Francis I onwards and greatly increased by Louis XIV, formed the nucleus of the national collection.

love (in tennis, squash, and some other sports) a score of zero; nil. This usage apparently comes from the phrase *play for love* (i.e. the love of the game, not for money); folk etymology has connected the word with French *l'oeuf* 'egg', from the resemblance in shape between an egg and a zero.

love see also ➤ *all's* FAIR *in love and war,* ➤ CALF *love,* ➤ *City of* BROTHERLY *Love,* ➤ *the* COURSE *of true love never did run smooth,* ➤ COURT *of love,* ➤ COURTLY *love,* ➤ CUPBOARD *love,* ➤ *the* FAMILY *of Love,* ➤ *it is best to be* OFF *with the old love before you are on with the new,* ➤ LABOUR *of love,* ➤ PITY *is akin to love,* ➤ PLATONIC *love,* ➤ QUEEN *of love,* ➤ *'tis* BETTER *to have loved and lost than never to have loved at all,* ➤ TOUGH *love,* ➤ TUNNEL *of love,* ➤ *when* POVERTY *comes in at the door love flies out of the window,* ➤ *whom the* GODS *love die young.*

love and a cough cannot be hid proverbial saying, early 16th century.

one cannot love and be wise proverbial saying, early 16th century.

love apple an old-fashioned term for a tomato, recorded from the late 16th century, and perhaps reflecting a belief that the plant was an aphrodisiac.

love begets love proverbial saying, early 16th century.

love in a cottage expression for a marriage made for love without sufficient means to sustain a household. The expression is recorded from the early 19th century, and probably derives from a play by George Colman the Elder (1732–94) and David Garrick (1717–79):

> Love and a cottage! Eh, Fanny! Ah, give me indifference and a coach and six!
> — George Colman, the Elder and David Garrick *The Clandestine Marriage* (1766)

love-in-a-mist a Mediterranean plant of the buttercup family, which has feathery foliage. It typically bears blue flowers surrounded by delicate thread-like green bracts, giving a hazy appearance to the flowers when seen from a distance.

love-in-idleness another term for heartsease; in Shakespeare's *Midsummer Night's Dream*, the magic flower with which Puck anoints the eyes of the lovers.

love is blind proverbial saying, late 14th century.

love-knot a knot or bow tied as a token of love.

love laughs at locksmiths proverbial saying, early 19th century.

love-lies-bleeding an amaranth with drooping purple-red flowering spikes.

love makes the world go round proverbial saying, mid 19th century, from a traditional French song.

love me little, love me long proverbial saying, early 16th century.

love me, love my dog proverbial saying, early 16th century; St Bernard in a sermon says '*qui me amat, amat et canem meum* [who loves me, also loves my dog].'

make love not war student slogan, 1960s.

love-spoon a wooden spoon, sometimes with a double bowl, carved for presentation to an intended wife.

love will find a way proverbial saying, early 17th century.

Ada, Countess of Lovelace (1815–52), English mathematician. The daughter of Lord Byron, in 1833 she met Charles Babbage, subsequently becoming his assistant. In 1843 she translated an Italian paper on Babbage's computer, adding significant and detailed notations as to how the machine could be programmed.

Richard Lovelace (1618–57), English poet. A Royalist, he was imprisoned in 1642, when he probably wrote his famous poem 'To Althea, from Prison'.

Robert Lovelace name of the principal male character in Richardson's *Clarissa*, whose prolonged seduction and ultimate rape of Clarissa leads to her death, taken as the type of a heartless seducer.

> If Arthur had been the most determined *roué* and artful Lovelace who ever set about deceiving a young girl, he could hardly have adopted better means.
> — W. M. Thackeray *Pendennis* (1850)

Lovell see ➤ *the* CAT, *the rat, and Lovell the dog, rule all England under the hog.*

lovelock a curl or lock of hair worn on the temple or forehead, originally fashionable in the time of Elizabeth I and James I.

James Lovelock (1919–), English scientist. He is best known for the ➤ GAIA *hypothesis,* first presented by him in 1972 and discussed in several popular books, including *Gaia* (1979).

lovely jubbly expressing delight or affirmation, especially in response to an anticipated success. The phrase derives ultimately from *lubbly Jubbly*, a 1950s advertising slogan for *Jubbly*, an orange-flavoured soft drink; it was recoined in the BBC television series *Only Fools and Horses* (1981–96) as a characteristic expression of Derek Trotter, or 'Del Boy', a Peckham market trader.

lovers ➤ St VALENTINE is the patron saint of *lovers*.
    See also ➤ JOVE *but laughs at lovers' perjury,* ➤ *the* QUARREL *of lovers is the renewal of love.*

loving cup a large, often silver, two-handled drinking-cup passed round at banquets, the guests successively drinking from it.

low see ➤ TOBY.

David Low (1891–1963), New-Zealand-born British cartoonist famous for his political cartoons and for inventing the character ➤ *Colonel* BLIMP.

Low Church of or adhering to a tradition within the Anglican Church (and some other denominations) which is Protestant in outlook and gives relatively little emphasis to ritual, sacraments, and the authority of the clergy.

the Low Countries the region of NW Europe comprising the Netherlands, Belgium, and Luxembourg. The term is first found in English in the mid 16th century.

Low German a vernacular language spoken in much of northern Germany, more closely related to Dutch than to standard German. Also called *Plattdeutsch.*

Low Latin medieval and later forms of Latin.

Low Mass in the Catholic Church, Mass with no music and a minimum of ceremony.

Low Sunday the Sunday after Easter, perhaps so named in contrast to the high days of Holy Week and Easter.

Low Week the week that begins with Low Sunday.

Lower Empire the later Roman Empire.

lower house the larger of two sections of a bicameral parliament or similar legislature, typically with elected members and having the primary responsibility for legislation.

L. S. Lowry (1887–1976), English painter. He painted small matchstick figures set against the iron and brick expanse of urban and industrial landscapes, settings provided by his life in Salford, near Manchester.

> Moving between, in and around them, were Lowry-like figures in black, shuffling their way to and from work.
> — C. Phillips *European Tribe* (1987)

Loyal North Lancashire Regiment the only British regiment to be given this appellation. Originally raised in 1793 as the Loyal Lincoln Volunteers by the 9th Earl of Lindsey, the regiment was given the family motto of *Loyaute m'oblige* [Loyalty compels me]. When the regiment became the 81st of Foot, it was allowed to keep the appellation 'Loyal', in recognition of the fact that it had volunteered en masse for the war with France.

loyal toast a toast proposed and drunk to the sovereign of one's country.

Loyalist a colonist of the American revolutionary period who supported the British cause.
    The name *Loyalist* is also given in Northern Ireland to a supporter of the union with Great Britain.

loyalty card an identity card issued by a retailer to its customers as part of a consumer incentive scheme, whereby credits are accumulated for future discounts every time a transaction is recorded.

lozenge in heraldry, a charge in the shape of a solid diamond, in particular one on which the arms of an unmarried or widowed woman are displayed.

l.s.d. a dated British term for money. The letters stand for Latin *librae* 'pounds', *solidi, denarii* (both denoting Roman coins).

LSD a synthetic crystalline compound, lysergic acid diethylamide, which is a powerful hallucinogenic drug.

Lubyanka a building in Moscow used as a prison and as the headquarters of the KGB and other Russian secret police organizations since the Russian Revolution.

Lucan (AD 39–65), Roman poet, born in Spain, who was forced to commit suicide after joining a conspiracy against Nero. His major work is *Pharsalia*, a hexametric epic in ten books dealing with the civil war between Julius Caesar and Pompey.

Lord Lucan a British peer who disappeared in mysterious circumstances in 1974 following an attack on his wife and the murder of the family nanny. Speculation about his survival and whereabouts continues to this day, and his name may be used allusively.

Lucanian ox an elephant; the name derives from the Latin phrase *Lucae boves*, meaning elephants, explained by Pliny as first seen during Pyrrhus's wars in Lucania, a district of southern Italy.

Lucifer the rebel archangel whose fall from heaven was supposed to be referred to in Isaiah 14:12, 'How art thou fallen from heaven, O Lucifer, son of the morning?'; *Lucifer* was traditionally interpreted as the name of Satan before his fall, and gives rise to the expression **proud as Lucifer**.

The name comes (in Old English) from Latin, 'light-bringing morning star', from *lux, luc-* 'light' + *-fer* 'bearing'. In poetic and literary use, *Lucifer* may designate the morning star, the planet Venus appearing in the sky before sunrise.

lucifer match an archaic term for a match struck by rubbing it on a rough surface.

Luciferian a member or adherent of a sect founded by Lucifer, bishop of Cagliari in the fourth century, who separated from the Church because it was too lenient (as he thought) towards Arians who repented of their heresy.

luciform having the quality of light, luminous; in particular, as a quality of the body which is the vehicle of the soul in the philosophy of ➤ NEOPLATONISM.

Lucina the Roman goddess who presided over childbirth, sometimes identified with Juno or Diana. In 16th-century poetry, the identification with Diana, the moon-goddess, meant that *Lucina* was occasionally used for the moon.

luck *luck* is sometimes used in names of objects on which the prosperity of a family is supposed to depend: this use originates with the ➤ LUCK *of Eden Hall*.

See also ➤ BEGINNER's *luck*, ➤ *the* DEVIL's *children have the devil's own luck*, ➤ DILIGENCE *is the mother of good luck*, ➤ FOOLS *for luck*, ➤ SALTASH *luck*, ➤ *see a* PIN *and pick it up, all the day you'll have good luck*.

there is luck in leisure proverbial saying, late 17th century.

there is luck in odd numbers proverbial saying, late 16th century.

the Luck of Eden Hall an oriental glass goblet (of the 15th century or earlier) in the possession of the

Musgraves of Eden, Cumberland, so called from a superstition embodied in the words, 'If this glass will break or fall, Farewell the luck of Eden-hall'.

Lucknow a city in northern India, which in 1775 became the capital of the province of Oudh. In 1857, during the Indian Mutiny, its British residency was twice besieged by Indian insurgents, and *The Relief of Lucknow* (1860, by the artist Thomas Jones Barker, 1815–82) was a popular Victorian painting.

lucky see also ➤ BORN *under a lucky star*, ➤ *it is* BETTER *to be born lucky than rich*, ➤ THIRD *time lucky.*

lucky at cards, unlucky in love proverbial saying, mid 18th century.

Lucky Country informal name for Australia, the title of a book by Donald Horne (1921–), published in 1964.

lucky stone a stone with a natural hole through it, regarded as an amulet or charm, and often worn as jewellery.

lucre money, especially when regarded as sordid or distasteful or gained in a dishonourable way; the phrase **filthy lucre** is with biblical allusion to Titus 1:11, 'Teaching things which they ought not, for filthy lucre's sake'.

Recorded from late Middle English, the word comes from French *lucre* or Latin *lucrum*, in the same sense.

Lucretia in Roman legend, a woman who was raped by a son of Tarquinius Superbus and took her own life; this led to the expulsion of the Tarquins from Rome by a rebellion under Brutus.

Lucretius (*c.*94–*c.*55 BC), Roman poet and philosopher. His didactic hexametric poem *On the Nature of Things* is an exposition of the materialist atomist physics of Epicurus, which aims to give peace of mind by showing that fear of the gods and of death is without foundation.

Lucullan (especially of food) extremely luxurious, from the name of Licinius Lucullus, Roman general of the 1st century BC, famous for giving lavish banquets.

lucus a non lucendo a paradoxical or otherwise absurd derivation; something of which the qualities are the opposite of what its name suggests. Recorded in English from the early 18th century, this

Latin phrase means 'a grove (so called) from the absence of *lux* (light)'; that is, a grove is named from the fact of its not shining, a proposition discussed by the Roman rhetorician Quintilian (AD *c*.35–*c*.96) in his *Institutio Oratoria*.

St Lucy (d. 304), virgin and martyr, who died at Syracuse in the persecution of Diocletian.

Her *eyes*, reputed to have been put out and miraculously restored, are the usual emblem of St Lucy.

☐ **FEAST DAY** Her feast day, 13 December, was the shortest day of the year according to the Julian calendar; John Donne's Poem 'A Nocturnal upon St Lucy's Day' begins ''Tis the year's midnight and it is the day's.' Especially in Sweden, St Lucy's day is associated with a festival of light.

Lud a mythical king of Britain, according to Geoffrey of Monmouth's *History* the eldest brother of Cassivellaunus. He built walls around the city of Brutus (Trinovantium) and renamed it Caerlud (Lud's city) from which it derives its modern name London. Geoffrey says that Gildas recounts at length the quarrel that ensued between Lud and his brother Nennius because of the impiety of renaming their father's city.

Luddite a member of any of the bands of English workers who destroyed machinery, especially in cotton and woollen mills, which they believed was threatening their jobs (1811–16). The name probably comes from Ned *Lud*, one of the participants in the destruction of machinery.

Ludgate the name (from its situation near the London City gate so called) of an ancient debtors' prison.

ludo a simple game in which players move counters round a board according to throws of a dice. The game originated in the late 19th century, and takes its name from Latin *ludo* 'I play'.

Ludolph's number the number π, which the German-born teacher *Ludolph* van Ceulen (1540–1610) evaluated to 35 decimal places.

Ludwig II (1845–86), king of Bavaria, reigned 1864–86. A patron of the arts, he became a recluse and built a series of elaborate castles. He was declared insane and deposed in 1886.

lues Boswellianae a biographer's tendency to magnify his or her subject, regarded as a disease

(*lues* in Latin means 'plague'). The phrase was coined by Macaulay in relation to Boswell's *Life of Samuel Johnson* (1791):

> Biographers, translators, editors,—all, in short, who employ themselves in illustrating the lives or the writings of others, are peculiarly exposed to the lues Boswellianae, or disease of admiration.
> — Lord Macaulay in *Edinburgh Review* January 1834

Lug in Irish mythology, the god who embodies the type of sacred kingship and who is associated with the sun.

Lughnasa in Ireland, 1 August, the first day of autumn and one of the four traditional quarter days. The name means 'festival of ➤ LUG' and would originally have been sacred to this god. In modern times *Lughnasa* has been associated with fairs; legends concerned with the day relate to St Patrick's defeat of paganism.

Bela Lugosi (1884–1956), Hungarian-born American actor famous for his roles in horror films such as *Dracula* (1931) and *The Wolf Man* (1940).

> Movies . . . in the Lugosi, cape-twitching tradition.
> — *Vanity Fair* April 1997

St Luke an evangelist, closely associated with St Paul and traditionally the author of the third Gospel and the Acts of the Apostles. A physician, he was possibly the son of a Greek freedman of Rome.

St Luke's emblem is an ox, one of the animals of the Tetramorph. He is the patron of artists as well as of physicians and surgeons, and in Flemish art of the 16th and 17th centuries is often portrayed painting the Virgin; he may also be shown with surgical instruments.

☐ **FEAST DAY** His feast day is 18 October, and the Sunday nearest to St Luke's day is sometimes known as ➤ HOSPITAL *Sunday*.

Luke Skywalker in the ➤ STAR *Wars* trilogy the boy who, unknown to himself, is the last inheritor of ➤ JEDI powers. Trained by Obi-Wan Kenobi and Yoda, he sets out on a quest in which he learns to master the Force, and in the end destroys the Empire and redeems his father ➤ DARTH *Vader*.

> Goalkeepers appeared to use 'The Force' to an extent Luke Skywalker himself would have been proud of.
> — *Stornoway Gazette* 13 July 1995

lulav a palm branch traditionally carried at the Jewish festival of Succoth.

Lumbini the wooded garden in which the Buddha was born (see ➤ MAYA¹).

Lumière Auguste Marie Louis Nicholas (1862–1954) and Louis Jean (1864–1948), French inventors and pioneers of cinema. In 1895 the brothers patented their 'Cinématographe', a cine camera and projector in one. They also invented the improved 'autochrome' process of colour photography.

lumpenproletariat (especially in Marxist terminology) the unorganized and unpolitical lower orders of society who are not interested in revolutionary advancement. The word was originally used by Karl Marx, the first element representing German *Lumpen* 'rag, rogue'.

Luna a series of Soviet moon probes launched in 1959–76. They made the first hard and soft landings on the moon (1959 and 1966).

Luna Park an amusement centre at Coney Island, Brooklyn, New York, which opened in 1903 with a ride called 'A Trip to the Moon', and was finally closed after a fire in 1946.

lunar of, determined by, or resembling the moon; the word is recorded from late Middle English, and comes from Latin *luna* 'moon'.

lunar month the period of the moon's revolution around the earth, especially a month measured between successive new moons (roughly 29½ days).

lunar race a legendary race of Indian kings supposed to have been descended from the moon.

lunar year a period of twelve lunar months (approximately 354 days).

Lunarian (in science fiction) an imagined inhabitant of the moon; the word is recorded from the early 18th century.

lunatic a person who is mentally ill, from the belief that the moon (in Latin, *luna*) caused intermittent insanity by its changes. The word, which is recorded from the late 13th century, is not now in technical use; the adjective *lunatic* occurs in the general sense 'extremely foolish, eccentric, or absurd'.

the lunatic fringe an extreme or eccentric minority within society or a group; the term was coined by Theodore Roosevelt (1858–1919) in 1913, 'There is apt to be a lunatic fringe among the votaries of any forward movement.'

lunch see ➤ LADIES *who lunch*.

Lunn see ➤ SALLY *Lunn*.

Luoyang an industrial city in east central China, in Henan province, formerly called *Honan*. Between the 4th and 6th centuries AD the construction of cave temples to the south of the city made it an important Buddhist centre.

Lupercalia an ancient Roman festival of purification and fertility, held annually on 15 February. Chosen celebrants, wearing the skins of sacrificed animals, ran through the streets, and for a woman to be struck by one of them was to increase her fertility. In Shakespeare's *Julius Caesar*, Caesar instructs his wife, the barren Calpurnia, to ensure that she is struck by Mark Antony, who is one of the runners.

Lupercus in ancient Rome, the equivalent of the Greek god Pan, in whose honour the festival of Lupercalia was held. It is likely that his name is connected with *lupus* 'wolf', and that he was seen as a protector of flocks from wolves.

lushburg a base coin made in imitation of the sterling or silver penny and imported from Luxembourg in the reign of Edward III (the name is an alteration of *Luxembourg*).

Lushington drunkenness; a drunkard, from the 'City of *Lushington*', a convivial society which met at the Harp Tavern, Russell Street, London (the name is probably from a punning allusion to *lush*). It had a 'Lord Mayor' and four aldermen, presiding over wards called Juniper, Poverty, Lunacy, and Suicide, and on the admission of a new member, the Lord Mayor lectured him on the dangers of alcohol.

the Lusiads an epic Portuguese poem on the history of Portugal by Luis de Camoëns (1524–80). It recounts the story of the descendants of *Lusus*, mythical companion of Bacchus and legendary founder of Lusitania, or Portugal, and celebrates particularly the exploits of the navigator Vasco da Gama. The first English translation was published in 1655 by the diplomatist and author Richard Fanshawe (1608–66).

Lusitania[1] an ancient Roman province in the Iberian peninsula, corresponding to modern Portugal, and supposedly founded by ➤ LUSUS.

Lusitania[2] a Cunard liner which was sunk by a German submarine in the Atlantic in May 1915 with the loss of over 1,000 lives. The anti-German feeling that this event generated in the US was a factor in bringing that country into the First World War.

lustrum a period of five years; the Latin word originally denoted a purificatory sacrifice after a quinquennial census.

lusus naturae a freak of nature; the phrase comes from Latin, and denotes a supposed sportive action of Nature to which the origin of marked variations from the normal type of an animal or plant was formerly ascribed.

lute see ➤ RIFT *within the lute.*

Lutetia the Roman name for what is now the city of Paris. It has given its name to **lutetium**, the chemical element of atomic number 71, a rare silverywhite metal of the lanthanide series, which was discovered in the early 20th century, and which was named for the home of its discoverer.

Martin Luther (1483–1546), German Protestant theologian, the principal figure of the German Reformation. He preached the doctrine of justification by faith rather than by works; his attack on the sale of indulgences with his ninety-five theses (1517) was followed by further attacks on papal authority, and in 1521 Luther was condemned and excommunicated at the ➤ DIET *of Worms*, where he is said to have declared, 'Here I stand. I can do no other.'

In 1530 he gave his approval to Melanchthon's ➤ AUGSBURG *Confession*, which laid down the Lutheran position. His translation of the Bible into High German (1522–34) contributed significantly to the spread of this form of the language and to the development of German literature in the vernacular.

Lutheran Church the Protestant Church accepting the Augsburg Confession of 1530, with justification by faith alone as a cardinal doctrine. The Lutheran Church is the largest Protestant body, with substantial membership in Germany, Scandinavia, and the US.

Lutine Bell a bell kept at Lloyd's in London and rung whenever there is an important announcement to be made to the underwriters. It was salvaged from HMS *Lutine*, which sank in 1799 with a large cargo of gold and bullion, which loss was borne by the underwriters, who were members of Lloyd's.

Edwin Lutyens (1869–1944), English architect. He established his reputation designing country houses, but is particularly known for his plans for New Delhi (1912), where he introduced an open garden-city layout, and for the Cenotaph in London (1919–21).

luvvy an actor or actress, especially one who is particularly effusive or affected. The use of the word developed in the early 1990s; it is also, in earlier usage, associated with actors and actresses who are short of work and have to accept parts with secondrate companies. It is now used increasingly to indicate the stage in general, and as the use has broadened it has become somewhat less derogatory.

> I try not to surround myself with actors or get sucked into the 'luvvy' scene.
> — *Radio Times* 28 August 1993

Luwian an ancient Anatolian language of the 2nd millennium BC, related to Hittite. It is recorded in both cuneiform and hieroglyphic scripts, and may have been the language spoken in Troy at the time of the Homeric war.

Lux Mundi Latin for the ➤ LIGHT *of the World.*

Luxor a city in eastern Egypt, on the east bank of the Nile, which is the site of the southern part of ancient Thebes and contains the ruins of the temple built by Amenhotep III and of monuments erected by Ramses II.

LXX the Roman numeral for 70; a symbol for ➤ SEPTUAGINT.

lyam in heraldry, a charge representing a leash for a dog.

lycanthropy the supernatural transformation of a person into a wolf, as recounted in folk tales. *Lycanthropy* is recorded from the late 16th century, as a supposed form of madness involving the delusion of being a wolf, with correspondingly altered behaviour:

> Lycanthropia . . . or Wolf-madness, when men run howling about graves and fields in the night, and will not be persuaded but that they are wolves or some such beasts.
> — Robert Burton *Anatomy of Melancholy* (1621)

The word comes from modern Latin *lycanthropia*, and ultimately from Greek *lukos* 'wolf' + *anthropos* 'man'.

Lycaon in Greek mythology, a king of Arcadia who sacrificed a child to Zeus and as punishment was turned into a wolf (Greek *lykos*); an alternative story was that the transformation was a punishment for his having offered Zeus human flesh to eat.

Lyceum the garden at Athens in which Aristotle taught philosophy; Aristotelian philosophy and its followers. The name comes via Latin from Greek

Lukeion, neuter of *Lukeios*, epithet of Apollo (from whose neighbouring temple the Lyceum was named).

The *Lyceum* was also the name of a theatre near the Strand in London, noted for the melodramatic productions staged there by Henry Irving and others.

lychgate a roofed gateway to a churchyard, formerly used at burials for sheltering a coffin until the clergyman's arrival. Recorded from the late 15th century, the word comes from Old English *līc* 'body' + *gate*.

lychway a path along which a corpse has been carried to burial, which was supposed in some districts to establish a right of way.

lycopodium a plant of a genus that includes the common clubmosses, so called because the claw-like shape of the root was thought to resemble a wolf's foot.

Lycurgus¹ a legendary Thracian king who persecuted the child Dionysus; he was consequently struck blind (or driven mad) so that he killed his own son, and he was then eaten alive by wild horses.

Lycurgus² (9th century BC), Spartan lawgiver. He is traditionally held to have been the founder of the constitution and military regime of ancient Sparta. The adjective **Lycurgan**, relating to his constitutional innovations, may also mean more generally harsh or severe.

Lydford law the summary procedure of certain local tribunals which had or assumed the power of inflicting sentence of death on thieves; the rule proverbially ascribed to them was, 'hang first, try afterwards'. *Lydford*, now a small town on the edge of Dartmoor, was formerly the chief town of the Stannaries.

John Lydgate (*c*.1370–*c*.1450), English poet and monk. His copious output of verse, often in Chaucerian style, includes the poetical translations the *Troy Book* (1412–20) and *The Fall of Princes* (1431–8).

Lydia an ancient region of western Asia Minor, south of Mysia and north of Caria. It became a powerful kingdom in the 7th century BC but in 546 its final king, Croesus, was defeated by Cyrus and it was absorbed into the Persian empire. Lydia was probably the first realm to use coined money, and allusions may refer to the wealth of Croesus.

Lydian mode in music, the mode represented by the natural diatonic scale F–F (containing an augmented 4th).

lying-in-state the display of the corpse of a public figure for public tribute before it is buried or cremated.

lyke wake a night spent watching over a dead body, typically acting as a celebration to mark the passing of the person's soul. Recorded from late Middle English, the phrase comes from *lyke* (from Old English *līc* 'body': compare with ➤ LYCHGATE) and the noun *wake*. It is probably best-known today from the traditional ballad, 'The Lyke-Wake Dirge'.

John Lyly (*c*.1554–1606), English prose writer and dramatist. His prose romance in two parts, *Euphues, The Anatomy of Wit* (1578) and *Euphues and his England* (1580) was written in an elaborate style that became known as *euphuism*.

Lynceus one of the Argonauts, famous for his keen eyesight. The adjective *lyncean* 'keen-sighted' (from the Greek word for *lynx*) may have been used by earlier writers with an intended reference to Lynceus.

lynch law the punishment or execution of alleged criminals by a group of people without a legal trial. It is named after Captain William *Lynch* (1742–1820), head of a self-constituted judicial tribunal in Virginia *c*.1780.

Lynn see ➤ RISING *was a seaport town and Lynn it was a wash.*

lynx this wild cat with tufted ears and spotted fur is traditionally alluded to for its keenness of sight; the expression **lynx-eyed** is recorded from the late 16th century.

Lyon the chief herald of Scotland. Also called **Lord Lyon, Lyon King of Arms**. *Lyon* is recorded from late Middle English, and is an archaic variant of *lion*, named from the lion on the royal shield.

Lyon Court the court over which the *Lyon King of Arms* presides.

Lyonesse in Malory, the region of origin for Tristram; the name is also geographical in Tennyson who makes it the place of the last battle between Arthur and Mordred. It is traditionally said to be a tract of land between Land's End and the Scilly Isles, now submerged.

Lyons see ➤ *the* BUTCHER *of Lyons.*

lyre a stringed instrument like a small U-shaped harp with strings fixed to a crossbar, used especially in ancient Greece. Modern instruments of this type are found mainly in East Africa.

Lysander (d.395 BC), Spartan general. He defeated the Athenian navy in 405 and captured Athens in 404, so bringing the Peloponnesian War to an end.

Trofim Denisovich Lysenko (1898–1976), Soviet biologist and geneticist. He was an adherent of

➤ LAMARCK's theory of evolution by the inheritance of acquired characteristics. Since his ideas harmonized with Marxist ideology he was favoured by Stalin and dominated Soviet genetics for many years.

Lysippus (4th century BC), Greek sculptor thought to be responsible for a series of bronze athletes, notably the Apoxyomenos (c.320–315). He is said to have introduced a naturalistic scheme of proportions for the human body into Greek sculpture.

M the thirteenth letter of the modern English alphabet and the twelfth of the ancient Roman one, corresponding to Greek *mū*, Semitic *mēm*.

In the ➤ *James* BOND novels and films, *M* is the initial by which the head of the Secret Service is known.

ma nishtana in the Passover Haggadah, the questions traditionally asked by the youngest member of a Jewish household on Seder Night; this part of the Passover celebrations. The name comes from the formulaic beginning of the questions, meaning 'What makes this night different from all other nights?', and the questions are, 'What is the meaning of the precepts, statutes, and laws which the Lord our God has given you?' (Deuteronomy 6:20), 'Why is this rite observed by you?' (Exodus 12:26), and 'What is this?' (Exodus 13:14).

Ma State informal name for New South Wales, the earliest Australian colony.

Maastricht Treaty a treaty on European economic and monetary union, agreed by the heads of government of the twelve member states of the European Community at a summit meeting in Maastricht in December 1991. Ratification was completed in October 1993.

Maat in Egyptian mythology, the goddess of truth, justice, and cosmic order, daughter of Ra. She is depicted as a young and beautiful woman, standing or seated, with a feather on her head.

Queen Mab in Shakespeare's *Romeo and Juliet*, *Queen Mab* is described as the 'fairies' midwife' who delivers the fancies of those who are dreaming; of tiny size, she travels in a coach made of an empty hazelnut. It has been suggested that she is to be identified with an Irish fairy *Mabh*.

Queen may be *quean*, a slattern or low woman, although in later use it was understood to mean the Queen of the Fairies; in Shelley's visionary poem *Queen Mab* (1813), Mab is the Fairy Queen.

Mabinogion a collection of Welsh prose tales of the 11th–13th centuries, dealing with Celtic legends and mythology, and preserved in The White Book of Rhydderch (1300–25) and The Red Book of Hergest (1375–1425). The four main stories cover events in the life and death of the legendary hero Pryderi, son of Pwyll.

These stories, together with a number of other tales from the Red Book of Hergest, were translated and published by Lady Charlotte Guest as the *Mabinogion* (1838–49).

macaroni an 18th-century British dandy affecting Continental fashions. The usage seems to have developed from the name of the **Macaroni Club**, a name which in turn was probably adopted to indicate the preference of the members for foreign food, macaroni being at that time little eaten in England. There is apparently no connection with the extended use of Italian *maccherone* in the senses 'blockhead, fool, mountebank' referred to in the *Spectator* of 1711, 'Those circumforaneous Wits whom every nation calls by the name of that Dish of Meat which it loves best…in Italy, *Maccaronies.*'

Macaroni Parson sobriquet applied to the clergyman William Dodd (1729–77), by *Town and Country Magazine*, 1773, when commenting on the life he was leading as a fashionable preacher. Dodd, deeply involved in debt, forged Lord Chesterfield's signature on a bond for an annuity in 1777; he was arrested and committed for trial in the same year. Sentenced to death on 26 May, he was executed a month later, despite great efforts to obtain a pardon. It was of Dr Dodd that Johnson, who had been active in these efforts, said, 'Depend upon it, Sir, when a man knows he is to be hanged in a fortnight, it concentrates the mind wonderfully.'

macaronic of or designating a burlesque form of verse in which vernacular words are introduced into the context of another language (originally and chiefly Latin), often with corresponding inflections and constructions; of or designating any form of verse in which two or more languages are mingled together. *Macaronic* meaning 'of the nature of a jumble or medley' is recorded in English from the early 17th century; the literary sense dates from the mid 17th century, and probably derives from the 'macaronic' poem (*Liber Macaronices*) published in 1517 by Teofilo Folengo, who explains (ed. 2, 1521) that the 'macaronic art' is so called from its resemblance to the traditional dish of macaroni in being a mix of ingredients.

Thomas Babington Macaulay (1800–59), English historian, essayist, and philanthropist. He was a civil servant in India, where he established a system of education and a new criminal code, before returning to Britain and devoting himself to literature and politics; he was the author of the popular *Lays of Ancient Rome*. Lord Melbourne (1779–1848) is said to have commented of him, 'I wish I was as cocksure of anything as Tom Macaulay is of everything'.

Macbeth (*c*.1005–57), king of Scotland 1040–57. He came to the throne after killing his cousin Duncan I in battle, and was himself defeated and killed by Duncan's son Malcolm III. Shakespeare's tragedy *Macbeth* considerably embroiders the historical events, especially in relation to the character of ➤ *Lady* MACBETH.

how many children had Lady Macbeth? title of an essay (1933) by L. C. Knights (1906–97), satirizing the style of criticism represented by A. C. Bradley's 'detective interest' in plot and emphasis on character; Knights took Lady Macbeth's line 'I have born children' as an example of how unhelpful it would be to base an approach to the play on exploring this point.

Lady Macbeth a remorseless or melodramatic woman, especially one leading or assisting a weak man, with allusion to the scene in Shakespeare's *Macbeth* in which Macbeth balks at returning to the room in which he has murdered Duncan to replace the daggers with which he killed the king, and so ensure that Duncan's attendants are believed to be his murderers. His wife undertakes the task, with the words 'Infirm of purpose! Give me the daggers'. After the murder, however, she is increasingly tormented by guilt, and in a sleep-walking scene obsessively tries to clean her hands of the blood she can still see.

Macbride principles the code of conduct, first advocated by the Irish diplomat Séan MacBride (1904–88) in 1976, that US firms or investors in Northern Ireland should pursue a policy of non-discrimination and ensure the employment of a balanced workforce.

Maccabee a member or supporter of a Jewish family of which ➤ JUDAS *Maccabaeus* was the leading figure, which led a religious revolt in Judaea against the Syrian Seleucid king Antiochus IV *c*.167 BC, as recorded in the Books of the ➤ MACCABEES. The term is occasionally found in extended use, the earliest of which as applied to the Methodists is recorded by John Wesley:

> They laid hold on a poor Chimney-sweeper they met, tho' no Maccabee, (as the common People call us here).
> — John Wesley diary, 30 August 1751

Maccabees each of four books of Jewish history and theology, of which the first two are included in the Apocrypha.

Joseph McCarthy (1909–57), American Republican politician. Between 1950 and 1954 he was the instigator of widespread investigations into alleged communist infiltration in US public life:

> I have here in my hand a list of two hundred and five [people] that were known to the Secretary of State as being members of the Communist Party and who nevertheless are still working and shaping the policy of the State Department.
> — Joseph McCarthy speech at Wheeling, West Virginia, 9 February 1950

McCarthyism a vociferous campaign against alleged communists in the US government and other institutions carried out under Senator Joseph McCarthy in the period 1950–4. Many of the accused were blacklisted or lost their jobs, though most did not in fact belong to the Communist Party. The campaign ended when McCarthy received public censure in December 1954.

McCoy see ➤ *the* REAL *McCoy*.

Flora MacDonald (1722–90), Scottish Jacobite heroine. She aided Charles Edward Stuart's escape from English pursuit, after his defeat at Culloden in 1746, by smuggling him from Benbecula to Skye in a small boat, disguised as her maid.

mace a staff of office, especially that which lies on the table in the House of Commons when the Speaker is in the chair, regarded as a symbol of the authority of the House. The *mace* is an ornamental version of a medieval weapon which consisted of a heavy staff or club, typically of metal and with a spiked head; the word comes from Old French *masse* 'large hammer'.

When Oliver Cromwell dismissed the Rump Parliament on 20 April 1653, he did so with the words, 'Take away that fool's bauble, the mace.'

Macedonia an ancient country in SE Europe, at the northern end of the Greek peninsula. In classical times it was a kingdom which under Philip II and Alexander the Great became a world power. In early sources, ancient Macedonia is referred to as **Macedon**, and Alexander himself as **the Macedon**.

Macedonia's Madman Pope's name for Alexander the Great:

> Heroes are much the same . . .
> From Macedonia's Madman to the Suede.
> — Alexander Pope *Essay on Man* (1734)

Macedonian Wars a series of four wars between Rome and Macedonia in the 3rd and 2nd centuries BC, which ended in the defeat of Macedonia and its annexation as a Roman province (148 BC). The first (214–205 BC) occurred when Philip V of Macedonia formed an alliance against Rome. The second (200–196), in which Philip was defeated, resulted in the extension of Roman influence in Greece; Philip's son Perseus was defeated in the third war (171–168). Macedonia was then divided into four republics, and after a fourth war (149–148) became a Roman province.

like Macfarlane's geese that liked their play better than meat Scottish traditional saying, recorded from the early 17th century. The suggested explanation is that James VI of Scotland had been watching the wild geese of Loch Lomond, which were said to have a connection with the family of Macfarlane, pursuing one another. When one of the geese was brought to table, and found to be tough and poorly fed, James made this comment.

William McGonagall (1830–1902), Scottish poet, author of naive yet entertaining doggerel which has won him a reputation as one of the worst poets in the world.

> Beautiful Railway Bridge of the Silv'ry Tay!
> Alas, I am very sorry to say
> That ninety lives have been taken away
> On the last Sabbath day of 1879,
> Which will be remembered for a very long time.
> — William McGonagall 'The Tay Bridge Disaster'

Macgregor name of the Scottish clan to which Robert MacGregor of Campbell ('Rob Roy'), highland freebooter, belonged, and which in the 17th century was twice proscribed.

where Macgregor sits is the head of the table proverbial saying, mid 19th century, sometimes attributed to 'Rob Roy'. Other names are used as well as Macgregor, and in the late 16th century in *Euphues and his England*, John Lyly has the story of Agesilaus' son who, when mocked for being placed at the lower end of the table, answered that the upper end was where he was sitting.

McGuffin an object or device in a film or a book which serves merely as a trigger for the plot. Recorded from the late 20th century, the word is a Scottish surname, said to have been borrowed by the English film director, Alfred Hitchcock, from a humorous story involving such a pivotal factor.

Mach number the ratio of the speed of a body to the speed of sound in the surrounding medium, deriving from the name of Ernst Mach (1838–1916), Austrian physicist and philosopher of science, who did important work on aerodynamics.

Captain Macheath the dashing highwayman who is the central character of John Gay's *The Beggar's Opera* (1728); he is betrayed by the informer ➤ PEACHUM, but ultimately escapes from Newgate.

> Everyone likes him. Some call him a bit of a scoundrel, a latter-day Macheath playing out his own *Threepenny Opera*.
> — *Premiere* July 1990

Machiavel a person compared to ➤ MACHIAVELLI for favouring expediency over morality; the term is recorded from the late 16th century.

> Francis Urquhart . . . was a machiavel who climbed on top of the greasy pole by means of blackmail and murder.
> — *Sunday Telegraph* (Review) 28 November 1993

Niccolò di Bernardo dei Machiavelli (1469–1527), Italian statesman and political philosopher. After being arrested (though later cleared) by the Medicis on suspicion of conspiracy, he withdrew from public life. His best-known work is *The Prince* (1532), which advises rulers that the acquisition and effective use of power may necessitate unethical methods.

machina see ➤ DEUS *ex machina*.

machine see ➤ *the* GHOST *in the machine*.

macho[1] showing aggressive pride in one's masculinity. Recorded from the 1920s, the word comes from Mexican Spanish, meaning 'masculine or vigorous'.

MACHO[2] a compact object, such as a brown dwarf, a low-mass star, or a black hole, of a kind which it is thought may constitute part of the dark matter in galactic haloes. The term is an acronym from *Massive (Astrophysical) Compact Halo Object*.

Machu Picchu a fortified Inca town in the Andes in Peru, which the invading Spaniards never found. Although it was not an important fortress, it is famous for its dramatic position, perched high on a steep-sided ridge. It contains a palace, a temple to the sun, and extensive cultivation terraces. Discovered in 1911, it was named after the mountain that rises above it.

Machzor a Jewish prayer book for use at festivals.

Alexander Mackenzie (1764–1820), Scottish explorer of Canada. He discovered the **Mackenzie River** in 1789 and in 1793 became the first European to reach the Pacific Ocean by land along a northern route.

mute as a mackerel completely silent and unforthcoming; proverbial expression, mid 18th century.

See also ➤ *a* SPRAT *to catch a mackerel.*

mackerel sky a sky dappled with rows of small white fleecy (typically cirrocumulus) clouds, like the pattern on a mackerel's back, recorded from the mid 17th century. It is traditionally believed to herald a change in the weather:

> Mackerel sky, mackerel sky,
> Never long wet, never long dry.
> — Traditional weather rhyme

John McKinlay (1819–72), Scottish-born explorer. He led an expedition (1861) to search for the missing explorers Burke and Wills. He found only traces of their party, but carried out valuable exploratory work in the Australian interior.

Charles Rennie Mackintosh (1868–1928), Scottish architect, designer, and painter. A leading exponent of art nouveau, he pioneered the new concept of functionalism in architecture and interior design. Notable among his designs is the Glasgow School of Art (1898–1909) and four Glasgow tea rooms (1897–1912), with all their furniture and equipment.

Donald Maclean (1913–83), British Foreign Office official and Soviet spy. After acting as a Soviet agent from the late 1930s he fled to the USSR with Guy Burgess in 1951, following a warning from Kim Philby of impending proceedings against him.

Marshall McLuhan (1911–80), Canadian writer and thinker. He became famous in the 1960s for his phrase 'the medium is the message' and his argument that it is the characteristics of a particular medium rather than the information it disseminates which influence and control society.

Macmillanite a member of the body subsequently known as the Reformed Presbyterian Church of Scotland. It was named for John *Macmillan* (1670–1753), the first ordained leader of the Church.

McNaghten rules rules or criteria for judging criminal responsibility where there is a question of insanity. The name applied to the answers given in the House of Lords in 1843 after the trial of Daniel McNaghten for the murder of Sir Robert Peel's secretary, Edward Drummond, when five questions were put respecting crimes alleged to have been committed by persons suffering from insanity.

According to the rules, the defendant must show that he or she is suffering from a defect of reason arising out of 'a disease of the mind', and that, as a result of this defect, was unaware of the 'nature and quality' of his or her acts.

macrocosm the universe, the cosmos; among ancient writers, the 'great world' as distinguished from the 'little world' (*microcosm*) represented by human nature. In extended use, *macrocosm* has come to mean whole of a complex structure, especially as represented or epitomized in a small part of itself (a microcosm).

The word is recorded in English from the early 17th century; an earlier usage in *The Assembly of Gods* (?1475) is a mistake for *microcosm*.

macumba a black religious cult practised in Brazil, using sorcery, ritual dance, and fetishes.

Macy's name of a New York department store, founded in 1858, which by 1924 comprised the tallest and largest store premises in the world, stretching from Broadway to Seventh Avenue. The prominence of Macy's was tacitly acknowledged by Lyndon Johnson when he said of a prospective assistant, 'I don't want loyalty. I want *loyalty*. I want him to kiss my ass in Macy's window at high noon and tell me it smells like roses.'

mad see ➤ *whom the* GODS *would destroy they first make mad.*

mad as a hatter completely mad. Hat-makers sometimes suffered from mercury poisoning as a result of the use of mercurous nitrate in the manufacture of felt hats, and the idea was personified in one of the two eccentric hosts (the **Mad Hatter**) at the 'mad tea party' in Lewis Carroll's *Alice's Adventures in Wonderland* (1865).

mad as a March hare completely mad; the allusion here is to the running and leaping of hares in the breeding season, and again was reinforced by the character created by Lewis Carroll.

> In that direction . . . lives a Hatter: and in that direction . . . lives a March Hare . . . they're both mad.
> — Lewis Carroll *Alice's Adventures in Wonderland* (1865)

mad cow disease informal term for ➤ BSE, deriving from the characteristic agitation and staggering caused by the disease. Originally popularized by journalists, the term caught the public imagination, and in the late 1980s and early 1990s a number of humorous variations were coined.

don't get mad, get even proverbial saying, late 20th century.

Mad Parliament a name [after the post-classical Latin *insane Parliamentum*, recorded in 1274] given to the meeting of the barons at Oxford in 1258, under the leadership of Simon de Montfort, which passed the 'Provisions of Oxford' in order to restrain Henry III's misrule. The term is first recorded in English in Stow's *Summarie of English Chronicles* (1580).

Madame a title given to female members of the French royal family, as the eldest daughter of the French king or of the dauphin, or (in the reign of Louis XIV) the wife of ➤ MONSIEUR, the king's only brother.

Madchester a colloquial name for Manchester, especially as a centre of the UK music scene in the late 1980s and early 1990s.

> The explosion of the Madchester scene in 1989 when the Stone Roses, 808 State and Happy Mondays all made it into the charts.
> — *DJ* 6 July 1995

Madeba Map a 6th-century coloured mosaic map of Palestine discovered in 1896 in a church at *Madeba*, to the east of the Dead Sea.

Mademoiselle see also ➤ *La* GRANDE *Mademoiselle*.

Mademoiselle from Armentiers British soldiers' song (1918) of the First World War.

madison a cycle relay race for teams of two or more riders, typically held over several days, and

named after *Madison* Square Gardens, New York, the site of the first such race in 1892.

Madison Avenue a street in New York City, centre of the American advertising business, often used in allusion to the world of American advertising agents.

> The campaign draws on an ancient Madison Avenue credo: make an irritating ad, and the product will walk off the shelf.
> — *Time* 6 January 1992

madness see ➤ METHOD *in one's madness*, ➤ MIDSUMMER *madness*.

Madog a 12th-century Welsh prince who in some stories is said to have been the discoverer of America. He does not appear in contemporary sources, and is first mentioned by a 15th-century bard in connection with a mysterious voyage. The claim that he discovered America was first made by David Powel in *The Historie of Cambria* (1584), and after this the story was accepted and elaborated by a number of scholars. It is the base of *Madoc* (1805), a narrative poem by Robert Southey.

Madonna the Virgin Mary, a name (from Italian, meaning 'my lady') recorded in English from the mid 17th century.

madrasa a college for Islamic instruction. The word is Arabic, and comes from *darasa* 'to study'.

Madrid conditions the set of conditions (laid down by UK Prime Minister Margaret Thatcher at the European summit held in Madrid in June 1989) for the entry of the UK into full participation in the European Monetary System.

madrigal a part-song for several voices, especially one of the Renaissance period, typically arranged in elaborate counterpoint and without instrumental accompaniment. Originally used of a genre of 14th-century Italian songs, the term now usually refers to songs of the late 16th and early 17th centuries, in a free style strongly influenced by the text.

The word comes from Italian *madrigale* (from medieval Latin *carmen matricalis* 'simple song') from *matricalis* 'maternal or primitive', from *matrix* 'womb'.

Mae West an inflatable life jacket, originally as issued to RAF personnel during the Second World War, from the name of the American film actress Mae West, noted for her large bust.

Gaius **Maecenas** (*c.*70–8 BC), Roman statesman. He was a trusted adviser of Augustus, a writer, and a notable patron of poets such as Virgil and Horace. From the mid 16th century, the name has been used for a generous patron.

> There would be neither respect nor money from any local Mæcenas.
>
> — *Opera Now* May 1990

Maeldune in early Irish literature, the hero of *Immram Curaig Máele Dúin* [*Voyage of Máel Dúin's Boat*], one of the stories of fabulous sea voyages (*immrams*) written in Ireland between the late 8th and 11th centuries.

In this poem, Maeldune, who has put to sea to avenge his father's murder, is blown off course and into uncharted waters; in the subsequent voyage he and his foster-brothers encounter marvels and Maeldune experiences a spiritual transformation. At the end of the voyage he is reconciled with the murderers and becomes a Christian, abandoning his quest for vengeance. Tennyson's 'Voyage of Maeldune' (1880) was based on the story.

maelstrom a powerful whirlpool in the sea or a river, named (in the late 17th century, from early modern Dutch) after a mythical whirlpool supposed to exist in the Arctic Ocean, west of Norway:

> There is between the said Rost Islands, and Lofoote, a whirle poole, called Malestrand, which . . . maketh such a terrible noise, that it shaketh the rings in the doores of the inhabitants houses of the said Islands, ten miles of.
>
> — A. Jenkinson (*c.*1560) in R. Hakluyt *Principall Navigations* (1589)

The use of *maelstrom* as a proper name seems to come from Dutch maps, for example in Mercator's *Atlas* (1595).

The figurative use of the word to denote a scene or state of confused and violent movement or upheaval is recorded from the mid 19th century.

maenad in ancient Greece, a female follower of Bacchus, traditionally associated with divine possession and frenzied rites. Recorded from the late 16th century, the word comes via Latin from Greek *Mainas, Mainad-*, from *mainesthai* 'to rave'.

> She sneered at him almost with a maenad fierceness.
>
> — W. Lewis *Revenge for Love* (1937)

Maera in Greek legend, name of a dog belonging to Erigone, daughter of Icarius. When Icarius was killed by drunken men for introducing them to wine, Maera helped Erigone to find his body.

Erigone, who hanged herself, was set among the stars in the constellation *Virgo*; Maera became the lesser Dog-star *Procyon*.

Maeve in Irish legend, the legendary and sexually voracious queen of Conacht (*Medb*), who is the implacable enemy of ➤ CUCHULAIN, and who instigates the cattle-raid on Ulster to capture the Brown Bull of Cuailgne (see ➤ TAIN-BO-CUAILGNE).

Mafeking a town in South Africa, in North-West Province. In 1899–1900, during the Second Boer War, a small British force under the command of Baden-Powell was besieged there by the Boers for 215 days; its eventual relief was greeted in Britain with widespread celebration. Although the town was of little strategic significance, its successful defence, at a time when the war was going very badly for the British, excited great interest. The archaic verb **maffick**, meaning to celebrate uproariously, especially on an occasion of national celebration, derives from this, originally as a journalistic invention.

Mafia an organized international body of criminals, operating originally in Sicily and now especially in Italy and the US and having a complex and ruthless behavioural code, developed during the 18th–19th centuries. The word comes from Italian (Sicilian dialect), originally in the sense 'bragging'.

Maga a familiar name for *Blackwood's Magazine* (1817–1980, originally the *Edinburgh Monthly Magazine*) first recorded in a letter of July 1820 from Sir Walter Scott.

Magadha an ancient kingdom situated in the valley of the River Ganges in NE India (modern Bihar) which was the centre of several empires, notably those of the Mauryan and Gupta dynasties, between the 6th century BC and the 8th century AD.

the **Magdalen** ➤ *St* MARY *Magdalen*; also called the **Magdalene**. The name comes, in late Middle English, via ecclesiastical Latin from Greek *(Maria hē) Magdalēnē* 'Mary of *Magdala*' (to whom Jesus appeared after his resurrection, as recounted in John 20:1–18).

She was commonly identified (probably wrongly) with the sinner of Luke 8:37, and was traditionally represented in hagiology as a reformed prostitute elevated to sanctity by repentance and faith; from this come the archaic uses of *magdalen* to mean a reformed prostitute and a house for reformed prostitutes.

the Magdalene another name for ➤ *the* MAGDALEN.

Magdalenian of, relating to, or denoting the final Palaeolithic culture in Europe, following the Solutrean and dated to about 17,000–11,500 years ago. It is characterized by a range of bone and horn tools, and by highly developed cave art.

The name comes from French *Magdalénien* 'from La Madeleine', a site in the Dordogne, France, where objects from this culture were found.

Centuriators of Magdeburg a group of 16th-century Protestant divines who under the supervision of Matthias Flacius Illyricus (1520–75), compiled a 13-volume Church History of which each volume embraced a century. From its third edition (1757) the work was entitled *Centuriae Magdeburgenses* 'Magdeburg Centuries'.

Magdeburg hemispheres a pair of copper or brass hemispheres joined to form a hollow globe from which the air can be extracted to demonstrate the pressure of the atmosphere, which then prevents them from being pulled apart. They are named after the German city of *Magdeburg*, home of the inventor, Otto von Guericke (1602–86).

mage archaic term for a magician or learned person. Recorded from late Middle English, the word is an Anglicized form of Latin *magus*.

Magellan an American space probe, named for ➤ *Ferdinand* MAGELLAN, launched in 1989 to map the surface of Venus, using radar to penetrate the dense cloud cover. The probe was deliberately burned up in Venus's atmosphere in 1994.

Ferdinand Magellan (*c*.1480–1521), Portuguese explorer. In 1519 he sailed from Spain, rounding South America through the strait which now bears his name, and reached the Philippines in 1521. He was killed in a skirmish on Cebu; the survivors sailed back to Spain round Africa, completing the first circumnavigation of the globe (1522).

Magellanic Clouds two diffuse luminous patches in the southern sky, now known to be small irregular galaxies that are the closest to our own.

Magen David a hexagram used as a symbol of Judaism. Recorded from the early 20th century, the term comes from Hebrew, and means literally

'shield of David', with reference to David, king of Israel.

magenta a light mauvish-crimson which is one of the primary subtractive colours, complementary to green. It is named after *Magenta* in northern Italy, site of a battle (1859) fought between Napoleon III and Austrian forces during the second War of Italian Independence shortly before the dye (of blood-like colour) was discovered.

Maggid an intinerant Jewish preacher. Recorded from the late 19th century, the word comes from Hebrew *maggīd* 'narrator'.

Maggie's drawers in US military slang, a red flag used to indicate a miss in target practice, said to be in reference to a song entitled *Those Old Red Flannel Drawers That Maggie Wore*.

maggot an archaic term for a whimsical fancy, deriving (in the early 17th century) from the idea of someone having maggots in their brain.

Magi the 'wise men' from the East, often referred to as the **Three Magi**, who brought gifts to the infant Jesus (Matthew 2:1), said in later tradition to be kings named Caspar, Melchior, and Balthasar who brought gifts of gold, frankincense, and myrrh. Recorded from Old English, the word is the plural form of ➤ MAGUS.

magic the power of apparently influencing the course of events by using mysterious or supernatural forces. Recorded from late Middle English, the word comes ultimately from Greek *magikē (tekhnē)* 'art of a ➤ MAGUS'; magi were regarded as magicians.

See also ➤ BLACK *magic*, ➤ NATURAL *magic*, ➤ WHITE *magic*.

magic carpet especially in stories set in Arabia, a mythical carpet that is able to transport people through the air.

magic circle an inner group of politicians viewed as choosing the leader of the Conservative Party before this became an electoral matter. The phrase was coined by Iain Macleod in a critical article in the *Spectator* on the 'emergence' of Alec Douglas-Home in succession to Harold Macmillan in 1963.

> It is some measure of the tightness of the magic circle on this occasion that neither the Chancellor of the Exchequer nor the Leader of the House of Commons had any inkling of what was happening.
> — Iain Macleod in *Spectator* 17 January 1964

magic mushroom any toadstool with hallucino-genic properties, especially the liberty cap and its relatives, traditionally consumed by American Indians in Mexico.

Great Magician a name for Sir Walter Scott, which Lockhart's *Life of Scott* records was first coined in 'a set of beautiful stanzas, inscribed to Scott by Mr Wilson under the title of 'The Magic Mirror'; the name afterwards became 'one of his standing titles'.

Little Magician nickname of the American states-man Martin van Buren (1782–1862), 8th President of the US (1837–41), and one of the founders of the Democratic Party. The sobriquet derived from his reputation for political cunning and skill; John Ran-dolph of Roanoke (1773–1833) said of him, 'he rowed to his objective with muffled oars.'

Magician of the North a nickname for Walter Scott.

Maginot Line a system of fortifications con-structed by the French along their eastern border between 1929 and 1934, widely considered impreg-nable, but outflanked by German forces in 1940. It was named after André *Maginot* (1877–1932), a French minister of war. The *Maginot Line* may now be referred to allusively to indicate a preoccupation with what is an illusory means of defence.

> It is far better to anticipate and plan a policy of managed realignment than to suffer the consequences of a deluded belief that we can maintain indefinitely an unbreachable Maginot Line of towering sea walls and flood defences.
> — *Daily Telegraph* 6 August 1998

magistrate see ➤ the BLIND *Magistrate*, ➤ GLAS-GOW *magistrate*.

Magna Carta a charter of liberty and political rights obtained from King John of England by his rebellious barons at Runnymede in 1215. Although often violated by medieval kings, it came to be seen as the seminal document of English constitutional practice, as shown by the comment of the English jurist Edward Coke (1552–1634) on the Lords' Amendment to the Petition of Right, 17 May 1628:

> Magna Charta is such a fellow, that he will have no sovereign.
> — Edward Coke in J. Rushworth (ed.) *Historical Collections* (1659)

magna cum laude chiefly in North America, with great distinction (with reference to university de-grees and diplomas). The phrase is Latin, and means literally, 'with great praise'.

Magna Graecia the ancient Greek cities of south-ern Italy, founded from *c.*750 BC onwards by colon-ists from Euboea, Sparta, and elsewhere in Greece. The cities thrived until after the 5th century BC; the Pythagorean and Eleatic systems of philosophy arose there. The name is Latin, and means literally 'Great Greece'.

magna mater Latin meaning 'great mother'; a mother-goddess; a fertility goddess, especially ➤ CYBELE.

the Magnanimous epithet of Alfonso V of Ara-gon (1396–1458), a translation of Spanish *el Magnánimo*, and Philip, Landgrave of Hesse (1504–47), translating German *der Grossmütige*.

magnet a piece of iron (or an ore, alloy, or other material) which has its component atoms so or-dered that the material exhibits properties of mag-netism, such as attracting other iron-containing objects or aligning itself in an external magnetic field.

The word (which comes via Latin from Greek *magnēs lithos* 'lodestone') is recorded from late Middle English denoting 'lodestone', and from the early 17th century with the current sense.

Magnet Mountain a legendary mountain in India which in Mandeville's *Travels* is said to have the power of destroying ships by causing iron bonds to break and nails to fly out. The tradition is also found in the *Arabian Nights*, in the story of a 'mountain of black stone' which is said to have des-troyed many ships through its attracting iron so strongly, that when any ship passed it the ship's sides opened and all the nails flew out and became stuck fast to the mountain.

Magnetic Island an island in the Cumberland Is-lands, off the coast of northeastern Queensland, so named by Captain Cook because he believed (wrongly) that iron deposits in its hills affected his ship's compass.

Magnificat a canticle used in Christian liturgy, es-pecially at vespers and evensong, the text being the hymn of the Virgin Mary (Luke 1:46–55). The literal meaning of *Magnificat* in Latin is 'magnifies', and the opening words of the canticle translate as 'my soul magnifies the Lord'.

the Magnificent an epithet of ➤ LORENZO *de' Medici* (1449–92), translating Italian *il Magnifico*, and other rulers.

City of Magnificent Distances an informal name for Washington, DC.

magnifico informal term for an eminent, powerful, or illustrious person, originally (in the late 16th century) used to denote a Venetian magnate.

magnolia a tree or shrub with large, typically creamy-pink, waxy flowers, named after Pierre Magnol (1638–1715), French botanist.

Magnolias are especially associated with the southern states of the US, and the term **Steel Magnolia**, epitomizing a southern woman who has a steely character beneath a feminine and apparently fragile exterior, was applied particularly to Rosalynn Carter, First Lady of the US, 1977–81.

Magnolia State informal name for Mississippi, the emblem of which is the magnolia flower.

magnum a wine bottle of twice the standard size. Recorded from the late 18th century, the word comes from Latin, neuter (used as a noun) of *magnus* 'great'.

magnum opus a large and important work of art, music, or literature, especially one regarded as the most important work of an artist or writer. Recorded from the late 18th century, the phrase means in Latin 'great work'.

St Magnus of Orkney (*c*.1075–1116), convert to Christianity and martyr; he was put to death by his cousin Haakon, co-earl of Orkney, accepting his violent death and praying for his killers. He was regarded as a martyr and became an important Scottish saint; he is said to have appeared promising victory to Robert Bruce on the night before Bannockburn.

    ☐ **EMBLEM** His emblem is an axe.
    ☐ **FEAST DAY** His feast day is 16 April.

Magnus effect the force exerted on a rapidly spinning cylinder or sphere moving through air or another fluid in a direction at an angle to the axis of spin. This force is responsible for the swerving of balls when hit or thrown with spin. It is named after the German scientist Heinrich G. *Magnus* (1802–70).

Magog see ➤ GOG *and Magog.*

magpie the *magpie* is used in similes or comparisons to refer to a person who collects things, especially things of little use or value, or a person who chatters idly, and in traditional belief was sometimes regarded as a bird of ill-omen.

The name is recorded from the late 16th century, and is probably a shortening of dialect *maggot the pie*, *maggoty-pie*, from Magot (Middle English pet form of the given name *Marguerite*) + *pie* (ultimately from Latin *pica* 'magpie').

See also ➤ ONE *for sorrow, two for mirth*

magus a member of a priestly caste in ancient Persia (of Akkadian or Median origin), which through its official status in western Iran became the principal protagonist of Zoroastrianism. The term was then extended to denote a person skilled in eastern magic and astrology; a magician or sorcerer.

See also ➤ MAGE, ➤ MAGI, ➤ SIMON *Magus.*

mah-jong a Chinese game played, usually by four people, with 136 or 144 rectangular pieces called tiles. The name is recorded in English from the early 20th century, and comes from Chinese dialect *ma-tsiang*, literally 'sparrows'.

Mahabharata one of the two great Sanskrit epics of the Hindus (the other is the *Ramayana*), that evolved over centuries, existing in its present form since *c*.400 AD. Probably the longest single poem in the world, it describes the civil war waged between the five Pandava brothers and their one hundred stepbrothers at Kuruksetra near modern Delhi; the numerous interpolated episodes include the *Bhagavadgita*.

Mahamad the body of trustees ruling a Sephardic synagogue.

mahant in Hinduism, a chief priest of a temple or the head of a monastery.

maharaja an Indian prince. The word is recorded in English from the late 17th century, and comes via Hindi from Sanskrit *mahā* 'great' + *rājan* 'raja'.

maharani a maharaja's wife or widow.

Maharishi a great Hindu sage or spiritual leader.

mahatma (in the Indian subcontinent) a person regarded with reverence or loving respect; a holy person or sage. The title was applied particularly to ➤ *Mahatma* GANDHI (1869–1948), known as **the Mahatma.**

Mahayana one of the two major traditions of Buddhism, now practised in a variety of forms especially in China, Tibet, Japan, and Korea. The tradition emerged around the 1st century AD and is typically concerned with personal spiritual practice and the ideal of the bodhisattva.

Mahdi in popular Muslim belief, a spiritual and temporal leader who will rule before the end of the world and restore religion and justice. Not part of orthodox doctrine, the concept of such a figure was introduced into popular Islam through Sufi channels influenced by Christian doctrine. Notable among those claiming to be this leader was Muhammad Ahmad of Dongola in Sudan (1843–85), whose revolutionary movement captured Khartoum and overthrew the Egyptian regime.

mahogany name for a Cornish drink made of gin and treacle, which Boswell in 1791 recorded as being drunk by Cornish fishermen.

Mahomet an archaic form of ➤ MUHAMMAD, recorded from late Middle English; the alternative *Mahound* is also found.

See also ➤ *if the* MOUNTAIN *will not come to Mahomet, Mahomet must go to the mountain.*

Mahomet's coffin according to a legend current in European sources and recorded from the medieval period, the coffin of Muhammad was suspended without visible supports, but by magnets or lodestones, from the ceiling of his tomb; Gibbon in *Decline and Fall of the Roman Empire* (1776–88) says that 'the Greeks and Latins have invented and propagated the…ridiculous story that Mohammed's iron tomb is suspended in the air at Mecca.' He refers to the 15th century Byzantine historian Laonicus Chalcocondyles, and points out that the Prophet was not buried at Mecca, and that his tomb at Medina, which has been visited 'by millions', is placed on the ground.

Mary Wollstonecraft in *The Rights of Women* (1792) uses the image (in a reference which indicates that she expected the story to be a familiar one, saying, 'women appear to be suspended by destiny, according to the vulgar tale of Mahomet's coffin') to evoke the notion of being held in a kind of limbo.

Maia in Greek mythology, the daughter of Atlas and mother of Hermes.

In Roman mythology, *Maia* is a goddess associated with Vulcan and also (by confusion with the Greek goddess) with Mercury, the Roman equivalent of Hermes. She was worshipped on 1 May and 15 May; that month is named after her.

maiasaur a genus of large duck-billed dinosaur, the members of which are notable for the association of some of their remains with nests containing eggs and young. The implication of parental care, and of colonial nesting at traditional sites,

prompted the name *good mother lizard* for the newly discovered genus: the word maiasaur comes from the Greek elements *maia* 'good mother' and *saura* 'lizard'.

maid see also ➤ HOLY *Maid of Kent*, ➤ *Maid* MARIAN.

Maid of Athens the heroine of Byron's poem of that name, said to have been based on the young daughter of a Mrs Makri, a widow whose husband had been vice-consul in Athens. She may be taken as the type of a romantic young girl.

Maid of Brittany Eleanor of Brittany, niece of King John, who after the murder of her brother Arthur (1187–1203) was kept in close confinement by her uncle.

Maid of Buttermere a name given to the local beauty Mary Robinson (also known as the *Buttermere Beauty*) by Wordsworth. She was bigamously married in 1802 by the forger and confidence trickster John Hatfield (1758–1803); arrested and charged with forgery, he was executed in the following year.

The story of Mary Robinson and John Hatfield has been the subject of a number of novels, plays, and poems, most recently *The Maid of Buttermere* (1996) by Melvin Bragg.

Maid of Norway Margaret of Norway (1283–90), granddaughter of Alexander III of Scotland, who on her grandfather's death was acknowledged queen of Scotland; she died in the Orkneys on her way to Scotland. She is the 'king's daughter o'Noroway' of the traditional ballad 'Sir Patrick Spens'.

Maid of Orleans name given to ➤ JOAN *of Arc*; 'Maid' here translates French *Pucelle*, and 'Orleans' represents the support given to her by the French royal and ducal house.

Maid of Saragossa Marí Augustín, who in the Peninsular War was one of the defenders of Zaragoza against the French siege of 1808–9; she is celebrated under this name in Byron's poem *Don Juan*.

Maida name of a deerhound belonging to Sir Walter Scott; she died in 1824, and Scott composed an epitaph for her which was translated into Latin by Lockhart.

See also ➤ CAMP.

Maida Vale a district of west London; the name derives ultimately from the battle of *Maida* in 1806.

maiden see also ➤ IRON *maiden*, ➤ RHINE *maiden*, ➤ SHIELD-*maiden*.

maiden Malcolm IV (1141–65), king of Scotland, was known as **the Maiden;** the Annals of Ulster praise him as a devoted Christian, but he was also an active and warlike king.

The **maiden** is also the name given to a form of the guillotine used in 16th and 17th century Scotland for beheading criminals of rank. According to tradition, it was introduced by James Douglas, Earl of Morton (d. 1581), Regent of Scotland, who was himself beheaded with it.

Maiden Castle a prehistoric site in Dorset, consisting of an enormous Iron Age earthwork surrounded by a series of ramparts; excavations in 1934–7 show that settlement there dated back to the Neolithic period.

maiden speech the first speech delivered in the House of Commons or House of Lords by a Member, an expression dating from the early 18th century. It was of the younger Pitt's maiden speech in February 1781 that Edmund Burke (1729–97), noting the resemblance to Chatham, commented, 'Not merely a chip of the old "block", but the old block itself.

the answer to a maiden's prayer an eligible bachelor; the phrase dates from the early 20th century, although an early 19th-century example of *the maid of all-work's prayer* is found.

maieutic of or denoting the Socratic mode of enquiry, which aims to bring a person's latent ideas into clear consciousness. Recorded from the mid 17th century, the word comes from Greek *maieutikos*, from *maieuesthai* 'act as a midwife', from *maia* 'midwife'.

maigre (in the Roman Catholic Church) denoting a day on which abstinence from meat is ordered; (of food) suitable for eating on maigre days. The word is French (literally 'lean'), and is recorded from the late 17th century.

Commissaire Maigret the pipe-smoking French detective in a series of novels by Georges Simenon (1903–89) beginning in 1931; Maigret relies on his understanding of the criminal's motives rather than scientific deduction to solve crimes and the novels show considerable insight into human psychology.

mail see ➤ COAT *of mail*.

mailed fist the threat or show of armed force, the display of political ruthlessness. Translating German *mit gepanzerter Faust*, the phrase is recorded from the late 19th century, as a report in the *Times* of 17 December 1897 of a speech by Emperor Wilhelm II of Germany, 'But should any one essay to detract from our just rights or to injure us, then up and at him with your mailed fist.'

Maillotin an insurgent in the Parisian uprising of 1382, in protest at levels of taxation; the name comes from the rioters having been armed with mauls (*maillets*).

mails and duties in Scottish usage, the rents of an estate; *mail* here means a payment, a tribute, as in the second element of ➤ BLACKMAIL.

Moses Maimonides (1135–1204), Jewish philosopher and Rabbinic scholar, born in Spain. He eventually settled in Cairo, where he became head of the Jewish community. His *Guide for the Perplexed* (1190) attempts to reconcile Talmudic scripture with the philosophy of Aristotle.

A later inscription on his tomb read, 'From Moses to Moses there was none like unto Moses.'

main (in the game of hazard) a number (5, 6, 7, 8, or 9) called by a player before dice are thrown. Recorded from the 16th century (and also used to designate a match between fighting cocks), the word probably comes from the phrase *main chance*, in the original sense 'the most important eventuality'.

See also ➤ *an* EYE *to the main chance*.

Main Plot the more important of two plots (the other was the ➤ BYE *Plot*) against the government of James I uncovered in 1603; the plan was to replace the king with the Lady Arabella Stuart.

Main Street chiefly in the US, used in reference to the materialism, mediocrity, or parochialism regarded as typical of small-town life, from the title of a novel (1920) by Sinclair Lewis.

> The President . . . was an amalgam of liberal traditions . . . and the values of Main Street.
> — B. Garfield *Line of Succession* (1972)

as Maine goes, so goes the nation American political saying, *c*.1840, asserting that electoral success in Maine was an indicator of national fortune; it was reworked by the American Democratic politician James Farley (1888–1976), to **as Maine goes, so goes Vermont**, after predicting correctly that Franklin Roosevelt would carry all but two states in the election of 1936.

Maine Law a law forbidding the manufacture or sale of intoxicating liquors, in particular, the prohibitory law passed in Maine in 1851.

maintenance see ➤ CAP *of maintenance*.

Madame de Maintenon (1635–1719), Françoise d'Aubigné, mistress and later second wife of the French king Louis XIV. In 1669 she became the governess of Louis's children by his previous mistress, ➤ *Madame de* MONTESPAN and married Louis after his first wife's death in 1683.

Maioli a French style of bookbinding with elaborate gold tooling, used for some of the books in the library of Thomas Mahieu (fl. 1549–72), French book-collector and secretary to Catherine de Medici (*Maioli* is a Latinized form of his name).

Maison Carrée a Roman temple at Nîmes in France, which according to an inscription was dedicated to Gaius and Lucius Caesar, grandsons and adopted heirs of the Emperor ➤ AUGUSTUS.

Maitland Club a club founded at Glasgow in 1828 for the publication of works on the literature and antiquities of Scotland.

Maitreya the Buddha who will appear in the future; a representation of this Buddha. The word is Sanskrit, from *mitra* 'friend or friendship'.

majesty the title given to a sovereign or a sovereign's wife or widow. Originally recorded (in Middle English) in the sense of 'greatness of God', the word comes ultimately from Latin *major* 'greater'.

While the current sense dates from late Middle English, it was not until the 17th century that **Your Majesty** entirely superseded the other customary forms of address to the sovereign in English; Henry VIII and Elizabeth I were often addressed as *Your Grace* and *Your Highness*.

See also ➤ APOSTOLIC *Majesty*.

Major Prophet each of the prophets, Isaiah, Jeremiah, and Ezekiel, for whom the three longer prophetic books of the Old Testament are named and whose prophecies they record.

majority see ➤ MORAL *Majority*.

makara a mythical crocodile or other sea-animal, variously represented in Indian art; the equivalent of Capricorn in the signs of the zodiac. The word is from Sanskrit.

make do and mend wartime slogan, 1940s.

make hay while the sun shines proverbial saying, mid 16th century.

as you make your bed, so you must lie on it proverbial saying, late 16th century.

Malabar Christians a group of Christians of SW India who trace their foundation to a mission of St Thomas the Apostle and have historically used a Syriac liturgy. Many now form a Uniate (Catholic) Church; others have links to the Syrian Orthodox or the Anglican Church.

Malachi a book of the Bible belonging to a period before Ezra and Nehemiah. The word in Hebrew means literally 'my messenger'; *Malachi* is probably not a personal name, though often taken as such.

Malachi Malagrowther the pseudonym under which Sir Walter Scott, in 1826, wrote three letters on the subject of the Scottish paper currency, to the *Edinburgh Weekly Journal*.

Malakoff a fort near Sevastopol captured by the French in 1855 in the Crimean War; the French general, Pélissier, took the title of Duc de Malakoff, and the name was also used for a suburb of Paris. At the capture of the fort, the French soldier and statesman the Comte de Macmahon (1808–93) is reputed to have said, '*J'y suis, j'y reste* [Here I am, and here I stay].'

malaprop the mistaken use of a word in place of a similar-sounding one, often with unintentionally amusing effect, as in, for example, 'dance a *flamingo*' (instead of *flamenco*), from the name of the character Mrs *Malaprop* in Sheridan's play *The Rivals* (1775).

Malbrouck s'en va-t-en guerre opening line of a traditional French song, said to have become fashionable through being sung as a cradle song by a nurse to one of the children of Louis XVI and Marie Antoinette; *Lesley Castle*, an unfinished novel in the juvenilia of Jane Austen, refers to the tune in the words, 'she might even…play Malbrook (which is the only tune I ever really like)'.

It is often said that *Malbrouck* stands for the Duke of Marlborough, but in fact the name is found in the *chansons de gestes* and other literature of the Middle Ages.

Malcolm III (*c*.1031–93), king of Scotland, son of Duncan I, reigned 1058–93; known as **Malcolm Canmore** (from Gaelic *Ceann-mor* great head). He came to the throne after killing Macbeth in battle (1057), and was responsible for helping to form Scotland into an organized kingdom.

Malcolm IV (1141–65), king of Scotland, reigned 1153–65; known as **Malcolm the Maiden**. His reign witnessed a progressive loss of power to Henry II of England; he died young and without an heir.

Malcolm X (1925–65), American political activist. He joined the Nation of Islam in 1946 and became a vigorous campaigner for black rights, initially advocating the use of violence. In 1964 after pilgrimage to Mecca he converted to orthodox Islam and moderated his views on black separatism; he was assassinated the following year.

Malebolge in Dante's *Inferno*, name of the eighth circle of Hell, consisting of ten rock-bound concentric circular valleys. The term came to be used in English to mean a pool of filth, a hellish place or condition.

François de Malherbe (1555–1628), French poet. An architect of classicism in poetic form and grammar, he criticized excess of emotion and ornamentation and the use of Latin and dialectal forms. The French critic and poet Nicolas Boileau (1636–1711) said of him, 'He was the first in France to give poetry a proper flow'.

Malibu a resort on the Pacific coast of southern California, immediately to the west of Los Angeles, noted for its beaches.

malice in law, wrongful intention, especially as increasing the guilt of certain offences; a person who refusing to plead in a court of law may be adjudged **mute of malice**. Recorded from Middle English, the word comes via Old French from Latin *malitia*, from *malus* 'bad'.

malice aforethought wrongful intent that was in the mind beforehand, especially as an element in murder.

Malignant a person who is disaffected towards constituted authority, a malcontent; especially (in Parliamentarian terminology), a supporter of the royalist cause during the English civil war. This may ultimately derive from established usage of the adjective in 16th-century Protestant polemic, as in the phrase **Church malignant**.

The first use of the noun in this sense is found in the 1642 *Declaration* of Charles I, 'That to be a Traitor (which is defined, and every Man undertands) should be no Crime; and to be called a Malignant (which no Body knows the Meaning of) should be Ground enough for close imprisonment?'

Maliki a member of one of the four sects of Sunni Muslims, following the rite of the Muslim jurist Malik ibn Anas (713–795).

malison archaic word for a curse.

malkin a designation (sometimes as if a proper name) for a cat or a hare.
See also ➤ GRIMALKIN.

the Mall a tree-bordered walk in St James's Park, London, so named in the late 17th century because it was the site of a *pall-mall* alley (see ➤ PALL *Mall*).

This gave rise (in the 18th century) to the sense of a sheltered walk or promenade, and finally to the modern sense of a **shopping mall**, a large enclosed shopping area from which traffic is excluded. In the US, young people frequenting malls for social purposes may be called **mall rats**.

mallam (in Nigeria and other parts of Africa) a learned man or scribe.

Mallard an express steam locomotive of the A4 pacific class, designed by the British railway engineer Nigel Gresley (1876–1941), which in 1938 achieved a world speed record of 126 mph.

mallard the duck which is the ancestor of most domestic ducks, the male having a dark green head and white collar. The name comes (in Middle English) from Old French 'wild drake', from *masle* 'male'.

The Mallard is a festival celebrated on 14 January at All Souls College, Oxford. The ceremony of the **Hunting of the Mallard** is traditionally performed once every hundred years on the same date in the first year of every new century.

mallecho mischief; the word occurs only in **miching mallecho**, in and after Shakespeare's *Hamlet*, 'Marry, this is miching mallecho; it means mischief.' The meaning and origin of the phrase are uncertain, but *miching* is usually taken to mean 'skulking'.

Malleus Maleficarum (or *Hexenhammer*), the 'Hammer of Witches', published in 1484 by Jakob Sprenger, the Dominican inquisitor of Cologne, and

Heinrich Krämer, prior of Cologne. It was the text-book of the day on witchcraft, setting out how it may be discovered and how it may be punished.

malmsey now, a fortified Madeira wine of the sweetest type. Originally, a strong, sweet white wine imported from Greece and the eastern Mediterranean islands. The word came into English from Middle Dutch via Old French from *Monemvasia*, the name of a port in SE mainland Greece.

George, Duke of Clarence (1449–78), brother of Edward IV, was said by contemporary chroniclers to have been drowned in a butt of malmsey while prisoner in the Tower of London.

Malone Society founded by Walter Wilson Greg in 1906 for the purpose of making accessible materials for the study of early English drama, by printing dramatic texts and documents. Its name is taken from the literary critic and Shakespearian scholar Edmond Malone (1741–1812).

Thomas Malory (d.1471), English writer. His major work, *Le Morte d'Arthur* (printed 1483), is a prose translation of a collection of the legends of King Arthur, selected from French and other sources.

Marcello Malpighi (c.1628–94), Italian microscopist. He discovered the alveoli and capillaries in the lungs and the fibres and red cells of clotted blood, and demonstrated the pathway of blood from arteries to veins.

Battle of Malplaquet a battle in 1709 during the War of the Spanish Succession, near the village of Malplaquet in northern France, on the border with Belgium. A force of allied British and Austrian troops under the Duke of Marlborough won a victory over the French.

Malta an island country in the central Mediterranean, which historically has been of great strategic importance. It has been held in turn by invaders including the Greeks, Arabs, Normans, and Knights Hospitallers or **Knights of Malta**. It was annexed by Britain in 1814 and was an important naval base until independence within the Commonwealth in 1964. During the Second World War the island was awarded the ➤ GEORGE *Cross* for its endurance under Axis air attack between 1940 and 1942. Besides Malta itself, the country includes two other inhabited islands, Gozo and Comino.

Maltese cross a cross with arms of equal length which broaden from the centre and have their ends indented in a shallow V-shape, so named because the cross was formerly worn by the Knights of Malta, a religious order.

Thomas Robert Malthus (1766–1834), English economist and clergyman. In *Essay on Population* (1798) he argued that without the practice of 'moral restraint' the population tends to increase at a greater rate than its means of subsistence, resulting in the population checks of war, famine, and epidemic.

Malvolio in Shakespeare's *Twelfth Night* (1601), the Puritan steward of Olivia who through his consciousness of moral superiority and personal worth is tricked by ➤ *Sir Toby* BELCH and his companions into believing that Olivia is in love with him; the behaviour into which they persuade him leads to his being confined for insanity.

> He smiled on me in quite a superior sort of way, such a smile as would have become the face of Malvolio.
> — Bram Stoker *Dracula* (1897)

Mamamouchi former term for a pompous-sounding title or a person assuming such a title, a ridiculous pretender to elevated dignity. The word is pseudo-Turkish, and comes from the title pretended to have been conferred by the Sultan upon M. Jourdain, in Molière's play *Le bourgeois gentilhomme* (1670).

> This ridiculous Mamamouchi [The Duke of Newcastle, Chancellor of Cambridge University].
> — Horace Walpole letter, 1749

Mambrino in Ariosto's *Orlando Furioso*, a pagan king whose magic helmet is acquired by Rinaldo. In Don Quixote (Part I) there is frequent mention of **Mambrino's helmet**. Don Quixote, seeing a barber riding with his brass basin upon his head, takes this for the golden helmet of Mambrino, and gets possession of it.

> Round-topped white manilla hat like Mambrino's helmet.
> — John Herschel letter, 28 November 1833

Mameluke a member of a regime that formerly ruled parts of the Middle East. Descended from slaves brought from the Caucasus and central Asia as bodyguards by the caliphs and sultans of Egypt, they ruled Syria (1260–1516) and Egypt (1250–1517), and continued as a ruling military caste in Ottoman Egypt until massacred by the viceroy Muhammad Ali in 1811.

The name comes from French *mameluk*, from

Arabic *mamlūk* (passive participle used as a noun meaning 'slave'), from *malaka* 'possess'.

Mammon wealth regarded as an evil influence or false object of worship and devotion. It was taken by medieval writers as the name of the devil of covetousness, and revived in this sense by Milton:

> Mammon, the least erected spirit that fell
> From heaven, for even in heaven his looks and thoughts
> Were always downward bent, admiring more
> The riches of heaven's pavement, trodden gold,
> Than aught divine.
> — John Milton *Paradise Lost* (1667)

See also ➤ *you cannot serve* God *and Mammon.*

the mammon of unrighteousness money, in a phrase from Luke 16:19, 'And I say unto you, Make to yourselves friends of the mammon of unrighteousness; that, when ye fail, they may receive you into everlasting habitations.'

mammoth a large extinct elephant of the Pleistocene epoch, typically hairy with a sloping back and long curved tusks. Recorded from the early 18th century, the word comes from Russian *mamo(n)t*, and is probably of Siberian origin. A gloss in an early 17th-century Russian-English dictionary at the word *maimanto* notes that the animal in question is 'as they say a sea elephant, which is never seene, but according to the Samyites he workes himself under grownde and so they finde his teeth or hornes or bones in Pechore and Nova Zemla.'

The adjectival use meaning 'huge' developed in the early 19th century.

Mammoth Cave in Kentucky, the largest known cave system in the world. It consists of over 480 km (300 miles) of charted passageways and contains some spectacular rock formations.

> The great cave in Kentucky is called the Mammoth Cave, although none of the remains of that animal have been found in it.
> — J. Flint *Letters from America* (1822)

man see also ➤ clothes *make the man,* ➤ Kentish *man,* ➤ *Man in the* Iron *Mask,* ➤ *Man of* Kent, ➤ *man of* wax, ➤ manners *maketh man,* ➤ midsummer *man,* ➤ *the* Mounties *always get their man,* ➤ mouse *and man,* ➤ red *man,* ➤ savage *man,* ➤ Selsdon *man,* ➤ Tollund *Man,* ➤ twelfth *man,* ➤ wild *man.*

am I not a man and a brother? the motto on the seal of the British and Foreign Anti-Slavery Society, 1787, depicting a kneeling slave in chains uttering these words.

man cannot live by bread alone proverbial saying, late 19th century, with biblical allusion:

> man shall not live by bread alone, but by every word that proceedeth out of the mouth of God.
> — Bible (AV) St Matthew ch. 4, v. 4

a man for all seasons a person who is ready for any situation or contingency, or adaptable to any circumstance; originally, as a description of St Thomas More:

> As time requireth, a man of marvellous mirth and pastimes, and sometime of as sad gravity, as who say: a man for all seasons.
> — Robert Whittington *Vulgaria* (1521)

Erasmus had applied the idea earlier, describing More in *In Praise of Folly* (1509) as 'a man of all hours'.

Man Friday in Daniel Defoe's novel *Robinson Crusoe* (1719), Crusoe's servant, whom he usually refers to as 'my man Friday':

> And first, I made him know his Name should be Friday, which was the Day I sav'd his Life.
> — Daniel Defore *Robinson Crusoe* (1719)

From the early 19th century the term has been used to designate a (male) helper or follower.

> She had become the superefficient man Friday to the executive director of a large foundation.
> — Louis Auchincloss *Book Class* (1984)

See also ➤ girl *Friday.*

whatever man has done, man may do proverbial saying, mid 19th century.

man in the moon a mythical person supposed to live in the moon. Inhabitants of the moon were postulated in ancient and Hellenistic Greek texts; the use in English, recorded from Middle English, derives from the imagined semblance of a person or a human face in the disc of the (full) moon. By the mid 16th century, the *man in the moon* had become proverbial as the type of someone too distant to have any understanding or knowledge of a person's circumstances.

a man is as old as he feels, and a woman as old as she looks proverbial saying, late 19th century.

man is the measure of all things proverbial saying, mid 16th century.

Man of December a nickname of Napoleon III, referring to December 1848, when he was elected President of the Second Republic.

Man of Destiny Napoleon I regarded as an instrument of destiny, a phrase first recorded in English in

Walter Scott's *The Life of Napoleon Buonaparte* (1827), 'The great plans which the Man of Destiny had been called upon earth to perform.'

Man of Ross a nickname of the philanthropist John Kyrle (1637–1724), eulogized by Pope in *Epistle III* (1736) 'But all our praises why should Lords engross? Rise honest Muse! and sing the Man of Ross.' Pope's poem stresses the point that while Kyrle's estate was not large, he spent little on himself and used his money for his charities.

Man of Sedan a nickname of Napoleon III, referring to his defeat by the Prussians at the Battle of Sedan in 1870, which marked the end of the French Second Empire.

man of sin a biblical phrase, in the second Epistle to the Thessalonians, which is generally understood to mean Antichrist:

> That day shall not come, except there come a falling away first, and that man of sin be revealed, the son of perdition.
> — Bible (AV) 2 Thessalonians ch. 2, v. 3

Man of Sorrows a name for Jesus Christ, deriving from a prophecy in Isaiah 53:3, 'He is despised and rejected of men; a man of sorrows, and acquainted with grief'; in art represented as an image of Christ surrounded by instruments of the Passion.

man of the match the player adjudged to have played best in a particular game (especially soccer and cricket).

man proposes, God disposes proverbial saying, mid 15th century.

man who broke the bank at Monte Carlo title of a popular Victorian music-hall song commemorating a feat of 1886.

the man who is born in a stable is not a horse proverbial saying, mid 19th century; sometimes attributed to the Duke of Wellington, who asserted that being born in Ireland did not make him Irish.

man's extremity is God's opportunity proverbial saying, early 17th century.

mana especially in Polynesian, Melanesian, and Maori belief, pervasive supernatural or magical power.

manaia a motif in Maori carving with a birdlike head and a human body.

Manannán the son of Lir, a highly popular god of the old Gaelic pantheon, the subject of many legends and the patron of sailors and merchants. The Isle of Man was his favourite abode, and is said to take its name from him. There he has degenerated into a legendary giant, with three legs (seen revolving in the coat of arms of the island).

Manasseh in the Bible, a Hebrew patriarch, son of Jacob. Also, the tribe descended from him.

Manasses see ➤ PRAYER *of Manasses*.

Manchester Martyrs three Fenians, William O'Meara Allen, Michael Larkin, and William O'Brien, who were hanged at Manchester in 1867, for their part in the rescue of Thomas Kelly and Timothy Deasy, two leading Fenians, in the course of which a police sergeant was shot dead.

In a statement from the dock, one of the accused, Edward Condon (convicted but not executed) used the phrase God save Ireland; this became the inspiration for Timothy Daniel Sullivan's nationalist song:

> 'God save Ireland!' said the heroes;
> 'God save Ireland', say they all;
> Whether on the scaffold high
> Or the battlefield we die,
> Oh, what matter when for Erin dear we fall.
> — Timothy Daniel Sullivan 'God Save Ireland' (1867)

Nine years later the nationalist leader Charles Stewart Parnell (1846–91), objecting to the expression 'the Manchester murders' in connection with the escape of Kelly and Deasy, asserted, 'I do not believe, and I never shall believe, that any murder was committed at Manchester.'

what Manchester says today, the rest of England says tomorrow proverbial saying, late 19th century.

Manchester School a group of liberal politicians and their followers led by Richard Cobden and John Bright, influential *c*.1840–1860, which met originally in Manchester to advocate free trade and the reduction of state intervention in commerce and industry.

manchet former term for a loaf of the finest kind of wheaten bread. Recorded from late Middle English, the word may come from obsolete *maine* 'flour of the finest quality' + obsolete *cheat*, denoting a kind of wheaten bread.

Manchu see also ➤ *Dr Fu Manchu.*

Manchu a member of a people originally living in Manchuria, who formed the last imperial dynasty of China (1644–1912). The name is from the Manchu language, and means literally 'pure'.

Manchukuo name given in 1932 to Manchuria, a mountainous region forming the NE portion of China, which was declared an independent state by Japan; it was restored to China in 1945.

mancus a money of account used in various parts of Western Europe between the 8th and 12th centuries, and in England equivalent to thirty silver pence.

Mancunian a native or inhabitant of Manchester; the name comes (in the early 20th century) from *Mancunium,* the Latin name of Manchester.

Mandaean a member of a Gnostic sect surviving in Iraq and SW Iran, who regard John the Baptist as the Messiah. They stress salvation through knowledge of the divine origin of the soul.

The name comes from Mandaean Aramaic *mandaia* 'Gnostics, those who have knowledge', from *manda* 'knowledge'.

mandala a circular figure representing the universe in Hindu and Buddhist symbolism; in psychoanalysis, such a symbol in a dream, representing the dreamer's search for completeness and self-unity. The word comes from Sanskrit *maṇḍala* 'disc'.

Mandalay a port on the Irrawaddy River in central Burma (Myanmar), founded in 1857, and until 1885 the capital of the Burmese kingdom. It is an important Buddhist religious centre.

mandamus a judicial writ issued as a command to an inferior court or ordering a person to perform a public or statutory duty. The word is Latin, and means literally 'we command'.

mandarin an official in any of the senior grades of the former imperial Chinese civil service. *Mandarins* were chosen by examination, and there were nine grades, each of which was distinguished by the material from which the round ornament or 'button' on top of the official headgear was made. From the early 18th century, *Mandarin* has also been used for the standard literary and official form of Chinese.

Recorded in English in the late 16th century, the word comes from Portuguese *mandarim,* via Malay, from Hindi *mantrī* 'counsellor'. The current transferred meaning of a powerful official or senior bureaucrat, especially one perceived as reactionary and secretive, developed in the early 20th century.

mandarin orange a small flattish citrus fruit with a loose skin, especially a variety with a yellow-orange skin, perhaps named from the colour of the fruit being likened to the official yellow robes of a ➤ MANDARIN.

mandate an official order or commission to do something; the authority to carry out a policy or course of action, regarded as given by the electorate to a party or candidate that is victorious in an election.

Recorded from the early 16th century, the word comes from Latin *mandatum* 'something commanded', and ultimately from *manus* 'hand' + *dare* 'give'. Historically, it was applied particularly to a commission from the League of Nations to a member state to administer a territory, as in 'the British mandate in Palestine'.

Nelson Mandela (1918–), South African statesman, President since 1994. He was sentenced to life imprisonment in 1964 as an activist for the African National Congress (ANC). Released in 1990, as leader of the ANC he engaged in talks on the introduction of majority rule with President F. W. de Klerk, with whom he shared the Nobel Peace Prize in 1993. He became the country's first democratically elected President in 1994, leaving office in 1999.

Mandelbrot set a particular set of complex numbers which has a highly convoluted fractal boundary when plotted. It is named after the Polish-born French mathematician Benoit Mandelbrot (1924–), who is known as the pioneer of fractal geometry.

John de Mandeville (14th century), English nobleman. He is remembered as the reputed author of a book of travels and travellers' tales which was actually compiled by an unknown hand from the works of several writers.

mandir a Hindu temple.

mandorla another term for ➤ VESICA *piscis*. The word is Italian, and means literally 'almond', referring to the pointed oval shape of the figure.

mandragora a poetic or literary term for the mandrake, especially when used as a narcotic. Recorded from Old English, the name comes via medieval Latin from Latin and Greek *mandragoras*.

> Not poppy, nor mandragora,
> Nor all the drowsy syrups of the world,
> Shall ever medicine thee to that sweet sleep
> Which thou owedst yesterday.
> — William Shakespeare *Othello* (1602–4)

mandrake a Mediterranean plant of the nightshade family, with white or purple flowers and large yellow berries. It has a forked fleshy root which supposedly resembles the human form and was formerly widely used in medicine and magic, being thought to promote conception. It was reputed to shriek when pulled from the ground and to cause the death of whoever uprooted it (a dog being therefore traditionally employed for the purpose). Recorded from Middle English, the name comes from medieval Latin *mandragora*, associated with man (because of the shape of its root) + *drake* in the Old English sense 'dragon'.

manes in Roman mythology, the deified souls of dead ancestors.

Manetho (3rd century BC), Egyptian priest. He wrote a history of Egypt from mythical times to 323, in which he arbitrarily divided the succession of rulers known to him into thirty dynasties, an arrangement which is still followed.

manga a Japanese genre of cartoons, comic books, and animated films, drawn with a meticulously detailed style, typically having a science-fiction or fantasy theme and sometimes including violent or sexually explicit material. The word is Japanese, from *man* 'indiscriminate' + *ga* 'picture'.

Mangi in the writings of ➤ *Marco* POLO, the name used for what is now South China.

Manhattan an island near the mouth of the Hudson River forming part of the city of New York. The site of the original Dutch settlement of New Amsterdam, it is now a borough containing the commercial and cultural centre of New York City. It is named after the Algonquin tribe from whom the Dutch settlers claimed to have bought the island in 1626.

Manhattan Project the code name for the American project set up in 1942 to develop an atom bomb. The project culminated in 1945 with the detonation of the first nuclear weapon, at White Sands in New Mexico.

Manichaeism a dualistic religious system with Christian, Gnostic, and pagan elements, founded in Persia in the 3rd century by Manes (*c*.216–*c*.276). The system was based on a supposed primeval conflict between light and darkness. It spread widely in the Roman Empire and in Asia, and survived in Chinese Turkestan until the 13th century.

manifest destiny phrase coined by the American journalist John L. O'Sullivan to encapsulate an expansionist policy for the United States, referring specifically here to opposition to the annexation of Texas:

> A spirit of hostile interference against us . . . checking the fulfilment of our manifest destiny to overspread the continent allotted by Providence for the free development of our yearly multiplying millions.
> — John L. O'Sullivan in *United States Magazine and Democratic Review* (1845)

maniple In the Western Church, a vestment formerly worn by a priest celebrating the Eucharist, consisting of a strip hanging from the left arm. The *maniple* is generally thought to derive from the folded napkin or handkerchief carried by Roman consuls as a rank ornament.

Maniple is also used (from the mid 16th century) for a subdivision of a Roman legion, containing either 120 or 60 men.

Recorded from late Middle English, the term comes via Old French from Latin *manipulus* 'handful, troop', from *manus* 'hand'.

manitou (among certain Algonquian North American Indians) a good or evil spirit as an object of reverence. The name comes in the late 17th century via French from an Algonquian language.

manna in the Bible, the substance miraculously supplied each day as food to the Israelites in the wilderness:

> And when the children of Israel saw it, they said one to another, It is manna: for they wist not what it was. And Moses said unto them, This is the bread which the Lord hath given you to eat.
> — Bible (AV) Exodus ch. 16, v. 15

This verse preserves the etymological tradition that the name originated from the question *man hū'* 'what is it' (in Aramaic or supposed archaic Hebrew).

The supposed nature of manna has been debated. In Exodus 16, it is described as 'a small round thing, as small as the hoar frost on the ground…It was like coriander seed, white: and the taste of it was like wafers made with honey.' It has thus been suggested that what was denoted was an exudation of the tamarisk, the word for which in Aramaic is *mannā*.

The extended use of *manna* to mean 'an unexpected or gratuitous benefit' (frequently in **manna from heaven**) is recorded from the early 17th century.

> His regular, technicoloured prose has been manna from heaven for hungry headline writers.
> — *Grocer* 12 September 1998

to the manner born naturally fitted for some position or employment; originally, as a quotation from Shakespeare's *Hamlet*, 'though I am native here, And to the manner born'.

Mannerism a style of 16th-century Italian art preceding the Baroque, characterized by unusual effects of scale, lighting, and perspective, and the use of bright, often lurid colours. It is particularly associated with the work of Pontormo, Vasari, and the later Michelangelo.

manners see also ➤ COMEDY *of manners,* ➤ EVIL *communications corrupt good manners.*

manners maketh man proverbial saying, mid fourteenth century; motto of William of Wykeham (1324–1404).

Manoa a fabulous city in South America; in his *Discoverie of Guiana* (1596), Walter Raleigh refers to it as 'the great and Golden Citie of Manoa (which the Spaniards call El Dorado)'.

manor in England and Wales, a unit of land, originally a feudal lordship, consisting of a lord's demesne and lands rented to tenants; in North America, an estate held in fee farm, especially one granted by royal charter in a British colony or by the Dutch governors of what is now New York State. Recorded from Middle English, the word comes from Anglo-Norman French *maner* 'dwelling', from Latin *manere* 'remain'.

See also ➤ LORD *of the manor.*

François Mansart (1598–1666) French architect. He rebuilt part of the château of Blois, which incorporated the type of roof (*mansard*) now named after him.

mansion a large impressive house; originally (in Middle English) the word denoted the chief residence of a lord.

the Mansion House the official residence of the Lord Mayor of London; it was built between 1739 and 1753.

Charles Manson (1934–), American cult leader. He founded a commune based on free love and complete subordination to him. In 1969 its members carried out a series of murders, including that of the American actress Sharon Tate, for which he and some followers received the death sentence (later commuted to life imprisonment).

Patrick Manson (1844–1922), Scottish physician, pioneer of tropical medicine. He discovered the organism responsible for elephantiasis and established that it was spread by the bite of a mosquito; he then suggested a similar role for the mosquito in spreading malaria.

Mansoul in Bunyan's *The Holy War* (1682), the stronghold which is assailed by the demonic forces of ➤ DIABOLUS.

> One watchword from our Armies,
> One answer from our Lands:—
> 'No dealings with Diabolus
> As long as Mansoul stands!'
> — Rudyard Kipling *The Holy War* (1917)

Gideon Algernon Mantell (1790–1852), English geologist. Mantell worked mainly as a surgeon in Sussex, but is best known as the first person to recognize dinosaur remains as reptilian. In 1825 he published a description of the teeth of a 'giant fossil lizard' which he named *Iguanodon*.

mantelletta a sleeveless vestment reaching to the knees, worn by cardinals, bishops, and other high-ranking Catholic ecclesiastics.

manticore a mythical beast typically depicted as having the body of a lion (occasionally a tiger), the face of a man, porcupine's quills, and the sting of a scorpion. Recorded from late Middle English, the name comes via Old French and Latin from Greek *mantikhōras*, corrupt reading in Aristotle for *martikhoras*, from an Old Persian word meaning 'maneater'.

In heraldry, the *manticore* is represented as a monster with the body of a beast of prey, the head of a man, sometimes with spiral or curved horns, and sometimes with the feet of a dragon.

mantis a slender predatory insect related to the cockroach. It waits motionless for prey with its large spiky forelegs folded like hands in prayer (also called **praying mantis**). The name comes (in the mid 17th century) via modern Latin from Greek, literally 'prophet'.

mantle an important role or responsibility that passes from one person to another, with allusion to the sign by which Elijah chose Elisha as his successor as prophet of Israel (2 Kings 2:13).

> He . . . found Elisha the son of Shaphat, who was plowing with twelve yoke of oxen before him, and he with the twelfth: and Elijah passed by him, and cast his mantle upon him.
> — Bible (AV) 2 Kings ch. 2, v. 13

mantra originally in Hinduism and Buddhism, a word or sound repeated to aid concentration in meditation. Also, a Vedic hymn. The word is Sanskrit and means literally 'instrument of thought', from *man* 'think'.

the Mantuan a name for Virgil, who was born near Mantua in northern Italy; he is also called the **Mantuan Muse** and the **Mantuan Swan**.

Manu the archetypal first man of Hindu mythology, survivor of the great flood and father of the human race. He is also the legendary author of one of the most famous codes of Hindu religious law, the *Manusmriti* (Laws of Manu), composed in Sanskrit and dating in its present form from the 1st century BC.

Manueline denoting a style of Portuguese architecture developed during the reign of Manuel I (1495–1521) and characterized by ornate elaborations of Gothic and Renaissance styles.

manumit release from slavery, set free. Recorded from late Middle English, the word comes from Latin *manumittere*, literally 'send forth from the hand'.

Manutius see ➤ ALDUS *Manutius*.

manvantara in Hindu cosmology: any of the fourteen periods, each presided over by a special Manu or cosmic god, which make up a *kalpa*.

manure animal dung used for fertilizing land; the word comes (as a verb in the sense 'cultivate land') from Old French *manouvrer* 'manoeuvre'.

Manx cat a cat of a breed having no tail or an extremely short one, originating on the Isle of Man.

many a mickle makes a little proverbial saying, mid 13th century.

many a mickle makes a muckle proverbial saying, late 18th century.

there's many a slip 'twixt cup and lip proverbial saying, mid 16th century.

many are called but few are chosen proverbial saying, early 17th century; originally with biblical allusion to Matthew 22:14.

many hands make light work proverbial saying, mid 14th century.

many-headed monster the people, the populace; after Horace *Epistles* 'the people are a many-headed beast.' The term is recorded in English since the 16th century; in *Arcadia* (1590) Philip Sidney remarks, 'O weak trust of the many-headed multitude', and Samuel Daniel in 1595 refers to 'This many-headed monster Multitude'. The expression was popularized by Pope in *Epistles of Horace* (1737), 'The many-headed Monster of the Pit'.

Mao Zedong (1893–1976), Chinese statesman, chairman of the Communist Party of the Chinese People's Republic 1949–76 and head of state 1949–59. A co-founder of the Chinese Communist Party in 1921 and its effective leader from the time of the Long March (1934–5), he eventually defeated both the occupying Japanese and rival Kuomintang nationalist forces to create the People's Republic of China in 1949, becoming its first head of state. At first Mao followed the Soviet Communist model, but from 1956 he introduced his own measures, such as the brief period of freedom of expression known as Hundred Flowers and the economically disastrous Great Leap Forward (1958–60). Despite having resigned as head of state Mao instigated the Cultural Revolution (1966–8), during which he became the focus of a personality cult.

Maori Wars a series of wars fought intermittently in 1845–8 and 1860–72 between Maoris and the colonial government of New Zealand over the enforced sale of Maori lands to Europeans, which was forbidden by the Treaty of Waitangi.

Maoritangi Maori culture, traditions, and way of life.

maple leaf the leaf of the maple, used as an emblem of Canada.

Mappa Mundi a famous 13th-century map of the world, now in Hereford cathedral, England. The map is round and typical of similar maps of the time in that it depicts Jerusalem at its centre. The name comes from medieval Latin, literally 'sheet of the world'.

mappemonde a medieval map of the world. See also ➤ MAPPA *Mundi*.

maquis dense scrub vegetation consisting of hardy evergreen shrubs and small trees, characteristic of coastal regions in the Mediterranean. The French resistance movement during the German occupation (1940–5), **the Maquis**, took their name from this.

Mar in Eastern Churches of the Syriac rite: an honorific title for a saint or a member of the higher clergy. Recorded from the early 17th century, the word comes from Aramaic 'sir'.

Mara in Buddhism, a devil or demon personifying death, desire, rebirth, and the totality of worldly existence. The name comes from Sanskrit *māra* 'slaughter', in Buddhist writings, 'the Destroyer, the Evil One'.

marabou a large African stork with a massive bill and large neck pouch, which feeds mainly by scavenging. The word comes (in the early 19th century) from French, from Arabic *murābiṭ* 'holy man' (see also ➤ MARABOUT), the stork being regarded as holy.

marabout a Muslim hermit or monk, especially in North Africa; a shrine marking the burial place of a Muslim hermit or monk. Recorded from the early 17th century, the word comes (like ➤ MARABOU) from Arabic *murābiṭ* 'holy man'.

marah in biblical allusions: bitterness, from Hebrew *mārāh* (feminine of *mar* bitter) used as a place name in Exodus 15:23, 'And when they came to Marah, they could not drink of the waters of Marah, for they were bitter: therefore the name of it was called Marah', and a personal name in Ruth 1:20, 'And she said unto them, Call me not Naomi, call me Mara: for the Almighty hath dealt very bitterly with me.'

Maranatha in biblical translations, a word representing an Aramaic phrase occurring in 1 Corinthians 16.22 and usually left untranslated, its exact interpretation being variously understood by scholars and translators. Current scholarship favours the interpretation 'Come, O Lord!'; the most widely advocated alternative being 'Our Lord has come.'

It has also often erroneously been regarded as forming part of a formula of imprecation in ➤ ANATHEMA *maranatha*.

Jean Paul Marat (1743–93), French revolutionary and journalist. A virulent critic of the moderate Girondists, he was instrumental (with Danton and Robespierre) in their fall from power in 1793. Marat, who suffered from a painful skin condition requiring the alleviation of medicinal baths, was assassinated in his bath by the Girondist Charlotte Corday. The *Death of Marat* (1793) by the painter David famously shows the scene.

Maratha a member of the princely and military castes of the former Hindu kingdom of Maharashtra in central India. The Marathas rose in rebellion against the Muslim Moguls and in 1674 established their own kingdom under the leadership of Shivaji. They came to dominate southern and central India but were later subdued by the British.

Marathon in ancient Greece, the scene of a victory over the Persians in 490 BC; the modern race (strictly one of 26 miles 38 yards or 42.195 km.) is based on the tradition that a messenger ran from Marathon to Athens (22 miles) with the news. The original account by Herodotus told of the messenger Pheidippides running 150 miles from Athens to Sparta before the battle, seeking help; on reaching Athens, he gasped out his dying words, 'Greetings, we win!'

Maravedi a name applied to the North African Berber rulers of Muslim Spain, from the late 11th century to 1145; the word is from Arabic meaning 'holy men', and came to mean a medieval Spanish copper coin and monetary unit.

marble see also ➤ ARUNDELIAN *marbles*, ➤ ELGIN *Marbles*, ➤ *I found* ROME *brick and leave it marble*, ➤ XANTHIAN *Marbles*.

Marble Arch a large arch with three gateways at the NE corner of Hyde Park in London, near the site of which ➤ TYBURN gallows once stood. Designed by John Nash, it was erected in 1827 in front of Buckingham Palace and moved in 1851 to its present site.

Marburg a city in the state of Hesse in west central Germany, which was the scene in 1529 of a debate between German and Swiss theologians, notably Martin Luther and Ulrich Zwingli, on the doctrine of consubstantiation.

marcassin in heraldry, a young wild boar with a limp tail, as a charge.

Marcel Marceau (1923–), French mime artist. He is known for appearing as the white-faced *Bip*, a character he developed from the French Pierrot character.

march see also ➤ HUNGER *march*, ➤ LONG *March*.

March the third month of the year, in the northern hemisphere usually considered the first month of spring. The name comes from Latin *Martius*, short for *mensis Martius* 'month of Mars', and at ancient Rome several festivals of Mars took place in March, presumably in preparation for the campaigning season, since Mars was a god of war.

See also ➤ *beware the* IDES *of March*.

march a frontier or border area (usually called **Marches**) between two countries or territories, especially between England and Wales (**the Welsh Marches**) or (formerly) England and Scotland.

The Marches is also used for a region of east central Italy, between the Apennines and the Adriatic Sea.

Recorded from Middle English, the word comes via Old French *marche*, and is ultimately of Germanic origin.

March borrowed from April three days, and they were ill traditional saying, mid 17th century; implying that bad weather in early April reflects the influence of March.

March comes in like a lion, and goes out like a lamb proverbial saying, early 17th century; meaning that weather is traditionally bad at the beginning of March, but calm at the end.

a peck of March dust is worth a king's ransom proverbial saying, early 16th century; meaning that March is traditionally a wet month, and dust is rare.

March hare a brown hare in the breeding season, noted for its leaping, boxing, and chasing in circles, and taken as the type of something mad.

See also ➤ MAD *as a March hare*.

so many mists in March, so many frosts in May proverbial saying, early 17th century; meaning that mist or fog in March presages frost in May.

on the first of March, the crows begin to search proverbial saying, mid 19th century; meaning that crows traditionally pair off on this day.

march to a different drum conform to different principles and practices from those around one; ultimately from Henry David Thoreau *Walden* (1854), 'If a man does not keep pace with his companions, perhaps it is because he hears a different drummer.

Let him step to the music which he hears, however measured or far away.'

Märchen in Germany, a folk-tale, a fairy tale.

marching season a season of processions or parades held annually throughout Northern Ireland from 12 July to 12 August, in which members of the ➤ ORANGE *Order* march in celebration of the defeat of the Catholic James II by ➤ WILLIAM *III* at the Battle of the Boyne in 1690. In recent years a number of marches through predominantly Catholic and Nationalist areas have been rerouted or banned.

> People [in Northern Ireland] don't march as an alternative to jogging. They do it to assert their supremacy. It is pure tribalism, the cause of troubles all over the world.
> — Gerry Fitt in *The Times* 5 August 1994

marchpane archaic spelling of ➤ MARZIPAN.

Marcionite an adherent of the rigorously ascetic sect founded in Rome in the 2nd cent. A.D. by Marcion of Sinope, who rejected the authority of the Old and New Testaments (with the exception of ten of the Epistles of St Paul and an edited recension of the Gospel of St Luke) on the grounds that the deity to which they referred was a God of Law rather than the God of Love.

Marco see ➤ *Marco* POLO.

Guglielmo Marconi (1874–1937), Italian electrical engineer, the father of radio. In 1912 Marconi produced a continuously oscillating wave, essential for the transmission of sound. He went on to develop short-wave transmission over long distances.

Marconi scandal in 1912, it was suggested that Lloyd George, chancellor of the exchequer, and Rufus Isaacs, attorney general, had used inside knowledge to buy shares in the American Marconi company at a favourable rate. In the following year a House of Commons select committee acquitted both ministers of acting otherwise than in good faith, but the reputations of both men suffered, and Isaacs (who was made Lord Chief Justice in October 1913) became the target of one of Kipling's bitterest poems:

> Well done, well done, Gehazi!
> Stretch forth thy ready hand.
> Thou barely 'scaped from judgement,
> Take oath to judge the land.
> Unswayed by gift of money
> Or privy bribe, more base,
> Of knowledge which is profit
> In any market-place.
> — Rudyard Kipling 'Gehazi' (1915)

Marcus see ➤ *Marcus* Aurelius.

Mardi Gras a carnival held in some countries on Shrove Tuesday, most famously in New Orleans. The (French) phrase means literally 'fat Tuesday', alluding to the last day of feasting before the fast and penitence of Lent.

Marduk the chief god of Babylon, who became lord of the gods of heaven and earth after conquering Tiamat, the monster of primeval chaos.

mare[1] the female of a horse or other equine animal. The word comes from Old English *mearh* 'horse', *mere* 'mare', from a Germanic base with cognates in Celtic languages meaning 'stallion'. The sense 'male horse' died out at the end of the Middle English period.

See also ➤ Flanders *Mare*, ➤ money *makes the mare to go*, ➤ nothing *so bold as a blind mare*.

mare[2] a large, level basalt plain on the surface of the moon, appearing dark by contrast with highland areas; the term (recorded from the mid 19th century) is a special use of the Latin word for 'sea', as these areas were once thought to be seas.

shoeing the wild mare a game played at Christmas and other festive seasons, in which a pole is suspended at either end above the floor and the 'rider' sits cross-legged on it and performs various antics or must pretend to shoe the mare by hammering the underside of the pole a certain number of times.

mare clausum the sea under the jurisdiction of a particular country (from Latin, 'closed sea').

the grey mare is the better horse proverbial saying, mid 16th century, meaning that the wife rules the husband; **the grey mare** can be used allusively for a woman who is the dominant partner in a marriage.

mare liberum the sea open to all nations (from Latin, 'free sea').

mare's nest an illusory discovery, originally in the phrase *to have found* (or *spied*) *a mare's nest* (i.e. something that does not exist), used in the sense 'to have discovered something amazing'. The expression is recorded from the late 16th century.

Marengo a decisive French victory of Napoleon's campaign in Italy in 1800, close to the village of Marengo, near Turin. After military reverses had all but destroyed French power in Italy, Napoleon crossed the Alps to defeat and capture an Austrian army, a victory which led to Italy coming under French control again.

Marengo also designates chicken or veal sautéed in oil, served with a tomato sauce, and traditionally garnished with eggs and crayfish. The dish is said to have been served to Napoleon after his victory at Marengo.

Margaret see also ➤ Lady *Margaret Hall*.

St Margaret of Antioch a saint who was the centre of much popular devotion in the Middle Ages, but who probably never existed as a historical person. She is a patroness of childbirth, and is recognized as one of the ➤ Fourteen *Holy Helpers*. Also called *Marina*.

Her feast day is on 13 July in the Eastern Church, and 20 July in the Western Church. She is often depicted spearing a dragon.

St Margaret of Scotland (*c*.1046–93), English princess and Scottish queen, wife of Malcolm III. She exerted a strong influence over royal policy during her husband's reign, and was instrumental in the reform of the Scottish Church. Feast day, 16 November.

Mari an ancient city on the west bank of the Euphrates, in Syria. Its period of greatest importance was from the late 19th to the mid 18th centuries BC; the vast palace of the last king, Zimri-Lin, has yielded an archive of 25,000 cuneiform tablets, which are the principal source for the history of northern Syria and Mesopotamia at that time. The city was sacked by Hammurabi of Babylon in 1759 BC.

Mari Lwyd 'Pale Mary', an important figure in traditional Welsh Christmas mumming plays, represented by the skull of a grey mare decked with ribbons, which is carried by young men as part of the Twelfth Night celebrations.

Maria see ➤ Ave *Maria*, ➤ Black *Maria*.

Maria Theresa (1717–80), Archduchess of Austria, queen of Hungary and Bohemia 1740–80. The daughter of the Emperor Charles VI, she succeeded to the Habsburg dominions in 1740 by virtue of the ➤ Pragmatic *Sanction*. Her accession triggered the War of the Austrian Succession (1740–8), which in turn led to the Seven Years War (1756–63).

Maid Marian in English folklore, the lover of ➤ Robin *Hood*; she is also a traditionally a female character in the morris dance and May game, and (in modern use) a named character in the Horn dance performed annually at Abbots Bromley in Staffordshire. Her appearance in later forms of the story of Robin Hood may be attributable to the fact that both were represented in the May Day pageants.

Marianne the French Republic personified; a proclamation of the Republic of 22 September 1792 announced that the symbol of the new regime would be a female figure representing the goddess of liberty. The name *Marianne* came popularly to be applied to the figure, typically represented wearing a Phrygian cap.

The image of *Marianne*, appearing on stamps and coins and as a bust in town halls, has since the 1960s been modelled on a living person (the first, in 1969, was inspired by Brigitte Bardot); in October 1999 the name of the latest Marianne, a Corsican model named Laetitia Casta, was announced. The new design will replace that based on the actress Catherine Deneuve and designer Inés de la Fressange.

The reason for the adoption of the name is not known. *La garisou de Marianno* is the name of an Occitan song composed by the Republican poet Guillaume Lavabre, probably in 1792; a song called *La Marianno* is said to have been sung at festivals in the mid 19th century in the town of Castres (Tarn), in front of a statue of the Republic known locally as 'La Marianno'.

marid a very powerful wicked jinn in Arabian stories and Muslim mythology. The word comes from Arab *mārid*, from *marada* 'to rebel'. It occurs once in the Koran with the sense 'rebel', but in later tradition denotes a fantastic being of a particular type, represented in the popular tales as being more powerful than an ➤ AFREET.

Marie Antoinette (1755–93), queen of France, wife of Louis XVI. A daughter of Maria Theresa, she married the future Louis XVI of France in 1770. Her extravagant lifestyle led to widespread unpopularity and, like her husband, she was executed during the French Revolution. The comment 'Let them eat cake', on being told that her people had no bread, is attributed to her, but it is much older; in his *Confessions* (1740) Rousseau refers to a similar remark being a well-known saying.

See also ➤ TRIANON.

Marie Celeste erroneous form of the name ➤ MARY *Celeste*.

Maries see ➤ *the* FOUR *Maries*.

marigold the name comes from the given name *Mary*, probably referring to the Virgin, + dialect *gold*, denoting the corn or garden marigold in Old English.

The flower possesses the property of opening when the sun shines, and this was often referred to by writers of the 16th and 17th centuries, as in Thomas Overbury's *Wife* (a. 1613) 'His wit, like the marigold, openeth with the sun.'

Marina green a greyish-green colour, named with reference to the colour of the going-away outfit worn by Princess Marina of Greece (1906–68) after her marriage to George, Duke of Kent in 1934.

mariner see also ➤ ANCIENT *Mariner*.

mariner's compass an archaic term for the compass.

marines see ➤ TELL *that to the (horse) marines*.

Filippo Tommaso Marinetti (1876–1944), Italian poet and dramatist. He launched the futurist movement with a manifesto (1909) which exalted technology, glorified war, and demanded revolution in the arts.

Mariolatry excessive reverence for the Virgin Mary, to the point of idolatrous worship. Recorded from the early 17th century, the term was coined as part of the vocabulary of Protestant polemic.

Maris lane in Cambridge, England, the original site of the Plant Breeding Institute; from this *Maris* is used in the names of varieties of potato, barley, and other crops developed by the Institute.

Marist a member of the Society of Mary, a Roman Catholic missionary and teaching order founded in Lyons in 1816.

Marist is also the name given to a member of the Little Brothers of Mary, a Roman Catholic teaching order.

the Maritimes the Canadian provinces of New Brunswick, Nova Scotia, and Prince Edward Island, with coastlines on the Gulf of St Lawrence and the Atlantic. These provinces, with Newfoundland and Labrador, are also known as the Atlantic Provinces.

Gaius Marius (*c*.157–86 BC), Roman general and politician. Elected consul in 107 BC, he defeated Jugurtha and invading Germanic tribes. After a power struggle with Sulla he was expelled from Italy; Plutarch records that arriving in North Africa, he was refused shelter by the local governor, and replied,

'Go tell him that you have seen Gaius Marius sitting in exile among the ruins of Carthage', an image of defeat to which later allusions are made. Marius returned to take Rome by force in 87 BC, but died shortly after.

> Here Bartleby makes his home . . . a sort of innocent and transformed Marius brooding among the ruins of Carthage.
> — Herman Melville *Bartleby* (1853)

Marivaudage exaggeratedly sentimental or affected style or language, regarded as characteristic of P. C. de *Marivaux* (1688–1763), French novelist and dramatist.

mark see ➤ CHARTER *Mark,* ➤ GOD *save the mark,* ➤ *Mark* ANTONY, ➤ MASON'*s mark.*

Mark in Arthurian legend, king of Cornwall, husband of ➤ ISEULT and uncle of ➤ TRISTRAM. In different versions of the story of Tristram and Iseult, he is represented as a noble king and trusting husband, or as the type of treachery and cowardice.

St Mark an Apostle, companion of St Peter and St Paul, traditional author of the second Gospel, sometimes identified with the John Mark whose mother's house in Jerusalem was a meeting-place for the Apostles. He is also sometimes said to have been the young man who according to Mark 14:51 followed Jesus after he had been arrested, but escaped capture.

Mark is patron of Venice, to which his body was brought in the 9th century. His symbol as an evangelist is a lion, one of the ➤ TETRAMORPH.

□ **FEAST DAY** His feast day is 25 April.
See also ➤ LION *of St Mark.*

the mark of the beast in Revelation 16:2, a sign placed on followers or worshippers of Antichrist. In extended use, the phrase was first used to mean an indicator or symptom of heresy, and then more generally a sign of infamy.

St Mark's Eve in the north of England it was customary to riddle the ashes on the hearth on St Mark's Eve as a method of divination.

market see ➤ BEAR *market,* ➤ BULL *market,* ➤ BUY *in the cheapest market and sell in the dearest,* ➤ IDOLS *of the tribe, cave, market, and theatre,* ➤ *the* MONEY-LESS *man goes fast through the market,* ➤ COMMON *Market.*

Marks and **Sparks** an informal and humorous name for the British retail chain Marks and Spencer

plc, originally founded as the **Marks and Spencer Penny Bazaars** by Michael *Marks*, Polish-born English retailer (1863–1907) and Thomas *Spencer*, English retailer (c.1852–1904).

burning marl the torments of hell, after the description of Satan in Milton's *Paradise Lost* (1667), 'His spear…He walked with to support uneasy steps Over the burning marl.'

Marlboro Man a cowboy character appearing in advertising campaigns for *Marlboro* cigarettes, often used allusively (and ironically) to denote the type of a tough outdoors man. **Marlboro Country** is similarly used for the natural home of such a person.

> Men are incomplete. Self-sufficiency is not tenable. Forget the Marlboro man. Let's get in touch with our feelings and get reconnected in dense relationships.
> — *New York Times Book Review* 9 January 1994

Duke of Marlborough (1650–1722), John Churchill, British general. He was commander of British and Dutch troops in the War of the Spanish Succession and won a series of victories (notably at Blenheim in 1704) over the French armies of Louis XIV, ending Louis's attempts to dominate Europe. Queen Anne funded the building of Blenheim Palace, his seat at Woodstock in Oxfordshire, in gratitude.

See also ➤ MALBROUCK *s'en va-t-en guerre.*

Bob Marley (1945–81), Jamaican reggae singer, guitarist, and songwriter. Having formed the trio the Wailers in 1965, in the 1970s he was instrumental in popularizing reggae. His lyrics often reflected his commitment to Rastafarianism.

Jacob Marley in Dickens's *A Christmas Carol,* Scrooge's late partner, whose chained ghost appears to Scrooge and warns him to change his miserly ways. **Marley's ghost** denotes the type of such a spectre.

> It was as if he'd woken up one day to find himself manacled like Marley's Ghost.
> — Sharyn McCrumb *Bimbos of the Death Sun* (1988)

Christopher Marlowe (1564–93), English dramatist and poet. As a dramatist he brought a new strength and vitality to blank verse; his work (notable for its sonorous language and violent plots) influenced Shakespeare's early historical plays.

In his own time, Marlowe was admired by other dramatists (Jonson refers to 'Marlowe's mighty line'), but he was also a controversial figure, suspected of atheism and perhaps involved in espionage. He was killed in a tavern brawl in Deptford, in

circumstances which have never been fully explained.

Philip Marlowe a fictional detective, created by
Raymond Chandler, who embodies the 'private eye'
qualities described by Chandler:

> Down these mean streets a man must go who is not
> himself mean, who is neither tarnished nor afraid.
> — Raymond Chandler in *Atlantic Monthly* December
> 1944 'The Simple Art of Murder'

Marne a river of east central France, which rises in
the Langres plateau north of Dijon and flows north
and west to join the Seine near Paris. Its valley was
the scene of two important battles in the First World
War. The first battle (September 1914) halted and repelled the German advance on Paris; the second
(July 1918) ended the final German offensive.

Maro, Prophet of the Gentiles in the Middle
Ages, the name under which the Roman poet
➤ VIRGIL (Publius Vergilius *Maro*) was commemorated at the Christmas Mass at Rouen and elsewhere;
the allusion is to the passage in his *Eclogues* which
was taken as an unconscious but divinely inspired
prophecy of Christ.

Marocco name of a 'dancing horse', owned by a
Scottish-born showman named Banks (fl.
1588–1637) which was exhibited at the Cross Keys in
Gracious Street, London, before 1588, and which
was said among other accomplishments to be able
to count money; it is referred to in Shakespeare's
Love's Labour's Lost (1595), 'how easy it is to put
"years" to the word "three", and study three years
in two words, the dancing horse will tell you.'

Maronite a member of a Christian sect of Syrian
origin, living chiefly in Lebanon and in communion
with the Roman Catholic Church. Maronites have
been prominent in Lebanese politics and traditionally hold the office of President. The name comes
ultimately from the name of John *Maro*, a 7th-cent.
Syrian religious leader, who may have been the first
Maronite patriarch.

Maroon a member of a group of black people living in the mountains and forests of Suriname and
the West Indies, descended from runaway slaves.
The name comes (in the mid 17th century) from
French *marron* meaning 'feral', from Spanish
cimarrón 'wild', (as a noun) 'runaway slave'.

maroon in the 17th century only, the name for a
large kind of chestnut, a word which comes from
French *marron* 'chestnut', via Italian from medieval

Greek *maraon*. This has given rise to two later senses
which are still current.

Maroon meaning a brownish-crimson colour,
held to resemble a chestnut, dates from the late 18th
century.

Maroon in the (chiefly British) sense of a firework
that makes a loud bang, used mainly as a signal or a
warning, is recorded from the early 19th century. It
is so named because the firework makes the noise of
a roast chestnut bursting in the fire.

Miss Marple a fictional detective created by Agatha Christie (1890–1976), whose apparently gentle
existence as an elderly spinster in an English village
(St Mary Mead) is belied by her frequent and successful investigations into murder and other crimes.
She typically solves mysteries by comparing actions
and events with her knowledge and experience of
village life.

Martin Marprelate the name assumed by the
authors of a number of anonymous pamphlets
which in 1588–9 were issued attacking the episcopal
system and defending Presbyterian discipline.
Marprelate derives from *mar* 'spoil' + *prelate*
'bishop'.

marque see ➤ LETTER *of marque*.

marquess a British nobleman ranking above an
earl and below a duke. The word is recorded from
the early 16th century, and is a variant of ➤ MAR-
QUIS.

Jacques Marquette (1637–75), French Jesuit missionary and explorer. Arriving in North America in
1666, he played a prominent part in the attempt to
Christianize the American Indians, and explored
the Wisconsin and Mississippi Rivers.

marquis in some European countries, a nobleman
ranking above a count and below a duke. Recorded
from Middle English, the word comes from Old
French *marchis*, reinforced by Old French *marquis*,
both from the base of ➤ MARCH, and meaning
someone who was in charge of a frontier territory.

Up to the beginning of the 20th century, *marquis*
was also used for a British nobleman; the preferred
spelling is now ➤ MARQUESS.

See also ➤ *the Marquis of* GRANBY.

Marrano (in medieval Spain) a christianized Jew
or Moor, especially one who merely professed conversion in order to avoid persecution. The name is
Spanish, and is of unknown origin, although various explanations have been suggested; these include

the earlier (10th-century) Spanish *marrano* 'hog', assuming the word to be used as a particularly offensive term of abuse, or Spanish Arabic *muḥarram* 'excommunicate'. This suggestion is based on the view that Jewish and Muslim converts would be suspected of practising their former religion in private, and would thus be excommunicates.

marriage see also ➤ DREAM *of a funeral and you hear of a marriage*, ➤ FLEET *marriage*, ➤ JACTITATION *of marriage*, ➤ LEFT-*handed marriage.*

marriage is a lottery proverbial saying, mid 17th century.

Marriage of the Adriatic a ceremony formerly held on Ascension Day in Venice to symbolize the city's sea power, during which the doge dropped a ring into the water from his official barge.

there goes more to marriage than four bare legs in a bed proverbial saying, mid 16th century.

marriages are made in heaven proverbial saying, mid 16th century.

married see also ➤ *a* YOUNG *man married is a man that's marred.*

married women ➤ *St* MONICA is the patron saint of married women.

Marrow Controversy in 18th century Scotland, a prolonged dispute centring on 'The Marrow of Modern Divinity', the title of a book by Edward Fisher (1645), and republished with notes by the Revd James Hog in 1718, which proposed a *via media* between legalistic and antinomian Calvinism, and which was condemned by the General Assembly of the Church of Scotland in 1720 as antinomian in tendency. *Marrow* meaning the vital or essential part, the essence, had been much used in the previous century in the titles of books.

never marry for money, but marry where money is proverbial saying, late 19th century.

marry in haste and repent at leisure proverbial saying, mid 16th century.

marry in May, rue for aye proverbial saying, late 17th century, but earlier in Latin. Ovid comments in his *Fasti* 'if proverbs influence you, the common people say it is bad luck to marry in May.'

marry over the broomstick go through a sham marriage ceremony in which the parties jump over a broom, a custom recorded from the late 17th century.

Mars in Roman mythology, the god of war and the most important Roman god after Jupiter. He was probably originally an agricultural god, and the month of March is named after him. His Greek equivalent is ➤ ARES. Legends of Mars include the story of his love for Venus, and the trap made for them by her husband Vulcan, and from early times this became a favourite subject for artists.

The wolf and the woodpecker were regarded as sacred to Mars.

Mars is the name given to a small reddish planet which is the fourth in order from the sun and is periodically visible to the naked eye. From its distinctive colour, which comes from its iron-rich minerals, it is known informally as the *red planet*.

In astrological belief, the influence of the planet Mars is associated with combative, aggressive, or masculine qualities; the popular *Men are from Mars, Women are from Venus* (1992, by John Gray) took this as a central image in its discussion of relationships.

See also ➤ CHAMP *de Mars.*

field of Mars another name for the ➤ CAMPUS *Martius* of ancient Rome.

hill of Mars the ➤ AREOPAGUS ('hill of Ares') of ancient Athens.

Marse Robert nickname ('Master Robert') for the Confederate general ➤ *Robert E.* LEE (1807–70).

Marseillaise the national anthem of France, written by Rouget de Lisle in 1792 on the declaration of war against Austria, and first sung in Paris by volunteer army units from Marseilles.

marshal an officer of the highest rank in the armed forces of some countries. Recorded from Middle English (denoting a high-ranking officer of state), the word comes from Old French *mareschal* 'farrier, commander', from late Latin *mariscalcus*, from Germanic elements meaning 'horse' and 'servant'.

See also ➤ EARL *Marshal.*

Marshall Plan a programme of financial aid and other initiatives, sponsored by the US, designed to boost the economies of western European countries after the Second World War. It was originally advocated by Secretary of State George C. Marshall and passed by Congress in 1948.

marshalsea in England, a court formerly held before the steward and the knight *marshal* of the royal household, originally to hear cases between the monarch's servants, but afterwards with wider jurisdiction. It was abolished in 1849.

The **Marshalsea** was the name of a former prison in Southwark, London, originally the prison of the Court of the Marshalsea, under the control of the knight marshal, and in later years used for the imprisonment of debtors. It was abolished in 1842.

The Marshalsea is the setting for a substantial part of Charles Dickens's *Little Dorrit* (1857), in which the imprisonment of Mr Dorrit lasts for so many years that he becomes known as the **Father of the Marshalsea**.

marshes see ➤ BAILIFF *of the marshes*, ➤ PONTINE *Marshes*.

Battle of Marston Moor a battle of the English Civil War, fought in 1644 on Marston Moor near York, in which the Royalist armies of Prince Rupert and the Duke of Newcastle suffered a defeat by the English and Scottish Parliamentary armies which fatally weakened Charles I's cause.

Marsyas in Greek mythology, a satyr who challenged Apollo to a contest in flute playing and was flayed alive when he lost; the river Marsyas in Asia Minor is said to have sprung either from his blood, or from the tears of his mourners.

The episode is the subject of one of Titian's best-known paintings, *The Flaying of Marsyas* (*c*.1570–6).

Martel nickname (meaning 'the hammer') of the Frankish ruler Charles Martel (*c*.688–741), grandfather of Charlemagne, who was so named from his crushing defeat of the Saracens at the battle of Poitiers in 732.

Martello tower any of numerous small circular forts that were erected for defence purposes along the SE coasts of England during the Napoleonic Wars.

The name comes from Cape *Mortella* in Corsica, site of a small circular fort which was recaptured with some difficulty by the English fleet on 8 February 1794; its design was then used as a basis for fortifications in the British Isles from 1804.

St Martha in the New Testament, the sister of Lazarus and Mary and friend of Jesus. She is taken as the type of a woman who is constantly busied with domestic affairs, from the story in Luke 10 in which she is seen as concerned with household chores while Mary sits and talks with Jesus.

According to medieval legend, Martha, Mary, and Lazarus travelled to Provence after the death of Jesus. Martha is said to have overcome a dragon at Tarascon by sprinkling it with holy water and tying her girdle about its neck; she then led it to Arles, where it was killed.

◻ **EMBLEM** Martha may be shown with a ladle, a broom, or a bunch of keys, for her housewifely skills, or with the dragon which she overcame.

◻ **FEAST DAY** Her feast day is 29 July in the West.

Martha Gunn a jug in the form of a woman, analogous to a toby jug, from the name of *Martha Gunn* (1727–1815), a female bathing-attendant celebrated for having dipped the Prince of Wales in the sea at Brighton.

Martha's Vineyard a resort island off the coast of Massachusetts, to the south of Cape Cod. Settled by the English in 1642, it became an important centre of fishing and whaling in the 18th and 19th centuries.

Martial (*c*.40–*c*.104 AD), Roman epigrammatist, born in Spain. His fifteen books of epigrams, in a variety of metres, reflect all facets of Roman life.

Martian a hypothetical or fictional inhabitant of Mars, later taken as the type of someone unfamiliar with what is generally considered to be normal or usual.

> I could sit on a beer crate in a gay bar and amuse myself for hours, drinking and laughing and doing 'Ludes, and never once feel like a Martian.
> — Armistead Maupin *Maybe the Moon* (1992)

martin see also ➤ *Martin* MARPRELATE, ➤ *the* ROBIN *and the wren are God's cock and hen; the martin and the swallow are God's mate and marrow*.

martin the name *martin* for a swift-flying songbird of the swallow family, is recorded from late Middle English and is probably a shortening of obsolete *martinet*, from French, probably from the name of ➤ *St* MARTIN *of Tours*.

St Martin de Porres (1579–1639), Dominican lay brother, who was the illegitimate son of a Spanish grandee and a freed black slave from Lima in Peru. He was noted for his dedication to the poor as for his undiscriminating charity to those of all races, and he is patron saint of the poor, and of race relations.

◻ **FEAST DAY** His feast day is 5 November.

St Martin of Tours (d.397), French bishop, and a patron saint of France. When giving half his cloak to a beggar he received a vision of Christ, after which he was baptized. He joined St Hilary at Poitiers and founded the first monastery in Gaul.

St Martin is often shown dividing his cloak with the beggar, or with a globe of fire above his head, seen one day when he said Mass. Another emblem, from the 15th century, is a goose, the migration of which often coincides with his feast.

   □ **FEAST DAY** His feast day (➤ Martinmas) is 11 November.

St Martin's beads cheap jewellery (the sanctuary of St *Martin*'s-le-Grand, London, was a noted resort of makers of sham jewellery).

St Martin's bird a name for the hen harrier.

St Martin's Lent the forty days between ➤ Martinmas and Christmas, formerly observed as a fast.

St Martin's summer a season of fine, mild weather occurring about ➤ Martinmas.

Harriet Martineau (1802–76), English writer on social, economic, and historical subjects; she is known for her twenty-five-volume series *Illustrations of Political Economy* (1832–4) and her translation of Auguste Comte's *Philosophie positive* (1853).

martinet a strict disciplinarian, especially in the armed forces. Recorded from the late 17th century, the word originally denoted a system of drill invented by Jean *Martinet* (d. 1672), a French soldier whose attention to drill and training as Inspector-General of the infantry helped to shape the regular army of Louis XIV.

Martinist an adherent of a form of mystical pantheism developed by the French philosopher L. C. de Saint-*Martin* (1743–1803).

Martinmas St *Martin*'s Day, 11 November, in Scotland, one of the two term-days recognized by common law. In many parts of England it was traditionally the time for hiring servants, and the day on which hiring fairs were held. It was also the time at which cattle and other farm animals were slaughtered, to be salted for the winter, and the phrases **Martinmas beef** and **Martinmas meat** refer to this, as does the proverbial saying, **every hog has its Martinmas**.

Martinus Scriblerus supposed author of the satirical *Memoirs of Martinus Scriblerus*, directed against 'false tastes in learning', initiated by the

➤ Scriblerus *Club* and written mainly by John Arbuthnot (1667–1735).

Martinware a type of brown salt-glazed, frequently elaborately modelled pottery made by the *Martin* brothers in Southall, near London, in the late 19th and early 20th centuries.

martlet in heraldry, a bird like a swallow without feet, borne (typically with the wings closed) as a charge or a mark of cadency for a fourth son.

martyr a person who is killed because of their religious or other beliefs. In the Roman Catholic liturgy, martyrs rank before all other saints.

   Recorded from Old English, the word comes via ecclesiastical Latin from Greek *martur* 'witness' (in Christian use, 'martyr').

   See also ➤ *the* blood *of the martyrs is the seed of the Church*, ➤ Manchester *Martyrs*, ➤ *St* Edmund *the Martyr*, ➤ *St* Edward *the Martyr*, ➤ *St* Justin, ➤ Tolpuddle *martyrs*.

the Martyr King Charles I, a title reflecting the beliefs of those members of the Anglican Church who regard his execution as an act of religious persecution; 30 January was formally instituted as a fast in his memory in 1660 (it was suppressed in 1859, although a lesser festival was reinstated in 1980).

martyrion a shrine or church erected in honour of a martyr; a building marking the site of a martyrdom or a martyr's relics.

Maruts in Hindu belief, the sons of Rudra. In the Rig Veda they are the storm gods, Indra's helpers. They are also called *Rudras*.

Captain Marvel cartoon character in American comics from 1940; a red-costumed superhero (resembling Superman), who has undergone a similar transformation. In real life he was Billy Batson, an orphan who was transformed into *Captain Marvel* with the utterance of the magic word ➤ Shazam.

Andrew Marvell (1621–78), English metaphysical poet. He was best known during his lifetime for his verse satires and pamphlets attacking the corruption of Charles II and his ministers; most of his poetry was published posthumously and was not recognized until the 20th century.

Karl Marx (1818–83), German political philosopher and economist, resident in England from 1849. The founder of modern communism with Friedrich Engels, he collaborated with him in the writing of the

Communist Manifesto (1848), and enlarged it into a series of books, most notably the three-volume *Das Kapital*.

Marx Brothers a family of American comedians, consisting of the brothers Chico (1886–1961), Harpo (1888–1964), Groucho (1890–1977), and Zeppo (1901–79). Their films, which are characterized by their anarchic humour, include *Duck Soup* (1933) and *A Night at the Opera* (1935).

Marxism the political and economic theories of Karl Marx and Friedrich Engels, later developed by their followers to form the basis for the theory and practice of communism.

Central to Marxist theory is an explanation of social change in terms of economic factors, according to which the means of production provide the economic *base* which influences or determines the political and ideological *superstructure*. Marx and Engels predicted the revolutionary overthrow of capitalism by the proletariat and the eventual attainment of a classless communist society.

I am a Marxist—of the Groucho tendency slogan found at Nanterre in Paris, 1968.

Mary see also ➤ Bloody *Mary*, ➤ Highland *Mary*, ➤ Little *Mary*, ➤ *Mary* Poppins, ➤ Philip *and Mary*, ➤ Queen *Mary toque*, ➤ *St Mary* Overie, ➤ Typhoid *Mary*.

Mary mother of Jesus, known as **the (Blessed) Virgin Mary**, **St Mary**, or **Our Lady**. According to the Gospels she was a virgin betrothed to Joseph at the time of the Annunciation and conceived Jesus by the power of the Holy Spirit. She has been venerated by Catholic and Orthodox Churches from the earliest Christian times.

▢ **FEAST DAY** Her feast days are, 1 January (Roman Catholic Church), 25 March (Annunciation), 15 August (Assumption), 8 September (Nativity), 8 December (Immaculate Conception).

See also ➤ seven *joys of Mary*, ➤ seven *sorrows of Mary*.

Mary Bell order a court order prohibiting the publication of information which might lead to the identification of a ward of court, from the name of *Mary Bell* (1957–), who in 1968 was convicted of the manslaughter of two younger children.

Mary Bell, who had been released from custody and was living under another name, gave birth to a daughter in 1984, and in order to protect the child's anonymity, the High Court made an order forbidding public identification of Mary Bell or her whereabouts.

In 1998, a further order was issued, following the publicity surrounding a book on the case by Gitta Sereny, in which Mary Bell had co-operated.

Mary Celeste an American brig that was found in the North Atlantic in December 1872 in perfect condition but abandoned. The fate of the crew and the reason for the abandonment of the ship remain a mystery. She is sometimes referred to incorrectly as the *Marie Celeste*.

St Mary Magdalene in the New Testament, a woman of Magdala in Galilee. She was a follower of Jesus, who cured her of evil spirits (Luke 8:2), and was present at the Crucifixion. She went with other women to anoint his body in the tomb and found it empty; she is the first of those in the Gospels to whom the risen Christ appeared.

Mary Magdalene is also traditionally identified with the 'sinner' of Luke 7:37 who anointed Jesus's feet with oil, and with Mary the sister of ➤ Martha and ➤ Lazarus. Although the identification is now rejected in the Roman Calendar, it is implicit in traditional legends and representations.

▢ **PATRONAGE** She is patron both of repentant sinners and of the contemplative life (in reference to the words of Jesus, 'Mary has chosen the better part', when Martha complained that Mary chose to sit and talk to him instead of helping her sister in the kitchen).

▢ **EMBLEM** She may be shown with a jar of ointment, or in a scene of the Crucifixion.

▢ **FEAST DAY** Her feast day is 22 July.

See also ➤ *the* Magdalen.

St Mary of Egypt 5th-century Egyptian saint who, according to her legend, after living as a prostitute was converted on a visit to Jerusalem and became a hermit. Taking three loaves for food, she withdrew to live in the desert, where she remained for the rest of her life, surviving on dates and berries. When she died, a lion helped to bury her body. She was sometimes referred to informally as **Mary Gypsy**.

▢ **EMBLEMS** Her usual emblems are the three loaves, and the lion.

▢ **FEAST DAY** Her feast day is usually 2 April, but may be celebrated on 9 or 10 April.

Mary, Queen of Scots (1542–87), daughter of James V, queen of Scotland 1542–67; known as **Mary Stuart**. Sent to France as an infant, she returned to Scotland in 1561 to resume personal rule. A devout

Catholic, she was unable to control her Protestant lords, and fled to England in 1567. She became the focus of several Catholic plots against Elizabeth I and was eventually beheaded.

Mary Rose a heavily armed ship, built for Henry VIII, that in 1545 sank with the loss of nearly all her company when going out to engage the French fleet off Portsmouth. The hull, with some of the ship's contents, was raised in 1982, and is now on public display in Portsmouth dockyard.

Mary Tudor (1516–58), daughter of Henry VIII, queen of England, reigned 1553–8; known as **Bloody Mary**. She married Philip II of Spain, and in an attempt to reverse the country's turn towards Protestantism she instigated the series of religious persecutions by which she earned her nickname.

marybud the bud of a marigold; now only with allusion to a line from a song in Shakespeare's *Cymbeline*, 'And winking marybuds begin to ope their golden eyes'.

Maryland a state of the eastern US, on the Atlantic coast, surrounding Chesapeake Bay, which was originally named after Queen Henrietta *Maria*, wife of Charles I.

Marylebone a district of London, formerly called ➤ TYBURN; the name comes from the church of 'St Mary on the bourn', the *bourn* being the stream from which *Tyburn* was also named.

Marymass a festival of the Virgin Mary, especially the Assumption, 15 August, or (formerly) Candlemas, 2 February.

marzipan layer the stockbroking executives ranking immediately below the partners in a firm. The expression, recorded from the early 1980s, makes figurative use of the layer of almond paste lying beneath the sugar icing of a cake. Although it is not the top layer, it is nevertheless rich and somewhat luxurious. **Marzipan set** is also used.

Masaccio (1401–28), Italian painter. The first artist to apply the laws of perspective (which he learned from Brunelleschi) to painting, he is remembered particularly for his frescoes in the Brancacci Chapel in Florence (1424–7).

Masada the site, on a steep rocky hill, of the ruins of a palace and fortification built by Herod the Great on the SW shore of the Dead Sea in the 1st

century BC. It was a Jewish stronghold in the Zealots' revolt against the Romans (AD 66–73) and was the scene in AD 73 of mass suicide by the Jewish defenders when the Romans breached the citadel after a siege of nearly two years.

The name may be used allusively of a readiness to anticipate threatened defeat by bringing about one's own destruction first.

> The rural Bosnians are slowly taking on the character of their enemies. Among them a kind of Masada complex predominates.
> — *New Yorker* 4 September 1995

Masaniello byname of Tommaso Aniello (1620–47), leader of a Neapolitan revolt against Spanish rule in 1647. Aniello was a young fisherman who in 1647 led a protest against a tax on fruit; although this was initially successful, when he tried to pursue a violent course against local nobles, he was assassinated.

mascle in heraldry, a lozenge voided, i.e. with a central lozenge-shaped aperture. The word comes (in late Middle English) from Anglo-Norman French, from Anglo-Latin *mascula* 'mesh'.

mascot a person or thing that is supposed to bring good luck or that is used to symbolize a particular event or organization. Recorded from the late 19th century, the word comes via French from modern Provençal *mascotto*, feminine diminutive of *masco* 'witch'.

masculine rhyme a rhyme between final stressed syllables, as *blow/flow* and *confess/redress*.

Mash from a novel (1968) by the American writer Richard Hooker, subsequently a film and (1973–84) a highly successful television series; *Mash* shows an American *Mobile Army Surgical Hospital* during the Korean War, staffed by *Hawkeye Pierce* and his colleagues. It is characterized by an irreverent and antimilitaristic spirit, and a realistic sense of the urgency, and capacity for invention and compromise, required in medical staff dealing with battlefield casualties.

Mashhad a city in NE Iran, close to the border with Turkmenistan. The burial place in AD 809 of the Abbasid caliph Harun ar-Rashid and in 818 of the Shiite leader Ali ar-Rida, it is a holy city of the Shiite Muslims.

mask see also ➤ *the Man in the* IRON *Mask*.

mason a builder or worker in stone; with capital initial, from the mid 17th century, a ➤ FREEMASON.

See also ➤ MASTER *mason*.

Perry Mason in the detective novels of the American writer Erle Stanley Gardner (1889–1970), a notably successful criminal lawyer who always appeared for the defence, and who revealed the true criminal in an exciting courtroom scene. Perry Mason was played in a long-running television series (1957–66) by the actor Raymond Burr.

> He paced around the courtroom in his best Perry Mason routine, unshackled by the customary rules of etiquette and procedure.
> — John Grisham *The Partner* (1997)

Mason–Dixon Line in the US, the boundary between Maryland and Pennsylvania, taken as the northern limit of the slave-owning states before the abolition of slavery; it is named after Charles *Mason* (1730–87) and Jeremiah *Dixon* (1733–77), English astronomers, who defined most of the boundary between Pennsylvania and Maryland by survey in 1763–7.

mason word in Scotland, the secret password or ritual of a Freemason.

mason's mark a distinctive device carved on stone by the mason who dressed it.

the Masorah the collection of information and comment on the text of the traditional Hebrew Bible by the Masoretes.

Masorete any of the Jewish scholars of the 6th to 10th centuries AD who contributed to the establishment of a recognized text of the Hebrew Bible, with pointing and accents to indicate its pronunciation, and to the compilation of the Masorah.

masque a form of amateur dramatic entertainment, popular among the nobility in 16th- and 17th-century England, which consisted of dancing and acting performed by masked players, originally in dumbshow and later with metrical dialogue.

Mass the Christian Eucharist or Holy Communion, especially in the Roman Catholic Church.

Mass was also formerly used for the feast day or festival of a specified saint; this usage now survives only as a suffix, as in *Candlemas, Christmas, Lammas*, and *Michaelmas*.

Recorded from Old English, the word comes from ecclesiastical Latin *missa*, from Latin *miss-* 'dismissed', from *mittere*, perhaps from the last words of the service, '*Ite, missa est* [Go, it is the dismissal]'.

See also ➤ MEAT *and mass*, ➤ TRIDENTINE *mass*.

mass observation the study and record of the social habits and day-to-day activities of large numbers of people.

Massachusetts a state in the north-eastern US, on the Atlantic coast, which was settled by the Pilgrim Fathers in 1620, and which was a centre of resistance to the British before becoming one of the original thirteen states of the Union (1788).

massacre see ➤ PETERLOO *massacre*, ➤ SHARPEVILLE *massacre*, ➤ *the Massacre of* GLENCOE, ➤ *the Massacre of St* BARTHOLOMEW, ➤ *St* VALENTINE'*s Day Massacre*, ➤ SEPTEMBER *massacres*.

Massacre of the Innocents the killing by order of Herod the Great, after the birth of Jesus, of all boy children under two years old (➤ *the* INNOCENTS) in Bethlehem.

In the 19th-century British parliament, the phrase was also used informally for measures which had to be 'sacrificed' at the end of a session for want of time.

master a man who has people working for him. The word is recorded in Old English (later reinforced by Old French *maistre*) and comes from Latin *magister*, probably related to *magis* 'more' (i.e. 'more important').

See also ➤ ANNALS *of the Four Masters*, ➤ *the* EYE *of a master does more work than both his hands*, ➤ JACK *is as good as his master*, ➤ JACK *of all trades and master of none*, ➤ LITTLE *Masters*, ➤ *Master of the* REVELS, ➤ NO *man can serve two masters*, ➤ SEVEN *Wise Masters*.

like master, like man proverbial saying, mid 16th century.

master mason a skilled or qualified mason; a fully qualified Freemason who has passed the third degree.

Master of Arts (a person who has been awarded) a degree (usually above a bachelor's degree) for a high level of proficiency in an arts subject or arts subjects.

master of ceremonies a person in charge of procedure at a state or public occasion.

Master of Stories a name given to Peter Comestor, Chancellor of the University of Paris (d. *c*.1179). The name is a translation of post-classical

Latin *Magister Historiarum* (1267), from the title of *Historia Scholastica*, his history of the world, founded on the Bible.

Master of the King's (or Queen's) Music (the title of) an officer appointed to supervise and conduct military music for the monarch.

Master of the Rolls (in England and Wales) the judge who presides over the Court of Appeal (Civil Division) and who was formerly in charge of the Public Record Office (see ➤ the ROLLS).

Master of the Sentences name given to Peter Lombard, bishop of Paris (d. 1160), translating post-classical Latin *Magister Sententiarum* (*c*.1343), from the title of his theological collection *Sententiarum libri quatuor*.

Masters Tournament a prestigious US golf competition, held in Augusta, Georgia, in which golfers (chiefly professionals) compete only by invitation on the basis of their past achievements. It has been held annually since 1934.

mastic tree in the Apocryphal story of ➤ SUSANNA and the two Elders who accuse her, Daniel detects that the accusation of her adultery is false through the inconsistency of their stories; in particular, in their naming of the tree under which she is said to have met her lover. In some translations, as the Douay Bible of the early 17th century, one of these is said to have been a *mastic tree*; this may be referred to allusively to suggest a story that is untrue.

> 'Whereabouts was I when I met her?'
> Woody gave up the effort. 'Under a mastic tree,' she
> said, laughing.
> — Christianna Brand *Green for Danger* (1945)

Mata Hari (1876–1917), Dutch dancer and secret agent. She became a professional dancer in Paris in 1905 and probably worked for both French and German intelligence services before being executed by the French in 1917. Her name is often used allusively for the type of a beautiful female spy.

matador a bullfighter whose task is to kill the bull. The word is Spanish, and means literally 'killer', from *matar* 'to kill', from Persian *māt* 'dead'.

matai in a Samoan extended family or clan, the person who is chosen to succeed to a chief's or orator's title and honoured as the head of the family.

match see ➤ HATCHES, *matches, and dispatches*, ➤ MAN *of the match*.

matchless see ➤ *the Matchless* ORINDA.

mate see ➤ SCHOLAR's *mate*.

mater see also ➤ ALMA *mater*, ➤ MAGNA *mater*.

mater dolorosa the Virgin Mary sorrowing for the death of Christ, especially as a representation in art. The phrase is Latin, and may originate in the verses ascribed to the Franciscan lay brother Jacopone da Todi (*c*.1230–1306) and others, '*Stabat mater dolorosa luxta crucem lacrimosa* [At the cross her station keeping, stood the sorrowful mother weeping].'

materia medica the body of remedial substances used in the practice of medicine; the study of the origin and properties of these substances. Recorded from the late 17th century, the phrase is modern Latin, translating Greek *hulē iatrikē* 'healing material', the title of a work by the 1st century Greek physician and pharmacologist Dioscorides.

materia prima primeval matter; fundamental substance. The phrase, which is Latin, is recorded in English from the mid 16th century.

materialism the philosophical doctrine that nothing exists except matter and its movements and modifications.

See also ➤ DIALECTICAL *materialism*.

Theobald Mathew (1796–1858), Irish Roman Catholic priest, known as the *Apostle of Temperance*. He took the pledge of total abstinence on 10 April 1838 with the words 'Here goes—in the name of the Lord.'

Mathurin a member of an order of regular canons (officially called Trinitarians) founded in 1198 by St John of *Matha* for the redemption of Christian captives.

Matilda see also ➤ WALTZING *Matilda*.

Matilda (1102–67), English princess, daughter of Henry I and mother of Henry II; known as **the Empress Maud** and **the Lady of England**. Henry's only legitimate child, she was named his heir, but her cousin Stephen seized the throne on Henry's death in 1135. She waged an unsuccessful civil war against Stephen until 1148.

matins a service forming part of the traditional Divine Office of the Western Christian Church, originally said (or chanted) at or after midnight, but historically often held with lauds on the previous evening. Also, a service of morning prayer in various Churches, especially the Anglican Church.

See also ➤ PARISIAN *matins*.

Henri Matisse (1869–1954), French painter and sculptor. His use of non-naturalistic colour led him to be regarded as a leader of the fauvists. His later painting and sculpture displays a trend towards formal simplification and abstraction, and includes large figure compositions and abstracts made from cut-out coloured paper.

matriculate be enrolled at a college or university. Recorded from the late 16th century, the word comes via medieval Latin from late Latin *matricula* 'register', diminutive of Latin *matrix* (see ➤ MATRIX).

matrix an environment or material in which something develops; a surrounding medium or structure; in mathematics, a rectangular array of quantities or expressions in rows and columns that is treated as a single entity and manipulated according to particular rules. Recorded from late Middle English, in the sense 'womb', the word comes from Latin *matrix* 'breeding female', later 'womb'.

matron a married woman, especially a dignified and sober middle-aged one; the marriage service in the *Book of Common Prayer* (1662) includes the prayer that the bride shall 'be a follower of holy and godly matrons.' (In the 15th and 16th centuries, *matron* in Christian usage also denoted a married female saint.)

The term was also sometimes used to denote a married woman with expert knowledge in matters of procreation, childbirth, and pregnancy; if a prisoner who had been sentenced to death pleaded pregnancy as a reason for stay of execution, a **jury of matrons** would be empanelled to examine her.

Recorded from late Middle English, the word comes via Old French from Latin *matrona*, from *mater, matr-* 'mother'.

Matronalia in ancient Rome, a festival in honour of the goddess Juno and her son Mars, celebrated by married women.

matsuri a solemn festival celebrated periodically at Shinto shrines in Japan.

matter see also ➤ COLD *dark matter*, ➤ *the* ROOT *of the matter*.

the Matter of Britain term used by Jean Bodel (late 12th–early 13th century) in a French verse romance about Charlemagne (dating from the late 12th century) to describe the subject-matter of the romances concerned with the Arthurian legends, as distinct from those concerned with classical stories (➤ *the* MATTER *of Rome*) or with Charlemagne and his circle (➤ *the* MATTER *of France*).

the Matter of England a term sometimes used by 20th-century scholars to refer to romances concerned with English heroes or localized in England (such as *King Horn* or *Havelok the Dane*) which therefore fall outside the three subject-matters said by Jean Bodel to be the only ones: the Matters of Britain, France, and Rome.

the Matter of France the term used by Jean Bodel, a late 12th-century romance writer, to refer to the romances based on stories about Charlemagne and his circle, as distinct from those based on Arthurian or classical legend.

the Matter of Rome the term used by Jean Bodel, a late 12th-century romance writer, to refer to those romances concerned with classical stories, as distinct from Arthurian or Charlemagne legends.

Matterhorn a mountain in the Alps, on the border between Switzerland and Italy, first climbed in 1865 by the English mountaineer ➤ *Edward* WHYMPER. It may be taken as the type of a difficult and dangerous ascent.

St Matthew an Apostle, a tax-gatherer from Capernaum in Galilee, traditional author of the first Gospel.

Matthew may be represented in art as the author of one of the Gospels, in which case his symbol is an angel, one of the ➤ TETRAMORPH. He may alternatively be shown with the instruments of his martyrdom (a spear, sword, or halberd), or with a money-bag or money-box as a sign of his occupation as tax-gatherer. He may also be shown wearing spectacles, perhaps so as to read his accounts.

☐ **FEAST DAY** His feast day is 21 September in the West and 16 November in the East.

Matthew Paris (*c*.1199–1259), English chronicler and Benedictine monk, noted for his *Chronica Majora*, a history of the world from the Creation to the mid 13th century, which is a valuable source for contemporary events.

Matthew principle the principle that more will be given to those who are already provided for. The allusion is to Matthew 25:29, 'Unto every one that hath shall be given, and he shall have abundance; but from him that hath not shall be taken away even that which he hath.' The term **Matthew effect** is also used.

Matthew's Bible an English translation issued in 1537, under the pseudonym of Thomas Matthew, by John Rogers (?1500–55). He was a friend of Tyndale, was converted to Protestantism, and prepared and annotated his version for publication. Rogers was burnt at Smithfield in Mary's reign.

St Matthias an Apostle, chosen by lot after the Ascension to replace Judas. He may be shown with an axe or a halberd as instruments of his martyrdom.
  □ **FEAST DAY** His feast day is 14 May in the Western Church and 9 August in the Eastern Church.

matzo a crisp biscuit of unleavened bread, traditionally eaten by Jews during Passover.

Mau Mau an African secret society originating among the Kikuyu that in the 1950s used violence and terror to try to expel European settlers and end British rule in Kenya. The British eventually subdued the organization, but Kenya gained independence in 1963. The term is Kikuyu, and in probably an application of *mau-mau* used to describe voracious devouring.

maudlin self-pityingly or tearfully sentimental. In Middle English *Maudlin* denotes ► St MARY *Magdalene*, and comes from Old French *Madeleine*, from ecclesiastical Latin *Magdalena*. The sense of the current adjective derives from allusion to pictures of Mary Magdalene weeping.

maulana a Muslim man revered for his religious learning or piety. The word comes from Arabic *mawlānā* 'our master'.

Maunder minimum a prolonged minimum in sunspot activity on the sun between about 1645 and 1715, which coincided with the Little Ice Age in the northern hemisphere. It is named after the English astronomer Edward W. *Maunder* (1851–1928).

Maundy in the UK, a public ceremony on the Thursday before Easter at which the monarch distributes ► MAUNDY *money*; the original form of this ceremony, in which a sovereign, senior cleric, or other eminent person washed the feet of a number of poor people (in commemoration of Christ's washing the Apostles' feet at the Last Supper: John 13), and usually distributed clothing, food, or money (also **Royal Maundy**).
  Recorded from Middle English, the word comes

via Old French from Latin *mandatum* 'commandment'. The words 'A new commandment (*mandatum novum*) give I unto you, that ye love one another' (John 13:34), from the discourse which followed the washing of the apostles' feet, were adopted as the first antiphon sung at the commemorative observance.

Maundy money specially minted silver coins distributed by the British sovereign on Maundy Thursday. The number of recipients and the face value in pence of the amount they each receive traditionally correspond to the number of years in the sovereign's age.
  The distribution of gifts of money has been part of the Royal Maundy ceremony in England since the 13th century. By the 16th century a specific amount of money and a purse to hold it had become part of the ceremony, and by the 18th century the Maundy distribution was made up of the four smallest silver coins, the 4, 3, 2, and 1 penny denominations.

Maundy Thursday the Thursday before Easter, observed in the Christian Church as a commemoration of the Last Supper.

Mauretania an ancient region of North Africa, corresponding to the northern part of Morocco and western and central Algeria. Originally occupied by the Moors (Latin *Mauri*), it was annexed by Claudius in the mid 1st century AD and conquered by the Arabs in the 7th century.
  The name is based on Latin *Mauri* 'Moors', by whom the region was originally occupied.

St Maurice 3rd-century soldier-saint, said to have been leader of the ► THEBAN *Legion* and martyred with them for refusing to sacrifice to the pagan gods. In medieval iconography he is often shown as an African.
  □ **FEAST DAY** His feast day is 22 September.

Maurist a member of the French Benedictine congregation founded in 1621 famous for its scholarship. It was named after St *Maurus*, 6th-century disciple of St Benedict, who was adopted as patron of the congregation.

Mauritania a country in West Africa with a coastline on the Atlantic Ocean, which was a centre of Berber power in the 11th and 12th centuries, at which time Islam became established in the region. Later, nomadic Arab tribes became dominant, while on the coast European nations, especially France, established trading posts.

Matthew Fontaine Maury (1806–73), American oceanographer. He conducted the first systematic survey of oceanic winds and currents, and published charts of his findings.

Maurya a dynasty which ruled northern India 321–*c*.184 BC. It was founded by ➤ CHANDRAGUPTA *Maurya*, who introduced a centralized government and uniform script, and developed a highway network which led to Mauryan control of most of the Indian subcontinent. The oldest extant Indian art dates from this era.

mausoleum a building, especially a large and stately one, housing a tomb or tombs. The word comes via Latin from Greek *Mausōlos*, the name of a king of Caria (4th century BC), to whose tomb in Halicarnassus, erected by his queen Artemisia and considered one of the ➤ SEVEN *Wonders of the World*, the name was originally applied.

maverick an unorthodox or independent-minded person; a person refusing to conform to a particular party or group. The word comes from the North American term for an unbranded calf or yearling, and dates in that sense from the mid 19th century, from the name of Samuel A. *Maverick* (1803–70), a Texas engineer and rancher who did not brand his cattle.

mavis a poetic or literary name for a song thrush. Recorded from late Middle English, the word comes from Old French *mauvis*, of unknown origin.

mawworm a hypocritical pretender to sanctity, from *Mawworm*, a character in Isaac Bickerstaffe's play *The Hypocrite*, 1769 (a *mawworm* is a parasitic worm).

Maxim gun the first fully automatic water-cooled machine gun, designed in Britain in 1884 and used especially in the First World War. In a satiric verse by Hilaire Belloc (1870–1953), it is seem as typifying the military power of a developed nation:

> Whatever happens we have got
> The Maxim Gun, and they have not.
> — Hilaire Belloc *The Modern Traveller* (1898)

Maxim's a fashionable restaurant in the rue Royale, Paris, opened in 1893, and forming a social and cultural centre.

> Jewelled ladies supping at Maxim's.
> — Cecil Beaton diary, August 1957

Maximilian (1832–67), Austrian emperor of Mexico 1864–7. Brother of Franz Josef, Maximilian was established as emperor of Mexico under French auspices in 1864. He was executed by firing squad with two companions after a popular uprising led by Benito Juárez; the scene was the subject of a painting by Manet, 'The Execution of the Emperor Maximilian of Mexico' (1867), influenced by Goya's ➤ *The 3rd of* MAY.

Maxwell's demon a hypothetical being imagined as controlling a hole in a partition dividing a gas-filled container into two parts, and allowing only fast-moving molecules to pass in one direction, and slow-moving molecules in the other. This would result in one side of the container becoming warmer and the other colder, in violation of the second law of thermodynamics. It is named after the Scottish physicist James Clerk *Maxwell* (1831–79).

May the fifth month of the year, in the northern hemisphere usually considered the last month of spring and harbinger of summer. From the late 16th century, *May* in poetic use also denotes one's bloom or prime.

Recorded from Old English, the name comes from Latin *Maius*, probably from the name of a deity cognate with the name of the goddess *Maia* and with *magnus* 'great'.

See also ➤ *here we go gathering* NUTS *in May*, ➤ APRIL *showers bring forth May flower*, ➤ KING *of the May*, ➤ MARRY *in May, rue the day*, ➤ *ne'er* CAST *a clout till May be out*, ➤ QUEEN *of the May*, ➤ SELL *in May and go away*, ➤ *so many mists in* MARCH, *so many frosts in May*.

the 3rd of May informal name for Goya's picture 'The 3rd of May 1808: The Execution of the Defenders of Madrid', painted to commemorate the execution by the French of Spanish insurgents against the invading Napoleonic forces; it later influenced Manet's depiction of the execution of the Emperor ➤ MAXIMILIAN.

May and January a young woman and an old man as husband and wife; the first instance of this image is found in Chaucer's *Merchant's Tale* (*c*.1395).

May ball at the University of Cambridge, a ball or similar entertainment held during ➤ MAY *Week*.

May basket originally in the US, a basket of flowers or (occasionally) confectionery, traditionally hung or left at the door of a loved one or friend on May Day as a token of affection.

May chickens come cheeping proverbial saying, late 19th century, meaning that the weakness of chickens born in May is apparent from their continuous feeble cries. The proverb has also been linked to the idea that marriage in May is unlucky, and that children of such marriages are less likely to survive.

May Day 1 May, celebrated in many countries as a traditional springtime festival or as an international day honouring workers.

Ill May Day a name for 1 May 1517, when London apprentices attacked foreign artisans and merchants. Also called *Evil May Day*.

May dew dew gathered in the month of May, especially on 1 May, popularly supposed to have medicinal and cosmetic properties.

May game a performance or entertainment (typically involving the characters of Robin Hood and Maid Marian) forming part of celebrations held on ➤ MAY *Day*; the merrymaking and sports associated with this. The term is recorded from the early 16th century; by the middle of the century, the phrase **make a May game of**, meaning make a laughing-stock of someone, had developed.

May garland a garland of flowers displayed during traditional celebrations of spring in Britain, especially on May Day, but on other days (such as ➤ GARLAND *Day*) according to region.

May meeting each of a succession of annual meetings of various religious and philanthropic societies formerly held during the month of May in Exeter Hall, London, and other buildings.

May Queen a pretty girl chosen and crowned with flowers in traditional celebrations of May Day; in 1591 an allegorical entertainment showing the *May Queen* being met by her nymphs was presented before Queen Elizabeth I.

May 7th designating an institution in the People's Republic of China in which study is combined with physical, typically agricultural, labour, so that cadres may experience the lifestyle of a peasant.

May the 4th Movement a demonstration held by students in Peking (now Beijing) on 4 May 1919, to protest against the Chinese government's failure to oppose the decision by the Versailles Peace Committee to allocate Germany's former possessions in China to Japan. This demonstration is generally seen as having been a catalyst for wider cultural and intellectual revolution in China.

May Week at Cambridge University, a week in late May or early June when intercollegiate boat races are held.

Maya[1] the mother of Siddhartha Gautama, the ➤ BUDDHA. According to Buddhist legend, the birth of her son was foretold in a dream in which she saw a white elephant with six tusks entering her side; she later gave birth in the wooded garden of Lumbini, standing with her right hand on the branch of a sal tree, while the child emerged from her right hip. The scenes of Maya and the elephant, and the birth of the Buddha, are frequently depicted in Buddhist art.

Maya[2] an American Indian people of Yucatán and elsewhere in Central America, with a civilization which developed over an extensive area of southern Mexico, Guatemala, and Belize from the 2nd millennium BC, reaching its peak *c.*300–*c.*900 AD. Its remains include stone temples built on pyramids and ornamented with sculptures. The Mayas had a cumbersome system of pictorial writing and an extremely accurate calendar system.

maya in Hinduism, the supernatural power wielded by gods and demons; in Hinduism and Buddhism, the power by which the universe becomes manifest; the illusion or appearance of the phenomenal world. The word comes from Sanskrit *māyā* 'create'.

Mayday an international radio distress signal used by ships and aircraft. Recorded from the 1920s, the word represents a pronunciation of French *m'aider*, from *venez m'aider* 'come and help me'.
    See also ➤ CQD, ➤ SOS.

Mayfair a fashionable and opulent district in the West End of London which includes the site of a fair which was held annually from the 17th century to the end of the 18th century in Brook fields near Hyde Park Corner; the area takes its name from this. **Mayfair boy** is a dated term for a gentleman crook of the 1930s.

Mayflower the ship in which the Pilgrim Fathers sailed from England to America. It arrived at Cape Cod on 21 November 1620 after a voyage of sixty-six days.

Mayflower Compact a document signed by 41 of the male passengers prior to their landing at Plymouth; it formed the signatories into a body politic for the purpose of establishing a government.

mayfly this short-lived slender insect with delicate transparent wings, living close to water, is proverbial for its brief existence.

> The integrated-intelligent-systems researchers have yet to build a machine with the survival ability of a mayfly.
> — *Scientific American* December 1991

mayhem violent or damaging disorder; chaos; as a legal term, the crime of maliciously injuring or maiming someone, originally so as to render the victim defenceless.

Recorded from the early 16th century, the word comes from Old French, from the same base as *maim*. The sense 'disorder, chaos' (originally US) dates from the late 19th century.

Maynooth a village in County Kildare in the Republic of Ireland, which is the site of St Patrick's College, a Roman Catholic seminary founded in 1795.

mayonnaise a thick creamy dressing consisting of egg yolks beaten with oil and vinegar and seasoned, probably from the feminine of *mahonnais* 'of or from Port Mahon', the capital of Minorca.

mayor the elected head of the municipal corporation of a city or borough. In some countries, such as England and Wales, the mayor is a ceremonial figure and is elected by the council; in other countries, such as the US and Canada, the mayor has substantial power and is elected by popular vote.

Recorded from Middle English, the word comes via Old French from the Latin adjective *major* 'greater', used as a noun in late Latin.

The Mayor of Garratt title of a play by the satirist Samuel Foote (1720–77), taking as its subject one of the mock elections which took place annually between 1747 and 1796 in the Garratt Lane district of Wandsworth.

Mayor of the Palace in the Frankish kingdoms, a nominal subordinate wielding the power of his titular superior, originally in the Frankish kingdoms under the later Merovingian kings. The title represents French *maire du palais* and post-classical Latin *major palatii*.

maypole a tall pole, traditionally decorated with flowers or greenery and often with painted spiral stripes, set up on a green or other open space, around which people dance during May or springtime celebrations; in the 17th century, it was one of the symbols of secular revelry particularly disliked by Puritans. The tradition of dancers holding long ribbons attached to the top of the pole dates from the 19th century.

See also ➤ MERRY *Mount*.

Mazar-e-Sharif a city in northern Afghanistan, whose name means 'tomb of the saint', and which is the reputed burial place of Ali, son-in-law of Muhammad.

Jules Mazarin (1602–61), Italian-born French statesman. Sent to Paris as the Italian papal legate (1634), he became a naturalized Frenchman, and entered the service of Louis XIII in 1639. He was made a cardinal in 1641 and then chief minister of France (1642). His administration during the minority of Louis XIV provoked the civil wars of the Fronde (1648–53).

Mazarin Bible the first printed bible, and probably the first book to be printed with movable type, *c*.1455, probably by Gutenberg in association with Fust and Schöffer. The first known copy was discovered in the Mazarine Library in Paris, the splendid library founded by Cardinal ➤ MAZARIN. It is also known as the *Forty-Two Line Bible* from the number of lines to the column.

Mazda see ➤ AHURA *Mazda*.

Mazdaism another term for ➤ ZOROASTRIANISM.

Giuseppe Mazzini (1805–72), Italian nationalist leader. He founded the patriotic movement Young Italy (1831) and was a leader of the Risorgimento. Following the country's unification as a monarchy in 1861, he continued to campaign for a republican Italy.

M.B. an abbreviation of Mark of the Beast, used especially in **M.B. waistcoat** with humorous allusion to the belief of some Anglicans that this garment was characteristically worn by clergymen influenced by or inclined to Roman Catholicism.

MCC Marylebone Cricket Club, founded in 1787, which has its headquarters at Lord's Cricket Ground in London. The tacitly accepted governing body of cricket until 1969, it continues to have primary responsibility for the game's laws.

ME short for myalgic encephalitis or ➤ CHRONIC *fatigue syndrome*.

mea culpa an acknowledgement of one's guilt or responsibility for an error; a Latin phrase, meaning literally '(through) my own fault', from the prayer of confession in the Latin liturgy of the Church.

mead an alcoholic drink of fermented honey and water. Recorded from Old English and of Germanic origin, the word is related to Dutch *mee* and German *Met*, from an Indo-European root shared by Sanskrit *madhu* 'sweet drink, honey' and Greek *methu* 'wine'.

Meal-tub Plot the name given to an alleged Catholic conspiracy of 1679 to assassinate Charles I and the Earl of Shaftesbury, documents concerning which were said to be concealed in a meal-tub in the house of Elizabeth Cellier, who was tried for high treason and acquitted. The affair was part of the ➤ POPISH *plot* concocted by Titus Oates and his associates.

meander (of a river or road) follow a winding course. The word comes (in the late 16th century) through Latin from Greek *Maiandros*, the name of a river noted for its winding course.

means see ➤ COMMITTEE *of Ways and Means*, ➤ *the* END *justifies the means*.

means test an official investigation into someone's financial circumstances to determine whether they are eligible for a welfare payment.

there is measure in all things proverbial saying, late 14th century.
See also ➤ MAN *is the measure of all things.*

meat an archaic expression for food of any kind. The word in this sense is recorded from Old English; the current sense of 'the flesh of an animal' dates from the Middle English period.
See also ➤ GOD *sends meat, but the Devil sends cooks,* ➤ QUICK *at meat, quick at work,* ➤ STRONG *meat.*

meat and mass never hindered man proverbial saying, early 17th century, indicating human need for physical and spiritual sustenance.

one man's meat is another man's poison proverbial saying, late 16th century; the Roman poet Lucretius (*c.*94–55 BC) in his *De Rerum Natura* has the comment, 'what is food to one person may be bitter poison to others'.

after meat, mustard a traditional comment, late 16th century, on some essential ingredient which is brought too late of be of use.

Mebyon Kernow Cornish, meaning 'Sons of Cornwall', name of the Cornish nationalist movement. The society first met on 6 January 1951 in Redruth, Cornwall, and became a political party by fielding a candidate in the general election of 1970.

Mec Vannin Manx, meaning 'Sons of (the Isle of) Man', a Manx nationalist party.

Mecca a city in western Saudi Arabia, an oasis town in the Red Sea region of Hejaz, east of Jiddah, considered by Muslims to be the holiest city of Islam. It was the birthplace in AD 570 of the prophet ➤ MUHAMMAD, and was the scene of his early teachings before his emigration to Medina in 622 (the ➤ HEGIRA). On Muhammad's return to Mecca in 630 it became the centre of the new Muslim faith. It is the site of the Great Mosque and the ➤ KAABA, and is a centre of Islamic ritual, including the haj pilgrimage which leads thousands of visitors to the city each year.

Meccano trademark name for a children's construction set for making mechanical models, consisting chiefly of metal girders, brackets, and other components. The product was marketed in 1902 under the name 'Mechanics Made Easy'; *Meccano* (perhaps an alteration of French *mécano* 'mechanic') was coined at some time during 1907. It had an Esperanto-like sound which was readily accepted by the growing international fraternity of Meccano model-builders.
    Meccano is often referred to as a toy particularly enjoyed by boys.

> Part of the whole oddity of being male, like obsessions with war and Meccano and cars.
> — Elspeth Barker *O Caledonia* (1991)

Mecklenburg Declaration of Independence signed in Charlotte, main city of Mecklenburg County in North Carolina, on 20 May 1775; it is still celebrated annually. Charlotte was named *the hornet's nest* by the British commander, Lord Cornwallis, when he occupied it in 1780, and this symbol has become the city's emblem.

medal see ➤ LEATHER *medal,* ➤ MILITARY *Medal,* ➤ PUTTY *medal,* ➤ *the* REVERSE *of the medal.*

medal chief in the colonial period, a North American Indian chief who received a medal from the British colonial or US authorities.

Medal of Honour in the US, an award for gallantry, instituted in 1862.

St Médard (*c.*470–*c.*560), bishop of Vermandois. It is popularly supposed (as with ➤ *St* SWITHIN) that the weather on his feast day determines the pattern for the succeeding 40 days, and he is also invoked against toothache.

☐ **FEAST DAY** His feast day is 8 June.

Medb Irish form of the name of ➤ MAEVE, legendary queen of Connacht in the Ulster cycle.

Mede a member of an Indo-European people who inhabited ancient Media, establishing an extensive empire during the 7th century BC, which was conquered by Cyrus the Great of Persia in 550 BC.

See also ➤ *law of the* MEDES *and Persians*.

Medea in Greek mythology, princess of Colchis and a sorceress, traditionally with a knowledge of poisons. She helped ➤ JASON to obtain the ➤ GOLDEN *Fleece* from her father Aeetes, and married him; assisting the Argonauts to escape from Colchis, she murdered her younger brother. When Jason deserted her for Creusa, the daughter of King Creon of Corinth, she took revenge by killing Creon, Creusa, and her own children, and fled to Athens. She is taken as the type of a vengeful and ruthless woman.

See also ➤ COLCHICUM.

law of the Medes and Persians in biblical allusion, a law, or system of laws, that cannot be altered. The reference, which has become proverbial, is to Daniel 6:15, 'the law of the Medes and Persians is, That no decree nor statute which the king establisheth may be changed.'

medical finger former term for the finger next to the little finger, especially of the left hand, traditionally so called because it is the finger used by physicians to handle ground salves. *Medical finger* is recorded from the mid 17th century and is a translation of 16th-century French *doigt medical* (the first appearance of *medical* in French) after classical Latin *digitus medicus* in the writings of Pliny. Other earlier names for this finger in English were *leech finger* and *medicinal finger*.

Medicean designating any of the four largest moons of Jupiter (Io, Europa, Ganymede, or Callisto), named by their discoverer Galileo in honour of his patron Cosimo II de' Medici.

Medici a powerful Italian family of bankers and merchants whose members effectively ruled Florence for much of the 15th century, and to whom belonged four popes, including Leo X (1513–21) and Clement VII (1523–34), and two queens of France;

from 1569 they were grand dukes of Tuscany.

See also ➤ CATHERINE *de' Medici*, ➤ COSIMO *de' Medici*, ➤ LORENZO *de' Medici*.

medicine a compound or preparation used for the treatment or prevention of disease, especially a drug or drugs taken by mouth. Recorded from Middle English, the word comes via Old French from Latin *medicina*, from *medicus* 'physician'.

See also ➤ COMPLEMENTARY *medicine*.

medicine man (among North American Indians and some other peoples) a person believed to have magical powers of healing; a shaman.

medieval Latin Latin of about AD 600–1500.

Medina a city in western Saudi Arabia, which was the refuge of Muhammad's infant Muslim community from its removal from Mecca in AD 622 until its return there in 630. It was renamed Medina, meaning 'city', by Muhammad and made the capital of the new Islamic state until it was superseded by Damascus in 661. It is Muhammad's burial place and the site of the first Islamic mosque, constructed around his tomb. It is considered by Muslims to be the second most holy city after Mecca, and a visit to the prophet's tomb at Medina often forms a sequel to the formal pilgrimage to Mecca.

Mediterranean an almost landlocked sea between southern Europe, the north coast of Africa, and SW Asia. It is connected with the Atlantic by the Strait of Gibraltar, with the Red Sea by the Suez Canal, and with the Black Sea by the Dardanelles, the Sea of Marmara, and the Bosporus.

The name comes from post-classical Latin *Mediterraneus*, and the notion expressed by it may originally have been 'the sea in the middle of the earth' rather than 'the sea enclosed by land'.

See also ➤ *the* LIGHTHOUSE *of the Mediterranean*.

Medmenham Abbey a ruined Cistercian abbey on the Thames near Marlow, rebuilt as a residence and notorious in the 18th century as the meeting-place of a convivial club known as the *Franciscans* or *Hell-fire Club*. This was founded by Francis Dashwood, and John Wilkes and Bubb Dodington were among its members. Its motto '*Fay ce que voudras*' was adopted from that of Rabelais's abbey of ➤ THÉLÈME.

Medusa the only one of the three ➤ GORGONS who was mortal, the sight of her head was so terrible that even after her death anyone who saw it was turned to stone. With the help of the gods, she was killed by ➤ PERSEUS; the winged horses ➤ PEGASUS and Chrysaor sprang from her blood as it was shed. Her name is used allusively with reference to her snaky hair and stony gaze.

Hans van Meegeren (1889–1947), Dutch painter and forger. He became famous after the Second World War, when it was revealed that he had forged a number of paintings attributed to Vermeer and other Dutch masters, many of which had been acquired by leading Nazis. Charged with collaboration, Van Meegeren confessed to an elaborate scheme for forging and disposing of paintings.

meeja non-standard spelling of *media*, used humorously in imitation of informal British speech. The form first cropped up in the mid 1980s, and became increasingly common, perhaps partly as a result of public debate about the role of the media, and especially the intrusion of journalists from the popular press into people's private lives.

meerschaum a soft white clay-like material consisting of hydrated magnesium silicate, found chiefly in Turkey, and much used in making tobacco pipes. The word in German means literally 'sea-foam', alluding to the frothy appearance of the silicate.

Meerut a city in northern India, in Uttar Pradesh north-east of Delhi, which was the scene in May 1857 of the first uprising against the British in the Indian Mutiny.

meet the challenge—make the change Labour Party slogan, 1989.

do not meet troubles half-way proverbial saying, late 19th century.

Meeting for Sufferings in the Society of Friends, an organization originally set up for investigating and relieving the hardships of those from whom payment of tithes was demanded.

Meg see ➤ LONG *Meg and her Daughters*, ➤ LONG *Meg of Westminster*, ➤ *Meg* MERRILIES.

Megaera in Greek mythology, one of the ➤ FURIES.

megalith a large stone that forms a prehistoric monument (e.g. a standing stone) or part of one (e.g. a stone circle or chambered tomb).

Megan's law a law passed in New Jersey, US, in 1994 which permits police to notify families if a convicted sex offender moves into their area; also, designating similar (proposed) laws in other states or countries, especially national legislation passed in the US in 1996, which makes notification of residents obligatory.

It was named after *Megan* Kanka, a 7-year-old girl who was murdered in 1994 in New Jersey, US, by a convicted child sex offender living near her home.

Megarian an inhabitant of the ancient Greek city of Megara, and in particular, a member or adherent of the school of philosophy founded *c*.400 BC by Euclides of Megara.

megaron the central hall of a large house in ancient Mycenae; its rectangular form is sometimes thought to be a precursor of the Doric temple.

Megiddo an ancient city of NW Palestine, situated to the south-east of Haifa in present-day Israel. Its commanding location made the city the scene of many early battles, and from its name the word *Armageddon* ('hill of Megiddo') is derived. It was the scene in 1918 of the defeat of Turkish forces by the British under General Allenby.

Megillah a book of the Hebrew scriptures (the Song of Solomon, Ruth, Lamentations, Ecclesiastes, and Esther) appointed to be read on certain Jewish notable days, especially the Book of Esther, read at the festival of Purim.

the whole megillah informal expression for something in its entirety, especially a complicated set of arrangements or a long-winded story. The phrase, which represents Yiddish *a gantse megile*, alludes to the length of the Megillah.

megrims an archaic term for depression, low spirits. Recorded from late Middle English, the word is a variant of *migraine*. Both come ultimately (in Middle English, via French and late Latin) from Greek *hēmikrania*, from *hēmi-* 'half' + *kranion* 'skull', in relation to the headache's typically affecting one side of the head.

Meiji the period when Japan was ruled by the emperor Meiji Tenno (1868–1912), marked by the modernization and westernization of the country.

Mein Kampf 'My Struggle', title of Hitler's autobiography, first published in German in two volumes in 1925 and 1927, and later widely translated. It embodies the principles of National Socialism which the author was later to put into practice.

meinie archaic term for a body of retainers or followers, a retinue. Recorded from Middle English, the word comes, via Old French, from the same Latin base as *mansion*; it was also influenced by *many* noun.

meiosis in rhetoric, another term for ➤ LITOTES. Recorded from the mid 16th century, the word comes via modern Latin, from Greek *meiōsis*, from *meioun* 'lessen', from *meiōn* 'less'.

Meissen fine hard-paste porcelain produced in Meissen, a city in Saxony, eastern Germany, since 1710, in Britain often called Dresden china. The name may be used allusively for the type of a woman whose looks evoke the delicacy of a Meissen figurine.

> Her face ... had the smooth, pleased prettiness of Meissen.
>
> — J. Wade *Back to Life* (1961)

Meistersinger a member of one of the guilds of German lyric poets and musicians which flourished from the 12th to 17th century. Their technique was elaborate and they were subject to rigid regulations, as depicted in Wagner's opera *Die Meistersinger von Nürnberg* (1868).

Mekhitarist a member of a congregation of Roman Catholic Armenian monks originally founded at Constantinople in 1701 by Mekhitar, an Armenian, and finally established by him in 1717 in the island of San Lazzaro, south of Venice.

the Mekon in the *Eagle* comic strip from *c.*1950, the adversary of ➤ *Dan* DARE, who constantly plots to dominate the solar system. His name is used allusively both for his cunning and powerful brain, and for his bald head.

> What Mekon minds they must have, these Labour men, manipulating the Tory factions to bash each other robotically like Punch and Judy.
>
> — *Daily Telegraph* 11 December 1996

mela in the Indian subcontinent, a fair or Hindu festival.

melampodium a former name for black hellebore, derived by Pliny from the name of *Melampos*, a mythical Greek soothsayer and healer.

melancholy a deep, pensive, and long-lasting sadness. In the Middle Ages, *melancholy* was also synonymous with ➤ *black* BILE, one of the four bodily humours.

The word comes ultimately from Greek *melas*

'black' + *kholē* 'bile', an excess of which was formerly believed to cause depression.

Melanchthon Greek name (meaning 'black earth') taken as a direct translation of his own surname by the German Protestant reformer Philipp Schwarzerd (1497–1560). He helped to systematize Luther's teachings in the *Loci Communes* (1521) and drew up the ➤ AUGSBURG *Confession* (1530).

Melba the name of the Australian operatic soprano Dame Nellie Melba (1861–1931), used in a number of figurative and allusive contexts. In Australia, the informal expression **do a Melba** refers to the repeated 'farewell' appearances made by her.

Melchior the traditional name of one of the ➤ MAGI, represented as a king of Nubia.

Melchizedek in the Bible, a priest and king of Salem (which is usually identified with Jerusalem). He was revered by Abraham, who paid tithes to him (Genesis 14:18), and he is described as bringing out bread and wine; this was later taken in the Christian Church as prefiguring the Eucharist.

Meleager[1] in Greek mythology, a hero at whose birth the Fates declared that he would die when a brand then on the fire was consumed. His mother Althaea seized the brand and kept it, but threw it back into the fire when he quarrelled with and killed her brothers in a hunting expedition, whereupon he died.

He is said to have hunted down and killed the ➤ CALYDONIAN *boar*, in the company of ➤ ATALANTA, with whom he was in love, and who first wounded the boar. He gave the spoils of the chase to her, and it was the attempt of his uncles to deprive her of them that brought about their deaths.

Meleager[2] (fl. 1st century BC), Greek poet, best known as the compiler of *Stephanos*, one of the first large anthologies of epigrams, he also wrote many epigrams of his own and short poems on love and death.

Meliboea an island forming part of ancient Syria, colonized from Thessaly, and famous for its purple dye.

Melicertes in Greek mythology, the son of Ino (➤ LEUCOTHEA), who became the sea-god Palaemon. According to tradition, his drowned mortal body was washed up on the Isthmus of Corinth, where the ➤ ISTHMIAN *Games* were founded in his memory.

Melkite originally, an Eastern Christian adhering to the Orthodox faith as defined by the councils of Ephesus (AD 431) and Chalcedon (AD 451) and as accepted by the Byzantine emperor. Now, an Orthodox or Uniate Christian belonging to the patriarchate of Antioch, Jerusalem, or Alexandria.

The name comes via ecclesiastical Latin from Byzantine Greek *Melkhitai* representing Syriac *malkāyā* 'royalists' (i.e. expressing agreement with the Byzantine emperor), from *malkā* 'king'.

mell supper in northern England, celebrating the completion of harvest; *mell* denotes the last sheaf of corn cut at harvest-time.

the Mellifluous Doctor in the *Golden Legend*, name given to St Bernard of Clairvaux (1090–1153), in recognition of his eloquence.

Sebastian Melmoth the name adopted by Oscar Wilde after his trial; *Melmoth the Wanderer* had been the title of a novel (1820) by Charles Robert Maturin (1782–1824).

melodrama originally, a stage-play (typically romantic and sensational in plot and incident) with songs interspersed and action accompanied by appropriate orchestral music. As the musical element ceased to be regarded as essential, the word came to mean a sensational dramatic piece with exaggerated characters and exciting events intended to appeal to the emotions.

Recorded from the early 19th century, the word comes via French from Greek *melos* 'music' + French *drame* 'drama'.

Melos a Greek island in the Aegean Sea, in the south-west of the Cyclades group. It was the centre of a flourishing civilization in the Bronze Age and is the site of the discovery in 1820 of a Hellenistic marble statue of Aphrodite, the Venus de Milo.

Melpomene in classical mythology, the Muse of tragedy. Her name, which is Greek, means literally 'singer'.

meltdown an accident in a nuclear reactor in which the fuel overheats and melts the reactor core or shielding; in figurative use, a disastrous event, especially a rapid fall in share prices.

meltemi a dry north-westerly wind which blows during the summer in the eastern Mediterranean. The name comes from modern Greek and Turkish.

melting pot a place where different elements, such as peoples, styles, or theories, are mixed together. The term is used particularly of a country seen as one in which diverse races and cultures are assimilated:

> America is God's Crucible, the great Melting-Pot where all the races of Europe are melting and reforming.
> — Israel Zangwill *Melting-Pot* (1909)

Melungeon a member of a people of mixed Black, White, and Amerindian descent inhabiting the southern Appalachian mountains in the eastern US. The name may be an alteration of *mélange*.

Mélusine in French medieval legend, a fairy, connected with various French princely houses, as the house of Lusignan. According to legend, although she appeared as a beautiful woman, she had the tail of a serpent.

member see ➤ UNRULY *member*.

memento mori an object serving as a warning or reminder of death, such as a skull. Recorded from the late 16th century, the Latin phrase means literally, 'remember (that you have) to die'.

Memnon a mythical king of the Ethiopians, son of Aurora and Tithonus, who fought for the Trojans at the siege of Troy and was killed by Achilles. He was associated by the ancients with various eastern lands, and in the 17th century **Memnonian** was used to mean 'oriental, Persian', as in Milton's *Paradise Lost* Susa is described as the 'Memnonian Palace' of Xerxes.

In the ancient world a colossus of Amenophis III at Thebes in Egypt was believed by the Greeks to be a statue of *Memnon*; it was said to give forth a musical sound when touched by the dawn.

Memorial Day in the US, a day on which those who died on active service are remembered, usually the last Monday in May, but on other days in some Southern states; it was originally a Union holiday after the Civil War of 1861–5.

memory see also ➤ *a* LIAR *ought to have a good memory*.

the Immortal Memory traditional toast to a revered person; ➤ GRAY's *Inn* on special guest nights drink to 'the pious, glorious and immortal memory' of Elizabeth I, and it is also drunk to Robert Burns (1759–96) at ➤ BURNS *Night* suppers.

down memory lane recalling a pleasant past; from *Down Memory Lane* (1949), the title of a compilation of Mack Sennett comedy shorts.

Memphis¹ an ancient city of Egypt, whose ruins are situated on the Nile about 15 km (nearly 10 miles) south of Cairo. It is thought to have been founded as the capital of the Old Kingdom of Egypt *c.*3100 BC by Menes, the ruler of the first Egyptian dynasty, who united the kingdoms of Upper and Lower Egypt. Associated with the god Ptah, it remained one of Egypt's principal cities even after Thebes was made the capital of the New Kingdom *c.*1550 BC. It is the site of the pyramids of Saqqara and Giza and the Sphinx.

Memphis² a river port on the Mississippi in the extreme south-west of Tennessee, named after the ancient city on the Nile because of its river location. Founded in 1819, it was the home in the late 19th century of blues music, the scene in 1968 of the assassination of Martin Luther King, and the childhood home and burial place of Elvis Presley.

men see also ➤ MEN *in buckram.*

men in black in the US, dark-clothed men of unknown identity or origin, who supposedly visit those who have seen a UFO or reported an alien encounter, in order to suppress any public account of the incident.

> CIA 'dirty trick' tactics included surveillance of UFO groups to make them look silly—the origin of the Men in Black legend.
> — *Daily Mail* 16 February 1998

men in (grey) suits powerful men within an organization who exercise their influence or authority anonymously.

> Margaret Thatcher was brought down by a brief, tacit alliance of 'men in grey suits' and Thatcher loyalists.
> — *Sunday Telegraph* 25 November 1990

men in white coats humorous term for psychiatrists or psychiatric workers (used to imply that somebody is mad or mentally unbalanced).

> I wondered just how much more stupid I could get before men in white coats would lead me away.
> — J. Curran *K2* (1987)

so many men, so many opinions proverbial saying, late 14th century, meaning that the greater the number of people involved, the greater the number of different opinions there will be.

See also ➤ QUOT *homines, tot sententiae.*

the more I see of men, the more I like dogs saying attributed to the French writer and revolutionary Madame Roland (1754–93); she was guillotined after the fall of the Girondists. In *L'Esprit des bêtes* (1847) the French writer A. Toussenel said, 'The more one gets to know of men, the more one values dogs.'

men's movement (chiefly in the US) a movement aimed at liberating men from traditional views about their character and role in society.

The term is first found in the 1970s, where it implies conscious contradistinction to the *women's movement* of the period. In the 1980s and 1990s the term found fresh currency, in particular through ➤ MYTHOPOETIC attempts to redefine the male role.

Menai Strait a channel separating Anglesey from the mainland of NW Wales. It is spanned by two bridges, a suspension bridge built by Thomas Telford 1819–26 and a second, built by Robert Stephenson 1846–50, which originally carried railway tracks within gigantic box girders but was rebuilt to a more conventional design as a combined road and rail bridge after being damaged by fire in 1970.

Menalcas personal name in Virgil's *Eclogues*, used allusively for a shepherd in 16th and 17th-century poetry.

Menander (*c.*342–292 BC), Greek dramatist. His comic plays deal with domestic situations and capture colloquial speech patterns. The sole complete extant play is *Dyskolos.*

Mencius (*c.*371–*c.*289 BC), Chinese philosopher. Noted for developing Confucianism, he believed that rulers should provide for the welfare of the people and that human nature is intrinsically good.

mend see ➤ MAKE *do and mend.*

Gregor Johann Mendel (1822–84), Moravian monk, the father of genetics. From systematically breeding peas he demonstrated the transmission of characteristics in a predictable way by factors (genes) which remain intact and independent between generations and do not blend, though they may mask one another's effects.

Menderes a river of SW Turkey, rising in the Anatolian plateau and entering the Aegean Sea south of the Greek island of Samos. Known in ancient times as the *Maeander,* and noted for its winding course, it gave its name to the verb ➤ MEANDER.

mendicant a member of a Christian religious order originally relying solely on alms, a **mendicant friar**. The most important of these orders in the Western Church (often referred to as the *Four Orders*) were the Franciscans, Dominicans, Carmelites, and Augustinian Hermits. Recorded from later Middle English, the term comes from Latin *mendicant-* 'begging', from the verb *mendicare*, from *mendicus* 'beggar', from *mendum* 'deficiency'.

From the early 17th century, the term was extended to Buddhists and members of other religions who lived a wandering life, relying upon alms.

Menelaus in Greek mythology, king of Sparta, husband of ➤ HELEN and brother of ➤ AGAMEMNON. Helen was stolen from him by Paris, an event which provoked the Trojan War. They were reunited after the fall of Troy.

Menes Egyptian pharaoh, reigned *c.*3100 BC. He founded the first dynasty that ruled Egypt and is traditionally held to have united Upper and Lower Egypt with Memphis as its capital.

menhir a tall upright stone of a kind erected in prehistoric times in western Europe. The word comes from Breton *men* 'stone' + *hir* 'long'.

Menin Gate a gateway to the town of ➤ YPRES which is a memorial to British soldiers of the First World War; on it are inscribed the names of those who have no known grave.

> Here was the world's worst wound. And here with pride
> 'Their name liveth for ever' the Gateway claims.
> Was ever an immolation so belied
> As these intolerably nameless names?
> — Siegfried Sassoon 'On Passing the New Menin Gate' (1928)

Menippus of Gadara (fl. 3rd century BC), Greek cynic philosopher and writer, whose work may be taken as a type of satirical writing.

> Most of my actual writing is Menippean satire, presenting the actual surface of the world we live in as a ludicrous image.
> — Marshall McLuhan letter, 3 February 1976

Mennonite chiefly in the US and Canada, a member of a Protestant sect originating in Friesland in the 16th century, emphasizing adult baptism and rejecting Church organization, military service, and public office. It is named after its founder, *Menno* Simons (1496–1561).

menology a calendar of the Greek Orthodox Church, containing biographies of the saints.

the Menorah a sacred candelabrum with seven branches used in the Temple in Jerusalem, originally that made by the craftsman Bezalel and placed in the sanctuary of the Tabernacle (Exodus 37:17 ff.). The Menorah framed by two olive branches is the emblem of the state of Israel.

The name *menorah* also denotes a candelabrum used in Jewish worship, especially one with eight branches used at Hanukkah.

mens sana in corpore sano Latin tag from the *Satires* of Juvenal (AD *c.*60–*c.*130) meaning 'a rational mind in a healthy body', quoted in English from the early 17th century, and frequently given as the ideal of education.

> *Mens sana in corpore sano* is an unwritten slogan of West Point.
> — *Independent* 16 November 1991

Mensa an international organization founded in England in 1945 whose members must achieve very high scores in IQ tests to be admitted. The name comes from Latin for 'table', with allusion to a round table at which all members have equal status.

Menshevik a member of the non-Leninist wing of the Russian Social Democratic Workers' Party, which proposed moderate reforms and opposed the Bolsheviks' advocacy of revolutionary action by a small political elite. They were defeated by the Bolsheviks after the overthrow of the tsar in 1917.

The name comes from Russian *Men' shevik* 'a member of the minority' from *men' she* 'less'. Lenin coined the name at a time when the party was (untypically) in the minority for a brief period.

mental illness ➤ *St* DYMPNA is the patron saint of those with mental illness.

Mentor in Homer's *Odyssey*, the character in whose guise Athena appears to the young Telemachus and acts as his guide and adviser; the familiarity of the story was reinforced by *Les Aventures des Télémaque* (1699) by the French theologian and writer Fénelon. From the mid 18th century, *mentor* has been used to mean an experienced and trusted adviser.

In the 18th and 19th centuries, *Mentor* was frequently used in book titles to denote a guide-book or book of advice.

Mephistopheles an evil spirit to whom Faust, in the German legend, sold his soul. The origin of the name, which appears first in German in the late 16th century, is uncertain.

Mercalli scale a twelve-point scale for expressing the local intensity of an earthquake, ranging from I (virtually imperceptible) to XII (total destruction). It is named (in the 1920s) after Giuseppe *Mercalli* (1850–1914), Italian geologist.

mercantilism belief in the benefits of profitable trading, in particular, the economic theory that trade generates wealth and is stimulated by the accumulation of profitable balances, which a government should encourage by means of protectionism. The theory was prevalent between 1500 and 1800, mainly in England and France.

Gerardus Mercator (1512–94), Flemish geographer and cartographer, resident in Germany from 1552. He invented the system of map projection that is named after him. The publication of his *Atlas* of part of Europe (1585) introduced the term *atlas* to refer to a book of maps.

Mercator projection a projection of a map of the world on to a cylinder in such a way that all the parallels of latitude have the same length as the equator, first published in 1569 and used especially for marine charts and certain climatological maps.

Mercedarians members of the *Order of the Blessed Virgin Mary of Mercy*, founded at Barcelona in 1218 by St Peter Nolasco (*c*.1182–1256) with the dual aims of tending the sick and rescuing Christians taken prisoner by the Muslims during the Crusades. The Mercedarians took vows which pledged them to offer their own lives, in need be, for those of the hostages. The order was also known as the *Order of Our Lady of Ransom*, and its members were called *Ransomers*, a name which survived even when the order later devoted itself to other charitable work.

The name derives from Latin *mercedem* meaning 'reward, fee, price paid to avert (an evil)', which in Christian Latin from the 6th century was often used in the sense of *misericordia*.

Merchant Adventurers an English trading guild which was involved in trade overseas, principally with the Netherlands (and later Germany) during the 15th–18th centuries. Established in 1407, it engaged chiefly in the lucrative business of exporting woollen cloth. It was formally disbanded in 1806.

merchants ► St Nicholas *of Myra* and St Homobonus (d. 1197), a merchant of Cremona, are the patron saints of merchants.

Mercia a former kingdom of central England. It was established by invading Angles in the 6th century AD in the border areas between the new Anglo-Saxon settlements in the east and the Celtic regions in the west.

the Merciless Doctor nickname of the English physician and physiologist John Haighton (1755–1826), noted for his many and ruthless physiological experiments; it was said that when a colleague disputed some of his results, Haighton killed a favourite spaniel to prove him in the wrong.

Merciless Parliament the parliament of 1388 in which the ► Lords *Appellant* and their supporters condemned the favourites of Richard II, bringing about the exile of Robert de Vere, Earl of Oxford, and Michael de la Pole, Earl of Suffolk.

Mercosur a free-trade agreement creating a common market between countries of the Southern Cone. The initial 'Treaty of Asuncion', was signed by Argentina, Brazil, Paraguay, and Uruguay on 26 March 1991. In 1996, both Chile and Bolivia signed trade accords with Mercosur.

mercurial formerly used to designate those born under the planet Mercury; having the qualities (identical with those assigned to or supposed to be inspired by the god Mercury) considered to be a consequence of this, as eloquence, ingenuity, aptitude for commerce.

In current usage, *mercurial* means subject to sudden or unpredictable changes of mood or mind; although these qualities were originally associated with the god, the allusion is now generally understood as referring to the properties of mercury as a metal.

Mercury in Roman mythology, the Roman god of eloquence, skill, trading, and thieving, herald and messenger of the gods, presider over roads, and conductor of departed souls to Hades, who was identified with ► Hermes. He is usually represented in art as a young man with winged sandals and a winged hat, and bearing the caduceus.

His function as a messenger gave rise to the use of his name in the titles of newspapers and journals, as *The Scotch Mercury* of 1643. (The '*English Mercury* (1588)', sometimes cited as the earliest English newspaper, was in fact an 18th-century forgery.)

In astronomy, *Mercury* is the name of a small planet that is the closest to the sun in the solar system, sometimes visible to the naked eye just after sunset.

From late Middle English, *mercury* was used to denote the chemical element of atomic number 80, a heavy silvery-white metal (also called *quicksilver*) which is liquid at ordinary temperatures. This application probably arose from an analogy between the fluidity of the metal at room temperature and the rapid motion held to be characteristic of the classical deity.

mercy see also ➤ SEVEN *corporal works of mercy*, ➤ SEVEN *spiritual works of mercy*, ➤ SISTER *of Mercy*.

Order of the Blessed Virgin Mary of Mercy the Order of ➤ MERCEDARIANS.

mercy seat the golden covering placed upon the Ark of the Covenant, regarded as the resting-place of God; the throne of God in Heaven. The term is found in Exodus 25:17, 'And thou shalt make a mercy seat of pure gold: two cubits and a half shall be the length and breadth thereof.'

Meredith, we're in catchphrase from *The Bailiff* (1907), a stage sketch by Fred Kitchen (1872–1950).

meridian a circle of constant longitude passing through a given place on the earth's surface and the terrestrial poles; in astronomy, a circle passing through the celestial poles and the zenith of a given place on the earth's surface.

In acupuncture and Chinese medicine, the term denotes each of a set of pathways in the body along which vital energy is said to flow. There are twelve such pathways associated with specific organs.

Recorded from late Middle English, the word comes via Old French from Latin *meridianum* (neuter, used as a noun) 'noon', from *medius* 'middle' + *dies* 'day'. The use in astronomy is due to the fact that the sun crosses a meridian at noon.

Order of Merit in the UK, an order founded in 1902, for distinguished achievement, with membership limited to twenty-four people, and in the sovereign's personal gift.

Merlin in Arthurian legend, the magician who guides the destinies of Arthur and his predecessor Uther; he later grows infatuated with Nimiane (Nimue or Vivien, the ➤ LADY *of the Lake*), who imprisons him in a forest of air in Broceliande where he dies. He is also linked to the Welsh bard Myrddhin and is credited, like him, with a series of prophecies, predicting to ➤ VORTIGERN the triumph of the Britons over the Saxons, as a gloss on the killing of a white dragon by a red one after the two

creatures are released by the digging of the foundations of a citadel from which Vortigern is to fight the Saxons.

In Geoffrey of Monmouth's *Historia Regum Britanniae*, he aids Uther in the deceit by which he marries Igraine and fathers Arthur, and he helps by magic to bring the great stones of Stonehenge from Naas in Ireland.

merlin a small dark falcon that hunts small birds; in the 15th-century Boke of St Albans, the *merlin* is listed in falconry as the bird for a lady. Recorded from late Middle English, the word comes from Anglo-Norman French, and is ultimately of Germanic origin.

merlion in heraldry, a bird with either no feet (identical with the heraldic martlet) or neither feet nor beak.

mermaid a fictitious or mythical half-human sea creature with the head and trunk of a woman and the tail of a fish, conventionally depicted (especially in heraldry) as beautiful and with long flowing golden hair, holding in the right hand a comb and in the left a mirror. In early use, the *mermaid* is often identified with the siren of classical mythology.

Recorded from Middle English, the word comes from *mere* with the obsolete sense 'sea' + *maid*.

the Mermaid Series a series of unexpurgated reprints of early English dramatists, published originally by Vizetelly, at the suggestion of Havelock Ellis, who edited the series from 1887 to 1889. It continued through various transformations, and became in 1964 the New Mermaid Series.

Mermaid Tavern a tavern that stood in Bread Street (with an entrance in Friday Street), London. One of the earliest of the English clubs, the *Friday Street Club*, started by Walter Raleigh, met there, and was frequented by Shakespeare, Selden, Donne, Beaumont, and Fletcher. Keats wrote 'Lines on the Mermaid Tavern', beginning 'Souls of poets dead and gone'.

Mermaid Theatre founded in the City of London in 1950 by Bernard Miles (1907–91) as a small Elizabethan-style playhouse.

merman a male of the mermaid kind, an imaginary partly human sea creature with the head and trunk of a man and the tail of a fish or cetacean; a representation of such a creature, especially (in heraldry) depicted with a trident in the right hand and a conch-shell trumpet in the left.

Meroe an ancient city on the Nile, in present-day Sudan north-east of Khartoum. Founded in *c.*750 BC, it was the capital of the ancient kingdom of Cush from *c.*590 BC until it fell to the invading Aksumites in the early 4th century AD.

meronym a term which denotes part of something but which is used to refer to the whole of it, e.g. *faces* when used to mean *people* in *I see several familiar faces present.*

Merope name of one of the ➤ PLEIADES; as the only one who married a mortal (Sisyphus), her star when the Pleiades were changed into a constellation was dimmer than the others, and she is known as *the lost Pleiad.*

Merovingian a member of the Frankish dynasty founded by Clovis and reigning in Gaul and Germany *c.*500–750. The word comes from the medieval Latin *Merovingi* 'descendants of Merovich' (semi-legendary 5th-century Frankish leader said to be the grandfather of ➤ CLOVIS).

merrier see ➤ *the* MORE *the merrier.*

merrill a game played on a board between two players, each with an equal number of pebbles, discs of wood or metal, pegs, or pins. Also called *nine men's morris.*

Meg Merrilies name of an old gypsy woman in Scott's *Guy Mannering* (1815), who is also the subject of a poem by Keats.

merrow in Irish folklore, a mermaid or merman.

merry now, cheerful and lively, but originally, pleasing and delightful; this sense is preserved in a number of fixed phrases, as ➤ MERRY *England.*

merry andrew a person who entertains people by means of antics and buffoonery, a clown or mountebank's assistant. Associated as a proper name with popular performances at Bartholomew Fair, probably those of one particular entertainer, whose persona was that of a fool, and who became the subject of at least one ballad and perhaps a puppet-show.

Merry Dancers a local name for the ➤ AURORA *borealis.*

Merry England England, originally as characterized by a pleasant landscape; (sometimes ironically, and with the pseudo-archaic spelling **merrie England**) England characterized by the cheerfulness or animation of its people, especially in a past golden age.

it is merry in hall when beards wag all proverbial saying, early 14th century, meaning when conversation is in full flow.

merry men the companions in arms or followers of an outlaw chief, recorded from late Middle English, and particularly associated with Robin Hood.

Merry Monarch a nickname of Charles II, deriving originally from a poem by Rochester (1647–80):

> A merry monarch, scandalous and poor.
> — Lord Rochester 'A Satire on King Charles II'

Merry Monday a former name for the Monday before Shrove Tuesday.

Merry Mount settlement at Mount Wollaston (now Quincy) in Massachusetts, founded by Captain Wollaston and Thomas Morton; in the spring of 1627 Morton set up a maypole there. Merry Mount was eventually suppressed by the Plymouth colony, under the leadership of Miles Standish, and Morton was arrested and sent back to England. Hawthorne used Merry Mount as a background for his allegorical story *The Maypole of Merrymount.*

Merry Widow an amorous or designing widow, from the English name of Franz Lehár's operetta *Die Lustige Witwe*, first produced in German in Vienna in 1905, and in English in London, 1907. The musical-comedy actress Lily Elsie (1886–1962), appearing in London in the title role, wore an ornate wide-brimmed hat designed by Lucy, Lady Duff Gordon ('Lucile'); **Merry Widow hats** are named from this.

Mersenne number in Mathematics, a number of the form $2^p - 1$, where p is a prime number. It is named (in the late 19th century) after Marin Mersenne (1588–1648), French mathematician.

Mersey the name of a river flowing to the Irish Sea near Liverpool, used (as in **Mersey beat**) to designate the kind of popular music associated with the Beatles and other groups from that area.

Merton see also ➤ SANDFORD *and Merton.*

Merton College the oldest college of Oxford University, founded in 1264, and named after its founder Walter de *Merton*, bishop of Rochester (d. 1277), whose surname probably implies birth or early residence at Merton in Surrey.

Mertonian School designates a school of mathematics and astronomy existing at the college in the 14th century.

Mount Meru in Hindu mythology, a mountain standing at the centre of the universe around which the planets revolve; it is the site of heaven (➤ SVARGA) and the gods are said to live on its summit.

Mesa Verde a high plateau in southern Colorado, with the remains of many prehistoric Pueblo Indian dwellings.

Franz Anton Mesmer (1734–1815), Austrian physician. Mesmer is chiefly remembered for introducing a therapeutic technique (**mesmerism**) involving hypnotism; it was bound up with his ideas about 'animal magnetism', however, and steeped in sensationalism, and Mesmer effectively retired following the critical report of a royal commission in 1784.

the Mesolithic the Middle Stone Age, which in Europe falls between the end of the last glacial period (c.8500 BC) and the beginnings of agriculture. Mesolithic people lived by hunting, gathering, and fishing, and the period is characterized by the use of microliths and the first domestication of an animal (the dog).

Mesopotamia an ancient region of SW Asia in present-day Iraq, lying between the Rivers Tigris and Euphrates. Its alluvial plains were the site of the civilizations of Akkad, Sumer, Babylonia, and Assyria.

The name comes from Greek *mesos* 'middle' + *potamus* 'river'. In the first recorded use in English, Scott's *Chronicles of the Canongate* (1827), it is taken as the type of a word which is long, pleasant-sounding, and incomprehensible:

> She resembled exactly in her criticism the devotee who pitched on the 'sweet word Mesopotamia', as the most edifying note which she could bring away from a sermon.
> — Walter Scott *Chronicles of the Canongate* (1st series, 1827)

From this the name can be used allusively to mean something which gives irrational or inexplicable comfort or satisfaction to the hearer.

> There are people who will swallow any sort of stuff that, so to speak, has the word Mesopotamia in it.
> — George Bernard Shaw *Platform and Pulpit* (1962)

mess the original sense (in Middle English) was 'a serving of food', also 'a serving of liquid or pulpy food', later 'liquid food for an animal'; this gave rise (in the early 19th century) to the senses 'unappetizing concoction' and 'predicament'. In late Middle English the term also denoted any of the small groups into which the company at a banquet was divided (who were served from the same dishes); hence, 'a group who regularly eat together' (recorded in military use from the mid 16th century).

mess of plottage a theatrical production with a poorly constructed plot; an alteration of ➤ MESS *of pottage*.

mess of pottage in the biblical story, the dish of lentils for which the hungry ➤ ESAU sold his birthright to his younger brother Jacob (Genesis 25); the expression is proverbial for a ridiculously small amount offered or taken for something of real value.

Although the proverbial use is recorded from 1526, it does not occur in the Authorized Version of 1611; it does however appear in the heading of chapter 25 in the Bibles of 1537 and 1539, and in the Geneva Bible of 1560.

> Some would say that the quarry lobby is selling the nation's birthright for a mess of pottage.
> — *Caribbean Week* April 1992

message see ➤ ON-*message*.

Messalina (c.22–48 BC), Roman empress, third wife of Claudius. She became notorious in Rome for the murders she instigated and for her extramarital affairs, and was executed on Claudius' orders, after the disclosure of her secret marriage with one of his political opponents.

Her name is used for the type of a licentious and scheming woman; in 1924 E. M. Delafield (1890–1943) published a novel based on the Thompson and Bywaters case, which in 1923 had resulted in the execution of Edith Thompson and her young lover Percy Bywaters for the murder of her husband, entitled *A Messalina of the Suburbs*.

> Yeah, a moviehouse Messalina with the instant hots for yours truly.
> — J. Torrington *Swing Hammer Swing* (1992)

messenger see ➤ CORBIE *messenger*.

the Messiah the promised deliverer of the Jewish nation prophesied in the Hebrew Bible; Jesus regarded by Christians as the Messiah of the Hebrew prophecies and the saviour of humankind.

Recorded from Old English (in the form *Messias*), the name comes via late Latin and Greek from Hebrew *māšīaḥ* 'anointed'.

From the mid 17th century, the word has developed a transferred use to denote an expected liberator or saviour of an oppressed people, country, or cause.

Messidor the tenth month of the French Republican calendar (1793–1805), originally running from 19 June to 18 July. The name comes (in French) from Latin *messis* 'harvest' + Greek *dōron* 'gift'.

Charles Messier (1730–1817), French astronomer. He discovered a number of nebulae, galaxies, and star clusters, which he designated by M numbers; the list had reached 103 items by 1784. Almost all of these designations, such as M1 (the Crab Nebula), are still in use today.

metacism the placing of a word with final *m* before a word beginning with a vowel, regarded as a fault in Latin prose composition. Also, the pronouncing of a final *m* which ought to be elided before a following vowel.

metal metals were traditionally divided into *noble* or *precious* metals (gold, silver, and platinum, which resist corrosion) and *base* or *imperfect* metals (such as lead). In heraldry, *metal* is used for the tinctures or (gold) and argent (silver).

Recorded from Middle English, the word comes via Old French or Latin, from Greek *metallon* 'mine, quarry, metal'.

See also ➤ Prince's *metal*.

metaphor a figure of speech in which a word or phrase is applied to an object or action to which it is not literally applicable. Recorded from the late 15th century, the word comes via French and Latin from Greek *metaphora*, from *metapherein* 'to transfer'.

metaphysical poets a group of 17th-century poets whose work is characterized by the use of complex and elaborate images or conceits, typically using an intellectual form of argumentation to express emotional states. Members of the group include John Donne, George Herbert, Henry Vaughan, and Andrew Marvell.

The application of *metaphysical* to these poets is first recorded from the mid 18th century (Pope remarks that Cowley has 'borrowed his metaphysical style from Donne'). The genesis of the specific use,

however, can be found a century earlier, in a comment by William Drummond of Hawthornden (1585–1649):

> In vaine have some men of late (Transformeres of evrye thing) consulted upon her [poesy's] reformation, and endevured to abstracte her to Metaphysicall Ideas, and Scholasticall Quidityes.
> — William Drummond *Letter on the True Nature of Poetry (a. 1641)*

Metaphysical Society founded in 1869 by the editor and architect James Thomas Knowles (1831–1908). It lasted until 1880 and brought together for discussion meetings most of the leaders of English thought of the period, of all shades of opinion, including Thomas Henry Huxley, Manning, Gladstone, and Tennyson.

metaphysics the branch of philosophy that deals with the first principles of things, including abstract concepts such as being, knowing, substance, cause, identity, time, and space. Metaphysics has two main strands: that which holds that what exists lies beyond experience (as argued by Plato), and that which holds that objects of experience constitute the only reality (as argued by Kant, the logical positivists, and Hume). Metaphysics has also concerned itself with a discussion of whether what exists is made of one substance or many, and whether what exists is inevitable or driven by chance.

Recorded from the mid 16th century, the word represents medieval Latin *metaphysica* (neuter plural), based on Greek *ta meta ta phusika* 'the things after the Physics', referring to the sequence of Aristotle's works: the title came to denote the branch of study treated in the books, later interpreted as meaning 'the science of things transcending what is physical or natural'.

metathesis the transposition of sounds or letters in a word.

Metatron in Jewish mystical theology, a supreme angelic being, usually identified with either Michael or Enoch.

Metawileh a sect of Shiite Muslims in Lebanon and Syria.

metempsychosis the supposed transmigration at death of the soul of a human being or animal into a new body of the same or a different species, chiefly in Pythagoreanism and certain Eastern religions.

Meteora a group of monasteries in north central Greece, in the region of Thessaly. The monasteries, built between the 12th and the 16th centuries, are perched on the summits of curiously shaped rock formations.

method acting a technique of acting in which an actor aspires to complete emotional identification with a part, based on the system evolved by Stanislavsky and brought into prominence in the US in the 1930s. Method acting was developed in institutions such as the Actors' Studio in New York City (founded 1947), notably by Elia Kazan and Lee Strasberg, and is particularly associated with actors such as Marlon Brando and Dustin Hoffman.

method in one's madness sense or reason in what appears to be foolish or abnormal behaviour; from Shakespeare, in the scene in which Hamlet feigns insanity:

> Though this be madness, yet there is method in't.
> — William Shakespeare *Hamlet* (1601)

Methodist a member of a Christian Protestant denomination originating in the 18th-century evangelistic movement of Charles and John Wesley and George Whitefield. The Methodist Church grew out of a religious society established within the Church of England, from which it formally separated in 1791. It is particularly strong in the US and now constitutes one of the largest Protestant denominations worldwide, with more than 30 million members. Methodism has a strong tradition of missionary work and concern with social welfare, and emphasizes the believer's personal relationship with God.

The term *Methodist* was first applied to members of a religious society (nicknamed 'the Holy Club') established at Oxford in 1729 by John and Charles Wesley, and having for its object the promotion of piety and morality; it later came to denote the adherents of those religious bodies originating from the evangelical movement led by the Wesleys. The original reason for the name is not clear, but it probably reflects the use of *Methodist* to mean someone who advocates a particular method or system of theological belief, especially with reference to doctrinal disputes about grace and justification.

St Methodius 9th-century Greek missionary, the brother of ➤ *St* CYRIL.

□ **FEAST DAY** His feast day, with St Cyril, is 11 May in the Eastern Church, 14 February (formerly 9 March or 7 July) in the Western Church.

methods see ➤ MILL's *Methods*.

Methuen Portuguese wine, from the name of John *Methuen* (c.1650–1706), English diplomat, who negotiated a commercial treaty between England and Portugal in 1703 by which the wine was originally imported, under a preferential duty.

Methuselah in the Bible, a patriarch, the grandfather of Noah, who is said to have lived for 969 years. His name is used allusively as the type of a very old person, and the expression **as old as Methuselah** is recorded from the early 16th century.

The name methuselah is used for a wine bottle of eight times the standard size.

Metis in Canada, a person of mixed race, especially the offspring of a white person and an American Indian. The name comes from French *métis*, from Latin *mixtus* 'mixed'.

Metonic cycle a period of 19 years (235 lunar months), after which the new and full moons return to the same day of the year. It was the basis of the ancient Greek calendar, and is still used for calculating movable feasts such as Easter.

metonymy the substitution of the name of an attribute or adjunct for that of the thing meant, for example *suit* for *business executive*, or *the turf* for *horse racing*.

Metroland the area around London served by the underground railway, especially as viewed nostalgically as an ideal suburban environment of the 1920s and 1930s. Evelyn Waugh used the name *Margot Metroland* for a key character in *Decline and Fall*, *Vile Bodies*, and other satiric novels.

metropolitan in the Christian Church, a bishop having authority over the bishops of a province, in particular (in many Orthodox Churches) one ranking above archbishop and below patriarch.

Prince Metternich (1773–1859), Austrian statesman, who was one of the organizers of the Congress of Vienna (1814–15), which devised the settlement of Europe after the Napoleonic Wars. He pursued policies which reflected his reactionary conservatism at home and abroad until forced to resign during the revolutions of 1848; he said of his own downfall, 'Nothing is altered. On 14 March 1848, there was merely one man fewer.'

meum and teum a Latin phrase meaning 'mine and yours', used to make the distinction between what is mine or one's own and what is yours or another's.

mews a group of stables, typically with rooms above, built round a yard or along an alley, and originally referring to the royal stables on the site of the hawk mews at Charing Cross, London; *mew* in falconry denotes a cage or building for trained hawks, especially while they are moulting, and derives ultimately from Old French *muer* 'to moult', from Latin *mutare* 'change'.

From the early 19th century, the term has been extended to cover a row or street of houses or flats that have been converted from stables or built to look like former stables.

Mexican War the war of 1846–8 between Mexico and the United States, mainly precipitated by the annexation of Texas by the US in 1845.

Mexican wave an effect resembling a moving wave produced by successive sections of the crowd in a stadium standing up, raising their arms, lowering them, and sitting down again. It is so named because of the repeated practice of this movement at the 1986 soccer World Cup finals in Mexico City.

Mezentius a mythical Etruscan king proverbial for his cruelty; Virgil's *Aeneid* relates how he had living people bound face to face with corpses and left to die.

> It did occur to me he could have driven the bike himself with the body lashed to his back looking like a pillion. It's a bit Mezentian, but possible.
> — Iain Banks *Crow Road* (1992)

mezuzah a parchment inscribed with religious texts and attached in a case to the doorpost of a Jewish house as a sign of faith. Recorded from the mid 17th century, the word comes from Hebrew *mĕzūzāh* 'doorpost'.

mezzanine financing financing which involves unsecured, higher-yielding loans that are subordinate to bank loans and secured loans but rank above equity. The usage is recorded from the mid 1970s, and represents a transference of *mezzanine* to mean a low storey between two others in a building.

Mezzofanti a person of exceptional linguistic ability, from the name of Giuseppe *Mezzofanti* (1774–1849), an Italian cardinal who reputedly mastered over fifty languages.

mezzotint a print made from an engraved copper or steel plate on which the surface has been partially roughened, for shading, and partially scraped smooth, giving light areas. The technique was invented by Ludwig von Siegen of Utrecht *c.*1640 and

was much used in the 17th, 18th, and early 19th centuries for the reproduction of paintings.

Micah (in the Bible) a Hebrew minor prophet. Also, a book of the Bible bearing his name, foretelling the destruction of Samaria and of Jerusalem.

Wilkins Micawber a character in Dickens's novel *David Copperfield* (1850), an eternal optimist who, despite evidence to the contrary, continues to have faith that 'something will turn up'.

> There is something engagingly Micawberish about the Philippines. Among the things the government is still hoping will turn up are the Marcos millions that the former dictator is supposed to have stashed away.
> — *Economist* 24 October 1992

mice see ➤ *the* BEST*-laid schemes of mice and men gant aft agley*, ➤ *a* CAT *in gloves catches no mice*, ➤ *when the* CAT*'s away the mice will play*.

St Michael one of the archangels (Jude 9) whose role is divine messenger and executor of God's judgements. His name means 'Who is like unto God?' In Revelations 12:7 he is shown as a warrior leading the hosts of heaven, 'There was war in heaven, Michael and his angels fought against the dragon.'

He is typically represented slaying a dragon, and he may also be shown weighing souls, sometimes as part of the Last Judgement.

☐ **FEAST DAY** His feast day (St Michael and All Angels, or ➤ MICHAELMAS *Day*) is 29 September.

Order of St Michael and St George (in the UK) an order of knighthood instituted in 1818, divided into three classes: Knight or Dame Grand Cross of the Order of St Michael and St George (GCMG), Knight or Dame Commander (KCMG/DCMG), and Companion (CMG).

Michael Fair in eastern Scotland, a livestock fair held at or around Michaelmas.

Michaelmas the feast of St ➤ MICHAEL and All Angels, 29 September, one of the quarter days in England, Ireland, and Wales.

Old Michaelmas the day that would have been called 29 September if the Old Style calendar had not been corrected.

Michaelmas goose traditionally eaten at a feast on Michaelmas day.

Michaelmas moon formerly a term for the harvest moon; also, in Scotland, booty from plundering border raids which were made at this season.

Michaelmas summer a period of warm weather before the onset of winter.

Michelangelo (1475–1564), Italian sculptor, painter, architect, and poet. A leading figure of the High Renaissance, Michelangelo established his reputation with sculptures such as the *Pietà* (*c.*1497–1500) and *David* (1501–4). Under papal patronage he decorated the ceiling of the Sistine Chapel in Rome (1508–12) and painted the fresco *The Last Judgement* (1536–41), both important mannerist works. His architectural achievements include the completion of St Peter's in Rome (1546–64).

Michelangelo is also the name of a virus affecting IBM-compatible computers, which was programmed to activate itself every year on 6 March, the birthday of Michelangelo, and to destroy any data on the hard disc.

Michelozzo (1396–1472), Italian architect and sculptor. In partnership with Ghiberti and Donatello he led a revival of interest in Roman architecture. One of the most influential palace designs of the early Renaissance is his Palazzo Medici-Riccardi in Florence (1444–59).

Michelson-Morley experiment an experiment performed in 1887 which attempted to measure the relative motion of the earth and the ether by measuring the speed of light in directions parallel and perpendicular to the earth's motion. The result disproved the existence of the ether, which contradicted Newtonian physics but was explained by Einstein's special theory of relativity.

Mick the Miller a racing greyhound who won many races in the UK from 1928 to 1931 and later starred in the film *Wild Boy* (1935).

Mickey Finn a surreptitiously drugged or doctored drink given to someone so as to make them drunk or insensible. Recorded from the 1920s, the origin of the expression is unknown, but it is sometimes said to be the name of a notorious Chicago saloonkeeper (*c.*1896–1906).

Mickey Mouse a Walt Disney cartoon character, who first appeared as Mortimer Mouse in 1927, becoming Mickey in 1928. During the 1930s he became established as the central Disney character, with Disney himself speaking the soundtrack for Mickey's voice. He is perhaps the most famous of the Disney cartoon characters; Disney himself is said to have commented, 'Fancy becoming known around the world for the invention of a mouse'.

Mickey Mouse is also used informally to indicate that something is of inferior quality.

> With 116 riders it was a bit Mickey Mouse and any lapped rider could easily have brought either of us down.
> — Cycling Weekly 16 January 1993

mickle see ➤ MANY *a mickle makes a little,* ➤ MANY *a mickle makes a muckle.*

microcosm among ancient writers, human nature considered as 'little world' as distinguished from the 'great world' (*macrocosm*); a community, place, or situation regarded as encapsulating in miniature the characteristic qualities or features of something much larger.

In the mid 18th century, a mechanical exhibition entitled 'The Microcosm, or, the World in Miniature' was presented as a travelling curiosity and attraction; it represented in sound and motion a number of celestial, mythological, and other scenes.

microlith a minute shaped flint, typically part of a composite tool such as a spear.

mid-Lent Sunday the middle or fourth Sunday in Lent, on which the severities of the Lenten fast are traditionally relaxed. The day is also called ➤ MOTHERING *Sunday* and ➤ SIMNEL *Sunday.*

Midas a king of Phrygia, who, according to one story, was given by Dionysus the power of turning everything he touched into gold. Unable to eat or drink, he prayed to be relieved of the gift and was instructed to wash in the River Pactolus. According to another story, he declared Pan a better flute player than Apollo, who thereupon gave him ass's ears. Midas tried to hide them but his barber whispered the secret to some reeds, which repeat it whenever they rustle in the wind.

Middle Ages the period of European history from the fall of the Roman Empire in the West (5th century) to the fall of Constantinople (1453), or, more narrowly, from *c.*1000 to 1453.

Middle America the middle class in the United States, especially when regarded as a conservative

political force; the Midwest of the United States regarded as the home of such people.

> How is Joe Paycheck in Middle America supposed to
> think of himself?
> — *Harper's Magazine* June 1998

Middle England the middle classes in England
outside London, especially as representative of conservative political views.

> Those matted dreadlocks, itchy just to look at, do not
> endear the eco-campaigners to middle England.
> — *Independent* 26 April 1995

Middle Kingdom[1] a period of ancient Egyptian
history (*c.*2040–1640 BC, 11th–14th dynasty).

Middle Kingdom[2] a former term for China or its
eighteen inner provinces. The name is a translation
of Chinese *zhongguo* 'central state', originally the
name given to the imperial state, in contrast to the
dependencies surrounding it; from 1911 onwards,
part of the official name of the Chinese state.

Middle Kingdom[3] the central region consisting of
the Low Countries, Alsace, Lorraine, Burgundy,
Provence, and Lombardy, and much of central Italy
given to the Frankish king Lothair I by the Treaty of
Verdun in 843.

middle passage the sea journey undertaken by
slave ships from West Africa to the West Indies, seen
as the middle part of the journey of the transportation of a slave from Africa to America. The term is
first recorded in *An Essay on the Impolicy of the African Slave Trade* (1788) by the abolitionist Thomas
Clarkson (1760–1846).

Middle Temple one of the two Inns of Court on
the site of the ➤ TEMPLE in London, England, the
other being the ➤ INNER *Temple*.

Middletown in the US, an archetypal middle-
class community. The term was popularized by R. S.
and H. M. Lynd's *Middletown: a study in contemporary American culture* (1929), said to be based on
Muncie, Indiana.

Midgard in Scandinavian mythology, the region,
encircled by the sea, in which human beings live; the
earth.

Midgard's serpent in Scandinavian mythology, a
monstrous serpent that was the offspring of Loki
and was thrown by Odin into the sea, where, with
its tail in its mouth, it encircled the earth.

midge see ➤ *the* MOTHER *of mischief is no bigger
than a midge's wing.*

midheaven on an astrological chart, the point
where the ecliptic intersects the meridian.

Midlothian see ➤ HEART *of Midlothian.*

midnight see also ➤ BURN *the midnight oil*,
➤ LAND *of the Midnight Sun.*

midnight appointment in US politics, an appointment made during the last hours of an administration, originally with particular reference to
those made by the 2nd President John Adams
(1735–1826):

> And then followed those scenes of midnight
> appointments, which have been condemned by all
> men.
> — Thomas Jefferson letter, 16 January 1811

midnight Mass a Mass celebrated at or shortly before midnight, especially on Christmas Eve.

Midrash an ancient commentary on part of the
Hebrew scriptures, attached to the biblical text. The
earliest Midrashim come from the 2nd century AD,
although much of their content is older.

midshipman a rank of officer in the Royal Navy,
above naval cadet and below sub lieutenant, and so
named because the officer was stationed amidships;
he was however allowed to walk the quarterdeck, to
which he aspired in promotion.

Midsummer another term for the Summer Solstice, and the period of time immediately surrounding it.

midsummer ale a festive gathering formerly held
at midsummer.

Midsummer Day 24 June, the feast of the Nativity
of St John the Baptist, a quarter day in England,
Wales, and Ireland, originally coinciding with the
summer solstice and in some countries marked by a
summer festival.

midsummer madness foolish or reckless behaviour, considered to be at its height at midsummer,
and sometimes attributed to the **midsummer moon**
of the lunar month in which Midsummer Day falls.

midsummer man traditionally, either of two specimens of orpine, symbolizing a young man and his
sweetheart, which were stuck up by girls on midsummer eve to prognosticate the course of their
love.

Battle of Midway in 1942, off the Midway Islands
in the central Pacific, a decisive sea battle in which

the US navy repelled a Japanese invasion fleet, sinking four aircraft carriers. This defeat marked the end of Japanese expansion in the Pacific during the Second World War.

midwife ➤ St Pantaleon and St Raymond Nonnatus (1204–40), said to have been born by Caesarian section, are the patron saints of midwives.

midwife toad a European toad, the male of which carries the developing eggs wrapped around his hind legs. The Austrian zoologist Paul Kammerer (1880–1926) showed specimens of the animal which appeared to support the evolutionary theories of ➤ Lamarck, but the apparent development of nuptial pads on the forefeet was shown to be fraudulent.

Ludwig Mies van der Rohe (1886–1969), German-born architect and designer. He designed the German pavilion at the 1929 International Exhibition at Barcelona and the Seagram Building in New York (1954–8), and was noted for his tubular steel furniture, notably the 'Barcelona Chair'. He was director of the Bauhaus 1930–3 before emigrating to the US in 1937.

He is now particularly associated with the saying ➤ less *is more*, although he did not coin it.

might is right proverbial saying, early 14th century.

mighty hunter in the Bible, an epithet applied to ➤ Nimrod.

> Even as Nimrod the mighty hunter before the Lord.
> — Bible (AV) Genesis ch. 10, v. 9

mihrab a niche in the wall of a mosque, at the point nearest to Mecca, towards which the congregation faces to pray.

mikado a title formerly given to the emperor of Japan. The word comes from Japanese *mi* 'august' + *kado* 'gate'; the title is a tranferred use of 'gate (to the Imperial palace)', an ancient place of audience.

It was usual for European writers prior to the Meiji Restoration of 1868 to describe the *Mikado* as a 'spiritual' emperor and the ➤ Shogun (who was the *de facto ruler* until 1867) as a second or 'temporal' ruler.

Milan an industrial city in NW Italy, capital of Lombardy region, which was in the past a powerful city, particularly from the 13th to the 15th centuries, as a duchy under the Visconti and Sforza families.

Milan steel was particularly known among armourers for the manufacture of mailcoats and swords.

See also ➤ Edict *of Milan.*

Milan decree issued by Napoleon on 17 December 1807 as part of the blockade with which he hoped to destroy British trade; the French, their allies, and neutral countries were forbidden to trade with Britain.

mile a unit of linear measure equal to 1,760 yards (approximately 1.609 kilometres); originally, a Roman measure of 1,000 paces (approximately 1,620 yards).

Recorded from Old English (in the form *mīl*) the word is based on Latin *mil(l)ia*, plural of *mille* 'thousand'; the original Roman unit of distance was *mille passus* 'a thousand paces'.

See also ➤ *a* miss *is as good as a mile.*

milecastle any of a series of forts erected by the Romans at intervals along a military wall, especially Hadrian's Wall across northern England.

miles gloriosus (in literature) a boastful soldier as a stock figure. The term, which is Latin, comes from the title of a comedy by Plautus (*c.*250–184 BC).

Milesian[1] of or pertaining to ancient ➤ Miletus, a city in Asia Minor, especially in ➤ Milesian *tale.*

Milesian[2] a native or inhabitant of ancient Ireland, from the legend that the ancient kingdom was conquered and reorganized about 1300 BC by the sons of *Milesius* (Miledh), a fabulous Spanish king.

Milesian tale the title of a collection of stories by Aristides (2nd century BC); probably so called because *Miletus* in Asia Minor was the traditional setting for the genre; an erotic short story of a type produced by ancient Greek and Roman novelists.

Miletus an ancient city of the Ionian Greeks in SW Asia Minor. In the 7th and 6th centuries BC it was a powerful port, from which more than sixty colonies were founded on the shores of the Black Sea and in Italy and Egypt. It was the home of the philosophers Thales, Anaximander, and Anaximenes. It was conquered by the Persians in 494 BC. By the 6th century AD its harbours had become silted up by the alluvial deposits of the Menderes River.

Milice in France, a force employed by the Vichy government of 1940–44 to repress internal dissent.

Il milione ('The milllion'), Italian title of what is known in English as *The Travels of Marco Polo.*

militant see also ➤ Church *Militant*.

Militant a Trotskyite political organization in Britain, which publishes the weekly newspaper *Militant*. During the early 1980s it attempted to infiltrate and express its views from within the Labour Party.

Military Cross (in the UK and Commonwealth countries) a decoration awarded for distinguished active service on land, instituted in 1914 (originally for officers).

military honours ceremonies performed by troops as a mark of respect at the burial of a member of the armed forces.

military-industrial complex a country's military establishment and those industries producing arms or other military materials, regarded as a powerful vested interest. The term derives from a speech by US President Eisenhower:

> In the councils of Government, we must guard against the acquisition of unwarranted influence, whether sought or unsought, by the military-industrial complex.
> — Dwight Eisenhower in *New York Times* 18 January (1961)

Military Medal (in the UK and Commonwealth countries) a decoration for distinguished active service on land, instituted in 1916 (originally for enlisted soldiers).

militia a military force that is raised from the civil population to supplement a regular army in an emergency.

Recorded from the late 16th century in the sense 'a system of military discipline and organization', in the 17th century the word came to be applied to the name of various military units and forces raised locally from the citizen body of an area, and distinguished from professional standing armies as these developed. The usage may derive from such instances as the 'Ordinance for settling the Militia of London' (1642, where the word was taken to refer specifically to the trained bands of London affected by the order).

Subsequently *militia* also developed the sense of a military force that engages in rebel or terror activities, typically in opposition to a regular army; most recently, this has been applied to the militias of East Timor.

milk see also ➤ *it is no use* crying *over spilt milk*, ➤ pigeon's *milk*, ➤ land *of milk and honey*.

milk for babes something easy and pleasant to learn; especially in allusion to 1 Corinthians 'I…speak unto you…even as unto babes in Christ. I have fed you with milk, and not with meat.'

milk of human kindness compassion, sympathy; originally from Lady Macbeth's expression of her anxiety that her husband lacked the necessary ruthlessness to kill King Duncan and seize the throne:

> Glamis thou art, and Cawdor; and shalt be
> What thou art promised. Yet I do fear thy nature;
> It is too full o' the milk of human kindness
> To catch the nearest way.
> — William Shakespeare *Macbeth* (1606)

In the 20th century, the critic Philip Guedalla extended the metaphor in his critique of James Barrie, referring to 'The cheerful clatter of Sir James Barrie's cans as he went round with the milk of human kindness'.

milk-white a spotless colour symbolizing purity.

Milky Way a faint band of light crossing the sky, clearly visible on dark moonless nights and discovered by Galileo to be made up of vast numbers of faint stars. It corresponds to the plane of our Galaxy, in which most of its stars are located.

The *Milky Way* was sometimes named from famous pilgrimage routes; as ➤ Walsingham *Way* and the *Way of St James* (the road to Santiago de Compostela).

mill a building equipped with machinery for grinding grain into flour, or more generally a device for grinding and crushing to powder; often in figurative contexts.

See also ➤ *all is* grist *that comes to the mill*.

John Stuart Mill (1806–73), English philosopher and economist. Mill is best known for his political and moral works, especially *On Liberty* (1859), which argued for the importance of individuality, and *Utilitarianism* (1861), which extensively developed Bentham's theory. He advocated representative democracy and criticized the contemporary treatment of women.

the mill cannot grind with the water that is past proverbial saying, early 17th century, meaning that an opportunity that has been missed cannot then be used.

Mill's Methods in logic, the five canons of inductive inquiry for discovering and establishing the validity of causal relations between phenomena, named for ➤ *John Stuart* Mill.

John Everett Millais (1829–96), English painter. A founder member of the Pre-Raphaelite Brotherhood, he went on to produce lavishly painted portraits and landscapes, although ➤ *John* Ruskin severely criticized his technique in the painting of ➤ *Sir* Isumbras.

Millbank a building on the embankment of the north side of the River Thames in Westminster, London, which since 1980 has been the headquarters of the British Labour Party, and which is particularly associated with the centralized control seen as typifying ➤ New *Labour*.

> Millbank's minions moaned that we were 'negative' and 'oppositional'.
> — *Earthmatters* Summer 1999

Mille see ➤ *Cecil B.* de *Mille*.

millefiori a kind of ornamental glass in which a number of glass rods of different sizes and colours are fused together and cut into sections which form various patterns, typically embedded in colourless transparent glass to make items such as paperweights.

millenarian relating to or believing in Christian millenarianism; in figurative usage, believing in the imminence or inevitability of a golden age of peace, justice, and prosperity; denoting a religious or political group seeking solutions to present crises through rapid and radical change.

millenarianism the doctrine of or belief in a future (and typically imminent) thousand-year age of blessedness, beginning with or culminating in the Second Coming of Christ. It is central to the teaching of groups such as Plymouth Brethren, Adventists, Mormons, and Jehovah's Witnesses.

The term may also be used more generally for belief in a future golden age of peace, justice, and prosperity.

Millenary Petition a petition presented by a number of Puritan ministers (represented as one thousand) to James I in London in April 1603, requesting certain changes in ecclesiastical ceremonial and practice.

millennium a period of a thousand years, especially when calculated from the traditional date of the birth of Christ. In the Christian Church, the term is also used for the period of one thousand years during which (according to one interpretation of Revelation 20:1–5), Christ will reign in person on earth.

Recorded from the mid 17th century, the word is modern Latin, from *mille* 'thousand', on the pattern of *biennium*.

millennium bug a problem with some computers arising from an inability of the software to deal correctly with dates of 1 January 2000 or later, through the misinterpretation of a two-digit number (as 87, 99) used to represent a year without specifying the century concerned.

Millennium Dome a large domed structure on the banks of the Thames, at Greenwich, London, designed to mark a national celebration of the 2nd millennium with exhibitions in the *Body Zone*, the *Spirit Zone*, and other themed areas; New Year's Eve celebrations were held at the Dome on 31 December 1999, and it opened to the general public the following day.

miller see ➤ Mick *the Miller*.

Millerite a believer in the doctrines of William Miller (1782–1849), an American preacher who interpreted the Scriptures as foretelling the imminent coming of Christ and the end of the world.

milliner a person who makes or sells women's hats, originally (in Middle English) in the sense 'native of *Milan*', and later 'a vendor of fancy goods from Milan'.

Bertram Mills (1873–1938), from 1920 proprietor of a British circus which he established and which continued until 1967. His father had been a coachbuilder and as a young man he had travelled over Europe exhibiting coaches at shows; after the first world war, when there was little coach-building work, he entered the circus business and between 1920 and 1937 put on an annual Christmas circus at Olympia. In 1929 his activities were extended to his tenting circus with which he toured the provinces.

Mills and Boon trademark name used to denote idealized and sentimental romantic situations of the kind associated with the type of fiction published by Mills & Boon Limited.

In his obituary, the chairman of the firm John Mills (1916–96) was quoted as saying of the popular and formulaic romantic novels issued by his firm, 'We ought to be prescribed by the NHS. We're better than valium.'

the mills of God grind slowly, yet they grind exceeding small proverbial saying, mid 17th century; ultimately from an anonymous verse in Sextus Empiricus *Adversus Mathematicos*, 'the mills of the gods are late to grind, but they grind small.' The exact wording of the current form of the proverb is a quotation from Longfellow:

> Though the mills of God grind slowly, yet they grind exceeding small;
> Though with patience He stands waiting, with exactness grinds He all.
> — Longfellow 'Retribution', translation of Friedrich von Logau (1604–55) *Sinnegedichte* (1654) no. 322

millstone each of two circular stones used for grinding corn; in figurative use, a heavy and inescapable responsibility, often with reference to Matthew 18:6, 'But whoso shall offend one of these little ones which believe in me, it were better for him that a millstone were hanged about his neck, and that he were drowned in the depth of the sea.'

See also ➤ NETHER *millstone*.

Milo of Croton a famous wrestler who lived towards the end of the 6th century BC. He is said to have died when his hand became trapped in the trunk of a tree which he was trying to split with his fist; held fast, he was eaten by wild animals.

> I was staying with nice people who had been very kind to me, then this hero turned up, like Milo of Croton looking for a tree to split with his fist.
> — Lindsey Davis *Time to Depart* (1995)

Caspar Milquetoast a cartoon character created by H. T. Webster in 1924 and named after the American dish *milk toast*. *Milquetoast* is now used as a term for a person who is timid or submissive.

> At sufficient volume Surgery turns even the mildest milquetoast into a raging bull . . . rock is—at its heart—for the body, not the brain.
> — *Magnet* May 1994

John Milton (1608–74), English poet. His three major works, completed after he had gone blind (1652), show his mastery of blank verse: they are the epic poems *Paradise Lost* (1667, revised 1674), on the fall of man, *Paradise Regained* (1671), on Christ's temptations, and the verse drama *Samson Agonistes* (1671), on Samson's final years. He was also a prolific writer of pamphlets concerned with civil and religious liberties.

mimamsa a leading system of Hindu philosophy, based on the interpretation of Vedic ritual and text. The name comes from a Sanskrit word meaning 'profound thought, consideration, investigation'.

Mimas in Greek mythology, a giant killed by Mars; one of the satellites of Saturn is named after him.

Mimir in Scandinavian mythology, the wisest of the Aesir and guardian of the sacred well, to whom

Odin sacrificed one eye in exchange for poetic inspiration; when he was killed by the Vanir, Odin preserved his decapitated head, which became oracular.

mimosa now chiefly an Australian acacia tree with delicate fern-like leaves and yellow flowers which are the mimosa of florists, but originally a plant of a genus that includes the sensitive plant; the name comes from Latin *mimus* 'mime', because the plant seemingly mimics the sensitivity of an animal.

minaret a slender tower, typically part of a mosque, with a balcony from which a muezzin calls Muslims to prayer. Recorded from the late 17th century, the word comes from French or Spanish and ultimately, via Turkish, from Arabic *manār(a* 'lighthouse, minaret', based on *nār* 'fire or light'.

mince pie a small round pie or tart containing sweet mincemeat, traditionally eaten at Christmas. *Mince pies* were originally *minced pies*, and were filled with minced meat or mincemeat.

Mincing Lane formerly the centre of the tea trade in London, and thus applied allusively to the auction room for tea and other commodities originally situated in this street. The name was earlier *Minchen Lane*; *minchen* here meant 'nun', and referred to the fact that the houses in the lane were owned by the nuns of St Helen's Priory in Bishopsgate.

mind see also ➤ GREAT *minds think alike*, ➤ LITTLE *things please little minds*, ➤ TIME *out of mind*, ➤ TRAVEL *broadens the mind*, ➤ YEAR*'s mind*.

mind one's P's and Q's be careful or particular in one's words or behaviour. The expression is recorded from the late 18th century, and may refer to the difficulty found by a child learning to write in distinguishing between the tailed letters *p* and *q*.

In the early 17th century, the dramatist Thomas Dekker has 'Now thou art in thy pee and cue'; *pee* here is a kind of coat, and *cue* means either a queue of hair, or possibly cue as a tail; it might however indicate an early currency of this expression through a punning allusion.

mine see ➤ FAIRY *of the mine*.

mineral see ➤ ANIMAL, *vegetable, and mineral*.

miners ➤ St BARBARA is the patron saint of miners.

Minerva in Roman mythology, the goddess, originally of weaving and other crafts, later of wisdom, creativity, and prowess in war, from ancient times identified with the Greek ➤ ATHENE; her symbol is an owl. She is said to have been born fully-armed from the head of Jupiter.

> When philosophy paints its grey on grey, then has a shape of life grown old . . . The owl of Minerva spreads its wings only with the falling of dusk.
> — G. W. F. Hegel *Philosophy of Right* (1821)

See also ➤ INVITA *Minerva*.

Minerva press (the name of) a printing press established by William Lane (*c.*1745–1814) formerly existing in Leadenhall Street, London; the series of light, romantic novels, characterized by a blend of sentiment and sensationalism, issued with the imprint of this press from *c.*1790.

Ming the dynasty ruling China 1368–1644. Also, Chinese porcelain made during the rule of the Ming dynasty, characterized by elaborate designs and vivid colours.

miniature (especially of a replica) of a much smaller size than normal. Recorded from the early 18th century, the word comes via Italian and medieval Latin from Latin *miniare* 'rubricate, illuminate', from *minium* 'red lead, vermilion' (used to mark particular words in manuscripts).

Minim Friar a member of the mendicant order founded, traditionally in 1435, by St Francis of Paola. The order was known as *Ordo Fratrum Minimorum* (literally, 'Order of the least brethren'), a reforming order of monks named in imitation, and emulation, of the Franciscan *Fratres Minores* or lesser brethren. By using the superlative in place of the comparative *minores*, the new order indicated their intention to exceed the humility professed by the original Franciscans.

minister originally, a person acting under the authority of another, one carrying out executive duties as the agent or representative of a superior. The word is from Latin *minister* 'servant' from *minus* 'less', formed after the correlative *magister* 'master'.

Minister of State (in the UK) a minister ranking below a Secretary of State; (in Canada) a federal government minister having responsibility for a certain policy area but without direct control over a department, a position superseded in 1993 by the creation of that of Secretary of State.

Minister of the Crown (in the UK and Canada) a member of the cabinet.

Minister without Portfolio (in the UK and some other countries) a government minister who has

cabinet status, but is not in charge of a specific department of state.

ministering angel a kind-hearted person, especially a woman, who nurses or comforts others. Recorded from the early 17th century, particularly with allusion to Shakespeare's *Hamlet* (1603), 'a ministering angel shall my sister be', the image of a tender and nurturing woman in this guise was reinforced by Scott:

> When pain and anguish wring the brow, A ministering angel thou!
> — Walter Scott *Marmion* (1808)

miniver plain white fur for lining or trimming clothes. Recorded from Middle English, the word comes from Old French *menu vair* 'little vair' (*vair* meaning 'squirrel fur').

Hermann Minkowski (1864–1909), Russian-born German mathematician. He worked on the properties of sets in multidimensional systems, and suggested the concept of four-dimensional space–time, which was the basis for Einstein's general theory of relativity.

Minnehaha in Longfellow's *The Song of Hiawatha* (1855), the beautiful Dakota girl whom Hiawatha marries, taken as the type of an American Indian woman.

> Up and down the boardwalk she stomped, humming a chant, trying to touch some ancient magic . . . Patricia and John chortled over the spectacle of Mother doing a Minnehaha in the dawn.
> — C. Wilkins *Wolf's Eye* (1992)

Minnesinger a German lyric poet and singer of the 12th–14th centuries, who performed songs of courtly love. The name comes (in the early 19th century) from German *Minnesinger* 'love-singer'.

minnie see ➤ MOANING *minnie*.

minnow this small freshwater fish, which typically forms large shoals, is often taken as the type of something which though great in number is weak in strength.

> Freedom for the pike is death for the minnows.
> — R. H. Tawney *Equality* (ed. 4, rev. ed. 1938)

See also ➤ TRITON *of the minnows*.

Minoan of, relating to, or denoting a Bronze Age civilization centred on Crete (*c.*3000–1050 BC), its people, or its language. This civilization had reached its zenith by the beginning of the late Bronze Age; impressive remains reveal the existence of large urban centres dominated by palaces. It is also noted for its script (see ➤ LINEAR *A*) and distinctive art and architecture, and greatly influenced the Mycenaeans, who succeeded the Minoans in control of the Aegean *c*.1400 BC.

It is named after the legendary king ➤ MINOS, to whom a palace excavated at Knossos was attributed.

minor orders the formal grades of Catholic or Orthodox clergy below the rank of deacon (most now discontinued).

Minor Prophet any of the twelve prophets after whom the shorter prophetic books of the Bible, from Hosea to Malachi, are named.

Minor Prophets			
Hosea	Obadiah	Nahum	Haggai
Joel	Jonah	Habakkuk	Zechariah
Amos	Micah	Zephaniah	Malachi

Minoress a Franciscan nun of the second order, a ➤ POOR *Clare*.

the Minories a street in the City of London, named from the convent of Franciscan nuns (*Minoresses*) outside Aldgate.

Minos in Greek mythology, a legendary king of Crete, son of Zeus and Europa. His wife Pasiphaë gave birth to the bull-headed ➤ MINOTAUR, which was kept in the ➤ LABYRINTH constructed by Daedalus. Minos exacted an annual tribute from Athens in the form of young people to be devoured by the monster; this came to an end when Theseus, son of the king of Athens, who had volunteered himself as one of the tribute party, killed the Minotaur.

Palace of Minos a complex of buildings excavated and reconstructed by Arthur Evans at Knossos, which yielded local coins portraying the labyrinth as the city's symbol and a ➤ LINEAR *B* religious tablet which refers to the 'lady of the labyrinth'.

Minotaur in Greek mythology, a creature who was half-man and half-bull, the offspring of Pasiphaë, wife of ➤ MINOS, and a bull with which she fell in love. Confined in Crete in a labyrinth made by ➤ DAEDALUS and fed on human flesh, it was eventually slain by Theseus.

minstrel a medieval singer or musician, especially one who sang or recited lyric or heroic poetry to a musical accompaniment for the nobility. Recorded from Middle English, the word comes from Old

French *menestral* 'entertainer, servant', via Provençal for late Latin *ministerialis* 'servant'.

See also ➤ CHRISTY *Minstrels*.

mint a place where money is coined, especially under state authority. Recorded from Old English (in form *mynet* 'coin', and of West Germanic origin) the word is related to Dutch *munt* and German *Münze*, from Latin *moneta* 'money'.

The Mint was a name given to a place of privilege formerly existing near the King's or Queen's Bench Prison in Southwark abolished by statute in 1723; to **send someone to the Mint** was to ruin them. The place took its name from a house which had been a 'mint of coynage' for Henry VIII, and so subject to royal privilege. Because it acted as a shelter for debtors it attracted a large number of poor and destitute people, and in mid-18th century poetry it was put on a similar level with Bedlam and Newgate:

> In durance, exile, Bedlam, or the Mint,
> Like Lee or Budgell, I will rhyme and print.

— Alexander Pope *Satires of Horace* (1733)

See also ➤ ROYAL *Mint*.

Minton pottery made at Stoke-on-Trent by *Thomas Minton* (1766–1836) or his factory. Minton's company popularized the ➤ WILLOW *pattern* design.

minuscule of or in a small cursive script of the Roman alphabet, with ascenders and descenders, developed in the 7th century AD. The name comes (in the early 18th century) via French from Latin *minuscula (littera)* 'somewhat smaller (letter)'.

minute a period of time equal to sixty seconds or a sixtieth of an hour; the word is also used to denote a sixtieth of a degree of angular measurement. Recorded from late Middle English, the word derives from medieval Latin *pars minuta prima* 'first minute part', the $\frac{1}{60}$ of a unit in a system of sexagesimal fractions originally derived from Babylon. The application of astronomical sexagesimal fractions to the measurement of time is first found in the *De Anni Ratione* (?1232) of John of Sacrobosto.

minute gun a gun fired at intervals of a minute, especially at a funeral.

minuteman a member of a class of militiamen of the American revolutionary period who volunteered to be ready for service at a minute's notice.

Minyan a member of a possibly historical ancient people said to have inhabited parts of central Greece (chiefly Orchomenus in Boeotia and Iolchus in

Thessaly), with whom the legends about Jason and the Argonauts are associated.

minyan a quorum of ten men over the age of 13 required for traditional Jewish public worship.

Miocene of, relating to, or denoting the fourth epoch of the Tertiary period, between the Oligocene and Pliocene epochs. This epoch lasted from 23.3 to 5.2 million years ago. During this time the Alps and Himalayas were being formed and there was diversification of the primates, including the first apes.

Miquelet originally, a member of an irregular Catalonian militia active in the Pyrenees from the secessionist revolt of 1640 to the Peninsular War. Later also, a member of a corps of irregular troops raised in Rousillon for service against the Spanish army by Louis XIV in 1689, or of a similar corps raised by Napoleon in 1808.

The name comes from Catalan *Miquel* (Michael); the *Miquelets* were traditionally said to have been called after a follower of Cesare Borgia named Miquel des Prats.

Mir a Soviet space station, launched in 1986 and designed to be permanently manned. The name is Russian, literally 'peace'.

Comte de Mirabeau (1749–91), French revolutionary politician. Pressing for a form of constitutional monarchy, Mirabeau was prominent in the early days of the French Revolution. He was made President of the National Assembly in 1791, but died shortly afterwards.

mirabile dictu Latin phrase, meaning 'wonderful to relate', perhaps originally as a tag from Virgil's *Georgics*.

> And for once, *mirabile dictu*, they all seem to be getting along.
> — Stephen King *Gerald's Game* (1993)

mirabilis see ➤ ANNUS *mirabilis*.

miracle a surprising and welcome event that is not explicable by natural or scientific laws and is therefore considered to be the work of a divine agency. Recorded from Middle English, the word comes via Old French from Latin *miraculum* 'object of wonder', from *mirari* 'to wonder', from *mirus* 'wonderful'.

miracle play a dramatization based on events in the life of Jesus or the legends of the saints, popular in the Middle Ages, a ➤ MYSTERY *play*.

the age of miracles is past proverbial saying; late sixteenth century.

mirage an optical illusion caused by atmospheric conditions, especially the appearance of a sheet of water in a desert or on a hot road caused by the refraction of light from the sky by heated air. The term comes (in the early 19th century) from French, from *se mirer* 'be reflected', from Latin *mirare* 'look at'.

Miranda[1] in Shakespeare's *The Tempest*, the daughter of Prospero; it is Miranda, first meeting the strangers shipwrecked on the island where she and her father are in exile, who utters the remark, 'O, brave new world, That has such people in't.'

Miranda[2] in the US, denoting or relating to the duty of the police to inform a person taken into custody of their right to legal counsel and the right to remain silent under questioning. The names comes (in the mid 20th century) from *Miranda* versus Arizona, the case that led to this ruling by the Supreme Court.

mirror see also ➤ HALL *of Mirrors*, ➤ LAO's *mirror*, ➤ SMOKE *and mirrors*.

Mirror of Diana a name (*Speculum Dianae*) given in ancient times to Lake Nemi, in recognition of the temple and grove of the goddess on its shores.

all done with mirrors an apparent achievement with an element of trickery, alluding to explanations of the art of a conjuror.

mirza originally (as a title) a Persian royal prince. Later, in Iran (Persia), a common honorific title for an official or man of learning who is not a member of the religious hierarchy.

miscreant now, a person who behaves badly or in a way that breaks the law, but originally, a heretic. The word is first recorded in Middle English (as an adjective in the sense 'disbelieving'), and comes from Old French *mescreire* 'disbelieve', the second element of which is from Latin *credere* 'believe'.

mise a grant, payment, or tribute formerly made to secure a liberty or immunity, as by the inhabitants of Wales to a new Lord Marcher, king, or prince on his first entrance into their country, or by the inhabitants of the County Palatine of Chester on a change of earl. The word is recorded in this sense from the mid 16th century, and from late Middle English in the sense 'the issue in a writ of right, a plea'.

miser a person who hoards wealth and spends as little money as possible. Recorded from the late 15th century (as an adjective in the sense 'miserly'), the word comes from Latin, meaning literally 'wretched'.

miserere a psalm in which mercy is sought, especially Psalm 51 (50 in the Vulgate), beginning '*Miserere mei Deus* [Have mercy upon me, O God]', or the music written for it.

misericord a ledge projecting from the underside of a hinged seat in a choir stall which, when the seat is turned up, gives support to someone standing. Medieval misericords were often decorated with elaborate and sometimes bawdy scenes from secular or religious life, visible when the seat was raised.

Dating in this sense from the early 16th century, *misericord* (denoting pity) is recorded from Middle English, and comes ultimately from Latin *misericordia*, from *misericors* 'compassionate', from the stem of *misereri* 'to pity' + *cor, cord-* 'heart'. Other early uses in English include an apartment in a monastery in which some relaxations of the monastic rule were permitted, and a small dagger used to deliver a death stroke to a wounded enemy.

misery loves company proverbial saying, late 16th century.

misfortunes never come singly proverbial saying, early 14th century.

Mishnah an authoritative collection of exegetical material embodying the oral tradition of Jewish law and forming the first part of the Talmud. The name is from Hebrew *mišnāh* and means 'teaching by repetition'.

misper police slang for a *missing person*, a phrase recorded from the 19th century. It seems likely that the contraction to *misper* by those trying to trace such people is of some duration, but the term came to public notice in Britain in 1994, when horrified attention was given to the discovery of the bodies of twelve young women in Gloucestershire, killed and buried over a period of years. Considerable publicity attended the arrest of a Gloucester builder, Frederick West (who committed suicide in prison), and the subsequent trial and conviction of his wife Rosemary on a number of charges. In discussions of the case, one of the main focuses of alarm was the realization of how many of the young women had become *mispers* without their disappearance being registered as a cause for concern.

Lord of Misrule traditionally a man presiding over games and other revelry over the Christmas season, especially in a wealthy household, at the Inns of Court, at Oxford and Cambridge Colleges, and at civic entertainments. Also called *Abbot of Misrule, Master of Misrule.*

miss a title prefixed to the name of an unmarried woman or girl, or to that of a married woman retaining her maiden name for professional purposes. Recorded from the mid 17th century, the word was originally an abbreviation of *mistress*.

See also ➤ *Miss* MARPLE, ➤ *Miss* PIGGY.

a miss is as good as a mile proverbial saying, early 17th century; the syntax has been distorted by abridgement: the original form was ' an inch in a miss is as good as an ell'.

you never miss the water till the well runs dry proverbial saying, early 17th century.

missal a book containing the texts used in the Catholic Mass throughout the year. Recorded from Middle English, the word comes from medieval Latin *missale*, neuter of ecclesiastical Latin *missalis* 'relating to the Mass', from *missa* 'Mass'.

missile see ➤ CRUISE *missile*, ➤ CUBAN *Missile Crisis.*

one of our aircraft is missing the title of a film (1941), an alteration of the customary formula used by BBC news in the Second World War, 'One of our aircraft failed to return.'

missing link a hypothetical fossil form intermediate between two living forms, especially between humans and apes, especially as sought by early evolutionary biologists. The term may also be applied pejoratively to a person held to resemble such a creature; D. H. Lawrence (1885–1930) recalled that a woman had written to him saying that he was 'a mixture of the missing-link and the chimpanzee'.

mission statement a formal summary of the aims and values of a company, organization, or individual; a concept which won an important place in the business jargon of the 1990s, although opinions were divided as to the effective value of such expressions of aspiration. On the positive side, *mission statements* are regarded as combining responsibility to the public and motivation for employees in their explicit statement of a company's aims and aspirations. On the debit side, a *mission statement* may be perceived as functioning as a publicity tool, but lacking the detail that would make it more than a general expression of intent.

missionary a person sent on a religious mission, especially one sent to promote Christianity in a foreign country.

➤ St FRANCIS *Xavier*, ➤ St TERESA *of Lisieux*, and the Franciscan St Leonard of Port Maurice (1676–1751), a noted preacher, are the patron saints of missionaries.

missionary bishops ➤ St PAUL and St Turibius (1538–1606), archbishop of Lima in Peru, are the patron saints of missionary bishops.

missionary position a position for sexual intercourse in which a couple lie face to face with the woman underneath the man, said to be so named because early missionaries advocated the position as 'proper' to primitive peoples, to whom the practice was unknown.

Mississippi a major river of North America, which rises in Minnesota near the Canadian border and flows south to a delta on the Gulf of Mexico. The river is known informally as the *Father of Waters*; when during the American Civil War the North regained control of the Mississippi by the capture of Vicksburg, 4 July 1863, Abraham Lincoln commented, 'the Father of Waters again goes unvexed to the sea.'

Mississippi bubble in 18th-century France, a financial scheme set up by the Scottish adventurer and econonomic theorist John Law, who in 1716 established the *Banque Générale*, which had the authority to issue notes. Speculative investment in Law's company for French development in the Mississippi Valley was followed by a major collapse in 1720.

Missolonghi a city in western Greece, on the north shore of the Gulf of Patras. It is noted as the place where the poet Byron, who had joined the fight for Greek independence from the Turks, died of malaria in 1824.

Missouri Compromise an arrangement made in 1820 which provided that Missouri should be admitted to the Union as a slave state, but that slavery should not be allowed in any new state lying north of 36° 30ʹ.

mistake see also ➤ SHOME *mistake, shurely?*.

if you don't make mistakes you don't make anything proverbial saying, late 19th century.

mistletoe a leathery-leaved parasitic plant which grows on apple, oak, and other broadleaf trees and bears white glutinous berries in winter. Pliny the Elder recorded that mistletoe was sacred to the druids, and it has a number of traditional and pagan associations. It is traditionally used in England to decorate houses at Christmas, when it is associated with the custom of **kissing under the mistletoe**.

In Scandinavian mythology, the shaft which Loki caused the blind Hod to throw at Balder, killing him, was tipped with mistletoe, which was the only plant that could harm him.

Recorded from Old English (in form *misteltā*), the word comes from *mistel* 'mistletoe' (of Germanic origin) + *tān* 'twig'.

The Mistletoe Bough a ballad by Thomas Bayly (1839), which recounts the story of a young bride who during a game hides herself in a chest with a spring-lock and is then trapped there; many years later her skeleton is discovered. Bayly based the ballad on a passage in Samuel Rogers' poem *Italy*; Rogers had commented, 'The story is, I believe, founded on fact; though the time and the place are uncertain. Many old houses lay claim to it.'

mistress originally, a woman having control or authority; a woman who is head of a household. *Mistress* was formerly used as a title prefixed to the name of a married woman, later abbreviated to *Mrs*; it is also the origin of ➤ MISS as a title for an unmarried woman.

The word is recorded from Middle English; from late Middle English, the sense also developed of a woman (other than a wife) having a sexual relationship with a married man.

Mistress of the Robes (in the English royal household) a woman of high rank in charge of the Queen's wardrobe.

Mistress of the World ancient Rome (perhaps as a translation of Livy).

mists see ➤ *so many mists in* MARCH, *so many frosts in May*

Mitanni an ancient kingdom which flourished in northern Mesopotamia in the 15th–14th centuries BC, thought to have had a Hurrian population but Indo-Iranian rulers.

Mitchell principles six recommendations arising from the investigations of the group chaired by George J. Mitchell (1933–), US lawyer and senator (1980–94), who from 1995–6 chaired a group investigating procedures by which disarmament in Northern Ireland could be achieved. The recommendations urged all sides involved in the conflict in Northern Ireland to renounce violence and to agree to a process of disarmament before entering into all-party negotiaions.

mite see ➤ WIDOW's *mite*.

Mithraeum a sanctuary or temple of the god ➤ MITHRAS.

Mithraism the cult of the god ➤ MITHRAS, which became popular among Roman soldiers of the later empire, and was the main rival to Christianity in the first three centuries AD. The sacrifice of a bull formed an important part of cult worship.

Mithras a god of light, truth, and honour, the central figure of the cult of ➤ MITHRAISM but probably of Persian origin; he is often shown slaying the sacred bull. He was also associated with merchants and the protection of warriors.

mithridate a medicine composed of many ingredients, and formerly supposed to be a universal antidote or preservative against poison and disease, named from ➤ MITHRIDATES, king of Pontus.

Mithridates (*c.*132–63 BC), king of Pontus 120–63; known as **Mithridates the Great**, whose expansionist policies led to three wars with Rome (88–85; 83–2; 74–66), and who was finally defeated by Pompey. He was said to have rendered himself proof against poisons by the constant use of antidotes.

Mitla an ancient city in southern Mexico, to the east of the city of Oaxaca, now a noted archaeological site. Believed to have been established as a burial site by the Zapotecs, it was eventually overrun by the Mixtecs in about AD 1000.

Mitnagged a religious opponent of the Hasidim; any Jew who is not a Hasid. The term was originally used by the Hasidim to designate their opponents, but is now used neutrally in the wider sense.

mitre a tall headdress worn by bishops and senior abbots as a symbol of office, tapering to a point at front and back with a deep cleft between. Recorded from late Middle English, the word comes from Old French via Latin from Greek *mitra* 'belt or turban'.

In the Anglican Church after the Reformation down to the time of George III, while the mitre was theoretically part of the episcopal insignia, it was generally only worn at coronations. More recently,

however, its use has been revived for ceremonial occasions.

Three *mitres* are the emblem of ➤ St BERNARDINO *of Siena*.

Mitre Tavern a tavern in Fleet Street, London, frequented by Johnson and Boswell among others.

mittimus a warrant committing a person to prison. The word is from Latin, literally 'we send', first used as the opening word of the writ which transferred records from one court to another (from the late Middle English period to the 18th century).

Walter Mitty a person who fantasizes about a life much more exciting and glamorous than their own life, from the name of the hero of James Thurber's short story *The Secret Life of Walter Mitty* (1939); the 1947 film was probably influential in popularizing the word.

> The Walter Mittys among us who have dreamed of piloting legendary airplanes.
> — *Air & Space Technology* November 1994

mitzvah in Judaism, a precept or commandment, a good deed done from religious duty.
See also ➤ BAR *mitzvah*, ➤ BAT *mitzvah*.

mixed metaphor a combination of two or more incompatible metaphors, which produces a ridiculous effect.

mixen see ➤ BETTER *wed over the mixen than over the moor*.

Mixolydian mode in music, the mode represented by the natural diatonic scale G–G (containing a minor 7th). The term is recorded from the late 16th century; *Mixolydian* comes from Greek *mixo-ludios* 'half-Lydian' (see ➤ LYDIAN *mode*).

Mizpah designating a ring, locket, or other piece of jewellery, given as an expression or token of association or remembrance, originally and especially one with 'Mizpah' inscribed on it. The allusion is biblical; in Genesis 31:49 Jacob and Laban give this name to a place as a sign that God should keep watch between them ('The Lord watch between me and thee').

Mizpah comes from Hebrew *Mispah* watchtower, used as the name of several places in ancient Palestine.

mnemonic a device such as a pattern of letters, ideas, or associations which assists in remembering something. Recorded from the mid 18th century (as an adjective), the word comes ultimately from Greek *mnēmonikos*, from *mnēmōn* 'mindful'.

Mnemosyne in Greek mythology, the mother of the Muses; one of the Titans, and the personification of memory.

moa a large extinct flightless bird resembling the emu, formerly found in New Zealand. One species, *Dinornis maximus* is the tallest known bird at over 3 m, but *Megalapteryx didinus*, which may have survived until the early 19th century, was much smaller. The name is from Maori.

Moab an ancient region east of the Dead Sea, the inhabitants of which, the **Moabites**, were said to be incestuously descended from Moab, son of Lot and Lot's daughter. There was regular contact between the Israelites and Moabites, and Naomi's daughter-in-law ➤ Ruth was a **Moabitess**.

In 19th-century slang, *Moab* was used for a kind of turban-shaped hat; the reference being to Psalms 40:8, 'Moab is my washpot' referring to the shape of the hat.

Moabite Stone a monument erected by Mesha, king of Moab, in *c*.850 BC which describes (in an early form of the Hebrew language) the campaign between Moab and ancient Israel (2 Kings 3), and furnishes an early example of an inscription in the Phoenician alphabet. It is now in the Louvre in Paris.

moaning minnie informal term for a kind of mortar or rocket launcher used by the German forces in the Second World War.

mob a large crowd of people, especially one that is disorderly and intent on causing trouble or violence. The word is recorded from the late 17th century is an abbreviation of the archaic *mobile*, short for Latin *mobile vulgus* 'excitable crowd'.

From the early 20th century, **the Mob** has been an informal term for the Mafia.

Mobilian a lingua franca or trade language formerly used in south-eastern North America, perhaps from *Mobile* a town in Alabama.

Moby Dick the great white whale in Herman Melville's novel of that name (1851), which is hunted by the vengeful Captain Ahab, and which eventually destroys the whaling ship the *Pequod*. The name is used allusively for something on a vast scale.

> A vast Moby Dick of a question that swallowed up all the ugly details.
> — R. Rosenbaum *Travels with Dr Death* (1990)

Mocha Dick name given to an actual white whale of the 1840s and 1850s, said to have caused the death of over thirty men, which may have been the original of ➤ Moby *Dick*.

Mock-Beggar Hall supposed name of a house which has the appearance of wealth, but which is either deserted or else inhabited by miserly or poor people. Also called *Mock-Beggar Manor*.

mockney a form of speech perceived as an affected imitation of cockney in accent and vocabulary. The name, which is a blend of *mock* and *Cockney*, is recorded from the late 1980s as a form of pseudo-Cockney often deliberately adopted to conceal a speaker's privileged background.

Mod[1] a meeting for Gaelic literary and musical competitions, in particular, the **Royal National Mod**, now held annually in Scotland.

Mod[2] in Britain (especially in the early 1960s) a young person of a subculture characterized by a smart stylish appearance, the riding of motor scooters, and a liking for soul music.

modality in scholastic and traditional logic: the fact or quality of being a modal proposition or syllogism; a qualification which confers this quality on a proposition.

moderation in all things proverbial saying, mid 19th century.

Moderations the first public examination in some faculties for the BA degree at Oxford University.

the Modern Babylon a name for London, deriving originally from Disraeli:

> London is a modern Babylon.
> — Benjamin Disraeli *Tancred* (1847)

Amedeo **Modigliani** (1884–1920), Italian painter and sculptor, resident in France from 1906. His portraits and nudes are noted for their elongated forms, linear qualities, and earthy colours.

modillion a projecting bracket under the corona of a cornice in the Corinthian and other orders.

Mods informal term for the ➤ Moderations examination at Oxford University.

Moesia an ancient country of southern Europe, corresponding to parts of modern Bulgaria and Serbia. Lying south of the lower Danube, it was bounded to the west by the River Drina, to the east by the Black Sea, and to the south by the Balkan

Mountains. It became a province of Rome in AD 15, remaining part of the Roman Empire until the 7th century.

Mogul a member of the Muslim dynasty of Mongol origin founded by the successors of Tamerlane, which ruled much of India from the 16th to the 19th century.

See also ➤ GREAT *Mogul*.

Moguntine of or pertaining to the city of Mainz, Germany, especially as an early centre of printing, from *Moguntia*, the Latin name for Mainz.

Mohács a river port and industrial town on the Danube in southern Hungary, close to the borders with Croatia and Serbia, which was the site of a battle in 1526 in which the Hungarians were defeated by a Turkish force under Suleiman I; as a result, Hungary became part of the Ottoman Empire. A site nearby was the scene of a further decisive battle fought in 1687 during the campaign that swept the Turks out of Hungary.

mohajir a Muslim emigrant who left India for Pakistan at the time of partition in 1947 or subsequently.

Mohammed see ➤ MUHAMMAD.

Mohawk a member of an American Indian people, originally inhabiting parts of what is now upper New York State. Recorded in English from the mid 17th century, the name comes from Narragansett *mohowawog*, literally 'maneaters'; an early variant spelling survives in ➤ MOHOCK.

From the 1980s in North America, *Mohawk* has also been used to denote a Mohican haircut.

Mohenjo-Daro an ancient city of the civilization of the Indus valley (*c*.2600–1700 BC), now a major archaeological site in Pakistan.

Mohican a member of an Algonquian people formerly inhabiting part of Connecticut, or their language; a Mohegan. Although the spelling *Mohegan* is now preferred, *Mohican* is also found in modern use after J. Fenimore Cooper's usage in *The Last of the Mohicans* (1826) and other novels.

From the 1960s, *Mohican* has been used to designate a hairstyle with the head shaved except for a strip of hair from the middle of the forehead to the back of the neck, typically stiffened to stand erect or in spikes. The style imitates a traditional deer-hair topknot worn by males of certain northeastern American Indian peoples, and is probably so named

from conventional illustrations of the writings of J. Fenimore Cooper.

the Last of the Mohicans in Fenimore Cooper's novel of that name (1826), the American Indian Uncas, the last survivor of his people; the term is used allusively for the sole survivor of a noble race or kind.

> One character is the spiritual leader of an alien race who chants messages to their gods. Imagine the last of the Mohicans with a touch of Yoda.
> — *Newsweek* 4 January 1993

Mohock a member of a band of aristocratic ruffians who roamed the streets of London at night in the early 18th century. The name was originally an extended use of ➤ MOHAWK, using a variant spelling.

Mohs' scale a scale of hardness used in classifying minerals. It runs from 1 to 10 using a series of reference minerals, and position on the scale depends on ability to scratch minerals rated lower.

The reference minerals used to define the scale are talc 1, gypsum 2, calcite 3, fluorspar 4, apatite 5, orthoclase 6, quartz 7, topaz 8, corundum 9, and diamond 10. It is named after Friedrich *Mohs*, (1773–1839), German mineralogist.

mohur a gold coin, originally Persian, used in India from the 16th century onward, and in the 19th century worth 15 rupees.

moi humorous exclamation, me? (used when accused of something that one knows one is guilty of). The usage was largely popularized through its use on television, especially by *The Muppets*, in which it was liberally used by the main female character, ➤ *Miss* PIGGY.

moidore a Portuguese gold coin, current in England in the early 18th century and then worth about 27 shillings. The name comes from Portuguese *moeda d'ouro* 'money of gold'.

mojo a magic charm, a talisman (chiefly in the US, and probably of African origin); compare with Gullah *moco* 'witchcraft'.

moksha (in Hinduism and Jainism) release from the cycle of rebirth impelled by the law of karma.

mole this small burrowing mammal with dark velvety fur, long muzzle, and very small eyes, is in proverbial use often referred to as the type of a blind creature. The mole was also toasted by Jacobites as the ➤ LITTLE *gentleman in black velvet*, in reference to the death of William III, said to have been caused by a fall from his horse which had stumbled on a molehill.

From the early 1920s, *mole* has been used allusively to designate a spy who achieves over a long period an important position within the security defences of a country, or someone within an organization who anonymously betrays confidential information.

molehill see ➤ *make a* MOUNTAIN *out of a molehill.*

Molière pseudonym taken by the French dramatist whose real name was Jean-Baptiste Poquelin (1622–73). He wrote more than twenty comic plays about contemporary France, developing stock characters from Italian *commedia dell'arte.*

moline in heraldry, (of a cross) having each extremity broadened, split, and curved back (a **cross moline**). The word comes from Anglo-Norman French *moliné*, from *molin* 'mill', because of a resemblance to the iron support of a millstone.

Molinism[1] the doctrine, propounded in 1588 by Luis de *Molina* (1535–1600), Spanish Jesuit, that human will remains free under the action of divine grace.

Molinism[2] ➤ QUIETISM, as propounded by Miguel de *Molinos* (1627–96), Spanish priest.

Moll see ➤ *Moll* CUTPURSE.

Mollweide projection a projection of a map of the world on to an ellipse, with lines of latitude represented by straight lines (spaced more closely towards the poles) and meridians represented by equally spaced elliptical curves. This projection distorts shape but preserves relative area. It is named after Karl B. *Mollweide* (1774–1825), German mathematician and astronomer, who first used it.

Molly Maguire a member of a secret society formed in Ireland in 1843 for the purpose of resisting evictions from land for the non-payment of rent. The name, which brings together a common Irish forename and surname, refers to a customary assumption of female disguise.

Molly Maguire was also the name for a member of a secret organization of coal miners supposedly responsible for acts of sabotage and terrorism in the anthracite coalfields of Pennsylvania and West Virginia from 1862–76.

Moloch a Canaanite idol to whom children were sacrificed; in extended usage, a tyrannical object of sacrifices. The Rabbinical story that children were burnt alive (being placed in the arms of the idol, whence they fell into the flames) appears to be unfounded, but is widely known, and has influenced the extended use. The deity is represented by Milton in *Paradise Lost* as one of the devils.

> A newspaper is a modern Moloch, craving blood sacrifice.
> — *Spectator* 28 January 1995

Vyacheslav Molotov (1890–1986), Soviet statesman, who as Commissar (later Minister) for Foreign Affairs (1939–49; 1953–6) negotiated the non-aggression pact with Nazi Germany (1939). The ➤ MOLOTOV *cocktail* is named after him.

Molotov cocktail a crude incendiary device typically consisting of a bottle filled with flammable liquid and with a means of ignition. The production of similar grenades was organized by Vyacheslav *Molotov* (1890–1986), during the Second World War.

moly a mythical herb with white flowers and black roots, endowed with magic properties, and said by Homer to have been given by Hermes to Odysseus as a charm against Circe. The name comes via Latin from Greek *mōlu.*

the moment of truth a crisis, a turning-point; a testing situation; from Spanish *el momento de la verdad* the time of the final sword-thrust in a bullfight.

Theodor Mommsen (1817–1903), German historian. He is noted for his three-volume *History of Rome* (1854–6; 1885) and his treatises on Roman constitutional law (1871–88).

Momus a person likened to *Momus*, the Greek god of censure and ridicule, who for his censures upon the gods was banished from heaven; a fault-finder, a captious or carping critic. Often in allusions to the story that when Hephaistos (or Zeus) had made a man, Momus blamed him for not having put a window in his breast.

Mona Lisa a painting (now in the Louvre in Paris) executed 1503–6 by Leonardo da Vinci. The sitter was the wife of Francesco del Giocondo; her enigmatic smile has become one of the most famous images in Western art.

monarch a sovereign head of state, especially a king, queen, or emperor. Recorded from late Middle English, the word comes via late Latin from Greek *monarkhēs*, from *monos* 'alone' + *arkhein* 'to rule'.

See also ➤ MERRY *Monarch.*

Monarchian a Christian heretic of the 2nd or 3rd century who denied the doctrine of the Trinity. The term was originally a nickname (*monarchiani*) applied by Tertullian to opponents of the doctrine of the Trinity, in reference to what he saw as their unintelligent use of the word *monarchia*. In early apologetics, 'the monarchy of God' was a current designation for Christian monotheism, and these heretics regarded themselves as defenders of this cardinal doctrine against the Trinitarians.

Monarcho in the 16th and 17th centuries, a person generally ridiculed for absurd pretensions, from Italian (= *monarca* monarch), a title assumed by an insane Italian who fancied himself emperor of the world.

monarchy see ➤ the DUAL *Monarchy*, ➤ FIFTH *Monarchy*, ➤ the JULY *monarchy*.

monasteries see ➤ DISSOLUTION *of the monasteries*.

George Monck (1608–70), English general, later Duke of Albemarle. Initially a Royalist, he became a supporter of Oliver Cromwell and later suppressed the Royalists in Scotland (1651). Concerned at the growing unrest following Cromwell's death (1658), Monck negotiated the return of Charles II in 1660.

Monday the day of the week before Tuesday and following Sunday. Recorded from Old English (in form *Mōnandæg*), the name originally meant 'day of the moon', a translation of late Latin *lunae dies*.

See also ➤ *Monday's* CHILD *is fair of face*.

Mondays	
Black Monday	the Monday after Easter Sunday; 19 October 1987
Blue Monday	the Monday before Shrove Tuesday; a Monday given over to celebration
Hock Monday	the second Monday after Easter Sunday
Merry Monday	the Monday before Shrove Tuesday
Nut Monday	the first Monday in August
Plough Monday	the first Monday after Epiphany
Rock Monday	the Monday after 6 January

Saint Monday used with reference to the practice among workmen of being idle on Monday, as a consequence of drunkenness on the Sunday, chiefly in the phrase **to keep Saint Monday.**

Monday club a right-wing Conservative club, formed in 1961, that originally held its meetings on Mondays.

Monday morning quarterback in North America, informal expression for a person who passes judgement on and criticizes something after the event, an armchair critic.

mondo used in reference to something very striking or remarkable of its kind (often in conjunction with a pseudo-Italian noun or adjective). The term comes from Italian *Mondo Cane*, literally 'dog's world', the title of a film (1961) depicting bizarre behaviour.

> I think it's going to be mondo weirdo this year.
> — Douglas Coupland *Generation X* (1991)

Claude Monet (1840–1926), French painter. A founder member of the Impressionists, his fascination with the play of light on objects led him to produce series of paintings of single subjects painted at different times of day and under different weather conditions, such as the *Water-lilies* sequence (1899–1906; 1916 onwards).

money *money* comes from Latin *moneta* 'mint', originally a title of a goddess (in classical times regarded as identical with Juno), in whose temple in Rome money was minted.

A money box (or moneybag) is the emblem of ➤ *St* MATTHEW and ➤ *St* NICHOLAS *of Myra*.

See also ➤ BAD *money drives out good*, ➤ *a* FOOL *and his money are soon parted*, ➤ LEND *your money and lose your friend*, ➤ MAUNDY *money*, ➤ PRIZE *money*, ➤ PROCLAMATION *money*, ➤ *a* RUN *for one's money*, ➤ SHIP *money*, ➤ SMART *money*, ➤ TIME *is money*.

money changer archaic term for a person whose business was the exchanging of one currency for another; often with biblical allusion, as to Matthew 21:12, 'And Jesus went into the temple of God, and cast out all them that sold and bought in the temple, and overthrew the tables of the moneychangers, and the seats of them that sold doves'.

> What will they say if he comes blighting the vine, flogging the money-changers out of the temple one day, and hobnobbing with the rich the next.
> — Robertson Davies *Fifth Business* (1970)

money has no smell proverbial saying, which in this form is recorded from the early 20th century. A translation of Latin *Pecunia non olet*, it derives from a comment made by the Emperor Vespasian (AD 9–79), when his son Titus objected to a tax levied on public lavatories. Vespasian is said to have held a coin to Titus's nose, and on being told that it did not smell, to have replied, '*Atque e lotio est* [Yes, that's made from urine]'.

money isn't everything proverbial saying, early 20th century.

money is power proverbial saying, mid 18th century.

money is the root of all evil proverbial saying, mid 15th century; with biblical allusion to 1 Timothy 6:10, 'The love of money is the root of all evil.'

money makes a man proverbial saying, early 16th century; translating the Latin tag, '*divitiae virum faciunt* [wealth makes the man]'.

money makes money proverbial saying, late 16th century, implying that those who are already wealthy are likely to become more so.

money makes the mare to go proverbial saying, late 15th century, referring to money as a source of power.

no money, no Swiss proverbial saying, late 16th century; the Swiss were particularly noted as mercenaries.

your money or your life a formula attributed to highwaymen in obtaining money from their victims.

money talks proverbial saying, mid 17th century.

moneybag a moneybag is the emblem of ➤ *St* MATTHEW and ➤ *St* NICHOLAS *of Myra*.

a moneyless man goes fast through the market proverbial saying, early 18th century; late 14th century in French.

Mongol a native or national of Mongolia, a Mongolian. In the 13th century AD the Mongol empire under Genghis Khan extended across central Asia from Manchuria in the east to European Russia in the west. Under Kublai Khan China was conquered and the Mongol capital moved to Khanbaliq (modern Beijing). The Mongol empire collapsed after a series of defeats culminating in the destruction of the Golden Horde by the Muscovites in 1380.

The term *mongol* was adopted in the late 19th century to refer to a person suffering from *Down's syndrome*, owing to the similarity of some of the physical symptoms of the disorder with the normal facial characteristics of East Asian people. In modern English, this use is now unacceptable and considered offensive.

Mongrel Parliament a name for the parliament summoned by Charles II at Oxford in 1681, in which the Protestant party, embracing both Whigs and Tories, pressed the king to name his illegitimate son Monmouth as his heir in preference to the Catholic Duke of York.

St Monica (332–*c*.387), mother of ➤ *St* AUGUSTINE *of Hippo*. She is often regarded as the model of Christian mothers for her patience with her son's spiritual crises, which ended with his conversion in 386. She is frequently chosen as the patron of associations of Christian mothers.

□ **FEAST DAY** Her feast day is 27 August (formerly 4 May).

monism a theory or doctrine that denies the existence of a distinction or duality in some sphere, such as that between matter and mind, or God and the world; the doctrine that only one supreme being exists.

monitor former term for a shallow-draught warship mounting one or two heavy guns for bombardment, named for a vessel developed by Swedish engineer John Ericsson for the Union forces. In a letter of 1862 he said that he proposed to name the new battery *Monitor* on the ground that 'The ironclad intruder will thus prove a severe monitor to those leaders [of the Southern rebellion].'

This prototype vessel engaged the Confederate ironclad *Virginia* in Chesapeake Bay in a battle that drew worldwide attention; after this a number of similar warships were built by the Union. The original *Monitor*, however, went down off Cape Hatteras in 1862.

monk a member of a religious community of men typically living under vows of poverty, chastity, and obedience; the earliest such communities were groups of hermits living in the desert. In England, the term was not applied before the Reformation to members of the mendicant orders, who were always called *friars*, but since that period the usage has widened to include members of those orders.

➤ *St* JOHN *the Baptist*, ➤ *St* ANTHONY *of Egypt*, and ➤ *St* BENEDICT are the patron saints of monks.

Recorded from Old English (in form *munuc*), the word is based on Greek *monakhos* 'solitary', from *monos* 'alone'.

See also ➤ BLACK *Monks*, ➤ *the* COWL *does not make the monk*, ➤ *the* DEVIL *was sick, the Devil a monk would be*, ➤ WHITE *Monk*.

monkey a *monkey* is proverbially taken as the type of a clever, artful, or amusing person. Monkeys were often in the past kept as domestic pets, and proprietors of barrel-organs were typically accompanied by a monkey, giving rise to an extended metaphor in which the monkey stands for the junior member of a disparaged partnership:

> If we complain about the tune, there is no reason to attack the monkey when the organ grinder is present.
> — Aneurin Bevan speech in the House of Commons, 16 May 1957

Recorded from the mid 16th century, the word is of unknown origin, perhaps from Low German; in the Middle Low German version of *Reynard the Fox* (1498), *Moneke* appears once as the name of the son of Martin the Ape.

See also ➤ *cold enough to freeze the balls off a* BRASS *monkey,* ➤ *the* HIGHER *the monkey climbs, the more he shows his tail,* ➤ *if you pay* PEANUTS *you get monkeys,* ➤ SOFTLY, *softly, catchee monkey.*

Monkey Trial a trial of a teacher for teaching evolutionary theories, contrary to the laws of certain States of the US, specifically that of J. T. Scopes in Dayton, Tennessee (10–21 July, 1925), with William Jennings Bryan for the prosecution, and Clarence Darrow for the defence. Scopes was convicted, and fined $100 dollars.

three wise monkeys a conventional sculptured group of three monkeys; used allusively to refer to a person who chooses to ignore or keep silent about wrongdoing. One monkey is depicted with its paws over its mouth (taken as connoting 'speak no evil'), one with its paws over its eyes ('see no evil'), and one with its paws over its ears ('hear no evil').

Monmouth a town in SE Wales, birthplace of ➤ HENRY V (**Henry of Monmouth**).
See also ➤ GEOFFREY *of Monmouth.*

Duke of Monmouth James Scott, Duke of *Monmouth* (1649–85), illegitimate son of Charles II. He became the focus of Whig supporters of a Protestant succession, and in 1685 he led a rebellion against the Catholic James II, but was defeated at the ➤ *Battle of* SEDGEMOOR and executed.
see also ➤ EXCLUSION *Bill.*

Monmouth cock a style of wearing a broad-brimmed hat turned up at the back and tipped over the eyes, fashionable for a few years from about 1667, and named for the ➤ *Duke of* MONMOUTH (1649–85).

monody an ode sung by a single actor in a Greek tragedy; a poem lamenting a person's death.

Monophysite a person who holds that there is only one inseparable nature (partly divine, partly and subordinately human) in the person of Christ,

contrary to a declaration of the Council of Chalcedon (451).

Monopoly trademark name for a board game in which players engage in simulated property and financial dealings using imitation money. It was invented in the US and the name was coined by Charles Darrow *c.*1935.

Monopoly money the imitation money provided in the game of ➤ MONOPOLY; in extended usage, currency having or perceived as having no real existence or value.

> It's a huge sum, but after a while it becomes like monopoly money.
> — *Daily Express* 8 June 1992

monopolylogue an entertainment in which a single performer sustains many characters, chiefly with reference to 'At Homes' performed from 1808 by the English actor Charles Mathews (1776–1835).

monopteros a classical temple consisting of a single circle of columns supporting a roof.

Monothelite an adherent of the doctrine that Jesus had only one will, proposed in the 7th century to reconcile Monophysite and orthodox parties in the Byzantine Empire but condemned as heresy.

James Monroe (1758–1831), American Democratic Republican statesman, 5th President of the US 1817–25. In 1803, while minister to France under President Jefferson, he negotiated and ratified the ➤ LOUISIANA *Purchase*; he is chiefly remembered, however, as the originator of the ➤ MONROE *doctrine.*

Marilyn Monroe (1926–62), American actress. Her film roles, largely in comedies, made her the definitive Hollywood sex symbol. She is thought to have died of an overdose of sleeping pills.

> So we think of Marilyn who was every man's love affair with America, Marilyn Monroe who was blonde and beautiful and had a sweet little rinky-dink of a voice and all the cleanliness of all the clean American backyards.
> — Norman Mailer *Marilyn* (1973)

Monroe doctrine a principle of US policy, originated by President James Monroe, that any intervention by external powers in the politics of the Americas is a potentially hostile act against the US.

> We owe it . . . to the amicable relations existing between the United States and those [European] powers to declare that we should consider any attempt on their part to extend their system to any portion of this hemisphere as dangerous to our peace and safety.
> — James Monroe annual message to Congress, 2 December 1823

Mons a town in southern Belgium, the scene in August 1914 of the first major battle of the First World War between British and German forces.

See also ➤ ANGELS *of Mons.*

Mons Gaudi the name (in post-classical Latin of the 10th century), meaning 'Mount of Joy', given by pilgrims to the mountain Rama, to the north-west of Jerusalem. The name was later applied to other elevations from which the holy city could be seen, and finally to any vantage point.

See also ➤ MONTJOIE.

Mons Meg a 15th-century gun in Edinburgh Castle, perhaps named from having been cast at ➤ MONS in Flanders (now Belgium).

Monseigneur a title of the Dauphin of France, originally conferred upon the Dauphin in the reign of Louis XIV (1643–1715). The word in French means literally 'my lord'.

Monsieur a title of the second son or the next younger brother of the King of France. The word in French means literally 'my lord'.

See also ➤ PEACE *of Monsieur.*

Monsignor the title of various senior Roman Catholic posts, such as a prelate or an officer of the papal court.

monsoon a seasonal prevailing wind in the region of the Indian subcontinent and SE Asia, blowing from the south-west between May and September and bringing rain (the **wet monsoon**), or from the north-east between October and April (the **dry monsoon**).

Recorded from the late 16th century, the word comes via Portuguese from Arabic *mawsim* 'season', from *wasama* 'to mark, brand'.

monster an imaginary creature that is typically large, ugly, and frightening. Recorded from late Middle English, the word comes via Old French from Lain *monstrum* 'portent or monster', from *monere* 'warn'.

See also ➤ BUG-*eyed monster,* ➤ *the* GREEN-*eyed monster,* ➤ LOCH *Ness Monster,* ➤ MANY-*headed monster.*

monstrance in the Roman Catholic Church, an open or transparent receptacle in which the consecrated Host is exposed for veneration. Recorded from late Middle English (also in the sense 'demonstration or proof'), the word comes via medieval Latin from Latin *monstrare* 'show'.

A monstrance is the emblem of ➤ *St* CLARE and

St Norbert, founder of the ➤ PREMONSTRATENSIANS.

monstre sacré a striking, eccentric, or controversial public figure. This French phrase became known in English from the title of Jean Cocteau's *Les monstres sacrés* (1940).

Mont St Michel a rocky islet off the coast of Normandy, NW France. An island only at high tide, it is surrounded by sandbanks and linked to the mainland, since 1875, by a causeway. It is crowned by a medieval Benedictine abbey-fortress.

Michel de Montaigne (1533–92), French essayist. Widely regarded as the originator of the modern essay, he wrote about prominent personalities and ideas of his age in his sceptical *Essays* (1580; 1588).

Montanism the tenets of a heretical millenarian and ascetic Christian sect that set great store by prophecy, founded in Phrygia by the priest *Montanus*, who claimed prophetic inspiration for himself and two female associates, in the middle of the 2nd century.

Marquis de Montcalm (1712–59), French general. He defended Quebec against British troops under General ➤ *James* WOLFE, but was defeated and fatally wounded in the battle on the Plains of Abraham.

Monte Albán an ancient city, now in ruins, in Oaxaca, southern Mexico. Occupied from the 8th century BC, it was a centre of the Zapotec culture from about the 1st century BC to the 8th century AD, after which it was occupied by the Mixtecs until the Spanish conquest in the 16th century.

Monte Carlo a resort in Monaco, forming one of the four communes of the principality; it is famous as a gambling resort and as the terminus of the annual Monte Carlo rally.

See also ➤ MAN *who broke the bank at Monte Carlo.*

Monte Carlo method a technique in which a large quantity of randomly generated numbers are studied using a probabilistic model to find an approximate solution to a numerical problem that would be difficult to solve by other methods. It is named after Monte Carlo with reference to its gambling casino.

Monte Cassino a hill in central Italy near the town of Cassino, the site of the principal monastery of the Benedictines, founded by St Benedict *c.*529. The monastery and the town were destroyed in 1944 during bitter fighting between Allied and German forces, but have since been restored.

monteith a deep ornamental bowl with a scalloped rim, usually made of silver, which was filled with iced water for the purpose of cooling wine glasses or, in later use, sometimes used as a punchbowl. From the name *Monteith*, probably of a 17th-century Scotsman who wore a cloak with a scalloped bottom edge.

Montem a festival celebrated (at first annually, later triennially) by the scholars of Eton College, who processed in fancy dress to 'Salt Hill', a mound near Slough, to raise money towards the expenses of the senior colleger (called the 'Captain of the Montem') when he went up to King's College, Cambridge. The last of these processions was held in 1844.

montero a cap of a type formerly worn in Spain for hunting, having a spherical crown and flaps that could be drawn down over the ears.

Marquise de Montespan (1641–1707), French noblewoman. She was mistress of Louis XIV from 1667 to 1679, and had seven illegitimate children by him. She subsequently fell from favour during the ➤ *Affair of the* POISONS, the king also becoming attracted to the children's governess, ➤ *Madame de* MAINTENON.

Montesquieu (1689–1755), French political philosopher. His reputation rests chiefly on *L'Esprit des lois* (1748), a comparative study of political systems in which he championed the separation of judicial, legislative, and executive powers as being most conducive to individual liberty.

Montessori a system of education for young children that seeks to develop natural interests and activities rather than use formal teaching methods, based on the ideas of the Italian educationist Maria Montessori (1870–1952), who in her book *The Montessori Method* (1909) advocated a child-centred approach to education, developed from her success with mentally handicapped children.

Claudio Monteverdi (1567–1643), Italian composer. His madrigals are noted for their use of harmonic dissonance; other important works include his opera *Orfeo* (1607) and his sacred *Vespers* (1610).

Lola Montez (1818–61), Irish dancer. She became the mistress of Ludwig I of Bavaria after performing in Munich in 1846 and exercised great influence over him until banished the following year.

Montezuma II (1466–1520), Aztec emperor 1502–20. The last ruler of the Aztec empire in Mexico, he was defeated and imprisoned by the Spanish under Cortés in 1519. He was killed while trying to pacify some of his former subjects during an uprising against his captors.

Simon de Montfort[1] (c.1165–1218), French soldier. From 1209 he led the Albigensian Crusade against the ➤ CATHARS in southern France.

Simon de Montfort[2] (c.1208–65), English soldier, born in Normandy, later Earl of Leicester. He led the baronial opposition to Henry III, defeating the king at Lewes in 1264 and summoning a Parliament (1265). He was defeated and killed by reorganized royal forces under Henry's son (later Edward I) at Evesham.

Montgolfier Joseph Michel (1740–1810) and Jacques Étienne (1745–99), French inventors and pioneers in hot-air ballooning. In 1782 they built a large balloon from linen and paper and successfully lifted a number of animals; the first human ascents followed in 1783.

month each of the twelve named periods into which a year is divided. Recorded from Old English (in form mōnaþ), and of Germanic origin, the word is related to ➤ MOON, and the primitive calendar month of many early civilizations began on, or on the day after, the day of the full moon.
See also ➤ FLAVOUR *of the month*.

month's mind in the Christian Church, the commemoration of a dead person by the celebration of a requiem mass or (later more widely) special prayers on the day one month after the date of the death or funeral.

months see ➤ MOTHER *of months*.

Montjoie in medieval French tradition, Charlemagne's ensign and war cry, representing ➤ MONS *Gaudi* from which Jerusalem was seen by pilgrims. *Montjoie* is the cry of Charlemagne's forces in the *Song of Roland*, and **Montjoie St Denis** (which appears in the old royal arms of France) was the national war-cry of the French.

Montmartre a district in northern Paris, on a hill above the Seine, much frequented by artists in the late 19th and early 20th centuries when it was a separate village. Many of its buildings have artistic associations, e.g. the Moulin de la Galette, which was painted by Renoir.

Montparnasse a district of Paris, on the left bank of the River Seine. Frequented in the late 19th century by writers and artists, it is traditionally associated with Parisian cultural life.

Montpellier a city in southern France, near the Mediterranean coast, which developed in the 10th century as a trading centre on the spice route from the Near East and was a stopover on the pilgrimage to Santiago de Compostela. A distinguished medical school and university, world-famous in medieval times, was founded there in 1221.

Montreux a resort town in SW Switzerland, at the east end of Lake Geneva, which since the 1960s has hosted annual festivals of both jazz and television; Golden, Silver, and Bronze Roses are awarded to winners at the light entertainment festival.

Marquis of Montrose (1612–50), James Graham, Scottish general. Montrose supported Charles I in the English Civil War and inflicted a dramatic series of defeats on the stronger Covenanter forces in the north (1644–5) before being defeated at Philiphaugh. In 1650 he attempted to restore Charles II, but was betrayed to the Covenanters and hanged.

Montserrat a mountain in the NW of Barcelona, known for an ancient wooden statue of the Virgin and Child, which had supposedly been carved by St Luke and brought to Spain by St Peter, and which was concealed in a cave there during the period of Moorish rule.

the full monty the full amount expected, desired, or possible. Of unknown origin, the phrase has only been recorded recently. Among various (unsubstantiated) theories, one cites the phrase *the full Montague Burton*, apparently meaning 'Sunday-best three-piece suit' (from the name of a tailor of made-to-measure clothing in the early 20th century); another recounts the possibility of a military usage, *the full monty* being 'the full cooked English breakfast' insisted upon by Field Marshal Montgomery.

Monty Python's Flying Circus an influential British television comedy series (1969–74), noted especially for its absurdist or surrealist style of humour and starring, among others, John Cleese.

> Conversations can seem like a shared hallucination scripted by Monty Python.
>
> — *Guardian* 24 November 1994

monument the word *monument* is recorded from Middle English, and originally denoted a burial place rather than the statue or building over it or commemorating a person or event; the word comes via French from Latin *monumentum*, from *monere* 'remind'.

the Monument a Doric column 202 feet in height, built in the City of London (1671–7) according to the design of Sir Christopher Wren, to commemorate the great fire of London of 1666, which originated in a house 202 feet from the site of the column.

Monumental City the city of Baltimore in Maryland, so called on account of the Washington Monument, the first monument erected to George Washington. Also called *Monument City*.

Moody and Sankey the American evangelist Dwight Moody (1837–1899) and hymnwriter Ira David Sankey (1840–1908), who collaborated on what became known as the 'Sankey & Moody' hymn book, first published in 1873. *Moody and Sankey* may be used to denote the style of such popular mission hymns.

moomba an annual pre-Lent festival held in Melbourne.

moon the natural satellite of the earth, visible (chiefly at night) by reflected light from the sun. Recorded from Old English (in form *mōna*) and of Germanic origin, related to *month*, the word comes from an Indo-European root shared by Latin *mensis* and Greek *mēn* 'month', and also Latin *metiri* 'measure' (the moon being used to measure time).

The constantly recurring changes and phases of the moon have caused it to be taken as a type of changeableness and inconstancy; they were also traditionally supposed to influence the health of body and mind, and to cause insanity.

The *moon* may also be personified as a goddess (for example, *Diana* or *Cynthia*), and as such symbolizes virginity:

> Chaste as cold Cynthia's virgin light.
>
> — Alexander Pope *Chorus of Youths and Virgins* (1722)

See also ➤ CYCLE *of the moon*, ➤ DARK *of the moon*, ➤ GALILEAN *moon*, ➤ GLIMPSES *of the moon*, ➤ HARVEST *moon*, ➤ MAN *in the Moon*, ➤ MICHAELMAS *moon*, ➤ MOUNTAINS *of the Moon*, ➤ OLD *moon*, ➤ *once in a* BLUE *moon*.

Moon Festival a Chinese festival held in the middle of the autumn, originally a family gathering after the completion of the harvest.

Moon Hoax a series of articles printed in the New York *Sun* of August 1835, purporting to reveal the discovery by the astronomer ➤ *John* Herschel of life on the moon, including mountains, forests, winged inhabitants, and beavers walking on two legs. The story, which excited great public interest and substantially increased the circulation of the paper, was revealed the following month as a hoax; the author was the British journalist Richard Adams Locke (1800–71).

believe that the moon is made of green cheese believe an absurdity, an expression recorded from the 16th century. The origin is not clear, but may refer to the mottled appearance of a cheese like sage Derby being held to resemble the variegated surface of the moon.

no moon, no man proverbial saying, late 19th century, recording the traditional belief that a child born at the time of the new moon or just before its appearance will not live to grow up.

mooncalf now, a foolish or stupid person, but originally, an abortive or misshapen fetus, regarded as being produced by the influence of the moon, and from that a term used for a creature regarded as a monster. Caliban in Shakespeare's *Tempest* is addressed as 'Mooncalf'.

Moonie informal and often derogatory term for a member of the Unification Church, from the name of its founder, Sun Myung *Moon*.

moonlight and roses romance; from the title of a song by Black and Moret, 1925.

> Chilly agreements in lawyerese, however sensible, can only detract from the moonlight and roses of the early years.
> — *Daily Telegraph* 2 February 1998

moonlighting in 19th-century Ireland, the perpetration by night of violence against the persons or property of tenants who had incurred the hostility of the Land League.

The term is now generally used for the practice of having a second job, typically secretly and at night, in addition to one's regular employment.

moonraker a native of the English county of Wiltshire, with reference to the Wiltshire story of men caught raking a pond for kegs of smuggled brandy, who feigned madness to fool the revenue men, by saying they were raking out the moon.

moonshine from late Middle English, *moonshine* has been taken as the type of something insubstantial or unreal (originally, in the phrase **moonshine in the water**). Later, the term was extended to mean foolish, nonsensical, or fanciful talk or ideas.

In North America, from the late 18th century, *moonshine* has been used to designate illicitly distilled or smuggled liquor.

moor see ➤ BETTER *wed over the mixen than over the moor.*

Moor a member of a NW African Muslim people of mixed Berber and Arab descent. In the 8th century they conquered the Iberian peninsula, but were finally driven out of their last stronghold in Granada at the end of the 15th century.

In the Middle Ages, and as late as the 17th century, the Moors were commonly supposed to be mostly black or very dark-skinned; the name was thus sometimes used in the sense 'a black person'.

The name comes from Old French *More*, via Latin from Greek *Mauros* 'inhabitant of Mauretania'.

Francis Moore (1657–*c.*1715), English physician, astrologer, and schoolmaster. His almanacs of meteorological and astrological predictions gave their name to the range of almanacs called 'Old Moore' available today.

Henry Moore (1898–1986), English sculptor and draughtsman. His work is characterized by semi-abstract reclining forms, large upright figures, and family groups, which Moore intended to be viewed in the open air.

John Moore (1761–1809), British general, who commanded the British army during the Peninsular War and was killed at Corunna. His burial, just before the British embarkation from the besieged city, was the subject of a famous poem by the Irish poet Charles Wolfe:

> We carved not a line, and we raised not a stone—
> But we left him alone with his glory.
> — Charles Wolfe 'The Burial of Sir John Moore at Corunna' (1817)

Thomas Moore (1779–1852), Irish poet and musician. He wrote patriotic and nostalgic songs set to Irish tunes, notably 'The Harp that once through Tara's Halls' and 'The Minstrel Boy', and is also known for the oriental romance *Lalla Rookh* (1817).

Moore's law an observation and prediction originally made in 1965 by Gordon Earle *Moore* (1929–), US microchip manufacturer, stating that a new type of microprocessor chip is released every 12 to 24 months, with each new version having approximately twice as many logical elements as its predecessor, and that this trend is likely to continue, resulting in an exponential rise in computing power per chip over a period of time.

Moors Murders name given to the sadistic serial killings of children carried out by Ian Brady (1938–) and his accomplice Myra Hindley (1942–), for which they were convicted in 1966; the name derived from their having buried the bodies of their victims on Saddleworth Moor in the Pennines. An additionally distressing feature of the case was that not all the bodies of those claimed to have been murdered have been located.

moot an assembly of people, especially one for judicial or legislative purposes. Chiefly associated with national and local administration from the Anglo-Saxon to the Early Modern period.

From the early 16th century, the term has also been used to designate a mock trial set up to examine a hypothetical case as an academic exercise. It was revived in the Inns of Court in the 19th century after falling into disuse, and introduced into universities where law is studied.

The use of *moot* as an adjective meaning 'subject to debate, dispute, or uncertainty, and typically not admitting a final decision' derives from the use of **moot court** to designate this kind of mock trial.

Recorded from Old English and of Germanic origin, the word is ultimately related to *meet*.

mop fair an annual fair or gathering at which servants seeking to be hired assembled together, a statute fair. The name is recorded from the late 17th century, and has been explained as deriving from the fact that those hoping to be hired would carry a mop, broom, or other implement indicating the work they did.

the moral Gower name given to the English poet John Gower (?1330–1408) by Geoffrey Chaucer:

> O moral Gower, this book I directe
> To the.
> — Geoffrey Chaucer *Troilus and Criseyde* (a. 1425)

moral concerned with the principles of right and wrong behaviour and the goodness and badness of human behaviour; as a noun and in plural, a person's standards of behaviour or beliefs concerning what is and is not acceptable for them to do.

Recorded from late Middle English, the word comes from Latin moralis, from *mos, mor-* 'custom',

(plural) *mores* 'morals'. As a noun the word was first used to translate Latin *Moralia* ('Morals'), the title of St Gregory the Great's moral exposition of the Book of Job, and was subsequently applied to the works of various classical writers.

Moral Majority the name of a political movement of evangelical Christians, founded in the US in 1979 by the Reverend Jerry Falwell, that advocates an ultra-conservative political and social agenda, especially on issues such as abortion and religious education. The choice of name may have been influenced by the title of Westely and Egstien's book *The Silent Majority* (1969).

Moral Rearmament an organization founded by the American Lutheran evangelist Frank Buchman (1878–1961) and first popularized in Oxford in the 1920s (hence until about 1938 called the *Oxford Group Movement*). It emphasizes personal integrity and confession of faults, cooperation, and mutual respect, especially as a basis for social transformation.

morality play a kind of drama with personified abstract qualities as the main characters and presenting a lesson about good conduct and character, popular in the 15th and early 16th centuries.

Morasthite in biblical translations and allusions, a native or inhabitant of Moresheth-Gath, a town near the Philistine city of Gath; **the Morasthite**, the prophet ➤ MICAH.

Moravian[1] a member of a Protestant Church founded in Saxony by emigrants from Moravia, and continuing the tradition of the Unitas Fratrum, a body holding Hussite doctrines, which had its chief seat in Moravia and Bohemia.

The virtual founder of the body was Count Zinzendorf (1700–60), who was the patron of the Moravian refugees, and embraced their doctrines. The Moravians early obtained many adherents in England and colonial North America.

Moravian[2] a native or inhabitant of Moray in NE Scotland (in early use, one of the great divisions of the country).

Moray see ➤ DINE *with St Giles and the Earl of Moray.*

Mordecai in the Bible, the cousin of Esther who is taken into favour by the king after the execution of his enemy ➤ HAMAN, the previously favoured counsellor. In the biblical story (Esther 5:13)

Haman's hatred of Mordecai is represented as obsessive, 'All this availeth me nothing, so long as I see Mordecai the Jew sitting at the king's gate.'

Mordred in the Arthurian legends, the nephew of King ➤ Arthur, the son of King Lot of Orkney and Arthur's sister ➤ Morgawse; Geoffrey of Monmouth makes him the son of Arthur and his sister. During Arthur's absence (and taking advantage of the king's loss of ➤ Lancelot) he treacherously seizes the queen and the kingdom; in the final battle in Cornwall he is slain by Arthur but deals the king his death blow.

more see also ➤ Less *is more*.

Thomas More (1478–1535), English scholar and statesman, Lord Chancellor 1529–32; canonized as **St Thomas More**. His *Utopia* (1516), describing an ideal city state, established him as a leading humanist of the Renaissance. He was imprisoned in 1534 after opposing Henry's marriage to Anne Boleyn, and beheaded for opposing the Act of Supremacy. Feast day, 22 June.

more people know Tom Fool than Tom Fool knows proverbial saying, mid 17th century. ➤ Tom *Fool* was a name given to the part of the fool in a play or morris dance, and the earliest recorded version of this proverb is 'more know the Clown, than the Clown knows' (S. Holland, *Wit and Fancy*, 1655).

the more the merrier proverbial saying, late 14th century.

the more you get, the more you want proverbial saying, mid 14th century; an earlier version is found in Horace's *Epistles*, 'quanto plura parasti, tanto plura cupis [you want as much again as you already have]'.

Morecambe Bay an inlet of the Irish Sea, on the NW Coast of England, the name of which derived in the 18th century from a reference by Ptolemy, 2nd-century Greek geographer, to *morī kambē*, from *mori cambo* 'great bay', the old Celtic name for the Lune estuary.

Morenu (an honorific title conferred on) a rabbi or Talmudic scholar, first used as an honorific title in Germany in the 14th century.

Moreton Bay a bay in Queensland, Australia, named in 1770 by Captain Cook from the name of James Douglas, 14th Earl of Morton (spelt *Moreton* by Cook), who had been instrumental in sending Cook in search of Australia.

Morgan see also ➤ de *Morgan's laws*.

Morgan le Fay in Arthurian romances, queen of Avalon, the daughter of Arthur's mother Igraine and therefore his half-sister; she is derived from a figure in Welsh and Irish mythology (the ➤ Morrigan), and has a curiously ambivalent attitude to Arthur. In Malory she attempts to kill Arthur through the agency of her lover Sir Accolon, but she is also the leader of the queens who carries him away to cure his wounds.

Morgana see ➤ Fata *Morgana*.

morganatic of or denoting a marriage in which neither the spouse of lower rank, nor any children, have any claim to the possessions or title of the spouse of higher rank.

Recorded from the early 18th century, the word comes from modern Latin *morganaticus*, from medieval Latin *matrimonium ad morganaticum* 'marriage with a morning gift', because a morning gift, given by a husband to his wife on the morning after the marriage, was the wife's sole entitlement in a marriage of this kind.

morganize in 19th-century America, assassinate secretly in order to prevent or punish disclosures, from the name of William *Morgan* (d. 1826) of the US, who was alleged to have been murdered by Freemasons.

Morgante Maggiore one of three giants in the poem of this name by the Florentine poet Luigi Pulci (1432–84); the poem retells the story of Orlando, who kills two of the giants, and having defeated the third, Morgante, takes him as a companion in arms. The first canto of the poem was translated by Byron.

Morgawse in Arthurian romances, half-sister of Arthur, the wife of King Lot of Orkney, and mother of Mordred, Gawain, Agravain, Gareth, and Gaheris. She seems to be in some ways identical in origin to ➤ Morgan *le Fay*; in later versions Arthur sleeps with her in disguise, thus begetting ➤ Mordred.

morgen a measure of land; originally (in the early 17th century) via Dutch from German *Morgen* 'morning', apparently from the notion of 'an area of land that can be ploughed in a morning'.

Morgiana in the Arabian Nights, the slave of ➤ Ali *Baba* who discovers the forty thieves in the oil jars, and contrives their deaths.

Morglay name of the sword of Bevis of Hampton, hero of a popular English medieval verse-romance telling of Bevis's adventures in Europe and the East, and of his revenge upon his father's murderer. In the late 16th and 17th centuries, *morglay* in extended use denoted a sword.

The name probably comes from an unattested Breton, Welsh, or Cornish compound, from *mor* 'great' + *clezeff* 'sword'; this may be compared with ➤ CLAYMORE, which contains the Scottish Gaelic equivalents of these words in reversed order.

Moriarty in Conan Doyle's stories of ➤ *Sherlock* HOLMES, the arch criminal who is Holmes's implacable enemy, described by Holmes in *The Memoirs of Sherlock Holmes* (1894) as 'the Napoleon of Crime'. His final attempt to murder Holmes resulted in their both falling into the abyss of the ➤ REICHENBACH *Falls*, apparently to their deaths, although the popularity of the character forced Conan Doyle to resurrect Holmes.

Morisonian a follower of James Morison (1816–93), a Scottish preacher who in 1841 was suspended from the office of minister of the United Secession Church at Kilmarnock for preaching against Calvinism, and founded a sect called the Evangelical Union.

Edward William Morley (1838–1923), American chemist. In 1887 he collaborated with Albert Michelson in an experiment to determine the speed of light, the result of which disproved the existence of the ether. See also ➤ MICHELSON–*Morley experiment*.

Mrs Morley the name assumed by Queen Anne in her correspondence with her favourite Sarah, Duchess of Marlborough ('Mrs Freeman').

mormaor in ancient Scotland, a high steward of a province. The word is Gaelic, and comes ultimately from *mòr* great + *maor* bailiff.

mormo An imaginary, terrifying monster, especially one which frightens children; a hobgoblin, a bugbear. The word comes from Greek *mormō* 'a hideous female monster'.

Mormon a member of the Church of Jesus Christ of Latter-Day Saints, a religion founded in the US in 1830 by Joseph Smith Jr.

Smith claimed to have found and translated *The Book of Mormon* by divine revelation. It tells the story of a group of Hebrews who migrated to America *c.*600 BC, and is taken as scriptural alongside the Bible. The Mormons came into conflict with the US government over their practice of polygamy (officially abandoned in 1890) and moved their headquarters from Illinois to Salt Lake City, Utah, in 1847 under Smith's successor, Brigham Young. Mormon doctrine emphasizes tithing, missionary work, and the Second Coming of Christ.

Mormon battalion a company of soldiers from Mormon communities in Iowa enlisted for service in the Mexican War.

Mormon Bible a translation of the Bible executed and used by the Mormons. Also called, the *Book of Mormon.*

Mormon City Salt Lake City, Utah.

Mormon trail the trail followed by Mormon migrants to Utah in 1847.

Mormon war the conflict between Utah Mormons and federal troops in 1857–8.

morning see also ➤ PRIDE *of the morning.*

northern morning a name for the aurora borealis.

morning dreams come true proverbial saying, mid 16th century.

morning star a planet, especially Venus, when visible in the east before sunrise; figuratively, someone or something regarded as the precursor of a new era. The term is particularly applied to Christ, after Revelation 22:16, 'I am the root and offspring of David, and the bright and morning star'.

See also ➤ LUCIFER.

Morning Star of the Reformation a name given to ➤ *John* WYCLIF.

morning watch the last of the three or four watches into which the night was divided by the Jews and Romans, used chiefly in translations of and allusions to the Bible.

Morningside in Scotland (of an accent or manners) affected and refined; from the name of a residential district in Edinburgh, Scotland.

Mornington Crescent the name of a station (closed for a number of years) on the London Underground, taken as the title of a spoof panel game on the BBC Radio comedy programme *I'm Sorry, I Haven't a Clue*. Panellists (according to a set of undisclosed rules) name underground stations in turn, the apparent aim being to reach *Mornington Crescent*.

morocco a kind of strong ale brewed at Levens Hall, Westmorland (now in Cumbria), by tradition according to a secret recipe; the best of the annual brewing was drunk on 12 May at the *Radish Feast*, when Milnthorpe Fair was opened. *Morocco* was offered to all present, and any stranger was expected to drink a full glass with the toast, 'Luck to Levens whilst the Kent flows'.

Morocco-man in the 18th century, an agent of an insurance broker, who took illegal side-bets on the British Government lotteries; the name has been explained by the fact of such agents carrying red morocco pocket-books with them.

Morpheus in Roman mythology, the son of Somnus (god of sleep), the god of dreams and, in later writings, also god of sleep. The phrase **in the arms of Morpheus** is recorded from the late 18th century.

morris a game played on a board between two players, each with an equal number of pebbles, discs of wood or metal, pegs, or pins. Recorded from the early 17th century, the word is an alteration of *merrills*, the counters or pieces used in the game.
    See also ➤ NINE *men's morris*.

William Morris (1834–96), English designer, craftsman, poet, and writer. A leading figure in the Arts and Crafts Movement, in 1861 he established Morris & Company, an association of craftsmen whose members included Edward Burne-Jones and Dante Gabriel Rossetti, to produce hand-crafted goods for the home. His Kelmscott Press (established 1890) printed limited editions of fine books. His many writings include *News from Nowhere* (1891), which portrays a socialist Utopia.

morris dance a lively traditional English dance performed out of doors by groups known as 'sides'. Dancers wear a distinctive costume that is mainly black and white and has small bells attached, and often carry handkerchiefs or sticks. At least one of the dancers is likely to represent a symbolic or legendary figure, as the fool, hobby horse, or Maid Marian.

The phrase is recorded from late Middle English; *morris* comes from a variant of *Moorish*, but the association with the Moors remains unexplained.

Morrison shelter a movable air-raid shelter, shaped like a table and used indoors, named after Herbert S. *Morrison* (1888–1965), British Labour politician and Secretary of State for Home Affairs and Home Security 1940–5, during which period the shelter was adopted.

Morse an alphabet or code in which letters are represented by combinations of long and short light or sound signals, named (in the mid 19th century) after Samuel F. B. *Morse* (1791–1872), American inventor.

Inspector Morse music-loving, beer-drinking Oxford policeman who is the central character in a series of detective novels by the British crime writer Colin Dexter (1930–), and who is played in the television series by John Thaw; in the most recent book (1999) Morse dies during his last investigation.

mortal coil see ➤ *shuffle off this mortal* COIL.

mortal sin in Christian theology, a grave sin that is regarded as depriving the soul of divine grace, often contrasted with a ➤ VENIAL *sin*.
    See also ➤ SEVEN *deadly sins*.

mortar board an academic cap with a stiff, flat, square top and a tassel, originally as an informal term likening its appearance to the small square board with a handle on the underside, used by bricklayers for holding mortar.

Le Morte D'Arthur the title, meaning 'the Death of Arthur' generally given to the lengthy cycle of Arthurian legends by Malory, finished in 1470 and printed by Caxton in 1485.

Morticia a member of the ghoulish ➤ ADDAMS *Family*, noted for her white complexion and shock of black hair.

> I'm also whipped into a nostalgic frenzy by the presence of so many ghoulishly white faces . . . Morticia Addams make-up masterclass graduates and raven-black hair mountains.
> — *Melody Maker* 25 March 1995

mortmain the status of lands or tenements held inalienably by an ecclesiastical or other corporation. Recorded from late Middle English, the term comes via Anglo-Norman French and Old French from medieval Latin *mortua manus* 'dead hand', probably alluding to impersonal ownership.

John Morton (*c*.1420–1500), English prelate and statesman. He was appointed Archbishop of Canterbury in 1486 and Chancellor under Henry VII a year later. The Crown's stringent taxation policies made the regime in general and Morton in particular widely unpopular.

Morton's Fork an argument used by John Morton as Chancellor in demanding gifts for the royal treasury: if a man lived well he was obviously rich and if he lived frugally then he must have savings. The phrase in this form dates from the mid 19th century, but Francis Bacon in his *Historie of the Raigne of King Henry the Seventh* (1622) says that, 'There is a tradition of a dilemma that Bishop Morton…used to raise up the benevolence to higher rates; and some called it his Fork.' The term is now found in wider allusive use.

> [He] is by no means the only academic in Britain to find himself in danger of being impaled on this peculiarly modern version of Morton's Fork.
> — *Daily Telegraph* 25 August 1988

he may remove Mortstone traditional Devonian comment expressing the view that only a man capable of such a feat could be master of his wife (*Mortstone* is a large rock off Morte Point in Devon).

mortuary a room or building in which dead bodies are kept, for hygienic storage or for examination, until burial or cremation. This sense dates from the mid 19th century; earlier (in late Middle English) the word denoted a gift claimed by a parish priest from a deceased person's estate.

Mosaic Law another name for the ➤ *Law of* MOSES.

Moses (fl. *c*.14th–13th centuries BC), Hebrew prophet and lawgiver, brother of Aaron. According to the biblical account, he was born in Egypt, and to escape a massacre was hidden by his mother in a basket among the bulrushes; found there by Pharaoh's daughter, he was adopted and brought up by her. Grown to manhood, he led the Israelites away from servitude in Egypt, across the desert towards the Promised Land. During the journey he was inspired by God on Mount Sinai to write down the ➤ TEN *Commandments* on tablets of stone (Exodus 20). In allusive use, the name may be used to denote someone held to resemble Moses, especially in his

character of lawgiver or leader.

> In nearly every territory in Asia and Africa a courageous Moses pleaded passionately for the freedom of his people.
> — Martin Luther King *Strength to Love* (1964)

See also ➤ *the* GOLDEN *calf*, ➤ HORNS *of Moses*, ➤ PLAGUES *of Egypt*.

Grandma Moses (1860–1961), name given to the American painter Anna Mary Robertson *Moses*, who took up painting as a hobby when widowed in 1927, producing more than a thousand paintings in naive style, mostly of American rural life.

Law of Moses the system of moral and ceremonial precepts contained in the Pentateuch; the ceremonial portion of the system considered separately.

Moses basket a carrycot or small portable cot made of wickerwork, with allusion to the biblical story of Moses, left in a basket among the bulrushes (Exodus 2:3).

Moses boat a former term in the US for a small boat, as a ship's boat, and in the Caribbean for a kind of broad flat-bottomed boat used especially to transport goods or passengers from between ship and shore. The reference may be to the biblical Moses or to *Moses* Lowell, a famous boat-builder at Salisbury, Massachusetts.

Oswald Mosley (1896–1980), English Fascist leader. Successively a Conservative, Independent, and Labour MP, he founded the British Union of Fascists, also known as the *Blackshirts*, in 1932. The party was effectively destroyed by the Public Order Act of 1936. In 1948 Mosley founded the right-wing Union Movement.

mosque a Muslim place of worship. Mosques consist of an area reserved for communal prayers, frequently in a domed building with a minaret, and with a niche (mihrab) or other structure indicating the direction of Mecca. There may also be a platform for preaching (minbar), and an adjacent courtyard in which water is provided for the obligatory ablutions before prayer. Since representations of the human form are forbidden, decoration is geometric or based on Arabic calligraphy.

See also ➤ PEARL *Mosque*, ➤ UMAYAD *Mosque*.

Great Mosque at ➤ MECCA, the mosque established by Muhammad as a place of worship and later extended; it was given its final form in the years 1572–7 in the reign of Sultan Selim II.

Mosquito Coast a sparsely populated coastal strip of swamp, lagoon, and tropical forest comprising the Caribbean coast of Nicaragua and NE Honduras, occupied by the Miskito people after whom it is named.

Mosquito State a former nickname for New Jersey.

Moss Bros name of a London firm of tailors and outfitters, often referred to as the type of an establishment from which formal clothes may be hired. The business was originally founded in two small shops by Moses Moses (later M. Moss), a dealer in second-hand clothes; the firm later moved to King Street, Covent Garden, and changed its name to *Moss Bross* at the end of the 19th century.

> I look forward to shuffling along in a Moss Bros morning suit behind Lester Piggott and in front of the woman who does out the Foreign Office.
> — Philip Larkin letter, 8 May 1965

Mossad[1] the Institution for the Second Immigration, an organization formed in 1938 for the purpose of bringing Jews from Europe to Palestine.

Mossad[2] the Supreme Institution for Intelligence and Special Assignments, the principal secret intelligence service of the state of Israel, founded in 1951.

mosstrooper a person who lived by plundering property in the Scottish Borders during the 17th century, making raids across the 'mosses' or peat-bogs.

mossy-back a person who hid during the American Civil War to avoid conscription for the Southern army. The name has been explained as meaning that such a fugitive was prepared to remain hiding in the swamps until the moss grew on his back.

Mostar a largely Muslim city in Bosnia–Herzegovina south-west of Sarajevo, the chief town of Herzegovina; its chief landmark, an old Turkish bridge across the River Neretva, was destroyed during the siege of the city by Serb forces in 1993.

a mote in a person's eye a fault observed in another person by a person who ignores a greater fault of his or her own; a *mote* is an irritating particle in the eye, and the allusion is to Matthew 7:3, 'Why beholdest thou the mote that is in thy brother's eye, but considerest not the beam that is in thine own eye?'

mother the word is of Germanic origin, from an Indo-European root shared by Latin *mater* and Greek *mētēr*.

The ➤ *Virgin* MARY, ➤ *St* GILES, and ➤ *St* MONICA are the patron saints of mothers.

See also ➤ *Mother* CAREY's *chicken*, ➤ *Mother* CAREY's *goose*, ➤ OLD *Mother Hubbard*, ➤ GOOD *mother lizard*, ➤ OLD *Mother Riley*, ➤ *Mother* SHIPTON, ➤ *Mother* TERESA, ➤ *tied to one's mother's* APRON *strings*.

Mother Ann name given to Ann Lee (1736–84), founder of the American Society of Shakers, as their spiritual head.

Mother Church the Church considered as a final arbiter.

Mother Earth the earth considered as the source of all its living beings and inanimate things, a phrase representing a personification recorded from the mid 16th century.

Mother Goose an old woman said to be the source of traditional nursery rhymes; she is often depicted as flying on the back of a gander. The name first appears in the title of *Mother Goose's Melody; or Sonnets from the Cradle*, published by John Newbery in 1781, but probably compiled around 1760. The ultimate origin is likely to be a fairy tale by Charles Perrault, *Contes de ma mère l'oye* [Tales of Mother Goose], a French expression meaning 'old wives' tale'.

There is a tradition in America that the real *Mother Goose* was an Elizabeth Goose, an inhabitant of Boston, but there is no evidence to substantiate this.

like mother, like daughter proverbial saying, early 14th century; the ultimate allusion is to a biblical one, to Ezekiel 16:44, 'As is the mother, so is her daughter'.

Mother of God a name given to the Virgin Mary (as mother of the divine Christ).

the mother of mischief is no bigger than a midge's wing proverbial saying, early 17th century, meaning that the origin of difficulties can be very small.

mother of months the moon; an expression recorded from the early 17th century.

Mother of Parliaments the British parliament, an expression coined by the English liberal politician and reformer John Bright (1811–89):

> England is the mother of Parliaments.
> — John Bright speech at Birmingham, 18 January 1865

mother-of-pearl a smooth shining iridescent substance forming the inner layer of the shell of some molluscs, especially oysters and abalones, used in ornamentation.

Mother of Presidents informal name for the state of Virginia, birthplace of Washington, Jefferson, and Monroe, and (later) Ohio, birthplace of Garfield and Taft.

Mother's Day a day of the year on which mothers are particularly honoured by their children. In North America it is the second Sunday in May; in Britain it has become another term for *Mothering Sunday.*

Mothering Sunday mid-Lent Sunday, traditionally the day on which children visited and gave presents to their parents.

motion the action or process of moving or being moved, in early use particularly applied to the movement of celestial bodies.

See also ➤ BROWNIAN *motion*, ➤ NEWTON's *laws of motion*, ➤ PERPETUAL *motion.*

motorists ➤ *St* CHRISTOPHER and St Frances of Rome (1384–1440), who for some years had a continuous vision of her guardian angel, are the patron saints of motorists.

Motown music released on or reminiscent of the US record label Tamla Motown. The first black-owned record company in the US, Tamla Motown was founded in Detroit in 1959 by Berry Gordy, and was important in popularizing soul music, producing artists such as the Supremes, Stevie Wonder, and Marvin Gaye.

motte-and-bailey denoting a castle consisting of a fort on a motte, or mound, surrounded by a bailey.

motto a short sentence or phrase chosen as encapsulating the beliefs or ideals guiding an individual, family, or institution; in heraldry, a phrase or sentence accompanying a coat of arms or crest, typically on a scroll. Recorded from the late 16th century, the word is from Italian 'word'.

motu propriu an edict issued by the Pope personally to the Roman Catholic Church or to a part of it. The phrase is Latin, and means literally 'of one's own volition'.

mould see ➤ BREAK *the mould.*

mouldwarp a name for the mole; recorded from Middle English, the word comes from a Germanic base literally meaning 'earth-thrower'.

Moulin Rouge a cabaret in Montmartre, Paris, a favourite resort of poets and artists around the end of the 19th century. Toulouse-Lautrec immortalized its dancers in his posters. In French, the literal meaning of the name is 'red windmill'.

mound originally (only in Middle English) the world, the earth as the abode of humankind. Later (from the mid 16th century), a globe forming part of royal regalia, usually of gold and often surmounted by a cross; an orb; in heraldry, this as a charge.

mount see also ➤ *Mount of* OLIVES, ➤ SERMON *on the Mount.*

mount in palmistry, any of various fleshy prominences on the palm of the hand regarded as significant of the degree of influence exercised by a particular planet.

mount of piety (in Italy and France) a pawnbroking establishment instituted and run by the state for providing loans to the poor at low interest.

Mount Vernon a property in NE Virginia, on a site overlooking the Potomac River. Built in 1743, it was the home of George Washington from 1747 until his death in 1799.

mountain see also ➤ DELECTABLE *Mountains*, ➤ FAITH *will move mountains*, ➤ MAGNET *Mountain*, ➤ OLD *man of the mountains.*

the Mountain an extreme party in the National Convention during the French Revolution, led by Robespierre and Danton, so called (*la Montagne*) from the fact that it occupied the most elevated position in the chamber of assembly.

mountain in labour great effort expended on little outcome, an allusion to the words of the Roman poet Horace (65–8 BC) in his *Ars Poetica*, '*Parturient montes, nascetur ridiculus mus* [Mountains will go into labour, and a silly little mouse will be born].'

> Considering the mountain of labour during the past year, it was a pathetic mouse for the prime minister to put before her new committee.
> — *Economist* 6 March 1982

make a mountain out of a molehill traditional description of laying unnecessary stress on a small matter, recorded from the 16th century.

Mountain State informal name for Vermont.

See also ➤ GREEN *Mountain State*.

Mountain time the standard time in a zone including parts of Canada and the US in or near the Rocky Mountains.

if the mountain will not come to Mahomet, Mahomet must go to the mountain proverbial saying, early 17th century, referring to a story of Muhammad recounted by Bacon in his *Essays*, in which the Prophet called a hill to him, and when it did not move, made this remark.

mountaineers ➤ *St* BERNARD *of Aosta* is the patron saint of mountaineers.

mountaineers' stick a mountaineers' stick is the emblem of ➤ *St* BERNARD *of Aosta*.

Mountains of the Moon the type of a very remote place; further than one can imagine, the ends of the earth. The term is also used by Ptolemy as the supposed source of the Nile, and is thought there to designate the Ruwenzori mountain range in central Africa.

mountebank a person who deceives others, especially in order to trick them out of their money; a charlatan; a person who sold patent medicines in public places.

Recorded from the late 16th century, the word comes from Italian *montambanco*, from the imperative phrase *monta in banco*! 'climb on the bench!', with allusion to the raised platform used to attract an audience.

the Mounties always get their man unofficial motto of the Royal Canadian Mounted Police.

mourning the expression of deep sorrow for someone who has died, typically involving following certain conventions such as wearing black clothes.

mouse in proverbial use, the *mouse* is often taken as the type of something small, weak, or insignificant, especially as contrasted with a larger, stronger animal.

A *mouse* is the emblem of ➤ *St* GERTRUDE *of Nivelles*.

In computing, a *mouse* is the name given to a small hand-held device which is moved over a flat surface to produce a corresponding movement of a pointer on a VDU screen.

See also ➤ CAT *and Mouse Act*, ➤ MICE, ➤ MICKEY *Mouse*, ➤ ONE *for the mouse, one for the crow*, ➤ *poor as a* CHURCH *mouse*.

country mouse a person from a rural area unfamiliar with urban life; the allusion is to one of Aesop's fables which contrasts the *country mouse* with the *town mouse*. In the fable each mouse visits the other, but is in the end convinced of the superiority of its own home.

town mouse an inhabitant of a city familiar with urban life; the allusion is to one of Aesop's fables which contrasts the *town mouse* with the *country mouse*. In the fable each mouse visits the other, but is in the end convinced of the superiority of its own home.

mouse and man an alliterative phrase for every living thing; it was probably popularized by Robert Burns in *To a Mouse* (1785), 'The best laid schemes o' Mice an' Men, Gang aft agley.'

a mouse may help a lion proverbial saying, mid 16th century; alluding to Aesop's fable of the lion and the rat, in which a rat saved a lion which had become trapped in a net by gnawing through the cords which bound it.

mouse potato a person who spends large amounts of leisure or working time operating a computer. An alteration of ➤ COUCH *potato*, the phrase is one of a cluster to terms which in the 1980s and 1990s developed in reference to an all-absorbing interest in computing (others include *propeller-head* and *otaku*).

Mouse Tower a tower on a rock in the Rhine near Bingen, according to legend the place where Archbishop ➤ HATTO *of Mainz* was eaten by mice in 913 for his wrongdoing.

mousse a brown frothy emulsion of oil and seawater formed by weathering of an oil slick; also called **chocolate mousse**. The term appears to have developed in relation to the ➤ TORREY *Canyon* disaster in 1967, and from initial usage in the popular press was taken up by specialists as a technical term (a water-in-oil emulsion of 50 to 80 per cent water content).

Mousterian of, relating to, or denoting the main culture of the Middle Palaeolithic period in Europe, between the Acheulian and Aurignacian periods (chiefly 80,000–35,000 years ago). It is associated with Neanderthal peoples and is typified by flints worked on one side only.

The name comes (in the late 19th century) from *Le Moustier*, a cave in SW France where objects from this culture were found.

mouth see ➤ *a* BONE *in her mouth*.

out of the mouths of babes— proverbial saying, late 19th century, meaning that young children may sometimes speak with disconcerting wisdom; with biblical allusion to Psalm 8, verse 2 (*Book of Common Prayer*), 'Out of the mouths of very babes and sucklings hast thou ordained strength, because of thine enemies', and Matthew 21:16, 'Jesus said unto them, Yea, have ye never read, Out of the mouths of babes and sucklings thou has perfected praise.'

moutons see ➤ REVENONS *à nos moutons*.

movable feast a religious feast day that does not occur on the same calendar date each year. The term refers most often to Easter Day and other Christian holy days whose dates are related to it.

move the goalposts unfairly alter the conditions or rules of a procedure during its course. The term has been current since the late 1980s, and provides a useful image for the idea of making an important (and usually unheralded) alteration to terms and conditions previously agreed. In contextual usage, there is often an implication that the process is undertaken with the deliberate intention of disadvantaging a particular person or group.

moved see ➤ WE *shall not be moved*.

mover and shaker a person who influences things, a person who gets things done; earliest in Arthur O'Shaughnessy's poem 'Ode' (1874), 'We are the movers and shakers Of the world for ever, it seems.'

movere see ➤ QUIETA *non movere*.

Mowgli in Kipling's *Jungle Books*, the boy who is reared with wolves.

Mozarabic of or relating to the Christian inhabitants of Spain under the Muslim Moorish kings. Recorded from the late 17th century, the word comes via Spanish from Arabic *musta'rib*, literally 'making oneself an Arab'.

The term **Mozarab** is used to designate a person who continued to practice Christianity, but who adopted many aspects of Islamic culture, including

language. Large Muslim cities such as Toledo, Cordoba, and Seville contained separate enclaves of Mozarabs forming wealthy communities including numerous artisans. The Islamic influence is evident in religious art of this time, and in architecture, esp. in the use of horseshoe-shaped arches and ribbed domes.

The **Mozarabic liturgy** denotes the ancient ritual of the Christian Church in the Iberian peninsula from the earliest times until the 11th century; a modified form of it is still used in some chapels in Spain.

Wolfgang Amadeus Mozart (1756–91), Austrian composer. A child prodigy as a harpsichordist, pianist, and composer, he came to epitomize classical music in its purity of form and melody. A prolific composer, he wrote more than forty symphonies, nearly thirty piano concertos, over twenty string quartets, and sixteen operas.

mozzetta a short cape with a hood, worn by the Pope, cardinals, and some other ecclesiastics. Recorded from the late 18th century, this Italian word is a shortened from of *almozzetta*, from medieval Latin *almucia* 'amice'.

mpret in Albania, a king or monarch; the word comes from Latin *imperator* 'emperor'.

Mr a title used before a surname or full name to address or refer to a man without a higher or honorific or professional title. Recorded from late Middle English, it was originally an abbreviation of *master*.

See also ➤ *Mr* CHAD, ➤ *Mr* CHIPS, ➤ *Mr* DARLING, ➤ *Mr* TURVEYDROP.

Mrs the title used before a surname or full name to address or refer to a married woman without a higher or honorific or professional title. Recorded from the early 17th century, it was originally an abbreviation of *mistress*.

See also ➤ *Mrs* FREEMAN, ➤ *Mrs* JELLYBY, ➤ *Mrs* MORLEY, ➤ like *Mrs* PARTINGTON *mopping up the Atlantic*.

mu the twelfth letter of the Greek alphabet (M, μ), transliterated as 'm'.

Much in the Robin Hood legend, the miller's son, who was one of the outlaw companions.

much cry and little wool proverbial saying, late 15th century, referring to a disturbance without tangible result; in early usage, the image was that of shearing a pig, which cried loudly but produced no wool.

much would have more proverbial saying, mid 14th century.

muck see also ➤ HIGH *muck-a-muck*.

where there's muck there's brass proverbial saying, late 17th century; *brass* here means 'money'.

muckraking the figurative use of *muckraking* to denote the searching out and publicizing of something discreditable can be traced back to Bunyan's description in *Pilgrim's Progress* (1684) of 'the Man with the Muck-rake' as an emblem of worldly gain; this was then alluded to and extended by Theodore Roosevelt:

> The men with the muck-rakes are often indispensable to the well-being of society; but only if they know when to stop raking the muck.
> — Theodore Roosevelt speech in Washington, 14 April 1906

Mudejar a subject Muslim during the Christian reconquest of the Iberian peninsula from the Moors (11th–15th centuries) who, until 1492, was allowed to retain Islamic laws and religion in return for loyalty to a Christian monarch. After 1492 such people were treated with less toleration, dubbed Moriscos, and forced to accept the Christian faith or leave the country.

The name is now used to designate a partly Gothic, partly Islamic style of architecture and art prevalent in Spain in the 12th to 15th centuries.

Mudejar is Spanish, and comes from Arabic *mudajjan* 'allowed to stay'.

mudge see ➤ FUDGE *and mudge*.

Mudie's Lending Library founded by Charles Edward Mudie (1818–90), who embarked on a career as bookseller, stationer, and lender of books in Bloomsbury; the lending proved so successful that he opened premises in Oxford Street in 1852, where the business prospered for many years, despite frequent complaints about Mudie's moral scruples in selecting his stock, which amounted, some claimed, to a form of censorship.

muesli belt a region held to be densely populated by prosperous middle-class people who consciously follow a healthy lifestyle.

muezzin a man who calls Muslims to prayer from the minaret of a mosque. Recorded from the late 16th century, the word is a dialect variant of Arabic *mu'addin*, active participle of *addana* 'proclaim'.

mufti[1] a Muslim legal expert who is empowered to give rulings on religious matters. Recorded from the late 16th century, the word comes from Arabic *muftī*, active participle of *'aftā* 'decide a point of law'.

In the Ottoman Empire, the *Mufti* (or **Grand Mufti**) was the name given to the official head of religion within the state, or to a deputy appointed by him as chief legal authority for a large city.

mufti[2] plain clothes worn by a person who wears a uniform for their job, such as a soldier or police officer. Recorded from the early 19th century, the word may come humorously from ➤ MUFTI[1], in a reference to a costume of dressing-gown, smoking-cap, and slippers, suggesting the appearance of a stage 'mufti'.

Muggletonian a member of a small Christian sect founded in England *c*.1651 by Lodowicke Muggleton (1609–98) and John Reeve (1608–58), who claimed to be the two witnesses mentioned in the book of Revelation (Revelations 11:3–6), 'And I will give power unto my two witnesses, and they shall prophesy a thousand two hundred and three-score days, clothed in sackcloth'. Despite many eccentric doctrines, the sect survived into the late 19th century.

mugwump in North America, a person who remains aloof or independent, especially from party politics. The term comes (in the mid 19th century) from Algonquian *mugquomp* 'great chief'.

Muhammad (*c*.570–632), Arab prophet and founder of ➤ ISLAM. He was born in Mecca, where *c*.610 he received the first of a series of revelations which, as the ➤ KORAN, became the doctrinal and legislative basis of Islam. His sayings (the *Hadith*) and the accounts of his daily practice (the *Sunna*) constitute the other main sources of guidance for most Muslims.

In the face of opposition to his preaching he and his small group of supporters were forced to flee to Medina in 622; this flight, known as the ➤ HEGIRA), is of great significance in Islam, and the Islamic calendar (which is based on lunar months) is dated from AD 622 (= 1 AH). Muhammad led his followers into a series of battles against the Meccans. In 630 Mecca capitulated, and by his death Muhammad had united most of Arabia.

See also ➤ MAHOMET.

Muhammad Ali[1] (1769–1849), Ottoman viceroy and pasha of Egypt 1805–49, possibly of Albanian descent. He modernized Egypt's infrastructure, making it the leading power in the eastern Mediterranean, and established a dynasty that survived until 1952.

Muhammad Ali[2] (1942–), American boxer; born *Cassius Marcellus Clay*, known for the catchphrase 'I'm the greatest', and for the summary of his boxing strategy (probably originated by his aide Drew 'Bundini' Brown), 'Float like a butterfly, sting like a bee'. He won the world heavyweight title in 1964, 1974, and 1978, becoming the only boxer to be world champion three times. He retired in 1981.

Muharram the first month of the year in the Islamic calendar, and an annual celebration in this month commemorating the death of Husayn, grandson of Muhammad, and his retinue. The name comes from Arabic *muḥarram* 'inviolable'.

Jean Muir (1933–95), English fashion designer. Her designs are noted for their subtle, restrained, and fluid styles.

mujtahid a person accepted as an original authority in Islamic law. Such authorities continue to be recognized in the Shia tradition, but Sunni Muslims accord this status only to the great lawmakers of early Islam. The word is Persian, from Arabic, active participle of *ijtahada* 'strive'.

mulatto dated term for a person with one white and one black parent. Recorded from the late 16th century, the word comes from Spanish *mulato* 'young mule or mulatto', formed irregularly from *mulo* 'mule'.

mulberry a small deciduous tree with broad leaves, native to the Far East and long cultivated elsewhere; the **white mulberry** was originally grown as a food-plant for silkworms.

mulberry bush a children's traditional singing game, with the refrain 'here we go round the mulberry bush'; the origin is unexplained, although it has been suggested that it refers ultimately to exercise in a prison yard.

Mulberry harbour code name for the prefabricated harbour used in the invasion of continental Europe by Allied forces in 1944.

Mulciber a name (meaning 'smelter of metals') for the Roman god ➤ VULCAN.

mule the offspring of a donkey and a horse (strictly, a male donkey and a female horse), typically sterile and used as a beast of burden. It is also

proverbially taken as the type of obstinacy.

Since the 1980s, *mule* has also been the informal name for a person (typically a young woman in need of money) recruited by a drug trafficker to carry drugs through airports and other customs points. Selected routes run through countries where penalties are particularly severe, but while the *mules* if caught are liable to such penalties, they are unlikely to have information about the wider organization, and are regarded as expendable by those who recruit them.

mullah a Muslim learned in Islamic theology and sacred law. Recorded from the early 17th century, the word comes from Persian, Turkish, and Urdu *mullā*, from Arabic *mawlā*.

Mulready a postage envelope with a design by the Irish painter William Mulready (1786–1863), the designer of the first penny postage envelope (1840).

multitude see ➤ CHARITY *covers a multitude*.

multum in parvo Latin tag meaning a great deal in a small compass (literally 'much in little'), recorded in English from the mid 18th century.

mum a kind of beer originally brewed in Brunswick; the tradition that the name comes from Christian *Mumme*, a brewer at Brunswick *c.*1487, has been discredited, and it is pointed out that the word resembles Italian *mommo*, a child's word for a drink.

mum's the word an injunction to say nothing; *mum* is recorded from late Middle English as an inarticulate sound made with closed lips, especially as an indication of inability or unwillingness to speak.

mumbo-jumbo language or ritual causing or intended to cause confusion or bewilderment. This sense dates from the late 19th century, and derives from the mid 18th-century form *Mumbo Jumbo*, name of a supposed African idol.

mumchance silent, tongue-tied, originally from a word in the 16th and 17th centuries denoting a game of dice.

mummers' play a traditional English folk play, of a type often associated with Christmas and popular in the 18th and early 19th centuries. The plot typically features Saint George and involves the miraculous resurrection of a character, possibly recalling pagan agricultural ceremonies.

Mummerset an imitation rustic West Country accent used by actors, from the name of an imaginary or idealized rustic county in the West of England.

The name probably comes from *mummer,* on the pattern of *Somerset.*

mummy especially in ancient Egypt, a body of a human being or animal that has been ceremonially preserved by removal of the internal organs, treatment with natron and resin, and wrapping in bandages. In Egypt the preservation of the body was regarded as important for the afterlife.

The idea of a mummy whose rest has been disturbed becoming an active and malevolent entity has become a staple of horror books and films, as in the Hammer Films *Curse of the Mummy's Tomb* (1964).

The word is recorded from late Middle English, denoting a substance taken from embalmed bodies and used in medicines; it comes from French *momie,* from medieval Latin *mumia* and Arabic *mūmiyā* 'embalmed body', perhaps from Persian *mūm* 'wax'.

Mumping-day St Thomas's Day, 21 December, when the poor used to go asking for alms; *mumping* here means 'begging'.

mumpsimus a traditional custom or notion adhered to although shown to be unreasonable; a person who obstinately adheres to such a custom or notion. The word represents an erroneous version of Latin *sumpsimus* in *quod in ore sumpsimus* 'which we have taken into the mouth' (Eucharist), in a story of an illiterate priest who, when corrected, replied 'I will not change my old mumpsimus for your new sumpsimus'.

Baron Munchausen the hero of a book of fantastic travellers' tales (1785) written in English by a German, Rudolph Erich Raspe. The original Baron Munchausen is said to have lived 1720–97, to have served in the Russian army against the Turks, and to have related extravagant tales of his prowess.

Munchausen's syndrome a mental disorder in which a person repeatedly feigns severe illness so as to obtain hospital treatment. **Munchausen's syndrome by proxy** is the term given to a mental disorder in which a person seeks attention by inducing or feigning illness in another person, typically a child. Both disorders are named for ➤ *Baron* MUNCHAUSEN as a type of fantasist.

Munchkin in the children's fantasy *The Wizard of Oz,* by L. Frank Baum (1856–1919), US writer: any of a race of small, child-like creatures who help Dorothy in her quest for the city of Oz; the term is used allusively for a small or mischievous person or a child. (Public familiarity with the Munchkins increased after the release of the film version of the story in 1939.)

mundane egg in Indian and other cosmogonies, a primordial egg from which the world was hatched (*mundane* here means 'relating to the cosmos or universe, cosmic').

mundi see ➤ ANIMA *mundi,* ➤ CURSOR *Mundi,* ➤ MAPPA *Mundi,* ➤ SIC *transit gloria mundi,* ➤ STUPOR *mundi,* ➤ THEATRUM *mundi.*

mundungus bad-smelling tobacco; the term comes (in the mid 17th century) from a humorous use of Spanish *mondongo* 'tripe, black pudding'.

St Mungo another name for ➤ St KENTIGERN; *mungo* in Celtic means 'my dear friend'.

muni especially in India, an inspired holy person; an ascetic, hermit, or sage. The word comes from Sanskrit, and means literally 'silent', from *man* 'think'.

Munich Agreement an agreement between Britain, France, Germany, and Italy, signed at Munich on 29 September 1938, under which the Sudetenland was ceded to Germany; Neville Chamberlain, on his return, famously and erroneously declared that he believed that he was bringing back 'peace for our time'. In extended use (and allusively as *Munich*), it may denote an agreement held to resemble this pact in representing mistaken or dishonourable appeasement.

Munro any of the 277 mountains in Scotland that are at least 3,000 feet high (approximately 914 metres), named (in the early 20th century) after Hugh Thomas *Munro* (1856–1919), who published a list of all such mountains in the *Journal of the Scottish Mountaineering Club* for 1891.

Munsell denoting a system of classifying colours according to their hue, value (or lightness), and chroma (or intensity of colour), named after the American painter Albert H. Munsell (1858–1918).

the Munsters monster family in an American TV series of the mid 1960s, of whom *Herman Munster* resembles ➤ FRANKENSTEIN's monster, his wife is a vampire, and their son a werewolf.

> The weight . . . is evenly distributed and you don't end up with sore shoulders that make you walk like a Munster.
>
> — *Face* June 1997

the **Muppets** a group of glove and rod puppets and marionettes, chiefly representing animals, and including such characters as ➤ KERMIT *the Frog* and ➤ *Miss* PIGGY, created by Jim Henson (1936–90). First popularized in the children's television programme *Sesame Street* (1969), they later appeared in *The Muppet Show* (1976–81).

mural crown a crown conferred by the Romans as a mark of honour on the first soldier to scale the walls of a besieged town, having an upper circumference crenellated to resemble a fortified wall.

Joachim Murat (*c.*1767–1815), French general, king of Naples 1808–15. Murat made his name as a cavalry commander in Napoleon's Italian campaign (1800) and was made king of Naples. He attempted to become king of all Italy in 1815, but was captured in Calabria and executed.

Muratorian fragment an 8th-century Latin manuscript fragment containing a translation from the Greek of the earliest surviving Western list of New Testament scriptures (*c.*A.D.170). It is named for L. A. *Muratori* (1672–1750), an Italian scholar who edited the fragment in his *Antiquites Italicae*.

murder see ➤ KILLING *no murder.*

the **murder in the Red Barn** the murder at Polstead, Suffolk, in 1827, of Maria Marten by her former lover; the case became a type of melodrama after the arrest, trial, and execution of William Corder.

Murder, Inc. in the US of the 1930s, originally and especially in New York, a network of gangsters controlling organized crime and carrying out assassinations for money.

murder will out proverbial saying, early 14th century.

murid a follower of a Muslim holy man, especially a Sufi disciple; (with capital initial) a member of any of several Muslim movements, especially one which advocated rebellion against the Russians in the Caucasus in the late 19th century. The name comes from Arabic *murīd*, literally 'he who desires'.

Bartolomé Esteban Murillo (*c.*1618–82), Spanish painter. He is noted for his genre scenes of urchins

and peasants and for his devotional pictures.

> Alleyn saw the satin skin and liquid eyes of a Murillo peasant.
>
> — Ngaio Marsh *Spinsters in Jeopardy* (1954)

Murphy's Law a supposed law of nature, expressed in various humorous popular sayings, to the effect that anything that can go wrong will go wrong. It is named for Captain Edward A. *Murphy*, who performed studies on deceleration for the US Air Force in 1949 (during which he noted that if things could be done wrongly, they would be).

murrain archaic term for a plague, epidemic, or crop blight, in particular, the potato blight during the Irish famine in the mid 19th century. Recorded from late Middle English, the word comes from Old French *morine*, based on Latin *mori* 'to die'.

Murray any of a series of guidebooks or railway timetables published by the British publisher John *Murray*, covering both foreign countries and various regions of Britain. The name comes from John *Murray* (1778–1843), London publisher, or his son, John *Murray* (1808–1892), also a publisher. John Murray, senior, published Mrs. Mariana Starke's 'Guide for Travellers on the Continent' in 1820, but the handbooks were primarily the result of the continental travels of his son.

murrey the deep purple-red colour of a mulberry; in heraldry, another term for ➤ SANGUINE. Recorded from late Middle English, the word comes via Old French from medieval Latin *moratus*, from *morum* 'mulberry'.

Mururoa a remote South Pacific atoll in the Tuamotu archipelago, in French Polynesia, used as a nuclear testing site since 1966.

Muscadin a dandy, a fop; a member of a moderate party in the early years of the French Revolution, composed chiefly of young men of the upper middle class. The word is French and represents a transferred use of *muscadin* 'musk-comfit'.

muscas see ➤ AQUILA *non captat muscas.*

Muscovy a medieval principality in west central Russia, centred on Moscow, which formed the nucleus of modern Russia. As Muscovy expanded, princes of Muscovy became the rulers of Russia; in 1472 Ivan III, grand duke of Muscovy, completed the unification of the country, and in 1547 Ivan the Terrible became the first tsar of Russia.

muscular Christianity a Christian life of brave and cheerful physical activity, especially as popularly associated with the writings of Charles Kingsley (1819–75) and with boys' public schools of the Victorian British Empire. The term is first recorded in the *Saturday Review* of 21 February 1857, in a reference to 'the task that Mr. Kingsley has made specially his own…that of spreading the knowledge and fostering the love of a muscular Christianity'.

Muse (in Greek and Roman mythology) each of nine goddesses, the daughters of Zeus and Mnemosyne, who preside over the arts and sciences.
See also ➤ *the* TENTH *Muse.*

Muses

Calliope	epic poetry
Clio	history
Euterpe	flute playing and lyric poetry
Terpsichore	choral dancing and song
Erato	lyre playing and lyric poetry
Melpomene	tragedy
Thalia	comedy and light verse
Polyhymnia	hymns, and later mime
Urania	astronomy

museum a building in which objects of historical, scientific, artistic, or cultural interest are stored and exhibited. Originally, the word denoted a university building, specifically one erected at Alexandria by Ptolemy Soter, *c.*280 BC; it comes via Latin from Greek *mouseion* 'seat of the Muses'.

mushroom a fungal growth that typically takes the form of a domed cap on a stalk, with gills on the underside of the cap; the type of a person or thing that appears or develops suddenly or is ephemeral.
See also ➤ MAGIC *mushroom,* ➤ SACRED *mushroom.*

mushroom cloud a mushroom-shaped cloud of dust and debris formed after a nuclear explosion.

music the art or science of combining vocal or instrumental sounds (or both) to produce beauty of form, harmony, and expression of emotion. Recorded from Middle English, the word comes via Old French and Latin from Greek *mousikē (tekhnē)* '(art) of the Muses'.
See also ➤ MASTER *of the King's (or Queen's) Music.*

music hall a form of variety entertainment popular in Britain from *c.*1850, consisting of singing, dancing, comedy, acrobatics, and novelty acts. Its popularity declined after the First World War with the rise of the cinema.

music of the spheres the harmonious sound supposed to be produced by the motion of the concentric, transparent, hollow globes imagined by the older astronomers as revolving round the earth and respectively carrying with them the several heavenly bodies (moon, sun, planets, and fixed stars).

musica ficta (in early contrapuntal music) the introduction by a performer of sharps, flats, or other accidentals to avoid unacceptable intervals.

musicians ➤ *St* CECILIA and ➤ *St* GREGORY are the patron saints of musicians.

musket a male sparrowhawk, which according to the 15th-century *Boke of St Albans* was in falconry to be flown by a 'holy water clerk'; the name is recorded from late Middle English, and comes ultimately (via Old French) from Latin *musca* 'fly', with diminutive suffix. Italian *moschetto* 'male sparrowhawk, crossbow bolt', from the same base, is ultimately the source of *musket* meaning 'an infantryman's light gun with a long barrel'.

musketeer a member of the household troops of the French king in the 17th and 18th centuries.
See also ➤ *the* THREE *Musketeers.*

Muslim a follower of the religion of Islam. Recorded from the early 17th century, the word comes from Arabic, the active participle of *'aslama* 'submit oneself to the will of God' (see also ➤ ISLAM).
See also ➤ BLACK *Muslim.*

Muslim Brotherhood an Islamic religious and political organization dedicated to the establishment of a nation based on Islamic principles. Founded in Egypt in 1928, it has become a radical underground force in Egypt and other Sunni countries, promoting strict moral discipline and opposing Western influence, often by violence.

Muslim calendar according to which the Islamic year is reckoned.

Muslim League one of the main political parties in Pakistan. It was formed in 1906 in India to represent the rights of Indian Muslims; its demands from 1940 for an independent Muslim state led ultimately to the establishment of Pakistan.

Muspelheim in Scandinavian mythology, the home of the fire-giant Surt.

Benito Mussolini (1883–1945), Italian Fascist statesman, Prime Minister 1922–43; known as **Il Duce** ('the leader'). He founded the Italian Fascist Party in 1919. He annexed Abyssinia in 1936 and entered the Second World War on Germany's side in 1940. Forced to resign after the Allied invasion of Sicily, he was rescued from imprisonment by German paratroopers, but was captured and executed by Italian communist partisans.

Mussulman an archaic name (from Persian) for a ➤ Muslim.

what must be, must be proverbial saying, late 14th century.

mustang an American feral horse which is typically small and lightly built. Recorded from the early 19th century, the word comes from a blend of Spanish *mestengo* (from *mesta* 'company of graziers') and *mostrenco*, both meaning 'wild or masterless cattle'.
   See also ➤ Pacing *Mustang*.

mustard a hot-tasting yellow or brown paste made from the crushed seeds of certain plants, typically eaten with meat or used as a cooking ingredient, and originally prepared with 'must' (new wine). It is frequently used to evoke ideas of warmth and enthusiasm, as in **keen as mustard**.
   See also ➤ *after* MEAT, *mustard*, ➤ CUT *the mustard*, ➤ *a* GRAIN *of mustard seed*.

Colonel Mustard one of the six stock characters constituting the murderer and suspects in the game of ➤ Cluedo.

> We lay people believed we would discover what really happened, as though a trial were a whodunit and the verdict the dénouement, that satisfying moment when the pieces fall together and Colonel Mustard's alibi goes down the tubes.
> — *Globe and Mail* (Toronto) 5 December 1991

grain of mustard seed a proverbial expression for something which, while small in itself, is capable of great development; the allusion is to Matthew 13:31, in which the kingdom of heaven is likened to a grain of mustard seed, tiny when it is sown, but becoming a tree when grown. (The plant referred to is thought to be the black mustard plant, which in Palestine grows to a great height.)

pass muster come up to the required standard on examination or inspection; originally, as a military expression, undergo muster or review without censure.

Mut in Egyptian mythology, a goddess who was the wife of Amun and mother of Khonsu.

mutatis mutandis (used when comparing two or more cases or situations) making necessary alterations while not affecting the main point at issue. The Latin tag, recorded in English from the early 16th century, means literally 'things having been changed that have to be changed'.

mutchkin a Scottish unit of capacity equal to a quarter of the old Scottish pint, or roughly three quarters of an imperial pint (0.43 litres). Recorded from late Middle English, the word comes from early modern Dutch *mudsekin*, diminutive of *mud* 'hectolitre'.

mutiny an open rebellion against the proper authorities, especially by soldiers or sailors against their officers. The word comes (in the mid 16th century) from obsolete *mutine* 'rebellion', from French *mutin* 'mutineer', based on Latin *movere* 'to move'.
   See also ➤ Curragh *mutiny*, ➤ Sepoy *Mutiny*.

mutiny on the Bounty a mutiny which took place in 1789 on the British navy ship HMS *Bounty*, when part of the crew, led by Fletcher Christian, mutinied against their commander, William Bligh, and set him adrift in an open boat with eighteen companions. Although a number of the mutineers were captured and executed, others (including Christian) reached the ➤ Pitcairn *Islands*, where they settled.

Mwami (the royal title of) any of the former kings of Ruanda and Urundi (now Rwanda and Burundi) in central Africa.

Mycenae an ancient city in Greece, situated near the coast in the NE Peloponnese, the centre of the late Bronze Age Mycenaean civilization. The capital of King Agamemnon, it was at its most prosperous in the period *c*.1400–1200 BC, which saw construction of the palace and the massive walls of Cyclopean masonry, including the 'Lion Gate', the entrance to the citadel (*c*.1250 BC). Systematic excavation of the site began in 1840, although the major discoveries were made by ➤ *Heinrich* Schliemann in the 1870s.

Mycenaean of, relating to, or denoting a late Bronze Age civilization in Greece represented by finds at Mycenae and other ancient cities of the Peloponnese; an inhabitant of Mycenae or member of the Mycenaean people.
   The Mycenaeans controlled the Aegean after the fall of the Minoan civilization *c*.1400 BC, and built fortified citadels and impressive palaces. They spoke a form of Greek, written in a distinctive script (see ➤ Linear *B*), and their culture is identified with

that portrayed in the Homeric poems. Their power declined during widespread upheavals at the end of the Mediterranean Bronze Age, around 1100 BC.

Myrmidon a member of a warlike Thessalian people whom, according to a Homeric story, Achilles led to the siege of Troy. In extended usage, the term is used for a hired ruffian or unscrupulous subordinate; **myrmidon of the law** is recorded as a derogatory term for a police officer or a minor administrative legal official.

Myron (fl. *c*.480–440 BC), Greek sculptor. None of his work is known to survive, but there are two certain copies, one being the *Discobolus* (*c*.450 BC), a figure of a man throwing the discus, which demonstrates a remarkable interest in symmetry and movement.

myrrh a fragrant gum resin obtained from certain trees and used, especially in the Near East, in perfumery, medicines, and incense. In early use (the word is recorded from Old English) it is almost always found with reference to the offering of *myrrh* made by the Magi to the infant Jesus, a gift which prefigured his death and entombment.

Myrrha in Greek mythology, the mother of ➤ ADONIS by her own father Cinyras; when Cinyras, finding that he had taken part in incest, was about to kill her, she was turned by the gods into a *myrrh-tree*.

myrrhophore a woman carrying spices to the sepulchre of Christ (according to Mark 16:1, 'Mary Magdalene, and Mary the mother of James, and Salome, had bought sweet spices, that they might come and anoint him') as represented in art.

myrtle an evergreen shrub which has glossy aromatic foliage and white flowers followed by purple-black oval berries. Myrtle was sacred to the goddess Venus and used as an emblem of love.

See also ➤ JEWS' *myrtle*.

mysteries the secret rites of Greek and Roman pagan religion, or of any ancient or tribal religion, to which only initiates are admitted.

See also ➤ ELEUSINIAN *mysteries*.

The Mysteries of Udolpho title of the influential gothic novel by ➤ Mrs RADCLIFFE (1764–1823), in which the heroine, who has been carried off by her aunt's husband to his castle in Italy, is menaced by terrors of apparently supernatural but actually human origin.

mysterium tremendum a great or profound mystery, especially the mystery of God or of existence; overwhelming awe felt by a person contemplating such a mystery. In theological contexts, the term is associated particularly with the German Protestant theologian Rudolf Otto (1869–1937).

mystery Something that is difficult or impossible to understand or explain; chiefly in Christian theology, a religious belief based on divine revelation, especially one regarded as beyond human understanding; an incident in the life of Jesus or of a saint as a focus of devotion in the Roman Catholic Church, especially each of those commemorated during recitation of successive decades of the rosary.

In secular reference, a handicraft or trade, especially when referred to in indentures; the practices, skills, or lore peculiar to a particular trade or activity and regarded as baffling to those without specialized knowledge.

Recorded from Middle English (in the sense 'mystic presence, hidden religious symbolism', the word comes via Old French and Latin from Greek *mustērion*, related to ➤ MYSTIC.

See also ➤ MYSTERIES.

mystery play a popular medieval play based on biblical stories or the lives of the saints. Mystery plays were performed by members of trade guilds in Europe from the 13th century, in churches or later on wagons or temporary stages along a route, frequently introducing apocryphal and satirical elements. Several cycles of plays survive in association with particular English cities and towns.

mystery religion a religion centred on secret or mystical rites for initiates, especially any of a number of cults popular during the late Roman Empire.

See also ➤ MYSTERIES.

mystic a person who seeks by contemplation and self-surrender to obtain unity with or absorption into the Deity or the absolute, or who believes in the spiritual apprehension of truths that are beyond the intellect.

➤ St JOHN *of the Cross* is the patron saint of mystics and mystic theologians.

Recorded from Middle English (in the sense 'mystical meaning'), the word comes via Old French or Latin from Greek *mustikos*, from *mustēs* 'initiated person' from *muein* 'close the eyes or lips', also 'initiate'. This sense of the noun dates from the late 17th century.

myth a traditional story, especially one concerning the early history of a people or explaining some natural or social phenomenon, and typically involving supernatural beings or events.

See also ➤ URBAN *myth*.

myth-kitty a body of myths known to and shared by the members of a society or community, a mythos, usually with allusion to Philip Larkin (1922–85), 'As a guiding principle I believe that every poem must be its own sole freshly-created universe, and therefore have no belief in "tradition" or a common myth-kitty.'

mythopoetic relating to or denoting a movement for men that uses activities such as storytelling and poetry reading as a means of self-understanding.

Myton see ➤ CHAPTER *of Myton*.

Nn

N the fourteenth letter of the modern English alphabet and the thirteenth of the ancient Roman one, representing the Greek *nū* and the Semitic *nūn*.

N or M the answer to the first question in the Catechism, 'What is your name?'

NAAFI the *Navy, Army, and Air Force Institutes*, an organization running canteens and shops for British service personnel.

Naaman in the Bible, the Syrian soldier who is healed of leprosy by the prophet ➤ ELISHA, who tells him to wash in the river of Jordan. Naaman does so, despite his initial protest (2 Kings 5:12), 'Are not Abana and Pharpar, rivers of Damascus, better than all the waters of Israel?'; being healed, he declares that henceforth he will worship the god of Israel, although he will still have to accompany his master the king to the temple of Rimmon.

> I went to church, and felt as Naaman must have felt on certain occasions when he had to accompany his master on his return after having been cured of his leprosy.
> — Samuel Butler *The Way of All Flesh* (1903)

See also ➤ BOW *down in the house of Rimmon*, ➤ GEHAZI.

Nabataean a member of an ancient Arabian people who from 312 BC formed an independent kingdom with its capital at Petra (now in Jordan). The kingdom was allied to the Roman Empire from AD 63 and incorporated as the province of Arabia in AD 106.

nabi a person inspired to speak the word of God; a prophet; in particular, a prophetical writer of the Old Testament and Hebrew Scriptures. The original meaning of the Hebrew word was probably, 'the man who calls or proclaims'.

Nabi Group a group of late 19th-century French painters, largely symbolist in their approach and heavily indebted to Gauguin. Members of the group included Maurice Denis, Pierre Bonnard, and Edouard Vuillard. The name comes from the Hebrew word for 'prophet'.

nabob a Muslim official or governor under the Mogul empire; especially in the 18th and 19th centuries, a person who returned from India to Europe with a fortune.

Nabonassar see ➤ ERA *of Nabonassar*.

Naboth in the Bible, the owner of a vineyard coveted by king Ahab; when Naboth refused to sell it, Ahab's wife ➤ JEZEBEL caused him to be falsely accused of blasphemy and stoned to death. On taking possession of the vineyard, Ahab was warned by ➤ ELIJAH that the sin would bring disaster on his dynasty and on Jezebel. The story is referred to allusively for situations in which one who is already wealthy covets the single possession of another.

> Canada, where Biblical references are still understood by quite a few people, sees itself suddenly as Naboth's vineyard.
> — Robertson Davies *The Merry Heart* (1996)

Nacht und Nebel a situation characterized by mystery or obscurity, specifically the name of a decree issued in Nazi Germany in December 1941, under which offending nationals in occupied countries disappeared suddenly and without trace, frequently during the night. The phrase, which is German, means 'night and fog'.

Ralph Nader (1934–), American lawyer and reformer. He campaigned on behalf of public safety and prompted legislation concerning car design (in 1965 he published a book with the title *Unsafe at Any Speed*), radiation hazards, food packaging, and insecticides. His researchers were popularly known as **Nader's Raiders**.

nadir the point on the celestial sphere directly below an observer; in general use, the lowest point in the fortunes of a person or organization. Recorded from late Middle English (in the astronomical sense) the word comes via French from Arabic *naẓīr (as-samt)* 'opposite (to the zenith)'.

Nægling the sword of ➤ BEOWULF, which breaks in his hand during his final fight with the dragon.

Nag's head an inn in Cheapside, which according to a scandalous story circulated in the 17th century was the place where Archbishop Matthew Parker (1504–75) and others were first admitted as bishops in an irregular ceremony.

naga[1] (in Indian mythology) a member of a semi-divine race, part human, part cobra in form, associated with water and sometimes with mystical initiation. The word comes from Sanskrit *nāga* 'serpent'.

naga[2] (in some Hindu sects) a naked wandering ascetic, in particular one belonging to a sect whose members carry arms and serve as mercenaries. The word comes from Hindi *nāgā* 'naked'.

Nagasaki a city and port in SW Japan, on the west coast of Kyushu island. It was the target of the second atom bomb, dropped by the United States on 9 August 1945, which resulted in the deaths of about 75,000 people and devastated one third of the city.

Nagelring in Germanic legend, name of the sword of Dietrich von Bern, forged by the dwarfs and given to him by their king.

Nagualism belief in a personal guardian spirit thought by some Central American Indians to reside in a bird, animal, or other embodiment. The word comes from Mexican Spanish *nagual, nahual* from Nahuatl *nahualli* guardian spirit, witch, literally 'disguise'.

nagware computer software which is free for a trial period and thereafter frequently reminds the user to pay for it.

Nahum (in the Bible) a Hebrew minor prophet. Also, a book of the Bible containing his prophecy of the fall of Nineveh (early 7th century BC).

naiad (in classical mythology) a water nymph said to inhabit a river, spring, or waterfall. The name comes via Latin from Greek *Naias, Naiad-*, from *naein* 'to flow'.

naiant (in heraldry, of a fish or marine creature) swimming horizontally. The word comes (in the mid 16th century) from Anglo-Norman French, variant of Old French *noiant* 'swimming'.

nail in devotion or meditation, *nails*, as used for the crucixion of Jesus, are taken as symbolizing the Passion.

Nails are the emblem of ➤ St JOSEPH *of Arimathea*, ➤ St LOUIS, and ➤ St WILLIAM *of Norwich*.

Livy records the belief in ancient Rome that a plague could be checked by the dictator driving a nail into the ➤ CAPITOL.

See also ➤ *for the* WANT *of a nail the shoe was lost*, ➤ ONE *nail drives out another*, ➤ *when all you have is a* HAMMER, *everything looks like a nail*.

on the nail immediately, at once (usually referring to the payment of money). The explanations associating this phrase with certain pillars of the Exchange at Limerick or Bristol are too late to be of any authority in deciding the question.

nail one's colours to the mast refuse to admit defeat; declare openly which side one favours. The allusion is to a sea-battle in which the colours nailed to the mast cannot be lowered in defeat.

naissant (in heraldry, of a charge, especially an animal) issuing from the middle of an ordinary, especially a fess. Recorded from the late 16th century, the word comes from French, and means literally 'being born'.

Najaf a city in southern Iraq, on the Euphrates, which contains the shrine of Ali, the prophet Muhammad's son-in-law, and is a holy city for the Shiite Muslims.

naked ape the human being, especially as viewed from a biological perspective. *The Naked Ape* was the title of a book (1967) by Desmond Morris.

naked truth the plain truth, perhaps originally with allusion to Horace's *nudaque veritas* (Odes), or to any of a number of fables in which Truth is shown personified as a naked woman in contrast to the elaborately dressed Falsehood.

Nam informal name for Vietnam in the context of the ➤ VIETNAM *War*.

namaskar a traditional Indian greeting or gesture of respect, made by bringing the palms together before the face or chest and bowing. The word comes via Hindi from Sanskrit *namaskāra*, from *namas* 'bowing' + *kāra* 'action'.

namaste a respectful greeting said when giving a ➤ NAMASKAR.

namby-pamby lacking energy, strength, or courage; feeble or effeminate in behaviour or expression. A fanciful formation based on the given name of *Ambrose* Philips (died 1749), an English writer whose pastorals were ridiculed by Carey and Pope. Henry Carey (?1687–1743) published 'Namby Pamby' in ridicule of Philips in 1729; by the middle of the century the term was being applied to literary compositions seen as sentimental or insipid, and further extension of the term soon followed.

name recorded from Old English and of Germanic origin, the word comes ultimately from a root shared by Latin *nomen* and Greek *onoma*.

See also ➤ CHRISTIAN *name*, ➤ EKE-*name*, ➤ *give a* DOG *a bad name and hang him*, ➤ *a* GOOD *name is better than a golden girdle*, ➤ *he that has an* ILL *name is half hanged*, ➤ NO *names, no packdrill*, ➤ *a* ROSE *by any other name would smell as sweet*, ➤ WE *name the guilty men*.

have one's name and number on it of a bullet, be destined to kill one; another version of ➤ *every* BULLET *has its billet*; the number here referred to is a military number.

name day the feast day of a saint after whom a person is named.

their name liveth for evermore from the Apocrypha, and employed as the standard inscription on the Stone of Sacrifice in each military cemetery of World War One. Its use was proposed by Rudyard Kipling as a member of the War Graves Commission.

namesake a person or thing that has the same name as another.

Namierian an adherent of the methods and theories of the Polish-born British historian Sir Lewis Namier (1886–1960), especially as concerning the influence of politics on the course of history.

Namur a province in central Belgium, which was the scene of the last German offensive in the Ardennes in 1945.

Nana in Barrie's *Peter Pan* (1911), name of the dog which is the children's nurse. Because Mr Darling has ordered Nana to be shut outside in her kennel, the nursery is left unguarded.

Nanak (1469–1539), Indian religious leader and founder of Sikhism; known as **Guru Nanak**. In 1499 he underwent a religious experience and became a wandering preacher. Not seeking to create a new religion, he preached that spiritual liberation could be achieved through meditating on the name of God. His teachings are contained in a number of hymns which form part of the ➤ ADI *Granth*.

Nancy a city in NE France, chief town of Lorraine, site of the battle in 1477 in which ➤ CHARLES *le Téméraire* of Burgundy was defeated and killed.

nancy story in the West Indies, a traditional African folk tale about ➤ ANANCY the spider, who overcomes others by cunning rather than physical strength.

Nandi in Hinduism, a bull which serves as the mount of ➤ SHIVA and symbolizes fertility.

Nanjing a city in eastern China, on the Yangtze River, formerly *Nanking*, which was the capital of various ruling dynasties and of China from 1368 until replaced by Beijing in 1421.

nankeen a yellowish cotton cloth, named from *Nanking* (now *Nanjing*) in China where it was first made.

nanny state government institutions and practices of the Welfare State collectively, perceived as overprotective, interfering, or excessively authoritarian, a term apparently coined by the Conservative politician Iain Macleod (1913–70) in the *Spectator* in 1965, 'The London County Council is dying, but the spirit of the Nanny State lives on.'

Fridtjof Nansen (1861–1930), Norwegian Arctic explorer. In 1888 he led the first expedition to cross the Greenland ice fields, and five years later he sailed from Siberia for the North Pole, which he failed to reach, on board the *Fram*. He received the Nobel Peace Prize in 1922 for organizing relief work among victims of the Russian famine.

Nansen passport a document of identification issued to stateless people after the First World War, named after ➤ *Fridtjof* NANSEN, who was responsible for its issue.

Nantes see ➤ EDICT *of Nantes*.

Nantucket an island off the coast of Massachusetts, south of Cape Cod and east of Martha's Vineyard. First visited by the English in 1602, it was settled by the Quakers in 1659, and was an important whaling centre in the 18th and 19th centuries.

naos the inner chamber or sanctuary of a Greek or other ancient temple. The term can also be applied to the main body or nave of a Byzantine church.

napalm a highly flammable sticky jelly used in incendiary bombs and flame-throwers, consisting of petrol thickened with special soaps; the use of *napalm* is associated particularly with the ➤ VIETNAM *War*, and the photograph (1972) of a young girl running screaming from a napalm attack became one of the enduring images of the conflict.

napery archaic term for household linen, especially tablecloths and napkins. The word comes (in Middle English) from Old French *naperie*, from *nape* 'tablecloth'.

Naphtali (in the Bible) a Hebrew patriarch, son of Jacob and Bilhah (Genesis 30:7–8); also, the tribe of Israel traditionally descended from him.

Napier's bones slips of ivory or other material divided into sections marked with digits, devised by the Scottish mathematician John *Napier* (1550–1617), inventor of logarithms, and formerly used to facilitate multiplication and division.

see Naples and die traditional saying, implying that after seeing Naples one could have nothing left to wish for.

Napoleon the name of three rulers of France, of the Bonaparte dynasty established by the Corsican-born Napoleon Bonaparte (1769–1821), emperor 1804–14 and 1815. In 1799 Napoleon joined a conspiracy which overthrew the Directory, becoming the supreme ruler of France as *First Consul*. He declared himself emperor in 1804, establishing an empire stretching from Spain to Poland. After defeats at Trafalgar (1805) and in Russia (1812), he abdicated and was exiled to the island of Elba (1814). He returned to power in 1815, but was defeated at Waterloo and exiled to the island of St Helena.

His son, the titular Napoleon II (1811–1832), given the title of *King of Rome* by his father, and later known as *Duke of Reichstadt*, who had gone into exile with his mother, Marie-Louise of Austria, had no active political role and died young. However, Louis-Napoleon Bonaparte (1808–73), a nephew of Napoleon I, was elected President of the Second Republic in 1848 and staged a coup in 1851; he ruled as Napoleon III, 1852–70, when forced to abdicate.

The name *Napoleon* is used particularly in allusion to someone who has the strategic and military capacities of Napoleon I; the belief on someone's part that they are Napoleon is sometimes cited as a type of derangement.

See also ➤ CODE *Napoléon*.

Napoleonic Wars a series of campaigns (1800–15) of French armies under Napoleon I against Austria, Russia, Great Britain, Portugal, Prussia, and other European powers. They ended with Napoleon's defeat at the Battle of Waterloo.

napoo in the First World War, British army slang for 'finished, done'. The word is a corruption of the French phrase *il n'y en a plus* 'there is no more'.

Nara a city in central Japan, on the island of Honshu, which was the first capital of Japan (710–84) and an important centre of Japanese Buddhism.

naraka in Hindu belief, hell; the opposite of ➤ SVARGA, where virtuous souls rest before being reincarnated.

Narcissus in Greek mythology, a beautiful youth who rejected the nymph Echo and fell in love with his own reflection in a pool. He pined away and was changed into the flower that bears his name. The term **narcissism** is thus used for excessive or erotic interest in oneself and one's physical appearance.

nark a police informer, from Romany *nāk* 'nose'.

Narmada a river which rises in Madhya Pradesh, central India, and flows generally westwards to the Gulf of Cambay; it is regarded by Hindus as sacred.

Narnia the fictional magic kingdom which is the setting for the Christian allegory of seven children's books by C. S. Lewis (1898–1963); in the first book, *The Lion, the Witch, and the Wardrobe* (1950) four children who reach Narnia through the back of a wardrobe are able, with the help of the lion ➤ ASLAN, to break the power of the witch Jadis and redeem Narnia from perpetual winter.

narrow seas the English Channel and the Irish Sea, the channels separating Great Britain from Ireland and Continental Europe.

Narrowdale-noon a former expression in Staffordshire for something done late in the day.

narthex an antechamber, porch, or distinct area at the western entrance of some early Christian churches, separated off by a railing and used by catechumens, penitents, and others; an antechamber or large porch in a modern church. Recorded from the late 17th century, the word comes via Latin from Greek *narthēx*.

narwhal a small Arctic whale, the male of which has a long forward-pointing spirally twisted tusk developed from one of its teeth; in the past this tusk was sometimes represented as or believed to be a unicorn's horn, with its magic properties.

NASA in the US, the National Aeronautics and Space Administration.

Petroleum V. Nasby fictional character and supposed author of the 'Nasby Letters' by the American humorist and Unionist supporter David Ross Locke (1833–88).

Naseby a major battle of the English Civil War, which took place in 1645 near the village of Naseby in Northamptonshire. The Royalist army of Prince Rupert and King Charles I was decisively defeated by the New Model Army under General Fairfax and Oliver Cromwell. Following this defeat Charles I's cause collapsed completely.

Beau Nash (1674–1761), the name given to *Richard Nash*, former gamester, who in 1705 settled in Bath where he established the Assembly Rooms, drew up a code of etiquette and dress, and became the unquestioned arbiter of Bath society.

John Nash (1752–1835), English town planner and architect. Under the patronage of the Prince Regent (later George IV), he planned the layout of Regent's Park (1811–25), Trafalgar Square (1826–c.1835), and many other parts of London, and designed the Marble Arch.

Nash equilibrium (in economics and game theory) a stable state of a system involving the interaction of different participants, in which no participant can gain by a unilateral change of strategy if the strategies of the others remain unchanged. It is named after John F. *Nash* (1928–), British mathematician.

Nashville the state capital of Tennessee, noted for its music industry and the Country Music Hall of Fame.

Nasier see ➤ ALCOFRIBAS *Nasier*.

Nasik in mathematics, used to designate magic squares which are pandiagonal (from the name of a town in India where the inventor, A. H. Frost, lived).

James Nasmyth (1808–90), British engineer. He invented the steam hammer (1839) for the forging industry, as well as a number of other steam-driven machines and railway locomotives. Nasmyth also became interested in astronomy, particularly the moon, producing a map of it in 1851, and a book twenty-three years later.

Naso name of ➤ OVID (Publius Ovidius Naso); the word means 'nose', to which Holofernes alludes in Shakespeare's *Love's Labours Lost*, 'Ovidius Naso was the man. And why, indeed, 'Naso' but for smelling out the oriferous flowers of fancy'.

Nasrani among Muslims, a Christian; the name comes ultimately from a Syriac word meaning 'of Nazareth'.

Nasrudin a semi-legendary Turkish sage and folk-hero, around whose name has gathered a body of jokes, stories, and anecdotes.

Nassau a former duchy of western Germany, centred on the small town of Nassau, from which a branch of the House of Orange arose. It corresponds to parts of the present-day states of Hesse and Rhineland-Palatinate.

Gamal Abdel Nasser (1918–70), Egyptian colonel and statesman, Prime Minister 1954–6 and President 1956–70. He deposed King Farouk in 1952 and President Muhammad Neguib in 1954. His nationalization of the Suez Canal brought war with Britain, France, and Israel in the ➤ SUEZ *Crisis* of 1956; he also waged two unsuccessful wars against Israel (1956 and 1967).

something nasty in the woodshed a traumatic experience or a concealed unpleasantness in a person's background. The phrase comes from Stella Gibbons' comic novel *Cold Comfort Farm* (1932), in which Ada Doom's dominance over her family is maintained by constant references to her having 'seen something nasty in the woodshed' in her youth; the details of the experience remain unexplained.

Natal a former province of South Africa, in 1994 renamed KwaZulu/Natal, originally *Terra Natalis* (Latin, 'land of the day of birth'), a name given by Vasco da Gama in 1497, because he sighted the entrance to what is now Durban harbour on Christmas Day.

Nathan in the Bible, a prophet of the time of ➤ DAVID, who rebuked the king for taking the wife of Uriah (see ➤ EWE *lamb*).

Nathaniel in the Bible, a disciple of whom Jesus said, 'Behold an Israelite indeed, in whom is no guile!' (John 1:47). He is sometimes identified with ➤ BARTHOLOMEW.

nation a large aggregate of people united by common descent, history, culture, or language, inhabiting a particular state or territory. In early examples the racial idea is usually stronger than the political or local; in later use the notions of occupation of the same territory and of political unity and independence are more prominent. The word comes (in Middle English) via Old French, and ultimately from Latin *nat-* 'born'.

See also ➤ *as* MAINE *goes the nation*, ➤ ONE *Nation*.

Nation of Islam an exclusively black Islamic sect proposing a separate black nation, founded in Detroit *c*.1930. It came to prominence under the influence of ➤ MALCOLM *X* (1925–65).

national anthem a solemn patriotic song officially adopted by a country as an expression of national identity. The term is first recorded as the title of a poem by Shelley, 'A New National Anthem' (1819); by the mid 19th century, it referred to a specific song.

National Assembly the elected legislature in France during the first part of the Revolution, 1789–91.

national curriculum a common programme of study in schools that is designed to ensure nationwide uniformity of content and standards in education. A national curriculum was introduced in state schools in England and Wales in 1990.

national debt the total amount of money which a country's government has borrowed, by various means. A government may raise money by means such as the selling of interest-bearing bonds to the public or borrowing from foreign creditors, often in order to support the national currency, pay for social programmes, or avoid the need to raise taxes.

National Front a right-wing UK political party, formed in 1967, with extreme reactionary views on immigration.

National Gallery an art gallery in Trafalgar Square, London, holding one of the chief national collections of pictures. The collection began in 1824, when Parliament voted money for the purchase of thirty-eight pictures from the J. J. Angerstein collection, and the present main building was opened in 1838 and has been extended several times, most recently by the addition of the Sainsbury wing (opened 1991).

national government a coalition government, especially one subordinating party differences to the national interest in a time of crisis, as in Britain under Ramsay MacDonald in 1931–5.

National Guard originally, an armed force (the *garde nationale*) existing in France at various times between 1789 and 1871, first commanded by the Marquis de Lafayette. Later, in the United States, a militia force largely maintained by individual states but available also for federal use.

National Hunt the body controlling steeplechasing and hurdle racing in Great Britain.

National Portrait Gallery an art gallery in London holding the national collection of portraits of eminent or well-known British men and women. Founded in 1856, it moved to its present site next to the National Gallery in 1896.

National Society (in full, the National Society for Promoting the Education of the Poor in the Principles of the Established Church throughout England and Wales), a society of the Church of England, founded in 1811 to promote the education of the poor.

National Trust a trust for the preservation of places of historic interest or natural beauty in England, Wales, and Northern Ireland, founded in 1895 and supported by endowment and private subscription. The National Trust for Scotland was founded in 1931.

nations see ➤ FIRST *Nations*, ➤ FIVE *Nations*, ➤ *the* GAIETY *of nations*, ➤ *the* LEAGUE *of Nations*, ➤ NIOBE *of nations*, ➤ SIX *Nations*, ➤ *the* TWO *nations*.

Native American a member of any of the indigenous peoples of North and South America and the Caribbean Islands. In the US, *Native American* is now the current accepted term in many contexts. The term *American Indian* is still used elsewhere, by American Indians themselves, among others.

   In turn, *Native American* itself has been seen by some as too all-embracing; members of such peoples from that part of the North American continent comprising Canada may choose to specify themselves as *Native Canadians*, and this has led to the proliferation of other forms, such as *Native Australian* and *Native Hawaiian*.

the Nativity the birth of Jesus Christ, celebrated in the Christian Church on 25 December; traditional representations of this show the stable, Mary and Jesus, Joseph (often a little to one side), an ox and an ass, and often the shepherds kneeling in adoration. Recorded from Middle English, the word comes via Old French from Latin, ultimately from *nativus* 'arisen by birth'.

Nattier blue dated term for a soft shade of blue, especially in fine textiles. Recorded from the early 20th century, it denotes a colour much used by Jean-Marc *Nattier* (1685–1766), French painter, a fashionable portraitist at the court of Louis XV.

Natty Bumppo in J. Fenimore Cooper's novels, the name of ➤ LEATHERSTOCKING.

Natufian of, relating to, or denoting a late Mesolithic culture of the Middle East, dated to about 12,500–10,000 years ago, which provides evidence for the first settled villages, and is characterized by the use of microliths and of bone for implements. The name comes from Wadi *an-Natuf*, the type site (a cave north-west of Jerusalem).

natura naturans Nature as creative; the essential creative power or act. This Latin phrase is found from the 12th century in translators of ➤ AVERROËS, and from the mid 13th century in a British source.

natura naturata Nature as created; the natural phenomena and forces in which creation is manifested.

naturae see ➤ FERAE *naturae*.

Natural History Museum a museum of zoological, botanical, palaeontological, and mineralogical items in South Kensington, London. It was originally formed from the natural history collections of the British Museum, where it was housed until 1881.

natural magic (in the Middle Ages) magic practised for beneficial purposes, involving the making of images, healing, and the use of herbs.

natural science a branch of science which deals with the physical world, e.g. physics, chemistry, geology, biology; the branch of knowledge which deals with the study of the physical world.

natural selection the process whereby organisms better adapted to their environment tend to survive and produce more offspring. The theory of its action was first fully expounded by Charles Darwin and it is now believed to be the main process that brings about evolution.

natural theology theology or knowledge of God based on observed facts and experience apart from divine revelation.

nature the phenomena of the physical world collectively, including plants, animals, the landscape, and other features and products of the earth, as opposed to humans or human creations; the physical force regarded as causing and regulating these phenomena, especially as personified as **Dame Nature**, **Mother Nature**.

Nature is also used for the basic or inherent features of something, especially when seen as characteristic of it; the innate or essential qualities or character of a person or animal. In the Middle Ages, and since in some theological use, these features were seen as given by God and arising out of his creation.

Recorded from Middle English (denoting the physical power of a person), the word comes via Old French from Latin *natura* 'birth'.

See also ➤ BALANCE *of nature*, ➤ *you can* DRIVE *out Nature, but she keeps on coming back*.

Nature abhors a vacuum proverbial saying, mid 16th century; the Latin phrase, *natura abhorret vacuum*, is quoted in Rabelais' *Gargantua* (1534) as an article of ancient wisdom.

nature and nurture heredity and environment as influences on, or the determinants of, personality or behaviour; there has been a long debate on which, if either, is dominant. The phrase in this form is recorded from the late 19th century, but Shakespeare's *Tempest* juxtaposes the concepts in the description of Caliban as one 'on whose nature Nurture can never stick'.

the nature of the beast the (undesirable but unchangeable) inherent or essential quality or character of the thing; an expression recorded from the late 17th century.

Nature red in tooth and claw a ruthless personification of the creative and regulative physical power conceived of as operating in the material world; the phrase is originally from Tennyson:

> Though Nature, red in tooth and claw
> With ravine, shrieked against his creed.
> — Lord Tennyson *In Memoriam A. H. H.* (1850)

naturopathy a system of alternative medicine based on the theory that diseases can be successfully treated or prevented without the use of drugs, by techniques such as control of diet, exercise, and massage.

Naturphilosophie the theory put forward, especially by Schelling (1775–1854) and other German philosophers, that there is an eternal and unchanging law of nature, proceeding from the absolute, from which all laws governing natural phenomena and forces derive.

naucrary in ancient Greece, any of the forty-eight political divisions of the Athenian people.

naughty but nice advertising slogan for cream-cakes in the first half of the 1980s; earlier, the title of a 1939 film.

naughty nineties the 1890s, regarded as a time of liberalism and permissiveness, especially in Britain and France; the term is first recorded in 1925.

naumachia in ancient Rome, an imitation sea battle staged for entertainment; a place, especially a building enclosing a stretch of water, specially constructed for such a battle. The first display of this kind was arranged by Julius Caesar on an artificial lake constructed in the Campus Martius in 46 BC.

Nauplios in Greek mythology, king of Euboea, son of Poseidon. A descendant of his, also called Nauplios, was one of the Argonauts.

Nausicaa in Greek mythology, the daugher of Alcinous, king of the Phaecians, who is found by the shipwrecked Odysseus playing at ball with her maids.

nautical mile a unit used in measuring distances at sea, equal to 1,852 metres (2,025 yards) approximately.

Nautilus a name given to Robert Fulton's 'diving boat' (1800), also to the fictitious submarine in Jules Verne's *Twenty Thousand Leagues under the Sea*. It became the name of the first nuclear-powered submarine, launched in 1954.
  Nautilus is a Latin word, from Greek *nautilos*, literally 'sailor'.

naval crown a crown conferred by the Romans as a mark of honour on the victor or a brave fighter in a sea battle.

Navaratri a Hindu autumn festival extending over the nine nights before Dussehra. It is associated with many local observances, especially the Bengali festival of the goddess ➤ Durga. The name comes from Sanskrit, meaning literally 'nine nights'.

Battle of Navarino a decisive naval battle in the Greek struggle for independence from the Ottoman Empire, fought in 1827 in the Bay of Navarino off Pylos in the Peloponnese. Britain, Russia, and France sent a combined fleet which destroyed the Egyptian and Turkish fleet.

Navarre an autonomous region of northern Spain, on the border with France; capital, Pamplona. It represents the southern part of the former kingdom of Navarre, which was conquered by Ferdinand in 1512 and attached to Spain, while the northern part

passed to France in 1589 through inheritance by ➤ Henri *IV*.

nave the central part of a church building, intended to accommodate most of the congregation. In traditional Western churches it is rectangular, separated from the chancel by a step or rail, and from adjacent aisles by pillars. Recorded from the late 17th century, the word comes from Latin *navis* 'ship'.

naveta a type of Bronze Age megalithic chambered tomb shaped like an upturned boat and found on the Balearic Island of Minorca.

the Navigator epithet of the Portuguese prince ➤ Henry *the Navigator* (1394–1460).

navy recorded from late Middle English (in the sense 'ships collectively, fleet'), the word comes via Old French and popular Latin from Latin *navis* 'ship'.
  See also ➤ Wavy *Navy*.

Navy List (in the UK) an official list of the commissioned officers in the Royal Navy and the Royal Marines.

nawab an Indian native governor during the time of the Mogul empire; a Muslim nobleman or person of high status.

Naxalite in the Indian subcontinent, a member of an armed revolutionary group advocating Maoist communism. The name comes from *Naxal(bari)*, a place name in West Bengal, India.

Naxos a Greek island in the southern Aegean, the largest of the Cyclades, where according to some legends ➤ Ariadne was abandoned by Theseus.

Nazarene Jesus Christ (**the Nazarene**); (chiefly in Jewish or Muslim use) a Christian. Also, a member of an early sect or faction of Jewish Christians, especially one in 4th-century Syria using an Aramaic version of the Gospels and observing much of the Jewish law.

Nazareth a historic town in lower Galilee, in present-day northern Israel. Mentioned in the Gospels as the home of Mary and Joseph, it is closely associated with the childhood of Jesus and is a centre of Christian pilgrimage.

can any good thing come out of Nazareth? in allusion to the question asked by ➤ Nathaniel

(John 1: 46) on being told of the ministry of Jesus, 'Can there any good thing come out of Nazareth?'

Nazca Lines a group of huge abstract designs, including representations of birds and animals, and straight lines on the coastal plain north of Nazca in southern Peru, clearly visible from the air but almost indecipherable from ground level. Made by exposing the underlying sand, they belong to a pre-Inca culture, and their purpose is uncertain; some hold the designs to represent a vast calendar or astronomical information. They have been preserved by the extreme dryness of the region.

Nazi a member of the National Socialist German Workers' Party, formed in Munich after the First World War. It advocated right-wing authoritarian nationalist government, and developed a racist ideology based on anti-Semitism and a belief in the superiority of 'Aryan' Germans. Its leader, Adolf Hitler, who was elected Chancellor in 1933, established a totalitarian dictatorship, rearmed Germany in support of expansionist foreign policies in central Europe, and so precipitated the Second World War.

Nazi salute a gesture or salute in which the right arm is inclined upwards, with the hand open and the palm down.

Nazirite an Israelite consecrated to the service of God, under vows to abstain from alcohol, let the hair grow, and avoid defilement by contact with corpses (Numbers 6).

ne plus ultra Latin, meaning 'not further beyond', the supposed inscription on the Pillars of Hercules prohibiting passage by ships.

Neaera in the poetry of Virgil and Horace, name for a female sweetheart; used in this way by Milton:

> To sport with Amaryllis in the shade,
> Or with the tangles of Neaera's hair.
> — John Milton 'Lycidas' (1638)

Neanderthal an extinct human that was widely distributed in ice age Europe between c.120,000–35,000 years ago, with a receding forehead and prominent brow ridges. The Neanderthals were associated with the Mousterian flint industry of the Middle Palaeolithic.

In figurative use, the name may be applied to someone considered uncivilized, unintelligent, or uncouth.

The name comes (in the mid 19th century) from *Neanderthal*, the name of a region in Germany,

where remains of Neanderthal man were found.

> Notwithstanding, if he could be reincarnated and placed in a New York subway—provided that he were bathed, shaved, and dressed in modern clothing—it is doubtful whether he would attract any more attention than some of its other denizens.
> — William L. Strauss and A. J. E. Cave in *Quarterly Review of Biology* Winter 1957

neap tide a tide just after the first or third quarters of the moon when there is least difference between high and low water. Recorded from late Middle English, *neap* was originally an adjective, from Old English *nēp*, first element of *nēflōd*, of unknown origin.

near-death experience an unusual experience taking place on the brink of death and recounted by a person on recovery, typically an out-of-body experience or a vision of a tunnel of light.

near is my kirtle, but nearer is my smock proverbial saying, mid 15th century, used as a justification for putting one's own interests first.

near is my shirt, but nearer is my skin proverbial saying, late 16th century, used as a justification for putting one's own interests first.

the nearer the bone, the sweeter the meat proverbial saying, late 14th century.

the nearer the church, the farther from God proverbial saying, early 14th century.

Nebel see ➤ NACHT *und Nebel*.

Nebo¹ in the Bible (Deuteronomy 32:49), the mountain in Moab from which Moses was told by God to look out over the Promised Land of ➤ CANAAN (which he himself would not enter).

Nebo² a Babylonian god, the processional worship of which is denounced by Isaiah (46:1), 'Bel boweth down, Nebo stoopeth, their idols were upon the beasts, and upon the cattle.'

Nebuchadnezzar (c.630–562 BC), king of Babylon 605–562 BC. He rebuilt the city with massive walls, a huge temple, and a ziggurat, and extended his rule over neighbouring countries. In 586 BC he captured and destroyed Jerusalem and deported many Israelites in what is known as the ➤ BABYLONIAN *Captivity*.

The name *Nebuchadnezzar* is given to a very large wine bottle, equivalent in capacity to about twenty regular bottles.

nebula a cloud of gas and dust in outer space, visible in the night sky either as an indistinct bright patch or as a dark silhouette against other luminous matter.

nebular theory the theory that the solar and stellar systems were developed from a primeval nebula.

nebulé (in heraldry) of a particular wavy form, used to represent clouds.

Necessitarian a person who maintains that all human action is necessarily determined by the law of causation, as opposed to one who believes in the doctrine of free will; a determinist.

necessity see also ➤ *make a* VIRTUE *out of necessity.*

necessity is the mother of invention proverbial saying, mid 16th century.

necessity knows no law proverbial saying, late 14th century.

Battle of Nechtansmere a battle which took place in 685 at Nechtansmere, near Forfar, Scotland, in which the Picts defeated the Northumbrians, stopping their expansion northward and forcing their withdrawal.

neck see also ➤ DERBYSHIRE *neck,* ➤ *would that the* ROMAN *people had but one neck.*

neck in south-western counties of England, the last handful or sheaf of corn cut at harvest-time. The word is of Norse origin, and is related to Danish *neg* 'sheaf'.

neck verse a Latin verse printed in black letter (usually the beginning of Psalm 51) by the reading of which a person's claim to benefit of clergy could be proved, and which therefore saved them from being hanged by the neck.

Jacques Necker (1732–1804), Swiss-born banker and director general of French finances (1777–81; 1788–9). In 1789 he recommended summoning the States General and was dismissed, this being one of the factors which resulted in the storming of the Bastille.

Necker cube a line drawing of a transparent cube, with opposite sides drawn parallel, so that the perspective is ambiguous, named (in the early 20th century) after L. A. *Necker* (1786–1861), Swiss naturalist.

necklace in Christian iconography, a *necklace* is the emblem of ➤ *St* ETHELDREDA.

In South Africa in the 1970s, *necklace* was used for a tyre doused or filled with petrol, placed round a victim's neck and set alight.

See also ➤ *Affair of the* DIAMOND *Necklace,* ➤ *the* FATAL *necklace,* ➤ *the necklace of* HARMONIA.

necromancy the supposed practice of communicating with the dead, especially in order to predict the future. The word comes from Middle English *nigromancie,* via Old French from medieval Latin *nigromantia,* changed (by association with Latin *niger* 'black') from late Latin *necromantia,* where the first element represented Greek *nekros* 'corpse'.

The translator ➤ *Philemon* HOLLAND (1552–1637) gave the name *Necromancy* to that part of the *Odyssey* (book 6) which describes Odysseus' visit to Hades.

nectar in Greek and Roman mythology, the drink of the gods. The word comes from Greek *nektar,* the ultimate origin of which is unexplained.

needle see also ➤ CLEOPATRA*'s Needles,* ➤ *the* EYE *of a needle,* ➤ GAMMER *Gurton's Needle.*

look for a needle in a haystack proverbial expression for attempting an impossible task; earlier versions (recorded from the mid 16th century) are **look for a needle in a meadow** and **look for a needle in a bottle of hay.**

needs must when the devil drives proverbial saying, mid 15th century.

Nefertiti (fl. 14th century BC), Egyptian queen, wife of ➤ AKHENATEN. She initially supported Akhenaten's religious reforms, although she may have withdrawn her support in favour of the new religion promoted by her half-brother Tutankhamen. She is best known from the painted limestone bust of her, now in Berlin, in which she is shown with a long and slender neck.

negative capability a phrase coined by Keats to describe his conception of the receptivity necessary to the process of poetic creativity. In a letter to Benjamin Bailey, 22 November 1817, he wrote, 'If a sparrow come before my window I take part in its existence and pick about the gravel', and a month later he wrote to his brothers George and Thomas defining his new concept:

> Negative Capability, that is when man is capable of being in uncertainties, mysteries, doubts, without any irritable reaching after fact and reason—.
>
> — John Keats letter, 22 December 1817

Keats regarded Shakespeare as the prime example of *negative capability*.

negative equity potential indebtedness arising when the market value of a property falls below the outstanding amount of a mortgage secured on it. The term had been in use in the US in financial jargon since the 1950s, but in the UK in the 1990s it acquired an extended sense applied specifically to property, as recession caused a drop in the previously buoyant housing market. House-owners were trapped by *negative equity*, a situation in which they were committed to high mortgage repayments on a house which as a capital asset had dropped in value, and which they could not sell.

Negritude the quality or fact of being of black African origin; the affirmation or consciousness of the value of black or African culture, heritage, and identity.

Negus a ruler, or the supreme ruler, of Ethiopia. Recorded in English from the late 16th century, the word comes from Amharic *n'gus* 'king'.

negus a hot drink of port, sugar, lemon, and spice, named after Colonel Francis *Negus* (died 1732), who created it.

Nehemiah (5th century BC) a Hebrew leader who supervised the rebuilding of the walls of Jerusalem (*c*.444) and introduced moral and religious reforms (*c*.432). His work was continued by ➤ EZRA.

Jawaharlal Nehru (1889–1964), Indian statesman, Prime Minister 1947–64; known as **Pandit Nehru**, and through his daughter Indira Gandhi (1917–84) founder of an Indian political dynasty. An early associate of ➤ *Mahatma* GANDHI, Nehru was elected leader of the Indian National Congress in 1929. He was imprisoned nine times by the British for his nationalist campaigns, but went on to become the first Prime Minister of independent India.

les neiges d'antan the snows of yesteryear, in François Villon's *Le Grand Testament* (1461), the type of things that are past and gone, '*Mais où sont les neiges d'antan*? [But where are the snows of yesteryear?].'

neighbour see also ➤ BEGGAR-*my-neighbour*.

what a neighbour gets is not lost proverbial saying, mid 16th century.

neighbourhood watch a scheme of systematic local vigilance by householders to discourage crime, especially burglary, originating in the US in the early 1970s.

neighbours see ➤ *the* GOOD *neighbours*.

Nell see ➤ BLACK *Nell*.

nelson a wrestling hold in which one arm is passed under the opponent's arm from behind and the hand is applied to the neck (**half nelson**), or both arms and hands are applied (**full nelson**). The word is apparently from the surname *Nelson*, but the reference is unknown.

Horatio Nelson (1758–1805), British admiral. Nelson became a national hero as a result of his victories at sea in the Napoleonic Wars, especially the Battle of Trafalgar, in which he was mortally wounded.

turn a Nelson eye turn a blind eye to, overlook, pretend ignorance of. The allusion is to the battle of Copenhagen in 1801, when the signal 'discontinue the action' was hoisted; Nelson is said to have clapped his telescope to his blind eye, and declared that he could not see the signal. In Southey's *Life of Nelson* (1813), he is reported as saying, 'I have only one eye,—I have a right to be blind sometimes...I really do not see the signal!'

Nelson touch a masterly or sympathetic approach to a problem, with allusion to the skills of Admiral Horatio Nelson. The expression was coined by Nelson himself:

> I am anxious to join the fleet, for it would add to my grief if any other man was to give them the Nelson touch, which *we* say is warranted never to fail.
>   — Horatio Nelson letter, 25 September 1805

Nelson's blood rum, as formerly officially issued in the Navy.

Nelson's Column a memorial to Lord Nelson in Trafalgar Square, London, consisting of a column 58 metres (170 feet) high surmounted by his statue.

Nelson's Pillar a monument in Dublin, erected 1808–9, which was blown up by Republicans in 1966.

nembutsu in Japanese Buddhism, the invocation and repetition of the name of the Buddha Amida for the purpose of salvation and spiritual unity; this invocation.

Nemean games one of the national festivals of ancient Greece, held at Nemea, a wooded district near

Argos, in the second and fourth years of each Olympiad.

Nemean lion a monstrous lion which terrorized the Nemean region until killed by Hercules as the first of his twelve labours.

Nemesis in Greek mythology, a goddess usually portrayed as the agent of divine punishment for wrongdoing or presumption (hubris). She is often little more than the personification of retribution or righteous indignation, although she is occasionally seen as a deity pursued amorously by Zeus and taking various non-human forms to evade him.

nemo dat the basic principle that a person who does not own property, especially a thief, cannot confer it on another except with the true owner's authority. The phrase, which is Latin, means literally 'no one gives (what he or she does not have)'.

nemo me impune lacessit Latin motto, meaning, 'no-one provokes me with impunity'; it is the motto of the Crown of Scotland, and of all Scottish regiments.

Nennius (fl. *c*.800), Welsh chronicler. He is traditionally credited with the compilation or revision of the *Historia Britonum*, which includes one of the earliest known accounts of King Arthur.

neoclassicism the revival of a classical style or treatment in art, literature, architecture, or music. As an aesthetic and artistic style this originated in Rome in the mid 18th century, combining a reaction against the late baroque and rococo with a new interest in antiquity. In music, the term refers to a return by composers of the early 20th century to the forms and styles of the 17th and 18th centuries, as a reaction against 19th-century Romanticism.

neodamode an enfranchised Helot in ancient Sparta; the word meant literally 'newly admitted citizen'.

Neogrammarian any of a group of 19th-century German scholars who, having noticed that sound changes in language are regular and that therefore lost word forms can be reconstructed, postulated the forms of entire lost languages such as Proto-Indo-European by the comparison of related forms in existing languages.

Neolithic of, relating to, or denoting the later part of the Stone Age, when ground or polished stone weapons and implements prevailed. In the Neolithic period farm animals were first domesticated and agriculture was introduced, beginning in the Near East by the 8th millennium BC and spreading to northern Europe by the 4th millennium BC. Neolithic societies in NW Europe left such monuments as causewayed camps, henges, long barrows, and chambered tombs.

neologism a newly coined word or expression. Recorded from the early 19th century, the word comes from French *néologisme*.

neomenia among the ancient Hebrews and Greeks: the time of the new moon, the beginning of the lunar month; the festival held at that time.

Neonomian a person maintaining that the gospel of Christ is a new law entirely supplanting the old or Mosaic law.

Neophron in Greek mythology, a man who was changed into a vulture, as recounted in the *Metamorphoses* of the Greek grammarian Antoninus Liberalis (fl. *c*.AD 150). The genus name of the Egyptian vulture, *Neophron percnopterus*, derives from this.

Neoplatonism a philosophical and religious system developed by the followers of Plotinus in the 3rd century AD. Neoplatonism combined ideas from Plato, Aristotle, Pythagoras, and the Stoics with oriental mysticism. Predominant in pagan Europe until the early 6th century, it was a major influence on early Christian writers, on later medieval and Renaissance thought, and on Islamic philosophy. It envisages the human soul rising above the imperfect material world through virtue and contemplation towards knowledge of the transcendent One.

Neoptolemus in Greek mythology, the son of Achilles and killer of Priam after the fall of Troy; in Homer's *Odyssey* he is said to have returned safely to his home at Scyros, and to have married Hermione, daughter of Menelaus and Helen.

nepenthes a drug described in Homer's *Odyssey* as banishing grief or trouble from a person's mind; the name may thus be applied to any drug or potion bringing welcome forgetfulness.

nephew a son of one's brother or sister, or of one's brother-in-law or sister-in-law. Recorded from Middle English, the word comes via Old French from Latin *nepos* 'grandson, nephew', from an Indo-European root.

nepotism the practice among those with power or influence of favouring relatives or friends, especially by giving them jobs. Recorded from the mid 17th century, the word comes via French from Italian *nepotismo,* from *nipote* 'nephew', with reference to privileges bestowed on the 'nephews' of popes, who were in many cases their illegitimate sons.

Neptune in Roman mythology, the god of the water and of the sea; his Greek equivalent is ➤ Po-seidon.

From the early 19th century, the traditional shipboard ceremony held when crossing the equator has included a sailor dressed as Neptune; the *Annual Register* of 1815 notes of Napoleon going into exile on St Helena that 'At the usual ceremony of passing the Line…Buonaparte made a present to old Neptune of one hundred Napoleons.'

Neptunism a theory propounded by A. G. Werner that the rocks of the earth's crust were formed primarily by crystallization from the sea, rather than by solidification of magma. The theory was popular at the end of the 18th and the beginning of the 19th century, but is now rejected.

nerd a foolish or contemptible person who lacks social skills or is boringly studious; the quintessential characteristic of the *nerd* is said to be a plastic pocket protector worn in the top pocket to prevent pens from soiling the fabric; it is nicknamed the **nerd pack**. Fashionable in the early 1980s, the word dates from the 1950s, but its origin is unknown.

Nereid in Greek mythology, any of the sea nymphs, daughters of Nereus. They include ➤ Thetis, mother of Achilles.

Nereus in Greek mythology, an old sea god, the father of the Nereids. Like Proteus he had the power of assuming various forms.

Nergal in Mesopotamian religion, a god of war and of the underworld.

Nero (AD 37–68), Roman emperor, whose patronage of the arts extended to appearing himself upon the stage. Infamous for his cruelty, he ordered the murder of his mother Agrippina in 59 and wantonly executed leading Romans. His reign witnessed a fire which destroyed half of Rome in 64; in Suetonius's *Lives of the Caesars,* it is said that after watching the fire, Nero dressed himself in his tragedian's costume and sang *The Fall of Ilium.* This story gave rise to the expression ➤ *to* fiddle *while Rome burns* (although

Nero's instrument would have been the lyre).

A wave of uprisings in 68 led to his flight from Rome and his eventual suicide; Suetonius says that his last words were '*Qualis artifex pero!* [What an artist dies with me!]'

neroli an essential oil distilled from the flowers of the Seville orange, used in perfumery. The name is said to come from that of Anna-Marie de la Tremoille, the wife of the Prince of *Nerola* in Italy, who is said to have discovered the oil *c.*1670.

Nerthus a Germanic earth goddess whose worship is described by Tacitus; she is said to have been worshipped by seven tribes, and her presence among her people is said to have engendered peace.

Marcus Cocceius Nerva (*c.*30–98 AD), Roman emperor 96–8. Appointed emperor by the Senate after the murder of Domitian, he returned to a liberal and constitutional form of rule after the autocracy of his predecessor. It was said by Tacitus (AD *c.*56–after 117), '*Res olim dissociabiles miscuerit, principatum ac libertatem* [He has united things long incompatible, the principate and liberty].'

Pier Luigi Nervi (1891–1979), Italian engineer and architect. A pioneer of new technology and materials, especially reinforced concrete, he co-designed the UNESCO building in Paris (1953) and designed the Pirelli skyscraper in Milan (1958) and San Francisco cathedral (1970).

Nessie informal name for the ➤ Loch *Ness monster.*

Nessus a centaur who was killed by Hercules; when dying, he told Hercules' wife Deianeira that if she ever doubted her husband's love, a robe smeared with Nessus's blood would ensure his constancy. Deianeira followed this advice, but the centaur's blood was a poison that consumed Hercules with fire.

The phrase **shirt of Nessus** is used for a destructive or expurgatory force or influence.

nest see ➤ mare's *nest,* ➤ *there are no* birds *in last year's nest*

nest egg a sum of money saved for the future; originally, a real or artificial egg left in a nest to induce hens to lay eggs there.

Nestor a king of Pylos in the Peloponnese, who in old age led his subjects to the ➤ Trojan *War.* His wisdom and eloquence were proverbial.

Nestorianism the Christian doctrine that there were two separate persons, one human and one divine, in the incarnate Christ. It is named after *Nestorius*, patriarch of Constantinople (428–31), and was maintained by some ancient Churches of the Middle East. A small Nestorian Church still exists in Iraq.

nests see ➤ BIRDS *in their little nests.*

net a net is the emblem of ➤ *St* PETER and ➤ *St* ANDREW.

the Net informal term for the ➤ INTERNET.
   See also ➤ SURF *the net.*

Net Book Agreement (in the UK) an agreement set up in 1900 between booksellers and publishers, by which booksellers will not, with certain exceptions, offer books for less than the price marked on the cover. The agreement effectively collapsed in September 1995 when several major publishers withdrew their support.

in vain the net is spread in the sight of the bird proverbial saying, late 14th century.

nether millstone the lower of a pair of millstones, as the type of something hard and unyielding, originally with biblical allusion to Job 41:24, 'his heart is as firm as a stone; yea, as hard as a piece of the nether millstone'.

netiquette the correct or acceptable way of using the Internet.

netizen a user of the Internet, especially a habitual or keen one.

Netscape trademark name for a browser used to access and display documents on the World Wide Web and other computer networks.

nettle see also ➤ GRASP *the nettle,* ➤ *in* DOCK, *out nettle.*

if you gently touch a nettle it'll sting you for your pains; grasp it like a lad of mettle, an' as soft as silk remains proverbial saying, late 16th century; recommending direct rather than hesitant action.

Neue Sachlichkeit a movement in the fine arts, music, and literature, which developed in Germany during the 1920s and was characterized by realism and a deliberate rejection of romantic attitudes.

John von Neumann (1903–57), Hungarian-born American mathematician and computer pioneer. He pioneered game theory and the design and operation of electronic computers.

Neustria the western part of the Frankish empire in the Merovingian period. The name probably represents an unrecorded Frankish toponym meaning 'new western dominion', referring to the Franks' conquest of northern Gaul in the 5th century.

Neutral Ground a nickname for Westchester County, New York, during the American War of Independence, because its residents' sympathies were divided and neither army occupied it for any length of time.

you've never had it so good a phrase associated with the Conservative politician Harold Macmillan (1894–1986), referring to a speech as Prime Minister on 20 July 1957, when he said, 'Let us be frank about it: most of our people have never had it so good.' 'You Never Had It So Good' was the Democratic Party slogan during the 1952 US election campaign.

never is a long time proverbial saying, late 14th century.

never knowingly undersold motto, from *c.*1920, of the John Lewis partnership.

never mind the quality, feel the width used as the title of a television comedy series (1967–9) about a tailoring business in the East End of London, ultimately probably an inversion of a cloth trade saying.

Never-Never in Australia, the unpopulated northern part of the Northern Territory and Queensland; the desert country of the interior of Australia, the remote outback. Recorded from the mid 19th century, the name has been variously explained as implying that one may never return from it, or will never wish to go back to it; it has also been suggested that the phrase is really a corruption of the Comeleroi *nievah vahs* signifying 'unoccupied land'.

Never-Never land an imaginary, illusory, or Utopian place, often with allusion to the ideal country in J. M. Barrie's *Peter Pan.*

it is never too late to learn proverbial saying, late 17th century.

it is never too late to mend proverbial saying, late 16th century.

never too old to learn proverbial saying, late 16th century.

new see also ➤ *New* COVENANT.

New Age a broad movement characterized by alternative approaches to traditional Western culture, with an interest in spirituality, mysticism, holism, and environmentalism. The term originated in and remained strongly associated with California and the West Coast of the US, but its influence subsequently spread throughout the rest of the US and northern Europe, and by the late 1980s was widely established.

The general theme of the **New Age Movement** was that in the harsh post-industrial world of the late 20th century, people had somehow become out of balance with their own spiritual selves and with nature and the environment as a whole. Some **New Agers** in response became **New Age travellers**, abandoning urban life to lead a nomadic existence.

New Albion name given (as *Nova Albion*) in 1579 by Francis Drake) to the area of land just north of modern San Francisco, which he claimed in the name of Queen Elizabeth; after Drake's landing no European set foot on the coast for a hundred years. The name *New Albion* was subsequently (*c.*1608) used for a province of Virginia.

New Amsterdam former name (until 1664) for New York city, capital of the New Netherlands.

The New Atlantis title of an unfinished treatise of political philosophy, written in the form of a fable, by Francis Bacon (1561–1626); it was published in 1627 after his death. The setting of the story is an imaginary island ('Bensalem') in the Pacific.

new brooms sweep clean proverbial saying, mid 16th century.

what is new cannot be true proverbial saying, mid 17th century.

New Comedy a style of ancient Greek comedy associated with Menander, in which young lovers typically undergo endless vicissitudes in the company of stock fictional characters.

New Commonwealth those countries which have achieved self-government within the Commonwealth since 1945.

New Criticism an influential movement in literary criticism in the mid 20th century, which stressed the importance of focusing on the text itself rather than

being concerned with external biographical or social considerations. Associated with the movement were John Crowe Ransom, who first used the term in 1941, I. A. Richards, and Cleanth Brooks.

New Deal the economic measures introduced by Franklin D. Roosevelt (1882–1945) in 1933 to counteract the effects of the Great Depression. It involved a massive public works programme, complemented by the large-scale granting of loans, and succeeded in reducing unemployment by between 7 and 10 million. Roosevelt had used the term when accepting the presidential nomination at the Democratic Convention in Chicago in 1932:

> I pledge you, I pledge myself, to a new deal for the American people.
> — Franklin Roosevelt speech to the Democratic Convention, 2 July 1932

New England an area on the NE coast of the US, comprising the states of Maine, New Hampshire, Vermont, Massachusetts, Rhode Island, and Connecticut. The name was given to it by the English explorer John Smith (1580–1631) in 1614.

New England theology a movement in American Congregationalism, also affecting other American Protestant bodies, repudiating much Calvinist doctrine.

New English Bible a translation into modern English published between 1961 and 1966.

New Forest an area of heath and woodland in southern Hampshire (*forest* here has the specialized sense of an area, typically owned by the sovereign and partly wooded, kept for hunting and having its own laws). It has been reserved as Crown property since 1079, originally by William I as a royal hunting area, and is noted for its ponies. William II was killed by an arrow when hunting there in 1100.

New Hampshire a state in the north-eastern US, on the Atlantic coast, which was settled from England in the 17th century and was one of the original thirteen states of the Union (1788).

New Harmony an estate on the Wabash river in Indiana, purchased in 1825 from a German colony which had set up a religious settlement there by Robert Owen for the implementation of his social and religious policies. The experiment failed, and the colony was disbanded after two years.

New International Version a modern English translation of the Bible published in 1973–8.

New Jersey a state in the north-eastern US, on the Atlantic coast. Colonized by Dutch settlers and ceded to Britain in 1664, it became one of the original thirteen states of the Union (1787).

New Jersey tea a ceanothus of eastern and central North America, the leaves of which have been used as a substitute for tea, especially (according to tradition) by colonists in the American Revolution.

New Jerusalem the abode of the blessed in heaven, with reference to Revelations 21:2, 'And I, John, saw the holy city, new Jerusalem, coming down from God out of heaven.'

New Jerusalem Church a Christian sect instituted by followers of Emanuel Swedenborg. It was founded in London in 1787.

New Kingdom a period of ancient Egyptian history (c.1550–1070 BC, 18th–20th dynasty).

New Labour that section of the Labour Party which actively supported the internal reforms initiated by Neil Kinnock (party leader, 1983–1992) and carried through by John Smith (party leader 1992–1994) and Tony Blair (party leader 1994–, Prime Minister 1997–); the Labour Party as a whole after the implementation of those reforms.

The phrase was sufficiently established for the Conservative Party to take **New Labour, new danger** as their slogan in 1996; since Labour's electoral success the term has increasingly been used to distinguish its adherents from those in the party holding to more traditional and left-wing *Old Labour* principles.

New Lad a (type of) young man who embraces sexist attitudes and the traditional male role as a reaction against the perceived effeminacy of the ➤ NEW *Man*; especially one who does so (or who claims to do so) knowingly and with a sense of ironic detachment.

new learning the studies, especially that of the Greek language, introduced into England in the 16th century. Also, the doctrines of the Reformation.

New Look a style of women's clothing introduced in 1947 by Christian Dior, featuring calf-length full skirts and a generous use of material in contrast to wartime austerity.

new lords, new laws proverbial saying, mid 16th century.

new man in Christian theology from the late Middle English period, this term has been used to designate someone regarded as morally or spiritually reformed or renewed, especially a convert or penitent. The phrase is often used with explicit biblical allusion, as to Ephesians 4:24, 'And that ye put on the new man, which after God is created in righteousness and holiness.'

In the 1980s, **New Man** has been used in a secular sense to designate a man who rejects sexist attitudes and the traditional male role, especially in the context of domestic responsibilities and childcare, and who is (or is held to be) caring, sensitive, and non-aggressive, the opposite of the ➤ NEW *Lad*.

New Model Army an army created in 1645 by Oliver Cromwell to fight for the Parliamentary cause in the English Civil War; it was of the foundation of this force that Cromwell commented, 'I would rather have a plain russet-coated captain that knows what he fights for, and loves what he knows, than that which you call "a gentleman" and is nothing else.' Led by Thomas Fairfax, it was a disciplined and well-trained army that defeated the Royalists, winning notable victories at Marston Moor and Naseby. It later came to possess considerable political influence.

New Netherlands former name (until 1664) of New York state.

new off the irons newly made or prepared; brand-new, *irons* are dies used in striking coins.

New Orleans a city and port in SE Louisiana, on the Mississippi, founded by the French in 1718 and named after the Duc d'Orléans, regent of France. It is noted for its annual Mardi Gras celebrations and for its association with the development of blues and jazz.

New Revised Standard Version a modern English translation of the Bible, based on the Revised Standard Version and published in 1990.

New Romantic denoting a style of popular music and fashion popular in Britain in the early 1980s in which both men and women wore make-up and dressed in flamboyant clothes.

New Spain a former Spanish viceroyalty established in Central and North America in 1535, centred on present-day Mexico City. It comprised all the land under Spanish control north of the Isthmus of Panama, including parts of the southern US. It also came to include the Spanish possessions in the Caribbean and the Philippines. The viceroyalty was abolished in 1821, when Mexico achieved independence.

New Style the method of calculating dates using the ➤ GREGORIAN *calendar*, which in England and Wales superseded the use of the Julian calendar in 1752.

New Territories part of Hong Kong on the south coast of mainland China, lying to the north of the Kowloon peninsula and including the islands of Lantau, Tsing Yi, and Lamma. It comprises 92 per cent of the land area of Hong Kong. Under the 1898 Convention of Peking the New Territories were leased to Britain by China for a period of ninety-nine years.

New Testament the second part of the Christian Bible, written originally in Greek and recording the life and teachings of Christ and his earliest followers. It includes the four Gospels, the Acts of the Apostles, twenty-one Epistles by St Paul and others, and the book of Revelation.

New Thought a theory of the nature of disease as caused by mistaken ideas and beliefs, and a method of healing based on hypnosis and suggestion formulated by Phineas P. Quimby (1802–66) of Portland, Maine, USA. Also, a religious sect following the principles of Quimby.

new wave a style of rock music popular in the 1970s, deriving from punk but generally more poppy in sound and less aggressive in performance. The term originated as a translation of French *nouvelle vague*.

you can't put new wine in old bottles proverbial saying, early 20th century; originally with biblical allusion to Matthew 9:17, 'Neither do men put new wine into old bottles: else the bottles break, and the wine runneth out, and the bottles perish.' The expression is often used in relation to the introduction of new ideas or practices.

new woman a woman aspiring to freedom and independence for women, a feminist; a woman successful in a traditionally male-dominated area.

New World North and South America regarded collectively in relation to Europe. The term was first applied to the Americas (also to other areas, e.g.

Australia), especially after the early voyages of European explorers.

See also ➤ BRAVE *new world*.

New World Order a vision of a world ordered differently from the way it is at present; in particular, an optimistic view of the world order or balance of power following the end of the Cold War. The term was given prominence in a speech by George Bush (1924–) when President of the US:

> And now, we can see a new world coming into view. A world in which there is the very real prospect of a new world order.
> — George Bush speech, 7 March 1991

New Year's Day the first day of the year; in the modern Western calendar, 1 January, although before the adoption of the ➤ GREGORIAN *calendar* in the 18th century, the legal beginning of the year was 25 March.

New Year's Eve in the modern Western calendar, 31 December.

New Year's gift a present given at New Year.

New York a state in the north-eastern US, and a major city and port in the south-east of New York State, situated on the Atlantic coast at the mouth of the Hudson River. In 1629 Dutch colonists purchased Manhattan Island from the American Indians for 24 dollars' worth of trinkets, establishing a settlement there which they called *New Amsterdam*. In 1664 it was captured by the British, who renamed it in honour of the Duke of York (later James II), who was at that time Lord High Admiral of England.

New Zealand an island country in the South Pacific, first sighted by the Dutch navigator Abel Tasman in 1642, and given its European name from the Dutch province of *Zeeland*.

John Newbery (1713–67), English publisher, especially of books for the young, who established his business in 1745 at the Bible and Sun in St Paul's Churchyard, London, where he combined bookselling with the selling of medicines. Newbery made his 'Juvenile Library' an important part of his publishing business (*Goody Two-Shoes* was one of his publications), and instituted the 'Lilliputian Magazine'.

Newbery Medal instituted in 1921 and named after ➤ *John* NEWBERY, an annual American prize for the best work of children's literature.

Newberry Library a private institute in Chicago, founded in 1887 with a bequest from a local banker Walter Loomis Newberry (1804–68). As a reference collection of rare books and manuscripts concentrating on the humanities, it emphasizes coverage of western Europe and America.

Newcastle see ➤ *carry* COALS *to Newcastle*.

Thomas Newcomen (1663–1729), English engineer, developer of the first practical steam engine. His beam engine to operate a pump for the removal of water from mines was first erected in Worcestershire in 1712. Newcomen's engine was later greatly improved by James Watt.

Newdigate Prize an English verse prize founded at Oxford University in 1805 by Roger Newdigate (1719–1806), MP for Oxford University.

Newfoundland a large island off the east coast of Canada, at the mouth of the St Lawrence River. It was discovered in 1497 by John Cabot and named 'the New Isle', '*Terra Nova*', or more commonly Newfoundland.

Newgate a former London prison, originally the gatehouse of the main west gate to the city, first used as a prison in the early Middle Ages. whose unsanitary conditions became notorious in the 18th century before the building was burnt down in the Gordon Riots of 1780. A new edifice was erected on the same spot but was demolished in 1902 to make way for the Central Criminal Court.

Newgate Calendar a publication issued from *c*.1774 until the mid 19th century that dealt with notorious crimes as committed by those who were prisoners in Newgate.

> I felt that I had committed every crime in the Newgate Calendar.
> — Charles Dickens *Our Mutual Friend* (1865)

Newgate hornpipe in the 19th century, informal term for a hanging.

Newgate novel a novel of a picaresque 19th-century genre involving criminal characters and often seen disapprovingly as sensational; in the mid 19th century, Thackeray's 'Catherine' in *Fraser's Magazine* has the sentence, 'The taste for Newgate literature is on the wane'.

John Newlands (1837–98), English industrial chemist. He proposed a form of periodic table shortly before Dmitri Mendeleev, based on a supposed **law of octaves** according to which similar chemical properties recurred in every eighth element. The significance of his idea was not understood until Mendeleev's periodic table had been accepted.

John Henry Newman (1801–90), English prelate and theologian. A founder of the ➤ OXFORD *Movement* with John Keble and Edward Pusey, he wrote twenty-four of the *Tracts for the Times*. (The term **Newmania** was used by some to indicate the enthusiasm felt by many for the revival.) In 1845 he converted to Roman Catholicism, and was made a cardinal in 1879.

See also ➤ APOLOGIA.

news newly received or noteworthy information, especially about recent or important events. Recorded from late Middle English, the word is the plural of *new*, translating Old French *noveles* or medieval Latin *nova* 'new things'.

See also ➤ BAD *news travels fast*, ➤ BE *good news*, ➤ NO *news is good news*.

newsgroup a group of Internet users who exchange e-mail messages on a topic of mutual interest.

newsletters a term specially applied to the manuscript records of parliamentary and court news, sent twice a week to subscribers from the London office of Muddiman in the second half of the 17th century.

newspeak the name of an artificial official language in George Orwell's *Nineteen Eighty-Four* (1949), now used to denote ambiguous euphemistic language used chiefly in political propaganda.

> In New Labour newspeak, she was 'disendorsed'.
> — *Guardian* 25 June 1998

Isaac Newton (1642–1727), English mathematician and physicist, considered the greatest single influence on theoretical physics until Einstein. In his *Principia Mathematica* (1687), Newton gave a mathematical description of the laws of mechanics and gravitation, and applied these to planetary motion. (According to tradition, the idea of universal gravitation occurred to him while watching an apple fall from a tree; this story is given in Voltaire's *Philosophie de Newton*, where the source is said to have been Newton's step-niece, Mrs Conduitt.)

Opticks (1704) records his optical experiments and theories, including the discovery that white light is made up of a mixture of colours. His work in mathematics included the binomial theorem and differential calculus.

The story that a dog by knocking over a candle set

fire to some papers and destroyed the almost finished work of some years, thereby eliciting the reproach, 'O Diamond! Diamond! thou little knowest the mischief done!' is probably apocryphal.

Newton's laws of motion three fundamental laws of classical physics. The first states that a body continues in a state of rest or uniform motion in a straight line unless it is acted on by an external force. The second states that the rate of change of momentum of a moving body is proportional to the force acting to produce the change. The third states that if one body exerts a force on another, there is an equal and opposite force (or reaction) exerted by the second body on the first.

next of kin a person's closest living relative or relatives, standing in the nearest degree of blood-relationship and entitled to a share in their personal estate in a case of intestacy.

next year in Jerusalem! traditionally the concluding words of the Jewish Passover service, expressing the hope of the ➤ DIASPORA that Jews dispersed throughout the world would once more be reunited.

Michel Ney (1768–1815), French marshal. He was one of Napoleon's leading generals, described by his master as 'the bravest of the brave', and commanded the French cavalry at Waterloo (1815). He was executed by the Bourbons despite attempts by Wellington and other allied leaders to intervene on his behalf.

Niagara Falls the waterfalls on the Niagara River, consisting of two principal parts separated by Goat Island: the Horseshoe Falls adjoining the west (Canadian) bank, which fall 47 m (158 ft), and the American Falls adjoining the east (American) bank, which fall 50 m (167 ft). They are a popular tourist venue, especially for honeymooners, and an attraction for various stunts. In 1859 Charles Blondin walked across on a tightrope and in 1901 Annie Edson Taylor was the first person to go over in a barrel.

Nibelung in Germanic mythology, a member of a Scandinavian race of dwarfs, owners of a hoard of gold and magic treasures, who were ruled by *Nibelung*, king of Nibelheim (land of mist).

The treasure was eventually taken by the hero Siegfried, and in the ➤ NIBELUNGENLIED, the name *Nibelung* is used for the later possessors of the hoard: Siegfried's supporters, or the Burgundians

who stole the treasure from him.

> He began digging like a demented Nibelung, choking only occasionally as his shovel released noxious airs.
> — George MacDonald Fraser *McAuslan in the Rough* (1974)

Nibelungenlied a 13th-century German poem, embodying a story found in the (Poetic) Edda, telling of the life and death of Siegfried, a prince of the Netherlands. There have been many adaptations of the story, including Wagner's epic music drama *Der Ring des Nibelungen* (1847–74).

➤ SIEGFRIED kills the dragon Fafner to seize the treasure of the Nibelungs; he then marries the Burgundian princess Kriemhild and uses trickery to help her brother Gunther win Brunhild, but is killed by Gunther's retainer Hagen. His wife Kriemhild agrees to marry Etzel (Attila the Hun) in order to be revenged, and beheads Hagen herself.

Nicaea an ancient city in Asia Minor, on the site of modern Iznik, which was important in Roman and Byzantine times. It was the site of two ecumenical councils of the early Christian Church (in 325 and 787). The first, the **Council of Nicaea** in 325, condemned Arianism and produced the Nicene Creed. The second, in 787, condemned the iconoclasts.

nice recorded from Middle English, the word originally denoted 'stupid', coming via Old French, from Latin *nescius* 'ignorant', from *nescire* 'not know'. Other early senses included 'coy, reserved', giving rise to 'fastidious, scrupulous'; this led both to the sense 'fine, subtle', and the main current senses of 'pleasant; agreeable; satisfactory'.

See also ➤ NAUGHTY *but nice*, ➤ NINEPENCE.

nice work if you can get it expressing envy of what is perceived to be another's more favourable situation, from a song (1937) by Gershwin:

> Holding hands at midnight
> 'Neath a starry sky,
> Nice work if you can get it,
> And you can get it if you try.
> — Ira Gershwin 'Nice Work If You Can Get It' (1937 song) in *Damsel in Distress*

Nicene Creed a formal statement of Christian belief which is very widely used in Christian liturgies, based on that adopted at the first Council of ➤ NICAEA in 325.

Nichiren a Japanese Buddhist sect founded by the religious teacher Nichiren (1222–82) with the Lotus

Sutra as its central scripture. There are more than 30 million followers in more than forty subsects, the largest now being Nichiren-Shoshu, which is connected with the religious and political organization Soka Gakkai.

St Nicholas of Myra (4th century), Christian prelate, said to have been bishop of Myra in Lycia; his relics were translated to Bari in Italy in 1087.

Legends of the saint include the stories that he gave three bags of gold as dowries to three girls about to be sold into prostitution, and that he restored to life three boys who had been murdered and pickled in a brine tub; he also saved from death three men who had been unjustly condemned, and three sailors off the coast of Turkey. He is patron saint of children, sailors, Greece, and Russia; of pawnbrokers (from the connection made between the ➤ *three* GOLDEN *balls* of a pawnbroker's sign and the three bags of gold given as dowries); and of perfumiers (because a fragrant substance is said to have been emitted from his shrine at Bari). The cult of *Santa Claus* (a corruption of his name) comes from the Dutch custom of giving gifts to children on his feast day.

   □ **EMBLEM** Three boys in a tub, three moneybags, and a ship, are all emblems of St Nicholas.

   □ **FEAST DAY** His feast day is 6 December.

St Nicholas of Tolentino (1245–1305), Augustinian friar, born in Ancona, and named for St Nicholas of Myra; he was renowned as a preacher, and for his care of the sick and destitute.

   □ **EMBLEM** His usual emblems are a basket of loaves of bread (traditionally given to the sick, or to women in labour) and a star.

   □ **FEAST DAY** His feast day is 10 September.

St Nicholas's bishop a boy-bishop traditionally elected by choirboys or schoolboys on or around St Nicholas' Day (6 December).

St Nicholas's clerks an archaic term for highwaymen and (formerly) poor scholars.

Nick see ➤ OLD *Nick*.

nickel a silvery-white metal. The name comes from a shortening of German *Kupfernickel*, the copper-coloured ore from which nickel was first obtained, which in turn was named from *Kupfer* 'copper' + *Nickel* 'demon' (with reference to the ore's failure to yield copper).

nickelodeon a theatre or cinema with an admission fee of one nickel; an amusement arcade, originally one containing nickel-in-the-slot machines.

nicker a supernatural being reported to live in the sea or other waters; a water-demon, a kelpie. Formerly also, a river-horse, (in Middle English) a siren or mermaid.

nickname a familiar or humorous name given to a person or thing instead of or as well as the real name. The word is recorded from late Middle English, and comes from *an eke name* (*eke* meaning 'addition') misinterpreted, by wrong division, as *a neke name*.

Nicky-nan Night in Cornish tradition, the evening preceding Shrove Tuesday.

Nicodemus in the Bible, the Pharisee and member of the council of the Sanhedrin who visited Jesus by night, and later assisted in Jesus's burial.

Nicolaitan a member of an early Christian sect advocating a return to pagan worship, mentioned in Revelation 2:6, 'But this thou hast, that thou hatest the deeds of the Nicolaitanes, which I also hate.' Formerly also, a married priest, an opponent of clerical celibacy.

nicotine the word *nicotine* comes from modern Latin *nicotiana* (*herba*) 'tobacco (plant)', named after Jaques *Nicot*, a 16th-century French diplomat who introduced tobacco to France in 1560.

Martin Niemöller (1892–1984), German Lutheran pastor. An outspoken opponent of Nazism, he organized resistance to Hitler's attempts to control the German Church and was imprisoned in Sachsenhausen and Dachau concentration camps (1937–45). He later advocated a united neutral Germany and nuclear disarmament.

nien hao a title given to (part of) the reign of a Chinese emperor, used in imperial China as a system of dating. Also, a mark (signifying the reign of a particular emperor) used on Chinese pottery or porcelain to indicate an object's period of manufacture.

Niflheim in Scandinavian mythology, an underworld of eternal cold, darkness, and mist inhabited by those who died of old age or illness, and ruled over by the goddess ➤ HEL.

nigger a contemptuous term for a black person, and one of the most racially offensive words in the language, sometimes referred to as 'the N-word'. It was first used as an adjective denoting a black person in the 17th century and has had strong offensive connotations ever since, although ironically it has acquired a new strand of use in recent years, being used by black people as a mildly disparaging way of referring to other black people.

night the period of darkness in each twenty-four hours; the time from sunset to sunrise; often taken as a type of darkness or blackness. Recorded from Old English, the word is of Germanic origin, and comes from an Indo-European root shared by Latin *nox* and Greek *nux*.

See ➤ CITY *of Dreadful Night,* ➤ QUEEN *of the night,* ➤ SHIPS *that pass in the night,* ➤ WATCHES *of the night.*

night brings counsel proverbial saying, late 16th century.

Night Journey in Muslim tradition, the journey through the air made by Muhammad, guided by the archangel Gabriel. They flew first to Jerusalem, where Muhammad prayed with earlier prophets including Abraham, Moses, and Jesus, before entering the presence of Allah in heaven.

night of the long knives a treacherous massacre or betrayal, especially the massacre of the Brownshirts on Hitler's orders in June 1934. Traditionally, the phrase is used to refer to the (legendary) massacre of the Britons by Hengist in 472, described by Geoffrey of Monmouth in his *Historia Regum Britanniae.*

The term has also been used to describe Harold Macmillan's dismissal of seven of his Cabinet on 13 July 1962, of which the Liberal politician Jeremy Thorpe commented, 'Greater love hath no man than this, that he lay down his friends for his life.'

nightingale a small migratory thrush with drab brownish plumage, noted for its rich melodious song which can often be heard at night. In Greek mythology, ➤ PHILOMELA was transformed into a nightingale.

See also ➤ SWEDISH *Nightingale.*

Florence Nightingale (1820–1910), English nurse and medical reformer. In 1854, during the Crimean War, she improved sanitation and medical procedures at the army hospital at Scutari, achieving a dramatic reduction in the mortality rate. She became known as the 'Lady of the Lamp' for her nightly rounds. She returned to England in 1856.

nightmare a frightening or unpleasant dream. In Middle English, the word denoted a female evil spirit thought to lie upon and suffocate sleepers.

nightshade see ➤ ENCHANTER*'s nightshade.*

nihil obstat (in the Roman Catholic Church) a certificate that a book is not open to objection on doctrinal or moral grounds. The phrase is Latin, and means literally 'nothing hinders'.

nihilism the rejection of all religious and moral principles, often in the belief that life is meaningless; extreme scepticism maintaining that nothing in the world has a real existence. This was the doctrine of an extreme Russian revolutionary party *c.*1900, which found nothing to approve of in the established social order.

Vaslav Nijinsky (1890–1950), Russian ballet dancer and choreographer. The leading dancer with Diaghilev's Ballets Russes from 1909, he went on to choreograph Debussy's *L'Après-midi d'un faune* (1912) and Stravinsky's *The Rite of Spring* (1913).

Nike in Greek mythology, the goddess of victory; a winged statue representing this goddess.

Nikkei index a figure indicating the relative price of representative shares on the Tokyo Stock Exchange. *Nikkei* is the Japanese abbreviation for *Nihon Keizai Shimbun,* the Japanese Economic Journal, Japan's principal financial daily newspaper.

nil admirari wonder at nothing. This Latin phrase comes originally from Horace's *Epistles,* in '*nil admirari (prope res est una…quae possit facere et servare beatum)* [to wonder at nothing (is just about the only way a man can become contented and remain so)].'

nil carborundum illegitimi cod Latin for 'Don't let the bastards grind you down', in circulation during the Second World War, though possibly of earlier origin; often quoted as, '*nil carborundum*' or '*illegitimi non carborundum*'.

nil desperandum do not despair; never despair. This Latin phrase comes originally from Horace's *Odes,* in *nil desperandum Teucro duce* 'no need to despair with Teucer as your leader'.

Nile a river in eastern Africa, the confluence of the ➤ BLUE *Nile* and the ➤ WHITE *Nile,* which flows northwards through Sudan and Egypt to the Mediterranean, and which is the longest river in the world; the search to discover the true source of the

Nile was pursued by a number of 19th-century explorers. It was in the course of such a journey that ➤ *David* LIVINGSTONE was for a time lost.

Nile is one of the oldest geographical names in the world, and comes via Latin from ancient Greek, and probably ultimately from Semitic–Hamitic *nagal* 'river'. It was called *Ar* or *Aur* 'black' by the ancient Egyptians, referring to the colour of the sediment when it is in full flood.

Battle of the Nile another name for the ➤ *Battle of* ABOUKIR *Bay*.

nimble see ➤ *nimble* NINEPENCE.

nimbus a luminous cloud or a halo surrounding a supernatural being or a saint. Recorded from the early 17th century, the word is Latin, and means literally 'cloud, aureole'.

Nimby a person who objects to the siting of something perceived as unpleasant or hazardous in their own neighbourhood, especially while raising no such objections to similar developments elsewhere. Recorded from the 1980s, the word is an acronym from the words *not in my back yard*.

niminy-piminy affectedly prim or refined; a fanciful coinage of the late 18th century.

Nimrod a skilful hunter, from the name of the great-grandson of Noah, traditional founder of the Babylonian dynasty, described in Genesis as 'a mighty hunter before the Lord'. The Hebrew name *Nimrōd*, literally 'let us rebel' or 'we will rebel', is probably a distortion of the name of the Mesopotamian war-god *Ninurta*, a mighty hunter and warrior.

Nimrud modern name of an ancient Mesopotamian city on the east bank of the Tigris south of Nineveh, near the modern city of Mosul. It was the capital of Assyria 879–722 BC. The city was known in biblical times as Calah (Genesis 10:11); the modern name arose through association in Islamic mythology with the biblical figure of ➤ NIMROD.

nine in medieval angelology there were traditionally *nine* orders to the ➤ CELESTIAL *hierarchy*; cats proverbially have *nine* lives; *nine* days or nights is the period during which a novelty is supposed to attract attention.

See also ➤ *a* CAT *has nine lives*, ➤ CAT *o' nine tails*, ➤ *on* CLOUD *nine*, ➤ PARSLEY *seed goes nine times to the Devil*, ➤ POSSESSION *is nine points of the law*, ➤ *a* STITCH *in time saves nine*.

Nine Days' Queen a name for ➤ *Lady Jane* GREY (1537–54), Queen of England for nine days following the death of Edward VI.

nine days' wonder a person who or thing which is briefly famous.

nine-killer traditional name for the shrike, which was believed to kill nine times before eating.

nine men's morris the game ➤ MERRILL, played on a board between two players, each with an equal number of pebbles, discs of wood or metal, pegs, or pins.

nine tailors make a man proverbial saying, early 17th century; the literal meaning is that a gentleman must select his attire from various sources; it is now also associated with bell-ringing: *tailors = tellers = strokes*, the number of strokes on the passing bell indicating the sex of the deceased.

Nine Worthies nine famous personages of ancient Jewish and classical and medieval Christian history and legend (Joshua, David, and Judas Maccabaeus; Hector, Alexander, and Julius Caesar; and King Arthur, Charlemagne, and Godfrey of Bouillon).

ninepence a sum of money used in several alliterative expressions; **nice as ninepence** means very smart, and **nimble ninepence**, as money which circulates swiftly, is said to be better than the slow shilling.

See also ➤ COMMENDATION *ninepence*, ➤ RIGHT *as ninepence*.

nineties see ➤ NAUGHTY *nineties*.

Nineveh an ancient city located on the east bank of the Tigris, opposite the modern city of Mosul, to which ➤ JONAH was sent to preach. It was the oldest city of the ancient Assyrian empire and its capital during the reign of Sennacherib until it was destroyed by a coalition of Babylonians and Medes in 612 BC.

St Ninian (*c*.360–*c*.432), Scottish bishop and missionary. According to Bede he founded a church at Whithorn in SW Scotland (*c*.400) and from there evangelized the southern Picts.

☐ **FEAST DAY** His feast day is 26 August.

Ninja see ➤ TURTLE.

ninjutsu the traditional Japanese technique of espionage, characterized by stealthy movement and camouflage. It was developed in feudal times for military purposes and subsequently used in the training of samurai.

Niño see ➤ El *Niño*.

Ninus Assyrian king and legendary founder of Nineveh, supposedly named after him.

Niobe the daughter of Tantalus, and mother of a large family. Apollo and Artemis, enraged because Niobe boasted herself superior to their mother Leto (who had only two children), slew her children and turned Niobe herself into a stone, and her tears into streams that trickled from it. She is taken as a type of mourning, as in 'Like Niobe, all tears' (Shakespeare *Hamlet*, 1601).

Niobe of nations Byron's name for Rome in *Childe Harold* (1818).

Nippon the Japanese name for Japan, literally 'land where the sun rises or originates'.

nirvana a transcendent state in which there is neither suffering, desire, nor sense of self, and the subject is released from the effects of karma. It represents the final goal of Buddhism.

The word comes from Sanskrit *nirvāṇa*, from *nirvā* 'be extinguished'.

Nirvana principle in psychoanalysis, yearning for a state of oblivion, as a manifestation of the death instinct.

Nisan in the Jewish calendar, the seventh month of the civil and first of the religious year, usually coinciding with parts of March and April.

nisei in North America, an American or Canadian whose parents were immigrants from Japan. The word comes (in the 1940s) from Japanese, meaning literally 'second generation'.

nisi prius a writ directing a sheriff to provide a jury at the Court of Westminster unless the assize judges came beforehand to the county from which the jury was to be drawn; the clause in such a writ of which the opening words are '*nisi prius*'.

Nisroch in the Bible, a Babylonian god worshipped by ➤ Sennacherib; it was when he was in Nisroch's temple that he was murdered by his sons.

Nissen hut a tunnel-shaped hut made of corrugated iron with a cement floor, named after Peter N. *Nissen* (1871–1930), the British engineer who invented it.

Nisus¹ in Greek mythology, king of Megara, on whose head grew a lock of purple hair with magical

powers of preservation for himself and his city. When the city was besieged by Minos of Crete, the lock of hair was cut off by Scylla, daughter of Nisus, who had fallen in love with Minos. The city fell, but Nisus was transformed into an osprey, and Scylla into a sea-bird.

Nisus² in Virgil's *Aeneid* the close friend and companion of Euryalus, who like him follows Aeneas to Italy, and is killed fighting there.

Nithsdale a long hooded riding cloak fashionable in the 18th century, named after the Countess of *Nithsdale*, who enabled her Jacobite husband to escape from the Tower in 1716 disguised in her cloak and hood.

nitre an early name for natron or saltpetre; used allusively with reference to natron employed as a cleansing agent, as in Jeremiah 22:2, 'For though thou wash thee with nitre, and take thee much soap, yet thine iniquity is marked before me'.

From the 17th century, *nitre* was also the name of a supposed volatile substance related to or present in saltpetre, formerly presumed to be present in the air and rain. It was used with reference to the use of saltpetre in gunpowder, or to the supposition that thunder and lightning were caused by nitre in the air.

Nitria a desert region in Egypt, west of Cairo, which in the 4th century was the site of a settlement of ascetic Christian hermits; it was said that early Christians liked the associations of the name with the words of Jeremiah, 'though thou wash thee with nitre, and take thee much soap, yet thine iniquity is marked before me, saith the Lord God.'

Nivose the fourth month of the French Republican calendar (1793–1805), originally running from 21 December to 19 January. The name comes from Latin *nivosus* 'snowy'.

nix a water sprite; the word comes (in the mid 19th century) from German, and is related to archaic English ➤ nicker.

nixie a female water sprite.

Richard Nixon (1913–94), American Republican statesman, 37th President of the US 1969–74. He had been Eisenhower's vice-president (described by Adlai Stevenson as ➤ *just a* heartbeat *away from the Presidency*), but had narrowly lost to John Fitzgerald Kennedy in the 1960 presidential election (their television debates, in which Nixon was said to have been disadvantaged by his heavy five o'clock shadow, were believed to have had considerable effect).

Nixon restored Sino-American diplomatic relations by his visit to China in 1972 and sought to end the ➤ VIETNAM *War*: the negotiations were successfully concluded by his Secretary of State, Henry Kissinger, in 1973. Re-elected in 1972, he became the first President to resign from office, owing to his involvement in the ➤ WATERGATE scandal; he said later, 'I brought myself down. I gave them a sword. And they stuck it in.'

Nizam the title of the hereditary ruler of Hyderabad.

Nizari a member of a Muslim sect that split from the Ismaili branch in 1094 over disagreement about the succession to the caliphate. The majority of Nizaris now live in the Indian subcontinent; their leader is the Aga Khan. Originally based in Persia, the Nizaris were known to those whom they opposed as *Hashshishin* or 'Assassins'.

Njord in Scandinavian mythology, the god of the wind and sea, father of ➤ FREY and ➤ FREYA.

no comment I do not intend to express an opinion; the traditional expression of refusal to answer journalists' questions.

no cure, no pay proverbial saying, late 19th century; expression used on Lloyd's of London's Standard Form of Salvage Agreement.

no man can serve two masters proverbial saying, early 14th century; with biblical allusion to Matthew 6:24.

no man is a hero to his valet proverbial saying, mid 18th century; originally said by the French society hostess Madame Cornuel (1605–94).

no-man's-land disputed ground between the front lines or trenches of two opposing armies; used particularly with reference to the First World War.

**No more Latin, no more French,
No more sitting on a hard board bench**
traditional children's rhyme for the end of school term.

no names, no packdrill proverbial saying, early 20th century, meaning that if nobody is named as being responsible, nobody can be blamed or punished (*packdrill* is a form of military punishment in which an offender is made to march up and down in full marching order). The expression is now used generally to express an unwillingness to provide detailed information.

no news is good news proverbial saying, early 17th century.

no pain, no gain proverbial saying, late 16th century.

no penny, no paternoster proverbial saying, early 16th century.

no surrender! Protestant Northern Irish slogan originating with the defenders of Derry against the Catholic forces of James II in 1689.

noa an expression substituted for a taboo word or phrase, from Hawaiian (Maori, Tahitian) meaning '(a thing) free from taboo, ordinary'.

Noah (in the Bible) a Hebrew patriarch represented as tenth in descent from Adam. According to a story in Genesis he made the ark which saved his family and specimens of every animal from the Flood, and his sons Ham, Shem, and Japheth were regarded as ancestors of all the races of humankind (Genesis 5–10). The tradition of a great flood in very early times is found also in other countries.

Noah's ark the ship in which Noah, his family, and the animals were saved from the Flood, according to the biblical account (Genesis 6–8); a children's toy representing this.

Alfred Bernhard Nobel (1833–96), Swedish chemist and engineer. He invented dynamite (1866), gelignite, and other high explosives, making a large fortune which enabled him to endow the prizes that bear his name.

Nobel Prize any of six international prizes awarded annually for outstanding work in physics, chemistry, physiology or medicine, literature, economics, and the promotion of peace. The Nobel Prizes, first awarded in 1901, were established by the will of Alfred Nobel, and are traditionally awarded on 10 December, the anniversary of his death. The awards are decided by members of Swedish learned societies or, in the case of the peace prize, the Norwegian Parliament.

noble a former English gold coin first issued in 1351.
    See also ➤ ROSE *noble*.

the **noble** art boxing.

noble gas any of the gaseous elements helium, neon, argon, krypton, xenon, and radon, occupying Group 0 (18) of the periodic table. They were long believed to be totally unreactive but compounds of xenon, krypton, and radon are now known.

noble hawk in falconry, a long-winged high-flying hawk (e.g. a peregrine or merlin) which swoops down on its prey rather than chasing or raking after it.

the **noble savage** a representative of primitive mankind as idealized in Romantic literature, symbolizing the innate goodness of humanity when free from the corrupting influence of civilization. The phrase itself comes from Dryden's *Conquest of Granada* (1672), 'When wild in woods the noble Savage ran'.

the **noble science** boxing; fencing.

noblesse oblige French phrase meaning, privilege entails responsibility.

Nobodaddy a disrespectful name for God, especially when regarded anthropomorphically; a person no longer held in esteem. The word, which was coined by the poet William Blake, is a blend of *nobody* and *daddy*.

Noctes Ambrosianae a series of dialogues which appeared in *Blackwood's Edinburgh Magazine* between 1822 and 1835, and which present a romanticized and whimsical view of Scotland.

noctuary an account of what happens during a particular night or particular nights; a term coined in the early 18th century from Latin *nox, noctis* after *diary*.

Nod see also ➤ LAND *of Nod*.

a **nod's as good as a wink to a blind horse** proverbial saying, late 18th century.

Noddy a character in the stories (1949–) of Enid Blyton, a toy figure of a boy with a head that nods when he speaks, whose brightly coloured clothes include a distinctive long blue cap with a bell at the tip, and whose simplicity and good intentions often lead to trouble.

nods see ➤ HOMER *sometimes nods*.

Noel Christmas, especially as a refrain in carols and on Christmas cards. Recorded from the early 19th century, the word comes from French *Noël* 'Christmas'.

See also ➤ NOWEL.

Emmy Noether (1882–1935), German mathematician. Despite prejudices against women mathematicians she inaugurated the modern period in algebraic geometry and abstract algebra.

Noh traditional Japanese masked drama with dance and song, evolved from Shinto rites. Noh dates from the 14th and 15th centuries, and its subject matter is taken mainly from Japan's classical literature. Traditionally the players were all male, with the chorus playing a passive narrative role.

Nok an ancient civilization of northern Nigeria, dated to the 5th–3rd centuries BC. It is characterized by the production of distinctive terracotta figurines and is significant for its development of iron-working.

noli me tangere a painting representing the appearance of Jesus to Mary Magdalen at the sepulchre (John 20:17), when the newly-risen Jesus warned his disciple 'do not touch me'.

Noll see ➤ OLD *Noll*.

nom de guerre an assumed name under which a person engages in combat or some other activity or enterprise, a French phrase meaning literally 'war name'.

nom de plume an assumed name used by a writer instead of their real name; a pen-name. Recorded from the early 19th century, the phrase was formed in English from French words, to render the sense 'pen name', on the pattern of *nom de guerre*.

nomarch the governor of an ancient Egyptian nome.

nombril in heraldry, the point halfway between fess point and the base of the shield. Recorded from the mid 16th century, the word is French, and means literally 'navel'.

Nome a city in western Alaska, on the south coast of the Seward Peninsula. Founded in 1896 as a gold-mining camp, it became a centre of the Alaskan gold rush at the turn of the century.

nome one of the thirty-six territorial divisions of ancient Egypt.

nomen in Roman history, the second personal name of a citizen of ancient Rome that indicates the gens to which he or she belonged, e.g. Marcus *Tullius* Cicero.

nominalism in philosophy, the doctrine that universals or general ideas are mere names without any corresponding reality. Only particular objects exist, and properties, numbers, and sets are merely features of the way of considering the things that exist. Important in medieval scholastic thought, nominalism is associated particularly with ➤ WILLIAM *of Occam*.

nominis umbra a name without substance; a thing which is not what the name implies. The phrase, which is Latin meaning 'the shadow or appearance of a name', comes from the Roman poet Lucan (AD 39–65), in his reference to Pompey in *Pharsalia*, 'Stat magni nominis umbra [There stands the shadow of a great name]'.

nomoli a small steatite figure of a human or animal of a type found in Sierra Leone.

clause of non-obstante a clause in a statute or letter patent, beginning 'non obstante', and conveying a dispensation from a monarch to perform an action despite any statute to the contrary (in England, first used by Henry III and abolished by the Bill of Rights in 1688); a similar clause issued by the Pope. The Latin phrase *non obstante* means literally 'not hindering'.

nonce (of a word or expression) coined for one occasion. The word derives (in Middle English) from *then anes* 'the one (purpose)', from *then* (obsolete form of *the*) + *ane* 'one', altered by misdivision.

Nonconformist originally (in the early part of the 17th century) a person adhering to the doctrine but not the usages of the Church of England; the first recorded usage relates to a defence of the surplice, the sign of the cross after baptism, and the custom of kneeling to receive Holy Communion. Later (especially after the passing of the ➤ *Act of* UNIFORMITY in 1662, and the consequent ejection from their livings of those ministers who refused to conform), a member of a Protestant Church which dissents from the established Church of England.

none see ➤ NONE *but the brave deserves the fair.*

nones in the ancient Roman calendar, the ninth day before the ides by inclusive reckoning, i.e. the 7th day of March, May, July, October, the 5th of other months. Recorded from late Middle English, the word comes via Old French from Latin *nonas*,

feminine accusative plural of *nonus* 'ninth'.

In the Christian Church, *nones* is the name for the fifth of the canonical hours of prayer, originally appointed for the ninth hour of the day (about 3 p.m.), and the office appointed for this hour.

Nonesuch chest a type of wooden chest of the 16th and 17th centuries, inlaid with stylized architectural designs supposedly representing ➤ NONSUCH *Palace.*

Nonjuror a member of the clergy who refused to take the oath of allegiance to William and Mary in 1689.

nonpareil an unrivalled or matchless person or thing; in printing, an old type size equal to six points (larger than ruby).

See also ➤ CLIFDON *nonpareil.*

Nonresistance the practice or principle of not resisting authority, even when it is unjustly exercised, especially with reference to those who, while considering William and Mary to be usurpers, did not offer resistance to the established authority.

Nonsuch Palace a Tudor palace near Cheam in Surrey, built by Henry VIII. It was not completed until 1557, but the name is first mentioned in the Exchequer Accounts for 1538. In the 17th century, the English Catholic priest Richard Lassels (1603?–68), in his posthumously published *The Voyage of Italy*, referred to Fontainebleu as 'the Nonsuch of France'. *Nonsuch Palace* was demolished in 1670.

noogenesis the growth or development of the mind or consciousness; the coming into being of the noosphere (frequently with reference to the writings of ➤ TEILHARD *de Chardin*).

noon twelve o'clock in the day; midday. In Old English, *nōn* means 'the ninth hour from sunrise', i.e. approximately 3 p.m., from Latin *nona (hora)* 'ninth hour'.

It was traditionally believed that the change in the time denoted by *noon*, from about 3 o'clock to about 12 o'clock, probably resulted from anticipation of the ecclesiastical office or of a meal hour; this view was based on the belief that the canonical hours were counted starting at 6 o'clock, and that in the Benedictine order *nones* would ordinarily be held at about 3 o'clock. Recent research, however, suggests that in the Benedictine order in Italy nones would have been held closer to 12 o'clock, and it is possible that this became the usual time for nones in several orders.

noon of night poetic expression for the time of night corresponding to midday; midnight.

noosphere the sphere or stage of evolutionary development characterized by (the emergence or dominance of) consciousness, the mind, and interpersonal relationships (frequently with reference to the writings of ➤ TEILHARD *de Chardin*).

Norbertine another term for ➤ PREMONSTRATENSIAN. The name comes (in the late 17th century) from St *Norbert* (*c*.1080–1134), founder of the order.

Norfolk see ➤ COKE *of Norfolk*, ➤ JOCKEY *of Norfolk*.

Norfolk Howard dated slang for a bedbug, from an advertisement in the *Times* of 26 June 1862, professing to be a declaration from one Joshua Bug that he had assumed the name of *Norfolk Howard*.

Norland trademark name used to designate a nurse or children's nanny trained at or according to the methods of the Norland Nursery Training College (formerly the Norland Institute) in London.

> Even a 20-year-old Norlander has the status of a seasoned expert.
> — *Daily Telegraph* 13 January 1999

Norman a member of a people of mixed Frankish and Scandinavian origin who settled in Normandy from about AD 912 and became a dominant military power in western Europe and the Mediterranean in the 11th century, in particular, any of the Normans who conquered England in 1066 or their descendants.

Norman Conquest the conquest of England by William of Normandy (William the Conqueror) after the Battle of Hastings in 1066.

William was crowned William I, founding a Norman dynasty that ruled until 1154, and had crushed most resistance by 1071. Under the Normans England prospered commercially and expanded its population, but most of the Saxon nobles were dispossessed or killed and the population was heavily taxed (the Domesday Book was compiled in 1086). Norman institutions and customs (such as feudalism) were introduced, and Anglo-Norman French and Latin adopted as the languages of literature, law, and government.

Norman French the northern form of Old French spoken by the Normans; the variety of this used in

English law courts from the 11th to 13th centuries; Anglo-Norman French.

the Norns in Scandinavian mythology, the three virgin goddesses of destiny (Urd or Urdar, Verdandi, and Skuld), who sit by the well of fate at the base of the ash tree ➤ YGGDRASIL and spin the web of fate.

Norroy (in the UK) the title (in full **Norroy and Ulster**) given to the third King of Arms, with jurisdiction north of the Trent and (since 1943) in Northern Ireland. The name comes (in late Middle English) from Old French *nord* 'north' + *roi* 'king'.

north the direction in which a compass needle normally points, towards the horizon on the left-hand side of a person facing east, or the part of the horizon lying in this direction.

In 19th-century America, **the North** was used for those northern states of the United States which were opposed to slavery in the Civil War, and which fought on the side of the Union. In current usage, **the North** often designates the industrialized and economically advanced nations of the world.

Names 'of the North'

NAME	PERSON OR PLACE
Addison of the North	Henry Mackenzie (1745–1831)
Alexander of the North	Charles XII of Sweden (1682–1718)
Ariosto of the North	Sir Walter Scott (1771–1832)
Athens of the North	Edinburgh
Cock of the North	Duke of Gordon
Lion of the North	Gustavus Adolphus of Sweden (1594–1632)
Magician of the North	Sir Walter Scott (1771–1832)
Venice of the North	St Petersburg
Wizard of the North	Sir Walter Scott (1771–1832)

The North Briton title of a weekly political periodical founded in 1762 by the radical ➤ *John* WILKES (1727–97); the intention was to counter the *Briton*, started by Wilkes's enemy Smollett under the patronage of Lord Bute.

In No. 45, Wilkes published a denunciation of the King's Speech, and was arrested for libel; according to tradition, he managed during the course of his arrest to pass a message to his collaborator Charles Churchill (1731–64), who took the hint to retire to the country and thus escaped.

North-East Passage a passage for ships along the northern coast of Europe and Asia, from the Atlantic to the Pacific via the Arctic Ocean, sought for many years as a possible trade route to the East; Richard Hakluyt (1552–1616) refers to 'Great probabilities of a North, Northwest, or Northeast passage'. It was first navigated in 1878–9 by the Swedish Arctic explorer Baron Nordenskjöld (1832–1901).

North German Confederation formed under Prussian influence in 1867, and comprising the German states north of the Main River.

North Pole the northern geographical pole of the earth, situated on the Arctic ice-cap; the northern celestial or magnetic pole.

North Star the Pole Star.

North Star State informal name for Minnesota.

North-West Frontier used particularly to designate the north-west frontier of British India (now Pakistan) and Afghanistan.

North-West Passage a sea passage along the northern coast of the American continent, through the Canadian Arctic from the Atlantic to the Pacific. It was (like the ➤ NORTH-*East Passage*) sought for many years as a possible trade route by explorers including Sebastian Cabot, Sir Francis Drake, and Martin Frobisher; it was first navigated in 1903–6 by Roald Amundsen.

Northampton stands on other men's legs traditional saying.

Northamptonshire for squires and spires traditional saying.

Northern Lights another name for the aurora borealis.

Northumbria an ancient Anglo-Saxon kingdom in NE England extending from the Humber to the Forth. The name comes from obsolete *Northumber*, denoting a person living beyond the Humber.

Norway see ➤ MAID *of Norway*.

Norwich see also ➤ JULIAN *of Norwich*.

Norwich School an English regional school of landscape painting associated with John Sell Cotman and John Crome.

nose see ➤ *don't* CUT *off your nose to spite your face.*

noshi a Japanese token of esteem, forming part of the wrapping of a gift, originally a piece of dried awabi but now usually a specially folded piece of paper.

nostalgia a sentimental longing or wistful affection for the past, typically for a period or place with happy personal associations. Recorded from the late 18th century (in the sense 'acute homesickness'), the word comes from modern Latin (translating German *Heimweh* 'homesickness'), from Greek *nostos* 'return home' + *algos* 'pain'.

nostalgia ain't what it used to be graffito; taken as the title of a book by Simone Signoret, 1978.

nostalgie de la boue a desire for degradation and depravity. The French phrase, meaning literally 'mud nostalgia', was coined by the French poet and dramatist Émile Augier (1820–89), in *Le Mariage d'Olympe* (1855). In response to the comment that a duck placed on a lake with swans will miss his pond and eventually return to it, the character Montrichard replies, '*La nostalgie de la boue!* [Longing to be back in the mud!]'

nostoc a micro-organism composed of beaded filaments which aggregate to form a gelatinous mass, growing in water and damp places and able to fix nitrogen from the atmosphere. It was formerly believed to be an emanation from the stars, and the name was invented by ➤ PARACELSUS.

nostos a homecoming or homeward journey, in particular, that of Odysseus and the other heroes from Troy.

Nostradamus (1503–66), French astrologer and physician; Latinized name of *Michel de Nostredame*. His cryptic and apocalyptic predictions in rhyming quatrains appeared in two collections (1555; 1558) and their interpretation continues to be the subject of controversy.

> Millennial cultists . . . believe that Nostradamus's reference to 'The Last Conflagration' dovetail neatly with the famous apocalyptic visions of Saint John the Divine.
>
> — Elizabeth Hand *Glimmering* (1997)

not see also ➤ *not* ANGLES *but angels,* ➤ *not by a long* CHALK, ➤ *not know a B from a* BATTLEDORE, ➤ *not* PROVEN.

not a day without a line proverbial saying traditionally attributed to the Greek artist Apelles (fl. 325 BC) by Pliny the Elder.

not in my backyard expressing an objection to the siting of something regarded as unpleasant in one's own locality, while by implication finding it acceptable elsewhere. The expression originated in the

United States in derogatory references to the anti-nuclear movement, and in Britain was particularly associated with reports of the then Environment Secretary Nicholas Ridley's opposition in 1988 to housing developments near his home; the acronym NIMBY derives from this.

Notables in France of the *ancien régime*, a body of prominent men summoned by the king as a deliberative assembly in times of national emergency.

notarikon a Kabbalistic method of interpreting the Hebrew Scriptures by making new words from letters taken from the beginning, middle, or end of the words in a sentence.

notation see ➤ BINARY *notation*.

note of the Church any of certain characteristics, as unity, sanctity, catholicity, and apostolicity (originally formulated in the Nicene Creed), by which the true Church may be known; a sign or proof of genuine origin, authority, and practice.

nothing comes of nothing proverbial saying, late 14th century.

nothing for nothing proverbial saying, early 18th century.

nothing is certain but death and taxes proverbial saying, early 18th century.

nothing is certain but the unforeseen proverbial saying, late 19th century.

there is nothing lost by civility proverbial saying, late 19th century.

there is nothing new under the sun proverbial saying, late 16th century; with biblical allusion to Ecclesiastes 1:9, 'There is no new thing under the sun'.

nothing should be done in haste but gripping a flea proverbial saying, mid 17th century.

nothing so bad but it might have been worse proverbial saying, late 19th century.

nothing so bold as a blind mare proverbial saying, early 17th century, meaning that those who know least about a situation are least likely to be deterred by it.

there is nothing so good for the inside of a man as the outside of a horse proverbial saying,

early 20th century; recommending the healthful effects of horseriding.

nothing succeeds like success proverbial saying, mid 19th century.

nothing venture, nothing gain proverbial saying, early 17th century.

nothing venture, nothing have proverbial saying, late 14th century.

Notre-Dame a Gothic cathedral church in Paris, dedicated to the Virgin Mary, on the Île de la Cité (an island in the Seine). It was built between 1163 and 1250 and is especially noted for its innovatory flying buttresses and sculptured facade. The French phrase means literally 'our lady'.

Notre Dame University a university in Notre Dame, near South Bend, northern Indiana, which was founded in 1842 by a French religious community affiliated with the Roman Catholic Church and was a men's college until 1972; it is noted for the success of its football team.

Notting Hill a district of NW central London, the scene of an annual Caribbean-style street carnival.

> Think traditional Notting Hill Carnival and you think of extravagant mas floats and costumes, parades, steel bands, reggae, a huge and colourful party on the move.
> — *Guardian* 26 August 1995

Notus in classical mythology, the god of the South Wind.

noughth week at Oxford University, the week in the academic calendar preceding the start of each term.

noughts and crosses a game in which two players seek to complete a row of either three noughts or three crosses drawn alternately in the spaces of a grid of nine squares.

noumenon (in Kantian philosophy) a thing as it is in itself, as distinct from a thing as it is knowable by the senses through phenomenal attributes. Recorded from the late 18th century, the word comes via German from Greek, and means literally '(something) conceived', from *noien* 'conceive, apprehend'.

noun a word (other than a pronoun) used to identify any of a class of people, places, or things (**common noun**), or to name a particular one of these (**proper noun**). Recorded from late Middle English, the word comes via Anglo-Norman French, from Latin *nomen* 'name'.

nous common sense; practical intelligence. Recorded from the late 17th century (in the sense 'mind or intellect'), the word comes from Greek, meaning 'mind, intelligence, intuitive apprehension'.

nous avons changé tout cela French phrase meaning 'we have changed all that', originally, a quotation from Molière (1622–73), in *Le Médecin malgré lui* (1667). The character Géronte has pointed out that the heart is on the left and the liver on the right, to which Sganarelle replies, '*Oui, cela était autrefois ainsi, mais nous avons changé tout cela, et nous faisons maintenant la médecine d'une méthode toute nouvelle* [Yes, in the old days that was so, but we have changed all that, and we now practise medicine by a completely new method]'.

nouveau see also ➤ ART *nouveau*, ➤ BEAUJOLAIS *nouveau*.

nouveau riche people who have recently acquired wealth, typically those perceived as ostentatious or lacking in good taste. Recorded in English from the early 19th century, the French phrase means literally 'new rich'.

nouveau roman a style of avant-garde French novel that came to prominence in the 1950s. It rejected the plot, characters, and omniscient narrator central to the traditional novel in an attempt to reflect more faithfully the sometimes random nature of experience.

nouvelle cuisine a modern style of cookery that avoids rich, heavy foods and emphasizes the freshness of the ingredients and the presentation of the dishes.

Nova Scotia a province of eastern Canada, comprising the peninsula of Nova Scotia and the adjoining Cape Breton Island, settled by the French in the early 18th century as *Acadia*. It changed hands several times between the French and English before being awarded to Britain in 1713, and became one of the original four provinces in the Dominion of Canada in 1867.

novel the word in the literary sense was originally (in the mid 16th century) applied to a tale or fictional narrative which with a number of others made up a larger work, as in the *Decameron* of Boccaccio or the *Heptameron* of Marguerite of Valois.

The current meaning developed in the 17th century, though in the 17th and 18th centuries a *novel* was frequently contrasted with a *romance*, as being shorter than this, and having more relation to real life, although overindulgence in such reading was likely to be viewed with suspicion:

> Very unlike a novel-reading Miss.
>
> — Eliza Parsons *Mysterious Visit* (1802)

Recorded from the mid 16th century, the word comes from Italian *novella (storia)* 'new (story)', and ultimately from Latin *novus* 'new'. It is also found from late Middle English until the 18th century in the sense 'a novelty, a piece of news', from Old French *novelle*.

See also ➤ CELEBRITY *novel*.

Ivor Novello (1893–1951), Welsh composer, songwriter, actor, and dramatist. In 1914 he wrote 'Keep the Home Fires Burning', which became one of the most popular songs of the First World War. Later he composed and acted in a series of musicals, including *King's Rhapsody* (1949).

November the eleventh month of the year, in the northern hemisphere usually considered the last month of autumn. Recorded from Old English, the name comes from Latin, from *novem* 'nine', being originally the ninth month of the Roman year.

November is used allusively with reference to the short, damp, cold, or foggy days regarded as characteristic of the northern hemisphere.

See also ➤ PLEASE *to remember the Fifth of November*.

novena (in the Roman Catholic church) a form of worship consisting of special prayers or services on nine successive days. Recorded from the mid 19th century, the phrase comes from medieval Latin, from Latin *novem* 'nine'.

Novgorod a city in NW Russia, on the Volkhov River at the northern tip of Lake Ilmen, which is Russia's oldest city; it was settled by the Varangian chief Rurik in 862 and ruled by Alexander Nevsky between 1238 and 1263, when it was an important centre of medieval eastern Europe.

Novial an artificial language created by Otto Jespersen in 1928 for use as an international auxiliary language.

novus homo in ancient Rome, a 'new man', the first man in a family to enter the senate, or the first man of senatorial family (or more especially, non-senatorial family) to reach the consulship.

nowed in heraldry, knotted, tied in a knot; (of a snake) displayed in the form of a horizontal figure of eight with the head and tail extending.

Nowel a word shouted or sung as an expression of joy, originally to commemorate the birth of Jesus. Now only as retained in Christmas carols. Recorded from late Middle English.

See also ➤ NOEL.

there's nowt so queer as folk proverbial saying, early 20th century.

noyade an execution carried out by drowning, especially a mass execution by drowning as carried out in France at Nantes in 1794. The word comes from French, and means literally 'drowning', from the verb *noyer*, from Latin *necare* 'kill without a weapon', later 'drown'.

nth denoting an unspecified member of a series of numbers or enumerated items; (in general use) denoting an unspecified item or instance in a series, typically the last or latest in a long series.

nu the thirteenth letter of the Greek alphabet (**N**, **ν**), transliterated as 'n'.

Nubia an ancient region of southern Egypt and northern Sudan, including the Nile valley between Aswan and Khartoum and the surrounding area. Much of Nubia is now drowned by the waters of Lake Nasser, formed by the building of the two dams at Aswan. Nubians constitute an ethnic minority group in Egypt.

nubile of a girl or young woman, sexually mature; suitable for marriage. Recorded from the mid 17th century, the word comes from Latin *nubilis* 'marriageable', from *nubere* 'cover or veil oneself for a bridegroom', from *nubes* 'cloud'.

nuclear see also ➤ CAMPAIGN *for Nuclear Disarmament.*

nuclear winter a period of abnormal cold and darkness predicted to follow a nuclear war, caused by a layer of smoke and dust in the atmosphere blocking the sun's rays.

nul points no points scored in a contest, especially as a hypothetical mark awarded for a failure or dismal performance. *Nul points* is the lowest score attainable by an entry in the Eurovision Song Contest, in which the compèring is delivered in both English and French. Although the term has been strongly

associated with Norway's 1978 entry *Mil etter Mil* by Kai Eide, sung by Jahn Teigen, which became the first song for eight years to score zero, scores of nul points were frequent under earlier scoring systems, especially in the early 1960s.

null and void having no legal or binding force.

null hypothesis (in a statistical test) the hypothesis that there is no significant difference between specified populations, any observed difference being due to sampling or experimental error.

Nullarbor Plain a vast arid plain in SW Australia, stretching inland from the Great Australian Bight. It contains no surface water, has sparse vegetation, and is almost uninhabited, from Latin *nullus arbor* 'no tree'.

nullifidian a person having no faith or religious belief. Recorded from the mid 16th century, the word comes from medieval Latin *nullifidius*, from *nullus* 'no, none' + *fides* 'faith'.

Numa Numa Pompilius (traditionally 715–673 BC), legendary second king of Rome, who claimed to have received instruction from the water goddess ➤ EGERIA; the name may be used allusively for someone likened to him, especially as a lawgiver:

> Titus Antoninus Pius has been justly denominated a second Numa.
> — Edward Gibbon *Decline and Fall of the Roman Empire* (1776)

number an arithmetical value, expressed by a word, symbol, or figure, representing a particular quantity and used in counting and making calculations and for showing order in a series or for identification.

See also ➤ ABUNDANT *number,* ➤ APOCALYPTIC *number,* ➤ CARDINAL *number,* ➤ CONCRETE *number,* ➤ GOLDEN *number,* ➤ have one's NAME *and number on it* ➤ LUDOLPH's *number,* ➤ MACH *number,* ➤ MERSENNE *number,* ➤ ORDINAL *number,* ➤ PERFECT *number,* ➤ PRIME *number,* ➤ TRIANGULAR *number.*

the number of the beast the number 666, numerologically representing the name of the Antichrist of the Revelation 13:18, 'Let him that hath understanding count the number of the beast: for it is the number of a man; and his number is Six hundred threescore and six.'

It has been suggested that the number given

could be a coded reference to Nero: the numerical value of *Nero Caesar*, written in Hebrew letters, adds up to 666.

Number Ten 10 Downing Street, the official London home of the British Prime Minister.

numbers see also ➤ AMICABLE *numbers*, ➤ QUATERNARY *of numbers*, ➤ *there is* LUCK *in odd numbers*, ➤ *there is* SAFETY *in numbers*.

Numbers the fourth book of the Bible, relating the experiences of the Israelites in the wilderness after Moses led them out of Egypt. It is named in English from the book's accounts of a census; the title in Hebrew means 'in the wilderness'.

numerals see ➤ ARABIC *numerals*, ➤ ROMAN *numerals*.

Numidia an ancient kingdom, later a Roman province, situated in North Africa in an area north of the Sahara corresponding roughly to present-day Algeria.

nun a member of a religious community of women, typically one living under vows of poverty, chastity, and obedience. The word comes (in Old English) from ecclesiastical Latin *nonna*, feminine of *nonnus* 'monk', reinforced by Old French.

The ➤ *Virgin* MARY and the 6th-century St Scholastica, sister of St Benedict and the first Benedictine nun, are the patron saints of nuns.

Nunc Dimittis the Song of Simeon (Luke 2:29–32) used as a canticle in Christian liturgy, especially at compline and evensong. The phrase is Latin, and represents the opening words of the canticle, '(Lord), now you let (your servant) depart'. In extended usage, *nunc dimittis* may now mean departure, dismissal.

nuncheon an archaic term for a drink taken in the afternoon; a light refreshment between meals, a snack. Recorded from late Middle English, the word comes from *noon* + obsolete *shench* 'cupful, drink (of liquor)'.

nuncio in the Roman Catholic Church, a papal ambassador to a foreign court or government. Recorded from the early 16th century, the word comes from Italian, from Latin *nuntius* 'messenger'.

nundinal letter each of the eight letters A to H used to indicate the days in ancient Rome of the market-day or **nundine**, held every eighth (by inclusive reckoning, ninth) day.

nuragh a type of massive stone tower found in Sardinia, dating from the Bronze and Iron Ages.

Nuremberg a city in southern Germany, in Bavaria, which in the 15th and 16th centuries was a leading cultural centre and was the home of Albrecht Dürer and Hans Sachs.

In the 1930s the Nazi Party congresses and annual rallies were held in the city and in 1945–6 it was the scene of the Nuremberg war trials, in which Nazi war criminals were tried by international military tribunal. After the war the city centre was carefully reconstructed, as its cobbled streets and timbered houses had been reduced to rubble by Allied bombing.

Nuremberg egg an early type of watch, made in Nuremberg in the 16th century. The term is a misnomer which derives from a misreading of *Uhrlein* 'little clock' for *Eierlein* 'little egg'.

Nuremberg laws in Nazi Germany, laws promulgated in 1935 barring Jews from German citizenship and forbidding intermarriage between Aryans and Jews.

Nuremberg rally a mass meeting of the German Nazi party, held annually in Nuremberg from 1933 to 1938, notable for their carefully stage-managed effects.

> The disco finale . . . did feel a bit like being in the lowest circle of hell as dreamed up by the designer of the Nuremberg Rally.
> — *City Life* 24 August 1994

Nuremberg trial any of a series of trials of former Nazi leaders for alleged war crimes, crimes against peace, and crimes against humanity, presided over by an International Military Tribunal representing the victorious Allied Powers and held in Nuremberg in 1945–6.

Rudolf Nureyev (1939–93), Russian-born ballet dancer and choreographer. He defected to the West in 1961, joining the Royal Ballet in London, where he began his noted partnership with Margot Fonteyn.

nursery rhyme a simple traditional song or poem for children. The term is first recorded in 1816, and probably derives from the title of Ann and Jane Taylor's *Rhymes for the Nursery* of 1806.

nurses St Camillus of Lellis (1550–1614), founder of the Ministers of the Sick, ➤ St ELIZABETH *of Hungary*, and ➤ St JOHN *of God* are the patron saints of nurses.

nut in Middle English a *nut* was sometimes taken as the type of something small and of little value; the English anchoress and mystic Julian of Norwich (1343–1416), in her *Revelations of Divine Love*, uses the image of a hazelnut in this way:

> He showed me something small, no bigger than a hazelnut, lying in the palm of my hand, as it seemed to me, and it was as round as a ball. I looked at it with the eye of my understanding, and thought: What can this be? I was amazed that it could last, for I thought that because of its littleness it would suddenly have fallen into nothing. And I was answered in my understanding: It lasts and always will, because God loves it; and thus every thing has being through the love of God.
> — Julian of Norwich *Revelations of Divine Love*

The children's nursery rhyme 'I had a little nut tree' relates that 'the King of Spain's daughter' came to visit the nut-tree's owner; it has been suggested that this is a reference to the visit to Henry VII's court made in 1506 by Juana of Castile, sister of Catherine of Aragon.

The hard shell of a nut also gives rise to expressions such as **a hard nut to crack** for a difficult problem.

See also ➤ *the* GODS *send nuts to those who have no teeth.*

Nut Monday the first Monday in August, in some localities traditionally observed as a holiday.

nut silver a payment formerly made in Northumberland in commutation of a manorial service of gathering nuts.

Nutcracker man the nickname of a fossil hominid with massive jaws and molar teeth, the maker of the oldest stone tools known, especially the original specimen found near Olduvai Gorge in 1959 by Mary Leakey.

nutmeg see also ➤ WOODEN *nutmeg.*

Nutmeg State informal name for Connecticut.

nutraceuticals another term for ➤ FUNCTIONAL *food*. The word is formed from a blend of *nutrition* and *pharmaceutical*, and is intended to express the dual nourishing and health-promoting role of such foods. (The alternative expression *pharmafood* has also been recorded.)

here we come gathering nuts in May refrain of a traditional children's singing game, recorded from the 19th century. It is a contest game, in which one side tries to 'fetch away' a member of the other side, and is associated with May celebrations. It has been suggested that the 'nuts' were originally 'knops' or buds.

nutshell traditionally regarded as the type of something extremely small in extent or capacity.

> I could be bounded in a nutshell, and count myself a king of infinite space, were it not that I have bad dreams.
> — William Shakespeare *Hamlet* (1601)

See also ➤ ILIAD *in a nutshell.*

nymph a mythological spirit of nature imagined as a beautiful maiden inhabiting rivers, woods, or other locations. Recorded from late Middle English, the word comes via Old French and Latin from Greek *numphē* 'nymph, bride', and is related to Latin *nubere* 'be the wife of'.

In literary use from the early 17th century, *nymph* may be used for a river or stream.

nymphaeum a grotto or shrine dedicated to a nymph or nymphs; a building or part of a building built to represent such a shrine.

Nynorsk a literary form of the Norwegian language, based on certain country dialects and constructed in the 19th century to serve as a national language more clearly distinct from Danish than Bokmål.

Nyx in Greek mythology, the female personification of the night, daughter of Chaos.

O the fifteenth letter of the modern English alphabet and the fourteenth of the ancient Roman one, corresponding to Greek *o*, representing the sixteenth letter of the Phoenician and ancient Semitic alphabet.

See also ➤ Fifteen *O's*, ➤ Giotto's *O*, ➤ Seven *O's of Advent*.

O' a prefix in Irish patronymic names such as *O'Neill*; recorded from the mid 18th century, it represents Irish *ó*, *ua* 'descendant'.

> Ireland her *O's*, her *Mac's* let Scotland boast.
> — Henry Fielding *Tom Thumb* (ed. 3, 1737)

O tempora, O mores! Latin phrase meaning, 'O, the times! Oh, the manners!', originally a quotation from the Roman orator and statesman Cicero (106–43 BC) in a speech from *In Catilinam*.

oaf a stupid, uncultured, or clumsy man. The word comes ultimately from Old Norse *álfr* 'elf', and the original meaning was 'elf's child, changeling', later 'idiot child' and 'halfwit', generalized in the current sense.

oak allusion is often made to the hardness and durability of the oak, and to the traditional use of oak timber for ships. In traditional rhymes, it may be linked and compared with other trees, as the *ash* and the *thorn*.

See also ➤ acorn, ➤ Heart *of Oak*, ➤ sport *one's oak*.

Oak-apple Day the anniversary of Charles II's restoration (29 May), when oak-apples or oak-leaves used to be worn in memory of his hiding in an oak after the battle of Worcester.

Oak-boy a member of an Irish rebel society of the 1760s, whose badge was a sprig of oak worn in the hat.

when the oak is before the ash, then you will only get a splash;
when the ash is before the oak, then you may expect a soak
proverbial saying, mid 19th century; meaning that if the oak comes out before the ash, it presages fine weather.

beware of an oak, it draws the stroke; avoid an ash, it counts the flash; creep under the thorn, it can save you from harm proverbial saying, late 19th century; on where to shelter from lightning.

Annie Oakley (1860–1926), American markswoman. In 1885 she joined Buffalo Bill's Wild West Show, of which she became a star attraction for the next seventeen years, often working with her husband, the marksman Frank E. Butler.

oaks see also ➤ little *strokes fell great oaks*, ➤ *a* reed *before the wind lives on, while mighty oaks do fall*.

the Oaks an annual flat horse race for three-year-old fillies run on Epsom Downs, over the same course as the Derby. It was first run in 1779, and is so called from the estate of the 12th Earl of Derby, owner of the first winner.

great oaks from little acorns grow proverbial saying, late 14th century.

oakum loose fibre obtained by untwisting old rope, used especially in caulking wooden ships. **Picking oakum** was a task formerly assigned to convicts and inmates of workhouses.

Recorded from Old English in the form *ācumbe*, literally 'off-combings', the current sense dates from Middle English.

Oannes in Babylonian mythology, a divine being with a fish's body but the head and feet of a man.

ply the labouring oar do much of the work. The **labouring oar** is the one hardest to pull, and the original allusion is to Dryden *Aeneis* (1697) 'three Trojans tug at ev'ry lab'ring oar'.

oasis a fertile spot in a desert, where water is found; in figurative use, a pleasant or peaceful area or period in the midst of a difficult, troubled, or hectic place or situation. Recorded from the early 17th century, the word comes via late Latin from Greek, and is apparently of Egyptian origin.

oast house a building containing an *oast*, a kiln used for drying hops, typically built of brick in a conical shape with a cowl on top.

Captain Lawrence Oates (1880–1912), English soldier and explorer, who took part in the Antarctic expedition of ➤ *Robert Falcon* SCOTT in 1912, and was one of the five members of the party who reached the South Pole. On 17 March, suffering from badly frostbitten feet and anxious that he was a risk to the other members of the party, he left their tent with the words 'I am just going outside and may be some time' (the words are recorded in Scott's diary, found with the bodies of the expedition). He was not seen again.

A cairn with a cross was subsequently erected near the site of his death; the inscription read, 'Hereabouts died a very gallant gentleman, Captain L. E. G. Oates of the Inniskilling Dragoons. In March 1912, returning from the Pole, he walked willingly to his death in a blizzard to try and save his comrades, beset by hardships.'

Titus Oates (1649–1705), English clergyman and conspirator, remembered as the fabricator of the ➤ POPISH *Plot*. Convicted of perjury in 1685, Oates was imprisoned in the same year, but subsequently released and granted a pension.

oath see ➤ HIPPOCRATIC *oath*, ➤ TENNIS-*court oath*, ➤ *Oath of* ABJURATION.

oats see ➤ SOW *one's wild oats*.

Obadiah (in the Bible) a Hebrew minor prophet; the shortest book of the Bible, bearing his name.

obeah a kind of sorcery practised especially in the Caribbean. Recorded from the mid 18th century, the word comes from Twi, from *bayi* 'sorcery'.

obelisk a stone pillar, typically having a square or rectangular cross section, set up as a monument or landmark, originally in ancient Egypt. Recorded from the mid 16th century, the word comes via Latin from Greek *obeliskos*, diminutive of *obelos* 'pointed pillar'.

obelus in printing, a symbol (†) used as a reference mark in printed matter, or to indicate that a person is deceased; also called *dagger*. *Obelus* is also the name for a mark (– or ÷) used in ancient manuscripts to mark a word or passage as spurious, corrupt or doubtful.

Recorded from late Middle English, the word comes via Latin from Greek *obelos* 'pointed pillar', also 'critical mark'.

Oberammergau a village in the Bavarian Alps of SW Germany, which is the site of the most famous of the few surviving passion plays, which has been performed by the villagers every tenth year (with few exceptions) from 1634 as a result of a vow made during an epidemic of plague. It is entirely amateur, the villagers dividing the parts among themselves and being responsible also for the production, music, costumes, and scenery.

Oberon name of the king of the fairies, husband of Titania in Shakespeare's *A Midsummer Night's Dream*; originally *Auberon*, the king of the elves who in the medieval French poem uses his magic powers to help ➤ HUON *of Bordeaux*. The spelling *Oberon* is used in Lord Berners's translation of *Huon de Bordeaux* (*c.*1530).

See also ➤ ALBERICH.

he that cannot obey cannot command proverbial saying, late 15th century.

obey orders, if you break owners proverbial saying, late 18th century; the saying is nautical, and means that orders should be followed even if it is clear that they are wrong.

Obi-Wan Kenobi in the first film of the ➤ STAR *Wars* trilogy, the ➤ JEDI master who finds and trains the young ➤ LUKE *Skywalker*, enabling him to set out on his quest.

> 'The disc you choose depends on the desired degree of "hyzer" you need for a particular shot,' says the Obi-Wan Kenobi of disc golf.
> — *Sports Illustrated* 14 June 1993

obit former term for a ceremony, typically a mass, commemorating, or commending to God, a deceased person, especially a founder or benefactor of an institution on the anniversary of his or her death; an annual or other regular memorial service.

obiter dictum a judge's expression of opinion uttered in court or giving judgement, but not essential to the decision and not part of the ratio decidendi. The phrase is Latin, from *obiter* 'in passing' + *dictum* 'something that is said'.

oblate a person dedicated to a religious life, but typically having not taken full monastic vows (as in, **Oblate of St Charles Borromeo**). In earlier times, *oblate* was also used for a child dedicated by his or her parents to a religious house and placed there to be brought up.

Recorded from the late 17th century, the word comes via French from medieval Latin *oblatus*, past participle (used as a noun) of Latin *offerre* 'to offer'.

obligation see ➤ DAY *of obligation.*

Oblomov an inactive, weak-willed, and procrastinating person, from the name of the hero of Ivan Goncharov's novel *Oblomov* (1855).

> Most people in the same day are Bonaparte and Oblomov by turns.
> — I. A. Richards *Principles of Literary Criticism* (1925)

obol an ancient Greek coin worth one sixth of a drachma, traditionally the coin placed in the mouth of the dead as a fee for ➤ CHARON to ferry them across the Styx. The word originally meant 'spit' or 'nail', and came to be used for a type of coin as in early times nails were used as money.

obosom any of various minor deities or spirits in the religious system of the Ashanti peoples of Ghana.

obscurum per obscurius another term for ➤ IGNOTUM *per ignotius.*

Observant a member of a branch of the Franciscans in which the friars follow a strict rule.

observation see ➤ MASS *observation.*

obsidian a hard, dark, glass-like volcanic rock formed by the rapid solidification of lava without crystallization. The name comes (in the mid 17th century) from Latin *obsidianus,* error for *obsianus,* from *Obsius,* the name (in Pliny) of the discoverer of a similar stone.

obsidional crown a wreath of grass or weeds conferred as a mark of honour on a Roman general who raised a siege. Recorded from late Middle English, it is a translation of Latin *corona obsidionalis; obsidio* in Latin means 'siege'.

cold obstruction death, rigor mortis; perhaps originally with allusion to Shakespeare:

> Ay, but to die, and go we know not where;
> To lie in cold obstruction and to rot.
> — William Shakespeare *Measure for Measure* (1604)

obverse the side of a coin or medal bearing the head or principal design.

oc see ➤ LANGUE *d'oc.*

Occam see also ➤ WILLIAM *of Occam.*

Occam a computer programming language devised for use in parallel processing, named after ➤ WILLIAM *of Occam.*

Occam's razor the principle (attributed to William of Occam) that in explaining a thing no more assumptions should be made than are necessary. The principle is often invoked to defend reductionism or nominalism.

occamy a metallic compound imitating silver. The word is an alteration of *alchemy.*

Occident formal or poetic name for the countries of the West, especially Europe and America. Recorded from late Middle English, the name comes via Old French from Latin *occident-* 'going down, setting' (referring to the sun), from the verb *occidere.*

Occitan the medieval or modern language of Languedoc, including literary Provençal of the 12th–14th centuries.

the occult supernatural, mystical, or magical beliefs, practices, or phenomena. Recorded from the late 15th century (as a verb, meaning 'to conceal'), the word comes from Latin *occultare* 'secrete', and is ultimately based on *celare* 'to hide'.

ocean a very large expanse of sea, in particular, each of the main areas into which the sea is divided geographically. Recorded from Middle English, the word comes via Latin from Greek *ōkeanos* 'great stream encircling the earth's disc'. 'The ocean' originally denoted the whole body of water regarded as encompassing the earth's single land mass.

See also ➤ SHEPHERD *of the Ocean.*

Ocean State informal name for Rhode Island.

Oceanid in Greek mythology, a sea nymph, any of the daughters of the sea-god ➤ OCEANUS, and his sister and wife ➤ TETHYS.

Oceanus in Greek mythology, the son of Uranus (Heaven) and Gaia (Earth), brother and husband of ➤ TETHYS, the personification of the great river believed to encircle the whole world.

Octarchy the supposed eight kingdoms of the Angles and Saxons in Britain in the 7th and 8th centuries.

Octateuch the first eight books of the Old Testament and Hebrew Scriptures collectively; the Pentateuch together with the books of Joshua, Judges, and Ruth.

law of octaves a supposed law of chemistry put forward by ➤ *John* NEWLANDS, the principle according to which, when the lighter elements (excluding hydrogen) are arranged in order of their atomic weights, similar properties recur at every eighth term of the series.

Octavian early name (until 27 BC) of Augustus (63 BC–AD 14), first Roman emperor.

octavo a size of book page that results from folding each printed sheet into eight leaves (sixteen pages). The name comes from the Latin phrase *in octavo*, used to designate such a book.

October the tenth month of the year, in the northern hemisphere usually considered the second month of autumn. Recorded from late Old English, the name comes from Latin, from *octo* 'eight', being originally the eighth month of the Roman year.

October Club a club of Tory MPs of Queen Anne's time, who met at the Bell (afterwards the Crown) in King Street, Westminster, to drink October ale, 'consult affairs and drive things on to extremes against the Whigs' (Swift, letter 10 February, 1710/11).

October crisis in Canada, a period of political unrest in 1970 in which the Front de Liberation du Quebec (FLQ) engaged in various terrorist activities to which the Canadian government responded with the mobilization of armed troops under the War Measures Act.

October Revolution the Russian Bolshevik revolution in November (October Old Style) 1917, in which the provisional government was overthrown, leading to the establishment of the USSR.

October surprise in the US, an unexpected but popular political act or speech made just prior to a November election in an attempt to win votes, used especially with reference to an alleged conspiracy in which members of the 1980 Republican campaign team are said to have made an arms deal with Iran to delay the release of US hostages in Iran until after the election.

October War Arab name for the ➤ YOM *Kippur War.*

Octobrist a member of the moderate party in the Russian Duma, which supported Tsar Nicholas II's reforming manifesto of 30 October 1905.

octonary a stanza of eight lines of verse, especially of Psalm 119 (118 in the Vulgate).

od¹ alteration of *God*, in archaic interjections and exclamatory phrases.

od² a hypothetical force proposed by Baron von Reichenbach (1788–1869) as pervading all nature, being manifest in certain people of sensitive temperament and accounting for the phenomena of mesmerism and animal magnetism. Also called *odyl.*

Oddfellow a member of a fraternity organized under this name, typically for social or benevolent purposes. The name 'Odd Fellows' appears to have been originally assumed by local social clubs formed in various parts of England during the 18th century, usually with rites of initiation, passwords, and secret ceremonies, supposed to imitate those of Freemasonry.

Various associations of these clubs have been formed from time to time for purposes of mutual recognition, of which the 'Independent Order of Oddfellows, Manchester Unity', formed about 1813, grew into an organization with many local branches or 'lodges' throughout the world, chiefly in Great Britain and the Commonwealth. An American lodge, founded in Baltimore in 1819, grew to become a distinct international association in North America and Europe, originally in connection with the Manchester Union but from 1842 separate from it.

ode a lyric poem, typically one in the form of an address to a particular subject, written in varied or irregular metre; a classical poem of a kind originally meant to be sung.

In classical times, odes written by Pindar were generally dignified or exalted in subject and style and were based on the odes sung by the chorus (choral odes) in Greek tragedy. Those written in Latin by Horace provide a simpler, more intimate model. Keats is among later poets to have written odes drawing on Horace, while Dryden, Wordsworth, and Coleridge wrote more elevated odes.

Recorded from the late 16th century, the word comes via French and late Latin from Greek *ōidē*, Attic form of *aoidē* 'song'.

odeon a cinema, from the name of a chain of large and lavish cinemas built by the company of Oscar Deutsch in the 1930s; *Odeon* here represented partly a variant of ➤ ODEUM, and partly an acronym from the initial letters of *Oscar Deutsch Entertains Our Nation.*

ODESSA an organization arranging the escape from Germany of high-ranking Nazis at the end of World War II. The name is an acronym from the initials of the German *Organisation der Ehemaligen*

SS *Angehörigen* Organization of former SS members, after *Odessa*, the name of a city and port on the south coast of the Ukraine.

odeum (especially in ancient Greece or Rome) a roofed building used for musical performances, a concert hall. The word comes via French or Latin from Greek *ōideion*, from *ōidē* 'song'.

Odin in Scandinavian mythology, the supreme god and creator, god of victory and the dead, married to Freya (Frigga) and usually represented as a one-eyed old man of great wisdom. He is said to have won the ➤ RUNES for humankind by hanging himself for nine nights and days on the world tree ➤ YGGDRASIL (because of which he is god of the hanged); he gave one eye to Mimir, guardian of the well of wisdom, in exchange for poetic inspiration.

odium theologicum a Latin phrase for the hatred which proverbially characterizes theological disputes. Recorded from the mid 18th century, it has given rise by imitation to many similar formulations, as **odium academicum** (academic) and **odium medicum** (medical).

odour of sanctity a sweet or balsamic odour reputedly emitted by the bodies of saints at or near death, and regarded as evidence of their sanctity.

Odysseus in Greek mythology, the king of Ithaca and central figure of the *Odyssey*, renowned for his cunning and resourcefulness; in Latin, he is known as *Ulysses*.

Odyssey a Greek hexameter epic poem traditionally ascribed to Homer, describing the travels of Odysseus during his ten years of wandering after the sack of Troy. He eventually returned home to Ithaca and killed the suitors who had plagued his wife Penelope during his absence.

Odysseus's adventures include amorous liaisons with Calypso and Circe, the hospitality of the Phaeacians, the evocation of the famous dead from the underworld, and encounters with a number of fabulous monsters, including the Cyclops Polyphemus and Scylla and Charybdis.

oecumene the inhabited world as known to a particular civilization, especially, the ancient Greeks; the Greeks and their neighbours regarded in the context of development in human society.

Oedipus in Greek mythology, the son of ➤ JOCASTA and of Laius, king of Thebes. Left to die on a mountain by Laius, who had been told by an oracle that he would be killed by his own son, the infant Oedipus was saved by a shepherd. Returning eventually to Thebes, Oedipus solved the riddle of the sphinx, but unwittingly killed his father and married Jocasta; their children were ➤ ANTIGONE, Ismene, ➤ POLYNICES, and Eteocles. On discovering what he had done he put out his own eyes in a fit of madness, while Jocasta hanged herself.

Oedipus complex (in Freudian theory) the complex of emotions aroused in a young child, typically around the age of four, by an unconscious sexual desire for the parent of the opposite sex and wish to exclude the parent of the same sex. (The term was originally applied to boys, the equivalent in girls being called the *Electra complex.*)

oeil-de-boeuf the name of an octagonal vestibule lighted by a small round window (a 'bull's eye') in the palace at Versailles; the expression has thus come to mean a small vestibule or antechamber in a palace, and figuratively, a royal household or court.

oenomel in ancient Greece, a drink made from wine mixed with honey; figuratively, language or thought in which strength and sweetness are combined.

Oenone a nymph of Mount Ida and lover of Paris, prince of Troy, who deserted her for Helen.

off-Broadway (of a theatre, play, or performer) located in, appearing in, or associated with an area of New York other than Broadway, typically with reference to experimental and less commercial productions. The term **off-off-Broadway** is now used for productions regarded as even more experimental, avant-garde, and informal.

it is best to be off with the old love before you are on with the new proverbial saying, early 19th century.

Offa (d.796), king of Mercia 757–96. He organized the construction of Offa's Dyke. After seizing power in Mercia he expanded his territory to become overlord of most of England south of the Humber.

Offa's Dyke a series of earthworks marking the traditional boundary between England and Wales, running from near the mouth of the Wye to near the mouth of the Dee, originally constructed by Offa in the second half of the 8th century to mark the boundary established by his wars with the Welsh.

offenders never pardon proverbial saying, mid 17th century.

office see ➤ Divine *Office*.

Official Secrets Act in the UK, the legislation that controls access to confidential information important for national security; the Act itself was passed in 1889.

in the offing likely to happen or appear soon; *offing* here means literally 'the more distant part of the sea in view'.

Oflag former term for a German prison camp for captured enemy officers; the name is German, and is a contraction of *Offizier(s)lager* 'officers' camp'.

Og in the Bible, the king of Bashan defeated by Moses and the Israelites.

ogbanje in Nigeria, a child believed to be a reincarnation of another dead child.

ogdoad in Gnosticism, a group of eight divine beings or aeons.

ogee in architecture, showing in section a double continuous S-shaped curve. The word comes (in late Middle English) from ➤ OGIVE, with which it was then synonymous; the current sense developed in the late 17th century.

ogham an ancient British and Irish alphabet, dating from the 4th century BC and consisting of twenty characters formed by parallel strokes on either side of or across a continuous line. Recorded from the early 18th century, the word comes from Irish *ogam*, connected with *Ogma*, the name of its mythical inventor.

Ogier the Dane in French medieval poetry, a hero (in Danish, *Holger Danske*) who is supposedly the son of the Danish king Gaufray, and who firsts fights against Charlemagne and then becomes one of his followers, noted for his skill in battle.

ogive a pointed or Gothic arch; the term is recorded from late Middle English, and comes from French, of unknown origin (see also ➤ OGEE).

Ogma in Irish legend, the reputed inventor of ogham, said to have been developed to provide signs for secret speech known only to the learned.

Ogopogo a water monster alleged to live in Okanagan Lake, British Columbia. The name is an invented word, and is said to be from a British music hall song (1924) by C. Clark, although no contemporary copy of this has been traced.

OGPU an organization for investigating and combating counter-revolutionary activities in the former Soviet Union, existing from 1922 (1922–3 as the GPU) to 1934 and replacing the Cheka.

ogre in folklore, a man-eating giant. The word comes from French, and was used by Charles Perrault in 1697; ultimately it derives from Latin *Orcus*, a name for Hades, god of the underworld; of unknown origin. In English, it is found first in an 18th-century translation of the *Arabian Nights*.

Ogyges name of a mythical Attic or Boeotian king; **Ogygian** is used to indicate great age and antiquity.

Ogygia in Homer's *Odyssey*, the island which is the home of the nymph ➤ CALYPSO.

Ogygian deluge a great flood supposed to have occurred in the reign of ➤ OGYGES.

Georg Simon Ohm (1789–1854), German physicist. In 1826 he published his law (Ohm's Law) on electricity but had to struggle to get due recognition for his work. The units ohm and mho are named after him, as is Ohm's Law on electricity.

Ohm's law a law stating that electric current is proportional to voltage and inversely proportional to resistance.

oil see ➤ CAULDRON *of oil*, ➤ BURN *the midnight oil*, ➤ PHIAL *of oil*, ➤ POUR *oil on troubled waters*.

oïl see ➤ LANGUE *d'oïl*.

ointment see ➤ *a* FLY *in the ointment*, ➤ JAR *of ointment*.

Oireachtas the legislature of the Irish Republic: the President, Dáil, and Seanad. The word is Irish, and means literally, 'assembly, convocation'.

OK used to express assent, agreement, or acceptance. Recorded from the mid 19th century (originally US), it is probably an abbreviation of *orl korrect*, humorous form of *all correct*, popularized as a slogan during President Martin Van Buren's re-election campaign of 1840 in the US; his nickname *Old Kinderhook* (derived from his birthplace) provided the initials.

Okhrana an organization set up in 1881 in Russia after the assassination of Alexander II to maintain State security and suppress revolutionary activities, replaced after the Revolution of 1917 by the Cheka.

Okie a derogatory term for a migrant agricultural worker from Oklahoma who had been forced to leave a farm during the depression of the 1930s.

St Olaf (*c*.995–1030), king of Norway as ➤ OLAF *II Haraldsson*.

Olaf I Tryggvason (969–1000), king of Norway, reigned 995–1000. According to legend he carried out extensive Viking raids before becoming king. Defeated by Denmark and Sweden at Svöld, he jumped overboard and was lost. His exploits and popularity made him a national legend.

Olaf II Haraldsson (*c*.995–1030), king of Norway, reigned 1016–30, canonized as **St Olaf** for his attempts to spread Christianity in his kingdom. He was forced into exile by a rebellion in 1028 and killed in battle at Stiklestad while attempting to return. He is the patron saint of Norway. Feast day, 29 July.

Olbers' paradox the apparent paradox that if stars are distributed evenly throughout an infinite universe, the sky should be as bright by night as by day, since more distant stars would be fainter but more numerous. This is not the case because the universe is of finite age, and the light from the more distant stars is dimmed because they are receding from the observer as the universe expands. It is named (in the 1950s) after Heinrich W. M. *Olbers* (1758–1840), the German astronomer who propounded it in 1826.

old see also ➤ BETTER *be an old man's darling than a young man's slave*, ➤ *the old* ADAM, ➤ *Old* BILL, ➤ *an old* CHESTNUT, ➤ *Old* COVENANT, ➤ *Old* MICHAELMAS, ➤ YOUNG *folks think old folks to be fools*, ➤ YOUNG *men may die, but old men must die*, ➤ YOUNG *saint, old devil*.

Old Bailey the Central Criminal Court in London, formerly standing in an ancient bailey of the London city wall. The present court was built in 1903–6 on the site of Newgate Prison.

Old Believer a member of a Russian Orthodox group which refused to accept the liturgical reforms of the patriarch Nikon (1605–81).

old boy network an informal system of support and friendship through which men are thought to use their positions of influence to help others who went to the same school or university as they did, or who share a similar social background.

Old Catholic a member of any of various religious groups which have separated from the Roman Catholic Church since the Reformation, especially the Church of Utrecht (which broke with Rome over the condemnation of Jansenism in 1724), and a number of German-speaking Churches which refused to accept papal infallibility after the First Vatican Council.

Old Church Slavonic the oldest recorded Slavic language, as used by the apostles Cyril and Methodius and surviving in texts from the 9th–12th centuries. It is related particularly to the Southern Slavic languages.

Old Colony informal name for Massachusetts.

Old Contemptibles the veterans of the British Expeditionary Force sent to France in the First World War (1914), so named because of the German Emperor's alleged exhortation to his soldiers to 'walk over General French's contemptible little army' (published in an annexe to B.E.F. Routine Orders of 24 September 1914).

the old country the native country of a person who has gone to live abroad, often particularly Great Britain.

Old Dart in Australia and New Zealand, an informal name for England, with *Dart* as a figurative use representing a pronunciation of *dirt*, from *pay dirt*.

Old Dominion an informal name for the state of Virginia.

Old English the language of the Anglo-Saxons (up to about 1150), an inflected language with a Germanic vocabulary, very different from modern English.

Old Faithful the name of a geyser in Yellowstone National Park, Wyoming, noted for the regularity of its eruptions.

> That fiery temper kept erupting just as predictably as Old Faithful.
> — J. Goodfield *Courier to Peking* (1973)

Old Glory an informal name for the US national flag, otherwise known as the ➤ STARS *and Stripes*. It is attributed to Captain William Driver (1803–86), who is reported to have said, 'I name thee Old Glory!', when saluting a new flag flown on his ship, the *Charles Dogget*, on leaving Salem, Massachusetts for the South Pacific in 1831.

Driver's actual flag is said to have been flown in the state capital of Nashville, Tennessee, 1862, after the city was recaptured by Union forces.

The Old Grey Whistle Test title of a 1970s BBC TV pop music series, supposedly from the practice of testing new pop songs on elderly grey-haired door-men; if the tune was then picked up and whistled, the song was thought to have popular appeal.

the old guard the original or long-standing members of a group or party, especially ones who are unwilling to accept change or new ideas.

old habits die hard proverbial saying, mid 18th century.

Old Harry a familiar name for the Devil, recorded from the late 18th century.

you cannot put an old head on young shoulders proverbial saying, late 16th century.

Old Hickory nickname given to Andrew Jackson (1767–1845), President of the US 1829–37.

Old Hundredth a hymn tune which first appeared in the Geneva psalter of 1551 and was later set to Psalm 100 in the 'old' metrical version of the Geneva Psalter (hymn 166 in 'Hymns Ancient and Modern'); the psalm itself.

Old King Cole traditional nursery-rhyme character said to have called for his pipe, his bowl, and his three fiddlers; as a 'merry old soul' he is a type of cheerfulness. The rhyme was known in the 18th century, and there was speculation as to its origin, with attempts to identify him with a king mentioned by Geoffrey of Monmouth, and with the founder of Colchester; in the 19th century, William Chappell put forward the theory that the song referred to a Reading clothier called Colebrook who was proverbially known as a wealthy man and was referred to as 'Old Cole'.

Old Kingdom a period of ancient Egyptian history (*c*.2575–2134 BC, 4th–8th dynasty).

Old Labour the Labour Party before the introduction of the internal reforms initiated by Neil Kinnock (party leader, 1983–1992) and carried through by John Smith (party leader 1992–1994) and his successor Tony Blair (Prime Minister 1997–); the term is now used for that section of the Labour Party which argues that the aims and ideals of ➤ NEW *Labour* represent an abandonment of socialist principles.

Old Lady of Threadneedle Street the nickname of the Bank of England, which stands in this street. The term dates from the late 18th century, as a caption to James Gillray's cartoon of 22 May 1797, 'Political Ravishment, or The Old Lady of Threadneedle-Street in danger!' showing the 'Old Lady' dressed in one-pound notes, seated on a strong-box containing her gold, with Pitt placing an arm round her waist and a hand in her pocket; he has dropped a scroll of forced 'loans'. The Old Lady is screaming, 'Murder! Murder! Rape! Murder!...Ruin, Ruin, Ruin!'

old leaven in Christian tradition, traces of the unregenerate state or prejudices that may be held by religious converts, referred to in 1 Corinthians 5:7, 'Purge out therefore the old leaven'.

See also ➤ LEAVEN.

Old Left a name given to the more left wing elements of the British Labour Party, as distinct from the more centrist elements who became dominant in the 1980s and 1990s.

Old Line State informal name for Maryland.

old maid a card game in which players collect pairs and try not to be left with an odd penalty card, typically a queen.

old man eloquent nickname for John Quincy Adams (1767–1848), sixth President of the United States.

old man of the mountains a name applied to the founder of the Assassins, who established a base for the sect at a mountain fortress in the region of what is now northern Iran, and his successors.

old man of the sea in the story of Sinbad the Sailor in the *Arabian Nights*, the sea-god who forced Sinbad to carry him on his shoulders for many days and nights until he was thwarted by being made so drunk that he toppled off.

Old Man River informal name for the Mississippi.

old man's beard a wild clematis which has grey fluffy hairs around the seeds; also known as ➤ TRAVELLER's *joy*.

old master a great artist of former times, especially of the 13th–17th century in Europe; the term is first recorded in 1696 in the diary of John Evelyn, who was shown 'a large book of the best drawings of the old masters' by Lord Pembroke.

old moon the moon in its last quarter, before the new moon.

Old Mother Hubbard nursery-rhyme character who found her cupboard bare when she went to fetch her dog a bone; the story is given in Sarah Catherine Martin's *The Comic Adventures of Old Mother Hubbard* (1805), based on a traditional rhyme. The character of *Mother Hubbard* is well-known in popular mythology since at least the late 16th century, and her name appears in the title of Spenser's satire on abuses in church and court, *Prosopopoia, or Mother Hubberds Tale* (1591).

Early nursery-rhyme illustrations often depicted *Mother Hubbard* in a loose-fitting cloak or dress, and her name was thus applied to this kind of garment. In allusive use, however, reference is likely to be made to the complete lack of resources typified by her empty cupboard, whereby 'the poor dog had none'.

> He invests his wedge in stocks and shares and probably shares a gaff with Old Mother Hubbard and the dog.
> — *Loaded* September 1996

Old Nick an informal name for the Devil, recorded from the mid 17th century ('For Roundheads Old Nick stand up now'). The name is unexplained, although it was once suggested to refer to the forename of ➤ *Niccoló* MACCHIAVELLI:

> Nick Machiavel had ne'r a Trick,
> (Though he gave 's Name to Old Nick).
> — Samuel Butler *Hudibras* (1678)

It has also been suggested that *Nick* may be a shortened form of *Iniquity*, another term for the Vice in the early modern English morality play; *Old Iniquity* is used by Ben Jonson in *The Devil is an Ass* (1616).

Old Noll a nickname for Oliver Cromwell, as in the title of the 17th-century pamphlet 'Oliver Cromwell's Ghost, or Old Noll newly revived'.

Old North State an informal name for North Carolina.

Old Pretender James Francis Edward Stuart (1688–1766), son of James II, whose birth as a Catholic male heir was a contributory cause to his father's being driven into exile. Referred to initially in anti-Jacobite circles as the *pretended Prince of Wales*, supposedly introduced into the Queen's bed in a ➤ WARMING *pan*, he then became known as **the Pretender**, a usage which Bishop Burnet attributes to James's half-sister Queen Anne:

> She also fixed a new Designation on the Pretended Prince of Wales, and called him the Pretender.
> — Gilbert Burnet *History of Our Own Time (a.* 1715)

The name *Old Pretender* developed later to distinguish James from his son, Charles Edward Stuart (1720–80), the ➤ YOUNG *Pretender*.

Old Q the nickname of William Douglas, 3rd Earl of March and 4th Duke of Queensberry (1724–1810), a friend of the prince of Wales, notorious for his escapades and dissolute life, much interested in horse-racing. He was satirized by Burns, and is the 'degenerate Douglas' of Wordsworth's sonnet.

Old Rough and Ready nickname of Zachary Taylor (1784–1850), 12th President of the USA, acquired during the war against the Seminole Indians in 1837. The nickname is preserved in a presidential campaign song of 1848:

> I think I hear his cheerful voice,
> 'On column! Steady! Steady!'
> So handy and so prompt was he,
> We called him Rough and Ready.
> — Whig presidential campaign song, 1848

Old Rowley nickname of Charles II as father of many (illegitimate) children; *Old Rowley* was the name of a stallion in the royal stud, noted for its many offspring.

Rowley Mile at Newmarket was named after Charles II.

Old Sarum a hill in southern England north of Salisbury, the site of an ancient Iron Age settlement and hill fort, and later of a Norman castle and town. It fell into decline after the new cathedral and town of Salisbury were established in 1220, and the site was deserted. As a famous ➤ ROTTEN *borough*, it returned two MPs until 1832.

old school tie a necktie with a characteristic pattern worn by the former pupils of a particular school, especially a public school; in transferred used, the behaviour and attitudes usually associated with the wearing of such a tie, especially conservatism and group loyalty.

> All of these initiatives ran up against the 'old school tie' attitudes of British management.
> — *Peace Magazine* May/June 1994

Old Scratch a name for the Devil, recorded from the mid 18th century; the name is an alteration of *scrat* 'a hobgoblin', from Old Norse *skratti* 'wizard, goblin, monster', perhaps also influenced by the verb 'to scratch'.

Old Serpent a name for the Devil, as in Revelation 20:2, 'And he laid hold on the dragon, that old serpent, which is the Devil'.

old sins cast long shadows proverbial saying, early 20th century. The image is developed earlier in Suckling's *Aglaura* 'Our sins, like to our shadows, When our day is in its glory scarce appear: Towards our evening how great and monstrous they are!' Current usage, however, is likely to refer to the wrong done by one generation affecting its descendants.

> 'The father was no good. Drove his poor wife into her grave.' 'So I understood.' 'Old sins cast long shadows.'
> — Caroline Graham *The Killings at Badger's Drift* (1987)

old soldiers never die proverbial saying, early 20th century; the lines 'Old soldiers never die, They simply fade away' (1920, by the British songwriter J. Foley) may reflect a folk-song from the First World War.

In 1951, in his message to Congress, Douglas MacArthur said, 'I still remember the refrain of one of the most popular barracks ballads of that day, which proclaimed most proudly that old soldiers never die; they just fade away. I now close my military career and just fade away.'

the Old South the Southern states of the US before the civil war of 1861–5. The term is recorded in *Harper's Magazine* of July 1873, 'Never in her most boastful days did the old South, under her cherished system of slave labour, produce better cotton.'

old Spanish custom an irregular practice in a company aimed at decreasing working hours or increasing financial rewards or perquisites. Recorded from the 1930s, the origin of the term has not been explained.

Old Style the method of calculating dates using the ➤ JULIAN *calendar*, which in England and Wales was superseded by the use of the Gregorian calendar in 1752.

Old Testament the first part of the Christian Bible, comprising thirty-nine books and corresponding approximately to the Hebrew Bible. Most of the books were written in Hebrew, some in Aramaic, between about 1200 and 100 BC. They comprise the chief texts of the law, history, prophecy, and wisdom literature of the ancient people of Israel.

Old Uncle Tom Cobleigh and all a name given to the last of a long list of persons, alluding to the ballad *Widdicombe Fair* (*c*.1800), 'Tom Pearce's old mare doth appear gashly white Wi' Bill Brewer, Jan Stewer, Peter Gurney, Peter Davy, Dan Whiddon, Harry Hawk, old Uncle Tom Cobleigh and all, Old Uncle Tom Cobleigh and all.'

Old Vic the popular name of the Royal Victoria Theatre in London, opened in 1818 as the Royal Coburg and renamed the Royal Victoria Theatre in honour of Princess (later Queen) Victoria in 1833. Under the management of Lilian Baylis from 1912 it gained an enduring reputation for its Shakespearean productions.

old wives' tale a widely held traditional belief that is now thought to be unscientific or incorrect. The phrase (and its earlier variant *old wives' fable*) is recorded from the 16th century, with the earliest example being from Tyndale's translation of the Bible (1526), in 1 Timothy 4:7, 'Cast away unghostly and old wives fables'. In Marlowe's *Faustus* (*a*. 1593) the usage is similarly dismissive, 'Tush, these are trifles and mere old wives' tales.'

Old World Europe, Asia, and Africa, regarded collectively as the part of the world known before the discovery of the Americas; the term is recorded from the late 16th century, in the poetry of John Donne.

Oldowan of, relating to, or denoting an early Lower Palaeolithic culture of Africa, dated to about 2.0–1.5 million years ago. It is characterized by primitive stone tools that are associated chiefly with *Homo habilis*. The name comes (in the 1930s) from *Oldoway*, alteration of ➤ OLDUVAI *Gorge*.

oldspeak normal English usage as opposed to technical or propagandist language, from George Orwell's *Nineteen Eighty-Four* (see ➤ NEWSPEAK).

Olduvai Gorge a gorge in northern Tanzania, in which the exposed strata contain numerous fossils (especially hominids) spanning the full range of the Pleistocene period.

'ole see ➤ BETTER *'ole*.

olio a hotchpotch, a mixture of heterogeneous elements; literally, a dish of Spanish and Portuguese origin, prepared from pieces of meat and poultry, bacon, pumpkin, cabbage, turnip, and other ingredients stewed and boiled with spices. The word comes (in the mid 17th century) from Spanish *olla* 'stew', from Latin *olla* 'cooking pot'.

Olivant name of Roland's horn, which was made of ivory (*oliphant*, or elephant ivory), and with which he finally summoned Charlemagne's army to Roncesvalles.

olive a small oval fruit with a hard stone and bitter flesh, green when unripe and bluish black when ripe, used as food and as a source of oil; the small evergreen tree which yields this fruit, a leaf, branch, or twig of which was traditionally regarded as an emblem of peace.

olive branch the branch of an olive tree, traditionally regarded as a symbol of peace (in allusion to the story of Noah in Genesis 8:1, in which a dove returns with an olive branch after the Flood).

> In a conciliatory mood, Microsoft's Mundie has extended an olive branch to his opponents.
> — *EE Times* 14 July 1997

olive crown a garland of olive leaves worn on the head as a symbol of victory.

Oliver see also ➤ BATH *Oliver*.

Oliver the companion of Roland in the *Chanson de Roland* and one of the paladins, who at Roncesvalles finally persuades his friend to summon Charlemagne to their aid by blowing the ivory horn ➤ OLIVANT.
　　See also ➤ *a* ROLAND *for an Oliver*.

Mount of Olives the highest point in the range of hills to the east of Jerusalem, a holy place for both Judaism and Christianity and frequently mentioned in the Bible. It was said to have been the site of Christ's ascension, and the Garden of Gethsemane is located nearby. Its slopes have been a sacred Jewish burial ground for centuries. It is also known as *Olivet*.

Olivet another name for the ➤ *Mount of* OLIVES.

Olivetan a member of a religious order founded in 1313 by John Tolomei of Siena, and following the Benedictine rule. The name comes from Monte *Oliveto* (or Uliveto) near Siena, the site of the mother house.

olla podrida another term for ➤ OLIO. The phrase comes from Spanish, and means literally 'rotten pot', from Latin *olla* 'jar' + *putridus* 'rotten'.

Olympia a plain in Greece, in the western Peloponnese. In ancient Greece it was the site of the chief sanctuary of the god Zeus, the place where the original Olympic Games were held.

Olympiad a period of four years between Olympic Games, used by the ancient Greeks in dating events.

Olympic Games an ancient Greek festival with athletic, literary, and musical competitions held at Olympia every four years, traditionally from 776 BC until abolished by the Roman emperor Theodosius I in AD 393.
　　In modern times, the phrase designates a sports festival held every four years in different venues, instigated by the Frenchman Baron de Coubertin (1863–1937) in 1896. Athletes representing nearly 150 countries now compete for gold, silver, and bronze medals in more than twenty sports.

Olympic village the place where the competitors in the modern Olympic games are housed for the duration of the event.

Olympus in Greek mythology, the home of the twelve greater gods and the court of Zeus, identified in later antiquity with Mount Olympus in Greece.

om in Hinduism and Tibetan Buddhism, a mystic syllable, considered the most sacred mantra. It appears at the beginning and end of most Sanskrit recitations, prayers, and texts. The word comes from Sanskrit, and is sometimes regarded as three sounds, *a-u-m*, symbolic of the three major Hindu deities.

om mane padme hum in Hinduism and Tibetan Buddhism, a mantra or auspicious formula, from Sanskrit, literally meaning 'oh (goddess) Manipadma', reinterpreted as 'oh jewel in the lotus'.

Omar I (*c*.581–644), Muslim caliph 634–44. Converted to Islam in 617, after becoming caliph he conquered Syria, Palestine, and Egypt, in the course of which (*c*.641) the library at Alexandria was burnt. In his account of this in *The Decline and Fall of the Roman Empire* (1776–8), Gibbon attributes to Omar the comment, 'If these writings of the Greeks agree with the book of God, they are useless and need not be preserved; if they disagree, they are pernicious and ought to be destroyed.'

Omar Khayyám (d.1123), Persian poet, mathematician, and astronomer. His *rubáiyát* (quatrains), found in *The Rubáiyát of Omar Khayyám* (translation by Edward Fitzgerald published 1859), are meditations on the mysteries of existence and celebrations of worldly pleasures.

ombre a trick-taking card game for three people using a pack of forty cards, popular in Europe in the 17th–18th centuries. The name comes from Spanish *hombre* 'man', with reference to one player seeking to win the pool.

ombudsman an official appointed to investigate individuals' complaints against maladministration, especially that of public authorities. The word comes (in the 1950s) from Swedish, meaning 'legal representative'.

Omdurman a city in central Sudan, on the Nile opposite Khartoum, which in 1885, following the victory of the Mahdi (Muhammad Ahmad) and his forces over the British, was made the capital of the Mahdist state of Sudan. In 1898 it was recaptured by the British after the Battle of Omdurman, Kitchener's decisive victory over the Mahdi's successor, which marked the end of the uprising.

omega the last letter of the Greek alphabet (Ω, ω), transliterated as 'o' or 'ō'; figuratively, the last of a series, the final development.

See also ➤ ALPHA *and omega.*

you cannot make an omelette without breaking eggs proverbial saying, mid 19th century; often used in the context of a regrettable political necessity which is said to be justified because it will benefit the majority.

omen an event regarded as a portent of good or evil. Recorded from the late 16th century, the word comes from Latin, but its ultimate origin is unknown.

See also ➤ BIRD *of ill omen.*

Omer in Judaism, a sheaf of corn or omer of grain presented as an offering on the second day of Passover; the period of 49 days between this day and Pentecost. The name comes from Hebrew '*ōmer*, an ancient Hebrew dry measure, the tenth part of an ephah.

counting of the omer the period of 49 days, formally counted by the Jews, from the offering of the sheaf on Passover, until Pentecost, as instructed in Leviticus 23:16, 'Even unto the morrow after the seventh sabbath shall ye number fifty days'.

omertà (as practised by the Mafia) a code of silence about criminal activity and a refusal to give evidence to the police. Recorded from the late 19th century, the word is Italian, and is either a regional variation of Italian *umiltà* 'humility' (with reference to the Mafia code which enjoins submission of the group to the leader as well as silence on all Mafia concerns), or Old Spanish *hombredad* 'manliness'.

omicron the fifteenth letter of the Greek alphabet (**O**, **o**), transliterated as 'o'.

omnibus from the early 19th century, a term for large public road vehicle for carrying numerous passengers; the word was introduced from French, and it has been suggested that it derives from vehicles run from 1825 by a former Napoleonic officer called Baudry from Nantes to a nearby bathing place which he owned; the idea for the name is said to have come from a tradesman with the surname Omnès who had the legend *Omnes omnibus* written

on the name-plate of his firm. Another suggestion is that the *omnibus* of the early 19th century may have been so named partly in order to make a distinction with the earlier *carosses* (first suggested by Pascal, and found from the late 17th century) which were more exclusive in the passengers they would accept.

From this developed the current use of a volume containing several novels or other items previously published separately.

French *omnibus* comes from Latin, literally 'for all', dative plural of *omnis*.

See also ➤ CLAPHAM *omnibus.*

omnium gatherum a collection of miscellaneous people or things. Recorded from the early 16th century, the phrase is mock Latin, from Latin *omnium* 'of all' and *gather* + the Latin suffix *-um.*

Omophore in Manichaean cosmology, the giant who carries the earth on his shoulders.

omophorion a vestment resembling the pallium of the Latin Church, worn by patriarchs and bishops.

OMOV abbreviation for, *one member, one vote,* a system of balloting within a trade union or political party whereby each member has a single vote rather than delegates casting block votes.

The slogan *one man, one vote* as advocating the principle of universal suffrage is recorded from the mid 19th century, but in modern times the understanding of 'man' to mean 'person' is less acceptable. The modification of *one member, one vote* developed in the 1980s, in association with a particular situation: the traditional block voting on behalf of their membership by Trade Union representatives within the Labour Party. *OMOV* as a slogan and principle became a focus of interest in the modernizing of the Labour Party.

Omphale in Greek mythology, queen of Lydia, to whom Hercules was sent by the Delphic Oracle to work as a slave for a year as punishment; he was forced to dress in women's clothes during his servitude, while Omphale wore his lion skin and wielded his club.

omphalos a conical stone (especially that at Delphi) representing the navel of the earth in ancient Greek mythology.

on-message in accordance with a planned or intended message; (of the actions or statements of a political party member) in accordance with official party policy; an expression recorded from the early 1990s.

> No government in history has been as obsessed with public relations as this one . . . Speaking for myself, if there is a message I want to be off it.
> — Jeremy Paxman in *Daily Telegraph* 3 July 1998

Onan in the Bible, a son of Judah (Genesis 38:9), who was ordered by his father to beget children with the wife of his brother who had died childless. He did not wish to beget children who would not belong to him, so he did not complete copulation but 'let his seed fall on the ground', for which God punished him with death. Although Onan's sin is taken by modern biblical scholars to have been his failure to fulfil the obligation of marrying his brother's widow, this passage has frequently been taken in the Christian (as in the Jewish) tradition to show divine condemnation of autoeroticism.

once see also ➤ ONCE *in a blue moon.*

once a—, always a— proverbial saying, the formula is found from the early 17th century.

once a priest, always a priest proverbial saying, mid 19th century.

once a whore, always a whore proverbial saying, early 17th century.

once bitten, twice shy proverbial saying, mid 19th century.

once upon a time a long time ago, the conventional opening to a narrative, and especially a fairy story, recorded from the late 17th century.

one see also ➤ *one man's* MEAT *is another man's poison,* ➤ *one* SWALLOW *does not make a summer,* ➤ ROUTE *One,* ➤ THREE *in One.*

when one door shuts, another opens proverbial saying, late 16th century.

one for sorrow; two for mirth; three for a wedding, four for a birth proverbial saying, mid 19th century; referring to the number of magpies seen at the same time.

one for the mouse, one for the crow, one to rot, one to grow proverbial saying, mid 19th century; referring to sowing seed.

one nail drives out another proverbial saying, mid 13th century.

One Nation a nation not divided by social inequality; in Britain in the 1990s, especially regarded as the objective of a branch of or movement within the Conservative Party, seen as originating in the paternalistic form of Toryism advocated by ➤ DISRAELI.

In 1950 a group of Conservative MPs, then in opposition, published under the title *One Nation* a pamphlet asserting their view of the necessity of greater commitment by their party to the social services; these ideas had great influence when the party returned to government in the following year.

In the 1990s, *One Nation* returned to prominence in the debate between the right and left wings of the Conservative Party on the effect of the Thatcherite policies of the 1980s.

See also ➤ TWO *nations.*

the one that got away traditional angler's description of a large fish that just eluded capture, from the comment 'you should have seen the one that got away.'

one year's seeding makes seven years' weeding proverbial saying, late 19th century; the allusion is to the danger of allowing weeds to grow and seed themselves.

Oneida Community a religious community, founded in New York State in 1848 and originally embracing primitive Christian beliefs and radical social and economic ideas, later relaxed. It became a joint-stock company in 1881.

The *Oneida* were an American Indian people formerly inhabiting upper New York State, one of the five peoples comprising the original Iroquois confederacy, and the name comes from a local word meaning 'erected stone', the name of successive principal Oneida settlements, near which, by tradition, a large syenite boulder was erected.

oneiromancy the interpretation of dreams in order to foretell the future. The word comes from Greek *oneiros* 'dream'.

ongon in the shamanist religion of the Buriats of Mongolia, an image of a god or spirit supposed to be endowed with a certain power; a fetish.

onion dome a dome which bulges in the middle and rises to a point, used especially in Russian church architecture.

onocentaur in Greek mythology, a centaur with the body of an ass, rather than of a horse; the first element comes from *onos* 'ass'.

onomancy divination from names or the letters of a name, as from the number of vowels or the sum of the numerical value of the letters.

onomatopoeia the formation of a word from a sound associated with what is named (e.g. *cuckoo*, *sizzle*). Recorded from the late 16th century, the term comes from Greek *onomatopoiia* 'word-making'.

Ontario a province of eastern Canada, between Hudson Bay and the Great Lakes, which was settled by the French and English in the 17th century, ceded to Britain in 1763, and became one of the original four provinces in the Dominion of Canada in 1867.

ontological argument in philosophy, the argument that God, being defined as most great or perfect, must exist, since a God who exists is greater than a God who does not.

ontology the branch of metaphysics dealing with the nature of being. Recorded from the early 18th century, the word comes from modern Latin ontologia, from Greek *ōn, ont-* 'being', + the suffix *-logy* denoting a subject of study or interest.

onycha an ingredient of incense used in Mosaic ritual, consisting of the opercula (the secreted plates closing the aperture of the shell when the animal is retracted) of marine molluscs. Recorded from late Middle English (in Wyclif's translation of the Bible) the word comes via Latin from Greek *onux* 'nail', from the resemblance of the molluscan operculum to a fingernail.

onymous having a name; (of a writing) bearing the name of the author; (of an author) giving his or her name. Recorded from the late 18th century, the word is a shortening of *anonymous*.

onyx a semi-precious variety of agate with different colours in layers. In the Bible it is one of the precious jewels said in Exodus 28:20 to have been set in the high priest's breastplate, and in Revelation 21:20 it is said to be one of the twelve jewels set in the wall of the New Jerusalem.

Oom Paul a nickname for President Kruger (1825–1904). (*Oom* in Afrikaans, meaning 'Uncle', was a traditional form of respectful address to an older or elderly man.)

Jan Hendrik Oort (1900–92), Dutch astronomer. He proved that the Galaxy is rotating, and determined the position and orbital period of the sun within it. Oort also proposed the existence of a cloud of incipient comets beyond the orbit of Pluto, now named after him.

oozlum bird in a nonsense rhyme by W. T. Goodge, a mythical bird displaying ridiculous behaviour:

> It's a curious bird, the Oozlum,
> And a bird that's mighty wise,
> For it always flies tail-first to
> Keep the dust out of its eyes!
> — W. T. Goodge *Hits! Skits! & Jingles!* (1899)

opal a gemstone consisting of a quartz-like form of hydrated silica, typically semi-transparent and showing many small points of shifting colour against a pale or dark ground; it is often referred to allusively to evoke the idea of changing colours.

The belief that opals are unlucky is recorded from the 19th century, and may originate with Walter Scott's novel *Anne of Geierstein* (1829), in which an opal brings ill fortune on its owner.

Open Brethren one of the two principal divisions of the Plymouth Brethren (the other is the Exclusive Brethren), formed in 1849 as a result of doctrinal and other differences. The Open Brethren are less rigorous and less exclusive in matters such as conditions for membership and contact with outsiders than the Exclusive Brethren.

open sesame in the tale of ➤ ALI *Baba* and the Forty Thieves, the magic words by which the door of the robbers' cave was made to fly open; the phrase is thus used for a means of securing access to what would normally be inaccessible.

Open University (in the UK) a university that teaches mainly by broadcasting, correspondence, and summer schools, and is open to those without formal academic qualifications. Introduced in the 1960s, an early name for it was the ➤ UNIVERSITY *of the Air*.

opera a dramatic work in one or more acts, set to music for singers and instrumentalists. Recorded for the mid 17th century, the word comes via Italian from Latin, meaning literally 'labour, work'. The earliest uses in English illustrate *opera* as an Italian word, as in this passage from the diarist John Evelyn:

> Streets . . . so incomparably fair and uniform, that you would imagine your self rather in some Italian *Opera*, where the diversity of scenes surprise the beholder, than in a real city.'
> — John Evelyn *State of France* (1652)

See also ➤ *the* BEGGARS' *Opera*, ➤ SOAP *opera*.

opéra bouffe a French comic opera, with dialogue in recitative and characters drawn from everyday life.

opera buffa a comic opera (usually in Italian), especially one with characters drawn from everyday life.

opéra comique an opera (usually in French) on a light-hearted theme, with spoken dialogue.

the opera isn't over till the fat lady sings proverbial saying, late 20th century.

opera seria an opera (especially one of the 18th century in Italian) on a serious, usually classical or mythological theme.

Ophelia the tragic heroine of Shakespeare's *Hamlet*, who is driven mad by the death of her father and Hamlet's rejection of her; while making garlands of flowers she falls into the river and is drowned. The image of Ophelia floating face upwards in the water, surrounded by her flowers, became a famous Pre-Raphaelite painting by Millais for which Lizzie Siddal was the model.

Ophir (in the Bible) an unidentified region, perhaps in SE Arabia, famous for its fine gold and precious stones.

Ophite a member of an early Gnostic sect which worshipped the serpent which tempted Eve to eat the apple (Genesis 3) as the liberator of humankind by bringing knowledge and revolt into the world.

Recorded from the early 17th century, the name comes via Latin from Greek *ophis* 'snake'.

Ophiuchus in astronomy, a large constellation (the Serpent Bearer or Holder), said to represent a man in the coils of a snake, and mentioned by Ptolemy. A misreading of the name may have given rise to the heraldic term ➤ OPINICUS.

Opimian wine a celebrated ancient Roman wine, mentioned by Pliny in his *History of the World*, laid down in the consulship of L. *Opimius* (121 BC).

opinicus a composite imaginary creature with the head and wings of an eagle or griffin and the body and legs of a lion. The term is recorded in heraldry books from the late 18th century, and may represent an error for ➤ OPHIUCHUS.

Opinionist a member of a sect in the 15th century who held that the only true Popes were those who practised voluntary poverty.

opinions see ➤ *so many* MEN, *so many opinions*.

opium a reddish-brown heavy-scented addictive drug prepared from the juice of the opium poppy and used illicitly as a narcotic; opium addiction is a strong theme in 19th century literature. In 1822 ➤ *Thomas De* QUINCEY had published his autobiographical *Confessions of an Opium Eater*, and the figure of John Jasper in Dickens's unfinished *The Mystery of Edwin Drood* (1870) is made more sinister by the account of his visit to the opium den kept by 'Her Royal Highness, the Princess Puffer'.

From the 17th century, the word has also been in figurative use, as in Tom Paine's comment on Parliament in *The Rights of Man* pt 2 (1792), 'The Minister, whoever he at any time may be, touches it as with an opium wand, and it sleeps obedience.'

Recorded from late Middle English, the word comes via Latin from Greek *opion* 'poppy juice', from *opos* 'juice', from an Indo-European root meaning 'water'.

opium of the people something regarded as inducing a false and unrealistic sense of contentment among people. The term originated as a translation of German *Opium des Volks*, used by Karl Marx in reference to religion:

> Religion is the sigh of the oppressed creature, the heart of a heartless world . . . It is the opium of the people.
> — Karl Marx *A Contribution to the Critique of Hegel's Philosophy of Right* (1843–4)

Opium Wars two wars involving China regarding the question of commercial rights. That between Britain and China (1839–42) followed China's attempt to prohibit the illegal importation of opium from British India into China. The second, involving Britain and France against China (1856–60), followed Chinese restrictions on foreign trade. Defeat of the Chinese resulted in the ceding of Hong Kong to Britain and the opening of five 'treaty ports' to traders.

oppidan at Eton College: a pupil not on the foundation who boards in a boarding-house (formerly with a private family in the town) rather than in the College itself, as opposed to a *colleger*. The word originally meant 'an inhabitant of a town', and comes from Latin *oppidum* 'town'.

oppidum an ancient Celtic fortified town, especially one under Roman rule. The word is Latin for 'town'.

opportunity see also ➤ LAND *of Opportunity*, ➤ WINDOW *of opportunity*.

opportunity makes a thief proverbial saying, early 13th century.

opportunity never knocks twice at any man's door proverbial saying, mid 16th century.

the **Opposition** in the UK, the principal parliamentary party opposed to that in office. The term 'His Majesty's Opposition' was first used in a debate by the radical politician John Cam Hobhouse (1786–1869), later Lord Broughton, 10 April 1826, when Hansard records that he said that 'For his own part, he thought it was more hard on his majesty's opposition (a laugh) to compel them to take this course.' In his *Recollections of a Long Life* (1865), Hobhouse recorded that when he invented the phrase Canning 'paid me a compliment on the fortunate hit'.

Grand Ole Opry (trademark name for) a concert of country music broadcast from Nashville, Tennessee; the type of music forming part of this. The name represents a dialect form of *opera*.

Ops in Roman mythology, goddess of abundance and harvest, associated with Saturn. She is referred to in *Paradise Lost* as Saturn's consort, and in Keats's *Hyperion* as one of the fallen Titans.

optime a person placed in the second or third class, called respectively senior and junior optimes, in the Mathematical Tripos at Cambridge. The phrase comes from Latin *optime disputasti* 'you have disputed very well'.

optimism hopefulness and confidence about the future; the philosophical doctrine, especially as set forth by Leibniz, that this world is the best of all possible worlds. Recorded from the mid 18th century, the word comes via French from Latin *optimum* 'best thing'.

opus Alexandrinum a pavement mosaic work widely used in Byzantium in the 9th century and later in Italy, consisting of coloured stone, glass, and semiprecious stones arranged in intricate geometric patterns.

opus anglicanum the fine pictorial embroidery produced in England in the Middle Ages, especially between *c.*1100 and *c.*1350, characterized by the depiction of lively human and animal figures, and the use of gold cloth, and used especially for ecclesiastical vestments.

Opus Dei a Roman Catholic organization of laymen and priests founded in Spain in 1928 with the aim of re-establishing Christian ideals in society through the implementation of them in the lives of its members.

opus Dei in the Christian Church, liturgical worship regarded as man's primary duty to God. The Latin phrase, meaning literally 'the work of God', is attributed to St Benedict but is attested from the 5th century in the sense of Divine Office or worship.

opus sectile an originally Roman floor decoration made up of pieces shaped individually to fit the pattern or design, as distinct from mosaic which uses regularly shaped pieces.

opus signinum an originally Roman flooring material consisting of broken tiles etc. mixed with lime mortar. The phrase, which is Latin, means 'work of *Signia*' a town (now *Segni*) in Central Italy famous for its tiles.

or gold or yellow, as a heraldic tincture. Recorded from the early 16th century, the word comes via French from Latin *aurum* 'gold'. It is one of the two metals used in heraldry, the other being ➤ ARGENT.

oracle a priest or priestess acting as a medium through whom advice or prophecy was sought from the gods in classical antiquity, or a place at which such advice or prophecy was sought; in extended use, the term may be used for a person or thing regarded as an infallible authority or guide on something. *Oracle* is also used to denote the response or message provided by such a source, especially one that is ambiguous or obscure.

Recorded from late Middle English, the word comes via Old French from Latin *oraculum*, from *orare* 'speak'.

See also ➤ DELPHIC *oracle*, ➤ SIBYLLINE *oracles*.

oracle bones the bones of a ritually-killed animal, carved with script and used in ancient China for divination.

Oral Law the part of Jewish religious law believed to have been passed down by oral tradition before being collected in the Mishnah.

Orange see also ➤ AGENT *Orange*, ➤ *all* LOMBARD *Street*.

House of Orange the Dutch royal house, originally a princely dynasty of the principality centred on the town of Orange in France in the 16th century.

Members of the family held the position of stadtholder or magistrate from the mid 16th until the late 18th century. In 1689 William of Orange became King William III of Great Britain and Ireland and the son of the last stadtholder became King William I of the United Netherlands in 1815.

See also ➤ WILLIAM *of Orange*, ➤ WILLIAM *the Silent*.

orange blossom flowers from an orange tree, traditionally worn by the bride at a wedding; *orange blossom* may thus be taken as a symbol of marriage. The custom appears to have been introduced to Britain in the 1820s from France, where it was said to be customary for a bride to wear a crown of orange buds and blossoms. Thackeray in *Vanity Fair* (1848) explains it as an emblem of 'female purity', but this interpretation of the symbolism appears to be his own.

Orange Free State an area and former province in central South Africa, situated to the north of the Orange River. First settled by Boers after the Great Trek, the area became a province of the Union of South Africa in 1910 and in 1994 became one of the new provinces of South Africa.

Orange Order a Protestant political society in Ireland, especially in Northern Ireland. The Orange Order was formed in 1795 (as the Association of Orangemen) for the defence of Protestantism and maintenance of Protestant ascendancy in Ireland, and was probably named from the wearing of orange badges as a symbol of adherence to William III (➤ WILLIAM *of Orange*), who defeated the Catholic James II at the Battle of the Boyne in 1690.

The ➤ ORANGE *Order*, organized as Freemasons' Lodges, spread beyond Ireland to Britain and many parts of the former British Empire. In the late 19th and early 20th centuries it was strengthened in the north of Ireland in its campaign to resist the Home Rule bill; in a letter of 1886 Lord Randolph Churchill commented that 'I decided some time ago that if the G. O. M. [Gladstone] went for Home Rule, the Orange card would be the one to play.' The Order has continued to form a core of Protestant Unionist opinion since; in the late 20th century, the annual ➤ MARCHING *season* of the Orange Lodges has increasingly been a focus of tension between Unionist and Nationalist groups.

Orangeman a member of the ➤ ORANGE *Order*.

oratio obliqua Latin phrase for indirect speech.

oratio recta Latin phrase for direct speech.

oration see ➤ CREWIAN *oration*.

Orator Henley nickname of John Henley (1692–1756), an eccentric London preacher, who in 1724 had been forced to leave London for the living of Chelmondiston in Suffolk. Believing his gifts to be unappreciated within the Church, from 1726 he rented rooms about the market-house in Newport Market, where each Sunday he preached a morning sermon, and each Wednesday delivered a lecture on 'some other science'. His preaching was accompanied by elaborate ritual, and his pulpit was decorated with gold and velvet. He regarded himself as one who had restored eloquence to the Church; Pope addressed him in the *Dunciad* as 'Oh great restorer of the good old Stage, Preacher at once, and Zany of thy age!'

Orator Hunt nickname of the radical politician Henry Hunt (1773–1835), described in the Dictionary of National Biography as 'a violent and stentorian, but impressive, speaker'.

Oratorian in the Roman Catholic Church, a priest who is a member of the ➤ ORATORY.

oratorio a large-scale, usually narrative musical work for orchestra and voices, typically on a sacred theme, performed without costume, scenery, or action. The form arose in the early 17th century, from the services of the ➤ ORATORY.

Oratory in the Roman Catholic Church, a religious society of secular priests founded in Rome in 1564 to provide plain preaching and popular services and established in various countries.

The Oratory of St Philip Neri was constituted at Rome in 1564 and recognized by the Pope in 1575. It was so named from the small chapel or oratory built over one of the aisles of the Church of St. Jerome, in which St Philip Neri (1515–95) and his followers, 'Fathers of the Oratory', carried on their work for six years before 1564. In 1577 the congregation moved to the new church (*Chiesa Nuova*) of the Valicella, in which were conducted the musical services thence called, in Italian, ➤ ORATORIO.

Oratory meaning 'a small chapel, especially for private worship', is recorded from Middle English, and comes ultimately from Latin *orare* 'pray, speak'.

orb a golden globe surmounted by a cross, forming part of the regalia of a monarch. Recorded from late Middle English in the sense 'circle', the word comes from Latin *orbis* 'ring'.

orbi see ➤ URBI *et orbi*.

orc in fantasy literature and games, a member of an imaginary race of human-like creatures, characterized as ugly, warlike, and malevolent. The word (denoting an ogre) is recorded from the late 16th century, perhaps from Latin *orcus* 'hell' or Italian *orco* 'demon, monster', influenced by obsolete *orc* 'ferocious sea creature' and by Old English *orcneas* 'monsters'. The current sense is due to the use of the word in Tolkien's fantasy adventures.

See also ➤ OGRE.

Orcades Latin name for the Orkney Islands.

Orcus in Roman mythology, a name (of unknown origin) for Dis, the god of the Underworld, or the Underworld itself; ultimately origin of the word ➤ OGRE and perhaps ➤ ORC.

ordeal an ancient test of guilt or innocence, especially among Germanic peoples, by subjection of the accused to severe pain, survival of which was taken as divine proof of innocence. In Anglo-Saxon and Norman England, until its abolition in 1215, it took four forms: fire ordeal, hot water ordeal, cold water ordeal, and trial by combat; later applied to analogous modes of determining innocence or guilt found in other societies.

Recorded in Old English and of Germanic origin, the word is related to German *urteilen* 'give judgement', from a base meaning 'share out'. The word is not found in Middle English (except once in Chaucer's *Troilus*); the modern use begins in late 16th-century accounts of these traditional tests.

order¹ any of the nine grades of angelic beings in the ➤ CELESTIAL *hierarchy* as formulated by Pseudo-Dionysius.

order² a society of monks, nuns, or friars living under the same religious, moral, and social regulations and discipline, such as **the Benedictine Order, the Franciscan Order.**

See also ➤ *Order of St* CLARE, ➤ *Order of the* AN-NUNCIATION, ➤ *Order of the* HOLY *Ghost,* ➤ *Order of the* VISITATION.

order³ a society of knights bound by a common rule of life and having a combined military and monastic character. Also, an institution founded by a monarch along the lines of certain medieval crusading monastic orders for the purpose of conferring an honour or honours for merit on those appointed to it.

See also ➤ *Order of* DANNEBROG, ➤ *Order of St* MICHAEL *and St George,* ➤ *Order of St* PATRICK, ➤ *Order of the* BATH, ➤ *Order of the* BRITISH *Empire,* ➤ *Order of the* ELEPHANT, ➤ *Order of the* GARTER, ➤ *Order of the* GOLDEN *Fleece,* ➤ *Order of the* THIS-TLE.

order⁴ any of the five classical styles of architecture (Doric, Ionic, Corinthian, Tuscan, and Composite)

based on the proportions of the columns and the type and amount of decoration.

Order! a call for silence or the observance of the prescribed procedures by someone in charge of a meeting or legislative assembly, such as the Speaker of the House of Commons.

Order in Council a sovereign's order on an administrative matter, given on the advice of the Privy Council.

Order Paper in the United Kingdom and Canada, a paper on which the day's business for a legislative assembly is entered; in the House of Commons, members traditionally wave their order papers to signify support for a speaker.

die on the Order Paper in Canada, (of a bill) fail to be voted on before the end of a legislative session.

Ordericus Vitalis (1075–1142/3), born near Shrewsbury of a Norman father and probably English mother, a monk of St Évroul in Normandy. He wrote between 1114 and 1141 his *Ecclesiastical History of England and Normandy* in Latin, covering events from the beginning of the Christian era down to 1141, which is one of the standard authorities for the Norman period. His accounts of the Conquest and other events show a lively sympathy with the English and a predominant interest in English matters.

orders see ➤ OBEY *orders, if you break owners.*

ordinal number a number defining a thing's position in a series, such as 'first', 'second', or 'third'. Ordinal numbers are used as adjectives, nouns, and pronouns.

Ordinary¹ those parts of a Roman Catholic service, especially the Mass, which do not vary from day to day.

Ordinary² the chaplain of Newgate prison, whose duty it was to prepare condemned prisoners for death.

ordinary in heraldry, any of the simplest principal charges used in coats of arms, usually having a basic geometrical shape (especially chief, pale, bend, fess, bar, chevron, cross, saltire).

ordnance mounted guns, cannon; from the late 15th century, the branch of government service dealing especially with military stores and materials, under the control of the **Master of the Ordnance.**

(The word was originally a variant of *ordinance*, and comes via Old French and medieval Latin from Latin *ordinare* 'put in order'.)

Ordnance Survey (in the UK) an official survey organization, originally under the direction of the Master of the Ordnance, preparing large-scale detailed maps of the whole country; it originated in a topographic survey (1784) of the Trigonometric Society.

oread in Greek and Roman mythology, a nymph believed to inhabit high mountains. The name comes ultimately from Greek *oros* 'mountain'.

Oregon Trail a route across the central US, from the Missouri to Oregon, some 3,000 km (2,000 miles) in length. It was used chiefly in the 1840s by settlers moving west.

Francisco de Orellana (*c*.1490–*c*.1546), Spanish soldier and first explorer of the Amazon River; on his return, his accounts of encounters with tribes led by women appears to have led to the naming of the river as the Amazon.

oremus in the Roman Catholic Church, a liturgical prayer introduced by the word *oremus*, Latin for 'let us pray.'

orenda invisible magic power believed by the Iroquois to pervade all natural objects as a spiritual energy. Recorded from the early 20th century, *orenda* was coined in English as the supposed Huron form of a Mohawk word.

Orestes the son of ➤ AGAMEMNON and ➤ CLYTEMNESTRA, and brother of ➤ ELECTRA. Having grown to manhood in exile, he returned to Argos and killed his mother and her lover Aegisthus to avenge the murder of Agamemnon; pursued by the avenging Furies for the crime of matricide he fled to the shrine of Apollo at Delphi, where ultimately he was pardoned by Athena. The story is the subject of Aeschylus's trilogy, the *Oresteia*.

orfèvrerie goldsmiths' work, and in medieval times, name for the goldsmiths' quarter in London. Recorded from Middle English, the word comes via French from popular Latin *aurifabrum* 'worker in gold, goldsmith'.

organ an organ is the emblem of ➤ St CECILIA, patron saint of music.

orgies secret rites used in the worship of Bacchus, Dionysus, and other Greek and Roman deities, celebrated with dancing, drunkenness, and singing. Recorded from the early 16th century, the word comes via French and Latin from Greek *orgia* 'secret rites or revels'.

orgone a supposed excess sexual energy or life force distributed throughout the universe which can be collected and stored for subsequent therapeutic use. Recorded from the 1940s, the word comes from the psychoanalytical theory of Wilhelm Reich (1897–1957).

orgulous a poetic and literary term for 'haughty'. Recorded from Middle English, and coming from Old French *orguillus*, from *orguill* 'pride', the word was rare from the 16th century until used by Robert Southey and Sir Walter Scott as a historical archaism and affected by 19th-century journalists.

Oriana a name frequently applied by poets to Elizabeth I; in the medieval Spanish or Portuguese romance *Amadis of Gaul*, the princess of Britain with whom the hero Amadis is in love is named *Oriana*.

orichalc a yellow metal prized in ancient times, probably a form of brass or a similar alloy, although some writers treated it as a fabulous metal. The name comes (in late Middle English, via Latin) from Greek *oreikhalkon*, literally 'mountain copper'.

oriel a large polygonal recess in a building, typically built out from an upper storey and supported from the ground or on corbels; a window in such a structure.

the Orient a poetic and literary name for the countries of the East, especially east Asia. The word comes (in late Middle English, via Old French) from Latin *orient*- 'rising or east', from *oriri* 'to rise'.

pearl of orient a pearl from the Indian seas, as distinguished from those of less beauty found in European mussels; generally, a brilliant or precious pearl.

Orient Express a train which ran between Paris and Istanbul and other Balkan cities, via Vienna, from 1883 to 1977; the name is also used for a successor to this train, following part of the original route. This train was the setting for one of Agatha Christie's best-known detective novels, *Murder on the Orient Express* (1934), in which the solution to the murder by multiple stabbing was that twelve people acting in concert had in turn passed through the compartment to stab the drugged and sleeping victim.

orientation the construction of a church with the longer axis running due east and west, and the chancel or chief altar at the eastern end; also, the burying of a body with the feet towards the east.

Oriflamme the sacred scarlet silk banner of St Denis given to early French kings on setting out for war by the abbot of St Denis; in extend use, a principle or ideal that serves as a rallying point in a struggle. Recorded from late Middle English, the word comes via Old French from Latin *aurum* 'gold' + *flamma* 'flame'.

Origen (*c*.185–*c*.254), Christian scholar and theologian, probably born in Alexandria. His most famous work was the *Hexapla*, an edition of the Old Testament with six or more parallel versions. His Neoplatonist theology, which taught the preexistence of souls, and that all rational beings, including the fallen angels, have free will and will ultimately be saved through God's love, was ultimately rejected by Church orthodoxy.

original sin the tendency to evil supposedly innate in all human beings, held to be inherited from Adam in consequence of the Fall. The concept of original sin was established by the writings of St Augustine and the view of some early theologians that the human will is capable of good without the help of divine grace was branded a heresy.

origo see ➤ FONS *et origo*.

the Matchless Orinda the poet Katherine Philips (1631–64) adopted the name of *Orinda* among her group of literary friends; after her early death from smallpox her collected poems were posthumously published as written by 'Mrs Katherine Philips, the Matchless Orinda' (London, 1667).

Orion in Greek mythology, a giant and hunter who was changed into a constellation at his death. His association with the constellation is very early, being mentioned in Homer.

The constellation itself, said to represent a hunter holding a club and shield, lies on the celestial equator and contains many bright stars, including Rigel, Betelgeuse, and a line of three that form **Orion's Belt**.

Orion's hound another term for the ➤ DOG *Star*.

orison archaic term for a prayer. Recorded from Middle English, the word comes via Old French from Latin *oratio(n-)* 'speech', from *orare* 'speak, pray'.

Orisha (in southern Nigeria) any of several minor gods. The term is also used in various black religious cults of South America and the Caribbean.

Orkhon any of a number of 8th century stone monuments discovered in northern Mongolia in 1889; the extinct Turkic language in which inscriptions on these monuments are written.

Orkney Islands a group of more than seventy islands off the NE tip of Scotland. Colonized by the Vikings in the 9th century, they came into Scottish possession in 1472, having previously been ruled by Norway and Denmark (together with Shetland) as security against the unpaid dowry of Margaret of Denmark after her marriage to James III of Scotland.

Orlando the Italian form of ➤ ROLAND, a hero of the romances of Charlemagne.

Orlando Furioso a poem by Ariosto, published in its complete form in 1532, designed to exalt the house of Este and its legendary ancestor Rogero (Ruggiero), and to continue the story of Orlando's love for Angelica begun in ➤ ORLANDO *Innamorato*.

Orlando Innamorato a poem by Boiardo published 1487, on the love of Orlando (➤ ROLAND in the Charlemagne romances) for Angelica, princess of Cathay.

orle in heraldry, a narrow border inset from the edge of a shield, a series of charges placed **in orle**. Recorded from the late 16th century, the word comes via French from Latin *ora* 'edge'.

Orleanist a person supporting the claim to the French throne of the descendants of the Duke of *Orleans* (1640–1701), younger brother of Louis XIV, especially Louis Philippe (1830–48), known as the ➤ CITIZEN *King*.

Orleans a city in central France on the Loire which in 1429 was the scene of Joan of Arc's first victory over the English during the Hundred Years War; *Orleans* was also one of the main royal duchies of medieval France, originally created in 1344 for the younger son of Philip VI of France, and associated particularly with the ➤ ORLEANIST dynasty descended from Louis XIV's younger brother.

See also ➤ CITIZEN *King*, ➤ ÉGALITÉ, ➤ MAID of *Orleans.*

Ormazd another name for ➤ AHURA *Mazda.*

The Ormulum a Middle English poem of which about 20,000 lines survive, composed by an Augustinian canon called Orm in the late 12th century. It purports to consist of gospel paraphrases, but is in fact a series of sermons.

ornaments rubric the rubric immediately preceding the Order for Morning and Evening Prayer in the *Book of Common Prayer,* referring to the ornaments to be used in the Church of England.

Orosius (fl. early 5th century), a priest of Tarragona in Spain, disciple of St Augustine and friend of St Jerome, author of the *Historia Adversos Paganos,* a universal history and geography which was translated by the circle of King Alfred in the 890s.

orpharion a stringed instrument of the 16th and 17th centuries, resembling a bandora but tuned like an ordinary lute. The name comes (in the late 16th century) from a blend of the names *Orpheus* and *Arion,* musicians in Greek mythology.

Orpheus in Greek mythology, a poet who could entrance wild beasts with the beauty of his singing and lyre playing. He went to the underworld after the death of his wife Eurydice and secured her release from the dead, but lost her because he failed to obey the condition that he must not look back at her until they had reached the world of the living. It was said that when he was killed by being torn to pieces by maenads, his severed head floated down the river Hebrus and reached the island of Lesbos, which became the home of lyric poetry.

Orphic egg the earth or the world, supposed in the doctrine of Orphism to be egg-shaped.

Orphism a mystic religion of ancient Greece, originating in the 7th or 6th century BC and based on poems (now lost) attributed to Orpheus, emphasizing the mixture of good and evil in human nature and the necessity for individuals to rid themselves of the evil part of their nature by ritual and moral purification throughout a series of reincarnations. It had declined by the 5th century BC, but was an important influence on Pindar and Plato.

orphrey an ornamental stripe or border, especially one on an ecclesiastical vestment such as a chasuble. Recorded from Middle English, the word comes via

Old French from a medieval Latin alteration of *auriphrygium,* from Latin *aurum* 'gold' + *Phrygius* 'Phrygian' (also used in the sense 'embroidered').

orrery a clockwork model of the solar system, or of just the sun, earth, and moon. It is named after Charles Boyle (1676–1731), fourth Earl of *Orrery,* for whom a copy of the machine invented by George Graham *c.*1700 was made by the instrument-maker John Rowley.

Tower of Orthanc in Tolkien's story of the ➤ LORD *of the Rings,* the tower of the wizard Saruman.

> Those mountains, they looked like a castle, those turrets, like the Tower of Orthanc.
> — Elizabeth Arthur *Antarctic Navigation* (1995)

orthodox (of a person or their views, especially religious or political ones, or other beliefs or practices) conforming to what is generally or traditionally accepted as right or true; established and approved. The word is recorded from late Middle English, and comes from Greek *orthodoxos* (probably via ecclesiastical Latin), from *orthos* 'straight or right' + *doxa* 'opinion'.

Orthodox Church a Christian Church or federation of Churches originating in the Greek-speaking Church of the Byzantine Empire, not accepting the authority of the Pope of Rome, and using elaborate and archaic forms of service.

The chief Orthodox Churches (often known collectively as the **Eastern Orthodox Church**) include the national Churches of Greece, Russia, Bulgaria, Romania, and Serbia. The term is also used by other ancient Churches, mainly of African or Asian origin, e.g. the Coptic, Syrian, and Ethiopian Churches.

Orthodox Judaism a major branch within Judaism which teaches strict adherence to rabbinical interpretation of Jewish law and its traditional observances. There are more than 600 rules governing religious and everyday life. Orthodox Jews maintain the separation of the sexes in synagogue worship.

Feast of Orthodoxy a festival celebrated in the Orthodox Church on the first Sunday in Lent.

Orthodoxy Sunday the first Sunday in Lent, when the ➤ *Feast of* ORTHODOXY is celebrated.

Orthrus in Greek mythology, name of a dog belonging to ➤ GERYON which is killed by Hercules.

ortolan a small Eurasian songbird that was formerly eaten as a delicacy, the male having an olive-green head and yellow throat; in Disraeli's *The Young Duke* (1831) the wish is expressed, 'Let me die eating ortolans to the sound of soft music!'

Arthur Orton (1834–98) English butcher; known as ➤ *the* TICHBORNE *claimant*. In 1866 he returned to England from Australia claiming to be the heir to the valuable Tichborne estate. He lost his claim and was tried and imprisoned for perjury.

Joe Orton (1933–67), English dramatist. He wrote a number of unconventional black comedies, examining corruption, sexuality, and violence; they include *Entertaining Mr Sloane* (1964) and *Loot* (1965). Orton was murdered by his homosexual lover, who then committed suicide.

Ortygia in Greek mythology, the island which was the birthplace of Apollo and Artemis, said to have been a floating island which was afterwards fixed to the seabed. It was later identified with ➤ DELOS.

Orvietan a composition which in the 17th and 18th centuries was held to be a universal antidote against poisons, so named from its inventor, Girolamo Ferrante, being a native of *Orvieto* in central Italy.

George Orwell pseudonym of the British novelist and essayist Eric Blair (1903–50). His work is characterized by his concern about social injustice. His most famous works are *Animal Farm* (1945), a satire on Communism as it developed under Stalin, and *Nineteen Eighty-four* (1949), a dystopian account of a future state in which every aspect of life is controlled by Big Brother. He fought for the Republicans in the Spanish Civil War.

> I cannot overstate how insidious and frightening, almost Orwellian, it was.
> — *Independent* 11 January 1993

os sacrum another term for the *sacrum*, triangular bone in the lower back formed from fused vertebrae and situated between the two hip bones of the pelvis. The phrase comes from Latin translating Greek *hieron osteon* 'sacred bone', from the belief that the soul resides in it.

John Osborne (1929–94), English dramatist. His first play, *Look Back in Anger* (1956), ushered in a new era of kitchen-sink drama; its hero Jimmy Porter personified contemporary disillusioned youth, the so-called 'angry young man'.

Oscan an extinct Italic language of southern Italy, related to Umbrian and surviving in inscriptions mainly of the 4th to 1st centuries BC.

Oscar the nickname (a trademark in the US) for a gold statuette given as an Academy award. One of the several speculative stories of its origin claims that the statuette reminded Margaret Herrick, an executive director of the Academy of Motion Picture Arts and Sciences, of her uncle Oscar.

Osiris in Egyptian mythology, a god originally connected with fertility, husband of Isis and father of Horus. He is known chiefly through the story of his death at the hands of his brother Seth and his subsequent restoration to a new life as ruler of the afterlife. Under Ptolemy I his cult was combined with that of Apis to produce the cult of Serapis.

Osman I (1259–1326), Turkish conqueror, founder of the Ottoman (**Osmanli**) dynasty and empire. Osman reigned as sultan of the Seljuk Turks from 1288, conquering NW Asia Minor. He assumed the title of emir in 1299.

Osmanli old-fashioned term for ➤ OTTOMAN, named after ➤ OSMAN *I*.

Osnabrück a city in NW Germany, in Lower Saxony. In 1648 the Treaty of Westphalia, ending the Thirty Years War, was signed there and in Münster.

osprey a large fish-eating bird of prey with long narrow wings and a white underside and crown, found throughout the world. The name comes (in late Middle English) from Old French *ospres*, apparently based on Latin *ossifraga* (mentioned by Pliny and identified with the lammergeier), from *os* 'bone' + *frangere* 'to break', probably because of the lammergeier's habit of dropping bones from a height to break them and reach the marrow.

Ossa a mountain in Thessaly, NE Greece, south of Mount Olympus. In Greek mythology the giants were said to have piled Mount Olympus and Mount Ossa on to Mount Pelion in an attempt to reach heaven and destroy the gods.

> The curious desire to add the Ossa of make-believe to the Pelion of solid achievement.
> — F. McLynn *Hearts of Darkness* (1992)

Ossi in Germany, an informal (often derogatory) term for a citizen of the former German Democratic Republic. The name is probably an abbreviation of *Ostdeutsche* 'East German'.

Ossian a legendary Irish warrior and bard, whose name became well known in 1760–3 when the Scottish poet James Macpherson (1736–96) published his own verse as an alleged translation of 3rd-century Gaelic tales. His Irish name is *Oisin*.

Ossining Correctional Facility official name for the American prison of ➤ SING *Sing*.

ossuary a container or room into which the bones of dead people are placed. Recorded from the mid 17th century, the word comes from late Latin *ossuarium*, formed irregularly from Latin *os* 'bone'.

Osten see ➤ DRANG *nach Osten*.

osteomancy divination by means of bones.

Ostia an ancient city and harbour which was situated on the western coast of Italy at the mouth of the River Tiber. It was the first colony founded by ancient Rome and was a major port and commercial centre.

Ostpolitik former term for the foreign policy of détente of western European countries with reference to the former communist bloc, especially the opening of relations with the Eastern bloc by the Federal Republic of Germany (West Germany) in the 1960s.

ostracize in ancient Greece, banish (an unpopular or too powerful citizen) from a city for five or ten years by popular vote. The word comes ultimately from Greek *ostrakon* 'shell or potsherd', on which names were written in such votes.

ostracon in ancient Greece, a potsherd used as a writing surface.

ostrich it was once popularly believed that ostriches bury their heads in the sand if pursued, through incapacity to distinguish between seeing and being seen, and this supposed habit is often referred to allusively. *Ostriches* are also proverbial for their indiscriminate voracity and liking for hard substances (which are swallowed to assist the gizzard in its functions).

Ostrogoth a member of the eastern branch of the Goths, who conquered Italy in the 5th–6th centuries AD.

Lee Harvey Oswald (1939–63), American alleged assassin of John F. Kennedy. He denied the charge of assassinating the president, but was murdered before he could be brought to trial.

St Oswald (d. 642), king of Northumbria and martyr, who was killed in battle against the pagan king Penda of Mercia; his body was mutilated as a sacrifice to Odin, and his relics were subsequently dispersed. His head was buried at Lindisfarne, and was taken with the body of ➤ CUTHBERT when the monks evacuated the island in 875.

Oswald was venerated as a warrior king who combined traditional Anglo Saxon heroism with Christian fortitude and sacrifice; his feast day was celebrated from the late 7th century.

　□ **PATRONAGE** He is a patron saint of *soldiers*.

　□ **EMBLEMS** His emblems are a *head* and a *raven*.

　□ **FEAST DAY** His feast day is 5 August.

St Oswald of York (d. 992), English prelate and Benedictine monk. As Archbishop of York, he founded several monasteries and, with St Dunstan, revived the Church and learning in 10th-century England.

　□ **FEAST DAY** His feast day is 28 February.

otaku in Japan, young people who are highly skilled in or obsessed with computer technology to the detriment of their social skills. Recorded in English from the early 1990s, the word in Japanese means literally 'your house', alluding to the reluctance of such young people to leave their houses.

Othello the 'Moor of Venice', central character of Shakespeare's tragedy (1602–4), shown as a great man and successful soldier who is driven by the machinations of ➤ IAGO to believe that his young wife Desdemona has been unfaithful to him; he kills her, and attempts to have her supposed lover murdered. *Othello* may be alluded to as a type of morbid jealousy.

> Psychiatrists call it the Othello syndrome because it makes men do the strangest things in pursuit of the ones they love.
> — *Independent* 25 July 1992

The Other Club a parliamentary cross-bench dining club founded by Winston Churchill and F. E. Smith, later Lord Birkenhead.

the other day originally this meant the second day, the following or next day.

other times, other manners proverbial saying, late 16th century.

Marcus Salvius Otho (AD 32–69), Roman emperor January–April 69. He was proclaimed emperor after he had procured the death of ➤ GALBA in a conspiracy of the praetorian guard, but the German legions, led by their imperial candidate, Vitellius, defeated his troops and Otho committed suicide.

Elisha Graves Otis (1811–61), American inventor and manufacturer. He produced the first efficient elevator with a safety device in 1852, and five years later installed the first public elevator for passengers in a New York department store.

ottava rima a form of poetry consisting of stanzas of eight lines of ten or eleven syllables, rhyming *abababcc*. The word comes (in the late 18th century) from Italian, literally 'eighth rhyme'.

otter *otters* are the emblem of ➤ *St* CUTHBERT.

Otto I (912–73), king of the Germans 936–73, Holy Roman emperor 962–73; known as **Otto the Great**. As king of the Germans he carried out a policy of eastward expansion and defeated the invading Hungarians in 955 and as Holy Roman emperor he established a presence in Italy to rival that of the papacy.

Ottoman of or relating to the Turkish dynasty of ➤ OSMAN *I* (Othman I); of or relating to the branch of the Turks to which he belonged, or to the Ottoman Empire ruled by his successors.

Ottoman Empire the Turkish empire, established in northern Anatolia by Osman I at the end of the 13th century and expanded by his successors to include all of Asia Minor and much of SE Europe. After setbacks caused by the invasion of the Mongol ruler Tamerlane in 1402, Constantinople was captured in 1453 and the empire reached its zenith under Suleiman in the mid 16th century. It had greatly declined by the 19th century and collapsed after the First World War; in its declining years it was nicknamed the ➤ SICK *Man of Europe*.

oubliette a secret dungeon with access only through a trapdoor in its ceiling. Recorded from the late 18th century, the word comes from French, from *oublier* 'forget'.

Battle of Oudenarde a battle which took place in 1708 during the War of the Spanish Succession, near the town of Oudenarde in eastern Flanders, Belgium. A force of allied British and Austrian troops under the Duke of Marlborough and the Austrian general Prince Eugene of Savoy defeated the French.

Ouida pseudonym of the English novelist Marie Louise de la Ramée (1839–1908), writer of popular novels which, like *Under Two Flags* (1867), are highly-coloured romances that are typically set in a fashionable world far removed from reality.

Ouija board a board with letters, numbers, and other signs around its edge, to which a planchette,

movable pointer, or upturned glass points supposedly in answer to questions from people at a seance. The word comes (in the late 19th century) from French *oui* 'yes' + German *ja* 'yes'.

ounce¹ a unit of weight of one sixteenth of a pound avoirdupois (approximately 28 grams); a unit of one twelfth of a pound troy or apothecaries' measure, equal to 480 grains (approximately 31 grams). Recorded from Middle English, the word comes via Old French from Latin *uncia* 'twelfth part (of a pound or foot)', also the base of ➤ INCH.

ounce² another name for the snow leopard. Recorded from Middle English, the word comes from Old French *once*, earlier *lonce* (the l- being misinterpreted as the definite article), based on Latin ➤ LYNX.

an **ounce** of practice is worth a pound of precept proverbial saying, late 16th century.

our see ➤ *Our* LADY.

out-Herod Herod outdo Herod in cruelty, evil, or extravagance. The reference is to the figure of Herod in the traditional mystery play, represented as a blustering tyrant, and the phrase is first used in Shakespeare's *Hamlet* in the scene in which Hamlet speaks to the Players and warns them against this kind of acting. Revived and popularized in the 19th century, the phrase later developed a weakened use meaning, be more extreme or outrageous than (often without the implication of savagery or cruelty).

out of debt, out of danger proverbial saying, mid 17th century.

out of God's blessing into the warm sun proverbial saying, mid 16th century; explained as implying a move from a better to a worse state.

out of sight, out of mind proverbial saying, mid 13th century.

out of the frying pan into the fire proverbial saying, mid 16th century; meaning that one has escaped from one danger into a worse one.

outing the practice or policy of revealing the homosexuality of a prominent person. *Outing* first came to public attention in the US in 1990, when public allegations about the sexual orientation of some celebrities were made as a political tactic by gay rights activists; they were concerned mainly by lack of support for victims of Aids, and about what they saw as the hypocrisy of secret gays legislating against other gays.

Outing causes considerable controversy because of its implications for personal privacy and the effects on partners and relatives, a controversy which was reawakened in the UK in the mid 1990s through the activities of the group **OutRage**.

Outremer a name applied to the medieval French crusader states, including Armenia, Antioch, Tripoli, and Jerusalem, from French *outre* 'beyond' + *mer* 'sea'.

outrun the constable overspend, get into debt; the *constable* was the law-officer whose duty was to arrest debtors.

the Oval the cricket ground at Kennington in London which is the headquarters of Surrey Cricket Club. In extended use, *oval* is thus used for an oval sports field, and (in Australia) a ground for Australian Rules football.

Oval Office the office of the US President in the west wing of the White House; in extended use, the Presidency.

> It's the kind of thinking that seems to elude the Oval Office.
> — *Newsweek* 4 May 1992

ovation a processional entrance into ancient Rome by a victorious commander, of lesser honour than a triumph. Recorded from the early 16th century, the word comes from Latin, from *ovare* 'to exult'.

Thomas Overbury (1581–1613), English poet and courtier, poisoned by agents of Frances Howard, Lady Essex, whose marriage to his patron Robert Carr he had opposed.

overpaid, overfed, oversexed, and over here of American troops in Britain during the Second World War; associated with Tommy Trinder, but probably not his invention.

Overlord the codename (in full, **Operation Overlord**) for the allied invasion of German-occupied Normandy in June 1944 (➤ D-*Day*).

St Mary Overie dedication of the priory church which later became Southwark Cathedral; *Overie* may mean 'over the river' or 'over the ferry', or represent a Saxon word meaning 'on the bank'; popular legend gave Mary 'of the ferry', daughter of a ferryman, as founder of the church.

Ovid (43 BC–*c*.17 AD), Roman poet. He is particularly known for his elegiac love poems (such as the *Amores* and the *Ars Amatoria*) and for the *Metamorphoses*, a hexametric epic which retells Greek and Roman myths. In AD 8 he was exiled to Tomis for offending Augustus.

Richard Owen (1804–92), English anatomist and palaeontologist. Owen made important contributions to evolution, taxonomy, and palaeontology and coined the word *dinosaur* in 1841. He was a strong opponent of Darwinism.

Robert Owen (1771–1858), Welsh social reformer and industrialist. A pioneer socialist thinker, he believed that character is a product of the social environment. He founded a model industrial community in Scotland, organized on principles of mutual cooperation, the first of a series of cooperative communities.

Jesse Owens (1913–80), American athlete. In 1935 he equalled or broke six world records in 45 minutes, and in 1936 won four gold medals at the Olympic Games in Berlin. The success in Berlin of Owens, as a black man, outraged Hitler.

owl the *owl* is taken as a symbol of wisdom (and was the emblem of ➤ ATHENE), but if a person is described as looking **owlish** it may imply that their solemn appearance is not matched by an inward intelligence or alertness.

See also ➤ STUFFED *owl*.

owl-jug a jug in the form of an owl, of a type originally made of faience and having a removable head used as a cup.

owl light in early use, the cover of night, the dark. Later: twilight, dusk; dim or poor light.

the owl was a baker's daughter traditional legend, alluded to by Shakespeare in *Hamlet*, that a baker's daughter once offered Jesus a very small piece of bread; in punishment for her niggardliness she was turned into an owl.

Till Owlglass the English name for ➤ *Till* EULENSPIEGEL.

score an own goal do something which has the unintended effect of harming one's own interests; an *own goal* is a goal scored by mistake against the scorer's own side.

owners see ➤ OBEY *orders if you break owners.*

on one's owney-oh on one's own, alone, after the words of a popular song *Antonio & his Ice-cream Cart* (1907).

ox a domesticated bovine animal kept for milk or meat; a cow or bull; a castrated male of this, formerly much used as a draught animal; the *ox* is proverbially a type of strength and fortitude, and of stupidity.

See also ➤ *the* DUMB *ox*, ➤ LUCANIAN *ox*.

the black ox misfortune, adversity, old age (originally in the traditional saying, **the black ox has trod on his foot**), recorded from the 16th century.

ox-bone an *ox-bone* is the emblem of ➤ St ALPHEGE, who was pelted to death with them by the Danes.

ox-eyed having large dark protuberant eyes like those of an ox; in references to classical literature, a particular epithet of ➤ JUNO.

Oxbridge Oxford and Cambridge universities regarded together; the expression is first recorded in Thackeray's novel *Pendennis* (1849), in which one of the characters refers to 'your dandy friends at Oxbridge'.

oxen see ➤ *put the* PLOUGH *before the oxen*.

Oxford accent supposedly characteristic of ➤ OXFORD *English*.

Oxford bags wide baggy trousers, fashionable in the UK in the 1920s.

Oxford blue¹ a dark blue, typically with a purple tinge.

Oxford blue² a person who has represented Oxford University in a particular sport.

the Oxford Blues the Royal Horse Guards, named in 1690 from their commander, the Earl of Oxford.

Oxford English spoken English marked by affected utterance, popularly supposed to be characteristic of members of Oxford University.

Oxford English Dictionary the largest dictionary of the English language, prepared in Oxford and originally issued in instalments (originally as the *New English Dictionary*) between 1884 and 1928.

Based on historical principles, it was edited by Sir James Murray from its inception in 1879 until his death in 1915. The original agreement between the Philological Society of London and Oxford University Press was for a four-volume dictionary, to be

completed in ten years. A second edition was published in 1989, and a third edition is being prepared.

Oxford Group a Christian movement popularized in Oxford in the late 1920s, advocating discussion of personal problems by groups. It was later known as ➤ MORAL REARMAMENT.

Oxford marmalade a kind of coarse-cut marmalade originally manufactured in Oxford.

Oxford Movement a Christian movement started in Oxford in 1833, seeking to restore traditional Catholic teachings and ceremonial within the Church of England. Its leaders were John Keble, Edward Pusey, and (until he became a Roman Catholic) John Henry Newman. Though it met with initial hostility, it contributed to social work and scholarship, and established the first Anglican religious communities. It formed the basis of the present Anglo-Catholic (or High Church) tradition.

Oxford University the oldest English university, comprising a federation of thirty-nine colleges, the first of which, University College, was formally founded in 1249. The university was established at Oxford soon after 1167, perhaps as a result of a migration of students from Paris. The first women's college, Lady Margaret Hall, was founded in 1878.

oxgang a former measure of land equivalent to an eighth of a ➤ CARUCATE; as much as one ox could plough in a year.

oxlip in early use, a hybrid between the cowslip and the primrose (now called the **false oxlip**); this is the flower mentioned by Shakespeare in *A Midsummer Night's Dream* and *The Winter's Tale*. The name is now properly applied to a woodland Eurasian primula with yellow flowers that hang down on one side of the stem; in Britain this is almost confined to parts of East Anglia, where it was discovered (at Great Barfield, Essex) in 1842.

Oxus ancient name for the Amu Darya river.

oxymoron a figure of speech in which apparently contradictory terms appear in conjunction (e.g. *faith unfaithful kept him falsely true*). Recorded from the mid 17th century, the word comes from Greek *oxumōron*, neuter (used as a noun) of *oxumōros* 'pointedly foolish', from *oxus* 'sharp' + *mōros* 'foolish'.

oxyrhynchus a fish with a pointed snout; in particular a mormyrid fish of the River Nile, venerated by the ancient Egyptians.

Oxyrhynchus papyri a number of ancient papyri which from the last decade of the 19th century have been discovered at Oxyrhyncus (El Bahnasa) in Upper Egypt.

oyer and terminer a commission formerly issued to judges on a circuit to hold courts. Recorded from late Middle English, the phrase comes from Anglo-Norman French, meaning literally 'hear and determine'.

oyez a call given, typically three times, by a public crier or a court officer to command silence and attention before an announcement. The word comes (in late Middle English) from Old French *oiez!*, *oyez!* 'hear!', ultimately from Latin *audire* 'to hear'.

oyster a bivalve mollusc with rough irregular shell, some kinds of which are eaten (especially raw) as a delicacy, and may be farmed for food and pearls. The *oyster* is also taken proverbially as the type of someone who is reserved and uncommunicative.

See also ➤ *the* WORLD *is one's oyster.*

oysters are only in season in the R months traditional saying, late 16th century; Harrison in his *Description of England* (1577) notes that 'our oysters are generally forborne in the four hot months of the year, that is, May, June, July, and August.'

Oz[1] informal name for Australia, recorded from the early 20th century.

Oz[2] the name of the fictional city and land in the children's fantasy *The Wonderful Wizard of Oz* by the US writer L. Frank Baum (1856–1919), widely popularized by the 1939 film *The Wizard of Oz*; in extended usage, any place thought to resemble Baum's city, especially any fantastic, ideal, or imaginary domain.

> San Francisco gleamed dusty white—an Oz mirage across the bay.
> — K. Green *Night Angel* (1989)

See also ➤ WIZARD *of Oz.*

Oz[3] title of a London magazine, founded in 1967 as an 'underground' publication, which was prosecuted for obscenity in a high-profile trial in 1971; the editors, who were found guilty, suffered a prison sentence.

Ozark Mountains a heavily forested highland plateau dissected by rivers, valleys, and streams, lying between the Missouri and Arkansas Rivers and within the states of Missouri, Arkansas, Oklahoma, Kansas, and Illinois.

Ozymandias a corruption (*Osymandias*) of the prenomen of Ramses II of Egypt (*c*.1304–*c*.1237 BC), of whom a colossal 57-foot statue, now surviving only in fragments, once stood at Thebes. The name became widely known from Shelley's sonnet of 1817 entitled *Ozymandias*, in which the poet describes 'the decay Of that colossal wreck, boundless and bare', and refers to the original inscription, 'My name is Ozymandias, king of kings: Look on my works, ye Mighty, and despair!' In allusive reference, *Ozymandias* is taken as a type of grandiose ambition and desire for lasting fame which ends in complete failure.

> There are ever-present lumps of concrete and glass which always contain 'The People' and 'Culture' in their titles, and seem to be part of some vast insecurity, some overpowering Ozymandian need to impose, on both the present and the past.
> — *Independent on Sunday* 11 February 1990

Pp

P the sixteenth letter of the modern English alphabet and the fifteenth of the ancient Roman one, corresponding to Greek *pi*, Phoenician and Semitic *pe*.
See also ➤ MIND *one's P's and Q's*.

pace with due respect to (someone or their opinion), used to express polite disagreement or contradiction; the word is Latin, and means literally 'in peace'.

it is the pace that kills proverbial saying, mid 19th century.

Pacific Ocean the largest of the world's oceans, lying between America to the east and Asia and Australasia to the west. Originally known as the South Sea, it was named the *Mar Pacifico* 'Pacific Sea' by Magellan following the calm seas he experienced on first reaching it in 1520.

David Pacifico (1784–1854), Greek trader of Portuguese Jewish extraction, who was born a British subject at Gibraltar in 1784, and who became the centre of the 'Don Pacifico' case which nearly evoked a European war. His house was burnt in a riot in Athens in 1847, and he made a large claim for compensation against the Greek government; when payment in this and other cases was delayed, Lord Palmerston sent the British fleet to the Piraeus, and all Greek ships and other vessels found in those waters were seized. Subsequent attempts by the French and English governments to arrange a settlement resulted in a quarrel between those two countries, and a vote of censure was passed on Palmerston's government in the Lords. The government was saved by a vote in the Commons, and Pacifico's compensation was finally paid; he spent his last years in England.

Pacing Mustang in the folk tales of the Western frontier, a legendary wild stallion famed for his beauty, size, strength, cunning, and untamability. He is referred to in *Moby Dick* as 'the White Steed of the Prairies', although in Ernest Thompson Seton's eponymous story he is said to be black.

pack a jury fill a jury with people likely to support a particular verdict or decision; the word probably comes from the obsolete verb *pact* 'enter into an agreement with', the final *-t* being interpreted as an inflection of the past tense.

pack up your troubles in your old kit-bag line from a British soldiers' song, 'Pack up your Troubles' (1915), of the First World War, written by George Asaf (1880–1951).

Kerry Packer (1937–), Australian media entrepreneur. He launched the 'World Series Cricket' tournaments (1977–9), engaging many leading cricketers in defiance of the wishes of cricket's ruling bodies.

a pad in the straw a lurking or hidden danger; a *pad* here is a toad, which was formerly believed to be venomous.

paddock archaic term for a toad, especially as the type of something venomous and unpleasant.

Paddy an informal and chiefly offensive name for an Irishman; the name is an Irish pet-form of *Padraig* or *Patrick*, and is recorded in this usage from the late 18th century.

Padishah a title of the Sultan of Turkey. The word was chiefly used as a title, meaning 'Great King' or 'Emperor': applied in Persia (later Iran) to the Shah, and in India (where often pronounced *bādshāh*) to the Great Mogul; it was also applied in India before 1948 to the British sovereign as Emperor of India.

padlock see ➤ WEDLOCK *is a padlock*.

Padmasambhava (fl. 8th century), the legendary Buddhist mystic who is credited with introducing Tantric Buddhism to Tibet.

padre informal term for a chaplain in any of the armed services. Recorded from the late 16th century, the word comes from Italian, Spanish, and Portuguese, literally 'father, priest', from Latin *pater* 'father'.

Padua a city in NE Italy, first mentioned in 302 BC as *Patavium*, which was the birthplace in 59 BC of the Roman historian Livy. A leading city from the 11th century AD, it was ruled by the Carrara family from 1318 until 1405, when it passed to Venice. Galileo taught at its university from 1592 to 1610.

See also ➤ St ANTHONY *of Padua*.

paean a song of praise or thanksgiving. Recorded from the late 16th century, the word comes via Latin from Greek *paian* 'hymn of thanksgiving to Apollo' (evoked by the name *Paian*, originally the Homeric name for the physician of the gods).

Pagan a town in Burma, situated on the Irrawaddy south-east of Mandalay, the site of an ancient city, founded in about AD 849, which was the capital of a powerful Buddhist dynasty from the 11th to the end of the 13th centuries.

pagan a person holding religious beliefs other than those of the main world religions. The word comes (in late Middle English) from Latin *paganus* 'villager, rustic' from *pagus* 'country district'. Latin *paganus* also meant 'civilian', becoming in Christian Latin 'heathen' (i.e. one not enrolled in the army of Christ).

Page Three a British trademark term for a feature which formerly appeared daily on page three of the *Sun* newspaper and included a picture of a topless young woman.

pagoda a Hindu or Buddhist temple or sacred building, typically a many-tiered tower, in India and the Far East. Recorded from the late 16th century, the word comes from Portuguese *pagode*, perhaps based on Persian *butkada* 'temple of idols', influenced by Prakrit *bhagodī* 'divine'.

pagoda-tree a mythical tree humorously supposed to produce *pagodas*, in this sense gold or silver coins formerly current in southern India; the expression **shake the pagoda-tree** meant to make a fortune in India under the East India Company.

Pahlavi[1] an Aramaic-based writing system used in Persia from the 2nd century BC to the advent of Islam in the 7th century AD. It was also used for the recording of ancient Avestan sacred texts.

Pahlavi[2] the name of two shahs of Iran, Reza (1878–1944), ruled 1925–41, an army officer who took control of the Persian government after a coup in 1921, and his son Mohammed Reza (1919–80), who came to power when his father abdicated in 1941 and ruled until 1979. Opposition to his regime culminated in the Islamic revolution of 1979 under Ayatollah Khomeini, and he was forced into exile and died in Egypt.

pain see ➤ PRIDE *feels no pain*, ➤ NO *pain, no gain*.

Thomas Paine (1737–1809), English political writer. His pamphlet *Common Sense* (1776) called for American independence and *The Rights of Man* (1791) defended the French Revolution. His radical views prompted the British government to indict him for treason and he fled to France, where he was imprisoned for opposing the execution of Louis XVI; it was in prison that he wrote *The Age of Reason* (1794–5).

He returned to the US in 1802, where he spent his remaining years, and was buried on his New Rochelle farm when consecrated ground was refused to him. In 1819 his bones were taken to England by William Cobbett, with the intention of erecting a monument to Paine; this never happened, and after Cobbett's own death the bones were lost.

pains see ➤ GENIUS *is an infinite capacity for taking pains*.

paint the town red enjoy oneself flamboyantly; an informal expression recorded first in the US in the mid 19th century.

painter an artist who paints pictures; ➤ St LUKE is the patron saint of painters.

See also ➤ JOHN *the Painter*.

painting see ➤ *painting the* FORTH *Bridge*, ➤ SAND *painting*.

pair a set of two things or people, in particular, either or both of two members of a legislative assembly on opposite sides who absent themselves from voting by mutual arrangement, leaving the relative position of the parties unaffected. The word in this sense is recorded from the early 19th century.

See also ➤ PIGEON *pair*.

paisley a distinctive intricate pattern of curved feather-shaped figures based on an Indian pine cone design, named after the town of *Paisley*, the original place of manufacture.

Paix des Dames an informal name for the Treaty of Cambrai in 1529, in allusion to its being negotiated by Louise of Savoy, regent of France and mother of Francis I, and Margaret of Austria, regent of the Netherlands and aunt of the Emperor Charles V.

pakapoo a Chinese form of lottery played with slips of paper marked with columns of characters. The name comes (in the early 20th century) from

Chinese, literally 'white pigeon ticket', perhaps with reference to a Cantonese competition which involved releasing pigeons and assessing distance flown and the number likely to return.

pakeha a white New Zealander, as opposed to a Maori. The word is from Maori.

Pakistan country in the Indian subcontinent, created as a separate country in 1947, following the British withdrawal from India. The name comes from *P*unjab, *A*fghan Frontier, *K*ashmir, Baluch*i*-*stan*, lands where Muslims predominated.

pal a friend, from Romany 'brother, mate', based on the Sanskrit *bhrātṛ* 'brother'. The word is recorded from the late 17th century.

palace the official residence of a sovereign, president, archbishop, or bishop. The word comes through Old French from Latin *Palatium*, the name of the Palatine hill in Rome, where the house of the emperor was situated.

See also ➤ CRYSTAL *Palace*, ➤ MAYOR *of the Palace*.

paladin any of the twelve peers of Charlemagne's court, of whom the *Count Palatine* was the chief; later, a knight renowned for heroism and chivalry. The word comes through Italian from Latin *palatinus* '(officer) of the palace'.

Palaemon in Greek mythology, a sea-god, representing the transformed ➤ MELICERTES, son of Ino (➤ LEUCOTHEA).

Palaeolithic the early phase of the Stone Age, lasting about 2.5 million years, when primitive stone implements were used. The Palaeolithic period extends from the first appearance of artefacts to the end of the last ice age (about 8,500 years BC). The period has been divided into the **Lower Palaeolithic**, with the earliest forms of humankind and the emergence of hand-axe industries (ending about 120,000 years ago), the **Middle Palaeolithic**, the era of Neanderthal man (ending about 35,000 years ago), and the **Upper Palaeolithic**, during which only modern Homo sapiens is known to have existed.

Palais Royal a theatre in Paris as characterized by a type of boisterous farce, popular in the late 19th century.

Palamedes in Greek mythology, the son of Nauplius, said to have invented some of the letters of the alphabet and the game of draughts. At the siege of Troy he was falsely accused by Odysseus of trying to

betray the Greeks to the Trojans for gold, and was stoned to death.

palatinate a territory under the jurisdiction of a Count Palatine; **the Palatinate** was a territory of the German Empire ruled by the Count Palatine of the Rhine.

Count Palatine in the later Roman Empire, a count (*comes*) attached to the imperial palace, and having supreme judicial authority in all causes that came to the king's immediate audience; later, a feudal lord having royal authority within a region of a kingdom; a high official of the Holy Roman Empire with royal authority within his domain.

County Palatine (in England and Ireland) a county in which royal privileges and exclusive rights of jurisdiction were held by its earl or lord.

pale¹ former term for an area within determined bounds, or subject to a particular jurisdiction, as in **the Pale**, used to designate the ➤ ENGLISH *Pale* in medieval Ireland, the territory of Calais in northern France when under English jurisdiction, and those areas of Tsarist Russia to which Jewish residence was restricted (known more fully as the **Pale of Settlement**).

The expression **beyond the pale**, meaning 'outside the bounds of acceptable behaviour', is recorded from the mid 19th century.

Pale in Middle English, meaning a wooden stake used as an upright along with others to form a fence, comes via Old French from Latin *palus* 'stake'.

pale² in heraldry, a broad vertical stripe down the middle of a shield.

pale horse the creature on which Death rides in the vision in Revelation, 'And I looked, and behold a pale horse: and his name that sat on him was Death, and Hell followed with him.' The phrase is often used allusively.

> What postilion can outride that pale horseman?
> — W. M. Thackeray *The Four Georges* (1861)

paleface a name supposedly used by the North American Indians for a white person. The term is recorded from the early 19th century.

Palenque the site of a former Mayan city in SE Mexico, south-east of present-day Villahermosa. The well-preserved ruins of the city, which existed from about AD 300 to 900, include notable examples of Mayan architecture and extensive hieroglyphic texts. The city's ancient name has been lost and it is now named after a neighbouring village.

Pales in Roman mythology, a god of flocks and shepherds, resembling Pan among the Greeks.

Palestine a territory in the Middle East on the eastern coast of the Mediterranean Sea, which in biblical times comprised the kingdoms of Israel and Judah. The land was controlled at various times by the Egyptian, Assyrian, Persian, and Roman empires before being conquered by the Arabs in AD 634; it was part of the Ottoman Empire from 1516 to 1918. The name Palestine was used as the official political title for the land west of the Jordan mandated to Britain in 1920; in 1948 the state of Israel was established in what was traditionally Palestine. The name continues to be used in the context of the struggle for territory and political rights of the displaced Palestinian Arabs.

The name *Palestine* comes from Greek *Palaistnē* (used in early Christian writing) from Latin *(Syria) Palaestina* (the name of a Roman province), from *Philistia* 'land of the Philistines'.

Giovanni Pierluigi da Palestrina (*c.*1525–94), Italian composer. Palestrina is chiefly known for his sacred music, including 105 masses, over 250 motets, and the *Missa Papae Marcelli* (1567).

Paleyan a follower or adherent of the English theologian William Paley (1743–1805) or of his rationalist and utilitarian moral philosophy, and his theology which styled God as the supreme craftsman in a mechanistic universe; ➤ *Richard* DAWKINS took his title *The Blind Watchmaker* (1986) from Paley's writings:

> Suppose I had found a *watch* upon the ground, and it should be enquired how the watch happened to be in that place . . . the inference, we think, is inevitable; that the watch must have had a maker, that there must have existed, at some time and at some place or other, an artificer or artificers, who formed it for the purpose which we find it actually to answer; who comprehended its construction, and designed its use.
> — William Paley *Natural Theology* (1802)

palfrey archaic term for a docile horse used for ordinary riding, especially by women. Recorded from Middle English, the word comes via Old French from medieval Latin alteration of late Latin *paraveredus*, from Greek *para* 'beside, extra' + Latin *veredus* 'light horse'.

Palgrave's Treasury an informal title for the anthology *The Golden Treasury of Songs and Lyrical Poems in the English Language* (1861) edited by Francis Turner Palgrave (1824–97), professor of poetry at Oxford 1886–95. This anthology originally contained no work by living poets, although such material was added in later revisions.

Pali an Indic language, closely related to Sanskrit, in which the sacred texts of southern Buddhism are written. Pali developed in northern India in the 5th–2nd centuries BC. As the language of the Buddhist sacred texts, it was brought to Sri Lanka and Burma (Myanmar), and, though not spoken there, became the vehicle of a large literature of commentaries and chronicles.

palimony compensation made by one member of an unmarried couple to the other after separation. The word comes (in the 1970s) from a blend of *pal* and *alimony*.

palimpsest a manuscript or piece of writing material on which later writing has been superimposed on effaced earlier writing; in figurative use, something reused or altered but still bearing visible traces of its earlier form. Recorded from the mid 17th century, the word comes via Latin from Greek *palimpsēstos*, from *palin* 'again' and *psēstos* 'rubbed smooth'.

palindrome a word, phrase, or sequence that reads the same backwards as forwards, e.g. *madam, nurses run,* or (in relation to Napoleon) *able was I ere I saw Elba*.

palinode a poem in which the poet retracts a view or sentiment expressed in a former poem.

Palinurus in Virgil's *Aeneid*, Aeneas's pilot, who is overcome by the god of sleep, falls overboard, and is murdered on the shore of Italy where he is washed up.

Palio a traditional horse race held in Siena twice a year, in July and August. The name is Italian, and comes from Latin *pallium* 'covering', with reference to the cloth, a banner of silk or velvet, given as the prize.

Palissy ware richly coloured earthenware decorated with reliefs of plants and animals, made by the French potter Bernard *Palissy* (*c.*1510–90) or those working in his style.

pall a cloth spread over a coffin, hearse, or tomb. The word is recorded in Old English as *pæll* 'rich (purple) cloth', 'cloth cover for a chalice', and comes from Latin *pallium* 'covering, cloak'. A **pall-**

bearer at a funeral, now a person either helping to carry or officially escorting the coffin, was originally someone who held up the edges of the pall.

Pall Mall a street in London built on the site of an alley for playing *pall-mall*, a 16th- and 17th-century game in which a boxwood ball was driven through an iron ring suspended at the end of a long alley.

Palladian of, relating to, or denoting the neoclassical style of Andrea Palladio, in particular with reference to the phase of English architecture from *c*.1715, when there was a revival of interest in Palladio and his English follower, Inigo Jones, and a reaction against the baroque.

Andrea Palladio (1508–80), Italian architect. He led a revival of classical architecture, in particular promoting the Roman ideals of harmonic proportions and symmetrical planning. A notable example of his many villas, palaces, and churches is the church of San Giorgio Maggiore in Venice.

Palladium in Greek legend, an image of the goddess Pallas (Athene), on which the safety of Troy was believed to depend; it was later said to have been taken to Rome.

Pallas in Greek mythology, one of the names (of unknown meaning) of ➤ ATHENE.

palliament in ancient Rome, a white gown worn by a candidate for the consulship.

pallium a woollen vestment conferred by the Pope on an archbishop, consisting of a narrow circular band placed round the shoulders with a short lappet hanging from front and back.

From the mid 16th century, the term has also been used to denote a man's large rectangular cloak, especially as worn by Greek philosophical and religious teachers.

Recorded from Old English, the word is Latin, and means literally 'covering'.

palm¹ an unbranched evergreen tree with a crown of very long feathered or fan-shaped leaves, and typically having old leaf scars forming a regular pattern on the trunk. The leaf of this tree was traditionally awarded as a prize or viewed as a symbol of victory or triumph.

In Christian symbolism, the *palm* is used as a festive emblem on Palm Sunday, and was also the sign of a pilgrim who was returning or had returned from the Holy Land (a ➤ PALMER). In northern countries, *palm* may be used for other shrubs, such as sallow or pussy willow, which are used on Palm

Sunday. A palm is also a symbol of virginity.

Recorded in Old English and of Germanic origin, the word is ultimately related to Latin *palma* 'palm (of a hand)', its leaf being likened to a spread hand.

palm² the inner surface of the hand between the wrist and fingers, the lines of which are supposed in ➤ PALMISTRY to allow interpretation of character or prediction of the future.

From the late 16th century, the *palm* has been proverbial in expressions relating to avarice and bribery.

The word comes (in Middle English) from Latin *palma*.

See also ➤ CROSS *someone's palm with silver*, ➤ ITCHING *palm*.

Palm Court a large room or patio, especially in a hotel, decorated with palm trees; the term **Palm Court music** is used to designate light orchestral music of a kind frequently played in a *Palm Court*.

Palm Sunday the Sunday before Easter, on which Christ's entry into Jerusalem is celebrated in many Christian churches by processions in which branches of palms are carried. The name is recorded from Old English.

See also ➤ SAD *Palm Sunday*.

palmer a pilgrim, especially one who had returned from the Holy Land with a palm branch or leaf as a sign of having undertaken the pilgrimage.

Samuel Palmer (1805–91), English painter and etcher. His friendship with William Blake resulted in the mystical, visionary landscape paintings, such as *Repose of the Holy Family* (1824), for which he is best known. He was leader of a group of artists called The Ancients, due to their love of the medieval, who were inspired by Blake's mysticism.

Lord Palmerston (1784–1865), Henry John Temple, 3rd Viscount, British Whig statesman, Prime Minister 1855–8 and 1859–65, informally known as 'Pam'. Palmerston declared the second Opium War against China in 1856, and oversaw the successful conclusion of the Crimean War in 1856 and the suppression of the Indian Mutiny in 1858. He maintained British neutrality during the American Civil War, but the quality most associated with him is a belief in the value of forceful diplomacy.

See also ➤ SCHLESWIG-*Holstein*.

palmetto flag the flag of South Carolina, which bears the figure of a cabbage palmetto tree.

Palmetto State informal name for South Carolina.

palmistry the art or practice of supposedly interpreting a person's character or predicting their future by examining the lines and other features of the hand, especially the palm and fingers.

Palmyra an ancient city of Syria, an oasis in the Syrian desert north-east of Damascus on the site of present-day Tadmur. First mentioned in the 19th century BC, Palmyra was an independent state in the 1st century BC, becoming a dependency of Rome between the 1st and 3rd centuries AD. A flourishing city on a trade route between Damascus and the Euphrates, it regained its independence briefly under ➤ ZENOBIA, who became queen of Palmyra in 267, until it was taken by the Emperor Aurelian in 272. The name is a Greek form of the city's modern and ancient pre-Semitic name *Tadmur* or *Tadmor,* meaning 'city of palms'.

Palookaville an imaginary town characterized by mediocrity, ineptitude, or stupidity. *Palooka* as a term for a stupid, clumsy, or ineffectual person, and in particular a mediocre prizefighter, has been current since 1920, and *Palookaville,* as the natural home of such a person, is found in Budd Schulberg's script for the film *On the Waterfront,* in a speech in which the character played by Marlon Brando looks back at his failed career as a boxer:

> And whadda I get? A one-way ticket to Palookaville.
> — Budd Schulberg *On the Waterfront* (film, 1954)

In 1990 the term achieved fresh currency, in a comment on the end of the boxing career of the former heavyweight champion Charles 'Sonny' Liston:

> The Liston-Wepner saga was Sonny's last stop on his sad, one-way ticket back to Palookaville.
> — *Boxing Illustrated* October 1990

palsgrave historical term for a ➤ *Count* PALATINE, in particular, the Count Palatine of the Rhine. Recorded from the mid 16th century, the word comes from early modern Dutch *paltsgrave,* from *palts* 'palatinate' + *grave* 'count'.

paludament a military cloak fastened at one shoulder with a brooch or clasp, worn by Roman generals and chief officers.

paly in heraldry, divided into equal vertical stripes. Recorded from late Middle English, the word comes from Old French *pale* 'divided by stakes', from *pal* 'pale, stake'.

Pam nickname of ➤ *Lord* PALMERSTON.

pam the jack of clubs, especially in certain versions of five-card loo in which this card is always the highest trump; in figurative use, a superlative or powerful person or thing, as in Pope's *Rape of the Lock* (1714), 'Ev'n mighty Pam that Kings and Queens o'erthrew'. The origin of the name is uncertain, but may come ultimately via French from Latin *Pamphilus* 'beloved of all'.

pamé in heraldry, (of a fish) having a gaping mouth.

pamphlet a small booklet or leaflet containing information or arguments about a single subject. The term was originally used of a short handwritten or printed document of several pages fastened together, having fewer pages than would constitute a book; it came particularly to be used of factual or informative documents. In the 17th century, *pamphlet* was used variously of issues of plays, romances, and chapbooks, and also of newspapers, newsletters, and other periodicals. In particular, in the 17th and 18th centuries, *pamphlet* denoted a work of a controversial, polemical, or political nature issued in this form; Milton in *The Reason of Church Government urged against Prelaty* (1641) refers to, 'These wretched projectors of ours that bescrawl their pamphlets everyday with new forms of government for our Church'.

Recorded from late Middle English, the word comes from *Pamphilet,* the familiar name of the highly popular 12th-century Latin love poem *Pamphilus, seu de Amore.*

pamphleteer a writer of pamphlets, especially ones of a political and controversial nature.

> The Squibs are those who in the common Phrase of the World are call'd Libellers, Lampooners and Pamphleteers.
> — *Tatler* No. 88 1709

Pamplona a city in northern Spain, capital of the former kingdom and modern region of Navarre, noted for the fiesta of San Fermin, held there in July, which is celebrated with the running of bulls through the streets of the city.

Pamyat a right-wing political movement in Russia, characterized by extreme nationalism and anti-Semitism. Recorded from the late 1980s, the word comes from Russian *pámyat* 'memory, remembrance'.

pan see also ➤ *a* FLASH *in the pan,* ➤ PETER *Pan.*

Pan in Greek mythology, a god of flocks and herds, native to Arcadia, typically represented with the horns, ears, and legs of a goat on a man's body. He was thought of as loving mountains, caves, and lonely places and as playing on the pan pipes. His sudden appearance was supposed to cause terror similar to that of a frightened and stampeding herd, and the word *panic* is derived from his name. He was identified by the Romans with ➤ FAUNUS.

Plutarch relates that during the reign of Tiberius (AD 14–37), passengers in a ship off the west coast of Greece heard a voice calling that the god Pan was dead; this story was associated in Christian legend with the birth and resurrection of Christ.

The name *Pan* was probably originally in the sense 'the feeder' (i.e. herdsman), although the name was regularly associated with Greek *pas* or *pan* (= 'all'), giving rise to his identification as a god of nature or the universe.

pan pipes a musical instrument made from a row of short pipes of varying length fixed together and played by blowing across the top, originally associated with the Greek rural god ➤ PAN.

panacea a solution or remedy for all difficulties or diseases. Recorded from the mid 16th century, the word comes via Latin from Greek *panakeia*, for *panakēs* 'all-healing'. In Spenser's *Faerie Queene*, the name *panacea* is given to a plant reputed to heal all ills (all-heal or woundwort).

panache a tuft or plume of feathers, especially for a headdress or as a decoration for a helmet; in later figurative usage, flamboyant confidence of style or manner. *Panache* is represented as the key quality of the hero of Rostand's play *Cyrano de Bergerac* (1897).

Recorded from the mid 16th century in its literal sense, the word comes via French and Italian from Latin *pinnaculum*, diminutive of *pinna* 'feather'.

Panama Canal a canal across the Isthmus of Panama, connecting the Atlantic and Pacific Oceans. Its construction, begun by Ferdinand de Lesseps in 1881 but abandoned in 1889, was completed by the US between 1904 and 1914. Control of the canal remained with the US until 1999, the date of its reversion to Panama.

pancake a thin, flat cake of batter, fried and turned in a pan and typically rolled up with a sweet or savoury filling; proverbially taken as the type of something flat and thin.

pancake-bell a bell traditionally rung on the morning of Shrove Tuesday.

Pancake Day Shrove Tuesday, when pancakes are traditionally made to use up eggs and fat before the beginning of Lent.

pancake race a race held in some places on Shrove Tuesday, in which the participants toss pancakes as they run.

Panchaea a mythical country mentioned in Ovid's *Metamorphoses*.

Panchen Lama a Tibetan lama ranking next after the Dalai Lama. The name comes from Tibetan *panchen*, abbreviation of *pandi-tachen-po* 'great learned one'. The Panchen Lama identifies the new Dalai Lama.

St Pancras (d. early 4th century), martyr, supposedly a Phrygian orphan brought to Rome and converted there. Relics of the saint were sent by the pope to Oswy, king of Northumbria, in the 7th century, and from this his name appears in Bede's martyrology. Six ancient churches in England were dedicated to St Pancras; the one in North London gave its name to the railway station.

☐ **FEAST DAY** His feast day is 12 May.

Pandarus a Lycian fighting on the side of the Trojans, described in the *Iliad* as breaking the truce with the Greeks by wounding Menelaus with an arrow. The role as the lovers' go-between that he plays in Chaucer's (and later Shakespeare's) story of Troilus and Cressida originated with Boccaccio and is also the origin of the word ➤ PANDER.

the Pandects a compendium in 50 books of the Roman civil law made by order of Justinian in the 6th century and systematized according to subject, to which he gave statutory force. The name comes via Latin from Greek *pandektēs* 'all-receiver'.

pandemonium wild and noisy disorder or confusion; uproar. Originally (in Milton's *Paradise Lost*) it denoted the capital of hell, containing the council chamber of the evil spirits:

> Pandemonium, the high capital
> Of Satan and his peers.
> — John Milton *Paradise Lost* (1667)

In extended use, *pandemonium* was used first for any place resembling this, and then more generally for wild and noisy disorder or confusion, uproar.

pander a person who assists the baser urges or evil designs of others. The term developed from the name of ➤ PANDARUS, first in the sense of someone who provides another with the means of sexual gratification, and then more generally.

pandit a Hindu scholar learned in Sanskrit and Hindu philosophy and religion, typically also a practising priest.

Pandora in Greek mythology, the first mortal woman. In one story she was created by Zeus and sent to earth with a jar or box of evils in revenge for Prometheus' having brought the gift of fire back to the world. Prometheus' simple brother Epimetheus married her despite his brother's warnings, and Pandora let out all the evils from the jar to infect the earth; hope alone remained to assuage the lot of humankind. In another account the jar contained all the blessings which would have been preserved for the world had they not been allowed to escape.

Pandora's box a process that generates many complicated problems as the result of unwise interference in something. The expression was once used in a notable mixed metaphor by the British Labour politician Ernest Bevin (1881–1851), on the Council of Europe, 'If you open that Pandora's Box, you never know what Trojan 'orses will jump out.'

pandour a member of an 18th-century military force that was originally the private army of a Croatian nobleman and later served under him as a regiment of the Austrian Army, where its members became feared for their rapacity and brutality; a brutal Croatian soldier. The name comes via French and German from Serbo-Croat *pandur* 'constable, bailiff', probably from medieval Latin *banderius* 'guard of cornfields and vineyards'.

Pandy a sepoy taking part in the Indian Mutiny of 1857–8, perhaps from the Indian surname *Paṇḍe*, common among high-caste sepoys in the Bengal army. One of those bearing the name was *Mangul Paṇḍe*, the first man to mutiny in the 34th Regiment.

panegyric a public speech or published text in praise of someone or something. Recorded from the early 17th century, the word comes via French and Latin from Greek *panēgurikos* 'of public assembly', from *pan* 'all' + *aguris* 'agora, assembly'.

panem et circenses Latin origin of the phrase ➤ BREAD *and circuses*, originally used by the Roman poet Juvenal (AD c.60–c.130).

panentheism the belief or doctrine that God is greater than the universe and includes and interpenetrates it.

Pangaea a vast continental area or supercontinent comprising all the continental crust of the earth, which is postulated to have existed in late Palaeozoic and Mesozoic times before breaking up into Gondwana and Laurasia.

The name is frequently stated to have been coined by A. Wegener 1914, in *Die Entstehung der Kontinente und Ozeane*, but it has not been found in the 1st edition of that book (actually published in 1915); *Pangäa* does occur in ed. 2 (1920), but with no indication that it is a coinage.

Pangloss name of the tutor and philosopher in Voltaire's *Candide* (1759), given to optimism regardless of circumstances.

> As factories moved out of the United States in the 1970s and 1980s, the Panglosses of the day called it progress and celebrated the transition to a 'service economy'.
> — *Harper's Magazine* September 1993

panhandle often in North American place names, a narrow strip of territory projecting from the main territory of one state into another.

panic sudden uncontrollable fear or anxiety, often causing wildly unthinking behaviour. The word comes from the name of the god ➤ PAN, noted for causing terror, to whom woodland noises were attributed.

Panini Indian grammarian. Sources vary as to when he lived, with dates ranging from the 4th to the 7th century BC. He is noted as the author of the *Eight Lectures*, a grammar of Sanskrit, outlining rules for the derivation of grammatical forms.

panjandrum a person who has or claims to have a great deal of authority or influence. The word comes from *Grand Panjandrum*, an invented phrase in a nonsense passage composed in 1755 by the English actor and dramatist Samuel Foote (1720–77) to test the vaunted memory of the actor Charles Macklin (1697?–1797):

> So she went into the garden to cut a cabbage-leaf to make an apple-pie; and at the same time a great she-bear coming up the street, pops its head into the shop. 'What! no soap?' So he died, and she very imprudently married the barber; and there were present the Picninnies, and the Joblillies, and the Garyulies, and the grand Panjandrum himself, with the little round button at top; and they all fell to playing the game of catch as catch can, till the gun powder ran out at the heels of their boots.
> — Samuel Foote nonsense passage

Pankhurst Emmeline (1858–1928), Christabel (1880–1958), and Sylvia (1882–1960), English suffragettes. In 1903 Emmeline and her daughters founded the Women's Social and Political Union, with the motto 'Votes for Women'. Following the imprisonment of Christabel in 1905, Emmeline initiated the militant suffragette campaign which continued until the outbreak of the First World War.

Panomphaean of or pertaining to the god Zeus, as sender of all oracular voices. Recorded from the early 17th century, the word comes from Greek *pan* 'all' + *omphē* 'voice of a god, oracular response'.

From a humorous use in French by Rabelais, the word may be found in translations of or allusions to Rabelais meaning 'suited to all', as in Urquhart's 1694 translation, '*Trinc* is a Panomphean word, that is, a word understood, us'd and celebrated by all nations, and signifies Drink.'

Panopticon the name given by Jeremy Bentham in 1790 to his proposal for an institutional building, especially a prison, of circular shape with the area occupied by the inmates disposed round and fully open to view from a central vantage point. A scheme for a penitentiary on these lines was accepted by Parliament in 1794, and a site at Millbank, London, was chosen, but, in the event, the new penitentiary (which opened in 1816) was not built to Bentham's plan. Among later prisons constructed on the panopticon principle, the Stateville Penitentiary at Joliet, Illinois, is still in use.

The word comes from Greek *pan* 'all' + *optikon*, neuter of *optikos* 'optic', and is recorded from the mid 18th century as a word for a kind of telescope.

Pantagruel the name of the last of the giants in Rabelais's *Pantagruel* (1532), represented as an extravagant and coarse humorist who deals satirically with serious subjects; **Pantagruelian** in extended usage means enormous, gigantic.

> The public appetite for celebrity and pseudo-event has grown to Pantagruelian proportions.
> — *New York Times* 4 December 1983

St Pantaleon 4th-century physician who was martyred under Diocletian; he is considered one of the ➤ FOURTEEN *Holy Helpers*, and from his cult in Venice his name may be the origin of ➤ PANTALOON.

☐ **FEAST DAY** His feast day is 27 July.

Pantaloon a Venetian character in Italian *commedia dell'arte*, typically represented as a foolish old man wearing spectacles, pantaloons, and slippers; in harlequinade or pantomime, he is shown as an old man, alternately foolish and scheming, who abets the clown in his tricks and provides a butt for his jokes.

Traditionally Pantaloon had the same role in both Italian and English harlequinade, as the father or guardian of the heroine (Columbine) who attempts to prevent her marriage to the hero (Harlequin).

The loose breeches extended below the knee, fashionable in the period following the Restoration, were known as *pantaloons*; the diarist John Evelyn (1620–1706) commented in 1661 that they had been taken by the French from the costume of the stage character of the period 'when the freak takes our Monsieurs to appear like so many Farces or Jack Puddings on the stage'.

Recorded in English from the late 16th century, the name comes originally via French from Italian *pantalone* 'a kind of mask on the Italian stage, representing the Venetian', supposed ultimately to be derived from the name of *San Pantaleone* or *Pantalone*, formerly a favourite saint of the Venetians.

Pantechnicon a building in Belgrave Square, London, constructed in the early 19th century to house an exhibition and sale of various arts and crafts, and later used as a furniture warehouse; it was destroyed by fire, with its contents, in 1874. From this the term was extended to mean any building housing a collection of shops or stalls offering a range of merchandise, and finally a large van for transporting furniture.

Pantelleria a volcanic Italian island in the Mediterranean, situated between Sicily and the coast of Tunisia, which was used as a place of exile by the ancient Romans, who called it *Cossyra*.

Panthalassa a universal sea or single ocean, such as would have surrounded Pangaea.

pantheism a doctrine which identifies God with the universe, or regards the universe as a manifestation of God.

Pantheon a large circular temple in Rome, dedicated to all the gods. It was begun by Agrippa *c*.25 BC as a conventional rectangular temple, but rebuilt as a larger, circular, domed building in the 2nd and 3rd centuries by Hadrian, Severus, and Caracalla. It was consecrated as a Christian church (Santa Maria Rotonda) in 609.

From this specific use the word was extended to mean a temple dedicated to all the gods (especially in ancient Greece and Rome) or a building in which the illustrious dead of a nation are buried on honoured. The term is now used for the gods of a people or religion collectively, or for a group or set of people particularly respected, famous, or important.

panther a leopard, especially a black one; originally, an exotic spotted wild cat believed to be distinct from the leopard. Fabulous accounts included the belief that the animal was a hybrid between the lion and the 'pard', and that the panther exhaled a sweet fragrance:

> The Panther's breath was ever fam'd for sweet.
>   — John Dryden *The Hind and the Panther* (1687)

In later literary use, the *panther* is also taken as the type of a fierce, powerful, and elusive creature.
    See also ➤ BLACK *Panther.*

pantheum see ➤ SIGNUM *pantheum.*

pantile a roof tile curved to form an S-shaped section, fitted to overlap its neighbour, probably suggested by Dutch *dakpan*, literally 'roof pan'. In the 18th century, the term was applied in a derogatory sense to rural Nonconformist chapels (sometimes, like ordinary cottages, roofed with pantiles), and to those who attended them.

Pantisocracy a form of utopian social organization in which all are equal in social position and responsibility. The term is used mainly to refer to the political ideas of a group of writers and intellectuals of the 1790s, including Robert Southey and Samuel Taylor Coleridge, and in particular to the community which Southey and Coleridge at one time planned to establish on the Susquehanna River in Pennsylvania. The word comes from Greek *panto-* 'all' + *isokratia* 'equality of power'.

Pantocrator a title of Christ represented as the ruler of the universe, especially in Byzantine church decoration. The name (recorded in English from the late 19th century) comes via Latin from Greek, 'ruler over all'.

pantomime a theatrical entertainment, mainly for children, which involves music, topical jokes, and slapstick comedy and is based on a fairy tale or nursery story, usually produced around Christmas. Modern British pantomime developed from the harlequinade and the cast typically includes a man in the chief comic female role ('principal dame'), a woman in the main male role ('principal boy'), and an animal played by actors in comic costume.
    Pantomime is recorded from the late 16th century, and was first used in the Latin form and in the sense of an actor in Roman mime expressing meaning through gestures accompanied by movement. The

current use developed in English in the mid 18th century.

Panurge roguish companion of ➤ PANTAGRUEL in the stories of Rabelais.

Panza see ➤ SANCHO *Panza.*

paolo an obsolete Italian silver coin, named after Pope Paul V, worth about five old pence.

papabile worthy of being or eligible to be pope.

papal of or relating to a pope or to the papacy; recorded from late Middle English, the word comes via Old French and medieval Latin from eccclesiastical Latin *papa* 'bishop of Rome'.
    See also ➤ BULL².

papal cross a cross with three transoms.

Papal States the temporal dominions belonging to the Pope, especially in central Italy, over which he exercised sovereignty from the 7th to the 19th centuries.

papal tiara an ornate cap with three coronets, used in the coronation of the Pope and as a symbol of the Pope's authority.

paparazzo a freelance photographer who pursues celebrities to get photographs of them. The name comes (in the mid 20th century, from Italian) from the name of a character in Fellini's film *La Dolce Vita* (1960).

> Outside her New York apartment building there are nearly always paparazzi and fans lying in wait.
>   — *Vanity Fair* April 1991

paper recorded from Middle English, the word comes via Anglo-Norman French from Latin *papyrus* 'paper-reed' (see ➤ PAPYRUS).
    The phrase **on paper** has been used increasingly to indicate something which is supposedly established by its written or printed form, but which in fact exists in theory rather than in actuality.
    See also ➤ COMMAND *Paper,* ➤ *a* SCRAP *of paper.*

paper over the cracks use a temporary expedient, create a mere semblance of order. The phrase is a translation of a German expression used by Otto von Bismarck in a letter of 1865, and early uses refer to this.

paper tiger a person or thing that appears threatening but is ineffectual. The expression became well-known in the West from its use by Mao Zhe

Dong in an interview in 1946, when he gave the view that 'all reactionaries are paper tigers'.

Paphian of or relating to Paphos, a Cypriot city held to be the birthplace of Aphrodite or Venus and formerly sacred to her; *Paphian* in literary use can thus mean relating to love and sexual desire.

Paphian Goddess Aphrodite, Venus.

Paphian Queen Aphrodite, Venus.

Pappus (fl. *c*.300–350 AD), Greek mathematician; known as **Pappus of Alexandria**. Little is known of his life, but his *Collection* of six books (another two are missing) is the principal source of knowledge of the mathematics of his predecessors. They are particularly strong on geometry, to which Pappus himself made major contributions.

papyrus a material prepared in ancient Egypt from the pithy stem of the water plant *papyrus*, a tall aquatic sedge native to central Africa and the Nile valley, used in sheets throughout the ancient Mediterranean world for writing or painting on and also for making articles such as rope, sandals, and boats.

To form a sheet of writing material, the stem of the papyrus plant was sliced into thin strips which were laid side by side, with another layer of similar strips crossing them, usually followed by a third parallel to the first. The whole was then soaked in water, pressed, and dried.

par in golf, the number of strokes a first-class player should normally require for a particular hole or course. The golf term dates from the late 19th century, and comes from the late 16th-century sense 'equality of value or standing', from Latin, 'equal' and 'equality'.

parabasis in ancient Greek comedy, a part unconnected with the action of the drama that was sung by the chorus to the audience in the poet's name; generally, a digression in which an author addresses the audience on personal or topical matters. The word comes from Greek, from *parabainein* 'go aside'.

parable a simple story used to illustrate a moral or spiritual lesson, as told by Jesus in the Gospels. Recorded from Middle English, the word comes via Old French from an ecclesiastical Latin sense 'discourse, allegory' of Latin *parabola* 'comparison', from Greek *parabolē* 'placing side by side, application'. Stories told by Jesus are often referred to by specific titles referring to their subjects, such as the **parable of the sower**.

parabolanus in the Church in Alexandria and Constantinople in the 5th and 6th centuries, a lay helper who attended the sick.

Paracelsus (*c*.1493–1541), Swiss physician: born Theophrastus Phillipus Aureolus Bombastus von Hohenheim. He developed a new approach to medicine and philosophy based on observation and experience. He saw illness as having a specific external cause (rather than an imbalance of the bodily humours), and introduced chemical remedies to replace traditional ones. Paracelsus' progressive view was offset by his overall occultist perspective.

Paraclete (in Christian theology) the Holy Spirit as advocate or counsellor (John 14:26, 'the Comforter, which is the Holy Ghost'). The name comes via late Latin from Greek *paraklētos* 'called in aid'.

Paradise heaven as the ultimate abode of the just; the abode of Adam and Eve before the Fall in the biblical account of the Creation; the garden of Eden. Recorded from Middle English, the word comes via Old French and ecclesiastical Latin from Greek *paradeisos* 'royal (enclosed) park', from Avestan *pairidaēza* 'enclosure, park'. The word was used first in Greek by Xenophon for a Persian enclosed park, orchard, or pleasure ground.

From late Middle English, *Paradise* was also used for an enclosed garden or orchard, or an enclosed area or court in front of a building, especially a church, and in the Middle Ages particularly a court in front of St Peter's, Rome. ➤ PARVIS derives from the same base as this.

See also ➤ EARTHLY *paradise*.

Paradise Lost title of Milton's epic poem (1667), which in twelve books relates the story of the Fall of Man, and which in its own words is intended to 'justify the ways of God to man'. *Paradise Regained* (1671), its sequel, relates in four books the story of the temptation of Jesus in the wilderness.

Paradise of Fools in Milton's *Paradise Lost*, a name for limbo.

paradox a statement or proposition which, despite sound (or apparently sound) reasoning from acceptable premises, leads to a conclusion that seems senseless, logically unacceptable, or self-contradictory; a seemingly absurd or self-contradictory statement or proposition which when investigated or explained may prove to be well founded or true.

Recorded from the mid 16th century (originally denoting a statement contrary to accepted opinion), the word comes via late Latin from Greek *paradoxon* 'contrary (opinion)'.

See also ➤ *the* LIAR *paradox,* ➤ OLBERS' *paradox,* ➤ RUSSELL'*s paradox.*

Paralympics an international athletic competition for disabled athletes, modelled on the Olympic Games, established during the 1950s. The name comes from a blend of *paraplegic* and *Olympics.*

paralysis St Osmund (d. 1099), bishop of Salisbury, noted for his healing miracles, is the patron saint of those suffering from paralysis.

Paramount a US film production and distribution company established in 1914. A major studio of the silent era, Paramount acted as an outlet for many of the films of Cecil B. De Mille and helped to create stars such as Mary Pickford and Rudolf Valentino.

Paranthropus a genus name often applied to robust fossil hominids first found in South Africa in 1938, and now usually included in the species *Australopithecus robustus.*

paraphernalia miscellaneous articles, especially the equipment needed for a particular activity. Recorded from the mid 17th century, the word originally denoted property owned by a married woman, and comes ultimately from Greek *parapherna* 'property apart from a dowry'. In later legal usage, the term became restricted to such purely personal possessions as clothing and jewellery, and from this developed the sense of miscellaneous objects.

parasite an organism which lives in or on another organism (its host) and benefits by deriving nutrients at the other's expense. Recorded from the mid 16th century denoting someone living at another's expense, the word originally comes from Greek *parasitos* denoting 'person who eats at another's table', and thus someone who lives at another's expense and repays them with flattery. The current meaning dates from the early 18th century.

Parcae in Roman mythology, the ➤ FATES.

parchment a stiff, flat, thin material of a yellowish colour made from the prepared skin of an animal, usually a sheep or goat, and used as a durable writing surface in ancient and medieval times. Recorded from Middle English, the word comes via Old French from a blend of late Latin *pergamina* 'writing material from Pergamum' and *Parthica pellis* 'Parthian skin' (a kind of scarlet leather).

parclose a screen or railing in a church enclosing a tomb or altar or separating off a side chapel.

pard poetic or literary term for a leopard; in heraldry, a representation of this animal. (In early use, the *pard* was sometimes thought to be a different animal from a leopard or panther.) Recorded from late Middle English, the word is often used with reference to Shakespeare's *As You Like It* (1599), 'bearded like the pard'.

pardon see ➤ OFFENDERS *never pardon.*

pardon-bell traditional name for the angelus bell (so called because special pardons were formerly granted to those who recited the angelus correctly on hearing it).

pardoner a person who was licensed to sell papal pardons or indulgences; in the Middle Ages, *pardoners* such as the character in Chaucer's *Canterbury Tales* were often represented as figures of dubious moral probity.

parens patriae the monarch, or any other authority, regarded as the legal protector of citizens unable to protect themselves. The phrase, which is Latin, means 'parent of the country', and is recorded in English from the late 16th century.

parentalia in ancient Rome, periodical observances in honour of dead parents or relations; in English, the term was sometimes used in the titles of books dedicated to or written about a person's parents or family.

our first parents Adam and Eve in relation to humankind.

pargeting plaster or mortar applied in a layer over a part of a building, especially ornamental plasterwork. The word comes ultimately from Old French *parjeter,* from *par-* 'all over' + *jeter* 'to throw'.

pariah a member of a low caste or of no caste in southern India. The word comes in the 17th century from Tamil 'hereditary drummer', from *parai* a drum (*pariahs* not being allowed to join in with a religious procession).

From the early 19th century, the term has been in general use for someone who is despised and shunned, an outcast.

Parian of or relating to ➤ PAROS or the fine white marble for which it is renowned; denoting a form of fine white unglazed hard-paste porcelain likened to Parian marble.

Parian chronicle an inscribed marble stele, originally set up on ➤ Paros, giving a record of ancient Greek history from the reign of Cecrops, the legendary first king of Athens, to the archonship of Astyanax at Paros and of Diognetus at Athens (*c.*264 BC); two fragments survive, one kept in the Ashmolean Museum at Oxford, the other on Paros itself.

Paris[1] in Greek mythology, a Trojan prince, the son of Priam and Hecuba. Appointed by the gods to decide who among the three goddesses Hera, Athene, and Aphrodite should win a prize for beauty, he awarded it to Aphrodite, who promised him the most beautiful woman in the world—Helen, wife of Menelaus king of Sparta. He abducted Helen, bringing about the Trojan War, in which he killed Achilles but was later himself killed.

Paris[2] the capital of France, on the River Seine. Paris was held by the Romans, who called it *Lutetia*, and the Franks (in the 5th century AD it fell to the Frankish king Clovis, who made it his seat of power), and was established as the capital in 987 under Hugh Capet. In the 19th century, the title of **Comte de Paris** was created for Philippe d'Orleans, grandson of the exiled former king Louis Philippe, who after his grandfather's death in 1850 became pretender to the French throne.

The city is named after the *Parisii*, a Gallic people who settled on the *Île de la Cité* in the Seine.

See also ➤ HERB *Paris*, ➤ MATTHEW *Paris*, ➤ PLASTER *of Paris.*

Paris club a group of the major creditor nations of the International Monetary Fund, meeting informally in Paris to discuss the financial relations of the IMF member nations.

Paris garden a noisy, disorderly place, from the name of a place at Bankside, Southwark, in London, where a bear garden was kept in Elizabethan and later times.

See also ➤ SACKERSON.

parish (in the Christian Church) a small administrative district typically having its own church and a priest or pastor. Also, a small country district; the smallest unit of local government, constituted only in rural areas.

St Jean-Baptiste Vianney (1786–1859), curé of Ars in France, is the patron saint of parish priests.

parish pump the pump supplying water to a parish, regarded as an informal place for meeting and discussion; used allusively to refer to matters of

limited scope and interest, especially in politics.

> Let us not be parish-pump . . . Let us recognize our diocesan responsibility.
> — *Church Times* 20 November 1998

Parisian matins the massacre of Huguenots throughout France (➤ *the Massacre of St* BARTHOLOMEW), begun without warning in Paris about 2 a.m. on the feast of St Bartholomew, 24 August, 1572. The term is recorded from the late 17th century, and is a translation of Middle French *matines parisiennes.*

Mungo Park (1771–1806), Scottish explorer. He undertook a series of explorations in West Africa (1795–7), among them the navigation of the Niger. He drowned on a second expedition to the Niger (1805–6).

Park Avenue name of a street in New York city, used allusively to denote the kind of fashionable and wealthy lifestyle typified by it.

> Somehow I can't imagine a Park Avenue matron shelling out $200,000 to hang this startling preconnubial portrait on her wall.
> — *Face* (BNC) 1990

park cattle animals of a breed of primitive cattle that are maintained in a semi-wild state in several parks in Britain, e.g. at Chillingham in Northumberland. They are typically white in colour with dark ears and muzzles. Also called **white park cattle**.

Park Lane name of a street in the West End of London, running alongside Hyde Park, used allusively to refer to the wealthy and aristocratic lifestyle traditionally typified by it.

> He drives around the streets of London in an old Volkswagen Beetle when he could purr along Park Lane in a Rolls-Royce.
> — *Sun* 26 April 1995

Charlie Parker (1920–55), American saxophonist, known as **Bird** or **Yardbird**. From 1944 he played with Thelonious Monk and Dizzy Gillespie, and became one of the key figures of the bebop movement.

Dorothy Parker (1893–1967), American humorist, literary critic, and writer. From 1927 Parker wrote book reviews and short stories for the *New Yorker* magazine, becoming one of its legendary wits; her fellow-writer Alexander Woollcott said of her:

> She is so odd a blend of Little Nell and Lady Macbeth. It is not so much the familiar phenomenon of a hand of steel in a velvet glove as a lacy sleeve with a bottle of vitriol concealed in its folds.
> — Alexander Woollcott *While Rome Burns* (1934)

Parkhurst a top-security British prison at Newport on the Isle of Wight, which was initially opened in 1838 as a model penal establishment for young offenders, taking boys who were later to be transported from the ➤ HULKS at Portsmouth.

Parkinson's law the notion that work expands so as to fill the time available for its completion. It is named after the English historian and journalist Cyril Northcote *Parkinson* (1909–93), who proposed it.

Parliament in the UK, the highest legislature, consisting of the Sovereign, the House of Lords, and the House of Commons; the members of this legislature for a particular period, especially between one dissolution and the next; a similar legislature in other nations and states. Recorded from Middle English, the word comes from Old French *parlement* 'speaking', from the verb *parler*.

A number of early Parliaments have acquired informal names reflecting their nature or actions.

See also ➤ GRATTAN'*s Parliament*, ➤ HIGH *Court of Parliament*, ➤ MOTHER *of Parliaments*.

Parliaments

NAME	YEAR
Addled Parliament	1614
Barebones Parliament	1653
Cavalier Parliament	1660
Convention Parliament	1660; 1688
Devil's Parliament	1459
Drunken Parliament	1661
Good Parliament	1376
Little Parliament	1653
Long Parliament	1640–53, 1659–60
Mad Parliament	1258
Merciless Parliament	1388
Mongrel Parliament	1681
Pensionary Parliament	1661–79
Rump Parliament	1648–53; 1659–60
Short Parliament	1640
Unlearned Parliament	1404
Unmerciful Parliament	1388
Useless Parliament	1625
Wonderful Parliament	1388

Parliament of Bats a parliament of 1426, held at Leicester during the minority of Henry VI, at which the Duke of Bedford as Regent attempted to settle a dispute between the Duke of Gloucester and the Chancellor, Beaufort; the name was given because the carrying of swords was forbidden, and many came instead armed with clubs or bludgeons.

Parliament of Dunces another name for the ➤ UNLEARNED *Parliament* of 1404, from which lawyers were excluded.

parliamentary train a train carrying passengers at a rate not exceeding one penny per mile, which, by a British Act of Parliament of 1844, every railway company was obliged to run daily each way over its system.

parlour a room in a monastery or convent that is set aside for conversation. Recorded from Middle English, the word comes from Anglo-Norman French *parlur* 'place for speaking'.

parlour game an indoor game, especially a word game; originally, a version of an outdoor game adapted for playing in a parlour.

Parmenides (fl. 5th century BC), Greek philosopher. Born in Elea in SW Italy, he founded the Eleatic school of philosophers. In his work *On Nature*, written in hexameter verse, he maintained that the apparent motion and changing forms of the universe are in fact manifestations of an unchanging and indivisible reality.

Parmentier cooked or served with potatoes, from the name of Antoine A. *Parmentier* (1737–1813), the French agriculturalist who popularized the potato in France.

Parnassian of or belonging to ➤ *Mount* PARNASSUS as the source of literary (especially poetic) inspiration.

The name *Parnassian* was also given to a group of French poets of the late 19th century who rejected Romanticism and emphasized strictness of form, named from the anthology *Le Parnasse contemporain* (1866).

Mount Parnassus a mountain in central Greece, just north of Delphi. Held to be sacred by the ancient Greeks, as was the spring of ➤ CASTALIA on its southern slopes, it was associated with Apollo and the Muses and regarded as a symbol of poetry.

Charles Stewart Parnell (1846–91), Irish nationalist leader. Parnell became leader of the Irish Home Rule faction in 1880 and raised the profile of Irish affairs through obstructive parliamentary tactics. He was forced to retire from public life in 1890 after being cited in the divorce of Katherine O'Shea, whom he married shortly before his death.

parody an imitation of the style of a particular writer, artist, or genre with deliberate exaggeration for comic effect. Recorded from the late 16th century, the word comes via late Latin from Greek *parōidia* 'burlesque poem'.

Paros a Greek island in the southern Aegean, in the Cyclades. It is noted for the translucent white Parian marble which has been quarried there since the 6th century BC.

Parousia in Christian theology, another term for ➤ Second *Coming;* the appearance of Christ in glory at the end of time. The word is Greek, and means literally 'being present'.

the Parquet (in France and French-speaking countries) the branch of the administration of the law that deals with the prosecution of crime. The word comes from French, meaning literally 'small park (i.e. delineated area)', and is the same word as *parquet* meaning flooring composed of wooden blocks arranged in a geometric pattern.

Thomas Parr (1483?–1635), known as **Old Parr**, and described as the 'old, old, very old man'. He became famous for his longevity in the 17th century, and in September 1635 was taken to London and presented to the king, Charles I, to whom he claimed that he had lived under ten kings and queens, from Edward IV to Charles himself. He died in November of that year and an autopsy of his body was performed by William Harvey; he was subsequently buried in Westminster Abbey.

parramatta a fine-quality twill fabric with a weft of worsted and a warp of cotton or silk, used originally as a dress material and now particularly in the making of rubber-proofed garments. It is named (in the early 19th century) after *Parramatta*, a city in New South Wales, Australia, which was the site of a prison whose inmates manufactured the cloth for clothing supplied to the convict servants of settlers.

parricide the killing of a parent or other near relative. The word comes (in the late 16th century) via French from Latin *parricidium* 'murder of a parent', with first element of unknown origin, but for long associated with Latin *pater* 'father' and *parens* 'parent'.

parrot the brightly-coloured *parrot*, often able to mimic the human voice, is referred to in speaking of a person who mechanically repeats the words or actions of another.

The name is recorded from the early 16th century,

and probably comes from dialect French *perrot*, diminutive of the male given name *Pierre* 'Peter'.

Parsee an adherent of Zoroastrianism, especially a descendant of those Zoroastrians who fled to India from Muslim persecution in Persia during the 7th–8th centuries. The name comes from Persian *pārsī* 'Persian'.

Parsifal another name for ➤ Perceval.

parsley a biennial plant with white flowers and aromatic leaves which are either crinkly or flat and are used as a culinary herb and for garnishing food. There is a traditional belief that it is unlucky to give a parsley-plant as a present; it was also said that girl children were found *in the parsley-bed*, as opposed to boy children being found *under the gooseberry bush*.

See also ➤ cow *parsley.*

parsley seed goes nine times to the Devil proverbial saying, mid 17th century; meaning that it is often slow to germinate.

parsnips see ➤ fine *words butter no parsnips.*

parson see also ➤ Macaroni *Parson.*

parson-and-clerk the running fiery spots observed on paper as it burns, especially in a children's game.

parson-has-lost-his-coat a forfeit game in which the players, under assumed names, accuse each other of stealing the parson's possession, and anyone who fails to answer pays a forfeit.

Parson's Pleasure at Oxford, a former bathing enclosure of the banks of the Cherwell restricted to men's use and later known for nude bathing.

Charles Parsons (1854–1931), British engineer, scientist, and manufacturer. He patented and built the first practical steam turbine in 1884, designed to drive electricity generators. He also developed steam turbines for marine propulsion, and his experimental vessel *Turbinia* caused a sensation in 1897.

part of speech a category to which a word is assigned in accordance with its syntactic functions. In English the main parts of speech are noun, pronoun, adjective, determiner, verb, adverb, preposition, conjunction, and interjection.

Partant pour la Syrie title ('Departing for Syria) of the official march of Second Empire French troops; it was said to have been the composition of

Queen Hortense, stepdaughter of Napoleon and mother of Napoleon III, but it is now thought that the words were composed by the Comte de Laborde (1774–1842), and the music chiefly by the Dutch flute player Philip Drouet (1792–1873).

Parthenon the temple of Athene Parthenos, built on the Acropolis in 447–432 BC by Pericles to honour Athens' patron goddess and to commemorate the recent Greek victory over the Persians. It was designed by Ictinus and Callicrates with sculptures by Phidias, including a colossal gold and ivory statue of Athene. It remains standing, despite being severely damaged by Venetian bombardment in 1687.

See also ➤ ELGIN *Marbles*.

Parthenope in Greek mythology, one of the sirens. The name was also that of a Greek colony from Cumae on the site of the modern Naples.

Parthenopean Republic the short-lived republic established in Naples by French revolutionary forces in 1799; the term is first used in a letter of Lord Nelson, 19 January 1799, 'the Parthenopien Republic is forming.'

Parthia an ancient kingdom which lay SE of the Caspian Sea in present-day Iran. From *c.*250 BC to *c.*230 AD the Parthians ruled an empire stretching from the Euphrates to the Indus. Established by the Parthians' rebellion against the Seleucids, the empire reached the peak of its power around the 2nd century BC. It was eventually eclipsed by the Sassanians. The Parthians were skilled horsemen, with a culture that contained a mixture of Greek and Persian elements.

Parthian shot a parting shot, so named because of the trick used by Parthians of shooting arrows backwards while in real or pretended flight.

particular see ➤ LONDON *particular*.

Particular Baptist a member of a Baptist denomination holding the doctrine of the election, or choosing by God for salvation, and redemption of some but not all people.

particularism the theological doctrine that some but not all people are elected and redeemed.

the parting of the ways the moment at which a choice must be made or at which two people must separate; after Ezekiel 21:21 'The king of Babylon stood at the parting of the ways.'

like Mrs Partington mopping up the Atlantic proverbial reference to a hopeless task, originating in a speech by Sidney Smith in 1831, in which he alluded to a Mrs Partington during a great storm at Sidmouth in 1824, when she tried to keep the sea out of her house with a mop; Smith likened the attempts of the Lords to impede the progress of reform to her efforts.

Dame Partlet a name for a hen, traditionally the mate of ➤ CHANTICLEER. The name comes from Old French *Pertelote*, a female proper name.

Parvati in Hindu mythology, a benevolent goddess, wife of Shiva, mother of Ganesha and Skanda, often identified in her malevolent aspect with Durga and Kali. The name comes from Sanskrit *Pārvatī*, literally 'daughter of the mountain'.

parvenu having recently achieved, or associated with someone who has recently achieved, wealth, influence, or celebrity despite obscure origins. Recorded from the early 19th century, the word comes from French, and means literally 'arrived'.

parvis an enclosed area in front of a cathedral or church, typically one that is surrounded with colonnades or porticoes. The word is based on late Latin *paradisus* 'paradise', in the Middle Ages denoting a court in front of St Peter's, Rome.

Blaise Pascal (1623–62), French mathematician, physicist, and religious philosopher. A child prodigy, before the age of 20 he had proved a geometric theorem and constructed the first mechanical calculator to be offered for sale. He founded the theory of probabilities and developed a forerunner of integral calculus, but is best known for deriving the principle that the pressure of a fluid at rest is transmitted equally in all directions. His *Lettres Provinciales* (1656–7) and *Pensées* (1670) argue for his Jansenist Christianity.

Pascal's triangle a triangular array of numbers in which those at the ends of the rows are 1 and each of the others is the sum of the nearest two numbers in the row above (the apex, 1, being at the top).

Pascal's wager the argument that it is in one's own best interest to behave as if God exists, since the possibility of eternal punishment in hell outweighs any advantage in believing otherwise.

Pasch the Christian festival of Easter; the Jewish festival of Passover. The name comes ultimately from Hebrew *pesaḥ* 'Passover'.

pasch-egg an egg dyed various colours and hard boiled, to be given as an Easter gift; an Easter egg. Also called *pace-egg*.

paschal candle a large candle blessed and lighted in the service of Holy Saturday and placed by the altar until Pentecost or (formerly) Ascension Day.

paschal lamb a lamb sacrificed at Passover; allusively, Christ.

Paschaltide in the Christian Church, the period following Easter Sunday.

pasha former title for a Turkish officer of high rank. There were three grades of pashas, distinguished by the number of horsetails they wore: three tails indicated a rank corresponding to commanding general; two, a rank corresponding to general of division; one, a rank corresponding to general of brigade; from this come the expressions **pasha of three tails** and **pasha of two tails**.

Recorded from the 17th century, the word comes from Turkish *paşa*.

> The pashas of three tails have those ensigns . . . placed in a very conspicuous manner before their tents.
> — Lady Mary Wortley Montagu letter, 17 May 1717

La Pasionaria nickname (meaning in Spanish 'passion-flower') of the Spanish Communist leader Dolores Ibarruri (1895–1975), renowned for her emotional oratory and colourful personality, and remembered particularly for her '*No pasarán* [They shall not pass]' in a radio broadcast from Madrid, 19 July 1936.

In extended usage, the term may denote a woman seen as having a similar popularity as a leader, as in Denis Healey's ironic comment on Margaret Thatcher as being 'La Pasionaria of middle-class privilege'.

Pasiphaë in Greek mythology, the wife of Minos and mother of the ➤ MINOTAUR, and of ➤ ARIADNE and Phaedra.

paso an image or group of images representing Passion scenes, carried in procession as part of Holy Week observances in Spain.

Pier Paolo Pasolini (1922–75), Italian film director and novelist. A Marxist, he drew on his experiences in the slums of Rome for his work, but became recognized for his controversial, bawdy literary adaptations such as *The Gospel According to St Matthew* (1964) and *The Canterbury Tales* (1973).

pasque flower a spring-flowering European plant related to the anemones, with purple flowers and fern-like foliage. Recorded (as *passeflower*) from the late 16th century, the name comes from French *passe-fleur*. The change in spelling of the first word was due to association with archaic *pasque* 'Easter' (because of the plant's early flowering).

pasquinade a satire or lampoon, originally one displayed or delivered publicly in a public place. The word comes through Italian from *Pasquino*, the name of a mutilated statue, or piece of ancient statuary, disinterred at Rome in 1501 and set up by Cardinal Caraffa at the corner of his palace near the Piazza Navona. Under his patronage, it became the annual custom on St. Mark's Day to 'restore' temporarily and dress up this torso to represent some historical or mythological personage of antiquity; on which occasion professors and students of the newly restored Ancient Learning saluted Pasquin in Latin verses which were usually posted or placed on the statue; in due course, these *pasquinate* or pasquinades tended to become satirical, and the term began to be applied, not only in Rome, but in other countries, to satirical compositions and lampoons, political, ecclesiastical, or personal, the anonymous authors of which often sheltered themselves under the conventional name of Pasquin.

According to an early collection of such verses, the name Pasquino or Pasquillo originated in that of a schoolmaster who lived opposite the spot where the statue was found; a later tradition makes him a caustic tailor or shoemaker; another calls him a barber.

pass see also ➤ PASS *the buck*.

sell the pass betray a cause (a pass is here viewed as a strategic entry to a country).

pass on the torch pass on a tradition; the expression comes originally from the Roman poet Lucretius (*c*.94–55 BC) in *De Rerum Natura*, 'Some races increase, others are reduced, and in a short while the generations of living creatures are changed and like runners relay the torch of life.' The reference is to the *torch-race* of classical antiquity, in which the runners carried lighted torches and (in some cases) passed them on to other runners stationed at certain points.

passade a movement performed in advanced dressage and classical riding, in which the horse performs a 180° turn, with its forelegs describing a large circle and its hind legs a smaller one.

passage see also ➤ BIRD *of passage,* ➤ MIDDLE *passage,* ➤ NORTH-*East Passage,* ➤ NORTH-*West Passage,* ➤ RITE *of passage.*

passage grave a prehistoric megalithic burial chamber of a type found chiefly in western Europe, with a passage leading to the exterior. Passage graves were originally covered by a mound, which in many cases has disappeared, and most date from the Neolithic period.

passant in heraldry, (of an animal) represented as walking, with the right front foot raised. The animal is depicted in profile facing the dexter (left) side with the tail raised, unless otherwise specified (e.g. as 'passant guardant').

Battle of Passchendaele a prolonged episode of trench warfare involving appalling loss of life during the First World War in 1917, near the village of Passchendaele in western Belgium. It is also known as the third Battle of Ypres.

passenger pigeon an extinct long-tailed North American pigeon, noted for its long migrations in huge flocks. It was relentlessly hunted, the last individual dying in captivity in 1914.

Passepartout name of Phileas Fogg's valet in Jules Verne's *Around the World in Eighty Days* (1873); the French word *passepartout* means literally something which goes or provides a means of going everywhere.

passim (of allusions or references in a published work) to be found at various places throughout the text. The word is Latin, and comes from *passus* 'scattered'.

passing bell in early use, a bell rung for a dying person at the point of death, as a signal for prayers for the departing soul; later, a bell rung immediately after a person's death.

passion see also ➤ RULING *passion,* ➤ *the* TENDER *passion.*

the Passion the suffering and death of Jesus, sometimes including his agony in Gethsemane. Recorded from Middle English, the word comes via Old French from late Latin *passio(n-)* (chiefly a term in Christian theology), from Latin *pati* 'suffer'.

Instruments of the Passion the objects associated with Christ's Passion, such as the Cross, the crown of thorns, and the nails.

passion flower an evergreen climbing plant of warm regions, which bears distinctive flowers with parts that supposedly resemble Instruments of the Passion. The three stigmas are said to correspond to the nails, the five stamens to the wounds, the corona to the crown of thorns, and the ten perianth segments to the apostles. The lobed leaves and tendrils of the plant were also said to represent the hands and scourges of Jesus' torturers.

passion play a dramatic performance representing Jesus's Passion from the Last Supper to the Crucifixion.

Passion Sunday the fifth Sunday in Lent, the beginning of Passiontide; the Sunday before Palm Sunday. In the Roman Catholic Church this was suppressed as a separate observance in the Second Vatican Council's revision of the Calendar in 1969; instead, the Passion is regarded as commemorated on Palm Sunday, now properly called Passion (Palm) Sunday.

Passion Week the week between Passion Sunday and Palm Sunday; formerly also, the week immediately before Easter, Holy Week.

Passionist a member of the Congregation of the Passion (formally the Congregation of the Discalced Clerks of the most Holy Cross and Passion of our Lord Jesus Christ), a religious order devoted to keeping alive the memory of Christ's Passion, founded by Paolo Francesco Danei (St Paul of the Cross) in Italy in 1720.

Passover the major Jewish spring festival which commemorates the liberation of the Israelites from Egyptian bondage, lasting seven or eight days from the 15th day of Nisan. The name comes from *pass over* 'pass without touching', with reference to the biblical story in Exodus 12 of how the Israelites escaped by marking their doorposts with the blood of a lamb, when the plague which destroyed their firstborn fell on the Egyptians.

things past cannot be recalled proverbial saying, late 15th century.

past master a person who is particularly skilled at a specified activity or art. The term is first recorded (in the mid 18th century) as denoting a person who has filled the office of master in a guild or Freemason's Lodge, and the figurative use may have arisen partly in allusion to the expertise resulting from having held such an office. It may however also refer to the expertise of someone who has passed the necessary training to qualify as a master in any art, science, or occupation.

Louis Pasteur (1822–95), French chemist and bacteriologist. He introduced pasteurization and made pioneering studies in vaccination techniques.

the Paston Letters a collection of letters preserved by the Pastons, a well-to-do Norfolk family, written between *c.*1420 and 1504. They are of great value for the evidence they give of the language of their time, but even more for the general historical, political, and social interest they provide. They concern three generations of the family, and most were written in the reigns of Henry VI, Edward IV, and Richard III. They are unique as historical material, showing the violence and anarchy of 15th-century England and the domestic conditions in which a family of this class lived.

pastoral a form of literature portraying an idealized version of country life, the earliest example of which is found in the Idylls of the Greek poet ➤ Theocritus (*c.*310–*c.*250 bc). The *pastoral* became popular during the Renaissance, and inspired particularly such prose romances as Sidney's *Arcadia*.

The word comes ultimately from Latin *pastor* 'shepherd'; in late Middle English, *pastoral* denoted a book on the cure or care of souls, often with reference to the title of St Gregory the Great's *Cura Pastoralis* ('Pastoral Care'), which had been translated into English by King Alfred.

Pastoral Epistles the books of the New Testament comprising the two letters of Paul to Timothy and the one to Titus, which deal chiefly with the duties of those charged with the care of souls.

pastoral letter an official letter from a bishop to all the clergy or members of his or her diocese.

pastoral staff a bishop's crozier.

pastoral theology Christian theology that considers religious truth in relation to spiritual needs.

Patagon former name for a member of a native South American people inhabiting a region in southern Argentina and Chile, alleged by early travellers to be the tallest known. The modern name of this region (*Patagonia*) derives from this name,

which comes from Spanish *patagon* 'large clumsy foot'.

Patarene a member of any of various heretical groups in the 12th century with extreme rigorous or Manichaean views, especially the Cathars; also used for a member of a group of craftsmen, peasants, and others, in 11th-century Milan, who opposed clerical concubinage and marriage The name probably comes ultimately from *Pattaria*, the ragmen's quarter of Milan.

Patavinian a native or inhabitant of the Roman town of *Patavium* (now ➤ Padua), especially the Roman historian Livy.

Patavinity the dialectal characteristics of the Latin of *Patavium* (now ➤ Padua), especially as found in Livy's writings.

patch a foolish person, a simpleton, said by T. Wilson (1553) and Heywood (1562), to have come from the nickname of Cardinal Wolsey's 'fool' or jester, his real surname being Sexton.

He is supposed by some to have been so called from his patched garb, or patched face; but the word may be an anglicized form of Italian *pazzo* 'fool'. It seems however to have been later associated or taken as identical with *patch* meaning 'a piece of cloth used for mending', as in Shakespeare's 'patch'd foole'.

patches see ➤ king of shreds *and patches.*

patent a government authority or licence to an individual or organization conferring a right or title for a set period, especially the sole right to make, use, or sell some invention. Recorded from late Middle English, the word comes via Old French from Latin *patent-* 'lying open'.

See also ➤ letters *patent.*

patent roll a parchment roll containing the ➤ letters *patent* issued in Britain (or formerly in England) in any one year.

paternoster (in the Roman Catholic Church) the Lord's Prayer, especially in Latin. Also, any of a number of special beads occurring at regular intervals in a rosary, indicating that the Lord's Prayer is to be recited. The name comes from Latin '*Pater noster* [our Father]', the first two words of the prayer in Latin.

See also ➤ *no* penny, *no paternoster,* ➤ say *an ape's paternoster,* ➤ say *the devil's paternoster.*

Paternoster Row a street in London near St Paul's, traditionally the site of booksellers and publishers.

Paterson's curse in Australia, a naturalized blue-flowered European plant which is variously regarded as a noxious weed, useful drought fodder, or a valuable honey plant; it is probably named after Richard Eyre *Patterson* (1844–1918), a grazier occupying various stations near Albury from *c.*1874.

path see ➤ EIGHTFOLD *path*, ➤ *a* LION *in the path*, ➤ PRIMROSE *path*, ➤ SHINING *Path*.

Charles Pathé (1863–1957), French film pioneer. In 1896 he and his brothers founded a company which came to dominate the production and distribution of films. It became internationally known for its newsreels, first introduced in France in 1909.

pathetic fallacy the attribution of human feelings and responses to inanimate things or animals, especially in art and literature. The term was coined by the critic John Ruskin (1819–1900):

> All violent feelings . . . produce . . . a falseness in . . . impressions of external things, which I would generally characterize as the 'Pathetic fallacy'.
> — John Ruskin *Modern Painters* (1856)

Pathfinder[1] in the novels of James Fenimore Cooper, one of the names given to ➤ NATTY *Bumppo*.

Pathfinder[2] an unmanned American spacecraft which landed on Mars in 1997, deploying a small robotic rover (Sojourner) to explore the surface and examine the rocks.

patience is a virtue proverbial saying, late 14th century.

Patmos a Greek island in the Aegean Sea, one of the Dodecanese group. It is believed that St John was living there in exile (from AD 95) when he had the visions described in Revelation.

patonce in heraldry, (of a cross) having limbs usually expanding in a curved form from the centre, with ends resembling those of the cross flory.

Patras an industrial port in the NW Peloponnese, on the Gulf of Patras. Taken by the Turks in the 18th century, it was the site in 1821 of the outbreak of the Greek war of independence. It was finally freed in 1828.

patria a person's native country or homeland; in extended use, heaven, regarded as the true home from which the soul is exiled while on earth. The word is Latin, and means literally 'fatherland'.

See also ➤ DULCE *et decorum est pro patria mori*.

patriarch the male head of a family or tribe; a person regarded as the oldest or most venerable of a group. The name is used particularly to denote any of those biblical figures regarded as fathers of the human race, especially ➤ ABRAHAM, ➤ ISAAC, and ➤ JACOB, and their forefathers, or the sons of Jacob.

Patriarch is also used for the title of a most senior Orthodox or Catholic bishop, in particular, a bishop of one of the most ancient Christian sees (Alexandria, Antioch, Constantinople, Jerusalem, and formerly Rome), and the head of an autocephalous or independent Orthodox Church.

Recorded from Middle English, the word comes via Old French and ecclesiastical Latin from Greek *patriarkhēs*, from *patria* 'family' + *arkhēs* 'ruling'.

See also ➤ ECUMENICAL *Patriarch*.

Patriarchal church each of the five great basilicas of Rome (St John Lateran, St Peter's, St Paul's outside the Walls, Santa Maria Maggiore, and St Laurence outside the Walls).

patriarchal cross a cross with two transverse pieces, the upper being the shorter, as an emblem of the patriarchs of the Greek Orthodox Church.

patrician a member of a noble family or class in ancient Rome. The rank was originally hereditary, but in Imperial Rome patricians could be appointed by the emperor. In the later Roman Empire and Byzantine Empire, *patrician* was an honorific title bestowed by the Emperor at Byzantium, introduced by Constantine I; it was also used for an officer, originally bearing this distinction, sent or appointed as representative of the Byzantine Emperor to administer the provinces of Italy and Africa.

In extended use, an aristocrat or nobleman, a member of a long-established wealthy family. Recorded from late Middle English, the word comes via Old French from Latin *patricius* 'having a noble father'.

St Patrick (5th century), Apostle and patron saint of Ireland. His *Confession* is the chief source for the events of his life. Of Romano-British parentage, he was taken as a slave to Ireland, where he experienced a religious conversion; having escaped to Britain, where he received training for the priesthood, he returned to Ireland to preach the Gospel *c.*435. He founded the archiepiscopal see of Armagh in about 454.

Legends of the saint include the tradition that he

used the shamrock to explain the nature of the Trinity, and that he was responsible for banishing snakes from Ireland.

☐ **FEAST DAY** His feast day is 17 March.

Order of St Patrick a former British order or knighthood instituted in 1783; its special epithet is 'most illustrious'.

St Patrick's cross a red diagonal cross on a white ground.

St Patrick's Purgatory a cavern on an island in Lough Derg, Co. Donegal, Ireland, where according to legend Christ appeared to St Patrick, and showed him a deep pit in which whoever spent one day and one night could see the torments of hell and the joys of heaven.

patrimonial seas an area extending beyond territorial waters, the natural resources of which belong to the coastal nation though vessels of other countries have freedom of passage through it.

patrimony of St Peter a name for territory held by the Pope; the ➤ PAPAL *States*.

patrin a trail left by gypsies, using arrangements of grass, leaves, and twigs, to indicate the direction taken. The word is Romany, and originally meant 'leaf'.

Patriots' Day in the US, the anniversary of the Battle of Lexington and Concord in the American War of Independence, 19 April 1775, observed since 1894 as a legal holiday in Maine and Massachusetts.

Patripassian a person who believes that God the Father suffered on the Cross in the person of the Son (a heresy of the 3rd century). The word comes from late Latin *patripassianus*, from *pater* 'father' + *passus* 'having suffered'.

patristics the branch of Christian theology that deals with the lives, writings, and doctrines of the early Christian theologians or Fathers of the Church.

Patroclus a Greek hero of the Trojan War, the close friend of Achilles. The *Iliad* describes how Patroclus' death at the hands of Hector led ➤ ACHILLES to return to battle, and to avenge his friend by killing Hector and dragging his body round the walls of Troy.

patron a person who gives financial or other support to a person, organization, cause, or activity; in early use, implying something of the superior relation in ancient Rome of a *patron*, a person of status or distinction who gave protection and aid to a client in return for certain services. The role of a patron was commented on notably by Samuel Johnson:

> Patron. Commonly a wretch who supports with insolence, and is paid with flattery.
> — Samuel Johnson *A Dictionary of the English Language* (1755)

patron saint a saint chosen or regarded as the special protector of or intercessor for a person, place, country, occupation, or institution.

Arms of Patronage in heraldry, arms derived from those of a patron or superior.

Patronage Secretary (in the UK) the member of the government through whom patronage is administered.

patronal festival the festival of a patron saint, especially the saint to whom a church is dedicated.

patronymic a name derived from the name of a father or ancestor, e.g. *Johnson, O'Brien, Ivanovich*.

patté in heraldry, (of a cross) having limbs which are nearly triangular, being very narrow where they meet and widening out towards the extremities.

patte de velours a cat's paw with the claws held in, as a symbol of resolution or inflexibility combined with apparent gentleness. The phrase is French, meaning 'velvet paw'.

patten historical term for a shoe or clog with a raised sole or set on an iron ring, worn to raise one's feet above wet or muddy ground when walking outdoors.

patter rapid or smooth-flowing continuous talk, such as that used by a comedian or salesman; rapid speech included in a song, especially for comic effect.

Patter is recorded from late Middle English, as a verb in the sense 'recite (a prayer or charm) rapidly'; it comes from ➤ PATERNOSTER. The noun in this sense dates from the 18th century.

patteroller in 19th-century America, a person who patrolled to restrict the movements of blacks at night in the southern US. The word was a variant of *patroller*.

Paul see also ➤ OOM *Paul*, ➤ *Paul* BUNYAN, ➤ ROB *Peter to pay Paul*.

St Paul[1] (d. *c*.64), missionary of Jewish descent; known as *Paul the Apostle*, or *Saul of Tarsus*, or *the Apostle of the Gentiles*. He first opposed the followers of Jesus, assisting at the martyrdom of St Stephen, but while travelling to Damascus he experienced a vision (and was temporarily struck blind), after which he was converted to Christianity; he became one of the first major Christian missionaries and theologians, and his epistles form part of the New Testament.

After a number of missionary journeys, Paul was arrested in Jerusalem for preaching against the Jewish Law; as a Roman citizen, he appealed to Caesar, and was sent for trial to Rome. He was martyred there during the persecution of Nero, traditionally on the same day as ➤ *St* PETER.

Paul's experience on the ➤ *road to* DAMASCUS has become proverbial as a life-changing revelation.

□ **EMBLEM** Paul's emblem is the sword with which he is said to have been executed.

□ **FEAST DAY** His feast day is 29 June; the feast of the Conversion of St Paul is 16 January.

St Paul[2] (d. *c*.345), said to have been the first Christian hermit, who had gone into the desert to escape persecution, and lived there for many years; Anthony of Egypt visited him there, and arranged for his burial; a raven is said to have dropped a loaf of bread beside them at their meeting. According to legend, his grave was dug by two lions at Anthony's request, and in art Paul is often shown with them, or with the palm-tree from which he gained food and shelter.

□ **EMBLEM** Paul may be shown with lions, a palm tree, and a crow or raven.

□ **FEAST DAY** His feast day is 10 January in the Western Church and 5 or 15 January in the Eastern Church.

Paul III (1468–1549), Italian pope 1534–49. He excommunicated Henry VIII of England in 1538, instituted the order of the Jesuits in 1540, and initiated the Council of Trent in 1545. Paul III was also a patron of the arts, commissioning Michelangelo to paint the Sistine Chapel and to design the dome of St Peter's Basilica.

Paul Jones a ballroom dance in which the dancers change partners after circling in concentric rings of men and women, named after John *Paul Jones* (1747–92), Scottish-born American admiral.

Paul Pry an inquisitive person, from the name of a character in a US song of 1820.

Paul the Deacon (*c*.725–97), a Lombard who was at one time an inmate of the Benedictine house of Monte Cassino, where he met Charlemagne. He is one of the best chroniclers of the Dark Ages, author of the *Historia Lombardorum*, and an important figure in the Carolingian Renaissance.

Children of Paul's a company of boy actors, recruited from the choristers of St Paul's Cathedral, whose performances enjoyed great popularity at the end of the 16th and beginning of the 17th centuries. They performed among others the works of Lyly. The *Children of the Chapel*, recruited from the choristers of the Chapel Royal, was another company enjoying popular favour at the same time. Their rivalry with men actors is alluded to in *Hamlet*.

Paul's cross a cross (destroyed in 1643) in the close of St. Paul's Cathedral, at which religious and political gatherings were often held. The sermon on the text 'bastard slips shall not take deep root' (Wisdom 4:3), which asserted the illegitimacy of Edward V and the consequent right to the crown of his uncle Richard of Gloucester, later Richard III, was preached here on 22 June 1483.

if Saint Paul's day be fair and clear, it will betide a happy year proverbial saying, late 16th century; the day in question is 16 January, the feast of the Conversion of St Paul.

Wolfgang Pauli (1900–58), Austrian-born American physicist. He made a major contribution to quantum theory with his *exclusion principle*, according to which only two electrons in an atom could occupy the same quantum level, provided they had opposite spins. In 1931 he postulated the existence of the neutrino, later discovered by Enrico Fermi.

Paulian a member of a sect founded by Paul of Samosata in the 3rd century AD, which rejected the separate personalities of the Logos and the Holy Spirit and denied Christ's pre-existence.

Paulician a member of a sect which arose in Armenia in the 7th century AD, having affinities with the Paulians and professing a modified form of Manichaeism.

Pauline (in the Roman Catholic Church) of or relating to Pope Paul VI, or the liturgical and doctrinal reforms pursued during his pontificate (1963–78) as a result of the Second Vatican Council.

Pauline privilege conceded by St Paul (1 Corinthians 7:15) to allow a newly converted Christian to contract a new marriage should the current non-Christian spouse wish to separate or seriously impede his or her Christian observance.

Linus Carl Pauling (1901–94), American chemist. He is renowned for his study of molecular structure and chemical bonding, for which he received the 1954 Nobel Prize for Chemistry. His suggestion of a helical structure for proteins formed the foundation for the elucidation of the structure of DNA. He was involved with attempts to ban nuclear weapons, for which he was awarded the Nobel Peace Prize in 1962.

Paumanok Indian name for Long Island, often used by Walt Whitman, as in the poem 'Starting from Paumanok'.

Pausanias (2nd century), Greek geographer and historian. His *Description of Greece* (also called the *Itinerary of Greece*) is a guide to the topography and remains of ancient Greece and is still considered an invaluable source of information.

pavane a stately dance in slow duple time, popular in the 16th and 17th centuries and performed in elaborate clothing. Recorded from the mid 16th century, the word is said to comes via French from Italian *pavana*, feminine adjective from *Pavo*, dialect name of Padua; an alternative explanation derives it from Spanish *pavo* 'peacock'.

pavis a large convex shield for protecting the whole body against arrows, used especially in sieges. The name comes ultimately from *Pavia*, a city in northern Italy where pavises were originally made.

Ivan Pavlov (1849–1936), Russian physiologist. He was awarded a Nobel Prize in 1904 for his work on digestion, but is best known for his studies on the conditioned reflex. He showed by experiment with dogs how the secretion of saliva can be stimulated not only by food but also by the sound of a bell associated with the presentation of food.

Anna Pavlova (1881–1931), Russian dancer, resident in Britain from 1912. Her highly acclaimed solo dance *The Dying Swan* was created for her by Michel Fokine in 1905. On settling in Britain she formed her own company, and embarked on numerous tours which made her a pioneer of classical ballet all over the world.

paw see ➤ CAT*'s paw*.

pawnbrokers ➤ St NICHOLAS *of Myra* is the patron saint of pawnbrokers, as the three bags of gold which he provided as dowries for three girls are seen as connected with the ➤ *three* GOLDEN *balls* of the pawnbrokers' sign.

pawn a chess piece of the smallest size and value, that moves one square forwards along its file if unobstructed (or two on the first move), or one square diagonally forwards when making a capture. Each player begins with eight pawns on the second rank, and can promote a pawn to become any other piece (typically a queen) if it reaches the opponent's end of the board. In figurative use, a *pawn* is a person used by others for their own purposes.

   Recorded from late Middle English, the word comes via Anglo-Norman French from medieval Latin *pedo* 'foot-soldier', from Latin *pes, ped-* 'foot'.

Pax in Roman mythology, the goddess of peace, equivalent of the Greek goddess Eirene.

pax (in the Christian Church) the kissing by all the participants at a mass of a tablet depicting the Crucifixion or other sacred object; the kiss of peace.

Pax Romana the peace which existed between nationalities within the Roman Empire. The *Pax Romana* is generally regarded as operating from the beginning of Augustus's reign (27 BC) to the death of Marcus Aurelius (AD 180), and in extended usage may apply to a widespread state of peace maintained under any jurisdiction.

   From the 19th century, various terms modelled on this are recorded, as **Pax Americana** and **Pax Britannica**.

> Within the Washington conference rooms where the strategic theorists decorate their maps with lines of force and arcs of crisis, the Pax Americana remains as it was in 1947, as permanent and serene as the dome on the Capitol or the stars in the flag.
> — *Harper's Magazine* May 1992

pax vobis in the Christian Church, the Latin phrase meaning 'peace be with you', reflecting Christ's greeting to the Apostles after his resurrection as recounted in John 20.

Joseph Paxton (1801–65), English gardener and architect. He became head gardener at Chatsworth House in Derbyshire in 1826 and designed a series of glass-and-iron greenhouses. He later reworked these in his design for the ➤ CRYSTAL *Palace* (1851).

pay beforehand was never well served proverbial saying, late 16th century.

he that cannot pay, let him pray proverbial saying, early 17th century.

paynim archaic term for a pagan; a non-Christian, especially a Muslim. Recorded from Middle English, the word comes ultimately from ecclesiastical Latin *paganismus* 'heathenism'.

payola in the US, the practice of bribing someone to use their influence or position to promote a particular product or interest. Recorded from the 1930s, the word comes from *pay* + *Victrola*, the name of a make of gramophone.

pays see also ➤ *he who pays the* PIPER *calls the tune.*

you pays your money and you takes your choice proverbial saying, mid 19th century.

Pazand a transcription of or the method of transcribing Persian sacred texts from the Pahlavi into the Avesta script. The name comes from Persian *pāzand* 'interpretation of the Zend' (see ➤ ZEND-*Avesta*).

PC 49 the central character of a children's radio series, 1946–53, *PC 49* was an untypical British police constable whose name was Archibald Berkeley Willoughby. From 1955 he appeared in a strip cartoon in the *Eagle*.

the princess and the pea a fairy-story by Hans Christian Andersen (1805–75), about a princess who can feel a pea even beneath twelve mattresses; she is taken allusively as a type of extreme sensitivity who is irked unbearably by something.

> It's the old fairy tale: I'm the princess, and the entire world is the pea.
> — *Mother Jones* January 1992

peace see also ➤ BREACH *of the peace,* ➤ CARTHAGINIAN *peace,* ➤ CONSERVATORS *of the peace,* ➤ JUSTICE *of the Peace,* ➤ the KISS *of peace,* ➤ *Peace of* UTRECHT, ➤ PIPE *of peace,* ➤ PRINCE *of Peace,* ➤ *Treaty of* PERPETUAL *Peace,* ➤ WAND *of peace.*

peace at any price name for a political philosophy which in the 19th century was particularly associated by their opponents (such as Lord Palmerston) with the liberal politicians John Bright (1811–89) and Richard Cobden (1804–65).

Peace Corps in the US, an organization (created by the Peace Corps Act of 1961) which sends young people to work as volunteers in developing countries.

peace dividend a (financial) benefit from reduced defence spending; a sum of public money which may become available for other purposes when spending on defence is reduced. The term was first recorded in the US in the late 1960s, at a time when the potential benefits of withdrawal from the war in Vietnam were increasingly acknowledged, and gained a high profile again in the early 1990s following the breakup of the Soviet Union. However, the Gulf War, involving massive use of US weaponry, followed the ending of the Cold War, and continuing conflict in areas such as the former Yugoslavia and the Middle East has meant that despite cuts in defence budgets, the *peace dividend* has remained elusive.

no peace for the wicked proverbial saying, with biblical allusion to Isaiah 48:22, 'There is no peace, saith the Lord, unto the wicked.'

Peace Garden State informal name for North Dakota.

peace in our time originally from the *Book of Common Prayer* (1662), 'Give peace in our time, O Lord', this phrase was famously used by Neville Chamberlain (1869–1940) on his return from Munich in 1938:

> This is the second time in our history that there has come back from Germany to Downing Street peace with honour. I believe that it is peace for our time.
> — Neville Chamberlain speech from 10 Downing Street, 30 September 1938

Peace of Monsieur signed in 1576 between the Huguenots and Henry III, king of France, arranged by the king's brother, the Duke of Alençon.

Peace Pledge Union a pacifist organization formed in 1936 and supported by a number of socialist writers and intellectuals including Bertrand Russell, Siegfried Sassoon, and Aldous Huxley.

if you want peace, you must prepare for war proverbial saying, mid 16th century; the 4th-century Roman military writer Vegetius had said, '*Qui desiderat pacem, praeparet bellum* [Let him who desires peace, prepare for war].'

peace process a series of initiatives, talks, and negotiations, designed to bring about a negotiated settlement between warring or disputing parties; in the 1990s, the term has been used with particular reference to attempts at a settlement in Northern Ireland.

peace with honour a phrase recorded from the 17th century, but used most famously by Benjamin Disraeli, Lord Beaconsfield, on his return from the Congress of Berlin:

> Lord Salisbury and myself have brought you back peace—but a peace I hope with honour.
> — Benjamin Disraeli speech, 16 July 1878

peach Melba a dish of ice cream and peaches with liqueur or sauce, originally created by the French chef Escoffier (1846–1935) in 1893 in honour of the singer Dame Nellie *Melba* when she was staying at the Savoy Hotel.

Peach State informal name for the US state of Georgia.

Peachum the receiver and informer who betrays the highwayman ➤ MACHEATH in John Gay's *The Beggar's Opera* (1728); his name comes from the informal verb *peach* 'inform on', a shortening of the archaic *appeach*, ultimately from the French base of *impeach*.

peacock a male peafowl, which has brilliant blue and green plumage and very long tail feathers that have eye-like markings and can be erected and expanded in display like a fan; in Greek mythology, the 'eyes' were those of the hundred-eyed ➤ ARGUS, placed there by Hera after Hermes killed him. The bird is proverbially taken as the type of an ostentatious, proud, or vain person; it may also be taken as a bird of ill-omen.

In the fable of the ➤ BORROWED *plumes*, a jay or jackdaw is said to have decked itself in peacock's feathers in an unsuccessful attempt to impress.

In Hindu tradition, a peacock may be shown as the mount of the war-god ➤ SKANDA.

Mrs Peacock one of the six stock characters constituting the murderer and suspects in the game of ➤ CLUEDO.

Peacock Alley the main corridor of the original Waldorf-Astoria Hotel in New York, so called because fashionable people paraded there.

> Seedy-respectable or Peacock Alley clothes.
> — John Dos Passos *42nd Parallel* (1930)

peacock in his pride in heraldry, a peacock represented as facing the spectator with the tail expanded and the wings drooping.

Peacock Throne the former throne of the Kings of Delhi, later that of the Shahs of Iran, adorned with precious stones forming an expanded peacock's tail. The throne was taken to Persia by Nadir Shah (1688–1747), king of Persia, who in 1739 captured Delhi and with it the *Peacock Throne* and the *Koh-i-noor* diamond.

peacock's feather one of the long tail feathers of the peacock, used figuratively as a symbol of ostentation or vainglory. It was traditionally believed that to bring a peacock's feather into the house would invite ill-luck.

peai among the Indians of Guiana and other parts of South America, a medicine man or witch-doctor.

Peak District a limestone plateau in Derbyshire, at the southern end of the Pennines, rising to 636 m (2,088 ft) at Kinder Scout. A large part of the area was designated a national park in 1951.

Peano axioms a set of axioms from which the properties of the natural numbers may be deduced, named after Giuseppe *Peano* (1858–1932), Italian mathematician.

Peanuts name of the comic strip (1950–99) by the American cartoonist Charles Schulz (1922–2000), featuring a range of characters including the likeable loser Charlie Brown, his dog ➤ SNOOPY, bossy Lucy, and the philosophical Linus.

if you pay peanuts, you get monkeys proverbial saying, mid 20th century.

pearl a hard, lustrous spherical mass, typically white or bluish-grey, formed within the shell of a pearl oyster or other bivalve mollusc and highly prized as a gem; in figurative use, a precious, noble, or fine thing, the finest or best member or part. There is also a tradition that pearls may portend tears; they were supposed to be unlucky for brides, and in Webster's *Duchess of Malfi* (*c*.1623), the doomed Duchess dreams that the diamonds in her coronet are changed to pearls.

In heraldry, *pearl* is used for the tincture argent in the fanciful blazon of arms of peers.

Recorded from late Middle English, the word comes from Old French *perle*, perhaps based on Latin *perna* 'leg', extended to denote a leg-of-mutton shaped bivalve.

Pearl Harbor a harbour on the island of Oahu, in Hawaii, the site of a major American naval base, where a surprise attack on 7 December 1941 by Japanese carrier-borne aircraft inflicted heavy damage and brought the US into the Second World War. The name may now be used allusively for a sudden and disastrous attack, mounted without warning.

Pearl Mosque a white marble mosque at Agra in Uttar Pradesh, northern India, built in the 17th century by the emperor Akbar (1542–1605).

do not throw pearls to swine proverbial saying, mid 14th century; with biblical allusion to Matthew 7:6, 'Give not that which is holy unto dogs, neither cast ye your pearls before swine, lest they trample them under their feet.'

Pearly Gates informal name for the gates of heaven; the term is first recorded in a hymn by Isaac Watts (1674–1748), and refers originally to Revelation 21:21, 'And the twelve gates were twelve pearls: every several gate was of one pearl.'

pearly king (also **pearly queen**), a London costermonger wearing traditional ceremonial clothes covered with pearl buttons.

pears see ➤ WALNUTS *and pears you plant for your heirs.*

Robert Edwin Peary (1856–1920), American explorer. He made eight Arctic voyages before becoming the first person to reach the North Pole, on 6 April 1909.

peas see ➤ DAVID *and Chad: sow peas good or bad.*

the Peasant Poet a name for the English poet ➤ *John* CLARE (1793–1864).

Peasants' Revolt an uprising in 1381 among the peasant and artisan classes in England, particularly in Kent and Essex. The rebels marched on London, occupying the city and executing unpopular ministers, but after the death of their leader, Wat Tyler, they were persuaded to disperse by Richard II, who granted some of their demands, though the government later went back on its promises.

peascod see ➤ WINTER-*time for shoeing, peascod-time for wooing.*

peccavi archaic expression used to express guilt or contrition, a Latin word meaning literally 'I have sinned'. The word features in the message supposedly sent by Charles Napier to Lord Ellenborough in 1843, announcing his conquest of the province of Sindh, '*Peccavi*—I have Sindh.' The 'message' appeared in *Punch*, 18 May 1844, and was in fact composed by Catherine Winkworth (1827–78).

peck a measure of capacity for dry goods, equal to a quarter of a bushel (2 imperial gallons = 9.092 l, or 8 US quarts = 8.81 l). The word is recorded from Middle English (used especially as a measure of oats for horses) and comes from Anglo-Norman French *pek*, of unknown origin.

See also ➤ *we must* EAT *a peck of dirt before we die*, ➤ *a peck of* MARCH *dust is worth a king's ransom.*

peckerwood in the US, an informal and often derogatory expression for a white person, especially a poor one. The term comes (in the 1920s) from a reversal of the elements of *woodpecker*, originally a dialect word for the bird, used commonly in Mississippi and Tennessee.

Pecksniff a hypocritical character in Dickens's novel *Martin Chuzzlewit* (1844); the name is used to denote an unctuous hypocrite who preaches morality while serving his own ends.

Pecos Bill in American folklore, a Texas cowboy from the region of the Pecos River who typified the values and stamina of the American frontier; he was said to have ridden a mountain lion, and to have used a rattlesnake as a lasso. His exploits were chronicled in *Century* magazine.

peculiar a parish or church exempt from the jurisdiction of the diocese in which it lies, through being subject to the jurisdiction of the monarch or an archbishop. Recorded from late Middle English (in the sense 'particular, special'), the word comes from Latin *peculiaris* 'of private property', and ultimately from *pecu* 'cattle' (cattle being private property). The current sense 'odd' dates from the early 17th century.

peculiar institution in 19th-century America, the system of Black slavery in the Southern States of the US.

peculiar people an evangelical fundamental Christian denomination founded in 1838 in London and relying on divine healing of disease. The term is originally a biblical one for God's chosen people, as in Deuteronomy 14:2, 'the Lord hath chosen thee to be a peculiar people unto himself, above all the nations that are upon the earth'.

Peculiars see ➤ COURT *of Peculiars*, ➤ DEAN *of peculiars.*

pecuniary of, relating to, or consisting of money. Recorded from the early 16th century, the word comes from Latin *pecuniarius*, and ultimately from *pecu* 'cattle, money'.

pedagogue a teacher, especially a strict or pedantic one. The word comes via Latin from Greek *paidagōgos*, denoting a slave who accompanied a child to school.

pede see ➤ *ex pede* HERCULEM.

pedlar a person who goes from place to place selling small goods. Recorded from Middle English, the word may be an alteration of synonymous dialect *pedder*, apparently from dialect *ped* 'pannier'.

peel a small square defensive tower of a kind built in the 16th century in the border counties of England and Scotland. The word comes from Anglo-Norman French *pel* 'stake, palisade', from Latin *palus* 'stake'.

Emma Peel cat-suited heroine of the television thriller series *The Avengers* (1961–8), played by Diana Rigg.

> Lady Sneerwell . . . strides around in black, wears shades and behaves like Emma Peel.
> — *20/20* July 1990

John Peel (1776–1854), the hero of the well-known hunting song 'D'ye ken John Peel?', was born at Caldbeck, Cumberland, and for over 40 years ran the famous pack of hounds that bore his name. The words of the song were composed by his friend John Woodcock Graves.

Robert Peel (1788–1850), British Conservative statesman, Prime Minister 1834–5 and 1841–6. As Home Secretary (1828–30) he established the Metropolitan Police (hence the nicknames *bobby* and *peeler*). His repeal of the Corn Laws in 1846 split the Conservatives and forced his resignation.

peeler a dated term for a police officer, from the name of Robert Peel (1788–1950), who as Home Secretary (1828–30) established the Metropolitan Police Force.

Peelite a Conservative supporting Robert Peel, especially with reference to the division in the Party resulting from his repeal of the Corn Laws (1846); after Peel's death, the *Peelites* still formed a discrete group intermediate between the Tory protectionists and the Liberals; their leaders, notably William Gladstone, eventually joined the Liberal Party.

Peenemunde a village in NE Germany, on a small island just off the Baltic coast, which during the Second World War was the chief site of German rocket research and testing.

Peep o' Day Boys a Protestant organization active in the north of Ireland *c.*1784–95, whose members clashed with Roman Catholic Defenders; the name supposedly arose from their practice of breaking into the houses of their Roman Catholic opponents at daybreak in search of arms.

Peeping Tom the man said to have watched Lady ➤ GODIVA ride naked through Coventry; his character is in fact a 17th-century addition to the story. From the late 18th century, *peeping Tom* has been used to denote a person who gets sexual pleasure from secretly watching people undressing or engaging in sexual activity; in the US, an act outlawing intrusive voyeurism is known as a **peeping Tom statute**.

peer a member of the nobility in Britain or Ireland, comprising the ranks of duke, marquess, earl, viscount, and baron. In the British peerage, earldoms and baronetcies were the earliest to be conferred; dukes were created from 1337, marquesses from the end of the 14th century, and viscounts from 1440. Such peerages are hereditary, although since 1958 there have also been non-hereditary life peerages.

Until the autumn of 1999, peers (debarred from election to the House of Commons) were entitled to a seat in the House of Lords and exemption from jury service. The initial reform established a limited number of hereditary peers (92), elected by their fellows, as having seats in the reformed Chamber; the final restructuring is still under consideration.

Former privileges included the right to a trial by one's peers instead of in the ordinary courts; this happened in the case of Earl Ferrers (1720–60), convicted of murder at his trial in Westminster Hall in April 1760 and subsequently hanged at Tyburn.

Recorded from Middle English, the word comes via Old French from Latin *par* 'equal'.

peerie folk in Scotland, fairies.

peg see ➤ *a* SQUARE *peg in a round hole*.

Pegasus in Greek mythology, a winged horse which sprang from the blood of ➤ MEDUSA when Perseus cut off her head. Pegasus was ridden by ➤ PERSEUS in his rescue of Andromeda, and by Bellerophon when he fought the ➤ CHIMERA; the spring ➤ HIPPOCRENE arose from a blow of his hoof.

Pegu a city and river port of southern Burma (Myanmar), on the Pegu River north-east of Rangoon. Founded in 825 as the capital of the Mon kingdom, it is a centre of Buddhist culture.

peine forte et dure a medieval form of torture in which the body was pressed with heavy weights, to death if necessary. It was used in England on prisoners who refused to accept jury trial; St Margaret Clitherow (1558–86), arrested for harbouring priests, refused to enter a plea, and died while undergoing this torture. The phrase is French, and means literally 'strong and hard suffering'.

Charles Sanders Peirce (1839–1914), American philosopher and logician. A founder of American pragmatism, he argued that the meaning of a belief is to be understood by the actions and uses to which it gives rise.

Peking earlier form of transliteration of the name of the Chinese capital Beijing.

Peking man a fossil hominid of the middle Pleistocene period, identified from remains found near Beijing in 1926.

Peking opera a stylized Chinese form of opera dating from the late 18th century, in which speech, singing, mime, and acrobatics are performed to an instrumental accompaniment.

Pelagius (*c*.360–*c*.420), British or Irish monk. He denied the doctrines of original sin and predestination, defending innate human goodness and free will. His beliefs were opposed by St Augustine of Hippo and condemned as heretical by the Synod of Carthage in about 418.

Pelasgian relating to or denoting an ancient people inhabiting the coasts and islands of the Aegean Sea and eastern Mediterranean before the arrival of Greek-speaking peoples in the Bronze Age (12th century BC).

Pele in Hawaiian mythology, the goddess of volcanoes. **Pele's hair** is the name given to fine threads of volcanic glass, formed when a spray of lava droplets cools rapidly in the air.

Peleus in Greek mythology, a king of Phthia in Thessaly, who was given as his wife the sea nymph Thetis; their child was ➤ ACHILLES.

pelf an archaic term for money, especially when gained in a dishonest or dishonourable way. The word comes (in late Middle English) from a variant of Old French *pelfre* 'spoils', of unknown origin.

pelican a large gregarious waterbird with a long bill, an extensible throat pouch for scooping up fish, and mainly white or grey plumage; the *pelican* is traditionally said to have fed its young on its own blood. (The story is told by Epiphanius and St Augustine; it appears to be of Egyptian origin, and to have referred originally to a different bird.)

Recorded from late Old English, the word comes via late Latin from Greek *pelekan*, probably based on *pelekus* 'axe', with reference to its bill.

pelican crossing (in the UK) a pedestrian crossing with traffic lights operated by pedestrians. The name comes (in the 1960s) from *pe(destrian) li(ght) con(trolled)*, altered to conform with the bird's name.

Pelican flag the state flag of Louisiana, which depicts a pelican.

pelican in her piety in heraldry and Christian art, the bird is typically depicted pecking its own breast as a symbol of Christ, from an ancient legend that the pelican fed its young on its own blood.

Pelican State informal name for Louisiana.

Pelion a wooded mountain in Greece, near the coast of SE Thessaly, which in Greek mythology was held to be the home of the centaurs, and the giants were said to have piled Mounts ➤ OLYMPUS and ➤ OSSA on its summit in their attempt to reach heaven and destroy the gods. This story has given rise to the phrase **pile Pelion on Ossa**, meaning to add an extra difficulty or task to something which is already difficult or onerous.

King Pellam in Arthurian legend, the *Maimed King*, father of the *Grail King*, ➤ PELLES. Wounded by the Dolorous Stroke of Balyn, he is healed by his great-grandson Galahad in the Grail Quest.

King Pelles in Malory, the *Grail King*, one of the Fisher Kings and said to be 'cousin nigh unto Joseph of Arimathie'. He is maimed for drawing the sword of David on the mysterious ship. Founded perhaps on ➤ PWYLL of Welsh mythology, he was the father of Elaine who was the mother of Galahad by Lancelot.

Pelmanism a system of memory training originally devised by the *Pelman* Institute for the Scientific Development of Mind, Memory, and Personality in London; a game based on memorizing cards or other objects placed before the players.

Peloponnesian War the war of 431–404 BC fought between Athens and Sparta with their respective allies, occasioned largely by Spartan opposition to the Delian League. It ended in the total defeat of Athens and the transfer, for a brief period, of the leadership of Greece to Sparta.

Pelops in Greek mythology, the son of ➤ TANTALUS, brother of ➤ NIOBE, and father of ➤ ATREUS. He was killed by his father and served up as food to the gods, but only one shoulder was eaten, and he was restored to life with an ivory shoulder replacing the one that was missing.

pen an instrument for writing or drawing with ink, typically consisting of a metal nib or ball, or a nylon tip, fitted into a metal or plastic holder. In Middle English the word denoted a feather with a sharpened quill as a writing instrument; it comes through Old French from Latin *penna* 'feather' (in late Latin, 'pen').

the pen is mightier than the sword proverbial saying, late 16th century.

Penal Laws various statutes passed in Britain and Ireland during the 16th and 17th centuries that imposed harsh restrictions on Roman Catholics. People participating in Catholic services could be fined and imprisoned, while Catholics were banned from voting, holding public office, owning land, and teaching. The laws were repealed by various Acts between 1791 and 1926.

Penang lawyer a kind of walking-stick, made from the stem of a dwarf palm which is a native of Penang and Singapore. In England it has often been misapplied to the Malacca cane.

The name apparently refers to the use of the weapon in settling disputes at Penang, although it has also been suggested that it is a corruption of Malay *pinang líyar* ' wild areca'.

penates in ancient Rome, household gods worshipped in conjunction with ➤ VESTA and the ➤ LARES; the name comes from Latin *penus* 'provision of food', related to *penes* 'within'.

penbard in Wales, a head or chief bard.

pence see also ➤ PETER's *pence*.

take care of the pence and the pounds will take care of themselves proverbial saying, mid 18th century.

pencil an instrument for writing or drawing, consisting of a thin stick of graphite or a similar substance enclosed in a long thin piece of wood or fixed in a metal or plastic case. In Middle English, the word denoted a fine paintbrush; it comes via Old

French from a diminutive of Latin *peniculus* 'brush', diminutive of *penis* 'tail'.

Pendragon a title given to an ancient British or Welsh prince holding or claiming supreme power. The word, which is Welsh, meant literally 'chief warleader', from *pen* 'head' + *dragon* 'standard'.

See also ➤ UTHER *Pendragon*.

pendulum see ➤ FOUCAULT.

Penelope in Greek mythology, the wife of ➤ ODYSSEUS, who was beset by suitors when her husband did not return after the fall of Troy. She put them off by saying that she would marry only when she had finished the piece of weaving on which she was engaged, and every night unravelled the work she had done during the day.

See also ➤ *Penelope's* WEB.

penetralia the innermost parts of a building; a sanctum; a secret or hidden place.

penguin the *penguin*, noted for its wings developed into flippers for swimming under water, may be referred to in relation to a clumsy, waddling walk; the black and white plumage has also given rise to the informal **penguin suit** to denote a man's evening dress of black dinner jacket worn with a white shirt.

Penguin Books paperback publishing imprint founded by Allen Lane in 1935; the first ten titles, published in 1936 and priced at sixpence each, included titles by Agatha Christie, Ernest Hemingway, and André Maurois. The non-fiction *Pelican* series was launched the following year with George Bernard Shaw's *Intelligent Woman's Guide to Socialism*; the *Puffin* brand for children was established in 1940. The distinctive covers were colour-coded; general fiction was orange and white, and green and white became the mark of crime fiction.

In 1960, Penguin published the first unexpurgated edition of D. H. Lawrence's *Lady Chatterley's Lover*; this led to a trial and acquittal at the Old Bailey.

Peninsular War a campaign waged on the Iberian peninsula between the French and the British, the latter assisted by Spanish and Portuguese forces, from 1808 to 1814 during the Napoleonic Wars. The French were finally driven back over the Pyrenees in an expedition led by Wellington.

penitent in the Christian Church, a person who confesses their sins to a priest and submits to the penance imposed; originally, this might include the performance of a punishment or discipline as an outward expression or token of repentance for and expiation of a sin. Those doing public penance might wear ➤ SACKCLOTH, or (when doing penance for fornication) be dressed in a white sheet.

➤ *St* MARY *Magdalene* is the patron saint of penitents.

Penitential Psalms seven psalms (6, 32, 38, 51, 102, 130, 143) which express penitence.

grand penitentiary a cardinal who presides over the penitentiary of the papal court and has the granting of absolution in cases reserved for the papal authority.

William Penn (1644–1718), English Quaker, founder of ➤ PENNSYLVANIA. Having been imprisoned in 1668 for his Quaker writings, he was granted a charter to land in North America by Charles II. He founded the colony of Pennsylvania as a sanctuary for Quakers and other Nonconformists in 1682. Penn also co-founded Philadelphia.

pennant a tapering flag on a ship, especially one flown at the masthead of a vessel in commission. The word is a blend of *pendant* and *pennon*.

pennies from heaven unexpected (financial) benefits, from a song by the American songwriter Johnny Burke (1908–64):

> Every time it rains, it rains
> Pennies from heaven.
> — Johnny Burke 'Pennies from Heaven' (1936)

In 1979 the Margaret Thatcher made allusive reference to the song, saying, 'Pennies don't fall from heaven. They have to be earned on earth.'

pennon another term for a *pennant*. Recorded from late Middle English, the word comes via Old French from a derivative of Latin *penna* 'feather'.

Pennsylvania a state of the north-eastern US, founded in 1682 by ➤ *William* PENN, which became one of the original thirteen states of the Union in 1787.

Pennsylvania Dutch the German-speaking inhabitants of Pennsylvania, descendants for the most part of 17th- and 18th-century Protestant immigrants from the Rhineland.

penny a British bronze coin and monetary unit equal (since decimalization in 1971) to one hundredth of a pound; formerly, to one twelfth of a shilling.

The penny has its origins in the Roman denarius. The English silver penny first appeared in the late 8th century and was the only coin in circulation for several centuries. The penny was minted in copper from 1797 and in bronze from 1860; coining of silver pennies ceased with the reign of Charles II, apart from a small regular issue as ➤ MAUNDY *money*.

Recorded from Old English and of Germanic origin, the word may be related to *pawn* 'deposit an object for money' and (with reference to its shape) *pan* 'a metal container for cooking'.

See also ➤ COCK-*penny,* ➤ NO *penny, no paternoster,* ➤ ROME-*penny.*

penny-a-liner a writer for a newspaper or journal who is paid at a penny a line, or at a low rate (usually implying one who manufactures 'paragraphs', or writes in an inflated style so as to cover as much space as possible); a poor or inferior writer for hire; a hack-writer for the press.

a bad penny always turns up proverbial saying, mid 18th century; the proverb refers to the inevitable return of an unwanted or disreputable person.

penny black the world's first adhesive postage stamp, issued in Britain in 1840. It was printed in black with an effigy of Queen Victoria, and had a value of one penny.

penny dreadful a cheap, sensational comic or storybook, so named because the original cost (in the 19th century) was one penny.

the penny drops understanding dawns (referring to the mechanism of a penny-in-the-slot machine).

penny-farthing an early type of bicycle, made in Britain, with a very large front wheel and a small rear wheel, current from the early 1870s to the mid 1890s, and often known as the *ordinary*.

a penny for the guy used by children to ask for money toward celebrations of Guy Fawkes Night.

a penny for your thoughts used in spoken English to ask someone what they are thinking about; recorded from the mid 16th century.

in for a penny, in for a pound proverbial saying, late 17th century; meaning that having embarked on a course, you are committed, whatever is involved.

a penny more and up goes the donkey inviting contributions to complete a sum of money (from the cry of a travelling showman); supposedly, once enough money is collected, the donkey will mount to the top of a pole or ladder.

penny plain, twopence coloured saying from the mid 19th century, with reference to prints of characters sold for toy theatres, costing one penny for black-and-white ones, and two pennies for coloured ones.

a penny post a system of carrying letters at a standard charge of one penny each regardless of distance, in particular the system established in the UK in 1840 at the instigation of Sir Rowland Hill.

a penny saved is a penny earned proverbial saying, mid 17th century.

not have a penny to bless oneself with be completely impoverished (with allusion to the cross on an old silver penny or to the practice of crossing a person's palm with silver for luck).

penny wedding a wedding at which each of the guests contributes money to the expenses of the entertainment; formerly customary in parts of Scotland and Wales.

penny wise and pound foolish proverbial saying, early 17th century.

pennyroyal either of two small-leaved plants of the mint family, used in herbal medicine. Recorded from the mid 16th century, the name comes from Anglo-Norman French *puliol* (based on Latin *pulegium* 'thyme') + *real* 'royal'.

pennyweight a unit of weight, 24 grains or one twentieth of an ounce troy.

pennywort any of a number of plants with rounded leaves.

pennyworth see ➤ ROBIN *Hood's pennyworth*.

Penrose tile any of a finite number of shapes that are components of a non-repeating two- or three-dimensional tiling, named after Roger *Penrose* (1931–), British mathematical physicist.

Penshurst Place a house in Kent which has been in the possession of the Sidney family since 1552, and was the birthplace of Philip Sidney. Many writers enjoyed its hospitality, including Jonson, who paid a graceful tribute in 'To Penshurst'.

pension originally (in Middle English) the word denoted a regular sum paid to retain allegiance.

Pension was also formerly used to denote a periodical payment levied upon each member of any of the Inns of Court or Chancery in London, or of the King's Inn in Dublin; it appears in this sense in the Black Book of Lincoln's Inn from 1433. Pensions were used to defray the standing charges of an Inn, such as maintenance and repair of buildings and gardens, salaries of officers, and wages of servants.

Grand Pensionary the first minister and magistrate of the province of Holland in the Seven United Provinces of the Netherlands (1619–1794).

The dignity was first created by Johan van Olden Barneveldt, under the title of Advocate of Holland and West Friesland; it attained great distinction when held by Johan de Witt 1653–72. The Grand Pensionary was by virtue of his office president of the legislature of the province, and permanent deputy to the States General. The position was abolished in 1795.

Pensionary Parliament the second Parliament of Charles II (1661–79), so called because of the alleged acceptance of bribes by its members.

pensioner a person who receives a pension or payment; in earliest (late Middle English) use, an officer who collected and kept record of pensions in any of the Inns of Court and Chancery in London, and in the King's Inn in Dublin.

The name *Pensioner* was also formerly used for a member of the body of gentlemen who act as guards or attendants to the British monarch within the royal palace; a gentleman-at-arms. This royal bodyguard was instituted by Henry VIII in 1509. Its members were originally called *Spears* or *Spearmen*, from 1539 *Pensioners*, and later *Gentlemen-Pensioners* or *Gentlemen-at-arms*.

At Cambridge University, an undergraduate without financial support from his or her college; the equivalent to a *commoner* at Oxford.

See also ➤ CHELSEA *pensioner*.

pentacle a talisman or magical object, typically disc-shaped and inscribed with a pentagram or other figure, and used as a symbol of the element of earth. *Pentacles* are also one of the suits in some tarot packs, corresponding to *coins* in others.

Recorded from the late 16th century, the word comes from medieval Latin *pentaculum*, apparently based on Greek *penta-* 'five'.

the Pentagon the pentagonal building serving as the headquarters of the US Department of Defense, near Washington DC. It was built in 1941–3.

Pentagonese euphemistic or cryptic language supposedly used among high-ranking US military personnel.

pentagram a five-pointed star that is formed by drawing a continuous line in five straight segments, often used as a mystic and magical symbol. The same figure can be formed by producing the sides of a pentagon both ways to their points of intersection; however, many mystical and occult systems ascribe particular efficacy to pentagrams drawn with a continuous line (i.e. without lifting the pen, etc., from the surface). According to some, a pentagram with a single point uppermost is a positive symbol, serving to ward off evil, whereas an 'inverted' pentagram, with two points uppermost, is negative.

In the Middle Ages, pentagrams were sometimes inscribed in clothing or hung in doors and windows to keep away evil spirits and the effects of witchcraft. The pentagram is now used as a symbol of Wicca and other neo-pagan movements, the five points often being taken to represent earth, water, air, fire, and spirit.

The Pentameron title of a book consisting of five imaginary conversations (1837) between Boccaccio and Petrarch, discussing Dante's works, by Walter Savage Landor.

Il Pentamerone name given to a collection of fairy stories, *Lo cunto de li cunti* (The story of stories), based on folktales by the Neapolitan writer Giambattista Basile (*c.*1575–1632); the stories included those of Puss in Boots, Cinderella, and Rapunzel, and the work was a source for Charles Perrault and the Grimm brothers.

pentameter a line of verse consisting of five metrical feet, or (in Greek and Latin verse) of two halves each of two feet and a long syllable.

Pentateuch the first five books of the Old Testament (Genesis, Exodus, Leviticus, Numbers, and Deuteronomy), relating the early history of the world and of the Hebrews up to the death of Moses, and including the Jewish law. Traditionally ascribed to Moses, it is now held by scholars to be a compilation from texts of the 9th to 5th centuries BC, incorporating older oral traditions.

See also ➤ SAMARITAN *Pentateuch.*

pentathlon an athletic event comprising five different events for each competitor, in particular, in ancient Greece, leaping, running, discus-throwing, spear-throwing, and wrestling; now, (also **modern pentathlon**) a men's event involving fencing, shooting, swimming, riding, and cross-country running.

Pentecost the Christian festival celebrating the descent of the Holy Spirit on the disciples of Jesus after his Ascension, held on the seventh Sunday after Easter. *Pentecost* also denotes the Jewish festival or Shavuoth.

Recorded in Old English, the word comes via ecclesiastical Latin from Greek *pentēkostē* (*hēmera*) 'fiftieth (day)', because the Jewish festival is held on the fiftieth day after the second day of Passover.

pentecostal in the Church of England: an offering formerly made at Whitsuntide by a parishioner to a priest, or by an inferior church to its mother church.

Pentecostal Church any of a number of Christian sects and individuals emphasizing baptism in the Holy Spirit, evidenced by 'speaking in tongues', prophecy, healing, and exorcism. Pentecostal sects are often fundamentalist in doctrine and are uninhibited and spontaneous in worship.

Penthesilea the queen of the Amazons, who came to the help of Troy after the death of Hector and was killed by Achilles.

peony a herbaceous or shrubby plant of north temperate regions, which has long been cultivated for its showy flowers. The name comes via Latin from Greek *Paiōn*, the name of the physician of the gods.

people see also ➤ CHOSEN *people,* ➤ OPIUM *of the people,* ➤ PECULIAR *people,* ➤ *People's* CHARTER, ➤ PLAIN *People,* ➤ POWER *to the people.*

like people, like priest proverbial saying, late 16th century; with biblical allusion to Hosea 4:9, 'And there shall be like people, like priest'.

the People's Princess informal name popularized by Tony Blair for Diana, Princess of Wales, on hearing of her death:

> She was the People's Princess, and that is how she will stay . . . in our hearts and in our memories forever.
> — Tony Blair in *Times* 1 September 1997

the People's William informal name for ➤ *William Ewart* GLADSTONE (1809–98), coined by the newspaper proprietor Edward Levy-Lawson (1833–1916).

Peoples of the Sea another term for ➤ SEA *Peoples.*

Peoria see ➤ IT *'ll play in Peoria.*

Pepin (*c*.714–68), known as **Pepin the Short**, son of Charles Martel and father of Charlemagne; he became the first king of the Frankish Carolingian dynasty on the deposition of the Merovingian Childeric III.

See also ➤ Donation *of Pepin.*

peplos a rich outer robe or shawl worn by women in ancient Greece, hanging in loose folds and sometimes drawn over the head.

pepper a pungent hot-tasting powder prepared from dried and ground peppercorns, commonly used as a spice or condiment to flavour food, and traditionally found in a number of allusive and proverbial expressions, such as **give someone pepper**, chiefly with reference to the biting, pungent, or inflaming qualities of pepper.

when your daughter is stolen, shut Pepper Gate traditional saying in Chester; *Peppergate* was a postern gate of the city.

peppercorn rent a very low or nominal rent, from the (formerly common) practice of stipulating the payment of a peppercorn as a nominal rent; the usage dates from the early 17th century.

Samuel Pepys (1633–1703), English diarist and naval administrator. He is particularly remembered for his *Diary* (1660–9), which describes events such as the Great Plague and the Fire of London as well as details of his personal life. Written in cipher, it was not deciphered until 1825.

Pepys became secretary of the Admiralty in 1672 but was deprived of his post in 1679 for his alleged complicity in the Popish Plot; he was reappointed in 1684.

perambulator a former machine for measuring distances, consisting of a large wheel of known circumference attached to a handle by which it is rolled over the ground, with a mechanism for recording the number of revolutions.

The later sense of baby's pram developed in the 19th century.

perception see ➤ Doors *of Perception.*

Perceval a legendary figure dating back to ancient times, found in French, German, and English poetry from the late 12th century onwards. He is the father of Lohengrin and the hero of a number of legends, some of which are associated with the Holy Grail. Also called *Parsifal.*

Spencer Perceval (1762–1812), British Tory statesman, Prime Minister 1809–12. He was shot dead in the lobby of the House of Commons by a bankrupt merchant who blamed the government for his insolvency.

perch former name for a measure of length, especially for land, equal to a quarter of a chain or 5½ yards (approximately 5.029 m). Recorded from Middle English, the word comes via Old French from Latin *pertica* 'measuring rod, pole'.

Percy family surname of the Dukes of Northumberland, and particularly associated with Henry Percy (1364–1403), known as *Hotspur* or *Harry Hotspur.* Son of the 1st Earl of Northumberland, he was killed at the battle of Shrewsbury during his father's revolt against Henry IV.

Percy's Reliques short title of a collection of traditional ballads, *Reliques of Ancient English Poetry,* made by Thomas Percy (1729–1811) and published in 1765.

Perdita in Shakespeare's *Winter's Tale,* the lost daughter of Leontes and Hermione who is brought up as a shepherdess; her name means 'the lost one'.

The actress Mary Robinson (1758–1800), mistress of George, Prince of Wales, afterwards George IV, was known as *Perdita* after her success in the part, as a result of which the prince fell in love with her.

perduellion in Roman and Scottish law, hostility against the state; treason. Recorded from the mid 16th century, the word comes from Latin *perduellis* 'a public or private enemy'.

Père Lachaise in Paris, the great cemetery on the site of a Jesuit foundation of 1626, which had been enlarged by Père Lachaise (1624–1709), confessor to Louis XIV. In May 1871, the forces of the Paris Commune made their last stand there against government troops.

peregrine falcon a powerful falcon found on most continents, breeding chiefly on mountains and coastal cliffs and much used for falconry. In the 15th-century *Boke of St Albans,* the *peregrine* is listed as the bird for a prince.

The name is a translation of the medieval Latin *falco peregrinus,* literally 'pilgrim falcon', because the bird was caught full-grown as a passage hawk, not taken from the nest. Recorded from late Middle

English, it comes from Latin *peregrinus* 'foreign', from *peregre* 'abroad'.

peregrine praetor in ancient Rome, a second praetor appointed at Rome to administer justice between Roman and non-Roman citizens ('peregrines' or pilgrims and foreigners) and between non-Roman citizens themselves.

peregrine tone one of the tones used in plainsong, used from the 9th century in the recitation of Psalm 114 (113 in the Vulgate), and later adopted as an Anglican chant. The term is sometimes explained as a reference to the reciting note, which changes ('wanders') halfway through.

perestroika (in the former Soviet Union) the policy or practice of restructuring or reforming the economic and political system. First proposed by Leonid Brezhnev in 1979 and actively promoted by Mikhail Gorbachev, *perestroika* originally referred to increased automation and labour efficiency, but came to entail greater awareness of economic markets and the ending of central planning. The word is Russian, and means literally 'restructuring'.

perfect see also ➤ PRACTICE *makes perfect.*

perfect number a number which is equal to the sum of its factors (not including itself).

perfect ruby a former term for the alchemists' ➤ ELIXIR.

perfection see also ➤ COUNSEL *of perfection.*

Perfectionist a member of the utopian Christian community established by John Humphrey Noyes at Putney, Vermont in 1841, and from 1847 at Oneida Creek, New York State.

Perfidious Albion England or Britain considered as treacherous in international affairs, in a rendering of the French phrase *la perfide Albion*, said to have been first used by the Marquis de Ximenès (1726–1817). Both terms are recorded in English from the mid 19th century.

perfume the word originally (in the mid 16th century) denoted pleasant-smelling smoke from a burning substance, especially one used in fumigation, and comes ultimately from obsolete Italian *parfumare*, literally 'to smoke through'.

perfumiers ➤ St NICHOLAS *of Myra* is the patron saint of *perfumiers.*

Pergamum a city in ancient Mysia, in western Asia Minor, situated to the north of Izmir on a rocky hill close to the Aegean coast. The capital in the 3rd and 2nd centuries BC of the Attalid dynasty, it was one of the greatest and most beautiful of the Hellenistic cities and was famed for its cultural institutions, especially its library, which was second only to that at Alexandria.

See also ➤ PARCHMENT.

peri (in Persian mythology) a mythical superhuman being, originally represented as evil but subsequently as a good or graceful genie or fairy. The name comes ultimately from Avestan (Zend) *pairikā*, any of several beautiful but malevolent female demons employed by Ahriman to bring comets and eclipses, prevent rain, and cause failure of crops and dearth.

Pericles (*c.*495–429 BC), Athenian statesman and general. A champion of Athenian democracy, he pursued an imperialist policy and masterminded Athenian strategy in the Peloponnesian War. He commissioned the building of the Parthenon in 447 and promoted the culture of Athens in a golden age that produced such figures as Aeschylus, Socrates, and Phidias.

> Banham had become to this deprecated, defamed, traduced, and disparaged metropolis what Pericles was to Athens.
> — *New Yorker* 26 September 1988

pericope an extract from a text, especially a passage from the Bible appointed for reading in public worship. Also, any of various short passages in the Gospels believed to have circulated independently before being incorporated by the gospel writers.

Recorded from the mid 17th century, the word comes via late Latin from Greek *perikopē* 'section'.

Perigord a district in the south-west of France, famous for its truffles.

Perillus legendary designer of a bronze bull in which Phalaris, tyrant of Acragas in Sicily (d. *c.*554 BC) roasted victims alive; Perillus was said to have been the first man to be executed by this means.

perilous see ➤ CASTLE *Perilous,* ➤ SIEGE *Perilous.*

Perilous Chair another name for ➤ SIEGE *Perilous.*

Peripatetic an Aristotelian philosopher (with reference to ➤ ARISTOTLE's practice of walking to and fro while teaching). The name is recorded from late

Middle English, and is the original sense of the word in English.

periphrasis the use of indirect and circumlocutory speech or writing; an indirect and circumlocutory phrase. The term is recorded from the mid 16th century, and comes via Latin from Greek, ultimately from *peri-* 'around' + *phrazein* 'declare'.

perish the thought used, often ironically, to show that one finds a suggestion or idea completely ridiculous; the phrase probably derives from *perish that thought!* in Colley Cibber's *Richard III* (1700).

periwinkle an Old World plant with flat five-petalled flowers and glossy leaves. Some kinds are grown as an ornamentals and some contain alkaloids used in medicine; it was popularly believed in the 16th and 17th centuries that *periwinkle* promoted conjugal love.

In early times, a garland of this flower was placed on the heads of persons on their way to execution, with which some have connected the Italian name *fiore di morte*, 'flower of death'.

permissive society the form of society supposed to have prevailed in the West since the mid-1960s (associated especially with the late 1960s and early 1970s), characterized by greater tolerance and more liberal attitudes in areas such as sexuality, abortion, drug use, and obscenity.

Perpendicular denoting the latest stage of English Gothic church architecture, prevalent from the late 14th to mid 16th centuries and characterized by broad arches, elaborate fan vaulting, and large windows with vertical tracery.

perpetual motion the motion of a hypothetical machine which, once activated, would run forever unless subject to an external force or to wear; although impossible according to the first and second laws of thermodynamics, the development of such a mechanism has been attempted by many inventors. The Dutch philosopher and inventor Cornelis Drebbel (1572–1634), in England in the early 17th century, was said to have perfected such a device, which he presented to the king, and which became one of the sights of the day.

Treaty of Perpetual Peace name given to a treaty between James IV of Scotland and Henry VII of England in 1502, whereby James ceased to support the Yorkist pretender ➤ *Perkin* WARBECK and married the English king's daughter; it was through his

descent from this marriage that James VI of Scotland inherited the English throne in 1603.

Charles Perrault (1628–1703), French writer. He is remembered for his *Mother Goose Tales* (1697), containing such fairy tales as 'Sleeping Beauty', 'Little Red Riding Hood', 'Puss in Boots', and 'Cinderella'. They were translated into English in 1729.

Jean Baptiste Perrin (1870–1942), French physical chemist, who provided the definitive proof of the existence of atoms, proved that cathode rays are negatively charged, and investigated Brownian motion.

persecutions see ➤ TEN *persecutions*.

Perseids an annual meteor shower with a radiant in the constellation *Perseus*, reaching a peak about 12 August; the name means 'daughters of Perseus'.

Persephone in Greek mythology, a goddess, the daughter of Zeus and Demeter. She was carried off by Hades and made queen of the underworld. Demeter, vainly seeking her, refused to let the earth produce its fruits until her daughter was restored to her, but because Persephone had eaten some pomegranate seeds in the other world, she was obliged to spend part of every year there. Her story symbolizes the return of spring and the life and growth of corn. Her Roman name is *Proserpina*.

Persepolis a city in ancient Persia, situated to the north-east of Shiraz. It was founded in the late 6th century BC by Darius I as the ceremonial capital of Persia under the Achaemenid dynasty. The city's impressive ruins include functional and ceremonial buildings and cuneiform inscriptions in Old Persian, Elamite, and Akkadian. It was partially destroyed in 330 BC by Alexander the Great, and though it survived as the capital of the Seleucids it began to decline after this date.

In the first part of Marlowe's *Tamburlaine the Great*, the name of the city is used to emphasize the greatness of the conqueror, in Tamburlaine's question, 'Is it not passing brave to be a king, And ride in triumph through Persepolis'.

Perseus in Greek mythology, the son of Zeus and ➤ DANAE, a hero celebrated for many achievements. Aided by gifts from the gods (a helmet which conferred invisibility from Pluto, wings for his feet from Hermes, and a mirror so that he could look indirectly at the gorgon from Athene) he cut off the head of the gorgon Medusa and gave it to Athene; riding the winged horse ➤ PEGASUS which sprang from the

gorgon's blood, he rescued and married Andromeda, and he became king of Tiryns in Greece.

A prophecy had said that he would kill his grandfather; this happened in Thessaly when his grandfather, who was attending some games there, was
accidentally killed by a discus thrown by Perseus.

Persia a former country of SW Asia, now called
Iran. The ancient kingdom of Persia, corresponding
to the modern district of Fars in SW Iran, became in
the 6th century BC the domain of the Achaemenid
dynasty, and under Cyrus the Great became the centre of a powerful empire which included all of western Asia, Egypt, and parts of eastern Europe; it was
eventually overthrown by Alexander the Great in
330 BC.

Persian Wars the wars fought between Greece and
Persia in the 5th century BC, in which the Persians
sought to extend their territory over the Greek
world.

The wars began in 490 BC when Darius I sent an
expedition to punish the Greeks for having supported the Ionian cities in their unsuccessful revolt
against Persian rule; the Persians were defeated by a
small force of Athenians at Marathon. Ten years
later Darius' son Xerxes I attempted an invasion. He
won a land-battle at Thermopylae and devastated
Attica, but Persian forces were defeated on land at
Plataea and in a sea battle at Salamis (480 BC), and
retreated. Intermittent war continued in various
areas until peace was signed in 449 BC.

Persians see ➤ *law of the* MEDES *and Persians.*

person a human being regarded as an individual.
The word comes (in Middle English, via Old
French) from Latin *persona* 'actor's mask, character
in a play', later 'human being'.

Peruvian bark in the mid 17th century, a name for
cinchona bark, from which quinine is made.

Pesach Jewish term for the Passover festival.

Peshitta the ancient Syriac version of the Bible,
used in Syriac-speaking Christian countries from
the early 5th century and still the official Bible of the
Syrian Christian Churches.

Peshwa the title of the chief minister of the Maratha princes from *c.*1660. Also, the hereditary monarch of the Maratha State from 1749 to 1818.

pest-house historical term for a hospital for
people suffering from infectious diseases, especially
the plague.

Johann Heinrich Pestalozzi (1746–1827), Swiss
educational reformer. He pioneered education for
poor children and had a major impact on the development of primary education.

Pestalozzi village any of several communities of
refugee and homeless children established in Switzerland after the war of 1939–45, on the principles
developed by ➤ *Johan Heinrich* PESTALOZZI.

pet name a name that is used instead of someone's
usual first name to express fondness or familiarity.
The term has been current since the early 19th century.

Philippe Pétain (1856–1951), French general and
statesman; in the First World War associated particularly with the defence of Verdun in 1916 (the slogan '*Ils ne passeront pas* [They shall not pass]' is
sometimes attributted to him).

As head of state 1940–2, he concluded an armistice with Nazi Germany in 1940 and established the
French government at Vichy (effectively a puppet
regime for the Third Reich) until the German occupation in 1942. After the war Pétain received a death
sentence for collaboration, but this was commuted
to life imprisonment.

hoist with one's own petard have one's plans to
cause trouble for others backfire on one, from
Shakespeare's *Hamlet*; *hoist* is in the sense 'lifted
and removed', and a *petard* is a small bomb made of
a metal or wooden box filled with powder, used to
blast down a door or make a hole in a wall.

petasus the winged hat which in Greek mythology
is represented as worn by the god ➤ HERMES.

Peter see also ➤ BLUE *Peter*, ➤ ROB *Peter to pay
Paul.*

St Peter an Apostle; born Simon. *Peter* ('stone') is
the name given him by Jesus, signifying the rock on
which he would establish his Church, although he
also fulfilled Jesus's prophecy that 'before the cock
crow twice, thou shalt deny me thrice' (Mark 14:30).

He is regarded by Roman Catholics as the first
bishop of the Church at Rome, where he is said to
have been martyred in about AD 67, traditionally by
being crucified upside down. He is often represented as the keeper of the door of heaven.
□ **EMBLEM** His emblem is a pair of keys.
□ **FEAST DAY** His feast day is 29 June.
See also ➤ PATRIMONY *of St Peter.*

the Gospel of Peter an apocryphal gospel of the
2nd century, known to ➤ ORIGEN.

Peter I (1672–1725), tsar of Russia 1682–1725; known as **Peter the Great**. Peter modernized his armed forces before waging the Great Northern War (1700–21) and expanding his territory in the Baltic. His extensive administrative reforms were instrumental in transforming Russia into a significant European power. In 1703 he made the new city of St Petersburg his capital.

St Peter ad Vincula church dedication meaning 'St Peter in chains', the reference is to the story in Acts 12, which tells of Peter's imprisonment 'bound with two chains', and of how he was miraculously released from his chains by an angel.

Peter Pan the hero of J. M. Barrie's play of the same name (1904), a motherless boy with magical powers who never grew up, and who takes the Darling children, Wendy and her brothers, from their unguarded nursery to Never Never Land where he and the Lost Boys struggle against the pirates and ➤ *Captain* Hook. After many adventures, the children go home, but Peter remains in Never Never Land, and Wendy visits him each year to spring-clean the house which he and the Lost Boys had built around her.

Peter Pan's name is used allusively for someone who retains youthful features, or who is immature.

> He's a prisoner of adolescence—unlike Peter Pan, he wants to grow up.
>
> — *New Yorker* 3 February 1992

See also ➤ *Captain* Hook, ➤ Nana, ➤ Wendy House.

Peter Principle the principle that members of a hierarchy are promoted until they reach the level at which they are no longer competent; named after Laurence J. *Peter* (1919–90), the American educationalist who put forward the theory.

Peter Rabbit the blue-coated rabbit who is one of the main characters in the series of children's stories by Beatrix Potter; *The Tale of Peter Rabbit* (published privately in 1900) was the first of these.

Peter-see-me a sweet white Spanish wine, from a corruption of *Pedro Ximenes*, the name of a celebrated Spanish grape, so called after its introducer.

Peter the Hermit c.1050–1115), French monk. His preaching on the First Crusade was a rallying cry for thousands of peasants throughout Europe to journey to the Holy Land; most were massacred by the Turks in Asia Minor. Peter later became prior of an Augustinian monastery in Flanders.

Peter the Painter name given to the supposed leader of the anarchist group at the centre of the ➤ *Siege of* Sidney *Street* in 1911; he was never captured or positively identified.

Peter the Wild Boy (1712–85), found living wild in the woods of Hanover in 1724, and believed by many to have been reared by animals; he was taken to England and presented to George I.

St Peter's fish any of several fishes having a mark on each side of the body, alluding to the touch of St Peter's thumb and finger when he caught the fish whose mouth contained the tribute-money (Matthew 17:27).

St Peter's keys the cross keys (one gold and one silver, representing the power to bind and loose) borne in the papal coat of arms.

Peter's pence an annual tax of one penny from every householder having land of a certain value, paid to the papal see at Rome from Anglo-Saxon times until discontinued in 1534 after Henry VIII's break with Rome; in the Roman Catholic Church, a name given to the collection taken in churches on the feast of St Peter and St Paul.

Peterborough see ➤ Ramsey, *the rich of gold and fee.*

Peterhouse the oldest college of Cambridge University, founded in 1284.

Peterloo massacre an attack by Manchester yeomanry on 16 August 1819 against a large but peaceable crowd. Sent to arrest the speaker at a rally of supporters of political reform in St Peter's Field, Manchester, the local yeomanry charged the crowd, killing 11 civilians and injuring more than 500.

Peters projection a world map projection in which areas are shown in correct proportion at the expense of distorted shape, using a rectangular decimal grid to replace latitude and longitude. It was devised in 1973 to be a fairer representation of equatorial (i.e. mainly developing) countries, whose area is under-represented by the usual projections such as ➤ Mercator's.

Petertide (the period around) 29 June, the feast of St Peter in the Church of England and of St Peter and St Paul in the Roman Catholic and Orthodox Churches.

petitio principii a fallacy in which a conclusion is taken for granted in the premises; begging the question. The phrase is Latin, and means literally 'laying claim to a principle'.

Petition see also ➤ MILLENARY *Petition*.

Petition of Right a parliamentary declaration of rights and liberties of the people presented to Charles I in a petition in 1627 and assented to by the monarch in 1628. Although not a formal statute or ordinance, this has traditionally been invested with the full force of law.

Petitioner any of those who signed the address to Charles II in 1680, petitioning for the summoning of Parliament (a move opposed by the *Abhorrers*).

Petra an ancient city of SW Asia, in present-day Jordan. The city, which lies in a hollow surrounded by cliffs, is accessible only through narrow gorges. Its extensive ruins include temples and tombs hewn from the red sandstone cliffs. It was the capital of the country of the Nabataeans from 312 BC until 63 BC, when they became subject to Rome.

> Match me such marvel, save in Eastern clime,—
> A rose-red city—half as old as Time!
> — John William Burgon *Petra* (1845)

Petrarch (1304–74), Italian poet. His reputation is chiefly based on the *Canzoniere* (*c*.1351–3), a sonnet sequence in praise of a woman he calls Laura. Petrarch was also an important figure in the rediscovery of Greek and Latin literature; he wrote most of his works in Latin. In 1341 Petrarch was crowned Poet Laureate.

Petrarchan denoting a sonnet of the kind used by the Italian poet Petrarch, with an octave rhyming *abbaabba*, and a sestet typically rhyming *cdcdcd* or *cdecde*.

Flinders Petrie (1853–1942), English archaeologist and Egyptologist. He began excavating the Great Pyramid in 1880. Petrie pioneered the use of mathematical calculation and became the first to establish the system of sequence dating, now standard archaeological practice, by which sites are excavated layer by layer and historical chronology determined by the dating of artefacts found *in situ*.

Petrobrusian a follower of Pierre de Bruys, who in southern France in the early 12th century rejected infant baptism, transubstantiation, and the authority of the Church, and opposed the building of churches and the observance of fasts.

Petroleum see ➤ *Petroleum V.* NASBY.

Gaius Petronius (d. AD 66), Roman writer; known as **Petronius Arbiter**. Petronius is generally accepted as the author of the *Satyricon*, a work in prose and verse satirizing the excesses of Roman society. According to Tacitus, Petronius was 'arbiter of taste' at Nero's court; he committed suicide after being accused of treason by Nero.

Petrushka name of a traditional Russian puppet (resembling Punch), who is the central figure in Stravinsky's ballet of that name.

Petticoat Lane popular name for Middlesex Street (formerly Hog Lane) in the City of London, a centre for dealers in second-hand clothes and other commodities.

Petty Bag former name for an office of the common-law jurisdiction of the Court of Chancery, which issued writs and commissions of various kinds.

Jasper Petulengro the principal gypsy character in Borrow's *Lavengro* and *The Romany Rye*, founded upon the Norfolk gypsy Ambrose Smith, with whom Borrow was acquainted in his youth. *Petulengro* means 'shoeing smith'.

peur see ➤ SANS *peur et sans reproche*.

Peutingerian table a map on parchment of the military roads of the ancient Roman Empire, supposed to be a copy of one constructed about AD 226, and named after K. *Peutinger* (1465–1547), of Augsburg, whose family owned the map until 1714.

Nikolaus Pevsner (1902–83), art historian, born in Germany and educated at the universities of Leipzig, Munich, Berlin, and Frankfurt. He lectured for four years at Göttingen before the rise of Hitler brought him to England, where he became in 1941 associated with Penguin Books, as editor of King Penguins and of his celebrated county-by-county series *The Buildings of England* (1951–74).

pew a long bench with a back, placed in rows in the main part of some churches to seat the congregation; an enclosure or compartment containing a number of seats, used in some churches to seat a particular worshipper or group of worshippers.

The word is recorded from late Middle English, and originally denoted a raised, enclosed place in a church, provided for particular worshippers; it comes via Old French from Latin *podia*, plural of *podium* 'elevated space'.

Pfister's Bible another name for the ➤ THIRTY-SIX-LINE BIBLE.

Phaeacian (in the *Odyssey*) an inhabitant of Scheria (Corfu), whose people were noted for their hedonism.

Phaedra in Greek mythology, the daughter of Minos of Crete and wife of ➤ THESEUS. She fell in love with her stepson ➤ HIPPOLYTUS, who rejected her, whereupon she hanged herself, leaving behind a letter which accused him of raping her. Theseus would not believe his son's protestations of innocence and banished him, leading to his death.

Phaedrus (*c*.15 BC–*c*. AD 50), Thracian slave and Roman fabulist, first writer to translate Greek fables into Latin.

Phaethon in Greek mythology, the son of Helios the sun god. He asked to drive his father's solar chariot for a day, but could not control the immortal horses and the chariot plunged too near to the earth until Zeus killed Phaethon with a thunderbolt in order to save the earth from destruction.

phalanx (in ancient Greece) a body of Macedonian infantry drawn up in close order with shields touching and long spears overlapping.

phallus a penis, especially when erect (typically used with reference to male potency or dominance); an image or representation of an erect penis, typically symbolizing fertility or potency.

Phanariot a Greek official in Constantinople under the Ottoman Empire. The name comes from *Phanar*, chief Greek quarter of Istanbul, from Greek *phanarion* 'lighthouse' (one being situated in this area).

Phansigar in 18th-century India, a professional robber and assassin of travellers and others; a Thug. The name comes from Hindi *phānsigār* 'strangler'.

Phantasiast a Docetist who held that Christ's body was only a phantasm, not a material substance.

Phantasmagoria the name of a London exhibition (1802) of optical illusions produced chiefly by magic lantern; the word from this was used to denote an optical device for rapidly varying the size of images on a screen. An earlier entertainment called a *fantasmagorie*, featuring projections of figures which moved or changed shape rapidly (often accompanied by sound effects), was presented in Paris by Étienne-Gaspard Robertson in 1798.

phantom a ghost. Recorded from Middle English (also in the sense 'illusion, delusion'), the word comes from Old French *fantosme* based on Greek *phantasma*, from *phantazein* 'make visible'.

Pharamond name of a legendary king of the Franks.

pharaoh a ruler in ancient Egypt; specifically in early use, any of those mentioned in the Old Testament and Hebrew Scriptures, under whom Joseph flourished and in whose time the oppression and Exodus of the Israelites took place.

Recorded from Middle English, the word comes via ecclesiastical Latin from Greek *Pharaō*, from Hebrew *par'ōh*, from Egyptian *pr-'o* 'great house'.

Pharaoh ant a small yellowish African ant that has established itself worldwide, living as a pest in heated buildings, so named because such ants were believed (erroneously) to be one of the plagues of ancient Egypt.

Pharaoh hound a hunting dog of a short-coated tan-coloured breed with large, pointed ears, so named because the breed is said to have been first introduced to Gozo and Malta by Phoenician sailors.

Pharaoh's chicken the Egyptian vulture.

Pharaoh's corn an ancient cultivar of wheat found in Egyptian tombs.

Pharaoh's serpent an indoor firework that produces ash in a coiled, serpentine form as it burns, named by association with Aaron's staff which turned into a serpent before Pharaoh (Exodus 7:9).

Pharisee a member of an ancient Jewish sect, distinguished by strict observance of the traditional and written law, and commonly held to have pretensions to superior sanctity; they are mentioned only by Josephus and in the New Testament. Unlike the Sadducees, who tried to apply Mosaic law strictly, the Pharisees allowed some freedom of interpretation. Although in the Gospels they are represented as the chief opponents of Christ they seem to have been less hostile than the Sadducees to the nascent Church, with which they shared belief in the Resurrection.

In general use, especially with allusion to the story in Luke of the Pharisee who gave thanks that he was 'not as other men', a self-righteous person, a hypocrite.

Recorded in Old English in the form *fariseus*, the

word comes via ecclesiastical Latin from Greek *Pharisaios*, from Aramaic *prīšayyā* 'separated ones'.

pharisee a fairy (in English regional use, perhaps as an alteration of *fairy*).

pharm a place where genetically modified plants or animals are grown or reared in order to producue pharmaceutical products. The word is formed from the first syllable of *pharmaceutical* with a punning play on *farm*, and references to *pharms* as sites for experiments in genetic engineering are found from the early 1990s.

pharmacopoeia a book, especially an official publication, containing a list of medicinal drugs with their effects and directions for their use.

pharmakos a scapegoat; in ancient Greece, one chosen in atonement for a crime or misfortune.

Pharos a lighthouse, often considered one of the ▶ SEVEN *Wonders of the World*, erected by Ptolemy II (308–246 BC) in *c.*280 BC on the island of Pharos, off the coast of Alexandria. It was destroyed in 1375.

Pharsalia the name of the region around about Pharsalus in Thessaly, and thus of the battle fought there in 48 BC, in which Pompey was defeated by Julius Caesar; in allusive use, a resounding defeat, a monumental failure.

pheasant a large long-tailed game bird native to Asia, the male of which typically has very showy plumage. Recorded from Middle English, the word comes via Old French and Latin from Greek *phasianos* '(bird of) Phasis', the name of a river in the Caucasus, from which the bird is said to have spread westwards.

Pheidippides (5th century BC), Athenian messenger, who was sent to Sparta to ask for help after the Persian landing at ▶ MARATHON in 490 and is said to have covered the 250 km (150 miles) in two days on foot.
  A second (probably legendary) story says that he ran from Athens to Marathon to take part in the battle, and then returned with news of the victory to Athens, making the announcement with the dying words, 'Greetings, we win!' This story is the basis of the modern marathon race.

phenakistoscope a toy consisting of a disc or drum with figures representing a moving object in successive positions arranged radially on it, to be viewed in such a way that an impression of actual motion is got when the disc or drum is rapidly rotated.

the infant phenomenon in Dickens's *Nicholas Nickleby* (1839), the girl actress Ninetta Crummles; the expression is found in extended (and ironic) usage.

salve the phenomenona reconcile observed facts with a theory or doctrine with which they appear to disagree; recorded from the early 17th century.

pheon a heraldic charge in the form of a broad arrowhead, especially one engrailed on the inner edge of each barb.

Phi Beta Kappa (in the US) an honorary society of undergraduates and some graduates to which members are elected on the basis of high academic achievement. The name comes from the initial letters of a Greek motto *philosophia biou kubernētēs* 'philosophy is the guide to life'.

phi the twenty-first letter of the Greek alphabet (Φ, φ), transliterated as 'ph' or (in modern Greek) 'f'.

phial of oil is the emblem of ▶ *St* REMIGIUS, ▶ *St* JANUARIUS, and the 8th-century English nun St Walburga.

Phidias (5th century BC), Athenian sculptor. He is noted for the Elgin marbles and his vast statue of Zeus at Olympia (*c.*430), which was one of the ▶ SEVEN *Wonders of the World*.

Philadelphia the chief city of Pennsylvania, on the Delaware River. Established as a Quaker colony by William Penn and others in 1681, it was the site in 1776 of the signing of the Declaration of Independence and in 1787 of the adoption of the Constitution of the United States. The name means, 'brotherly love', and *City of Brotherly Love* is an informal name for Philadelphia.

Philadelphia lawyer a very shrewd lawyer expert in the exploitation of legal technicalities, originally with reference to Andrew Hamilton of Philadelphia, who successfully defended John Zenger (1735), an American journalist and publisher, from libel charges.

philander (of a man) readily or frequently enter into casual sexual relationships with women, from the earlier noun *philander* 'man, husband', often used in literature as the given name of a lover.

philanthropine a school founded in Germany in 1774 by John Bernhard Bassedau (1723–90) to educate children in the principles of philanthropy, natural religion, and cosmopolitanism.

Kim Philby (1912–88), British Foreign Office official and spy. While working at the British Embassy in Washington DC (1949–51), Philby was asked to resign on suspicion of being a Soviet agent, although there was no firm evidence to this effect. He defected to the USSR in 1963 and was officially revealed to have spied for the Soviets from 1933.

Philemon in Greek mythology, a good old countryman living with his wife ➤ BAUCIS in Phrygia who offered hospitality to Zeus and Hermes when the two gods came to earth, without revealing their identities, to test people's piety. Philemon and Baucis were subsequently saved from a flood which covered the district.

Epistle to Philemon a book of the New Testament, an epistle of St Paul to a well-to-do Christian living probably at Colossae in Phrygia.

Philip see also ➤ *Philip* MARLOWE.

St Philip[1] an Apostle. In art he is shown either with a cross as the instrument of his martyrdom, or with loaves of bread as symbolizing his part in the feeding of the five thousand.
□ **FEAST DAY** His feast day (with St James the Less) is 1 May.

St Philip[2] a deacon of the early Christian Church, also known as **St Philip the Evangelist**. He was one of seven deacons appointed to superintend the secular business of the Church at Jerusalem (Acts 6:5–6).
□ **FEAST DAY** His feast day is 6 June.

Philip and Mary Philip of Spain, consort of Mary Tudor, and Mary herself, as represented on coinage issued in 1555.

appeal from Philip drunk to Philip sober proverbial saying, implying that an opinion or decision reflects only a passing mood. The original allusion is to Philip, King of Macedon, father of Alexander the Great, who is said to have been the subject of such an appeal.

Philip of Valois (1293–1350), king of France (as Philip VI) from 1328. The founder of the Valois dynasty, Philip came to the throne on the death of Charles IV, whose only child was a girl and barred from ruling. His claim was challenged by Edward III of England; the dispute developed into the Hundred Years War.

Philip the Bold name given to Philip III of France (1245–85).

Philip the Fair name given to Philip IV of France (1268–1314), king of France from 1285. His influence secured the appointment of Clement V as pope and the move of the papal seat to Avignon (1309–77). Philip also persuaded Clement to dissolve the powerful and wealthy order of the Knights Templars in 1312.

Philip the Handsome name given to Philip I of Spain (1478–1506). Son of the Holy Roman emperor Maximilian I, in 1496 Philip married the infanta Joanna, daughter of Ferdinand of Aragon and Isabella of Castile; their son Charles V established the Habsburgs as the ruling dynasty in Spain.

Philip the Tall name given to Philip V of France (1293–1322).

King Philip's War the fighting in 1675–6 between English colonists and Wampanoag and other New England Indians; *King Philip* was the English name for Metacomet (d. 1676), the Wampanoag chief.

Philippi a city in ancient Macedonia, the scene in 42 BC of two battles in which Mark Antony and Octavian defeated Brutus and Cassius. The ruins lie close to the Aegean coast in NE Greece, near the port of Kaválla (ancient Neapolis).

Epistle to the Philippians a book of the New Testament, an epistle of St Paul to the Church at Philippi in Macedonia.

philippic a bitter attack or denunciation, especially a verbal one; from (via Latin) Greek *philippikos*, the name given to Demosthenes' speeches against Philip II of Macedon, also to those of Cicero against Mark Antony.

philippina a nut with two kernels. Also, a custom of German origin in which a gift may be claimed by the first of two people who have shared a nut with two kernels to say 'philippina' at their next meeting; a gift claimed in this way.

Philippine a member of a religious society of young unmarried poor women whose patron was St Philip Neri (1515–95), founder of the ➤ ORATORY.

Philistine a member of a non-Semitic people of southern Palestine in ancient times, who came into conflict with the Israelites during the 12th and 11th centuries BC. The Philistines, from whom the country of Palestine took its name, were one of the ➤ SEA *Peoples* who, according to the Bible, came from Crete and settled the southern coastal plain of Canaan in the 12th century BC.

The word (usually in the form *philistine*) has come to mean a person who is hostile or indifferent to culture and the arts, or who has no understanding of them. This sense arose as a result of a confrontation between town and gown in Jena, Germany, in the late 17th century; a sermon on the conflict quoted: 'the Philistines are upon you' (Judges 16), which led to an association between the townspeople and those hostile to culture. The term was notably used in 1997 by the Labour politician Gerald Kaufman, as Chairman of a House of Commons select committee, commenting unfavourably on the management of Covent Garden Opera House:

> We would prefer to see the House run by a philistine with the requisite financial acumen than by the succession of opera and ballet lovers who have brought a great and valuable institution to its knees.
> — Gerald Kaufman report, 3 December 1997

Phillips curve a supposed inverse relationship between the level of unemployment and the rate of inflation, named after Alban W. H. *Phillips* (1914–75), New Zealand economist.

Phillis a pretty country girl or a sweetheart; originally, a generic proper name in pastoral poetry. Also, a pretty, neat, or dexterous female servant, after Milton's *L'Allegro* (1632), 'Herbs, and other country messes, Which the neat-handed Phillis dresses'.

Philo Judaeus (*c.*15 BC–*c.*50 AD), Jewish philosopher of Alexandria. He is particularly known for his commentaries on the Pentateuch (written in Greek), which he interpreted allegorically in the light of Platonic and Aristotelian philosophy.

Philoctetes in Greek mythology, a famous archer, who by shooting Paris helped to bring about the fall of Troy. Although he had originally set out for Troy with the other Greeks, he had been bitten by a snake at Tenedos, and because of the smell of the suppurating wound that resulted he had been left by his companions on the desolate coast of Lesbos. After a prophecy that Troy would not fall without Philoctetes he was brought to the siege; his wound

was healed and he killed Paris.

> Embrocation, cough linctus, arnica and Vicks wafted from him according to his need or the time of year, as though, like Philoctetes, he concealed some suppurating sore about his person.
> — D. M. Greenwood *A Grave Disturbance* (1998)

Philomel the daughter of Pandion, king of Athens. She was turned into a swallow and her sister Procne into a nightingale (or, in Latin versions, into a nightingale with Procne the swallow) when they were being pursued by the cruel Tereus, who had married Procne and raped Philomel.

philosopher a person engaged or learned in philosophy, especially as an academic discipline.

➤ *St* JUSTIN and ➤ *St* CATHERINE *of Alexandria* are the patron saints of philosophers.

See also ➤ LAUGHING *philosopher,* ➤ WEEPING *philosopher.*

philosopher kings (in the political theory of Plato) the elite whose knowledge enables them to rule justly.

philosopher's egg a medicine made of egg-yolk and saffron, formerly thought to cure the plague.

philosopher's stone a mythical substance supposed to change any metal into gold or silver and, according to some, to cure all diseases and prolong life indefinitely. Its discovery was the supreme object of alchemy.

philosopher's tree the branched tree-like amalgam precipitated by mercury from a solution of nitrate of silver, also called *Diana's tree, tree of Diana.*

Philosophes the collective name of a group of 18th-century writers and thinkers united by their faith in the efficacy of reason and their dislike of repressive traditions. Its most significant representatives included Montesquieu, Voltaire, Diderot, Rousseau, Buffon, Condillac, and Helvétius. They inclined to scepticism in religion, materialism in philosophy, and hedonism in ethics.

philosophia perennis a core of philosophical truths which is hypothesized to exist independently of and unaffected by time or place.

philosophia prima (the branch of inquiry that deals with) the most general truths of philosophy, in particular, (the branch of inquiry that deals with) the divine and the eternal.

philosophical radical a member of a group of 19th-century radicals advocating political reform based on Benthamite utilitarian philosophy.

philtre a drink supposed to excite sexual love in the drinker; a love potion. Recorded from the late 16th century, the word comes via French and Latin from Greek *philtron*, from *philein* 'to love'.

Phiz pseudonym of the English illustrator Hablot Knight Browne (1815–82), who in 1836 was chosen to illustrate Dickens's *Pickwick Papers*, and took his pseudonym to complement Dickens's 'Boz'.

Phlegethon the name of a mythological river of fire, one of the five rivers of Hades.

phlegm in medieval science and medicine, one of the four bodily ➤ HUMOURS, believed to be associated with a calm, stolid, or apathetic temperament; the adjective *phlegmatic* derives from this.

Recorded from late Middle English, the word comes via Old French from late Latin *phlegma* 'clammy moisture (of the body)', from Greek *phlegma* 'inflammation', from *phlegein* 'to burn'.

phlogiston a substance supposed by 18th-century chemists to exist in all combustible bodies, and to be released in combustion. The **phlogiston theory** was discredited when Antoine Lavoisier showed the true nature of oxygen.

Phobos in Greek mythology, a son of the war god ➤ ARES.

St Phocas a 4th-century saint and martyr of Sinope on the Black Sea; a hermit, he was noted as a gardener, and used his produce to feed pilgrims. He is the patron saint of gardeners and agricultural workers, and sailors (perhaps because his name resembles Greek *phoce* 'a seal'), and his emblem is a spade.

☐ **FEAST DAY** His feast day is celebrated on various dates, especially, 22 September or 14 July.

Phoebe in Greek mythology, a Titaness, daughter of Uranus (Heaven) and Gaia (Earth). She became the mother of Leto and thus the grandmother of Apollo and Artemis. In the later Greek writers her name was often used for Selene (Moon).

Phoebus an epithet of Apollo, used in contexts where the god was identified with the sun. The name comes from Greek *Phoibos*, literally 'bright one'.

Phoenicia an ancient country on the shores of the eastern Mediterranean, corresponding to modern Lebanon and the coastal plains of Syria. It consisted of a number of city states, including Tyre and Sidon, and was a flourishing centre of Mediterranean trade

and colonization during the early part of the 1st millennium BC.

Phoenician a member of a Semitic people inhabiting ancient Phoenicia and its colonies. The Phoenicians prospered from trade and their trading contacts extended throughout Asia, and reached westwards as far as Africa (where they founded Carthage), Spain, and possibly Britain. The Phoenicians continued to thrive until the capital, Tyre, was sacked by Alexander the Great in 332 BC. The Phoenicians invented an alphabet which was borrowed by the Greeks and passed down into Western cultural tradition.

phoenix (in classical mythology) a unique bird, resembling an eagle but with rich red and gold plumage, that lived for five or six centuries in the Arabian desert (it is also known as the *Arabian bird*), after this time burning itself on a funeral pyre ignited by the sun and fanned by its own wings, and rising from the ashes with renewed youth to live through another cycle.

A variation of the myth stated that the phoenix burnt itself on the altar of the temple of Helios (the Sun) at Heliopolis (Egypt), and that a worm emerged from the ashes and became the young phoenix.

phoenix company derogatory term for an insolvent company which is placed into voluntary liquidation by its directors, trading being resumed soon afterwards under a different company name. The usage is recorded from the early 1990s.

The Phoenix of these Late Times title under which an account of the recluse Henry Welby (d. 1636) was published in 1637; Welby had lived in seclusion for 44 years before his death, but had constantly been charitable to poorer neighbours.

Phoenix Park Murders the murder in Phoenix Park, Dublin, with surgical knives, of the newly arrived Irish chief secretary, Lord Frederick Cavendish, and under-secretary T. H. Burke by Irish Invincibles in 1882. The assassination caused wide public outrage in England, and embarrassment to supporters of Home Rule; in 1887, the Irish journalist and forger ➤ *Richard* PIGOTT published a letter in the *Times* purporting to show the complicity of ➤ PARNELL (the forgery was shown up in a subseqent trial for libel).

phoney war the period of comparative inaction at the beginning of the Second World War between the

German invasion of Poland (September 1939) and that of Norway (April 1940).

phossy jaw informal term for gangrene of the jaw-bone caused by phosphorus poisoning; recorded from the late 19th century, this industrial disease often affected workers in match factories.

Photius (*c.*820–*c.*891), Byzantine scholar and patri-arch of Constantinople. His most important work is the *Bibliotheca*, a critical account of 280 earlier prose works and an invaluable source of information about many works now lost.

photo finish a close finish of a race in which the winner is identifiable only from a photograph taken as the competitors cross the line; the phrase is fre-quently found in extended use.

Phrygia an ancient region of west central Asia Minor, to the south of Bithynia. Centred on the city of Gordium, it dominated Asia Minor after the de-cline of the Hittites in the 12th century BC, reaching the peak of its power in the 8th century under King Midas. It was eventually absorbed into the kingdom of Lydia in the 6th century BC.

The term **Phrygian**, meaning a native or inhabit-ant of ancient Phrygia, is also sometimes used for a member of the ➤ MONTANISTS, because they origin-ated in Phrygia.

Phrygian bonnet a conical cap with the top bent forwards, worn in ancient times and now identified with the ➤ CAP *of liberty*. Also called *Phrygian cap*.

Phrygian mode the mode represented by the nat-ural diatonic scale E–E (containing a minor 2nd, 3rd, 6th, and 7th). Said to be warlike in character, it is supposed to have been derived from the ancient Phrygians.

Phryne name of a famous Greek courtesan of the 4th century BC, noted for her beauty and said to have been the model for Apelles's painting of Aph-rodite Anadyomene and Praxiteles's statue of Aph-rodite.

> These were the classy courtesans, descendants of . . . Phryne who was the model for her lover Praxiteles's statue of Aphrodite.
> — *Independent* 19 May 1992

phylactery a small leather box containing Hebrew texts on vellum, worn by Jewish men at morning prayer as a reminder to keep the law.

The two boxes are worn on the arm (usually the left) and the forehead, with the same four texts in-serted into each. These are Deuteronomy 6:4–9 and 13–21 and Exodus 13:1–10 and 11–16.

Recorded from late Middle English, the word comes via late Latin from Greek *phulaktērion* 'amu-let', from *phulassein* 'to guard'.

physician a person qualified to practise medicine, especially one who specializes in diagnosis and medical treatment as distinct from surgery. Re-corded from Middle English, the word comes via Old French from Latin *physica* 'things relating to nature'.

the beloved physician in the Bible, epithet of St Luke, as used by Paul in Colossians 4:14, 'Luke, the beloved physician, and Demas greet you'. Luke is thus a patron saint of doctors.

physician-assisted suicide ➤ ASSISTED *suicide* carried out with the help of a doctor.

physician finger the finger next to the little finger, the ring finger; another term for the ➤ MEDICAL *fin-ger*.

physician, heal thyself proverbial saying, early 15th century, meaning that before attempting to cor-rect others you should make sure that you are not guilty of the same faults; with biblical allusion to Luke 4:23, 'And he said unto them, Ye will surely say unto me this proverb, Physician, heal thyself: what-soever we have heard done in Capernaum, do also here in thy country.'

physics the branch of science concerned with the nature and properties of matter and energy. The subject matter of physics, distinguished from that of chemistry and biology, includes mechanics, heat, light and other radiation, sound, electricity, mag-netism, and the structure of atoms.

Recorded from the late 15th century, the word originally denoted natural science in general, espe-cially the Aristotelian system, and comes ultimately from Greek *phusika* 'natural things' from *phusis* 'nature'.

physiocrat a member of an 18th-century group of French economists who believed that agriculture was the source of all wealth and that agricultural products should be highly priced. Advocating ad-herence to a supposed natural order of social insti-tutions, they also stressed the necessity of free trade.

pi the sixteenth letter of the Greek alphabet (Π, π), transliterated as 'p'. Also, the numerical value of the ratio of the circumference of a circle to its diameter (approximately 3.14159).

Jean Piaget (1896–1980), Swiss psychologist. Piaget's work on the intellectual and logical abilities of children provided the single biggest impact on the study of the development of human thought processes. He described the mind as proceeding through a series of fixed stages of cognitive development, each being a prerequisite for the next.

piano nobile in architecture, the main storey of a large house (usually the first floor), containing the principal rooms. The phrase is Italian, and means literally 'noble floor'.

Piarist a member of a Roman Catholic secular order, founded in Rome *c.*1600 and devoted to teaching the young. The name comes from Italian *Piaristi* from modern Latin *patres scholarum piarum* 'fathers of the religious schools'.

piblokto among Eskimos, a condition characterized by episodes of hysterical excitement or frenzy followed by depression or stupor, affecting especially women in winter; hysteria in a dog or other animal.

Picardy a region and former province of northern France, centred on the city of Amiens, which was the scene of heavy fighting in the First World War. One of the soldiers' songs of the First World War was entitled 'Roses of Picardy' (1916).

picaresque of or relating to an episodic style of fiction dealing with the adventures of a rough and dishonest but appealing hero. The picaresque novel originated in Spain in the 16th century, *La Vida de Lazarillo de Tormes* (*c.*1554) usually being cited as the earliest example. In English, the genre is associated particularly with 18th-century writers such as Daniel Defoe, Henry Fielding, and Tobias Smollett.

Recorded from the early 19th century, the word comes via French from Spanish *picaresco*, from *picaro* 'rogue'.

Pablo Picasso (1881–1973), Spanish painter, sculptor, and graphic artist, resident in France from 1904. His prolific inventiveness and technical versatility made him the dominant figure in avant-garde art in the first half of the 20th century. Following his Blue Period (1901–4) and Rose Period (1905–6), *Les Demoiselles d'Avignon* (1907) signalled his development of cubism (1908–14). In the 1920s and 1930s he adopted a neoclassical figurative style and produced semi-surrealist paintings using increasingly violent imagery, notably *The Three Dancers* (1935) and *Guernica* (1937), his response to the destruction of the Basque capital by German bombers.

picayune petty, worthless. The word is recorded from the 19th century, from French *picaillon* denoting a Piedmontese copper coin, also used to mean 'cash', from Provençal *picaioun*, of unknown ultimate origin.

Piccadilly a street in central London, extending from Hyde Park eastwards to Piccadilly Circus, noted for its fashionable shops, hotels, and restaurants. The name was originally applied to a house, Pickadilly Hall, thought to be named from the obsolete word *piccadil* 'a decorative border inserted on the edge of an article of dress', either because piccadils were manufactured there or because houses built there were on the outskirts of the developed area in the 16th century.

Mary Pickford (1893–1979), Canadian-born American actress. She was a star of silent films, usually playing the innocent young heroine, as in *Pollyanna* (1920). She also co-founded United Artists (1919).

Pickwickian of or like Mr Pickwick in Dickens's *Pickwick Papers*, especially in being jovial, plump, or generous. *Pickwickian* can also refer to a word being used misunderstood or misused, especially to avoid offence:

> The Chairman felt it his imperative duty to demand . . . whether he had used the expression . . . in a common sense. Mr. Blotton had no hesitation in saying, that he had not—he had used the word in its Pickwickian sense.
> — Charles Dickens *Pickwick Papers* (1837)

Pict a member of an ancient people inhabiting northern Scotland in Roman times. Roman writings of around 300 AD apply the term *Picti* to the hostile tribes of the area north of the Antonine Wall. Their origins are uncertain, but they may have been a loose confederation of Celtic tribes. According to chroniclers the Pictish kingdom was united with that of the southern Scots under Kenneth I in about 844, and the name of the Picts as a distinct people gradually disappeared. The name comes from late Latin *Picti*, perhaps from *pict-* 'painted, tattooed', or perhaps influenced by a local name.

Picts' house any of various ancient dwellings in northern Scotland and the northern and western Isles, formerly thought to have been built by the Picts.

picture see also ➤ DEVIL's *picture books*.

picture hat a woman's highly decorated hat with a wide brim, as shown in pictures by 18th-century

English painters such as Reynolds and Gainsborough.

one picture is worth ten thousand words proverbial saying, early 20th century (there is no basis for an ascription of Chinese origin).

every picture tells a story proverbial saying, early 20th century; in *Jane Eyre* (1847), Charlotte Brontë had written for the child Jane, 'The letter-press…I cared little for…Each picture told a story'.

pidgin a grammatically simplified form of a language, typically English, Dutch, or Portuguese, with a limited vocabulary, some elements of which are taken from local languages, used for communication between people not sharing a common language. Pidgins are not normally found as native languages, but arise out of language contact between speakers of other languages. The word comes from a late 19th-century Chinese simplification of English *business*.

Pidyon Haben a Jewish ceremony performed thirty days after the birth of a first-born male child to redeem him from being nominally committed to the service of the priesthood. The ceremony is based upon Exodus 13:2–16 and Numbers 18:15, and is not required if either parent is a Cohen or a Levite. The name represents Hebrew *pidyōn habēn* 'redemption of a son'.

pie¹ a baked dish of fruit, or meat and vegetables, typically with a top and base of pastry. Recorded from Middle English, the word is probably the same as ➤ PIE², the various combinations of ingredients being compared to objects randomly collected by a magpie.

    See also ➤ COCK-*and-pie*, ➤ *have a* FINGER *in every pie*, ➤ PUMPKIN *pie*, ➤ PROMISES, *like pie-crust, are made to be broken*.

pie² used in names of birds that resemble the magpie, especially in having black-and-white plumage, e.g. **sea-pie**, **tree pie**. Recorded from Middle English, the word comes via Old French from Latin *pica* 'magpie', related to Latin *picus* 'green woodpecker'.

pie³ a confused mass of printers' type; recorded from the mid 17th century, the term may represent a transferred use of ➤ PIE¹, with reference to its miscellaneous contents.

pie in the sky something that is pleasant to contemplate but is very unlikely to be realized, from a song by the American labour leader Joe Hill (1879–1915):

> Work and pray, live on hay,
> You'll get pie in the sky when you die.
> — Joe Hill 'The Preacher and the Slave' (1911)

piece of eight a Spanish dollar, equivalent to 8 reals, and marked with the figure 8. The phrase is notably associated with Robert Stevenson's *Treasure Island* (1883); ➤ LONG *John Silver*'s parrot constantly repeats 'Pieces of eight! Pieces of eight!' as a reminder of the pirates' treasure.

Pied Piper the central character of *The Pied Piper of Hamelin*, a poem by Robert Browning (1842), based on an old German legend. The piper, dressed in particoloured costume, rid the town of Hamelin (Hameln) in Brunswick of rats by enticing them away with his music, and when refused the promised payment he lured away the children of the citizens.

    In extended usage, the term is used for a person who entices people to follow, especially to their doom.

> Nonbelievers worry that Witten may be a Pied Piper, leading his followers away from reality and into a phantasmagoria of pure mathematics.
> — *Scientific American* November 1991

Piedfort a coin that is thicker than a normal issue, made as a collector's item. The name comes from French *pied* 'foot' + *fort* 'strong'.

Piedmont a region of NW Italy, in the foothills of the Alps. Dominated by Savoy from 1400, it became a part of the kingdom of Sardinia in 1720, and was the centre of the movement for a united Italy in the 19th century.

    See also ➤ PRINCE *of Piedmont*.

Piepowders see ➤ COURT *of Piepowders*.

Pierian belonging to Pieria, a district in northern Thessaly, that in classical mythology was reputed home of the Muses and the location of a spring sacred to them; in figurative usage, the **Pierian spring** is the source of poetic inspiration.

> Next these, learn'd Jonson, in this list I bring,
> Who had drunk deep of the Pierian spring.
> — Michael Drayton 'To Henry Reynolds, of Poets and Poesy' (1627)

Pierrot a stock male character in French pantomime, usually played as a sentimental lovesick youth with a sad white-painted face, a loose white costume with a neck ruff, and a pointed hat. The character derives from *Pedrolino* of the Italian

Commedia dell'Arte; originally a robust but simple-minded servant, the victim of pranks practised by his fellow comedians, he was gradually transformed by his interpretation in the French theatre.

Piero della Francesca (1416–92), Italian painter. He used perspective, proportion, and geometrical relationships to create ordered and harmonious pictures in which the figures appear to inhabit real space. He is best known for his frescoes, notably a cycle in Arezzo depicting the story of the True Cross (begun 1452).

Piers Plowman central character of Langland's poem *The Vision of Piers Plowman*; in the vision shown to the narrator, Piers is first shown leading the Pilgrimage to Truth.

pietà a picture or sculpture of the Virgin Mary holding the dead body of Christ on her lap or in her arms. The word is Italian, and comes from Latin *pietas* 'dutifulness'.

Pietism a movement within the German Lutheran Church in the late 17th century originated by the minister Philipp Jakob Spener (1635–1705) who, in reaction to the rigidity of standard orthodoxy at the time, organized devotional meetings for prayer and Bible reading in order to foster Christian values and spirituality in members of the church. *Pietism* also influenced other emerging movements, notably Wesleyan Methodism in the Anglican Church.

The name **Pietist** was originally applied mockingly to followers of Spener, in reference to the *collegia pietatis*, or unions for mutual religious edification, formed by them.

piety see ➤ MOUNT *of piety*, ➤ PELICAN *in her piety*.

Piffer informal name for a member of the Punjab Irregular Frontier Force (a military unit raised in 1849 and employed especially to police the North-West Frontier of India) or of one of the regiments that succeeded it; the name came from the initials of the force.

pig the pig family is descended from the wild boar and was domesticated over 8,000 years ago; the *pig* is proverbial as a type of obstinacy and greed.

A *pig* is the emblem of ➤ St ANTHONY *of Egypt*.

See also ➤ *if you would be happy for a* WEEK, ➤ LONG *pig*, ➤ St ANTHONY'*s pig*, ➤ *what can you expect from a* PIG *but a grunt?*.

Pig and Whistle a traditional public-house sign; it has been suggested that the name represents *piggin* 'small pail' and *wassail* 'be in health'. *Pig* denoted an earthenware crock or pitcher; the expression **go to pigs and whistles**, meaning fall into ruin and disrepair, is recorded from the late 17th century.

pig in a poke something that is bought or accepted without knowing its value or seeing it first (a *poke* here is a bag).

pig Latin an invented language formed by systematic distortion of a source language; a secret language formed from English by transferring the initial consonant or consonant cluster of each word to the end of the word and adding a vocalic syllable (usually *-ay*): so *igpay atinlay*.

pigeon in allusion to its harmlessness and to the fact that it is easily caught, *pigeon* in extended use means a person who is easily swindled, a dupe.

See also ➤ PASSENGER *pigeon*, ➤ STOOL *pigeon*.

pigeon-hole a small compartment, open at the front and forming part of a set, where letters or messages may be left for someone, resembling a roosting recess in a loft for domestic pigeons; in figurative use, a category to which someone or something is assigned. In verbal use, to *pigeon-hole* may now apply assignment to a category or class in a manner that is too rigid or exclusive.

pigeon pair a boy and girl as twins, or as the only children in a family.

pigeon's blood a type of precious stone (usually a ruby or opal) of a dark red colour.

pigeon's milk an imaginary article for which a child or a gullible person is sent as a joke.

pigeons see ➤ BLACK *pigeons*, ➤ *put the* CAT *among the pigeons*.

Miss Piggy the flamboyant and demanding ➤ MUPPET whose conviction of her own attractions is not always shared by her companions.

piggy bank a money box, especially one shaped like a pig; savings. In the past, children's *piggy banks* were often made of earthenware with a small slot for inserting coins, and had to be smashed in order to retrieve the savings.

Richard Pigott (1828?–89), Irish journalist and forger, who in April 1887 published a letter in the *Times* purporting to implicate Charles Stewart Parnell in the ➤ PHOENIX *Park Murders*. In 1889, after a libel action in which the forgery of this and other papers was demonstrated, Pigott committed suicide.

pigs see also ➤ Hogs *Norton where pigs play the organ.*

Bay of Pigs a bay on the SW coast of Cuba, scene of an unsuccessful attempt in 1961 by US-backed Cuban exiles to invade the country and overthrow the regime of Fidel Castro.

pigs in clover a game in which a number of marbles are rolled into a recess or pocket in a board by tilting the board itself.

pigs may fly, but they are very unlikely birds proverbial saying, indicating incredulity or impossibility.

pigtail a plait or tail of hair, denoting especially a single tail of hair hanging down the back and worn by soldiers and sailors in the late 18th and early 19th centuries, and the long plait of hair formerly worn by the Chinese.

Pike in California and other Pacific states of the US, a name given in the 19th century to a perceived class of poor white migrants from the southern states of the US; the name comes from *Pike County,* Missouri, from which the first people of this kind were said to have come to California.

pike a long-bodied predatory freshwater fish with a pointed snout and large teeth; the name comes from *pike* as a weapon, and refers to the fish's pointed jaw.

The *pike* may be referred to as a type of lurking ferocity, as in the comment by the Irish politician T. M. Healy (1855–1931) on seeing Lord Hartington apparently asleep on the Opposition bench: 'There is the noble Marquis. Like a pike at the bottom of a pool.'

pikestaff see ➤ plain *as a pikestaff.*

Acts of Pilate apocryphal work which tells the story of the trial, death, and resurrection of Christ.

Pontius Pilate (d. *c.*36 AD), Roman procurator of Judaea *c.*26–*c.*36. He is remembered for presiding at the trial of Jesus Christ and authorizing his crucifixion, as recorded in the New Testament, although ritually washing his hands to show that he was innocent of Jesus's blood. *Pilate* appeared as a character in medieval mystery plays, and from this his name was used as a term of reproach for a corrupt or lax person, or one evading responsibility for their actions.

Pilate was later recalled to Rome following a massacre of Samaritans in 36. According to one tradition he subsequently committed suicide.

Mount Pilatus name of a mountain in Switzerland above Lausanne, said to be haunted by the ghost of *Pontius Pilate* (who had been exiled to Vienne) either because he drowned in the Rhône at Vienne or because he is buried near Lausanne; in Alpine Europe, Pilate was traditionally linked with mountains, pools, and bad weather.

pile it high, sell it cheap slogan coined by Jack Cohen (1898–1979), founder of the Tesco supermarket chain.

pilgrim a person who journeys to a sacred place for religious reasons. The word comes (in Middle English) from Provençal *pelegrin,* from Latin *peregrinus* 'foreign' (cf. *peregrine*).

➤ *St* James *the Great* and the 4th-century Egyptian martyr St Mennas, whose shrine near Alexandria was a popular pilgrimage centre, are the patron saints of pilgrims.

pilgrim bottle a flat bottle with a ring on each side of the neck by which it may be hung from the waist and carried, as used on a pilgrimage.

pilgrim city in the US, a city associated with the Pilgrim Fathers, in particular Boston and Plymouth, Massachusetts.

Pilgrim Fathers the pioneers of British colonization of North America. A group of 102 people led by English Puritans fleeing religious persecution sailed in the *Mayflower* and founded the colony of Plymouth, Massachusetts, in 1620.

pilgrim's hat a type of broad-brimmed hat as worn by pilgrims, the emblem of ➤ *St* James *the Great.*

The Pilgrim's Progress allegorical story (1678–84) by ➤ *John* Bunyan, of which the first part tells of the journey of Christian to the Celestial City, and the second the journey of his wife Christiana, guided by Greatheart.

The story takes the form of a dream in which the narrator sees Christian (accompanied by Faithful) fleeing from the City of Destruction, and passing through such snares of the world as the Slough of Despond, Vanity Fair (where Faithful is put to death), the Valley of the Shadow of Death, and Doubting Castle, before reaching the Delectable Mountains, Beulah, and the Celestial City. Sustained by Evangelist, and his later companion

Hopeful, he faces Giant Despair, Apollyon, and many enemies on his way.

pilgrim's shell a ➤ SCALLOP *shell* carried by a pilgrim as a sign of having visited a shrine, in particular that of ➤ St JAMES *the Great* at Compostela in Spain.

pilgrimage a journey made to some sacred place, as an act of religious devotion.

Pilgrimage of Grace a series of popular risings in northern England in 1536 and 1537 opposing the dissolution of the monasteries and other features of the Reformation.

pill see also ➤ BITTER *pill*, ➤ GILD *the pill*, ➤ POISON *pill*.

the Pill a contraceptive pill; the expression dates from the 1950s, when the first oral contraceptives containing synthetic female hormones were introduced.

pillar a tall vertical structure of stone, wood, or metal used as a support for a building or as an ornament or monument; a *pillar* as that to which Jesus was bound during the Flagellation is thus one of the symbols of the ➤ PASSION.

In the 16th and 17th centuries, a *pillar* denoted a small column carried as a symbol of dignity or office; this was used by Cardinal Wolsey (*c*.1475–1530) and Cardinal Pole (1500–1558), but not recorded elsewhere. Representations of Wolsey's pillars appear in the decorations of Christ Church, Oxford. Those of Pole are represented in the illumination on the first page of his Register of Wills at Somerset House; they appear as Corinthian columns with capital and base, about the size of Roman fasces.

See also ➤ ASOKA *pillar*, ➤ FIVE *Pillars of Islam*, ➤ NELSON*'s Pillar*, ➤ POMPEY*'s pillar*.

pillar apostle each of the Apostles Peter, James, and John (with allusion to Galatians 2:9), where they are described as 'pillars' by Paul.

pillar of salt in the Bible, the wife of Lot (see ➤ LOT[1]) turned back to look at Sodom, from which they were fleeing before its destruction; for this disobedience, she was turned into a pillar of salt.

pillar of society a person regarded as a particularly responsible citizen, a mainstay of the social fabric. *Pillar* in the sense of a person regarded as a mainstay or support for something is recorded from Middle English; *Pillars of Society* was the English title (1888) of a play by Ibsen.

from pillar to post from one place to another in an unceremonious or fruitless manner. The phrase (in its earlier form **from post to pillar**) originally referred to the rapid movement of a ball around the court in real tennis. The rhyming constructions with *tost* or *tossed* which are found in a number of early uses make reference to this.

pillarist an ascetic who lives on a pillar; a ➤ STYLITE.

Pillars of Hercules an ancient name for two promontories on either side of the Strait of Gibraltar (the Rock of Gibraltar and Mount Acho in Ceuta), held by legend to have been parted by the arm of Hercules.

Piller see ➤ ANTON *Piller order*.

pillory a wooden framework with holes for the head and hands, in which an offender was imprisoned and exposed to public abuse. In Great Britain the punishment of the pillory was abolished, except for perjury, in 1815, and totally in 1837. In Delaware, US, it was not abolished till 1905.

Recorded from Middle English, the word comes from Old French *pilori*, and probably from Provençal *espilori* (associated by some with a Catalan word meaning 'peephole', of uncertain origin).

pilot the word came into English in the early 16th century, denoting a person who steers a ship, via French from medieval Latin *pilotus*, an alteration of *pedota*, based on Greek *pēdon* 'oar' (plural) 'rudder'.

drop the pilot abandon a trustworthy adviser; after a a cartoon by John Tenniel in *Punch* 20 March 1890 depicting the recent dismissal of Bismarck from the Chancellorship of Germany by the new young German Emperor William II; the caption read 'dropping the pilot'.

Pilsen see ➤ *as much akin as* LENSON *Hill to Pilsen Pen*.

Piltdown man a fraudulent fossil composed of a human cranium and an ape jaw, allegedly discovered near *Piltdown*, a village in East Sussex, and presented in 1912 as a genuine hominid of the early Pleistocene, but shown to be a hoax in 1953.

> Alas, we historians have so little scandal. We are not palaeontologists to display our Piltdowns.
> — Angus Wilson *Anglo-Saxon Attitudes* (1956)

pily in heraldry, of a field: divided into a (usually specified) number of piles.

Pimlico a district of London, originally the name of a place of resort (perhaps called after its proprietor) at Hogsdon (now Hoxton), a suburb of London, formerly celebrated for its ale and cakes.

Pimm's trademark name for any of four different spirit-based mixed drinks, sometimes drunk neat but usually mixed with lemonade, ginger ale, or soda water, and served with ice as a summer drink.

pimpernel see ➤ SCARLET *Pimpernel*.

pin see also ➤ *it's a* SIN *to steal a pin*.

see a pin and pick it up, all the day you'll have good luck; see a pin and let it lie, bad luck you'll have all day proverbial saying, mid 19th century.

pin money traditional term for an allowance to a woman for dress and other personal expenses from her husband.

Mount Pinatubo a volcano on the island of Luzon, in the Philippines. It erupted in 1991, killing more than 300 people and destroying the homes of more than 200,000.

pincers are the emblem of St Apollonia, a 3rd-century martyr whose sufferings included having her teeth wrenched from her jaws, ➤ *St* AGATHA, ➤ *St* DUNSTAN, and ➤ *St* ELOI.

pinchbeck an alloy of copper and zinc resembling gold, used in watchmaking and cheap jewellery, named after Christopher *Pinchbeck* (died 1732), English watchmaker and toymaker in Fleet Street, London, who invented it. An advertisement in the *Daily Post* of 27 November 1732 referred to 'toys made of the late ingenious Mr Pinchbeck's curious metal', and *pinchbeck* was in general use two years later.

pinches see ➤ *I know best where the* SHOE *pinches*.

pinda in Hinduism, a cake or ball of rice offered to the memory of one's ancestors, especially as part of funerary rites.

Pindar (*c*.518–*c*.438 BC), Greek lyric poet, born at Thebes in Boeotia, and sometimes referred to as the *Theban bard*. He is famous for his odes (the *Epinikia*), which celebrate victories in athletic contests at Olympia and elsewhere and relate them to religious and moral themes. The odes are often in the form of choral hymns, written in an elevated style and imbued with religious significance.

See also ➤ THEBAN *eagle*.

Peter Pindar pseudonym of the satirical writer John Wolcot (1738–1819).

Pindari a member of a body of mounted raiders active in Central India in the 17th and 18th centuries.

Pindaric verse poetry characteristic of or used in emulation of the style of Pindar.

Pine Tree State informal name for the state of Maine (so called from its extensive pineforests).

pink¹ a plant with sweet-smelling pink or white flowers and slender, typically grey-green leaves. The name may be short for *pink eye*, literally 'small or half-shut eye'; compare with the synonymous French word *oeillet*, literally 'little eye'.

In figurative usage, *pink* denotes the finest example of excellence, as in Shakespeare's *Romeo and Juliet*, 'I am the very pink of courtesy'; from this developed **in the pink of condition** to denote the best possible state of health and spirits.

pink² of a colour intermediate between red and white, as of coral or salmon. The word comes (in the mid 17th century) from ➤ PINK¹, the early use of the adjective being to describe the colour of the flowers of this plant.

Politically, *pink* is used as a mildly derogatory informal term for a person of left-wing tendencies.

See also ➤ HUNTING *pink*, ➤ SKY-*blue pink*.

pink elephants hallucinations supposedly typical of those experienced by a person who is drunk.

pink pound the perceived buying power of homosexuals as a consumer group, recognized in the 1980s; by the 1990s, the **pink economy** was seen as a substantial element of the business world.

pink triangle a triangular piece of pink cloth sewn on to clothing to identify homosexual men in Nazi concentration camps; in later use, a symbol indicating support for homosexual freedom and rights.

Pink 'Un informal name for the *Sporting Times* (1865–1931), which from April 1876 was printed on pink paper.

Allen Pinkerton (1819–84), Scottish-born American detective, who in 1850 established the first American private detective agency. He served as chief of the secret service for the Union side in the Civil War, later becoming involved in anti-trade union activity, particularly in the coal industry (1877).

Pinkster in the US, dialect term for Whitsuntide. The name comes (in the mid 18th century) from Dutch 'Pentecost', from celebrations in areas of former Dutch influence, such as New York.

Pinocchio puppet hero of the story by the Italian author and journalist Carlo Lorenzini (1824–90), in 1940 the subject of one of Disney's cartoons. *Pinocchio* has longings to be human; one of his characteristics is that whenever he tells a lie, his nose grows longer.

> My gambling friends call them 'tells': signs that tell you someone's bluffing. Think Pinocchio's nose, only more subtle.
>
> — *Cosmopolitan* February 1999

pint a unit of liquid or dry capacity equal to one eighth of a gallon, in Britain equal to 0.568 litre and in the US equal to 0.473 litre (for liquid measure) or 0.551 litre (for dry measure); in **pint-sized**, taken as the type of something very small.

See also ➤ *you cannot get a* QUART *into a pint pot*.

Pinyin the standard system of romanized spelling for transliterating Chinese, which superseded the earlier ➤ WADE–*Giles* system. Recorded from the 1960s, the term comes from Chinese *pīn-yīn*, literally 'spell-sound'.

pioneer a person who is among the first to explore or settle a new country or area. Recorded from the early 16th century (as a military term denoting a member of the infantry), the word comes ultimately (via French) from Latin *pedo*, the same base as ➤ PAWN.

Pioneer is the name of a series of American space probes launched between 1958 and 1973, two of which provided the first clear pictures of Jupiter and Saturn (1973–79).

See also ➤ *the* ROCHDALE *Pioneers*.

Pious epithet applied to ➤ AENEAS and the Roman emperor ➤ ANTONINUS *Pius*; **the Pious** was also the byname of Louis I (778–840), son of Charlemagne, king of the West Franks and Holy Roman Emperor 814–40.

pip a small shape or symbol, as any of the spots on a playing card, dice, or domino; in extended use, a star (1–3 according to rank) on the shoulder of an army officer's uniform.

Pip, Squeak, and Wilfred names of three animal characters, a dog, a penguin, and a baby rabbit, featured in a children's comic strip in the *Daily Mirror* from 1920 onwards. The baby rabbit, Wilfred, could say only 'gug' and 'nunc' (= uncle), and from this

the league of *Gugnuncs* was set up for his fans.

The names were later used for a trio of objects or persons; in particular, a series of campaign medals and medal ribbons, the 1914–15 Star, the War Medal, and the Victory Medal, awarded to British soldiers during and at the conclusion of the war of 1914–18.

pip emma post meridiem: First World War signallers' name for the letters pm.

pipe see also ➤ PLAGUE-*pipe*.

pipe dream an unattainable or fanciful hope or scheme, referring to a dream experienced when smoking an opium pipe.

pipe of peace a North American Indian peace pipe; a ➤ CALUMET; the term is first recorded in the late 17th century.

Pipe Roll the annual accounts kept by the Exchequer from the 12th to the 19th century; apart from an isolated roll in 1130, the series begins in 1156 and continues with a few interruptions until 1832. The name probably derives from the subsidiary documents having been rolled in pipe form.

piper see also ➤ PIED *Piper*.

he who pays the piper calls the tune proverbial saying, late 19th century.

pippin see ➤ RIBSTON *pippin*.

pir a Muslim saint or holy man. The word comes from Persian *pīr* 'old man, chief of a sect'.

St Piran (d. *c*.480), monk from Ireland or Wales who settled in north Cornwall, giving his name to Perranporth. He was the patron of Cornish tinminers.

☐ **FEAST DAY** His feast day is 5 March.

Giovanni Battista Piranesi (1720–78), Italian engraver. His interest in classical Roman architecture is reflected in his prints, in which he relied on atypical viewpoints and dramatic chiaroscuro to aggrandize its power and scale.

Pisa see ➤ LEANING *Tower of Pisa*.

Pisan see ➤ *Christine* DE *Pisan*.

Pisano[1] Andrea (*c*.1290–*c*.1348) and Nino, his son (died *c*.1368), Italian sculptors. Andrea created the earliest pair of bronze doors for the baptistery at

Florence (completed 1336). Nino was one of the earliest to specialize in free-standing life-size figures.

Pisano[2] two Italian sculptors, Nicola (*c*.1220–*c*.1278) and his son Giovanni (*c*.1250–*c*.1314). Nicola's work departed from medieval conventions and signalled a revival of interest in classical sculpture. His most famous works are the pulpits in the baptistery at Pisa and in Siena cathedral. Giovanni's works include the richly decorated facade of Siena cathedral.

Pisces a large constellation (the Fish or Fishes), said to represent a pair of fishes tied together by their tails. In Astrology, the twelfth sign of the zodiac, which the sun enters about 20 February.

piscina a stone basin near the altar in Catholic and pre-Reformation churches for draining water used in the Mass.

Pisgah the name of a mountain range east of Jordan, used with allusion to Deuteronomy 3:27, in which Moses is allowed to view the Promised Land, which he himself will not enter, from Mount Pisgah.

> Sir James Murray planned and led to within a Pisgah sight of completion a larger and more scientifically organized work of linguistic reference than Dr Johnson could have produced.
> — *Notes and Queries* February 1979

pishogue an Irish word for the power or skill of sorcery.

Pisistratus (*c*.600–*c*.527 BC), tyrant of Athens. He reduced aristocratic power in rural Attica and promoted the financial prosperity and cultural preeminence of Athens.

piskun a North American Indian trap for buffalo, consisting of a run along which buffalo were stampeded into a V-shaped natural or artificial canyon, into an enclosure, or over a steep drop.

pistic nard in biblical translations and allusions, ➤ SPIKENARD; figuratively, relating to faith and trust rather than reason. *Pistic* comes via Latin from Greek, but the ultimate meaning is uncertain ('genuine' or 'pure' has been suggested).

pistol a small firearm designed to be held in one hand. The word, which is mid 16th century, comes via French and German from Czech *pišt'ala*, of which the original meaning was 'whistle', hence 'a

firearm' by the resemblance in shape.
> See also ➤ a SMOKING *pistol*.

pit and gallows in Scottish law, the privilege, formerly conferred on barons, of executing male thieves or other felons by hanging on a gallows and female thieves or other felons by drowning in a pond or pool.

Pitcairn Islands a British dependency comprising a group of volcanic islands in the South Pacific, east of French Polynesia. Pitcairn Island was discovered in 1767, and remained uninhabited until settled in 1790 by mutineers from HMS *Bounty* and their Tahitian companions, some of whose descendants still live there.

pitch see also ➤ CONCERT *pitch*, ➤ QUEER *a person's pitch*.

pitch-and-toss a gambling game in which the player who manages to throw a coin closest to a mark gets to toss all the coins, winning those that land with the head up.

he that touches pitch shall be defiled proverbial saying, early 14th century; with allusion to Ecclesiasticus 13:1, 'he that toucheth pitch, shall be defiled therewith'.

pitched battle a relatively static battle fought between large formations of troops, originally denoting a planned military encounter on a prearranged battleground.

the pitcher will go to the well once too often proverbial saying, mid 14th century.

pitchers see also ➤ LITTLE *pitchers have large ears*.

pitchfork see ➤ *you can* DRIVE *out Nature with a pitchfork, but she keeps on coming back*.

Pithecanthropus a former genus name applied to some fossil hominids found in Java in 1891. Also called *Java man*. The term was originally coined as a name for a hypothetical creature bridging the gap in evolutionary development between apes and man, and came from Greek *pithēkos* 'ape' + *anthropos* 'man'.

Isaac Pitman (1813–97), English inventor of a shorthand system, published as *Stenographic Sound Hand* (1837). Pitman shorthand is still widely used in the UK and elsewhere.

Pitt see also ➤ DIAMOND *Pitt*.

William Pitt[1] (1708–78), Earl of Chatham, known as **Pitt the Elder**. As Secretary of State (effectively Prime Minister), he headed coalition governments 1756–61 and 1766–8. He brought the Seven Years War to an end in 1763 and also masterminded the conquest of French possessions overseas, particularly in Canada and India.

William Pitt[2] (1759–1806), Prime Minister 1783–1801 and 1804–6, the son of Pitt the Elder; known as **Pitt the Younger**. The youngest-ever Prime Minister, he introduced financial reforms to reduce the national debt.

Pitt diamond bought by Thomas Pitt (1653–1726), from which he received the sobriquet of ➤ DIAMOND *Pitt*.

Augustus Pitt-Rivers (1827–1900), English archaeologist and anthropologist. He developed a new scientific approach to archaeology. His collection of weapons and artefacts from different cultures formed the basis of the ethnological museum in Oxford which bears his name.

Pitti an art gallery and museum in Florence, housed in the Pitti Palace (built 1440–*c*.1549). Its contents include masterpieces from the Medici collections and Gobelin tapestries.

pity is akin to love proverbial saying, early 17th century.

Pius see also ➤ ANTONINUS *Pius*.

Pius XII (1876–1958), pope 1939–58. He upheld the neutrality of the Roman Catholic Church during the Second World War, maintaining diplomatic relations with both Allied and Axis governments, and was criticized after the war for failing to condemn Nazi atrocities.

pixie a supernatural being in folklore and children's stories, typically portrayed as small and human-like in form, with pointed ears and a pointed hat.

Francisco Pizarro (*c*.1478–1541), Spanish conquistador. He defeated the Inca empire and in 1533 set up a puppet monarchy at Cuzco, building his own capital at Lima (1535), where he was assassinated.

Place Act an Act of Parliament excluding people holding office under the Crown from sitting in the House of Commons.

a place for everything, and everything in its place proverbial saying, mid 17th century; often associated with Samuel Smiles and Mrs Beeton.

place in the sun a position of favour or advantage. The phrase is traceable to Pascal *Pensées*, translated by J. Walker in 1688: '*Ce chien est à moi, disaient ces pauvres enfants; c'est là ma place au soleil; voilà le commencement et l'image de l'usurpation de la terre.* [This Dog is mine, said those poor Children; That's my place in the Sun: This is the beginning and Image of the Usurpation of all the Earth].'

In later use, it is associated with the German Chancellor Bernhard von Bülow, who in 1897 said in a speech, 'We desire to throw no one into the shade, but we also demand our own place in the sunlight.'

there's no place like home proverbial saying, late 16th century.

Placebo in the Roman Catholic Church, Vespers for the Dead, from the first word of the first antiphon (*Placebo Domino in regione vivorum*); *placebo* in Latin means 'I shall be acceptable or pleasing'.

placebo a pill, medicine, or procedure prescribed more for the psychological benefit to the patient of being given a prescription than for any physiological effect.

Placemakers' Bible the second edition of the ➤ GENEVA *Bible*, 1562, with 'placemakers' misprinted for 'peacemakers' in the Beatitudes.

placeman a person appointed to a position, especially in government service, for personal profit and as a reward for political support. The term is recorded from the mid 18th century.

plagiarism the practice of taking someone else's work or ideas and passing them off as one's own. Recorded from the early 17th century, the word comes from Latin *plagiarius* 'kidnapping'.

plague a contagious bacterial disease characterized by fever and delirium, typically with the formation of buboes (as *bubonic plague*). Recorded from late Middle English, the word comes from Latin *plaga* 'stroke, wound', probably from Greek (Doric dialect) *plaga*, from a base meaning 'strike'.

➤ *St* ROCH and ➤ *St* SEBASTIAN are traditionally invoked against plague.

See also ➤ BLACK *Death*, ➤ BUBONIC *plague*, ➤ GAY *plague*, ➤ GREAT *Plague*, ➤ WHITE *plague*.

a plague on all their houses! animadversion in recent use echoing the words of the mortally wounded Mercutio in Shakespeare's *Romeo and Juliet*, 'A plague o' both your houses'.

plague-pipe a small clay pipe in which tobacco was smoked as a supposed disinfectant against the plague.

plague-pit a deep pit for the common burial of plague victims.

plague-water an infusion of various herbs and roots in purified alcohol, supposedly giving protection against the plague.

Plagues of Egypt ten plagues, described in Exodus 7 to Exodus 12, visited on the Egyptians to persuade them to release the Israelites.

Plagues of Egypt

PLAGUE	NUMBER
rods into serpents	first
rivers turned into blood	second
frogs	third
lice	fourth
flies	fifth
murrain	sixth
boils	seventh
hail	eighth
locusts	ninth
death of the firstborn	tenth

Plaid Cymru the Welsh Nationalist party, founded in 1925 and dedicated to seeking autonomy for Wales. It won its first parliamentary seat in 1966, and since 1974 has maintained a small number of representatives in Parliament; it is more strongly represented in the current Welsh Assembly. The name is Welsh, and means 'party of Wales'.

plain see also ➤ CITIES *of the Plain*, ➤ PENNY *plain, twopence coloured.*

the Plain the moderate party in the French National Convention of 1792–5; the members sat on benches opposite to those of *the Mountain*.

plain as a pikestaff very plain. The phrase was originally (in the mid 16th century) **plain as a packstaff**, a *packstaff* being the staff on which a pedlar supported his wares while resting. Dickens in *Pickwick Papers* (1837) alters the phrase by a punning reference to Salisbury Plain, 'it's as plain as Salisbury'.

plain living and high thinking a frugal and philosophic lifestyle; the original allusion is to Wordsworth:

> Plain living and high thinking are no more:
> The homely beauty of the good old cause
> Is gone.
> — William Wordsworth 'O friend! I know not which way
> I must look' (1807)

See also ➤ *the good old* CAUSE.

Plain People the Amish, the Mennonites, and the Dunkers, three strict Christian sects emphasizing a simple way of life.

plain sailing used to describe a process or activity which goes well and is easy and uncomplicated. The phrase, which is mid 18th century, is probably a popular use of *plane sailing*, denoting the practice of determining a ship's position on the theory that it is moving on a plane.

Plains Indian a member of any of various North American Indian peoples who formerly inhabited the Great Plains area. Although a few of the Plains Indian peoples were sedentary farmers, most, including the Blackfoot, Cheyenne, and Comanche, were nomadic buffalo hunters, who gathered in tribes during the summer and dispersed into family groups in the winter. They hunted on foot until they acquired horses from the Spanish in the early 18th century. The introduction of the horse also led to other peoples, such as the Sioux and the Cree, moving into the Plains area.

Plains of Abraham a plateau beside the city of Quebec, overlooking the St Lawrence River. It was the scene in 1759 of a battle in which the British army under General Wolfe, having scaled the heights above the city under cover of darkness, surprised and defeated the French. The battle led to British control over Canada, but both Wolfe and the French commander Montcalm died of their wounds.

plainsong unaccompanied church music sung in unison in medieval modes and in free rhythm corresponding to the accentuation of the words, which are taken from the liturgy. Recorded from late Middle English, the word is a translation of Latin *cantus planus*.

planchette a small board supported on castors, typically heart-shaped and fitted with a vertical pencil, used for automatic writing and in seances.

Max Planck (1858–1947), German theoretical physicist who founded quantum theory, announcing the radiation law named after him in 1900.

Planck's constant a fundamental constant, equal to the energy of a quantum of electromagnetic radiation divided by its frequency, with a value of 6.626 $\times$ 10^{-34} joules.

Planck's law a law, forming the basis of quantum theory, which states that electromagnetic radiation from heated bodies is not emitted as a continuous flow but is made up of discrete units or quanta of energy, the size of which involve a fundamental physical constant (*Planck's constant*).

planet a celestial body moving in an elliptical orbit round a star; originally, each of the seven major celestial bodies visible from the earth which move independently of the fixed stars and were believed to revolve the earth in concentric spheres centred on the earth (in order of their supposed distance from the earth in the Ptolemaic system, the moon, Mercury, Venus, the sun, Mars, Jupiter, and Saturn). In astrology, a celestial body distinguished from the fixed stars by having an apparent motion of its own (including the moon and sun), especially with reference to its supposed influence on people and events.

The nine planets of the solar system are either gas giants—Jupiter, Saturn, Uranus, and Neptune—or smaller rocky bodies—Mercury, Venus, Earth, Mars, and Pluto.

Recorded from Middle English, the word comes via Old French and late Latin from Greek *planētēs* 'wanderer, planet', from *planan* 'wander'.

See also ➤ JOY *of a planet*, ➤ RULING *planet*.

planet-struck afflicted by the supposed malign influence of a planet (sometimes used in reference to paralytic or other sudden physical disorders).

planetary hour in astrological belief, each hour as ruled by a planet. Planetary derives (in the early 17th century) from late Latin *planetarius*, properly an adjective meaning 'belonging to a planet or planets', but recorded only as a noun meaning 'astrologer'.

Plantagenet name of the English royal dynasty which held the throne from the accession of Henry II in 1154 until the death of Richard III in 1485. The name comes from Latin *planta genista* 'sprig of broom', said to be worn as a crest by and given as a nickname to Geoffrey, count of Anjou, the father of Henry II. The name is first recorded in late Middle English, in the Chronicle of Robert of Gloucester, where mention is made of Geoffrey's death.

Plantation colonization or the settlement of English and then Scottish families in Ireland in the 16th–17th centuries under government sponsorship. A settler in one of these colonies was known as a **Planter**:

> For the house of the planter
> Is known by the trees.
> — Austin Clarke 'The Planter's Daughter' (1929)

plantation an estate on which crops such as coffee, sugar, and tobacco are grown, especially in former colonies and as once worked by slaves.

plantation song a song of the kind formerly sung by black slaves on American plantations.

Plantin designating any of a class of old-face types based on a 16th century Flemish original, named after Christophe *Plantin* (1514–89), printer, of Antwerp. The first of these types was designed by F. H. Pierpont for the Monotype Corporation in 1913.

planting see ➤ CHURCH-*planting*.

plantocracy a population of planters regarded as the dominant class, especially in the West Indies.

Plassey a village in NE India, in West Bengal, north-west of Calcutta. It was the scene in 1757 of a battle in which a small British army under Robert Clive defeated the forces of the nawab of Bengal, establishing British supremacy in Bengal.

plaster see also ➤ COURT *plaster*.

plaster of Paris a hard white substance made by the addition of water to powdered and partly dehydrated gypsum, used for holding broken bones in place and making sculptures and casts. It is so called because it was originally prepared from the gypsums of Montmartre.

plaster saint a person who makes a show of being without moral faults or human weakness, especially in a hypocritical way. Recorded from the late 19th century, the allusion is to a plaster statuette of a saint.

Battle of Plataea a battle in 479 BC, during the Persian Wars, in which the Persian forces were defeated by the Greeks near the city of Plataea in Boeotia.

plate a silver or gold dish or trophy awarded as a prize in a race or competition. The word dates from Middle English as meaning a thin piece of precious metal or silver and gold utensils; this specific use is recorded first in a letter of 1639 recording the success of a particular horse.

River Plate a wide estuary on the Atlantic coast of South America at the border between Argentina and Uruguay, formed by the confluence of the Rivers Paraná and Uruguay, and with the cities of Buenos Aires and Montevideo on its shores; in 1939 it was the scene of a naval battle in which the British defeated the Germans.

plateresque (especially of Spanish architecture) richly ornamented in a style suggesting silverware. The term comes from Spanish *plateresco*, from *platero* 'silversmith', from *plata* 'silver'.

platform the declared policy of a political party or group; the term has developed from the literal sense (recorded from the mid 19th century) of an area of raised flooring from which a speaker addresses an audience or on which the organizers or supporters of a meeting sit.

This sense is distinct from the earlier, now obsolete, sense of *platform* to mean 'a plan of political action', first recorded in a letter of 1587 of Queen Elizabeth's favourite Robert Dudley (1532–88), in which he refers to 'their late platform, led by faction and conspiracy'.

Plato (*c*.429–*c*.347 BC), Greek philosopher. A disciple of Socrates and the teacher of Aristotle, he founded the Academy in Athens. An integral part of his thought is the theory of 'ideas' or 'forms', in which abstract entities or *universals* are contrasted with their objects or *particulars* in the material world. His philosophical writings are presented in the form of dialogues, with Socrates as the principal speaker; they include the *Symposium* and the *Timaeus*. Plato's political theories appear in the *Republic*, in which he explored the nature and structure of a just society.

Platonic love love which is intimate and affectionate but not sexual. The term is recorded in English from the mid 17th century; the equivalent Latin term *amor platonicus* was used synonymously with *amor socraticus* by Ficinus (the Florentine Marsilio Ficino, 1433–99), president of Cosmo de' Medici's *Accademia Platonica*, to denote the kind of interest in young men with which Socrates was credited.

Platonic solid one of five regular solids (i.e., having all sides and all angles equal), a tetrahedron,

cube, octahedron, dodecahedron, or icosahedron. Formerly also called **Platonic body**.

Platonic year a cycle, imagined by some ancient astronomers, in which the heavenly bodies were supposed to go through all their possible movements and return to their original relative positions, after which, according to some, all history would repeat itself (sometimes identified with the period of precession of the equinoxes, about 25,800 years). Also called *great year*.

Platonism the philosophy of Plato or his followers; any of various revivals of Platonic doctrines or related ideas, especially ➤ NEOPLATONISM and Cambridge Platonism (a 17th–century attempt to reconcile Christianity with humanism and science).

Plattdeutsch another term for ➤ Low *German*. The name comes via German from Dutch *Platduitsch*, from *plat* 'low' + *Duitsch* 'German'.

Titus Maccius Plautus (*c*.250–184 BC), Roman comic dramatist. His plays, such as *Rudens*, are modelled on Greek New Comedy. Fantasy and imagination are more important than realism in the development of his plots, and his stock characters, which follow Greek types, are often larger than life and their language is correspondingly exuberant.

play see also ➤ FAIR *play's a jewel*, ➤ *the* SCOTTISH *play*.

play it again, Sam popular misquotation of Humphrey Bogart in *Casablanca* (1942), subsequently used as the title of a play (1969) and film (1972) by Woody Allen. In the film, Humphrey Bogart says, 'If she can stand it, I can. Play it!'; earlier in the film Ingrid Bergman says, 'Play it, Sam. Play *As Time Goes By*.'

play the—card introduce a specified (advantageous) factor; the term derives from a comment made in 1886 by Lord Randolph Churchill on Gladstone's handling of the Irish Home Rule question, 'I decided some time ago that if the G. O. M. [Grand Old Man = Gladstone] went for Home Rule, the Orange card would be the one to play.'

In 1995, commenting on the defence team's change of strategy at the trial of O. J. Simpson, the American lawyer Robert Shapiro said, 'Not only did we play the race card, we played it from the bottom of the deck.'

play the game behave in a fair or honourable way; abide by the rules or conventions. Recorded from the late 19th century, the phrase is particularly associated with the appeal to public-school values enshrined in Henry Newbolt's poem:

> And it's not for the sake of a ribboned coat,
> Or the selfish hope of a season's fame,
> But his Captain's hand on his shoulder smote—
> 'Play up! play up! and play the game!'
> — Henry Newbolt 'Vitaï Lampada' (1897)

play to the gallery act in an exaggerated or histrionic manner, especially in order to appeal to popular taste; the *gallery* here is the highest of the galleries in a theatre, containing the cheapest seats.

if you play with fire you'll get burnt proverbial saying, late 19th century.

play within a play a play acted as part of the action of another play; often with reference to *Hamlet*, in which Hamlet arranges for the Players to perform a play ('the Mouse-trap') which shows the circumstances of his father's murder.

Playfair a code or cipher in which successive pairs of letters are replaced by pairs chosen in a prescribed manner from a matrix of 25 letters, usually arranged in accordance with a keyword, named after Lord *Playfair* (1818–98), British chemist and administrator.

> Here's a cipher message. Probably Playfair.
> — Dorothy L. Sayers *Have His Carcase* (1932)

John Playfair (1748–1819), Scottish mathematician and geologist. A friend of ➤ *James* HUTTON, he summarized the latter's views for a wider readership in his *Illustrations of the Huttonian Theory of the Earth* (1802), which presented Hutton's views on geology—and some of his own—in a concise and readable form.

pleas see also ➤ COMMON *Pleas*.

Pleas of the Crown legal proceedings in which the Crown had a financial interest, as by exacting a fine, as distinct from those involving claims between subjects; legal proceedings including all criminal proceedings, as involving conduct held to be committed against the Crown (in Scotland, limited to proceedings concerned with murder, rape, robbery, and arson).

you can't please everyone proverbial saying, late 15th century.

**Please to remember the Fifth of November, Gunpowder Treason and Plot.
We know no reason why gunpowder treason
Should ever be forgot.**
traditional rhyme on the ➤ GUNPOWDER *Plot* (1605).

pleased see also ➤ *as pleased as* PUNCH.

pleasure see also ➤ BUSINESS *before pleasure*.

pleasure principle in psychoanalysis, the instinctive drive to seek pleasure and avoid pain, expressed by the id as a basic motivating force which reduces psychic tension. The term was used originally in Freudian analysis.

plebeian (in ancient Rome) a commoner, as opposed to the patricians, senators, and knights. Recorded from the mid 16th century, the word comes from Latin *plebs, pleb-* 'the common people'.

plebiscite (in ancient Rome) a law enacted by the plebeians' assembly; now, the direct vote of all the members of an electorate on an important public question such as a change in the constitution.

pledge a solemn promise or undertaking; originally (in Middle English) denoting a person acting as surety for another. The word comes via Old French from medieval Latin *plebium*, perhaps related to the Germanic base of *plight*.

From the mid 19th century, **the pledge** has denoted a solemn undertaking to abstain from alcohol.

Pledge of Allegiance (in the US) a solemn oath of loyalty to the United States, declaimed as part of flag-saluting ceremonies, composed by the American clergyman and editor Francis Bellamy (1856–1931):

> I pledge allegiance to the flag of the United States of America and to the republic for which it stands, one nation under God, indivisible, with liberty and justice for all.
> — Francis Bellamy *The Pledge of Allegiance to the Flag* (1892)

the Pleiad a group of eight or more Greek writers of tragedy living in Alexandria in the reign of Ptolemy II Philadelphus (285–246 BC).

Pleiades the seven daughters of the Titan Atlas and the Oceanid Pleione, the eldest of whom, Merope, was 'the lost Pleiad', and not represented by a star. They were pursued by the hunter Orion until Zeus changed them into stars. Their name has been given to a cluster of stars (usually spoken of as seven and also called ➤ SEVEN *Sisters*) in the constellation Taurus; six stars are visible to the naked eye but there are actually some five hundred present, formed very recently in stellar terms.

Les Pléiades a group of seven 16th-century French writers, led by Pierre de Ronsard, who aimed to elevate French literary language to classical standards.

plenary indulgence a full and complete ➤ INDULGENCE granted by the Pope of remission of the temporal punishment in purgatory.

plene of or pertaining to a system of full orthographic notation in Hebrew, whereby vowel sounds are indicated by certain vocalic signs; of or pertaining to similar conventions in other Middle Eastern and oriental languages.

plenipotentiary a person, especially a diplomat, invested with the full power of independent action on behalf of their government, typically in a foreign country. Recorded from the mid 17th century, the word comes from medieval Latin *plenipotentiarius*, from *plenus* 'full' + *potentia* 'power'.

plenty see ➤ HORN *of plenty*.

Pleven an industrial town in northern Bulgaria, north-east of Sofia. An important fortress town and trading centre of the Ottoman Empire, it was taken from the Turks by the Russians in the Russo-Turkish War of 1877, after a siege of 143 days.

Plimsoll line a marking on a ship's side showing the limit of legal submersion when loaded with cargo under various sea conditions. It is named after Samuel *Plimsoll* (1824–98), the English politician whose agitation in the 1870s resulted in the Merchant Shipping Act of 1876, ending the practice of sending to sea overloaded and heavily insured old ships, from which the owners profited if they sank.

Plinian relating to or denoting a type of a volcanic eruption in which a narrow stream of gas and ash is violently ejected from a vent to a height of several miles. The word comes (in the mid 17th century) from Italian *pliniano*, with reference to the eruption of Vesuvius in AD 79, in which Pliny the Elder died.

Pliny the Elder (23–79), Roman statesman and scholar. His *Natural History* (77) is a vast encyclopedia of the natural and human worlds and is one of the earliest known works of its kind. He died while observing the eruption of Vesuvius.

Pliny the Younger (*c*.61–*c*.112), Roman senator and writer, nephew of Pliny the Elder. He is noted

for his books of letters which deal with both public and private affairs and which include a description of the eruption of Vesuvius in 79 which destroyed the town of Pompeii and in which his uncle died. The letters also contain one of the earliest descriptions of non-Christian attitudes towards Christians.

Plon Plon nickname of Prince Napoleon (1822–91), cousin of Napoleon III.

plonk cheap wine of inferior quality. Recorded as an informal Australian term from the 1930s, it is probably originally an alteration of *blanc* in French *vin blanc* 'white wine'.

plot a plan made in secret by a group of people to do something illegal or harmful. This sense of the word, which dates from the late 16th century, is associated with Old French *complot* 'dense crowd, secret project', the same term being used occasionally in English from the mid 16th century.
    See also ➤ COBHAM's *Plot*, ➤ GUNPOWDER *Plot*, ➤ MAIN *Plot*, ➤ MEAL-*tub Plot*, ➤ POPISH *Plot*, ➤ RYE *House Plot*, ➤ SCOTCH *Plot*, ➤ SCREW *Plot*, ➤ WATSON's *plot*.

the plot thickens the situation becomes more difficult and complex; from George Villiers *The Rehearsal* (1671), 'Ay, now the plot thickens very much upon us.'

Plotinus (*c*.205–70), philosopher, probably of Roman descent. He was the founder and leading exponent of Neoplatonism; his writings were published after his death by his pupil Porphyry.

plough a large farming implement with one or more blades fixed in a frame, drawn originally by animals and used for cutting furrows in the soil and turning it over, especially to prepare for the planting of seeds; often used emblematically, as in **follow the plough** meaning be a ploughman or farmer.
    From late Middle English, **the Plough** has been the name given to a prominent formation of seven stars in the constellation Ursa Major (the Great Bear), containing the Pointers that indicate the direction to the Pole Star. Also called (in North America) the *Big Dipper* and (formerly, in Britain) *Charles's Wain*.
    See also ➤ *God* SPEED *the plough*, ➤ *put one's* HAND *to the plough*.

plough a lonely furrow carry on without help or companionship. The earliest recorded form of this phrase is found in Lord Rosebery's speech of July

1901 on his remaining outside the Liberal Party leadership, 'I must plough my furrow alone'.

put the plough before the oxen reverse the natural or proper order of things; an early alternative to *put the cart before the horse*.

Plough Monday the first Monday after Epiphany, formerly marked by popular festivals or observances in some regions, especially the north and east of England, named from the custom of dragging a plough through the streets to mark the beginning of the ploughing season.

plough the sands undertake an impossible task; first recorded in Robert Greene's *Never Too Late* (1590), 'With sweating brows I long have ploughed the sands…Repent hath sent me home with empty hands'.

plough with someone's heifer concern oneself with a person's affairs, follow someone's practices. The phrase is mainly used with allusion to Judges 14:18, 'If ye had not ploughed with my heifer, ye had not found out my riddle'.

> One never knows what heifers the young are ploughing with.
> — Rudyard Kipling *Complete Stalky & Co* (1929) 'The Propagation of Knowledge'

ploughshare the main cutting blade of a plough, often with biblical allusion to Isaiah 2:4, 'They shall beat their swords into ploughshares, and their spears into pruning-hooks.'

plover a short-billed gregarious wading bird, typically found by water but sometimes frequenting grassland, tundra, and mountains. The name comes (in Middle English) from Anglo-Norman, and is based on Latin *pluvia* 'rain'. The connection with rain has been variously explained, including the suggestion (in the mid 16th century) that the birds were so called because they were most easily taken in rainy weather.

Plowden see also ➤ *the* CASE *is altered, quoth Plowden*.

pluck spirited and determined courage; recorded as a term in boxing from the 18th century, and deriving from the literal sense of the word 'the heart, liver, and lungs of an animal'.

plug-ugly a thug or villain, by association with the verb *plug* in the informal sense 'hit with the fist'.

plum see ➤ *a* CHERRY *year, a merry year; a plum year, a dumb year.*

Professor Plum one of the six stock characters constituting the murderer and suspects in the game of ➤ CLUEDO.

plumed serpent a mythical creature depicted as part bird, part snake, in particular Quetzalcóatl, a god of the Toltec and Aztec civilizations having this form.

plumes see ➤ BORROWED *plumes*.

plumetty in heraldry, (of a field) charged with overlapping feathers.

plunder steal goods from (a place or person), typically using force and in a time of war or civil disorder. The word comes (in the mid 17th century) from German *plündern*, literally 'rob of household goods', from Middle High German *plunder* 'household effects'.

Early use of the verb was with reference to the Thirty Years War (reflecting German usage); on the outbreak of the Civil War in 1642, the word and activity were associated with the forces under Prince Rupert; the poet Thomas May (1595–1650), in his *History of the Long Parliament* (1647) wrote, 'Many Townes and Villages he [Prince Rupert] plundered, which is to say robb'd, for at that time first was the word plunder used in England, being borne in Germany.'

The well-known comment 'What a place to plunder!' is a misquotation (*was für plündern*) of the comment of the Prussian Field-Marshal Blücher (1742–1819) on London, as seen from the Monument in June 1814, '*Was für Plünder!* [What rubbish!]'

E Pluribus Unum Latin phrase, 'out of many, one', selected as the motto for the American national seal in 1776 by a committee consisting of Thomas Jefferson, John Adams, and Benjamin Franklin. In 1988, Jesse Jackson, at the Democratic National Convention, said, 'The genius of America is that out of the many, we become one.'

plus fours baggy knickerbockers reaching below the knee, worn by men for hunting and golf, and so named because the overhang at the knee requires an extra four inches of material.

plus royaliste que le roi a French phrase meaning 'more of a royalist than the king', now used in a number of variants to indicate that a person has adopted or developed the characteristics of a specified group or individual to an exaggerated degree.

Plutarch (*c.*46–*c.*120), Greek biographer and philosopher. He is chiefly known for *Parallel Lives*, a collection of biographies of prominent Greeks and Romans in which the moral character of his subjects is illustrated by a series of anecdotes.

Pluto[1] in Greek mythology, the god of the underworld, ➤ HADES; *Pluto* is the Latin form (used in English) of the Greek name *Ploutōn*, meaning 'wealth-giver', because wealth is seen as coming from the earth.

The name *Pluto* was given to the most remote known planet of the solar system, ninth in order from the sun, discovered in 1930 by Clyde Tombaugh.

Pluto was also the name of the black cartoon dog which made its first appearance with Mickey Mouse in Walt Disney's *The Chain Gang*, 1930.

Pluto[2] (the code-name for) a system of pipelines laid in 1944 to carry petrol supplies from Britain to Allied forces in France. The name is an acronym for *Pipe Line Under The Ocean*.

Plutonian of or associated with the underworld or the god Pluto; infernal; gloomy and dark.

> Tell me what thy lordly name is on the Night's Plutonian shore!
> — Edgar Allen Poe 'The Raven' (1834)

Plutus in Greek mythology, the personification of wealth, son of Demeter and Iasion. His name can be used allusively to indicate great riches; a character in Shakespeare's *Timon of Athens* (1616), describing Timon's wealth, says of him, 'Plutus, the god of gold Is but his steward.'

Pluviose the fifth month of the French Republican calendar (1793–1805), originally running from 20 January to 18 February. The name comes via French from Latin *pluviosus* 'rainy'.

Plymouth Brethren a strict Calvinistic religious body formed at Plymouth in Devon *c.*1830, having no formal creed and no official order of ministers. Its teaching emphasizes an expected millennium and members renounce many secular occupations, allowing only those compatible with New Testament standards. As a result of doctrinal and other differences, a split in 1849 resulted in the formation of the Exclusive Brethren and the Open Brethren.

Plymouth Rock a granite boulder at Plymouth, Massachusetts, on to which the Pilgrim Fathers are said to have stepped from the *Mayflower*.

Pnyx the public place of assembly in ancient Athens, a semicircular level cut out of the side of a small hill west of the Acropolis.

an old poacher makes the best gamekeeper proverbial saying, late 14th century.

Pocahontas (*c.*1595–1617), American Indian princess, daughter of an Algonquian chief in Virginia. According to an English colonist, John Smith, Pocahontas rescued him from death at the hands of her father. In 1613 she was seized as a hostage by the English and she later married another colonist, John Rolfe. In 1616 she and her husband visited England, where she died.

pocket see ➤ *the* DEVIL *dances in an empty pocket.*

pocket borough (in the UK) a borough in which the election of political representatives was controlled by one person or family. Such boroughs were abolished by the Reform Acts of 1832 and 1867.

pocket veto in the US, an indirect veto of a legislative bill by the President or a State governor, by retaining the bill unsigned until it is too late for it to be dealt with during the legislative session.

pockets see ➤ SHROUDS *have no pockets.*

Pocomania a Jamaican folk religion combining revivalism with ancestor worship and spirit possession.

Podarge (meaning 'Swiftfoot'), mentioned by Homer as the name of one of the harpies.

podestà originally, a governor appointed by Frederick I (Holy Roman Emperor 1155–90, and King of Germany 1152–90) over one or more cities of Lombardy; an elected chief magistrate of a medieval Italian town or republic. Later, a subordinate judge or magistrate in an Italian municipality; an administrative head of an Italian commune.

Podsnappery the behaviour or outlook characteristic of Dickens's Mr Podsnap in *Our Mutual Friend* (1864–5); insular complacency and blinkered self-satisfaction.

> Masochists may get their kicks from national self-denigration, but for the rest of us there is neither much fun nor much enlightenment in such bouts of inverted Podsnappery.
> — *Independent* 24 February 1992

Podunk in the US, informal name for a hypothetical small town regarded as typically dull or insignificant. Recorded from the mid 19th century, it is a place name of southern New England, of Algonquian origin.

Edgar Allan Poe (1809–49), American short-story writer, poet, and critic. His fiction and poetry are Gothic in style and characterized by their exploration of the macabre and the grotesque.

poet see also ➤ the ARCH-*poet*, ➤ the AYRSHIRE *Poet*, ➤ CYCLIC *poet*, ➤ the QUAKER *poet*, ➤ WATER *Poet*.

a poet is born, not made proverbial saying, late 16th century.

Poet Laureate an eminent poet appointed as a member of the British royal household. The first Poet Laureate in the modern sense was Ben Jonson, but the title became established with the appointment of John Dryden in 1668. The Poet Laureate was formerly expected to write poems for state occasions, but since Victorian times the post has carried no specific duties.

It was the implied abandonment of radical principles in Wordsworth's acceptance of the laureateship that caused Robert Browning to write:

> Just for a handful of silver he left us,
> Just for a riband to stick in his coat.
>
> — Robert Browning 'The Lost Leader' (1845)

Poet Squab a nickname of the poet John Dryden (1631–1700), said to reflect his appearance (*squab* here means a young pigeon); a contemporary epigram said of him 'A sleepy eye he had and no sweet feature'.

poetaster a paltry or inferior poet; a writer of poor or trashy verse. The word, which is modern Latin, was coined by Erasmus in a letter of 1521; it is first found in English in Ben Jonson's *Fountain of Self-Love* (1599).

poetic justice the fact of experiencing a fitting or deserved retribution for one's actions; the phrase is often found as an allusion to Pope's *The Dunciad* (1728), 'Poetic Justice, with her lifted scale'.

poetic licence the freedom to depart from the facts of a matter or from the conventional rules of language when speaking or writing in order to create an effect; originally, as a quotation from Byron's *Don Juan* (1819), 'This liberty is a poetic licence'.

poetry see also ➤ BOLLINGEN *Prize in Poetry*, ➤ CONCRETE *poetry*.

poets ➤ St COLUMBA and ➤ St JOHN *of the Cross* are the patron saints of poets.

Poets' Corner part of the south transept of Westminster Abbey where several distinguished poets are buried or commemorated; the name is recorded from the mid 18th century, but *poetical quarter* is earlier:

> In the poetical Quarter [of Westminster Abbey] I found there were Poets who had no Monuments, and Monuments which had no Poets.
>
> — Joseph Addison *Spectator* 1711 No. 26

pogrom an organized massacre of a particular ethnic group, in particular that of Jews in Russia or eastern Europe. The word comes (in the early 20th century) from Russian, meaning literally 'devastation'.

Poictesme a fictional medieval country, setting of *Jurgen* and other books by James Branch Cabell (1879–1958).

poilu informal historical term for an infantry soldier in the French army, especially one who fought in the First World War. The word is French, and means literally 'hairy', by extension 'brave', whiskers being associated with virility.

Jules-Henri Poincaré (1854–1912), French mathematician and philosopher of science, who transformed celestial mechanics and was one of the pioneers of algebraic topology. He proposed a relativistic philosophy which implied the absolute velocity of light, which nothing could exceed.

point see also ➤ CARDINAL *point*, ➤ *point the* BONE *at*.

point of no return a point in a journey (especially by air) or enterprise at which it becomes essential or more practical to continue to the end.

the Pointers (in the northern hemisphere) two stars of the Plough or Big Dipper in Ursa Major, through which a line points nearly to the Pole Star.

pointillism a technique of neo-Impressionist painting using tiny dots of various pure colours, which become blended in the viewer's eye. It was developed by Seurat with the aim of producing a greater degree of luminosity and brilliance of colour. Recorded from the early 20th century, the word comes from French *pointillisme*, from *pointiller* 'mark with dots'.

points see ➤ ARMED *at all points*, ➤ FOURTEEN *Points*, ➤ SIX *points*.

Hercule Poirot a fictional Belgian private detective, living in England, in the crime stories of Agatha Christie; Poirot is notable for his dapper appearance, his waxed moustaches, and his powers of deduction using his ➤ *little* GREY *cells*.

poison a substance that when introduced into or absorbed by a living organism causes death or injury, especially one that kills by rapid action even in a small quantity. In Middle English the word denotes a harmful medicinal draught; it comes from Old French 'magic potion' from Latin *potio(n-)* 'potion', related to *potare* 'to drink'.

See also ➤ *one man's* MEAT *is another man's poison.*

poison pen letter an anonymous letter that is libellous, abusive, or malicious; the term *poison pen* is recorded from the early 20th century.

poison pill a tactic used by a company threatened with an unwelcome takeover bid to make itself unattractive to the bidder. The use arose in the US financial markets in the early 1980s, and was allegedly coined by the US lawyer Martin Lipman in his defence of El Paso Natural Gas in 1982; it was shortly afterwards adopted as a device and a term on the British Stock Exchange. Despite attempts to limit the practice it remained popular in a number of markets and generated several variants; another name for a similar type of defence is a *shark repellent.*

poisoned chalice an assignment, award, or honour which is likely to prove a disadvantage or source of problems to the recipient; the phrase is found originally in Shakespeare's *Macbeth* (1606), in a speech in which Macbeth flinches from the prospective murder of Duncan: 'This even-handed justice Commends th'ingredience of our poison'd chalice To our own lips.'

Affair of the Poisons a notorious criminal case of 17th-century France, when it was revealed by the investigation of the ➤ CHAMBRE *Ardente* that well-to-do and aristocratic people in Paris, including the ➤ *Marquise de* MONTESPAN, had been resorting to witches and fortune-tellers not only to predict the future, but to obtain and use poison. Over 30 people

were sentenced to death by the tribunal, and many more arrested and imprisoned.

Siméon-Denis Poisson (1781–1840), French mathematical physicist. His major contributions were in probability theory, in which he greatly improved Laplace's work and developed several concepts that are now named after him.

Poisson d'Avril in France, the equivalent of April Fool (literally, 'April fish').

Poitiers a city in west central France, capital of the former province of Poitou. It was the site in AD 507 of the defeat of the Visigoths by Clovis and in 732 of Charles Martel's victory over the invading Muslims. In 1356 the city fell to the English forces of Edward, the Black Prince, but was reclaimed by the French some thirteen years later.

Poitou a former province of west central France, formerly part of Aquitaine, which was held by the French and English in succession until it was finally united with France at the end of the Hundred Years War.

poke a small bag or pouch; now chiefly in phrase ➤ *a* PIG *in a poke.*

poke-bonnet a bonnet with a projecting brim, originally fashionable in the early 19th century, and later traditionally worn by women members of the Religious Society of Friends (Quakers) and the Salvation Army.

poker a card game played by two or more people who bet on the value of the hands dealt to them. A player wins the pool either by having the highest combination at the showdown or by forcing all opponents to concede without a showing of the hand, sometimes by means of bluff. Recorded from the mid 19th century, the word is of US origin, and may be related to German *pochen* 'to brag'.

poker-face an impassive expression that hides one's true feelings, as typical of a poker player.

Pol Pot (*c*.1925–98), Cambodian communist leader of the Khmer Rouge, Prime Minister 1976–9. During his regime the Khmer Rouge embarked on a brutal reconstruction programme in which many millions of Cambodians were killed. Overthrown in 1979, Pol Pot led the Khmer Rouge in a guerrilla war against the new Vietnamese-backed government until his official retirement in 1985.

Polack (now chiefly in North America), a deroga-tory term for a person from Poland or of Polish des-cent. The name is recorded from the late 16th century, and in Shakespeare's *Hamlet* (1603) refer-ence is made to 'a preparation gainst the Polack'.

Polaris[1] the Pole Star; the name comes (in the mid 19th century) from medieval Latin *polaris* 'heav-enly', from Latin *polus* 'end of an axis'.

Polaris[2] a type of submarine-launched ballistic missile designed to carry nuclear warheads, for-merly in service with the US and British navies.

pole[1] a long, slender, rounded piece of wood or metal, typically used with one end placed in the ground as a support for something; from the late 15th century, of definite length, and used as a meas-ure. From this, *pole* came to mean a measure of length, equivalent to a ➤ PERCH. Recorded from Old English, the word is of Germanic origin, ultimately based on Latin *palus* 'stake'.

See also ➤ BARBER's *pole*.

pole[2] either of the two locations (**North Pole** or **South Pole**) on the surface of the earth (or of a ce-lestial object) which are the northern and southern ends of the axis of rotation. Recorded from late Middle English, the name comes from Latin *polus* 'end of an axis', from Greek *polos* 'pivot, axis, sky'.

pole position the most favourable position at the start of a motor race, from a 19th-century use of *pole* in horse racing, denoting the starting position next to the inside boundary fence.

Pole Star a fairly bright star located within one de-gree of the celestial north pole, in the constellation Ursa Minor; in figurative usage, something which serves as a guide or governing principle, a lodestar.

> Price went to southern California (as always the Pole Star for American eccentrics) and organised . . . the Deluge Geology Society.
> — *New Scientist* December 1986

from pole to pole throughout the world.

> Oh Sleep! it is a gentle thing,
> Beloved from pole to pole.
> — Samuel Taylor Coleridge 'The Rime of the Ancient Mariner' (1798)

policy wonk someone who takes an unnecessary interest in minor details of policy. The term is re-corded from the mid 1980s, in terms of the Ameri-can political scene, and there is often an implication that the high level of theoretical knowledge involved

has unfitted the *policy wonk* for dealing with prac-tical matters.

> She has the lawyerly, analytical mind; he likes to wander off into the thickets of policy wonkdom.
> — *Newsweek* 28 December 1992

Polish Corridor a former region of Poland which extended northwards to the Baltic coast and separ-ated East Prussia from the rest of Germany, granted to Poland after the First World War to ensure Polish access to the coast. Its annexation by Germany in 1939, with the German occupation of the rest of Pol-and, precipitated the Second World War. After the war the area was restored to Poland.

Polish notation in logic and computing, a system of formula notation without brackets or special punctuation, frequently used to represent the order in which arithmetical operations are performed in many computers and calculators. In the usual form (**reverse Polish notation**), operators follow rather than precede their operands.

Politburo the principal policy-making committee of the former USSR, founded in 1917; also called (1952–66) the ➤ PRESIDIUM. The name comes from Russian *politbyuro*, from *polit(icheskoe) byuro* 'polit-ical bureau'.

politeness see ➤ PUNCTUALITY *is the politeness of princes.*

politic see ➤ BODY *politic.*

political animal a person viewed as living and act-ing with others; a follower of or participant in polit-ics, translating Greek *politikon zōon*, in the works of Aristotle:

> Man is by nature a political animal.
> — Aristotle *Politics*

political correctness the avoidance of forms of expression or action that are perceived to exclude, marginalize, or insult groups of people who are so-cially disadvantaged or discriminated against.

Politically correct meaning 'appropriate to the prevailing political or social circumstances' has been recorded from the late 18th century, but did not become a fixed phrase until the early 1970s, when it received a dramatic impetus in the feminist literature of the time, and the campaign against a perceived gender bias. In the 1980s, an increased awareness of the way in which use of language could perpetuate inequalities on a broad range of sensitive issues, engendered movement to a *political correct-ness* which would reflect appropriate sensitivity.

However, by the late 1980s the view also developed that this in itself could represent a puritanical approach which was a potential enemy to freedom of thought and expression; its proponents were held by some to be proponents of a new kind of bigotry, which might become as pernicious as the prejudices they sought to overturn.

By the early 1990s, use of the term political correctness was nearly always pejorative, while the labels **politically incorrect** and **political incorrectness** often suggested the notion that the idea or statement described was bravely formulated. The abbreviation **PC**, which is widely found, is nearly always pejorative or ironic.

> I believe that political correctness can be a form of linguistic fascism, and it sends shivers down the spine of my generation who went to war against fascism.
> — P. D. James in *Paris Review* 1995

political economy economics as a branch of knowledge or academic discipline. The term is a translation of French *économie politique*, and is recorded from the late 17th century.

politics makes strange bedfellows proverbial saying, mid 19th century.

politique a member of a moderate Catholic group, founded in France after the *St Bartholomew's Day Massacre*, which regarded peace and national unity as more important than the religious war between Ultramontane Catholics and Huguenots.

polka a lively dance of Bohemian origin in duple time. The name comes (in the mid 19th century) via French and German from Czech *půlka* 'half-step'. First danced at Prague in 1835, it subsequently became popular in the fashionable centres of Europe.

poll the process of voting in an election. The word is recorded from Middle English in the sense 'head', and hence 'an individual person among a number', from which developed the sense 'number of people ascertained by counting of heads' and then 'counting of heads or of votes' (17th century).

See also ➤ DEED *poll*, ➤ GALLUP *poll*.

poll tax a tax levied on every adult, without reference to their income or resources. Poll taxes have often been extremely unpopular because they weigh disproportionately heavily on poorer people. Such taxes were levied in England in 1377, 1379, and 1380; the last of these is generally regarded as having contributed to the 1381 Peasants' Revolt.

From the mid 1980s, the term was used informally for the ➤ COMMUNITY *charge*, a usage which reflected the tax's deep unpopularity.

Pollaiuolo Antonio (*c*.1432–98) and Piero (1443–96), Italian sculptors, painters, and engravers. Both brothers worked on the monuments to Popes Sixtus IV and Innocent VIII in St Peter's, and Antonio is particularly known for his realistic depiction of the human form.

Jackson Pollock (1912–56), American painter. He was a leading figure in the abstract expressionist movement and from 1947 became the chief exponent of the style known as action painting, whereby he poured, splashed, or dripped paint on to the canvas.

Pollux in Greek mythology, the twin brother of Castor (see ➤ CASTOR *and Pollux*); also called *Polydeuces.*

Pollyanna an excessively cheerful or optimistic person, from the name of the optimistic heroine created by Eleanor Hodgman Porter (1868–1920), American author of children's stories.

> He comes from a baseball family, and is a family man himself. He is positively Pollyannaish about the game he loves to play.
> — *Economist* July 1995

Marco Polo (*c*.1254–*c*.1324), Italian traveller. With his father and uncle he travelled to China and the court of Kublai Khan via central Asia (1271–75). He eventually returned home (1292–5) via Sumatra, India, and Persia. His book recounting his travels spurred the European quest for Eastern riches.

Polonius in Shakespeare's *Hamlet*, the sententious lord chamberlain who is the father of ➤ OPHELIA and Laertes, and whose good intentions and well-meant advice do nothing to avert the tragedy to his family.

> Less like Marcus Aurelius than like a prosy Polonius.
> — Wallace Stegner *The Spectator Bird* (1976)

Polonnaruwa a town in NE Sri Lanka, which succeeded Anuradhapura in the 8th century as the capital of Ceylon, and became an important Buddhist centre in the 12th century; it was subsequently deserted until a modern town was built there in the 20th century.

Poltava a city in east central Ukraine which was besieged unsuccessfully in 1709 by Charles XII's Swedish forces; they were defeated by the Russians under Peter the Great.

poltergeist a ghost or other supernatural being supposedly responsible for physical disturbances such as making loud noises and throwing objects about. The term comes (in the mid 19th century) from German *Poltergeist*, from *poltern* 'create a disturbance' + *Geist* 'ghost'.

poltroon poetic and literary term for an utter coward. The word comes (in the early 16th century) via French from Italian *poltrone*, and may come ultimately from *poltro* 'sluggard'.

Polybius (*c*.200–*c*.118 BC), Greek historian. After an early political career in Greece he was deported to Rome. His forty books of *Histories* (only partially extant) chronicled the rise of the Roman Empire from 220 to 146 BC.

St Polycarp (*c*.69–*c*.155), Greek bishop of Smyrna in Asia Minor. The leading Christian figure in Smyrna, he was arrested during a pagan festival, refused to recant his faith, and was burnt to death. His followers wrote an account of his martyrdom, one of the oldest such records to survive.

□ **FEAST DAY** His feast day is 23 February.

Polyclitus (5th century BC), Greek sculptor, known for his statues of idealized male athletes. Two Roman copies of his works survive, the *Doryphoros* (spear-bearer) and the *Diadumenos* (youth fastening a band round his head).

Polycrates (d. *c*.522 BC), tyrant of Samos and friend of Amasis of Egypt, who was trapped and executed by the Persian satrap Oroetes. According to Herodotus, Polycrates's apparent good fortune had earlier so alarmed his friend Amasis that he advised him to throw away something that he valued. Polycrates accordingly threw a ring he treasured into the sea, but shortly afterwards the ring was returned to him by a fisherman; a sign that the attempt to avert ill-fortune would be unsuccessful.

Polydeuces another name for ➤ POLLUX.

Polyglot Bible edited in 1653–7 by Brian Walton (?1600–61), bishop of Chester, with the help of many scholars. It contains various oriental texts of the Bible with Latin translations, and a critical apparatus.

See also ➤ COMPLUTENSIAN *Polyglot*.

Polyhymnia the ➤ MUSE of the art of mime. The name comes via Latin from Greek, and means literally 'she of many hymns'.

Polynices in Greek mythology, son of ➤ OEDIPUS and Jocasta, and leader of the ➤ SEVEN *against*

Thebes; his sister ➤ ANTIGONE was sentenced to death by their uncle Creon for burying his ritually unburied body.

Polyphemus in Greek mythology, a Cyclops who trapped Odysseus and some of his companions in a cave, from which they escaped by putting out his one eye while he slept. In another story Polyphemus loved the sea nymph Galatea, and in jealousy killed his rival ➤ ACIS.

pomander a ball or perforated container of sweet-smelling substances such as herbs and spices, placed in a cupboard or room to perfume the air or (formerly) carried as a supposed protection against infection. The word comes (in the late 15th century) via Old French from medieval Latin *pomum de ambra* 'apple of ambergris'.

pomegranate an orange-sized fruit with a tough golden-orange outer skin and sweet red gelatinous flesh containing many seeds. The *pomegranate* was the badge of Catherine of Aragon (1485–1536), first wife of Henry VIII, and is a symbol of fertility.

In Greek mythology, ➤ PERSEPHONE was forced to remain for half the year in the Underworld, because during her captivity there she had eaten some pomegranate seeds.

Recorded from Middle English, the word comes from Old French *pome granate*, from *pome* 'apple' + *grenate* 'pomegranate' (from Latin *(malum) granatum* '(apple) having many seeds', from *granum* 'seed').

Pomerania a region of northern Europe, extending along the south shore of the Baltic Sea between Stralsund in NE Germany and the Vistula in Poland. The region was controlled variously by Germany, Poland, the Holy Roman Empire, Prussia, and Sweden, until the larger part was restored to Poland in 1945, the western portion becoming a part of the German state of Mecklenburg-West Pomerania.

pomfret cake an archaic variant of ➤ PONTEFRACT *cake*.

pommel a rounded knob on the end of the handle of a sword, dagger, or old-fashioned gun; the upward curving or projecting part of a saddle in front of the rider. In Middle English the word denotes a ball or finial at the top point of a tower or corner of an altar; it comes through Old French from a diminutive of Latin *pomum* 'fruit, apple'.

Pommy in Australia, an informal (derogatory) term for a British person. It is said by some to derive from *pomegranate*, as a near rhyme to *immigrant*, but evidence is lacking.

Pomona in Roman mythology, the goddess of fruit and fruit-trees, wife of Vortumnus.

Marquise de Pompadour (1721–64), Jeanne Antoinette Poisson, known as **Madame de Pompadour**. In 1744 she became the mistress of Louis XV, gaining considerable influence at court, but she later became unpopular as a result of her interference in political affairs. She was a notable patron of the arts and founded the porcelain factory at Sèvres.

The name *pompadour* is used for various items of costume fashionable, or resembling those fashionable, in the time of the Marquise, especially (in the US) a men's hairstyle in which the hair is combed back from the forehead without a parting, and a woman's hairstyle in which the hair is turned back from the forehead in a roll.

Pompeii an ancient city in western Italy, southeast of Naples. The city was buried by an eruption of Mount Vesuvius in 79 AD in which ➤ PLINY *the Elder* was killed; excavations of the site began in 1748, revealing well-preserved remains of buildings, mosaics, furniture, and the personal possessions of the city's inhabitants.

Pompey[1] (106–48 BC), Roman general and statesman, known as **Pompey the Great**. He founded the First Triumvirate, but later quarrelled with ➤ *Julius* CAESAR, who defeated him at the battle of Pharsalus. He then fled to Egypt, where he was murdered.

Pompey[2] informal name for the town and dockyard of the British city of Portsmouth, in Hampshire. Recorded from the late 19th century, the origin is unknown.

Pompey's Pillar name given to a marble column in Alexandria; actually dedicated to the Emperor Diocletian.

Pompidou Centre a modern art gallery, exhibition centre, and concert hall in Paris, designed by Richard Rogers and the Italian architect Renzo Piano (1937–) and opened in 1977. The design features brightly coloured pipes, ducts, and elevators, on the outside of the exterior walls, giving the building an industrial appearance. It is named after the French statesman Georges Pompidou (1911–74).

the pomps and vanities of this wicked world ostentatious display as a type of worldly temptation; after the answer in the *Catechism*. *Pomps* here meant originally the public shows and spectacles associated with or sanctioned by pagan worship, then, more vaguely, any 'shows' held to be under the patronage of the devil, and finally (from the 17th century) tacitly transferred to those of 'the world' and associated with its 'vanities'.

Juan Ponce de León (*c*.1460–1521), Spanish explorer. He accompanied Columbus on his second voyage to the New World in 1493, became governor of Puerto Rico (1510–12), and landed on the coast of Florida in 1513, claiming the area for Spain and becoming its governor the following year.

pongal the Tamil New Year festival, celebrated by the cooking of new rice. The name comes from Tamil *poṅkal*, literally 'boiling, swelling', with reference to the cooking process of rice.

pongo originally, a large anthropoid African ape, variously identified with the chimpanzee or gorilla. Recorded from the early 20th century, the word comes from Congolese *mpongo*. In British military slang (used especially by the Royal Navy or RAF) it means a soldier.

pons asinorum the point at which many learners fail, especially a theory or formula that is difficult to grasp. The term is Latin for 'bridge of asses', taken from the fifth proposition of the first book of Euclid.

Ponsonby rule a rule by which the Government may authorize an agreement without parliamentary approval, named after Arthur A. W. H. *Ponsonby* (1871–1946), English politician; it is said to have originated in a departmental minute dated 1 February 1924, signed by Ponsonby when Under-Secretary of State for Foreign Affairs.

Pont du Gard an arched structure built by the Romans *c*.14 AD over the River Gard in southern France as part of an aqueduct carrying water to Nîmes. Three tiers of limestone arches of diminishing span support the covered water channel at a height of 55 metres (180 ft) above the valley. In the 18th century the lowest tier was widened to form a road bridge, which is still in use.

Pontefract cake a flat, round liquorice sweet, named after *Pontefract* (earlier *Pomfret*), a town in Yorkshire where the sweets were first made.

pontianak in Malayan folklore: a vampire, especially one that is the ghost of a still-born child. The word comes from Malay and means literally 'child-killer'.

Pontifex Maximus (in ancient Rome) the head of the principal college of priests; (in the Roman Catholic Church) a title of the Pope. The title means literally in Latin 'supreme high priest'.

pontiff the Pope. The name comes (in the late 17th century) via French from Latin *pontifex* 'high priest'.

pontificals a bishop's or priest's robes; the vestments and insignia of a bishop, cardinal, or abbot.

Pontine Marshes an area of marshland in western Italy, on the Tyrrhenian coast south of Rome. It became infested with malaria in ancient Roman times, and it was not until 1928 that an extensive scheme to drain the marshes was begun. Several new towns have since been built in the region, which is now a productive agricultural area.

Pontius see ➤ *Pontius* PILATE.

Erik Pontoppidan (1698–1764), Danish author and bishop of Bergen in Norway. His principal works are *Gesta et vestigia Danorum extra Daniam* (1740), and a *Natural History of Norway* (1755), frequently mentioned on account of its description of the ➤ KRAKEN.

Pontus an ancient region of northern Asia Minor, on the Black Sea coast north of Cappadocia. It reached its height between 120 and 63 BC under Mithridates VI, when it dominated the whole of Asia Minor; by the end of the 1st century BC it had been defeated by Rome and absorbed into the Roman Empire.

pony see also ➤ JERUSALEM *pony*, ➤ SHANKS*'s pony*.

Pony Express (in the US) a system of mail delivery operating from 1860–1 between St Joseph in Missouri and Sacramento in California, using continuous relays of horse riders. Buffalo Bill (William Cody) was one of its riders.

Ponzi scheme a form of fraud in which belief in the success of a non-existent enterprise is fostered by the payment of quick returns to the first investors from money invested by later investors. It is named after Charles *Ponzi* (died 1949), who carried out such a fraud (1919–20).

poodle see ➤ BALFOUR*'s poodle*.

Pooh see ➤ WINNIE-*the-Pooh*.

pooh-bah a person having much influence or holding many offices at the same time, especially one perceived as pompously self-important, from the name of a character in W. S. Gilbert's *The Mikado* (1885).

> Any inside look at the game's pooh-bahs would be valuable.
> — *Sports Illustrated* 14 March 1994

Poohsticks a game in which each player throws a stick over the upstream side of a bridge into a stream or river, the winner being the person whose stick emerges first from under the bridge. The name comes (in the 1920s) from ➤ WINNIE-*the-Pooh*, the toy bear in the children's books of A. A. Milne.

pooka in Irish mythology, a hobgoblin. Recorded from the early 19th century, the name comes from Irish *púca*.

Poona an industrial city in Maharashtra, western India, in the hills south-east of Bombay, which was a military and administrative centre under British rule; the name is used allusively for Army officers supposedly typical of that period.

> They're county people, all frightfully toffee-nosed and Poona.
> — Nevil Shute *Pastoral* (1944)

poor ➤ St ANTHONY *of Padua* and ➤ St MARTIN *de Porres* are the patron saints of the poor.
See also ➤ *poor as a* CHURCH *mouse*, ➤ POOR *as Job*.

Poor Clare a member of an order of Franciscan nuns founded by St ➤ CLARE *of Assisi* in *c.*1212; the name is recorded from the early 17th century.

it is a poor dog that's not worth whistling for proverbial saying, mid 16th century.

it is a poor heart that never rejoices proverbial saying, mid 19th century.

Poor Law a law relating to the support of the poor. Originally the responsibility of the parish, the relief and employment of the poor passed over to the workhouses in 1834. In the early 20th century the Poor Law was replaced by schemes of social security.

poor little rich girl a girl or young woman whose wealth brings her no happiness; mainly from the title of a song (1925) by Noel Coward; although the phrase had been used earlier in the title, *The Poor Little Rich Girl*, of a film (1917) starring Mary Pickford, and based on a play with the same title (1913) by Eleanor Gates.

poor man's weather-glass the scarlet pimpernel, so named because its flowers close before rain.

Poor Richard's Almanack (1733–58), American ➤ ALMANAC by ➤ *Benjamin* FRANKLIN; the character of the supposed author *Poor Richard* is originally a foolish astronomer, but is changed to that of the sensible and quiet country-dweller who is a rich source of proverbs and sayings.

Poor Robin's Almanack a British ➤ ALMANAC first published in 1661 or 1662; *Poor Robin* was the supposed author of a number of publications of the period, including *Poor Robin's Jests, c.*1669.

Pooter a person resembling Charles Pooter, whose mundane and trivial lifestyle is the subject of George and Weedon Grossmith's *Diary of a Nobody* (1892); a narrow, fastidious, or self-important person.

> He is Pooterishly suspicious of the upper classes and the rich (whom he always calls 'wealthy').
> — *Independent on Sunday* 19 September 1993

Pop goes the weasel refrain of a popular song now regarded as a children's rhyme:

> Up and down the City Road,
> In and out the Eagle,
> That's the way the money goes—
> Pop goes the weasel!
> — W. R. Mandale 'Pop Goes the Weasel' (1853 song); also attributed to Charles Twiggs

The Eagle was a public house in the City Road, London.

In the mid 19th century, **Pop goes the weasel** was also the name of a popular country dance, in which one dancer would dance under the arms of the others to his or her partner to the tune of the rhyme.

Pope title of the Bishop of Rome as head of the Roman Catholic Church, and seen as in direct succession from St Peter; in extended use, a person who assumes or is credited with a position, authority, or infallibility like that of the Pope.

Recorded from Old English, the word comes via ecclesiastical Latin from ecclesiastical Greek *papas* 'bishop', patriarch', variant of Greek *pappas* 'father'.

➤ *St* PETER and ➤ *St* GREGORY *the Great* are the patron saints of popes.

See also ➤ BLACK *Pope*, ➤ GIANT *Pope*, ➤ *it is ill* SITTING *at home and striving with the Pope*, ➤ RED *Pope*, ➤ *Pope* JOAN, ➤ KISS *the pope's toe.*

Pope's eye a lymphatic gland in a sheep's thigh, which is surrounded with fat and regarded by some

as a delicacy. It is called in German *pfaffensbisschen* 'priest's bit', probably as being a tit-bit which the priest was supposed to claim; in French *œil de Judas* Judas's eye; 'eye' referring apparently to its rounded form.

Popemobile informal name for a bulletproof vehicle with a raised viewing area, used by the Pope on official visits.

Popeye cartoon character created by Elzie Segar in 1926 for the cartoon strip originating as 'Thimble Theatre' in 1919 and featuring *Olive Oyl, J. Wellington Wimpy,* and *Eugene the Jeep. Popeye,* the sailor whose immense strength derived from eating spinach, became Olive's accepted suitor after defeating various rivals.

popinjay a parrot; in archery, a target made of bunches of plumage fixed to a pole of different heights. From the early 16th century, *popinjay* is used, with reference to the bird's gaudy plumage, for a vain or conceited person, especially one who dresses or behaves extravagantly.

The word comes (in Middle English) from Old French *papingay,* via Spanish from Arabic *babbagā.* The change in the ending was due to association with *jay.*

Popish Plot a fictitious Jesuit plot concocted by ➤ *Titus* OATES in 1678, involving a plan to kill Charles II, massacre Protestants, and put the Catholic Duke of York on the English throne. The 'discovery' of the plot led to widespread panic and the execution of about thirty-five Catholics.

poplar see ➤ WHITE *poplar.*

Poplarism the policy of giving out-relief on a generous or extravagant scale, as practised by the board of guardians of *Poplar* in the 1920s.

Mary Poppins the brisk fictional nanny with magic powers created by P. L. Travers in *Mary Poppins* (1934), and further popularized by the Walt Disney film of the same name in 1964.

> You can't go around with that tatty green canvas thing. You look like some sort of Mary Poppins person who's fallen on hard times.
> — Helen Fielding *Bridget Jones's Diary* (1996)

poppy the striking appearance of the flower as a cornfield weed has led to the figurative use of the *poppy* as the type of something where the showy look is not matched by real worth:

> He little dreamt then that the weeding-hook of
> reformation would after two ages pluck up his glorious
> poppy from insulting over the good corn.
> — John Milton *The Reason of Church Government urged
> against Prelaty* (1641)

References are also made to the story of the legendary Roman king Tarquin the Proud (see ➤ TAR-
QUINIUS), who is said to have demonstrated how to
deal with presumption or rebellion by silently striking off the heads of a row of poppies.

From the 19th century, the scarlet poppy has been
seen as emblematic of those who have died in war;
in *The Folk-Lore of Plants* (1889), T. F. Thiselton
Dyer noted the tradition that the red poppies which
grew on the field of Waterloo after it was ploughed
sprang from the blood shed during the battle of
1815. In the 20th century, the *poppy* as a symbol has
been associated particularly with the dead of the
two World Wars.

See also ➤ FLANDERS *poppy*, ➤ TALL *poppy syndrome*.

Poppy Day another name for ➤ REMEMBRANCE
Sunday.

poppy head an ornamental top on the end of a
church pew. The term is recorded from late Middle
English, and although it has been suggested that the
first element represents French *poupée* 'baby, puppet', or English *poppet*, *puppet*, this appears to be
without foundation.

Popski's Private Army in the Second World War, a
British group for raiding and reconnaissance led by
Lieutenant Colonel Vladimir Peniakoff (1897–1951).

> A message came on the wireless for me. It said: 'SPREAD
> ALARM AND DESPONDENCY'. So the time had come, I
> thought, Eighth Army was taking the offensive. The
> date was, I think, May 18th, 1942.
> — Vladimir Peniakoff *Private Army* (1950)

popular front a party or coalition representing
left-wing elements, in particular (**the Popular Front**)
an alliance of communist, radical, and socialist
elements formed and gaining some power in countries such as France and Spain in the 1930s. In
France such an alliance won elections in 1936, under
the leadership of Léon Blum. In Spain the Popular
Front government was in office 1936–9, and fought
the Spanish Civil War against Franco and the Nationalists. In Chile a Popular Front government
ruled from 1938 to 1946.

populist a member or adherent of a political party
seeking to represent the interests of ordinary people,

originally referring to a party formed in the US in
1892 to represent the interests of all of the people.
The policies of the Populists included public control
of railways, limitation of private ownership of land,
extension of the currency by free coinage of silver
and increased issue of paper money, and a graduated income tax.

porcelain a white vitrified translucent ceramic;
china. Recorded from the mid 16th century, the
word comes via French from Italian *porcellana* 'cow-
rie shell', hence 'chinaware' (from its resemblance
to the dense polished shells).

the Porch another name for ➤ *the* STOA, the public
ambulatory in the agora of ancient Athens in which
the philosopher Zeno and his pupils met.

porcupine a large rodent with defensive spines or
quills on the body and tail, which was traditionally
believed to defend itself by discharging its quills at
its enemy. The *porcupine* was the personal badge of
Louis XII, king of France (1462–1515).

Recorded from late Middle English, the name
comes via Old French and Provençal from Latin
porcus 'pig' + *spina* 'thorn'. An early variant,
porpentine, is now likely to be known from its use by
Shakespeare, as in *Hamlet*, 'Like quills upon the
fretful porpentine'.

pork the flesh of a pig used as food, especially when
uncured; the word comes (in Middle English) via
Old French from Latin *porcus* 'pig'.

pork barrel in North America, used in reference to
the use of government funds for projects designed
to please voters or legislators and win votes. The
term, which is recorded from the early 20th century
in this sense, refers to the use of such a barrel by
farmers, to keep a reserve supply of meat.

Person from Porlock according to his note on
'Kubla Khan', the casual visitor who was responsible
for Coleridge's being unable to finish the poem.
While working on it he was 'unfortunately called
out by a person on business from Porlock, and detained by him above an hour'; on returning to the
poem, he was unable to recall the opium dream on
which it had been based.

> I would look at it again, and see if it had been totally
> destroyed. At least no person from Porlock was likely to
> interrupt me today.
> — Mary Stewart *Stormy Petrel* (1992)

porphyria a rare hereditary disease in which there
is abnormal metabolism of the blood pigment
haemoglobin. Porphyrins are excreted in the urine,

which becomes dark; other symptoms include mental disturbances and extreme sensitivity of the skin to light. It has been suggested that George III suffered from *porphyria*.

Porphyry (*c*.232–303), Neoplatonist philosopher. He was a pupil of Plotinus, whose works he edited after the latter's death.

porphyry a hard igneous rock containing crystals of feldspar in a fine-grained, typically reddish groundmass, used in ancient Egypt as a building stone. The word comes (in late Middle English) via medieval Latin from Greek *porphuritēs*, from *porphura* 'purple'.

porphyrogenite a member of the imperial family at Constantinople, reputedly born in a purple-hung or porphyry chamber. Later, a child born after his or her father's accession to a throne; a member of an imperial or royal reigning family; belonging to the highest or most privileged ranks of an organization.

Ferdinand Porsche (1875–1952), Austrian car designer. In 1934 he designed the Volkswagen ('people's car'), while his name has since become famous for the high-performance sports and racing cars produced by his company, originally to his designs.

Lars Porsena (6th century BC), a legendary Etruscan chieftain, king of the town of Clusium. Summoned by Tarquinius Superbus after the latter's overthrow and exile from Rome, Porsena subsequently laid siege to the city, but did not succeed in capturing it; during this period the exploits of ➤ SCAEVOLA and ➤ HORATIUS took place.

Porson's rule the metrical rule that in a Greek tragic iambic trimeter where the last word forms a cretic, the preceding syllable is short, from the name of Richard *Porson* (1759–1808), the English classical scholar who formulated it.

port the side of a ship or aircraft that is on the left when one is facing forward; the opposite of ➤ STARBOARD. Originally it probably meant the side turned towards the port.

any port in a storm in adverse circumstances any source of relief or escape is welcome; saying recorded from the mid 18th century.

Port-Royal A 17th-century lay Jansenist community housed in the convent of *Port-Royal des*

Champs near Versailles, known for its educational work especially in logic and grammar; the wider educational and philosophical community adhering to the work of this institution.

Port Sunlight a village on the south bank of the Mersey. Founded and built in the 1880s by Viscount Leverhulme, it provided model housing for the employees of his 'Sunlight' soap factory.

portate in heraldry, represented in a sloping position, as if carried on the shoulder.

Porte in full, the **Sublime Porte** or the **Ottoman Porte**: the Ottoman court at Constantinople. The name dates from the early 17th century, and comes from French *la Sublime Porte* 'the exalted gate', translation of the Turkish title of the central office of the Ottoman government.

Porteous riot in Edinburgh in 1736, centring on the lynching of Captain Porteous, captain of the City Guard. At the execution of Andrew Wilson, an Edinburgh merchant, Porteous had ordered his men to fire on the crowd; several of those present were killed. Tried, condemned to death, and reprieved, he was taken out of the prison by a mob, and hanged from a signpost near where the gallows was usually erected. Despite a subsequent rigorous investigation, no one was ever convicted of the crime. The episode features in Walter Scott's *Heart of Midlothian*.

porter's knot historical term for a double shoulder pad and forehead loop used for carrying loads.

portfolio see ➤ MINISTER *without Portfolio*.

Porthos name of one of the ➤ THREE *Musketeers* who befriend ➤ D'ARTAGNAN in Dumas' novel.

Portia name of the heroine in Shakespeare's *Merchant of Venice*, who, dressed in men's clothes, successfully defends her husband's friend Antonio from the prosecution of ➤ SHYLOCK; her name may be used allusively for a female advocate or barrister.

the Portico another name for ➤ *the* STOA or ➤ *the* PORCH.

portion see ➤ BENJAMIN'*s portion*.

Portland Place (the directorship of) the BBC, whose headquarters are in Portland Place, a street in London.

Portland vase a dark blue Roman glass vase with white decoration, dating from around the 1st century AD. Acquired in the 18th century by the Duchess of *Portland*, it is now in the British Museum; smashed in 1845, it was skilfully and carefully restored.

portmanteau word a word blending the sounds and combining the meanings of two others, for example *motel* or *brunch*. The term was coined by Lewis Carroll:

> Well, 'slithy' means 'lithe and slimy' . . . You see it's like a portmanteau—there are two meanings packed up into one word.
> — Lewis Carroll *Through the Looking-glass* (1872)

Porto Novo the capital of Benin, a port on the Gulf of Guinea close to the border with Nigeria, which was a Portuguese settlement in the 17th century, and became a centre of the Portuguese slave trade.

Portobello a port in South America, captured by Admiral Vernon in 1739 during the war with Spain; the *Portobello* district in Edinburgh and Portobello Road in London were named for it.

Porton Down the British Ministry of Defence's chemical and biological research establishment near Salisbury in Wiltshire.

> I was dosing the greenfly . . . with that frightfully good aerosol defoliant that Picarda got the recipe for from some boffin on the run from Porton Down.
> — Richard Ingrams and John Wells *The Other Half* (1981)

portreeve originally, the ruler or chief officer of a town or borough, after the Norman Conquest often identified with or of the status of a mayor; a borough-reeve. Later, an officer subordinate to a mayor; a bailiff.

Portsoken ward a ward of the city of London; *portsoken* is a former term for the jurisdiction of a port or town, especially the district outside a city or borough over which its jurisdiction extended.

posada in Mexico, each of a series of visits traditionally paid to different friends before Christmas, representing Mary and Joseph's search for a lodging in Bethlehem. The word is Spanish, and means literally a resting-place, an inn.

Poseidon in Greek mythology, the god of the sea, water, earthquakes, and horses, son of Cronus and Rhea and brother of Zeus. He is often depicted with a trident in his hand. His Roman equivalent is ►NEPTUNE.

poser a difficult or perplexing question or problem; in earlier use, a person who set testing questions (an *apposer*).

posh informal expression meaning elegant or stylishly luxurious. Early 20th century, perhaps from slang *posh*, denoting a dandy. There is no evidence to support the folk etymology that *posh* is formed from the initials of *port out starboard home* (referring to the practice of using the more comfortable accommodation, out of the heat of the sun, on ships between England and India).

positive vetting a process of exhaustive inquiry into the background and character of a candidate for a Civil Service post that involves access to secret material.

positivism a philosophical system which holds that every rationally justifiable assertion can be scientifically verified or is capable of logical or mathematical proof, and which therefore rejects metaphysics and theism.

posse originally (also **posse comitatus**), the body of men above the age of fifteen in a county (excluding peers, the clergy, or the infirm), whom the sheriff could summon to repress a riot or for other purposes. Later (in the US), a body of men summoned by a sheriff to enforce the law.

possession is nine points of the law proverbial saying, early 17th century. Although it does not reflect any specific legal ruling, in early use the satisfaction of ten (sometimes twelve) points was commonly asserted to attest to full entitlement or ownership; possession, represented by nine (or eleven) points is therefore the closest substitute for this.

POSSLQ abbreviation for *person of the opposite sex sharing living quarters* (used to refer to a live-in sexual partner); the expression was apparently coined in 1978 by Arthur J. Norton, a member of the US Census Bureau, but was never officially adopted by them.

play possum pretend to be asleep or unconscious when threatened (in allusion to the opossum's habit of feigning death when threatened or attacked); recorded from the early 19th century.

post see also ► *by* RETURN *of post*, ► FIRST *past the post*, ► *from* PILLAR *to post*.

post captain former term for a Royal Navy officer holding the full rank of captain, as opposed to a commander with the courtesy title of captain.

post-bellum occurring or existing after a war, in particular the American Civil War.

> The Greenbackers, the Grangers, the Knights of Labor and other dissident groups of the post-bellum era.
> — Alan Brinkley *Voices of Protest* (1982)

post-haste with great speed or immediacy; from the direction 'haste, post, haste', formerly given on letters; in this direction, *post* means the courier who was carrying the letters.

post hoc, ergo propter hoc proverbial Latin saying, 'after this, therefore on account of this', expressing the fallacy that a thing which follows another is therefore caused by it.

post-Impressionism the work or style of a varied group of late 19th-century and early 20th-century artists including Van Gogh, Gauguin, and Cézanne. They reacted against the naturalism of the Impressionists to explore colour, line, and form, and the emotional response of the artist, a concern which led to the development of expressionism.

post meridiem after midday; between noon and midnight; abbreviated as *pm*. The expression is first recorded in the mid 17th century:

> I would erect a Figure of Heaven the sixt of January 1646, one hour thirty minutes afternoon, or P.M, that is Post Meridiem.
> — William Lilly *Christian Astrology* (1647)

post-mortem an examination of a dead body to determine the cause of death; figuratively, an analysis or discussion of an event held soon after it has occurred, especially in order to determine why it was a failure. The use is recorded from the mid 19th century, and derives from the mid 18th century use of the Latin phrase meaning literally 'after death'.

post-obit a bond given by a borrower to a lender which secures a sum to be paid to the lender on the death of a specified person from whom the borrower expects to inherit.

post-structural an extension and critique of structuralism, especially as used in critical textual analysis. Emerging in French intellectual life in the late 1960s and early 1970s, post-structuralism embraced Jacques Derrida's deconstructionism and the later work of Roland Barthes, the psychoanalytic theories of Jacques Lacan, and the historical critiques of Michel Foucault. It departed from the claims to objectivity and comprehensiveness made by structuralism and emphasized instead plurality and deferral of meaning, rejecting the fixed binary oppositions of structuralism and the validity of authorial authority.

post-traumatic stress disorder a condition of persistent mental and emotional stress occurring as a result of injury or severe psychological shock, typically involving disturbance of sleep and constant vivid recall of the experience, with dulled responses to others and to the outside world.

Post-traumatic stress disorder was identified as a specific syndrome in the early 1970s; the term entered the general language in the 1980s, especially in relation to Vietnam War veterans suffering from stress-related illnesses. Symptoms of the disorder are now associated particularly with the long-term effects on survivors of such events as the sinking of the passenger ferry the *Herald of Free Enterprise* at Zeebrugge, the terrorist bombing in Oklahoma City, and the mass shooting of schoolchildren at Dunblane in Scotland. Members of the emergency services attending such disasters may be similarly traumatized.

a postern door makes a thief proverbial saying, mid 15th century; referring to the opportunity offered by a back or side entrance.

postmillennial (especially in Christian doctrine) following the millennium, relating to the belief that the Second Coming of Christ will occur after the millennium.

postmillennialism (among fundamentalist Christians) the doctrine that the Second Coming of Christ will be the culmination of the prophesied millennium of blessedness.

postnatus a person born after a particular event; in particular, in Scotland, one born after the uniting of the Scottish and English crowns (1603); in the US, one born after the Declaration of Independence (1776).

posy a short motto or line of verse inscribed inside a ring, typically in patterned language such as an acrostic. The word is a contraction (in late Middle English) of *poesy*.

pot see ➤ DEATH *in the pot*, ➤ *a* LITTLE *pot is soon hot*, ➤ *the* WATCHED *pot never boils*.

the pot calling the kettle black proverbial saying, late 17th century; of a person who accuses or blames another while being guilty of the same offence.

pot-hook a curved stroke in handwriting, especially as made by children learning to write.

pot-pourri a mixture of dried petals and spices placed in a bowl or small sack to perfume clothing or a room. Originally (in the early 17th century) denoting a stew made of different kinds of meat, it comes from French, literally 'rotten pot'.

potato originally, the plant which is now known as the sweet potato, which was introduced to Spain by Columbus in 1492, and was cultivated there and in other warmer parts of Europe thereafter. The name comes in the mid 16th century from Spanish *patata*, variant of Taino 'sweet potato'.

The plant which is known as *potato* in English today was introduced to Spain *c.*1570 and thence to Italy and the Low Countries. It may have been introduced to England independently of the continental stock in 1590, and is first mentioned by Gerard as 'Virginia Potatoes' in 1596. In 1693 its introduction into Ireland was attributed to Sir Walter Raleigh 'after his return from Virginia' (where he never was); but no contemporary statement associating Raleigh's name with the potato has been found. This plant slowly became more widely cultivated in Britain and the rest of temperate Europe, and as it became a more important food source, became 'the potato', while the original plant became 'the sweet potato'.

See also ➤ COUCH *potato*, ➤ MOUSE *potato*.

Potato Famine the famine which occurred in Ireland in 1846–7, after the failure of the potato crop, which resulted in widescale deaths; the nationalist leader Daniel O'Connell said in 1846, 'a NATION is starving', and the government's failure or inability to alleviate conditions remained a longstanding source of bitterness.

In 1997, the British Prime Minister Tony Blair issued an official statement which was read at the Famine commemoration at Millstreet, County Cork:

> Those who governed in London at the time failed their people through standing by while a crop failure turned into a massive human tragedy. We must not forget such a dreadful event. It is also right that we should pay tribute to the ways in which the Irish people have triumphed in the face of this catastrophe.
>
> — Tony Blair statement, 1 June 1997

See also ➤ *the* FAMINE *Queen*.

Potato War informal name for the War of the Bavarian Succession (1778–9); deriving from the fact that the combatants were more concerned with blocking each other's communications and supplies than with direct fighting. The name is a translation of German *Kartoffelkrieg*.

potboiler an informal term for a book, painting, or recording produced merely to make the writer or artist a living by catering to popular taste. The expression is recorded from the early 19th century.

poteen Irish alcohol made illicitly, typically from potatoes. The word comes (in the early 19th century) from Irish *(fuisce) poitín* 'little pot (of whiskey)'.

Potemkin[1] having a false or deceptive appearance, especially one presented for the purpose of propaganda. The word comes (in the 1930s) from Grigori Aleksandrovich *Potyomkin* (often transliterated *Potemkin*), a favourite of Empress Catherine II of Russia, who reputedly gave the order for sham villages to be built for the empress's tour of the Crimea in 1787.

Potemkin[2] a battleship whose crew mutinied in the Russian Revolution of 1905 when in the Black Sea, bombarding Odessa before seeking asylum in Romania. The incident, commemorated in Eisenstein's 1925 film *The Battleship Potemkin*, persuaded the tsar to agree to a measure of reform.

potent in heraldry, (of a cross) having the limbs terminating in potents; (of a fur) consisting of interlocking T-shaped areas of alternating tinctures and orientations; (of a line) formed into an open T-shape at regular intervals.

potichomania a hobby (fashionable in the 19th century) involving the transformation of glass vases into imitation porcelain by the application of paint or images printed on paper. The word comes from French, from an irregular formation on *potiche* 'an oriental porcelain vase'.

Potiphar (in the Bible) an Egyptian officer whose wife tried to seduce ➤ JOSEPH and then falsely accused him of attempting to rape her (Genesis 39).

potlatch (among North American Indian peoples of the northwest coast) an opulent ceremonial feast at which possessions are given away or destroyed to display wealth or enhance prestige.

Potomac a river of the eastern US, which rises in the Appalachian Mountains in West Virginia and flows about 459 km (285 miles) through Washington DC into Chesapeake Bay on the Atlantic coast. The report 'All quiet along the Potomac' is attributed to the Union general George B. McClellan (1826–85) at the time of the Civil War, although the phrase is also found in a poem by Ethel Lynn Beers (1827–79):

> All quiet along the Potomac to-night,
> No sound save the rush of the river,
> While soft falls the dew on the face of the dead—
> The picket's off duty forever.
> — Ethel Lynn Beers 'The Picket Guard' (1861)

Potsdam a city in eastern Germany, the capital of Brandenburg, situated just south-west of Berlin on the Havel River. It is the site of the rococo Sans Souci palace built for Frederick II between 1745 and 1747, and is associated particularly with the military strength of Prussia.

> Frederick William, the half-mad recruiter of the big Potsdam grenadiers.
> — Arthur Conan Doyle *Duet* (1899)

Potsdam Conference a meeting held in Potsdam in the summer of 1945 between US, Soviet, and British leaders, which established principles for the Allied occupation of Germany following the end of the Second World War. From this conference an ultimatum was sent to Japan demanding unconditional surrender.

potsherd a broken piece of ceramic material, especially one found on an archaeological site.

pottage see ➤ MESS *of pottage.*

Harry Potter hero of the children's fantasy stories by J. K. Rowling, *Harry Potter,* who has been grudgingly brought up by his aunt and uncle, attends a boarding school for wizards to learn how to fight the evil Lord Voldemort who has caused his parents' death.

The first books in the projected seven-book series have been enormously popular with children and adults, although in October 1999 it was reported that parents in South Carolina were trying to have the books banned from school libraries because of the death and violence they contained.

See also ➤ HOGWARTS.

Beatrix Potter (1866–1943), English writer for children. She is known for her series of animal stories, illustrated with her own delicate watercolours, which began with *The Tale of Peter Rabbit* (first published privately in 1900).

potter's field a burial place for paupers and strangers, with biblical allusion to Matthew 27:7, 'And they took counsel, and bought with them the potter's field, to bury strangers in.' The field was bought with the thirty pieces of silver paid to Judas for the betrayal of Jesus by the priests, and which the repentant and despairing Judas had returned to them. It is also called *Aceldama.*

the Potteries the area around Stoke-on-Trent, Staffordshire, where the English pottery industry is based.

potwalloper in an English borough before the 1832 Reform Act: a man qualified for a parliamentary vote by virtue of being a householder and so having his own fireplace on which a pot could be boiled; a man able to feed and house himself and his family, whether a landowner or tenant. This system of determining the electorate was one of the abuses criticized by electoral reformers in the early 19th century.

Poujadism the conservative political philosophy and methods advocated by the French publisher and bookseller Pierre *Poujade* (b. 1920), who in 1954 founded a movement for the protection of artisans and small shopkeepers, protesting chiefly against the French tax system then in force.

poult a young domestic chicken, turkey, pheasant, or other fowl being raised for food. The word is recorded from late Middle English, and is a contraction of *pullet.*

poulter a poulterer; now only as the name of one of the London City Companies.

poulter's measure in prosody, a fanciful name for a metre consisting of lines of 12 and 14 syllables alternately (corresponding to the modern 'short metre').

pound a unit of weight equal to 16 oz. avoirdupois (0.4536 kg), or 12 oz. troy (0.3732 kg); the basic monetary unit (also **pound sterling**) of the UK, equal to 100 pence (prior to decimalization, 20 shillings or 240 pence). Recorded from Old English, the word is of Germanic origin, and comes ultimately from Latin *(libra) pondo,* denoting a Roman 'pound weight' of 12 ounces.

In the UK in the late 20th century the *pound* as a monetary unit has become emblematic of a desire to preserve British currency from the European standardization already applied by metrication to weights and measures.

See also ➤ *in for a* PENNY, *in for a pound,* ➤ PENNY *wise and pound foolish,* ➤ PINK *pound,* ➤ *take care of the* PENCE *and the pounds will take care of themselves,* ➤ TOWER *pound.*

one's pound of flesh something one is strictly or legally entitled to, but which it is ruthless or inhuman to demand. The allusion is to Shakespeare's *Merchant of Venice,* and the bond between Antonio and ➤ SHYLOCK by which Antonio pledges a pound of his own flesh if he defaults on the bill. Shylock's insistence (defeated by Portia) on holding to the letter of the agreement is taken as a type of rapacity and ferocity.

pound Scots a former Scottish monetary unit, originally of the same value as the pound sterling, but debased to one twelfth of that by the time of the Union of the Crown in 1603.

poundage see ➤ TONNAGE *and poundage.*

pour oil on troubled waters proverbial expression, mid 19th century; try to settle a disagreement or dispute with words intended to placate or pacify those involved. In 1774 the *Philosophical Transactions* of the Royal Society included a paper headed 'of the stilling of waves by means of oil'; the paper referred to an account given by Pliny of how seamen in his time poured oil into the water in the belief that this would calm the waves in a storm.

Nicolas Poussin (1594–1665), French painter. He is regarded as the chief representative of French classicism and a master of the grand manner. His subject matter included biblical scenes (*The Adoration of the Golden Calf, c.*1635), classical mythology (*Et in Arcadia Ego, c.*1655), and historical landscapes.

when poverty comes in at the door, love flies out of the window proverbial saying, mid 17th century.

poverty is no disgrace, but it is a great incovenience proverbial saying, late 16th century.

poverty is not a crime proverbial saying, late 16th century.

put your trust in God, and keep your powder dry proverbial saying, mid 19th century; attributed

to Oliver Cromwell, but not traced to a contemporary source. The earliest recorded instance to date is found in the poem 'Oliver's Advice' by the Anglo-Irish Valentine Blacker (1728–1823), in which the refrain runs, 'Put your trust in God, my boys, and keep your powder dry'.

powder of projection in alchemy, the powder of the ➤ PHILOSOPHER'*s stone.*

power see also ➤ BALANCE *of power,* ➤ BLACK *Power,* ➤ *the* CORRIDORS *of power,* ➤ KNOWLEDGE *is power,* ➤ MONEY *is power,* ➤ RED *Power.*

power corrupts proverbial saying, late 19th century; now commonly used in allusion to Lord Acton (1834–1902):

> Power tends to corrupt and absolute power corrupts absolutely.
> — Lord Acton letter to Bishop Mandell Creighton, 3 April 1887

power of attorney a document, or clause in a document, giving a person the authority to act for another person in specified or all legal or financial matters.

power dressing a style of dressing for business popular in the mid-1980s, intended to convey an impression of efficiency and self-assertive confidence. The term has been applied predominantly to women's clothing, and is frequently characterized by the use of shoulder pads.

power of the keys in the Roman Catholic Church, the spiritual authority believed to have been transmitted from Christ to St. Peter and so to subsequent popes; the authority of priests.

power to the people slogan of the Black Panther movement, from *c.*1968 onwards.

powers in traditional Christian angelology, the sixth-highest order of the ninefold celestial hierarchy.

the powers that be the authorities concerned, the people exercising political or social control, with allusion to Romans 13:1, 'For there is no power but of God: the powers that be are ordained of God.'

powwow a North American Indian ceremony involving feasting and dancing; in extended usage, a conference or meeting for discussion, especially among friends or colleagues.

Recorded from the early 17th century, the word

comes from Narragansett *powah, powwaw* 'magician' (literally 'he dreams').

Powys a former Welsh kingdom. At its most powerful in the early 12th century, Powys was divided in 1160 into two principalities. It was conquered by the English in 1284 after the death of the Welsh Prince Llewelyn in 1282.

Poynings' law a series of statutes, passed at Drogheda in 1494–5 and repealed in 1782, by which the Irish parliament was subordinated to the English Crown. They are named after Sir Edward *Poynings* (1459–1521), Lord Deputy in Ireland, 1494–6.

Poznań a city in NW Poland. An area of German colonization since the 13th century, it was under German control almost continuously until the First World War, and was overrun by the Germans again in 1939. It was severely damaged during the Second World War.

practice makes perfect proverbial saying, mid 16th century.

practise what you preach proverbial saying, late 14th century.

pradakshina in Hinduism and Buddhism, the circumambulation of a thing to be revered in which the thing is kept always on one's right-hand side, carried out as a religious ceremony in which the holiness of the thing itself is affirmed and the spiritual state of the worshipper enhanced.

Prado the Spanish national art gallery in Madrid, established in 1818. The name came originally from Spanish *Prado* (from Latin *pratum* 'meadow'), the proper name of the public park of Madrid.

praemunientes a clause (opening with the Latin word *praemunientes*, 'warning') in the writ of Edward I by which bishops and abbots summoned to Parliament were required to summon representatives of the lesser clergy to attend with them.

praemunire a writ charging a sheriff to summon a person accused of one of several possible offences which deny or violate the supremacy of the sovereign; also, the original statute of 16 Richard II (1392–3), or any of the later statutes amending it, in accordance with which this writ is issued.

   The offence originally dealt with was that of prosecuting in a foreign court a suit cognizable by the law of England; later, asserting or maintaining papal jurisdiction in England, so denying the ecclesiastical supremacy of the sovereign was added; later still the statute was applied to other actions seen as questioning or diminishing the royal jurisdiction.

Praenestine of or pertaining to Praeneste, an ancient city in Latium (the modern Palestrina, near Rome) from which come the earliest known examples of Latin.

praenomen an ancient Roman's first or personal name, for example *Marcus* Tullius Cicero.

praetor in ancient Rome, originally, the consul commanding the army; after BC 366, the annually elected magistrate; later, each of two magistrates ranking below consul.
   See also ➤ PEREGRINE *praetor*.

Praetorian Guard in ancient Rome, the bodyguard of the Roman praetor or (later) emperor; in extended use, a group using its power and influence to support or defend a leader or central figure, or an established system.

> Rarely since the Praetorian Guard has there been such an unattractive manifestation of testosterone.
> — *Observer* 29 March 1987

Pragmatic Sanction a document drafted in 1717 by the Emperor Charles VI providing for his daughter Maria Theresa to succeed to all his territories should he die without a son. It was accepted by Austria, Hungary, and the Austrian Netherlands in 1720–3, but opposition to it led to the War of the Austrian Succession on Charles's death in 1740.

pragmatism a philosophical approach that assesses the truth of meaning of theories or beliefs in terms of the success of their practical application.

Prague the capital of the Czech Republic, which was the capital of Bohemia from the 14th century, and the scene of much religious conflict.
   See also ➤ DEFENESTRATION *of Prague*.

Prague School a group of linguists established in Prague in 1926 who developed distinctive feature theory in phonology and communicative dynamism in language teaching. Leading members were Nikolai Trubetzkoy (1890–1938) and Roman Jakobson.

Prague Spring a brief period of liberalization in Czechoslovakia, ending in August 1968, during which a programme of political, economic, and cultural reform was initiated.

Prairial the ninth month of the French Republican calendar (1793–1805), originally running from 20 May to 18 June. The name, which is French, comes from *prairie* 'meadow'.

prairie schooner a covered wagon used by the 19th-century pioneers in crossing the North American prairies.

Prairie Province the Canadian province of Manitoba.

Prairie Provinces the Canadian provinces of Manitoba, Saskatchewan, and Alberta.

Prairie State an informal name for the state of Illinois.

Prairie States the States of Illinois, Wisconsin, Iowa, Minnesota, and others to the south.

praise see also ➤ DAMN *with faint praise*, ➤ SACRIFICE *of praise (and thanksgiving)*, ➤ SELF-*praise is no recommendation.*

praise the child, and you make love to the mother proverbial saying, early 19th century.

praise the Lord and pass the ammunition Second World War saying by the American naval chaplain Howell Forgy (1908–83), at Pearl Harbor, 7 December 1941, as he moved along a line of sailors passing ammunition by hand to the deck; the words later became the title of a song (1942) by Frank Loesser.

prajna direct insight into the truth taught by the Buddha, as a faculty required to attain enlightenment.

Prakrit any of the ancient or medieval vernacular dialects of north and central India which existed alongside or were derived from Sanskrit.

prakriti in Hinduism, matter as opposed to spirit, primordial matter; in Sankhya philosophy, the passive principle (personified as female) which with the active (male) principle produces the universe.

pralaya in Hinduism, a process of dissolution and destruction of the world supposed to take place at the end of each age, preceding a new creation and emanation.

prasad in Hinduism, a devotional offering made to a god, typically consisting of food that is later shared among devotees.

Prater a large wooded park in Vienna. The name, which is German, comes from Italian *prato* 'meadow'.

pratique permission granted to a ship to have dealings with a port, given after quarantine or on showing a clean bill of health.

pratyahara in yoga, withdrawal of the senses; restraint of response to external stimuli.

Pravda a Russian daily newspaper, founded in 1912 and from 1918 to 1991 the official organ of the Soviet Communist Party. Banned twice under President Yeltsin, the paper is now regarded as being broadly representative of the views of communists in Russia. The name is Russian, and means literally 'truth'.

prawn cocktail offensive humorous term for the campaign of action instituted by the then Shadow Chancellor, John Smith, in the run-up to the British General Election of 1992, to reassure the City as to the budgetary intentions of an incoming Labour government.

praxis practice, as distinguished from theory; accepted practice or custom. Recorded from the late 16th century, the word comes via medieval Latin from Greek, literally 'doing'.

Praxiteles (mid 4th century BC), Athenian sculptor, only one of whose works, *Hermes Carrying the Infant Dionysus*, survives. He is also noted for a statue of Aphrodite, of which there are only Roman copies.

pray see also ➤ *he that cannot* PAY *let him pray.*

pray a tales summon substitute jurors from among those present in court where the original jury has become deficient in number by challenges, exemptions, or other causes. *Tales* here represents the plural of Latin *talis* 'such', in the phrase *tales de circumstantibus* 'such persons from those standing about'.

prayer see also ➤ COMMON *Prayer*, ➤ *a* WING *and a prayer.*

Prayer of Manasses a book of the Apocrypha consisting of a penitential prayer put into the mouth of Manasseh, king of Judah. His life and reign are described at 2 Kings 21:1–18.

prayer wheel a small revolving cylinder inscribed with or containing prayers, a revolution of which symbolizes the repetition of a prayer, used by Tibetan Buddhists.

the family that prays together, stays together motto devised by Al Scalpone for the Roman Catholic Family Rosary Crusade, 1947.

Pre-Adamite a name given by Isaac de la Peyrère in his *Præadamitæ*, 1655, to a race of men, the progenitors of the Gentile peoples, supposed by him to have existed long before Adam, whom he held to be the first parent of the Jews and their kindred only.

pre-embryo a human embryo or fertilized ovum in the first fourteen days after fertilization, before implantation in the womb has occurred. The term is recorded from the 1980s in this sense, and subsequently recognition of the human *pre-embryo* as an entity distinct from the *embryo* influenced the legal and ethical debate about the use of the human embryo in genetic and medical research.

Pre-Raphaelite a member of a group of English 19th-century artists, including Holman Hunt, Millais, and D. G. Rossetti, who consciously sought to emulate the simplicity and sincerity of the work of Italian artists from before the time of Raphael.

Seven young English artists and writers founded the **Pre-Raphaelite Brotherhood** in 1848 as a reaction against the slick sentimentality and academic convention of much Victorian art. Their work is characterized by strong line and colour, naturalistic detail, and often biblical or literary subjects. The group began to disperse in the 1850s, and the term became applied to the rather different later work of Rossetti, and that of Burne-Jones and William Morris, in which a romantic and decorative depiction of classical and medieval themes had come to predominate.

preach see ➤ PRACTISE *what you preach*.

preachers ➤ St JOHN *Chrysostom* and ➤ *St* BERNARDINO *of Siena* are the patron saints of preachers.

prebend the portion of the revenues of a cathedral or collegiate church formerly granted to a canon or member of the chapter as his stipend. The term

comes (in late Middle English) via Old French from late Latin *praebenda* 'things to be supplied, pension'.

precentor a person who leads a congregation in its singing or (in a synagogue) prayers; a minor canon who administers the musical life of a cathedral.

precept see ➤ EXAMPLE *is better than precept*.

preceptory a subordinate community of the Knights Templar; the provincial estate or manor supporting such a community; the buildings in which such a community was housed.

Les Précieuses derogatory term for women affecting a refined delicacy of language and taste, with particular reference to the circle of the Marquise de Rambouillet in 17th-century France. The usage was popularized by Molière in *Les Précieuses ridicules* (1659), a comedy in which those frequenting the literary salons of Paris were satirized.

precious blood the blood of Jesus, as shed for the redemption of humankind; the phrase (first recorded in Wyclif's translation of the Bible) is frequently used in the names of religious orders and feast days.

precious stone a highly attractive and valuable piece of mineral, used especially in jewellery; a gemstone.

predella a step or platform on which an altar is placed; also, a raised shelf above an altar, a painting or sculpture on this, typically forming an appendage to an altarpiece. The word is Italian, and means literally 'stool'.

predestination (as a doctrine in Christian theology) the divine foreordaining of all that will happen, especially with regard to the salvation of some and not others. It has been particularly associated with the teachings of St Augustine of Hippo and of Calvin.

predicant archaic term for a preacher, especially a Dominican friar.

predikant in South Africa, a minister of the Dutch Reformed Church.

predynastic of or relating to a period before the normally recognized dynasties, especially in ancient Egypt before about 3000 BC.

pregnancy ➤ *St* MARGARET *of Antioch* is the patron saint of pregnant women.

prelapsarian in theology, or poetic and literary use, characteristic of the time before the Fall of Man; innocent and unspoilt.

prelate a bishop or other high ecclesiastical dignitary. Recorded from Middle English, the word comes, via Old French, from medieval Latin *praelatus* 'civil dignitary', and ultimately from Latin *praeferre* 'carry before', also 'place before in esteem'.

Premier a Prime Minister or other head of government; the term is recorded in this sense from the early 18th century.

ce n'est que le premier pas qui coûte saying attributed to the French literary hostess Mme Du Deffand (1697–1780). Commenting on the legend that St Denis, carrying his head in his hands, walked two leagues, she wrote in a letter to Jean Le Rond d'Alembert, 7 July 1763, '*La distance n'y fait rien; il n'y a que le premier pas qui coûte* [The distance is nothing; it is only the first step that is difficult].'

premillennialism (among Christian fundamentalists) the doctrine that the prophesied millennium of blessedness will begin with the imminent Second Coming of Christ.

Premonstratensian a member of an order of regular canons founded at Prémontré in France in 1120, or of the corresponding order of nuns. The Premonstratensians wear white habits and follow a strict form of the Augustinian rule, combining contemplative life with active ministry. The order had several abbeys in Britain before the Reformation and still exists in Europe.

The name comes from medieval Latin *Praemonstratensis*, from *Praemonstratus* (literally 'foreshown'), the Latin name of the abbey of Prémontré, so named because the site was prophetically pointed out by the order's founder, St Norbert, (*c*.1080–1134).

preppy (chiefly in the US), an informal term for a pupil or graduate of an expensive preparatory school or a person resembling such a pupil in dress or appearance.

Presbyterianism a form of Protestant Church government in which the Church is administered locally by the minister with a group of elected elders of equal rank, and regionally and nationally by representative courts of ministers and elders.

Presbyterianism was first introduced in Geneva in 1541 under John Calvin, on the principle that all believers are equal in Christ and in the belief that it best represented the pattern of the early church. There are now many Presbyterian Churches (often called Reformed Churches) worldwide, notably in the Netherlands and Scotland (the Church of Scotland being the only nationally established Presbyterian Church) and in countries with which they have historic links (including the United States and Northern Ireland). They typically subscribe (more or less strictly) to the Calvinist theology set out in the Westminster Confession.

presence see ➤ REAL *presence*.

present see ➤ *no* TIME *like the present*, ➤ SACRAMENT *of the present moment*.

presenteeism the practice of being present at one's place of work for more hours than is required by one's terms of employment. The term is recorded intermittently from the 1930s, but current usage is associated with the anxieties of the 1990s, when increasing job insecurity has appeared to result in some employees working for much longer hours than required by their contractual obligations. The phenomenon of *presenteeism*, in its more extreme forms, is regarded by many as counter-productive, with belief in the need to be observably present at work for as many hours as possible resulting in an overtired and overstrained workforce, but not necessarily in a significant increase in what is achieved.

preservation see ➤ SELF-*preservation is the first law of nature*.

Presidency see ➤ *just a* HEARTBEAT *away from the Presidency*

Presidential Medal of Freedom (in the US) a medal constituting the highest award that can be given to a civilian in peacetime.

Presidents see ➤ MOTHER *of Presidents*.

Presidium the standing executive committee in the former USSR, which functioned as the legislative authority when the Supreme Soviet was not sitting.

Elvis Presley (1935–77), American rock-and-roll and pop singer, who was the dominant personality of early rock and roll with songs such as 'Heartbreak Hotel' and 'Blue Suede Shoes' (both 1956), and who was known particularly for the vigour and frank sexuality of his performances.

Presocratic of, relating to, or denoting the speculative philosophers active in the ancient Greek world in the 6th and 5th centuries BC (before the time of Socrates), who attempted to find rational explanations for natural phenomena. They included Parmenides, Anaxagoras, Empedocles, and Heraclitus; their work survives only in fragments or in references by later writers.

press see also ➤ YELLOW *press*.

Press Council a body established in the UK in 1953 to raise and maintain professional standards among journalists.

press gang in the 18th and 19th centuries, a body of men employed to enlist men forcibly into service in the army or navy.

pressed see ➤ *one* VOLUNTEER *is worth two pressed men*.

prester a mythical serpent, the bite of which caused death by swelling; the word, which is Greek, is also the name for a scorching whirlwind.

Prester John a legendary medieval Christian king of Asia, said to have defeated the Muslims and to be destined to bring help to the Holy Land. The legend spread in Europe in the mid 12th century. He was later identified with a real king of Ethiopia; another theory identifies him with a Chinese prince who defeated the sultan of Persia in 1141.

prestidigitation magic tricks performed as entertainment. The word comes (in the mid 19th century) via French, from *preste* 'nimble' + Latin *digitus* 'finger'.

prestige widespread respect and admiration felt for someone or something on the basis of a perception of their achievements or quality. Originally (in the mid 17th century) the word means 'illusion, conjuring trick' The transference of meaning occurred by way of the sense 'dazzling influence, glamour', at first depreciatory.

Dr Presto punning nickname allegedly given to Jonathan Swift by the Duchess of Shrewsbury.

Preston a city in NW England, the administrative centre of Lancashire, on the River Ribble, which has been a spinning and weaving centre since the 15th century, and was the site in the 18th century of the first English cotton mills.

Battle of Prestonpans a battle in 1745 near the town of Prestonpans just east of Edinburgh, the first major engagement of the Jacobite uprising of 1745–6. The Jacobites routed the Hanoverians, leaving the way clear for Charles Edward Stuart's subsequent invasion of England.

presumptive see ➤ HEIR *presumptive*.

pretence see ➤ ESCUTCHEON *of pretence*.

pretender see ➤ OLD *Pretender*, ➤ YOUNG *Pretender*.

pretext a reason given in justification of a course of action that is not the real reason. The word comes (in the early 16th century) from Latin *praetextus* 'outward display', from the verb *praetexere* 'to disguise'.

prevaricate speak or act in an evasive way. The word comes (in the mid 16th century, in the sense 'go astray, transgress') from Latin *praevaricat-* 'walked crookedly, deviated', from the verb *praevaricari*, from *prae* 'before' + *varicari* 'straddle', from *varus* 'bent, knock-kneed'.

prevention is better than cure proverbial saying, early 17th century.

Previous Examination former name for the first examination for the degree of BA at Cambridge University.

previous question (in parliamentary procedure) a motion to decide whether to vote on a main question, moved before the main question itself is put.

Priam in Greek mythology, the king of Troy at the time of its destruction by the Greeks under ➤ AGAMEMNON. The father of Paris and Hector and husband of ➤ HECUBA, he was killed after the fall of Troy by Neoptolemus, son of Achilles.

Priapus in Greek mythology, a god of fertility, whose cult spread to Greece (and, later, Italy) from Turkey after Alexander's conquests. He was represented as a distorted human figure with enormous genitals. He was also a god of gardens and the patron of seafarers and shepherds.

price see ➤ EVERY *man has his price*, ➤ PEACE *at any price*, ➤ *the price of* ADMIRALTY.

prick¹ (of the sovereign) select (a person) for office, especially that of sheriff, by scoring through or putting a mark against a name on a list.

prick² stick a pin in the skin of (a person suspected of witchcraft) to see if a spot could be discovered which did not bleed. The term is first recorded in the *Daemonologie* of James I.

prick-eared in the 17th century, designating a person with ears made prominent or conspicuous as a result of the hair being short and close-cropped, in a style favoured by Puritan supporters of Parliament in the English Civil War; later, in figurative usage, priggish, puritanical.

> Fred Vincy had called Lydgate a prig, and now Mr Chichely was inclined to call him prick-eared.
> — George Eliot *Middlemarch* (1872)

prick of conscience compunction, remorse, guilt; used as the title of a devotional treatise by the English mystic Richard Rolle of Hampole (*c.*1290–1349).

prick-song music sung from notes written or pricked, as opposed to music sung from memory or by ear; a written descant or accompanying melody to a plainsong or simple theme.

pricking of one's thumbs an intuitive feeling, a foreboding, often with allusion to the words of the Second Witch in Shakespeare's *Macbeth*:

> By the pricking of my thumbs,
> Something wicked this way comes.
> — William Shakespeare *Macbeth* (1606)

It was customary to fold the thumb into the palm of the hand as a precaution against the supernatural; Ovid's *Fasti* refers to a person pointing 'with his closed fingers, and his thumb Put in the midst, lest ghosts should near him come.'

pride In earliest use, a feeling of inordinate pleasure or satisfaction derived from one's own achievements, with resulting contempt for others, unbridled self esteem; in this sense, counted as the first of the ➤ SEVEN *deadly sins.*

See also ➤ PEACOCK *in his pride.*

pride feels no pain proverbial saying, early 17th century; implying that inordinate self-esteem will not allow the admission that one might be suffering.

pride goes before a fall proverbial saying, late 14th century; with biblical allusion to Proverbs 16:18, 'Pride goeth before destruction, and an haughty spirit before a fall'.

a pride of lions a group of lions forming a social unit; the term is recorded in late Middle English, and was revived in the early 20th century.

pride of place in falconry, the high position from which a falcon or similar bird swoops down on its prey; the term is first recorded in Shakespeare's

Macbeth in the description of a reversal of the natural order which has accompanied the killing of Duncan:

> A falcon, tow'ring in her pride of place,
> Was by a mousing owl hawkd'd at and kill'd.
> — William Shakespeare *Macbeth* (1606)

pride of the morning dialect term for mist or drizzle at sunrise, supposedly indicating a fine day to come.

Pride's Purge the exclusion or arrest of about 140 members of parliament likely to vote against a trial of the captive Charles I by soldiers under the command of Colonel Thomas *Pride* (d.1658) in December 1648. Following the purge, the remaining members, known as the ➤ RUMP *Parliament*, voted for the trial which resulted in Charles's execution.

prie-dieu a piece of furniture for use during prayer, consisting of a kneeling surface and a narrow upright front with a rest for the elbows or for books. Recorded from the mid 18th century, the phrase is French and means literally 'pray God'.

priest see also ➤ *like* PEOPLE, *like priest,* ➤ ONCE *a priest, always a priest.*

priest's hole a hiding place for a Roman Catholic priest during times of religious persecution; these secret cupboards and passages, constructed especially in the Elizabethan period in the houses of Catholic gentry, were intended to provide refuge if necessary for days and even weeks. Some of the most ingenious were constructed by the Jesuit Nicholas Owen (d. 1606, while undergoing questioning in the Tower), who may well have been a builder by trade.

priestess a female priest of a non-Christian religion; the term is currrently sometimes used by those most strongly opposed to the ordination of women to reflect the view that it is impossible for a woman to be a priest.

Joseph Priestley (1733–1804), English scientist and theologian. Priestley was the author of about 150 books, mostly theological or educational. His chief work was on the chemistry of gases, in which his most significant discovery was of 'dephlogisticated air' (oxygen) in 1774; he demonstrated that it was important to animal life, and that plants give off this gas in sunlight.

prig a self-righteously moralistic person who behaves as if they are superior to others. Recorded from the 16th century, the origin of the word is unknown. The earliest sense was 'tinker' or 'petty thief', whence 'disliked person', especially 'someone who is affectedly and self-consciously precise' (late 17th century).

prima donna the chief female singer in an opera or opera company; in extended use, a very temperamental person with an inflated view of their own talent or importance.

> I also wanted him to see me as a nice person, someone far too magnanimous to pull a prima donna number, however justified, on some dizzy film student.
> — Armistead Maupin *Maybe the Moon* (1992)

primal scene (in Freudian theory) the occasion on which a child becomes aware of its parents' sexual intercourse, the timing of which is thought to be crucial in determining predisposition to future neuroses.

primal scream a release of intense basic frustration, anger, and aggression, especially that rediscovered by means of primal therapy.

primal therapy a form of psychotherapy which focuses on a patient's earliest emotional experiences and encourages verbal expression of childhood suffering, typically using an empty chair or other prop to represent a parent towards whom anger is directed.

primary colour any of a group of colours from which all other colours can be obtained by mixing. The primary colours for pigments are red, blue, and yellow. The primary additive colours for light are red, green, and blue; the primary subtractive colours (which give the primary additive colours when subtracted from white light) are magenta, cyan, and yellow.

primate in the Christian Church, the chief bishop or archbishop of a province. In England both the archbishops are primates, the Archbishop of Canterbury being entitled **Primate of All England** and the Archbishop of York **Primate of England**. In Ireland, both the Roman Catholic and the Anglican Archbishops of Armagh are styled **Primate of All Ireland**. Before the Reformation, the Archbishop of St Andrews was (from 1487) **Primate of Scotland**. In France there were formerly three primates, the archbishops of Lyons, Bourges, and Rouen.

prime[1] in the Christian Church, a service forming part of the Divine Office of the Western Church, traditionally said (or chanted) at the first hour of the day (i.e. 6 a.m.), but now little used. In monastic

rules such as the *Regula Magistri* and the Rule of St Benedict (both dating from the 6th century), *prima* is the first of the Little Hours (the others are *tierce*, *sext*, and *none*). It is believed to have been introduced by Cassian at his monastery in Bethlehem in the late 4th century. *Prime* is not included in the reordered breviary of the Divine Office issued by Pope Paul VI in 1971.

Recorded in Old English (in the form *prīm*), the word comes from Latin *prima (hora)* 'first (hour)'.

prime[2] a state or time of greatest strength, vigour, or success in a person's life. This derives from the use of *prime* to mean the first season of the year (when this began at the vernal equinox); spring; from this developed the phrase *the prime of youth*, the time of early adulthood as the springtime of a person's life.

prime minister the head of an elected government; the principal minister of a sovereign or state. In Britain Robert Walpole is regarded as having been the first Prime Minister in the modern sense. By the middle of the 19th century the term had become common in informal use, and in 1905 it was formally recognized. In current use, the terms *Premier* and *Prime Minister* refer to the same office in Britain, but in Canada and Australia the government of a province or state is headed by a Premier, that of the federal government by a Prime Minister. In countries such as France, where the President has an executive function, the Prime Minister is in a subordinate position.

See also ► UNKNOWN *Prime Minister*.

prime number a number that is divisible only by itself and unity (e.g. 2, 3, 5, 7, 11). Formerly also, the ► GOLDEN *number*.

prime-sign mark (a person) with the sign of the cross before baptism; make (a person) a catechumen (from ecclesiastical Latin *prima signatio* literally 'the first signing'.

primed prepared for a situation or task, typically by having been supplied with relevant information; the allusion is to a firearm or explosive device having been made ready for firing or detonation.

primer in the late Middle Ages and the 16th century, a prayer book or devotional manual for the use of educated lay people. Also, a book of hours. In current use, an elementary textbook that serves as an introduction to a subject of study or is used for teaching children to read.

Recorded from late Middle English, the word

comes from medieval Latin *primarius (liber)* 'primary (book)' and *primarium (manuale)* 'primary (manual)'.

primero a gambling card game, an ancestor of poker, which was very popular in England in the 16th and early 17th centuries. The game is played with a forty-card pack, and players bet on the combinations of the cards they are dealt.

primicere the first candle-bearer or chief office-holder before a bishop. The name comes from late Latin *primicerius*, literally, the first of those whose names are inscribed on the wax-coated tablets; in medieval Latin, a precentor.

primipilus in ancient Rome, the chief centurion of the first maniple of the third rank in a legion; the Latin word comes from *primi pili centurio* 'centurion of the first body of pikemen'.

Primitive Baptist in the US, a member of an association of conservative Baptists, formed by secession from the Baptist Church.

Primitive Church the Christian Church in its earliest times.

Primitive Methodist a member of a society of Methodists which was formed in 1811 and joined the united Methodist Church in 1932.

Miguel Primo de Rivera (1870–1930) Spanish general and statesman, head of state 1923–30. He assumed dictatorial powers after leading a military coup. His son, **José Antonio Primo de Rivera** (1903–36), founded the ➤ FALANGE in 1933 and was executed by Republicans in the Spanish Civil War.

right of primogeniture the right of succession belonging to the firstborn child, especially the feudal rule by which the whole real estate of an intestate passed to the eldest son. The word comes (in the early 17th century) from medieval Latin *primogenitura*, from Latin *primo* 'first' + *genitura* 'geniture'.

primordial soup a solution rich in organic compounds in the primitive oceans of the earth, from which life is thought to have originated. Also called *primeval soup*.

primrose in early figurative use, this yellow springtime flower is taken as the type of the first and best.

The name is recorded from late Middle English, and means literally 'first rose'.

Primrose Day the anniversary of the death of Benjamin Disraeli (19 April 1881), whose favourite flower was reputedly the primrose.

Primrose League a political association, formed in memory of Benjamin Disraeli in 1883, to promote and sustain the principles of Conservatism as represented by him.

primrose path the pursuit of pleasure, especially when it is seen to bring disastrous consequences. The original allusion is to the reference in Shakespeare's *Hamlet* to 'the primrose path of dalliance'.

primum mobile (in the medieval version of the Ptolemaic system) an outer sphere supposed to move round the earth in 24 hours carrying the inner spheres with it. The name comes from medieval Latin, meaning literally 'first moving thing'.

primus the presiding bishop of the Scottish Episcopal Church, elected by the bishops from among their number.

prince the son of a monarch; a close male relative of a monarch, especially a son's son; a male royal ruler of a small state, actually, nominally, or originally subject to a king or emperor. The word comes (in Middle English) via Old French from Latin *princeps, princip-* 'first, chief, sovereign', from *primus* 'first' + *capere* 'take'.

See also ➤ BLACK *Prince*, ➤ BONNIE *Prince Charlie*, ➤ CROWN *prince*, ➤ *Prince* RUPERT, ➤ *Prince* TITI, ➤ PUNCTUALITY *is the politeness of princes*, ➤ RED *Prince*.

Prince Charming a fairy-tale hero who first appears as in French *Roi Charmant*, hero of the Comtesse d'Aulnoy's *L'Oiseau Bleu* (1697), and in English as *King Charming* or *Prince Charming* by James Robinson Planché (1796–1880). The name was later adopted for the hero of various fairy-tale pantomimes, especially the *Sleeping Beauty* and *Cinderella*.

Prince Imperial title of the heir apparent (1854–79) of ➤ NAPOLEON *III*. Exiled with his parents after his father's abdication, in 1879 he joined the British expedition to Zululand, where he was killed.

Prince of Darkness a name for the Devil, recorded from the early 17th century; in recent usage, it has been taken as a humorous appellation for the Labour politician Peter Mandelson (1953–), in tribute to his perceived mastery of the 'black art' of spin-doctoring.

> The man known variously as the Prince of Darkness, Sultan of Spin or plain Minister Sinister.
> — *Independent* 7 August 1998

prince of demons in the New Testament, a designation of ➤ BEELZEBUB.

Prince of Peace a title given to Jesus Christ, in allusion to the prophecy in Isaiah 9:6, 'his name shall be called Wonderful, Counsellor, The mighty God, The everlasting Father, The Prince of Peace.'

Prince of Piedmont title of the heir to the throne of Italy.

Prince of the Apostles a name for St Peter.

Prince of the Asturias title of the heir to the throne of Spain.

Prince of the (Holy Roman) Church a title given to a Cardinal.

Prince of Wales a title traditionally granted to the heir apparent to the British throne (usually the eldest son of the sovereign) since Edward I of England gave the title to his son in 1301 after the conquest of Wales.

Prince of Wales' feathers a plume of three ostrich feathers, first adopted as a crest by the eldest son of Edward III, Edward Plantagenet (1330–76), the ➤ BLACK *Prince*.

Prince Regent a prince who acts as regent, in particular the title of the future George IV, who was regent from 1811 until he became king in 1820.

Prince's metal an alloy, resembling brass, of about three parts copper and one zinc, used especially for cheap jewellery, named after ➤ *Prince* RUPERT.

Princely States in the Indian subcontinent, any of those States that were ruled by an Indian prince before the Indian Independence Act of 1947.

Princes in the Tower the young sons of Edward IV, namely Edward, Prince of Wales (b.1470) and Richard, Duke of York (b.1472), supposedly murdered in the Tower of London in or shortly after 1483 (in that year Edward reigned briefly as Edward V on the death of his father but was not crowned). They were taken to the Tower of London by their uncle (the future Richard III) and are generally assumed to have been murdered, but whether at the instigation of Richard III (as Tudor propagandists claimed) or of another is not known; two skeletons

discovered in 1674 are thought to have been those of the princes.

princess see also ➤ the PEOPLE*'s Princess.*

Princess Royal the eldest daughter of a reigning monarch (especially as a title conferred by the British monarch).

princesse lointaine an ideal but unattainable woman. The expression is French, literally 'distant princess', and comes from the title of a play by ➤ *Edmond* ROSTAND (1868–1918), based on a theme of the poetry of the 12th-century troubadour Jaufré Rudel.

> She lay there, the unachievable *princesse lointaine.*
> — Margaret Drabble *Waterfall* (1969)

principal boy the leading male role in a pantomime, especially when played by a woman; the phrase is recorded from the late 19th century.

principalities (in traditional Christian angelology) the fifth-highest order of the ninefold celestial hierarchy.

the Principality a name for Wales.

principle see ➤ MACBRIDE *principles,* ➤ MATTHEW *principle,* ➤ MITCHELL *principles,* ➤ NIRVANA *principle,* ➤ PETER *Principle,* ➤ PLEASURE *principle,* ➤ SULLIVAN *principles,* ➤ VALDEZ *Principles.*

print see ➤ SMALL *print.*

printer's devil an errand-boy or junior assistant in a printing office; a *devil* is a person employed in a subordinate position to work under the direction of or for a particular person.

printer's mark a monogram or other device serving as a printer's trademark.

printers ➤ *St* AUGUSTINE and ➤ *St* JOHN *of God* are the patron saints of printers.

Printers' Bible an early 18th century edition with the misreading 'Printers have persecuted me without a cause' in Psalm 119, 'printers' being substituted for 'princes'.

Printing House Square a small square in London, the former site of the *Times* newspaper office.

> Is, indeed, anyone, anywhere, truly worthy of The Times? This was the awfully solemn thought which . . . sometimes oppressed Printing House Square.
> — Claud Cockburn *In Time of Trouble* (1956)

prion a protein particle that is believed to be the cause of brain diseases such as BSE, scrapie, and CJD. Prions are not visible microscopically, contain no nucleic acid, and are highly resistant to destruction.

prior the male head of a house or group of houses of certain religious orders, in particular, the man next in rank below an abbot, the head of a house of friars. Recorded from late Old English, the word comes from a medieval Latin noun use of Latin *prior* 'elder, former'.

priory see ➤ ALIEN *priory.*

St Prisca a Roman lady of the early centuries, traditionally venerated as a martyr; she is sometimes shown with two lions, who according to her Acts refused to attack her.

☐ **FEAST DAY** Her feast day is 18 January.

Priscian (6th century AD), Byzantine grammarian. His *Grammatical Institutions* became one of the standard Latin grammatical works in the Middle Ages.

break Priscian's head violate the rules of grammar; the expression is recorded from the early 16th century, in John Skelton's *Speke Parrot* (*c.*1525).

Priscillianist a disciple of Priscillian, bishop of Avila in the 4th century, who taught doctrines alleged to be Gnostic or Manichaean.

prisms see ➤ PRUNES *and prisms.*

prisoner a person who is a captive; ➤ *St* DISMAS, ➤ *St* LEONARD, and ➤ *St* ROCH are the patron saints of prisoners.

See also ➤ *prisoner of* CONSCIENCE.

Prisoner of Chillon the anti-Savoyard Genevan patriot François Bonivard (1493–1570), who was imprisoned for 6 years in the castle of Chillon; he was the subject of a poem by Byron, *The Prisoner of Chillon*, published in 1816.

Prisoner of the Vatican a name for the Pope between 1870 (when Pius IX withdrew into the Vatican on the occupation of Rome) and the Lateran Treaty of 1929.

prisoner's dilemma (in game theory) a situation in which two players each have two options whose outcome depends crucially on the simultaneous choice made by the other, often formulated in terms of two prisoners separately deciding whether to confess to a crime.

prisoner's friend in the armed services, an officer who represents a defendant at a court martial; the term is recorded from the early 20th century.

private see ➤ PUBLIC *key.*

private bill a legislative bill affecting the interests only of a particular body or individual.

Private Eye title of a British satirical magazine, founded in 1962; some of its ironical euphemisms, such as *Ugandan affairs* and *tired and emotional*, have passed into the language.

private eye a private detective. The term is first recorded in a story (1938) by Raymond Chandler, 'We don't use any private eyes in here.' It has been suggested that the origin of the expression was the American detective agency founded by Allan Pinkerton; their motto (*c.*1855) was 'We never sleep', and the agency was informally known as 'The Eye'.

private member's bill (in the UK, Canada, Australia, and New Zealand) a legislative bill that is introduced by a private Member of Parliament and is not part of a government's planned legislation. In the British House of Commons, members ballot for the right to present such bills, which however rarely become law; a notable exception was the bill for the abolition of the death penalty, sponsored in 1964 by the Labour politician Sydney Silverman (1895–1968).

privateer between the 17th and 19th centuries, an armed ship owned and officered by private individuals holding a government commission and authorized for use in war, especially in the capture of merchant shipping. The word is recorded from the mid 17th century, and is formed from *private*, on the pattern of *volunteer*.

privilege (especially in a parliamentary context) the right to say or write something without the risk of incurring punishment or legal action for defamation.

See also ➤ PAULINE *privilege.*

privileged communication a communication which a witness cannot be legally compelled to divulge; a communication made between such people and in such circumstances that it is not actionable.

priviligentsia a class of intellectuals and party bureaucrats in Communist states seen as enjoying certain social and economic privileges over ordinary citizens. The term is recorded chiefly between the 1960s and the 1980s.

Privy Council a body of advisers appointed by a sovereign or a Governor General (now chiefly on an honorary basis and including present and former government ministers).

In Britain, the Privy Council originated in the council of the Norman kings. A select body of officials met regularly with the sovereign to carry on everyday government, known from the 14th century as the Privy (= 'private') Council. In the 18th century the importance of the cabinet, a smaller group drawn from the Privy Council, increased and the full Privy Council's functions became chiefly formal.

privy seal in the UK, a seal affixed to documents that are afterwards to pass the Great Seal or that do not require it. Recorded from Middle English, the name means 'private seal'.

Prix de Rome a prize awarded annually by the French government in a competition for artists, sculptors, architects, and musicians; it was founded by Louis XIV in 1666 for painters and sculptors, and extended in 1720 to include architects, and in 1803 musicians and engravers. The name, literally 'prize of Rome', was given because the winner of the first prize in each category is funded for a period of study in Rome.

Prix Goncourt an award given annually for a work of French literature, named after the ➤ *de* GON-COURT brothers.

prize see also ➤ BOOKER *Prize*, ➤ NOBEL *Prize*, ➤ PULITZER *Prize*.

prize court a naval court that adjudicated on the distribution of ships and property captured in the course of naval warfare.

prize money money realized by the sale of a prize, especially a ship or ship's cargo taken in war, and distributed among the captors.

prize ring a ring or enclosed space (now a square area enclosed by poles and ropes) for prizefighting; in extended usage, boxing.

pro bono publico Latin, meaning for the public good; recorded in English from the late 17th century.

Pro bono publico has traditionally been used as a signature to an open letter to a newspaper, where the writer wishes to signal support for the public interest:

> She was inclined to think, that an 'Ode to an early Rosebud,' in the corner devoted to original poetry, and a letter in the correspondence department, signed 'Pro Bono Publico,' were her husband's writing.
> — Elizabeth Gaskell *Christmas Storms & Sunshine* (1848)

In North America, the phrase (usually in form *pro bono*) denotes work undertaken for the public good without charge, especially legal work for a client on a low income.

problem see ➤ DELIAN *problem*, ➤ *if you're not part of the* SOLUTION, *you're part of the problem.*

proclaim from the housetops announce loudly, originally with biblical allusion, from Luke 12:3 'that which ye have spoken in the ear in closets shall be proclaimed upon the housetops'.

proclamation see also ➤ EMANCIPATION *Proclamation.*

proclamation money in 18th-century America, coin valued according to a royal proclamation of 1704, according to which the Spanish dollar of 17½ pennyweight was to be rated at six shillings in all the colonies.

Procne in Greek mythology, the sister of ➤ PHILOMEL and wife of Tereus; when her sister was raped by Tereus, Procne in vengeance murdered her son Itys and served his flesh to her husband.

proconsul a governor of a province in ancient Rome, having much of the authority of a consul.

In 1933, the name *Proconsul* was given to a fossil hominoid primate found in Lower Miocene deposits in East Africa, one of the last common ancestors of both humans and the great apes.

Procopius (*c.*500–*c.*562), Byzantine historian, born in Caesarea in Palestine. He accompanied Justinian's general Belisarius on his campaigns between 527 and 540. His principal works are the *History of the Wars of Justinian* and *On Justinian's Buildings*. The authenticity of his attack on Justinian, the *Secret History,* has often been doubted but is now generally accepted.

procrastination is the thief of time proverbial saying, mid 18th century; from *Night Thoughts* (1742–5) by the English poet and dramatist Edward Young (1683–1765).

Procris in Greek mythology, the wife of ► CEPHALUS with whom ► Eos (the dawn) fell in love. Hiding in a thicket to keep watch on her husband, the jealous Procris was mistaken by him for an animal and killed by a thrown spear. In the mechanicals' play in Shakespeare's *Midsummer Night's Dream*, 'Shafalus' and 'Procrus' refer to Cephalus and Procris.

Procrustes in Greek mythology, a robber who forced travellers to lie on a bed and made them fit it by stretching their limbs or cutting off the appropriate length of leg; ► THESEUS eventually killed him with his own device.

> Patients with severe habitual migraine seemed to me so various . . . that I despaired of putting them in a single category, unless I played Procrustes.
> — Oliver Sacks *Migraine* (1970)

proctor an officer (usually one of two) at certain universities, appointed annually and having mainly disciplinary functions; the word is a late Middle English contraction of *procurator*.

See also ► KING's *Proctor*, ► QUEEN's *Proctor*.

Proctor order a system of classification by geographical origin and chronology for early printed books, first used in the *Index to the Early Printed Books in the British Museum* (1898–1938), begun by the English bibliographer Robert George Collier *Proctor* (1863–1903).

procurator an agent representing others in a court of law in countries retaining Roman civil law; (in Scotland) a lawyer practising before the lower courts. The word is recorded from Middle English (denoting a steward), and comes ultimately from Latin, meaning 'administrator, finance agent'.

procurator fiscal (in Scotland) a local coroner and public prosecutor.

Procyon the eighth-brightest star in the sky, and the brightest in the constellation Canis Minor. In Greek, the name means 'before the dog', because it rises before Sirius, the Dog Star.

prodigal a person (also **prodigal son** or **prodigal daughter**) who leaves home and behaves extravagantly and wastefully, but later makes a repentant return. The allusion is to the parable in Luke 15: 11–32, in which the younger son of a wealthy man wastes his substance abroad until he is reduced to sharing 'the husks that the swine do eat'. Returning, repentant, to his home, he finds that while his elder brother grudges the welcome offered, his father rejoices and ► *kills the* FATTED *calf* to make a celebratory feast.

> Most Samaritans would draw the line at the sort of boondoggle enjoyed by the prodigal son. You run off and waste your substance on riotous living with a fast crowd in Galilee, you shouldn't expect to come home and get a feast and a ring and a big hug.
> — Garrison Keillor *We Are Still Married* (1989)

prodigy a person, especially a young one, endowed with exceptional qualities or abilities. The term is recorded from the late 15th century, denoting something extraordinary considered to be an omen, and comes from Latin *prodigium* 'portent'.

Producer Choice a policy of the BBC, instituted under John Birt (Director-General 1992–2000) in 1993, giving programme makers control over their budget, allowing them to purchases services from other departments, or from outside the Corporation; the introduction of the system, based on the principles of the marketplace, was and remains controversial.

profane not relating or devoted to that which is sacred or biblical; secular rather than religious. Originally (in late Middle English) the word meant 'heathen', via Old French from Latin *profanus* 'outside the temple, not sacred'.

profile an outline of something, especially a person's face, as seen from one side. The word comes (in the 17th century) via Italian from Latin *filum* 'thread'.

profiling the recording and analysis of a person's psychological and behavioural characteristics, so as to assess or predict their capabilities in a certain sphere or to assist in identifying a particular subgroup of people.

In the 1980s and 1990s, profiling became a staple of forensic investigation, with the technique of **DNA profiling**, or *genetic fingerprinting*, frequently employed to establish the unique physical characteristics of an individual. More controversially, *psychological profiling* has been used to build up an outline of the likely offender. It was initially welcomed with public enthusiasm (the technique formed a key theme in the hit television thriller series *Cracker*), but criticism in the course of at least one highly publicized murder trial has led to the process being viewed more cautiously.

John Profumo (1915–), British Conservative politician. In 1960 he was appointed Secretary of State for War under Harold Macmillan. Three years later news broke of his relationship with the mistress of a Soviet diplomat, Christine Keeler, raising fears of a security breach and precipitating his resignation, after it became apparent that his formal denial of the relationship to the House of Commons could not stand. The **Profumo affair** was seen as deeply damaging to the Conservative government.

profundis see ➤ DE *profundis*.

programme music music that is intended to evoke images or convey the impression of a definite series of objects, scenes, or events.

Progressive Conservative Party a Canadian political party advocating free trade and holding moderate views on social policies. Founded in the mid 19th century but operating under its present name since 1942, the party was in power 1984–93 under Brian Mulroney.

prohibited see ➤ *prohibited* DEGREES.

Prohibition the prevention by law of the manufacture and sale of alcohol, especially in the US between 1920 and 1933. In the US, it was forbidden by the 18th Amendment to the Constitution, but led to widespread bootlegging of illicit liquor by organized gangs, and was repealed by the 21st Amendment.

Prohibition Party a political party in the US, formed in 1869 to nominate or support advocates of the prohibition of alcohol.

projection in alchemy, the throwing of an ingredient into a crucible; especially, the casting of the powder of philosopher's stone on a molten metal to effect its transmutation into gold or silver; the transmutation of metals.
See also ➤ MERCATOR *projection*, ➤ PETERS *projection*, ➤ POWDER *of projection*.

prolegomenon a critical or discursive introduction to a book. The word is recorded from the mid 17th century and comes via Latin from Greek, ultimately from *prolegein* 'say beforehand'.

proletarian revolution (in Marxist theory) the predicted stage of political development when the proletarians overthrow capitalism.

proletariat the lowest class of citizens in ancient Rome; workers or working-class people, regarded collectively (often used with reference to Marxism).
See also ➤ DICTATORSHIP *of the proletariat*.

promenade concert a concert of classical music at which a part of the audience stands in an area without seating, for which tickets are sold at a reduced price. The most famous series of such concerts is the annual BBC Promenade Concerts (known as **the Proms**), instituted by Sir Henry Wood in 1895 and held since the Second World War chiefly in the Albert Hall in London.

Promethean in the 19th century, a match made from a flammable mixture of sugar and potassium chlorate wrapped in a paper roll around a small glass bulb of sulphuric acid, and igniting when the bulb is fractured (superseded by the friction match).

Promethean fire in Greek mythology, stolen from the Gods by ➤ PROMETHEUS; in extended usage, inspiration.

> I must confess, they seemed to me to lack something of the Promethean fire.
> — J. T. James diary, 1816

Prometheus a demigod, one of the Titans, who was worshipped by craftsmen; he is said in one legend to have made humankind out of clay. When Zeus hid fire away from man Prometheus stole it by trickery and returned it to earth. As punishment Zeus chained him to a rock where an eagle fed each day on his liver, which (since he was immortal) grew again each night; he was eventually rescued by Hercules.

> A careless mortal . . . who, Prometheus-like, will scale heaven.
> — Thomas Carlyle *Miscellaneous Essays* (1847)

promise see also ➤ BREACH *of promise*.

bow of promise a rainbow; in allusion to God's promise, in Genesis 9:13, 'I do set my bow in the cloud, and it shall be for a token of a covenant between me and the earth,' that there would not be a second Flood.

the Promised Land in the Bible, the land of Canaan, as promised by God to Abraham and his descendants in Genesis 12:7, 'Unto thy seed will I give this land.' In extended usage, *the Promised Land* is often used with the implication that it remains just out of reach.

> You never reach the promised land. You can march towards it.
> — James Callaghan in a television interview, 20 July 1978

promises, like pie-crust, are made to be broken proverbial saying, late 17th century.

pronaos in classical antiquity, the space in front of the body of a temple, enclosed by a portico and projecting side-walls. Also, a narthex.

proof a trial impression of a page, taken from type or film and used for making corrections before final printing.

See also ➤ BURDEN *of proof.*

the proof of the pudding is in the eating proverbial saying, early 14th century.

proof spirit a mixture of alcohol and water containing (in the UK) 57.1 per cent alcohol by volume or (in the US) 50 per cent alcohol by volume, used as a standard of strength of distilled alcoholic liquor.

prop a portable object other than furniture or costumes used on the set of a play or film. The word, which dates from the mid 19th century, is an abbreviation of *property.*

propaganda originally (as *Propaganda*) a committee of cardinals of the Roman Catholic Church responsible for foreign missions, founded in 1622 by Pope Gregory XV. The word is Italian and comes from modern Latin *congregatio de propaganda fide* 'congregation for propagation of the faith'.

In the early 20th century what is now the main current sense developed: information, especially of a biased or misleading nature, used to promote or publicize a particular political cause or point of view. An early definition was suggested by Francis M. Cornford in *Microcosmographia Academica* (1922 ed.), 'That branch of the art of lying which consists in very nearly deceiving your friends without quite deceiving your enemies.'

propeller-head a person who has an obsessive interest in computers or technology, probably with reference to a beanie hat with a propeller on top, popularized by science-fiction enthusiasts.

> Three or four years ago, those of us using the Internet were nerds and propeller-heads.
> — *Computer Weekly* 10 February 1994

Proper Bostonian another name for a ➤ BOSTON Brahmin.

proper lesson a bible passage appointed for a particular day, occasion, or season.

proper psalm a psalm appointed for a particular day, occasion, or season.

Sextus Propertius (*c.*50–*c.*16 BC), Roman poet. His four books of elegies are largely concerned with

his love affair with a woman whom he called Cynthia, though the later poems also deal with mythological and historical themes.

prophet a person regarded as an inspired teacher or proclaimer of the will of God; among Muslims, **the Prophet** means Muhammad, and among Mormons, Joseph Smith or one of his successors. The word comes (in Middle English) via Old French and Latin from Greek *prophētēs* 'spokesman'.

in Christian use, **the Prophets** designates the books of Isaiah, Jeremiah, Ezekiel, Daniel, and the twelve minor prophets; in Jewish use, **the Prophets** is one of the three canonical divisions of the Hebrew Bible, distinguished from the Law and the Hagiographa, and comprising the books of Joshua, Judges, Samuel, Kings, Jeremiah, Ezekiel, Isaiah, and the twelve minor prophets.

See also ➤ EVANGELICAL *Prophet,* ➤ *is* SAUL *also among the prophets,* ➤ MAJOR *Prophet,* ➤ MINOR *Prophet,* ➤ ZWICKAU *prophets.*

a prophet is not without honour save in his own country proverbial saying, late 15th century, meaning that a person's gifts and talents are rarely appreciated by those close to him; in Matthew 13:57, the words are attributed to Jesus.

Prophet's flower a plant of the borage family, native to the regions west of the Upper Indus, which has a yellow corolla bearing evanescent purple spots, believed to be the marks of Muhammad's fingers.

Former Prophets in Judaism, the books of Joshua, Judges, 1 & 2 Samuel, and 1 & 2 Kings, which with the Latter Prophets make up one of the three canonical divisions of the Hebrew Scriptures.

Latter Prophets in Judaism, the books of Isaiah, Ezekiel, Jeremiah, and the twelve shorter prophetic books from Hosea to Malachi, which with the Former Prophets make up one of the three canonical divisions of the Hebrew Scriptures.

the Law and the Prophets the Old Testament Scriptures or their content (especially as referred to in the New Testament).

Propylaeum the entrance to the Acropolis at Athens.

proscenium the part of a theatre stage in front of the curtain; the stage of an ancient theatre.

proscribe originally: condemn to death or banishment, outlaw; later, forbid, especially by law. The word comes from Latin *proscribere* 'write before the world, publish by writing', and refers to the public notification of a person's sentence.

prose written or spoken language in its ordinary form, without metrical structure; the word comes (in Middle English via Old French) from Latin *prosa (oratio)* 'straightforward (discourse)'.

A notable definition of the difference between prose and poetry is attributed to Jeremy Bentham (1748–1832), 'Prose is when all the lines except the last go on to the end. Poetry is when some of them fall short of it.' Earlier, in Molière's *Le Bourgeois Gentilhomme* (1671), M. Jourdain made the discovery, 'For more than forty years I have been speaking prose without knowing it.'

prosecution see ➤ CROWN *Prosecution Service*.

proselyte a person who has converted from one opinion, religion, or party to another, especially recently. Recorded from late Middle English, the word comes via late Latin from Greek *prosēluthos* 'stranger'.

Proserpina in Roman mythology, the Roman name for ➤ PERSEPHONE.

prosit an expression used in drinking a person's health. The word comes via German from Latin, and means literally 'may it benefit'.

prospective glass in the 16th and 17th centuries, a magic glass or crystal, supposedly used to foretell the future.

prosper see ➤ CHEATS *never prosper*.

prosperity see ➤ *Prosperity* ROBINSON.

Prospero in Shakespeare's *The Tempest*, the exiled Duke of Milan who exercises magical powers over the island on which he lives, and over ➤ ARIEL and ➤ CALIBAN who are constrained to serve him. At the end of the play, preparing to return to Milan, he promises to break his staff and drown his book: symbols of his magical prowess.

prostitute ➤ St MARY *Magdalen*, St Margaret of Cortona, 13th-century penitent and reformed prostitute, and ➤ St MARY *of Egypt* are the patron saints of repentant prostitutes.

protagonist the leading character or one of the major characters in a drama, film, novel, or other fictional text, originally used in connection with ancient Greek drama, as in 'the main character in a play'. In the early 20th century a new sense arose

meaning 'a supporter of a cause'; this new sense probably arose by analogy with *antagonist*, the *pro*- being interpreted as meaning 'in favour of'. In fact, the *prot*- in *protagonist* derives from the Greek root meaning 'first'. For this reason some traditionalists regard the newer use as incorrect, although it is now widely accepted in standard English.

protectionism the theory or practice of shielding a country's domestic industries from foreign competition by taxing imports.

Protector a regent in charge of a kingdom during the minority, absence, or incapacity of the sovereign. The term in this sense is recorded from late Middle English, at the time of the minority of Henry VI (1421–71), and was later used by Richard of Gloucester (before assuming the throne as ➤ RICHARD *III*) and ➤ *Oliver* CROMWELL.

See also ➤ LORD *Protector of the Commonwealth*.

Protestant a member or follower of any of the Western Christian Churches that are separate from the Roman Catholic Church in accordance with the principles of the Reformation, including the Baptist, Presbyterian, and Lutheran Churches.

Protestants are so called after the declaration (*protestatio*) of Martin Luther and his supporters dissenting from the decision of the Diet of Spires (1529), which reaffirmed the edict of the Diet of Worms against the Reformation. All Protestants reject the authority of the papacy, both religious and political, and find authority in the text of the Bible, made available to all in vernacular translation.

See also ➤ *Protestant* FLAIL.

Protestant Ascendancy the domination by the Anglo-Irish Protestant minority in Ireland, especially in the 18th and 19th centuries. The phrase is first recorded in a letter of 1792 by ➤ *Edmund* BURKE, referring to the Lord Mayor of Dublin and the Speaker of the Irish parliament who 'recommend the preservation of the Protestant ascendancy'.

Protestant ethic the view that a person's duty and responsibility is to achieve success through hard work and thrift. The term renders German *die protestantische Ethik*, coined (1904) by the economist Max Weber in his thesis on the relationship between the teachings of Calvin and the rise of capitalism.

Proteus in Greek mythology, a minor sea god, son of Oceanus and Tethys, who had the power of prophecy but who would assume different shapes to avoid answering questions; his name can be applied allusively to a changing, varying, or inconstant person or thing.

In 1989, the name *Proteus* was given to a satellite of Neptune, the sixth closest to the planet, discovered by the Voyager 2 space probe.

> I give the benefit of the doubt to this modern Proteus, and suggest that he is an astute hypocrite.
> — *Broadcast* December 1976

Protevangelium the name given to an apocryphal gospel, attributed to St James the Less. In later use, *Protevangelium* is applied to the promise concerning the seed of the woman implied in the curse upon the serpent (Genesis 3:15, 'it shall bruise thy head, and thou shalt bruise his heel'), regarded as the earliest intimation of the gospel.

prothalamium a song or poem celebrating a forthcoming wedding, from *Prothalamion* (1596), title of a poem by Edmund Spenser, on the pattern of *epithalamium*.

protocol the official procedure or system of rules governing affairs of state or diplomatic occasions. The word is recorded from late Middle English, denoting the original minute of an agreement, forming the legal authority for future dealings relating to it; it comes via Old French and medieval Latin from Greek *prōtokollon* 'first page, flyleaf'.

The current sense also derives directly from French *protocole*, the collection of set forms of etiquette to be observed by the French head of state, and the name of the government department responsible for this (in the 19th century).

Protocols of the Learned Elders of Zion a fraudulent, anti-Semitic document printed in Russia in 1903 and purporting to be a report of a series of meetings held in 1897 to plan the overthrow of Christian civilization by Jews and Freemasons.

protomartyr the first martyr for a cause, especially the first Christian martyr, St Stephen.

the Proud epithet of various rulers, including Tarquin II of Rome (*Tarquinus Superbus*).

the proud duke nickname of Charles Seymour, 6th Duke of Somerset (1662–1748), cited by Horace Walpole as the type of aristocratic arrogance and parental despotism.

Joseph Louis Proust (1754–1826), French analytical chemist. He proposed the law of constant proportions, demonstrating that any pure sample of a chemical compound (such as an oxide of a metal) always contains the same elements in fixed proportions.

Marcel Proust (1871–1922), French novelist, essayist, and critic. He devoted much of his life to writing his novel *À la recherche du temps perdu* (published in seven sections between 1913 and 1927). Its central theme is the recovery of the lost past and the releasing of its creative energies through the stimulation of unconscious memory, as the narrator recalls in *Du côté de chez Swann* (Swann's Way, 1913), 'And suddenly the memory revealed itself. The taste was that of the little piece of madeleine which on Sunday mornings at Combray…my aunt Léonie used to give me, dipping it first in her own cup of tea or tisane.'

William Prout (1785–1850), English chemist and biochemist. He developed the hypothesis that hydrogen is the primary substance from which all other elements are formed, which although incorrect stimulated research in atomic theory.

Provençal a Romance language closely related to French, Italian, and Catalan; it is sometimes called *langue d'oc* (or *Occitan*), though strictly speaking it is one dialect of this. In the 12th–14th centuries it was the language of the troubadours and cultured speakers of southern France, but the spread of the northern dialects of French led to its decline.

not proven in Scots law, a verdict that there is insufficient evidence to establish guilt or innocence.

Provence a former province of SE France, on the Mediterranean coast east of the Rhône. Settled by the Greeks in the 6th century BC, the area around Marseilles became, in the 1st century BC, part of the Roman colony of Gaul. It was united with France under Louis XI in 1481.

proverb a short pithy saying in general use; a concise sentence, often metaphorical or alliterative in form, stating a general truth or piece of advice.

Proverbs a book of the Bible containing maxims attributed mainly to Solomon.

Providence God or nature as providing protective care.

Providence is always on the side of the big battalions proverbial saying, early 19th century; earlier versions are attributed to the Comte de Bussy-Rabutin (1618–93), 'God is usually on the side of the big squadrons against the small,' and Voltaire

(1694–1778), 'God is on the side not of the heavy battalions but of the best shots.'

provincial in the Christian Church, the ecclesiastical head of a province; the chief of a religious order in a district or province.

provincials in Canada, sporting contests held between teams representing the country's administrative divisions.

proxime accessit used to name the person who comes second in an examination or is runner-up for an award. The phrase is Latin, and means literally 'came very near'.

proxy sitting in spiritualism, a sitting arranged with a medium and attended by one person at the request of another, usually unknown, person who hopes for news of someone recently dead.

Prozac trademark name for fluoxetine, a synthetic compound which inhibits the uptake of serotonin in the brain and is taken to treat depression. *Prozac* was heralded in the late 1980s as an effective new treatment for depression and was increasingly prescribed; used also to treat some forms of compulsive behaviour, it came to be regarded by many as a wonder drug. However, more latterly concern has been expressed about its perceived effects on mood and personality in some individuals. Although now widely used, it cannot be universally administered.

Prozymite (a derogatory name used by Western Churches for) a member of any of the Eastern Christian Churches which administer the Eucharist with leavened bread.

prudhomme in the Middle Ages, a man of valour and discretion; a knight or freeholder summoned to sit on the jury or serve in the king's council.

Prufrockian resembling or characteristic of the timid, passive Prufrock and his world of middle-class conformity and unfulfilled aspirations, from the central character of T. S. Eliot's poem *The Love Song of J. Alfred Prufrock* (1917), who has 'measured out his life with coffee spoons':

> I grow old . . . I grow old . . .
> I shall wear the bottoms of my trousers rolled.
> — T. S. Eliot 'The Love Song of J. Alfred Prufrock (1917)

prunella a strong silk or worsted fabric used formerly for barristers' gowns and the uppers of women's shoes. Recorded from the mid 17th century, the word may come from French *prunelle* 'sloe', because of its dark colour.

See also ➤ *all* LEATHER *or prunella*.

prunes and prisms a phrase spoken aloud in order to form the mouth into an attractive shape, from the advice offered by Mrs General in Dickens's *Little Dorrit*:

> You will find it serviceable in the formation of a demeanour, if you sometimes say to yourself in company or on entering a room, 'Papa, potatoes, poultry, prunes, and prism, prunes and prism.'
> — Charles Dickens *Little Dorrit* (1857)

From this, the phrase is used allusively to designated a prim and affected speech, look, or manner.

Prussia a former kingdom of Germany. Originally a small country on the SE shores of the Baltic, under Frederick the Great it became a major European power covering much of modern NE Germany and Poland. After the Franco-Prussian War of 1870–1 it became the centre of Bismarck's new German Empire, but following Germany's defeat in the First World War the Prussian monarchy was abolished.

Prussian is sometimes used to convey a sense of the rigid (military) discipline held to typify 19th-century Prussia.

Prussian blue a deep blue pigment used in painting and dyeing, made from or in imitation of ferric ferrocyanide; the deep blue colour of this pigment. The name comes from its having been accidentally discovered by Diesbach, a colour-maker in Berlin, in 1704, and announced as a pigment in the Berlin *Miscellanies* for 1710.

pry see ➤ PAUL *Pry*.

prytaneum in ancient Greece, the public hall of a Greek State or city, in which a sacred fire was kept burning; especially in Athens, the hall in which distinguished citizens, foreign ambassadors, and successive presidents of the senate were entertained at the public charge.

prytanis (in ancient Greece) each of the ten divisions of the Athenian Council of Five Hundred; a period of five weeks for which each division presided in turn.

Przewalski's horse a stocky wild Mongolian horse with a dun-coloured coat and a dark brown erect mane, now extinct in the wild. It is the only true wild horse, and is the ancestor of the domestic horse. It is named after Nikolai M. *Przheval'sky* (1839–88), Russian explorer.

psalm a sacred song or hymn, in particular any of those contained in the biblical Book of Psalms and used in Christian and Jewish worship. Recorded from Old English, the word comes via ecclesiastical

Latin from Greek *psalmos* 'song sung to harp music', from *psallein* 'pluck'.

See also ➤ Abecedarian *psalm*, ➤ Bay *Psalm Book*, ➤ proper *psalm*.

George Psalmanazar (1679?–1763), literary impostor supposedly born in Formosa, a native of the south of France whose real name is unknown; he adapted his pseudonym from the biblical character Shalmaneser.

He came to London at the end of 1703 and became a centre of interest, presenting Bishop Compton with the catechism in 'Formosan' (his invented language), and talking volubly in Latin to Archbishop Tillotson; he published in 1704 a *Description of Formosa*, with an introductory autobiography. After the withdrawal of a confederate who was his mentor, he was unable to sustain the imposture unaided, and passed from ridicule to obscurity, although he still found patrons. He renounced his past life after a serious illness in 1728, became an accomplished Hebraist, wrote *A General History of Printing*, and contributed to the *Universal History*.

Psalms a book of the Bible comprising a collection of religious verses, sung or recited in both Jewish and Christian worship. Many are traditionally ascribed to King David; their numbering varies between the Hebrew, Latin, and Greek versions of the Bible.

See also ➤ Penitential *Psalms*.

Psalter the Book of Psalms; a copy of the biblical Psalms, especially for liturgical use.

Jesus psalter a form of devotion consisting of 15 petitions, each beginning with a tenfold repetition of the name Jesus (which is thus said as many times as there are psalms in the Psalter).

Our Lady's psalter the rosary (so called on account of its containing as many Aves as there are psalms in the Psalter); a book containing this.

Psammead the prickly-tempered 'sand-fairy' in the children's story *Five Children and It* (1902) by E. Nesbit. Discovered by the children, it is constrained to grant them one wish a day, but its literal interpretation of the form in which the wishes are expressed means that the fulfilment is seldom enjoyable.

pschent the double crown of ancient Egypt, combining the white crown of Upper Egypt with the red crown of Lower Egypt, used after the union of the two kingdoms under ➤ Menes (*c.*3000 BC). The

word came into use through the discovery of the ➤ Rosetta *Stone* in 1798, and derives through Greek from Egyptian *sekhet*.

pseudepigrapha spurious or pseudonymous writings, especially Jewish writings ascribed to various biblical patriarchs and prophets but composed within approximately 200 years of the birth of Christ.

Pseudo-Dionysius (6th century AD), the unidentified author of important theological works formerly attributed to *Dionysius the Areopagite* (see ➤ Dionysius⁴).

psi the twenty-third letter of the Greek alphabet (Ψ, ψ), transliterated as 'ps'.

Psmith name of an elegant, imperturbable character created by P. G. Wodehouse; *Psmith*, who first appears as a schoolboy in *Mike* (1909), explains that he has created this version of the name as best suited to his style and character.

> Rupert D'Oyly Carte was a friend of P. G. Wodehouse, and said to be the model for his unflappable, unwrongable Psmith.
> — *Guardian* 15 May 1999

Psyche in Greek mythology, a Hellenistic personification of the soul as female, or sometimes as a butterfly. The allegory of Psyche's love for Cupid is told in *The Golden Ass* by Apuleius.

In the story, Cupid, who had become Psyche's lover, visited her in the dark and forbade her to try to see him; when (urged on by her sisters) she disobeyed, he left her in anger. Psyche, searching for him, had to perform superhuman tasks set by his mother, Venus, before she could be reunited with her lover; in achieving the final task, she opened a casket said to contain beauty, and was overcome by a deadly sleep. Finally rescued by the intervention of Jupiter, she was brought to heaven to be married to Cupid. Allusions to Psyche often refer to the curiosity which brings her into danger.

> I couldn't walk away from it any more than Jack could have refrained from exchanging his mother's cow for the magic beans, or Psyche from opening the magic box.
> — Robert Hellenga *Sixteen Pleasures* (1994)

psyche the human soul, mind, or spirit. The word comes (in the mid 17th century) via Latin from Greek *psukhē* 'breath, life, soul'.

psychedelic relating to or denoting drugs (especially LSD) that produce hallucinations and apparent expansion of consciousness; relating to or denoting a style of rock music originating in the mid 1960s, characterized by musical experimentation and drug-related lyrics; denoting or having an intense, vivid colour or a swirling abstract pattern.

psychological moment the moment at which something will or would have the greatest psychological effect. The phrase is a translation of French *moment psychologique*, which arose in Paris in December 1870, during the Siege, when it was asserted to have been used by the German *Kreuz Zeitung* in reference to the bombardment of the city, and explained to mean that, as the bombardment had as its aim to act upon the imagination of the Parisians, it was necessary to choose the very moment when this imagination, already shaken by famine and perhaps by civil dissension, was in the fittest state to be effectively acted upon.

psychology see ➤ GESTALT *psychology*.

psychomachia conflict of the soul; an instance or allegorical representation of this. The word comes from late Latin, and is the title of a poem by the 4th-century Christian Latin poet Prudentius.

Ptah in Egyptian mythology, an ancient deity of Memphis, creator of the universe, god of artisans, and husband of Sekhmet. He became one of the chief deities of Egypt, and was identified by the Greeks with ➤ HEPHAESTUS.

ptarmigan a northern grouse of mountainous and Arctic regions, with feathered legs and feet and plumage that typically changes to white in winter. The name comes (in the late 16th century) from Scottish Gaelic *tàrmachan*; the spelling with *p-* was introduced later, suggested by Greek words starting with *pt-*.

Ptolemaic system the theory (see ➤ PTOLEMY²) that the earth is the stationary centre of the universe, with the planets moving in epicyclic orbits within surrounding concentric spheres.

Although heliocentric models of planetary motion had been proposed before Ptolemy, his geocentric model was so accurate in predicting the positions of the planets that it became the standard model until challenged by Copernicus. A heliocentric system was not generally accepted until ➤ KEPLER developed his laws of planetary motion, and the Ptolemaic system was only finally disproved following Galileo's observations of the phases of the planet Venus.

Ptolemy[1] the name of all the Macedonian rulers of Egypt, a dynasty founded by Ptolemy, the close friend and general of Alexander the Great, who took charge of Egypt after the latter's death and declared himself king (Ptolemy I) in 304 BC. The dynasty ended with the death of Cleopatra in 30 BC.

Ptolemy[2] (2nd century), Greek astronomer and geographer. His teachings had enormous influence on medieval thought, the geocentric view of the cosmos (the ➤ PTOLEMAIC *system* outlined in his major work *Almagest*) being adopted as Christian doctrine until the late Renaissance. Ptolemy's *Geography*, giving lists of places with their longitudes and latitudes, was also a standard work for centuries, despite its inaccuracies.

the public ordinary people in general; the community. The expression, which represents Latin *res publica*, is first recorded in the Translator's Preface to the Authorized Version (1611), 'Whosoever attempteth any thing for the public'.

See also ➤ JOE *Public*.

public bill a bill of legislation affecting the public as a whole.

public enemy number one a person who poses the greatest threat to the welfare or security of a community or nation; (especially in the US), the first on a list of notorious wanted criminals. The term is first recorded in the *Chicago Tribune*:

> Al Capone, public enemy No. 1 . . . was reported to have returned to Chicago from his winter estate at Miami.
> — *Chicago Tribune* 22 February 1931

public-house sign a sign displaying the name of the establishment, usually with a pictorial representation.

public key a cryptographic key that can be obtained and used by anyone to encrypt messages intended for a particular recipient, such that the encrypted messages can be deciphered only by using a second key that is known only to the recipient (the *private key*).

Although in theory such encrypted messages can be broken, in practice they can employ such large numbers in the keys that it is believed that there is insufficient computational power in the world's computers to crack them in any reasonable time. The US government has prohibited the export of systems which employ long, safe keys (classing them as munitions of war) but has come under great pressure to relax its embargo so that an international system of secure electronic transfer of financial information can be put in place.

public lending right (in the UK) the right of authors to receive payment when their books or other works are lent out by public libraries; although the first Bill aimed at creating this was drafted in 1960, legislation was not passed until 1979.

public safety see see ➤ COMMITTEE *of Public Safety.*

public school (in the UK) a private fee-paying secondary school, especially one for boarders; the oldest of these foundations were originally grammar schools founded or endowed for public use and subject to public management and control. In North America, the term denotes a school managed by public authority for the use of the community of a defined district, as part of a free local education system; it has been used in New England and Pennsylvania from the 17th century.

Public school represents Latin *publica schola,* which goes back under the Roman Empire to the fourth (and by implication, the first) century AD, and also appears in the Capitula of Louis the Pious AD 829, in the sense of a school maintained at the public expense, national or local. The English form *public school* is recorded from the late 16th century.

publican in ancient Roman and biblical times, a collector or farmer of taxes. The word is used chiefly in biblical translations and allusions, as in reference to Matthew 11:9, 'And when the Pharisees saw it, they said unto his disciples, Why eateth your Master with publicans and sinners?'

any publicity is good publicity proverbial saying; early 20th century.

publishers ➤ St JOHN *the Apostle* is the patron saint of publishers.

Giacomo Puccini (1858–1924), Italian composer. Puccini's sense of the dramatic, gift for melody, and skilful use of the orchestra have contributed to his enduring popularity.

the Pucelle a name (meaning 'the Maid') for ➤ JOAN *of Arc,* recorded from late Middle English.

Puck another name for ➤ ROBIN *Goodfellow;* more generally (from the Old English period), *puck* meant a mischievous and evil sprite. The use of the name for one particular spirit seems to derive from

the character in Shakespeare's *Midsummer Night's Dream* (1600), and has been reinforced by Kipling's *Puck of Pook's Hill* (1906).

pudding see ➤ *the* PROOF *of the pudding is in the eating*

puddle see ➤ *the* SUN *loses nothing by shining into a puddle.*

pueblo a town or village in Spain, Latin America, or the south-western US, especially an American Indian settlement. The word is Spanish, meaning literally 'people', from Latin *populus.*

puff a review of a work of art, book, or theatrical production, especially an excessively complimentary one; an advertisement, especially one exaggerating the value of the goods advertised. *Puff* meaning undue or extravagant praise is recorded from the early 17th century; in 1742, the *London Magazine* noted, 'Puff is a cant word for the applause that writers and Book-sellers give their own books &c. to promote their sale.'

puffball a fungus that produces a spherical or pear-shaped fruiting body which ruptures when ripe to release a cloud of spores; in figurative use, someone blown up with their own self-importance, a pompous and lightweight person.

Puffin trademark name for a variety of children's paperback books published by ➤ PENGUIN *Books.* The first editor of the series, Eleanor Graham, determined that it should offer '*new* classics for the new generation', and its influence on children's reading was considerable.

Augustus Welby Pugin (1812–52), English architect, theorist, and designer. He believed that the Gothic style was the only proper architectural style because of its origins in medieval Christian society. He is known particularly for his work on the external detail and internal fittings for the Houses of Parliament, designed by Sir Charles Barry; he is recorded as having said that, 'There is nothing worth living for but Christian Architecture and a boat'.

Captain Pugwash rotund pirate hero of the children's cartoon of this name.

> A script that makes 'Captain Pugwash' look like Joseph Conrad.
>
> — *Time Out* 31 March 1993

Pugwash conferences a series of international conferences first held in Pugwash (a village in Nova Scotia) in 1957 by scientists to promote the peaceful application of scientific discoveries.

puha (in American Indian religion) supernatural or spiritual power.

puisne (in the UK and some other countries) denoting a judge of a superior court inferior in rank to chief justices. The word is recorded from the late 16th century, as a noun, denoting a junior or inferior person, and comes from Old French, from *puis* (from Latin *postea* 'afterwards') + *ne* 'born' (from Latin *natus*); the same base as the English adjective *puny* 'weak'.

puja a Hindu ceremonial offering; the word comes from Sanskrit *pūjā* 'worship'.

pujari a Hindu priest.

pukka of or appropriate to high or respectable society. The word, which comes from Hindi *pakkā* 'cooked, ripe, substantial', is used first (in the mid 17th century) of a weight or measure, meaning full, good; in extended usage, this came (in the late 18th century) to mean sure, certain, reliable. The expression **pukka sahib** came to be used for a person of good family and credentials whose behaviour was beyond reproach.

Joseph Pulitzer (1847–1911), Hungarian-born American newspaper proprietor and editor. A pioneer of campaigning popular journalism, he owned a number of newspapers, including the *New York World*. Through his journalism he aimed to reform social and economic inequalities by the exposure of extreme examples; the following words, attributed to him, are inscribed on the gateway to the Columbia School of Journalism in New York: 'A cynical, mercenary, demagogic, corrupt press will produce in time a people as base as itself.' He made provisions in his will for the establishment of the annual Pulitzer Prizes.

Pulitzer Prize an award for an achievement in American journalism, literature, or music, of which there are thirteen made each year.

pull see also ➤ *a* LONG *pull, a strong pull, and pull all together*, ➤ *pull someone's* CHESTNUTS *out of the fire*.

pull Devil, pull baker traditional saying, recorded from the 18th century; the origin has not been explained.

it is easier to pull down than to build up proverbial saying, late 16th century.

Pullman a railway carriage affording special comfort, typically with a lounge interior and meals service at the passengers' seats. It is named after the designer, George F. *Pullman* (1831–97) of Chicago.

pulpit a raised enclosed platform in a church or chapel from which the preacher delivers a sermon. The word comes (in Middle English) from Latin *pulpitum* 'scaffold, platform', in medieval Latin 'pulpit'.

bully pulpit a public office or position of authority that provides its occupant with an outstanding opportunity to speak out on any issue, apparently from an original use by ➤ *Theodore* ROOSEVELT to explain his personal view of the presidency:

> I have got such a bully pulpit!
> — Theodore Roosevelt in *Outlook* (New York) 27 February 1909

The remark was referred to by Nancy Reagan (1923–), commenting on the role of First Lady:

> If the President has a bully pulpit, then the First Lady has a white glove pulpit . . . more refined, restricted, ceremonial, but it's a pulpit all the same.
> — Nancy Reagan in *New York Times* 10 March 1988

pulpitum a stone screen in a church separating the choir from the nave, frequently surmounted by an organ loft.

pulsar a celestial object, thought to be a rapidly rotating neutron star, that emits regular pulses of radio waves and other electromagnetic radiation at rates of up to one thousand pulses per second. The first *pulsar* was discovered in 1967. The name comes from *puls(ating st)ar*, after the pattern of *quasar*.

Pulver Wednesday a former name for ➤ ASH *Wednesday*; *pulver* means 'powder' or 'dust'.

pumpernickel dark, dense German bread made from coarsely ground wholemeal rye. Recorded from the mid 18th century, the word is a transferred use of German *Pumpernickel* 'lout, bumpkin', of unknown ultimate origin (the word seems not to have been known at the time of Fynes Moryson's *Itinerary* (1617), in which this bread is described).

pumpkin in the fairy-story of *Cinderella*, the golden coach provided by the fairy godmother was a transformed pumpkin, which on the stroke of midnight would turn back into the fruit.

It is traditional at ➤ HALLOW'EEN to make a lantern from a hollowed-out pumpkin with holes cut for eyes, nose, and mouth so that it resembles a face.

pumpkin pie pie made with a filling of pumpkin and traditionally eaten on ➤ THANKSGIVING *day* in the US and Canada.

pumpkinification literally, transformation (after death) into a pumpkin; extravagant or absurdly uncritical glorification. The term refers to the travesty (ascribed to Seneca) of the apotheosis of the Roman emperor Claudius Caesar under the title of '*Apocolocyntosis* [Transformation into a pumpkin]'.

pun a joke exploiting the different possible meanings of a word or the fact that there are words which sound alike but have different meanings. Recorded from the mid 17th century, the word may be an abbreviation of obsolet *pundigrion*, as a fanciful alteration of *punctilio*, a fine or petty point of conduct or procedure.

Punch a grotesque, hook-nosed humpbacked buffoon, the chief male character of the ➤ PUNCH *and Judy* show. Punch is the English variant of a stock character derived ultimately from Italian *commedia dell'arte* (he is also called *Punchinello*), and his self-satisfaction in his doings have given rise to the expressions **as pleased as Punch** and **as proud as Punch**.

Punch also gave his name to the title of the weekly comic magazine first published in London in 1841 as *Punch, or the London Charivari*; 'Mr Punch' was the supposed editor of the journal.

punch a drink made from wine or spirits mixed with water, fruit juices, and spices, and typically served hot. Recorded from the mid 17th century, the word apparently comes from Sanskrit *pañca* 'five, five kinds of', because the drink had five ingredients (water, fruit juices, spices, fruit, and sugar).

Punch and Judy an English puppet show presented on the miniature stage of a tall collapsible booth traditionally covered with striped canvas. The show was probably introduced from the Continent in the 17th century. Punch is on the manipulator's right hand, remaining on stage all the time, while the left hand provides a series of characters—baby, wife (Judy), priest, doctor, policeman, hangman— for him to nag, beat, and finally kill. His live dog, Toby, sits on the ledge of the booth.

Punchbowl see ➤ DEVIL'*s Punchbowl.*

Punchinello another name for ➤ PUNCH.

punctuality is the politeness of princes proverbial saying, mid 19th century.

punctuality is the soul of business proverbial saying, mid 19th century.

pundit an expert in a particular subject or field who is frequently called upon to give their opinions about it to the public. The word comes from Sanskrit *paṇḍita* 'learned'.

Punic of or relating to ancient Carthage; the word comes from Latin *Punicus* (earlier *Poenicus*), and ultimately from Greek *Phoinix* 'Phoenician'.

Punic apple a former name for the ➤ POMEGRANATE.

Punic faith treachery, from the character attributed to the Carthaginians by the Romans, as in Philemon Holland's translation (1600) of *Livy's Romane Historie*, 'Crueltie most savage and inhumane, falshood and trecherie more than Punicke'.

Punic Wars three wars between Rome and Carthage, which led to the unquestioned dominance of Rome in the western Mediterranean. In the first Punic War (264–241 BC), Rome secured Sicily from Carthage and established herself as a naval power; in the second (218–201 BC), the defeat of Hannibal (largely through the generalship of Fabius Cunctator and Scipio Africanus) put an end to Carthage's position as a Mediterranean power; the third (149–146 BC) ended in the total destruction of the city of Carthage.

punishment see ➤ CAPITAL *punishment.*

Punjab a region of NW India and Pakistan, a wide, fertile plain traversed by the Indus and the five tributaries which gave the region its name (from Hindi *panj* 'five' + *āb* 'waters').

punk an admirer or player of a loud, fast-moving, and aggressive form of rock music popular in the late 1970s, typically characterized by coloured spiked hair and clothing decorated with safety pins or zips; also, this form of music. The terms **punk rocker** and **punk rock** are also used.

The word is recorded from the late 17th century in the sense 'soft crumbly wood that can be used as timber', and from the early 20th century in the sense 'a worthless person'; it may also be related to archaic *punk* 'prostitute' and *spunk,* 'courage'.

puppy a young dog; originally (in the late 15th century) the word denoted a lapdog, and derived from Old French *poupee* 'doll, plaything'. Subsequently the sense of a conceited and callow young man also developed.

puppy love intense but relatively shallow romantic attachment, typically associated with adolescents; also called *calf love*.

Purana any of a class of Sanskrit sacred writings on Hindu mythology and folklore of varying date and origin, the most ancient of which dates from the 4th century AD. The name comes from Sanskrit *purāṇa* 'ancient (legend)'.

Purbeck marble a hard limestone from *Purbeck* in Dorset, which is polished and used for decorative parts of buildings, fonts, and effigies.

Henry Purcell (1659–95), English composer, who was organist for Westminster Abbey (1679–95) and the Chapel Royal (1682–95). He composed choral odes and songs for royal occasions as well as sacred anthems for the Chapel Royal. His main interest was music for the theatre; he composed the first English opera *Dido and Aeneas* (1689) and the incidental music for many plays. His instrumental music includes a series of *Fantasias* for the viol (1680).

purchase see ➤ GADSDEN *Purchase*, ➤ LOUISIANA *Purchase*.

purdah the practice among women in certain Muslim and Hindu societies of living in a separate room or behind a curtain, or of dressing in all-enveloping clothes, in order to stay out of the sight of men or strangers. The word comes (in the early 19th century) from Urdu and Persian *parda* 'veil, curtain'.

pure see also ➤ SIMON-*pure*.

to the pure all things are pure proverbial saying, mid 19th century; originally with biblical allusion to Titus 1:15, 'Unto the pure all things are pure, but unto them that are defiled, and unbelieving, is nothing pure.'

purgatory (in Catholic doctrine) a place or state of suffering inhabited by the souls of sinners who are expiating their sins before going to heaven. Recorded from Middle English, the word ultimately comes (via Anglo-Norman French or medieval Latin) from late Latin *purgatorius* 'purifying'.
See also ➤ St PATRICK's *Purgatory*.

purge see ➤ PRIDE's *Purge*.

Purification (of the Virgin Mary) the purification of the Virgin Mary after the birth of Jesus, culminating in her presentation of Jesus in the temple; the feast (2 February, also called *Candlemas*) commemorating this.

Purim a lesser Jewish festival held in spring (on the 14th or 15th day of Adar) to commemorate the defeat of ➤ HAMAN's plot to massacre the Jews as recorded in the book of Esther. The name is a Hebrew word, plural of *pūr*, explained in the book of Esther (3:7, 9:24) as meaning 'lot', with allusion to the casting of lots by Haman to select the day on which the Jews were to be killed.

Puritan a member of a group of English Protestants of the late 16th and 17th centuries who regarded the Reformation of the Church under Elizabeth as incomplete and sought to simplify and regulate forms of worship.
The Puritans were Protestants who, dissatisfied with the elements of Catholicism retained by the Elizabethan religious settlement, sought a further purification of the Church from supposedly unscriptural forms. At first they tried to rid the Church of ornaments, vestments, and organs; from 1570 the more extreme attacked the institution of episcopacy itself, wishing to substitute government by Church elders (Presbyterianism). Oppressed under James I and Charles I, in particular by Archbishop Laud, many (such as the Pilgrim Fathers) emigrated to the Netherlands and America. The Civil War of the 1640s led to the temporary pre-eminence of Puritanism. Soon, however, the movement fragmented into sects, and the term *Puritan* began to be less used; after the Restoration such people tended to be called Dissenters or Nonconformists.

Puritan spoon a type of silver spoon with a flat plain stem and an oval bowl, made in the 17th century.

purlieu originally, a tract on the border of a forest, especially one earlier included in it and still partly subject to forest laws; in extended usage, the area near or surrounding a place. Recorded from the late 15th century, the word is probably an alteration (suggested by French *lieu* 'place') of Anglo-Norman French *puralee* 'a going round to settle the boundaries'.

purple originally, a crimson dye obtained from some molluscs, formerly used for fabric worn by an emperor or senior magistrate in ancient Rome or Byzantium; in figurative use, imperial, royal. In later use, *purple* came to be used for a colour intermediate between red and blue.

Purple as a colour has symbolic connotations of penitence and mourning, especially as an ecclesiastical colour; in literary and poetic use, it may refer to the colour of blood.

Recorded from Old English (describing the clothing of an emperor) the word comes via Latin *purpura* 'purple' from Greek *porphura*, denoting molluscs that yielded a crimson dye, or cloth dyed with this.

See also ➤ BORN *in the purple*, ➤ TYRIAN *purple*.

purple airway informal name for a route reserved for an aircraft on which a member of royalty is flying.

Purple Heart (in the US) a decoration for those wounded or killed in action, established in 1782 and re-established in 1932. *Purple heart* was also a slang term for amphetamines (from their colour and shape) in the 1960s.

purple passage an elaborate or excessively ornate passage in a literary composition; an alternative name is **purple patch**. The term is a translation of Latin *purpureus pannus*, and comes from the Roman poet Horace's *Ars Poetica*, 'Works of serious purpose and grand promises often have a purple patch or two stitched on, to shine far and wide.'

purse a purse is the emblem of St Antoninus of Florence (389–1459), who as a Christian moralist taught that money invested in commerce was true capital, and that therefore interest could be claimed on it without the sin of usury, ➤ *St* LAWRENCE, and St John the Almsgiver (fl. *c.*620), patriarch of Alexandria.

See also ➤ FORTUNATUS *'s purse*.

pursuivant an officer of the College of Arms ranking below a herald. The four ordinary pursuivants are *Rouge Croix*, *Bluemantle*, *Rouge Dragon*, and *Portcullis*. The word is recorded from late Middle English, denoting a junior heraldic officer, and comes ultimately from Old French *pursivre* 'follow after'.

From the early 16th century, *pursuivant* denoted a royal or State messenger with power to execute warrants; it refers especially in the 16th and 17th centuries to those who pursued the Catholic priests harboured by ➤ RECUSANTS.

purveyance in Britain, the former prerogative of the sovereign to buy provisions and use horses and

vehicles for a fixed price lower than the market value.

Edward Bouverie Pusey (1800–82), English theologian. In 1833, while professor of Hebrew at Oxford, he founded the ➤ OXFORD *Movement*, and became its leader after the withdrawal of ➤ *John Henry* NEWMAN (1841). His many writings include a series of *Tracts for the Times*.

Puseyite a follower or supporter of Dr E. B. *Pusey* (1800–82) and his associates in the Oxford Movement who advocated the revival of Catholic doctrine and observance in the Church of England.

push the envelope approach or extend the limits of what is possible, originally as aviation slang, relating to graphs of aerodynamic performance on which the *envelope* is the boundary line representing an aircraft's capabilities.

pushmi-pullyu an imaginary creature resembling a llama or an antelope, but with a head at both ends, as invented by Hugh Lofting (1886–1947) in *Doctor Dolittle* (1922); in extended usage, something which is ambivalent or incoherent. It was widely popularized by the film version of *Doctor Dolittle* (1967).

> The constitutional division of war powers is not intended to produce a pushmipullyu, with two minds to make up.
> — *New Yorker* 7 August 1995

puss informal name for a cat; recorded from the mid 16th century, it is a word common to a number of Germanic languages, usually as a call-name for a cat. From the mid 17th century, the word has also been applied to a hare.

Puss in Boots the central character of a story by Perrault, in which a miller bequeaths his three sons respectively his mill, his ass, and his cat. The youngest, who inherits the cat, laments his ill-fortune. But the resourceful cat, by a series of unscrupulous ruses, in which he represents his master to the king as the wealthy marquis of Carabas, secures for him the hand of the king's daughter.

puss in the corner a children's game in which a player in the centre tries to capture one of the other players' 'dens' or 'bases' as they change places.

pussyfoot an advocate or supporter of prohibition, a teetotaller, from the nickname given to W. E. ('Pussyfoot') Johnson (1862–1945), given to him on account of his stealthy methods as a magistrate.

See also ➤ *Pussyfoot* JOHNSON.

never put off till tomorrow what you can do today proverbial saying, late 14th century.

putsch a violent attempt to ovethrow a government; a coup. The word is Swiss German, originally 'knock, thrust, blow', and is recorded from the early 20th century; it is used particularly in connection with Hitler's unsuccessful attempt at an uprising in Munich, 1923–4.

putty medal a worthless reward for insignificant service or achievement; recorded from the late 19th century.

putz in Pennsylvanian Dutch homes, a representation of the Nativity scene traditionally placed under a Christmas tree.

Pwyll in Welsh mythology, prince of Dyfed and 'Head of Hades', the subject of the first story in the *Mabinogion*, in which he changes places for a year with ➤ ARAWN.

Pygmalion in Greek mythology, a king of Cyprus who fashioned an ivory statue of a beautiful woman and loved it so deeply that in answer to his prayer Aphrodite gave it life. The woman (later named *Galatea*) bore him a daughter, Paphos.

Pygmalion was used as the name of a play (1916; the musical *My Fair Lady* was based on it) by George Bernard Shaw, in which the phonetician Henry Higgins teaches the Cockney flower-seller Eliza Doolittle to pass herself off as a society woman. Before her transformation is fully achieved, Eliza utters the words 'not bloody likely', which caused a public sensation at the time of the first London production; as a result, *Pygmalion* became a humorous euphemism for 'bloody'.

> My immediate reaction was to say, 'Not Pygmalion likely.'
> — *Times* 18 March 1976

pygmy originally (in late Middle English) denoting a mythological race of small people; in later use, a member of certain peoples of very short stature in equatorial Africa and parts of SE Asia. The word comes via Latin from Greek *pugmaios* 'dwarf', from *pugmē* 'the length measured from elbow to knuckles'.

pyjamas a suit of loose trousers and jacket for sleeping in. The word comes (in the early 19th century) from Urdu and Persian, from *pāy* 'leg' + *jāma* 'clothing'.

Pylades in Greek mythology, the friend and companion of Orestes; his name may be used allusively for a close friend.

> Ha, Softhead! my Pylades—my second self!
> — Edward Bulwer-Lytton *Not so Bad* (1851)

pylagore in ancient Greece, either of the two deputies sent by each constituent State to the Amphictyonic Council, from *Pulai* 'Thermopylae' (the older place of assembly of the Pythian Amphictyony) + *agora* 'assembly'.

pylon a monumental gateway to an ancient Egyptian temple formed by two truncated pyramidal towers.

In the early 20th century, the term was extended to cover a tall tower-like structure used for carrying electricity cables high above the ground; the word may be used (as in **Pylon Poets**) to designate those poets of the 1930s (chiefly W. H. Auden, C. Day Lewis, Louis MacNeice, and Stephen Spender) who used industrial scenes and imagery as themes of their poetry, after Spender's poem *The Pylons* (1933).

The word comes (in the early 19th century) from Greek *pulōn*, from *pulē* 'gate'.

Pylos in Greek mythology, the legendary kingdom of ➤ NESTOR in the Peloponnese.

pyramid a monumental structure with a square or triangular base and sloping sides that meet in a point at the top, especially one built of stone as a royal tomb in ancient Egypt.

Pyramids were built as tombs for Egyptian pharaohs from the 3rd dynasty (*c*.2649 BC) until *c*.1640 BC. The early step pyramid, with several levels and a flat top, developed into the true pyramid, such as the three largest at Giza near Cairo (**the Pyramids**, including the Great Pyramid of Cheops) which were one of the Seven Wonders of the World. Monuments of similar shape are associated with the Aztec and Maya civilizations of *c*.1200 BC–AD 750, and, like those in Egypt, were part of large ritual complexes.

Pyramus a Babylonian youth, lover of Thisbe. Forbidden to marry by their parents, who were neighbours, the lovers conversed through a chink in a wall and agreed to meet at a tomb outside the city. There, Thisbe was frightened away by a lioness coming from its kill, and Pyramus, seeing her bloodstained cloak and supposing her dead, stabbed himself. Thisbe, finding his body when she returned, threw herself upon his sword. Their blood stained a mulberry tree, whose fruit has ever since been black when ripe, in sign of mourning for them.

The story of Pyramus and Thisbe is the subject of the mechanicals' play in Shakespeare's *Midsummer Night's Dream.*

Pyrenees a range of mountains extending along the border between France and Spain from the Atlantic coast to the Mediterranean, said to be named after *Purēnē* daughter of Bebryx, beloved of Hercules, said to be buried there. The comment '*Il n'y a plus de Pyrénées* [The Pyrenees are no more]' is attributed to Louis XIV of France, on the accession of his grandson to the throne of Spain in 1700.

pyrography the art or technique of decorating wood or leather by burning a design on the surface with a heated metallic point. Also called *pokerwork.*

pyromancy divination by signs derived from fire.

Pyrrha in Greek mythology, the wife of ➤ Deucalion, who with her husband survived a flood sent by Zeus.

pyrrhic dance a war dance of the ancient Greeks, incorporating the movements of actual warfare, performed in armour to a musical accompaniment. It is said to have been named after its inventor, *Purrhikos.*

Pyrrhic victory a victory gained at too great a cost; the phrase refers to the exclamation attributed to ➤ Pyrrhus after the battle of Asculum in Apulia (in which he routed the Romans but suffered a great number of casualties), 'One more such victory and we are lost.'

Pyrrho (*c.*365–*c.*270 BC), Greek philosopher, regarded as the founder of scepticism. He is credited with arguing that happiness comes from suspending judgement because certainty of knowledge is impossible.

Pyrrhus (*c.*318–272 BC), king of Epirus *c.*307–272. After invading Italy in 280, he defeated the Romans at Asculum in 279, but sustained heavy losses; the term *Pyrrhic victory* derives from this.

Pythagoras (*c.*580–500 BC), Greek philosopher; known as **Pythagoras of Samos**. Pythagoras sought to interpret the entire physical world in terms of numbers, and founded their systematic and mystical study; he is best known for the theorem of the right-angled triangle. His analysis of the courses of the sun, moon, and stars into circular motions was not set aside until the 17th century.

Pythagoras also founded a secret religious, political, and scientific sect in Italy: the Pythagoreans

held that the soul is condemned to a cycle of re-incarnation, from which it may escape by attaining a state of purity.

Pythagoras' theorem the theorem attributed to Pythagoras that the square on the hypotenuse of a right-angled triangle is equal in area to the sum of the squares on the other two sides.

Pythagorean letter the Greek letter Y, used by Pythagoras as a symbol of the two divergent paths of virtue and of vice.

Pythagorean system the system of astronomy proposed by Pythagoras, in which all celestial bodies, including the earth, were held to revolve around a central fire (not the sun, but presumably identified with the sun, resulting in the system being assumed identical with the Copernican system).

Pythia the priestess of Apollo at Delphi in ancient Greece. The name comes from Greek *Puthō*, a former name of Delphi.

Pythiad in ancient Greece, the four-year period between two celebrations of the Pythian games.

Pythian games one of the four national festivals of ancient Greece, celebrated near Delphi in the third year of each Olympiad.

Pythias in Greek mythology, the friend and companion of ➤ Damon.

See also ➤ Knight *of Pythias.*

python a large heavy-bodied non-venomous snake occurring throughout the Old World tropics, killing prey by constriction and asphyxiation. The name comes from Greek *Puthōn*, a huge serpent killed by Apollo near Delphi; in some legends, it was the original guardian of the oracle there.

Pythonesque after the style of or resembling the absurdist or surrealist humour of *Monty Python's Flying Circus*, a British television comedy series (1969–74).

See also ➤ Monty *Python's Flying Circus.*

pythoness a female soothsayer or conjuror of spirits. Recorded from Middle English, the term comes via Old French from late Latin *pythonissa*, based on Greek *puthōn* 'soothsaying'.

pyx[1] in the Christian Church, the container in which the consecrated bread of the Eucharist is kept.

pyx[2] (in the UK) a box at the Royal Mint in which specimen gold and silver coins are deposited to be tested annually at the **trial of the pyx** by members of the Goldsmiths' Company.

Qq

Q the seventeenth letter of the modern English alphabet and the sixteenth of the ancient Roman one, in the latter an adoption of the κ (*koppa*) of some of the early Greek alphabets, in turn derived from the Phoenician letter used to represent voiced uvular.

Q was the pseudonym of the English writer and critic Arthur Quiller-Couch (1863–1944), which he originally adopted as a student at Oxford when writing parodies of English poets for the *Oxford Magazine*.

Q also denotes the hypothetical source of the passages shared by the gospels of Matthew and Luke, but not found in Mark; *Q* here probably comes from German *Quelle* 'source'.

In the James Bond films, *Q* is the name of the elderly technician responsible for the development of Bond's customized cars and other gadgets.

See also ➤ MIND *one's P's and Q's*, ➤ OLD *Q*.

Q-ship a merchant ship with concealed weapons, used by the British in the First and Second World Wars in an attempt to destroy submarines. The term dates from the First World War, from *Q* as a non-explicit symbol of the type of vessel.

QED abbreviation for ➤ QUOD *erat demonstrandum*.

> The Brunello fragrance is an immediate QED of the advantages of the pursuit of riches.
> — Saul Bellow *It All Adds Up* (1993)

qigong a Chinese system of physical exercises and breathing control related to t'ai chi.

Qin a dynasty that ruled China 221–206 BC and was the first to establish rule over a united China. The construction of the Great Wall of China was begun during this period. Also *Ch'in*.

Qing a dynasty established by the Manchus that ruled China 1644–1912. Its overthrow in 1912 by Sun Yat-sen and his supporters ended imperial rule in China. Also *Ch'ing*.

quack a person who dishonestly claims to have special knowledge and skill in some field, typically in medicine. The word is recorded from the mid 17th century and is an abbreviation of earlier *quacksalver*, from Dutch, probably from obsolete

quacken 'prattle' + *salf, zalf* 'salve, ointment'. A *quacksalver* may have been someone who 'quacked' or boasted about the virtues of his remedies; it has however been suggested that *quack-* may mean 'to work incompetently'.

Quadragesima the forty days of ➤ LENT. The name comes from ecclesiastical Latin, ultimately from Latin *quadraginta* 'forty'.

Quadragesima Sunday the first Sunday in Lent.

the Quadrant in London, two rows of shops with projecting colonnades extending from Glasshouse Street to Piccadilly, designed by John Nash (1752–1835); the colonnades were removed in 1848 at the request of shopkeepers.

Quadrantids an annual meteor shower with a radiant in the constellation Boötes, reaching a peak about 3 January.

quadriga a chariot drawn by four horses harnessed abreast; especially, representation of this in sculpture or on a coin.

Quadrilateral[1] the area in northern Italy lying between and defended by the four fortresses of Mantua, Verona, Peschiera, and Legnano.

Quadrilateral[2] the essence of Anglicanism comprising four essential principles, originally enunciated in 1870 and approved by the Lambeth Conference of 1888 as a basis for the reunion of the Christian Church; the key points are, the Bible as the word of God, the Apostles' and the Nicene Creed, the two sacraments of baptism and communion, and the rule of episcopacy. Also called **Lambeth Quadrilateral**.

quadrille[1] a trick-taking card game for four players using a pack of forty cards (i.e. one lacking eights, nines, and tens), fashionable in the 18th century.

quadrille[2] a square dance performed typically by four couples and containing five figures, each of which is a complete dance in itself; in Carroll's *Alice* *in Wonderland* (1865) the Gryphon and the Mock Turtle describe the **Lobster Quadrille** to Alice.

quadrivium a medieval university course involving the 'mathematical arts' of arithmetic, geometry, astronomy, and music; with the ➤ TRIVIUM comprising grammar, rhetoric, and logic, these subjects formed the ➤ SEVEN *liberal arts*. The name is Latin, and means literally 'the place where four roads meet'.

quadroon a person whose parents are a mulatto and a white person and who is therefore one-quarter black by descent.

Quadruple Alliance a union or association between four powers or states, notably that formed in 1813 between Britain, Russia, Austria, and Prussia in order to defeat Napoleon and to maintain the international order established in Europe at the end of the Napoleonic Wars.

quaestor in ancient Rome, any of a number of officials who had charge of public revenue and expenditure; *quaestor* is also the name for the chief financial officer of St Andrews University, formerly, of other (especially Scottish) universities. The word is Latin, from an old form of *quaesit-* 'sought'.

Quai d'Orsay a riverside street on the left bank of the Seine in Paris; the French ministry of foreign affairs, which has its headquarters in this street.

> He . . . was said to have more power at the Quai d'Orsay than the minister himself.
> — W. Somerset Maugham *On Chinese Screen* (1922)

quail a small short-tailed Old World game bird resembling a tiny partridge, typically having brown camouflaged plumage; in 17th- and 18th-century usage, often referred to with allusion to the supposed amorousness of its disposition.

Quaker a member of the Religious Society of Friends, a Christian movement founded by George Fox *c.*1650 and devoted to peaceful principles. Central to the Quakers' belief is the doctrine of the 'Inner Light', or sense of Christ's direct working in the soul. This has led them to reject both formal ministry and all set forms of worship.

The name may refer to George Fox's direction to his followers to 'tremble at the name of the Lord', or from fits supposedly experienced by worshippers when moved by the Spirit, and this is suggested by a passage in his journal; however, there is a record of 1647 of the name having previously been applied to members of a foreign religious sect, a group of women who were 'called Quakers, and these swell, shiver, and shake'. *Quaker* is not used by the Friends themselves, but is not now regarded as derogatory.

Members of the Society of Friends typically wore very plain clothes, and this may be referred to allusively.

Quaker City informal name for the city of Philadelphia.

the Quaker poet nickname of the English poet Bernard Barton (1784–1849), born of Quaker stock, who was a friend of Robert Southey and Charles Lamb. He worked as a clerk in a bank in Woodbridge, but at one point considered giving this up to support himself by his pen; Lamb advised against it with the words, 'Keep to your bank, and the bank will keep you.'

Quaker State informal name for the state of Pennsylvania.

quality see also ➤ NEVER *mind the quality, feel the width*.

quality time time spent in giving another person one's undivided attention in order to strengthen a relationship, especially with reference to a working parent and their child or children. The concept of *quality time*, pioneered in the US, has found many supporters, although the sceptical view has also been expressed that it is often little more than a euphemism for a child's having limited time with a parent who is anyway, at the end of a working day, too tired to provide the productive and creative attention envisaged by proponents of *quality time*.

quango chiefly derogatory term for a semi-public administrative body outside the civil service but with financial support from and senior appointments made by the government. Recorded from the 1970s, the term is an acronym from *quasi* (or *quasi-autonomous*) *non-government(al) organization*.

Mary Quant (1934–), English fashion designer. She was a principal creator of the '1960s look', launching the miniskirt in 1966 and promoting bold colours and geometric designs. She was also one of the first to design for the ready-to-wear market.

> Perfect '70s Mary Quant with these little PVC floral appliqué earrings that looked like antiskid bathtub stickers from a gay Hollywood tub circa 1956.
> — Douglas Coupland *Generation X* (1991)

Quarant' Ore another term for the ➤ FORTY *hours*.

quarantain former term (from French) for a period of forty days or nights; **King's quarantain**, a compulsory forty days' truce between quarrelling parties in France, in force especially during the reign of Louis IX in the 13th century.

quarantine a state, period, or place of isolation in which people or animals that have arrived from elsewhere or been exposed to infectious or contagious disease are placed. The use developed in the 17th century, from the original (early 16th-century) meaning of a period of forty days during which a widow who is entitled to a dower has the right to remain in her deceased husband's main dwelling.

quarantine flag a yellow flag used in signalling the presence of disease on a ship.

quare impedit a writ issued in cases of disputed presentation to a benefice, requiring the defendant to state why he hinders the plaintiff from making the presentation. The phrase is Latin and means literally, 'why he impedes or hinders'.

quark in physics, any of a number of subatomic particles carrying a fractional electric charge, postulated as building blocks of the hadrons. Quarks have not been directly observed but theoretical predictions based on their existence have been confirmed experimentally. The name (originally *quork*) was invented in the 1960s by Murray Gell-Mann; it was changed by association with the line 'Three quarks for Muster Mark' in Joyce's *Finnegans Wake* (1939).

quarrel[1] an angry argument or disagreement, typically between people who are usually on good terms. Recorded from Middle English, the word originally meant 'reason for disagreement with a person', and comes ultimately (via Old French) from Latin *queri* 'complain'.
See also ➤ *it takes* TWO *to make a quarrel.*

quarrel[2] a short heavy square-headed arrow or bolt used in a crossbow or arbalest. Recorded from Middle English, the word comes from Old French, based on Latin *quadrus* 'square'; a 16th-century alteration of the word to *quarry* meaning 'a lattice windowpane' also then gave rise to *quarry tile* for an unglazed floor tile.

the quarrel of lovers is the renewal of love proverbial saying, early 16th century.

quarry[1] an animal which is being hunted. Originally, the term denoted the parts of a deer that were placed on the hide and given as a reward to the hounds; the word comes (in Middle English) from Old French *cuiree*, an alteration, influenced by *cuir*

'leather' and *curer* 'clean, disembowel', of *couree*, based on Latin *cor* 'heart'.

quarry[2] a place, typically a large, deep pit, from which stone or other materials are or have been extracted. The word comes from a variant of medieval Latin *quareria*, based on Latin *quadrum* 'a square'.

you cannot get a quart into a pint pot proverbial saying, late 19th century.

quarter in heraldry, each of four or more roughly equal divisions (*dexter chief, sinister chief, dexter base*, and *sinister base*) of a shield separated by vertical and horizontal lines; a square charge which covers the top left (dexter chief) quarter of the field.

quarter day each of four days fixed by custom as marking off the quarters of the year, on which some tenancies begin and end and quarterly payments of rent and other charges fall due.

In England and Ireland the quarter days are Lady Day (March 25), Midsummer Day (June 24), Michaelmas (September 29), and Christmas (December 25). The name is also sometimes applied to the Scottish terms of Candlemas (Feb. 2), Whit Sunday (May 15), Lammas (August 1), and Martinmas (November 11).

quarter sessions (in England, Wales, and Northern Ireland) a court of limited criminal and civil jurisdiction and of appeal, usually held quarterly in counties or boroughs, and replaced in 1572 by crown courts.

Quarter horse a horse of a small stocky breed noted for agility and speed over short distances. It is reputed to be the fastest breed of horse over distances of a quarter of a mile.

quarterback see ➤ MONDAY *morning quarterback.*

quarterdeck the part of a ship's upper deck near the stern, traditionally reserved for officers. The term was originally (in the early 17th century) used for a smaller deck situated above the *half-deck*, covering about a quarter of the vessel.

quartered divided into quarters; in heraldry, (of a shield or arms) divided into four or more parts by vertical and horizontal lines.
See also ➤ HANGED, *drawn, and quartered.*

The Quarterly Review a magazine (1809–1967), founded by John Murray as a Tory rival to the Whig *Edinburgh Review*, and particularly critical of Keats, Shelley, and others. It was supported by Sir Walter

Scott, whose son-in-law and biographer John Gibson Lockhart (1794–1854), noted as a savage critic under the pseudonym of 'The Scorpion', became its second editor in 1825.

quartermaster a regimental officer, usually commissioned from the ranks, responsible for administering barracks, laying out the camp, and looking after supplies; a naval petty officer with particular responsibility for steering and signals.

Quartier Latin the ➤ LATIN *Quarter* of Paris.

quarto a size of book page resulting from folding each printed sheet into four leaves (eight pages). Quarto-sizes range from 15 × 11 inches (**imperial quarto**) to 7⅝ × 6⅜ (**pot quarto**), according to the size of the original sheet.

Quartodeciman any of a group of early Christians who celebrated Easter on the day of the Jewish Passover (the 14th of Nisan), whether this was a Sunday or not. The practice (chiefly observed in Proconsular Asia) was condemned by the Council of Nicaea, AD 325.

quasar a massive and extremely remote celestial object, emitting exceptionally large amounts of energy, which typically has a starlike image in a telescope; it has been suggested that quasars contain massive black holes and may represent a stage in the evolution of some galaxies. Recorded from the 1960s, the word is a contraction of *quasi-stellar*.

Quashee in Caribbean English, a personal name adopted as a general term for a black person. Recorded from the late 17th century, the word comes from Ashantee or Fantee *Kwasi*, a name commonly given to a child born on a Sunday.

quasi that is to say, as it were. The word is Latin, and means literally, 'as if, almost'.

Quasimodo name of the hunchback bellringer in Victor Hugo's novel *Notre-Dame de Paris* (1831), sometimes taken as a type of courage and kindness behind an unattractive exterior.

From the 1960s, *Quasimodo* has been used in surfing for an act of riding on a wave in a crouched position with one arm forward and one arm back.

Quasimodo Sunday the Sunday after Easter, Low Sunday, from Latin *quasi modo*, the first words of the introit for this day, *quasi modo geniti infantes* 'as if new-born babes'.

quassia the wood, bark, or root of a South American shrub or small tree related to ailanthus, yielding a bitter medicinal tonic, insecticide, and vermifuge. It is named after Graman *Quassi*, an 18th-century Surinamese slave who discovered its medicinal properties in 1730.

quaternary of numbers former term for the ➤ TETRACTYS of Pythagoreanism; ten (= 1 + 2 + 3 + 4).

Quatorze Juillet the anniversary of the storming of the Bastille on 14 July 1789, celebrated as a national holiday in France; Bastille Day.

quatrain a stanza of four lines, especially one having alternate rhymes. Recorded from the late 16th century, the word comes from French, from *quatre* 'four'.

quatrefoil an ornamental design of four lobes or leaves as used in architectural tracery, resembling a flower or clover leaf.

the quattrocento the 15th century as a period of Italian art or architecture. The word comes from Italian, literally '400 (shortened from *milquattrocento* '1400'), used with reference to the years 1400–99.

Que sais-je? French for 'What do I know?'; in the *Essays* of Montaigne (1533–92), summarizing the position of the sceptic.

queen the female ruler of an independent state, especially one who inherits the position by right of birth; the wife of a king. The word is recorded from Old English (in form *cwēn*) and is of Germanic origin.

See ➤ *the* FAMINE *Queen*, ➤ GOD *save the Queen*, ➤ MAY *queen*, ➤ NINE *Days' Queen*, ➤ PEARLY *queen*, ➤ SNOW *Queen*, ➤ WINTER *Queen*.

queen and country the objects of allegiance for a patriot whose head of State is a queen. The term is first recorded in Farquhar's *The Recruiting Officer* (1706), 'I endeavour by the example of this worthy gentleman to serve my Queen and country at home', from the reign of Queen Anne (1665–1714).

Queen Anne denoting a style of English furniture or architecture characteristic of the early 18th century. The furniture is noted for its simple, proportioned style and for its cabriole legs and walnut veneer; the architecture is characterized by the use of red brick in simple, basically rectangular designs.

In architecture, referring frequently to a style of

building popularized by R. N. Shaw (1831–1912), which drew on period sources actually dating from the mid-seventeenth century.

See also ➤ ANNE.

Queen Anne's Bounty duties called 'first fruits and tenths', payable originally to the Pope but made payable to the Crown by Henry VIII, and directed by Queen Anne in 1704 to be used to augment the livings of the poorer clergy.

Queen Anne is dead a phrase implying stale news; it is first recorded in the mid 19th century, in Barham's *Ingoldsby Legends* (1840), series 1, 'Lord Brougham, it appears, isn't dead, though Queen Anne is'; an earlier variant appears in Swift's *Complete Collection of Genteel and Ingenious Conversation* (1738), 'Why, Madam, Queen Elizabeth's dead'.

queen bee the single reproductive female in a hive or colony of honeybees; in extended usage, the chief or dominant woman in an organization or social group.

Queen City in the US, the pre-eminent city of a region.

queen consort the wife of a reigning king.

Queen Dick derogatory nickname for Richard Cromwell (1626–1712), who was briefly ➤ *Lord Protector of the* COMMONWEALTH on the death of his father Oliver Cromwell.

queen dowager the widow of a king.

Queen Elizabeth's pocket pistol a large cannon for the defence of Dover Castle; the name is recorded from the late 17th century.

Queen in Council (in the UK) the Privy Council as issuing Orders in Council or receiving petitions when the reigning monarch is a queen.

Queen Mary toque a variety of toque popularized by Queen Mary (1867–1953), wife of King George V, who favoured the hat because it enabled the public to see her face clearly.

queen mother the widow of a king and mother of the sovereign.

Queen of glory an epithet of the Virgin Mary.

Queen of Hearts nickname of Elizabeth of Bohemia (1598–1662), daughter of James I of England,

who with her husband Frederick (the 'Winter King') had briefly occupied the throne of Bohemia before being driven into exile.

The *Queen of Hearts*, who 'made some tarts', is a well-known nursery-rhyme character dating from the late 18th century; in the 19th century she becomes one of the leading playing-card characters in Lewis Carroll's *Alice's Adventurers in Wonderland* (1865); her favourite exclamation is 'Off with his (or her) head!'

In the late 20th century the name was applied to Diana, Princess of Wales (1961–97), following an interview she gave in 1995:

> I'd like to be a queen in people's hearts but I don't see myself being Queen of this country.
> — Diana, Princess of Wales interview on *Panorama*, BBC1 TV, 20 November 1995

Queen of heaven an epithet of the Virgin Mary.

queen of love in classical mythology, an epithet of Aphrodite or Venus.

Queen of the May another term for ➤ MAY *Queen*; also called the *May Lady*.

queen of the night the moon.

Queen of the West an informal name for Cincinnati.

queen of tides the moon; the phrase is first recorded in Byron's *Childe Harold* (1812), 'the Queen of tides on high consenting shone'.

queen regnant a queen ruling in her own right.

the Queen's Bays another name for ➤ *the* BAYS.

Queen's College a college of Oxford University, founded in 1340 in honour of Queen Philippa (1314?–69), wife of Edward III.

Queen's Proctor in the UK, an official who has the right to intervene in probate, divorce, and nullity cases when collusion or the suppression of facts is alleged.

queen's weather fine weather, first recorded in 1851 in the reign of Queen Victoria.

Queenomania in the early 19th century, a rare term for devotion to the cause of Caroline of Brunswick (1768–1821), estranged wife of King George IV, who excited strong popular feeling by his public criticism of her, and by his attempts to have their marriage dissolved and to force her to renounce her title and live in exile.

queens see also ➤ VALLEY *of the Queens.*

the Queens the Cunard passenger liners, 'Queen Mary' and 'Queen Elizabeth'.

Queens' College a college of Cambridge University, founded by Margaret of Anjou (1430–82), wife of the Lancastrian Henry VI, and refounded by Elizabeth Woodville (1437?–92), wife of the Yorkist Edward IV.

Queensberry Rules the standard rules of boxing, originally drawn up in 1867 to govern the sport in Britain, named after John Sholto Douglas (1844–1900), 8th Marquess of *Queensberry,* who supervised the preparation of the rules; in figurative use, standard rules of polite or acceptable behaviour.

queensware a type of fine, cream-coloured Wedgwood pottery, said to have been named in honour of Queen Charlotte (wife of George III), who had been presented with a set in 1765.

queer see also ➤ *queer as* DICK'*s hatband,* ➤ *there's* NOWT *so queer as folk.*

queer a person's pitch interfere with or spoil someone's affairs or opportunities; a *pitch* here was originally a tradesman's or showman's pitch.

Queer Nation the name of a campaigning lesbian and gay rights organization founded in the US in 1990, reflecting a militant form of gay activism which set out deliberately to reclaim the contemptuous slang use of queer to mean a homosexual by transmuting what was originally regarded as pejorative into a force for asserting the rights of the group concerned.
See also ➤ QUEERCORE.

Queer Street an imaginary street where people in difficulties are supposed to reside; the term is recorded from the early 19th century, and is now used particularly in relation to financial difficulty.

queercore a cultural movement among young homosexuals which deliberately rebels against and dissociates itself from the established gay scene, having as its primary form of expression an aggressive type of punk-style music.
See also ➤ QUEER *Nation.*

quemadero in Spain and former Spanish territories during the Inquisition, a place where convicted heretics were executed by burning. The word comes from Spanish, from *quemar* 'to burn'.

Querno an Apulian poet of the early 16th century, in Pope's *Dunciad* described as 'the Antichrist of Wit', and as such compared with the actor and dramatist Colley Cibber (1671–1757). The original Querno is supposed to have been made poet laureate for a joke by Pope Leo X (1475–1521).

quest see ➤ VISION *quest.*

the Questing Beast in *Le Morte d'Arthur*, a monstrous creature hunted by Palomydes the Saracen; the name (a translation of ➤ GLATYSANT *Beast*) refers to its making a noise in its belly 'as hit had bene a thirty couple of howndis'.

question in the British House of Commons, used as an interjection to recall a speaker to the subject under discussion.
See also ➤ ASK *a silly question and you'll get a silly answer,* ➤ ASK *no questions and you'll be told no lies,* ➤ BEG *the question,* ➤ *a* CIVIL *question deserves a civil answer,* ➤ CROSS-*questions and crooked answers,* ➤ FOOLS *ask questions that wise men cannot answer,* ➤ PREVIOUS *question,* ➤ RHETORICAL *question,* ➤ SIXTY-*four thousand dollar question,* ➤ STARRED *question,* ➤ TWENTY *questions,* ➤ WEST *Lothian question.*

question time in the UK, a period during parliamentary proceedings in the House of Commons when MPs may question ministers.

questionist a habitual or professed questioner, particularly in theological matters; in early usage, applied to certain schoolmen, as ➤ *St* THOMAS *Aquinas* and ➤ *John* DUNS *Scotus.*
At Cambridge and Harvard universities, a name formerly given to an undergraduate in the last term before final examinations.

Quetzalcóatl the plumed serpent god of the Toltec and Aztec civilizations. Traditionally the god of the morning and evening star, he later became known as the patron of priests, inventor of books and of the calendar, and as the symbol of death and resurrection. His worship involved human sacrifice. Legend said that he would return in another age, and when Montezuma, last king of the Aztecs, received news of the landing of Cortés and his men in 1519, he thought that Quetzalcóatl had returned.

quetzalcoatlus a giant pterosaur of the late Cretaceous period, which was the largest ever flying animal with a wingspan of up to 15 m.

Queuetopia a designation for Great Britain under Labour or Socialist rule, supposedly characterized by universal queueing; the word is said to have been coined by Winston Churchill.

Qufu a small town in Shandong province in eastern China, where ➤ CONFUCIUS was born in 551 BC and lived for much of his life.

the quick and the dead the living and the dead; the phrase comes from the Apostles' Creed in the *Book of Common Prayer* (1662), 'From thence he shall come to judge the quick and the dead'.

quick at meat, quick at work proverbial saying, early 17th century.

the quick brown fox jumps over the lazy dog traditional sentence used by keyboarders to ensure that all letters of the alphabet are functioning.

quicklime lime which has not been slaked, and in which the bodies of executed criminals were traditionally buried.

quickly come, quickly go proverbial saying, late 16th century.

quicksand loose wet sand that yields easily to pressure and sucks in anything resting on or falling into it; from the late 16th century, the word has been used for something having the absorbent, yielding, or treacherous character of quicksand.

> That campaign lies dulled and all but buried in the quicksand of a severely faltering US economy.
> — *Christian Science Monitor* 10 January 1992

quickset hedging, especially of hawthorn, grown from slips or cuttings.

quicksilver the liquid metal mercury, used in similes and metaphors to describe something that moves or changes very quickly, or that is difficult to hold or contain.

Quicunque vult another term for ➤ ATHANASIAN *Creed*, from Latin *quicunque vult (salvus esse)* 'whosoever wishes (to be saved)', the opening words of the creed.

Quid a name given to a section of the American Republican party in 1805–11; the term is an abbreviation of ➤ TERTIUM *quid*, and is first recorded in a letter of 1805 by Thomas Jefferson (1743–1826), 'Those called the third party, or Quids'.

quid slang term for one pound sterling; the term is recorded from the late 17th century (denoting a sovereign), but the origin is unknown.

quid pro quo a favour or advantage granted in return for something; the phrase is Latin, and means literally 'something for something'.

quiddity the inherent nature or essence of someone or something; a distinctive feature or peculiarity. Recorded from late Middle English, the word comes from medieval Latin *quidditas*, from Latin *quid* 'what'.

quidnunc an archaic term for an inquisitive and gossipy person; someone who is always asking 'What now?' or 'What's new'. Recorded from the early 18th century, the word comes from Latin *quid* 'what' + *nunc* 'now'.

quiet see also ➤ *the best* DOCTORS *are Dr Diet, Dr Quiet, and Dr Merryman.*

quiet American a person suspected of being an undercover agent or spy; with allusion to Graham Greene's *The Quiet American* (1955).

> There never was much 'reality' about Washington's presence in Vietnam from the moment when the first quiet Americans moved in.
> — *Times* 11 January 1973

a quiet conscience sleeps in thunder proverbial saying, late 16th century; meaning that someone with an untroubled conscience will sleep undisturbed whatever the noise.

quieta non movere proverbial expression meaning, ➤ *let* SLEEPING *dogs lie*; recorded from the late 18th century, the Latin phrase means literally, 'not to move settled things'.

Quietism (in the Christian faith) devotional contemplation and abandonment of the will as a form of religious mysticism. Recorded from the late 17th century, the term originally denoted the religious mysticism based on the teachings of the Spanish priest Miguel de Molinos (*c*.1640–97); also called *Molinism*.

quietus death or something that causes death, regarded as a release from life. The expression dates from late Middle English, and represents an abbreviation of medieval Latin *quietus est* 'he is quit', originally used as a form of receipt or discharge on payment of a debt.

quilombo in 18th- and 19th-century Brazil, an organized community of escaped slaves, usually in a remote area. The word probably comes ultimately from Mbundu *ki'lombo* 'settlement'.

Quincey see ➤ DE *Quincey*.

quincunx in astrology, an aspect of 150°, equivalent to five zodiacal signs, first referred by the English astrologer William Lilly (1602–81):

> One Kepler, a learned man, hath added some new ones, as follow, viz.: A Quincunx Vc consisting of 150 degrees.
>
> — William Lilly *Christian Astrology* (1647)

Quincunx is also used for an arrangement of five objects with four at the corners of a square or rectangle and the fifth at its centre, used for the five on a dice or playing card, and in planting trees (this sense, which is also found in Latin, apparently derives from the use of five dots or dashes, arranged in this way, to denote five twelfths of an ➤ AS).

The word is Latin, and means literally 'five twelfths'.

quindecemvir in ancient Rome, any of the fifteen priests in charge of the Sibylline books.

quindene in ecclesiastical usage, the fifteenth (later fourteenth) day after a church festival.

quinine a bitter crystalline compound present in ➤ CINCHONA bark, used as a tonic and formerly as an antimalarial drug; the word comes (in the early 19th century) from Spanish *quina* 'cinchona bark'.

Quinquagesima Sunday the Sunday before the beginning of Lent. *Quinquagesima* comes from medieval Latin, from Latin *quinquagesimus* 'fiftieth', on the pattern of ➤ QUADRAGESIMA, because it is ten days before the forty penitential days of Lent.

Quinquatria in ancient Rome, the festival of ➤ MINERVA (March 19–23), starting five (*quinque*) days after the Ides, which may be the origin of the name. The festival was celebrated by those, such as spinners, weavers, and dyers, under the patronage of the goddess. Also called *Quinquatrus*.

quinquereme an ancient Roman or Greek galley of a kind believed to have had three banks of oars, the oars in the top two banks being rowed by pairs of oarsmen and the oars in the bottom bank being rowed by single oarsmen.

The word comes from Latin, from *quinque* 'five' + *remus* 'oar'; the significance of the number five continues to be debated. In current usage, *quinquereme* may be employed to evoke a romantic vision of the ancient world.

> I wanted everyone ... to dance all day to cymbals and tambourines ... until they sank exhausted on the seashore as quinqueremes arrived bring gods and heroes to enact the ancient ritual before the sinking sun.
>
> — *Descant* Summer 1991

quinsy inflammation of the throat, especially an abscess in the region of the tonsils. The illness has a key role in the plot of Conan Doyle's Sherlock Holmes story 'A Case of Identity' (1891), in which Miss Mary Sutherland's missing suitor turns out to have been her stepfather in disguise; his whispering voice, an important feature of this, he had attributed to a weak throat resulting from having 'the quinsy' when young.

Recorded from Middle English, the word comes via medieval Latin, from Greek *kunankhē* 'canine quinsy', from *kun-* 'dog' + *ankhein* 'throttle'.

the quintain the medieval military exercise of tilting at a post set up as a mark in tilting with a lance, typically with a sandbag attached that would swing round and strike an unsuccessful tilter. Recorded from late Middle English, the word comes from Old French *quintaine*, and is perhaps based on Latin *quintana*, a street in a Roman camp separating the fifth and sixth maniples, where military exercises were performed (from *quintus* 'fifth').

See also ➤ TILT *at the quintain*.

quintessence (in classical and medieval philosophy) a fifth substance in addition to the four elements, thought to compose the heavenly bodies and to be latent in all things; it was believed that this essence could be extracted by alchemy.

From the late 16th century, *quintessence* has also meant the most perfect or typical example of a quality or class, as in the title of George Bernard Shaw's *The Quintessence of Ibsenism* (1891).

The word comes (in late Middle English) via French from medieval Latin *quinta essentia* 'fifth essence'.

quintile in astrology, an aspect of 72° (one fifth of a circle).

Quintilian (*c*.35–*c*.96 AD), Roman rhetorician. He is best known for his *Education of an Orator*, a comprehensive treatment of the art of rhetoric and the training of an orator which was highly influential in the Middle Ages and the Renaissance.

quintuplet each of five children born to the same mother at one birth; the first documented such set known to have survived birth were the ➤ DIONNE *Quintuplets*, born in Canada in 1934.

quip a witty remark; in archaic use, a verbal equivocation. The word is recorded from the mid 16th century, and may come from Latin *quippe* 'perhaps, forsooth'.

quipu an ancient Inca device for recording information, consisting of variously coloured threads knotted in different ways; the word comes from Quechua *khipu* 'knot'.

Quirinal one of the Seven Hills on which the ancient city of Rome was built. From the 17th century, *Quirinal* has also been the name of the summer palace of the popes on the Quirinal Hill in Rome, which later became the palace first of the monarchs and then of the presidents of Italy; later, the name denoted the Italian court, monarchy, or government, especially as distinguished from that of the Vatican.

> The complete accord which exists in practice between the Vatican and the Quirinal.
> — *Contemporary Review* November 1922

quis custodiet ipsos custodes? Latin phrase, meaning literally 'who will guard those appointed to guard?', from the work of the Roman satirist Juvenal (AD *c*.60–*c*.130).

> Mr. Swinburne is of the same way of thinking as what may be termed the English literary radicals generally as to the propriety of the oppressors of Bulgaria 1285 being chastised by the oppressors of Poland. They enquire, 'Quis custodiet ipsos custodes?'
> — Henry James in *The Nation* 11 January 1877

quisling a traitor who collaborates with an enemy force occupying their country, from the name of Major Vidkun *Quisling* (1887–1945), the Norwegian army officer and diplomat who ruled Norway on behalf of the German occupying forces (1940–45), and who was executed for treason.

quit-rent a rent, typically a small one, paid by a freeholder or copyholder in lieu of services which might be required of them.

Don Quixote the hero of a romance (1605–15) by Cervantes, a satirical account of chivalric beliefs and conduct. The character of Don Quixote, the poor gentlemen devoted to the ideal of chivalry, who christens his peasant lady-love ➤ DULCINEA, and

seeks adventures wearing rusty armour and riding his old horse ➤ ROSINANTE, is typified by a romantic vision and naive, unworldly idealism.

> The latest Don Quixote to joust with the Rice Curtain, Japan's barrier to offshore grain imports
> — *Time* 28 September 1992

See also ➤ TILT *at windmills*.

quiz an odd or eccentric person; a person who mocks, ridicules or engages in banter; a practical joke. The word is sometimes said to have been invented (in the late 18th century) by a Dublin theatre proprietor who, having made a bet that a nonsense word could be made known within 48 hours throughout the city, and that the public would give it a meaning, had the word written up on walls all over the city, but there is no evidence to support this theory.

Qumran a region on the western shore of the Dead Sea; the ➤ DEAD *Sea Scrolls* were found (1947–56) in caves at nearby *Khirbet Qumran*, the site of an ancient Jewish settlement. *Qumran* also denotes the religious community located in Khirbet Qumran during the beginning of the Christian era, which preserved the scrolls.

quo vadis Latin for, 'where are you going?'; according to a legend first found in the apocryphal Acts of St Peter, the apostle Peter, fleeing the persecutions in Rome, met Christ on the Appian Way and asked him '*Domine, quo vadis* [Lord, where are you going]'. Receiving the reply that Christ was going to be crucified again, Peter understood that this would be in his place; he accordingly turned back, and was martyred.

quod erat demonstrandum used to convey that a fact or situation demonstrates the truth of one's theory or claim, especially to mark the conclusion of a formal proof; the Latin phrase, meaning literally 'which was to be demonstrated', is a translation of the Greek phrase used in a number of ➤ EUCLID's propositions. It is frequently abbreviated to *QED*.

quodlibet originally (from late Middle English) a question proposed as an exercise in philosophical or theological debate; a scholastic debate, thesis, or exercise. Later (from the early 19th century) a light-hearted combination of several tunes, a fantasia, a medley.

The word is Latin, from *quod* 'what' + *libet* 'pleases'.

quondam that once was; former; according to Malory's *Le Morte d'Arthur*, used in the Latin inscription on the tomb of ➤ ARTHUR:

> And many men say that there is written upon his tomb this verse: *Hic iacet Arthurus, rex quondam rexque futurus* [Here lies Arthur, the once and future king].
> — Thomas Malory *Le Morte d'Arthur* (1485)

Quonset hut a North American trademark name for a building made of corrugated metal and having a semicircular cross section. It was named (in the Second World War) after *Quonset* Point, Rhode Island, where such huts were first made.

Quorn former name of a village in Leicestershire (now *Quorndon*), surviving in **the Quorn**, a famous hunt centred there.

From the 1980s, *Quorn* has also been (from *Quorn* Specialities Ltd of Leicester) the trademark name for a type of textured vegetable protein made from an edible fungus and used as a meat substitute in cooking.

quorum originally, a select body of justices of the peace, every member of which had to be present to constitute a deciding body. Later, the minimum number of members of an assembly or society that must be present at any of its meetings to make the proceedings of that meeting valid.

Recorded from late Middle English, the word comes from the text of commissions for committee members designated by the Latin words *quorum vos…unum esse volumus* 'of whom we wish that you…be one'.

quot homines, tot sententiae Latin proverbial saying from *Phormio* by the Roman comic dramatist Terence (*c.*190–159 BC), '*Quot homines tot sententiae: suus cuique mos* [There are as many opinions as there are people: each has his own correct way].'

quote see ➤ *the* DEVIL *can quote Scripture for his own ends.*

quotidian (of a fever) recurring every day, in particular, designating the malignant form of malaria. The word comes ultimately from Latin *cotidie* 'daily'.

qwerty denoting the standard layout on English-language typewriters and keyboards, having *q, w, e, r, t,* and *y* as the first keys from the left on the top row of letters.

Rr

R the eighteenth letter of the modern English alphabet and the seventeenth of the ancient Roman one, derived through early Greek ρ from Phoenician, representing the twentieth letter of the early Semitic alphabet.

See also ➤ OYSTERS *are only in season in the R months*, ➤ *the* THREE *R's.*

R is the dog's letter proverbial saying, referring to the sound of the letter resembling the snarl of a dog; Ben Jonson in *The English Grammar* (1636) comments, 'R is the dog's letter, and hurreth in the sound, the tongue striking the inner palate, with a trembling about the teeth.'

Ra in Egyptian mythology, the sun god, the supreme Egyptian deity, worshipped as the creator of all life and typically portrayed with a falcon's head bearing the solar disc. He appears travelling in his ship with other gods, crossing the sky by day and journeying through the underworld of the dead at night. From earliest times he was associated with the pharaoh.

rabbi a Jewish scholar or teacher, especially one who studies or teaches Jewish law. Recorded from late Old English, the word comes via ecclesiastical Latin and Greek from Hebrew *rabbī* 'my master'.

rabbit a burrowing gregarious plant-eating mammal, with long ears, long hind legs, and a short tail. The *rabbit* is often taken to typify timidity and the word is used for someone who is a poor performer in a sport; the animal is also noted for its prolific breeding, a quality referred to disapprovingly by Queen Victoria in a letter to her elder daughter:

> I fear the seventh granddaughter and fourteenth grandchild becomes a very uninteresting thing—for it seems to me to go on like the rabbits in Windsor Park!
> — Queen Victoria letter to the Crown Princess of Prussia, 10 July 1868

A **rabbit's foot** has traditionally been taken as a good-luck charm, and the word *rabbits* spoken on the first day of the month, was supposed to bring good luck. *Rabbits* are also alluded to as typically made to appear or disappear by a conjuror.

See also ➤ PETER *Rabbit,* ➤ WHITE *Rabbit.*

Brer Rabbit hero of many of the ➤ *Uncle* REMUS stories by Joel Chandler Harris, which typically centre on the unavailing efforts of Brer Fox to outwit and catch the cunning *Brer Rabbit*, who describes himself in the story of 'How Mr Rabbit was too Sharp for Mr Fox' as 'Bred en bawn in a brier-patch!'

François Rabelais (*c.*1494–1553) French satirist, whose writings are noted for their earthy humour, their parody of medieval learning and literature, and their affirmation of humanist values.

> A fat Frenchwoman of middle age, a Rabelaisian figure with a broad, obscene laugh.
> — W. Somerset Maugham *Of Human Bondage* (1915)

See also ➤ GARGANTUA, ➤ PANTAGRUEL, ➤ PANURGE.

race see also ➤ CLASSIC *race.*

the race is not to the swift, nor the battle to the strong proverbial saying, mid 17th century; originally with allusion to Ecclesiastes 9:11.

race relations relations between members or communities of different races within one country; ➤ *St* MARTIN *de Porres* and St Peter Claver (1580–1654), a Spanish Jesuit priest who worked particularly at Cartagena (now Colombia) when it was the centre of the slave trade, are the patron saints of *race relations*. Although the term is recorded from the early 20th century, it is since the 1960s that the concerns which it embodies have been at the centre of public attention (in the UK, the **Race Relations Act**, penalizing incitement to racial hatred, was passed in 1965).

rache archaic term for a hunting dog which pursues its prey by scent, occasionally taken as the type of a merciless pursuer; the word is recorded from Old English, and is related to Old Norse *rakki* 'dog'.

Rachel in the Bible, the younger daughter of ➤ LABAN, loved by ➤ JACOB, who serves his uncle Laban for seven years for the right to marry her. Tricked into marrying her elder sister Leah, Jacob served another seven years for Rachel, who afterwards became the mother of ➤ Joseph and ➤ Benjamin.

According to tradition, Rachel's tomb was in Rama, and in connection with this she is a figure of the mother mourning for Israel:

> In Rama was there a voice heard, lamentation and weeping, and great mourning, Rachel weeping for her children, and would not be comforted, because they are not.
>
> — Bible (AV) St Matthew ch. 2, v. 18

rachel a light, tannish shade (originally and chiefly of face-powder), taken from the stage name of the French tragedian Élisabeth Rachel Félix (1821–58).

Rachmanism the exploitation and intimidation of tenants by unscrupulous landlords, named after Peter *Rachman* (1919–62), a London landlord whose practices became notorious in the early 1960s.

Jean Racine (1639–99), French dramatist, the principal tragedian of the French classical period, who in his work drew on many sources, including Greek and Roman literature and the Bible. Central to most of his tragedies is a perception of the blind folly of human passion, continually enslaved and unsatisfied.

rack an instrument of torture consisting of a frame on which the victim was stretched by turning rollers to which the wrists and ankles were tied; it is first recorded in English in Caxton's translation of *Reynard the Fox* (1481), and is sometimes found in the expression **come rack, come rope**.

go to rack and ruin gradually deteriorate in condition because of neglect: fall into disrepair; *rack* here is a variant (recorded from the late 16th century) of *wrack* 'damage, disaster'.

rack-rent an extortionate or very high rent; in legal usage, a rent equal to or close to the annual value of the property. Recorded from the early 17th century, the expression was particularly associated with the ➤ Protestant *Ascendancy* in Ireland by the publication in 1800 of Maria Edgeworth's novel *Castle Rackrent*, telling the story of the decline, through three generations, of the Rackrent family and their property.

racketeer a person who engages in dishonest and fraudulent business dealings; the term was particularly used of the ➤ Prohibition period in America.

Arthur Rackham (1867–1939), English illustrator, noted for his illustrations of books, as the Grimm brothers' *Fairy Tales* (1900), which established his reputation as an artist of imagination and Gothic invention. His pictures, which were displayed in galleries worldwide, also appear in books such as *Rip Van Winkle* (1905) and *Peter Pan* (1906).

> Illustrations . . . that are reminiscent of Authur Rackham's drollery and exquisite draughtsmanship.
> — Judith Saltman *Modern Canadian Children's Books* (1987)

Rada a group of deities of West African derivation venerated in Haiti. The name apparently represents *Allada*, a former principality of Dahomey (now Benin).

radar a system for detecting the presence, direction, distance, and speed of aircraft, ships, and other objects, by sending out pulses of high-frequency electromagnetic waves which are reflected off the object back to the source. Introduced in the 1940s, the system was named from the first letters of *(ra)dio d(etection) a(nd) r(anging)*.

Mrs Ann Radcliffe (1764–1823), English novelist, a leading exponent of the ➤ Gothic *novel*, who in novels such as *The Mysteries of Udolpho* (1794) influenced Byron, Shelley, and Charlotte Brontë.

Radcliffe Camera a circular building in Oxford, built by the Scottish architect James Gibbs (1682–1754) as the **Radcliffe Library** with a bequest from the English physician John *Radcliffe* (1650–1714); it was originally intended as a medical library, but now houses part of the ➤ Bodleian collection.

St Radegund (518–87), queen of the Franks and wife of Clotaire, son of Clovis; born a princess of Thuringia, she had been captured at the age of twelve and later married to Clotaire. Leaving the court after six years of marriage, she took the veil, and later founded a monastery at Poitiers. Soon after her death, miracles were reported at her tomb; she became one of the first ➤ Merovingian saints, and her feast was celebrated in France from the 9th century.

☐ **FEAST DAY** Her feast day is 13 August.

Radha in Hinduism, the favourite mistress of the god ➤ Krishna, and an incarnation of ➤ Lakshmi. In devotional religion she represents the longing of the human soul for God.

radical advocating thorough or complete political or social reform; representing or supporting an extreme or progressive section of a political party; the word in this sense is first recorded in the Shelley's

Oedipus Tyrannus (1820), 'Kings and laurelled Emperors, Radical butchers'. In a letter of 1832, John Stuart Mill refers to, 'Several friends of mine, radical-utilitarians of a better than the ordinary sort.'

Radical is recorded from late Middle English (in the senses 'forming the root' and 'inherent'), and comes ultimately from Latin *radix, radic-* 'root'.

See also ➤ PHILOSOPHICAL *radical*.

radical chic the fashionable affectation of radical left-wing views or an associated style of dress or life; coined by the American writer Tom Wolfe (1931–):

> Radical Chic . . . is only radical in Style; in its heart it is part of Society and its tradition—Politics, like Rock, Pop, and Camp, has its uses.
> — Tom Wolfe in *New York* 8 June 1970

Radical Jack a nickname of the British reformist politician John George Lambton, 1st Earl of Durham (1792–1840).

radiocarbon dating another term for ➤ CARBON *dating*.

radiologists ➤ *St* MICHAEL is the patron saint of radiologists.

Radish Feast held annually in Westmorland on 12 May to mark the opening of Milnthorpe Fair; the occasion on which ➤ MOROCCO ale was drunk.

radium the chemical element of atomic number 88, a rare radioactive metal of the alkaline earth series, which was formerly used as a source of radiation for radiotherapy, but which has now largely been replaced by other substances. The name comes (in the late 19th century) from Latin *radius* 'ray'.

Henry Raeburn (1756–1823), Scottish portrait painter. The leading Scottish portraitist of his day, he depicted the local intelligentsia and Highland chieftains in a bold and distinctive style.

Rafferty's rules in Australia and New Zealand, informal expression meaning no rules at all; *Rafferty* is probably an English dialect alteration of *refractory*.

A. J. Raffles a debonair cricket-loving gentleman burglar, hero of *The Amateur Cracksman* (1899) and other books by E. W. Hornung (1866–1921); his name is used allusively for a man of good birth who engages in crime, especially burglary.

> An educated renegade . . . in the classic *Raffles* tradition.
> — *John o'London's* 31 March 1960

Stamford Raffles (1781–1826), British colonial administrator. As Lieutenant General of Sumatra he persuaded the East India Company to purchase the undeveloped island of Singapore (1819), undertaking much of the preliminary work for transforming it into an international port and centre of commerce.

rag originally (in the early 19th century) a noisy disorderly scene or dispute, carried on in defiance of authority or discipline; a rowdy celebration. Now usually, a programme of stunts, parades, and other entertainments organized by students to raise money for charity. The term comes from *rag* verb, make fun of in a loud boisterous manner, play a practical joke on.

rag-and-bone man an itinerant dealer in old clothes, furniture, and small, cheap second-hand items; the synonymous **rag-and-bone picker** is first recorded by Henry Mayhew in *London Labour* (1851). In late 20th century Britain, the term is likely to be immediately associated with the father and son featured in the television comedy ➤ STEPTOE *and Son*.

the Rag and Famish nickname of the Army and Navy Club in London, first recorded in Trollope's novel *The Three Clerks* (1858). The name is said in one source to have been coined by a Captain William Duff of the 23rd Fusiliers, in reference to the food offered when he arrived for supper late one night.

ragamuffin a person, typically a child, in ragged, dirty clothes. The term is recorded from Middle English as the name of a demon; and is probably based on *rag* as a piece of old and torn cloth, with a fanciful suffix.

a ragged colt may make a good horse proverbial saying, early 16th century; meaning that an unpromising youngster may still turn out well.

ragged robin a pink-flowered European campion of damp grassland, with divided petals that give it a tattered appearance; occasionally in 19th-century literary use, a ragged person.

ragged school in the 19th century, informal term for a free school for poor children.

ragged staff a depiction of a staff with projecting knobs (usually in reference to the crest of the Earls of Warwick).

See also ➤ BEAR *and ragged staff*.

raglan an overcoat having sleeves continuing in one piece up to the neck of a garment, without a shoulder seam; named after Lord *Raglan* (1788–1855), a British commander in the Crimean War.

Ragman roll a set of rolls (formerly preserved in the Tower of London, now in the Public Record Office), in which are recorded the instruments of homage made to Edward I by the Scottish king (John de Baliol, ➤ *Toom* TABARD, 1249–1315) and nobles in 1296; *Ragman*, the origin of which is not explained, was the name orginally given to a statute of 4 Edward I, which in 1276 appointed justices to hear and determine complaints of injuries done during the preceding 25 years.

Ragnarök in Scandinavian mythology, the destruction or twilight of the gods; the final battle between the gods and the powers of evil, in which gods and men will be defeated by monsters and the sky will grow dark, the Scandinavian equivalent of the *Götterdämmerung*. The original Old Norse form is *ragna rök*, from *ragna* 'of the gods' + *rök* 'destined end', but the variant *Ragna rökr* (*rökr* 'twilight'), which occurs in the prose ➤ EDDA, has influenced understanding of the name.

> An all-out race war would be triggered, a final, bloody Ragnarok of the races.
> — *Time* 26 July 1993

ragtag and bobtail a group of people perceived as disreputable or undesirable; the expression dates from the early 19th century, and derives from the earlier (16th-century) phrase *tag and rag*.

ragtime music characterized by a syncopated melodic line and regularly accented accompaniment, evolved by black American musicians in the 1890s and played especially on the piano; it is now seen as the immediate precursor of jazz.

raguly in heraldry, having an edge with oblique notches like a row of sawn-off branches.

Ragusa the Italian name, generally used until 1918, of Dubrovnik on the Adriatic coast; in the 16th and 17th centuries, Ragusa was a flourishing city-state and a centre of Croat culture.

Rahu in Hindu tradition, the evil being who is responsible for eclipses.

rai a style of music fusing Arabic and Algerian folk elements with Western rock. Recorded from the 1980s, the name may come from Arabic *ha er-ray*,

literally 'that's the thinking, here is the view', a phrase frequently found in the songs.

raid a rapid surprise attack on an enemy by troops, aircraft, or other armed forces in warfare. Recorded from late Middle English as a Scots variant of *road*, the word originally meant 'journey on horseback, foray'. It became rare from the end of the 16th century but was revived by Sir Walter Scott.

See also ➤ DAWN *raid*.

railroad see ➤ UNDERGROUND *Railroad*.

the Railway King nickname of George Hudson (1800–71), who in 1827 invested a large bequest in North Midland Railway shares, and who subsequently became chairman of first the York and North Midland and then a number of other railway companies. By 1844 (the keenest period of railway speculation) his personal influence was unrivalled, and he acquired this sobriquet. Three years later, with the fall in the value of railway property, his power declined; in 1849 he resigned his chairmanships, and in 1865 he was briefly imprisoned for debt.

rain see also ➤ ACID *rain*, ➤ RIGHT *as rain*, ➤ BLESSED *are the dead that the rain rains on*, ➤ *if in* FEBRUARY *there be no rain 'tis neither good for hay nor grain*, ➤ *Saint* SWITHIN*'s day, if thou be fair*.

rain before seven, fine before eleven proverbial saying, mid 19th century.

rain cats and dogs rain very heavily; the phrase is first recorded in 1738, used by Jonathan Swift, but the variant **rain dogs and polecats** was used earlier in Richard Brome's *The City Witt* (1653). The origin is not known, although explanations adduced include a connection with the supernatural (cats were associated with witches, believed to be able to raise storms), as well as the suggestion that in earlier times heavy rain would have resulted in the bodies of drowned dogs and cats floating in the streets and gutters. Cats and dogs are also proverbial for the enmity between them.

take a rain check said when politely refusing an offer, with the implication that one may take it up at a later date (a **rain check** is a ticket given for later use when a sporting fixture or other outdoor event is interrupted or postponed by rain).

rain from the east: wet two days at least proverbial saying; mid 17th century.

rain, rain, go to Spain: fair weather come again proverbial saying; mid 17th century.

rainbow an arch of colours formed in the sky in certain circumstances, and caused by the refraction and dispersion of the sun's light by rain or other water droplets in the atmosphere. The colours of the rainbow are generally said to be red, orange, yellow, green, blue, indigo, and violet.

A *rainbow* is often taken as a symbol of hope or a promise for peace, traditionally with allusion to Genesis 9:13–16, referring to God's setting a rainbow in the sky as a sign of his covenant with his chosen people (see also ➤ *bow of* PROMISE). It may also more generally be a sign of something distant and (perhaps) unattainable:

> Somewhere over the rainbow
> Way up high
> There's a land that I heard of
> Once in a lullaby.
> — E. Y. ('Yip') Harburg 'Over the Rainbow' (1939 song)
> in *The Wizard of Oz*

at the end of the rainbow used to refer to something much sought after but impossible to attain, with allusion to the story of a crock of gold supposedly to be found by anyone reaching the end of a rainbow.

Rainbow Bridge a bridge of natural rock, the world's largest natural bridge, situated in southern Utah, just north of the border with Arizona. Its span is 86 m (278 ft).

rainbow coalition (especially in the US) a political alliance of differing groups, typically one comprising minority peoples and other disadvantaged groups; a phrase originally coined by Jesse Jackson:

> When I look out at this convention, I see the face of America, red, yellow, brown, black, and white. We are all precious in God's sight—the real rainbow coalition.
> — Jesse Jackson speech at Democratic National Convention, Atlanta, 19 July 1988

Rainbow in this context was used more sombrely in 1998 by Winnie Madikizela-Mandela, at the funeral of a black child reportedly shot dead by a white farmer, 'Maybe there is no rainbow nation after all because it does not have the colour black.'

a rainbow in the morning is the sailor's warning;
a rainbow at night is the sailor's delight
proverbial saying, mid 16th century.

rainbow serpent a widely venerated spirit of Australian Aboriginal mythology, a large snake associated with water.

Rainbow Warrior name of a ship belonging to ➤ GREENPEACE which in 1985 was sunk in Auckland harbour after two bomb explosions; it had been about to sail for Mororua Atoll to protest against French nuclear testing there, and it was subsequently revealed that French intelligence agents had planted the bombs. The French Minister of Defence resigned as a result, and the head of the intelligence service was dismissed.

rainmaker a person who attempts to cause rain to fall, either by rituals or by a scientific technique such as seeding clouds with crystals; in figurative use, a person who is highly successful, especially in business.

it never rains but it pours proverbial saying, early 18th century.

if it rains when the sun is shining, the devil is beating his wife proverbial saying, mid 17th century.

it is easier to raise the Devil than to lay him proverbial saying, mid 17th century.

the Raj British sovereignty in India before 1947 (also called, **the British Raj**). The word is from Hindi *rāj* 'reign'.

raja an Indian king or prince; a title extended to petty dignitaries and nobles in India during the British Raj.

See also ➤ WHITE *Raja*.

Bhagwan Shree Rajneesh (1931–90), Indian guru, known as *the Bhagwan* (Sanskrit, 'lord'). He founded an ashram in Poona, India, and a commune in Oregon, becoming notorious for his doctrine of communal therapy and salvation through free love. He was deported from the US in 1985 for immigration violations.

Rajput a member of a Hindu military caste claiming ➤ KSHATRIYA descent.

Rajputana an ancient region of India consisting of a collection of princely states ruled by dynasties. Following independence from Britain in 1947, they united to form the state of Rajasthan, parts also being incorporated into Gujarat and Madhya Pradesh.

Rajya Sabha the upper house of the Indian parliament.

rake's progress a progressive deterioration, especially through self-indulgence, from the title of a series of engravings by William Hogarth (1735), showing the rake's life progressing from its wealthy and privileged origins to debt, despair, and death on the gallows.

rakhi a cotton bracelet, typically bearing elaborate ornamentation, given at Raksha Bandhan by a girl or woman to a brother or to a close male friend who must then treat and protect her as a sister.

Raksha Bandhan (in the Indian subcontinent) a popular festival of friendship occurring annually in August, during which a girl or woman gives cotton bracelets (rakhis) to brothers and close male friends.

rakshasa in Hinduism, a malignant demon, especially any of a band at war with ➤ RAMA and ➤ HANUMAN.

Walter Raleigh (*c*.1552–1618), English explorer, courtier, and writer. A favourite of Elizabeth I (he is said once to have spread his new cloak for her to walk over a muddy road), he organized several voyages of exploration and colonization to the Americas, and introduced potato and tobacco plants to England.

Imprisoned in 1603 by James I on a charge of conspiracy, he was released in 1616 to lead an expedition up the Orinoco River in search of El Dorado, but was executed on the original charge when he returned empty-handed.

ram an uncastrated male sheep, often taken as a type of virility; **the Ram** is the name of the zodiacal sign or the constellation Aries. The word is recorded from Old English, and is of Germanic origin.

it is possible for a ram to kill a butcher proverbial saying, mid 17th century.

Rama the hero of the ➤ RAMAYANA, husband of ➤ SITA. He is the Hindu model of the ideal man, the seventh incarnation of Vishnu, and is widely venerated, by some sects as the supreme god.

See also ➤ ADAM*'s Bridge*.

Ramadan the ninth month of the Muslim year, during which strict fasting is observed from sunrise to sunset. The name comes from Arabic *ramaḍān*, from *ramaḍa* 'be hot'. The lunar reckoning of the Muslim calendar brings the fast eleven days earlier each year, eventually causing Ramadan to occur in any season; originally it was supposed to be in one of the hot months.

Ramakrishna (1836–86), Indian yogi and mystic. He condemned lust, money, and the caste system, preaching that all religions leading to the attainment of mystical experience are equally good and true.

Chandrasekhara Venkata Raman (1888–1970), Indian physicist. He discovered the ➤ RAMAN *effect*, one of the most important proofs of the quantum theory of light.

Raman effect a change of wavelength exhibited by some of the radiation scattered in a medium. The effect is specific to the molecules which cause it, and so can be used in spectroscopic analysis.

Ramapithecus a fossil anthropoid ape of the Miocene epoch, known from remains found in SW Asia and East Africa, and probably ancestral to the orang-utan; it is named from ➤ RAMA + Greek *pithēkos* 'ape'.

Ramayana one of the two great Sanskrit epics of the Hindus, composed *c*.300 BC. It describes how ➤ RAMA, aided by his brother and the monkey Hanuman, rescued his wife Sita from Ravana, the ten-headed demon king of Lanka.

See also ➤ ADAM*'s Bridge*.

Marie Rambert (1888–1982), British ballet dancer, teacher, and director, born in Poland. In 1913 she joined Diaghilev's Ballets Russes as a teacher of eurhythmics, and after moving to London in 1917 she formed and directed the Ballet Club, which became known as the Ballet Rambert in 1935.

the Ramblas a broad avenue in Barcelona; in Spanish, the word *rambla* in the singular originally denoted a broad street built on a shallow watercourse, and comes ultimately from Arabic *ramla* 'sandy ground'.

Rambo an exceptionally tough, aggressive man, from the name of the hero of David Morrell's novel *First Blood* (1972), a Vietnam war veteran represented as macho, self-sufficient, and bent on violent retribution. The character was popularized in the films *First Blood* (1982) and *Rambo: First Blood Part II* (1985).

Hotel de Rambouillet town house of Catherine de Vivonne, marquise de *Rambouillet* (1588–1665), near the site of the Palais-Royal, and the intellectual centre of fashionable Paris in the first half of the 17th century. Mme de Rambouillet exerted a refining influence on French language and literature. Although

Molière, Boileau, and Racine reacted against her salon, it was the inaugurating example of what became a French cultural institution for over two centuries.

Ramessid a member of the Egyptian royal family during the 19th and 20th dynasties (*c*.13th to 11th centuries); the name comes from *Rameses*, variant of ➤ RAMSES.

Battle of Ramillies a battle in the ➤ *War of the* SPANISH *Succession* which took place in 1706 near the village of Ramillies, north of Namur, in Belgium, when British army under Marlborough defeated the French.

Santiago Ramón y Cajal (1852–1934), Spanish physician and histologist. He was a founder of the science of neurology, identifying the neuron as the fundamental unit of the nervous system.

rampant in heraldry, (of an animal) represented standing on one hind foot with its forefeet in the air (typically in profile, facing the dexter (left) side, with right hind foot and tail raised, unless otherwise specified).

Allan Ramsay (1713–84), Scottish portrait painter who became much in demand in London as a portraitist in the 1750s. His style is noted for its French rococo grace and sensitivity, particularly in his portraits of women. In 1767 he was appointed painter to George III.

William Ramsay (1852–1916), Scottish chemist, discoverer of the noble gases. He first discovered argon, helium, and (with the help of M. W. Travers, (1872–1961)) neon, krypton, and xenon, determing their atomic weights and places in the periodic table. In 1910, with Frederick Soddy and Robert Whytlaw-Gray (1877–1958), he identified the last noble gas, radon.

Ramses II (died *c*.1225 BC), Egyptian pharaoh, reigned *c*.1292–*c*.1225 BC; known as **Ramses the Great**. The third pharaoh of the 19th dynasty, he built vast monuments and statues, including the two rock temples at ➤ ABU *Simbel*.
See also ➤ OZYMANDIAS.

Ramses III (died *c*.1167 BC), Egyptian pharaoh, reigned *c*.1198–*c*.1167 BC. The second pharaoh of the 20th dynasty, he fought decisive battles against the Libyans and the ➤ SEA *Peoples*. After his death the power of Egypt declined.

Alf Ramsey (1920–99), English footballer and manager, who managed England from 1963 to 1974, winning the World Cup in 1966.

Ramsey, the rich of gold and of fee;
Thorney, the flower of the fen country.
Crowland, so courteous of meat and of drink;
Peterborough the proud, as all men do think.
And Sawtrey, by the way, that old abbey
Gave more alms in one day than all they
traditional rhyme on East Anglian abbeys, variants of which are recorded from the early 17th century.

Rana (the title of) a member of the family of ➤ RAJPUT origin which virtually ruled Nepal from 1846 to 1951.

the Rand another name for *Witwatersrand*, a goldfield district near Johannesburg; from this came the name *rand* for the base monetary unit of South Africa.

Randlord in the first part of the 20th century, a mining tycoon on the Rand.

random access in computing, the process of transferring information to or from memory in which every memory location can be accessed directly rather than being accessed in a fixed sequence.

random walk in physics, the movements of an object or changes in a variable that follow no discernible pattern or trend.

Ranelagh Gardens in Chelsea, a place of public amusement opened in 1742 in the grounds of the earl of Ranelagh. It had a famous Rotunda, 150 feet in diameter, with an orchestra in the centre, and boxes round it, where people promenaded. The gardens were closed in 1804. They now form part of Chelsea Hospital Gardens.

ranger a keeper of a park, forest, or area of countryside; a person or thing that wanders or ranges. *Ranger* is also the name of a series of nine American moon probes launched between 1961 and 1965, the last three of which took many photographs before crashing into the moon.
See also ➤ LONE *Ranger*, ➤ ROGERS' *Rangers*, ➤ SLOANE *Ranger*, ➤ TEXAS *Ranger*.

rangoli traditional Indian decoration and patterns made with ground rice, particularly during festivals.

Rangoon the capital of Burma (Myanmar), a port in the Irrawaddy delta, which for centuries has been a Buddhist religious centre, and is the site of the

➤ SHWE *Dagon* Pagoda, built over 2,500 years ago. The Burmese name of the city is *Yangon*.

rani a Hindu queen, either by marriage to a raja or in her own right.

Ranjit Singh (1780–1839), Indian maharaja, founder of the Sikh state of Punjab; known as the **Lion of the Punjab**. He proclaimed himself maharaja of Punjab in 1801, and went on to make it the most powerful state in India. Most of his territory was annexed by Britain after the Sikh Wars which followed his death.

Kumar Shri Ranjitsinhji Vibhaji (1872–1933), Maharaja Jam Sahib of Navanagar, Indian cricketer and statesman. He made his cricketing debut for Sussex in 1895, and scored a total of 72 centuries as a batsman for Sussex and England. In 1907 he succeeded his cousin as maharaja of the state of Navanagar.

J. Arthur Rank (1888–1972), English industrialist and film executive. In 1941 he founded the Rank Organization, a film production and distribution company that acquired control of the leading British studios and cinema chains in the 1940s and 1950s.

rank and file the ordinary members of an organization as opposed to its leaders (referring to the 'ranks' and 'files' into which privates and non-commissioned officers form on parade).

Rankenian Club one of the most influential 18th-century Edinburgh clubs, founded *c*.1717 by a group of radical divinity students who were admirers of the moral and political writings of the third earl of Shaftesbury; its leading members later rose to prominence in the universities, the Church, medicine, and the law, and were influential in the improvement of literary style in Edinburgh. Lord Auchinleck, father of Boswell, was a member.

ransom a sum of money or other payment demanded or paid for the release of a prisoner. The word comes from the same root as *redemption*, and early use occurs in theological contexts expressing 'deliverance' and 'atonement'.

Arthur Ransome (1884–1967), English novelist and journalist, best known for the children's classic *Swallows and Amazons* (1930) and its sequels, which depict the imaginative world of children while reflecting a keen interest in sailing, fishing, and the countryside.

Ransomers informal name for the ➤ MERCEDARIANS.

ranz-des-vaches a type of Swiss Alpine melody, originally sung or played on an Alpenhorn to call cows on the mountainside, and consisting of irregular phrases made up of the harmonic notes of the horn.

rape see also ➤ DATE *rape*.

rape any of the six ancient divisions of Sussex. The word comes from an Old English variant of *rope*, with reference to the fencing-off of land.

the Rape of the Lock title of a mock-heroic poem (1714) by Alexander Pope, based on an incident in which Lord Petre cut off a lock of hair from the head of a celebrated beauty, his distant cousin Arabella Fermor.

the Rape of the Sabine Women in Roman mythology, the forcible carrying off of the ➤ SABINE women by ➤ ROMULUS, to provide wives for his men of the new settlement of Rome, at a spectacle to which the Sabines had been invited.

Raphael[1] in the Bible, one of the seven archangels in the apocryphal Book of Enoch. He is said to have 'healed' the earth when it was defiled by the sins of the fallen angels.

Raphael[2] (1483–1520), Italian painter and architect, regarded as one of the greatest artists of the Renaissance, and particularly noted for his madonnas.

rapparee a bandit or irregular soldier in Ireland in the 17th century. The word comes from Irish *rapaire* 'short pike'.

Rappite a member of a 19th-century communistic Christian sect founded by George *Rapp* (1757–1847), in Pennsylvania; a Rappist, a Harmonist.

raptor a dromaeosaurid dinosaur, especially velociraptor or utahraptor. The word *raptor* (from Latin, meaning 'bird of prey') is recorded in English from the 19th century, but in this sense comes directly from a shortened form of *velociraptor*, used originally by palaeontologists and popularized by Michael Crichton's thriller *Jurassic Park* and the Spielberg film (1993) based on it.

rara avis Latin phrase meaning literally a 'rare bird'; a phenomenon, a prodigy. The expression comes from the Roman satirist Juvenal (AD *c*.60–*c*.130), '*Rara avis in terris nigroque simillima* *cycno* [A rare bird on this earth, like nothing so much as a black swan].'

rare (of meat, especially beef) lightly cooked, so that the inside is still red. The word is a late 18th-century variant of obsolete *rear* 'half-cooked', used to refer to soft-boiled eggs, from the mid 17th to mid 19th centuries.

Rare Ben a nickname of Ben Jonson; Sir John Young, a visitor to the Westminster Abbey who had seen the slab over his grave, caused the words 'O rare Ben Jonson' to be cut in it.

rare bird an exceptional person or thing, a ➤ RARA *avis.*

raree-show a form of entertainment, especially one carried in a box, such as a peep show; the term is recorded from the late 17th century, and apparently represents *rare show*, as pronounced by Savoyard showmen.

Ras an Ethiopian king, prince, or feudal lord; the word comes originally from Amharic *rās* 'head'.

rasa in Hinduism, the essence or characteristic quality of something, in particular the flavour or juice of a foodstuff. The word comes from Sanskrit and means literally, 'juice'.

rasa a traditional Indian dance, originally performed by ➤ KRISHNA and the ➤ GOPIS in Hindu mythology; a festival celebrating this. The word comes from Sanskrit *rāsa* 'sport'.

rascal a mischievous or cheeky person or child (typically used in an affectionate way); originally (in Middle English) meaning 'a mob', 'member of the rabble'.

Raskolnik a member of a Russian Orthodox group which refused to accept the liturgical reforms of the patriarch Nikon (1605–81); an ➤ OLD *Believer.*

Grigori Rasputin (1871–1916), Russian monk. He came to exert great influence over Tsar Nicholas II and his family by claiming miraculous powers to heal the heir to the throne, who suffered from haemophilia. This influence, combined with his reputation for debauchery, steadily discredited the imperial family, and he was assassinated by a group loyal to the tsar; the murder was first attempted by poison, to which he proved impervious, and he was finally shot.

Rastafarian a member of a religious movement of Jamaican origin holding that blacks are the chosen

people. *Rastafarians* believe that Emperor Haile Selassie of Ethiopia (who from 1916–30 was known as *Ras Tafari*) was the Messiah, and that black people will eventually return to their African homeland. They have distinctive codes of behaviour and dress, including the wearing of dreadlocks, the smoking of cannabis, and the rejection of Western medicine, and they follow a diet that excludes pork, shellfish, and milk.

rat a rodent that resembles a large mouse, typically having a pointed snout and a long sparsely haired tail; some kinds have become cosmopolitan and are sometimes responsible for transmitting diseases; in particular (in the case of the black rat) plague. The rat has traditionally been taken as the type of a cunning and vicious animal, especially (as in the saying that ➤ RATS *desert a sinking ship*) one ready to betray a cause, or **to rat.**

> Anyone can rat, but it takes a certain amount of ingenuity to re-rat.
> — Winston Churchill on rejoining the Conservatives, c.1924, twenty years after leaving them for the Liberals.

See also ➤ *the* CAT, *the rat, and Lovell the dog,* ➤ IRISH *rat,* ➤ *you* DIRTY *rat.*

Tahupotiki Wiremu Ratana (1873–1939), Maori political and religious leader. He founded the **Ratana Church** (1920), a religious revival movement which aimed to unite all Maori people.

rate see ➤ CROW *rate.*

rath[1] in ancient Ireland, a strong circular earthen wall forming an enclosure and serving as a fort and residence for a tribal chief.

rath[2] in the Indian subcontinent, a chariot, especially one used to carry an idol in a ceremonial procession.

rath yatra in Hinduism, a ceremonial procession centred around a chariot carrying an idol, specifically the procession of the ➤ JUGGERNAUT.

rathe poetic and literary term for prompt and eager; (of flowers or fruit) blooming or ripening early in the year.

rational dress a style of women's dress introduced in the late 19th century, characterized by the wearing of knickerbockers or bloomers in place of a skirt.

rats see also ➤ *the* DESERT *Rats,* ➤ *Grand Order of* WATER *Rats,* ➤ RHYME *rats to death.*

rats desert a sinking ship proverbial saying, late 16th century; sometimes used allusively, as in Beaverbrook's comment, in *Men and Power* (1956) on Lord Curzon, 'Often undecided whether to desert a sinking ship for one that might not float, he would make up his mind to sit on the wharf for a day.'

raven the raven is traditionally regarded as a bird of ill-omen, and one that as a carrion-bird feeds on corpses, especially of those who have been killed in battle or hanged. Danish vikings had the symbol of a raven on their flag. In Scandinavian mythology, Odin has two ravens, Hugin and Munin, who are his messengers.

A raven is the emblem of ➤ *St* BENEDICT and ➤ *St* OSWALD; ravens are also said to have brought bread to the prophet Elijah when he was living east of the Jordan (1 Kings 17:6), and during the ➤ FLOOD a raven was sent out of the ark by Noah.

the croaking raven bodes misfortune proverbial saying, late 16th century.

raven-stone a place of execution, the gallows, the gibbet; the expression is a translation of German *rabenstein*, and refers to ravens feeding on the corpses of those who have been executed.

Ravenna a city near the Adriatic coast in NE central Italy, which became the capital of the Western Roman Empire in 402 and then of the Ostrogothic kingdom of Italy, afterwards serving as capital of Byzantine Italy. It is noted for its ancient mosaics dating from the early Christian period.

Ravi a river in the north of the Indian subcontinent, one of the headwaters of the Indus, which rises in the Himalayas and is one of the five rivers that gave ➤ PUNJAB its name.

ravissant in heraldry, in the half-raised posture of a wolf beginning to spring on its prey.

rawhead and bloody bones proverbial type of something terrifying, recorded from the mid 16th century, perhaps associated with the idea that the apparition of a murdered man is traditionally supposed to haunt the scene of his murder.

John Ray (1627–1705), English naturalist. Ray was the first to classify flowering plants into monocotyledons and dicotyledons, and he established the species as the basic taxonomic unit. His systematic

scheme was not improved upon until that of Linnaeus.

Man Ray (1890–1976), American photographer, painter, and film-maker. A leading figure in the New York and European Dada movements, he is perhaps best known for his photograph the *Violin d'Ingres* (1924), which achieved the effect of making the back of a female nude resemble a violin.

John Rayleigh (1842–1919), English physicist. He established the electrical units of resistance, current, and electromotive force. With William Ramsay he discovered argon and other inert gases.

Rayleigh scattering the scattering of light by particles in a medium, without change in wavelength. It accounts, for example, for the blue colour of the sky, since blue light is scattered slightly more efficiently than red.

rayonnant relating to or denoting a French style of Gothic architecture prevalent from *c.*1230 to *c.*1350, characterized by distinctive rose windows. The word is French and means literally 'radiating', from the pattern of radiating lights in the windows.

rayonné in heraldry, (of a division between parts of the field) having alternate straight and wavy sided pointed projections and depressions.

razor see ➤ OCCAM's *razor*.

razzia a hostile raid for purposes of conquest, plunder, and capture of slaves, especially one carried out by Moors in North Africa. The word comes (in the mid 19th century) via French from Algerian Arabic *ġāziya* 'raid'.

read see also ➤ *he that* RUNS *may read*.

read my lips in US politics, a catch-phrase promoted during the Republican presidential campaign of George Bush (1924–) to emphasize commitment to lower taxes; accepting the Republican nomination in August 1988, Bush said, 'Read my lips: no new taxes'.

read oneself in enter office as incumbent of a benefice in the Church of England by reading publicly the Thirty-nine Articles and making the Declaration of Assent.

reader the general term for someone who reads aloud has different specific meanings in various professions. In ecclesiastical usage, the term is used for a ➤ LAY *reader*; in the Inns of Court, the word denotes a lecturer on law (*readers* were traditionally appointed to deliver explanatory dissertations on statutes). In British universities, *Reader* is the title given to a university lecturer of the highest grade below professor.

ready, steady, go used to announce the beginning of a race.

the real McCoy the real thing, the genuine article; it is suggested that this originated from the phrase *the real Mackay*, an advertising slogan used by G. Mackay and Co, whisky distillers in Edinburgh in 1870. The form *McCoy* appears to be of US origin.

real presence in Christian theology, the actual presence of Christ's body and blood in the Eucharistic elements.

realism the philosophical doctrine that universals or abstract concepts have an objective or absolute existence. The theory that universals have their own reality is sometimes call **Platonic realism** because it was first outlined by Plato's doctrine of 'forms' or ideas.

In art and literature, *realism* denotes the movement or style of representing familiar things as they actually are. While realism in art is often used in the same contexts as naturalism, implying a concern to depict or describe accurately and objectively, it also suggests a deliberate rejection of conventionally beautiful or appropriate subjects in favour of sincerity and a focus on simple and unidealized treatment of contemporary life. Specifically, the term is applied to a late 19th-century movement in French painting and literature represented by Gustave Courbet in the former and Balzac, Stendhal, and Flaubert in the latter.

See also ➤ SOCIALIST *realism*.

realo a member of the pragmatic, as opposed to the radical, wing of the Green movement; often contrasted with *fundie*. The word comes in the 1980s from German *Realist* 'realist'.

realpolitik a system of politics or principles based on practical rather than moral or ideological considerations. The word is German, and is recorded in English from the early 20th century.

reap see ➤ *as you* SOW *so shall you reap*.

reaper see ➤ GRIM *Reaper*.

rearmament see ➤ MORAL *Rearmament*.

rearmouse an archaic term for a bat; the first element may represent the stem of an Old English verb meaning 'to move'.

reason see also ➤ FEAST *of reason*, ➤ TEMPLE *of Reason*.

age of reason in the late 17th and 18th centuries in western Europe, during which cultural life was characterized by faith in human reason, the ➤ ENLIGHTENMENT.

the Goddess of Reason in Revolutionary France, the central figure of a system of thought intended to replace Christianity; the first ceremony of celebration, in which an actress, dressed in white and wearing a ➤ PHRYGIAN *bonnet*, represented Liberty bowing before the flame of Reason, was held in Notre-Dame Cathedral (renamed the *Temple of Reason*) on 10 November 1793.

Temple of Reason during the French Revolutionary period, the name given to the cathedral of ➤ NOTRE-*Dame*.

there is reason in the roasting of eggs proverbial saying, mid 17th century; meaning that however odd an action may seem, there is a reason for it.

René Antoine Ferchault de Réaumur (1683–1757), French naturalist. He is chiefly remembered for his thermometer scale (the **Réaumur scale**), now obsolete, which set the melting point of ice at 0° and the boiling point of water at 80°. Réaumur also carried out pioneering work on insects and other invertebrates.

Reb[1] a traditional Jewish title or form of address, corresponding to Sir, for a man who is not a rabbi (used preceding the forename or surname).

Reb[2] informal name for a Confederate soldier in the American Civil War, recorded from 1862. Also *Johnny Reb*.

Rebecca in the Bible, the wife of ➤ ISAAC and mother of ➤ ESAU and ➤ JACOB.

According to the story in Genesis 24:60, when she left her parents' home for her marriage her family blessed her, saying, 'let thy seed possess the gate of those which hate them.' From this, the name *Rebecca* was given to the leader, dressed as a woman, of a group of rioters who demolished toll-gates in South Wales in 1843–4.

Rebekah a member of a women's society resembling that of the Oddfellows and founded in Indiana in 1851; the name (following the spelling of the Authorized Version) is in allusion to Genesis 24:60, in which ➤ REBECCA was told that she would be 'the mother of thousands of millions'.

rebel see also ➤ *rebel without a* CAUSE.

rebel yell a shout or battle cry used by the Confederates during the American Civil War.

rebellion see ➤ BACON'*s Rebellion,* ➤ GREAT *Rebellion,* ➤ SHAYS'*s Rebellion,* ➤ TAIPING *Rebellion.*

rebus a puzzle in which words are represented by combinations of pictures and individual letters; for instance, *apex* might be represented by a picture of an ape followed by a letter *X*.

Madame Récamier (1777–1849), a Frenchwoman whose salon during the Napoleonic years and the Restoration was frequented by the most brilliant society of the day; she was portrayed by David in a reclining position on a chaise-longue, and her name is used allusively both for the kind of couch, and for the posture in which she is shown.

received pronunciation the standard form of British English pronunciation, based on educated speech in southern England, widely accepted as a standard elsewhere.

official receiver a person or company appointed by a court to manage the financial affairs of a business or person that has gone bankrupt.

receiver of wrecks a port official to whom all objects recovered from the sea or from sunken ships must be delivered for adjudication of ownership.

if there were no receivers there would be no thieves proverbial saying, late 14th century.

recessional a hymn sung while the clergy and choir process out of church at the end of a service; in 1897, Kipling gave the title 'The Recessional' to his poem which begins, 'The tumult and the shouting dies—The captains and the kings depart'.

Rechabite (in the Bible) a member of an Israelite family, descended from Rechab, who refused to drink wine or live in houses (Jeremiah 35). Now, a member of the Independent Order of Rechabites, a benefit society of teetotallers, founded in 1835.

recherche du temps perdu an evocation of one's early life; a French phrase, literally 'in search of the lost time', title of Proust's novel sequence of 1913–27 (in English translation of 1922–31, 'Remembrance of things past').

recipe a set of instructions for preparing a particular dish, including a list of the ingredients required; formerly also, a medical prescription, where it was

first used as an instruction (the word is Latin, and means literally 'receive').

reck pay heed to something (an archaic term, usually in negative contexts). An Old English word, of Germanic origin, *reck* became common in rhetorical and poetic language in the 19th century.

reckon establish by counting or calculation. Early senses included 'give an account of items received' and 'mention things in order', which gave rise to the notion of 'calculation' and hence of 'coming to a conclusion'.

reckoning see ➤ DAY *of reckoning,* ➤ SHORT *reckonings make long friends.*

he that reckons without his host must reckon again (twice) proverbial saying, late 15th century.

Recollet a member of a reformed branch of the Franciscan order, founded in France in the late 16th century. The name comes from French *récollet*, from medieval Latin *recollectus* 'gathered together', expressing a notion of concentration, and absorption in thought.

take heed of reconciled enemies (and of meat twice boiled) proverbial saying, late Middle English.

reconciliation see ➤ DAY *of the Vow,* ➤ TRUTH *and Reconciliation Commission.*

Reconstruction the period 1865–77 following the American Civil War, during which the Southern states of the Confederacy were controlled by federal government and social legislation, including the granting of new rights to black people, was introduced. There was strong white opposition to the new measures, and when a new Republican government returned power to white Southern leaders a policy of racial segregation was introduced.

record a thing constituting a piece of evidence about the past, especially an account of an act or occurrence kept in writing or some other permanent form. As a noun it was earliest used in law to denote the fact of being written down as evidence. As a verb it originally meant 'narrate orally or in writing', also 'repeat so as to commit to memory'.

Recorder in England and Wales, a barrister appointed to serve as a part-time judge.

recording angel an angel that is believed to register each person's good and bad actions; the term is recorded from the late 16th century.

recreant a coward, an apostate; the word comes (in Middle English) from Old French, literally 'surrendering'.

recreational drugs drugs taken on an occasional basis for enjoyment, especially when socializing. The term, which encompasses a wide range of narcotic and hallucinogenic drugs, was originally used literally to distinguish the form of use from that of medical necessity, but in the 1980s it came increasingly to reflect the view that it was possible to have intermittent and pleasurable recourse to stimulants of this kind without the user becoming addicted, or being seen as part of the 'drug scene'. Recreational drug users, or RDUs, are not those who followed the 1960s injunction to 'tune in, turn on, and drop out', but those who regard the preferred drug as something which could enhance without damaging the chosen lifestyle.

recusant a person, especially a Roman Catholic, who refused to attend the services of the Church of England at a time when this was legally required.

The Act of Uniformity of 1558 first imposed fines on all non-attenders of a parish church, but Roman Catholics were the specific target of the Act against Popish Recusants of 1592; subsequent acts through the 17th century imposed heavy penalties on Catholic recusants, the exaction of which persisted up to the Second Relief Act of 1791. Particular pressure was put on Roman Catholics after 1570, when the papal bull 'Regnans in Excelsis' excommunicated Elizabeth I.

red a colour at the end of of the spectrum next to orange and opposite violet, as the colour of blood, fire, or rubies. As a ➤ LITURGICAL *colour, red* is used for Passion Sunday and Pentecost, and for the feasts of martyrs; figuratively it is associated with the emotions of anger and embarrassment, and in political terms is the colour of radicalism.

Recorded from Old English (as *rēad*), the word is of Germanic origin, from an Indo-European root shared by Latin *rufus*, Greek *eruthros*, and Sanskrit *rudhira* 'red'.

See also ➤ BETTER *dead than red,* ➤ ERIC *the Red,* ➤ LITTLE *Red Riding-hood,* ➤ *the* MURDER *in the Red Barn,* ➤ PAINT *the town red,* ➤ *the* THIN *red line.*

Admiral of the Red in the British navy, former title of the Admiral of the Red squadron (one of the three divisions of the Royal Navy made in the 17th century).

Red Army originally, the army of the Bolsheviks, the Workers' and Peasants' Red Army; later, the army of the Soviet Union, formed after the Revolution of 1917. The name was officially dropped in 1946. *Red Army* has also been used for the army of China or some other Communist countries.

Red Army Faction a left-wing terrorist group in former West Germany, active from 1968 onwards. It was originally led by Andreas Baader (1943–77) and Ulrike Meinhof (1934–76), and was also called the ➤ BAADER-*Meinhof Group.*

Red Arrows in the UK, the aerobatic display team of the Royal Air Force.

Red Baron a nickname for the German fighter pilot Manfred, Freiherr von ➤ RICHTHOFEN (1882–1918), who flew a distinctive bright red aircraft.

a red beard and a black head, catch him with a good trick and take him dead proverbial saying, late 16th century; perhaps referring to ➤ RED *hair* as associated with Judas.

red book the title given to any of various official books of economic or political significance (*red* being the conventional colour of the binding of official books); as *Red Book,* a popular name for the 'Royal Kalendar, or Complete...Annual Register' (published from 1767 to 1893).

See also ➤ LITTLE *Red Book.*

The Red Book of Hergest a Welsh manuscript of the late 14th to early 15th centuries (now the property of Jesus College, Oxford), containing the tales known as the ➤ MABINOGION and other pieces in prose and verse.

Red Book of the Exchequer in England, a MS volume compiled in the 13th century, recording charters, statutes, and surveys (published in 1896 in the Rolls Series); in Ireland, a book of record of the Irish court of the exchequer.

red box in the UK, a box, typically covered with red leather, used by a Minister of State to hold official documents.

Red Branch in Irish epic tradition, the name (translating Gaelic *Craebh Ruaid*) of the most famous of the royal houses of Ulster; the **House of the Red Branch** at the capital of ➤ EMAIN *Macha* was the place where the arms of defeated enemies were stored.

Red Brigades an extreme left-wing terrorist organization based in Italy, which from the early 1970s was responsible for carrying out kidnappings, murders, and acts of sabotage. A former Prime Minister of Italy, Aldo Moro, was killed by the Red Brigades in 1978.

red button in the Chinese empire, distinguishing the highest class of mandarin.

red card (in soccer and some other games) a red card shown by the referee to a player who is being sent off the field.

red carpet a long, narrow red carpet laid on the ground for a distinguished visitor to walk along when arriving.

red cent the smallest amount of money (the US one-cent coin was formerly made of copper).

Red Chamber the Senate chamber of the Canadian Parliament Building in Ottawa, so called because of its red carpet and draperies; the Senate itself.

the Red Comyn John Comyn (d. 1306), of Badenoch, son of one of the claimants to the Scottish throne, killed in an affray with ➤ *Robert* BRUCE in the church at Dumfries; in 1307, Bruce and his associates were excommunicated by the papal legate as a result.

Red Crescent a national branch in Muslim countries of the International Movement of the Red Cross and the Red Crescent. The name was adopted in 1906.

red cross an upright red cross on a white ground; the symbol of ➤ *St* GEORGE, especially as the national emblem of England, and as the badge and emblem of Christian forces in the Crusades.

In the 17th century, the sign of a *red cross* was placed on the door of a house to indicate the presence within the house of plague; in the mid 19th century, it was taken as the internationally agreed badge of a nursing and ambulance service.

The *Red Cross* was set up in 1864 at the instigation of the Swiss philanthropist Henri Dunant (1828–1910) according to the Geneva Convention, and its headquarters are at Geneva. The International Movement of the Red Cross and the Red Crescent is now an international humanitarian organization bringing relief to victims of war or natural disaster.

See also ➤ REDCROSSE *Knight*.

red dragon in heraldry, the badge of Wales, also known as the **red dragon of Cadwallader**.

red duster informal term for the ➤ RED *ensign*.

red ensign a red flag with the Union Jack in the top corner next to the flagstaff, flown by British-registered ships.

red-eye flight chiefly in North America, a flight on which a passenger cannot expect to get much sleep on account of the time of departure or arrival, especially when a time zone is crossed. In the late 1980s, with transatlantic commuting a reality, it became a fashionable term among British business executives for the overnight flight from New York to London; arriving at breakfast time on such a flight, the traveller has a full business day ahead and a time difference of five or six hours to cope with.

red flag the symbol of socialist revolution or a warning of danger; the anthem of Britain's Labour Party, a socialist song with words written in 1889 by the Irish socialist James M. Connell (1852–1929) and sung to the tune of the German song 'O Tannenbaum':

> Then raise the scarlet standard high!
> Within its shade we'll live or die.
> Tho' cowards flinch and traitors sneer,
> We'll keep the red flag flying here.
> — James M. Connell 'The Red Flag' (1889)

In Britain, the song is still sung at the conclusion of the annual Labour Party Conference.

red gold traditional (chiefly poetic) expression for gold; in modern usage, the term for an alloy of gold and copper.

Red Guard any of various radical or socialist groups, in particular an organized detachment of workers during the Russian Revolution of 1917 and a militant youth movement in China (1966–76) which carried out attacks on intellectuals and other disfavoured groups as part of Mao Zedong's Cultural Revolution.

red hair traditionally regarded as unlucky or dangerous; it was the medieval belief that ➤ JUDAS *Iscariot* had red hair.

red hand the arms or badge of Ulster, a red left hand (also called *bloody hand*) cut off squarely at the wrist, originally a badge of the O'Neill family.

red hat a cardinal's hat, especially as the symbol of a cardinal's office; in Christian art, a red hat is often shown in depictions of ➤ *St* JEROME as a ➤ DOCTOR *of the Church*.

red herring something, especially a clue, which is or is intended to be misleading or distracting (so named from the practice of using the scent of a dried smoked herring in training hounds).

See also ➤ *neither* FISH *nor fowl nor good red herring.*

Red Indian an old-fashioned term for an American Indian. First recorded in the early 19th century, it has largely fallen out of use, being associated with an earlier period and the corresponding stereotypes of cowboys and Indians and the ➤ WILD *West.*

red-letter day a day that is pleasantly noteworthy or memorable, from the practice of highlighting a saint's day or other festival in red on an ecclesiastical calendar. The term is recorded from the early 18th century.

red-light district an area of a town or city containing many brothels, strip clubs, and other sex businesses, from the use of a red light as the sign of a brothel.

red man in alchemical belief, an obsolete term for a red substance mystically represented as a male principle.

Red Pope in the Roman Catholic Church, informal name for the Prefect of the Propaganda.

Red Power a movement in support of rights and political power for American Indians.

Red Prince a nickname for Prince Frederick Charles of Prussia (1828–85), said to be from the colour of the uniform which he usually wore.

Red Queen a main character in Lewis Carroll's *Through the Looking Glass* (1871), who tells Alice that 'it takes all the running you can do to stay in the same place'.

> I felt that I had spent my academic career like the Red Queen, running as fast as I could just to stay in the same place.
> — *American Scientist* July 1995

Red Queen hypothesis the hypothesis that organisms are constantly struggling to keep up with one another in an evolutionary race between predator and prey species, named from Lewis Carroll's ➤ RED *Queen.*

like a red rag to a bull an object, utterance, or act which is certain to provoke someone, from the traditional belief (recorded from the late 16th century)

that this colour is particularly irritating to the animal.

Red Republic a republic based on socialist principles, in particular, the French Second Republic, proclaimed in 1848.

red rose traditionally, the emblem of the ➤ *House of* LANCASTER (as opposed to the ➤ WHITE *rose* of the Yorkists. In the late 20th century, a *red rose* has also been used as a symbol of the British Labour Party.

red route denoting a scheme intended to facilitate the smooth flow of urban traffic by the imposition of severe penalties for stopping and parking along roads marked with a red line, introduced in Britain in the 1990s.

Red Sea a long, narrow landlocked sea separating Africa from the Arabian peninsula, and now linked to the Indian Ocean in the south by the Gulf of Aden and to the Mediterranean in the north by the Suez Canal.

In the biblical account, the Israelites led by Moses escaped from Egypt when the waters of the *Red Sea* were miraculously parted; the army and chariots of the pursuing Egyptians were drowned when the waters once more closed over them. The name here should properly be translated 'Sea, or Lake, of Reeds'; it may in fact refer to the marshes of Lake Timsah, now part of the Suez Canal.

red shift in astronomy, the displacement of spectral lines towards longer wavelengths (the red end of the spectrum) in radiation from distant galaxies and celestial objects.

red sky at night, shepherd's delight; red sky in the morning, shepherd's warning proverbial saying, late 14th century; meaning that good and bad weather respectively is presaged by a red sky at sunset and dawn.

Red Square a large square in Moscow next to the Kremlin. In existence since the late 15th century, under Communism the square was the scene of great parades celebrating May Day and the October Revolution.

red tape excessive bureaucracy or adherence to rules and formalities, especially in public business; the expression refers to the reddish-pink tape which is commonly used for securing legal and official documents.

Red Tory (in Canada) a member of a political group who, while maintaining some conservative principles, supports many liberal and socialist policies.

redbreast an informal name for the robin, recorded from late Middle English; in the mid 19th century, *Redbreast* was used as a nickname for ➤ Bow *Street Runners*, who habitually wore bright scarlet waistcoats.

See also ➤ ROBIN *redbreast*.

redbrick (designating) a British university founded in the late 19th or early 20th century, usually in a large industrial city, and especially as contrasted with Oxford and Cambridge.

redcoat a traditional name for a British soldier (so named because of the colour of the uniform). In the Civil War the term was commonly applied to the Parliamentary forces, although there were red-uniformed soldiers on both sides.

In the UK from the 1950s, *redcoat* has been used for an organizer and entertainer at a Butlin's holiday camp, who on duty wore a scarlet blazer.

Redcrosse Knight in the first book of Spenser's *Faerie Queene*, St George, the patron saint of England; the Knight and the heroine Una (the true religion) are finally betrothed, after he has killed the dragon which besieged her parents' castle.

redding stroke traditionally suffered by someone trying to make peace between two combatants, and believed to be particularly dangerous; *redding* here comes from the verb *redd* 'to separate combatants'.

rede an archaic term for advice or counsel given by one person to another.

the Redeemer Christ, who has saved humankind from the effects of sin.

redemptioner in the late 18th and 19th centuries, an emigrant who received his passage to America on the condition that his services there should be disposed of by the master or owners of the vessel, until the passage-money and other expenses were repaid out of his earnings.

Redemptionist a member of a Christian order dedicated to redeeming Christian captives from slavery, a ➤ MERCEDARIAN.

Redemptorist a member of the Roman Catholic Congregation of the Most Holy Redeemer, founded at Naples in 1732 by St Alphonsus Liguori, and devoted chiefly to work among the poor.

redneck informal and derogatory term for a working-class white person from the southern US, especially a politically reactionary one; the term is recorded from the mid 19th century.

reductio ad absurdum a method of proving the falsity of a premise by showing that its logical consequence is absurd or contradictory; a Latin phrase, meaning 'reduction to the absurd' recorded in English from the mid 18th century.

reductio ad impossibile a method of proving a proposition by drawing an absurd or impossible conclusion from its contradictory; a Latin phrase, meaning 'reduction to the impossible', recorded in English from the mid 16th century.

reduplicate repeat (a syllable or other linguistic element) exactly or with a slight change (e.g. *hurly-burly*, *see-saw*).

reed see also ➤ BROKEN *reed*.

a reed before the wind lives on, while mighty oaks do fall proverbial saying, late 14th century.

a reed shaken by the wind the type of something easily moved and insubstantial, with biblical allusion as to Matthew 11:7, 'What went ye out into the wilderness to see? A reed shaken by the wind?'

the Reef in South Africa, another term for ➤ *the* RAND.

Reekie see ➤ AULD *Reekie*.

reeve a local official, in particular the chief magistrate of a town or district in Anglo-Saxon England; in Canada, the president of a village or town council. Recorded from Old English (in the form *rēfa*), the second syllable of ➤ SHERIFF comes from this word.

referendum a general vote by the electorate on a single political question which has been referred to them for a direct decision; the process of referring a political question to the electorate for this purpose.

reflexology a system of massage used to relieve tension and treat illness, based on the theory that there are reflex points on the feet, hands, and head linked to every part of the body.

reform see also ➤ *the* FATHER *of Reform*.

Reform Act an act framed to amend the system of parliamentary representation, especially those introduced in Britain during the 19th century.

The first Reform Act (1832) disenfranchised various rotten boroughs and lowered the property qualification, widening the electorate by about 50 per cent to include most of the male members of the upper middle class. The second (1867) doubled the electorate to about 2 million men by again lowering the property qualification, and the third (1884) increased it to about 5 million.

Reform Club a London club in Pall Mall, founded in 1836 to promote political reform.

Reform Judaism a form of Judaism, initiated in Germany by the philosopher Moses Mendelssohn (1729–86), which has reformed or abandoned aspects of Orthodox Jewish worship and ritual in an attempt to adapt to modern changes in social, political, and cultural life.

the Reformation a 16th-century movement for the reform of abuses in the Roman Church ending in the establishment of the Reformed and Protestant Churches. The roots of the Reformation go back to the 14th-century attacks on the wealth and hierarchy of the Church made by groups such as the Lollards and the Hussites. But the *Reformation* is usually thought of as beginning in 1517 in Wittenberg, when ➤ *Martin* LUTHER issued ninety-five theses criticizing Church doctrine and practice. In Denmark, Norway, Sweden, Saxony, Hesse, and Brandenburg, supporters broke away and established Protestant Churches, while in Switzerland a separate movement was led by Zwingli and later Calvin.

See also ➤ COUNTER-*Reformation*, ➤ MORNING *Star of the Reformation*.

Reformed Church a Church that has accepted the principles of the Reformation, especially a Calvinist Church (as distinct from Lutheran).

See also ➤ DUTCH *Reformed Church*.

refresher an extra fee payable to counsel in a prolonged case; the term is recorded from the early 19th century.

Refreshment Sunday the fourth Sunday in Lent, so called because the Gospel for the day is from John 6, which tells the story of the feeding of the five thousand. Also called *Refection Sunday*.

refuge see ➤ CITY *of refuge*.

refusenik a Jew in the former Soviet Union who was refused permission to emigrate to Israel.

Refusés see ➤ SALON *des Refusés*.

regardant in heraldry, (typically of a lion) looking backwards over the shoulder.

regatta a sporting event consisting of a series of boat or yacht races. The word comes (in the early 17th century) from Venetian dialect, literally 'fight, contest'.

Regency in the UK, the period from 1811–20 when, during the incapacity of ➤ GEORGE *III*, the country was ruled by his eldest son as Regent; in particular, relating to or denoting British architecture, clothing, and furniture of the period (1811–20) or, more widely, of the late 18th and early 19th centuries. *Regency* style was contemporary with the ➤ EMPIRE style and shares many of its features: elaborate and ornate, it is generally neoclassical, with a generous borrowing of Greek and Egyptian motifs.

See also ➤ *the* GOOD *Regent*, ➤ PRINCE *Regent*.

Regent's Park in London, established by George IV when Prince Regent; it was designed and developed by the architect ➤ *John* NASH as a royal park.

reggae a style of popular music with a strongly accented subsidiary beat, originating in Jamaica. Reggae evolved in the late 1960s from ska and other local variations on calypso and rhythm and blues, and became widely known in the 1970s through the work of Bob Marley; its lyrics are much influenced by Rastafarian ideas. The term may be related to Jamaican English *rege-rege* 'quarrel, row'.

regia see ➤ AQUA *regia*.

regicide any of those who took part in the trial and execution of Charles I; after the ➤ RESTORATION, several of the *regicides* were tried and executed, and the bodies of ➤ *Oliver* CROMWELL, his son-in-law Henry Ireton, Bradshaw, and Pride, were ordered to be dug up, drawn on a hurdle to Tyburn, and there first displayed in their coffins on the scaffold, and finally buried under the gallows.

regimental colour (in the UK) a regimental standard in the form of a silk flag, carried by a particular regiment along with its Queen's colour.

regimental nickname often alluding to a particular event in the history of a regiment, as the ➤ BLOODY *Eleventh*.

Regina the reigning queen (used following a name or in the titles of lawsuits, e.g. *Regina v. Jones*, the Crown versus Jones).

See also ➤ Salve *Regina*.

Regina Coeli a Latin epithet ('Queen of Heaven') of the Virgin Mary.

Johannes Regiomontanus (1436–76), German astronomer and mathematician. Regiomontanus is considered the most important astronomer of the 15th century. He translated Ptolemy's *Mathematical Syntaxis*, with revisions and comments, and wrote four monumental works on mathematics (especially trigonometry) and astronomy.

register see also ➤ Annual *Register*.

Register House in Scotland, the house appointed for the keeping of the registers, now a special building (the **General Register House**) in Princes Street, Edinburgh.

regium donum an annual grant made from public funds to Nonconformist clergy in Britain and Ireland from the late 17th to the mid 19th century; the phrase is Latin, and means literally 'royal gift'.

Regius professor (in the UK) the holder of a university chair founded by a sovereign (especially one at Oxford or Cambridge instituted by Henry VIII) or filled by Crown appointment.

regnal year a year reckoned from the date or anniversary of a sovereign's accession.

Marcus Atilius Regulus Roman soldier and politician of the 3rd century BC; captured by the Carthaginians, he is said in the *Odes* of Horace to have been sent by them to negotiate a peace with Rome, but instead to have advised them to continue the war. He then fulfilled the agreement he had made by returning to Carthage, where he was tortured to death.

Rehoboam son of Solomon, king of ancient Israel *c*.930–*c*.915 BC. His reign witnessed the secession of the northern tribes and their establishment of a new kingdom under Jeroboam, leaving Rehoboam as the first king of Judah (1 Kings 11–14).

From the late 19th century, the word *rehoboam* has been used for a wine bottle of about six times the standard size.

Reich the former German state, most often used to refer to the Third Reich, the Nazi regime from 1933

to 1945. The **First Reich** was considered to be the Holy Roman Empire, 962–1806, and the **Second Reich** the German Empire, 1871–1918, but neither of these terms are part of normal historical terminology.

See also ➤ Third *Reich*, ➤ Thousand-*Year Reich*.

Reichenbach Falls in Switzerland, one of the highest falls in the Alps, and scene of the final struggle between ➤ Sherlock Holmes and his arch-enemy Professor ➤ Moriarty. Conan Doyle had originally decided that Sherlock Holmes's career would end with his death here, but he was persuaded by popular demand to allow the detective to emerge from the *Reichenbach Falls* alive.

Reichstag the main legislature of the German state under the Second and Third Reichs; the building in Berlin in which this met, which was badly damaged by fire on the Nazi accession to power in 1933, an event believed by many to have been contrived by the Nazis to justify suppression of opposition and the assumption of emergency powers.

In April 1999, the renovated Reichstag building, parliament of reunited Germany, was formally opened, its new interior having been created by the British architect Norman Fowler.

reign name the symbolic name adopted by a Japanese or (formerly) Chinese ruler.

Reign of Terror the period of remorseless repression or bloodshed (➤ *the* Terror) during the French Revolution.

reim-kennar a person skilled in magic rhymes; a pseudo-archaism of Sir Walter Scott, apparently formed on German *Reim* 'rhyme' + *Kenner* 'knower'.

Reims a city of northern France, which was the traditional coronation place of most French kings and is noted for its fine 13th-century Gothic cathedral.

la reine le veult the queen wishes it; formula by which the queen gives her ➤ royal *assent* to a bill. *Le roy le veult* is the equivalent when the sovereign is a king.

la reine s'avisera the queen will consider; formula by which the queen can exercise her right of veto over a bill. It was last used in 1707, when Queen Anne refused her assent to a Scottish militia bill. *Le roy s'avisera* is the equivalent when the sovereign is a king.

reins archaic term for the kidneys; the loins; in biblical use, the seat of feelings or affections, the heart.

reinvent the wheel be forced by necessity to construct a basic requirement again from the beginning; the *wheel* taken as an essential requirement of modern civilization.

reiter a German cavalry soldier, especially one who fought in the wars of the 16th and 17th centuries; the word is German for 'rider, trooper'.

John Reith (1889–1971), 1st Baron, Scottish administrator and politician, first general manager (1922–7) and first director general (1927–38) of the BBC. He played a major part in the growth of the BBC and championed the moral and intellectual role of broadcasting in the community. In 1948 the BBC established the **Reith Lectures**, broadcast annually, in his honour.

> The new ITV licenses began on January 1, ushering in, as everyone agreed, a more competitive, less Reithian, commercial television system.
> — *Guardian* 1 July 1993

relativism the doctrine that knowledge, truth, and morality exist in relation to culture, society, or historical context, and are not absolute.

relegation in ancient Rome, banishment to a certain place or distance from Rome for a limited time and without loss of civil rights.

In 20th-century Britain, *relegation* in sporting terms is used for the transfer of a team to a lower division of a league.

relic in religious use, especially in the Greek and Roman Catholic Churches, a part of a deceased holy person's body or belongings kept as an object of reverence. Recorded from Middle English, the word (like ➤ RELIQUARY) comes ultimately from Latin *reliquus* 'remaining'.

Relief Church a Scottish ecclesiastical body, founded by Thomas Gillespie and others in 1761 in assertion of the right of congregations to elect their own ministers and in protest against the aggressions of the General Assembly; in 1847 it amalgamated with the United Secession to form the United Presbyterian Church.

Most Religious King epithet of the king of England.

Religious Society of Friends official name for the ➤ QUAKERS.

reliquary a container, as a box or shrine, for holy ➤ RELICS; *reliquaries* are often richly ornamented.

Reliques see ➤ PERCY's *Reliques*.

Rembrandt (1606–69), Dutch painter. He made his name as a portrait painter with the *Anatomy Lesson of Dr Tulp* (1632). With his most celebrated painting, the *Night Watch* (1642), he used chiaroscuro to give his subjects a more spiritual and introspective quality, a departure which was to transform the Dutch portrait tradition. Rembrandt is especially identified with the series of more than sixty self-portraits painted from 1629 to 1669.

remedies see ➤ DESPERATE *diseases must have desperate remedies.*

there is a remedy for everything except death proverbial saying, mid 15th century.

Remember! supposedly the last word said by Charles I on the scaffold to Bishop William Juxon (1582–1663), who attended him (at the ➤ RESTORATION, Juxon was made archbishop of Canterbury).

Remembrance Day another term for ➤ REMEMBRANCE *Sunday.*

Remembrance Sunday (in the UK) the Sunday nearest 11 November, when those who were killed in the First and Second World Wars and later conflicts are commemorated.

Remembrancetide the period immediately preceding Remembrance Sunday, considered as part of the liturgical year.

St Remigius (d. 533), bishop, of Gaulish parentage, who became known as the *Apostle of the Franks*; he baptized ➤ CLOVIS, king of the Franks, whose queen Clotild was a Christian.

Remigius, who died at Reims on 13 January, was later said to have had the power of touching for the ➤ KING's *evil*; this ability supposedly passed from him to Clovis, and was later claimed by ➤ EDWARD *the Confessor* and the Norman kings of England. It was also said that a miraculous dove had brought the chrism for the baptism of Clovis; until the Revolution, what was left of this, known as the ➤ *la* SAINTE *ampoule*, was kept in Reims Cathedral.

☐ **FEAST DAY** His feast day is 13 January; his translation is celebrated on 1 October.

remittance man an emigrant supported or assisted by payments of money from home; typically a disgraced man of good position or family who has been sent abroad by his family and whose payments depend on his remaining there.

the Remonstrance a document drawn up in 1610 by the Arminians of the Dutch Reformed Church, presenting the differences between their doctrines and those of the strict Calvinists.

the Grand Remonstrance the formal statement of grievances presented by the House of Commons to the Crown in 1641.

Remonstrant a member of the Arminian party in the Dutch Reformed Church.

removals see ➤ THREE *removals are as bad as a fire.*

Remus in Roman mythology, the twin brother of ➤ ROMULUS; he is said to have quarrelled with his brother over the building of the walls of Rome, and to have been killed by him.
    See also ➤ UNCLE *Remus.*

Renaissance the revival of art and literature under the influence of classical models in the 14th–16th centuries; the culture and style of art and architecture developed during this era.
    The Renaissance is generally regarded as beginning in Florence, where there was a revival of interest in classical antiquity. Important early figures are the writers Petrarch, Dante, and Boccaccio and the painter Giotto. Music flourished, from madrigals to the polyphonic masses of Palestrina, with a wide variety of instruments such as viols and lutes. Classical techniques and styles were studied in Rome by the sculptor Donatello as well as by the architects Bramante and Brunelleschi, who worked on the theory of perspective, which was developed in the innovative frescoes and paintings of Masaccio.
    The period from the end of the 15th century has become known as the **High Renaissance**, when Venice and Rome began to share Florence's importance and Botticelli, Cellini, Raphael, Leonardo da Vinci, and Michelangelo were active. Renaissance thinking spread to the rest of Europe from the early 16th century, and was influential for the next hundred years.
    See also ➤ CAROLINGIAN *Renaissance.*

Renaissance man a person with many talents or interests, especially in the humanities, supposedly exhibiting the virtues of an idealized man of the ➤ RENAISSANCE.

renegade originally (in the late 16th century) an apostate from any form of religious faith, especially a Christian who became a Muslim; the general use

to mean someone who deserts and betrays an organization or country developed in the mid 17th century. The word is an anglicization of Spanish *renegado* and comes from medieval Latin *renegatus* 'renounced'.

Rennes an industrial city in NW France, originally established as the capital of a Celtic tribe, the *Redones*, from whom it derives its name, later becoming the capital of the ancient kingdom and duchy of Brittany.

John Rennie (1761–1821), Scottish civil engineer. He is best known as the designer of the London and East India Docks (built *c.*1800), the Inchcape Rock lighthouse (1807–*c.*1811), and Waterloo Bridge, Southwark Bridge, and London Bridge (1811–31).

Reno a city in western Nevada noted as a gambling resort and for its liberal laws enabling quick marriages and divorces. During the ➤ ABDICATION *Crisis* in Britain, when Mrs Simpson's divorce was granted in an Ipswich court, it was reported that an American newspaper had carried the headline, 'King's Moll Reno'd in Wolsey's home town.'

Auguste Renoir (1841–1919), French painter. An early Impressionist, he developed a style characterized by light, fresh colours and indistinct, subtle outlines. In his later work he concentrated on the human, especially female, form.

rent see ➤ ANTI-*Rent War,* ➤ PEPPERCORN *rent,* ➤ RACK-*rent,* ➤ SIN-*rent.*

repetitive strain injury a condition in which the prolonged performance of repetitive actions, typically with the hands, causes pain or impairment of function in the tendons and muscles involved (the abbreviation **RSI** is frequently used).
    A rapid increase in the number of keyboard users generated by the advent of computers brought the phenomenon of repetitive strain injury to public attention in the early 1980s; legal controversy subsequently developed as the condition was cited as grounds for industrial compensation, and this in turn brought media attention. Initially (while recognizing the components of the condition) the medical profession was divided on the question of whether the physical symptoms were evidence of permanent physical injury; *RSI* is however now widely acknowledged as an occupational health problem.

House of Representatives the lower house of the US Congress and some other legislatures.

reprobate in Calvinist theology, an archaic term for a sinner who is not of the elect and is predestined to damnation. The word comes ultimately from Latin *reprobat-* 'disapproved'.

Humphrey Repton (1752–1818), English landscape gardener. His parks were carefully informal after the model of Capability Brown. Important designs include the park at Cobham in Kent (*c.*1789–*c.*1793) and the house and grounds at Sheringham Hall in Norfolk (1812).

republic a state in which supreme power is held by the people and their elected representatives, and which has an elected or nominated president rather than a monarch. **The Republic** is the English title of Plato's most famous work.

See also ➤ BANANA *republic*, ➤ BATTLE *Hymn of the Republic*, ➤ FIRST *Republic*, ➤ FOURTH *Republic*.

Republic Day the day on which the foundation of a republic is commemorated, in particular (in India) 26 January.

the republic of letters the collective body of those engaged in literary pursuits; the field of literature itself.

republican see also ➤ FRENCH *Republican Calendar*.

Republican Party one of the two main US political parties (the other being the Democratic Party), favouring a right-wing stance, limited central government and tough, interventionist foreign policy. It was formed in 1854 in support of the anti-slavery movement preceding the Civil War.

request see ➤ COURT *of Requests*, ➤ *no* FLOWERS *by request*.

requeté a member of a Carlist militia that took the Nationalist side during the Spanish Civil War of 1936–9. The name, which is Spanish, is perhaps an abbreviation of *requetefiel*, from the intensive prefix *requete-* and *fiel* 'loyal'.

requiem (especially in the Roman Catholic Church) a Mass for the repose of the souls of the dead. Recorded from Middle English, the word comes from Latin (the first word of the Mass), accusative of *requies* 'rest'.

reredos an ornamental screen covering the wall at the back of an altar. The word comes (in late Middle English) via Anglo-Norman French from Old French *areredos*, from *arere* 'behind' + *dos* 'back'.

Resh Galuta another name for ➤ EXILARCH, from Aramaic *rēš gālūṯā* literally 'chief of the exile'.

the Resistance the underground movement formed in France during the Second World War to fight the German occupying forces and the Vichy government. The Resistance was composed of various groups which were coordinated into the *Forces Françaises de l'Intérieur* in 1944, which joined with Free French forces in the liberation of Paris and northern France.

the line of least resistance an option avoiding difficulty or unpleasantness; the easiest course of action.

respond in architectural use, a half-pillar or half-pier attached to a wall to support an arch, especially at the end of an arcade.

responsa prudentum the opinions and judgements of learned lawyers, originally as forming part of Roman civil law; the phrase is Latin, and means literally 'the answers of the learned'.

the Resolute Doctor nickname of the Carmelite and scholar John Baconthorpe (d. 1346), perhaps from the tenacity with which he maintained his Averroist principles.

rest see also ➤ *a* CHANGE *is as good as a rest*, ➤ DAY *of rest*, ➤ *rest on one's* LAURELS.

the rest is silence in Shakespeare's play, the final words of Hamlet himself.

the Restoration the re-establishment of ➤ CHARLES *II* as King of England in 1660. After the death of ➤ *Oliver* CROMWELL in 1658, his son Richard (1626–1712) proved incapable of maintaining the Protectorate, and General Monck organized the king's return from exile. The term itself is first recorded in the early 18th century.

Restoration comedy a style of drama which flourished in London after the Restoration in 1660, typically having a complicated plot marked by wit, cynicism, and licentiousness; principal exponents include ➤ *William* CONGREVE, William Wycherley, George Farquhar, ➤ *John* VANBRUGH, and Aphra Behn. The genre marked the first appearance of women, most notably ➤ *Nell* GWYN, on stage in Britain.

the Resurrection in Christian belief, Christ's rising from the dead; the rising of the dead at the Last Judgement.

resurrection man in the 18th and 19th centuries, a person who illicitly retrieved corpses to be sold for dissection from rivers, scenes of disaster, or burial grounds.

retainer a fee paid in advance to someone, especially a barrister, in order to secure or keep their services when required.

retiarius an ancient Roman gladiator who used a net to trap his opponent; he was typically also armed with a trident for use on his entangled victim. The name comes from Latin, from *rete* 'net'.

retreatants ➤ *St* IGNATIUS *of Loyola* is the patron saint of those taking part in a religious retreat.

day of retribution the day on which divine reward or punishment will supposedly be assigned to humans; the phrase is recorded from the early 16th century.

return see also ➤ POINT *of no return*.

by return of post originally, this meant by return of the 'post' or courier who brought the dispatch.

Reuben in the Bible, a Hebrew patriarch, eldest son of ➤ JACOB and Leah; in the story of ➤ JOSEPH, it is Reuben who persuades his brothers not to kill the boy by prophesying that if they do his blood will be required of them. Later, Reuben loses his birthright as the eldest son because he has slept with his father's concubine; Jacob on his deathbed (Genesis 49:4) says to him, 'Unstable as water, thou shalt not excel.'

From the early 19th century in North America, the name *Reuben* has been used to suggest the conventionally conceived figure of a farmer or rustic, a country bumpkin (there is no evident link with the biblical figure).

Reuters an international news agency founded in London in 1851 by Paul Julius Reuter (1816–99). The agency pioneered the use of telegraphy, building up a worldwide network of correspondents to produce a service used today by newspapers and radio and television stations in most countries.

reveille a signal sounded especially on a bugle or drum to wake personnel in the armed forces. The word comes, in the mid 17th century, from French *réveillez!* 'wake up', ultimately based on Latin *vigilare* 'keep watch'.

the Revelation of St John the Divine the last book of the New Testament, recounting a divine revelation of the future to ➤ *St* JOHN. Also known as **Revelations**.

Master of the Revels an officer appointed to superintend masques and other entertainments at court. He is first mentioned in the reign of Henry VII. The first permanent master of the revels was Sir Thomas Cawarden, appointed in 1545. Holders of the office in Shakespeare's day were Edmund Tilney, 1579–1610, and Sir George Buc, 1610–22 (he had been deputy master since 1603).

revenant a person who has returned, especially supposedly from the dead. The word, which is French, and means literally 'returning', is recorded from the early 19th century.

revenge is a dish that can be eaten cold proverbial saying, late 19th century.

revenge is sweet proverbial saying, mid 16th century.

revenge tragedy a style of drama, popular in England during the late 16th and 17th centuries, in which the basic plot was a quest for vengeance and which typically featured scenes of carnage and mutilation, real or feigned insanity, and the appearance of ghosts. Examples of the genre include Thomas Kyd's *The Spanish Tragedy* (1592) and John Webster's *The Duchess Of Malfi* (1623).

revenons à nos moutons traditional saying meaning, let us return to the matter in hand; this French phrase, literally 'let us return to our sheep', originally alludes to a confused court scene in the Old French *Farce de Maistre Pierre Pathelin* (*c.*1470).

Paul Revere (1735–1818), American patriot. In 1775 he rode from Boston to Lexington to warn fellow American revolutionaries of the approach of British troops, a feat immortalized in Longfellow's poem 'Paul Revere's Ride' (1863).

reverend used as a title or form of address to members of the clergy.

reverse engineering the reproduction of another manufacturer's product following detailed examination of its construction or composition; the term developed especially with the growth of the market for computer software, and in 1993 the European Union published its European Software directive outlawing all *reverse-engineering* except in certain well-defined circumstances.

the reverse of the medal the other side of the coin; an earlier expression, the obsolete *the medal is reversing* implied that the change was for the worse.

Revised Standard Version a modern English translation of the Bible, published in 1946–57 and based on the American Standard Version of 1901.

Revised Version an English translation of the Bible published in 1881–95 and based on the Authorized Version.

revival of learning the ➤ RENAISSANCE in its literary aspect; also called *revival of letters.*

revolution ➤ BLOODLESS *Revolution,* ➤ CULTURAL *Revolution,* ➤ DAUGHTERS *of the American Revolution,* ➤ FEBRUARY *Revolution,* ➤ FRENCH *Revolution,* ➤ *the* JULY *Revolution,* ➤ OCTOBER *Revolution,* ➤ PROLETARIAN *revolution,* ➤ RUSSIAN *Revolution,* ➤ VELVET *revolution.*

Revolutions	
Bloodless Revolution	England, 1688
Cultural Revolution	China, 1966
February Revolution	Russia, 1917
French Revolution	France, 1789
Glorious Revolution	England, 1688
July Revolution	France, 1830
October Revolution	Russia, 1917
Velvet Revolution	Czechoslovakia, 1989

Revolutionary Tribunal a court established in Paris in October 1793 to try political opponents of the French Revolution. There was no right of appeal and from June 1794 the only penalty was death. A principal instrument of the Terror, it existed until May 1795 and was responsible for ordering more than 2,600 executions.

revolutions are not made with rosewater proverbial saying, early 19th century.

Revolutions of 1848 a series of revolts against monarchical rule in Europe during 1848, springing from a shared background of autocratic government, lack of representation for the middle classes, economic grievances, and growing nationalism. Revolution occurred first in France, where socialists and supporters of universal suffrage caused the overthrow of King ➤ LOUIS *Philippe,* and in the German and Italian states there were uprisings and demonstrations; in Austria rioting caused the flight of the emperor and of ➤ *Prince* METTERNICH, and

peoples subject to the Habsburg empire, notably the Hungarians, demanded autonomy. All the revolutions ended in failure and repression, but some of the liberal reforms gained as a result (such as universal male suffrage in France) survived, and nationalist aims in Germany and Italy were achieved.

Revudeville a form of continuous variety performance presented at the ➤ WINDMILL *Theatre* between 1932 and 1964.

reward see ➤ VIRTUE *is its own reward.*

Rex the reigning king (used following a name or in the titles of lawsuits, e.g. *Rex v. Jones*: the Crown versus Jones).

Rexism a right-wing Roman Catholic political movement established in 1935 in Belgium; the name comes from Latin *(Christus) Rex* '(Christ) the King'.

Reynard a name for a fox; originally, that of the central character, **Reynard the Fox**, in the *Roman de Renart*, a series of popular satirical fables written in France *c.*1175–1250, in which he represents the man who preys on society and is brought to justice, but who escapes by his cunning.

rhabdomancy divination by means of a rod or wand; the art of discovering ores or springs of water in the earth by means of a divining-rod.

Rhadamanthus in Greek mythology, the son of ➤ ZEUS and Europa, and brother of ➤ MINOS, who, as a ruler and judge in the underworld, was renowned for his justice. In poetic and literary usage, **Rhadamanthine** means showing stern and inflexible judgement.

rhapsody (in ancient Greece) an epic poem, or part of it, of a suitable length for recitation at one time. The word comes (in the mid 16th century) via Latin from Greek, ultimately from *rhaptein* 'to stitch' + *ōidē* 'song, ode'.

Rhea in Greek mythology, one of the Titans, wife of ➤ CRONUS and mother of ➤ ZEUS, Demeter, Poseidon, Hera, and Hades. Frightened of betrayal by their children, Cronus ate them; Rhea rescued Zeus from this fate by hiding him and giving Cronus a stone wrapped in blankets instead.

Rhea Silvia in Roman mythology, princess of Alba Longa, mother of ➤ ROMULUS and Remus by the god Mars.

Rheims see ➤ *the* JACKDAW *of Rheims,* ➤ REIMS.

Rhemish Bible an English translation of the New Testament by Roman Catholics of the English college at Reims, published in 1582.

Rhesus a mythical king of Thrace, son of the muse Terpsichore, whose name was arbitrarily used to name the *rhesus monkey*; he is said in the *Iliad* to have brought his army to support the Trojans, but to have been murdered by a trick by Odysseus and Diomedes.

rhesus factor an antigen occurring on the red blood cells of many humans (around 85 per cent) and some other primates. It is particularly important as a cause of haemolytic disease of the newborn and of incompatibility in blood transfusions. It was named in the 1940s for the *rhesus monkey* in which the antigen was first observed.

rhetoric the art of effective or persuasive speaking or writing, especially the exploitation of figures of speech and other compositional techniques; language designed to have a persuasive or impressive effect on its audience, but which is now often regarded as lacking in sincerity or meaningful content.

In the Middle Ages, *rhetoric* was counted as one of the ➤ SEVEN *liberal arts*; the word comes via Old French and Latin from Greek.

rhetorical question a question asked not for information but to produce an effect, e.g. *who cares?* for *nobody cares.*

rheumatism ➤ St JAMES *the Great* is the patron saint of those suffering from rheumatism.

Rhiannon in Celtic mythology, the Welsh equivalent of the Gaulish horse goddess Epona and the Irish goddess Macha; she is also associated with the underworld, and has power over the dead. In the *Mabinogion*, she is the wife of Pwyll.

Rhine the name of the chief river of Germany, forming the German-Swiss border and flowing through Germany to the Netherlands.

See also ➤ CONFEDERATION *on the Rhine*, ➤ *the* WATCH *on the Rhine.*

Rhine maiden each of three water maidens in Wagner's opera *Der Ring des Nibelungen* who are guardians of the Rhine's golden treasure (the 'Rheingold'); a woman with the fair hair and large physique with which the *Rhine maidens* are usually portrayed.

rho the seventeenth letter of the Greek alphabet (**P**, **ρ**), transliterated as 'r' or (when written with a rough breathing) 'rh'.

Rhode Island a state in the north-eastern US, on the Atlantic coast, which was settled from England in the 17th century and was one of the original thirteen states of the Union (1776). It is named after an island in Narragansett Bay, which was one of the original settlements.

Rhodes the largest of the Dodecanese Islands in the SE Aegean, which in the late Bronze Age became a significant trading nation and dominant power; its capital, *Rhodes*, a port on the northernmost tip of the island, founded *c.*408 BC, was the site of the ➤ COLOSSUS *of Rhodes.*

From 1309 to 1522 it was the headquarters of the order of the ➤ KNIGHTS *Hospitallers.*

See also ➤ APOLLONIUS *of Rhodes.*

Cecil Rhodes 1853–1902), British-born South African statesman, Prime Minister of Cape Colony 1890–6. He expanded British territory in southern Africa, annexing Bechuanaland (now Botswana) in 1884 and developing Rhodesia from 1889. By 1890 he had acquired 90 per cent of the world's production of diamonds, but he was forced to resign as Premier by his involvement in the Jameson Raid of 1895. His reported last words were, 'So little done, so much to do.'

Rhodes Scholarship any of several scholarships awarded annually and tenable at Oxford University by students from certain Commonwealth countries, South Africa, the United States, and Germany. They are named after ➤ *Cecil* RHODES, who founded the scholarships in 1902.

Rhodesia the former name of a large territory in central southern Africa which was divided into Northern Rhodesia (now Zambia) and Southern Rhodesia (now *Zimbabwe*). It was originally named after ➤ *Cecil* RHODES (1853–1902), British-born South African statesman.

Rhodian law an early system of maritime law, originally relating to the island of ➤ RHODES as a maritime power in the ancient world.

Rhondda an urbanized district of South Wales, extending along the valleys of the Rivers Rhondda Fawr and Rhondda Fach, which was formerly noted as a coal-mining area.

rhopalic verse (of a line or passage of verse) in which each word contains one syllable more than the one immediately preceding it, or each line is a foot longer than the one before. Recorded from the late 17th century, the word comes via late Latin from Greek *rhopalos* 'club, tapered cudgel'.

rhubarb informal term for the noise made by a group of actors to give the impression of indistinct background conversation or to represent the noise of a crowd, especially by the random repetition of the word 'rhubarb' with different intonations. The word in this sense is recorded from the 1930s.

rhyme correspondence of sound between words or the endings of words, especially when these are used at the ends of lines of poetry. The word was recorded in Middle English in the form *rime*; the current spelling was introduced in the early 17th century under the influence of *rhythm*, and both forms come ultimately via Latin *rhythmus* from Greek *rhuthmos*, related to *rhein* 'to flow'.

rhyme or reason good sense or logic; the phrase (which is found chiefly in negative contexts) is recorded from the mid 17th century.

rhyme rats to death proverbial saying, late 16th century; with reference to a legend that Irish rats were killed or expelled by rhyme.

rhymer see ➤ CORN *Law Rhymer*, ➤ THOMAS *the Rhymer*.

Rhymers Club a group of poets that met at the Cheshire Cheese in Fleet Street for two or three years, from 1891, to read poetry. Members and associates included W. B. Yeats and Ernest Dowson.

rhyming slang a type of slang that replaces words with rhyming words or phrases, typically with the rhyming element omitted. For example *butcher's*, short for *butcher's hook*, means 'look' in Cockney rhyming slang.

rhythm method a method of avoiding conception favoured by the Roman Catholic Church, by which sexual intercourse is restricted to the times of a woman's menstrual cycle when ovulation is least likely to occur.

rhyton a type of drinking container used in ancient Greece, typically having the form of an animal's head or a horn, with the hole for drinking from located at the lower or pointed end. The word comes from Greek *rhuton*, related to *rhein* 'to flow'.

Rialto an island in Venice, containing the old mercantile quarter of medieval Venice; the **Rialto Bridge**, completed in 1591, crosses the Grand Canal between Rialto and San Marco islands. In Shakespeare's *The Merchant of Venice* (1596–8), Shylock asks, 'What news on the Rialto?'

rib see ➤ ADAMS *'s rib*, ➤ *smite under the* FIFTH *rib*.

riband see ➤ BLUE *Riband*.

ribbon knots of coloured ribbon traditionally displayed the wearer's support for a cause, and it has recently become the fashion to wear or display ribbons of certain colours to demonstrate one's sympathies, as, a **red ribbon** for Aids sufferers, or a **yellow ribbon** for the release of prisoners.

See also ➤ BLUE *Ribbon Army*, ➤ BLUE *Ribbon of the Turf*, ➤ GREEN *ribbon*.

ribbon development in the UK, the building of houses along a main road, especially one leading out of a town or village.

Ribbon Society a Roman Catholic nationalist secret society formed in the north and northwest of Ireland in the 19th century and associated with agrarian violence.

Ribston pippin a variety of eating apple prized for its rich flavour, supposedly originating from a pip brought from France about 1707, and named for *Ribston* Park between Knaresborough and Wetherby.

> I said to Heart, 'How goes it?' Heart replied:
> 'Right as a Ribstone Pippin!' But it lied.
> — Hilaire Belloc 'The False Heart' (1910)

Ricardian a supporter of the view that ➤ RICHARD *III* was a just king who was misrepresented by Shakespeare and other writers on the basis of antagonistic Tudor propaganda.

rice traditionally thrown over a bridal couple to bring them luck.

rice-Christian derogatory term for a person who adopts Christianity for material benefits.

rich see also ➤ *one* LAW *for the rich and another for the poor*, ➤ POOR *little rich girl*.

Penelope Rich (*c*.1562–1607), sister of Robert Devereux, Earl of Essex, and the model for Sidney's 'Stella' in *Astrophel and Stella*.

the rich man has his ice in the summer and the poor man gets his in the winter proverbial saying, early 20th century.

Richard see also ➤ Poor *Richard's Almanack*.

Richard I (1157–99), king of England, reigned 1189–99; known as **Richard Coeur de Lion** or **Richard the Lionheart**. He led the Third Crusade, defeating Saladin at Arsuf (1191), but failing to capture Jerusalem. Returning home, he was held hostage by the Holy Roman emperor Henry VI until being released in 1194 on payment of a huge ransom. He was fatally wounded during the siege of the castle of Châlus on a campaign against Philip II of France.

Richard III (1452–85), king of England, brother of Edward IV, reigned 1483–5. He served as Protector to his nephew Edward V, who, after two months, was declared illegitimate and subsequently disappeared. Richard's brief rule ended at Bosworth Field, where he was defeated by Henry Tudor and killed. Many historians argue that the picture of Richard as a hunchbacked cut-throat usurper was Tudor propaganda.

Cliff Richard (1940–), British pop singer. With his group the Drifters (later called the Shadows) he recorded such songs as 'Living Doll' (1959) and 'Bachelor Boy' (1961). He also acted in several musicals, such as *Summer Holiday* (1962). Since the 1970s he has combined a successful solo pop career with evangelism.

Richard's himself again said to indicate that a person is restored to their usual physical and mental state; originally, a line inserted by ➤ *Colley* Cibber in his version (1700) of Shakespeare's *Richard III*, 'Conscience avaunt; Richard's himself again.'

Richelieu (1585–1642), Armand Jean du Plessis, duc de Richelieu, French cardinal and statesman. As chief minister of Louis XIII (1624–42) he dominated French government. He destroyed the power base of the Huguenots in the late 1620s and supported Gustavus Adolphus in the Thirty Years War from 1635. In 1635 he established the Académie française.

Richmond¹ earldom held by ➤ Henry *VII* before becoming king.

Richmond² the state capital of Virginia, a port on the James River, which during the American Civil War was the Confederate capital from July 1861 until its capture in 1865.

Richmond Park a large park in Greater London, formerly the site of *Richmond Palace*, built by Henry VII on the site of the earlier *Shene Palace*, and named by him for his earldom of *Richmond* in Yorkshire.

Richter scale a numerical scale for expressing the magnitude of an earthquake on the basis of seismograph oscillations. The more destructive earthquakes typically have magnitudes between about 5.5 and 8.9; it is a logarithmic scale and a difference of one represents an approximate thirtyfold difference in magnitude. It is named after Charles F. *Richter* (1900–85), American geologist.

Manfred von Richthofen (1882–1918), Freiherr von Richthofen, German fighter pilot; known as **the Red Baron**. He joined a fighter squadron (informally known as a *Flying Circus*) in 1915, flying a distinctive bright red aircraft. He was eventually shot down after destroying eighty enemy planes.

rickshaw a light two-wheeled hooded vehicle drawn by one or more people, chiefly used in Asian countries; the word is an abbreviation of Japanese *jinricksha*, from *jin* 'man' + *riki* 'strength' + *sha* 'vehicle'.

riddle¹ a question or statement intentionally phrased so as to require ingenuity in ascertaining its answer or meaning, typically presented as a game. The word is recorded from Old English (in form *rǣdels(e)*) 'opinion, conjecture, riddle'.

riddle² an amount (thirteen bottles) of claret; *riddle* here means a coarse-meshed sieve, and is said to derive from the wine being brought in on an actual riddle.

riddle-me-ree here's a riddle!, answer this puzzle; a fanciful variant of *riddle me a riddle, riddle my riddle*, and similar phrases.

ride a-cock-horse ride (as) on a child's hobby-horse; recorded from the mid 16th century, and apparently a nursery term applied to anything that a child rides astride upon. It is not clear whether *cock-horse* was originally the name of the plaything, as it appears to have become by the late 16th century.

he will ride backwards up Holborn Hill proverbial expression, late 16th century; meaning that a person will be drawn up ➤ Holborn Hill in a cart to be hanged at Tyburn.

you might ride to Romford on it proverbial allusion to *Romford* in Essex as a place famous for making breeches.

if you can't ride two horses at once, you shouldn't be in the circus proverbial saying, mid 20th century; the British Labour politician James Maxton (1885–1946) is often quoted as saying, 'if you cannot ride two horses you have no right in the bloody circus'.

rider see also ➤ CIRCUIT *rider*, ➤ ROUGH *Rider*.

he who rides a tiger is afraid to dismount proverbial saying, late 19th century.

Riding each of three former administrative divisions of Yorkshire, usually known as the East, North, and West Ridings; the word is recorded in Old English in the form *trithing*, from Old Norse *þriðjungr* 'third part'. The initial *th-* was lost due to assimilation with the preceding *-t* of *East*, *West*, or with the *-th* of *North*.

Nicolas Ridley (*c.*1500–55), English Protestant bishop and martyr. He was appointed bishop of Rochester (1547) and then of London (1550). He opposed the Catholic policies of Mary I, for which he was burnt at the stake in Oxford; his fellow martyr Hugh Latimer encouraged him, 'Be of good comfort Master Ridley, and play the man. We shall this day light such a candle by God's grace in England, as (I trust) shall never be put out.'

ridotto an entertainment or ball with music and dancing, frequently in masquerade, popular in the 18th century; the word comes from Italian.

Lucie Rie (1902–95), Austrian-born British potter. Her pottery and stoneware were admired for their precise simple shapes and varied subtle glazes.

Leni Riefenstahl (1902–), German film-maker and photographer. She is chiefly known for *Triumph of the Will* (1934), a depiction of the 1934 Nuremberg Nazi Party rallies, and *Olympia* (1938), a documentary of the 1936 Berlin Olympic Games. Though she was not working for the Nazi Party, outside Germany her work was regarded as Nazi propaganda.

Bernhard Riemann (1826–66), German mathematician. He founded Riemannian geometry, which is of fundamental importance to both mathematics and physics. The **Riemann hypothesis**, about the complex numbers which are roots of a certain transcendental equation, remains an unsolved problem.

Riemannian geometry a form of differential non-Euclidean geometry developed by Riemann, used to describe curved space. It provided Einstein with a mathematical basis for his general theory of relativity.

riff-raff disreputable or undesirable people; the term is recorded from the late 15th century as *riff and raff*, and comes ultimately from Old French *rif et raf* 'one and all, every bit'.

rift within the lute an apparently minor piece of damage likely to have fatal consequences; the phrase comes originally from a poem by Tennyson:

> It is the little rift within the lute,
> That by and by will make the music mute.
> — Alfred, Lord Tennyson *Idylls of the King* 'Merlin and Vivien' (1859)

Rig Veda in Hinduism, the oldest and principal of the Vedas, composed in the 2nd millennium BC and containing a collection of hymns in early Sanskrit.

rigadoon a lively dance for couples, in duple or quadruple time, of Provençal origin, perhaps named after its inventor, said to be a dance teacher called *Rigaud*.

right see ➤ *the* CUSTOMER *is always right*, ➤ DO *right and fear no man*, ➤ DIVINE *right of kings*, ➤ MIGHT *is right*, ➤ PETITION *of Right*.

right as a trivet quite all right; in reference to a trivet's always standing firm on its three legs.

right as ninepence quite all right; perhaps a variant of the alliterative *nice as ninepence*.

right as rain perfectly fit and well; reinforced by alliteration.

Right Bank a district of the city of Paris, situated on the right bank of the River Seine, to the north of the river. The area contains the Champs Élysées and the Louvre.

Right Honourable a title given to certain high officials such as Privy Counsellors and government ministers.

right of common in English law, a person's right over another's land, e.g. for pasturage or mineral extraction.

somewhere to the right of Genghis Khan holding right-wing views of the most extreme kind; *Genghis Khan* taken as the type of a repressive and tyrannical ruler.

right of way the legal right, established by usage or grant, to pass along a specific route through grounds or property belonging to another. It was often locally believed that a funeral procession taking a direct route to a graveyard could cross private ground, and in so doing establish a permanent right of way.

right-to-life another term for ➤ PRO-*life*.

righteousness see ➤ SUN *of Righteousness*.

Rights see also ➤ BILL *of Rights*, ➤ DECLARATION *of Rights*.

rights of man rights held to be justifiably belonging to any person; human rights. The phrase is associated with the Declaration of the Rights of Man and of the Citizen, adopted by the French National Assembly in 1789 and used as a preface to the French Constitution of 1791.

rigmarie former term for a Scottish coin of small value, said to originate from the billon coins struck during the reign of Queen Mary, inscribed with the words *Reg. Maria*.

rigmarole a long, rambling story or statement, apparently an alteration of *ragman roll*, originally denoting a legal document recording a list of offences.

Rijksmuseum the national art gallery of the Netherlands, in Amsterdam. Established in the late 19th century and developed from the collection of the House of Orange, it contains the most representative collection of Dutch art in the world.

Riksmål another term for ➤ BOKMÅL.

the life of Riley a comfortable pleasant carefree existence; the phrase is said to originate in a late 19th-century song, but this has not so far been traced. To date the earliest version is found in H. Pease's song *My Name is Kelly* (1919), 'my name is Kelly Michael Kelly, But I'm living the life of Reilly.'

Arthur Rimbaud (1854–91), French poet. Known for poems such as 'Le Bateau ivre' (1871) and the collection of symbolist prose poems *Une Saison en enfer* (1873), and for his stormy relationship with Paul Verlaine, he stopped writing at about the age of 20 and spent the rest of his life travelling.

Rimini see ➤ FRANCESCA *da Rimini*.

Rimmon (in the Bible) a deity worshipped in ancient Damascus (2 Kings 5: 18).
   See also ➤ BOW *down in the house of Rimmon*.

Rinaldo a central character in the Charlemagne cycle (also called *Renaud*), who later appears in *Orlando Furioso* and *Gerusalemme Liberata*. He is at first an enemy of Charlemagne, but is pardoned by the king on condition that he goes on Crusade to Palestine, and gives up his horse Bayard (although he agrees to the terms, it turns out that the horse will allow no other rider to mount him).

ring see also ➤ *ring the* BELL, ➤ *ring the* BELLS *backward*, ➤ *ring the* CHANGES.

ring a small circular band, typically of precious metal and often set with one or more gemstones, worn on a finger as an ornament or a token of marriage, engagement, or authority. A ring can also be seen as a particularly personal possession, as in the story of ➤ POLYCRATES and his attempt to avert ill-fortune.
   In traditional legends such as that of the ➤ NIBELUNGENLIED a ring may be an object of power; ➤ TOLKIEN drew on this for his fantasy *The Lord of the Rings*, in which magic rings made for dwarves, elves, and men are under the control of **One Ring** of power.
   A ring is the emblem of ➤ *St* CATHERINE *of Alexandria*, ➤ *St* CATHERINE *of Siena*, and ➤ *St* EDWARD *the Confessor*.
   See also ➤ *the* BRASS *ring*, ➤ CLADDAGH *ring*, ➤ CRAMP *ring*, ➤ CUP-*and-ring*, ➤ ETERNITY *ring*, ➤ FISHERMAN'*s ring*, ➤ SOLOMON'*s ring*.

ring-a-ring o' roses a singing game played by children, in which the players hold hands and dance in a circle, falling down at the end of the song. It is said to refer to the inflamed ('rose-coloured') ring of buboes, symptomatic of the plague; the final part of the game is symbolic of death.

the Ring Cycle informal name for Wagner's cycle of operas based on the ➤ NIBELUNGENLIED.

ring finger the finger next to the little finger, especially of the left hand, on which the wedding ring is worn.

ring fort a prehistoric earthwork, especially an Iron Age hill fort, defended by circular ramparts and ditches.

ring of iron the defensive cordon created around Bilbao by the Basques in the Spanish Civil War; the term is a translation of Spanish *cinturón de hierro*.

ring of steel a security cordon built around (part of) a city, typically as an anti-terrorist measure, employing roadblocks and surveillance procedures; in the UK, the possibility was raised of establishing a *ring of steel* round the City of London after the IRA's bombing of the Baltic Exchange in 1992.

Ringerike a style of late Viking decorative art, characterized by abundant use of foliage patterns, named after a district centred on Honefoss, north of Oslo in Norway.

rings see ➤ LORD *of the Rings*.

Rinpoche a religious teacher held in high regard among Tibetan Buddhists (often used as an honorific title). The word is Tibetan, literally 'precious jewel'.

Rio Grande a river of North America which rises in the Rocky Mountains of Colorado and flows southeastwards to the Gulf of Mexico, forming the US–Mexico frontier from El Paso to the sea.

riot see also ➤ ASTOR *Place riot*, ➤ GORDON *Riots*, ➤ PORTEOUS *riot*.

Riot Act an Act passed by the British government in 1715 (in the wake of the Jacobite rebellion of that year) and repealed in 1967, designed to prevent civil disorder. The Act made it a felony for an assembly of more than twelve people to refuse to disperse after being ordered to do so and having been read a specified portion of the Act by lawful authority.

read the Riot Act formally read the specified portion of the act as a notification to an assembly to disperse.

riot girl a member of a movement of young feminists expressing their resistance to the sexual harassment and exploitation of women, especially through aggressive punk-style rock music.

RIP abbreviation of Latin *requiescat in pace*, 'may he (or she) rest in peace' or *requiescant in pace*, 'may they rest in peace', used in memorial notices and inscriptions.

Rip van Winkle the hero of a story in Washington Irving's *Sketch Book* (1819–20), a good-for-nothing

who fell asleep in the Catskill Mountains and awoke after twenty years to find the world completely changed. Often found in extended allusive usage.

> Religious Rip Van Winkles who have slept through a generation of progress in moral theology.
> — Dorothy Rowe *Wanting Everything* (1991)

ripe see ➤ SOON *ripe, soon rotten*.

ripper a murderer who mutilates victims' bodies; the term was first used in the late 19th century connection with ➤ JACK *the Ripper*, and in the late 1970s began to be used of the **Yorkshire Ripper**, the name given to Peter Sutcliffe (1946–), who murdered 13 women in northern England and the Midlands before being captured in January 1981.

rise see also ➤ EARLY *to bed and early to rise*.

rise from the ashes be renewed after destruction, perhaps alluding to the legend of the ➤ PHOENIX, fabled to burn itself to ashes on a funeral pyre ignited by the sun and fanned by its own wings, only to emerge from the ashes with renewed youth.

rishi a Hindu sage or saint.

rising see also ➤ EASTER *Rising*, ➤ LAND *of the Rising Sun*.

Rising was a seaport town, and Lynn it was a wash,

but now Lynn is a seaport town, and Rising fears the worst
traditional rhyme, mid 19th century.

a rising tide lifts all boats proverbial saying, mid 20th century; in America the expression was particularly associated with John Fitzgerald Kennedy (1917–63):

> As they say on my own Cape Cod, a rising tide lifts all boats. And a partnership, by definition, serves both partners, without domination or unfair advantage.
> — John Fitzgerald Kennedy address, 25 June 1963

Risorgimento a movement for the unification and independence of Italy, which was achieved in 1870. The restoration of repressive regimes after the ➤ NAPOLEONIC *Wars* led to revolts in Naples and Piedmont (1821) and Bologna (1831). With French aid, the Austrians were driven out of northern Italy by 1859, and the south was won over by ➤ GARIBALDI. Voting resulted in the acceptance of Victor Emmanuel II as the first king of a united Italy in 1861.

The name is Italian, and means literally, 'resurrection'.

rite of passage a ceremony or event marking an important stage in someone's life, especially birth, initiation, marriage, and death. The term is a translation of French *rite de passage*, coined by Arnold van Gennep as the title of a book, *Les rites de passage*, in 1909.

ritter a German or Austrian knight or mounted warrior; a member of the German or Austrian minor nobility. The word is German, and is a variant of ➤ REITER.

Ritterkreuz the Knight's Cross of the Iron Cross, a German decoration instituted by Adolf Hitler and awarded for distinguished service in war.

Ritualism a derogatory term coined in the 19th century, by those who opposed Catholic forms of worship in the Church of England, for the beliefs and practices of the High Church party.

ritzy expensively stylish; from the name of the Swiss-born hotelier César *Ritz* (1850–1918), given to his luxury hotels in Paris, London, New York, and elsewhere.

rival a person or thing competing with another for the same objective or for superiority in the same field of activity; the word comes (in the late 16th century) from Latin *rivalis*, originally in the sense 'person using the same stream as another', from *rivus* 'stream'.

river see also ➤ OLD *Man River*, ➤ ROW *someone up Salt River*, ➤ SABBATICAL *river*, ➤ *the* SEA *refuses no river*, ➤ SELL *down the river*.

up the river in the US, to or in prison, originally referring to ➤ SING *Sing* prison, situated up the Hudson River from the city of New York.

**River of Dart! O river of Dart!
every year thou claimest a heart**
traditional rhyme, mid 19th century.

river of white a white line or streak down a printed page where spaces between words on consecutive lines are close together.

> Oh those proofs, those proofs! Imagine . . . sticking in words to make the printing look decent—to get the rivers of white out of it!
> — George Bernard Shaw letter, 5 January 1898

all rivers run into the sea proverbial saying, early 16th century; originally with biblical allusion to Ecclesiastes 1:7, 'All the rivers run into the sea; yet the sea is not full; unto the place from whence the rivers come, thither they return again'.

the Riviera part of the Mediterranean coastal region of southern France and northern Italy, extending from Cannes to La Spezia, famous for its beauty, mild climate, and fashionable resorts. The name is Italian, and means literally 'seashore'.

road see also ➤ *all roads lead to* ROME, ➤ BURMA *Road*, ➤ CORDUROY *road*, ➤ *road to* DAMASCUS, ➤ ROMAN *road*, ➤ RULE *of the road*, ➤ SILK *Road*, ➤ *there is no* ROYAL *road to learning*, ➤ WILDERNESS *Road*.

road rage violent anger caused by the stress and frustration of driving a motor vehicle; especially (an act of) violence committed by one motorist against another which is provoked by the supposedly objectionable driving of the victim.

Road rage is probably the best known of the forms of *rage* which have become a feature of modern urban life; but in recent years the growing familiarity of the term has occasioned some anxiety, in case the attribution of violent behaviour to *road rage* should seem to lessen the responsibility of the aggressor.

> Advice on how to deal with road rage is to be included in the new edition of the Highway Code in July.
> — *Daily Telegraph* 27 May 1996 (electronic edition)

the road to hell is paved with good intentions proverbial saying, late 16th century; earlier forms of the proverb omit the first three words, as in a letter from St Francis de Sales in which he attributed to St Bernard the saying, 'Hell is full of good intentions or desires.'

Roanoke Island an island off the coast of North Carolina, first settled unsuccessfully in 1584 by Richard Grenville; this was the site of the ➤ LOST *Colony*.

roaring boy archaic term for a young man living in a noisy and riotous manner; **roaring girl** is also found, as in the title of Middleton and Dekker's play *The Roaring Girl: or Moll Cutpurse* (1611).

roaring forties stormy ocean tracts between latitudes 40° and 50° south; the name is recorded from the late 19th century.

roaring game a name for curling, perhaps from the sound made by the stones sliding along the ice; in a poem of 1786 (*Vision*), Robert Burns refers to the curlers' 'roaring-play'.

Roaring Meg another name for ➤ Mons *Meg*, recorded from the late 16th century.

roaring twenties the decade 1920–29 (with reference to its post-war buoyancy).

roast see also ➤ RULE *the roast*.

cry roast meat be foolish enough to announce to others a piece of private luck or good fortune, recorded from the mid 17th century.

rob Peter to pay Paul traditional saying, late Middle English; meaning to take away from one person or cause in order to give to another. In early examples, the use of *Peter* and *Paul* apparently represents no more than a conjunction of alliterative names, but in later use the phrase seems to have been influenced by the association of the apostles Peter and Paul as leaders of the early Church and fellow martyrs.

Rob Roy (1671–1734), Scottish outlaw and member of the proscribed ➤ MACGREGOR family, whose reputation as a Scottish ➤ ROBIN *Hood* was coloured by Sir Walter Scott's novel *Rob Roy* (1817).

Robben Island a small island off the coast of South Africa, near Cape Town, the site of a prison which was formerly used for the detention of political prisoners, including ➤ *Nelson* MANDELA. On New Year's Eve, 1999, as part of South Africa's millennial celebrations, Nelson Mandela lit a candle in his former cell.

> As restrictions on studying by correspondence were eased, Robben Island became known . . . as the University. In truth, it was known as Mandela University.
> — *New York Review of Books* 2 February 1995

robbery see ➤ *a fair* EXCHANGE *is no robbery*.

Robbia see ➤ *Luca* DELLA *Robbia*.

Robert see also ➤ HERB *Robert*, ➤ MARSE *Robert*.

Robert I (1274–1329), king of Scotland, reigned 1306–29; known as **Robert the Bruce**. He campaigned against Edward I, after the death of ➤ *William* WALLACE in 1305, and despite initial setbacks (and excommunication following the death of the ➤ RED *Comyn*), finally defeated the English forces under Edward II at ➤ BANNOCKBURN (1314). He re-established Scotland as a separate kingdom, negotiating the Treaty of Northampton (1328).

Robert the Devil byname of Robert, Duke of Normandy, father of ➤ WILLIAM *the Conqueror*; according to legend, his mother, who was childless, had

prayed to the devil for the gift of a son. The historical Robert in fact died on pilgrimage in 1035.

Robert's Rules of Order an American manual of parliamentary procedure, first produced in 1876, and more widely used as a guide for formal meetings.

> I realize this isn't a board meeting where Robert's Rules apply, but could you take it from where we left off in Rowbottom's office this morning?
> — Jack Batten *Blood Count* (1991)

Robertian a follower or successor of *Robert the Strong* (d. 866), count of Anjou and Blois, whose descendants replaced the ➤ CAROLINGIANS as kings of France in the 10th century.

robes see ➤ MISTRESS *of the Robes*.

Paul Robeson (1898–1976), American singer and actor. His singing of 'Ol' Man River' in the musical *Showboat* (1927) established his international reputation. His black activism and Communist sympathies led to ostracism in the 1950s.

Maximilien Robespierre (1758–94), French revolutionary, described by Thomas Carlyle in his *History of the French Revolution* (1837) as 'the seagreen Incorruptible'. As leader of the radical Jacobins in the National Assembly he backed the execution of Louis XVI, implemented a purge of the Girondists, and initiated the ➤ TERROR, but the following year he fell from power and was guillotined.

Robin see also ➤ BATMAN, ➤ CHRISTOPHER *Robin*, ➤ POOR *Robin's Almanack*.

robin a small brown bird with a red breast, which legendarily was coloured by the blood of Christ. The robin is traditionally taken as a harbinger of death; there was also a tradition that robins would cover the bodies of the unburied dead with leaves. The name comes (in late Middle English, as **robin redbreast**) from Old French, pet form of the given name *Robert*.

See also ➤ COCK *robin*, ➤ RAGGED *robin*, ➤ ROUND *robin*.

the robin and the wren are God's cock and hen; the martin and the swallow are God's mate and marrow

proverbial saying, late 18th century (*marrow* in the second line means 'companion'); there was a traditional belief that the robin and the wren were sacred birds, and that to harm them in any way would be unlucky.

Robin Goodfellow a mischievous sprite or goblin believed, especially in the 16th and 17th centuries, to haunt the English countryside; he is also called ➤ PUCK.

Robin Hood a semi-legendary English medieval outlaw, reputed to have robbed the rich and helped the poor. Although he is generally associated with Sherwood Forest in Nottinghamshire, it seems likely that the real Robin Hood operated in Yorkshire in the early 13th century.

Robin Hood, with his lover ➤ MAID *Marian*, is traditionally also a leading figure in the ➤ MORRIS *dance*.

> The Robin Hood myth is eternal, whether it's *Star Wars* or a samurai movie—a group of underdogs who are unclothed, virtually, take on the machine and win.
> — *Premiere* July 1990

many that never shot with his bow speak of Robin Hood traditional saying, late Middle English; meaning that people often speak familiarly of someone with whom in fact they are little acquainted.

Robin Hood could brave all weathers but a thaw wind proverbial saying, mid 19th century; a *thaw wind* is a cold wind which accompanies the breaking up of frost.

> I dread the melting wind which makes seas of rivers and lakes of valleys. Robin Hood feared little above ground, but he feared the thaw-wind.
> — John Buchan *The Blanket of the Dark* (1931)

round **Robin** Hood's barn by a circuitous route; *Robin Hood's barn* here represents the type of an out-of-the-way place.

Robin Hood's pennyworth something sold at well below its real value; the phrase is recorded from the mid 16th century.

robin redbreast an informal name for a ➤ ROBIN.

Robinocracy the regime of ➤ *Robert* WALPOLE (1676–1745), the predominant figure in British politics between 1721 and 1742; the clique led by Walpole; the period of Walpole's supremacy.

Robinson see also ➤ BROWN, *Jones, and Robinson*, ➤ *Robinson* CRUSOE.

Prosperity Robinson nickname of Frederick John Robinson, Lord Goderich (1782–1859); the name was applied to him by ➤ *William* COBBETT on account of his sanguine view of the economy as Chancellor of the Exchequer; in 1825, bringing in his third budget, he congratulated the house on the prosperity of the country, while proposing (and carrying) a reduction of duty on coffee, sugar, wine, and spirits,

although the ensuing months in fact saw a developing commercial crisis.

Robinsonade a novel with a subject similar to that of *Robinson Crusoe*; a story about shipwreck on a desert island. The term was coined by J. G. Schnabel in the preface to *Die Insel Felsenburg* (1731), although it is not recorded in English until the mid 19th century.

robot (especially in science fiction) a machine resembling a human being and able to replicate certain human movements and functions automatically. The term (from Czech *robota* 'forced labour') was coined in K. Čapek's play *R.U.R.* 'Rossum's Universal Robots' (1920).

Amy Robsart (1532–60), English noblewoman, wife of Robert Dudley, Earl of Leicester. Her mysterious death at her home in Cumnor, Oxfordshire aroused suspicions that her husband had had her killed so that he could be free to marry Queen Elizabeth I; the story is the basis of Sir Walter Scott's novel *Kenilworth* (1821).

roc a mythical bird of Eastern legend, supposed to be of great size and strength; it is first referred to in ➤ *Marco* POLO's account of Madagascar, but in English use it is known chiefly from the ➤ ARABIAN *Nights*; in the story of ➤ SINBAD it is said to be able to lift elephants in its claws.

roc's egg in the story of ➤ SINBAD, the *roc's egg* is said to be so large that it is fifty paces round; in extended usage, it may be taken as the type of something rare and fabulous.

> Roc's eggs are cheap today.
> — Dorothy L. Sayers *Gaudy Night* (1936)

rocaille an 18th-century artistic or architectural style of decoration characterized by elaborate ornamentation with pebbles and shells, typical of grottos and fountains. The word (which is French) comes from *roc* 'rock'; by humorous alteration, it gave rise to ➤ ROCOCO.

Rocambole a character created by the French author Ponson du Terrail (1829–71), renowned for being the subject of improbable and fantastic adventures.

> An exemplary surrealistic life . . . which included a *rocambolesque* episode . . . in which he kidnapped his Bulgarian mistress from her husband.
> — *New Society* 13 May 1976

St Roch (*c*.1350–*c*.80), hermit, much invoked against the plague; he is said to have caught the plague himself and to have recovered while alone in the woods in Piacenza, where he was brought food by a dog. He is often shown with a plague sore on his leg, or accompanied by a dog with a loaf of bread in its mouth.

□ **PATRONAGE** He is patron saint of invalids and prisoners.

□ **FEAST DAY** His feast day is 16 August.

Rochdale Pioneers the founders of the first commercially successful co-operative store, the **Rochdale Society of Equitable Pioneers**, founded in 1844; their first shop, in Toad Lane, Rochdale, is now the site of a museum in which the original store is preserved.

Edward Rochester in Charlotte Brontë's *Jane Eyre* (1847) the dark and Byronic owner of Thornfield Hall by whom Jane is employed as a governess and with whom she falls in love; their marriage is at first frustrated by the revelation that Mr Rochester's first wife, a madwoman, is still alive, kept under restraint in the attic rooms of Thornfield. After Jane has fled from Thornfield Bertha Rochester, escaping her keeper, sets fire to the Hall; she is killed and Rochester blinded in the conflagration. The subsequent marriage of Jane and Rochester is reported by Jane in the words, 'Reader, I married him.'

Lord Rochester (1647–80), John Wilmot, Earl of Rochester, English poet and courtier. Notorious for his dissolute life at the court of Charles II, he wrote sexually explicit love poems and verse satires; he coined the name the ➤ MERRY *Monarch* for the king, and was the author of a proposed epitaph on Charles:

> Here lies a great and mighty king
> Whose promise none relies on;
> He never said a foolish thing,
> Nor ever did a wise one.
> — Lord Rochester 'The King's Epitaph'

Charles himself is said to have responded, 'This is very true: for my words are my own, and my actions are my ministers'.'

rochet a vestment resembling a surplice, used chiefly by bishops and abbots; the word comes (in Middle English) from Old French, a diminutive from a Germanic base shared by German *Rock* 'coat'.

rock the solid mineral material forming part of the surface of the earth and other similar planets, exposed on the surface or underlying the soil; a mass of such material projecting above the earth's surface

or out of the sea. In figurative usage, *rock* may be taken as the type of something providing a sure foundation and support, as in the words of Jesus Christ to Peter:

> And I say also unto thee, That thou art Peter, and upon this rock I will build my church; and the gates of hell shall not prevail against it.
> — Bible (AV) St Matthew ch. 16, v. 18

In the parable in Matthew 7 of the two houses, it is the house built on sand which falls, and the house built on rock which stands.

A *rock* in biblical contexts may also be a source of sustenance (with allusion to Numbers 20:11, in which water issued from the rock struck by the staff of Moses), and a shelter, as in Isaiah 32:2, 'the shadow of a great rock in a weary land'.

A *rock* (especially with the notion of one on which a ship may be wrecked) can also be taken as a sign of danger, as in **rocks ahead**.

See also ➤ DOME *of the Rock*, ➤ EDDYSTONE *Rocks*, ➤ PLYMOUTH *Rock*.

the Rock an elliptical name for the ➤ *Rock of* GIBRALTAR.

rock and roll a type of popular dance music originating in the 1950s, characterized by a heavy beat and simple melodies. Rock and roll was an amalgam of black rhythm and blues and white country music, usually based around a twelve-bar structure and an instrumentation of guitar, double bass, and drums.

Rock English the mixed English of ➤ GIBRALTAR.

Rock of Ages symbolizing the foundation of Christian belief; the phrase is now probably best-known from the hymn 'Rock of Ages, cleft for me' (1773), by the English clergyman Augustus Toplady (1740–78).

Rock Monday the Monday after 6 January; supposedly the day on which women traditionally resumed their spinning, after the festivities of Christmas (see also ➤ *St* DISTAFF's *day*).

Rock scorpion a military nickname for a civilian inhabitant of ➤ GIBRALTAR (a *rock scorpion* is literally another name for a rock lizard).

John D. Rockefeller (1839–1937), American industrialist and philanthropist. He founded the Standard Oil Company in 1870 and by 1880 he exercised a virtual monopoly over oil refining in the US; both he and his son, John D. Rockefeller Jr (1874–1960), established many philanthropic institutions, including the Rockefeller Foundation (1913) and the Rockefeller Center in New York (1939). The name *Rockefeller* is now used allusively as the type of a very rich person.

> That uncle, whom I still think of as a Mellon, a Rockefeller . . . would collapse in awe of my annual grocery bill today.
> — *New York Times* 30 September 1979

Rocket the name of the steam locomotive (1829) built by George Stephenson (1781–1848) and his son Robert, the prototype for all future steam locomotives.

Rockite a member of an Irish organization associated with agrarian disorders in the earlier part of the 19th century, from the assumed name of Captain *Rock*, the organization's supposed leader.

Norman Rockwell (1894–1978), American illustrator. Known for his typically sentimental portraits of small-town American life, he was an illustrator for *Life* and the *Saturday Evening Post*, for whom he created 317 covers (1916–63).

> Some people later took Quayle's words to be fatuous white-bread truisms—Norman Rockwell evocations of an America long gone.
> — *Time* 1 June 1992

rococo (of furniture or architecture) of or characterized by an elaborately ornamental late baroque style of decoration prevalent in 18th-century Continental Europe, with asymmetrical patterns involving motifs and scrollwork; extravagantly or excessively ornate, especially (of music or literature) highly ornamented and florid. Recorded from the mid 19th century, the word comes from French, as a humorous alteration of ➤ ROCAILLE.

rod in former British usage, a unit of measurement, the equivalent of a ➤ PERCH.

See also ➤ BLACK *Rod*, ➤ DIVINING *rod*, ➤ SPARE *the rod and spoil the child*.

Anita Roddick (1943–), English businesswoman, who in 1976 opened a shop selling cosmetics with an emphasis on environmentally conscious products. This developed into the *Body Shop* chain.

Roderick (d. 711), the last Visigothic king of Spain, killed in the Moorish invasion; he is a figure in the work of several Romantic writers, including Walter Scott in his poem *The Vision of Don Roderick* (1811) and Robert Southey in his narrative poem *Roderick, the last of the Goths* (1814). According to legend, Roderick had dishonoured the daughter of one of his nobles, who in revenge brought the Moors into Spain.

Richard Rodgers (1902–79), American composer. He worked with librettist Lorenz Hart (1895–1942) before collaborating with Oscar Hammerstein II on a succession of popular musicals, including *Oklahoma!* (1943) and *The Sound of Music* (1959).

Auguste Rodin (1840–1917), French sculptor. He was chiefly concerned with the human form, as in *The Thinker* (1880) and *The Kiss* (1886). His first major work, *The Age of Bronze* (1875–6), was considered so lifelike that Rodin was alleged to have taken a cast from a live model.

Rodomont the boastful Saracen leader in ➤ OR-LANDO *Innamorato* and ➤ ORLANDO *Furioso*; from the late 16th century, *rodomont* came to be used to mean a braggart or boaster.

rodomontade boastful or inflated talk or behaviour; the word comes (in the early 17th century) via French from the Italian form of ➤ RODOMONT.

Roe see ➤ *John* DOE *and Richard Roe.*

Roedean the name of an independent public school for girls in Brighton, on the south coast of England, taken as the type of an exclusive girls' boarding school for the aristocratic and wealthy.

> The Betty Ford Clinic; that Roedean of drying out.
> — *Sunday Times* 8 September 1991

rogation (in the Christian Church) a solemn supplication consisting of the litany of the saints chanted on the three days before Ascension Day. The name comes (in late Middle English) from Latin *rogatio(n-)*, from *rogare* 'ask'.

Rogation Days (in the Western Christian Church) the three days before Ascension Day, traditionally marked by fasting and prayer, particularly for the blessing of the harvest (after the pattern of pre-Christian rituals).

Rogation flower the milkwort, which was formerly woven into garlands and carried in procession in Rogation week.

Rogation Sunday the Sunday preceding the Rogation Days.

Rogation week the week in which Ascension Day falls.

roger your message has been received and understood (used in radio communication); informally, used to express assent or understanding.

See also ➤ JOLLY *Roger,* ➤ *Sir Roger de* COVERLEY.

Roger of Wendover (d. 1236), monk and chronicler at St Albans; his *Flores Historiarum* was a history of the world from the creation to AD 1235, compiled from many different sources. He was succeeded as chronicler by Matthew Paris.

Rogerene a member of a small religious sect founded by John *Rogers* (1648–1721) in Connecticut, opposed to some of the formal practices of churches and participation in military service.

Ginger Rogers (1911–95), American actress and dancer, known particularly for her dancing partnership with Fred Astaire, during which she appeared in musicals including *Top Hat* (1935).

Richard Rogers (1933–), British architect. A leading exponent of high-tech architecture, his major works include the Pompidou Centre in Paris (1971–7), designed with the Italian architect Renzo Piano, and the Lloyd's Building in London (1986).

Rogers' Rangers a body of soldiers commanded by Robert *Rogers* (1727–1800) in the war with the French in North America, 1755–60.

Peter Roget (1779–1869), English scholar. He worked as a physician but is remembered as the compiler of *Thesaurus of English Words and Phrases*, a catalogue of synonyms first published in 1852, and commonly known as **Roget's Thesaurus**.

rogue a dishonest or unprincipled man. Recorded in the mid 16th century meaning 'an idle beggar', the word probably comes from Latin *rogare* 'beg, ask', and is related to obsolete slang *roger* 'beggar' (many such cant terms were introduced towards the middle of the 16th century).

rogue's march a tune played when someone is drummed out of a camp or garrison.

rogues' gallery a collection of photographs of known criminals, used by police to identify suspects.

rogues' Latin another term for ➤ THIEVES' *Latin*.

roi fainéant any of the later ➤ MEROVINGIAN kings of France, whose power was merely nominal; the phrase is French, and means literally 'sluggard king'.

roi soleil a title ('sun king') commonly used to designate Louis XIV of France, derived from a heraldic device used by him, and intended to convey his pre-eminence as a ruler.

Cecil Harmsworth King, the *roi soleil* of Long Acre.
— *Guardian* 31 December 1966

roid rage (an outburst of) heightened aggression manifested as a side-effect of anabolic steroid use; the term may be a conscious alteration of ➤ ROAD *rage*. Instances have been reported since the early 1990s among athletes and bodybuilders; it appears that as well as increasing muscle size, *roids* (anabolic steroids) produce an excess of aggression.

Roland see also ➤ CHILDE *Roland*.

Roland the most famous of ➤ CHARLEMAGNE'S paladins, hero of the *Chanson de Roland* (12th century) and other medieval romances. He is said to have become a friend of Oliver, another paladin, after engaging him in single combat in which neither won. Roland was killed in a rearguard action at the Battle of ➤ RONCESVALLES, refusing until too late to blow the horn ➤ OLIVANT to summon Charlemagne to his aid.

See also ➤ *the* SONG *of Roland*.

a **Roland for an Oliver** an effective or adequate retort or response, taking ➤ ROLAND and his comrade ➤ OLIVER as the type of a match in skill and courage; the phrase is recorded from the early 17th century.

Rolfing a massage technique aimed at the vertical realignment of the body, and therefore deep enough to release muscular tension at skeletal level, which can contribute to the relief of long-standing tension and neuroses. It is named after Ida P. *Rolf* (1897–1979), American physiotherapist.

roll see ➤ BATTLE *Abbey Roll*, ➤ EXULTET *Roll*, ➤ PATENT *roll*, ➤ PIPE *Roll*.

rolling news a service in which a channel or station is dedicated entirely to news reports, which are broadcast 24 hours a day. In the UK, the term came to the fore just after the Gulf War of 1991, during which almost continuous news broadcasts and assessments had been given; it has been particularly associated with ➤ BIRTISM.

a **rolling stone gathers no moss** proverbial saying, mid 14th century.

Rolling Stones an English rock group formed *c*.1962, featuring singer Mick Jagger and guitarist Keith Richards. They became successful with a much-imitated rebel image and evolved a simple, derivative, yet distinctive style.

Rollo name of the Viking leader (*Hrolf*) said to be ancestor of the Dukes of Normandy; he established himself in Normandy in the early 10th century.

rollover the process whereby a jackpot which has not been won in the weekly draw of the British National Lottery is carried over to the following week. The amount of money in the **rollover jackpot** thus created has been a particular factor in increasing existing anxieties about the size of lottery wins.

Rollright Stones a circle of prehistoric stones on the Oxfordshire–Warwickshire border.

the Rolls the former buildings in Chancery Lane in which the records in the custody of the Master of the Rolls were kept.

See also ➤ CHAPEL *of the Rolls*, ➤ MASTER *of the Rolls*, ➤ RAGMAN *rolls*.

Charles Stewart Rolls (1877–1910), English motoring and aviation pioneer. He and Henry Royce formed the company Rolls-Royce Ltd in 1906. Rolls was the first Englishman to fly across the English Channel, and made the first double crossing in 1910 shortly before he was killed in an air crash. The Rolls-Royce company established its reputation with luxury cars such as the Silver Ghost and the Silver Shadow, and produced aircraft engines used in both world wars.

romaji a system of romanized spelling used to transliterate Japanese. The word comes (in the early 20th century) from Japanese, from *rōm* 'Roman' + *ji* 'letter(s)'.

Roman alphabet the alphabet used for writing Latin, English, and most European languages, developed in ancient Rome.

Roman Britain Britain during the period AD 43–410, when most of Britain was part of the Roman Empire. The frontier of the Roman province of Britain was eventually established at Hadrian's Wall; the more northerly Antonine Wall was breached and abandoned (*c*.181). Roman settlers and traders built villas, and Roman towns including London (Londinium), York (Eboracum), Lincoln (Lindum Colonia), St Albans (Verulamium), and Colchester (Camulodunum) were established or developed.

Roman candle a firework giving off a series of flaming coloured balls and sparks; the name is recorded from the mid 19th century.

Roman Catholic Church the part of the Christian Church which acknowledges the Pope as its head, especially as it has developed since the Reformation, and which is the largest Christian Church, dominant particularly in South America and southern Europe. Roman Catholicism differs from Protestantism in the importance it grants to tradition, ritual, and the authority of the Pope as successor to the Apostle St Peter, and especially in its doctrines of papal infallibility (formally defined in 1870) and of the Eucharist (➤ TRANSUBSTANTIATION), its celibate male priesthood, its emphasis on confession, and the veneration of the Virgin Mary and other saints. Much modern Roman Catholic thought and practice arises from scholastic theology and from the response to the Reformation made by the Council of Trent (1545–63). It became less rigid after the Second Vatican Council (1962–5), but its continuing opposition to divorce, abortion, and artificial contraception remains controversial.

The name is recorded from the late 16th century as a translation of Latin *(Ecclesia) Romana Catholica (et Apostolica)* 'Roman Catholic (and Apostolic Church)'. It was apparently first used as a conciliatory term in place of the earlier *Roman, Romanist,* or *Romish,* considered derogatory.

Roman de la Rose an extremely influential French poem of the 13th century, an allegorical romance embodying the aristocratic ethic of courtly love. It was composed by two different authors some forty years apart.

Roman Empire the empire established by Augustus in 27 BC, which was divided after the death of Theodosius I (AD 395) into the Western Empire and the Eastern or Byzantine Empire (centred on Constantinople). At its greatest extent Roman rule or influence extended from Armenia and Mesopotamia in the east to the Iberian peninsula in the west, and from the Rhine and Danube in the north to Egypt and provinces on the Mediterranean coast of North Africa.

Peace was maintained largely by the substantial presence of the Roman army, and a degree of unity was achieved by an extensive network of roads, a single legal system, and a common language (Latin in the West, Greek in the East). Eventually, the sheer extent of the territories led to the collapse of the Western Empire: Rome was sacked by the Visigoths under Alaric in 410, and the last emperor of the West, Romulus Augustulus, was deposed in 476. The Eastern Empire, which was stronger, lasted until 1453.

See also ➤ HOLY *Roman Empire*.

Roman holiday an occasion on which entertainment or profit is derived from injury or death; originally a holiday for a gladiatorial combat, as in Byron's poem:

> There were his young barbarians all at play,
> There was their Dacian mother—he, their sire,
> Butchered to make a Roman holiday.
> — Lord Byron *Childe Harold's Pilgrimage* (1812-18)

Roman law the law code of the ancient Romans forming the basis of civil law in many countries today.

Roman numeral any of the letters representing numbers in the Roman numerical system: I = 1, V = 5, X = 10, L = 50, C = 100, D = 500, M = 1,000. In this system a letter placed after another of greater value adds (thus XVI or xvi is 16), whereas a letter placed before another of greater value subtracts (thus XC is 90).

would that the Roman people had but one neck! saying attributed to ➤ CALIGULA (Roman emperor AD 37–41) in Suetonius's *Lives of the Caesars*.

Roman Republic the ancient Roman state from the expulsion of the Etruscan monarchs in 509 BC until the assumption of power by Augustus (Octavian) in 27 BC. The republic was dominated by a landed aristocracy, the ➤ PATRICIANS, who ruled through the advisory Senate and two annually elected chief magistrates or consuls; the ➤ PLEBEIANS or common people had their own representatives, the tribunes, who in time gained the power of veto over the other magistrates. During the life of the republic Rome came to dominate the rest of Italy and, following the Punic and Macedonian Wars, began to acquire extensive dominions in the Mediterranean and Asia Minor. Dissatisfaction with the Senate's control of government led to civil wars, which culminated in ➤ JULIUS *Caesar*'s brief dictatorship. This established the principle of personal autocracy, and after Caesar's assassination another round of civil war ended with Octavian's assumption of authority.

Roman road following the line of one made under the Roman empire; typically of military origin, and where possible following the straight route of marching legions.

Roman type a plain upright kind of type used in ordinary print, especially as distinguished from ➤ ITALIC and ➤ GOTHIC.

Romana see ➤ PAX *Romana*.

Romance the group of Indo-European languages descended from Latin, principally French, Spanish, Portuguese, Italian, Catalan, Occitan, and Romanian. In Middle English, *Romance* denoted the vernacular language of France as opposed to Latin; the word comes via Old French from Latin *Romanicus* 'Roman'.

Romanes Lectures annual lectures founded at Oxford in 1891 by the scholar and scientist George John *Romanes* (1848–94), to be given on subjects related to science, art, and literature; the first lecture, on 'Mediaeval Universities', was delivered by William Ewart Gladstone on 24 October 1892.

Romanesque a style of architecture which prevailed in Europe *c.*1000–1200, although sometimes dated back to the end of the Roman Empire (5th century). *Romanesque* architecture is characterized by round arches and massive vaulting, and by heavy piers, columns, and walls with small windows. Although disseminated throughout western Europe, the style reached its fullest development in France and Germany; the equivalent style in England is often called *Norman*.

Romanorum see ➤ GESTA *Romanorum*.

Romanov a dynasty that ruled in Russia from the accession of Michael Romanov (1596–1645) in 1613 until the overthrow of the last tsar, Nicholas II, in 1917.

Romans see also ➤ KING *of the Romans*.

Epistle to the Romans a book of the New Testament, an epistle of St Paul to the Church at Rome.

Romansh the Rhaeto-Romance language spoken in the Swiss canton of Grisons by fewer than 30,000 people. It has several dialects, and is an official language of Switzerland.

Romanticism a movement in the arts and literature which originated in the late 18th century, emphasizing inspiration, subjectivity, and the primacy of the individual. Romanticism was a reaction against the order and restraint of classicism and neoclassicism, and a rejection of the rationalism which characterized the ➤ ENLIGHTENMENT. In music, the period embraces much of the 19th century, with composers including Schubert, Schumann, Liszt, and Wagner, and (in the opinion of some critics) Beethoven. Writers exemplifying the movement include Wordsworth, Coleridge, Byron, Shelley, and Keats; among romantic painters are such stylistically diverse artists as William Blake, J. M. W. Turner, Delacroix, and Goya. In its implicit idea of an artist as an isolated misunderstood genius the movement has not yet ended.

Romanus see ➤ CIVIS *Romanus sum.*

Romany the language of the gypsies, which is an Indo-European language related to Hindi. It is spoken by a dispersed group of about 1 million people, and has many dialects. The name comes (in the early 19th century) from Romany *Romani*, feminine and plural of the adjective *Romano*, from *Rom* 'man, husband'.

Romany rye a man who is not a gypsy by birth, but who lives with gypsies; the phrase is first recorded in George Borrow's *Lavengro* (1851), an account of a wandering life apparently based on Borrow's own; the sequel, published in 1857, was called *The Romany Rye*. (*Rye* here represents Romany *rai* 'gentleman'.)

Rome the capital of Italy and of the Lazio region, situated on the River Tiber. According to tradition the ancient city was founded by Romulus (after whom it is named) in 753 BC on the Palatine Hill; as it grew it spread to the other six hills of Rome (Aventine, Caelian, Capitoline, Esquiline, and Quirinal). Rome was ruled by kings until the expulsion of Tarquinius Superbus in 510 BC led to the establishment of the Roman Republic and the beginning of the Roman Empire.

By the time of the empire's fall the city was overshadowed politically by Constantinople, but emerged as the seat of the papacy and as the spiritual capital of Western Christianity. In the 14th and 15th centuries Rome became a centre of the Renaissance. It remained under papal control, forming part of the Papal States, until 1871, when it was made the capital of a unified Italy.

In allusive use, *Rome* is traditionally seen as standing for the Roman Empire or the Roman Catholic Church: the heart and emblem of a major power.

> While stands the Coliseum, Rome shall stand;
> When falls the Coliseum, Rome shall fall;
> And when Rome falls—the World.
>
> — Lord Byron *Childe Harold's Pilgrimage* (1812–18)

See also ➤ FIDDLE *while Rome burns*, ➤ KING *of Rome*, ➤ *the* MATTER *of Rome*, ➤ PRIX *de Rome*, ➤ SEE *of Rome*, ➤ SEVEN *Hills*, ➤ SWORD *of Rome.*

all roads lead to Rome proverbial saying; late 14th century; earlier in Latin.

Treaty of Rome a treaty setting up and defining the aims of the European Economic Community. It was signed at Rome on 25 March 1957 by France, West Germany, Italy, Belgium, the Netherlands, and Luxembourg.

> The Treaty [of Rome] is like an incoming tide. It flows into the estuaries and up the rivers. It cannot be held back.
>
> — Lord Denning comment, 1975

I found Rome brick, I leave it marble according to Suetonius's *Lives of the Caesars*, ➤ AUGUSTUS (63 BC–AD 14) could say of Rome that 'he inherited it brick and left it marble'.

when in Rome, do as the Romans do proverbial saying, late 15th century; ➤ St AMBROSE, the 4th-century bishop of Milan, wrote in a letter, 'When I go to Rome, I fast on Saturday, but here [Milan] I do not. Do you also follow the custom of whatever church you attend.'

Rome has spoken translation of '*Roma locuta est; causa finita est.* [Rome has spoken; the case is concluded]', traditional summary of words found in the *Sermons* of St Augustine (AD 354–430) published in Antwerp in 1702.

Rome-penny another term for ➤ PETER*'s pence.* Also called *Rome-scot.*

Rome was not built in a day proverbial saying, mid 16th century.

Romeo hero of Shakespeare's romantic tragedy *Romeo and Juliet*, who falls in love with ➤ JULIET, daughter of the enemy house of Capulet, when he first sees her, and in the end dies by suicide with her. From the mid 18th century, the name has been used for an attractive, passionate male seducer and lover.

romer a small piece of plastic or card bearing perpendicularly aligned scales or (if transparent) a grid, used to determine the precise reference of a point within the grid printed on a map. It is named after Carrol *Romer* (1883–1951), its British inventor.

Romford see ➤ *you might* RIDE *to Romford.*

Erwin Rommel (1891–1944), German Field Marshal; known as *the Desert Fox*. As commander of the Afrika Korps he deployed a series of surprise manoeuvres and succeeded in capturing Tobruk (1942), but was defeated by Montgomery at El Alamein later that year. He was forced to commit suicide after being implicated in the officers' conspiracy against Hitler in 1944.

George **Romney** (1734–1802), English portrait painter, who in the late 18th century rivalled Gainsborough and Reynolds for popularity. From the early 1780s he produced over fifty portraits of ➤ *Emma* HAMILTON in historical costumes and poses.

Romulus the legendary founder of Rome, one of the twin sons of Mars by the Vestal Virgin ➤ RHEA *Silvia*; he and his brother Remus were exposed at birth in a basket on the River Tiber but were found and suckled by a she-wolf and later brought up by a shepherd family.

Grown to manhood, the twins avenged themselves and their mother on their great uncle, king of Alba Longa, and founded a new settlement on the spot at which they had been washed ashore from the Tiber. An augury in the form of a flight of birds indicated that Romulus should be king, but during the building of the walls of Rome the brothers quarrelled, and Remus was killed.

The new city was settled by Romulus and his men, and the population was increased by the addition of runaway slaves and criminals. To find wives for his followers, Romulus is said to have invited the neighbouring ➤ SABINES to witness a spectacle; in the course of this, the Sabine women were carried off (the *Rape of the Sabines*). The fighting which followed was eventually settled without the women returning to their own people.

Ronald chestnut charger ridden by Lord Cardigan at the Charge of the Light Brigade.

Battle of Roncesvalles a battle which took place in 778 at a mountain pass in the Pyrenees, near the village of Roncesvalles in northern Spain. The rearguard of ➤ CHARLEMAGNE's army was attacked by the Basques and massacred; one of the paladins, ➤ ROLAND, was killed, an event celebrated in the *Chanson de Roland* (in which the attackers are wrongly identified as the Moors).

ronin (in feudal Japan) a wandering samurai who had no lord or master.

rood a crucifix, especially one positioned above the rood screen of a church or on a beam over the entrance to the chancel. Recorded from Old English (in the form *rōd*), the word is related to German *Rute* 'rod'.

See also ➤ HOLY *Rood Day*.

the Roof of the World the Pamirs; later also, Tibet, the Himalayas.

rooinek in South Africa, an informal derogatory term among Afrikaners for an English person or an English-speaking person. The word is Afrikaans, and means literally 'redneck'.

rook[1] a crow with black plumage and a bare face, nesting in colonies in treetops; in traditional belief, associated with death. From the mid 16th century, *rook* also denoted a cheat or swindler, especially in gaming.

rook[2] a chess piece, typically with its top in the shape of a battlement, that can move in any direction along a rank or file on which it stands; a *castle*. Each player starts the game with two rooks at opposite ends of the first rank.

The word is recorded from Middle English and comes from Old French *rock*, based on an Arabic word of which the sense remains uncertain.

rookery a breeding colony of rooks, typically seen as a collection of nests high in a clump of trees; a dense collection of housing, especially in a slum area.

there is always room at the top proverbial saying, early 20th century; as a response to being advised against joining the overcrowded legal profession, it is also attributed to the American politician and lawyer Daniel Webster.

have no room to swing a cat very little room; the *cat* originally referred to may be a ➤ CAT-*o'-nine-tails.*

> Mrs. Crupp had indignantly assured him that there wasn't room to swing a cat there; but, as Mr. Dick justly observed to me, . . . 'You know, Trotwood, I don't want to swing a cat. I never do swing a cat.'
> — Charles Dickens *David Copperfield* (1850)

roorback in the US, a political slander or false report; from the name of Baron von *Roorback*, fictitious author of a mid 19th-century book of travels.

Franklin D. Roosevelt (1882–1945), American Democratic statesman, 32nd President of the US 1933–45, known as **FDR**. His ➤ NEW *Deal* of 1933 helped to lift the US out of the Great Depression, and he played an important part in Allied policy during the Second World War. He was the only American President to be elected for a third term in office.

See also ➤ ROUGH *Rider.*

Theodore Roosevelt (1858–1919), American Republican statesman, 26th President of the US

1901–9; known as **Teddy Roosevelt**. He was noted for his antitrust laws and successfully engineered the American bid to build the Panama Canal (1904–14). The ➤ TEDDY *bear* is named after him, with reference to his bear-hunting.

root see also ➤ IDLENESS *is the root of all evil*, ➤ MONEY *is the root of all evil.*

root and branch used to express the thorough or radical nature of a process or operation; originally with biblical allusion to Malachi 4:1 'the day cometh that shall burn them up…that it shall leave them neither root nor branch'. The phrase derives directly from the London petition of 11 December 1640 for the total abolition of episcopal government, 'That the said government, with all its dependencies, roots, and branches, be abolished'.

the root of the matter the essential part of something; the expression comes originally from Job 19:28, 'But ye should say, Why persecute we him, seeing the root of the matter is found in me?'

give a man rope enough and he will hang himself proverbial saying, mid 17th century.

never mention rope in the house of a man who has been hanged proverbial saying, late 16th century.

rope of sand the type of something having no coherence or binding power, recorded from the 17th century.

roquelaure a cloak reaching to the knee worn by men during the 18th century and the early part of the 19th century, named after the Duc de *Roquelaure* (1656–1738).

Rorschach test a type of projective test used in psychoanalysis, in which a standard set of symmetrical ink blots of different shapes and colours is presented one by one to the subject, who is asked to describe what they suggest or resemble. Also called *ink-blot test*. It is named after Hermann *Rorschach* (1884–1922), Swiss psychiatrist.

Salvator Rosa (1615–73), Italian painter and etcher. The picturesque and 'sublime' qualities of his landscapes, often peopled with bandits and containing scenes of violence in wild natural settings, were an important influence on the romantic art of the 18th and 19th centuries.

Rosamond see ➤ FAIR *Rosamond.*

rosary (in the Roman Catholic Church) a form of devotion in which five (or fifteen) decades of Hail Marys are repeated (a *decade* is a set of ten), each decade preceded by an Our Father and followed by a Glory Be; a string of beads for keeping count in such a devotion or in the devotions of some other religions, in Roman Catholic use 55 or 165 in number.

The word comes (in late Middle English, in the sense 'rose garden') from Latin *rosarium* rose-garden, from *rosa* 'rose'. In the 16th century (from which this meaning dates) the word was also used as the title of a book of devotion.

Rosary Sunday in the Roman Catholic Church, the first Sunday in October, when the victory over the Turks at Lepanto in 1571 was sometimes celebrated.

Roscius (d. 62 BC), a phenomenally successful comic actor, he later became identified with all that was considered best in acting. A number of famous English actors from the 16th century onwards, notably ➤ *David* GARRICK, were nicknamed *Roscius* in reference to his great skill.

In 1761, the English poet Charles Churchill (1732–64) published the satirical poem *The Rosciad*, describing the attempt to find a worth successor to Roscius.

the Young Roscius nickname of William Betty (1791–1874), boy actor, who made his debut in Belfast in 1803. In 1804 he appeared at Drury Lane; he was presented to the king, and it is said that on one occasion the Commons was adjourned so that members could see his appearance as Hamlet. His final appearance as a boy actor was in 1808, at Bath.

rose a prickly bush or shrub that typically bears red, pink, yellow, or white fragrant flowers. In allusive or emblematic use, the *rose* typifies surpassing qualities of beauty, fragrance, and colour (Hamlet is described as 'the expectancy and rose of the fair state'); it may also be referred to in contrast or relation to its thorns.

Roses are the emblem of ➤ *St* TERESA *of Lisieux*, ➤ *St* ELIZABETH *of Hungary*, and the Peruvian St Rose of Lima (1586–1617).

See also ➤ DAMASK *rose*, ➤ DESERT *rose*, ➤ DOG *rose*, ➤ GOLDEN *rose*, ➤ LENTEN *rose*, ➤ MOONLIGHT *and roses*, ➤ RED *rose*, ➤ RING-*a-ring o'roses*, ➤ ROMAN *de la Rose*, ➤ TOKYO *Rose*, ➤ TUDOR *rose*, ➤ VIE *en rose*, ➤ WARS *of the Roses*, ➤ WHITE *rose*.

the last rose the last flowering of an era, with allusion to the song by the Irish songwriter Thomas Moore (1779–1852):

> 'Tis the last rose of summer
> Left blooming alone;
> All her lovely companions
> Are faded and gone.
> — Thomas Moore *Irish Melodies* (1807) ''Tis the last rose of summer'

under the rose in secret, in strict confidence, ➤ SUB *rosa*; the expression dates from the late 16th century.

Rose Bowl a football stadium at Pasadena, California, used to designate a football match played between rival college teams annually on New Year's Day at the conclusion of the local Tournament of Roses. The ➤ SUPER *Bowl* is named after this.

not the rose but near it not ideal but approaching or near this; the earliest version in English is found in an early 19th century translation of the *Gulistan* by the Persian poet Sadi (*c.*1213–*c.*1291), 'I was a worthless piece of clay, but having for a season associated with the rose, the virtue of my companion was communicated to me.'

a rose by any other name allusive reference to Shakespeare's *Romeo and Juliet* (1597), 'That which we call a Rose, By any other name would smell as sweet.'

rose-coloured spectacles indicating that a person's view of something is unduly favourable, optimistic, or idealistic; recorded from the mid 19th century.

rose noble a gold coin current in the fifteenth and sixteenth centuries, being a variety of the noble with the figure of a rose stamped upon it, and of varying value at different times and places.

rose of Jericho a cruciferous plant of deserts in North Africa and the Middle East, the dried fronds of which unfold under the influence of moisture; also called **resurrection plant**.

rose of Sharon an unidentified flower, translating a Hebrew phrase in the Song of Solomon 2:1, 'I am the rose of Sharon, and the lily of the valleys.' (The translators of the Revised Version explain the flower as 'the autumn crocus'.)

rose-red city the ancient city of ➤ PETRA, from a poem by the English clergyman John William

Burgon (1813–88), with which he won the ➤ NEWDIGATE *Prize*:

> Match me such marvel, save in Eastern clime,—
> A rose-red city—half as old as Time!
> — John William Burgon *Petra* (1845)

Rose Sunday a former name for the fourth Sunday in Lent, as the day on which ➤ GOLDEN *roses* were blessed by the pope.

no rose without a thorn traditional saying; late Middle English.

Rose Tavern in Russell Street, Covent Garden, a favourite place of resort in the 17th and early 18th centuries, frequently referred to in the literature of the period.

Rose Theatre a theatre in Southwark, London, built in 1587. Many of Shakespeare's plays were performed there, some for the first time. Remains of the theatre, which was demolished *c.*1605, were uncovered in 1989.

rose window a circular window with mullions or tracery radiating in a form suggestive of a rose.

rosemary an evergreen aromatic shrub of the mint family, native to southern Europe. The narrow leaves are used as a culinary herb, in perfumery, and as an emblem of remembrance; in this connection, it is particulary associated with the words of ➤ OPHELIA in Shakespeare's *Hamlet*, 'There's rosemary for remembrance'.

In traditional belief, rosemary grows best in the garden of a woman who dominates her husband; it is also associated with the Virgin Mary on the Flight into Egypt (as in the story that on the way, having washed her clothes, she hung her blue robe on a rosemary bush to dry).

The name is recorded from Middle English (in form *rosmarine*), and is based on Latin *ros marinus* 'dew of the sea'; it was later understood as primarily associated with *rose* and *Mary* (for the Virgin).

Rosetta Stone an inscribed stone found near Rosetta on the western mouth of the Nile in 1799. Its text, a decree commemorating the accession of Ptolemy V (reigned 205–180 BC), is written in three scripts: hieroglyphic, demotic, and Greek; the deciphering of the hieroglyphs by Jean-François Champollion in 1822 led to the interpretation of many other early records of Egyptian civilization. The *Rosetta Stone* is sometimes taken as the type of a mysterious cryptogram which, when decoded, will unlock other mysteries.

> The problem is there's no Rosetta stone to help you crack the code and ferret out the best.
> — *Gourmet* June 1997

rosewater see ➤ REVOLUTIONS *are not made with rosewater*.

Rosh Chodesh a Jewish half-holiday observed at the appearance of the new moon, the beginning of the Jewish month. The name means in Hebrew 'head of the month'.

Rosh Hashana the Jewish New Year festival, held on the first (and sometimes the second) day of Tishri (in September). It is marked by the blowing of the shofar, and begins the ten days of penitence culminating in ➤ YOM *Kippur*. The literal meaning in Hebrew is 'head (i.e. beginning) of the year'.

Rosherville Gardens a pleasure-garden of the 19th century, established in 1840 by Jeremiah *Rosher* in a disused chalk-pit at Northfleet beside the Thames; it became a place of resort for Londoners, many of whom visited it by paddle-steamer.

> [He] dragged him by sheer muscular strength to Rosherville every gala night.
> — Albert R. Smith *The Fortunes of the Scattergood Family* (1845)

Roshi the spiritual leader of a community of Zen Buddhist monks; the word is from Japanese.

Rosicrucian a member of a secretive 17th- and 18th-century society devoted to the study of metaphysical, mystical, and alchemical lore, especially that concerning the transmutation of metals, prolongation of life, and power over the elements. An anonymous pamphlet of 1614 about a mythical 15th-century knight called Christian *Rosenkreuz* is said to have launched the movement, the emblem of which was a ➤ ROSY CROSS.

Rosinante the name of Don Quixote's horse, taken as the type of a poor, worn-out, and elderly horse.

Roskilde a port in Denmark, on the island of Zealand, which was the seat of Danish kings from *c.*1020 and the capital of Denmark until 1443; it is also the site of a museum of Viking ships, which had been sunk in the harbour.

Ross see also ➤ MAN *of Ross*.

Betsy Ross (1752–1836), American seamstress, who according to legend made the first ➤ STARS *and Stripes*.

James Clark Ross (1800–62, British explorer. He discovered the north magnetic pole in 1831, and headed an expedition to the Antarctic from 1839 to 1843, in the course of which he discovered Ross Island, Ross Dependency, and the Ross Sea. He was the nephew of John Ross.

John Ross (1777–1856), British explorer. He led an expedition to Baffin Bay in 1818 and another in search of the North-West Passage between 1829 and 1833.

Ronald Ross (1857–1932), British physician. Ross confirmed that the *Anopheles* mosquito transmitted malaria, and went on to elucidate the stages in the malarial parasite's life cycle.

Ross herald one of the six Scottish heralds, named for the county of Ross in northern Scotland.

Dante Gabriel Rossetti (1828–82), English painter and poet. A founder member of the ➤ PRE-*Raphaelite* brotherhood (1848), he is best known for his idealized images of women, including *Beata Beatrix* (*c.*1863) and *The Blessed Damozel* (1871–9).

His wife Elizabeth Siddal (model for Millais' picture of the drowned ➤ OPHELIA) died from an overdose of laudanum in 1862, and the grief-stricken Rossetti gave his manuscript poems to be buried with her; in 1869, however, he was persuaded to retrieve them, and the coffin was disinterred.

Gioacchino Antonio Rossini (1792–1868), Italian composer, one of the creators of Italian bel canto. He wrote over thirty operas, including *The Barber of Seville* (1816) and *William Tell* (1829).

Edmond Rostand (1868–1918), French dramatist and poet. He romanticized the life of the 17th-century soldier, duellist, and writer ➤ CYRANO *de Bergerac* in his poetic drama of that name (1897).

rostrum a raised platform on which a person stands to make a public speech, receive an award or medal, play music, or conduct an orchestra. The word was originally used (at first in the plural *rostra*) to denote part of the Forum in Rome, which was decorated with the beaks (*rostra*) of captured galleys, and was used as a platform for public speakers.

Roswell a town in New Mexico, the scene of a mysterious crash in July 1947. Controversy has surrounded claims (apparently supported by photographic evidence) by some investigators that the crashed object was a UFO.

rosy cross an equal-armed cross with a rose at its centre, the emblem of the ➤ ROSICRUCIANS.

rosy-fingered having rose-coloured fingers; chiefly (as a translation of Homer) as an epithet of the dawn.

> The Rosy finger'd Morn appears.
> — John Dryden *Albion & Albanius* (1685)

the rot set in a rapid succession of (usually un-accountable) failures began; *rot* in cricket, a rapid fall of wickets during an innings. The term is re-corded from the mid 19th century.

rota from Latin (literally 'a wheel'); in the mid 17th century, **The Rota** was the name of a political club, founded in 1659 by the political theorist James Harrington (1611–77), which advocated rotation in the offices of Government, and which in 1660 pub-lished Harrington's 'The Censure of the Rota upon Mr Milton's Book, entituled, The Ready and Easie way to Establish a Free Common-wealth'.

> As full of tricks,
> As Rota-men of Politicks.
> — Samuel Butler *Hudibras* (1664)

The Rota is also the title (recorded in English since the late 17th century) of the supreme ecclesi-astical and secular court of the Roman Catholic Church.

Rotary a worldwide charitable society of clubs for businessmen and women and professional people; the first of these was formed in Chicago in 1905, and met at each other's premises in rotation.

Rothesay the name of an ancient castle in the is-land of Bute in Scotland, used in the title of ➤ ROTHESAY *herald*, one of the six Scottish heralds; since the 14th century, *Rothesay* has been a royal duchy, held by the heir to the throne.

Rothschild a famous Jewish banking house estab-lished in Frankfurt at the end of the 18th century by Meyer *Rothschild* (1744–1812) and spreading its op-erations all over western Europe; *Rothschild* (like ➤ ROCKEFELLER and ➤ VANDERBILT) is often used as the type of someone who is exceptionally wealthy, a millionaire.

> I had wealth—not a Rothschild or Vanderbilt fortune but enough to assure me ease and luxury.
> — W. J. Locke *Simon the Jester* (1910)

rotisserie a game, originally using baseball stat-istics but in later use extended also to other sports, in which participants create imaginary teams by 'buying' actual players and scoring points according to their real performances. It is called after *La Rotis-serie*, a restaurant in Manhattan, New York City, where the league was devised.

the rotten apple injures its neighbour proverb-ial saying, mid 14th century.

small choice in rotten apples proverbial saying, late 16th century.

rotten borough a borough that was able to elect an MP though having very few voters. Before the ➤ REFORM *Act* of 1832, in which such boroughs were largely disenfranchised, elections in rotten bor-oughs were rarely contested and the choice of MP was often in the hands of one person or family. The term derives from the borough's being found to have 'decayed' to the point of no longer having a constituency.

something is rotten in the state of Denmark an expression of moral, social, or political corruption, originally as spoken by the ghost in *Hamlet*, reveal-ing to his son the story of his brother Claudius's fratricide and usurpation.

> I suppose something's rotten in the state of Denmark . . . and I don't want him around much longer, if we can help it.
> — Kurt Vonnegut 'The Package' (1952)

Rotten Row a road in Hyde Park, extending from Apsley Gate to Kensington Gardens, much used as a fashionable resort for horse or carriage exercise; the name was formerly applied to a number of streets in different towns, although the reason for this is not clear. Now usually called *the Row*.

rotulorum see ➤ CUSTOS *rotulorum*.

roué a debauched man, especially an elderly one. The word comes from French, where it means lit-erally 'broken on a wheel', referring to the instru-ment of torture thought to be deserved by such a person, and was first given (*c*.1720) to the profligate companions of the Duke of Orleans.

Rouen a port on the River Seine in NW France, chief town of Haute-Normandie. Rouen was in English possession from the time of the Norman Conquest until captured by the French in 1204, and again 1419–49; in 1431 ➤ JOAN *of Arc* was tried and burnt at the stake there.

rouge see also ➤ BONNET *rouge*, ➤ KHMER *Rouge*, ➤ MOULIN *Rouge*.

Rouge Croix one of the four pursuivants of the English College of Arms, so named from the red cross design on the badge worn by the pursuivant.

Rouge Dragon one of the four pursuivants of the English College of Arms, so named from the red dragon design on the pursuivant's badge.

rouge et noir a gambling card game in which cards are turned up on a table marked with red and black diamonds, upon which the players place their stakes according to the colour they favour.

rough see also ➤ OLD *Rough and Ready*.

rough music noisy uproar as intended to display public outrage or discontent at the behaviour of others; *rough music* was traditionally produced by banging together pots, pans, and other domestic utensils; it was likely to accompany the ➤ SKIMMINGTON procession.

Rough Rider an irregular cavalryman; in particular, a member of a volunteer cavalry force during the Spanish-American War, the *Rough Riders*, raised and commanded by ➤ *Theodore* ROOSEVELT.

> When finally the Generals of Division and Brigade began to write in formal communications about our regiment as the 'Rough Riders', we adopted the term ourselves.
> — Theodore Roosevelt in *Scribner's Magazine* 1899

roulette a gambling game in which a ball is dropped on to a revolving wheel with numbered compartments, the players betting on the number at which the ball comes to rest. The name comes (in the mid 18th century) from French, the diminutive of *rouelle* 'wheel', and ultimately from Latin *rota*.

See also ➤ RUSSIAN *roulette*.

roumi in Arabic-speaking countries, a foreigner, especially a European (from Arabic *(al-)Rūm* inhabitants of the late Roman or Byzantine Empire); the term is recorded from the late 16th century.

round robin a petition, especially one with signatures written in a circle to conceal the order of writing; the term was originally (in the mid 18th century) used by sailors, and was frequently referred to as a nautical term.

Round Table the table at which King Arthur and his knights sat so that none should have precedence, and which came to represent their chivalric fellowship. It was first mentioned in Wace's *Roman de Brut* (1155); from the 15th century, the name has

been given to a large circular table preserved at Winchester, bearing the names of Arthur and his most famous knights.

Round Table was also subsequently used for something regarded as resembling Arthur's Round Table as an institution, such as an assembly of knights for the purpose of holding a tournament and festival, especially that instituted by King Edward III in 1345. The name has also been applied to various natural or artificial antiquities seen as having associations with King Arthur.

Since 1927, *Round Table* has also been the name of an organization for professional people between the ages of 18 and 40, intended to promote community service and international understanding.

See also ➤ ALGONQUIN *Round Table*, ➤ KNIGHT *of the Round Table*.

round tower a high tower of circular plan tapering from the base to a conical roofed top, typically found in Ireland; the purpose of such *round towers* has been debated, but it seems likely that they were intended as the sign of dominance of an area rather than having strategic importance in themselves.

roundabout a merry-go-round, a carousel; the term in this sense is recorded from the mid 18th century.

See also ➤ SWINGS *and roundabouts*.

roundel in heraldry, a plain filled circle as a charge, often with a special name according to colour.

roundelay a short simple song with a refrain; a circle dance. Recorded from late Middle English, the term comes from Old French *rondelet*, ultimately from *ronde* 'round'; the change in ending was due to association with the final syllable of ➤ VIRELAY.

Roundhead a member or supporter of the Parliamentary party in the English Civil War, so called from their custom of wearing the hair close cut. The name is recorded from 1641, and Rushworth's *Historical Collections* (1692) attributes the coinage to an officer called David Hide who, in December 1641, apparently threatened 'to cut the throat of those roundheaded dogs that bawled against bishops'. In Sellar's and Yeatman's *1066 and All That* (1930), the name was used in their well-known and terse summary of the opposing sides in the Civil War, 'The Cavaliers (Wrong but Wromantic) and the Roundheads (Right but Repulsive).'

roundsman in the 19th century a labourer in need of parochial relief, who was sent round from one farmer to another for employment, partly at the expense of the farmer and partly at the cost of the parish.

roup in Scotland and northern England, an auction. The word is of Scandinavian origin, probably related to Old Norse *raupa* 'boast, brag'.

Henri Rousseau (1844–1910), French painter, known as *le Douanier* ('customs officer'). After retiring as a customs official in 1893, he created bold and colourful paintings of fantastic dreams and exotic jungle landscapes, such as *Sleeping Gypsy* (1897) and *Tropical Storm with Tiger* (1891).

Jean-Jacques Rousseau (1712–78), French philosopher and writer, born in Switzerland. From 1750 he came to fame with a series of works highly critical of the existing social order, such as *Émile* (1762) and *The Social Contract* (1762). He believed that civilization warps the fundamental goodness of human nature, but that the ill effects can be moderated by active participation in democratic consensual politics; the ➤ NOBLE *savage* is a concept particularly associated with his thought.

Route One in soccer, the use of a long kick upfield as an attacking tactic. The term comes from a phrase used in the 1960s television quiz show *Quizball*, in which questions (graded in difficulty) led to scoring a goal, *Route One* being the direct path.

routier a member of a band of mercenaries in France in the late medieval period; the word comes from French *route* 'road' From the mid 20th century, routier has also denoted a long-distance lorry-driver.

rove travel constantly without a fixed destination; wander. This was originally (in the 15th century) a term in archery in the sense 'shoot at a casual mark of undetermined range', perhaps from dialect *rave* 'to stray', probably of Scandinavian origin. The object of *roving* in this sense was apparently to give practice in finding the range of a mark, while practice at the *butts* taught accuracy.

row see also ➤ DEATH *row*, ➤ ROTTEN *Row*, ➤ SAVILE *Row*, ➤ SKID *row*.

row someone up Salt River defeat a political opponent, send to oblivion, probably with reference to an attributive use of the name of a river (possibly one in Kentucky) to designate inhabitants of the American backwoods region.

rowan a small deciduous tree of the rose family, with compound leaves, white flowers, and red berries, which traditionally is a protection against witchcraft. The name (which is recorded from the late 15th century, originally Scots and northern English) is of Scandinavian origin.

rowan tree and red thread make witches tine their speed proverbial saying, mid 19th century, relating to a way of defeating a witch's power; a sprig or cross of rowan tied with red thread across a barn door would secure it against witches (*tine* here means 'lose' and *speed* means 'success').

Thomas Rowlandson (1756–1827), English painter, draughtsman, and caricaturist. Some of his watercolours and drawings satirizing Georgian manners, morals, and occupations feature in a series of books known as *The Tours of Dr Syntax* (1812–21).

Rowley see also ➤ OLD *Rowley*.

Rowley Poems fraudulent poems, supposedly the work of a 15th-century monk and poet called *Thomas Rowley*, composed by ➤ *Thomas* CHATTERTON, who also provided apparent supporting documentary evidence in the form of forged letters from and to Rowley. Despite Chatterton's suicide in 1770, the *Rowley Poems* were published in 1777, and debate over their possible authenticity lasted for a number of years.

Rowntree a family of English business entrepreneurs and philanthropists. Joseph (1801–59) was a grocer who established several Quaker schools. His son Henry Isaac (1838–83) founded the family cocoa and chocolate manufacturing firm in York, while his brother Joseph (1836–1925) became Henry's business partner in 1869 and founded three Rowntree trusts (1904) to support research into social welfare and policy.

Rowton house a type of cheap lodging house, aiming to provide accommodation of a decent standard for poor single men, named after Montague Lowry-Corry, Lord *Rowton* (1838–1903), English social reformer.

Roxburghe Club the first of the book-clubs, founded in 1812 and named for the 3rd Duke of *Roxburghe* (1740–1804), an ardent bibliophile, at a dinner arranged to celebrate the sale of the duke's edition of Boccaccio to the Marquis of Blandford.

le roy le veult the king wishes it; formula by which the king gives his ➤ ROYAL *assent* to a bill. *La reine le veult* is the equivalent when the sovereign is a queen.

le roy s'avisera the king will consider; formula by which the king can exercise his right of veto over a bill. The veto was last exercised by the sovereign in 1707.

See ➤ *la* REINE *s'avisera*.

royal see also ➤ ASTRONOMER *Royal*, ➤ CAFÉ *Royal*, ➤ *the* CHAPEL *Royal*, ➤ FISH *royal*, ➤ PALAIS *Royal*, ➤ PRINCESS *Royal*.

royal a paper size, 636 x 480 mm; a book size, 234 x 156 mm or 312 x 237 mm; the term dates from the late 15th century.

Royal Academy of Arts an institution established in London in 1768, whose purpose was to cultivate painting, sculpture, and architecture in Britain. Sir Joshua Reynolds was its first president and he instituted a highly influential series of annual lectures. Although it became increasingly unrepresentative of modernist tendencies (and often at odds with new talent), it still commands considerable influence and prestige.

Royal American Regiment original name of the King's Royal Rifle Corps, raised in 1754 on the outbreak of war between French and English settlers in North America.

the Royal and Ancient St Andrews Golf Club, formed at St Andrews in Fife, Scotland, in 1754 as the *Society of St Andrews Golfers*; originally for 'noblemen and gentlemen'. The name **The Royal and Ancient Golf Club of St Andrews** was adopted in 1834 by permission of William IV, and in the 19th century the Club became the recognized authority on rules of golf.

Royal Arms used by the sovereign of a country, and generally including dynastic emblems and other traditional badges; the present *Royal Arms* of the United Kingdom, for example, show the leopards of England and lion rampant of Scotland with a harp for Ireland; the supporters, a lion and a unicorn, represent England and Scotland respectively, and the ground beneath the shield and its supporters has the rose of England, the thistle of Scotland, the Irish shamrock, and the Welsh leek. At earlier periods, they have included the lilies of France and the white horse of Hanover.

Royal Ascot a four-day race meeting held at Ascot in June, traditionally attended by the sovereign; it was initiated in 1711 by Queen Anne.

royal assent assent of the sovereign to a Bill which has been passed by Parliament, and which thus becomes an Act of Parliament. *Royal assent* by the sovereign (in person or through commissioners of the Crown) is required before a Bill (or a Measure passed by the General Synod of the Church of England) can come into force as law, but it has not been withheld since 1707.

Royal Exchange originally founded by ➤ *Thomas* GRESHAM (1518–79); 'Burse' or Exchange was built in 1566, and received the name *Royal Exchange* from Queen Elizabeth; a name which was retained by the newer building which later housed it. In the 17th century, the two were sometimes respectively referred to as the **Old Exchange** and the **New Exchange**; the older building was burnt in the Great Fire of London. The second *Royal Exchange*, which was opened in 1669, was also destroyed by fire (in 1838); it was finally closed as an institution in 1939.

royal flush a straight flush including ace, king, queen, jack, and ten all in the same suit, which is the hand of the highest possible value in poker when wild cards are not in use; the term is recorded from the mid 19th century.

Royal Greenwich Observatory the official astronomical institution of Great Britain. It was founded at Greenwich in London in 1675 by Charles II, and the old buildings now form part of the National Maritime Museum. The Observatory headquarters were moved to Herstmonceux Castle in East Sussex in 1948 and to Cambridge in 1990. Because of poor viewing conditions in Britain the 2.5-metre Isaac Newton telescope and the 4.2-metre William Herschel telescope are sited at La Palma in the Canary Islands.

Royal Highness title of a prince or princess regarded as being of royal rank; up to the 17th century, ➤ HIGHNESS was the title of English kings and queens. In current British usage, *Royal Highness* is limited to the children, and grandchildren through the male line, of the sovereign.

Royal Institution a British society founded in 1799 for the diffusion of scientific knowledge. It organizes educational events, promotes research, and maintains a museum, library, and information service.

royal jelly a substance secreted by honeybee workers and fed by them to larvae which are being raised as potential queen bees; in figurative use, the quality which means that someone can succeed in a pre-eminent role.

> Politics is not a cult of personality, but leadership is an essential quality in the game. Mr Charest has the royal jelly that Daniel Johnson lacked.
> — *Globe & Mail* 6 March 1998

Royal Mint the establishment responsible for the manufacture of British coins. Set up in 1810 in London, it moved in 1968 to Llantrisant in South Wales.

there is no royal road to learning proverbial saying, early 19th century; the expression comes ultimately from a saying attributed to ➤ EUCLID in the *Commentary on Euclid* by the 5th-century Greek philosopher Proclus, 'there is no royal short-cut to geometry'.

royal sign-manual the sovereign's signature as authenticating a document.

Royal Society the oldest and most prestigious scientific society in Britain. It was formed by followers of Francis Bacon (including Robert Boyle, John Evelyn, and Christopher Wren) to promote scientific discussion especially in the physical sciences, and received its charter from Charles II in 1662. Past presidents include Isaac Newton and Joseph Banks. Its *Philosophical Transactions*, founded in 1665, is the oldest scientific journal.

Royal Victorian Chain (in the UK) an order founded by Edward VII in 1902 and conferred by the sovereign on special occasions.

Royal Victorian Order (in the UK) an order founded by Queen Victoria in 1896 and typically conferred for great service rendered to the sovereign.

royal 'we' the use of 'we' instead of 'I' by a single person, as traditionally used by a sovereign.

Royalist a supporter of the King against Parliament in the English Civil War; the term is first used in the Puritan pamphleteer William Prynne's *The Sovereign Power of Parliaments and Kingdoms* (1643), 'His Majesty and all Royalists must necessarily yield…that the ports, forts, navy…are not his, but the kingdom's'.

royaliste see ➤ PLUS *royaliste*.

Royals see ➤ BLUES *and Royals*.

a Royston horse and a Cambridge master of arts will give way to no-one traditional saying, late 16th century; *Royston* is a town in Cambridgeshire.

there's the rub there's the difficulty, originally from Shakespeare's *Hamlet*; a *rub* here is literally an impediment in bowls by which a bowl is hindered in or diverted from its proper course.

rub of the green good fortune, especially as determining events in a sporting match, luck; literally, the lie of the green in golf as determining the way a ball will run.

Rub' al Khali a vast desert in the Arabian peninsula, extending from central Saudi Arabia southwards to Yemen and eastwards to the United Arab Emirates and Oman. It is also known as the Great Sandy Desert and the Empty Quarter.

rubáiyát an Arabic word meaning literally 'quatrains', as in the title of Edward Fitzgerald's version (first published in 1859) of the verses by ➤ OMAR *Khayyám*.

rubber[1] a tough elastic polymeric substance made from the latex of a tropical plant or synthetically. The original sense was 'an implement (such as a hard brush) used for rubbing and cleaning', and because an early use of the elastic substance (previously known as *caoutchouc*) was to rub out pencil marks, *rubber* in the late 18th century gained the sense 'eraser'. The sense was subsequently (mid 19th century) generalized to refer to the substance in any form or use, at first often differentiated as **India rubber**.

rubber[2] a contest consisting of a series of successive matches (typically three or five) between the same sides or people in cricket, tennis, and other games. The origin is unknown, although the early use was as a term in bowls.

the rubber chicken circuit the circuit followed by professional speakers; referring to what is regarded as the customary menu for the lunch or dinner preceding the speech.

> He spent the winter making speeches on the rubber-chicken circuit.
> — *Rolling Stone* 5 May 1977

Rube Goldberg designating a device that is unnecessarily complicated, impractical, or ingenious, from the name of Reuben ('*Rube*') Lucius

Goldberg (1883–1970), US humorous artist, whose illustrations often depicted such devices.

> Orchids are Rube Goldberg machines; a perfect
> engineer would certainly have come up with
> something better.
> — *Nature* 9 November 1978

Peter Paul Rubens (1577–1640), Flemish painter. The foremost exponent of northern Baroque, he is best known for his portraits and mythological paintings featuring voluptuous female nudes, as in *Venus and Adonis* (*c*.1635).

> The artless gesture of the ingénue, inappropriate for
> this Rubensesque wife and mother.
> — Len Deighton *Twinkle, Twinkle, Little Spy* (1976)

Rübezahl in Germanic folklore, a mountain spirit of the Riesengeberg mountain; he is called 'Prince of the Gnomes' in a Silesian folk tale, and sometimes (like Puck) may play the part of a trickster.

Rubicon a stream in NE Italy which marked the ancient boundary between Italy and Cisalpine Gaul. ➤ Julius *Caesar* led his army across it into Italy in 49 BC, breaking the law forbidding a general to lead an army out of his province, and so committing himself to war against the Senate and Pompey; the ensuing civil war resulted in victory for Caesar after three years.

In general use, *rubicon* came in the 17th century to mean a boundary or limit, and from the late 19th century, in the card-game of piquet, to denote an act of winning a game against an opponent whose total score is less than 100, in which case the loser's score is added to rather than subtracted from the winner's.

cross the Rubicon pass a point of no return, as Caesar led his army across the river forming the ancient boundary between Italy and Cisalpine Gaul; the expression has been current since the 17th century.

> It is clear the Rubicon early hominids crossed wasn't the
> large brain or toolmaking, but bipedality.
> — *Post* (Denver) 5 September 1995

Rubik's cube a puzzle in the form of a plastic cube covered with multicoloured squares, which the player attempts to twist and turn so that all the squares on each face are of the same colour. It is named after Erno *Rubik* (1944–), its Hungarian inventor, and had a great vogue when first introduced in the 1980s.

Helena Rubinstein (1882–1965), American beautician and businesswoman. Her organization became an international cosmetics manufacturer and distributor.

rubric a heading on a document; in particular, a direction in a liturgical book as to how a church service should be conducted. The word (in late Middle English in form *rubrish*) originally refers to a heading or section of text written in red for distinctiveness (see also ➤ RED *letter day*); it comes via Old French from Latin *rubrica (terra)* 'red (earth or ochre as writing material)', from the base of *rubeus* 'red'.

From the mid 19th century, the word was used for a descriptive heading or designation, and then for a set of instructions on an examination paper.

ruby a precious stone consisting of corundum in colour varieties varying from deep crimson or purple to pale rose (the term ➤ PIGEON's *blood* is sometimes used of ruby of a particularly deep shade); the name may also be used for the less valuable **spinel ruby**, a deep red variety of the mineral spinel. The *ruby* may also be taken as the type of something exceedingly precious, as in the biblical passage:

> Who can find a virtuous woman? for her price is far
> above rubies.
> — Bible (AV) Proverbs ch. 31, v. 10

See also ➤ BLACK *Prince's ruby*, ➤ PERFECT *ruby*.

ruby wedding the fortieth (or occasionally, the forty-fifth) anniversary of a wedding; the name is recorded from the early 20th century.

rudder see ➤ *who won't be* RULED *by the rudder must be ruled by the rock*.

ruddock dialect name for the robin, referring to its red colouring, and recorded from Old English. In Shakespeare's *Cymbeline* (1609–10), with reference to the belief that a robin would cover an unburied body with flowers and leaves, Arviragus says, 'the ruddock would, With charitable bill…bring thee all this'.

Rudge see ➤ BARNABY *Rudge*.

Rudolphine tables a series of astronomical calculations published by ➤ KEPLER in 1627 and named after his patron the Emperor Rudolph II of Austria.

Rudra in the ➤ RIG *Veda*, a Vedic minor god, associated with the storm, father of the ➤ MARUTS. In Hinduism, *Rudra* is also one of the names of ➤ SHIVA.

rue a perennial evergreen shrub with bitter strong-scented lobed leaves which are used in herbal medicine; the name has often been used with punning allusion to *rue* meaning 'sorrow, regret', which may have given rise to the alternative name ➤ HERB *of grace*. *Rue* is a symbol of grief and repentance.

Rufai a dervish (also called **howling dervish**) belonging to an order practising the repeated calling out of chants to induce trance. The order is named after its 12th-century founder.

ruff a card game of the 16th and 17th century; the name came from Old French, and perhaps ultimately from an alteration of Italian *trionfo* 'a trump'.

Rufus see ➤ WILLIAM *Rufus*.

Rugby see also ➤ ARNOLD *of Rugby*.

rugby a team game played with an oval ball that may be kicked, carried, and passed from hand to hand. Points are scored by grounding the ball behind the opponents' goal line (thereby scoring a try) or by kicking it between the two posts and over the crossbar of the opponents' goal.

The game is named after *Rugby* School in Warwickshire, where it was first played; according to tradition, in 1823 a pupil named William Webb Ellis, playing in a football match, picked up the ball and ran with it. Although precise details of the origin are a matter of debate, by 1846 the school had published rules for rugby, and subsequently it was widely played.

Ruggiero the legendary ancestor of the house of Este (also called *Rogero*), son of a Christian knight and a Saracen; he accepts baptism, and fights for Charlemagne. His deeds are celebrated in *Orlando Furioso*.

rule see also ➤ DIVIDE *and rule*, ➤ EXCEPTION *that proves the rule*, ➤ FREEDOM *of the Rule*, ➤ GOLDEN *rule*, ➤ PONSONBY *rule*, ➤ PORSON'*s rule*, ➤ SIMPSON'*s rule*, ➤ TEN-*minute rule*, ➤ THIRTY-*year rule*.

St Rule (?4th century), a Scottish saint who supposedly brought the relics of St Andrew to Scotland; he is said to have been a native of Patras in the Peloponnese, who was instructed in a dream to set out with the relics; when he reached Fife, he was similarly told to stop, and there he built a church. This was said to be the origin of the name *St Andrews*.

◻ **FEAST DAY** His feast day is 17 October (and also, through confusion with St Regulus of Senlis, 30 March).

Rule, Britannia name given to the song from *Alfred: A Masque* (1740), attributed to the Scottish poet James Thomson (1700–48); the name comes from the concluding lines of the verse, 'Rule, Britannia, rule the waves; Britons never will be slaves.'

By the end of the 19th century, the singing of *Rule Britannia* was associated with a particularly assertive patriotism:

> When you've shouted 'Rule Britannia', when you've
> sung 'God save the Queen',
> When you've finished killing Kruger with your mouth.
> — Rudyard Kipling *The Absent-Minded Beggar* (1898)

Rule 43 (in the UK) a prison regulation whereby prisoners, typically sex offenders, can be isolated or segregated for their own protection.

> None of the other Rule 43s on the wing had ventured
> out under the governor's new scheme to integrate
> them.
> — G. F. Newman *Law & Order* (1993)

rule of the road a custom or law regulating the direction in which two vehicles (or riders or ships) should move to pass one another on meeting, or which should give way to the other, so as to avoid collision; the expression is recorded from the late 19th century.

rule of three a method of finding a number in the same ratio to a given number as exists between two other given numbers; recorded from the late 16th century, it is also called the *golden rule*.

rule of thumb a broadly accurate guide or principle, based on experience or practice rather than theory; the expression dates from the late 17th century:

> What he doth, he doth by rule of thumb, and not by art.
> — William Hope *The Compleat Fencing-Master* (ed 2,
> 1692)

rule the roast be in charge, have full authority; the expression is found frequently from the mid 16th century on, but the precise origin is unclear. The (now more common) form **rule the roost** is recorded from the mid 18th century.

who won't be ruled by the rudder must be ruled by the rock proverbial saying, mid 17th century; meaning that a ship which is not being steered on its course will run on to a rock.

ruler of the choir archaic term for a ➤ CANTOR, recorded from the late 15th century.

rules see ➤ McNAGHTEN *rules*, ➤ QUEENSBERRY *Rules*, ➤ RAFFERTY'*s rules*, ➤ ROBERT'*s Rules of Order*.

Rules Committee a house of a US federal or state legislature responsible for expediting the passage of bills.

ruling elder a nominated or elected lay official of any of various Christian Churches, especially of a Presbyterian Church; the term is recorded from the late 16th century.

ruling passion an interest or concern that occupies a large part of someone's time and effort; initially perhaps as a quotation from Alexander Pope (1688–1744):

> The ruling passion, be it what it will,
> The ruling passion conquers reason still.
> — Alexander Pope *Epistles to Several Persons* 'To Lord Bathurst' (1733)

ruling planet in astrology, a planet which is held to have a particular influence over a specific sign of the zodiac, house, or aspect of life.

rum an alcoholic spirit distilled from sugar-cane residues or molasses, which in the British navy was formerly regulation issue for sailors; in Australia during the early days of New South Wales it was also an important medium of exchange.

In North America, from the early 19th century, *rum* has been used generically for intoxicating liquor, particularly by those advocating temperance.

See also ➤ GROG, ➤ NELSON'*s blood*.

Rum Hospital a hospital in Sydney, Australia, the building of which was undertaken in return for the granting of a monopoly on the import of spirits from 1810 to 1814.

Rum Rebellion the rebellion against William Bligh, Governor of New South Wales, by officers of the New South Wales Corps (the **Rum (Puncheon) Corps**) in 1808, when Bligh had attempted to limit the importation of spirits into the Colony.

rum-runner during Prohibition in the US, one smuggling or landing prohibited liquor.

Rumelia the territories in Europe which formerly belonged to the Ottoman Empire, including Macedonia, Thrace, and Albania. The name comes from Turkish *Rumeli*, 'land of the Romans'.

ruminate think deeply about something; the word comes from from Latin *ruminat-* 'chewed over'.

Rump Parliament the part of the Long Parliament which continued to sit after Pride's Purge in 1648, and voted for the trial which resulted in the execution of Charles I. Dissolved by Oliver Cromwell in 1653, the Rump Parliament was briefly reconvened in 1659 but voted its own dissolution early in 1660.

The origin of the name is uncertain; it is said to derive from *The Bloody Rump*, the name of a paper written before the trial, the word being popularized after a speech by Major General Brown, given at a public assembly; it is alternatively said to have been coined by Clem Walker in his *History of Independency* (1648), as a term for those strenuously opposing the king.

See also ➤ BAUBLE.

Rumpelstiltskin the name of a vindictive dwarf in one of Grimm's fairy tales; he initially appears beneficent, helping a miller's daughter to fulfil her father's boast to the king that she can spin straw into gold, but as a price on three successive nights he takes her necklace, her ring, and finally the promise of her first child. After she has married the king and born a son, *Rumpelstiltskin* returns for his forfeit; the only way in which she can save the child is to discover the dwarf's name. Over the next three days she sends out messengers to discover names; it is only on the final day that one of the messengers overhears the dwarf gloating that the queen will never discover that 'Rumpelstiltskin is my name'. When the dwarf appears for his prize, the queen is able to name him; Rumpelstiltskin tears himself in two in his frustrated rage.

run see also ➤ CRESTA *Run*, ➤ *we must learn to* WALK *before we can run*.

if you run after two hares you will catch neither proverbial saying, early 16th century; meaning that one must decide on one's goal.

a run for one's money a satisfactory period of success in return for one's exertions or expenditure; originally from racing, and recorded from the late 19th century.

run the gauntlet undergo the military punishment of receiving blows while running between two rows of men with sticks; alteration (in the mid 17th century) of *gantlope* (from Swedish *gatlopp*, from *gata* 'lane' + *lopp* 'course') by association with *gauntlet*.

you cannot run with the hare and hunt with the hounds proverbial saying, mid 15th century.

runcible a nonsense word used by Edward Lear in formations such as **runcible cat** and (especially) **runcible spoon**; this term was later applied to a fork curved like a spoon, with three broad prongs, one of which has a sharpened outer edge for cutting, although Lear's own illustrations for his books of verse give no warrant for this. The word was perhaps suggested by late 16th-century *rouncival*, denoting a large variety of pea.

> They dined on mince, and slices of quince,
> Which they ate with a runcible spoon.
> — Edward Lear 'The Owl and the Pussy-Cat' (1871)

rune a letter of an ancient Germanic alphabet, related to the Roman alphabet; the original runic alphabet dates from at least the 2nd or 3rd century, and was formed by modifying the letters of the Roman or Greek alphabet so as to facilitate cutting them upon wood or stone.

In Scandinavian mythology, *runes* (supposedly won for humankind by ➤ ODIN) were also seen as having magical powers; in current British usage, the phrase **read the runes** means to try to forecast the outcome of a situation by analysing all the significant factors involved.

The word comes from Old English *rūn* 'a secret, a mystery', not recorded between Middle English and the late 17th century, when it was reintroduced under the influence of Old Norse *rúnir, rúnar* 'magic signs, hidden lore'.

rune-staff a magic wand inscribed with runes.

rune stone a large stone carved with runes by ancient Scandinavians or Anglo-Saxons; a small stone or piece of bone, marked with a rune and used in divination.

runner see ➤ Bow *Street Runner*.

running footman a footman employed as a messenger to run on errands; sometimes also one who ran before or beside a coach in livery as part of a formal progression.

Runnymede a meadow on the south bank of the Thames near Windsor. It is famous for its association with Magna Carta, which was signed by King John in 1215 there or nearby.

runo an ancient Finnish poem or song on an epic or legendary subject, in particular, any of the songs of the ➤ KALEVALA.

he that runs may read proverbial saying, late 16th century; originally with biblical allusion to Habakkuk 2:2, 'That he may run that readeth it', reinforced by John Keble's 'Septuagesima' in *The Christian Year* (1827), 'There is a book, who runs may read, Which heavenly truth imparts'.

Damon Runyon (1884–1946), American author and journalist. His short stories about New York's Broadway and underworld characters are written in a highly individual style with much use of colourful slang. His collection *Guys and Dolls* (1932) formed the basis for the musical of the same name (1950).

Prince Rupert (1619–82), English Royalist general, son of Frederick V (elector of the Palatinate) and Elizabeth Stuart, the ➤ WINTER *Queen*, and nephew of Charles I, also known as **Rupert of the Rhine**. The Royalist leader of cavalry, he initially won a series of victories, but was defeated by Parliamentarian forces at Marston Moor (1644) and Naseby (1645). After the Restoration he settled in England; he was one of the founders of the ➤ HUDSON's *Bay Company* and (reflecting his interest in science) of the ➤ ROYAL *Society*.

See also ➤ PRINCE's *metal*.

Rupert Bear cartoon character created by the illustrator Mary Tourtel, a white bear with a red jacket and black and yellow checked scarf; under the title 'Rupert, the Adventures of a Little Lost Teddy Bear', the cartoon appeared in the *Daily Express* in 1920, and was the first comic strip for children to appear in an adult newspaper.

Rupert of debate a description by the British novelist and politician Edward Bulwer-Lytton (1803–73) of Edward Stanley, later 14th Earl of Derby, likening his parliamentary style to the dashing cavalry charges of ➤ *Prince* RUPERT.

> Here Stanley meets,—how Stanley scorns, the glance!
> The brilliant chief, irregularly great,
> Frank, haughty, rash,—the Rupert of Debate!
> — Edward Bulwer-Lytton *The New Timon* (1846)

Prince Rupert's drop a pear-shaped bubble of glass with a long tail, made by dropping melted glass into water. *Prince Rupert's drops* have the property, due to internal strain, of disintegrating explosively when the tail is broken off or the surface scratched.

Rupert's Land a historical region of northern and western Canada, roughly corresponding to what is now Manitoba, Saskatchewan, Yukon, Alberta, and the southern part of the Northwest Territories. It was originally granted in 1670 by Charles II to the Hudson's Bay Company and named after ➤ *Prince* RUPERT, the first governor of the Company; it was purchased by Canada in 1870. Also called *Prince Rupert's Land*.

Rurik a member of a dynasty that ruled Muscovy and much of Russia from the 9th century until the death of Fyodor, son of Ivan the Terrible, in 1598. It was reputedly founded by a Varangian chief who settled in Novgorod in 862.

Ruritania an imaginary kingdom in SE Europe used as a fictional background for the adventure novels of courtly intrigue and romance written by Anthony Hope (1863–1933), notably *The Prisoner of Zenda* (1894) and *Rupert of Hentzau* (1898).

Rus a people of Scandinavian or perhaps Slavonic origin whose settlement around Kiev and the Dnieper in the 9th century gave rise to the Russian principalities.

rus in urbe an illusion of countryside created by a building or garden within a city. The phrase, which is Latin and means literally 'country in the city', was coined originally by the Spanish-born Latin epigrammatist Martial (AD *c.*40–*c.*104).

Rush see ➤ FRIAR *Rush.*

rush-bearing an annual ceremony in northern districts of carrying rushes and garlands to the church and strewing the floor or decorating the walls with them; usually made the occasion of a general holiday. The term is recorded from the early 17th century.

Salman Rushdie (1947–), Indian-born British novelist. His work, chiefly associated with magic realism, includes *Midnight's Children* (Booker Prize, 1981) and *The Satanic Verses* (1988). The latter, regarded by Muslims as blasphemous, caused Ayatollah Khomeini to issue a fatwa in 1989 condemning Rushdie to death.

Mount Rushmore a mountain in the Black Hills of South Dakota, noted for its giant busts of four US Presidents—George Washington, Thomas Jefferson, Abraham Lincoln, and Theodore Roosevelt—carved (1927–41) under the direction of the sculptor Gutzon Borglum (1867–1941).

> A face and frame of such grave solidity that they look fit for Mount Rushmore already.
> — *Guardian* 11 October 1995

John Ruskin (1819–1900), English art and social critic, whose writings profoundly influenced 19th-century opinion and the development of the Labour movement. He was a champion of the painter J. M. W. Turner (at that time a controversial figure), the ➤ PRE-*Raphaelite* Brotherhood, and of Gothic architecture, which (following Pugin) he saw as a religious expression of medieval piety. His *Fors*

Clavigera (1871–8) or 'Letters to the Workmen and Labourers of Great Britain' was an attempt to spread his notions of social justice, coupled with aesthetic improvement. His religious and philanthropic instincts also expressed themselves in the founding of the Guild of St George in 1871, a major contribution to the Arts and Crafts Movement.

Russell see also ➤ JACK *Russell.*

Bertrand Russell (1872–1970), 3rd Earl Russell, British philosopher, mathematician, and social reformer. In *Principia Mathematica* (1910–13) he and A. N. Whitehead attempted to express all of mathematics in formal logic terms. He expounded logical atomism in *Our Knowledge of the External World* (1914) and neutral monism in *The Analysis of Mind* (1921). A conscientious objector during the First World War, he also campaigned for women's suffrage and against nuclear arms.

Russell's paradox a logical paradox stated in terms of set theory, concerning the set of all sets that do not contain themselves as members, namely that the condition for it to contain itself is that it should not contain itself. It is named after ➤ *Bertrand* RUSSELL.

russet a coarse homespun reddish-brown or grey cloth traditionally used for simple clothing; *russet* may be taken as a symbol of simplicity and honesty, as in a letter written by ➤ *Oliver* CROMWELL:

> I would rather have a plain russet-coated captain that knows what he fights for, and loves what he knows, than that which you call a 'gentleman' and is nothing else.
> — Oliver Cromwell letter to William Spring, September 1643

Russian see also ➤ SCRATCH *a Russian and you find a Tartar,* ➤ WHITE *Russian.*

Russian Civil War a conflict fought in Russia (1918–21) after the Revolution, between the Bolshevik ➤ RED *Army* and the counter-revolutionary ➤ WHITE *Russians.*

Russian doll each of a set of brightly painted hollow wooden dolls of varying sizes, designed to fit inside each other.

> Like a Russian doll, the task of reform has many layers.
> — Will Hutton *The State We're In* (rev. ed., 1996)

Russian Orthodox Church the national Church of Russia, a branch of the Eastern ➤ ORTHODOX *Church.*

Russian Revolution the revolution in the Russian empire in 1917, in which the tsarist regime was overthrown and replaced by Bolshevik rule under Lenin.

There were two phases to the Revolution: the first, in March (Old Style, February, whence *February Revolution*), largely supported by the liberal Mensheviks; it was sparked off by food and fuel shortages during the First World War and began with strikes and riots in Petrograd (St Petersburg). The tsar abdicated, and a provisional government was set up. The second phase, in November 1917 (Old Style, October, whence *October Revolution*), was marked by the seizure of power by the Bolsheviks in a coup led by Lenin. After workers' councils or *soviets* took power in major cities, the new Soviet constitution was declared in 1918.

Russian Revolution of 1905 Popular discontent, fuelled by heavy taxation and the country's defeat in the Russo-Japanese War, led to a peaceful demonstration in St Petersburg, which was fired on by troops. The crew of the battleship *Potemkin* mutinied and a soviet was formed in St Petersburg, prompting Tsar Nicholas II to make a number of short-lived concessions including the formation of an elected legislative body or Duma.

Russian roulette the practice of loading a bullet into one chamber of a revolver, spinning the cylinder, and then pulling the trigger while pointing the gun at one's own head, said to have originated among Russian officers in the early 20th century.

Russian scandal another name for ➤ CHINESE *whispers*.

Russo-Finnish War another term for the ➤ WINTER *War*.

Russo-Japanese War a war between the Russian empire and Japan 1904–5, caused by territorial disputes in Manchuria and Korea. Russia suffered a series of humiliating defeats which contributed to the Revolution of 1905, and the peace settlement gave Japan the ascendancy in the disputed region.

Russo-Turkish War a series of wars between Russia and the Ottoman Empire, fought largely in the Balkans, the Crimea, and the Caucasus in the 19th century. The treaty ending the war of 1877–8 freed the nations of Romania, Serbia, and Bulgaria from Turkish rule.

Rust Belt a part of a country considered to be characterized by declining industry, ageing factories,

and a falling population, especially the American Midwest and NE states. Coinage of the term is often attributed to the US Democratic politician Walter Mondale, who opposed Ronald Reagan in the presidential election of 1984, and criticized his opponent's economic policies by saying that 'His…policies are turning our great industrial Midwest…into a rust bowl.' This was picked up by the media and repeated as *Rust Belt*, and the term survived the failure of the Mondale campaign.

rusticate suspend a student from a university as a punishment (used chiefly at Oxford and Cambridge). Recorded from the late 15th century (in the sense 'countrify' the word comes from Latin *rusticat-* '(having) lived in the country'.

Ruth a book of the Bible telling the story of *Ruth*, a Moabite woman, who when her husband died resolved to accompany her mother-in-law Naomi back to Judah, with the words:

> Intreat me not to leave thee, or to return from following after thee: for whither thou goes, I will go; and where thou lodgest, I will lodge: thy people shall be my people, and thy God my God.
> — Bible (AV) Ruth ch. 1, v. 16

The two women returned to Judah, and through Naomi's agency Ruth married her deceased husband's kinsman Boaz and bore a son who became grandfather to King David. *Ruth* together with Naomi may be taken as a type of devotion; the image of Ruth herself, in her early days in Judah, may also be that of a lonely stranger:

> Through the sad heart of Ruth, when, sick for home, She stood in tears amid the alien corn.
> — John Keats 'Ode to a Nightingale' (1820)

Babe Ruth (1895–1948), American baseball player. He played for the Boston Red Sox (1914–19) and the New York Yankees (1919–35), setting a record of 714 home runs which remained unbroken until 1974.

Ernest Rutherford (1871–1937), New Zealand physicist, regarded as the founder of nuclear physics. As a result of his experiments on the scattering of alpha particles, he proposed that the positive charge in an atom, and virtually all its mass, is concentrated in a central nucleus.

Rutland a county in the east Midlands, the smallest county in England; which between 1974 and 1997 was part of Leicestershire.

Ruwenzori a mountain range in central Africa, on the Uganda–Zaire border between Lake Edward and Lake Albert, which is generally thought to be the

➤ MOUNTAINS *of the Moon* mentioned by Ptolemy, and as such the supposed source of the Nile.

Ruy Lopez in chess, an opening in which White moves the king's bishop to the fifth rank, usually on the third move, named after *Ruy López* de Segura (fl. 1560), Spanish priest and chess expert, who developed this opening.

Sue Ryder (1923–), English philanthropist. She co-founded an organization to care for former inmates of concentration camps, which expanded to provide homes for the mentally and physically disabled.

Ryder Cup a golf tournament held every two years and played between teams of male professionals from the US and Europe (originally Great Britain), first held in 1927. It is so named because the trophy was donated by Samuel *Ryder* (1859–1936), English seed merchant.

rye see ➤ ROMANY *Rye*.

Rye House Plot a conspiracy in 1683 to murder Charles II and his heir, his brother James, duke of York as they passed the Rye House, near Hoddesdon in Hertfordshire, on their way back from Newmarket to London; the owner of the Rye House, the republican conspirator Richard Rumbold (1622?–85), was said to have referred to the prospective assassination as *lopping*. The plan was not in fact put into action, and one of the conspirators revealed its existence to the government in June 1683. Rumbold was indicted for high treason, although he temporarily escaped overseas, and several others, including Algernon Sidney and William Russell, were executed.

Gilbert Ryle (1900–76), English philosopher. In *The Concept of Mind* (1949) he attacks the mind–body dualism of ➤ DESCARTES. He was a cousin of the astronomer Martin Ryle.

Martin Ryle (1918–84), English astronomer. His demonstration that remote objects appeared to be different from closer ones helped to establish the ➤ BIG *bang* theory of the universe.

ryu a school or style in Japanese arts, especially in the martial arts.

Ss

S The nineteenth letter of the modern English alphabet and the eighteenth of the ancient Roman one, derived from a Semitic (Phoenician) character.

Saba an ancient kingdom in SW Arabia, famous for its trade in gold and spices; the biblical ➤ SHEBA, which Greek and Roman writers believed to be the name of the capital city of the kingdom.

Sabaean a member of an ancient Semitic people who ruled ➤ SABA in SW Arabia until overrun by Persians and Arabs in the 6th century AD.

Sabaism the worship of stars or of spirits in them, especially as practised in ancient Arabia and Mesopotamia; the term comes (in the early 18th century) via French from Hebrew *ṣābā* 'hosts (of heaven)', after the presumed etymology of ➤ SABIAN.

Sabaoth the hosts of heaven, in the biblical title **Lord (God) of Sabaoth**; a Hebrew word, literally 'armies, hosts', retained untranslated in the English New Testament (as in the original Greek and in the Vulgate) and in the *Te Deum*. English versions of Old Testament passages in which the word occurs have the rendering 'The Lord of Hosts'.

sabbatarian a Christian who strictly observes Sunday as the sabbath; a Jew who strictly observes the sabbath. The term is recorded from the early 17th century, and was formerly also used to designate a sect, founded towards the end of the 16th century, which maintained that the Sabbath should be observed on the seventh and not on the first day of the week, a *seventh-day Baptist*.

the Sabbath a day of religious observance and abstinence from work, kept by Jews from Friday evening to Saturday evening, and by most Christians on Sunday; the idea that the ➤ LORD's *Day* is a 'Christian Sabbath' or a substitute for the Sabbath occurs in theological writings from the 4th century onwards, but was not popularly current before the Reformation. In English, *Sabbath* as a synonym for 'Sunday' did not become common until the 17th century.

Recorded from Old English, the name comes via Latin and Greek from Hebrew *šabbāt*, from *šābat* 'to rest'. 'Remember the sabbath day, to keep it holy' is the fourth (or in medieval reckoning, the third) of the ➤ TEN *Commandments*.

See also ➤ *Monday's* CHILD *is fair of face*, ➤ WITCHES' *sabbath*.

Sabbath day's journey the distance (equivalent to 1225 yards) which (according to Rabbinical prescription in the time of Christ) was the utmost limit of permitted travel on the Sabbath; in Acts 1:12, the distance from Mount Olivet to Jerusalem is described as being 'a Sabbath day's journey'.

Sabbathaism the doctrines of *Sabbathai Zebi*, born at Smyrna in 1626, who proclaimed himself to be the Messiah.

Sabbatian a member of a 4th-century Christian sect founded by a former Novatianist, *Sabbatius*, who held ➤ QUARTODECIMAN views.

Sabbatical river an imaginary river celebrated in Jewish legend, said to stop flowing on the Sabbath; in an alternative version of the story, it was in full stream only on the seventh day.

Sabbatical year every seventh year, prescribed by the Mosaic law to be observed as a 'sabbath', during which the land was to be fallow and all debtors were to be released; from this, *sabbatical* is the name given to a period of paid leave granted to a university teacher for study or travel, traditionally one year for every seven years worked.

Sabellian[1] a member of a group of Oscan-speaking peoples of ancient Italy, including the Sabines and Samnites. Also, any of the Osco-Umbrian languages thought to have been used by these peoples.

Sabellian[2] of or relating to the teachings of *Sabellius* (*fl. c.*220 in North Africa), who developed a form of the modalist doctrine that the Father, Son, and Holy Spirit are not truly distinct but merely aspects of one divine being. The doctrine was eventually condemned as heretical by the councils of the Church.

sabi in Japanese art, a quality of simple and mellow beauty expressing a mood of spiritual solitude recognized in Zen Buddhist philosophy.

Sabian of or relating to a non-Muslim sect classed in the Koran with Jews, Christians, and Zoroastrians as having a faith revealed by the true God. It is not known who the original Sabians were, but the name was adopted by some groups in order to escape religious persecution by Muslims; it is said by some Arabic writers that the Sabians were professedly Christian, but secretly worshippers of the stars, the etymology of *Sabian* being presumed to be Hebrew *ṣābā'* 'hosts (of heaven)' (see ➤ Sabaism).

Sabine of, relating to, or denoting an ancient Oscan-speaking people of the central Apennines in Italy, north-east of Rome, who feature in early Roman legends and were incorporated into the Roman state in 290 BC. The Sabines were renowned in antiquity for their frugal and hardy character and their superstitious practices, the latter perhaps reflected in the Latin proverb *Sabini quod volunt somniant* 'the Sabines dream what they will' (recorded by the 3rd-century Latin grammarian Festus).

The (unhistorical) legend of the ➤ Rape *of the Sabine Women* reflects the early intermingling of Romans and Sabines; some Roman religious institutions were said to have a Sabine origin.

sable the heraldic term for black, recorded from Middle English. The word comes from Old French, and is generally taken to be identical with *sable* as the name for a marten with a short tail and dark brown fur, native to Japan and Siberia and valued for its fur. Although sable fur is in fact dark brown, it has been suggested that it may have been customary to dye sable-fur black, perhaps in order to heighten the contrast with ermine, with which it was often worn.

sabotage the malicious damaging or destruction of an employer's property by workmen during a strike or the like; any disabling damage deliberately inflicted, especially that carried out clandestinely in order to disrupt the economic or military resources of an enemy. The word is recorded from the early 20th century, and comes from French, from *saboter* 'kick with sabots, wilfully destroy'.

sabra a Jew born in Israel (or before 1948 in Palestine). The word comes from modern Hebrew *ṣabbār* 'opuntia fruit' (opuntias being common in coastal regions of Israel).

sabreur see ➤ beau *sabreur*.

Sabrina a poetic name for the river Severn; in Geoffrey of Monmouth's *History*, from the name of king Locrine's daughter, who was put to death by drowning in the Severn. In Milton's *Comus*, Sabrina is the nymph of the River Severn:

> Sabrina fair,
> Listen where thou art sitting
> Under the glassy, cool, translucent wave.
> — John Milton *Comus* (1637) 'Song'

sac and soke a modernized form of an expression used in charters from the reign of ➤ Cnut onward to denote certain rights of jurisdiction which by custom belonged to the lord of a manor, and which were specified (along with others) as included in the grant of a manor by the crown.

Sacco and Vanzetti Case the Italian-born Nicola *Sacco* and Bartolomeo *Vanzetti*, American anarchists, were tried for and convicted of murder and robbery in 1927; their trial and execution became a cause célèbre, and the subject of a poem (1928) by the American writer Edna St Vincent Millay, 'Justice Denied in Massachusetts'.

Saccharissa poetic name for Dorothy Sidney, later Countess of Sunderland, coined by Edmund Waller (1608–87), her unsuccessful suitor.

sachem (among some American Indian peoples) a chief; in informal usage, a boss, a leader.

> Most party sachems are lining up behind either incumbent Abraham Beame or Governor Hugh Carey's choice.
> — *Time* 18 July 1977

Sacheverell affair in which the political preacher Henry *Sacheverell* (1674?–1724) was impeached for two sermons preached in 1709 on 'the perils of false brethren in church and state'; in the second sermon, preached at St Paul's in November, he had been particularly critical of the Whig ministers as pretended friends and actual enemies of the Church. In December the sermons were declared by the Commons to be 'malicious, scandalous, and seditious libels, highly reflecting upon Her Majesty and her government, the late happy revolution, and the protestant succession', and Sacheverell was impeached.

The trial, which began in February 1710, caused great public disquiet, and consequent unpopularity for the Whig government; his conviction, which resulted only in his suspension from preaching for 3 years and the order that his sermons be burnt by the hangman, was viewed as a victory for the High Church and Tory party.

Hans Sachs (1494–1576), German poet and dramatist. Some of his poetry celebrated Luther and furthered the Protestant cause, while other pieces were comic verse dramas. Forgotten after his death, he was restored to fame in a poem by Goethe, and Wagner made him the hero of his opera *Die Meistersinger von Nürnberg* (1868).

sack see ➤ EMPTY *sacks will never stand upright,* ➤ SAD *sack.*

sackcloth and ashes used with biblical allusion to the wearing of sackcloth and having ashes sprinkled on the head as a sign of penitence or mourning, as in Matthew 11:21, 'if the mighty works, which were done in you, had done in Tyre and Sidon, they would have repented long ago in sackcloth and ashes'.

> Technologists who say 'There is no answer today, but trust us, there will be an answer in time', are harder to credit than the people wearing sackcloth and ashes whose prophecies of inevitable doom excuse our torpor.
> — *Computer Language* October 1990

Sackerson name of a bear kept in the ➤ PARIS *garden* in the 16th century; it is referred to in Joyce's *Ulysses*:

> The flag is up on the playhouse by the bankside. The bear Sackerson growls in the pit near it, Paris Garden.
> — James Joyce *Ulysses* (1922)

Via Sacra the ➤ SACRED *Way*, a street of ancient Rome leading to the Forum and passing a number of sacred buildings, including the temple of Vesta.

sacrament a religious ceremony or act of the Christian Church which is regarded as an outward and visible sign of inward and spiritual divine grace, in particular (in the Roman Catholic and many Orthodox Churches) the seven rites of *baptism, confirmation,* the *Eucharist, penance, anointing of the sick, ordination,* and *matrimony,* and among Protestants, the two rites of *baptism* and the *Eucharist.* In Catholic usage, *sacrament* (or the **Holy Sacrament** or the **Blessed Sacrament**) also denotes the consecrated elements of the Eucharist, especially the bread or Host.

The word comes (in Middle English) via Old French from Latin *sacramentum* 'solemn oath' (ultimately from *sacer* 'sacred'), used in Christian Latin as a translation of Greek *mustērion* 'mystery'.

See also ➤ SEVEN *sacraments.*

sacrament of reconciliation (chiefly in the Roman Catholic Church) the practice of private confession of sins to a priest and the receiving of absolution.

sacrament of the present moment every moment regarded as an opportunity to receive divine grace.

sacrament of the sick in the Roman Catholic Church, the anointing of the sick, ➤ EXTREME *unction.*

Sacrament Sunday a Sunday on which the Eucharist is celebrated (in the Presbyterian Church and especially in Scotland formerly only once or twice a year).

Sacramentarian a name given by Luther to a Protestant theologian (such as Ulrich Zwingli (1484–1531), see ➤ ZWINGLIAN) who maintained that it is merely in a 'sacramental' or metaphorical sense that the bread and wine of the Eucharist are called the body and blood of Christ. The name was thus used in the 16th century (by opponents) as a general name for those who denied the doctrine of the ➤ REAL *Presence.*

Sacred Band in ancient Greece, a body of 300 young nobles, who formed part of the permanent military force of Thebes from 379 BC.

Sacred Blood the blood of Christ.

Sacred College another term for the ➤ COLLEGE *of Cardinals.*

See also ➤ DEAN *of the Sacred College.*

sacred cow an idea, custom or institution held, especially unreasonably, to be above criticism (with reference to the Hindus' respect for the cow as a holy animal). The term is recorded in English in its literal sense from the late 19th century, and in figurative use from the early 20th.

> Physicists were stunned to see one of their most sacred cows slain by an idea straight out of a Sixties TV series.
> — *Express* 10 June 1999

sacred geese in ancient Rome, kept as guardians of the Capitol; they gave warning of attack by the Gauls in 390 BC, and saved the Capitol when the rest of the city fell.

See also ➤ VAE *victis.*

Sacred Heart an image representing the heart of Christ, used as an object of devotion among Roman Catholics. In the Roman Catholic Church, the **Feast of the Sacred Heart** is observed on the Friday in the week following ➤ CORPUS *Christi.*

sacred ibis a mainly white ibis with a bare black head and neck and black plumes over the lower back, native to Africa and the Middle East, and venerated by the ancient Egyptians.

sacred mushroom another term for ➤ MAGIC *mushroom.*

sacred scarab another term for the ➤ SCARAB.

sacred thread a cord worn over the left shoulder and right hip, with which Brahmins and Parsees are invested at initiation.

Sacred War in ancient Greece, each of three wars of the 6th, 5th, and 4th centuries BC waged by the league of neighbouring states of Delphi in punishment for alleged sacrilege of Apollo's shrine.

Sacred Way a route used traditionally for religious processions or pilgrimages; in particular, in ancient Rome, the *Via Sacra*, a street leading to the Forum and passing a number of sacred buildings, including the temple of ➤ VESTA, from which it took its name.

sacrifice an act of slaughtering an animal or person or surrendering a possession as an offering to God or to a divine or supernatural figure; also, the offering itself. In its primary use, a *sacrifice* implies an altar on which the victim is placed, an association often retained in figurative and metaphorical use.

In the Christian Church, the term is used for Christ's offering of himself in the Crucifixion, or for the Eucharist regarded either (in Catholic terms) as a propitiatory offering of the body and blood of Christ or (in Protestant terms) as an act of thanksgiving. The word is recorded from Middle English, and comes ultimately from Latin *sacer* 'holy'.

sacrifice of praise (and thanksgiving) in the Christian Church, an offering of praise to God, often with biblical allusion, as to Leviticus 7:12, 'He shall offer with the sacrifice of thanks giving unleavened cakes mingled with oil', and Jeremiah 27:26, 'Bringing sacrifices of praise unto the house of the Lord.' The expression was further reinforced by its use in the Communion Service in the Book of Common Prayer.

sacring bell a bell rung in some Christian churches at certain points during the Mass or Eucharist, especially at the elevation of the consecrated elements.

Sad Palm Sunday in *Polyolbion* by Michael Drayton (1563–1631), a name for 29 March 1461, the day (*Palm Sunday*) of the battle of Towton, near York, in which the Lancastrians were decisively defeated by the Yorkists.

sad sack an inept blundering person, originally the name of a cartoon character invented by the American cartoonist G. Baker in 1942.

saddle see ➤ BOOT *and saddle.*

Sadducee a member of a Jewish sect or party of the time of Christ that denied the resurrection of the dead, the existence of spirits, and the obligation of oral tradition, emphasizing acceptance of the written Law alone. The name is occasionally used allusively for someone of a sceptical and materialist temperament.

Recorded from Old English, the word comes via late Latin and Greek from Hebrew *ṣĕḏōqī* in the sense 'descendant of Zadok' (2 Samuel 8:17). The prevailing modern view is that the Zadok referred to is the high-priest of ➤ DAVID's time, from whom the priesthood of the Captivity and later periods claimed to be descended, and the late Jewish notion of a post-exilian Zadok as the founder of the sect is regarded as baseless.

> You needn't overdo this Sadducee attitude, Charles.
> — Dorothy L. Sayers *Clouds of Witness* (1926)

sadhu in the Indian subcontinent, a holy man, sage, or ascetic.

Sadie Hawkins day a day early in November on which, according to a 'tradition' in the cartoon strip *Li'l Abner* by the US cartoonist Alfred Gerald Caplin (1909–79), a woman may propose marriage to or demand a date from a man; *Sadie Hawkins* herself is a character in the series.

sadism the tendency to derive pleasure, especially sexual gratification, from inflicting pain, suffering, or humiliation on others. The term comes from the name of the French writer and soldier the Marquis de *Sade* (1740–1814), whose career as a cavalry officer was interrupted by periods of imprisonment for cruelty and debauchery, and who while in prison wrote a number of sexually explicit works.

Sadler's Wells a London theatre opened by Lilian Baylis in 1931, known for its ballet and opera companies. Although the Sadler's Wells Ballet moved to the Covent Garden Theatre in 1946, a second company, the Sadler's Wells Theatre Company, and a ballet school were set up at the theatre, the three merging as the Royal Ballet in 1956; in 1968 the opera company moved to the Coliseum in London as the English National Opera.

Sadler's Wells was named after Thomas *Sadler*, who discovered a medicinal spring at the original site in 1683.

Safaitic designating an ancient Semitic language known only from inscriptions discovered near *Safa*, probably of the first centuries AD.

safari an expedition to observe or hunt animals in their natural habitat, especially in East Africa. The word comes from Kiswahili, from Arabic *safara* 'to travel'.

Safavid a member of a dynasty which ruled Persia 1502–1736 and installed Shia rather than Sunni Islam as the state religion. The name comes from Arabic *ṣafawī* 'descended from the ruler Sophy'.

safe see also ➤ BETTER *be safe than sorry*, ➤ *it is* BEST *to be on the safe side*, ➤ JUST *when you thought it was safe to go back in the water.*

safe bind, safe find proverbial saying, mid 16th century.

safe haven a protected zone in a country designated for members of a religious or ethnic minority, especially by the United Nations. The term in this sense came to public attention in the aftermath of the Gulf War of 1991 when (following further persecution) *safe havens* were established in northern Iraq for the Kurds, many of whom fled to Turkey and Iran after coming under attack by Saddam Hussein's troops.

Subsequently, events in the former Yugoslavia, and in particular the implementation of ➤ ETHNIC *cleansing*, resulted in supposed *safe havens* being set up for minority groups, although the practical difficulties of providing real protection for those seeking shelter then became clear.

Committee of Safety a body of 23 members appointed in October 1659 by the parliamentary army to conduct the government of England during the interregnum following the practical deposition of Richard Cromwell.

See also ➤ COMMITTEE *of Public Safety.*

there is safety in numbers proverbial saying, late 17th century; perhaps ultimately with biblical allusion to Proverbs 11:14, 'In the multitude of counsellors there is safety', but now with the implication that a number of people will be unscathed where an individual might be in danger.

saga a long story of heroic achievement, especially a medieval prose narrative in Old Norse or Old Icelandic, embodying the traditional histories of the Norse families who first settled Iceland or of the kings of Norway. The word is recorded in English from the early 18th century, and comes from Old Norse, literally 'narrative'.

From the mid 19th century, the use of the term has widened to cover stories regarded as resembling traditional sagas, in particular (as with Galsworthy's *The Forsyte Saga*) dealing with the history of a family through several generations. *Saga* may also be used loosely for a long, involved story, account, or series of incidents.

> Eventually, the two girls have children, their children have children, and the novel turns into a family saga.
> — *Private Eye* 13 March 1992

sagamore (among some American Indian peoples) a chief; a sachem.

Sagan in ancient Judaism, the deputy of the Jewish high priest; the captain of the Temple. The word comes ultimately via Hebrew from Akkadian *šaknu* 'governor'; in the Bible the Hebrew word denotes a civil governor.

sage[1] an aromatic plant with greyish-green leaves that are used as a culinary herb, native to southern Europe and the Mediterranean; in traditional belief, the plant grows best either under the care of the dominant partner of a marriage, or when the wife is dominant.

Sage was formerly regarded as having medicinal properties, and the name comes (in Middle English via Old French) from Latin *salvia* 'healing plant', from *salvus* 'safe'.

sage[2] a profoundly wise man, especially one who features in ancient history or legend; the word comes (in Middle English, as an adjective, via Old French) from Latin *sapere* 'be wise'.

See also ➤ SEVEN *Sages.*

Sagebrush State informal name for the state of Nevada.

Sagittarius a large constellation (the Archer), said to represent a ➤ CENTAUR carrying a bow and arrow. In astrology, the ninth sign of the zodiac, which the sun enters about 22 November; a person born between 22 November and 21 December is in astrological belief thought to be under its influence.

The name is Latin, from *sagitta* 'arrow'.

> Sagittarians are a bit like cats; playful but cruel.
> — *Independent on Sunday* 27 July 1997

sagittary a ➤ CENTAUR; in particular, the centaur who according to medieval romance fought in the Trojan army against the Greeks at the siege of Troy.

Sahara a vast desert in North Africa, extending from the Atlantic in the west to the Red Sea in the east, and from the Mediterranean and the Atlas Mountains in the north to the Sahel in the south, the largest desert in the world. Often used figuratively.

sahib in the Indian subcontinent, a polite title or form of address for a man. The word comes from Urdu, via Persian, from Arabic ṣāḥib 'friend, lord'.

Sahidic a dialect of Coptic spoken in Thebes and Upper Egypt, in which a version of the Bible is extant. The name comes from Arabic meaning literally 'the Fortunate', a name for Upper Egypt.

said see ➤ THEY *haif said: Quhat say they? Lat thame say.*

sail under false colours disguise one's true nature or intentions; the *colours* are the flag which signals a ship's nationality.

sailor ➤ *St* NICHOLAS *of Myra*, St Francis of Paola (1416–1507), founder of the ➤ MINIM *Friars* and author of a number of miracles connected with the sea, and ➤ *St* PHOCAS are the patron saints of *sailors*.

See also ➤ HEAVEN *protects children, sailors, and drunken men*, ➤ *a* RAINBOW *in the morning is the sailor's warning*, ➤ SINBAD *the Sailor*.

the Sailor King nickname for ➤ WILLIAM *IV* of England, who had served in the Navy.

sainfoin a pink-flowered plant of the pea family, which is native to Asia and grown widely for fodder. The name comes (in the mid 17th century) via French from modern Latin *sanum foenum* 'wholesome hay', with reference to its medicinal properties.

saint a person acknowledged as holy or virtuous and typically regarded as being in heaven after death; (in the Catholic and Orthodox Churches) a person formally recognized or canonized by the Church after death, who may be the object of veneration and prayers for intercession. In pictorial representations, a saint is typically shown with a ➤ HALO, and often with a symbol particularly associated with them.

The word comes (in Middle English, via Old

French) from Latin *sanctus* 'holy'.

See also ➤ PATRON *saint*, ➤ SAINTS, ➤ WEEPING *saint*. For names of individual saints, as ➤ *St* LUKE, ➤ *St* PAUL, see under the personal name.

the Saint nickname of Simon Templar, a fictional character created by the thriller writer Leslie Charteris (1907–93) and first appearing in *Meet the Tiger* (1928) and *Enter the Saint* (1930). The *Saint*, a debonair criminal whose lawbreaking excludes such areas as treason and drug-running, signifies his intervention in a case by leaving the sketch of a stick figure surmounted by a halo. He was played in a long-running television series by the actor Roger Moore.

St Helena a solitary island in the South Atlantic, a British dependency, which from 1659 until 1834 was administered by the East India Company. It is famous as the place of ➤ NAPOLEON's exile (1815–21) and death.

St James's see ➤ COURT *of St James's*.

St Leger an annual flat horse race at Doncaster for three-year-olds, held in September, and named after Colonel Barry *St Leger* (1737–89), who instituted the race in 1776.

Saint-Simon[1] (1760–1825), Claude-Henri de Rouvroy, Comte de Saint-Simon, French social reformer and philosopher. Later claimed as the founder of French socialism, he argued that society should be organized by leaders of industry and given spiritual direction by scientists.

Saint-Simon[2] (1675–1755), Louis de Rouvroy, Duc de Saint-Simon, French writer. He is best known for his *Mémoires*, a detailed record of court life between 1694 and 1723, in the reigns of Louis XIV and XV.

St Sophia the key monument of Byzantine architecture, originally a church, at Istanbul. Built by order of ➤ JUSTINIAN and inaugurated in 537, its enormous dome is supported by piers, arches, and pendentives and pierced by forty windows. In 1453, when the Turks invaded, orders were given for St Sophia's conversion into a mosque and minarets were added. In 1935 Atatürk declared it a museum. It is also known as *Hagia Sophia* and *Santa Sophia*.

St Trinian's a fictional girls' school invented by the English cartoonist Ronald Searle (1920–) in 1941, whose pupils are characterized by unruly behaviour, ungainly appearance, and unattractive school uniform; *St Trinian's* later also became known through associated books and films.

> The network would appeal to the iconoclastic enrollees of Ronald Searle's fictional British citadel of mayhem, St Trinian's.
> — *New York Times* 8 November 1980

saint's day a day on which a saint is particularly commemorated in the Christian Church; the term is recorded from late Middle English.

la sainte ampoule the 'holy ampoule' or vessel containing the oil with which kings of France were anointed at their coronation; it was said to have been brought from heaven by a dove at the coronation of ➤ Clovis. The English diarist John Evelyn recorded in 1660 being shown it, but it was destroyed during the French Revolution.

Sainte Chapelle a royal chapel in Paris, noted for its stained glass, built in 1248 in high Gothic style by ➤ *St* Louis to house Christ's Crown of Thorns and other relics of the Passion.

saints see also ➤ communion *of saints*, ➤ ice *saints*, ➤ Latter-*Day Saints*.

Land of Saints and Scholars a name for Ireland, alluding to the holiness and learning associated with the early Celtic Church.

All Saints' Day a Christian festival in honour of all the saints in heaven, held (in the Western Church) on 1 November; it is sometimes also known as ➤ *All* Hallows.

Saiva a member of one of the main branches of modern Hinduism, devoted to the worship of the god ➤ Shiva as the supreme being.

saker a large falcon with a brown back and whitish head, used in falconry, which according to the 15th-century *Boke of St Albans* was to be flown by a knight. The word comes (in late Middle English, via Old French) from Arabic *ṣaḳr* 'falcon', although it was sometimes taken to mean 'sacred falcon' through a confusion with Latin *sacer* 'sacred'.

The word *saker* was applied by transferred use to an early form of small cannon, much used in sieges and on ships.

Saki pseudonym of the British short-story writer Hector Hugh Munro (1870–1916), whose stories encompass the satiric, comic, macabre, and supernatural, and frequently depict animals as agents seeking revenge on humankind; he was killed in action during the First World War. The name *Saki* is

taken from that of the cupbearer in the *Rubaáiyát*:

> And when like her, O Saki, you shall pass
> Among the guests star-scattered on the grass,
> And in your joyous errand reach the spot
> Where I made one—turn down an empty glass!
> — Edwarrd Fitzgerald *The Rubáiyát of Omar Khayyám*
> (4th ed., 1879)

Sakta a member of one of the principal Hindu sects which worships the *Sakti* or divine energy, especially as this is identified with Durga, the wife of ➤ Shiva.

salad days the period when one is young and inexperienced, one's time of youth; originally as a quotation from Shakespeare in the words of Cleopatra:

> My salad days,
> When I was green in judgment, cold in blood,
> To say as I said then!
> — William Shakespeare *Antony and Cleopatra* (1606-7)

Saladin (1137–93), sultan of Egypt and Syria 1174–93. Saladin invaded the Holy Land and reconquered Jerusalem from the Christians in 1187, but he was defeated by ➤ Richard *I* at Arsuf (1191) and withdrew to Damascus, where he died. He earned a reputation not only for military skill but also for honesty and chivalry.

Saladine tax a tax, consisting of the tenth of a man's income, first imposed in 1188 on England and France for the support of the crusade against ➤ Saladin.

salamander a mythical lizard-like creature said to live in fire or to be able to stand its effects. The word is recorded from Middle English; from the early 17th century, *salamander* has been used for a newt-like amphibian that typically has bright markings, once thought able to endure fire. The *salamander* may be taken as the type of something able to endure great heat unscathed; it is also found in heraldry as an emblem, for example that of Francis I of France.

salami tactics piecemeal attack on or elimination of (especially political) opposition, in which an opponent's strengths are systematically sliced away.

Salamis an island in the Saronic Gulf in Greece, to the west of Athens. The strait between the island and the mainland was the scene in 480 bc of a crushing defeat of the Persian fleet under ➤ Xerxes *I* by the Greeks under ➤ Themistocles.

salary a fixed regular payment, typically paid on a monthly basis but often expressed as an annual sum, made by an employer to an employee, especially a professional or white-collar worker. The word comes (in Middle English) via Anglo-Norman French from Latin *salarium*, originally denoting a Roman soldier's allowance to buy salt, from *sal* 'salt'.

Salem a city and port in NE Massachusetts, on the Atlantic coast north of Boston. First settled in 1626, it was the scene in 1692 of a notorious series of witchcraft trials, in which initially three women were accused by a number of children of having bewitched them; ultimately 19 people were hanged, and many others imprisoned. The convictions were later annulled by the Massachusetts' state legislature, and indemnities granted to the families of those who had been put to death.

Arthur Miller's play *The Crucible* (1952), based on the story of the Salem trials, uses the story of the mass hysteria which developed as an illustration of the phenomenon of ➤ McCarthyism.

In the Bible (Genesis 14:18) *Salem* is a place-name understood to to be another name for Jerusalem and to mean 'peace'. It was later (chiefly in the nineteenth century) adopted by Methodists, Baptists, and others as the name of a particular chapel or meeting-house, and thus was sometimes used as a synonym for a nonconformist chapel.

Salerno a port on the west coast of Italy, which was formerly the site of a famous medical school.

Salesian a member of a Roman Catholic educational religious order founded near Turin in 1859 and named after ➤ St Francis *de Sales*.

Salian a member of the *Salii*, a 4th-century Frankish people living near the River Ijssel, from whom the ➤ Merovingians were descended. Also called *Salic*.

Salic law a law excluding females from dynastic succession, especially as the alleged fundamental law of the French monarchy. Such a law was used in the 14th century by the French to deny Edward III's claim to the French throne (based on descent from his Capetian mother Isabella), so initiating the ➤ Hundred *Years War*.

The ancient text which under the name of the *Salic law* was adduced in favour of the succession of Philip V in 1316, and afterwards used to combat the claims of Edward III of England (and his successors) to the French crown, was really a quotation from the *Lex Salica*, a Frankish law-book, written in Latin, and extant in five successively enlarged recensions of

Merovingian and Carolingian date. The words however have no reference to succession to the crown, but merely state that a woman can have no portion of the inheritance of 'Salic land' (*terra Salica*); the precise meaning of this term is disputed, and in the earliest form of the code the word 'Salic' is omitted.

Antonio Salieri (1750–1825), Italian composer. Salieri was hostile to Mozart and a rumour arose that he poisoned him, though the story is now thought to be without foundation.

Salii the priests of Mars in ancient Rome, whose rite involved performing a ritual dance wearing battledress; the name in Latin means literally, 'leapers, dancers'.

Salisbury a city in southern England, in Wiltshire, noted for its 13th-century cathedral, whose spire, at 123 m (404 ft), is the highest in England. Its diocese is known as ➤ Sarum, an old name for the city.

See also ➤ Shepherd *of Salisbury Plain*.

Sallee-man former name for a Moorish pirate-ship; the name comes (in the mid 17th century) from *Sallee*, the name of a Moroccan seaport which was then of piratical repute.

Sallust (86–35 BC), Roman historian and politician. As a historian he was concerned with the political and moral decline of Rome after the fall of Carthage in 146 BC. His chief surviving works deal with the ➤ Catiline conspiracy and the Jugurthine War.

Sally see also ➤ Aunt *Sally*.

Sally Lunn a sweet, light teacake, typically served hot, said to be from the name of a woman selling such cakes in Bath *c*.1800.

sally port a small exit point in a fortification for the passage of troops when making a sally.

Salmanazar a very large wine bottle, named from *Salmanasar* late Latin (Vulgate) form of *Shalmaneser* King of Assyria (2 Kings 17–18).

salmon a salmon with a ring is the emblem of ➤ St Kentigern.

salmon and sermon have their season in Lent traditional saying, mid 17th century; referring to Lent as a penitential period.

Salome (in the New Testament) the daughter of Herodias, who danced before her stepfather Herod Antipas. Given a choice of reward for her dancing, she asked for the head of ➤ St John *the Baptist* and thus caused him to be beheaded. Her name is given by Josephus; she is mentioned but not named in the Gospels.

> Communist heads on a silver platter. Not salami tactics but Salome tactics.
> — *New York Review of Books* 16 August 1990

the Salon an annual exhibition of the work of living artists held by the Royal Academy of Painting and Sculpture in Paris, originally in the Salon d'Apollon in the Louvre in 1667.

Salon des Refusés an exhibition in Paris ordered by Napoleon III in 1863 to display pictures rejected by the Salon. The artists represented included Manet, Cézanne, Pissarro, and Whistler.

Salop another name for Shropshire, and the official name of the county 1974–80. The name comes from an abbreviation of Anglo-Norman French *Salopesberie*, a corruption of Old English *Scrobbesbyrig* 'Shrewsbury'.

salt a white crystalline substance which gives seawater its characteristic taste, is obtained by evaporating seawater or by mining rock salt deposits, and is used for seasoning or preserving food; in proverbial use, it is taken as the type of a necessary adjunct to food, and hence as a symbol of hospitality (as in the expression, **to eat a person's salt**).

See also ➤ ATTIC *salt*, ➤ BARREL *of salt*, ➤ BELOW *the salt*, ➤ PILLAR *of salt*.

with a grain of salt sceptically; a translation of the modern Latin phrase *cum grano salis*, recorded from the mid 17th century.

> Words of love are ricocheting all over the place, and although you'd love to believe in them, you must take them with the proverbial pinch of salt.
> — *Sugar* June 1996

help you to salt, help you to sorrow proverbial saying, mid 17th century; salt regarded as a sign of bad luck (especially if spilt at table).

Salt Lake City the capital of Utah, situated near the south-eastern shores of the Great Salt Lake, founded in 1847 by Brigham Young. The city is the world headquarters of the Church of Latter-Day Saints (Mormons).

the salt of the earth a person or group of people of great kindness, reliability, or honesty; originally with biblical allusion:

> Ye are the salt of the earth: but if the salt have lost his savour, wherewith shall it be salted?
> — Bible (AV) St Matthew ch. 5, v. 13

put salt on a bird's tail in allusion to humorous advice traditionally given to children on how to catch birds, recorded from the late 16th century.

> Will I write a foreword? Will I put salt on its tail!
> — D. H. Lawrence letter, January 1926

Salt River see ➤ ROW *someone up Salt River*.

carry salt to Dysart and puddings to Tranent traditional Scottish saying, early 17th century; meaning to take commodities to a place where they are already plentiful.

Saltash luck a thankless or fruitless task that involves getting wet through, named after *Saltash*, a fishing port in Cornwall, whose fisherman were traditionally said to be unlucky.

Mr Salteena the society man who is the hero of the child author Daisy Ashford's *The Young Visiters* (1919); he is described by the author as 'an elderly man of 42'.

Saltero see ➤ DON *Saltero's Coffee House*.

saltire a diagonal cross as a heraldic ordinary.
See also ➤ CROSS *saltire*.

the salutation the angel Gabriel's greeting to the Virgin Mary (cf. Luke 1:28–9), which forms the first part of the ➤ AVE *Maria*; it is also called **the angelic salutation**. In art, the virgin is often shown sitting reading; her posture in response to Gabriel may be startled or quiescent. A branch or pot of lilies, for purity, often appears.

Salvation Army a worldwide Christian evangelical organization on quasi-military lines, established by ➤ *William* BOOTH (1829–1912).

The name was adopted in 1878 (the body until then was styled 'the Christian Mission'). The officers bear military titles ('general', 'captain', etc.). In its early years, open-air evangelistic services, featuring its famous brass bands, were the most prominent feature of the *Salvation Army*'s work; it has since become notable for its charitable service among the poor and homeless.

Salvatorian a member of the Society of the Divine Saviour, a Roman Catholic congregation founded in Rome in the late 19th century.

salve see ➤ *salve the* PHENOMENON.

Salve Regina a Roman Catholic hymn or prayer said or sung after compline, and after the Divine Office from Trinity Sunday to Advent. The phrase is from the opening words in Latin, 'hail (holy) queen'.

Salzburg a city in western Austria, near the border with Germany. It is noted for its annual music festivals, one of which is dedicated to the composer Mozart, who was born in the city in 1756.

Sam see ➤ PLAY *it again, Sam,* ➤ SOAPY *Sam,* ➤ UNCLE *Sam.*

Sam Browne a leather belt with a supporting strap that passes over the right shoulder, worn by army and police officers, named after Sir Samuel J. Brown(e) (1824–1901), the British military commander who invented it.

Sam Slick a type of smooth-spoken sharp-practising New Englander, a resourceful trickster, from the hero of a series of stories by T. C. Haliburton (1796–1865), Nova Scotian judge and political propagandist.

Sam Spade fictional private eye of the hard-boiled school of detective fiction, created by Dashiell Hammett (1894–1961) in *The Maltese Falcon* (1930), and played by Humphrey Bogart in the film.

Sama Veda one of the four ➤ VEDAS, a collection of liturgical Hindu chants chanted aloud at the sacrifice. Its material is drawn largely from the ➤ RIG *Veda.*

samadhi in Hinduism and Buddhism, a state of intense concentration achieved through meditation. In yoga this is regarded as the final stage, at which union with the divine is reached (before or at death).

Samanid a member of a Muslim dynasty which ruled in Persia in the 9th and 10th centuries, the first native dynasty following the Muslim Arab conquest.

Samaria an ancient city of central Palestine, founded in the 9th century BC as the capital of the northern Hebrew kingdom of Israel; the ancient site is situated in the modern West Bank, north-west of Nablus. Also, the region of ancient Palestine around this city, between Galilee in the north and Judaea in the south.

Samaritan a member of a people inhabiting Samaria in biblical times, or of the modern community claiming descent from them, adhering to a form of Judaism accepting only its own ancient version of the Pentateuch as Scripture.

In the New Testament, the enmity between the Jews and the Samaritans gave especial point to the story (in John ch. 4) of Jesus's asking for water from the woman of Samaria although (in her words) 'Jews have no dealings with Samaritans', and to the parable of the ➤ *good* SAMARITAN.

In the UK, **the Samaritans** (taking their name from the parable) are an organization which counsels the suicidal and others in distress, mainly through a telephone service.

good Samaritan a charitable or helpful person, with reference to the parable told by Jesus in Luke ch. 10, in which 'a certain man went down from Jerusalem to Jericho, and fell among thieves'. Stripped and wounded, he was left lying by the side of the road, and the first two people who saw him, a priest and a Levite, 'passed by on the other side'. It was the third traveller, a Samaritan, who (despite the traditional enmity between them) took pity on him and succoured him.

Samaritan Pentateuch a recension used by ➤ SAMARITANS of which the manuscripts are in archaic characters.

Samarkand a city in eastern Uzbekistan, one of the oldest cities of Asia, founded in the 3rd or 4th millennium BC. It grew to prominence as a prosperous centre of the silk trade, situated on the Silk Road, and in the 14th century became the capital of ➤ TAMERLANE's Mongol empire; it may be taken as the object of an arduous but worthwhile journey, as in Flecker's poem:

> For lust of knowing what should not be known,
> We take the Golden Road to Samarkand.
> — James Elroy Flecker *The Golden Journey to Samarkand* (1913)

Samarra a city in Iraq, on the River Tigris north of Baghdad; its 17th-century mosque is a place of Shiite pilgrimage.

appointment in Samarra an unavoidable meeting with death or fate, from a story by Somerset Maugham in the play *Sheppey* (1933), in which a man sees Death in Baghdad and flees to distant Samarra to escape, not realizing that Death had always intended to meet him that night in Samarra.

Samhain the first day of November, celebrated by the ancient Celts as a festival marking the beginning of winter and the Celtic new year. The name is Irish, from Old Irish *samain.*

Samhita a continuous version of a Vedic text, involving phonetic liaison between, and alteration of, the words; more generally, any of the basic collections of Vedic texts.

Sami the Lapps of northern Scandinavia. *Sami* (a Lappish word of unknown origin) is the term by which the Lapps themselves prefer to be known. Its use is becoming increasingly common, although *Lapp* is still the main term in general use.

Samian letter the letter Y, used by ➤ PYTHAGORAS as an emblem of the different roads of Virtue and Vice.

samite a rich silk fabric interwoven with gold and silver threads, used for dressmaking and decoration in the Middle Ages. In literary use, it is particularly associated with the story of King Arthur; when the sword ➤ EXCALIBUR is finally thrown back into the lake, the arm that reaches out of the water to catch and grasp it is clothed in white samite.

The word comes (in Middle English) via Old French and medieval Latin from medieval Greek, and ultimately from Greek *hexa* 'six' + *mitos* 'thread'; this may mean that the original *samite* was woven of thread consisting of six strands of silk.

samizdat the clandestine copying and distribution of literature banned by the state, especially formerly in the communist countries of eastern Europe. Recorded from the 1960s, the word is Russian and means literally 'self-publishing house'.

Samnite a member of an Oscan-speaking people of southern Italy in ancient times, who spent long periods at war with republican Rome in the 4th to 1st centuries BC.

Samos an island in the Aegean Sea, situated close to the coast of western Turkey; the birthplace of ➤ PYTHAGORAS.

Sampford ghost a supposed poltergeist whose activities were described by the English writer and clergyman Charles Caleb Colton (1780?–1832); his sermon entitled a 'Plain and Authentic Narrative of the Sampford Ghost' was published in 1809.

samsara in Hinduism and Buddhism, the material world, the cycle of death and rebirth to which life in the material world is bound.

samskara in Hinduism, a purificatory ceremony or rite marking a major event in one's life.

Samson an Israelite leader (probably 11th century BC) famous for his strength (Judges 13–16). He fell in

love with Delilah and confided to her that his strength lay in his uncut hair. She betrayed him to the Philistines who cut off his hair and blinded him, but his hair grew again, and he pulled down the pillars of a house, destroying himself and a large gathering of Philistines.

The name *Samson* is used allusively with reference to his enormous strength, his having been blinded 'Eyeless in Gaza at the mill with slaves', as in Milton's *Samson Agonistes* (1671), or his final destruction of his enemies at the price of his own life.

> Saddam may also be contemplating what Middle East experts have dubbed the Samson scenario, lashing out in desperate attempts to relieve the siege, even if his efforts pull him down too.
> — *Time* 3 September 1990

Samuel in the Bible, a Hebrew prophet who rallied the Israelites after their defeat by the Philistines and became their ruler; either of two books of the Bible covering the history of ancient Israel from Samuel's birth to the end of the reign of David. It was Samuel who anointed ➤ SAUL as king of Israel, and after his death Saul invoked his ghost through the ➤ WITCH *of Endor* in an attempt to discover if the Israelites would defeat the Philistines.

samurai a member of a powerful military caste in feudal Japan.

See also ➤ SEVEN *samurai*.

samyama in Hinduism and Buddhism, the three final stages of meditation in yoga, which lead to *samadhi* or the state of union.

San Andreas fault a fault line extending through the length of coastal California. Seismic activity is common along its course and is due to two crustal plates sliding past each other along the line of the fault. The city of San Francisco lies close to the fault, and such movement caused the devastating earthquake of 1906 and a further convulsion in 1989.

San Francisco a city and seaport on the coast of California. The city suffered severe damage from an earthquake in 1906, and has been frequently shaken by less severe earthquakes since. Founded as a mission by Mexican Jesuits in 1776, it was taken by the US in 1846. The fine natural harbour of San Francisco Bay is entered by a channel known as the Golden Gate, which is spanned by a noted suspension bridge (built 1937).

San Marino a republic forming a small enclave in Italy, near Rimini. It is perhaps Europe's oldest state, claiming to have been independent almost continuously since its foundation in the 4th century. It is said to be named after *Marino*, a Dalmatian stonecutter who fled there to escape the persecution of Christians under Diocletian.

José de San Martin (1778–1850), Argentinian soldier and statesman. Having assisted in the liberation of his country from Spanish rule (1812–13), he went on to aid Bernardo O'Higgins in the liberation of Chile (1817–18) and Peru (1820–4). He was also involved in gaining Peruvian independence and was Protector of Peru 1821–2.

sanbenito under the Spanish Inquisition, a penitential garment of yellow cloth, resembling a scapular in shape, ornamented with a red St Andrew's cross before and behind, worn by a confessed and penitent heretic; also, a similar garment of a black colour ornamented with flames, devils, and other devices (sometimes called a *samarra*) worn by an impenitent confessed heretic at an auto-da-fé.

Sanchi the site in Madhya Pradesh of several well-preserved ancient Buddhist stupas. The largest of these was probably begun by the Emperor Asoka in the 3rd century BC.

Sancho Panza the squire of Don Quixote, who accompanies the latter on his adventures. He is an uneducated peasant but has a store of proverbial wisdom, and is thus a foil to his master.

sanction see ➤ PRAGMATIC *sanction*.

sanctity see ➤ ODOUR *of sanctity*.

sanctuary a place of refuge or safety; originally, a church or other sacred place where a fugitive was immune, by the law of the medieval Church, from arrest. By English common law, a fugitive charged with any offence but sacrilege and treason might escape punishment by taking refuge in a sanctuary, and within forty days confessing his crime and taking an oath which subjected him to perpetual banishment.

Certain places, chiefly actual or reputed precincts of former royal palaces, such as Whitefriars, the Savoy, and the Mint, continued to be sanctuaries in civil cases until their privilege was abolished by the acts in 1696–7 and 1722. The abbey of Holyrood is still by law a sanctuary for debtors, but the abolition of imprisonment for debt has rendered the privilege useless.

The word is recorded from Middle English in the sense a holy place, a temple, or the inmost recess or holiest part of such a place; it comes ultimately from Latin *sanctus* 'holy'.

sanctuary lamp a candle or small light left lit in the sanctuary of a church, especially (in Catholic churches) a red lamp indicating the presence of the reserved Sacrament.

sanctum sanctorum the ➤ HOLY *of holies* in the Jewish temple.

Sanctus in the Christian Church, a hymn beginning *Sanctus, sanctus, sanctus* (Holy, holy, holy) forming a set part of the Mass.

sanctus bell another term for ➤ SACRING *bell*.

Sancy diamond a famous diamond, of Indian origin, first recorded as in the possession of ➤ CHARLES *le Téméraire* of Burgundy (1433–77). It was bought in Constantinople, *c*.1570, by the French ambassador Nicolas Harlay de Sancy, for whom it is named, and was later owned by James I; after the execution of Charles I, his widow Henrietta Maria sold it in France. In the 20th century it was the property of ➤ *Nancy* ASTOR.

sand see also ➤ BURY *one's head in the sand*, ➤ PLOUGH *the sands*, ➤ ROPE *of sand*.

built on sand lacking a firm foundation, unstable, ephemeral; often with biblical allusion to the parable in Matthew 7, in which of two houses it is the house built on rock which withstands the floods, and the house *built on sand* which falls.

George Sand pseudonym of the French novelist Amandine-Aurore Lucille Dupin, Baronne Dudevant (1804–76); her earlier novels portray women's struggles against conventional morals.

sand-blind partially sighted; the first element probably represents an alteration of Old English *sam-*, from the base of *semi-*.

sand painting an American Indian ceremonial art form using coloured sands, used especially in connection with healing ceremonies.

Sande a secret tribal cult for women, based on secret rites of initiation, and widespread in Sierra Leone and Liberia.

Sandemanian a member of a religious sect developed by Robert Sandeman (1718–71) from the

► Glassites. Sandeman emigrated to New England, where he established his sect, in 1764.

Sandford and Merton heroes of the children's story of that name by Thomas Day (1748–89); the intention of the book, which contrasts the kind and upright Harry Sandford with the rich and spoilt Tommy Merton, was to illustrate that reform may be accomplished and goodness developed by education and example.

Sandgroper in Australia, informal term for a non-Aboriginal Western Australian, so named because of the large amount of sand in Western Australia.

Sandhurst a training college at Camberley, Surrey, for officers for the British army. It was formed in 1946 from an amalgamation of the Royal Military College at Sandhurst in Berkshire and the Royal Military Academy at Woolwich, London.

sandman a fictional man supposed to make children sleep by sprinkling sand in their eyes (because they rub their eyes when sleepy).

Sandow a phenomenally strong man, from the name of Eugen *Sandow* (1867–1925), Russo-German exponent of physical culture.

> I'm Sandow to what I was when I left the prison camp.
> — Noël Coward *Peace in Our Time* (1947)

Sandringham House a country residence of the British royal family, north-east of King's Lynn in Norfolk. The estate was acquired in 1861 by Edward VII, then Prince of Wales.

the sands (of time) are running out the allotted time is nearly at an end; the expression, recorded from the mid 16th century (in *Tottel's Miscellany* (1557), 'I saw, my time how it did run, as sand out of the glass'), refers to the sand in an hourglass running from one chamber to the other.

sandwich an item of food consisting of two pieces of bread with meat, cheese, or other filling between them, eaten as a light meal, named after the 4th Earl of *Sandwich* (1718–92), an English nobleman who once spent twenty-four hours at the gaming-table without other refreshment than some slices of cold beef placed between slices of toast.

The story is given in Grosley's *Londres* (1770); Grosley was living in London in 1765, and he speaks of the word as having then lately come into use. The first recorded instance in English is from Gibbon's journal of 24 November, 1762, where he refers to

dining at the Cocoa-Tree and seeing, 'Twenty or thirty…of the first men in the kingdom…supping at little tables…upon a bit of cold meat, or a sandwich.'

See also ► Dagwood *sandwich*.

sang-de-boeuf a deep red colour, typically found on old Chinese porcelain. The phrase, which is French, means literally 'ox blood'.

Sangam any of three important Tamil literary academies in southern India which flourished until the 4th century AD.

Sanger's Circus founded by the English circus proprietor and showman, 'Lord' George Sanger (1825–1911). George and his brother John started a travelling show and circus which first appeared at King's Lynn in February 1854; from these modest beginnings, *Sanger's Circus* developed to outstrip American and British rivals. George Sanger bought Astley's Amphitheatre in Westminster Road in 1871; in 1886 he put on the spectacle of 'The Fall of Khartoum and Death of General Gordon', which brought on to the stage 100 camels and 200 horses as well as the fifes and drums of the grenadiers and the pipers of the Scots Guards. Sanger, who finally disposed of his circus in 1905, was regarded as the British head of his profession.

sangha the Buddhist monastic order, including monks, nuns, and novices. The word comes from Sanskrit *saṃgha* 'community'.

Sanglamore in Spenser's *Faerie Queene*, name of the sword belonging to ► Braggadochio.

sangoma (in southern Africa) a traditional healer or diviner; a witch doctor; the word comes from Zulu *isangoma*.

Sangrado a medical practitioner held to resemble Dr *Sangrado*, a character in Lesage's *Gil Blas* (1715–35), a physician whose sole remedies were bleeding and the drinking of hot water; his name was suggested by Spanish *sangrador* bleeder.

> One is sadly off in France and Italy, where the Sangrados are of such low reputation, that it were a shame even to be killed by them.
> — Sir Walter Scott letter, 1820

sangrail another term for the ► Grail; recorded from late Middle English, the word comes from Old French *sant graal* 'Holy Grail', although a later spurious etymologies suggested that the original form was *sang roial* 'royal blood' or *Sangreal*, refer-ring to the actual blood of Christ.

sangre azul the purity of blood claimed by certain ancient Castilian families, which professed to be free from Moorish or Jewish ancestry (the phrase is Spanish, and means literally 'blue blood').

sanguine (in medieval science and medicine) of or having the constitution associated with the pre-dominance of blood among the bodily humours, supposedly marked by a ruddy complexion and an optimistic disposition; the modern use of *sanguine* to mean cheerfully optimistic derives from this.

In heraldry, *sanguine* is the name for a blood-red stain used in blazoning.

Sanhedrin the highest court of justice and the su-preme council in ancient Jerusalem, with seventy-one members. The word comes via late Hebrew from Greek *sunedrion* 'council', from *sun-* 'with' + *hedra* 'seat'.

The title *Sanhedrin* was used by Napoleon as a designation for an assembly of representatives of Jewish rabbis and laymen convened in 1807 to re-port on certain points of Jewish law.

Sankey see ➤ MOODY *and Sankey*.

sannyasi a Hindu religious mendicant, especially, a Brahmin in the fourth stage of his life. The word comes from Sanskrit *saṃnyāsin* 'laying aside, as-cetic'.

Madame Sans-Gêne nickname of Madame Lefebvre, wife of one of Napoleon's marshals (1755–1820); *sans-gêne* in French means literally dis-regard of the ordinary forms of civility or politeness.

sans peur et sans reproche without fear and without reproach; the description '*Chevalier sans peur et sans reproche* [Fearless, blameless knight]' was used in contemporary chronicles of ➤ *Pierre* BAYARD (1476–1524).

sans phrase without more words; after '*la mort, sans phrases* [Death, without rhetoric]', attributed to the French abbot and statesman Emmanuel Sieyès (1748–1836), voting in the French Convention for the death of Louis XVI, 16 January 1793. Sieyès afterwards repudiated the qualification, and *Le Moniteur* 20 January 1793 records his vote simply as '*La mort*'.

Sans Souci see also ➤ ENFANTS *Sans Souci*.

Sans Souci name of the French rococo palace (in French, literally 'Carefree') built near Berlin by ➤ FREDERICK *the Great* of Prussia (1740–86).

sansculotte a lower-class Parisian republican in the French Revolution; the name, meaning literally 'without knee-breeches', is usually explained as someone wearing trousers as opposed to knee-breeches. The term is first recorded in English in the *Annual Register* for 1790.

sansculottid each of the five (in leap years six) complementary days added at the end of the month ➤ FRUCTIDOR of the French Republican calendar (more fully **sansculottid day**).

sansei an American or Canadian whose grandpar-ents were immigrants from Japan; a third-generation Japanese American, born of ➤ NISEI parents.

Sanskrit an ancient Indo-European language of India, in which the Hindu scriptures and classical Indian epic poems are written and from which many northern Indian (Indic) languages are de-rived.

Sanskrit was spoken in India roughly 1200–400 BC, and continues in use as a language of religion and scholarship. It is written from left to right in the Devanagari script. The suggestion by Sir William Jones (1746–94) of its common origin with Latin and Greek was a major advance in the development of historical linguistics.

Jacopo Tatti Sansovino (1486–1570), Italian sculptor and architect. He was city architect of Ven-ice, where his buildings, including the Palazzo Cor-ner (1533) and St Mark's Library (begun 1536), show the development of classical architectural style for contemporary use.

sant in Hinduism and Sikhism, a saint; the word comes from Hindi *santah* 'venerable men'.

Santa see also ➤ SEMANA *Santa*.

Santa Claus another name for ➤ FATHER *Christ-mas*; originally, a US usage, recorded from the late 18th century, an alteration of Dutch dialect *Sante Klaas* 'St Nicholas'.

Santa Fe Trail a famous wagon trail from Inde-pendence, Missouri, to Santa Fe, New Mexico; an important commercial route in the 19th century.

santeria a pantheistic Afro-Cuban religious cult developed from the beliefs and customs of the Yor-uba people and incorporating some elements of the

Catholic religion, which was established in Cuba at the time African slaves were brought there.

Santiago de Compostela a city in NW Spain, capital in Galicia, named after ➤ *St* JAMES *the Great* (Spanish *Sant Iago*), whose remains, according to Spanish tradition, were brought there after his death. According to later accounts, the relics were rediscovered in 813, when a hermit named Pelayo noticed a star hovering above the previously hidden tomb. The story gave rise to a popular folk etymology, in which *Compostela* was seen to mean *campus stellae* 'field of the star', rather than being related to *compostum* 'burial place'.

From the 9th century, when the relics were discovered, the city became the centre of a national and Christian movement against the Moors and an important place of pilgrimage.

santon (chiefly in Provence) a figurine adorning a representation of the manger in which Jesus was laid.

saphie a North African or Arabic charm; the word comes in the late 18th century from Mandingo *safaye*.

Sapir–Whorf hypothesis a hypothesis, first advanced by the German-born American linguistics scholar Edward *Sapir* (1884–1939) in 1929 and subsequently developed by the American linguist Benjamin *Whorf* (1897–1941), that the structure of a language determines a native speaker's perception and categorization of experience.

sapphics verse in a metre associated with ➤ SAP-PHO; the term is first used in Philip Sidney's *Arcadia* (1590).

Sapphira in the Bible, the wife of ➤ ANANIAS; in Acts 5:1–11, the pair attempted to deceive Peter by keeping back the price of something they had sold, and died of shock when the truth was revealed; the name of either may be used allusively for a liar.

sapphire a transparent precious stone, typically blue, which is a variety of corundum (aluminium oxide). *Sapphire* was the second jewel in the walls of the New Jerusalem, as described in Revelations 21:19, and the prophet Ezekiel in his vision (Ezekiel 1:26) refers to 'the likeness of a throne, as the appearance of a sapphire stone'.

The word comes (in Middle English, via Old French and Latin) from Greek *sappheiros*, probably denoting lapis lazuli.

sapphire wedding a forty-fifth wedding anniversary.

Sappho (early 7th century BC), Greek lyric poet who lived on Lesbos. The centre of a circle of women on her native island of Lesbos, she mainly wrote love poems in her local dialect. Many of her poems express her affection and love for women, and have given rise to her association with female homosexuality, from which the words *lesbian* and *sapphic* in this sense derive.

Saqqara a vast necropolis at the ancient Egyptian city of Memphis, with monuments dating from the 3rd millennium BC to the Graeco-Roman age, notably a step pyramid which is the first known building made entirely of stone (*c*.2650 BC).

Sara in one legend of the arrival of ➤ ST MARTHA with Lazarus and Mary in Provence, *Sara* is said to have been Martha's black maidservant who settled at Les Saintes, and became patroness of gypsies.

Sarabaite any of a class of monks in the early Christian Church who lived together in small bands without rule or superior. The 4–5th century monk and theologian Cassianus says that the word is Egyptian, but this origin has not been traced.

Saracen an Arab or Muslim, especially at the time of the Crusades; originally, among the later Greeks and Romans, a name for the nomadic peoples of the Syro-Arabian desert which harassed the Syrian confines of the Empire.

The name comes (in Middle English, via Old French and late Latin) from late Greek *Sarakēnos*, perhaps from Arabic *šarḳī* 'eastern'. In medieval times the name was often associated with ➤ SARAH, the wife of Abraham; ➤ *St* JEROME identifies the Saracens with the *Agareni* (Hagarens, descendants of ➤ HAGAR) 'who are now called Saracens, taking to themselves the name of Sara'.

Saracen's head a conventionalized depiction of the head of a Saracen as a heraldic charge or inn sign; recorded from the early 16th century.

Saragossa a city in northern Spain, capital of Aragon; the name is an alteration of *Caesaraugusta*, the name given to the ancient settlement on the site, taken by the Romans in the 1st century BC.

See also ➤ MAID *of Saragossa*, ➤ *St* VINCENT *of Saragossa*.

Sarah in the Bible, the wife of ➤ ABRAHAM and mother (in her old age) of ➤ ISAAC. When she herself had a son, she forced Abraham to drive away the maidservant ➤ HAGAR with their child ➤ ISHMAEL.

Sarajevo the capital of Bosnia–Herzegovina, which was taken by the Austro-Hungarians in 1878, and which became a centre of Slav opposition to Austrian rule. It was the scene in June 1914 of the assassination by a Bosnian Serb named Gavrilo Princip of Archduke Franz Ferdinand (1863–1914), the heir to the Austrian throne, an event which triggered the outbreak of the First World War.

Battle of Saratoga either of two battles fought in 1777 during the War of American Independence, near the modern city of Saratoga Springs in New York State. The British defeats are conventionally regarded as the turning point in the war in favour of the American side.

sarcophagus a stone coffin, typically adorned with a sculpture or inscription and associated with the ancient civilizations of Egypt, Rome, and Greece. Recorded from late Middle English, the word comes via Latin from Greek *sarkophagos* 'flesh-consuming'; the stone of which these coffins was made was originally believed to be able to consume the flesh of the dead bodies deposited in it.

Sardanapalus the name given by ancient Greek historians to the last king of Assyria (died before 600 BC), portrayed as being notorious for his wealth and sensuality. It may not represent a specific historical person.

> I have always been well paid—though not . . . on the scale of Sardanapalian profusion.
> — Robertson Davies *The Cunning Man* (1994)

sardines a children's game based on hide-and-seek, in which one child hides and the other children, as they find the hider, join him or her in the hiding place, packed together as sardines are packed in a tin, until just one child remains.

Sardinia a large Italian island in the Mediterranean Sea to the west of Italy. In 1720 it was joined with Savoy and Piedmont to form the kingdom of Sardinia; the kingdom formed the nucleus of the ➤ RISORGIMENTO, becoming part of a unified Italy under Victor Emmanuel II of Sardinia in 1861.

Sardis an ancient city of Asia Minor, the capital of Lydia, whose ruins lie near the west coast of modern Turkey, to the north-east of Izmir; in the Bible, its

Church was one of the ➤ SEVEN *Churches of Asia* referred to in Revelations. It was destroyed by ➤ TAMERLANE in the 14th century.

sardius a red precious stone mentioned in the Bible (e.g. Exodus 28:17, as adorning the breastpiece of the high priest, and Revelations 21:20, as set in the wall of the New Jerusalem) and in classical writings, probably ruby or carnelian.

sardonic grimly mocking or cynical, from French via Latin, and ultimately from Greek *sardonios* 'of Sardinia', alteration of *sardanios*, used by Homer to describe bitter or scornful laughter. The usage derives from the idea that eating a 'Sardinian plant' (Latin *herba Sardonia*) would produce facial convulsions resembling horrible laughter, usually followed by death.

sardonyx onyx in which white layers alternate with sard, a yellow or brownish-red variety of chalcedony; in Revelations 21:20; it is said to be the fifth of the precious stones adorning the walls of the New Jerusalem.

Sardoodledom well-written but trivial or morally objectionable plays considered collectively; the milieu in which these are admired. The word is a fanciful formation from the name of Victorien *Sardou* (1831–1908), French dramatist, *doodle*, and the suffix *-dom*, coined by George Bernard Shaw.

> It is rather a nice point whether Miss Ellen Terry should be forgiven for sailing the Lyceum ship into the shallows of Sardoodledom for the sake of Madame Sans-Gêne.
> — George Bernard Shaw in *Saturday Review* 17 April 1897

Sargasso Sea a region of the western Atlantic Ocean between the Azores and the Caribbean, so called because of the prevalence in it of floating sargasso seaweed; known for its usually calm conditions, its name is often used allusively for a congested and stagnant situation.

The novelist Jean Rhys used the title *Wide Sargasso Sea* (1966) for her story, set in Dominica and Jamaica in the 1830s, of the Creole heiress who was to become the mad first wife of Charlotte Brontë's ➤ *Edward* ROCHESTER.

> He looks out on a sargasso sea of extras who are providing the smoky atmosphere in which the wordless scene plays itself out.
> — *Premiere* October 1991

John Singer Sargent (1856–1925), American painter. He is best known for his portraiture in a style noted for its bold brushwork; an anonymous comment on the dangers of sitting to a portraitist of his perspicacity was, 'It's taking your face in your hands'. He was much in demand in Parisian circles in the 19th century, but following a scandal over the supposed eroticism of *Madame Gautreau* (1884) he moved to London. In the First World War he worked as an official war artist.

Sargon (2334–2279 BC), the semi-legendary founder of the ancient kingdom of Akkad.

Sargon II (d.705 BC), king of Assyria 721–705. He was probably a son of Tiglath-pileser III and is famous for his conquest of cities in Syria and Palestine and transportation of many peoples, including Israelites. He may have been named after the semi-legendary King ➤ SARGON, or after Sargon I of Assyria (*c*.1860 BC).

Sargonid a member of the Assyrian dynasty founded by ➤ SARGON *II*, in power until the fall of Assyria in 607 BC.

sarong a garment consisting of a long piece of cloth worn wrapped round the body and tucked at the waist or under the armpits, traditionally worn in SE Asia and now also by women in the West. The word comes from Malay and means literally 'sheath'.

saros in astronomy, a period of about 18 years between repetitions of solar and lunar eclipses. The name comes (in the early 19th century) from Greek, from Babylonian *šār(u)* '3,600 (years)', the sense apparently based on a misinterpretation of the number.

sarsen a silicified sandstone boulder of a kind which occurs on the chalk downs of southern England. Such stones were used in constructing ➤ STONEHENGE and other prehistoric monuments. They consist of a form of quartzite, and were probably formed as a duricrust in the Pliocene period. The word is recorded from the late 17th century, and is apparently a variant of ➤ SARACEN.

sarsenet a fine soft silk fabric, used as a lining material and in dressmaking; the word is recorded from late Middle English, and may come ultimately from Old French *drap sarrasinois* 'Saracen cloth'.

Andrea del Sarto (1486–1531), Italian painter, who worked chiefly in Florence, where his works include fresco cycles in the church of Santa Annunziata and the series of grisailles in the cloister of the Scalzi

(1511–26); his life is the subject of a dramatic monologue (1855) by Robert Browning, in which the artist compares his technical competence with the supreme achievements of the greater artists who have given up material gain for their art.

Jean-Paul Sartre (1905–80), French philosopher, novelist, dramatist, and critic. A leading existentialist, he dealt in his work with the nature of human life and the structures of consciousness. He refused the Nobel Prize for Literature in 1964, but was still regarded as a towering figure; asked in the 1960s to have him arrested, De Gaulle said, 'One does not put Voltaire in the Bastille'.

Sarum an old name for ➤ SALISBURY, still used as the name of its diocese; in particular, denoting the order of divine service used before the Reformation in the diocese of Salisbury and, by the 15th century, in most of England, Wales, and Ireland.

Sarum comes from medieval Latin, perhaps from an abbreviated form of Latin *Sarisburia* 'Salisbury'.

See also ➤ OLD *Sarum*.

sarvodaya the economic and social development of the community as a whole, especially as advocated by ➤ *Mahatma* GANDHI. The word is Sanskrit, from *sarva* 'all' + *udaya* 'prosperity'.

sash see ➤ BLACK *Sash*.

Sasquatch another term (a Salish name) for ➤ BIGFOOT.

Sassanian of or relating to a dynasty that ruled Persia from the early 3rd century AD until the Arab Muslim conquest of 651; also called *Sassanid*. The name comes from *Sasan*, name of the father or grandfather of Ardashir, the first Sassanian.

Sassenach Scottish term for an English person. Recorded from the early 18th century, the word comes from Scottish Gaelic *Sasunnoch*, Irish *Sasanach*, from Latin *Saxones* 'Saxons'.

Satan the Devil, Lucifer. Recorded from Old English, the name comes via late Latin and Greek from Hebrew *śāṭān*, literally 'adversary', from *śāṭan* 'plot against'.

In the Old Testament, the Hebrew word usually denotes a human enemy, but in some of the later books is found as the designation of an angelic being hostile to humankind.

get thee behind me, Satan as a rejection of temptation; originally, with biblical allusion to the words of Jesus in Matthew 16:23 in which he re-buked Peter for denying the prophecy that Jesus would be put to death in Jerusalem.

Satan rebuking sin proverbial expression; re-corded from the early 17th century in the form, 'when vice rebuketh sin'; the meaning is that when this happens, the worst possible stage has been reached. In later use, the emphasis is an ironic com-ment on the nature of the person delivering the re-buke.

the Satanic School the name given by Robert Southey (1774–1843) to Byron, Shelley, and associ-ated poets regarded as exemplifying a defiant im-piety and pleasure in the portrayal of lawless passion:

> The school which they have set up may properly be called the Satanic school; for . . . their productions . . . are more especially characterized by a Satanic spirit of pride and audacious impiety.
> — Robert Southey *Vision of Judgement* (1821)

Sati in Hinduism, the wife of ➤ SHIVA, reborn as Parvati. According to some accounts, she died by throwing herself into the sacred fire, giving rise to the custom of ➤ SUTTEE.

satire the use of humour, irony, exaggeration, or ridicule to expose and criticize people's stupidity or vices, particularly in the context of contemporary politics and other topical issues. The word comes (in the early 16th century) from French, or from Latin *satira*, later form of *satura* 'poetic medley'.

satispassion in Christian theology, atonement by an adequate degree of suffering; the word comes from the Latin phrase *satis pati* 'to suffer enough'.

satnav navigation dependent on information re-ceived from satellites. Recorded from the 1970s, the word is a blend of *satellite* and *navigation*.

satori in Buddhism, sudden enlightenment; the word is Japanese, and means literally 'awakening'.

satrap a provincial governor in the ancient Persian empire; in general usage, any subordinate or local ruler. The word comes (in late Middle English) from Old French or Latin, ultimately based on Old Persian *kšathra-pāvan* 'country-protector'.

satsang in the Indian subcontinent, a spiritual discourse or sacred gathering; the word comes from Sanskrit *satsaṅga* 'association of good men'.

Saturday the day of the week before Sunday and following Friday, and (together with Sunday) form-ing part of the weekend. Recorded from Old English

(in form *Sætern(es)dæg*) the name is a translation of Latin *Saturni dies* 'day of Saturn'.

See also ➤ *Monday's* CHILD *is fair of face.* ➤ BLACK *Saturday,* ➤ EGG *Saturday,* ➤ HOLY *Saturday.*

Saturdays	
Black Saturday	10 September 1547; 4 August 1621
Egg Saturday	Saturday before Shrove Tuesday
Holy Saturday	Saturday before Easter Sunday

Saturday night special in North America, infor-mal term for a cheap low-calibre pistol or revolver, easily obtained and concealed.

Saturn in Roman mythology, an ancient god (Latin *Saturnus* may come from Etruscan), origin-ally regarded as a god of agriculture, but in classical times identified with the Greek ➤ CRONUS, deposed by his son Zeus (Jupiter). His festival in December, ➤ SATURNALIA, eventually became one of the elem-ents in the traditional celebrations of Christmas.

Saturn was the name given to the most remote of the seven planets known to ancient astronomy (now known to be the sixth planet from the sun in the solar system). In astrology, on account of its re-moteness and slowness of motion, Saturn was sup-posed to cause coldness, sluggishness, and gloominess of temperament in those born under its influence, and in general to have a baleful effect on human affairs.

Saturn is also the name of a series of American space rockets, of which the very large **Saturn V** was used as the launch vehicle for the Apollo missions of 1969–72.

Saturnalia the ancient Roman festival of ➤ SAT-URN in December, which was a period of general merrymaking and was the predecessor of Christ-mas; the unrestrained revelry of the original festival extended even to slaves.

Saturnian reign in poetic use, a golden age, sup-posedly the time of the reign of the god Saturn (Latin *Saturnia regna*).

Saturnian verses verses making use of the metre used in early Roman poetry before the introduction of Greek metres.

saturnine (of a person or their manner) slow and gloomy; (of a person or their features) dark in col-ouring and moody or mysterious. The word is re-corded from late Middle English (as a term in astrology) and comes via Old French from Latin

Saturninus 'of Saturn' (identified with lead by the alchemists and associated with slowness and gloom by astrologers).

satyaghra a policy of passive political resistance, especially that advocated by ➤ *Mahatma* GANDHI against British rule in India. The word is Sanskrit, from *satya* 'truth' + *āgraha* 'obstinacy'.

satyr in Greek mythology, one of a class of lustful, drunken woodland gods. In Greek art they were represented as a man with a horse's ears and tail, but in Roman representations as a man with a goat's ears, tail, legs, and horns.

In English translations of the Bible the word is applied to the hairy demons or monsters of Semitic superstition, supposed to inhabit deserts, as in Isaiah 13:21, 'wild beasts of the desert shall lie there…and satyrs shall dance there'.

sauce see also ➤ HUNGER *is the best sauce.*

what's sauce for the goose is sauce for the gander proverbial saying, late 17th century; meaning that what is suitable for a woman is also suitable for a man.

saucer a shallow dish, typically having a circular indentation in the centre, on which a cup is placed, originally (in Middle English) a dish for *sauce*. The current sense is recorded from the early 18th century.

See also ➤ FLYING *saucer.*

saudade a feeling of longing, melancholy, or nostalgia that is supposedly characteristic of the Portuguese or Brazilian temperament; the word is Portuguese.

Saudi Arabia a country in SW Asia occupying most of the Arabian peninsula, which was the birthplace of Islam in the 7th century; as a modern country it became an independent kingdom in 1932, and is ruled along traditional Islamic lines.

Saul (in the Bible) the first king of Israel (11th century BC); chosen as king and anointed by the prophet ➤ SAMUEL. In later life Saul lost God's favour; he became violently jealous of his former favourite ➤ DAVID, who was to succeed him as God's chosen king after the death of Saul and his son Jonathan in battle against the Philistines.

is Saul also among the prophets? proverbial saying, expressing scepticism of someone's capacity; originally, with allusion to 1 Samuel 10:11, the first

response from bystanders when they saw the newly anointed ➤ SAUL prophesying among a group of prophets as a sign of God's favour.

Saul of Tarsus in the Bible, the original name of ➤ *St* PAUL[1].

savage see also ➤ *the* NOBLE *savage.*

Savage Club a club with strong literary and artistic connections founded in 1857, with the journalist George Augustus Henry Sala (1828–96) as one of the founder members; it was named after the poet Richard *Savage* (*c.*1697–1743).

savage man a primitive person as represented in heraldry and pageantry; a human figure naked or surrounded by foliage.

See also ➤ WOODWOSE.

save the whale environmental slogan associated with the alarm over the rapidly declining whale population which led in 1985 to a moratorium on commercial whaling; now often used allusively to refer to environmental concerns.

> Spot an old-fashioned push lawnmower these days, and I bet you'll find a sandal-wearing Green with 'Save the Whale' posters plastering the windows of his Morris Minor.
>
> — *Practical Gardening* June 1996

save us from our friends proverbial saying, late 15th century; developed in the early 19th century by the British Tory statesman George Canning (1770–1827):

> Give me the avowed, erect and manly foe;
> Firm I can meet, perhaps return the blow;
> But of all plagues, good Heaven, thy wrath can send,
> Save me, oh, save me, from the candid friend.
> — George Canning 'New Morality' (1821)

saved see ➤ *a* PENNY *saved is a penny earned.*

Thomas Savery (*c.*1650–1715), English engineer; known as **Captain Savery**. He patented an early steam engine that was later developed by ➤ *Thomas* NEWCOMEN.

Savile Club founded in 1868 as the Eclectic Club, renamed in 1869 the New Club, and from 1871, when it moved to independent premises in Savile Row, known as the Savile Club. It moved to its present home, 69 Brook Street, in 1927. The club has always had a strong literary tradition; members have included Robert Louis Stevenson, Thomas Hardy, W. B. Yeats, and Henry James.

Savile Row a street in London which has traditionally been the centre of fashionable and expensive tailoring.

saving see also ➤ DAYLIGHT *saving*.

saving grace in Christian belief, the redeeming grace of God; generally, a redeeming quality or characteristic.

the Saviour a name for Jesus Christ, as the rescuer of humankind from sin and its consequences; recorded from Middle English.

Girolamo Savonarola (1452–98), Italian preacher and religious reformer. A Dominican monk and strict ascetic, he became popular for his passionate preaching against immorality and corruption, and his apocalyptic prophecies. Savonarola became virtual ruler of Florence (1494–5) but made many enemies; in 1497 he was excommunicated and later executed as a heretic.

> The magazine had arrogated to itself . . . a Savonarolan role at home to thwart the efforts of Communists.
> — Robert Manning *The Swamp Root Chronicle* (1992)

Savonnerie carpet a hand-knotted pile carpet, originally made in 17th-century Paris. The name comes from the French for 'soap factory', referring to the original building on the site, converted to carpet manufacture.

Savoy an area of SE France bordering on NW Italy, a former duchy ruled by the counts of Savoy from the 11th century. In 1720 Savoy was joined with ➤ SARDINIA and Piedmont to form the kingdom of Sardinia, but in 1861, when Sardinia became part of a unified Italy, Savoy was ceded to France.

the Savoy a district of London, adjacent to the Strand, originally land belonging to Peter of Savoy (d. 1268), uncle of Eleanor of Provence, queen of Henry III; it was the site of the **Savoy Palace**, later the residence of ➤ JOHN *of Gaunt*, and was burnt down in 1381 during the Peasants' Revolt. It was rebuilt by Henry VII in 1505 as a hospital, but of this only the royal chapel survives. As the precinct of a former royal palace, *the Savoy* continued to be a ➤ SANCTUARY in civil cases until the privilege was formally abolished.

Savoy Conference a conference held at the Savoy Palace in London between the Episcopalians and Presbyterians after the ➤ RESTORATION in 1661 to consider revisions to the *Book of Common Prayer*; in the event, few of the suggestions from the Puritan side were incorporated in the final text of 1662.

Savoy Hill in London; from 1923 to 1932 (prior to the move to ➤ PORTLAND *Place*) home of the British Broadcasting Corporation.

Savoy Opera any of Gilbert and Sullivan's operas, originally presented at the *Savoy Theatre*, London, by the D'Oyly Carte company.

> Savoy opera . . . was snuffed out by the deplorable death of my distinguished collaborator, Sir Arthur Sullivan.
> — W. S. Gilbert in *Daily Mail Year Book* (1907)

sawbuck in informal North American usage, a $10 note, from association of the X-shaped ends of a sawhorse with the Roman numeral X (=10).

Sawbwa former title of the hereditary ruler of a Shan state in eastern Burma (Myanmar).

Saxe-Coburg-Gotha the name of the British royal house 1901–17. The name dates from the accession of Edward VII, whose father Prince Albert, consort of Queen Victoria, was a prince of the German duchy of Saxe-Coburg and Gotha. During the First World War, with anti-German feeling running high, George V changed the family name to Windsor.

saxifrage a low-growing plant of poor soils, bearing small white, yellow, or red flowers and forming rosettes of succulent leaves or hummocks of mossy leaves, many of which are grown as alpines in rockeries. The Latin name (*saxifraga*, in Pliny *saxifragum*), which means 'rock-breaking', was probably given because so many species are found growing among stones and in clefts; Pliny however took it to imply that the plant had the medicinal property of breaking up stones in the bladder, and this gained a good deal of popular belief.

Saxo Grammaticus a 13th century Danish historian, author of the *Gesta Danorum*, a partly mythical Latin history of the Danes (which contains the *Hamlet* story).

Saxon a member of a people that inhabited parts of central and northern Germany from Roman times, many of whom conquered and settled in much of southern England in the 5th–6th centuries. The name comes ultimately from late Latin and Greek *Saxones* (plural), of West Germanic origin; related to Old English *Seaxan, Seaxe* (plural), perhaps from the base of *seax* 'knife'.

In modern English usage (primarily as a term used by Celtic speakers), *Saxon* means an English person as distinct from someone of Welsh, Irish, or

Scots origin, a ➤ SASSENACH.
   See also ➤ ANGLO-*Saxon.*

Saxon Shore the coast of Britain, from Norfolk to Hampshire, as fortified by the Romans.
   See also ➤ COUNT *of the Saxon Shore.*

say see also ➤ DO *as I say, not as I do,* ➤ SIMON *Says.*

say an ape's paternoster chatter with cold; recorded from the early 17th century.

say it with flowers slogan of the Society of American Florists, first used in 1918; often in general and figurative use.

> Is your group too fulsome in its praise or does it damn you fairly? Does your circle say it with flowers or with forked tongue?
> — *Freelance Writing & Photography* Winter 1990

say the devil's paternoster speak a muttered imprecation, especially to oneself, grumble; *devil's paternoster* in this sense is first recorded in Chaucer.

Dorothy L. Sayers 1893–1957), English novelist and dramatist, chiefly known for her detective fiction featuring the aristocratic amateur detective and bibliophile ➤ *Lord Peter* WIMSEY.

who says A must say B proverbial saying, mid 19th century; only recorded in English from North American sources.

sayyid a Muslim claiming descent from ➤ MUHAMMAD through Husayn, the prophet's younger grandson. The word is Arabic, and means literally 'lord, prince'.

Scaevola ('left-handed'), traditionally the name given to the legendary Roman hero Gaius Mucius, who is said to have saved Rome from the Etruscan king ➤ LARS *Porsena, c.*509 BC, during the attempt to restore the Tarquins to rule in Rome. Captured in the Etruscan camp while planning to kill Lars Porsena, and threatened with torture, Gaius Mucius showed his lack of fear by thrusting his right hand into the fire. The king, impressed by such fortitude, ordered his release.

scale see also ➤ BEAUFORT *scale,* ➤ KELVIN *scale,* ➤ LIKERT *scale,* ➤ MERCALLI *scale,* ➤ RÉAUMUR, ➤ RICHTER *scale.*

scales an instrument for weighing, originally a simple balance (**a pair of scales**); the notion of a soul's good and evil deeds being weighed after death is present in number of early religions. In ancient

Egypt, the heart of a dead person was weighed by the god ➤ ANUBIS; in Zoroastrianism, a person's good and bad deeds were thought to be weighed against each other.
   The Scales is the name given to the zodiacal sign or constellation Libra.
   Scales (in which souls are weighed) are the emblem of the ➤ *Virgin* MARY and ➤ *St* MICHAEL. Justice personified is shown blindfolded and with a pair of scales.

the scales fall from someone's eyes someone is no longer deceived; originally with biblical reference to Acts 9:18, in which Saul of Tarsus (see ➤ *St* PAUL[1]), blinded by his vision on the road to Damascus, received back his sight at the hand of God:

> And immediately there fell from his eyes as it had been scales: and he received sight forthwith, and arose, and was baptized.
> — Bible (AV) Acts ch. 9, v. 18

Joseph Justus Scaliger (1540–1609), French scholar, son of Julius Caesar Scaliger, often regarded as the founder of historical criticism. His *De Emendatione Temporum* (1583) gave a more scientific foundation to the understanding of ancient chronology by comparing and revising the computations of time made by different civilizations, including those of the Babylonians and Egyptians.

Julius Caesar Scaliger (1484–1558), Italian-born French classical scholar and physician. Appointed physician to the bishop of Agen, he became a French citizen in 1528. Besides polemical works directed against ➤ ERASMUS (1531, 1536) he wrote a long Latin treatise on poetics, a number of commentaries on botanical works, and a philosophical treatise.

scallop shell a scallop shell is the emblem of ➤ *St* JAMES *the Great,* and from this association with the shrine at ➤ SANTIAGO, was often used as a pilgrim's badge:

> Give me my scallop-shell of quiet,
> My staff of faith to walk upon,
> My scrip of joy, immortal diet,
> My bottle of salvation,
> My gown of glory, hope's true gage,
> And thus I'll take my pilgrimage.
> — Walter Raleigh 'The Passionate Man's Pilgrimage' (1604)

scallywag a disreputable person; in the US, a derogatory term for a white Southerner who collaborated with northern Republicans during the post-Civil War reconstruction period.

scandal an action or event regarded as morally or legally wrong and causing general public outrage. The word comes in Middle English, in the sense 'discredit to religion (by the reprehensible behaviour of a religious person)', via Old French from ecclesiastical Latin *scandalum* 'cause of offence' from Greek *skandalon* 'snare, stumbling block'.

See also ➤ RUSSIAN *scandal*.

scandalum magnatum the utterance or publication of a malicious report against any person holding a position of dignity. The phrase, which is medieval Latin, literally 'scandal of magnates', was suggested by the wording of a statute of the reign of Richard II which provides penalties for the offence, although the Anglo-Norman French of the statute does not contain a directly equivalent expression.

Scapa Flow a strait in the Orkney Islands, Scotland, which was an important British naval base, especially in the First World War. The German High Seas Fleet was interned there after its surrender, and was scuttled in 1919 as an act of defiance against the terms of the Versailles peace settlement.

scapegoat in the Bible, a goat sent into the wilderness after the Jewish chief priest had symbolically laid the sins of the people upon it, as in Leviticus 16:22, 'And the goat shall bear upon him all their iniquities unto a land not inhabited: and he shall let the goat go into the wilderness.' In the Mosaic ritual of the Day of Atonement, this was the one of two goats that was chosen to be sent alive into the wilderness, while the other was sacrificed.

The English term *scapegoat* appears to have been coined by Tyndale from archaic *scape* 'escape' + goat; that is, the goat which was not to be sacrificed.

In the early 19th century, the word acquired the more general meaning of a person who is blamed for the wrongdoings, mistakes, or faults of others, especially for reasons of expediency.

scapular a short monastic cloak covering the shoulders; a symbol of affiliation to an ecclesiastical order, consisting of two strips of cloth hanging down the breast and back and joined across the shoulders. The word comes (in the late 15th century) from late Latin *scapulare*, from *scapula* 'shoulder'.

scarab a large dung beetle of the eastern Mediterranean area, regarded as sacred in ancient Egypt; also called *sacred scarab*. The term is also used for an ancient Egyptian gem cut in the form of this beetle,

sometimes depicted with the wings spread, and engraved with hieroglyphs on the flat underside.

Scaramouch a stock character in Italian *commedia dell' arte*, a cowardly and foolish boaster usually represented as a Spanish don, wearing a black costume; the name is an adaptation of Italian *scaramuccia* 'skirmish'.

Scarborough warning very short notice, no notice at all. It was traditionally believed that this referred to the surprise of Scarborough Castle by the rebel Thomas Stafford in April 1557, but the expression is in fact recorded from 1546.

scarce as hen's teeth very scarce; originally a US expression, recorded from the mid 19th century.

scarlet a brilliant red colour. The word comes (in Middle English, originally denoting any brightly coloured cloth) via Old French from medieval Latin *scarlata*, which in turn comes via Arabic and medieval Greek from late Latin *sigillatus* 'decorated with small images', from *sigillum* 'small image'.

Miss Scarlet one of the six stock characters constituting the murderer and suspects in the game of ➤ CLUEDO; the traditional accusation of a named character in a specific location and with a particular weapon is parodied in the film *Sleepless in Seattle* (1993) as 'Miss Scarlet—in the broom closet—with the radio'.

Will Scarlet traditionally the name of one of ➤ ROBIN *Hood*'s companions.

scarlet hat another term for a cardinal's ➤ RED *hat*.

Scarlet Lancers nickname for the 16th Lancers, from their distinctive red tunic.

scarlet letter a representation of the letter *A* in scarlet cloth which persons convicted of adultery were condemned to wear, as described in the novel (1850) by Nathaniel Hawthorne, in which Hester Prynne, convicted of adultery in 17th-century New England, is sentenced to wear the *scarlet letter* on the breast of her gown for the rest of her life.

> Your date turns out to wear a scarlet letter.
> — Scott Turow *Burden of Proof* (1990)

Scarlet Pimpernel the name assumed by Sir Percy Blakeney, the hero of a series of novels by Baroness Orczy (1865–1947), a dashing but elusive Englishman, hiding his true nature beneath a lazy and foppish exterior, who rescued potential victims of the French Reign of Terror; the scarlet pimpernel is the emblem which he often leaves behind to infuriate his baffled enemies.

> A war-time Scarlet Pimpernel organisation which rescued thousands of Eastern European Jews from the Nazis.
> — *Guardian* 24 May 1961

scarlet woman an abusive epithet applied to the Roman Catholic Church, in allusion to Revelation 17:3–4, 'And I saw a woman sit upon a scarlet coloured beast...And the woman was arrayed in purple and scarlet colour.'

scarp in heraldry, a diminutive of the bend sinister, one-half its width; the word comes from Old French *escharpe*, literally 'sash'.

scat singing improvised jazz singing in which the voice is used in imitation of an instrument. Recorded from the 1920s, the term is probably imitative.

scavage a toll formerly levied by the mayor, sheriff, or corporation of London and other towns on foreign merchants, on goods offered for sale within the town's precincts; it was prohibited by an act of Henry VII.

scavenger an animal that feeds on carrion, dead plant material, or refuse. The term originally denoted an officer who collected ➤ SCAVAGE, a toll on foreign merchants' goods offered for sale in a town, later a person who kept the streets clean.

Scavenger's daughter another name for ➤ SKEVINGTON*'s daughter*.

sceptic an ancient or modern philosopher who denies the possibility of knowledge, or even rational belief, in some sphere. The leading ancient sceptic was Pyrrho, whose followers at the Academy vigorously opposed Stoicism. Modern sceptics have held diverse views: the most extreme have doubted whether any knowledge at all of the external world is possible (see ➤ SOLIPSISM), while others have questioned the existence of objects beyond our experience of them.

The term comes (in the late 16th century) via French or Latin from Greek *skeptikos*, from *skepsis* 'inquiry, doubt'.

sceptre an ornamented staff carried by rulers on ceremonial occasions as a symbol of sovereignty; in England, the traditional way of signifying the royal assent to a bill was by the sovereign's touching it with the sceptre. The word comes (in Middle English) via Old French and Latin from Greek *skēptron*, from *skēptein* 'lean on'.

Schadenfreude pleasure derived by someone from another person's misfortune; the word is German, and comes from *Schaden* 'harm' + *Freude* 'joy'.

Scheherazade in the *Arabian Nights*, the daughter of the vizier of King Shahriyar, who married the king and escaped the death that was the usual fate of his wives by telling him the tales which compose that work, interrupting each one at an interesting point, and postponing the continuation till the next night.

> Her lieutenants were probably only too happy to see her leave town . . . so that she could tell her Scheherazade escape stories to fresh faces.
> — Wilfred Sheed *Frank and Maisie* (1985)

schemes see ➤ *the* BEST*-laid schemes of mice and men gang aft agley*.

Schengen a town in Luxembourg where an agreement on border controls was signed in June 1985 by France, (West) Germany, Belgium, the Netherlands, and Luxembourg, and later by a number of other countries.

Elsa Schiaparelli (1896–1973), Italian-born French fashion designer, who introduced the vivid shade now known as 'shocking pink' in 1947.

Friedrich von Schiller (1759–1805), German dramatist, poet, historian, and critic. Initially influenced by the *Sturm und Drang* movement, he was later an important figure of the Enlightenment.

Oskar Schindler (1908–74), German industrialist. He saved more than 1,200 Jews from concentration camps by employing them first in his enamelware factory in Cracow and then in an armaments factory that he set up in Czechoslovakia in 1944. This was celebrated in the film *Schindler's List* (1993), based on a novel by Thomas Keneally.

> Chiune Sugihara—the 'Japanese Schindler'—a World War II diplomat who risked his career by directly violating official Japanese policy to save the lives of more than 10,000 Jews fleeing Hitler's Germany.
> — *New York Review of Books* 28 November 1996

schism the formal separation of a Church into two Churches or the secession of a group owing to doctrinal and other differences. The word comes ultimately from Greek *skhizein* 'to split'.

See also ➤ GREAT *Schism*.

August Wilhelm von Schlegel (1767–1845), German romantic poet and critic, who was among the founders of art history and comparative philology.

schlemiel Yiddish term for an awkward, clumsy person, a blunderer, perhaps from Hebrew *Shelumiel*, name of a person in the Bible said by the Talmud to have met with an unhappy end; perhaps influenced by the name of the eponymous hero of A. von Chamisso's *Peter Schlemihls wundersame Geschichte* (1814).

Schleswig-Holstein a state of NW Germany, occupying the southern part of the Jutland peninsula, comprising the former duchies of Schleswig and Holstein, annexed by Prussia in 1866. The complexity of the **Schleswig-Holstein question** in 19th-century politics was notably commented on by ➤ *Lord* PALMERSTON, who said that only three men in Europe had ever understood it, and of these the Prince Consort was dead, a Danish statesman (unnamed) was in an asylum, and he himself had forgotten it.

Schlieffen plan a plan or model for the invasion and defeat of France formulated by the German general Alfred, Graf von *Schlieffen* (1833–1913) before 1905 and applied, with modifications, in 1914.

Heinrich Schliemann (1822–90), German archaeologist. In 1871 he began excavating the mound of Hissarlik on the NE Aegean coast of Turkey, where he discovered the remains of nine superimposed cities, identifying the second oldest as Homer's ➤ TROY, although it was later found to be pre-Homeric. He subsequently undertook excavations at ➤ MYCENAE (1876).

The gold treasure discovered in Turkey by Schliemann, believed by him to be ➤ PRIAM's treasure, and which was initially on display in Berlin, disappeared after the Second World War; it is currently in the Pushkin Museum in Moscow.

schola cantorum the papal choir at Rome, established by Gregory the Great (*c.*540–604).

scholar's mate in chess, mate in which the second player is checkmated in the opponent's fourth move.
See also ➤ CHECKMATE.

scholars ➤ *St* BEDE and ➤ *St* JEROME are the patron saints of scholars.
See also ➤ *Land of* SAINTS *and Scholars*.

scholasticism the system of theology and philosophy taught in medieval European universities, based on Aristotelian logic and the writings of the early Christian Fathers and having a strong emphasis on tradition and dogma.
See also ➤ SCHOOLMAN.

scholiast a commentator on ancient or classical literature; recorded from the late 16th century, the word comes ultimately from medieval Greek *skoliazein* 'write scholia' (i.e. marginal notes or explanatory comments).

school see also ➤ EXPERIENCE *keeps a dear school*, ➤ RAGGED *school*.

school of hard knocks the experience of a life of hardship, considered as a means of instruction; the term is originally US, and is recorded from the early 20th century.

every schoolboy knows it is a generally known fact (that); the expression is recorded from the mid 17th century, but is often particularly associated with a use by Macaulay:

> Every schoolboy knows who imprisoned Montezuma, and who strangled Atahualpa.
> — Lord Macaulay *Essays Contributed to the Edinburgh Review* (1843) vol. 3 'Lord Clive'

schoolboys ➤ *St* NICHOLAS *of Myra* and the Piedmontese St John Bosco (1815–88), who established schools and workshops for the destitute urban young, are the patron saints of schoolboys.

schoolgirls ➤ *St* CATHERINE *of Alexandria* and ➤ *St* URSULA are the patron saints of schoolgirls.

the schoolmaster is abroad Lord Brougham's assertion, in the House of Commons in 1828, of the spread of education; sometimes quoted as 'Look out, gentlemen, the schoolmaster is abroad!', which Brougham is said to have used in a speech at the Mechanics' Instute, London, in 1825:

> The schoolmaster is abroad! and I trust more to the schoolmaster, armed with his primer, than I do to the soldier in full military array, for upholding and extending the liberties of his country.
> — Lord Brougham speech in the House of Commons, 29 January 1828

schoolman any of a number of writers, from between the 9th and the 14th centuries, who deal with logic, metaphysics, and theology as taught in the medieval universities of Italy, France, Germany, and England; a scholastic theologian.

Arthur Schopenhauer (1788–1860), German philosopher, according to whose philosophy, as expressed in *The World as Will and Idea*, the will is identified with ultimate reality and happiness is only achieved by abnegating the will (as desire).

John Schorne (d. *c.*1315), English parish priest, popularly regarded as a saint, who was said to have divined a perpetual spring for his parish in a time of drought and to have trapped the Devil in his boot; an exploit recorded in the iconography of some Norfolk churches. His cult, centred on North Marston in Buckinghamshire, continued down to the time of the Reformation.

Schrödinger's cat a paradox suggested in 1935 by the Austrian theoretical physicist Erwin Schrödinger (1887–1961), to illustrate the conceptual difficulties of quantum mechanics. Schrödinger described an experiment in which a cat is put into a sealed box containing a lethal device triggered by radioactive decay; an outside observer cannot know whether the device has been set off and the cat killed. According to quantum mechanics the cat is in an indeterminate state, some combination of alive and dead, until the box is opened, at which point it will be found to be one or the other.

Franz Schubert (1797–1828), Austrian composer. His music is associated with the romantic movement for its lyricism and emotional intensity, but belongs in formal terms to the classical age.

Charles Schulz (1922–2000), American cartoonist. He is remembered as the creator of the *Peanuts* comic strip (originally entitled 'Li'l Folks') which featured a range of characters including the boy Charlie Brown and the dog Snoopy. The comic strip was first published in 1950 and has since appeared in many publications around the world.

E. F. Schumacher (1911–77), German economist. His most famous work is *Small is Beautiful: Economics as if People Mattered* (1973), which argues that economic growth is a false god of Western governments and industrialists, and that mass production needs to be replaced by smaller, more energy-efficient enterprises.

Robert Schumann (1810–56), German composer. He was a leading romantic composer, particularly noted for his songs (including settings of poems by Heine and Burns) and piano music.

schwa in phonetics, the unstressed central vowel (as in *a* mom*e*nt *a*go), represented by the symbol ə in the International Phonetic Alphabet (from Hebrew *šĕwā*').

Albert Schweitzer (1875–1965), German theologian, musician, and medical missionary, born in Alsace. In 1913 he qualified as a doctor and went as a missionary to Gabon, where he established a hospital; he was awarded the Nobel Peace Prize in 1952. He is cited as a type of selfless devotion to healing and charitable work.

> The hack pack like to picture themselves as a hybrid of Oscar Wilde and Albert Schweitzer; we like to think we will listen to criticism with humility and tolerance.
> — Julie Burchill *Sex and Sensibility* (1992)

sciapod a monster having the form of a man with a single large foot, in medieval iconography frequently represented with the foot raised as a sunshade, and believed to be from a race found in Libya. The name comes ultimately from Greek *skia* shadow + *pod-*, *pous* foot.

science the intellectual and practical activity encompassing the systematic study of the structure and behaviour of the physical and natural world through observation and experiment.

See also ➤ BLIND *with science*, ➤ CHRISTIAN *science*, ➤ CREATION *science*, ➤ *the* DISMAL *science*, ➤ *the* GAY *science*, ➤ *the* NOBLE *science*, ➤ SEVEN *sciences*.

scientific misconduct action which wilfully compromises the integrity of scientific research, such as plagiarism or the falsification or fabrication of data.

scientist a person with expert knowledge of a science or using scientific methods. The term was coined in the mid 19th century by the British Association for the Advancement of Science; the *Quarterly Review* for 1834 carried a summary of the debate over the previous three years, in which, having rejected *philosophers* as 'too wide and too lofty' and *savans* as 'rather assuming', it was suggested that *scientists* could be formed by analogy with *artists*.

➤ St ALBERTUS *Magnus* is the patron saint of scientists.

Scientology trademark name for a religious system based on the seeking of self-knowledge and spiritual fulfilment through graded courses of study and training. It was founded by American science-fiction writer L. Ron Hubbard (1911–86) in 1955.

sciomancy divination by means of shadows; divination by communication with the ghosts of the dead.

Scipio Aemilianus (*c.*185–129 BC), Roman general and politician, adoptive grandson of Scipio Africanus. He achieved distinction in the siege of Carthage (146) during the third Punic War and in his campaign in Spain (133). His opposition to the reforms introduced by his brother-in-law Tiberius Gracchus may have led to his death, possibly by poison.

Scipio Africanus (236–*c*.184 BC), Roman general and politician. He was successful in concluding the second Punic War, firstly by the defeat of the Carthaginians in Spain in 206 and then by the defeat of ➤ HANNIBAL in Africa in 202; his victories pointed the way to Roman hegemony in the Mediterranean.

Sciron in Greek mythology, a brigand on the cliff road from Athens to Megara; he forced travellers to wash his feet, and then kicked them into the sea. He was killed by ➤ THESEUS who threw him over the cliff.

scold's bridle an instrument of punishment for a scolding woman, consisting of an iron framework for the head and a sharp metal gag for restraining the tongue; a ➤ BRANKS.

sconce a candle holder that is attached to a wall with an ornamental bracket; a flaming torch or candle secured in such a candle holder. The word comes (in late Middle English, originally denoting a portable lantern with a screen to protect the flame) from a shortening of Old French *ensconse*, or from medieval Latin *sconsa* from Latin *absconsa (laterna)* 'dark (lantern)'.

Scone an ancient Scottish settlement to the north of Perth, believed to be on the site of the capital of the Picts, where the kings of medieval Scotland were crowned on the ➤ STONE *of Scone*.

Scopes trial the ➤ MONKEY *Trial* in Dayton, Tennessee, in 1925, when the teacher J. T. *Scopes* was prosecuted for teaching the theory of evolution.

scorched earth policy a military strategy of burning or destroying crops or other resources that might be of use to an invading enemy force; the term is first used in English in 1937 in a report of the Sino-Japanese conflict, and is apparently a translation of Chinese *jiāotǔ (zhèngcè)* 'scorched earth (policy)'.

score see also ➤ *score an* OWN *goal*.

score a group or set of twenty or about twenty. The word comes in late Old English from Old Norse *skor* 'notch, tally, twenty', of Germanic origin.

Scorpio the eighth sign of the zodiac (the Scorpion), which the sun enters about 23 October; a person born under this sign.

scorpion a terrestrial arachnid which has lobster-like pincers and a poisonous sting at the end of its jointed tail, which it can hold curved over the back, living in tropical and subtropical areas; the intense pain cause by its sting is proverbial.

In traditional belief, the flesh of the scorpion was thought to be a cure for its own sting; it is also said by ancient writers that when surrounded by fire, a scorpion will commit suicide by stinging itself:

> And we are left, as scorpions ringed with fire.
> What should we do but strike ourselves to death?
>
> — Percy Shelley *The Cenci* (1819)

See also ➤ ROCK *scorpion*.

a whip (or lash) of scorpions originally with biblical allusion, as to 1 Kings 12:11, 'my father hath chastised you with whips, but I will chastise you with scorpions'; *scorpion* here is taken to denote a kind of whip made of knotted cords, or armed with pieces of lead or steel spikes. The allusive force was subsequently reinforced by Milton in *Paradise Lost* (1667) 'Least with a whip of scorpions I pursue Thy lingring'.

Scot a member of a Gaelic people that migrated from Ireland to Scotland around the late 5th century. The name is recorded in Old English (as *Scottas*, plural) and comes from late Latin *Scottus*, of unknown ultimate origin.

Down to the reign of Alfred, *Scottas* was the ordinary word for Irishmen (as *Scotland* for Hibernia). In the next reign there were relations between the Anglo-Saxon kingdom and the kingdom of the Scots in North Britain, and from that time onward the name was no longer associated with Ireland except in historical statements.

scot archaic term for a payment corresponding to a modern tax, rate, or other assessed contribution; the word comes (in late Old English) from Old Norse *skot* 'a shot', reinforced by Old French *escot*, of Germanic origin.

See also ➤ CHURCH-*scot*.

scot ale a festival at which ale was drunk at the invitation of the lord of the manor or of a forester or other bailiff, for which a forced contribution or *scot* was levied.

scot and lot a tax levied by a municipal corporation on its members for the defraying of expenses; the figurative expression **pay (off) scot and lot**

meant to pay out thoroughly, to settle with:

> I'll pay you off scot and lot by and bye.
> — Charles Dickens *Martin Chuzzlewit* (1844)

Scotch old-fashioned term for ➤ SCOTTISH. The use of *Scotch* to mean 'of or relating to Scotland or its people' was widely used in the past by Scottish writers such as Robert Burns and Sir Walter Scott. In the 20th century it has become less common; it is disliked by Scottish people (as being an 'English' invention) and is now regarded as old-fashioned in most contexts other than in such fixed expressions as *Scotch egg* and *Scotch whisky*.

See also ➤ BROAD *Scotch*.

scotch decisively put an end to; render (something regarded as dangerous) temporarily harmless. The sense 'render temporarily harmless' is based on an emendation of Shakespeare's *Macbeth* as 'We have scotch'd the snake, not kill'd it', originally understood as a use of the homonym *scotch* with the meaning 'cut or score the skin of'.

Scotch Plot a supposed Jacobite plot of 1703 for a Stuart restoration.

Scotist a follower or adherent of ➤ *John* DUNS *Scotus*, a scholastic philosopher and theologian of the 13th century.

Scotland ➤ *St* ANDREW is patron saint of Scotland.

See also ➤ CHURCH *of Scotland*, ➤ CONSTABLE *of Scotland*, ➤ CURSE *of Scotland*, ➤ *St* MARGARET *of Scotland*.

Scotland Yard the headquarters of the London Metropolitan Police, situated from 1829 to 1890 in Great Scotland Yard off Whitehall, from 1890 until 1967 in New Scotland Yard on the Thames Embankment, and from 1967 in New Scotland Yard, Westminster.

Scots see also ➤ POUND *Scots*, ➤ *the Scots* GREYS.

Scots-Irish of or pertaining to those inhabitants of Northern Ireland descended fron Scottish settlers or their immediate descendants in other countries; of mixed Scots and Irish descent.

Scotsman see ➤ FLYING *Scotsman*.

Michael Scott (*c*.1175–*c*.1235), a Scottish scholar, born at Balwearie who studied at Oxford, Bologna, and Paris, and was attached to the court of Frederick II at Palermo, probably in the capacity of official astrologer. Because the science he studied was

astronomy, legends of his magical powers grew up and served as a theme for many writers from Dante to Sir Walter Scott.

Robert Falcon Scott (1868–1912), English explorer, also known as **Scott of the Antarctic**. In 1910–12 Scott and four companions made a journey to the South Pole ('Great God! this an awful place', Scott wrote in his diary of 17 January 1912) by sled, arriving there in January 1912 to discover that Roald Amundsen had beaten them by a month. Scott and his companions (including ➤ *Captain Lawrence* OATES) died on the journey back to base; their bodies and diaries were discovered eight months later. The attempt has become a symbol of courageous endurance and endeavour, typified by the last 'Message to the Public':

> Had we lived, I should have had a tale to tell of the hardihood, endurance, and courage of my companions which would have stirred the heart of every Englishman. These rough notes and our dead bodies must tell the tale.
> — Robert Falcon Scott 'Message to the Public' in late editions of *The Times* 11 February 1913

Sir Walter Scott (1771–1832), Scottish novelist and poet, also known as the **Magician of the North** and the **Wizard of the North**, terms which reflect his great contemporary popularity. He established, through *Waverley* (1814) and many subsequent books, the form of the historical novel in Britain and was influential in his treatment of rural themes and use of regional speech and revival of archaic terms. He collected and imitated old Borders tales and ballads, while among his original works is *The Lady of the Lake* (1810).

Scottish of or relating to Scotland or its people; in modern usage, a term now preferred to ➤ SCOTCH, which is disliked by many Scottish people (as being an 'English' invention) and is now regarded as old-fashioned in most contexts.

the Scottish play Shakespeare's *Macbeth*; in theatrical tradition, it is unlucky to mention this play by name.

Scottsboro case an American cause célèbre of 1931, in which nine black men were charged with the rape of two white girls on a freight train in Alabama. Eight of the nine men were originally sentenced to death; after a series of appeals and a retrial, charges against five of the men were dropped, although four received sentences equivalent to life imprisonment.

Scotus see ➤ *John* DUNS *Scotus*.

Scourer in the 17th and 18th centuries, a member of a group of violent young men who habitually roamed the streets at night, breaking windows and beating the watch; the word is ultimately an alteration of *discoverer*, later confused with the verb *to scour*.

scourge a whip used as an instrument of punishment; a scourge is the emblem of ➤ *St* GUTHLAC.

the Scourge of God translation of Latin *flagellum Dei*, the title given by historians to Attila, the leader of the Huns in the 5th century; the term is recorded in English from the 14th century.

Scouse the dialect or accent of people from Liverpool; a native or inhabitant of Liverpool. Recorded in this sense from the mid 20th century, the word is a shortening of *lobscouse*.

scout a soldier or other person sent out ahead of a main force so as to gather information about the enemy's position, strength, or movements. The word comes (in late Middle English, as a verb) via Old French from Latin *auscultare* 'listen'.

Scout Association a worldwide youth organization founded for boys in 1908 by Lord Baden-Powell with the aim of developing their character by training them in self-sufficiency and survival techniques in the outdoors. Called the Boy Scouts until 1967, the Scout Association admitted girls as members from 1990.

The name was explained by Baden-Powell in *Scouting for Boys* (1908) as deriving from the Boer War, 'We had an example of how useful Boy Scouts can be on active service, when a corps of boys was formed in the defence of Mafeking.'

Scrabble trademark name for a game in which players build up words on a board from small lettered squares or tiles.

a scrap of paper a document containing a treaty or pledge which one does not intend to honour. The phrase (a translation of German *ein Fetzen Papier*) is attributed to the German Chancellor, Theobald von Bethmann Hollweg (1856–1921), in connection with German violation of Belgian neutrality in August 1914; in a letter of 8 August 1914, Sir Edward Goschen recorded the German Chancellor's words as, 'just for a scrap of paper, Great Britain is going to make war on a kindred nation who desires nothing better than to be friends with her'.

scratch a Russian and you find a Tartar proverbial saying, early 19th century.

scratch card a card with a section or sections coated in an opaque waxy substance which may be scraped away to reveal a symbol indicating whether a prize has been won in a competition. *Scratch cards* were introduced in America in the early 1980s, and have since become familiar both when sold as a gambling device (in Britain, particularly as linked to the National Lottery), and as a consumer incentive, when issued free.

screen see ➤ *the* SILVER *screen*.

screw see also ➤ ARCHIMEDEAN *screw*.

Screw Plot an imaginary plot to destroy Queen Anne and the Court on Thanksgiving Day, 1710, by the removal of some of the iron bolts from the timbers of the roof of St Paul's in order to cause its fall.

Scribe in biblical contexts, an ancient Jewish record keeper; a member of a class of professional interpreters of the Jewish Law after the return from the Captivity; in the Gospels, often coupled with the ➤ PHARISEES as upholders of ceremonial tradition.

Scriblerus Club an association of which Swift, Pope, and Gay were members, and the earl of Oxford (Robert Harley) a regularly invited member. The group appears to have met from January to July 1714, though various members later collaborated on joint projects. Its object was to ridicule 'all the false tastes in learning', but nothing was produced under the name of ➤ MARTINUS *Scriblerus* for some years.

scrimshaw adorn (shells, ivory, or other materials) with carved or coloured designs. Recorded from the early 19th century, the word may be influenced by the surname *Scrimshaw*.

Scriptores Decem short title for *Historia Anglicanae Scriptores Decem*, edited by the historical antiquary Roger Twysden (1597–1672), and published in 1652.

scriptorium a room set apart for writing, especially one in a monastery where manuscripts were copied; in the 19th and 20th centuries, the name was used by Sir James Murray for the study (at his house in Oxford, actually a separate structure erected in the garden) in which the ➤ OXFORD *English Dictionary* was compiled.

Scripture the sacred writings of Christianity contained in the Bible; also, the sacred writings of another religion. Recorded from Middle English, the word comes from Latin *scriptura* 'writings'.

See also ➤ *the* DEVIL *can quote scripture for his own ends.*

Scroll of the Law another name for the ➤ SEFER *Torah.*

scrolls see ➤ DEAD *Sea Scrolls.*

Ebenezer Scrooge a miserly curmudgeon in Charles Dickens's novel *A Christmas Carol* (1843); his initially grudging and scornful attitude, typified by his characteristic exclamation 'Bah, humbug!', is changed in the course of the book after the warning he receives from the ghost of his late partner ➤ *Jacob* MARLEY.

> Wonderful flowery antique cards with syrupy greetings that can melt the heart of the most Scrooge-ish.
> — *Atlanta Journal & Constitution* 20 December 1992

scruple a feeling of doubt or hesitation with regard to the morality or propriety of a course of action; formerly also, a unit of weight equal to 20 grains used by apothecaries. The term comes (in late Middle English, from French *scrupule* or Latin *scrupula*) from Latin *scrupus*, literally 'rough pebble', figuratively 'anxiety'.

scry divine, especially by crystal-gazing or looking in a mirror or water; recorded from the early 16th century.

Scullabogue in the Irish Insurrection of 1798, scene of a massacre by insurgents when 200 Protestant prisoners were burnt to death in a barn.

sculls see ➤ *the* DIAMOND *Sculls.*

scuola in Venice, any of the buildings in which the medieval religious confraternities or guilds used to meet, a guildhall.

scutage in feudal society, money paid by a vassal to his lord in lieu of military service. The word comes (in late Middle English) from medieval Latin *scutagium*, from Latin *scutum* 'shield'.

Scutari a former name for Üsküdar near Istanbul, site of a British army hospital in which ➤ *Florence* NIGHTINGALE worked during the Crimean War.

> The world is full of Miss Nightingales, and we sick and wounded in our private Scutaries, have countless nurse-tenders.
> — W. M. Thackeray *The Newcomes* (1855)

Scylla¹ in Greek mythology, a female sea monster who devoured sailors when they tried to navigate

the narrow channel between her cave and the whirlpool ➤ CHARYBDIS. In later legend *Scylla* was a dangerous rock, located on the Italian side of the Strait of Messina.

Scylla² in Greek mythology, the daughter of king Nisus of Megara (see ➤ NISUS¹), who betrayed her father and his city to ➤ MINOS of Crete, and who was drowned in punishment.

between Scylla and Charybdis between two dangers or pitfalls, as between the cave of the sea-monster and the whirlpool.

> The difficulty now is to navigate between the Scylla of authoritarian taste and the Charybdis of slop.
> — *Prospect* March 1996

scytale¹ a snake mentioned by ancient writers, described as resembling a round staff of uniform thickness and having colourful markings; a figure of this as a heraldic bearing.

scytale² in ancient Greece, a Spartan method of transmitting secret messages by writing on a strip of parchment wound spirally round a cylindrical or tapering staff or rod, the message being legible only when the parchment was wound round an identical staff; a secret dispatch conveyed by this method; a rod used for this.

scythe a tool used for cutting crops such as grass or corn, with a long curved blade at the end of a long pole attached to one or two short handles; often shown as a symbolic attribute of Time or Death.

A scythe is the emblem of St Juthwara and St Sidwell, sisters, and reputed British virgin martyrs with cults in the south west of England, St Walstan, an English saint with a local cult in Norfolk among farmers and farm labourers of the Middle Ages, and ➤ *St* ISIDORE *the Farmer.*

Scythian of or pertaining to an ancient region of SE Europe and Asia. The Scythian empire, which existed between the 8th and 2nd centuries BC, was centred on the northern shores of the Black Sea and extended from southern Russia to the borders of Persia.

Scythism a movement among Russian intellectuals soon after the Revolution of 1917 favouring peasant values associated with eastern Russia over those of western European civilization.

sea see ➤ *all* RIVERS *run into the sea,* ➤ *the* BRIDE *of the Sea,* ➤ DEAD *Sea,* ➤ *the* FOUR *seas,* ➤ HANDS *across the sea,* ➤ *the* HIGH *seas,* ➤ KEEP *your own guts for your own sea-maws,* ➤ PATRIMONIAL *seas,* ➤ RED *Sea,* ➤ SARGASSO *Sea,* ➤ SEVEN *seas,* ➤ *there are as good* FISH *in the sea as ever came out of it.*

sea-beggar a seaman of a small fleet organized by ➤ WILLIAM *the Silent* (1533–84) in 1572 to combat the Spaniards; the phrase is a translation of French *gueux de mer*.

sea-born born in or of the sea; in particular, an epithet of ➤ VENUS.

sea-born city Venice, in Byron's *Beppo* (1817), 'That sea-born city was in all her glory'.

sea change a profound or notable transformation; originally with allusion to the song in Shakespeare's *Tempest* (1611) which envisages the physical changes that will come to Ferdinand's supposedly drowned father:

> Full fathom five thy father lies;
> Of his bones are coral made:
> Those are pearls that were his eyes:
> Nothing of him that doth fade,
> But doth suffer a sea-change
> Into something rich and strange.
> — William Shakespeare *The Tempest* (1611)

sea dog in heraldry, a mythical beast like a dog with fins, webbed feet, and a scaly tail.

he that would go to sea for pleasure would go to hell for a pastime proverbial saying, late 19th century.

the sea-green Incorruptible Carlyle's name for ➤ ROBESPIERRE.

sea lion in heraldry, a mythical beast formed of a lion's head and foreparts and a fish's tail.

Sea Lord either of two senior officers in the Royal Navy (**First Sea Lord**, **Second Sea Lord**) serving originally as members of the Admiralty Board (now of the Ministry of Defence).

Sea Peoples any or all of the groups of invaders, of uncertain identity, who encroached on Egypt and the eastern Mediterranean by land and sea in the late 13th century BC. The Egyptians were successful in driving them away, but some, including the Philistines, settled in Palestine. Also called *Peoples of the Sea*.

the sea refuses no river proverbial saying, early 17th century.

sea serpent a legendary serpent-like monster of great size, traditionally reported to have been seen at sea.

> To believe all that has been said of the sea-serpent, or the Kraken, would be credulity.
> — Oliver Goldsmith *History of the Earth* (1774)

Seabee a member of one of the construction battalions of the Civil Engineer Corps of the US Navy. The name represents a pronunciation of the letters *CB* (from *construction battalion*).

seal[1] a fish-eating aquatic mammal with a streamlined body and feet developed as flippers, returning to land to breed or rest; in folklore, seals (as in the legend of the ➤ SELKIE) were believed able to take human form. The name is recorded from Old English, and is of Germanic origin.

seal[2] a piece of wax, lead, or other material with an individual design stamped into it, attached to a document to show that it has come from the person who claims to have issued it. Recorded from Middle English, the word comes via Old French from Latin *sigillum* 'small picture', diminutive of *signum* 'a sign'.

See also ➤ GREAT *Seal,* ➤ KEEPER *of the Great Seal,* ➤ KEEPER *of the Privy Seal,* ➤ LORD *Privy Seal,* ➤ SOLOMON'*s seal*.

seal of the confessional in the Catholic Church, the obligation on a priest not to disclose any part of a person's confession.

sealing-wax see ➤ STRING *and sealing-wax*.

seals of office (in the UK) engraved seals held during tenure of an official position, especially that of Lord Chancellor or Secretary of State, and symbolizing the office held.

> There are two supreme pleasures in life. One is ideal, the other real. The ideal is when a man receives the seals of office from his Sovereign. The real pleasure comes when he hands them back.
> — Lord Rosebery *Sir Robert Peel* (1899)

Seanad the upper House of Parliament in the Republic of Ireland, composed of sixty members, of whom eleven are nominated by the Taoiseach and forty-nine are elected by institutions. Also called *Seanad Eireann*. The name is Irish, and means 'Senate'.

SEAQ (in the UK) Stock Exchange Automated Quotations (the computer system on which dealers trade shares and seek or provide price quotations on the London Stock Exchange).

searcher of men's hearts God; chiefly with allusion to Romans 8:27, 'And he that searcheth the hearts knoweth what is in the mind of the Spirit.'

Ronald Searle (1920–), English artist and cartoonist, famous for creating the schoolgirls of ➤ ST *Trinian's.*

Sears Tower a skyscraper in Chicago, the tallest building in the world when it was completed in 1973. It is 443 m (1,454 ft) high and has 110 floors.

season each of the four divisions of the year (spring, summer, autumn, and winter) marked by particular weather patterns and daylight hours, resulting from the earth's changing position with regard to the sun. The word is recorded from Middle English, and comes via Old French from Latin *satio(n-)* 'sowing', later 'time of sowing'.

See also ➤ CLOSE *season,* ➤ *a* MAN *for all seasons,* ➤ *the* SILLY *season.*

seasonal affective disorder depression associated with late autumn and winter and thought to be caused by a lack of light; it is characterized by loss of motivation, a tendency to sleep for abnormally long periods, and often a craving for foods rich in carbohydrates.

seat see ➤ ARTHUR'S *Seat,* ➤ *in the* CATBIRD *seat.*

Sebastian see ➤ *Sebastian* MELMOTH.

St Sebastian (late 3rd century), Roman martyr. According to legend he was a soldier who was shot by archers on the orders of Diocletian, but who recovered, confronted the emperor, and was then clubbed to death.

Sebastian is the patron saint of archers and is often (like ➤ *St* ROCH) invoked against plague.

☐ **FEAST DAY** His emblem is an arrow (symbolizing plague).

☐ **FEAST DAY** His feast day is 20 January.

Sebastopol a fortress and naval base in Ukraine, near the southern tip of the Crimea. The focal point of military operations during the Crimean War, it fell to Anglo-French forces in September 1855 after a year-long siege.

Sebat (in the Jewish calendar) the fifth month of the civil and eleventh of the religious year, usually coinciding with parts of January and February.

Secession the withdrawal of eleven Southern states from the US Union in 1860, leading to the Civil War; the term **War of Secession** is sometimes used for the American Civil War. In a letter of

March 1861, the American general Winfield Scott, hoping to avoid civil war, had advised, 'Say to the seceded states, "Wayward sisters, depart in peace." ' James Russell Lowell, however, in *E Pluribus Unum* (1861) commented, 'Rebellion smells no sweeter because it is called Secession.'

second the ordinal number constituting number two in a sequence, coming after the first in time or order. The word comes (in Middle English, via Old French) from Latin *secundus* 'following, second', from the base of *sequi* 'follow'.

second Adam (in Christian thought) Jesus Christ, with reference to 1 Corinthians 15:45, 'The first Adam was made a living soul; the last Adam was made a quickening spirit'; the actual phrase *second Adam* is first recorded in a marginal gloss on this passage from the Geneva Bible (1587), 'To wit, with the Spirit of God, which descendeth from Christ the second Adam, into us.'

Second Advent another term for the ➤ SECOND *Coming.*

Second Adventist a member of a sect holding millenarian views, in particular, a ➤ MILLERITE.

a second bite at the cherry more than one attempt or opportunity to do something; a *cherry* as the type of something to be consumed in a single bite (in original proverbial use, to **take two bites at the cherry** indicated a person's behaving with affected nicety).

second chamber the upper house of a parliament with two chambers.

Second Coming the prophesied return of Christ to Earth at the Last Judgement; the term itself is recorded from the late 16th century.

Second Empire the imperial government in France of Napoleon III, 1852–70.

Second Republic the republican regime in France from the deposition of King Louis Philippe (1848) to the beginning of the Second Empire (1852).

second sight the supposed ability to perceive future or distant events; clairvoyance. Reports of the faculty (recorded from the early 17th century) have traditionally been much associated with those of Scottish ancestry.

second thoughts are best proverbial saying, late 16th century.

Second World the former communist block consisting of the Soviet Union and some countries in eastern Europe.

Second World War a war (1939–45) in which the ➤ AXIS Powers (Germany, Italy, and Japan) were defeated by an alliance eventually including the United Kingdom and its dominions, the Soviet Union, and the United States.

secret see also ➤ DISCIPLINE *of the Secret*, ➤ OFFICIAL *Secrets Act*, ➤ THREE *may keep a secret, if two of them are dead.*

Secret Intelligence Service in the UK, the official name for MI6.

secret service a government department concerned with espionage; the term is recorded from 1737, in a reference in the *Gentleman's Magazine* to 'The prodigious increase of Secret Service Money in the late Reign [i.e., that of George II]'.

In the US, the *Secret Service* is a branch of the Treasury Department, dealing with counterfeiting and providing protection for the President.

Secreta Secretorum comprising pronouncements on political and ethical matters, written in Syriac in the 8th century AD and claiming to be advice from Aristotle to Alexander. It reached Europe through Arabic and 12th-century Hispano-Arabic. The main version in Latin was translated in Spain *c.*1230 and was influential on poets from then until the 16th century. It influenced in particular the tradition of writing works of advice to kings; it was translated in part by Lydgate.

secretaries ➤ *St* MARK and St Genesius of Arles, a 4th-century martyr whose early legend says that he was a notary (a later legend makes him an actor), are the patron saints of secretaries.

secretary hand a style of handwriting used chiefly in legal documents from the 15th to the 17th centuries.

sect a group of people with somewhat different religious beliefs (typically regarded as heretical) from those of a larger group to which they belong.

See also ➤ CLAPHAM *Sect.*

section see also ➤ GOLDEN *section.*

Section 28 in the UK, a clause in the Local Government Act (1988) prohibiting local authorities from the promotion of homosexuality or the teaching in maintained schools of the acceptability of homosexuality as a family relationship; government

plans in 1999 to repeal the clause, on the grounds that it may inhibit necessary counselling, have aroused considerable controversy.

secular denoting attitudes, activities, or other things that have no religious or spiritual basis; (of a member of the clergy) not bound by a religious rule, not belonging to or living in seclusion with a monastic or other order. Recorded from Middle English, the word comes via Old French from Latin *saeculum* 'generation, age', used in Christian Latin to mean 'the world' (as opposed to the Church).

the secular arm the legal authority of the civil power as invoked by the Church to punish offenders; the phrase is a translation of medieval Latin *brachium seculare*, and is recorded from late Middle English.

secular games in ancient Rome, games continuing three days and three nights celebrated once in an 'age' or period of 120 years; the phrase is a translation of Latin *ludi saeculares.*

secularism the doctrine that morality should be based solely on regard to the well-being of mankind in the present life, to the exclusion of all considerations drawn from belief in God or in a future state, especially, as the name of a definitely professed system of belief, promulgated by George Jacob Holyoake (1817–1906).

Securitate the internal security force of Romania, set up in 1948 and officially disbanded during the revolution of December 1989.

Security Council a permanent body of the United Nations seeking to maintain peace and security. It consists of fifteen members, of which five (China, France, the UK, the US, and Russia) are permanent and have the power of veto. The other members are elected for two-year terms.

security risk a person or situation which poses a possible threat to the security of something. The term is first recorded from the period of ➤ MCCARTHYISM in the US, in a report of the dismissal of ten State Department employees as *security risks* in the late 1940s.

Security Service in the UK, official name for MI5.

sedan an enclosed chair for conveying one person, carried between horizontal poles by two porters. The word may represent an alteration of an Italian dialect word, based on Latin *sella* 'saddle', from *sedere* 'sit'.

Battle of Sedan a battle fought in 1870 near the town of Sedan in NE France, in which the Prussian army defeated a smaller French army under Napoleon III, opening the way for a Prussian advance on Paris and marking the end of the French Second Empire.

See also ➤ MAN *of Sedan.*

sede vacante during the vacancy of an episcopal see; the phrase is Latin, and means literally 'the seat being vacant'; it is first used in English in a letter of ➤ *Thomas* CRANMER.

Sedevacantist a member of a conservative faction of the Catholic Church, which denies the legitimacy of those popes elected since the ➤ *Second* VATICAN *Council* (1962–5), and claims that the See of Rome has been vacant since this period.

Seder a Jewish ritual service and ceremonial dinner for the first night or first two nights of Passover. The name comes from Hebrew *sēḏer* 'order, procedure'.

sederunt (in Scotland) a sitting of an ecclesiastical assembly or other body; the word comes from Latin, and means literally '(the following persons) sat'.

Act of Sederunt in Scottish law, an act for regulating the forms of procedure before the Court of Session.

Battle of Sedgemoor a battle fought in 1685 on the plain of Sedgemoor in Somerset, in which the forces of the rebel ➤ *Duke of* MONMOUTH, who had landed in Dorset as champion of the Protestant cause and pretender to the throne, were decisively defeated by James II's troops.

See also ➤ BLOODY *Assizes.*

Adam Sedgwick (1785–1873), English geologist. He specialized in the fossil record of rocks from North Wales, assigning the oldest of these to a period that he named the *Cambrian.*

sedilia a group of stone seats for clergy in the south chancel wall of a church, usually three in number and often canopied and decorated. The word is recorded from the late 18th century, and comes from Latin, meaning 'seat'.

sedulous ape frequently in **play the sedulous ape**, try diligently to conform to the principles and style

of, with reference to Robert Louis Stevenson:

> I have thus played the sedulous ape to Hazlitt, to Lamb, to Wordsworth, to Sir Thomas Browne, to Defoe, to Hawthorne, to Montaigne, to Baudelaire and to Obermann.
> — Robert Louis Stevenson *Memories and Portraits* (1887)

see see also ➤ *see* NAPLES *and die*, ➤ *see the* ELEPHANT.

see the place in which a cathedral church stands, identified as the seat of authority of a bishop or archbishop. The word comes (in Middle English, via Anglo-Norman French) from Latin *sedes* 'seat'.

See also ➤ HOLY *See.*

what you see is what you get proverbial saying, late 20th century; the origin of ➤ WYSIWYG.

see no evil, hear no evil, speak no evil proverbial saying, early 20th century; conventionally represented by 'the three wise monkeys' covering their eyes, ears, and mouth respectively with their hands.

See of Rome another term for the ➤ HOLY *See.*

seed a flowering plant's unit of reproduction, capable of developing into another such plant; in figurative use (with allusion to the ➤ *parable of the* SOWER, Matthew ch. 13) applied to religious teaching in the light of the fruitfulness of its result.

In sport (especially tennis), *seed* denotes any of a number of stronger competitors in a sports tournament who have been assigned a specified position in an ordered list with the aim of ensuring that they do not play each other in the early rounds.

See also ➤ *the* BLOOD *of the martyrs is the seed of the Church.*

good seed makes a bad crop proverbial saying, mid 16th century.

seeding see ➤ ONE *year's seeding makes seven years' weeding.*

Seeing Eye trademark name in the US for an organization training guide dogs for the blind, originally with biblical allusion to Proverbs 20:12, 'The hearing ear, and the seeing eye, the Lord hath made even both of them.'

seeing is believing proverbial saying, early 17th century.

seek and ye shall find proverbial saying, mid 16th century; originally with biblical allusion to Matthew 7:7, 'Ask, and it shall be given you; seek, and ye shall find.'

Seeker a member of a class of sectaries in the 16th and 17th centuries who assumed this name:

> Many . . . go under the name of Expecters and Seekers & doe deny that there is any true Church, or any true Minister, or any Ordinances: some of them assume the Church to be in the wildernesse, and they are seeking it there: others say it is in the smoke of the Temple, & that they are groping for it there.
> — Ephraim Pagitt *Heresiography* (1645)

seem see ➤ BE *what you would seem to be.*

seen see ➤ CHILDREN *should be seen and not heard.*

Sefer a book of Hebrew religious literature; a scroll containing the Torah or Pentateuch (usually **Sefer Torah**). The name comes from Hebrew *sēper tōrāh* 'book of (the) Law'.

Sehnsucht poetic and literary expression for yearning; wistful longing; recorded from the mid 19th century, the word is German.

seicento the style of Italian art and literature of the 17th century. The word is Italian for '600', shortened from *mille seicento* '1600', used with reference to the years 1600–99.

seigneur see ➤ DROIT *de seigneur,* ➤ GRAND *Seignior.*

Seikan Tunnel the world's longest underwater tunnel, linking the Japanese islands of Hokkaido and Honshu under the Tsungaru Strait. Completed in 1988, the tunnel is 51.7 km (32.3 miles) in length.

seisin possession, especially of land; a grant of freehold possession; what is so held. In popular usage, *seisin* has sometimes been understood to mean an actual object, such as a turf, a key, or a staff, handed over as a token of possession. The word comes (in Middle English) from Old French, ultimately from *saisir* 'seize'.

sejant in heraldry, in a sitting posture, especially (of a quadruped) sitting with the forelegs upright.

Sejm the lower house of parliament in Poland.

Sekhmet in Egyptian mythology, a ferocious lioness-goddess, counterpart of the gentle cat-goddess ➤ BASTET and wife of ➤ PTAH at Memphis. Her messengers were fearsome creatures who could inflict disease and other scourges upon humankind.

sekos a sacred enclosure in an ancient Egyptian temple; the word comes from Greek, meaning 'pen, enclosure'.

selah in the Bible, occurring frequently at the end of a verse in Psalms and Habakkuk, probably as a musical direction.

selamlik former term for the public procession of the Turkish Sultan to a mosque on Friday at noon. Now, a room in a Turkish Muslim house set aside for business or the reception of male friends; the part of a Turkish Muslim house reserved for men.

select committee a small parliamentary committee appointed for a special purpose; recorded from the mid 17th century.

selectman a member of a board of officers elected annually to manage various local concerns in a 'town' or 'township' in New England.

Selene in Greek mythology, the goddess of the moon, identified with ➤ ARTEMIS. She fell in love with ➤ ENDYMION and asked Zeus to grant him a wish. Endymion chose immortality and eternal youth, which Zeus granted, but only on condition that Endymion remain forever asleep. In another story, Selene visited Endymion nightly as he lay asleep, and bore him fifty daughters.

selenite from the mid 16th century, the name given to a stone variously described by ancient writers, perhaps in part identifiable with the mineral now so called, but said to have fabulous properties, such as that of growing and decreasing as the moon waxes and wanes, or of giving the faculty of prediction or of reconciling lovers. In the 17th and 18th centuries it was often identified with stones described by travellers or existing in collections.

From the mid 17th century, *Selenite* has also been used for a hypothetical inhabitant of the moon.

Seleucid a member of a dynasty ruling over Syria and a great part of western Asia from 311 to 65 BC. Its capital was at Antioch. The name comes from *Seleucus* Nicator (the founder, one of Alexander the Great's generals).

self-denying ordinance a resolution (1645) of the ➤ LONG *Parliament* depriving members of parliament of civil and military office.

self-determination the process by which a country determines its own statehood and forms its own allegiances and government.

self-praise is no recommendation proverbial saying, early 19th century.

self-preservation is the first law of nature proverbial saying, mid 17th century.

the selfish gene hypothesized as the unit of heredity whose preservation is the ultimate explanation of and rationale for human existence; from the title of a book (1976) by Richard Dawkins, which did much to popularize the theory of sociobiology.

selicha a Jewish penitential prayer recited on a fast-day, before Rosh Hashanah, and before and on Yom Kippur.

Seljuk a member of any of the Turkish dynasties which ruled Asia Minor in the 11th to 13th centuries, successfully invading the Byzantine Empire and defending the Holy Land against the Crusaders. The name comes from Turkish *seljūq*, the name of the reputed ancestor of the dynasty.

selkie an imaginary sea creature resembling a seal in the water but able to assume human form on land; it was traditionally believed unlucky to kill a seal in case it might in fact be at least partially human.

> I am a man upon the land,
> I am a selkie in the sea;
> When I am far and far from land,
> My home it is the Sule Skerry.
>   — 'The Great Selkie of Sule Skerry' (traditional ballad)

Alexander Selkirk (1676–1721), Scottish sailor. While on a privateering expedition in 1704 Selkirk quarrelled with his captain and was put ashore, at his own request, on one of the uninhabited Juan Fernandez Islands, where he remained until 1709. His experiences formed the basis of Daniel Defoe's novel ➤ *Robinson* CRUSOE (1719).

sell see also ➤ PILE *it high, sell it cheap,* ➤ *sell the* PASS.

sell by the candle dispose of by auction in which bids are received so long as a small piece of candle burns, the last bid before the candle goes out securing the article; the custom was apparently French in origin.

sell down the river in 19th-century America, sell (a troublesome slave) to the owner of a sugar-cane plantation on the lower Mississippi, where conditions were harsher than in the northern slave States.

sell in May and go away stockmarket saying.

> 'Sell in May and go away,' says the old adage. This year it has been right on the button: a bad June for world stockmarkets is being followed by a worse July.
>   — *Economist* 11 July 1992

sell the skin before one has caught the bear traditional saying, mid 16th century; meaning that someone is unwisely taking a successful outcome for granted.

Sellafield the site of a nuclear power station and reprocessing plant on the coast of Cumbria in NW England. It was the scene in 1957 of a fire which caused a serious escape of radioactive material. It was formerly (1947–81) called *Windscale.*

Sellenger's Round an old country round dance. The name represents a pronunciation of the surname *St Leger.*

Peter Sellers (1925–80), English comic actor. He made his name in *The Goon Show,* a radio series of the 1950s, but is best known for the 'Pink Panther' series of films of the 1960s and 1970s, in which he played the bumbling French detective ➤ *Inspector* CLOUSEAU.

selling race a horse race after which the winning horse must be auctioned.

Frederick Courteney Selous (1851–1917), English explorer, naturalist, and soldier. From 1890 he was involved in the British South Africa Company, negotiating mineral and land rights. The Selous Game Reserve in Tanzania is named after him.

Selsdon man an advocate or adherent of the policies outlined at a conference of Conservative Party leaders held at the *Selsdon* Park Hotel 30 January–1 February 1970; the term was coined by Harold Wilson in 1970, 'Selsdon Man is designing a system of society for the ruthless and the pushing.'

Sem in ancient Egypt, an officiating priest who wore a distinctive robe made from a leopard's skin.

Semana Santa in Spain and Spanish-speaking countries, Holy Week.

semantron in Orthodox churches, especially in Greece, a wooden or metal bar struck by a mallet used to summon worshippers to service.

Semele in Greek mythology, the mother, by ➤ ZEUS, of ➤ DIONYSUS. The fire of Zeus's thunderbolts killed her but made her child immortal.

Semiramis in Greek mythology, the daughter of an Assyrian goddess who married an Assyrian king. After his death she ruled for many years and became one of the founders of Babylon. She is thought to have been based on the historical queen Sammuramat (*c.*800 BC).

Semite a member of any of the peoples who speak or spoke a Semitic language, including in particular the Jews and Arabs. The name comes via Latin from Greek *Sēm* 'Shem', son of Noah in the Bible, from whom these people were traditionally supposed to be descended.

Semitic relating to or denoting a family of languages that includes Hebrew, Arabic, and Aramaic and certain ancient languages such as Phoenician and Akkadian, constituting the main subgroup of the Afro-Asiatic family.

semper eadem ever the same (Latin phrase, the motto of Elizabeth I).

semper fidelis always faithful (Latin phrase, the motto of the US Marine Corps).

Senate the state council of the ancient Roman republic and empire, which shared legislative power with the popular assemblies, administration with the magistrates, and judicial power with the knights. In modern usage, *Senate* is the title of various legislative or governing bodies, in particular the smaller upper assembly in the US, US states, France, and other countries; the governing body of a university or college.

The name comes (in Middle English, via Old French) from Latin *senatus*, from *senex* 'old man'.

senatus consultum a decree of the ancient Roman senate; the term was also used for decrees of in France under Napoleon I and Napoleon III.

send see ➤ *send to* COVENTRY.

sendal former term for a fine, rich silk material, chiefly used to make ceremonial robes and banners; the word comes (in Middle English, via Old French) from Greek *sindōn*.

Lucius Annaeus Seneca (*c*.4 BC–AD 65), Roman statesman, philosopher, and dramatist; known as **Seneca the Younger**. Son of Seneca the Elder, he became tutor to Nero in 49 and was appointed consul in 57, retiring in 62. His implication in a plot on Nero's life led to his forced suicide. His *Epistulae Morales* is a notable Stoic work.

Marcus (or Lucius) Annaeus Seneca (*c*.55 BC–*c*.39 AD), Roman rhetorician, born in Spain; known as **Seneca the Elder**. Father of Seneca the Younger, he is best known for his works on rhetoric, only parts of which survive.

senex in literature, especially comedy, an old man as a stock figure; the word is Latin for 'old man'.

Senior Service in the UK, the Royal Navy (as distinguished from the army); the term is recorded from the late 19th century.

Sennacherib (d. 681 BC), king of Assyria 705–681, son of Sargon II. He devoted much of his reign to suppressing revolts in various parts of his empire, including Babylon (689). In 701 he put down a Jewish rebellion, laying siege to Jerusalem but sparing it from destruction (according to 2 Kings 19:35). He also rebuilt the city of ➤ NINEVEH and made it his capital.

Sennacherib is the Assyrian who 'came down like a wolf on the fold' on Israel, as described in Byron's poem 'The Destruction of Sennacherib' (1815); he was forced to break off his campaign when his army was devastated by divine intervention (2 Kings 35). On his return to Nineveh he was assassinated by his sons.

sennachie in Ireland and the Scottish Highlands: a professional recorder and reciter of family or traditional history and genealogy, attached to the household of a clan chieftain or person of noble rank. Now, a teller of traditional Gaelic heroic tales.

sennet (in the stage directions of Elizabethan plays) a call on a trumpet or cornet to signal the ceremonial entrance or exit of an actor. The word is recorded from the late 16th century, and may be a variant of *signet*.

sennight a week, seven nights; the word is recorded from Old English.

sennin in oriental tradition, originally in Taoism, an elderly recluse who has achieved immortality through meditation and self-discipline; a human being with supernatural powers, a reclusive mystic or teacher. The word is Japanese, meaning 'wizard, recluse', from Chinese *hsien-jên* 'an immortal man'.

sensei (in martial arts) a teacher; the word is Japanese, and comes from *sen* 'previous' + *sei* 'birth'.

sensibility see ➤ DISSOCIATION *of sensibility*.

sensuous relating to or affecting the senses rather than the intellect. The word is thought to have been invented by Milton (1641) in a deliberate attempt to avoid the sexual overtones of *sensual*:

> The Soule . . . finding the ease she had from her visible, and sensuous colleague the body in performance of Religious duties . . . shifted off from her selfe, the labour of high soaring any more.
> — John Milton *Of Reformation* (1641)

The usage was subsequently reinforced by Coleridge:

> Thus, to express in one word what belongs to the senses, or the recipient and more passive faculty of the soul, I have reintroduced the word *sensuous*, used, among many others of our elder writers, by Milton.
> — Samuel Taylor Coleridge *Principles of Genial Criticism* (1814)

sentence see ➤ MASTER *of the Sentences*.

Senussi a member of a North African Muslim religious fraternity founded in 1837 by Sidi Muhammad ibn Ali es-Senussi (d. 1859).

Separatist a member of any of the sects separated from the Church of England in the 17th century, especially the Independents and those who agreed with them in rejecting all ecclesiastical authority outside the individual congregations.

Sephardi a Jew of Spanish or Portuguese descent. They retain their own distinctive dialect of Spanish (Ladino), customs, and rituals, preserving Babylonian Jewish traditions rather than the Palestinian ones of the ➤ ASHKENAZIM. The name is modern Hebrew, from *sĕpārad̠*, a country mentioned in Obadiah 20 ('the captivity of Jerusalem, which is in Sepharad') and taken to be Spain.

sephira in the ➤ KABBALAH, each of the ten attributes or emanations surrounding the Infinite and by means of which it relates to the finite. They are represented as spheres on the ➤ TREE *of life*.

sepoy former term for an Indian soldier serving under European orders. The word comes from Urdu and Persian *sipāhī* 'soldier', from *sipāh* 'army'.

Sepoy Mutiny another term for the ➤ INDIAN *Mutiny*; the name is recorded from the mid 19th century.

seppuku another term for ➤ HARA-*kiri*; the word is Japanese, and comes from *setsu* 'cut' + *fuku* 'abdomen'.

sept a clan, originally one in Ireland; the term is recorded from the early 16th century, and is probably a variant of *sect*.

September the ninth month of the year, in the northern hemisphere usually considered the first month of autumn. The name comes (in late Old English) from Latin, from *septem* 'seven' (being originally the seventh month of the Roman year). The native Old English name was *hærfestmōnaþ* ➤ HARVEST *month*.

September blow soft, till the fruit's in the loft proverbial saying, late 16th century.

September massacres a mass killing of political prisoners in Paris on 2–6 September 1792, an event which initiated the ➤ TERROR.

> I thought of those September Massacres,
> Divided from me by a little month.
> — William Wordsworth *The Prelude* (1805-6)

Septembrist in Portugal, a supporter of the (successful) insurrection of September 1836 in favour of the restoration of the constitution of 1822.

Septembrizer any of those who took part in or advocated the massacre of the political prisoners in Paris on September 2nd–5th, 1792; Byron in *Don Juan* (1824) subsequently used the name punningly for someone who shoots partridges in September:

> Some deadly shots too, Septembrizers, seen
> Earliest to rise, and last to quit the search
> Of the poor partridge.
> — Lord Byron *Don Juan* (1824)

Septentrion the constellation of the Great Bear (the ➤ PLOUGH) or the Little Bear. Formerly also, the north; the northern regions of the earth or the heavens. Recorded from late Middle English, the name comes from Latin, originally *septem triones* (the seven stars of the Great Bear), from *septem* 'seven' + *triones* 'plough-oxen'.

septentrional signs in astronomy, the first six signs of the zodiac.

Septuagesima Sunday the Sunday before Sexagesima. The name comes (in late Middle English) from Latin 'seventieth (day)', probably named by analogy with ➤ QUINQUAGESIMA, although it has also been suggested that it refers to 'the seventieth day' before the octave of Easter. Both conjectures were recorded by Alcuin in the 8th century.

Septuagint a Greek version of the Hebrew Bible (or Old Testament), including the Apocrypha, made for Greek-speaking Jews in Egypt in the 3rd and 2nd centuries BC and adopted by the early Christian Churches.

The name is recorded from the mid 16th century (originally denoting the translators themselves), from Latin *septuaginta* 'seventy', because of the tradition that it was produced, under divine inspiration, by seventy-two translators working independently.

sepulchre a small room or monument, cut in rock or built of stone, in which a dead person is laid or buried; the word comes (in Middle English) from Latin *sepulcrum* 'burial place'.

See also ➤ EASTER *Sepulchre*, ➤ HOLY *Sepulchre*, ➤ WHITED *sepulchre*.

Sequoia National Park a national park in the Sierra Nevada of California, east of Fresno. It was established in 1890 to protect groves of giant sequoia trees, of which the largest, the General Sherman Tree, is thought to be between 3,000 and 4,000 years old.

Sequoya the name of the Cherokee Indian (c.1770–1843) who invented the Cherokee syllabary; the sequoia (redwood) tree is named after him.

seraglio the women's apartments (harem) in a Muslim palace. **The Seraglio** was also formerly the term for a Turkish palace, especially the Sultan's court and government offices at Constantinople. The word comes (in the late 16th century) via Italian and Turkish from Persian *sarāy* 'palace'.

Serapeum a temple of ➤ SERAPIS; in particular, the great precinct near Memphis, where the sacred ➤ APIS bulls were buried, and a temple in Alexandria.

seraph an angelic being, regarded in traditional Christian angelology as belonging to the highest order of the ninefold celestial hierarchy, associated with light, ardour, and purity. Also, a conventional representation of such a being, typically as a human face or figure with six wings, as described in Isaiah 6:2, 'each one had six wings; with twain he covered his face, and with twain he covered his feet, and with twain he did fly.'

The word is recorded from Old English, and comes ultimately from the Hebrew (plural) *śĕrāpīm*; before the mid 17th century, the singular *seraph* is rare.

Seraphic Doctor a title given to ➤ St BONAVENTURA (in Spain also popularly to ➤ St TERESA *of Ávila*).

Seraphic Father a title given to ➤ St FRANCIS.

Seraphic Hymn another name for the ➤ SANCTUS; with reference to the vision in Isaiah 6:3, in which the seraphim are heard crying 'Holy, holy, holy'.

Serapis in Egyptian mythology, a god whose cult was developed by Ptolemy I at Memphis as a combination of ➤ APIS and ➤ OSIRIS, to unite Greeks and Egyptians in a common worship.

seraskier the title of commander-in-chief and minister of war of the Ottoman Empire. The word is Turkish, and comes from Persian *sar'askar* 'head (of the) army'.

Serbonian bog Milton's name for Lake Serbonis in Lower Egypt, a marshy tract (now dry) covered with shifting sand:

> A gulf profound as that Serbonian Bog
> Betwixt Damiata and mount Casius old,
> Where Armies whole have sunk.
> — John Milton *Paradise Lost* (1667)

From this, the term is sometimes used allusively.

> The Serbonian bog of Egyptian finance.
> — John Morley *Life of Gladstone* (1903)

serdab a secret passage or chamber in an ancient Egyptian tomb.

Serendib a former name (also *Serendip*) for Sri Lanka.

serendipity the occurrence and development of events by chance in a happy or beneficial way. The word was coined (in 1754) by Horace Walpole, and was suggested by *The Three Princes of Serendip*, the title of a fairy tale in which the heroes 'were always making discoveries, by accidents and sagacity, of things they were not in quest of'.

drop serene in *Paradise Lost* (1667), Milton's term for partial or total blindness, translating modern Latin *gutta serena*, 'so thick a drop serene hath quencht their orbs'.

Serene Highness a title given to members of some European royal families, or used in addressing them.

Serengeti a vast plain in Tanzania, to the west of the Great Rift Valley. In 1951 the Serengeti National Park was created to protect the area's large numbers of wildebeest, zebra, and Thomson's gazelle.

Serenissima a historic title for Venice or the former Venetian republic; Italian for 'the most serene (city)'.

Seres the inhabitants of the Far Eastern countries from which silk reached Europe overland during ancient times; the Chinese and Tibetans.

St Sergius (1314–92), Russian monastic reformer and mystic. He founded forty monasteries, re-establishing the monasticism which had been lost through the Tartar invasion, and inspired the resistance which saved Russia from the Tartars in 1380.

□ **FEAST DAY** His feast day is 25 September.

serial killer a murderer who repeatedly commits the same offence, typically following a characteristic, predictable behaviour pattern. The term was originally a technical one used by the Federal Bureau of Investigation in America; it came to public notice in the 1980s in the wake of a number of notorious cases, notably the crimes eventually traced to Theodore Bundy and John Wayne Gacy.

The FBI's institution for profiling serial killers, set up during this period, was brought famously to public attention by the novel (later an Oscar-winning film) *The Silence of the Lambs* by Thomas Harris, featuring the cannibalistic serial killer ➤ HANNIBAL *Lecter.*

serjeant in official lists, a sergeant in the Foot Guards.

See also ➤ COMMON *Serjeant.*

serjeant-at-arms originally, a knight or armed officer in the service of the monarch or a lord; now, an official of a legislative assembly whose duty includes maintaining order and security.

serjeant-at-law in the UK, former term for a barrister of the highest rank.

serjeanty a form of feudal tenure conditional on rendering some specified personal service to the monarch. A **grand serjeanty** entailed an important service, often as a soldier, and a **petty serjeanty** entailed a minor one.

sermon a talk on a religious or moral subject, especially one given during a church service and based on a passage from the Bible; the term comes (in Middle English, also in the sense of 'speech, discourse') via Old French from Latin *sermo(n-)* 'discourse, talk'.

See also ➤ ACTION *Sermon,* ➤ LION *Sermon,* ➤ SPITTLE *sermon.*

Sermon on the Mount the discourse of Christ recorded in Matthew 5–7, including the Beatitudes and the Lord's Prayer; it is introduced by the words, 'he went up into a mountain…and taught them, saying'. The title *Sermon on the Mount* is first recorded in a marginal gloss of the ➤ RHEMISH *Bible* (1582).

serpent a large snake; a dragon or other mythical snake-like reptile. The word is recorded from Middle English, and comes via Old French from Latin *serpent-* 'creeping'.

In proverbial and allusive reference, a *serpent* is taken as the type of cunning, treachery, and malignancy. The figure of a serpent with its tail in its mouth is a symbol of eternity.

In the Bible, **the Serpent** is a special designation of Satan, as in Genesis 3:1, 'Now the serpent was more subtil than any beast of the field', and Revelation 20:2, 'the dragon, that old serpent, which is the Devil'.

See also ➤ MIDGARD'*s serpent,* ➤ OLD *Serpent,* ➤ PLUMED *serpent,* ➤ RAINBOW *serpent,* ➤ SEA *serpent.*

brazen serpent the figure of a brass serpent on a pole; with reference to the story in Numbers ch. 21, in which, when the people of Israel were punished by 'fiery serpents', Moses was told by God to mount a serpent of brass on a pole. If anyone who had been bitten by a snake looked at this, they would be healed.

serpent-stone an artificial stone or bead traditionally supposed to be a remedy for snake venom, and often resembling a snake in shape or markings.

serpent-wand another name for the ➤ CADUCEUS.

the Serpentine a winding lake in Hyde Park, London, constructed in 1730, as part of the laying out of the gardens by the royal gardener Charles Bridgman (d. 1738); it was in the Serpentine, in 1816, that the body of the poet ➤ SHELLEY's first wife Harriet was found.

serpentine verse a metrical line beginning and ending with the same word (in allusion to the representation of a serpent with its tail in its mouth).

servant St Zita, a 13th-century Luccan serving-maid, is the patron saint of servants.

See also ➤ FIRE *is a good servant but a bad master.*

is thy servant a dog biblical saying, with reference to 2 Kings 8:13, in which the Syrian Hazael protests against Elisha's prophecy that he will do harm to Israel, 'Is thy servant a dog, that he should do this great thing?'

servant of the servants of God a title of the Pope, first assumed by ➤ GREGORY *the Great,* a translation of Latin *servus servorum Dei.*

if you would be well served, serve yourself proverbial saying, mid 17th century.

Servian wall a wall encircling the ancient city of Rome, said to have been built by Servius Tullius, the semi-legendary sixth king of ancient Rome (fl. 6th century BC).

Servite a friar or nun of the Catholic religious order of the Servants of Blessed Mary, founded in 1233.

sesame see ➤ OPEN *sesame*.

sesquipedalian (of a word) polysyllabic; long; the term comes originally from the Roman poet Horace's phrase *sesquipedalia verba* 'words a foot and a half long'.

session see ➤ COURT *of Session*.

sestina a poem with six stanzas of six lines and a final triplet, all stanzas having the same six words at the line-ends in six different sequences; the word is Italian, from *sesto* 'a sixth'.

set-aside the policy of taking land out of production to reduce crop surpluses. The term has been used in the US since the 1940s, but in the UK it came to public notice in the 1980s, in the context of attempts by the European Community to reduce such produce surpluses as the 'beef' and 'butter mountains' and the 'wine lake'. The policy involved payment of subsidies to farmers for taking land out of production; while there has been an agreed environmental benefit in terms of wildlife, some hostility has been shown towards what has been seen as paying for work not to be done.

set the Thames on fire do something marvellous, work wonders (usually in negative contexts); the expression is recorded from the late 18th century.

Setebos in Shakespeare's *Tempest*, the god worshipped by ➤ CALIBAN's mother Sycorax; *Setebos* was a Patagonian deity, and his name appears in accounts of Magellan's voyages.

Seth[1] in Egyptian mythology, an evil god who murdered his brother ➤ OSIRIS and wounded Osiris's son ➤ HORUS. Seth is represented as having the head of an animal with a long pointed snout.

Seth[2] in the Bible, the son of ➤ ADAM who according to Genesis was the father of ➤ NOAH and thus of the existing race of humankind; in Genesis 5:25, Eve says of him 'God…hath appointed me another seed instead of Abel, whom Cain slew.'

Sethian a member of a Gnostic sect of the 2nd century AD, holding Seth (see ➤ SETH[2]) in great veneration, and believing that Jesus was Seth revived.

Act of Settlement a statute of 1701 that vested the British Crown in Sophia of Hanover (granddaughter of James I of England and VI of Scotland) and her Protestant heirs, so excluding Roman Catholics, including the Stuarts, from the succession. Sophia's son became George I.

settler's clock in Australia, a name for the kookaburra.

seven the number *seven* is often used symbolically, denoting completion or perfection, especially in echoes of biblical phraseology.

See also ➤ *at* SIXES *and sevens*, ➤ *give me a* CHILD *for the first seven years, and you may do what you like with him afterwards*, ➤ *Group of* SEVEN, ➤ RAIN *before seven, fine before eleven*, ➤ *you should* KNOW *a man seven years before you stir his fire*.

Seven against Thebes in Greek mythology, the expedition against Thebes led by Polynices, son of ➤ OEDIPUS, against his brother Eteocles. When both young men are killed, their uncle Creon decrees that ➤ POLYNICES is not to be buried because he has attacked his own city; his niece ➤ ANTIGONE defies the order.

Seven Bishops Archbishop Sancroft, and Bishops Ken, Lake, Lloyd, Trelawney, Turner, and White in 1688 protested against the ➤ DECLARATION *of Indulgence* of James II; it was the imprisonment of the bishops which led to the popular lines, later incorporated by the English clergyman and poet R. S. Hawker (1803–75) in his 'Song of the Western Men':

> And shall Trelawny die?
> Here's twenty thousand Cornish men
> Will know the reason why!
> — traditional song, late 17th century

seven bodies terrestrial in astrology, another term for ➤ SEVEN METALS.

Seven Champions the national saints of England, Scotland, Wales, Ireland, France, Spain, and Italy, respectively George, Andrew, David, Patrick, Denis, James, and Anthony.

Seven Churches of Asia the seven churches addressed by John in Revelation, the Churches of Ephesus, Smyrna, Pergamos, Thyatira, Sardis, Philadelphia, and Laodicea.

seven corporal works of mercy as enumerated in medieval theology, taken from Matthew 25:35–37 and Tobit 12:12; they are feeding the hungry, giving the thirsty to drink, sheltering the stranger, clothing the naked, visiting the sick, comforting the prisoner, and (from Tobit) burying the dead.

Seven Deacons as mentioned in Acts 6:5, chosen by the apostles as 'seven men of honest report' to minister to the early Church; their names are given as Stephen, Philip, Prochorus, Nicanor, Timon, Parmenas, and Nicolas.

seven deadly sins (in Christian tradition) the sins of pride, covetousness, lust, anger, gluttony, envy, and sloth. They are listed (with minor variation) by the monk John Cassian (d.435), St Gregory the Great, and St Thomas Aquinas.

Seven Dials a district of Holborn in London, once known as a thieves' quarter, the centre of which is the meeting place of seven streets. It was originally named for a column with seven dials which stood there until 1773.

Seven Dwarfs in the story of ➤ SNOW *White*, the dwarfs living in a hut in the forest who shelter the fugitive princess from her stepmother; in the Walt Disney cartoon film (1937), they are named Happy, Sleepy, Doc, Bashful, Sneezy, Grumpy, and Dopey.

seven gifts of the Holy Spirit wisdom, understanding, counsel, fortitude, knowledge, piety, and fear of the Lord. The list is taken from Isaiah 11:2; six as in the AV 'And the spirit of the Lord shall rest upon him, the spirit of wisdom and understanding, the spirit of counsel and might, the spirit of knowledge and of the fear of the Lord,' with piety (*pietas*) added from the Vulgate text.

seven heavens recognized in later Jewish and in Muslim belief; the highest being the abode of God and the most exalted angels. The division may have been of Babylonian origin, and founded on astronomical theories.

City of the Seven Hills an informal name for Rome.

Seven Hills of Rome the seven hills on which the ancient city of Rome was built: Aventine, Caelian, Capitoline, Esquiline, Quirinal, Viminal, and Palatine.

Seven Joys of Mary special occasions for joy on the part of the Virgin Mary, as traditionally enumerated; the Annunciation, Visitation, Nativity, Epiphany, Finding in the Temple, Resurrection, and Ascension. The medieval church reckoned five (although lists differ); an early 14th century poem gives the Annunciation, Nativity, Epiphany, Resurrection, and the Assumption of the Virgin, with later Roman Catholic writers adding the Visitation and the Finding as the second and fifth respectively, and making the seventh the Ascension.

Seven Last Words the last seven utterances of Christ on the Cross: 'Father, forgive them, for they know not what they do' (Luke 23:34); 'Woman, behold thy son!' (John 19:26); 'Behold thy mother!'

(John 19:27); 'Eli, Eli, lama sabachthani? [My God, my God, why has thou forsaken me?]' (Matthew 27:46); 'I thirst' (John 19:28); 'It is finished' (John 19:30); 'Father, into thy hands I commend my spirit' (Luke 23:46, a quotation from Psalm 31:5). Also known as the **Seven Words**.

seven-league boots the boots which in the fairy story of ➤ HOP *o' my Thumb* enabled their wearer to cover seven leagues at each step.

> This antique superhighway went straight as a ruler from Boston to Newburyport, taking the hills as if with seven-league boots.
> — John Updike *Toward the End of Time* (1997)

seven liberal arts in the Middle Ages, the ➤ QUADRIVIUM and the ➤ TRIVIUM, a course of seven subjects of study introduced in the 6th century and regarded as essential grounding for more advanced studies: they are arithmetic, geometry, astronomy, music, grammar, rhetoric, and logic. Also known as the *seven sciences*.

seven metals in alchemy, seven metals were regarded as corresponding to seven planets.

Seven Metals	
METAL	PLANET
copper	Venus
gold	the Sun
iron	Mars
lead	Saturn
quicksilver	Mercury
silver	the Moon
tin	Jupiter

Seven O's of Advent the seven anthems traditionally sung on the days preceding Christmas and containing an invocation to Christ beginning with O, as **O Sapientia** and **O Adonai**.

Seven Pillars of Wisdom title of T. E. Lawrence's account (1926) of the Arab Revolt during the First World War and his own part in it; it derives from Proverbs 9:1, 'Wisdom hath builded her house, she hath hewn out her seven pillars.'

seven sacraments the sacraments as enumerated in Christian belief, a list thought to have been formulated first by Peter Lombard in the 12th century: Baptism, Confirmation, the Eucharist, Penance, Extreme Unction, Holy Orders, and Matrimony. Since the Reformation, Protestant usage has generally recognized two sacraments, Baptism and the Eucharist or Lord's Supper.

Seven Sages seven wise Greeks of the 6th century BC, to each of whom a moral saying is attributed. The seven, named in a traditional list found in Plato, are Bias, Chilon, Cleobulus, Periander, Pittacus, Solon, and Thales.

seven samurai *The Seven Samurai* was the title of a Japanese film (1954) depicting a group of warriors who come together to protect a village against marauding bandits (it was remade in 1960 as an American film, *The Magnificent Seven*). In extended usage, the term may be used for a number of individuals who decide to act together when conventional systems, and protection, have failed.

> A group of astronomers (nicknamed the Seven Samurai for their challenge to conventional wisdom).
> — Joseph Silk *Big Bang* (1989)

seven sciences another name for the ➤ SEVEN *liberal arts.*

seven seas all the oceans of the world (conventionally listed as the Arctic, Antarctic, North Pacific, South Pacific, North Atlantic, South Atlantic, and Indian Oceans).

Seven Sisters the star cluster of the ➤ PLEIADES, traditionally believed to represent the seven daughters of the Titan Atlas and the Oceanid Pleione.

In early 16th-century Scotland, *Seven Sisters* was the name given to seven cannon, resembling each other in size and make, cast by Robert Borthwick and used at the ➤ *Battle of* FLODDEN in 1513.

In the late 20th century, the seven international oil companies noted for their dominant influence on the production and marketing of petroleum, Exxon, Mobil, Gulf, Standard Oil of California, Texaco, British Petroleum, and Royal Dutch Shell, became known as the *Seven Sisters.*

Seven Sleepers (in early Christian legend) seven noble Christian youths of Ephesus who fell asleep in a cave while fleeing from the Decian persecution and awoke 187 years later. The legend was translated from the Syriac by Gregory of Tours (6th century) and is mentioned in other sources, including the Koran.

Seven Sorrows of Mary seven particular griefs of the Virgin Mary, as enumerated in medieval theology: the prophecy of Simeon (see ➤ SIMEON², 'a sword shall pierce through thy own soul also', Luke 2:35); the flight into Egypt; the three-day loss of the child Jesus in Jerusalem; the meeting with Jesus on the way to Calvary; the Crucifixion; the taking down from the Cross; and the entombment of Jesus.

The Servite order, founded in the 13th century, was devoted to meditation on the sorrows of the Virgin, and the enumeration developed from this.

seven spiritual works of mercy as enumerated in Christian belief: conversion of the sinner, instruction of the ignorant, counselling the doubtful, comforting the sorrowful, patient endurance of wrong, forgiveness of injuries, and prayer for the living and the dead.

seven stars former name for the ➤ PLEIADES and the ➤ GREAT *Bear.*

Seven Weeks' War another name for the Austro-Prussian War of 1866, in which Prussia defeated an alliance between Austria, Bavaria, Hanover, Saxony, and other minor German states; this was an important stage in ➤ BISMARCK's planned unification of Germany.

Seven Wise Masters a cycle of Arabic and Persian stories, ultimately probably of Indian origin, in which seven learned men in turn foil the attempts of a wicked queen to discredit her stepson in the eyes of his father; each of the seven stories she tells is countered by a tale which centres on female deceit. The text is included in *The Thousand and One Nights.*

Seven Wonders of the World the seven most spectacular man-made structures of the ancient world. Traditionally they comprise (1) the pyramids of Egypt, especially those at Giza; (2) the Hanging Gardens of Babylon; (3) the Mausoleum of Halicarnassus; (4) the temple of Artemis at Ephesus in Asia Minor, rebuilt in 356 BC; (5) the Colossus of Rhodes; (6) the huge ivory and gold statue of Zeus at Olympia in the Peloponnese, made by Phidias *c.*430 BC; (7) the Pharos of Alexandria (or in some lists, the walls of Babylon). The earliest extant list of these dates from the 2nd century BC.

seven year itch originally (in literal use, recorded from the late 19th century) a condition lasting for or recurring after seven years; now, a supposed tendency to infidelity after seven years of marriage; in modern usage, the term was reinforced by Billy Wilder's film *The Seven Year Itch* (1955), starring Marilyn Monroe.

Seven Years War a war (1756–63) which ranged Britain, Prussia, and Hanover against Austria, France, Russia, Saxony, Sweden, and Spain. Its main issues were the struggle between Britain and France for supremacy overseas, and that between Prussia and Austria for the domination of Germany. The British made substantial gains over France abroad, capturing (under James Wolfe) French Canada and (under Robert Clive) undermining French influence in India. On the Continent, the war was most notable for the brilliant campaigns of Frederick the Great of Prussia against converging enemy armies. The war was ended by the Treaties of Paris and Hubertusburg in 1763, leaving Britain the supreme European naval and colonial power and Prussia in an appreciably stronger position than before in central Europe.

Sevener a member of the smaller of the two Shia sects (the 'Seveners' and the 'Twelvers'), acknowledging only seven ➤ Imams.

Seventh-Day Adventist a member of a strict Protestant sect which preaches the imminent return of Christ to Earth (originally expecting the Second Coming in 1844) and observes Saturday as the sabbath.

in **seventh** heaven in a state of ecstasy; the term relates to the concept of ➤ seven *heavens* in late Jewish and Muslim theology.

seventh wave the wave traditionally regarded as the biggest in an increasing swell of the sea; in figurative use, a culminating act or experience.

seventy the number equivalent to the product of seven and ten; ten less than eighty; 70; traditionally regarded as the natural span of human life (see ➤ threescore *years and ten*).
   The Seventy is the name given to the 70 disciples whose mission is recorded in Luke 10:1, 'After these things the Lord appointed other seventy also, and sent them two and two before his face into every city'. It is also used for the interpreters of the ➤ Septuagint.
   See also ➤ Group *of Seventy-Seven*.

Septimius Severus (146–211), Roman emperor 193–211. He reformed the imperial administration and the army, and in 208 he led an army to Britain to suppress a rebellion in the north of the country; he later died at York.
   See also ➤ Wall *of Severus*.

Seville see ➤ *the* Barber *of Seville*.

Sèvres a type of fine porcelain characterized by elaborate decoration on backgrounds of intense colour, made at Sèvres in the suburbs of Paris.

sex and shopping designating novels of a popular type concerning wealthy and glamorous characters typically indulging in frequent sexual relationships and extravagant spending; the genre relies on blending the elements of commercial success and high fashion with scenes of explicit sexuality. *Sex and shopping* novels had their main success in the expansionist 1980s. With the coming of recession, much of their unquestioned bestseller status was relinquished to the more domestic world of the ➤ Aga *saga*.

Sexagesima Sunday the Sunday before ➤ Quinquagesima, and (like ➤ Septuagesima) probably named on analogy with it.

sextile in astrology, an aspect of 60° (one sixth of a circle); the term is recorded from the mid 16th century.

sexton a person who looks after a church and churchyard, typically acting as bell-ringer and gravedigger; in early use, often the sacristan in a religious house or cathedral, having charge of the vestments, sacred vessels, and relics. The word comes via Anglo-Norman French from medieval Latin *sacristanus* 'sacristan'.

Sexton Blake name of a fictional detective first introduced in a magazine story of 1898, and subsequently appearing in a number of stories and books by various authors; he is distinguished by his powers of deduction as well as his physical prowess.

> We don't want you playing Son of Sexton Blake . . . You could get hurt.
>   — Rhona Petrie *Thorne in the Flesh* (1971)

the **Sezession** a radical movement involving groups of avant-garde German and Austrian artists who, from 1892, organized exhibitions independently of the traditional academies. The **Vienna Secession** founded by Gustav Klimt in 1897 helped to launch the Jugendstil.

sgraffito a form of decoration made by scratching through a surface to reveal a lower layer of a contrasting colour, typically done in plaster or stucco on walls, or in slip on ceramics before firing. The word comes (in the mid 18th century) from Italian, literally 'scratched away'.

Shabaka (d. 698 bc), Egyptian pharaoh, founder of the 25th dynasty, reigned 712–698 bc; known as **Sabacon**. He promoted the cult of Amun and revived the custom of pyramid burial in his own death arrangements.

Shabbat (among Sephardic Jews and in Israel) the Sabbath; **Shabbat shalom** 'peaceful Sabbath' is a form of salutation used on this day.

Shabbos among Ashkenazic Jews, the Sabbath.

shabti each of a set of wooden, stone, or faience figurines, in the form of mummies, placed in an ancient Egyptian tomb to do any work that the dead person might be called upon to do in the afterlife. They were often 365 in number, one for each day of the year.

Ernest Henry Shackleton (1874–1922), British explorer. During one of his Antarctic expeditions (1914–16), Shackleton's ship *Endurance* was crushed in the ice. Shackleton and his crew eventually reached an island, from where he and five others set out in an open boat on a 1,300-km (800-mile) voyage to South Georgia to get help.

Shaddai one of the names given to God in the Hebrew Bible. The name is translated as 'Almighty' in English versions of the Bible, but is of uncertain meaning.

the Shades in poetic and literary usage, the underworld, Hades; the realm of disembodied spirits (*shade* here meaning the visible but impalpable form of a dead person, a ghost). From this developed the humorous invocation of a deceased person, who would supposedly be shocked or amazed by the thing specified; loosely, a reference to a person or thing in the past of which a present event is reminiscent.

From the early 19th century, *The Shades* was a name for wine and beer vaults with a bar, either underground or sheltered from the sun by an arcade; the term later came to be used as a name for a retail liquor shop, or a bar attached to a hotel.

shadow see also ➤ COMING *events cast their shadows before them.*

shadow Cabinet the opposition counterpart of government ministers; the term is first recorded in a letter from the Conservative statesman Arthur James Balfour (1848–1930), in the year after his party had suffered a major electoral defeat:

> If we are to have, as you suggest, a Committee consisting of members selected from the Front Bench in both Houses, ... what we should really have would be a shadow Cabinet once a week.
> — Arthur James Balfour letter, 1906

the shadow of death a place or period of intense gloom or peril; often with reference to Psalm 23:4, 'Yea, though I walk through the valley of the shadow of death, I will fear no evil'. The term in biblical usage represents a Hebrew expression which is a poetic word for intense darkness; in English, however, it is likely to be used in a context denoting the sorrow and fear associated with approaching death.

Lord Shaftesbury (1801–85), Anthony Ashley Cooper, English philanthropist and social reformer. A dominant figure of the 19th-century social reform movement, he inspired much of the legislation designed to improve conditions for the large working class created as a result of the Industrial Revolution. His reforms included the introduction of the ten-hour working day (1847).

shaggy-dog story a long, rambling story or joke, typically one that is amusing only because it is absurdly inconsequential or pointless. The expression comes from an anecdote of this type, about a shaggy-haired dog (1945).

shagroon an early settler in Canterbury, New Zealand, from anywhere except Britain, especially one from Australia. The word may come from Irish *seachrán* 'wandering'.

shah a title of the former monarch of Iran; *shah* is a Persian title equivalent to 'king', and is recorded in English from the mid 16th century in reference to the ruler of Persia.

shahada the Muslim profession of faith ('there is no god but Allah, and Muhammad is the messenger of Allah').

shahanshah a title given to the Shah of Iran (Persia); it means literally 'King of Kings'.

shahid a Muslim martyr; the word comes from Arabic *šhīd* 'witness, martyr'.

Shaitan (in Muslim countries) the Devil, Satan, or an evil spirit.

Shaka (*c.*1787–1828), Zulu chief 1816–28. He reorganized his forces and waged war against the Nguni clans, subjugating them and forming a Zulu empire in SE Africa. Shaka's military campaigns led to a huge displacement of people and a lengthy spell of clan warfare. He was assassinated by his two half-brothers. Also called **Chaka**.

shaken, not stirred popular summary of the directions for making the perfect martini given by ➤ *James* BOND:

> A medium Vodka dry Martini—with a slice of lemon peel. Shaken and not stirred.
> — Ian Fleming *Dr No* (1958)

shaker see also ➤ MOVER *and shaker.*

Shaker a member of an American religious sect, the United Society of Believers in Christ's Second Coming, established in England *c*.1750 and living simply in celibate mixed communities, so named from the wild, ecstatic movements engaged in during worship. The first of the American communities was founded by Ann Lee (1736–84), who emigrated from England in 1774.

Shakescene a derogatory term applied to ➤ *William* SHAKESPEARE by the rival poet and dramatist Robert Greene (*c*.1560–92):

> For there is an upstart crow, beautified with our feathers, that with his tiger's heart wrapped in a player's hide, supposes he is as well able to bumbast out a blank verse as the best of you; and being an absolute *Johannes fac totum*, is in his own conceit the only Shake-scene in a country.
> — Robert Greene *Groatsworth of Wit Bought with a Million of Repentance* (1592)

William Shakespeare (1564–1616), English dramatist. He probably began to write in the late 1580s; although his plays were widely performed in his lifetime, many were not printed until the First Folio of 1623. His plays are written mostly in blank verse and include comedies, such as *A Midsummer Night's Dream* and *As You Like It*; historical plays, including *Richard III* and *Henry V*; the Greek and Roman plays, which include *Julius Caesar* and *Antony and Cleopatra*; enigmatic comedies such as *All's Well that Ends Well* and *Measure for Measure*; the great tragedies, *Hamlet*, *Othello*, *King Lear*, and *Macbeth*; and the group of tragicomedies with which he ended his career, such as *The Winter's Tale* and *The Tempest*. He also wrote more than 150 sonnets, published in 1609.

His name is used allusively for a person seen as comparable to him in a particular sphere, especially as being pre-eminent in it.

See also ➤ BACONIAN *theory*, ➤ FOLGER *Shakespeare Memorial Library*, ➤ SHAKESCENE, ➤ SWAN *of Avon.*

Shakti in Hinduism, the female principle of divine energy, especially when personified as the supreme deity. The name comes from Sanskrit *śakti* 'power, divine energy'.

shaku a flat narrow board of wood or horn on which a Japanese court noble formerly would note memoranda, later carried as a mark of honour in the presence of the emperor, by the emperor himself, or by a Shinto priest.

shale see ➤ BURGESS *Shale.*

shallal a West Country term for ➤ ROUGH *music*, the origin is echoic.

Shalmaneser III (d.824 BC), king of Assyria 859–824. Most of his reign was devoted to the expansion of his kingdom and the conquest of neighbouring lands. According to Assyrian records (though it is not mentioned in the Bible) he defeated an alliance of Syrian kings and the king of Israel in a battle at Qarqar on the Orontes in 853 BC.

shalom used as salutation by Jews at meeting or parting, meaning 'peace'.

shallop in historical and poetic use, a light sailing boat; the word in this sense is first recorded in Spenser's *Faerie Queene* (1590), and comes via French from Dutch *sloep* 'sloop'.

> The shallop flitteth silken-sail'd
> Skimming down to Camelot.
> — Lord Tennyson *The Lady of Shalott* (1832)

Shalott see ➤ *the* LADY *of Shalott.*

sham Abraham feign illness or insanity, an expression recorded from the mid 18th century (especially in nautical contexts); the allusion is to ➤ ABRAHAM *man*, a beggar who was or who pretended to be insane.

shaman a person regarded as having access to, and influence in, the world of good and evil spirits, especially among some peoples of northern Asia and North America. Typically such people enter a trance state during a ritual, and practise divination and healing.

shamash an extra candle used for lighting the candles at the festival of ➤ HANUKKAH.

shambles a state of total disorder. The word comes (in late Middle English, in the sense 'meat market') as a plural of earlier *shamble* 'stool, stall', of West Germanic origin, from Latin *scamellum*, diminutive of *scamnum* 'bench'. The current meaning is a transferred usage from the sense 'a scene of carnage', from the earlier meaning 'a butcher's slaughterhouse'.

shamefaced feeling or expressing shame or embarrassment. The word is an alteration (in the 16th century, in the sense 'modest, shy') of the archaic *shamefast*, by association with *face*.

shamrock a low-growing clover-like plant with three-lobed leaves, used as the national emblem of Ireland, and traditionally said to have been employed by ➤ *St* PATRICK to explain the nature of the Trinity. The *shamrock* of legend has been identified with a number of different related plants, in particular the lesser yellow trefoil, which is the plant most frequently worn as an emblem on St Patrick's day.

The word is recorded in England from the late 16th century, and comes from Irish *seamróg* 'trefoil', diminutive of *seamar* 'clover'.

drown the shamrock drink in honour of the shamrock on St Patrick's day, 17 March.

Shan Van Vocht one of the names of Ireland conceived as a feminine entity ('the little old woman'), and used as the title of a nationalist song of 1798. Also called *Sean Bhean Bhocht*.

Shandy see ➤ TRISTRAM *Shandy*.

Shang a dynasty which ruled China during part of the 2nd millennium BC, probably the 16th–11th centuries. The period encompassed the invention of Chinese ideographic script and the discovery and development of bronze casting.

shanghai force (someone) to join a ship lacking a full crew by drugging them or using other underhand means; more widely, coerce or trick (someone) into a place or position or into doing something. The term is recorded from the late 19th century, and is taken from the name of *Shanghai*, a port on the estuary of the Yangtze on the east coast of China, which was opened for trade with the west in 1842.

Shango a religious cult originating in western Nigeria and now practised chiefly in parts of the Caribbean; *Shango* is also the name of an African god of thunder significant to this cult.

Shangri-La a Tibetan utopia in James Hilton's novel *Lost Horizon* (1933); the term is now used for a place regarded as an earthly paradise, especially when involving a retreat from the pressures of modern civilization.

> Over there, it looked like Shangri-La, a lush valley hidden in high mountains.
> — Elizabeth Arthur *Antarctic Navigation* (1995)

Shanks's pony used humorously to refer to one's own legs and the action of walking as a means of conveyance; recorded from the late 18th century.

Claude Elwood Shannon (1916–), American engineer. He was the pioneer of mathematical communication theory, which has become vital to the design of both communication and electronic equipment. He also investigated digital circuits, and was the first to use the term *bit* to denote a unit of information.

Shannon's theorem a theorem defining the maximum capacity of a communication channel to carry information with no more than an arbitrary error rate, given the bandwidth and signal-to-noise ratio.

shanti in the Indian subcontinent, peace; the word is repeated three times at the end of an ➤ UPANISHAD as a prayer for the peace of the soul, and was incorporated by T. S. Eliot into *The Waste Land* (1923).

shanty a song with alternating solo and chorus, of a kind originally sung by sailors while performing physical labour together. Recorded from the mid 19th century, the word probably comes from French *chantez*! 'sing!'

Sharawaggi variety, asymmetry, or irregularity of an aesthetically pleasing nature, especially with regard to landscape gardening and architecture. The term was first recorded in the late 17th century by William Temple (1628–99) as being a Chinese word; this is not etymologically sustainable, although the true origin is not known. The Chinese association, however, was popularly believed; in the late 18th century, Horace Walpole wrote that, 'I am almost as fond of the Sharawaggi, or Chinese want of symmetry, in buildings, as in grounds or gardens.'

With a change of fashion, the word *Sharawaggi* lapsed from use and is not recorded in the 19th century; it was revived as a historical term in the 1930s.

shard-beetle archaic term for a dor-beetle; *shard* here means a patch of dung, and a *shard-born beetle* is thus a beetle born in dung; the occurrence in Shakespeare's *Macbeth* as 'The shard-borne beetle with his drowsy hums' was subsequently misinterpreted as meaning a beetle carried on *shards* or wings.

sharecropper in the US, a tenant farmer who gives a part of each crop as rent.

sharia Islamic canonical law based on the teachings of the Koran and the traditions of the Prophet (Hadith and Sunna), prescribing both religious and secular duties and sometimes retributive penalties for lawbreaking. It has generally been supplemented by legislation adapted to the conditions of the day, though the manner in which it should be applied in modern states is a subject of dispute between Islamic fundamentalists and modernists.

sharif a descendant of ➤ MUHAMMAD through his daughter ➤ FATIMA, entitled to wear a green turban or veil. The word comes from Arabic *šarīf* 'noble', from *šarafa* 'be exalted'.

shark a long-bodied chiefly marine fish with a prominent dorsal fin. Most sharks are predatory, and the shark has become a type for predatory ruthless behaviour, as in ➤ FEEDING *frenzy*; the image of the great white shark typifying particular ferocity was established in the public mind by the film *Jaws* (1975) and its sequels. The word is recorded from late Middle English, although the origin is unknown.
    See also ➤ *a* DOVER *shark and a Deal savage*, ➤ JUST *when you thought it was safe to go back in the water*.

Sharon a fertile coastal plain in Israel, lying between the Mediterranean Sea and the hills of Samaria, mentioned in Chronicles for its pasturage and the Song of Solomon for its flowers.
    See also ➤ ROSE *of Sharon*.

Sharp see also ➤ BECKY *Sharp*.

Cecil Sharp (1859–1924), English collector of folk songs and folk dances. From 1904 onwards he published a number of collections of songs and dances, stimulating a revival of interest in English folk music. Sharp also founded the English Folk Dance Society in 1911.

the sharper the storm, the sooner it's over proverbial saying, late 19th century.

Sharpeville massacre the killing of sixty-seven anti-apartheid demonstrators by security forces at Sharpeville, a black township south of Johannesburg, on 21 March 1960. Following the massacre, the South African government banned the African National Congress and the Pan-Africanist Congress.

shastra (in Hinduism and some forms of Buddhism) a work of sacred scripture.

Shavuoth a major Jewish festival held on the 6th (and usually the 7th) of Sivan, fifty days after the second day of Passover. It was originally a harvest festival, but now also commemorates the giving of the Law (the ➤ TORAH). The name comes from Hebrew *šābū'ōt* 'weeks', with reference to the weeks between Passover and Pentecost.

Shazam the magic word (originally the name of a wizard) with which the orphan Billy Batson is transformed into the superhero ➤ *Captain* MARVEL; the letters stood for the wisdom of Solomon, the strength of Hercules, the stamina of Atlas, the power of Zeus, the courage of Achilles, and the speed of Mercury.

Shays's Rebellion (1786–87), an insurrection of Massachusetts farmers led by Daniel Shays (1747–1825), former officer in the War of Independence, in opposition to high land taxes and harsh economic conditions following on the Revolution.

She Bible the second of two issues of the Bible printed in 1611, in which the last words of Ruth 3:15 are, 'and she went into the city', where the ➤ HE *Bible* has, 'and he went into the city'.

She-Wolf of France a name for Isabella of France (1292–1358), queen of Edward II, who overthrew her husband and connived in his murder.

shears see ➤ SIEVE *and shears*.

Sheba the biblical name of ➤ SABA in SW Arabia, whose queen, having heard of the wisdom of Solomon, 'came to prove him with hard questions' (1 Kings 10:1); her verdict was, 'behold, the half was not told me: thy wisdom and prosperity exceedeth the fame which I heard' (1 Kings 10:7).
    In Matthew 12:42, Jesus referred to the journey she had made to Jerusalem, as a model for the scribes and Pharisees of his own day:

> The queen of the south shall rise up in judgement with this generation, and shall condemn it: for she came from the uttermost parts of the earth to hear the wisdom of Solomon; and, behold, a greater than Solomon is here.
> — Bible (AV) St Matthew ch. 12, v. 42

The **Queen of Sheba** is sometimes taken as a type of beauty and splendour.

> Now you look like the Queen of Sheba, beautiful sister.
> — Mtutuzeli Matshoba *Call me not Man* (1979)

shebeen (especially in Ireland, Scotland, and South Africa) an unlicensed establishment or private house selling alcoholic liquor and typically regarded as slightly disreputable. The word comes (in the late 18th century) from Anglo-Irish *sibín*, from *séibe* 'mugful'.

shechita the method of slaughtering animals that fulfils the requirements of Jewish law.

Sheela-na-gig a medieval stone figure of a naked female with the legs wide apart and the hands emphasizing the genitals, found in churches in Britain and Ireland. The name comes from Irish *Síle na gcíoch* 'Julia of the breasts'.

sheep the sheep is proverbial for its tendency to follow others in the flock, and for its timidity and inoffensiveness.

In biblical allusions, the people of Israel are likened to *sheep* without a shepherd (Matthew 9:6); in Acts 8:32, the words 'He was led as a sheep to the slaughter' describe the death of Jesus.

See also ➤ BELL *sheep*, ➤ BLACK *sheep*, ➤ *a* BLEAT-ING *sheep loses a bite*, ➤ JACOB *sheep*, ➤ *might as well be* HANGED *for a sheep as a lamb*, ➤ *a* WOLF *in sheep's clothing*.

separate the sheep from the goats divide the good from the bad, with biblical allusion to the parable of the Last Judgement in Matthew 25:32–3, when all the nations will be gathered before God, and 'he shall separate them one from another, as a shepherd divideth his sheep from the goats.'

sheep-shearing the time or occasion of the festival (now rarely held) celebrating the shearing of sheep; in Shakespeare's *Winter's Tale*, the Clown has to 'buy spices for our sheep-shearing'.

Sheer Thursday another name for ➤ MAUNDY *Thursday*; *Sheer* (meaning 'blameless, clear') is an allusion to the purification of the soul by confession on that day, in preparation for ➤ GOOD *Friday*, and perhaps also to the traditional washing of the altars.

in a white sheet dressed for formally doing penance, originally for fornication.

sheet lightning lightning with its brightness diffused by reflection within clouds.

sheets see also ➤ THREE *sheets*.

Sheffield plate copper plated with silver by rolling and edging with silver film and ribbon, especially as produced in Sheffield between 1760 and 1840. The process was superseded by electroplating.

shehecheyanu a Jewish benediction pronounced on the evening of a principal holy day and on new occasions of thanksgiving; the word comes from Hebrew, and means literally, 'that has sustained us'.

sheikh an Arab leader, in particular the chief or head of an Arab tribe, family, or village; the word, which is recorded from the late 16th century, is based on Arabic *šayk* 'old man, sheikh'.

In the 1920s the word (chiefly with the spelling *sheik*) came to mean a strong, romantic lover; this derived from the novel *The Sheik* (1919) by E. M. Hull, filmed in 1921 as *The Sheikh*, starring Rudolph Valentino as the desert hero who kidnaps the English girl whose lover he becomes.

shekel silver coin and unit of weight used in ancient Israel and the Middle East; informally, **shekels** is used to mean money, wealth, perhaps originally as a quotation from Byron:

> No land of Canaan, full of milk and honey,
> Nor (save in paper shekels) ready money.
> — Lord Byron *The Age of Bronze* (1823)

Shekinah in Jewish and Christian theology, the glory of the divine presence, conventionally represented as light or interpreted symbolically (in Kabbalism as a divine feminine aspect). Recorded from the mid 17th century, the word comes from late Hebrew, from *šākan* 'dwell, rest'.

Sheldonian Theatre name of the Senate House of Oxford University; built for the purpose by Gilbert Sheldon (1598–1677), archbishop of Canterbury, when Chancellor of the University; designed by Christopher Wren, it was built entirely at Sheldon's own expense, and was opened on 9 July 1669.

shell a (scallop) shell is the emblem of ➤ *St* JAMES *the Great*.

See also ➤ PILGRIM's *shell*, ➤ SCALLOP *shell*.

Mary Shelley (1797–1851), English writer, daughter of William Godwin and Mary Wollstonecraft, who eloped with Percy Bysshe Shelley in 1814 and married him in 1816; she is also remembered as the author of the Gothic novel *Frankenstein, or the Modern Prometheus* (1818). After her husband's death, discussing the education of their son, she is said to have exclaimed, 'Teach him to think for himself? Oh, my God, teach him rather to think like other people!'

Percy Bysshe Shelley (1792–1822), English poet, a leading figure of the romantic movement with radical political views; he married ➤ *Mary* SHELLEY as his second wife after his first wife Harriet was found drowned in the Serpentine. His poem *Adonais* (1821) was an elegy on the death of Keats, and Shelley himself was drowned when sailing from Leghorn to Spezzia on 8 July 1822.

Shelta an ancient secret language used by Irish and Welsh tinkers and gypsies, and based largely on altered Irish or Gaelic words. The name is recorded from the late 19th century, but is of unknown origin.

Shem (in the Bible) a son of ➤ NOAH (Genesis 10:21), traditional ancestor of the Semites.

Shema a Hebrew text consisting of three passages from the Pentateuch (Deuteronomy 6:4, 11:13–21; Numbers 15:37–41) and beginning 'Hear O Israel, the Lord our God is one Lord'. It forms an important part of Jewish evening and morning prayer and is used as a Jewish confession of faith. The word is Hebrew, and means literally 'hear'.

shen (in Chinese thought) the spiritual element of a person's psyche.

Shenandoah a river of Virginia. Rising in two headstreams, one on each side of the Blue Ridge Mountains, it flows some 240 km (150 miles) northwards to join the Potomac at ➤ HARPERS *Ferry*.

sheogue in Ireland, a fairy.

Sheol the Hebrew underworld, abode of the dead, envisaged as a subterranean region clothed in thick darkness, return from which was impossible. In the Authorized Version, it was translated variously as 'hell', 'grave', or 'pit'.

shepherd in biblical usage, the image of the shepherd caring for his flock is a strong one; God is seen as the shepherd of his people, and in Luke 2:8 the shepherds to whom the announcement of the Nativity is made are described as 'abiding in the field, keeping watch over their flock by night'. ➤ *St* CUTHBERT and ➤ *St* BERNADETTE are the patron saints of shepherds.

In French history, **The Shepherds** (a translation of French *les Pastoureaux*) is the name given to those who took part in the peasant insurrections of 1251 and 1320.

In pastoral poetry, *shepherd* is a designation of one of the rustic characters; from this, in 16th-century poetry adopting the pastoral convention,

the name is often used for the writer and his friends and fellow poets.

See also ➤ *the* ETTRICK *Shepherd*, ➤ *the* GENTLE *Shepherd*, ➤ *the* GOOD *Shepherd*, ➤ RED *sky at night, shepherd's delight.*

Shepherd Kings a name for the ➤ HYKSOS, deriving from a misinterpretation of Greek *Huksōs* by ➤ MANETHO, Egyptian priest of the 3rd century BC.

Shepherd Lord byname of Henry, Lord Clifford (?1455–1523), used by Wordsworth in 'Song at the Feast at Brougham Castle' (1807). Henry Clifford's father had been killed fighting for the Lancastrians at Towton in 1461; he was subsequently attainted and his estates forfeited, while his son was brought up as a shepherd. The Clifford estates were restored after Bosworth, on Henry VII's accession to the throne.

Shepherd of Banbury John Claridge, shepherd, supposed original author of *The Shepherd of Banbury's Rules to judge of the Changes of the Weather*, first published in 1670 and frequently reprinted up to 1827.

Shepherd of Hermas a Christian text of the 2nd century, for a time regarded as part of scripture, and written by the Hermas to whom Paul in Romans 16:14 sends greetings.

Shepherd of Salisbury Plain idealized character created in a tract by the religious writer Hannah More (1745–1833); the original is said to have been a man named Saunders, of Cherrill Down, who lived on a shilling a day and never complained of hunger because he 'lived upon the promises'.

Shepherd of the Ocean epithet for ➤ *Walter* RALEIGH coined by Edmund Spenser (1552–99); Raleigh subsequently used the appellation of himself.

shepherd's calendar a calendar containing weather lore for shepherds (apparently proverbially regarded as an unreliable source of information).

shepherd's weather-glass a name for the scarlet pimpernel, which is said to close as a sign that it is going to rain.

Jack Sheppard (1702–24), thief, noted for his daring prison escapes; originally condemned to death at the Old Bailey on 14 August 1724, he escaped (and was recaptured) twice before he was finally executed at Tyburn on 16 November.

> The same qualities could be found in legendary bandits like Jack Sheppard or Robin Hood.
>
> — Robert Murphy *Smash and Grab* (1993)

Sheraton (of furniture) designed, made by, or in the simple, delicate, and graceful style of the English furniture-maker Thomas Sheraton (1751–1806).

Richard Brinsley Sheridan (1751–1816), Irish dramatist and Whig politician. His plays are comedies of manners; they include *The Rivals* (1775) and *The School for Scandal* (1777). In 1780 he entered Parliament, becoming a celebrated orator and holding senior government posts.

sheriff (in England and Wales) the chief executive officer of the Crown in a county, also known as the **high sheriff**, having various administrative and judicial functions; originally (in Anglo-Saxon England) the *shire-reeve* (Old English *scīrgerēfa*) was the representative of royal authority in a shire, and was responsible for the administration of the royal demesne and the execution of the law. The office was continued after the Conquest, the title being retained in English documents. The function of the sheriff was restricted by successive legal changes.

In the US, the *sheriff* is an elected officer in a county, responsible for keeping the peace; in films and books set in towns of the ➤ WILD *West*, the sheriff is often a key figure.

Sherlock informal term for a person who investigates mysteries or shows great perceptiveness; the term comes (in the early 20th century) from the name of Conan Doyle's fictional detective ➤ *Sherlock* HOLMES.

> When it's our turn to be a statistic, we demand promptness, patience, politeness, and Sherlockian insight.
>
> — *Esquire* October 1997

William Tecumseh Sherman (1820–91), American general, who in 1864 in the American Civil War became chief Union commander in the west. He set out with 60,000 men on a march through Georgia, during which he crushed Confederate forces and broke civilian morale by his policy of deliberate destruction of the territory he passed through; he is reported as saying in 1864, 'War is the remedy our *enemies* have chosen, and I say let us give them all they want.'

After the war, Sherman was invited to stand as Republican candidate in the 1884 presidential election; his telegram of refusal was comprehensive: 'I will not accept if nominated, and will not serve if elected.'

> General Schwarzkopf was briskly Shermanesque when a cadet asked him what his plans were after he retires from the Army in August: 'If you are asking me if I am going to run for political office, the answer is, *Absolutely not!*'
>
> — *US News and World Report* 27 May 1991

Sherpa a member of a Himalayan people living on the borders of Nepal and Tibet, renowned for their skill in mountaineering; the name is used figuratively of a civil servant or diplomat who undertakes preparatory political work prior to a summit conference.

> Felipe González, the sherpa who amazingly has become the Spanish head of state.
>
> — *American Spectator* February 1994

sherry a fortified wine originally and mainly from southern Spain, often drunk as an aperitif. The name comes (in the late 16th century) from an alteration of archaic *sherris* (understood as a plural), from Spanish *(vino de) Xeres* 'Xeres (wine)', *Xeres* being the former name of ➤ JEREZ.

shewbread twelve loaves of unleavened bread placed every Sabbath in the Jewish Temple and eaten by the priests at the end of the week. David, when in flight from Saul (1 Samuel 21:4–6) once ate the *shewbread* himself; in Matthew 12:3–4, Jesus cites this to the Pharisees to justify his disciples picking and eating ears of corn on the Sabbath.

Recorded in English from the mid 16th century, the term, suggested by German *Schaubrot*, represents Hebrew *leḥem pānīm*, literally 'bread of the face (of God)'.

Shia one of the two main branches of Islam, followed especially in Iran, that rejects the first three Sunni caliphs and regards Ali, the fourth caliph, as ➤ MUHAMMAD's first true successor. The name comes from Arabic *šīʿa* 'party of Ali'.

shiatsu a form of therapy of Japanese origin based on the same principles as acupuncture, in which pressure is applied to certain points on the body using the hands. The word is Japanese and means literally 'finger pressure'.

shibboleth a custom, principle, or belief distinguishing a particular class or group of people, especially a long-standing one regarded as outmoded or no longer important. Of biblical origin, the word comes from the Hebrew word meaning 'ear of corn', used as a test of nationality by its difficult pronunciation:

> Then said they unto him, Say now Shibboleth: and he said Sibboleth: for he could not frame to pronounce it right. Then they took him, and slew him.
> — Bible (AV) Judges ch. 12, v. 14

shield a broad piece of metal or another suitable material, held by straps or a handle attached on one side, used in ancient and medieval warfare as a protection against blows or missiles. In the Middle Ages the armorial bearings of a knight were depicted on his shield; decorated shields, made for display rather than use, were often hung on walls in churches or other buildings as a memorial of a knight or noble. The word is recorded from Old English (in form *scild*) and is of Germanic origin; it comes ultimately from a base meaning 'divide, separate'.

two sides of a shield two ways of looking at something, two sides to a question; an expression recorded from the mid 19th century.

shield-maiden a female warrior, an Amazon; a ➤ Valkyrie.

you cannot shift an old tree without it dying proverbial saying, early 16th century.

Shiite an adherent of the ➤ Shia branch of Islam.

shikhara a pyramidal tower on a Hindu temple, sometimes having convexly curved sides.

shikimi a small evergreen tree of Japan and Korea, which has aromatic leaves used in Buddhist funeral rites.

shillelagh a thick stick of blackthorn or oak used in Ireland, typically as a weapon. The word is recorded from the late 18th century, and comes from the name of *Shillelagh*, a town in County Wicklow, and a wood near it.

shilling a former British coin and monetary unit equal to one twentieth of a pound or twelve pence; the word is recorded from Old English (in form *scilling*), and was traditionally used in emphatic or rhetorical statements when the speaker wished to be understood as reckoning or accounting for the cost of every item:

> I will not engage to pay one shilling more than the expenses really incurred by Hanover.
> — Duke of Wellington dispatches, 1815

See also ➤ King's *shilling*, ➤ York *shilling*.

little shilling a term used in 1826 by the political reformer William Cobbett (1763–1835) to designate a

proposed silver ⟨...⟩ value; the express⟨...⟩ Macaulay in referen⟨...⟩

shilly-shally fail to act re⟨...⟩ ginally from a reduplication,⟨...⟩ in Congreve's *Way of the Worla⟨...⟩*

> I don't stand shill I, shall I, then; if ⟨...⟩
> — William Congreve *The Way ⟨...⟩* ⟨...⟩00)

Shin a major Japanese Buddhist sect teac⟨...⟩ng salvation by faith in the Buddha Amida and emphasizing morality rather than orthodoxy. The word is Japanese, and means 'genuine, authentic'.

Shin Bet the principal security service of Israel, concerned primarily with counter-espionage. The name is modern Hebrew, the initial letters of the first two words of *šērūṭ biṭṭāhōn kĕlālī* '(general) security service'.

hang out one's shingle begin to practise one's profession (in North American usage, a *shingle* is a signboard or nameplate of a lawyer, doctor, or other professional person).

Shingon a Japanese Buddhist sect founded in the 9th century and devoted to esoteric Buddhism. The word is Japanese and means 'true word, mantra'.

knight in shining armour an idealized or chivalrous man who comes to the rescue of a woman in a difficult situation; the term is recorded (in informal or ironic use) from the mid 20th century.

> Those who resisted the temptation to redirect the group's work stuck to their guns. Knights in shining armour . . . kept the organisation afloat till the tide turned in the mid-1980s, with a boomtime for green organisations.
> — *Earth Matters* Summer 1996

improve the shining hour make good use of time, make the most of one's time; originally with allusion to Isaac Watts's *Divine Songs for Children* (1715), 'How doth the little busy bee Improve each shining hour'; a verse parodied by Lewis Carroll in Alice's Adventures in Wonderland (1865), 'How doth the little crocodile Improve his shining tail.'

Shining Path a Peruvian Maoist revolutionary movement and terrorist organization, founded in 1970 and led by Abimael Guzmán (1934–) until his capture and imprisonment in 1992. At first the movement operated in rural areas, but in the 1980s it began to launch terrorist attacks in Peruvian towns and cities.

the US and Australia, a banknote
...ory note regarded as having little or no
...e, so named because of the resemblance to a
square piece of paper soaked in vinegar and used to
bandage the shin; the expression is used similarly in
Canada of a twenty-five cent bill.

Shinto a Japanese religion dating from the early
8th century and incorporating the worship of ancestors and nature spirits and a belief in sacred power
(*kami*) in both animate and inanimate things. It was
the state religion of Japan until 1945. The word is
Japanese, and comes from Chinese *shen dao* 'way of
the gods'.

ship in figurative and allusive phrases, a *ship* traditionally typifies the fortunes or affairs of a person,
or the person themselves in regard to them. A ship is
also the emblem of ➤ St ANSELM, ➤ St NICHOLAS *of
Myra*, and ➤ St URSULA, and the 7th-century French
abbot St Bertin, whose monastery of Sithiu (Saint-
Bertin) in northern France was originally accessible
only by water.

See also ➤ the FACE that launched a thousand
ships, ➤ FIRST *Four Ships*, ➤ *one* HAND *for oneself
and one for the ship*, ➤ RATS *desert a sinking ship*,
➤ *ship's* HUSBAND, ➤ WHITE *Ship*, ➤ *a* WOMAN *and a
ship ever want mending*.

when one's ship comes home traditional saying,
mid 19th century; referring to a future state of prosperity which will exist when a cargo arrives.

> One [customer] always says he'll give me a ton of taties
> when his ship comes home.
> — Henry Mayhew *London Labour* (1851)

do not spoil the ship for a ha'porth of tar proverbial saying, early 17th century; *ship* = a dialectal
pronunciation of *sheep*, and the original literal sense
was 'do not allow sheep to die for the lack of a trif-
ling amount of tar', tar being used to protect sores
and wounds on sheep from flies.

ship money a tax raised in England in medieval
times to provide ships for the navy; originally levied
on ports and maritime towns and counties. It was
revived (with an extended application to inland
counties) by Charles I in 1634 without parliamentary consent and abolished by statute in 1640; the
actual term is first recorded in William Prynne's
Remonstrance against Shipmoney of 1636.

ship of fools a ship whose passengers represent
various types of vice or folly; the expression comes
from the title of Sebastian Brant's satirical work *Das*

Narrenschiff (1494), translated into English by Alexander Barclay as ship *The shyp of folys of the worlde*
(1509). In the 20th century, the American writer
Katherine Anne Porter (1890–1980) used *The Ship of
Fools* as the title of a novel (1962) depicting a group
of passengers (mostly German) on a long voyage in
which the ship is a microcosm of contemporary life.

the ship of state the state and its affairs, especially
when regarded as being subject to adverse or changing circumstances; a *ship* is taken here as the type
of something subject to adverse or changing weather. The phrase (as **ship of the state**) is first recorded in English in a 1675 translation of
Machiavelli's *The Prince*, in a reference to 'when
times are tempestuous, and the ship of the State has
need of the help…of the subject'.

ship of the desert a camel; in his *Relation of a
Journey* (1615), recounting his travels in Turkey and
Egypt, the English poet George Sandys wrote,
'Camels. These are the ships of Arabia, their seas are
the deserts.'

ship of the line a sailing warship of the largest size,
used in the ➤ LINE *of battle*; the term is recorded
from the early 18th century.

ships that pass in the night people whose ac-
quaintance is necessarily transitory; the phrase
comes originally from a poem by Longfellow:

> Ships that pass in the night, and speak each other in
> passing;
> Only a signal shown and a distant voice in the darkness.
> — Henry Wadsworth Longfellow *Tales of a Wayside Inn*
> (1874) 'The Theologian's Tale: Elizabeth'

shipshape see ➤ *all shipshape and* BRISTOL *fashion*.

Mother Shipton (fl. 1530), reputed prophetess,
perhaps a completely mythical personage; the earliest reference to her is found in 1641, in an anonymous tract entitled 'The Prophecie of Mother Shipton
in the Raigne of King Henry 8th, foretelling the
death of Cardinall Wolsey, the Lord Percy, and
others, as also what should happen in insuing
Times'. The pamphlet was widely circulated, and
Mother Shipton's prophetic powers became proverbial; William Lilly, in his 'A Collection of Ancient
and Modern Prophesies' (1645) discussed eighteen
prophecies associated with her, the majority of
which had already been fulfilled. Twenty years later,
Samuel Pepys recorded in his diary that when
Prince Rupert, sailing up the Thames on 20 October
1666, heard of the outbreak of the Fire of London,

'all he said was, now Shipton's prophecy was out'.

A purported account of her life and death was published by Richard Head; according to this she was the daughter of the devil, hideous to look at, and with the power of prophesying disaster. An expanded version of Head's biography, published in 1686, claimed to identify her as having been born Ursula Sonthiel in 1488, to have married a carpenter named Shipton, and to have died at Clifton in 1561.

Her prophecies were subsequently frequently reprinted and added to; a version in 1862 included some verses (actually written by Charles Hindley) implying that she had foretold the invention of the steam-engine, the electric telegraph, and the end of the world (in 1881).

Shiraz a city in SW central Iran, an important cultural centre since the 4th century BC, noted for the school of miniature painting based there between the 14th and 16th centuries, and for the manufacture of carpets and the production of wine.

Shiraz is also the name of a variety of black wine grape, and a red wine made from this; it is an alteration of French *syrah*, apparently reflecting the belief that the vine was brought from Iran by the Crusades.

shire an administrative district in medieval times ruled jointly by an ➤ ALDERMAN and a ➤ SHERIFF, and consisting of a number of smaller districts (*hundreds* or *wapentakes*); the name comes from Old English *scīr* 'care, official charge, county'.

Since the late 18th century, **the Shires** has been used in reference to parts of England regarded as strongholds of traditional rural culture, especially the rural Midlands.

See also ➤ KNIGHT *of the shire*, ➤ NORTHAMPTON-SHIRE *for squires and shires*.

shire horse a heavy powerful horse of a draught breed, originally from the English Midlands; the name is recorded from the late 19th century.

shirt see also ➤ *the* DIRTY *Shirts*, ➤ NEAR *is my shirt, but nearer is my skin*, ➤ *shirt of* NESSUS.

from shirtsleeves to shirtsleeves in three generations proverbial saying, early 20th century; meaning that wealth gained in one generation will be lost by the third. The saying is often attributed to ➤ *Andrew* CARNEGIE but is not found in his writings.

shittah tree in the Authorized Version of the Bible, a kind of acacia, from which **shittim wood**, which in Exodus 25:5 was one of the offerings the people of Israel were commanded to make to God, was obtained.

shiur in Judaism, a Talmudic study session, usually led by a rabbi. The word comes from Hebrew *šĭʿūr* 'measure, portion'.

Shiva (in Indian religion) a god associated with the powers of reproduction and dissolution. Perhaps a later development of the Vedic god Rudra, Shiva is regarded by some as the supreme being and by others as forming a triad with ➤ BRAHMA and ➤ VISHNU. He is worshipped in many aspects: as destroyer, ascetic, lord of the cosmic dance, and lord of beasts, and through the symbolic lingam. His wife is ➤ PARVATI, and their two sons, Ganesha and Skanda. His mount is the bull Nandi. Typically, Shiva is depicted with a third eye in the middle of his forehead, wearing a crescent moon in his matted hair and a necklace of skulls at his throat, entwined with live snakes, and carrying a trident.

shiva in Judaism, a period of seven days' formal mourning for the dead, beginning immediately after the funeral. The word comes from Hebrew *šiḇʿāh* 'seven'.

Shivaji (1627–80), Indian raja of the Marathas 1674–80. He raised a successful Hindu revolt against Muslim rule in 1659 and expanded Maratha territory. After being crowned raja he blocked Mogul expansionism by forming an alliance with the sultans in the south.

the Shoah another term for the Holocaust; the word is modern Hebrew, and means literally 'catastrophe'.

shock see also ➤ CULTURE *shock*, ➤ FUTURE *shock*, ➤ SHORT, *sharp shock*.

shock-headed Peter an English name for ➤ STRUUWELPETER.

shock jock a disc jockey on a talk-radio show who expresses opinions in a deliberately offensive or provocative way. The phenomenon developed in America in the late 1980s and then crossed the Atlantic, although while it attained a high profile in Britain it was ultimately less successful.

William Shockley (1910–89), American physicist. Shockley and his researchers at Bell Laboratories developed the transistor in 1948 and in 1958 he shared with them the Nobel Prize for Physics. He later became a controversial figure because of his views on a supposed connection between race and intelligence.

shoe shoes are the emblems of ➤ St Crispin and ➤ St Crispinian.

See also ➤ *it's* ill *waiting for dead men's shoes.*

if the shoe fits, wear it proverbial saying, late 18th century; chiefly in the US.

I know best where the shoe pinches proverbial saying.

shoemaker ➤ *St* Crispin and ➤ *St* Crispinian are patron saints of shoemakers.

the shoemaker's son always goes barefoot proverbial saying, mid 16th century.

Shoemaker–Levy 9 a comet discovered in March 1993, when it had just broken up as a result of passing very close to Jupiter. In July 1994 more than twenty separate fragments impacted successively on Jupiter, causing large explosions in its atmosphere. It is named after Carolyn (1929–) and Eugene *Shoemaker* (1928–97), American astronomers, and David *Levy* (1948–), Canadian astronomer, discoverers of the comet.

shofar a ram's-horn trumpet used by Jews in religious ceremonies and as an ancient battle signal.

shogun a hereditary commander-in-chief in feudal Japan. Because of the military power concentrated in his hands and the consequent weakness of the nominal head of state (the mikado or emperor), the shogun was generally the real ruler of the country until feudalism was abolished in 1867.

By successive usurpations of power, the shogun or tycoon had become the real ruler of Japan, though nominally the subject of the mikado, and acting in his name. This state of things was misunderstood by Europeans, and it was erroneously supposed that there were two emperors in Japan, the mikado (who was the object of a loyalty of the nature of religious devotion) being called 'the spiritual emperor', and the shogun 'the temporal emperor'.

shome mistake, shurely? catch-phrase in *Private Eye* magazine, from the 1980s, as in a bracketed comment 'shome mistake, shurely? Ed.'

shooting see also ➤ drive-*by shooting.*

shooting star a small, rapidly moving meteor burning up on entering the earth's atmosphere; in literary use, sometimes an image for a glorious position that cannot be sustained.

> I see thy glory like a shooting star
> Fall to the base earth.
> — William Shakespeare *Richard II* (1597)

shop see also ➤ keep *your shop.*

the Shop informal military term for the former Academy at Woolwich.

shopkeeper see ➤ *the* English *are a nation of shopkeepers.*

shopping see ➤ sex *and shopping.*

— shopping days to Christmas the imminence of Christmas expressed in commercial terms.

shore see ➤ Saxon *Shore.*

Shoreditch a district of London, erroneously said to have been named after Jane *Shore* (d. 1527), mistress of Edward IV; the name is recorded before her time.

short see also ➤ *short* shrift.

a short horse is soon curried proverbial saying, mid 14th century; meaning that a slight task is soon completed.

Short Parliament the first of two parliaments summoned by Charles I in 1640 (the other being the ➤ Long *Parliament*). Due to its insistence on seeking a general redress of grievances against him before granting the money he required, Charles dismissed it after only three weeks; one of the main topics considered was ➤ ship-*money*, with the king demanding subsidies against the abandonment of the unpopular tax.

short reckonings make long friends proverbial saying, mid 16th century; meaning that the swift settlement of any debt ensures that a friendship will not be damaged.

short, sharp shock a brief but harsh custodial sentence handed down to an offender in an attempt to discourage them from committing further offences. The term attained a high profile in the UK in the early 1980s, following a recommendation to the 1979 Conservative Party Conference of the introduction of a regime of this kind to be applied to young offenders. The *short, sharp shock* policy, typically featuring a tough military-style discipline, soon became a staple of the law-and-order debate, but there was increasing scepticism as to its effectiveness in deterrence.

Shorter Catechism a form of catechism issued by the Westminster Assembly of Divines and used by the Presbyterian churches; the image of a teacher of the principles of the Christian religion using this catechism was incorporated by the poet the poet W. E. Henley (1849–1903) in a description of Robert Louis Stevenson:

> A deal of Ariel, just a streak of Puck,
> Much Antony, of Hamlet most of all,
> And something of the Shorter-Catechist.
> — W. E. Henley 'In Hospital' (1888)

a shot in the locker a thing in reserve but ready for use; in literal use, the *locker* here is the compartment in which ammunition is kept.

Shotokan the style of karate which is now the most widespread in the UK and a number of other countries. The word is Japanese, from *shō* 'true' + *to* 'way' + *kan* 'mansion'.

shotten herring a herring that has spawned; in archaic use, a weakened or dispirited person, originally with allusion to Shakespeare's *1 Henry IV*, 'If manhood…be not forgot upon the face of the earth, then am I a shotten herring'. *Shotten* here is the archaic past participle of *shoot*, in the specialized sense 'discharge (spawn)'.

shoulder see also ➤ *a* CHIP *on one's shoulder*, ➤ IVORY *shoulder*.

shovel hat a black felt hat with a low round crown and a broad brim turned up at the sides, formerly worn especially by clergymen; the term is recorded from the early 19th century, in a usage by Thomas Carlyle, 'Does not the very sight of a shovel-hat in some degree indispose me to the wearer thereof?'

show see also ➤ GREATEST *Show on Earth*, ➤ *show the white* FEATHER.

Show Me State informal name for Missouri; 'Show Me' here refers to what was regarded as the characteristically sceptical approach of the people of Missouri.

Showa the period (1926–89) when Japan was ruled by the emperor ➤ HIROHITO; *Showa*, his reign-title (given on his death) comes from Japanese *shō* 'bright, clear' + *wa* 'harmony'.

showboat (in the US) a river steamer on which theatrical performances are given, recorded from the mid 19th century; *Showboat* (1927), starring Paul

Robeson, was a musical by Oscar Hammerstein and Jerome Kern depicting life on such a boat.

shower a shower of rain is the emblem of ➤ *St* SWITHIN.

In North America, *shower* denotes a party at which presents are given to someone, typically a woman who is about to get married or have a baby.

See also ➤ APRIL *showers bring forth May flowers.*

shradh a Hindu ceremony to honour and make offerings to a deceased relative.

king of shreds and patches used allusively after Shakespeare's *Hamlet*, in which Hamlet describes his usurping uncle as 'a king of shreds and patches'; later reinforced by *The Mikado*:

> A wandering minstrel I—
> A thing of shreds and patches.
> — William Schwenck Gilbert *The Mikado* (1885)

shrew the shrew was popularly believed to be dangerous, and especially venomous; in his *Herball* (1551) the English physician and botanist William Turner (d. 1568) refers to 'the poyson of…the feld mouse called a shrew'. The name is recorded in Old English (in form *scrēawa*, *scrǣwa*, of Germanic origin); related words in Germanic languages have senses such as 'dwarf', 'devil', or 'fox'.

From the Middle English period, *shrew*, with regard to the animal's reputation, was used to designate a malignant or vexatious person, and from this developed the particular sense of a bad-tempered or aggressively assertive woman.

by Shrewsbury clock (of a specified length of time) exactly, precisely; with allusion to Shakespeare's *1 Henry IV*, in which ➤ FALSTAFF untruthfully asserts that he and Hotspur 'fought a long hour by Shrewsbury clock'.

short shrift rapid and unsympathetic dismissal; curt treatment; the phrase originally meant little time for a criminal to make his confession and be *shriven* between condemnation and execution or punishment.

Shriner a member of the Order of Nobles of the Mystic Shrine, a charitable society founded in the US in 1872.

shrive (of a priest) hear the confession of, assign penance to, and absolve; recorded in Old English (in form *scrīfan*) the word is of Germanic origin, and comes ultimately from the same base as Latin *scribere* 'write'.

shroud see also ➤ TURIN *Shroud*.

shrouds have no pockets proverbial saying, mid 19th century; meaning that worldly wealth cannot be kept and used after death.

Shrove Tuesday the day before ➤ ASH *Wednesday*, on which people would be *shriven* in preparation for Lent. Though named for its former religious significance, it is chiefly marked by feasting and celebration, which traditionally preceded the observance of the Lenten fast.

Shrovetide Shrove Tuesday and the two days preceding it, when it was formerly customary to attend confession.

shuffle see ➤ *shuffle off this mortal* COIL.

shut see also ➤ *a* DOOR *must either be shut or open*.

a shut mouth catches no flies proverbial saying, late 16th century.

shuttle diplomacy negotiations conducted by a mediator who travels between two or more parties that are reluctant to hold direct discussions; the concept was particularly associated with ➤ Henry KISSINGER.

Shylock a Jewish moneylender in Shakespeare's *Merchant of Venice*, who lends money to Antonio but demands in return a pound of Antonio's own flesh should the debt not be repaid on time; when the debt falls due, and Shylock enforces the penalty, Antonio is saved by ➤ PORTIA, who pleads successfully that if the flesh is taken it must be done without shedding blood, which is not mentioned in the deed.

In Shakespeare's play Shylock's ill-treatment at the hands of the Christian merchants, and his resentment of it, are vividly portrayed, but in allusive use his name is used for a moneylender who charges extortionate rates of interest.

si quis archaic term for a public intimation, notice, or bill, frequently one exhibited on a post or door, requesting or giving information about a missing or absent person or thing; in ecclesiastical use, a notice indicating that a candidate seeks ordination, and asking if anyone knows of an impediment. The phrase is recorded from the late 16th century, and comes from Latin, meaning literally 'if anyone', the opening words of the notice when written in Latin.

Siamese twins twins that are physically joined at birth, sometimes sharing organs, and sometimes separable by surgery (depending on the degree of fusion). The term originated with the *Siamese* men Chang and Eng (1811–74), who, despite being joined at the waist, led an active life.

Jean Sibelius (1865–1957), Finnish composer. His affinity for his country's landscape and legends, especially the epic *Kalevala*, is expressed in a series of symphonic poems including *The Swan of Tuonela* (1893) and *Finlandia* (1899).

Siberia a vast region of Russia, extending from the Urals to the Pacific and from the Arctic coast to the northern borders of Kazakhstan, Mongolia, and China. Noted for the severity of its winters, it was traditionally used as a place of exile.

> She and her family are still living in the projects—exiled to an urban Siberia where shop, banks, and other amenities of city living are few and far between.
> — *Washington City Paper* 21 February 1992

sibyl a woman in ancient times supposed to utter the oracles and prophecies of a god; in later times the number of sibyls was usually given as ten, living at different times and places in Asia, Africa, Greece, and Italy. Among them were the **Erythraean Sibyl**, who was said to have prophesied to ➤ HECUBA, and the **Cumaean Sibyl**, said in Virgil's *Aeneid* to have been visited by ➤ AENEAS.

It was the *Cumaean Sibyl* who was said to have offered nine books of oracles to Tarquin the Proud (see ➤ TARQUINIUS), the last king of Rome; when he repeatedly refused to pay the price she asked, she burned six of the nine ➤ SIBYLLINE *books* before his eyes.

She was also said to have asked the god Apollo for longevity, which was granted, but to have forgotten at the same time to ask for eternal youth; a character in Petronius's *Satyricon* says that he has seen her in her extreme old age:

> 'I saw the Sibyl at Cumae'
> (One said) 'with mine own eye.
> She hung in a cage, and read her rune
> To all the passers-by.
> Said the boys, "What wouldst thou, Sibyl?"
> She answered, "I would die." '
> — Dante Gabriel Rossetti translation of Petronius
> *Satyricon*

Sibylline books books containing the prophecies of the ➤ *Cumaean* SIBYL, three of which she supposedly sold to Tarquinius Superbus, king of ancient Rome, at the price of the original nine.

Sibylline oracles a collection imitating the ➤ SIBYLLINE *books*, probably written by early Christian or Jewish authors.

sic et non a method of argument used by ➤ *Peter* ABELARD, 12th-century French theologian and philosopher, and later Scholastics, in which contradictory passages of scripture are presented without commentary in order to stimulate readers to resolve the contradictions themselves. The phrase is Latin, and means literally 'yes and no'.

sic transit gloria mundi thus passes the glory of the world; a Latin sentence spoken during the coronation of a new Pope, while flax is burned to represent the transitoriness of earthly glory. It was first used at the coronation of Alexander V in Pisa, 7 July 1409, but is earlier in origin; it may ultimately derive from '*O quam cito transit gloria mundi* [Oh how quickly the glory of the world passes away]' in the *De Imitatione Christi* of ➤ THOMAS *à Kempis*.

sicarius a member of a sect of assassins active during the zealot disturbances in Palestine in the 1st century; the word comes from Latin, from *sica* 'dagger'.

Sicilian Vespers a massacre of French inhabitants of Sicily, which began near Palermo at the time of vespers on Easter Monday in 1282. The ensuing war resulted in the replacement of the unpopular French Angevin dynasty by the Spanish House of Aragon.

Sicilies see ➤ Two *Sicilies*.

sick ➤ *St* MICHAEL, St Camillus (1550–1614), founder of the Ministers of the Sick, and other saints, are patron saints of the sick.

See also ➤ *the* DEVIL *was sick, the Devil a monk would be*, ➤ SACRAMENT *of the sick*.

sick building syndrome a condition affecting office workers, typically marked by headaches and respiratory problems, attributed to unhealthy or stressful factors in the working environment such as poor ventilation.

Sick Man of Europe a nickname for Ottoman Turkey deriving from a reported conversation between Tsar Nicholas I of Russia and Sir George Seymour at St Petersburg on 21 February 1853; in the Annual Register for 1853, the Tsar is quoted as saying, 'I am not so eager about what shall be done when the sick man dies, as I am to determine with England what shall not be done upon that event taking place.'

sickle see ➤ HAMMER *and sickle*.

siddha in Hinduism, an ascetic who has achieved enlightenment.

Siddhartha Gautama name of the Indian prince who was given the title of ➤ BUDDHA.

Mrs Sarah Siddons (1755–1831), English actress. She was an acclaimed tragic actress, noted particularly for her role as Lady Macbeth, and was a formidable figure; when Samuel Rogers suggested that he might 'make open love' to Mrs Siddons, Richard Sheridan replied, 'To her! To that magnificent and appalling creature! I should as soon have thought of making love to the Archbishop of Canterbury!'

Siddur a Jewish prayer book containing prayers and other information relevant to the daily liturgy. The name is Hebrew, and means literally 'order'.

side see also ➤ DISTAFF *side*, ➤ *a* THORN *in one's side*, ➤ *two sides of the* SHIELD.

sideburns a strip of hair grown by a man down each side of the face in front of his ears. The term was originally *burnside*, from the name of General Burnside (1824–81), who affected this style.

I am on the side of the angels an assertion by Benjamin Disraeli in the debate on evolution following the publication of Darwin's *Origin of Species*; in a speech at Oxford, 25 November 1864, Disraeli said, 'Is man an ape or an angel? Now I am on the side of the angels.'

Sidhe the fairy people of Irish folklore, said to live beneath the hills and often identified as the remnant of the ancient ➤ TUATHA *Dé Danann*. The name is Irish, and comes from *aos sidhe* 'people of the fairy mound'.

Philip Sidney (1554–86), English poet, courtier, and soldier. Generally considered to represent the apotheosis of the Elizabethan courtier, he was a leading poet and patron of Edmund Spenser. His best-known work is *Arcadia* (published posthumously in 1590), a pastoral prose romance including poems and pastoral eclogues in a wide variety of verse forms.

Sidney was killed in battle at Zutphen, and from the circumstances of his death may be taken as a type of chivalry; Fulke Greville related in his memoir (1652) of his friend that the wounded and dying Sidney, although parched with thirst, passed his water-bottle to another wounded soldier with the words, 'Thy necessity [often quoted as need] is greater than mine.'

Siege of Sidney Street in January 1911, a gun battle centring on 100 Sidney Street, in which members of an anarchist group suspected of murder and robbery were besieged by the police supported by the army; the then Home Secretary, Winston Churchill, visited the site in person. The house itself was burnt to the ground (two bodies were found in the wreckage) and other gang members arrested, although the supposed leader, 'Peter the Painter', was never found or positively identified.

Sidon a city in Lebanon, on the Mediterranean coast south of Beirut, which was founded in the 3rd millennium BC, it was a Phoenician seaport and city state; in New Testament times it was known for its luxury and wealth.

sidra in Jewish liturgy, a section of the Torah read at a Sabbath morning synagogue service.

Sieg Heil a victory salute used originally by Nazis at political rallies; the words are German, and mean literally 'Hail victory'.

Siege of Troy in Greek mythology, the 10-year siege of the city of Troy by ➤ AGAMEMNON and his forces, after Paris, son of Priam king of Troy, had abducted ➤ HELEN, wife of Menelaus of Sparta, brother of Agamemnon; the ➤ TROJAN *War* finally resulted in the fall and destruction of Troy.

Siege Perilous the vacant seat at King Arthur's ➤ ROUND *Table* which could be occupied without peril only by the knight destined to achieve the ➤ GRAIL.

Siegfried the hero of the first part of the *Nibelungenlied*. A prince of the Netherlands, Siegfried obtains a hoard of treasure by killing the dragon Fafner; he marries the Burgundian Kriemhild, and helps her brother Gunther to win Brunhild before being killed by Hagen. His Norse equivalent is ➤ SIGURD.

Siegfried Line the line of defence constructed by the Germans along the western frontier of Germany before the Second World War, named for the Germanic hero ➤ SIEGFRIED. In September 1939 the *Times* questioned 'What song is to be the "Tipperary" of this war?' and answered its own question by suggesting 'We're gonna hang out the washing on the Siegfried line…if the Siegfried line's still there',

but after the fall of France in 1940, this song was little sung by British soldiers.

Siena a city in west central Italy, in Tuscany, which in the 13th and 14th centuries was the centre of a flourishing school of art. Its central square is the venue for the noted ➤ PALIO horse race.

See also ➤ St CATHERINE *of Siena*.

Sierpinski triangle in mathematics, a fractal based on a triangle with four equal triangles inscribed in it. The central triangle is removed and each of the other three treated as the original was, and so on, creating an infinite regression in a finite space. It is named after the Polish mathematician Waclaw Sierpiński (1882–1969).

sierra (especially in Spanish-speaking countries or the western US) a long jagged mountain chain; the word comes through Spanish from Latin, meaning 'saw'.

sieve and shears divination by the turning of a sieve held on a pair of shears; also called *coscinomancy*.

sigh see ➤ BRIDGE *of Sighs*.

sight see ➤ SECOND *sight*.

sigma the eighteenth letter of the Greek alphabet (Σ, σ), transliterated as 's'.

signature tune a distinctive piece of music associated with a particular programme or performer on television or radio; the term is first recorded in the *Daily Mail* of 1932, in an account of three tunes selected by Henry Hall for his new BBC Dance Band, 'to be used every time the band begins or concludes a broadcast'.

doctrine of signatures the belief (common in medieval times and originally advocated by Pliny) that the form or colouring of a medicinal plant in some way resembled the organ or disease it was used to treat.

the Signet the royal seal formerly used for special purposes in England and Scotland, and in Scotland later as the seal of the Court of Session. The word comes (in late Middle English, meaning a small seal used instead of or with a signature to give authentication to an official document) from Old French or medieval Latin diminutive of *signum* 'token, seal'.

See also ➤ WRITER *to the Signet*.

signum see also ➤ ECCE *signum*.

signum pantheum in classical antiquity, a statue combining the figures, symbols, or attributes of several gods.

Sigurd in Norse legend the equivalent of the Germanic ➤ Siegfried, the last of the ➤ Volsungs who kills the dragon Fafnir and takes his treasure; betrothed to the Valkyrie Brynhild, he is tricked into forgetting her and marrying the Nibelung princess ➤ Gudrun. He wins Brynhild for Gudrun's brother Gunnar, but when Brynhild discovers the part he has played, she incites Gunnar and his brother Hogni into killing Sigurd.

The stories of Sigurd are told in a number of poems in the ➤ *Poetic* Edda. William Morris made him the subject of his long narrative poem, *The Story of Sigurd the Volsung and the Fall of the Niblungs* (1876); Morris described the story as 'the Great Story of the North which should be to our race what the Tale of Troy was to the Greeks'.

Bill Sikes the violent burglar in Dickens's *Oliver Twist*, an associate of ➤ Fagin who in the end murders his mistress Nancy and hangs himself while attempting to escape from the mob across the rooftops.

Sikh Wars a series of wars between the Sikhs and the British in 1845 and 1848–9, culminating in the British annexation of Punjab.

Sikhism a monotheistic religion founded in Punjab in the 15th century by Guru Nanak. Sikh teaching centres on spiritual liberation and social justice and harmony, though the community took on a militant aspect during early conflicts. The last guru, Gobind Singh (1666–1708), passed his authority to the scripture, the ➤ Adi *Granth*, and to the ➤ Khalsa, the body of initiated Sikhs.

Silat the Malay art of self-defence, practised as a martial art or accompanied by drums as a ceremonial display or dance.

Silbury Hill a Neolithic monument near Avebury in Wiltshire, a flat-topped conical mound more than 40 m (130 ft) high, which is the largest man-made prehistoric mound in Europe.

Silchester a modern village in Hampshire, situated to the south-west of Reading, near which is the site of an important town of pre-Roman and Roman Britain, known to the Romans as Calleva Atrebatum. The site was abandoned at the end of the Roman period, and recent excavations suggest it may have been ritually cursed.

silence see also ➤ *the* REST *is silence*, ➤ SPEECH *is silver, but silence is golden*, ➤ TOWER *of silence*, ➤ TWO-*minute silence*.

silence is a woman's best garment proverbial saying, mid 16th century; in earlier references, Sophocles in *Ajax* has 'silence is a woman's best ornament', and 1 Corinthians 14:34 reads, 'Let your women keep silence in the churches, for it is not permitted to them to speak'.

silence means consent proverbial saying, late 14th century; translation of a Latin tag, '*qui tacet consentire videtur* [he who is silent seems to consent]', said to have been spoken by Thomas More (1478–1535) when asked at his trial why he was silent on being asked to acknowledge the king's supremacy over the Church. The principle is not accepted in modern English law.

silent see ➤ William *the Silent*.

Silenus in Greek mythology, an aged woodland deity, one of the *sileni*, who was entrusted with the education of Dionysus. He is depicted either as dignified and musical, or as an old drunkard. In general use, a *silenus* denotes a woodland spirit, usually depicted in art as old and having ears like those of a horse, similar to the satyrs.

> The reeling old Silenus of a baronet.
> — W. M. Thackeray *Vanity Fair* (1848)

silhouette the dark shape and outline of someone or something visible against a lighter background, especially in dim light; a representation of someone or something showing the shape and outline only, typically coloured in solid black. It is named (although the reason remains obscure) after Étienne de *Silhouette* (1709–67), French author and politician.

Silicon Valley a name given to an area between San Jose and Palo Alto in Santa Clara County, California, USA, noted for its computing and electronics industries.

> East Germany is a combination of backward agriculture and rustbelt which makes the most blighted parts of northern England and central Scotland look like Silicon Valley.
> — *Punch* 27 July 1990

silk a fine, strong, soft lustrous fibre produced by silkworms in making cocoons and collected to make thread and fabric; the type of something soft, rich, and luxurious. Recorded in Old English (in form *sioloc, seolec*) the word comes via Latin from Greek *Sēres*, the name given to the inhabitants of the Far

Eastern countries from which silk first came over-land to Europe.

See also ➤ *we are all* ADAM*'s children (but silk makes the difference).*

take silk become a Queen's (or King's) Counsel; a barrister of this rank has the right to wear a silk gown.

you can't make a silk purse out of a sow's ear proverbial saying, early 16th century; meaning that inherent nature cannot be overcome by nurture.

> One disadvantage of being a hog is that at any moment some blundering fool may try to make a silk purse out of your wife's ear.
> — J. B. Morton ('Beachcomber') *By the Way* (1931)

Silk Road an ancient caravan route linking Xian in central China with the eastern Mediterranean. Skirting the northern edge of the Taklimakan Desert and passing through Turkestan, it covered a distance of some 6,400 km (4,000 miles). It was established during the period of Roman rule in Europe, and took its name from the silk which was brought to the west from China. It was also the route by which Christianity spread to the East. A railway (completed in 1963) follows the Chinese part of the route, from Xian to Urumqi.

> The idea of an American *res publica*—of the commonwealth preserved by the civic virtue of an informed citizenry—seems as distant as the silk road to Cathay.
> — *Harper's Magazine* February 1994

silly having or showing a lack of common sense or judgement; absurd and foolish. In late Middle English the word meant 'deserving of pity or sympathy', and was an alteration of dialect *seely* 'happy', later 'innocent, feeble', from a West Germanic base meaning 'happiness'. The sense 'foolish' developed via the stages 'feeble' and 'unsophisticated, ignorant'.

Silly Billy a nickname of William IV; the Oxford historian C. R. L. Fletcher, author of *A History of England* (1911) for schools, recalled a story told him by his grandfather of William's visiting Bedlam to be shown one of the inmates:

> The lunatic pointed at him and called out 'Silly Billy! Silly Billy!' 'By Gad he knows me,' said William. 'Oh yes,' said the keeper, 'he has his lucid intervals.'
> — Peter Sutcliffe *The Oxford University Press: an Informal History* (1978)

In the 20th century, the catchphrase *Silly Billy*, originally as used by the comedian Mike Yarwood, was associated with the Labour politician Denis Healey (1917–).

the silly season summer regarded as the season when newspapers often publish trivial material because of a lack of important news; the term is first recorded in the *Saturday Review* of 13 July 1861, 'We have observed this year very strong symptoms of the Silly Season of 1861 setting in a month or two before its time.'

Silly Suffolk a traditional name for Suffolk, recorded from the mid 19th century.

Siloam (in the New Testament) a spring and pool of water near Jerusalem, where a man born blind was told by Jesus to wash, thereby gaining sight (John 9:7).

Silurian of or belonging to the ancient British tribe of the Silures, or the south-eastern part of Wales inhabited by them.

In the mid 19th century, *Silurian* was used to denote the third period of the Palaeozoic era, between the Ordovician and Devonian periods, which lasted from about 439 to 409 million years ago. The first true fish and land plants appeared, and the end of the period is marked by the climax of the Caledonian mountain-forming.

Silurist epithet taken by the poet Henry Vaughan, who was born in Brecknockshire, part of the area originally inhabited by the Silures; in 1650 he published, 'Silex Scintillans: or Sacred Poems and private Ejaculations, by Henry Vaughan, Silurist.'

Silvanus in Roman mythology, an Italian woodland deity identified with ➤ PAN.

silver a precious shiny greyish-white metal, in general use ranking next to gold, found in nature in its uncombined state as well as in ores, and valued for use in jewellery and other ornaments as well as formerly in coins. *Silver* is also a tincture in heraldry, but is more usually called ➤ ARGENT. The word is recorded in Old English (in form *seolfor*), and is ultimately of Germanic origin.

See also ➤ ALE*-silver*, ➤ ANGLE *with a silver hook*, ➤ CROSS *someone's palm with silver*, ➤ *every* CLOUD *has a silver lining*, ➤ LARK*-silver*, ➤ LONG *John Silver*, ➤ NUT *silver*, ➤ THIRTY *pieces of silver*.

silver age in classical Greek and Roman literature, the second age of the world, inferior to the simplicity and happiness of the first or ➤ GOLDEN *age*; in general use, a period regarded as notable but inferior to a golden age, such as that of so-called silver Latin literature.

silver cord used in biblical allusion to Ecclesiastes 12:6 to indicate the dissolution of life, 'Or ever the silver cord be loosed, or the golden bowl broken'.

silver-fork designating a school of novelists of about 1830 distinguished by an affectation of gentility; the *Examiner* of 18 November 1827 had noted that, 'A writer of this accomplished stamp…also informs you that the quality eat fish with silver forks.'

Silver Lady an epithet applied to Miss Elizabeth Baxter (d. 1972), philanthropist, from her custom of giving silver coins to the down-and-outs of the Embankment in London, used attributively to describe a charitable organization (and its appurtenances) which distributes food and hot drinks to vagrants.

silver Latin literary Latin from the death of Augustus (AD 14) to the mid second century.

the silver screen the cinema; originally, a cinematographic projection screen covered with metallic paint to produce a highly reflective silver-coloured surface; the term is recorded from the 1920s, in its earliest literal use in a letter of 1921 from Mary Pickford, 'It is not always easy to take a classic like "Little Lord Fauntleroy" and place it on the cold, silver screen.'

Silver Star a decoration for gallantry awarded to members of the US Army and Navy.

Silver State informal name for Nevada, referring to its silver mines.

Silver Stick (the bearer of) a silver-tipped rod borne on State occasions by a particular officer of the Life Guards or their successors the Household Cavalry Regiment.

silver streak the English Channel; recorded from the late 19th century.

silver-tongued eloquent and persuasive in speaking; recorded from the late 16th century.

silver wedding the twenty-fifth anniversary of a wedding.

Silverstone a motor-racing circuit near Towcester in Northamptonshire, built on a disused airfield after the Second World War.

Silvia see ➤ RHEA *Silvia*.

Simchat Torah the final day of the Jewish festival of ➤ SUCCOTH, on which the annual cycle of the reading of the Torah is completed and begun anew.

Simeon[1] in the Bible, a Hebrew patriarch, son of Jacob and Leah (Genesis 29:33); also, the tribe of Israel traditionally descended from him.

Simeon[2] in the Bible, the singer of the ➤ NUNC *Dimittis*, who recognized the child Jesus in the Temple and gave thanks that he had seen the ➤ MESSIAH; he also prophesied to Mary that a sword would pierce her heart (one of the ➤ SEVEN *Sorrows of Mary*).

St Simeon Stylites (*c*.390–459), Syrian monk. After living in a monastic community he became the first to practise an extreme form of asceticism which involved living on top of a pillar; this became a site of pilgrimage.

similia similibus curantur proverbial Latin saying, meaning 'like cures like'; it is the motto of homeopathic medicine, though not found in this form in the writings of C. F. S. Hahnemann (1755–1843), founder of the homeopathic movement. The Latin is found in an anonymous sidenote in the *Opera Omnia* (*c*.1490–1541) of ➤ PARACELSUS.

Simla a city in NE India, situated in the foothills of the Himalayas, which served from 1865 to 1939 as the summer capital of British India, and is now a popular hill resort.

> A handsome parish church, with a tower; a shopping street called The Mall; a town hall, several half-timbered post offices, 'Tudorbethan' villas with names like Rose Cottage, an amateur dramatics society with its own little theatre, the Gaiety: all these Simla had.
> — *Independent on Sunday* 29 June 1997

Lambert Simnel (*c*.1475–1525), English pretender and rebel. He was trained by Yorkists to impersonate firstly one of the Princes in the Tower and subsequently the Earl of Warwick in an attempt to overthrow Henry VII. He was crowned in Dublin in 1487 but when the Yorkist uprising was defeated he was given a menial post in the royal household.

simnel cake a rich fruit cake, now typically with a marzipan covering and decoration, traditionally eaten on ➤ MID-*Lent Sunday*; the custom is recorded from the 17th century.

Simnel was originally (in Middle English) a kind of bread or bun made of fine flour; the word comes via Old French from Latin *simila* or Greek *semidalis* 'fine flour'.

Simnel Sunday another name for ➤ MID-*Lent Sunday*.

Simon original name of the Apostle ➤ St PETER. See also ➤ SIMPLE *Simon*.

St **Simon** an Apostle; known as **Simon the Zealot**. According to one tradition he preached and was martyred in Persia along with St Jude.

□ **FEAST DAY** His feast day (with St Jude) is 28 October.

Simon Magus a magician, who in Acts 8 was baptized by Philip, and who tried to buy the power of the Holy Spirit from Peter and Paul, and was rejected by them:

> And Peter said unto him, Thy money perish with thee, because thou hast thought that the gift of God may be purchased with money.
> — Bible (AV) Acts ch. 8, v. 20

According to legend, *Simon Magus* was killed attempting to fly to demonstrate his superior magic powers.

See also ➤ SIMONY.

Simon of Cyrene in the Bible, a man from Cyrene who in Mark 15:21 was made by the Roman soldiers to carry the Cross on the way to Calvary; Simon helping Jesus with his burden is one of the ➤ STATIONS *of the Cross*.

simon-pure completely genuine, authentic, or honest, from *(the real) Simon Pure*, a character in Centlivre's *Bold Stroke for a Wife* (1717), who for part of the play is impersonated by another character.

Simon Says a children's game in which players must obey the leader's instructions if (and only if) they are prefaced with the words 'Simon says'.

Simonides (*c*.556–468 BC), Greek lyric poet, who wrote for the rulers of Athens, Thessaly, and Syracuse. Much of his poetry, which includes elegies, odes, and epigrams, celebrates the heroes of the Persian Wars, and includes verse commemorating those killed at Marathon and Thermopylae.

simony the buying or selling of ecclesiastical privileges, for example pardons or benefices, from the name of ➤ SIMON *Magus*, in reference to his attempt to buy the power of the Holy Spirit from Peter and Paul.

the **Simple** epithet of Charles III of France (879–929), who became the first Carolingian ruler to be deposed and who died in captivity.

Simple Simon a foolish or gullible person, probably from the name of a character who features in various nursery rhymes; the first known is recorded

in a chapbook of the mid 18th century, but it is suggested that the name may be earlier by several centuries.

simplicity see ➤ VOLUNTARY *simplicity*.

Simplon a pass in the Alps in southern Switzerland, consisting of a road built by Napoleon in 1801–5 and a railway tunnel (built in 1922) which links Switzerland and Italy.

Simpson see also ➤ BART *Simpson*, ➤ HOMER *J. Simpson*.

O. J. Simpson (1947–), American football player, actor, and celebrity. He was arrested in 1994, accused of murdering his wife and her male companion, but was acquitted after a lengthy, high-profile trial.

> A handful of lawyers make enormous fees from representing celebrity jocks like O. J. Simpson.
> — *Daily Press* 23 August 1995

Wallis Simpson (1896–1986), American wife of Edward, ➤ *Duke of* WINDSOR (Edward VIII); born Wallis Warfield. Her relationship with the king caused a scandal in view of her impending second divorce and forced the king's abdication in 1936; a contemporary children's rhyme ran:

> Hark the herald angels sing
> Mrs Simpson's pinched our king.
> — quoted in letter from Clement Attlee, 26 December 1938

It is said that when her divorce was granted in an Ipswich court, an American paper carried the headline 'King's Moll Reno'd in Wolsey's Home Town'.

Simpson's rule an arithmetical rule for estimating the area under a curve where the values of an odd number of ordinates, including those at each end, are known. It is named after Thomas *Simpson* (1710–61), English mathematician.

simurg in Persian mythology, a large mythical bird of great age, believed to have the power of reasoning and speech; the name comes ultimately from Pahlavi *sēn* 'eagle' + *murg* 'bird'.

sin an immoral act considered to be a transgression against divine law; an act regarded as a serious or regrettable fault, offence, or omission. The word is recorded from Old English (in form *synn*), and is probably related to Latin *sons, sont-* 'guilty'.

See also ➤ MAN *of Sin*, ➤ ORIGINAL *sin*, ➤ SATAN *rebuking sin*, ➤ SINS.

sin against the Holy Ghost in theological debate, the only sin which may be beyond forgiveness, as indicated in the words of Jesus:

> And whosoever speaketh a word against the Son of man, it shall be forgiven him: but whosoever speaketh against the Holy Ghost, it shall not be forgiven him, neither in this world, neither in the world to come.
> — Bible (AV) St Matthew ch. 13, v. 32

An early usage of the phrase is found in 1565 by the Protestant divine Thomas Becon (1512–67), 'Only the sin against the Holy Ghost…is irremissible and never forgiven.'

In extended modern usage, the phrase may be used for the one thing in a particular context which is seen as beyond toleration.

> The sin against the Holy Ghost is to be average, never to have the will to break our impermeable boundaries.
> — Edward Dahlberg *Reasons of the Heart* (1965)

sin-eater someone traditionally hired to take upon themselves the sins of a deceased person by means of food eaten beside the dead body; the term is recorded from the mid 17th century, in *Remains of Gentilism and Judaism* by the antiquary John Aubrey (1626–97).

sin lieth at the door biblical saying, from Genesis 4:7, God's words to the murderer ➤ Cain, 'and if thou doest not well, sin lieth at the door.'

sin-offering in traditional Jewish practice, an offering of an animal for sacrifice, made as an atonement for sin, as in Leviticus 4:3, 'then let him bring for his sin…a young bullock without blemish unto the Lord for a sin offering.'

Sin On Bible an edition of 1716, the first English-language Bible to be printed in Ireland, in which John 5:14 reads 'sin on more' instead of 'sin no more'.

it's a sin to steal a pin proverbial saying, late 19th century; meaning that even if what is stolen is of little value, the action is still sinful.

Mount Sinai a mountain in the south of the Sinai peninsula in NE Egypt, the place, according to the Bible, where Moses received the Ten Commandments (Exodus 19–34).

Sinanthropus a former genus name applied to some fossil hominids found in China in 1926 (see ➤ Peking *man*).

Sinbad the Sailor the hero of one of the tales in the *Arabian Nights*, who relates the fantastic adventures he meets with in his voyages; in one of them, he is abandoned on an island where he finds a roc's

egg, 'fifty good paces' round, and in another he unwisely offers to carry on his back the sheikh who turns out to be the ➤ Old *Man of the Sea*, and who is only dislodged by a trick.

sindonology the branch of knowledge that deals with the ➤ Turin *Shroud*, thought by some to be the shroud in which the body of Jesus was wrapped. The word comes from *sindon*, a fine thin fabric traditionally used for shrouds.

sinecure a position requiring little or no work but giving the holder status or financial benefit. The word comes (in the mid 17th century) from Latin *sine cura* 'without care'.

the sinews of war the money and equipment needed to wage a war; the phrase is first used in English in the mid 16th century, and refers to the *Fifth Philippic* of the Roman orator and statesman Cicero (106–43 BC), 'Nervos belli, pecuniam infinitam [The sinews of war, unlimited money].' Francis Bacon (1561–1626) in his essay 'Of the True Greatness of Kingdoms' disagreed: 'Neither is money the sinews of war (as it is trivially said).'

sing see also ➤ little birds *that can't sing and won't sing must be made to sing.*

sing before breakfast, cry before night proverbial saying, early 17th century.

Sing Sing a New York State prison, built in 1825–8 at *Ossining* village on the Hudson River and formerly notorious for its severe discipline.

singeing of the king of Spain's beard the attack by ➤ *Francis* Drake on the Spanish fleet in Cadiz harbour in 1587, during which he sank or burnt 33 Spanish ships; the phrase is recorded by Francis Bacon in *Considerations touching a War with Spain* (1629).

singer ➤ *St* Cecilia and ➤ *St* Gregory are patron saints of *singers*.

See also ➤ sweet *singer of Israel*.

Singh a title or surname adopted by certain warrior castes of northern India, especially by male members of the Sikh Khalsa. The word comes from Punjabi *singh* 'lion'.

singing see ➤ all-*singing all-dancing*.

singing bread former term for the wafer used in the celebration of the Mass; the verb *sing* formerly meant, 'chant or intone, in the performance of divine service, say Mass'.

single see also ➤ *single* BLESSEDNESS.

single currency a currency used by all the members of an economic federation, specifically, the single European currency proposed for use by the member states of the European Union, originally having a planned implementation date of 1999 (when the ➤ EURO was in fact introduced).

Although the topic of a *single currency* is at present strongly associated with the current debate on the political and economic relationships of the member states of the European Union, the proposition is far from new. In a letter of 6 May 1807, to his brother Louis, ➤ NAPOLEON *I* wrote, 'I want the whole of Europe to have one currency; it will make trading much easier.'

Single-speech Hamilton nickname of the politician William Gerard Hamilton (1729–96), who on 13 November 1755 made a celebrated maiden speech in the House of Commons; Horace Walpole, giving a glowing account of it, concluded, 'You will ask, what could be beyond this? Nothing but what was beyond what ever was, and that was Pitt!' Hamilton did in fact make other speeches in the House, but none outdid the reputation of the first, from which he was named.

single tax originally, a tax on that part of land value known as unearned profit (*produit net*), proposed by François Quesnay (1694–1774) and favoured by the ➤ PHYSIOCRATS. Later, a tax on land value as the sole source of public revenue, proposed by Henry George (1839–97); the name **Single Tax Party** was given in English to a Danish political party inspired by the principles of Henry George.

Sinis in Greek mythology, a brigand killed by Theseus; it was *Sinis*'s custom to murder those he robbed by fastening them to two pine trees bent down to the ground; when the branches were released, the trees sprang upright, and the victim was torn in two.

sinister originally (in late Middle English) *sinister* meant 'malicious, underhand'; in the late 16th century, the sense of 'inauspicious, unfavourable' developed, especially as denoting omens seen on the left hand, which was regarded as the unlucky side. From this in turn developed the current sense, giving the impression that something harmful or evil is happening or will happen.

In heraldry, of, on, or towards the left-hand side (in a coat of arms, from the bearer's point of view, i.e. the right as it is depicted); the opposite of ➤ DEXTER.

See also ➤ BEND *sinister*.

sinking fund a fund formed by periodically setting aside money for the gradual repayment of a debt or replacement of a wasting asset. Sinking funds were established by the British Government in 1716, 1786, and 1875 for reducing the National Debt. In an Act of George I (1716) it is termed 'a General Yearly Fund'.

Sinn Fein a political movement and party seeking a united republican Ireland. Founded in 1905, Sinn Fein became increasingly committed to Republicanism after the failure of the Home Rule movement. Having won a majority of Irish seats in the 1918 general election, its members refused to go to Westminster and set up their own parliament in Ireland in 1919. After a split in the 1920s, when many of its members joined Fianna Fáil, the party began to function as the political wing of the IRA. The name represents Irish *sinn féin* 'we ourselves', often given as 'ourselves alone'.

sinner see ➤ *the* GREATER *the sinner, the greater the saint.*

Sino-Japanese Wars two wars (1894–5, 1937–45) fought between China and Japan. The first war, caused by rivalry over Korea, was ended by a treaty in Japan's favour and led to the eventual overthrow of the Manchus in 1912. In the second war Japanese expansionism led to trouble in Manchuria in 1931 and to the establishment of a Japanese puppet state (➤ MANCHUKUO) a year later.

sins see ➤ CHARITY *covers a multitude of sins,* ➤ OLD *sins cast long shadows,* ➤ SEVEN *deadly sins.*

sir used as a polite or respectful way of addressing a man, especially one in a position of authority; it is used as a title before the forename of a knight or baronet. The word is recorded from Middle English, and is a reduced form of ➤ SIRE.

Al Sirat in Muslim prophetic tradition, a bridge over Hell leading to Paradise; although *Al Sirat* is not mentioned by name in the Koran, the verse in Sura 19 'Not one of you but will Pass over it' has been interpreted to refer to it, and to mean that the souls passing into Paradise must see Hell on their way (by another interpretation, 'you' refers to the souls of the wicked).

Sirdar in the Indian subcontinent and other Eastern countries, a military or political leader; formerly in particular, the British commander-in-chief of the Egyptian army.

sire in archaic usage, a respectful form of address for someone of high social status, especially a king. Recorded from Middle English, the word comes via Old French from an alteration of Latin *senior*, and is the origin of ➤ SIR.

siren in Greek mythology, each of a number of women or winged creatures whose singing lured unwary sailors on to rocks; when Odysseus sailed past their rock, he made his men block their ears with wax, and had himself lashed to the mast. The English writer and physician Sir Thomas Browne (1605–82) took 'what song the sirens sang' as one of his types of difficult question:

> What song the Sirens sang, or what name Achilles assumed when he hid himself among women, though puzzling questions, are not beyond all conjecture.
> — Sir Thomas Browne *Hydriotaphia* (Urn Burial, 1658)

In the early 19th century, *siren* was the name given to an acoustical instrument (invented by Cagniard de la Tour in 1819) for producing musical tones and used in numbering the vibrations in any note; the term was then extended to an instrument, made on a similar principle but of a larger size, used on steamships for giving fog-signals and warnings. The word thus came to be used more generally for a device which produces a piercing note (frequently of varying tone), used as an air-raid warning, or to signify the approach of a police car.

The name comes from Greek and is recorded from Middle English; in earliest use, it designates an imaginary type of snake, from glossarial explanations of Latin *sirenes* in the Vulgate text of Isaiah 13:22, where the Wycliffite versions have 'wengid edderes' and 'fliynge serpentis', and the Authorized Version, 'dragons'.

siren suit a one-piece garment for the whole body which is easily put on or taken off, originally designed for use in air-raid shelters, when warning had been given by the piercing whistle or ➤ SIREN.

Sirius the brightest star in the sky, south of the celestial equator in the constellation Canis Major. It is a binary star with a dim companion, which is a white dwarf. Sirius is conspicuous in the winter sky of the northern hemisphere, apparently following on the heels of the hunter Orion, and is also known as the ➤ DOG *Star*. It was important to the ancient

Egyptians, as its heliacal rising coincided with the season of flooding of the Nile.

sirloin the choicer part of a loin of beef. Recorded from late Middle English and coming from Old French, the name means simply 'above the loin', but traditional folk etymology provides the story that a piece of such beef was set before a king (variously Henry VIII, James I, and Charles II), who acknowledged its excellence by knighting it as 'Sir Loin'.

sirvente a poem or lay, typically a satirical one, recited by a medieval troubadour.

Sister Dora a nurse's cap tied under the chin, named after Dorothy ('*Dora*') Pattison (1832–78), a famous nurse.

Sister of Mercy a member of an order of women founded for educational or charitable purposes, especially that founded in Dublin in 1827.

sisters see also ➤ *the* FATAL *Sisters*, ➤ SEVEN *Sisters*, ➤ *the* WEIRD *sisters*.

the three sisters the three goddesses of destiny, the ➤ FATES.

Sistine Chapel a chapel in the Vatican, built in the late 15th century by Pope *Sixtus IV*, for whom it is named, containing a painted ceiling and fresco of the Last Judgement by Michelangelo and also frescoes by Botticelli and other painters. It is used for the principal papal ceremonies and also by the cardinals when meeting for the election of a new pope.

Sisyphus in Greek mythology, the son of Aeolus, punished in Hades for his misdeeds in life by being condemned to the eternal task of rolling a large stone to the top of a hill, from which it always rolled down again.

> A Sisyphean struggle for security against the thieves who repeatedly break into his home in the Bronx.
> — *New York Times* 17 January 1993

Sita in the Ramayana, the wife of ➤ RAMA; she is the Hindu model of the ideal woman, an incarnation of Lakshmi.

sitting see also ➤ ARE *you sitting comfortably*, ➤ *it is as* CHEAP *sitting as standing*, ➤ PROXY *sitting*.

it is ill sitting at Rome and striving with the Pope proverbial saying, early 17th century; meaning that one should not disagree with someone on their own ground.

Sitting Bull (*c.*1831–90), Sioux chief. As the main chief of the Sioux peoples from about 1867, Sitting

Bull led the Sioux in the fight to retain their lands; this resulted in the massacre of General Custer and his men at Little Bighorn. He later became an advocate of the Ghost Dance cult, and was killed in an uprising.

sitzkrieg a war, or a phase of a war, in which there is little or no active warfare; formed on the analogy of ➤ BLITZKRIEG, from German *sitzen* 'to sit', the term was applied particularly in the Second World War to the ➤ PHONEY *war* of September 1939 to May 1940.

Sivan (in the Jewish calendar) the ninth month of the civil and third of the religious year, usually coinciding with parts of May and June.

six the name **Les Six** was given to a group of six Parisian composers (Louis Durey, Arthur Honegger, Darius Milhaud, Germaine Tailleferre, Georges Auric, and Francis Poulenc) formed after the First World War, whose music represents a reaction against romanticism and Impressionism.

The name **The Six** designates the six original member countries forming the Common Market, Belgium, France, Germany, Italy, Luxembourg, and the Netherlands.

Six Acts repressive measures for the regulation of political activity, in particular the restriction of meetings and the regulation of political publications, passed in 1819, in the wake of the ➤ PETERLOO *massacre.*

> Every man that dared to open his mouth against the Castlereagh and Sidmouth despotism must have set the Six Acts at defiance.
> — *Times* 22 April 1834

Six Articles passed in 1539, enforcing the doctrines of transubstantiation, communion of one kind, celibacy of the clergy, vows of chastity, private masses, and auricular confession.

Six Clerks the six official clerks formerly connected with the Court of Chancery.

Six Counties the counties of Northern Ireland, Antrim, Down, Londonderry, Tyrone, and Fermanagh, which by the Treaty of 1920 were constituted as a separate province.

Six Day War a war, 5–10 June 1967, in which Israel occupied Sinai, the Old City of Jerusalem, the West Bank, and the Golan Heights and defeated an Egyptian, Jordanian, and Syrian alliance. Arab name ➤ JUNE *War.*

Six Dynasties the Chinese dynasties belonging to the period AD 220–589, the dynasties of Ch'en, Eastern Chin, Liang, Liu-Sung, Southern Ch'i, and Wu; this period of Chinese history.

six hours sleep for a man, seven for a woman, and eight for a fool proverbial saying, early 17th century.

Six Nations the peoples of the Iroquois confederacy, the Mohawks, the Oneidas, the Onondegas, the Cayugas, the Senecas, and the Tuscaroras. The term is first recorded in English in a translation of a letter of 1710, 'And as a sure token of the sincerity of the Six Nations, we do…present our great Queen with these belts of wampum.'

six of one and half a dozen of the other traditional saying, mid 19th century; meaning that there is little or nothing to choose between two sides.

six points regarded as the essential points of ritualism by proponents of the 19th-century Anglo-Catholic revival; they are altar lights, eucharistic vestments, communion in both kinds, the use of incense, unleavened bread, and the eastward position.

at sixes and sevens a state of confusion or disorder; originally denoting the hazard of one's whole fortune, or carelessness as to the consequences of one's actions; in later use, meaning the creation or existence of, or neglect to remove, confusion, disorder, or disagreement.

The original form of the phrase, *to set on six and seven* (from Chaucer's *Troylus and Criseyde*), is based on the language of dicing, and is probably a fanciful alteration of *to set on cinque and sice*, these being the two highest numbers.

sixpack see ➤ JOE *Sixpack.*

sixteen see also ➤ SWEET *sixteen.*

Sixteen-string Jack nickname of the highwayman John Rann, executed at Tyburn in 1774; according to the New Newgate Calendar (1780), the name came from his 'wearing breeches with eight strings at each knee'.

> He looked like Sixteen-string Jack on his way to Tyburn, keenly conscious of his position.
> — George MacDonald Fraser *The General Danced at Dawn* (1970)

sixty cardinal number equivalent to the product of six and ten; ten more than fifty.

See also ➤ *the* SWINGING *sixties.*

sixty-four thousand dollar question something that is not known and on which a great deal depends; originally (1940s) *sixty-four dollar question*, from a question posed for the top prize in a broadcast US quiz show.

sizar an undergraduate at Cambridge University or at Trinity College, Dublin, receiving financial help from the college and formerly having certain menial duties. The word comes (in the late 16th century) from the obsolete word *size* 'ration of bread, beer, etc.'

Sizewell a village on the Suffolk coast, the site of two nuclear power stations including a pressurized-water reactor.

sizing at Cambridge University or at Trinity College, Dublin, the action or practice of procuring 'sizes' (see ➤ SIZAR) from the buttery or kitchen; a portion or quantity so obtained.

SJ initials standing for the Society of Jesus.

skald in ancient Scandinavia, a composer and reciter of poems honouring heroes and their deeds; the complex syllabic and rhyme structure of most **skaldic** verses make it likely that the majority of them have come down from oral tradition uncorrupted. Typically, skalds of the 10th and 11th centuries were court poets, providing praise-poems for the Norse rulers of Norway, Denmark, the Orkneys, and the Viking kingdoms of York and Dublin.

Skanda the Hindu war god, first son of ➤ SHIVA and ➤ PARVATI and brother of Ganesha. He is depicted as a boy or youth, sometimes with six heads and often with his mount, a peacock.

Skanderbeg byname of the Albanian leader George Castriota (1403–68); who as a boy became a hostage of Turkey; having converted to Islam, he was named *Iskander* (after ➤ ALEXANDER *the Great*) and given the rank of bey by the Sultan. After a Turkish defeat in 1443 he reconverted to Christianity and moved back to Albania, where he organized Albanian resistance to Turkish rule.

Skara Brae a late Neolithic (3rd millennium BC) settlement on Mainland in the Orkney Islands, overwhelmed by a sand dune and first uncovered by a storm in the mid 19th century. The settlement consists of a group of one-room stone dwellings with built-in stone shelves, chests, and hearths

skean-dhu a dagger worn in the stocking as part of Highland dress. Recorded from the early 19th century, the term comes from *skean* 'dagger formerly used in Scotland and Ireland' + Scottish Gaelic *dubh* 'black'.

skeleton army a 19th-century group who attempted to disrupt the activities of the Salvation Army or Church Army.

> The Salvation Army was marching that way, and . . . yells and cat-calls behind showed that the Skeleton Army was on its way to meet them.
> — Charlotte M. Yonge *Beechcroft at Rockstone* (1888)

skeleton at the feast a reminder of serious or saddening things in the midst of enjoyment, originally in allusion to an ancient Egyptian custom recorded in Herodotus's *Histories*, which tells of a carved and painted wooden corpse in a coffin being carried round the room at parties, and shown to guests with the words, 'Look on this, for this will be your lot when you are dead.'

Skeleton Coast an arid coastal area in Namibia, which comprises the northern part of the Namib desert, and extends from Walvis Bay in the south to the border with Angola.

skeleton in the cupboard a discreditable or embarrassing fact that someone wishes to keep secret (brought into literary use by Thackeray but probably already an existing expression).

Skevington's daughter an instrument of torture which so compressed the body as to force blood from the nose and ears, named after Leonard *Skevington*, Lieutenant of the Tower in the reign of Henry VIII, who invented the instrument. Also called *Scavenger's daughter*.

Skidbladnir in Scandinavian mythology, the magic ship made by the dwarfs for ➤ FREY; it was large enough to carry all the Aesir, but when not at sea it could be taken to pieces and folded up like a cloth to be put into one's pocket.

skid row a run-down part of a town frequented by vagrants and alcoholics. The term comes from an alteration of *skid road*, originally a part of a town frequented by loggers.

skiffle a kind of folk music with a blues or jazz flavour that was popular in the 1950s, played by a small group and mainly with a rhythmic accompaniment to a singing guitarist or banjoist, often incorporating improvised instruments such as washboards. Also, a style of 1920s and 1930s jazz deriving from blues, ragtime, and folk music, using both improvised and conventional instruments.

skimmington a procession made through a village intended to bring ridicule on and make an example of a nagging wife or an unfaithful husband. Recorded from the early 17th century, the term may come from *skimming-ladle*, used as a thrashing instrument during the procession.

skin see ➤ BEAUTY *is only skin deep*, ➤ SELL *the skin before one has caught the bear*.

Skinfaxi in Scandinavian mythology, the name, 'Shining mane', of the horse of the day.

Skinner during the American War of Independence, a marauder who committed depredations on the neutral ground between the British and American lines.

Skinner box an apparatus for studying instrumental conditioning in animals (typically rats or pigeons) in which the animal is isolated and provided with a lever or switch which it learns to use to obtain a reward, such as a food pellet, or to avoid a punishment, such as an electric shock. It is named after Burrhus Frederic *Skinner* (1904–90), American behaviourist psychologist, who promoted the view that the proper aim of psychology should be to predict behaviour, and hence be able to control it.

the Skins informal name for the 5th Royal Inniskilling Dragoon Guards, from an alteration of *Inniskilling*.

skittle see ➤ LIFE *isn't all beer and skittles*.

skookum an evil spirit (especially among northwest North American Indians). The word is Chinook Jargon.

skothending in skaldic verse, rhyme formed with the same consonant or consonant cluster preceded by differing vowels; half-rhyme.

Skraeling an Inuit or other indigenous inhabitant of Greenland or ➤ VINLAND (on the NE coast of North America) at the time of early Norse settlement.

skull and crossbones a representation of a skull with two thigh bones crossed below it as an emblem of piracy or death.

> The nuclear submarine . . . [was] flying the Jolly Roger to denote their success in sinking the Argentine cruiser . . . The Skull-and-Crossbones denotes a 'kill'.
> — *Times* 5 July 1982

skunkworks an experimental laboratory or department of a company or institution, typically smaller than and independent of its main research division; *Skunk Works* was originally the trademark name of an engineering and design technical consultancy service provided by the Lockheed Advanced Development Company.

The term is said to derive from the fact that the original operation was located next to a plastics factory which reminded workers there of the outdoor still called the 'Skonk Works' in the 'L'il Abner' comic strip by the cartoonist, Al Capp, in which one of the characters, Injun Joe, would make 'kickapoo joy juice' from old shoes and dead skunk. To avoid infringement of copyright, the first vowel was changed when the name was registered.

sky see also ➤ MACKEREL *sky*, ➤ PIE *in the sky*.

if the sky falls we shall catch larks proverbial saying, mid 15th century; meaning that something will be attainable only in the most unlikely circumstances.

sky-blue pink a non-existent colour; recorded from the mid 20th century.

skyhook an imaginary or fanciful device by which something could be suspended in the air; the first recorded usage, reported in *Aeroplane* 10 March 1915, appeared in 'this machine is not fitted with sky-hooks', a response to the command, 'remain aloft awaiting orders'.

Skylab an American orbiting space laboratory launched in 1973, used for experiments in zero gravity and for astrophysical studies until 1974.

Skylon a spire resembling a spindle in shape, especially that originally designed for the South Bank exhibition in London at the Festival of Britain in 1951.

slam in bridge, a **grand slam** (all thirteen tricks) or **small slam** (twelve tricks), for which bonus points are scored if bid and made. Recorded from the early 17th century, and originally the name of a card game, the word may come from obsolete *slampant* 'trickery'.

See also ➤ GRAND *slam*.

slang a type of language that consists of words and phrases that are regarded as very informal, are more common in speech than writing, and are typically restricted to a particular context or group of people. The word is recorded from the mid 18th century, but the ultimate origin is unknown.

See also ➤ BACK *slang*, ➤ RHYMING *slang*.

slapstick comedy based on deliberately clumsy actions and humorously embarrassing events; a device consisting of two flexible pieces of wood joined together at one end, used by clowns and in pantomime to produce a loud slapping noise.

slash a genre of science fiction, chiefly published in fanzines, in which any of various male pairings from popular films or books is portrayed as having a homosexual relationship. The term, which refers to an oblique printed stroke / used between the adjoining names or initials of the characters concerned, seems to have originated among fans of the 1960s science-fiction series ➤ STAR *Trek*, in stories centring on the relationship between *Captain Kirk* and *Mr Spock* (*K/S* is an alternative name for the genre).

the Slashers a nickname for the 28th Foot, acquired during the American War of Independence.

Slaughter's Coffee House opened by Thomas Slaughter in 1692 on St Martin's Lane, and the favourite resort of artists including Hogarth, Gainsborough, and Haydon.

Slav a member of a group of peoples in central and eastern Europe speaking Slavic languages. The name comes from medieval Greek and late Latin, and is also the base of ➤ SLAVE.

Slava (among Orthodox Serbs) a festival of a family saint. The word is Serbo-Croat, and means literally 'renown, honour'.

slave a person who is the legal property of another and is forced to obey them. The word comes in Middle English from a shortening of Old French *esclave*, equivalent of medieval Latin *sclava* 'Slavonic (captive)': the Slavonic peoples had been reduced to a servile state by conquest in the 9th century.

See also ➤ WHITE *slave*.

Slave Coast part of the west coast of Africa, between the Volta River and Mount Cameroon, from which slaves were exported in the 16th–19th centuries.

Slave King a member of a dynasty founded by a former slave, Qutb uddin Aibak, which ruled the Delhi Sultanate from 1206 to 1290.

Slave of the Lamp in the story of ➤ ALADDIN, a genie summoned by rubbing a magic lamp and

bound to perform the wishes of the lamp's possessor.

Slave State any of the Southern states of the US in which slavery was legal before the Civil War.

Slavonic see ➤ CHURCH *Slavonic*.

sleaze factor the sleazy or sordid aspect of a situation as applied to political scandals and alleged corruption involving officials of an administration. The term was applied initially, in US politics, to scandals and alleged corruption involving officials of the Reagan administration; in the UK in the 1980s and 1990s it was applied to a number of political scandals, resignations, and instances of alleged malpractice, such as the ➤ CASH *for questions* affair.

sleep see ➤ *an* HOUR*'s sleep before midnight is worth two after,* ➤ SIX *hours sleep for a man, seven for a woman, and eight for a fool*.

sleepers see ➤ SEVEN *Sleepers*.

Sleeping Beauty the heroine of a fairy-tale, Charles Perrault's *La belle au bois dormant*, who is put under a curse by a resentful fairy who has not been invited to her christening; as a result, the princess pricks her finger on a spindle and falls into a sleep which last for a hundred years, while a hedge of briars grows up around the sleeping palace. Finally a young prince finds his way into the castle and wakes the princess with a kiss.

> It has been a Sleeping Beauty story so far. Treasure for the winning—a thorn hedge—and slain lovers!
> — Mrs Humphrey Ward *Daphne* (1909)

let sleeping dogs lie proverbial saying, late 14th century.

Sleepy Hollow in Washington Irving's *Sketch Book* (1820), a name given to a place with a soporific atmosphere or characterized by torpidity (from the name of a valley near Tarrytown (Irving's home) in Westchester county, New York State).

> Taking over CentCom two years ago, he whipped a Sleepy Hollow headquarters into fighting trim.
> — *Newsweek* 11 March 1991

sleeve see also ➤ *an* ACE *up one's sleeve,* ➤ *a* CARD *up one's sleeve,* ➤ HIPPOCRATES*' sleeve,* ➤ STRETCH *your arm no further than your sleeve will reach*.

sleeveless archaic term meaning, pointless, unprofitable; a **sleeveless answer** was originally one that was irrelevant or trivial; a **sleeveless errand** was sometimes one invented to get someone out of the way for a time.

Sleipnir in Scandinavian mythology, the name of Odin's eight-legged horse, son of ➤ SVADILFARI and the god ➤ LOKI in the shape of a mare.

sleuth-hound old-fashioned term for a bloodhound. The first element originally meant 'track' or 'trail', and the animal was used for tracking fugitives.

a slice off a cut loaf isn't missed proverbial saying, late 16th century.

the best thing since sliced bread a particularly notable invention or discovery.

slick see ➤ SAM *Slick*.

slip see ➤ *there's* MANY *a slip 'twixt cup and lip*.

slipper see ➤ HUNT *the slipper*.

Hans Sloane (1660–1753), Irish physician and naturalist. He purchased the manor of Chelsea and endowed the Chelsea Physic Garden. His collections were purchased by the nation and his books and specimens formed the basis of the British Museum Library and the Natural History Museum in London.

Sloane Ranger a fashionable upper-class young person (typically a woman) of independent means, especially one living in London. The term was coined in the 1970s, from *Sloane* Square, London + Lone *Ranger*, the name of a fictitious cowboy hero.

slogan a short and striking or memorable phrase used in advertising; a motto associated with a political party or movement or other group. The word originally meant 'a Scottish Highland war cry', and comes (in the early 16th century) from Scottish Gaelic *sluagh-ghairm*, from *sluagh* 'army' + *gairm* 'shout'.

slop slang term for a policeman; from an alteration of *ecilop*, back-slang for *police*, recorded from the mid 19th century.

Dr Slop nickname given to John Stoddart (1773–1856) during his editorship of 'The New Times' (*c*.1817–28); he was the subject of several satires, such as 'A Slap at Slop' (1820). At an earlier period, the name had been applied to the antiquary and physician John Burton (1710–71), who was satirized as *Dr Slop* in Sterne's *Tristram Shandy* (1759–67).

Sloper see ➤ ALLY *Sloper*.

Slough of Despond a deep boggy place in John Bunyan's *The Pilgrim's Progress* (1678) between the City of Destruction and the gate at the beginning of ➤ CHRISTIAN's journey; in extended use, the term is used for any general condition of hopelessness and gloom.

> Its release was strategically sandwiched between the two most hyped movies of the summer . . . evidently judged to be the Slough of Despond slot, when American moviegoers would be walking around with seven dollars burning a hole in their pockets and wondering what in the world to do with themselves.
> — *New York Review of Books* 19 September 1996

slow-belly archaic term for a lazy or indolent person, a sluggard; the term is recorded from the early 17th century, and refers to Tyndale's version of Titus 1:12 (followed by the Authorized Version) 'the Cretians are…slow bellies', a rendering of Greek *gasteres argai*, literally 'slothful bellies'.

slow but sure proverbial saying, late 17th century; sure here means 'sure-footed, deliberate'. The related saying **slow and steady wins the race** is recorded from the mid 18th century.

slow-worm the *slow-worm* (also called the ➤ BLINDWORM) was traditionally regarded as venomous; the first element in Old English was *slā* (of uncertain origin), and was not associated with the adjective *slow* before the 16th century. In early glossaries, the name is used to render various Latin names for snakes.

slugabed a lazy person who stays in bed late; the first element represents the rare verb *slug* 'be lazy or slow'.

slughorn a trumpet; from a misunderstanding by ➤ *Thomas* CHATTERTON (1752–70) of an earlier variant of *slogan* 'a war-cry'; Chatterton's *Battle of Hastings* has, 'Some caught a slughorne, and an onsette wounde.' The term was famously used by Browning:

> Dauntless the slug-horn to my lips I set,
> And blew. '*Childe Roland to the Dark Tower came.*'
> — Robert Browning 'Childe Roland to the Dark Tower Came' (1855)

slype a covered way or passage between a cathedral transept and the chapter house or deanery. Recorded from the mid 19th century, the word may be a variant of dialect *slipe* 'long narrow piece of ground'.

Smalcaldic alliance an alliance of Protestant States formed at *Schmalkalden*, a town in Thuringia in central Germany, in 1534.

small see also ➤ the BEST things come in small packages, ➤ small choice in ROTTEN apples.

small beer a thing that is considered unimportant, from an archaic term for weak beer. The figurative use may originally have referred to Shakespeare's *Othello* (1602–4), 'To suckle fools and chronicle small beer'.

small deer archaic expression for small creatures collectively, *deer* having originally been used for any quadruped; the archaic use may allude to Shakespeare's *King Lear* (1605–6), 'But mice and rats, and such small deer, Hath been Tom's food for seven long year.'

Small-endian in Swift's *Gulliver's Travels* (1726), a member of the faction (opposed to the ➤ BIG-endians) who believed that eggs should be broken at the smaller end before they are eaten.

the small hours the early hours of the morning after midnight, denoted by the low numbers one, two, and so on; the term is first recorded in Dickens's *Sketches by Boz* (2nd series, 1836), in a reference to guests 'who used to come at ten o'clock, and begin to get happy about the small hours'.

small is beautiful proverbial saying, late 20th century, expressing the belief that small-scale organizations are more efficient and effective than large-scale ones; originally the title of a book (1973) by E. F. Schumacher.

small print printed matter in small type; inconspicuous details or conditions printed in an agreement or contract, especially ones that may prove unfavourable.

> Read the small print carefully and you'll see that with one company, even with insurance cover, you're liable to a £13 administration fee if you cancel within six weeks of departure.
>
> — *Holiday Which?* March 1991

smallpox an acute contagious viral disease, with fever and pustules usually leaving permanent scars. It was effectively eradicated through vaccination by 1979. Recorded from the early 16th century, the term represents the plural of *small-pock*, each of the pustules characterizing the illness. It was originally written as two words, to distinguish the illness from the *great pox*, or syphilis.

Smalls informal name at Oxford University for the former examination officially called *Responsions*; the name is recorded from the mid 19th century,

and may perhaps reflect an association of the obsolete Latin expressions *in parvisiis* or *in parviso* (*parvis* here meaning 'a public or academic conference or disputation') with *parvis* ablative plural of *parvus* 'small'.

smaragd archaic term for a precious stone of a bright green colour, an emerald; the word comes (in Middle English) via Old French *smaragde* or Latin *smaragdus*, from the base of ➤ EMERALD.

smart alec a person considered irritating because they know a great deal or always have a clever answer to a question; the term is recorded from the mid 19th century, and is originally US.

smart bomb a radio-controlled or laser-guided bomb, often with inbuilt computer. The concept of such missiles which could home in on a target with very high levels of accuracy dates from the early 1970s, but enjoyed considerable exposure during the Gulf War of 1991.

smart card a plastic bank card or similar device with an embedded microprocessor, used in conjunction with an electronic card-reader to authorize or provide particular services, especially the automatic transfer of funds between bank accounts.

smart money originally (in the late 17th century), money paid to sailors, soldiers, and others as compensation for disablement or injuries received while on duty or at work; *smart* here meant 'physical pain'.

In the modern usage of *smart money*, money bet or invested by people with expert knowledge, recorded from the 1920s, *smart* is the adjective meaning 'quick-witted'.

Smectymnus the collective pen-name, formed from their initials, of five Presbyterian divines, Stephen Marshall, Edmund Calamy, Thomas Young, Matthew Newcomen, and William Spurstow, who in 1641 published an attack on episcopacy, *An Answer to a Book*, in answer to Bishop Hall's *Humble Remonstrance*.

smell the faculty or power of perceiving odours or scents by means of the organs in the nose; one of the five senses.

See also ➤ MONEY has no smell.

smell of the lamp show signs of laborious study and effort; the reference is to an oil-lamp, and according to Plutarch the criticism was once made of the work of ➤ DEMOSTHENES, 'His impromptus smell of the lamp', meaning that his speeches were written rather than spoken orations.

smellfungus a discontented person, a grumbler, a fault-finder, from Sterne's name for Smollett, with reference to the carping tone of Smollett's *Travels through France and Italy* (1766).

> Smellfungus people, who love to torment themselves.
> — Frances Trollope *Visit to Italy* (1842)

smells and bells derogatory term for rituals of Christian worship such as the burning of incense and ringing of bells, especially as characterizing High Anglican worship.

Smersh the popular name for the Russian counter-espionage organization, originating during the Second World War, responsible for maintaining security within the Soviet armed and intelligence services.

Bedřich Smetana (1824–84), Czech composer. Regarded as the founder of Czech music, he was dedicated to the cause of Czech nationalism, as is apparent in his operas, such as *The Bartered Bride* (1866), and in the cycle of symphonic poems *Ma Vlast ('My Country'* 1874–9). He died from syphilis, which had left him completely deaf in 1874.

Samuel Smiles (1812–1904), British writer, author of *Self-Help* (1859) and other works on self-improvement by personal effort and initiative.

> Religion was Smilesian—heaven looked with favour on those who strove to improve themselves—unto him that hath shall be given.
> — George Mackay Brown *Orkney Tapestry* (1969)

smiley a symbol which, when viewed sideways, represents a smiling face, formed by the characters :-), an ➤ EMOTICON used in electronic communications to indicate that the writer is pleased or joking.

smite see ➤ *smite under the* FIFTH *rib*.

smith see also ➤ WAYLAND *the Smith*.

Adam Smith (1723–90), Scottish economist and philosopher. Often regarded as the founder of modern economics, he advocated minimal state interference in economic matters and discredited mercantilism; he is the author of an early use of the expression *nation of shopkeepers*:

> To found a great empire for the sole purpose of raising up a people of customers, may at first sight appear a project fit only for a nation of shopkeepers. It is, however, a project altogether unfit for a nation of shopkeepers; but extremely fit for a nation whose government is influenced by shopkeepers.
> — Adam Smith *Wealth of Nations* (1776)

John Smith (1580–1631), English soldier and colonist, who claimed in his memoirs to have been rescued from death by the Algonquian princess ➤ POCAHONTAS.

Joseph Smith (1805–44), American religious leader and founder of the Church of Jesus Christ of Latter-Day Saints (the Mormons). In 1827, according to his own account, he was led by divine revelation to find the sacred texts written by the prophet Mormon, which he published as *The Book of Mormon* in 1830. He founded the Mormon Church in the same year and later established a large community in Illinois, where he was arrested and murdered by the local militia.

the Smith of Smiths Macaulay's name for the English clergyman and wit Sydney Smith (1771–1845):

> Down I went, and to my utter amazement beheld the Smith of Smiths, Sydney Smith.
> — Lord Macaulay letter to his father, 21 July 1826

Smith Square a square in Westminster, London, the location since 1958 of the headquarters of the British Conservative Party and (between 1928 and 1980) of the Labour Party (see ➤ TRANSPORT *House*). *Smith Square* has thus been used for the leadership of the Conservative Party (and occasionally, for the leadership of both parties).

> According to ministers there is almost as much dead wood in Smith Square as in Kew Gardens.
> — *Independent* 27 September 1987

smithereens small pieces or fragments into which something is broken or smashed; first recorded (in the early 19th century) in Irish contexts, and probably from Irish *smídirín*.

Smithfield a locality in London, long the site of a cattle and horse market and then a meat-market; the name was originally *Smethefield*, from *smethe* 'smooth'. In the 16th century, it was also the place where heretics were executed at the stake.

Smithsonian Institution a US foundation for education and scientific research in Washington DC, opened in 1846 and now responsible for administering many museums, art galleries, and other establishments. It originated in a £100,000 bequest in the will of the English chemist and mineralogist James *Smithson* (1765–1829).

smog fog or haze intensified by smoke or other atmospheric pollutants; the word is recorded from the early 20th century, and is a blend of *smoke* and *fog*.

the Smoke archaic term for a big city, especially London, with reference to its many smoking chimneys.; cf. ➤ AULD *Reekie*.

See also ➤ BIG *Smoke*.

smoke and mirrors deception, dissimulation, bluff; especially, an obscuring or embellishment of the truth with misleading or irrelevant information; originally, with reference to the illusion created by conjuring tricks.

> The grandstanding of Congress, claiming taxpayer money will no longer fund these types of caucuses, is in fact so much smoke and mirrors.
> — *New Jersey* April 1995

smoke-farthing a Whitsuntide offering traditionally made by the householders of a diocese to the cathedral church; a hearth-tax.

smoke-filled room regarded as the characteristic venue of those in control of a party meeting to arrange a political decision, from Kirke Simpson news report, filed 12 June 1920, '[Warren] Harding of Ohio was chosen by a group of men in a smoke-filled room early today as Republican candidate for President'; usually attributed to Harry Daugherty, one of Harding's supporters, who appears merely to have concurred with this version of events, when pressed for comment by Simpson.

from the smoke into the smother from one evil to an even worse one; often with allusion to Shakespeare's *As You Like It* (1598), 'Thus must I from the smoke unto the smother; From tyrant duke unto a tyrant brother.'

no smoke without fire proverbial saying, late Middle English.

Smokey Bear the name of an animal character used in US fire-prevention advertising and characteristically wearing a wide-brimmed hat; *Smokey Bear* was then used in the US as a name for a state policeman, since the hats worn by state troopers resembled those in the cartoon.

smoking can seriously damage your health government health warning now required by British law to be printed on cigarette packets; in form 'Smoking can damage your health' from early 1970s.

a smoking pistol a piece of incontrovertible incriminating evidence; on the assumption that a person found with a smoking pistol or gun must be the guilty party; particularly associated with Barber B. Conable's comment on a Watergate tape revealing President Nixon's wish to limit FBI involvement in the investigation: 'I guess we have found the smoking pistol, haven't we?'

smother see ➤ *from the* SMOKE *into the smother*.

Jan Christiaan Smuts (1870–1950), South African statesman and soldier, Prime Minister 1919–24 and 1939–48. He led Boer forces during the Second Boer War, but afterwards supported the policy of Anglo-Boer cooperation. He commanded Allied troops against German East Africa (1916) and later helped to found the ➤ LEAGUE *of Nations*, the necessity for which in the wake of the First World War he outlined in a pamphlet of 1919:

> Mankind is once more on the move. The very foundations have been shaken and loosened, and things are again fluid. The tents have been struck, and the great caravan of humanity is once more on the march.
> — Jan Christiaan Smuts pamphlet, 1919

snail mail the ordinary postal system as opposed to electronic mail; the term is recorded from the first half of the 1980s.

snake proverbial allusions to the snake focus on its venomous bite as representing a lurking danger; it is a type of deceit and treachery, as with reference to the fable by Aesop, in which the man who had warmed a chilled snake in his own bosom was bitten for his pains. The word is recorded from Old English (in form *snaka*) and is of Germanic origin.

Snakes are the emblems of ➤ St PATRICK, who was said to have banished them from Ireland.

See also ➤ AESCULAPIAN *snake*, ➤ SERPENT.

snake charmer an entertainer who appears to make snakes move by playing music, although the snake is in fact following the movement of the player's instrument rather than the sound of the music. The image is of longstanding, as in the biblical reference in Psalm 58:4–5 to the 'deaf adder…Which will not hearken to the voices of charmers: charming never so wisely.'

snake in the grass a treacherous or deceitful person. The expression comes originally from Virgil's *Eclogues*: '*latet anguis in herba* [there is a snake in the grass].'

snake oil a substance with no real medicinal value sold as a remedy for all diseases.

snake-stone dialect term for an ammonite; also, a porous or absorbent substance traditionally regarded as efficacious in curing snake-bite or as a remedy against poison.

snakepit a pit containing poisonous snakes; in early legends, used as a means of execution, as in the story of ➤ GUNNAR, who is said to have been put to death in this way by Atli.

In the 20th century, the term has been used for a scene of vicious behaviour or ruthless competition, and specifically (after the title of a novel (1947) by M. J. Ward), a mental hospital.

snakes and ladders a children's game in which players move counters along a board, gaining an advantage by moving up pictures of ladders or a disadvantage by moving down pictures of snakes; the game was put on the market in the early part of the 20th century.

snakes in Iceland an allusive phrase referring to something posited only to be dismissed as nonexistent; the reference is to Dr Johnson's comment on Horrebow's *Natural History of Iceland* (1758):

> Johnson had said that he could repeat a complete chapter of 'The Natural History of Iceland', from the Danish of *Horrebow*, the whole of which was exactly thus:—'Chap. lxxii. *Concerning Snakes*. There are no snakes to be met with throughout the whole island'.
> — James Boswell *Life of Samuel Johnson* (1791)

snallygaster a mythical monster supposedly found in Maryland; the name comes from German *schnelle geister* 'quick spirits'.

snap, crackle, and pop an advertiser's 1950s catchphrase for the breakfast cereal Rice Krispies, representing the sound produced when milk is added to the bowl.

snapdragon a plant bearing spikes of brightly coloured two-lobed flowers which gape like a mouth when a bee lands on the curved lip; the name is recorded from the late 16th century.

In the 17th and 18th centuries, *snapdragon* also denoted a representation of a dragon, especially one constructed so as to open and shut its mouth, used in mayoral or civic shows or possessions.

Snapdragon is also recorded, from the early 18th century, as a game (typically played at Christmas) which consisted of snatching raisins out of a bowl or dish of burning brandy and eating them while still alight.

snare a trap for catching birds or mammals, typically one having a noose of wire or cord; often in figurative and allusive use, as in Psalms 91:3, 'Surely he shall deliver thee from the snare of the fowler'.

snark an imaginary animal (used to refer to someone or something that is difficult to track down);

the name is a nonsense word coined by Lewis Carroll in *The Hunting of the Snark* (1876).

> I have yet to glimpse a live snark, but many a rare or shy forest animal has first been described to science on the basis of its remains in a hunter's pot.
> — *New Scientist* 28 May 1994

sneeze an act or the sound of involuntarily expelling air from the nose and mouth due to irritation of one's nostrils. The custom of blessing or wishing a person well when they sneeze is of long-standing; the *Golden Legend* suggests that it derives from a time of plague which afflicted Christians in Rome, in which a sneeze was a sign that someone had caught the plague, but Pliny in his *Natural History* (AD 77) refers to Tiberius Caesar following the custom.

A traditional rhyme, recorded in the mid 19th century, links sneezing with divination:

> If you sneeze on a Monday, you sneeze for danger;
> Sneeze on a Tuesday, kiss a stranger;
> Sneeze on a Wednesday, sneeze for a letter;
> Sneeze on a Thursday, something better;
> Sneeze on a Friday, sneeze for sorrow;
> Sneeze on a Saturday, see your sweetheart tomorrow.
> Sneeze on a Sunday, and the devil will have domination over you all the week!
> — in *Athenaeum* 1848

See also ➤ COUGHS *and sneezes spread diseases.*

Hannah Snell (1723–92), female soldier, who is said to have enlisted in the army in 1745 in search of her missing husband. Unjustly sentenced to five hundred lashes by a hostile sergeant, she deserted, but at Portsmouth joined the marines, and subsequently served as a common sailor. She was said to have been in action on the coast of Coromandel, and to have been wounded in the campaign.

In 1750, hearing of her husband's death, she left the ship when it was paid off, and shortly afterwards a narrative of her adventures was published under the title of 'The Female Soldier: or the Surprising Adventures of Hannah Snell'.

In later life, she remarried, took a public house at Wapping which she named 'The Female Soldier', and finally died insane in the Bethlehem hospital at the age of sixty-nine.

Snellen test an eyesight test using rows of letters printed in successively decreasing sizes (the **Snellen scale**) of which patients are asked to read as many as they can. It is named after Hermann *Snellen* (1834–1908), Dutch ophthalmologist.

snipe a wading bird of marshes and wet meadows, with brown camouflaged plumage, a long straight bill, and typically a drumming display flight; in literary use, *snipe* has occasionally been employed as a derogatory term for someone regarded as trivial or contemptible.

snood an ornamental hairnet or fabric bag worn over the hair at the back of a woman's head; originally, a ribbon or band worn by unmarried women in Scotland to confine their hair.

Snoopy cartoon character, a frustrated beagle given to fantasies, from Charles M. Schulz's comic strip ➤ PEANUTS.

Snorri Sturluson (1178–1241), Icelandic historian and poet. A leading figure of medieval Icelandic literature, he wrote the *Younger Edda* or *Prose Edda* and the *Heimskringla*, a history of the kings of Norway from mythical times to the year 1177.

snow atmospheric water vapour frozen into ice crystals and falling in light white flakes or lying on the ground as a white layer; often taken as a type of whiteness and brightness.

See also ➤ DRIVEN *snow*, ➤ *Our* LADY *of the Snows*.

Snow Queen a cold-hearted woman, from the chief character in a Hans Christian Andersen fairy tale with this title; the cruel but beautiful queen who carries off Kay to her frozen kingdom, from which he is ultimately rescued by his playmate Gerda.

> She gave me the inscrutable Snow Queen smile.
> — Len Deighton *Spy Story* (1974)

Snow White in the traditional fairy story, the princess whose wicked stepmother attempts to murder her, and who finds refuge with the ➤ SEVEN *Dwarfs*. The queen, whose magic mirror has told her that Snow White is still 'the fairest in the land', seeks out the dwarfs' cottage in the guise of a pedlar and tries to kill her stepdaughter, with a poisoned lace, a poisoned comb, and finally a poisoned apple, one bite of which apparently kills her. The Dwarfs, who cannot revive her, place her in a coffin of glass; she is found there by a prince who raises her so that the piece of apple falls from her lips and she regains consciousness. The story was filmed by Disney in 1937.

Snowdon a mountain in NW Wales, the highest mountain in Wales, the Welsh name of which is *Yr Wyddfa*.

Snowdon herald the title of one of six Scottish heralds; *Snowdon* here may be a name for Stirling,

or may refer to the castle of *Snowdoune* in the county of Ross.

snowman see ➤ ABOMINABLE *Snowman*.

snuff movie a pornographic film or video recording of an actual murder (the name refers to the *snuffing out* of life which such a film or video portrays). Privately circulated *snuff videos* were allegedly known to the police in the 1970s, and figured briefly in the news in 1990 in reports of a paedophile ring involved in the production of such films; the crimes were linked with the disappearance of a number of young boys in the UK in the 1980s.

John Soane (1753–1837), English architect. His later work avoided unnecessary ornament and adopted structural necessity as the basis of design. His designs included the Bank of England (1788–1833, since rebuilt) and his house in London, now a museum.

soapbox a box or crate, originally one in which soap had been packed, used as a makeshift stand by a public speaker. Although the soapbox as a device for public speaking is associated with the first half of the 20th century, it had a brief renaissance in the British general election of 1992, when the Conservative Prime Minister John Major, faced with unfavourable polls, reverted to it as his personal means for making speeches on the hustings.

soap opera a television or radio drama serial dealing typically with daily events in the lives of the same group of characters, so named (in the 1930s) because such serials were originally sponsored in the US by soap manufacturers.

Soapy Sam nickname of Bishop Samuel Wilberforce (1805–73), applied after Lord Westbury in the House of Lords had described his synodical judgement on 'Essays and Reviews' as 'a well-lubricated set of words, a sentence so oily and saponaceous that no one can grasp it'. Wilberforce himself declared that he owed his nickname to the fact that 'though often in hot water, he always came out with clean hands'.

Sobieski see ➤ JOHN *Sobieski*.

socage a feudal tenure of land involving payment of rent or other non-military service to a superior. Recorded from Middle English, the word comes from Anglo-Norman French *soc*, a variant of ➤ SOKE.

Social and **Liberal Democrats** (in the UK) a political party formed in 1988 from a majority of the membership of the Liberal Party and the Social Democratic Party. It was officially renamed in 1989 as the Liberal Democrats.

social chapter the section of the ➤ MAASTRICHT *Treaty* dealing with social policy, and in particular workers' rights and welfare. It originated in the *social charter* of December 1989, signed by eleven European member states, and dealing in particular with workers' rights and welfares. The *social chapter*, which developed from this, recommended among other things the adoption of a minimum wage.

socialism a political and economic theory of social organization which advocates that the means of production, distribution, and exchange should be owned or regulated by the community as a whole. The early history of the word is somewhat obscure, but the first use of French *socialisme* appears to have been in the Globe of 13 February 1832, where it was used in contrast to *personnalité*; in its modern sense it has been variously attributed to Leroux or Reybaud, writing a few years after this. An alternative theory is that the word was coined in 1835 in the discussions of a society founded by ➤ *Robert* OWEN.

socialist realism the theory of art, literature, and music officially sanctioned by the state in some Communist countries (especially in the Soviet Union under Stalin), by which artistic work was supposed to reflect and promote the ideals of a socialist society.

society the sense of society to denote 'the aggregate of people living together in a more or less ordered community' is recorded from the mid 17th century; it was however famously questioned in the 1980s by Margaret Thatcher:

> There is no such thing as Society. There are individual
> men and women, and there are families.
> — *Woman's Own* 31 October 1987

Society of Jesus official name for the ➤ JESUITS.

Socinian a member of a sect founded by Laelius and Faustus *Socinus*, two Italian theologians of the 16th century, who denied the divinity of Christ.

sock a light shoe worn by comic actors on the ancient Greek and Roman stage; hence used allusively to denote comedy or the comic muse.

> The comic Sock that binds thy Feet.
> — William Collins *Odes* (1747)

sock and **buskin** comedy and tragedy, the drama or theatrical profession as a whole.

> He was a critic upon operas, too,
> And knew all niceties of the sock and buskin.
> — Lord Byron *Beppo* (1817)

Socrates (469–399 BC), ancient Athenian philosopher. As represented in the writings of his disciple Plato, he engaged in dialogue with others in an attempt to reach understanding and ethical concepts by exposing and dispelling error (the **Socratic method**). Charged with introducing strange gods and corrupting the young, Socrates was sentenced to death and died by drinking hemlock.

Socratic elenchus refutation by short questions eliciting from the proponent of a thesis its absurd or unacceptable implications.

Socratic irony a pose of ignorance assumed in order to entice others into making statements that can then be challenged.

from soda to hock from beginning to end; in the game of faro, *soda* is the exposed top card at the beginning of a deal, and *hock* is the last card remaining in the box after all the others have been dealt.

Frederick William Soddy (1877–1956), English physicist. He assisted William Ramsay in the discovery of helium and formulated a theory of isotopes, the word *isotope* being coined by him in 1913, after work on radioactive decay.

Sodom a town in ancient Palestine, probably south of the Dead Sea, which according to Genesis 19:24 was destroyed by fire from heaven, together with Gomorrah, the other of the two ➤ CITIES *of the Plain*, for the wickedness of its inhabitants.

The term *sodomy* derives from the late Latin *peccatum Sodomiticum* 'sin of Sodom', since it is implied in Genesis 19:5 that the men of Sodom practised homosexual rape.

See also ➤ APPLE *of Sodom*.

Sodor a medieval diocese comprising the Hebrides and the Isle of Man; **Sodor and Man** has been the official name for the Anglican diocese of the Isle of Man since 1684. The name comes from Norse *Sudhr-eyjar* 'southern isles'; the islands belonged formerly to Norway.

a soft answer turneth away wrath proverbial saying, late 14th century; with biblical allusion to Proverbs 15:1.

softly, softly, catchee monkey proverbial saying, early 20th century, advocating caution or guile as the best way to achieve an end.

software the programs and other operating information used by a computer; the term is recorded from 1960, and is formed after *hardware*.

Soho the name of a district in the West End of London, noted for its foreign population, prostitutes, and restaurants, and latterly for its night clubs, striptease shows, and pornography shops.

soho a call used by huntsmen to direct the attention of the dogs or of other hunters to a hare which has been discovered or started, or to encourage them in the chase.

soil see ➤ BLOOD *and soil.*

Soka Gakkai a political and lay religious organization founded in Japan in 1930, based on the teachings of the Nichiren Buddhist sect.

Sokol a Slav gymnastic society aiming to promote a communal spirit and physical fitness, originating in Prague in 1862.

Sol in Roman mythology, the sun, especially when personified as a god; recorded in English from late Middle English.

solander a box made in the form of a book, for holding botanical specimens, maps, or other papers, and named after D. C. *Solander* (1736–82), Swedish botanist.

solar an upper chamber in a medieval house; the word comes (in Middle English, via Anglo-Norman French) from Latin *solarium* 'gallery, terrace'.

soldier ➤ *St* GEORGE, ➤ *St* MAURICE, ➤ *St* OsWALD, and ➤ *St* JAMES *the Great* are patron saints of soldiers.

Recorded from Middle English, the word comes via Old French *sould* '(soldier's) pay', from Latin *solidus* 'a gold coin of the later Roman Empire'.

See ➤ OLD *soldiers never die,* ➤ UNKNOWN *Soldier.*

soldier of fortune a person who works as a soldier for any country or group that will pay them; a mercenary; the term is first recorded in Robert Boyle's *Some Considerations touching the Style of the Holy Scriptures* (1661), 'war…is wont as well to raise soldiers of fortune as to ruin men of fortune'.

what the soldier said isn't evidence proverbial saying, mid 19th century; originally as a reference to Dickens:

> 'Little to do, and plenty to get, I suppose?' said Sergeant Buzfuz, with jocularity. 'Oh, quite enough to get, sir, as the soldier said ven they ordered him three hundred and fifty lashes,' replied Sam. 'You must not tell us what the soldier, or any other man, said, sir,' interposed the judge; 'it's not evidence.'
> — Charles Dickens *Pickwick Papers* (1837)

solecism a grammatical mistake in speech or writing; a breach of good manners, or piece of incorrect behaviour. The word is recorded from the mid 16th century, and comes ultimately from Greek *soloikismos*, from *soloikos* 'speaking incorrectly'.

Solemn League and Covenant an agreement made in 1643 between the English Parliament and the Scottish ➤ COVENANTERS during the English Civil War, by which the Scots would provide military aid in return for the establishment of a Presbyterian system in England, Scotland, and Ireland. Although the Scottish support proved crucial in the Parliamentary victory, the principal Presbyterian leaders were expelled from Parliament in 1647 and the covenant was never honoured.

Solemn Mass another term for ➤ HIGH *Mass.*

solicitor a member of the legal profession qualified to deal with conveyancing, the drawing up of wills, and other legal matters. A solicitor may also advise clients, instruct barristers, and represent clients in some courts.

The word is recorded from late Middle English, denoting an agent or deputy; it comes ultimately via Old French from Latin *sollicitare* 'agitate'.

Solicitor General (in the UK) the Crown law officer below the Attorney General or (in Scotland) below the Lord Advocate.

solid South the politically united Southern states of America, traditionally regarded as giving unwavering electoral support to the Democratic Party. The phrase was used in 1876 in a letter by the former Confederate general John Singleton Mosby (1833–1916).

Solidarity an independent trade union movement in Poland which developed into a mass campaign for political change and inspired popular opposition to Communist regimes across eastern Europe. Formed in 1980 under the leadership of Lech Wałęsa, it was banned in 1981 following the imposition of martial law. Legalized again in 1989, it won a majority in the elections of that year. The name is a translation of Polish *Solidarność*.

doctor solidus et copiosus contemporary description of the Franciscan Richard Middleton (fl.1280), whose name is inscribed on the tomb of ➤ *John* DUNS *Scotus* at Cologne as one of the fifteen doctors of his order; the words are Latin, and mean literally 'solid and abundant doctor'.

solipsism the view or theory that the self is all that can be known to exist; the word is recorded from the late 19th century, and comes from Latin *solus* 'alone' + *ipse* 'self'.

solitaire in the early 18th century, a person living in seclusion, a recluse; also, a precious stone, usually a diamond, set by itself.

From the mid 18th century, the term was also given to a game for one player, as a form of patience, or a game played by removing pegs one at a time from a board by jumping others over them from adjacent holes, the object being to be left with only one peg.

The word comes from Latin *solitarius* 'solitary'.

Solnhofen a village in Bavaria, Germany, near which there are extensive, thinly stratified beds of lithographic limestone dating from the Upper Jurassic period. These beds are noted as the chief source of ➤ ARCHAEOPTERYX fossils.

Solomon son of David, king of ancient Israel *c.*970–*c.*930 BC, builder of the first Jewish ➤ TEMPLE in Jerusalem. In the Bible Solomon is traditionally associated with the Song of Solomon, Ecclesiastes, and Proverbs, while his wisdom is illustrated by the ➤ JUDGEMENT *of Solomon*. Discontent with his rule, however, led to the secession of the northern tribes in the reign of his son Rehoboam.

See also ➤ WISDOM *of Solomon*.

the English Solomon James I and VI (also called *British Solomon*, *Scotch Solomon*).

Solomon's ring a magic ring belonging to ➤ SOLOMON, which according to the ➤ HAGGADA was thrown into the river and retrieved from a fish that had swallowed it.

Solomon's seal a figure like the Star of David. Also, a widely distributed plant of the lily family, having arching stems that bear a double row of broad leaves with drooping green and white flowers in their axils; the name has been variously explained as referring to markings seen on a transverse section of the rootstock, to the round scars left by the decay

of stems, or to the use of the root 'to seal and close up green wounds'.

Solon (*c.*630–*c.*560 BC), Athenian statesman and lawgiver. One of the ➤ SEVEN *Sages*, he revised the code of laws established by Draco (see ➤ DRACO¹), making it less severe. His division of the citizens into four classes based on wealth rather than birth laid the foundations of Athenian democracy.

> Our Solons are not convened in the District of Columbia to spell out a new moral code for us.
> — *Audubon* January 1996

solstice either of the two times in the year, the ➤ SUMMER *solstice* and the ➤ WINTER *solstice*, when the sun reaches its highest or lowest point in the sky at noon, marked by the longest and shortest days. Recorded from Middle English, the word comes via Old French from Latin *solstitium*, from *sol* 'sun' + *stit-* 'stopped, stationary'.

if you're not part of the solution, you're part of the problem proverbial saying, late 20th century.

Alexander Solzhenitsyn (1918–), Russian novelist. He spent eight years in a labour camp for criticizing Stalin and began writing on his release. From 1963 his books were banned in the Soviet Union, and he was exiled in 1974, eventually returning to Russia in 1994.

soma an intoxicating drink prepared from a plant and used in Vedic ritual, believed to be the drink of the gods.

Somerset House in London, on the site of the house built by the Duke of *Somerset*, Lord Protector for Edward VI; the current neoclassical building dates from the late 18th century, and was built by the Scottish architect Sir William Chambers (1723–96); since 1990 it has housed the Courtauld Institute Galleries. Between its establishment in 1837 and 1990, the national registry for births, marriages, and deaths was at *Somerset House*.

Somerville for women see ➤ LADY *Margaret Hall for ladies*.

something see also ➤ *something is* ROTTEN *in the state of Denmark*.

you don't get something for nothing proverbial saying, late 19th century.

something is better than nothing proverbial saying, mid 16th century.

Somme a river of northern France, the upper valley of which was the scene of heavy fighting in the First World War.

Battle of the Somme a major battle of the First World War between the British and the Germans, on the Western Front in northern France July–November 1916. Following a bombardment of German lines the British advanced from their trenches on foot to face the German machine guns; although the Germans retreated a few kilometres they took refuge in the fortified Hindenburg Line. More than a million men on both sides were killed or wounded.

son et lumière an entertainment held by night at a historic monument or building, telling its history by the use of lighting effects and recorded sound.

son of a gun a jocular or affectionate way of addressing or referring to someone (with reference to the guns carried aboard ships: the epithet is said to have been applied originally to babies born at sea to women allowed to accompany their husbands).

Son of Heaven a title given to the Emperor of China, translating Chinese *tiānzǐ*.

Son of Man a title of Jesus Christ, as in Matthew 8:20, 'The foxes have holes…but the Son of man hath not where to lay his head'.

horny-handed son of toil a labourer; originally coined by Lord Salisbury (1830–1903):

> The peculiar virtues of the horny-handed sons of toil received a severe shock in 1848, and finally collapsed in 1871.
> — Lord Salisbury in *Quarterly Review* October 1873

The expression was popularized in the US by Denis Kearney (1847–1907).

my son is my son till he gets him a wife, but my daughter's my daughter all the days of her life proverbial saying, late 17th century.

Sonderbund a league formed by the Roman Catholic cantons of Switzerland in 1843 and defeated in a civil war in 1847; in German, the name means 'special league, separate association'.

Sonderkommando in Nazi Germany, a detachment of prisoners in a concentration camp responsible for the disposal of the dead; a member of such a detachment; the name in German means 'special detachment'.

song a short poem or other set of words set to music or meant to be sung, often taken as the type

of something very cheap and inexpensive; Horace Walpole in a letter of 1751 commented of a sale that, 'The whole-length Vandykes went for a song!'

What! all this for a song? reported comment of the courtier and politician William Cecil, Lord Burghley (1529–98) to Queen Elizabeth I on being told to give a gratuity of £100 to the poet ➤ *Edmund* SPENSER in return for some poems. The anecdote is reported in 'The Life of Mr Edmund Spenser' (1751) by Thomas Birch.

a song in one's heart a feeling of joy or pleasure; originally with allusion to Lorenz Hart 'With a Song in my Heart', 1930 song. The phrase was used by the Labour politician Hugh Dalton (1887–1962) when Chancellor:

> I will find, and find with a song in my heart, whatever money is necessary to finance useful and practical proposals for developing these areas.
> — Hugh Dalton speech in the House of Commons, 9 April 1946

Song of Ascents each of the ➤ GRADUAL *psalms*, in the Revised Version entitled 'A Song of Ascents'.

Song of Degrees each of the ➤ GRADUAL *psalms*, in the Authorized Version entitled 'A Song of Degrees'.

The Song of Roland the medieval chanson which tells of the death of the paladin ➤ ROLAND at ➤ RONCESVALLES.

Song of Songs a book of the Bible containing an anthology of Hebrew love poems traditionally ascribed to ➤ SOLOMON but in fact dating from a much later period. Jewish and Christian writers have interpreted the book allegorically as representing God's relationship with his people, or with the soul.

Song of the Three Holy Children a book of the Apocrypha, an addition to the book of Daniel, telling of three Hebrew exiles, Ananias, Azarias, and Misael, thrown (with Daniel) into a furnace by Nebuchadnezzar; protected by God from the flames, they sang the words which in the Anglican service of matins is the canticle of the ➤ BENEDICITE, 'O all ye works of the Lord, bless ye the Lord'.

The story of the ➤ BURNING *fiery furnace* is also told in the book of Daniel; here the three cast into the fire (without Daniel) are named Shadrach, Meshach, and Abednego.

sons see also ➤ CLERGYMEN's *sons always turn out badly.*

sons of Belial evildoers. The original reference is biblical (from 1 Samuel 2:12), and was reinforced in the 17th century both by a reference in the 1663 *Book of Common Prayer* to the execution of Charles I, 'In permitting cruel men, sons of Belial (as on this day) to imbrue their hands in the blood of thine Anointed', and then by Milton:

> And when night
> Darkens the streets, then wander forth the sons
> Of Belial, flown with insolence and wine.
> — John Milton *Paradise Lost* (1776) bk. 1

sons of liberty an association of American nationalists during the colonial period; John Adams, in his diary of 1 July 1770, records that he 'Came home and took a pipe after supper with landlord, who is a staunch, zealous son of liberty'.

sons of thunder epithet of the apostles James and John, the sons of Zebedee, given as the translation of ➤ BOANERGES.

sons of Uisneach in the Ulster cycle, Naoise, husband of ➤ DEIRDRE, and his brothers, all killed by Conchobar in punishment for Naoise's elopement with Deirdre, Conchobar's promised wife.

soon ripe, soon rotten proverbial saying, late 14th century.

the sooner begun, the sooner done proverbial saying, late 16th century.

Sooner State informal name for Oklahoma. *Sooner* here is in the sense 'one who acts prematurely', i.e. a person who tried to get into the frontier territory of Oklahoma before the US government opened it to settlers in 1889.

soonest see ➤ LEAST *said, soonest mended.*

sooterkin an imaginary kind of afterbirth formerly attributed to Dutch women, and first recorded in John Cleveland (1613–58) in *The character of a diurnall-maker*, as 'There goes a report of the Holland women, that together with their children, they are delivered of a sooterkin, not unlike to a rat, which some imagine to be the offspring of the stoves.'

give a sop to Cerberus in allusion to the story in the *Aeneid* of the descent of Aeneas into the underworld; he was able to pass safely by the monstrous watchdog ➤ CERBERUS by drugging him with a specially prepared cake.

> Clintonite spinmeisters will hail this 'sop to Cerberus' as a summit triumph.
> — *Post* (Denver) 7 May 1995

St Sophia legendary mother of three virgin martyrs, Faith, Hope, and Charity; she supposedly died three days after their death, while praying at their tomb. The legend originated in the Eastern Church, and can be understood as an allegory of Divine Wisdom (*Haga Sophia*) from whom proceed the virtues of faith, hope, and charity.

☐ **FEAST DAY** Her feast day is 30 September.
See also ➤ ST *Sophia.*

sophist a paid teacher of philosophy and rhetoric in Greece in the Classical and Hellenistic periods, associated in popular thought with moral scepticism and specious reasoning. Recorded from the mid 16th century, the word comes ultimately via Latin from Greek *sophizesthai* 'devise, become wise', from *sophos* 'wise'.

sophisticated developed to a high degree of complexity; aware of and able to interpret complex issues; having, revealing, or proceeding from a great deal of worldly experience and knowledge of fashion and culture; these current uses are recorded from the 19th and 20th centuries. *Sophisticate* is recorded from late Middle English, as an adjective in the sense 'adulterated', and as a verb in the sense 'mix with a foreign substance'; it comes from medieval Latin *sophisticatus* 'tampered with'. The shift of sense probably occurred first in the adjective unsophisticated, from 'uncorrupted' via 'innocent' to 'inexperienced, uncultured'.

Sophocles (*c.*496–406 BC), Greek dramatist. His seven surviving plays are notable for their complexity of plot and depth of characterization, and for their examination of the relationship between mortals and the divine order.

sophomore in North America, a second-year university or high-school student. The word is recorded from the mid 17th century (originally, as a second-year student at Cambridge University), and comes from *sophum*, *sophom*, obsolete variants of *sophism* 'a fallacious argument, especially one used deliberately to deceive and serving as a University exercise'.

Sophonisba the daughter of Hasdrubal, a Carthaginian general, who avoided captivity by taking poison at the instigation of her betrothed Masinissa;

she was the subject of several plays. The notorious line 'Oh! Sophonisba! Sophonisba! Oh!', which occurs in the version by James Thomson (1730) was altered to 'Oh Sophonisba, I am wholly thine' in later editions, and parodied by Henry Fielding in *Tom Thumb* as 'O Huncamunca, Huncamunca O!'

Sophy a former title for the ruler of Persia associated especially with the ➤ SAFAVID dynasty; in early sources the title the **Grand Sophy** is also used. The word comes from Arabic *Ṣafī-al-dīn* 'pure of religion', given to Ismail Safi, the founder of the dynasty.

Thomas Sopwith (1888–1989), English aircraft designer. During the First World War he designed the fighter biplane the **Sopwith Camel**, while in the Second World War, as chairman of the Hawker Siddeley company, he was responsible for the production of aircraft such as the Hurricane fighter.

Sorbonne the seat of the faculties of science and literature of the University of Paris. It was originally a theological college founded by Robert de *Sorbon*, chaplain to Louis IX, *c*.1257.

sorcerer a person who claims or is believed to have magic powers; a wizard. Recorded from late Middle English, the word comes ultimately, via Old French, from Latin *sors, sort-* 'lot, fortune'.

sorcerer's apprentice a person who instigates a process or project which they are then unable to control without assistance. The phrase is a translation of French *l'apprentit sorcier*, the title of a symphonic poem by Paul Dukas (1897), after *der Zauberlehrling*, a ballad by Goethe (1797), in which the apprentice through the use of spells instigates processes which he cannot control.

> The new bureaucracy doubles every year—exponentially, people claim, it is like the Sorcerer's Apprentice, it is like a fungus devouring everything.
> — Doris Lessing *African Laughter* (1992)

sorites in logic, a series of propositions in which the predicate of each is the subject of the next, the conclusion being formed of the first subject and the last predicate. Recorded from the mid 16th century, the word comes via Latin from Greek *sōreitēs*, from *sōros* 'heap'.

Soroptimist a member of an international association of clubs for professional and business women founded in California in 1921. The name comes from Latin *soror* 'sister' + *optimist*.

Sorrel name of the favourite horse of ➤ WILLIAM *III*, which stumbled on a molehill in the park of Hampton Court and threw the king, 20 February 1702, leading to his death.

See also ➤ LITTLE *gentleman in black velvet*.

sorrow see ➤ *help you to* SALT, *help you to sorrow*, ➤ MAN *of Sorrows*, ➤ ONE *for sorrow, two for mirth*, ➤ SEVEN *sorrows of Mary*.

sortes divination, or the seeking of guidance, by chance selection of a passage in the Bible (**sortes Biblicae**) or another text regarded as authoritative (**sortes Virgilianae**). Recorded from the late 16th century, the word is Latin, and means 'chance selections (of the Bible or other chosen work)'.

A popular story recorded in the early 18th-century *Memoirs* of James Wellwood (1652–1727) gives an account of Charles I and Lord Falkland visiting the Bodleian Library, and trying the *sortes Virgilianae*. Charles is said to have received Dido's curse on Aeneas, predicting the outbreak of war, while Falkland (who was killed fighting for the King), found Evander's lament for his son Pallas, killed in battle. The story became widely known, although accounts of it vary; Archbishop Sancroft (1617–93) said it took place at Windsor, and Aubrey attributes it to the Prince of Wales when in France.

sorts see ➤ *it takes* ALL *sorts to make a world*.

SOS an international code signal of extreme distress, used especially by ships at sea. The letters were chosen as being easily transmitted and recognized in Morse code; by folk etymology they are taken as an abbreviation of *save our souls*. The earlier and original distress call for shipping (as used by the ➤ TITANIC) was *CQD*.

soteriology the doctrine of salvation; the word comes from Greek *sōtēria* 'salvation'.

Sothic of or relating to ➤ SIRIUS (the Dog Star), especially with reference to the ancient Egyptian year fixed by its heliacal rising. The word comes (in the early 19th century), from Greek *Sōthis*, from an Egyptian name of the Dog Star.

Soto one of the three branches of Zen Buddhism (the others being Obaku and Rinzai) founded in the 9th century in the Ts'ao and Tung monasteries in China, and transmitted to Japan in 1227 by Dōgen (1200–53).

soul the spiritual or immaterial part of a human being or animal, regarded as immortal. The word is recorded from Old English (in form *sāwol, sāw(e)*), and is of Germanic origin.

See also ➤ BODY *and soul,* ➤ CONFESSION *is good for the soul,* ➤ *the* EYES *are the window of the soul,* ➤ FLOW *of soul,* ➤ *the* IRON *entered his soul,* ➤ SOULS.

soul and conscience in Scottish law, the formula by which medical testimony in writing is authenticated.

soul-cake a specially prepared cake or bun distributed especially to parties of children in various northern or north-midland counties of England on All Souls' Day, when it is customary to go 'souling', or asking for alms.

soul-candle in Judaism, a candle lit on the eve of the anniversary of a parent's death, and also on the eve of Yom Kippur. The name is a translation of Yiddish *neshome licht* 'soul light'.

soul-catcher among various North American Indian peoples, a hollowed bone tube used by a medicine man to contain the soul of a sick person.

Soul City informal term for the Harlem area of New York city, with reference to the prevalence of ➤ SOUL *music.*

soul-house a model or representation of a house placed by the ancient Egyptians in a tomb to receive the soul of a dead person.

soul music a kind of music incorporating elements of rhythm and blues and gospel music, popularized by American blacks. Characterized by an emphasis on vocals and an impassioned improvisatory delivery, it is associated with performers such as Marvin Gaye, Aretha Franklin, James Brown, and Otis Redding.

the soul of the world the animating principle of the world, according to early philosophers (after Latin *anima mundi*, Greek *psukh tou kosmou*).

souls see also ➤ ALL *Souls,* ➤ CORPORATIONS *have neither bodies to be punished nor souls to be damned,* ➤ TRANSMIGRATION *of souls.*

the Souls a late 19th-century aristocratic circle with predominantly cultural and intellectual interests; the name was said to have been given by Lord Charles Beresford in 1888. Members of the group included Curzon, Arthur Balfour, and Margot Tennant (later Margot Asquith).

sound bite a short extract from a recorded interview, chosen for its pungency or aptness, or a one-liner deliberately produced to be used in this way. Use of the technique and the term, first recorded in the 1980s, has steadily increased, with the US presidential campaigns of 1988 and 1992 making great use of the *sound bite* to carry their messages to the public. The view has also developed that the concentration on crafting a sentence to catch a few minutes of air time has had an adverse effect on the quality of public debate; the veteran Labour politician Tony Benn (1925–), has also commented 'A quotation is what a speaker wants to say—unlike a soundbite which is all that an interviewer allows you to say.'

sour grapes an expression or attitude of deliberate disparagement of a desired but unattainable object, alluding to Aesop's fable of 'The Fox and the Grapes', in which a fox, unable to reach a tempting bunch of grapes, comforted himself with the reflection that the fruit was probably sour and was therefore no loss.

sourdough an experienced prospector in Alaska, the Yukon, and similar places; the name alludes to the use of *sourdough*, or fermenting dough used as leaven, to raise bread baked during the winter.

souterrain an underground chamber or passage. The word comes (in the mid 18th century) from French, from *sous* 'under' + *terre* 'earth'.

south the direction towards the point of the horizon 90° clockwise from east, or the point on the horizon itself. In literary contexts, it is often contrasted as a region with the more temperate *north*:

> O tell, her, Swallow, thou that knowest each,
> That bright and fierce and fickle is the South,
> And dark and true and tender is the North.
> — Lord Tennyson *The Princess* (1847)

In 1861, warning the people of Texas against secession, the American politician Samuel Houston (1793–1863) wrote:

> The North is determined to preserve this Union. They are not a fiery, impulsive people as you are, for they live in colder climes. But when they begin to move in a given direction . . . they move with the steady momentum and perseverance of a mighty avalanche.
> — Samuel Houston warning given in 1861

From the late 20th century, *south* has been used as a collective term for the industrially and economically less advanced countries of the world, typically situated to the south of the industrialized nations.

See also ➤ *the* DEEP *South,* ➤ EMPIRE *State of the South,* ➤ SOLID *South.*

South Bank the southern bank of the Thames, noted for the cultural complexes and public gardens developed between Westminster and Blackfriars bridges for and since the ▶ FESTIVAL *of Britain* in 1951.

▶ SOUTH *Bank* is also used with reference to the policy of the Anglican diocese of Southwark to re-express traditional beliefs and practices in ways that would make them better suited to contemporary life.

South Sea Bubble a speculative boom in the shares of the **South Sea Company**, which had been incorporated in 1711 for the purpose of exclusive trade with the South Seas, and of taking up the unfunded National Debt. The Prospectus for the Company is said to have included the words, 'A Company for carrying on an undertaking of Great Advantage, but no one to know what it is.'

The **South Sea Scheme** was a stock-jobbing scheme inaugurated in 1720 for taking up the whole National Debt; it ended in the same year with the failure of the company and a general financial collapse. The *South Sea Bubble* has become a type of a superficially attractive but disastrous investment scheme associated with sudden public enthusiasm.

> The rage for genes reminds us of Tulipomania and the South Sea Bubble.
> — *New York Review of Books* 28 May 1992

Joanna Southcott (1750–1814), a former Wesleyan Methodist who announced herself as the woman spoken of in Revelation 12, who is seen 'clothed with the sun, and the moon under her feet', and who will bear a son to rule the nations, and will be protected against the dragon.

Having begun to make prophecies, she developed the practice of sealing up her writings, to be opened when the predicted events had matured. She also published numerous books and pamphlets. In 1813 she announced that she was pregnant with a Messiah ('Shiloh'), and in March 1814 the imminent birth was apparently confirmed; however, no child was born, and Joanna herself died in December of that year.

Joanna Southcott's box was a locked and sealed box said to contain her prophecies, which was supposed to be opened in a time of national emergency and in the presence of the Anglican bishops. A number of appeals to open the box were made to Randall Davidson when Archbishop of Canterbury (1903–28). It was finally opened (although not by Davidson) in 1927; a woman's nightcap and a lottery ticket were among its contents.

southerly buster in Australia, a sudden, strong, cool wind from the south, affecting the south-eastern coast.

Southern blot a procedure for identifying specific sequences of DNA, in which fragments separated on a gel are transferred directly to a second medium on which assay by hybridization may be carried out. It is named after the British biochemist Edwin M. *Southern* (1938–).

Southern Cross the constellation *Crux Australis*, four stars of which form a cross; the name **land of the Southern Cross** has been used for Australia since the late 19th century. *Southern Cross* is also a name for the ▶ EUREKA *flag*.

Southern Lights another name for the *aurora australis*.

southpaw a left-handed boxer who leads with the right hand; in baseball, a left-handed pitcher. The term comes from the mid 19th century (denoting the left hand or a punch with the left hand); the usage in baseball is from the orientation of the diamond to the same points of the compass, causing the pitcher to have his left hand on the south side of his body.

sovereign a supreme ruler, especially a monarch; in early use, applied to God in relation to created things.

From the early 16th century, *sovereign* also denoted a gold coin, originally, one minted in England from the time of Henry VII to Charles I and at first of the value of 22s. 6d.; later, a British coin worth one pound sterling, now only minted for commemorative purposes.

The word is recorded from Middle English and comes from Old French *soverain*, based on Latin *super* 'above'; the change in ending was due to association with *reign*.

the sovereign good the greatest good, especially that of a state or its people; the phrase is recorded from Middle English.

> The inquiry of truth, which is the love-making, or wooing of it, the knowledge of truth, which is the presence of it, and the belief of truth, which is the enjoying of it, is the sovereign good of human nature.
> — Francis Bacon *Essays* (1625) 'Of Truth'

sow see also ➤ DRUNK *as David's sow,* ➤ *you cannot make a* SILK *purse out of a sow's ear.*

have the right sow by the ear have the correct understanding of the situation; recorded from the mid 16th century, the phrase has been attributed to Henry VIII, when in 1529 ➤ *Thomas* CRANMER suggested that in the question of the projected divorce from Catherine of Aragon, the king should consult divines at the universities. Henry is said in *Foxe's Book of Martyrs* (ed. 2, 1570) to have declared, 'That man hath the sow by the right ear.'

sow dry and set wet proverbial saying, mid 17th century.

a sow may whistle, though it has an ill mouth for it proverbial saying, early 19th century.

sow one's wild oats go through a period of wild or promiscuous behaviour while young, late 16th century; *wild oat,* a wild grass related to the cultivated oat which was traditionally a weed of cornfields, is recorded from the mid 16th to the early 17th century as a name for a dissolute young man.

as you sow, so you reap proverbial saying, late 15th century; originally with biblical allusion to Galatians 6:7, 'whatsoever a man soweth, that shall he also reap'.

they that sow the wind shall reap the whirlwind proverbial saying, late 16th century; originally with biblical allusion to Hosea 8:7, 'For they have sown the wind, and they shall reap the whirlwind.'

sowbread a cyclamen with pale pink or white flowers and leaves that do not appear until late summer after flowering, native to southern Eurasia; it is so named because the roots are reputedly eaten by wild boars in Sicily.

parable of the sower in the Bible (Matthew 13:3–8), the story told by Jesus of how 'a sower went forth to sow', and of how some seed was eaten by birds, some fell on stony ground, and some was choked by weeds, but some 'fell into good ground' and germinated; the parable illustrates the varying readiness of those he taught to receive Jesus's message.

Soweto a large urban area, consisting of several townships, in South Africa south-west of Johannesburg. In 1976 demonstrations against the compulsory use of Afrikaans in schools resulted in violent

police activity and the deaths of hundreds of people.

> Soweto—that is not even a name. It is an acronym for South Western Townships, and it stands as a monument to the greed and rapacity of those who rule our beloved land.
> — P. Magubane et al. *Soweto* (1990)

Alexis Benoît Soyer (1809–58), French-born cook to fashionable society in England, who subsequently worked for Irish famine-relief and with the British army in Crimea, and developed the **Soyer stove**, a tabletop cooking-range or field stove.

Soyuz a series of manned Soviet orbiting spacecraft, used to investigate the operation of orbiting space stations.

Spa a small town in eastern Belgium, south-east of Liège, which has been celebrated since medieval times for the curative properties of its mineral springs; the use of the word *spa* to mean a mineral spring developed from this in the early 17th century.

space see ➤ WATCH *this space!*

Spade see ➤ SAM *Spade.*

spade¹ a tool with a sharp-edged, typically rectangular, metal blade and a long handle, used for digging and cutting earth and turf; a *spade* is the emblem of ➤ *St* FIACRE and ➤ *St* PHOCAS. Recorded from Old English (in form *spadu, spada*), the word is of Germanic origin and is ultimately (like ➤ SPADE²) related to Greek *spathē* 'blade, paddle'.

spade² one of the four suits in a conventional pack of playing cards, denoted by a black inverted heart-shaped figure with a small stalk. The word is recorded from the late 16th century, and comes from Italian *spade,* plural of *spada* 'sword', ultimately from Greek *spathē* (cf. ➤ SPADE¹).

Spades are the highest-ranking suit in Bridge, and from this comes the informal **in spades**, very much, extremely.

call a spade a spade speak plainly without avoiding unpleasant or embarrassing issues. The expression is recorded in English from the mid 16th century, and derives ultimately from Plutarch's *Apophthegmata,* which uses Greek *skaphē* 'basin'. Erasmus, perhaps confusing this with derivatives of *skaptein* 'dig', rendered this as Latin *ligo* 'mattock', and Nicholas Udall, translating Erasmus in 1542, used the word *spade*:

> The Macedonians . . . had not the witte to calle a spade by any other name then a spade.
> — Nicholas Udall tr. *Erasmus Apophthegmes* (1542)

spade guinea a guinea of the pattern coined 1787–1800, so called from the form of the escutcheon on the reverse.

spaghetti junction a complex multi-level road junction, especially one on a motorway, and originally applied to a major interchange on the M6 near Birmingham in the UK.

spaghetti western informal term for a western film made cheaply in Europe by an Italian director.

spaghettification in physics, the process by which (in some theories) an object would be stretched and ripped apart by gravitational forces on falling into a black hole.

spagyric of or pertaining to alchemy, alchemical. Recorded from the late 16th century, the word comes from modern Latin *spagiricus*, used and probably invented by ➤ PARACELSUS.

spahi former term for a member of the Turkish irregular cavalry or a member of the Algerian cavalry in French service. Recorded from the mid 16th century, the word comes ultimately from Persian *sipāhī*, from the same base as ➤ SEPOY.

Spain see ➤ APOSTLE *of Spain*, ➤ CASTLES *in Spain*, ➤ KING *of Spain's trumpeter*, ➤ RAIN, *rain, go to Spain*, ➤ SINGEING *of the king of Spain's beard*

Lazzaro Spallanzani (1729–99), Italian physiologist and biologist. He is known today for his experiments in subjects such as the circulation of the blood and the digestive system of animals. He also disproved the theory of spontaneous generation.

spam to send irrelevant or inappropriate messages on the Internet to a large number of newsgroups or users, often for the purpose of advertising. The term is recorded from the first half of the 1990s and derives from *Spam*, trademark name for a type of tinned meat, apparently in allusion to a sketch by the British *Monty Python* comedy group, set in a café in which every item on the menu includes Spam.

Spanglish hybrid language combining words and idioms from both Spanish and English, often as spoken in Latin America.

spaniel a dog of a breed with a long silky coat and drooping ears, used in similes and metaphors as a symbol of devotion or obsequiousness. The word is recorded from Middle English and comes from Old

French *espaigneul* 'Spanish (dog)', from Latin *Hispaniolus*.

Spanish see also ➤ OLD *Spanish custom*.

Spanish-American War a war between Spain and the United States in the Caribbean and the Philippines in 1898. American public opinion having been aroused by Spanish atrocities in Cuba and the destruction of the warship *Maine* in Santiago harbour, the US declared war and destroyed the Spanish fleets in both the Pacific and the West Indies before successfully invading Cuba, Puerto Rico, and the Philippines, all of which Spain gave up by the Treaty of Paris (1898).

Spanish flu influenza caused by an influenza virus of type A, in particular that of the pandemic which began in 1918.

> Some strains can kill people before they have enough antibodies to subdue the infection. The Spanish flu strain in 1918, for example, killed 20 million people.
> — *New Scientist* 13 August 1994

Spanish fly a bright green European blister beetle with a mousy smell; a toxic preparation of the dried bodies of these beetles, formerly used in medicine as a counterirritant and sometimes taken as an aphrodisiac.

Spanish Inquisition an ecclesiastical court established in 1478 and directed originally against converts from Judaism and Islam but later also against Protestants. It operated with great severity, especially under its first inquisitor, Torquemada, and was not suppressed until the early 19th century.

nobody expects the Spanish Inquisition from a *Monty Python* script, in which the Inquisitors consistently fail to make a successful announcement of their arrival and identity: 'Nobody expects the Spanish Inquisition! Our chief weapon is surprise—surprise and fear…fear and surprise…our two weapons are fear and surprise—and ruthless efficiency…our *three* weapons are fear and surprise and ruthless efficiency and an almost fanatical devotion to the Pope…our *four*…no…*Amongst* our weapons—amongst our weaponry—are such elements as fear, surprise…I'll come in again.'

Spanish Main the former name for the NW coast of South America between the Orinoco River and Panama, and adjoining parts of the Caribbean Sea.

Spanish Mission denoting a style of architecture characteristic of the Catholic missions in Spanish America.

Spanish practice another term for ➤ OLD *Spanish custom.*

War of the Spanish Succession a European war (1701–14), provoked by the death of the Spanish king Charles II without issue. The Grand Alliance of Britain, the Netherlands, and the Holy Roman emperor threw back a French invasion of the Low Countries, and, although the Peace of Utrecht confirmed the accession of a Bourbon king in Spain, prevented Spain and France from being united under one crown.

sparagmos the dismemberment of a victim, forming a part of some ancient rituals and represented in Greek myths and tragedies. The word is Greek, and means literally 'tearing'.

spare at the spigot, and let out the bung-hole proverbial saying, mid 17th century; referring to the practice of being overcareful on the one hand, and carelessly generous on the other.

spare the rod and spoil the child proverbial saying, early 11th century; often with biblical allusion to Proverbs 13:24, 'he that spareth his rod hateth his son'.

spare well and have to spend proverbial saying, mid 16th century.

sparrowhawk a small Old World woodland hawk that preys on small birds; in the 15th-century *Boke of St Albans*, the *sparrowhawk* is listed in falconry as appropriate for a priest.

Spartacist a member of the ➤ SPARTACUS *League*.

Spartacus (died *c*.71 BC), Thracian slave and gladiator. He led a revolt against Rome in 73, increasing his army from some seventy gladiators at the outset to several thousand rebels, but was eventually defeated by Crassus in 71 and crucified.

Spartacus League a German revolutionary socialist group (the *Spartacists*) founded in 1916 by Rosa Luxemburg and Karl Liebknecht (1871–1919) with the aims of overthrowing the government and ending the First World War; they took their name from the Thracian slave and revolutionary ➤ SPARTACUS. At the end of 1918 the group became the German Communist Party, which in 1919 organized an uprising in Berlin that was brutally crushed.

Spartan a citizen of Sparta, a powerful city state in the 5th century BC, which defeated its rival Athens in the Peloponnesian War to become the leading city of Greece until challenged by Thebes in 371 BC.

The ancient Spartans were renowned for the military organization of their state and for their rigorous discipline, courage, and austerity.

Spasmodic School a name given by W. E. Aytoun to a group of poets chiefly represented by Alexander Smith, Philip James Bailey, and Sydney Dobell; his dramatic poem 'Firmilian' (1854) was written in ridicule of their extravagant themes and style.

spatulamancy divination by means of the shoulder-blade of an animal.

speak see also ➤ THINK *first and speak afterwards.*

never speak ill of the dead proverbial saying, mid 16th century; earlier versions are 'speak no evil of the dead', as attributed to the Sparton ephor Chilon of the 6th century BC, and the Latin tag '*de mortuis nil nisi bonum* [say nothing of the dead but what is good]'.

speak not of my debts unless you mean to pay them proverbial saying, mid 17th century.

speakeasy in the US, an illicit liquor shop or drinking club; the term is in fact recorded from the late 19th century, but is particularly associated with the period of ➤ PROHIBITION.

Speaker the presiding officer in a legislative assembly, especially the House of Commons; the first person mentioned as formally holding the office in the English Parliament is Sir Thomas de Hungerford (d. 1398), although Sir Peter de la Mare had preceded him in the post in the ➤ GOOD *Parliament* of 1376, but without the title.

One of the best remembered Speakers of the British House of Commons was William Lenthall (1591–1662), who was presiding on 4 January 1642 when Charles I attempted to arrest the ➤ FIVE *Members*. In response to the king's question as to whether he saw any of the members present, Lenthall replied, 'I have neither eye to see, nor tongue to speak here, but as the House is pleased to direct me.'

everyone speaks well of the bridge that carries him over proverbial saying, late 17th century.

spear a *spear* is the emblem of ➤ St THOMAS *the Apostle.*

pass under the spear be sold at auction, rendering Latin *sub hasta vendere*; first recorded in Philemon Holland's translation of *Livy's Roman*

History (1600), 'The rest of the inhabitants were sold at the speare in ouvert market like slaves'. In a letter of 12 August 1689, the diarist John Evelyn referred to 'The noblest…library, that ever passed under the spear'. It was the custom in ancient Rome to set up a spear where an auction was to be held.

spear-carrier an actor with a walk-on part; an unimportant participant in something.

spear side the male side or members of a family, the opposite of the *distaff side.*

Special Branch in the UK, the police department dealing with political security.

Special Operations Executive a secret British military service during the Second World War, set up in 1940 to carry out clandestine operations and coordinate with resistance movements in Europe and later the Far East. Abbreviation, **SOE.**

special pleading argument in which the speaker deliberately ignores aspects that are unfavourable to their point of view; the term was originally (in the late 17th century) used for a legal pleading drawn with particular references to the circumstances of a case, as opposed to general pleading.

the special relationship the relationship between Britain and the US, regarded as particularly close in terms of common origin and language. The expression is associated with Winston Churchill, as in the House of Commons 7 November 1945, 'We should not abandon our special relationship with the United States and Canada.'

specie money in the form of coins rather than notes. The term derives from the Latin phrase *in specie,* meaning (in the mid 16th century) in the real, precise, or actual form identified; this then came to mean, 'in actual coin or money', and finally *specie* was used for coin or coined money itself.

species a group of living organisms consisting of similar individuals capable of exchanging genes or interbreeding. The species is the principal natural taxonomic unit, ranking below a genus and denoted by a Latin binomial, e.g. *Homo sapiens.*

See also ➤ *the* FEMALE *of the species is more deadly than the male.*

spectre see ➤ BROCKEN *spectre.*

if you don't speculate, you can't accumulate proverbial saying, mid 20th century.

speech the expression of or the ability to express thoughts and feelings by articulate sounds; one of the ➤ FIVE *senses.*

See also ➤ SINGLE-*speech Hamilton.*

speech is silver, but silence is golden proverbial saying, mid 19th century.

speed see ➤ *more* HASTE, *less speed.*

God speed the plough traditional saying, late Middle English.

Speenhamland system a system of poor relief first adopted in the late 18th century and established throughout rural England in succeeding years, named after the village of *Speenhamland* near Newbury, Berkshire, where the system was adopted by the magistrates in 1795.

Speewah an imaginary Australian cattle station or place used as a setting for tall stories of the outback; recorded from the late 19th century.

speleologists ➤ *St* BENEDICT is patron saint of speleologists.

spell a form of words used as a magical charm or incantation. Recorded from Old English, the word originally meant 'narration', and is of Germanic origin; the current sense is found first in late Middle English, in **night-spell**, a spell intended as a protection against harm at night.

Spencean a follower of the political theorist Thomas Spence (1750–1814), bookseller and author of a scheme of land nationalization. His views were first published in a paper, 'The Real Rights of Man', presented to the Philosophical Society in 1775; he was subsequently expelled from the society for hawking the paper about like a ballad. Spence issued further pamphlets, including one entitled the 'Constitution of Spensonea, a country in Fairyland'. He died in 1814, and in 1816 the Society of Spencean Philanthropists was instituted, to promote his ideas on land reformation; Harriet Martineau in *England during the Thirty Years' Peace* (1849) reported that they also 'openly meddled with sundry grave questions…and, amongst other notable projects, petitioned parliament to do away with machinery'.

spencer a short, close-fitting jacket, worn by women and children in the early 19th century, probably named after the second Earl *Spencer* (1758–1834), English politician.

Herbert Spencer (1820–1903), English philosopher and sociologist. He sought to apply the theory of natural selection to human societies, developing social Darwinism and coining the phrase the ➤ SURVIVAL *of the fittest* (1864).

Stanley Spencer (1891–1959), English painter. He is best known for his religious and visionary works in the modern setting of his native village of Cookham in Berkshire, such as *Resurrection: Cookham* (1926) and the sequence of panels portraying the Clyde shipyards during the Second World War when he was an official war artist. The English novelist and critic Wyndham Lewis (1882–1957) described the figures in his paintings as 'Angels in jumpers'; Spencer himself is quoted as saying, 'Painting is saying "Ta" to God'.

Spencerian of or relating to a style of sloping handwriting widely taught in American schools from around 1850, and named after the US calligrapher Platt Rogers *Spencer* (1800–64).

spend see also ➤ SPARE *well and have to spend.*

what you spend, you have proverbial saying, early 14th century.

Oswald Spengler (1880–1936), German philosopher. In his book *The Decline of the West* (1918–22) he argues that civilizations undergo a seasonal cycle of a thousand years and are subject to growth and decay analogous to biological species.

> Even if we accept some Spenglerian Cycle routine, the cycle never comes back to exactly the same place, nor does it ever exactly repeat itself.
> — William S. Burroughs letter, 18 August 1954

Edmund Spenser (*c.*1552–99), English poet, best known for his allegorical romance the *Faerie Queene* (1590; 1596), celebrating Queen Elizabeth I and written in the ➤ SPENSERIAN *stanza.*

Spenserian stanza the stanza used by Spenser in the *Faerie Queene*, consisting of eight iambic pentameters and an alexandrine, with the rhyming scheme *ababbcbcc.*

spero see ➤ DUM *spiro spero.*

sphairistike an early form of lawn tennis, first played in 1873; it is named from Greek *sphairistikē (tekhnē)* 'skill in playing at ball'.

sphere each of a series of revolving concentrically arranged spherical shells in which celestial bodies were formerly thought to be set in a fixed relationship.

See also ➤ ARMILLARY *sphere*, ➤ CRYSTALLINE *sphere*, ➤ MUSIC *of the spheres.*

Sphinx in Greek mythology, a winged monster of Thebes, having a woman's head and a lion's body. It propounded a riddle about the three ages of man, killing those who failed to solve it, until Oedipus was successful, whereupon the Sphinx committed suicide.

The name *sphinx* was later used for the sculptured or carved figure of an imaginary creature with a human head and breast and the body of a lion, in particular, an ancient Egyptian stone figure having a lion's body and a human or animal head, especially the huge statue near the Pyramids at Giza.

The word is recorded from late Middle English (and comes via Latin from Greek, apparently from *sphingein* 'draw tight'); from the early 17th century, the name is used for a person held to resemble the sphinx, in posing difficult questions, or in being of a mysterious or inscrutable nature.

spice see ➤ VARIETY *is the spice of life.*

Spice Islands former name for the Molucca Islands, from which spices were traditionally imported to the west; the name is recorded from the early 18th century.

spick and span neat, clean, and well looked after; smart and new. The phrase comes (in the late 16th century, meaning 'brand new') from *spick and span new*, emphatic extension of *span new*, from Old Norse *spán-nýr*, from *spán* 'chip' + *nýr* 'new'; *spick* influenced by Dutch *spiksplinternieuw*, literally 'splinter new'.

spider an eight-legged predatory arachnid with an unsegmented body consisting of a fused head and thorax and a rounded abdomen; spiders have fangs which inject poison into their prey, and most kinds spin webs in which to capture insects.

In proverbial and traditional allusion, references are made to the cunning, skill, and industry of the spider, as well as its power of secreting or emitting poison; in a traditional story of ➤ *Robert the* BRUCE watching a spider in a cave attempting to spin a thread long enough to reach another piece of rock, it becomes a type of perseverance.

A spider is also said to have helped ➤ MUHAMMAD. According to the story, the Prophet and his friend ➤ Abu-*Bakr* were in flight from the men of Mecca and took shelter in a cave; to protect them, pigeons built their nests and a spider spun its web across the mouth of the cave, so that the pursuers assumed that it was undisturbed.

In Greek mythology, the weaver ➤ Arachne who challenged Athene to a contest of skill was changed into a spider by the angry goddess.

See also ➤ *if you want to* Live *and thrive, let the spider run alive.*

Spiderman name of an American comic-strip hero first appearing in 1952; *Spiderman* is the alter ego of a shy bookish teenager called Peter Parker, who develops arachnid powers after being bitten by a radio-active spider.

spigot see ➤ Spare *at the spigot, and let out at the bung-hole.*

spikenard a costly perfumed ointment much valued in ancient times, obtained from the rhizome of a Himalayan plant of the valerian family; in John 12:3, Mary 'took…a pound of ointment of spikenard, very costly, and anointed the feet of Jesus'. Her action was criticized by ➤ Judas, on the grounds that the ointment could have been sold and the money given to the poor, calling forth the response from Jesus, 'the poor always ye have with ye; but me ye have not always'.

spillikins a game played with a heap of small rods of wood, bone, or plastic, in which players try to remove one at a time without disturbing the others; the term is recorded from the mid 18th century.

spin a yarn tell a long far-fetched story; the expression is a nautical one, and is recorded from the early 19th century.

spin doctor a spokesperson employed to give a favourable interpretation of events to the media, especially on behalf of a political party. The term comes from US politics, and originated in a sporting metaphor, with the idea of the *spin* put on the ball, for example by a pitcher in baseball.

> We should put the spin-doctors in spin clinics, where they can meet other spin patients and be treated by spin consultants. The rest of us can get on with the proper democratic process.
> — Tony Benn in *Independent* 25 October 1997

spinach see ➤ Gammon *and spinach.*

spindle side another name for *distaff side.*

spinster an unmarried woman, typically an older woman beyond the usual age for marriage; in current usage, the term carries overtones of a stereotypical woman in this situation who is regarded as prissy and repressed.

Spinster is first recorded in late Middle English in the sense of 'a woman who spins', and in early use it was appended to the names of women to denote their occupation. From the 17th century the word was appended to names as the official legal description of an unmarried woman (as in, **spinster of this parish**); the current sense dates from the early 18th century.

spires see ➤ *City of* Dreaming *Spires.*

spirit[1] the non-physical part of a person which is the seat of emotions and character; the soul; such a part regarded as a person's true self and as capable of surviving physical death or separation, or manifested as an apparition after their death; a ghost. The word is recorded in Middle English, and comes via Anglo-Norman French from Latin *spiritus* 'breath, spirit'.

See also ➤ Great *Spirit,* ➤ Holy *Spirit,* ➤ Sword *of the Spirit.*

spirit[2] a former term meaning, kidnap in order to transport to the plantations in America; the term is recorded from the mid 17th century.

the spirit moves me I am inclined to do something; a phrase originally in Quaker use with reference to the ➤ Holy *Spirit.*

spiritual see ➤ Seven *spiritual works of mercy.*

spiritualism a system of belief or religious practice based on supposed communication with the spirits of the dead, especially through mediums; the word in this sense is recorded from the mid 19th century.

spiro see ➤ Dum *spiro spero.*

spit and polish extreme neatness or smartness, originally with allusion to the cleaning and polishing duties of a serviceman.

Spitalfields the name of a district in the east of London, so called from the church of St Mary Spital; the word is used of silk and velvet traditionally made up there, or to the weavers (originally Huguenot refugees) involved in this trade.

See also ➤ Spittle *sermon.*

spitting from classical times it was believed that the action of spitting would bring good fortune or avert evil; Pliny in his *Natural History* refers to the habit of spitting to repel contagion.

spitting image the exact double of (another person or thing); the term is recorded from the early 20th century, and is an alteration of *spitten image*, which itself is an alteration of *split and image*.

In Britain in the 1980s and 1990s, *Spitting Image* was the title of a satirical television programme, featuring puppets of British politicians and the British royal family.

spittle sermon any of the sermons traditionally preached on Easter Monday and Tuesday from a special pulpit at St Mary Spital in ➤ SPITALFIELDS outside of Bishopsgate (afterwards at St Bride's and finally at Christ Church in the City); *spittle* here represents an aphetic form of *hospital*, and meant originally a foundation for the reception of the poor and ill, especially those with leprosy or similar diseases.

splatter denoting or referring to films featuring many violent and gruesome deaths; such films have been recognized as a genre since the early 1980s.

spleen an abdominal organ involved in the production and removal of blood cells in most vertebrates and forming part of the immune system, which in earlier belief was held to be the seat of such emotions as bad temper and spite; *spleen* thus came to be used in these senses.

splendid see ➤ *the* VISION *splendid*.

splice join or connect (a rope or ropes) by interweaving the strands at the ends; the word is recorded from the early 16th century, and by the mid 18th century the slang sense 'to join in matrimony, to marry' had developed.

splice the mainbrace in naval use, serve an extra ration of rum (the *mainbrace* was the brace attached to the main yard).

split infinitive a construction consisting of an infinitive with an adverb or other word inserted between *to* and the verb, e.g. *she seems to really like it*. Although it is still widely held that such a construction is wrong, the dislike of it is not well-founded, being based on an analogy with Latin, where infinitives consist of only one word.

In English, the placing of an adverb may be extremely important in giving a particular emphasis;

in some cases, splitting an infinitive can only be avoided at the cost of losing such emphasis—a situation in which Raymond Chandler presumably found himself when he said, 'When I split an infinitive, God damn it, I split it so it will stay split.' It is now increasingly the view that in standard English the principle of allowing split infinitives is broadly acceptable as both normal and useful.

Benjamin McLane Spock (1903–98), American paediatrician and writer; known as **Dr Spock**. His influential manual *The Common Sense Book of Baby and Child Care* (1946) challenged traditional ideas of discipline and rigid routine in child-rearing in favour of a psychological approach.

> These days, even icons of seventies macraméd indulgence have gone chaste. Wizened old Dr Spock no longer condemns the spanking of children.
> — *New York Magazine* 1 September 1997

Mr Spock a character in the science fiction series ➤ STAR *Trek*; a ➤ VULCAN who is characterized by his use of logic, lack of emotions, and pointed ears.

> Popular belief has it that science is the preserve of logical Mr Spocks.
> — *New Scientist* 27 July 1996

See also ➤ SLASH.

Spode fine pottery or porcelain made at the factories of the English potter Josiah *Spode* (1755–1827) or his successors, characteristically consisting of ornately decorated and gilded services and large vases. Spode invented what became standard English bone china by combining china clay with bone ash.

spoil see ➤ *do not spoil the* SHIP *for a ha'porth of tar*, ➤ *spoil the* EGYPTIANS.

spoils system the practice of a successful political party giving public office to its supporters; the term is recorded from mid 19th-century America, and the first use of *spoils* in this sense is in a letter of 1833 which refers to 'the idolatrous "spoils party" of the day'.

put a spoke in someone's wheel prevent someone from carrying out a plan; the expression is recorded from the late 16th century in the form 'I will sett a spoke to your cogge'; the current form became established in the early 17th century. *Spoke* here is probably a mistranslation of Dutch *spaak* meaning 'bar, stave'.

sponge see ➤ THROW *up the sponge*.

sponging house in the 18th and 19th centuries, a preliminary place of detention for debtors kept by a bailiff or sheriff's officer; the name comes from the use of *sponge* verb as meaning 'to press or squeeze someone for money'.

spontaneous combustion the ignition of organic matter (e.g. hay or coal) without apparent cause, typically through heat generated internally by rapid oxidation. Alleged reports of human death caused by such a phenomenon have long been the subject of controversy; in Dickens's *Bleak House* (1853), the rag-and-bone man Krook dies in this way.

spontaneous generation the supposed production of living organisms from non-living matter, as inferred from the apparent appearance of life in some infusions. Also called *abiogenesis*.

spoon see also ➤ APOSTLE *spoon*, ➤ *he who* SUPS *with the devil should have a long spoon*, ➤ PURITAN *spoon*, ➤ RUNCIBLE *spoon*, ➤ WOODEN *spoon*.

make a spoon or spoil a horn proverbial saying, early 19th century; referring to spoons being made of horn, and meaning that either success or failure will be the result of endeavour.

spoonerism a verbal error in which a speaker accidentally transposes the initial sounds or letters of two or more words, often to humorous effect, as in the sentence *you have hissed the mystery lectures*. The word comes (in the early 20th century) from the Revd William Archibald *Spooner* (1844–1930), Warden of New College, an English scholar who reputedly made such errors in speaking, although many of those now attributed to him are probably apocryphal.

> It is no unusual experience for the members of New College to hear their late Dean give out in chapel a well-known sentence in the unintelligible guise of 'Kinkering Kongs their tykles tate'.
>
> — *Echo* 4 May 1892

the sport of kings proverbial phrase for hunting and (now, most usually) horse-racing, although the earliest uses of the expression related to war, as in Dryden's *King Arthur* (1691), 'War is the Trade of Kings, that fight for Empire'.

sport of nature a former term for a ➤ LUSUS *naturae*, recorded from the mid 17th century.

sport one's oak shut a heavy wooden outer door (especially of a set of university rooms) as a sign that one does not wish to be disturbed; the term is recorded from the late 18th century.

spots see ➤ *the* LEOPARD *does not change his spots*.

spouse a husband or wife, considered in relation to their partner; the term is recorded from Middle English, and comes ultimately (via Old French) from Latin *spondere* 'betroth'.

SPQR *Senatus Populusque Romanus*, the Senate and People of Rome, used in documents and inscriptions (as on standards) in ancient Rome.

sprat see also ➤ JACK *Sprat*.

sprat to catch a mackerel a small expenditure made, or a small risk taken, in the hope of a large or significant gain, recorded from the mid 19th century.

spread eagle a representation of an eagle with body, legs, and both wings displayed, especially as the emblem of various states or rulers, as of imperial Russia or Germany, or as an inn sign.

spree killer a person who kills in a sudden, random, and apparently unpremeditated manner, especially one killing a number of people at a single location in such an attack. Since the early 1980s, criminologists have identified two kinds of multiple murderer, the ➤ SERIAL *killer* and the spree killer. In the 1990s, a number of incidents of **spree killing**, such as that at Dunblane in March 1996, were the subject of wide media coverage and public attention.

spring the season after winter and before summer, in which vegetation begins to appear, in the northern hemisphere from March to May and in the southern hemisphere from September to November; in figurative usage, a time of youth and strength, associated with fresh growth. The word is recorded in Middle English in the obsolete sense of 'the first sign of day, the beginning of a season'; as a name for the season, it dates from late Middle English.

See also ➤ PRAGUE *Spring*.

spring forward, fall back a reminder that clocks are moved *forward* in *spring* and *back* in the *fall* (autumn).

spring tide a tide just after a new or full moon, when there is the greatest difference between high and low water.

it is not spring until you can plant your foot upon twelve daisies proverbial saying, mid 19th century.

Springfield the state capital of Illinois, the home and burial place of ➤ *Abraham* LINCOLN.

Bruce Springsteen (1949–), American rock singer, songwriter, and guitarist, noted for his songs about working-class life in the US.

spruce neat in dress and appearance. Recorded from the late 16th century, the word may come from *spruce* in the obsolete sense 'Prussian', in the phrase *spruce (leather)* jerkin.

spruce beer originally (early 16th century) beer from Prussia; later, a fermented drink using spruce twigs and needles as flavouring.

sprung rhythm a poetic metre approximating to speech, each foot having one stressed syllable followed by a varying number of unstressed ones. The term was coined by ➤ *Gerard Manley* HOPKINS, who used the metre.

> Why do I employ sprung rhythm at all? Because it is the nearest to the rhythm of prose, . . . the least forced, the most rhetorical and emphatic of all possible rhythms.
> — Gerard Manley Hopkins letter to Robert Bridges, 1877

spur a device with a small spike or a spiked wheel that is worn on a rider's heel and used for urging a horse forward; ➤ GILDED *spurs* were a distinctive mark of knighthood.

See also ➤ BATTLE *of the Spurs,* ➤ WIN *one's spurs.*

spur-royal a gold coin worth fifteen shillings, chiefly struck in the reign of James I & VI and having on its reverse a sun with rays, resembling a *spur-rowel* (the spiked wheel forming part of a spur).

sputnik each of a series of Soviet artificial satellites, the first of which (launched on 4 October 1957) was the first satellite to be placed in orbit. The Russian word means literally 'fellow-traveller'.

I spy strangers! in the British House of Commons, the formula used by a member in demanding the expulsion of strangers from the House; the use of stranger in this sense is recorded from the journal of the House of Commons, 31 October 1705, in an order that 'the Serjeant at Arms attending this House do from time to time take into his Custody any Stranger or Strangers that he shall see or be inform'd of…while the House or any Committee of the whole House is Sitting.'

Spy Wednesday the Wednesday before Easter, as the anniversary of the day on which ➤ JUDAS secretly visited the Jewish authorities to betray Jesus.

squab see also ➤ POET *Squab.*

squab pie pigeon pie (a *squab* is a young unfledged pigeon); formerly also, a pie with a thick crust containing mutton, pork, onions, and apples.

squad see ➤ AWKWARD *squad.*

squander-bug a symbol of reckless extravagance; a person who recklessly squanders money. The *squander-bug*, introduced in 1943 by the National Savings Committee, appeared in Ministry of Information posters as a devilish insect inciting to reckless spending.

> Beware the treacherous Squander Bug! He's the prince of fifth-columnists—doesn't believe in a nest-egg for the future—doesn't believe in making money fight for Britain. . . . Join a Savings Group to defeat the Squander Bug!
> — advertisement in *Times* 8 January 1943

square a plane figure with four equal straight sides and four right angles; in astrology, an aspect of 90° (one quarter of a circle).

From the late 16th century, *square* was the term for a body of infantry drawn up in rectangular formation, as on a battlefield or parade ground.

From the late 17th century, *square* has been used (often as part of a place-name) for an open space or area in a town or city, especially one of approximately quadrilateral and rectangular shape enclosed by houses.

See also ➤ RED *Square,* ➤ SMITH *Square,* ➤ TIANANMEN *Square,* ➤ TRAFALGAR *Square,*

on the square having membership of the Freemasons, in accordance with the Masonic code.

Square Mile an informal name for the City of London.

back to square one back to the starting-point, with no progress made (*square one* may be a reference to a board-game such as Snakes and Ladders, or derive from the notional division of a football pitch into eight numbered sections for the purpose of early radio commentaries).

square the circle construct a square equal in area to a given circle (a problem incapable of a purely geometrical solution); thus, do something that is considered to be impossible.

> For a fleeting moment he thought he had found it, the philosopher's stone that would square the circle.
> — E. Toman *Dancing in Limbo* (1995)

squarson former term for an Anglican clergyman who also held the position of squire in his parish. The word, coinage of which has been attributed to Bishop Samuel Wilberforce (1805–73), Sydney Smith, and others, is formed from a blend of *squire* and *parson*, and is recorded from the late 19th century.

squatter sovereignty in the US, the right claimed by settlers of newly formed territories to decide for themselves the question of slavery and other matters.

squeak see ➤ BUBBLE *and squeak*.

the squeaking wheel gets the grease proverbial saying, mid 20th century; meaning that the person who complains aloud is likely to receive help and sympathy.

squeegee merchant a person who cleans the window of a car stopped in traffic and solicits payment from the driver. *Squeegee merchants* have been a feature of urban life since the mid 1980s, and the development of such terms as **squeegee bandit** and **squeegee thug** suggest that the 'service' provided is not always a welcome one, with the unasked-for attention being regarded as an implicitly aggressive act.

squint an oblique opening through a wall in a church permitting a view of the altar from an aisle or side chapel.

Dr Squintum nickname under which the evangelist George Whitefield (1714–70) was burlesqued by Samuel Foote in his comedy *The Minor* (1760), a satire on Methodists.

squire in feudal times, a young nobleman acting as an attendant to a knight before becoming a knight himself; from the late 16th century, a young man attending or escorting a lady, a gallant or lover.

From the 17th century, *squire* came to denote a man of high social standing who owns and lives on an estate in a rural area, especially the chief landowner in such an area.

The word is recorded from Middle English, and is originally a shortening of Old French *esquier* 'esquire'.

See also ➤ NORTHAMPTONSHIRE *for squires and spires.*

Squirearchy the influential literary circle, composed principally of critics and poets, which surrounded the English poet and man of letters John Collings *Squire* (1884–1958), especially during his editorship of the *London Mercury* (1919–43).

Sri in the Indian subcontinent, a title of respect used before the name of a man, a god, or a sacred book. The word comes from Sanskrit *Śrī* 'beauty, fortune', used as an honorific title.

SS the Nazi special police force, the *Schutzstaffel* 'defence squadron'. Founded in 1925 by Hitler as a personal bodyguard, the SS provided security forces (including the Gestapo) and administered the concentration camps. It was headed by Heinrich Himmler 1929–45.

Stabat Mater a medieval Latin hymn on the suffering of the Virgin Mary at the Crucifixion, named from the opening words *Stabat mater dolorosa* 'Stood the mother, full of grief'.

stable see also ➤ AUGEAN *stables,* ➤ *the* MAN *who is born in a stable.*

it is too late to shut the stable-door after the horse has bolted proverbial saying, mid 14th century.

Stableford a form of stroke-play golf in which points are awarded according to the number of strokes taken to complete each hole. It is named after Frank B. *Stableford* (1870–1959), the American doctor who devised it.

stadium originally (in late Middle English) an ancient Roman or Greek measure of length, about 185 metres, which was the traditional length for a racecourse for foot-racing. From this the word *stadium* was extended to mean a track for a foot-race or chariot-race in ancient Greece or Rome, and finally developed its current meaning of an athletic or sports ground with tiers of seats for spectators.

stadtholder (from the 15th century to the late 18th century) the chief magistrate of the United Provinces of the Netherlands; a title which from the mid 16th until the late 18th century was held by a member of the ➤ *House of* ORANGE; in 1815 the son of the last stadtholder became King William I of the United Netherlands.

Madame de Staël (1766–1817), French novelist and critic, a precursor of the French romantics, born Anne Louise Germaine Necker. Her best-known critical work, *De l'Allemagne* (1810), introduced late 18th-century German writers and thinkers to France; it was banned by Napoleon.

staff a staff (with the child Jesus) is the emblem of ➤ *St* CHRISTOPHER.

See also ➤ BEAR *and ragged staff*, ➤ JACOB'*s staff*, ➤ PASTORAL *staff*, ➤ RAGGED *staff*.

the staff of life bread; the usage probably derives from the biblical translation of a Hebrew phrase meaning 'cut off the supply of food', as in Leviticus 26:26, 'And when I have broken the staff of your bread'. The use of *staff of life* to mean bread is recorded from the mid 17th century.

Stafford knot in heraldry, a half-hitch or over-hand knot used as a badge originally by the *Stafford* family, Dukes of Buckingham in the 15th and 16th centuries.

stag a male deer, especially a male red deer after its fifth year; a *stag* is the emblem of ➤ *St* EUSTACE, ➤ *St* GILES, ➤ *St* HUBERT, and St Osyth (d. *c.*700), supposedly protected from the unwanted attentions of her husband by a white stag. The word is recorded from Middle English, and is related to Old Norse *steggr* 'male bird' and Icelandic *steggi* 'tomcat'.

From the mid 19th century, stag has been used in Stock Exchange jargon for a person who applies for shares in a new issue with a view to selling at once for a profit.

stag night a celebration held for a man shortly before his wedding, attended by his male friends only.

stage whisper a loud whisper uttered by an actor on stage, intended to be heard by the audience but supposedly unheard by other characters in the play.

> His bedroom scene, spoken throughout in an oppressively ostentatious stage whisper, is an intolerable blunder.
> — H. Morley diary, 17 December 1864

the Stagirite the philosopher Aristotle, who was born at Stagira, a city of Macedonia.

> No lofty wing,
> Plumed by Longinus or the Stagyrite.
> — Lord Byron *Don Juan* (1824)

spirit of the staircase English term for the ➤ ESPRIT *de l'escalier*.

stake a wooden post to which a person was tied before being burned alive as a punishment; **the**

stake was thus used for the punishment of death by burning, especially in times of religious persecution.

Stake of Zion in the Mormon Church, a territorial division; the jurisdiction of a Mormon bishop.

Stakhanovite a worker in the former USSR who was exceptionally hard-working and productive; an exceptionally hard-working or zealous person. From the name of Aleksei Grigorevich *Stakhanov* (1906–1977), Russian coal miner.

> The new Labour Government was displaying a Stakhanovite level of energy in the production of policies designed to implement its vision of a world-class education service.
> — *Education Review* Summer 1998

Stalag (in the Second World War) a German prison camp, especially for non-commissioned officers and privates. The word is German, a contraction of *Stammlager*, from *Stamm* 'base, main stock' + *Lager* 'camp'.

stalemate in chess, a position counting as a draw, in which a player is not in check but cannot move except into check. The word comes (in the mid 18th century) from obsolete *stale* (from Anglo-Norman French *estale* 'position', from *estaler* 'be placed'), + *mate*.

Joseph Stalin (1879–1953), Soviet statesman, General Secretary of the Communist Party of the USSR 1922–53. Born *Iosif Vissarionovich Dzhugashvili*, his adoptive name Stalin means 'man of steel'. Having isolated his political rival Trotsky, by 1927 Stalin was the uncontested leader of the Communist Party. In 1928 he launched a succession of five-year plans for rapid industrialization and the enforced collectivization of agriculture; as a result of this process some 10 million peasants are thought to have died. His large-scale purges of the intelligentsia in the 1930s were equally ruthless. After the victory over Hitler in 1945 he maintained a firm grip on neighbouring Communist states.

Battle of Stalingrad a long and bitterly fought battle of the Second World War, in which the German advance into the Soviet Union was turned back at Stalingrad in 1942–3. The Germans surrendered after suffering more than 300,000 casualties. (*Stalingrad* is the former name (1925–61) of Volgograd, an industrial city in SW Russia, which until 1925 had been called Tsaritsyn.)

stalker a person who harasses or persecutes someone with unwanted and obsessive attention; the phenomenon of **stalking** has become increasingly high-profile in recent years, with a concern that the end of the obsession may well be violence against the victim.

stalking horse a screen traditionally made in the shape of a horse behind which a hunter may stay concealed when stalking prey. Later, a false pretext concealing someone's real intentions; a candidate in an election for the leadership of a political party who stands only in order to provoke the election and thus allow a stronger candidate to come forward.

Stalky nickname of Lionel Corkran, the leader of three schoolboys in Kipling's *Stalky & Co* (1899); the name implies the character's high degree of stealth and cunning, and had originally belonged to Kipling's schoolfriend Lionel 'Stalky' Dunsterville.

the Stammerer nickname of Lambert *(le) Bègue* (= 'the Stammerer'), 12th-century priest of Liège who founded the Beguine order.

Stamp Act an act regulating stamp duty, especially that imposing the duty on the American colonies in 1765 and repealed in 1766; in his diary of 18 December 1765, John Adams referred to it as, 'That enormous engine, fabricated by the British Parliament, for beating down all the rights and liberties of America, I mean the Stamp Act.'

stand see also ➤ UNITED *we stand, divided we fall.*

stand and deliver! a highwayman's traditional order to travellers to halt and hand over their money and valuables; the expression is recorded from the early 18th century.

standard the authorized exemplar of a unit of measurement, in particular, the prescribed weight of fine metal in gold or silver coins; a system by which the value of a currency is defined in terms of gold or silver or both.

    The word is recorded from Middle English and comes ultimately from Old French *estendre* 'extend'; from the same period (influenced by the verb to stand) it denoted also a flag raised on a pole as a rallying point, typically carrying the distinctive badge of a sovereign, leader, nation, or city. The word appears first in English with reference to the ➤ BATTLE *of the Standard.*

    See also ➤ GOLD *standard.*

standard-bearer a soldier whose duty is to carry a standard, especially in battle; in extended usage, a conspicuous advocate of a cause, one who is in the forefront of a political or religious party.

standard gauge a railway gauge of 4 ft 8½ inches (1.435 m), standard in Britain and many other parts of the world.

standard time a uniform time for places in approximately the same longitude, established in a country or region by law or custom, and given a particular name, as *Eastern Standard Time, Greenwich Mean Time.*

Standing Fishes Bible an edition of 1806, in which *Ezekiel* 47:10 reads 'And it shall come to pass that the fishes shall stand upon it,' instead of, 'the fishers shall stand upon it.'

standing stone another term for a ➤ MENHIR.

Lady Hester Stanhope (1776–1839), English traveller. Granted a pension on the death of her uncle, Pitt the Younger, she settled in a ruined convent in the Lebanon Mountains in 1814 and participated in Middle Eastern politics for several years. She died in poverty after her pension was stopped by Lord Palmerston.

Stanhope press a printing-press invented by the 3rd Earl *Stanhope* (1753–1816, father of ➤ *Lady Hester* STANHOPE), and which he later gave to the delegates of the Clarendon Press at Oxford, who had in 1805 acquired his process of stereotyping.

staniel the kestrel; also used as a term of contempt for a person, with allusion to the uselessness of the kestrel for falconry. The name is recorded in Old English in form *stān(e)gella*, and means literally 'stone-yeller'.

St Stanislaus (1030–79), patron saint of Poland, known as **St Stanislaus of Cracow**. As bishop of Cracow (1072–79) he excommunicated King Boleslaus II. According to tradition Stanislaus was murdered by Boleslaus while taking Mass.

    ☐ **FEAST DAY** His feast day is 11 April (formerly 7 May).

Konstantin Stanislavsky (1863–1938), Russian theatre director and actor. He trained his actors to take a psychological approach and use latent powers of self-expression when taking on roles; his theory and technique were later developed into method acting.

Henry Morton Stanley (1841–1904), Welsh explorer. As a newspaper correspondent he was sent in 1869 to central Africa to find ➤ *David* LIVINGSTONE;

two years later he found him at Lake Tanganyika. After Livingstone's death in 1873 Stanley continued his explorations in Africa, charting Lake Victoria, tracing the course of the Congo, and mapping Lake Albert; the name the ➤ DARK *Continent* for Africa is first recorded in his book *Through the Dark Continent* (1878).

Stanley Cup a trophy awarded annually to the North American ice-hockey team that wins the championship in the National Hockey League. It is named after Lord *Stanley* of Preston (1841–1908), the Governor General of Canada who donated the trophy in 1893.

the Stannaries the districts comprising the tin mines and smelting works of Cornwall and Devon, formerly under the jurisdiction of stannary courts. The name is recorded from late Middle English, and comes ultimately from late Latin *stannum* 'tin'.

Stannary Court a legal body for the regulation of tin miners in the stannaries. The phrase *Stannaria curia* is found in a charter of 1337; by the Stannaries Courts Abolition Act of 1896 the jurisdiction of these courts was transferred to the County Court.

stap me! archaic interjection; *stap* here represents an affected pronunciation of *stop*, given to a character in Vanbrugh's play *The Relapse* (1696).

staple former term for a centre of trade, especially in a specified commodity, such as wool; originally, a town or place, appointed by royal authority, in which was a body of merchants with exclusive right of purchase for certain classes of goods destined for export. An ordinance of Edward III in 1353, the **Statute of the Staple**, established *staples* in a number of English towns as well as at Carmarthen, Dublin, Waterford, Cork, and Drogheda.

At various times the chief staple was overseas; from about 1390 to 1558 it was at Calais, which was sometimes called **the Staple**.

star in allusive or proverbial use, a type of brightness and remoteness, or as representing an innumerable host or multitude.

A *star* is the emblem of ➤ St DOMINIC, ➤ *St* THOMAS *Aquinas*, ➤ *St* VINCENT *Ferrer*, and ➤ *St* NICHOLAS *of Tolentino*.

In astrology, the *stars* denote the planets and zodiacal constellations which are supposed to influence human affairs or (from their position at the time of a person's birth) affect their destiny.

See also ➤ BORN *under a lucky star*, ➤ DARK *star*, ➤ DAY-*star*, ➤ DOG *Star*, ➤ FALLING *star*, ➤ HITCH *one's wagon to a star*, ➤ MORNING *star*, ➤ NORTH *Star*, ➤ POLE *Star*, ➤ SEVEN *stars*, ➤ SHOOTING *star*, ➤ SILVER *Star*, ➤ YELLOW *star*, ➤ STARS.

Star Chamber an English court of civil and criminal jurisdiction that developed in the late 15th century, trying especially those cases affecting the interests of the Crown. It was noted for its arbitrary and oppressive judgements and was abolished in 1641.

In Sir Thomas Smith's *Commonwealth of England* (1610), it is suggested that the name was given 'because at first all the roofe thereof was decked with images of starres gilted'; while this is likely, there is no confirmatory evidence. The alternative suggestion by Blackstone that *starrs* (Jewish deeds or bonds) were deposited there, and so gave rise to the name, is not regarded seriously; the 'sterred chambre' is first mentioned in 1398, while *starr* is not recorded until the early 17th century.

star-crossed (of a person or a plan) thwarted by bad luck; often with allusion to Shakespeare's *Romeo and Juliet* 'a pair of star-crossed lovers'.

Star of Bethlehem a plant of the lily family with star-shaped flowers which typically have green stripes on the outer surface, found in temperate regions of the Old World.

Star of David a six-pointed figure consisting of two interlaced equilateral triangles, used as a Jewish and Israeli symbol; the ➤ MAGEN *David*.

the Star of India a former British Order of knighthood.

Star of the Sea a title of the Virgin Mary, an English translation of ➤ STELLA *Maris*.

Star-spangled Banner a song written in 1814 with words composed by Francis Scott Key (1779–1843) and a tune adapted from that of a popular English drinking song, *To Anacreon in Heaven*.

> 'Tis the star-spangled banner; O long may it wave
> O'er the land of the free, and the home of the brave!
> — Francis Scott Key 'The Star-Spangled Banner' (1814)

It was officially adopted as the US national anthem in 1931.

Star Trek title of a cult science-fiction drama series created by Gene Roddenberry (1921–91); the series chronicled 'the voyages of the starship *Enterprise*', whose five-year mission was 'to boldly go where no man has gone before', and which was commanded by Captain James Kirk.

See also ➤ *Mr* SPOCK, ➤ TREKKIE.

Star Wars[1] title of the first (1977) of a trio of films by George Lucas; the films told the story of the young Luke Skywalker who with the training of ➤ OBI-*Wan Kenobi*, last of the Jedi knights, plays the key role in resisting the Imperial forces under the command of ➤ DARTH *Vader*.

Star Wars[2] popular name for *Strategic Defense Initiative*, a projected US system of defence against nuclear weapons, proposed by President Reagan in 1983, using satellites armed with lasers to intercept and destroy intercontinental ballistic missiles.

starboard the side of a ship or aircraft that is on the right when one is facing forward. The word comes from Old English *stēorbord* 'rudder side', because early Teutonic sailing vessels were steered with a paddle over the right side.

stargazy pie a kind of fish pie traditionally made in Cornwall, with the heads of the fish appearing through the crust.

starling a wooden pile erected with others around or just upstream of a bridge or pier to protect it from the current or floating objects; the word is recorded from the late 17th century, and may be an alteration of dialect *staddling* 'staddle'.

Ernest Henry Starling (1866–1927), English physiologist and founder of the science of endocrinology. He demonstrated the existence of peristalsis, and coined the term *hormone* for the substance secreted by the pancreas which stimulates the secretion of digestive juices.

starred question a question asked in the House of Lords to obtain a spoken answer, marked with an asterisk on the order paper.

Stars and Bars the flag of the Confederate States, which had two horizontal red bars separated by a narrow white bar, and in the top left-hand corner, a circle of eleven white stars on a blue background for the eleven states of the Confederacy.

> Forty flags with their silver stars,
> Forty flags with their crimson bars.
> — John Greenleaf Whittier *Barbara Frietchie* (1863)

Stars and Stripes the national flag of the US. When first adopted by Congress (14th June 1777) it contained 13 stripes and 13 stars, representing the 13

states of the Union; it now has 13 stripes and 50 stars. An informal name for the flag is ➤ OLD *Glory*.

Starvation Dundas nickname given to Henry Dundas (1742–1811), in reference to a speech made about the prospect of famine in the American colonies resulting from a bill of 1775 restraining trade and commerce with the New England colonies; he had said in a debate on 6 March 1775 that he was 'afraid' that the famine spoken of 'would not be produced by this Act'. It was said that this was the first use of the word *starvation* in English, although it does not occur in Dundas's actual speech.

Stasi the internal security force of the former German Democratic Republic, abolished in 1989.

> I've heard a prominent figure in television news suggest that the media have become the new Stasi: the place that informers turn to in order to spill the secrets of—well, the newsworthy.
> — *New Yorker* 25 August 1997

state see ➤ CLOTH *of state*, ➤ COUNSELLOR *of State*, ➤ NANNY *state*, ➤ SHIP *of state*, ➤ STATES.

State Department (in the US) the department in the government dealing with foreign affairs, presided over by the Secretary of State.

State of the Union message a yearly address delivered in January by the President of the US to Congress, giving the administration's view of the state of the nation and plans for legislation. The expression itself is recorded only from 1945, but the requirement for such an address is enshrined in the Constitution of 1787, 'He shall from time to time give to the Congress information of the state of the union'. Also called **State of the Union address**.

stately home a large and fine house that is occupied or was formerly occupied by an aristocratic family; originally in allusion to a poem (1827) by Felicia Hemans, 'The stately homes of England, How beautiful they stand', which was parodied by Noël Coward:

> The Stately Homes of England,
> How beautiful they stand,
> To prove the upper classes
> Have still the upper hand.
> — Noël Coward 'The Stately Homes of England' (1938)

Staten Island an island borough of New York City, which was named by early Dutch settlers after the *Staten* or States General of the Netherlands.

States see also ➤ CONFEDERATE *States*, ➤ UNITED *States*.

the States informal name for the ➤ UNITED *States* of America, first recorded in a letter of John Adams:

> The enemy are in possession of the Head of Elk . . . in which they found a quantity of corn and oats belonging to the States.
>
> — John Adams letter, 1777

the States General the legislative body in the Netherlands from the 15th to 18th centuries, and in France until 1789, representing the three estates of the realm (i.e. the clergy, the nobility, and the commons).

The States General in France was first convened by King Philip IV in 1302 but was called upon only occasionally until it was revived as a political device against the Huguenots during the French Wars of Religion. It met in 1614 but then not again until 1789, when it was urgently summoned to push through much-needed financial and administrative reforms. The same voting methods as in 1614 were used and as a result the radical Third Estate (the commons) gained control and formed themselves into a National Assembly, helping to precipitate the French Revolution.

station the place where someone or something stands or is placed. Early uses of this word referred generally to 'position', especially 'position in life, status', and specifically, in ecclesiastical use, to 'a holy place of pilgrimage (visited as one of a succession)'.

Stationers' Hall the hall of the Stationers' Company in London, formerly used for the registration of books for purposes of copyright.

Stationery Office (in the UK) a government department that publishes governmental publications and provides stationery for government offices.

Stations of the Cross fourteen pictures or carvings representing successive incidents during Jesus' progress from Pilate's house to his crucifixion at Calvary, before which devotions are performed in some Churches. They are, in order: Jesus before Pilate, Jesus carrying the Cross, Jesus falling for the first time, Jesus meeting the Virgin Mary, Jesus with Simon of Cyrene helping to carry the Cross, St Veronica wiping the face of Jesus, Jesus falling for the second time, Jesus and the weeping Women of Jerusalem, Jesus falling for the third time, Jesus stripped of his clothing, Jesus nailed to the Cross, Jesus's death on the Cross, the taking down of Jesus's body, and the entombment of Jesus.

Publius Papinius Statius (*c.*45–96 AD), Roman poet. He is best known for the *Silvae*, a miscellany of poems addressed to friends, and the *Thebais*, an epic concerning the bloody quarrel between the sons of Oedipus. His work, which often uses mythological or fantastical images, was much admired in the Middle Ages.

Stator Latin word for 'sustainer, supporter', primarily an epithet of ➤ JUPITER.

statue see ➤ *Statue of* LIBERTY.

statute originally, a law or decree made by a monarch or a legislative authority, a divine law. Later, a decree or enactment passed by a legislative body, and expressed in a formal document, an Act of Parliament. The word is recorded from Middle English and comes ultimately (via Old French and late Latin) from Latin *statuere* 'set up' from *status* 'standing'.

Bloody Statute a name given to an Act of 1539, enforcing the ➤ SIX *Articles* and imposing severe penalties on all who disputed certain articles of faith.

statute book the book containing the statutes of a nation or state; a nation's laws regarded collectively.

statute cap a cap of wool ordered by statute in 1571 to be worn by citizens on official holidays for the benefit of the cappers' trade.

statute fair another name for a ➤ HIRING *fair.*

Statute of Labourers name given to the medieval statute *De Servientibus*, regulating the rate of wages.

stave church a church of a type built in Norway from the 11th to the 13th century, the walls of which were constructed of upright planks or staves.

steady state an unvarying condition in a physical process, especially as in the theory that the universe is eternal and maintained by constant creation of matter. The steady state theory postulates that the universe maintains a constant average density, with more matter continuously created to fill the void left by galaxies that are receding from one another. The theory has now largely been abandoned in favour of the ➤ BIG *bang* theory and an evolving universe.

steal see ➤ STEAL *someone's thunder.*

one man may steal a horse, while another may not look over a hedge proverbial saying, mid 16th century.

stealth bomber an aircraft designed in accordance with technology which makes detection by radar or sonar difficult; the *stealth bomber* or **B2 bomber** was first seen in operation by the general public during the Gulf War of January—February 1991. Detection is made less likely by the use of a shape with proportions and angles that are not easily visible on radar and materials which evade infrared sensing.

Stedman in bell-ringing, relating to or denoting a method of change-ringing devised by the English printer Fabian *Stedman* (fl. 1670).

steel see ➤ DAMASCUS *steel*, ➤ MAGNOLIA, ➤ RING *of steel*.

Steelboy a member of a group of Irish insurgents, calling themselves 'the Hearts of Steel', involved in agrarian violence 1772–4.

Richard Steele (1672–1729), Irish essayist and dramatist. He founded and wrote for the periodicals the *Tatler* (1709–11) and the *Spectator* (1711–12), the latter in collaboration with ➤ *Joseph* ADDISON.

Steelyard the place on the north bank of the Thames above London Bridge where the Merchants of the ➤ HANSE had their establishment; the Hanseatic Merchants collectively.

Steenie James I's nickname for his favourite George Villiers (1592–1628), later Duke of Buckingham, from a perceived resemblance to a picture of St Stephen.

steeple-house a building with a steeple, especially (as a derogatory term) in early Quaker usage; the English founder of the Society of Friends, George Fox (1624–91), uses the term in describing the effect on him of seeing the spires of Lichfield:

> I . . . espied three steeple-house spires, and they struck at my life.
> — George Fox journal, 1651

steeplechase a horse race run on a racecourse having ditches and hedges as jumps, originally so called because a *steeple* marked the finishing point across country; the term is first recorded in the *Sporting Magazine* of April 1793 of a race of this kind run near Galloway.

stela an upright stone slab or column typically bearing a commemorative inscription or relief design, often serving as a gravestone.

Stella Maris a female protector or guiding spirit at sea (a title sometimes given to the Virgin Mary); the phrase is Latin, and means 'Star of the Sea', and is first attested as an epithet of the Virgin in St Jerome.

Stellenbosch transfer to a post of minimal responsibility as a response to incompetence or lack of success, from the name of a town in Cape Province, South Africa, traditionally the place selected for command by unsuccessful military personnel.

Georg Wilhelm Steller (1709–46), German naturalist and geographer. Steller was a research member of Vitus Bering's second expedition to Kamchatka and Alaska. Following their shipwreck on Bering Island (1741) he made a large collection of specimens but had to abandon it, though he later described many new birds and mammals, several of which now bear his name.

Nicolaus Steno (1638–86), Danish anatomist and geologist. His ideas on the geological history of the earth are now regarded as fundamental—that fossils are the petrified remains of living organisms, that many rocks arise from consolidation of sediments, and that such rocks occur in layers in the order in which they were laid down.

Stentor name of a Greek herald in the Trojan War, 'whose voice was as powerful as fifty voices of other men'; in extended use, a person with a powerful voice.

step- denoting a relationship resulting from a remarriage. This combining form comes (in Old English) from a Germanic base meaning 'bereaved, orphaned'.

one step at a time proverbial saying, mid 19th century.

it is the first step that is difficult see ➤ *ce n'est que le* PREMIER *pas qui coûte*.

St Stephen (died *c.*35), Christian martyr. One of the original seven deacons in Jerusalem appointed by the Apostles, he was charged with blasphemy and stoned, thus becoming the first Christian martyr. Saul of Tarsus (see ➤ *St* PAUL[1]) was present at his execution.

    ☐ **PATRONAGE** He is patron of deacons, bricklayers, and those suffering from headaches.

    ☐ **EMBLEM** His emblem is a stone, as a sign of his martyrdom.

    ☐ **FEAST DAY** His feast day is (in the Western Church) 26 December; (in the Eastern Church) 27 December.

St **Stephen** of Hungary (*c.*977–1038), king and patron saint of Hungary, reigned 1000–38. The first king of Hungary, he united Pannonia and Dacia as one kingdom and took steps to Christianize the country.

 ☐ **FEAST DAY** His feast day is 2 September or (in Hungary) 20 August.

 See also ➤ Crown *of St Stephen.*

St **Stephen's** occasional former name for Parliament, from the chapel of *St Stephen* in which the Commons used to sit.

> For what end at all are men . . . sent to St Stephen's . . . kept talking, struggling, motioning and counter-motioning?
> — Thomas Carlyle *Chartism* (1839)

wicked **stepmother** traditional fairy-tale figure of evil, as in the story of ➤ Snow *White.*

> The wicked stepmother-witch we know best, the one in 'Snow White,' was a mother in the original story the brothers Grimm collected. They changed it in the printed version, thinking her behavior unnatural.
> — Alison Lurie *Don't Tell the Grown-ups* (1990)

Steptoe and Son British television comedy series (1964–73) about a ➤ rag-*and-bone man* father and son, in which Harold Steptoe's social aspirations are constantly frustrated by his father's contentment with their current lifestyle; the name *Steptoe* may be used allusively for a dealer in second-hand goods.

> The result is booming business for Berlin's Steptoes, and it is almost impossible to find a secondhand car in Berlin.
> — *New Scientist* 19 January 1991

Stercoranist derogatory nickname for a person holding that the consecrated elements in the Eucharist undergo digestion in, and evacuation from, the body of the recipient. The word comes (in the mid 16th century) ultimately from Latin *stercor-*, *stercus* 'dung'.

sterling British money. Recorded from Middle English, the word probably comes from *steorra* 'star' + *-ling* (because some early Norman pennies bore a small star). Until recently one popular theory was that the coin was originally made by *Easterling* moneyers (from the 'eastern' Hanse towns), but the stressed first syllable would not have been dropped.

a **stern** chase is a long chase proverbial saying, early 19th century; a *stern chase* is a chase in which the pursuing ship follows directly in the wake of the pursued.

Stern Gang the British name for a militant Zionist group that campaigned in Palestine during the 1940s for the creation of a Jewish state. Founded by Avraham Stern (1907–42) as an offshoot of Irgun, the group assassinated the British Minister for the Middle East, Lord Moyne, and Count Bernadotte, the UN mediator for Palestine.

be made of **sterner stuff** be more resolute, be less inclined to yield (originally with reference to Shakespeare's *Julius Caesar*):

> When that the poor have cried, Caesar hath wept;
> Ambition should be made of sterner stuff.
> — William Shakespeare *Julius Caesar* (1599)

Sternhold and Hopkins informal name for a metrical version of the Psalms, prepared by Thomas *Sternhold* (d. 1548) and John *Hopkins* (d. 1570).

stet let it stand (Latin word used as an instruction on a printed proof to indicate that a correction or alteration should be ignored).

Stetson a hat with a high crown and a very wide brim, traditionally worn by cowboys and ranchers in the US, named after John B. *Stetson* (1830–1906), American hat manufacturer.

Stevengraph a type of small picture made from brightly coloured woven silk, produced during the late 19th century; it is named after Thomas Stevens (1828–88), English weaver, whose firm made them.

Robert Louis Stevenson (1850–94) Scottish novelist, poet, and travel writer, author of *Treasure Island* (1883), *Kidnapped*, and *The Strange Case of Dr Jekyll and Mr Hyde*. His later life was spent in Samoa, where he was given the name *Tusitala*, 'teller of tales'.

steward a person employed to manage another person's property, especially a large house or estate; in the UK, an officer of the royal household, especially an administrator of Crown estates. Recorded from Old English (in form *stīweard*), the word comes from *stig* (probably in the sense 'house, hall') + *weard* 'ward'.

unjust steward in a parable from Luke 16, a rich man's steward who, accused by his master of being thriftless and fearing destitution from being dismissed, arranges with his master's debtors to reduce the apparent amount of the debts they owe. He is commended for this by his master, 'for the children of this world are in their generation wiser than the children of light.'

Lord High Steward of England a high officer of State, appointed since the 15th century only on the occasion of a coronation, at which he presides, or formerly (prior to 1948), for the trial of a peer, at which he presided in the House of Lords.

Lord High Steward of Scotland the principal officer of the Scottish sovereign in early times in charge of administering Crown revenues, supervising the royal household, and having the privilege of standing in the army in battle second only to the sovereign.

Lord Steward of the King's (or Queen's) Household a peer in charge of the management of the sovereign's household and presiding at the ➤ Board *of Green Cloth*.

steward of the manor a person who transacted the financial and legal business of a manor on behalf of the lord and whose chief functions were to hold the manor-court in the lord's absence, and to keep the court rolls.

Stewart an alternative spelling of the name ➤ Stuart.

See also ➤ Walking *Stewart*.

The Stewartry the Kirkcudbright district of Galloway; a *stewartry* was a former territorial division of Scotland (abolished in 1747) under the jurisdiction of a steward.

stick see also ➤ big *stick*, ➤ Gold *Stick*, ➤ Silver *Stick*.

stick-and-carrot a method of persuasion combining the threat of punishment with the promise of reward; a *carrot* dangled in front of a donkey was a proverbial method of tempting the animal to move.

it is easy to find a stick to beat a dog proverbial saying, mid 16th century; meaning that it is easy to find reasons to criticize someone who is vulnerable.

sticking-place a place in which something stops and holds fast; in allusion to Shakespeare's *Macbeth*, where the reference seems to be to the screwing-up of the peg of a musical instrument until it becomes tightly fixed in the hole.

> But screw your courage to the sticking-place,
> And we'll not fail.
> — William Shakespeare *Macbeth* (1606)

stickit in Scotland, designating a member of a trade or profession who has relinquished their intended calling from want of ability or means to pursue it.

stickler a person who insists on a certain quality or type of behaviour. The word comes (in the mid 16th

century, in the sense 'umpire') from obsolete *stickle* 'be umpire', alteration of obsolete *stightle* 'to control', frequentative of Old English *stiht(i)an* 'set in order'.

sticks see also ➤ *the* DEVIL *on two sticks*, ➤ LAND *of the Little Sticks*.

the sticks informal and derogatory term for rural areas far from cities and civilization; recorded (originally in the US) from the early 1900s.

sticks and stones may break my bones, but words will never hurt me proverbial saying, late 19th century.

sticky wicket a cricket pitch that has been drying after rain and is difficult to bat on; a tricky or awkward situation. The term is recorded in its literal sense from 1882, in a reference to the Australians finding themselves on a sticky wicket; the first figurative example is found in the 1950s:

> Mr Churchill was batting on a very sticky wicket in Washington.
> — *National News-Letter* 24 January 1952

stigma originally (in the late 16th century) a mark made on the skin by pricking or branding, as punishment for a criminal or a mark of subjection, a brand; in extended usage, a mark of disgrace associated with a particular circumstance, quality, or person. The word comes via Latin from Greek *stigma* 'a mark made by a pointed instrument, a dot'; its plural form gives ➤ stigmata.

stigmata (in Christian tradition) marks corresponding to those left on Christ's body by the Crucifixion, said to have been impressed by divine favour on the bodies of ➤ St Francis *of Assisi* and others; the word (plural of ➤ stigma) is recorded in this sense from the early 17th century.

Stiles see ➤ John-*a-Stiles*.

still life a painting or drawing of an arrangement of objects, typically including fruit and flowers and objects contrasting with these in texture, such as bowls and glassware. The term is recorded from the late 17th century, in John Dryden's translation of Du Fresnoy's *De Arte Graphica* (1695), and was influenced by Dutch *stilleven* in the same sense.

still room originally, a room in a house where a *still* was kept for the distillation of perfumes and cordials; later, a room in a large house which was used by the housekeeper for the storage of preserves, cakes, and liqueurs and the preparation of tea and coffee. The term is recorded from the early 18th century.

a still tongue makes a wise head proverbial saying, mid 16th century.

still waters run deep proverbial saying, early 15th century.

stilo novo appended to a date: = 'New Style', i.e. according to the reformed (or ➤ GREGORIAN) calendar; the phrase is Latin, and is recorded from the early 17th century. *Stilo vetere* is the corresponding phrase for 'Old Style'.

See also ➤ DOLCE *stil nuovo*.

Stilton trademark name for a kind of strong rich cheese, often with blue veins, originally made at various places in Leicestershire, and so named because it was formerly sold to travellers at a coaching inn in Stilton (now in Cambridgeshire).

the more you stir it [a turd] the worse it stinks proverbial saying, mid 16th century.

Stir-up Sunday the Sunday next before Advent, so called from the opening words of the collect for the day:

> Stir up, we beseech thee, O Lord, the wills of thy faithful people; that they, plenteously bringing forth the fruit of good works, may of thee be plenteously rewarded.
> — The Book of Common Prayer *Collects* The five and twentieth Sunday after Trinity (1662)

The name also became associated with the stirring of the Christmas mincemeat, which it was customary to begin making that week.

James Stirling (1692–1770), Scottish mathematician. His main work, *Methodus Differentialis* (1730), was concerned with summation and interpolation. A formula named after him, giving the approximate value of the factorial of large numbers, was actually first worked out by the French-born mathematician Abraham De Moivre (1667–1754).

James Fraser Stirling (1926–92), Scottish architect. Working at first in a brutalist style, he became known for his use of geometric shapes and coloured decoration in public buildings such as the Neuestaatsgalerie in Stuttgart (1977).

stirrup the device probably originated in the Asian steppes around the 2nd century BC, and was of great military value. The word comes (in Old English) from the Germanic base of obsolete *sty* 'climb' +

rope, indicating that the original stirrup must have been a looped rope.

The expression **hold the stirrup**, as in helping a person to mount, indicates an expression of homage or reverence, and is sometimes used to refer to a formal sign of respect paid by an emperor to the Pope.

stirrup cup a cup of wine or other alcoholic drink offered to a person on horseback who is about to depart on a journey.

a stitch in time saves nine proverbial saying, early 18th century; it was originally a couplet, with *nine* chosen as the number for assonance.

stiver a small coin formerly used in the Netherlands, equal to one twentieth of a guilder, taken as the type of a small or insignificant amount. The word comes from Dutch *stuiver*, denoting a small coin, probably related to the noun *stub*.

the Stoa the great hall in Athens in which the ancient Greek philosopher ➤ ZENO *of Citium* gave the founding lectures of the philosophic school of ➤ STOICISM. Also known as *the Porch*.

stock originally (in Old English) this meant 'trunk, block of wood, post'; proverbially taken as the type of what is lifeless and motionless, and thus a senseless or stupid person.

See also ➤ STOCKS *and stones*.

stock dove a grey Eurasian and North African pigeon, resembling a small wood pigeon without white markings, and nesting in holes in trees; also called *stock pigeon*. The name probably comes from its habit of nesting in hollow trees, although it has been suggested that it implies that it is the 'stock' or ancestral form of the domestic pigeon.

Stock Exchange a market in which securities are bought and sold; the level of prices in such a market. The term is first used (in the late 18th century) of the London *Stock Exchange* in Threadneedle Street, which replaced ➤ JONATHAN's coffee house in Exchange Alley, the former mart for stockjobbers.

> Yesterday the Brokers and others at New Jonathan's, came to a resolution, that instead of being called New Jonathan's, it should be named 'The Stock Exchange', which is to be wrote over the door.
> — *London Chronicle* 13–15 July 1773

stockbroker a broker who buys and sells securities on a stock exchange on behalf of clients; the term is recorded from the early 18th century.

stockbroker belt an affluent residential area outside a large city, supposedly typical of the lifestyle of a successful stockbroker.

Stockbroker's Tudor a style of mock-Tudor architecture associated with a ➤ STOCKBROKER *belt*; the term was first recorded in *Homes Sweet Homes* (1939), by the English cartoonist and writer Osbert Lancaster (1908–86).

stockfish cod or a similar fish split and dried in the open air without salt, used formerly by the Vikings as food for sea voyages, and now popular as a gourmet food; in allusive and figurative use, the *stockfish* is the type of something mute and lifeless.

Stockholm syndrome feelings of trust or affection felt in many cases of kidnapping or hostage-taking by a victim towards a captor, with reference to the aftermath of a bank robbery in Stockholm.

stocking originally, a long sock; sometimes used as a purse or a receptacle for savings, and thus coming formerly to mean 'a store of money'.

See also ➤ CHRISTMAS *stocking*.

hang up one's stocking on Christmas Eve, put an empty stocking ready as a receptacle for small gifts, supposedly to be filled by Santa Claus.

stockjobber in the UK, archaic term for a principal or wholesaler who dealt only on the Stock Exchange with brokers, not directly with the public; a ➤ JOBBER.

stocks and stones a derogatory term for gods of wood and stone, as in Wisdom 14:21, 'men…did ascribe unto stones and stocks the incommunicable name'.

Stoicism an ancient Greek school of philosophy founded at Athens by ➤ ZENO of Citium, and named for ➤ *the* STOA in which he taught. The school taught that virtue, the highest good, is based on knowledge; the wise live in harmony with the divine Reason (also identified with Fate and Providence) that governs nature, and are indifferent to the vicissitudes of fortune and to pleasure and pain.

Bram Stoker (1847–1912), Irish novelist and theatre manager. He was secretary and touring manager to the actor Henry Irving but is chiefly remembered as the author of the vampire story *Dracula* (1897).

Leopold Stokowski (1882–1977), British-born American conductor, of Polish descent. He is best known for arranging and conducting the music for Walt Disney's film *Fantasia* (1940), which sought to bring classical music to cinema audiences by means of cartoons.

stole a priest's silk vestment worn over the shoulders and hanging down to the knee or below. Recorded from Old English (in the senses 'long robe' and 'priest's vestment'), the word comes via Latin from Greek *stolē* 'clothing'.

See also ➤ GROOM *of the Stole*.

stolen fruit is sweet proverbial saying, early 17th century; the proverb (which is found in a number of forms) is often used with direct allusion to the temptation of ➤ EVE by the serpent in the Garden of Eden.

stolen waters are sweet proverbial saying, late 14th century.

Stolypin car a type of railway carriage for the transport of prisoners, introduced after the Russian Revolution of 1905. It was named for the Russian conservative statesman Pyotr Arkadyevich *Stolypin* (1862–1911), who was assassinated by a revolutionary while attending a performance of the opera in the company of the Tsar.

Stolypin's necktie a hangman's noose, like the ➤ STOLYPIN *car* named for the Russian conservative statesman.

stomach see ➤ *an* ARMY *marches on its stomach*.

stone a *stone* may be the type of motionlessness or fixity, or of hardness, and thus insensibility (as in **stone-blind**) or stupidity; in Ezekiel 36:26, a 'stony heart' is contrasted with a 'heart of flesh'.

A stone is the emblem of ➤ St STEPHEN and ➤ St JEROME.

See also ➤ BLARNEY *Stone*, ➤ BLOWING *Stone*, ➤ CAST *the first stone*, ➤ CONSTANT *dropping wears away a stone*, ➤ CORONATION *Stone*, ➤ EAGLE-*stone*, ➤ JACOB'*s stone*, ➤ LEAVE *no stone unturned*, ➤ LOGAN *stone*, ➤ LONDON *stone*, ➤ LUCKY *stone*, ➤ *mark with a* WHITE *stone*, ➤ MOABITE *Stone*, ➤ PHILOSOPHER'*s stone*, ➤ PRECIOUS *stone*, ➤ RAVEN-*stone*, ➤ *a* ROLLING *stone*, ➤ ROSETTA *Stone*, ➤ SERPENT-*stone*, ➤ SNAKE-*stone*, ➤ TREATY *Stone*, ➤ *you cannot get* BLOOD *from a stone*; ➤ STONES.

Stone Age a prehistoric period when weapons and tools were made of stone or of organic materials such as bone, wood, or horn. The Stone Age covers a period of about 2.5 million years, from the first use of tools by the ancestors of man (*Australopithecus*) to the introduction of agriculture and the first towns. It is subdivided into the Palaeolithic, Mesolithic, and Neolithic periods, and is succeeded in Europe by the *Bronze Age* (or, sometimes, the *Copper Age*) about 5,000–4,000 years ago.

Stone Age may be used generally to designate something or someone regarded as primitive or reactionary; it was notably employed by the American Air Force General Curtis LeMay (1906–90) in 1965 in his comments on the North Vietnamese:

> They've got to draw in their horns and stop their aggression, or we're going to bomb them back into the Stone Age.
> — Curtis E. LeMay *Mission with LeMay* (1965)

stone-dead hath no fellow proverbial saying, mid 17th century.

Stone of Scone the stone on which medieval Scottish kings were crowned at ➤ SCONE. It was brought to England by Edward I and preserved in the coronation chair in Westminster Abbey, and returned to Scotland in 1996. Also called *Coronation stone*, *Stone of Destiny*.

Stonehenge a megalithic monument on Salisbury Plain in Wiltshire. Completed in several constructional phases from *c*.2950 BC, it is composed of a circle of sarsen stones surrounded by a bank and ditch and enclosing a circle of smaller bluestones. Within this inner circle is a horseshoe arrangement of five trilithons with the axis aligned on the midsummer sunrise, an orientation that was probably for ritual purposes.

Stonehenge is popularly associated with the Druids, although this connection is now generally rejected by scholars; the monument has also been attributed to the Phoenicians, Romans, Vikings, and visitors from other worlds. Geoffrey of Monmouth says that the main stones were brought from Ireland by the magic of ➤ MERLIN.

The second element of the name may have meant something 'hanging or supported in the air'. A spurious form *Stanhengest* is found in some (*a*. 1500) Latin chronicles, with a story associating Stonehenge with a massacre of British nobles by the Saxon leader ➤ HENGIST (see also ➤ NIGHT *of the long knives*).

stones see ➤ DRIVE *gently over the stones*, ➤ ROLLRIGHT *Stones*, ➤ *you buy* LAND, *you buy stones*.

Stonewall[1] nickname of Thomas Jonathan Jackson (1824–63), Confederate general during the American Civil War. It derives from a comment by his fellow Confederate general Barnard Elliott Bee (1823–61) at the battle of Bull Run, in which Bee himself was killed:

> There is Jackson with his Virginians, standing like a stone wall. Let us determine to die here, and we will conquer.
> — Barnard Elliott Bee comment, 21 July 1861

Stonewall[2] a gay bar in Greenwich Village where in 1969 those present responded violently to a police raid; the riot has subsequently been commemorated annually during Gay Pride week in June, both in America and in a number of other countries.

stony see ➤ FALL *on stony ground*.

stool see also ➤ BETWEEN *two stools one falls to the ground*, ➤ CUCKING *stool*, ➤ CUTTY-*stool*, ➤ DUCKING *stool*.

stool of repentance traditionally in the Presbyterian Church, on which a person sat to do formal penance before the rest of the congregation.

stool pigeon a police informer, a person acting as a decoy, so named from the original use in wildfowling of a pigeon fixed to a stool as a decoy.

stop-me-and-buy-one slogan for Wall's ice cream, from spring 1922.

stop of the exchequer the suspension of payment of the Government debt to the London goldsmiths in 1672, a national act of bankruptcy by which the government obtained over a million pounds.

Marie Stopes (1880–1958), Scottish birth-control campaigner. Her book *Married Love* (1918) was a frank treatment of sexuality within marriage. In 1921 she founded the pioneering Mothers' Clinic for Birth Control in London.

stories see ➤ MASTER *of Stories*.

stork a very tall long-legged wading bird with a long heavy bill, characteristically with white and black plumage. The white stork is traditionally known as the bringer of children, and other legends associate the bird as a bringer of luck to houses where it nests.

King Stork in Aesop's fable of Jupiter and the frogs who asked for a king, the harsh ruler who replaces the inert ➤ *King* Log.

storm see also ➤ *any* port *in a storm*, ➤ Cape *of Storms*, ➤ Desert *Storm*, ➤ gowk *storm*, ➤ *the* sharper *the storm, the sooner it's over.*

storm cock the mistle thrush (from its continuing to sing in stormy weather); the name is first recorded by the naturalist Gilbert White (1720–93) in a letter of 1769, noting that the name is used in Hampshire and Sussex.

Stormont Castle a castle in Belfast which was, until 1972, the seat of the Parliament of Northern Ireland and in 1999 became the headquarters of the Northern Ireland Assembly.

stormy see also ➤ *it was a* dark *and stormy night.*

stormy petrel a small seabird of the open ocean, typically having blackish plumage and a white rump, and formerly believed to be a harbinger of bad weather; a person who causes or presages unrest.

Storting the Norwegian parliament; the name comes from Norwegian *stor* 'great' + *ting* 'assembly'.

story see ➤ *every* picture *tells a story.*

one story is good till another is told proverbial saying, late 16th century.

stoup a basin for holy water, especially on the wall near the door of a Roman Catholic church for worshippers to dip their fingers in before crossing themselves. Recorded from Middle English, the word originally denoted 'pail, small cask'.

put a stout heart to a stey brae proverbial saying, late 16th century; meaning that determination is needed to climb a steep ('stey') hillside.

collapse of stout party standard dénouement in Victorian humour; the phrase is supposed to come from *Punch*, as the characteristic finishing line of a joke, but no actual example has been traced, although the character *Stout Party* appeared in a cartoon of 1855.

stovepipe hat a silk hat resembling a top hat but much taller, popular in the mid 19th century.

Strabo (*c*.63 bc–*c*.23 ad), historian and geographer of Greek descent. His only extant work,

Geographica, in seventeen volumes, provides a detailed physical and historical geography of the ancient world during the reign of Augustus.

Lytton Strachey (1880–1932), English biographer. A prominent member of the ➤ Bloomsbury *Group*, he achieved recognition with *Eminent Victorians* (1918), which attacked the literary Establishment through its satirical biographies of Florence Nightingale, General Gordon, and others.

> What was once Stracheyesque subversion has become simply the way that everybody writes about public figures.
> — *Independent on Sunday* 28 August 1994

Antonio Stradivari (*c*.1644–1737), Italian violinmaker. He devised the proportions of the modern violin, giving a more powerful and rounded sound than earlier instruments possessed. About 650 of his celebrated violins, violas, and violoncellos are still in existence.

Stradivarius a violin or other stringed instrument made by Antonio *Stradivari* or his followers; sometimes informally shortened to **Strad**.

strafe attack repeatedly with bombs or machine-gun fire from low-flying aircraft; humorous adaptation of the German First World War catchphrase *Gott strafe England* 'may God punish England', coined by the German writer Alfred Funke (b. 1869).

Straffordian any of the fifty-nine members of the House of Commons who in 1641 voted against the bill impeaching the English statesman Thomas Wentworth, Earl of *Strafford* (1593–1641); the name was initially used on a list posted up at Westminster by their opponents on 3rd May 1641 to show who had supported the king's minister. Strafford was executed on 11 May.

See also ➤ Black *Tom*, ➤ Thorough.

straight from the horse's mouth expression for the original, authentic source of information; recorded from the 1920s, and probably referring to the ideal source for a racing tip.

strain at a gnat and swallow a camel proverbial saying, late 16th century; meaning that one will make great difficulty over accepting a trivial matter, but will accept something serious without question. The phrase derives from Matthew 23:24, 'Ye blind guides, which strain at a gnat and swallow a camel'; in which *strain* has been misunderstood as 'make violent effort', rather than indicating that the liquor would be strained if a gnat were found in it.

Strait of Magellan between the South American mainland and Tierra del Fuego; it is named after the Portuguese explorer ➤ *Ferdinand* MAGELLAN (*c.*1480–1521).

strand see also ➤ *you're never* ALONE *with a Strand.*

the Strand a street in London; originally so called as occupying, with the gardens belonging to the houses, the 'strand' or shore of the Thames between the cities of London and Westminster; the name is recorded from the mid 13th century.

Dr Strangelove a person who ruthlessly considers or plans nuclear warfare, from the character in the film of that name (1963).

> A bearded, friendly fellow who votes Democratic, Kent Johnson embodies the outward diversity of lab culture: no Dr. Strangelove clones here.
> — *Mother Jones* April 1995

strangers see ➤ *I* SPY *strangers!*.

strappado a form of punishment or torture in which the victim was secured to a rope and made to fall from a height almost to the ground before being stopped with an abrupt jerk; the instrument used for inflicting this punishment or torture. The word is recorded from the mid 16th century, and comes (via French) ultimately from Italian *strappare* 'to snatch'.

Strasbourg a city in NE France, in Alsace, close to the border with Germany, which was annexed by Germany in 1870, it was returned to France after the First World War. It is the headquarters of the Council of Europe and of the European Parliament.

> MPs may be jealous of Strasbourg's power, but British voters will not understand why Euro-MPs should be able to block laws they dislike.
> — *Economist* 2 November 1991

Strasbourg goose a goose fattened in such a way as to enlarge the liver for use in pâté de foie gras.

Stratford-upon-Avon a town in Warwickshire, on the River Avon, famous as the birth and burial place of William Shakespeare, which is also the site of the Royal Shakespeare Theatre.

straw dried stalks of grain, used especially as fodder or as material for thatching, packing, or weaving; in proverbial or allusive use, something of small value, lack of substance or value, or inflammability.

See also ➤ *a* DROWNING *man will clutch at a straw,* ➤ *it is the* LAST *straw that breaks the camel's back,* ➤ *a* PAD *in the straw,* ➤ *you cannot make* BRICKS *without straw.*

Jack Straw name of one of the main leaders of the ➤ PEASANTS' *Revolt* of 1381; after the suppression of the rising his head (with ➤ *Wat* TYLER's) was exposed on London Bridge. He is referred to in Chaucer's *Nun's Priest's Tale.*

man of straw originally, a dummy or image made of straw; from this, a person compared to a straw image, a sham; a sham argument set up to be defeated.

straw poll an unofficial ballot conducted as a test of opinion. The term is recorded from the mid 20th century; the earlier **straw vote** dates (in the US) from 1866.

strawberry a sweet soft red fruit with a seed-studded surface; the low-growing plant which produces this fruit, having white flowers, lobed leaves, and runners, and found throughout north temperate regions. The English physician William Butler (1535–1618) said of it, 'Doubtless God could have made a better berry, but doubtless God never did.'

In the 17th century, the term was used attributively in such compounds as **strawberry preaching** and **strawberry sermon**, in allusion to a sermon preached in 1549 by the Protestant divine and future martyr Hugh Latimer (1485?–1555):

> The preaching of the word of God unto the people is called meat . . . Not strawberries, that come but once a year and tarry not long.
> — Hugh Latimer *Sermon on the Ploughers* (1549)

Strawberry Hill a house in Twickenham rebuilt after the Gothic style between 1750 and 1770 by Horace Walpole, which gave its name to an early phase of the Gothic revival inspired and epitomized by this house. Walpole himself said of his house that it was 'a little plaything-house that I got out of Mrs Chevenix's shop, and is the prettiest bauble you ever saw'.

> These terraces are adorned with two curious turrets, resting on baroque basements and crowned by swallow-tailed crenellations—a fantastic reversion to mediaevalism, more suggestive of 'Strawberry Hill Gothic' than of the Italian seventeenth century.
> — Edith Wharton *Italian Villas* (1904)

strawberry leaves the row of conventional figures of the leaf on the coronet of a duke, marquis, or earl.

strawberry mark a soft red birthmark resembling a strawberry; in traditional stories, often the means by which a lost member of a family can be identified.

straws in one's hair a state of insanity, from the supposed characteristic practice of a deranged person; the first explicit reference to the expression is found in Lewis Carroll's description of the illustration by Tenniel of the ➤ MARCH *Hare* in *Alice in Wonderland*:

> That's the March Hare, with the long ears, and straws mixed up with his hair. The straws showed he was mad—I don't know why. Never twist up straws among *your* hair, for fear people should think you're mad!
> — Lewis Carroll *Nursery 'Alice'* (1890)

straws tell which way the wind blows proverbial saying, mid 17th century; in *Table-talk* (1689), John Selden recommended, 'Take a straw and throw it up in the Air, you shall see by that which way the wind is.'

a stream cannot rise above its source proverbial saying, mid 17th century.

stream of consciousness a person's thoughts and conscious reactions to events, perceived as a continuous flow. The term was introduced by William James in his *Principles of Psychology* (1890); a literary style in which a character's thoughts, feelings, and reactions are depicted in a continuous flow uninterrupted by objective description or conventional dialogue. James Joyce, Virginia Woolf, and Marcel Proust are among its notable early exponents.

street see also ➤ CORONATION *Street*, ➤ QUEER *Street*.

street Arab archaic term for a raggedly dressed homeless child wandering the streets; the use of Arab in this sense dates from the mid 19th century.

streets paved with gold proverbial view of a city in which opportunities for advancement are easy; as in George Colman the Younger's *The Heir at Law* (1797) 'Oh, London is a fine town, A very famous city, Where all the streets are paved with gold.'

strength see also ➤ TOWER *of strength*, ➤ UNION *is strength*.

strength through joy the promotion of physical and cultural recreational activities among working people, from the name of *Kraft durch Freude*, a movement founded in Germany by the National Socialist Party in 1933.

Strephon the shepherd whose lament for his lost Urania forms the opening of Sidney's Arcadia. *Strephon* has been adopted as a conventional name for a rustic lover.

stretch your arm no further than your sleeve will reach proverbial saying, mid 16th century.

everyone stretches his legs according to the length of his coverlet proverbial saying, late 13th century.

strike while the iron is hot proverbial saying, late 14th century.

strikes see ➤ LIGHTNING *never strikes twice in the same place*, ➤ THREE *strikes*.

Strine the English language as spoken by Australians; the Australian accent, especially when considered pronounced or uneducated. The name represents an alleged Australian pronunciation of *Australian*, coined by A. A. Morrison (1911–) in 1964:

> New light on the Strine language, by Afferbeck Lauder, Professor of Strine Studies, University of Sinny.
> — heading in *Sydney Morning Herald* 19 December 1964

string and sealing-wax (the type of) simple or unpretentious scientific equipment, with which great scientific discoveries may yet be made; the *Daily Telegraph* of 5 March 1962 prophesied that, 'The traditional British method of scientific research with "string and sealing wax" will pay rich dividends'. The physicist Ernest Rutherford (1871–1937) had earlier commented in a similar context, 'We haven't got the money, so we've got to think!'

strip-jack-naked another name for ➤ BEGGAR-*my-neighbour*.

stripes see ➤ FORTY *stripes*.

striptease a form of entertainment in which a performer gradually undresses to music in a way intended to be sexually exciting; the term is recorded from 1936, with an earlier related usage in *Variety* of 1 October 1930, 'The girls have the strip and tease down to a science'.

stroke see also ➤ DIFFERENT *strokes for different folks*, ➤ REDDING *stroke*.

stroke the oar or oarsman nearest the stern of a boat, setting the timing for the other rowers, recorded from the early 19th century; *stroke* in this sense appears in 'All rowed fast, but none so fast as stroke', a famous misquotation of a passage from Desmond Coke's novel *Sandford of Merton* (1903), in which it is said of the oarsman that 'his oar was dipping into the water nearly *twice* as often as any other'.

Stromboli a volcanic island in the Mediterranean, the most north-easterly of the Lipari Islands, whose volcano is typified by continual mild eruptions in which lava fragments are ejected.

strong see also ➤ the RACE *is not to the swift, nor the battle to the strong,* ➤ YORKSHIRE *born and Yorkshire bred, strong in the arm and weak in the head.*

strong meat something acceptable only to strong or instructed minds; often with biblical allusion to Hebrews 5:12, 'ye…are become such as have need of meat, and not of strong meat'.

strong verb a verb (of Germanic origin) forming the past tense and past participle by means of a change of vowel in the stem rather than by the addition of a suffix (e.g. *swim, swam, swum*).

stronger see ➤ *a* CHAIN *is no stronger than its weakest link.*

strophe the first section of an ancient Greek choral ode or of one division of it; a turn in dancing made by an ancient Greek chorus. Recorded from the early 17th century, the word comes from Greek *strophē*, literally 'turning', from *strephein* 'to turn'. The term originally denoted a movement from right to left made by a Greek chorus, or lines of choral song recited during this.

Struldbrug in Swift's *Gulliver's Travels* (1726), given as the native appellation of 'the immortals' in the kingdom of Luggnagg, who were incapable of dying, but after the age of eighty continued to exist in a state of miserable decrepitude, regarded as legally dead, and receiving a small pittance from the state.

> There is a danger lest the aged pensioner at home should sink into the condition of a Struldbrug.
> — *Contemporary Review* December 1908

Struwwelpeter a character in a collection of children's stories of the same name by Heinrich Hoffmann (1809–94), with long thick unkempt hair standing out from his head and extremely long fingernails; also known as *shock-headed Peter*.

> Marz standing in the doorway, Struwwelpeter hair combed for once.
> — Elizabeth Hand *Glimmering* (1997)

Stuart the royal family (also called *Stewart*) ruling Scotland 1371–1714 and Britain 1603–1649 and 1660–1714. The name of the royal house comes ultimately from ➤ STEWARD, and the accession in 1371 to the throne of Scotland as Robert II of Robert the Steward, grandson of Robert the Bruce by Bruce's daughter Marjory and her husband Walter, Steward of Scotland.

Charles Edward Stuart (1720–88), son of ➤ *James Francis Edward* STUART, pretender to the British throne; known as the ➤ YOUNG *Pretender* or ➤ BONNIE *Prince Charlie*. He led the Jacobite uprising of 1745–6. However, he was driven back to Scotland by the Duke of Cumberland and defeated at the Battle of Culloden (1746). He died in exile in Rome.

James Francis Edward Stuart (1688–1766), son of James II, pretender to the British throne; known as the ➤ OLD *Pretender*. He arrived in Scotland too late to alter the outcome of the 1715 Jacobite uprising and left the leadership of the 1745–6 uprising to his son ➤ *Charles Edward* STUART.

all Stuarts are not sib to the king Scottish proverb, early 18th century; meaning that the possession of a famous name is not in itself an indication of a shared bloodline.

studium generale in the Middle Ages, a university attended by scholars from outside as well as within its own locality.

stuffed owl referring to poetry which treats trivial or inconsequential subjects in a grandiose manner. The phrase comes from the title of Wyndham Lewis's *The Stuffed Owl: an anthology of bad verse* (1930), and ultimately alludes to Wordsworth:

> The presence even of a stuffed owl for her
> Can cheat the time.
> — William Wordsworth *Miscellaneous Sonnets* (1827)

stumbling block a circumstance that causes difficulty or hesitation; especially with biblical allusion to Romans 14:13, 'That no man put a stumbling block or an occasion to fall in his brother's way'; a phrase first used in Tyndale's translation.

stump see also ➤ *beyond the* BLACK *stump*, ➤ BOS-TON *Stump*.

stump in early US use (from the late 18th century), the stump of a large felled tree used as a stand or platform for a speaker; from this came the expression **to go on the stump** meaning to make a campaigning tour throughout a region. The Democratic politician Adlai Stevenson (1900–65) said of Richard Nixon that he was 'the kind of politician who would cut down a redwood tree, and then mount the stump and make a speech on conservation'.

Stundist a member of a large Evangelical sect which arose among the peasantry of South Russia about 1860, as a result of contact with German Protestant settlers, and in opposition to the doctrine and authority of the Russian Orthodox Church. The name comes ultimately from German *Stunde* 'hour', said to be used by the German settlers as the name for their religious meetings.

stupa a round, usually domed, structure erected as a Buddhist shrine.

Stupor mundi Latin phrase meaning the marvel of the world, an object of admiring bewilderment and wonder; it was originally used by the 13th-century chronicler Matthew Paris to describe the Emperor Frederick II of Germany (1194–1250).

sturdy beggar archaic term for an able-bodied beggar or vagabond, especially a violent one.

sturgeon a very large primitive fish with bony plates on the body. It occurs in temperate seas and rivers of the northern hemisphere, especially central Eurasia, and is of commercial importance for its caviar and flesh. A sturgeon is a royal fish. The name is recorded from Middle English, and is ultimately of Germanic origin.

Sturm und Drang a literary and artistic movement in Germany in the late 18th century, influenced by ➤ *Jean-Jacques* ROUSSEAU and characterized by the expression of emotional unrest and a rejection of neoclassical literary norms. The phrase is German, and means literally 'Storm and Stress'.

Stygian of or relating to the River ➤ STYX or to the underworld of classical mythology; in extended usage, dark and gloomy.

Stygian Jove a term for Pluto, as god of the underworld.

style a manner of doing something, a distinctive appearance. The word is recorded from Middle English, denoting a ➤ STYLUS, also a literary composition, an official title, or a characteristic manner of literary expression, and comes via Old French from Latin *stilus*.

the style is the man proverbial saying, early 20th century; from the French naturalist Buffon (1707–88):

> Style is the man himself.
> — Comte de Buffon *Discours sur le style* (address given to the Académie Française, 25 August 1753)

In a covering letter of 2 February 1891 to the *Daily Telegraph*, Oscar Wilde wrote of a letter on 'Fashion in Dress' which he enclosed, 'I don't wish to sign my name, though I am afraid everybody will know who the writer is: one's style is one's signature always.'

stylite an ascetic living on top of a pillar, especially in ancient or medieval Syria, Turkey, and Greece in the 5th century AD. Recorded from the mid 17th century, the word comes ultimately from ecclesiastical Greek *stulos* 'pillar'.

See also ➤ *St* SIMEON *Stylites*.

stylus an ancient writing implement, consisting of a small rod with a pointed end for scratching letters on wax-covered tablets, and a blunt end for obliterating them. The word is recorded from the early 18th century, and is a misspelling of Latin *stilus*.

stymie in golf, a situation on the putting green in which a player's ball lies between another player and the hole, forming a possible obstruction to play; in general usage, *stymie* now means prevent or hinder the progress of. The origin of the word is unknown.

Stymphalian birds in Greek mythology, harmful birds which infested *Stymphalus*, a district in Arcadia, and were destroyed by Hercules as the fifth of his twelve labours.

Styx in Greek mythology, one of the nine rivers in the underworld, over which ➤ CHARON ferried the souls of the dead, and by which the gods swore their most solemn oaths. It was into the Styx that his mother Thetis dipped the child ➤ ACHILLES to make his body invulnerable. The name comes from Greek *Stux*, from *stugnos* 'hateful, gloomy'.

> Hong Kong . . . will change owners from one of the world's most liberal empires to its most repressive . . . Hong Kong is crossing this political Styx with lavish provisions.
> — *Times* 13 November 1996

sub Jove frigido under the chilly sky, in the open air; Latin phrase, in occasional literary use from the early 19th century; *Jove* is taken here as the god of the sky.

sub judice a legal term meaning, under judicial consideration and therefore prohibited from public discussion elsewhere; the phrase is Latin, and means literally 'under a judge'.

sub rosa happening or done in secret; the phrase (recorded from the mid 17th century) is Latin, and means literally 'under the rose', taken as an emblem of secrecy.

See also ➤ *under the* ROSE.

be subdued to what one works in become reduced in capacity or ability to the standard of one's material, in allusion to Shakespeare:

> My nature is subdued
> To what it works in, like the dyer's hand.
> — William Shakespeare Sonnet 111

subfusc the formal clothing worn for examinations and formal occasions at some universities; in poetic and literary use, *subfusc* as an adjective means 'dull, gloomy'. The term, recorded from the early 18th century, comes from Latin *subfuscus*, from *sub-* 'somewhat' + *fuscus* 'dark brown'.

subject in philosophy, a thinking or feeling entity; the conscious mind; the ego, especially as opposed to anything external to the mind; the usage derives from the employment of *subjectum* for the mind or ego considered as the subject of all knowledge.

Sublapsarian another term for an ➤ INFRALAP-SARIAN, recorded from the mid 17th century.

sublime see also ➤ *egotistical* SUBLIME, ➤ *the Sublime* PORTE, ➤ *the Sublime Society of* BEEF *Steaks*.

On the Sublime the title of a Greek literary treatise, supposedly by the 1st century Greek scholar Longinus (see ➤ LONGINUS²), which influenced the English ➤ AUGUSTAN writers.

from the sublime to the ridiculous is only a step proverbial saying, late 19th century; in *The Age of Reason* (1795) ➤ *Thomas* PAINE had said, 'One step above the sublime, makes the ridiculous; and one step about the ridiculous, makes the sublime again.' A remark attributed to ➤ NAPOLEON *I*, on the retreat from Moscow in 1812, is 'There is only one step from the sublime to the ridiculous'.

submerged tenth the supposed fraction of the population permanently living in poverty, implicitly

contrasted with the ➤ UPPER *ten*: the term was used by the Salvationist William Booth (1829–1912) in his account of the 'army of nearly two millions belonging to the submerged classes':

> This Submerged Tenth—is it, then, beyond the reach of the nine-tenths in the midst of whom they live?
> — William Booth *In Darkest England* (1890)

subpoena a writ ordering a person to attend a court; originally, a writ issued by chancery ordering a person to answer a matter alleged against them. The word is recorded from late Middle English and comes from Latin *sub poena* ('under penalty'), the first words of the writ.

subsidiarity the principle that a central authority should have a subsidiary function, performing only those tasks which cannot be performed effectively at a more immediate or local level. The word has been recorded since the mid 1930s, but was then used primarily in discussions of ecclesiastical polity, with particular reference to the role of the papacy. In the early 1980s, however, it came to prominence in the debate on the European Union, and the question of how national sovereignties can be reconciled with any proposed federal structure; the principle was asserted by Britain as a condition of her ratification of the ➤ MAASTRICHT *Treaty*.

the Subtle Doctor informal name (a translation of Latin *Doctor Subtilis*) for the schoolman ➤ *John* DUNS *Scotus*.

subtopia unsightly, sprawling suburban development, named from a blend of *suburb* and *utopia*, an ironic term for suburbia considered as an ideal environment:

> There will be no real distinction between town and country. Both will consist of a limbo of shacks, bogus rusticities, wire and aerodromes, set in some fir-poled fields ... Upon this new Britain the *Review* bestows a name in the hope that it will stick—*Subtopia*.
> — Ian Nairn in *Architectural Review* 1955

if at first you don't succeed, try, try, try again proverbial saying, mid 19th century.

success has many fathers, while failure is an orphan proverbial saying, mid 20th century; in his diary for 9 September 1942, the Italian fascist politician Galeazzo Ciano, son-in-law of Mussolini, noted, 'Victory has a hundred fathers, but no-one wants to recognize defeat as his own'.

succession see also ➤ APOSTOLIC *succession*, ➤ *War of the* AUSTRIAN *Succession*.

Act of Succession (in English history) each of three Acts of Parliament passed during the reign of Henry VIII regarding the succession of his children.

The first (1534) declared Henry's marriage to Catherine of Aragon to be invalid and disqualified their daughter Mary from succeeding to the throne, fixing the succession on any child born to Henry's new wife Anne Boleyn. The second (1536) cancelled this, asserting the rights of Jane Seymour and her issue, while the third (1544) determined the order of succession of Henry's three children, the future Edward VI, Mary I, and Elizabeth I.

Succoth a major Jewish festival held in the autumn (beginning on the 15th day of Tishri) to commemorate the sheltering of the Israelites in the wilderness. It is marked by the erection of small booths covered in natural materials. Also called *Feast of Tabernacles.*

succubus a female demon believed to have sexual intercourse with sleeping men; recorded from late Middle English, the word comes from medieval Latin *succubus* 'prostitute'.

never give a sucker an even break proverbial saying, early 20th century; often associated with W. C. Fields.

sudarium in the Roman Catholic Church, a cloth supposedly impressed with an image of Christ's face, with which ➤ St VERONICA is said to have wiped his face on the way to Calvary. Recorded from the early 17th century, the word comes from Latin, literally 'napkin', from *sudor* 'sweat'.

Sudetenland an area in the north-west part of the Czech Republic, on the border with Germany. Allocated to Czechoslovakia after the First World War, it became an object of Nazi expansionist policies and was ceded to Germany as a result of the Munich Agreement of September 1938; in a speech in Berlin on 26 September 1938, Adolf Hitler said, 'It is the last territorial claim which I have to make in Europe'. In 1945 the area was returned to Czechoslovakia.

Sudra a member of the worker caste, lowest of the four Hindu castes.

sue a beggar and catch a louse proverbial saying, mid 17th century.

suede leather, especially kidskin, with the flesh side rubbed to make a velvety nap, from French *(gants de) Suède* '(gloves of) Sweden'.

Suetonius (*c.*69–*c.*150 AD) Roman biographer and historian. His surviving works include *Lives of the Caesars,* covering Julius Caesar and the Roman emperors who followed him, up to Domitian.

Suez Canal a shipping canal connecting the Mediterranean at Port Said with the Red Sea. It was constructed between 1859 and 1869 by Ferdinand de Lesseps. In 1875 it came under British control; its nationalization by Egypt in 1956 prompted the Suez crisis.

Suez Crisis a short conflict following the nationalization of the Suez Canal by President Nasser of Egypt in 1956. Britain and France made a military alliance with Israel to regain control of the canal, but international criticism forced the withdrawal of forces. The British writer and politician Harold Nicolson described the affair (which resulted in the resignation of the British Prime Minister, Anthony Eden) as 'a smash and grab raid that was all smash and no grab'.

sufferings see ➤ MEETING *for Sufferings.*

sufficient unto the day is the evil thereof proverbial saying, mid 18th century; originally a quotation from Matthew 6:34.

Suffolk see ➤ SILLY *Suffolk.*

Suffolk punch a draught-horse of a short-legged thickset breed, originally bred largely in Suffolk.

suffragan an assistant or subsidiary bishop peforming episcopal functions in a certain diocese but having no jurisdiction; in the Church of England, a bishop appointed to help a diocesan bishop. *Suffragan bishops* take their title from certain towns specified in a 16th century Act of Parliament or (according to the Suffragans Nomination Act of 1888) from 'such other towns as Her Majesty may...by Order in Council direct shall be taken'. The word is recorded from late Middle English, and comes ultimately from medieval Latin *suffraganeus* 'assistant bishop'.

suffrage originally (in late Middle English); suffrage meant 'intercessory prayers'; from this developed *suffrages,* which in the Book of Common Prayer are the intercessory petitions pronounced by a priest in the Litany.

The (archaic) sense of a vote given in assent to a proposal or in favour of the election of a particular person is recorded from the mid 16th century. The current sense of the right to vote in political elections dates from the late 18th century; the first recorded use is in the *Constitution of the United States* (1789), 'No state shall be deprived of its equal suffrage in the Senate.'

suffragette a woman seeking the right to vote through organized protest; the term is recorded from 1906, in an account in the *Daily Mail* of 10 January of a meeting between 'Mr Balfour and the Suffragettes'.

The *suffragettes* were more formally members of the Women's Suffrage Movement, an organization which initiated a campaign of demonstrations and militant action, under the leadership of the Pankhursts, after the repeated defeat of women's suffrage bills in Parliament. ('The argument of the broken window pane is the most valuable argument in modern politics' is a comment attributed to ➤ *Emmeline* PANKHURST).

Sufi a Muslim ascetic and mystic. The word is recorded from the mid 17th century and comes from Arabic, perhaps ultimately from *ṣūf* 'wool', referring the the woollen garment worn by such a person.

Sufism the mystical system of the Sufis, the esoteric dimension of the Islamic faith, the spiritual path to mystical union with God. It is influenced by other faiths, such as Buddhism, and reached its peak in the 13th century. There are many Sufi orders, the best-known being the dervishes, each founded by a devout individual and each having different devotional practices.

suggestio falsi a misrepresentation of the truth whereby something incorrect is implied to be true. The phrase (recorded from the early 19th century) is modern Latin and means literally 'suggestion of what is false'; it is often coupled with ➤ SUPPRESSIO *veri*.

Sui a dynasty which ruled in China AD 581–618 and reunified the country, preparing the ground for the cultural flowering of the succeeding Tang dynasty.

sui generis unique; a Latin phrase recorded in English from the late 18th century, and meaning literally, 'of one's or its own kind'. The demagogic American Democratic politician Huey Long (1893–1935), nicknamed the ➤ KINGFISH, is said to have told journalists attempting to analyse his political personality, 'Oh hell, say that I am *sui generis* and let it go at that'.

suicide the action of killing oneself intentionally; a person who does this. The term is recorded from the mid 17th century, and comes ultimately from Latin *sui* 'of oneself' and *caedere* 'kill'.

In Christian theology, suicide is regarded as a sin; it was also formerly a criminal act in the UK (see ➤ FELO *de se*). A person who had killed themselves was regarded as someone whose ghost might walk; there was a traditional belief that this could be averted by a stake through the heart, or by the body's being buried at a crossroads. Suicides were also buried at the north side of a churchyard, as referred to in *A Shropshire Lad* (1896):

> North, for a soon-told number,
> Chill graves the sexton delves,
> And steeple-shadowed slumber
> The slayers of themselves.
> — A. E. Housman *A Shropshire Lad* (1896) 'Hughley
> Steeple'

suit informal term for a high-ranking executive in a business or organization, typically one regarded as exercising influence in an impersonal way.

> The 'suits' in Nashville told him his first album was too country.
> — *Reason* December 1991

See also ➤ MEN *in suits*.

Suleiman I (*c*.1494–1566), sultan of the Ottoman Empire 1520–66; also known as **Suleiman the Magnificent** or **Suleiman the Lawgiver**. The Ottoman Empire reached its fullest extent under his rule; his conquests included Belgrade (1521), Rhodes (1522), and Tripoli (1551), in addition to those in Iraq (1534) and Hungary (1562). He was also a noted administrator and patron of the arts.

Lucius Cornelius Sulla (138–78 BC), Roman general and politician. Sulla became involved in a power struggle with ➤ MARIUS and in 88 marched on Rome. After a victorious campaign against Mithridates VI, Sulla invaded Italy in 83. He was elected dictator in 82 and implemented constitutional reforms in favour of the Senate.

Arthur Sullivan (1842–1900), English composer. His fame rests on the fourteen light operas which he wrote in collaboration with the librettist ➤ W. S. GILBERT, many for Richard D'Oyly Carte's company at the Savoy Theatre.

Sullivan principles a set of principles concerning the employment of personnel in South Africa by US companies, formulated to counter racial discrimination, and named after Leon H. *Sullivan* (1923–), US businessman and minister.

Sulpician a member of a congregation of secular Roman Catholic priests founded in 1642 by a priest of St Sulpice, Paris, mainly to train candidates for holy orders.

sultan a Muslim sovereign; **the Sultan** was the title given to the sultan of Turkey. The word is recorded in English from the mid 16th century, and comes (via French or medieval Latin) from Arabic *sulṭān* 'power, ruler'.

Sumer an ancient region of SW Asia in present-day Iraq, comprising the southern part of Mesopotamia. From the 4th millennium BC it was the site of city states which became part of ancient Babylonia.

Sumerian a member of the indigenous non-Semitic people of ancient Babylonia.

The Sumerians had the oldest known written language, whose relationship to any other language is unclear. Theirs is the first historically attested civilization and they invented cuneiform writing, the sexagesimal system of mathematics, and the socio-political institution of the city state with bureaucracies, legal codes, division of labour, and a form of currency. Their art, literature, and theology had a profound influence long after their demise *c*.2000 BC.

summa archaic term for the summary of a subject; recorded from the early 18th century, the word comes from Latin 'sum total'.

summer the warmest season of the year, in the northern hemisphere from June to August and in the southern hemisphere from December to February. Recorded from Old English (in form *sumor*), the word is of Germanic origin, and is ultimately related to Sanskrit *samā* 'year'.

See also ➤ *All* HALLOWS *summer*, ➤ INDIAN *summer*, ➤ MICHAELMAS *summer*, ➤ *one* SWALLOW *does not make a summer*, ➤ *St* MARTIN*'s summer*.

Summer Palace a palace (now in ruins) of the former Chinese emperors near Beijing.

summer solstice the occasion of the longest day in the year, when the sun reaches its greatest altitude north of the equator, on approximately 21 June (or in the southern hemisphere, south of the equator, on approximately 21 December).

summer time time as adjusted to achieve longer evening daylight in summer by setting clocks an hour ahead of the standard time; originally introduced in the UK in 1916, from 21 May to 30 September, and subsequently adopted for ➤ DAYLIGHT *saving* from March to October.

The principle of adjusting clocks in this way was suggested first by Benjamin Franklin in an essay of 1784; the notion of ➤ DAYLIGHT *saving* was the originator of the English builder William Willett (1856–1915).

See also ➤ DOUBLE *Summer Time*.

Summist the author of a summa of religious doctrine, e.g. Thomas Aquinas, author of *Summa theologiae*, *Summa contra gentiles*; generally, a medieval scholastic writer.

summit a meeting between heads of government; the term is first recorded in a comment by Winston Churchill in the *Times* of 15 February 1950, 'It is not easy to see how things could be worsened by a parley at the summit, if such a thing were possible'.

summum bonum the highest good, especially as the ultimate goal according to which values and priorities are established in an ethical system. The phrase, which is Latin, is recorded from the mid 17th century.

sumpsimus a correct expression taking the place of an incorrect but popular one (➤ MUMPSIMUS). The terms were notably juxtaposed in this way by Henry VIII, in a speech of 24 December 1545 to his parliament:

> Some be too stiff in their old Mumpsimus, other be too busy and curious, in their new Sumpsimus.
> — Henry VIII speech to Parliament, 24 December 1545

The word comes from Latin, and means 'we have taken' (see ➤ MUMPSIMUS).

sumptuary relating to or denoting laws that limit private expenditure on food and personal items. The word is recorded from the early 17th century, and comes ultimately from Latin *sumptus* 'cost, expenditure' from *sumere* 'take'.

sun the star round which the earth orbits and from which it receives light and warmth; it is the central body of the solar system and provides the light and energy that sustains life on earth, and its changing position relative to the earth's axis determines the terrestrial seasons.

In the ancient and medieval world, it was believed (in accordance with the ➤ PTOLEMAIC *system*) that the earth is the stationary centre of the universe. The heliocentric theory was proposed by the Polish astronomer ➤ COPERNICUS (1473–1543) in *De Revolutionibus Orbium Coelestium* (1543), and later supported by ➤ GALILEO (1564–1642); although he was forced to recant by the Inquisition, the theory continued to gain ground.

The sun has been an object of worship in a number of religions, and has thus been personified as a male being, sometimes identified with a particular god, especially ➤ APOLLO, who in classical mythology was believed to drive his chariot across the sky.

Proverbially the sun is a type of brightness and clearness, and in literary and poetic usage often stands for a person or thing regarded as a source of glory, inspiration, or understanding; the word may also be used with reference to someone's success or prosperity.

Recorded from Old English (in form *sunne*), the word is of Germanic origin, and comes ultimately from an Indo-European root shared by Greek *hēlios* and Latin *sol*.

See also ➤ CROWN *of the sun*, ➤ CYCLE *of the sun*, ➤ *if it* RAINS *when the sun is shining, the devil is beating his wife*, ➤ LAND *of the Midnight Sun*, ➤ PLACE *in the sun*, ➤ *there is* NOTHING *new under the sun*.

never let the sun go down on your anger proverbial saying, mid 17th century; originally with biblical allusion to Ephesians 4:26, 'Let not the sun go down on your wrath'.

sun in splendour in heraldry, the sun as heraldically blazoned, depicted with rays and often a human face; the *sun in splendour* was an emblem of the ➤ *House of* YORK.

when the sun is over the yardarm originally in nautical usage the time of day (noon) when it is permissible to begin drinking; the earlier variant **when the sun is over the foreyard** dates from the mid, and this from the late, 19th century.

Sun King a designation of Louis XIV of France, a translation of French ➤ ROI *soleil*.

the sun loses nothing by shining into a puddle proverbial saying, early 14th century, of classical origin; the comment 'the sun shines into dung but is not tainted' is attributed to the Greek philosopher ➤ DIOGENES, and ➤ TERTULLIAN has, 'the sun spreads his rays even into the sewer, and is not stained'.

on which the sun never sets (of an empire, originally the Spanish, later the British) worldwide. The first reference in English is found in John Smith's *Advertisements for the Unexperienced Planters of New England* (1631), 'Why should the brave Spanish soldiers brag; the sun never sets in the Spanish dominions, but ever shineth on one art or other we have conquered for our king.' The term as applied to Britain is first used by the Scottish writer Christopher North (1785–1854), in Blackwood's Magazine, April 1829, 'His Majesty's dominions, on which the sun never sets.'

Sun of Righteousness an epithet of Jesus Christ, after Malachi 4:2, 'But unto you that fear my name shall the Sun of righteousness arise with healing in his wings'.

Sun Yat-sen (1866–1925), Chinese Kuomintang statesman, provisional President of the Republic of China 1911–12 and President of the Southern Chinese Republic 1923–5. He organized the Kuomintang force and played a vital part in the revolution of 1911 which overthrew the Manchu dynasty. Following opposition, however, he resigned as President to establish a secessionist government at Guangzhou.

sunbelt a strip of territory receiving a high amount of sunshine, especially the southern US from California to Florida.

Sunday the day of the week before Monday and following Saturday, observed by Christians as a day of rest and religious worship and (together with Saturday) forming part of the weekend. Recorded in Old English as *Sunnandæg* 'day of the sun', the name is a translation of Latin *dies solis*.

Sundays ■ See box opposite.

Sunday school a class held on Sundays to teach children about Christianity; such schools are now intended only for religious instruction, but originally also taught some secular subjects. The reformer Robert Raikes (1735–1811) of Gloucester was the promoter of Sunday Schools in England; in 1783, as proprietor of the *Gloucester Journal*, he inserted in the paper a short notice of the success of his first school, set up in July 1780.

Sunday's child a child born on Sunday, traditionally greatly blessed or favoured; the belief is the culmination of the rhyme ➤ *Monday's* CHILD *is fair of face*.

sundowner in Australia, a tramp arriving at a sheep station in the evening under the pretence of seeking work, so as to obtain food and shelter; the term is recorded from the mid 19th century.

Sundays

NAME	DAY
Advent Sunday	first Sunday in Advent
Bloody Sunday	30 January 1972
Cantate Sunday	4th Sunday after Easter
Care Sunday	5th Sunday in Lent
Carling Sunday	5th Sunday in Lent
Egg Sunday	Sunday before Shrove Tuesday
Fig Sunday	Sunday before Easter
Garland Sunday	last Sunday in July
Hosanna Sunday	Sunday before Easter
Hospital Sunday	Sunday nearest to St Luke's day
Laetare Sunday	4th Sunday in Lent
Lost Sunday	Sunday before Sexagesima
Low Sunday	Sunday after Easter
Mid-Lent Sunday	4th Sunday in Lent
Mothering Sunday	4th Sunday in Lent
Orthodoxy Sunday	1st Sunday in Lent
Palm Sunday	Sunday before Easter
Passion Sunday	5th Sunday in Lent
Quadragesima Sunday	1st Sunday in Lent
Quasimodo Sunday	Sunday after Easter
Quinquagesima Sunday	Sunday before Lent
Refreshment Sunday	4th Sunday in Lent
Remembrance Sunday	Sunday nearest 11 November
Rogation Sunday	Sunday preceding Rogation days
Rosary Sunday	1st Sunday in October
Rose Sunday	4th Sunday in Lent
Sacrament Sunday	Sunday on which the Eucharist is celebrated
Sad Palm Sunday	29 March 1461
Septuagesima Sunday	Sunday before Sexagesima
Sexuagesima Sunday	Sunday before Quinquagesima
Simnel Sunday	4th Sunday in Lent
Stir-up Sunday	Sunday next before Advent
Trinity Sunday	Sunday next after Pentecost
Whit Sunday	7th Sunday after Easter

Sunflower State informal name for Kansas.

Sung a dynasty that ruled in China AD 960–1279. The period was marked by the first use of paper money and by advances in printing, firearms, shipbuilding, clockmaking, and medicine. Also **Song**.

sunlight see ➤ PORT *Sunlight*.

Sunna the traditional portion of Muslim law based on Muhammad's words or acts, accepted (together with the Koran) as authoritative by Muslims and followed particularly by ➤ SUNNI Muslims. The word is Arabic, and means literally 'form, way, course, rule'.

Sunni one of the two main branches of Islam, commonly described as orthodox, and differing from ➤ SHIA in its understanding of the ➤ SUNNA and in its acceptance of the first three caliphs. The word is Arabic, and means literally, 'custom, normative rule'.

Sunningdale agreement an agreement negotiated on 9 December 1973 by the British and Irish governments and representatives of Northern Irish political parties following the suspension of the Stormont parliament in 1972. The intention was to set up a power-sharing executive, but the initiative foundered in the strike subsequently called by the Ulster Workers' Council, and the agreement was never ratified.

Sunny Jim a cheerful or good-natured person, from an energetic character used to advertise a brand of breakfast cereal:

> High o'er the fence leaps Sunny Jim
> 'Force' is the food that raises him.
> — advertising slogan for breakfast cereal (1903); coined by Minnie Hanff (1880–1942)

ride off into the sunset achieve a happy ending, from the conventional closing scene of many films.

Sunset Boulevard a road which links the centre of Los Angeles with the Pacific Ocean 48 km (30 miles) to the west. The eastern section of the road between Fairfax Avenue and Beverly Hills is known as **Sunset Strip**.

Sunshine State any of the states of New Mexico, South Dakota, California, and Florida.

sunyata in Buddhism, the doctrine that phenomena are devoid of an immutable or determinate intrinsic nature. It is often regarded as a means of gaining an intuition of ultimate reality. The word comes from Sanskrit *śūnyatā* 'emptiness'.

Super Bowl (in the US) the National Football League championship game played annually between the champions of the National and the American Football Conferences; the title is after ➤ ROSE *Bowl*.

Super Tuesday in the US, a day on which several states hold primary elections for the presidential nominations.

superbug a term recorded from the mid 1970s and reflecting the development of biotechnology; it is used both for a microbe which is useful in biotechnology, especially one which has been genetically engineered to enhance its usefulness, and for a strain of bacteria which has become resistant to antibiotic drugs, or an insect that is difficult to control or eradicate because it has become immune to insecticides.

supererogation see ➤ WORKS *of supererogation.*

superhighway see ➤ INFORMATION *superhighway.*

Superman a US cartoon character having great strength, the ability to fly, and other extraordinary powers, who conceals his true nature behind the identity of mild-mannered reporter Clark Kent. Superman was created in 1938 in a comic strip by writer Jerry Siegel (1914–96) and artist Joe Shuster (1914–92).

> Faster than a speeding bullet! . . . Look! Up in the sky! It's a bird! It's a plane! It's Superman! Yes, it's Superman! Strange visitor from another planet . . . Who can change the course of mighty rivers, bend steel with his bare hands, and who—disguised as Clark Kent, mild-mannered reporter for a great metropolitan newspaper—fights a never ending battle for truth, justice and the American way!
> — *Superman* (US radio show, 1940 onwards) preamble

superman in philosophy, the ideal superior man of the future; the term in English originally a translation of German *Übermensch* in the philosophy of Nietzsche (1844–1900):

> I teach you the superman. Man is something to be surpassed.
> — Friedrich Nietzsche *Also Sprach Zarathustra* (1883) prologue

supernaculum a high quality wine; the term was originally used in reference to the practice of turning up the emptied cup or glass on one's left thumbnail, to show that all the liquor has been drunk. The word is modern Latin, and is a rendering of German *auf den nagel* 'on to the nail', in the phrase *auf den nagel trinken* 'to drink off liquor to the last drop'.

supper see ➤ BUMP *supper,* ➤ CHURN *supper,* ➤ LAST *Supper,* ➤ LORD's *supper,* ➤ MELL *supper.*

supplies in the UK, a grant of money by Parliament for the costs of government not provided for by the revenue; a term recorded from the early 17th century.

supply day the day on which the House of Commons debates an Opposition motion criticizing the Government's proposed expenditure; the term is recorded from the 1940s.

suppressio veri a misrepresentation of the truth by concealing facts which ought to be made known. Recorded from the mid 18th century, the term is modern Latin, and means 'suppression of what is true'; it is often linked with ➤ SUGGESTIO *falsi.*

Act of Supremacy (in English history) either of two Acts of Parliament of 1534 and 1559 (particularly the former), which established Henry VIII and Elizabeth I as supreme heads of the Church of England and excluded the authority of the Pope. The term is used particularly with reference to the Act of 1534.

supreme sacrifice the laying down of one's life for one's country; the term is particularly associated with the First World War.

> These young men have gone down not only to the horror of the battlefield but to the gates of death as they made the supreme sacrifice.
> — W. M. Clow *Evangel of Strait Gate* (1916)

he who sups with the devil should have a long spoon proverbial saying, late 14th century.

sura a chapter or section of the Koran.

Surat a city in the state of Gujarat in western India, a port on the Tapti River near its mouth on the Gulf of Cambay, which was the site of the first trading post of the East India Company, established in 1612.

sure see ➤ SLOW *but sure,* ➤ *sure as* EGGS *is eggs.*

Sûreté the French police department of criminal investigation; the name is recorded in English from the late 19th century, and means in French, 'surety, security'.

surf the net move from site to site on the ➤ INTERNET, an expression recorded from the first half of the 1990s, which in 1997 was referred to by the Queen as typifying the developing technology of recent years:

> Think what we would have missed if we had never . . . surfed the Net—or, to be honest, listened to other people talking about surfing the Net.
> — Elizabeth II speech at luncheon celebrating her golden wedding, 18 November 1997

The usage probably comes from *channel-surfing*, the activity of switching between channels on a television set to see what is available.

surgeon a medical practitioner qualified to practice surgery; ➤ St LUKE, and St Cosmas and St Damian, martyrs of the early Church said in a late legend to have been twin brothers who were doctors, are patron saints of *surgeons*.

Recorded from Middle English, the word is ultimately (via Anglo-Norman French and Old French) based on Latin *chirurgia*, from Greek *kheirourgia* 'handiwork, surgery'.

See also ➤ BARBER.

surgical instrument *surgical instruments* are the emblem of ➤ *St* LUKE, and of St Cosmas and St Damian, martyrs of the early Church said in a late legend to have been twin brothers who were doctors.

surname a hereditary name common to all members of a family, as distinct from a Christian or other given name. Formerly also, a name, title, or epithet added to a person's name, especially one indicating their birthplace or a particular quality or achievement. The word is recorded from Middle English, and is a partial translation of Anglo-Norman French *surnoun*, suggested by medieval Latin *supernomen*.

surplice a loose white linen vestment varying from hip-length to calf-length, worn over a cassock by clergy and choristers at Christian church services. The word is recorded from Middle English, and comes via Old French from medieval Latin *superpellicium*, from *super-* 'above' + *pellicia* 'fur garment'.

surprise see ➤ OCTOBER *surprise*.

surrealism a 20th-century avant-garde movement in art and literature which sought to release the creative potential of the unconscious mind, for example by the irrational juxtaposition of images. Launched in 1924 by a manifesto of André Breton and having a strong political content, the movement grew out of symbolism and Dada and was strongly influenced by Sigmund Freud. In the visual arts its most notable exponents were André Masson, Jean Arp, Joan Miró, René Magritte, Salvador Dali, Max Ernst, Man Ray, and Luis Buñuel.

surrender see ➤ NO *surrender!*

Surrey see ➤ WHITE *Surrey.*

surrogate mother a woman who bears a child on behalf of another woman, either from her own egg fertilized by the other woman's partner, or from the implantation in her womb of a fertilized egg from the other woman.

The practice of **surrogacy**, which first developed in the US in the late 1970s, was the subject of heated legal and moral debate in the 1980s, centring on the ethics of an arrangement whereby a woman agreed to carry and bear a child for others in return for a fee, on condition that she handed over the baby after birth. In a famous case in the US (known as the case of Baby M) the surrogate mother was reluctant to relinquish the child after bonding with her at birth, and a custody battle ensued. In the UK a committee considered the ethics of surrogacy, and recommended (in July 1984) that it be made illegal. In the US a distinction has now been made between **host surrogacy**, in which a fertilized egg from the biological parents is implanted in the surrogate mother's womb, and *surrogacy*, where the surrogate mother's own egg is used for fertilization.

Sursum corda in Latin Eucharistic liturgies, the words addressed by the celebrant to the congregation at the beginning of the Eucharistic Prayer; in English rites, the corresponding versicle, 'Lift up your hearts'.

> Sursum corda, thought Van der Valk; get up off the floor.
> — Nicholas Freeling *Over the High Side* (1971)

Robert Smith Surtees (1805–64), English journalist and novelist. He is best remembered for his comic sketches of Mr Jorrocks, the sporting Cockney grocer, collected in *Jorrocks's Jaunts and Jollities* (1838). Other famous caricatures, all set against a background of English fox-hunting society, include Mr Soapy Sponge of *Mr Sponge's Sporting Tour* (1849; 1853).

Surtr in Scandinavian mythology, a fire-bearing giant; at ➤ RAGNARÖK he will lead the forces of evil from the east to do battle with the gods.

Surtsey a small island to the south of Iceland, formed by a volcanic eruption in 1963, and named for the fire-giant ➤ SURTR of Scandinavian mythology.

Surveyor a series of unmanned American spacecraft sent to the moon between 1966 and 1968, five of which successfully made soft landings.

survival of the fittest the continued existence of organisms which are best adapted to their environment, with the extinction of others, as a concept in the Darwinian theory of evolution. The phrase was coined by the English philosopher and sociologist

➤ *Herbert* Spencer (1820–1903):

> This survival of the fittest which I have here sought to express in mechanical terms, is that which Mr Darwin has called 'natural selection, or the preservation of favoured races in the struggle for life'.
>
> — Herbert Spencer *Principles of Biology* (1865)

➤ *Charles* Darwin commented on this in *On the Origin of Species* (1869 ed.), 'The expression often used by Mr Herbert Spencer of the Survival of the Fittest is more accurate [than Struggle for Existence], and is sometimes equally convenient'.

survivalism the practising of outdoor survival skills as a sport or hobby, a pastime which developed through channels such as military reserve training and outward bound courses, and which by the mid 1980s had developed considerable popularity. The proliferation of dangerous weapons with which the hobby was often associated had occasioned some public concern when, in August 1987, the ➤ Hungerford massacre, carried out by a keen **survivalist** named Michael Ryan, occurred. While the circumstances of this tragedy were of course unique, it affected public perception of *survivalism* as a hobby.

Surya the sun god of later Hindu mythology, originally one of several solar deities in the Vedic religion. The name comes from Sanskrit *sūrya* 'sun'.

Susanna in the Apocrypha, a woman of Babylon falsely accused of adultery by two Elders but saved by the sagacity of ➤ Daniel, who questioned the accusers and demonstrated that their accounts were contradictory, in particular in the name of the tree under which she was alleged to have met her lover. The story of Susanna is told in the Apocryphal book of this name.

See also ➤ mastic *tree*.

suspicion see ➤ Caesar*'s wife*.

Sussex won't be druv proverbial saying, early 20th century.

susuhunan formerly, (the title of) the ruler of Surakarta and of Mataram in Java.

Sutlej a river of northern India and Pakistan which rises in the Himalayas in SW Tibet. It is one of the five rivers that gave ➤ Punjab its name.

sutra a rule or aphorism in Sanskrit literature, or a set of these on grammar or Hindu law or philosophy; also, a Buddhist or Jainist scripture. The word comes from Sanskrit *sūtra* 'thread, rule', from *siv* 'sew'.

See also ➤ Kama Sutra.

suttee the former Hindu practice of a widow immolating herself on her husband's funeral pyre; a widow who committed such an act. The word, which is Hindi, comes from Sanskrit *satī* 'faithful wife', from *sat* 'good'.

Sutton Hoo the site in Suffolk of a Saxon ship burial of the 7th century AD, containing magnificent grave goods including jewellery, decorated weapons, and gold coins, which are now in the British Museum.

Helen Suzman (1917–), South African politician, of Lithuanian-Jewish descent. From 1961 to 1974 she was the sole MP opposed to apartheid.

Svadilfari in Scandinavian mythology, the horse belonging to a giant who agreed to build a wall around ➤ Asgard for the gods; if he completed his work within the stated time, the goddess Freya, and the sun and moon, would be his reward. When it appeared he would succeed, ➤ Loki delayed the work by changing himself into a mare and decoying *Svadilfari* away. Odin's magic horse ➤ Sleipnir was born of their union.

Svarga in Hinduism, the heaven presided over by Indra, where virtuous souls reside before reincarnation; it is situated on ➤ Mount Meru.

Svengali a person who exercises a controlling or mesmeric influence on another, especially for a sinister purpose, from the name of a musician in George du Maurier's novel *Trilby* (1894) who trains ➤ Trilby's voice and controls her stage singing hypnotically; his influence over her is such that when he dies her voice collapses and she loses her eminence.

> Bush and his election-year Svengali, former secretary of state Jim Baker.
>
> — *Washington Post* 26 October 1992

Swaddler in Ireland, a nickname for a Methodist, especially a preacher; later, for any Protestant. In his diary for 10 September 1747, ➤ *John* Wesley notes that the name was explained to him as deriving from the Protestant divine John Cennick (1718–55) and his frequent references to 'the babe that lay in the manger, the babe that lay in Mary's lap, the babe that lay in swaddling clouts'; from this he was supposed to have been nicknamed *Swaddler* and **Swaddling John**, and the first name to have been applied to Methodists generally.

An alternative explanation is that *Swaddler* as the derogatory name for an itinerant preacher came from the name of the long round bag for clothes and effects fastened to the back of the preacher's saddle.

Swadeshi an Indian nationalist movement of the first part of the 20th century advocating the use of home-produced materials in industry and the boycott of foreign goods. The word comes via Hindi from Sanskrit *svadeśīya* 'of one's own country'.

swagger portrait a commissioned portrait of a prominent or wealthy person, representing his or her role, power, or status, in a striking, often flamboyant, manner.

swagger stick a short cane carried by a military officer.

swagman in Australia and New Zealand, a person carrying a swag or bundle of personal belongings; an itinerant worker, especially one in search of employment, or a tramp.

swallow a migratory swift-flying songbird with a forked tail and long pointed wings, feeding on insects in flight, popularly regarded as a harbinger of summer, and taken as a type of swift movement.

In classical mythology, a *swallow* was one of the birds (the other was a nightingale) into which Procne and her sister Philomel were turned.

See also ➤ *the* ROBIN *and the wren are God's cock and hen; the martin and the swallow are God's mate and marrow.*

one swallow does not make a summer proverbial saying, mid 16th century.

it is idle to swallow the cow and choke on the tail proverbial saying, mid 17th century; meaning that when a serious matter has been accepted, there is no point in quibbling over a trifle.

swami a Hindu male religious teacher; often used as a title. The word comes from Hindi *swāmī* 'master, prince" from Sanskrit *svāmin.*

Jan Swammerdam (1637–80), Dutch naturalist and microscopist. He classified insects into four groups and was the first to observe red blood cells.

Swamp Fox sobriquet of Francis Marion (1732–95), soldier and South Carolina guerrilla fighter against the British in the American War of Independence; he was given the name by the British in reference to his elusive tactics.

swan swans have numerous legendary associations, including the story in Irish mythology that the ➤ *Children of* LIR were changed into swans by enchantment, and the Finnish belief that the swan sings once before it dies. In classical mythology the swan was sacred to Apollo and to Venus (occasionally, as by Shakespeare, also ascribed to Juno).

In reference to its pure white plumage and graceful appearance, the *swan* is often taken as a type of faultlessness or excellence.

A swan is the emblem of ➤ *St* HUGH *of Lincoln.*

See also ➤ BLACK *swan*, ➤ DIRCAEAN *swan*, ➤ *the* KNIGHT *of the Swan*, ➤ MANTUAN, ➤ SWANS.

swan maiden in a number of Norse and Germanic folk tales, a girl who has the power of transforming herself into a swan by means of a dress of swan's feathers or of a magic ring or chain.

swan-neck a neck like that of a swan in being long and graceful; in 11th-century England, *Swanneshals* (= Swan's Neck) was the epithet of Eadgyth, mistress of Harold Godwinsson, later ➤ HAROLD *II.*

Swan of Avon a name for ➤ SHAKESPEARE, deriving from Ben Jonson:

> Sweet Swan of Avon! What a sight it were
> To see thee in our waters yet appear,
> And make those flights upon the banks of Thames
> That so did take Eliza, and our James!
> — Ben Jonson 'To the Memory of My Beloved, the Author, Mr William Shakespeare' (1623)

Swan of Lichfield a name for the English poet Anna Seward (1747–1809), who lived there from the age of ten. She had a good deal of contemporary popularity and was in touch with literary circles of her day, although Mary Russell Mitford described her as 'all tinkling and tinsel—a sort of Dr Darwin in petticoats'.

Swan River a river of Western Australia, which was the site of the first free European settlement in Western Australia.

swan-upping the action or practice of 'upping' or taking up swans and marking them with nicks on the beak in token of being owned by the crown or some corporation.

swanimote a forest assembly held three times a year in accordance with the Forest Charter of 1217, probably originally to organize the periodic pasturing and clearance of certain animals in the forest at various times of year.

swans see ➤ *all one's* GEESE *are swans.*

swansong a song fabled to be sung by a dying swan, originally as translating German *Schwangen(ge)sang*; in extended usage, a person's final public performance or professional activity.

Swaraj former term for self-government or independence for India; the word comes from Sanskrit *svarājya*, from *sva* 'own' + *rājya* 'rule'.

a swarm in May is worth a load of hay; a swarm in June is worth a silver spoon; but a swarm in July is not worth a fly proverbial beekeepers' saying, mid 17th century.

swartrutter a kind of irregular trooper, with black dress and armour and blackened face, active in the Netherlands in the 16th and 17th centuries.

swashbuckle engage in daring and romantic adventures with ostentatious bravado or flamboyance; a **swashbuckler** was originally a person who made a noise by striking his own or his opponent's shield with his sword.

swastika an ancient symbol in the form of an equal-armed cross with each arm continued at a right angle, used (in clockwise form) as the emblem of the German Nazi party. The word is recorded in English from the late 19th century, and comes ultimately from Sanskrit *svasti* 'well-being'.

swear see ➤ *swear like a* TROOPER.

sweat ➤ BLOOD, *toil, tears and sweat.*

sweating sickness any of various fevers with intense sweating, epidemic in England in the 15th–16th centuries.

Swedenborgian an adherent or follower of Emanuel *Swedenborg* (1688–1772), Swedish scientist, philosopher, and mystic. The spiritual beliefs which he expounded after a series of mystical experiences blended Christianity with pantheism and theosophy. His ideas anticipated nebular theory, crystallography, and flying machines, and he was prompted by a series of mystical experiences (1743–5) to turn to expounding his spiritual beliefs, which blended Christianity with elements of pantheism and theosophy. His followers founded the New Jerusalem Church in 1787.

Swedish Nightingale nickname of the Swedish opera singer Jenny Lind (1820–87).

Sweeney Todd legendary barber who murdered his customers, the central character of a play by George Dibdin Pitt (1799–1855) and of later plays; from the mid 1930s, *Sweeney* was used by rhyming slang as a name for the Flying Squad. The original *Sweeney Todd* was said to kill his victims by cutting their throats while they sat waiting to be shaved; the bodies were then disposed of through a trapdoor and made into sausages.

> Sweeney Todd with a cut-throat razor welcoming you into your last chair would better personify urban death than yon undernourished gink with the scythe.
> — J. Torrington *Swing Hammer Swing!* (1992)

if every man would sweep his own doorstep the city would soon be clean proverbial saying, early 17th century.

Sweeps informal name for the Rifle Brigade, from its dark-coloured uniform and facings.

sweeps in the US, a survey of the ratings of television stations, carried out at regular intervals to determine advertising rates.

sweepstake a form of gambling, especially on horse races, in which all the stakes are divided among the winners; the word originally (from the late 14th century) meant someone who 'sweeps', or takes the whole of, stakes in a game; in figurative usage, someone who took or appropriated everything. From the 15th to the 17th century, *Sweepstake* was often used as a ship's name.

From the late 18th century, the word meant a prize won in a race or contest in which the whole of the stakes contributed by the competitors were taken by the winner or a limited number of them; the current meaning developed from this.

sweet see also ➤ REVENGE *is sweet*, ➤ *sweet* FANNY *Adams*.

Sweet Adeline a group or organization of female barber-shop singers, from the title of a popular close harmony song, R. H. Gerard's 'You're the Flower of my Heart, Sweet Adeline' (1903).

sweet singer of Israel a member of a sect or sects flourishing in the late 17th century, apparently with reference to 2 Samuel 23:1, where David is called the 'sweet psalmist of Israel'.

sweet sixteen regarded as the characteristic age of girlish beauty; the term is recorded from the early 19th century.

from the sweetest wine, the sharpest vinegar proverbial saying, late 16th century.

sweetness and light social or political harmony; a phrase taken from originally Swift:

> Instead of dirt and poison, we have rather chosen to fill our hives with honey and wax, thus furnishing mankind with the two noblest of things, which are sweetness and light.
> — Jonathan Swift *The Battle of the Books* (1704), preface

The term was taken up and used with aesthetic or moral reference, initially by Matthew Arnold:

> The pursuit of perfection, then, is the pursuit of sweetness and light . . . He who works for sweetness and light united, works to make reason and the will of God prevail.
> — Matthew Arnold *Culture and Anarchy* (1869)

Sweyn I (d.1014), king of Denmark *c.*985–1014; known as **Sweyn Forkbeard**. From 1003 he launched a series of attacks on England, finally driving Ethelred the Unready to flee to Normandy at the end of 1013. Sweyn then became king of England but died five weeks later. His son Canute was later king of England, Denmark, and Norway.

swift see also ➤ *the* RACE *is not to the swift, nor the battle to the strong.*

Jonathan Swift (1667–1745), Irish satirist, poet, and Anglican cleric; known as **Dean Swift**. He is best known for *Gulliver's Travels* (1726), a satire on human society in the form of a fantastic tale of travels in imaginary lands. He also wrote political pamphlets, such as *A Modest Proposal* (1729), ironically urging that the children of the poor should be fattened to feed the rich.

swim see ➤ *don't go near the* WATER *until you learn how to swim.*

swindle use deception to deprive (someone) of money or possessions; obtain (money) fraudulently. The word comes (in the late 18th century) as a back-formation from *swindler*, and then from German *Schwindler* 'extravagant maker of schemes', from *schwindle* ' be giddy', also 'tell lies'.

swine see also ➤ *do not throw* PEARLS *to swine*, ➤ GADARENE *swine*, ➤ *on Saint* THOMAS *the Divine, kill all turkeys, geese and swine.*

swing a style of jazz or dance music with an easy flowing but vigorous rhythm; the term is recorded from the end of the 19th century.

Captain Swing the fictitious instigator of a system of intimidation practised in agricultural districts of the South of England in 1830–1, consisting in sending to farmers and landowners threatening letters over the signature of 'Captain Swing', followed by the incendiary destruction of their ricks and other property.

Three pretended lives of Swing appeared, *The Life and History of Swing, the Kent Rick-burner, written by himself*, 1830, *A Short Account of the Life and Death of Swing, the Rick-burner, written by one well acquainted with him*, by H. N. Coleridge, and *The Genuine Life of Mr. Francis Swing*, 1831. A review of the first of these, by Gen. P. Thompson, entitled 'On Machine-breaking', in the Westminster Review, January 1831, was republished in pamphlet form, 'In answer to "Swing".'

swing the lead malinger, shirk one's duty; originally, with nautical allusion to the lump of lead suspended by a string, slowly lowered to ascertain the depth of water.

swinging sixties the 1960s as a period free from convention.

swings see also ➤ *what you* LOSE *on the swings you gain on the roundabouts.*

Swiss Confederation the confederation of cantons forming Switzerland, originating from a pact signed on the field of the Rutli in 1291, pledging mutual assistance against aggression; in 1991, the Swiss celebrated the 700th anniversary of the agreement.

Swiss guard Swiss mercenaries employed as a special guard, formerly by sovereigns of France, now only at the Vatican. They have been the pope's personal guard since 1506 (many of them were killed during the sack of Rome in 1527 by Spanish troops).

St Swithin (d. 862), English ecclesiastic. He was bishop of Winchester from 852. The tradition that if it rains on St Swithin's Day it will do so for the next forty days may have its origin in the heavy rain said to have occurred when his relics were to be transferred to a shrine in Winchester cathedral.
　☐ **FEAST DAY** His feast day is 15 July.

Saint Swithin's day, if thou be fair, for forty days it will remain; Saint Swithin's day, if thou bring rain, for forty days it will remain proverbial saying, early 17th century; Saint Swithin's day is 15 July.

sword a weapon with a long metal blade and a hilt with a handguard, used for thrusting or striking and now typically worn as part of ceremonial dress; it is taken as a symbol of warfare and massacre, as in

Matthew 10:34, 'I came not to send peace, but a sword'.

A sword is the emblem of ➤ *St* PAUL and many other saints executed by a sword.

See also ➤ FIRE *and sword*, ➤ FLAMING *sword*, ➤ *he who* LIVES *by the sword dies by the sword*, ➤ *the* PEN *is mightier than the sword*, ➤ *whosoever* DRAWS *his sword against the prince must throw the scabbard away*.

Swords

SWORD	OWNER
Arondight	Lancelot
Balisard	Ruggiero
Cortana	Ogier the Dane
Durindana	Roland
Excalibur	King Arthur
Floberge	Renaud
Fusberta	Rinaldo
Gram	Sigurd
Hauteclaire	Oliver
Morglay	Bevis of Hampton
Nægling	Beowulf
Nagelring	Dietrich von Bern
Sanglamore	Braggadochio

sword-and-sorcery a genre of fiction characterized by heroic adventures and elements of fantasy; the related term *sword-and-sandal*, centring on this form of fiction set in the ancient world, is also recorded.

sword dance a dance in which the performers brandish swords or step around swords laid on the ground, originally as a tribal preparation for war or as a victory celebration. The term is first recorded in English in the early 17th century, in the punning line in Marston's *The Malcontent* (1604), 'Here's a knight shall…Do the sword dance with any morrisdancer in Christendom'.

sword dollar name for a Scottish silver coin of James VI, of the value of 30 shillings Scotch, with the figure of a sword on the reverse.

sword of Damocles in classical mythology, the sword suspended over the head of ➤ DAMOCLES.

Sword of God nickname of Khalid ibn al-Walid (d. 642), Islamic military leader under ➤ MUHAMMAD and his successors,

Sword of Rome nickname of Marcus Claudius Marcellus (*c*.268–208 BC), Roman general of the Second Punic War who captured Syracuse.

Sword of State a sword borne before the sovereign on State occasions.

the sword of the Lord and of Gideon in the Bible, the battle-cry of ➤ GIDEON in his attack on the Midianites and Amalekites (Judges 7:20).

> The padre, his Hebridean paganism surging up through his Calvinistic crust, swung into the M.O., and the latter, his constitution undermined by drink and peering through microscopes, mistimed him and received him heavily amidships. The padre simply cried, 'The sword of the Lord and of Gideon!' and danced on, but the M.O. had to be taken to the rear.
> — George Macdonald Fraser *The General Danced at Dawn* (1970)

Sword of the Spirit biblical phrase for the word of God; originally with reference to Ephesians 6:17, 'And take the helmet of salvation, and the sword of the Spirit, which is the word of God.'

sybarite a person who is self-indulgent in their fondness for sensuous luxury. Originally (in the mid 16th century) the word denoted an inhabitant of *Sybaris*, an ancient Greek city in southern Italy, noted for luxury.

sycophant a person who acts obsequiously towards someone in order to gain advantage; a servile flatterer. The term is recorded from the mid 16th century, as denoting an informer, especially in ancient Athens; Plutarch suggests that the Greek word *sukophantēs* 'informer' derives from *sukon* 'fig', and refers to the practice of informing against the illegal exportation of figs, but this is not substantiated. The current sense is recorded from the late 16th century.

Sydney see also ➤ *Sydney* CARTON.

Sydney Opera House a striking building at Sydney harbour the roof of which is composed of huge white shapes resembling sails or shells. Designed by the Danish architect Jörn Utzon (1918–) and opened in 1973, it contains a concert hall, theatres, and a cinema.

Sydney or the bush Australian expression meaning all or nothing; originally, it was used in the context of someone who gambled on the prospect of making a fortune which would bring with it an easy urban life; failure meant that work would have to be sought in the outback.

syllogism an instance of a form of reasoning in which a conclusion is drawn (whether validly or not) from two given or assumed propositions (premises) that each share a term with the conclusion, and that share a common or middle term not present in the conclusion (e.g. *all dogs are animals; all animals have four legs; therefore all dogs have four legs*).

sylph a member of a race of beings or spirits supposed to inhabit the air (originally in the system of ➤ Paracelsus); the word is recorded from the mid 17th century, coming from modern Latin *sylphes*, *sylphi*, and the German plural *Sylphen*, and may ultimately be based on Latin *sylvestris* 'of the woods' + *nympha* 'nymph'. From the mid 19th century, the term has been applied to a slender and graceful woman or girl.

Sylva see ➤ Carmen *Sylva*.

sylvan in classical mythology, an imaginary being believed to haunt woods or groves; a spirit of the woods.

sylvester a spirit of the woods (in the system of ➤ Paracelsus).

Sylvester Eve New Year's Eve, from St *Sylvester* (d. 335), Pope from 314 to 335; his feast-day is 31 December.

symbol originally (in late Middle English), *symbol* denoted a formal authoritative statement or summary of the religious belief of the Christian Church, in particular, the ➤ Apostles' *Creed*. This use is first found in the writing of Cyprian, bishop of Carthage (*c*.250), who used Latin *symbolum* for the baptismal Creed, this Creed being the mark or sign of a Christian as distinguished from a heathen.

The current meaning, a thing that represents or stands for something else, especially a material object representing something abstract, is recorded from the late 16th century.

The word comes via Latin *symbolum* 'symbol, Creed' from Greek *sumbolon* 'mark, token'.

Symbolism an artistic and poetic movement or style using symbolic images and indirect suggestion to express mystical ideas, emotions, and states of mind. It originated in late 19th century France and Belgium, with important figures including Mallarmé, Maeterlinck, Verlaine, Rimbaud, and Redon.

symphony see ➤ Unfinished *Symphony*.

symposium originally (in the late 16th century) a drinking party or convivial discussion, especially as held in ancient Greece after a banquet (and notable

as the title of a work by Plato); the word comes ultimately from Greek *sumpotēs* 'fellow drinker'.

From the late 18th century, the word has been used to denote a conference or meeting to discuss a particular subject, and from the mid 20th century, a publication consisting of essays or papers on a given subject by a number of contributors.

synagogue the regular assembly of Jews for religious observance and instruction; a building or place of worship for this purpose. The word is recorded from Middle English and comes via Old French and late Latin from Greek *sunagōgē* 'meeting'.

In religious controversy from the Middle Ages, the word was given derogatory use as a term for an assembly of the wicked or heretical; in medieval iconography, *Synagogue* may be shown as a blindfolded figure contrasted with the sighted *Church*.

See ➤ Great *Synagogue*.

Synchromism an artistic movement resembling ➤ Orphism, founded by the US painters Stanton Macdonald-Wright (b. 1890) and Morgan Russell (1886–1953), with emphasis on the abstract use of colour.

syndicalism a movement for transferring the ownership and control of the means of production and distribution to workers' unions. *Syndicalism* was closer in philosophy to anarchism than to socialism, perceiving the state as an inevitable tool of oppression. Influenced by Proudhon and by the French social philosopher Georges Sorel (1847–1922), syndicalism developed in French trade unions during the late 19th century and was at its most vigorous between 1900 and 1914, particularly in France, Italy, Spain, and the US.

syndrome see also ➤ China *syndrome*, ➤ Desert *Storm syndrome*, ➤ Stockholm *syndrome*.

synechdoche a figure of speech in which a part is made to represent the whole or vice versa, as in *there were several new faces at the meeting* (meaning 'new people') or *England lost by six wickets* (meaning ' the English cricket team').

synod an assembly of the clergy of a particular Church, nation, province, or diocese, sometimes with representatives of the laity, duly convened for discussing and deciding ecclesiastical affairs. The term is recorded from late Middle English, and

comes via late Latin from Greek *sunodos* 'meeting'.
See also ➤ General *Synod,* ➤ *Synod of* Whitby.

synonym a word or phrase that means exactly or
nearly the same as another word or phrase in the
same language, for example *shut* is a synonym of
close.

Synoptic Gospels the Gospels of Matthew, Mark,
and Luke, which given an account of the events
from the a similar point of view, as contrasted with
that of John.

Synoptic problem the question of the relationship between the ➤ Synoptic *Gospels.* The general
view is that Mark is the earlier text and that Matthew and Luke draw on it; it is widely thought that
they also had access to a hypothetical source (➤ Q),
from which comes the material which is not in
Mark. An alternative explanation is that Luke's Gospel was written from a knowledge of both Mark and
Matthew.

syntax the arrangement of words and phrases to
create well-formed sentences in a language. Recorded from the late 16th century, the word comes
via French or late Latin from Greek *suntaxis,* from
sun- 'together' + *tassein* 'arrange'.

syphilis a chronic bacterial disease that is contracted chiefly by infection during sexual intercourse, but also congenitally by infection of a
developing fetus. The word is recorded in English
from the early 18th century, and is modern Latin,
originally from the title of a poem, *Syphilis, sive
Morbus Gallicus,* published 1530 by Girolamo
Frastoro or Hieronymus Fracastorius (1483–1553), a
physician, astronomer, and poet of Verona; it was
translated by Nahum Tate in 1686 with the title
'Syphilis: or, a Poetical History of the French Disease'. The illness was known from the early 16th
century as the *great pox,* to distinguish it from
smallpox.

Syphilis was used as the name of the disease in the
poem itself; the subject is the shepherd 'Syphilus',
the first sufferer from the illness. (The ultimate origin of his name is disputed; it has been suggested
that it is a corrupt medieval form of *Sipylus,* a son of
➤ Niobe.)

➤ *St* Fiacre and ➤ *St* George are patron saints of
those suffering from syphilis.

Syrinx in Greek mythology, the name of a nymph
loved by Pan, who was changed into a reed in order
to escape him; the set of pan pipes created by him
were named *syrinx* for her.

Tt

T the twentieth letter of the modern English alphabet and the nineteenth of the ancient Roman one, corresponding to Greek *tau*, Hebrew *taw*.

See also ➤ DOT *the i's*.

the taal in South Africa, Afrikaans; the word comes from the Dutch word for language, speech.

tabard a coarse sleeveless jerkin consisting only of front and back pieces with a hole for the head as the outer dress of medieval peasants and clerics, or worn as a surcoat over armour; a herald's official coat emblazoned with the arms of the sovereign.

Toom Tabard nickname (meaning 'Empty Jacket') given by the Scots to John de Baliol (1249–1315), titular king of Scotland, who was crowned at ➤ SCONE in November 1292, and the next month did homage to Edward I of England. In 1296, Edward invaded Scotland; Baliol, who had attempted to renounce his fealty, was taken prisoner to England. On his release, he went to France, where he spent the rest of his life, without any attempt to recover Scotland. He was also called by the variant **Tyne Tabard** ('Lose Coat').

Tabard Inn in Chaucer's *Canterbury Tales*, the inn in Southwark at which the pilgrims meet before setting out for Canterbury.

tabby a grey or brownish cat mottled or streaked with dark stripes, said to be so named from its striped markings, after the name for a kind of silk taffeta, originally striped, later with a watered finish. The word comes (in the late 16th century) via French from the Arabic name of the quarter of Baghdad where *tabby* was manufactured.

taberdar a former name for certain scholars of Queen's College, Oxford, from the gown they wore; still surviving in the name of some of the scholarships of that college.

tabernacle in biblical use, a fixed or movable habitation, typically of light construction; a tent used as a sanctuary for the Ark of the Covenant by the Israelites during the Exodus and until the building of the Temple. The word is recorded from Middle English, and comes via French from Latin *tabernaculum* 'tent', diminutive of *taberna* 'hut, tavern'.

From the late 15th century, the term has also been used to denote an ornamented receptacle or cabinet in which a pyx containing the reserved sacrament may be placed in Catholic churches, usually on or above an altar.

See also ➤ TIN *tabernacle*.

Feast of Tabernacles another name for ➤ SUCCOTH.

Tabitha in the Bible (Acts 9:36:42), name ('which by interpretation is called Dorcas') of the charitable woman at Joppa who was raised from the dead by Peter. *Tabitha* is the Aramaic form of the Greek *Dorcas*, and means 'gazelle'.

table see also ➤ CREDENCE *table*, ➤ PEUTINGERIAN *table*, ➤ ROUND *Table*, ➤ TABLES.

first table the first of two divisions of the ➤ TEN *Commandments*, relating to religious duties.

second table the second of two divisions of the ➤ TEN *Commandments*, relating to moral duties.

table d'hôte a restaurant meal offered at a fixed price and with few if any choices. The term originally (in the early 17th century) denoted a table in a hotel or restaurant where all guests ate together, hence a meal served there at a stated time and for a fixed price.

Table Office an office in the British House of Commons where the civil servants who prepare the notice papers and the order book work.

table-rapping the production of raps or knocking sounds on a table without apparent physical means; by spiritualists ascribed to the agency of departed spirits, and used as a supposed means of communication with them.

> The matter has been explained to us thus . . . Table-turning and table-rapping are designed to call attention to the existence and presence of superhuman powers.
>
> — *Spiritual Herald* April 1856

table-turning a process or phenomenon in which a table is turned or moved supposedly by spiritual agency acting through a group of people who have placed their hands on its surface.

tableau vivant a silent and motionless group of people arranged to represent a scene or incident, or a well-known painting or sculpture, especially as a theatrical device in the 19th century; the phrase is French, and means literally 'living picture'.

tables see ➤ RUDOLPHINE *tables*, ➤ TWELVE *Tables*.

tablets see ➤ KEEP *taking the tablets*.

taboo a social or religious custom prohibiting or restricting a particular practice or forbidding association with a particular person, place, or thing. The word comes (in the late 18th century) from Tongan *tabu* 'set apart, forbidden', and was introduced into English by Captain Cook (1728–79):

> Not one of them would sit down, or eat a bit of any thing . . . On expressing my surprize at this, they were all *taboo*, as they said; which word has a very comprehensive meaning; but, in general, signifies that a thing is forbidden.
> — James Cook *A Voyage to the Pacific Ocean* (1784)

Mount Tabor traditionally regarded as the site of Christ's ➤ TRANSFIGURATION (Mark 9:2), although this is held to be unlikely; it does not conform to the 'high mountain' of Mark's description.

Taborite a member of the extreme party of the ➤ HUSSITES. The name comes ultimately from Czech *tábor* from Hungarian = 'camp, encampment', so called from their encampment on a craggy height; it may also allude to ➤ *Mount* TABOR.

tabouret a low backless seat or stool for one person; at the French court, *tabouret* denoted the right of certain ladies to be seated on such a stool in the presence of the king or queen.

tabula gratulatoria a list in a Festschrift of the people and institutions who have subscribed to the publication; the phrase is modern Latin, and means literally 'congratulatory tablet'.

tabula rasa an absence of preconceived ideas or predetermined goals; a clean slate; the human mind, especially at birth, viewed as having no innate ideas. The phrase, which is Latin, means literally 'scraped tablet', denoting a tablet with the writing erased.

tace is Latin for a candle proverbial saying, late 17th century; *tace* in Latin means 'be silent' (in implicit contrast to the illumination provided by a candle) and the saying was traditionally used as an indication that a person should stop talking.

tachi in Japan, a long single-edged samurai sword with a slightly curved blade, worn slung from the belt.

Tacitus (*c.*56–*c.*120 AD), Roman historian. His *Annals* (covering the years 14–68) and *Histories* (69–96) are major works on the history of the Roman Empire.

tacks see ➤ *get down to* BRASS *tacks*.

Tadpole and Taper in Disraeli's Coningsby (1844), two politicians of whom it is said that, 'they too had lost their seats since 1832; but being men of business, and accustomed from early life to look about them, they had already commenced the combinations which…were to bear them back to the assembly where they were so missed.' Their names have been used allusively to describe political schemers or party hacks, as by Winston Churchill in 1905:

> The Cabinet was packed with nonentities, Tadpoles and Tapers from the Whips' room.
> — Winston Churchill in *Daily Chronicle* 13 May 1905

It is Taper in *Coningsby* who provides the definition of a sound Conservative government: 'Tory men and Whig measures'.

tae kwon do a modern Korean system of unarmed combat developed chiefly in the mid 20th century, combining elements of karate, ancient Korean martial art, and kung fu, differing from karate in its wide range of kicking techniques and its emphasis on different methods of breaking objects.

taedium vitae weariness of life; disgust with life; extreme ennui or inertia, often as a pathological state with a tendency to suicide. The phrase is Latin, and recorded from the mid 18th century.

Taegu a city in SE South Korea, nearby to which is the Haeinsa temple, established in AD 802, which contains 80,000 Buddhist printing blocks dating from the 13th century, engraved with compilations of Buddhist scriptures.

taffeta a fine lustrous silk or similar synthetic fabric with a crisp texture. Recorded from late Middle English, the word (originally denoting a plainweave silk) comes via Old French or medieval Latin from Persian *tāftan* 'to shine'.

Taffia any supposed network of prominent or influential Welsh people, especially one which is strongly nationalistic; the word is recorded from the 1980s, and is a blend of ➤ TAFFY and ➤ MAFIA.

Taffy a mid-17th century term (informal, and often offensive) for a Welshman, representing a supposed Welsh pronunciation of the given name *Davy* or *David* (Welsh *Dafydd*).

tag a brief and usually familiar quotation added for special effect; a much used quotation or stock phrase. The word in this sense is recorded from the early 18th century.

> I don't talk in tags of Latin, which might be learned by a schoolmaster's footboy.
> — George Eliot *Felix Holt* (1866)

tag day North American term for a ➤ FLAG *day*.

tagati among some South African peoples, an evil witch or wizard.

Tages name of an Etruscan god, a boy with the face of a wise old man who sprang originally from the ploughed fields and who is said to have taught the Etruscans how to predict the future. In his translation of Camden's *Britannia* (1610), Philemon Holland makes transferred use of the name, by referring to Merlin as 'the Tages of the Britans'; *Tages* is glossed as 'diviner or prophet'.

Taghairm a method of divination said to have been practised in the Scottish Highlands; the precise method varied, but it involved invocation by a sorcerer of some natural element.

> Brian an augury hath tried,
> Of that dread kind which must not be
> Unless in dread extremity,
> The Taghairm call'd; by which, afar,
> Our sires foresaw the events of war.
> — Sir Walter Scott *The Lady of the Lake* (1810)

tahara in Jewish ritual, an act of washing a corpse before burial. The word comes from Hebrew *ṭohŭrāh* 'purification'.

t'ai chi¹ a Chinese martial art and system of callisthenics, consisting of sequences of very slow controlled movements. It is believed to have been devised by a Taoist priest in the Sung dynasty.

t'ai chi² in Chinese philosophy, the ultimate source and limit of reality, from which spring yin and yang and all of creation. The concept occurs first in the *I Ching*.

Taig originally (from the mid 17th century), *Teague* and its variant *Taig*, Anglicized spellings of the Irish name *Tadhg*, were used as derogatory nicknames for an Irishman, as in the anti-Jacobite song ➤ LILLI-BURLERO, which was intended to parody Irish speech:

> Ho, Brother Teague, dost hear de decree?
> Lilli burlero bullen a la.
> Dat we shall have a new Debity,
> Lilli burlero bullen a la.
> — Thomas, Lord Wharton 'A New Song' (written 1687)

Taig is recorded from the 1970s as a derogatory term used among Protestants for a Catholic in Northern Ireland.

Taillefer a minstrel in the army of William the Conqueror who (according to the *Carmen de Hastingae Proelio* and to Henry of Huntingdon and Gaimar) marched in front of the army at Hastings, singing of the deeds of ➤ ROLAND to encourage the Normans.

tailors ➤ St HOMOBONUS is patron saint of tailors. See also ➤ DEVIL *among the tailors*, ➤ NINE *tailors make a man*, ➤ THREE *Tailors of Tooley Street*.

tails see ➤ HEADS *or tails*.

Tain-Bo-Cuailgne the 'Cattle Raid of Cooley', the chief epic of the Ulster cycle of Irish mythology, the story of the raid of Queen Maeve of Connaught to secure the Brown Bull of Cuailgne (pronounced 'Cooley'), and her defeat by ➤ CUCHULAIN.

Taiping Rebellion a sustained uprising against the Qing dynasty in China 1850–64. The rebellion was led by Hong Xinquan (1814–64), who had founded a religious group inspired by elements of Christian theology and proposing egalitarian social policies. His large army captured Nanjing in 1853 but was eventually defeated at Shanghai at the hands of an army trained by the British general Charles Gordon. The rebellion was finally defeated after the recapture of Nanjing, some 20 million people having been killed, but the Qing dynasty was severely weakened as a result. The name comes from Chinese *T'ai-p'ing-wang* 'Prince of great peace', a title given to Hong Xinquan.

taisch in Scottish folklore, the apparition of a living person who is about to die; generally, something perceived by second sight. The word is first recorded in English in accounts of Dr Johnson's travels in Scotland:

> By the term Second sight, seems to be meant a mode of seeing, superadded to that which Nature generally bestows. In the Earse it is called Taisch; which signifies likewise a spectre, or a vision.
> — Samuel Johnson *Journey to the Western Islands* (1775)

Taisho the period of rule of the Japanese emperor Yoshihito (1912–26). The name *Taishō* means in Japanese 'great righteousness'.

Taj Mahal a mausoleum at Agra built by the Mogul emperor Shah Jahan (1592–1666) in memory of his favourite wife, completed *c*.1649. Set in formal gardens, the domed building in white marble is reflected in a pool flanked by cypresses.

In 1992, when she and her husband visited India, ➤ DIANA, *Princess of Wales* was famously photographed sitting alone in front of the *Taj Mahal*, an image which became a symbol of her troubled marriage.

take see also ➤ GIVE *a thing and take a thing, to wear the devil's gold ring,* ➤ GIVE *and take is fair play,* ➤ *take away* ABERDEEN *and twelve miles round, and where are you?.*

take me to your leader catch-phrase from science-fiction stories.

> To be sure, a DOMB (dead old Martian bacterium) isn't the same as a bald humanoid with pointy ears saying 'Take me to your leader'.
> — *New Yorker* 19 August 1996

take the goods the gods provide proverbial saying, late 17th century; perhaps originally as a quotation from Dryden:

> Lovely Thais sits beside thee,
> Take the goods the gods provide thee.
> — John Dryden *Alexander's Feast* (1697)

An earlier classical form is found in Plautus, 'you may keep what good the gods give'.

Fox Talbot (1800–77), English pioneer of photography. He produced the first photograph on paper in 1835. Five years later he discovered a process for producing a negative from which multiple positive prints could be made, though the independently developed daguerreotype proved to be superior.

talaria in Roman mythology, winged sandals or small wings attached to the ankles of some gods and goddesses, especially ➤ MERCURY. The word is Latin, and comes ultimately from *talus* 'ankle'.

tale a fictitious or true narrative or story, especially one that is imaginatively recounted. The word is recorded from Old English (in form *talu*) in the sense 'telling, something told', of Germanic origin; it is related to Dutch *taal* 'speech' and German *Zahl* 'number'.

See also ➤ CANTERBURY *tale,* ➤ DEAD *men tell no tales,* ➤ WINTER'*s tale.*

a tale never loses in the telling proverbial saying, mid 16th century.

a tale of a tub an apocryphal story; mid 16th century. The phrase was used as the title of a comedy (1633) by Ben Jonson, and then in 1696 (published 1704) as the title of a prose satire by Swift; the allusion was to Hobbes's *Leviathan* and its criticism of contemporary religion and government:

> Sea-men have a Custom when they meet a Whale, to fling him out an empty Tub . . . to divert him from laying violent Hands upon the Ship . . . It was decreed, that in order to prevent these Leviathans from tossing and sporting with the Commonwealth (which of it self is too apt to fluctuate) they should be diverted . . . by a Tale of a Tub.
> — Jonathan Swift *A Tale of a Tub* (1704), preface

talent originally (in Old English, in the form *talente, talentan*) this denoted an ancient unit of weight, especially one used by the Athenians and Romans, equivalent to nearly 57 lb (26 kg), or such a weight of silver or (occasionally) gold used to represent a sum of money.

The **parable of the talents** (Matthew 25:14–30) tells the story of a wealthy man who, before going on a journey, gave each of his servants a certain number of talents. According to the story, the man who had received five talents and the man who had received two doubled them by trading, but the man who had been given one talent buried it for safety. When their master returned he commended those who had increased their talents as good and faithful, but the man who had buried his was condemned as wicked and slothful, and ordered to hand over his one talent to the man who had ten, 'For unto every one that hath shall be given…but from him that hath not shall be taken away even that which he hath.'

From this parable, *talent* in late Middle English came to mean a person's mental ability or particular faculty regarded as something divinely entrusted to them for their use and improvement; this developed (in the early 17th century) to the current sense of natural aptitude or skill.

Administration of All the Talents ironical name for the ministry of Lord Grenville (1806–7), implying that it combined all possible talents in its members; the term is recorded from 1807:

> The general impression upon the public mind, relative to the recent change in administration, seems to be, that the downfall of 'All the Talents' was occasioned by the unbending perverseness of my Lord H-w-k . . . and the deference which Lord G-n-lle paid to Lord H-w-k.
>
> — *All Talents in Ireland!* (1807)

tales a writ for summoning substitute jurors when the original jury has become deficient in number; a list of people who may be summoned as substitute jurors. The term comes from Latin *tales (de circumstantibus)* 'such (of the bystanders)', the first words of the writ.

See also ➤ PRAY *a tales.*

never tell tales out of school proverbial saying, mid 16th century.

Taliban a fundamentalist Muslim movement whose militia took control of much of Afghanistan from early 1995, and in 1996 took Kabul and set up an Islamic state. The name comes from Pashto or Dari, from Persian, literally 'students, seekers of knowledge'.

Taliesin a British bard of the 6th century, perhaps a mythic personage, first mentioned in the *Saxon Genealogies* appended to the *Historia Britonum* (*c.*690).

talisman an object, typically an inscribed ring or stone, that is thought to have magic powers and to bring good luck. The word is recorded from the mid 17th century, and is based on Arabic *ṭilsam*, apparently from an alteration of late Greek *telesma* 'completion, religious rite'.

talk see also ➤ CHALK *and talk,* ➤ IT*'s good to talk,* ➤ *talk* TURKEY.

talk is cheap proverbial saying, mid 19th century; an early 17th century source has, 'words are but words, and pay not what men owe'.

talk of the Devil, and he is bound to appear proverbial saying, mid 17th century.

tall see also ➤ PHILIP *the Tall.*

tall poppy syndrome a perceived tendency to discredit or disparage those who have achieved notable wealth or prominence in public life; with allusion to the idea of the ➤ POPPY as a flower whose showy appearance does not represent real worth.

Charles Maurice de Talleyrand (1754–1838), French statesman. Involved in the coup that brought Napoleon to power, he became head of the new government after the fall of Napoleon (1814) and was later instrumental in the overthrow of Charles X and the accession of Louis Philippe (1830); he is said to have commented that treason 'is a question of dates'.

Thomas Tallis (*c.*1505–85), English composer. Organist of the Chapel Royal jointly with William Byrd, he served under Henry VIII, Edward VI, Mary, and Elizabeth I. His works include the forty-part motet *Spem in Alium.*

tallith a fringed shawl traditionally worn by Jewish men at prayer. The word comes ultimately from biblical Hebrew *ṭillel* 'to cover'.

tally a current score or amount; the original meaning (in late Middle English) was a stick or rod of wood scored across with notches for the items of an account; it was customary for the debtor and creditor to split the piece of wood in half lengthways through the notches, each party keeping one piece. The word comes via Anglo-Norman French from Latin *talea* 'twig, cutting'.

tally-ho a huntsman's cry to the hounds on sighting a fox. The term is recorded from the late 18th century; it is apparently an alteration of French *taïaut*, of unknown origin.

Talmud the body of Jewish civil and ceremonial law and legend comprising the Mishnah and the Gemara. There are two versions of the Talmud: the Babylonian Talmud (which dates from the 5th century AD but includes earlier material) and the earlier Palestinian or Jerusalem Talmud.

Talmud Torah the field of study that deals with the Jewish law.

Talos in Greek mythology, a bronze man made by Hephaestus and given by him to ➤ MINOS of Crete; as guardian of the island, he defended it against strangers by making himself red-hot and scorching them to death in his embrace.

> He stood there, swaying gigantically in the gloom, like Talos the Man of Brass.
>
> — George Macdonald Fraser *The Sheikh and the Dustbin* (1988)

Talus in Spenser's *Faerie Queene*, an iron man who represents the executive power of government; armed with an iron flail, he punishes falsehood and reveals truth.

Tam o' Shanter the hero of Robert Burns's poem of that name, a Scottish farmer who on his way home from an alehouse comes across witches dancing, and is chased by them; the name *tam o'shanter* is used for a round woollen or cloth cap of Scottish origin, with a bobble in the centre, of a kind formerly worn by Scottish ploughmen.

See also ➤ Cutty *Sark*.

tamagotchi trademark name for an electronic toy displaying a digital image of a creature, which has to be looked after and responded to by the 'owner' as if it were a pet.

Tamerlane (1336–1405), Mongol ruler of Samarkand 1369–1405; Tartar name *Timur Lenk* ('lame Timur'). Leading a force of Mongols and Turks, he conquered Persia, northern India, and Syria and established his capital at Samarkand; he was the ancestor of the Mogul dynasty in India. He is also known as *Tamburlaine*, the spelling used by Marlowe in *Tamburlaine the Great* (1590).

From the late 16th century, *Tamerlane* has been referred to as the type of a savage conqueror or despot.

See also ➤ Persepolis.

Tamil Tigers a Sri Lankan guerrilla organization founded in 1972 that seeks the establishment of an independent state (Eelam) in the north-east of the country for the Tamil community.

Tammany Hall in the US, a powerful organization within the Democratic Party that was widely associated with corruption. Founded as a fraternal and benevolent society in 1789, it came to dominate political life in New York City in the 19th and early 20th centuries, before being reduced in power by Franklin D. Roosevelt in the early 1930s.

> The New York lawyer surprised his detractors by running an Administration of un-Tammany-like integrity.
>
> — *New Yorker* 21 October 1996

Tammuz a Mesopotamian god, lover of Ishtar and similar in some respects to the Greek Adonis. He became the personification of the seasonal death and rebirth of crops.

Tamworth Manifesto (in English history) an election speech by Sir Robert Peel in 1834 in his Tamworth constituency, in which he accepted the changes instituted by the Reform Act and expressed his belief in moderate political reform. The manifesto is widely held to signal the emergence of the Conservative Party from the old loose grouping of Tory interests.

Tanagra an ancient Greek city in Boeotia, site of a battle in 457 BC during the Peloponnesian War. It has given its name to a type of terracotta figurine, often of a young woman, made there and elsewhere mainly in the 4th and 3rd centuries BC.

Tanaiste the deputy prime minister of the Republic of Ireland; in use since 1938, the word is from the Irish base of ➤ tanist.

Tancred a Norman hero of the First Crusade, who figures in *Jerusalem Delivered* as one of the principal knights serving Godfrey of Bouillon; taken as the type of a Crusader.

> It speaks to him of Baldwin, and Tancred, the princely Saladin, and great Richard of the Lion Heart.
> — Mark Twain *The Innocents Abroad* (1869)

Tang a dynasty ruling China 618–*c.*906, a period noted for territorial conquest and great wealth and regarded as the golden age of Chinese poetry and art.

Kenzo Tange (1913–), Japanese architect. His work, for example the Peace Centre at Hiroshima (1955), is characterized by the use of modern materials while retaining a feeling for traditional Japanese architecture.

tango see ➤ *it takes* two *to tango*.

tangram a Chinese geometrical puzzle consisting of a square cut into seven pieces which can be arranged to make various other shapes.

tanist the heir apparent to a Celtic chief, typically the most vigorous adult of his kin, elected during the chief's lifetime. The word comes (in the mid 16th century) from Irish, Scottish Gaelic *tánaiste*, literally 'second in excellence' (see also ➤ Tanaiste).

tanist stone any of a number of large monoliths in Scotland, popularly supposed to mark the spot where tanists were elected.

tank a heavy armoured fighting vehicle carrying guns and moving on a continuous articulated metal track. The name comes from the use of *tank* as a secret code word during manufacture in 1915.

See also ➤ *a* tiger *in one's tank*.

tanka[1] a Japanese poem in five lines and thirty-one syllables, giving a complete picture of an event or mood.

tanka² a Tibetan religious painting on a scroll, hung as a banner in temples and carried in processions.

tankard originally (in Middle English) a large tub for carrying liquid; from the late 15th century, this came to mean a drinking-vessel, first one made of wooden staves and hooped, then a tall beer mug, now typically made of silver or pewter, with a handle and sometimes a hinged lid.

tanner former informal name for a silver sixpence; recorded from the early 19th century, but of unknown origin.

Tannhäuser (c.1200–c.1270), German poet. In reality a Minnesinger whose works included lyrics and love poetry, he became a legendary figure as a knight who visited Venus's grotto (see ➤ Venusberg) and spent seven years in debauchery, then repented and sought absolution from the Pope.

Tans see ➤ Black and Tans.

Tantalus in Greek mythology, a Lydian king, son of Zeus and father of Pelops. For his crimes (which included killing Pelops) he was punished by being provided with fruit and water which receded when he reached for them. His name is the origin of the word *tantalize*.

Tantivy in the 17th and 18th centuries, a derogatory term for a post-Restoration High-Churchman, regarded as a likely convert to Roman Catholicism. The term developed c.1680–81, when a caricature was published in which a number of High Church clergymen were represented as mounted upon the Church of England and 'riding tantivy', or at full gallop, to Rome, behind the Duke of York.

tantony bell a hand-bell; a small church bell; a bell here is an emblem of ➤ St Anthony of Egypt, whose hospitallers used to ring little bells to attract alms; these bells were then hung round the necks of animals to protect them. *Tantony* is from an alteration of the saint's name.

tantony pig the smallest pig of a litter; a pig here is the emblem of ➤ St Anthony of Egypt, who is represented as the patron of swineherds, and often shown accompanied by a pig. *Tantony* is from an alteration of the saint's name.

tantra a Hindu or Buddhist mystical or magical text, dating from the 7th century or earlier. The word is Sanskrit, and means literally 'loom, groundwork, doctrine', from *tan* 'stretch'.

Tantum ergo (a setting of) the last two stanzas of the Latin hymn of St Thomas Aquinas *Pange lingua gloriosi Corporis mysterium* 'Now, my tongue, the mystery telling', sung especially at the service of benediction.

Tao in Chinese philosophy, the absolute principle underlying the universe, combining within itself the principles of yin and yang and signifying the way, or code of behaviour, that is in harmony with the natural order. The interpretation of Tao in the Tao-te-Ching developed into the philosophical religion of Taoism.

Tao-te-Ching the central Taoist text, ascribed to Lao-tzu, the traditional founder of Taoism. Apparently written as a guide for rulers, it defined the Tao, or way, and established the philosophical basis of Taoism.

tao-tieh a mythical fierce and voracious Chinese monster with a head but no body; a representation of this, found typically on metalware of the Zhou period.

Taoiseach the Prime Minister of the Irish Republic, a title in use from 1938; the word is Irish, and means literally 'chief, leader'.

Taoism a Chinese philosophy based on the writings of Lao-tzu, advocating humility and religious piety. The central concept and goal is the Tao, and its most important text is the Tao-te-Ching. Taoism has both a philosophical and a religious aspect. Philosophical Taoism emphasizes inner contemplation and mystical union with nature; wisdom, learning, and purposive action should be abandoned in favour of simplicity and *wu-wei* (non-action, or letting things take their natural course). The religious aspect of Taoism developed later, c.3rd century AD, incorporating certain Buddhist features and developing a monastic system.

taonga in Maori culture, an object or natural resource which is highly prized.

tape see ➤ RED tape.

Taper see ➤ Tadpole and Taper.

tapestry see ➤ Bayeux Tapestry.

Mark Tapley a character in Dickens's *Martin Chuzzlewit* (1843–4), notable for optimism in the most hopeless circumstances.

> If we were all Mark Tapleys, it would be difficult to be jolly under the influence of the pea-soup weather we have been enduring.
> — *Spirit of the Times* 19 January 1878

Simon Tappertit a conceited apprentice in Dickens's *Barnaby Rudge* (1841).

> Had they been, there would not have been any procession of Tappertitian playboys.
> — St John Ervine *Craigavon* (1949)

tappit hen in Scotland, a drinking-vessel having a lid with a knob, specifically one containing a Scotch quart; a *tappit hen* was literally a hen with a crest or topknot.

tar see also ➤ *do not spoil the* SHIP *for a ha'porth of tar.*

tar and feather smear with tar and then cover with feathers as a punishment, a practice originally imposed by an ordinance of Richard I in 1189 as a punishment in the navy for theft. In 18th-century America in particular, the punishment was sometimes inflicted by the mob on an unpopular or scandalous character.

tar baby a difficult problem which is only aggravated by attempts to solve it, with allusion to the doll smeared with tar as a trap for ➤ *Brer* RABBIT, in J. C. Harris's *Uncle Remus* (1880).

Tar Heel State informal name for North Carolina, with allusion to tar as a principal product of that state.

Tara a hill in County Meath in the Republic of Ireland, site in early times of the residence of the high kings of Ireland and still marked by ancient earthworks.

tarantella a rapid whirling dance originating in southern Italy. The word comes (in the late 18th century) from Italian, from the name of the seaport *Taranto*; so named because it was thought to be a cure for ➤ TARANTISM, the victim dancing the tarantella until exhausted.

Quentin Tarantino (1963–), American film director, screenwriter, and actor. He came to sudden prominence with *Reservoir Dogs* (1992), followed in 1994 by *Pulp Fiction*. Both aroused controversy for their amorality and violence but also won admiration for their wit and style.

tarantism a psychological illness characterized by an extreme impulse to dance, prevalent in southern Italy from the 15th to the 17th century, and widely believed at the time to have been caused by the bite of a tarantula.

tarantula a large black wolf spider of southern Europe, whose bite was formerly believed to cause tarantism.

Tardis the time machine, resembling a police box, of the science fiction hero ➤ *Doctor* WHO.

> This is a perfect description of Dr Who's Tardis, whose police-box exterior belied its roomy interior.
> — *Express* 10 June 1999

tare and tret the two deductions used in calculating the net weight of goods; *tare* being the weight of a wrapping, container, or receptacle in which goods are packed, and *tret* an allowance to compensate for waste during transportation.

Targum an ancient Aramaic paraphrase or interpretation of the Hebrew Bible, of a type made from about the 1st century AD when Hebrew was ceasing to be a spoken language.

tariff reform the reform of a tariff, or of existing tariff conditions; (in the US) a reform in favour of reducing import duties, and generally moving away from protectionism; (in Britain in the early 20th century) a reform in favour of the extension of tariffs on imports, as opposed to free trade.

tarn-cap a magic cap, securing the invisibility of the wearer; the word represents German *tarnkappe*.

> Rings of Gyges, coats of darkness, tarn-caps, and other means of invisibility.
> — R. A. Vaughan *Hours with Mystics* (1860)

the Tarot playing cards, traditionally a pack of 78 with five suits, used for fortune telling and (especially in Europe) in certain games. The suits are typically swords, cups, coins (or pentacles), batons (or wands), and a permanent suit of trumps. The name is recorded from the late 16th century, and comes via French from Italian *tarocchi*; the ultimate origin is unknown.

Tarpeia in Roman mythology, one of the Vestal Virgins, the daughter of a commander of the Capitol in ancient Rome. According to legend she betrayed the citadel to the Sabines in return for whatever they wore on their arms, hoping to receive their golden bracelets; however, the Sabines killed her by throwing their shields on to her.

Tarpeian Rock a cliff in ancient Rome, at the south-western corner of the Capitoline Hill, named for ➤ TARPEIA, over which murderers and traitors were hurled.

Tarquinius the name of the semi-legendary Etruscan kings of ancient Rome; anglicized name *Tarquin*. One of these, **Tarquinius Priscus**, is said to have reigned *c*.616–578 BC; according to tradition he was murdered by the sons of the previous king.

His son or grandson **Tarquinius Superbus**, 'Tarquin the Proud', reigned *c*.534–510 BC. Noted for his cruelty, he was expelled from the city after his son's rape of ➤ LUCRETIA, and the Republic was founded. He repeatedly, but unsuccessfully, attacked Rome, assisted by ➤ *Lars* PORSENA.

See also ➤ ATTUS *Navius*, ➤ POPPY, ➤ SIBYL.

tarroo-ushtey in Manx mythology, a water-bull.

Tarsus an ancient city in southern Turkey, the capital of Cilicia and the birthplace of ➤ *St* PAUL[1], originally known as **Saul of Tarsus**.

tartan a woollen cloth woven in one of several patterns of coloured checks and intersecting lines, especially of a design associated with a particular Scottish clan. (The attribution of particular designs is comparatively modern, dating from around 1800.)

Recorded from the late 15th century, the word may come from Old French *tertaine*, denoting a kind of cloth; compare with *tartarin*, a rich fabric formerly imported from the east through Tartary.

Tartar a member of the combined forces of central Asian peoples, including Mongols and Turks, who under the leadership of ➤ GENGHIS *Khan* conquered much of Asia and eastern Europe in the early 13th century, and under Tamerlane (14th century) established an empire with its capital at Samarkand.

➤ SCRATCH *a Russian and you find a Tartar*.

Tartarus a part of the underworld where the wicked suffered punishment for their misdeeds, especially those such as ➤ IXION and ➤ TANTALUS who had committed some outrage against the gods.

Tartary a historical region of Asia and eastern Europe, especially the high plateau of central Asia and its NW slopes, which formed part of the Tartar empire in the Middle Ages.

Tartuffe a religious hypocrite, or a hypocritical pretender to excellence of any kind, from the name of the principal character (a religious hypocrite) in Molière's *Tartuffe* (1664).

> Jeff Simpson's recent rant about the outrageous salaries accorded Canadian captains of industry had a Tartuffish whiff to it.
> — *Frank* 8 May 1996

Tarzan a fictitious character created by Edgar Rice Burroughs. Tarzan (Lord Greystoke by birth) is orphaned in West Africa in his infancy and reared by apes in the jungle; he is noted for his agility and powerful physique (typified by the image of his swinging himself through the trees, or at the end of a liana stem), and for his yodelling call.

The character is associated with one of the best-known misquotations of a (supposed) film line, 'Me Tarzan, you Jane', supposedly the words in which Tarzan introduced himself to his future bride. In fact the words were used by Johnny Weissmuller (1904–84), summing up his role in *Tarzan the Ape Man* (1932 film); they do not occur in the film or the original novel by Edgar Rice Burroughs.

In the late 1980s and 1990s, *Tarzan* was used by the popular press as a nickname for the Conservative politician Michael Heseltine (1933–).

> The Tarzan of British politics is now swinging in the highest branches of the political tree.
> — *Daily Telegraph* 4 August 1995

Tasaday a member of a small group of people living on the Philippine island of Mindanao, formerly said to represent a long-isolated Stone Age people discovered only in the 1960s.

Tashi Lama another name for ➤ PANCHEN *Lama*.

Tashkent the capital of Uzbekistan, in the far north-east of the country in the western foothills of the Tien Shan mountains, an important centre on the trade route between Europe and the Orient, which became part of the Mongol empire in the 13th century.

Abel Tasman (1603–*c*.1659), Dutch navigator. Sent in 1642 by the Governor General of the Dutch East Indies, Anthony van Diemen (1593–1645), to explore Australian waters, he reached Tasmania (which he named Van Diemen's Land) and New Zealand, and in 1643 arrived at Tonga and Fiji.

Tass the official news agency of the former Soviet Union, renamed ITAR-Tass in 1992.

Torquato Tasso (1544–95), Italian poet, known for his epic poem *Gerusalemme liberata* (1581).

taste see ➤ EVERY *man to his taste*, ➤ *there is no* ACCOUNTING *for tastes*.

tastes differ proverbial saying, early 19th century.

Tate Gallery a national museum of art at Millbank, London, founded in 1897 by the sugar manufacturer Sir Henry *Tate* (1819–99) to house his collection of modern British paintings, as a nucleus for a permanent national collection of modern art. In the

20th century modern foreign paintings and sculpture (both British and foreign) were added.

Tathagata an honorific title of a Buddha, especially the Buddha Gautama, or a person who has attained perfection by following Buddhist principles.

Jacques Tati (1908–82), French film director and actor. He introduced the comically inept character ➤ *Monsieur* HULOT in *Monsieur Hulot's Holiday* (1953), seen again in films including the Oscar-winning *Mon oncle* (1958).

Tattersalls an English firm of horse auctioneers founded in 1776 by the horseman Richard *Tattersall* (1724–95), originally sited at Hyde Park Corner.

tattoo[1] an evening drum or bugle signal recalling soldiers to their quarters. The word is recorded in this sense from 1644, in a military order decreeing that anyone found 'tippling or drinking in any tavern, inn, or alehouse after nine of the clock at night', when the tattoo sounded, would be fined two shillings and sixpence.

From the mid 18th century, the word has also denoted an entertainment consisting of music, marching, and the performance of displays and exercises by military personnel.

tattoo[2] mark a person or a part of the body with an indelible design by inserting pigment into punctures in the skin; the word comes (in the mid 18th century) from Tahitian, Tongan, and Samoan *ta-tau* or Marquesan *ta-tu*.

tau the nineteenth letter of the Greek alphabet. It was sometimes used in the sense 'last letter', as *tau* was originally in Greek, and continued to be in Hebrew (see ➤ TAW).

The word is also used for the ➤ ANKH of ancient Egyptian symbolism.

tau cross a T-shaped cross, both as a sacred symbol and in heraldry.

A *tau-cross* is the emblem of ➤ St ANTHONY *of Egypt*.

Tauchnitz a publishing house founded by Christian Berhard von Tauchnitz (1816–95), which in 1843 began to issue piratically, then from 1843 to 1943 by sanction or copyright, a series of English-language publications.

Taurus in astronomy, a constellation (the Bull), said to represent a bull with brazen feet that was tamed by Jason. Its many bright stars include Aldebaran (the bull's eye), and it contains the star clusters of the Hyades and the Pleiades, and the Crab Nebula. In astrology, Taurus is the second sign of the zodiac, which the sun enters on about 21 April.

tautology the saying of the same thing twice over in different words, generally considered to be a fault of style (e.g. *they arrived one after the other in succession*).

Tavern see ➤ AMBROSE's *Tavern*, ➤ MERMAID *Tavern*, ➤ MITRE *Tavern*, ➤ ROSE *Tavern*.

John Taverner (*c*.1490–1545), English composer, an influential writer of early polyphonic church music.

Taverner's Bible a revision of ➤ MATTHEW's *Bible*, printed in 1539. Richard *Taverner* (?1505–75) was a religious author who was patronized by Wolsey and Cromwell and was sent to the Tower on the latter's fall, but subsequently obtained the favour of Henry VIII.

taw the final letter of the Hebrew alphabet; the corresponding letter in any of various ancient Semitic alphabets.

tawdry showy but cheap and of poor quality. Recorded from the early 17th century, the word is short for *tawdry lace*, a fine silk lace or ribbon worn as a necklace in the 16th–17th cents, contraction of *St Audrey's lace*: *Audrey* was a later form of ➤ *St* ETHELDREDA (died 679), patron saint of Ely where tawdry laces, along with cheap imitations and other cheap finery, were traditionally sold at a fair.

tax see ➤ POLL *tax*, ➤ SALADINE *tax*, ➤ SINGLE *tax*, ➤ *there is* NOTHING *certain but death and taxes*, ➤ WINDOW *tax*.

tax-collectors ➤ *St* MATTHEW is patron saint of tax-collectors.

taxi-drivers ➤ *St* FIACRE is patron saint of taxi-drivers.

tazia a representation, often made of paper and elaborately decorated, of the tombs of Hassan and Hussein (grandsons of Muhammad) carried in procession during Muharram. Also, a play commemorating the suffering and death of Hassan and Hussein, performed especially on the anniversary of the event each year. The word comes from Arabic *ta'ziya* 'consolation, mourning'.

Te Deum a Latin hymn beginning *Te Deum laudamus*, 'We praise Thee, O God', sung at matins or on special occasions such as a thanksgiving.

Te igitur the first prayer in the canon of the Mass in the Roman and some other Latin liturgies, beginning with the words, 'thee therefore'.

tea a hot drink made by infusing the dried, crushed leaves of the tea plant in boiling water, and usually adding a small amount of milk. The word comes (in the mid 17th century, probably via Malay) from Chinese (Min dialect) *te*. It is related to Mandarin *chá*, which has given rise directly to the informal *char*.

The pattern of tea-leaves left at the bottom of a cup is sometimes used for fortune-telling.

See also ➤ BOSTON *Tea Party*.

tea and sympathy kind and attentive behaviour towards someone who is upset or in trouble; the phrase was used as a film title in 1956.

not for all the tea in China there is nothing at all that could induce one to do something; an emphatic expression recorded from the mid 20th century.

you can't teach an old dog new tricks proverbial saying, mid 16th century.

don't teach your grandmother to suck eggs proverbial saying, early 18th century.

teacher ➤ *St* JOHN *Baptist de la Salle* is patron saint of *teachers*.

See also ➤ EXPERIENCE *is the best teacher*.

Teachta Dála (in the Republic of Ireland) a member of the Dáil or lower House of Parliament.

Teague see ➤ TAIG.

Teapot Dome the name of a naval oil reserve in Wyoming, irregularly leased by the US government in 1922, and referred to allusively in connection with the resulting political scandal.

> In an era of Teapot Dome and bathtub gin, he [Lindbergh] seemed to Americans a cleaner, sharper version of themselves.
> — *Time* 23 May 1977

teapoy a small three-legged table or stand, especially one that holds a tea caddy; the word comes (in the early 19th century) from Hindi *tī*- 'three' + Urdu and Persian *pāī* 'foot', the sense and spelling influenced by ➤ TEA.

tears see ➤ BLOOD, *toil, tears and sweat*, ➤ CROCO-DILE *tears*, ➤ *the* GATE *of Tears*, ➤ TRAIL *of Tears*, ➤ VALE *of tears*.

Tebet in the Jewish calendar, the fourth month of the civil and tenth of the religious year, usually coinciding with parts of December and January.

teddy bear a soft toy bear; the *teddy bear* came into vogue about 1907, and was so called in humorous allusion to ➤ *Theodore* ROOSEVELT (US President 1901–9), whose bear-hunting expeditions occasioned a celebrated comic poem, accompanied by cartoons, in the *New York Times* of 7 January 1906, concerning the adventures of two bears named 'Teddy B' and 'Teddy G'. These names were transferred to two bears (also known as the 'Roosevelt bears') presented to Bronx Zoo in the same year; finally the fame of these bears was turned to advantage by toy dealers, whose toy 'Roosevelt bears', imported from Germany, became an instant fashion in the US.

teddy bears' picnic an occasion of innocent enjoyment; from the title of a song (*c.*1932) by Jimmy Kennedy and J. W. Bratton.

Teddy boy (in the 1950s) a young man of a subculture characterized by a style of dress based on Edwardian fashion (typically with drainpipe trousers, bootlace tie, and hair slicked up in a quiff) and a liking for rock-and-roll music.

teeth see ➤ DRAGON's *teeth*.

teetotal choosing or characterized by abstinence from alcohol. Recorded from the mid 19th century, the word is an emphatic extension of *total*, apparently first used by Richard Turner, a worker from Preston, in a speech (1833) urging total abstinence from all alcohol, rather than mere abstinence from spirits, advocated by some early temperance reformers.

teetotum a small spinning top spun with the fingers, especially one with four sides lettered to determine whether the spinner has won or lost.

Teflon-coated having an undamaged reputation, in spite of scandal or misjudgement; able to deflect criticism on to others, so that nothing sticks to oneself.

> Ronald Reagan . . . is attempting a great breakthrough in political technology—he has been perfecting the Teflon-coated Presidency. He sees to it that nothing sticks to him.
> — Patricia Schroeder speech in the US House of Representatives, 2 August 1983

Teian Muse a name for the Greek lyric poet ➤ ANACREON, who was born in the ancient Ionian city of Teos, on the western coast of Asia Minor north of Ephesus.

teil a lime-tree; in the Bishops' Bible of 1568 and the Authorized Version of 1611, used in Isaiah 6:13 to translate Hebrew *ēlāh* (elsewhere rendered 'oak' and once 'elm'). Other translations have *terebinth*.

Teilhard de Chardin (1881–1955), French Jesuit philosopher and palaeontologist. He is best known for his theory, blending science and Christianity, that man is evolving mentally and socially towards a perfect spiritual state. The Roman Catholic Church declared his views were unorthodox and his major works (e.g. *The Phenomenon of Man*, 1955) were published posthumously.

Pope Pius XII (1876–1958) is said to have commented, on being asked to proscribe his works, 'One Galileo in two thousand years is enough.'

tekoteko in New Zealand, a carved human figure, typically one placed on a gable. The word is from Maori.

Tel Aviv a city on the Mediterranean coast of Israel which was founded as a suburb of Jaffa by Russian Jewish immigrants in 1909 and named Tel Aviv a year later.

telamon a male figure used as a pillar to support an entablature or other structure, from the name of *Telamon*, a hero of Greek mythology, king of Salamis and father of ➤ AJAX and ➤ TEUCER.

telecommunications ➤ *St* GABRIEL is patron saint of telecommunications.

Telegonus in post-Homeric legend, the son of ➤ ODYSSEUS by ➤ CIRCE, who when grown to manhood went in search of his father in Ithaca. Not recognizing Odysseus, he fought with him and killed him; his spear had been tipped with the sting of a stingray, and this fulfilled the prophecy in the Odyssey that Odysseus's death would come 'from the sea'.

telegram ➤ KRUGER *telegram*.

telegraph ➤ BUSH *telegraph*.

Telemachus in Greek mythology, the son of ➤ ODYSSEUS and ➤ PENELOPE, who grows up while his father is away, and is guided and advised by Athena in the guise of ➤ MENTOR. When Odysseus returns, Telemachus assists him in defending their house against Penelope's suitors.

teleology the explanation of phenomena by the purpose they serve rather than by postulated causes; in theology, the doctrine of design and purpose in the material world.

telepathy the supposed communication of thoughts or ideas by means other than the known senses; the term was coined in the late 19th century by the poet and essayist Frederic William Henry Myers (1843–1901), who in 1882 became one of the founding members of the Society for Psychical Research.

televangelist chiefly in the US, an evangelical preacher who appears regularly on television to promote beliefs and appeal for funds. With the renewed fashion for fundamentalist doctrine during the early 1980s in the US, *televangelists* such as Jim Bakker, Jimmy Swaggart, and Oral Roberts achieved considerable fame and political influence. In the later 1980s, a number of financial and sexual scandals involving televangelists brought them into the news in a more negative way.

television ➤ *St* CLARE *of Assisi* is patron saint of television.

tell see also ➤ *Tell el-*AMARNA.

William Tell a legendary hero of the liberation of Switzerland from Austrian oppression. He was required to hit with an arrow an apple placed on the head of his son, which he did successfully. The events are placed in the 14th century, but there is no evidence for a historical person of this name, and similar legends are of widespread occurrence.

tell it not in Gath saying enjoining discretion; originally with biblical allusion to 2 Samuel 1:20, as part of David's lament for Jonathan and Saul, 'Tell it not in Gath, publish it not in the streets of Askelon, lest the daughters of the Philistines rejoice.'

tell that to the horse marines a scornful expression of disbelief; the *horse marines* are taken as an imaginary corps of mounted marine soldiers (out of their natural element); the phrase is now often found as *tell that to the marines*.

tell the truth and shame the Devil proverbial saying, mid 16th century.

teller in the UK, each of the four officers of the Exchequer responsible for the receipt and payment of moneys.

Tellus in Roman mythology, the goddess of the earth; the name is also used for the earth personified, the planet Earth.

Telstar the first of the active communications satellites (i.e. both receiving and retransmitting signals, not merely reflecting signals from the earth). It was launched by the US in 1962 and used in the transmission of television broadcasting and telephone communication.

temenos a piece of ground surrounding or adjacent to a temple; a sacred enclosure or precinct. The word is recorded from the early 19th century, and comes from Greek, from the stem of *temnein* 'cut off'.

Téméraire an English battleship, named after a captured French ship (the word in French means 'bold' or 'rash'), which was built in 1798. She took part in the battle of Trafalgar (1805), where she was the second ship of the line, closely following the Victory; her share in the action was considered notable. The *Téméraire* was broken up in 1838; her final journey was the subject of one of Turner's most famous paintings, *The Fighting Téméraire* (1838), and of a poem by Newbolt:

> Now the sunset breezes shiver,
> And she's fading down the river,
> But in England's song for ever
> She's the Fighting Téméraire.
> — Henry Newbolt 'The Fighting Téméraire' (1897)

See also ➤ CHARLES *le Téméraire*.

Tempe a beautiful valley or delightful rural spot, from the name of a valley in Thessaly, Greece, traditionally noted for its beauty.

> The gay solitude of my own little Tempe.
> — Horace Walpole letter, 17 July 1770

temper see ➤ GOD *tempers the wind to the shorn lamb*.

tempera a method of painting with pigments dispersed in an emulsion miscible with water, typically egg yolk. The method was used in Europe for fine painting, mainly on wood panels, from the 12th or early 13th century until the 15th, when it began to give way to oils.

temperance see ➤ *Theobald* MATHEW.

tempest-tossed thrown violently about (as) by a tempest; originally used with allusion to Shakespeare's *Romeo and Juliet* and *Macbeth*. In the 19th century, the phrase was used by the American poet Emma Lazarus in the lines inscribed on the ➤ *Statue of* LIBERTY:

> Send these, the homeless, tempest-tossed, to me:
> I lift my lamp beside the golden door.
> — Emma Lazarus 'The New Colossus' (1883)

Templar a member of the ➤ KNIGHTS *Templars*.

temple a building devoted to the worship, or regarded as the dwelling place, of a god or gods or other objects of religious reverence. The word is recorded from Old English (in form *temp(e)l*), and was reinforced in Middle English by Old French *temple*; both come from Latin templum 'open or consecrated ground'.

The Temple is the name given to either of two successive religious buildings of the Jews in Jerusalem. The first (957–586 BC) was built by Solomon and destroyed by Nebuchadnezzar; it contained the Ark of the Covenant. The second (515 BC–AD 70) was enlarged by Herod the Great from 20 BC and destroyed by the Romans during a Jewish revolt; all that remains is the Wailing Wall. Also called **Temple of Solomon**.

A group of buildings in Fleet Street, London, which stand on land formerly occupied by the headquarters of the Knights Templars is also known as **the Temple**; the Inner Temple and the Outer Temple, two of the ➤ INNS *of Court*, are located there.

See also ➤ *Temple of* REASON.

Temple Bar the name of the barrier or gateway closing the entrance into the City of London from the Strand; removed in 1878. Heads of those executed for treason were traditionally exposed there; Dr Johnson in 1773 commented on seeing the heads of two Jacobites who had been executed in 1746.

tempora see also ➤ O *tempora! O mores!*.

tempora mutantur, et nos mutamur in illis Latin proverbial saying, meaning 'Times change, and we change with them'; in William Harrison's *Description of Britain* (1577), it is attributed to the Emperor Lothar I (795–855) in the form *Omnia mutantur, nos et mutamur in illis* [All things change, and we change with them]'.

temporal power the power of a bishop or cleric, especially the Pope, in secular matters.

temps perdu the past, contemplated with nostalgia and a sense of irretrievability; a French phrase, literally 'time lost', originally with allusion to Proust (see ➤ RECHERCHE *du temps perdu*).

the Temptation the tempting of Jesus by the Devil, as told in Matthew 4, when Jesus was challenged to demonstrate his miraculous powers, firstly in the wilderness by turning stones into bread, and then in the holy city, by flinging himself from a pinnacle of the temple. Lastly he was taken up into a high mountain and shown the kingdoms of the world, all of which he was promised if he would worship the Devil.

The expression is also used to refer to the tempting of certain medieval saints, as in the **Temptation of St Anthony**, in which demons in the form of beautiful women tried to tempt the hermit ➤ St Anthony *of Egypt*; this was a favourite subject of early paintings.

the Tempter the Devil; the appellation is recorded from late Middle English.

tempus fugit Latin proverbial saying, meaning 'time flies'; it comes originally from a line from Virgil's *Georgics*, '*Sed fugit interea, fugit inreparabile tempus* [But meanwhile it is flying, irretrievable time is flying].'

temura a Kabbalistic method of interpreting the Hebrew Scriptures by the systematic replacement of the letters of a word with other letters.

ten a cardinal number equivalent to the product of five and two; one more than nine. Recorded from Old English (in form *tēn, tīen*) and of Germanic origin, the word comes ultimately from an Indo-European root shared by Latin *decem*.
  See also ➤ Council *of Ten*, ➤ Number *Ten*, ➤ Ten *Words*, ➤ upper *ten thousand*.

Ten Commandments in the Bible, the divine rules of conduct given by God to Moses on Mount Sinai, according to Exodus 20:1–17. The commandments are generally enumerated as: have no other gods; do not make or worship idols; do not take the name of the Lord in vain; keep the sabbath holy; honour one's father and mother; do not kill; do not commit adultery; do not steal; do not give false evidence; do not covet another's property or wife.

ten-gallon hat a large, broad-brimmed hat, traditionally worn by cowboys.

ten-minute rule a rule of the House of Commons allowing brief discussion of a motion to introduce a bill, each speech being limited to ten minutes; the standing order imposing this limitation was passed in 1888.

ten persecutions persecutions of the early Church, as enumerated by 5th-century writers; ➤ Orosius popularized the idea of ten Roman emperors as persecutors, namely Nero, Domitian, Trajan, Marcus Aurelius, Septimius Severus, Maximinus Thrax, Decius, Valerian, Aurelian, and Diocletian, although in fact treatment of Christians in the different reigns varied widely.

tenant a person who occupies land or property rented from a landlord. The word is recorded from Middle English and comes from Old French, literally 'holding'.

tenant at will a tenant who can be evicted without notice.

tenant right the right of a tenant to continue a tenancy at the termination of the lease.

Tendai a Buddhist sect introduced into Japan from China by the monk Saichō (767–822), founded by Zhi Yi (515–97) and characterized by elaborate ritual, moral idealism, and philosophical eclecticism.

tender passion romantic love; the term dates from the late 18th century and is first recorded in Sheridan's *Duenna* (1775), 'I delight in the tender passions.'

tenderloin in the US, informal name for a district of a city where vice and corruption are prominent. Recorded from the late 19th century, the name was originally a term applied to a district of New York, seen as a 'choice' assignment by police because of the bribes offered to them to turn a blind eye to criminal activity.

La Tène the second cultural phase of the European Iron Age, following the Halstatt period (*c*.480 BC) and lasting until the coming of the Romans. This culture represents the height of Celtic power, being characterized by hill forts, rich and elaborate burials, and distinctively crafted artefacts.
  The name is recorded from the late 19th century, and comes from the name of a district in Switzerland, where remains of the culture were first identified.

Tenebrae in the Roman Catholic Church, matins and lauds for the last three days of Holy Week, at which candles are successively extinguished, in memory of the darkness at the Crucifixion. Several composers have set parts of the office to music. The word is Latin, and means literally 'darkness'.

John Tenniel (1820–1914), English illustrator and cartoonist, who illustrated Lewis Carroll's *Alice's Adventures in Wonderland* (1865) and *Through the Looking Glass* (1871). He was also the author of the cartoon on the fall of ➤ Bismarck from which the phrase ➤ *drop the* pilot derives.

tennis see ➤ anyone *for tennis*.

tennis-court oath the pledge given on June 20, 1789, by members of the States General of France that they would not separate before a constitution was granted; the meeting was held on the tennis court at Versailles.

Tenno the Emperor of Japan viewed as a divinity.

Alfred, Lord Tennyson (1809–92), English poet, Poet Laureate from 1850. His reputation was established by *In Memoriam* (1850), a long poem concerned with immortality, change, and evolution, written in memory of his friend Arthur Hallam. He had earlier published a series of twelve Arthurian poems, *Idylls of the King*, written after Hallam's death and published in 1842; the second edition (1862) was dedicated to the memory of ➤ *Prince* AL-BERT.

Tenochtitlán the ancient capital of the Aztec empire, founded *c*.1320. In 1521 the Spanish conquistador Cortés, having deposed the Aztec emperor Montezuma and overthrown his empire, destroyed it and established Mexico City on its site.

tenson a contest in verse-making between troubadours; the word comes via French from Provençal *tenso* 'poetical contest'.

Tenterden steeple is the cause of Goodwin Sands traditional saying, early 16th century; from the story that the land represented by these quicksands was submerged (about 1100) because the abbot of St Augustine's Canterbury had used the stones of the seawall for the tower of Tenterden church.

on tenterhooks in a state of suspense or agitation because of uncertainty about a future event; a *tenterhook* was originally a hook used to fasten cloth on a drying frame or *tenter*.

the tenth Muse a person or thing considered to be a source of inspiration comparable to one of the mythological Muses, especially in a particular field; the term is recorded from the early 17th century, in one of Shakespeare's *Sonnets*, and was used in 1650 by the poet Anne Bradstreet (1612–72) in the title of her collection of poems, 'The tenth Muse lately sprung up in America, or several poems compiled with great variety of wit and learning'.

tenth wave it was formerly thought that every tenth wave was larger than the nine preceding waves; the belief is recorded from the late 16th century.

tenths the tenth part of produce or profits, or of the estimated value of personal property, appropriated as a religious or ecclesiastical due or a royal subsidy. The tenth part of every living in the kingdom was originally paid to the pope, but by an act of Henry VIII (1534) was transferred to the Crown, and was afterwards made part of the fund known as ➤ QUEEN *Anne's Bounty*.

Tenzing Norgay (1914–86), Sherpa mountaineer. In 1953, as members of the British expedition, he and Sir Edmund Hillary were the first to reach the summit of Mount Everest.

teocalli a temple of the Aztecs or other Mexican peoples, typically standing on a truncated pyramid. The word is American Spanish and comes from Nahuatl *teo:kalli*, from *teo:tl* 'god' + *kalli* 'house'.

Teotihuacán the largest city of pre-Columbian America, situated about 40 km (25 miles) north-east of Mexico City. Built *c*.300 BC, it reached its zenith *c*.300–600 AD, when it was the centre of an influential culture which spread throughout Meso-America.

teraphim small images or cult objects used as domestic deities or oracles by ancient Semitic peoples.

teratology mythology relating to fantastic creatures and monsters. The term is recorded from the late 17th century, and comes from Greek *teras, terat-* 'monster'.

terce a service forming part of the Divine Office of the Western Christian Church, traditionally said (or chanted) at the third hour of the day (i.e. 9 a.m.). The word is recorded from late Middle English, and comes via Old French from Latin *tertia*, feminine of *tertius* 'third'.

tercel in falconry, the male of a hawk, especially a peregrine or a goshawk. Recorded from Middle English, the word comes via Old French from Latin *tertius* 'third', perhaps from the belief that the third egg of a clutch produced a male.

tercel-gentle the male of the falcon; recorded from the late 15th century, the name is after ➤ FALCON-*gentle*; after Shakespeare, it is also found in figurative and allusive use:

> O for a falconer's voice,
> To lure this tassel-gentle back again.
> — William Shakespeare *Romeo and Juliet* (1595)

Terence (*c*.190–159 BC), Roman comic dramatist. His six surviving comedies are based on the Greek New Comedy; they use the same stock characters as are found in Plautus, but are marked by more realism and a greater consistency of plot.

Mother Teresa (1910–97), Roman Catholic nun and missionary, born in what is now Macedonia of

Albanian parentage. She became an Indian citizen in 1948. She founded the Order of Missionaries of Charity, which became noted for its work among the poor in Calcutta and now operates in many parts of the world.

St Teresa of Ávila (1515–82) Spanish Carmelite nun and mystic, who combined vigorous activity as a reformer with mysticism and religious contemplation. She instituted the 'discalced' reform movement with St John of the Cross, establishing the first of a number of convents in 1562. In 1970 she became the first woman to be declared a ➤ DOCTOR *of the Church.*

□ **EMBLEMS** Her emblems are a fiery arrow or a dove above her head.

□ **FEAST DAY** Her feast day is 15 October.

St Teresa of Lisieux (1873–97), French Carmelite nun. Her cult grew through the publication of her autobiography *L'Histoire d'une âme* (1898) in which she taught that sanctity can be attained through continual renunciation in small matters, and not only through extreme self-mortification. She is represented in her Carmelite habit and holding roses, as a sign of her promise to 'let fall a shower of roses' of miracles and other favours.

□ **FEAST DAY** Her feast day is 3 October.

Valentina Tereshkova (1937–), Russian cosmonaut, who in June 1963 became the first woman in space.

termagant a harsh-tempered or overbearing woman; originally (in the early 13th century) the name of an imaginary deity held in medieval Christendom to be worshipped by Muslims: in the mystery plays represented as a violent overbearing personage. In ➤ LAYAMON's *Brut,* the name is used for the gods of the Romans and the heathen Saxons.

the Terminator the deadly robot who in the film *Terminator* (1984) and its sequel is sent back from the future to find and kill the humans who are destined to provide the leadership for human resistance to the 21st-century computer Skynet. His promise is, 'I'll be back.'

> Biocontrol insects can seem like smart bombs, able to home in on a pest with Terminator-like efficiency.
> — *New Scientist* 15 January 2000

terminator gene in a genetically modified crop, a gene which ensures that nothing can be grown from the seeds of a plant; the commercial development of

such a gene has been one of the points of dispute in the ➤ GM debate.

> It also condemns 'suicide seeds' that contain a terminator gene which makes the next generation of seeds sterile, forcing farmers to buy new seed every year.
> — *Guardian* 10 May 1999

terminer see ➤ OYER *and terminer.*

terminological inexactitude a humorous euphemism for a lie, first used by Winston Churchill in a Commons speech in 1906:

> It cannot in the opinion of His Majesty's Government be classified as slavery in the extreme acceptance of the word without some risk of terminological inexactitude.
> — Winston Churchill speech in the House of Commons, 22 February 1906

terminus in ancient Rome, a boundary marker consisting of a figure of a human bust or an animal ending in a square pillar from which it appears to spring. *Terminus* was originally the name of the deity who presided over boundaries and landmarks.

terms see ➤ EAT *one's terms.*

Terpsichore in Roman mythology, the Muse of lyric poetry and dance.

terra firma dry land; the ground as distinct from the sea or air. Recorded from the early 17th century, the phrase denoted originally the territories on the Italian mainland which were subject to the state of Venice.

terra incognita unknown or unexplored territory; the term is first recorded in John Smith's *Description of New England* (1616), in a reference to the supposed southern continent (➤ AUSTRALIA):

> The Spaniards know . . . not so much as the true circumference of Terra Incognita, whose large dominions may equalize the greatness and goodness of America.
> — John Smith *Description of New England* (1616)

Terran in science fiction, of or relating to the planet Earth or its inhabitants.

Terrapin State an informal name for Maryland.

terrier[1] a small dog of a breed originally used for turning out foxes and other burrowing animals from their earths, sometimes taken as the type of determined aggression. The name, which is recorded from late Middle English, comes from Old French *(chien) terrier* 'earth dog', and ultimately from Latin *terra* 'earth'.

terrier[2] a register of the lands belonging to a landowner, originally including a list of tenants, their holdings, and the rents paid, later consisting of a description of the acreage and boundaries of the property. The word is recorded from the late 15th century, and comes via Old French from medieval Latin *terrarius (liber)* '(book) of land', and ultimately from Latin *terra* 'earth'.

terror see also ➤ KING *of Terrors,* ➤ REIGN *of Terror,* ➤ WHITE *Terror.*

the Terror the period of the French Revolution between mid 1793 and July 1794 when the ruling Jacobin faction, dominated by Robespierre, ruthlessly executed anyone considered a threat to their regime; it ended with the fall and execution of ➤ ROBESPIERRE.

Terry Alt a member of a secret agrarian association active in western Ireland in the 1830s. According to a manuscript diary of 1831, quoted in the *Times Literary Supplement* of 29 September 1932, *Terry Alts* was the name of an innocent bystander suspected of an act of violence.

tertiary a lay associate of certain Christian monastic organizations, as of the Franciscan ➤ THIRD *Order.*

tertium quid a third thing that is indefinite and undefined but is related to two definite or known things; *tertium quid* was used by alchemists for a third substance which was different from its two constituents. The phrase is recorded from the early 18th century and comes from late Latin, a translation of Greek *triton ti* 'some third thing'.

Tertullian (*c.*160–*c.*240), early Christian theologian. His writings include Christian apologetics and attacks on pagan idolatry and Gnosticism. He later joined the Montanists, urging asceticism and venerating martyrs.

terza rima an arrangement of triplets, especially in iambic pentameter, that rhyme *aba bcb cdc* etc. as in Dante's *Divine Comedy.*

test see also ➤ ACID *test,* ➤ BETA *test.*

Test Act in the UK, an act in force between 1673 and 1828 that made an oath of allegiance to the Church of England and the supremacy of the monarch as its head and repudiation of the doctrine of transubstantiation a condition of eligibility for public office.

Test Act also designates an act of 1871 relaxing restrictions on university entrance for candidates who were not members of the Church of England.

Test-Ban Treaty an international agreement not to test nuclear weapons in the atmosphere, in space, or under water, signed in 1963 by the US, the UK, and the USSR, and later by more than 100 governments.

test match an international cricket or rugby match, typically one of a series, played between teams representing two different countries; the term is first recorded in an account of five cricket *test matches* played between England and Australia in the season of 1861–2.

testament see ➤ NEW *Testament,* ➤ OLD *Testament.*

tester dated slang term for a sixpence, deriving from an alteration of ➤ TESTON.

teston the French name of a silver coin struck at Milan by Galeazzo Maria Sforza (1468–76), bearing a portrait or head of the duke, and called in Italian *testone*; then of the similar coin struck by Louis XII after his conquest of Milan, for currency in Italy, and by Francis I (1515–47) for use in France. Both in Italy and France, the name was soon applied to equivalent silver coins without a portrait; but always to pieces heavier than the *gros.*

testudo in ancient Rome, a screen on wheels and with an arched roof, used to protect besieging troops; a protective screen formed by a body of troops holding their shields above their heads in such a way that the shields overlap. Recorded from late Middle English, the word is Latin, and means literally 'tortoise', from *testa* 'tile, shell'.

Tet the Vietnamese lunar New Year.

Tet offensive (in the Vietnam War) an offensive launched in January–February 1968 by the Vietcong and the North Vietnamese army. Timed to coincide with the first day of the Tet, it was a surprise attack on South Vietnamese cities, notably Saigon. Although repulsed after initial successes, the attack shook US confidence and hastened the withdrawal of its forces.

tête-bêche (of a postage stamp) printed upside down or sideways relative to another. The (French) term comes from *tête* 'head' and *bêche*, contraction of obsolete *béchevet* 'double bedhead'.

Tethys in Greek mythology, a goddess of the sea, daughter of ➤ URANUS (Heaven) and ➤ GAIA (Earth), and consort of ➤ OCEANUS.

In astronomy, *Tethys* was the name given to a satellite of Saturn, the ninth closest to the planet and probably composed mainly of ice, discovered by Cassini in 1684. In geology, it is the name of an ocean formerly separating the supercontinents of Gondwana and Laurasia, the forerunner of the present-day Mediterranean.

tetractys a set of four; the number four; especially, the Pythagorean name for the sum of the first four numbers ($1 + 2 + 3 + 4 = 10$) regarded as the source of all things (formerly also called the *quaternary of numbers*).

Tetragrammaton the Hebrew name of God transliterated in four letters as *YHWH* or *JHVH* and articulated as *Yahweh* or *Jehovah*. The word is Greek, the neuter of *tetragrammatos* 'having four letters'.

tetralogy a series of four ancient Greek dramas, three tragic and one satyric, originally presented together at the festival of Dionysus at Athens; from this, the term has come to mean a series of four linked dramatic or literary works.

tetramorph in painting or sculpture, the representation of the iconographical symbols of the four evangelists.

Tetramorph

EVANGELIST	SYMBOL
Matthew	Angel
Mark	Lion
Luke	Ox
John	Eagle

tetrarch in the Roman Empire, the governor of one of four divisions of a country or province; later, more generally, a subordinate ruler.

Teucer in Greek mythology, the legendary ancestor of the Trojan kings through his daughter, the wife of Dardanus.

Teucer is also the name of the son of Telamon and half-brother of Ajax, who fought as an archer with the Greeks at the siege of Troy.

teum see ➤ MEUM *and teum*.

Teuton a member of a people who lived in Jutland in the 4th century BC and fought the Romans in France in the 2nd century BC; from the mid 19th century, the term was used generally to denote Germanic-speaking races and peoples.

Teutonic cross a cross potent, the badge of the Teutonic Knights.

Teutonic Knights a military and religious order of German knights, priests, and lay brothers, originally enrolled *c.*1191 as the **Teutonic Knights of St Mary of Jerusalem**. They took part in the Crusades from a base in Palestine until expelled from the Holy Land in 1225. Abolished by Napoleon in 1809, the order was re-established in Vienna as an honorary ecclesiastical institution in 1834 and maintains a titular existence.

Texas Ranger a member of the Texas State police force (formerly, of certain locally mustered regiments in the federal service during the Mexican War).

William Makepeace Thackeray (1811–63), British novelist. He established his reputation with *Vanity Fair* (1847–8), a satire of the upper middle class of early 19th-century society.

Thaddaeus an apostle named in Matthew 10:3 as 'Lebbaeus, whose surname was Thaddaeus'; he is traditionally identified with ➤ *St* JUDE.

Thais Athenian courtesan who is said to have caused Alexander the Great to set fire to ➤ PERSEPOLIS.

> Thais led the way,
> To light him to his prey,
> And, like another Helen, fired another Troy.
> — John Dryden *Alexander's Feast* (1697)

thalassa in Greek, the sea. In ➤ XENOPHON's account of the war between Artaxerxes II of Persia and his younger brother Cyrus, he relates how retreating Greek soldiers of the defeated Cyrus fought their way through the Armenian mountains and finally reached the Black Sea; when they first saw the sea, they cried out, '*thalassa, thalassa!*'

Thales (*c.*624–*c.*545 BC), Greek philosopher, mathematician, and astronomer, living at Miletus. One of the ➤ SEVEN *Sages* listed by Plato and judged by Aristotle to be the founder of physical science, he is also credited with founding geometry. He proposed that water was the primary substance from which all things were derived.

Thalestris name of a legendary queen of the Amazons, who is said to have met Alexander the Great on the border of India.

Thalia in Greek mythology, the Muse of comedy and idyllic poetry; in classical mythology, she is also one of the three Graces. The name is Greek, and means literally 'rich, plentiful'.

thalidomide a drug formerly used as a sedative, but withdrawn in the UK in the early 1960s after it was found to cause congenital malformation or absence of limbs in children whose mothers took the drug during early pregnancy.

Thames a river of southern England, flowing eastwards from the Cotswolds in Gloucestershire through London to the North Sea; in literary use, sometimes personified as **Father Thames**.

> In vain on Father Thames she calls for aid.
> — Alexander Pope *Windsor-Forest* (1713)

See also ➤ SET *the Thames on fire.*

Thammuz (in the Jewish calendar) the tenth month of the civil and fourth of the religious year, usually coinciding with parts of June and July. Also called *Tammuz.*

Thamudic an ancient language, allied to early Arabic and known only from graffiti inscriptions dating from the 5th to the 1st centuries BC discovered in northern and central Arabia.

Thamyris in Greek mythology, a Thracian poet blinded by the Muses because of his boast that he could surpass them in song.

Thanatos in Greek mythology, the god of Death, brother of Hypnos (Sleep); in Freudian theory, *Thanatos* is used for the death instinct (often contrasted with ➤ EROS).

thane in Anglo-Saxon England, a man who held land granted by the king or by a military nobleman, ranking between an ordinary freeman and a hereditary noble; in Scotland, a man, often the chief of a clan, who held land from a Scottish king and ranked with an earl's son.

See also ➤ THEGN.

General Thanksgiving a form of thanksgiving in the *Book of Common Prayer* or the Alternative Service Book; in its Prayer-book form it opens, 'We bless thee for our creation, preservation, and all the blessings of this life.'

Thanksgiving Day (in North America) an annual national holiday marked by religious observances and a traditional meal including turkey. The holiday commemorates a harvest festival celebrated by the ➤ PILGRIM *Fathers* in 1621, and is held in the US on the fourth Thursday in November. A similar holiday is held in Canada, usually on the second Monday in October.

Thathanabaing the chief Buddhist dignitary in Myanmar (Burma).

thaumatrope a scientific toy that was devised in the 19th century, consisting of a disc having a different picture on each of its two sides, these appearing to combine into one image when the disc is rapidly rotated. The name comes from Greek *thauma* 'marvel' + *-tropos* 'turning'.

thaumaturge a worker of wonders and performer of miracles; a magician; the word is recorded from the early 18th century, and comes ultimately from Greek *thauma* 'marvel' + *-ergos* '-working'.

theatre in ancient Greece or Rome, a place constructed in the open air for viewing drama or other spectacles (the word comes ultimately from Greek *theasthai* 'behold'). It was in the form of the segment of a circle, with the auditorium typically excavated fom a hillside and the seats in tiers; the orchestra, occupied by the chorus, separated the stage from the auditorium.

Theatre in modern use, meaning a building constructed for putting on plays and other performance, is recorded from the late 16th century, and was apparently first used as the name of a particular playhouse in Shoreditch, outside the City of London, built in 1576.

See also ➤ IDOLS *of the tribe, cave, market, and theatre,* ➤ MERMAID *Theatre,* ➤ ROSE *Theatre,* ➤ SHELDONIAN *Theatre,* ➤ WINDMILL *Theatre.*

patent theatre a theatre established or licensed by royal letters patent (the first two of which were granted in 1603). Their exclusive privileges were abolished in 1843.

Theatre of Cruelty drama intended to communicate a sense of pain, suffering, and evil through the portrayal of extreme physical violence; the phrase is a translation of French, originally in *Manifeste du théâtre de la cruauté* (1932) by A. Artaud.

Theatre of the Absurd drama using the abandonment of conventional dramatic form to portray the futility of human struggle in a senseless world. Major exponents include Samuel Beckett, Eugène Ionesco, and Harold Pinter.

theatrum mundi the theatre thought of as a presentation of all aspects of human life (the phrase is Latin, and means 'theatre of the world'); it particularly designates a form of mechanical automaton, first constructed in Nuremberg at the end of the 17th century, which provided a traditional afterpiece for marionette theatres and depicted a number of scenes by means of movable figures on rails.

Theban bard a name for the Greek poet ➤ PINDAR (*c.*518–*c.*438 BC), a native of Thebes in Boeotia.

Theban eagle a name for ➤ PINDAR, as in Thomas Gray's *Progress of Poesy*:

> Nor the pride, nor ample pinion,
> That the Theban eagle bear
> Sailing with supreme dominion
> Thro' the azure deep of air.
>
> — Thomas Gray *The Progress of Poesy* (1757)

The name derives from three passages in poems by Pindar in which an eagle is mentioned without its connection to the context being clear; traditionally, the bird has been taken as an image of the poet.

Theban Legion a Roman legion said to have been recruited near Thebes in Egypt and composed solely of Christians; with their leader, the soldier saint ➤ *St MAURICE*, they are said to have been massacred *c.*287 when during an expedition against the Gauls, the emperor Maximian commanded his army to sacrifice to the gods for success. When the Theban Legion refused to obey, they were first decimated, and then massacred.

Thebes¹ the Greek name for an ancient city of Upper Egypt, whose ruins are situated on the Nile about 675 km (420 miles) south of Cairo. It was the capital of ancient Egypt under the 18th dynasty (*c.*1550–1290 BC) and is the site of the major temples of Luxor and Karnak. Its monuments (on both banks of the Nile) were the richest in the land, with the town on the east bank and the necropolis, with tombs of royalty and nobles, on the west bank. It was already a tourist attraction in the 2nd century AD.

Thebes² a city in Greece, in Boeotia, north-west of Athens, birthplace of the poet ➤ PINDAR. Traditionally founded by ➤ CADMUS and the seat of the legendary king ➤ OEDIPUS, Thebes became a major military power in Greece following the defeat of the Spartans at the battle of Leuctra in 371 BC. It was destroyed by Alexander the Great in 336 BC.

See also ➤ SEVEN *against Thebes*.

St Thecla of Iconium virgin martyr and in the Eastern Church one of the most popular saints of the 1st century, supposedly converted by St Paul. Her cult was suppressed in the Roman Catholic Church in 1969.

□ **FEAST DAY** Her feast day is 23 September in the Western Church, 24 September in the Eastern Church.

thegn an English thane. The word is a modern representation of Old English *theg(e)n*, adopted to distinguish the Old English use of ➤ THANE from the Scots use made familiar by Shakespeare in *Macbeth*.

theism belief in the existence of a god or gods, especially belief in one god as creator of the universe, intervening in it and sustaining a personal relation to his creatures. The word is recorded from the late 17th century, and comes from Greek *theos* 'god'.

Abbey of Thélèma in the work of ➤ RABELAIS, the abbey founded by ➤ GARGANTUA, in which the only law was '*Fay ce que vouldras*' 'Do what you like'.

Thellusson Act passed in 1800 to prohibit further schemes of bequest such as that by which Peter Thellusson (1737–97) had assigned a substantial part of his fortune to trustees to accumulate during the lives of his sons and their sons, and of their issue alive at the time of his death. On the death of the last survivor the estate was to be divided equally among the eldest male lineal descendants of his three sons then living; if there were no heir, the property would go to the extinction of the national debt.

The will, while widely criticized, was found to be valid, which gave rise to the passing of the *Thellusson Act*.

theme park an amusement park with a unifying setting or idea, the first examples of which were modelled on the American Disneyland in the 1960s. By the 1980s the concept had become popular enough to be applied in other concepts; in the UK, *theme pubs* and *theme restaurants* were set up, in which each aspect of design and atmosphere was related to a particular unifying theme. Despite their public popularity, the phrase *theme park* is now often used with a conscious allusion to the artificiality of the experience offered.

> Castle Howard could become a sort of Albion theme park, embracing everything that evokes the chirpy spirit of Britain, from stately home to corporate hospitality suites and adventure playground.
>
> — *Times* 19 October 1991

Themis in Greek mythology, a goddess, daughter of ➤ URANUS (Heaven) and ➤ GAIA (Earth). In Homer she was the personification of order and justice, who convened the assembly of the gods.

Themistian a member of a Monophysite sect founded by *Themistius*, 6th-century deacon of Alexandria, which attributed to Christ imperfect knowledge.

Themistocles (*c.*528–462 BC), Athenian statesman, who helped build up the Athenian fleet (see

➤ WOODEN *walls*), and defeated the Persian fleet at Salamis in 480. He was ostracized in 470, and eventually fled to the Persians in Asia Minor; after his defeat at Waterloo in 1815 Napoleon, writing to the Prince Regent, compared himself with Themistocles at the mercy of a former enemy.

Theocritus (*c.*310–*c.*250 BC), Greek poet, born in Sicily. He is chiefly known for his *Idylls*, hexameter poems presenting the lives of imaginary shepherds which were the model for Virgil's *Eclogues*.

> I am a shepherd of the Theocritean breed.
> — Louis MacNeice 'Eclogue by a Five-Barred Gate'
> (1935)

Theodora (*c.*500–48), Byzantine empress, wife of ➤ JUSTINIAN, said to have been an actress, and the daughter of a bearkeeper. As Justinian's closest adviser, she exercised a considerable influence on political affairs and the theological questions of the time. She is depicted in the mosaics of the church of San Vitale at Ravenna.

Theodoric (*c.*454–526), king of the Ostrogoths 471–526; known as **Theodoric the Great**. At its greatest extent his empire included Italy, which he invaded in 488 and conquered by 493, Sicily, Dalmatia, and parts of Germany. He established his capital at Ravenna.

Theodosian Code a collection of laws, including those banning paganism and penalizing heresy, made under the Roman emperor Theodosius II (408–450), and published 438.

Theodosius I (*c.*346–95), Roman emperor 379–95, known as **Theodosius the Great**. Proclaimed co-emperor by the Emperor Gratian in 379, he took control of the Eastern Empire and ended the war with the Visigoths. A pious Christian, in 391 he banned all forms of pagan worship.

theologians ➤ St AUGUSTINE, ➤ St JOHN *the Apostle*, ➤ St THOMAS *Aquinas*, and St Alphonsus Liguori (1696–1787), Doctor of the Church, are patron saints of theologians.

theological virtues the three virtues of faith, hope, and charity, as enumerated in 1 Corinthians 13:13, 'And now abideth faith, hope, charity, these three;' they were traditionally distinguished from the ➤ CARDINAL *virtues* of Plato and classical philosophers, and were particularly studied by ➤ *St* THOMAS *Aquinas* and the schoolmen.

theology see also ➤ COVENANT *Theology,* ➤ LIBERATION *theology.*

theology of hope a theory, popularized by German theologians in the 1960s, which regards Christian hope as the basis for human action and eschatological salvation.

theomancy a kind of divination based on the prophecies of oracles or oracular beings.

Theon a 4th-century Greek mathematician and astronomer, father of ➤ HYPATIA.

Theophrastus (*c.*370–*c.*287 BC), Greek philosopher and scientist, the pupil and successor of Aristotle, whose method and researches he continued, with a particular emphasis on empirical observation. The most influential of his works was *Characters*, a collection of sketches of psychological types.

theor in ancient Greece, an ambassador sent on behalf of a State, especially to consult an oracle or perform a religious rite.

theorem in physics and mathematics, a general proposition not self-evident but proved by a chain of reasoning; a truth established by means of accepted truths. The term is recorded from the mid 16th century, and comes ultimately from Greek *theōrēma* 'speculation, proposition'.

See also ➤ FERMAT'*s last theorem.*

theosophy any of a number of philosophies maintaining that a knowledge of God may be achieved through spiritual ecstasy, direct intuition, or special individual relations, especially the movement founded in 1875 as the Theosophical Society by Helena Blavatsky (1831–91) and Henry Steel Olcott (1832–1907), following Hindu and Buddhist teachings and seeking universal brotherhood.

Catherine Théot (1716–94) a French visionary of the revolutionary period, who proclaimed ➤ ROBESPIERRE as the prophet of the New Dawn.

theotokion in the Orthodox Church, a short hymn or stanza addressed or referring to the Mother of God, usually the last stanza in a series.

Theotokos Mother of God (used in the Eastern Orthodox Church as a title of the Virgin Mary); the word is ecclesiastical Greek, and comes from *theos* 'god' + -*tokos* 'bringing forth'.

Thera a Greek island in the southern Cyclades. The island suffered a violent volcanic eruption in about

1500 BC; remains of an ancient Minoan civilization have been preserved beneath the pumice and volcanic debris.

Theramenes (d. 403/4 BC), Athenian politician of moderate views regarded as shifting in his allegiance, who was nicknamed 'Buskin' or 'Cothurnus' after the thick-soled laced boot, fitting either foot, worn by Athenian actors. Initially appointed as one of the ➤ THIRTY *Tyrants*, he was later put to death.

Therapeutae a sect of Jewish mystics residing in Egypt in the first century AD, described in a book attributed to Philo.

Theravada the more conservative of the two major traditions of Buddhism (the other being Mahayana), which developed from Hinayana Buddhism. It is practised mainly in Sri Lanka, Burma (Myanmar), Thailand, Cambodia, and Laos.

therblig in time-and-motion study, a unit of work or absence of work into which an industrial operation may be divided, or a symbol representing this. The word is an anagram of the name of F. B. *Gilbreth*, American engineer (1868–1924), who invented it.

theriac archaic name for an ointment or other medicinal compound used as an antidote to snake venom or other poison. The word is recorded from late Middle English, and comes from Latin *theriaca*, from the Greek base of ➤ TREACLE.

It was traditionally believed that the flesh of a viper was a necessary ingredient of the antidote to its venom, as recorded in Topsell's *History of Serpents*:

> Theriac or treacle, not only because it cureth the venomous biting of serpents, but also because the serpents themselves are usually mingled in the making thereof.
>
> — Edward Topsell *History of Serpents* (1608)

Thermidor the eleventh month of the French Republican calendar (1793–1805), originally running from 19 July to 17 August. Also, a reaction of moderates following a revolution, such as that which occurred in Paris on 9 Thermidor (27 July 1794) and resulted in the fall of ➤ ROBESPIERRE. The name is French, and comes from Greek *thermē* 'heat' + *dōron* 'gift'.

Thermidorian any of those who took part in the overthrow of Robespierre on the 9th Thermidor (27 July) 1794.

laws of thermodynamics laws describing the general direction of physical change in the universe; the **first law of thermodynamics** states the equivalence of heat and work and reaffirms the principle of conservation of energy; the **second law of thermodynamics** states that heat does not of itself pass from a cooler to a hotter body (another, equivalent formulation of the second law is that the entropy of a closed system can only increase); the **third law of thermodynamics** states that it is impossible to reduce the temperature of a system to absolute zero in a finite number of operations.

> If someone points out to you that your pet theory of the universe is in disagreement with Maxwell's equations—then so much the worse for Maxwell's equations. If it is found to be contradicted by observation—well, these experimentalists do bungle things sometimes. But if your theory is found to be against the second law of thermodynamics I can give you no hope; there is nothing for it but to collapse in deepest humiliation.
>
> — Arthur Eddington *The Nature of the Physical World* (1928)

Thermopylae a pass between the mountains and the sea in Greece, about 200 km (120 miles) northwest of Athens, originally narrow but now much widened by the recession of the sea. In 480 BC it was the scene of the defence against the Persian army of Xerxes I by 6,000 Greeks; among them were 300 Spartans, all of whom, including their king ➤ LEONIDAS, were killed:

> Go, tell the Spartans, thou who passest by,
> That here obedient to their laws we lie.
>
> — epitaph, attributed to Simonides, for the 300 Spartans killed at Thermopylae; Herodotus *Histories*

The pass was the traditional invasion route from northern Greece and was subsequently used by the Gauls in 279 BC and by Cato the Elder in 191 BC.

Thersites a member of the Greek forces at the siege of Troy, noted for his scurrilous and backbiting tongue; he was killed by ➤ ACHILLES after Thersites had jeered at him for mourning the death of the Amazon queen ➤ PENTHESILEA.

thesaurus originally, a dictionary or encyclopedia; after the publication of ➤ ROGET*'s Thesaurus*, the meaning narrowed to its current sense of a book that lists words in groups of synonyms and related concepts. Recorded in English from the late 16th century, the word comes via Latin from Greek *thēsauros* 'storehouse, treasure'.

Theseus in Greek mythology, the legendary hero of Athens, son of Poseidon (or, in another account,

of Aegeus, king of Athens) and husband of ➤ Phaedra.

Aegeus had left the child Theseus and his mother
at her father's court in Troezen, with the instruction
that when the boy was old enough to lift a certain
rock, he was to come to Athens with the sword and
sandals he would find beneath it; it was on this journey that he encountered and killed such bandits as
➤ Procrustes and ➤ Sinis.

At Athens, he became one of the boys and girls
sent as tribute to Crete; there he slew the Cretan
➤ Minotaur with the help of ➤ Ariadne, and returned to Athens. Forgetting an earlier agreement
with his father, he did not change his ship's sails
from black to white in token of success, and Aegeus
is said to have killed himself in despair on seeing the
black-sailed ship. Theseus became king of Athens;
his many subsequent adventures (often in the company of ➤ Hercules) included the capture of the
Amazon queen ➤ Hippolyta.

Thesmophoria in ancient Greece, a fertility festival held by women in honour of the goddess
➤ Demeter. The name comes from Greek
thesmophoros 'law-bearing', an epithet of Demeter.

Thespis (6th century BC), Greek dramatic poet, regarded as the founder of Greek tragedy; Aristotle
named him the originator of the role of the actor in
addition to the traditional chorus. His name gives
rise to the word *thespian*.

Epistle to the Thessalonians either of two books
of the New Testament, the earliest letters of St Paul,
written from Corinth to the new Church at Thessalonica.

Thestylis name for a young country girl in pastoral poetry, as in Milton's *L'Allegro*:

> Her bow'r she leaves,
> With Thestylis to bind the sheaves.
> — John Milton *L'Allegro* (1632)

theta the eighth letter of the Greek alphabet (Θ,
θ), transliterated as 'th'. In ancient Greece, on the
ballots used in voting upon a sentence of life or
death, this character stood for *thanatos* 'death',
which gave rise to allusive uses:

> Setting his *theta* or mark of condemnation upon them.
> — Samuel Daniel *A Defence of Ryme* (1603)

Thetis in Greek mythology, a sea nymph, mother
of ➤ Achilles.

theurgy originally (in the mid 16th century) a system of magic as practised by Egyptian Neoplatonists
to procure communication with beneficent spirits;

in later use, ➤ white *magic* as distinct from
➤ black *magic*. The word comes via late Latin from
Greek *theourgia* 'sorcery', from *theos* 'god' + *-ergos*
'working'.

From the mid 19th century, *theurgy* has denoted
the operation or effect of a supernatural or divine
agency in human affairs.

they haif said: Quhat say they? Lat thame say
motto of the Earls Marischal of Scotland, inscribed
at Marischal College; a similarly defiant motto in
Greek has been found engraved in remains from
classical antiquity.

thief ➤ *St* Dismas, otherwise the **Good Thief**, is
patron saint of thieves.

See also ➤ hang *a thief when he's young, and he'll
no' steal when he's old,* ➤ *if there were no* receivers
there would be no thieves, ➤ little *thieves are
hanged, but great ones escape,* ➤ opportunity
makes a thief, ➤ *a* postern *door makes a thief,*
➤ procrastination *is the thief of time,* ➤ *there is*
honour *among thieves.*

set a thief to catch a thief proverbial saying, mid
17th century.

**when thieves fall out, honest men come by
their own** proverbial saying, mid 16th century.

thieves' Latin the secret language or 'cant' of
thieves; the term is recorded from the early 19th century.

thigh see ➤ smite hip *and thigh*.

thimble a metal or plastic cap with a closed end,
worn to protect the finger and push the needle in
sewing. The word comes from Old English 'finger-
stall', from the base of ➤ thumb; the current meaning is recorded from late Middle English.

Thimble and Bodkin Army in the English Civil
War, a pejorative name for the forces of Parliament,
referring to the fact that even silver thimbles and
similar articles had been offered and accepted as
contributions to the cause:

> The poorer sort, like that Widow in the Gospel,
> presented their Mites also; insomuch that it was a
> common Jeer of men disaffected to the Cause, to call it
> the Thimble- and Bodkin-Army.
> — Thomas May *The History of the Parliament of England*
> (1647)

thimblerig a game involving sleight of hand, in
which three inverted thimbles or cups are moved
about, contestants having to spot which is the one
with a pea or other object underneath. Recorded

from the early 19th century, the name means literally 'thimble trick'.

thin see also ➤ *thin as* BANBURY *cheese.*

the thin blue line the police as a defensive barrier of the law; from an alteration of ➤ *the* THIN *red line.*

thin end of the wedge proverbial expression for a small beginning which it is hoped or feared may lead to something greater; the term is recorded from the mid 19th century.

the thin red line the British army (in reference to the traditional scarlet uniform); the phrase first occurs in the war correspondent William Howard Russell's book *The British Expedition to the Crimea* (1877) of the Russians charging the British at Balaclava, 'They dashed on towards that thin red line tipped with steel'. Russell's original dispatch to *The Times*, 14 November 1854, had read 'That thin red streak topped with a line of steel', although the infantry were described as an 'impenetrable red line' in a letter from Fanny Duberly, 8 June 1855.

Use of the phrase was reinforced by Kipling in 1890:

> It's 'Thin red line of 'eroes' when the drums begin to roll.
>
> — Rudyard Kipling 'Tommy' (1890)

thing see also ➤ ALL *things are possible with God,* ➤ ALL *things come to those who wait,* ➤ *be* ALL *things to all men.*

Thing in Scandinavian countries or settlements: a public meeting or assembly, especially, a legislative council, a parliament, a court of law.

if a thing's worth doing, it's worth doing well proverbial saying, mid 18th century.

when things are at the worst, they begin to mend proverbial saying, mid 18th century.

think first and speak afterwards proverbial saying, mid 16th century.

thinking see ➤ PLAIN *living and high thinking.*

third age the period in life between middle age and old age, about 55 to 70; the term is a translation of French *troisième âge.*

See also ➤ UNIVERSITY *of the Third Age.*

third estate the common people as part of a country's political system. The first two estates were formerly represented by the clergy, and the barons and knights; later the Lords spiritual and the Lords temporal.

third eye in Hinduism and Buddhism, the 'eye of insight' in the forehead of an image of a deity, especially the god Shiva.

third-generation (of a computer) distinguished by the introduction of integrated circuits and operating systems and belonging essentially to the period 1960–70.

third man an unidentified third participant in a crime; the phrase in this sense derives from the screenplay (1949) by Graham Greene, later filmed by Carol Reed, in which the plot centres on the doings of this shadowy figure. After the flight in 1951 of the Soviet agents ➤ *Guy* BURGESS and Donald Maclean to Moscow, the phrase was used in connection with the third party (later demonstrated to be ➤ *Kim* PHILBY) who was thought to have warned them.

> Kim Philby was finally identified as the 'Third Man', in 1963, when he too fled to Moscow.
>
> — M. Green *Children of the Sun* (rev. ed., 1977)

Third Order an order for lay members retaining the secular life and not subject to the strict rule of the regular orders, originated by St Francis of Assisi and now established among Franciscans, Dominicans, and others.

third party a person or group besides the two primarily involved in a situation, especially a dispute; the phrase is recorded from the early 19th century.

Third Programme one of the three national radio networks of the BBC from 1946 until 1967, when it was replaced by Radio 3; the name was often used allusively to qualify what was considered intellectually superior or highbrow.

> She had fine eyes but a rather ugly despairing sort of mouth, as if she came out of one of those Greek Tragedies on the Third Programme.
>
> — J. B. Priestley *Festival at Farbridge* (1951)

third reading a third presentation of a bill to a legislative assembly, in the UK to debate committee reports and in the US to consider it for the last time.

Third Reich the Nazi regime, 1933–45, considered as succeeding the Holy Roman Empire (962–1806) and the German Empire (1871–1918) as the previous periods of empire (see ➤ REICH). The name, which is a translation of German *drittes Reich*, is recorded in English from 1930, in an interview in the *Times* of 26 September 1930 with Hitler.

Third Republic the republican regime in France between the fall of Napoleon III (1870) and the German occupation of 1940.

third time lucky proverbial saying, mid 19th century.

the third time pays for all proverbial saying, late 16th century.

Third Wave the American writer Alvin Toffler's term for the current phase of economic, social and cultural change (following the agrarian *First Wave* and the industrial *Second Wave*) in which knowledge (especially as stored and disseminated by information technology) is the primary productive force.

third way in politics, a middle way between conventional right- and left-wing ideologies or policies; an ideology founded on political centrism or neutrality. In the 1990s the *third way* became identified with the political programmes of centre-left parties in Western Europe and North America, characterized by both market-driven economic policy and a concern for social justice; in this context it is conceived of as an alternative to, rather than a compromise between, conventional right- and left-wing ideologies, and in the UK has become particularly associated with the premiership of Tony Blair.

Third World the developing countries of Asia, Africa, and Latin America. The phrase was first applied in the 1950s by French commentators who used *tiers monde* to distinguish the developing countries from the capitalist and Communist blocs.

thirteen the number *thirteen* has been widely regarded as unlucky; there is a traditional belief that if thirteen people sit down to table, the first to get up will die. This may go back to the ➤ LAST *Supper*, at which Jesus, sitting at table with the twelve disciples, told them that one of them (Judas) would betray him.

Thirteen Colonies the British colonies that ratified the Declaration of Independence in 1776 and thereby became founding states of the US.

Thirteen Colonies

Connecticut	New Hampshire	Pennsylvania
Delaware	New Jersey	Rhode Island
Georgia	New York	South Carolina
Maryland	North Carolina	Virginia
Massachusetts		

Thirty-nine Articles a series of points of doctrine historically accepted as representing the teaching of the Church of England. Adopted in 1571, the Articles often allow a wide variety of interpretation.

thirty pieces of silver the price for which ➤ JUDAS betrayed Jesus to the Jewish authorities, as told in Matthew 26:15, 'and they covenanted with him for thirty pieces of silver'. In the following chapter 27:3–10), Judas is said to have repented and to have thrown down the money in the temple before killing himself. Because it was regarded as blood money it could not be returned to the treasury; it was therefore used to purchase the ➤ POTTER*'s field*.

In extended usage, *thirty pieces of silver* is used for a material gain for which a principle has been betrayed.

> The money for the bunting, what was left of it, lay like thirty pieces of silver on the counter.
> — E. Toman *Dancing in Limbo* (1995)

Thirty-Six-Line Bible a typographic resetting of the ➤ FORTY-*Two-Line Bible*, printed in Bamberg, formerly attributed to Gutenberg.

thirty-something an unspecified age between thirty and forty; the term was widely publicized by the successful US television series *Thirtysomething* which from 1987 recounted the ups and downs and family lives of a group who had reached their thirties in the 1980s.

Thirty Tyrants the magistrates imposed by Sparta on Athens at the end of the Peloponnesian War; their repressive rule was ended when Critias, leader of the oligarchy, was killed, and democracy restored.

thirty-year rule a rule that public records may be open to inspection after a lapse of thirty years.

Thirty Years War a European war of 1618–48 which broke out between the Catholic Holy Roman emperor and some of his German Protestant states and developed into a struggle for continental hegemony with France, Sweden, Spain, and the Holy Roman Empire as the major protagonists. It was ended by the Treaty of Westphalia.

Thisbe in Roman mythology, a Babylonian girl, lover of ➤ PYRAMUS.

thistle a widely distributed herbaceous plant of the daisy family, which typically has a prickly stem and leaves and rounded heads of purple flowers; a plant of this type as the Scottish national emblem.

In biblical use, *thistle* is also generally used as the type of an unrewarding crop, as in God's words to

Adam (Genesis 3:17–18), 'Cursed is the ground for thy sake…Thorns also and thistles shall it bring forth unto thee.'

Order of the Thistle the highest order of Scottish knighthood, instituted by James II in 1687 and revived by Queen Anne in 1703.

thivish in Irish folklore, a ghost, a spectre.

Thomas see also ➤ *St Thomas à* BECKET, ➤ *Thomas* MORE.

St Thomas an apostle, known as **Doubting Thomas**. He earned his nickname by saying that he would not believe that Christ had risen again until he had seen and touched his wounds (John 20:24–9). According to tradition he preached in SW India.

A non-canonical gospel of Thomas, found in a Coptic text, is apparently a Gnostic work.

☐ **FEAST DAY** His feast day is 21 December.

Thomas à Kempis (*c*.1380–1471), German theologian. An Augustinian canon in Holland, he is the probable author of *On the Imitation of Christ* (*c*.1415–24), a manual of spiritual devotion.

St Thomas Aquinas (1225–74), Italian philosopher, theologian, and Dominican friar; known as *the Angelic Doctor*. He is regarded as the greatest figure of scholasticism; one of his most important achievements was the introduction of the work of Aristotle to Christian western Europe. His works include commentaries on Aristotle as well as the *Summa Contra Gentiles*, intended as a manual for missionaries, and *Summa Theologiae*, the greatest achievement of medieval systematic theology. He also devised the official Roman Catholic tenets as declared by Pope Leo XIII.

☐ **FEAST DAY** His feast day is 28 January.

on Saint Thomas the Divine kill all turkeys, geese and swine proverbial saying, mid 18th century; St Thomas the Apostle's feast is on 21 December, traditionally the time at which animals were slaughtered before the winter.

Thomas the Rhymer nickname of the seer and poet Thomas of Erceldoune (fl. ?1220–?97); he was popularly said to have foreseen both the death of Alexander III of Scotland and the battle of Bannockburn.

Thomasing the traditional begging of alms on St. Thomas's day (21 December). Also called *corning*, *doling*, or *gooding*.

Thomism the theology of ➤ *St* THOMAS *Aquinas* or of his followers.

Thor in Scandinavian mythology, the god of thunder, the weather, agriculture, and the home, the son of Odin and Freya (Frigga). He is represented as armed with a hammer. Thursday is named after him.

Henry David Thoreau (1817–62), American essayist and poet, and a key figure in Transcendentalism. He is best known for his book *Walden, or Life in the Woods* (1854), an account of a two-year experiment in self-sufficiency. His essay on civil disobedience (1849) influenced Mahatma Gandhi's policy of passive resistance.

thorn see also ➤ *beware of an* OAK, *it draws the stroke; avoid an ash, it counts the flash; creep under the thorn, it can save you from harm*, ➤ CHRIST'S *thorn*, ➤ CROWN *of thorns*, ➤ GLASTONBURY *thorn*, ➤ *no* ROSE *without a thorn*.

thorn an Old English and Icelandic runic letter, þ or ꝥ. It was eventually superseded by the digraph *th*, but has been used as a phonetic symbol for the voiceless dental fricative.

thorn in the flesh a constant affliction, a source of continual trouble and annoyance; often with biblical allusion to 2 Corinthians 12:7, 'Lest I should be exalted above measure…there was given to me a thorn in the flesh'. The phrase **thorn in the side** is also frequently used.

Thorough the thorough-going actions and policy pursued by Strafford (see ➤ STRAFFORDIAN) and ➤ LAUD in the reign of Charles I; the first recorded use is by Laud himself, in a letter to Strafford, *c*.1643, 'And for the state, indeed, my lord, I am for Thorough.'

thoroughbred a horse of pure breed, especially of a breed originating from English mares and Arab stallions and widely used as racehorses.

Thoth in Egyptian mythology, a moon god, the god of wisdom, justice, and writing, patron of the sciences, and messenger of Ra, identified by the Greeks with Hermes. He is most often represented in human form with the head of an ibis surmounted by the moon's disc and crescent.

thought see ➤ JUST *when you thought it was safe*, ➤ PERISH *the thought*, ➤ SECOND *thoughts*.

thought is free proverbial saying, late 14th century.

thoughtcrime an instance of unorthodox or controversial thinking, considered as a criminal offence or as socially unacceptable, from George Orwell's *Nineteen Eighty-Four* (1949).

Thousand and One Nights another name for the ➤ ARABIAN *Nights.*

Thousand-Year Reich the German ➤ THIRD *Reich* (1933–45), as a regime envisaged by the Nazis as established for an indefinite period; in the *Times* of 6 September 1934, a proclamation of Hitler's that 'there will be no further revolution in Germany for a thousand years' was reported.

thread see also ➤ *the* FATAL *thread,* ➤ SACRED *thread.*

thread and thrum each length of the warp-yarn, and the tuft where it is fastened to the loom; in figurative terms, the whole of anything, good and bad together.

thread of life in classical mythology, the extent of a person's life, as spun, measured, and cut off by the ➤ FATES.

Threadneedle Street a street in the City of London containing the premises of the Bank of England, which is also known as the ➤ OLD *Lady of Threadneedle Street. Threadneedle* here comes from *three-needle,* possibly from a tavern with the arms of the city of London Guild of Needlemakers.

threatened men live long proverbial saying, mid 16th century.

three see also ➤ GROUP *of Three,* ➤ PAGE *Three,* ➤ RULE *of three,* ➤ SONG *of the Three Holy Children,* ➤ *three* BOYS *in a tub,* ➤ *three* GOLDEN *balls,* ➤ *three* SISTERS, ➤ *three wise* MONKEYS.

three acres and a cow regarded as the requirement for self-sufficiency; as a political slogan associated with the radical politician Jesse Collings (1831–1920) and his land reform campaign begun in 1885. Collings used the phrase in the House of Commons, 26 January 1886; it had also been used earlier by Joseph Chamberlain in a speech at Evesham (reported in the *Times* of 17 November 1885). It quickly became proverbial.

three ages the Stone, Bronze, and Iron Ages as basic divisions of the prehistoric period.

Three Choirs Festival an annual festival held by Gloucester, Worcester, and Hereford, and taking place at each city in turn.

three-decker literally (from the late 18th century) a three-decked line-of-battle ship; in the 19th century *three-decker* was used as an informal term for a novel in three volumes.

three-field system a method of agriculture in which three fields are worked on a three-course system of two crops and a fallow.

the three F's in 19th-century Ireland, fair rents, fixity of tenure, and free sale.

the Three Graces in Greek mythology, three beautiful goddesses (Aglaia, Thalia, and Euphrosyne), daughters of Zeus. They were believed to personify and bestow charm, grace, and beauty.

Three Hours a devotional service lasting from 12 to 3 p.m. on Good Friday, intended to represent the hours of the Crucifixion.

Three in One in Christian thought, the Trinity.

Three Kings the ➤ MAGI, who came from the East to worship the new-born Christ. They are also known as **The Three Kings of Cologne**, from a prevalent belief that their bodies were preserved at that city, having been removed thither in 1164 from Milan, where they were alleged to have been discovered in 1158.

three may keep a secret, if two of them are dead proverbial saying, mid 16th century.

Three Mile Island an island in the Susquehanna River near Harrisburg, Pennsylvania, site of a nuclear power station. In 1979 an accident caused damage to the reactor core, provoking strong reactions against the nuclear industry in the US.

three-mile limit the limit of territorial waters for Britain, America, and other states.

Three Musketeers in Dumas' novel *Les Trois Mousquetaires* (1844), Athos, Porthos, and Aramis, the musketeers who befriend the young ➤ D'ARTAGNAN, and assist him in defeating the scheming agent of Cardinal Richelieu; in extended use, three close associates.

> James Bolton is the last of these three musketeers, a likely lad with a divorced mum and a strong right hook.
> — *Scotsman* 21 October 1995

the three R's reading, writing, and (a)rithmetic; a phrase said to have originated in a toast by Sir William Curtis (1752–1829).

three removals are as bad as a fire proverbial saying, mid 18th century.

three sheets in the wind very drunk; a *sheet* is a rope or chain attached to the lower corner of a sail for securing the sail or altering its direction relative to the wind.

three strikes legislation which provides that an offender's third felony is punishable by life imprisonment or other severe sentence, a phrase which developed in the US in the 1980s, and which comes from the terminology of baseball, in which a batter who has had three strikes, or three fair opportunities of hitting the ball, is out. While the **three-strikes-you're-out** legislation was popular with the conservative right, the system has been criticized not only on the general grounds of the danger to civil liberties, but more specifically in that the definition of what constitutes a serious felony may result in inappropriately draconian punishment for offenders.

Three Tailors of Tooley Street proverbial example of a small group claiming to speak for the whole of society; the tailors were said to have addressed a petition to the House of Commons beginning, 'We, the people of England'.

three things are not to be trusted; a cow's horn, a dog's tooth, and a horse's hoof proverbial saying, late 14th century.

the three tongues former term for Latin, Greek, and Hebrew, the three languages inscribed on the Cross.

Three Wise Men another name for the ➤ MAGI.

threescore years and ten the age of seventy as one's allotted span, with biblical allusion to Psalm 90, 'The days of our age are threescore years and ten.'

thrift is a great revenue proverbial saying, mid 17th century.

thrive see also ➤ *if you want to* LIVE *and thrive, let the spider run alive.*

he that will thrive must first ask his wife proverbial saying,

throat see also ➤ *have a* FROG *in one's throat.*

throat ➤ *St* BLAISE is patron saint of those with illnesses of the throat.

Throgmorton Street the name of the street in the City of London where the Stock Exchange is located, used allusively for the Stock Exchange or its members.

> What could Worlington Dodds know at Dunsloe which was not known in Throgmorton Street?
> — Arthur Conan Doyle *The Green Flag* (1900)

throne a ceremonial chair for a sovereign, bishop, or similar figure. Recorded from Middle English, the word comes via Old French and Latin from Greek *thronos* 'elevated seat'.
See ➤ CHRYSANTHEMUM *Throne*, ➤ PEACOCK *Throne*.

Great White Throne the throne of God, with allusion to Revelation 20:11, 'And I saw a great white throne, and him that sat on it.'

throne and altar the established civil and ecclesiastical systems in a State; the phrase is recorded from the early 19th century.

Throne of Grace the place where God is conceived as sitting to answer prayer, as in Hebrews 4:16, 'Let us therefore come boldly unto the throne of grace, that we may obtain mercy.'

thrones (in traditional Christian angelology) the third-highest order of the ninefold celestial hierarchy.

throw see also ➤ *throw down the* GAUNTLET, ➤ *throw* DIRT *enough and some will stick*, ➤ *throw the* BONES.

don't throw out your dirty water until you get in fresh proverbial saying, late 15th century.

throw someone to the wolves sacrifice another person in order to avert danger or difficulties for oneself; probably in allusion to stories of wolves in a pack pursuing travellers in a horse-drawn sleigh.

don't throw the baby out with the bathwater proverbial saying, mid 19th century.

throw up the sponge abandon a contest or struggle, submit, give in; in boxing, throw up the sponge used to wipe a contestant's face as a sign that a fight has been abandoned.

thrum in weaving, each of the ends of the warp-threads left unwoven and remaining attached to the loom when the web is cut off.

See also ➤ THREAD *and thrum*.

Thucydides (*c*.455–*c*.400 BC), Greek historian. He is remembered for his *History of the Peloponnesian War*, which analyses the origins and course of the war, and includes the reconstruction of political speeches of figures such as Pericles; he fought in the conflict on the Athenian side, but having failed successfully to defend a valuable colony, was condemned in his absence and exiled.

> Exiled Thucydides knew
> All that a speech can say
> About Democracy,
> And what dictators do.
> — W. H. Auden 'September 1, 1939' (1940)

Thug a member of a religious organization of robbers and assassins in India, also called ➤ PHANSIGAR. Devotees of the goddess ➤ KALI, the Thugs waylaid and strangled their victims, usually travellers, in a ritually prescribed manner. They were suppressed by the British in the 1830s. The name is recorded from the early 19th century and comes from Hindi *ṭhag* 'swindler, thief', based on Sanskrit *sthagati* 'he covers or conceals'.

Thule a country described by the ancient Greek explorer Pytheas (*c*.310 BC) as being six days' sail north of Britain, variously identified with Iceland, the Shetland Islands, and most plausibly, Norway. It was regarded by the ancients as the northernmost part of the world.

See also ➤ ULTIMA *Thule*.

thumb the breadth of the thumb, taken as equal to an inch, was formerly used as a measure; in the cloth trade, it was customary to allow a *thumb* in addition to each yard of cloth measured. The word is recorded from Old English (in form *thūma*), of West Germanic origin; it comes ultimately from an Indo-European root shared by Latin *tumere* 'swell'.

See also ➤ *all* FINGERS *and thumbs*, ➤ BITE *one's thumb at*, ➤ HOP-*o'-my-thumb*, ➤ PRICKING *of one's thumbs*, ➤ RULE *of thumb*, ➤ TOM *Thumb*.

thumbs up (or down) an indication of satisfaction or approval (or of rejection or failure), with reference to the signal of approval or disapproval, used by spectators at a Roman amphitheatre; the sense has been reversed, as the Romans used 'thumbs down' to signify that a beaten gladiator had performed well and should be spared, and 'thumbs up' to call for his death.

thumbscrews an instrument of torture for crushing the thumbs.

Thummim see ➤ URIM *and Thummim*.

thunder a loud rumbling or crashing noise heard after a lightning flash due to the expansion of rapidly heated air; traditionally regarded as the destructive agent producing the effects usually attributed to lightning. In biblical phrases, *thunder* denotes great force and energy, as in Job 39:19, 'Hast thou clothed his neck with thunder?'

See also ➤ BLOOD-*and-thunder*, ➤ SONS *of thunder*.

steal someone's thunder win praise for oneself by pre-empting someone else's attempt to impress. The phrase comes from an exclamation from the English dramatist John Dennis (1657–1734), on hearing his new thunder effects used at a performance of *Macbeth*, following the withdrawal of one of his own plays after only a short run: 'Damn them! They will not let my play run, but they steal my thunder!'

thunderbolt a supposed bolt or shaft believed to be the destructive agent in a lightning flash, especially as an attribute of a god such as Jupiter or Thor.

the Thunderer epithet of a deity regarded as causing thunder, such as Jupiter or Thor; recorded from late Middle English.

From the mid 19th century, the *Thunderer* became the nickname of the *Times* newspaper, initially with reference to the writing of the journalist Edward Sterling (1773–1847). The phrase 'we thundered out' was used in a leader of 11 February 1829, and on 15 February 1830 the *Morning Herald* carried a reference to 'the office of *The Thunderer*, Printing-House-square'.

Thundering Legion a name for the 12th Roman Legion, said to come from their having saved themselves and the whole army in an expedition under Marcus Aurelius against the Germanic tribes. Parched with thirst, the Christians among them successfully prayed for rain; their prayers also caused lightning and thunderbolts to fall on the enemy.

James Thurber (1894–1961), American humorist and cartoonist. His collections of essays, stories, and sketches include *My World—And Welcome to It* (1942), which contains the story 'The Secret Life of Walter Mitty'.

Thursday the day of the week before Friday and following Wednesday. The name comes from Old English *þu(n)resdæg* 'day of thunder', translation of late Latin *Jovis dies* 'day of Jupiter' (god associated with thunder).

Thursday's child see ➤ *Monday's* CHILD *is fair of face.*

Thursdays	
NAME	**DAY**
Black Thursday	6 February 1851
Bloody Thursday	5 July 1934
Green Thursday	Thursday before Easter
Holy Thursday	Thursday before Easter
Maundy Thursday	Thursday before Easter
Sheer Thursday	Thursday before Easter

thurse a goblin, a hobgoblin. Formerly also, a giant; the Devil, a demon.

Thyad in classical Greece, a Bacchante.

Thyestes in Greek mythology, the brother of ➤ ATREUS and father of ➤ AEGISTHUS, whose brother tricked him into eating the flesh of his own children at a feast; part of the curse on the house of Atreus.

thyine in biblical translations and allusions, epithet of a tree providing valuable wood referred to in Revelation 12:18, 'all manner vessels of ivory, and all manner thyine wood'; it is thought to be the thuja, a coniferous tree with fragrant wood.

thymele the altar of Dionysus in the centre of the orchestra in an ancient Greek theatre; the word comes ultimately from Greek *thuein* 'to sacrifice'.

thyrsus in ancient Greece and Rome, a staff or spear tipped with an ornament like a pine cone and sometimes wreathed with ivy or vine branches, carried by ➤ BACCHUS and his followers.

Ti in early Chinese philosophy, (an honorific title given to) the supreme being, God (and formerly also, to an early Chinese ruler).

Tiahuanaco a ruined ceremonial site south of Lake Titicaca in Bolivia, from which a pre-Incan culture of the first millennium AD in South America is named.

Tiamat in Babylonian mythology, a monstrous she-dragon who was the mother of the first gods. She was slain by Marduk.

Tiananmen Square a square in the centre of Beijing adjacent to the Forbidden City, the largest public open space in the world. In spring 1989 it was occupied by hundreds of thousands of student-led protesters of the emerging pro-democracy movement. Government troops opened fire there on unarmed protesters, killing over 2,000.

> The real test will be instability in China . . . Another Tiananmen Square could really upset the applecart.
> — *Business Age* June 1996

tiara originally, a turban worn by ancient Persian kings; the word is recorded from the mid 16th century. From the early 17th century, the term was also used for a high diadem encircled with three crowns and worn by a pope; more fully the ➤ PAPAL *tiara*, also known as the *triple crown*.

on Tib's Eve never, an expression recorded from the late 18th century; there is no saint of this name, and so (like *latter Lammas* and the *Greek calends*) this is a day that will never come.

Tiber a river of central Italy, upon which Rome stands. It is supposedly named after the legendary hero *Tiberinus*, who was drowned in its waters; he was traditionally said to be either the son of the god Janus, or a descendant of Aeneas.

The *Tiber* figures in the doom-laden prophecy of Virgil's *Aeneid*, book 6, 'I see wars, horrible wars, and the Tiber foaming with much blood', a line referred to by the Conservative politician Enoch Powell (1912–98) in April 1968 when he predicted disastrous results for Britain's immigration policy:

> Like the Roman, I seem to see 'the River Tiber foaming with much blood'.
> — Enoch Powell speech, 20 April 1968

Lake Tiberias another name for the ➤ *Sea of* GALILEE. *Tiberias* was the name given to the city founded by Herod Antipas as his new capital on its western shore; it was named in honour of the Emperor ➤ TIBERIUS.

Tiberius (42 BC–AD 37), Roman emperor AD 14–37. The adopted successor of his stepfather and father-in-law Augustus, he became increasingly tyrannical and his reign was marked by a growing number of treason trials and executions. In 26 he retired to Capri, never returning to Rome.

Tibert name of the cat in the apologue of Reynard the Fox, thus used as a name for any cat. In *Romeo and Juliet*, Shakespeare identifies it with the name of *Tybalt*, who is mockingly called 'ratcatcher' and 'king of cats' by Mercutio.

Tibetan Buddhism the religion of Tibet, a form of Mahayana Buddhism. It was formed in the 8th century AD from a combination of Buddhism and the indigenous Tibetan religion. The head of the religion is the Dalai Lama.

Albius Tibullus (*c*.50–19 BC), Roman poet. He is known for his elegiac love poetry and for his celebration of peaceful rural life in preference to the harsh realities of military campaigning.

Little Tich stage name of the music-hall comedian Harry Relph, who was given the nickname as a child because of a resemblance to the ➤ TICHBORNE *claimant*.

Tichborne claimant name given to➤ *Arthur* ORTON (1834–98), English butcher, who in 1866 returned to England from Australia claiming to be Sir Roger Tichborne (lost at sea in 1854) and thus heir to the valuable Tichborne estate in Hampshire. Roger Tichborne's mother, who had never accepted his death, had continued to advertise widely for him in English and colonial papers; when she heard of Orton's claim, she accepted him as her son, although she was the only member of the family to do so. When the case finally came to court, Orton lost his claim and was tried and imprisoned for perjury.

Tichborne dole on the Tichborne estate in Hampshire, alms traditionally given on 25 March.

ticket of leave a document granting certain concessions, especially leave, to a prisoner or convict who had served part of their time.

tiddler see ➤ TOM *Tiddler's ground*.

tiddy oggy in naval slang, a Cornish pasty; the name probably comes from West Country dialect *tiddy* 'potato' and Cornish *hogen* 'pastry'.

tide a particular time, season, or festival of the Christian Church; *tide* meaning 'time, period, era' is recorded from Old English (in form *tīd*) and is of German origin, ultimately related to German *Zeit*.

From late Middle English, the word has also meant (now the current meaning) the alternate rising and falling of the sea, usually twice in each lunar day at a particular place, due to the attraction of the moon and sun.

See also ➤ QUEEN *of tides*, ➤ *a* RISING *tide lifts all boats*, ➤ TIME *and tide wait for no man*.

Tidewater in the US, eastern Virginia, as typifying an area affected by tides.

tidy neat, orderly. The original meaning was 'timely, opportune'; it later had various senses expressing approval, usually of a person, including 'attractive', 'healthy', and 'skilful'; the sense 'orderly, neat' dates from the early 18th century.

Giovanni Battista Tiepolo (1696–1770), Italian painter. He painted numerous rococo frescoes and altarpieces characterized by dramatic foreshortening, translucent colour, and settings of theatrical splendour; they include the *Antony and Cleopatra* frescoes in the Palazzo Labia, Venice (*c*.1750), and the decoration of the residence of the Prince-Bishop at Würzburg (1751–3).

> At least the drawings in this new Bible are beautiful, in a Tiepolo-ish kind of way, curving bodies and voluptuous clothing.
> — *Church Times* 8 March 1996

tiffany thin gauze muslin. The word comes (in the early 17th century) via Old French and ecclesiastical Latin from Greek *theophaneia* 'epiphany' It is usually taken to be short for *Epiphany silk* or *muslin*, i.e., that worn on Twelfth Night, but may be a humorous allusion to *epiphany* in the sense 'manifestation', tiffany being semi-transparent.

Louis Comfort Tiffany (1848–1933), American glass-maker and interior decorator, whose father Charles Louis Tiffany founded the New York jewellers Tiffany and Company. A leading exponent of American art nouveau, he established an interior decorating firm in New York which produced stained glass, vases, lamps, and mosaic.

tiffin a light meal, especially lunch. Recorded from the early 19th century, the word apparently comes from dialect *tiffing* 'sipping', of unknown origin.

tiger the *tiger* is proverbial for its ferocity and cunning; in Shakespeare's *3 Henry VI* (1592) Queen Margaret is addressed as 'O tiger's heart wrapped in a woman's hide', and **the Tiger** was the nickname of both Tipu Sultan (*c*.1750–99) who said that he would rather live two days like a tiger, than two hundred years like a sheep, and the French statesman Georges Clemenceau (1841–1929).

See also ➤ *he who* RIDES *a tiger is afraid to dismount*, ➤ PAPER *tiger*, ➤ TAMIL *Tigers*.

tiger economy a dynamic economy of one of the smaller East Asian countries, especially that of Singapore, Taiwan, or South Korea, or of Hong Kong; these original **Four Tigers** of the early 1980s were later joined by Malaysia, Thailand, and the Philippines, before economic problems in the 1990s sharply reduced the strength and dominance of the region. By this time, however, the figurative use of *tiger* in an economic sense was established; the successful Irish economy of the last years has frequently been designated as the **Celtic Tiger**.

put a tiger in your tank advertising slogan for Esso petrol, 1964.

Tiger Tim cartoon character, leader of a group of animals known as the Bruin Boys, who first appeared in the *Daily Mirror* in 1904, and subsequently in the *Children's Encyclopaedia* monthly reissue from 1910 and *Rainbow* (1914–56). He has also figured in a number of annuals.

Bengal Tigers nickname of the 17th Foot, from their tiger badge.

Tigger the irrepressible and bouncy tiger character created by A. A. Milne as one of ➤ WINNIE-*the-Pooh*'s companions; he makes his first appearance in *The House at Pooh Corner* (1928).

Tikal an ancient Mayan city in the tropical Petén region of northern Guatemala, with great plazas, pyramids, and palaces. It flourished AD 300–800, reaching its peak towards the end of that period.

Tilbury now the principal container port of London and SE England, on the north bank of the River Thames; in 1588, the point at which troops for the defence of England against the Armada were assembled, and the site of ➤ ELIZABETH *I*'s speech to her forces.

Tilbury Town fictitious setting of many poems by the American poet Edwin Arlington Robinson, a conventional and materialistic place, thought to be modelled on his home town of Gardiner in Maine.

tilde an accent (˜) placed over Spanish *n* when pronounced *ny* (as in *señor*) or Portuguese *a* or *o* when nasalized (as in *São Paulo*), or over a vowel in phonetic transcription, indicating nasalization.

till see ➤ *till* DEATH *us do part*, ➤ *Till* EULENSPIEGEL, ➤ *Till* OWLGLASS.

tilt at the quintain practice jousting by aiming one's lance at a post set up as a mark, typically with a sandbag attached that would swing round and strike an unsuccessful tilter.
    See also ➤ QUINTAIN.

tilt at windmills attack imaginary obstacles, in the manner of ➤ *Don* QUIXOTE, who mistook a group of windmills in the distance for giants.

Tim see ➤ TIGER *Tim*, ➤ TIRED *Tim*.

Timbuctoo a distant or remote place, from the name of *Timbuktu*, a town in northern Mali which was founded by the Tuareg in the 11th century, and which became a Muslim centre of learning. It was formerly a major trading centre for gold and salt on the trans-Saharan trade routes, reaching the height of its prosperity in the 16th century but falling into decline after its capture by the Moroccans in 1591.

time see also ➤ BORROWED *time*, ➤ EQUATION *of time*, ➤ *a* GOOD *time was had by all*, ➤ GREENWICH *Mean Time*, ➤ PEACE *in our time*, ➤ PROCRASTINATION *is the thief of time*, ➤ QUALITY *time*, ➤ *there is always a* FIRST *time*, ➤ *there's a* GOOD *time coming*.

Father Time the personification of time, typically as an old man with a scythe and hourglass, and sometimes also bald but with a forelock.

there is a time and a place for everything proverbial saying, early 16th century.

time and tide wait for no man proverbial saying, late 14th century.

take time by the forelock proverbial expression, meaning that one should seize an opportunity when it is offered.

time flies proverbial saying, late 14th century; English equivalent of ➤ TEMPUS *fugit*.

there is a time for everything proverbial saying, late 14th century; with biblical allusion to Ecclesiastes 3:1, 'To every thing there is a season.'

time-honoured Lancaster in Shakespeare's *Richard II* (1595), a name for ➤ JOHN *of Gaunt*, Duke of Lancaster.

time immemorial a period beyond human memory.

time is a great healer proverbial saying, late 14th century.

time is money proverbial saying, late 16th century.

no time like the present proverbial saying, mid 16th century.

time out of mind another term for ➤ TIME *immemorial*.

time will tell proverbial saying, mid 16th century.

time works wonders proverbial saying, late 16th century.

time's arrow the direction of travel from past to future in time considered as a physical dimension. The phrase comes from Arthur Eddington (1882–1944) *The Nature of the Physical World* (1928) 'Let us draw an arrow arbitrarily. If as we follow the arrow we find more and more of the random element in the world, then the arrow is pointing towards the future; if the random element decreases the arrow points towards the past…I shall use the phrase 'time's arrow' to express this one-way property of time which has no analogue in space.'

timeo Danaos et dona ferentes Latin quotation from Virgil's *Aeneid* meaning, 'I fear the Greeks even when they bring gifts'; the warning given to the Trojans that they should not trust the ➤ TROJAN *Horse*.

times see also ➤ OTHER *times, other manners,* ➤ TRACTS *for the Times.*

times change and we with time proverbial saying, late 16th century; English equivalent of ➤ TEMPORA *mutantur, et nos mutamur in illis.*

Times Square a square in Manhattan, New York City, at the intersection of Broadway, 42nd Street, and Seventh Avenue; it is named after the building formerly occupied by the *New York Times*, which still transmits news flashes in lights on its façade. It is often taken as the type of an area of the entertainment industry in a major city.

> Ridley Scott's bleak vision of the future as a giant, sleazoid Times Square . . . is the best dystopia yet.
> — *Premiere* August 1992

Timoleon (d. *c.*336 BC), Corinthian statesman and general, who when his own brother attempted to make himself tyrant helped to kill him; he was later sent by Corinth with a mercenary army to Syracuse, in response to that city's appeal for help against the tyrant Dionysius II. He is sometimes referred to as the type of a lover of freedom and democracy.

Timon of Athens semi-legendary Athenian misanthrope, who according to a story in Plutarch became a recluse because of the ingratitude of his friends, refusing to see anyone but Alcibiades. Shakespeare's play (*c.*1607) is based on Plutarch.

Epistle to Timothy either of two books of the New Testament, epistles of St Paul addressed to St Timothy.

St Timothy (1st century AD), convert and disciple of St Paul. Traditionally he was the first bishop of

Ephesus and was martyred in the reign of the Roman emperor Nerva.

☐ **FEAST DAY** His feast day is January 22 or 26.

Timur Tartar name of ➤ TAMERLANE.

Timurid a descendant of Timur (➤ TAMERLANE); a member of the Turkic dynasty founded by him, which ruled in central Asia until the 16th century.

little tin god a person, especially a minor official, who is pompous and self-important; an object of unjustified veneration or respect.

tin Lizzie in North America, a dated informal expression for a motor car, in particular a very early Ford.

Tin Man in the story of the ➤ WIZARD *of Oz*, one of Dorothy's companions in the search for the magician.

Tin Pan Alley the name given to a district in New York (28th Street, between 5th Avenue and Broadway) where many songwriters, arrangers, and music publishers were formerly based. The phrase is now used for the world of composers and publishers of popular music, particularly with reference to the works of such composers as Irving Berlin, Jerome Kern, George Gershwin, Cole Porter, and Richard Rodgers.

tin tabernacle in the 19th century, a disparaging term for a Nonconformist chapel, often made partly of corrugated iron.

tin wedding in the US, a 10th wedding anniversary.

Tina acronym for the phrase *There Is No Alternative*, associated with Margaret Thatcher and her policies as Prime Minister (1979–90). The acronym is said to be an abbreviation formulated and adopted by the Young Conservatives; the phrase originally came from a speech of Margaret Thatcher's to the Conservative Women's Conference, 21 May 1980, when she said, 'I believe people accept there is no alternative.'

Nikolaas Tinbergen (1907–88), Dutch zoologist. From his studies he found that much animal behaviour was innate and stereotyped, and he introduced the concept of displacement activity. This work helped to establish ethology as a distinct discipline, with relevance also to human psychology and sociology.

tinderbox a box containing tinder, flint, a steel, and other items for kindling fires. It is central to one of Hans Andersen's fairy stories, in which a soldier summons three magic dogs, each one with huge eyes, to do his bidding and protect him, by striking a light with the tinderbox.

the Tins a nickname of the Household Cavalry, from their cuirasses.

Tinseltown Hollywood, or the superficially glamorous world it represents.

Tintagel a village on the coast of northern Cornwall. Nearby are the ruins of Tintagel Castle, the legendary birthplace of King Arthur and a stronghold of the Earls of Cornwall from the 12th to the 15th centuries.

Tintin boy reporter and detective, cartoon character created by the Belgian artist Hergé (1907–83); *Tintin* and his dog Snowy first appeared in 1929 in the Belgian newspaper *Le Vingtième Siècle*.

Tintoretto (1518–94), Italian painter. His work was typified by a mannerist style, including unusual viewpoints and chiaroscuro effects. Primarily a religious painter, he is best known for the huge canvas *Paradiso* (after 1577) in the Doges' Palace in Venice, and for his paintings (1576–88) in the Scuola di San Rocco in Venice.

tip-and-run an informal way of playing cricket in which the batsman must run after every hit; from 1918, the term is also recorded as an expression for a short, sudden wartime attack.

tip of the iceberg the small perceptible part of a much larger situation or problem that remains hidden, as the larger part of an iceberg remains submerged; the expression was used by the Conservative politician Nigel Lawson (1932–), following his resignation as Chancellor, to describe an article by Alan Walters, Margaret Thatcher's economic adviser, criticizing the Exchange Rate Mechanism:

> It represented the tip of a singularly ill-concealed iceberg, with all the destructive potential that icebergs possess.
> — Nigel Lawson speech in the House of Commons, 31 October 1989

Tipperary a county in the province of Munster, made famous by the song (1912) by Jack Judge and Harry Williams, popular as a British soldiers' song in the First World War:

> It's a long way to Tipperary,
> It's a long way to go;
> It's a long way to Tipperary,
> To the sweetest girl I know!
> Goodbye, Piccadilly,
> Farewell, Leicester Square,
> It's a long, long way to Tipperary,
> But my heart's right there!
> — Jack Judge and Harry Williams 'It's a Long Way to Tipperary' (1912)

In the mid 19th century the German travel writer Johann Georg Kohl (1808–78) noted 'We had now entered the notorious county of Tipperary, in which more murders and assaults are committed in one year than in the whole Kingdom of Saxony in five,' a view that was later echoed by Anthony Trollope:

> 'It's in Tipperary—not at all a desirable country to live in.'
> 'Oh, dear, no! Don't they murder the people?'
> — Anthony Trollope *The Eustace Diamonds* (1872)

Michael Tippett (1905–98), English composer. He established his reputation with the oratorio *A Child of Our Time* (1941), which drew on jazz, madrigals, and spirituals besides classical sources.

tippler a habitual drinker of alcohol; originally (in late Middle English), the word meant 'a retailer of alcoholic liquor'.

tipstaff a sheriff's officer; a bailiff. Originally (in the mid 16th century) the word denoted a metal-tipped staff: contraction of *tipped staff* (carried by a bailiff).

Tir-nan-Og a land of perpetual youth, the Irish equivalent of Elysium; the name means literally in Irish, 'land of the young'.

> Don't talk to me about the Isles of Youth. These are the Isles of Senescence, of Inactivity . . . I do not want to sleep or dream of Tir n'an Og.
> — Louis MacNeice *I Crossed the Minch* (1938)

tirailleur a sharpshooter; originally, a skirmisher employed in the wars of the French Revolution.

tired and emotional humorous phrase, associated particularly with the British satirical magazine *Private Eye*, used euphemistically to indicate that someone is drunk; an earlier variant was **tired and overwrought**:

> Mr Brown had been tired and overwrought on many occasions.
> — *Private Eye* 29 September 1967

tired businessman ironic phrase alluding to the short working hours and pleasure-loving habits popularly ascribed to businessmen; first recorded in

1913, the expression is said to have been used earlier by Mark Twain.

tired Tim a tramp, a work-shy person, with allusion to two tramps (the other is *weary Willie*), characters in the comic magazine *Illustrated Chips*.

Tiresias a blind Theban prophet, so wise that even his ghost had its wits and was not a mere phantom. Legends account variously for his wisdom and blindness; some stories hold also that he spent seven years as a woman. He was said to have been asked by Zeus and Hera whether a man or a woman derived more pleasure from the act of love; when he answered that a man did, Hera blinded him, but Zeus gave him in recompense a gift for unfailing prophecy.

Tironian notes a system of shorthand in use in ancient Rome, said to have been invented or introduced by Tiro, a freedman of Cicero.

> Shorthand systems had not been much improved since the invention of Tironian notes.
> — Johanna Drucker *The Alphabetical Labyrinth* (1995)

tirshatha (the title of) a viceroy or prefect of ancient Persia; in the Old Testament and Hebrew Scriptures, Nehemiah, who was governor of Judah, as in 'and Nehemiah, which is the Tirshatha' (Nehemiah 8:9).

Tirthankara in the Jain religion, one of the twenty-four founding prophets or Jinas, venerated as having successfully crossed the stream of time and having made a path for others to follow; the name in Sanskrit means 'maker of a ford'.

Tisha b'Av the ninth day of the month Ab, on which both the First and the Second Temples are said to have been destroyed, observed by Jews as a day of mourning.

Tishri (in the Jewish calendar) the first month of the civil and seventh of the religious year, usually coinciding with parts of September and October.

Tisiphone one of the ➤ FURIES; the name is Greek, and means literally 'avenger of blood'.

Titan in Greek mythology, any of the older gods who preceded the Olympians and were the children of ➤ URANUS (Heaven) and ➤ GAIA (Earth). Led by ➤ CRONUS, they overthrew Uranus; Cronus' son, ➤ ZEUS, then rebelled against his father and eventually defeated the Titans.

In early poetry, *Titan* is used as a name for the sun-god, or for the sun personified, or for the elder brother of Cronus as the first-born of the race. From the early 19th century, *titan* has denoted a person or thing of very great strength, intellect, or importance.

> The $80 million beachhead of William H. Gates's campaign to create a global network of brain factories for his software industry titan.
> — *New York Times* 18 January 1998

Titania the name of the queen of the fairies in Shakespeare's *A Midsummer Night's Dream*; in the play she has quarrelled with her husband Oberon, and in revenge he causes her by enchantment to fall in love with ➤ BOTTOM *the Weaver*. The name is used by Ovid in *Metamorphoses* to designate Diana, Circe, and others as descended from the Titans.

Titanic a British passenger liner, the largest ship in the world when she was built and supposedly unsinkable, that struck an iceberg in the North Atlantic on her maiden voyage in April 1912 and sank with the loss of 1,490 lives. Her name is now used allusively for an enterprise which is seen as doomed to failure, as in the comment of President Ford's campaign manager having lost five out of six primaries:

> I'm not going to rearrange the furniture on the deck of the Titanic.
> — Rogers Morton in *Washington Post* 16 May 1976

titch a small person; the word comes from *Little Tich*, stage name of Harry Relph (1868–1928), an English music-hall comedian of small stature. He was given the nickname because he resembled Arthur Orton, the *Tich*borne claimant.

tithe one tenth of annual produce or earnings, formerly taken as a tax for the support of the Church and clergy. The practice derived from Jewish custom, as recorded in Jacob's vow at Bethel, Genesis 28:22, 'and of all that thou shalt give me I will surely give the tenth unto thee'.

tithing in medieval England, a group of ten householders who lived close together and were collectively responsible for each other's behaviour.

Tithonus a Trojan prince with whom the goddess Aurora fell in love. She asked Zeus to make him immortal but omitted to ask for eternal youth, and he became very old and decrepit although he talked perpetually. Tithonus prayed her to remove him from this world and she changed him into a grasshopper, which chirps ceaselessly.

> A Tithonian sort of immortality that no sane man would covet.
> — H. Kuttner *Fury* (1947)

Prince Titi Frederick, Prince of Wales (1707–51), eldest son of George II and Caroline of Ansbach, who was on bad terms with his parents, wrote or instigated the writing in 1735 of *Histoire du Prince Titi* (of which two English translations appeared the following year) in which the king and queen were grossly caricatured.

Queen Caroline said of her son:

> My dear firstborn is the greatest ass, and the greatest liar, and the greatest *canaille*, and the greatest beast in the whole world, and I heartily wish he was out of it.
> — Caroline of Ansbach quoted in *Dictionary of National Biography* (1917–)

Titian (*c*.1488–1576), Italian painter. The most important painter of the Venetian school, he experimented with vivid colours and often broke conventions of composition. He painted many sensual mythological works, including *Bacchus and Ariadne* (*c*.1518–23). The term *Titian* as applied to hair, meaning bright golden auburn, developed by association with the bright auburn hair portrayed in many of his works.

Titivil name for a devil said to collect fragments of words dropped, skipped, or mumbled in the recitation of divine service, and to carry them to hell, to be registered against the offender; hence, a name for a demon or devil in the mystery plays. Also called *Tutivillus*.

titmouse another term for *tit*, a small songbird that searches acrobatically for insects among foliage and branches. Originally composed of *tit*, a word used in compound in the names of various small birds and *mose*, the original name of this bird; the change in the ending took place in the 16th century due to association with *mouse*, probably because of the bird's size and quick movements.

tittle a tiny amount or part of something; a small written or printed stroke or dot. Recorded from late Middle English, the word comes from Latin *titulus* 'title', in medieval Latin 'small stroke, accent'; the phrase ➤ *not one* JOT *or tittle* is from Matthew 5:18.

titular bishop in the Roman Catholic Church, a bishop deriving his title from an ancient see lost to the control of the Roman pontificate.

Titus (AD 39–81), Roman emperor, son of ➤ VESPASIAN. In 70 he ended a revolt in Judaea with the conquest of Jerusalem; he fell in love with the Jewish Queen Berenice, daughter of Herod Agrippa, who accompanied him back to Rome, although he was forced by the disapproval of his own people to send her away.

It was to Titus that his father Vespasian made the comment, ➤ MONEY *has no smell*; Titus himself is said in Suetonius's *Lives of the Caesars* to have lamented 'Friends, I have lost a day' on reflecting that he had done nothing to help anyone all day.

Arch of Titus a triumphal arch, commemorating the capture of Jerusalem by ➤ TITUS, erected in the Forum at Rome by Titus's brother and successor ➤ DOMITIAN.

Epistle to Titus a book of the New Testament, an epistle of St Paul addressed to St Titus.

St Titus (1st century AD), Greek churchman. A convert and helper of St Paul, he was traditionally the first bishop of Crete.

☐ **FEAST DAY** His feast day is (in the Eastern Church) 23 August; (in the Western Church) 6 February.

Titus Tatius name of a legendary Sabine king who was reconciled with Romulus after the rape of the Sabine women, and who became joint king over the combined peoples.

tityre-tu any of a group of well-to-do ruffians on the streets of London in the 17th century. The name comes from Latin *Tityre tu* 'you Tityrus', the first two words of Virgil's first eclogue, addressed to a man lying at ease beneath a tree.

Tityrus in Virgil's first Eclogue, the name of a shepherd, from whom the ➤ TITYRE-*tus* derived their name.

The word (said to represent 'satyr' in Doric) is also used for a fictitious monster supposed to be bred between a sheep and a goat.

Tityus in Greek mythology, a giant, the son of ➤ GAIA, who was killed by Zeus (or by Apollo and Artemis) for assaulting ➤ LETO. It is said in the *Odyssey* that Odysseus, on his visit to the underworld, saw Tityus, his body covering nine acres of ground, lying with two vultures tearing at his liver in punishment for his wrongdoing.

tmesis the separation of parts of a compound word by an intervening word or words, used mainly in informal speech for emphasis (e.g. *can't find it any-blooming-where*).

toad the toad, which typically has dry warty skin that can exude poison, is traditionally taken as the type of something unpleasant, as in Philip Larkin's poem *Toads* (1955), 'Why should I let the toad work Squat on my life?'

In Kenneth Grahame's *The Wind in the Willows*

(1908), the wealthy, boastful, spoiled, but ultimately good-hearted *Toad* needs to be rescued and redeemed from his self-indulgent ways by Ratty, Mole, and Badger:

> The clever men at Oxford
> Know all that there is to be knowed.
> But they none of them know one half as much
> As intelligent Mr Toad!
>
> — Kenneth Grahame *The Wind in the Willows* (1908)

See also ➤ PAD *in the straw*, ➤ PADDOCK.

toadstone a gem, fossil tooth, or other stone formerly supposed to have been formed in the body of a toad, and credited with therapeutic or protective properties.

> Sweet are the uses of adversity,
> Which like the toad, ugly and venomous,
> Wears yet a precious jewel in his head;
>
> — William Shakespeare *As You Like It* (1599)

toady a person who behaves obsequiously to someone important. Recorded from the early 19th century, the word is said to be a contraction of *toad-eater*, a charlatan's assistant who ate toads; toads were regarded as poisonous, and the assistant's survival was thought to be due to the efficacy of the charlatan's remedy.

toast the practice of drinking a toast in honour of a person or thing goes back to the late 17th century, and originated in naming a lady whose health the company was requested to drink, the idea being that the lady's name flavoured the drink like the pieces of spiced toast that were formerly placed in drinks such as wine.

See also ➤ LOYAL *toast*.

tobacco a preparation of the nicotine-rich leaves of an American plant, which are cured by a process of drying and fermentation for smoking or chewing. The word comes (in the mid 16th century) from Spanish *tabaco*; said to be from a Carib word denoting a tobacco pipe or from a Taino word for a primitive cigar, but perhaps from Arabic.

Hostility to tobacco is recorded from an early period, notably by James I:

> A custom loathsome to the eye, hateful to the nose, harmful to the brain, dangerous to the lungs, and in the black, stinking fume thereof, nearest resembling the horrible Stygian smoke of the pit that is bottomless.
>
> — James I *A Counterblast to Tobacco* (1604)

Tobias night a night during which the consummation of a marriage is postponed, translating German *Tobiasnacht*, with allusion to the story of ➤ TOBIT's son Tobias and his bride and cousin Sara in Tobit 8:1–3, in which Tobias with angelic help defeats the demonic spirit which has killed her previous husbands on their wedding nights.

Tobit a pious Israelite living during the Babylonian Captivity, described in the Apocrypha; the book of the Apocrypha telling the story of Tobit and his son Tobias, from whom ➤ TOBIAS *night* is named.

Tobruk a port on the Mediterranean coast of NE Libya, which was the scene of fierce fighting during the North African campaign in the Second World War.

Toby see also ➤ *Sir Toby* BELCH.

Toby the name of the trained dog introduced (in the first half of the 19th century) into the ➤ PUNCH *and Judy* show, which wears a frill round its neck.

toby archaic term for the public highway, especially in **the high toby**, highway robbery by a mounted thief, and **the low toby**, robbery by a footpad. The word is apparently an alteration of Shelta *tobar* 'road'.

toby jug a jug or mug in the form of a stout old man wearing a long and full-skirted coat and a three-cornered hat. The term comes from the mid 19th century (as a pet form of the given name *Tobias*), and is said to come from an 18th-century poem about *Toby Philpot* (with a pun on *fill pot*), a soldier who liked to drink.

Toc H in the UK, a society, originally of ex-service personnel, founded after the First World War by the Australian-born British clergyman Philip 'Tubby' Clayton (1885–1972) for promoting Christian fellowship and social service; in the admission ceremony the chairman asks, 'What is service?' and the candidate replies, 'The rent we pay for our room on earth.'

The name comes from *toc* (former telegraphy code for *T*) and *H*, from the initials of *Talbot House*, a soldier's club established in Belgium in 1915.

Tocharian either of two extinct languages (**Tocharian A** and **Tocharian B**) spoken by this people, the most easterly of known ancient Indo-European languages, surviving in a few documents and inscriptions and showing curious affinities to Celtic and Italic languages.

tocsin an alarm bell or signal. The word is recorded from the late 16th century and comes via Old French from Provençal *tocasenh*, from *tocar* 'to touch' + *senh* 'signal bell'.

tod a northern dialect word for a fox, recorded from the 12th century, but of unknown origin.

on one's tod on one's own, from rhyming slang *Tod Sloan*, the name of an American jockey (1873–1933).

today you; tomorrow me proverbial saying, mid 13th century.

toddy a drink made of spirits with hot water, sugar, and sometimes spices. Recorded from the early 17th century, denoting the sap of some kinds of plant, fermented to produce arrack, the word comes via Marathi and Hindi from a Sanskrit word meaning 'palmyra'.

toga a loose flowing outer garment worn by the citizens of ancient Rome, made of a single piece of cloth and covering the whole body apart from the right arm. The word is Latin, and is related to *tegere* 'to cover'.

toga praetextra a toga with a broad purple border worn by children, magistrates, persons engaged in sacred rites, and later by emperors.

toga virilis the toga of manhood, assumed by boys at puberty.

tohubohu (chiefly in North America), a state of chaos; utter confusion. The term comes from Hebrew *tōhū wa-bōhū* 'emptiness and desolation', translated in Genesis 1:2 (Authorized Version) as 'without form and void'.

toil see ➤ BLOOD, *toil, tears and sweat.*

toisech in Celtic Scotland, a dignitary or official ranking below a mormaor: corresponding to the later chief of a clan or thane. The word, which comes from Gaelic *tòisech* 'lord chief', is related to ➤ TAOISEACH.

Hideki Tojo (1884–1948), Japanese military leader and statesman, Prime Minister 1941–4. He initiated the Japanese attack on ➤ PEARL *Harbor* and by 1944 he had assumed virtual control of all political and military decision-making. After Japan's surrender he was tried and hanged as a war criminal.

Tok Pisin an English-based creole used as a commercial and administrative language by over 2 million people in Papua New Guinea. The name in Tok Pisin means literally 'pidgin talk'.

token a characteristic or distinctive sign or mark, especially a badge or favour worn to indicate allegiance to a particular person or party. In early biblical translations, *token* is used to denote an act which demonstrates divine power or authority, as Psalms 135:9 (Authorized Version), 'Who sent

tokens and wonders into the midst of thee, O Egypt'.

The word is recorded from Old English (in form *tā(e)n*) and is of Germanic origin, related to *teach*.

tokenism the practice of making only a perfunctory or symbolic effort to do a particular thing, especially by recruiting a small number of people from under-represented groups in order to give the appearance of sexual or racial equality within a workforce.

tokoloshe in African folklore, a mischievous and lascivious hairy water sprite.

Tokugawa the last shogunate in Japan (1603–1867), founded by Tokugawa Ieyasu (1543–1616). This period was marked by internal peace, stability, and economic growth, rigid feudalism, and almost complete international isolation. The shogunate was followed by the restoration of imperial power under Meiji Tenno.

Tokyo Rose the name given by American servicemen in the Second World War to a woman broadcaster of Japanese propaganda; the name in fact covered a number of women broadcasting Japanese propaganda, although one Japanese-American, Iva Toguri, was tried and convicted of treason after the war. Later evidence suggested that she and others had in fact tried to subvert the propaganda effort, and in 1977 she was pardoned by President Ford.

Toledo a city in central Spain on the River Tagus, which from the first century was famous for its steel and sword blades; from the late 16th century, *Toledo* was used for a sword made there, or for one of that kind.

Toleration Act an act of 1689 granting freedom of worship to dissenters (excluding Roman Catholics and Unitarians) on certain conditions. Its real purpose was to unite all Protestants under William III against the deposed Roman Catholic James II.

J. R. R. Tolkien (1892–1973), British novelist and literary scholar. He is famous for the fantasy adventures *The Hobbit* (1937) and *The Lord of the Rings* (1954–5), set in Middle Earth, an imaginary land peopled by mythical creatures, and for which he devised languages with considerable thoroughness.

> Most modern fantasy just rearranges the furniture in Tolkien's attic.
>
> — Terry Pratchett in Stan Nicholls (ed.) *Wordsmiths of Wonder* (1993)

tollbooth a booth, stall, or office at which tolls, duties or customs are collected; a custom house. In

Scotland, the word denoted a town hall or guildhall, and consequently also a town gaol (formerly often consisting of cells under the town hall).

Tollund Man the well-preserved corpse of an Iron Age man (*c.*500 BC–AD 400) found in 1950 in a peat bog in central Jutland, Denmark. Around the neck was a plaited leather noose, indicating that Tollund Man had met his death by hanging, a victim of murder or sacrifice.

Tolpuddle martyrs six farm labourers from the village of Tolpuddle in Dorset who attempted to form a trade union and were sentenced in 1834 to seven years' transportation on a charge of administering unlawful oaths. Their harsh sentences caused widespread protests, and two years later they were pardoned and repatriated from Australia.

Leo Tolstoy (1828–1910), Russian writer, best known for his novels *War and Peace* (1863–9), an epic tale of the Napoleonic invasion, and *Anna Karenina* (1873–7).

> I feel—everybody, if they're honest, feels—that it would be lovely to have one absolutely great Tolstoyian passion before one dies.
> — *Daily Telegraph* 3 April 1997

Tom see also ► BLACK *Tom*, ► GREAT *Tom of Oxford*, ► LONG *Tom*, ► MORE *people know Tom Fool than Tom Fool knows*, ► OLD *Uncle Tom Cobleigh and all*, ► PEEPING *Tom*, ► UNCLE *Tom*.

tom the male of various animals, especially a domestic cat. This dates from the 18th century, and may derive from 'The Life and Adventures of a Cat' (1760), an anonymous story which became very popular. The hero, a male or 'ram' cat, bore the name of Tom, and is commonly mentioned as 'Tom the Cat', as 'Tybert the Catte' is in Caxton's *Reynard the Fox*. Thus Tom became a favourite allusive name for a male cat.

Tom and Jerry names of the two chief characters in Egan's *Life in London*, 1821, and its continuation, 1828; whence in various allusive and attributive uses, especially as name of a compound alcoholic drink, a kind of highly-spiced punch. The title of Egan's original work (1821) is 'Life in London, or Days and Nights of Jerry Hawthorne and his elegant friend Corinthian Tom'; that of the continuation of 1828 is 'Finish to the Adventures of Tom, Jerry, and Logic', whence apparently the order of the names in *Tom and Jerry*.

Tom and Jerry are also the names of the cat and mouse cartoon characters (created by William

Hanna and Joseph Barbera) who first appeared in *Puss Gets the Boot* (1939); in their constant and violent battles, the large black-and-white cat is in the end outwitted by the adroit mouse.

Tom, Dick, and Harry used to refer to ordinary people in general; the phrase in this form is recorded from the mid 18th century, but Shakespeare in *1 Henry IV* (1597) has 'Tom, Dick, and Francis' in a similar sense.

Tom-noddy a foolish or stupid person, recorded from the early 19th century; 'My Lord Tomnoddy' appears as a character in R. H. Barham's *Ingoldsby Legends* (1840), and Robert Barnabas Brough's *Songs of the Governing Classes* (1855), which looks forward to his future as a legislator in the House of Lords:

> Office he'll hold and patronage sway;
> Fortunes and lives he will vote away;
> And what are his qualifications?—ONE!
> He's the Earl of Fitzdotterel's eldest son.
> — Robert Barnabas Brough *Songs of the Governing Classes* (1855)

Tom o'Bedlam a madman, a deranged person discharged from Bedlam and licensed to beg; in Shakespeare's *King Lear* (1605–6), the banished Edgar disguises himself as the mad 'Poor Tom'.

Tom quad the main quadrangle of Christ Church, Oxford, named for the bell ► GREAT *Tom of Oxford*.

Tom Thumb the hero of an old children's story, the son of a ploughman in the time of King Arthur who was only as tall as his father's thumb; the story of his life was popular as a chapbook publication, and was the subject of Fielding's mock-heroic *Tom Thumb, a Tragedy* (1730).

Tom Tiddler's ground name of a children's game. One of the players is *Tom Tiddler*, his territory being marked by a line drawn on the ground; over this the other players run, crying 'We're on Tom Tiddler's ground, picking up gold and silver'. They are chased by Tom Tiddler, the first, or sometimes the last, caught taking his place. *Tom Tiddler's ground* is used allusively for a place which offers a rich choice of items to be gathered up.

> The French naval yard, an undreamed-of Tom Tiddler's ground strewn with cordage, sailcloth, and spars of every dimension.
> — Patrick O'Brian *The Mauritius Command* (1977)

Tom tower a tower in which a great bell hangs; at Oxford, the western tower of Christ Church.

Tom's Coffee House situated in Russell Street, Covent Garden, and named after Thomas West, its landlord. It was frequented by the best company after the play, and patrons included Dr Johnson, Goldsmith, and Garrick.

tomahawk a light axe used as a tool or weapon by American Indians. The word is recorded in English from the early 17th century and comes from a Virginia Algonquian language; John Smith in his *Map of Virginia* (1612) gives *tomahacks* as a word for *axes*.

tombola a game in which people pick tickets out of a revolving drum and certain tickets win immediate prizes, typically played at a fête or fair. The word is recorded in English from the late 19th century, and comes via French or Italian from Italian *tombolare* 'turn a somersault'.

the Tombs informal name for New York City prison, recorded from the mid 19th century.

Tommy Atkins a name for the typical private soldier in the British army; deriving from the casual use of *Thomas Atkins* in the specimen forms given in official regulations from 1815 onwards; although other names were also used, *Thomas Atkins* became best known as used in all forms for privates in the cavalry and infantry.

> *Tommy Atkins* is recorded from 1883, but is now particularly associated with Rudyard Kipling:

> O it's Tommy this, an' Tommy that, an' 'Tommy, go away';
> But it's 'Thank you, Mister Atkins,' when the band begins to play.
> — Rudyard Kipling 'Tommy' (1890)

tomorrow see also ➤ *never* PUT *off till tomorrow what you can do today*.

tomorrow is another day proverbial saying, early 16th century; more recently, particularly associated with Scarlett O'Hara, Southern heroine of Margaret Mitchell's *Gone With the Wind* (1936); the closing line of the book is Scarlett's encouragement to herself, 'After all, tomorrow is another day.'

tomorrow never comes proverbial saying, early 16th century.

Thomas Tompion (*c*.1639–1713), English clock and watchmaker. He made one of the first balance-spring watches to the design of Robert Hooke, and made two large pendulum clocks for the Royal Greenwich Observatory which needed winding only once a year. Tompion also collaborated with Edward Barlow (1636–1716) in patenting the horizontal-wheel cylinder escapement needed to produce flat watches.

Wolfe Tone (1763–98), Irish nationalist. Having helped to found the Society of United Irishmen in 1791, in 1794 he induced a French invasion of Ireland to overthrow English rule, which failed. Tone was captured by the British during the Irish insurrection in 1798 and committed suicide in prison by cutting his throat; having accidentally severed his windpipe instead of his jugular, thus lingering for several days before dying, he is said to have commented, 'I find, then, I am but a bad anatomist.'

Mount Tongarira a mountain in North Island, New Zealand, which is held sacred by the Maoris.

tongs tongs are the emblem of ➤ *St* DUNSTAN and ➤ *St* ELOI.

tongue see also ➤ CONFUSION *of tongues*, ➤ *a* STILL *tongue makes a wise head*.

the tongue always returns to the sore tooth proverbial saying, late 16th century.

the gift of tongues in the Christian Church, the ability to speak in a language unknown to the speaker, or to vocalize freely, usually in the context of religious (especially pentecostal or charismatic) worship, identified as a gift of the Holy Spirit.

tonic sol-fa a system of naming the notes of the scale (usually *doh, ray, me, fah, soh, lah, te*) used especially to teach singing, with doh as the keynote of all major keys and lah as the keynote of all minor keys.

Gulf of Tonkin an arm of the South China Sea, bounded by the coasts of southern China and northern Vietnam. An incident there in 1964 led to increased US military involvement in the area prior to the Vietnam War.

tonnage originally (in late Middle English) the word derived from *tun*, and denoted a duty or tax of so much per tun levied on wine imported to England in tuns or casks between the 14th and 18th centuries. From the early 16th century, however, further senses were formed on *ton*, denoting a charge for the hire of a ship of so much per ton of capacity per week or month, and later a charge or duty payable at so much per ton on cargo or freight.

The sense of ships collectively, shipping (considered in respect of carrying capacity, or of weight of cargo carried), is recorded from the early 17th century, and from the early 18th century the word has denoted the internal capacity of a ship expressed in tons of 100 cubic feet or 2.83 cubic metres (originally, the number of tun casks of wine which a merchant ship could carry).

tonnage and poundage duties first levied in the 14th century, and granted for life to several sovereigns, beginning with Edward IV. They were abolished in 1787.

tonsure a part of a monk's or priest's head left bare on top by shaving off the hair. In the Eastern church the whole head is shaven (the **tonsure of St Paul**), in the Roman Catholic Church, the tonsure consists of either a circular patch on the crown, or the whole upper part of the head so as to leave only a fringe or circle of hair (the **tonsure of St Peter**), and in the ancient Celtic Church, the head was shaved in the front of a line drawn from ear to ear (the **tonsure of St John**).

Recorded from late Middle English, the word comes from Old French or from Latin *tonsura*, from *tondere* 'shear, clip'.

tontine an annuity shared by subscribers to a loan or common fund, the shares increasing as subscribers die until the last survivor enjoys the whole income. The word comes (in the mid 18th century) from French, and is named after Lorenzo *Tonti* (1630–95), a Neapolitan banker who started such a scheme to raise government loans in France (*c*.1653).

Tonton Macoute a member of a notoriously brutal militia formed by President François Duvalier of Haiti, active from 1961–86. The name is Haitian French, apparently with reference to an ogre of folk tales.

Tony (in the US) any of a number of awards given annually for outstanding achievement in the theatre in various categories. The name comes from the nickname of Antoinette Perry (1888–1946), American actress and director.

you can have too much of a good thing proverbial saying, late 15th century.

Toom see ➤ *Toom* TABARD.

tooth see ➤ DOG-*tooth*, ➤ *an* EYE *for an eye and a tooth for a tooth*, ➤ *the* TONGUE *always returns to the sore tooth*, ➤ WISDOM *tooth*.

toothache St Apollonia, a 3rd-century martyr whose sufferings included having her teeth

wrenched from her jaws, ➤ *St* MÉDARD, and St Osmund (d. 1099), noted for his healing miracles, are patron saints of those suffering from toothache.

Top End in Australia, the northern part of the Northern Territory.

Tophet a term for hell, from the name of a place in the Valley of Hinnom near Jerusalem used for idolatrous worship, including the sacrifice of children (after which, according to Jeremiah 19:6, it was decreed by God that 'this place shall no more be called Tophet, nor The valley of the son of Hinnom, but The valley of slaughter'), and later for burning refuse.

> Energy is generated in a central inner core hotter than Tophet itself.
> — Alexander Theroux *The Primary Colours* (1994)

Topkapi Palace the former seraglio or residence in Istanbul of the sultans of the Ottoman Empire, last occupied by Mahmut II (1808–39) and now a museum.

toponym a place name, especially one derived from a topographical feature.

Topsy name of the young slave girl in Harriet Beecher Stowe's *Uncle Tom's Cabin* (1852), who says of herself 'I s'pect I growed. Don't think nobody never made me.' From this, *Topsy* is taken as the type of something which seems to have grown of itself without anyone's intention or direction.

> The story, like Topsy, grows and grows.
> — *Toronto Life* January 1995

topsy-turvy upside down; a jingle apparently based on *top* and obsolete *terve* 'overturn'.

Torah in Judaism, the law of God as revealed to Moses and recorded in the first five books of the Hebrew scriptures (the ➤ PENTATEUCH).
See also ➤ SIMCHAT *Torah*, ➤ TALMUD *Torah*.

torana a sacred Buddhist gateway, consisting of a pair of uprights with one or more (typically three) crosspieces and elaborate carving. The word comes from Sanskrit *toraṇa* 'gate, arched portal'.

torc a neck ornament consisting of a band of twisted metal, worn especially by the ancient Gauls and Britons.

torch a portable means of illumination such as a piece of wood or cloth soaked in tallow or an oil lamp on a pole, sometimes carried ceremonially; figuratively, *the* valuable quality, principle, or cause, which needs to be protected and maintained.

Torch was the codename for the Allied landings on the western coast of North Africa in 1942.

See also ➤ PASS *on the torch.*

torii the gateway of a Shinto shrine, with two uprights and two crosspieces.

torma a sacrificial offering burned in a Tibetan Buddhist ceremony.

Toronto the capital of Ontario and the largest city in Canada, originally named *York* but renamed *Toronto* in 1834, from a Huron word meaning 'meeting place'.

Toronto blessing a manifestation of religious ecstasy, typically involving mass fainting, with speaking in tongues, laughter, or weeping, associated with a charismatic revival among evangelical Christians which originated in a fellowship meeting at *Toronto* airport chapel in 1994.

Torpids at Oxford University, boat races rowed in the Lent term between the second crews of colleges; the term, which is recorded from 1838, originally designated the boats.

Tomás de Torquemada (*c.*1420–98), Spanish cleric and Grand Inquisitor. A Dominican monk, he became confessor to Ferdinand and Isabella, whom he persuaded to institute the Inquisition in 1478, and was also the prime mover behind the expulsion of the Jews from Spain in and after 1492. His name is used allusively for someone in the role of a ruthless inquisitor.

> The Torquemada of television . . . skewered his victim with gotcha questions.
>
> — *Life* June 1993

Torrey Canyon name of the oil-tanker which in March 1967 struck the rocks off the Isles of Scilly; the resulting pollution devastated the Cornish coastline, and the ship itself, which continued to lose oil, was finally bombed to destroy the cargo and prevent further damage to the environment.

Evangelista Torricelli (1608–47), Italian mathematician and physicist. He invented the mercury barometer, with which he demonstrated that the atmosphere exerts a pressure sufficient to support a column of mercury in an inverted closed tube.

Torschlusspanik a sense of alarm or anxiety at the passing of life's opportunities, said to be experienced in middle age; the word is German, and means literally 'shut door panic'.

torso the trunk of a statue, without or considered independently of the head and limbs; the trunk of the human body. The word is recorded from the late 18th century and comes from Italian, literally 'stalk, stump', from the Latin base of ➤ THYRSUS.

See also ➤ BELVEDERE *Torso.*

tortoise the *tortoise* is taken (as in the story of ➤ *the* HARE *and the tortoise*) as the type of something which moves slowly and laboriously, but with determination.

According to an anecdote, the Greek dramatist ➤ AESCHYLUS was killed when an eagle dropped a tortoise on to his bald head.

See also ➤ ACHILLES *and the tortoise.*

Tory now (in the UK) a member or supporter of the Conservative Party; originally, a member of the English political party opposing the exclusion of James II from the succession. It remained the name for members of the English, later British, parliamentary party supporting the established religious and political order until the emergence of the Conservative Party in the 1830s.

The name comes (in the mid 17th century, denoting Irish peasants dispossessed by English settlers and living as robbers) from Irish *toraidhe* 'outlaw, highwayman', from *tóir* 'pursue'; it was then extended to other marauders especially in the Scottish Highlands. It was then adopted *c.*1679 as an abusive nickname for supporters of the Catholic James, Duke of York, later James II.

tosafist a medieval writer of critical and explanatory notes on the Talmud.

toss see ➤ PITCH-*and-toss.*

totem a natural object or animal that is believed by a particular society to have spiritual significance and that is adopted by it as an emblem. The word is recorded from the mid 18th century, and comes from Ojibwa *nindoodem* 'my totem'.

totem pole a pole on which totems are hung or on which the images of totems are carved; in figurative use, a hierarchy.

Totentanz in Germany, the ➤ DANCE *of death.*

Totten trust a tentative trust in the form of a savings account opened by one person acting as trustee for another, but revocable by the former at any time. It is named after H. B. *Totten*, party to a court case in 1902 concerning an estate of which he was administrator.

touch see also ➤ *if you gently touch a* NETTLE *it'll sting your for your pains,* ➤ NELSON *touch,* ➤ *touch a* CHORD.

touch not the cat but a glove Scottish proverbial saying, early 19th century; *but* here means 'without'.

touch of nature a manifestation of human feeling with which others sympathize, from a misinterpretation of Shakespeare's *Troilus & Cressida* (1602), 'One touch of nature makes the whole world kin'.

touch wood traditional formula for luck, from the superstition that touching wood was a charm to avert ill-fortune; recorded from the early 19th century.

touchstone a piece of fine-grained dark schist or jasper formerly used for testing alloys of gold by observing the colour of the mark which they made on it; in figurative usage, something which acts as a test of genuineness, a criterion.

Touchstone is also the name of the fool in Shakespeare's *As You Like It*, who loyally accompanies Rosalind and Celia into exile.

touchy-feely openly expressing affection or other emotions, especially through physical contact. In its literal senses, *touchy-feely* is associated with the development in the 1960s and 1970s of encounter groups in which participants sought psychological benefit through close contact with one another. By the 1990s, the figurative use of the term was strongly established; it is often used to sum up the attitude implicit in the 'caring nineties' and the values of a ➤ NEW *Age* society.

tough see also ➤ *when the* GOING *gets tough, the tough get going.*

tough love promotion of a person's welfare, especially that of an addict, child, or criminal, by enforcing certain constraints on them, or requiring them to take responsibility for their actions. The concept developed in America in the early 1980s as an appropriate way for family members in co-operation with professional carers to deal with children and young adults affected by drug abuse; the climate of the times was sympathetic to a view

that true concern was best expressed by the setting of standards rather than by showing indulgence.

Henri Toulouse-Lautrec (1864–1901), French painter and lithographer. His reputation is based on his colour lithographs from the 1890s, depicting actors, music-hall singers, prostitutes, and waitresses in Montmartre: particularly well known is the *Moulin Rouge* series (1894).

Tour de France a French race for professional cyclists held annually since 1903, covering approximately 4,800 km (3,000 miles) of roads in about three weeks, renowned for its mountain stages. The overall leader after each stage wears the famous yellow leader's jersey.

Tourist Trophy a motorcycle-racing competition, often abbreviated to **TT**, held annually on roads in the Isle of Man since 1907.

Tournai a town in Belgium, on the River Scheldt near the French frontier, which became the Merovingian capital in the 5th century and was the birthplace of the Frankish king ➤ CLOVIS.

tournament in the Middle Ages, a sporting event in which two knights (or two groups of knights) jousted on horseback with blunted weapons, each trying to knock the other off, the winner receiving a prize. According to the chronicler Roger of Hoveden, the practice was first introduced into England by Richard I. Tournaments continued up to the 16th century; Henri II of France (1519–59) died of wounds accidentally sustained while jousting.

Tours a city in western France, said by Geoffrey of Monmouth to derive its name from a nephew of Brutus called Turonus.

Toussaint l'Ouverture (*c.*1743–1803), Haitian revolutionary leader. One of the leaders of a rebellion (1791) that emancipated the island's slaves, he was appointed Governor General by the revolutionary government of France in 1797. In 1802 Napoleon (wishing to restore slavery) took over the island and Toussaint died in prison in France. He was the subject of a sonnet by Wordsworth, 'To Toussaint L'Overture' (1807), of which the closing lines are, 'Thy friends are exultations, agonies, And love, and man's unconquerable mind'.

tout passe, tout casse, tout lasse French saying, meaning 'everything passes, everything perishes, everything palls'; recorded from the mid 19th century.

towel see ➤ CHUCK *in the towel.*

tower a *tower* is the emblem of ➤ *St* BARBARA.
See also ➤ IVORY *tower,* ➤ LEANING *Tower of Pisa,* ➤ LIEUTENANT *of the Tower,* ➤ MARTELLO *tower,* ➤ PRINCES *in the Tower,* ➤ ROUND *tower,* ➤ *Tower of* BABEL, ➤ TOWN *and tower.*

Towers	
Bloody Tower	London
Devil's Tower	Wyoming
Eiffel Tower	Paris
Mouse Tower	Bingen
Sears Tower	Chicago
Tom Tower	Oxford
White Tower	London

Tower Bridge a bridge across the Thames in London, famous for its twin towers and for the two bascules of which the roadway consists, able to be lifted to allow the passage of large ships. It was completed in 1894.

Tower of London a fortress by the Thames just east of the City of London. The oldest part, the White Tower, was begun in 1078. It was later used as a state prison, and is now open to the public as a repository of ancient armour and weapons, and of the Crown jewels (which have been kept there since the time of Henry III).

tower of silence a tall open-topped structure on which Parsees traditionally place and leave exposed the body of someone who has died.

tower of strength a source of strong and reliable support; perhaps originally alluding to the *Book of Common Prayer* 'O Lord…be unto them a tower of strength.'

Tower pound a pound weight of 5400 grains (= 11¼ Troy ounces), which was the legal mint pound of England prior to the adoption of the Troy pound of 5760 grains in 1526.

town an urban area with a name, defined boundaries, and local government, that is larger than a village and generally smaller than a city. Originally (in Old English) the word meant 'enclosed piece of land, homestead, village', of Germanic origin, related to Dutch *tuin* 'garden' and German *Zaun* 'fence'.
See also ➤ *the* FIVE *Towns,* ➤ *town* MOUSE.

town and gown the permanent residents of a university town and the members of the university, especially as seen in opposition to one another.

town and tower inhabited parts of a country or region; an alliterative phrase recorded from late Middle English.

town crier a person traditionally employed to make public announcements in the streets or marketplace of a town; the type of someone who will spread information far and wide.

toxophilite a student or lover of archery. The word comes (in the late 18th century) from *Toxophilus,* a name invented by Roger Ascham, used as the title of his treatise on archery (1545), from Greek *toxon* 'bow' + *-philos* 'loving'.

toy boy a male lover who is much younger than his partner; an expression developed in the early 1980s as a regular feature in the language of the tabloids.

toyi-toyi in South Africa, a dance step characterized by high-stepping movements, typically performed at protest gatherings or marches. The name comes from Ndebele and Shona; it was probably introduced into South Africa by ANC exiles returning from military training in Zimbabwe.

Arnold Toynbee[1] (1852–83), English economist and social reformer. He taught both undergraduates and workers' adult education classes in Oxford and worked with the poor in London's East End. He is best known for his pioneering work *The Industrial Revolution* (1884).

Arnold Toynbee[2] (1889–1975), English historian. He is best known for his twelve-volume *Study of History* (1934–61), in which he traced the pattern of growth, maturity, and decay of different civilizations; he concluded that contemporary Western civilization is in decay.

Toytown setting for the children's stories of S. G. Hulme Beatman (1886–1932), first published in 1925 and in 1929 adapted for Children's Hour on radio; *Toytown,* inhabited by ➤ LARRY *the Lamb* and his friends, is referred to allusively as a type of small or insignificant town.

Tractarianism another name for ➤ OXFORD *Movement;* from the title *Tracts for the Times.*

tractate a treatise. Recorded from the late 15th century, the word comes from Latin *tractatus* 'handling, treatment, discussion', from *tractare* 'to handle'.

Tracts for the Times the title of a series of pamphlets on theological topics started by ➤ *John Henry* NEWMAN and published in Oxford 1833–41, which set out the doctrines on which the ➤ OXFORD *Movement* or *Tractarianism* was based.

Dick Tracy American plainclothes detective with a jutting jaw whose slogan (like the FBI's) is 'Crime doesn't pay', and who is ready to use violence in the service of right, in the cartoon strip created in 1931 by the American cartoonist Chester Gould (1900–85).

> A doughty, sawed off thirty-year-old Army sergeant with a lantern jaw and Dick Tracy-esque mug
> — *Esquire* December 1993

William de Tracy (d. 1173), one of the four knights who killed ➤ *Thomas à* BECKET.

trade see also ➤ EVERY *man to his trade*, ➤ JACK *of all trades and master of none*, ➤ *there are* TRICKS *in every trade*, ➤ TWO *of a trade never agree*.

trade follows the flag proverbial saying, late 19th century.

trade union an organized association of workers in a trade, group of trades, or profession, formed to protect and further their rights and interests. Although prefigured by the medieval artisans' guilds, trade unions were a product of the Industrial Revolution in Britain. They expanded in size and importance during the 19th century, despite being subject, particularly in the earlier years, to repressive legislation such as the Combination Acts. The Trades Union Congress first met in 1868, and the position of unions in Britain was legally recognized by the Trade Union Act of 1871; the unions began assuming a more assertive and politicized outlook towards the end of the century, playing a central role in the formation of the Labour Party. The trade union movement achieved true national importance in the early 20th century, with smaller unions tending to amalgamate into larger national organizations and white-collar workers joining in greater numbers. After confrontations between the government and unions in the 1960s and 1970s the Thatcher government severely restricted the powers of the trade unions in Britain.

trade wind a wind blowing steadily towards the equator from the north-east in the northern hemisphere (the **north-east trade wind**) or the south-east in the southern hemisphere (the **south-east trade wind**), especially at sea. Two belts of trade winds encircle the earth, blowing from the tropical high-pressure belts to the low-pressure zone at the equator; the system is seasonally displaced respectively to the north and south of the equator in the northern and southern summers.

trademark a symbol, word, or words, legally registered or established by use as representing a company or product.

John Tradescant (1570–1638), English botanist and horticulturalist. He was the earliest known collector of plants and other natural history specimens, and took part in collecting trips to western Europe, Russia, and North Africa; he also set up his own garden and museum in Lambeth, London. His son John (1608–62) added many plants to his father's collection, which was eventually bequeathed to Elias Ashmole.

traduttore traditore an Italian saying, meaning, 'translators, traitors'.

Battle of Trafalgar a decisive naval battle fought on 21 October 1805 off the cape of Trafalgar on the south coast of Spain during the Napoleonic Wars. The British fleet under Horatio Nelson (who was killed in the action) defeated the combined fleets of France and Spain, which were attempting to clear the way for Napoleon's projected invasion of Britain. Napoleon was never again able to mount a serious threat to British naval supremacy.

Trafalgar Day 21 October, the anniversary of the Battle of Trafalgar.

Trafalgar Square a square in central London, planned by John Nash and built between the 1820s and 1840s. It is dominated by Nelson's Column, a memorial to Lord Nelson.

tragedy in classical and Renaissance drama, a serious verse play (originally a Greek lyric song), written in an elevated style, in which the protagonist (usually a political leader or royal personage) is drawn to disaster or death by an error or fatal flaw. Later, a drama of a similarly serious nature and unhappy ending but typically dealing with an ordinary person or people. Recorded from late Middle English, the word comes ultimately via Old French and Latin from Greek *tragōidia*, apparently from *tragos* 'goat' + *ōidē* 'song'.

See also ➤ KENTUCKY *Tragedy*, ➤ REVENGE *tragedy*.

tragelaph any of various antelopes or other horned animals vaguely known to ancient writers; a mythical or fictitious composite animal represented as a combination of a goat and a stag.

tragic flaw a less technical term for ➤ HAMARTIA.

Thomas Traherne (1637–74), English religious writer and metaphysical poet. His major prose work *Centuries* (1699) was rediscovered in 1896 and re-published as *Centuries of Meditation* (1908). It consists of brief meditations showing his joy in creation and in divine love and is noted for its description of his childhood.

trahison des clercs a betrayal of intellectual, artistic, or moral standards by writers, academics, or artists. The (French) phrase, literally 'treason of the scholars', is the title of a book by Julien Benda (1927).

Trails

Appalachian Trail	Mormon Trail
Chisholm Trail	Oregon Trail
Freedom Trail	Santa Fe Trail

Trail of Tears the forced removal, in 1838–9, of the Cherokee people from their homeland and sent on a march from Georgia to Oklahoma; many died on the journey.

trail one's coat deliberately provoke a quarrel or fight (said to be from the earlier *drag his coat-tails, so that someone may tread on them*, attributed to Irishmen at ➤ DONNYBROOK *Fair*).

train see ➤ LET *the train*.

trainband a division of civilian soldiers in London and other areas, in particular in the Stuart period; during the Civil War the *trainbands* were important to the Parliamentary defence of London. The word comes from a contraction of *trained band*.

trainspotter a person who obsessively studies the minutiae of any minority interest or specialized hobby; the interest and knowledge brought by the *trainspotter* to their chosen hobby are seen as negated by the trivial nature of the selected subject area (as, collecting train or locomotive numbers).

Traitors' Gate the gate to the ➤ TOWER *of London* by which state prisoners brought by river entered.

Trajan (*c.*53–117) AD), Roman emperor 98–117. His reign is noted for the many public works undertaken and for the Dacian wars (101–6), which ended in the annexation of Dacia as a province, and which are illustrated on ➤ TRAJAN*'s Column* in Rome.

Arch of Trajan a monumental arch at Benevento, decreed or dedicated *c.* 115 AD, and showing Trajan's achievements at home and abroad.

Trajan's Column monument erected 106–113 AD in Rome, commemorating his successful Dacian campaign; his ashes were deposited at its base.

tram a passenger vehicle powered by electricity conveyed by overhead cables, and running on rails laid in a public road; formerly also, a low four-wheeled cart or barrow used in coal mines. Recorded from the early 16th century (denoting a shaft of a barrow), the word comes from Middle Low German and Middle Dutch 'beam, barrow shaft'. In the early 19th century the word denoted the parallel wheel tracks used in a mine, on which the public tramway was modelled, and from this came (in the late 19th century) the current sense.

The civil engineer Benjamin Outram (1764–1805) was much concerned with producing iron railways for colliery traffic, and folk etymology suggested wrongly that *tram* came from his name.

tramontana a cold north wind blowing in Italy or the adjoining regions of the Adriatic and Mediterranean. The word is Italian, and means 'north wind, Pole Star' (see ➤ TRAMONTANE).

tramontane originally (in Middle English) a name for the Pole Star, ultimately from Latin *transmontanus* 'beyond the mountains'. Later (in the late 16th century) a person who lives on the other side of mountains, used in particular by Italians to refer to people beyond the Alps, who were regarded as strange and barbarous.

tramps the French-born St Benedict Labre (1748–83), who after living as a pilgrim visiting shrines on the way to Rome, spent his last nine years there as a homeless person among the destitute, is patron saint of tramps.

Trans-Siberian Railway a railway running from Moscow east around Lake Baikal to Vladivostok on the Sea of Japan. Begun in 1891 and virtually completed by 1904, it opened up Siberia and advanced Russian interest in eastern Asia.

Transcendental Club a group of American intellectuals who met informally for philosophical discussion at Emerson's house and elsewhere during some years from 1836, the embodiment of a movement of thought, philosophical, religious, social, and economic, produced in New England between 1830 and 1850 by the spirit of revolutionary Europe, German philosophy, and Wordsworth, Coleridge, and Carlyle.

Its social and economic aspects took form in the Brook Farm Institute of George Ripley, a self-supporting group of men and women, who shared in manual labour and intellectual pursuits.

transept in a cross-shaped church, either of the two parts forming the arms of the cross shape, projecting at right angles from the nave.

the Transfiguration Christ's appearance in radiant glory to three of his disciples, Peter, James, and John; they are said to have seen with him Moses and Elijah (Matthew 17:2 and Mark 9:2–3).

Translator General Thomas Fuller's name for Philemon Holland (1552–1637), who translated the work of Livy, Pliny, Plutarch, Suetonius, and others into English; Fuller, who named him the 'translator general in his age' said of his translations that 'these books alone of his turning into English will make a country gentleman a competent library'. He was admired also by writers of a later period; Southey says that 'Philemon…for the service which he rendered to his contemporaries and to his countrymen, deserves to be called the best of Hollands'.

transmigration of souls the doctrine of the passage of the soul at death into another body; ➤ MET-EMPSYCHOSIS.

Transport House a building in ➤ SMITH *Square*, Westminster, London, between 1928 and 1980 the headquarters of the British Labour Party until the move to ➤ MILLBANK.

transubstantiation the conversion of the substance of the Eucharistic elements into the body and blood of Christ at consecration, only the appearances of bread and wine still remaining. The belief was defined at the Lateran Council of 1215, based on Aristotelian theories on the nature of 'substance', and is the official doctrine of the Roman Catholic Church; the word itself has been used from the mid 16th century. It was rejected by Luther, Zwingli, and other Protestant reformers.

Trappist a member of a branch of the Cistercian order of monks founded in 1664 at *La Trappe* in Normandy and noted for an austere rule including a vow of silence.

Traskite a follower of John *Trask*, who *c.*1617 began to advocate certain Jewish ceremonies, including the observance of the seventh-day Sabbath; now represented by the Seventh-day Baptists.

travel broadens the mind proverbial saying, early 20th century; G. K. Chesterton's comment on this was, 'They say travel broadens the mind, but you must have the mind.'

Traveller name of the grey horse ridden during the American Civil War by Robert E. Lee; it was said that after the war he lost many hairs from his tail to admirers who wanted souvenirs. His bones were on display for many years at Washington College, where Lee spent his final years, but are now buried near the grave of General Lee.

traveller's joy a tall scrambling clematis with small creamy white fragrant flowers and tufts of grey hairs around the seeds. Native to Eurasia and North Africa, it grows chiefly in hedges and on wasteland on calcareous soils; the name was given to it by the English herbalist John Gerard (1545–1612) for its trailing over and adorning wayside hedges. Also called *old man's beard*.

travellers ➤ *St* CHRISTOPHER, ➤ *St* JULIAN, and the ➤ MAGI (venerated as saints in the Middle Ages) are patron saints of travellers.

he travels fastest who travels alone proverbial saying, late 19th century.

By Tre, Pol, and Pen,
you shall know the Cornish men
traditional rhyme, referring to the typical first syllables of Cornish surnames.

treacle originally (in Middle English) any of various medicinal salves formerly used as antidotes to poisons or venomous bites; the word comes via Old French and Latin from Greek *thēriakē* 'antidote against venom', ultimately from *thērion* 'wild beast'.

The current sense of uncrystallized syrup dates from the late 17th century.

See also ➤ THERIAC.

Treacle Bible another name for the ➤ BISHOPS' *Bible*, in which *Jeremiah* 8:22 reads 'Is there no tryacle in Gilead?' where the Authorized Version has, 'Is there no balm in Gilead?'

treason the crime of betraying one's country, especially by attempting to kill or overthrow the sovereign or government. Formerly, there were two types of crime to which the term *treason* was applied: **petty treason**, the crime of murdering one's master, and **high treason**, the crime of betraying one's country. The crime of **petty treason** was abolished in 1828 and in modern use the term **high treason** is now often simply called *treason*.

The word is recorded from Middle English and comes via Anglo-Norman French from Latin *traditio(n-)* 'handing over'.

treason of the clerks another term for
➤ TRAHISON *des clercs*.

treasure originally, wealth or riches stored or accumulated, especially in the form of precious metals; later, a quantity of precious metals, gems, or other valuable objects. The word is recorded from Middle English, and comes ultimately from the Greek base of ➤ THESAURUS.

In biblical allusions, *treasure* often denotes something valued by a person above all else, as in Matthew 6:21, 'Where your treasure is, there will your heart be also.'

Treasure State informal name for Montana, noted for its gold, silver, copper, and coal mines.

treasure trove valuables of unknown ownership that are found hidden (as opposed to lost or abandoned) and declared the property of the Crown; the British law of *treasure trove* was abolished in 1996. Recorded from late Middle English, the term comes from Anglo-Norman French *tresor trové*, literally 'found treasure'.

Treasury originally, a room or building in which precious or valuable objects are kept, the funds or revenue of a state; later (in some countries), the government department responsible for budgeting for and controlling public expenditure, management of the national debt, and the overall management of the economy.

First Lord of the Treasury in Britain, the Prime Minister.

Secretary of the Treasury the head of the US Treasury Department.

Treasury Bench in the UK, the front bench in the House of Commons occupied by the Prime Minister, the Chancellor of the Exchequer, and other members of the government.

treat see ➤ TRICK *or treat*.

treaty see also ➤ *City of the* VIOLATED *Treaty*, ➤ TEST-*Ban Treaty*,

Treaties	
TREATY	PARTIES
Treaty of Dover	England and France, 1670
Treaty of Limerick	Jacobite and Williamite forces in Ireland, 1691
Treaty of Maastricht	European Community members, 1993
Treaty of Perpetual Peace	England and Scotland, 1502
Treaty of Rome	France, West Germany, Italy, Belgium, the Netherlands, and Luxembourg, 1957
Treaty of Versailles	Allies and the Central Powers, 1919
Treaty of Waitangi	British and Maori leaders, 1840
Treaty of Westphalia	France, Sweden, Spain, and Holy Roman Empire, 1648

treaty port a port bound by treaty to be open to foreign trade, especially in 19th and early 20th-century China and Japan.

Treaty Stone the stone on which the ➤ *Treaty of* LIMERICK (3 October 1691) was reputedly signed by representatives of the Jacobite and Williamite forces; it became a symbol of English failure to honour the terms of the treaty.

> Remember Limerick and the broken treatystone.
> — James Joyce *Ulysses* (1922)

Trebizond former name of *Trabzon*, a port on the Black Sea in northern Turkey, which was founded by Greek colonists in 756 BC. Its ancient name was *Trapezus*. In 1204, after the sack of Constantinople by the Crusaders, an offshoot of the Byzantine Empire was founded with Trebizond as its capital, which was annexed to the Ottoman Empire in 1461.

Treblinka a Nazi concentration camp in Poland in the Second World War, where a great many of the Jews of the Warsaw ghetto were murdered.

tree a woody perennial plant, typically having a single stem or trunk growing to a considerable height and bearing lateral branches at some distance from the ground, sometimes taken as the type of height and strength. In poetic use, the *tree* may refer to the cross on which Christ was crucified; the word may also be used for the gallows.

From Middle English, the word has also been used for a genealogical table or **family tree**, in which the original ancestor is seen as the root, and the various lines of descent as the branches.

The word is recorded from Old English (in form *trēow, trēo*), and comes from a Germanic variant of an Indo-European root shared by Greek *doru* 'wood, spear', *drus* 'oak'.

See also ➤ *the* APPLE *never falls far from the tree*, ➤ *as the* TWIG *is bent, so is the tree inclined*, ➤ BARK *up the wrong tree*, ➤ *between the* BARK *and the tree*, ➤ BO *tree*, ➤ CHRISTMAS *tree*, ➤ GREGORIAN *tree*, ➤ JESSE *tree*, ➤ JOSHUA *tree*, ➤ JUDAS *tree*, ➤ *not see the* WOOD *for the trees*, ➤ PAGODA-*tree*, ➤ PHILO-SOPHER'*s tree*, ➤ SHITTAH *tree*, ➤ UPAS *tree*, ➤ *you cannot* SHIFT *an old tree without it dying.*

as a tree falls, so shall it lie proverbial saying; mid 16th century, meaning that one should not change from one's long established practices and customs because of approaching death, although contextual use suggests the meaning that one should die and be buried where one has lived. The original allusion is biblical, to Ecclesiastes 11:3, 'If the tree fall toward the South, or toward the North, in the place where the tree falleth, there let it lie.'

tree-goose a former name for the ➤ BARNACLE *goose*, which was traditionally believed to grow on trees in the form of barnacles.

tree-hugger a (derogatory) term for an environmental campaigner, used in reference to the practice of embracing a tree in an attempt to prevent it from being felled.

the tree is known by its fruit proverbial saying, early 16th century, meaning that a person is judged by what they do and produce; originally with biblical allusion to Matthew 12:33, 'The tree is known by his fruit.'

tree of knowledge in the Bible, the 'tree of the knowledge of good and evil' (Genesis 2:9) in the Garden of Eden, the fruit of which was forbidden to Adam and Eve, but which they ate as a result of the serpent's temptation of Eve.

tree of liberty a tree (or a pole) planted in celebration of a revolution or victory securing liberty; often in reference to the French Revolution.

> The tree of liberty must be refreshed from time to time with the blood of patriots and tyrants. It is its natural manure.
> — Thomas Jefferson letter, 13 November 1787

tree of life in the Bible, a tree in the Garden of Eden whose fruit imparts eternal life; in Genesis 3:24, God judges that disobedient man must be expelled from Eden 'lest he put forth his hand, and take also of the tree of life, and eat, and live for ever'.

The phrase *tree of life* is used for an imaginary branching, tree-like structure representing the evolutionary divergence of all living creatures; in the Kabbalah, it is a diagram in the form of a tree bearing spheres, each of which represents a ➤ SEPHIRA.

trefoil an ornamental design of three rounded lobes like a clover leaf, used typically in architectural tracery.

Tregeagle in Cornwall, a spirit hunted over the moors by the Devil and his hounds, noted for his roaring and howling.

trek see ➤ GREAT *Trek*.

Trekkie informal term for a fan of the cult US science-fiction television programme ➤ STAR *Trek*.

trench a ditch dug by troops to provide a place of shelter from enemy fire, often as part of a connected system of such ditches forming an army's line; **the trenches** is the term used for the battlefields of northern France and Belgium in the First World War.

trench fever a highly contagious rickettsial disease transmitted by lice, that infested soldiers in the trenches in the First World War.

trench foot a painful condition of the feet caused by long immersion in cold water or mud and marked by blackening and death of surface tissue, often suffered by soldiers in the trenches in the First World War.

Council of Trent an ecumenical council of the Roman Catholic Church, held in three sessions between 1545 and 1563 in Trento. Prompted by the opposition of the Reformation, the council clarified and redefined the Church's doctrine, abolished many ecclesiastical abuses, and strengthened the authority of the papacy. These measures provided the Church with a solid foundation for the Counter-Reformation.

Trent affair during the American Civil War, an incident in which two Confederate commissioners were seized by the Union navy from the *Trent*, a neutral British ship; the British govenment demanded an apology, and to avert war the Secretary of State William Seward acknowledged that the matter should have been brought to adjudication.

> And Palmerston being insolent
> To Lincoln and Seward over the *Trent*.
> — Alice Duer Miller *The White Cliffs* (1941)

See also ➤ ALABAMA *claims*.

tressure in heraldry, a thin border inset from the edge of a shield, narrower than an orle and usually borne double.

tret an allowance of extra weight formerly made to purchasers of certain goods to compensate for waste during transportation; the word is recorded from the late 15th century and comes from an Old French variant of *trait* 'draught'.

See also ➤ TARE *and tret*.

Tretyakov Gallery an art gallery in Moscow, one of the largest in the world. It houses exhibits ranging from early Russian art to contemporary work, and has a huge collection of icons. It is named after P. M. Tretyakov (1832–98), who founded it in 1856.

Richard Trevithick (1771–1833), English engineer. His chief contribution was in the use of high-pressure steam to drive a double-acting engine. Trevithick built the world's first railway locomotive (1804) and many stationary engines.

tria juncta in uno Latin motto of the ➤ *Order of the* BATH, 'three joined in one'; the motto appears to date from the early 17th century, and may symbolize the union of the crowns of England and France (at this time the English royal arms still carried the traditional claim to French sovereignty adopted during the Hundred Years' War) with Scotland under James I.

triad a group or set of three connected people or things, as, a Welsh form of literary composition with an arrangement of subjects or statements in groups of three.

The name *Triad* is used for a secret society originating in China, typically involved in organized crime; it comes from Chinese *San Ho Hui*, literally 'triple union society', which was said to mean 'the union of Heaven, Earth, and Man'. The original society was formed in the early 18th century, with the alleged purpose of ousting the ➤ MANCHU dynasty.

trial a formal examination of evidence by a judge, typically before a jury, in order to decide guilt in a case of criminal or civil proceedings. The word is recorded from late Middle English, and comes from Anglo-Norman French, or from Latin *triallum*.

See also ➤ PYX², ➤ SCOPES *trial*.

triangle see ➤ BERMUDA *Triangle*, ➤ *the* GOLDEN *Triangle*, ➤ PASCAL'*s triangle*, ➤ SIERPINSKI *triangle*.

triangular number any of the series of numbers (1, 3, 6, 10, 15, etc.) obtained by continued summation of the natural numbers 1, 2, 3, 4, 5, etc.

Trianon either of two small palaces in the great park at Versailles in France. The larger was built by Louis XIV in 1687; the smaller, the **Petit Trianon**, built by Louis XV 1762–8, was used first by his mistress Madame du Barry (1743–93) and afterwards by ➤ MARIE *Antoinette*. Both *Trianon* and *Petit Trianon* may be used allusively to refer to the imitation of peasant life practised there by Marie Antoinette and her court.

> Any 'simplicity' of Tony's would be the purest artifice, a Petit Trianon of titled milkmaids and silver churns.
> — James Merrill *A Different Person* (1993)

tribe see also ➤ IDOLS *of the tribe, cave, market, and theatre*.

City of the Tribes an informal name for Galway; the term *tribes of Galway* was used for Irish families or communities having the same surname.

Tribes of Israel the twelve divisions of ancient Israel, each traditionally descended from one of the twelve sons of Jacob. Ten of the tribes (Asher, Dan, Gad, Issachar, Levi, Manasseh, Naphtali, Reuben, Simeon, and Zebulun, known as the **Lost Tribes**) were deported to captivity in Assyria *c.*720 BC, leaving only the tribes of Judah and Benjamin. Also called ➤ TWELVE *Tribes of Israel*.

See also ➤ LOST *Tribes of Israel*, ➤ TWELVE *Tribes of Israel*.

Tribuna an octagonal room in the ➤ UFFIZI at Florence containing many famous paintings and statues; it is first mentioned in English in the diary of John Evelyn (1620–1706).

tribunal see ➤ REVOLUTIONARY *Tribunal*.

tribune an official in ancient Rome (also known as the **tribune of the people**) chosen by the plebeians to protect their interests; in extended and figurative usage, a popular leader, a champion of the people. The word is recorded from late Middle English, and comes from Latin *tribunus*, literally 'head of a tribe'.

Tribune Group a left-wing group within the British Labour Party consisting of supporters of the views put forward in the weekly journal *Tribune*.

in a trice in a moment, very quickly. In late Middle English, *trice* meant 'a tug', figuratively 'an instant';

the word comes from Middle Duch *trīsen* 'pull sharply', related to *trīse* 'pulley'.

trick or treat a children's custom of calling at houses at Halloween with the threat of pranks if they are not given a small gift (often used as a greeting by children doing this); the practice is first recorded in the US in the mid 20th century.

trickle-down of an economic system, in which the poorest gradually benefit as a result of the increasing wealth of the richest.

> Trickle-down theory—the less than elegant metaphor that if one feeds the horse enough oats, some will pass through to the road for the sparrows.
> — John Kenneth Galbraith *The Culture of Contentment* (1992)

there are tricks in every trade proverbial saying, mid 17th century; meaning that the practise of every skill is likely to involve some trickery or dishonesty.

tricolour a flag with three bands or blocks of different colours, especially the French national flag (adopted at the Revolution) with equal upright bands of blue, white, and red.

tricorn an imaginary creature with three horns.

tricoteuse a woman who sits and knits, used in particular in reference to a number of women who did this, during the French Revolution, while attending meetings of the Convention or watching public executions.

> Exhausted sunflowers rested their heads on broken necks while the snails gathered below like *tricoteuses*.
> — Douglas Coupland *Generation X* (1991)

trident a three-pronged spear, especially as an attribute of ➤ POSEIDON (Neptune) or ➤ BRITANNIA.

Tridentine of or relating to the ➤ *Council of* TRENT (1545–63), especially as the basis of Roman Catholic doctrine; the name comes from *Tridentum*, Latin name of the city of Trent in the Tyrol.

Tridentine mass the Latin Eucharistic liturgy used by the Roman Catholic Church from 1570 until the changes instituted by the ➤ *Second* VATICAN *Council* (1962–5) came into effect.

trieteric in ancient Greece or Rome, a festival, especially one in honour of ➤ BACCHUS, celebrated every third year.

triffid in the science fiction novel *The Day of the Triffids* (1951) by John Wyndham, the *triffids* are a race of predatory plants which are capable of growing to a gigantic size and are possessed of locomotor ability and a poisonous sting. The name is used allusively of plants showing vigorous growth, or more widely to denote invasive and rapid development.

The name is probably an alteration of *trifid* 'divided into three', as the original plants were supported on 'three bluntly-tapered projections'.

> River banks are being colonised by the giant hogweed, a triffid-like exotic with big umbrellas for leaves.
> — *World* (BBC) April 1992

triforium a gallery or arcade above the arches of the nave, choir, and transepts of a church. The Anglo-Latin term is found first in the chronicle of Gervase of Canterbury, *c*.1185, and originally referred only to Canterbury Cathedral; it was mentioned by Viollet-le-Duc in his *Dictionnaire d'Architecture* (1868) as having been introduced into architectural nomenclature by the English archaeologists, and from the 19th century was extended as a general term. The origin of the word is unknown.

trigon in astrology, a former term for ➤ TRINE.

Trilby name of the heroine of George du Maurier's eponymous novel (1894), a beautiful artist's model who becomes a successful singer under the tutelage of ➤ SVENGALI. The *trilby* hat, a soft felt hat with a narrow brim and indented crown, is named for her, as such a hat was worn in the stage version, and in the first part of the 20th century feet were informally known as *trilbies*, as du Maurier's heroine was admired for her feet.

> Erich . . . conducted her to a couch, black Svengali to her Trilby, and started to Germantalk some life into her.
> — F. Leiber *Big Time* (1961)

trilogy in ancient Greece, a series of three tragedies performed one after the other and originally connected in subject, performed at Athens at the festival of Dionysus; in extended usage, a group of related novels, plays, films, operas, or albums.

the Trimmer nickname of the English politician and essayist Lord Halifax (1633–95), in the sense of one who inclines to each of two opposite political sides as interest dictates; Halifax himself, however, accepted the term in the sense of one who kept the ship of state on an even keel:

> This innocent word *Trimmer* signifieth no more than this, that if men are together in a boat, and one part of the company would weigh it down on one side, another would make it lean as much to the contrary.
> — Lord Halifax *Character of a Trimmer* (1685, printed 1688)

Trimurti in Hinduism, the trinity of ➤ Brahma, ➤ Vishnu, and ➤ Shiva; the word comes from Sanskrit *tri* 'three' + *mūrti* 'form'.

trine in astrology, denoting the aspect of two heavenly bodies 120° (one third of the zodiac) apart. Formerly also called *trigon.*

Trinian see ➤ St *Trinian's.*

Trinitarian a person who believes in the doctrine of the Trinity. The word in this sense is recorded from the mid 16th century, and in its earliest uses is applied to those whose belief in the Trinity was not regarded as orthodox.

the Trinity the three persons of the Christian Godhead; Father, Son, and Holy Spirit. The term is recorded from Middle English, and comes ultimately from Latin *trinus* 'threefold'.

Trinity Brethren the members of ➤ Trinity House.

Trinity House a guild or fraternity originally established at Deptford, incorporated in the reign of Henry VIII, formerly having the official regulation of British shipping, and now chiefly concerned with the licensing of pilots and the erection and maintenance of lighthouses, buoys, and other aids to navigation, on the coasts of England and Wales.

Trinity Sunday the next Sunday after Pentecost, observed in the Western Christian Church as a feast in honour of the Holy Trinity.

Trinity term a session of the High Court beginning after Easter; (in some universities) the term beginning after Easter.

trip see ➤ clunk, *click, every trip*, ➤ *trip the light* fantastic.

the Tripitaka the sacred canon of ➤ Theravada Buddhism, written in the Pali language. The name comes from Sanskrit, meaning literally 'the three baskets or collections'.

Triple Alliance a union or association between three powers or states, in particular that made in 1668 between England, the Netherlands, and Sweden against France, and that in 1882 between Germany, Austria-Hungary, and Italy against France and Russia.

triple crown[1] a name for the ➤ papal *tiara*, recorded from the mid 16th century, and referred to in Shakespeare's *2 Henry VI* (1592), 'I would the college of the Cardinals Would choose him Pope, and carry him to Rome, And set the triple crown upon his head.'

triple crown[2] in horse-racing, the winning of the Two Thousand Guineas, the Derby, and the St Leger by the same horse.

Triple Entente an early 20th-century alliance between Great Britain, France, and Russia. Originally a series of loose agreements, the Triple Entente began to assume the nature of a more formal alliance as the prospect of war with the Central Powers became more likely, and formed the basis of the Allied powers in the First World War.

triple-witching hour in the US, informal name for the unpredictable final hour of trading on the US Stock Exchange before the simultaneous expiry of three different kinds of options; the term is a development of ➤ witching *hour.*

tripos the final honours examination for a BA degree at Cambridge University. The word comes (in the late 16th century) from an alteration of Latin *tripus* 'tripod', with reference to the stool on which a designated graduate (known as the 'Tripos') sat to deliver a satirical speech at the degree ceremony. A sheet of humorous verses (at one time composed by the Tripos) was published on this occasion until the late 19th century, on the back of which the list of successful candidates for the honours degree in mathematics was originally printed; hence the current sense.

trippant in heraldry, (of a stag or deer) represented as walking.

Triptolemus in Greek mythology, a young man selected by the goddess Demeter to teach the skills of agriculture to humankind.

triptych a picture or relief carving on three panels, typically hinged together vertically and used as an altarpiece. The word is recorded from the mid 18th century, and denoted originally a set of three writing tablets, hinged or tied together; it is formed from *tri-* 'three' on the pattern of *diptych.*

Trisagion a hymn, especially in the Orthodox Church, with a triple invocation of God as holy. The word is recorded from late Middle English and comes from Greek, from *tris* 'three times' + *hagios* 'holy'.

triskaidephobia extreme superstition regarding the number thirteen; the word is recorded from the early 20th century.

triskelion a Celtic symbol consisting of three legs or lines radiating from a centre, as in the emblem of the Isle of Man.

Trismegistus an epithet, meaning 'thrice-greatest', of the Egyptian god Hermes (see ➤ HERMES *Trismegistus*).

Tristram in medieval legend, a knight (also called *Tristan*) who was the lover of ➤ ISEULT and nephew of her husband king Mark of Cornwall; sent by the king to Ireland to bring the princess to Cornwall, Tristram falls in love with her, a love which is reinforced by the love potion which they accidentally drink, and which binds them to one another.

Despite their fated love, Tristram leaves Cornwall, and later marries Iseult of Brittany; in some versions of the story, he returns to Cornwall and is killed by the jealous Mark, in others (used by Wagner) he falls ill, and asks that Iseult of Ireland be sent for. The ship bringing her is to fly a white sail if she is on board; his jealous wife tells him that it is black, and Tristram dies before Iseult of Ireland can reach him.

The story of Tristram is now seen as one of the Arthurian romances, but it was incorporated at a late stage.

Tristram Shandy paradox a paradox of infinity, named after the eponymous hero of Sterne's novel *Tristram Shandy* (1759–67), who concluded that it was hopeless to attempt writing his biography since at the end of two years he had recorded the events of only the first two days of his life.

tritheism in Christian theology, the doctrine of or belief in the three persons of the Trinity as three distinct gods.

Triton in Greek mythology, a minor sea god usually represented as a man with a fish's tail and carrying a trident and shell-trumpet.

Triton of the minnows the type of something large or great contrasted with something small and insignificant, often with reference to Shakespeare, from the scene in which Coriolanus furiously rejects the pretensions of the tribunes:

> Hear you this Triton of the minnows? mark you
> His absolute 'shall'?
> — William Shakespearre *Coriolanus* (1608)

triumph the processional entry of a victorious general with his army and spoils of the campaign into ancient Rome, permission for which was granted by the senate in honour of an important achievement in war. Recorded from late Middle English, the word comes via Old French from Latin

triump(h)us, probably from Greek *thriambos* 'hymn to Bacchus'.

triumph-gate the gate through which a triumphal procession entered ancient Rome.

triumvir in ancient Rome, each of three public officers jointly responsible for overseeing any of the administrative departments.

trivet see ➤ RIGHT *as a trivet.*

Trivia name by which John Gay invoked a 'goddess of the highways' in his poem *Trivia, or the Art of Walking the Streets of London* (1716), from Latin *trivium* 'place where three roads meet'.

The modern word *trivia* 'details, considerations, or pieces of information of little importance or value' dates from the early 20th century.

Trivial Pursuit trademark name for a board game in which players advance by answering general knowledge questions in various subject areas.

> It is easy to dismiss such learning as fact-loading for a Trivial Pursuit marathon.
> — *Saturday Night* June 1993

trivium an introductory course at a medieval university involving the study of grammar, rhetoric, and logic; with the ➤ QUADRIVIUM, forming the ➤ SEVEN *liberal arts.* The word comes from Latin, and means literally 'place where three roads meet'.

trochilus a small Egyptian bird (not certainly identified) said by the ancients to pick the teeth of the crocodile.

> When the crocodile yawns, the trochilus flies into his mouth and cleans his teeth.
> — Aristotle *Historia Animalium*

troglodyte especially in prehistoric times, a person who lived in a cave; in figurative use, a person who is regarded as being deliberately ignorant or old-fashioned. The word is recorded from the late 15th century, and comes via Latin from Greek *trōglodutēs*, alteration of the name of an Ethiopian people, influenced by *trōglē* 'hole'.

Troilus a Trojan prince, the son of ➤ PRIAM and Hecuba, killed by ➤ ACHILLES. In medieval legends of the Trojan war he is portrayed as the forsaken lover of Cressida.

true as Troilus completely devoted; with allusion to Troilus's speech to Cressida in Shakespeare's play:

> Yet, after all comparisons of truth,
> As truth's authentic author to be cited,
> 'As true as Troilus' shall crown up the verse.
> — William Shakespeare *Troilus and Cressida* (1602)

Trojan Horse in Greek mythology, a hollow wooden statue of a horse in which the Greeks are said to have concealed themselves in order to enter and capture Troy; despite the warning of ➤ LAOCOON, the Trojans breached the city walls to draw the horse inside, so that the Greeks were able the following night to overrun and sack the city.

Trojan Horse in figurative use denotes a person or thing intended secretly to undermine or bring about the downfall of an enemy or opponent; in computing, it is a program designed to breach the security of a computer system while ostensibly performing some innocuous function.

See also ➤ TIMEO *Danaos et dona ferentes.*

Trojan War the legendary ten-year siege of Troy by a coalition of Greeks led by ➤ AGAMEMNON, described in Homer's *Iliad.* The Greeks were attempting to recover ➤ HELEN, wife of Menelaus, who had been abducted by the Trojan prince Paris. The war ended with the capture of the city by a trick: the Greeks ostensibly ended the siege but left behind a group of men concealed in a hollow wooden horse (the ➤ TROJAN *Horse*) so large that the city walls had to be breached for it to be drawn inside.

troll[1] a mythical, cave-dwelling being depicted in folklore as either a giant or a dwarf, typically having a very ugly appearance. The word was adopted in English from Scandinavian in the middle of the 19th century, but in Shetland and Orkney, where the form is now *trow,* it has survived from the Norse dialect formerly spoken there.

troll[2] send (an e-mail message or posting on the Internet) intended to provoke a response from the reader by containing errors. The word is a figurative use of the verb *troll* 'fish by trailing a baited line along behind a boat'.

Anthony Trollope (1815–82), English novelist. He worked for the General Post Office from 1834 to 1867 and introduced the pillar box to Britain. He is best-known for the six 'Barsetshire' novels, including *The Warden* (1855) and *Barchester Towers* (1857), and for the six political 'Palliser' novels; W. H. Auden said of him, 'Of all novelists in any country, Trollope best understands the role of money. Compared with him, even Balzac is too romantic.'

trompe l'œil visual illusion in art, especially as used to trick the eye into perceiving a painted detail as a three-dimensional object. The term is French, and means literally 'deceive the eye'.

Trondheim a fishing port in west central Norway which was the capital of Norway during the Viking period.

troop the colour perform the ceremony of parading a regiment's flag along ranks of soldiers as part of the ceremonial of the mounting of the guard; the first standing order on the subject (although it does not contain the word) is dated May 1755, but the name may date back to the time of Marlborough.

In Britain a ceremony of **trooping the colour** is carried out on the monarch's official birthday.

> Even during the annus horribilis, Trooping the Colour took place on Horse Guards Parade in June: the Queen in her uniform reviewed her brightly arrayed troops.
> — *New York Times Magazine* 13 June 1993

trooper a soldier in a troop of cavalry; the term was used in connexion with the Covenanting Army which invaded England in 1640, and was used in the English Army in 1660. In the first establishment of Horse Regiments after the Restoration, the strength of a troop of horse was 1 Captain, 1 Lieutenant, and 60 Troopers.

The expression **swear like a trooper** meaning 'swear profusely' is recorded from the mid 18th century.

trope a figurative or metaphorical use of a word or expression. The word is recorded from the mid 16th century and comes via Latin from Greek *tropos* 'turn, way, trope', from *trepein* 'to turn'.

Trophonius in Greek mythology, an architect, sometimes said to be the son of Apollo, who with his brother Agamedes reputedly built the temple of Apollo at Delphi; worshipped as a god, he had an oracle in a cave in Boeotia, which was said to affect those who entered with such awe that they never smiled again.

> There is great danger that they who enter smiling into this Trophonian cave, will come out of it sad and serious conspirators.
> — Edmund Burke *Two Letters on the Proposals for Peace with the Regicide Directory* (1796)

trophy in ancient Greece or Rome, the weapons of a defeated army set up as a memorial of victory, originally on the field of battle, later in any public place. The term was then extended to mean a spoil or prize won in war or hunting, especially one kept or displayed as a memorial, and finally a cup or other object serving as a prize or memento of victory or success.

The word is recorded from the late 15th century,

and comes via French and Latin from Greek tropaion, from *tropē* 'a rout', from *trepein* 'to turn'.

trophy wife a young, attractive wife regarded as a status symbol for an older man; the term is recorded from the late 1980s.

tropic the parallel of latitude 23°26′ north (**tropic of Cancer**) or south (**tropic of Capricorn**) of the equator; **the tropics** is the name given to the region between the tropics of Cancer and Capricorn. The word is recorded from late Middle English, denoting the point on the ecliptic reached by the sun at the solstice.

Leon Trotsky (1879–1940) Russian revolutionary. He helped to organize the October Revolution with Lenin, and built up the Red Army. He was expelled from the party by Stalin in 1927 and exiled in 1929. He settled in Mexico in 1937, where he was later murdered with an ice-pick by a Stalinist assassin.

Trotskyism the political or economic principles of Leon Trotsky, especially the theory that socialism should be established throughout the world by continuing revolution.

troubador a French medieval lyric poet composing and singing in Provençal in the 11th to 13th centuries, especially on the theme of courtly love. The word is French, and comes from Provençal *trobador*, from *trobar* 'find, invent, compose in verse'.

a trouble shared is a trouble halved proverbial saying, mid 20th century; meaning that discussing a problem will lessen its impact.

never trouble trouble till trouble troubles you proverbial saying, late 19th century; another version of the advice that one should let well alone.

troubles see also ➤ *do not meet* TROUBLES *halfway*, ➤ PACK *up your troubles in your old kit-bag*.

the Troubles any of various periods of civil war or unrest in Ireland, especially in 1919–23 and (in Northern Ireland) since 1968; the expression is first recorded in the 19th century as referring to the Irish rebellion of 1641.

trouvère a medieval epic poet in northern France in the 11th–14th centuries; the word comes from Old French *trovere*, from *trover* 'to find'.

Troy in Homeric legend, the city of King ➤ PRIAM, besieged for ten years by the Greeks during the

➤ TROJAN *War*. It was regarded as having been a purely legendary city until ➤ *Heinrich* SCHLIEMANN identified the mound of Hissarlik on the NE Aegean coast of Turkey as the site of Troy. Schliemann's excavations showed the mound to be composed of nine main strata, dating from the early Bronze Age to the Roman era. The stratum known as Troy VIIa is believed to be that of the Homeric city; the city was apparently sacked and destroyed by fire in the mid 13th century BC, a period coinciding with the Mycenaean civilization of Greece.
    See also ➤ SIEGE *of Troy*.

Troy town a scene of disorder or confusion, a bewildering place, a maze; perhaps originally with reference to the destruction of captured Troy.

troy weight a system of weights used mainly for precious metals and gems, with a pound of 12 ounces or 5,760 grains. The expression comes (in late Middle English) from a weight used at the fair of *Troyes* in northern France.

Troyes see ➤ CHRÉTIEN *de Troyes*.

Troynovant poetic and literary name for London, supposedly founded by the legendary Trojan ➤ BRUTUS.

truce see also ➤ FLAG *of truce*.

truce of God a suspension of hostilities between armies, or of private feuds, ordered by the Church during certain days and seasons in medieval times.

Truck Acts in the UK, a series of Acts directed, from 1830 onwards, against the system whereby workers received their wages in the form of vouchers for goods redeemable only at a special shop (often run by the employer). The Acts required wages to be paid in cash.

true see also ➤ *the* COURSE *of true love never did run smooth*, ➤ *true as* TROILUS, ➤ *what* EVERYBODY *says must be true*, ➤ *what is* NEW *cannot be true*.

true bill a bill of indictment found by a grand jury to be supported by sufficient evidence to justify the hearing of a case; in allusive use, a true statement or charge.

true-blue in early use (from the mid 17th century), applied to the Scottish Presbyterian or Whig party, the Covenanters having adopted *blue* as their colour in contradistinction to the royal *red*. Later (in the current sense), staunchly loyal to the Tory, or Conservative, Party; in the US, extremely loyal or orthodox.

true-love knot a kind of knot with interlacing bows on each side, symbolizing the bonds of love.

many a true word is spoken in jest proverbial saying, late 14th century.

truepenny archaic term for a trusty or honest person, meaning someone who is like a coin of genuine metal.

Harry S. Truman (1884–1972), American Democratic statesman, who as Vice-president became 33rd President of the US on the death of Franklin Roosevelt in 1945. He subsequently fought and won the election of 1948, although the *Chicago Tribune* of 3 November 1948, unwisely relying on early polls, was published with the headline 'Dewey defeats Truman'.

As President, Truman authorized the use of the atom bomb against Hiroshima and Nagasaki, introduced the Marshall Plan of emergency aid in 1948 to war-shattered European countries, and involved the US in the Korean War. He is associated with two political sayings, 'The buck stops here' (motto on his desk), and 'If you can't stand the heat, get out of the kitchen.'

Truman doctrine the principle that the US should give support to countries or peoples threatened by Soviet forces or Communist insurrection. First expressed in 1947 by US President Truman in a speech to Congress seeking aid for Greece and Turkey, the doctrine was seen by the Communists as an open declaration of the cold war.

trump see also ➤ LAST *trump*.

trump in bridge, whist, and similar card games, a playing card of the suit chosen to rank above the others, which can win a trick where a card of a different suit has been led; (in a tarot pack) any of a special suit of 22 cards depicting symbolic and typical figures and scenes. The word is an alteration of *triumph*, once used in card games in the same sense.

See also ➤ TURN *up trumps*.

trumpery attractive articles of little value or use; practices or beliefs that are superficially or visually appealing but have little real value or worth. The

term comes (in late Middle English, denoting trickery) from Old French *tromperie*, from *tromper* 'deceive'.

trumpet see also ➤ DRUM-*and-trumpet history*.

trumpeter see ➤ KING *of Spain's trumpeter*.

feast of trumpets a Jewish autumn festival observed at the beginning of the month Tishri, characterized by the blowing of trumpets.

trust see ➤ BRAINS *trust*, ➤ *put your trust in God, and keep your* POWDER *dry*.

truth the quality or state of being true, that which is true or in accordance with fact or reality; in biblical allusion, often with reference to the account in John 18:38 of the examination of Jesus by Pilate, when 'Pilate saith unto him, What is truth?' This is alluded to in Francis Bacon's 'Of Truth' (*Essays*, 1625), 'What is truth? said jesting Pilate; and would not stay for an answer.'

See also ➤ ECONOMICAL *with the truth*, ➤ FOUR *noble truths*, ➤ *the* GREATER *the truth, the greater the libel*, ➤ *the* MOMENT *of truth*, ➤ NAKED *truth*, ➤ TELL *the truth and shame the Devil*.

Sojourner Truth (*c.*1797–1883), American evangelist and reformer. Born into slavery, she was sold to an Isaac Van Wagener, who released her in 1827. She became a zealous evangelist, preaching in favour of black rights and women's suffrage. In 1864 she was received at the White House by Abraham Lincoln.

Truth and Reconciliation Commission a commission set up by a South African Parliamentary Act on 26 July 1995 to investigate claims of abuses during the Apartheid era.

truth drug a drug supposedly able to induce a state in which a person answers questions truthfully.

there is truth in wine proverbial saying, mid 16th century; meaning that a person who is drunk is more likely to speak the truth.

truth is stranger than fiction proverbial saying, early 19th century; originally with reference to Byron's *Don Juan* (1823), 'Truth is always strange, Stranger than fiction.'

truth lies at the bottom of a well proverbial saying, mid 16th century; in earlier classical sources, the saying 'we know nothing certainly, for truth lies in the deep' is attributed to Democritus, and 'truth lies sunk in a well' is attributed to the 3rd–4th century Latin author Lactantius.

the truth, the whole truth, and nothing but the truth the absolute truth, without concealment or addition; part of the formula of the oath taken by witnesses in court.

truth will out proverbial saying, mid 15th century; meaning that in the end what has really happened will become apparent.

tsaddik in Judaism, a man of exemplary righteousness; a Hasidic spiritual leader or sage.

tsar an emperor of Russia before 1917. The Russian word *tsar* reprents Latin *Caesar*; it is first recorded in English in the mid 16th century. In Russia itself it was partially used by the Grand Duke Ivan III (1462–1505) and his son, but was formally assumed by Ivan IV in 1547. Peter the Great introduced the title *imperator* 'emperor' and the official style shortly before the Revolution of 1917 was 'Emperor of all the Russias, Tsar of Poland, and Grand Duke of Finland', but the Russian popular appellation was still *tsar*.

The title *tsar* was also used by Serbian rulers of the 14th century, as Tsar Stephen Dushan.

tsarevich the eldest son of an emperor of Russia.

tsitsith the tassels on the corners of the Jewish tallith or prayer-shawl. Also, (the tassels on each corner of) a small tasselled rectangular garment with a large hole in the middle, worn under the shirt by orthodox Jews.

Tsongdu the national assembly of Tibet.

tsunami a long high sea wave caused by an earthquake or other disturbance; the word is Japanese, and comes from *tsu* 'harbour' + *nami* 'wave'.

tsung a Chinese ritual artefact, typically of jade, consisting of a hollow cylinder with central rectangular casing, usually thought to symbolize the fertility of the earth.

Tsushima a Japanese island in the Korea Strait, between South Korea and Japan, which in 1905 was the scene of a defeat for the Russian navy during the Russo-Japanese War.

Tu Fu (AD 712–70), Chinese poet, noted for his bitter satiric poems attacking social injustice and corruption at court.

tu quoque an argument which consists of turning an accusation back on the accuser; the phrase is Latin, and means literally 'thou also'.

Tuatha Dé Danann in Irish mythology, the members of an ancient race said to have inhabited Ireland before the historical Irish. Formerly believed to have been a real people, they are credited with the possession of magical powers and great wisdom. The name is Irish, literally 'people of the goddess Danann'.

tub a tub is the emblem of ➤ St NICHOLAS *of Myra*. See also ➤ *a* TALE *of a tub*, ➤ *three* BOYS *in a tub*.

every tub must stand on its own bottom proverbial saying, mid 16th century; meaning that it is necessary to support oneself by one's own efforts.

throw out a tub to the whale create a diversion, especially in order to escape a threatened danger; the term is first used by Swift (see ➤ *a* TALE *of a tub*) explaining the nautical custom of throwing an empty tub over the side when a whale is encountered to divert it from the ship itself.

tub-thumping expressing opinions in a loud and violent or dramatic manner (in the mid-17th century, *tub* was a derogatory term for a pulpit, especially one used by a nonconformist preacher).

Friar Tuck a member of ➤ ROBIN *Hood*'s company, a fat and jovial friar who despite his order is noted for his pugnacity.

Tuckahoe a local nickname for the lowlands of Virginia and for an inhabitant of this district, from the name of a root or other underground plant part formerly eaten by North American Indians.

one's best bib and tucker one's smartest clothes, an expression recorded from the mid 18th century; a *tucker* was a piece of lace or linen worn in or around the top of a bodice or as an insert at the front of a low-cut dress.

Tudor name of the English royal dynasty which held the throne from the accession of Henry VII in 1485 until the death of Elizabeth I in 1603; they were descended from the Welsh Owen Tudor, who married Catherine, widowed queen of Henry V.

See also ➤ STOCKBROKER's *Tudor*.

Tudor rose a conventionalized, typically five-lobed figure of a rose used in architectural and other decoration in the Tudor period, in particular a combination of the red and white roses of Lancaster or York adopted as a badge by Henry VII.

Tudorbethan of a contemporary house or architectural design, imitative of Tudor and Elizabethan styles.

Tuesday the day of the week before Wednesday and following Monday. In Old English the form of the word was *Tīwesdæg* named after the Germanic god *Tīw* (associated with Mars); translation of Latin *dies Marti* 'day of Mars'.

See also ➤ *Monday's* CHILD *is fair of face.*

Tuesdays

Hock Tuesday	the second Tuesday after Easter Sunday
Shrove Tuesday	the day before Ash Wednesday
Super Tuesday	in the US, the day on which several states hold primary elections

---

tuffet a tuft or clump of something; (perhaps from a misunderstanding of the nursery rhyme, 'Little Miss Muffet sat on a tuffet') a footstool or low seat.

Tugendbund a secret political organization founded in Königsberg in 1808 to promote Prussian nationalism and anti-Napoleonic feeling within Germany (the society was officially disbanded in 1809). The name is German, and means literally 'league of virtue'.

tughra a Turkish ornamental monogram incorporating the name and title of the Sultan.

Tuileries formal gardens next to the Louvre in Paris, laid out by André Le Nôtre in the mid 17th century. The gardens are all that remain of the Tuileries Palace, a royal residence begun in 1564 by Catherine de' Medici and burnt down in 1871 during the Commune of Paris. The name is French and means literally 'tile-works', as the palace was built on the site of an ancient tile-works.

Tula the ancient capital city of the Toltecs, generally identified with a site near the town of Tula in Hidalgo State, central Mexico.

tulchan derogatory term for a titular bishop appointed in Scotland immediately after the Reformation, in whose names the revenues of the sees were drawn by the lay barons. The word is Gaelic, and meant literally a calf's skin placed beneath a cow to make her yield milk freely.

tulip the first mention of the plant by a Western European is by the Emperor's ambassador on the way from Adrianople to Constantinople, *c.*1554. It was grown by the Fuggers at Augsburg (where it was seen and described in 1561), and was introduced successively in Vienna, Mechlin, France, and England.

The name (recorded from the late 16th century, when it was introduced into Western Europe from Turkey) comes via French and Turkish from Persian *dulband* 'turban', from the shape of the expanded flower.

tulipomania the excessive enthusiasm for tulips current in Holland in the 17th century, during which tulip bulbs became the subject of much financial investment and speculation, resulting in the crash of 1637.

Jethro Tull (1674–1741), English agriculturalist. In 1701 he invented the seed drill, a machine which could sow seeds in accurately spaced rows at a controlled rate. This made possible the control of weeds by horse-drawn hoe, reducing the need for farm labourers.

tulsi a kind of basil, sacred to ➤ VISHNU, which is cultivated by Hindus as a sacred plant.

Tulsidas (*c.*1543–1623), Indian poet. A leading Hindu devotional poet, he is chiefly remembered for the *Ramcaritmanas* (*c.*1574–7), a work consisting of seven cantos based on the Sanskrit epic the Ramayana. The poet's expression of worship or bhakti for Rama led to the cult of Rama (rather than that of Krishna) dominating the Hindu culture of northern India.

tumbaga an alloy of gold and copper commonly used in pre-Columbian South and Central America.

Tumbledown Dick a nickname for Richard Cromwell, briefly Protector after the death of his father ➤ *Oliver* CROMWELL; the *Verney Memoirs* for 1659 note that he 'retired into complete obscurity…with the people's nickname of Tumbledown Dick.'

tumbler a drinking glass with straight sides and no handle or stem (originally, such a glass had a rounded bottom so as not to stand upright).

tumbril an open cart that tilted backwards to empty out its load, in particular one used to convey condemned prisoners to the guillotine during the French Revolution.

tummler in the US, a person who makes things happen, in particular a professional entertainer whose function is to encourage an audience to participate in the entertainments or activities. The word comes via Yiddish from German *tummeln* 'to stir'.

tumulus an ancient burial mound; a barrow. Recorded from late Middle English, the word is from Latin, and is related to *tumere* 'to swell'.

Tunbridge Wells a spa town in Kent, founded in the 1630s after the discovery of iron-rich springs, the town was patronized by royalty throughout the 17th and 18th centuries, frequently appearing in the humorous phrase **Disgusted of Tunbridge Wells**. The popular coupling of *disgusted* with *Tunbridge Wells* (often portrayed as home to the reactionary, conservative middle-class), probably originates from a 1978 BBC radio program called *Disgusted, Tunbridge Wells*.

tune see also ➤ *he who pays the* PIPER *calls the tune,* ➤ *why should the* DEVIL *have all the best tunes.*

the tune the old cow died of traditional description of a series of unmusical or discordant sounds; the expression dates from the early 19th century, and is said to refer to an old ballad in which a piper who had nothing else to give his starving cow played it a tune on his pipe.

tunnel See also ➤ CHANNEL *Tunnel,* ➤ LIGHT *at the end of the tunnel,* ➤ SEIKAN *Tunnel.*

tunnel of love a fairground amusement involving a romantic train- or boat-ride through a darkened tunnel.

Tupperism a saying or generalization characteristic of those in Martin F. Tupper's *Proverbial Philosophy* (1838–42), a moralistic work popular in the 19th century.

> The gradual degeneration of a poetic faith into a ritual of unimaginative Tupperisms.
> — James Russell Lowell *Among my Books* (1870)

Tupperware trademark name for a range of plastic containers used chiefly for storing food, tradionally sold at parties in private homes for prospective purchasers; sometimes referred to allusively as characteristic of middle-class suburbia.

> She neither plays golf nor holds Tupperware parties, but she is big in flower arrangement.
> — *Punch* 16 July 1986

turcopole a soldier of the Order of St John of Jerusalem with light weapons or armour; the name comes via medieval Latin from Byzantine Greek *Tourko-* Turk + *pōlos* 'foal, child', applied to children of a Turkish or Saracen father and a Greek mother. These soldiers were commanded by a *turcopolier.*

the turf horse racing or racecourses, from the grassy track or course over which a race takes place; the term is recorded from the mid 18th century.

turf war an acrimonious dispute between rival groups over territory or a particular sphere of influence. The phrase comes (in the 1970s) from the notion of a *war* over *turf* in the informal sense 'area regarded as personal territory' (originally the area controlled by, for example, a street gang or criminal).

Turin a city in NW Italy on the River Po, which was the capital of the kingdom of Sardinia from 1720 and became the first capital of a unified Italy (1861–4).

Turin Shroud a relic, preserved at Turin since 1578, venerated as the winding-sheet in which Christ's body was wrapped for burial. It bears the imprint of the front and back of a human body as well as markings that correspond to the traditional stigmata. Scientific tests carried out in 1988 dated the shroud to the 13th–14th centuries.

Alan Mathison Turing (1912–54), English mathematician. He developed the concept of a theoretical computing machine, a key step in the development of the first computer, and carried out important code-breaking work in the Second World War. He also investigated artificial intelligence. Turing committed suicide after being prosecuted for homosexuality and forced to undergo hormone treatment.

Turing machine a mathematical model of a hypothetical computing machine which can use a predefined set of rules to determine a result from a set of input variables.

Turing test a test for intelligence in a computer, requiring that a human being should be unable to distinguish the machine from another human being by using the replies to questions put to both.

Turk archaic term for a member of the ruling Muslim population of the Ottoman Empire, or for a member of any of the ancient central Asian peoples who spoke Turkic languages, including the Seljuks and Ottomans; in extended usage, the name was applied to anyone regarded as showing the harshness or cruelty associated with the Turks by Western Europeans.

See also ➤ BYERLEY *Turk,* ➤ YOUNG *Turk.*

the Grand Turk the Ottoman Sultan; also called the *Great Turk.*

turkey a large mainly domesticated game bird native to North America, having a bald head and (in the male) red wattles; it is prized as food, especially on festive occasions such as Christmas and (in the US) Thanksgiving. The name (recorded from the mid 16th century) is short for *turkeycock* or *turkeyhen*, originally applied to the guineafowl (which was imported through Turkey), and then erroneously to the American bird.

See also ➤ COLD *turkey*, ➤ *on Saint* THOMAS *the Divine, kill all turkeys, geese, and swine.*

talk turkey talk frankly and informally; a US expression recorded from the early 19th century, which originally could also mean talk agreeably or affably. The origin is not clear, but *turkey* appears to stand for something of substance (the 'meat') needing to be said.

turkey, heresy, hops, and beer came into England all in one year proverbial saying, late 16th century; perhaps referring to 1521. The *turkey*, found domesticated in Mexico in 1518, was soon afterwards introduced into Europe, in 1521, the Pope conferred on Henry VIII the title ➤ DEFENDER *of the Faith*, in recognition of his opposition to the Lutheran *heresy*, the *hop*-plant is believed to have been introduced into the south of England from Flanders between 1520 and 1524, and *beer* as the name of hopped malt liquor became common only in the 16th century.

Turkish bath a cleansing or relaxing treatment (originally introduced from the East) that involves a period of time spent sitting in a room filled with very hot air or steam, generally followed by washing and massage; a building or room where such a treatment is available.

turn see also ➤ *one* GOOD *turn deserves another*, ➤ *turn a* BLIND *eye*, ➤ TURN *the other cheek*.

turn about is fair play proverbial saying, mid 18th century.

turn over a new leaf adopt a different (now always a better) line of conduct; *leaf* is here the leaf of a book.

a turn-up for the book a completely unexpected (especially welcome) result or happening; *turn-up* the turning up of a particular card or die in a game; *book* as kept by a bookie on a race-course.

turn up trumps turn out better than expected; be very successful or helpful; in allusion to card-playing.

turncoat a person who deserts one party or cause in order to join an opposing one; the term dates from the mid 16th century, and reflects the idea that the person's outer clothing carries the badge of their allegiance.

J. M. W. Turner (1775–1851), English painter. He made his name with landscapes and stormy seascapes, becoming increasingly concerned with depicting the power of light by the use of primary colours, often arranged in a swirling vortex.

> The sky ahead was aglow with a Turneresque riot of colour, framed in East Anglian space.
> — Sybil Marshall *A Nest of Magpies* (1993)

Turpin in a number of chansons de geste, archbishop of Rheims and friend and companion of ➤ CHARLEMAGNE, killed at ➤ RONCESVALLES.

> The padre, full of the lust of holy slaughter like Archbishop Turpin at Roncesvalles.
> — George Macdonald Fraser *The General Danced at Dawn* (1970)

Dick Turpin (1706–39), English highwayman. He was a cattle and deer thief before entering into partnership with Tom King, a notorious highwayman. Turpin eventually fled north, and was hanged at York for horse-stealing. His escapades (often featuring his horse Black Bess, and including a dramatic ride from London to York) were romanticized by Harrison Ainsworth in his novel *Rookwood* (1834).

turtle[1] archaic name for a ➤ TURTLE *dove*, as in the Song of Solomon 2:12, 'the voice of the turtle is heard in the land'.

turtle[2] the name *turtle* is an alteration (originally by English sailors) of *tortoise*. The flesh of various species of the turtle is used as food, and it was traditionally regarded as a feature of civic banquets; in the late 19th century the term **turtledom** was coined for aldermen as consumers of turtle-dinners.

The *Turtles* are a group of four fantasy characters for children, in full, (in the US) **Teenage Mutant Ninja Turtles** or (in the UK) **Teenage Mutant Hero Turtles**, in the form of terrapins who have supposedly been mutated through being covered with radioactive slime in a New York sewer.

In Terry Pratchett's ➤ DISCWORLD series, the world is said to be supported by four elephants carried on the back of a giant turtle; the idea of the universe supported on a turtle's back is derived from Hindu mythology.

turtle dove a small Old World dove with a soft purring call, noted for the apparent affection shown for its mate. The name comes ultimately from Latin *turtur*, of imitative origin.

See also ➤ TURTLE[1].

Mr Turveydrop a character in Dickens's *Bleak House*, who poses as a perfect model of deportment.

> He showed himself a past master in deportment and might be envied by Court Chamberlains, Gold Sticks, Masters of Ceremonies, and the whole of Turveydropdom.
> — *Pall Mall Gazette* 21 June 1892

Tuscan order a classical order of architecture resembling the Doric but lacking all ornamentation.

Tusitala nickname ('teller of tales') given by the Samoans to ➤ *Robert Louis* STEVENSON.

Madame Tussaud (1761–1850), French founder of Madame Tussaud's waxworks, resident in Britain from 1802. She took death masks in wax of prominent victims of the French Revolution and later toured Britain with her wax models. In 1835 she founded a permanent waxworks exhibition in Baker Street, London.

See also ➤ CHAMBER *of Horrors*.

Tutankhamen (died *c*.1352 BC), Egyptian pharaoh of the 18th dynasty, reigned *c*.1361–*c*.1352 BC. He abandoned the worship of the sun god instituted by ➤ AKHENATEN, reinstating the worship of Amun and making Thebes the capital city once again.

His tomb, containing a wealth of rich and varied contents, was discovered virtually intact by the English archaeologist Howard Carter in 1922, who when asked if he could see anything on first looking into the tomb is said to have replied simply, 'Yes, wonderful things'. Lord Carnarvon, who had sponsored the excavation, died the following year of blood-poisoning following a mosquito bite in the Valley of the Kings; this gave rise to the belief that to open the tomb had been unlucky.

Tuthmosis III (died *c*.1450 BC), son of Tuthmosis II, Egyptian pharaoh of the 18th dynasty *c*.1504–*c*.1450, initially joint ruler with his aunt Hatshepsut. His reign was marked by extensive building; the monuments he erected included ➤ CLEOPATRA*'s Needles* (*c*.1475).

Tutsi a people forming a minority of the population of Rwanda and Burundi but who formerly dominated the Hutu majority. Historical antagonism between the peoples led 'n 1994 to large-scale ethnic violence, especially in Rwanda.

Desmond Tutu (1931–), South African clergyman, archbishop of Cape Town 1986–96. As General Secretary of the South African Council of Churches (1979–84) he became a leading voice in the struggle against apartheid, calling for economic sanctions against South Africa and emphasizing non-violent action. He became a member of the Truth and Reconciliation Commission set up in 1995.

tuxedo a man's dinner jacket (chiefly in the US). The term comes (in the late 19th century) from *Tuxedo Park*, the site of a country club in New York, where it was first worn.

Tuzla a town in NE Bosnia, which as a Muslim enclave suffered damage and heavy casualties when besieged by Bosnian Serb forces between 1992 and 1994.

Mark Twain pseudonym of the American novelist and humorist Samuel Langhorne Clemens (1835–1910), author of *The Adventures of Tom Sawyer* (1876) and *The Adventures of Huckleberry Finn* (1885). He is one of the most widely quoted writers, and one to whom many apocryphal remarks have also been attributed; his well-known comment in the *New York Journal* 2 June 1897 'The report of my death was an exaggeration' is usually given in the pithier form, 'Reports of my death have been greatly exaggerated.'

tweed a rough-surfaced woollen cloth, typically of mixed flecked colours, originally produced in Scotland. Recorded from the mid 19th century, the word was originally a misreading of *tweel*, Scots form of *twill*, influenced by association with the river *Tweed*.

Tweed Ring the political group which under 'Boss' *Tweed* (1823–78) controlled the municipal government of New York, *c*.1870.

> The infamous Tweed Ring engaged in mere old-fashioned vote-buying.
> — Michael Lind *The Next American Nation* (1995)

Tweedledum and **Tweedledee** originally names applied to the composers Bononcini (1670–1747) and Handel, in a 1725 satire by John Byrom (1692–1763):

> Strange all this difference should be,
> 'Twixt Tweedle-dum and Tweedle-dee.
> — John Byrom *Handel and Bononcini* (1725)

The nursery rhyme featuring Tweedledum and Tweedledee, and their agreement to 'have a battle', is recorded from the early 19th century, and they were later developed as two identical characters in Lewis Carroll's *Through the Looking Glass* (1872).

The names generally designate a pair of people or things that are virtually indistinguishable and interchangeable.

twelfth the phrase **The Twelfth** denotes both 12 July, celebrated by upholders of Protestant supremacy in Ireland as the anniversary of William III's victory over James II at the Battle of the Boyne, and (in the UK) 12 August, the day on which the grouse-shooting season begins.

See also ➤ *the* GLORIOUS *Twelfth.*

Twelfth cake a large cake traditionally made for ➤ TWELFTH *Night* festivities, typically iced and decorated, and with a bean or coin baked inside it; the person who was given the slice with the bean or coin within was made 'king' or 'queen' of the feast.

Twelfth Day an archaic term for ➤ TWELFTH *Night.*

twelfth man in cricket, a player nominated to act as a reserve in a game, typically carrying out duties such as fielding as a substitute and taking out drinks.

Twelfth Night 6 January, the feast of the Epiphany. Strictly, this denotes the evening of 5 January, the eve of the ➤ EPIPHANY and formerly the twelfth and last day of Christmas festivities.

twelve the number of certain well known sets or groups, as the twelve Apostles, the twelve Labours of Hercules, and the twelve signs of the zodiac.

Recorded from Old English (in form *twelf(e)*, the word is of Germanic origin and comes from the base of *two* + a second element probably expressing the sense 'left over'.

the twelve days of Christmas the traditional period of Christmas festivities, from Christmas Day to the feast of the Epiphany.

twelve good men and true the twelve members of a jury; the expression is recorded from the mid 17th century.

> Submitting myself to be try'd by my Country, and allowing any Jury of 12 good Men and true, to be that Country.
>
> — Richard Steele *Tatler* 1709

Twelve Tables a set of laws drawn up in ancient Rome in 451 and 450 BC, embodying the most important rules of Roman law and forming the chief basis of subsequent legislation; they were originally learned by heart by Roman schoolboys.

Twelve Tribes of Israel the twelve divisions of ancient Israel, each traditionally descended from one of the twelve sons of Jacob. Ten of the tribes (Asher, Dan, Gad, Issachar, Levi, Manasseh, Naphtali, Reuben, Simeon, and Zebulun, known as the *Lost Tribes*) were deported to captivity in Assyria *c.*720 BC, leaving only the tribes of Judah and Benjamin.

Twelver a member of the larger of the two Shiah sects (the 'Twelvers' and the 'Seveners'), a follower of the twelve Imams or prophets.

twenties see ➤ *the* ROARING *twenties.*

twenty the cardinal number equivalent to the product of two and ten; ten less than thirty; 20. Recorded from Old English (in form *twentig*) the word comes from the base of *two* + *-ty.*

twenty-one until 1970 in the UK a person's coming-of-age.

twenty questions a parlour game in which a participant has twenty questions (answered by either 'yes' or 'no') to identify a chosen object. The first recorded reference is in a letter from Hannah More of 1786, 'Mrs Fielding and I diverted ourselves with teaching Sir Joshua and Lord Palmerston the play of twenty questions'; in the 20th century, *Twenty Questions* became the name of a popular radio panel game.

Twenty-six Counties the counties constituting the Republic of Ireland, separated from the ➤ SIX *Counties* of Northern Ireland by the peace agreement of 1921–22 from which the Irish Free State was formed.

twenty-twenty the Snellen fraction for normal visual acuity, expressed in feet; used informally to denote good eyesight.

twenty-two see ➤ CATCH-22.

twice see also ➤ *he* GIVES *twice who gives quickly.*

twice-born having undergone a renewal of faith or life, in particular, (of a Hindu) belonging to one of the three highest castes, especially as an initiated Brahmin; (of a Christian) born-again.

Twickenham originally a village in Middlesex, site of Horace Walpole's ➤ STRAWBERRY *Hill*, and from 1718 home of ➤ *Alexander* POPE (1688–1744). It is now known primarily as the site of the English Rugby Football Union's ground, acquired in 1907.

as the twig is bent, so is the tree inclined proverbial saying, early 18th century; meaning that early influences have a permanent effect. There is a related comment of the mid 16th century, 'a man may bend a wand while it is green and make it straight though it be never so crooked,' but the current form comes originally from Pope:

'Tis education forms the common mind,
Just as the twig is bent the tree's inclined.
— Alexander Pope *Epistles to Several Persons* (1732)

twigloo a tree-house built and occupied by environmental protesters; the word is probably formed from a blend of *twig* and *igloo*, a coinage which suggests both the material and the shape of the construction.

The word first came to public attention in Britain in 1995, in reports of controversy surrounding the construction of the Newbury bypass in Hampshire. Protesters against the scheme established themselves in a number of encampments within the threatened woodland, in temporary structures which included *benders*, or ground-level erections with a superstructure of branches which have been bent over, and *twigloos*, houses with a similar superstructure, but with a flooring of tarpaulin over netting.

twilight see also ➤ CELTIC *twilight*.

twilight of the gods in Scandinavian and Germanic mythology, the destruction of the gods and the world in a final conflict with the powers of evil, ➤ RAGNARÖK, ➤ GÖTTERDAMMERUNG; the phrase is first recorded in English in Thomas Gray's note to his *Descent of Odin* (1768), 'Lok is the evil Being who continues in chains till the Twilight of the Gods approaches.'

Twin Cities two cities that are very close neighbours; in the US, Minneapolis and St Paul in Minnesota; in Canada, Fort William and Port Arthur.

Twinkie defence a legal defence of diminished responsibility in which irregular behaviour is attributed to an unbalanced diet of convenience food, from a proprietary name for a brand of cupcake with a creamy filling.

The *Twinkie defence* was first employed in 1979 in a San Francisco Supreme Court murder trial, when it was alleged that the defendant's compulsive consumption of sugar through cupcakes, coca cola, and similarly sweet foods had aggravated a chemical imbalance in his brain. The *Twinkie defence* was disallowed as a legal defence by the US Congress in 1981, and it is now likely to be referred to as the type of a defence which seeks to exculpate wrongdoing by the evasion of responsibility.

in the twinkling of an eye in an instant, very quickly; recorded from Middle English, but often with biblical allusion to Corinthians 15:51, 'In a moment, in the twinkling of an eye, at the last trump'.

The English dramatist Thomas Shadwell (*c*.1642–92) varied the expression in *The Virtuoso* (1676), 'Instantly, in the twinkling of a bedstaff'.

twins see also ➤ SIAMESE *twins*.

the Twins the zodiacal sign or constellation ➤ GEMINI; the name is recorded from late Middle English.

twist the lion's tail provoke the resentment of the British (taking a *lion* as the symbol of the British Empire); the expression is first recorded in the late 19th-century US, in a remark that 'Twisting the lion's tail is a regular electioneering maneuver'.

Jemmy Twitcher name of a character in the *Beggar's Opera* who betrays his associate Macheath; it was used as a nickname for Lord Sandwich (1718–92) who was active in collecting evidence against the radical John Wilkes despite their past friendship, and who gained the nickname from Macheath's line in the last scene 'That Jemmy Twitcher should peach me, I own surprised me.'

Twm Shon Catti according to Welsh legend, a Robin Hood-like figure who is said after his bandit days to have married an heiress and become a magistrate and finally high sheriff; the name is in fact a sobriquet for the Welsh bard and genealogist Thomas Jones (1530–1620?), whose youthful exploits and knowledge of what was regarded as the occult subject of heraldry won him his reputation as an outlaw and magician.

two recorded from Old English (in form *twā*) and of Germanic origin, the word comes ultimately from an Indo-European root shared by Latin and Greek *duo*.

See also ➤ GOODY *Two-shoes*, ➤ *two* BOYS *are half a boy*, ➤ *two-headed* EAGLE, ➤ YEAR 2000 *problem*.

two bites at the cherry more than one attempt or opportunity to do something; originally (from the mid 17th century) with the implication of behaving with an affectation of restraint.

two blacks don't make a white proverbial saying, early 18th century.

two cultures literature and science as disciplines that tend to be mutually incompatible or hostile; the term was coined by the novelist and scientist C. P. Snow (1905–80) in 'The two cultures and the scientific revolution', title of The Rede Lecture given at Cambridge in 1959. It was Snow's view that the gulf between 'literary intellectuals' and 'physical scientists' was wide and growing wider, so that the two sides could no longer communicate with one another.

two heads are better than one proverbial saying, late 14th century.

two is company, but three is none proverbial saying, early 18th century; often used with the alternative ending 'three's a crowd.'

two-minute silence observed on the anniversary of Armistice Day (11 November 1918), or on Remembrance Sunday; the *Times* of 12 November 1919 recorded that 'At 11 o'clock yesterday morning the nation, in response to the King's invitation, paid homage to the Glorious Dead by keeping a two minutes' silence.'

Later sources refer to a silence of two minutes' duration having been observed by Canadian railways and churches in memory of those Canadians who drowned in the *Titanic* disaster of 1912, but contemporary use of the phrase is not recorded.

two nations the rich and poor members of a society seen as effectively divided into separate nations by the presence or absence of wealth; the phrase comes from Disraeli:

> Two nations, between who there is no intercourse and no sympathy, who are as ignorant of each other's habits, thoughts, and feelings, as if they were . . . inhabitants of different planets . . . the rich and the poor.
> — Benjamin Disraeli *Sybil* (1845)

See also ➤ One *Nation.*

two of a trade never agree proverbial saying, early 17th century; meaning that close association with someone makes disagreement over policy and principles more likely.

if two ride on a horse, one must ride behind proverbial saying, late 16th century; meaning that of two people engaged on the same task, one must take a subordinate role.

Two Sicilies the former kingdom of Naples and Sicily. Originally a single state uniting the southern peninsula of Italy with Sicily, it was divided in the 13th century between the Angevin dynasty on the mainland territory and the Aragonese dynasty on the island; both claimed title to the kingdom of Sicily. In the mid 15th century the state was reunited under Alfonso V of Aragon, who took the title '*rex Utriusque Siciliae* [king of the Two Sicilies]'. The name was used intermittently until 1815, when it was officially established; it was subsequently merged with a united Italy.

there are two sides to every question proverbial saying, early 19th century.

it takes two to make a bargain proverbial saying, late 16th century.

it takes two to make a quarrel proverbial saying, early 18th century.

it takes two to tango proverbial saying, mid 20th century.

two wrongs don't make a right proverbial saying, late 18th century.

twopenny post the London post (1801–39) for the conveyance of letters at an ordinary charge of twopence each.

> Marianne . . . requested the footman . . . to get that letter conveyed to the two-penny post.
> — Jane Austen *Sense and Sensibility* (1811)

twopenny tube informal name for the Central London Railway, opened in 1900, on which the fare was originally twopence for any distance.

add one's twopennyworth contribute one's opinion; *twopennyworth* taken as the type of a paltry or insignificant amount.

Tybalt a character in Shakespeare's *Romeo and Juliet*; his name is identified by Shakespeare with that of ➤ Tibert, the cat in the apologue of Reynard the Fox.

Tyburn a place in London, near Marble Arch, where public hangings were held *c.*1300–1783. It is named after a tributary of the Thames, which flows in an underground culvert nearby.

See also ➤ Dance *the Tyburn jig.*

Tyburn ticket a certificate formerly granted to one who secured the conviction of a felon, exempting the holder from all parochial duties in the parish where the offence was committed.

Tyburnia a former literary name for the residential district built in the nineteenth century and extending along the Bayswater Road from Marble Arch to Lancaster Gate and northwards.

tychism the doctrine that account must be taken of the element of chance in reasoning or explanation of the universe. The term comes from Greek *tukhē* 'chance'.

Tycho see ➤ *Tycho* Brahe.

tycoon a title applied by foreigners to the shogun of Japan in power between 1857 and 1868; the word comes from Japanese *taikun* 'great lord'.

In the US, *Tycoon* was used as a nickname of
➤ *Abraham* LINCOLN; it subsequently developed the
current general meaning of a wealthy and powerful
person in business or industry.

Wat Tyler (d.1381), English leader of the Peasants'
Revolt of 1381. He captured Canterbury and went on
to take London and secure Richard II's concession
to the rebels' demands, which included the lifting of
the newly imposed poll tax. He was killed by royal
supporters.

Tylwyth Teg in Welsh folklore, a fairy people who
might bring good fortune but who could be dangerous; the name in Welsh means 'the fair people', and
it is held to be unlucky to refer to them directly.

William Tyndale (*c*.1494–1536), English translator
and Protestant martyr, who is said to have asserted
to an opponent, 'If God spare my life, ere many
years I will cause a boy that driveth the plough shall
know more of the scripture than thou doest!'

Faced with ecclesiastical opposition to his project
for translating the Bible into English, Tyndale left
England in 1524. His translations of the Bible later
formed the basis of the Authorized Version. He was
burnt at the stake as a heretic in Antwerp, his last
words reportedly being, 'Lord, open the king of
England's eyes!'

Tyndale's Bible the translation of the New Testament from Greek to English made by William Tyndale and printed at Worms 1525–6; in 1530 his
translations from Hebrew of the Pentateuch and the
Book of Jonah were printed at Marburg.

Tynwald the parliament of the Isle of Man. It
meets annually and consists of the governor (representing the sovereign) and council acting as the
upper house, and an elected assembly called the
House of Keys. The name comes from Old Norse
þing-vǫllr 'place of assembly'; the place-names
Tinwald in Dumfriesshire and *Dingwall* in Ross-
shire have the same source.

Typhoeus in Greek mythology, a monster with a
hundred serpent heads, fiery eyes, and a tremendous voice, born to Tartarus and Gaia after the Titans were defeated by Zeus. Also called *Typhon*.

Typhoid Mary the nickname of *Mary* Mallon
(died 1938), an Irish-born cook who as an unwitting
carrier of the disease transmitted typhoid fever in

the US; she has become the type of a person who
transmits undesirable opinions, sentiments, or attitudes.

> Bill Clinton is the Typhoid Mary of American politics.
> — *Post* (Denver) 20 November 1994

typhoon a tropical storm in the region of the Indian or western Pacific oceans. The word comes (in
the late 16th century) partly via Portuguese from
Arabic (perhaps from Greek *tuphōn* 'whirlwind');
reinforced by Chinese dialect *tai fung* 'big wind'.

Tyr in Scandinavian mythology, the god of battle,
identified with Mars, after whom ➤ TUESDAY is
named; he is one-handed, the other hand having
been bitten off by the wolf ➤ FENRIR when it was
shackled by the gods.

tyrannosaur a very large bipedal carnivorous
dinosaur of the late Cretaceous period, with powerful jaws and small claw-like front legs; **Tyranno-
saurus rex** is the best-known species. The name is
modern Latin, and is formed from Greek *turannos*
'tyrant' + *sauros* 'lizard', on the pattern of *dinosaur*.

tyrant especially in ancient Greece, a ruler who
seized absolute power without legal right, an absolute ruler. The word is recorded from Middle English, and comes from Greek *turannos*.

See also ➤ VIOLET *on the tyrant's grave.*

Tyre a port on the Mediterranean in southern
Lebanon, founded in the 2nd millennium BC as a
colony of Sidon, it was for centuries a Phoenician
port and trading centre. Its prosperity did not decline until the 14th century.

Tyrian purple ➤ PURPLE or crimson dye traditionally made at ancient Tyre.

Tyrtaeus a Greek elegiac poet of the 7th century
BC, living at Sparta and probably of Spartan birth,
noted for his martial songs.

Mike Tyson (1966–), American boxer. He became
undisputed world heavyweight champion in 1987,
winning the WBA, WBC, and IBF titles. He was imprisoned in 1992 for rape; after his release in 1995 he
reclaimed the WBC and WBA titles in the following
year.

tzolkin the cycle of two hundred and sixty days
constituting a year in the Mayan sacred calendar.

Uu

U the twenty-first letter of the modern English alphabet and the twentieth of the ancient Roman one, a differentiated form of the letter V. Latin manuscripts written in capitals have V only, but other Latin manuscripts also have a modified form of this, resembling u. Both forms occur in OE manuscripts: capital V represents either V or U, and the modified form usually represents the vowel u. In ME the symbols u and v both occur, but without formal distinction of use.

During the 16th century continental printers began to distinguish lower case u as the vowel symbol and v as the consonant symbol, and by the mid 17th century this was also the case in English. Capital V continued to be used for both V and U into the 17th century, but in the course of that century it was replaced, for the vowel, by capital U. From about 1700 the regular forms have been U u for the vowel, and V v for the consonant. However, many dictionaries continued into the 19th century to give items beginning with u or v in a single alphabetic sequence.

U is used (of language or social behaviour) to mean characteristic of or appropriate to the upper social classes. The expression is an abbreviation of upper class, and was coined in 1954 by Alan S. C. Ross, professor of linguistics, the term was popularized by its use in Nancy Mitford's *Noblesse Oblige* (1956).

Übermensch the ideal superior man of the future who could rise above conventional Christian morality to create and impose his own values, originally described by Nietzsche in *Thus Spake Zarathustra* (1883–5). Nietzsche thought that such a being could arise when any man of superior potential shook off the conventional Christian morality of the masses to create and impose his own values.

See also ➤ SUPERMAN.

ubi sunt a Latin phrase meaning 'where are', the opening words or refrain of certain medieval Latin works; the expression is used in literary criticism to designate a literary theme or passage lamenting the mutability of things.

ubiquitarian a person, typically a Lutheran, who believes that Christ's body is everywhere present at all times. The term is recorded from the mid 17th century, and comes ultimately from Latin *ubique* 'everywhere'.

udal a kind of freehold tenure based on uninterrupted possession, formerly practised in northern Europe and still in use in Orkney and Shetland. The word is recorded from the late 15th century, and comes from Old Norse *oðal*, land(s) in Orkney or Shetland held by the old native form of freehold tenure.

Udolpho see ➤ MYSTERIES *of Udolpho*.

uffish Lewis Carroll's alteration of *huffish* in 'Jabberwocky' (1871), 'And as in uffish thought he stood'.

Uffizi an art gallery and museum in Florence, housing one of Europe's finest art collections. Italian Renaissance painting is particularly well represented, although the collection also contains sculptures, drawings, and Flemish, French, and Dutch paintings. The building, the Uffizi palace, was designed by Giorgio Vasari c.1560 as offices for the Medici family.

UFO a mysterious object seen in the sky (an *Unidentified Flying Object*) for which it is claimed no orthodox scientific explanation can be found. UFO incidents range from sightings of unidentified lights in the sky to accounts of supposed abductions by alien beings. Of the thousands of reported cases, only a controversial minority resists explanation in terms of known phenomena or artefacts. It is often supposed that UFOs, if real, must be vehicles carrying extraterrestrials, although other theories are put forward.

See also ➤ ROSWELL.

Ugarit an ancient port and Bronze Age trading city in northern Syria, founded in Neolithic times and destroyed by the Sea Peoples in about the 12th century BC. Late Bronze Age remains include a palace, temples, and private residences containing legal, religious, and administrative cuneiform texts in Sumerian, Akkadian, Hurrian, Hittite, and Ugaritic languages. Its people spoke a Semitic language written in a distinctive cuneiform alphabet.

ugly American an American who behaves offensively when abroad; the phrase was originally used as the title of a book in 1954.

> It quickly became clear that this was not the place to demonstrate my Ugly American routine of wolfing down a quick meal and promptly sacking out.
> — *Ski* March 1991

ugly duckling a person who turns out to be beautiful or talented against all expectations. The term comes from the title of one of Hans Christian Andersen's fairy tales, in which the 'ugly duckling' is in fact a cygnet which becomes a swan.

uht-song in pre-Conquest England, the ecclesiastical office (nocturns, matins) celebrated just before daybreak; the word comes from Old English *ūhte* 'early morning, part of the night just before daybreak' + *sang* 'song'.

Uhuru national independence of an African country, in particular, Kenya; the word is Swahili, and means 'freedom'.

Uisneach see ➤ SONS *of Uisneach*.

Uitlander a British immigrant living in the Transvaal of the late 19th century who was denied citizenship by the Boers for cultural and economic reasons; the word is Afrikaans and comes from Dutch *uit* 'out' + *land* 'land'.

ujigami in feudal and pre-feudal Japan, the ancestral deity of a family (the *uji*), or (later) the tutelary deity of a particular village or area.

ukase in tsarist Russia, a decree with the force of law; more generally, an arbitrary or peremptory demand. The word comes from Russian *ukaz* 'ordinance, edict', from *ukazat'* 'show, decree'.

ulema a body of Muslim scholars who are recognized as having specialist knowledge of Islamic sacred law and theology. The word comes from the plural of Arabic *'ulamā* 'learned', from *'alima* 'know'.

Ulfilas (*c*.311–*c*.381), bishop and translator. Believed to be of Cappadocian descent, he became bishop of the Visigoths in 341. His translation of the Bible from Greek into Gothic (of which fragments survive) is the earliest known translation of the Bible

into a Germanic language. Ulfilas is traditionally held to have invented the Gothic alphabet, based on Latin and Greek characters. Also called **Wulfila**.

ullage the amount by which a container falls short of being full, typically the volume of air between the cork and the level of wine in a bottle or cask. The word comes (in late Middle English) via Anglo-Norman French from Old French *euillier* 'fill up', based on Latin *oculus* 'eye', with reference to a container's bunghole.

Ulloa see ➤ CIRCLE *of Ulloa*.

Ulpian (died *c*.228), Roman jurist, born in Phoenicia. His numerous legal writings provided one of the chief sources for ➤ JUSTINIAN's *Digest* of 533.

Ulster a former province of Ireland, in the north of the island; with Leinster, Munster, and Connaught one of the original four provinces, the 'four green fields' of Ireland. The nine counties of Ulster are now divided between Northern Ireland (Antrim, Down, Armagh, Londonderry, Tyrone, and Fermanagh) and the Republic of Ireland (Cavan, Donegal, and Monaghan). The name is also used generally for Northern Ireland, particularly in a political context, as in Lord Randolph Churchill's public letter of 7 May 1886 over the question of Irish home rule, 'Ulster will fight; Ulster will be right.'

Ulster King of Arms formerly the chief heraldic officer for Ireland; since 1943, the office has been united with that of *Norroy King of Arms*.

ultima Thule a distant unknown region; the extreme limit of travel and discovery; the Latin phrase means 'furthest Thule' (see ➤ THULE).

> The occasional conga is the *Ultima Thule* of expressiveness at most golf club dances.
> — *Daily Telegraph* 22 May 1995

Ultor Latin epithet (meaning 'avenger') given to the Roman god ➤ MARS.

Ultra in the Second World War, codename given to the project at ➤ BLETCHLEY *Park* in which British crytographers broke the German Enigma code.

ultracrepidarian a person who goes beyond their proper province or gives opinions on matters beyond their knowledge. The word comes from the Latin phrase *ultra crepidam* 'beyond the last', in allusion to the advice of Apelles to a cobbler (see ➤ *let the* COBBLER *stick to his last*).

ultramarine a brilliant deep blue pigment originally obtained from lapis lazuli. The word comes (in the late 16th century) from medieval Latin *ultramarinus* 'beyond the sea'; the name of the pigment is from obsolete Italian *(azzurro) oltramarino*, literally '(azure) from overseas'.

ultramontane advocating supreme papal authority in matters of faith and discipline. Recorded from the late 16th century, the name originally denoted a representative of the Roman Catholic Church north of the Alps.

ultreya in the Spanish Roman Catholic Church, a regular discussion group held by participants in a *cursillo* or course of religious study. The word is Spanish, apparently recalling the medieval cry *(E)ultreya* 'onward!', 'forward!' in the hymn sung by pilgrims to ➤ SANTIAGO *de Compostela*.

Ulysses the Roman name for ➤ ODYSSEUS; he is referred to as the type of a traveller or adventurer, and also of a crafty and clever schemer.

> I had been dreaming of foreign parts . . . and here on a Glasgow stairhead I had found Ulysses himself.
> — John Buchan *Salute to Adventurers* (1915)

Ulysses' bow able to be bent by ➤ ULYSSES alone; on his return to Ithaca, he finds that his wife Penelope has agreed that she will marry whichever of her suitors can bend and string the bow, and only Ulysses can achieve this.

> Who now can bend Ulysses bow, and wing
> The well-aim'd arrow thro' the distant ring.
> — Alexander Pope tr. Homer *Odyssey* (1726)

Umayyad a member of a Muslim dynasty that ruled the Islamic world from AD 660 (or 661) to 750 and Moorish Spain 756–1031. The dynasty claimed descent from *Umayya*, a distant relative of Muhammad.

Umayyad Mosque a mosque in Damascus, Syria, built AD 705–15 on the site of a church dedicated to St John the Baptist. Within the mosque is a shrine believed to contain the relic of the saint's head.

Umbanda a Brazilian folk religion combining elements of macumba, Roman Catholicism, and South American Indian practices and beliefs.

umbrage offence or annoyance. Recorded from late Middle English, in the sense 'shade or shadow, especially as cast by trees', the word comes via Old French from Latin *umbra* 'shadow'. An early sense was 'shadowy outline', giving rise to 'ground for suspicion', whence the current notion of 'offence'.

umbrella originally (in the early 17th century) a light portable screen or shade, usually circular, and supported on a central rod, for protection against the sun; the word comes from Italian *ombrella*, diminutive of *ombra* 'shade', from Latin *umbra*.

The term is recorded from a travel writer of the mid 17th century as a protection against rain, now a device consisting of a circular canopy of cloth on a folding metal frame supported by a central rod; according to the *Dictionary of National Biography*, the traveller and philanthropist Jonas Hanway (1712–86), was the first man who customarily used an umbrella in the streets of London, and did so despite jeers for thirty years before he saw it generally adopted.

Umbrian School a Renaissance school of Italian painting developed in Umbria in central Italy in the 15th century, to which Raphael and Perugino belonged.

Umbriel a sprite in *The Rape of the Lock* by Alexander Pope, after whom one of the satellites of the planet Uranus is named.

umlaut the process in Germanic languages by which the quality of a vowel was altered in certain phonetic contexts, resulting for example in the differences between modern German *Mann* and *Männer* or (after loss of the inflection) English *man* and *men*.

umma the whole community of Muslims bound together by ties of religion. The word is Arabic and means literally, 'people, community'.

umpty an indefinite, usually fairly large, number; the word comes from a humorous formation after such cardinal numbers as *twenty* and *thirty*, and may originally be after military slang representative of the dash in Morse code.

Umwelt in ethology, the world as it is experienced by a particular organism. The word is German, and means literally 'environment'.

House Un-American Activities Committee a committee of the US House of Representatives established in 1938 to investigate subversives. It became notorious for its zealous investigations of alleged communists, particularly in the late 1940s, although it was originally intended to pursue Fascists also.

See also ➤ McCARTHYISM.

Una in Spenser's *Faerie Queene*, the personification of single-minded adherence to true religion, and the antithesis of the falsity of ➤ DUESSA.

> The impression of this figure of Margaret—with all Margaret's character taken out of it, as completely as if some evil spirit had got possession of her form—was so deeply stamped upon his imagination, that when he wakened he felt hardly able to separate the Una from the Duessa.
> — Elizabeth Gaskell *North and South*

Unabomber the media nickname for a terrorist who carried out a series of bomb attacks in the US between 1978 and 1995 as part of an anarchist, anti-technology personal crusade; because the attacks were made on academic institutions (and particularly scientists), the name *Unabomber*, a blend of *university* and *bomber*, was coined. A suspect, Theodore Kaczynski, was finally arrested and charged in 1996; in 1998 he was sentenced to four life terms of imprisonment.

Unam Sanctam a bull (its Latin name means 'One Holy') issued in 1302 by Boniface VIII, formulating the content of the papal office.

unbecoming see ➤ CONDUCT *unbecoming*.

uncertainty see ➤ *the* GLORIOUS *uncertainty*.

uncial of or written in a majuscule script with rounded unjoined letters which is found in European manuscripts of the 4th–8th centuries and from which modern capital letters are derived. The term is recorded from the late 17th century and comes from late Latin *unciales littera* 'uncial letters', the original application of which is unclear. (One explanation has been that the phrase stands for 'letters of an inch long' from Latin *uncia* 'inch'; the emendations *initiales* 'initial' and *uncinales* 'hooked, bent' have also been suggested.)

uncle the brother of one's father or mother or the husband of one's aunt; the word comes (in Middle English, via Old French) from a late Latin alteration of Latin *avunculus* 'maternal uncle'.

From the mid 18th century, *uncle* has been used as an informal name for a pawnbroker, perhaps as a humorous reference to the relationship implied by the pawnbroker's taking charge of a person's possessions.

See also ➤ BOB's *your uncle*, ➤ DUTCH *uncle*, ➤ OLD *Uncle Tom Cobleigh and all*, ➤ WELSH *uncle*.

Uncle Joe British wartime nickname for ➤ *Joseph* STALIN as the personification of Soviet Russia; the name is first recorded in a comment made by Winston Churchill to Franklin Roosevelt in 1943, 'The castigation we have both received from Uncle Joe…was naturally to be expected'.'

Uncle Remus the elderly slave who is the narrator of Joel Chandler Harris's ➤ *Brer* RABBIT stories; the first book in the series (published 1880) was entitled *Uncle Remus, his songs and his sayings; the folk-lore of the old plantation*.

Uncle Sam a personification of the federal government or citizens of the US. Recorded from the early 19th century, it is said (from the time of the first recorded instances) to have arisen as a facetious expansion of the letters US.

Uncle Tom a black man considered to be excessively obedient or servile, from the name of the hero of Harriet Beecher Stowe's *Uncle Tom's Cabin* (1852). The book was seen at the time as dramatizing the question of abolition; Abraham Lincoln, on meeting Mrs Stowe, is said to have greeted her, 'So you're the little woman who wrote the book that made this great war!'

> Uncle Toms . . . control the Negro community on behalf of the white power structure.
> — Eldridge Cleaver *Soul on Ice* (1967)

unclubbable not friendly or gregarious; first used by Dr Johnson of Sir John Hawkins (1719–89), 'Sir John was a most unclubbable man!'

the unco guid Scottish term for those who are professedly strict in matters of morals and religion; *unco* (an alteration of *uncouth*) means 'extremely, remarkably', and the expression comes from the title of Robert Burns's 'Address to the Unco Guid, or the Rigidly Righteous' (1786).

the unconscious the part of the mind which is inaccessible to the conscious mind but which affects behaviour and emotions; the term in this sense was first used by Freud in 1912 in *Proceedings of the Society for Psychical Research*.

unction see ➤ EXTREME *unction*.

St Uncumber another name for ➤ *St* WILGEFORTIS, said by St Thomas More to refer to the belief that if an offering of oats were made at her shrine by an unhappy wife, the saint would relieve her of her troubles: 'For a peck of oats she will not fail to uncumber them of their husbands.'

☐ **FEAST DAY** Her feast day is 20 July.

Underground Railroad in the US, a secret network for helping slaves escape from the South to the North and Canada in the years before the American Civil War. Escaped slaves were given safe houses, transport, and other assistance, often by members of the free black community.

undersold see ➤ NEVER *knowingly undersold.*

undertaker a person whose business is preparing dead bodies for burial or cremation and making arrangements for funerals; the word in this sense is recorded from the late 17th century, and comes from the earlier general sense of someone who undertakes to carry out business for another, a contractor.

underworld the mythical abode of the dead, imagined as being under the earth; in classical mythology, various heroes such as ➤ ODYSSEUS and ➤ AENEAS were said to have visited the underworld and to have returned.

underwriter a person who signs and accepts liability under an insurance policy, thus guaranteeing payment in case loss or damage occurs.

undine a female spirit or nymph imagined as inhabiting water, a water-nymph; recorded from the early 19th century, the word comes from modern Latin *Undina* (in Paracelsus *De Nymphis*), from Latin *und*a 'wave'.

the unexpected always happens proverbial saying, late 19th century.

Unfinished Symphony informal name for Schubert's *Symphony in B Minor* (1822).

unforeseen see ➤ NOTHING *is certain but the unforeseen.*

Uniate denoting or relating to any community of Christians in eastern Europe or the Near East that acknowledges papal supremacy but retains its own liturgy. The name comes via Russian from Latin *unio(n-)* 'unity'.

unicorn a mythical animal typically represented as a horse with a single straight horn projecting from its forehead; a heraldic representation of such an animal, with a twisted horn, a deer's feet, a goat's beard, and a lion's tail.

The unicorn has at various times been identified or confused with the rhinoceros, with various species of antelope, or with other animals having a horn (or horns) or horn-like projection from the head. According to Pliny it had a body resembling that of a horse, the head of a deer, the feet of an elephant, and the tail of a lion, with one black horn projecting 'two cubits' from the middle of the forehead. In biblical translation, *unicorn* may be used for a kind of wild ox.

The horn of this animal was reputed to possess medicinal or magical properties, especially as an antidote to or preventive of poison. It was also said that it could only be captured by a virgin.

In heraldry, the unicorn is a supporter of the ➤ ROYAL *Arms* of the United Kingdom.

unicorn's horn a horn regarded as or alleged to be obtained from the legendary unicorn, but in reality that of the rhinoceros, narwhal, or other animal, frequently mounted or made into a drinking cup and employed as a preventive of or charm against poison.

Unification Church an evangelistic religious and political organization founded in 1954 in Korea by Sun Myung Moon.

Act of Uniformity in British history, any of four acts (especially that of 1662) establishing the foundations of the English Protestant Church and securing uniformity in public worship and use of a particular Book of Common Prayer. The first two Acts were passed in the reign of Edward VI but repealed under his Catholic successor Mary I; a third was passed in the reign of Elizabeth I, and a final Act in 1662 after the Restoration.

Unigenitus a papal bull of 1713, issued by Clement XI, condemning the doctrines of ➤ JANSENISM.

Unilateral Declaration of Independence the declaration of independence from the United Kingdom made by Rhodesia under Ian Smith in 1965. Abbreviation, **UDI**.

the Union in 19th century America, a term for the United States; in a speech in 1844 the American politician Henry Clay (1777–1852) said, 'If any man wants the key of my heart, let him take the key of the Union, and that is the key to my heart.'

Act of Union in British history, either of the parliamentary acts by which the countries of the United Kingdom were brought together as a political whole. By the first Act of Union (1707) Scotland was joined with England to form Great Britain. The second Act of Union (1801) established the United Kingdom of Great Britain and Ireland. Wales had been incorporated with England in 1536.

Union flag the national flag of the United Kingdom, consisting of red and white crosses on a blue background and formed by combining the flags of St George, St Andrew, and St Patrick; the name ➤ UNION *Jack* is now frequently used.

union is strength proverbial saying, mid 17th century; early classical versions include Homer's *Iliad* 'even weak men have strength in unity' and the Latin tag 'force united is stronger'.

Union Jack originally and properly a small ➤ UNION *flag* flown as the *jack* of a ship (a small version of a national flag flown at the bow of a vessel in harbour to indicate its nationality); more generally, the ➤ UNION *flag* in any size or adaptation, regarded as the national ensign.

Unitarian a person, especially a Christian, who asserts the unity of God and rejects the doctrine of the Trinity; a member of a Church or religious body maintaining this belief and typically rejecting formal dogma in favour of a rationalist and inclusivist approach to belief.

unite an English gold coin first issued by James I in 1604, originally current at the value of 20 shillings, and raised in 1611 to 22 shillings. The coin was named in allusion to the Union of the Crowns under James I, coins of the original issue bearing on the obverse the inscription *Faciam eos in gentem unam* (Ezekiel 37:22, 'I will make them one nation').

United Artists a US film production company founded in 1919 by Charlie Chaplin, Douglas Fairbanks, Mary Pickford, and D. W. Griffith, formed to make films without the artistic strictures of the larger companies; on hearing that Chaplin and others had taken over the running of the company the American film producer Richard Rowland (*c*.1881–1947) is said to have commented, 'The lunatics have taken charge of the asylum.' United Artists owned no studios or cinemas. It produced many literary adaptations in the 1930s and 1940s and the James Bond series in the 1960s.

United Empire Loyalist any of those who after the American War of Independence left their home in one of the American colonies and settled in Canada.

United Free Church a Presbyterian Church in Scotland formed in 1900 by the union of the Free Church of Scotland with the United Presbyterian Church. In 1929 the majority of its congregation joined the established Church of Scotland.

United Irishman a member of the Society of United Irishmen, a political association, originally formed to promote union between Protestants and Catholics, which became a separatist secret society

and took part in organizing the rebellion of 1798.

> What have you got in your hand?
> A green bough.
> Where did it first grow?
> In America.
> Where did it bud?
> In France.
> Where are you going to plant it?
> In the crown of Great Britain.
> — oath of the United Irishmen, *c*.1797

United Kingdom a country of western Europe consisting of England, Wales, Scotland, and Northern Ireland. England (which had incorporated Wales in the 16th century) and Scotland have had the same monarch since 1603, when James VI of Scotland succeeded to the English crown as James I; the kingdoms were formally united by the Act of Union in 1707. An Act of Parliament joined Great Britain and Ireland in 1801, but the Irish Free State (later the Republic of Ireland) broke away in 1921.

United Nations an international organization of countries set up in 1945, in succession to the ➤ LEAGUE *of Nations*, to promote international peace, security, and cooperation. Its members, originally the countries that fought against the Axis Powers in the Second World War, now number more than 150 and include most sovereign states of the world, the chief exceptions being Switzerland and North and South Korea. Administration is by a secretariat headed by the Secretary General. The chief deliberative body is the General Assembly, in which each member state has one vote; recommendations are passed but are not binding on members, and in general have had little effect on world politics.

United Presbyterian Church a Presbyterian Church in Scotland formed in 1847. In 1900 it joined with the Free Church of Scotland to form the United Free Church.

United Provinces the seven northern provinces of the Netherlands, which in 1579 declared their independence of Spain and were united by the Union of Utrecht into the United Provinces of the Netherlands (the 'Dutch Republic'); in 1814 the United Provinces became the kingdom of the Netherlands.

United Reformed Church a Church formed in 1972 by the union of the Congregational Church in England and Wales with the Presbyterian Church in England.

United States the US originated in the ➤ *War of* AMERICAN *Independence*, the successful rebellion of the British colonies on the east coast in 1775–83; The original thirteen states (see ➤ THIRTEEN *Colonies*) which formed the Union drew up a federal constitution in 1787, and George Washington was elected the first President in 1789. In the 19th century the territory of the US was extended across the continent through the westward spread of pioneers and settlers (at the expense of the American Indian peoples), by the purchase of the Louisiana territory from France (1803) and Florida from Spain (1819), and acquisitions such as that of Texas and California from Mexico in the 1840s.

The ➤ AMERICAN *Civil War* (1861–5), between the northern states and the southern Confederacy, which wished to secede over the issues of slavery and states' rights, ended in defeat for the South and the abolition of slavery in the US. Arizona became the 48th state of the Union in 1912, completing the organization of the coterminous territory; Alaska, purchased from Russia in 1867, and Hawaii, annexed in 1898, achieved statehood in 1959.

See also ➤ BROTHER *Jonathan*, ➤ UNCLE *Sam*.

united we stand, divided we fall proverbial saying, late 18th century; originally with reference to the American politician John Dickinson (1732–1808):

> Then join hand in hand, brave Americans all,—
> By uniting we stand, by dividing we fall.
> — John Dickinson 'The Liberty Song' (1768)

unity see ➤ DRAMATIC *unities*.

universal see also ➤ CONCRETE *universal*.

Universal Declaration of Human Rights declaration adopted by the United Nations in 1948, the first article of which states, 'All human beings are born free and equal in dignity and rights.'

Universal Doctor nickname, translating Latin *Doctor Universalis*, of ➤ St ALBERTUS *Magnus* (c.1200–80) and Alain de Lille (1114–1203), theologian and poet.

universe the universe is believed to be at least 10 billion light years in diameter and contains a vast number of galaxies; it has been expanding since its creation in the big bang about 13 billion years ago.

Ancient and medieval philosophers followed the Ptolemaic system, which placed the earth at the centre of the universe with the celestial bodies orbiting it on idealized crystal spheres. It later gave way to the Copernican system, placing the sun at the centre. This was in turn displaced by the realization (due to William Herschel) that the Milky Way was a great host of stars, of which our sun was but one. Only in the 20th century was it conclusively shown that there are billions of other star systems or galaxies, many bigger than our own.

university a high-level educational institution in which students study for degrees and academic research is done. The word is recorded from Middle English and comes via Old French from Latin *universitas* 'the whole', in late Latin 'society, guild', from Latin *universus* 'combined into one'.

university lecturers the Polish priest St John of Kanti (1390–1473), noted for his learning, and ➤ *St* THOMAS *Aquinas* are patron saints of university lecturers.

University of the Air an organization providing courses of (higher) education partly through radio and television broadcasts; in particular, an early name for the Open University, as used by the Labour Prime Minister Harold Wilson.

> Mr Wilson . . . suggested the broadcasting time for the 'university of the air' could be obtained by allocation of the fourth television channel.
> — *Glasgow Herald* 9 September 1963

University of the Third Age an organization providing courses of education for retired or elderly people, founded in 1981.

the unkindest cut of all the most hurtful thing that could be done or said; originally as a quotation from Shakespeare's *Julius Caesar* (1598), 'Through this the well-beloved Brutus stabb'd…This was the most unkindest cut of all.'

unknowing see ➤ *the* CLOUD *of Unknowing*.

unknown see also ➤ GREAT *Unknown*.

unknown god an unidentified god, especially one to whom an altar has been set up so no god would feel overlooked; in Acts 17:23, St Paul sees an altar in Athens with the inscription 'to the Unknown God', and proclaims to the Athenians that this God is in fact Jesus Christ.

Unknown Prime Minister the Canadian-born British Conservative statesman Andrew Bonar Law (1858–1923), Prime Minister 1922–3, who having succeeded Lloyd George died unexpectedly after only a year in office; He was buried in Westminster Abbey and his predecessor Herbert Asquith commented, 'It is fitting that we should have buried the

Unknown Prime Minister by the side of the Unknown Soldier.'

Unknown Soldier an unidentified representative member of a country's armed forces killed in war, given burial with special honours in a national memorial; also called the *Unknown Warrior*. In Britain the tomb of the *Unknown Soldier* is in Westminster Abbey:

> The Unknown Warrior . . . was brought to London by night . . . He lay . . . awaing burial today in the Abbey among the greatest of his race.
>   — *Times* 11 November 1920

Unlearned Parliament the parliament (also known as the *Parliament of Dunces*) convened by Henry IV at Coventry in 1404, from which all lawyers were excluded; the name is a translation of Latin *Parliamentum indoctorum*.

Unmerciful Parliament another name for the ➤ MERCILESS *Parliament*, which in 1388 condemned the favourites of Richard II.

unparliamentary language contrary to the rules or procedures of parliament; the term is used more generally to cover what is regarded as an offensive form of speech.

the late unpleasantness the war that took place recently; the phrase was used originally of the American Civil War.

Unprofor abbreviation for United Nations Protection Force; a multinational peace-keeping force administrated by the United Nations, instituted in 1992 to mediate in the conflict in former Yugoslavia.

the Unready epithet of Ethelred II (d. 1016); the word is an alteration of *unredy* and means *redeless* or without counsel, having no resource in a difficulty.

Unrighteous Bible an edition printed in Cambridge in 1653, with the misreading 'Know ye not that the unrighteous shall inherit the Kingdom of God?' Also called the *Wicked Bible*.

unrighteousness see ➤ *the* MAMMON *of unrighteousness*.

unruly member the tongue; with biblical allusion to James 3:8 'the tongue is a little member…the tongue can no man tame; it is an unruly evil.'

untouchable a member of the lowest-caste Hindu group or a person outside the caste system. Contact with untouchables is traditionally held to defile members of higher castes. The term *untouchable*

and the social restrictions accompanying it were declared illegal in the constitution of India in 1949 and of Pakistan in 1953.

unwashed see ➤ GREAT *unwashed*.

Up Guards and at them! order attributed to Wellington at Waterloo, from a letter from an officer in the Guards, 22 June 1815, in *The Battle of Waterloo* by a Near Observer [J. Booth] (1815); the quotation was later denied by Wellington himself.

Up-Helly-Aa an annual festival held at Lerwick in the Shetland Islands, celebrated as the revival of a traditional midwinter fire festival. The name comes from a variant of Scots *Uphaliday*, denoting Epiphany as the end of the Christmas holiday, and the current festival dates from the late 19th century.

what goes up must come down proverbial saying, early 20th century; meaning that success is likely to be followed by failure.

up to a point, Lord Copper quotation from Evelyn Waugh's *Scoop* (1938) used to indicate limited agreement with a policy or proposition; Lord Copper in the novel is the overbearing proprietor of the popular newspaper *The Beast*.

Upanishad each of a series of Hindu sacred treatises written in Sanskrit *c.*800–200 BC, expounding the ➤ VEDAS. The *Upanishads* mark the transition from ritual sacrifice to a mystical concern with the nature of reality; polytheism is superseded by a pantheistic monism derived from the basic concepts of atman and Brahman.

upas tree in folklore, a Javanese tree alleged to poison its surroundings and said to be fatal to approach. An account of the tree was given in the *London Magazine* of 1783, and was said to be translated from one written in Dutch by Mr Foersch, a surgeon at Samarang in 1773. The physician Erasmus Darwin (1731–1802) adopted and gave currency to the fiction, but it was in fact invented by the writer and critic George Steevens (1736–1800).

> Fierce in dread silence on the blasted heath
> Fell Upas sits, the Hydra-Tree of death.
>   — Erasmus Darwin *The Loves of Plants* (1789)

upper house the higher house in a bicameral parliament or similar legislature; **the Upper House** (in the UK) the House of Lords.

upper room in the Bible, the room in which the ➤ *Last Supper* was celebrated, and in which the Holy Spirit descended to the disciples at ➤ PENTECOST.

upper ten thousand the aristocracy; the term is first recorded in the US in 1844.

upsilon the twentieth letter of the Greek alphabet (Υ, υ), transliterated as 'u' or (chiefly in English words derived through Latin) as 'y'.

upstage (of an actor) move towards the back of a stage to make (another actor) face away from the audience; in extended usage, divert attention from (someone) towards oneself, outshine.

Ur an ancient Sumerian city formerly on the Euphrates, in southern Iraq. It was one of the oldest cities of Mesopotamia, dating from the 4th millennium BC, and reached its zenith in the late 3rd millennium BC.

In the Bible (Genesis 12:31), **Ur of the Chaldees** is named as the original home of Abraham (the connection with the Chaldeans may be of later date). *Ur of the Chaldees* is sometimes referred to as the type of a place from the infinitely distant past.

> A pair of tweezers and a head-scratcher from Ur of the Chaldees.
> — J. B. Priestley *They Walk in the City* (1936)

uraeus a representation of a sacred serpent as an emblem of supreme power, worn on the headdresses of ancient Egyptian deities and sovereigns. The word comes (in the mid 19th century, via modern Latin) from Greek *ouraios*, representing the Egyptian word for 'cobra'.

Urania in classical mythology, the Muse of astronomy; the name is Greek, and means literally, 'heavenly female'.

Uranus in Greek mythology, a personification of heaven or the sky, the most ancient of the Greek gods and first ruler of the universe. He was overthrown and castrated by his son ➤ CRONUS.

urban myth an entertaining story or piece of information circulated as though true, especially one purporting to involve someone vaguely related or known to the teller. *Urban myths* or **urban legends** have been recognized as a form since the early 1980s, but the kind of story covered by the term is likely to be of very long standing.

urbi et orbi Latin phrase meaning, 'to the city (of Rome) and to the world', as used in papal proclamations and blessings.

Urdu an Indic language closely related to Hindi but written in the Persian script and having many loanwords from Persian and Arabic. It is the official language of Pakistan, and is also widely used in India and elsewhere, with about 50 million speakers worldwide.

Uriah see also ➤ *Uriah* HEEP.

Uriah in the Bible, a Hittite officer in David's army, whom David, desiring his wife Bathsheba, caused to be killed in battle by giving the order (2 Samuel 11:15) to his commander, Joab, 'Set ye Uriah in the forefront of the hottest battle, and retire ye from him, that he may be smitten, and die.'

Uriel in the Apocrypha (2 Esdras 4) the name of an archangel who appears in a vision to Esdras; he appears in Milton's *Paradise Lost*, where he is described as 'Regent of the Sun, and held The sharpest sighted spirit of all in heaven'.

Urim and Thummim two objects of a now unknown nature, possibly used for divination, worn on the breastplate of a Jewish high priest. They are first mentioned in the Bible at Exodus 28:30, and the role of Urim is hinted at in Numbers 27:21 ('he shall stand before Eleazar the priest, who shall ask counsel for him after the judgement of Urim before the Lord') and I Samuel 28:6 ('And when Saul enquired of the Lord, the Lord answered him not, neither by dreams, nor by Urim, nor by prophets').

urisk in Scottish Highland folklore, a supernatural creature haunting mountain streams and other lonely places.

Urnes a style of late Viking decorative art, characterized by the use of animal motifs and complex interlacing. The term comes from the town of *Urnes* in western Norway, site of an 11th-century stave church decorated in this style.

uroboros a circular symbol depicting a snake, or less commonly a dragon, swallowing its tail, as an emblem of wholeness or infinity. The word comes from Greek *(drakōn) ouroboros* '(snake) devouring its tail'.

Ursa Major one of the largest and most prominent northern constellations (the *Great Bear*). The seven brightest stars form a familiar formation variously called the Plough, Big Dipper, or Charles's Wain, and include the Pointers.

Boswell's father, Lord Auchinleck (1706–82) gave the name *Ursa Major* to Dr Johnson.

Ursa Minor a northern constellation (the *Little Bear*), which contains the north celestial pole and the pole star Polaris. The brightest stars form a shape that is also known as the Little Dipper.

Urschleim in early biological studies, a term for the earliest form of life, conceived as amorphous protoplasm; the word is German, and was first used by George Bernard Shaw in his preface to *Back to Methuselah* (1921).

St Ursula a legendary British saint and martyr, said to have been put to death with 11,000 virgins after being captured by Huns near Cologne while on a pilgrimage. The legend probably developed from an incident of the 4th century or earlier.

❑ **FEAST DAY** Her feast day 21 October.

Ursuline a nun of an order founded by St Angela Merici (1470–1540) at Brescia in 1535 for nursing the sick and teaching girls. It is the oldest teaching order of women in the Roman Catholic Church.

urtext an original or the earliest version of a text, to which later versions can be compared; a work of literature considered as the foundation or prototypical text in a genre or a movement; the word is German, and is recorded in English from the early 1930s.

Uruk an ancient city in southern Mesopotamia, to the north-west of Ur. One of the greatest cities of Sumer, it was built in the 5th millennium BC and is associated with the legendary hero Gilgamesh. Excavations begun in 1928 revealed great ziggurats and temples dedicated to the sky god Anu.

used see ➤ *would you buy a used* CAR *from this man.*

Useless Parliament the first Parliament of Charles I, 18 June to 12 August 1625.

user-friendly (of a machine or system) easy to use or understand. *User-friendly* was a coinage of the late 1970s which started purely as a computing term to describe systems which incorporated a user interface geared to the needs of the non-specialist; the term became so popular and so widely known, that it became the model for a multitude of other formations ending in *-friendly*.

usher a person who shows people to their seats, especially in a theatre or cinema or at a wedding. Recorded from late Middle English (denoting a doorkeeper), the word comes via Anglo-Norman French and medieval Latin from Latin *ostiarius*, from *ostium* 'door'.

From the early 16th century, the word was used for an assistant to a schoolmaster or headteacher, an assistant master.

See also ➤ YEOMAN *Usher.*

Gentleman Usher of the Black Rod the formal title of ➤ BLACK *Rod.*

Usher of the Green Rod an officer attached to the Order of the Thistle.

Usonian of or relating to the United States, in particular, relating to or denoting the style of buildings designed in the 1930s by Frank Lloyd Wright, characterized by inexpensive construction and flat roofs. The word is recorded from 1915, and is a partial acronym, from the initial letters of *United States of North America* + *-ian.*

usquebaugh chiefly in Ireland and Scotland, whisky. The word is recorded from the late 16th century, and comes from Irish and Scottish Gaelic *uisge beatha* 'water of life'.

Ustashe the members of a Croatian extreme nationalist movement that engaged in terrorist activity before the Second World War and ruled Croatia with Nazi support after Yugoslavia was invaded and divided by the Germans in 1941.

Utgard in Scandinavian mythology, the home of the giants.

Uther Pendragon in Arthurian legend, king of the Britons and father of ➤ *King* ARTHUR.

utilitarianism the doctrine that actions are right if they are useful or for the benefit of a majority; the doctrine that an action is right in so far as it promotes happiness, and that the greatest happiness of the greatest number should be the guiding principle of conduct.

The most famous exponents of utilitarianism were Jeremy Bentham and J. S. Mill. It has been criticized for focusing on the consequences rather than the motive or intrinsic nature of an action, for the difficulty of adequately comparing the happiness of different individuals, and for failing to account for the value placed on concepts such as justice and equality.

Utnapishtim in Babylonian mythology, a figure equivalent to ➤ NOAH who survives a devastating flood.

Utopia an imagined place or state of things in which everything is perfect. The word was first used as the name of an imaginary island, governed on a perfect political and social system, in the book *Utopia* (1516) by Sir Thomas More. The name in modern Latin is literally 'no-place', from Greek *ou* 'not' + *topos* 'place'.

Utraquist another term for ➤ CALIXTINE; the name comes from Latin *utraque* 'each, both'.

Peace of Utrecht a series of treaties (1713–14) ending the War of the Spanish Succession. The disputed throne of Spain was given to the French Philip V, but the union of the French and Spanish thrones was forbidden. The House of Hanover succeeded to the British throne and the former Spanish territories in Italy were ceded to the Habsburgs.

Uzziel name of an angel who in Milton's *Paradise Lost* is described as 'next in power' to ➤ GABRIEL.

V v

V the twenty-second letter of the modern English alphabet and the twentieth of the ancient Roman one, of which U is a differentiated form.

V-chip a computer chip installed in a television receiver that can be programmed by the user to block or scramble material containing a special code in its signal indicating that it is deemed *violent* or sexually explicit.

V-1 a small flying bomb powered by a simple jet engine, used by the Germans in the Second World War. Also called *doodlebug*.

V-2 a rocket-powered flying bomb, which was the first ballistic missile, used by the Germans in the Second World War.

V-sign a sign resembling the letter V made with the first two fingers pointing up and the palm of the hand facing outwards, used as a symbol or gesture of victory; a similar sign made with the back of the hand facing outwards, used as a gesture of abuse or contempt.

vacuum see ➤ NATURE *abhors a vacuum*.

vade mecum a handbook or guide that is kept constantly at hand for consultation. The phrase is Latin and means 'go with me'; it is first used (in the early 17th century) as the title of a book.

Vader see ➤ DARTH *Vader*.

vadis see ➤ QUO *vadis*.

vae victis woe to the conquered (Latin proverbial saying); it is said by Livy to have been uttered by the Gallic king, Brennus, on capturing Rome in 390 BC (the occasion on which the Capitol was saved by the warning given by the ➤ SACRED *geese*).

vagina dentata the motif of a vagina with teeth, occurring in folklore and fantasy and said to symbolize male fears of the dangers of sexual intercourse.

vahana in Indian mythology, the mount or vehicle of a god.

Vaishnava a member of one of the main branches of modern Hinduism, devoted to the worship of the god ➤ VISHNU as the supreme being.

Vaisya a member of the third of the four Hindu castes, comprising the merchants and farmers.

vajra in Buddhism and Hinduism, a thunderbolt or mythical weapon, especially one wielded by the god Indra. Being struck by such a weapon is said to bring spiritual illumination.

Valdez Principles a set of guidelines drawn up in 1989, designed to regulate and monitor the conduct of corporations in matters relating to the environment. They are named after the Exxon *Valdez*, an oil tanker which ran aground off the Alaskan coast in 1989, causing considerable environmental damage.

vale a written or spoken farewell; the word is Latin, and means literally 'be well'.

See also ➤ AVE *atque vale*.

vale of tears the world as a place of sorrow and difficulty; the expression dates from the mid 16th century, and earlier variants are *vale of woe* and *vale of weeping*.

valentine originally (in late Middle English), a person chosen (sometimes by lot) to be one's sweetheart. Later, a card sent, often anonymously, on ➤ *St* VALENTINE's Day, 14 February, to a person one loves or is attracted to; a person to whom one sends such a card or whom one asks to be one's sweetheart.

Valentine cards first appeared in the 18th century and were made by the sender. In the 19th century shop-made valentines were first produced and became increasingly elaborate, adorned with lace, real flowers, feathers, and moss; their dispatch was aided by the introduction of the penny post.

St Valentine either of two early Italian saints (who may have been the same person) traditionally commemorated on 14 February—a Roman priest martyred *c*.269 and a bishop of Terni martyred at Rome. St Valentine was regarded as the patron of lovers, a tradition which may be connected with the old belief that birds pair on 14 February or with the pagan fertility festival of ➤ LUPERCALIA (15 February).

☐ **FEAST DAY** His feast day is 14 February.

St Valentine's Day Massacre the shooting on 14th February 1929 in Chicago by some of ➤ *Al* CAPONE's men, disguised as policemen, of seven members of the rival gang of 'Bugsy' Moran's.

Rudolph Valentino (1895–1926), Italian-born American actor. He played the romantic hero in silent films such as *The Sheikh* (1921) and *Blood and Sand* (1922), and is often taken as the type of a dashing and romantic lover; his sudden death at the age of 31 shocked his fans worldwide, and his funeral attracted a crowd of thousands.

Valera see ➤ *Eamon* DE *Valera*.

Valerian (d.260), Roman emperor 253–60, who renewed the persecution of the Christians initiated by Decius. He died after being captured while campaigning against the Persians of the Sassanian dynasty.

valet see ➤ NO *man is a hero to his valet*.

Valhalla in Scandinavian mythology, a palace in which heroes killed in battle were believed to feast with Odin for eternity. The name is from modern Latin, and comes from Old Norse *Valhǫll*, from *valr* 'the slain' + *hǫll* 'hall'.

> This Valhalla for the weary record collector carries hot jazz, zydeco, Cajun, and more.
> — *Wired* May 1996

Valkyrie in Scandinavian mythology, each of Odin's twelve handmaids who conducted the slain warriors of their choice from the battlefield to Valhalla. The name comes from Old Norse *Valkyrja*, literally 'chooser of the slain'.

Valletta the capital and chief port of Malta, named after Jean de *Valette*, Grand Master of the Knights of St John, who built the town after the victory over the Turks in 1565.

valley see also ➤ DEATH *Valley*, ➤ LILY *of the valley*, ➤ SILICON *Valley*.

Valley Forge the site on the Schuylkill River in Pennsylvania, about 32 km (20 miles) to the northwest of Philadelphia, where George Washington's

Continental Army spent the winter of 1777–8, during the War of American Independence, in conditions of extreme hardship.

Valley Girl informal term for a fashionable and affluent teenage girl, often using ➤ VALSPEAK, from the San Fernando valley in southern California.

Valley of the Kings a valley near ancient Thebes in Egypt where the pharaohs of the New Kingdom (*c*.1550–1070 BC) were buried. Most of the tombs, typically consisting of a richly decorated chamber at the end of a long series of descending corridors, were robbed in antiquity; the exception was the tomb of ➤ TUTANKHAMEN, almost untouched until discovered in 1922.

Valley of the Queens a valley near ancient Thebes in Egypt where the wives and daughters of pharaohs of the 20th dynasty were buried.

Vallombrosan a member of a strictly contemplative Benedictine order established at *Vallombrosa* in Italy in the 11th century by St John Gualberto (d. 1073).

Valois the French royal house from the accession of Philip VI, successor to the last Capetian king, in 1328 to the death of Henry III (1589), when the throne passed to the Bourbons.

valour see ➤ DISCRETION *is the better part of valour*.

Valspeak a variety of slang originating among teenage girls (➤ VALLEY *Girls*) in the San Fernando Valley of southern California and characterized by the use of filler words such as *like* and *totally* and a limited group of adjectives expressing approval or disapproval.

vampire in European folklore, a corpse supposed to leave its grave at night to drink the blood of the living by biting their necks with long pointed canine teeth. The word comes (in the mid 18th century) via French from Hungarian *vampir*, perhaps from Turkish *uber* 'witch'.

The 20th-century *vamp* for a woman who uses sexual attraction to exploit men is an abbreviation of this word.

Van Diemen's land former name (until 1855) for Tasmania (see ➤ *Abel* TASMAN).

Anthony Van Dyck (1599–1641), Flemish painter. He is famous for his portraits of members of the English court prior to the Civil War, noted for their refinement of style and elegant composition, which determined the course of portraiture in England for more than 200 years; the last words attributed to the artist Thomas Gainsborough (1727–88) are, 'We are all going to Heaven, and Van Dyck is of the company.'

See also ➤ VANDYKE.

Jan Van Eyck (*c*.1370–1441), Flemish painter. He made innovative use of oils, bringing greater flexibility, richer and denser colour, and a wider range from light to dark, in such paintings as *The Adoration of the Lamb* (known as the Ghent Altarpiece, 1432) in the church of St Bavon in Ghent and *The Arnolfini Marriage* (1434).

Vincent Van Gogh (1853–90), Dutch painter. He is best known for his post-Impressionist work, influenced by contact with Impressionist painting and Japanese woodcuts after he moved to Paris in 1886. His most famous pictures include several studies of sunflowers and *A Starry Night* (1889). Suffering from severe depression, he cut off part of his own ear and eventually committed suicide.

John Vanbrugh (1664–1726), English architect and dramatist. His comedies include *The Relapse* (1696) and *The Provok'd Wife* (1697); among his architectural works are Castle Howard in Yorkshire (1702) and Blenheim Palace in Oxfordshire (1705), both produced in collaboration with Nicholas Hawksmoor.

George Vancouver (1757–98), English navigator. He led an exploration of the coasts of Australia, New Zealand, and Hawaii (1791–2), and later charted much of the west coast of North America between southern Alaska and California. Vancouver Island and the city of Vancouver are named after him.

Vandal a member of a Germanic people that ravaged Gaul, Spain, Rome (455), and North Africa in the 4th–5th centuries, destroying many books and works of art. They were eventually defeated by the Byzantine general Belisarius (*c*.505–65), after which their North African kingdom fell prey to Muslim invaders.

The name is recorded in English from the mid 16th century; from the mid 17th century, the word *vandal* is used for a person who deliberately destroys or damages public or private property.

Cornelius Vanderbilt (1794–1877), American businessman and philanthropist. He amassed a fortune from shipping and railroads, and made an endowment to found Vanderbilt University in Nashville, Tennessee (1873). Subsequent generations of his family increased the family wealth and continued his philanthropy.

> Today . . . a *SatEvePost* rejection, my 2nd semester bill, and your forwarding of my check balance all came, and it is enough to make Vanderbilt wince.
> — Sylvia Plath letter to her mother, 27 January 1955

Vandyke a broad lace or linen collar with an edge deeply cut into large points (in imitation of a style frequently depicted in portraits by ➤ *Anthony* VAN Dyck), fashionable in the 18th century.

Vanessa female given name originally coined for *Esther Van*homrigh (1690–1723) by Jonathan Swift; *Vanessa* was later adopted as modern Latin as the name of a genus of butterfly.

vanilla having no special or extra features; ordinary. The term is a figurative use of *vanilla* as the default or standard flavour of ice-cream; it was used first with reference to sexual activity, and then from the early 1980s was applied particularly to computing equipment in the form supplied as standard by the manufacturer, without any optional additions or extra equipment.

Vanir in Scandinavian mythology, a race of gods responsible for commerce and fertility while the ➤ AESIR were responsible for war; ➤ NJORD and ➤ FREY were two of the Vanir.

Vanist an ➤ ANTINOMIAN, in particular a member of a 17th-century New England sect, from the name of the regicide Henry *Vane* (1613–62), English parliamentarian, Puritan, and governor of Massachusetts (1636–7).

vanitas a still-life painting of a 17th-century Dutch genre containing symbols of death or change as a reminder of their inevitability.

vanitas vanitatum vanity of vanities, futility (frequently as an exclamation of disillusionment or pessimism). The phrase is late Latin and comes from the Vulgate translation of Ecclesiastes 1:2.

vanities see ➤ POMPS *and vanities*.

Vanity Fair the world regarded as a place of frivolity and idle amusement, originally with reference to Bunyan's *Pilgrim's Progress* (1678), and the fair set up by Apollyon and named Vanity Fair 'because the town where 'tis kept is lighter than vanity'. The pilgrims have to pass through the fair on their way to the Celestial City, and it is there that Faithful is put to death.

Thackeray used the title for his satirical novel (1847–8) of 19th-century society life, in which the hopes and expectations of all his characters are to a greater or lesser degree disappointed.

Vanzetti see ➤ Sacco *and Vanzetti Case.*

Chad Varah (1911–), English clergyman, founder of the Samaritans in 1953 after recognizing a widespread need for an anonymous counselling service.
See also ➤ Samaritan.

Varanasi a city on the Ganges, in Uttar Pradesh, northern India, which is a holy city and a place of pilgrimage for Hindus, who undergo ritual purification in the Ganges.

Varangian any of the Scandinavian voyagers who travelled by land and up rivers into Russia in the 9th and 10th centuries AD, establishing the Rurik dynasty and gaining great influence in the Byzantine Empire. The name comes from medieval Latin *Varangus,* ultimately from Old Norse, and probably based on *vár* 'pledge'.

Varangian guard the bodyguard of the later Byzantine emperors, comprising Varangians and later also Anglo-Saxons.

Varden see ➤ Dolly *Varden.*

vardo a gypsy caravan; the word is from Romany.

variation see ➤ elegant *variation.*

variety is the spice of life proverbial saying, late 18th century; originally as a quotation from the English poet William Cowper (1731–1800):

> Variety's the very spice of life,
> That gives it all its flavour.
> — William Cowper *The Task* (1785)

An earlier version is found in the *The Rover* (1681) by the dramatist Aphra Behn (1640–89), 'Variety is the soul of pleasure.'

variorum an edition of an author's works having notes by various editors or commentators, and often including variant readings from manuscripts or earlier editions. The word is Latin, and comes (in the early 18th century) from *editio cum notis variorum* 'edition with notes by various (commentators)'.

varlet see ➤ *an* ape's *an ape.*

varna each of the four Hindu castes, Brahman, Kshatriya, Vaisya, and Sudra. In the Vedic religion of the ancient Aryans, the first three classes of society were Brahman, Kshatriya, and Vaisya. The fourth class, Sudra, was probably added later after contact with the indigenous people of the subcontinent.

Each class was considered equally necessary to the social order, the separate functions being complementary.

varnishing day another term for ➤ vernissage.

Marcus Terentius Varro (116–27 BC), Roman scholar and satirist. His works covered many subjects, including philosophy, agriculture, the Latin language, and education; he has given his name to *varroa,* a microscopic mite which is a debilitating parasite of the honeybee, with reference to his work on beekeeping.

varsity (especially of a sporting event or team) of or relating to a university, especially Oxford or Cambridge. The word comes (in the mid 17th century) from a shortening of *university,* reflecting an archaic pronunciation.

vartabed a member of an order of celibate priests in the Armenian Church. The word is Armenian, and is recorded in English from the early 18th century.

Varuna in Hinduism, one of the gods in the Rig Veda. Originally the sovereign lord of the universe and guardian of cosmic law, he is known in later Hinduism as god of the waters.

Vasa name of a Swedish dynasty, descended from an Uppland family, ruling Sweden between 1523 and 1818.

Giorgio Vasari (1511–74), Italian painter, architect, and biographer. His *Lives of the Most Excellent Painters, Sculptors, and Architects* (1550, enlarged 1568) laid the basis for later study of art history in the West. His own work includes frescoes depicting the history of Florence in the Palazzo Vecchio in Florence and the design of the Uffizi palace.

vassal a holder of land by feudal tenure on conditions of homage and allegiance; the word comes (in late Middle English, via Old French) from medieval Latin *vassalius* 'retainer', of Celtic origin.

VAT value-added tax; a tax on the amount by which the value of an article has been increased at each stage of its production or distribution. The introduction of the tax into the UK in the 1960s gave rise to the informal **VATman** for a customs and excise officer who deals with *VAT,* and to *zero-rated* to describe those items which are exempted from the tax.

Vaterland Germany as the Fatherland; the name is recorded from the mid 19th century.

Vathek central character of the oriental romance of that name by ➤ *William* Beckford (1760–1844), originally written in French and translated with the author's assistance by Samuel Henley; the Argentinian writer Jorge Luis Borges (1899–1986) said of Henley's work, 'The original is unfaithful to the translation.'

the Vatican the palace and official residence of the Pope in Rome, built on and named for the Vatican Hill; the administrative centre of the Roman Catholic Church. The name is recorded in English from the mid 16th century.

See also ➤ PRISONER *of the Vatican.*

Vatican City an independent papal state in the city of Rome, the seat of government of the Roman Catholic Church. It covers an area of 44 hectares (109 acres) around St Peter's Basilica and the palace of the Vatican. Having been suspended after the incorporation of the former Papal States into Italy in 1870, the temporal power of the Pope was restored by the Lateran Treaty of 1929.

Vatican Council each of two general councils of the Roman Catholic Church, held in 1869–70 and 1962–5. The first (**Vatican I**) proclaimed the infallibility of the Pope when speaking *ex cathedra*; the second (**Vatican II**) made numerous reforms, abandoning the universal Latin liturgy and acknowledging ecumenism.

vaudeville a type of entertainment popular chiefly in the US in the early 20th century, featuring a mixture of speciality acts such as burlesque comedy and song and dance. The word is recorded in English from the mid 18th century, originally in the sense a light popular song; it comes from French, earlier as *vau de ville* (or *vire*), said to be a name given originally to songs composed by Olivier Basselin, a 15th-century fuller born in *Vau de Vire* in Normandy.

Vaudois in France and French-speaking countries, a member of the ➤ WALDENSES religious sect.

Vauxhall an area of London in the neighbourhood of Lambeth, the site of **Vauxhall Gardens**, a popular pleasure resort originally laid out in 1661, as recorded by John Evelyn:

> I went to see the New Spring Garden at Lambeth, a pretty contriv'd plantation.
> — John Evelyn *Diary* 2 July 1661

The gardens were finally closed on 25 July 1859.

vavasour under the feudal system, a vassal owing allegiance to a great lord and having other vassals under him; the word is recorded from Middle English and comes via French from medieval Latin

vavassor, perhaps from *vassus vassorum* 'vassal of vassals'.

VE day the day (8 May) marking the Allied victory in Europe in 1945.

Thorstein Veblen (1857–1929), American economist and social scientist, whose works include the critique of capitalism and *The Theory of the Leisure Class* (1899), in which he coined the term *conspicuous consumption.*

> The eighties were to mark the blossoming of what Thorstein Veblen might have called the Conspicuous Friendship: a relationship or bond pursued not because of the psychological rewards it offered but because of the opportunity it provided individuals for enhanced status through mutual association.
> — John Taylor *Circus of Ambition* (1989)

Veda the most ancient Hindu scriptures, written in early Sanskrit and containing hymns, philosophy, and guidance on ritual for the priests of Vedic religion. Believed to have been directly revealed to seers among the early Aryans in India, and preserved by oral tradition, the four chief collections are the Rig Veda, Sama Veda, Yajur Veda, and Atharva Veda. In its wider sense, the term also includes the Brahmanas and the mystical Aranyakas and Upanishads.

Vedanta a Hindu philosophy based on the doctrine of the Upanishads, especially in its monistic form.

Vedic religion the ancient religion of the Aryan peoples who entered NW India from Persia *c.*2000–1200 BC. It was the precursor of Hinduism, and its beliefs and practices are contained in the Vedas.

Its characteristics included ritual sacrifice to many gods, especially Indra, Varuna, and Agni; social classes (varnas) that formed the basis of the caste system; and the emergence of the priesthood which dominated orthodox Brahmanism from *c.*900 BC. Transition to classical Hinduism began in about the 5th century BC.

veduta a realistic, detailed picture of a town scene with buildings of interest, especially one belonging to the genre represented by 18th-century Italian artists such as Canaletto and Piranesi; a **veduta ideata** is a picture in this style but showing an imaginary scene, especially one by Pannini.

Lope de Vega (1562–1635), Spanish dramatist and poet, regarded as the founder of Spanish drama. He is said to have written 1,500 plays, of which several hundred survive.

vegan a person who does not eat or use animal products. The word was coined in 1944 as the existing terms *vegetarian* and *fruitarian* were 'already associated with societies that allow the "fruits" of cows and fowls' (i.e. dairy products); the new expression was intended to convey adherence to much stricter principles.

vegetable see ➤ ANIMAL, *vegetable, and mineral.*

Vehmgericht a form of secret tribunal which exercised great power in Westphalia from the end of the 12th to the middle of the 16th century; the word is German, and means literally 'punishment court'.

> 'Was Rebecca guilty or not?' The Vehmgericht of the servants' hall had pronounced against him.
> — William Makepeace Thackeray *Vanity Fair* (1848)

veil see ➤ BEYOND *the veil.*

Diego Rodríguez de Silva y Velázquez (1599–1660), Spanish painter, court painter to Philip IV. His portraits humanized the formal Spanish tradition of idealized figures.

Diego Velázquez de Cuéllar (*c.*1465–1524), Spanish conquistador. After sailing with Columbus to the New World in 1493, he began the conquest of Cuba in 1511; he later initiated expeditions to conquer Mexico.

Velikovskianism the (controversial) theories of cosmology and history propounded by the Russian-born psychologist Immanuel *Velikovsky* (1895–1979), based on the hypothesis that other planets have approached close to the earth in historical times.

> Velikovsky's vision of the solar system has now been relegated to that corner of the scientific attic where sit ancient astronauts, the Piltdown man . . . and all the other playmates of the pseudoscientist.
> — J. L. Casti *Paradigms Lost* (1989)

Velleius Paterculus (*c.*19 BC–*c.*30 AD), Roman historian and soldier. His *Roman History,* covering the period from the early history of Rome to AD 30, is notable for its rhetorical manner and for its eulogistic depiction of ➤ TIBERIUS.

velociraptor a small dromaeosaurid dinosaur of the late Cretaceous period, given great prominence in the novel and film *Jurassic Park*; the current general use of ➤ RAPTOR for this kind of dinosaur comes from a shortening of ➤ VELOCIRAPTOR.

velvet see ➤ BLACK *velvet,* ➤ *an* IRON *hand in a velvet glove,* ➤ LITTLE *gentleman in black velvet,*

velvet divorce the non-violent split of the former state of Czechozlavakia in 1992 into the Czech Republic and Slovakia.

velvet revolution a non-violent political revolution, especially the relatively smooth change from Communism to a Western-style democracy in Czechoslovakia at the end of 1989.

> There may be, as one commentator has proposed, a kind of velvet revolution in which the change in Britain will be greater and more immediate than the Labour manifesto suggests.
> — *Independent on Sunday* 27 April 1997

Vendean an inhabitant of the Vendée (*La Vendée*), a maritime department in western France, who took part in the insurrection of 1793 against the Republic.

Vendemiaire the first month of the French Republican calendar (1793–1805), originally running from 22 September to 21 October. The name is French, and comes from Latin *vindemia* 'vintage'.

vendetta a blood feud in which the family of a murdered person seeks vengeance on the murderer or the murderer's family, especially as traditionally prevalent in Corsica and Sicily. Recorded from the mid 19th century, the word is Italian, and comes from Latin *vindicta* 'vengeance'.

venerable accorded a great deal of respect, especially because of age, wisdom, or character; (in the Anglican Church) a title given to an archdeacon; (in the Roman Catholic Church) a title given to a deceased person who has attained a certain degree of sanctity but has not been fully beatified or canonized.

the Venerable Bede traditional name for ➤ *St* BEDE.

Venetian School a school of painting, noted for its mastery of colouring, which originated in Venice in the 15th century and reached its climax with artists such as Titian in the 16th century.

Veni, Sancte Spiritus opening words ('Come, Holy Spirit') of a medieval Latin hymn, used on Whit Sunday; it is attributed to Stephen Langton (d. 1228), Archbishop of Canterbury, as well as to others, notably Pope Innocent III, and is sometimes known as the *Golden Sequence.*

veni, vidi, vici Latin for 'I came, I saw, I conquered', an inscription displayed in Julius Caesar's

Pontic triumph (according to Suetonius) or (according to Plutarch), written in a letter by Caesar, announcing the victory of Zela (47 BC) which concluded the Pontic campaign.

venial in Christian theology, denoting a sin that is not regarded as depriving the soul of divine grace. The word comes ultimately (in Middle English, via Old French) from late Latin *venia* 'forgiveness'.

Venice a city in NE Italy, situated on a lagoon of the Adriatic and built on numerous islands that are separated by canals and linked by bridges. It was a powerful republic in the Middle Ages and from the 13th to the 16th centuries a leading sea power, controlling trade to the Levant and ruling parts of the eastern Mediterranean.

Venice glass a very fine and delicate kind of glass, originally manufactured at Murano, near Venice.

Venice treacle an electuary composed of many ingredients, supposed to possess universal properties as an antidote to poison and a preservative.

venison meat from a deer; originally the flesh of any animal killed by hunting and used as food. The word comes (in Middle English, via Old French) from Latin *venatio(n-)* 'hunting'.

Venite Psalm 95 used as a canticle in Christian liturgy, chiefly at matins; *venite* is Latin for 'come ye', and is the first word of the psalm.

Venn diagram a diagram representing mathematical or logical sets pictorially as circles or closed curves within an enclosing rectangle (the universal set), common elements of the sets being represented by intersections of the circles. It is named after John *Venn* (1834–1923), English logician.

Thomas Venner (d. 1661), English preacher and revolutionary, leader (in January 1661) of a rising by the ➤ FIFTH-*Monarchy-Men*. The rising failed, and Venner, who was captured, was hanged in front of his meeting-house on 19 January.

Ventose the sixth month of the French Republican calendar (1793–1805), originally running from 19 February to 20 March. The word is French and comes from Latin *ventosus* 'windy'.

ventre à terre at full speed (used especially of a horse's movement or its representation in painting). The phrase comes from French, and means literally '(with) belly to the ground'.

ventriloquist a person who can speak or utter sounds so that they seem to come from somewhere else, especially an entertainer who makes their voice appear to come from a dummy of a person or animal. The word comes (in the mid 17th century) from modern Latin *ventriloquium*, from Latin *venter* 'belly' + *loqui* 'speak'.

venture see ➤ NOTHING *venture, nothing gain*, ➤ NOTHING *venture, nothing have*.

Robert Venturi (1925–), American architect, pioneer of postmodernist architecture. Among his buildings are the Humanities Classroom Building of the State University of New York (1973) and the Sainsbury Wing of the National Gallery in London (1991).

Venus in Roman mythology, a goddess, worshipped as the goddess of love in classical Rome though apparently a spirit of kitchen gardens in earlier times. She is the mother of ➤ CUPID and (though wife of Hephaestus), lover of ➤ MARS. Her Greek equivalent is ➤ APHRODITE.

Venus Anadyomene Venus portrayed rising from the sea, according to Pliny's *Natural History* in a picture by the Greek artist ➤ APELLES, and represented in Botticelli's The Birth of Venus.

Venus de Medici a classical sculpture in the Uffizi Gallery at Florence.

Venus de Milo a classical sculpture of Aphrodite dated to *c.*100 BC. It was discovered on the Greek island of Melos in 1820 and is now in the Louvre in Paris, having formed part of the war loot acquired by Napoleon on his campaigns.

Venus Genetrix Venus as a symbol of marriage and motherhood.

Venus Verticordia Venus as one who turns hearts.

Venus Victrix Venus as goddess of victory.

Venusberg in German legend, the court of Venus, said to have been visited by the poet ➤ TANN-HÄUSER; in transferred use, any environment whose primary environment is sensual pleasure.

> *Tartarus of Maids* is a descent into a sexual underworld, both inferno and Venusberg.
> — Camille Paglia *Sexual Personae* (1990)

venville a special form of tenure obtaining in parishes adjoining Dartmoor, by which the tenants enjoy certain privileges in the use of the moor. The origin of the word is unknown; the suggestion that it represents an alteration of *fines villarum* is not supported by earlier forms.

vera causa (in Newtonian philosophy) the true cause of a natural phenomenon, by an agency whose existence is independently evidenced; the phrase is Latin, and means literally 'real cause'.

verb. sap. used to express the absence of the need for a further explicit statement; an abbreviation of Latin *verbum sapienti sat est* 'a word is enough for a wise person'. The saying comes originally from the Roman comic dramatist Plautus (*c.*250–184 BC), '*Dictum sapienti sat est* [A sentence is enough for a sensible man]'.

verbatim in exactly the same words as were used originally; the word is recorded from the late 15th century, and comes ultimately from Latin *verbum* 'word'.

Vercingetorix Gallic leader of a revolt against Rome; defeated by Julius Caesar in the ➤ GALLIC *Wars*, he was put to death in 46 BC.

verderer a judicial officer of a royal forest; the word is recorded from the mid 16th century, and comes from Anglo-Norman French, based on Latin *viridis* 'green'.

Giuseppe Verdi (1813–1901), Italian composer. His many operas, such as *La Traviata* (1853), *Aida* (1871), and *Otello* (1887), emphasize the dramatic element, treating personal stories on a heroic scale and often against backgrounds that reflect his political interests. He is also famous for his *Requiem* (1874).

Battle of Verdun a long and severe battle in 1916, during the First World War, at the fortified town of Verdun in NE France, in which the French, initially unprepared, eventually repelled a prolonged German offensive but suffered heavy losses. Their slogan, '*Ils ne passeront pas* [They shall not pass]' has been variously attributed to Marshal Pétain and to General Robert Nivelle.

> The battlefields that made the name Verdun synonymous with the horrors of the Great War.
> — *Homiletic & Pastoral Review* October 1993

verger an official in a church who carries a rod before a bishop or dean as a symbol of office; an officer who carries a rod before a bishop or dean as a symbol of office. The word is recorded from Middle English, and comes ultimately from Latin *virga* 'rod'.

vergobret the chief magistrate among the Aedui, a people of ancient Gaul.

Jan Vermeer (1632–75), Dutch painter. He generally painted domestic genre scenes, for example *The*

Kitchen-Maid (*c.*1658). His work is distinguished by its clear design and simple form.

vermilion a brilliant red pigment made from mercury sulphide (cinnabar). Recorded from Middle English, the word comes via Old French and ultimately from Latin *vermiculus*, diminutive of *vermis* 'worm'.

Vermont see ➤ *as* MAINE *goes, so goes the nation.*

Jules Verne (1828–1905), French novelist. One of the first writers of science fiction, he often anticipated later scientific and technological developments, as in *Twenty Thousand Leagues under the Sea* (1870).

Verner's law the observation that voiceless fricatives in Germanic predicted by Grimm's Law became voiced if the preceding syllable in the corresponding Indo-European word was unstressed. It is named after Karl A. *Verner* (1846–96), Danish philologist.

vernicle a vernicle, or cloth supposedly impressed with Christ's face, is the emblem of ➤ *St* VERONICA.

vernissage a private view of paintings before public exhibition. The word is French (literally 'varnishing'), and originally referred to the day prior to an exhibition when artists were allowed to retouch and varnish hung work.

Paolo Veronese (*c.*1528–88), Italian painter. He gained many commissions in Venice, including the painting of frescoes in the Doges' Palace. He is particularly known for his richly coloured feast scenes (for example *The Marriage at Cana*, 1562).

St Veronica according to tradition, a woman of Jerusalem who offered her headcloth to Christ on the way to Calvary, to wipe the blood and sweat from his face. The cloth is said to have retained the image of his features, and is called a *vernicle* or *veronica* in her honour.

The term veronica also denotes the movement of a matador's cape away from a charging bull; this is said to be by association of the attitude of the matador with the depiction of St Veronica holding out a cloth to Christ.

Verrazano-Narrows Bridge a suspension bridge across New York harbour between Brooklyn and Staten Island, the longest in the world when it was completed in 1964. It was named after Giovanni da *Verrazano* (1485–1528), Italian explorer.

vers de société verse dealing with topics provided by polite society in a light, witty style; the French phrase is recorded in English from the late 18th century.

vers libre French term for *free verse*.

Gianni Versace (1946–97), Italian fashion designer noted for his glitzy and extravagant styles, who was shot dead outside his home in Miami.

> She was only taken seriously in male-dominated Hollywod once blanded out, Versace'd up and slimmed down.
>
> — *Cosmopolitan* June 1999

Versailles a palace built for Louis XIV near the town of Versailles, south-west of Paris. It was built around a château belonging to Louis XIII, which was transformed by additions in the grand French classical style.

Much interior work was carried out by Charles Lebrun and André-Charles Boulle (1642–1732), while the elaborate gardens were laid out by André Le Nôtre. Later extensions were added during the reigns of Louis XIV and Louis XV. The palace's active life terminated when Louis XVI was forced out by the Paris revolutionaries in October 1789, but Versailles was restored and turned into a museum by King Louis Philippe.

Treaty of Versailles a treaty which terminated the War of American Independence in 1783; a treaty signed in 1919 which brought a formal end to the First World War.

The treaty of 1919 redivided the territory of the defeated Central Powers, restricted Germany's armed forces, and established the League of Nations. It left Germany smarting under what it considered a vindictive settlement while not sufficiently restricting its ability eventually to rearm and seek forcible redress; the French general Ferdinand Foch (1851–1929) is said to have remarked at the signing of the Treaty, 'This is not a peace treaty, it is an armistice for twenty years.'

versal a capital letter in an ornate style used to start a verse or paragraph in a manuscript, typically built up by inking between pen strokes and with long, rather flat serifs. The word comes from Latin *vers-* 'turned', influenced by *verse*.

verse see ➤ CHAPTER *and verse*.

versicle a short sentence said or sung by the minister in a church service, to which the congregation gives a response.

verso a left-hand page of an open book, or the back of a loose document. The word is Latin, and comes from the phrase *verso (folio)* 'on the turned (leaf)'.

vert green, as a heraldic tincture. The word is recorded from Middle English (as an adjective), and comes via Old French from Latin *viridis* 'green'.

vervain a widely distributed herbaceous plant with small blue, white, or purple flowers and a long history of use as a magical and medicinal herb; the name is recorded from late Middle English, and comes ultimately from Latin *verbena* 'sacred bough'.

Verwoerdian in South Africa, of or relating to apartheid, especially as it involved geographically based racial segregation. It is named after Hendrik *Verwoerd* (1901–66), South African statesman, who developed the segregation policy of apartheid, and who as Premier banned the ANC and the Pan-Africanist Congress in 1960, following the ➤ SHARPEVILLE massacre. He was assassinated by a parliamentary messenger.

Vesak the most important Buddhist festival, taking place at the full moon when the sun is in the zodiacal sign of Taurus, and commemorating the birth, enlightenment, and death of the Buddha. Also, the month in which this festival occurs.

Andreas Vesalius (1514–64, Flemish anatomist, the founder of modern anatomy. His major work, *De Humani Corporis Fabrica* (1543), contained accurate descriptions of human anatomy, but owed much of its great historical impact to the woodcuts of his dissections.

vesica piscis a pointed oval figure (also called *mandorla*) used as an architectural feature and as an aureole enclosing figures such as Christ or the Virgin Mary in medieval art. The term is Latin, and means literally 'fish's bladder'; the reason for the name is not clear, although it may refer to the shape.

Vespasian (AD 9–79), Roman emperor 69–79 and founder of the Flavian dynasty, father of ➤ TITUS. He was acclaimed emperor by the legions in Egypt during the civil wars following the death of Nero and gained control of Italy after the defeat of Vitellius. His reign saw the restoration of financial and military order and the initiation of a public building programme (in the course of which he is said to have pointed out to his son that ➤ MONEY *has no smell*). His last words, according to Suetonius, were 'An emperor ought to die standing.'

Vesper in poetic and literary use, Venus as the evening star; Hesper, Hesperus.

vespers a service of evening prayer in the Divine Office of the Western Christian Church (sometimes said earlier in the day). In modern Roman Catholic use, the services for Sundays and solemn feasts begin on the preceding evening with first vespers and end with second vespers.

See also ➤ *the* FATAL *Vespers*, ➤ SICILIAN *Vespers*.

Amerigo Vespucci (1451–1512), Italian merchant and explorer. He travelled to the New World, reaching the coast of Venezuela on his first voyage (1499–1500) and exploring the Brazilian coastline in 1501–2. The Latin form of his first name is believed to have given rise to the name of *America*.

vessel see ➤ EMPTY *vessels make the most sound*, ➤ *the* WEAKER *vessel*.

Vesta in Roman mythology, the goddess of the hearth and household. She was worshipped in a round building in the Forum at Rome, probably an imitation in stone of an ancient round hut. Her temple in Rome contained no image but a fire which was kept constantly burning and was tended by the Vestal Virgins.

Vestal Virgin in ancient Rome, a virgin consecrated to Vesta and vowed to chastity, sharing the charge of maintaining the sacred fire burning on the goddess's altar; there were originally four, and later six, of these priestesses.

vestry a room or building attached to a church, used as an office and for changing into ceremonial vestments; a meeting of parishioners, originally in a vestry, for the conduct of parochial business; a body of parishioners meeting in such a way.

Vesuvius an active volcano near Naples, in southern Italy, 1,277 m (4,190 ft) high. A violent eruption in AD 79 buried the towns of ➤ POMPEII and Herculaneum.

> A political Vesuvius had erupted which made the Milan corruption scandals look like a middle-sized tremor.
> — *Independent on Sunday* 4 April 1993

veteran a person who has had long experience in a particular field, especially military service. Recorded from the early 16th century, the word comes ultimately from Latin *vetus* 'old'.

veteran car in the UK, an old style or model of car, specifically one made before 1916, or (strictly) before 1905.

Veterans Day in the US, a public holiday held on the anniversary of the end of the First World War (11 November) to honour US veterans and victims of all wars. It replaced ➤ ARMISTICE *Day* in 1954.

veto a constitutional right to reject a decision or proposal-made by a law-making body. The word comes (in the early 17th century) from Latin, meaning literally 'I forbid', used by Roman tribunes of the people when opposing measures of the Senate.

In late 18th century France, **Monsieur Veto** and **Madame Veto** were nicknames given to Louis XVI and Marie Antoinette.

See also ➤ POCKET *veto*.

vexillum a Roman military standard or banner, especially one of a maniple; a body of troops under such a standard. The word is Latin, and comes from *vehere* 'carry'.

vi et armis violently, forcibly; with unlawful violence; the phrase is Latin, and means literally 'with force and arms'.

via a road or highway; in particular, one of the great Roman roads (in Latin *via* means 'road' or 'way').

The preposition *via*, travelling through (a place) en route to a destination, comes (in the late 18th century) from Latin, ablative of *via* 'way, road'.

via affirmativa in theology, the approach to God through positive statements about his nature.

Via Appia Latin name for the ➤ APPIAN *Way*.

Via Crucis Latin name for the ➤ WAY *of the Cross*.

via dolorosa the route believed to have been taken by Christ through Jerusalem to Calvary. The name is Latin, and means literally 'painful path'.

Via Flaminia Latin name for the ➤ FLAMINIAN *Way*.

Via Lactea Latin name for the ➤ MILKY *Way*.

via media a middle way; the term is Latin, recorded in English from the mid 19th century.

via negativa in theology, a way of describing something by saying what it is not, especially denying that any finite concept of attribute can be identified with or used of God or ultimate reality.

vials of wrath stored-up anger, originally with allusion to Revelation 15:7, 'seven golden vials full of the wrath of God'.

viatical settlement an arrangement whereby a person with a terminal illness sells their life insurance policy to a third party for less than its mature value, in order to benefit from the proceeds while alive; the system (referred to informally as *death futures*) developed with the spread of Aids and the heightened awareness of the possibility of long-drawn-out terminal illness requiring nursing care for previous healthy young people.

The term is recorded from the 1990s, and comes from Latin *viaticus* 'relating to a journey or departing'.

viaticum the Eucharist as given to a person near or in danger of death; the word comes (in the mid 16th century) from Latin, ultimately from *via* 'road'.

vicar (in the Church of England) an incumbent of a parish where tithes formerly passed to a chapter or religious house or layman; (in other Anglican Churches) a member of the clergy deputizing for another; (in the Roman Catholic Church) a representative or deputy of a bishop; (in the US Episcopal Church) a clergyman in charge of a chapel. The word is recorded from Middle English, and comes ultimately from Latin *vicarius* 'substitute'.

See also ➤ *Vicar of* BRAY.

vicar apostolic a Roman Catholic missionary; a titular bishop.

vicar choral a member of the clergy or choir appointed to sing certain parts of a cathedral service.

vicar general an Anglican official serving as a deputy or assistant to a bishop or archbishop; (in the Roman Catholic Church) a bishop's representative in matters of jurisdiction or administration.

Vicar of Christ (in the Roman Catholic Church) a title of the Pope, as Christ's representative on earth, dating from the 8th century.

Vicar of Hell nickname given to the courtier and translator Francis Bryan (d. 1550) by Thomas Cromwell, shortly after Bryan had accepted a pension formerly in the possession of one of the men implicated in the fall of Bryan's cousin Anne Boleyn. It is likely to be Bryan to whom Milton refers in *Areopagitica* (1644) 'I name not him for posterity's sake, whom Henry VIII named in merriment his Vicar of Hell.'

vice immoral or wicked behaviour; often personified, especially as a character in a morality play.

> I hate when vice can bolt her arguments,
> And virtue has no tongue to check her pride.
> — John Milton *Comus* (1634)

vice versa with the main items in the preceding statement the other way round. The phrase is Latin, recorded in English from the early 17th century, and means literally 'in-turned position'.

Gil Vicente (*c*.1465–*c*.1536), Portuguese dramatist and poet. He is regarded as Portugal's most important dramatist; many of his works were written to commemorate national or court events and include religious dramas, farces, pastoral plays, and satirical comedies.

Vichy a town in south central France which during the Second World War was the headquarters of the regime (1940–4) that was set up under Marshal Pétain after the German occupation of northern France, to administer unoccupied France and the colonies. Never recognized by the Allies, the regime functioned as a puppet government for the Nazis and continued to collaborate with the Germans after they had moved into the unoccupied parts of France in 1942.

> Dirty fragments of the past constantly surface and are used, often dirtily, in current political disputes. For France, the historian Henry Rousso has described this vividly as the 'Vichy Syndrome'.
> — *New York Review of Books* 19 February 1998

vicious circle a sequence of reciprocal cause and effect in which two or more elements intensify and aggravate each other, leading inexorably to a worsening of the situation.

vicisti, Galilaee Latin for 'You have won, Galilean'; supposed dying words of Julian the Apostate (AD *c*.332–363), who as emperor had restored paganism as the state cult in place of Christianity, a move which was reversed after his death.

Vicksburg a city on the Mississippi River, in western Mississippi. In 1863, during the American Civil War, it was successfully besieged by Union forces under General Grant. It was the last Confederate-held outpost on the river and its loss effectively split the secessionist states in half.

> Marty, in the fruition of the best-laid campaign since Grant took Vicksburg, has finally . . . won Hannah.
> — *TV Guide* 23 February 1991

Giambattista Vico (1668–1744), Italian philosopher. In *Scienza Nuova* (1725) he asserted that civilizations are subject to recurring cycles of barbarism, heroism, and reason, accompanied by corresponding cultural, linguistic, and political modes. His historicist approach influenced later philosophers such as Marx.

Victor Emmanuel II (1820–78), ruler of the kingdom of Sardinia 1849–61 and first king of united Italy 1861–78. He hastened the drive towards Italian unification by appointing Cavour as Premier of Piedmont in 1852. In 1859 he defeated the Austrians at the battles of Magenta and Solferino, and in 1860 he joined forces with ➤ GARIBALDI in the papal territories around French-held Rome. After being crowned king of Italy he added Venetia to the kingdom in 1866 and Rome in 1870.

victor ludorum a boy or man who is the overall champion in a sports competition, especially at a school or college. The phrase is Latin, and means literally 'victor of the games'.

Victoria (1819–1901), queen of Great Britain and Ireland 1837–1901 and empress of India 1876–1901. Inheriting the throne at the age of 18 (she said as a child, on being shown a chart of the line of succession, 'I will be good'), she took an active interest in the policies of her ministers, but largely retired from public life after Prince Albert's death in 1861. Her reign was the longest in British history and she is often seen as embodying the unyielding virtues of the 'Victorian' years, and typified by the attributed remark, 'We are not amused.'

Victoria and Albert Museum a national museum of fine and applied art in South Kensington, London, having collections principally of pictures, textiles, ceramics, and furniture. Created in 1852 out of the surplus funds of the Great Exhibition, the museum moved to its present site in 1857.

Victoria Cross a decoration awarded for conspicuous bravery in the Commonwealth armed services, instituted by Queen Victoria in 1856. The medals were originally struck from the metal of Russian guns captured at Sebastopol during the Crimean War.

Victoria Day in Canada, the Monday preceding May 24, observed as a national holiday to commemorate the birthday of Queen Victoria.

Victoria Falls a spectacular waterfall 109 m (355 ft) high, on the River Zambezi, on the Zimbabwe–Zambia border, discovered in 1855 by David Livingstone. Its native name is *Mosi-oa-tunya* 'the smoke that thunders'.

Victorian see also ➤ ROYAL *Victorian Order*.

Victorian values a phrase associated with the Margaret Thatcher's Conservative government of the 1980s, embodying aspirations for what were seen as the 19th-century virtues of self-reliance and morality; the term was used by Margaret Thatcher in a speech of July 1983, explaining a reference she had made in an earlier interview: 'I was asked whether I was trying to restore Victorian values. I

said straight out I was. And I am.'

> That whole decade, with all its fading fantasies—Reagan, Thatcher, Scargill, Kinnock, 'Victorian values', 'sustained economic growth'.
> — *Guardian* 24 July 1993

victoriate an ancient Roman silver coin stamped with the image of the goddess of Victory, equal to half a denarius.

victorine a founder or adherent of the type of mysticism developed at the monastery of St Victor near Paris in the 12th and 13th centuries.

victory See also ➤ CADMEAN *victory*, ➤ PYRRHIC *victory*, ➤ WINGED *Victory*.

Victory the flagship of Lord Nelson at the Battle of Trafalgar, launched in 1765. It has been restored, and is now on display in dry dock at Portsmouth.

Victory Medal awarded to British soldiers at the conclusion of the First World War; with the 1914–15 Star and the War Medal, sometimes known as ➤ PIP, *Squeak, and Wilfred*.

victory sign a signal of triumph or celebration made by holding up the hand with the palm outwards and the first two fingers spread apart to represent the letter V; also known as the ➤ V-*sign*.

Vicwardian in a style characteristic of the reigns of Queen Victoria (1837–1901) and King Edward VII (1901–10), blending Victorian and Edwardian styles.

Vidar in Scandinavian mythology, the son of ➤ ODIN who will avenge his father at Ragnarök by killing the wolf ➤ FENRIR.

videlicet more formal term for ➤ VIZ.; the word is Latin, and comes from *videre* 'to see' + *licet* 'it is permissible'.

vie de Bohème French expression for an unconventional or informal way of life, especially as practised by an artist or writer, a ➤ BOHEMIAN life.

vie en rose a life seen through rose-coloured spectacles (the phrase apparently comes from a French song by Edith Piaf containing the line '*je vois la vie en rose*').

Vie Parisienne Parisian life, from *La Vie Parisienne*, a popular French magazine, used to denote a characteristic of voluptuous appeal.

Congress of Vienna an international conference held 1814–15 to agree the settlement of Europe after the Napoleonic Wars. Attended by all the major

European powers, it was dominated by Prussia, Russia, Britain, Austria, and France. The guiding principle of the settlement was the restoration and strengthening of hereditary and sometimes despotic rulers; the result was a political stability that lasted for three or four decades. It was of the *Congress of Vienna* that the Belgian soldier Charles-Joseph, Prince de Ligne (1735–1814) commented, '*Le congrès ne marche pas, il danse* [The Congress makes no progress; it dances].'

Vienna Circle a group of empiricist philosophers, scientists, and mathematicians active in Vienna from the 1920s until 1938, including Rudolf Carnap and Kurt Gödel. Their work laid the foundations of logical positivism.

Vietnam War a war between Communist North Vietnam and US-backed South Vietnam.

Since the partition of Vietnam in 1954 the Communist North had attempted to unite the country as a Communist state, fuelling US concern over the possible spread of Communism in SE Asia. After two US destroyers were reportedly fired on in the Gulf of Tonkin in 1964, a US army was sent to Vietnam, supported by contingents from South Korea, Australia, New Zealand, and Thailand, while American aircraft bombed North Vietnamese forces and areas of Cambodia.

The Tet Offensive of 1968 damaged US confidence in its ability to win the war, which was arousing immense controversy and resentment at home, and US forces began to be withdrawn, finally leaving in 1973.

view see ➤ DISTANCE *lends enchantment.*

Élisabeth Vigée-Lebrun (1755–1842), French painter. She is known for her portraits of women and children, especially Marie Antoinette and Lady Hamilton.

Vigenere a polyalphabetic cipher first described in 1586 by Blaise de *Vigenère* (1523–96), French scholar and student of ciphers.

vigilante a member of a self-appointed group of citizens who undertake law enforcement in their community without legal authority, typically because the legal agencies are thought to be inadequate. The word comes (in the mid 19th century) from Spanish, and means literally 'vigilant'.

Viking any of the Scandinavian seafaring pirates and traders who raided and settled in many parts of NW Europe in the 8th–11th centuries. The name

comes from Old Norse *vik* 'creek' or Old English *wīc* 'camp, dwelling place'.

The name *Viking* was also given to either of two American space probes sent to Mars in 1975, each of which consisted of a lander that conducted experiments on the surface and an orbiter.

vila in southern Slavonic mythology, a fairy, a nymph, a spirit.

Pancho Villa (1878–1923), Mexican revolutionary. After playing a prominent role in the revolution of 1910–11 he overthrew the dictatorial regime of General Victoriano Huerta in 1914 together with Venustiano Carranza, but then rebelled against Carranza's regime with Emiliano Zapata.

villain originally (in Middle English) a rustic, a boor; later, a person with ignoble ideas or instincts, a scoundrel; a person guilty or capable of a crime or wickedness. The word comes via Old French from Latin *villa* a country residence, the same base as ➤ VILLEIN.

the villain of the piece the main culprit; the character in a play or novel, important to the plot because of his or her evil motives or actions. The first recorded use of *villain* in this sense is from Charles Lamb's *Elia* (1822); *villain of the piece* is recorded from the mid 19th century.

villanelle a pastoral or lyrical poem of nineteen lines, with only two rhymes throughout, and some lines repeated. The word is French, and comes ultimately from the diminutive of Italan *villano* 'peasant'.

villein in medieval England, a feudal tenant entirely subject to a lord or manor to whom he paid dues and services in return for land. The word is recorded from Middle English, and is a variant of ➤ VILLAIN.

François Villon (fl. *c.*1460), French poet, best known for *Le Lais* or *Le Petit testament* (1456) and the longer, more serious *Le Grand testament* (1461). Criminal behaviour led eventually to the death sentence in Paris (1462), but it was commuted to banishment.

vim an informal word for energy and enthusiasm, perhaps deriving from Latin, the accusative of *vis* 'energy'.

vimana in Indian mythology, a heavenly chariot.

Battle of Vimy Ridge an Allied attack on the German position of Vimy Ridge, near Arras, during the

First World War. One of the key points on the Western Front, it had long resisted assaults, but on 9 April 1917 it was taken by Canadian troops in fifteen minutes, at the cost of heavy casualties.

Vinalia in ancient Rome, each of two wine festivals, held in April and August. The first marked the opening of casks filled the previous August; the second was for the inauguration of the grape harvest.

vinaya (the scripture containing) the code of conduct that regulates Buddhist monastic life.

St Vincent de Paul (1581–1660), French priest. He devoted his life to work among the poor and the sick and established institutions to continue his work, including the Congregation of the Mission (1625) and the Daughters of Charity (Sisters of Charity of St Vincent de Paul) (1633).

   □ **FEAST DAY** His feast day is 19 July.

St Vincent of Saragossa (d. 304), Spanish deacon and martyr, who is said to have been tortured on a gridiron, and who was the centre of a widespread early cult; he is typically shown either with a palm as a sign of being a deacon, or with a gridiron.

   □ **EMBLEM** A vine, a palm, and a gridiron are all emblems of St Vincent of Saragossa.

   □ **FEAST DAY** His feast day is 22 January.

Vincentian another name for ➤ LAZARIST.

Vinci see ➤ LEONARDO *da Vinci*.

Vincula see ➤ *St* PETER *ad Vincula*.

vindaloo a highly spiced hot Indian curry made with meat or fish. The name probably comes from Portuguese *vin d'alho* 'wine and garlic (sauce)', from *vinho* 'wine' + *alho* 'garlic'.

vine in Christian iconography, the *vine* sometimes stands for Jesus Christ, in allusion to John 15:1 'I am the true vine' and John 15:5, 'I am the vine, ye are the branches'.

   A *vine* is the emblem of ➤ *St* VINCENT *of Saragossa*.

   The word is recorded from Middle English and comes via Old French from Latin *vinea* 'vineyard, vine' from *vinum* 'wine'.

vinegar *vinegar* is taken as the type of something sour and acrid-tasting, as in Proverbs 10:26, 'As vinegar to the teeth, and as smoke to the eyes'. *Vinegar* was offered to Christ on the Cross in response to his words 'I thirst'; this was later sometimes understood as an infliction of further suffering.

According to Livy, Hannibal cleared a way over the Alps by felling trees, burning logs on the rocks to heat them, and then pouring *vinegar* over them to make them crumble; the Roman poet Juvenal has the lines, 'Then nature bars his path with the snowy Alps; by vinegar's aid he splits the rocks and shatters the mountain.'

   In figurative use, *vinegar* denotes sourness or peevishness of behaviour, character, or speech.

   See also ➤ HONEY *catches more flies than vinegar*.

Vinegar Bible an edition of 1717 by John Baskett, in which one of the running-heads for *Luke* reads 'The parable of the vinegar' instead of 'The parable of the vineyard'.

Vinegar Hill in the Irish insurrection of 1798, this was the main rebel encampment, successfully stormed on 21 June, and remembered as the Wexford rebel forces' decisive defeat.

> And if for want of leaders we lost at Vinegar Hill,
> We're ready for another fight and love our country still.

> We are the Boys of Wexford who fought with heart and hand
> To burst in twain the galling chain, and free our native land.
> — Robert Dwyer Joyce 'The Boys of Wexford' (1908)

Vinegar Joe nickname of the American general Joseph Stilwell (1883–1946), noted for his acid tongue.

vineyard in figurative usage, a sphere of action or labour, as in biblical allusion to Matthew 20:1 'For the kingdom of heaven is like unto a man that is an householder, which went out early in the morning to hire labourers into his vineyard' and 21:28, 'go work today in my vineyard'.

   In the **parable of the vineyard** in Luke's gospel, which gave its name to the ➤ VINEGAR *Bible*, the vineyard stands for the world created by God. The parable tells the story of a man who planted a vineyard and let it out to husbandmen while he was away. On his return, he sent his servants (the prophets) for the fruit, but they were beaten and driven away; when he sent his son (Jesus Christ), the husbandmen said, 'This is the heir; come, let us kill him that the inheritance may be ours.'

   See also ➤ MARTHA*'s Vineyard*, ➤ NABOTH.

vingt-et-un the card game pontoon or blackjack, in which the object is to make the number twenty-one or as near this as possible; the term is first recorded in the Duchess of Northumberland's diary for 7 June 1772, 'We play'd…at Vingt et un till supper time.'

Vinland the region of the NE coast of North America which was visited in the 11th century by Norsemen led by Leif Ericsson. It was so named from the report that grapevines were found growing there. The exact location is uncertain: sites from the northernmost tip of Newfoundland, where Viking remains have been found, to Cape Cod and even Virginia have been proposed.

Vinland Map supposedly a 15th century map, first published in 1965, showing the northeastern coastline of the North American continent as an island named Vinland, with an inscription describing its discovery by Leif Eiriksson; the authenticiy of the map is debated.

vintage the harvesting of grapes for winemaking; the grapes or wine produced in a particular season.

vintage car an old style or model of car, specifically one made between 1917 and 1930.

the Vintry a large wine-store formerly existing in the City of London; also, the immediate neighbourhood of this as a part of the city. The name survives in the designation of the church St Martin Vintry, now united with St. Michael Paternoster Royal and All Hallows the Great and Less.

City of the Violated Treaty name given to Limerick, with reference to the ➤ *Treaty of* LIMERICK.

violet a herbaceous plant of temperate regions, typically having purple, blue, or white five-petalled flowers; traditionally regarded as a flower of spring, the *violet* is also sometimes taken as emblematic of modesty and shyness.

City of the Violet Crown poetic name for Athens, translating an epithet used by Pindar and Aristophanes.

the violet on the tyrant's grave reference in Tennyson's 'Aylmer's Field' (1864), 'Pity, the violet on the tyrant's grave' to a legend that flowers were secretly scattered on the grave of Nero. Byron in *Don Juan* has, 'Some hands unseen strewed flowers upon his tomb,' and the story can be traced back to *Suetonius's Lives of the Caesars*, 'Yet there were some who for a long time decorated his tomb with spring and summer flowers.'

vipassana (in Theravada Buddhism) meditation involving concentration on the body or its sensations, or the insight which this provides.

viper a venomous snake with large hinged fangs, typically having a broad head and stout body, with dark patterns on a lighter background; although it is taken as the type of malignancy and treachery, its flesh was formerly believed to have great nutritive or restorative properties, and was used medicinally.

Early allusive references include some to the statement in Pliny's *Natural History* that the female viper was killed by her young eating their way out at birth:

> I am no viper, yet I feed
> On mother's flesh which did me breed.
> — William Shakespeare *Pericles* (1609)

The viper is in fact viviparous, as its name suggests; recorded from the early 16th century, the word comes ultimately from Latin *vivus* 'alive' + *parere* 'bring forth'.

viper-broth a soup made by boiling vipers, formerly supposed to be highly nutritious.

viper in one's bosom a person who betrays those who have helped them; from the fable (found in Aesop) of the viper which was reared or warmed in a person's bosom, and which ended by biting its nurturer.

viper-wine wine with an added extract obtained from vipers, formerly taken as a restorative.

virago a domineering, violent, or bad-tempered woman; formerly, a woman of masculine strength or spirit; a female warrior. The word is recorded in Old English (used only as the name given by Adam to Eve, following the Vulgate), from Latin 'heroic woman, female warrior', from *vir* 'man'. The current sense dates from late Middle English.

virelay a short lyric poem of a type originating in France in the 14th century, consisting of short lines arranged in stanzas with only two rhymes, the end rhyme of one stanza being the chief one of the next.

virgate a varying measure of land, typically 30 acres; recorded from the mid 17th century, the word comes ultimately from Latin *virga* 'rod'.

Virgil (70–19 BC), Roman poet. He wrote three major works: the *Eclogues*, ten pastoral poems, blending traditional themes of Greek bucolic poetry with contemporary political and literary themes; the *Georgics*, a didactic poem on farming, treats the relationship of human beings to nature, and the

Aeneid is an epic poem about the Trojan Aeneas.

Virgil was highly regarded in the Middle Ages, a passage in his fourth *Eclogue* being taken as a prophecy of the birth of Christ, 'Now has come the last age…Now too the virgin goddess returns, the golden days of Saturn's reign return, now a new race is sent down from high heaven.' In Dante's poem Virgil guides the poet through Hell and Purgatory.

See also ➤ Maro, *Prophet of the Gentiles.*

Virgilian lots a method of divination by selecting a passage of Virgil at random in the *sortes Virgilianae* (see ➤ sortes).

virgin originally (in ecclesiastical usage) an unmarried woman esteemed for her chastity and piety within the Christian Church; a woman (especially a young woman) who remains in a state of inviolate chastity (in early use chiefly of **the Virgin** or the ➤ Virgin *Mary* as the mother of Jesus).

Virgin was then used of a girl or young woman, as one likely to be chaste; it is used in this sense in the parable of the **wise and foolish virgins** (Matthew 25:1–13), in which ten young women taken their lamps and go out in a bridal party to meet the bridegroom. Five of them are wise and take extra oil for their lamps; the five who are foolish do not, and when the bridegroom is delayed their lamps run dry. Going to buy more oil, they miss their opportunity to join the wedding feast. In the context a **wise virgin** is someone who has ensured that they have adequate supplies of the necessary commodity.

The ➤ *Virgin* Mary is patron saint of virgins.

See also ➤ Purification *of the Virgin Mary.*

Virgin Birth the doctrine of Christ's birth from a mother, Mary, who was a virgin.

Virgin Queen Queen Elizabeth I of England, who died unmarried; the state of ➤ Virginia takes its name from this epithet.

virgin's garland garland of flowers and coloured paper formerly carried at a virgin's funeral.

virginals an early spinet with the strings parallel to the keyboard, typically rectangular, and popular in 16th and 17th century houses, perhaps so called because usually played by young women.

Virginia a state of the eastern US, on the Atlantic coast, which was the site of the first permanent European settlement in North America in 1607, and was named in honour of Elizabeth I, the 'Virgin Queen'. It was one of the original thirteen states of the Union (1788).

make a Virginia fence walk drunkenly; in the US, a *Virginia fence* is a rail fence made in a zigzag pattern.

Virgo a large constellation (the Virgin), said to represent a maiden or goddess associated with the harvest. It contains several bright stars, the brightest of which is Spica, and a dense cluster of galaxies.

In astrology, Virgo is the sixth sign of the zodiac, which the sun enters about 23 August.

virtue a quality considered morally good or desirable in a person; the important virtues are traditionally the four ➤ cardinal *virtues*, justice, prudence, temperance, and fortitude, valued by the classical philosophers and adopted by the scholastic philosophers, and the three ➤ theological *virtues* of faith, hope, and charity, enumerated by St Paul.

See also ➤ patience *is a virtue.*

virtue is its own reward proverbial saying, early 16th century; meaning that the satisfaction of knowing that one has observed appropriate moral standards should be all that is sought.

make a virtue of necessity proverbial saying, late Middle English; meaning that one should do with a good grace what is unavoidable.

virus originally, the venom of a snake; the word came (in Middle English) from Latin, and meant literally 'slimy liquid, poison'.

From the early 18th century, the word had the earlier medical sense (now superseded as a result of improved scientific understanding) of a substance produced in the body as the result of disease, especially one that is capable of infecting others with the same disease.

In the late 19th century, the current meaning developed: an infective agent that typically consists of a nucleic acid molecule in a protein coat, is too small to be seen by light microscopy, and is able to multiply only within the living cells of a host. Most recently, this has developed the transferred sense of a piece of computer code which is capable of copying itself and typically has a detrimental effect, such as corrupting the system or destroying data.

vis inertiae the resistance naturally offered by matter to any force tending to alter its state in respect of rest or motion; tendency on the part of someone to remain inactive or unprogressive. The phrase is Latin, and means literally 'strength of inertia'.

viscount a British nobleman ranking above a baron and below an earl; in early use also, a person acting as the deputy or representative of a count or earl in the administration of a district.

Vishnu a god, originally a minor Vedic god, now regarded by his worshippers as the supreme deity and saviour, by others as the preserver of the cosmos in a triad with ➤ BRAHMA and ➤ SHIVA. His consort is Lakshmi, his mount the eagle Garuda. Vishnu is considered by Hindus to have had nine earthly incarnations or avatars, including Rama, Krishna, and the historical Buddha; the tenth avatar will herald the end of the world.

Visible Church the Church as consisting of its publicly professed members, as distinguished from the ➤ CHURCH *Invisible*.

Visigoth a member of the branch of the Goths who invaded the Roman Empire between the 3rd and 5th centuries AD and ruled much of Spain until overthrown by the Moors in 711. The name comes from Latin *Visigothus*, and the first element may mean 'west' (as the ➤ OSTROGOTHS were members of the eastern branch of Goths).

vision see also ➤ BEATIFIC *vision*.

vision quest an attempt to achieve a vision of a future guardian spirit, traditionally undertaken at puberty by boys of the Plains Indian peoples, typically through fasting or self-torture.

the vision splendid the dream of some glorious imagined time; the phrase is originally a quotation from Wordsworth:

> And by the vision splendid
> Is on his way attended.
> — William Wordsworth 'Ode. Intimations of
> Immortality' (1807)

vision thing a political view encompassing the longer term as distinct from short-term campaign objectives. The expression comes from the response of the American Republican statesman George Bush (1924–), who in 1987 responded to the suggestion that he turn his attention from short-term campaign objectives and look to the longer term by saying, 'Oh, the vision thing'.

Visitandine a nun belonging to the ➤ *Order of the* VISITATION.

the Visitation the visit of the Virgin Mary to her cousin Elizabeth related in Luke 1:39–56, during which, on being greeted by Elizabeth, 'whence is this…that the mother of my Lord should come to me?', Mary responded with the words which form the ➤ MAGNIFICAT.

Order of the Visitation an order of nuns founded in 1610 by St Jane Frances de Chantal under the direction of St Francis de Sales; they are known as *Visitandines*.

visiting fireman in the US, a visitor to an organization given especially cordial treatment on account of his or her importance. The usage is recorded from the 1920s, but there is a much earlier literal example on record, in an account in an 1855 Baltimore paper of the hospitality offer by the firemen of Baltimore to their colleagues of Rochester.

vita nuova a fresh start or new direction in life, especially after some powerful emotional experience. The phrase is Italian, literally 'new life', the title of a work by Dante describing his love for Beatrice.

vital statistics quantitative data concerning the population, such as the number of births, marriages, and deaths; informally, the measurements of a woman's bust, waist, and hips. The expression is recorded from the mid 19th century, although the informal sense did not develop until the 1950s.

Vitoria a city in NE Spain, capital of the Basque Provinces, site of a battle in 1813 in which Wellington defeated a French force and thus freed Spain from French domination.

Vitruvius (fl. 1st century BC), Roman architect and military engineer. He wrote a comprehensive ten-volume treatise on architecture which includes matters such as acoustics and water supply as well as the more obvious aspects of architectural design, decoration, and building.

St Vitus (d. *c.*300), Christian martyr, who is said to have been martyred during the reign of Diocletian. He was invoked against rabies and as the patron of those who suffered from epilepsy and certain nervous disorders, including ➤ St VITUS's *dance*. He is traditionally regarded as one of the ➤ FOURTEEN *Holy Helpers*.

  ☐ **FEAST DAY** His feast day is 15 June.

St Vitus's dance an old-fashioned term for Sydenham's chorea, a neurological disorder in children characterized by jerky involuntary movements; it is so named because appealing to ➤ St VITUS was believed to alleviate the disease.

viva voce (especially of an examination) oral rather than written. The term is recorded from the mid 16th century, and comes from medieval Latin, literally 'with the living voice'.

vivat a word of acclamation, as in **vivat rex**, **vivat regina**; the word is Latin, and means 'long live'.

Swami Vivekananda (1863–1902), Indian spiritual leader and reformer. He spread the teachings of the Indian mystic Ramakrishna and introduced Vedantic philosophy to the US and Europe.

Vivien in the Arthurian legend, an enchantress (otherwise Nimue or Niniane) who entrapped ➤ Merlin and imprisoned him in a tower of air in the forest of Broceliande.

vivimus see ➤ DUM *vivimus vivamus*.

vixen a female fox. The word comes from late Middle English *fixen*, perhaps from the Old English adjective *fyxen* 'of a fox'; the *v-* is from the form of the word in southern English dialect. From the late 16th century, *vixen* has been used of a quarrelsome woman, a termagant.

viz. namely; in other words (used especially to introduce a gloss or explanation). The expression (dating from the mid 16th century) is an abbreviation of ➤ VIDELICET; the *z* represents the ordinary medieval Latin symbol of contraction for *et*.

vizier a high official in some Muslim countries, especially in Turkey under Ottoman rule. The word is recorded from the mid 16th century and comes via Turkish from Arabic *wazīr* 'caliph's chief counsellor'.

VJ day the day (15 August) in 1945 on which Japan ceased fighting in the Second World War, or the day (2 September) when Japan formally surrendered.

vodun a fetish, typically one connected with the snake-worship and other rites practised first in Dahomey (now Benin) and later introduced by slaves especially to Haiti and Louisiana.

vogue the prevailing fashion or style. The word comes (in the late 16th century, in *the vogue*, denoting the foremost place in popular estimation) via French from Italian *voga* 'rowing, fashion', from *vogare* 'row, go well'.

voice see also ➤ *a* VOICE *in the wilderness*.

Voice of America an official US radio station founded in 1942, operated by the Board for International Broadcasting, that broadcasts around the world in English and other languages.

the voice of the people is the voice of God proverbial saying, early 15th century; English version of ➤ VOX *populi, vox dei*.

voivode a local governor or ruler in various parts of central and eastern Europe, in particular an early semi-independent ruler of Transylvania.

volant in heraldry, represented as flying.

Volapük an artificial language devised in 1879 for universal use by a German cleric, Johann M. Schleyer, and based on extremely modified forms of words from English and Romance languages, with complex inflections.

volcano a mountain or hill, typically conical, having a crater or vent through which lava, rock fragments, hot vapour, and gas are or have been erupted from the earth's crust; in figurative usage, an intense suppressed emotion; a situation liable to burst out suddenly. Recorded from the early 17th century, the word comes from Italian, from Latin *Volcanus* ➤ VULCAN.

Völkerwanderung German word for the migration of Germanic and Slavonic peoples into and across Europe from the second to the eleventh centuries.

Volkslied the national anthem of the 19th-century Transvaal Republic; the word is Afrikaans, and means literally 'People's song'.

Volscian a member of an ancient Italic people who fought the Romans in Latium in the 5th and 4th centuries BC until absorbed into Rome after their final defeat in 304 BC.

Volstead Act a law which enforced alcohol prohibition in the US from 1920–33. It is named after Andrew J. *Volstead* (1860–1947), American legislator.

Volsung in Scandinavian mythology, a dynasty of heroes (including ➤ SIGURD) whose deeds are the subject of *Volsunga Saga* and a number of Eddic poems.

Voltaire pseudonym of the French writer, dramatist, and poet François-Marie Arouet ((1694–1778). He was a leading figure of the Enlightenment, and frequently came into conflict with the Establishment as a result of his radical views and satirical writings. He spent a period in exile in England (1726–9) and was introduced there to the theories of Isaac Newton and the empiricist philosophy of John Locke. He also became acquainted with British political institutions, and extolled them as against the royal autocracy of France.

A famous quotation attributed to Voltaire, 'I disapprove of what you say, but I will defend to the death your right to say it,', supposedly said to the French philosopher Helvétius following the burning of *De l'esprit* in 1759, is actually a later summary of Voltaire's attitude.

See also ➤ CANDIDE, ➤ *pour* ENCOURAGER *les autres*.

volte-face an act of turning round so as to face in the opposite direction; an abrupt and complete reversal of attitude, opinion, or position. The term comes (in the early 19th century) from French, from Italian *voltafaccia*, based on Latin *volvere* 'to roll' + *facies* 'appearance'.

volume originally (in late Middle English) denoting a roll of parchment containing written matter; the word comes via Old French from Latin *volumen* 'a roll', from *volvere* 'to roll'; this came to mean a single book or bound collection of printed sheets, and then a book forming part of a work or series.

In the 16th and 17th centuries volume meant 'size or extent (of a book)'; this gave rise to the current sense of the amount of space that a substance or object occupies.

Volund in Norse mythology, a Lappish prince and skilled worker in metal who is the equivalent of the Anglo-Saxon ➤ WAYLAND. Bereft of his swan-maiden wife, he is captured by the king of Sweden and held prisoner to work with the king's gold. By cunning, he escapes, after killing the king's sons and leaving his daughter pregnant.

voluntary school (in the UK) a school which, though not established by the local education authority, is funded mainly or entirely by it, and which typically encourages a particular set of religious beliefs; originally such schools were maintained by voluntary bodies.

voluntary simplicity a philosophy or way of life that rejects materialism in favour of human and spiritual values, and is characterized by minimal consumption, environmental responsibility, and community cooperation.

one volunteer is worth two pressed men proverbial saying, early 18th century; a *pressed man* was someone forcibly enlisted by the ➤ PRESS *gang*.

Volunteer State informal name for Tennessee, given in allusion to the large number of volunteers contributed by Tennessee to the Mexican War of 1847.

vomit see ➤ *the* DOG *returns to its vomit*.

voodoo a black religious cult practised in the Caribbean and the southern US, combining elements of Roman Catholic ritual with traditional African magical and religious rites, and characterized by sorcery and spirit possession. The word comes (in the early 19th century) from Louisiana French, from Kwa *vodū*.

Voortrekker a member of one of the groups of Dutch-speaking people who migrated by wagon from the Cape Colony into the interior from 1836 onwards, in order to live beyond the borders of British rule. The word is Afrikaans and comes from Dutch *voor* 'fore' + *trekken* 'travel'.

Vorticist a member of a British artistic movement of 1914–15 influenced by cubism and futurism and favouring machine-like forms. The name comes from Latin *vortex, vortic-* 'eddy'; the origin was explained by Ezra Pound in *Fortnightly Review* September 1914, 'The image is not an idea. It is a radiant node or cluster; it is what I can… call a *Vortex*, from which…ideas are constantly rushing…And from this necessity came the name "vorticism".'

Vortigern a legendary 5th-century British king traditionally said to have invited the Saxons under ➤ HENGIST and Horsa into Britain and to have married Hengist's daughter Rowena; according to Geoffrey of Monmouth's chronicle he was defeated and killed by ➤ AMBROSIUS *Aurelianus*, leader of Romano-British resistance to the Saxon invasion.

Vortigern and Rowena was the title of an alleged Shakespeare play which the forger William Henry Ireland (1777–1835) pretended to have discovered; it was produced by Kemble in 1796, but was derided by the public.

Vortumnus a Roman deity, perhaps of Sabine origin; a god of the changing year, who presided over orchards and fruit, husband of ➤ POMONA.

vote early and vote often American election slogan, already current when quoted by the American politician William Porcher Miles (1822–96):

> 'Vote early and vote often,' the advice openly displayed on the election banners in one of our northern cities.
> — William Porcher Miles in the House of Representatives, 31 March 1858

Votes for Women slogan of the women's suffrage movement from 13 October 1905, adopted when it proved impossible to use a banner with the longer slogan 'Will the Liberal Party Give Votes for Women?' made by Emmeline Pankhurst (1858–1928), Christabel Pankhurst (1880–1958), and Annie Kenney (1879–1953).

vow see also ➤ Day *of the Vow.*

vows a set of solemn promises committing one to a prescribed role, calling, or course of action, typically to marriage or a monastic career. Recorded from Middle English, *vow* comes via Old French from the Latin base of *vote.*

vox et praeterea nihil proverbial saying meaning, 'a voice and nothing more'; the phrase is found in Plutarch's *Moralia*, and describes a nightingale.

> The fellow is not worth her—a poor groatsworth of a man, vox et praeterea nihil.
> — Patrick O'Brian *The Far Side of the World* (1984)

vox pop popular opinion as represented by informal comments from members of the public, especially when broadcast or published; the term is recorded from the 1960s, and is an abbreviation of ➤ vox *populi.*

vox populi the opinions or beliefs of the majority; the Latin phrase is recorded in English from the mid 16th century.

vox populi, vox Dei Latin proverbial saying, the voice of the people is the voice of God; cited by the Anglo-Saxon scholar and theologian Alcuin (*c.*735–804), '*Nec audiendi qui solent dicere, Vox populi, vox Dei, quum tumultuositas vulgi semper insaniae proxima sit* [And those people should not be listened to who keep saying the voice of the people is the voice of God, since the riotousness of the crowd is always very close to madness].'

The American Union general William Tecumsah Sherman (1820–91) took a similarly sceptical view in a letter to his wife, 2 June 1863, '*Vox populi, vox humbug*'.

voyage see ➤ *Voyage of* Maeldune.

Voyager either of two American space probes launched in 1977 to investigate the outer planets. Voyager 1 encountered Jupiter and Saturn, while Voyager 2 reached Jupiter, Saturn, Uranus, and finally Neptune (1989).

voyageur in 18th- and 19th-century Canada, a boatman employed by the fur companies in transporting goods and passengers to and from the trading posts on the lakes and rivers.

vril an imaginary form of energy supposedly discovered by the people described in E. Bulwer-Lytton's *The Coming Race* (1871).

See also ➤ Bovril.

Vulcan[1] in Roman mythology, the god of fire; equivalent of the Greek ➤ Hephaestus. His lameness, and his betrayal by his wife ➤ Venus for ➤ Mars, are both subjects for literary allusion; he is also taken as the type of a blacksmith or metalworker.

Vulcan[2] in the ➤ Star *Trek* science fiction series, a member of the race to which ➤ *Mr* Spock belongs, characterized by their logic, lack of emotion, and mental prowess, as well as by their pointed ears and green-tinged skin. In the mid 1990s, **the Vulcan** began to be used as a nickname for the British Conservative politician John Redwood, former Secretary of State for Wales.

> 'The Vulcan's' mixture of free-market capitalism, family values, Euro-scepticism and public spending cuts, which may yet conquer the rest of Britain, has been tried in Wales.
> — *Independent on Sunday* 2 July 1995

Vulcanian Islands another name for the volcanic ➤ Lipari *Islands* between Sicily and Italy.

Vulcanist a supporter of the theory (now accepted) that rocks such as granite were formed by solidification from the molten state, as proposed by the Scottish geologist James Hutton and others, rather than by precipitation from the sea.

vulgar Latin informal Latin of classical times; vulgar in this sense means 'in ordinary use, used by the people', and comes ultimately from *vulgus* 'common people'.

Vulgate the principal Latin version of the Bible, prepared mainly by St Jerome in the late 4th century, and (as revised in 1592) adopted as the official text for the Roman Catholic Church. The name comes from Latin *vulgata (editio)* '(edition) prepared for the public'.

vulpine of or relating to a fox or foxes; crafty, cunning. The word comes from Latin *vulpes* 'fox', the base of Italian *Volpone*, the crafty schemer in Jonson's play (1607).

vulture a large bird of prey with the head and neck more or less bare of feathers, feeding chiefly on carrion and reputed to gather with others in anticipation of the death of a sick or injured animal or person; a contemptible person who preys on or exploits others.

Vulture may also be used allusively for something that preys on one's mind, such as a consuming or torturing passion, especially with reference to the punishment inflicted on ➤ Tityus.

See also ➤ culture *vulture.*

W The twenty-third letter of the modern English alphabet, originating from a ligature of the Roman letter represented by *U* and *V* of modern alphabets.

Waac a member of the British Women's Army Auxiliary Corps (1917–19) or the American force of the same name (now the WAC) formed in 1942.

Waaf in the UK, a member of the Women's Auxiliary Air Force (1939–48, subsequently reorganized as part of the Women's Royal Air Force).

Wade–Giles a system of romanized spelling for transliterating Chinese, devised by the British diplomat Sir Thomas Francis Wade (1818–95), professor of Chinese at Cambridge, and modified by his successor Herbert Allen Giles (1845–1935). It has been largely superseded by Pinyin. It produces spellings such as *Peking*, *Mao Tse-tung* rather than *Beijing*, *Mao Zedong*.

Wade's boat a reference in the *Canterbury Tales*; Wade was the father of ➤ WAYLAND, who in Norse legend built a famous boat to escape his pursuers.

Wafd an Egyptian nationalist organization and later a political party, formed in 1918 and reconstituted as the New Wafd in 1978. The name comes from Arabic *wafd* delegation (in full *al-wafd al-miṣrī* the Egyptian delegation), from *wafada* 'come, travel, especially as an envoy'

wafer a thin disc of unleavened bread used in the Eucharist; the term is recorded first in an injunction of Elizabeth I in 1559, 'the usual bread and wafer, heretofore named singing cakes, which served for the use of the private Mass'.

Waffen SS the combat units of the ➤ SS in Nazi Germany during the Second World War; *Waffen* is German and means 'armed'.

wag dated term for a person who makes facetious jokes. The word is recorded from the mid 16th century (denoting a young man or mischievous boy, also used as a term of endearment to an infant); it probably comes from obsolete *waghalter* 'person likely to be hanged'.

wager a more formal term for a bet; recorded from Middle English, the word originally meant also a solemn pledge or undertaking, and comes ultimately from Anglo-Norman French *wager* 'to wage'.
  See also ➤ PASCAL*'s wager*.

wager of battle a form of trial by which someone's guilt or innocence was decided by personal combat between the parties or their champions.

wager of law a form of trial in which the defendant was required to produce witnesses who would swear to his or her innocence.

Richard Wagner (1813–83), German composer. He developed an operatic genre which he called music drama, synthesizing music, drama, verse, legend, and spectacle, as in *The Flying Dutchman* (opera, 1841).
  Wagner was forced into exile after supporting the German nationalist uprising in Dresden in 1848; in the same year he began writing the text of *Der Ring des Nibelungen* (*The Ring of the Nibelungs*), a cycle of four operas (*Das Rheingold*, *Die Walküre*, *Siegfried*, and *Götterdämmerung*) based loosely on ancient Germanic sagas. The *Ring* cycle is notable for its use of leitmotifs and orchestral colour to unify the music, dramatic narrative, and characterization.
  The term Wagnerian is used figuratively of something having the enormous dramatic scale and intensity of a Wagner opera.

wagon see also ➤ CHARLEMAGNE*'s wagon*, ➤ CONESTOGA *wagon*.

wagon train a convoy or train of covered horse-drawn wagons, as used by pioneers or settlers in North America.

wagoner former term for a book of charts for nautical use; originally, the atlas of charts published by Lucas Janssen Waghenaer in 1584 under the title *Spieghel der Zeevaerdt* (English translation *The Mariners Mirror*, by Sir A. Ashley, 1588).

Wahhabi a member of a strictly orthodox Sunni Muslim sect founded by Muhammad ibn Abd al-Wahhab (1703–92). It advocates a return to the early Islam of the Koran and Sunna, rejecting later innovations; the sect is still the predominant religious force in Saudi Arabia.

Abd al-Wahhab called for a return to the earliest doctrines and practices of Islam as embodied in the Koran and Sunna, and opposed mystical groups such as the Sufis. Followers and allies of Abd al-Wahhab forged a state which came to encompass most of the Arabian peninsula; this was eventually conquered by the Ottomans, but formed the basis for the state of Saudi Arabia (1932), which is still dominated by Wahhabi doctrines.

Wailing Wall a high wall in Jerusalem said to stand on the site of the Jewish Temple, where Jews traditionally pray and lament on Fridays.

wain see ➤ CHARLES'*s Wain*.

wait and see habitual expression of the British Liberal statesman Herbert Asquith (1852–1928); 'We had better wait and see' was a phrase used repeatedly in speeches in 1910, referring to the rumour that the House of Lords was to be flooded with new Liberal peers to ensure the passage of the Finance Bill.

Treaty of Waitangi a treaty signed in 1840 at the settlement of Waitangi in New Zealand, which formed the basis of the British annexation of New Zealand. The Maori chiefs of North Island accepted British sovereignty in exchange for protection, and direct purchase of land from the Maoris was forbidden. Subsequent contraventions of the treaty by the British led to the Maori Wars.

Waitangi Day the anniversary of the signing of the Treaty of Waitangi, celebrated as a public holiday in New Zealand on 6 February since 1960.

waiting see ➤ WATCHFUL *waiting*.

waits between the Middle Ages and the 18th century, a small band of musicians maintained by a city or town at the public charge; they played especially on ceremonial and festive occasions, and Oliver Goldsmith in his *Life of Richard Nash* (1762) notes that, 'Upon a stranger's arrival at Bath he is welcomed by…the voice and music of the city waits.'

The city *waits* often played through the streets, and from the late 18th century the name was used for street singers of Christmas carols.

wake see also ➤ HEREWARD *the Wake*.

wake a watch or vigil held beside the body of someone who has died, sometimes accompanied by

ritual observances including eating and drinking.

See also ➤ LYKE *wake*.

wake-robin another term for the cuckoo-pint, perhaps referring to its supposedly aphrodisiac qualities; in *Loves Metamorphosis* (1601), John Lyly has, 'They have eaten so much wake-robin, that they cannot sleep for love.'

wakeman in the 15th and 16th centuries, a member of a class of municipal officers in Ripon, Yorkshire, whose duties included attendance on the shrine of St Wilfrid. Until 1604, *wakeman* was also the title of the chief magistrate of the borough, when it was exchanged for the title of mayor.

wakes in some parts of the UK, a festival and holiday held annually in a rural parish, originally on the feast day (originally the *wake* or vigil before the festival) of the patron saint of the church.

Wakes Week in northern England, an annual holiday in towns such as Leeds, traditionally when mills closed for a stated period.

wakon another name for the ➤ MANITOU; the word comes from Dakota, meaning 'being with supernatural power'.

wakon-bird a mythical bird venerated by some North American Indians.

Waldenses a puritan religious sect based originally in southern France, now chiefly in Italy and America, founded *c*.1170 by Peter *Valdes* (d. 1205), a merchant of Lyons.

waldo a remote-controlled device for handling objects, named after *Waldo* F. Jones, a fictional inventor described by Robert Heinlein in a science-fiction story.

Wales a principality of Great Britain and the United Kingdom, to the west of central England; Welsh name *Cymru*.

The Celtic inhabitants of Wales successfully maintained independence against the Anglo-Saxons who settled in England following the withdrawal of the Romans in the 5th century, and in the 8th century Offa, king of Mercia, built an earthwork (*Offa's Dyke*) marking the frontier. The country remained divided between rival rulers and chieftains until the death of the younger ➤ LLEWELYN, and Edward I's conquest (1277–84). Edward began the custom of making the English sovereign's eldest son Prince of Wales.

Wales was formally brought into the English legal

and parliamentary system by Henry VIII (1536), but has retained a distinct cultural identity. In 1997 a referendum narrowly approved proposals for a Welsh assembly without tax-raising powers.

See also ➤ DIANA, *Princess of Wales,* ➤ GERALD *of Wales,* ➤ PRINCE *of Wales.*

Lech Wałęsa (1943–), Polish trade unionist and statesman, President 1990–5. The founder of Solidarity (1980), he was imprisoned 1981–2 after the movement was banned. After Solidarity's landslide victory in the 1989 elections he became President.

walk see also ➤ COCK-*of-the-walk,* ➤ LAMBETH *Walk.*

we must learn to walk before we can run proverbial saying, mid 14th century; meaning that a solid foundation is necessary for faster progress.

walkabout a journey on foot undertaken by an Australian Aboriginal in order to live in the traditional manner; from the 1970s in the UK the word has also been used for an informal stroll among a crowd conducted by an important visitor.

Walker Cup a golf tournament held every two years and played between teams of male amateurs from the US and from Great Britain and Ireland, first held in 1922. The tournament was instituted by George Herbert *Walker,* a former President of the US Golf Association.

Walkerite a member of an extreme Calvinistic sect founded in Ireland by John *Walker* (1768–1833).

walking see also ➤ DEAD *man walking.*

walking gentleman an actor playing a nonspeaking part requiring gentlemanlike appearance; the term is recorded from the late 18th century, in a letter from the actor Charles Mathews recording 'asked me if I would like to play walking gentleman'.

Walking Stewart nickname of the traveller and explorer John Stewart (1749–1822), whose journeys were largely carried out on foot; he became a noted figure in his day, and De Quincey wrote two articles about him. The actor and composer Michael Kelly, meeting him in Vienna in 1784, noted that he had walked there from Calais and was about to set out for Constantinople.

Walkyrie in Anglo-Saxon England, any of a group of supernatural female warriors supposed to ride through the air over battlefields and decide who should die, the equivalent of the Scandinavian ➤ VALKYRIE; the word in Old English is found as

rendering the name of the Roman war-goddess ➤ BELLONA, or designating the ➤ FURIES or ➤ GORGONS of classical mythology.

wall see also ➤ ANTONINE *Wall,* ➤ BERLIN *Wall,* ➤ CHINESE *wall,* ➤ *a* FLY *on the wall,* ➤ GREAT *Wall of China,* ➤ SERVIAN *wall,* ➤ WAILING *Wall,* ➤ *the* WEAKEST *go to the wall,* ➤ WESTERN *Wall,* ➤ WOODEN *walls,* ➤ *the* WRITING *on the wall.*

wall eye an eye with a streaked or opaque white iris; an eye squinting outwards. The term comes, in the early 16th century, as a back-formation from the earlier *wall-eyed,* from Old Norse *vagleygr,* related to Iceland *vagl* 'film over the eye'.

Wall of Death a fairground sideshow in which a motorcyclist uses gravitational force to ride around the inside walls of a vertical cylinder.

Wall of Severus the rampart strengthening ➤ HADRIAN's *Wall* in northern Britain, constructed during the reign of the emperor ➤ SEVERUS.

Wall Street a street at the south end of Manhattan, where the New York Stock Exchange and other leading American financial institutions are located, used allusively to refer to the American money market or financial interests. It is named after a wooden stockade which was built in 1653 around the original Dutch settlement of New Amsterdam.

> Most Wall Streeters expect Asia's turmoil to knock about half a percentage point from America's growth rate this year.
> — *Economist* 17 January 1998

Wall Street Crash the collapse of prices on the New York Stock Exchange in October 1929, a major factor in the early stages of the ➤ DEPRESSION; many investors became bankrupt, and there were a number of suicides from high-rise Wall Street buildings.

Wallace name of the cheese-loving inventor ➤ WALLACE, owner of the dog ➤ GROMIT, in Nick Park's claymation films of his two plasticine figures.

William Wallace (*c.*1270–1305), Scottish national hero. He was a leader of Scottish resistance to Edward I, defeating the English army at Stirling in 1297 and mounting campaigns against the north of England. After Edward's second invasion of Scotland in 1298 Wallace was defeated and subsequently executed.

See also ➤ BRAVEHEART.

Wallace Collection a museum in Manchester Square, London, containing French 18th-century paintings and furniture, English 18th-century portraits, and medieval armour. The collection was built up by the fourth marquis of Hertford and Richard Wallace (1819–90), his illegimate son or half-brother; Richard Wallace's widow gave it to the nation in 1897.

Wallace's line a hypothetical line, proposed by Alfred Russel Wallace, marking the boundary between the Oriental and Australian zoogeographical regions. Wallace's line is now placed along the continental shelf of SE Asia. To the west of the line Asian mammals such as monkeys predominate, while to the east of it the fauna is dominated by marsupials.

wallah in Indian or informal English, a person concerned or involved with a specified thing or business. The word comes from the Hindi suffix -*wālā* 'doer' (commonly interpreted in the sense 'fellow'), from Sanskrit *pālaka* 'keeper'.

Raoul Wallenberg (1912–?), Swedish diplomat. In 1944 in Budapest he helped many thousands of Jews to escape death by issuing them with Swedish passports. In 1945 he was arrested by Soviet forces and imprisoned in Moscow. Although the Soviet authorities stated that Wallenberg had died in prison in 1947, his fate remains uncertain.

Fats Waller (1904–43), American jazz pianist, songwriter, bandleader, and singer. He was the foremost exponent of the New York 'stride school' of piano playing.

wallflower a southern European plant with fragrant yellow, orange-red, dark red, or brown flowers, cultivated for its early spring blooming; from the early 19th century, informal term for a person who has no one to dance with.

Barnes Wallis (1887–1979), English inventor. His designs include the bouncing bomb used against the Ruhr dams in Germany in the Second World War.
See also ➤ Dambusters' *raid*.

walls have ears proverbial saying, late 16th century; meaning that care should be taken for possible eavesdroppers.

walnut the large wrinkled edible seed of a deciduous tree, consisting of two halves contained within a hard shell which is enclosed in a green fruit; the *walnut tree* produces a valuable ornamental timber used chiefly in cabinetmaking and for gun stocks. The word is recorded from late Old English in form *walh-hnutu*, from a Germanic compound meaning 'foreign nut'.
See also ➤ *a* woman, *a dog, and a walnut tree, the more you beat them the better they be.*

walnuts and pears you plant for your heirs proverbial saying, mid 17th century; meaning that both trees are slow growing, so that the benefit will be felt by future generations.

Horace Walpole (1717–97), English writer and Whig politician, son of Sir Robert Walpole. He wrote *The Castle of Otranto* (1764), one of the first Gothic novels, and is also noted for his contribution to the Gothic revival in architecture, converting his ➤ Strawberry *Hill* home at Twickenham, near London, into a Gothic castle (*c*.1753–76).

Robert Walpole 1676–1745), British Whig statesman, First Lord of the Treasury and Chancellor of the Exchequer 1715–17 and 1721–42, father of Horace Walpole. Walpole is generally regarded as the first British ➤ Prime *Minister*, having presided over the cabinet for George I and George II.

Walpurgis Night (in German folklore) the night of April 30 (May Day's eve), when witches meet on the ➤ Brocken mountain and hold revels with the Devil. It is named after St *Walburga*, an English nun who in the 8th century helped to convert the Germans to Christianity; her feast day coincided with an ancient pagan festival whose rites were intended to give protection from witchcraft.

Walsingham a village in Kent which is the site of the shrine of *Our Lady of Walsingham*, a popular place of pilgrimage in the Middle Ages.

Francis Walsingham (*c*.1530–90), English politician. As Secretary of State to Queen Elizabeth I he developed a spy network that gathered information about Catholic plots against Elizabeth I and intelligence about the Spanish Armada. In 1586 Walsingham uncovered a plot involving Mary, Queen of Scots; he subsequently exerted his judicial power to have Mary executed.

Walsingham way the Milky Way, as fancifully supposed to have been used as a guide by pilgrims travelling to the shrine of Our Lady of Walsingham.

Walt see ➤ *Walt* Disney.

Walter see ➤ *Walter* Mitty.

Izaak Walton (1593–1683), English writer. He is chiefly known for *The Compleat Angler* (1653; largely rewritten, 1655) which combines practical information on fishing with folklore, interspersed with pastoral songs and ballads. He also wrote biographies of John Donne (1640) and George Herbert (1670).

Waltzing Matilda an Australian song with words by Andrew Barton Paterson (1864–1941). To 'waltz

Matilda' is to travel with a bushman's bundle of belongings. The tune is that of a march arranged from an adaptation of 'The Bold Fusilier', a song that was popular with British soldiers in the early 18th century.

wampum a quantity of small cylindrical beads made by North American Indians from shells, strung together and worn as a decorative belt or other decoration or used as money. The word comes from Algonquian *wampumpeag*, from *wap* 'white' + *umpe* 'string' + the plural suffix *-ag*.

wand of peace in Scottish law, a silver-topped baton carried by a king's messenger as a symbol of his office, and traditionally delivered to an outlaw as a sign of his restoration to the King's peace.

wander-year a year of travel by an apprentice to improve in skill and knowledge; the word is a direct translation of German *Wanderjahr* in this sense.

wandering fire another name for ➤ WILL o' the wisp; used figuratively by Tennyson in *The Holy Grail* (1869), 'This chance of noble deeds will come and go Unchallenged, while ye follow wandering fires Lost in the quagmire!'

wandering Jew a legendary person said to have been condemned by Christ to wander the earth until the second advent; according to a popular belief recorded from the 13th century and current at least until the 16th, he was said to have insulted Jesus on his way to the Cross. In the earliest versions of the story he is called Cartaphilus, but in the best-known modern version it is given as Ahasuerus.

Wandervogel a member of a German youth organization founded at the end of the 19th century for the promotion of outdoor activities and folk culture. The name is German and means literally, 'bird of passage'.

wannabe a person who tries to be like someone else or to fit in with a particular group of people. Coined in the 1980s, the word represents a pronunciation of *want to be*.

Wansdyke an ancient east-west fortification system running from near Portishead to near Marlborough, and probably constructed as a defence against Saxon invasion.

if you want a thing done well, do it yourself proverbial saying, mid 16th century; in 1975, Margaret Thatcher was quoted as modifying this to, 'In politics, if you want anything said, ask a man. If you want anything done, ask a woman.'

for the want of a nail the shoe was lost; for want of a shoe the horse was lost; and for want of a horse the man was lost proverbial saying, early 17th century; late 15th century in French. The saying is often quoted allusively to imply that one apparently small circumstance can result in a large-scale disaster.

Wantley see ➤ the DRAGON of Wantley.

wapentake in the UK, a subdivision of certain northern and midland English counties, corresponding to a hundred in other counties. Recorded from late Old English, the word comes from Old Norse *vápnatak*, from *vápn* 'weapon' + *taka* 'take', perhaps with reference to voting in an assembly by a show of weapons.

wappenschawing a periodical muster or review of the men under arms within a particular lordship or district; the term is recorded from late Middle English, and means literally 'weapon showing'.

war see also ➤ ARTICLES of War, ➤ the COLD war, ➤ COUNCILS of war never fight, ➤ the DOGS of war, ➤ HONOURS of war, ➤ if you want PEACE, you must prepare for war, ➤ make LOVE not war, ➤ the SINEWS of war.

Wars ■ See box overleaf.

war dance a ceremonial dance performed before a battle or to celebrate victory; associated particularly with North American Indian peoples.

war game a military exercise carried out to test or improve tactical expertise; a simulated military conflict carried out as a game, leisure activity, or exercise in personal development. The term is recorded from the early 19th century, and is the equivalent of the German ➤ KRIEGSPIEL.

War of 1812 a conflict between the US and the UK (1812–14), prompted by restrictions on US trade resulting from the British blockade of French and allied ports during the Napoleonic Wars, and by British and Canadian support for American Indians trying to resist westward expansion. It was ended by a treaty which restored all conquered territories to their owners before outbreak of war. The main area of operations was the Canadian border, which US forces tried repeatedly but unsuccessfully to breach. The Americans captured Detroit and won a series of engagements between single ships, while the British took Washington and burned public buildings (including the White House).

Wars

NAME	DATE
American Civil War	1861–5
Barons' War	1264–7
Chaco War	1932–5
Crimean War	1853–6
First World War	1870–1
Great Northern War	1700–21
Gulf War	1991
Hundred Years War	1337–1453
Iran–Iraq War	1980–8
June War	1967
King Philip's War	1675–6
Korean War	1950–3
Mexican War	1846–8
Mormon War	1857–8
October War	1973
Peloponnesian War	431–404 BC
Peninsular War	1808–1814
Potato War	1778–9
Russian Civil War	1918–21
Sacred War	6th, 5th, and 4th centuries BC
Second World War	1939–45
Seven Weeks War	1866
Seven Years War	1756–63
Six Day War	1967
Spanish-American War	1898
Thirty Years War	1618–48
Vietnam War	1964–73
Winter War	1939–40
Yom Kippur War	1973

War of the Brown Bull in Irish legend, another name for the *Cattle Raid of Cooley*, as related in the ➤ TAIN-*Bo-Cuailgne.*

war to end wars a war which is intended to make subsequent wars impossible; in particular, applied to the First World War. Lloyd George, in a speech to the House of Commons on 11 November 1918, announcing the end of the First World War had said, 'I hope we may say that thus…came to an end all wars;' *The War That Will End War* (1920) was the title of a book by H. G. Wells.

war will cease when men refuse to fight pacifist slogan, from *c.*1936; often quoted as 'Wars will cease…'

Perkin Warbeck (1474–99), Flemish claimant to the English throne, who in a Yorkist attempt to overthrow Henry VII, claimed to be one of the

➤ PRINCES *in the Tower.* After an abortive revolt he was captured and imprisoned in the Tower of London in 1497 and later executed.

Aby Warburg (1866–1929), German art historian. From 1905 he built up a library in Hamburg, dedicated to preserving the classical heritage of Western culture. In 1933 it was transferred to England and housed in the *Warburg Institute* (part of the University of London).

Ward in Cumberland, Northumberland, and some Scottish counties: any of the administrative districts into which these counties were formerly divided.

Artemus Ward pseudonym of the American humorist Charles Farrar Browne (1834–67).

warden an old variety of cooking pear; the arms of Wardon or Warden Abbey in Bedfordshire were 'argent, three warden pears or', probably with punning intention.

wardroom a commissioned officers' mess on board a warship.

Wardour Street originally used as a modifier denoting the pseudo-archaic diction affected by some modern writers of historical novels, and later used allusively to refer to the British film industry. It is the name of a street in central London, formerly mainly occupied by dealers in antique furniture, now the site of the central offices of the British film industry.

> Hitler had the best admen: nasty 'creatives' whose designs and slogans worked better than anything dreamed up in Wardour St.
> — *Independent* 7 September 1996

Ware see ➤ GREAT *Bed of Ware.*

Andy Warhol (*c.*1928–87), American painter, graphic artist, and film-maker. A major exponent of pop art, he achieved fame for a series of silk-screen prints and acrylic paintings of familiar objects (such as Campbell's soup tins) and famous people (such as Marilyn Monroe), treated with objectivity and precision. He is particularly remembered for the comment (1968), 'In the future everybody will be world famous for fifteen minutes.'

> Burckhardt and Curtius lived and died before the Age of Warhol, when so many are famous for fifteen minutes each.
> — Harold Bloom *The Western Canon* (1994)

warlock a man who practises witchcraft; a sorcerer. In Old English *wǣrloga* meant 'traitor, scoundrel, monster', and also 'the Devil', from *wǣr* 'covenant' + an element related to *lēogan* 'belie, deny'. From its application to the Devil, the word was transferred in Middle English to a person in league with the devil, and hence a sorcerer. It was chiefly Scots until given wider currency by Sir Walter Scott.

warming pan a wide, flat brass pan on a long handle, filled with hot coals and used for warming a bed, formerly used in allusion to the story that James II's son, afterwards called the ➤ OLD *Pretender*, was a supposititious child introduced into the Queen's bed in a warming pan.

warning see ➤ SCARBOROUGH *warning*.

warpaint a pigment or paint traditionally used in some societies, especially those of North American Indians, to decorate the face and body before battle.

warrant see ➤ DEATH *warran*.

warrantable (of a stag) regarded as old enough to be hunted (5 or 6 years old).

Wars of the Roses the 15th-century English civil wars between the Houses of York and Lancaster, represented by white and red roses respectively, during the reigns of Henry VI, Edward IV, and Richard III. The struggle was largely ended in 1485 by the defeat and death of the Yorkist king Richard III at the Battle of Bosworth and the accession of the Lancastrian Henry Tudor (Henry VII), who united the two houses by marrying Elizabeth, daughter of Edward IV.

Warsaw Pact a treaty of mutual defence and military aid signed at Warsaw on 14 May 1955 by Communist states of Europe under Soviet influence, in response to the admission of West Germany to NATO.

warts and all including features or qualities that are not appealing or attractive; the term derives from a request supposedly made by ➤ *Oliver* CROMWELL to the portraitist Peter Lely; it is in fact a popular summary of Cromwell's words as reported by Horace Walpole:

> Mr Lely, I desire you would use all your skill to paint my picture truly like me, and not flatter me at all; but remark all these roughnesses, pimples, warts, and everything as you see me; otherwise I will never pay a farthing for it.
> — Horace Walpole *Anecdotes of Painting in England* (1763)

Earl of **Warwick** (1428–71), English statesman; known as **Warwick the Kingmaker**. During the Wars

of the Roses he fought first on the Yorkist side, helping Edward IV to gain the throne (1461), and then on the Lancastrian side, briefly restoring Henry VI to the throne (1470). Warwick was killed at the battle of Barnet.

the Wash an inlet of the North Sea on the east coast of England between Norfolk and Lincolnshire; *wash* in this sense means a sandbank or tract of land alternately covered and exposed by the sea.

one does not wash one's dirty linen in public proverbial saying, early 19th century; meaning that discreditable matters should be dealt with privately.

wash one's hands of disclaim responsibility for; the original allusion is to the biblical story of ➤ *Pontius* PILATE who, when he was forced to condemn Jesus, sent for a bowl of water and ritually washed his hands as a sign that he was inncoent of 'this just person' (Matthew 27:24). In proverbial usage, the attempt at avoiding guilt is often seen as futile.

Booker T. Washington (1856–1915), American educationist. A leading commentator for black Americans, Washington established the Tuskegee Institute in Alabama (1881). His support for segregation and his emphasis on black people's vocational skills attracted criticism from other black leaders.

George Washington (1732–99), American general and statesman, 1st President of the US 1789–97. Washington helped win the War of Independence by keeping his army together through the winter at Valley Forge and winning a decisive battle at Yorktown (1781). He chaired the convention at Philadelphia (1787) that drew up the American Constitution and subsequently served two terms as President, following a policy of neutrality in international affairs.

Allusions to Washington refer either to his readiness to relinquish power and retire into private life, or to the legend that in childhood he cut down a cherry tree, and when questioned said, 'I can't tell a lie.'

Bird of Washington the American baldheaded eagle as a national symbol.

Wasp an upper- or middle-class American white Protestant, considered to be a member of the most powerful group in society. The word is an acronym from *white Anglo-Saxon Protestant*.

wassail spiced ale or mulled wine drunk during celebrations for Twelfth Night and Christmas Eve;

lively and noisy festivities involving the drinking of plentiful amounts of alcohol; revelry. The word comes from Middle English *wæs hæil* 'be in (good) health', from Old Norse *ves heill*. The drinking formula *wassail* (and the reply *drinkhail* 'drink good health') were probably introduced by Danish-speaking inhabitants of England, and then spread, so that by the 12th century the usage was considered by the Normans to be characteristic of Englishmen.

wassail bowl a large bowl in which wassail was made and from which it was dispensed for the drinking of toasts.

Wassermann test a diagnostic test for syphilis using a specific antibody reaction of the patient's blood serum, named after August P. *Wassermann* (1866–1925), German pathologist.

waste see also ➤ HASTE *makes waste*, ➤ WILFUL *waste makes woeful want*.

waste not, want not proverbial saying, late 18th century.

wat a dialect name for a hare; probably a shortened form of the given name *Walter*, and recorded from the late 15th century.

watch see also ➤ BLACK *Watch*, ➤ NEIGHBOUR-HOOD *watch*

the watch a watchman or group of watchmen who patrolled and guarded the streets of a town before the introduction of the police force.

watch and ward the performance of the duty of a watchman or sentinel, especially as a feudal obligation. It has traditionally been suggested that *watch* referred to service by night and *ward* to service by day, but there is no evidence for this as an original meaning.

Watch Committee formerly in the UK, the committee of a county borough council dealing with policing and public lighting.

The Watch on the Rhine a German patriotic song, *Die Wacht am Rhein* (1840), written by Max Schneckenburger, which was set to music by Karl Wilhelm in 1854, and became a popular Prussian soldiers' song in the ➤ FRANCO-*Prussian War*.

watch this space! be alert for further news of a particular topic; *space* here is a portion of a newspaper or journal available for a specific purpose, especially for advertising; room which may be acquired for this.

a watched pot never boils proverbial saying, mid 19th century; meaning that to pay to close an attention to the development of desired event appears to inhibit the result.

the watches of the night the night-time; *watch* originally each of the three or four periods of time, during which a watch or guard was kept, into which the night was divided by the Jews and Romans.

watchful waiting phrase used by Woodrow Wilson to describe American policy towards Mexico during Mexico's revolutionary period, 1913–20:

> Our policy of watchful waiting.
> — Woodrow Wilson State of the Union address, 2 December 1913

Watchnight originally a religious service extending over midnight held monthly by Wesleyan Methodists; in later use a service held (by Methodists and others) on New Year's eve, lasting until midnight; also, the night upon which the service is held.

watchword originally, a military password; now, a word or phrase expressing a person's or group's core aim or belief; the comment 'Our watchword is security' is attributed to William Pitt, Earl of Chatham (1708–78).

water *water* was one of the four elements in ancient and medieval philosophy and in astrology (considered essential to the nature of the signs Cancer, Scorpio, and Pisces).

The word is recorded from Old English (in form *wæter*) and is of Germanic origin; it comes from an Indo-European root shared by Lain *unda* 'wave' and Greek *hudōr* 'water'.

See also ➤ BLOOD *is thicker than water*, ➤ BREAD *and water*, ➤ CHINESE *water torture*, ➤ CLEAR *blue water*, ➤ DIRTY *water will quench fire*, ➤ JUST *when you thought it was safe to go back in the water*, ➤ KING *over the Water*, ➤ *the* MILL *cannot grind with the water that it past*, ➤ PLAGUE-*water*, ➤ WATERS, ➤ *you can take a* HORSE *to water but you cannot make him drink*, ➤ *you never* MISS *the water till the well runs dry*.

bitter water in the Bible, offered to a woman suspected of adultery, as in Numbers 5:17–27; it consists of holy water with dust from the floor of the tabernacle, and a guilty woman who drinks it becomes subject to a ritual curse.

of the first water the highest grade of diamond. The three highest grades of diamond were formerly known as first, second, and third water, and the phrase *of the first water* is used generally to indicate the finest possible quaility. The usage may come ultimately from Arabic, where this sense of water is a particular application of 'lustre, splendour' (e.g., of a sword).

the **Water Bearer** the zodiacal sign or constellation ➤ AQUARIUS.

water birth a birth in which the mother spends the final stages of labour in a birthing pool, with delivery taking place either in or out of the water.

water-bull in Manx folklore, a semi-aquatic animal resembling a bull.

the **Water Carrier** the zodiacal sign or constellation ➤ AQUARIUS.

water-horse in Scottish folklore, a water-spirit appearing in the form of a horse, a ➤ KELPIE.

Water Poet title adopted by the poet John Taylor (1580–1653), who had worked as a Thames waterman. A supporter of the king against Parliament, in 1645 he took over a public-house called the Crown which he renamed the Mourning Crown after the king's execution; when this was condemned as 'malignant', he put up his own portrait for the Poet's Head in its place.

Grand Order of Water Rats a philanthropic show-business society, a British association of music-hall performers originating in 1889 from a Thames river party to celebrate the success of a racehorse called Water Rat.

water under the bridge used to refer to events or situations that are in the past and consequently no longer to be regarded as important or as a source of concern.

don't go near the water until you learn how to swim proverbial saying, mid 19th century; advising against overconfidence.

Watergate a US political scandal in which an attempt to bug the national headquarters of the Democratic Party (in the Watergate building in Washington DC) led to the resignation of President Nixon (1974).

Five men hired by the Republican organization campaigning to re-elect Richard Nixon President were caught with electronic bugging equipment at the offices. The attempted cover-up and subsequent inquiry gravely weakened the prestige of the government and finally led to the resignation of President Nixon in August 1974, before impeachment proceedings against him could begin.

See also ➤ *a* SMOKING *pistol*.

Waterlander a member of a moderate or liberal grouping of Mennonites, from *Waterland* a district in the northern Netherlands.

Battle of Waterloo a battle fought on 18 June 1815 near the village of Waterloo (in what is now Belgium), in which Napoleon's army was defeated by the British (under the Duke of Wellington) and Prussians. The allied pursuit caused Napoleon's army to disintegrate entirely, ending his bid to return to power; *Waterloo* is often used as a word for a decisive defeat or failure.

> Without uttering a word, she communicated to him that she was pleased to see he had at last met his Waterloo.
> — Joanna Trollope *The Rector's Wife* (1991)

Waterloo ball a frivolous entertainment preceding a serious occurrence (with reference to a ball given in Brussels by the Duchess of Richmond on the eve of the Battle of Waterloo).

> I now see these dances as a succession of Waterloo Balls, a rapturously gay company, rapturously doomed.
> — Philip Toynbee *Friends Apart* (1954)

Waterloo Cup in coursing, a race held annually at Altcar, near Liverpool.

waterman a licensed wherryman of London, plying for hire on the river; the term is recorded from late Middle English.

watermark a faint design made in some paper during manufacture that is visible when held against the light and typically identifies the maker.

waters see ➤ *the* FATHER *of Waters*, ➤ FISH *in troubled waters*, ➤ POUR *oil on troubled waters*, ➤ STILL *waters run deep*, ➤ STOLEN *waters are sweet*.

Watford a town in Hertfordshire, SE England, used with allusion to the view attributed to Londoners that north of the metropolis there is nothing of any significance to English national or cultural life.

> A man who, until he made the journey from London, thought that woad began at Watford.
> — Godfrey Talbot *Ten Seconds from Now* (1973)

Watier's a club founded at 81 Piccadilly, at the suggestion of the Prince Regent, by Watier, the Prince's chef, as a dinner club, noted for its elaborate cooking. It was frequented by men of fashion (including Brummell), became a gambling centre, and was closed about 1819.

Watling Street a Roman road (now largely underlying modern roads) running north-westwards across England, from Richborough in Kent through London and St Albans to Wroxeter in Shropshire. The predominant form of the name in Old English is *Wæclinga stræt*; the first element may represent a (real or imaginary) family or clan.

Dr Watson a doctor who is the companion and assistant of ➤ *Sherlock* HOLMES in detective stories by Arthur Conan Doyle; his good nature and lack of perspicacity make him a foil to the more difficult but brilliant Holmes. It is customary for Watson to have the truth revealed to him by his friend, although ➤ ELEMENTARY, *my dear Watson* does not occur in any of Conan Doyle's stories.

> The story is told by the detective's *fidus Achates* or (to use the modern term) his Watson.
> — Dorothy L. Sayers *Unpopular Opinions* (1946)

Watson's plot another name for the ➤ BYE *Plot*, from the English secular priest and conspirator William *Watson* (1559–1603), executed at Winchester 9 December 1603.

bet like the Watsons wager large sums, an informal Australian expression apparently referring to two brothers known at the beginning of the 20th century for making large bets.

Jean Antoine Watteau (1684–1721), French painter, of Flemish descent. An initiator of the rococo style, he is also known for his invention of the *fête galante*. The light-hearted imagery of his painting contrasted with the serious religious and classical subject matter approved by the Royal Academy.

Wattle Day in Australia, an annual celebration, the date of which varies locally, of the blossoming of the wattle, the floral emblem of Australia.

wave see also ➤ MEXICAN *wave*, ➤ SEVENTH *wave*, ➤ TENTH *wave*, ➤ THIRD *Wave*.

wave of the future the inevitable future fashion or trend; the coming thing, from the title of a book (1940) by Anne Morrow Lindbergh.

Waverer any of a group of peers who were willing to make terms with the Reform government of 1832 rather than wreck the Upper House.

Waverley Novels the novels of Sir Walter Scott; *Waverley* was the title of his first novel (1814), set in the Jacobite rising of 1745.

WAVES the women's section of the US Naval Reserve, established in 1942, or, since 1948, of the US Navy.

Wavy Navy former colloquial term for the Royal Naval Volunteer Reserve; from the wavy braid worn by officers on their sleeves prior to 1956.

waw the sixth letter of the Hebrew alphabet; the corresponding letter in the Arabic and other Semitic alphabets.

man of wax former expression meaning, as faultless as if modelled in wax.

wax and wane undergo alternate increases and decreases.

waxen image an effigy in wax representing a person whom it is desired to injure by witchcraft; it was believed that the victim would waste away as the wax melted in the fire, and feel pain if the figure was pricked or pierced.

way see also ➤ COMMITTEE *of Ways and Means*, ➤ DUNSTABLE *way*, ➤ *the* LONGEST *way round is the shortest way home*, ➤ LOVE *will find a way*, ➤ MILKY *Way*, ➤ *the* PARTING *of the ways*, ➤ SACRED *way*, ➤ THIRD *way*, ➤ WALSINGHAM *way*, ➤ *where there's a* WILL *there's a way*, ➤ *a* WILFUL *man must have his way*.

the Way in the Acts of the Apostles, the Christian religion; with allusion to John 24:6, 'I am the Way…no man cometh to the Father but by me.'

way of all flesh death; **go the way of all flesh**, meaning 'die', is an early variant of the biblical 'go the way of all the earth', as in 1 Kings 2:2 (the ➤ DOUAY *Bible* has 'I enter the way of all flesh' in this verse). The *way of all flesh* is also sometimes used to mean the experience common to humankind in its passage through life.

the Way of the Cross a series of images representing the Stations of the Cross, ranged round the interior of a church, or on the road to a church or shrine; the series of devotions prescribed to be used at these stations in succession.

Wayland the Smith in Anglo-Saxon mythology, a smith with supernatural powers, in English legend supposed to have his forge in a Neolithic chambered tomb (**Wayland's Smithy**) on the downs in SW Oxfordshire. His Norse equivalent is ➤ VOLUND.
> See also ➤ WADE's *boat*.

the way to a man's heart is through his stomach proverbial saying, early 19th century.

waymark a conspicuous object which serves as a guide to travellers; perhaps originally with allusion to Jeremiah 31:21, 'Set thee up waymarks.'

there are more ways of killing a cat than choking it with cream proverbial saying, mid 19th century.

there are more ways of killing a dog than choking it with butter proverbial saying, mid 19th century.

there are more ways of killing a dog than hanging it proverbial saying, late 17th century.

John Wayne (1907–79), American actor, known as **the Duke**. Associated with the film director John Ford from 1930, Wayne became a Hollywood star with *Stagecoach* (1939) and appeared in classic westerns such as *Red River* (1948).

wayzgoose an annual summer dinner or outing held by a printing house for its employees. The term is recorded from the mid 18th century, as an alteration of the earlier *waygoose*; there is no evidence as to its etymology (there is, for instance, nothing to suggest that *goose* was eaten at the dinner).

we used in formal contexts by a sovereign or ruler of a country, or by a writer or editor (as supported by an editorial staff collectively), to refer to himself or herself.

See also ➤ *we are all* ADAM's *children, but silk makes the difference*, ➤ *we must* EAT *a peck of dirt before we die*, ➤ *we will not go to* CANOSSA.

we are all guilty supposedly typical of the liberal view that all members of society bear responsibility for its wrongs; used particularly as a catch-phrase by the psychiatrist 'Dr Heinz Kiosk' in the *Daily Telegraph* satirical column of 'Peter Simple' (pseudonym of Michael Wharton).

we are not amused comment attributed to Queen Victoria; recorded in Caroline Holland *Notebooks of a Spinster Lady* (1919), and popularly regarded as typifying the repression associated with the Victorian age.

we name the guilty men a cliché of investigative journalism; *Guilty Men* (1940) was the title of a tract by Michael Foot, Frank Owen, and Peter Howard, published under the pseudonym of 'Cato', which attacked the supporters of Munich and the appeasement policy of Neville Chamberlain.

we shall not be moved title of labour and civil rights song (1931), adapted from an earlier gospel hymn.

we shall overcome title of song, originating from before the American Civil War, adapted as a Baptist hymn ('I'll Overcome Some Day', 1901) by C. Albert Tindley; revived in 1946 as a protest song by black tobacco workers, and in 1963 during the black Civil Rights Campaign.

the weaker vessel a wife, a female partner; originally in allusion to 1 Peter 'Giving honour unto the wife, as unto the weaker vessel'.

weakest see also ➤ *a* CHAIN *is no stronger than its weakest link*.

the weakest go to the wall proverbial saying, early 16th century; usually said to derive from the installation of seating around the walls in churches of the later Middle Ages. *Go to the wall* in figurative use means, succumb in a conflict or struggle.

the Weald a formerly wooded district including parts of Kent, Surrey, and East Sussex.

Wealden denoting a style of timber house built in the Weald in the late medieval and Tudor periods.

weapon-salve an ointment superstitiously believed to heal a wound by sympathetic agency when applied to the weapon by which the wound was made.

wear see also ➤ BETTER *to wear out than to rust out*, ➤ *wear the* WILLOW.

wear one's heart on one's sleeve make one's feelings apparent; perhaps originally with reference to Shakespeare's *Othello*, 'For I will wear my heart upon my sleeve, For daws to peck at'.

Wearing of the Green Irish nationalist song, dating from the end of the 18th century; ➤ GREEN had been recognized as the national colour of Ireland since the 17th century, and was adopted particularly by the United Irishmen at the time of the insurrection of 1798:

> I met wid Napper Tandy, and he took me by the hand,
> And he said, 'How's poor ould Ireland, and how does she stand?'
> She's the most disthressful country that iver yet was seen,
> For they're hangin' men an' women for the wearin' o' the Green.
> — 'The Wearin' o' the Green' (*c*.1795 ballad); James Napper Tandy (*c*.1737–1803) was a prominent Irish nationalist

In Kipling's story 'Namgay Doola' (1891), the Irish origin of Namgay is recognized by the narrator when he realizes that Namgay's children are singing the final line of this verse.

weary see ➤ *be the* DAY *weary, or be the day long, at last it ringeth to evensong*.

weary Willie the tramp who is the companion of ➤ TIRED *Tim*.

weasel the *weasel* as a small and agile carnivore is taken as a type of cunning; a deceitful or treacherous person.

> I'm . . . as sharp as a ferret, and as cunning as a weasel.
> — Charles Dickens *The Old Curiosity Shop* (1841)

See also ➤ POP *goes the weasel.*

weasel words words or statements that are intentionally ambiguous or misleading; the expression was popularized by the American Republican statesman Theodore Roosevelt (1858–1919):

> One of our defects as a nation is a tendency to use what have been called 'weasel words'. When a weasel sucks eggs the meat is sucked out of the egg. If you use a 'weasel word' after another, there is nothing left of the other.
> — Theodore Roosevelt speech in St Louis, 31 May 1915

weather see also ➤ CLERK *of the Weather*, ➤ POOR *man's weather-glass*, ➤ QUEEN*'s weather*, ➤ ROBIN *Hood could brave all weathers but a thaw wind*, ➤ SHEPHERD*'s weather-glass.*

weather-breeder a day of exceptionally sunny and calm weather, popularly suppposed to be a presage of a coming storm; the term is recorded from the mid 17th century.

weathercock a weathervane in the form of a cockerel, which turns with its head to the wind; traditionally taken as a symbol of mutability or fickleness.

Weatherman a member of a violent revolutionary group in the US, founded *c.*1970, and apparently named from a line in a song by Bob Dylan, 'You don't need a weatherman to know which way the wind blows'.

weave form (fabric) by interlacing long threads passing in one direction with others at a right angle to them. Recorded in Old English (*wefan*) and of Germanic origin, the word comes from an Indo-European root shared by Greek *huphē* 'web' and Sanskrit 'spider'.

In classical mythology, weaving was a particular skill of the goddess ➤ ARIADNE, in which she was unwisely challenged by ➤ ARACHNE; it was also the means by which ➤ PENELOPE kept her suitors waiting for many years.

weaver ➤ *St* MAURICE and ➤ *St* BERNARDINO *of Siena* are patron saints of weavers.

See also ➤ BOTTOM *the Weaver.*

the Web short for the ➤ WORLD *Wide Web.*

Penelope's web in the Greek legend, woven every day by ➤ PENELOPE, wife of Odysseus, and unravelled every night; she had told the many suitors who had gathered in Odysseus's absence that she would not marry again until the work was finished.

> How long shall we be constrained to weave Penelope's web?
> — John Wesley diary, 6 September 1771

the web of life supposedly woven, and cut, by the ➤ FATES.

Daniel Webster (1782–1852), American lawyer and politician, noted for his oratory. Although opposed to slavery, he saw the preservation of the Union as paramount, and was bitterly criticized by abolitionists. The response 'There is always room at the top', on being advised against joining the overcrowded legal profession, has been attributed to him.

Noah Webster (1758–1843), American lexicographer. His *American Dictionary of the English Language* (1828) in two volumes was the first dictionary to give comprehensive coverage of American usage, and was so well-known as to form the basis of the joke in Johnny Burke's title-song in the film *The Road to Morocco* (1942), 'Like Webster's Dictionary, we're Morocco bound.'

wed formal or archaic term meaning 'marry'. Old English *weddian* comes from the Germanic base of Scots wed 'a pledge', related to Latin *vas* 'surety' and *gage*.

See also ➤ BETTER *wed over the mixen than over the moor.*

wedding see also ➤ PENNY *wedding.*

wedding anniversary many wedding anniversaries are designated with particular names, as *china wedding, silver wedding*. The tradition is recorded (in reference to golden and silver weddings) from the mid 19th century, as a custom borrowed from Germany.

Wedding anniversaries

NAME	ANNIVERSARY
china wedding	20th
crystal wedding	15th
diamond wedding	60th or 75th
golden wedding	50th
ruby wedding	40th (occasionally, 45th)
sapphire wedding	45th
silver wedding	25th
tin wedding	10th
wooden wedding	5th

wedding breakfast a celebratory meal eaten just after a wedding (at any time of day) by the couple and their guests; the term is recorded from the mid 19th century.

one wedding brings another proverbial saying, mid 17th century.

wedding-finger another name for the ➤ RING-*finger*; it was traditionally believed (and is recorded by Aulus Gellius, 2nd century AD) that a particular nerve runs from the fourth finger of the left hand to the heart. The use of the ring-finger is directed in the ➤ SARUM rite for this reason.

wedge see ➤ THIN *end of the wedge*, ➤ WOODEN *wedge*.

Wedgwood trademark name for ceramic ware made by the English potter Josiah Wedgwood (1730–95) and his successors. Wedgwood is most associated with the powder-blue stoneware pieces with white embossed cameos that first appeared in 1775.

wedlock see also ➤ WINTER *and wedlock tames man and beast*.

wedlock is a padlock proverbial saying, late 17th century.

Wednesday the day of the week before Thursday and following Tuesday. Recorded from Old English (in the form *Wōdnesdæg*) it is named after the Germanic god *Odin*, and is the equivalent of late Latin *Mercurii dies*.

Wednesdays

Ash Wednesday	the first day of Lent
Black Wednesday	16 September 1992
Pulver Wednesday	the first day of Lent
Spy Wednesday	the Wednesday before Easter
White Wednesday	16 September 1992

Wednesday's child see ➤ *Monday's* CHILD *is fair of face*.

the wee folk the fairies; the term is recorded from the early 19th century, in Irish usage.

Wee Free a member of the minority group nicknamed the **Wee Free Kirk** which stood apart from the Free Church of Scotland when the majority amalgamated with the United Presbyterian Church to form the United Free Church in 1900. The group continued to call itself the Free Church of Scotland after this date.

weeding see ➤ ONE *year's seeding makes seven years' weeding*.

weeds see ➤ ILL *weeds grow apace*, ➤ WIDOW'S *weeds*.

week see ➤ EIGHTS *Week*, ➤ HOLY *Week*, ➤ MAY *Week*, ➤ SEVEN *Weeks' War*.

Feast of Weeks another term for the Jewish festival of ➤ SHAVUOTH.

weep see ➤ LAUGH *and the world laughs with you, weep and you weep alone*.

weeper a hired mourner at a funeral (recorded from late Middle English); also, a figure in the niche of a funeral monument, typically one of a number representing mourners.

Weeping Cross a wayside cross for penitents to pray at; *Weeping Cross* occurs as a place-name in a number of English counties, and is likely to represent the original site of such a cross. A *weeping cross* at Banbury in Oxfordshire is said to have been removed in 1841, and one at Ludlow in 1826. Other suggestions for the origin of the name are that the cross was in the vicinity of a place of execution, or that it marked the point at which a body being carried to burial was set down for the bearers to rest.

The expression **come home by Weeping Cross**, meaning suffer grievous disappointment or failure, is recorded from the late 16th century.

weeping philosopher a nickname for Heraclitus of Ephesus, Greek philosopher of the 5th century, which explicitly contrasted him with the ➤ LAUGH-ING *philosopher*, Democritus; Heraclitus, who was noted for misanthropy, was thought of as weeping at the spectacle presented by human life.

weeping saint traditional name (recorded in Camden's *Remaines*, 1605) for ➤ *St* SWITHIN, in relation to the association of his feast-day with rain.

weeping willow a Eurasian willow with trailing branches and foliage reaching down to the ground, widely grown as an ornamental in waterside settings and regarded as symbolical of mourning.

wegotism obtrusive or excessive use of the first person plural by a speaker or writer; an expression, a blend of *we* and *egotism*, coined in the late 18th century.

Wehrmacht the German armed forces, especially the army, from 1921 to 1945. The name is German, and means literally 'defensive force'.

Wei the name of several dynasties which ruled in China, especially that of AD 386–535.

weighed in the balance and found wanting biblical saying, from Daniel 5:27, 'thou art weighed in the balances and found wanting'; part of the message of the ➤ WRITING *on the wall* which prophesied imminent destruction to the king of Babylon.

Weimar a city in Thuringia, central Germany, which was famous in the late 18th and early 19th century for its intellectual and cultural life; both Goethe and Schiller lived and worked there.

Weimar Republic the German republic of 1919–33, so called because its constitution was drawn up at Weimar. The republic was faced with huge reparation costs deriving from the Treaty of Versailles as well as soaring inflation and high unemployment. The 1920s saw a growth in support for right-wing groups and the Republic was eventually overthrown by the Nazi Party of Adolf Hitler, after his appointment as Chancellor by President Hindenburg.

Wein, Weib, und Gesang in Germany, wine, women, and song, proverbially considered the essential ingredients for carefree entertainment and pleasure by men; the expression was popularized as the title of a Strauss waltz (1869), and probably comes ultimately from a couplet inscribed in the Luther room in the Wartburg, '*Wer nich liebt Wein, Weib und Gesang, Der bleibt ein Narr sein Leben lang* [Who loves not woman, wine, and song Remains a fool his whole life long]'.

weird a person's fate or destiny (now chiefly in Scottish use); the word is recorded from Old English (in form *wyrd*), and is of Germanic origin; it was used in plural form to mean ➤ *the* FATES.

See ➤ DREE *one's weird*.

the weird sisters originally (in late Middle English) ➤ *the* FATES; from the early 17th century, used for the three witches in Shakespeare's *Macbeth* (1606), with the meaning that they had the power to control destiny; this in turn gave rise (in the early 19th century) to *weird* as meaning 'unearthly'.

Welch variant spelling of *Welsh*, now surviving only in **Royal Welch Fusiliers**.

welfare state a system whereby the state undertakes to protect the health and well-being of its citizens, especially those in financial or social need, by means of grants, pensions, and other benefits. The foundations for the modern welfare state in the UK were laid by the Beveridge Report of 1942; proposals

such as the establishment of a National Health Service and the National Insurance Scheme were implemented by the Labour administration in 1948.

welkin the sky, heaven, especially in the phrase **make the welkin ring**, make a very loud sound. The word is recorded from Old English (in form *wolcen*, meaning 'cloud, sky') and is of Germanic origin.

well a well is the emblem of St Juthwara and St Sidwell, sisters, and reputed British virgin martyrs with a cult in the south west of England. *Wells*, representing springs of natural water, are often associated with holy sites, as that of the shrine of ➤ *St* WINEFRIDE in Wales.

See also ➤ *the* PITCHER *will go to the well once too often*, ➤ TRUTH *lies at the bottom of a well*, ➤ WISHING *well*.

well begun is half done proverbial saying, early 15th century; emphasizing the importance of a successful beginning to the completion of a project.

Well-beloved epithet of Louis XV of France and other rulers; the term is also used in letters or decrees of a sovereign as part of the formal address to a trusted councillor.

well-dressing the decoration of wells with flowers, an ancient custom at Whitsuntide especially in Derbyshire.

all's well that ends well proverbial saying, late 14th century.

Wellerism a form of humorous comparison in which a familiar saying or proverb is identified with something said by a person in a specified but inapposite situation, from the name of Samuel *Weller* or his father, characters in Dickens's *Pickwick Papers*.

Duke of Wellington Arthur Wellesley (1769–1852), British soldier and Tory statesman, Prime Minister 1828–30 and 1834; also known as **the Iron Duke**. He served as commander of the British forces in the ➤ PENINSULAR *War* (1808–14) and in 1815 defeated ➤ NAPOLEON at the Battle of Waterloo, so ending the Napoleonic Wars.

Wellington is associated with a number of well-known quotations, including 'Publish and be damned', his response to a blackmail threat prior to the publication of the *Memoirs* of the English courtesan Harriette Wilson (1789–1846).

Wells, Fargo, & Co. a US transportation company founded in 1852 by the businessmen Henry Wells

(1805–78) and William Fargo (1818–81) and others. It carried mail to and from the newly developed West, founded a San Francisco bank, and later ran a stage-coach service (having bought the *Pony Express* system) until the development of a transcontinental railway service.

Welsh of or relating to Wales, its people, or their Celtic language. Old English *Welisc*, *Wælisc* comes from a Germanic word meaning 'foreigner', from Latin *Volcae*, the name of a Celtic people; the Welsh name for Wales is *Cymru* and for its people, *Cymry*.

Welsh aunt a parent's first female cousin.

Welsh dragon a red heraldic dragon as the emblem of Wales.

Welsh harp another name for the triple harp, a large harp without pedals and with three rows of strings, the middle row providing sharps and flats; the name is recorded from the mid 17th century, in Ben Jonson's *Masque, for Honour of Wales.*

Welsh main a term in cockfighting; a series of matches organized as a knockout competition.

> Laying schemes for massacring men on Palm Sunday, as if he were backing a Welsh main, where all must fight to the death.
> — Sir Walter Scott *The Fair Maid of Perth* (1828)

Welsh rarebit a dish of melted and seasoned cheese on toast, sometimes with other ingredients; the term is a late 18th century alteration of the earlier *Welsh rabbit* (early 18th century), but the reason for the use of *rabbit* is unknown.

Welsh uncle a parent's first male cousin.

Welsh Wizard a nickname for the Welsh politician and British Prime Minister David Lloyd George (1863–1945), who was described by John Maynard Keynes as, 'This extraordinary figure of our time, this syren, this goat-footed bard, this half-human visitor to our age from the hag-ridden magic and enchanted woods of Celtic antiquity'.

Weltanschauung a particular philosophy or view of life; the world view of an individual or group. The word is German, and comes from *Welt* 'world' + *Anschauung* 'perception'.

welterweight a weight in boxing and other sports intermediate between lightweight and middleweight, which in the amateur boxing scale ranges from 63.5–67 kg. It is recorded from the early 19th century, but the origin of *welter* is unknown.

Weltpolitik international politics; world affairs from a political standpoint; a particular country's

policy towards the world at large. The word is German, and is recorded in English from the early 20th century.

Weltschmerz a feeling of melancholy and world-weariness. Recorded in English from the late 19th century, the word is German, and comes from *Welt* 'world' + *Schmerz* 'pain'.

wely a Muslim saint; the shrine of a Muslim saint.

Wembley Stadium a sports stadium in Wembley, NW London, where the FA Cup Final and the England football team's home matches are played; it was the venue for the 1966 World Cup Final.

wen see also ➤ GREAT *Wen*.

wen a runic letter, used in Old and Middle English, later replaced by *w*.

St Wenceslas (*c*.907–29), Duke of Bohemia and patron saint of the Czech Republic; also known as **Good King Wenceslas**. He worked to Christianize the people of Bohemia but was murdered by his brother; he later became venerated as a martyr and hero of Bohemia. The story told in the Christmas carol 'Good King Wenceslas' appears to have no basis in fact.

    ☐ **FEAST DAY** His feast day is 28 September.

Wendy house a toy house large enough for children to play in, named after the house built around *Wendy* by the Lost Boys and ➤ PETER *Pan*.

werejaguar in Olmec mythology, a creature partly human and partly feline.

werewolf in myth or fiction, a person who changes for periods of time into a wolf, typically when there is a full moon. Recorded from late Old English, in form *werewulf*; the first element has usually been identified with Old English *wer* 'man'. In modern use the word has been revived through folklore studies.

wergeld in Germanic and Anglo-Saxon law, the price put on a man according to his rank, payable as a fine or compensation by a person guilty of homicide or certain other crimes.

Abraham Gottlob Werner (1749–1817), German geologist. He was the chief exponent of the theory of ➤ NEPTUNISM, eventually shown to be incorrect, and attempted to establish a universal stratigraphic sequence.

Wertherism morbid sentimentality, regarded as characteristic of *Werther*, the hero of Goethe's romance 'Die Leiden des jungen Werther' (1774), a sensitive artist who is at odds with the world and unhappily in love, and who commits suicide. The cult of *Wertherism* was held up to ridicule by Thackeray:

> Werther had a love for Charlotte
> Such as words could never utter;
> Would you know how first he met her?
> She was cutting bread and butter.
> — William Makepeace Thackeray 'Sorrows of Werther'
> (1855)

John Wesley (1703–91), English preacher and co-founder of Methodism. Wesley was a committed Christian evangelist who won many working-class converts, often through open-air preaching. The opposition they encountered from the Church establishment led to the Methodists forming a separate denomination in 1791. His brother Charles (1707–88) was also a founding Methodist, and both wrote many hymns.

Wessel see ➤ HORST *Wessel Song*.

Wessex the kingdom of the West Saxons, established in Hampshire in the early 6th century and gradually extended by conquest to include much of southern England. Under Alfred the Great and his successors it formed the nucleus of the Anglo-Saxon kingdom of England. Athelstan, Alfred's grandson, became king of England. The name was revived in the 19th century by Thomas Hardy to designate the south-western counties of England (especially Dorset) in which his novels are set.

Wessi a term used in Germany (especially since reunification) to denote a citizen of the former Federal Republic of Germany; a West German as opposed to an East German or ➤ OSSI.

west the direction towards the point of the horizon where the sun sets at the equinoxes, on the left-hand side of a person facing north, or the part of the horizon lying in this direction. The word is recorded from Old English and is of Germanic origin; it comes from an Indo-European root shared by Greek *hesperos*, Latin *vesper* 'evening'.

From the Middle Ages **the West** has designated Europe (and later America) as seen in contrast to other civilizations; in the 20th century, the term also denoted the non-Communist states of Europe and America contrasted with the former Communist states of eastern Europe. **The West** was also traditionally used for the western part of the United States, especially the states west of the Mississippi.

The *west* is also referred to allusively as the place of the sun's setting.

See also ➤ EAST, *west, home's best*, ➤ GO *west, young man*, ➤ MAE *West*, ➤ QUEEN *of the West*.

West Bank a region west of the River Jordan and north-west of the Dead Sea. It contains Jericho, Hebron, Nablus, Bethlehem, and other settlements. It became part of Jordan in 1948 and was occupied by Israel following the Six Day War of 1967. In 1993 an agreement was signed which granted limited autonomy to the Palestinians, who comprise 97 per cent of its inhabitants; withdrawal of Israeli troops began in 1994.

West End the entertainment and shopping area of London to the west of the City; the name is recorded from the late 18th century.

West Lothian question a rhetorical question that identifies the constitutional anomaly that arises from devolved assemblies being established for Scotland and for Wales but not for England, i.e. that MPs for Scottish and Welsh constituencies are unable to vote on Scottish or Welsh matters that have been devolved to those assemblies, but are able to vote on equivalent matters concerning England, whilst MPs for English constituencies have no reciprocal influence on Scottish or Welsh policy.

West Lothian is the name of a former parlimentary constituency in Central Scotland, whose MP, Tam Dalyell, persistently raised this question in Parliament in debates on Scottish and Welsh devolution during 1977–8.

West Point the US Military Academy, founded in 1802, located on the site of a former strategic fort on the west bank of the Hudson River in New York State.

West Side the western part of any of several North American cities or boroughs, especially the island borough of Manhattan, New York.

Western Church the part of the Christian Church historically originating in the Latin Church of the Western Roman Empire, including the Roman Catholic Church and the Anglican, Lutheran, and Reformed Churches, especially as distinct from the Eastern Orthodox Church.

Western Empire the western part of the Roman Empire, after its division in AD 395.

Western Front the zone of fighting in western Europe in the First World War, in which the German army engaged the armies to its west, i.e.

France, the UK (and its dominions), and, from 1917, the US. For most of the war the front line stretched from the Vosges mountains in eastern France through Amiens to Ostend in Belgium.

Western Wall another name for the ➤ WAILING Wall.

Westminster an inner London borough which contains the Houses of Parliament and many government offices; often used in reference to the British Parliament.

> Devolutionists in both Wales and Scotland are increasingly taking what they call 'the Westminster by-pass' to set up their own missions in Brussels.
> — *Independent* 24 January 1997

See also ➤ LONG *Meg of Westminster.*

Palace of Westminster the building in Westminster in which the British Parliament meets; the Houses of Parliament. The present building, designed by Sir Charles Barry, was formally opened in 1852. The original palace, a royal residence supposed to date from the 11th century until it was damaged by fire in 1512, was destroyed by a fire in 1834.

Statute of Westminster a statute of 1931 recognizing the equality of status of the dominions as autonomous communities within the British Empire, and giving their legislatures independence from British control.

Westminster Abbey the collegiate church of St Peter in Westminster, originally the abbey church of a Benedictine monastery. The present building, begun by Henry III in 1245 and altered and added to by successive rulers, replaced an earlier church built by Edward the Confessor. Nearly all the kings and queens of England have been crowned in Westminster Abbey; it is also the burial place of many of England's monarchs and of some of the nation's leading figures.

Westminster Assembly appointed by the Long Parliament in 1643, to help in establishing the government and liturgy of the Church of England.

Westminster chimes the pattern of chimes struck at successive quarters by Big Ben in the Houses of Parliament, used for other clocks and door chimes; the chime uses four bells struck in five different four-note sequences, each of which occurs twice in the course of an hour.

Westminster Confession a Calvinist doctrinal statement which was issued by the synod appointed to reform the English and Scottish Churches in 1643,

and became widely accepted among Presbyterian Churches.

Weston see ➤ AGGIE *Weston's.*

Treaty of Westphalia the peace accord (1648) which ended the ➤ THIRTY *Years War*, signed simultaneously in Osnabrück and Münster.

Westralia in Australia, an informal name for Western Australia.

wetback a Mexican living in the US, especially one who is an illegal immigrant, so named from the practice of swimming the Rio Grande to reach the US.

grey wethers any large boulders which resemble sheep in the distance; especially, the sarsen stones of Wiltshire.

wetware chiefly in science fiction, computer technology in which the brain is linked to artificial systems, or used as a model for artificial systems based on biochemical processes.

Rogier van der Weyden (*c.*1400–64), Flemish painter. His work, mostly portraits and religious paintings, became widely known in Europe during his lifetime, and he was particularly influential in the development of Dutch portrait painting.

Mr W. H. the 'onlie begetter' to whom Shakespeare's sonnets (in 1609) were dedicated; he has variously been identified with the Earl of Southampton (Henry Wriothesley), the Earl of Pembroke (William Herbert), and others.

wh-question a question in English introduced by a wh-word, that requires information in answer, rather than *yes* or *no.*

whale a very large marine mammal with a stream-lined hairless body, a horizontal tail fin, and a blow-hole on top of the head for breathing, which in early translations of the Bible is given as the 'great fish' which swallowed Jonah. A whale is the emblem of ➤ *St* BRENDAN and the 6th–7th bishop St Malo, who is regarded as the apostle of Brittany.

See also ➤ SAVE *the whale,* ➤ *throw out a* TUB *to a whale.*

whammy see ➤ DOUBLE *whammy.*

wheatear a mainly Eurasian and African songbird related to the chats, with black and buff or black and white plumage and a white rump. Recorded from the late 16th century, the name apparently comes from *white* assimilated to *wheat* + *arse* assimilated to *ear.*

wheel a wheel is the emblem of ➤ *St* Catherine *of Alexandria* and ➤ *St* Christina.

See also ➤ break *a butterfly on a wheel*, ➤ Catherine *wheel*, ➤ Ferris *wheel*, ➤ fifth *wheel*, ➤ Fortune's *wheel*, ➤ prayer *wheel*, ➤ *put a* spoke *in someone's wheel*, ➤ reinvent *the wheel*, ➤ *the* squeaking *wheel gets the grease*, ➤ *the wheel has come full* circle.

wheel of Fortune the wheel which ➤ Fortune is fabled to turn, as an emblem of mutability. Also called *Fortune's wheel*.

wheelbarrow a *wheelbarrow* is the emblem of the 8th-century Anglo-Saxon hermit St Cuthman, who is said to have made a wheeled bed for his invalid mother out of a wheelbarrow.

wheels within wheels used to indicate that a situation is complicated and affected by secret or indirect influences; perhaps originally after the description of the vision of four creatures in Ezekiel 1:16, 'their work was as it were a wheel in the middle of a wheel'.

where's the beef advertising slogan for Wendy's Hamburgers in campaign launched 9 January 1984, and subsequently taken up by Walter Mondale in a televised debate with Gary Hart from Atlanta, 11 March 1984: 'When I hear your new ideas I'm reminded of that ad, "Where's the beef?" '

Whetstone of Witte a treatise by the Welsh mathematician Robert Recorde (1510?–58), which is said to be the first English book containing the symbols '+' and '-'.

whiffler an attendant armed with a javelin, battle-axe, sword, or staff and employed to keep the way clear for a procession or other public spectacle. Whifflers formed a regular part of the Corporation procession at Norwich till 1835; they were employed also on 11 September 1848, when the Duke of Cambridge attended the triennial musical festival.

The word is recorded from the mid 16th century, and may come ultimately from *wifle* 'javelin, axe'.

Whig originally, an adherent of the Presbyterian cause in Scotland in the 17th century; the name is probably a shortening of Scots ➤ Whiggamore. At the end of the 17th century, *Whig* designated a person who opposed the succession of the Catholic James II to the crown; an exclusioner.

From the early 18th century, *Whig* was used for a member of the British reforming and constitutional party that after 1688 sought the supremacy of Parliament and was eventually succeeded in the 19th century by the Liberal Party. The name was further applied, again in the early 18th century, to an American colonist who supported the American Revolution.

Whig historian a historian who interprets history as the continuing and inevitable victory of progress over reaction; the term is first recorded in George Bernard Shaw's preface to *St Joan* (1924), where he comments that Joan's 'ideal biographer…must understand the Middle Ages…much more intimately than our Whig historians have ever understood them'.

Whiggamore a member of a body of rebels from the western part of Scotland who in 1648 marched on Edinburgh in opposition to Charles I. The name comes from *whig* 'to drive' + *mare* 'female horse', and is probably the origin of ➤ Whig.

whip an official of a political party appointed to maintain parliamentary discipline among its members, especially so as to ensure attendance and voting in debates. The term is recorded from the mid 19th century, and is a shortening of *whipper-in*, literally a huntsman's assistant who keeps the hounds from straying by driving them back with the whip into the main body of the pack.

The British Tory statesman Lord Canning (1770–1827), is said to have commented that the duty of a whip is 'to make a House, and keep a House, and cheer the minister'.

See also ➤ three-*line whip*.

whipping boy a person who is blamed or punished for the faults or incompetence of others; an extended use of the original term (mid 17th century) denoting a boy educated with a young prince or other royal person and punished instead of him.

whirling dervish a member of an order of ➤ dervishes known for their dancing ritual.

whisky a spirit distilled from malted grain, especially barley or rye. The name comes (in the early 18th century) from an abbreviation of obsolete *whiskybae*, variant of ➤ usquebaugh.

whisky insurrection an outbreak in Pennsylvania in 1794 against an exercise duty on spirits imposed by Congress in 1791.

whisky money the proportion of the beer and spirit duty which was allocated to technical education by the Local Taxation (Customs and Excise) Act of 1890.

whisky ring in the US, a combination of distillers and revenue officers formed in 1872 to defraud the government of part of the tax on spirits.

whispering campaign a systematic circulation of a rumour, typically in order to damage someone's reputation; the term originated in US politics of the early 20th century.

whispering gallery a typically circular or elliptical gallery situated under a dome, whose acoustic properties are such that a whisper may be heard round its entire circumference; there is a famous example in the dome of St Paul's Cathedral in London.

whispers see ➤ Chinese *whispers*.

whist a card game, usually for two pairs of players, in which points are scored according to the number of tricks won and (in some forms) by the highest trumps or honours held by each pair. Recorded from the mid 17th century (earlier as *whisk*), the name may allude to whisking away the tricks.

whistle see ➤ bells *and whistles*, ➤ blow *the whistle on*, ➤ Pig *and Whistle*, ➤ *a* sow *may whistle though it has an ill mouth for it.*

whistle down the wind let something go; abandon something, originally meaning to turn a trained hawk loose by casting it off with the wind, instead of against the wind in pursuit of prey.

whistle for a wind traditional practice among sailors; it was believed that whistling would bring a wind during a calm spell, and that refraining from whistling could calm a gale, and the English antiquary and biographer John Aubrey in his *Remaines* (1686–7) notes that 'the seamen will not endure to have one whistle on shipboard, believing that it raises winds'.

James McNeill Whistler (1834–1903), American painter and etcher, who mainly painted in one or two colours and sought to achieve harmony of colour and tone. He was the centre of a famous libel case in which he sued the critic John Ruskin for his comment on Whistler's *Nocturne in Black and Gold*,

'I never expected to hear a coxcomb ask two hundred guineas for flinging a pot of paint in the public's face.' Whistler won the case, but the jury awarded him only one farthing damages.

a whistling woman and a crowing hen are neither fit for God nor men proverbial saying, early 18th century; both the woman and the hen are considered unnatural, and therefore unlucky.

Whit Sunday the seventh Sunday after Easter, a Christian festival commemorating the descent of the Holy Spirit at ➤ Pentecost (Acts 2). The name is recorded from Old English, in form *Hwīta Sunnandæg*, literally 'white Sunday', probably with reference to the white robes of those newly baptized at Pentecost.

Whit walk a traditional ➤ Whitsuntide event in which church congregations walk in procession through the streets.

Synod of Whitby a conference held in Whitby in 664 that resolved the differences between the Celtic and Roman forms of Christian worship in England, in particular the method of calculating the date of Easter. The Northumbrian Christians had followed the Celtic method of fixing the date while those of the south had adopted the Roman system. King Oswy (612–70) of Northumbria decided in favour of Rome, and England as a result effectively severed the connection with the Celtic Church.

white a colour or pigment of the colour of milk or fresh snow, due to the reflection of all visible rays of light; the opposite of black, traditionally taken as the colour of innocence and purity.

From the 17th century, white was specially associated with royalist and legitimist causes, as in the ➤ white *cockade* of the Jacobites and the ➤ white *flag* of the Bourbons.

See also ➤ angry *white male*, ➤ big *white chief*, ➤ dead *white European male*, ➤ Great *White Way*, ➤ *in a white* sheet, ➤ men *in white coats*, ➤ park *cattle*, ➤ river *of white*, ➤ show *the white feather*, ➤ Snow *White*, ➤ *white* crow.

Admiral of the White Admiral of the White squadron (one of the three divisions of the Royal Navy made in the 17th century).

Gilbert White (1720–93), English clergyman and naturalist. He wrote many letters to friends on aspects of natural history (especially ornithology) in his native village of Selborne, Hampshire; these were published in 1789 as *The Natural History and*

Antiquities of Selborne, which has remained in print ever since.

Mrs White one of the six stock characters constituting the murderer and suspects in the game of ➤ Cluedo.

White Army any of the armies which opposed the Bolsheviks during the Russian Civil War of 1918–21.

white bird in Irish folklore, a bird of fairyland.

White Boar the personal badge of Richard III (1452–85), alluded to in the political rhyme beginning ➤ *the* cat, *the rat, and Lovell the dog.*

white-bread of, belonging to, or representative of the white middle classes; not progressive, radical, or innovative; the term (which is recorded from the late 1970s, originally in North America) refers to the colour and perceived blandness of white bread as a commodity, and may also be a pun on 'white bred'.

white Christmas Christmas with snow on the ground, a term first recorded in Charles Kingsley *Two Years Ago* (1857), 'We shall have a white Christmas, I expect. Snow's coming.', and popularized by Irving Berlin:

> I'm dreaming of a white Christmas,
> Just like the ones I used to know.
> — Irving Berlin 'White Christmas' (1942 song)

white cliffs of Dover the chalk cliffs on the Kent coast near Dover, taken as a national and patriotic symbol, and popularized as such in the patriotic wartime song by Nat Burton:

> There'll be blue birds over the white cliffs of Dover,
> Tomorrow, just you wait and see.
> — Nat Burton 'The White Cliffs of Dover' (1941 song)

white coal flowing water as a source of energy; the term is recorded from the late 19th century.

white cockade a Jacobite badge, worn by the supporters of Charles Edward Stuart; according to a note in Boswell's *Life of Samuel Johnson*, in 1745 Boswell himself 'wore a white cockade, and prayed for King James'.

white-collar of or relating to the work done or those who work in an office or other professional environment; denoting non-violent crime committed by white-collar workers, especially fraud. References to a *white collar* as the sign of a clerical or non-manual worker are found from the 1920s.

White Company name of a mercenary company led by John Hawkwood (d. 1394), who were active in Italy in the mid 14th century; it is suggested that the name reflected the splendour of their equipment.

White Devil in John Webster's *The White Devil* (1612), the name given to the central character, Vittoria Corombona, who connives at the murder of her husband and her lover's wife, and who is finally herself murdered; the play is based on the historical character Vittoria Accoramboni (1557–85).

white dwarf a small very dense star that is typically the size of a planet. A white dwarf is formed when a low-mass star has exhausted all its central nuclear fuel and lost its outer layers as a planetary nebula.

white elephant a possession that is useless or troublesome, especially one that is expensive to maintain or difficult to dispose of, from the story that the kings of Siam gave such animals as a gift to courtiers considered obnoxious, in order to ruin the recipient by the great expense incurred in maintaining the animal.

See also ➤ King *of the White Elephant.*

white ensign a white flag carrying a St George's cross with the Union Jack in the top corner next to the flagstaff, flown by the Royal and most Commonwealth navies (other than that of Canada) and the Royal Yacht Squadron.

White Father a member of the Society of Missionaries of Africa, a Roman Catholic order founded in Algiers in 1868; the term is a translation of the French *Père Blanc*, for the white habits worn by the order.

white flag a white flag or cloth used as a symbol of surrender, truce, or a desire to parley; Livy's *Roman Histories* refer to a Carthaginian ship displaying white flags as a sign of peace. The *white flag* was also the flag of the house of Bourbon, and thus the national flag of pre-Revolutionary France.

one white foot, buy him; two white feet, try him; three white feet, look well about him; four white feet, go without him proverbial saying, late 19th century; on horse-dealing.

White Friar a ➤ Carmelite monk, so named because of the white habits worn by the monks.

White Goddess in the poetic thought of Robert Graves (1895–1985), as detailed in his book *The White Goddess* (1948), the triple mother goddess as the source of poetic inspiration.

White Guard a member of a force fighting for the government in the Finnish civil war of 1918; a member of a counter-revolutionary force fighting in the Russian civil war of 1918–21.

White Hart the personal badge of Richard II (1306–1400), shown wearing a golden collar; his mother's personal badge had been a white hind.

white heat the temperature or state of something that is so hot that it emits white light; a state of intense passion or activity. Since the 1960s the term has been associated with the phrase 'the white heat of technology', a popular misquotation of a passage from a speech by Harold Wilson:

> The Britain that is going to be forged in the white heat of this revolution will be no place for restrictive practices or for outdated methods on either side of industry.
> — Harold Wilson speech at the Labour Party Conference, 1 October 1963

White Highlands an area in western Kenya formerly (1909–59) reserved for Europeans.

White Horse the figure of a white horse, reputed (by later writers) as the ensign of the Saxons when they invaded Britain, and the heraldic ensign of Brunswick, Hanover, and Kent; also, the figure of a horse cut on the face of chalk downs in England, and popularly supposed to represent the 'white horse' of the Saxons; notably that near Uffington in Berkshire.

white horses white-crested waves at sea; the term is recorded from the mid 19th century, and in poetry is often used in an extended metaphor, as in Arnold's *The Forsaken Merman* (1849), 'The wild white horses play, Champ and chafe and toss in the spray'.

White House the official residence of the US president in Washington DC. The White House was built 1792–9 of greyish-white limestone from designs of the Irish-born architect James Hoban (*c.*1762–1831). The building was restored in 1814 after being burnt by British troops during the War of 1812, the smoke-stained walls being painted white. It was first formally designated the *White House* in 1902.

white information positive information about a person's creditworthiness held by a bank or similar institution; the term is recorded from the late 1980s, and is the opposite of the kind of *black information* which might cause a person to be blacklisted. Both terms are now established, although the contextual use often indicates uneasiness about the ethical aspect of disclosure of what is effectively confidential information, whether or not it is favourable.

white knight a hero or champion; in allusion to the amiable and confused White Knight in Lewis Carroll's *Through the Looking-Glass* (1872), a term for an amiable but ineffectual person. Later, the phrase was used without irony in Stock Exchange slang to mean a company which comes to the aid of another which is facing an unwelcome take-over bid.

   The *White Knight* is one of three hereditary Irish titles (the others being the ➤ *Knight of* GLIN and the ➤ *Knight of* KERRY). The title of the *White Knight* (which is currently in abeyance) was granted to the Fitzgibbon family in the 14th century when Maurice Fitzgibbon was reputedly knighted by Edward III after distinguishing himself at the battle of Halidon Hill in Scotland in 1333.

white lady a spectre in the form of a woman dressed in white, traditionally regarded as a sign of death; the *white lady* is particularly associated with Germanic folklore, and may be a survival of the mythological ➤ BERCHTA.

white lie a harmless or trivial lie, especially one told to avoid hurting someone's feelings; the term is first recorded in the *Gentleman's Magazine* of 1741, in a reference to 'a certain Lady of the highest Quality' who made a judicious distinction between the two forms of lie.

white-livered feeble-spirited, cowardly; reflecting the traditional belief that a light-coloured liver indicated a deficiency of bile or ➤ CHOLER, and thus of vigour, spirit, or courage.

white magic magic used only for good purposes, the opposite of ➤ BLACK *magic.*

white man's burden the supposed task of whites to spread the benefits of civilization. The term derives from a poem by Kipling (1899), written with particular reference to the colonial role of the US in the Philippines:

> Take up the White Man's burden—
> Send forth the best ye breed—
> Go, bind your sons to exile
> To serve your captives' need.
> — Rudyard Kipling 'The White Man's Burden' (1899)

white man's grave equatorial West Africa considered as being particularly unhealthy for whites; recorded from the mid 19th century.

White Monk a ➤ CISTERCIAN monk, so named (in late Middle English) because of the habits of undyed wool worn by the monks.

white night a sleepless night; the phrase is a translation of French *nuit blanche.*

White Nile the name for the main, western branch of the ➤ NILE between the Ugandan–Sudanese border and its confluence with the Blue Nile at Khartoum.

White Paper in the UK, a government report giving information or proposals on an issue; (prior to 1940), an Order Paper of the House of Commons which was a corrected and revised version of one (a *Blue Paper*) issued earlier the same day.

white plague an archaic term for tuberculosis, reflecting the perception of it as a widespread and often fatal disease.

white poplar the nymph Leuce, daughter of Oceanus, was taken to the underworld by Hades; after her death, she was changed into a white poplar.

White Rabbit a character in Lewis Carroll's *Alice's Adventures in Wonderland* (1865), who was always running from fear of being late; his typical ejaculation is 'Oh my ears and whiskers!'

White Raja any of the three Rajas belonging to the English family of Brooke who ruled Sarawak from 1841 to 1941.

white rose the emblem of the House of York in the ➤ WARS *of the Roses* or (later) of Yorkshire, directly opposed to the ➤ RED *rose* of Lancaster. In the 18th century, the *white rose* was adopted as an emblem by the Jacobites.

White Russian a Belorussian; an opponent of the Bolsheviks during the Russian Civil War.

White Sands an area of white gypsum salt flats in central New Mexico, designated a national monument in 1933. It is surrounded by a large missile-testing range, which, in 1945, as part of the ➤ MANHATTAN *Project*, was the site of the detonation of the first nuclear weapon.

White Ship name of the ship which in November 1120 foundered in the channel with the loss of nearly all on board, including Henry I's only legitimate son.

White Sister a member of the Congregation of the Missionary Sisters of Our Lady of Africa, founded in 1869 to assist the White Fathers, or of the Congregation of the Daughters of the Holy Ghost, founded in 1706 in Brittany.

white slave a white person treated like a slave, especially a woman tricked or forced into prostitution, typically one taken to a foreign country for this purpose; the term is first recorded in the debates of the US Congress, 13 May 1789, in a reference to 'the white slaves…who were imported from all the jails of Europe'.

white staff any of various royal or governmental offices symbolized by a white staff; an official holding such an office.

mark with a white stone regard as specially fortunate or happy (with allusion to the ancient practice of using a white stone as a memorial of a happy event).

White Surrey name of Richard III's horse, which he rode at the battle of ➤ BOSWORTH.

White Terror any of various periods of persecution by counter-revolutionaries, in particular, that in Hungary in 1919–20 and in China in the years following 1927.

White Tower the keep which is the oldest part of the ➤ TOWER *of London.*

white wedding a wedding at which the bride wears a formal white dress, traditionally as a sign of virginity.

White Wednesday a Eurosceptic name for ➤ BLACK *Wednesday.*

white witch a person, typically a woman, who practises magic for altruistic purposes, one who practises *white magic.*

White's a chocolate-house in St James's Street, London, started in 1697 by Francis White. The first number of *The Tatler* announced that accounts of gallantry, pleasure, and entertainment would emanate from White's Chocolate House. It was taken over by Arthur (the founder of Arthur's Club) and converted into a club, which became a celebrate gaming centre. The present clubhouse, with its bay window (associated with Brummell), dates from 1755, though much altered inside and out.

Whiteboy in 18th- and 19th-century Ireland, a member of an illegal agrarian association, so called because they wore white shirts as distinctive clothing.

Whitechapel a district in the East End of London, scene of the ➤ JACK *the Ripper* murders in 1888.

whited sepulchre a hypocrite, an ostensibly virtuous or pleasant person who is inwardly corrupt; originally as a biblical reference to Matthew 23:27, 'Woe unto you, scribes and Pharisees, hypocrites! for ye are like unto whited sepulchres, which indeed appear beautiful outward, but are within full of dead men's bones.'

Whitehall a street in Westminster, London, in which many government offices are located, used as an allusive reference to the British Civil Service. The name is taken from the former royal palace of *White Hall*, originally a residence of Cardinal Wolsey.

> For decades, the nuclear industry, and its followers in Whitehall and Westminster, had a simple answer to these questions: Micawberism. Something, they believed, would turn up.
> — *Independent on Sunday* 15 March 1998

Whitewatergate the political scandal arising from the Clintons' alleged connection with the Whitewater property venture and with related incidents. *Whitewater* was the name of a 1980s property development corporation based in Arkansas, in which US president Bill Clinton and his wife Hillary Rodham Clinton were partners, and attempts to investigate the matter led to the affair being likened to ➤ WATERGATE.

Whitley Council a negotiating body for discussing and settling matters of industrial relations, pay and conditions, and related issues, named after John H. *Whitley* (1866–1935), chairman of a committee (1916) which recommended such bodies.

Eli Whitney (1765–1825), American inventor, who conceived the idea of mass-producing interchangeable parts. This he applied in his fulfilment of a contract (1797) to supply muskets.

Whitsun ale a parish festival formerly held at Whitsuntide, marked by feasting, sports, and merrymaking.

Whitsuntide the weekend or week including ➤ WHIT *Sunday*.

Dick Whittington (d. 1423), English merchant and Lord Mayor of London; full name Sir Richard Whittington. Whittington was a mercer who became Lord Mayor three times (1397–8; 1406–7; 1419–20) and left legacies for rebuilding Newgate

Prison and establishing a city library.

The legend of his early life as a poor orphan was first recorded in 1605. According to the popular story, he was a kitchen boy who was so badly treated that he was about to run away, when he heard the bells of London ringing as though saying, 'Turn again Whittington, Lord Mayor of London'; later, through the ratcatching skills of his cat, he made enough money to set himself up in business, and later to make his fortune.

> What Mr Theodore Roszak has called the 'counterculture' and Professor Lionel Trilling the 'adversary culture' is the Dick Whittington's cat that brings in this sort of wealth.
> — Saul Bellow *Israel* (1967)

Whittington chimes a pattern of eight chimes (traditionally supposed to have been heard by Whittington in London), used in some chiming clocks.

Frank Whittle (1907–96), English aeronautical engineer, test pilot, and inventor of the jet aircraft engine. He took out the first patent for a turbojet engine in 1930 and in 1941 the first flight using Whittle's jet engine was made.

Doctor Who central character of a long-running British television science fiction series beginning in 1963, played first by William Hartnell and later by others including Tom Baker; the time-travelling *Doctor Who* is a Time Lord whose survival includes regular changes of physical appearance. He travels in the *Tardis* (Time And Relative Dimensions In Space) which resembles an old-fashioned London police telephone box.

who dares wins motto of the British Special Air Service regiment, from 1942.

who goes home? formal question asked by the doorkeeper when the House of Commons adjourns.

who he? an editorial interjection after the name of a (supposedly) little-known person, associated particularly with Harold Ross (1892–1951), editor of the *New Yorker*; repopularized in Britain by the satirical magazine *Private Eye*.

Who's Who an annual biographical dictionary of contemporary men and women. It was first issued in 1849 but took its present form in 1897, when it incorporated material from another biographical work, *Men and Women of the Time*; earlier editions of *Who's Who* had consisted merely of professional lists, etc. The entries are compiled with the assistance of the subjects themselves, and contain some agreeable eccentricities particularly in the section labelled 'Recreations'.

The first *Who Was Who 1897–1916* appeared in 1920, and the seventh (1971–80) in 1981. These decennial volumes contain the biographies removed from *Who's Who* on account of death, with final details and date of death added.

whodunnit informal term for a story or play about a murder in which the identity of the murderer is not revealed until the end; the term is recorded from 1930.

whole see also ➤ COMMITTEE *of the Whole House*, ➤ *the whole* CABOODLE, ➤ *the whole* MEGILLAH.

wholesale see ➤ COOPERATIVE *Wholesale Society*.

whore see ➤ ONCE *a whore.*

Whore of Babylon derogatory name for the Roman Catholic Church, first recorded in Tyndale's *The Practyse of Prelates* (1530), where it is applied to the Pope; originally with biblical allusion to Revelation 17:1 'I will show unto thee the judgement of the great whore' and 17:5–6 'And the woman was arrayed in scarlet…And upon her head was a name written, Mystery, Babylon the Great, the Mother of Harlots'.

Edward Whymper (1840–1911), English mountaineer. After seven attempts he finally succeeded in climbing the Matterhorn in 1865, but on the way down four of his fellow climbers fell to their deaths.

Wicca the religious cult of modern witchcraft, especially an initiatory tradition founded in England in the mid 20th century and claiming its origins in pre-Christian pagan religions. *Wicca* as a modern term is recorded from the late 1950s; it represents Old English *wicca* 'witch'.

wich former (local) name for a salt-works or salt-pit, in the salt-manufacturing district of Cheshire and neighbouring parts; the original meaning may have been the group of buildings connected with a salt-pit.

wicked evil and morally wrong; the word (which dates from Middle English) probably comes from Old English *wicca* 'witch'.

In US slang, *wicked* (like *mean* in British English) has been used in the sense of 'formidable' since the end of the 19th century; a famous example occurs in F. Scott Fitzgerald's *This Side of Paradise* (1920), when Sloane calls for music and announces, 'Phoebe and I are going to shake a wicked calf.' In the early 1980s, wicked was taken up among young people as a fashionable term of approval, often preceded and emphasized by *well*. This usage spread widely, with a children's weekend television programme in the UK taking up the theme in its title *It's Wicked!*.

no peace for the wicked no rest or tranquillity for the speaker, incessant activity, responsibility, or work; originally with reference to Isaiah 48:22, 'There is no peace, saith the Lord, unto the wicked', and 57:21, 'There is no peace, saith my God, to the wicked.'

Wicked Bible another name for the ➤ UNRIGHTEOUS *Bible.*

widdershins in a direction contrary to the sun's course, considered as unlucky; anticlockwise. The term is recorded from the early 16th century, chiefly in Scottish sources, and comes ultimately from Middle High German *widersinnes*, from *wider* 'against' + *sin* 'direction'; the second element was associated with Scots *sin* 'sun'.

Widecombe Fair an annual fair held in the Devon village of Widecombe-in-the-Moor; in the traditional ballad the intended destination of ➤ OLD *Uncle Tom Cobleigh and all.*

widow a woman who has lost her husband by death and has not married again. The word comes (in Old English) from an Indo-European root meaning 'be empty', and may be compared with Sanskrit *vidh* 'be destitute', Latin *viduus* 'bereft, widowed', and Greek *ēitheos* 'unmarried man'.

The widow is an informal term for champagne, from a translation of French *la Veuve* Clicquot, a firm of wine merchants.

➤ *St* MONICA, mother of ➤ *St* AUGUSTINE *of Hippo*, and the 5th-century Roman widow St Paula, pupil of ➤ *St* JEROME, are patron saints of widows.

See also ➤ BLACK *widow*, ➤ GRASS *widow*, ➤ MERRY *Widow.*

the Widow at Windsor Queen Victoria after the death of the Prince Consort, in reference to her prolonged withdrawal from public life; the phrase was used as the title of a poem by Rudyard Kipling (1890).

Widow Twankey in H. J. Byron's dramatization of the story of ➤ ALADDIN as a pantomime, Aladdin's mother was named *Widow Twankay* in reference to a kind of green tea which was then popular (Byron's play had a number of jokes about China tea). *Widow*

Twankey is now one of the stock characters for this pantomime.

> Alice, in a long Chinese garment of bright colours with a funny flowered toque, had overtones of Widow Twankey.
> — Cecil Beaton diary, 11 November 1944

widow's cruse an apparently small supply that proves inexhaustible, with biblical allusion to 1 Kings 17:10–16, in the story of the widow to whom Elijah was sent for sustenance. When he asked her for bread, she replied that all she had for herself and her son was 'an handful of meal in a barrel, and a little oil in a cruse'; Elijah told her to make a cake of it for him first, and then to make food for herself and her son, since the Lord had decreed that 'the barrel of meal shall not waste, neither shall the cruse of oil fail'.

widow's men fictitious crewmen whose names were entered on a ship's books, their pay being credited to a widows' pension fund; the term is recorded from the late 18th century.

widow's mite a small monetary contribution from someone who is poor, with biblical allusion to Mark 12:42–44 which tells the story of a poor widow who gave to the Temple treasury 'two mites, which make a farthing'; Jesus, who saw her, told his disciples that she had given more than the richest contributor, because she had given all that she had.

widow's peak a V-shaped growth of hair towards the centre of the forehead, especially one left by a receding hairline in a man; held to resemble the peak of a cap traditionally worn by a widow.

widow's weeds black clothes worn by a widow in mourning, traditionally including a crape veil and broad white cuffs or 'weepers'.

Simon Wiesenthal (1908–), Austrian Jewish investigator of Nazi war crimes. After spending three years in concentration camps he began a campaign to bring Nazi war criminals to justice, tracing some 1,000 unprosecuted criminals including Adolf Eichmann. Through the Wiesenthal Centre in Vienna he continued to track down Nazi criminals when other countries had ceased to pursue their cases.

wife a married woman considered in relation to her husband. The word comes from Old English *wīf* 'woman', of Germanic origin.

See also ➤ *all the* WORLD *and his wife*, ➤ *a* BLIND *man's wife needs no paint*, ➤ CAESAR's *wife must be above suspicion*, ➤ *if you would be* HAPPY *for a week take a wife*, ➤ TROPHY *wife*.

Wife-hater Bible an edition of 1810 in which *Luke* 14:26 has the misreading 'If any man come to me, and hate not his father, and mother…yea, and his own wife also'.

Wife of Bath a character in Chaucer's *Canterbury Tales*, notable for her sexual appetites and outspoken tongue.

> Alison sings, a great lusty Wife of Bath woman.
> — Ruth Rendell *A Sleeping Life* (1978)

wig a covering for the head made of real or artificial hair, typically worn by judges and barristers in law courts or by people trying to conceal their baldness. The word comes (in the late 17th century) from a shortening of *periwig*.

See also ➤ CAMPAIGN *wig*.

wight archaic or dialectal term for a person of a specified kind; in poetic and literary usage, a spirit, ghost, or other supernatural being. The word comes from Old English *wiht* 'thing, creature', of Germanic origin; related to Dutch *wicht* 'little child' and German *Wicht* 'creature'.

Wightman Cup an annual tennis contest between women players of the US and Britain, inaugurated in 1923 and suspended in 1990. The competition was suspended in 1990 because the standard of British tennis was felt to be insufficiently high. It was named after Mrs H. H. *Wightman* (1886–1974), the American tennis player who donated the trophy.

wigs on the green violent or unpleasant developments, ructions; the term is recorded from the mid 19th century, and suggests literally a physical fight in which wigs may be dislodged or pulled off.

wigwam a dome-shaped hut or tent made by fastening mats, skins, or bark over a framework of poles, used by some North American Indian peoples. The word is recorded from the early 17th century, and comes from Ojibwa *wigwaum*, Algonquian *wikiwam* 'their house'.

Wilberforce see also ➤ SOAPY *Sam*.

William Wilberforce (1759–1833), English politician and social reformer. He was a prominent campaigner for the abolition of the slave trade, his efforts resulting in its outlawing in the British West Indies (1807) and in the 1833 Slavery Abolition Act.

wild blue yonder the far distance; a remote place; from R. Crawford *Army Air Corps* (song, 1939) 'Off we go into the wild blue yonder, Climbing high into the sun.'

Wild Boy of Aveyron a boy of about eleven found living in the woods in Aveyron in southern France, c.1801; the French physician Jean-Marc-Gaspard Itard (1775–1838), who worked particularly with deaf-mutes, tried to train and educate him.

See also ➤ PETER *the Wild Boy.*

Wild Children term used to describe children who in different places and at different periods have been discovered apparently living independently in the wild, and perhaps reared or nurtured by animals; ➤ PETER *the Wild Boy* and the ➤ WILD *Boy of Aveyron* are two historical examples. Although there are a number of well-documented cases of such discoveries, how the children concerned reached the state in which they were found remains a matter of conjecture; it has been suggested that in a number of cases the child had in fact been abandoned comparatively recently by its parents.

Children reared in the wild by animals (especially wolves) have a long fictional history, from ➤ ROMULUS and Remus of Roman mythology, to ➤ MOWGLI and ➤ TARZAN in the 19th and 20th centuries.

wild geese a name for the Irish Jacobites who emigrated to the Continent after the defeat of James II, especially after the ➤ *Treaty of* LIMERICK. The name is first found in a verse by Michael Joseph Barry (1817–89):

> The wild geese—the wild geese,—'tis long since they
> flew,
> O'er the billowy ocean's bright bosom of blue.
> — Michael Joseph Barry in *Spirit of the Nation* (Dublin,
> 1845)

wild goose chase a foolish and hopeless search for or pursuit of something unattainable; originally, a kind of horse-race or sport in which all competitors had to follow accurately the course of the leader (at a definite interval), like a flight of wild geese.

Wild Huntsman a phantom huntsman of Teutonic legend, fabled to ride at night through the fields and woods with shouts and baying of hounds (the ➤ WISH-*hounds*).

wild man the image of a primitive or uncivilized man as a symbol of the wild side of human nature or of seasonal fertility.

wild man of the woods dated term for an orangutan; the name of which comes (in the late 17th century) from Malay *orang huan* 'forest person'.

Wild West the western US in a time of lawlessness in its early history. The Wild West was the last of a succession of frontiers formed as settlers moved gradually further west. The frontier was officially declared closed in 1890, and the Wild West disappeared with the ending of hostilities with the American Indians, the building of the railways, and the establishment of settled communities.

wildcat a small native Eurasian and African cat that is typically grey with black markings and a bushy black-tipped tail, noted for its ferocity and taken as a type of savagery and hot temper, especially in a woman.

From the early 19th century *wildcat* has been used to designate a person engaging in a risky or unsafe enterprise, or an unsound business undertaking. It was applied specifically to banks in the western US which, before the passing of the National Bank Act of 1863, fraudulently issued notes supported by little or no capital; the use of the name is said to derive from the fact that the notes of a bank in Michigan carried the device of a panther or 'wild cat'.

Oscar Wilde (1854–1900), Irish dramatist, novelist, poet, and wit. His advocacy of 'art for art's sake' is evident in his only novel, *The Picture of Dorian Gray* (1890). As a dramatist he achieved success with the comedies *Lady Windermere's Fan* (1892) and *The Importance of Being Earnest* (1895). Wilde was imprisoned (1895–7) for homosexual offences and died in exile.

Battle of the Wilderness in the American Civil War (5–7 May, 1864), a battle between the Union army under Grant and the Confederates under Robert E. Lee. Fighting took place in a wooded area, known as the Wilderness, and many of the wounded died in the burning undergrowth. After two days, Grant moved his troops on to Spotsylvania.

in the wilderness of a politician or political party, out of office, removed from influence; originally with allusion to Numbers 14:33, 'And your children shall wander in the wilderness forty years.'

a voice in the wilderness an unheeded advocate of reform, originally in allusion to the words of John the Baptist in John 1:23, 'I am the voice of one crying in the wilderness.'

Wilderness Road a pioneer route blazed by Daniel Boone in 1775 from eastern Virginia through the Cumberland Gap to Kentucky, used by many frontier settlers in the first great westward migration.

wildfire a combustible liquid such as Greek fire that was readily ignited and difficult to extinguish, used especially in warfare.

Wildfire is also used for various kinds of fire or flame which are naturally rather than artificially produced; it is a less common term for ➤ WILL-*o'-the-wisp*, and is used also for lightning, especially sheet lightning.

St Wilfrid (*c.*633–709), Northumbrian-born bishop of York and afterwards of Hexham, who at the ➤ *Synod of* WHITBY in 664 was a chief proponent of the case for calculating the date of Easter by the Roman rather than the Celtic method.
   ☐ **FEAST DAY** His feast day is 12 October.

Wilfridian a member of a religious fraternity founded by Father F. W. Faber (1814–63) for his fellow converts to Roman Catholicism; the fraternity was later united with the oratory of St Philip Neri, Birmingham.

a wilful man must have his way proverbial saying, early 19th century.

wilful waste makes woeful want proverbial saying, early 18th century.

St Wilgefortis virgin and martyr, legendary daughter of a pagan king of Portugal, who grew a beard to discourage an unwanted suitor. Also known as ➤ *St* UNCUMBER.
   ☐ **FEAST DAY** Her feast day is 20 July.

Wilhelm II (1859–1941), emperor of Germany 1888–1918, grandson of Queen Victoria; known as *Kaiser Wilhelm*. After forcing Bismarck to resign in 1890 he proved unable to exercise a strong or consistent influence over German policies, which became increasingly militaristic. He was vilified by Allied propaganda as the author of the First World War. In 1918 he abdicated and went into exile.

Wilhelmina (1880–1962), queen of the Netherlands 1890–1948. During the Second World War she maintained a government in exile in London, and through frequent radio broadcasts became a symbol of resistance to the Dutch people. She returned to the Netherlands in 1945.

Wilhelmstrasse the name of a street in Berlin, the site of the German foreign office until 1945; hence used for the pre-war German foreign office and its policies.

> What remains of Czechoslovakia . . . must subordinate her foreign policy to that of the Wilhelmstrasse.
> — Harold Nicolson diary, 21 September 1938

wili in Slavonic and eastern German legends, a spirit of a betrothed girl who has died from grief at being jilted by her lover (used especially with reference to the ballet *Giselle*).

will see also ➤ LIVING *will*, ➤ *Will* SCARLET.

he that will not when he may, when he will he shall have nay proverbial saying, late 10th century.

will-o'-the-wisp a phosphorescent light seen hovering or floating at night on marshy ground, thought to result from the combustion of natural gases. Recorded from the early 17th century, the expression was originally *Will with the wisp*, the sense of *wisp* being 'handful of (lighted) hay'.

will the real — please stand up? catchphrase from an American TV game show (1955–66) in which a panel was asked to identify the 'real' one of three candidates all claiming to be a particular person; after the guesses were made, the compère would request the 'real' candidate to stand up.

where there's a will, there's a way proverbial saying, mid 17th century.

Will's Coffee House at No. 1 Bow Street, at the corner of Russell Street, and named after its proprietor William Unwin; it was frequented in the 17th and 18th centuries by authors.

William see ➤ *also the* PEOPLE's *William*.

William I (*c.*1027–87), reigned 1066–87, the first Norman king of England; known as **William the Conqueror**. Claiming that Edward the Confessor had promised him the English throne, he invaded England and defeated and killed ➤ HAROLD *II* at the Battle of Hastings (1066). He introduced Norman institutions and customs (including feudalism) and instigated the ➤ DOMESDAY *Book*.

William II (*c.*1060–1100), son of William I, reigned 1087–1100; known as **William Rufus**. William crushed rebellions in 1088 and 1095 and also campaigned against his brother Robert, Duke of Normandy (1089–96), ultimately acquiring the duchy. He was killed by an arrow while out hunting; whether he was assassinated or whether his death was an accident remains unclear.

William III (1650–1702), grandson of Charles I, husband of Mary II, reigned 1689–1702; known as **William of Orange**. In 1688 he deposed James II at the invitation of disaffected politicians and, having accepted the Declaration of Rights, was crowned along with his wife Mary. He defeated James's supporters in Scotland and Ireland (1689–90), and thereafter devoted his energies towards opposing the territorial ambitions of Louis XIV of France.

William IV (1765–1837), son of George III, and brother of George IV, reigned 1830–7; having served in the Royal Navy, he was known as the *Sailor King*. Although an opponent of the first ➤ REFORM *Act* (1832), William reluctantly agreed to create fifty new peers to overcome opposition to it in the House of Lords.

See also ➤ SILLY *Billy*.

William of Malmesbury (d. 1143?), monk and historian, who in a treatise described himself as being of 'the blood of two races' (Norman and English). He was the author of *Gesta Regum Anglorum* (a history of England, 449–1190) and *Gesta Pontificorum Anglorum* (an ecclesiastical history of England, 597–1125), having said that 'not satisfied with the writings of old, I began to write myself'.

St William of Norwich said to have been murdered in 1144, supposedly by Jews for ritual purposes; his anti-Semitic cult, resembling that of ➤ *Little St* HUGH, had a local popularity, and images of him survive in screen paintings in East Anglia.

William of Occam (*c*.1285–1349), English philosopher and Franciscan friar. A defender of nominalism, he is known for the maxim called *Occam's razor*, that 'entities should not be multiplied beyond necessity', i.e. that in explaining a thing no more assumptions should be made than are necessary. His views on property and papal authority brought him into conflict with the Vatican and he was excommunicated in 1328.

William of Orange ➤ WILLIAM *III* of Great Britain and Ireland or ➤ WILLIAM *the Silent*.

William of Wykeham (1324–1404), bishop of Winchester and chancellor of England, founder of Winchester College school and of New College at Oxford; his motto was the proverbial saying ➤ MANNERS *maketh man*.

William Rufus nickname of ➤ WILLIAM *II* of England.

William the Conqueror epithet of ➤ WILLIAM *I* of England.

William the Lion name given to William I (1143–1214), king of Scotland from 1165, who in 1189 established Scotland as independent of the overlordship of England.

William the Silent name given to William I (1533–84), prince of the house of ➤ ORANGE, first stadtholder (chief magistrate) of the United Provinces of the Netherlands (1572–84). He led a revolt against Spain from 1568 and was assassinated by a Spanish agent.

> As long as he lived, he was the guiding-star of a whole brave nation, and when he died the little children cried in the streets.
> — John Lothrop Motley *The Rise of the Dutch Republic* (1856)

Williamite in 17th-century Ireland, a supporter of ➤ WILLIAM *III* and opponent to the Jacobite cause.

Williamsburg a city in SE Virginia, between the James and York Rivers. First settled as Middle Plantation in 1633, it was the state capital of Virginia from 1699, when it was renamed in honour of William III, until 1799, when Richmond became the capital. A large part of the town has been restored and reconstructed so that it appears as it was during the colonial era.

Willie see also ➤ HOLY *Willie*, ➤ WEARY *Willie*, ➤ WOODBINE *Willie*.

willow a tree or shrub of temperate climates which typically has narrow leaves, bears catkins, and grows near water. Its pliant branches yield osiers for basketry, and the timber is used for making cricket bats.

Willow is traditionally a symbol of unrequited love, or of mourning or loss, as in **wear the willow** and **the willow garland**.

See also ➤ WEEPING *willow*.

willow pattern a conventional design representing a Chinese scene in blue on white pottery, typically showing three figures on a bridge, with a willow tree and two birds above; a pattern introduced by the English potter Thomas Turner (1749–1809).

William John Wills (1834–61), English explorer. In 1860 he was a member, with two others, of Robert Burke's expedition to cross Australia from south to north. They became the first white people to make this journey but Wills died of starvation on the return journey.

he who wills the end, wills the means proverbial saying, late 17th century.

willy-nilly whether one likes it or not; the term is recorded from the early 17th century, and comes from the expression *will I, nill I* (or *will he, nill he, will ye, nill ye*), 'be I (he, ye) willing or unwilling'.

willy-willy in Australia and New Zealand, a whirlwind or dust storm; the name comes from Yindjibarndi, an Aboriginal language of western Australia.

Wilton House in Wiltshire, seat of the earls of Pembroke, associated with Philip Sidney, who is said to have written much of the first version of the *Arcadia* there while staying with his sister Mary, countess of Pembroke. According to Aubrey, 'In her time Wilton house was like a College, there were so many learned and ingeniose persons.' She was undoubtedly a literary patroness, but the claim made to W. J. Cory in 1865 that Shakespeare was her guest and that *As You Like It* was performed there before James I has never been confirmed.

Wimbledon an annual international tennis championship on grass for individual players and pairs, held at the headquarters of the All England Lawn Tennis and Croquet Club in the London suburb of Wimbledon. Now one of the world's major tennis championships, it has been played since 1877; women were first admitted in 1884, and professionals in 1968.

> New Yorkers love it when you spill your guts out there [at Flushing Meadow]. Spill your guts at Wimbledon and they make you stop and clean it up.
> — Jimmy Connors in *Guardian* 1984 'Sports Quotes of the Year'

wimmin non-standard spelling of 'women' adopted by some feminists to avoid the word ending *-men*. The first examples date from the 1970s, and by the mid 1980s, it had come to be associated particularly with militant feminism.

WIMP[1] in computing, a set of software features and hardware devices (such as *windows, icons, mice, and pull-down menus*) designed to simplify or demystify computing operations for the user.

WIMP[2] a hypothetical subatomic particle of large mass which interacts only weakly with ordinary matter, postulated as a constituent of the dark matter of the universe. The term is recorded from the 1980s, and is an acronym for *weakly interacting massive particle*.

Lord Peter Wimsey aristocratic fictional amateur detective created by Dorothy L. Sayers (1893–1957); Wimsey is a duke's son who is a keen bibliophile and expert on wine; he also suffers from a degree of war-induced nervous insomnia.

> He reeled off down the road, pretending to lift the bottle to his lips, upending it in the process. When I think, Kate said to herself, that Lord Peter Wimsey wouldn't even let anyone *dust* a bottle of wine.
> — Amanda Cross *The James Joyce Murders* (1967)

win see also ➤ *let them* LAUGH *that win*.

you win a few, you lose a few proverbial saying, mid 20th century.

win one's spurs gain a knighthood by an act of bravery; Froissart's *Chronicle*, referring to the Black Prince at the battle of Crécy in 1346, refers to the instruction given by his father Edward III that those with the prince should 'suffre hym this day to wynne his spurres', often quoted as 'Let the boy win his spurs.'

you can't win them all proverbial saying, mid 20th century.

Winchester a city in southern England, the county town of Hampshire. Known to the Romans as Venta Belgarum, it became capital of the West Saxon kingdom of Wessex in 519. It is the site of Winchester College, the oldest public school in England, founded by the bishop of Winchester ➤ WILLIAM *of Wykeham* (1324–1404) in 1382.

Winchester measure a system of dry and liquid measure the standards of which were originally deposited at Winchester.

Winchester school a style of manuscript illumination of the 10th and 11th centuries originating at Winchester.

wind the perceptible natural movement of the air, especially in the form of a current of air blowing from a particular direction, especially (in **the four winds**) blowing from each of the points of the compass, and often personified as such. The wind is traditionally taken as a type of swift light movement; it can also stand for mutability, and as a force that cannot be predicted or controlled.

In classical mythology, the winds were counted as gods; in Greece, ➤ BOREAS (the North Wind) and ➤ ZEPHYR (the West Wind) were of particular importance. Virgil in the *Aeneid* describes the winds as being under the control of ➤ AEOLUS, who had been given charge of them by Zeus and who kept them confined in a cave.

See also ➤ CAPFUL *of wind*, ➤ GONE *with the wind*, ➤ *it's an* ILL *wind that blows nobody any good*, ➤ *a* REED *before the wind*, ➤ *a* REED *shaken by the wind*, ➤ STRAWS *tell which way the wind blows*, ➤ *they that* sow *the wind shall reap the whirlwind*, ➤ TRADE *wind*, ➤ WHISTLE *down the wind*, ➤ WHISTLE *for a wind*.

wind farm an area of land with a group of energy-producing windmills or wind turbines; the idea is that wind can be farmed to produce energy. *Wind farms* were introduced at the beginning of the 1980s and were initially regarded with enthusiasm as a source of power that could be obtained without environmental damage. However, as they have become more common, some adverse opinion has been expressed as to their visual impact and the possible noise pollution resulting from their operation.

when the wind is in the east, 'tis neither good for man nor beast proverbial saying, early 17th century.

wind of change an influence or tendency to change that cannot be resisted; the phrase in this sense derives from a speech by the Conservative politician Harold Macmillan (1894–1986) about the current of unstoppable change he was seeing in Africa:

> The wind of change is blowing through the continent, and, whether we like it or not, this growth of national consciousness is a political fact.
> — Harold Macmillan speech at Cape Town, 3 February 1960

windfall an apple or other fruit blown down from a tree or bush by the wind; a piece of unexpected good fortune, typically one that involves receiving a large amount of money.

windigo (in the folklore of the northern Algonquian Indians) a cannibalistic giant; a person who has been transformed into a monster by the consumption of human flesh. The name comes from Ojibwa *wintiko*.

windmill see also ➤ TILT *at windmills*.

Windmill Theatre popular variety theatre of the 1930s and 1940s near Piccadilly Circus in London, which between 1932 and 1964 presented its *Revudeville* (named from a blend of *revue* and *vaudeville*), a continuous variety performance. The Windmill Theatre's wartime motto was, 'We Never Closed'.

window see also ➤ JESSE *window*, ➤ JUDAS *window*.

a window of opportunity a free or suitable interval or period of time for a particular event or action; the expression was first used in connection with the US–Soviet arms race in the early 1980s.

window tax a tax on windows or similar openings that was imposed in the UK in 1695 and abolished in 1851; while it was in force, a number of windows in larger houses were bricked up to escape the tax.

Windrush a former troopship, the 'Empire Windrush', which in 1948 brought the first organized party of Caribbean immigrants, many of whom were former British servicemen, to Britain; the term **Windrush generation** is now used allusively to refer to this group and the period of their arrival.

> The classic novel of the 'Windrush generation' of postwar migrants from the Caribbean.
> — *Guardian* 22 June 1995

Windscale former name (1947–81) for ➤ SELLA-FIELD; associated particularly with the fire which occurred there in 1957.

Windsor name (from the royal residence of ➤ WINDSOR *Castle*) of the British royal house from 1917, changed as a result of anti-German feeling; the previous name was ➤ SAXE-*Coburg-Gotha*.

See also ➤ KNIGHT *of Windsor*, ➤ *the* WIDOW *at Windsor*.

Duke of Windsor the title conferred on ➤ EDWARD *VIII* on his abdication in 1936.

Windsor Castle a royal residence at Windsor, founded by William the Conqueror on the site of an earlier fortress and extended by his successors, particularly Edward III. The castle was severely damaged by fire in 1992.

Windsor herald an officer whose duties are now performed by Garter King of Arms.

Windy City informal name for Chicago, recorded from the late 19th century.

wine St Amand (*c*.584–*c*.675), French monk and missionary, and ➤ *St* VINCENT are patron saints of the wine trade.

See also ➤ *from* SWEETEST *wine, the sharpest vinegar*, ➤ *there is* TRUTH *is wine*, ➤ VIPER-*wine*, ➤ *you can't put* NEW *wine in old bottles*.

when the wine is in, the wit is out proverbial saying, late 14th century.

good wine needs no bush proverbial saying, early 15th century, meaning that there is no need to advertise or boast about something of good quality as people will always discover its merits; the expression refers to the fact that a bunch of ivy was formerly the sign of a vintner's shop.

St Winefride (7th century), Welsh virgin, supposedly killed by a rejected suitor and then raised from the dead to become a nun. The chapel and well at Holywell, where she is said to have been abbess, became an important pilgrimage centre.

In 1138 her relics were translated to the abbey of Shrewsbury, one account of which is given in the first of the popular ➤ *Brother* CADFAEL mysteries by Ellis Peters.

☐ **FEAST DAY** Her feast day is 3 November, and her translation is celebrated on 2 June.

wing see also ➤ *a* BIRD *never flew.*

a wing and a prayer reliance on hope or the slightest chance in a desperate situation; the phrase comes from a song by the American songwriter Harold Adamson (1906–80), derived from the contemporary comment of a wartime pilot, speaking from a disabled plane to ground control:

> Comin' in on a wing and a pray'r.
> — Harold Adamson title of song (1943)

Winged Victory a winged statue of ➤ NIKE, the Greek goddess of victory, especially the Nike of Samothrace (*c*.200 BC) preserved in the Louvre in Paris.

winged words highly apposite or significant words (travelling swiftly as arrows to the mark); the phrase comes originally from Homer's *Iliad.*

wink see ➤ *a* NOD*'s as good as a wink to a blind horse.*

Winnie-the-Pooh Christopher Robin's bear in the stories by A. A. Milne; *Winnie-the-Pooh* (1926) is the first of the books, and Pooh, the 'bear of very little brain' with his liking for honey, is the central character of the nursery animals.

Winnie was originally the name of a black bear which was the mascot of a Canadian regiment, and which was brought to London zoo (where it remained) while the regiment was fighting in France in the First World War; *Pooh* was borrowed from the name first given by Christopher Robin to a swan.

Winston is back message sent to the Fleet when Winston Churchill returned to office as First Lord of the Admiralty in September 1939 (he had previously been First Lord 1910–15).

winter the coldest season of the year, in the northern hemisphere from December to February and in the southern hemisphere from June to August. In figurative and allusive usage, *winter* can stand for old age, or a time or state of affliction or distress.

The word is recorded from Old English, and is of Germanic origin.

See also ➤ BLACKTHORN *winter,* ➤ NUCLEAR *winter.*

winter and wedlock tames man and beast proverbial saying, late 16th century.

winter never rots in the sky proverbial saying, early 17th century; meaning that the arrival of winter is not delayed.

Winter Olympics an international contest of winter sports held every four years at a two year interval from the summer games. They have been held separately from the main games since 1924.

Winter Palace the former Russian imperial residence in St Petersburg, stormed in the Revolution of 1917 and later used as a museum and art gallery.

Winter Queen name given to Elizabeth Stuart (1596–1662), princess of Great Britain, married to Frederick, Elector Palatine of the Rhine; he was elected king of Bohemia in 1619 but driven out the following year, and they spent the rest of their lives in exile.

winter solstice the solstice at midwinter, at the time of the shortest day, about 22 December in the northern hemisphere and 21 June in the southern hemisphere.

winter-time for shoeing, peascod-time for wooing proverbial saying, mid 19th century.

Winter War the war between the USSR and Finland in 1939–40. Heavily outnumbered by invading Soviet troops, the Finns were defeated and forced to cede western Karelia to the Soviet Union.

winter's tale former alternative name for an old wives' story. Recorded from the late 16th century, it has become particularly well-known as the title of Shakespeare's play *The Winter's Tale* (1610–11), in which the child prince Mamilius, offering to tell a story, says:

> A sad tale's best for winter.
> I have one of sprites and goblins.
> — William Shakespeare *The Winter's Tale* (1610-11)

winterbourne British expression for a stream, typically on chalk or limestone, which flows only after wet weather and especially in winter.

Franz Xavier Winterhalter (1806–73), German painter. He painted many portraits of European royalty and aristocracy. His subjects included Napoleon III, the emperor Franz Josef, and Queen Victoria and her family.

> The background for the first part is Winterhalter, with jewels glittering and court uniforms ablaze with medals.
> — *New York Review of Books* 15 January 1998

wireless broadcasting or telegraphy using radio signals; the term, which is now dated, refers originally to a system of **wireless telegraphy** (such as that patented by Guglielmo Marconi in 1897) in which no conducting wire is used between the transmitting and receiving stations, the signals or messages being transmitted through space by means of electric waves.

Wirtschaftswunder an economic miracle, especially the economic recovery of the Federal Republic of West Germany after the Second World War. The word is German, and comes from *Wirtschaft* 'economics or economic theory' + *Wunder* 'wonder'.

Wisden short name for *Wisden's Cricketers' Almanack*, an annual publication which first appeared in 1864, published by the English cricketer John *Wisden* (1826–84).

wisdom see also ➤ EXPERIENCE *is the father of wisdom.*

wisdom literature the biblical books of Job, Proverbs, Ecclesiastes, Song of Songs, Wisdom of Solomon, and Ecclesiasticus collectively; similar works, especially from the ancient Near East, containing proverbial sayings and practical maxims.

Wisdom of Solomon a book of the Apocrypha ascribed to Solomon and containing a meditation on wisdom. The book is thought actually to date from about 1st century BC to the 1st century AD.

wisdom tooth each of the four hindmost molars in humans which usually appear at about the age of twenty; the phrase (in plural) represents Latin *dentes sapientiae*, as the teeth were said by the ancient Greek physician ➤ HIPPOCRATES not to appear until years of discretion were reached.

wise see also ➤ *a* FOOL *may give a wise man counsel*, ➤ *one cannot* LOVE *and be wise*, ➤ SEVEN *Wise Masters*, ➤ THREE *Wise Men*, ➤ *three wise* MONKEYS, ➤ *a* WORD *to the wise is enough.*

the Wise epithet of various rulers, as Alfonso the Wise (1221–84), king of Castile and León from 1252.

Thomas James Wise (1859–1937), noted scholar and bibliographer who compiled the ➤ ASHLEY *Library*; in 1934 the publication of Carter and Pollard's *An Enquiry into the Nature of Certain 19th-Century Pamphlets* demonstrated (with the assistance of the new science of carbon-dating) that a substantial number of the rare pamphlets authenticated by Wise were actually forgeries.

it is easy to be wise after the event proverbial saying, early 17th century.

it is a wise child that knows its own father proverbial saying, late 16th century.

Wise Men of Gotham fools (➤ GOTHAM was proverbial for the folly of its inhabitants).

Wise Men of Greece another name for the ➤ SEVEN *Sages*.

wise use environmental policy which favours stricter controls on existing methods of exploiting natural resources, as opposed to policies which seek either to find alternative resources or to prevent such exploitation altogether.

wise woman a woman considered to be knowledgeable in matters such as herbal healing, magic charms, or other traditional lore.

wiseacre a person with an affectation of wisdom or knowledge, regarded with scorn or irritation by others; a know-all. The word comes (in the late 16th century) from Middle Dutch *wijsseger* 'soothsayer', probably from the Germanic base of *wit*. The assimilation to *acre* remains unexplained.

the Wisest Fool in Christendom nickname of James I of England and VI of Scotland (1566–1625); attributed both to Henri IV of France (1553–1610) and to his minister Sully (1559–1641).

wish-hounds local name for a ghostly pack of hounds popularly believed to hunt over Dartmoor (Devon) by night, led by the ➤ WILD *Huntsman*; *wish* means 'uncanny, supernatural'.

the wish is father to the thought proverbial saying, late 16th century.

wishbone a forked bone (the furcula) between the neck and breast of a bird. According to a popular custom, this bone from a cooked bird is broken by two people, the holder of the longer portion that results being entitled to make a wish.

if wishes were horses, then beggars would ride proverbial saying, early 17th century.

wishing well a well into which one drops a coin and makes a wish.

Wissenschaft the systematic pursuit of knowledge, learning, and scholarship (especially as contrasted with its application). The word is German, and means literally 'knowledge'.

wit see ➤ BREVITY *is the soul,* ➤ CONNECTICUT *Wits,* ➤ *when the* WINE *is in the wit is out.*

witan another term for ➤ WITENAGEMOT; the name represents the Old English plural of *wita* 'wise man'.

witch a person, typically a woman, who practises magic or sorcery and was traditionally thought to have evil magic powers; such witches are popularly depicted as wearing a black cloak and pointed hat, and flying on a broomstick, and are associated with ➤ HALLOWEEN.
     In the Middle Ages and the 16th and 17th centuries, ➤ WITCHCRAFT was a capital offence and there were numerous trials and executions of suspected witches; sometimes a whole community became involved, as in ➤ SALEM, Massachusetts, in 1692.
     In the 20th century, the term *witch* is now used also for a follower or practitioner of modern witchcraft; a Wiccan priest or priestess.
     See also ➤ ROWAN *tree and red thread make witches tine,* ➤ WHITE *witch.*

witch ball a ball of decorated, typically coloured or silvered blown glass, originally used as a charm against witchcraft.

witch doctor among tribal peoples, a magician credited with powers of healing, divination, and protection against the magic of others.

witch-hunt a search for and subsequent persecution of a supposed witch; a campaign directed against a person or group holding unorthodox or unpopular views.

Witch of Endor in the Bible, the woman of whom (in 1 Samuel 27:7) Saul was told, 'Behold there is a woman that hath a familiar spirit at En-dor', and who with its help conjured up the spirit of the dead prophet Samuel for Saul. She is taken as a type of this kind of divination, and when during the First World War Kipling wrote a poem warning against

the dangers of trying to get in touch with the dead, he used the biblical story:

> Oh, the road to En-dor is the oldest road
> And the craziest road of all!
> Straight it runs to the Witch's abode
> As it did in the days of Saul,
> And nothing has changed of the sorrow in store
> For such as go down on the road to En-dor!
> — Rudyard Kipling 'En-dor' (1914–19)

witchcraft the practice of magic, especially black magic; the use of spells and the invocation of spirits. Persecution of witches, part of the old Roman law, was in the early Middle Ages discouraged by Charlemagne, but in later centuries the Inquisition dealt with witchcraft if it was connected with heresy.
     ➤ MALLEUS *Maleficarum* ('Hammer of Witches'), published in the late 15th century, gave details of the supposed customs of witches, including attendance at ➤ WITCHES' *sabbaths,* shapeshifting, and the casting of spells, and in the 16th and 17th centuries persecution of those supposed to follow such practices increased.

witches' sabbath a supposed annual midnight meeting of witches with the Devil; belief in the occurrence of such meetings fuelled the persecution of witchcraft in the 16th and 17th centuries.

the witching hour midnight; the time when witches are proverbially active; after Shakespeare's *Hamlet* ''Tis now the very witching time of night, When churchyards yawn and hell itself breathes out Contagion to this world.'
     See also ➤ TRIPLE-*witching hour.*

witenagemot an Anglo-Saxon national council or parliament. The name is Old English, and comes from *witena,* genitive plural of *wita* 'wise man' + *gemōt* 'meeting'. The name ➤ WITAN is also used.

withers see also ➤ WRING *the withers.*

the five wits the five (bodily) senses of hearing, sight, smell, taste, and touch; the term is recorded from Middle English.

Wittenberg a town in eastern Germany, on the River Elbe north-east of Leipzig, which was the scene in 1517 of Martin Luther's campaign against the Roman Catholic Church, a major factor in the rise of the Reformation.

Ludwig Wittgenstein (1889–1951), British philosopher, born in Austria. His two major works,

Tractatus Logico-Philosophicus (1921) and *Philosophical Investigations* (1953), examine language and its relationship to the world.

unhappy wives ➤ *St* WILGEFORTIS and St Rita of Cascia (1377–1447), a widow and Augustinian nun who had endured 18 years of marriage to a violent and unfaithful husband, are patron saints of women who are unhappily married.

wives see ➤ OLD *wives' tale*.

wiving see ➤ HANGING *and wiving go by destiny.*

wizard a man who has magical powers, especially in legends and fairy tales. Recorded from late Middle English, the word originally meant 'philosopher, sage', and comes from *wise*; the sense of a person skilled in the occult arts dates from the mid 16th century.

See also ➤ CARPATHIAN *wizard.*

Wizard of Oz in *The Wonderful Wizard of Oz* (1900) by L. Frank Baum, the orphaned Dorothy, who has been carried by a cyclone to the land of Oz, joins the Cowardly Lion, the Scarecrow, and the Tin Man in their search for the magician who can give them their heart's desire, although the wizard's power is in the end illusory. The story was filmed in 1939 with Judy Garland as Dorothy.

> No one has ever met directly with me. I'm not the godfather type. The Wizard of Oz is more my style.
> — Kate Green *Night Angel* (1989)

Wizard of the North nickname of Sir Walter Scott.

woad a yellow-flowered European plant of the cabbage family, formerly widely grown in Britain as a source of blue dye, which was extracted from the leaves after they had been dried, powdered, and fermented. It is often referred to allusively as typifying an early and uncivilized era in which the skin was patterned with woad; Caesar in his *Gallic Wars* noted that, 'all the Britons dye themselves with woad'.

> He will . . . conquer that country again, in despite of all you savage chiefs smeared with woad!
> — Marion Zimmer Bradley *The Mists of Avalon* (1982)

Wobblies informal name for members of ➤ INDUSTRIAL *Workers of the World.*

P. G. Wodehouse (1881–1975), English writer. His best-known works are humorous stories of the upper-class world of Bertie Wooster and his valet Jeeves, the first of which appeared in 1917. During the Second World War Wodehouse was interned by the Germans but was later accused in Britain of being a traitor after making radio broadcasts from Berlin.

Woden another name for ➤ ODIN.

woebegone sad or miserable in appearance. Recorded from Middle English (in the sense 'afflicted with grief'), from *woe* + *begone* 'surrounded' (past participle of obsolete *bego* 'go around, beset').

wolf a wild carnivorous mammal which is the largest member of the dog family, living and hunting in packs, which is native to both Eurasia and North America, but is much persecuted and has been widely exterminated. The last wolf in Britain was killed in 1740.

In figurative and allusive use, the *wolf* is often taken as the type of savagery and rapacity, explicitly or implicitly contrasted with the meek and vulnerable sheep. From the mid 19th century, the term has also been used as an informal designation of a sexually aggressive male.

A *wolf* is the emblem of ➤ *St* EDMUND *the Martyr*, ➤ *St* FRANCIS *of Assisi*, and (as a play on his name) the 10th-century Swabian bishop St Wolfgang.

See also ➤ LONE *wolf,* ➤ SHE-*Wolf of France*, ➤ THROW *someone to the wolves.*

cry wolf call for help when it is not needed, with the effect that one is not believed when one really does need help, with allusion to the fable of the shepherd boy who deluded people with false cries of 'Wolf!'; when he was actually attacked and killed, his genuine appeals for help were ignored.

see a wolf be lost for words, from the traditional belief, referrred to in Virgil's pastoral poetry, that on seeing a wolf a person lost their voice.

have a wolf by the ears be in a precarious position; the expression is of classical origin, and means that the present situation can neither be maintained nor safely ended.

keep the wolf from the door have enough money to avert hunger or starvation; the *wolf* here is a type of something that will devour and destroy, as hunger or famine.

a wolf in sheep's clothing a person or thing that appears friendly or harmless but is really hostile; often with biblical allusion to Matthew 7:15, 'Beware of false prophets, which come to you in sheep's clothing, but inwardly they are ravening wolves.'

wolf's head an outlaw, from *cry wolf's head*, in Anglo-Saxon England uttering a cry for the pursuit of an outlaw as one to be hunted down like a wolf.

James Wolfe (1727–59), British general. One of the leaders of the expedition sent to seize French Canada, he commanded the attack on the French capital, Quebec (1759). He was fatally wounded while leading his troops to victory on the Plains of Abraham, the scene of the battle which led to British control of Canada; his last words are recorded as, 'Now God be praised, I will die in peace.'

George II (1683–1760), to whom the Duke of Newcastle had complained that Wolfe was a madman, is said to have replied, 'Mad, is he? Then I hope he will *bite* some of my other generals.'

Tom Wolfe (1931–), American writer. Having been a news reporter for the *Washington Post* and the *Herald Tribune*, he examined contemporary American culture in *The Electric Kool-Aid Acid Test* (1968) and the novel *The Bonfire of the Vanities* (1988).

Wolfenden Report a study produced in 1957 by the Committee on Homosexual Offences and Prostitution in Britain which recommended the legalization of homosexual relations between consenting adults.

Wolfian a follower or adherent of the German classical scholar and philologist Friedrich August *Wolf* (1759–1824), or his theory that the Homeric poems are texts deriving from an oral tradition rather than being the unified work of a single author.

Isaac Wolfson (1897–1991), Scottish businessman and philanthropist. Chairman of Great Universal Stores, he established the Wolfson Foundation in 1955 for promoting and funding medical research and education. Colleges in both Oxford and Cambridge now bear his name.

Mary Wollstonecraft (1759–97), English writer and feminist, of Irish descent. Her best-known work, *A Vindication of the Rights of Woman* (1792), defied assumptions about male supremacy (Horace Walpole called her 'that hyena in petticoats') and championed educational equality for women; the popularly quoted summary of her views is 'Mind has no sex.' In 1797 she married William Godwin

and died shortly after giving birth to their daughter Mary Shelley.

Thomas Wolsey (*c*.1474–1530), English prelate and statesman; known as *Cardinal Wolsey*. Wolsey dominated foreign and domestic policy in the early part of Henry VIII's reign, but incurred royal displeasure through his failure to secure the papal dispensation necessary for Henry's divorce from Catherine of Aragon. He was arrested on a charge of treason and died on his way to trial; he is said to remarked on his deathbed that, 'Had I but served God as diligently as I have served the King, he would not have given me over in my grey hairs.'

Wolverine State informal name for Michigan, where wolverines are found.

woman see also ➤ Bird *Woman*, ➤ *never* choose *your women or your linen by candlelight*, ➤ scarlet *woman*, ➤ silence *is a woman's best garment*, ➤ *a* whistling *woman and a crowing hen.*

a woman, a dog, and a walnut tree, the more you beat them the better they be proverbial saying, late 16th century; the walnut tree was beaten firstly to bring down the fruit, and then to break down long shoots and encourage short fruit-bearing ones.

a woman and a ship ever want mending proverbial saying, late 16th century; 2nd century BC in Plautus, 'whoever wants to acquire a lot of trouble should get himself a ship and a woman. For neither of them is ever sufficiently equipped, and there is never enough means of equipping them.'

a woman's place is in the home proverbial saying, mid 19th century.

a woman's work is never done proverbial saying, late 16th century.

women beneath a cloak a group of women beneath a cloak is the emblem of ➤ *St* Ursula, who was said to have been put to death with 11,000 virgins.

Women's Institute an organization of women, especially in rural areas, who meet regularly and participate in crafts, cultural activities, and social work. Now worldwide, it was first set up in Ontario, Canada, in 1897, and in Britain in 1915.

women's liberation the liberation of women from inequalities and subservient status in relation to men, and from attitudes causing these (now generally replaced by the term *feminism*).

wonder see also ➤ NINE *days' wonder*, ➤ SEVEN *Wonders of the World*, ➤ TIME *works wonders*.

eighth wonder of the world a particularly impressive person or thing, regarded as an addition to the ➤ SEVEN *Wonders of the World*; Maria Edgeworth makes ironical use of the phrase in a letter of 20 January 1831, referring to 'a spoiled child of 30 whose mother and father have not been able to conceal from him that they think him the 8th wonder of the world'.

wonder-rabbi in Hasidic Judaism, a ➤ TSADDIK.

wonderful Parliament the Parliament, otherwise known as the ➤ MERCILESS *Parliament*, which in 1388 condemned the favourites of Richard II; it was also called the *wonder-working Parliament* in recognition of its achievement. The antiquary John Stow (1525?–1605) notes in his *Summarie of Englyshe Chronicles* (1580) that 'This Parliament was named the Parliament that wrought wonders.'

wonderland a land or place full of wonderful things, a fairyland; the term is recorded from the late 18th century, but is most frequently used with reference to the country which Alice found down a rabbit-hole in Lewis Carroll's *Alice's Adventures in Wonderland* (1866).

wonders will never cease proverbial saying, late 18th century.

wood see also ➤ BABES *in the wood*, ➤ CHILDREN *in the Wood*, ➤ TOUCH *wood*.

not see the wood for the trees fail to grasp the main issue or gain a general view among a mass of details; the term is recorded from the mid 16th century.

Wood's halfpence copper coinage introduced into Ireland in 1722 by the English ironmaster William *Wood* (1671–1730), under a license from George I; as a result of ➤ *The* DRAPIER*'s Letters*, a series of critical pamphlets by Swift, the coinage had to be withdrawn, and Wood compensated by the government.

Woodbine Willie nickname of the English priest and poet Geoffrey Studdert Kennedy (1883–1929), who once described his wartime chaplain's ministry as taking 'a box of fags in your haversack and a great deal of love in your heart'; *Woodbine* here is the trademark name of a brand of cigarettes.

wooden horse the ➤ TROJAN *Horse*:

> Odysseus's great stratagem of the wooden horse.
> — John Barth *Tidewater Tales* (1987)

The Wooden Horse (1949) was the account by the writer Eric Williams of how he and two companions, when prisoners of war in Germany, successfully used a wooden vaulting horse to disguise the escape tunnel which they constructed over four and a half months.

In the 17th and 18th centuries, *wooden horse* also denoted an instrument of military punishment, a structure with a sharply ridged back on which offenders were made to sit astride, sometimes with their hands bound and weights on their feet (**riding the wooden horse**).

wooden nickel in the US, a worthless or counterfeit coin; the term is recorded from the early 20th century.

wooden nutmeg in the US, a false or fraudulent thing; a fraud, cheat, or deception; originally, a piece of wood sold to the credulous as a nutmeg. The story of this fraud was recounted in the *Clockmaker* (1836) by the Canadian humorist 'Sam Slick' (T. C. Haliburton, 1796–1865).

See also ➤ NUTMEG *State*.

wooden spoon a real or imaginary prize given in fun to the person who is last in a race or competition; originally a spoon given to the candidate coming last in the Cambridge mathematical tripos, a custom recorded from the early 19th century.

wooden walls the wooden ships of the Royal Navy, considered as Britain's defences. The term derives from a story in Herodotus of how the Athenian statesman ➤ THEMISTOCLES (*c*.528–*c*.462 BC) interpreted the words of the Delphic oracle before the battle of ➤ SALAMIS, that 'the wooden wall' would help them. Themistocles is said to have told the Athenians, 'The wooden wall is your ships.'

wooden wedding in the US, a 5th wedding anniversary, on which it is appropriate to give presents made of wood.

wooden wedge the student coming last in the classical tripos list at Cambridge University; the term derives from the fact that in the first classical tripos (1824) the last man was Wedgwood of Christ's College, afterwards famous as an English etymologist.

William Woodfall (1746–1803), parliamentary reporter and dramatic critic. In 1789 he established the 'Diary', and was thus the first to publish reports of parliamentary debates on the morning after they had taken place; he became known for the remarkable memory which enabled him to do this, and it is said that when he visited Dublin crowds followed him in the streets because he was supposed to be 'endowed with supernatural powers'.

Woodhenge a prehistoric henge, near Stonehenge, in the form of a circular bank and ditch believed to have contained a circular timber structure; the first of its kind to be discovered.

Woodser see ➤ JIMMY *Woodser.*

woodshed see ➤ *something* NASTY *in the woodshed.*

Woodstock a small town in New York State, situated in the south-east near Albany. It gave its name in the summer of 1969 to a huge rock festival held some 96 km (60 miles) to the south-west.

woodwose a wild man of the woods; a savage; a satyr, a faun; the representation of such a being, as a decoration or as a heraldic bearing or supporter. The term is recorded from late Old English, and the first element *wood* means 'mad'.

happy's the wooing that is not long doing proverbial saying, late 16th century.

wool see also ➤ DYED *in the wool.*

many go out for wool and come home shorn proverbial saying, late 16th century; meaning that many who hope to succeed in an enterprise fall victim to the success of others.

Virginia Woolf (1882–1941), English novelist, essayist, and critic. A member of the Bloomsbury Group, she gained recognition with *Jacob's Room* (1922). Subsequent novels, such as *Mrs Dalloway* (1925) and *To the Lighthouse* (1927), characterized by their poetic Impressionism, established her as an exponent of modernism.

woollen see ➤ BURIED *in woollen.*

Woolsack in the UK, the Lord Chancellor's wool-stuffed seat in the House of Lords. It is said to have been adopted in Edward III's reign as a reminder to the Lords of the importance to England of the wool trade.

Woolton pie a type of vegetable pie, named after F. J. Marquis (1883–1964), Lord *Woolton*, who was Minister of Food during the war of 1939–45 when the pie was publicized.

Woolwich the old dockyard and the Royal Arsenal in Woolwich, an area of Greater London (formerly in Kent).

Frank Winfield Woolworth (1852–1919), American businessman. He opened his first shop selling low-priced goods in 1879 and from this built a large international chain of stores. The British Labour politician Aneurin Bevan (1897–1960) once used the image of the 'Sixpenny Store' to criticize the oratorical prowess of the Conservative Neville Chamberlain, saying, 'Listening to a speech by Chamberlain is like paying a visit to Woolworth's: everything in its place and nothing above sixpence.'

Woolworth Building on Broadway in New York, built in 1913; it was for a time the tallest building in the world.

Woomera a town in central South Australia, the site of a vast military testing ground used in the 1950s for nuclear tests and since the 1960s for tracking space satellites. The name (which comes from Dharuk *wamara*) means 'an Aboriginal stick used to throw a dart or spear more forcibly'.

woopie an affluent retired person able to pursue an active lifestyle; the term, which is from the acronym for *well-off older person*, is recorded from the mid 1980s, and is one of a number of terms modelled on the earlier ➤ YUPPIE.

Bertie Wooster fictional character created by P. G. Wodehouse, a pleasant, affluent, and idle young man about town who is much persecuted by his aunts, but who is usually protected by his valet ➤ JEEVES.

> The popular view of a gentleman is poised somewhere between the imbecile parasite and the villainous one: between Woosteresque chinless wonders, and those heartless capitalist toffs who are . . . the stock-in-trade of television.
> — *Daily Telegraph* 24 May 1996

wop an offensive term for an Italian or other southern European. Recorded from the early 20th century (originally US), the word may come from Italian *guappo* 'bold, showy', from Spanish *guapo* 'dandy'.

Worcester a cathedral city in western England, on the River Severn, the scene in 1651, during the English Civil War, of a battle in which Oliver Cromwell defeated a Scottish army under Charles II.

word a single distinct meaningful element of speech or writing, used with others (or sometimes alone) to form a sentence and typically shown with a space on either side when written or printed; re-corded from Old English, *word* is of Germanic origin, and comes ultimately from an Indo-European root shared by Latin *verbum* 'word'.

From the mid 16th century, **the Word** or **the Word of God** has been a term used for the Bible, as embodying divine revelation, often with allusion to John 1:1, 'In the beginning was the Word, and the Word was with God, and the Word was God.'

See also ➤ ACTIONS *speak louder than words,* ➤ *an* ENGLISHMAN*'s word is his bond,* ➤ FINE *words butter no parsnips,* ➤ FOUR-*letter word,* ➤ GHOST *word,* ➤ HARD *words break no bones,* ➤ LONG *word,* ➤ MUM*'s the word,* ➤ NONCE-*word,* ➤ *one* PICTURE *is worth ten thousand words,* ➤ PORTMANTEAU *word,* ➤ SEVEN *last words,* ➤ WEASEL *words,* ➤ WINGED *words.*

a word to the wise is enough proverbial saying, early 16th century; earlier in Latin (see ➤ VERB. *sap.*).

Ten Words an archaic expression (recorded from late Middle English) for the ➤ TEN *Commandments.*

world of words former term for a dictionary; used initially (in 1598) by John Florio as the title for his 'Worlde of Wordes, Or Most copious, and exact Dictionarie in Italian and English'.

William Wordsworth (1770–1850), English poet. Much of his work was inspired by the Lake District. His *Lyrical Ballads* (1798), which was composed with Coleridge and included 'Tintern Abbey', was a landmark in romanticism. He was appointed Poet Laureate in 1843.

See also ➤ LAKE *Poets,* ➤ *the* LOST *Leader,* ➤ STUFFED *owl.*

work see also ➤ *the* END *crowns the work,* ➤ NICE *work if you can get it,* ➤ WOMEN'S *work is never done.*

all work and no play makes Jack a dull boy proverbial saying, mid 17th century.

work expands so as to fill the time available proverbial saying, mid 20th century; the view, which was formulated by the English historian and journalist C. Northcote Parkinson (1909–93), is commonly known as ➤ PARKINSON*'s Law.*

it is not work that kills, but worry proverbial saying, late 19th century.

if you won't work you shan't eat proverbial saying, mid 16th century.

worker see ➤ *a* BAYONET *is a weapon with a worker at each end of it.*

workers ➤ *St* JOSEPH is patron saint of workers.

workers of the world, unite usual rendering of the closing words of Marx and Engels's *The Communist Manifesto* (1848), 'the proletarians have nothing to lose but their chains. They have a world to win. WORKING MEN OF ALL COUNTRIES, UNITE!'

working see also ➤ LABOUR *isn't working.*

working class the social group consisting of people who are employed for wages, especially in manual or industrial work; the term is recorded from 1789, in a reference to 'the clergyman and the schoolmaster, and to other persons superior to the working class'.

workman see ➤ *a* BAD *workman blames his tools.*

works see also ➤ COVENANT *of Works.*

works of supererogation in the Roman Catholic Church, the performance of good works beyond what God commands or requires, which are held to constitute a store of merit which the Church may dispense to others to make up for their deficiencies.

Workshop of the World informal term for England in the 19th century; the expression was used by Disraeli in the House of Commons in 1838, in reference to the British manufacturing and industrial capacity.

world see also ➤ BRAVE *new world,* ➤ *eighth* WONDER *of the world,* ➤ *the* END *of the world,* ➤ FIRST *World,* ➤ FOURTH *World,* ➤ KING *of the World,* ➤ LAUGH *and the world laughs with you,* ➤ LIBERTY *Enlightening the World,* ➤ *the* LIGHT *of the World,* ➤ LOVE *makes the world go round,* ➤ MISTRESS *of the World,* ➤ OLD *World,* ➤ *the* ROOF *of the World,* ➤ SECOND *World,* ➤ SEVEN *Wonders of the World,* ➤ *the* SOUL *of the world,* ➤ THIRD *World,* ➤ WORKSHOP *of the World,* ➤ *world of* WORDS.

all the world and his wife everyone; the term is first recorded in Swift's Polite Conversation (1738), when in response to the question 'who were the Company?' Lady Smart answers, 'there was all the World, and his Wife.'

World Bank an international banking organization established to control the distribution of economic aid between member nations, and to make loans to them in times of financial crisis.

World Council of Churches an association established in 1948 to promote unity among the many different Christian Churches. Its member Churches number over 300, and include virtually all Christian traditions except Roman Catholicism and Unitarianism. Its headquarters are in Geneva.

world English the English language including all of its regional varieties, such as North American, Australian, New Zealand, and South African English.

World Heritage Site a natural or man-made site, area, or structure recognized as being of outstanding international importance and therefore as deserving special protection. Sites are nominated to and designated by the World Heritage Convention (an organization of UNESCO).

the world is one's oyster the world is one's prize; the whole world is available to one; perhaps originally with allusion to Shakespeare's *Merry Wives of Windsor* (1597), ' the world's mine oyster, which I, with sword will open'.

World Series the professional championship for major league baseball, played at the end of the season between the champions of the American League and the National League. It was first played in 1903.

World Service a service of the British Broadcasting Corporation that transmits radio programmes in English and over thirty other languages around the world twenty-four hours a day. A worldwide television station was established in 1991 on a similar basis.

the world, the flesh, and the devil all forms of temptation to sin; the phrase comes from the ➤ LITANY, 'From all the deceits of the world, the flesh, and the devil, Good Lord, deliver us.'

World Trade Center a complex of buildings in New York featuring twin skyscrapers 110 storeys high, designed by Minoru Yamasaki and completed in 1972.

the world turned upside down the natural order of things reversed; *The World Turned Upside Down* was the title of a Royalist of *c.*1646, and was also the title of the tune played when the British army under Cornwallis surrendered at Yorktown in 1781.

World War I another term for ➤ FIRST *World War.*

World War II another term for ➤ SECOND *World War.*

World Wide Fund for Nature an international organization established (as the World Wildlife Fund)

in 1961 to raise funds for projects including the conservation of endangered species or of valuable habitats. Its headquarters are in Gland, Switzerland. Its symbol is a panda, typifying endangered species.

World Wide Web a widely used information system on the Internet, which provides facilities for documents to be connected to other documents by hypertext links, enabling the user to search for information by moving from one document to another.

world without end for ever, eternally; a translation of Late Latin *in saecula saeculorum* to the ages of ages, as used in *Morning Prayer* and other services, 'As it was in the beginning, is now, and ever shall be: world without end.'

worm in archaic use, a serpent, snake, or dragon; in Shakespeare's *Antony and Cleopatra* (1606–7), Cleopatra calls the asp which kills her 'the pretty worm of Nilus'. Recorded from Old English (in form *wyrm*) the word originally also meant any animal which creeps or crawls, a reptile or insect.

The current meaning of an earthworm or other creeping or burrowing limbless invertebrate animal with a long slender soft body also dates from Old English, and gives rise to the allusive uses of worm as the type of weakness, humility, or nakedness.

Worm has also been used from Old English for a maggot, or in popular belief, an earthworm, supposed to eat dead bodies in the grave; in biblical allusion, this becomes one of the pains of hell, as in Mark 9:48, 'Where their worm dieth not, and their fire is not quenched.'

See also ➤ *a* CAN *of worms,* ➤ *the* EARLY *bird catches the worm.*

even a worm will turn proverbial saying, mid 16th century; meaning that even a meek person will resist or retaliate if pushed too far.

Worms an industrial town in western Germany, on the Rhine north-west of Mannheim, which was the scene in 1521 of the condemnation of Martin Luther's teaching, at the ➤ DIET *of Worms.*

wormwood a woody shrub with a bitter aromatic taste, used as an ingredient of vermouth and absinthe and in medicine; in figurative use, a state or source of bitterness or grief, originally with biblical allusion, as to Deuteronomy 29:18, 'lest there should be among you a root that beareth gall and wormwood'.

The word is recorded from Old English, in form

wermōd; the change in spelling in late Middle English was due to association with *worm* and *wood*.

Wormwood Scrubs a prison in the Hammersmith district of London.

> A group of lads she doesn't care about . . . Next stop Wormwood Scrubs, that little lot.
> — Pauline Glen Winslow *Death of an Angel* (1975)

worry see also ➤ *it is not* WORK *that kills.*

worry beads a string of beads that one fingers and moves in order to calm oneself.

worship the feeling or expression of reverence and adoration for a deity; the acts or rites that make up a formal expression of reverence for a deity; a religious ceremony or ceremonies. The word is recorded from Old English in form *weorthscipe* 'worthiness, acknowledgement of worth'.

worst see ➤ *when* THINGS *are at their worst.*

worsted a fine smooth yarn spun from combed long-staple wool; fabric made from such yarn, having a close-textured surface with no nap. The word comes (in Middle English) from *Worstead*, the name of a parish in Norfolk, England.

Charles Frederick Worth (1825–95), English couturier, resident in France from 1845. He opened his own establishment in Paris in 1858 and soon gained the patronage of the empress Eugénie. Regarded as the founder of Parisian *haute couture*, he is noted for designing gowns with crinolines and for introducing the bustle.

worth see also ➤ *if a* THING*'s worth doing.*

the worth of a thing is what it will bring proverbial saying, mid 16th century.

worthies see ➤ NINE *Worthies.*

Wotan another name for ➤ ODIN.

would see ➤ DO *as you would be done by.*

wound a wound in the head is the emblem of St Peter the Martyr, a 13th-century Dominican friar and priest born in Verona, who was attacked and killed while travelling from Como to Milan; he was wounded in the head with an axe, while the friar who was with him was stabbed.

Battle of Wounded Knee the last major confrontation (1890) between the US Army and American Indians, at the village of Wounded Knee on a reservation in South Dakota. More than 300 largely unarmed Sioux men, women, and children were

massacred. A civil rights protest at the site in 1973 led to clashes with the authorities.

Five Wounds the wounds in the hands, feet, and side of the crucified Jesus; devotion to the *Five Wounds* developed during the Middle Ages, and they are symbolized by five signs of the cross made over the host during a Mass, five grains of incense in a Paschal candle, and five crosses inscribed on an altar.

wraith a ghost or ghostlike image of someone, especially one seen shortly before or after their death. The term is recorded from the early 16th century (originally in Scottish sources), but is of unknown origin.

wrangler at Cambridge University, a person placed in the first class of the mathematical tripos; a *wrangler* in this sense is a debater or a disputant.

wreath see ➤ ADVENT *wreath.*

wrecker a person on the shore who tried to bring about a shipwreck in order to plunder or profit from the wreckage; the term is first recorded in Washington Irving's *Sketch Book* (1820) in a reference to a crowd watching a shipwreck, 'The good people…thronged like wreckers to get some part of the noble vessel'.

wrecks see ➤ RECEIVER *of wrecks.*

wren the *wren* is proverbial for its small size. It was traditionally regarded as a sacred bird, and Pliny notes that there was antipathy between the wren and the eagle because the wren had been given the title of the 'king of the birds'; this relates to the fable in which the wren concealed itself on the eagle's back, and could thus claim that it had flown higher than the eagle.

In the UK, *Wren* (as a partial acronym) is a name for a member of the former *Women's Royal Naval Service.*

See also ➤ *the* ROBIN *and the wren are God's cock and hen.*

Christopher Wren (1632–1723), English architect. Following the Fire of London (1666) Wren was responsible for the design of the new St Paul's Cathedral (1675–1711) and many of the city's churches. Other works include the Greenwich Observatory (1675) and a partial rebuilding of Hampton Court (1689–94). He was a founder member and President (1680–2) of the Royal Society.

Y the twenty-fifth letter of the modern English alphabet and the twenty-second of the ancient Roman one, representing Greek *upsilon*, a differentiated form of the early Greek vowel-symbol, now also represented by U and V.

Y chromosome in humans and other mammals, a sex chromosome which is normally present only in male cells, which are designated XY.

yahoo a rude, noisy, or violent person, from the name of an imaginary race of brutish creatures in Swift's *Gulliver's Travels* (1726).

From the mid 19th century *yahoo* (perhaps a different word in origin) has also been used in Australia for a mythical creature resembling a big hairy man, said to haunt eastern Australia.

Yahweh a form of the Hebrew name of God used in the Bible. The name came to be regarded by Jews (*c.*300 BC) as too sacred to be spoken, and the vowel sounds are uncertain. Compare with ➤ JEHOVAH.

Yahwist the postulated author or authors of parts of the first six books of the Bible, in which God is regularly named *Yahweh*. Compare with ➤ ELOHIST.

yajna in Hinduism, a ritual sacrifice with a specific objective; the word comes from Sanskrit *yajña* 'worship, sacrifice'.

Yajur Veda in Hinduism, one of the four Vedas, based on a collection of sacrificial formulae in early Sanskrit used in the Vedic religion by the priest in charge of sacrificial ritual.

yaksha in Indian mythology, any of a class of demigods or nature spirits often serving as tutelary guardians, especially one ministering to Kubera, the Hindu god of wealth.

Yale University a university at New Haven, Connecticut, one of the most prestigious in the US. It was founded in 1701 at Killingworth and Saybrook, Connecticut, by a group of Congregational ministers. In 1716 it moved to its present site at New Haven and soon afterwards was renamed Yale College after Elihu *Yale* (1649–1721), a notable benefactor. In 1887 it became Yale University.

Yalta Conference a meeting between the Allied leaders Churchill, Roosevelt, and Stalin in February 1945 at Yalta, a Crimean port on the Black Sea. The leaders planned the final stages of the Second World War and agreed the subsequent territorial division of Europe.

Yama in Hindu mythology, the first man to die. He became the guardian, judge, and ruler of the dead, and is represented as carrying a noose and riding a buffalo.

Isoroku Yamamoto (1884–1943), Japanese admiral. As Commander-in-Chief of the Combined Fleet (air and naval forces) from 1939, he was responsible for planning the Japanese attack on ➤ PEARL *Harbor* (1941). He then attempted to gain control of the Pacific, but was thwarted by the defeat of his fleet at the ➤ *Battle of* MIDWAY (1942).

Minoru Yamasaki (1912–86), American architect. He designed the influential barrel-vaulted St Louis Municipal Airport Terminal (1956) and the World Trade Center in New York (1972).

Yamato-e a style of decorative painting in Japan during the 12th and early 13th centuries, characterized by strong colour and flowing lines; the name comes from Japanese *Yamato* 'Japan' + *e* 'picture'.

yang in Chinese philosophy, the active male principle of the universe, characterized as male and creative and associated with heaven, heat, and light. Contrasted with ➤ YIN.

Yangshao a Neolithic civilization of northern China, dated to *c.*5000–2700 BC and preceding the Longshan period. It is marked by pottery painted with naturalistic designs of fish and human faces and abstract patterns of triangles, spirals, arcs, and dots. It is named after *Yang Shao Cun*, the first settlement of this period to be excavated (1921).

Yankee an often derogatory term for a person who lives in, or is from, the US, especially, an inhabitant of New England or one of the northern states, or a Federal soldier in the Civil War. The term is recorded from the mid 18th century but the origin is uncertain; it may come (as a nickname) from Dutch *Janke*, diminutive of *Jan* 'John'.

Yankee Doodle Dandy a song popular during the War of American Independence, now regarded as a national song; the tune is said to have been composed in 1755 by Dr Richard Shuckburgh, a British surgeon in Lord Amherst's army, in derision of provincial troops:

> Yankee Doodle came to town
> Riding on a pony,
> He stuck a feather in his hat
> And called it Macaroni.
>
> Yankee Doodle keep it up,
> Yankee Doodle dandy,
> Mind the music and the step,
> And with the girls be handy.
> — Anonymous soldiers' song, *c.*1755

Yankee State an informal name for Ohio.

yantra a geometrical diagram, or any object, used as an aid to meditation in tantric worship. The word is from Sanskrit, and means literally 'device for holding or fastening'.

in yarak of a trained hawk, fit and in a proper condition for hunting. Recorded from the mid 19th century, the expression may come from Persian *yārakī* 'strength, ability' or from Turkish *yaraǧ* 'readiness'.

yarborough in bridge or whist, a hand with no card above a nine. It is named after the Earl of *Yarborough* (died 1897), said to have bet 1000 to 1 against its occurrence.

yarmulke a skullcap worn in public by Orthodox Jewish men or during prayer by other Jewish men.

yarn see ➤ SPIN *a yarn*.

Yasa a codification of Mongolian customary laws ascribed to Genghis Khan (1162–1227), used as the basis of law in much of Asia under Mongol rule.

yashmak a veil concealing all of the face except the eyes, worn by some Muslim women in public; the word comes (in the mid 19th century) via Arabic from Turkish.

Yates's correction in statistics, a correction for the discreteness of the data that is made in the chi-square test when the number of cases in any class is small and there is one degree of freedom, named after the English statistician Frank *Yates* (1902–94).

yatra in the Indian subcontinent, a procession or pilgrimage, especially one with a religious purpose; the word comes from Sanskrit *yātrā* 'journey'.

Yayoi a Japanese culture following the Jomon period and dated to *c.*300 BC–AD 300. It was marked by the introduction of rice cultivation, and the appearance of large burial mounds has suggested the emergence of an increasingly powerful ruling class. It is named after a street in Tokyo where its characteristic pottery (chiefly wheel-made) was first discovered.

Yazoo frauds in late 18th-century America, a land speculation scheme in which four companies bribed the state legislature of Georgia in order to obtain large grants of land, to some of which the state had doubtful claims. The sale was revoked in the following year.

yclept archaic adjective meaning 'by the name of'; the word represents Old English *gecleopod*, past participle of *cleopian* 'call'.

ye pseudo-archaic term for *the*. In origin this is a graphic variant; in late Middle English the letter þ (see ➤ THORN) came to be written identically with y, so that *the* could be written *ye*. This spelling (usually y^e) was kept as a convenient abbreviation in handwriting down to the 19th century, and in printers' types during the 15th and 16th centuries, but it was never pronounced as 'ye'.

Chuck Yeager (1923–), American pilot. He became the first person to break the sound barrier when he piloted the Bell X-1 rocket research aircraft at high altitude to a level-flight speed of 670 mph in 1947.

year the time taken by the earth to make one revolution around the sun. The length of the year depends on the manner of calculation. For ordinary purposes the important period is the **tropical year** (also called **astronomical year**, **equinoctial year**, or **solar year**) which is the time between successive spring or autumn equinoxes, or winter or summer solstices, roughly 365 days, 5 hours, 48 minutes, and 46 seconds in length. This period thus marks the regular cycle of the seasons.

The **calendar year** or **civil year** is the period of 365 days (or 366 days in leap years) starting from the first of January, used for reckoning time in ordinary affairs.

The word is recorded from Old English (in form *gē(a)r*) and is of Germanic origin; it comes from an

Indo-European root shared by Greek *hōra* 'season'.

See also ➤ *a* CHERRY *year, a merry year,* ➤ FORTY *years on,* ➤ HOLY *Year,* ➤ LEAP *year,* ➤ LIGHT *year,* ➤ LOCUST *years,* ➤ PLATONIC *year,* ➤ REGNAL *year,* ➤ SABBATICAL *year,* ➤ SEVEN *year itch,* ➤ SEVEN *Years War,* ➤ THREESCORE *years and ten.*

a year and a day a legal period constituting a term for certain purposes, in order to ensure the completion of a full year.

year, day, and waste a prerogative (abolished in 1870) whereby the sovereign was entitled to the profits for a year and a day of a tenement held by a person attainted of petty treason or felony, with the right of allowing the property to deteriorate.

year of grace year — AD, suggested by medieval Latin *anno gratiae,* used by chroniclers to indicate the year as reckoned from the birth of Christ.

year of Our Lord year — AD, as reckoned from the birth of Christ; ➤ ANNO *domini.*

Year 2000 problem another name for the ➤ MILLENNIUM *bug.*

year's mind the anniversary of a person's death or burial, as an occasion for special prayers; a Requiem Mass held on such an anniversary; the term is recorded from the 11th century.

yearbook an annual publication giving current information and listing events or aspects of the previous year, especially in a particular field; in North America, a book containing photographs of the senior class in a school or university and details of school activities in the previous year.

yeast a microscopic fungus consisting of single oval cells that reproduce by budding, and capable of converting sugar into alcohol and carbon dioxide; a greyish-yellow preparation of this obtained chiefly from fermented beer, used as a fermenting agent, to raise bread dough, and as a food supplement; in figurative usage, ➤ LEAVEN.

W. B. Yeats (1865–1939), Irish poet and dramatist. His play *The Countess Cathleen* (1892) and his collection of stories *The Celtic Twilight* (1893) stimulated Ireland's theatrical, cultural, and literary revival.

Yeibichai a Navajo curative or initiation ceremony performed by masked dancers representing deities. The name comes from Navajo *Ye'ii Bichaii* literally 'Grandfather of the Giants', from *yé'ii* fearful one, giant + *bicheii, -aii* his maternal grandfather.

Yekaterinburg an industrial city in central Russia, in the eastern foothills of the Urals, where the last tsar, Nicholas II, and his family were shot in 1918.

yell see ➤ REBEL *yell.*

yellow of the colour between green and orange in the spectrum, a primary subtractive colour complementary to blue; coloured like ripe lemons or egg yolks. *Yellow* is traditionally the colour associated with jealousy and cowardice.

Recorded from Old English (in form *geolu, geolu*) the word is of West Germanic origin, and is related to ➤ GOLD.

yellow admiral in the British navy, a post captain promoted to the rank of rear admiral on retirement without having actually served at that rank; the term is recorded from the late 18th century, and the use of *yellow* indicates that the officer concerned is not attached to a particular squadron (red, white, or blue, as in ➤ *Admiral of the* RED).

yellow alert the preliminary stage of an alert, when danger is thought to be near but not actually imminent; a warning of such a situation.

Yellow Book an illustrated literary periodical published quarterly in the UK between 1894 and 1897, associated with the Aesthetic Movement. Often controversial, it contained contributions from writers including Max Beerbohm, Henry James, Edmund Gosse, Arnold Bennett, and H. G. Wells. The art editor was Aubrey Beardsley. It was so named because of its distinctive yellow binding.

yellow boy an informal term for a gold coin, a guinea; the phrase is recorded from the mid 17th century.

yellow card in soccer and some other games, a yellow card shown by the referee to a player being cautioned.

yellow-dog contract in the US, an agreement by which an employee undertakes not to join a union, as a condition of employment; *yellow dog* here implies something regarded as of little account. Contracts of this kind were common in the 1920s; they were prohibited in 1932.

yellow-dog Democrat in the US, a diehard Democrat, who will vote for a Democratic candidate, regardless of their personal qualities; the term implies someone who would vote for even a *yellow dog* if it were on the party ticket.

yellow fever a tropical virus disease affecting the liver and kidneys, causing fever and jaundice and often fatal, which is transmitted by mosquitoes. It was also known informally as *yellow jack.*

yellow flag a ship's yellow or quarantine flag (denoting the letter Q), indicating a request for customs clearance when flown alone.

yellow jack archaic term for ➤ YELLOW *fever*; also, a ship's yellow quarantine flag.

yellow jersey in a cycling race involving stages, a yellow jersey worn each day by the rider who is ahead on time over the whole race to that point, and presented to the rider with the shortest overall time at the finish of the race.

Yellow Pages in the UK, a telephone directory, or a section of one, printed on yellow paper and listing businesses and other organizations according to the goods or services they offer. Its advertising slogan of the 1960s, 'Let your fingers do the walking', has become well-known, as has ➤ *J. R.* HARTLEY, the character on whom a later television advertisement for *Yellow Pages* centred.

yellow peril dated and derogatory term for the supposed danger posed by Asiatic peoples to the rest of the world; the expression is recorded from 1900.

yellow press newspapers of an unscrupulously sensational character; journalists working on such papers. The use of *yellow* in this sense derives from the appearance in 1895 of a number of the *New York World* in which a child in a yellow dress ('The Yellow Kid') was the central figure of the cartoon, an experiment in colour-printing designed to attract purchasers.

Yellow River the second-largest river in China, which rises in the mountains of west central China and flows over 4,830 km (3,000 miles) in a huge semicircle before entering the gulf of Bo Hai.

yellow star a piece of yellow cloth bearing the Star of David, which the Nazis required Jews to wear.

yellowback a cheap novel in a yellow board binding, sold in late 19th-century railway bookstalls.

yellowhammer a common Eurasian bunting, the male of which has a yellow head, neck, and breast; its song is traditionally said to represent the call, 'a little bit of bread and no cheese!'

Yellowhammer State informal name for Alabama.

Yellowstone National Park a national park in NW Wyoming and Montana. Named after the Yellowstone River, a tributary of the Missouri which runs through it, the park was established in 1872 and was the first national park in the US. It is noted for its many geysers, hot springs, and mud volcanoes, especially Old Faithful, a geyser which erupts every 45 to 80 minutes to a height of about one hundred feet.

yen informal term for a longing or yearning; the term comes (in the late 19th century, in the sense 'craving (of a drug addict) for a drug') from Chinese *yǎn.*

Yenan designating the period 1936–49 in the history of the Chinese Communist Party, during which Yenan was its headquarters, or principles and policies evolved by the Party at that time.

yeoman a man holding and cultivating a small landed estate; a freeholder; a person qualified for certain duties and rights, such as to serve on juries and vote for the knight of the shire, by virtue of possessing free land of an annual value of 40 shillings. The term is recorded from Middle English, and probably comes from *young + man.*

Yeoman of the Guard a member of the British sovereign's bodyguard, first established by Henry VII, now having only ceremonial duties and wearing Tudor dress as uniform. Also called *Beefeater.*

Yeoman Usher in the United Kingdom, the deputy of ➤ BLACK *Rod.*

Yeoman Warder a warder at the Tower of London.

Yerkish a sign language devised for chimpanzees, based on geometric symbols, named after R. M. *Yerkes* (1876–1956), US primatologist.

yeti a large hairy creature resembling a human or bear, said to live in the highest part of the Himalayas; it is informally known as the ➤ ABOMINABLE *Snowman.* The term is recorded in English from the

1930s, and comes from Tibetan *yeh-teh* 'little man-like animal'.

Yevgeni Yevtushenko (1933–), Russian poet. *Third Snow* (1955) and *Zima Junction* (1956) were regarded as encapsulating the feelings and aspirations of the post-Stalin generation, and he incurred official hostility because of the outspoken nature of some of his poetry, notably *Babi Yar* (1961), a poem on the massacre of Jews from Kiev at ➤ BABI *Yar* in 1941.

yew a coniferous tree which has red berry-like fruits, and most parts of which are highly poisonous. Yews are linked with folklore and superstition (Macbeth's witches included 'Slips of yew Slivered in the moon's eclipse' in their cauldron) and can live to a great age; they are often planted in churchyards, and from this are regarded as symbolizing loss and grief. The timber is used in cabinetmaking and (formerly) to make longbows.

> What of the bow?
> The bow was made in England,
> Of true wood, of yew wood,
> The wood of English bows.
> — Arthur Conan Doyle *The White Company* (1890) 'Song of the Bow'

Yggdrasil a huge ash tree located at the centre of the earth, with three roots, one extending to ➤ NIFLHEIM (the underworld), one to ➤ JOTUNHEIM (land of the giants), and one to ➤ ASGARD (land of the gods). Although threatened by a malevolent serpent that gnaws at its roots and by deer eating its foliage, the tree survives because it is watered by the Norns from the well of fate.

The name is Old Norse, and apparently comes from *Yggr* 'Odin' + *drasill* 'horse'; Odin hanged himself on the tree for nine nights and days to win the runes for humankind.

Yiddish a language used by Jews in central and eastern Europe before the ➤ HOLOCAUST. It was originally a German dialect with words from Hebrew and several modern languages, and still has some 200,000 speakers, mainly in the US, Israel, and Russia. The name is recorded from the late 19th century, and comes from Yiddish *yidish (daytsh)* 'Jewish German'.

yin in Chinese philosophy, the passive female principle of the universe, characterized as female and sustaining and associated with earth, dark, and cold. Contrasted with ➤ YANG.

Yinglish a form of English containing many Yiddishisms.

Yishuv the Jewish community or settlement in Palestine during the 19th century and until the formation of the state of Israel in 1948. The name comes from Hebrew *yiššūḇ* 'settlement'.

Yizkor a memorial service held by Jews on certain holy days for deceased relatives or martyrs. The word is from Hebrew *yizkōr*, literally 'may (God) remember'.

ylem in the ➤ BIG *bang* theory the primordial matter of the universe, originally conceived as composed of neutrons at high temperature and density. The word comes (in the 1940s) from late Latin *hylem* (accusative) 'matter'.

Ymir in Scandinavian mythology, the primeval giant killed by ➤ ODIN and the other gods, from whose body they created the world; his blood formed the seas, and his bones the rocks.

yod the tenth and smallest letter of the Hebrew alphabet; the name comes from Hebrew and is related to *yaḏ* 'hand'.

In astrology, *yod* is another term for ➤ FINGER *of God*.

Yoda in the second film of the ➤ STAR *Wars*, the last surviving master of ➤ JEDI skills who trains *Luke Skywalker* to master the Force. In appearance he is a small creature with blinking eyes and large pointed ears; he is characterized also by a reversed word order in his sentences, 'Your father he is' for 'He is your father'.

> You saw Bill Gates as some sort of oracular Yoda perched on a misty summit of cyber wisdom to whom even a lowly journalist can gain access via the miracle of cyberspace.
> — John Seabrook *Deeper* (1997)

yodel practise a form of singing or calling marked by rapid alternation between the normal voice and falsetto.

yoga a Hindu spiritual and ascetic discipline, a part of which, including breath control, simple meditation, and the adoption of specific bodily postures, is widely practised for health and relaxation; the name comes from Sanskrit, and means literally 'union'.

The yoga widely known in the West is based on **hatha yoga**, which forms one aspect of the ancient Hindu system of religious and ascetic observance and meditation, the highest form of which is **raja**

yoga and the ultimate aim of which is spiritual purification and self-understanding leading to *samadhi* or union with the divine.

See also ➤ KARMA *yoga*.

Yogacara a school of Mahayana Buddhism which teaches that only consciousness is real.

yogh a Middle English letter (3) used mainly where modern English has *gh* and *y*. The name is recorded from Middle English, but the origin is unknown.

Yogi Bear a cartoon bear, the central character of a series set in *Jellystone Park* and created by William Hanna (1910–) and Joseph Barbera (1911–); *Yogi Bear*, with his companion *Boo-Boo*, spends his time trying to circumvent the *Ranger* and steal or beg food from tourists.

yogic flying a technique used chiefly by Transcendental Meditation practitioners which involves thrusting oneself off the ground while in the lotus position.

pass under the yoke in ancient Rome, a captive or conquered enemy was forced to pass under device consisting of two spears fixed upright in the ground with another on the top of them, in token of submission.

stone yoke an ancient Mexican carving representing a yoke, supposed to have been placed on the necks of victims when sacrificed.

yokozuna a grand champion sumo wrestler. The word is Japanese and comes from *yoko* 'crosswise' + *tsuna* 'rope' (originally denoting a kind of belt presented to the champion).

Yom Kippur the most solemn religious fast of the Jewish year, the last of the ten days of penitence that begin with ➤ ROSH *Hashana* (the Jewish New Year). It is also called the ➤ DAY *of Atonement*.

Yom Kippur War the Israeli name for the Arab--Israeli conflict in 1973.

The war lasted for less than three weeks; it started on the festival of Yom Kippur (in that year, 6 October) when Egypt and Syria simultaneously attacked Israeli forces from the south and north respectively. The Syrians were repulsed and the Egyptians were surrounded. A ceasefire followed and disengagement agreements over the Suez area were signed in 1974 and 1975.

yomp of a soldier, march with heavy equipment over difficult terrain. The term, which is of unknown origin, is recorded from the 1980s, and first

became widely known during the ➤ FALKLANDS *War*, in accounts of marines **yomping** across difficult ground.

yoni in Hinduism, the vulva, especially as a symbol of divine procreative energy conventionally represented by a circular stone. The word is Sanskrit, and means literally 'source, womb, female genitals'.

yonks a very long time, recorded from the 1960s and perhaps related to ➤ DONKEY's *years*.

yoof non-standard spelling of *youth*, used humorously or ironically to refer to young people collectively. The term is recorded from the mid 1980s, when **yoof culture** was often used to sum up a category of the contemporary scene, particularly in the field of broadcasting.

York see also ➤ DUKE *of York's Column*, ➤ GRAND *Old Duke of York*, ➤ *St* OSWALD *of York*.

Archbishop of York the archbishop of the northern province of the Church of England. The office carries the title of Primate of England, being first in precedence after the Archbishop of Canterbury, and dates from AD 735. The archbishop's cathedral church is York Minster.

House of York the English royal house which ruled England from 1461 (Edward IV) until the defeat and death of Richard III in 1485, with a short break in 1470–1 (the restoration of Henry VI).

Descended from Edmund of Langley (1341–1402), 1st Duke of York and 5th son of Edward III, the House of York fought the ➤ WARS *of the Roses* with the ➤ *House of* LANCASTER, both houses being branches of the Plantagenet line. Lancaster eventually prevailed, through their descendants, the Tudors, but the houses were united when the victorious Henry VII married Elizabeth, the eldest daughter of Edward IV (1486).

The Yorkist emblem was a ➤ WHITE *rose*.

York shilling a coin formerly used in New York, worth about 12½ cents; the term is recorded from the early 19th century.

yorker in cricket, a ball bowled so that it pitches immediately under the bat, perhaps originally introduced by Yorkshire players.

Yorkist an adherent or a supporter of the ➤ *House of* YORK, especially in the Wars of the Roses. The term is recorded from the early 17th century.

Yorkshire see also ➤ RIPPER.

Yorkshire born and Yorkshire bred, strong in the arm and weak in the head proverbial saying, mid 19th century; the names of other (chiefly northern) English counties and towns are also used instead of Yorkshire

Yorkshire tyke traditional name for a native or inhabitant of Yorkshire, perhaps originally derogatory; it may derive from the fact that in Yorkshire *tyke* is often used for *dog*.

Yosemite National Park a national park in the Sierra Nevada in central California. It includes Yosemite Valley, with its sheer granite cliffs and Yosemite Falls, the highest waterfall in the US.

young see also ➤ BRIGHT *young thing*, ➤ *the* GOOD *die young*, ➤ *whom the* GODS *love die young*, ➤ *the Young* CHEVALIER, ➤ *Young* ROSCIUS

Brigham Young (1801–77), American Mormon leader. He succeeded Joseph Smith as the leader of the Mormons in 1844, and established their headquarters at Salt Lake City, Utah.

Thomas Young (1773–1829), English physicist, physician, and Egyptologist. His major work in physics concerned the wave theory of light. He also played a major part in the deciphering of the ➤ ROSETTA *Stone*.

Young England name assumed by a group of Tory politicians in the early part of the reign of Queen Victoria.

Young Europe a group of associations of various republican activists arising after the July revolution in France in 1830, as *Young France*, *Young Germany*.

young folks think old folks to be fools, but old folks know young folks to be fools proverbial saying, late 16th century.

the young idea the child's mind, from James Thomson's *The Seasons* (1746), 'Delightful task! to rear the tender thought, To teach the young idea how to shoot.'

Young Ireland a group of Irish activists about 1840–50; the poet Thomas Davis (1814–45) was one of their leaders, and the revival of national culture one of their aims.

Young Italy a movement founded by Giuseppe Mazzini in 1831 to work towards a united Italian republic. In the 1830s and 1840s the movement plotted against the Italian governments. It failed to gain popular support but was nevertheless a significant stimulus to the ➤ RISORGIMENTO.

a young man married is a young man marred proverbial saying, late 16th century.

young men may die, but old men must die proverbial saying, mid 16th century.

Young Pretender ➤ *Charles Edward* STUART (1720–80), as son of the ➤ OLD *Pretender*; the name is first recorded from 1745 (the year of the second Jacobite Rising):

> The Young Pretender . . . has got a march on General Cope.
> — Horace Walpole letter, 1745

young saint, old devil proverbial saying, early 15th century; meaning that good and moral behaviour at an early age may change in later life.

Young Turk a member of a revolutionary party in the Ottoman Empire who carried out the revolution of 1908 and deposed the sultan Abdul Hamid II; in extended usage, a young person eager for radical change to the established order.

> The young turks of neo-conservatism are on the march . . . They are a more urbane lot, often with wonkish tendencies and Ivy League pretensions.
> — *Globe &Mail* (Toronto) 5 February 1994

youth the 16th-century Italian Jesuit St Aloysius Gonzaga (1568–91), noted for his early piety, and the Piedmontese St John Bosco (1815–88), who established schools and workshops for the destitute urban young, are patron saints of the young.

See also ➤ FOUNTAIN *of Youth*, ➤ GILDED *youth*.

thy youth is renewed like the eagle's biblical saying, from Psalm 103:5; it was traditionally believed that when the eagle grew old it flew up to the sun to burn off its heavy wings and blinded eyes, and then plunged down into a spring of pure water; by immersing itself three times, its youth was renewed.

if youth knew; if age could traditional saying, early 17th century; meaning that by the time a person is wise enough to know the right course of action, they may be too old to effect it.

youth must be served proverbial saying, early 19th century.

Ypres a town in NW Belgium, near the border with France, in the province of West Flanders, the scene of some of the bitterest fighting of the First World War, and now site of the ➤ MENIN *Gate*.

Battle of Ypres each of three battles on the Western Front near Ypres during the First World War in 1914, 1915, and 1917.

In the first battle (October–November 1914) Allied forces prevented the Germans breaking through to the Channel ports; the second battle (April–May 1915) was an inconclusive trench conflict in which poison gas was used for the first time, while the third battle (1917) was the slaughter of ➤ PASSCHEN-DAELE.

Yuan a dynasty that ruled China AD 1279–1368, established by the Mongols under Kublai Khan. It preceded the Ming dynasty.

yuga in Hindu belief, any of the four ages of the life of the world.

Yugoslavia a federation of states in SE Europe, in the Balkans, formed as the Kingdom of Serbs, Croats, and Slovenes in the peace settlements at the end of the First World War. It comprised Serbia, Montenegro, and the former South Slavic provinces of the Austro-Hungarian empire, and assumed the name of Yugoslavia in 1929; after the Second World War and the ending of German occupation it emerged as a non-aligned Communist state under the rule of Marshal Tito (1892–1980).

In 1990 Communist rule was formally ended. Four of the six constituent republics (Slovenia, Croatia, Bosnia–Herzegovina, and Macedonia) then seceded amid serious civil and ethnic conflict (see ➤ ETHNIC *cleansing*). The two remaining republics,

Serbia and Montenegro, declared a new federal republic of Yugoslavia in 1992. The term **former Yugoslavia** has been in frequent use since the early 1990s.

Yukon Territory a territory of NW Canada, on the border with Alaska, a sparsely inhabited, largely undeveloped Arctic region, isolated by mountains, the population of which increased briefly during the Klondike gold rush (1897–9).

Yule archaic term for *Christmas*. The name comes from Old English *gēol(a)* 'Christmas Day'; compare with Old Norse *jól*, originally applied to a heathen festival lasting twelve days, later to Christmas.

See also ➤ *a* GREEN *Yule makes a fat churchyard*.

yule log a large log traditionally burnt in the hearth on Christmas Eve.

Yuletide the time of Yule, Christmas.

yuppie informal and derogatory term for a well-paid young middle-class professional who works in a city job and has a luxurious lifestyle. The term is recorded from the 1980s, seen as the period at which such people flourished, and is an elaboration of the acronym from *young urban professional*. It has generated a number of similar terms, of which ➤ WOOPIE is only one.

Zz

Z the last letter of the modern English alphabet and of the ancient Roman one, corresponding to Gk ζ and Hebrew *zayin*.

Zacchaeus in the Bible (Luke 19:1–10) a tax collector who was 'little of stature' and so could not see Jesus in the crowds; he climbed a tree for a better view, but was called down by Jesus, who visited his house.

Zacharias in the Bible, the father of ➤ JOHN *the Baptist*, to whom the archangel Gabriel foretold his son's birth; Zacharias from that moment was unable to speak until the moment when the child was to be named, and he wrote the words 'His name is John' (Luke 1:63).

Zadkiel pseudonym of the inventor and astrologer Richard Morrison (1795–1874), who published his annual astrological predictions under the title of *Zadkiel's Almanac*. *Zadkiel* is the name of an angel listed in Kabbalistic tradition.

> As devoutly as any superstitious washerwoman ever read Zadkiel or Old Moore.
> — George Bernard Shaw comment, 1896, in *Our Theatres in the Nineties* (1932)

Zadok in the Bible, name of the priest who supported Solomon's accession to the throne of David and anointed him as king (1 Kings 1:39); *Zadok the Priest* is the title of one of the coronation anthems composed by Handel for the coronation of George II.

Zadokite a member of a Jewish sect established in the 2nd century BC and tracing its leaders' authority back to ➤ ZADOK.

zakat obligatory payment made annually under Islamic law on certain kinds of property and used for charitable and religious purposes. The word comes via Persian and Urdu from Arabic *zakā(t)* 'almsgiving'.

zany an erratic or eccentric person; originally, a comic performer partnering a clown, whom he imitated in an amusing way. The word comes (in the late 16th century) from French *zani* or Italian *zan(n)i*, Venetian form of *Gianni, Giovanni* 'John', stock name of the servants acting as clowns in the *commedia dell'arte*.

Emiliano Zapata (1879–1919), Mexican revolutionary. When the leader of the 1910–11 revolution Francisco Madero failed to redistribute land to the peasants, Zapata attempted to implement his programme of agrarian reform by means of guerrilla warfare. From 1914 he and ➤ *Pancho* VILLA fought against the regimes of General Huerta and Venustiano Carranza.

Zapata moustache a type of moustache in which the two ends extend downwards to the chin., as worn by Marlon Brando in the film *Viva Zapata!* in 1952.

Zar in several North African countries, a malignant spirit, possession by which is traditionally held to explain attacks of madness.

Zarathustra the Avestan name for the Persian prophet ➤ ZOROASTER, used in the title of Nietzsche's *Also Sprach Zarathustra* [Thus Spake Zarathustra] (1883).

Zealot a member of an ancient Jewish sect aiming at a world Jewish theocracy and resisting the Romans until AD 70. The name is recorded from the mid 16th century, and comes via ecclesiastical Latin from Greek *zēlōtēs*, from *zēloun* 'be jealous', from *zēlos* 'zeal'.

The extended sense of *zealot* as a person who is fanatical and uncompromising in pursuit of their religious, political, or other ideals is recorded from the mid 17th century.

See also ➤ *St* SIMON.

Zebulun in the Bible, a Hebrew patriarch, son of Jacob and Leah (Genesis 30:20); also, the tribe of Israel traditionally descended from him.

Zechariah a Hebrew minor prophet of the 6th century BC. Also, a book of the Bible including his prophecies, urging the restoration of the Temple, and some later material.

Zedekiah in the Bible, the last king of Judaea, who rebelled against Nebuchadnezzar and was carried off to Babylon into captivity (2 Kings 24–5, 2 Chronicles 36).

zeitgeber a cue given by the environment to reset the internal body clock. The term is German, and comes from *Zeit* 'time' + *Geber* 'giver'.

zeitgeist the defining spirit or mood of a particular period of history as shown by the ideas and beliefs of the time. Recorded from the mid 19th century, the word is German, and comes from *Zeit* 'time' + *Geist* 'spirit'.

Zem Zem name of a sacred well near Mecca, said to have been revealed to Hagar when she and her son ➤ ISHMAEL were dying of thirst in the desert.

zemstvo an elective district or provincial council in Russia for purposes of local government, created by Alexander II in 1864.

Zen a Japanese school of Mahayana Buddhism emphasizing the value of meditation and intuition rather than ritual worship or study of scriptures. Zen Buddhism was introduced to Japan from China in the 12th century, and has had a profound cultural influence. The aim of Zen is to achieve sudden enlightenment (satori) through meditation in a seated posture (zazen), usually under the guidance of a teacher and often using paradoxical statements (koans) to transcend rational thought.

zenana in India and Iran, the part of a house for the seclusion of women; the word comes from Persian and Urdu *zanānah*, from *zan* 'woman'.

Zend an interpretation of the Avesta, each Zend being part of the ➤ ZEND-*Avesta*; the word comes from Persian *zand* 'interpretation'.

Zend-Avesta the Zoroastrian sacred writings, comprising the ➤ AVESTA (the text) and ➤ ZEND (the commentary).

Zendik among Muslims, a heretic, especially one who does not believe in revealed religion. The name comes via Arabic from Persian *zandīk* 'fire-worshipper, heretic'.

zenith the highest point reached by a celestial or other object; the point in the sky or celestial sphere directly above an observer; in figurative usage, the time at which something is most powerful or successful. Recorded from late Middle English, the word comes via Old French from medieval Latin *cenit*, based on Arabic *samt (ar-ra's)* 'path (over the head)'.

Zeno (fl. 5th century BC), Greek philosopher. A member of the Eleatic school, he defended Parmenides' theories by formulating paradoxes which appeared to demonstrate the impossibility of motion, one of which shows that once Achilles has given a tortoise a start he can never overtake it, since each time he arrives where it was, it has already moved on.

Zeno of Citium (*c.*335–*c.*263 BC), Greek philosopher, founder of Stoicism. He founded the school of Stoic philosophy, but all that remains of his treatises are fragments of quotations.

Zenobia (3rd century AD), queen of Palmyra *c.*267–272. She conquered Egypt and much of Asia Minor. When she proclaimed her son emperor, the Roman emperor Aurelian attacked, defeated, and captured her. She was later given a pension and a villa in Italy.

Zephaniah a Hebrew minor prophet of the 7th century BC; a book of the Bible containing his prophecies.

Zephyr in classical mythology, the god of the west wind; from the late 17th century, *zephyr* has also been a literary term for a soft gentle breeze.

Zeppelin a large German dirigible airship of the early 20th century, long and cylindrical in shape and with a rigid framework. Zeppelins were used during the First World War for reconnaissance and bombing, and after the war as passenger transports until the 1930s; their popularity decreased sharply after the *Hindenburg* disaster of 1937, when the dirigible, which had completed its first transatlantic crossing, burst into flames while landing at Lakehurst, New Jersey, with considerable loss of life.

Ferdinand Zeppelin (1838–1917), Count von Zeppelin, German aviation pioneer. An army officer until his retirement in 1890, he devoted the rest of his life to the development of the dirigible airship named after him. It made its maiden flight in 1900.

Zermatt an Alpine ski resort and mountaineering centre near the Matterhorn, in southern Switzerland.

> Zermatt was put on the map by British alpinists who began to visit it in winter at the end of the last century.
> — *World Magazine* No. 46 1990

zero no quantity or number; nought; the figure 0. The word is recorded from the early 17th century, and comes via French or Italian from Old Spanish and ultimately from Arabic *ṣifr* 'cypher'.

See also ➤ ABSOLUTE *zero*.

zero hour the time at which a planned operation, typically a military one, is set to begin.

zeta the sixth letter of the Greek alphabet (Z, ζ), transliterated as 'z'.

zeugma a figure of speech in which a word applies to two others in different senses (e.g. *John and his driving licence expired last week*) or to two others of which it semantically suits only one (e.g. *with weeping eyes and hearts*).

Zeus in Greek mythology, the supreme god, the son of ➤ CRONUS (whom he dethroned) and Rhea, and husband of Hera, traditionally said to have his court on ➤ OLYMPUS. Zeus was the protector and ruler of humankind, the dispenser of good and evil, and the god of weather and atmospheric phenomena (such as rain and thunder). His Roman equivalent is *Jupiter*.

Zeuxis (fl. late 5th century BC), Greek painter, born at Heraclea in southern Italy. His works are known only through the reports of ancient writers, who make reference to monochrome techniques and his use of shading to create an illusion of depth, while his verisimilitude is the subject of many anecdotes.

Zhou a dynasty which ruled in China from the 11th century BC to 256 BC.

The dynasty's rule is commonly divided into **Western Zhou** (which ruled from a capital in the west of the region near Xian until 771 BC) and **Eastern Zhou** (which ruled after 771 BC from a capital based in the east). The rule of the Eastern Zhou, although weak and characterized by strife, saw the Chinese classical age of Confucius and Lao-tzu.

ziggurat in ancient Mesopotamia, a rectangular stepped tower, sometimes surmounted by a temple. Ziggurats are first attested in the late 3rd millennium BC and probably inspired the biblical story of the ➤ *Tower of* BABEL (Genesis 11:1–9).

Zimri in the Bible, (1 Kings) *Zimri* is a captain who kills the king of Israel and makes himself king; he himself in turn is defeated and killed. In 2 Kings 10:31, ➤ JEZEBEL refers to the story, greeting Jehu who will kill her with the words, 'Had Zimri peace,

who slew his master?' *Zimri* is thus a type of treachery, and in Dryden's ➤ ABSALOM *and Achitophel*, the name is given to Buckingham.

Zingaro a gypsy; the name probably comes from the Italian equivalent of Greek *Athigganoi*, name of an oriental people. It is recorded in English from the early 17th century; **I Zingari** (or **The Zingari**) is the name of an amateur cricket club founded in 1845.

Zinoviev letter a letter published in the press in 1924 as having been sent by the Soviet politician Grigori *Zinoviev* (1883–1936) to British Communists, inciting them to subversion; it was later discovered to be a forgery.

Zion the hill of Jerusalem on which the city of David was built; the citadel of ancient Jerusalem; (in Christian thought) the heavenly city or kingdom of heaven. Also, the Jewish people or religion.

See also ➤ DAUGHTER *of Zion*, ➤ PROTOCOLS *of the Learned Elders*.

Zionism a movement for (originally) the re-establishment and (now) the development and protection of a Jewish nation in what is now Israel. It was established as a political organization in 1897 under Theodor Herzl, and was later led by Chaim Weizmann.

zip code in the US, a postal code consisting of five or nine digits, the first element being an acronym from *zone improvement plan*.

zodiac a belt of the heavens within about 8° either side of the ecliptic, including all apparent positions of the sun, moon, and most familiar planets, which is divided into twelve equal divisions or signs (Aries, Taurus, Gemini, Cancer, Leo, Virgo, Libra, Scorpio, Sagittarius, Capricorn, Aquarius, Pisces). The supposed significance of the movements of the sun, moon, and planets within the zodiacal band forms the basis of astrology. However, the modern constellations do not represent equal divisions of the zodiac, and the ecliptic now passes through a thirteenth (Ophiuchus).

Owing to precession, the signs of the zodiac now roughly correspond to the constellations that bear the names of the *preceding* signs.

The word is recorded from late Middle English and comes via Old French and Latin from Greek *zōidiakos*, from *zōidion* 'sculptured animal figure', diminutive of *zōion* 'animal'.

Zodiac: Signs of the Zodiac

Aries	the Ram
Taurus	the Bull
Gemini	the Twins
Cancer	the Crab
Leo	the Lion
Virgo	the Virgin
Libra	the Scales
Scorpio	the Scorpion
Sagittarius	the Archer
Capricorn	the Goat
Aquarius	the Water-carrier
Pisces	the Fish

Zohar the chief text of the Jewish ➤ KABBALAH, presented as an allegorical or mystical interpretation of the Pentateuch. The name comes from Hebrew *zōhar*, literally 'light, splendour'.

Zoilus (4th century BC), Greek Cynic philosopher, rhetorician, and critic, famous for his severe criticism of Homer; his name has thus been used for a censorious, malignant, or envious critic.

Émile Zola (1840–1902), French novelist and critic. His series of twenty novels collectively entitled *Les Rougon-Macquart* (1871–93), including *Nana* (1880) and *Germinal* (1885), attempts to show how human behaviour is determined by environment and heredity. In 1898 he published *J'accuse*, a pamphlet in support of ➤ *Alfred* DREYFUS.

Zollverein a union, originally between certain states of the German empire, but after 1833 including all the states, for the maintenance of a uniform rate of customs duties from other countries and of free trade among themselves; in general usage, an association resembling this.

zombie a corpse said to be revived by witchcraft, especially in certain African and Caribbean religions. Recorded from the early 19th century, the word is of West African origin.

zoot suit a man's suit of an exaggerated style, characterized by a long loose jacket with padded shoulders and high-waisted tapering trousers, popular in the 1940s. The name was originally a rhyming formation on *suit*.

Zoroaster (*c.*628–*c.*551 BC), Persian prophet and founder of Zoroastrianism; Avestan name *Zarathustra*. Little is known of his life, but traditionally he was born in Persia and began to preach the tenets of

what was later called Zoroastrianism after receiving a vision from ➤ AHURA *Mazda*.

Zoroastrianism a monotheistic pre-Islamic religion of ancient Persia founded by Zoroaster in the 6th century BC. According to the teachings of Zoroaster the supreme god, ➤ AHURA *Mazda*, created twin spirits, one of which chose truth and light, the other untruth and darkness. Later writings present a more dualistic cosmology in which the struggle is between Ahura Mazda (Ormazd) and the evil spirit ➤ AHRIMAN. The scriptures of Zoroastrianism are the Zend-Avesta. It survives today in isolated areas of Iran and in India, where followers are known as Parsees.

Zorro fictional character ('The Fox') created by Johnston McCulley in a 1919 magazine story; *Zorro* is the pseudonym of Diego de la Vida, the apparently weak son of a landowning Spanish family in California who seeks to protect the weak against tyranny, and whose swashbuckling habits include the cutting of a Z (the **mark of Zorro**) with his sword as a signature.

Zouave a member of a light-infantry corps in the French army, originally formed of Algerians and long retaining their oriental uniform. The name comes (in the mid 19th century) via French, from Kabyle *Zouaoua*, the name of a tribe.

zounds archaic expression of surprise or indignation. The word comes (in the late 16th century) from a contraction of *(God)'s wounds* (i.e. those of Christ on the Cross). In Shakespeare's *Richard III*, when Buckingham, stressing his apparent anger at Richard's initial refusal of the crown, cries out 'Zounds, I'll entreat no more', Richard responds, 'O, do not swear, my lord of Buckingham.'

zucchetto a Roman Catholic cleric's skullcap: black for a priest, purple for a bishop, red for a cardinal, and white for the Pope. Recorded from the mid 19th century, the word comes from Italian *zucchetto*, diminutive of *zucca* 'gourd, head'.

Zulu a member of a South African people living mainly in KwaZulu/Natal province. The Zulus formed a powerful military empire in southern Africa during the 19th century before being defeated in a series of engagements with white Afrikaner and British settlers. In recent years the Zulu Inkatha movement has been drawn into violent clashes with other black groups in South Africa, particularly the Xhosa.

Zuleika according to Muslim tradition, the name of ➤ POTIPHAR's wife.

Zurich see ➤ GNOMES *of Zurich*.

Zurich Bible published in Zurich in 1529. Also called the ➤ CANNON *Bible*.

Zwickau prophets in the early 16th century, a radical religious reform group based in Zwickau in Saxony, who claimed to have had divine revelations about the impending end of the world.

Zwinglian an adherent or supporter of the Swiss Protestant reformer Ulrich *Zwingli* (1484–1531), the principal figure of the Swiss Reformation. He was minister of Zurich from 1518, where he sought to carry through his political and religious reforms. He rejected papal authority and many orthodox doctrines, and although he had strong local support in Zurich, his ideas met with fierce resistance in some regions. Zwingli was killed in the civil war that resulted from his reforms.

Index of Boxed Entries

Acknowledgements

Entries from the following Oxford University Press publications have been used in this title. We are grateful to the copyright holders for permission to reproduce material from these entries.

From *The Oxford Companion to English Literature*, revised 5th edition, edited by Margaret Drabble, © Margaret Drabble and Oxford University Press 1985, 1995

album amicorum
Annales Cambriae
Apostles, The
Boar's Head Inn
Café Royal
Carmina Burana
Coffee House
Garsington Manor
Grosvenor Gallery
Hutchinsonians
Liverpool Poets
Matter of Britain, the
Merlin
Morgan le Fay
negative capability
Pellam, King
Philosophes
Revels, Master of the
Roxburghe Club
Scriblerus Club
Taillefer
Wilton House

Alcuin Club
Annual Register
Atellan fables
Boots Library
Cambridge Platonists
Cheshire Cheese
Cruden, Alexander
Glatysant Beast, the
Henty, G. A.
Jack Horner
Llangollen, the Ladies of
Matter of England, the
Mermaid Series, the
Morgawse
Ordericus Vitalis
Pelles, King
Psalmanazar, George
Reynard
Savage Club
Secreta Secretorum
Tauchnitz

Ambrose's Tavern
Anson, George
Battle Abbey Roll, The
Britomart
Camden Society
Cloud of Unknowing
Forman, Simon
Golden Cockerel Press
Herne the Hunter
Jack of Dover
London Library
Matter of France, the
Metaphysical Society
Mudie's lending Library
Paston Letters, the
Penshurst Place
Rambouillet, Hotel de
Rhymers Club
Savile Club
Slaughter's Coffee House
Tom's Coffee House

Angria and Gondal
Apollodorus
Bedford Coffee-House
Burnell the Ass
Camlann
Cock Lane Ghost
Franklin, John
Gregynog Press
Hogarth Press
Little Gidding
Malone Society
Matter of Rome, the
Modred
Nasrudin
Paul the Deacon
Pevsner, Nikolaus
Rankenian Club
Roger of Wendover
Scott, Michael
Sophonisba
Transendental Club

From *The Oxford Companion to American Literature*, 6th edition, by James D. Hart, © 1995 by Oxford University Press, Inc. Used by permission of Oxford University Press Inc.

Algonquin Round Table
Anti-Rent War
Atlanta
Bird Woman
Bread and Cheese Club
Chaco War
Chisholm Trail
Connecticut Wits
Deadwood Dick

federal theology

Fox Sisters
Goudy, Frederick W.
Hall of Fame
Kentucky Tragedy

Lost Colony
Mocha Dick
New Amsterdam
Newberry Library
Paumanok
Rappite

Sandemanian
Tilbury Town
Wilderness Road

Amherst College
Armory Show
Bancroft Library
Booth, John Wilkes
Bridger, James
Chancellorsville, Battle of
Come-outer
Covenant Theology
Dewey decimal
   classification
Fink, Mike

Gastronia strike
Greek Revival
Haymarket Riot
Know-nothing

manifest destiny
Moon Hoax
Harmony, New
Oneida Community
Phi Beta Kappa
Roanoke Island

Scopes trial
Webster, Daniel
Williamsburg

Andersonville
Astor Place riot
Beacon Hill
Boston Athenaeum
Bryn Mawr College
Charleston
Comstock lode
Crockett almanacs
Donner Party

Folger Shakespeare
   Memorial Library
go west, young man
Green Mountain Boys
Hudson River school
Lewis and Clark
   Expedition
Merry Mount
Nasby, Petroleum V.
New Netherlands
Pacing Mustang
Philip's War, King
Robert's Rules of
   Order
Scottsboro case
Webster, Noah
Yazoo frauds

Anthology Club
Astoria
Bent's Fort
Bowery
Carson, Kit
Chicago
Concord
Dare, Virginia
Dorchester Company
   of Adventurers
Ford Foundation

Good Gray Poet
Grolier
Humanism
Little Giant

Mexican War
Neutral Ground
Newbery Medal
Paine, Thomas
Poictesme
Sacco and Vanzetti
   Case
Shays's Rebellion
West Point